A AND AS LEVEL

ACTIVE PSYCHOLOGY

LONGMAN

EDITED BY IRENE TAYLOR

Pearson Education Limited
Edinburgh Gate
Harlow
Essex CM20 2JE, England

Printed in Singapore

ISBN 0582 05195 9

The Publisher's policy is to use paper manufactured from
sustainable forests.

Contents

Introduction

This book represents the work, over many years, of a large number of teachers and examiners. All are united in the pursuit of psychological knowledge and have tried to convey their own fascination with the subject through their writing.

The major theme of the book is the *active* learning of psychology. The writers have tried to take the student reader inside the research process and to foster a critical understanding of the reasoning and significance of empirical findings. As experienced teachers we encourage the interaction of the student with the text content, which we have tried to ensure is as easy to read and understand as we could make it.

Approach of the book

This text includes topics ranging across all the psychological areas covered at pre-degree level. It sets out both to represent current areas of interest and to encompass the central core of psychology. The main research areas of social, comparative, biopsychology, cognitive, developmental and abnormal psychology are sandwiched between a section introducing perspectives on psychology, and research methods and analysis at the end of the book - the tools of the psychological researcher.

Study aids

Each unit includes:

- Learning objectives which allow the reader to have an outline of the core concepts of the unit.
- Activities which are central to the unit content and facilitate the development of psychological knowledge through discovery learning.
- Self-assessment questions of varying difficulty designed to consolidate the learning of central concepts.
- Terms to define at the end of each unit, to enable the reader to check their understanding of central terms and to become familiar with the vocabulary of psychology. These are shown in bold, and are given full definitions in the Glossary at the end of the book.
- Further reading is suggested at the end of each unit. These texts have been selected from a wide range of books and journals to enhance and extend the knowledge gained from each unit.
- A summary concludes the unit by reviewing the main topics and concepts introduced.
- Suggested answers are available at the end of each unit to allow distance learning and help readers who may not have regular contact with tutors.

The book also includes tables, figures, photographs, drawings and cartoons which are referred to regularly and cross-referenced when they prove useful to other subject areas.

To the reader

It is the wealth of interest provided by psychology which has motivated the authors to write this book and to continue to teach the subject to our students. We are aware that you, the reader, will spend a long time reading and interacting with this book. We hope you will enjoy it.

Authors' acknowledgements

As writers we tend to consider the book as 'ours' but it actually belongs to a large number of people. Reviewers, who have read the successive versions of the text, have provided us with social reinforcers and maintained our enthusiasm during such a long project. Many colleagues helped by reading drafts of the units and suggesting changes.

We would also thank our families and friends for their support, consideration, patience and tolerance, without which the book would not have been completed.

Finally we must not forget the early work done by Graham Davies and the writers acknowledged below, who originated the concept of *active* learning which remains central to the teaching of psychology, as portrayed in this book: David Bosworth, Liz Conroy, Nancy Cowley, Peter Hull, Lorna Jones, Tony Malim, Darren Meer, Peter Reddy, Judith Silver, Jill Smith, Darrell de Souza, Jennifer Taylor, Sandie Taylor, Regina Teahan and Lance Workman.

Irene Taylor (1999)

Acknowledgements

We are grateful to the following for permission to reproduce copyright material:

Figure 3.6, The Bateson Model, *New Scientist*; 5.4, 15.30, Baron, R A and Byrne, D (1997) *Social Psychology*, 8th edn, Allyn and Bacon; 8.4a, 8.4b, Durrell, G (1982) *The Amateur Naturalist*, Hamish Hamilton; 8.5, 9.7, Ridley, M (1995) *Animal Behaviour*, Blackwell; 9.4, Cronin, H (1991) *The Ant and the Peacock*, Cambridge University Press; 9.6, Halliday, T R *Sex and Evolution*, Eds. Slater, P J B and Halliday, T R (1994) *Behaviour and Evolution*, Cambridge University Press; 12.1, 12.8a, 13.15, 13.17, 13.19, 15.2, 15.14, Pinel, J P J (1997) *Biopsychology*, 3rd edn, Allyn and Bacon; 12.2, 12.8b, 13.6, 13.13, Carlson, N R and Buskist, W (1997) *Psychology the Science of Behaviour*, Allyn and Bacon; 12.3, 12.4a, Atkinson et al (1996) *Hilgard's Introduction to Psychology*, 12th edn, Harcourt Brace & Co; 12.9, Parents Against Drug Abuse; 13.20b, Pinel, J P J (1997); 14.1, 14.6, 15.27, Baron, R A (1996) *Essentials of Psychology*, Allyn & Bacon; 14.2, Horne, J A (1988) *Why We Sleep: The Functions of Sleep in Humans and Other Mammals*, Oxford University Press; 15.15, LeDoux (1989), 16.3, Gregory, R and Ganbrick, E H (1973) *The Confounded Eye*, Illusion in Nature and Art, Duckworth; 17.7, Results of Johnston and Wilson's 1980 study on divided attention; 18.5a, Baddeley, A D (1996) *Your Memory A Users Guider*, Prion; 19.5, 19.6, 19.7, Smyth, M M et al (1994) *Cognition in Action*, 2nd edn, Psychology Press; 19.8, Eysenck, M W (1993) *Principles of Cognitive Psychology*, Laurence Erlbaum; 21.6, Butterworth, G and Harris, M (1994) *Principles of Developmental 4*, Laurence Erlbaum; 23.10, Sunday Observer Magazine (25.4.1993);

We are grateful to the following for permission to reproduce photographs:

Bubbles pages 535 centre left (L.J Thurstun), 535 centre right (Jennie Woodcock); Collections page 535 below left (Sandra Lousada), 535 below right, 727, 728 below (Anthea Sieveking); Mary Evans Picture Library pages 911, 957; Sally & Richard Greenhill page 760; Hutchison Library pages 741 left (Maurice Harvey), 741 right (S. Errington); Panos Pictures/J. Hartley page 741 centre; Pictor International page 458; Popperfoto page 931; Janine Wiedel pages 535 above left & above right, 728 above.

Though every effort has been made to trace the owners of copyright material this has proved impossible in the following cases and we would welcome any information enabling us to do so:

Figure 13.4, 13.10, Matlin and Foley (1992); 13.20a, Springer and Deutch (1993); 15.21, Gross, R (1996); 15.22, Looker and Gregson (1990); 19.12, Bruner et al (1956); 21.2, Taylor and Hayes (1990); 21.8, Smith, P K and Cowie, H (1991); 21.22, Turkheimer and Farace (1992); 22.13, American Association of University Women (1991).

Perspectives

Unit 1

Approaches to Psychology

Nancy Cowley and Sara Nadin

This unit covers:

The contributions and applications of major approaches in psychology

The nature of the person in psychology

By the end of this unit, you should be able to:

- understand the basic principles of the five main approaches covered; biological, psychodynamic, behaviourist, cognitive and humanistic

- evaluate the contributions of the five main approaches

- understand the debates of free will and determinism, reductionism, and nature versus nurture

- understand the relevance of these debates to current psychological theory and practice.

Unit 1   Contents

Introduction

Just as a wide range of different coloured spotlights can focus on a performer on stage, so have the influences of a wide range of viewpoints focused on the study of mind and behaviour. Since 1879, when Wundt set up the first psychology laboratory at Leipzig in Germany, the discipline has developed a range of schools of thought, each favouring a particular view of what it is important for psychology to study. The unifying theme between all these approaches is their concern with the understanding of mind and behaviour. These different approaches reflect influences from a diversity of disciplines, each of which has contributed its own distinctive flavour to the subject.

This unit begins by reviewing some of the differing approaches to psychology which have been developed. It then goes on to discuss some of the major debates within psychology which have inevitably emerged from such a diversity of approaches – debates which still seem far from being finally resolved.

The contributions and applications of major approaches in psychology

This unit outlines five of the major approaches to psychology, focusing on their historical links and practical applications. These approaches sometimes overlap and where this happens, we consider how this occurs.

Whilst the various different approaches may appear confusing to the new student of psychology, this in itself is a reflection of the complexity of human behaviour. Behaviour is determined by numerous different factors, with the different approaches emphasising the influence of certain factors over others. Thus whilst one approach may focus on the role of genetics in the determination of behaviour, another may focus upon the role of childhood experience. This difference in focus is also reflected in the methods adopted by the different approaches. The five approaches to be covered here are:

- the biological approach
- the psychodynamic approach
- the behaviourist approach
- the cognitive approach
- the humanist approach.

This list is not exhaustive, but it does represent the most influential viewpoints dominating psychology over the past century. This section begins with a look at the biological approach.

The biological approach

Whilst the bulk of this section focuses upon neurobiological explanations of behaviour, other explanations of human behaviour fall under the general heading of biological approaches. These include sociobiology and comparative psychology.

■ Sociobiology

This approach is strongly influenced by Darwin's theory of evolution and the need to ensure genetic survival. One of the most influential proponents of the theory is Wilson (1975, 1978) who argued that all aspects of human culture and behaviour are contained in our genes, which have themselves been moulded by natural selection. Behaviour can be understood in terms of 'inclusive fitness' where actions are taken to maximise the chance of survival of one's own genes, through protection of our children or close relatives. This approach has been influential in offering explanations of human aggression and altruism.

However, sociobiology has been strongly criticised for offering a **eurocentric** view of behaviour, explanations which are inadequate for understanding behavioural patterns in other cultures. The explanatory power of sociobiological theories within western culture is also limited. Adoption is an obvious example, representing a behaviour which involves a heavy investment of resources, an investment which cannot be explained genetically. Thus it would seem that explanations other than sociobiological ones are needed in order to understand this and many other complex behaviours.

Another emotive body of criticism is that which points out the potentially oppressive implications of sociobiological explanations. These include asserting the 'naturalness' of male domination and aggression, and the desire to further the survival of one's own group, possibly at the expense of other groups. The danger here is of regarding and accepting discriminatory practices and racism as natural in the fight for the survival of the fittest. Viewing genes as the basic determinants of human behaviour is thus a potentially dangerous position to advocate, and one which is pure speculation (Rose *et al.*, 1984). (This issue is also covered in the section on controversial issues in psychology.)

In spite of such criticisms, although not overtly sociobiological in influence, there has been an enormous increase in the past decade in genetic explanations of behaviour. This is principally due to the biological mapping of DNA, with scientists claiming the existence of genes which determine, among other traits, sexual orientation, criminal tendencies and even religiosity (Nelkin and Lindee, 1995). Such research will ensure that genetic explanations of behaviour continue to attract attention from a wide audience.

■ Comparative psychology
This is covered in depth and detail in Units 8–11. However, it is useful here to explore briefly the basic assumptions within the broader context of biological explanations of behaviour. The comparative approach has its roots in ethology which aimed to study animal behaviour in naturalistic settings using observational methods. This is in contrast to the dominant approach of the behaviourists who investigated animal behaviour in artificial experimental situations (see figure 1.3).

It was the study of patterns of animal behaviour which formed the basis of explanations for similar patterns of behaviour observed in humans, for example aggressive and territorial behaviour. Again, this approach has been heavily influenced by Darwin's theory of evolution with human beings having evolved from other species. As a result, the understanding of animal behaviour (especially higher order mammals) could have important implications for the understanding of human behaviour.

Perhaps most well known is the early research of Lorenz in the 1930s. Lorenz identified the processes of imprinting, which in turn influenced the early theories of attachment and bonding in humans. The comparative study of animals has also had a strong influence on the study of language development (see Gardner and Gardner, 1969), and has been marked most recently by research into the emotional lives of animals (Masson and McCarthy, 1994). This has, in turn, informed ethical debates concerning the use of animals in psychological research, with questions also being raised as to the relevance of using animals as the basis for explaining human behaviour, especially where more complex cognitive processes are concerned. In spite of these criticisms, the naturalistic settings and observational methods used by ethologists have been advocated by many psychologists as the most appropriate methods for the study of humans.

■ Neurobiological explanations of behaviour
The neurobiological approach tries to relate behaviour to the electrical and chemical events which occur inside the body.

This perspective is seen variously as:
■ the ultimate solution to the problem of the duality of mind and body
■ the perspective offering the fullest explanation of human behaviour, into which all other perspectives will eventually be incorporated
■ a limited, reductionist account of human activity and ability, which misses the richness and complexity of human meanings and purposes.

Research in this field focuses upon the role of the nervous system (predominantly the brain) and the role of the endocrine system (responsible for the release of hormones) in the determination of behaviour.

The link between brain and behaviour is not new, but during the 1980s and 1990s great advances were made in brain research.

Technological developments such as CT scans and PET scans have enabled scientists to study the structural and electro-chemical connections of the brain and their relationship to behaviour in humans and non-human species.

Links have been established between structures and circuitry in specific brain areas and human abilities or behaviour patterns, for example motor activity, reactions of anger or pleasure, and facial expression. Damage or malfunction in specific brain locations has been associated with language and speech deficits as well as with faults in perceptual organisation and memory. Fore brain structures have been identified as areas where thinking, planning and calculation take place. Although many of the links between structures and functions are incompletely understood, the implication is that the need to describe 'mind' has been eliminated by the ability to describe the brain. Not all mental activities are accounted for, but there is hope that these will eventually be revealed.

This prospect may be exciting, but sceptics object because although such research may show us the mechanism (the 'how'), it fails to show us the meaning (the 'why') or the content (the 'what') of behaviour – both essential parts of 'mind'.

If a genetic condition, like phenylketonuria (PKU), can cause severe mental retardation, which in turn will affect learning ability and social experience, it is a short step to infer that all abilities and characteristics must stem from physiological sources. Not all of these will have such drastic effects as the enzyme deficiency causing PKU, but Eysenck suggested that personality springs from the responsiveness of our nervous system. The receptivity of neurons in the central and autonomic nervous systems will influence the speed with which we become conditioned by experience.

This approach reduces all abilities and characteristics, including motivation, to a physio-logical base. It makes virtually no recognition of non-deterministic factors such as rationality or imagination. It is often viewed as the ultimate reductionist perspective (see page 25).

■ Contributions of the neurobiological approach

Although many psychologists do not agree with neurobiological explanations of behaviour, regarding them as reductionist, the approach has had, and continues to have, a strong influence on psychological research. The approach as a whole has contributed immensely to our understanding of mind and behaviour. This contribution is obvious in a wide range of research areas, including:

■ the study of sleep and consciousness
■ the study of emotion, motivation and stress
■ the study of sensory processes such as visual perception
■ the diagnoses and treatment of mental illness.

As can be seen from the research carried out in these areas, the most commonly adopted methodological approach is the controlled experiment. So, although we may object to having all the qualities we take to be uniquely human (for example, sensitivity, intelligence, creativity) explained in terms of neurophysiological states, it is unwise to ignore neurophysiological accounts of psychological phenomena. The examples of autism and dyslexia in figure 1.1 illustrate the important and continuing contributions neurophysiological explanations can make.

Do neurophysiological explanations exclude environmental influences? Few genetic characteristics are totally immune from environmental influences, for example nutrition and hospitable conditions are basic necessities for the development of any organism. Light was found to be necessary for the normal functioning of retinal cells; Riesen's experiments with chimpanzees reared in the dark (1947) and other research into visual perception clearly show the vital role of the environment in developing innate mechanisms.

When it comes to human personality and patterns of behaviour, the range of influencing factors is enormous. Genes, nervous systems, social experience, opportunities and interactions, historical events and individual life experiences are all meshed together (see figure 1.2).

1.1 Neurophysiological explanations of autism and dyslexia

Autism is still a poorly understood condition, although it is now more generally acknowledged to have a physiological base. Early experiments blamed the mother for her supposed failure to give sufficient love and attention to the child; an explanation which arose because of the social withdrawal and speech deficits of autistic children.

Dyslexia is another poorly understood condition. Not all reading difficulties stem from it, but for many years educationalists believed that it was caused by emotional problems or a lack of intelligence, dyslexia being a word used by middle-class parents to cover up the fact that their child was a slow learner. Now that there is some understanding that certain atypical brain or cell structures may make the neural coding of language difficult, it becomes possible to devise techniques to help.

1.2 Hyperactivity – interactional factors

It has been suggested that certain food additives may adversely affect some children's metabolism, producing hyperactivity. Hyperactivity is difficult to control and is a generally antisocial behaviour. Given a physiological base for this behaviour, the cure seems deceptively simple – cut out the additives. However, problems may occur:

1   The child enjoys crisps, fish fingers, orange squash – all forbidden items – and refuses to eat the recommended fresh fruit, vegetables and unsweetened drinks.
2   Mother and child are faced with a battle of wills. The child sees other children eating crisps and drinking orange squash, so is unlikely to understand the mother's reasons for banning these treats.
3   Confrontations ensue and hostilities are likely to prolong the behavioural patterns already built up through the hyperactivity.
4   These patterns have developed from interactions between the child, the mother and all other significant people in the child's environment. Thus other people will be predisposed to continue to react to the child as a problem. Their attitudes to the child trigger off all the former maladaptive interactions.
5   By the time treatment starts, the child will have formed a self concept. This will be difficult to change because it is built up slowly by experiences and by the reactions of others. Also, the hyperactive behaviour may have intrinsic rewards, as the difficult child has much power and may enjoy the attention its behaviour brings.

■ Evaluation of the neurobiological approach

If human activity is reduced to a neurophysiological explanation, emotions, imagination and subjective experiences all lose the special qualities we like to give them. The medical model of mental illness tends to regard the patient's motives, statements and actions as mere symptoms of the condition. Humanistic perspectives deplore this loss of meaning. Szasz (1972) wrote that Christ would, in this model, be classified as a paranoid schizophrenic. It is also hard to give a reductionist explanation of the 'spiritual uplift' experienced when listening to music, looking at paintings or engaging in some artistic or creative activity.

Looking back at figure 1.2, it is difficult to see how all forms of psychology can be incorporated within the neurophysiological model. For some things a physiological level is adequate, but for most things it may only be a starting point. However, higher levels of explanation or understanding, for example cognitive and social considerations, seem to be crucial in obtaining full information about the sources and directions of behaviour. In spite of these higher levels of explanation, however, humanistic psychologists remain dissatisfied. The whole approach is seen as too deterministic. Human personality and activity are dynamic and the outcome of any interaction cannot be known or explained by universal principles.

Despite strong objections to the deterministic nature of biological explanations of human behaviour, this approach still enjoys much popularity. Developments in genetic research have resulted in renewed genetic explanations of a variety of behavioural traits, and with it, renewed controversy concerning the validity and implications of such theories. Research concerning the complex interaction of mind and body has also highlighted how psychological factors may affect our biological state, for example the effect of stress upon blood pressure. Such valuable research will certainly continue, maintaining the important contribution biological explanations can make in developing a thorough and complete understanding of human behaviour.

The psychodynamic approach

The psychodynamic approach is derived from Freud's *psychoanalytical* theories in which the central concept is the *unconscious mind* as the determinant of motivation and personality. The technique most commonly associated with this approach is the case study method conducted within a clinical setting. Post-Freudians and psychodynamic theorists, whilst agreeing with Freud's basic principles, vary in terms of the emphasis placed upon sexual drives and in the degree of control they give the conscious part of the mind over the unconscious part.

American psychoanalysis, influenced by Horney and Adler, tends to be more optimistic about ego control (self control) of the impulses and drives of the id (basic biological drives) and recovery from trauma experienced during childhood conflicts. Freud stressed that the first five years of life are crucial to the formation of adult personality. The id must be controlled in order to satisfy social demands; this sets up a conflict between frustrated wishes and social sanctions. Conceptual structures of ego and superego (the embodiment or moral rules) develop in order to exercise this control and direct the need for gratification into socially acceptable channels.

Gratification centres on different areas of the body at different stages of growth, making the quality of the conflict different at each *psychosexual stage*. The ego comes under pressure from the demands of both id and superego, developing defence mechanisms to deflect otherwise intolerable levels of conflict.

It is important to note two further points about these processes. No individual is perfectly adjusted, but will always have some residual conflict; and all characteristics are traceable back to experiences in the first five years of life, by which time children should have identified with their own sex.

Psychosexual or psychosocial? Most of those who parted company with Freud but remained within the framework of psychoanalysis thought that the need for social integration took precedence over the satisfaction of biological drives. Erikson disagreed with Freud's emphasis on sex as the primary motivating force and outlined growth in terms of *psychosocial* development. He characterised the outcomes of conflicts at eight stages as social qualities such as trust, initiative, identity and altruism. Erikson's view is that development continues throughout life and that bad experiences in childhood can be retrospectively compensated for. The dynamics of personality are more far reaching than Freud's and less deterministic.

Psychodynamic theories differ from learning perspectives by dealing with qualitative aspects of experience rather than understanding behaviour as the acquisition of mechanistic responses. To understand what this means, look at what happens in Erikson's first stage of psychosocial development: the conflict in the first stage is related to 'trust versus mistrust'. The quality of trust developed in a child will reflect the quality of interactions and experiences of the child with significant others.

Trust will acquire some sort of meaning for the child but bad experiences will give it a negative quality, for example that it is unsafe to trust anyone.

In contrast, behaviourists would explain the development of social relationships without reference to the psychological component, and in terms of certain patterns of behaviour being reinforced or punished by external stimuli.

■ Contributions of the psychodynamic approach

This approach has had a strong influence in many different areas of psychology, the most obvious being the study of child development, personality development and the study of atypical behaviour.

■ Practical applications of the psychodynamic approach

Freud's theory contributes to our understanding and gives insights into the underlying forces of motivation by citing the psychosexual origins of, for example:

- hostility to authority (Oedipal conflict)
- fastidious life styles (anal fixation)
- gluttony or alcoholism (oral fixation)

and seeing faults in others when they are really our own (projection).

Freud's work caused children's behaviour and antisocial or criminal acts to be regarded more tolerantly than before. For instance, the stormy interactions of teenagers and parents, seen through the Freudian perspective, become not only normal but also as a necessary stage in achieving independent adult identity. The underlying anxieties and tensions created in all of us, by the inherent and continual conflict between our biological drives and social demands, not only explain why each of us may sometimes explode with anger or behave cruelly towards someone we love, but also suggest how it is that extreme situations can cause depression or neurotic conditions like agoraphobia.

Probably one of the biggest influences psychodynamic theories have had is in the treatment of psychological problems and disorders. This is especially true of the US where psychoanalysis is a popular form of therapy.

■ Evaluation of the psychodynamic approach

Does Freud explain too much? A less positive effect of Freudian theory is the way in which it tends to draw inferences about the meaning of every action, thought or motive. All actions, however trivial, are assigned to a cause arising in the unconscious mind. Causes are located, more specifically, in the two instinctual drives of *eros* (life) and *thanatos* (death). Accidents or slips of the tongue are believed to reveal unconscious wishes, just as dreams disguise the true preoccupations and wishes of the dreamer within a system of symbols.

However, Freudian theory has some attractions. At a general level, Freud brought attention to the importance of childhood, especially the first five years, in determining adult behaviours. Few psychologists today would deny the strong influence of childhood experience. It can also be comforting to think that we can blame our parents for our shortcomings and that responsibility for our actions can be evaded by pleading unconscious motivation! On the other hand, we are less happy to have all our actions and endeavours reduced to psychosexual motives, even though we often like to ascribe such base motives to other people. If we feel, like many neo-Freudians, that Freud overemphasised sexual drive, we can still acknowledge that he was largely responsible for freeing sexuality from its socially unacceptable image. Sexual interests and activity, even in young children, are today more readily accepted.

Is Freudian theory scientific? This depends on the perspective of the critic. Popper rejected its claims to scientific status, as the size and nature of the sample Freud used was too restricted to be representative; his clinical data was unreliable and lacked controls; the concepts are untestable because of the difficulty of designing suitable experiments and they cannot be submitted to 'falsification', that is, the possibility of being proved wrong. There is, Popper (1960) said, *no* evidence that Freud would accept as refutation of his theory. A female patient, who recounted dreams which could not be interpreted as 'wish fulfilment', was unable to provide a challenge to his theory.

Freud's explanation was that the lady's principal wish was to prove him wrong. The atypical dreaming was therefore performing the same function as 'wish fulfilment' and Freud was right all along!

Is the falsification principle necessary to a science? Kubie (1953) argued that scientific knowledge can be obtained by carefully sifting data to eliminate inconsistencies. The adherents of psychoanalysis argue that it does not aim for **nomothetic** (universal) explanations and predictions but examines individual case studies to understand an individual's present state in terms of past experiences. Opponents of psychoanalysis are critical of its claims to give **idiographic** (individual) explanations through using case studies. These case studies are carried out over long periods, but the theoretical perspective is heavily reductionist and deterministic. Psychoanalysis has a disputed success rate. Eysenck (1953) rejected all psychoanalytical claims and believed that a two-year period is usually sufficient for most neuroses to be cured spontaneously.

Is it all 'in the mind'? One of the frustrations when undergoing Freudian analysis is the therapist's reaction to a patient who disputes or rejects a Freudian interpretation of events. Dora, an early patient of Freud, angrily rejected his explanation of her anxiety neurosis and walked out, leaving analysis incomplete. Freud took this as confirmation of his analysis; Dora had simply found the truth unpalatable.

Refusal to accept the patient's account of events at face value may not only be annoying to the patient but also possibly damaging. Freud refused to accept the large number of childhood seduction stories recounted to him by women patients. These, he decided, were fantasies reflecting their unconscious desires and were not real actions by the adult males involved. The concept of infantile sexuality arose from this interpretation, yet Masson (1984) questioned Freud's integrity here. Did Freud suppress the evidence or genuinely believe his interpretation? Today, although incest and sexual abuse of children are accepted as being more common than was previously thought, some women have complained that psychoanalysts have

not only disbelieved their accounts of sexual abuse but have assumed that these 'fantasies' are the source of their 'neurosis'.

Although therapies based solely on psychodynamic principles are still used to treat the underlying causes of childhood problems, depression or disorders like anorexia nervosa, these techniques may form only part of modern treatment programmes, or may not be used at all. Often the greatest value of psychoanalysis to the therapist lies in the concept of the unconscious mind harbouring unresolved conflicts which are obscurely related to observable behaviour. This brings attention to the experiences encountered in childhood, and the impact the internalisation of these events have upon later behaviour. Sexual drives are emphasised less in modern psychodynamic theory. However, the self-destructive drive has much explanatory value when attempting to explain irrational aggression. Whatever our reactions to psychodynamic theories, these approaches have profoundly affected many aspects of life in western cultures.

The behaviourist approach

The main principles underlying the behaviourist approach are those of *association learning*. Learning is defined as a permanent change in behaviour resulting from repeated reinforcement of associations between environmental stimuli and the organism's response.

The predominant method of study adopted by behaviourists are the experiments, many of which have been laboratory based, concerned with the conditioning of animal behaviour. More recent research has shifted to more naturalistic settings, seen most obviously in research related to behavioural therapies involving human participants.

Behaviourists consider that *classical* and *operant conditioning* are the principal forms of learning but it is important to note two points. Firstly, there are several variations of learning theories, put forward by Pavlov, Thorndike, Skinner, Hull, and Tolman.

Secondly, the major exponent of behaviourism, Skinner, rejected the idea of 'theory' and referred consistently to 'principles' instead.

Behaviourists do not look for underlying causes of behaviour such as psychoanalysts might. They assume that antisocial or maladaptive learning can be extinguished and a new set of associations trained in. Genetic influences are largely ignored, although some learning theorists accept biological factors as generalised motivational or potential elements. These can affect the nature of associations made, or the speed with which learning is acquired, for example Hull's drive theory or Eysenck's personality theory.

Behaviourism overlaps with two of the models commonly used by psychologists for research purposes: the human animal model (figure 1.3) and the mechanistic model (figure 1.4). However, it is worth noting that the **mechanistic** model incorporates aspects of cognitive psychology and can cause confusion.

1.3 Comparative psychology and ethology

Comparative psychologists make use of laboratory studies with animals, pioneered by Pavlov, Thorndike, Watson, and Skinner, although based on Darwinian assumptions, concentrate on controlled experiments. Their aim is to isolate the basic units of learning in less sophisticated animals in order to illuminate the processes of learning in humans.

Ethologists criticise this because of the artificiality of laboratory conditons and the restricted range of species used. They say that only by observing an animal's natural responses to normal conditions can we understand the reasons as well as the mechanisms underlying learning. Comparative psychologists distrust the uncontrolled research conditions of ethologists. However, because of the common aim of both approaches, compromises are now often made, for example Tinbergen's introduction of experimental techniques into the natural environment with his studies of herring gulls.

1.4 Modern learning theory and cognitive psychology

The mechanistic view of modern learning theories and the cognitive psychologist's view of humans as computers or information processors overlap. In experimental psychology, it can be quite difficult to see where behaviourism ends and cognitive psychology begins. Often it is simply a matter of complexity. Modern learning theorists go beyond simply using stimulus-response connections and are prepared to concede that intervening variables are involved. However, they tend not to study these variables in themselves, whereas for the cognitive psychologist it is precisely these internal, intellectual or cognitive processes which are paramount in importance.

■ Contributions of the behaviourist approach

Behaviourism has had a strong influence upon many areas of psychology, the most obvious being theories of learning and the understanding and treatment of atypical behaviour. A great strength of these theories is the relative ease with which they can be practically applied and also the vast claims for the success of these applications. Learning occurs through the implicit and explicit use of behaviour modification techniques, some examples of which follow.

In child rearing, or in the classroom, desirable behaviour is reinforced by positive rewards, and undesirable behaviour discouraged either by ignoring it, by punishment or by negative reinforcement.

Programmed learning, pioneered by Skinner, breaks material to be learned into logical, small steps, reinforcing the learner at each stage for correct responses before moving on. Irrelevancies or confusions are thus eliminated as each item is fully mastered before the next is encountered. These principles are also applied to skills learning, especially where muscular coordination is needed, for example the mastery of games such as tennis.

Accident or stroke victims can be encouraged to regain physical functions by using reinforcement schedules and the principles or behaviour *shaping* by successive approximation.

Token economies, the offering or withholding of tokens according to the appropriateness of the behaviour, are often used in institutional environments with mentally and physically handicapped people. Tokens can later be exchanged for some desired reward. This system is helpful in encouraging independence and in the breakdown of institutionalised attitudes. *Time out*, whereby a person is removed from the social group following bad behaviour, is another technique used in institutions. These approaches also claim success with the severely physically handicapped, who previously would have been classified as beyond help.

The foregoing techniques are based on operant conditioning, but classical conditioning is also used in behaviour therapy. Wolpe's technique of *systematic desensitisation* gradually allows a phobic to respond positively to an object of fear, whereas *flooding* continuously presents a feared object or event until the patient's nervous system is fatigued and extinction of the fear occurs. *Aversion therapy* relies on introducing a new, noxious association into a pleasurable, but damaging, association. It is used to combat problems like drug or alcoholism but could, in principle, be used (or misused) to create aversions to almost anything.

■ Evaluation of the behaviourist approach

Although widely used, behavioural techniques may sometimes be overrated or given credit for cures and improvements which may have come about for other reasons. A child who continues bedwetting beyond the age when it would be expected to stop can be given a pad and buzzer. The buzzer rings when the pad becomes damp, the child awakens, goes to the toilet and is subsequently dry. Some children do not respond to this method of conditioning. A Freudian therapist would explain this by saying that bedwetting occurs because of deep-seated problems between mother and child and unless these are identified and resolved, bedwetting will continue. Alternatively, another problem may subsequently arise even if the bedwetting appeared to be cured.

Programmed learning does not lend itself to literature or history, which are not easily broken down into logical sequences. Other subjects, including science, would need a broader approach than programmed learning packages could offer.

It is not clear what is happening during therapies like systematic desensitisation. It is assumed to be a form of retraining. The relaxation which is part of the technique brings about *reciprocal inhibition*, that is, relaxation and anxiety cannot occur simultaneously. However, Weitzman (1980) suggested that what goes on during the quiet periods of relaxation is a profound, internal process closer to a psychodynamic (Freudian) experience. He cited the following statement from a patient with an obsessive fear of his mother's eventual death:

> *'It was as if my feelings about my mother were transformed . . . what I really felt was a fear of my being deserted by her. Now if I think of her dying, I feel sorry for her. For the first time, I feel sorry for her instead of myself.'*

Token economics and 'time out' procedures can be seen as alternative terms for bribes and threats, which many parents use when socialising their children. Ethical reservations aside, such treatments have limited effectiveness, for example how can a naughty child be persuaded to behave well when no bribe is available and no threat a deterrent? A long-term situation may arise where bribes have to be made more attractive or threats have to be made more fearful before the desired behaviour occurs. Sometimes good behaviour may have been trained in before such escalation is necessary, but it may depend on the strength of the forbidden attraction, or on the consistency of the parent to forbid it.

There is also a problem with punishment being used as a behavioural deterrent. For some children, punishment may be the only form of attention they receive, and it may thus act as a positive reinforcer, with children behaving naughtily in order to receive such attention. There is a need to look beyond the child's behaviour and to understand the context in which it occurs.

One anxiety about using behaviour modification concerns its misuse. Skinner was fiercely attacked after publication of *Beyond Freedom and Dignity* (1973) for his failure to consider who would do the programming in his behaviourist 'Utopia'. Aldous Huxley faced this problem in his satire *Brave New World* (1932) depicting a perfectly ordered society where every person was conditioned, or brainwashed, into accepting their place in it. Huxley's 'Savage', who had somehow escaped early conditioning, was almost alone in being able to see the inequality and injustice of this smoothly running structure. The only other people who really understood what was going on were the programmers themselves, who were enjoying all the privileges. Skinner was criticised for putting the regulation of behaviour above any other consideration, not examining the sources of the social order, and having an overdeterministic view of human learning.

While much of our behaviour may be acquired by classical and operant conditioning, by no means all of it is. Behaviourism sees life as rather static and human beings as relatively passive. Creativity, purposefulness and meaningfulness in human life are virtually ignored in an effort to avoid referring to inner processes.

Is there a future for behaviourism? It is easy to belittle the *stimulus-response* (S-R) patterns involved, but behaviourists have gained from avoiding descriptions of the unobservable. By leaving intangible mental processes uncharted, they have been able to link up with research in artificial intelligence and neurophysiology. Learning theory can build on its previous work and extend its explanatory power by reference to brain functions and other processes known to science.

The cognitive approach

Although the cognitive approach was one of the earliest perspectives in psychology, it was virtually eclipsed by behaviourism until after the Second World War. Wundt (1879) investigated the structure of mental processes, but his introspective method was unreliable. Watson's argument was that it was too subjective and that the study of behaviour was the only way to achieve scientific objectivity.

In the 1920s and 1930s, *Gestalt* theorists proposed that the brain operated by organising external stimuli into whole patterns and that these

external stimuli were represented by corresponding patterns within the brain. A great deal of their work focused on visual perception. Although they met similar reactions to their ideas and principles as Wundt had, it is worth noting that links can be made from these studies to later theories. For example, Hubel and Wiesel (1959) discovered that cells in the visual cortex were specialised to respond to specific features of environmental stimuli.

Cognitive psychology has grown in importance since the Second World War, superseding behaviourism as the dominant research area in modern psychology. Two principal reasons lie behind this development. Firstly, there has been increasing dissatisfaction with behaviourist assumptions about learning. Tolman's *cognitive maps* (1946) suggested simple S-R sequences were inadequate to account for all forms of learning: for example, latent learning refers to the ability to register and store information not directly relevant at the time of learning. Also, studies of problem solving and logical thinking strongly suggested some internal processing of information. Secondly, the development of techniques and instruments, especially the computer, encouraged models to be created for the investigation of internal cognitive processes (see figure 1.5).

Modern cognitive psychology is much broader than theories of learning or logical rule following. Contemporary research is predominantly based upon the use of experiments with human participants, which has resulted in the rapid expansion of cognitive-based theories in a number of areas. Eysenck (1984) wrote: 'Anyone attempting to come to grips with the booming, buzzing confusion that is contemporary cognitive psychology is likely to be left with an actual or metaphorical headache.'

Part of the problem of defining cognitive psychology is that much experimentation in areas like attention, perception and memory, language learning, thinking, and intelligence is more accurately described in behaviourist terms. Another difficulty is that cognitive psychologists are divided between those who consider physiological explanations to be unnecessary to their research and others who see the explanation of a process as

1.5 The computer model of intelligence

Two significant factors of computer functioning are logical processing and pattern recognition. Whilst computers may possess functions resembling human thought processes, there are nevertheless doubts as to the adequacy of this model of human intelligence. For example, it is unclear:

- whether humans think in logical sequences all or even most of the time. Wason and Johnson-Laird (1972), investigating logical thinking, suggested that it may not be a very natural process

- whether a computer can, or would ever be able to, understand the meanings behind the logical exercises or the pattern recognition. Could it understand the meanings of the symbols it manipulates or does it simply follow a set of rules logically and predictably? Could it tell the difference between herrings and stones if it were asked to carry out some exercise using these items? Would it know that herrings were food? What could food mean to a computer in any case?

incomplete without including the underlying physiological structures.

Eysenck (1984) described three basic characteristics of modern cognitive psychology (see figure 1.6).

At some point, all cognitive research comes up against the realisation that social and cultural environments can shape or even distort the recognition and interpretation of information. Cognition is susceptible to influences initially separated from its innate mechanisms. Visual illusions and social prejudice are examples of cognitive reactions shaped by social and cultural influences.

Environmental effects are so strong that they have given rise to a belief that all perception is learned. The early nativist versus empiricist debate has changed over the years towards accepting the mutual interaction between innate mechanisms and the environment. Experience is mapped onto the brain or wired into the circuitry, predisposing the individual to make predictable interpretations of external stimuli; a process known as *set*.

The problem of internal processes and their nature is ignored by behaviourists, whereas for the cognitive psychologists these processes are the core of their science. Cognitive psychologists say there must be a representational level (that is, mind) within human beings between information input and behaviour output which cannot be adequately described in terms of brain cells. This means that if introspection is necessary to find out about the ideas, images and schemata used by an individual, cognitive psychologists are back with the problem Wundt faced in his early psychology laboratory of identifying these concepts objectively. Also, Freudian theorists would be critical of the status given to information provided by the so-called rational part of the brain, when unconscious motivation may have more significance. Only the use of models, computers and controlled experiments gives modern cognitive psychology its greater scientific credibility.

1.6 Research in modern cognitive psychology

- Research tends to be laboratory based rather than relating to everyday life. However, there are some signs of broadening into real-life areas, for example eye-witness reliability and dyslexia.
- The focus of research tends to be on specific, rather than on general problems. Experiments are conducted on such items as the articulatory loop (memory) and monocular dominance (perception). This can fragment or bias the body of knowledge, although it can be argued that more information will eventually accrue from this narrowing of research focus.
- Emotional and motivational influences are generally regarded as complicating and confusing experimental findings and, in general, there is an attempt to minimise or eliminate them.

■ Contributions of the cognitive approach

Research in cognitive psychology has been of great value in many practical areas such as study and learning techniques, language development and reading ability, the relevance of imagery to memory, attitude formation and the treatment of depressives.

No discussion of cognitive psychology could ignore Piaget's cognitive developmental theories, which have had tremendous impact on educational methods, particularly in primary schools. In contrast to the behaviourist view of learning as a collection of associations, Piaget's theory emphasises the fundamentally rational nature of human beings and also sees immature reasoning and intellectual functioning as being profoundly different from that of mature adults (see figure 1.7).

Will cognitive psychology ultimately merge with neurobiological approaches? Most cognitive psychologists would resist this at present. They would argue that more understanding of higher intellectual functioning has come from studies of analogue computers with their parallel processing than from what is currently understood from studies of the human brain. Although it may seem absurd to see ourselves as more like a machine than an animal, we need only consider cognitive models like Atkinson and Shiffrin's memory model (1971) to understand how this approach can lead towards a closer picture of the real thing.

■ Evaluation of the cognitive approach

Humans characteristically seek to understand the world, including their own actions. Cognitive psychologists characteristically ask how it is that we understand. Although cognitive psychologists largely ignore motivational and emotional aspects of behaviour, which humanists feel so important, they do not ignore thinking processes, like the behaviourists – or ignore the nature of thinking, like the psychoanalysts. However, perhaps due to the fact that there is no one single important theorist, there is little integration between explanations of, for example, problem solving and emotion.

Another problem arises from explaining human behaviour in terms of computer functioning. Input, storage and retrieval all refer to memory. However, computers do not forget – or ignore information, whereas humans do both. Also, computer errors have external causes while human errors have internal ones. Some believe that the explanatory power of any computer metaphor is ultimately limited as computers are unable to 'think' creatively or innovatively. They are limited to preprogrammed data and instructions and are unable to generate truly unique thoughts, unlike humans.

In spite of these criticisms, research in areas of cognitive psychology has expanded rapidly over recent years and it is not unreasonable to expect an expansion of the explanatory power of theories within the field.

1.7 Developmental approaches

Developmental theories are based on recognising human beings as biological organisms which grow to maturity through various maturational stages. Like biology, this approach accepts that organisms have inbuilt features, not obvious at birth, which will unfold according to pre-set patterns and time scales until maturity is reached. It is also important to note that environmental conditions will affect the growth and final nature of the organisms.

Nature and *nurture*, therefore, both contribute but there is implicit acceptance of an optimum point for growth beyond which organisms decline and die.

Two major developmental theories are those of *Freud* (and neo-Freudians like Erikson), these are psychodynamic theories, and of *Piaget*, his is a cognitive developmental theory. Both are stage based and claim that children are qualitatively different from adults. Freud's theory is centred largely on emotional and social development; personality is shaped by the conflict between basic animal instincts and society's demands and all conscious motivation arises from unconscious sources. Piaget's concern is with intellectual growth which he sees as arising from an interaction between biological growth and environmental stimulation; children progress through various fixed stages as they develop an understanding of the physical and social world. Each stage is characterised by a different set of cognitive strategies which children use to understand and structure information.

The humanistic or phenomenological approach

Humanistic or **phenomenological** perspectives suggest that the world is differently perceived by individuals because of their unique experiences. Most humanistic approaches share this view and differ from Freudian or behaviourist approaches in that they believe human nature to be basically benevolent, rational and altruistic. If humans are basically benevolent, it may be difficult to see how or why problems arise for the individual.

According to Maslow, *self-actualisation* is the ultimate goal of human striving. This state cannot begin to be achieved if more basic needs remain unfulfilled. Maslow's hierarchy of needs is presented like a pyramid, reflecting an increasing awareness of the universe. Lower levels of needs must be satisfied before a person can progress to higher levels of the hierarchy. Besides outlining a generalised baseline of human potential, the humanistic perspective lays down no general laws about individual development. Above all, the humanist accredits the individual with **free will** and the ability to initiate action, or alter circumstances, as opposed to deterministic perspectives which reduce an individual to a largely passive role.

The humanistic perspective is a fresh and optimistic approach which offers individuals some hope of controlling their destiny. However, it also offers the bleak absurdity of the extreme **existentialist** position which insists on the freedom of the individual to make choices no matter what the circumstances. This position was taken by the French philosopher Sartre who went so far as to argue that a concentration camp inmate still had freedom to choose a course of action!

Most people would agree that physical coercion severely restricts freedom to choose or to develop a potential, but the deterministic psychologist is not usually talking about physical coercion. A behaviourist or Freudian believes that an individual is shaped by external or internal forces, while the humanistic psychologist says that the human can become independent of the constraints imposed from outside or from biological drives, although no one suggests this will be easy. Full responsibility for your own life and personality is in your own hands, according to the humanistic perspective.

There is some risk in accepting this view of freedom which involves accepting full responsibility for yourself and your actions, unlike deterministic explanations, which 'let you off the hook' and allow you to blame parents, circumstances or biological pressures for your shortcomings. Fromm (1941) called this the 'fear of freedom'.

Can humanistic psychologists find evidence to support their views? 'Evidence' usually implies the need for objective experimentation. The scientific method, however, is difficult to apply to a non-deterministic approach; experiments are valueless because of interference to an individual's free choice and autonomy. For the humanist, an experimental conclusion would have no more significance than any other account of what had taken place. It would have no predictive value and could not generate general laws or principles.

Commenting upon this, Bannister and Fransella (1986) wrote that many psychologists seem to see others not as persons, but as many objects or mechanisms. At the same time, the psychologists appear to exempt themselves from the causal and deterministic explanations they give of their participants' abilities and activities. How can determined subjects study other people? Consistent with a highly individualistic view of mind and behaviour, the method most commonly adopted by humanist researchers is the case study, emphasising minimal interference from the psychologist. This can be observed most obviously in humanistic approaches to counselling.

▪ Contributions of the humanistic approach

Despite rejecting many traditional research methods, the humanistic paradigm has had considerable impact on practice within social psychology. Controlled experimentation in the laboratory was probably always the most controversial method for investigating social interactions, for reasons of validity and ethical justification.

Many therapeutic systems set up or inspired by humanistic psychology are used today for childhood and family problems and the mentally ill. They are also applied to human relationships within institutions, industry and commercial concerns.

What do group and family therapies offer? One of the hardest consequences for a person seeking help through humanistic psychology is to find that the therapist's role is to encourage you to make your own decisions and be responsible for the changes you make in your life, rather than tell you what to do. The view is that if you need help, it is largely because you have so far failed to take control of your life. Naturally, it is going to be hard if you are this type of person because if this had been possible before the therapy, then therapy would not have been needed.

One humanistic psychologist, Rogers, emphasised that individuals must set their own goals and standards, refusing to follow and fulfil the demands and expectations of others. This is to urge the individual to develop integrity of purpose and a clear sense of identity rather than to encourage a selfish style of life. Only by doing this can we establish real communication with each other and avoid involvement in other people's 'games'. The therapist, in turn, accepts the client as being a person worthy of respect and thus encourages openness and recognition of the emotional defences which prevent full growth. Whether individual or group forms of therapy are used, the principle remains that it is not for the therapist to solve the problems but for the client to gain insights and take control.

Stress is an area of concern to both medical practitioners and psychologists because of the interaction between mental and bodily responses. In the humanistic perspective, stress arises from the way reality is construed. Perhaps the stressful situation calls for anger or more assertion. An overdemanding boss, an unreasonable spouse or friend should be challenged with a view to protecting the basic human rights of the stressed person. Perhaps the stress has arisen from setting an unattainable goal. Understanding personal strengths and limitations will reduce stress because more realistic self-expectations are adopted.

■ Evaluation of the humanistic approach

Is it all in our own hands? Despite much success claimed for these therapeutic methods, flaws remain. Cases have been known where group therapy has adversely affected one of its participants. There is no guarantee that a group's perception of a person is accurate, yet if a majority decides that, for example, a person is behaving aggressively, the judgement may stick, no matter how strongly it is denied, and damage to self-esteem may result.

Although there are good arguments to suppose that the dynamic nature of interactions is the reverse of deterministic explanations, the humanistic approach can sometimes be guilty of overestimating an individual's control over events. For example, a single parent, about to be evicted for non-payment of rent, with nowhere to turn, might be told that the stress experienced is purely a matter of how reality is construed. This is unlikely to relieve the situation!

Like the psychodynamic approach, the humanistic perspective does not interest itself in prediction, but, unlike the psychodynamic approach, an individual is accorded the potential for self-development and complete conscious control of motives and actions.

Conclusions

The aim of this unit so far has been to outline the five main approaches which have dominated the discipline of psychology during the 20th century. These are not the only approaches to have made significant contributions to the study of psychology, and this section could easily be expanded to include both developmental and social psychology. Important developments within social psychology and psychology as a whole have led to the emergence of the **socio-cultural perspective**. This explores the impact of social factors and cultural diversity upon psychological theory and practice, often highlighting the inappropriateness of western psychological theory when applied to other cultures. See figure 1.8 for a summary of this perspective.

The relevance of cultural factors in the development of psychological theory is also explored in Unit 2. It is important to recognise that whilst there may be conflicting views between the different approaches, no single perspective can offer a full explanation of psychological phenomena. There is necessary overlap between different approaches which reflects the richness and complexity of human behaviour.

1.8 The socio-cultural perspective

The socio-cultural perspective questions the focus within psychology upon the study of the individual and explanations of behaviour in terms of biological, cognitive or unconscious drives. It focuses instead upon the way people are affected by the social context, exploring how cultural values and political systems affect everyday experience. All of us tend to underestimate the influence of a particular situations in which we find ourselves. We are like fish that are unaware they live in water, so obvious is water in their lives. Socio-cultural psychologists study the water, and ask how it affects everything that swims in it.

Those who emphasise the 'socio' side of the socio-cultural perspective may explore how standards of masculinity and femininity influence the expression of emotion, or how being in a group affects attitudes and conformist behaviour. They also study how we are affected by other people such as peers, parents, strangers and lovers. They may also study how features of the physical environment (such as our working conditions) affect our behaviour.

Those who emphasise the cultural side of the socio-cultural perspective explore the way in which cultures affect their members. The beliefs, values and rules of a culture affect all aspects of psychological functioning and it is only by understanding the cultural context that meaningful explanations can be generated. For example, people from western cultures that emphasise individualism differ from people in Asian and Latino cultures that emphasise group loyalty and cooperation.

By placing the study of the individual human being in historical, social, situational and cultural context, the socio-cultural perspective has made psychology a more fully representative and scientific endeavour.

Source: Adapted from Tavris and Wade (1995, pp. 23–4).

Activity 1

Draw a table comparing the five main approaches. Use the following headings to structure your information:

Approach	Basic premise	Method	Strengths	Weaknesses
Biological	Behaviour is determined by nervous systems and endocrine system	Controlled experimentation	Made important contributions to explanations of disorders, e.g. autism, dyslexia	Too reductionist; fails to do justice to the complexity of human behaviour

(Suggested answers on page 33.)

Activity 2

Rank the five approaches outlined in Activity 1, in terms of which you think make the most important contribution to furthering our understanding of the human mind and human behaviour. Give reasons for your answer.

(Suggested answer on page 34.)

Activity 3

Below are a number of statements. State which approach each statement is referring to.
a   Behaviour is a response to external stimuli.
b   Behaviour is motivated by the desire to fulfil potential.
c   This approach seeks to generate explanatory models of internal processes such as thinking.

Activity 3 *cont'd*

d   This approach emphasises the importance of childhood experience.
e   Supporting evidence is provided through the use of controlled experimentation.
f   Individuals have the free will to take control of their actions.
g   Genes are the building blocks of behaviour.
h   This approach is criticised for failing to explain emotional aspects of behaviour.
i   The case study is the preferred method of this approach.
j   This approach incorporates both the human animal model and the mechanistic model.

(Suggested answers on page 34.)

Self-assessment questions

1   Certain approaches are criticised for being mechanistic and reductionist.
    a   Explain what the terms 'mechanistic' and 'reductionist' mean.
    b   Which approaches have these labels been applied to?
2   How do the ideas of contemporary psychoanalysts differ from the original ideas of Freud?
3   Cognitive theorists attempt to explain what the behaviourists do not. What is meant by this?
4   Fromm (1941) talked of 'fear of freedom'. What was he referring to?

(Suggested answers on page 34.)

The nature of the person in psychology

The contrasting approaches within psychology offer differing explanations of human behaviour. Underlying many of the approaches are basic philosophical positions concerning the fundamental nature of people as a whole.

This section covers three of these debates. One way of contrasting theories is according to how deterministic they are with their varying positions being set within the debate on free will versus **determinism**. **Reductionism** is another perspective, with behaviour being broken down and understood in terms of its component parts. There is also the nature/nurture debate which continues to weave its way through much psychological theory, past and present. Whilst these three debates are distinct in their own right, there is some common ground between them which will be commented upon where relevant.

Free will and determinism

The philosophical debate about free will and determinism is complex, but for the psychologist the problem can be summarised in the questions: 'Do human beings control their destinies?' and 'To what extent are events inevitable?'

Determinists believe that events and behaviour occur in a causal sequence and a certain set of circumstances can only produce a specific outcome. The physical sciences operate mainly on this basis, but there are objections to explaining human behaviour in this way. Kelly (1955) put the objections like this: 'Behaviour is man's way of changing his circumstances, not proof that he has submitted to them.'

Given that many psychological theories are reductionist and aim to explain behaviour in physical terms, the question arises as to whether we are subject to physical laws and regularities in the same way as natural phenomena. Behaviour is perceived as having come about from conscious, free choice, but is this an illusion?

■ The concept of consciousness

What is *consciousness*? Each psychological approach defines it differently (see figure 1.9).

Whether or not conscious choice is illusory, we *do* have the powerful feeling that we make decisions and act as a result of our own judgements; that if we plan a course of action, we can control what happens and this is not reducible to mechanistic explanations. We are indignant at being told we are merely puppets conditioned by forces outside our control, but there is a reason, apart from our anger, for objecting to the suggestion that human beings are incapable of self-determination.

Westland (1978) expressed it neatly:

'To treat other human beings as mere mechanisms creates a serious logical problem since it follows that the scientist himself is no more than a machine also.'

■ Laws of behaviour

Can laws of behaviour be identified? We can relate to the physical and social environments we live in only because we assume that they operate in generally stable patterns. Positivistic science relies upon the ability to identify these patterns, but the philosophy of science has questioned our ability to know 'facts'. Phenomenology draws attention to the ways in which we select information to suit our

1.9 Psychological interpretations of consciousness

- A reductionist or neurobiological account of consciousness refers to the level of arousal of the nervous system, which can be measured in terms of brain-wave frequencies or responses to external stimuli.
- Freud's psychoanalytical theory ascribes some consciousness to the ego, whose functions are to disguise and partially satisfy the demands of id and superego by devising an apparently rational and socially acceptable form of behaviour. The ego is only partially conscious but operates on the 'reality principle', which means that it is aware of the physical and social worlds.
- Behaviourist approaches dismiss the concept of consciousness, describing it as nothing more than a side-effect of brain functioning.

Philosophically, this is known as **epiphenomenalism**. Skinner, for example, dealt with the problem of thought by explaining it as internalised 'verbal behaviour'.
- Cognitive psychology also considers consciousness as a by-product of brain function but differs from the reductionist view in that this process is believed to influence behaviour directly. Conscious reflection on behaviour interacts with brain mechanisms and thus can control actions. Modern cognitive and humanistic psychology both accredit the human being with voluntary control over decisions and actions, although humanistic psychology does not concern itself with underlying mechanisms.

purposes, relativity and quantum theories have challenged our fundamental assumptions that even natural phenomena work on a regular basis, obeying universal laws. Humanistic psychologists argue that the dynamic, interactional nature of life means that truth is elusive and prediction impossible. These arguments are also applicable to the physical sciences and as a consequence old certainties about fixed causal sequences have been abandoned.

Broadbent (1964) wrote that no two behavioural sequences carried out to achieve the same goal are ever, in fact, identical. He was critical of the 'habit of mind amongst researchers who look for a constant rule of behaviour which will apply to all people . . . on all occasions'.

Do these arguments destroy determinism? Rather than demolishing the determinist viewpoint they suggest that science, including psychology, has often been too sweeping in its generalisations, or too specific about its predictions concerning single events. When an individual acts there is usually a range of possible outcomes. This may be what gives the appearance of free choice, but determinists would insist that whatever 'choice' was made, it could not have been otherwise, given the nature and history of the individual who made it.

Again, although there is a strong belief that events are not random but within an individual's control, other points are worth considering. Firstly, some events are accepted as being beyond an individual's control. Individuals believing that they have unlimited control, either over themselves or other people or events, would probably be regarded as mentally disturbed. Secondly, cultures foster different attitudes in their members. Some Arabic cultures, for example, encourage a highly fatalistic outlook, whereas others, like the North American 'fixer' mentality, strongly believe that they can take control of practically everything that occurs and change circumstances to suit themselves. Rotter (1966) designed a 'locus of control' scale in which subjects select from pairs of statements referred to as 'internals' or 'externals', that is, one statement suggests that people are responsible for their achievements or misfortunes whilst the other suggests that it is luck that is mainly responsible.

Cognitive and humanistic branches of psychology offer more support to our notions of freedom of will than do psychoanalytical and behaviourist theories, which seem to suggest that early learning is either impossible or difficult to shake off. One ascribes all behaviour to unconsciously directed motives; the other ascribes it to automatic reactions to familiar stimuli (see table 1.10, which compares different psychological explanations of motivation). Information processing, as understood by the cognitive psychologist, implies the capacity to change in response to altered situations and to think out logical solutions to problems. Like consciousness, motivation is differently explained within different psychological approaches. Some of these are highly deterministic, seeing the human as motivated 'only by the action of some force either external or internal upon him' (Heather, 1976).

Activity 4

You are asked to recommend a treatment programme for an individual who behaves aggressively. What would you suggest if you were:

a   a biological determinist
b   an environmental determinist
c   a psychic determinist?

(Suggested answers on page 34.)

Is it psychologically important to believe in freedom of will? No one has resolved the argument satisfactorily, but psychologists have noted two important reactions related to a belief in free will. Firstly, people tend to overestimate the degree of control they have over their lives; secondly, stress, and sometimes depressive illness, can follow if people believe they have lost control of their lives.

Seligman (1974) investigated the phenomenon of *learned helplessness* where, in non-human subjects, repeated unpleasant events from which escape was impossible led to the animal becoming dispirited or withdrawn, The apathy displayed by the animal can be likened to that of a depressed person who feels trapped in an unhappy situation or relationship. Wortman and Brehm (1975) claimed that the reaction to helplessness depends on whether an individual expects to have control. More distress is experienced in those

Table 1.10

Approach	Explanation of motivation	Free will or determinism
Biological	A neurobiological approach understands motivation in terms of the physiological needs to maintain a steady internal environment for effective functioning. *Homeostasis* is the mechanism behind drives or purposive behaviour. Hunger, thirst and body temperature are some of the basic homeostatic mechanisms, the principle being that when the body's organs signal a deficit, a person or animal is impelled to seek appropriate items from the environment in order to restore the internal equilibrium. Many experiments have been carried out to try to establish the determining physiological factors involved in this process, for example research into the mechanisms of the brain and digestive organs underlying the regulation of eating (e.g. Friedman and Stricker, 1976). According to ethologists, the main springs of motivation are evolutionary. Courtship and mating, for example, are species-specific rituals determined by hormonal factors but developed through the processes of natural selection.	*Biological determinism:* actions are controlled by internal biological, physiological and genetic mechanisms
Behaviourist	A behaviourist approach suggests that non-homeostatic drives are acquired through *reinforcement*. Learned drives may become so powerful that they can interfere with the operation of homeostatic drives, for example the pleasure of eating may override the mechanism controlling the food intake so that a person may overeat and become obese. Olds and Milner (1954), investigating the mechanisms of reinforcement, identified 'pleasure centres' in the brain. The interesting thing about this discovery is that it runs counter to Hull's (1943) theory that motivation is based on the need to reduce a drive. Olds (1958) noted that rats would press a lever many times per minute in order to stimulate one of these pleasure centres.	*Environmental determinism:* behaviour is controlled by external stimuli which act as reinforcers
Psychoanalytical	Motivation in psychoanalytic terms comes from unconscious drives, mainly the *libido*. The reduction or satisfaction of these drives is restricted by social taboos, the residual energy being sublimated (channelled into some more socially acceptable substitute).	*Psychic determinism:* all actions are controlled by unconscious motives and drives
Humanistic	Humanistic psychologists do not accept that the determinants of human motivation can be inferred from investigation of biological drives in non-human animals. According to Maslow, self-actualisation or the need for self-development is the chief motivational factor. Satisfaction of needs rises hierarchically from biological necessities to fulfilment of individual potential. Personality growth need not proceed smoothly through a set of predetermined stages, or according to a rigid pattern. The essence of humanistic psychology, such as that of Rogers (1959), is that individuals can 'take control of their own lives'.	*Free will:* individuals are free to behave as they choose
Cognitive	This approach, like the humanistic approach, construes motivation as directed by the individual. Heider (1946), for example, suggested that humans are motivated by the desire or need for cognitive consistency; Murray (1938) proposed that motivation arises from the need for achievement. Atkinson (1964) later argued that fear of failure could modify a person's perception of what it is possible to achieve.	*Free will:* individuals make choices based upon rational cognitive processes

Theories of motivation

situations where an individual expects a high degree of control than when outside agencies, whether social or godlike, are seen as the controlling forces.

The apparent contradiction between the sense of free will and the deterministic explanations given by the scientist is often avoided by making the distinction between reasons and causes. What this means is, in effect, that we cause our own behaviour by choosing from a number of alternatives. This indeterministic viewpoint implies that alternative courses of available action exist until a decision to act is made. This decision is made on the basis of free will, but having chosen a particular option, this necessitates a course of action which is determined by the selected end goal. For example, I may choose either to do some homework, go swimming or do some shopping. Which ever option I do choose will then set in motion a course of predictable actions necessary to reach my end goal. This less extreme view of determinism acknowledges the freedom of the individual to make rationally based choices.

Freud, who called himself an 'arch determinist', would have dismissed the substitution of reasons for causes since he believed our 'reasons' to be

rationalisations made by the ego to enable the id to satisfy, at least partially, its socially unacceptable aims.

However, going back to the notion of rational choice, Heather (1976) referred to the philosophical device of describing humans as 'rule-following animals'. What this means is that regularities in human behaviour are governed by rules which are socially designed and therefore flexible. A response is predictable but by no means inevitable and a variety of responses can be equally 'lawful'. A mundane conversational gambit like 'Nice day, isn't it?' could produce a range of responses. 'Yes', or 'No, I don't think so', are very predictable but 'It's all right if you can stand the heat', or 'Pity it wasn't like this when we had the barbecue' are perfectly reasonable. Responses such as 'I'm going to plant some potatoes' or even 'Trust you to ignore the real problem' would be difficult or impossible to predict. This approach, known as **soft determinism**, offers a way out of the logical difficulty mentioned by Westland (1978) (see page 21). It accepts that lawful sequences of behaviour do occur, but in recognising that prediction is limited, it gives freedom and even creativity to human actions.

Self-assessment questions

5   How does the concept of consciousness relate to the debate about free will and determinism?

6   Define what is meant by: (a) psychic determinism; (b) biological determinism; (c) environmental determinism.

7   What are the dangers of believing in free will?

8   What is 'soft determinism'?

(Suggested answers on page 34.)

Reductionism

You are invited to dine at an elegant restaurant. You select a delicious meal and enjoy some wine with it. The company is good and you realise at the end of the evening that you have fallen in love. You would probably consider that you had just had a

rather special experience, one that you would remember for years to come.

How would you react to the following alternative account of this experience? The equilibrium of your nervous system has been restored by the food and drink, although you took rather an elaborate way to satisfy these homeostatic drives. Your sensory appreciation of the food was heightened by the anticipation and consumption of specially prepared dishes and you were fulfilling your affiliation needs by eating in company. The heightened sensory state contributed to a general high level of arousal of central and autonomic nervous systems and, with hormones coursing round your blood stream, and your heart rate noticeably above normal, your intentions towards your companion become rationalised into a socially acceptable framework.

This account is not meant to be taken too seriously but two points can be made. Firstly, what you think or say you were doing can be explained more simply in terms of the underlying biological mechanisms. Secondly, reducing your activity and your sensations to these simpler components appears to take away the quality and significance of your experience.

Reductionism is a mode of explanation which implies that the apparent complexity of your behaviour and motives can be simplified by describing their basic units. However, as with deterministic accounts, we feel belittled and cheated out of what seems to be a much richer and more meaningful experience. The powerful feeling of consciousness that gives the impression of an ability to plan and choose what we do also gives us the conviction that our experiences have meaning and personal significance. We feel we have purposes, hopes and intentions independent of the mechanisms which operate our bodies.

Reductionism works by analysing and explaining complex activity in terms of drives and the nervous system or species-specific patterns related to survival. It regards individuality, like consciousness, as something of an illusion; individual variation is reduced to a position within a normal range of performance.

Not all psychological theories are reductionist but let us look now at five types of reductionism within some psychological perspectives.

Homeostatic mechanisms versus personal accounts

If asked to explain something we are doing, we usually answer without referring to the state of our nervous system. Physiological psychologists identify the driving mechanisms of behaviour in terms of the physical systems of brain and body. They sometimes claim that the whole causal pattern can be explained without reference to a personal account of behaviour. The laws of parsimony, often referred to as Occam's Razor, are frequently invoked as justification of reductionist explanations of this kind. Occam was a medieval monk who first put forward the principles of economy of explanation in science. If a homeostatic mechanism can sufficiently explain why a piece of behaviour occurred, then why complicate the issue with additional details given by the subject?

Reductionism and mental illness

The *medical model* of mental illness could be said to be a form of reductionist explanation. This suggests that physical illness may be caused by bacteria, viruses or malfunction of bodily mechanisms. Likewise, mental disorders like manic depression or schizophrenia can be understood as conditions caused by genetic factors or a neurochemical imbalance. The quickest way, therefore, to persuade manics that they lack superhuman powers or to convince schizophrenics that they are not controlled by forces from another planet is to administer a drug that will restore the chemical imbalance to normal.

Phylogeny and reductionism

Sociobiology derives from an ethological perspective and purports to explain societies in evolutionary terms. Wilson (1976) expounded this view and Morris has popularised it through his books *The Naked Ape* (1967) and *Manwatching* (1978). Hierarchical systems, such as caste or class, are explained by reference to dominance systems observable in animal species; male and female social roles are understood as extensions of their biological roles. At the same time as their popularity, sociobiological explanations evoke tremendous hostility from political and philosophical groups which argue that social structures are as likely to come from social and political sources as they are to arise from biological origins.

Behaviourism and reductionism

Behaviourist theories deriving from Pavlov, Hull and Skinner reduce learning to basic units and universal laws. Whatever can be learned is understood as the result of a systematic association between stimuli and responses, even where differences between species limit the range of learning, so that dogs, for example, are not able to learn to write. Modern learning theories extend the range of mechanisms involved either by linking up with computer models or with the neurobiologist's study of the physiological bases of learning. Either way, the approach remains reductionist because the learner remains no more than a collection and combination of all past conditioning or programming, but the mind itself is simply explained away.

Reductionism and Freudian theory

Although Freud's case study method necessarily involved careful consideration of an individual's unique experience, especially in childhood, the subjective meaning of these events is always reinterpreted in terms of universal laws and the processes of psychoanalytical theory. Dream interpretation illustrates this well, where the 'manifest' (actual) content is translated into the 'latent' (symbolic) content in order to reveal the true meaning of the dream. Psychoanalysts do not attempt to interpret the symbols independently of the dreamer's life and circumstances but, nevertheless, the rich variety of images produced by the dreamer's own brain is reduced to universal biological preoccupations.

Evaluation of reductionism

Although we tend to feel indignant about having the meaning of our actions changed into something which removes their significance, it can be comforting to have some of our less edifying behaviour explained as a conditioned reflex, a malfunction of our nervous system or a deep-seated, but universally experienced, unconscious drive. It removes the responsibility from us, which is useful if we are not proud of what we have done. However, whether we like it or not, the question remains: 'Can reductionism adequately explain behaviour?'

Activity 5

Imagine you are cycling to have tea with a friend whose company you always enjoy. The sun is shining, the view at the top of a hill is breathtaking and you pause for a while to enjoy it. How can you describe your feelings in terms of muscular and nervous activity? In what other ways could you describe your feelings? (Now read on.)

(Suggested answer on page 34.)

Were your feelings adequately described in terms of muscular activity, neural connections in the brain and arousal mechanisms in the autonomic nervous system? These reactions all happen and it is arguable that without them you would experience no emotions at all. Yet if you want to convey your inner experience in all its intensity, it is not enough to describe it in units of physiological reactions or associative learning. Cognitive explanations are also necessary but would need to be elaborated by social or cultural factors and your own individual interpretation would provide the final reference.

Rose's concept of a *hierarchy of levels* (1976) best expresses the argument here. Reductionist accounts need not be rejected provided they are used appropriately. Philosophical discussions about the nature of explanation often take the dining table as an example. The physicist and chemist may describe the table in terms of atoms and molecules. The artist might depict it in terms of shape, colour or its relation to other objects in an arrangement for painting. Most of us would understand it in terms of its function and some of us might regard it affectionately as the one we used to turn upside-down and use as an imaginary boat. Depending on the purpose for describing the table, any one of these levels might be adequate. Looked at in this way, reductionism may be seen as having a part to play, but it is an incomplete explanation in itself (see figure 1.11).

Reductionism resembles determinism in that it questions the voluntary nature of human behaviour. The consequence of attributing sources or behaviour to underlying organic causes is that intellect (or consciousness) cannot be seen as independent of homeostatic processes or past conditioning. For example, the conscious thoughts of a schizophrenic may be delusions reflecting some physiological malfunction. However, once all the reasons, thoughts and intentions expressed by a schizophrenic are dismissed as symptoms of the illness, there is a danger that essential information or truths may be lost or ignored. As a psychological explanation, reductionism cannot stand alone.

1.11 Levels of explanation in emotion

Psychological explanations of emotion recognise three components: the physiological, the behavioural and the subjective experience. The James-Lange theory argues that subjective experience is inferred from physiological and behavioural reactions (we have run away from a bear and are now in a high state of physiological arousal, therefore we must be afraid). One problem here is how we know that it is fear we feel, rather than anger or pleasant excitement. Ax (1953) attempted to identify specific physiological differences underlying different emotions and suggested that adrenaline was associated with fear and noradrenaline with anger.

Schachter and Singer (1964) found that injections of adrenaline did not produce subjective feelings of emotion unless the environmental situation was manipulated to offer an explanation for the agitation. Conversely, research has shown that subjects experience emotional reactions even though the connections between viscera (internal organs) and brain have been severed (Dana, 1921; Cannon, 1927).

In our present state of knowledge, it seems that cognitive processes are necessary to enable us to define a generalised, undifferentiated state of arousal. If, however, specific neurochemical bases for different emotions should be identified in future research, the role of cognitive processes could be seen as that of trigger rather than interpreter. Izard (1977) took this view and argued that autonomic arousal is a consequence rather than a determinant of emotion. Cognitive or intellectual reactions are faster than visceral changes, and milder emotions may not stir the internal environment very deeply.

It seems that cognitive and physiological factors interact to reproduce emotional experience. Individual motivation or personality complete the description. It is useful to remind ourselves here of the *Gestalt* view that the 'whole is greater than the sum of its parts'.

Self-assessment questions

9 Why is the medical model of mental illness reductionist?

10 When might reductionist explanations be useful to us?

11 Explain the concept of 'hierarchy of levels' and the implications of this for reductionist explanations.

(Suggested answers on page 35.)

Nature versus nurture

Variously known as the '**nativist** versus **empiricist**' or the 'innate versus learning' debate, nature/nurture is one of the most persistent controversies in psychology. It has changed its focus over the years but it will not go away. Simply stated, the problem is this: given that physical characteristics are biologically determined by the genetic structure of an organism, is it probable that personality, individual abilities and even day-to-day behavioural patterns are also inherited?

The difficulty is that much of our behaviour is clearly acquired through learning. If this was not the case, humans would have rigid behaviour patterns like those of primitive species. Recognition that learning is central to human behaviour, coupled with the disrepute brought to the concept of 'instinct' by McDougall (1908), who claimed that 18 instincts could explain all behaviour, led in one direction towards nurture. On the other hand, recognition that biological organisms develop and change as they mature, led in the other direction towards nature. Behaviourism, which dominated psychology from the early 20th century until the 1950s rejected the concept of innate patterns of behaviour and largely discounted the impact of biological factors on learning. By virtually excluding genetic differences, this approach, pioneered by Watson (1904), suggests that we all start from more or less the same base point. The kind of person we become and the types and levels of ability we acquire will depend entirely on what happens to us and the way we are brought up or taught.

■ The nativist approach

Both developmental and ethological approaches stress the importance of nature in determining behaviour. Since inherited characteristics largely determine our constitution and physical appearance, it seems reasonable to suppose we also inherit our parents' abilities, talents, limitations and temperaments. All these genetic bases will determine our responses to environmental experiences ensuring that we will mature into the kind of adult our genes dictate.

Activity 6

Study figure 1.12. How do we know that the answer to the first question is 'no' and why do we remain unsure how to answer the second question? (Read on.)

(Suggested answer on page 34.)

Part of the explanation is that the mechanisms underlying the growth of the beard are known. We can point to the universality of the male experience

1.12 Learning or maturation?

1   A boy of three does not have a beard. When the boy reaches puberty and a beard starts to grow, he has already spent many years learning or observing that men grow beards. Has he therefore learned to grow one himself?

2   A girl of four has a musical family but she cannot yet play the piano. By the age of 16, she can play more competently than her brother or sister, both of whom are older. Did she have an innate talent for piano playing?

of growing a beard, and demonstrate that one would grow even if the boy had never seen one on anyone else. In the second case, these explanations do not apply. The girl had to be introduced to piano-playing in order to be able to play at all, but why does she play so much better than her older brother or sister, who may have practised just as hard? This is where an argument might develop between nativists and empiricists, and in our current state of knowledge, this debate cannot be settled. A piano is neither a natural object that we know automatically how to play nor could we learn to play it without inheriting flexible fingers, a brain to control them and an understanding of musical techniques. Therefore, it is evident that both innate and learned factors are involved, although we do not know the proportions of each. Such evidence has been explored in research into topics such as the development of visual perception, the determinants of intelligence, language acquisition, the origins of personality, the causes of mental illness and the nature of human nature.

Some of these areas have become slanted towards one side of the nativist versus empiricist argument. For example, language is more commonly accepted today as a largely innate, programmed ability, even though perhaps not in as detailed a way as Chomsky suggested with his concept of a language acquisition device. Other areas, such as the origin of male and female abilities, fluctuate between the nativist and the empiricist approach in response to the latest research and perhaps the latest popular trends (figure 1.13).

Whatever the emphasis, it is vital to remember that no behaviour can be either all innate or all learned. Several types of evidence show this. The *genotype* consists of two genes governing each characteristic (one gene from each parent). Its effect can only be seen when it is manifested during development in what we call the *phenotype* (for example to display blue eyes or brown eyes).

Some genes (dominant) mask the effect of others (recessive), so the phenotype cannot always show us what the genotype is like. We can tell the genotype of a brown-eyed child with one blue-eyed parent, but brown-eyed people may have a mixture of dominant and recessive genes for eye colour, or dominant ones only.

Rothenbühler (1964), who cross-bred 'hygienic' and 'non-hygienic' bees, revealed that external patterns of behaviour do not necessarily show the presence of a gene, especially if its effect is suppressed by groupings of genes (figure 1.14).

■ The empiricist approach

Work by Riesen (1953), who reared chimpanzees in the dark to investigate the effects of learning on perceptual ability, found that the environment, in the form of light falling on the retina, was fundamental to the development of visual ability. Later work by Hubel and Wiesel (1959) and Blakemore (1969) showed that although specific neural receptors may be present at birth, their functioning depends upon the correct environmental stimulation within a critical period of time. Without this, they will be to all intents and purposes non-existent. Hubel and Wiesel (1963) demonstrated that if one eye of a kitten is kept covered after the other eye has opened around the first two weeks of life, neural connections between retina and visual cortex are developed at the expense of the covered eye. Monocular deprivation (one eye covered) was shown to have more drastic effects than binocular deprivation (both eyes covered). The earlier the deprivation, the more serious the effects, although Kratz *et al.* (1976) demonstrated that the covered eye can still function, but only if the eye which was allowed to develop normally is removed. Blakemore (1969) had also demonstrated with kittens reared in an environment of vertical lines that receptors specialised for responding to horizontal stimuli failed to develop, making the kittens functionally blind for these stimuli.

1.13 Gender differences: nature or nurture?

Why do women seldom if ever become grand chess masters, although they play the game? Women's tennis is separated from men's tennis on the grounds of physical strength – but this could not apply to chess. Also, why, when women's musicianship is equal to men's in terms of playing musical instruments, are there so few women composers?

It has been relatively easy to suggest social and cultural reasons to explain, for example, the small number of women engineers. Traditional ideas of social roles also deterred men from entering the nursing profession.

However, research into variations between male and female spatial and verbal abilities seems to indicate strongly that there are innate differences. What exactly those innate factors are is less clear. Waber (1976) suggested that the slower maturation rate of the male brain delays lateralisation, thus allowing greater development of the right hemisphere which governs spatial ability. This indicates that the genetic effect is to confer a slower maturation rate rather than a superior spatial ability in itself.

Kolb and Whishaw (1985) pointed out that there are six explanations commonly advanced to account for sex differences: differential brain organisation; hormonal effects on brain function; genetic sex linkage; maturation rate; environment; and preferred cognitive mode.

It is also important to recognise that this evidence is correlational (cause and effect cannot be established) and has to take account of the fact that learning and practice can cancel out genetic advantage.

1.14 Hygienic and non-hygienic bees

'Hygienic bees' are so called because they uncap and clear out cells in which larvae have died. Those colonies of bees which did not engage in this practice were thought to have a specific gene deficiency. When Rothenbühler crossed hygienic and non-hygienic bees, he discovered that the hybrids were all unhygienic, suggesting the effect of a single gene. When he cross-bred the hybrids with hygienic colonies, he discovered that there were in fact two types of hygienic gene: one for uncapping and one for clearing out. Both of these were recessive and were only able to release the hygienic activity if paired with another recessive gene.

Evidence from cross-cultural studies reveals a wide range of human behaviour reflecting the powerful influence of the different learning environments of different cultures. On the other hand, studies of monozygotic (MZ) twins, whose genotypes are identical because they developed from a single fertilised egg, have tended to favour innate factors. Correlations in intelligence quotients (IQ), talents and mental illness have been recorded in MZ twins who have been brought up in different environments. However, a correlation is insufficient to explain the source of the similarity and the validity of twin studies is often questioned, particularly because of difficulty in tracing a large enough number of MZ twins reared in sufficiently differing backgrounds. Also, concordance rates between MZ twins reared either together or apart are never 100 per cent, which means that genes alone cannot give us the full picture.

If it is so difficult to distinguish environmental and genetic effects, why do we try? One reason why nature/nurture arguments become polarised is fear of the social consequences. Some psychologists question the motivation behind efforts to measure the relative effects of nature and nurture. Wahlsten (1990) believed that 'the only practical application of the heritability coefficient is to predict the results of a programme of selective breeding' (cited in Nelkin and Lindee, 1995). The concept of inherited intelligence is an example of the controversial consequences of 'nature/ nurture' research. When children's IQs were believed to reflect inherited potential, the education and subsequently the occupational and social opportunities of children with low IQs were restricted. Slow learning children were considered impossible to help and scarce resources were considered better spent on innately bright children. It is hard to realise that before this, delinquent or difficult children were regarded as inherently wicked and the phrase 'bad blood' was taken literally. Injustices such as these led to stressing the role of the environment. On the other hand, it is possible to go to the other extreme and create injustice by insisting that the environment is wholly responsible for behaviour, ability or characteristics.

After all, we do not blame parents for short-sightedness in children. We accept that this may be a genetic condition and prescribe artificial lenses to correct the defect. Work on learning difficulties is not helped by refusing to take account of possible genetic origins. Nor is it helped by assuming that, because we have been unable to identify specific physiological factors, the problems must arise from, for example, a parent's failure to give the right kind of loving care. A child with learning problems may also have emotional problems, but these may be the *effects* of the cognitive difficulty rather than the cause. Here again, a physiological condition giving rise to learning difficulties can have a genetic source, for example Down's Syndrome, or be the outcome of exposure to a poisonous environment, for example lead-polluted atmospheres, which are known to be linked to mental retardation.

It is virtually impossible to disentangle the proportions of inborn and acquired factors contributing to individual personalities. At present, we are also unable to specify the mechanisms underlying many aspects of human life and personality.

Psychologists could be said to have a dual aim in continuing to pursue questions related to the nature/nurture debate. Firstly, they could aim to identify, wherever possible, the mechanisms – both innate and environmental – which go towards optimum development. Secondly, they could attempt to ensure that knowledge is used to benefit individuals, not to restrict their growth or life opportunities. This second point raises the question of the accountability of psychologists, and those from other research disciplines, for the consequences and applications of their research. This will become an ever more important question as research into the heritability of psychological traits increases in range and scope.

Conclusions

Issues relating to free will and determinism, reductionism, and nature/nurture have permeated the whole history of psychology.

Most psychologists today would avoid adopting extreme positions in acknowledgement of the sheer variety and complexity of human thought and behaviour which renders extreme positions too simplistic. This has resulted in positions such as soft determinism and acceptance of the role of both genes and environment in the determination of behaviour. Thankfully there is still certainly enough scope for differing positions to be adopted, illustrated by the five different approaches explored in the first part of this unit. This variety will help to ensure the continued role of rigorous debate within psychology, essential for the progression of psychological theory and practice.

Self-assessment questions

12 Give examples of the psychological attributes and behaviours to which the nature/nurture debate has been applied.

13 What is the main difficulty faced in the nature/nurture debate?

14 What are the possible advantages and disadvantages associated with establishing the effects of nature or nurture?

(Suggested answers on page 35.)

Unit summary

- Psychology is characterised by a variety of *different approaches*, each emphasising different factors in their explanations of mind and behaviour. There are five main approaches: biological, psychodynamic, behaviourist, cognitive and humanist.
- *Biological approaches* include sociobiology, comparative psychology and neurobiological explanations. *Sociobiology* explains behaviour in evolutionary terms, the ultimate aim being the survival of one's gene pool. It has been criticised for being eurocentric and for justifying inequalities as 'natural'.
- *Comparative psychology* is the study of animal behaviour in naturalistic settings forming the basis of explanations of similar patterns of human behaviour.

- The *neurobiological approach* explores the role of the nervous system and the endocrine system in the determination of behaviour. Despite being criticised as reductionist, this approach has made important contributions to our understanding of many behaviours and disorders.
- The *psychoanalytical approach* explains behaviour in terms of unconscious drives and the dynamics of the id, ego and superego. For Freud, sex was the central motivating force, although subsequent psychoanalysts preferred to emphasise the importance of social factors.
- Popular in the US, *psychoanalysis* highlights the importance of childhood experience and this provides the basis for explanations and treatment of psychological problems and atypical behaviours.

Summary cont'd.

- *Behaviourism* explains behaviour in terms of stimulus-response relations brought about through the reinforcement of associations between an organism and its environment. Although criticised as mechanistic, reductionist and too simplistic, the principles of behaviourism have been applied to great effect in a variety of settings.
- *Cognitive psychologists* focus upon the role of mental processes in activities such as learning and visual perception. Through the use of controlled experiments, explanatory models are proposed representing cognitive activities.
- *Cognitive theories* have been applied widely, for example to aid memory and learning or to the treatment of people with depression. Cognitive explanations are criticised for being too mechanistic, failing to account for things such as emotional behaviour or creativity.
- The *humanist approach* focuses upon an individual's experiences and free will in determining actions. People are rational, benevolent, altruistic beings whose purpose is to fulfill a potential.
- *Humanistic psychology* has made significant contributions to therapy, where the emphasis is on the individual taking responsibility for decisions and initiating change. Critics argue that often individuals do not have the control humanists assume they have, and that this approach fails to acknowledge constraining external factors.
- Underlying the different approaches in psychology are ideas about the *fundamental nature of the person*. These ideas include debates about free will and determinism, reductionism and nature/nurture.
- *Determinists* believe behaviour occurs in a causal sequence subject to physical laws and regularities as in the natural sciences. The influence of consciousness on behaviour is negated.
- Approaches to psychology considered deterministic include psychoanalysis, (psychic-determinism), biological approach (biological determinism) and behaviourism (environmental determinism).
- The perspective of *free will* suggests that we have the freedom to choose our own destiny, with individuals having ultimate control over their thoughts and actions. Humanist and cognitive theories advocate the notion of free will.
- *Soft determinism* is a less extreme position which accepts that there may be lawful sequences of behaviour, although people may choose what those behaviours are, making predictions difficult.
- *Reductionism* refers to the explanation of behaviour in terms of its simplest component parts, usually in terms of biological drives and the nervous system. Examples of reductionism in psychology include the medical model of mental illness, behaviourism and Freudian theory.
- The *nature/nurture debate* has persisted throughout the history of psychology in relation to attributes such as intelligence, visual perception and language. This debate is complicated as often both innate and learned factors are involved in behaviour.
- The persistence of the nature/nurture debate is questioned by some. Establishing that a behaviour is 'natural' serves only to justify social inequalities. Alternatively, it would not be beneficial to ignore the effect of genetic factors where it is obvious that they have an impact upon behaviour.

Terms to define

determinism
empiricist
epiphenomenalism
eurocentric
existentialist
free will
idiographic

mechanistic
nativist
nomothetic
phenomenological
reductionism
socio-cultural perspective
soft determinism

Further reading

Eysenck, M W (1994) *Perspectives on Psychology,* Laurence Erlbaum, Hove.

A very accessible overview of the different approaches and major issues, with an interesting account of the historical roots of psychology.

Malum, T, Birch, A and Wadeley, A (1992) *Perspectives in Psychology,* Macmillan, London.

An accessible and enjoyable review of the different perspectives in psychology.

Answers

▓ Suggested answers to activities

1

Examples of information to include in table:

Behaviourist approach
Basic permise: behaviour is a learned response to external stimuli.
Method: controlled experimentation, often using animals
Strengths: successfully applied in a range of settings in order to modify behaviour.
Weaknesses: cannot explain all behaviours such as creativity; also criticised for being reductionist and mechanistic.

Psychodynamic approach
Basic premise: behaviour is the result of subconscious forces moulded through childhood experience.
Method: clinical case study.
Strengths: strongly influenced ideas about personality development and has informed treatments of those with personality problems; highlighted the role of childhood experience in shaping the adult.
Weaknesses: many concepts remain untestable; it lacks in empirical support.

Cognitive approach
Basic premise: understanding the internal processes of the mind (such as decision making, memory and attention processes); is crucial in understanding behaviour.
Method: controlled experimentation.
Strengths: offers explanations of unobservable thought in processes which guide our actions; has been successfully applied to the treatment of depression.
Weaknesses: cannot explain emotional aspects of behaviour; presents a mechanistic view of behaviour.

Humanistic approach
Basic premise: people have the free will to determine their own actions and strive to fulfil their potential(s).
Method: case study.
Strengths: accredits the individual with the potential for self-development and attempts to facilitate this in counselling situations.
Weaknesses: can overestimate the degree of control an individual has over situations.

2

There are no right or wrong answers to this question, just personal preferences. The aim is to get you to think about the kind of psychology which you are most interested in and also to appreciate that no single approach can adequately explain all aspects of behaviour.

3
a   behaviourism
b   humanistic
c   cognitive
d   psychoanalytical
e   behaviourism, cognitive and psychobiology
f   humanistic
g   biological approaches (sociobiology)
h   cognitive
i   humanistic and psychoanalytical
j   behaviourism

4
a   A biological determinist would focus on altering the biology of the individual through the use of, for example, drugs, electric shock treatment (or psychosurgery!).
b   An environmental determinist would seek to change the environment of the individual to one which would not trigger aggression or to one in which aggression would not be tolerated, perhaps through the use of reinforcement.
c   A psychic determinist would seek to access the unconscious meaning behind the aggressive behaviour using psychotherapy.

5

The issues related to this activity are discussed in the text following the activity. The aim is to get across the understanding that it is possible to have explanations at a variety of levels and that a reductionist explanation alone would provide an inadequate representation of an experience.

6

The issues emerging from this activity are discussed in the text following the activity. The aim is to gain an appreciation of the difficulties in attempting to assess the relative influence of both innate and environmental factors.

■ Suggested answers to self-assessment questions

1
a   *Mechanistic:* explains behaviour in mechanical terms, failing to do justice to the complexity of behaviour (such as the influence of emotions and personal desires).

Reductionist: breaks down behaviour into its separate component parts. This offers only simplistic explanations of behaviour and does not help us understand the whole person.
b   Both labels have been applied to neurobiological psychology, behaviourism and cognitive psychology.

2

Contemporary psychoanalysts do not put as much emphasis upon the role of sexual drives in the development of the person. Erikson, for example, places more emphasis upon psychosocial development.

3

Behaviourists focus upon stimulus-response relationships and are not interested in the thought processes which may go on in between. In contrast, cognitive theorists focus upon the internal thought processes and how these influence our behaviour.

4

'Fear of freedom' (Fromm, 1941) refers to a reluctance to accept full responsibility for one's life and to take control of events. Security is found in denying the self that freedom by putting the responsibility elsewhere, for example by blaming parents, circumstances or biological pressures.

5

The concept of consciousness is important as the degree of consciousness relates to the degree of choice one is seen to have. So, if someone is said to have made 'a conscious decision', this suggests he or she has actively chosen a particular option. Alternatively, consciousness may be dismissed as simply a by-product of other processes.

6
a   Actions are controlled by unconscious motives and drives.
b   Actions are controlled by internal biological, physiological and genetic mechanisms.
c   Actions are controlled by external stimuli which act as reinforcers.

7

The potential dangers of accepting that individuals have free will is that people tend to overestimate the degree of control they have over their lives, and that a feeling of loss of control may cause stress and/or result in depression.

8

Soft determinism is a less extreme form of determinism which accepts that there may be lawful sequences to behaviour although people have the freedom to choose what those behaviours are, thus making prediction difficult.

9

The medical model of mental illness is described as reductionist because it explains mental illnesses in terms of basic biological mechanisms such as neurochemical or genetic factors.

10

Reductionist explanations might be useful in situations where we do not want to accept responsibility for certain behaviour, explaining it instead as a conditioned reflex, as a malfunction of the nervous system or as a deep-seated but universally experienced unconscious drive.

11

This acknowledges that a phenomenon/event/action can be interpreted at a variety of different levels. A reductionist account may represent one of those levels, although it would be an incomplete explanation by itself.

12

The nature/nurture debate has been applied to the study of intelligence, personality, language, gender differences (for example child-rearing practices), visual perception; mental illness.

13

The main difficulty with the nature/nurture debate is that for most behaviours and psychological attributes, both environmental and innate factors will play a part. It is very difficult to assess the relative influence of each of these, or determine possible interactions between biology and environment.

14

The advantages of the nature/nurture debate lie in pinpointing the mechanisms responsible for producing particular behaviours. This reveals the potential for beneficial change or adaptation of behaviours, as well as the form (i.e. whether it is environmental or biological) any desired interentions may take.
The disadvantages lie in the justification of inequalities as 'natural' and in potentially endorsing the practice of genetic engineering.

Unit 2

Controversies in Psychology

Sara Nadin

This unit covers:

Controversial applications of research

Scientific status of psychology

Biases in psychological theory and practice

By the end of this unit, you should be able to:

- understand the psychology underlying persuasive tactics used in advertising, propaganda and warfare

- recognise the controversies surrounding the use of psychometric tests

- discuss arguments surrounding the scientific status of psychology

- show, with examples, some of the gender and cultural biases in psychological research.

Unit 2   Contents

Introduction

It would be useful to begin this unit by thinking about the following questions:

- What is psychology?
- Does it serve a purpose?
- Who, if anyone, benefits?

Activity 1

Write a short paragraph summarising your answer to the above questions. (Now read on.)

Your answer may have been something like the following paragraph:

> Psychology is presented as a way of understanding the human mind and behaviour. Such understanding serves to illuminate what it is to be human and should be harnessed to the benefit of all. Through the conduct of unbiased, scientific research the body of knowledge we have come to know as psychology gets richer, increasing the potential advantage of such knowledge.

The aim of this unit is to dispel this somewhat idealistic picture, questioning many hidden assumptions implicit within psychological research and practice.

In the first section on tactics of persuasion, we explore how psychological principles can and have been used in an exploitative manner in order to manipulate behaviour. The psychological principles of persuasion have been applied in the fields of advertising, usually with the aim of getting us to buy particular products. An extension of such practices is seen in the use of propaganda which aims to convince us of the merits of a particular view, regardless of the actual factual basis of those views. These practices then serve to justify actions which would otherwise be considered unacceptable. An extreme form of such manipulative tactics is seen in the context of warfare, with serious consequences for those involved. This section concludes with a look at **cults**, another contemporary example which

illustrates just how effective persuasive techniques can be.

The next section explores the controversial debate over the scientific status of psychology. Whilst much theory and research has progressed along the model of the natural sciences, we explore at what cost, questioning the appropriateness of the model of science used and the motives of those attempting to emulate this model.

The final section aims to bring to the fore some of the hidden assumptions upon which much of psychology is based. The white, middle-class, western male is taken as the representative unit of analysis across much of psychology. The result is a psychology which implicitly devalues the psychological reality of those who do not fall into this category. The impact of this is explored in relation to women and non-western cultures serving to highlight the dangers of such biases.

Whilst this may all sound like a very negative attack upon psychology as a whole, it is only by being aware of these issues and actively exploring them that psychology can progress. Pretending that such controversies do not exist will ultimately result in a psychology which is of limited relevance and more readily open to abuse. As psychologists, we must take responsibility if we aspire to a psychology which is representative, unbiased and to be used for the benefit of all.

Controversial applications of research

Tactics of persuasion

Psychology has done much to contribute to our understanding of persuasion (for example the field of attitude change). The aim of this section is not to reiterate that wealth of theory and research but to explore how these findings and theories have both informed persuasive practices and helped us to understand them.

Some may question the aims of psychology in attempting to explain different persuasive techniques, arguing that such research is only valuable to those who wish to abuse that knowledge. However, it is only by increasing awareness of the different techniques of persuasion that people can recognise them and actively seek to minimise their influence.

In our high-tech world of mass communication we are constantly bombarded with messages and information, much of which attempts to persuade us in one way or another. As control over the massive machinery of the mass media increasingly rests in the hands of a powerful few, there is an added need to understand how the presentation of information may manipulate our beliefs and control our behaviour.

Persuasion tactics operate at a variety of different levels from the seemingly innocuous to the overtly dangerous. It would be wrong to conclude that all uses of persuasive techniques represent an abuse of psychological principles and are evidence of exploitation. We all use, and are subject to, persuasion in one form or another in our everyday lives (think of college open days you may have been involved in, for example). However, it would also be equally naive to assume that all techniques of persuasion are legitimate and pose no cause for concern. The difficulty comes in determining at what point persuasive messages and techniques become unacceptable.

Activity 2

List the different situations you have experienced where you have been exposed to persuasive messages.
Would you consider the tactics used to be acceptable?
Using the examples you have thought of, try to say what distinguishes an acceptable persuasive communication from an unacceptable one.

(Suggested answers on page 72.)

This section focuses upon three areas in which persuasive techniques have been intentionally and systematically applied: advertising, **propaganda** and cults.

■ The role of psychology in advertising

Advertising is probably the most obvious example of an intention to influence in order to encourage a particular type of behaviour (usually to buy something).

Contemporary explanations of the persuasive tactics used in advertising have developed from the basic principles of at least one of three schools of thought in psychology: psychoanalysis, behaviourism and cognitive psychology.

Psychoanalysis was one of the earliest psychological approaches used in advertising. Advertising designed along psychoanalytical principles attempts to appeal to our deepest motivations which unconsciously drive our behaviour. Thus attention is directed at the symbolic meaning of adverts rather than their overt content. Although popular in the 1950s, the ineffectiveness of this approach has since rendered it obsolete. Contemporary notions of appeals to the unconscious are now manifest in the notion of **subliminal advertising** (see page 43).

By contrast, the principles of learning theory have informed techniques of persuasion for almost a century. In 1917 Walter Dill Scott wrote a textbook recommending that advertisers increase the remembering of their adverts by using repetition (repeat the advert over and over), association (link content to recipients' experiences), intensity (using bright and loud adverts) and ingenuity (make the advert distinctive). The behaviourist, J B Watson, also had an influential role in the introduction of rigorous research techniques whilst working in a marketing company. Examples of behaviourist concepts utilised in advertising today include the following:

■ *Association*: where a product is often associated with a pleasant feeling. Banyard (1996) gave the example of the Andrex toilet paper advert where a labrador puppy is used to create an 'ahhh' response. Whilst puppies have very little to do with toilet paper, the advert works by encouraging viewers to associate warm feelings with this brand of paper.

■ *Generalisation*: advertisers will seek to generalise a response to other brands of products by making them appear as similar as possible in terms of packaging. This is often seen in supermarkets which sell their own brand of products. Hopefully, customers will generalise the qualities associated with the brand of product they usually buy to the other brand, and then choose the 'copy cat' brand because the only discriminating feature appears to be cost (i.e. supermarket own brands tend to be cheaper).

■ *Imitation*: advertisers will aim to encourage an imitation effect where people will copy the behaviour of others in terms of the use and purchase of particular products. Usually used to establish a market for new products, whilst initial sales may be low, the effect of imitation will hopefully result in ever increasing sales as the product becomes ever more popular (Banyard, 1996).

The concept of reward or positive reinforcement underlies behaviourist explanations of persuasion: a persuasive message is learned and accepted if it is rewarding to do so (Pratkanis and Aronson, 1992).

The cognitive psychology approach emerged in the late 1960s in response to some of the criticisms of the behaviourist approach. Rather than perceiving people as passive receptors who obeyed the principles of learning theory, they were regarded as having a more active role in the persuasion process. Emphasis was placed on the interpretation of the message and associated cognitive processes. One of the most influential theories examining the role of a person's thought processes in persuasive communication is that of cognitive dissonance (Festinger, 1957). Dissonance emerges when there is inconsistency between different beliefs or between beliefs and behaviour. This creates a high degree of discomfort which we seek to reduce by restoring consonance. In effect this means that we will distort, filter and adapt incoming messages to fit with our existing beliefs or to justify our behaviour. Alternatively we may change our beliefs or behaviour to be consistent with the new message and alleviate the discomfort

associated with that message. One example here is the charity appeal which triggers the emotional response of guilt by showing people in situations of distress. In order to alleviate the uncomfortable feelings this arouses in us, we may be prompted to donate to that particular charity. Another example is when, after making a purchase such as a car, people will pay more attention to subsequent adverts about their own car, ignoring adverts which extol the benefits of other makes and models. This selective processing of information serves to justify the original behaviour of buying that car. It also explains why car manufacturers find it very difficult to get people to change their choice of make of car.

Banyard (1996) suggested that the use of psychology by advertisers relates to four stages of consumer behaviour (figure 2.1). Encouraging specific behaviours within these four stages is done using a wide variety of psychological tactics all designed to elicit a desirable response. Some make appeals at the behavioural levels, others at the cognitive and emotional levels. Pratkanis and Aronson (1992) discussed a range of tactics used by advertisers, a selection of which are summarised in figure 2.2.

2.1 Advertiser/consumer relationship: four stages of consumer behaviour (Banyard, 1996)

Stage 1: developing a need – convincing people that they want or need a particular product. Without this there will be little incentive to purchase the product.

Stage 2: noticing the product – making the product stand out from all others that are available.

Stage 3: purchasing the product – having got the product noticed, how to get people to buy it.

Stage 4: behaviour after the purchase – having bought the product, understanding what encourages us to make a repeat purchase or to recommend it to others.

2.2 Tactics used by advertisers (Pratkanis and Aronson, 1992)

■ Emotional appeals: fear and guilt

Evidence suggests that all other things being equal, the more frightened a person is by a communication, the more likely he or she is to take positive preventive action. Fear is often used in health advertising campaigns urging people to stop smoking, not to take drugs or to avoid unsafe sexual practices. For such campaigns to change behaviour successfully, however, fear alone is not enough. There should also be a specific recommendation for overcoming the threat, comprising of actions which the perceiver feels he or she is capable of performing. Similarly, by inducing feelings of guilt, people will respond in a way to alleviate those feelings. One possible response is to donate money to a charity in response to an appeal; the converse of this is reflected in the National Lottery which makes much of its charitable contributions. For many, this serves to justify behaviour which may otherwise be interpreted as blatant self-interest and greed. People need no longer feel guilty about gambling!

■ Repetition

Continually repeating the same message in advertisements is an effective strategy for increasing sales. As demonstrated experimentally by Zajonc (cited in Pratkanis and Aronson, 1992), all other things being equal, the more a person is exposed to an item, the more attractive it is. Repetition is a good way of introducing a new product and to remind consumers of the value of an older brand. Often advertisers will continue with the same commercial because it is a proven winner, so avoiding the risk and expense of changing it.

■ Faulty heuristics

Modern living is characterised by decreasing leisure time, increasing information and increasing choices. Consequently, people often resort to the use of heuristics as a guide for action. Heuristics provide us with simple cues which usually associate particular qualities with different products. Three of the most common heuristics used to infer product quality associated with a particular brand are price, store image and brand name. Whilst the use of heuristics may give us a practical solution to dealing with an overload of information, their use does have certain dangers. Heuristics may actually be faulty and the qualities associated with particular products may have no reliable basis in fact. Cereal boxes can be designed to make the contents appear 'healthy', applause or laughter can be dubbed into TV ads, all of which give a false impression aimed to increase desirability.

■ Scarcity

The more scarce and unavailable a product is, the more desirable it becomes. This is based upon the simple heuristic that if it is rare, if it is unavailable, it must be valuable. Advertisers often exploit this by emphasising the scarcity and uniqueness of particular products, stressing that they are a 'limited edition', 'unavailable in stores' and 'available for a limited time only' (Pratkanis and Aronson, 1992 p. 188). The increasing desirability of the unobtainable is reflected by the often enormous success of censored items such as CDs or books. Songs barred from radio stations and TV shows often end up topping the charts, and Salman Rushdie's novel *The Satanic Verses*, for example, was elevated to the status of a best-seller once it had been condemned by the Iranian leader Ayatollah Khomeini, who called for the assassination of the author.

The tactics summarised in figure 2.2 are not only used in advertising. As will be seen in the discussion of propaganda, many of the persuasive strategies used are, in principle, exactly the same.

Activity 3

Select a number of TV advertisements. Try to discern what strategies and tactics each advert is using.

This section concludes with a discussion of the popular notion of *subliminal advertising* which attempts to influence people through messages presented subconsciously.

Can we really be persuaded by a message or image which is presented to us below our threshold of recognition? If so, this certainly raises serious questions surrounding the use and abuse of such methods. One early test proclaiming the success of subliminal advertising was conducted by James Vicary in the 1950s. During a screen show at a cinema the words 'Eat popcorn' and 'Drink coke' were flashed onto the screen at a speed of 1/3000 of a second, well below conscious recognition. Vicary claimed that this increased popcorn sales by 57.7 per cent and coke sales by 18.1 per cent. Not surprisingly, these results aroused a great deal of attention and concern. Such concerns have been perpetuated by much media attention on a few isolated examples, resulting in a legal ban upon the use of subliminal messages. Little attention, however, has been paid to empirical data subsequent to Vicary's study, which in fact reveal no support for the efficacy of subliminal advertising. As Pratkanis and Aronson (1992) reported:

'We have been collecting published articles on subliminal processes, gathering more than 150 articles from the mass media and more than 200 academic articles on the topic. In none of these papers is there clear evidence in support of the proposition that subliminal messages influence behaviour. Many of the studies fail to find an effect, and those that do are either fatally flawed on methodological grounds or cannot be reproduced. Other reviewers of this literature have reached the same conclusion.' (p. 201)

Such conclusions are further substantiated by the reported admission by Vicary that his original study was in fact a fabrication, designed to increase customers for his marketing business (Pratkanis and Aronson, 1992, p. 202).

Whilst there is nothing to say that effective strategies for subliminal influence cannot be developed in the future, at present research might more fruitfully focus on other subtle influences used in advertising, such as the use of colour, scents and music to evoke certain moods and behaviours.

◼ Propaganda and warfare

In its original form the word 'propaganda' was a value-free term used to describe a particular type of persuasive message, or particular religious doctrine. Today, however, the term 'propaganda' has strong negative connotations. This is principally a result of the two world wars where 'propaganda' was used to describe the 'enemy's' attempts to persuade others by manipulative means of their legitimacy. This is reflected by the fact that in Nazi Germany Josef Goebbels headed the Propaganda Bureau, whereas the US used labels such as 'information' and 'communication' agencies to describe comparable organisations. Taylor (1992), commenting on the Gulf War, noted that this distinction still continues: 'Propaganda, to most people, means lies or at best half truths. In wartime, "they" – the enemy – conduct propaganda, whereas "we" deal with honest news and information' (p. 18).

As Taylor pointed out, due to the association of the term 'propaganda' with totalitarian regimes such as Nazi Germany and communist Russia, democracies have been careful to distance themselves from the term adopting a variety of euphemisms, such as 'political education', 'publicity' and 'media management'.

So, what actually constitutes propaganda? According to a definition given in the *Encyclopedia of Psychology* (2nd edition), propaganda is the advancement of a position or view in a manner that attempts to persuade rather than to present a balanced overview (Winick, 1994). This may involve among other methods the deliberate selection and omission of accurate information as well as falsehoods (Taylor, 1992). As such, propaganda is simply another process of persuasion, with a very thin line separating it from other persuasive techniques such as those used in advertising. Indeed, marketing, public relations and advertising strategies are themselves a form of propaganda, presenting selective information in an effort to increase sales.

A useful distinction between education and propaganda is made by Brown (1963): whereas education teaches people how to think, propaganda teaches them what to think (cited in Taylor, 1992, p. 21).

Winick (1994) made a similar distinction: 'Propaganda, seeking to effect attitude change, can be contrasted with education, which seeks to communicate knowledge' (p. 129).

The use of propaganda in war situations has, and continues to serve, two main functions:

- to convince the public of the legitimacy of new political powers
- to be used as a weapon of psychological warfare, alongside other military operations, to subvert the morale of the enemy in an attempt to get them to surrender or desert.

A clear example of the use of propaganda in a war situation is found in Hitler's Nazi Germany during the Second World War. This case is summarised in figure 2.3.

Many essential and valuable lessons can be learnt from the atrocities of the Second World War. It must not be forgotten that the death of 6 million Jews (along with 3 million gypsies, homosexual and disabled people) resulted from the propaganda-induced prejudice of the Nazi movement. We must ourselves be careful of concluding that all that is history now, assuming a moral highground by virtue of our distance in time from those events. Whilst the Nazi experience provides a very graphic example of the consequences of dogma and the abuse of persuasion, such tactics are still employed in situations of conflict today. As Taylor (1992) revealed in his analysis of the 1990 Gulf War, the propaganda of warring democracies takes more subtle forms, veiled in the guise of legitimate news or government agencies. It is the subtlety of such messages which renders them dangerous and highlights the need for awareness of the strategies and techniques of persuasion employed. It is only by increasing this awareness that we can recognise such messages for what they are and attempt to minimise their manipulative impact.

2.3 Propaganda and the Nazi movement

The control and manipulation of information on a mass scale played a crucial role in Hitler's advance across Europe in the Second World War. Reflecting on Germany's defeat in the First World War, Hitler realised the importance of the war of persuasion, learning much from the tactics employed by the Allies. On obtaining power in 1933, Hitler soon set his propaganda machinery up and running. Hitler's strategy involved the following:

1 Josef Goebbels was appointed as Minister of Popular Enlightenment and Propaganda (1933).
2 Goebbels and Hitler then set about establishing control over all media outlets, including radio, cinema, the press and the theatre. The result was that at every possible opportunity, people were repeatedly bombarded with the Nazi image of the ideal society and citizen. Well educated in the tactics of persuasion, Hitler himself commented that: 'Only constant repetition will finally succeed in imprinting an idea on the memory of the crowd' (from Mein Kampf in Cohen and Cohen, 1971, p. 155).
3 Simplified labels and slogans were created (i.e. easily available heuristics) which expressed the distinct Nazi identity: Hitler was known as the Führer and the swastika symbol was adopted; followers loyal to the Nazi party wore brown shirts.
4 Displays of confidence and social support: when appearing to a mass audience, Hitler was always supported by cheering, saluting Nazi supporters; slogans expressed an air of confidence such as 'Fight with us' or 'Adolf Hitler is victory'; even architecture was designed to a certain style and on a grand scale, symbolising the power of the state over the individual.
5 Defining the 'enemy': finally, perhaps the most barbaric piece in Hitler's propaganda jigsaw were the lies about the Jews, blaming them for all the nation's problems. This myth, perpetuated through propaganda films, exploited the emotion of fear in order to establish a united identity among Nazis/Germans against the common enemy, i.e. the Jews. This strategy was very effective in legitimising the activities of the holocaust.

A contemporary example of the systematic use of information in specific ways to achieve military goals is that known as **psychological operations** (PSYOP). A description of modern applications of psychological operations as used by the US military is given in figure 2.4. This is adapted from an article written by an advocate of psychological operations, Scott Rodgers, who is head of the Psychological Operations Branch of the United States Air Force.

Whilst a very legitimate view of PSYOP is given by Rodgers, a number of questions can be raised about the assumptions made. Despite the emphasis on presenting the truth, surely this is contradicted by the presentation of selected information. Is withholding truthful information any more legitimate than telling lies?

As Rodgers stated, truth is necessary for the practical purpose of maintaining credibility; thus it would seem the job of PSYOP is to determine how far the definitions of truth can be pushed, without sacrificing credibility. The fact that this is aided by the thorough and indepth analyses of the target audiences and their perceived reactions merely adds to the clever and manipulative bent of the communication strategy – in principle, if a target audience were to react in a different way, then this would presumably change the definition of the truth it would then receive. Also, if the measure of an acceptable message is whether or not it has been discredited, presumably messages based upon lies and distortions are acceptable as long as they remain credible. Whilst Rodgers would certainly like to distance PSYOP from the label of

2.4 Psychological operations – a US perspective

The official definition of psychological operations is:

Planned operations to convey selected information and indicators to foreign audiences to influence their emotions, motives, objective reasoning, and ultimately the behaviour of foreign governments, organisations, groups and individuals. The purpose of psychological operations is to induce or reinforce foreign attitudes and behaviour favourable to the originator's objectives.

Examples of behaviour which PSYOP attempts to induce include: surrender of the enemy; the cessation of resistance; encouraging people to stay off the main roads; delaying the deployment of enemy troops.

A high level of official approval is necessary before PSYOP programmes are given the go-ahead. This is to ensure that the PSYOP planned are consistent with national policies and objectives.

Credibility is the key to the success of PSYOP. The audience must believe that the message being communicated is the truth. This reliance on the truth is not for moral reasons, but out of practicality; social psychology research has shown that to influence behaviour you must have credibility with your audience. Maximum effectiveness comes from understanding the target group's perception of reality. This entails understanding the history, culture, language, customs, mores, values and communication patterns of the target group. The result is indepth analyses of target audiences and the perceived reactions of those audiences.

It is important to point out what PSYOP is not. It is not brainwashing nor is it lies or false information. PSYOP is based on truth, at least on most of the truth. As soon as a PSYOP programme is discredited, its effects are lost and it becomes at best propaganda. The overall PSYOP programme must be based on credibility or truth projection. PSYOP is not deception operations. By definition, deceptive measures are designed to mislead by manipulation, distortion, or falsification. Although both involve perception management, once the target group believes it has been tricked, credibility vanishes and the effectiveness of the psychological operation is neutralised. Properly used, PSYOP is a significant combat multiplier and peacetime contributor: decreasing the levels of lethal force needed, saving lives, and producing a quicker accomplishment of the mission.

Source: adapted from Rodgers (1997).

propaganda, in terms of the definitions talked about earlier, it is an appropriate label.

The overlap between the official definition of PSYOP as given in figure 2.4 and the following definition of propaganda is self evident:

'Propaganda is the advancement of a position or view in a manner that attempts to persuade rather than to present a balanced overview. Propaganda, seeking to effect attitude change, can be contrasted with education, which seeks to communicate knowledge. (Winick, 1994, p.' 129)

Readers are strongly encouraged to read the original article by Rodgers in order to make up their own minds!

■ Persuasion in cults

This section concludes with a look at the role of persuasion in cults. It is the alarming proliferation of cults and the often tragic extremes of their behaviour, such as mass suicides, which underlie the importance of understanding the conditions under which such groups emerge and exert such an influence.

The past few years have been marked by a massive increase in cult membership across the globe. Whilst the number of cults has increased, so

too has the number of mass suicides associated with such groups (figure 2.5).

Given the obvious influence cults yield over their members, a question with important implications is from where do they derive such power?

Whilst the activities of some of these cult groups make for startling headlines, the persuasive strategies used in cults are the same as those employed in other propaganda situations. Cults simply use these techniques in a more systematic and complete manner. Pratkanis and Aronson (1992) suggested seven tactics used by cult leaders when creating and maintaining a cult (figure 2.6).

As can be seen, there is nothing particularly startling about the tactics used in cults to encourage recruitment and continued commitment of members. It is simply the intensity of their application which inhibits the consideration of any alternative ideas or beliefs which makes them so powerful.

Examining cults provides an interesting but alarming window into the potential power of propaganda and the abuse of psychological tactics of persuasion. Given their increasing popularity, it is a power that none of us can afford to ignore.

2.5 Cult deaths, 1978–97

Cult deaths
- *November 18, 1978:* The Rev Jim Jones, an American, led 914 followers to their deaths at Jonestown, Guyana, by drinking a cyanide-laced fruit drink. Those who refused were shot.
- *December 1991:* A minister and 29 followers died as toxic fumes filled their church in Mexico.
- *April 19, 1993:* At least 70 Branch Davidian cult members killed in fire and shootout with federal agents at compound near Waco, Texas.
- *October 1993:* 53 villagers in remote Vietnamese hamlet committed mass suicide with primitive weapons believing they would go to heaven.
- *October 1994:* Burnt bodies of 48 Solar Temple members found in Switzerland; five bodies found in Quebec.
- *December 1995:* 16 Solar Temple members found dead near Grenoble.
- *March 23, 1997:* In Saint Casimir, Quebec, the charred bodies of three women and two men were found inside a house owned by a member of the Solar Temple.
- *March 27, 1997:* In Santa Fe, California, 39 members of the Heavens Gate sect were found dead following a mass suicide at a luxurious mansion they occupied.

Source: *The Times* (1997), 28 March, p. 16.

2.6 The seven tactics used by cult leader

1 *Creating a social reality*: eliminate all sources of information other than those provided by the cult. Usually this means severing all contact with the outside world such that cult members only have contact with each other. Concepts of reality are then replaced with the cult's own view of the world or belief system.

2 *Creation of an ingroup and outgroup identity*: members should be encouraged to identify with each other and see themselves as a collective social unit. This reinforces the break with the older world and membership of the new. All those who are not cult members become outgroups who represent evil which should be avoided.

3 *Commitment through dissonance reduction*: encourage members to show small acts of commitment. In order to justify/rationalise this initial commitment, an even bigger commitment is made. This sets up a spiral of escalating commitment as each act is rationalised by carrying out a larger act.

4 *Establish the leaders' credibility and attractiveness*: if the leader is afforded a superior status such as the son of God, then he (or she) is much less likely to be disobeyed.

5 *Conversion of the unredeemed*: preaching the cults message to non-members serves two functions: (a) to obtain new recruits and, (b) to further convince members of the cult's beliefs by promoting it and defending it if criticised.

6 *Distract members from thinking undesirable thoughts*: prevent members questioning the rationale behind the conditions and beliefs of the cult by never leaving members on their own and keeping them engaged in constant activity such as chanting or working for the collective benefit of the group.

7 *Fixate members' vision on a phantom*: keep members striving for the promised land, a better world, or a higher state. This acts as a powerful motivator, giving the group a sense of purpose and a mission, inhibiting individuals from showing any lack of commitment should this hinder their attainment of their goal.

Source: Adapted from Pratkanis and Aronson (1992) pp. 241–9.

Psychometric testing

Issues related to the use of **psychometric tests** are significant simply for the fact that such tests are used to make important decisions affecting individuals and society. Tests are used in a variety of settings to aid selection in education and work and for diagnosis for those with learning difficulties and psychological problems. As mentioned in the section on socially sensitive research (Unit 3), it is research which may have a direct impact upon people and society which gives rise to the greatest concerns. The importance of such issues is further reinforced by the increased use of psychometric tests (especially within the workplace) and the highly commercialised context surrounding their development and use.

This popularity may in part stem from the conclusion that, in spite of their limitations, 'tests represent the best, most accurate and fairest technology available for making important decisions about individuals' (Murphy and Davidshofer, 1991, p. 2).

Having said this, tests alone give only a partial representation of the psychological attribute being measured and to base any decisions solely upon test results is a mistake. In order sensibly to evaluate the outcomes of psychological tests, it is necessary to be familiar with the principles and techniques of psychological measurement and to interpret results within the context of other relevant factors. To this end the British Psychological Society has a certification scheme through which all test users in the psychological community should pass, and which is designed to equip test users with the appropriate knowledge and skills. The Level A certificate is for those using ability tests, and the Level B certificate for those using personality tests. However, whilst the need for such skills is recognised within the psychological community, such awareness has not kept pace with the ever expanding development and use of tests, which, despite attempts at control, are widely available. This is especially true of testing in occupational settings, an area which has seen significant growth in the use of tests. Whilst occupational psychologists may have the appropriate training and knowledge for test use, they represent a small proportion of all those using such tests. Other test users include personnel managers, management consultants, careers counsellors and training advisers, many of whom are not psychologists and may have no background or training in testing (Bartram, 1995). The massive increase in testing has resulted in some dubious tests promising unrealistic solutions, which are bought by those who cannot distinguish between a good and bad test (Bartram, 1995). It is observations of such practices which have contributed to the negative image of psychometric testing, a situation which was summarised by Kline (1993):

'Much of their misuse and public approbrium arises from impossible expectations of tests on the part of testers, who in many cases are not well versed in psychometrics. In Great Britain, at least, psychometrics can be used with very little training' (p. 309).

■ Range of tests

Psychometric tests are widely used in three main settings. Table 2.7 summarises what the tests typically measure within these settings.

For those brought up in western educational systems it is probably true to say that they will be subject to some form of psychometric assessment which will inform important decisions about their educational future.

■ Criticisms of psychometric tests

Summarised below are a number of criticisms made of psychometric tests and the uses to which they are put. These issues are explored in greater detail in the following sections in relation to ability tests and personality tests.

- *Philosophical reaction to the quantification of psychological attributes.* Some critics disagree with the basic notion of the measurement and quantification of psychological attributes. It simply reflects the dominant model of science in western culture with greater credibility afforded to statistical representations of what may otherwise be viewed as non-scientific subjects of study. This move to greater objectification reduces people to the status of objects, as the science of psychometrics becomes increasingly divorced from the reality of the individual.
- *Labelling effects.* Many critics point to the dangerous **labelling effects** of test outcomes. The application of a label on the basis of test

Table 2.7	
Setting	Application
Educational	Assess ability and academic progress for purposes of allocation to suitable educational level and also for diagnosis and treatment of educational difficulties. Usually involve use of ability tests which may be general, or specific to particular skills. Personality and motivational tests may be used in assessments of children with educational difficulties.
Industrial/Occupational	Used for selection and placement of workers, measuring attributes such as management potential, cognitive and psychomotor ability, and ability to do specific job-related tasks, as well as assessing general training needs.
Clinical	Tests are used for diagnosis and assessment of treatment. They may include measures of intelligence, psychopathology and neuropsychological assessments. These may take a variety of forms from ability tests and personality questionnaires to projective tests.

results may set in motion a self-fulfilling prophecy where the individual increasingly behaves in a way consistent with that label. The most famous example of this is Rosenthal and Jacobson's (1968) experiment involving disadvantaged school children. Teachers were informed that, on the basis of test scores, certain children would be expected to improve considerably. Later, when tested again, these children had improved in spite of the fact that they were actually randomly assigned to the 'improvement' group and had not performed better on the first tests as originally reported. Goffmann (1968) was particularly critical of such effects in a clinical setting. Once patients are diagnosed and labelled as having a particular disorder, then behaviour consistent with this role is reinforced and perpetuated. Supporters of psychometric tests, whilst acknowledging the potentially negative impact of labelling, argue that when applied sensitively and appropriately such information is very useful in terms of curbing unrealistic expectations and informing interventions.

- *Biases in tests.* Probably the strongest attack upon psychometric testing comes from research showing that tests are biased, with certain groups performing systematically better on tests than others. In ability tests, scores vary as a function of socioeconomic status, sex and race, with white middle/upper-class males generally obtaining superior scores. For some this simply indicates the desire to maintain existing power structures by designing selective mechanisms which favour those in power, to the detriment of those without it. Further fuelling this debate are arguments that these differences are indicative of the genetic superiority of whites, asserting that such scores are immutable and cannot be changed. Such arguments divert attention away from consideration of other possible causes of test score differences and have provided credibility for systematic programmes of discrimination. (See ability testing below.)
- *Potential for mis-use.* The increased use of psychometric testing has increased the potential for misuse, especially in areas where regulations

for the use of such tests exert little force, for example in occupational/industrial settings. Lack of knowledge on behalf of the test user may lead to the assessment of inappropriate traits using inadequate measures constituting unnecessary invasions of privacy. Test results may then themselves be open to abuse if the confidentiality of the participant is not protected. Test users must make every attempt to protect the well-being of test participants throughout every stage of the testing process, from test selection to feedback and follow-up. Such protection is best assured both by a thorough understanding of the principles of psychometric testing and through recognised training in test administration.

■ Ability testing

Ability tests were among the first psychometric tests to be developed and controversy has consistently surrounded their use. Binet and Simon (1905) first developed tests in France to determine who was most likely to benefit from education. Revisions to the Binet–Simon Scale resulted in the concept of 'mental age', an easily understandable concept which significantly increased the popularity of ability testing. Further developments of the tests (for example by Terman in 1916) produced the concept of intelligence quotient (IQ) and resulted in one of the currently most widely used tests, the Stanford Binet Scale. Research into the psychometric assessment of intelligence has been the focus of many eminent psychologists over the last century including Spearman, Burt, Cattell and Eysenck. Popular tests used today include the Weschler Scales, the British Ability Scales and Raven's Progressive Matrices.

Historically, controversy has surrounded the use of such tests as many were developed on the assumption that intelligence was genetically determined. Such arguments were used to support the view that nothing could be done to improve an individual's intelligence, having drastic implications for those obtaining low IQ scores. In the US a number of states brought in sterilisation laws for those who scored very low on IQ tests. Between 1924 and 1972 more than 7000 people with low IQs were sterilised in the state of Virginia. In 1912, low IQ scores were used to restrict access to immigrants entering the US, and again in 1924 the Immigration Restriction Act limited the number of Jewish refugees eligible to enter the United States leaving them to perish in the concentration camps of Nazi Germany (Colman, cited in Roth, 1990). As Colman concluded: 'The writings of American psychometricians, while not a direct cause of these deplorable measures, lent intellectual credibility to them, (cited in Roth, 1990, p. 345).

In the field of education Cyril Burt was a strong and influential advocate of psychometric assessment of abilities, arguing that selection was necessary due to the innate nature of intelligence. As a consequence, the eleven plus exam was introduced which was largely compiled of IQ tests. Those who passed the tests went on to grammar schools and were prepared for higher education, whilst those who failed went to academically inferior secondary modern schools. Jensen (1969) suggested that genetic differences were the cause of the consistently lower IQ scores observed in non-white racial groups. In practice, this meant that little could be done to improve the intelligence of those children labelled as having inferior intelligence. Such arguments have been used to explain why compensatory education programmes have little long-term effect, diverting attention away from consideration of other potential causes of low IQ scores.

Recent controversies surrounding ability testing relate to the systematic differences in test scores attained by different groups in society. The biases revealed by researchers can be summarised as follows:

- Test scores from children and adults in the middle and upper classes tend to be higher than those of children and adults in the lower socioeconomic classes.
- White children tend to receive higher scores than ethnic minorities.
- Males receive systematically higher scores on some tests and systematically lower scores on other tests than females. (Murphy and Davidshofer, 1991, p. 256.)

Critics point out that such differences are the result of bias in test items which are used to inform decisions which are ultimately unfair. Note here that criticisms of testing relate to both biases within the actual tests used, and uses to which those tests are put. In our culture, because test scores are used to make important decisions, any systematic differences in test scores have important societal consequences, providing strong arguments for the reduction of test bias.

■ Test bias and attempts to reduce it

Typical examples of bias in test items come from items relating to previously learned information and items using verbal information, typically English, which require reading and writing. Even when such tests are translated into the native language of the participants, questions are still raised over the cultural equivalence of certain items (Zindi, 1994). Differences in understanding and ways of thinking go far deeper than simply language differences, as is summed up by Laosa (1977):

'Standardised tests are biased and unfair to persons from cultural and socio-cultural minorities since most tests reflect largely middle class values and attitudes and they do not reflect the experiences and the linguistic, cognitive and cultural styles and values of minority persons.' (Cited in Zindi, 1994, p. 550)

Even tests which explicitly attempt to be culture fair have been questioned. On one such test, the Raven's Progressive Matrices, and on others, the performance of Asian immigrants has been found to improve over a five-year period by an average of 15–20 points (Roth, 1990). What such tests demonstrate, therefore, is that minorities will be disadvantaged in taking them until they learn different ways of approaching them (Roth, 1990).

In an attempt to highlight cultural biases in test items, Williams (1972) produced the Black Intelligence Test of Cultural Homogeneity (BITCH test) which was heavily loaded in favour of black minorities. Using this test, it is black people who tend to receive consistently higher test scores than whites (Matarazzo and Weins, 1977, cited in Murphy and Davidshofer, 1991).

Whilst many do acknowledge the role of test bias in producing systematic group differences in test scores, there is also the danger of masking any actual differences in cognitive ability which do exist when scores are levelled out. As Murphy and Davidshofer (1991) point out:

'There is considerable controversy over the meaning, causes and modifiability of these differences, but there is little doubt that some of the differences in test scores reflect real differences in ability' (p. 267).

The sensitivity of this issue should not deter an open and informed analysis of why these differences exist, and the negative labelling of lower test scores as a failure of one group to meet another group's standards should be avoided. A more positive approach, exploring the value of such differences and recognising those attributes and abilities not typically measured by ability tests, should be adopted.

Alternative ways of reducing the effects of test bias are to change the way in which the tests are used and to employ other methods of assessment in parallel with testing. One example of modification of test use is to use the tests to discriminate positively in favour of those scoring lower. Alternatively, scoring systems may be changed, reducing group difference scores and decreasing the likelihood of unfair treatment of minority groups on the basis of lower test scores.

The most effective way to reduce the effects of test bias is to complement their use with other methods of assessment such as interviews and observations. As pointed out at the beginning of this unit, a single test cannot give the whole picture, and testing should form only part of a wider assessment programme. In this way the potential impact of biased test items is reduced.

■ Personality testing

Historically, the psychometric assessment of personality is strongly linked to the study of psychopathology. One of the first taxonomies proposed suggested that personalities could be described on a continuum from schizophrenic to manic depressive. As psychology developed, the study of personality became an area of study in its own right and efforts concentrated on the categorisation and measurement of normal behaviour. Today, personality assessments are mainly used in clinical settings, with their use in occupational settings increasing. They may also be used in educational settings in assessing individuals with learning problems and are still widely used and developed within academic and research settings. Examples of well-known personality tests developed by psychologists include Cattell's 16PF and the Eysenck Personality Questionnaire (EPQ).

In terms of regulating the use of personality tests, test users should have obtained the Level B competency award which aims to ensure appropriate knowledge of the different tests available and practical competencies in the use of such tests. (Personality tests used in clinical settings for diagnostic purposes are subject to greater controls.)

■ Personality testing in the workplace

Such tests are becoming increasingly popular within the largely unregulated environment of the workplace, which raises some rather pertinent ethical issues.

The fact that the use and development of such tests is on the increase has resulted in the production of some rather dubious measures used for rather dubious means. Before using such tests it is first important to ask: what relevance is the measurement of one's personality for this assessment exercise? If no relevance can be demonstrated, then personality assessments should not be used. This is particularly important in occupational settings where often personality has no bearing on the individual's ability to do the job for which he or she has been or are being employed. Establishing the relevance of personality testing is especially important given the often sensitive and personal nature of the questions asked, which may cause distress and constitute unwarranted invasions of privacy, especially if tests are badly designed. There is a clear ethical responsibility upon test users in terms of:

■ assessing what attributes it is appropriate to measure

■ selecting the most valid and reliable measures

- administering the tests appropriately and ensuring the maximum protection for participants.

Thus, assurances of confidentiality should be upheld and feedback of test results should be done in a sensitive way to minimise distress and potential misuse of the test results. Unless these issues are negotiated from the outset between the test users and the employer requesting them to carry out the testing, the test users may later find themselves in a difficult situation with the conflicting interests of employer and employees. Many of these issues are summarised in the newspaper article in figure 2.8.

Problems associated with personality testing

As well as the issues raised in the section above on the use of personality tests in the workplace, there are a number of other problems related to their use.

Figure 2.8

Experts from the watchdog British Psychological Society have criticised the use of personality tests, which are widely used by British companies. One adviser to the BPS, Pat Frankish, has called for test use to be restricted: 'I personally think that a lot of tests can be as dangerous as the misuse of drugs, and I would like to see them regulated in a similar sort of way.

Any personality test is potentially dangerous. People have a sense of self worth. If they believe in the validity of a test – and it tells them something they didn't think they were – it is destroying their personality.' Another BPS adviser, John Toplis, says: 'I have come across plenty of examples of personality questionnaires being used inappropriately. I feel there is a lot of bad practice around.'

The experts are concerned not so much about the tests themselves – although they concede there are a lot of poor ones on the market – but rather about the way they are used.

Seven out of ten British companies use personality questionnaires in processes ranging from selection and development to redundancy. Yet there is little regulation. Only 10 per cent of test users are members of the British Psychological Society – and the professional body admits it is a 'somewhat toothless' watchdog.

So while the market in testing grows, so do the concerns. On today's *Money Programme* on BBC2, employees of Anglian Water speak out for the first time about the way a personality test was used in a restructuring that led to the loss of 900 jobs. Some staff were upset at the computer-generated personality profiles they were given after the test. The profile was used when they reapplied for the remaining jobs.

One woman says the personality profile left her distraught: 'I ended up in tears. I felt very, very vulnerable. I felt that my whole personality, my whole life, had been stripped to the bone.'

A man who failed to get a job in the reorganisation is unhappy at the way his profile was used in an interview: 'I felt that the negative statements were not backed up by any facts about myself.

'I was also concerned that the report was written in the style of a reference by someone who knew you well – but in fact was generated completely by a computer.'

Anglian Water defends its use of the questionnaire by saying that each process was carefully tailored in conjunction with leading consultants and the staff union.

But when the BBC programme presents its evidence about the way the tests were used at Anglian to Mr Toplis at the BPS, his verdict is that the process was 'far removed from best practice'.

'What I think they have done is to give the questionnaire, and to some extent psychology, a bad name,' he says.

The BBC also investigated the use of a personality questionnaire in a recent redundancy programme by Southwark Council in south London. Staff had to answer a questionnaire that asked their views on sex, religion and family life. Among the statements they had to address were the following: 'Most people worry too much about sex'; 'I like tall women'; and 'I dread the thought of earthquakes'.

Sacked employee Kareena Barry says she was given no option but to take the test: 'I said I felt very vulnerable. I didn't want to do it. I had tears in my eyes, a lump in my throat. I was told I just had to take it. That, or go.'

The programme reveals that since that test was used at Southwark, the test suppliers have dropped 153 questions they judged to be intrusive or discriminatory.

The council insists no one was sacked on the basis of the personality test alone, and that it tried to be fair and objective. But some employees are taking the local authority to an industrial tribunal – in the first test of these questionnaires in Britain.

Former employee Ms Barry says: 'I've actually asked them to explain how they have come to their conclusions, via these testing papers, and I've had no answers. So I'm challenging it. I'm very angry.'

Source: Spiller, S (1994) 'Bosses warned on mind games: watchdog seeks curbs on personality tests', *The Independent on Sunday*, 13 November, p. 7.

One issue worth mentioning is the increased use of computer-based test interpretations for personality measures. Software is widely available which produces a computer-generated profile from an individual's completed questionnaire, a seemingly efficient and attractive way of getting results. Kline (1993) is wary of such techniques as they offer broad descriptions based around the categories of high, average and low scores. Such crude interpretations fail to do justice to the uniqueness of an individual's profile, with different scores often generating the same generalised statements because they fall into that category. Another problem relates to the feedback process itself.

> *'If subjects are, just for example, low on intelligence and high on anxiety, fascistic tendencies and schizophrenia, a computer printout informing them of these results is not a pleasant thing. Clearly there are different ways of conveying information without causing offence or deflating egos.' (Kline, 1993, p. 86)*

One alternative is to go through the computer printout with the individual item by item, although this then calls into question the purpose of having a computer printout in the first instance. Whilst computer interpretations may give added convenience, this is at the expense of quality and protection of the participants.

Another criticism of personality testing relates to the underlying assumption of stability inherent in such measures. This concerns the person–situation debate, and questions whether people do actually behave consistently across a range of situations. If the view is accepted that behaviour is not consistent across situations, then any attempt to measure personality would be meaningless. Most psychologists accept a moderate position, i.e. that whilst behaviours may be unstable across situations, broad patterns can be identified, and as such, personality measures are valuable. This issue, however, does alert us to the need to consider the impact of situational factors upon personality assessments. If a close relative has recently died, it is reasonable to expect this to affect responses to personality type questions. If this is not taken into account, then conclusions drawn about the personality type of an individual may be misleading.

Kline reviewed a number of other problems associated with the type of questions typically found on personality questionnaires. These are summarised below.

■ Typically respondents are asked simply to reply 'yes' or 'no' to very simplistic statements. This affronts their intelligence and creates poor cooperation in the testing process.

■ **Response sets** refer to the effect where people are likely to respond in certain ways. These include:
  – acquiescence: the tendency to agree with items regardless of content
  – social desirability: to respond to items in what is believed to be a socially desirable way
  – converging to neutral or extremes: certain subjects will consistently opt for the middle/undecided choice, whilst others will adopt extreme scores simply because they are extreme.

Whilst all of these responses may indicate something about the individual's personality, the point is that it is not necessarily anything to do with the personality attribute being measured.

■ It is extremely difficult to establish the validity of personality constructs simply due to the lack of established, external criteria. Having determined the dimensions which constitute personality (which is itself open to debate), the problem then is of deriving statements about behaviour, values and attitudes which are valid indicators of those dimensions. Consequently, whilst it is relatively easy to generate *reliable* tests and to establish norms, establishing the *validity* of a test is much harder and is often ignored.

■ Conclusion

Having critically discussed psychometric testing, it would be easy to come to very negative conclusions about their development and use, at the expense of recognising their strengths. When used properly, psychometric tests do provide the fairest and most accurate technology available for making important decisions about people. This 'proper use' is dependent upon a number of factors in the testing process:

- the professional *development* of tests by people who possess the relevant skills and expertise
- the *selection* of appropriate tests, again by people who have the expertise to distinguish between a good and a bad test
- the appropriate *interpretation* of test results, again by experts who will also consider other factors in putting together the whole picture
- appropriate use of the test, ensuring as far as is

possible that the testing process is not abused and that the well-being of test participants is protected.

The increased use of testing produces greater potential for standards like these to be compromised. It is only by raising awareness within the testing communities and introducing tighter regulation in currently unregulated areas that abuses of psychometric testing can be limited.

Self-assessment questions

1 Explain how behaviourist principles have been applied in advertising.

2 Summarise the contribution of cognitive psychology to our understanding of advertising behaviour.

3 What are the four stages of consumer behaviour?

4 What is subliminal advertising and does it work?

5 Distinguish between propaganda and education.

6 Explain how Hitler used propaganda to great effect in the Second World War.

7 Do psychological operations constitute propaganda? Give reasons for your answer.

8 What advice would you give a cult leader who wanted to encourage total commitment from his or her devotees?

9 As psychologists, why should we be concerned about the use of psychometric tests?

10 What are the three main settings in which psychometric tests are used?

11 Summarise the four criticisms made against psychometric testing.

12 Give an example of discriminatory practices which have been supported by scores on ability tests.

13 Which groups are likely to achieve higher scores on ability tests?

14 How can test bias and its effects be reduced?

15 What concerns have been raised about the increase in use of personality tests in the workplace?

16 What are the dangers and limitations of computer-based personality profiles?

17 Summarise Kline's (1993) criticisms common to many personality tests.

(Suggested answers on pages 72–74.)

Scientific status of psychology

Questions surrounding the scientific status of psychology have long been debated with still no consensus in sight. Such debate, however, plays a crucial role in revealing many important issues related to the production of scientific knowledge, issues which have very real implications for psychology as a whole. This section begins by exploring what science is, and reviewing the main philosophical theories which have influenced this question. Attention then focuses on whether, in the light of what science is, psychology can be labelled as a science and indeed whether such a label is desirable.

Science and its current status in western culture

Modern usage of the term 'science' refers both to a *type of knowledge* which is trustworthy and to a *method* of arriving at that type of knowledge. The scientific method is accepted as the vehicle through which scientific knowledge is obtained. Slife and Williams (1995) identified a number of characteristics and assumptions about science and the scientific method which afford it almost universal credibility:

1 The **scientific method** is grounded in *objective observations* of phenomena, observations which are uninfluenced by the values, expectations and desires of the scientist. This is in contrast to the earlier influence of rationality as the basis of knowledge.

2 These observations are conducted under *controlled conditions*, often *experimental*, where scientists seek to reveal *cause and effect* relationships through the isolation of different variables/factors.

3 This enables the *prediction* of outcomes under specified conditions.

4 Such predictions are then *applied* to real settings through the vehicle of technology, with the outcomes of research often realised in the form of some sort of technological advance. The enormous contribution science has made to the rapid technological advances of the past century have strongly added to its credibility.

5 Science is also assumed to be *accessible*, with the public, in theory, being able to scrutinise the methods and results, and repeat the results themselves if desired.

6 Finally, there is the assumed *similarity between science and mathematics*. Because science often uses mathematical language, for example equations, it is automatically assumed by many to have the precise properties of mathematical problems which result in certain and correct solutions. This certainty is generalised to the outcomes of science.

In everyday life science is held in high regard. Science is assumed to be the pursuit of truth through the use of rigorous techniques which measure and record phenomena in an objective way. The label of 'science' is often used as a sign of credibility. One example here is in advertisements which often assert that their product is 'scientifically proven' to be better, to get the washing whiter, the surfaces cleaner, etc. Similarly, in academic settings supporters of different disciplines are often keen to stress the scientific nature of their subject, presumably in an effort to imply that the methods used are as firmly based and as potentially useful as those used in physics (Chalmers, 1982). Different subjects are held in a state of **physics envy** as they seek to emulate the 'role model' of scientific theory and practice. Thus, the more scientific something can be said to be, the more highly regarded and acceptable it is. In western culture at least, the label of science adds status and value.

Background to contemporary notions of science

Popular ideas about science and the scientific method are strongly influenced by the inductivist notions of science first espoused in the seventeenth century. Subsequent theories, however, have questioned many of the basic assumptions of inductivist explanations, offering alternative accounts of what science actually is. This section gives brief summaries of some of the most influential of these theories, which include:

- inductivist explanations of science
- the falsificationist view of science
- Kuhn's theory of scientific paradigms.

Inductivist explanations of science

Inductivism was popularised in the scientific revolution of the seventeenth century. The philosopher Francis Bacon rejected Aristotelian ideas of deductive knowledge based on *reason* alone. The source of knowledge lay in *observations* of nature which we experience through our senses (i.e. sight, touch, hearing, etc.). Thus, science begins with observation with the scientist faithfully recording what he or she sees in a value-free way. These individual observations, known as *singular statements*, then form the basis of the laws and theories which constitute science, known as *universal statements*. Certain conditions must be satisfied in order to produce legitimate universal statements:

- The number of observation statements forming the basis of the generalisation must be large.
- The observations must be repeated under a wide variety of conditions.
- No accepted observation statement should conflict with the derived universal law (Chalmers, 1982, p. 4).

This process of going from singular statements to universal statements is known as *inductive reasoning*. It is through this process that scientific theories progress and develop to encompass an ever wider range of phenomena, all of which is founded on the basis of objective observation and experimentation. The general laws resulting from inductive reasoning then provide the basis for further explanation and predictions based upon *deductive reasoning*. In order for such deductions to be true, however, it is essential that they are based upon valid universal laws. Deductions derived from invalid universal laws will themselves be incorrect despite being logically valid.

Whilst influential, inductivism has been heavily criticised. Two of these criticisms are as follows:

- Induction is based on invalid logic. No amount of accurate observations under varying conditions guarantees that subsequent observations will be the same. We may observe that swans all around the world are white, yet this does not rule out the possibility that the next swan we see

may be black. Also, at what point is the number of observations large enough and the range of circumstances of the observations varied enough.
- Observations are not objective and value free – they are influenced by the expectations, knowledge and values of the observer. Observation involves interpretation.

Criticisms of inductivist explanations have provided the basis for alternative accounts of science, with debates concerning the assumed objectivity of observation giving rise to the most contemporary theories about the development of science.

The falsificationist view of science: Karl Popper

The influential philosopher, Karl Popper, rejected deterministic notions of objective observations arguing that a theory could never be 'proven' right as it might be contradicted by the next observation. In this way a theory could, however, be proven wrong. Thus all scientific knowledge is provisional and 'true until further notice'. The test of any good theory is that it can be subject to such testing and the possibility of **falsification**. If the theory is a valid one, then it will withstand the rigours of such testing. In instances where contradictory observations are made, the theory is said to have been refuted and is rejected on the grounds of this, with a new theory taking its place which should be able to explain the latest contradictory findings. In this way science progresses through the processes of *conjecture*, i.e. making inferences on the basis of incomplete evidence, and *refutation*, i.e. disproving theories on the basis of evidence gathered.

Probably the biggest criticism of this explanation of scientific progress is the fact that it is not accurate. A look at the history of the development of some of the most influential scientific theories shows that this is not the way science has progressed. Inconsistent observations have been recorded which contradict many influential scientific theories; nevertheless these theories were not rejected and abandoned (which, as Chalmers (1982) commented, is just as well in many cases). Examples of such theories include Newton's theory of gravity, Bohr's theory of the atom and the Copernican Revolution. A quick look at the historical development of these theories reveals that Popper's falsificationist theory offers a far too simplistic account of scientific progress.

■ Kuhn's theory of scientific paradigms

An alternative to Popper's theory which attempts to account for the complexity of the development of scientific knowledge is Thomas Kuhn's (1970) theory of **scientific paradigms**. Kuhn attempts to offer an account of scientific progress which bears resemblance to the actual historical development of science. Central to Kuhn's account is the revolutionary nature of scientific progress and the influence of the sociological characteristics of the scientific communities. Kuhn proposes that science progresses through the following stages in an open-ended manner:

pre-science → normal science → crisis → revolution → new normal science → new crisis

The state of *pre-science* is characterised by a lack of consistency among theoretical ideas, having no unifying structure and direction. As this mix of ideas develops, a single *paradigm* emerges which represents the theoretical assumptions, laws and methodological techniques associated with that particular 'world view' or body of thought. Once a paradigm is established, a state of *normal science* exists in which scientists further develop their paradigm through scientific investigation. During this period, inconsistent or *anomalous* findings will occur and scientists will seek to adapt their theories in order to account for such findings. This is in contrast to the suggestion by Popper that at this stage theories would be rejected. Kuhn maintains that scientific communities are actually reluctant to throw away their ideas and theories in the light of contradictory evidence and will, as far as possible, attempt to accommodate such findings within their existing theoretical framework(s). If, however, such anomalies become too great for a paradigm to accommodate (for example, perhaps they question the basic principles underlying that paradigm of thought), then a state of *crisis* emerges. This state resolves itself through the process of a *revolution* when a new paradigm emerges which attracts the allegiance of more and more scientists and the old

paradigm is rejected. Thus a state of *new normal science* exists until the anomalies thrown up by scientific activity again forces it into crisis, which is in turn followed by a new revolution.

Kuhn's theory is significant in acknowledging the influence of social factors in defining what is science. The fact that scientific communities will seek to defend their ideas in the light of apparently contradictory evidence is in sharp contrast to the notions of value-free observations so crucial to the inductivist. This forms the basis of contemporary *post-modern* views of science which argue that the status of all knowledge is relative to the social and cultural context and should not be judged by the hallmark of accepted western notions of science. The value of knowledge is relative in time and place. Different cultures value different types of knowledge (such as witchcraft/magic), and notions of what is accepted as knowledge change historically. Thus any debate concerning the definitions of science must acknowledge the impact of this cultural and historical context. This brings us back to the question of what actually constitutes science (Is it meaning? Is it method? Is it both?), the answers to which directly impact upon the scientific status afforded to psychology.

Activity 5

State which of the three theories each statement below is referring to:
a   When faced with a contradictory finding, a theory is modified rather than rejected.
b   This theory emerged in response to criticisms of deductionism.
c   Science is influenced by the sociological characteristics of the different scientific communities.
d   No number of consistent observations can ever prove a theory right, yet one contradictory observation can prove a theory wrong.
e   Value-free objective observations form the basis of science.
f   Science progresses through the processes of conjecture and refutation.

(Suggested answers on page 72.)

Is psychology a science?

The answer to this question will obviously depend upon what is accepted as science. As we can see from the range of theories outlined above, the criteria of what actually constitutes science can vary greatly. Generally speaking, however, it is explanations within the inductivist tradition utilising empirical methods which have gained widespread acceptance. Slife and Williams (1995) suggested that accepted notions of science can be usefully broken down into two components in attempting to assess the status of psychology and other behavioural sciences (figure 2.9).

In relation to definition 1 in figure 2.9, psychology would fail principally because it has not demonstrated the degree of prediction and control observed in the natural sciences (although it may be argued that some branches of psychology are more successful at doing this than others). The complexity of human life with its subtle and uncontrollable range of variables makes it doubtful that psychology will ever be labelled a science on this basis.

There is a greater possibility of psychology being labelled a science by definition 2, with the experimental method being fundamental to many areas of psychological research. As Koch (1959, cited by Slife and Williams, 1995) observed, at the turn of the century, because logical positivism was the dominant view in the natural sciences

this was automatically adopted by psychology, which was then in its developmental stages. Indeed, the emphasis upon the scientific method seemed to take precedence over all other considerations:

'In psychology, unlike the natural sciences, researchers settled on methods before they developed their questions – that is, they did not decide psychology was a science because they were faced with questions that seemed to require a scientific method to answer. Rather, psychologists seem to have first made the decision to use scientific methods and then framed their disciplinary questions according to what could be studied using that method.' (Slife and Williams, 1995, on Sigmund Koch's observations, p. 179)

Thus, the boundaries of psychology were defined by what was appropriate to be studied using the scientific method. Thankfully, a look at psychology 100 years on reveals a very different picture, with many psychologists within different fields of psychology rejecting the assumption that the scientific experiment is the most appropriate method for studying human behaviour (see Unit 27 for an overview of the criticisms of the experimental method).

This reminds us of the enormous difficulty in answering questions relating to psychology as a whole. Whilst some approaches rely heavily on the scientific method and experimentation, and would thus by this definition constitute a science, other approaches which do not use the scientific method would not.

Figure 2.9

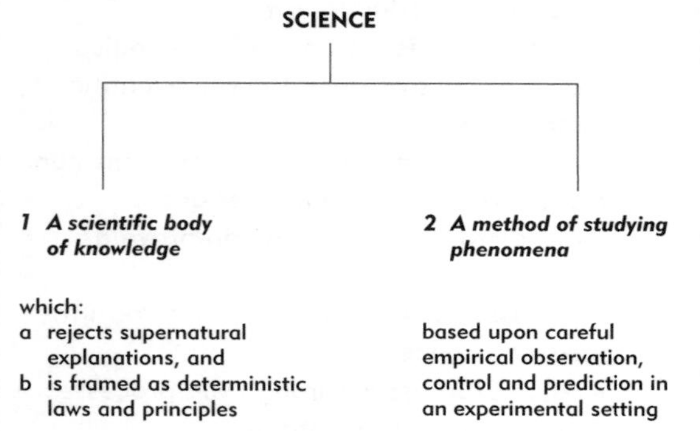

SCIENCE

1 **A scientific body of knowledge**

which:
a rejects supernatural explanations, and
b is framed as deterministic laws and principles

2 **A method of studying phenomena**

based upon careful empirical observation, control and prediction in an experimental setting

Notions of science (Slife and Williams, 1995)

Activity 6

Using this methodology-based definition of science, generally speaking, which branches of psychology are most likely to be defined as scientific and which are not?

(Suggested answer on page 72.)

In acknowledging the plurality within psychology, Michael Eysenck (1994) provided a useful comparison of the contrasting approaches within psychology of psychoanalysis, behaviourism and humanism in terms of their scientific merits. This comparison is summarised figure 2.10.

As can be seen from table 2.10, credibility as a science can be assessed against a number of criteria: the quality and extent of understanding provided; the degree of prediction and control afforded; the rigour and objectivity of the methodology adopted. Not surprisingly, different approaches within psychology offer these characteristics to varying degrees.

Commenting on this variety within psychology, Devalle (1996) noted the tendency to label the less 'scientific' branches of psychology as 'pseudo-science' in an attempt to denigrate the status of a particular approach (psychoanalysis is an example of a field of psychology where such as label has been applied). Such labelling is used to undermine competing views, but perhaps more harmful is the assertion that 'such a characterisation of science and non/pseudo science pays homage to an illusory monolithic method (i.e. the scientific

experiment), and maintains all the sciences in a state of "physics envy"' (Kitzinger, 1990, cited in Devalle, 1996, p. 123).

Eysenck (1994) suggested that the very restricted view of a science as defined by the experimental method is a view which philosophers of science have demonstrated as untenable. It is now accepted that science can progress in a number of different ways, which is reflected in the range of different research methods adopted by psychologists to test their scientific theories.

■ An alternative notion of science: hermeneutics

An alternative view of what constitutes science – **hermeneutics** – defines it not in terms of the research methodology, but in terms of the meaning generated by a systematic approach to studying different things. Thus the emphasis is on interpretation and the meaning generated by the study of a particular phenomenon rather than

Table 2.10

	Why the theory *is* scientific	Why the theory is *not* scientific
Psychoanalysis Freud	Freud attempted to enhance our understanding of human behaviour; he believed in a direct cause and effect relationship between childhood experience and adult behaviour; he sought techniques which attempted to control the behaviour of the neurotic.	Did not collect data using systematic objective measures and did not conduct experiments. His concepts were difficult to test due to their hypothetical nature, and the fact that they allowed for such a variety of interpretations his theories were always supported (they were not open to falsification).
Behaviourism Skinner Watson	Strong emphasis on empirical methods and focus upon observable behaviour. Highly deterministic – all behaviour is caused by external stimuli. Theoretical assumptions detailed direct cause and effect relationships through concepts such as stimulus and response. Strong belief in concept of behaviour control, i.e. through use of external stimuli.	Provided only limited understanding of human behaviour. Failed to do justice to the complexity of many functions by reducing them to the measurement of overt responses.
Humanism Maslow Rogers	Strong interest in understanding the complexity of human behaviour – the emphasis is upon the individual and experiences that are unique to that person.	Rejected the scientific method; not concerned with issues of prediction and control. Rejected external deterministic explanations and emphasised the role of individual free will.

Comparison of contrasting approaches within psychology (Eysenck, 1994)

upon the 'absolute truth'. Such a view openly acknowledges the *social construction* of meaning and warns against the absolutist assumptions of the scientific method.

Psychological approaches sitting firmly within this hermeneutic tradition include phenomenological approaches, such as humanistic psychology, and many areas of social psychology which acknowledge the reactivity of any research situation, regardless of how scientific it may purport to be. The focus is on the perception and experience of events and what they actually mean to people, rather than upon the measurement of some objective reality. Similarly, meaning is created within a psychoanalytical framework in the interpretation of the 'data' of the mind (for example dreams). The rise of the socio-cultural perspective within psychology also highlights the context-specific definitions of scientific theory, raising serious questions about the appropriateness of the supposed scientific method and the relevance of much supposed scientific knowledge, with its misplaced assumed universality.

Thus, the answer to any question regarding the scientific status of psychology is contingent upon the assumptions of what science is, assumptions which are often implicit in the question. Perhaps the question needs to be qualified in order to clarify these assumptions. It may be more useful to break the question up into a series of different ones:

1   Are we talking about psychology as a whole and asking whether it is a *unified discipline*? If so, then according to Kuhn, psychology would most definitely be in a state of pseudo-science or pre-science.
2   Are we asking whether psychology is a science in terms of the *methods of study* it employs? If so, then this will obviously depend upon the 'branch' of psychology under consideration.
3   Are we asking is psychology (or any branch within it) is scientific on the basis of its ability to *predict and control*?
4   Are we asking whether psychology (or any branch within it) is scientific in terms of its ability to *increase understanding*?

It is only by making explicit the assumptions of what we mean when we talk about science that any meaningful answer to the question of whether psychology is a science can be generated.

■ *Should* psychology be a science?

In western culture the status of science is perceived as desirable. This section questions the desirability of such a label, examining briefly the possible dangers of holding the concept of science in such high esteem.

Perhaps the biggest danger is the unquestioning respect often given to research which can be defined as scientific. Results are accepted and applied, having a significant impact upon the lives of many people in our society, people who are often in vulnerable positions. This is seen perhaps most obviously within the fields of medical science with the development of new treatment techniques, drugs and therapies.

This situation is perpetuated within the culture of scientific research environments, where the pressure to publish meaningful research in respected journals is ever increasing. Publications in such journals reward authors with greater respectability as well as often having a direct impact upon the funding awarded in order to further those areas of research. As academic institutions become increasingly dependent upon funding from private sources, issues of impartiality versus the vested interest of the funding body cannot be ignored.

One of the most extreme consequences of the pressure to produce scientifically respectable research has been in the production, publication and application of fraudulent data. Two examples of such research are detailed in figure 2.11.

Whilst fraudulent research represents an obvious attempt to mislead, that which is not fraudulent may also be misleading if presented under the guise of respectability associated with science. The recent reporting of controversial research suggesting a biological basis for gender differences in the sociability of children has been heavily criticised by Orbach and Schwartz (1997). They argued that the interpretation of the research

2.11 The pressure to produce 'science': two examples of fraudulent research

Perhaps the most famous example is the case of Cyril Burt and his research on genetic inheritance of intelligence in the 1950s and 1960s. Thirty years after its publication Burt's data revealing strong correlations supporting the idea that intelligence was genetically determined, were found to be too good to be true. (Leon Kamin (1974) who uncovered Burt's fraud, also revealed how Burt had invented fictitious co-authors.) Burt's work was accepted by the scientific community contributing significantly to the eugenics movement, popular at that time, and exerting a strong influence upon educational policy of the time.

Heller (1986) argued that the fraud could have been detected by any qualified researcher and the fact that it took 30 years to do so is partly a reflection of the unwillingness in academic circles to question the research of eminent people. It also reveals how the values of the researcher may influence research findings, with Burt himself a 'fanatical believer in inequality' (Heller, 1986). (It is worrying to note Hans Eysenck's purported response to Kamin's revelations: in a letter to Burt's sister he wrote that the disclosures were 'just a determined effort on the part of some very left wing environmentalists determined to play a political game with scientific facts' (Broad and Wade, 1985, cited in Heller, 1986).

A more recent example of fraudulent research is that cited by Jones (1995). In the 1980s Stephen Brenning reported a series of findings in which the IQ scores of mentally retarded patients doubled when the patients were taken off a particular drug. These findings had a strong influence upon drug treatment programmes with the drug being withdrawn from many patients (even though the drug helped to control violent behaviour). Brenning's colleagues became suspicious when, like Burt, his publishing record was just too good to be true. Between 1980 and 1983 he had published 24 articles representing one-third of *all* literature on that subject. A closer look at his research record revealed that he was carrying out studies in one city whilst also working in another, and that the data gathered by different observers were too consistent. Unable to produce his raw data, Brenning admitted his fraud and resigned. He was convicted in 1988 on two counts of false grant statements. (Case reported by Sise, 1991, cited in Jones, 1995).

as *scientific* is misleading and you could be forgiven for assuming that the results were the work of geneticists working on the human genome project. A closer look at the research reveals that the data were based on parents' assessments of their own children's behaviour and that the actual differences between scores given to boys and girls, whilst statistically significant, were in fact quite small. As Orbach and Schwartz (1997) pointed out, 'the assumption that the difference in scorings is due to a gene or genes that somehow code for behaviour is only an assumption – one that finds resonance in our culture for reasons that are unconnected to its validity'. Commenting upon the unquestioning acceptance of science, they conclude by asking, 'Why does a report in *Nature* [a respected and widely read scientific journal] automatically command an "it must be right attitude?" as though science were a different kind of activity than any other?'

The question here is at what expense do we strive for the unquestioned status of being labelled scientific? If such a label means that we are 'blinded by science' and are unable to look beyond and question its claims, then we must ask, is such a state actually desirable for psychology? Questions must be asked within scientific communities about the status of research produced under the influence of a range of factors (for example personal values; pressure to publish; sources of funding for research), which together define what is accepted as scientific knowledge.

Self-assessment | questions

18 What are the characteristics of science which give it a high degree of credibility?

19 What is meant by 'physics envy'?

20 Slife and Williams (1995) suggested two interpretations of what it is to be scientific. What are they?

21 Why is the question 'Is Psychology a Science?' too simplistic?

22 What are the possible dangers of science having such a high status?

(Suggested answers on pages 74–75.)

Biases in psychological theory and practice

Psychology as we know it is, by and large, a western (predominantly US) discipline. The hallmark of 'normal' behaviour is that of the white, middle-class, western male, and this has been the standard against which the behaviour of all others has been measured. The result is a bias in research and practice which favours the white western male at the expense of other groups such as women and different ethnic groups. The impact of such bias upon these two groups is the focus of the next two sections.

Cultural diversity

Within psychology there is increasing recognition of the need to address explicitly the reality of cultural diversity, both at the practical and theoretical levels. As the population of the US and other western countries becomes increasingly diverse, psychological theory must respond and reflect these changes if it is to retain any relevance. Similarly, as the popularity of psychology grows around the world, it is becoming ever more apparent that many of the concepts of western theory provide an inadequate basis for the explanation of cross-cultural behaviours. Owusu-Bempah and Howitt

(1995) questioned the **assumed universality** of western psychological theory pointing out how the interpretation of African culture through the belief systems of western psychology simply serves to denigrate that culture and fails to do justice to the strengths or advantages of the cultural differences. One example here is the Eurocentric notion of individualism which many African cultures are 'lacking'. Whilst highly favoured and encouraged in western culture, individualism is seen as an undesirable trait in Malawi, threatening the overall well-being of the community. Instead of recognising the possible benefits for that culture (as well as highlighting the selfish nature of western culture) this is interpreted very negatively by western psychologists (for example Carr and MacLachlan, 1993), indicating the 'pull down' motive which ultimately inhibits the 'progress' of development in Malawi.

It is observations such as these which have led many to question two implicit assumptions associated with psychology:

- that there is a universal acceptable conception of psychological science
- that all cultures should emulate psychology as practised in the US (Gergen *et al.*, 1996).

There are now strong calls for **indigenous psychology** where culture is given primacy in understanding behaviour. Most of traditional psychology to date has either been culturally blind, or, where cultural variations have been acknowledged, has de-emphasised their influence or bracketed them together for later study (Gergen *et al.*, 1996).

■ Three examples: India; Maori culture; Turkey

Figure 2.12 explores the inappropriateness of western psychological concepts and the damaging impact they have when applied to three different cultures: India, Maori culture (New Zealand) and Turkey. This issue is relevant to therapeutic approaches (see Unit 26, page 978).

2.12 The effects of applying western psychological concepts to non-western cultures

■ India

The colonial condition of India meant that for a long time the focus of psychology was on testing western theories and concepts. Indian intellectual and cultural traditions were ignored even though such practices were central to the daily lives of Indian people. Culture was regarded as an intrusion which simply impeded the development of universal scientific generalisations, with their strong emphasis on individualism, mechanism and objectivity. The effect has been a debilitating one which has misconstrued the realities of different cultures and disregarded psychologies that are non-western. 'Consequently, when people from other cultures are exposed to Western psychology, they find their identities placed in question and their conceptual repertoires rendered obsolete' (Misra, 1996).

The response from the academic community in India has been a call for an indigenous psychology based upon Indian (Hindu) construals of psychological functioning. Examples of concepts such a psychology would embrace include: a holistic-organic world view, coherence and order across all life forms, the socially constituted nature of the person, control that is distributed rather than personalised, a belief in multiple worlds (material and spiritual).

Another avenue of development has been the alternative construing of western psychological concepts to complement and reflect Indian culture. This has occurred within social psychological, clinical and organisational contexts.

This illustrates the point made by Misra that understanding the impact of culture does not mean abandoning all of western psychology. The way forward is to generate an integrative approach to psychology which appreciates alternatives and explores the intersections of concepts relating to different cultures.

■ Maori culture (New Zealand)

Andrew Lock (1996) suggested that the use of psychology in New Zealand simply serves to perpetuate the western oppression of the Maoris and , as a result, psychology is practised in a highly politicised environment. This position is summed up by Lawson-Te Aho:

'Psychology, and clinical psychology in particular, has created the mass abnormalisation of Maori people by virtue of the fact that Maori people have been on the receiving end of psychological practice as the helpless recipients of English defined labels and treatments . . .' (1993, cited in Lock, 1996).

The fact that psychiatric admission rates are two to three times higher for Maoris than non-Maoris adds weight to the predominantly negative impact of western psychology. As Lock pointed out, there is a clash between Maori and white New Zealand cultures in which the concept of the self is completely different and incommensurable. This renders many concepts associated with western psychology irrelevant – 'Why would a Maori want to measure intelligence, or sanity, for example? Western schools and Western asylums are not the Maori way of education or treatment for the troubled' (Lock, 1996, p. 499). Lock suggested that the future of psychology lies in making it practically relevant to the cultural context. This itself is dependent upon the adoption of appropriate methodological and theoretical frameworks such as those provided within the **narrative tradition**. This approach focuses upon the unfolding of the stories surrounding the phenomenon under study, attempting to generate contextualised understandings through the examination of the discourse used in a particular culture.

2.12 The effects of applying western psychological concepts to non-western cultures *cont'd*

■ Turkey

Psychology is developing rapidly in Turkey, being heavily influenced by western theory and practice. Whilst the limitations of western psychology, in terms of its cultural inappropriateness, have been noted for some time, there has been a reluctance to abandon western theory and practice, with the focus upon adapting western theories, measures and concepts to the Turkish context.

The danger here lies in the inherent acceptance of positivist-empiricist notions of science, and the injustice in failing to recognise local intelligibilities because they do not conform to the imported western definitions. Examples of these disparities include conceptualisations of mental health, child development and the family whose implicit western values clashed with those of Turkish culture. Gulerce (1996) adds:

> 'additionally many other theoretical assumptions relying on a view of rational, materialist, pragmatic, functionalist, self-centred, and self-contained human beings fall short in application to understanding of much Turkish behaviour. A guiding model is required that leaves room for the irrational, spiritual, altruistic, conservative, other centred, community oriented, and interdependent human being' (p. 501).

Such concepts should be the focus of indigenous psychology, which would not only provide culturally valid theories, but may also have valuable contributions to make in the revision of western theories.

■ Redressing the balance

Criticisms such as those outlined above have led to increasing recognition of the limits of western psychology, and with it moves to develop more culturally relevant theories and practice. Tavris and Wade (1995) noted the rise of the '*socio-cultural perspective*', referring to the substantial body of work which examines the impact of social and cultural factors upon psychological phenomena. In May 1996 the journal of the American Psychological Association, *American Psychologist*, launched a new section called 'International Perspectives in Psychology'. This emerged out of recognition of the growing limitations of US Psychology, as both the US itself becomes more culturally diverse and the practice and study of psychology becomes more popular around the globe. As pointed out by Mays *et al.* (1996), failure to respond to the demands for more culturally relevant theories and applications will result in western psychology becoming ever more fragmented, irrelevant and redundant. The way forward is to expand the boundaries of psychology as we know it and acknowledge the psychologies of different cultures. In this way: 'US psychology through the influence of the professional development of psychology of other countries will grow to become a more inclusive and responsive psychology that is poised to meet the challenges of the next century' (Mays *et al.*, 1996, p. 486).

Gender biases in psychological research

Just as psychology has failed adequately to represent the experiences of cultural/ethnic minorities, so too has it failed adequately to represent the experiences of women. Psychology as we know it is, by and large, the psychology of the western male. Many widely accepted theories speak of behaviour in a gender neutral way, implying that the theory is representative of all. This often belies the fact that the theory is based upon the observations of totally male samples. In this way male behaviour becomes the norm against which all others are measured.

Where the experiences of women are given separate consideration, this is often couched in terms of what women are missing, or in terms of how far they deviate from the norm. Thus, women become the 'other' and many theoretical developments stemming from the study of women alone remain peripheral to the 'main' (male) body of psychological knowledge. This is apparent in the vast body of research into sex differences which dates back to the beginning of the twentieth century. 'Then, as now, men served as the unmarked reference group, and male behaviour was the norm or standard of comparison. The implicit question was whether women are the same as, different from, or even as good as men' (Hare-Mustin and Marecek, 1994, p. 531). Thus, by definition, any difference is an indication of inferiority, with such theories serving to perpetuate and justify the inferior status occupied by many women in all different sectors of society.

Reflecting upon the literature addressing the issue of gender bias, Denmark *et al.* (1988) concluded that the bias pervades all stages of the research process: question formulation, research design, data analysis and interpretation, and conclusion formulation. Specific examples of biases at these particular stages are given in figure 2.13, which also provides a non-sexist solution to each example.

(Figure 2.13 includes only a small selection of the problems highlighted by Denmark *et al.* (1988). Readers are encouraged to read their original paper.)

The collective impact of these biases inherent in the research process is the production of theories which give invalid accounts of women's experiences, which may justify discriminatory practices and have a serious detrimental impact upon the way women are treated.

2.13 Examples of biases at different stages in the research process (Denmark et al., 1988)

■ Stage 1: Question formulation

Problem: Gender stereotypes that are associated with the topic being studied can bias question formulation and research outcomes.

Example: Some studies have defined leadership only in terms of dominance, aggression and other styles that emphasise characteristics congruent with a male stereotype.

Solution: Recognise the existence of a range of leadership styles, including those that emphasise egalitarian relationships, negotiation, conflict resolution and consideration of others. The limits of any definition should be specified.

■ Stage 2: Research methods

Problem: The selection of research participants is based on stereotypic assumptions and does not allow for generalisations to other groups.

Example: On the basis of stereotypes about who should be responsible for contraception, only females are looked at in studies of contraception.

Solution: Both sexes should be studied before conclusions are drawn about the factors that determine use of contraception.

■ Stage 3: Data analysis and interpretation

Problem: Serendipitous gender differences are reported, but no report is made when differences are not found. Care must be taken to avoid giving a skewed image of the actual data.

Example: 'In analysing data, we found that males and females differed significantly on . . .'

Solution: Any non-hypothesised sex or gender differences should be reported and the need for replication indicated to assure that the difference is not artifactual. When gender differences are not found and where such an observation is relevant, this too should be reported so that future research could confirm or disconfirm the lack of any non-hypothesised gender differences.

■ Stage 4: Conclusions

Problem: Differential opportunities for males and females are advocated on the basis of statistically significant sex difference findings.

Example: Gender differences in group means for mathematics ability tests are used to justify denying women opportunities for training in advanced mathematics.

Solution: Equality of opportunity is a basic tenet of our society. Group scores should not be used to justify discrimination against individuals who may or may not score well.

A look at a number of research areas illustrates the extent of gender bias inherent in many, widely accepted, psychological theories.

Theories of motivation. The established textbook theories on motivation have little to say about women; they appear to assume that men and women are a homogeneous group in this regard. This is illustrated by the early explanations of work motivation. F W Taylor's study of the male manual worker in the steel and manufacturing processes influenced many ideas of work motivation, ideas which were generalised to all, inspite of the fact that no women were observed. Similarly, in the famous Hawthorne studies of the mid-1920s there were substantial gender differences in terms of the treatment of participants and the outcomes of the research. Whilst the men were observed under normal working conditions, the female group was pressured by male supervisors into an experimental situation, and whilst output was increased by the women, it was restricted by the men. In spite of this, the overall findings were generalised to all of the workers (Wilson, 1995).

Maslow's theory of motivation has also been criticised for being gender blind. Motivation is explained in terms of satisfying a hierarchical pyramid of needs, the ultimate aim of which is self actualisation (see Unit 15 page 526). Some have argued that self actualisation reflects stereotypical male traits and defines concepts such as risk taking in ways that reflect male experiences (Kasten, 1972, cited in Wilson, 1995, p. 129; Cullen, 1992). In assessing the relevance of Maslow's theory to women, Betz (1982, 1984) concluded that, whilst working women supported the ordering of the needs in Maslow's hierarchy, women homemakers diverged considerably. Similar critical observations are made of McClelland's achievement theory:

'David McClelland's initial theory of achievement concerned men as men were compatible with his theoretical predictions. When female subjects did not respond to the instructions designed to arouse their achievement motivation, it was suggested that they were less motivated than men (Veroff et al., 1953). A

different theory, McClelland suggested, would have to be developed for females (McClelland, 1966). The researchers did not seem to think it important that under relaxed conditions females actually scored higher than males in the achievement motivation test (Betz and Fitgerald, 1987). For the next decade or so only males were used in the achievement motivation research. Males tended to be treated as the norm and women regarded as members of a non-standard population of lesser interest.' (Spence et al., 1985). (Wilson, 1995, pp. 132–3)

Theories of power and leadership. Definitions of what it is to be powerful or a good leader concentrate on characteristics associated with the typical male stereotype. Research into leadership has typically focused on male leaders, affirming assumptions that all leaders are not only male, but also quite masculine. This is consistent with Miller's suggestion that power in most organisations has meant the ability to advance one's self and simultaneously to control, limit and if possible, destroy the power of others. By contrast is the 'relational' basis of stereotypical notions of women's power, in which the emphasis is upon 'taking care', being supportive and facilitative (Cassell and Walsh, 1993). Unfortunately, although relational power may be very effective, it is largely invisible, with such behaviours deemed as inappropriate expressions of power in competitive, male-dominated environments. Ironically, it is also often deemed inappropriate when women exhibit accepted powerful behaviours, such as assertiveness and initiative, with such women often labelled as 'super bitches'. By defining power in gender specific ways, i.e. male, this ensures that power remains the exclusive right of that gender, i.e. men. This relationship is illustrated in figure 2.14, using Wilson's (1995) analysis of French and Raven's (1959) popular theory of power.

In an attempt to help rectify the situation Cassell and Walsh (1993) suggested a feminising of the concept of power, a redefinition which does not automatically value male and devalue female behaviours. This means acknowledging the strengths of relational aspects of power, thus broadening the range of acceptable behaviours for

2.14 Gender biases in definitions of power: French and Raven's theory

French and Raven (1959) differentiated power into five types:

1 *Expert power*: refers to the ability to perceive and influence because you possess superior skills or knowledge. This is more likely to be perceived as belonging to men.
2 *Referent power*: this is charismatic power, and again is more likely to be possessed by men. A study of role models (cited in Kahn, 1984) found that while both sexes typically listed a member of their own sex as a role model, females listed a male role model ten times more frequently than males listed a female role model.
3 *Reward power*: refers to the ability to mediate rewards such as money, food, promotion and affection. Since men are more likely to work, and are paid more for equal work, we can expect men to have more monetary reward than women and to have more reward power. The personal rewards such as affection should be equally available to men and women.
4 *Coercive power*: refers to the ability to mediate punishment. Since men are, on average, larger and stronger than women and have more rewards to withhold, men typically possess more coercive power.
5 *Legitimate power*: refers to the formal power associated with a role. Men have more legitimate power as they are socialised to believe they have the right to influence and this is supported by our language, laws and institutions which privilege the male.

Source: Adapted from Wilson (1995) p. 168.

both men and women in positions of power, and in turn increasing opportunities for those who exhibit such behaviour.

■ Factors perpetuating gender bias

Janet Hyde (1994) identified a number of factors in academic research environments which perpetuate gender biases in psychological theory (figure 2.15).

Taken together, the factors shown in figure 2.15 illustrate the complicated web of forces which ultimately define what is accepted as psychological knowledge. As well as raising questions related to the inherent biases these forces may introduce, fundamental questions must also be asked about the nature of scientific enquiry and definitions of 'truth'. This issue is covered in the earlier section on psychology as a science (pages 58–61).

2.15 Factors perpetuating bias in psychological theory

1 *Publication bias*: common to the whole of psychology, this is where significant results are more likely to get published than non-significant ones. As a result, those studies which find significant gender differences are likely to be published whereas those that do not are not. The result of this bias is a general impression that there is a multitude of psychological gender differences and few gender similarities, because the latter tend not to be reported.
2 *Unreplicated findings of gender differences*: often a single report of a significant finding receives much attention both from the media and from academic communities. However, if attempts are then made to replicate these findings and they fail (i.e. they reveal non-significant results), these studies will receive very little attention. As a result, the original study stands as authoritative, with no recognition of contradictory evidence.
3 *Failure to report effect sizes*: often differences found are very small yet findings are treated as if the differences are huge.
4 *Findings of gender differences are often interpreted as indicating female deficits*: for example, research into self-confidence – on

2.15 Factors perpetuating bias in psychological theory *cont'd*

tasks such as estimating how many points they think they earned in an exam, females consistently report lower marks than males. This is taken as an indication of a self-confidence deficit in females. However, in reality female estimates are much closer to their actual scores then male estimates, which is more indicative of males' inflated self-confidence than a deficit in females.

5   *Findings of gender differences, when not reported and applied carefully, may be used in a manner that is harmful to females*: one example here is the research by Benbow and Stanley (1980) which made much of a lop-sided ratio (far more males than females) in their sample of highly mathematically gifted seventh graders. The media made much of this report, which was found to influence mothers' ratings of their daughters' mathematical ability in a subsequent study by Jacobs and Eccles (1985). Mothers who

had heard the media coverage were likely to give significantly lower estimates of their daughters' ability than those who had not heard the media coverage. The importance of this is that a mother's confidence in her daughter's abilities plays a crucial role in developing the daughter's own self-confidence. Thus, the reporting and interpretation of results from studies such as those conducted by Benbow and Stanley can have a harmful effect on females.

6   *Gender differences are often interpreted as being due to biological factors in the absence of appropriate biological data*: researchers may speculate or media reports suggest that observed differences between the sexes are due to biological factors, even though no biological measures have actually been collected. (This point was made by Orbach and Schwartz (1997). (See pages 60–61 of this unit.)

■ The way forward

Some psychologists have argued that the study of sex differences should be abandoned and other more relevant questions should be asked. Research solely into difference serves artificially to exaggerate differences which do exist at the expense of recognising similarities. Thus, there is value in asking what are the similarities between men and women, rather than what are the differences.

Others feel that this does not go far enough, questioning the validity and relevance of dualistic comparisons between men and women regardless of whether similarities or differences are being researched. The parameters of the debate about gender need redefining in a way which complements the multitude of social realities present in contemporary society. Attention should be focused on how the concept of gender becomes established as a social fact in different situations. Thus the emphasis is on contextual factors such as the institutions, practices, beliefs and language within a culture/subculture and the role they play

in determining reality for members of different groups within that culture/subculture.

Consistent with this is the acknowledgement that women do not represent a single homogeneous gender group who share a common set of experiences. Research into sex differences which continues within the predetermined, dualistic categories of men and women simply highlights ways in which men differ from women. This ignores the differences among both men and women assuming each shares a common experience, which again is predominantly that of the white middle-class man or woman. This issue supports calls for a shift in mainstream psychology to recognise the complexity of gender relations. Questions need to be asked as to how notions of masculinity and femininity are created and changed, a process which will be aided by the wider adoption of more qualitative methods such as ethnography and discourse analysis.

Whilst this debate goes on, research into sex differences will most certainly continue. Indeed, the current intensity of interest in genetic research underlies the important role psychology has to play in countering more deterministic, and potentially more damaging, explanations of gender differences (Eagly, 1994; Hyde, 1994). There is a strong need to try and ensure that psychological research which is conducted is non-sexist, thus minimising the possible detrimental effect of such research. To this end, Hyde (1994) proposed six guidelines for non-sexist research on gender differences:

■ Researchers should routinely conduct the appropriate significance tests for gender differences for all major measures in their study. Furthermore, researchers should take responsibility for reporting and publishing findings of non-significant gender differences, so they are reported on an equal basis with significant gender differences.

■ Journal editors should take care to publish findings of non-significant gender differences, provided the study meets the appropriate scientific standards.

■ Researchers should be required to report an effect size for all findings on gender differences, whether significant or not, so that the reader is informed of the magnitude of the difference.

■ Researchers should be alert to the manner in which they interpret findings of gender differences. Interpretations implying a female deficit should always be questioned to see whether there is an equally tenable interpretation that does not imply a female deficit.

■ Biological explanations for gender differences should be made with great caution. Biological explanations should not be invoked when no biological measures have been taken.

■ Researchers should apply appropriate scientific standards of conduct in ensuring that their data are appropriately interpreted so that the risk of the data being used inappropriately, in a manner detrimental to women, is minimised as much as possible.

Whilst this section has focused upon culture and gender bias in psychology, the issues discussed are relevant to all minority groups. Psychology can no longer continue to be the psychology of the white middle-class male. The diversity within and between societies must be recognised and represented, especially as psychology grows in popularity both in academia and in applied settings. Failure to recognise this diversity has, and will continue to have, negative consequences for those in minority groups. As such diversity increases, a psychology which remains that of the white middle-class will become increasingly redundant.

Self-assessment questions

23 What is the fundamental source of cultural bias in psychology?

24 Why can psychology no longer afford to be culturally biased?

25 What is meant by indigenous psychology?

26 Give an example of the inappropriateness of western psychology when applied to a different culture.

27 Summarise how gender bias is inherent in the research process.

28 Explain how the psychological concept of power is gender biased.

29 What can psychologists do in an attempt to reduce gender bias in psychological research?

(Suggested answers on page 75.)

Unit summary

- Controversy surrounds the application of some areas of psychological research such as the *persuasive* techniques used in advertising and propaganda.

- *Advertising* has used principles based upon psychoanalytical, behaviourist and cognitive psychology often with the aim of encouraging the audience to purchase a particular product. There is little evidence to suggest *subliminal advertising* works.

- *Propaganda* is the attempt to persuade on the basis of inaccurate, false or selective information. It has been and continues to be used in situations of warfare.

- The power of persuasion is shown in the examples of *cults*. The tactics used by cult leaders are similar in principle to other techniques of persuasion, only applied with greater intensity to the exclusion of all other sources of information.

- *Psychometric testing* gives cause for concern because important decisions are made on the basis of test results and their use is on the increase in educational, occupational and clinical settings.

- *Ability tests* are widely used to assess IQ, although tests are biased to favour certain groups in society. 'Culture fair' tests have been produced in response to this bias.

- Personality testing is on the increase although the relevance of such tests, especially in occupational settings, has been questioned. Other concerns include the *validity* of such tests, the *crudeness* of computer generated feedback and the *simplicity* of test items.

- The value of psychometric testing depends upon the appropriate development, selection and interpretation of tests. Checks should be in place to ensure that the testing process is not abused and that participants are protected.

- *Science* is held in high regard in our culture. Common sense notions of what it is to be scientific are based upon inductivist theory and the emphasis upon empirical methods.

- Notions within psychology of what it is to be scientific vary, encompassing: the method used; the quality of understanding produced; the degree of prediction and control afforded.

- The question of *whether psychology is a science* is dependent upon what is meant by science and what is meant by psychology (for example, are we talking about psychology as a whole).

- There are dangers of holding science in such high regard including the devaluation of other forms of knowledge not acquired using rigorous experimentation. We should not blindly accept that asserting the scientific status of psychology is desirable.

- Biases in psychological theory stem from the fact that the 'norm' is the white, middle-class male. This has resulted in both culture and gender bias.

- *Culture bias* has become increasingly apparent as psychology has become more popular around the world. This has often had a damaging effect resulting in the devaluation of the experiences of those in other cultures.

- Culture bias is being recognised as seen in the rise of the *socio-cultural* perspective and with calls for '*indigenous psychologies*' to represent non-western cultures.

- Women are treated in psychology in terms of how far they deviate from the male norm with *gender biases* permeating all stages of the research process. Examples of gender bias in psychological theory include notions of power and theories of motivation.

- A range of factors have been identified in academic and research environments which perpetuate gender bias. Whilst some have suggested a shift to focus on gender similarities rather than differences, others suggest we look at the whole complex range of different groups in society getting away from the basic male/female comparison.

- If psychology fails to recognise the increasing diversity in terms of both gender and ethnicity, as well as potentially damaging these minority groups, it ultimately runs the risk of becoming increasingly redundant.

Terms to define

assumed universality
cults
falsification
faulty heuristics
hermeneutics
indigenous psychology
inductivism
labelling effects
narrative tradition

physics envy
propaganda
psychological operations
psychometric tests
response sets
scientific method
scientific paradigms
subliminal advertising

Further reading

Banyard, P (1996) 'Psychology and advertising', *Psychology Review*, September, pp. 24–7.

Both Banyard's and Wadeley's articles provide good, readable summaries of research in these areas.

Devalle, D (1996) 'Dacapo: science and social psychology', in R Sapsford (ed.) *Issues for Social Psychology*, Open University, Milton Keynes.

Whilst the issues raised are discussed in relation to social psychology, many are important to psychology as a whole.

Gergen, J, Gulerce, A, Lock, A and Misra, G (1996) 'Psychological science in cultural context', *American Psychologist, 51(5)*, pp. 496–503.

A useful article on cultural bias.

Kitzinger, C (1994) (ed.) 'Should psychologists study sex differences', *Feminism and Psychology, 4(4)*.

For the topic of gender bias this special feature includes two particularly useful articles: Hyde, pp. 507–512, 'Should psychologists study gender differences? Yes, with some guidelines'.
Hare-Mustin, R T and Marecek, J, pp. 531–7, 'Asking the right questions: feminist psychology and sex differences'.

Mays, V M, Rubin, J, Sabourin, M and Walker, L (1996) 'Moving towards global psychology: changing theories and practice to meet the needs of a changing world', *American Psychologist, 51(5)*, pp. 485–7.

Another useful article on cultural bias.

Murphy, K R and Davidshofer, C O (1991) *Psychological Testing: Principles and Practice*, 2nd edn, Prentice Hall, Englewood Cliffs, NJ.

A thorough and critical review of all aspects of psychometric testing. This is a good text to dip into even if at first the length of it may be off-putting.

Pratkanis, A R and Aronson, E (1992) *Age of Propaganda: The Everyday Use and Abuse of Persuasion*, W H Freeman, New York.

An excellent analysis of different persuasive techniques applied across a variety of settings. Whilst quite detailed, it is very accessible, bringing the reader's attention to a wide range of important issues.

Slife, B D and Williams, R N (1995) *What's Behind the Research? Discovering Hidden Assumptions in the Behavioral Sciences*, Sage, Beverly Hills, CA.

Contains an excellent chapter on psychology as a science.

Wadeley, A (1996) 'Persuasion and propaganda', *Psychology Review*, November, pp. 17–19.

A good readable summary.

Answers

■ Suggested answers to activities

2

Responses to this activity will obviously vary. Some common examples may include: television adverts; being persuaded by friends to join them in a particular activity; attending school/college open days when deciding where to go; being persuaded by parents to do housework or tidy bedroom.

Whether these were considered acceptable may relate to issues of fairness. Was all the information presented? Was all the information given true? Did you feel pressured into doing something you didn't want to? Did you feel blackmailed or bribed – or was it just gentle encouragement which actually helped you make up your mind?

4

Responses may focus upon the type of knowledge generated – whether it is factual or not; the way that knowledge is produced – whether the experimental method is used; how useful the knowledge is – whether it has any application to real life.

5

a   Kuhn
b   Inductivism
c   Kuhn
d   Popper/criticism of inductivism
e   Inductivism
f   Popper

6

In terms of methodology, the branches of psychology most likely to be considered scientific are: neurobiological approaches, cognitive and behaviourist approaches – most research within these areas is based upon controlled experimentation.

■ Suggested answers to self-assessment questions

1

The behaviourist principles used by advertisers include:
■   positive reinforcement: a persuasive message is learned and accepted if it is rewarding to do so
■   association: when a product is associated with a pleasant feeling
■   generalisation and discrimination: when products are packaged very similarly so qualities of more expensive brands are generalised to other cheaper brands, with the only remaining discrimination feature being cost
■   imitation: where advertisers encourage consumers to copy the behaviour of others in the use and purchase of particular products.

2

Cognitive psychology explains the strength of persuasive messages in terms of the way people interpret a particular message and the associated cognitive processes. One such explanation is provided by the theory of cognitive dissonance which occurs when there is an inconsistency between beliefs and behaviour. If advertisers can create dissonance in their audience, this may encourage them to engage in a particular behaviour in order to reduce that dissonance, for example emotional charity appeals may create feelings of guilt, the discomfort of which is reduced by making a donation. Other cognitive explanations include the use of faulty heuristics – simple cues associated with a particular product aimed to cut through the overload of information faced in today's modern world. Emphasising the scarcity of a particular product also increases the value and desirability of that product in the mind of the perceiver.

3

The four stages of consumer behaviour are:
Stage 1: developing a need – convincing people that they need or want a particular product.
Stage 2: noticing the product – making the product stand out from others available.
Stage 3: purchasing the product – getting people to buy it.
Stage 4: behaviour after the purchase – getting people to make repeat purchases.

4

Subliminal advertising is the presentation of persuasive advertising messages below the threshold of recognition. Whilst the work of Vicary (1950s) reported how effective subliminal advertising was, subsequent research has found little evidence supporting its effectiveness (Pratkanis and Aronson, 1991). Future research may more fruitfully focus on other subtle influences in advertising such as the use of colour, scents and music to evoke certain moods.

5

Whereas education teaches people how to think, propaganda teaches people what to think (Brown, 1963); propaganda seeks to effect attitude change, education seeks to communicate knowledge (Winick, 1994).

6

Hitler operated a highly organised and oppressive propaganda machine. This involved: appointing Goebbels as minister for popular enlightenment and propaganda; establishing control over all media outlets, bombarding people with Nazi messages and images at every opportunity; using simplified slogans and labels expressing the distinct Nazi identity; orchestrating large-scale public displays of support; defining the Jews as the enemy; establishing a common united Nazi identity.

7

It could be argued that psychological operations is not propaganda principally because it is based on truth. It does not set out to deceive, distort or falsify – this is the view of Rodgers (1997). It could also be argued that psychological operations is propaganda. Truthful information may be withheld. The message delivered is dependent upon an indepth analysis of how it is likely to be perceived. Any information which is likely to conflict with the desired perception to be created is simply left out. By Winick's definition of propaganda then, psychological operations can be classified as such: 'Propaganda is the advancement of a position or view which attempts to persuade rather then present a balanced overview'.

8

A range of measures can be taken in order to increase commitment of cult members:
- create a social reality which is that of the cult, severing all links with the outside world
- establish fellow cult members as the 'in-group' and all others as the evil 'out-group'
- encourage displays of commitment to the group – these should escalate, showing ever greater levels of commitment
- establish the leader's credibility and attractiveness
- get members to convert the unconverted
- distract members from thinking undesirable thoughts by keeping them constantly engaged in cult activities and never leave them alone
- keep members striving for a promised land, a better world, a higher state – this gives a sense of purpose in which they are all united.

9

We should be concerned about the use of psychometric tests because important decisions are made on the basis of test scores, and because their use is on the increase, although not necessarily by those suitably qualified to administer the tests.

10

The three main settings in which tests are used are:
- educational – ability tests to measure abilities and academic progress
- industrial/occupational – for selection, placement and training of workers, measuring a range of abilities
- Clinical – ability and personality tests used for diagnosis and assessment of treatment.

11

Summary of four main criticisms of psychometric tests:
- Objection to the quantification of psychological attributes – this reduces the status of people to objects and does not reflect the reality of the individual.
- Labelling effects – a person may be labelled on the basis of test results which may set in motion a self-fulfilling prophecy where they behave, and are encouraged to behave, in a way which is consistent with that label.
- Tests are biased with certain groups performing systematically better on tests than others. Scores vary as a function of socioeconomic status, sex and race.
- Greater use of tests has increased the potential for mis-use especially in occupational/industrial settings where there are few or no regulations governing the use of such tests.

12

Examples of discriminatory practices resulting from ability test scores include the following:
- The use of compulsory sterilisation – between 1924 and 1972 more than 7000 people with low IQ scores were sterilised in the state of Virginia.
- Low IQ scores have been used in the US as the basis for restricting access to immigrants.
- In Britain, those who failed the eleven plus exam were denied access to a grammar school education.

13

The group which scores consistently higher on IQ tests is white, middle-class, males.

14

Ways of reducing test bias include:
- developing culture fair tests which measure abilities relevant to that particular culture in a way which is culturally appropriate

- modifying tests to discriminate positively in favour of those scoring lower
- changing scoring systems to reduce group difference scores thus reducing the likelihood of unfair treatment of minority groups on the basis of lower test scores
- linking the tests to other modes of assessment, for example interviews and observations, such that a more complete picture is obtained and abilities other than those measured on tests are taken into consideration.

The way in which test results are used could also be changed – where there are differences in test scores, the value of these differences should be explored and the attributes and abilities not typically measured by ability tests should be positively recognised.

15

The use of personality tests in the workplace is largely unregulated. Whilst their use is on the increase, personality often bears no relevance to one's ability to do a particular job. Unless this relevance can be demonstrated people may be refused jobs or promotions which they are perfectly capable of doing. The tests may also be unwarranted invasions of privacy and it may be difficult to guarantee confidentiality. Not all tests are well designed and not all test users are suitably qualified to be able to select a good test or to administer tests and give feedback of test results.

16

Computer-based test interpretations give rather crude, broad descriptions which fail to do justice to the uniqueness of an individual's profile. Also, having a computer printout as feedback can be insensitive and may cause unnecessary distress.

17

Summary of Klines' criticisms common to many personality tests:
- Items can be too simple, affronting the intelligence of those completing them.
- Response sets: acquiescence – tendency to agree with items; social desirability – tendency to respond in desirable way; some people are consistently neutral on all items, others will always opt for the extreme choice.
- Difficult to find valid tests (even though they may be reliable).

18

The characteristics of science giving it a high degree of credibility include: the objective observation of phenomena carried out under controlled experimental conditions in an attempt to identify cause and effect relationships; the findings are applied, for example technological advances; the findings of science are in theory accessible to all to be scrutinised; science is assumed to have the correctness of mathematics due to the similarities in language used.

19

Subjects which seek to be defined as scientific are said to be in a state of 'physics envy' as physics is the role model of science which they seek to emulate.

20

The two interpretations of the label 'science' suggested by Slife and Williams are:
- as a scientific body of knowledge which rejects supernatural explanations of behaviour and seeks to establish deterministic laws and principles
- as a method of studying phenomena based upon careful empirical observation, control and prediction in an experimental setting.

21

The question 'Is psychology a science?' is too simplistic for two main reasons:
- There are a variety of interpretations about what it is to be a science. Is it the method of study employed?; is it the ability to predict and control? Is it the quality and extent of understanding provided? Is it whether or not the discipline is unified?
- Psychology itself is characterised by a plurality of approaches, some of which may be regarded as more scientific than others.

So, it is necessary to define what is meant by science and whether we are talking about psychology as a whole or certain approaches within it.

22

The dangers of science having such a high status include the following:
- Findings may go unquestioned because they are labelled 'scientific'. The implications of this are serious given that many scientific findings are applied and have a direct impact upon people's lives.
- There is pressure within scientific communities to produce and publish research, research which is increasingly funded by private sources – this brings into question the impartiality and objectivity of research conducted.
- In aspiring to attain recognition within scientific communities, researchers may be tempted to

produce fraudulent research or may seek to give the impression that their research is the result of rigorous, objective methods when it in fact is not.

■ More generally, seeking to aspire to the label of science by definition devalues those approaches deemed to be less scientific.

23

The fundamental source of cultural bias in psychology derives from the fact that research and theories are based largely upon an analysis of western males and the theories which emerge are founded within the cultural value systems of the western world.

24

Psychology can no longer afford to be culturally biased because of the increasing ethnic diversity within the US and the global spread of psychology. It risks becoming irrelevant and ultimately redundant.

25

Indigenous psychology is that which takes account of the culture of those being studied resulting in psychological theory and practice which is consistent with and complements the specific cultural context.

26

Examples of the inappropriateness of western psychological theory when applied to other cultures include the following:

■ The concept on 'individualism' when applied to the African culture of Malawi – whilst individualism is valued in western culture, it is not in Africa.

■ Many concepts from western psychology, for example individualism, the emphasis on mechanistic models and objectivity, are irrelevant when applied to India.

■ In Maori culture (New Zealand) the concept of the self is completely different to that of western culture and psychology.

■ Western conceptualisations of mental health, child development and the family are irrelevant to the cultural context of Turkey, as is the western emphasis upon rationality, materialism, pragmatism and the individual self.

27

Gender bias is inherent in all stages of the research process. This includes question formulation, research methods, data analysis and interpretation, conclusions and applications.

28

The psychological concept of power is gender biased because definitions of power are based upon stereotypically masculine behaviours, i.e. to dominate and to advance one's self at the expense of others. Relational aspects of power such as being supportive and facilitative (behaviours typically associated with women) are invisible even though they are very effective behaviours. Thus to be powerful is to show 'male' behaviours such as assertion, aggression and competitiveness. Defining power in this way helps ensure that it remains the exclusive preserve of the gender upon whose behaviour the definition is based, i.e. men. This is supported by French and Raven's (1959) theory of power with men much more likely to exhibit the behaviours defined in their various definitions of power.

29

Psychology can seek to become less gender biased by:

■ abandoning research into sex differences and focusing upon similarities instead

■ abandoning all dualistic comparisons between men and women as they are too simplistic – we need to look at how gender comes to be defined for a whole range of different groups in our society, recognising that not all men share common experiences and neither do all women

■ following the guidelines suggested by Hyde (1994):

– Routinely test for sex differences in all studies and report non-significant ones as well as significant ones.

– Journals should publish findings showing non-significant differences.

– The magnitude of any difference found between the sexes should be reported.

– Interpretations of results implying a female deficit should be questioned to see if there is as valid an interpretation which does not imply such a deficit.

– Biological interpretations should only be done when appropriate biological measures have been used.

– Researchers should help ensure their results are interpreted and applied appropriately and not applied in a detrimental manner.

Unit 3

Ethical Issues in Psychology

Sara Nadin

This unit covers:

Ethics and their place in psychology

The British Psychological Society and its code of conduct

Research involving human participants

The ethics of animal experimentation

The ethics of socially sensitive research

By the end of this unit, you should be able to:

- understand the central importance of ethical issues in all areas of psychological research

- understand the British Psychological Society's Code of Conduct, Ethical Principles and Guidelines – and apply these in the evaluation of psychological research

- demonstrate an awareness of alternative techniques which attempt to reduce the potential discomfort participants may experience

- recognise the practical and ethical debate concerning animal experimentation

- show an awareness of possible alternatives to the use of animals

- identify areas of socially sensitive research recognising the responsibility of researchers to protect minority groups which may be represented in their research.

Unit 3 Contents

Introduction

What are **ethics**? The study of ethics has its roots in philosophy and is concerned with the acceptability of human behaviour, with right and wrong, with what is good and bad conduct. Ethical ideas shape the moral values held by an individual, group or society, guiding their thought and action. These moral values often form the basis of a moral code which classifies those behaviours which are deemed acceptable for members of a particular group. Anyone who is a member of that group is expected to abide by the moral code held. The ethical principles specific to psychology are designed to ensure protection and respect for participants, both human and animal, as well as ensuring concern for the impact any research may have on wider society.

Ethics and their place in psychology

The very nature of psychological research and practice demands a high concern for ethical issues. Most research within psychology involves human participants. Psychologists/researchers thus have a duty to look after the well-being of their participants ensuring they do not come to any harm or experience discomfort. Similarly, psychological research using animals demands a strong concern for ethical issues. For some, this means ensuring minimal discomfort for any animals used; for others, this means a total ban on the use of animals in psychological research.

Concern simply for the ethical conduct of research is not enough. Psychologists must also be aware of the consequences of their research. What applications could the research result in, and are these applications themselves ethical? This is especially true of **socially sensitive research** where results of studies may be used to the disadvantage of certain groups or individuals in society. Even if researchers are themselves conducting research for legitimate reasons, they must consider how their findings could be (mis-) used to support oppressive practices.

These issues are explored in the next few pages. Examples of previous research are used to illustrate a range of ethical dilemmas, showing that we have a lot to learn from previous research, beyond the original research aims of those studies. The danger here is that by using very obvious examples of research (for example Milgram's obedience studies), it is easy to assume that such issues are not the concern of the relatively mundane studies carried out at undergraduate level. Don't be fooled! Ethical concerns should be paramount in the minds of all students of psychology, with ethical issues arising whenever psychological research is carried out.

Neither should this awareness be restricted to the carrying out of research, to the specific chapter in a book or to a specific part of a syllabus. Awareness of ethical issues should permeate your whole understanding and evaluation of psychological research and practice. So, with each psychology study you come across, ask yourself: Was this study conducted with full consideration of all relevant ethical issues?

The British Psychological Society and its code of conduct

The **British Psychological Society (BPS)** is the professional body representing psychologists, which appropriately qualified psychologists can join. All members are expected to adhere to the society's code of conduct which details expected norms of behaviour for psychologists as a whole. There are also ethical principles set out specifically for the conduct of research with human participants, as well as ethical guidelines specifically for the use of animals in research. All of these are contained in the booklet, *Code of Conduct, Ethical Principles and Guidelines* (1996) (BPS 198), which is freely available to all members of the BPS. It is these guidelines and principles which are referred to in the following two sections.

Research involving human participants

The code of conduct adopted by the BPS begins by stating that in their work psychologists should seek to establish the highest ethical standards, ensuring scientific integrity and the protection of participants or others involved in the receipt of their services. The code of conduct then details four other areas of concern for all practising psychologists. These are summarised in figure 3.1.

This code of conduct is supplemented by the 'Ethical Principles for Conducting Research with Human Participants' (figure 3.2), which specifically addresses the above issues of consent and confidentiality. The importance of competence and personal conduct should also be stressed. This is especially true at more introductory levels of psychology where students may not fully appreciate the level of skill and expertise necessary to implement research ideas they may have.

Studies highlighting ethical issues

Guidelines such as those outlined in figure 3.2 are regularly revised in the light of new research findings and in accordance with the changing moral climate. Ironically, the need for ethical guidelines is largely a response to studies which, in retrospect, were considered ethically dubious. Classic examples here include Milgram's (1974) research into obedience to authority, and Zimbardo's (1973) prison simulation. These studies and others are summarised in figure 3.3. Together they illustrate a range of ethical dilemmas faced in psychological research.

3.1 Summary of code of conduct adopted by the BPS

■ **Competence**
Psychologists should endeavour to maintain and develop their professional competence, to recognise and work within their own limitations. They should not lay claims to qualifications and competences they do not hold and should not seek to practise in areas for which they are not appropriately prepared or qualified. They should also ensure that those under their supervision comply with these standards.

■ **Obtaining consent**
Psychologists shall normally carry out investigations only with the valid consent of participants, having taken all reasonable steps to ensure that they have understood the nature of the investigation or intervention and its anticipated consequences.

■ **Confidentiality**
Psychologists shall take all reasonable steps to preserve the confidentiality of information acquired through their practice and to protect the privacy of individuals or organisations about whom information is held.

■ **Personal conduct**
Psychologists should conduct themselves in their professional activities in a way that does not damage the interest of the recipients of their service or participants in their research and does not undermine public confidence in their ability to carry out their professional duties.

Source: Adapted from BPS (1996) pp. 1–4.

3.2 Summary of 'Ethical Principles for Conducting Research with Human Participants'

■ 1 Introduction
Good research is based upon mutual respect and confidence between investigators and participants. There are some areas of human experience or behaviour which are beyond the reach of psychological investigations and the guidelines are necessary to clarify the conditions under which psychological research is acceptable. All BPS members and those under their supervision should abide by the principles and members should be aware of the legal implications of alleged misconduct.

■ 2 General
In all circumstances investigators must consider the ethical implications and psychological consequences for the participants in their research. Essentially, consideration must come from the standpoint of all those involved in the research. This means recognising the impact of the research on participants from a range of different ethnic, social and age groups. Often such knowledge can only be obtained from the population from which the participants of the research have been drawn.

■ 3 Consent
Whenever possible, participants should be informed of the objectives of the investigation. They should be told everything which may influence their willingness to participate. Where full disclosure of research aims is not possible, additional safeguards are necessary to protect the welfare and dignity of participants (see 4 below). For research involving children or participants who have impairments which limit their understanding such that they are unable to give their real consent, consent should be sought from parents or from those *in loco parentis*.

■ 4 Deception
Withholding information or misleading participants is unacceptable if participants are typically likely to show unease once debriefed. If in doubt, consultation should be sought from those who share the social and cultural background of the participants, or from ethics committees or experienced and disinterested colleagues. Intentional deception over the purpose and general nature of an investigation should be avoided, and participants should never be deliberately misled without extremely strong scientific or medical justification.

■ 5 Debriefing
Investigators should provide participants with necessary information to complete their understanding of the research. They should discuss the experience of participation with participants in order to monitor for any unforeseen negative effects or misconceptions. Debriefing does not provide justification for any unethical aspects of the research.

■ 6 Withdrawal from the investigation
Investigators should make it clear to participants that they have a right to withdraw at any stage of the research, irrespective of any payment or inducement that has been offered. Following involvement in the investigation or a debriefing, participants have the right to withdraw retrospectively, requiring that their own data be destroyed.

■ 7 Confidentiality
Subject to legislation and the Data Protection Act, information obtained about a participant during an investigation is confidential unless otherwise agreed in advance. Identification of participants should not be possible if research is published and in cases where anonymity cannot be guaranteed, participants should be warned of this before agreeing to participate.

■ 8 Protection of participants
Investigators have a primary responsibility to protect participants from physical and mental harm during the investigation. The risk of harm should be no greater than the risks normally associated with the life-styles of the participants. Participants should be asked about any factors which may create a risk in the procedure, such as a pre-existing medical condition, and they must be advised of any special action they should take to avoid risk.

3.2 Summary of 'Ethical Principles for Conducting Research with Human Participants' cont'd.

■ 9 Observational research

Studies based upon observation must respect the privacy and psychological well-being of the individuals studied. Unless consent is obtained, observational research is only acceptable in situations where those observed would expect to be observed by strangers. Particular account should be taken of local cultural values.

■ 10 Giving advice

During research, if evidence is obtained of psychological and physical problems of which a participant is apparently unaware, the investigator has a duty to inform the participant if by not doing so the participant's future well-being may be endangered. If the problem is serious and the investigator is not qualified to offer assistance, then the appropriate source of professional advice should be recommended.

■ 11 Colleagues

Investigators share the responsibility of the ethical treatment of research participants with their collaborators, assistants, students and employees. A psychologist who believes that another psychologist may be conducting research that is not in accordance with the ethical principles should encourage that researcher to re-evaluate the research.

Source: Adapted from BPS (1996) pp. 7–11.

3.3 Studies highlighting ethical issues in psychological research

■ Milgram (1974): obedience studies

Participants were recruited via a newspaper advertisement asking people to take part in a study of memory performance and learning. Participants were apparently randomly assigned to the role of 'teacher' and 'learner', with the teachers having to administer electric shocks to learners should they respond incorrectly to a word-pair question. The voltage of each shock given increased with every mistake the learner made, up to a maximum labelled 'XXX'. In reality the 'learners' were confederates of the experimenter who did not receive any electric shocks although they behaved as if they had, crying out in pain and pleading to be released. Approximately two-thirds of Milgram's participants obeyed the experimenter administering the highest level of electric shock. This was in spite of the obvious distress of the victim and the obvious distress they themselves were experiencing. (See Unit 6 pages 180–2.)

■ Zimbardo (1973): prison simulation study

Student participants were paid to take part in a role play where they were randomly assigned to the positions of prisoner or guard. Made to be as realistic as possible, prisoners were arrested by uniformed officers and taken to a 'cell' in the basement of a university building. Neither prisoners nor guards were given any instructions on how to behave. Although the study was originally planned to last two weeks, it was abandoned after six days due to the extreme behaviour of the participants. Some prisoners became depressed, tearful and apathetic, others became angry and rebellious, with half of them pleading to be let out after a few days. Many of the guards relished their new-found power, abusing prisoners and treating them cruelly. Whilst most of the prisoners were relieved when the study was called off, many of the guards were disappointed and actually wanted to continue. (See Unit 6 pages 186–8.)

3.3 Studies highlighting ethical issues in psychological research *cont'd.*

Studies of helping behaviour

In the following studies participants were not informed as to the real aims, with confederates playing the parts of injured people as needed:

- Latane and Darley (1968). This study examined the impact of having others present upon helping behaviour. Whilst participants were sitting in a room completing a questionnaire, smoke began pouring in through a vent in the wall. Participants were more likely to report this when working on their own than when working with two others in the room.
- Latane and Rodin (1969). On hearing the experimenter cry out and fall in the adjacent room, participants were much faster to react when alone than when others were present.
- Pilliavin *et al.* (1969). In field experiments on the New York subway, student experimenters collapsed in the subway train compartments and waited to see if they were helped. The students varied their appearance (and in one condition had fake blood coming from their mouth) to see if this affected helping behaviour. Confederates observed the helping behaviour of members of the public. (See Unit 7 pages 209–14.)

Personal space

- Felipe and Sommer (1966): a field study which took place in the library. The experimenter wanted to observe reactions from female students sitting in the library when somebody sat 'too close' to them. The discomfort often caused students to either leave, move away or erect barriers between themselves and the space invader. Similar studies were carried out on unsuspecting citizens sitting on park benches where experimenters sat 6 inches from people on an otherwise empty bench.

Learned helplessness

- Seligman's (1975) theory of learned helplessness is based upon studies using people and animals who are exposed to discomfort which they cannot escape (with humans this was intolerable noise; the animals were exposed to electric shocks). When the 'participants' were then put into similar situations of discomfort, only this time from which they could escape, the majority failed to do so. These findings have been used to explain depression in humans. (See Unit 25 page 935.)

Studies involving children

- Ainsworth *et al.* (1978) studied attachment in 1-year-olds using 'The Strange Situation'. This is where the mother and a stranger left and returned to the room in episodes lasting 3 minutes. The babies were observed to see how they reacted to the absence of their mother and the presence of the stranger. The majority of children experienced distress of some sort when placed in this situation. (See Unit 20 page 730.)
- Bandura (1965) conducted famous studies on imitation learning in children. Under various conditions, children watched a film of an adult behaving aggressively towards a bo-bo doll. The children were then placed in a room containing toys (one of which was a bo-bo doll) and their behaviour was observed for imitative acts of aggression. When the children were rewarded for imitative behaviour, they all showed high levels of aggression. (See Unit 22 page 813.)
- Watson and Rayner (1920) deliberately conditioned a fear response in Little Albert. This was done by striking a metal bar, which Albert was scared of, whilst at the same time showing Albert a white rat. The result was that Albert came to fear the rat, a response which he generalised to other animals and objects. It is not known whether Little Albert was ever desensitised. (See Unit 24 page 900.)
- Rosenthal and Jacobson (1968): 'Pygmalion in the Classroom'. In this study teachers were told that certain pupils could be expected to make superior academic progress over the next year. When tested at the end of the year, the 'selected' pupils showed significantly greater gains in IQ compared to their classmates. The pupils were in fact randomly assigned to the superior or normal group. The study demonstrated the self-fulfilling prophecy where the teachers' beliefs resulted in expected behaviour.

Activity 1

a   For each of the studies detailed in figure 3.3 list briefly the relevant ethical issues raised. It will be helpful to use the BPS guidelines in figure 3.2.
b   Find some other examples of research which may be considered ethically dubious. Give a brief summary of each study and the ethical principles violated.

(Suggested answers on pages 104–5.)

Ethical issues highlighted by research

The research examples described in figure 3.3 raise a number of concerns in respect of the welfare and rights of the participants. These include: the issue of consent; the use of deception and the role of debriefing; problematic cases such as field studies; and the participant's right to withdraw from the study.

■ Consent

Participants should be able to make an informed decision about whether or not to participate in a psychological investigation. This means making available to the potential participant as much information as possible as to the aims of the study and the research procedures involved. Participants who agree to take part in a study based upon partial information cannot be considered to have given **informed consent**. Special consideration must be given where prospective participants may not be in a position to give consent. This includes studies involving children, people with a mental handicap, prisoners and other 'captive' populations (for example persons in homes for the aged, or students on a course). The issues are whether they can rationally, knowingly and freely give informed consent (Robson, 1993). With children, in addition to fully informing the child who may well understand much of what is going on, consent must be obtained from the parent or guardian. For other groups, care must be taken not to abuse their

potentially powerless position. Relevant ethical committees and review boards should be consulted whenever possible.

■ Use of deception

Sometimes when carrying out investigations the researchers decide it is necessary to deceive participants, and withhold information, usually in relation to the real aims of the study. In such instances, informed consent is impossible. For example, in Milgram's study (see figure 3.3), had participants known about the real aims of the study, this would most certainly have affected their behaviour. Similarly, in the bystander intervention studies of Pilliavin *et al.* and Latane and Darley (see figure 3.3), had the participants known that confederates were faking collapse or accidents, again this would have affected the participants' responses. According to Aronson (1992), this highlights the dynamics of the investigation as a social situation in its own right. If people know they are being observed, and more specifically, what aspect of their behaviour is being observed, then that behaviour will change, usually to try and enhance the perception of the participants by behaving 'good'. The same is true of less 'sensational' experiments where the deception used seems fairly innocuous. These include investigations into memory research, where researchers are often interested in a person's ability to remember information which he or she has not been explicitly asked to remember. Coolican (1994) summarised a number of other examples:

> 'Some participants are told a baby is male, others that it is female, and their descriptions of it are compared. Participants performing a sensory motor task, where the true aim is to record the effect of an observer on performance, are told that the observer is present to note details of the skilled behaviour involved. Children are told not to play with a toy because it belongs to another child who is next door. Students are told their experimental rats are 'bright'. Even the use of placebos is a deception' (Coolican, 1994, p. 397).

Given these examples, the question of whether to deceive or not to deceive is not a simple one.

Eysenck (1994) suggested that three factors need to be considered when determining whether or not deception is justified:

1 The *less potentially damaging* the consequences of the deception, the more acceptable it is.

2 Deception is easier to justify in studies that are *important in scientific terms* than in those that are trivial in nature.

3 Deception is more justifiable when there are *no alternative, deception-free, ways* of investigating an issue.

Activity 2

Many of the studies summarised in figure 3.3 involved deception. Apply Eysenck's guidelines to each of these studies and come to a conclusion as to whether the deception was justified. If you can think of an alternative, deception-free way of conducting the study, give a brief explanation.

(Suggested answers on page 105.)

Although the guidelines suggested by Eysenck (1994) may seem like straightforward principles to follow, the reality of human behaviour means that principles 1 and 2 may actually contradict each other. Research which is of important scientific interest and has the greatest potential to benefit society is that which is most likely to require deception and that which is most likely to cause participants distress and discomfort (Aronson, 1992). There is thus a conflict of interests between the individuals participating in such research and wider society which may benefit from the findings of such research. Examples here include research into bystander intervention, conformity and obedience. This research has resulted in profound psychological insights, much of which defied commonsense prediction, with many findings being dependent upon the use of deception.

An alternative to the use of deception is **role playing**. Here participants are requested to behave in ways which they think they would naturally do, had they known nothing about the research. The value of the role-play method in psychological research is questionable. Aronson (1992) argued that once people know they are being observed, they will behave in a socially desirable way. The artificiality of the situation results in superficial behaviour failing to provide insights into the reality of human behaviour. Supporters of the role-play method use the example of Zimbardo's prison study (see figure 3.3) to counter claims that the technique results in socially desirable, superficial behaviours. However, this then prompts the question of the added value afforded by the use of the role play in terms of the protection of participants. The participants in Zimbardo's mock prison study were all volunteers who had given informed consent. However, many behaved in ways they themselves did not anticipate, with the guards showing excessive brutality and many of the prisoners experiencing distress.

Where a researcher comes to the decision that it is impossible to conduct a study without the use of deception, then steps should be taken to ensure that the deception is used appropriately. Robson (1993) suggested a number of useful questions any researcher should ask when considering situations where deception is involved or when informed consent is not obtained:

- Will the study involve people in *doing things they would not otherwise do*? If not, then the study will be less of an infringement and therefore less questionable.
- What degree of *inconvenience* will be caused to those who participate (especially those who unknowingly do so)?
- What is the likelihood of *emotional involvement* of participants?

With these last two questions, obviously the higher the degree of inconvenience and likelihood of emotional involvement, the more questionable such practices are.

Two possible ways of controlling the potentially negative impact of deception is by **presumptive consent** and **prior general consent**:

- With *presumptive consent*, views regarding the acceptability of the deception are obtained from a sample of the population to be involved in the study (these people will not participate themselves). If they believe that the deception used is acceptable, then it can be presumed that this will also be the reaction of the participants who will actually be involved.

- With prior general consent, all potential subjects are contacted and asked if they would be willing to take part in research in which they would be misled about its purpose. Only those agreeing are asked to participate.

Where researchers come to the conclusion that prior consent must be sought, it has become increasingly popular to use 'informed consent' forms with potential participants. However, although these clarify the mutual obligations of the participant and researcher, reinforcing the rights of the participant, researchers may be legally obliged to provide this information, along with other research information, should the situation arise. This situation is most likely to occur when conducting research on socially sensitive issues such as drug abuse or Aids (Robson, 1993). Similarly, in the field of occupational psychology, employees may be providing information on the understanding that it is confidential. However, should that employee then become involved in a work-related dispute which goes to court, researchers may be legally obliged to disclose the information provided by the employee. At present, this is an area of some ambiguity in need of urgent clarification given the potential consequences of possible situations.

Debriefing

There are two aims to debriefing participants after they have taken part in a study: firstly, to ensure they leave the study in the same state they entered; and secondly, to provide them with sufficient information for their experience to have some educational value to them.

It is the responsibility of the researcher to determine if there were any unforeseen consequences of the procedures used and to provide participants with the opportunity to contact them should there be any long-term effects or concerns related to their involvement in the research.

The importance of debriefing is obvious in studies involving deception. It is essential that participants know that anagrams they were asked to solve were unsolvable; that electric shocks they were asked to administer were faked; that having words arranged in categories produces superior recall – it is not that they have a terrible memory. The debriefing should give complete reassurance to the participants, which in some cases may necessitate elaborate debriefing programmes. In Milgram's experiment (see figure 3.3) this consisted of reuniting participants with 'electrocuted' confederates, reassuring them that no electric shock had been delivered. Participants were also reassured that their behaviour, whether they had inflicted pain or not, was normal and that others had happily behaved in the same way. Coolican (1994), however, is sceptical that such a procedure would ensure that participants left the study in the same state they had entered: 'at least 26 out of 40 participants knew, when they left, that they were capable, under pressure, of inflicting extreme pain, if not death, on an innocent human being' (p. 398).

Milgram, however, obtained an independent psychiatrist's assessment of 40 participants one year after the studies were complete. None of these participants showed any signs of being psychologically harmed by their involvement. The results of a questionnaire distributed to all participants also reflected this. With a response rate of 92 per cent, 84 per cent of participants were glad to have participated, with 80 per cent agreeing that more experiments of this sort should be carried out. Only 1.3 per cent were 'sorry' or 'very sorry' they had taken part.

Whilst the results from Milgram's debriefing are offered as strong defence against those who criticise his research, this is not to say that debriefing justifies unethical practices. Nor does it mean that debriefing is only important in studies involving deception. Debriefing is an essential component in all studies and should be an integral part of the research methodology.

Problematic cases

Often in field studies it is impossible to debrief participants as they are not aware that they are participating in research. This was the case in the passive bystander studies of Pilliavin *et al.* (1969) (see figure 3.3). Similarly, Sommer carried out a series of studies in the 1960s which involved the deliberate invasion of people's personal space in a variety of public settings. The anxiety or discomfort caused by the researcher's behaviour resulted in individuals trying to distance themselves from the experimenter. Given that both these studies may have caused anxiety to people who had not consented to participate, and that there was no opportunity for debriefing which might have helped to alleviate some of this anxiety, then the methodologies would most certainly be considered unacceptable practice today.

■ The right to withdraw

It should be made clear to participants at the outset of an experiment that they have the right to withdraw at any time, irrespective of whether or not they have received payment for participating. It would be naive, however, not to acknowledge the power differential which often exists between participants and researchers and the added sense of obligation this may place upon participants to continue to participate, or to behave in a particular way. Often in US universities participation in research is a requirement for course completion. Indeed, the fact that Milgram's research was carried out by academics at the distinguished Yale University was a reason cited by participants for not withdrawing from the study at an earlier stage. Robson (1993) summed up the nature of this relationship:

> *'The situation can lead to researchers and participants taking on employer and employee roles respectively. The employer has to guard against the notion that payment justifies placing the participant at risk. On the employee's side there is the likely tendency to "give them whatever I think I am being paid for"* ' (Robson, 1993, p. 33).

Even where an inducement is not being offered to participants, researchers must acknowledge the added obligation they may put upon participants simply by being in the position of the researcher, a position which they should not seek to exploit.

Keeping participants aware of their right to withdraw at any stage of the research is one way of doing this. In longitudinal research it may be necessary to remind participants of this right as the research continues and necessarily evolves. It is also the duty of the researcher to give participants the option to withdraw retrospectively from the study and to have their own data destroyed.

The objective of the ethical guidelines is the *protection of participants*. Whilst obtaining consent and debriefing do offer some protection, there is also the explicit obligation not to expose participants to any mental and physical harm throughout the research, beyond that which they would normally encounter in their everyday lives.

Conclusions

No serious student or practitioner of psychology can afford to ignore the very real ethical implications of psychological research. Whilst we have learnt much from the previous research in terms of what is acceptable and unacceptable practice, it is easy to criticise in retrospect. Ethical dilemmas will continue to emerge as research progresses, the challenge being to eliminate as far as possible the negative consequences of such research, both in terms of the participants taking part and in terms of the implications such research may have. The crux of many of these dilemmas will be the rights of the individual versus the benefit to society. Making the right decisions when facing these dilemmas will only be achieved through greater awareness of ethical issues generally and through continued debate about what is acceptable practice. The BPS guidelines are not set in stone and must themselves be open to debate and, where necessary, revision. The ever-increasing popularity of psychology in both academic and applied settings strongly reinforces the need to maintain ethical standards, ensuring that those who participate in research, those who conduct research, and the discipline as a whole, are respected.

The ethics of animal experimentation

Animals are used in psychology for a number of reasons. Perhaps most contentious is the rationale that you can subject animals to procedures which it would be unethical to subject humans to. Such procedures also allow a high degree of experimental control enabling cause and effect relationships to be established more clearly. These findings are often then extrapolated to humans on the basis that there are sufficient similarities (for example, in the nervous systems) to make such generalisations. The shorter life cycle of many animals also allows for the study of **generational effects** and genetic transmission.

A good example of research which illustrates these points is the work on maternal deprivation by Harry Harlow (1959) using rhesus monkeys (figure 3.4).

Activity 3

Justify the procedures Harlow used in investigating attachment processes.

(Suggested answer on page 105.)

Animals were among the earliest 'subjects' to be used in psychological experiments. The pioneering work of the behaviourists Pavlov and Skinner was carried out on dogs and rats. Other experiments include the executive monkey experiments (Brady, 1958); Harlow's (1959) studies of maternal deprivation; visual deprivation studies using cats

3.4 Harlow's (1959) experiments on maternal deprivation using rhesus monkeys

Harlow conducted a range of experiments over a 20-year period in order to investigate attachment processes. Rhesus monkeys were reared on their own in a cage with two faked surrogate mothers. Both mothers were of the same size and general shape of an adult monkey although one mother was made of wire mesh and the other was covered in soft towelling. Harlow discovered that, regardless of which mother provided food, the monkeys spent most of their time clinging to the soft mother. This affirmed the importance of 'contact comfort' in attachment processes. The long-term impact of these procedures on the monkeys was dramatic. Having spent their 'childhood' reared in isolated cages with no contact with other real monkeys, the monkeys were then placed in a large compound of normally reared monkeys. They were unable to interact with their peers becoming withdrawn and displaying anxious behaviour. Once sexually mature, the adult males were unable to mate. The females who were successful in producing offspring themselves made inadequate mothers, failing to nurse and comfort them properly. (See Unit 20 page 722.)

and chimps (Hubel and Wiesel, 1962, 1968). Whilst it is easy to condemn much previous research with hindsight, this preempts the conclusion that all animal research is bad and should be phased out. Indeed, unless you have specifically covered the areas of comparative and biological psychology, you may well come to the conclusion that the use of animals in psychology is largely a thing of the past. The study of animals, however, still constitutes a very important part of psychology. Animal studies (although not necessarily experiments) form the basis of **comparative psychology** and **ethology**, important fields of study which seek to understand patterns of animal behaviour, making comparisons between different animals and between animals and humans. Also more recently, **sociobiology** has emerged, which seeks to explain the biological basis of social behaviour within the framework of evolutionary biology.

Neurobiological approaches to psychology also rely heavily upon research involving animals on the basis that all mammals share the same basic neurochemical processes (for example nervous system responses, synapse transmission, etc.). Animals are thus usually used in the early stages of research, with the intention of later generalising to humans. This is often the rationale underlying much medical research where medicines are tested and developed on animals before being tested on humans.

Animal rights: their impact upon psychology

The debate concerning the use of animals in scientific research came under ever-increasing public and political attention throughout the 1980s and 1990s. Objections were raised against once-accepted scientific practices, objections which stemmed from many sectors of society, not just the 'traditional' animal rights groups. The popularity of this debate reinforced the transient and political nature of ethical issues.

The impact of the increasing concern for the welfare of animals has been a significant decline in the use of animals across science generally and specifically within psychology. In the UK, Netherlands and Germany the total number of animals used in laboratory experiments has fallen by half since the 1970s. In Canada mammals have largely been replaced by fish and in the USA the use of dogs and cats is down by half, although primate use has remained constant. (However, the overall use of animals used in Canada and the USA remains fairly constant, at 2 million and 18–22 million respectively) (all figures cited in Mukerjee, 1997, p. 70).

In relation specifically to psychology, students are now preferring to opt for degree courses which do not involve animal experimentation, which, in turn, has a knock-on effect on the interests of post-graduate students, and, eventually, departments as a whole. Thomas and Blackman (1991) reported an overall decrease of 31 per cent in the use of animal experiments between 1977 and 1989. Of the animal experiments still conducted, there was a marked increase (26 per cent) in the number of observational/non-experimental studies conducted. To summarise Thomas and Blackman's findings, their survey revealed an overall decline in the number of studies involving animals; a decline in the range of animals used; and a decline in the use of experimental (as opposed to non-experimental) procedures.

New legislation has also affected the use of animals for experimentation. Under the Animal (Scientific Procedures) Act of 1986, people intending to carry out research which may potentially entail harm or suffering to animals must first obtain a project licence from the Home Office for the specific procedures to be used. In 1989, the number of academic staff holding such licences was 68 per cent of the number who held 'equivalent' licences in 1977; the figure for post-graduate students fell to 38 per cent (Thomas and Blackman, 1991).

Thomas and Blackman lamented the decline in animal-based psychological research, arguing that a lot will be lost if animal research disappears altogether. At present, research based on animals contributes to our understanding of behaviour processes (see for example Mackintosh, 1983; Rescorla, 1990), with fruitful applications of animal models of behaviour to important practical problems such as drug addiction and the alleviation of anxiety (see Miller, 1985). This line of argument suggests that, for Thomas and Blackman, benefit to humans in terms of furthering understanding and reducing human suffering is substantial justification for the continued use of animals.

Activity 4

List as many examples as you can which show how humans have benefited from research with animals.

(Suggested answer on page 105.)

BPS guidelines for research using animals

As well as the 1986 legislation, the BPS also has its own 'Guidelines for the use of animals in research', published by the Scientific Affairs Board in 1985. These are summarised in figure 3.5. Treating animals appropriately necessitates knowing a lot about the natural habitats and behaviours of those animals. To this end the BPS give additional sources of information relating to most of their guidelines, encouraging researchers to inform themselves thoroughly before commencing with research.

3.5 Summary of 'Guidelines for the use of animals in research'

There is a general obligation to avoid, or at least minimise, discomfort to living animals. To this end, researchers should discuss carefully with colleagues who are experts details of any proposed experimentation. They should also seek independent advice as to whether the likely scientific contribution of the work they intend justifies the use of living animals, and whether the scientific point they wish to make may not be made without the use of animals.

■ 1 The law
Members should familiarise themselves with the law. Failure to comply has resulted in prosecution. (References to the laws protecting animals are given in the Universities' Federation for Animal Welfare Handbook (1978).)

■ 2 Ethical considerations
If the animal is to be constrained, confined, harmed or stressed in any way, the investigator must consider if the knowledge to be gained justifies the procedure. Some knowledge is trivial, and experiments must not be done simply because it is possible to do them. Alternatives to animal experimentation should also be considered.

■ 3 Species
When confining animals or using a procedure that is likely to cause pain and discomfort, the investigator should be aware that members of some species are less likely to suffer than members of others. Choosing an appropriate subject usually requires knowledge of the species' natural history as well as its special needs.

■ 4 Number of animals
Laboratory studies should use the smallest number of animals necessary. Careful thought should be given to the design of the experiment and the statistical techniques used as these can often reduce the number of animals required.

■ 5 Members of endangered species
These should not be collected or manipulated in the wild except as part of a serious attempt at conservation.

■ 6 Animal suppliers
Animals should only be obtained from reputable suppliers and full records kept of their provenance and history.

■ 7 Caging and social environment
Caging conditions should take into account the social behaviour of the species. An acceptable density of animals of one species may constitute overcrowding for a different species. In social animals, caging in isolation may have undesirable effects.

3.5 Summary of 'Guidelines for the use of animals in research' cont.

■ 8 Fieldwork

Fieldworkers should disturb the animals they study as little as possible. Even simple observations on wild animals can have marked effects on their breeding and survival. If animals are marked for identification or radio transmitters attached, they may be intolerant of the marks or transmitters, and stressed by the capture and recapture. The stress involved varies greatly with the type of technique used and the species studied.

■ 9 Aggression and predation including infanticide

The fact that pain and injury may come to animals in the wild is not a defence for allowing it to occur in the laboratory. Wherever possible, field studies of natural encounters should be used in preference to staged encounters.

■ 10 Motivation

When arranging schedules of deprivation, the experimenter should consider the animal's normal eating and drinking habits and its metabolic requirements. Differences in species must be borne in mind: a short period of deprivation for one species may be unacceptably long for another.

■ 11 Aversive stimulation and stressful procedures

Procedures that cause pain or distress to animals are illegal in the UK unless the experimenter holds a Home Office licence and the relevant certificate. The investigator should be satisfied that there are no alternatives to the use of painful stimuli. If alternatives are not available, the investigator has

the responsibility of ensuring that any suffering is kept to a minimum and that it is justified by the expected scientific contribution of the experiment.

■ 12 Surgical and pharmacological procedures

It is illegal to perform any surgical or pharmacological procedure on vertebrates in the UK without a Home Office licence and the relevant certificate. Such procedures should only be performed by experienced staff. Experimenters must be familiar with the technical aspects of anaesthesia, as well as the behavioural effects and toxicity of any drugs being used.

■ 13 Anaesthesia, analgesia and euthanasia

Animals must receive adequate post-operative care and any suffering must be minimised by suitable nursing and anaesthetics where appropriate. If the animal is found to be suffering severe and enduring pain, it must be killed.

■ 14 Independent advice

If an experimenter is ever in any doubt about the condition of an animal, a second opinion should be obtained, preferably from a qualified veterinarian, but certainly from someone not directly involved in the experiments concerned.

■ 15 Asking for help

Members with further questions or comments are advised to contact other advisory bodies via the BPS.

Source: BPS (1985, 1996) pp.12–15.

Activity 5

How can psychologists best protect the welfare of any animals used in their research?

(Suggested answer on page 105.)

Can the use of animals be justified?

Arguments concerning the use of animals in research relate to both practical and ethical issues. So, for example, someone opposing animal research may argue that it is ethically wrong to use animals because they are our equals and should be treated as such. They may also raise practical objections to animal research pointing to the artificiality of the experimental environment and the dangers in extrapolating from animals to humans. Both the practical and ethical sides of this debate are explored below.

The ethical debate

Most people would agree that intentionally to cause psychological or physical harm to an animal purely for the sake of it is ethically wrong. Some would argue that in certain circumstances, however, subjecting an animal to physical or psychological pain can be justified. Yet others would argue that there is no justification for causing pain (psychological or physical) to animals in the name of research.

A strong supporter of the use of animals in psychological research is Jeffrey Gray (1987). The question of whether or not to use animals in research confronts us with an ethical dilemma – should animals be used to the benefit of humans? Gray suggests that when faced with such a dilemma it becomes necessary to weigh up the suffering of the animals against the human suffering their use will alleviate. The basic premise of Gray's position is that we owe a special duty to members of our own species and it is therefore acceptable to use animals in research if humans will benefit. For Gray, the difficulty comes in trying to assess/measure and compare degrees of suffering, which is further compounded by the fact that the benefits of such research are not usually immediate (a lot of experimentation has to go into the research phase before human applications are made). Gray acknowledges that there will be a point where the degree of suffering inflicted upon animals is too great to be worth the avoidance of lesser suffering by people. The difficulty faced by scientists and ethical committees is in deciding exactly where that point is.

A contrasting view is held by, among others, Peter Singer. Singer (1991) argues that there can be no justification for inflicting harm upon another (whether human or non-human), irrespective of

any benefits such harm may generate. Singer accuses Gray of **speciesism**, that is, discrimination and exploitation based upon a difference in species. Whereas Gray accepts that the suffering of animals can be justified, Singer argues that if we are to accept the basic moral principle of equality, this requires that the suffering of any one being be counted equally with the like suffering of any other being (human or non-human). It is only in situations where there is not the capacity to suffer (for example, with inanimate objects) that such concerns do not apply. Thus, anything which can be described as **sentient** (i.e. that which has the capacity to suffer or experience enjoyment or happiness) deserves equal consideration. This is a view also held by Ryder (1991) who advocated a move to 'sentientism', with sentiency being the basis of morality. A powerful argument proposed by Singer is that the unequal treatment of different species is no different in principle to racism:

'Racists violate the principle of equality by giving greater weight to the interests of members of their own race when there is a clash between their interests and those of another race. Racists of European descent typically have not accepted that pain matters as much when it is felt by Africans, for example, as when it is felt by Europeans. Similarly, those I would call speciesist give greater weight to the interests of members of their own species when there is a clash between their interests and those of other species. Human speciesists do not accept that pain is as bad when it is felt by pigs or mice as when it is felt by humans' (Singer, 1993, p. 58).

The practical debate

Supporters of animal research in psychology (for example Miller, 1985) point to the important practical benefits research with animals has produced. The principles of classical and operant conditioning form the basis of many interventions which attempt to encourage 'appropriate' behaviour: for example, the principles of classical conditioning are used in 'aversion therapy' to deter smoking or excessive drinking; behaviour modification techniques are based upon operant conditioning which are used to train animals to behave in a desired way (for example, pigeons trained in air–sea rescue are able to signal when they have spotted a coloured life-raft; pigs have been trained to control their own lighting conditions to suit their own preferences). Programmed learning techniques (used in learning environments) and token economy systems (often used in prisons) are also based upon the principles of operant conditioning.

Early research into imprinting has led to new techniques to reintegrate birds bred in captivity by placing the eggs with wild surrogate parents before they hatch.

Many successful medical treatments would not have been developed without the use of animals. For example, Green (1994) pointed out that anaesthetics, anti-cancer drugs, anti-Aids treatments, anti-epilepsy, anti-anxiety and anti-depressants simply could not have been developed without the use of animals.

Other supporters of animal experimentation point out that many animal experimenters are also animal lovers, with researchers choosing to use animals because they feel it is the only way to help humans. Mukerjee (1997) reported the case of a veterinarian at the Rockerfeller University's (USA) animal centre who runs a shelter to which he takes cats that are no longer needed for research. Botting and Morrison (1997), two scientists active in the defence of animal research since the 1980s, suggested an interesting challenge for some of their critics: take an example of an advance dependent on animal experiments and detail how an alternative procedure could provide the same material benefit.

Also pointed out are the inconsistencies in the public's view of the unnecessary use of animals. Why, when there is a vast range of alternatives available, do people still choose to 'eat meat and in the same gulp condemn experimentation . . . shielding themselves from the reality behind dinner'? (Mukerjee, 1997, p. 71, reporting the views of J L Owens).

Whilst many supporters of animal research point to the success of behaviourism in validating the use of animals, such theories also did a lot of damage in terms of the way animals were perceived by scientists. By reducing animals to 'stimulus response bundles' with the focus of attention clearly on behaviour as opposed to any internal processes, animals were effectively denied any degree of emotional expression such as pain. The actions of animals were interpreted in terms of the lowest psychological faculties possible (for example a physiological response to an environmental stimulus), with animals unable to experience feelings. Thus, as Rollins (1989) argued, the animal psyche went from being impossible to measure to being non-existent (cited in Mukerjee, 1997). More recent research has sought to invalidate such **anthropocentric** assumptions, which, although having great public appeal, the view that animals experience emotion, still struggles to gain acceptance in the world of scientists. As Jeffrey Masson commented:

> 'The interest is certainly budding, but as yet no prominent scientist has undertaken a sustained treatment of animal emotions. It is to be hoped, for the sake of animals as well as humans, that scientists will be persuaded to look more seriously at the feelings of animals who share the world with us' (Masson, 1994, p. 17).

The rationale underlying much animal research is that there is a sufficient similarity between the animals being studied and humans. This assumption, however, is also the source of many practical objections. Some critics argue that the assumed similarities do not exist, with findings from such studies merely reflecting the unique biology of that species, the unnatural interventions being manipulated and the stressful environment of the laboratory (Barnard and Kaufman, 1997). As such, **extrapolation** from animals to humans is invalid.

Researchers who assume that such similarities do exist (therefore validating comparisons made with humans) have also been accused of **anthropomorphism**, that is, attributing animals with characteristics which may be specific to humans. The irony of this argument, however, is that such assumed similarities reinforce the need to respect the rights of animals (especially primates) as they are as capable of experiencing emotion as humans are.

Also questioned is the ecological validity of many animal studies, much of which take place under controlled experimental conditions. These conditions bear little resemblance to the natural habitats of those animals or the environments of humans.

Critics also remain unconvinced by historical arguments pointing to the pivotal role of animal experimentation in past scientific advances. Had animal experimentation been outlawed, then scientists would have had to have been more creative in devising alternative methods to resolve the problems they faced. Dependence upon the use of animals has thus hindered the development of such alternatives. Besides, the issue of what role, if any, animal experimentation played in *past* discoveries is not relevant to what is necessary *now* for research (Barnard and Kaufman, 1997).

The repetition of many animal experiments for the purpose of generating consistent findings with a large enough sample is also criticised as unnecessary. Such unnecessary use of animals can be cut down through the development and use of statistical techniques and through eliminating research which simply seeks to support already well established findings.

'Harry Harlow's famous monkey experiments, conducted in the 1960s at the University of Wisconsin, involved separating infant monkeys from their mothers and keeping some of them in total isolation for a year. The experiments, which left the animals severely damaged emotionally, served primarily as graphic illustrations of the need for maternal contact – a fact already well established from observations of human infants' (Barnard and Kaufman, 1997, p. 66; author's emphasis).

Activity 6

The psychology course you have chosen at university has a compulsory module involving animal experimentation. You must present your arguments in writing as to why you disagree with animal experimentation and therefore do not want to take part in the module.

(Suggested answer on page 105.)

The current state of play

Given the arguments for and against animal testing, decisions about whether or not to use animals can be difficult. In an attempt to resolve such difficult decisions, Bateson (1986) suggested that three criteria need to be taken into consideration:

- The certainty of benefit: how likely is it that research will have a beneficial impact? Such questions are complicated by the fact that the beneficial results are not always immediate and are often part of wider research programmes.
- The quality of research: the BPS guidelines emphasise the need for well-designed research in terms of the methods and the statistical techniques used. The fact that most British universities have their own ethics committees helps to ensure that research using animals is of a high standard.
- The degree of animal suffering: obviously the less suffering the better, but the difficulty here is in actually trying to measure suffering. Increasing our knowledge of different species will help us to identify how different species respond in stressful situations.

Each of these criteria represent dimensions, along which every situation involving the use of animals should be assessed. The outcome of this assessment tells you whether or not the research should proceed. This is illustrated in figure 3.6.

Thus in a situation where the certainty of benefit is low, the quality of research is low and the degree of suffering is high, the research should most definitely not proceed. This is indicated by the solid area in the diagram. The ideal situation for animal research is when the certainty of benefit is high, the quality of research is high and the degree of suffering is low. The formula also allows for 'in-between' situations where the degree of suffering is medium, but the quality of research and the certainty of benefit are high; and where the quality of research is high, the degree of suffering is low but the certainty of benefit is low.

Activity 7

Evaluate Harlow's research with monkeys using Bateson's model. Do the same with two other examples of animal research in psychology.

(Suggested answer on page 106.)

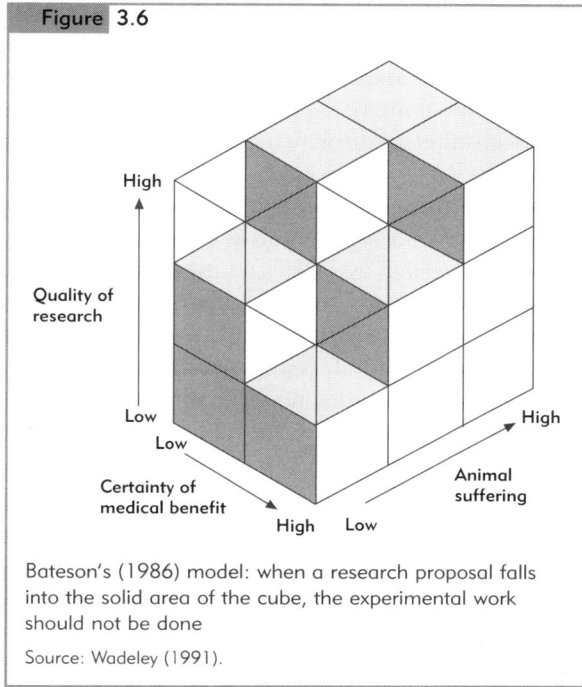

Figure 3.6

Bateson's (1986) model: when a research proposal falls into the solid area of the cube, the experimental work should not be done

Source: Wadeley (1991).

Whilst this model certainly provides a useful heuristic for determining the appropriateness of conducting research with animals, judgements may still be based on speculation and subjective opinion. This is especially true for the dimension of degree of animal suffering, the measurement of which is crucial to the whole debate about the use of animals. In the context of Gray's argument, at what point does animal suffering become too much to justify the benefits? And, for Singer, at what point is an animal sentient enough to experience pain?

Whilst this debate continues, at the policy level there has been a settling on the middle ground, a position which can be summarised as follows:

- Animal research is needed when no alternatives can be found.
- It is preferable to use certain animals rather than others.
- The benefits of the research should outweigh the costs.

Interpretations of this middle ground position vary between different countries. In many institutions throughout Europe, Canada, Australia and New Zealand pain scales have been developed in which experimental procedures are assigned a grade. These countries also require a cost–benefit analysis to be performed before an animal experiment can proceed. Similarly, in the USA the 1966 Animal Welfare Act was amended in 1985 establishing institutional animal care and use committees at each facility using regulated animals. This required, for example, that dogs had to be exercised and that the psychological well-being of primates should be looked after. However, whilst regulatory measures such as these are in place, it is difficult to assess how effective they are. In the USA there are 69 inspectors, yet more than 1300 regulated laboratories with many abuses of the regulations being brought to the fore by 'whistle blowers' (Mukerjee, 1997).

The search for alternatives

One response to the concern for animal welfare has been increased focus on the search for alternative methods. Such ideas, however, are not new, with contemporary ideas owing much to the earlier work of Russell and Burch (1959). Russell and Burch proposed the principle of the 'three Rs':

- *Replace* – to replace the use of animals by test tube or in vitro methods.
- *Reduce* – to reduce the number of animals needed using statistical techniques.
- *Refine* – to refine the techniques used in the experiment in order to reduce the suffering.

Bodies set up to help attain such goals have gradually received more funding over the past 20 years. In 1992 the European Centre for the Validation of Alternative Methods was founded; 1993 saw the first World Congress on Alternatives held in the USA, followed by the second in 1996 held in the Netherlands.

This emphasis on the need for alternatives has resulted in a number of progressive developments (figure 3.7). Some seek to replace animals with an alternative, others either to minimise the number of animals used or to change the condition under which they are studied.

Ensuring that research involving animals continues to progress in the right direction depends on two things: one is changing the mindset of scientists, challenging the often accepted wisdom that animal experimentation is essential. To this end, since 1985 in the Netherlands scientists

3.7 Methods to reduce or eliminate the use of animals in scientific research

- **Protocol changes**: reductions in the required number of animals upon which a drug has to be tested.
- **Data mining**: sifting through existing mountains of data to come up with relevant new findings.
- The development of test tube alternatives.
- Increasing use of naturalistic observation techniques and field-based research.

starting research on animals have been required to take a three-week course. As well as learning hands-on procedures, they learn the three Rs, and, having designed an animal experiment, are required to design an alternative which does not use animals (Mukerjee, 1997). Secondly, it is essential that research into the animals themselves continues in order to find out as much as is possible about the different species. As well as their biology and physiology, this also means learning about their communication abilities, their social structures and their emotional repertoires. It is only in gaining such an understanding that we can fully appreciate (and thereby minimise) the negative impact any research procedure may have upon that species.

Self-assessment questions

5 What impact has the animal rights movement had upon the prevalence of experiments involving animals?

6 Distinguish between the practical and ethical sides of the debate concerning animal experimentation.

7 What arguments does Gray use in defence of animal experimentation?

8 Singer suggests that speciesism is no different to racism. Explain what he means.

9 What is meant by *anthropocentric assumptions*? Illustrate your answer with an example.

10 Explain the three Rs.

(Suggested answers on page 106–7.)

The ethics of socially sensitive research

This section is concerned with the impact of psychological research on wider society. There is obvious overlap here with Unit 2 Controversies in Psychology, particularly the sections on biases in theory and research (pages 62ff.), and psychometric testing (pages 47ff.). The message common to each of these units is the increasing impact psychology is having in many sectors of society. Often this is on potentially vulnerable groups, whose marginal, and often disempowered position, may leave them open to exploitation. There is increasing awareness within psychology of the need to ensure that the impact any research may have is as beneficial as possible and that those who are affected are adequately protected.

What is socially sensitive research?

Before exploring specific ethical problems, it is worth defining what actually constitutes socially sensitive research:

'Socially sensitive research refers to studies in which there are potential social consequences or implications, either directly for the participants in the research or for the class of individuals represented by the research' (Sieber and Stanley, 1988, p. 49).

Examples of such research include that which links race to psychological attributes such as IQ; research on the determination of gender differences; research into sexual orientation; and research into the explanation and treatment of atypical behaviours from psychosis to aggression and social deviancy/criminal behaviour. Such research can have a significant impact upon different groups in society, which in the past has not always been positive.

Currently, the BPS's *Code of Conduct, Ethical Principles and Guidelines* (1996) does not specifically address the issues associated with socially sensitive research. However, encompassed within the general guidelines and principles there is specific mention of the need for sensitivity in relation to culturally diverse/minority populations:

'Investigators should recognise that, in our multi-cultural and multi-ethnic society and where investigations involve individuals of different ages, gender and social background, the investigators may not have sufficient knowledge of the implications of any investigation for the participants. It should be borne in mind that the best judge of whether an investigation will cause offence may be members of the population from which the participants in the research are to be drawn' (BPS, 1996, p. 7).

Whilst such references raise awareness of the need for extra sensitivity to protect *participants* who may be members of minority groups, no mention is made of the wider social implications of research and the need to consider/protect 'the class of individuals *represented* by the research' (Sieber and Stanley, 1988, p. 49; author's italics). Also, as Condor (1991, cited in Gale, 1994) pointed out, by focusing upon the relationship between the experimenter and the participant, this neglects the possibility that the research might be offensive to particular groups. One example Condor used is the use of pornographic material in the study of

male aggression. Whilst male participants might not object to it, its very use is an insult to women (Gale, 1994).

Examples of socially sensitive research

▪ Race-related research

An early example of this is research asserting the biological basis of IQ. Supported by many influential psychologists (for example Louis Terman), several states in the USA passed laws requiring compulsory sterilisation of certain undesirable categories of people, including those with low IQ. This debate has rumbled on in psychology precisely because of the serious implications such research has. In 1969, Harvard psychologist Arthur Jensen published a famous essay, 'How much can we boost IQ and scholastic achievement?' Jensen, supported by Hans Eysenck (1971), argued that the higher scores obtained by white people on IQ tests compared to black people was due to genetic differences. Nelkin and Lindee (1995) pointed out that despite critical reactions to this research, support for the views of Jensen has continued: Jensen, Herrnstein and Bouchard published supporting articles in popular magazines as a way of gaining public acceptance and legitimacy for their claims.

More recently in the 1990s these views have become ever more popular with the increase in genetic-based research:

- At the annual meeting of the American Psychological Association in 1990, J Rushton presented a paper arguing that black people have smaller brains than white people which accounts for the differences in their educational performance.
- Michael Levin in 1990 argued that black people were not as intelligent as white people, and thus opposed affirmative action programmes as genetic predispositions could not be altered.
- In 1994, Herrnstein and Murray published *The Bell Curve*, again in support of the genetic determination of intelligence. The book became an immediate best-seller (Nelkin and Lindee, 1995).

The point here is that the popularity and acceptance of research will influence political and social policy agendas, with such 'respected' research providing the much-needed evidence to support discriminatory practices and prejudiced assumptions. This also highlights the role of the media in publishing and popularising 'newsworthy' research, which often results in a biased or partial presentation of the outcomes, with little or no opportunity to redress the issue (see comments of Orbach and Schwartz in Unit 2 pages 60–61).

■ Psychology and social control

Findings and theories within psychology have often been used to legitimise different forms of social control in a variety of settings such as psychiatric institutions and prisons. Research into the treatment of psychiatric disorders has resulted in a wide range of therapies, many of which raise ethical questions about the way in which people with such disorders are treated.

Early therapies often meant psychosurgery where lesions were made in the frontal lobes of patients' brains. Such techniques became popular ways of treating schizophrenics and depressives in the USA and UK in the 1940s and 1950s. This was in spite of the very serious side-effects which included apathy, lethargy, epilepsy, intellectual impairment and even death. Taylor (1992) highlighted the systematic abuse of this technique.

Not surprisingly, psychosurgery has been superseded by more humane therapeutic approaches, although these too raise a number of ethical considerations. (See Unit 26.) The principles of behaviourism pioneered by Skinner have strongly influenced the treatment of psychological disorders and other areas where changes in behaviour are required. The basic premise of these behaviourist approaches is that behaviour can be controlled by the use of rewards and punishment. Whilst some would support these developments with reference to the success of behaviour modification programmes and token economy systems, strong concerns have been voiced. Critics argue that the use of reinforcement and reward to control behaviour essentially denies people freedom and dignity. We are also alerted to the potential for abuse should such techniques be used in an exploitative manner. Wider questions should be asked in relation to what constitutes desirable or normal behaviour. Who is making these decisions and on what basis? Such questions have led to changes in approach to the treatment of adolescent offenders. Instead of being people upon whom the decisions of experts are imposed, they are now more likely to be consulted about their treatment (Gale, 1994).

The changing status of homosexuality similarly questions definitions of 'normal behaviour'. Remember, it was not long ago, in the mid-1970s, that *aversion therapy* based on behaviourist principles was used to administer punishment in the treatment of homosexuals. Whilst Eysenck (1994) reassured us that there is no real prospect of Skinner's reinforcement controlled society coming about, the fact that such principles form the basis of treatment for many disadvantaged people on a daily basis means we cannot afford to be complacent and ignore the ethical responsibility upon psychologists to limit potential abuses. (See Unit 26 pages 964–8.)

■ Research into alternative sexuality

Other important socially sensitive research is that related to sexual orientation, which predominantly focuses upon the causes of homosexuality. Such research has had, and continues to have, a strong influence upon public attitudes and social policy. Explanations of what has largely been regarded as undesirable sexual behaviour have varied throughout history. The earliest contributory explanations from the field of psychology came in the late nineteenth century when homosexuality was defined as a medical condition which could be cured through psychoanalysis, aversive conditioning (for example electric shock treatment) and drug therapy. The American Psychiatric Association included homosexuality as a category of mental illness in the Diagnostic and Statistical Manual (DSM), having serious consequences for those 'patients' presenting with the 'disorder', both in terms of the treatments administered, and in encouraging homophobia due to the stigmatisation of homosexuals as diseased. (Gay rights activists were successful in convincing the American Psychiatric Association that homosexuality should be removed from the DSM scale in 1973.)

Today the debate centres upon the genetic determination of homosexuality. Influential work by LeVay (1993) reported differences in the size of the hypothalamus between heterosexual and homosexual men. Hamer *et al.* (1993) reported to have located genes on the X chromosome which predisposed men to homosexuality. What is interesting is the response to this research and the consequences for the homosexual population. Some sectors of the gay community have welcomed the research, as they can no longer be blamed for their sexual preference. It is something determined beyond their control, just like any other genetically inherited characteristic. This will help to encourage the social legitimation of homosexuality, thereby reducing prejudice.

Others, however, are not so optimistic. As LeVay (1996) asserted, many people hold the view that homosexuals are inferior, and scientific findings asserting the biological determination of homosexuality should be used to eradicate homosexuality through, for example, genetic engineering. Thus many fear the rise of anti-gay eugenics, with 'gay' foetuses being aborted or embryos being manipulated to eradicate the 'gay gene'.

Activity 8

Draw a table with two columns. In the first column briefly describe each area of socially sensitive research. Next to each description in the second column, state the negative consequences this research has had or could have.

(Suggested answer on page 106.)

Issues emerging from socially sensitive research

The recognition of socially sensitive research highlights a number of trends: firstly, the increasing application of psychological research; and secondly, greater awareness of the rights of the individual in society. Psychology must necessarily keep pace with the changing socio-cultural context if it is to be of any use. This means conducting research into contemporary issues, whilst also acknowledging the specific ethical problems this research may give rise to. It is worth looking at two such areas in greater detail: one is research into Aids and related behaviour; the other is the recent revival in popularity of genetic-based explanations of behaviour (figure 3.8).

3.8 Contemporary areas of psychological research giving rise to special ethical concerns

■ Research into Aids

Central to Aids research is the dilemma involved in balancing individual rights with public health benefits. Melton and Gray (1988) explored some of the difficulties associated with this research: the biggest threat to those taking part in research is a breach of confidentiality, which can at present be legally enforced. The nature of the research also represents an intrusion of privacy and a threat to personal dignity, requiring the disclosure of information of a very personal nature. Direct harm may be caused with questions about one's status as a patient with a grave illness likely to cause distress. Harm may also result if the identity of participants is disclosed due to the social stigma attached to the disease. Unless participants can be sure that they will be adequately protected, then they will be reluctant to take part in this much-needed

3.8 Contemporary areas of psychological research giving rise to special ethical concerns *cont.*

research. Melton and Gray (1988) concluded that legislation is needed in order to protect the privacy of those taking part in research. Failure to ensure this will result in a stagnation of research into Aids-related behaviour which will be of benefit to no one.

■ Genetic research

The past decade has been marked by a surge in genetic explanations for a whole range of behaviours. These include among others: sociability, creativity, criminal tendencies, sexual orientation, child-rearing tendencies, dominance, personality and, of course, intelligence. The implications of such genetic explanations is that biology is accepted as destiny. Differences which exist between, for example, different racial groups and between the

sexes will be accepted as 'natural' and remain unchallenged. Attention is diverted away from the role social factors play in determining behaviour. It is a recipe for non-intervention, as genetically determined characteristics (such as intelligence and resulting educational performance) cannot be altered. An important point which often gets lost in the furore of excitement surrounding genetic research is that it is, at best, inconclusive with many claims openly disputed. Some of the more sinister but very real implications of genetic research are highlighted in the newspaper article shown in figure 3.9. Remember, these are the views of a lecturer in psychology at Edinburgh University not that long ago! Moreover, he is not alone. Similar views have been expressed by psychology Professor Richard Lynn (1996).

Figure 3.9

Black people are less intelligent than white people, and single mothers should be encouraged to breed with higher-IQ males to escape the poverty trap. So runs the wisdom of Chris Brand, a lecturer in psychology at Edinburgh University and author of *The g Factor* . . .

'I am perfectly proud to be a racist in the scientific sense,' he said yesterday. 'It is scientific fact that black Americans are less intelligent than white Americans and the IQ of Asians is higher than blacks.'

Mr Brand, who never gained a doctorate but formulated his ideas as a prison psychologist, said his book represents a stand against the 'high priests of egalitarianism and political correctness'. He argues that understanding that people have different levels of 'g', or general intellectual ability, could eradicate the problem of single mothers.

'The only way to get away from the explosion of single parenting is to persuade these girls to postpone babies before finding a more suitable husband.' They would then widen the gene pool of their offspring with a decent scattering of intelligent ancestry. 'They should be encouraged to have sex with higher-IQ boys. There need be

no compulsion, but we could teach these girls that it would be highly advantageous.'

He is also convinced of the intellectual inequality of different races. For example, 'Hong Kong is as advanced as many western cities. Africa, however, remains the utterly dark continent.'

But the answer is not mixed breeding to improve the blacks' gene pool. 'There are plenty of intelligent African men for black girls to be having sex with. It is just black intelligence is more polarised. There are many very successful blacks, particularly in areas like baseball or music, but at the other end of the scale there is squalor and degradation.'

Other psychologists find this not only repellent, but misconceived. Michael Howe, professor of psychology at Exeter University, said: 'His views are dangerous, but more importantly, they are wrong. It is true that certain groups score less well in IQ testing than others, but a score doesn't assess the fundamental quality of a person – indeed, the nature of the tests themselves says a lot about cultural expectations.'

Source: Wynne-Jones (1996).

Examples of how psychology has kept pace with social change can be seen in the definitions and treatment of homosexuality referred to earlier. Also, increasing respect for those who take part in

research is reflected by now defining them as 'participants' rather than 'subjects'. This indicates the shift in the perception of participant from 'object' to 'person', from 'it' to 'you' (Gale, 1994).

▨ Ethical responsibility for the consequences of research

In terms of ethical responsibilities, psychologists have a duty to protect both those directly involved in research and those who may be affected by the research. Even if the researchers themselves claim to have no political or social agenda, they cannot afford to divorce themselves completely from the consequences of their research. This in itself brings its own difficulties as often research which can be applied to positive effect can equally be applied to negative effect. Gale (1994) cited a number of examples of such research: conditioning principles, which have had a very positive effect in the rehabilitation of psychiatric patients, might also be used in the torturing of political prisoners; theories and research on attitude change can be used not only positively in health education programmes (for example to prevent smoking), but also for the promotion of political extremism, such as the promotion of ethnic cleansing (see Unit 26 pages 964–8).

Some have suggested that checks should be introduced to prevent the abuse of research findings (for example Hamer (1996) suggested that the use of genetic testing for homosexuality should be restricted and that relevant DNA sequences should be patented preventing the development of commercial blood testing). However, it is difficult to see how such checks and controls could be introduced across the whole of psychology, biology and medicine, especially as it is often difficult to predict in advance exactly what will be made of the research findings.

Difficulties faced in conducting socially sensitive research

Due to the ethical difficulties often associated with socially sensitive research, many are deterred from conducting it, avoiding the potentially controversial position they may be placing themselves in. Such a reaction is with due justification, as those who do explicitly address sensitive issues risk ostracisation from colleagues and other sectors of society, should they come up with the 'wrong' answers. Examples here include Milgram, whose shocking findings about obedience resulted in heavy criticism from colleagues and the press, and harassment from the public for a number of years. (This is in contrast to his participants a year after the study of whom only 1 per cent regretted taking part in the research (Sieber and Stanley, 1988).) Scarr (1988) detailed the harassment and threats Jensen received for many years after coming to the controversial conclusion that black people may be genetically inferior to others in intelligence. Scarr herself refused to be deterred from asking 'dangerous questions' concerning racial differences, although conceded that she would emigrate should she find a link between African ancestry and low intellectual skills (Scarr, 1988). Other pressures deterring the conduct of socially sensitive research come from ethical review committees which are more likely to find fault with socially sensitive research protocols. Ceci, Peters and Plotkin (1985, cited in Sieber and Stanley, 1988) found that socially sensitive research proposals were twice as likely to be rejected by review committees than similarly designed non-sensitive proposals.

In spite of the factors deterring the carrying out of socially sensitive research, there are strong arguments for the need for this research to continue. Choosing to ignore any differences that exist between different groups does nothing to help members of those groups or further our understanding of why those differences exist. Also needed is a shift in the belief systems of psychologists which have so far failed to investigate the *strengths* of underrepresented groups, with questions about minorities framed in terms of what is wrong with, deficient about or needs improving upon. 'If the standard for good behaviour is always the white male group, then the behaviour of women and ethnic minorities is likely to seem negative' (Scarr, 1988, p. 57). Such assumptions also underlie much research into ageing, with the emphasis being on what is lost as we 'degenerate' into old age, thus helping to perpetuate the stereotypes of the elderly as incompetent (Gale, 1994). Given our current demographic structure, it is not difficult to see how such negative views may have a detrimental impact upon the way the elderly are regarded and treated in our society.

The way forward

The way forward is certainly not to retreat and pretend that issues of a socially sensitive nature do not exist or do not warrant investigation. If psychology is restricted to those areas unlikely to raise socially sensitive issues, then there will be at least two undesirable consequences:

■ Psychology will be limited to the study of relatively unimportant issues.
■ The disadvantages characterising many minority groups will remain unquestioned.

There is a need for good quality research in which the assumptions underlying any method or theory are made explicit. Psychologists must acknowledge their relationship with wider society, clearly stating the limits of the generalisability of their findings. There is a need to build positive links with policymakers and the media which may help to ensure the appropriate interpretation and application of research findings.

Self-assessment questions

11 Define what socially sensitive research is and why such areas generate special ethical concerns.

12 What changes have brought attention to the issues associated with socially sensitive research?

13 What are the difficulties psychologists face in attempting to protect those who may be affected by the outcomes of their research?

14 Should research into ethically sensitive issues be encouraged? Justify your answer.

(Suggested answers on page 107.)

Unit summary

■ *Ethics* concern what is acceptable human behaviour. In the context of psychology, ethics relate to what is considered acceptable practice for psychologists in both research and applied settings.

■ Ethical practice is essential in all psychological research involving both humans and animals, regardless of the level of the research. Psychologists should also be aware of the potential disadvantages research may result in, especially in dealing with issues of a socially sensitive nature.

■ The BPS has a *code of conduct* and ethical principles and guidelines which psychologists should follow in order to ensure adequate protection for research participants.

■ Previous studies highlight some of the ethical dilemmas often faced by psychologists. These dilemmas centre around the *issues of consent*, the use of *deception, debriefing* and the *right to withdraw.*

■ Consent should be *informed,* which means participants should know the real aims of the study. Care needs to be taken to protect those who may not be in a position to give informed consent, for example children, those with a mental handicap.

■ Deception of participants should be avoided. Deception is more easily justified when the potential harm is minimal, when the findings of the research are important and when there are no alternative deception-free ways of investigating the issue.

■ Debriefing should ensure participants leave the study in the same state they entered and provide participants with information so they can benefit educationally. It is especially important where deception is used. Debriefing does not justify the use of unethical practices.

Summary cont'd.

- Participants should be made aware of their right to withdraw and care must be taken not to exploit the power base inherent in the researcher/participant relationship. Participants also have the right to withdraw retrospectively from a study.
- Animals have been and are used in many areas of psychology, for example behaviourism; neurobiological approaches; comparative psychology; sociobiology. However, their use in experimental settings has declined greatly since the 1970s.
- Students are preferring psychology degree courses which do not involve animal experimentation. Where animals are used, this use is controlled by law and by the BPS which has guidelines for the use of animals in research.
- The arguments surrounding animal experimentation relate to both *practical* and *ethical* issues. The ethical debate surrounds the notion of equality – if we accept animals as our equals, then they should not be used in experiments. If, on the other hand, we accept that we owe a special duty to our own species as opposed to any other, then their use can be justified.
- Supporters of animal experimentation point out the practical benefits resulting from such research, with both humans and the animals themselves often benefiting.
- Critics suggest more harm than good has been done in denying that animals are capable of feeling emotion. *Extrapolating* from animals to humans is also questioned on the basis that they are not sufficiently similar.
- In deciding whether to proceed with research involving animals, three things need assessing: the likelihood of benefit from the research; the quality of the research; the degree of animal suffering.
- Negative reaction to animal experimentation has led to a focus on alternatives and attempts to reduce the number of animals and experiments needed. Such moves include protocol changes; data mining; the development of test-tube alternatives; increasing field research/naturalistic observations.
- Ensuring the adequate protection of animals in the future means educating scientists in the need for alternatives and learning as much as possible about different species such that the negative impact of any research procedures is minimal.
- *Socially sensitive research* is that which has potential social consequences or implications for those involved in the research or for those represented by the research. Examples include research which links intelligence to race; research supporting the need to control certain behaviour; research into sexual orientation.
- Research supporting the link between race and IQ has long been used to justify *discriminatory practices* (such as denial of educational opportunity). The way these researchers used the media to popularise such ideas highlights the dangers associated with 'newsworthy' research.
- Psychological research has been used to legitimise the *social control* of various behaviours, for example psychosurgery used to control people with schizophrenia; the application of behaviourist principles to treat homosexuality.
- Recent research asserting the genetic basis of homosexuality has important implications: it may reduce prejudice, with homosexuality being seen as the same as any other genetically determined trait, or it may result in anti-gay eugenics.
- Psychologists cannot ignore the social and political implications of their research. The paradox is that research applied to positive effect can also be applied to negative effect.
- Many are deterred from conducting socially sensitive research due to the risk of being ostracised should they find the 'wrong' thing. It is also more difficult to get proposals for socially sensitive research passed by ethics committees.
- There is a need for socially sensitive issues to be explored. Avoiding these issues will result in a psychology which studies relatively unimportant issues with the disadvantages faced by minority groups remaining unquestioned.

Terms to define

anthropocentric
anthropomorphism
British Psychological Society (BPS)
comparative psychology
data mining
ethics
ethology
extrapolation
generational effects

informed consent
presumptive consent
prior general consent
protocol changes
role playing
sentient
socially sensitive research
sociobiology
speciesism

Further reading

All students of psychology should read the BPS *Code of Conduct, Ethical Principles and Guidelines.* This is available through the BPS.

Gale, A (1994) 'Ethical issues in psychological research', in A Colman (ed.) *Companion Encyclopedia of Psychology,* vol. 2, Routledge, London.

This is an excellent chapter which covers a range of contemporary issues relevant to research with humans and animals and in relation to socially sensitive issues. Highly recommended!

Scientific American (1997) 276 (2) February, pp. 63–77.

This contains a number of articles debating the issue of the benefits and ethics of animal research. It provides an up-to-date readable summary of arguments both for and against animal research.

Answers

■ Suggested answers to activities

1

a   The ethical guidelines violated in each study include the following:

■   Milgram (1963). Deception – 'informed consent' was not possible because participants didn't know the aims of the study; withdrawal from the study – participants were pressured to continue rather than being offered the opportunity to leave; inadequate protection of participants, many of whom experienced discomfort and stress.

■   Zimbardo (1973). Protection of participants – many participants experienced extreme distress; the fact that the study continued for 6 days questions whether the researchers made it clear to participants that they had a right to withdraw. The respect (principle 1) researchers should show participants is lacking.

■   In the three studies of helping behaviour, deception is used. All three studies also put participants in a stressful situation, a situation which they had not consented to, and arguably, a situation which they would not ordinarily encounter. This again violates the respect researchers should show their participants.

■   In the studies on personal space, people are involved in studies without first consenting to that involvement. The studies resulted in discomfort for those involved, and, because it was a field study, there was no opportunity to debrief people.

■   Seligman (1965). The experimental situation caused discomfort to participants. This discomfort would certainly have been exacerbated when participants realised they could not escape it. This questions whether the researchers made participants adequately aware of their right to withdraw. The resulting learned helplessness is evidence enough of the negative effect the experimental procedure had upon the participants.

■ Ainsworth (1978). Could the babies be said to have been adequately protected if they were put into a situation which would foreseeably cause them distress? Would they have agreed to take part if they understood what was going to happen?

■ Bandura (1965). The children were not told the aims of the study. It is also irresponsible deliberately to reinforce acts of aggression with rewards and this could cause confusion for the children outside of the experimental situation.

■ Watson and Rayner (1920). The well-being of Little Albert was totally violated. 'Debriefing' doesn't appear to have happened. A blatant abuse of the power relationship between the experimenter and the unsuspecting participant.

■ Rosenthal and Jacobson (1968). Deception was used giving the teachers false information and not revealing the aim of the study. Consent was denied the children who knew nothing of the study. The study deliberately affects the real academic performance of children – this is an area of behaviour which should be beyond the reach of psychological investigations of this type (principle 1).

2

■ Milgram's study arguably revealed important insights; also difficult to see how this could be done without deception. The distress caused to participants would be the main reason this study would not get the go-ahead today.

■ Studies on helping behaviour – it could be argued that the potential distress caused is minimal, especially in relation to what was revealed about helping behaviour. However, it could also be argued that similar insights could be made by observing natural situations.

■ Seligman's experiment(s) provided important insights into the nature of depression. One possible alternative would be to explore the notion of learned helplessness using participants who already suffered from depression. Their performance across different tasks could be compared with the performance of a control group who were not depressed.

■ Rosenthal and Jacobson's study highlighted the impact of teacher expectations on children's performance – an important insight which arguably justifies the deception. It could also be argued, however, that the study, given its effect on the participants, added little to what was already known about self-fulfilling prophecies and the effects of labelling.

3

It would be unethical to subject humans to the experimental conditions. Generational effects could be studied in a controlled setting. There are sufficient similarities between humans and monkeys for generalisations to be made. Harlow's studies did much to further our understanding of the effects of maternal deprivation.

4

Possible examples of benefits resulting from research with animals include: behaviourist applications for therapeutic and educational purposes; the trialing of new medical treatments; the training of helper dogs to help people with disabilities; benefits to the animals themselves in terms of preserving the species or developing more humane ways of treating them.

5

The welfare of animals used in studies can best be protected by following the BPS guidelines. These can be summarised as follows: abiding by the law; ensuring the knowledge to be gained is important enough to justify the use of animals; ensuring informed selection of appropriate animals through knowledge of different species; keeping the number of animals used to a minimum; using endangered species in the wild for conservation purposes only; obtaining animals from reputable suppliers only; ensuring the environment is appropriate for the species; in fieldwork, ensuring minimum disruption of the species; avoiding staged displays of aggression; ensuring any deprivation is appropriate for the species; keeping any necessary suffering to a minimum and only when a Home Office licence is held; for surgical procedures a Home Office licence must be held, and they should be conducted only by those appropriately qualified; animals must receive appropriate post-operative care; in any doubt a second opinion must be sought; any questions should be addressed to appropriate advisory bodies via the BPS.

6

Taking the form of a letter, the points made should be based on rational arguments, not just emotive opinions! Examples of points to include are:

■ Animals are our equals.

■ We should not assume that animals do not feel pain as we do.

■ Using animals devalues their status, reducing them to mechanistic, stimulus-response bundles.

■ The assumed similarities between humans and animals do not exist, therefore extrapolating is invalid.

■ Low ecological validity renders the use of animals irrelevant.

■ There are alternatives, for example the use of statistical techniques, avoiding research into what we already know, as is likely in the module proposed.

It would be helpful to suggest alternatives; for example, base the module around the search for alternatives to the proposed animal experiments.

7

One possible evaluation of Harlow's research using Bateson's model:
Harlow's research could be said to be moderately beneficial in terms of highlighting the consequences of maternal deprivation (although as Barnard and Kaufman (1997) suggested, these facts were already established). Whilst Harlow's study may have been well designed from an experimental point of view in terms of control over conditions, the experimental situation bore no resemblance to the normal social and environmental conditions of the monkeys. The degree of suffering in Harlow's study was high with many of the monkeys in distress, resulting in permanently dysfunctional behaviour. With moderate benefits, questionable quality and high levels of suffering the study should not proceed.

8

Summary table should include the following information:

- *Research area*: race and IQ – asserts the genetic basis of intelligence, with black people having inferior intelligence to white people.
  Negative impact: support for compulsory sterilisation programmes and immigration restrictions in the USA; the opposition of affirmative action programmes designed to help racial minorities achieve educational success; general reinforcement of racist attitudes supporting the notion of the superiority of white people.
- *Research area*: social control – attempts to manage and control the behaviour of those displaying undesirable behaviour, for example people with psychiatric disorders, offenders.
  Negative impact: early psychosurgery often resulted in lethargy, epilepsy, intellectual impairment and death. Behaviourist treatments imposed definitions of acceptable behaviour, denying people their freedom and dignity (as late as the 1970s, people who were homosexual were subjected to punishment regimes based on behaviourist principles).
- *Research area*: alternative sexuality and the causes of homosexuality. Early research defined homosexuality as abnormal behaviour requiring treatment. Recent research asserts the genetic basis of homosexuality,
  Negative impact: early research resulted in 'treatments' including electric shock therapy designed to 'cure' the individual of the condition. Treating it as a disorder also fuelled homophobic attitudes. Genetic research could possibly result in anti-gay eugenics.

Suggested answers to self-assessment questions

1

The BPS helps to ensure ethical practice through its code of conduct which all members should follow.

Supplementing the code of conduct are ethical guidelines for the conduct of research with both humans and animals. It is in the interests of psychologists (in terms of affiliation to the BPS) and psychology as a whole (in terms of its professional standing in society) that the code of conduct is adhered to.

2

The potentially harmful effects of deception can be minimised by:
- finding an alternative, deception-free way of investigating the issue, for example role play
- obtaining presumptive consent
- obtaining prior general consent
- ensuring that participants are sufficiently debriefed such that they leave the study in the same state they entered.

3

Obtaining consent can be problematic in cases where deception is used – people don't know what they are consenting to. It is also difficult in observational studies in the field where the emphasis is on 'participants' behaving naturally. Care also needs to be taken not to exploit those people who may not be in a position to give consent, for example children, people with a mental handicap.

4

The power relationship between the researcher and the participant may inhibit the participant from withdrawing from the study should he or she wish to. The researcher may also be tempted to exploit his or her own position, even if unknowingly. Robson (1993) suggested that it can turn into an employer/employee situation, especially where an incentive for participating is offered.

5

The animal rights movement has resulted in a reduction in the number of animals used for experimental purposes (for example, in the UK, Netherlands and Germany, the total number of animals used in laboratory experiments has fallen by half since the 1970s; students are opting for psychology courses which do not involve animal experiments; there has been a shift away from experimental procedures to observational/field studies).

6

The ethical debate centres around the view that animals are our equals and should therefore not be used for experiments versus the view that we owe a special duty to our own species and it is therefore acceptable to use animals for the benefit of humans.
The practical debate centres around the practical benefits realised through animal experimentation, although this is disputed.

7
    Gray argues that we owe a special duty to our own species and that the suffering of animals in experiments is justified if it is to alleviate the suffering of humans. Gray does acknowledge that there is a point where the degree of suffering inflicted upon animals is too great to be worth the avoidance of lesser suffering by people – the problem is in how to assess and compare degrees of suffering.

8
    Just as racists give greater weight to the interests of members of their own race, speciesists give greater weight to the interests of their own species. For racists, pain felt by members of another race does not matter as much as pain felt by members of their own race; for speciesists, pain felt by another species does not matter as much as pain felt by their own species.

9
    Anthropocentric assumptions are the assumptions that humans lie at the centre of all things, setting the standards against which all other things are measured. One example is in denying that animals are capable of experiencing emotions – behaviour is explained in reductionist terms, for example physiological responses to environmental stimuli, as in behaviourism.

10
    The principle of the 'three Rs' was proposed by Russell and Burch (1959) in an attempt to reduce the unnecessary suffering of animals used in experiments. The three Rs stand for:

- *replace* – replace use of animals with in vitro or test tube methods

- *reduce* – reduce the number of animals used using statistical techniques
- *refine* – refine experimental techniques in order to reduce suffering.

11
    Socially sensitive research is research which has social consequences or implications for those involved in the research or those represented by the research. Such research raises ethical concerns because it may directly impact on people's lives, with such people often occupying vulnerable or minority positions in our society.

12
    Awareness of socially sensitive issues has emerged due to the increasing application of psychological research to real life, along with increasing recognition in society of the rights of the individual. Also, there are new areas of research which pose their own ethical problems, for example research into Aids.

13
    One problem psychologists face in attempting to protect those who may be affected by their research is that it may be difficult to foresee all the consequences of their research. Also, research which can be applied to positive effect can usually also be applied to negative effect. It is also difficult to see how any controls over the applications of research can be realistically enforced.

14
    Research into sensitive issues should be encouraged if psychology is to deal with important issues and if disadvantages faced by different groups are to be questioned.

Social Psychology

Unit 4

Social Cognition

Penny Cortvriend, Sandie Taylor and Regina Teahan

This unit covers:

Social and cultural influences upon perception

Attribution theories

Prejudice and discrimination

By the end of this unit, you should be able to:

■ explain how social groups and cultures influence our perception

■ explain and understand various attribution theories

■ explain the origins and maintenance of prejudice and discrimination

■ understand the concept of stereotyping

■ evaluate recommendations for the reduction of prejudice and discrimination.

Unit 4 Contents

Introduction

In order to understand the term 'social cognition' as a particular approach in social psychology, consider what is meant by cognition. Cognition, broadly speaking, is the action or faculty of knowing, and cognitive psychology looks at how people acquire knowledge or information, organise and use it. Thus the central concerns of cognitive psychology are perception, attention, memory, language and thought. *Social cognition* is also concerned with these processes, but in a social context – in other words, the role played by cognitive factors in our social behaviour. It is also concerned with how different social situations and contexts influence cognitive processes in people.

In this unit we look at social and cultural influences upon perceptions and examine social and cultural identity theories. Social and cultural factors consider how membership of social groups and cultures can influence perception of and determine reactions to other people. Following this, the theory of social representations examines how socially shared beliefs develop and are transmitted in social groups and in society as a whole. This theory is an important aspect of social cognition because our social representations help us to make sense of our world.

Attribution is also considered in this unit. Attribution is the process by which we judge the actions of others. It is concerned with the perception and calculation of causes – why a particular behaviour occurs. Some of the biases identified in the attribution process are also covered.

Finally, we look at the origin and maintenance of prejudice and discrimination and consider ways of reducing them.

Social and cultural influences upon perception

The various areas of social cognition have their roots in post-war Europe. After the Second World War European social psychology circles were uneasy about the growing dependency on the US lead in defining the field, theories and methods of social psychology. There was also concern over the strongly individualist approach taken by many US theorists of social behaviour which ignored the context in which the behaviour took place. Among the first to voice this unease and to search for the identity of social psychology in Europe were Tajfel and Moscovici. Their concern was for a more *social* social psychology than the self-contained individualism of the US approach. Tajfel emphasised the social dimension of individual and group behaviour. In other words, the emphasis was on the degree to which behaviour and experience is embedded and shaped by the culture and society one lives in. Society has its own structure which, according to Moscovici, is not definable in terms of the characteristics of individuals. Therefore,

> 'social psychology can and must include in its theoretical and research preoccupations a direct concern with a relationship between human psychological functioning and the large-scale social processes and events which shape this functioning and are shaped by it' (Tajfel, 1989).

Given the diversity of social and cultural backgrounds characteristic of Europe, this greater concern for the social context of both social behaviour and psychological investigation is not surprising. It is with this background in mind that we now turn to the theories regarded as representing the school of thought known as European Social Psychology: **social identity theory**, **social representation theory** and **cultural identity theory**.

Social identity theory

The question 'Who am I?' can be asked in relation to the context of self concept. However, the question also relates to social identity theory: analysis of people's answers to the question often reveals several references to group affiliations. These can be either explicit (for example 'I am a member of the National Trust'), or implicit through reference to social roles ('I am a librarian'), to gender ('I am a man'), or to nationality ('I am Welsh').

It is very likely that, if not the majority, then at least several self descriptions refer to group membership. Why do we classify ourselves as a member of groups? One explanation is that categorisation, i.e. classifying people and things into groups or categories, is a fundamental aspect of human perception. Segmenting the world into a manageable number of categories simplifies it and helps us make sense of it. Classifying people into groups in society is known as **social categorisation** and cuts down on the amount of information that must be processed (social categorisation is in fact the basis of stereotyping, i.e. the attribution of certain traits and characteristics to *all* members of a social category). Classification into social groups also serves another important function. It helps define who we are. Not only do we classify others as members of certain groups but we also place ourselves in groups. This is why our sense of identity is so closely allied with our various group memberships. As well as a personal identity (a sense of who one is, based on individual traits and unique history), people also develop social identities based on roles in society, nationality, religion, ethnicity, etc. 'Social identities are important because they give people a feeling of place and position in the world. Without them most people would feel like loose marbles rolling around in an unconnected universe' (Tavris and Wade, 1995).

The idea that social identity derives from group membership is not new, but it was not until quite recently that it was realised that social identity processes might have implications for intergroup behaviour. In an attempt to assess the effect of group membership on behaviour we now turn to the work of Tajfel.

One phenomenon associated with categorisation is an enhanced homogeneity within groups. Items or members of the same group are seen as similar to one another. This accompanies an accentuation of differences between categories or groups. Tajfel and Wilkes (1963) demonstrated the powerful effect of categorisation on the perception of lengths of lines. Lines of different lengths which had not been labelled were perceived quite accurately, but when lines were put randomly into the same category (or group) they were seen as being more similar than those in different categories (category A or B) – even when the participants in the experiment knew they had been categorised randomly. This shows that when stimuli are placed in categories, the stimuli in each category are perceived to be more similar than they actually are. If objective stimuli such as lines are perceived to differ in length according to how they are categorised, then social stimuli, since they are more ambiguous, are even more susceptible to the effect of categorisation. Social categorisation therefore results in the development of two important perceptual sets: first of all, in the social world people perceive a greater degree of similarity between themselves and others who they perceive to be similar to themselves; and secondly, greater differences than actually do exist between themselves and people they think of as different to themselves. Hence members of the same group are seen as very similar to one another. This effect was particularly noticeable during the Second World War, when the media emphasised 'the British people' as a courageous, inventive group in contrast with outgroup enemies. What is interesting about this perception of homogeneity is that it is assymetrical, 'they' – the *outgroup* – are all the same, but 'we' – the *ingroup* – though similar, are distinguishable from one another. Perhaps we process more thoroughly information about those who belong to the ingroup.

Activity 1

Think of a group that you consider to be an outgroup. In what ways do members of that group seem to be the same? Make a list. Now think of a group which you consider to be the ingroup and to which you belong. In what ways are its members distinguishable?

Tajfel's research illustrates another phenomenon associated with categorisation which is that social categorisation results in ingroup favouritism, and negative outgroup bias. School children aged 14–15 years were randomly divided into two groups. Each child was told he or she could give money to his or her own group but they had also to give money to members of the other group (outgroup). The children did not know the identity of the members of either group. No face-to-face interaction took place between group members and no conflict of interest was said to exist between the two groups. These conditions are called the **minimal group paradigm**. Tajfel found strong evidence of ingroup–outgroup discrimination. The children allocated monetary rewards making the difference between the two groups as great as possible, even if this meant that the ingroup was disadvantaged. For example, the child could choose between the two following options: (a) allocating 20 coins to a member of the ingroup and 15 coins to a member of the outgroup (difference of 5 coins); or (b) allocating 15 coins to a member of the ingroup and 8 coins to a member of the outgroup (difference of 7 coins). The children were more likely to choose the latter option, demonstrating that they discriminated as much as possible between the two groups.

Activity 2

Why do you think children chose the latter option? Write down your thoughts before reading on.

It is the ingroup which come off best in intergroup perceptions, judgements and resource allocations. This brings us to another aspect of the theory, the search for positive self-esteem. People make social comparisons, i.e. they evaluate and compare themselves with reference to their own group, in search of a positive social identity. Since part of our self concept or identity is defined in terms of group affiliations, it follows that people make social comparisons and that there will be a preference to view their own group (ingroup) positively rather than negatively. The outcome of such intergroup comparisons is critical because if

the ingroup can be perceived as clearly superior on some dimension of value, then this indirectly contributes to self-esteem. Because of the need for a positive self concept it follows that there will be a bias in these comparisons to look for ways in which the ingroup can be distinguished favourably from the outgroups. Tajfel calls this the 'establishment of positive distinctiveness' (Tajfel, 1978).

Sometimes it happens that, under certain circumstances, it is impossible for group members to find a positive basis for social comparison, for example groups which have low status in society. Tajfel suggests three possible strategies: first, the members might seek new bases for comparison which might give a more favourable outcome (*social creativity*), for example emphasising the liveliness of the group's language; secondly, they might leave the group and join another with more positive qualities (*social mobility*), for example if one is unhappy about being one of the 'unemployed' voluntary work may be sought; and thirdly, they might seek to change the attributes of their group so that it might be more favourably evaluated in future (*social change*), for example the 'black is beautiful' movement in the USA in the late 1960s.

Activity 3

When evaluating social identity theory, you need to consider its reliability and validity. (If you are not certain what these terms mean check these out now).
Jot down some of your thoughts regarding the reliability and validity of this theory before reading on.

One criticism that has been levelled against minimal group experiments is that members of such groups as Tajfel's may have been demonstrating demand characteristics and felt that discrimination against outgroup members was required of them. However, the findings from minimal group studies have been replicated many times in the UK and in other individualist countries, for example Doise *et al.* (1972) using

German soldiers, Simon *et al.* (1990) using Dutch students, and Hogg and Sutherland (1991) using Australian students as participants. Another criticism is that the theory's validity may be restricted to more individualist cultural groups. Studies by Wetherell (1992) reported rather more complex results from New Zealand. She studied white and Polynesian children in New Zealand and found the latter to be much more generous toward the outgroup, perhaps reflecting cultural norms which emphasised cooperation. However, because the giving of gifts to others is highly esteemed within the traditional Polynesian culture, by rewarding the outgroup the Polynesian child could in fact be assuring his or her positive social identity.

Further support for the theory's validity is provided by Oakes and Turner (1986). Participants in a minimal group experiment who were not given the usual opportunity to make intergroup reward allocations showed lower self-esteem than those who were. A follow-up experiment confirmed this result and established that it was indeed the opportunity to display intergroup discrimination that resulted in an increase in self-esteem. Control participants who, having been categorised, could only distribute rewards between two ingroup members or two outgroup members or who could not distribute rewards at all showed lower self-esteem than participants who were allowed to make intergroup decisions (Lemyre and Smith, 1985). Another strength of the theory is that its applicability is not limited simply to contrived experimental situations. It has also been used to explain a wide range of phenomena in naturalistic settings, for example differences in wages between associated groups of workers, endeavours by ethnic groups to maintain the standard of their native language and discriminations between nurses holding differing qualifications (Brown, 1988). The theory can also account for the ways in which members of existing social groups perceive one another. Numerous studies have shown that members of different ethnic groups often maintain stereotyped beliefs about the positive qualities of their own group and negative qualities of other groups.

Cultural identity

We have already seen how a person's sense of identity, an idea of oneself as unique, is rooted in the groups to which the person belongs. One such group is that of culture, 'the man-made part of the environment' (Segall *et al.*, 1990). This definition of culture covers not only material human-made objects such as houses but also social institutions such as marriage and employment. Such institutions are regulated by laws, norms and rules. However, the problem with this definition is that it does not suggest how to draw boundaries between cultures. How much difference is required before two populations are two different cultures? No definitive agreement is possible as to how to distinguish between cultures. Rohner (1984) suggests that the concept of culture should be restricted to what things mean to a group of people. Culture is defined as 'an organised system of meanings which members of that culture attribute to the persons and objects that make up that culture' (Rohner, 1984). This brings us to the most important aspect of a definition of culture, i.e. a relatively organised system of shared meanings.

How do these systems of shared meanings influence perception and how does a sense of cultural identity affect how one behaves towards others? We will deal with these two aspects in order. In looking at how a sense of cultural identity affects how one behaves towards members of one's cultural group and outgroup members, we revisit social identity theory.

One of the most important ways in which cultures differ has to do with whether the individual or the group is given the greater emphasis. This in turn, affects people's basic concepts of the self and personality. In individual-centred cultures, the self is defined as a collection of personality traits such as 'I am ambitious, friendly, outgoing'. In collectivist or group-centred cultures, the 'self' is seen as something embedded in a community and defined that way, for example 'I am the son of Fred and Doris who came to Shetland at the turn of the century and farmed ponies'.

Markus and Kitayama (1991) have introduced the terms *'independent self'* and *'interdependent self'* to differentiate those who consider themselves independent agents, as often found in western individualist countries, from those who consider themselves interdependent, as often found in more collectivist countries. Individuals in collectivist cultures perceive themselves and others in more situational terms. Shweder and Bourne (1982) compared free descriptions of their peers by 70 Indian and 17 white American adults: 72 per cent of the white Americans' descriptions were context-free personality trait attributions; only 50 per cent of the Indian statements were such. A large proportion of the Indian statements specified the social context. Thus, where a typical statement would be 'He is selfish', the equivalent Indian statement might be 'He is reluctant to give money to his family'. Korten (1974) found a similar effect when comparing the perceptions of others by Ethiopian and American students. The Ethiopians included more context-related descriptions, for example 'He likes to socialise with other students' than did the Americans.

In 1984, Miller presented white American and Indian participants with an account of a motorcycle accident (see below). Participants were asked to explain why they thought the key person in the incident acted as they did.

Activity 4

Read the episode below and consider your own explanations.

'The back wheel burst on the motorcycle. The passenger sitting on the rear jumped. The moment the passenger fell, he struck his head on the pavement. The driver of the motorcycle – who is an attorney – as he was on his way to court for some work, just took the passenger to a local hospital and went on and attended to his court work. The driver left the passenger there without consulting the doctor about the seriousness of the injury – the gravity of the situation – whether the passenger should be shifted immediately – and he went on to court. So ultimately the passenger died.'

Miller cites three responses given by white American participants and three responses given by Indian participants.

American responses:
1 He was obviously irresponsible.
2 He must have been in a state of shock.
3 He was aggressive in pursuit of his career.

Indian responses:
1 It was his duty to be in court for the client he was representing.
2 He might have become nervous or confused.
3 The injured man might not have looked as seriously injured as he was.

Activity 5

Consider how the explanations given by the white Americans differ from the explanations given by the Indians.
Are your explanations more in line with white American or Indian responses?
Explain your answer.

Although the above study did show differences between white American and Indian participants in that the white Americans gave significantly more personality explanations whilst the Indians gave more situational ones, this is not to say that the white Americans did not provide situational explanations of behaviour or that the Indians did not provide personality traits as explanations. The differences were simply differences in frequency. This suggests that the people in the two cultural groups direct their attention differently. It does not suggest that the processes of social cognition were fundamentally different. Those with interdependent values would give more attention to the context or situation whilst those with independent values would focus primarily on the actions of themselves and others.

One of the limitations of the studies quoted is that rarely was any measure of the participants' independent or interdependent values taken. Hence one can only speculate as to why these differences were found.

In looking at how our sense of cultural identity affects how one behaves towards members of one's own cultural group and outgroup members, we need to revisit Tajfel's minimal group theory which accounts for ways in which members of existing social groups perceive themselves and others. A number of studies have shown that members of different cultural groups often hold positive beliefs of their own group and negative beliefs about other groups. Further, some of these studies show a complete reversal of the pattern of attributions usually made about an individual's pattern of behaviour. In one such study conducted by Taylor and Jaggi, 30 Hindu clerks were asked to explain and evaluate a series of events. Some of the events were desirable such as a shop-keeper being generous to customers. Others were undesirable, for example the shop-keeper cheating customers. The actions presented to the participants were said to have been carried out by either a Hindu or an outgroup Muslim. Positive behaviours of the Hindu (an ingroup member) were explained as internal dispositions, negative behaviours were seen to be the result of some external forces. Explanations of these same behaviours carried out by a Muslim (an outgroup member) went in the opposite direction (Taylor and Jaggi, 1974).

Social representations

One of the challenges to any theory of cognition is that cognition does not depend on the objective characteristics of objects, but involves a mental reconstruction of that which is real. For any individual, this mental reconstruction is based on past experiences, needs and intentions. However, because of the social life we lead, which involves many forms of communication and influence, much information and many meanings are collectively shared by groups of individuals or societies. In other words, our perception is determined by the social context in which we exist and the meanings of events are thus not constructed by the individual but are culturally shared social representations. In the process of socialisation we come to understand that particular events or situations have a particular meaning within our culture. This understanding in turn enables us to relate better to the social activities of our cultural group members, and vice versa. Moscovici has defined **social representations** as follows:

'by social representations we mean a set of concepts, statements and explanations originating in daily life in the course of inter-individual communications. They are equivalent in our society to the myths and belief systems of traditional societies; they might even be said to be the contemporary version of common sense' (Moscovici, 1981).

Activity 6

Working within a group, consider social representations of (a) work and (b) what is appropriate to eat. Compare the group's social representations with what you think might be the social representations of other cultures.

One could say that the study of social representations is the study of the transformation from knowledge to common sense or how the strange and the unfamiliar become in time the familiar (Farr and Moscovici, 1984). A couple of examples will make this clearer. Moscovici and Hewstone (1984) reported how the scientific split-brain studies became transformed into social representations. Although scientists were talking about some differences between the two cerebral hemispheres, people came up with different theories, for example that one side of the brain was more intuitive, caring and gentle than the other. Moscovici (1961) showed how psychoanalytic theory had come to be adopted in France by the lay public as an everyday explanation of behaviour. In a study, 45 per cent of the students were trying to understand and explain their colleagues' behaviour through the term 'having a complex'. What began as a scientific theory restricted to professional scientists became changed and modified by society to meet that society's need to explain a particular kind of behaviour. This common knowledge is termed by psychologists 'lay epistemology' (epistemology means 'the theory of knowledge').

There are two main functions of social representations. One is to help the individual master and make sense of the world and the other is to facilitate communication. To realise these two functions people use two main processes: **anchoring** and **objectifying**. People anchor new ideas into a pre-existing system and the abstract is made concrete by the process of objectifying. For example, although most of us probably know nothing about the theory of relativity, we probably associate the theory with the name of Einstein. This is called personification, i.e. a theory or idea is linked to a particular name, and this is one aspect of objectifying. The second aspect of objectifying is figuration, for example the visualisation of the relativity equation $E = mc^2$. All this 'knowledge' is enough not to remain silent during conversation at a dinner party. The absence of precise knowledge does not prevent people from discussing such a matter. Shared social representations held by a group or society allow its members to communicate effectively. These interactions can be based on metaphors such as the use of sexual metaphors used by Austrians to explain conception (Wagner *et al.*, 1995). Social representations also provide us with a way of understanding our own experience, for example when given a short story to read about passive, abused peasants, it was found that the story had far more personal relevance for Hungarians than Danes because it was connected with an established and traditional Hungarian social representation (Larsen and Laszlo, 1990). Social representations can also be brought about and perpetuated by implicit, unspoken means. For example, in a particular area of France a system of 'care in the community' was participated in by families in the area who housed and cared for mentally ill individuals. The families explicitly expressed the opinion that they believed this was the best course of action for such individuals, but the families actually washed the patients' cutlery and bedding separately, as though they were contagious in some way – thus this was an implicit social representation or shared meaning of that particular group of people (Jodelet, 1991). According to Moscovici, these shared social representations are created and recreated by individuals in interaction with each other, for example in the course of a conversation.

But not only do social representations make ideas conventional and familiar, in so doing they also guide social action. In 1980, Di Giacomo studied social representations in a student protest movement at a Belgian University. The social representations held by the leaders of the protest movement were different from those held by the majority of students. The leaders believed that there were parallels between what they were doing and industrial action, whereas the social representations shared by the ordinary students made no connection between student and industrial action. It is not surprising therefore that the student leaders' attempts to call a strike met with complete failure.

Because many of the most fundamental social representations exist in our cultural group long before we are born, it is most unlikely that any one individual will create substantial change. Although one might argue that major historical figures such as Gandhi or Martin Luther King did do so, it could be the case that changes occurred because the time was ripe for change. Other representations, might be much more amenable to change.

This change often results in *social consensus*, which means that representations are shared and agreed by all of the individuals who hold those representations. A change in social consensus can come about by means of major social events such as was found after the Chernobyl disaster (Galli and Nigro, 1987).

Sperber (1985) distinguishes three types of social representations. Cultural representations would be the most lasting, for example the caste system in Hindu society, a social system dating from ancient times which does not allow for any upward or downward mobility. Traditional representations such as respect for authority, would last through several generations. Fashions, for example diet, encompass the rapidly changing representations which have become highly characteristic of contemporary societies dominated by the mass media. The latter, of course, reflects social and economic changes, but the source of change is everyday conversation and explanations.

Self-assessment questions

1   How can social identity theory help explain the tendency for people to display intergroup discrimination in the minimal group paradigm?

2   In 1973, Herzlich, in a study of medical social representations, showed that some doctors tended to see patients' problems as having physical causes. Others saw patients' problems as the result of psychological causes. How might these different social representations influence treatments?

3   With reference to Taylor and Jaggi's study (1974) (see page 118) and social identity theory, explain why identification with the Hindu cultural group resulted in the pattern of attributions found.

4   Define and differentiate between individualist and collectivist cultures.

(Suggested answers on page 140.)

Attribution theories

We have seen how perception is influenced by social and cultural factors but let us now turn to our perception of others in behavioural situations. That is, how and why do we attribute causes of behaviour to others?

Attribution is the process by which we judge the actions of others. It is therefore concerned with the perception and calculation of cause – why a particular behaviour occurs. This may appear to be straightforward but when an action is individualised by relating it to internal or external factors, the possible explanations for that action greatly increase. A perceived *internal* cause of a behaviour may be something to do with the personality, motives or intentions of the person carrying out the action. A perceived *external* cause would be something to do with another person or the environment. Internal attributions usually lead us to infer some trait or characteristic in a person, whereas external attributions tell us little, if anything, about that person.

This area of study is commonly expressed as being the psychology of man as the lay psychologist, who attributes reasons for actions based on stereotyping and implicit personality theory. Three attribution theories are discussed below, each with a slightly different emphasis of approach. Heider focused on the antecedents of people's perceptions of the causes of events. Jones and Davis considered the fact that people already

have preconceptions, possibly biased, about the causes of events. Kelly concentrated on the consequences these attributions have for the actor (the person who made them) involved.

Heider's attribution theory

Heider's attribution theory (1932, 1958) makes comparisons between the lay and professional psychologist, both of whom use observational techniques to study behaviour and to formulate beliefs or theories about human nature. The major difference is that professional psychologists use logical deduction methods and remain aloof from their observations by excluding, as far as possible, both personal biases and subjective interpretations. On the other hand, lay psychologists base their beliefs on a few observed instances of behaviour (Kahneman and Tversky, 1972).

The way things are seen may affect the consequence of an attribution for an actor but the function of the attribution process, whether by the lay or professional psychologist, remains the same. This function is to understand and explain a world which would otherwise be strange and to control and predict events which would otherwise appear chaotic. When we look for conditional relationships between people's behaviours (such as the possible relationship between giving money to the blind but not to the deaf), we assign cause along a dimension extending from external factors, which relate to the situation (for example collection envelope provided) and internal ones, which relate to the person (for example concern for a relative who is blind).

Heider stressed the importance of intentionality as a vital criterion for the attribution of external and internal causes. Causes are attributed internally if the behaviour is seen as being intended by the actor. For example, if one person replaces a colleague at work onlookers may attribute the takeover to internal factors, perceiving that person as being manipulative and back-handed and intentionally taking the colleague's position. On the other hand, if they perceive the cause as external, they may attribute the takeover to external factors, such as the employer needing an excuse to sack the colleague.

Another factor Heider stressed is the **covariation** principle which examines conditions, where two or more variables occur consistently together. This enables possible conclusions to be drawn about how they affect one another. For example, if white clothes change colour every time a certain garment is washed with them, then it would be reasonable to assume that this garment causes the problem (i.e. covarying takes place). If the whites change colour when this garment is not in the wash, then this particular covariation does not take place and the cause cannot be attributed to the garment.

Activity 7

Jot down occasions which you have enjoyed and others which you have not. To what did you attribute your enjoyment (or lack of it)? Are these attributions internal or external?

Correspondent inference theory

Correspondent inference theory (Jones and Davis, 1965) extends Heider's attribution theory to incorporate factors enabling specific predictions about people to be made on the basis of present behaviour. It involves making inferences about people's intentions and personality, for example perceiving a person as aggressive because he or she is portraying aggressive behaviour. Opinions or behaviour are regarded as accurate guides to what a person is really like. If these are judged as intentional, then the likelihood of an attribution relating to an internal quality, such as the person's temperament, increases. In other words, an *attribution of intention* (whether or not the behaviour was deliberate) is made before an *attribution of disposition* (whether the behaviour resulted because of the person). If an act is seen as being intentional, then perceivers begin to consider the consequences this has for the actor, at the expense of evaluating other possible acts. For example, someone might intentionally choose to type an essay using an electric typewriter. You might think that this is less efficient than using a wordprocessor and that the person concerned was not really considering the issues of time and expense.

An alternative evaluation, however, is possible: that the person does not have access to a wordprocessor and by implication is forced to work less efficiently. In this case, little is known about the person's character and more can be said about the person's predicament.

Jones and Davis (1965) also considered the issue of *normative behaviour* which relates to how most people behave in given situations. Imagine a person frantically running away from a lion. It is easy to understand why he or she is doing this and you would probably do the same. In this case, information about the person's character is limited, as the normative behaviour would be to run away. However, if the person ran away from a labrador, is it now possible to infer information about the person? Yes, but only if the person runs away from all dogs, or if nobody else runs away from this dog. If the normative behaviour is to run away from this dog, then we can infer that there is something unusual or frightening about the dog. If the person only runs away from this particular dog, then this is further evidence for the dog being unusual.

Nisbett and Ross (1980) and Markus and Zajonc (1985) have argued that more information about a person can be obtained from dispositional attributions than from situational attributions. Both are, however, valuable for making predictions about future behaviour. Unfortunately, the lay psychologist often makes the **fundamental attribution error**, attributing cause to a person rather than to a situation (Ross, 1977).

Correspondent inference occurs when observers are asked to make attributions about people's behaviour, unless this behaviour is overtly and directly under the control of another person or establishment. In Milgram's (1959) experiment on obedience, for example, participants played the role of 'teacher' and gave dummy electric shocks (which they thought were real) to a confederate of the researcher. Observers of this situation were found to attribute the participants' behaviour to a personality characteristic more often than to the situation they found themselves in. Harvey *et al.* (1975) found evidence to support these predictions. Observers felt that participant volunteers could quit the experiment if and when they wanted to. Correspondent inferences are made with strong emphasis on internal causes. For example, if a person acts aggressively, then correspondent inference would attribute the aggression to an innate aggressiveness, when in reality it may occur as a result of a situation warranting such a response. In other words, little attention is paid towards unchosen behaviours and their consequences (Ross and Fletcher, 1985).

Kelley's ANOVA model

Kelley's ANOVA model (1963, 1967) focuses on the judgements made of internal and external causes in the attribution process. The aim of the model is to explain cases where we have knowledge of how the person being studied usually behaves in a range of situations and how others usually behave in a range of situations. The principle of covariation suggests that if two events occur together repeatedly, then cause is more likely to be inferred

than if they occur together rarely. Kelly identifies three kinds of cause (see figure 4.1).

Kelley believed that an attribution of the cause of behaviour to internal or external factors may then be made, depending on whether levels of consensus, distinctiveness and consistency are high or low (see figure 4.2).

Kelley acknowledges that we very often make inferences about people using limited information. Preconceptions, in the form of **stereotypes** and implicit personality theory, fill the missing gaps. Using Kelley's assumptions, several researchers have studied the effects of each component of the ANOVA model through the control of behavioural episodes. Generally, support for Kelley's theory has been forthcoming, for example from McArthur (1972) who gave participants 12 brief descriptions of behavioural episodes, each being accompanied by information that was high or low with regard to consensus, consistency and distinctiveness. She found that attributions of cause were applied to a person, the situation or a combination of these in the ways that Kelley predicted.

A major problem with Kelley's approach is that people are less logical than he would have us believe. People often correlate unrelated sets of behaviour and falsely interpret correlations in terms of cause and effect. For example, people may wrongly attribute sickness to having eaten seafood, when a virus could have been responsible instead. In other words, people correlate variables that they feel *should* be related, even though this may blind them to the real cause (Spears *et al.*, 1986).

4.1 Consensus, distinctiveness and consistency

Consensus is concerned with the extent to which other people react in the same way to a stimulus or event as the person under consideration.

Distinctiveness is concerned with the extent to which the person reacts in a similar way to different stimuli or events.

Consistency is concerned with the extent to which the person's reaction to a stimulus or event is stable over time.

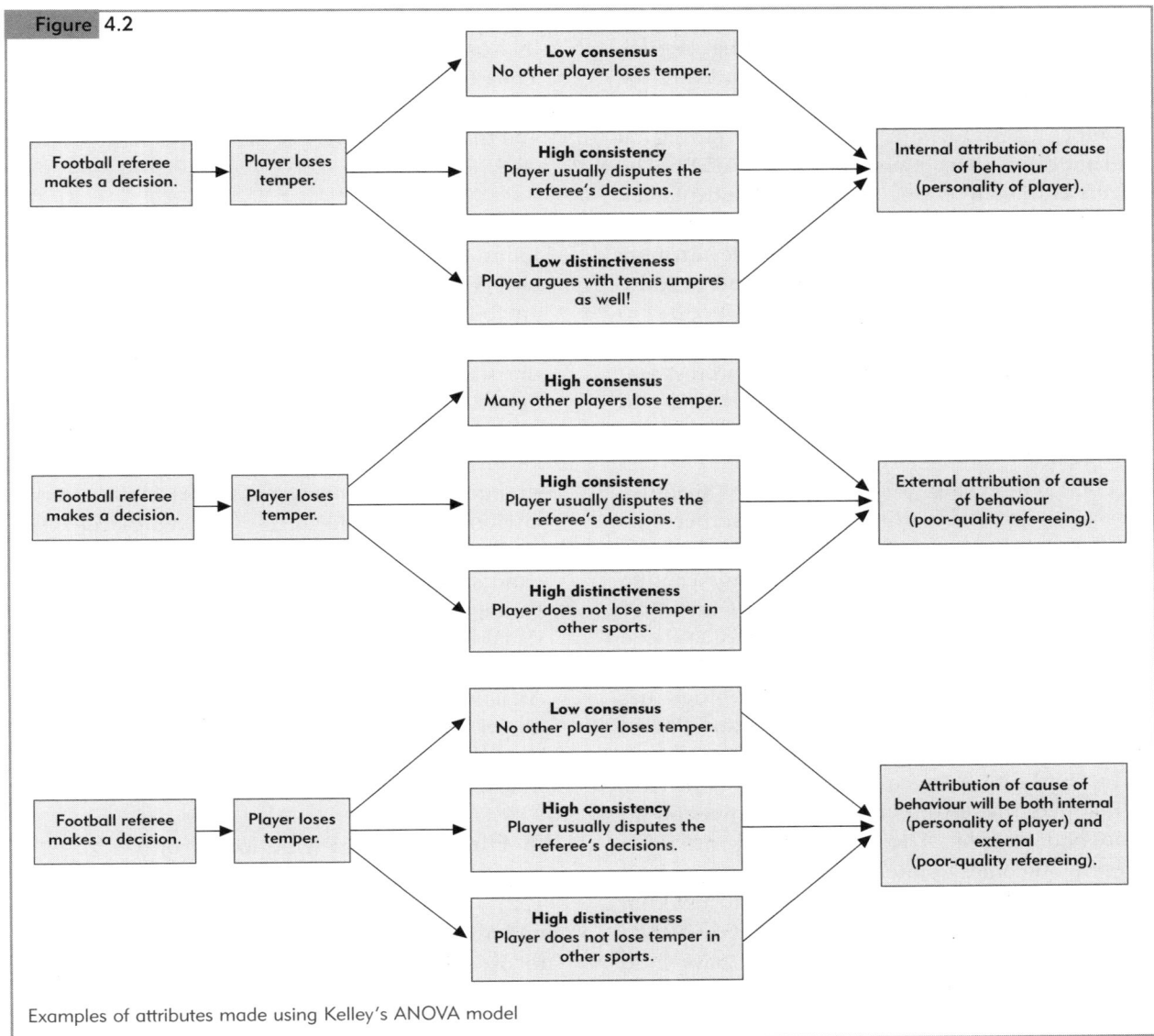

Examples of attributes made using Kelley's ANOVA model

Biases and errors in attributional processes

The theories described thus far suggest that attribution is a reasonably logical process involving cognitive steps to assimilate information about a person and his or her actions and then to reach decisions relating to events and behaviour. However, several biases and/or errors can occur in

this process. These are described below. These errors can have a significant impact on social issues.

■ The self-serving bias

A **self-serving bias** is activated to restore self-esteem and operates by attributing desirable actions to the self (internal causes) and undesirable actions to the situation (external causes). For example, passing an exam could be attributed to the candidate's own efforts (i.e. an internal cause) whereas failure could be attributed to the external cause of poor teaching (Rotter, 1966). Attributing cause can, however, be complicated by other factors, for example sex. Girls are more likely to perceive failure as having an internal cause than boys are (Weiner, 1978). The origins of the self-serving bias have been explained by means of cognitive and motivational factors. The cognitive explanation suggests that 'we attribute positive outcomes to internal causes and negative outcomes to external causes because we *expect* to succeed': on the other hand, the motivational explanation suggests that 'we need to protect and enhance our self-esteem, or the related desire to look good in the eyes of others' (Baron and Byrne, 1997, p. 59).

The self-serving bias can have negative consequences within the area of interpersonal relationships. For example, we may attribute success on a joint task mainly to ourselves, thus causing some friction with colleagues. Also, we can lead ourselves to believe that our own success has been brought about by internal causes and therefore deserves praise, but that the success of others has been brought about by external causes and should therefore not be deserving of as much credit.

In addition, research in this area has highlighted the inverse of this phenomenon in depressed people. These individuals attribute negative outcomes to internal causes (such as their lack of ability) and positive outcomes to external causes (such as fate) (Baron and Byrne, 1997). These people therefore feel that they have little control over their lives and so remain passive and depressed. Cognitive behavioural therapy (see Unit 26) has been one of the main and most successful focuses in encouraging those who are depressed to change their attributions.

■ False consensus

People often overestimate the extent to which others agree with their own views, another factor leading to interpersonal friction. They fail to see that their behaviour, feelings and thoughts are not necessarily shared by another person. This phenomenon has been described as *false consensus* and has been investigated by van der Pligt (1984)

in terms of judgement on energy conservation and by Ross *et al.* (1977) on views concerning tennis. They found that people assume that others have the same opinions regarding energy conservation and that their favourite sport (tennis) is enjoyed by all.

■ The actor-observer effect

Jones and Nisbett (1971) examined the **actor-observer effect** in terms of external and internal attributions of cause. They found that actors attribute their actions to external causes such as the situation, whereas observers attribute actors' behaviour to personality. Also, Storms (1973) claimed that actors would make external attributions concerning their conversation with a stranger, whereas observers would make internal attributions. Differences between the two attributions were explained in terms of visual field, experience of 'know thyself' and access to current feelings and thoughts. In other words, an actor's visual field is dominated by a stranger, but that of an observer is dominated by an actor's behaviour. An actor also has past experience with strangers to go on and is able to review current feelings and thoughts, unlike observers who rely upon interpreting the overt behaviour shown.

■ Fundamental attribution error

Finally, fundamental attribution error (see page 122) involves an observer's tendency to underestimate the impact of situational factors and to overestimate the importance of internal ones (Ross, 1977). For example, if a young, attractive woman, with blonde hair, who was late for a meeting, which consisted mainly of men, tripped over, dropped the pile of papers she was carrying and in the process knocked over a cup of coffee, the men in the room might attribute her behaviour to clumsiness and disorganisation (they may also describe her as a 'dizzy blonde' – a common stereotype). Although they might be correct, it is also very possible that they were explaining the woman's actions in terms of internal (dispositional) causes rather than external (situational) causes. The woman might have been the new chairperson of the company who was late because she had been held up by traffic congestion; she may have tripped over a briefcase belonging to one of the men which in turn caused her to knock over the coffee.

The fundamental attribution may occur because we tend to focus on people's actions rather than the overall context or we do notice situational factors but lend more weight to dispositional ones (Gilbert and Jones, 1986). Whatever the reason, this error has significant consequences within society because we may tend to perceive those who

are disadvantaged (such as homeless individuals) as lazy, irresponsible and ill-educated, when, it may have been their situational context that caused them to be homeless, for example dysfunctional family life or ineffective educational opportunities.

Thus attribution theory has led to a greater understanding of person and self-perception. It has generated research in these areas. It has been used to explain many social phenomena, such as interpersonal attraction and altruistic behaviour, and offers an explanation for attitude change.

Self-assessment questions

5 Complete a table comparing and contrasting Heider's attribution theory with correspondent inference theory.

6 Outline what Kelley meant by 'consensus', 'distinctiveness' and 'consistency'.

7 What are two of the likely sources of error in attribution?

(Suggested answers on page 140.)

Prejudice and discrimination

Forming likes and dislikes about people when we first meet them is understandable, but it is harder to understand why we feel strongly attracted to, or repulsed by, someone we have never met. However, such prejudice is a prejudgement which frequently occurs. Psychological studies have tried to investigate the conditions under which prejudice can occur.

Activity 8

Everyone is prejudiced in some way, whether they are aware of it or not. Make a list of anything you are prejudiced for or against. Keep it with you when you work through the rest of this unit and see if you can identify the cause of some of your prejudices.

Case studies

In the 1930s in the USA, there were strong feelings against oriental people. La Piere (1934) carried out an investigation in which he travelled with a Chinese couple, stopping at 251 hotels and restaurants throughout the USA. He was only refused service once. Later, La Piere wrote to each of these places asking the proprietors if they would accept Chinese patrons: 128 of them replied, and over 90 per cent said they would not!

Word et al. (1974) asked white college students to interview both black and white job applicants. Their behaviour differed depending on who they were interviewing. They sat further away from, made more speech errors, and held shorter interviews with the black applicants than with the white applicants.

The 'Robber's Cave' study, carried out by Sherif et al. (1971) at a boys' summer camp in Oklahoma, deliberately manipulated events to create prejudice in two groups of 11 boys. For the first week, the groups were totally oblivious to each other's presence and worked on tasks within their own groups so that, by the end of the week, they had really gelled together as units. One group called itself the Rattlers; the other the Eagles. Once they were allowed to become aware of each other's existence, they were informed that there would be a sports tournament between the groups. A great rivalry built up, which soon developed into hostility when the Eagles burned the Rattlers' flag after defeating them in a tug-of-war. Each boy held a stereotyped view of the members of the two groups, seeing their own group favourably and the other group unfavourably. They overestimated the achievements of their own group – the ingroup – and underestimated the achievements of the other group – the outgroup.

The feelings did not alter by putting the two groups together in pleasant situations. Only when Sherif introduced frustrating situations, which required all boys to cooperate to achieve mutually desirable outcomes, did the hostilities eventually disappear.

> ### Activity 9
>
> What do *you* think were the reasons for the prejudices in the above studies? Jot down a possible reason for each one before reading on to see if you were right.

What, then, is **prejudice**? Allport (1954) defines it as 'an antipathy based on a faulty and inflexible generalisation directed towards a group as a whole, or towards an individual because he is a member of that group. It may be felt or expressed'.

Prejudice is thus an attitude, but differs from other attitudes because it is based on a *prejudgement* of the *attitude object*. We judge some people before we have firm knowledge of them, and thus our attitude is often unjustified. When we do this to identifiable groups of people, such as orientals, blacks, Russians and women in managerial positions, we are dealing with stereotypes, which involve widespread, oversimplified and probably erroneous beliefs.

We can be prejudiced in favour of something too, such as when a mother assumes her child can do no wrong, or when a teenager defends a favourite rock star from criticism without knowing the circumstances. Alternatively, we can be prejudiced against something, such as labelling young people as lazy and as expecting everything handed to them on a plate.

Social psychologists are interested in such problem areas and their research has focused on issues such as racial prejudice or sexual discrimination. The bulk of this research was initiated after the Holocaust of the Second World War. Subsequently, their main interest has been prejudice against groups such as ethnic minorities, particularly those involving colour prejudice; although prejudice has been found in every society.

Discrimination is the behavioural expression of prejudice. For example, a person prejudiced against orientals might not allow them into an establishment. A person prejudiced against black people might not sit next to a black person on a bus. A male primary school teacher might be given a headship, not because he is the best person for the job, but simply because the school governors think there should be a male influence in primary schools.

Theories as to the causes of prejudice have been formed on many levels, for example historical, economic and sociological levels, but psychologists are concerned with the nature of prejudice in the individual rather than in society at large.

The components of prejudice

Prejudice comprises three components that are common to all attitudes:

- *Cognitive* – this involves the individual's knowledge about the facts of the attitude object, i.e. what we know about something.
- *Affective* – this involves feelings of liking or disliking, approval or disapproval for the attitude object, i.e. how we feel about it.

■ *Behavioural* – this involves how we behave towards the attitude object, verbally or non-verbally, i.e. what we do about it.

We look now at how individuals acquire prejudices, and then try to specify some of the causes.

The acquisition of prejudice

We are not born with our prejudices intact, or any other attitude for that matter. We acquire them over the years in the same way that we acquire any other behaviour – through conditioning and observation. The processes of *classical conditioning*, *operant conditioning* and *observational learning* are simple but powerful ways in which prejudices can be acquired.

■ The role of classical conditioning
Pavlov (1927) discovered that if a new stimulus is repeatedly associated with a stimulus which elicits a reflex response, then the new stimulus will soon elicit the same response on its own. This kind of association is called classical conditioning.

Take the example of parents who are strongly prejudiced against skinheads. Their children may frequently hear them refer to skinheads with negative words such as 'hate', 'bad', or 'dirty'. To start with, the word 'skinhead' has no specific meaning for the children and evokes no particular reaction. However, after repeated pairings with such negative words, it soon acquires a negative association. Consequently, children feel negatively about skinheads whenever the word is mentioned, just as they had before when the words 'hate, 'bad' and 'dirty' were mentioned (see figure 4.3).

Classical conditioning can exert a strong impact on our feelings towards an attitude object. If stimuli, which can evoke positive or negative feelings, are repeatedly associated with a certain attitude object, then the attitude object itself will, in time, be capable of evoking such feelings.

This process has been demonstrated in the laboratory by Staats and Staats (1958). Over a number of trials, they projected the name of one of

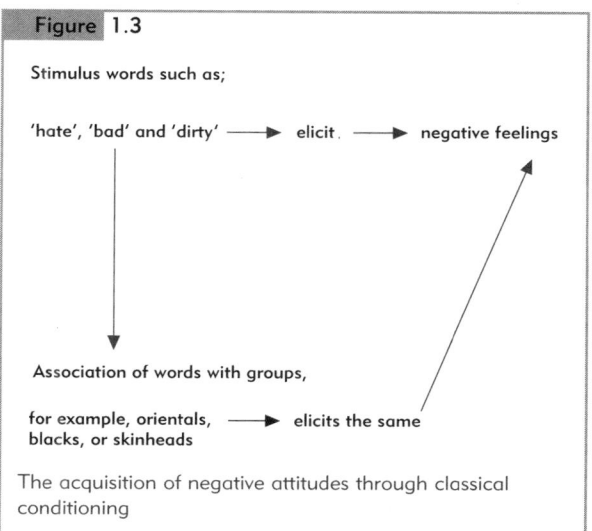

Figure 1.3

Stimulus words such as;

'hate', 'bad' and 'dirty' ⟶ elicit ⟶ negative feelings

Association of words with groups,

for example, orientals, ⟶ elicits the same
blacks, or skinheads

The acquisition of negative attitudes through classical conditioning

two nationality groups – Dutch or Swedish – onto a screen and, whilst the name was being shown, the experimenter said either a positive word (such as happy, sacred, gift), or a negative word (such as failure, ugly, bitter). Participants were then required to rate the two nationalities. The nationality paired with negative words received more negative ratings than the one paired with positive words. Although the strength of such reactions is minimal, the fact that such negative attitudes could be quickly created in the laboratory makes it possible that very strong prejudices might be created in real life. Here, a much larger number of pairings may occur over a much longer period of time, and under a much greater variety of circumstances.

Activity 10

Without looking back, see if you can remember and write down the three components of prejudice. (If you have any difficulty, turn back to page 126 and recap.)

■ The role of operant conditioning
If a particular response to a stimulus or situation is associated with a reinforcement, such as a pleasant

outcome, that response will tend to be repeated when any similar stimulus or situation is present. This basic principle of operant conditioning can be applied to the acquisition of prejudices. Throughout their early years, children are usually keen to please their parents. They agree with them and adopt their attitudes on most issues, liking what they like and disliking what they dislike. They will defend their parents' principles without necessarily understanding them. Parents are keen for their children to adopt the 'right' attitudes towards things and so reinforce these quite happily when they express an opinion or behave in a way that is in accordance with their own feelings. Reinforcements may take the form of praise, affection or approval or something more tangible, such as sweets or hiring a video rather than, say, playing with the Jones children down the street (see figure 4.4). Whatever the reinforcement is, the effect is the same, and the children start to exhibit the same prejudices as their parents. By adolescence, these may often be so strong that they are very resistant to change.

The operant conditioning of attitudes and prejudices has been demonstrated in the laboratory. Singer (1961) identified participants with authoritarian and anti-democratic tendencies through administering Adorno et al.'s (1950) F- and E-scales (the F-scale was designed to measure implicit authoritarian and anti-democratic trends in personality, i.e. potentiality for fascism; the E-scale measured ethnocentrism, that is, a view whereby one's own group is perceived to be the centre of everything and others are compared and rated with reference to that group). Some months later, an experimental group was reinforced every time they expressed an anti-authoritarian opinion or disagreed with an authoritarian statement. The control group was given no such reinforcement. The experimental group showed a 30 per cent gain in pro-democratic opinions, compared with the control group.

Kerpelman and Himmelfarb (1971) rewarded participants for describing an imaginary group of people in favourable terms, by telling them that their guesses concerning the characteristics of the group were correct. The more consistently their responses were rewarded, the more positive was their attitude towards the group when later measured by an attitude questionnaire. Again, it is hardly surprising that, in real life, when parents have much greater control over much more important forms of reward, and for a much longer time, prejudices can develop which are highly resistant to change.

■ The role of observational learning

Bandura et al. (1963) reported that children who observed an adult behave aggressively towards a large, inflatable doll also acted aggressively towards it when put in a room with toys which included such a doll. Those who had seen an adult behave non-aggressively towards the doll also behaved non-aggressively towards it. This research became recognised as landmark study in observational learning.

Classical and operant conditioning cannot account for the transmission of prejudices which adults *do not wish* to impart to their children. An adult may, for example, be prejudiced towards black people, but believe that it is not right to feel this way and try not to show it in front of the children. In cases like this, observational learning can play a crucial role. New responses can be acquired simply by observing the actions and outcomes of others. In the example in figure 4.5 the child might notice an apparent avoidance, or change in facial expression or tone of voice in the presence of particular people. In this case, actions

4.4 The acquisition of negative attitudes through operant conditioning

A *stimulus* elicits a *response* which may be reinforced.

Stimulus →	Response →	Reinforcement
The Jones children are playing in the street.	'They're dirty children. I don't want to play with them.'	'Quite right. Come on, let's go in and have an ice-cream.'

4.5 Negative attitudes can be acquired through observational learning

Observation of the *stimulus* and the *response* given (e.g. by the mother) results in the *outcome*.

Stimulus →	*Response* →	*Outcome*
Black people.	Avoiding sitting next to them on the bus.	Child learning to avoid black people.

speak louder than words and the child is likely to imitate the parent.

Classical conditioning, operant conditioning and observational learning may act separately or in a complementary way. Initially, children may acquire negative feelings towards members of a particular group, disliked by their parents, through classical conditioning. Once these are acquired, they may then observe their parents' prejudiced behaviour and, as they then go on to voice the same prejudices, they will be rewarded by their parents for expressing the 'right' views. If this continues for many years, it is likely to result in deep-set prejudices. Individuals can also learn prejudices in the same way from people other than their parents, as the research mentioned indicates.

Activity 11

Describe one experiment in which 'prejudice' was induced in participants.

The roots of prejudice

Activity 12

Now take out the paper on which you listed your own prejudices (see Activity 8 on page 125). Are you any clearer yet about how you acquired them? (You may find the next section helpful.)

In trying to establish the causes of prejudice, psychologists have examined the reasons for a person's acceptable *social distance*, or their acceptable degree of relationship with members of a given group. If a white person rejects black people, is it because of an assumption that the black people hold different *values*, or is it simply that they are *black* and belong to a different race of people?

Allport (1946) argued that we should not be looking for a single cause of prejudice; rather, prejudice is likely to have a number of roots. If, however, the root cause can be found, it can help towards an understanding. Consequently, psychologists have attempted to search for causes of prejudice both internally, within individuals, and externally, from social factors, in the hope of reducing it. The main factors which have been found to be related to a greater or lesser extent to prejudice are stereotyping, personality, conformity to group norms and frustration leading to scapegoating. We shall look at each of these factors in turn.

■ Social stereotyping

We have already mentioned 'stereotyping' several times but what does this word mean and how is it different from prejudice? Stereotyping comes about naturally as a means of dealing with the vast amount of stimuli which bombard us daily. We cannot deal with all these stimuli individually, as there is too much information to make this possible. However, by categorising information, we are able to deal with it more easily. Similarly, it is difficult to deal with every single person with whom we come into contact as a unique individual. If we categorise people, we feel better able to predict their behaviour.

By expecting certain characteristics to go together, and certain groups of people to display certain characteristics, we are better able to predict our world and cope with it. Through stereotyping, we assume that individuals belonging to a particular group possess the characteristics of that group. However, what usually happens is that as we meet individual members of a particular group, we realise that they possess other attributes and the effects of stereotyping break down. Stereotyping is therefore different from prejudice, in which new knowledge, giving different or conflicting evidence, does *not* cause people to change their attitudes. Prejudiced people see the new evidence as wrong – not their own perceptions.

Activity 13

Write down the stereotype of a group of which you know some members (such as students). Identify the extent to which the members you know fit the stereotype.

Gender, sex, ethnicity, age, education and wealth can all form the basis for a stereotype. We have already seen when discussing social identity theory that we like to favour our own group as a means of increasing and maintaining self-esteem (see pages 115–16). Thus it is easy to see that this is one factor contributing to the use of social stereotypes. Other ingroup/outgroup comparisons also serve to reinforce social stereotypes such as 'beneficence' (believing the ingroup to be more generous and kind than the outgroup), or 'competence' (believing the ingroup to be more intelligent, successful, wealthy, etc.). In addition, stereotypes function amongst groups in society 'to allow those who hold them to reduce their uncertainty about what members of other groups are likely to want, to believe and to' (Smith and Bond, 1993, p. 169).

Therefore, we can surmise that stereotypes are a form of cognitive schema which save us time. We use these means of social cognition as shortcuts in order to free up our cognitive capacity so that we can save time and have the space to concentrate on other factors. Support for this suggestion has been provided by Macrae *et al.* (1994) who found that when stereotypes were activated by means of labelling photographs of people (e.g. doctor, artist), participants performed better in a simultaneous listening task than when photographs were not labelled and so did not activate stereotypes. Therefore, social cognition tactics such as stereotyping save us energy and that is why they are used so readily by people.

However, more recent research suggests that cognitive factors, or beliefs, actually work hand in hand with affect. Jussim *et al.* (1995) provided participants with information about strangers who were presented as either rock musicians or child abusers. On the basis of word definitions allegedly written by these people, participants were asked to rate the strangers according to dimensions of creativity and mental illness. Also, they were asked to point out their feelings and beliefs about the strangers. Stereotypes became apparent, i.e. rock musicians were described as being more creative and less mentally ill than the child abusers. However, when feelings were held constant, the impact of stereotypes became reduced, therefore implying that feelings play some part in stereotypes; if beliefs (or cognitions) were the only factor involved in stereotypes then the impact of stereotypes should have remained the same. In relation to this perspective, research has also discovered that people who are in a good mood are more unwilling to exert cognitive effort into reducing stereotypes, possibly because they do not want to spoil their pleasant affective state, and therefore offer stronger stereotypical beliefs than those feeling less positive affect (Bodenhausen *et al.*, 1994). This research is in the early stages of development but the studies cited above do offer strong support for the supposition that affect contributes to stereotypical effect.

Activity 14

Write down six characteristics that you associate with each of five nationalities. Ask some friends to do the same. Compare your answers for similarities and differences. Can you explain any stereotypes which emerge? What evidence is there, if any, for the existence of these stereotypes?

■ Personality

Is a strong need to categorise related to personality?

Adorno *et al.* (1964) investigated anti-Semitism in Nazi Germany during the Second World War, devising the F-scale (see page 128) as a way of doing so. From their results, they identified a group of personality characteristics which became known as the *authoritarian personality syndrome*. This included characteristics such as deference to superiors, hostility towards inferiors and the upholding of conventional values, all of which show authoritarian tendencies (see figure 4.6). The authoritarian personality is not only descriptive of anti-Semitism, but also indicates prejudice towards many groups.

The F-scale has been criticised for measuring only political right-wing authoritarianism, and not left-wing as well. Rokeach (1960) tried to solve this problem by developing the *dogmatism scale*. This identifies individuals with a rigid outlook of life and who are intolerant of those who disagree with them, be they right- *or* left-wing. Scores distinguish between open and closed minds. High scorers show closed minds and authoritarianism and lack flexibility. Such a personality is predisposed to be prejudiced.

■ Conformity to group norms

People show conformity to norms that are established within a society.

> ### Activity 15
>
> Before reading any further, list some of the ways in which *you* conform to society.

To conform is to be a member of an ingroup, whereas not to do so is to be a member of an outgroup. If a group is prejudiced against a minority culture, then the consequences of deviation from the group, of not being a part of it, may be viewed as too great for an individual to adopt. So the individual must also be prejudiced in order to remain a member of the ingroup. Pettigrew (1958) pointed out that people who called for racial integration in the early 1960s in the southern US states, were threatened, harassed and received burning crosses. Could conformity to group norms be one of the factors involved in the anti-Semitism of Nazi Germany in the 1930s? It has been suggested that conformity to group norms can be the cause of milder prejudices but that it also helps existing, strong prejudices within a society to be maintained.

Pettigrew (1958) showed that prejudice against black people in the USA and South Africa was more closely related to measures of general conformity to group norms than to measures on the F-scale – those more likely to conform to the norms of their society were also the most prejudiced. Adorno had claimed that the authoritarian personality was a generalised attitude. Thus, someone who was prejudiced against one minority group should also be prejudiced against other minority groups. Yet Pettigrew did *not* find that people from the southern states of the USA, who are more anti-black than people from the north, were also more anti-Semitic than the northerners. Similarly, in 1959, he demonstrated that there was no difference in

4.6 Examples from the F-scale

Participants have to indicate their degree of agreement/disagreement on each item on a six-point scale.

1. Obedience and respect for authority are the most important virtues children should learn.
2. If people would talk less and work more, everybody would be better off.
3. The businessman and the manufacturer are much more important to society than the artist or the professor.
4. Young people sometimes get rebellious ideas, but as they grow up they ought to get over them and settle down.
5. Nobody ever learned anything really important except through suffering.
6. A person who has bad manners, habits and breeding can hardly expect to get along with decent people.
7. What youth needs most is strict discipline, rugged determination and the will to work and fight for family and country.
8. People can be divided into two distinct classes: the weak and the strong.
9. An insult to our honour should always be punished.

(Source: Adorno et al., 1964)

measures of authoritarianism between people from the northern states and those from the southern states. The relationship between personality and prejudice is, therefore, not clear-cut.

■ Frustration and scapegoating

This idea rests on the assumption that frustration gives rise to aggression. If an individual is frustrated in some goal – for example, a school leaver cannot get a job, or a child cannot answer his or her parents back – feelings of aggression are created, which, if they cannot be vented against the cause of the aggression (the companies applied to for a job; the parent) are then displaced on to something or someone else. In the case of prejudice, this could be some kind of ethnic minority group. In other words, a *scapegoat* is found.

Frustration resulting in scapegoating was found to exist when a classic study by Hovland and Sears was carried out in 1940. They found that the majority of lynchings in the USA between 1882 and 1930 occurred in 14 southern states and that most of the victims were African Americans. An immediate conclusion might be that the lynchings occurred because of racial prejudice alone. However, the researchers discovered that the number of lynchings was higher during times of economic decline and therefore reflected 'displaced aggression', i.e. the frustration felt by those experiencing economic hardship was taken out on African Americans because the perpetrators could not express their aggression against the economic system. Today, social psychologists believe that economic decline results in an escalation of racial prejudice caused by increased competition for resources and that violence occurs because of this prejudice rather than displaced aggression (Baron and Byrne, 1997). (Note that this an example of research which makes use of archival information, i.e. data stored about historical social events.)

Studies vary in their findings of whether frustration does lead to prejudice. On the one hand, Allport and Kramer (1946) showed that Catholic students who complained of being discriminated against because of their religion were more anti-black and more anti-Semitic than other Catholics. Epstein and Kamorita (1965), on the other hand, found that children whose parents were highly punitive were no more prejudiced towards minority groups than children whose parents were less punitive.

One factor that may play a part in the apparent discrepancies between the findings of such studies is the distinction between shared threats and personal threats. *Shared threats* have the effect of bringing people together, as Sherif *et al.* (1971) found in the *'Robber's Cave'* experiment (see page 125). In one situation, a stalled truck could only be started by both groups of boys joining forces to pull on a rope. This led to a marked reduction in hostility. *Personal threats*, as frustration theory would predict, seem to augment prejudice.

■ Social distance

How far people can accept other people, their attitudes or beliefs affects the social distance between them. Rokeach (1961) argued that people are more likely to increase social distance when they think others hold different beliefs, than when they belong to a different race. Participants were asked to indicate the extent to which they felt they could be friends with a person, on a nine-point scale from:

■ 'I *can't* see myself being friends with such a person.'

to:

■ 'I can very easily be friends with such a person.'

Hypothetical descriptions were presented in pairs, where either the beliefs were held constant, for example:

■ A white person who believes in God.
■ A black person who believes in God.

or the race was held constant, for example:

■ A white person who believes in God.
■ A white person who is an atheist.

Rokeach found that similarity of values or beliefs was more important.

Byrne and Wong (1962) showed that people tend to assume more dissimilarity of beliefs when individuals are of a different race than when they are of the same race.

Triandis (1961) criticised Rokeach's work because the scales used were measures of friendship rather than prejudice. According to Triandis, friendship relationships are measures of small social distance, whereas prejudice is more relevant to relationships with large social distances, such as accepting someone as a neighbour or into one's club. Triandis used all distances, from marrying someone to lynching someone, and found membership of a particular race to be more important than similarity of beliefs.

A study by Stein *et al.* (1965) seemed to reconcile these different findings. For less-intimate relationships, such as who a person would like as a companion, differences in values were much more likely to account for rejection of black people than differences in race. However, with more intimate activities, such as inviting someone home for dinner or dating one's sister, or when no information regarding the other person's values was available, race *did* have an important effect.

This study was also criticised by Triandis and Davies (1965) because only positive behaviour (for example invitation home for dinner; being a member of social group) and not the more negative behaviours of exclusion which involved lack of acceptance (for example would not eat with; would exclude from the neighbourhood) were investigated. However, when they carried out an investigation taking this into account, they drew similar conclusions to Stein. The main difference was that Stein found beliefs to be important for most people throughout the social distance scale, whereas Triandis found differences (see figure 4.7).

Do these findings hold true in *real-life* settings? Rokeach carried out two investigations on a university campus and one in a state-employment service using men seeking employment as participants. In all situations, real participants met four strangers who were actually stooges. Two were black and two were white. They participated in a group discussion about an important or relevant topic. One white and one black stooge agreed with the participant and one white and one black stooge disagreed. The participant then had to choose which of the four strangers he or she would prefer to be with in the coffee break (in the case of the students), or work with (in the case of the men seeking employment).

In all three situations, the two strangers who held the same beliefs or values as the participant were chosen more frequently. Out of the total 118 cases, only seven chose the two people of the same race. This should be repeated, however, with behaviours more intimate than drinking coffee (for example dating) if a complete picture is to be gained.

La Piere (see page 125) had demonstrated that what people say in writing can be very different from what they do in face-to-face situations. In looking at this question, studies vary in their findings. Many studies indicate that the two are positively related. For example, Green (1968) carried out a study based on photographs of mixed-race couples in varying degrees of intimacy. Participants were asked if they would agree to pose for similar photographs which would then be published in different sorts of magazines. When they were later given a racial attitude scale, it was found that their attitudes were related to the degree of intimacy of behaviour shown on the photo release form.

Other studies are inconsistent with this finding. In a study by Weitz (1972), white participants at a summer school were expected to interact with a white or black stranger. Attitude measures (pencil and paper) were taken, and then behaviour was observed. Participants sat further away from their partners, selected less-intimate working tasks and adopted a different voice tone when interacting with black students, compared to white students.

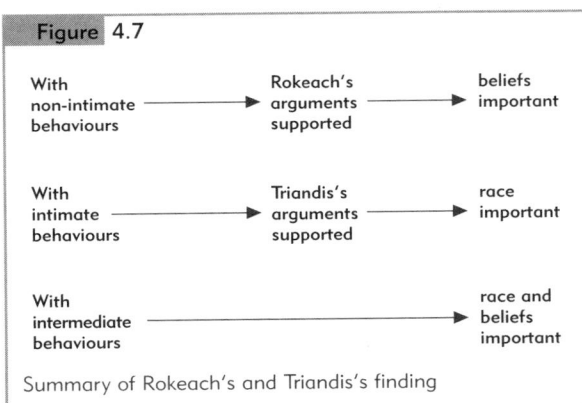

Figure 4.7

With non-intimate behaviours	→	Rokeach's arguments supported	→	beliefs important
With intimate behaviours	→	Triandis's arguments supported	→	race important
With intermediate behaviours	→		→	race and beliefs important

Summary of Rokeach's and Triandis's finding

Although the attitude response indicated favourableness, the behavioural response indicated rejection. Why should there be a difference in the findings of such studies? Perhaps one reason could be in the *timing* of the measures. In Green's study, the behaviour was noted first, *then* the pencil and paper measure taken. Bem (1967) proposed that behaviour may cause the attitude, rather than the attitude lead to the behaviour as one might traditionally expect. Having agreed to behave in a certain way, if an individual then has to state in writing the degree of prejudice felt, he or she might think 'Well I can't be that prejudiced if I've agreed to do that'. In the Weitz study, the participants had to fill in an attitude questionnaire, then carry out a certain task in which they were unaware of being observed. In this case, the pencil and paper measure came *before* the behaviour.

The situations in both studies were also very different and may account for some of the differences in the findings. In the La Piere study (see page 125), the people who received the Chinese guests in person may not have been the same people who then wrote in response to La Piere's letter! It is not as though these studies replicate each other. They are very different and may be looking at different aspects of prejudice.

In general, studies carried out in the laboratory find greater consistency than those carried out in the field. Perhaps in real life the relationship is diluted by other factors, such as environmental situations. For example, how do you account for the white person who is prejudiced against black people, yet sits next to one on the bus? Perhaps this person's behaviour belies his or her attitude because it is the only seat on the bus! This example illustrates the problem of using one-off measures of behaviour when other information, such as interests, motives, personality or abilities, is lacking.

The social context of prejudice and discrimination

The explanations of prejudice and discrimination looked at so far have considered aspects of the individual and relationships between people and between groups, but have largely ignored the social context in which both attitudes and behaviour occur. In this section we consider the social context in which prejudice and discrimination occur. By social context is meant such factors as culture/subculture, institutions (for example education and justice) and general economic factors. Such factors support and maintain racism, sexism, etc. and make the reduction of prejudice and discrimination more problematic. Cultural aspects include changes in the way society operates. Increased urbanisation, mechanisation, unemployment and competition for jobs, the increased importance of training and qualifications, the increasing power of the media, changes in the structure of the family and in standards of morality, and the upward mobility of some groups are all factors which may produce breeding grounds for racial prejudice.

Institutional aspects such as the law and education may also help to maintain and perpetuate racism and sexism. In 1972, Jones stated that there were two principal ways in which educational institutions were racist in America:

- By means of inferior education given to black children who were thought to be 'dumb and incapable of learning'.
- By means of miseducation about racial history and heritage, i.e. by denigrating African history and culture and glorifying western Anglo-American history.

More recently, and closer to home, the Scarman Report (1982) on the Brixton riots in April 1981 recommended teachers be given 'awareness' training in different cultural backgrounds. This was in response to dissatisfaction expressed by West Indian parents about poor school discipline, the failure by teachers to appreciate the value of different cultural practices, lack of contact between parents and schools, and a failure of teachers to provide motivation resulting in the underachievement of their children at school.

It may be that these observations and recommendations were taken on board. It can be seen that racial discrimination does not operate as blatantly as it used to do both in such institutions and in the broader context of society where people from different races are no longer segregated.

Unfortunately this does not appear to be true for disabled individuals (Swain *et al.*, 1993). However, Baron and Byrne (1997) asserted that more subtle forms of prejudice and discrimination still operate in society. For example, Swim *et al.* (1995) suggested that what is often termed 'modern racism' functions according to three main components:

■ Denial that discrimination still exists (for example 'discrimination against Asians is no longer a problem in the UK').

■ Antagonism to the demands of minorities for equal treatment (for example 'individuals from ethnic minorities are getting too demanding in their push for equal rights').

■ Resentment concerning special favours for minority groups (for example 'the media and the government are giving too much attention and respect to minority groups in Britain').

On the other hand, other researchers propose a more favourable view and suggest that young people are less prejudiced and are optimistic about eliminating prejudice and discrimination (Martin and Parker, 1995).

The justice system also reveals how prejudice in the form of racism may be created and perpetuated. US statistical data in 1972 demonstrated that the average white population of 65 per cent produced the average white police population of 95 per cent in major US cities (Jones, 1972). Given such a skewed statistic it is perhaps unsurprising that residents of black urban communities can at times view police officers as 'occupation forces'. The Scarman Report (1982) revealed that the police both as an institution and as individuals enforcing the law (for example, 'stop and search' in a discriminatory way on blacks) were seen to contribute to the Brixton riots. The recommendation was for more recruitment of ethnic minorities into the police force, 'sensitivity training in law enforcement for new policemen and liaison committees between the police and local community'.

Loosely linked with these issues is some interesting research surrounding the conflict felt by individual police officers who are also gay which can be extended to other social contexts. Burke (1995) stated that previous researchers have indicated that conflict exists for black, gay men

between sexual orientation and racial identity, resulting in 'multiple prejudice' from society: racism from gay communities and homophobia from black communities. Burke's own research uncovered the conflict felt by gay policemen and women who feared or experienced prejudice from the police community because they were gay and prejudice from the gay community because they were members of the police force. He found that 53 per cent of his sample had not 'come out' as gay in the police service or as police officers in the non-heterosexual community, thus suggesting that they lived 'double lives' which resulted in feelings of distress.

Women are also discriminated against in the social context. Whilst open discrimination is illegal in many countries, females still receive lower salaries than males and occupy lower-paid, lower-status jobs. This could be due to the role of expectations, i.e. people tend to get what they expect from life, and women expect to be employed in lower-status jobs than men and receive lower salaries so this is what happens. In addition, women seem to be less self-confident than men in a number of situations and this attribute is noticed by women themselves, colleagues and managers (Baron and Byrne, 1997). Even when women do achieve high-status positions they tend to be viewed more negatively than men (Eagly *et al.*, 1992), perhaps because they display aggressive, autocratic behaviour which challenges our stereotypes of submissive, passive women. Recent research has also discovered that women are not prevented from reaching the top of their professions by men but by developmental opportunities during their rise to the top. That is, job-related experiences that prepare people for high-status jobs are not as readily available for women as for men, such as key assignments; thus prejudice is operating at lower levels of the work place (Ohlott *et al.*, 1994).

Finally, a look at ageism. Recent research has found that stereotypes we have about elderly people can become self-fulfilling and thus induce a physical effect. Levy and Langer (1994) suggested that beliefs we accept unconditionally about becoming older, such as loss of memory, can become self-fulfilling. These stereotypes are sometimes culturally specific, for example Americans associate old age with negative attributes such as loss of memory, poor mental and physical health whereas Chinese people view older people as wise and knowledgeable. When participants were compared cross-culturally, it was found that older American individuals did not perform as well as Chinese people on a memory test, thus supporting the idea that prejudices concerning older people become self-fulfilling.

By taking the social context into account we can see the complexity of both prejudice and discrimination, though whether such factors create or simply maintain prejudice is impossible to determine. The following section looks at a number of factors which have been found to influence the maintenance and reduction of prejudice. In looking at these factors, the role of social context should be borne in mind.

The maintenance and reduction of prejudice

A number of factors have been found to influence the maintenance and reduction of prejudice. The most important include personal contact, equality of status and common goals.

■ Personal contact

Evidence suggests that personal contact with an attitude object decreases prejudice towards it. It is possible to see links here between similarity and attraction which are discussed in Unit 5. In La Piere's study (page 125), the Chinese patrons were accepted when they appeared in person. Evidence shows, however, that this reduction in prejudice is only in the contact situation and does not generalise to other situations.

Contact in the work situation does not generalise to personal friendships. Harding and Hargrofe (1952) showed that white department store assistants accepted black assistants but did not have black people as personal friends.

A number of studies involving integrated housing projects show that those living in such housing are less prejudiced than those living in segregated housing. Deutsch and Collins (1951) found that a high proportion of white housewives living in a biracial project had black people as friends, whereas in segregated housing whites and blacks did not mix. Stouffer et al. (1949) found that prejudice between black and white soldiers was reduced in a combat situation but, back in camp, hostility increased. It seems, therefore, that prejudice will only break down completely if individuals become personally acquainted with members of the prejudiced group.

Baron and Byrne suggested that the following requirements be met before the *contact hypothesis* can work, offering explanations as to why some contact situations cannot be generalised to all circumstances:

■ The groups or people interacting must be roughly equal in social, economic, or task-related status.
■ Cooperation and interdependence must be involved whereby people work towards the same goals (as in the 'Robber's Cave' experiment described on page 125).
■ Contact must be informal so that people can get to know each other as individuals.
■ The setting in which contact takes place must favour group equality as the norm.
■ Interaction must involve the allowance of disconfirmation of negative, stereotyped beliefs held about one another.
■ The individuals involved must see one another as typical of their respective groups.

Unfortunately, these requirements are not often met. When they are, prejudices do seem to decrease, as has been evidenced when different factions in Northern Ireland have made contact and when people from mixed races have integrated as in the study by Deutsch and Collins cited above.

■ Recategorisation as a means of reducing prejudice

We have seen how prejudices occur between groups and how the ingroup/outgroup phenomenon can influence the maintenance of prejudices. One way of combating this situation might be to shift the boundaries between 'us' and 'them'. The *common ingroup identity* model (Gaertner *et al.*, 1989, 1993) suggests that changing boundaries between groups results in members of two or more groups seeing themselves as a single social entity and so favourable attitudes prevail. One way of creating a single social entity is for groups to work together towards collective goals which are important to the groups concerned. Therefore, if two football teams from the same college compete against each other, there may exist prejudices between the two teams and their supporters. However, if one team wins and goes forward into a regional tournament, the boundaries between the two teams disintegrate or shift so that both groups become a single social entity; this group will now be in the ingroup and the rival regional team will be the outgroup. This theory does not therefore abolish our need to see our group as more positive than others, as posited in social identity theory (see pages 113–16), but can work in reducing prejudices in some circumstances.

■ Tokenism

This concept has been introduced in society in order to reduce discrimination. In the workplace, people from minority groups who might experience prejudice are employed as a 'token gesture' to society to prove that the employer is not practising discrimination. If you are the employed person and realise that you have been employed merely for this purpose, you may feel quite distressed, experience low self-esteem and confidence. Your colleagues may also perceive you in negative terms, believing you to be less competent (Summer, 1991; Heilman *et al.*, 1992). Thus, whilst offered as an explanation for reducing discrimination, it can be seen that, in fact, tokenism can do more damage than good.

■ Breaking down stereotypes

Earlier in the unit we discussed how stereotypes can have a powerful impact on prejudices. Some researchers have suggested that it may be possible to weaken stereotyped beliefs by means of cognitive interventions.

One means of changing the cognitive processes inherent in stereotyping is to ask people to think carefully about another person, that it is important for them to do so; thus interfering in their attributional processes. In this way people will tend to look past stereotypes and focus on more accurate information about others (Neuberg, 1989).

Another method of reducing the impact of stereotypes can be brought about by asking people to focus on the processes which occur in order to reach an outcome, in much the same way as it is possible to combat the fundamental attribution error. Instead of designing our own 'story' about how someone reached a particular outcome, we need to examine what really happened. Therefore, instead of relying on stereotypical judgements about people, for example 'the dizzy blonde who has been promoted', we can try to focus on the outcome, i.e. a person has been promoted because she is, in fact, competent and hard working (Baron and Byrne, 1997).

At the beginning of this section, we saw how prejudices built up through learning processes. These processes are also at work in prejudice reduction. If cooperation results in success, then the success acts as a reward. If people are of equal status, then it means personal contact and acquaintance are more likely to occur and individuals can gain rewards from others, as they seek to do from all relationships. Reduction of prejudice can, therefore, be seen as being dependent on receiving rewards from others.

Prejudice has neither a single cause nor is there one way to reduce it. It is a complex process, built up on complex levels and serving complex purposes. The vast amount of research in this area has led to a better understanding of its nature and causes and this may lead to a greater likelihood that the prejudices, and the damage they do, will break down. However, the extent to which this can be achieved is dependent on prejudice being reduced in society as a whole.

Self-assessment questions

8   This unit discussed *three* ways in which prejudices might be acquired. Name these and then provide a brief outline of one of them.

9   Explain the concept of stereotyping and describe how affect is implicated in this process.

10 Briefly examine how frustration and scapegoating have been associated with prejudice, giving *two* examples of research related to this area.

11 Discuss *two* examples of ways in which prejudice and discrimination might be reduced.

12 Why might the increasing tendency for people to live in large cities result in prejudice towards ethnic minorities? State *three* points and try to include psychological terminology in your answer.

(Suggested answers on page 140.)

Unit summary

- *Social and cultural identity theory* and the *theory of social representation* have developed from a European social psychology background that evolved during the 1960s as a backlash against the individualist approach taken in the USA.

  These theories help us to understand how people from different social groups and cultures make sense of their own, unique, social world – that is, their own social reality.

- By identifying with groups and cultures we can make decisions about other people and about ourselves. The social groups and cultures to which we belong can help to determine the kind of interpersonal relationships we form and can also affect our sense of self-esteem and motivation to be who we choose to be.

- *Social representations* are at the basis of social belief systems – our collective interpretations of reality. These representations are a means of guiding social action and it is not difficult to see how they can be linked with the identity theories.

- *Attribution theories* attempt to explain how we make inferences about a person's behaviour by means of ascribing characteristics or behaviour to that person. Thus, an individual observes the behaviour of another engaging in some behaviour, makes an inference about that behaviour based on perceived actions and then attributes some underlying motivational trait to the person which they believe is consistent with that behaviour.

- Attribution is subject to several forms of error, including the *fundamental attribution error*, the *actor-observer effect* and the *self-serving bias*. These errors can have significant consequences within society and help to shape social policy.

- *Prejudices* can be acquired throughout the developmental process by means of *classical and operant conditioning* and also by means of observations from people in our social world. Prejudice is a negative attitude towards a social group or individual which can be expressed by means of *discrimination*, i.e. negative behaviour towards the object of prejudice. Whilst discrimination has been made illegal in many countries, there is still evidence that it operates in more subtle forms.

- The *roots of prejudice* can be found in *stereotypes* which can be defined as a set of widely shared generalisations about the characteristics of a group or class of people. Once in place, they can act as *cognitive* short-cuts which save us time and reduce cognitive effort, thus, they can be difficult to break down. In addition, prejudice can be associated with personality types, conformity to group norms, social distance and frustration and *scapegoating*.

Summary cont'd.

There are significant difficulties inherent in reducing prejudice and discrimination as so many conditions have to be met in order to influence successful outcomes, for example *equal status, cooperation* and so on when contact is made.

■ *Recategorisation* has been suggested as a way forward, in order to shift boundaries between groups. However, this cannot prevent ingroup/outgroup biases in all cases.

■ *Tokenism* has been one way of attempting to reduce discrimination, for example 'affirmative action projects' in the workplace, but evidence has demonstrated that this can be damaging to employees and their colleagues.

Terms to define

actor-observer effect
anchoring
attribution
correspondent inference theory
covariation
cultural identity
discrimination
fundamental attribution error

minimal group paradigm
objectifying
prejudice
self-serving bias
social categorisation
social identity theory
social representations
stereotype

Further reading

Baron, R A and Byrne, D (1997) *Social Psychology*, 8th edn, Allyn & Bacon, Boston, chapters 2 and 6.

A modern text which covers some very recent evidence in the areas of attribution, prejudice and discrimination.

Burke, M (1995) 'Identities and disclosure: the case of lesbian and gay police officers', *The Psychologist*, pp.543–47.

Takes a close look at prejudice and discrimination in practice and how it affects the lives of people in a particular social group.

Hayes, N (1996) 'Social representation', 'Social identity theory', 'Cultural identity', a series of articles in *Psychology Review*, September 1997 onwards.

An excellent introduction to these theories aimed at A-level students, which are informative, easy to read, yet providing enough depth and breadth to cover this part of the syllabus.

Smith, P B and Bond, M H (1993) *Social Psychology Across Cultures: Analysis and Perspectives*, Harvester Wheatsheaf, Trowbridge.

A very well-written analysis covering an interesting range of social and cultural theories in depth.

Answers

■ Suggested answers to activities

Base your answers on information in the text and your own ideas, as appropriate.

■ Suggested answers to self-assessment questions

1

Allocated to two equally meaningless groups. There is nothing to differentiate them except group labels and the fact that they themselves are in one group and not the other. They are referred to by code and this leads to feelings of anonymity. Their only source of identity is their ingroup. However, this ingroup is initially indistinguishable from the other group and contributes little to the self-esteem of its members. The pressures of distinctiveness come into play and the members of both groups seek to differentiate their own group positively from the other by the only means possible, i.e. by allocating more money to their ingroup members. They will also do this even at the cost of some absolute gain to the group, i.e. by maximising the difference between ingroup and outgroup.

2

A doctor who believes that illness mainly arises from physical causes would probably prescribe treatment which aimed at a direct physical effect, whereas a doctor who interpreted the problem as psychological would seek to alleviate the psychological problem, for example stress.

3

Results are consistent with social identity theory. Hindu clerks would have been able to sustain a positive social identity since they perceived the causes of behaviours by the ingroup and outgroup members in ways that favoured their group over the other.

4

Individualist cultures place more emphasis on personal goals and personal autonomy.

Collectivist cultures stress group goals, loyalty to groups and emotional dependence on groups.

5

Factors to be included:
For *Heider's attribution theory* – distinguishes between lay and professional psychologists; behaviours are assigned along a continuum from external to internal causes; stresses importance of intentionality of cause; covariation explains how events affect each other.
For *correspondent inference theory* – occurs when observers

asked to make attributions of another's behaviour; enables predictions to be made about people based on their present behaviour; attributions of intention are made before attributions of disposition; normative behaviour allows comparisons to be made both with other people's behaviour or other behaviours of the person concerned; correspondent inferences are made with strong emphasis on internal causes – which may lead to fundamental attribution errors.

6

For definitions of Kelley's 'consensus', 'distinctiveness' and 'consistency', see page 122.

7

Two likely sources of error in attribution could include an outline of any of the following:
fundamental attribution error; self-serving bias; actor-observer effect.

8

Ways in which prejudices might be acquired include:
classical conditioning; operant conditioning; observational learning.

9

Explanation of stereotyping is given on page 129. Affect is implicated as demonstrated by Jussim *et al.* (1995) and Bodenhausen *et al.* (1994) on page 130; it is not only cognitive beliefs which influence stereotyping.

10

Frustration and scapegoating is explained on pages 131–2. Examples of research include:
■ Allport and Kramer (1946).
■ Epstein and Kamorita (1965).
■ Hovland and Sears (1940).
■ Baron and Byrne (1997).

11

Examples of ways in which prejudice and discrimination might be reduced include:
personal contact; recategorisation; tokenism; changing cognitive processes.

12

Increasing tendency for people to live in large cities may result in prejudice towards ethnic minorities because cities are impersonal and generally stressful places to live in. Such factors lead to scapegoating. Social identity becomes relevant in such environments. Strong ethnic affiliations emerge in the sense of group superiority which results in strong group conflict.

Unit 5

Social Relationships

Penny Cortvriend and Regina Teahan

This unit covers:

Affiliation and attraction

The development, maintenance and breakdown of relationships

The effects of interpersonal relationships on mental health and happiness

By the end of this unit, you should be able to:

- show some understanding of why individuals seek out, and are attracted to, others
- understand and explain the formation, maintenance and breakdown of interpersonal relationships
- define and be knowledgeable about the components of relationships
- understand the effects of interpersonal relationships on mental health and happiness.

Unit 5   Contents

Introduction

Probably most of us can identify people we want to be with much of the time; people we can be friendly with, but would not like to be close to; also people we do not like and seek to avoid. This unit is about social relationships. We are, by our very nature, social animals, yet the nature of relationships is quite complex. Why do we seek out some people and avoid others? How do relationships develop and how do we keep them going? Why do some relationships break down? Are relationships important? This unit attempts to provide some answers to the above questions.

First, we look at the different kinds of association that form when people are attracted to each other. Associations of this kind come under the umbrella term of affiliation. We then consider some of the theories of **interpersonal relationships** and explanations and research evidence relating to the formation, maintenance and dissolution of relationships. Social relationships have been likened to games involving cooperative behaviour which leads to the attainment of goals by play within rules. An understanding of such components of relationships sheds light on the successful maintenance of relationships or their subsequent breakdown. In addition, throughout this unit, we reflect upon individual differences in relationships and how relationships vary in different societies and cultures. Finally, the main reason for psychologists' interest in relationships is the strong link with health and happiness and this, too, is examined.

Affiliation and attraction

The term **affiliation** refers to associations or relationships which are made between people who cooperate with each other. Some associations are quite casual, with cooperation being limited to such things as a smile and nod in passing. Others are closer and take the form of friendships, in which the participants enjoy each other's company and share interests, thoughts and feelings. Yet others are closer still, taking the form of long-term partnerships, such as marriage.

Most people prefer to be on friendly terms with those they come into contact with. In fact, Wright (1984) has suggested that people are innately motivated to form enjoyable relationships, and Newcomb (1990) suggested further that this basic human need derives from early attachment to others in infancy and childhood (cited in Flanagan, 1994). McAdams and Losoff (1984) found that children with high friendship motivation, who felt the need to establish warm and friendly relationships, knew more about their friends than children with lower friendship motivation. They were also rated as friendly, affectionate, cooperative, happy and popular by their teachers.

Social psychologists have researched the factors that determine who we are attracted to and make friends with, how strong the friendships will be and how long they will last. First of all, let us look at the need for affiliation.

The need for affiliation

There may be some support for an innate or inborn origin for the need for affiliation. Classic studies by Schachter (1959) have demonstrated that people find total isolation almost impossible to bear. When participants were offered $50 to remain completely alone in a room with no windows, books, telephone, television or radio and no contact whatsoever with another person, it was found that eight days was the longest period of time any one person could remain in such a state. One participant left after only 20 minutes. These experiences were described as inducing feelings of uneasiness and nervousness.

De Waal (1989) described a tendency in primates to make friends, resolve conflicts and live in peace. Primates are the species closest to humans in evolutionary terms, but although such evidence merits consideration, it is dangerous to generalise behaviour from one species to another because of the different life styles involved. Research has demonstrated that individuals differ in their need for affiliation and that, in addition, people indicate an explicit (self-attributed) and/or implicit (unconscious) need to affiliate. For example, Craig *et al.* (1994) found that when college students were asked to keep a diary for a week, detailing their social interactions, those with high explicit needs to affiliate interacted with many people, whilst those with high implicit needs interacted closely with only a few people, usually in two-person situations. This research demonstrates that we can meet affiliation needs by having several or few contacts with others.

A need for affiliation can, however, be manifested in different ways. Hill (1987) recognised four different types, each having a clearly different function (see figure 5.1).

5.1 Four types of affiliation need (Hill, 1987)

Social comparison: comparing self to others in order to reduce uncertainty about how well something is being done

Positive stimulation: wishing to have interesting interactions with others and find out about them

Emotional support: interacting with others when they are experiencing problems

Attention: liking to be the centre of attention

It appears that we can extend the types of affiliation need beyond those identified by Hill. It seems that affiliation needs may also be aroused by events such as external experiences, for example the experience provided by people living in a town close to the epicentre of the 1989 California earthquake:

'After the earthquake there was a strange mixture of elation and despair. Neighbors gathered for an impromptu party on the lawn. We needed to hold on through the terrifying aftershocks and reassure one another that loved ones whom we couldn't reach would be fine. Our bodies were intact, but the interiors of our homes were a mangled mess of broken glass, *splintered furniture, and uncertain underpinnings. We united as friends.' (Humphriss, 1989.)*

More recently, in Great Britain, these kinds of experiences were also commonly reported after the death of Diana, Princess of Wales in 1997.

Additionally, affiliation need can be motivated by a desire to obtain informed knowledge. For example, Kulik and Mahler (1989) studied the need for affiliation in patients about to undergo major heart surgery. Prior to the surgery, the patients showed a preference to be with people who had already experienced similar surgery rather than with those who were also about to experience it.

The factors which determine attraction

What exactly is **attraction**?

Activity 1

Write down the factors that you think would be important for attraction to occur between two people. Keep your notes by you and compare them with what you discover in this unit.

We are constantly meeting new people – at work, in the pub, at shops, even walking down the street. Some we may actively dislike; to others we remain completely indifferent. However, we also feel drawn towards some people: we like the look of them; we want to get to know them better; we want to spend time with them. In short, we are attracted to them. Attraction, however, is more than just knowing facts about someone; it involves our feelings as well.

For many years social psychologists have been interested in determining what is involved in attraction. They have found a number of factors to be important in determining whether or not attraction between two people will occur. The six main factors are:

- proximity
- similarity
- familiarity
- competence
- reciprocal liking
- physical attractiveness.

Did the list you compiled in Activity 1 contain any of these factors?

Activity 2

Look again at the six factors listed above. Place them in order of importance, from most to least, if you think that attraction is to occur. (How do your ideas compare with the findings on the following pages?)

Looking in more detail at several of these factors, we assess below the evidence of their importance in establishing liking for another person.

■ Proximity

Proximity means nearness. The idea that how far apart two people live is an important determinant of whether or not they will make friends (or even get married) is well established. Evidence to support this has come from studies of the relationship between proximity and marriage selection in specific communities. Such studies show a *negative correlation* between the two factors, that is, as the distance between potential marriage partners increases, the number of marriages decreases. Note that correlational research cannot conclude that proximity *causes* attraction, it can only conclude that a relationship exists (see Unit 27). It may be that other variables are involved such as the consideration that people who live close to each other are of the same religion, social class, ethnic background and so on, which may contribute to attractiveness.

Festinger (1950) carried out a study in a new housing project for married veteran students in the USA. He discovered that people who lived close to each other became friends, whilst those who lived further apart on the project did not. He also found that:

- 76 per cent of marriages were between persons living within 20 blocks of each other
- 35 per cent of marriages were between persons living within five blocks of each other.

In addition, when students were asked to name the three people they saw most often socially:

- 41 per cent named neighbours living in the apartment next door
- 22 per cent named neighbours living two doors away
- only 10 per cent named neighbours living at the end of the hall.

Further research in this area has found that manipulation of seating arrangements in the classroom has resulted in the reinforcement of the premise that proximity leads to familiarity and in turn to liking (Baron and Byrne, 1997). If you would prefer not to make friends in a new classroom situation, you would do well to sit at the back of the classroom as far from others as possible (Pedersen, 1994).

However, although proximity appears to be the *best* single predictor of whether or not two people will be friends, people do not *always* like each other when they first meet. Sometimes the opposite occurs! What happens to the relationship then?

Schiffenbauer and Schiavo (1976) showed that when the initial reaction of one person to another was positive, proximity increased the liking. However, if the initial reaction was negative, the effect of proximity was to increase the dislike. This evidence supports the idea that, over close distances, proximity intensifies the quality of the initial interaction. Increasing distances reduce the likelihood of two individuals meeting in the first place and it is difficult to be friends with someone you have not met. Perhaps the essence of why proximity should have such an impact on the liking one individual may have for another is that proximity increases the opportunity to meet each other, which then leads to greater familiarity.

■ Familiarity

How can familiarity lead to attraction? From the student housing project (see above), Festinger observed that the routes participants took on leaving or entering their home, or wandering about the neighbourhood, provided opportunities for casual meetings with others. If such brief meetings occurred frequently, the individuals concerned became more familiar with each other. They started to nod when they passed someone they recognised, then spoke to someone they nodded to and, once they had started speaking to someone, friendships could blossom.

Zajonc (1968) referred to this increased opportunity for interaction as *exposure*. His **mere exposure hypothesis** implies that someone will prefer one person to another simply because he or she has been exposed to that person more often. This hypothesis seems to contradict the well-known adage 'Familiarity breeds contempt'. Zajonc exposed participants to pictures of faces and then asked them to evaluate the people in the pictures. The more often a particular face was seen, the more the participants said they thought they would like that person (see figure 5.2). The lowest ratings were given by participants who had not seen the photograph before.

Moreland and Beach (1992) asked four research assistants to join a class of students on differing occasions and for a different number of times each, during one semester. At the end of this time, the assistants were asked to visit the class and the students rated them in terms of how much they were liked. The results supported the familiarity-repeated exposure phenomenon as the assistant who had attended the class the greatest number of times was liked the most. (Note that none of the assistants had interacted with the class, therefore this could not have been a confounding variable.)

Proximity and familiarity are two very powerful factors in interpersonal attraction. If you fancy someone from a distance, therefore, it may pay you to move in next door and maintain a high profile by going out on countless errands!

■ Similarity

Another familiar saying 'Opposites attract' also appears not to hold true. There is much evidence to suggest that attraction is more likely to occur, and be maintained, between individuals who are similar rather than dissimilar. Similarity refers to both sociological and psychological characteristics. Atkinson *et al.* (1993) reported that over 99 per cent of married couples in the United States were of the same race or ethnic group; 94 per cent were of the same religion.

Similarity of such sociological characteristics is unsurprising. Many religions demand that their members marry someone of the same religion; most people marry someone of their own race or ethnic group. It is also true that, despite living in an era of the 'sugar daddy' and the 'toyboy', relationships with large age gaps are considered abnormal by many.

Studies have also shown that similarity of psychological characteristics is more conducive to both initial attraction and to longer-lasting relationships. Hill *et al.* (1976) carried out an investigation of 200 couples. After two years, half of these had split up. Hill found that those who were still dating, engaged or married, were more similar on a variety of attributes (see figure 5.3).

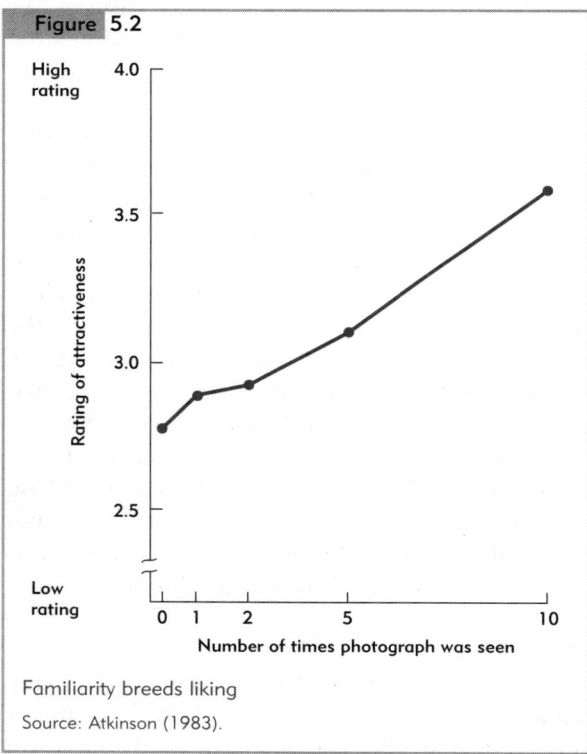

Figure 5.2

Number of times photograph was seen

Familiarity breeds liking
Source: Atkinson (1983).

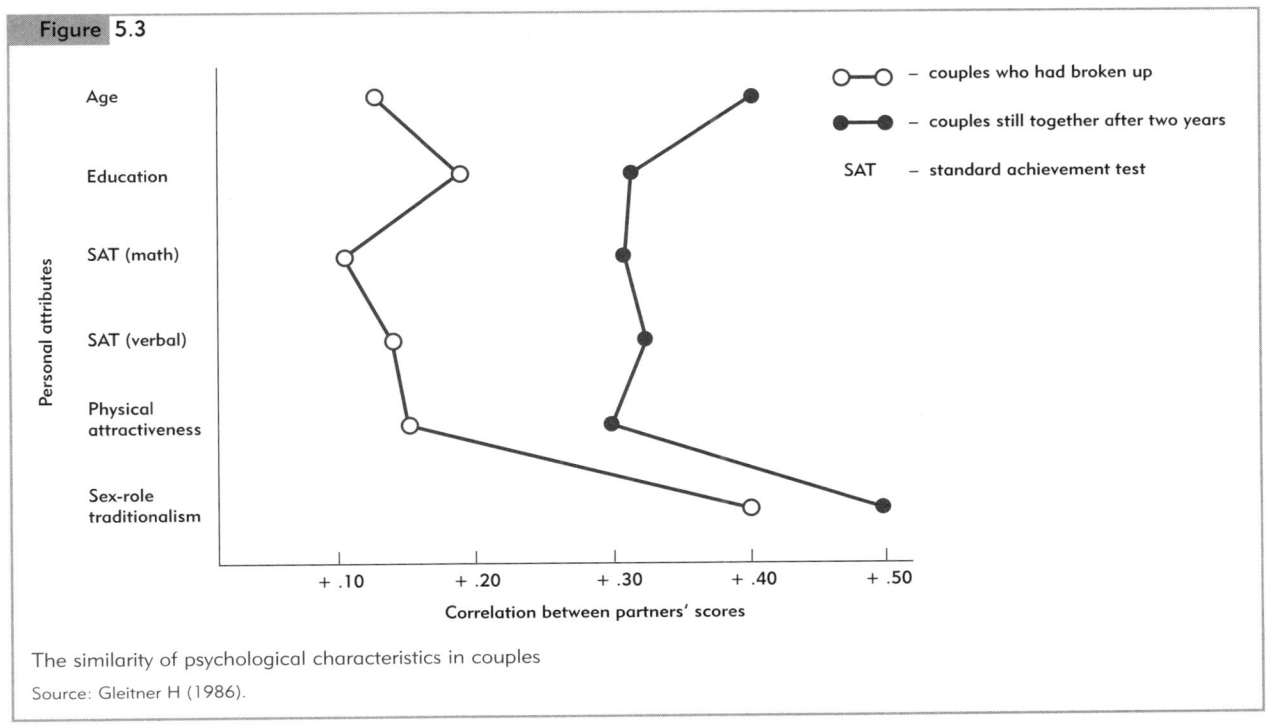

Figure 5.3

The similarity of psychological characteristics in couples

Source: Gleitner H (1986).

In a classic study, Newcomb (1961) watched the attraction process unfold over a two-year period. By offering free rent for completion of a questionnaire each week, he recruited male students who were transferring to the University of Michigan from other colleges. On the basis of these questionnaires and certain tests, Newcomb assigned some students who were similar, and some who were dissimilar, to be room mates. After a few months, he found that friendship patterns of varying degrees had developed. Those students who were similar tended to like each other and end up as friends. Those who were dissimilar tended to dislike each other and did not end up as friends. However, in a repeat study with different students in the second year, Newcomb found the familiarity factor to be more powerful as room mates had grown to like each other more, regardless of whether they were initially similar or dissimilar.

The above are examples taken from an expansive amount of research conducted in this area during the 1960s and 1970s. More recent studies suggest that the similarity effect is still in evidence today, as those using the e-mail system prefer to be in contact with those who share similar views (Schwartz, 1994).

Critics of the similarity effect have argued that similar attitudes are irrelevant and that, in essence, we like everyone we meet but gradually increase our dislike of them as we find out about the attitudes they hold which are dissimilar from our own. This argument is called the repulsion hypothesis (Rosenbaum, 1986). However, this explanation of attraction was soon disputed and found to be inaccurate as a study. Smeaton *et al.* (1989) found that when dissimilar attitudes were held constant and similar attitudes varied in proportion, the liking of a person varied according to that proportion.

Another criticism aimed at similarity as a factor contributing to attraction has been raised by Duck (1992) who argued that similarity of attitudes, proximity and familiarity are only superficial features of a first meeting, or meetings of two people, and that when people actually interact and get to know each other these factors become less important.

Proximity, familiarity and similarity thus combine to enhance interpersonal attraction. Perhaps not only should you move next door to someone you fancy, but you should also get a job at the same place and join the same sports club!

Activity 3

Try to recall what 'mere exposure hypothesis' means. (If in doubt, turn back to page 146.)

■ Physical attractiveness

It hardly seems fair that something so far beyond our control as physical attractiveness should have such an effect on our interactions with other people. The importance of physical attractiveness in a wide variety of interpersonal processes is, however, inescapable and this is confirmed by the huge amount of research that exists in this area.

Despite the platitude *'Beauty is only skin deep'*, the importance of physical attractiveness begins early on in our development, verifying its existence as a cultural and social phenomenon. Physical attractiveness can and does affect the course of children's lives, impacting upon their relationships during infancy and adulthood (Erwin, 1993). Preference is given for, and more sociably acceptable behaviour is exhibited towards, attractive care-givers over those who are thought to be unattractive by babies and young children (Samuels and Ewy, 1985; Langlois *et al.*, 1990). That a physical attractiveness stereotype is built upon during infancy has wide implications for all of us as we develop. For example, 'cute' babies are given more attention and preferred to unattractive babies. The implication is that unattractive children will be treated perhaps more negatively than attractive children. In addition, the relationships between attractive care-givers and their attractive children will be different and perhaps more positive than those between unattractive or 'mixed' pairs. Erwin (1993) contended that there is 'ample

evidence to support the notion that physically attractive individuals are treated differently and do grow to be different from their less attractive peers on a number of characteristics'. One example of the physical attractiveness stereotype during adulthood is the way in which people who are deemed to be attractive are also thought to be good and automatically associated with many other positive qualities; this is known as the 'halo effect' (Deaux *et al.*, 1993).

But what do we mean when we talk about physical attractiveness? This differs from culture to culture and historically has included chipped teeth, bound feet and breasts, corseted waists and plump, voluptuous women. Western culture today favours the slim ideal in women and a toned, muscular form in men, both images of which are reinforced by the media (Grogan, 1998). Favoured facial characteristics of women are 'cute' with full lips, a small nose and rounded eyes whilst men are preferred if they possess a thick-set jawline with more rugged features. These features are thought to be attractive by some because of evolutionary and socio-biological factors. For example, 'cute' looking women with a small waist to hip ratio appear to be younger and more fertile which means they would be able to provide their mate with offspring to keep the genetic line intact; women are less interested in looks, they are more concerned that their mate can provide for them materially (Buss, 1989; Singh, 1993; Kenrick *et al.*, 1994).

Other findings which have evolved from research in the 1960s and 1970s indicate that in reality we tend to be similar in terms of physical attractiveness to our partners because we adhere to balanced **social exchanges** (see social exchange theory, pages 151–2). This is commonly known as the **matching hypothesis**. This finding began to develop when Walster *et al.* (1966) set up a 'computer dance' where participants were unknowingly and randomly assigned to partners. The partners had been rated independently for physical attractiveness, and personality test scores had been obtained. During an interval at the dance, the participants were asked to evaluate their dates. It was found that personality was not related to whether or not a person liked their dates. The greatest determinant of whether dates were asked out again was how attractive they were.

However, further research undertaken by Bersheid *et al.* (1971) found that participants asked for dates who matched themselves in attractiveness when asked to specify the characteristics they hoped to find in a date. The difference between this and the Walster study was that participants stated their preferences before having a date. Perhaps less-attractive people fear rejection and so lower their aspirations in the hope that they will be less likely to be rejected. 'Computer dance' studies involve couples who have had little or no interaction. Therefore, they may lack validity. They do not involve people attracted to each other over months or years. However, Price and Vandenberg (1979) showed that when it comes to marriage, the matching hypothesis does occur. They asked participants to rate photographs of individuals on a scale of attractiveness and found that photographs of couples were indeed matched in terms of attractiveness.

Activity 4

Write down a real-life example illustrating how each of the following interactions might occur. The first one has been completed for you.

Initial influence on attraction		Resultant influence on attraction
1 Familiarity	→	proximity

On the first day at college, whilst waiting to go into the psychology class, a girl recognises one face only, a boy she saw when she attended for interview. She goes to stand near him, remarks on the fact that they were both successful at the interview, walks into class with him and sits next to him.

2 Proximity	→	familiarity
3 Proximity	→	similarity
4 Similarity	→	proximity
5 Similarity	→	familiarity
6 Familiarity	→	similarity
7 Physical attractiveness	→	proximity

Self-assessment questions

1 List the possible reasons why Walster's 'computer dance' participants did not fit in with the matching hypothesis.

2 Describe the distinctions to be made between affiliation and attraction.

3 Note briefly the findings of two studies investigating proximity/exposure/familiarity.

(Suggested answers on page 169.)

The development, maintenance and breakdown of relationships

Theoretical models of interpersonal relationships

You have now looked at the major factors which determine attraction and have seen that these factors interact. Newcomb (1961) among others, suggests that different factors are important at the different stages of a relationship. At first, surface-level factors are important, for example physical attractiveness and proximity, as this is usually the only information initially available to us. We have seen how proximity, familiarity and similarity interact. As we find out more about a person, personal qualities start to count also.

Newcomb suggested that attraction is basically a matter of rewards: we like people who provide us with many rewards and few costs. If we like people who reward us, it becomes obvious why physical attractiveness is initially so important as it is thought in western cultures that prestige is gained from being seen with an attractive partner and hence attractiveness becomes a reward. We have already seen how physical attractiveness can be construed in terms of reward, for example the evolutionary theory discussed on page 148. Many of the theories connected with explanations of how relationships function are based on a reward-cost application and attempt to explain why certain factors are important in the development of relationships and what makes a relationship develop further, what factors influence the root of relationships and what factors might be accountable in the dissolution of relationships.

■ Byrne's affect-centred model of attraction

This theory has evolved from earlier reinforcement theories proposed by Lott and Lott (1969), Byrne and Clore (1970) and Byrne (1971). These theories of interpersonal attraction stem from behaviourist ideas surrounding classical and instrumental conditioning (see Unit 4). Reinforcement from another person (either in the form of reward or punishment) will result in the like or dislike of that person. Therefore, rewarding reinforcement such as similar attitudes, will result in positive affect and this positive affect can be extended to another person or object associated with that person.

Before we begin a more detailed discussion about this theory, we should make sure we understand the terminology involved and ask, first of all, what is 'affect'? In psychological terms it usually means a feeling, emotion or desire. We also talk about the intensity of affect, that is, the weakness and strength of emotions, and the direction of affect, that is, whether it is positive or negative. Research has demonstrated that we are inclined to find people or events that make us feel good pleasant and find them unpleasant if they make us feel bad (Downey and Damhave, 1991, cited in Baron and Byrne, 1997). For example, if we are walking along a corridor and drop all our books and someone helps us to pick them up, we will probably associate that person with positive feelings and thus come to like them.

Byrne (1992) proposed that positive and negative affect can be induced by a person we meet because of their actions, observable attributes and other variables that might be present at the time. So we like the person we meet because he or she has helped us pick up our books; if, in addition, we find the person to be physically attractive (an observable attribute), our positive affect towards them is likely to be stronger. However, this theory does not just take affect into account, it is also concerned with cognitive process. The observable attribute of physical attractiveness has to be processed cognitively before we can evaluate this attribute and we therefore rely on previous experiences, attitudes and stereotypes which form schemas we have about people to help us to decide what direction and intensity of affect we are going to experience in relation to the person we meet.

It should be noted that stereotypes and prejudices can play an important part in the development of positive and negative affect. If we are prejudiced towards those from a different ethnic background to ourselves, then this will obviously produce a negative affect towards the person who helps us pick up our books, if the person is white and we are black-Caribbean for example. Even if a stigma is removed (such as an obese person dieting and hence becoming slim), the individual concerned will still produce negative affect if it is known that he or she was once obese – perhaps we should not mention these past stigmas to people, even though honesty is supposed to be the best policy!

Byrne further added that a neutral object or event can influence whether we like a person or not. Therefore, in our example, if we were experiencing a hangover at the time of meeting the person in the corridor, then this stimulus (which was negative) would induce negative affect towards that person. On the other hand, if it was a beautiful summer's day and we had just eaten some chocolate (positive stimuli), then positive affect would be aroused further by that person. These theories concerning associations are based on classical conditioning and are illustrated in figure 5.4.

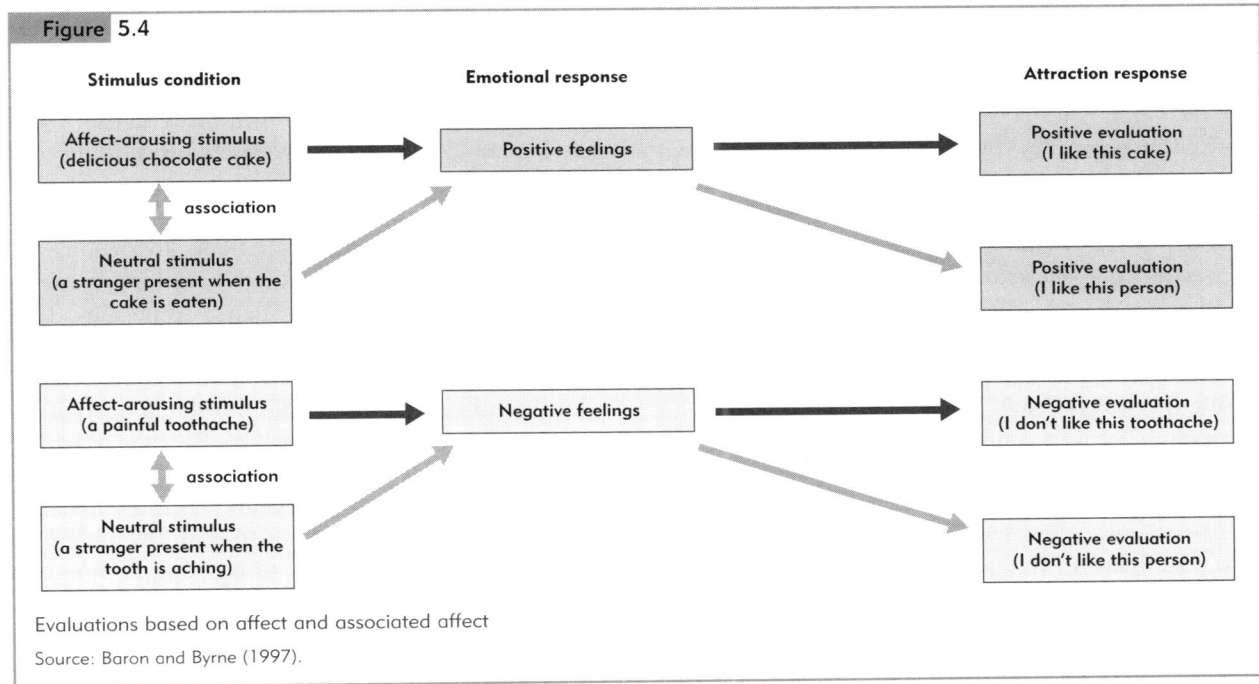

Figure 5.4

Evaluations based on affect and associated affect

Source: Baron and Byrne (1997).

It can be concluded from various research projects that whilst it might be possible to anticipate or predict behaviour in respect of attraction, it is nevertheless quite often irrational:

■ Researchers attempted several chat-up lines aimed at those of the opposite sex in a singles bar. It was found that those using flippant and superficial chat-up lines, such as 'Hi. I'm easy, are you?' or 'Bet I can out-drink you' induced negative affect (particularly among women). The most successful lines, which induced positive affect, included those that were simple and direct such as 'Do you want to dance?' or 'Where are you from?' (Kleinke *et al.*, 1986; Cunningham, 1989).

■ A stranger's photograph paired with pleasant or unpleasant subliminal pictures has been found to influence affect (Krosnick *et al.*, 1992), thus upholding the part of the theory that states that neutral events or objects are associated with affect.

■ Researchers have manipulated a number of variables to determine whether or not they influenced the liking or disliking of a member

of the opposite sex. For example, Baron *et al.* (1992) used pleasant lighting in a social setting which produced positive affect towards those of the opposite sex whilst unpleasant lighting produced negative affect.

■ Rozin *et al.* (1986) found that when a freshly cleaned and ironed shirt was worn by someone whom the participant in the study disliked, then the shirt itself produced a negative affect and vice versa for the same kind of shirt worn by a person who was liked! This illustration serves to emphasise how illogical our attitudes and behaviour can be.

■ Social exchange and equity theory

Social exchange theory seeks to explain when relationships are likely to develop and when to end. The theory also takes into account interaction between people in a relationship rather than focusing solely on the characteristics of one person and ignoring the other. Thibaut and Kelley (1959) developed the hypothesis that everyone tries to make social interaction as profitable as possible. This would mean that we constantly weigh up the rewards gained from an interaction and the costs one must pay. If rewards outweigh costs, the relationship should continue. If the costs are greater, then the relationship is likely to end. Take, for example, physical attractiveness and proximity. A handsome man from a poor area meets a pretty girl from an affluent area some distance away. Rewards are the same for both in terms of physical attractiveness and the prestige associated with it. Are there other rewards for him which will counteract the time, effort and cost involved in dating her? Does she receive enough rewards from other areas (similarity or competence, for example) to outweigh the costs of being dated by a poor man? Satisfaction in a relationship is determined not just by actual rewards received but by comparing them with the rewards expected. If a girl is expecting to be wined and dined and given flowers and chocolates regularly, but is only taken to the pub for half a pint on a Saturday night, then the relationship is not likely to last! However, if all a girl is expecting is to go to the pub in the evening and return home before *Match of the Day*, then the relationship could be a winner! It is only likely to end if better alternatives are available.

Equity theory (Walster *et al.,* 1978) can be described as an evolvement from social exchange theory. This later theory argues that rewards and costs do not have to be shared equally or exactly balanced between those participating in a relationship so long as there exists a sense of 'fairness' or 'equity'. In business or acquaintance relationships, the rewards and costs are quite often evenly matched, usually based on a strict exchange of benefits to each. However, in closer relationships between friends, kin and partners, the rewards and costs may be more unevenly balanced, but this does not mean that happiness cannot be achieved. In a closer relationship, the fact that rewards and costs are imbalanced is a consideration which is accounted for and accepted. For example, in friendship we may go to help our friend in times of trouble without expecting anything in return. Or, the girl who expects to be wined and dined in the example above may settle for these rewards irregularly because she finds other attributes rewarding in her partner which are taken into consideration when weighing up the whole relationship.

An inequitable relationship can cause great distress, obviously for the person who is losing out. This person will try to restore a sense of fairness and put as much effort as possible into doing so. However, the relationship is likely to dissolve or end when this person feels it is no longer worth expending such effort on such a futile aim. This can often be seen in partnerships where one partner has been unfaithful, although repentant, but the other partner cannot put the affair behind himself or herself, and so cracks appear which cannot mended.

Equity theory often finds couples trading resources that are quite different, in order to retain a sense of justice. For example, in our westernised culture, which is primarily male-dominated in terms of its economic system, there are apparent differences between males and females. In 1987, Buss found that the attractiveness of wives is correlated with their husbands' occupational prestige; the implications here are that both partners are seeking some kind of equitable status. It would be interesting to compare these findings with relationship concerns in matriarchal societies and to further research in our own society as economic changes are made which affect women.

■ Balance theory

Newcomb (1971) showed how balance theory could be used to explain how relationships are likely to develop when there are contradictory feelings. Balance theory looks at the relationship between the feelings two people have for each other and for something or someone else: the three relationships in figure 5.5 can occur.

A balanced state explains why the factor of similarity between individuals can have such an impact on the attraction between them. An imbalanced state creates problems for the relationship. If a disagreement occurs, it may result in a lessening of intimacy; if X is something very important to A and B, then the relationship could break down altogether. It may also provide

Figure 5.5

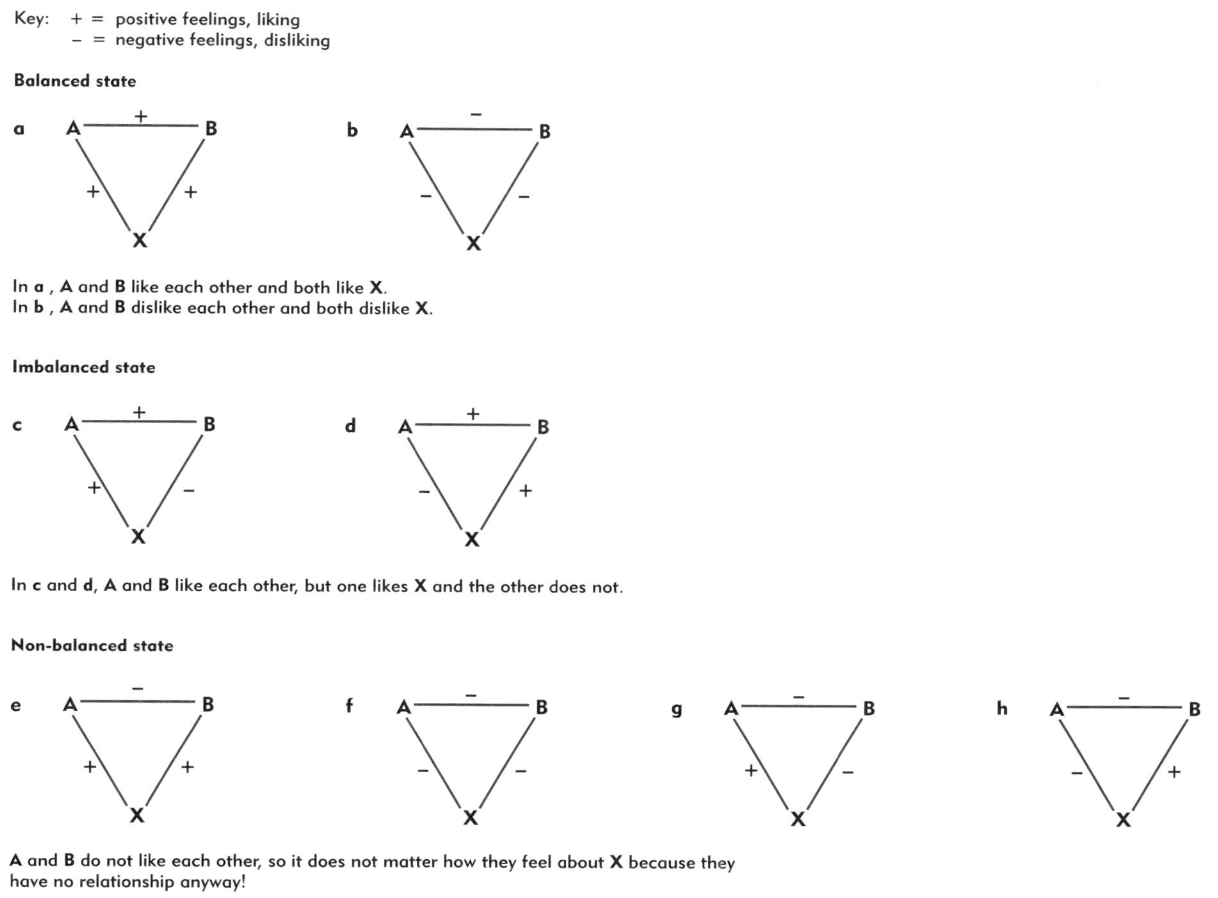

Key: + = positive feelings, liking
     − = negative feelings, disliking

Balanced state

In **a**, **A** and **B** like each other and both like **X**.
In **b**, **A** and **B** dislike each other and both dislike **X**.

Imbalanced state

In **c** and **d**, **A** and **B** like each other, but one likes **X** and the other does not.

Non-balanced state

A and **B** do not like each other, so it does not matter how they feel about **X** because they have no relationship anyway!

Balanced, imbalanced and non-balanced states

motivation for the individuals to restore the balance in their relationship (Orive, 1988).

This theory supports the matching hypothesis discussed on page 148 as it seems that physical attractiveness is not the only similarity factor involved in whether we like one another or not and that attitudes are indeed important. Research has demonstrated that other characteristics are also found to be similar in friendships and intimate relationships such as sociability (Joiner, 1994), expressing emotions (Alliger and Williams, 1991), smoking marijuana (Eisenman, 1985), having similar self concepts (LaPrelle *et al.*, 1990) and accepting traditional gender roles (Smith *et al.*,

1995). Surprisingly (or not!), sense of humour was found in one study to be more important than shared attitudes (Cann *et al.*, 1995).

Rushton (1989, 1990) agreed with the above findings and suggested that all these characteristics that are found to be similar in friendships or partnerships are cues we look for in order to develop relationships with those who are genetically similar to ourselves. His research found that not only are people in such relationships similar in terms of attitudes but they also have inherited characteristics in common such as blood type. Helping and being friends with similar others is an unconscious means of protecting our genetic inheritance and therefore ensuring that our genes will be passed on to the next generation.

Activity 5

Look at figure 5.5 and think about your own relationships. When you experience 'imbalance' in a relationship, does that necessarily result in problems? Do you experience 'balance' with all your friends? Discuss these issues in groups of three.

■ **Filter models and self-disclosure (Duck, 1988)**

Duck suggested that much of the laboratory-based research which has concentrated on similarity of various characteristics, whilst of considerable value, is nevertheless somewhat false and lacks ecological validity (i.e. this is not what happens in the 'real world'). Duck argued that 'the business of initial attraction is not just one of *matching* our attitudes or characteristics with someone else's but of *communicating* about them' (1992, p. 72).

Duck proposed that we discover whether we like other people and hence commence a relationship with them, by means of experiencing several 'filters', such as non-verbal behaviours and progressive interaction, which lead us to a point where we can evaluate a person based on knowledge we have gathered about him or her and then decide whether or not we want to form a relationship with the person. Van Lear and Trujillo (1986) put forward a four-stage model of 'filtering' as follows:

1. We start with a sense of uncertainty which involves a need to discover more about the person.
2. We then explore affect and feeling towards that person.
3. We then develop personal growth in relation to that person.
4. We then turn to issues of interpersonal stability.

In this model, the partnership entails not only discovery about feelings but developing the relationship by attending to different issues throughout the relationship's growth. In this way,

we may begin a relationship by means of being physically attracted to a person. We then discover a broad overview of that person by finding out how his or her attitudes and values compare to our own; these discoveries become more finely tuned as the relationship progresses and so we get to know more about our partner's deepest fears and how we can cheer up the individual and so on.

This form of discovery involves **self-disclosure**. Initially (upon first communicating), people are guarded in how much they give away about themselves in case it 'puts people off'. Yet, if a relationship is to develop, the people in it must reveal to each other more and more private and personal information. People begin by giving away superficial information, but, gradually, disclosures become more intimate. As this happens, disclosures by one partner are matched by those of the other in both breadth and depth. Timing is also important. Disclosures from one partner need to be met fairly immediately by disclosures from the other, until the relationship is better established. When this happens, there is less need for immediate reciprocation.

Attraction therefore is not just a question of *'love at first sight'* or of *'body chemistry'*. Relationships can develop through other factors, even when there appears to be no initial, immediate attraction. However, the fact that the vast majority of people do marry or establish other long-term relationships means that there is hope for all of us!

Attachment patterns and their influence on relationships throughout life

So far, in this unit, we have discussed factors which can influence how and why we might become attracted to others and thus begin relationships. We have also looked at various theories concerned with the development of relationships and how these relationships might be sustained and/or annulled. We have seen how relationships can be influenced by our own cognitive processes, situations we might find ourselves in and various interactions which take place at different stages in a relationship. However, we must remember that relationships are not created solely on the basis of these factors and that our earliest memories and experiences can also affect relationship patterns in childhood, adolescence and adulthood. It is to this dimension of relationship inquiry that we now turn.

> 'The early bond of attachment of a child to a parent or primary care-giver exerts a major influence on later relationships. It is on the foundation of this primary relationship that the conduct and expectations of all other relationships are built' (Erwin, 1993).

Patterns of attachment are said to be the product of specific parenting styles which include secure attachment, insecure-avoidant attachment and insecure-resistant attachment. These patterns are discussed in more depth in Unit 20 and there is a growing body of research which suggests that these attachment patterns have a significant effect on the patterns of relationships established in later life. Each individual has a different set of expectations of what relationships should be like based on their early attachment with significant others. These sets of expectations have been termed 'working models of relationships' by Bowlby (1969). Therefore, we build future relationships on the basis of early working models brought about by early relationships and our own experiences of attachment patterns (Sroufe and Fleeson, 1986). One implication of this view point is that the child who has experienced an early relationship of neglect will subsequently develop a working model of relationships which involves feelings of unworthiness and thus cannot expect to be treated positively by others. This child may find it difficult to develop and maintain future relationships.

Most of the research in this area has focused on relationships in young children which has demonstrated that children securely attached to their mothers at 12–19 months of age show positive social behaviours at ages three to four. They are found to be confident, more socially skilled and less dependent than insecurely attached infants (Erickson *et al.*, 1985). In addition they appear to be more popular and have more friends (LaFreniere and Sroufe, 1985).

In 1981, Pastor examined the behaviour of secure, anxious-avoidant and anxious-resistant infants towards an unknown securely attached infant. Their patterns of attachment had been resolved by the strange situation test at 18 months of age. The secure children were found to display more sociability and orientation towards peers; in addition, they resolved conflicts over a toy more easily than others. The anxious-avoidant chidren participated actively but did not demonstrate as much orientation towards their peers and evoked more aggression from playmates. Finally, the anxious-resistant children were found to lack social skills, were unsettled by the situation and made few peer offers. More recent research suggests that these kinds of pattern are evident in less superficial situations where children are observed in more 'natural' situations (Park and Waters, 1989).

It should also be noted that the parenting styles discussed in Unit 20 can affect relationships in adulthood, for example authoritative parenting has been found to induce psychological well-being and peer popularity in later life (Roopnarine, 1987), whilst permissive parenting has been associated with low self-esteem and aggressiveness in adolescence (Dean *et al.*, 1986), characteristics which are obviously going to have some bearing on the development and maintenance of relationships.

Recent studies of attachment styles and formation of relationships has focused on how the attachment patterns in infancy relate to self and other image. Griffin and Bartholomew (1994) suggested that attachment patterns influence whether we have a positive or negative image of ourselves and/or others and that this in turn affects our relationships. For example, a secure attachment pattern in childhood will result in a positive image of ourselves and others, resulting in us seeking closeness to others; those experiencing an avoidant or fearful attachment pattern in childhood will result in negative images of self and others, thus resulting in avoidance of rejection by avoiding closeness with others.

Future research needs to concentrate more on adult relationships in relation to working models of relationships, but the research thus far does suggest that adult relationships are not constructed in isolation but influenced by other past and present relationships.

■ The cultural aspect of attachment research

It should be noted that most of the research in this area has focused on middle-class 'nuclear' families in western industrialised society. The inferences made from such research do not always reflect the attachment styles and subsequent relationship behaviour in other societies and cultures. Each culture has its own values and goals to which individuals or groups aspire and this includes relationship patterns.

In relation to different patterns in western societies Ogbu (1981) stated that children in urban ghettoes of America need and demonstrate very different patterns to those who are brought up in a middle-class background. Gang membership and being 'street-wise' are important characteristics of these societies and academic qualifications are of little importance. Parents in these areas are generally found to use parenting styles which are more suited to this way of life.

In addition, as our own society changes and incorporates many different types of *reconstructed* families (as opposed to only the nuclear family), researchers are beginning to look at the affect of different care-givers' attachment and parenting styles, instead of focusing solely on the natural mother and/or father as the primary care-givers (Ladd, 1991).

Staying in love

If we successfully negotiate all the interactional hurdles and develop a stable, close and intimate relationship with another person, how do we successfully maintain this bond? Studies of romantic relationships have proposed that there are several ways of doing this.

Hatfield (1988) makes a distinction between 'passionate' and 'companionate' love. Passionate love can be described as a strong, intense emotional response to another person – we talk about being 'blinded by love', 'falling head over heels' and 'love at first sight'. This kind of love is all-consuming and might be described by observers as 'infatuation'. Passionate love is too extreme to last and if the relationship is maintained, this kind of impulsive love usually transforms itself into companionate love where two people care for each other, are still attracted, demonstrate mutual respect but are more realistic about their relationship – they do not remain blind to each other's faults, they are aware of problems that might beset them and make attempts to sort out these problems.

Several strategies employed by couples in order to maintain a relationship and combat any problems arising are cited by Hayes (1994):

■ When accounts were collected from a wide variety of adults, it was found that the strategies they used for maintaining their relationships fell into three categories:

a *Avoidance strategies* – when one person wants the relationship to develop further and the other does not, the latter partner avoids discussion of the relationship's future.

b *Balance strategies* – when one person wants the relationship to dissolve, he or she tends to put less effort into it. However, the partner will then attempt to restore balance by doing good turns for the other, for example.

c *Directness strategies* – these involve talking directly about the relationship and stating a desire to keep things as they are (Ayres, 1983). Individual differences seem to be apparent in the strategies employed, for example women tend to use directness strategies when they wish to maintain the relationship as it currently exists but their male partner wishes the relationship to intensify (Shea and Pearson, 1986).

■ Dindia and Baxter (1987) interviewed 50 married couples about the maintenance strategies they employed and identified the existence of 49 such strategies. These included tactics such as 'talking about the day' and 'spending time together with friends'. The maintenance strategies used highlighted the employment of joint activity or interaction, whereas tactics used when the relationship encountered problems focused more on the relationship itself such as 'offering an ultimatum'. These researchers also found that long-term relationships did not use as many maintenance strategies as those who had been engaged in short-term relationships. It may be that long-term relationships do not require as much effort because the partners understand each other better or that the relationships are maintained more through force of habit. Linked to this is Morgan's observation (1986) that it is only when a relationship dissolves that partners begin to notice the amount of insignificant interaction involved in their relationship. These small things may help to maintain the relationship if they are thought to be positive by the people involved. However, if they are seen to be negative, they may play a significant part in the breakdown of the relationship.

■ Societal factors affecting relationship maintenance

Whilst divorce is becoming more prevalent today, it is nevertheless true that heterosexual couples still prefer to marry, and the majority of those that do divorce, remarry (resulting in a wide variety of family 'types'). Nowadays, therefore, it is becoming more important for such couples to adjust to changing parenting and economic patterns as both partners follow a career and some find themselves living apart from their 'natural' children and taking on the role of parents to their new partner's offspring. These marital patterns are stressful and difficult to operate (Argyle, 1992). In relation to this issue, research has found that the female partner in a heterosexual relationship still does much more than 50 per cent of the housework. It has been found that only lesbian couples tend to share housework chores evenly (Baron and Byrne, 1997).

Until very recently, most of the research concerned with personal relationships has focused on heterosexual relationships. Kitzinger and Coyle (1995) attacked this state of affairs and suggested that there is a great need for psychology to investigate *homosexual relationships*. On the subject of relationship maintenance, Kitzinger suggested that difficulties are inherent in homosexual relationships because of the lack of social, religious and legal support they receive (that is, homosexual

relationships are not socially sanctioned). She further stated that lesbian and gay male couples are often forced to remain invisible to their families and the workplace where prejudices and stereotypes still exist in full force. For example, in the workplace it is usual for heterosexuality to be displayed openly in the form of wedding rings, photographs of spouses on the desk, flirtation, discussions of weekend acitivities and so on. However, gay couples are still regarded as being deviant and feel unable to disclose information about their relationships for fear of being ostracised. This affects their ability to develop and maintain a relationship as it is put under strain.

Components of interpersonal relationships

Activity 6

a   Before reading any further, make a list of social relationships. Some commonly listed relationships are given below. Make sure your list includes some of the following:
 • friends
 • marriage (and other kinds of cohabitation)
 • parent-child relations
 • work relations
 • neighbours.
b   Apart from regular social encounters with certain people over a period of time, did you consider casual encounters and acquaintances when compiling your list of relationships?

Another perspective taken by psychologists which has helped us to gain insight into how relationships can be maintained or why they break up, is by analysing the components of interpersonal alliances. Argyle and Henderson (1985) believed that some marriages and other relationships break up because people do not understand the true nature of these relationships, for example that conflict is inevitable in marriage. There are differences between the forms of relationships, for example, in different social classes, cultures and for men and women.

In many cases there will be an 'attachment' or 'bonding' and distress if the relationship has ended, but this is not an essential feature. For example, there does not seem to be much attachment (in the sense that the other is missed when absent) to many people at work or to neighbours. Some relationships are associated with positive emotions, such as spouse, kin and friends, but this is not the case in all relationships. Finally, some relationships, though superficial, such as contacts with postmen/women, bus drivers and hairdressers, are important for isolated or lonely individuals.

Social relationships are therefore complex and whilst they may have some things in common, there are also differences between them. Argyle (1992) likened relationships to games. In order to understand a game and to be able to play, first and foremost one needs to know the rules that must be followed and the goals that are being pursued (how to win). The rules make attainment of goals possible, set limits as to how the goals are to be pursued and define roles which players should enact. There are different rules for different games and different rules for different relationships, reflecting the nature of each relationship and culture norms. However, relationships are also unlike games in that in most cases they are cooperative rather than competitive. No one is trying to win.

■ Goals

Activity 7

Think of three people with whom you have a relationship. You could include friends, family, colleagues, etc. For each, list the goals, or in other words what are you trying to achieve in the relationship, why are you in it and what are the sources of satisfaction. Compare the goals for each relationship.

Argyle and Furnham (1983) carried out studies in which people listed the most important **goals** in their relationship. The following three were the most common:

- own physical well-being
- social acceptance and related factors
- task goals specific to the situation.

A look at sources of satisfaction received from relationships sheds some light as to the goals of the relationship. In the same way that people will not play a game unless they receive sufficient satisfaction from doing so, and satisfactions that are greater than the costs involved, people will not stay in a relationship for these reasons.

Argyle and Furnham (1983) asked participants about their degree of satisfaction with a number of relationships. They found three important dimensions of satisfaction:

- material and instrumental help
- social and emotional support
- common interests.

They found that the spouse is the greatest source of satisfaction especially where material and instrumental help is concerned. Neighbours and work associates were found to be poor sources of satisfaction. Friends are particularly important and are often the main source of social support. Where instrumental and material help is concerned, friends are generally not as important as family, though among the young (before marriage) and old (the over 60s after retirement and widowhood) and in some cultures, friends are an important source of help. Shared activities, especially in the form of joint leisure, is the explanation of why friends are a major source of happiness (Larson, 1990) particularly because of the enjoyable things friends do together and partly because of the exchange of positive non-verbal signals, that is smiling, gazing, touching, tone of voice (Argyle, 1987).

In most cultures, kinship is the main basis of relationships, but the importance of kinship, the sources of satisfaction and the forms this takes varies. In a study of three generations in Minneapolis, Hill found that 50 per cent of parents help their children with childcare, 47 per cent with household management and 41 per cent with economic concerns. As well as parents, siblings are also major sources of satisfaction in material and instrumental help. A lot of this help is provided by women, and this is particularly important in third world cultures where the kinship network replaces the public sources of help such as social security in developed cultures. Kinship networks are much more extensive in Africa, India and the rest of the third world, where the kinship network is the best place to turn for any kind of help, even jobs. In Britain, social and emotional support is important, especially that received by women who rely on it from their mothers or sisters. Working-class people tend to keep closer kinship ties in most cultures. One reason is that working-class kin live much closer together; children do not seek jobs or education in different places and do not move away.

■ Rules

A great deal of human behaviour is governed by **rules**. To take one example, when driving, the rule of the road enables us to travel safely. Some rules are formally outlined and legally sanctioned such as most laws. Others are more informl, relating to norms rather than legal penalties. Queuing makes it possible for people to obtain whatever they are queuing for in an orderly and fair manner. Rules are developed so that people's goals can be attained. Whilst they may sometimes appear restrictive, for example observing a speed limit, they are beneficial. The rules of queuing are clearly aimed at avoiding common difficulties. Argyle and Henderson (1985) defined rules as 'shared opinions and beliefs about what should and should not be done'. We are concerned here with the informal rules applying to relationships. Although there are laws applying to relationships, for example it is not allowed in Britain to be married to two people at the same time, the informal rules deal with styles of behaviour or ways of handling relationships. Relationships involve others, so routes to goals will be collective solutions including the necessary coordination of some behaviours and the exclusion of other behaviours by means of rules. Unless coordination is achieved, group goals will not be attained.

Activity 8

Look back at Activity 7 on page 158. What are the informal rules that apply to each relationship? Try to list as many as you can. To enable you to do this task think of the *behaviours* that you believe should or should not be performed.

Argyle, Henderson and Furnham (1985) compiled a list of 33 rules which would apply to most relationships, for example rules about what should or should not be discussed in conversation. They also drew up a list of 22 common relationships ranging from intimate, for example husband–wife, to professional relationships, for example teacher–pupil. They asked 180 British-born men and women from different occupational and social class backgrounds to rate how important the rules were in six to eight of these relationships on a nine-point rating scale. In order to overcome gender bias, equal numbers of both genders completed each questionnaire, and age-generation differences were also taken into account in the design of the study. In order to find out whether or not the rules of the relationships were culture specific, 300 Japanese, 280 Hong Kong Chinese, and 230 Italians also participated in the study.

Four rules were rated as important in virtually all of the 22 relationships in all four cultures. These were:

- should respect the other's privacy
- should look the other person in the eye during conversation
- should not discuss that which is said in confidence with the other person
- should not criticise the other person publicly.

The most important rule across all relationships and cultures is the rule about privacy, rated as very important in 60 per cent of cases and fairly important in another 30 per cent. What this means in effect is that the above rules are believed to be important by people from very different cultures in dealing with relationships ranging from the very temporary and task orientated, for example householder and salesperson, to the very intimate and long term, for example husband and wife. The researchers also found rules that were common to more than half of the 22 relationships in all four countries. Some of these were:

- should stand up for the other person in their absence
- should not disclose to the other person one's feelings and personal problems
- should not ask the other person for material help.

Cultural differences

In both Italy and Britain, the relationships with the highest number of important rules attached to them were the more intimate ones. In Hong Kong, these intimate relationships also have a large number of important rules but, in addition, work superiors and work subordinates have as many rules. In Japan, these work relationships have a greater number of important rules applied to them, more than any of the intimate relationships. Rules concerned with expressing emotion, self-disclosure, discussing intimate topics and making requests for material help or personal advice are more strongly applied among the two European groups, particularly Italy. Such intimate behaviour is actually proscribed in Hong Kong and Japan, particularly for professional and work relationships. Japanese rules tend to be more formal, for example those about not swearing, neat dress, first name usage, particularly in work relationships. Japanese culture also emphasises the control of an outward show of emotions in public, ideally, to show an expressionless face to the world, especially in situations of great anxiety. Hence, there are rules in Japan about *not* showing distress or anxiety or expressing anger. Only in the marital relationship should one express anxiety or distress, and not even then in the case of anger. The same applies to Hong Kong. In Britain and Italy, it is deemed more important to discuss and express potentially negative emotions or topics that may lead to conflict, whilst in the eastern cultures, potential sources of conflict are to be avoided in line with strong social conformity and harmonious group behaviour (Argyle and Henderson, 1985).

Purpose of rules

Argyle proposed that rules have two major functions in relationships. The first purpose is to regulate behaviour to minimise potential sources of conflict which may disrupt the relationship. Such rules function to *maintain* the relationship. Secondly, rules provide for an exchange of rewards that motivate the individuals to remain in the relationship. Such rules allow for the relationship to *grow*.

A couple of examples should illustrate these different functions. In a householder–repairman/woman relationship, the main goal of the relationship is task orientated. There are few relevant rewarding rules and little need for relationship growth. The main rules will be regulatory: ones that allow the relationship to continue long enough and with the minimum of conflict to complete the task. But for intimate relationships, for example husband–wife relationship, many regulating and rewarding rules are involved. Because large amounts of time are spent in close contact, over long periods of time, with a high level of emotional involvement, there are substantial potential sources of conflict which may disrupt the relationship. Therefore many regulating rules are thought important to provide the basis on which reward rules can operate.

The importance of rules in relationships cannot be overestimated. Some rules when broken lead to the collapse or disruption of the relationships. To illustrate this point we consider below the rules of friendship.

Activity 9

Before examining the findings below consider first which rules you think are important for good friends.

According to Argyle (1992), the following are some of the most important rules for friendship:

- volunteer help in time of need
- respect the friend's privacy
- keep confidences
- trust and confide in each other

- don't criticise each other in public
- don't be jealous or critical of his or her other relationships
- don't nag
- share news of success
- engage in joking or teasing with a friend.

Relationships break down when friends do not keep the rules. Argyle asked 150 people to think of a specific relationship that had lapsed because of something to do with the relationship (there are factors other than the actual relationship that can cause the breakdown of a friendship such as the friend moving away). Certain rules, presented below, were seen as contributing to the breakdown:

- being jealous or critical of your other relationships
- discussing with others what was said in confidence
- not volunteering help in time of need
- not showing postive regard
- not showing emotional support.

It is interesting to note that both men and women agreed on these rules, though women were much more likely than men to stress the importance of two rules: not showing positive regard and not showing emotional support.

There is a lot that can be learnt about relationships and much of this information is contained in rules which, if broken, as we have seen in looking at the rules of friendship, can lead to a disruption of the relationship. Part of education for relationships is learning the rules, for example in marital-skills training partners may be trained to be better senders and receivers of non-verbal cues for emotions (show emotional support – a rewarding rule is regarded as very important in marriage). For people who complain about difficulties in making friends, social-skills training focuses on the positive non-verbal signals and the reduction of egocentricity.

■ Rules and power

Systems based on rules implicitly allocate roles to the participants. In other words, rules define roles. To return to the analogy with games, just as in cricket there are a number of distinct parts to be played such as batter, bowler, wicket-keeper, so too relationships are role systems. To take one example, for a long time in marriage and in most cultures, wives had an 'expressive' and nurturant role inside the home whilst husbands had an 'instrumental' role in being the provider (Argyle, 1988).

An important part of occupying a role is the power which the occupant has over those in other roles. In the traditional family, the husband often had a career and was able to pursue his ambitions, whereas the wife had to play a secondary role. Granted that if her husband was successful, she shared in the benefits of increased income and greater status. However, it was the husband rather than she who had the success. Many studies have found that the partner who earns the most money, has the more prestigious job or is better educated, has the more power. In virtually all cultures, primitive and industrialised, men have had more power than women both inside and outside families. During the depression of the 1930s, many husbands earned less or lost their jobs. The result was a large increase in the power of their wives.

With the increased education and aspirations of women, more wives have jobs and careers than before and sometimes better jobs than their husbands. There has been a gradual rise in the power of women. However, although it is true that more women do have paid employment outside the home, many of these jobs are part time, temporary and poorly paid. Pressure from women for equal say in decisions, to have careers and for husbands to share the housework is causing marital roles to change. Better-educated wives not only have more power based on their education but are also more likely to have jobs and earn money, have husbands who accept equality of the sexes and be socially skilled. Studies have found that many wives do want more power than they have and are happier with their marriage when they do have more power. A number of American studies have found that egalitarian marriages are the happiest.

■ Conflict

As stated earlier, one of the functions of rules is to minimise potential sources of conflict. Informal rules partly reduce conflict at work. Some rules are directly concerned with maintaining cooperation over work and being cooperative with regard to the shared physical working conditions, for example light, temperature and noise and being willing to help when requested. Many of the other rules are concerned with maintaining positive relations and preventing common causes of friction, for example keep confidences and stand up for the co-worker in his or her absence. Friction may occur when fairness, cooperation, help, mutual support and privacy are brought into question.

One of the central features of marriage is the high level of conflict that occurs in it. There are a number of features of marriage that makes conflict so common, such as living at very close quarters, which means that agreements have to be made over a wide range of issues such as changing jobs, moving home. Because husbands and wives usually occupy different marital roles, they will hold different opinions on many issues. Finally, because there is a high level of emotional involvement with each other, it is easy to become upset at the other's behaviour. Part of the solution is to keep the informal rules which it is generally believed should be followed in marriage.

Relationship breakdown

Activity 10

Write down three reasons why you think a romantic relationship might begin to break down and compare your reasons with the findings below.

What happens if we find we cannot stick to the rules that Argyle discussed? What if we cannot keep the relationship in balance and no longer feel positive affect when communicating with our partner? We have seen how rule breaking can affect friendships, but let us now consider what happens when an intimate and loving relationship malfunctions.

There are a multitude of reasons why a relationship might begin to deteriorate which have been summarised by Baron and Byrne (1997):

- Most partners overestimate how much they agree and often do not realise how much their views differ even when communicating. This can lead to conflict if this realisation becomes apparent when problems occur.
- Partners who have the same responses to stress are more satisfied. This is often not the case as men tend to respond to a stressful situation by avoiding conflict rather than confronting it.
- Individual differences in the way people interact in terms of hostility, defensiveness and depression are important determinants of satisfaction in relationships. For example, those who are able to express their emotions are found to be happiest in their marriages.
- Jealousy is a common problem and sex differences are apparent with regards to this emotion. A man is most jealous when his partner is sexually unfaithful, but a woman is most jealous when her partner becomes emotionally involved with another person.
- Changes in attitudes or values can damage a relationship. As people develop and grow, they may change their mind about an issue which is of great importance to their partner, such as politics or religion, and this can detrimentally affect a long-term relationship.
- Important attitudes may not be apparent when two people first live together, but when they do surface, they may cause conflict.
- Relationships can simply become boring. Daily routines (including sexual patterns of behaviour) can lead either partner to believe himself or herself to be in a rut. If only one partner becomes bored the partners will each have different goals, leading to the possible breakdown of the relationship.
- Lack of sexual satisfaction can lead to disharmony and negative affect.
- Work-related issues can spill over into family life and vice versa. Sex differences can be noted here: women experience more positive affect when away from the home, whilst men feel happiest when in the home.

When a relationship does fail a significant amount of distress is felt by both partners. Particularly prevalent is a feeling of anger. This is justified when partners have put a great deal of time and commitment into making the relationship work. Men and women react differently at the end of a relationship: women seek the social support of their friends and confide in them whilst men look for a new relationship as soon as possible (Sorenson *et al.*, 1993).

Rusbult and Zembrodt (1983) suggested that there are two ways in which partners respond to an unhappy relationship. The first is an active response which can involve ending the relationship (exiting) or trying to improve it (voicing their concerns and plan of action, for example marital counselling). The second is a passive response which entails either waiting for improvement (loyalty) or waiting for the inevitable break up (neglect). Exit and neglect are the least constructive in terms of attempting to sustain the relationship whereas voicing concerns is the most constructive. Loyalty can be misinterpreted or remains unnoticed.

Duck (1988) has proposed a model which identifies four phases in the breakdown of a close relationship:

1 In the *intra-psychic* phase, one partner becomes increasingly dissatisfied with the relationship, although communication of this dissatisfaction to the partner may not go beyond hinting. If the dissatisfied partner concludes that the costs of relationship outweigh the benefits, then the second phase may begin.

2 When the second phase – the *dyadic* phase – is entered, the other partner in the relationship becomes involved, either through direct confrontation or through avoidance by the dissatisfied partner. At this stage, the partners may attempt to renegotiate the relationship or, alternatively, they may progress to the third phase.

3 The *social* phase is characterised by a working out of the possible social consequences of the breakdown in the relationship. Friends or relatives may be consulted in order to try to justifying leaving. If, however, the breakdown of the relationship can be considered inevitable, then the fourth and final phase is entered.

4 The final stage is the *grave-dressing* phase, in which the partners endeavour to get over the breakdown in their relationship. The former partners will tell their own social circles their own versions of events – this serves to provide a socially acceptable account of the relationship breakdown, and also helps to justify the original commitment made. In relation to this phase, Gray and Silver (1990) surveyed 45 couples who had been married for an average of ten years but had filed for divorce. Both men and women were equally likely to protect their self-esteem by providing their own perceived version of events which placed them in a more favourable light than their ex-partner. For example, when talking about the 'other woman' one couple described the situation as thus:
Man: 'I met another woman that I liked better than my spouse . . . My new wife is younger and better looking . . .'
Woman: '. . . a real bimbo . . . her elevator doesn't go quite to the top.'

Self-assessment questions

4 How have early attachment patterns been linked with later relationships?

5 Briefly summarise two of the theories of interpersonal relationships.

6 Suggest three strategies which might be used to sustain a loving relationship.

7 Give two rules that Argyle *et al.* (1985) found were important in most important relationships in the four cultures they investigated. What was considered to be the most important rule?

8 List three possible reasons why a relationship might break down. Support your answers with psychological research.

(Suggested answers on pages 169–78.)

The effects of interpersonal relationships on mental health and happiness

Why are relationships important? According to Argyle (1985), 'The answer is simple: they are good for us. If we have the right kind of social attachments we are likely to live longer, to have better physical and mental health and to feel happier'. Studies of positive life events, that is events that make people happy, have revealed that gaining a relationship was estimated to be a very positive social event (measured by asking a sample of respondents to rate a number of pleasant events on a scale from zero to 100, according to how much happiness, satisfaction or well-being they believed each would bring to most people). In a study involving over 100 000 people, Freedman (1978) found that for single women 'friends and social life' and 'being in love' were ranked as the events that gave greatest happiness. For single men, these events also ranked high in importance. For married men and women, 'friends and social life' were ranked at eight on the scale with 'being in love', 'marriage' and 'partner's happiness' receiving higher ratings. What this study suggests is that health and happiness are affected by social relationships.

Mental health

A simple definition of mental health is the absence of anxiety, depression or other symptoms commonly found in people admitted to psychiatric units. Such a definition is not very helpful in that it does not identify characteristics which people should possess in order for them to be considered healthy. A more positive definition of mental health has been suggested by Jahoda (1958):

'Success or adaptation in the areas of love, work, play, inter-personal relationships, situational requirements, ability to adapt and problem solving.' Because marriage, cohabitation and similar relationships are found to be most important, much of the research that has considered the link between mental health and social relationships has compared the widowed and the divorced/separated with the still married. Results of such research have found that the divorced and separated are more likely to suffer mental ill health or commit suicide (which is linked with depression) than the married (Argyle and Henderson, 1985). The effect is greater for men and is more for the divorced/separated. In addition, the consequences for the children from these broken alliances are negative long-term effects on their health and their lifespans (Friedman *et al.*, 1995).

Activity 11

Suggest possible explanations for the above findings.

One of the difficulties in interpreting the findings of research concerns the direction of the effect. Part of the explanation of this high rate for the separated and divorced could be that many of them get divorced because of these mental disturbances. However, single people, those who have never married, also have higher rates of mental disorder than the married. Again, one might argue that the lower rate of mental illness for the married is because they are less disturbed than the single in the first place. However, this is unlikely given that the widowed (and divorced) also have higher rates of mental illness than the single. Argyle believes that a more likely explanation is that marriage in some way provides protection against stress. Single people are more vulnerable to the effects of stress, partly because they are alone or if they do live with others such as parents, there is less social support provided and more conflict than most spouses. What these people are suffering from in the majority of cases is depression, one of the main causes of which is lack of a close relationship.

Many studies have found that there is a link between high stress, low social support and mental ill health. It seems that stress affects health when there is low social support. What is suggested is a **buffering hypothesis**, that is, social support comes into action when it is needed. There is quite a lot of support for such a hypothesis. In a study of working-class women in South London, Brown and Harris (1978) found that women who reported stressful experiences were likely to become clinically depressed. However, the effect was much reduced if the spouse acted as a confidant. It is the quality of the relationship which counts. More recently lack of support from a spouse or partner was found to be related to poor mental well-being, anxiety and depression among construction managers (Sutherland and Davidson, 1989). The number of days lost in the working world due to stress-related illnesses has risen exponentially since the early 1980s (Sutherland and Cooper, 1990). Whilst stress might be attributable to a number of factors, it is plain to see from stress scales that many of these factors can be attributable to problems concerned with relationships. For example, the Holmes and Rahe social readjustment rating scale (1967) lists several life changing events which cause stress and are concerned with relationships such as death of spouse, divorce, marriage, gain of new family member, trouble with boss and so on.

Studies of patients diagnosed as mentally ill have found that they are particularly short of family relationships rather than friends. Contact with siblings and other close kin are important since they are the main source of help in times of need. Disturbance in adolescence is associated with stressful life events and lack of support from the family.

In a similar vein, research has found that where friends are concerned, it is the quality not the quantity of social interactions, that is, the level of intimacy, amount of self-disclosure, pleasantness of contact and satisfaction derived, which is important. Neighbours and local organisations are regarded as the weakest kind of relationship, providing least in the way of benefits. However,

their role can in fact be underestimated. For the elderly, good contacts with neighbours and local organisations does in fact have some effect on mental health and well-being. Likewise, for members of ethnic minority groups interaction with and attachment to the neighbourhood can be important as a source of help.

Why is the buffering effect particularly due to such close relationships? Several explanations have been put forward. It seems that when people are in trouble and need help, it is usually only families and kin who are prepared to do this. Where emotional trouble is involved, it is only those in close family relationships in whom the person is willing to confide. Another explanation is that of simply being loved (an innate dependence on love and protection) derived from the first bond of attachment of infants with their mothers. A further explanation is that this kind of support increases self-esteem and feelings of mastery.

Activity 12

Think of three recent occasions when you have felt in need of help. To whom did you turn? Were these people helpful?

Some of these findings are complicated by the fact that mental disorder also predicts later lack of social support. Experiments have been carried out in which some patients have been given social support as a form of treatment. Results have been inconclusive reporting mixed success, possibly because the amount of support in some cases has been rather weak. It seems from the above that social support produces benefits for mental health. Most people when asked what action they take when feeling depressed say that they turn to others for help, sympathy and advice.

Recent research has produced even more complications. One study has shown that neurotic mental illness is due to the perception of social support as inadequate which in turn is related to a neurotic disposition (Henderson and Duncan-Jones. A study by Saracon and Saracon (1984) has shown that a rigid and authoritarian personality may be linked with a weak social network, and of course, depression, or other negative states may lead to a weakening of the social network. It must also be remembered that relationships with others are a source of costs as well as rewards and that social support can have negative consequences in the form of reducing self-reliance, distracting attention from tackling the problems which in itself can create worry and more stress.

Finally, other studies have found that social support has a direct effect even at low levels of stress, though the effects are weaker, for example a good social network may prevent certain events taking place such as strong support from work mates reducing hostility on the part of the boss.

Many studies in Britain, the USA and elsewhere have found higher rates of mental ill health among the working classes, one of which has already been discussed (Brown and Harris, 1978). The same researchers subsequently stated, in 1982, that they had found a threefold difference in depression rates between working-class women and their professional counterparts. Townsend *et al.* (1992) suggested that there is growing evidence that social isolation and poor social support (in terms of quality and quantity) provide the explanation for poor mental and physical health in working-class women and that a close or confiding relationship may protect health. These authors also point out that the unemployed suffer greater health problems and higher numbers of attempted suicides than the employed indicating the importance of work-based relationships which form an integral part of social networks. Indeed, studies which have investigated the health of people who have erratic working patterns have found that minor psychiatric illnesses were more prevalent in this group when unemployed than when they were employed.

Happiness

Research on happiness is relatively new in psychology. The concern here is the effect of relationships on happiness. Before looking at some of this research, we need to consider what happiness is.

> **Activity 13**
>
> What does happiness mean to you? Write three words you associate with the word 'happiness'.

Generally, if people are asked what they mean by happiness, they give two kinds of answer: (a) positive emotions such as joy, fun, euphoria (b) satisfaction and contentment with life as a whole. There are a number of problems connected with research into happiness. Do people give a truthful and accurate account of their levels of satisfaction? Reported satisfaction is found to vary a lot with the immediate situation. How can one be sure that respondents are not deceiving the interviewer or themselves when reporting their satisfaction? To quote one example, most people report very high levels of marital satisfaction, but then 35 per cent or more get divorced (Argyle, 1982).

Happiness is not simply the opposite of unhappiness, just as joy is not the opposite of depression. If this were so, then research into happiness would not be required, one would simply turn to the research on depression. As a result of a number of studies, research into happiness has identified the main components, loosely correlated with one another:

- the frequency of experience of joy and its intensity
- level of satisfaction with life as a whole
- the absence of depression, anxiety or other negative states.

The most common source of joy is being with friends. Spouses also cause each other joy, but the main effect is satisfaction rather than joy.

> **Activity 14**
>
> Which components of happiness do friends provide you with?

Several explanations have been advanced for joy in friendship: friends do things together such as going to parties, drinking, have a great deal of fun and laughter together, etc. These are all enjoyable activities requiring the cooperation of others. Friends also send positive non-verbal signals to one another, for example smiling, which is rewarding.

In looking at satisfaction, research has found that the spouse is by far the greatest source of satisfaction followed by close relations and friends. Many studies have confirmed the effects of marriage on happiness. As with mental health, studies have compared married and unmarried people of the same age both with and without children. Again married men and women are happier than the unmarried, especially couples without children. A study by Harding (1985) has found that women with children experience negative emotions such as boredom, aggression and loneliness. It is of course possible that it is happiness that causes marriage (happy people are found to be more attractive) but the effects of ending marriage by death, separation or divorce are very strong. Among the divorced and separated only 33 per cent say they are satisfied with life as a whole compared with 89 per cent of young married women without children. For men, the corresponding figures are 42 per cent and 72 per cent. Research into loneliness shows that people who report feeling lonely also feel unhappy, depressed, worthless and lacking in self-esteem. Feeling lonely is mainly due to lack of friends or other social attachments and is most common in adolescence. How can all these findings be explained? Argyle (1991) proposed that since humans are basically sociable and cooperative, cooperation has acquired rewards to motivate it. Losing a relationship denies those rewards and so life is felt as incomplete and less meaningful. Other relationships also contribute to satisfaction, for example friends, from shared interests and activities, kin, as sources of material help, and work mates as major sources of help and cooperation.

Relationships can be a source of stress and conflict. Marriage, as well as causing satisfaction, is the greatest source of conflict. Nevertheless, relationships continue to provide the greatest single source of happiness (Argyle, 1987).

Self-assessment questions

9 Define mental health and give two reasons why it might be affected by relationships.

10 Outline some empirical evidence which suggests that social support is of value in deterring mental health problems.

11 How is happiness implicated in the study of relationships?

(Suggested answers on page 170.)

Unit summary

■ Studies have found that human beings find it very difficult to remain alone for significant periods of time with no means of communication. One explanation for the need to *affiliate* with other human beings has been put forward by socio-biologists who state that we seek human contact in order to maintain evolutionary balance. External events, such as earthquakes, can also arouse our need to make contact with others and can involve an increase in cooperation between individuals and groups.

■ Apart from seeking mere human contact, we also decide who we like and dislike, and these positive and negative affects can be influenced by a number of factors which determine attraction. These determinants include *proximity, similarity, familiarity and physical attractiveness* and can often be combined to produce a longer lasting and more intense impact upon us.

Summary cont'd.

- Several theories have been put forward to explain the fundamental reasoning behind interpersonal relationships, most of which are based on a *reward-cost principle*. These theories include: the affect-centred model, social exchange/equity theory, balance theory and filter models and self-disclosure.

- *Childhood attachment* patterns have recently been investigated with regard to adult relationships. The link between these patterns and later relationships suggests that those experiencing *secure attachment* in infancy will later experience happy, satisfying and stable relationships. However, those experiencing *insecure-avoidant* and *resistant* attachment patterns in early childhood will have more difficulty in developing later relationships and may suffer more emotional upheaval and dysfunction in these later encounters.

- The successful *maintenance of relationships* has been found to rely on several strategies used by couples in order to combat problems they might encounter. Many maintenance strategies involve joint activities which appear to be used more by those who are engaged in long-term relationships. Factors which hinder healthy relationship maintenance in westernised societies today include changing economic patterns, the formation of untraditional family types and attitudes towards homosexual partners.

- Other factors involved in successful relationships have been found to involve their components such as rules, goals and conflicts. Breaking of rules and changes of goal posts can lead to *relationship breakdown*. Dissolution of relationships can occur for a number of reasons including differing stress responses in partners or simple boredom, and Duck (1988) suggested that there exist four stages of relationship breakdown which each couple experiences before 'moving on'.

- Most research appertaining to health and relationships has focused on comparisons of those people who are married and those who are not. The latter group has been found to suffer more mental ill health. The results suggest some ambiguity, for example do people get divorced because they suffer from mental distress or do people suffer from mental distress because they have been divorced?

- The *buffering hypothesis* suggests that there are lower instances of mental ill health in those that have a supportive spouse or social network who can help to protect them in times of stress. These findings lead us to the obvious conclusion that the happiest of us are those who develop and maintain satisfying and successful relationships.

Terms to define

affiliation
attraction
buffering effect/hypothesis
goals
interpersonal relationships
matching hypothesis

mere exposure hypothesis
proximity
rules
self-disclosure
social exchanges

Further reading

Argyle, M (1992) *The Social Psychology of Everyday Life*, Routledge, London.

An excellent primary source for an explanation of the components of relationships and their meaning.

Baron, R A and Byrne, D (1997) *Social Psychology*, 8th edn, Allyn & Bacon, Boston, MA, chapters 7 and 8.

An up-to-date American text which covers many of the topic areas discussed in this unit in an interesting, informative and 'easy to read' style.

Duck, S (1992) *Human Relationships*, 2nd edn, Sage, London.

Puts forward an enjoyable and clear account of human relationships as experienced in everyday life, with a strong focus on the role of communication.

Erwin, P (1993) *Friendship and Peer Relations in Children*, John Wiley, Chichester.

Child relationships are focused on in depth and many examples of empirical evidence are provided to support the text. Discusses issues related to social and cognitive aspects of peer relationships and their influence on later development.

Answers

▊ Suggested answers to activities

Base your answers on information in the text and your own ideas, as appropriate.

▊ Suggested answers to self-assessment questions

1

Firstly, Walster's participants were not in the position of having to try to get a partner and possibly being turned down. If a person fears rejection, they are perhaps more likely to be realistic in their desires in order to avoid this, and so ask for someone similar to themselves.
Walster's participants, however, were in the position of already having a desirable date and had to state if they would like to see the date again. They were not in a position of feeling threatened by possible rejection and so would, perhaps, be more likely to try to get the best deal they could.
Secondly, the participants were freshmen at university. In looking for partners, they were, perhaps, full of hope of getting their ideal partners, and were not prepared, at that early stage, to settle for something less than that ideal.

Finally, much prestige is gained from having an attractive partner. Perhaps prestige is more important than anything else to 18-year-olds starting university. Also, perhaps, it is more important to them than it is to older adults.

2

Refer to pages 143–9.

3

Possible studies could include:
▪ Festinger (1950) (see page 145)
▪ Schiffenbauer and Schiavo (1976) (see page 145)
▪ Zajonc (1968) (see page 146)
▪ Moreland and Beach (1992) (see page 146).

4

Securely attached children have been found to experience stable, satisfying relationships during later developmental periods. Those with insecure attachment patterns have been found to endure some problems with regard to the establishment and development of later relationships. Evidence cited: Erikson *et al.* (1985); LaFreniere and Sroufe (1985); Pastor (1981); Griffin and Bartholomew (1994) (see pages 154–156).

5

Theories of attraction include:
- Byrne's affect-centred model
- balance theory
- equity/social exchange theory
- filter models and self-disclosure.
 (See pages 149–54.)

6

Strategies could include the following:
- avoidance, balance, directness strategies (Ayres, 1983).
- joint activity strategies, tactics focusing on the relationship itself (Dindia and Baxter, 1987).
 (See pages 156–7.)

7

Relationship rules found to be most important in the four cultures were:
a should respect the other's privacy
b should look the other person in the eye during conversation
c should not discuss that which is said in confidence with the other person
d should not criticise the other person publicly.
The most important rule was (a).

8

Possible reasons for relationship breakdown include:
- loss or lack of positive affect (Byrne, 1992, see pages 150–1)

- lack of equity (equity theory, see page 152)
- imbalance (balance theory, see pages 152–4)
- lack of communication (self-disclosure, see page 154)
- insecure attachment patterns in early infancy (see pages 154–5)
- societal factors (see page 157)
- rule breaking (Argyle, see pages 160–1)
- see other reasons from Baron and Byrne on page 162.

9

For definitions of mental health, see page 164. Reasons why mental health might be affected by relationships:
a Marriage, cohabitation and other close relationships have been found to offer protection from mental ill health.
b Stress scales demonstrate that most causes of stress are concerned with relationship problems.
c The buffering hypothesis – it is not only close relationships that protect people from ill health but also the wider social network which includes work mates.

10

See pages 164–6.

11

The most common source of joy is being with friends.
Spouses offer the greatest source of satisfaction.
Therefore, without relationships people become unhappy and depressed (see pages 166–7).

Unit 6

Social Influence in Interaction

Penny Cortvriend, Tony Malim and Regina Teahan

This unit covers:

Social facilitation

Conformity, compliance and obedience

Social power

Leadership

By the end of this unit, you should be able to:

- understand theories of, and research into, coaction and audience effects
- evaluate studies on social influence, including norm formation, conformity and obedience to authority
- understand the relationships between power and social influence
- evaluate the concept of collective behaviour and crowd interaction
- understand research on the emergence and effectiveness of leaders and the importance of followership.

Unit 6 Contents

Introduction

It is a hot summer's day. The candidates for the job wait in an anteroom, getting hotter and more nervous as time passes. All wear suits and ties with shirt-collars buttoned up. No one wants to spoil the image by loosening a jacket or tie. It is a formal interview and formality is expected. Finally, one candidate can bear it no longer and takes the initiative. With a sigh of relief, the others follow the candidate's example and remove their jackets.

Why was it so hard to be the first to do what was after all a very sensible thing? What appeared to be necessary was for someone else to be the first – to *facilitate* the behaviour.

This unit endeavours to show that individuals seldom, if ever, operate alone without reference to others. A smoker's decision whether or not to light a cigarette at a social gathering may be determined by what other people are doing. If one acts as a leader and lights up, others may follow.

Conformity, compliance and obedience

Psychologists are interested in the influences which cause people to behave in particular ways. This section examines the way in which **norms** are set up within a social group. The behaviour of members of the group concerned will tend to conform to these norms, or at least they will be seen to comply with them if they are to remain members of the group. We also discuss the distinction between conformity and compliance, describing some of the better known studies in these areas. We then consider obedience to authority.

Norm formation

We can often predict how others will behave because we know they are likely to be influenced by the norms of the group to which they belong. For example, city workers would probably go to work in a suit, maybe also carrying an umbrella. Someone wearing jeans and a T-shirt would probably feel uncomfortable among them. Established norms govern not only clothing but also things like behaviour on trains and relationships with fellow-commuters. If the norm is to hide behind a newspaper and speak to no one there is great pressure to do the same, even though you may occupy the same seat on the same train for five days a week, 48 weeks in a year. Anyone trying to engage in small talk may find sanctions applied against them, for example glares of disapproval. Human behaviour is governed by a whole network of such norms and maintained by the processes of reward and punishment.

If a group is to stay together and remain a group, its members, whether or not they have deliberately elected to become members of that group, have to adhere to that group's norms. If not, the group will cease to provide the degree of predictability that ensures psychological protection for its members and will consequently disintegrate. The coherence of a group is determined by the extent of firmness with which members adhere to its norms. Members of exclusive clubs often establish a great range of norms, for instance which chairs to sit in. Some of these will be formally enshrined as rules, others will simply be the 'done thing', for example what topics are taboo over the dinner table. Where a group is less exclusive and less coherent, norms will be fewer and the sanctions against breaching them less rigorous. If, however, an individual will not conform to the norms, it becomes impossible to remain a group member.

Conformity

Conformity can be defined as the tendency to allow one's opinions, attitudes, actions and even perceptions to be affected by prevailing opinions, attitudes, actions and perceptions (Reber, 1985). The more conformity there is to group norms, the more a group will remain cohesive. It is in the interests of group members to retain the same norms because individuals who share these and who are group members have more security.

Mann (1969) described conformity as yielding to group pressures. Group members may yield to group norms because they are convinced the norms are good ones, or they may conform in order to avoid sanctions which the group may apply. In this case, group norms are openly accepted but have not been internalised and privately individual views are maintained. This is called **compliance** rather than conformity. Mann suggested three types of conformity (figure 6.1).

Non-conformity may also occur where individuals do not conform to group norms. This may be a deliberate statement of independence but carries a risk because non-conforming individuals are then exposed as different and therefore insecure. Alternatively, there may be **anti-conformity**, a rebellion against group norms for the sake of rebellion.

6.1 The forms of conformity suggested by Mann

Normative conformity
Yielding to threats of sanctions or to promises of reward to accept group norms. This may be true conformity, or compliance.

Informational conformity
WHEN individuals in novel situations are uncertain how to respond and look to those around them for a lead. What these say and do gives them clues for their own behaviour.

Ingratiational conformity
WHEN a person feels the need to impress or gain acceptance from a superior, thus conforming to the norms set by that superior. It is likely that in this case there is no identification with the superior, and so there is no internalisation of conformity. It is compliance only.

Activity 1

Without looking back, try to describe the difference between compliance and conformity. (If you have difficulty, re-read the section on conformity and compliance, above.)

■ Research on conformity

The *autokinetic effect* is an illusion of movement which occurs when a stationary pinpoint of light in a darkened room appears to move. Sherif (1935) brought participants individually into a darkened room and asked them to estimate the movement of such a light. Their judgements varied considerably, unsurprising in a situation where no movement actually took place. When tested in groups, however, estimates of movement began to converge to a compromise estimate. Each group produced different, group-unique estimates which were attributed to the influence of the individual group members making their judgements aloud in each other's company.

If you concluded that this was informational conformity you would have been right. The situation was novel (the light was not really moving

anyway) and in the absence of any other information they looked to each other's judgement for support and a lead.

This experiment could be criticised on the grounds that the experimental task is ambiguous (i.e. there is no correct or incorrect answer). Therefore it is hard to draw any firm conclusions from it about conformity.

Asch (1951) set up an experiment in which groups of six to nine people were seated either in a straight line or around a table. In each group there was one genuine participant and six to eight stooges (confederates of the experimenter) who had been primed beforehand what answer to give. The participants were shown cards (as in figure 6.2) and asked which of the three comparison lines was the same length as the standard line.

Answers were given verbally by each person, with the genuine participant answering last, or last but one, in each case. In 12 out of the 18 problems the stooges agreed beforehand with the experimenter to give the same wrong answer. On average, participants gave a conforming wrong answer about a third of the time. Seventy six per cent of participants went along with group answers at least once, thus conforming to a group norm

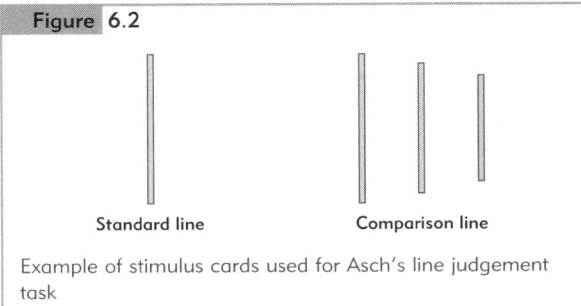

Figure 6.2

Standard line   Comparison line

Example of stimulus cards used for Asch's line judgement task

which had been established (despite the group answer being clearly incorrect). In contrast, less than five per cent of participants made errors in control trials where they were tested on their own.

In follow-up studies, Asch then attempted to isolate the factors which governed the extent of the conformity. (These are outlined in figure 6.3.)

A recent study by Baron *et al.* (1996) sought to investigate further the factor of task difficulty. These researchers hypothesised that social influence would be moderated by task difficulty whereby high task importance would result in lower social influence (or conformity) when the task was easy and higher social influence when the task was difficult. This 'conflict model' seeks to explain the conflicting pressures faced by people when exposed to social influences in different situations.

To test this hypothesis the researchers asked two groups of participants to view black ink drawings of male figures and the groups were told that they were involved in an eye witness ability task. Task difficulty was manipulated by the length of exposure of the drawings (that is, minimum exposure equalled high difficulty). Task importance was manipulated by telling participants in one group that their performance was a verified measure of eye witness ability and that those whose accuracy placed them in the top 12 per cent of scores would receive $20 (this was the high importance group). The other group of participants were told that this was a pilot study (low importance). There were also two control groups which did not contain confederates whose data was needed to measure error rates for the tasks and establish the effectiveness of the difficulty manipulation.

The results confirmed that when the task was easy, incentives for accuracy reduced conformity,

6.3 Factors governing strength of conformity (after Asch)

Task difficulty
When the comparison lines were nearly equal in length to the test lines, conformity was greater. This could have been informational conformity (following the lead given because of uncertainty).

Number of confederates
Asch systematically varied the number of confederates who deliberately gave wrong answers. With two confederates the conformity was greater than with one; and greater with three than with two. Beyond that, conformity remained the same. This suggests that it is unanimity of group responses which is the important factor rather than the actual number of confederates.

Unanimity of confederates
Even if just one confederate gave the right answer, the level of conformity dropped to minimal levels.

Decisiveness
This is an important factor. In some trials Asch arranged that one confederate at first answered correctly, as did the genuine participant. Then there was a change of mind; the confederate joining the majority in giving an incorrect response. Conformity rose to the same level as in the original experiment.

Status
Where stooges were regarded as being of high status, conformity was more likely.

Privacy
In some of Asch's trials the confederates were not brought face to face with the genuine participants, decisions were simply reported to them. In these cases, conformity was markedly lower.

i.e. participants did not agree with confederates. However, in a second, similar, study when the task difficulty was increased, individuals conformed more to inaccurate confederate decisions even when incentives for accuracy were high. This latter finding illustrates that when applied to real situations participants suffer conflict when faced with a difficult task. Stress is induced because of the difficulty of the task and the desire to remain independent because of high reward incentives, but, nevertheless, people give in to group norms and pressure even under these circumstances.

Asch's research has received a great deal of attention and some criticisms:

- Firstly, the distribution of responses was *positively skewed*, that is it did not follow a *normal distribution*. It would have been better in these circumstances to have used the *median* as the average rather than the mean. Using the median would have brought the level of conformity down to 25 per cent (Dobson *et al.*, 1981). If you do not understand these terms, turn to Unit 29 for guidance.

- Secondly, there was no question in these trials of the participants being able to reserve judgement, that is to say 'I'm not sure'. They had to decide immediately in favour of one answer or another. They could not ask advice or voice an opinion which they might have been able to do in real-life situations. Another important issue was the necessity to respond in public. To overcome this problem Deutsch and Gerard (1955) used partitions which shielded respondents from other participants. Conformity was lower than in Asch's study. Ross *et al.* (1976) suggested that participants did not want to appear stupid by responding differently from the others.

- Thirdly, the experiment has been criticised as rather trivial and therefore lacking validity. Who after all goes about judging the length of lines? Crutchfield (1954) attempted to meet some of these criticisms by designing a more realistic experiment. Participants included army officers who were taking part in a three-day assessment programme as part of their training. They worked in individual cubicles. Each participant was presented with a variety of tasks. A series of lights provided feedback on how others had supposedly responded to the tasks. In each case, the participants were led to believe that they were the last to respond.

Test materials used were much more varied than simply judging the length of lines. They included, besides Asch-type perceptual problems, statements of attitude such as 'I believe we are made better by the trials and hardships of life'. Thirty per cent disagreed with this statement when the lights indicated that four others also disagreed. In control conditions there was 100 per cent agreement. On the other tasks, the level of conformity varied, although it tended to be higher when the task was more difficult.

These key studies of conformity raise important issues. Conformity does not occur at the same level in all situations or in all people. In fact it is important to remember that in Asch's research 24 per cent of participants never conformed; many others conformed on only a few of the trials.

Activity 2

To what extent do you think the level of conformity in the experiments discussed here was a reflection of the experimental situation rather than of how things happen in everyday life?

Is conformity a negative trait or can it be positive?

The above experiments all involved the deliberate deception of participants. How would you feel if you had taken part in one of these experiments? Do you think the value of the knowledge obtained justifies the means? Discuss these questions with a group of friends and try to identify whether you are conforming or not in response to any influences.

■ Factors influencing conformity

Table 6.4 summarises various factors that can influence whether individuals conform or not, together with examples of supporting evidence.

Table 6.4

Factor	Supporting evidence	Level of conformity
The judgement or opinion issue is difficult	• Asch (1951) – when the distinction between length of lines was minimal, conformity increased. • Baron et al. (1996) – when task difficulty was high in an eye witness ability task, conformity increased (see page 175).	High
People face a unanimous group consensus	Asch (1956) – conformity rates dropped to under 10% when only one confederate disagreed with the majority.	High
Group size	Milgram et al. (1969) – groups of different numbers of confederates stood in the street and looked upwards. The percentage of passers-by who imitated the confederates increased as group size increased to five persons; the number imitating then levelled off.	High (when group size five or above)
Admiration of group/group cohesiveness (the degree of attraction felt by an individual toward an influencing group)	Crandall (1988) – female students who became friendly conformed more to 'other' behaviour, in this case binge-eating.	High
Personality	• Snyder (1979) – *High self-monitors* are keen to be accepted in every situation and control their behaviour accordingly. *Low self-monitors* like to be genuine and sincere, they present themselves as they really are. • Snyder and Fromkin (1980) – *desire for uniqueness (or individuation)*; people do not want to appear to be 'ordinary'. This includes people who feel they are unique anyway such as those from a minority group or redheads.	High Low Low
Being strongly committed to an initial viewpoint	Moscovici (1985) – studies on minority influence (see further discussion on pages 185–6).	Low

Factors affecting conformity

A further important factor which influences conforming behaviour is one which perhaps needs to be discussed in more detail in order to gain an understanding. This factor concerns the difference between norms, not in the sense of formal and informal norms but in the sense of descriptive and injunctive norms (Reno *et al.*, 1993). **Descriptive norms** are those which denote what most people do in a given situation. They tell us about what is generally effective or adaptive behaviour in a situation. **Injunctive norms**, on the other hand, tell us about what ought to be done, i.e. what is approved or disapproved of in a situation. Reno *et al.* believed that injunctive norms can influence behaviour more in certain situations because of the pressures put on individuals to do what is right. In

addition, people would rather behave in a manner which seems desirable to themselves – a kind of self-approval.

To investigate whether such norm differences occur in reality, Reno *et al.* (1993) designed a series of clever and interesting studies. People walking through a car park saw an accomplice of the researchers either dropping litter or picking litter up; the car park was either heavily littered or had been cleaned up by the researchers before the participants walked through the car park. These investigators measured the participants' tendency to drop litter by placing an advertising flyer on their windscreen. The researchers found that seeing a person drop litter activated a descriptive norm, i.e. the participants concerned would notice whether the car park was heavily littered or not, and if the car park was clean they would refrain from dropping litter. However, when the participants saw someone else picking up litter, an injunctive norm would be activated, i.e. they would think about what ought to be done and society's disapproval of litter bugging. In these cases the participants refrained from dropping litter whether the car park was clean or not. When applied to other situations it is easy to see that when people already behave in a pro-social manner, this behaviour can be reinforced by reminding people that others do indeed behave in this way (activation of descriptive norms). On the other hand, when people do not already behave in a pro-social manner, reminding people of how they *should* behave might be more effective (activation of injunctive norms).

Compliance

Compliance is a form of social influence that is perhaps used the most frequently. We all use different tactics in order to get others to do something for us. Compliance involves giving into another person, often on the basis of a direct request. However, its effects are seldom permanent. For example, some of the participants in Asch's studies admitted to giving an incorrect answer so that they did not 'spoil' the experiment and were not subject to derision from the rest of the group. However, their own private views did not change. So an individual might comply with another person or group of people in order to avoid conflict or mockery although this apparent change in perspective is not permanent to him or her.

Activity 3

Before reading on, list some of the tactics you think you use to get others to do things for you. Think about different people and different situations, for example borrowing money from parents or friends, or asking for help on an assignment from fellow students, colleagues or tutors.

Outlined briefly below are some of the most commonly used strategies for inducing compliance in others.

■ Ingratiation

This technique involves getting another person to like you before changing his or her behaviour or viewpoint to fit in with your preferred outcome. It can involve the following strategies:

- *Self-enhancing tactics* – these include impression management techniques such as improving our appearance, non-verbal cues such as smiling, and making known to the other person our association with people or events.
- *Other-enhancing tactics* – these include flattery, doing favours for the other person, bestowing gifts, listening and showing an interest in the other person and agreeing with him or her.

■ The 'foot-in-the-door' technique

This is a tactic often used by salespersons, fundraisers and advertisers. It involves making, initially, a small, inconsequential request before moving on to what the person really wants. This tactic plays on the premise of the need to be consistent in individuals. Once a person has agreed to a small request he or she does not like to be seen to be indecisive or unhelpful and so is more likely to then agree to the second, usually more costly, request.

Supporting evidence for this technique came from a famous study by Freedman and Fraser in 1966. One member of the research team telephoned participants, explaining that he was a member of a consumer's group, and asked them a few questions about the kinds of soap they used. A few days later he telephoned the participants again asking them if they would mind if a group of people visited them to conduct a two-hour inventory of the products in their home. Results confirmed that 52.8 per cent of these participants agreed to the second, larger, request compared with only 22.2 per cent of those who were asked to comply with the larger request 'cold'.

Another technique related to the foot-in-the-door approach is the *lowball procedure*. This is often used by car salespersons when they initially offer an excellent deal to a customer but after the customer's acceptance something happens which makes the deal less attractive, such as an error in calculations by the salesperson. It is usually the case that the customer will still accept the deal.

Finally, Cialdini (1994) has identified the *bait-and-switch tactic*. An example of this tactic might be a retailer who advertises a bargain. However, when the customer reaches the retail outlet the product offered has either sold out or is of inferior quality. In this case the customer will still buy a more expensive, but similar, item. Because the customer has exerted a great deal of effort in travelling to the shop, having already made a commitment to buying the item, he or she feels it would be too difficult to change his or her initial course of action.

■ Tactics based on mutuality or reciprocity

The following techniques are based on the premise that when someone does something for us we usually feel obliged to return the favour.

■ The *door-in-the-face technique* could be described as being the opposite of the foot-in-the-door technique. In these instances people start with an unusually large request and after its expected rejection (the door-in-the-face), make a much smaller request which is often acceptable and the one the requester wanted compliance with all along.

■ The *that's-not-all technique* is another technique often used by car salespersons when the salesperson feels the buyer is very close to agreeing to the terms offered on a sale. In this case the salesperson will offer an added extra incentive before the buyer has time to say 'yes' or 'no' such as free petrol for a limited time period.

■ The *foot-in-the-mouth technique* relies heavily on forming a link or relationship (however tenuous) between the 'salesperson' and the 'buyer'. If the 'buyer' can sense some kind of mutual relationship between himself or herself and the 'salesperson', he or she will be more willing to show consideration for that person and so want to help him or her. This tactic was shown to be effective by Aune and Basil (1994). They asked a female confederate to act as fund-raiser on a college campus. In the control condition they just asked participants (passers-by) to contribute to a well-known charity. In another condition they asked participants if they were students and then said, 'Oh, that's great, so am I.' After this comment they asked for funds for the charity. When a tenuous relationship was established in the latter condition, 25.5 per cent of participants donated, compared to only 9.8 per cent in the control condition.

After working in several professions that might use the above tactics (and others), Cialdini (1994) suggested that compliance rests on the following six basic principles which can be identified in some of the tactics described above:

1 *Friendship or liking* – we are more willing to comply with friends or people we like than strangers or those we dislike.

2 *Commitment/consistency* – once committed to a course of action, we wish to remain consistent with our initial position and are therefore more willing to comply with requests consistent with that commitment.

3 *Scarcity* – we like to secure opportunities that are rare or decreasing; we are therefore more likely to comply when made aware of this factor.

4 *Reciprocity* – we are more likely to comply when we feel obligated to return a favour or someone has previously offered us a concession.

5 *Social validation* – if we believe that persons similar to ourselves will take a course of action, then we will do the same because we want to be correct and one way of validating our behaviour is to compare it with others.

6 *Authority* – we value authority and will comply with requests from a legitimate authority or someone whom we believe or perceive to be legitimate.

Obedience to authority

We saw above that the sixth principle underlying compliance, according to Cialdini, is 'authority'. It is to this principle that we now turn our attention as we begin to focus on 'obedience'.

Obedience may be defined as complying to the rules set by a recognised authority, which may impose sanctions for disobedience. Although obedience is considered by many people to be desirable, it was used at Nazi war crimes trials as a justification for genocide. In Vietnam, the massacre of a whole village at Mi Lai was claimed by its perpetrator to have resulted from obeying orders.

■ Research on obedience to authority

Milgram (1963) was interested in this sort of tragic event in human history, and set out to determine the level of obedience people tend to give to a powerful authority figure. He recruited male participants through advertisements offering payment of $4.50 to take part in an experiment on what he claimed was a study of memory and learning. This was in fact a deception. Participants were introduced to the experimenter, who was wearing a white coat, and to a confederate who was introduced as another participant. The experimenter explained that the investigation was on the effects of punishment on learning and that lots would be drawn as to which of them would take the part of a 'learner' and which the part of 'teacher' in the experiment. In fact, the drawing of lots was rigged and the confederate was always assigned the role of 'learner'.

The 'learner' and the 'teacher' were seated in adjoining rooms, the 'learner' being strapped into a chair and attached to electrodes. An impressive machine purported to generate electric shocks between 15 and 450 volts, but unknown to the participant this did no such thing. On Milgram's instruction, the participant was asked to administer shocks of increasing severity to the 'learner' every time he or she failed to produce a correct response to a question.

In one of a series of experiments, the 'learner' was heard crying out in pain and asking to be released as the 'shocks' increased in severity. If participants expressed doubts about continuing, the 'teacher' was simply told that the experiment must continue. Most participants did continue, even though some expressed the view that something bad must have happened. At 330 volts, the administration of the shock resulted in silence from the next room. It seemed the learner had collapsed, but still the participant was instructed to continue.

Prior to the experiment a group of staff at Yale University had estimated that only 0.1 per cent of the participants would continue to 450 volts; in fact, 65 per cent did. Many of these participants experienced considerable discomfort, three even had uncontrollable seizures.

Participants were debriefed after the experiment, told its real purpose and that the 'learner' was in fact an actor. Interviews also tried to ascertain why obedience levels were so high. As a result, several variations on the original experiment were carried out:

■ To test the effect of the experimenter's proximity to the participant three conditions were used:
- the original condition with the experimenter only a few metres away
- a condition where the experimenter was present at first, then left the room and gave instructions by phone
- a condition where the experimenter was absent, but left instructions on a tape recording.

It was found that the level of obedience was almost three times greater in the original condition than in the one where the experimenter was absent.

■ To test the effect of 'learner' proximity to the participant there were again three conditions studied:
- the original condition with the learner in an adjoining room
- a condition where the learner was only 45 centimetres away and the participants could see and hear the results of the shocks (40 per cent still completed the trial)
- a condition where the participant had to hold the learner's hand on to a plate to receive the shock (even in this condition 30 per cent still obeyed).

■ There was also a variation where the participant had two 'partners' (confederates) who also had to administer shocks to the 'learners' and who withdrew halfway through. Ninety per cent of the participants also withdrew at this point.

Why do people obey?

Milgram believed that the experimenter's position of legitimate authority was an important factor. When the experimenter was absent and participants had to take responsibility for their own actions, obedience was markedly lower. Status seemed to be important, not only the status of Milgram himself in his white coat but also the prestige of the institution, Yale University itself. Further studies were carried out in a run-down building in a poor part of town. Obedience was found to be less, but at 47.5 per cent still significant.

In 1973 Milgram developed a theory to explain why usually independent and self-determining people obeyed others even when they consciously believed their actions to be wrong. He proposed that we have two modes of social consciousness which have evolved from living in a predominantly hierarchical society:

- the **autonomous state** – whilst in this state of consciousness individuals act according to their own values and ideals. Therefore, people in this state behave honestly, pro-socially and compassionately.
- the **agentic state** – whilst in this state, in contrast to the autonomous state, individuals see themselves acting as agents on behalf of someone else, the person in authority. Therefore, in this state pro-social qualities are suppressed and people will begin to behave aggressively, dishonestly and anti-socially.

Milgram believed that suppression of the autonomous state results in lack of hostility and competition, thus ensuring leaders are not continuously threatened. In addition, the agentic state can become internalised which results in greater control, for example parental authority can result in children internalising the need for obedience so that disobedience becomes a difficult course of action. One of the most important consequences of moving into an agentic state is that people feel they are no longer responsible for their actions; they can place the blame on those in higher authority and are therefore 'let off the hook', so to speak (Hayes, 1993).

Criticisms of Milgram

Milgram's experiments have attracted a great deal of comment and criticism. Baumrind (1964) criticised them on the grounds of ethics and generality. The ethics of the experiments are doubtful; participants were deceived as to the purpose of the research and many experienced extreme trauma. Milgram's justification was that participants were fully debriefed afterwards and so should not suffer any lasting harm. In any case, he thought that the resulting insights gained into human nature justified any disturbance caused. Whether it is possible to accept that the ends justify the means must remain doubtful.

Activity 4

Write down your own thoughts about the ethical implications of Milgram's experiment.

The study was also thought to be of questionable generality. Could the disturbing findings really be generalised to real-life situations? There does seem to be evidence that ordinary people are prepared to do things when obeying authority that they would never do otherwise, for example think about the Tiananmen Square demonstration in 1989 and the alleged killings of their own people in Iraq by Saddam Hussein's followers during the Gulf War.

It was also claimed that the participants were an unrepresentative sample, being paid volunteers (who are known to exhibit special characteristics). *Demand characteristics* may also have played a part: these are the tendency for participants to act in particular ways as a result of the research situation.

Activity 5

Given the ethical issues which arose with the original investigation, do you think the follow-up studies can be justified?

A more realistic study of obedience was carried out by Hofling *et al.* (1966). Nurses in a hospital were instructed by a 'doctor' over the telephone to administer 20 mg of the drug Astrofen to a patient, Mr Jones. The doctor would be up in 10 minutes to see the patient and sign for the drug. In fact, both doctor and patient were confederates of the experimenter. Administering the drug would break several rules:

- Nurses were not allowed to administer drugs except on a doctor's *written instructions*.
- A check must be made on a doctor's authenticity.
- The maximum prescribed dose for Astrofen, written on the bottle, was 10 mg.

Despite these rules 21 out of 22 nurses showed themselves willing to comply with the telephoned request.

It might be argued that nurses in a hospital context are atypical of the population but it still suggests a great willingness to obey orders.

Rebellion against authority

One study, which was performed much later than Milgram's, found that rebellion does occur in some cases. Gamson *et al.* (1982) told volunteers that they were participating in a market research project concerning community standards and legal cases. They were asked to discuss in groups of about nine people the case of a man who was suing a company for terminating his franchise on a garage because he was cohabiting with someone. Throughout the group debate the experimenters would enter the room and ask the participants to argue the case in a certain way, for example they might ask three individuals to argue the case as if they were offended by the man's behaviour. Eventually, participants were asked to sign a legal document stating that they would allow videotapes of the discussions to be used as evidence in court and that the tapes could be edited by the company being sued as they saw fit. During this procedure the participants gradually realised that they were being manipulated. Because of this realisation, only one out of 33 groups continued until the end of the procedure. There were differences between the groups as to how far they went along with the

manipulation. Those who had expressed anti-authoritarian attitudes when completing a pre-experimental questionnaire rebelled earlier, whilst those who expressed pro-authoritarian attitudes conflicted enough with the other group members to sign the legal document.

There were some important differences between this and previous studies, for example the fact that the participants were in groups as opposed to acting alone and therefore more support was available. In addition, as mentioned above, the study took place at a much later time historically than Milgram's and so people may have been more aware of the effects of obedience (Hayes, 1993). It is to the question of time and place that the next section of this unit turns its focus.

The socio-cultural perspective on conformity and obedience

Milgram's theory of the autonomous and agentic states (explained on page 181) proposes that these states are of evolutionary origin, that we have adapted to these means of behaviour due to our ancestral hierarchical history. Hayes (1995) argued that there are several things wrong with this theory, one being that, in fact, social hierarchies are not as usual as Milgram believed at the time of propounding his theory. Subsequent research has suggested that dominance hierarchies are quite rare (Appleby, 1985).

In addition, Milgram described the behaviour of those participants in his study who refused to obey, but does not actually do much to explain it; he just says they were in 'autonomous mode'. Hayes suggested that this is a gross oversimplification as these participants were willing to cooperate where other parts of the experiment were concerned. It was only when they were asked to administer painful shocks that they discontinued.

Finally, Hayes criticised the research on the basis of it being interpreted in purely individualistic terms. That is, Milgram did not take into account the power relations that exist within a complex society. The example that Hayes used to explain this criticism is that of soldiers who refuse to obey orders. If orders were disobeyed, the soldiers would be subject to army discipline which, in the main, members of society would probably take for granted, even if members of that society thought the soldiers were right to disobey. Army discipline is in place to stop soldiers disobeying in order that they become more frightened of this course of action than killing other people. What is clear from these arguments is that all research takes place at a certain stage and place in time when there exist differing social, economic, cultural and political values from other times. These are arguments which are put forward by the new wave of European social psychologists who battle against the old traditional (often American) form of social psychology.

Obedience studies undertaken in different countries, and therefore different cultures, offer a surface view that suggests there are variations in the number of people willing to obey in these cultures. Table 6.5 shows the percentage of participants who administered shocks up to the highest level of volts (450) under Milgram's 'baseline' experimental condition.

This table serves to show how difficult it is to exactly replicate another piece of research and draw comparative conclusions and generalities from several studies. There are a number of factors which make this problematical which are discussed by Humphreys (1994). For example, notice the types of subject samples used; Milgram found no sex differences in 1963, but would differences have been found in the later studies (Schurz, 1985; Meeus and Raaijmakers, 1986) when societal changes might have induced differences between the behaviour of the sexes? Also, the 'victims' in the studies were sometimes different. In the Australian study the victim was a long-haired student; in other studies the victim was dressed smartly in a business suit. In Milgram's study the victim was male but in the Australian scenario both 'victim' and 'teacher' were female. The Dutch experiment did not use electric shocks as a variable but instead the participant was instructed to badger and criticise a person completing a job application form. These differences serve to inform us of the different social contexts that individuals function in and their differing views towards authority figures and the meaning of obedience.

When focusing on conformity, Smith and Bond remind us that Friend et al. (1990) studied over 99 American social psychology texts and found 'an increasing trend over time to concentrate upon the fact that one third of the judgements were erroneous, and to use this as evidence of how widespread is the process of conformity in society' (Smith and Bond, 1993, p. 17). This is the opposite of what Asch himself attempted with success to

Table 6.5			
Study	Country	Subjects	Percentage obedient
Milgram (1963)	USA	Male general population	65
		Female general population	65
Rosenhan (in Milgram, 1974)	USA	Students	85
Ancona and Pareyson (1968)	Italy	Students	85
Mantell (1971)	Germany	Male general population	85
Kilham and Mann (1974)	Australia	Male students	40
		Female students	16
Burley and McGuiness (1977)	UK	Male students	50
Shanab and Yahya (1978)	Jordan	Students	62
Miranda et al. (1981)	Spain	Students	over 90
Schurz (1985)	Austria	General population	80
Meeus and Raaijmakers (1986)	Holland	General population	92

Studies of destructive obedience to authority (from Smith and Bond, 1993)

demonstrate: that most judgements were in fact correct and individuals did not tend to conform. Is a 37 per cent conformity rate to be considered high? Perhaps it has been interpreted as being high by American text authors as the individualistic American culture values independence. Any conformity rate above 10 per cent, therefore, might be construed as being high in this cultural context. In a collectivist culture the perspective might be somewhat different.

Independence and minority influence

■ Independence

If conformity is yielding to group pressure, what is the opposite?

Many think in terms of 'non-conformity' without reflecting on two different types of opposing non-conformity responses: **independence** and **anti-conformity**. Independence is the maintenance of expressions of behaviour without regard to group norms, i.e. the person does his or her own thing. In contrast, in anti-conformity the individual is opposed to the majority on all occasions. Such a person is not really independent at all but just as dependent on the group as the conformer. The only difference is that the conformer feels obliged to follow the group whilst the 'rebel' goes against it. In both cases it is the group which is determining the individual's behaviour. Clearly two people may behave in the same way by non-conforming but may in fact reflect different motives.

Activity 6

Give examples of non-conformity demonstrated by you. What were the motives in each case? Separate your examples into 'independent' and 'anti-conformity'.

Between 1950 and 1953 during the Korean War, approximately 3600 American soldiers were captured by the North Korean and Communist Chinese forces and imprisoned in China. Whilst in prison they were subjected to constant pressure to change their attitudes and behaviour and collaborate with the Chinese. Most of the prisoners of war did not collaborate with their Communist Chinese captors and two types of resisters were identified, i.e. soldiers who did not give in (Schein, 1957; Kinkhead, 1959):

■ The first group was characterised by a long history of unwillingness to accept any kind of authority. Soldiers in this group had not conformed to commands in the American Army and neither were they prepared to obey their Chinese captors. This group of individuals would be classified as anti-conformists.

■ The second group felt it would be wrong to collaborate with the enemy. These prisoners held to the standards they believed in. This is an example of independence: behaviour which ignores group pressures and norms. Throughout history there are many examples of people who have not obeyed orders or conformed to ideas they believed to be misguided or immoral. Sometimes they have even resisted them, for example the Quakers and other white abolitionists believed in the inherent evil of slavery and risked their lives to help African–Americans escape their captors before the American Civil War. Deeply held moral values and personal feelings for the victims motivated some gentiles to rescue Jews during the Holocaust (Fogelman, 1994). Thus one reason why people are willing to take independent action is in part a matter of personal belief and conscience. In the Milgram study, the people who were unwilling to give high levels of shock took responsibility for their actions and refused to continue to obey orders as a matter of conscience or principle. A 32-year-old engineer is reported to have said,

'One of the things I think is very cowardly is to try and shove the responsibility onto someone else. See, if I now turned round and said "It's your fault . . . it's not mine". I would call that cowardly' (Milgram, 1974).

The use of the terms 'conformist', 'anti-conformist' and 'independent' seems to suggest we can classify people into these categories, thereby implying that a person who conforms in one situation will conform in all other situations. Research in this area has found that the conforming personality is not so easily pinned down. Crutchfield (1955), in studying a group of businessmen and military officers, did report that independent subjects showed more intellectual effectiveness, ego, strength, leadership ability and maturity of social relations together with an absence of inferiority feelings, rigid and excessive self-control and authoritarian attitudes. However, the consistency of conformity behaviour across a wide variety of situations has been much less impressive, and the search for a single conforming type of person has proved futile. What research has in fact demonstrated is that situational factors are of importance in eliciting conformity behaviour or otherwise. According to Willis, whether our response in one situation is conformist, independent, or anti-conformist will depend largely on our perception of the situation. According to evidence from many fields and laboratory studies, there are a number of situational factors that predict independent behaviour:

- The individual *has an ally*. In Asch's experiment the presence of one other person who did not go along with the group's opinion was enough to overcome conformity. In Milgram's experiment, the presence of a peer who disobeyed the authority figure enabled participants to do what they thought was right rather than obey instructions.

- The individual *weighs the costs* of getting involved as opposed to going along with the group. The cost of protesting might be embarrassment and wasted time, lost income and friends, even personal danger. The cost of remaining silent might be guilt, blame from others, loss of honour, even responsibility for the injury or death of others. Three courageous individuals from Rockwell International tried to inform NASA that the space shuttle Challenger was not safe, but the authorities remained silent. No one was prepared to take responsibility for the costly decision to postpone the launch.

- The individual *feels competent*. People who remain independent feel they have the skills and knowledge to do so. Perrin and Spencer (1980) when involving mathematics, engineering and science students as participants, found conformity on only one trial out of 396. This result can be

explained partly by independence based on confidence that their perceptions were correct.

Thus there are social conditions that make individual protest more likely to occur.

■ The minority influence

It is clear from the above section that a group can contain one or more 'social deviants', individuals who will stand their ground for whatever reason. The French social psychologist Moscovici was interested in questioning whether this one 'social deviant' or a small minority in a group could exert any influence on the rest of the group. Does the majority always rule? The answer, apparently, is no. This is obvious when we think about historical figures who have persuaded a large and often antagonistic majority to come round to their theoretical perspective, such as Darwin or Freud. Other minority examples include environmentalists who first alerted us to holes in the ozone layer, but when they first expounded their views the majority of people saw them as radicals.

Moscovici (1976) undertook a number of studies to determine whether a minority influence had any impact within a group, i.e. could they persuade the rest of the group to come round to their way of thinking. In 1969 Moscovici *et al.* conducted an experiment which was, in essence, a reversal of the Asch experiments. Participants in this experiment were initially tested for colour blindness and then shown 36 slides which were all blue although differing in intensity. The participants were asked to say aloud the colour they saw on the slides. Two of the participants were confederates seated in the first and second or first and fourth position. In the 'consistent condition' these participants stated that they saw green on all trials. In the 'inconsistent condition' they stated that they saw green 24 times and blue 12 times. There was also a control condition containing no confederates. In the latter condition only 0.25 per cent of the responses given were 'green'. In the inconsistent minority condition 1.25 per cent of responses were 'green', but in the consistent condition this percentage was significantly different at 8.42.

This study differs from the Asch studies because there existed a minority of two and a majority of two, whereas in the Asch studies there existed a minority of one and a majority of six. Moscovici *et al*.'s study therefore demonstrates that when one member of the majority moves over to the minority camp, this highlights to other group members that the minority may have a point worth considering and so a tendency might appear to follow this opinion.

Further research suggests that certain conditions must be met in order for the minority to succeed in swaying other group members:

- The minority must be *consistent* in their approach; if they show signs of giving into the minority their position will be damaged.
- Members of the minority must demonstrate some *flexibility* and not be seen to be rigid in their views.
- The minority will be more successful in changing the majority perspective if it is *in line with current social trends*, for example liberal views at a time of growing liberalism.

Research by Nemeth (1986) has found that when people first hear minority views that may sound quite ludicrous, they may take more note because they have to use cognitive processes in order to understand where these people 'are coming from'. People therefore scrutinise carefully what the minority is saying. Once they have exerted this effort they sometimes realise that the minority actually makes sense. Baker and Petty (1994), in an attempt to investigate this possibility in more depth, found that in fact individuals do not automatically give more attention to minorities or majorities. The recipients' end viewpoint is dependent on the source and the message when deciding which side to take. When the source and the message are surprising, people spend more effort in scrutinising the message which could be an explanation of why people take notice of minority perspectives since their views and opinions are quite often surprising to us.

Self-assessment questions

1 List some of the factors and their effects which appeared to influence the level of conformity in Asch's studies.

2 With reference to Milgram's work, make a table of the factors which influenced the level of obedience to authority, and their effects.

3 Make a table of factors associated with independent behaviour. Divide the table into situational factors and dispositional factors.

(Suggested answers on page 203)

Social power

Collins and Raven (1969) saw *social power* as the way in which a person exercises influence over someone else. This influence involves some change in a person's cognition, behaviour or emotional state. This power could be any one of six kinds (see figure 6.6).

Research on social power

An illustration of the exercise of power and its effects on the individuals concerned is contained in a study by Zimbardo (1973). Twenty-five participants (all exclusively tested to ascertain their suitability, particularly in terms of emotional stability) were recruited from about 100 volunteer applicants. The study was carried out as a simulation of a prison. Participants were assigned to the roles of either prisoner or guard by tossing a coin. A generous fee was paid. The experiment is outlined in figure 6.7.

Was it all worth it? Two points may be made. First, it attracted sufficient publicity to provide a focus for criticism of the existing prison system. There were, however, departures from actual prison procedures which made the research less useful than it could have been. Second, there was

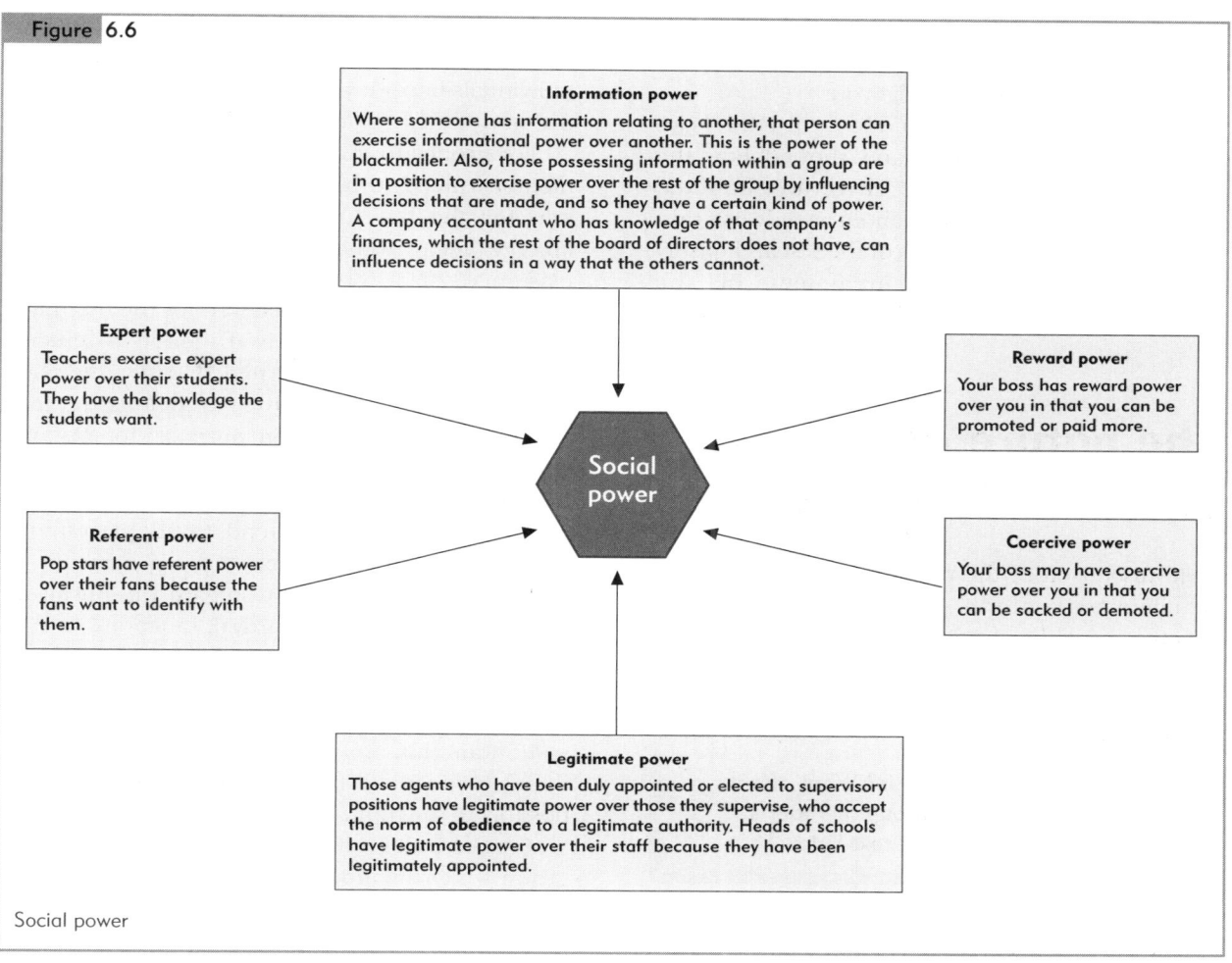

Figure 6.6

Information power

Where someone has information relating to another, that person can exercise informational power over another. This is the power of the blackmailer. Also, those possessing information within a group are in a position to exercise power over the rest of the group by influencing decisions that are made, and so they have a certain kind of power. A company accountant who has knowledge of that company's finances, which the rest of the board of directors does not have, can influence decisions in a way that the others cannot.

Expert power

Teachers exercise expert power over their students. They have the knowledge the students want.

Reward power

Your boss has reward power over you in that you can be promoted or paid more.

Referent power

Pop stars have referent power over their fans because the fans want to identify with them.

Coercive power

Your boss may have coercive power over you in that you can be sacked or demoted.

Social power

Legitimate power

Those agents who have been duly appointed or elected to supervisory positions have legitimate power over those they supervise, who accept the norm of **obedience** to a legitimate authority. Heads of schools have legitimate power over their staff because they have been legitimately appointed.

Social power

6.7 The Stanford prison experiment (Zimbardo, 1973)

At the beginning of the experiment the prisoners were 'arrested' and charged with felony. They were often made to go through all the degrading procedures that accompany arrest – strip searching, delousing, being given a prison uniform and even a manacle on one ankle.

The guards wore military-style uniforms, reflective sunglasses to prevent eye contact and carried whistles, clubs, handcuffs and keys. They were allowed to shout at the prisoners and push them about if requests were not complied with quickly enough, but other physical contact was not permitted. Whilst the prisoners were locked up round the clock, the guards worked eight-hour shifts.

Soon the relationship which developed between the prisoners and guards became distorted. The guards became more aggressive, the prisoners more passive. Within 36 hours one prisoner had to be released because he had broken down and was suffering symptoms of depression. Other prisoners developed symptoms of stress, and the whole experiment, scheduled to last a fortnight, had to be aborted in six days.

no attempt made to separate out those aspects of the situation which had the greatest effect. The analysis was not sufficiently rigorous.

This study did uncover hidden evil tendencies in ordinary human beings and showed how the exercise of power corrupts. There are, however, ethical questions to be asked about a study like this. For instance, do the purposes of the research justify the humiliation and maltreatment of the participants?

The nature of groups and their formation

From discussion of the pressures placed on group members to conform, we now turn to group structure and the dynamics of how groups form and evolve.

Activity 7

What do you think a group is? What effect does a group have on a group member's behaviour? (Answers in the text below.)

Before answering these questions, we consider the differences in interaction between small or large groups meeting together. For example, a group of two people may have a fairly limited range of interaction, whereas a group of 30 people may have even less or none at all. In this latter case, the scope that exists for each group member to communicate with all the others is limited and communication is likely to be one-way; for example a leader or manager telling others what they need to know.

Do six people waiting for a bus constitute a group? They might, but only if the bus is delayed or if something happens whilst they are waiting to unite them into a group. Otherwise there will probably be little interaction and they will remain a collection of individuals.

Bales (1950) suggested that provided each group member receives some impression of every other member that is sufficiently distinct for them to allow personalised reactions, then a collection of individuals becomes a group. This implies a group size of not more than 12.

For groups to form, *interactions* between group members need to be sustained. If there is a long wait for the bus to arrive then a group might emerge. There also has to be some *perception* of the existence of a group and of the members belonging to it. A prolonged wait for the bus might allow some kind of perceived identity to emerge among the people concerned. Usually, members already perceive themselves as belonging to a group owing to a common purpose; for instance people meeting to plan action against a proposed library closure.

Members of a group tend to adopt common norms of behaviour, which may or may not be expressed. Members who disregard the norms lay themselves open to disapproval, sanctions or even removal from the group. In the library example mentioned above, the protesters may provide a roster for a sit-in at the library. The norm would be to honour this. Any members who failed to take their turn would be open to disapproval and possibly to sanction.

Certain roles will tend to develop within the group which members will adopt, either formally or informally, for example chair, food preparer or joker. Patterns of liking and disliking will emerge among group members. These are known as *affective relations*. Each relationship will develop its own set of norms.

A group needs to have *shared goals* before it forms or remains a group. These goals may be either internally or externally set; even in the latter case they will be open to interpretation and re-interpretation. Additional goals may be generated in accordance with group norms, as these develop.

There are clearly many kinds of group. It is a pity that so many reported studies are based on laboratory groups, brought together only for study purposes. Out of 2000 studies reported by McGrath and Altman (1966), only 5 per cent could be said to have been carried out on naturally formed groups in natural settings.

Cohesiveness

Why do group members stick together and what binds them in the first place? It seems obvious that group members who like each other, who are seeking common goals and find satisfaction from being a member of that particular group, will be more 'cohesive' than if these requirements were not met. On the surface, then, it might appear that just liking other group members leads to cohesiveness, but Hogg and Haines (1996) have found that cohesiveness actually involves what they term 'depersonalised attraction', i.e. liking other group members simply because they belong to the group and represent that particular group's main characteristics.

The cohesiveness of groups used to be measured in terms of 'high' or 'low', but more recently its measurement has developed into something more complex. Cohesiveness ranges along two primary dimensions:

- *task–social* – this relates to how far group members are committed to the goals of the group (task) or the social relationships in the groups (social)
- *individual–group* – this dimension refers to how far group members are committed to the group or other members of the group.

Apart from these primary dimensions, there also exist secondary dimensions such as those relating to different kinds of groups. For example, military groups may be bound together by status with higher-ranking individuals having higher cohesiveness than the lower ranks (Cota *et al.*, 1995).

Group structure

Within a group there are several well-defined structures which may be either formal or informal:

- An *affective structure* governs the patterns of likes and dislikes within a group.
- A *communication structure* governs the patterns of communication that exist.
- A *power structure* might be considered in terms of the individuals in the group and their positions within it.

Affective structures within groups

Affective structures have been examined by *sociograms*. Individual group members are asked questions such as, 'Whom among the members of the group do you most enjoy working with?' The results are then mapped, as in figure 3.8.

This is a very simplified example of how a sociogram might highlight the affective relationships within a group. It is possible to see who the most popular individuals are, who the odd one out is and where sub-groups are emerging even within the group.

> ### Activity 8
> Try to identify the popular individuals from figure 6.8.
> (Answers in the text below)

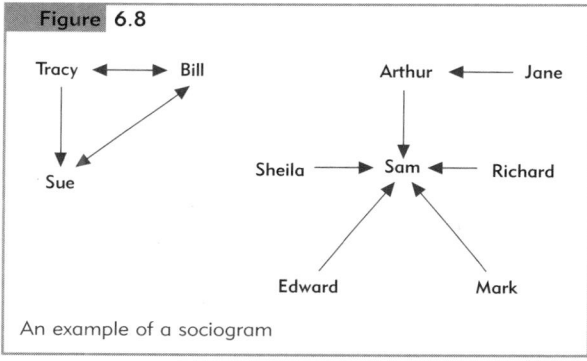

Figure 6.8

An example of a sociogram

Clearly, Tracy, Sue and Bill are forming a group on their own with no real affective link with the others. Jane is possibly an odd one out. Sam is the acknowledged centre of popularity, although not with Tracy's group.

Power structure

Bales (1970) developed the Interaction Process Analysis (IPA) to examine the roles adopted by group members. Trained observers recorded each piece of group behaviour and categorised it as in table 6.9.

Two distinct types of group leader emerged. Bales concluded that there were task leaders,

Table 6.9

Bales's categories:

Socio-emotional responses	Emotionally positive responses:
	1 Shows solidarity, raises other's morale, gives help or reward.
	2 Shows tension release, jokes, laughs, shows satisfaction.
	3 Agrees, shows passive acceptance, understands, concurs, complies.
	Emotionally negative responses:
	4 Gives suggestion, direction, implying autonomy for others.
	5 Gives opinion, evaluation, analysis, expresses feelings and wishes.
	6 Gives orientation, information, repeats, clarifies, confirms.
Task centred responses	Problem-solving responses, answers:
	7 Asks for orientation, information, repetition, confirmation.
	8 Asks for opinion, evaluation, analysis, expression of feeling.
	9 Asks for suggestion, direction, possible ways of action.
	Problem-solving responses, questions:
	10 Disagrees, shows passive rejection, formality, withholds help.
	11 Shows tension, asks for help, withdraws out of the field.
	12 Shows antagonism, deflates another's status, defends or asserts self.

System of categories used in IPA (from Bales and Slater, 1955)

whose main function was the advancement of the task and achieving the goals of the group, and socio-emotional leaders, whose function was to maintain group well-being.

Decision making

■ Groupthink or over-conformity

We have already seen how individuals conform within groups, but when groups are discussing important issues and attempting to reach decisions, Janis (1972) has identified a bias within groups to over-conformity or **groupthink**. This involves a group reaching a decision without having evaluated the issue thoroughly, i.e. not considering all possible alternatives before reaching their decision. This can occur when group members are deeply committed to the group and its norms and the pressure to conform becomes too great to withstand. It can also occur when the group is in competition with or feeling threatened by another group.

Groupthink can obviously be damaging to decision making and it is therefore useful to be aware of the following conditions under which groupthink can emerge:

■ when the group has no habit of evaluating information in an open-minded manner
■ when the group is very cohesive
■ when the group lacks expert opinion or has become isolated
■ when the group leader does not encourage evaluation but demands group loyalty at all cost
■ when the group is under stress. (Tysoe, 1988)

■ Group polarisation

This is another form of bias which can occur when groups are involved in a decision-making process. **Group polarisation** means that members become more biased or shift towards one end of the 'pole' of a topic during group discussion. In other words, if a group member is cautiously in favour of a viewpoint at the beginning of a discussion, he or she moves towards an extreme and becomes strongly in favour of this viewpoint by the end of the discussion (and vice-versa). Note that it does not mean that the group splits itself to opposite ends of a 'pole', which the term might imply at face value. This kind of bias can result in the *risky shift effect* whereby group members will move closer towards a decision which carries a great deal of risk even though they began the discussion at a much less risky point. This phenomenon can also, of course, lead a group to err too far on the side of caution.

Polarisation can occur because of *social comparison*. This involves individuals maintaining a positive self-image which they attain by comparing themselves favourably with others. Therefore, if a group member begins the discussion by offering an extreme view, the others may believe themselves to be ordinary or average. Because each member wants to be viewed favourably all the group members will shift towards the extreme.

Another reason for polarisation is the power of *persuasive argument*. If an extreme argument is put forward that has not been heard before, this new argument will be explained by its proponent. Because it is new to the other group members, they may be persuaded to change their minds somewhat and then move further towards this line of argument, thus enhancing group polarisation.

So far in this section there has been a focus on groups which seem to have a set function or purpose and the dynamics of such groups. In the next section we turn our attention to 'collective behaviour' and the notion of 'crowds' as opposed to groups in an effort to distinguish between the two.

Collective behaviour

Collective behaviour might be considered as being synonymous with 'the crowd'. Partly for historical reasons and partly because researchers are more likely to study the problems presented by crowds, the term 'collective behaviour' has in fact become associated with difficult rather than peaceful types of crowd. As a starting point it may be helpful to separate crowds into several types:

- *Casual crowd*: this is a mere accidental grouping of people who happen to be at the same place, for example a throng of people lying on a beach. They do not necessarily have any interest

that unites them and their only connection with the type of behaviour being discussed is that they are in close proximity. The behaviour expected of people in such situations is known and usually conformed to.

- *Conventional crowd* – this is an orderly crowd meeting according to custom, best examplified by an audience. It is called conventional because it is following social conventions, for example in response to speakers or entertainers.

- *Active crowd* – occasionally the conventional crowd can begin to merge into more of an active crowd, for example at a football game. Fights may break out during or after the game. Under such circumstances, when the audience is keyed up a few individuals who start a fight might attract others to join in the mêlée or simply to urge them on. 'Active crowd' is thus the name for the type of crowd usually thought of first in collective behaviour, i.e. group actions that are somewhat spontaneous and unpredictable, behaviour not well regulated by conventional norms. It is the name given to violent crowds as mobs (which usually form in pursuit of one individual or with some limited objective in mind) or riots (in which large numbers of people take part usually over a considerable area and with rather diffuse aims of action).

Collective behaviour is concerned with such things as panics of escape, mob lynchings, riots, crazes of acquisition, and fads. One might indeed wonder why such diverse collective activities should be seen as examples of the same phenomenon except that they all seem to involve large numbers of people behaving in an extraordinary and irrational fashion simultaneously. Perhaps Roger Brown did put it aptly when he stated 'collective behaviour is seen popularly as collective misbehaviour'. Moreover, what seems to be involved in such situations is:

- a large number of interacting persons
- individuals do not necessarily engage in face-to-face interaction but simply influence one another

- the crowd is not constituted according to some principal of membership: it simply appears to emerge
- there are no pre-established norms or rules governing the behaviour, but patterns of action again seem simply to emerge.

■ *Orgiastic crowds*: these are crowds that engage in particularly wild celebrations, for example a party that has got out of hand with inebriated people entertaining themselves by throwing things and by boisterous behaviour or even fights. The worst instances of orgiastic crowds have been connected with wars when troops entering a city have been completely out of control looting, killing civilians and raping women.

■ *Expressive crowds*: these are crowds of people not trying to accomplish any aim but simply engaged in spontaneous expression, as in revival meetings or at rock concerts.

Activity 9

This task might be best done as a group. Scan newspapers and record examples of crowd behaviour. Try and classify each example into one of the above categories. Discuss difficulties of classification. What kind of crowd seems to get most coverage and why?

Of the types of crowd analysed above, it has been the active crowd which has received most attention. Casual crowds are so typical of everyday living that we hardly notice them. However, crowds that have come together for a particular purpose often take on a different 'collective' character.

One of the earliest attempts to explain crowd behaviour was *La Foule* (the crowd) by Gustave Le Bon in 1895, some 20 years after the insurrection of the Paris Commune. According to Le Bon, the significant social and political changes in his recent times had been brought about by the action of mobs. Le Bon's thinking was mainly influenced by revolutions and the crowds which brought them about.

What did Le Bon have to say about 'the crowd'? It is important at this stage to remember that he was limiting his discussion to mobs. The mob man, he believed, is 'fickle', 'incredulous' and 'intolerant', and shows the violence and ferocity of 'primitive beings'. The list of 'primitive beings' were women, savages, children and the lower classes! These inferior forms of life, in Le Bon's view, regularly manifested the emotionality and irrationality to which civilised man might give way when he was in a crowd.

Le Bon even attempted to offer a neurological theory of the mob mind and the primitive mind it resembled, operating 'under the influence of the spinal chord'. In other words, once in the grip of the law of mental unity of crowds, the individual undergoes an important transformation. Primitive, irrational behaviour emerges, the individual loses self-control and acts in an impulsive, irrational, possibly bestial manner doing things which he or she would never tolerate if alone. The individual is taken over by 'the collective mind', incapable of reasoning and showing an absence of judgement and critical spirit.

Le Bon was writing at a time when testing or verifying theories empirically was of little concern. In the late 1920s, social psychology turned from discussion to an empirical approach which attempted to be reliable, quantitative and, wherever possible, experimental. However, crowd behaviour is not easily studied in an experimental way. Crowds are spontaneous, mobile and dynamic entities with changing moods, purposes and composition, making them hardly amenable to study. Those studies of crowds which have been attempted, such as Mann's (1981), have tended to be culturally specific.

Nevertheless, Le Bon's theory of 'mob psychology' and subsequent observations of the diverse behaviours subsumed under 'collective behaviour' have given rise to a series of experimental investigations into the question of anonymity given by crowds.

In 1969 Zimbardo suggested that people in crowds have the experience of *deindividuation*, that is, identification with the mob and a loss of personal identity. As a result, they are no longer in touch with their individual consciences, and anti-social behaviour becomes more likely.

Zimbardo tested his theory experimentally. College women were asked to deliver electric shocks to others. Some of the women were dressed in bulky coats and their faces were obscured. Other women were dressed normally. As predicted, Zimbardo found that the women made anonymous by their dress gave shocks twice as strong as those delivered by participants dressed normally.

A major criticism of this study was that the bulky coats with hoods were similar to the well-known gear of the Ku Klux Klan (an extreme racist organisation) and hence very suggestive of aggression. Perhaps the women were responding to the role suggested by the uniform and not to the process of deindividuation.

In fact a follow-up study by Johnson and Downing (1979) supported this interpretation of the results. Their participants were divided into three groups with one group wearing the Ku Klux Klan costume, one wearing their own clothes and the third group wearing nurses' uniforms. The participants wearing nurses' uniforms gave fewer and less severe shocks than the other two groups. Thus terms such as 'deindividuation' and the 'collective mind' seem to have exaggerated the phenomena, though it seems to be the case that the individual in the crowd is more suggestible to ideas than is usually the case.

There are a number of problems with the 'mob psychology' perspective on the behaviour of crowds. First of all, the theory as proposed by Le Bon reflected the spirit of the times but has since been used to justify heavy-handed control of mass demonstrations. More seriously, such views about mob behaviour have predisposed those in authority, such as the police, to believe that a crowd is a mob and therefore unable to listen to reason. It was such a mentality that contributed to the disaster at the Hillsborough football stadium (Banyard, 1989).

Secondly, the assumption that people in crowds are not able to think rationally is highly controversial. Such explanations have been advanced for riots, that people suddenly go mad and are pawns in the hands of a mere handful of

radicals and outside agitators. That ignores the fact that there are causes for riots. Blaming a few individuals is an easy solution to the problem of explaining riots rather than society having to take the blame for tolerating the social conditions that led to the riots. It is easier to attribute the cause to individuals than to the social system. Moreover, the behaviour of people in conditions of disaster is usually more rational than common stereotypes suggest. Most descriptions of earthquakes and tornadoes include scenes of neighbours helping one another, rescue units taking control and very little, if any, looting or disorder.

Thirdly, a study by Marsh et al. (1978) of football fans found that, contrary to the belief that fans' behaviour is impulsive and unbridled, a football crowd has its own form of self-regulation and behavioural norms. The crowd had a pattern of accepted behaviour which was regarded as legitimate, for example chasing rival fans to the railway station after the match but without any intention of the activity escalating into violence. The study in fact suggested that outbreaks of uncontrolled violence are more likely if the crowd's self-regulating behaviour is interfered with by police action.

Finally, there are more examples of peaceful crowds than violent crowds, but these are rarely studied. However, in 1987, Benewick and Holton did interview several participants in a large crowd which attended an open-air Mass during Pope John Paul II's visit to Britain in 1982. The picture presented was very different to that of Le Bon's mob psychology. Participants reported a sense of unity and an uplifting spiritual experience which strengthened their *personal* commitment.

Smelser (1962) drew attention to the fact that crowds which become violent do so in a social context. He proposed a series of determinants of collective behaviour in which each stage must be reached successively:

1 The social system must be conducive to collective behaviour, for example in totalitarian countries there is little rioting because such behaviour is not tolerated.
2 Perception of strain – this is the belief that things are no longer acceptable, that injustices

exist, for example in the case of urban riots in the black ghettos a gap has existed between the needs of the ghetto and society's ability to fill those needs, as well as a gap between what society preaches and practises.

3   Spread and growth of a belief – participants must come to see the strain in a similar manner and so have a shared view of the problem.

4   Structural conduciveness refers to the possibility of taking action: forming groups or gathering together. Crowding of people as in the ghetto is one type of conduciveness; ready and rapid communication of events is another.

5   A specific event, for example an arrest or fight, will most often trigger the collective behaviour. Waddington et al. (1987) studied 'flashpoints' in political demonstrations and found that flashpoint incidents have their effect mainly because they provide an example to the crowd of something 'typical' to their more general sources of grievance, so the incidents erupt into violence. Antagonism between the authorities and both Republican and Loyalist communities in Northern Ireland has provided many examples of this phenomenon over the last 30 years. Perhaps the most vivid example in recent years was the stand-off between police and Loyalists at Drumcree, when police attempted to re-route a Loyalist Protestant march away from a predominantly Catholic Republican area, and local Republican crowds reacted angrily when this decision was reversed under pressure from the Loyalists.

6   Resolution to the collective action, for example police may break up the demonstration or make mass arrests or the purpose of the group has been achieved.

What this shows is that seemingly spontaneous crowds and riots do not materialise out of nothing, but certain social, psychological and environmental conditions must exist before collective behaviour arises. Argyle (1998) managed to highlight the importance of these conditions succinctly when he made a distinction between football and religious crowds. Drawing on sociological research, he pointed out that the

violent behaviour sometimes exhibited in football crowds is often due to the social origins, subcultures and historical contexts from which violent fans are drawn. Some of the extraordinary behaviours exhibited by religious crowds, on the other hand, such as uninhibited emotional arousal, stem from physiological arousal, dependence on the religious leader and methods of inducing religious feelings such as music and ritual. These findings reiterate what has already been a main theme throughout the units in this book focusing on social psychology; that is, the importance of the social context in which people behave.

Activity 10

Follow a current case of collective behaviour in the newspapers and magazines. Analyse the social situation that has given rise to the event.

In conclusion, we can see that studies of crowd or collective behaviour were strongly influenced by Le Bon's model of 'mob psychology'. Although this captured certain important aspects of crowd behaviour, such as the process of deindividuation, it is important to bear in mind that most gatherings of people are peaceful. From time to time crowds do become violent, but a broader awareness of social context and precipitating factors is necessary.

Self-assessment questions

4   From memory, list and define six types of social power.

5   What ethical questions emerged from Zimbardo's study?

6   List the criteria needed for a group to develop. Think about any groups of people you may be involved with, and consider which criteria they match up to.

7   Define 'deindividuation' and outline one study supporting this concept.

(Suggested answers on page 203)

Leadership

Leadership can be defined as a phenomenon whereby 'one person (the leader) is consciously trying to get other people (the followers) to do something the leader wants them to do' (de Alberdi, 1990, p. 46). The issues that this section considers surround questions such as: what kind of people are likely to make the best leaders? Is it best to appoint them, or should they just be allowed to emerge? Do some tasks demand very different leadership styles from others?

Leadership and personality

Activity 11

Do good leaders possess certain personality characteristics? What are these?

The approach taken by social psychologists has generally been to examine the personality characteristics of those who are regarded as good leaders by common consent. This approach is often known as the *trait theory* perspective and rests on the assumption that leaders possess certain traits, or personality characteristics, which differentiate them from their *followers*.

Stogdill (1948) reviewed the then current literature on the relationship between personality and leadership, and concluded that the factors associated with leadership can be classified under the five headings shown in figure 6.10.

More recently, after several decades of further research on personality, it has been found that leaders do indeed demonstrate that they possess some characteristics to a greater extent than others. These include drive, honesty, self-confidence, cognitive ability, flexibility and creativity (Kirkpatrick and Locke, 1991). However, it is important to note that it is now generally agreed among social psychologists

6.10 Five factors associated with personality and leadership (after Stogdill, 1948)

Capacity: intelligence, alertness, verbal facility, originality, judgement.

Achievement: scholarship, knowledge, athletic accomplishments.

Responsibility: dependability, initiative, persistence, aggressiveness, self-confidence, the desire to excel.

Participation: activity, sociability, cooperation, adaptability, humour.

Status: socio-economic position, popularity.

that whilst these traits have some bearing on leadership they are only part of the picture. If you have read the other units in this book focusing on social psychology, you will be aware that any social behaviour does not stand alone; it is part of a network of complicated interactions between various other factors. It is to some of these other factors that we now turn our attention.

Situational factors and leadership

Do situational factors make someone a good leader in one context, not so good in another? Perhaps the first question relating to situation is how the leader came to be in that position. An *assigned* leader is appointed to that position by some external authority, whereas an *emergent* leader gradually assumes that position. Leaders should also be considered in the light of their functions. Leaders who are primarily decision makers may not have interpersonal relations as a major requirement of their role. The primary role of other leaders, however, may be successfully interacting with their subordinates, directing and controlling their progress towards group goals and maintaining morale. Emergent leaders exercise their leadership purely because of their personal qualities, for example intelligence and verbal ability.

Rice *et al.* (1980) illustrated the situational factor in leadership by making groups of male cadets at West Point Military Academy in the USA perform tasks under the leadership of either a male or a female cadet. Half of the participants had liberal attitudes towards women and their position, half were more conservative. The responses of the liberal cadets to male and female leaders were very similar. On the other hand, the conservative cadets responded better when the leader was a male. Where women-led groups succeeded this was ascribed to luck; where male-led groups were successful it was ascribed to the hard work and cooperation of the group members.

Fiedler's contingency model

The **contingency model** of leadership (Fiedler, 1964, 1967) attempts to link factors relating to the situation with the leader's and the followers' personalities. Leaders were asked to evaluate their 'least preferred co-workers' (LPC) on a number of scales. If this evaluation gave high scores and leaders thought quite positively even of their least favourite colleagues, this was held to be characteristic of a friendly, permissive and accepting leadership style. On the other hand, if the LPC scores were low and leaders held a very poor opinion of their least favourite colleagues, their style of leadership was described as aloof, demanding and task-orientated. The situation was also evaluated as favourable or unfavourable, depending on the ease with which a leader could control and direct the group members. This seemed to be dependent upon three factors (see figure 6.11).

Fiedler found that where the situation was either very favourable or very unfavourable, low LPC leaders were the most effective. When the situation was intermediate between the two extremes, high LPC leaders did better (see figure 6.12).

6.11 Factors influencing the ease with which a leader can control group members

1 *Leader–member relationships*: if a leader enjoyed the loyalty and confidence of the group there was a favourable situation.
2 The clearer the *structure of the task*, the more favourable the situation was held to be.
3 *Power of the leader* was important, as the more rewards and sanctions were controlled and power was assumed by the leader, the more favourable the situation was held to be.

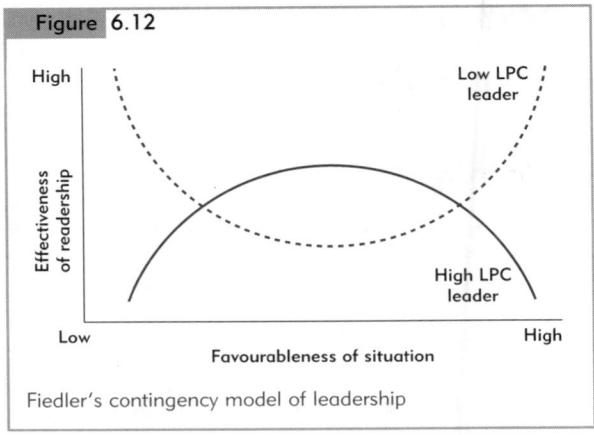

Figure 6.12

Fiedler's contingency model of leadership

■ Criticisms of Fiedler's model

Fishbein *et al.* (1969) criticised Fiedler's model. They suggested that high and low LPC leaders might well have different types of least preferred co-workers in mind when they made their judgements. If a high LPC leader is irked by highly intelligent, pushy, dogmatic individuals and the low LPC leader is annoyed by unfriendly, hostile, unpleasant and unwholesome individuals, the differences between them are going to be blurred.

Having briefly outlined the trait approach it is also worth mentioning at this point that the personality of an individual can vary over time and within different situations (Mischel, 1968). This factor does not appear to be taken into account by Fiedler. In addition, further research has provided evidence to suggest that there exists low reliability for test/retest reliability of LPC scores (Rice, 1978). Finally, Hogg and Vaughan (1995) noted that although this theory examines the interaction between the person and situation, it fails to take into account the group processes which might occur leading to the rise or fall of leaders.

Normative theory

On the basis of previous research into the personality and situational factors related to leadership, Vroom and Yetton (1973) developed a decision-based theory (**normative theory**) of how leaders might behave given the situation whilst also taking into account their followers. Therefore, according to Vroom and Yetton leaders should be flexible and adaptable to each different situation, deciding how much they should allow their followers to participate in the decision-making process. The level of participation will therefore vary according to the situation, and level of participation is determined by which leadership style should be used in different situations (autocratic, consultative or based on group decision making). Vroom (1984) outlined 11 different situation analysis questions which would be involved in the leader's decision of which leadership style to use to make his or her leadership most effective. These questions have been adapted by Hayes (1994, p. 568) and are presented in table 6.13.

Leadership: functions and role

Activity 12

Without looking back, try to remember the difference between low LPC and high LPC. (If you have any difficulty, turn back to page 196 and read the paragraph beginning 'The contingency model of leadership' again.)

Table	6.13
A	Is it necessary to produce a quality solution to the problem?
B	Do I have enough information to make a high-quality decision?
C	Is the problem structured?
D	Is acceptance of the decision by my subordinates important for its effective implementation?
E	If I were to make the decision by myself, is it reasonably certain that it would be accepted by my subordinates?
F	Do my subordinates share the organisational goals to be attained in solving this problem?
G	Is conflict among my subordinates over preferred solutions likely?
H	How much prior information and ability do my subordinates have?
I	Is there a time constraint on solving this problem?
J	How important is my subordinates' development in this?
K	How valuable is time in this situation?

Vroom's situation analysis questions

What seem to be the main functions that leaders perform? The function of leadership might be defined as 'to move a group towards the realisation of its goals'. Leadership might emanate from one or more individuals in a group, or be evenly spread throughout it.

Studies of leadership in a wide variety of contexts, from bomber crews to undergraduates in laboratory studies, seem to result in the establishment of two main categories of leader: the task leader and the socio-emotional leader. This largely follows Bales's (1970) division (see pages 189–90).

There seem to be certain well-defined roles relating to leadership which exist independently of the people occupying them. Verba (1961) suggested that the separation of roles might be exaggerated in the case of laboratory groups of participants. In such groups, the leader lacks the institutional legitimacy of having been appointed or assigned to a leadership position. An appointed leader can exercise legitimate power unavailable to leaders in laboratory groups. Verba used real groups, as opposed to laboratory groups, to show that the dual roles of task and socio-emotional leaders were combined more often than Bales had suggested (see pages 189–90). After all, if your head of department is seen to be providing the legitimate goals, which this function demands, not only will subordinates be loyal but they will also tend to get greater job satisfaction. Verba's view was confirmed by Burke (1972) using laboratory groups and Bales's IPA (see pages 189–90), to attempt to compare activities which had either high or low legitimacy. Only in the low legitimacy cases did there appear to be a clear separation between the two kinds of leadership.

Leadership styles

What are the virtues and defects of particular styles of leadership? To some degree the styles which leaders adopt tend to affect the situation. Lewin *et al.* (1939) tested the effect of different styles of leadership upon group members. Their participants were ten-year-old members of boys' clubs with similar social backgrounds and intelligence levels. Leaders were instructed to operate three distinct leadership styles. They were trained so that they performed similarly apart from the leadership styles they were to operate. They moved from one club to another every six weeks, changing their leadership style with each move. The idea was that the boys should react to the styles rather than to the personalities of those who were leading them.

Notes were taken of the ways in which the boys reacted and behaved under each of the leadership styles described in figure 6.14.

Under autocratic leadership, more work was achieved than under either of the other styles. Group solidarity was poorer than under democratic leadership and there was less originality and motivation to work. When the leader was absent there was a tendency for work to stop and apathy and disruption to ensue. Morale was low and levels of aggression and destructiveness were higher than in the democratic condition.

6.14 Leadership styles (after Lewin *et al.*)

The **autocratic leader** would give orders, discourage communication or participation on the part of the boys; praise or blame was administered without any explanation.

The *laissez-faire leader* left the boys to their own devices. No orders or suggestions were given except when the boys asked specifically, which was not often.

The **democratic leader** helped the boys plan, made suggestions, seemed concerned with their welfare and participated in group life. Reasons for praise or blame were fully explained.

With laissez-faire leadership (which seemed to be the poorest of the three styles), the boys were more aggressive to each other than in the democratic condition, although less aggressive than in the autocratic condition. Very little work was done whether the leader was there or not and they were easily discouraged.

Morale under democratic leadership was higher than in the other conditions. Boys seemed to like each other more and to get on better. Slightly less work was done than in the autocratic condition but relations with the leader were generally good. When the leader was absent, the boys carried on working and were more independent than in the other conditions.

Another dimension has evolved since the research undertaken by Lewin *et al.* which focuses on the directive–permissive leadership style (Muczyk and Reimann, 1987). This dimension concentrates on how far leaders instruct their followers when undertaking a certain task (directive) or how far they allow them the freedom to work in any way they desire (permissive). Therefore, leaders can demonstrate a style that cuts across the autocratic–democratic and directive–permissive dimensions by taking one of the following approaches: permissive–democratic; directive–democratic; permissive–autocratic or directive–autocratic.

It is perhaps difficult to translate findings such as these into the context of leadership in an organisation such as a company but work by Yukl (1971) does seem to bear some relation to leadership style, or at least by styles of decision making. Yukl proposed that there were three dimensions along which a leader might vary. *Consideration* reflects the leader's concern and respect for subordinates. *Initiating structure* concerns the way in which a leader directs subordinates towards the attainment of group goals. *Decision centralisation* relates to the extent to which decisions are taken centrally and handed down. These are similar to the task-orientation and person-orientation dimensions discussed by Baron and Byrne (1997) where the leader is more concerned with getting the task done or more interested in maintaining good relations with his or her followers.

These dimensions seemed to be independent of one another, at least in theory. In practice, perhaps, there might be a relationship between the kind of leader who is concerned about subordinates and a tendency to decentralise decision making.

Lowin (1968) argued that *participative decision making*, where decisions are taken close to the point where they must be executed, meets the needs both of the organisation and of the subordinates better than a *hierarchical structure of decision making*. Heller and Yukl (1969) suggested that a manager's decision-making style depended to some extent upon the position held in the organisation. Senior managers were likely to allow more scope to their subordinates than supervisors and junior managers who are closer to them in the management structure. Perhaps senior managers enjoy greater security than their juniors.

There seems to be no firm way in which you can be certain which type of leader will be the most effective. There are clearly personality characteristics which go along with leadership, but they are very wide ranging. On that basis you might claim that almost anyone is capable of being a leader!

Situational considerations are also important and it seems that the interaction between the personality of leaders and the situations in which they find themselves will determine whether or not they will be successful. Leadership roles and functions also seem to be determined by such considerations as their legitimacy and the task that has to be accomplished. It is clearly a very complex issue and still a long way from resolution.

Leadership and followership

So far 'leader' and 'leadership' have been used perhaps seemingly interchangeably but it has probably become apparent that leadership and leader are not synonymous. Leadership is a process and a leader is a person. Granted the leader fills a central role in the process of leadership, but leadership is not just the task of the leader. Other people and the characteristics of the particular situation represent important elements of the process. A major view of leadership in social psychology nowadays stresses the functions to be fulfilled in a situation and the role of the followers as well as the activities and the characteristics of the leader. According to Hollander, the process of leadership implies the existence of a particular influence relationship between these individuals, with one or more called 'leaders' and the others considered their 'followers' (Hollander, 1976). The three elements involved in leadership, i.e. the leader, followers and situation in which they interact, can be represented graphically (see figure 6.15).

There are several features worthy of comment:
- The locus of leadership is represented by the area of overlap, i.e. the leader and followers are bound together in a relationship within a situation.
- Each of the three elements has characteristics or components which can affect both leadership and its outcomes.
- The system is an interacting one.
- The leaders and followers are mainly within the situation, i.e. their involvement in the situation is partial, not total.

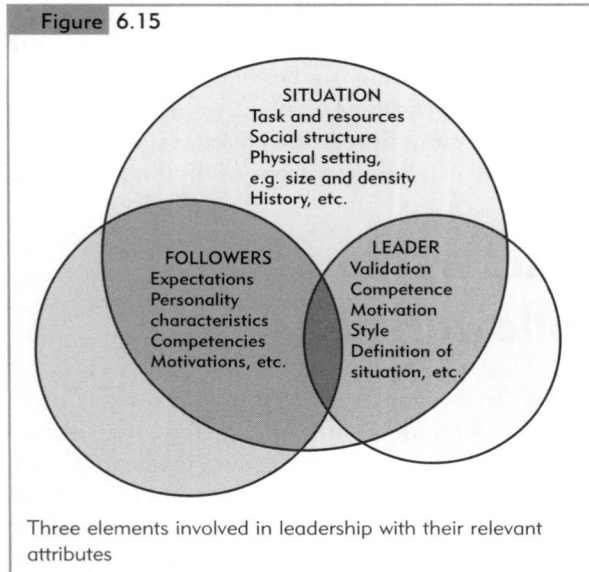

Figure 6.15

SITUATION
Task and resources
Social structure
Physical setting,
e.g. size and density
History, etc.

FOLLOWERS
Expectations
Personality
characteristics
Competencies
Motivations, etc.

LEADER
Validation
Competence
Motivation
Style
Definition of
situation, etc.

Three elements involved in leadership with their relevant attributes

- The leaders and followers are represented as having a relationship in the area designated 'leadership'.

Thus leadership can be viewed as involving a transaction between the leader and followers. The traditional view of leadership was one of the leader as the main actor, with influence over others. But as Homans (1961) states, 'Influence over others is purchased at the price of allowing oneself to be influenced by others'. What seems to be operating is a process of social exchange in which the leader gives something and gets something in return. '. . . the person in the role of leader who fulfils expectations and achieves group goals provides rewards for others which are reciprocated in the form of status, esteem, and heightened influence' (Hollander and Julian, 1969). Leadership cannot therefore be considered independently of the followers. The leader may be expected to set goals in certain situations and to effectively communicate these to the group. In a study by Burke (1966), it was found that the leader's failure to provide goal orientations to the followers resulted in antagonism, tension and absenteeism. In other words, the followers' expectations had not been fulfilled.

The idea that some members of a group have 'leadership qualities' and that followers are a passive group of 'non-leaders' has limited plausibility. Hollander and Webb (1955) in a study of leaders and followers have confirmed that leaders and followers are by no means different types. The participants in their study, all military men, were asked to (a) select which members of their group they would prefer to have for group leader and (b) if they were the leader, who would they select as followers. The researchers found a high correlation between the two groups. The men preferred for leadership roles were the first to be named as followers. In organisations there is an expectation that *active* followership will be exhibited throughout the hierarchy. Walt Kelly cited the case of an applicant who impressed an admissions tutor by stating that she was a 'good follower'. So many applicants had indicated that they were 'leaders' that it was felt by the tutor it would be a good thing to have at least one follower applying for the course. Although there are very real distinctions made between leaders and followers, especially in what is expected of them, namely directing the activity of others and organising action to achieve goals in the case of leaders, leadership is not a solo activity. Much depends on the cooperative effort of the followers.

It is clear from the above that followership can also be linked to obedience. Staub (1992), cited by Humphreys (1994), discussed mass killing in the context of obedience but stated that motivation to obey a leader who orders mass killing does not come from the followers' desire to obey but from their motivation of a desire to follow a leader, to be a member of a group and respect authority. In most cases followers have a general acceptance of their leader's ideologies and share in his or her beliefs because of a wider social contextual situation. Staub believed that Milgram's studies of obedience have hampered psychological research by focusing only on the issue of obedience rather than examining more closely the issue of followership.

Activity 13

Make an attempt to rate leadership, for example in college, school or clubs in terms of effectiveness. Analyse the process in terms of the interaction between the leaders, followers and situation.

Self-assessment questions

8   Make a diagram showing some of the personality characteristics which have been associated with leadership.

9   Make short notes identifying the key features of the contingency model of leadership.

10 Outline Vroom and Yetton's normative theory of leadership.

11 List the three elements involved in leadership and describe how they interact.

12 Outline Hollander and Webb's research and try to explain why it found followership to be as important as leadership.

(Suggested answers on pages 203–4.)

Unit summary

- *Conformity* can be described as behaviour which is brought about by yielding to group pressures. A significant amount of research in this area was undertaken by Solomon Asch who placed confederates within groups. These confederates gave incorrect answers when questioned about the lengths of lines which induced participants to conform. Despite criticism, Asch's work is still of significant importance.

- *Compliance* describes behaviour which involves a person attempting to get another person to do something for them, often on the basis of a direct request. People use any one of a number of techniques in order to gain compliance from another including ingratiation, the foot-in-the-door technique and tactics based on reciprocity.

- *Obedience* involves complying with rules set by a recognised authority. Disobedience can result in sanctions being imposed. The forefather of obedience research was Milgram who designed a famous experiment involving participants who were instructed to give electric shocks to 'learners' who gave the wrong answers. A significant number of participants obeyed to an alarming degree. Milgram believed that people obeyed because they were in an agentic state, acting as agents on someone else's behalf.

- However, many psychologists today believe the social and historical context of obedience should be taken into account and other researchers have suggested that people do not always obey but sometimes rebel against authority. In addition, factors such as *independence*, *non-conformity* and *minority influence* need to be included in the equation.

- Groups can often exert a significant amount of *power* and so their formation, structure and processes need to be examined carefully. For groups to form there really needs to be sustained interaction between group members and a perception that the group and group members exist. Groups tend to adopt explicit or implicit norms of behaviour which must be adhered to for fear of sanctions or disapproval.

- Within groups there are certain structures binding the group together such as communication and affective structures. Decision making is one of the functions of groups, and *groupthink* and *polarisation* are two terms used to describe how decision making can go wrong because of group processes.

- *Collective behaviour* can be considered as being synonymous with 'a crowd'. Several types of crowd have been defined which have differing functions. Much of the research in this area has focused on unruly crowds and was first instigated by Le Bon in 1895 based on observations made at the time of the French Revolution. Zimbardo (1969) suggested that individuals in crowds experience *deindividuation*, i.e. they lose their sense of personal identity. It is generally believed that certain

Summary cont'd.

social, psychological and environmental conditions must exist before collective behaviour arises.

- There are several theories of *leadership*. One of these is the 'trait theory' which assumes that all leaders possess certain personality characteristics which make such individuals 'good leaders'. However, this theory has been criticised for not taking account of the situation in which leaders find themselves.

- One of the main situational theories is *Fiedler's contingency model* which suggests that leaders will be more effective in certain situations depending on the interactions involved with subordinates.

- A later theory of leadership was developed by Vroom and Yetton which is based on a *decision-making* model. This approach contends that the leader should be adaptable to different styles of leadership depending upon the decision that has to be made. In conclusion, it should be noted that leaders would be nothing without their followers.

Terms to define

agentic state
anti-conformity
autocratic leader
autonomous state
compliance
conformity
contingency model (of leadership)
democratic leader

descriptive norms
group polarisation
groupthink
independence
injunctive norms
normative theory
norms
obedience

Further reading

Baron, R A and Byrne, D (1997) *Social Psychology*, 8th edn, Allyn & Bacon, Boston, MA, chapters 9 and 12.

As stated in other social psychology units, a well-written, informative and up-to-date text, well worth reading if interested in this area of psychology.

de Alberdi, L (1990) *People, Psychology and Business*, Cambridge University Press, Cambridge.

An excellent text exploring many aspects relating to groups and leadership which go beyond the present text, but easy to digest and to the point.

Hayes, N (1995) *Psychology in Perspective*, Macmillan, Basingstoke, chapters 5 and 6.

These two chapters serve as a good introduction to understanding the differences between traditional social psychology and European social psychology. The explanations are clear and the rest of the book offers interesting insights with regard to other areas of psychology.

Answers

■ Suggested answers to activities

Base your answers on information in the text and your own ideas, as appropriate.

■ Suggested answers to self-assessment questions

1

Did you include the following?
Unanimity of confederates – 76 per cent conformed if confederates unanimous; if one dissenter was present, conformity dropped to minimum levels.
Task difficulty – harder tasks make conformity more likely.
Number of confederates – more conformity with two confederates than one, and more with three than two. Beyond three confederates, conformity remained at a similar level.
Status of confederates – high-status confederates produced greater conformity.
Privacy – reduced conformity.

2

Did you include the following?
Proximity of experimenter to the participant – obedience three times higher than when experimenter absent.
Proximity of learner to the participant – at a distance of 45 cm obedience reduced to 40 per cent.
Participant holding learner's hand on to a plate to receive shock – obedience reduced to 30 per cent.
Presence of other participants (actually confederates of the experimenter) who withdrew during the experiment – 90 per cent of participants withdrew at the same time.
Absence of experimenter – obedience reduced.
Status of institution – obedience reduced to 47.5 per cent when the experiment took place in a run-down building in a poor area rather than in a university.

3

Situational	Dispositional
Presence of a supporter	Deeply held moral values – conscience
Costs versus benefits	Personal belief system
Task difficulty	Intellectual effectiveness
	Ego strength
	Leadership ability

4

Information power: where someone has power based on information relating to another.

Reward power: where someone has the power to provide with something valued in the form of a reward.
Coercive power: where someone has the power to punish.
Legitimate power: where someone has the power associated with a supervisory position.
Referent power: power that is achieved through a wish to identify with the person concerned.
Expert power: where someone has power based on knowledge that is wanted by another.

5

Consent – particularly the issue of informed consent.
Conduct – did the ends justify the means? The extent to which the participants were degraded. Self-discovery by the participants of what they were prepared to do.

6

Did you include:
– sustained interaction between people
– the scope for group members to communicate
– perception of the existence of a group identity
– common norms of behaviour
– the formal/informal roles of group members
– the affective relationships between group members
– the shared goals of group members?

7

Look back to pages 192–3.

8

Did you include: capacity, achievement, responsibility, participation, status, situational characteristics, group characteristics, the characteristics of followers?

9

Attempts to link situational factors with the personalities of the leader and of the followers. Leaders requested to identify least preferred co-workers (LPCs) on a series of scales. High scores indicated positive views of their LPCs and a friendly, permissive and accepting leadership style. Low scores indicated negative views of their LPCs and an aloof, demanding and task-orientated leadership style. Favourable or unfavourable situations were determined by how easily a leader could control group members. The most effective were low LPC leaders when the situation was either very favourable or very unfavourable; and high LPC leaders when a situation was intermediate between these two extremes.

10

Normative theory is based on decisions made by leaders, based on the situation and how much participation they believe their followers should have. Participation varies according to the situation and also the leadership style used in the situation. For more detail see page 197.

11

The three elements involved in leadership are: the leader, the followers and the situation. Interaction of the three elements is described on pages 199–200.

12

Hollander and Webb's research is described in detail on page 200.

Unit 7

Pro- and Anti-social Behaviour

Penny Cortvriend, Judith Silver, Regina Teahan and Lance Workman

This unit covers:

- Pro-social behaviour
- Anti-social behaviour
- Individual, social and cultural diversity in pro- and anti-social behaviour
- The reduction and control of aggression

By the end of this unit, you should be able to:

- show knowledge and understanding of research and theories about pro- and anti-social behaviour
- be able to evaluate the effects of the media on helping and aggressive behaviour
- offer explanations of individual, social and cultural diversity in pro- and anti-social behaviour
- show some understanding of how aggression can be controlled or reduced.

Unit 7 Contents

Introduction

This unit is about pro- and anti-social behaviour: what exactly do these terms mean?

Anti-social behaviour violates the social norms of a particular group, society or culture. Such behaviour is likely to attract moral censure and punishment. This may happen informally, through group pressure on a member who doesn't keep to the social rules of that particular group, or where behaviour is defined by law as 'criminal', via formal legal procedures.

Pro-social behaviour helps others promote harmony in society. The most extreme form of pro-social behaviour is altruism. This is unselfish behaviour, where the benefit of others is put above any possible costs to oneself. *Socialisation* is the process of learning to conform to the rules of our particular society, that is, to behave in a 'pro-social' rather than an 'anti-social' manner.

Social psychologists seek to understand the causes of pro- or anti-social behaviour. They hope to apply this understanding to prevent violations of the social order, such as burglaries, murders, football violence or prison riots and also to create social conditions which encourage people to behave positively and helpfully towards others.

Why do people behave in a pro- or anti-social manner? Social psychologists have been particularly interested in isolating the *situational* factors which determine such behaviour. For example, is it possible to predict under what circumstances onlookers will or will not come to the rescue of a victim of a crime? Such research takes a nomothetic approach; it attempts to predict how people will behave on average.

Psychologists also ask questions about *dispositional* factors in pro- and anti-social behaviour. What motivates exceptional individuals who are prepared to sacrifice their own lives to save those of other people? This focus on the individual characteristics of atypical people is known as idiographic research.

In this unit we examine **bystander behaviour** and **aggression** as two forms of anti-social behaviour and take helping and altruism as our models of pro-social behaviour. Our approach is interactionist; we recognise that a social event rarely has one simple cause but is triggered off by complex interactions between individuals and their social surroundings.

The section on pages 231–6 focuses on the influences of individual personality and historical, social and cultural contexts on pro- and anti-social behaviour. Recent research suggests that what is happening in society at a particular historical moment can have a powerful impact on individual and group behaviour. It may be that human subjectivity colours research itself. We must therefore be careful when making assumptions about human behaviour based on studies that do not reflect our own society or culture.

Pro-social behaviour

Pro-social behaviour includes a wide spectrum of activities, from saving someone's life at great risk to oneself, to everyday helping of others through courtesy, cooperation, sharing and sympathy. In this section, we first examine a dramatic type of failure of pro-social behaviour which has been termed bystander apathy. We then move on to consider research and theories about active helping and altruism, including the influence of the media.

Bystander behaviour

Bystander refers to an onlooker who witnesses an incident. This section examines research and theories addressing the failure of onlookers to help the victims of a crime or accident.

■ Bystander apathy

The media regularly report incidents in which onlookers fail to act to save an individual from danger. A woman is attacked on a roadside verge and this is witnessed by hundreds of passing motorists, yet no one stops; a young man is mugged in a rail carriage and fellow passengers fail to intervene. During the Second World War, people in Nazi-occupied Europe lived in villages immediately adjacent to concentration camps, where Jews, Gypsies, mentally handicapped people and political dissenters were being systematically murdered. Some of these people claimed after the war that they knew nothing at all about what was going on inside. The expression bystander apathy refers to the apparently unfeeling behaviour of onlookers in such situations.

In 1964, a murder was committed in the Queens District of New York. At about 3 am, Kitty Genovese was attacked and killed in a protracted assault that continued for about half an hour. During this time she screamed repeatedly. It emerged in the police investigation that the attack had been witnessed by 38 separate neighbours, yet none had intervened or phoned the police during the period. The extract below is from the *New York Times*, in which the crime was recalled by residents of Queens District.

It flashes through Margaret Swinchoski's mind, each time she walks past the Kew Gardens, Queens, train station: this was where Kitty Genovese met her killer. Even in the small town in Vermont where Miss Swinchoski grew up, Catherine Genovese's case became a shocking symbol of apathy.

Now Miss Swinchoski lives in the same quiet, middle-class neighbourhood where Miss Genovese was slain 20 years ago as she tried to make her way from her car, parked in the train station lot, to her apartment on Austin Street.

'What might happen'
For more than half an hour that night, Miss Genovese's killer stalked and stabbed her, again and again, as 38 of her neighbours silently turned away from her cries.

'I walk here during the day but not at night,' said Miss Swinchoski, a 25-year-old flutist, 'because of what happened then and because of what might happen now.'

The killer, Winston Moseley, had followed Miss Genovese into the parking lot at 3.20 a.m. on 13 March 1964. Mr Mosely, a 29-year-old machine operator and family man, was convicted after he confessed that he had been cruising around, planning 'to rape and to rob and to kill a girl'. He is serving a

life sentence in Green Haven state prison, and was recently denied parole.

Mr Moseley attacked Miss Genovese for the first time in front of the Austin Book Shop as she ran up the street, apparently toward a police call box. 'Oh, my God, he stabbed me,' she screamed into the early-morning stillness. 'Please help me!' Windows opened and lights went on in the building across the street.

'Let that girl alone,' yelled a man on the seventh floor. Mr Moseley walked toward his car. As he later told the police, 'I had a feeling this man would close his window and go back to sleep and then I would return.'

Miss Genovese staggered around the corner and fell inside the lobby of the first unlocked building she could find.

As witnesses watched from behind their curtains – one couple pulled up a chair to the window and turned out the light to see better – Mr Moseley came back and calmly poked into doors until he found his victim. He stabbed her eight more times and sexually molested her.

First call to police
It was 3.50 a.m. when the police received their first call – from a man who said he did not want to 'get involved'.

Bernard Titowsky, owner of the Austin Book Shop, recalls coming in the next morning and finding blood near the door. 'Time and rain washed most of it away,' he said Saturday, sitting on a stool behind his antique cash register.

Mr Titowsky and many other long-time residents remain sensitive about the case and say the residents were unfairly portrayed as callous. 'No one wants to give the people that lived here any credit,' he said. 'They just want to use it as a sociology lesson.'

A woman who remembers
Most of the witnesses have moved away, or died. One who remembers is an 83-year-old woman, who lived next door to Miss Genovese. She was awakened at 3.30 a.m. that night when a friend called to say he had seen the attack but was intoxicated and did not want to deal with the police.

She put on a coat over her nightgown and went down the street to find a door ajar and Miss Genovese crumpled behind it. 'She was dying,' the woman recalled. 'She was making noises like "Uh, uh, uh," like she couldn't breathe'. The woman then went to a neighbour, who called the police.

The woman said she wished people would forget. 'We weren't apathetic,' she said. 'There are good people here. There's so much else bad in the world. Poor Kitty.'

Source: 'The night that 38 stood by as a life was lost', New York Times, 12 March 1984.

Activity 1

Why did no one intervene?

What could you have done if you had been an onlooker?

(Suggested answers on page 241.)

■ Laboratory studies of bystander behaviour

The puzzle of the Kitty Genovese murder was that she received no help despite the presence of so many onlookers. Two American social psych-

ologists, Latane and Darley (1968) set out to investigate this phenomenon. In a series of carefully controlled experiments, they systematically varied the number of witnesses to a simulated accident or emergency, in order to see how this affected the chances of the victim receiving any help.

These experiments all involved the deliberate *deception* of participants. The participants were either volunteer students, who were given false information about the real purpose of the research, or unsuspecting members of the general public, who were not aware that their behaviour was being monitored. The case study below gives an account of one such experiment.

A similar inverse relationship between the number of bystanders and the likelihood and speed of intervention was found in many subsequent studies. Some of these findings are presented in table 7.1.

Latane and Nida (1981) reviewed fifty six research studies of this type and identified a

---

Case study – the effect of different conditions on bystander behaviour

Darley and Latane (1968) invited 72 male and female undergraduates of New York University to participate in confidential discussion about the problems of student life. Each participant was placed in an individual room and invited to chat over an intercom system with an invisible fellow student, whom they believed was in an adjacent room. This other student was actually a confederate of the experimenter. As the conversation continued, the confederate indicated that he was having an epileptic seizure and started to cry out for help. The researchers varied the information given to the participant about the number of other students who were supposedly participating in the discussion from their separate rooms and would presumably be equally able to hear the sounds of distress. In reality these other students were just tape-recordings. Participants were led to believe either that they were in discussion alone with the seizure victim, or with one other person apart from the victim, or with four others.

The results of this study confirmed the researchers' prediction that the presence of additional witnesses to the emergency would inhibit helping. The response rate was 85 per cent when the participants thought they were alone, 62 per cent when they believed one other person was aware of the emergency and only 31 per cent where they thought that four other people could hear the victim's cries. The speed of participants' reactions to the incident also depended on the number of fellow witnesses they believed were present. Participants who thought they were alone reacted on average in 52 seconds. This was only one-third of the reaction time (166 seconds) of those participants who believed they were facing the emergency in the company of four other people.

Table 7.1

Authors	Date	Nature of simulated emergency	Experimental conditions	Intervention rate
Darley and Latane	1968	Confederate pretends to have an epileptic seizure	– participant is alone	85%
			– participant believes there is one other witness	63%
			– participant believes there are are four other witnesses	31%
Latane and Darley	1968	'Smoke' fills a room	– participant is alone	75%
			– two other participants in the room	38%
			– two confederates in the room, who don't react	18%
Latane and Rodin	1969	A confederate pretends to fall off a chair and break her ankle	– participant is alone	70%
			– participants are in pairs	40%
			– a non-reactive confederate is present	7%
Latane and Darley	1970	Staged 'theft' of a beer barrel in a liquor store	– one customer (a member of the public) witnesses the theft	65%
			– two customers witness the theft	

The bystander effect: experimental results showing inverse relationship between the number of onlookers and the probability of intervention

consistent trend. As the number of bystanders *increased*, so the probability of the victim getting help *decreased*. This paradoxical bystander effect is a good example of a counter-intuitive finding in psychology, i.e. one that turns out to be contrary to our common sense theories.

The researchers took care to debrief their participants after the experiments, explaining the real purpose of the study. Participants often thought the emergency had been a real one. Sometimes they indicated that they had been uncertain how to interpret this situation or that they realised things were serious but had not intervened in case they should embarrass the victim.

Activity 2

Do you think these research studies were worthwhile?
Did they advance scientific understanding?
Were the experiments ethically acceptable, in view of the deception that took place?

(Suggested answers on page 241.)

One of this series of experiments (Latane and Darley, 1968) consisted of a mock-up of a fire emergency. Male undergraduates from Columbia University were asked to fill out a questionnaire in a small room that had a one-way mirror for observation purposes. After a few moments, smoke was poured into the room through a small vent in the wall. The experiment had three conditions: either a single participant was alone in the room, or the true participant was placed together with two 'passive' confederates who did not react to the smoke, or a group of three genuine participants were placed in the room. The participants who were alone reacted to the smoke as a genuine sign of fire in 70 per cent of cases and tended to respond very rapidly to the emergency. Those participants who were together with others seemed to be inhibited in their responses.

In debriefing interviews, those participants who did not respond

'. . . *uniformly said they had rejected the idea that it was a fire. Instead they hit upon an astonishing variety of alternative explanations, all sharing the common characteristic of interpreting the smoke as a non-dangerous event'.*

Participants interpreted the smoke as steam, or air-conditioning vapours, 'smog to simulate an urban environment' or even 'truth gas' to make them answer the questionnaire accurately.

Activity 3

Why do you think increasing the number of bystanders inhibited helping?
What social influences could have led the participants in this experiment to reinterpret such a potentially dangerous situation as a safe one?

(Suggested answers on page 241.)

■ Explaining bystander behaviour

Latane and Darley suggested three social cognitive processes which they thought might be involved in the typical passive behaviour of bystanders:

■ *Diffusion of responsibility*. When many others were present, each individual tended to assume that someone else was helping and was in control of the situation.

■ *Pluralistic ignorance*. Each individual observed the behaviour of the other onlookers and took his or her cue from others. If no one else moved or reacted, then the interpretation was made that this situation could not be urgent or dangerous.

■ *Audience inhibition*. People were concerned about what others might think of them. They did not want to risk social embarrassment by over-reacting to what might prove a false alarm.

■ A cognitive model to explain bystander apathy

Latane and Darley (1970) put these ideas about social influence together to propose a more complex model of the factors which tend to bias the behaviour of onlookers towards inaction. They suggested that there were five conditions necessary in order for an onlooker to take positive action:

■ The individual must *notice* that something unusual was happening. You may recall from research on eyewitness testimony that we simply fail to 'register' many of the events that go on

around us. City-dwellers, especially, tend to develop 'tunnel vision' and do not pay attention to anything which is not personally significant. Milgram (1970) termed this phenomenon urban overload.

■ The individual must *interpret* the situation as an emergency. It is here that social comparison processes operate. If the signals from others are all negative then we get that collective misinterpretation of the situation known as pluralistic ignorance.

■ The onlooker must perceive the situation as one where he or she has a *personal responsibility* to help.

■ The individual must believe he or she is *competent* to help out. Bandura (1977) coined the term self-efficacy to refer to the mind-set of someone who believes in general terms that he or she will cope or have the capacity to manage in difficult situations.

■ The individual must be *prepared to intervene despite possible social costs* or physical danger. Such people are not deterred by the possibility of making a fool of themselves!

Figure 7.2 presents this model in the form of a five-step decision tree. Five separate decisions must be taken and if only one of these is negative, no help will be given.

Table 7.3 on page 213 summarises some further research studies which have tested out the propositions of Latane and Darley's cognitive decision-making model.

Latane and Darley's cognitive model has proved useful but also has certain limitations. It focuses on circumstances where people do *not* give help to others (Schroeder *et al.*, 1995). It doesn't give much insight into cases where whole communities have pulled together in rescue efforts under crisis circumstances. Nor does it seem to explain why some exceptional, altruistic individuals have been willing to sacrifice their own lives in order to save those of others.

■ Social behaviour in cities

You are now familiar with a number of controlled experiments which all demonstrate the bystander effect as the inverse relationship between the

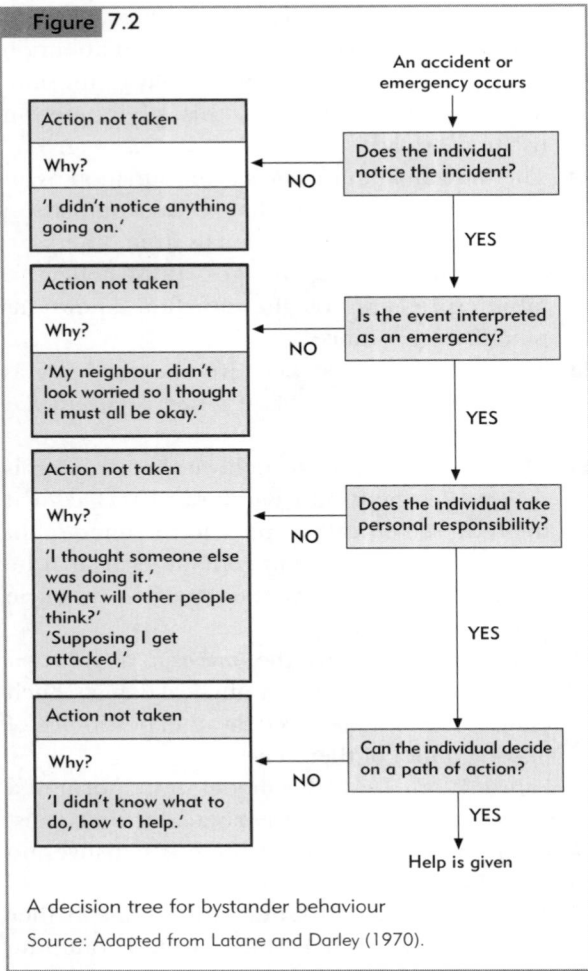

Figure 7.2

An accident or emergency occurs

Does the individual notice the incident?

NO → **Action not taken**

Why?

'I didn't notice anything going on.'

YES

Is the event interpreted as an emergency?

NO → **Action not taken**

Why?

'My neighbour didn't look worried so I thought it must all be okay.'

YES

Does the individual take personal responsibility?

NO → **Action not taken**

Why?

'I thought someone else was doing it.'
'What will other people think?'
'Supposing I get attacked,'

YES

Can the individual decide on a path of action?

NO → **Action not taken**

Why?

'I didn't know what to do, how to help.'

YES

Help is given

A decision tree for bystander behaviour

Source: Adapted from Latane and Darley (1970).

number of onlookers to an emergency and the chances of a victim getting help. But all these studies were highly contrived simulations of real-life scenarios, using elaborate deceptions. The number of bystanders that the researchers manipulated was typically small; maybe between one and a dozen. How far are the findings from such studies ecologically valid, i.e. valid in the complicated real world outside the laboratory? Could it be that the size of the wider social community in which we live, as opposed to the number of immediate witnesses to an incident, also has an effect on our tendency to help others?

Amato (1983) studied readiness to help in Australian communities ranging in size from villages of under 1000 inhabitants to large conurbations of over 300 000 people. He reported that a range of helpful acts, such as picking up a dropped envelope, giving to charity, and correcting inaccurate street directions became less likely as community size increased. Smith and Bond (1993) found, similarly, that help was more forthcoming in rural districts than in large cities in the USA, Canada and Turkey. Lavrakas (1982) reported that people feel safer in suburban neighbourhoods than in an urban environment.

What is it about large cities, apart from sheer physical size, that may inhibit our pro-social behaviour? Milgram (1970) proposed that in urban environments our senses are over-stimulated, so we narrow the focus of our attention and ignore strangers. This urban overload hypothesis is supported by the findings of McCauley *et al.* (1977), who found that there is less eye contact between strangers in large cities than in small towns.

More recently, Dunbar (1993), an evolutionary biologist, speculated that a 'natural' group size, to which the 'social intelligence' of the human brain is optimally adapted, may be around 150–200 people. He suggested it is no accident that prehistoric hunter-gatherer and farming communities, army units, small commercial enterprises, and even the number of names in our personal address books, all tend to be of this order of magnitude. Beyond a group size of about 150, it becomes hard to keep track of people and relate to them on a personal basis. If this line of argument is accepted, our dysfunctional behaviour in large cities arises because we are trying to operate outside the range of environments to which we are adapted as animals.

However, it could be misleading to assume that a disintegration of social behaviour in large cities is somehow inevitable. Korte *et al.* (1975) found no differences in helpfulness between rural and urban communities in Holland. This finding has been attributed to a strong norm for 'civility' in Dutch society.

Could the effects of big cities be mitigated by giving people a greater sense of belonging within their local community? The notion of territory is important here. Coleman (1986) surveyed 4099

Table 7.3

Researchers and date	Research question	Method and findings
Shotland and Stebbins (1980)	*Are people less likely to interpret a situation as an emergency if they can hear what is going on but can't see anything?*	A simulated attack on a woman in a deserted area of a college campus. Half the participants see a struggle in the distance. Actors then disappear into a room. All the participants hear realistic taped sounds of violence from within.
		Experimental condition — *Intervention rate* Participants both see and hear the violence — 95% ***Control condition*** Participants hear the tape, but see nothing — 13%
Darley et al. (1973)	*Is it more likely that witnesses to an event will take action if they are able to see one another?*	A simulated accident. Sounds of pain emerge from the room adjacent to the participants.
		Experimental condition — *Help rate* Participants in pairs, facing each other — 75% ***Control condition*** Participants back to back — 20%
Moriarty (1975)	*Will a stranger intervene to stop your belongings being stolen if you ask him or her to guard your possessions?*	Field experiment on a New York beach. Sunbather (a confederate) departs to swim, leaving possessions behind. Seconds later, thief (another confederate) steals his transistor radio.
		Experimental condition — *Intervention rate* Confederate asks participant to guard his possessions — 95% ***Control condition*** Confederate asks participant for a match — 20%
Pantin and Carver (1982)	*Does provision of first aid training make people more likely to intervene in a medical emergency?*	92 female undergraduates shown films about emergency first aid, then exposed three weeks later to a situation where a confederate stages a choking fit.

Mean response latencies (seconds)

No. of bystanders	***Experimental group***	***Control group*** (no first aid film seen)
2	77.07	77.80
6	71.4	159.82

Further research studies to test out Latane and Darley's cognitive decision-making model blocks of flats and over 4000 individual houses to assess the effect of physical design features on social problems such as litter, graffiti, vandalism to property and violence to people. Aerial walkways and 'confused space' of unclear ownership were particularly associated with problems. Relatively minor changes dramatically reduced crime as well as improving morale, for example fences around individual gardens, removal of walkways. Such environmental psychology research has changed housing design. 'Community architects' now consult future occupants and take psychological aspects of the environment into account at the planning stage. Design changes, such as orientating dwellings inward onto a courtyard instead of in a line along a corridor, can help deter criminals and make it more difficult for the bystanders of the future to overlook danger or trouble.

Helping and altruism

Having looked at non-responsiveness to victims of ill-fortune and the decisions involved, we now turn to the reasons for and against helping and the notion of **altruism**. Altruism can be defined as 'the elevation of the welfare, happiness, interests or even the survival of others above one's own'. Whilst helping behaviour can occur when there is no risk involved to the helper, altruistic behaviour involves the helper in selfless acts which jeopardise the helper's welfare, happiness, interests or even life. Theorists have been particularly interested in trying to determine whether or not there is such a thing as true altruism or whether altruistic behaviour is, in fact, an egotistical act, i.e. one which concentrates on self-interest. In this section we first of all examine some of these theories and then turn to other factors which might be involved in helping and altruistic behaviour, such as psychological and physical mediators.

■ The arousal: cost–reward model

This model suggests that bystanders weigh up the potential rewards and costs of intervention and non-intervention. In 1969, Piliavin staged a field experiment on a New York subway in which a confederate appeared to collapse and to need help: 95 per cent of onlookers helped a blind person carrying a white cane but only 50 per cent helped an alcoholic who smelled of liquor and was carrying a bottle in a brown paper bag. Clearly the sense of disgust onlookers felt for the alcoholic added to the perceived costs of helping.

Suppose you witness an armed theft in the china department of a large shop. How would this make you feel? Would you be distressed, frightened, or would you feel sympathy for the retailer? Should you intervene? The costs include the risk of getting hurt by thieves, breaking more china and even having to face police questioning. Also, if by any chance you are mistaken, this could prove embarrassing. The possible rewards in this case may seem very slight: you may gain the gratitude of the store owner, but the costs almost certainly outweigh this small benefit.

Activity 4

Before reading on, can you think of any costs associated with non-intervention?

The arousal: cost–reward model basically consists of two factors that are interdependent in order to explain helping and altruism:

■ *Arousal in response to the need of others* – this is an emotional response which is experienced as distressing and unpleasant to the helper, thus motivating the helper to act in order to reduce his or her own distress. This emotional response can induce the bystander to feel empathic towards the victim (i.e. he or she has an understanding and awareness of the emotions and feelings of another), thus more motivation to help emerges. Arousal has been measured in several studies by taking physiological measures in bystanders such as heart-rate and skin conductance.

■ *Cost–reward factor* – this involves the bystander weighing up the helping situation in terms of costs and rewards to himself or herself by means of a series of cognitive processes. Costs and rewards may be perceived in terms of:

– those received for helping the victim (such as the amount of effort or physical danger involved, unfamiliarity with helping task, admiration from others, fame, monetary reward). As costs for helping increase, helping decreases and as potential rewards increase, so intervention increases.

- costs for not helping the victim (such as self-blame, public censure). When costs for helping are low, helping increases as the costs for no help to the victim increase. Helping tends to increase when appeal for help is strong, and when it comes verbally from the victim or third party's request (Dovidio *et al.*, 1991).

In a review of this model by Dovidio *et al.* in 1991 the authors suggested that whilst this model is useful it is not necessarily a clear-cut one as there are so many factors involved which serve to make it extremely complex. It is an egotistical model because it suggests that, generally, helpers intervene for selfish motives, i.e. to reduce negative emotional arousal and to gain rewards. Next we examine another egotistical model suggesting altruistic behaviour is based purely on selfish motives.

■ The socio-biological perspective of altruistic behaviour

According to this theory there is no such thing as altruism, only 'apparent altruism', because human beings have evolved behaviours which serve to protect the species. Therefore any altruistic action is a purely selfish one which serves only to protect the helper and ultimately his or her genetic lineage.

'Stating that a behaviour pattern "evolves" is emphasising the adaptive nature of that behaviour' (Davies, 1995, p. 6). For example, spinal reflexes are adaptive responses enabling us to make a fast response so that we may remove ourselves from a dangerous situation. This response has been inherited from our ancestors who fled from dangerous animals when hunting for instance. Some evolved behaviour patterns may become maladaptive as cultures and societies change, therefore providing an explanation for some behaviours which seem to be at odds with the welfare of a particular species.

Altruism, then, is explained as an adapted behaviour which serves to maintain the reproduction of humans. People who fail or choose not to produce children, or neglect the children they have created, or fail to care for their close family relatives do not abide by the simple biological law which assumes the procreation of the genetic lineage is of paramount importance. These acts are generally uncommon and it is a more prevailing finding that people act favourably towards their close relatives. Altruism aimed towards close family members increases *inclusive fitness*, i.e. the probability that helping the family will lead to the further reproduction of their genes, thus the continued survival of those closest to us.

Helping our families is quite understandable when taking a socio-biological approach. But how can it explain why we help strangers? If we save a stranger from a blazing fire and are injured ourselves, how does this necessarily ensure the survival of our genes? Surely this helps the victim to survive genetically and not the helper. Socio-biologists propose that this kind of behaviour is **reciprocal altruism**. In other words, as a highly complex species with highly evolved elaborate brain networks we recognise those who are familiar to us (i.e. other human beings – the other members of our species), whether related or not, and, in addition, form alliances for combined action resulting in help being given freely to one another. In this way help is given on the understanding that it will be reciprocated in some way by another member of the 'coalition', if needed in the future. Therefore, altruistic behaviour is not, in fact, altruistic, as the helper is aiming for the survival of his or her own genes and ultimately ensuring the survival of the species.

■ The empathy–altruism hypothesis

This theory claims that 'feeling empathy evokes motivation with an ultimate goal of benefiting the person for whom empathy is felt' (Batson and Oleson, 1991). In other words, its proponents believe that highly empathic individuals feel compelled to help no matter what the situation. Therefore, according to this theory, altruistic behaviour is not egoistic, it does not depend on increasing our own welfare and contradicts the assumption that helping behaviour is self-serving. Further, the empathy–altruism hypothesis claims that we do care about the well-being of the victim for his or her own sake and not merely our own.

Experiments which have served to test this theory have generally used participants who are either high or low in **empathy**. In some experiments high or low empathy has been induced in participants by asking them to take an affective perspective, i.e. to focus on the feelings of the victim (high empathy) or by asking them to take a cognitive perspective, i.e. to focus on the thoughts of others and objectiveness of the situation (low empathy). In other experiments empathy in participants has been measured as an inherent characteristic of the participant by means of a psychological questionnaire. These experiments have sought to manipulate various other variables in order to ascertain whether highly empathic individuals do in fact behave altruistically or not. Two of these variables are discussed below:

- *Ease or difficulty of escape from the helping situation* – the arousal : cost–reward model explained on pages 214–5 suggests that we feel distress when faced with a helping situation and seek to dispense with this distress in some way in order to reduce arousal. This distress can be brought about by feelings of empathy. Therefore, if it is easy to escape from the helping situation this will reduce arousal and hence distress. However, the empathy–altruism hypothesis suggests that when a bystander is highly empathic he or she will not escape from the situation even when escape is made easy. When Batson (1987) summarised five experiments which had made escape either easy or difficult, those who were highly empathic still displayed altruistic behaviour even when escape was easy, thus upholding the premise put forward by this theory.

- *Socially or self administered punishment* – manipulation of this variable explores the premise that socialisation leads us to help because this is the 'right thing to do' and we therefore feel morally obligated to help. If we do not help others we will be evaluated negatively by society and face public disapproval. In addition, we may evaluate ourselves negatively by feeling shame and guilt

because we have not done 'the right thing'. Experimental research has found that when social evaluation is low (i.e. there is not much chance of others finding out that we have not helped) highly empathic individuals will still help, as demonstrated in the following study: Fultz *et al.* (1986) induced participants to feel more, or less, *empathy* for a lonely young woman who they were given an opportunity to help. To manipulate social evaluation some participants were told that the experimenter and the young woman would know if they did not help (high social evaluation) and others were told that nobody would know if they did not help (low social evaluation). It was found that even under the low social evaluation scenario those with high empathy were willing to help.

There are, however, limits to this theory which are acknowledged by Batson and Oleson (1991). These concerns focus on the extent of empathy and the concession that empathy can be 'a fragile flower, easily crushed by self-concern' (Batson *et al.*, 1983, p. 718). In addition, more recently Cialdini *et al.* (1997) have sought to reinterpret this theory. These researchers have suggested that when we feel empathy for another we identify with him or her and in this way become part of that person in that our own self concept overlaps with the self of the victim. This phenomena results in self–other overlap which the investigators describe as 'oneness'. Therefore, we are still behaving in order to benefit ourselves. This suggestion has been refuted by Batson (1997) and there appears to be a continued debate in this area (Batson *et al.*, 1997; Neuberg *et al.*, 1997) which should entice all readers to 'watch this space'!

Additional factors mediating helping behaviour

Thus far this unit has discussed issues with regard to pro-social behaviour concerning bystander intervention or non-intervention and the decisions surrounding action; in addition, the previous section deliberated the notion of whether altruistic behaviour does, in fact, exist. We are now going to turn to other issues which might compromise the effects of 'helping decisions' and helping or altruistic behaviour. These factors include: the effect of temporary states of mind which may affect the willingness of the helper, the personal attributes of the victim which might determine the readiness of others to help him or her, the kind of characteristics which might be involved in help seeking behaviour and, finally, the notion of the altruistic personality.

■ Psychological states and helping

Most of the research in this area has been concerned with the mood state of the helper or bystander. Common sense might tell us that positive affect – being in a 'good mood' – might generate more instances of helping behaviour; however, we will discover below that research in this field of inquiry uncovers another paradox.

Baron and Thornley (1992) found that when individuals experienced an environment in which they could sense a pleasant odour, such as a floral or lemon fragrance, then pro-social behaviour became more pronounced as positive affect was induced in the helper. To test the effect of positive mood on pro-social behaviour in everyday life, Baron (1995) arranged for a stooge to drop a pen or ask for change from a same sex consumer in a busy shopping centre. Help was sought either outside a shop which smelt agreeable, such as a coffee shop or bakery, or one which was neutral in terms of odour, such as a clothing retail outlet. Considerably more helping behaviour was found to occur when a pleasant smell was sensed.

However, alternative research has discovered that people who experience positive affect feel powerful and when the situation is somewhat ambiguous for the bystander, helping behaviour is not as prevalent because the helper feels sufficiently powerful to say 'no'. In addition, if there is a threat that one's happiness will be spoiled by helping, then the helper will also refuse to help under these circumstances (Baron and Byrne, 1997).

The effect of negative mood states is also contradictory. Once again, common sense would intimate that people in a 'bad mood' would refrain from helping and this has indeed been found to be the case in a number of studies (for example Rogers et al., 1982; Amato, 1986).

However, if it is believed by a bystander that helping someone will significantly improve his or her mood then the bystander is considerably more likely to help (Cialdini et al., 1982). This kind of response will only take place, however, if certain conditions are present such as an interesting helping situation that is not too difficult to deal with or one in which the emergency is obvious (Baron and Byrne, 1997).

Linked with this issue is the interesting finding that those who have consumed even moderate amounts of alcohol are likely to help more than their sober counterparts. This is because not only do people feel less inhibited when having consumed alcohol, but individuals affected by alcohol are less likely than others to perceive any ambiguities in the situation, which, as we have already seen, may affect the decisions made in a helping situation (Steele et al., 1985).

■ Characteristics of the victim

Some victims are more likely to receive help than others because of their personal or physical characteristics and the attitudes the helper holds about these characteristics. For example, *attractiveness* plays a significant role in the helping relationship. We have already seen some evidence of this in Unit 5. The more attractive we find a person to be, the more likely we are to help him or her.

Activity 5

How do you think prejudice might affect helping?

Shaw et al. (1994) hypothesised that prejudices towards homosexuals (a personal characteristic) would affect pro-social behaviour. In order to test their supposition research assistants were asked to call several telephone numbers at random and explain to the person called that they were using their last coin to speak to either their girlfriend 'Lisa', or their boyfriend 'Rick' (the research assistant was male) and had dialled the wrong number in error. The assistants then asked the person they were speaking to if they would kindly call their girl/boyfriend for them as they had a flat tyre and would be late for their first anniversary celebration with Lisa or Rick. They then gave the person called their telephone number in order to ascertain whether the recipient did or did not make the call to their girl/boyfriend as requested. The results are illustrated in figure 7.4 and demonstrate that when people believed the research assistant to be homosexual the majority of people called did not exhibit pro-social behaviour.

Gender has also been implicated in studies of pro-social behaviour and it may be assumed on the findings of such studies that we should expect

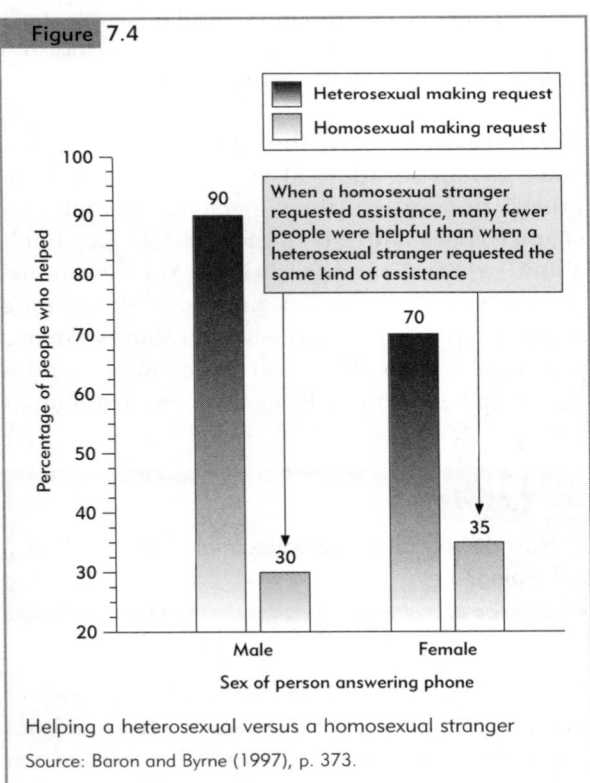

Figure 7.4

Helping a heterosexual versus a homosexual stranger
Source: Baron and Byrne (1997), p. 373.

more help from someone of the opposite sex. For example, in an American study of several police departments it was found that female officers issued more driving offence tickets than warnings to female drivers and a similar pattern was found to occur when investigating male officers. It was believed by the investigators that issuing driving tickets was of a less pro-social inclination than issuing warnings. This study provides evidence that certainly in most cases it is opportune to be stopped whilst driving by a police officer who is of the opposite sex.

However, other studies have found that it pays to be similar to your helper when seeking help. The helper may be able to envisage himself or herself more easily in the same situation as the victim if he or she is very similar in terms of sex, age, ethnic background and so on. This finding is especially true in rape cases and can be linked to attribution which was discussed in Unit 4. Bell *et al.* (1994) found that women felt themselves to be more similar to a female rape victim and attributed more blame to the rapist, whereas men felt themselves to be similar, at least in some respects, to the rapist and attributed blame to the victim. In cases such as these it may be that women are more likely to help a female rape victim than men. On the other hand, if a female considers herself to be similar to a rape victim she may not help as she may be fearful that this terrible attack could happen to her simply because she is similar. In this case the woman might escape from the distressed arousal state by attributing blame to the victim or repressing what had happened (Baron and Byrne, 1997).

From the research discussed here it might be surmised that we can expect more help if we are physically attractive, of the opposite sex from the helper, do not present any stigma inducing prejudice in the helper and are attributed no blame for our plight. A tall order by anyone's standards, particularly when we bear in mind that the helper might have to run through a second checklist considering such factors as cost, reward, what kind of mood he or she is in, whether he or she is empathic and how much he or she wants to protect the human species!

■ Who seeks help?

Some individuals are more likely to seek help than others. This section examines the characteristics of this differential in people. These differentials can be affected by situational, personality and demographic variables, and the differences found between individuals can be due to gaining benefits, such as easing suffering or task completion, and psychological costs, such as threatened self competence and independence (Nadler, 1991).

One of the first attributes to be considered is *gender*. Studies have generally indicated that females are more prone to seek help than males at a ratio of approximately two to one, although these studies have focused predominantly on help of an emotional nature. When it comes to problems of an instrumental nature males tend to seek help more readily. It could be that the difference comes about because of the western socialisation process during which males are defined as strong and independent and females as weak and dependent.

Self-esteem also plays an important part in help seeking behaviour – individuals high in self-esteem seek less help than those low in self-esteem. Several arguments have been proposed for this difference. One is that high self-esteem individuals find it difficult to seek help because of their positive self-image and so only seek help when exposure of weakness is low and when they can maintain a positive view of themselves. Because high self-esteem individuals seek less help, they fare more poorly on tasks which require reliance on other's help. Low self-esteem individuals, on the other hand, might label themselves as dependent on others and hence seek help. The consequences of this when applied to reality may result in high self-esteem individuals not seeking help when necessary and low self-esteem individuals overutilising helping resources.

Other attributes are summarised briefly below:

- *Age* – older people are less likely to ask for help than young people.
- *Socio-economic background* – higher socio-economic individuals make more requests for help but during these encounters seek less help than lower socio-economic individuals.

- *Shyness* – shy individuals are far less likely to seek the help of others, particularly when the helper is of the opposite sex. This attribute can be considered in a positive light in that shy people may be more motivated to help themselves and therefore become more successful problem solvers. (Nadler, 1991)

■ Is there an altruistic personality?

Steven Spielberg's film *Schindler's List* (1993) movingly describes the audacious rescue of Jews from certain death in Nazi extermination camps, by a German, Oskar Schindler. He managed to keep 1300 Jews alive throughout the war by purchasing a munitions factory in Krakow, Poland, and persuading his superiors with bribes and lies to allow him to employ Jews with 'essential skills'. Schindler, then, was no conventional 'do-gooder'. Before the war he had been a feckless gambler and drinker with many mistresses. He took great risks and seemed to thrive on the excitement and danger of his actions. He was defiant of convention, yet was at the same time illuminated by compassion which transcended barriers of race and religion. 'If you saw a dog going to be crushed under a car,' he said later of his wartime actions, 'wouldn't you help?'. After the war, he didn't really manage to adapt to civilian life and ended his days in decrepitude.

There have been several formal research studies which indicate that the minority of people who overcome the social pull towards bystander apathy and help those in need, have special personality traits: Bierhoff *et al.* (1991) compared individuals who witnessed a traffic accident and administered first aid to a victim, with those who took no action. The researchers proposed that the following five 'altruistic personality' traits were characteristic of those who took action:

- Empathy.
- A strong belief in a 'just world' (Lerner, 1980).
- A strong sense of social responsibility.
- Internal 'locus of control' (Rotter, 1966). People who possess an internal locus of control believe they are in control of most events and can make a difference to their own lives. This is a similar concept to 'self-efficacy' (Bandura, 1977). Individuals with external locus of control

tend to believe that events happen by luck, fate, or other forces outside their own control.

■ A low level of egocentrism; i.e. they were not self-absorbed or preoccupied with competing with others.

Oliner and Oliner (1988) studied 406 brave individuals who, like Schindler, had risked their own lives during the Second World War in order to rescue Jews in Nazi-occupied Europe. They compared them with a matched sample of non-rescuers who had lived throughout the war in similar circumstances but had not intervened. The researchers used in-depth structured interviews to probe the childhood upbringing, important life events, personalities and values of their respondents. They found that though rescuers and non-rescuers had similar information available to them about Nazi treatment of Jews (for example being forced to wear a yellow star, being 'deported' in closed railway trucks to unknown destinations), they differed in important ways in their interpretation of that information. Non-rescuers were very vague about what had happened and psychologically distanced themselves from events. Rescuers, on the other hand, were so moved by the suffering they witnessed that they felt as if they had no choice but to involve themselves. There were many other telling differences between the responses of rescuers and non-rescuers to the same desperate circumstances. These are summarised in table 7.5.

Media influences on pro-social behaviour

■ Television

Debates concerning the influence of the media on behaviour stress the potentially harmful effects of television. But can the media have good effects too? Some television programmes, it is claimed, are pro-social, such as 'Sesame Street', 'Lassie' and 'Blue Peter'. They try to encourage children to be constructive, imaginative and cooperative. Some, such as the annual 'Blue Peter appeal', encourage sharing and helping too. In order to assess the role

of the media in pro-social behaviour we need to look at some of the research findings. In one study, exposure to an episode of 'Lassie' in which a boy helped a dog, meant the willingness of children to help puppies in distress in a test situation increased (Sprafkin et al., 1975). Moriarty and McCabe (1977) studied 259 children and youths engaged in organised team sports – little league baseball, lacrosse and ice hockey. The pro-social behaviour of the players on the field was measured before, during and after experimental treatment. The treatment consisted of providing pro-social and control video presentations of the relevant sport. The pro-social material included: altruism (helping, encouraging and team work); sympathy (compassion, pity and caring for another's plight); courtesy (displays of respect); reparation (correcting a wrong or apologising); affection (expressing positive feelings towards another). The level of pro-social behaviour on the part of hockey and lacrosse players heightened following exposure to pro-social television content. No effects were found for baseball players.

Activity 6

Suggest reasons for the different outcomes for the three sports as a result of exposure to the pro-social material.

The results of the Friedrich and Stein (1973) study (see case study on page 222) do suggest some positive effects from watching programmes with pro-social rather than aggressive content but some effects are not statistically significant or, as already shown, go in the opposite direction. The researchers carried out many analyses and tried to emphasise the 'desired' findings in their report. Nevertheless, such mixed findings must give rise to some scepticism. Further, the learning of pro-social behaviour through modelling does not appear to generalise to different situations. Paulson (1974) found that the modelling of cooperative behaviour on 'Sesame Street' produced cooperation in young children but did not have more general effects on pro-social behaviour.

Table 7.5	Non-rescuers	Rescuers
Opportunity to help		
Did they live near Jews before the war?	57%	59%
Had they seen Jews wearing a yellow star?	93%	99%
Where they aware of Nazi intentions towards Jews?	◄——————— Similar proportions ———————►	
Had they witnessed Nazi brutality towards Jews and others?	◄——————— Similar proportions ———————►	
Did they take risks if they sheltered Jews?	◄——————— Similar proportions ———————►	
What material resources had they? Food? Spare rooms in their house?	◄——————— Similar proportions ———————►	
What was their social class background?	◄——————— Similar distribution ———————►	
Interpretation of information	Talked of vague rumours	Knew exactly what was going on
	Emphasised their own ignorance and impotence	Felt obliged to act, take personal responsibility
Were they asked for help?	25% had been asked; 10% of respondents had refused such requests. Help where given tended to be brief	Frequently asked for help, often through intermediaries. They also spontaneously volunteered help
Attitude towards the Nazi threat	Often a passive one of fear, hopelessness and uncertainty	Their over-riding concern was compassion for the victims
Values and personality		
Social and ethical values	'Equity' values: Working hard Getting a good job Being thrifty	'Care' values: Giving out to other people Universalistic orientation-regarding all humans as equal
Moral feelings		Moved by pain, sadness or helplessness in other people
Attitude towards religion	◄——————— Religious observance in similar proportions ———————►	
'Locus of Control' (Rotter, 1966)	External	Internal
'Social Responsibility' scale (Berkowitz, 1963)	Lower scores	Higher scores
Childhood and upbringing	Family relationships often passive and distant	Family relationships close, warm and affectionate
	Stress on obedience and physical punishment	'Inductive' approach to discipline (discussing reasons for prohibitions with the child) (Hoffman, 1975/6)
Attitudes and activities after the war	Didn't talk to their children about the war period	Talked freely to their children
		'Warm glow' of satisfaction in describing their rescue activities
	Low level of community involvement	Often engaged in community work, such as care for the old and sick, teaching and counselling

Is there an 'altruistic personality'? (Oliner, 1988). Comparison of circumstances and personality of rescuers of Jews in Nazi-occupied Europe

Case study – Friedrich and Stein (1973)

Friedrich and Stein (1973) studied 4-year-old children enrolled in a nine-week summer nursery school programme. In the first three weeks of the programme baseline observations of the 100 children were collected. The children were then assigned to three groups: 30 into the 'aggressive' condition, 30 into the 'pro-social' condition and 40 into the 'neutral' condition. For the next four weeks children were exposed to various television programmes. The children in the aggressive condition saw 'Batman' and 'Superman' cartoons. Those in the pro-social condition were exposed to 'Mister Roger's Neighbourhood' which promoted themes of cooperation, sympathy and friendship. Those in the neutral conditions were exposed to neutral fare (factual films with little aggressive or pro-social content).

During the four-week period and also the two final weeks the children's free-play behaviour was closely observed. The children who watched the pro-social programmes were scored as more patient (tolerance of delay) than the children who watched the aggressive programmes and tended to be more persistent at tasks and more spontaneously helpful or obedient. Children initially high in aggression showed a decrease in aggressive behaviour following pro-social and neutral programmes. For children low in aggression no significant effect was observed. However, results of the study are mixed. For pro-social behaviour it was found that this increased only in lower income children who watched pro-social programmes. It also increased in children from higher social class families who watched the aggressive programmes.

More recently, however, Forge and Phemister (1987) have demonstrated that when pre-school children have watched pro-social programmes such as 'Sesame Street', they are much more likely to engage in pro-social behaviour than those who do not. Baron and Byrne (1997) claimed that studies in general consistently demonstrate that social modelling on television has been found to have had a profound effect on pro-social behaviour.

■ Computers

Another aspect of media influence that is becoming more prominent is that concerning computer games, and no doubt there will soon be an influx of research concerning the internet. Computers and game consoles now play a significant role in many children's lives and there has been ongoing debate concerning their benefits, if any. Many authors believe that such games are an important and beneficial part of the modern child's educational process. For example, Silvern (1986) suggested that classroom computer games are fun and that some children may only be drawn into learning through this process, and Surrey (1982) stated that video games are good because they introduce children to modern technology.

Perhaps a more convincing argument, particularly as we are concerned here with pro-social behaviour, is that of Brown (1989). He argued that electronic games arouse the biological functions of the regulation of arousal which can be described as a decrease through escape or recreation or an increase through competition; the preparation for reality; the regulation of confidence which can affect other decisions. According to Brown, therefore, computer games may deter individuals from exhibiting violent behaviour because of these beneficial effects.

Other supporters of this type of media outlet have found that such games promote social interaction and growth. Mitchell (1983) found that families generally believe that computer games promote family interaction beneficially by means of cooperation and competition. In addition, Creasey and Myers (1986) explored the relationship between computer games and children's leisure activities, school work and peer contacts. None of these activities were affected and therefore the researchers concluded that video game machines do not produce a detrimental effect.

In conclusion, however, these sparse findings have not all been tested empirically. In addition, the findings do not relate specifically to the use of computer games and pro-social behaviour *per se* and therefore more research is necessary in this area before any firm conclusions can be reached.

Self-assessment questions

1 Imagine that you are being attacked, have fallen through the ice on a pond or are in a burning building. Use the decision-making model to suggest things that you could do or say to bring others to your aid.

2 Criticise the use of controlled experimentation as a method of investigating bystander behaviour. Can you suggest an alternative method?

3 How far do you consider the socio-biological perspective gives us useful insights into altruism in humans?

4 Briefly outline one theory of pro-social behaviour.

5 Explain the paradox concerning both positive and negative affect as a psychological state involved in helping behaviour.

6 What evidence is there that exposure to pro-social behaviour on television is likely to influence pro-social behaviour?

(Suggested answers on pages 241–2.)

Anti-social behaviour

We turn now from apathy and helping behaviour – which do not carry any overt wish to hurt – to the other side of the coin, to those forms of behaviour which do hurt. In studying the research evidence in this section of the unit, you may find it helpful to keep in mind the following questions:

- What situational factors triggered off the anti-social behaviour?
- How could the situation be changed in order to reduce and control the anti-social behaviour and encourage pro-social behaviour?

Aggression and violence

In everyday usage **aggression** and violence are frequently treated as interchangeable terms. To the psychologist, however, violence is only one aspect of aggression. Archer (1988) identified three components of aggression:

- an internal emotional state (anger),
- an intent (to harm), and
- a behavioural response (the violence itself).

Violence is frequently the way in which an aggressive act is expressed but the behavioural response may, however, be expressed in other ways as well.

Activity 7

Make a list of the aggressive responses which are possible from a feeling of anger and an intent to harm (then read on).

Did you include such things as glaring, name calling and putting people down? Psychologists commonly divide aggressive behaviour into hostile (with intent to harm) and instrumental (goal-orientated). A rigid classification such as this may be misleading, since aggressive behaviour will often involve costs (in particular from retaliation). Thus aggressive acts which do not gain benefits are unlikely to be repeated. Furthermore, it is difficult to imagine aggressive behaviour which lacks hostility.

Theories of aggression

Psychologists do not agree on how aggressive and violent behaviours develop. Theories of aggression perceive hostile behaviours as biological, social or cognitive phenomena. The main biological approach is that concerning instinct which can very loosely be linked to the more recent socio-biological perpective. The latter theory is similar in approach to the one discussed in the section on pro-social behaviour. Three, in some cases overlapping, socially based theories are discussed here as well as the cognitive theories which are prevalent in many areas of psychology today.

■ The instinctive theory of aggression

The instinctive theory of aggression emphasises the biological roots of violent behaviour and may be traced back to the two widely separate disciplines of *psychoanalysis* and *ethology*. Freud (1933), a psychoanalyst, saw aggression as originating from the thanatos, a powerful death instinct which is initially aimed inwards at the self but which gradually becomes directed outward towards others. The hostile impulses generated by the thanatos build up over time, in much the same way that hunger pangs gradually increase in the absence of food. Aggression needs to be released periodically and the longer the period prior to release of aggression, the greater the ultimate hostility.

In contrast to Freud's approach, the ethologist Lorenz (1966) marshalled developments in evolutionary theory to create an attractive hypothesis. He believed that aggression in both humans and non-human animals is a fighting instinct which is directed against members of the *same* species. The key difference, according to Lorez, between aggression in human and in non-human animals is that it is *ritualised* in non-human animals. In non-human animals, aggression is

discharged in stereotyped, ritualised ways which results in the loser from a contest suffering relatively little physical damage. For example, many species use appeasement gestures (dogs expose the vulnerable throat and stomach to prevent attack) which allow dominance hierarchies to become established.

> ### Activity 8
>
> Make a list of the appeasement gestures that you think humans may use. (Answers are in the following paragraph.)

Human appeasement gestures include smiling, cowering and begging for mercy. So what is it that is significantly different in human aggression? Lorenz believed that in humans, the evolution of cognitive abilities has outstripped the evolution of the ritualistic mechanisms which serve to inhibit aggression – hence the frightening potential of human beings to destroy each other. The distances at which bombs and missiles can kill make smiling or begging for mercy ineffective strategies!

The view that aggression in non-human animals is ritualised is over-simplified. Although this is often the case, many examples of violent aggression occur, such as the killing of males in a rival group of chimpanzees (Goodall, 1978) and infanticide (for example among lions and bears).

Socio-biologists today agree, in part, with Lorenz's contention that aggression, as a social behaviour, is the result of an evolutionary process which contributes to the reproduction of the human genetic lineage. Aggression is males, therefore, helps the male of a species to procure a mate, and the main tenets of natural selection suggest that aggression is a natural phenomenon in humans and non-humans, particularly among males.

Baron and Byrne (1997) argued that these instinct theories use 'circular reasoning' which does not appear to be logical. The proponents of these theories begin by proposing that aggression is a common type of behaviour. The theorists then go on to observe that aggression stems from universal, innate or evolved urges or tendencies. In conclusion, they suggest the high incidence of aggressive acts is due to these urges or tendencies.

In addition, it has been found that studies which compare various cultures and societies note that aggression does not appear to be a universal phenomenon. Different types and levels of aggression are apparent in different areas of the world, for example in some developing countries rates of aggressive crime are much higher than in some developed countries and vice-versa (Osterman *et al.*, 1994). These differences lead to the observation that social and cultural factors must surely influence aggressive tendencies and we must remember that instinct theories remain somewhat unconvincing.

■ The frustration–aggression hypothesis

The frustration–aggression hypothesis was developed by Dollard *et al.* (1939) as an alternative to the instinctive theory. It also developed from the Freudian notion that aggression occurs in response to the blocking of a pleasurable drive or expectation. It attempts to restate these views in terms acceptable to learning theory. Basically, in its initial form, the hypothesis stated that aggression is *always* a consequence of frustration, and that frustration *always* leads to some form of aggression.

In common with the instinctive theory, internal drive is regarded as an important component, but in the frustration–aggression hypothesis such a drive is related to frustration caused by goal blocking rather than to a gradual increase in aggression irrespective of external circumstances. The critical point of this hypothesis is an unfulfilled expectancy. If people do not expect to receive rewards they are far less affected than if one is promised and then withheld. This external blocking of a perceived goal sets up a state of frustration which is, in turn, expressed as anger and aggression. Thus there is a clear shift from a purely internal to an external situation-dependent explanation.

Evidence in favour of the frustration–aggression hypothesis is found in the experimental literature. Rats subjected to repeated electric shocks will engage in long-lasting fights (O'Kelly and Steckle, 1939). Furthermore, rats, pigeons and squirrel-monkeys which have been reinforced on a learning task with food, will show aggression towards a nearby target when food is no longer forthcoming. Similarly, aggression develops rapidly in children who are frustrated by being deliberately denied access to attractive toys (Barker *et al.*, 1941). Aggression frequently follows defeat in sport; and most of us will have felt angry at missing a bus or train.

Activity 9

Can you think of examples of aggression that do not result from frustration? (Some ideas are in the following text.)

You may have thought of such examples as carrying out military orders or gaining rewards from being a professional wrestler. In its initial format, therefore, it became obvious that the frustration–aggression hypothesis was overstated. Miller (1941) noted that although frustration can make aggression more likely, aggression is not an inevitable consequence of it. He therefore regarded frustration as an instigator of aggression – which might be held in check through learned responses such as fear of retaliation.

Also, despite the relationship between frustration and aggression observed in animals, a great deal of aggression occurs in the absence of any clear frustrating block. This raises two problems. Firstly, what constitutes frustration? Should pain or discomfort be classified as frustrating agents, since they give rise to immobility and dependency? The second problem concerns the measurement of frustrating agents which is difficult both in terms of quality and quantity, since both human and other animal participants will bring differing expectations with them.

The frustration–aggression hypothesis has been modified more recently by Berkowitz (1993) who suggested that frustration may not be the only arousing factor which drives individuals to become aggressive. He suggests that arousal induced by any negative affect can lead us to behave aggressively and 'the stronger the displeasure, the stronger will be the resulting instigation to aggression'. Berkowitz suggested various inciters of negative affects which might influence aggressive tendencies, some of which are outlined below:

■ Effects of insults or threats to one's esteem – such detrimental acts tarnish one's self-image in such a way that the injured party may become aggressive.

■ Sadness and depression can result in hostile thoughts, angry feelings and lead to aggressive tendencies. It is quite common for individuals who have been bereaved to feel anger resulting in hostility.

■ It can be recognised that even a mild headache can induce a feeling of irritability and hence illness induces aggressive inclinations.

Berkowitz continues to state that studies similar to the ones described earlier in this unit concerning positive affect and helping behaviour have demonstrated that negative affect induced by foul odours, high temperatures and so on can induce aggression. However, it should be remembered that this negative affect can produce a flight or fight type of behaviour and therefore aggression is not always inevitable and may be defensive in nature. In addtion, as negative affect can conjure up thoughts, feelings and behaviour that have been learned in our social environment, it is necessary to be acquainted with social learning theory to which we now turn.

■ Social learning theory

Contemporary social learning theory models emphasise the modification of hostile responses through learning. They acknowledge both the biological bases of aggression and the existence of frustration. The two main models, reinforcement and modelling, are discussed in this section.

Under the reinforcement hypothesis, a child allowed to attain a goal through aggression will be more likely to show hostility in the future. Research has shown that parents of highly aggressive children frequently (unintentionally) reinforce violent behaviour, for instance by responding positively to their demands (for example Littman and Bricker, 1967). Furthermore, children subjected to physical punishment often use violence themselves in later life. Bandura (1973) and Baron and Richardson (1994) reported that,

within the family setting, physical punishment from parents correlates significantly with aggression and delinquency in the children. Also, adults who have themselves received high levels of physical punishment as children are far more likely to physically abuse their own children (for example Strauss et al., 1980).

Although there appears to be strong support for the reinforcement theory, there are problems. Followers of the instinctive theory might argue that social learning theory mixes up cause and effect. For example, instinctive theorists might say children are innately aggressive. Since parents and offspring share each other's genes, both may be biologically prone to violence. Also, aggressive children will elicit a greater degree of punishment from their parents – and violent citizens will need tougher control from the police.

Children may learn aggression by *modelling*, which provides **vicarious reinforcement** and involves imitating the actions of those around them, in particular friends, teachers and television characters. Bandura (1961) showed that children imitated adults who hit and kicked at a bobo doll.

In general boys imitate more readily than girls but both sexes will copy adults in preference to other children (Bandura, 1986). However, this research has been criticised on the grounds of artificiality. Firstly, it is argued that children know they are attacking a bobo doll and therefore harming no one. Secondly, independent observers (for example Burton-Jones, 1972) have, through analysis of facial expression, re-classified much of this 'aggression' as rough-and-tumble play. It has also been suggested that participants do not understand what they are supposed to be doing and are simply fulfilling the expectations of the experimenters (Archer, 1989). This last criticism has been levelled at laboratory-based investigations in general which, in turn, has led to a movement towards field or naturalistic studies.

Beynon and Delamont (1984) and Beynon (1989) conducted naturalistic studies of aggression by integrating themselves into the school system to observe the effects of modelling in routine violence. Pupils were observed to model their responses upon their teachers' behaviour. The teachers used violence to gain respect from their pupils, then, as with their teachers, boys were seen to use violence as a means to achieve respect from their peers. In addition to increasing their personal standing within the school, Beynon also frequently observed aggressive behaviour as a way of relieving boredom, a finding which appears to lend support to the frustration–aggression hypothesis.

Despite research which supports the premise that *'violence breeds violence'*, Peterson and Brown (1994) have developed an *'integrative model'* which they have applied to maltreatment of children but which can be applied to other forms of aggression. Their model states that not only do people who have been abused themselves as children follow this pattern in adulthood and abuse their own or other children, but that there are also a number of other significant variables involved such as socio-cultural factors, child-based determinants and considerations surrounding the care-giver. Figure 7.6 summarises these variables and presents a more holistic picture of the complex social factors involved.

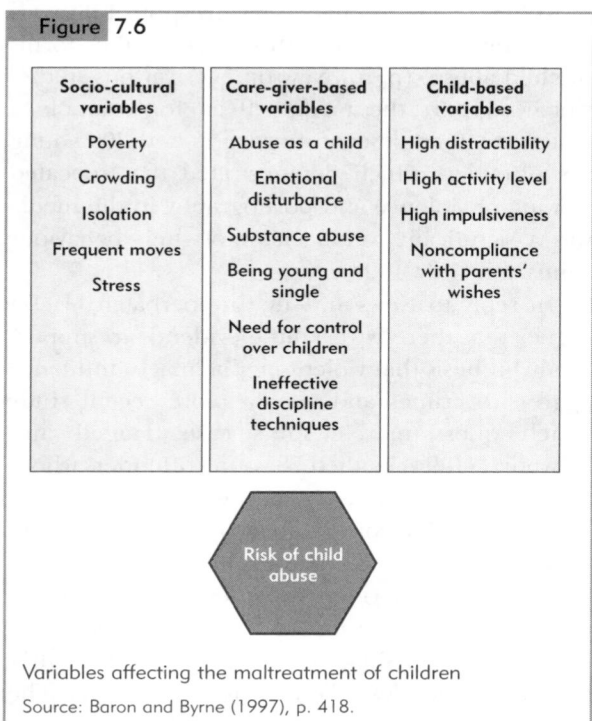

Figure 7.6

Socio-cultural variables	Care-giver-based variables	Child-based variables
Poverty	Abuse as a child	High distractibility
Crowding	Emotional disturbance	High activity level
Isolation	Substance abuse	High impulsiveness
Frequent moves	Being young and single	Noncompliance with parents' wishes
Stress	Need for control over children	
	Ineffective discipline techniques	

Risk of child abuse

Variables affecting the maltreatment of children

Source: Baron and Byrne (1997), p. 418.

Cognitive theories

Imagine you are in a very busy shopping centre just before Christmas carrying several bags full of gifts for family and friends. You are just about to enter a department store and try to squeeze in behind someone who is just going through the door, but the person slams the door in your face causing you to drop your bags. How do you feel?

Activity 10

Think about what your course of action might be and make a note of several possibilities before reading on.

According to cognitive theories of aggression (Huesmann, 1988, 1994; Berkowitz, 1993; Anderson *et al.*, 1995) your decision concerning what action to take might depend on one or all of the following factors:

- *'Scripts' or 'cognitive programmes'* – these are scripts or behaviour patterns that are influenced by past events or socialisation patterns which determine what you think you ought to do in any given situation or setting. In the case of the above example, you might decide not to behave in a hostile manner in this situation because your script for Christmas shopping does not involve retaliating against another shopper, particularly at a time of 'goodwill to all men'.

- **Hostile attributional bias** – this involves a tendency in individuals to perceive others' actions as being intentionally antagonistic even when the situation is ambiguous, which can lead to aggressive retaliation for a purely accidental act. Going back to our example, if we held a hostile attributional bias ourselves we would not accept that the other shopper had slammed the door accidentally because the person was overloaded with shopping and could not control the swing of the door, but we would infer that the shopper had done this purposefully. In this case, therefore, we would retaliate.

- *Appraisal* – this involves weighing up the situation and deciding why another person has behaved in a certain way. Therefore, whilst appraising, we seek to rule out any ambiguities and think through why an incident might have occurred. If involved in the shopping scenario, we might consider whether the other shopper was apologetic or not, or realise that someone else had in fact bumped into the shopper, thus causing the event to occur. Following this appraisal, we may make a second appraisal which determines our behaviour by weighing up the pros and cons of any subsequent action we might take next.

■ *Negative affect* – we have already seen on page 226 how negative affect can produce arousal which causes us to flee from a situation or stay and fight. Having a door slammed in our face would induce negative affect and this may influence our behavioural pattern: we might choose to stay in the shopping centre and retaliate aggressively or decide we have had enough and go home.

The media and aggression

In November 1993 two juveniles were convicted in an English Crown Court of the brutal murder of a 2-year-old boy who was killed after being lured away from his mother in a shopping centre. The trial judge suggested that the killers may have been influenced by violent videos.

The extent to which there was a link between violent videos and the crime may never be known. The police involved in the case believed that the attack could not simply be blamed on video 'nasties'. However, a film rented by the father of one of the convicted children contained scenes which bore some resemblances to the boy's death, although it was said in Court that the child had not seen it.

It is a popularly held notion that violence portrayed by the media and, in particular, on television and videos encourages aggressive behaviour in young people. However, the vast amount of research in this area provides a great deal of ambiguity. Some psychologists believe that a *'media effect'* does exist whilst others do not and believe that we should look at other factors in society which help to mediate violence and aggression.

The work carried out by social learning theorists on aggression (for example Bandura, 1961) has shown that modelling can be a powerful factor in the acquisition of aggressive behaviour. Much of the research supports the finding that exposure to television programmes showing violence leads to *more* aggression, not a cathartic reduction of it. Therefore, we might expect that the media, particularly television and videos, are powerful sources of aggressive role models.

Elizabeth Newson (1994) is a strong supporter of the 'media effects' theory. She believes that watching violent videos and film 'nasties' leads to violent behaviour in viewers and states that 'Many of us hold our liberal ideals of freedom of expression dear, but now begin to feel that we were naive in our failure to predict the extent of damaging material and its all too free availability to children . . . By restricting such material from home viewing, society must take on a necessary responsibility in protecting children from this as from other forms of child abuse' (p. 5). Newson cites various studies which support the media effect, for example a review of 40 adolescent murderers and 200 young sex offenders which demonstrated that repeated viewing of violence and pornography in the media was a significant causal factor of their behaviour (Sims and Gray, 1993).

In reply to Newson, Guy Cumberbatch (1997) argues that there is very little evidence to support the hypothesis that violent media images influence aggressive crimes and cites a more recent study which questions Newson's case. Hagell and Newburn (1994) studied 78 young offenders whose average of arrests in one year was nearly five. When compared with a control group of school children, it was found that the offenders had fewer television sets or access to video recorders and had more difficulty in naming a favourite television personality who they would wish to be like; they were also much less likely to visit the cinema. The offenders were more likely to be too busy offending outside the home than remaining at home watching violent videos. Cumberbatch also claims that, ironically, it is the media itself which creates the moral panics fuelling speculation about media violence and aggression.

This is, however, a difficult area to research. Many of the studies are correlational in nature and therefore fail to establish cause and effect. Another difficulty concerns the elimination of other variables when conducting research, for example reinforcement from parents.

Much of the research in this area has been undertaken in the USA where, it can be argued, there is a wider choice of programmes. However, in the light of the Bulger case of 1993 described above, more research is being undertaken in Britain. Gauntlett (1997) believes that the Hagell and Newburn study approached the problem from the best angle – instead of investigating the media first (and its content) the investigation centred on the offenders. Gauntlett suggests that there are ten things wrong with the media effects model including treating children as inadequate and unable to criticise the media and the artificiality of such studies, for example the content of programmes used for such studies.

Activity 11

How much violence would you judge there is on British television?

In table 7.7 are the results of two studies which have analysed the content of British programmes.

It would appear from these statistics that there is more violence on television today and that television is permeated by violence. However, Gunter and Harrison pointed out that statistics can be misleading. First of all, we should note that the Cumberbatch study probably did not contain BSkyB programmes. In addition, the authors of the latter study stated that nearly half the violence occurred in only 2 per cent of programmes which tended to fall into main categories: contact sports such as boxing and wrestling and late night movies usually found on subscription movie channels.

Activity 12

Do you think violence in cartoons counts as aggression?

In the Gunter and Harrison study it may be noted that a substantial percentage (24 per cent) of children's programmes contained violent acts. Out of 4700 hours of television viewed altogether, 7 hours were occupied by violence during children's programmes. From a total of over 2000 programmes viewed for the study, 368 children's programmes contained some violence. However, approximately one-third of the violence

Table 7.7

	Cumberbatch (1987)	Gunter and Harrison (1995)
	Time span: 4 separate weeks during	Time span: 4 separate weeks during
	1986	1994–95
Programmes containing some violence	30%	37%
Percentage of violent episodes per total programme time	1%	1%
Violent acts per programme	1.14	unknown
Violent acts per hour	1.68	4–5
Percentage of violent acts resulting in death	26%	unknown

Content analysis of television programmes in 1987 and 1995

occurred in only 20 programmes, the majority of which were cartoons broadcast on Sky One and the American programmes *Power Rangers* and *VR Troopers*.

These writers were not suggesting that there is an insignificant amount of violence on television but that it is possible for a television viewer to view very little violence during an average day's viewing.

Several studies, as we noted earlier, support the 'media effects' model and have found significant correlations between the amount of aggression viewed on television and that displayed by children. For example, Huesmann and Eron (1986) found that seven- to nine-year-olds, in five countries over a period of three years, displayed more hostile behaviour when correlated with the amount of violence watched on television. Aggression was measured using self-evaluation questionnaires and peer ratings. Critics may argue that aggressive children prefer to watch aggressive or violent television programmes. However, a study which compared communities of children aged six to eleven, who either watched only one channel, several channels or had only recently been introduced to television, found that aggression increased in the latter community but there were no changes in behaviour in the other two communities (Williams, 1986).

Very recent studies in Britain suggest opposite findings. Professor Tony Charlton is involved in a longitudinal study on the remote island of St Helena in the South Atlantic which is investigating the inception of broadcast television. Whilst this research is ongoing, Charlton (1997) has published some early results. He investigated children's behaviour both before and after the introduction of television to the island. It is now possible to watch television 24 hours a day in St Helena on a variety of channels. The research uses several quantitative and qualitative measures including teacher observations, content analysis of programmes, video recordings of children's playground behaviour, ratings of parental mediation, identification with television characters, and group and individual interviews. Findings to date reveal that children's behaviour on the island has remained exemplary since the inception of television. Charlton tentatively concludes at this point that the social context on the island is a caring and 'watchful' one where parents mediate the viewing patterns of their children, coview with them and discuss children's viewing with them. In addition, he proposes that 'it could be reasoned that most behaviours . . . are rooted within the home, the wider community and the peer group' (p. 59). In other words, television viewing is rooted within a social context and does not stand alone. Perhaps this will lead to more meaningful research.

The research findings of another important investigation, commissioned by the Home Office in the light of the Bulger case, have also recently been published. Browne and Pennell (1998) compared three groups: 54 violent offenders, 28 non-violent offenders and a control group of 40 non-offender students. Participants were asked about their viewing habits and shown a violent video film. They were interviewed regarding their recollections and interpretations of the film immediately after viewing and again after both a four- and ten-month interval. They were also assessed with regard to family background, predisposition towards anger, empathic concern and moral maturity. The findings agree somewhat with Charlton in that the social context of violent and non-violent offenders seems to play a significant part in their behaviour (little difference was found between these two groups). The authors put forward a tentative model which depicts a pathway from having a violent home background, to being an offender, to being more likely to prefer violent films and violent actors. Personal characteristics such as low empathy for others, low moral development and distorted perceptions of violent behaviour all enhance the likelihood of offending and preference for viewing violent films.

The findings from these recent studies need to be followed up and conclusions made accordingly. However, they are likely to have important implications when considering methods for controlling and reducing aggression and violence (see pages 236–8).

Self-assessment questions

7   Explain reinforcement and modelling as appertaining to the social learning theory of aggression.

8   Briefly describe two components of the cognitive theory of aggression.

9   Provide one example of evidence for and one against the 'media effects' model of aggression.

(Suggested answers on pages 242–3.)

Individual, social and cultural diversity in pro- and anti-social behaviour

The individual and personality

So far the study of pro- and anti-social behaviour has mainly focused on the individual in terms of processes within the individual which explain such behaviour and situational factors that lead an individual to behave in a predictable way. As well as the hostile attributional bias which we have already discussed, there are other aspects concerned with the individual personality which need to be examined, focusing mainly on the question of whether people aggress because they have an *aggressive personality*.

■ The Type A personality

Research has demonstrated that there exists both a Type A and a Type B personality (Matthews, 1982; Strube, 1989). Type As are found to be excessively competitive, to be particularly hostile and aggressive, to be always in a hurry and to be prone to heart disease. Type Bs, on the other hand, possess none of these characteristics. There are also, of course, those who fall somewhere in between the two at varying points. Several studies have found that Type As tend to be much more aggressive than their Type B counterparts. For example, Carver and Glass (1978) found that Type A individuals were more aggressive towards people who were perceived to be competing with them on an important task. Type A personalities have also been found to be more likely to engage in child and spouse abuse (Strube *et al.*, 1984). A more recent investigation has discovered that the Type A personality can also work hand in hand with another variable: testosterone levels. Berman *et al.* (1993) used participants who were known to be either Type A or Type B and exposed them to growing levels of provocation from a stranger – the stranger set gradually stronger shocks for the participants in a competitive reaction time test where the loser on each trial received a shock set for him by his opponent. In addition to this the participants' testosterone (male sex hormone) levels were measured before the task began. Results provided evidence that Type As who also had high levels of testosterone administered the strongest shocks available, thus both variables (Type A personality and testosterone) play a significant role in determining aggression.

■ The 'big five' dimensions of personality

A growing body of research claims that each individual's personality centres around five basic dimensions: extraversion, agreeableness, conscientiousness, emotional stability and openness to experience (for example Costa and McCrae, 1994).

Many studies have been undertaken which support this proposal, for example people meeting strangers for the first time can place individuals on the five dimensions (Funder and Colvin, 1991).

But how is this linked to aggression? Caprara and his colleagues, during a European based study in 1994, identified two of the dimensions that are linked to aggressive individuals: agreeableness and emotional stability. Traits such as irritability (found at the 'hostile' end of the agreeableness–hostile dimension), emotional reactivity and rumination (found at the unstable end of the emotional stability dimension) can all be linked to these two dimensions and were found to exist in aggressive individuals.

Social and cultural contexts

Such an emphasis on the individual approach has been criticised for overlooking how social contexts shape social behaviour. We have already seen how some researchers have placed emphasis on the social context when studying violence and the media (see page 220). In addition, reference has already been made to Tajfel's belief that behaviour is embedded in and shaped by the nature of the **culture** and society we live in and a number of studies support the view that the expression of aggression reflects cultural norms. (Culture refers to a programme of shared rules that govern the behaviour of members of a community or society, and a set of values, beliefs and attitudes shared by most members of that community.)

Research mainly done in the US has found that groups are more aggressive than individuals. Jaffe and Yinon (1983) found a similar effect in Israel where groups were more willing to administer shocks to participants in an experiment than were individuals. On the basis of such evidence, one might be tempted to conclude that group membership results in a lessening of control over one's behaviour and an increase in anti-social behaviour. This can be linked to deindividuation which is the process by which group members come to lose part of their individual identity. By becoming undifferentiated from those around them, individuals feel less concerned with, and hence less restricted by, social norms (Prentice-Dunn and Rogers, 1983). As a group becomes larger, so the degree of anonymity increases. This, in turn, means that people may behave in uncharacteristically aggressive ways compared to their normal behaviour. The anonymity experienced may reduce the risk of identification and therefore their fear of punishment as well (Gergen and Gergen, 1981).

However, studies by Rabbie (1982) in Holland show that such an analysis is an oversimplification. Where norms favour aggression a group will indeed be more aggressive than individuals and conversely where norms favour restraint a group will show more restraint than an individual. The expression of aggression thus varies with the social context; the culture and society we live in both shape and reflect social behaviour.

■ Class

Newson and Newson (1968) in a large study of child-rearing practices in Nottingham found social class differences in parental attitudes to aggression. Working-class parents actively encouraged their children to stand up for themselves and fight back whilst middle-class parents objected to such behaviour. In a similar vein, Miller and Swanson (1960) in a large-scale study in Detroit investigated the links between methods of child-rearing, social class and means of resolving inner conflict. The social class position of boys was determined by father's occupation and education. It was predicted that middle-class boys would be more inclined to inhibit the direct expression of aggression than working-class boys. There were three stages to the experiment. In the first of these stages, boys wrote endings for three stories (in each story an adult does something to a boy which, though well intentioned, is very frustrating and tends to make the boy angry). In the next stage of the experiment, the experimenter aroused the hostility of the boys by telling them that their mothers as a group felt that 'their sons were once attractive children with bright futures and were now neither providing the pleasures of the past nor fulfilling their early promise'. In the final stage of the experiment, the boys were requested to write endings for three more stories. Three criteria were used to identify defences against aggression:

1   The main character in the ending of the story must not express his anger directly.
2   The main character must distort his interpretation of the frustrating act of the individual.
3   The distortion must result in socially acceptable behaviour.

The number of defences was counted in the stories told by each boy, before and after the arousal of hostility. It was found that after the arousal of hostility, the sons of middle-class workers exceeded the sons of working-class workers in making increased use of defences against the direct expression of aggression. Such findings remind us of the malleability of human nature and that any individual readiness to aggress can be modified by the 'norms' of society.

Activity 13

Discuss in class the ethical issues raised by the above study.

■ Drugs

One factor which is of particular relevance in today's social context is the use of drugs, especially among adolescents and young adults. A study similar to the one described on page 231 (Berman *et al.*, 1993) has found that low doses of alcohol (one cocktail) reduce a tendency towards aggression compared with a no alcohol control group. Larger doses of alcohol (three cocktails) have the opposite effect; participants were found to administer stronger shocks in this condition and hence display more aggression (Taylor *et al.*, 1976). Marijuana, on the other hand, appears to suppress aggressive behaviour and high doses decrease a person's willingness to retaliate against an aggressor (Myerscough and Taylor, 1985).

It is widely accepted that substance abuse, particularly where heroin, cocaine and alcohol are concerned, can be correlated with high crime rates, many involving hostility and aggression

(Davidson and Neale, 1994). Problems to be identified for the diagnosis of substance abuse according to the DSM IV (see Unit 24 page 909), include persistent social or interpersonal problems, such as arguments with spouse, and legal problems, such as arrest for disorderly conduct or traffic violations. Dr Anne Jasper (1998) from the Adolescent Forensic Service in Manchester has studied approximately 300 girls over a six-year period who have been referred to the service with emotional and behavioural disorders and have broken the law. The girls were, on average, 14 years old. Sixty-eight per cent had deliberately injured another person, 76 per cent had harmed themselves deliberately and 40 per cent were regular drug abusers. When comparing girls who had been violent with those who had not, Jasper found that no more of the violent girls had been physically or sexually abused than the non-violent girls but that there was a link between violent behaviour and drug abuse. It is obvious that more research is needed in this area in order to identify just how much drug abuse can account for aggression or even pro-social behaviour in today's society.

■ Cross-cultural studies

Whilst a number of theorists argue that aggression is instinctively or biologically rooted, the fact is that there are large variations in expressed aggression amongst different cultures of the world. In fact anthropologists report a few societies in which no aggressive behaviour is manifested, such as isolated communities in the US and Canada. One such community, the Hutterites, advocate a life of pacifism and any aggressive acts that might occur go unrewarded (Eaton and Weil, 1955). Gover (1968) has reviewed anthropological evidence of societies whose goal is peaceful isolation and found several characteristics of such communities that seem to facilitate the development and maintenance of non-aggressive behaviour:

■   They tend to exist in rather inaccessible places so there is little likelihood of their territory being invaded by other groups. If this does occur, the response is to retreat into even more inaccessible areas.

- Everyday existence is orientated towards the concrete pleasures, for example eating, drinking and sex. Achievement and power needs are not encouraged.
- Few distinctions are made between males and females. Although differences between male and female roles exist, there is no attempt to project an image of a brave, aggressive masculinity.

To take another example of cultural variation, statistics show that the murder rate is currently seven times higher in the US than in Britain, and in South Africa it is 35 times higher. This suggests that aggression, if instinctive, is channelled in different ways within different cultures. However, Landau (1984) has looked at factors which might affect murder rates. Based on Dollard's proposition that frustration always leads to aggression, it was predicted that murder rates would rise in countries where social support systems were failing and stress was increasing. He compared reported statistics for murder and other crimes for 13 countries over a decade. As a measure of stress he selected the rate of inflation and as a measure of social support he used the ratio of divorces to marriages. His predictions were supported in all countries except Japan where he found a rising suicide rate rather than murder rate.

This interesting study can be criticised first of all on some rather substantial assumptions made regarding what constitutes valid measures of stress and a failing support system. Secondly, the study was influenced by the frustration–aggression hypothesis formulated to account for the aggressive behaviour of individuals. We cannot be sure it has validity at the level of comparisons across cultures. Finally, the study examined links between the variables. It is of course possible that murder rates, divorce rates and inflation rates are linked to one another for other reasons.

Most investigations studying cultural differences in aggression have focused on adults who, obviously, have become enculturated into their own society's norms and mores. A recent study sought to discover whether such differences occur among children and found that it was true that even young children displayed aggression according to their own cultural norms. Osterman *et*

al. (1994) interviewed several hundred eight-year-old children individually from five different ethnic backgrounds. The children were asked a variety of questions about physical, verbal and indirect forms of aggression whilst being shown photos of their class peers. For example, 'Who hits when they get angry with others?'; the child would then point to the photo of the student who aggressed in this way the most. Very large differences were found to exist between the groups, with African-American children being the most aggressive followed by Caucasian American children; the least aggressive were those from Poland and Finland. Osterman did not delve into the whys and wherefores of such behaviour but it could be speculated that African-American children are more aggressive because they come from inner-city neighbourhoods where they are exposed to much aggression, thus supporting the social learning modelling theory. For example, it has been suggested that by their mid-teens approximately half of these children have witnessed someone being shot (Shakoor and Chalmers, 1991). There is also some support that American norms dictate that individuals generally tend to settle interpersonal differences aggressively when compared with other cultures (Baron and Byrne, 1997).

We can see therefore that there are social and cultural influences upon how and indeed whether aggression is expressed. However, in looking at social and cultural diversity in anti-social behaviour, a complicating factor is interpreting whether or not a particular behaviour constitutes aggression. The judgement of an action as aggressive or violent depends on the beliefs and attitudes of the person making the judgement. One post-modern theory, **social constructionism**, holds that knowledge is not so much discovered as constructed or invented. Social constructionism is the view that there are no universal truths about human nature because people construct reality differently depending on their culture, the historical moment and power arrangements (Tavris and Wade, 1995). Camino and Trocolli (reported in Leyens and Fraczek, 1984) found that in Brazil, those who believed in a just world were less likely to judge police action to have been violent. Strong criticism from one's boss might not be judged aggressive in a high power distance culture. Bond *et al.* (1985) asked students in Hong Kong and the US to evaluate an episode in which a manager insults either a superior or a subordinate who is either inside or outside the manager's own department. The judgements made by the Chinese students were much more influenced by who was receiving the insult than were American judgements. For example, the Chinese perceived the insult to a subordinate within one's own department as a 'scolding' and saw less reason to dislike the superior who delivered it than the American students. The Chinese also differentiated more between insults to ingroup members and outgroup members, possibly related to the higher collectivism of Hong Kong compared to the United States. Members of collectivist groups favour other members of their group more strongly and treat them more equally.

Activity 14

What might be the implications for research of 'social constructionism'. Jot down some ideas before reading on.

There are several implications of such a post-modern theory. One, which we have already raised, is that rather than restrict research to try to establish patterns of individual behaviour, *researchers should study the social being.* A further implication concerns the meaning of knowledge and methods of research. Traditionally knowledge was equated with some 'reality' existing 'out there', the way to find it was to be objective and the purpose of a theory was to reflect this reality. These fundamental assumptions are being questioned by supporters of the post-modernist view. They argue that detached objectivity is a myth and that the observer's values and judgements affect how events are studied and interpreted. Because researchers do their work at a particular time and in a cultural context, they bring with them shared assumptions and views that influence what they regard as important and what parts of reality they notice. In other words, they are not exempt from human

subjectivity. Knowledge is not so much discovered as constructed or invented, so our understanding of 'reality' does not so much mirror what is 'out there' but *organises and orders it.*

This can be quite a demoralising view. Not only does this amount to an attack on traditional methods of research, but psychologists, whose goal is understanding the behaviour and mental processes of human beings, are also being asked to analyse their own behaviour and to examine how their own values and cultural experiences affect their conclusions. However, as Tavris and Wade (1995) have pointed out, these new ideas of looking at knowledge and of doing research can in fact help to expand and enrich our understanding of human behaviour. Ultimately, what we know about human behaviour is inseparable from how we know it.

Cultural differences in pro-social behaviour

The earlier section on social behaviour in cities discusses rural-urban differences in pro-social behaviour. The Dutch study by Korte *et al.* (1975) suggested that the culture of a particular country can moderate such differences. Studies investigating cultural diversity have a number of limitations.

One is that few studies have been reported which made direct comparisons of pro-social behaviours using identical procedures in different cultures. Another is that the meaning of, helpfulness varies widely. Although we know that responding 'helpfully' to strangers in the street may well be widespread, we do not know the nature of the help nor the reasons why it was given or withheld. Further, the above reported studies all involved help requested by local nationals. Some interesting findings emerge when the help is requested by foreigners. Fieldman (1967) found that foreigners who asked a favour in Athens received more help than Greeks asking the same favour and in the same place. The reverse was found to be the case in Boston and Paris. A study by

Collett and O'Shea involved foreigners asking directions to two non-existent sites as well as sites that did exist. In Tehran and Isfahan (both in Iran) the foreigner was given directions to the non-existent sites as well as the existent ones. Thus the seemingly helpful response was of no help at all. (What seemed to matter was that the semblance of helpfulness was preserved.) Such spurious 'helpfulness' did not occur in London. What these studies show is that in some collective cultures foreigners are treated, perhaps out of deference and politeness, in a manner which would in fact suggest that they are in some way more important and worthy of help than those who are local, possibly reflecting cultural norms about the types of behaviour regarded as desirable. Thus we can see that the social convention of helpfulness is culturally mediated.

Self-assessment questions

10 Outline reasons why the social context should be taken into account when considering social behaviour.

11 What evidence is there to suggest that a Type A personality might be more aggressive than a Type B?

12 How does research concerning aggression in different cultures refute the instinctive theory of aggression?

(Suggested answers on page 243.)

The reduction and control of aggression

Activity 15

Before reading further, suggest ways of controlling violent behaviour that breaks out between two children aged ten; two teenagers; a mother and father; two rival gangs.

There are several possible ways of reducing and controlling aggression. Which method individuals support is likely to be shaped by their view of the cause of aggression. A biological perspective will carry with it the belief that aggression, as a drive, is inevitable and as such should be redirected. Favouring a socially based theory would imply a belief that behaviour is highly modifiable. This perhaps allows for a more optimistic view of the control of violence.

There are three main strategies which are currently used to reduce or moderate aggression: control, **catharsis** and empathy training.

■ Control

Control procedures rely upon punishing and confining violent individuals. Such an approach frequently stems from a desire to protect the community and is linked to the biological theory that certain individuals are innately aggressive. Since such aggression often gives rise to deviance, altering the social context is seen as an unlikely method of rehabilitation. Most punishment is used as a deterrent to reduce the motivation to act aggressively in future.

Research in this area is conflicting. Bower and Hilgard (1981) have shown that punishment can be effective if it is prompt, intense and probable. This means that it must be carried out as soon as possible after the aggressive behaviour, it must be aversive to the people receiving it and the likelihood of receiving it after aggressive behaviour must be high if it is to be effective.

You may have considered problems here such as long delays between arrest and conviction and that the likelihood of receiving punishment is improbable in many cases. Research into the effects of imprisonment does not lend strong support for the view that punishment is an effective deterrent. Ross and Fabiano (1985) have found no significant correlation between the number of crimes committed and levels of punishment. Similar studies have been shown to shift the location or type of crime rather than reduce it. Most other studies agree that when punishment does reduce violent crime, it does so only temporarily.

■ Catharsis

Catharsis may be defined as the indirect release of aggression. Followers of catharsis propose that hostile feelings may be released by observing or taking part in any physical and emotion-draining activity, for example sport. The rationale for catharsis stems from a belief that aggression is a biological or psychological drive which may be kept in check by draining off socially acceptable amounts at regular intervals. People are less likely to engage in aggression subsequently.

Studies of the value of catharsis, however, have not produced promising results. For example, Holdstein and Arms (1971) measured the level of aggression in football fans and found that supporters of both winning and losing teams showed an increase in aggression when compared to pre-match levels. Studies of the players themselves bear this out. Teams which have met each other several times during a season have been shown to increase their levels of aggression with each meeting. Also, Ebbesen *et al.* (1975) found that more aggressive countries played more combative games. There is also some evidence that aggression may actually increase after watching violence (Geen, 1978) or the attacking of inanimate objects on television (Mallick and McCandless, 1966).

From both theoretical and practical perspectives it should be noted that this increase in aggression would be predicted by social learning theorists. It should, however, be mentioned that positive cathartic affects have been demonstrated under very specific circumstances. In particular, they may work temporarily through anxiety, which inhibits further aggression (Atkinson *et al.*, 1993)

or when aggressive participants are shown the harm that they have caused to others (Koneci, 1975). Clearly, the mixed evidence does not bode well for the future of catharsis as a means of moderating violence. It appears to be less effective than many people assume.

■ Empathy and social skills training

Aggressive feelings may be lessened by reactions or emotional states which are incompatible, such as empathy, mild sexual arousal or humour (for example Baron, 1993). Empathy training is designed to introduce and develop alternative responses such as these to help people overcome aggressive behaviour in themselves.

The relationship between empathy and aggression is well established. Children who show high empathy levels are unlikely to exhibit high levels of aggression and vice versa (Feshbach and Feshbach, 1969). If there is a causal link in such a correlation then it can be argued that increasing a hostile child's empathy level should result in a reduction of aggression. Followers of empathy training generally view aggression as a socially learned response and one reason why people become involved in aggressive encounters may be because they do not have the *social skills* to avoid such behaviour. For example, they do not know how to give negative criticism without threat to another's well-being, or to express their wishes without aggression. They have an abrasive style of self-expression and appear insensitive to the overt signs of other's emotions. Social skills can be improved in a matter of a few hours by means of social modelling, i.e. watching other people who demonstrate effective and ineffective social behaviours (Schneider, 1991).

Empathy trainers believe that the cure for wrongly learned social skills lies in developing more socially acceptable ones, i.e. empathic ones.

Research indicates that an apology can be a useful way to reduce retaliation. It is difficult to be angry with someone who admits blame and says he or she is sorry. Ohbuchi *et al.* (1989) demonstrated that participants who had been provoked by an 'assistant' who spoiled their performance felt less aggressive toward him when they received an apology from him, than when they received no apology. Also, a public apology which accepted blame (said in front of the experimenters) was slightly more effective than a private apology to the participant alone.

In another study highlighting support for empathy training, when participants who were administering electric shocks were asked to attempt to understand how the other person was feeling, weaker shocks were given by those in whom empathy was induced than those in whom it was not. Thus, empathy did appear to reduce levels of aggression (Richardson *et al.*, 1994).

Empathy training involves a great deal of small-group work, including various exercises designed to increase children's awareness of their actions upon others. They generally include activities such as group discussion, problem-solving games and role-playing (where participants are asked to assess the feelings of others and act out a suitable response). In this way, it is anticipated that disruptive children will gain understanding of their companions' feelings.

Field studies which have followed up empathy training have produced promising results. Children taking part in such schemes demonstrate significantly lower levels of aggression than matched children who have received no training. Advocates of other regimes for modifying aggression may claim that the reduced level of hostility simply reflects the degree of small-group attention the participants received irrespective of their level of empathy. Such a criticism should not be ignored on theoretical grounds but, for practical purposes, if there is a long-term lowering of hostile behaviour then the underlying reason for this is of little consequence.

■ Cognitive interventions

We have already seen how an apology can change the way we react to provocative behaviour (see above). Cognitive therapists believe that admissions of error such as apologies and excuses can act as cognitive tactics to reduce aggression and help to determine whether we retaliate in any given situation. If the apology is sincere we are not likely to do so (Baron, 1989). Also, if the excuses made

centre around being beyond the antagonist's control, they are much more likely to be acceptable than if they are deemed to be in the person's control (Weiner *et al.*, 1987).

If we are able to change our cognitions about aggressive behaviour (whether perceived or real), then we may be able to keep our own aggressive tendencies in check. When we experience extreme anger we use up much of the cognitive capacity that we possess and are left with little space in our cognitive system. We may, therefore, react aggressively without being able to think things through. However, if we employ strategies to help us to combat this problem before becoming angry in the first place, we may reduce or eliminate our need to retaliate. Zillman (1993) suggested two techniques which might be useful:

■ *Preattribution* – this means attributing annoying behaviours to unintentional causes before the behaviour actually occurs. If, for example, you have to work closely with someone who annoys you on a project at work, then you must remind yourself beforehand that that person does not really mean to annoy you, it is merely a result of the person's unfortunate manner.

■ *Rumination prevention* – this involves preventing yourself from pondering over real or imagined events where you have felt wronged. Prevention can be achieved by distracting yourself by, for example, watching a humorous film, thus allowing for a cooling-off period. During this time hostility can disintegrate and cognitive capacity can be 're-aligned' in tune with your 'normal' cognitive control. In this way aggressive behaviour can be avoided.

Throughout this unit we have looked at several theories, interpretations, causes and therapies concerning pro- and anti-social behaviour. It is often difficult to separate these issues out and disregard the situational, social or cultural aspects of behaviour whilst focusing only on the personal (or vice-versa). Therefore, as in many other areas of psychology, it is often necessary to take an interactional approach to these dilemmas and consider taking a look at what is happening at each level of explanation before making any firm conclusions.

Self-assessment questions

13 List the ways in which punishment might (a) reduce and (b) increase aggressive behaviour.

14 Imagine you are playing a board game but your opponents become very heated and you feel that the game is going to degenerate into violence at any moment. Suggest how you might seek to reduce the growing aggressive tendencies of your fellow players.

15 How might cognitive therapists suggest you reduce or eliminate aggressive tendencies?

(Suggested answers on page 243.)

Unit summary

- The murder of Kitty Genovese highlights the paradoxical numbers effect regarding *bystander intervention*. Thirty-eight neighbours witnessed her attack and yet not one intervened to help her. Research indicates that the more bystanders involved, the less help will be offered to a victim because of one key factor – diffusion of responsibility; each bystander believes that one of his or her many counterparts will intervene. The decision-making model suggests that if one negative decision out of four is made then an individual will not help a victim.

- One theory of pro-social behaviour is the *arousal: cost–reward model* which suggests that bystanders weigh up the rewards and costs of intervention and non-intervention based on two interdependent factors: arousal in response to the need of others and a cost–reward factor. A second theory involves the premise that we help others in order to protect the genetic lineage of those close to us and others of the same species – this is known as the *socio-biological approach*. In addition, there exists the *empathy–altruism hypothesis* which proposes that feeling empathy for a victim motivates us to help that person for his or her benefit and to act selflessly. Other mediating factors that must be considered include the psychological state of the helper, his or her attitude toward the victim and whether the helper possesses an 'altruistic personality'.

- Research focusing on the *effects of television* and pro-social behaviour has produced mixed results. Studies have found that watching pro-socially biased programmes such as 'Sesame Street' has resulted in improved helping behaviour and more tolerance towards peers, whilst other results have found some effect on behaviour such as cooperation but no effect on pro-social actions. Studies to date on computer games have found that they can have several positive effects such as deterring violent behaviour by regulating arousal.

- The debate concerning the media and aggressive behaviour centres around the *media effects model* which proposes that violence depicted in the media induces violence in individuals. However, recent studies have produced evidence to refute this proposal and suggest that other social factors influence aggressive behaviour, such as family involvement and violence in the family setting.

- One biological approach upholds that *aggression is instinctive*, i.e. originating from a death instinct inherent in all of us which is initially aimed at the self but gradually directs itself outwards towards others. On the other hand, the *frustration–aggression hypothesis* holds that frustration leads to aggression due to perceived goal blocks. This theory has been modified and it is now suggested that arousal induced by any negative affect can produce aggressive behaviour. Social learning theory focuses on *reinforcement*, whereby parents reinforce violent behaviour in their child, for

Summary cont'd.

example, and *modelling* which involves mimicry by a child of others' aggressive behaviour. More recently *cognitive theories* have proposed that aggressive behaviour is dependent on cognitive programmes within us, appraisal of the situation and negative affect.

■ Factors such as *personality*, for example the altruistic personality, Type A individuals and the 'big five' dimensions can play an important role in pro- and anti-social behaviour. *Societal factors* also play a key role including, for example, socio-economic background and, today, drugs. In addition, *cultures* are found to define and display aggression differently. Social constructionism holds that researchers should be aware of the historical background to their research, what is influencing them at the time of their investigation and the assumptions they are making.

■ There are several strategies which can be used to *reduce and control aggression* and sometimes an eclectic approach can provide the best answer.

Punishment and confinement must be immediate, intense and probable if it is to be successful, and nowadays this is often not the case where the judicial system is concerned. *Catharsis* may then be the answer which involves the release of hostile feelings through observation or participation in some sort of activity, such as sport. Unfortunately, studies have found this to be ineffective, unlike *empathy and social skills training* which produce very good results. If people are asked to try and imagine how their victim is feeling or offered effective models of how to improve their social skills (lack of which can lead people to become aggressive) then behaviour is soon found to improve. Finally, *cognitive interventions* can also be successful – like most cognitive therapies these attempt to change the thought patterns of individuals to help them to react and behave in different ways. Where aggression is concerned this can involve strategies such as *preattribution* and *rumination prevention*.

Terms to define

aggression
altruism
anti-social behaviour
bystander behaviour
catharsis
culture
empathy

hostile attributional bias
pro-social behaviour
reciprocal altruism
social constructionism
vicarious reinforcement

Further reading

Berkowitz, L (1993) *Aggression: Its Causes, Consequence and Control*, McGraw Hill, New York.

Comprehensive, readable coverage of aggression. This book focuses mainly on the views of its author but offers some interesting and worthwhile insights including a chapter on violence and the media.

Charlton, T and David, K (eds) (1997) *Elusive Links: Television, Video Games and Children's Behaviour*, Park Published Papers.

A slim, easy to read volume containing several up-to-date British papers on pro- and anti-social behaviour and the media.

Clark, M S (ed.) (1991) *Prosocial Behaviour*, Sage, Newbury Park.

An interesting and informative read from several authors providing a broad range of sub-topics in this area.

Answers

▥ Suggested answers to activities

1

If you read the *New York Times* article carefully, you may
have noted that some of the onlookers did notice
something amiss and made attempts to help, for example
one resident called out to the attacker from a window to
leave the girl alone. At least two individuals did eventually
call the police, but by this time it was too late. You may
have found it hard to account for the lack of any *effective*
intervention to save Kitty. It is natural to think that the
chances of a victim of a crime getting help would increase
as the number of witnesses increased. But here, it looks as
if the presence of a large number of onlookers actually
inhibited any natural human tendency to help. Perhaps
people, taking their cue from the inaction of others,
found it hard to believe they were really witnessing a
brutal attack and instead created an innocent
interpretation for what they saw and heard. They may also
have assumed that, as so many other people were present,
someone must have the situation under control. Or
maybe people were simply afraid of getting hurt
themselves if they intervened. The research studies which
follow on pages 209–11 represent systematic attempts to
investigate the situational factors which might inhibit
helping in such circumstances.

2

Only a well-controlled experiment permits us to infer a
causal relationship between two variables with reasonable
confidence. A controlled experiment has *internal validity*,
i.e. we can make valid inferences about the direction of
causality *within the particular context* of the experiment. In
this instance, the finding that increasing the number of
witnesses *decreased* helping was well *replicated*.
Do we have here some sort of universal law of social
behaviour? Probably not. The disadvantage of
experimental method is that the more carefully contrived
and meticulously controlled the experiment, the more it
can come to be unlike real-life situations. We cannot
legitimately generalise experimental results outside the
particular context of the experiment; this is often
described as a weakness in *ecological validity*. In addition,
social psychology experiments in which the participants
are themselves psychology students are particularly liable
to *demand effects*. This means that the behaviour we
observe may be caused merely by a participant's
knowledge that he or she is taking part in an experiment.
The British Psychological Society's ethical guidelines for
research with human participants (BPS, 1990) propose
that, wherever possible, researchers should obtain
informed consent from potential participants. This implies
that researchers should strive to avoid *deception*.

Researchers should also protect participants from *physical
or psychological harm*. The more realistic the simulation of
an emergency the more likely it seems that some
participants might become scared or upset. It is also
conceivable that some participants might suffer
embarrassment or shame about their own behaviour
when they learn that they have been tricked.
You may feel that this constitutes socially useful research,
and that the results could be used to make people more
aware of the dangers of bystander apathy. Do the socially
useful goals of this research justify the deception and
potential psychological harm to participants? There is no
one 'right' answer to this moral dilemma. Those who take
an *absolute* moral position would say that no scientific
advance can ever justify hurting another human being.
On the other hand, *moral relativists* might argue that
deception could *sometimes* be justified, if the issue was
socially important and there was no alternative method of
investigating the problem. (For fuller discussion of ethical
issues in psychological research see Unit 3).

3

The researchers suggested that increasing the number of
bystanders increased the chances that each individual
would misread the social situation. See page 211, for an
explanation of three separate social cognitive processes –
diffusion of responsibility, pluralistic ignorance and *audience
inhibition* – which might be involved.

▥ Suggested answers to self-assessment questions

1

If you thought you were about to be mugged, what about
hurling the largest possible rock or other object, not at
your attacker, but through the nearest illuminated house
window? This would ensure that the situation was *noticed*:
this was the first step in Latane and Darley's 'decision
tree' (1970), (page 212). The suggestion recognises that
people are more likely to act upon threats to their own
well-being than threats to others. On the same principle,
you could try calling 'Fire!', rather than 'Help!'. This
unambiguously defines the emergency and again enlists
self-interest. These are just some suggestions. You can
probably think of others for yourself.

2

We discussed in the answer to Activity 2 (see above) how
laboratory experiments may have limited *ecological validity*,
i.e. validity in the world outside. However, student samples
are rather unlikely even to represent the population of

their own society, let alone the behaviour of people in other cultures, where social norms may be very different. We also discussed how social psychology experiments are susceptible to *demand effects* and explored some of the *ethical dilemmas* that may arise in experimental research. It is therefore essential to use other methods to complement information gained from experimentation. One alternative is to interview people who have been crime victims or have intervened on behalf of others: Huston *et al.* (1981) interviewed individuals who had intervened in real-life muggings and armed bank robberies. They were compared with a matched group of individuals who had failed to 'act to prevent' in such crimes. Those who intervened were more likely to have had some sort of training that involved dealing with emergencies, for example first aid or self-defence training. They were more likely to have been members of the police force or medical professions. In addition, those who responded to crimes were taller, heavier and more likely to describe themselves as strong, aggressive, emotional and principled.

3

It can be fascinating to analyse human behaviour from a socio-biological perspective. However, socio-biology seems to suggest that our higher human activities, even moral choices, are somehow *determined* by the genes we happen to inherit. This *reductionism* has been strongly criticised:

- The 'selfish gene theory' applies to *instinctive* behaviour, i.e. inherited, stereotyped and inflexible behaviour patterns common to all species members. Such behaviour does not have to be learned, and it appears in complete form on first occurrence. However, humans have to *learn* to behave in a pro-social manner, and our capacity for altruism varies immensely between individuals. Human altruism involves conscious reasoning processes, which are mediated by the cerebral hemispheres of the brain. So the comparison with behaviour in lower animals is potentially misleading. Human altruism and (apparent) animal altruism may appear superficially similar, but are not really the same type of phenomenon at all.
- The 'selfish gene theory' proposes genes for altruism, but this goes way beyond biochemical knowledge. It involves premature reductionism. Biochemists have succeeded in chemically identifying genes with certain units of the DNA molecule. However, the genes whose actions we understand so far, form a code for very simple chemical building-blocks of the body, such as the amino-acids that make up proteins. It is quite unlikely that these

simple units of inheritance could cause abstract behaviours like altruism in any straightforward way. We are a long way from understanding how this might be possible.

4

You could have included an explanation of one of the following, all of which are detailed on pages 214–6:
- the arousal: cost–reward model
- the socio-biological perspective
- the empathy–altruism hypothesis.

5

Research has found that inducing positive affect results in people behaving more altruistically (see Baron and Thornley (1992) study on page 217). However, a paradox is in evidence as positive affect has also resulted in people feeling so good about themselves that they feel able to turn down people needing help. Other studies have found the same kind of paradox occurs when inducing negative affect (see page 217 for details of studies).

6

You could have included any of the following studies in your answer (all are described on pages 220–22):
- the 'Lassie' study by Sprafkin *et al.* (1975)
- the 'team sports' study by Moriarty and McCabe (1977)
- Friedrich and Stein's 'nursery programme' study (1973)
- the 'Sesame Street' study by Forge and Phemister (1987).

7

Reinforcement of aggression occurs when a child is allowed to attain a goal by means of aggressive behaviour; a parent will often, unintentionally, positively reinforce the aggression by allowing the child to 'get their own way' even when the child behaves aggressively.
Modelling occurs when children imitate the aggressive actions of those around them, particularly role models such as parents, peers, teachers or television characters.

8

You could have included a description of any of the following cognitive factors in your answer (all are described on pages 227–28):
- 'scripts' or 'cognitive programmes'
- hostile attributional bias
- appraisal
- negative affect.

9

Support *for* the *media effects* model of aggression comes from the following psychologists:

- *Sims and Gray (1993)* demonstrated that young offenders' behaviour was caused by repeated viewing of violence.
- *Huesmann and Eron (1986)* found that children in five different countries behaved more aggressively when watching violence on television.

Support *against* comes from the following:

- *Hagell and Newburn (1994)* found that offenders had less access to television than non-offenders.
- *Charlton (1997)* suggested that it is not television or its content that causes violence but the social context that children are brought up in.
- *Browne and Pennell (1998)* agreed with Charlton and suggested that coming from a social background which contains violence leads children to prefer watching violence on television.

10

Possible points:

- Behaviour, particularly social behaviour, occurs in a social context.
- Evidence that behaviour is embedded in and shaped by the society and culture we live in.
- Individual approach is incomplete.
- Social constructionism.

Make sure you back up points with research. Try to discuss the evidence. Though the question which asks for an outline does not demand this, it is good practice for the examination.

11

Carver and Grass (1978) found Type A individuals to be more hostile and aggressive when competing with others. Strube *et al.* (1984) found that Type A personalities are more likely to participate in child and spouse abuse. Berman *et al.* (1993) found that people with high testosterone levels are more likely to be Type A individuals who exhibit more aggressive behaviour. Type B personalities, on the other hand, are not found to exhibit violent behaviour.

12

There are numerous studies suggesting that it is the culture we live in and the social context of our lives which determines whether we will be aggressive. These studies therefore dispute the assumption that aggression is an instinctive behaviour (see pages 232–35 for more details).

13

Punishment may deter aggressive behaviour in the future but it might only suppress it in the specific situation – not all the time. Did you also include that punishment must be prompt, intense and probable? Punishment might increase aggressive behaviour through role modelling and through reinforcement.

14

One answer would be to remain calm yourself and to use your knowledge of your companions to acknowledge their feelings. Suggest a change of game.

15

You might have included Zillman's (1993) ideas in your answer: *preattribution* and *rumination prevention*. (For more detail see page 238.)

Comparative Psychology

Unit | 8

Evolutionary Determinants of Behaviour

Gillian Lang

This unit covers:

The evolution of behaviour in animals

Competition for resources

Predator–prey and cooperative relationships

Adaptationism

By the end of this unit, you should be able to:

- demonstrate knowledge of the principles of Darwin's theory of natural selection, the ways in which it is studied, and its relevance to understanding the behaviour of non-human animals

- show awareness of the nature of competition for resources both within and between species, when such competition is likely to occur and the advantages of ritualised aggression

- demonstrate understanding of the evolutionary consequences of the predator–prey relationship; also of symbiotic relationships and of how cooperation between species might evolve

- understand the advantages and limitations of the adaptationist approach.

Unit 8 Contents

The evolution of behaviour in animals

The world as we know it contains millions of different organisms varying enormously in shape and size. These include insects, arthropods, fish, reptiles, birds and mammals. Taking birds alone there are innumerable forms, each distinguishable from the other. Thus robins are different from chaffinches, crows different from blackbirds and swans different from geese. Each of these is known as a species. A species can be defined as a group of organisms that can breed with one another. Robins breed with robins, wrens breed with wrens and so on.

Offspring resemble their parents. Occasionally, closely related species may breed but their young are unlikely to be fertile as, for instance, when a male donkey mates with a mare and produces a mule. Biologists believe that the innumerable species alive today developed through a process of evolution where parents pass characteristics which have survival value on to their young. They believe also that species are still evolving, although this is a very slow process.

The study of evolution

Darwin was not the first to propose a theory of evolution. Scientists in general were agreed that fossils were the petrified remains of organisms which had lived hundreds of millions of years ago. The fossil record provides evidence that organisms which had once lived on earth were very different from those alive today. The fossil record indicated, therefore, that life forms had changed over the millennia, and that species alive today differ from their ancestors. Scientists developed theories as to how and why this had taken place.

By the time Darwin's book *The Origin of Species* was published in 1859, the idea of change taking place slowly over very long periods was accepted by some. Erasmus Darwin, Darwin's grandfather, had proposed a theory of evolution in 1794, and another was put forward by Lamarck in 1809. The fossil record has made an important contribution to evolutionary theory. Darwin, however, stressed that *behaviour* as well as form evolved. Today biologists and evolutionary psychologists agree with Darwin and believe that the behaviour as well as the physiology of animals has changed through evolution. Physiological adaptation is unlikely to have evolutionary consequences unless it is paralleled by a change in behaviour. Behavioural and physical changes tend to occur together. Behaviour, however, is not preserved. Fossilised animals are dead; they do not *behave*, although it is often possible to make inferences about how a fossilised animal might have behaved on the basis of its remains. Thus the teeth of a fossilised animal indicate the type of food it ate. If the teeth suggest that it was a grazing animal, then perhaps its behaviour resembled that of grazing animals alive today. The function of head ornaments found on dinosaur remains has been inferred from the behaviour of living species which have similar ornaments, such as deer and stag beetles (Molnar, 1977). Fossilised patterns of footprints are compared with tracks made by living animals and conclusions drawn about those long dead.

Gastropods, for example, may leave fossil evidence of their behaviour on the basis of the holes they leave in the shells of their prey. Examination of such fossilised prey may reveal whether a predatory attempt was made on it and whether it succeeded, and also the size of the predator. Careful study of the tiny changes which occur over millions of years reveals how the prey and predators evolved (Kitchell, 1986).

However, these are inferences only and, although based on careful observation and interpretation, are not facts. Another approach taken by evolutionary theorists involves comparing the behaviour of present-day species. This makes it possible to deduce how their common ancestor is likely to have behaved, and what changes have taken place over the generations as the new species evolved. For instance, Lorenz (1941) made a detailed analysis of 47 behaviour patterns among 20 species of geese and ducks. By identifying which of these behavioural patterns occurred most often in these birds, he was able to trace their evolution from a probable ancestor.

Evolution is also studied by experiment in natural or artificial conditions. Differences in survival or reproductive success can be investigated in relation to a group of animals that differ with regard to a particular characteristic, for example Kettlewell's famous study on the peppered moth *Biston betularia* (Kettlewell, 1965) which is outlined below.

There are two main types of the peppered moth: light and dark. The light form has speckled greyish-white wings. The difference is inherited. The moths are eaten by birds which hunt by sight, and initially more of the light form survived because it was less visible against lichen-covered trees. As parts of Britain became industrialised, soot killed the lichen and darkened the trees. The dark form was now better camouflaged and less likely to be seen by predators than the light form. Consequently, the proportion of dark relative to light coloured moths increased in the industrial areas of Britain, while a higher proportion of light moths remained in the non-industrial areas.

Kettlewell investigated this by breeding large numbers of the light and dark (melanic) forms. He marked them, then released equal numbers in an area of high pollution (Birmingham) where 90 per cent of existing moths were dark, and in an area of low pollution where no dark moths had been observed. He recaptured samples of moths using light traps. In Birmingham the number of marked dark moths recaptured was double that of the light forms. In Dorset light forms were recaptured at twice the frequency of the dark.

Activity 1

Write down three ways in which evolution may be studied.

(Suggested answer on page 275.)

Natural selection

In the natural environment selection occurs because some animals possess characteristics which enable them to live longer and therefore produce more offspring than animals which lack these features. The natural environment includes climate (which is liable to change), availability of food and shelter, and predation.

You will realise that in the natural world life often involves a struggle to survive, let alone breed. Some animals possess traits which enable them to survive longer than others. Since they are more likely to survive, they are also more likely to reproduce. The example of the peppered moth above demonstrates that aspects of the environment determine which of an animal's characteristics will contribute to its survival. In a sense then, the environment can be said to *select* those traits which help an individual to survive. Since individuals with such traits are the most likely to reproduce, and since the traits are likely to be inherited by their young, in time more and more of the population will possess these traits.

The natural environment is liable to change. Kettlewell's work with the peppered moth demonstrates that in a polluted sooty environment the proportion of dark moths in the population increased; the dark colour was favoured or *selected* by this environment. Over many generations this process may produce changes in the form and behaviour of animals, eventually resulting in the development of new species. Darwin called this *natural selection*. Kettlewell's study of the peppered moth reveals natural selection in action.

For evolution to occur through natural selection three conditions are necessary:

- that the individuals within a species differ from one another: they have slightly different physical or behavioural characteristics; this is often referred to as **genetic variation**
- that this variation is inherited, that is, the individuals vary in their *genetic makeup*
- that animals of all species produce more offspring than can survive.

Darwin was influenced by the work of Malthus. Malthus had calculated that populations have the potential to increase geometrically: that a population doubles in a certain length of time, doubles again and so on. If populations grew at such a rate, the world would be overrun with rats, frogs, elephants, people and so on. But this does not happen. Malthus realised that several factors restrict the growth of such populations: competition for food, illness, predation. Malthus's (1798) essay contributed to Darwin's realisation that in the natural environment most animals fail to survive long enough to reproduce. This led him to ask why some animals survive whilst others do not. He concluded that the survivors would be those best fitted to their ecological niche (this refers to their particular requirements of food and shelter). Thus, if a long beak helps a bird to feed, it will be more likely to survive than those with shorter beaks.

Darwin calculated that if a single pair of elephants were to breed between the ages of 30 and 90 years, producing six young, after about 750 years they would have nearly 19 million descendants! (Providing they all survived, of course!) Darwin chose the elephant since it was '. . . reckoned the slowest breeder of all known animals' (Darwin, 1859).

Activity 2

You can test this for yourself. Take a species of animal you are familiar with, such as rabbits or cats, and calculate how many young a female might produce in a year. Do the same for her offspring from the age at which they are reproductively mature. (Follow the example given in table 8.1, but note that rabbits, for instance, breed more rapidly than the example given in table 8.1, which has an average litter size of four. Females are able to produce their first litter at three months.)

■ Genetic variation

It is clear therefore that many offspring will die. If any inherit a characteristic that makes them more likely to survive and to reproduce, then this characteristic is passed on. The offspring with this trait will compete more successfully for resources, they will leave more offspring similar to themselves, and the next generation will contain more individuals with this trait (variant) than did the previous generation. The population will have changed slightly. If the variant continues to aid survival, it is likely to increase until

Table 8.1

Month	Breeding females	Females born	Males born	Total females	Total males	Total
January	0	0	0	(1)	(1)	2
				The male and female above are the breeding pair. The young are conceived, but not yet born.		
March	1	2	2	(3)	(3)	6
		First litter is born.				
June	3	6	6	(9)	(9)	18
September	9	18	18	(27)	(27)	54
December	27	54	54	(81)	(81)	162
March	81	162	162	(243)	(243)	486

Reproduction and the pattern of a hypothetical population through a year the entire population consists of individuals with this trait.

Genes are complex chemical units holding the code which controls physical traits specific to any particular species. There are two genes for each trait which form a pair, one contributed by the mother and one by the father of an individual. Take genes for eye colour, for example. One of each pair of genes will be passed on to any offspring via the gametes (egg and sperm – see Unit 9 page 284). Parents produce offspring which are similar to themselves in general terms but different in detail. This is due to the fact that thousands of genes are needed to produce even the simplest organism.

Sometimes a gene becomes altered and manifests itself in a different way. Such changes are called **mutations**, and it is possible for these to be inherited by offspring. Genetic mutations may be harmful, such as the mutation which causes haemophilia. Some, and some only, of these variations benefit the animals which possess them. In such instances the animal is described as better adapted. Thus the peppered moth with the genetic variation of dark colouring is better adapted to the polluted (dark) environment than the moth with light colouring. An animal with a greater capacity for storing water is better adapted to a desert environment than the animal with a smaller capacity.

The lungfish is a good example of a beneficial mutation. All fish have air-filled swim bladders which keep them buoyant, but are unconnected to the outside air. Lungfish, however, have inherited a mutated gene which allows air to reach the swim bladder directly from the atmosphere. This has enabled them to survive even when the water level has receded and left them stranded on the ground. Without this inherited gene, other stranded fish will die.

The benefits of such a genetic variation may be very small, but result in those animals which possess them being better adapted than those which do not; they live a little longer, and leave a greater number of offspring. The work of Benkman and Lindholm (1991) revealed that even a very small variation can provide survival value (see figure 8.2).

Darwin's theory of evolution offers an explanation as to why some animal species have been successful and have survived, whereas others have been unsuccessful and have become extinct. He suggests that those animals which are best adapted to the environments in which they live are most likely to survive.

8.2 Benkman and Lindholm's investigation of crossbills (1991)

'If it could be demonstrated that any complex organ existed which could not possibly have been formed by numerous, slight modifications my theory would absolutely break down.' (Darwin, *The Origin of Species*, 1859.)

Benkman and Lindholm (1991) carried out an investigation on seven species of crossbill, which reveals that even a tiny change can benefit an organism. These birds feed on pine cones and have a crossed beak which allows its owner to prise open cones which are tightly closed. Benkman and Lindholm trimmed off the crossed part of the bill, thus, in effect, uncrossing the bill (this causes the birds no pain). The birds were still able to extract seeds from open pine cones, but could no longer manage the closed cones.

Little by little, as their beaks grew back, the birds did better with the cones, gradually succeeding with the more difficult ones. The importance of this finding for Darwin's theory of natural selection is that the finches began to improve at opening the cones when the crossover of their beaks was still so little it could not be seen. Thus even a small amount of crossing provides a benefit. The benefit increases gradually as the bill grows, and the crossover is increased.

This suggests how such a bill could evolve over successive generations, each generation of birds doing a little better than the one before because of their greater ability to feed from pine cones.

Fitness and inclusive fitness

The concept of **fitness** often causes problems because the term has been used in different ways. Fitness is generally used to refer to the capacity to survive and to reproduce. Reproductive success is more important than individual success as it ensures the passing on of genes.

For Darwin, what mattered was how well the individual was adapted to the life style of its species. Thus the fittest grazing animals would be those with the hardest and most effective teeth. The fittest hunting animals would be the fastest, and with the sharpest teeth and claws. Such animals would be the most likely to survive and to reproduce.

Parents feed and protect their young and, by so doing, ensure that their genes are passed on. However, this is not the only way in which this may be achieved. Their near relatives share their genes, so an inherited tendency to help a brother or sister to reproduce could be favoured by natural selection. Thus, while genes for the care of the young could spread in the population, so also would genes for a tendency to help a sibling reproduce. Hamilton (1984) suggested that the term *inclusive* fitness might be used to refer to success in leaving offspring, including offspring of a close relative. Is there evidence for this?

Young jackals sometimes help their parents rather than breed. Moehlman (1979) suggested that when there are insufficient suitable breeding sites, young jackals are unable to find anywhere to breed. In such instances they stay and help their parents, thus ensuring that their genes are passed on. Young male wolves remain celibate until they acquire a territory. In the meantime they help close relatives to feed and to rear their young. Woolfenden and Fitzpatrick (1984) reported that when there is a shortage of nest sites, Florida scrub jays help adult birds in the defence of the nest and in rearing the young. The majority of the helpers are male and tend to be sons of the birds they help. Their defence of the nest increases the number of fledglings the parents can rear successfully. In both these examples the helpers are ensuring that genes they share with close relatives are passed on. (The concept of inclusive fitness is relevant to altruistic behaviour; see Unit 10.)

Activity 3

Darwin (1859) described a possible situation involving a pack of wolves. Food was in short supply, with deer the main prey available. These deer were able to run fast. Write down some of the variations in body form and behaviour likely to be found in a pack of wolves, and suggest which characteristics would contribute to the adaptedness of the wolves.

(Suggested answer on page 275.)

Selection pressure

A fit individual, then, is one that survives and reproduces. The concept of natural selection implies that *nature*, in the form of such things as climate and competition, picks out the animals that will survive. To describe an animal as being under selection pressure means that something in its environment is putting it into competition for survival with other members of its *own* or *another* species. For example, if one animal's food is destroyed by insecticides then, if it can adapt successfully, this animal may start to eat food normally eaten by another species. There will now be two species of animal in competition for the same food source, and both will be put under selection pressure. Unless further adaptation takes place, with one of the two species finding an alternative source of food, the competition is likely to result in one of the two becoming extinct. The one most likely to survive is the one which is most efficient at obtaining what food there is.

Climatic changes, especially if rapid, may put species under severe pressure. For example, a climatic change has been suggested as contributing to the extinction of the dinosaurs. Under the effects of a climate change these creatures were unable to adjust and consequently died. (Read about the effects of El Niño in figure 8.3.)

Thus some animals are more fit than others because they possess certain physical or behavioural characteristics which are well adapted to the environment. Fish possess streamlined bodies and gills; these are well adapted to the

8.3 Changing eco-systems and the risk of extinction

Eco-systems may change slowly over thousands of years, or more rapidly due to human activity or such events as flood or drought.

The El Niño of 1997–8 affected weather in many parts of the world. In some areas it produced drought, in others high rainfall. Unseasonal high temperatures and rainfall threatened to change the eco-systems of the Galápagos, home to unique animals and plants made famous by Darwin.

A similar El Niño event occurred in 1982–3, resulting in much higher than average rainfall and significantly higher sea temperatures than average for the time of year. The high rainfall caused heavy growth of plants which encouraged the multiplication of pests such as fire ants and rats. Flightless cormorants, found only in the Galápagos, dropped by 45 per cent and 78 per cent of the Galápagos penguins died.

The 1998 El Niño seems to have had similar devastating effects. For example, many seabirds, including the waved albatross, failed to nest. In previous years native species have recovered, but biologists fear that the 1998 El Niño might cause populations of native species to crash. This would allow alien species which have invaded the islands to gain such a firm foothold that native species will not recover. The eco-system of the Galápagos may change forever (Pain, 1998).

environment. The polar bear is superbly adapted to the Arctic environment. But both animals will be in competition with other members of their own species. Thus those fish which are better at escaping possible predators, those polar bears with better hunting skills, might survive when their **conspecifics** do not.

The same principle applies to behaviour. The nurture and care shown by parents who produce immature and helpless offspring is well adapted to the needs of their young. However, the care given by parents will vary slightly in quality; better care is likely to result in a greater number of young being reared.

Stasis and sudden change

Over countless generations the better adapted animals survive, whilst those less well adapted will gradually disappear. The term *evolution* mean gradual. However, this does not necessarily mean that evolution is a steady and continuous process. There are gaps in the fossil record where there appear to be periods of little or no evolutionary change (stasis) interspersed by periods of rapid change (sudden appearance). Gould and Eldredge (1972) referred to this **punctuated equilibria**.

There is disagreement among biologists as to whether the gaps in the fossil record are due to missing information or to evolution not proceeding smoothly, but in sudden bursts punctuating long periods without change. This is the view of Gould and Eldredge.

Gould (1970) believes that there are two major modes in evolution:

- phyletic transformation, where an entire population changes gradually over time
- *speciation*, where new species branch off from a continuing parental stock (two species produced from one ancestral species).

Gould argues that speciation is responsible for most evolutionary change. There are two forms of speciation:

- Allopatric speciation occurs when two populations become geographically separated. Thus a landslide might cause a stream to change course and divide a population of snails. The two populations would diverge until they form two distinct species of snail.
- Sympatric or 'same place' speciation occurs when organisms inhabit the same area but become separated for reasons other than geographical barriers. Thus, for some reason, the two groups do not breed together. This might happen when some individuals in a population become able to deal with a new food source. If these individuals prefer to mate only

with others with the same food habits, the species would gradually split from the parent stock.

Maynard-Smith (1958) offers an example. Domestic pigeons are descended from rock pigeons; London pigeons are descended from domestic pigeons. London pigeons prefer to nest on buildings rather than cliffs, thus maintaining a separation from the wild forms of the domestic pigeon. In time this might lead to London pigeons evolving as a separate species (there are many kinds of domestic pigeon – see figure 8.4).

Thus for speciation to occur, it is necessary that two groups within a population no longer interbreed, whether this is brought about by physical separation or behaviour. It is not known whether sympatric or allopatric speciation is more likely to occur. It would seem likely that forms which are in contact are less likely to form a new species than those separated physically. When different forms are in contact, some interbreeding is likely; this mixing of the genes lowers the likelihood of genetic divergence into new species (Hauffe and Searle, 1992).

Clearly more research needs to be done to determine whether evolutionary change proceeds smoothly, or in small jerks interspersing long periods of stasis. However, this uncertainty does not challenge Darwin's theory of evolution through natural selection.

Darwin's finches

In his role as naturalist on the research ship *Beagle*, Darwin visited the Galápagos Islands. They are of volcanic origin and generally inaccessible for land animals and plants. Darwin noted that the islands differed environmentally, some being large, some very small; some mountainous, others much flatter. The extent of rainfall also varied significantly. Darwin recorded that the islands were populated by species of finch and tortoise which differed from one island to another. Although he did not realise the significance at the time, when he later began to analyse his findings he realised their importance. He noted that many of the species on the Galápagos (the finches, for instance) had evolved

from a common ancestor, and had adapted to the conditions on each island. There has been disagreement as to how many species or subspecies the finches represent, but it is now generally agreed that there are 13 related species of which four groups are particularly closely related.

Since the islands differ environmentally, they also differ with regard to vegetation and the insects and seeds upon which the birds feed. These different environments require different characteristics in a species if it is to survive. Today the finches vary in several ways, one of which is in the size and shape of the beak. These variations are appropriate to the different food available on the islands. When the birds first colonised the islands, those with beaks best adapted to the food supply of a particular island would survive; those less well adapted would not. Darwin surmised that over many generations natural selection had resulted in the evolution of different species of finch, each well adapted to the food supply on its particular island.

Darwin himself bred pigeons, and used the wide variation in domestic pigeons to illustrate how such variety could develop from a single ancestral species.

Activity 4

Looking at figure 8.4, compare Darwin's finches with the illustrations of domestic pigeons all descended from a single ancestor, the Eurasian rock dove. Which of the domestic pigeons do you feel differ most from their wild ancestor? In what aspects do the pigeons vary from each other? And in what ways do the finches vary? How might these differences have evolved?

(Suggested answers on page 275.)

■ Artificial selection

The pigeons are an example of artificial selection. Darwin used the term *natural* **selection** to distinguish it from *artificial* **selection**, a process with which, as he pointed out, we are all familiar. The principles of artificial selection provide the basis for understanding natural selection.

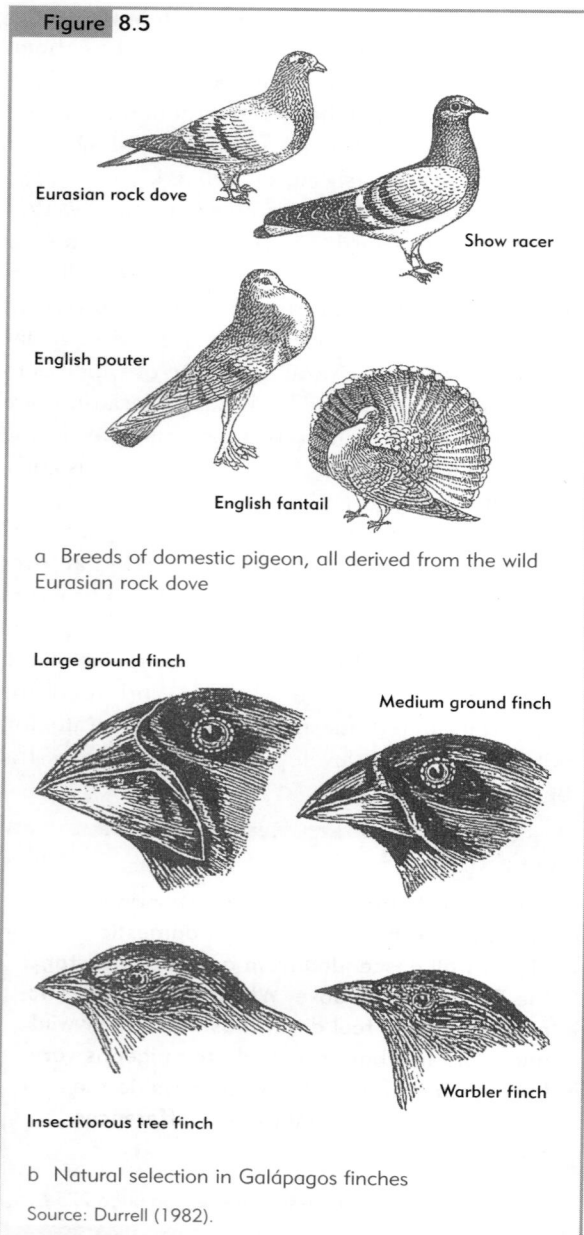

Figure 8.5

Eurasian rock dove

Show racer

English pouter

English fantail

a Breeds of domestic pigeon, all derived from the wild Eurasian rock dove

Large ground finch

Medium ground finch

Insectivorous tree finch

Warbler finch

b Natural selection in Galápagos finches

Source: Durrell (1982).

Human beings have kept and bred animals for thousands of years. Selective breeding has been carried out to produce desired characteristics in these animals. Some of these are physical such as the ability of cows and goats to produce plenty of milk, and speed or strength in horses. But behavioural characteristics are also important, for example docility in farm animals, aggression in hunting and guard dogs, and so on.

It is probable that all the breeds of dog in existence today are descended from a wolf ancestor. Humans have achieved this through selective breeding: the breeder selects animals with desired heritable characteristics, and only allows these to breed. Consider the characteristics existing in their wolf ancestors in relation to the variety of dogs today, from the chihuahua to the great dane, the dachshund to the bulldog! The breeders did not induce the genetic variation; they *selected* and bred from those animals which had the characteristics they wanted. Thus a greater proportion of the succeeding generations would possess these features. Darwin would, of course, expect natural selection to be a very much slower process than artificial selection.

Activity 5

Imagine that you have some dogs which are very attractive but are too aggressive to keep as pets. Describe how you would use artificial selection to produce friendly and docile animals. You are not allowed to use genetic engineering or outbreeding (crossing with another breed of dog).

(Suggested answer on page 275.)

Phylogeny and ontogeny

When we talk about the evolution of behaviour, we are implying that the way in which organisms behave has been shaped over countless generations, and that the way they behave is influenced by their genes. Behaviour patterns do not only exist because they have been passed on through the generations. Some become modified by experience gained during an animal's lifetime. When we consider the relative importance of phylogeny and ontogeny, we are, in effect, trying to determine how much of an animal's behaviour is inherited, and how much is learned, that is acquired during its lifetime. *Phylogeny* is a term used to refer to the evolution of a behaviour or trait within a species. For example, horses have changed in size and shape over the centuries; they are characterised by the fact that they run on the tips of their toes; these have become elongated and strengthened through evolution. The nails at the end of these lengthened toes have enlarged, and become hard. They are known as hooves. Horses run on the toe which was originally the middle toe of five. The remaining four have virtually disappeared (Dawkins, 1986). The human stance has changed from stooped to upright. Complex behaviour patterns as found in some insects (see the mason wasp below) have developed over many generations.

The term *ontogeny* was defined by McFarland (1987) as 'the elaboration and perfection of behaviour as an individual grows up'. Dawkins (1989) defines ontogeny as the process of individual development. This refers to how behaviour develops within the individual's lifetime. For example, a chimpanzee learns how to crack nuts, a child learns how to dress himself or herself, to talk, to interact with others. Ontogeny is linked to learning and memory.

The behaviour of an organism is influenced by both its genetic inheritance and the environment in which it develops. However, the nature of the interaction betwen genetic and environmental factors is very complex. If an organism can carry out behaviour without previous experience, then it would seem to be inherited, an example of phylogenesis. An instance of this is the mason wasp described by Manning and Stamp-Dawkins (1992). The female wasp builds a series of between eight and ten cells inside the hollow stem of a plant. She builds a wall of mud and saliva, lays an egg, then hunts for, and returns with, a caterpillar which she has paralysed with her sting on which the newly hatched offspring will feed. She places several of these in the cell with the egg and builds another wall, thereby completing the first cell and beginning a second. She lays an egg, sets out for more caterpillars and so on. An egg is laid in each cell, and food is supplied for her young.

The mason wasp lives for a few weeks only. From the time she emerges from the cell she lives a solitary existence apart from mating. She could not carry out such a complex sequence if she had to learn such behaviour. She relies on pre-set, unlearned responses which have evolved over many generations. However, the mason wasp has some ability to learn. She has to identify and locate the stem in which her eggs are laid, so that she can return to them with the caterpillars.

The sudden appearance of seemingly fully formed behaviour occurs in many species. In some cases this has been shown to be resistant to experience and to changes in the environment. The head-bobbing lizard is an example of this. Each species of this lizard has a characteristic pattern of head-bobbing suggesting that this behaviour is inherited and predetermined. The name of these lizards derives from the fact that when they meet, the males respond with rhythmic head bobbing movements which act as signals. Research indicates that less than 7 per cent of the variance in these displays is due to experience. This, plus the fact that the behaviour occurs in all members of the species, suggests that this behaviour is largely inherited.

However, even an animal which depends largely on predetermined (inherited) behaviour can reveal the capacity to learn. The newly hatched cockroach with no experience of wind, will turn away from a puff of air. This escape behaviour is fully formed, as accurate as that of the adult, and would seem to be innate. If a cockroach loses one of its two cerci (structures sensitive to wind) this behaviour loses its accuracy, and the cockroach will turn into the wind rather than away from it. Gradually, however, the cockroach succeeds in again turning away from the wind. Thus, even when a behaviour pattern is innate and does not depend on experience, it can be modified.

Like many insects, much of the behaviour of the honeybee is based on inheritance. Even so, bees have a great capacity to learn, although the nature of their learning is influenced by genetic factors. Thus when foraging the worker bee learns the location of the hive, the direction and distance of the food source, and which flowers are most likely to yield nectar and pollen (see Unit 11 page 374).

Thorpe (1961) demonstrated that isolated male chaffinches develop a basic song which shows little variation between individuals. This is the inherited, the genetic basis of the song. The song of wild chaffinches is considerably more complex and varied, however. These variations are due to experience, to hearing the song of adult chaffinches. Marler and Tamura (1964) found that male white-crowned sparrows also have a basic song, but acquire local dialects by listening to adult birds. Young white crowned sparrows seem to be highly selective in what they learn. Also, Marler *et al.* (1984) found that young swamp sparrows and song sparrows, when hearing the adult song for the first time, will select the song rhythms of their own species to copy.

Such research findings indicate that some species of bird have an inherited tendency to imitate song patterns of their own species. Thus genes predispose animals to behave in certain ways. Blue tits, for instance, can learn how to open bottles of milk. This behaviour closely resembles the natural behaviour involved in pulling bark from trees so as to reach the insects underneath (Sherry and Galef, 1982). Appropriate environmental conditions are necessary if these tendencies are to be expressed.

The interaction between genes and environment is clearly illustrated by those animals which change colour in response to certain environmental conditions. Ermine is a white fur obtained from the stoat. In summer the stoat has reddish brown fur, but in winter this changes to white, except for the tip of the tail, which is black. Although the colouring is genetically determined, the environmental changes due to approaching winter are required if it is to be expressed.

The ontogeny of behaviour in some species appears to be due mainly to learning, with no inherited component. African elephants live in matriarchal groups headed by a mature female and her daughters and their offspring. All the individuals know and recognise each other. The young elephants slowly acquire adult patterns of behaviour, necessary for survival. The behaviour of individual elephants and of groups varies, suggesting that the behaviour is acquired through experience during the lifetime of individuals. Manning and Stamp-Dawkins (1992) cited research which exemplified this. Douglas-Hamilton and Douglas-Hamilton (1975) recorded the behaviour of a group of African elephants. They were more nocturnal than elephants in general, and unusually aggressive towards humans. Why did

they behave like this? It was discovered that attempts had been made to shoot the whole group in 1919. Although elephants are long lived, it is uncertain whether any from that original group were still alive, but the group still showed behaviour patterns which had helped the original group to survive attempts to kill them. It seemed that these behaviours had been transmitted and passed down to other members of the group.

Elephants do, however, possess some innate patterns of behaviour such as those involved in feeding and reproduction. Indeed, several aspects of behaviour which develop early in life would seem to be preprogrammed, based on genetic instruction. If an organism did not start life with some innate, predetermined responses such as feeding behaviour, it could easily starve to death. Such behaviour is often based on reflex responses, the rooting reflex in human neonates, for instance. However, even reflexes do not occur in isolation; they occur in response to a stimulus of some kind.

Activity 6

See if you can find out how many reflex responses are present in the human neonate. How many of them have survival value?

(Suggested answer on pages 275–6.)

It is difficult to determine the relative contributions made to behaviour by learning and inheritance. The ontogeny of predatory behaviour in mammals suggests that both learning and heredity are involved. Eibl-Eibesfeldt (1951) studied the ontogeny of nut opening in squirrels. Young squirrels without previous experience of opening nuts have innate movements for gnawing and investigating, but become much more efficient with experience. We have all, surely, seen kittens playing, and noted how similar this is to the hunting behaviour of the adult.

It is not possible to determine precisely how much of an animal's behaviour is phylogenetically determined and how much is due to learning. Research is continuing and clarifying some areas of doubt. It has been found, for example, that tool use in chimpanzees is cultural, acquired through observational learning (Matsuzawa, 1996). Tool use, then, has not evolved over many generations.

What has evolved, however, is the level of intelligence needed to learn in this way.

Self-assessment questions

1 a Explain why the fossil record gives us only limited information on the evolution of behaviour.
   b Outline one experimental investigation into natural selection.
   c Explain why the tendency of animals to overproduce themselves is an important factor in evolution through natural selection.

2 a Explain the following terms: (i) adaptive behaviour, (ii) mutation, (iii) selection (environmental) pressure, (iv) fitness.
   b Give an example of when the same mutation can be (i) an advantage, and (ii) a disadvantage.

3 Explain the difference between artifical selection and natural selection.

4 a Outline the difference between phyletic transformation and speciation.
   b Explain why geographical separation is more likely to result in the formation of new species than same place speciation.

5 a Define the terms phylogeny and ontogeny.
   b Give an example of behaviour which is (i) largely phylogenetic, (ii) largely genetic, and (iii) reveals the interaction of heredity and learning. Include reasons for your choice.

(Suggested answers on pages 276–7.)

Competition for resources

You will remember that an important factor in evolution is the tendency of animals to reproduce themselves in larger numbers than can survive. This leads to competition for resources, both within and between species. In many cases this will involve aggression. Aggression refers to behaviours involving attack or hostility, and is shown by all species. It occurs in self-defence, predatory activity and competition for resources. Although some forms of aggression may result in serious or fatal injury, much aggression is substantially ritualised.

Most competition for resources takes place between animals of the same species (**intra-specific aggression**). Darwin believed that this was the most important factor in producing evolution.

Aggressive behaviours directed towards other species (**inter-specific aggression**) typically differ from those towards the same species. For example,

a cat will attack a rat by biting its neck, but will fight another cat with its claws. Deer fight each other with their horns or antlers, but attack potential predators with their hooves. Generally, rivals are threatened by ritualised behaviour patterns; enemies, such as potential predators, by all-out attack if escape is impossible.

Activity 7

Aggression against members of the same species is different to that against members of a different species. As you read the following pages, find examples of these differences.

It is not difficult to imagine how the tendency of animals to overproduce themselves leads, for instance, to competition over a supply of food. Even when food is plentiful, animals compete for the best or preferred food items. Indeed, you may even have witnessed this yourself if you put out food for birds in winter. In the natural environment such competition may lead to severe depletion of the food supply. Some animals may starve. Those most likely to survive are those which compete successfully for what there is, or those which are able to cope with an alternative kind of food.

> ### Activity 8
>
> In winter many birds will come into your garden if you put out food for them. Spend 10–15 minutes watching them, and record examples of within-species and between-species competition.

Some animals eat very restricted diets. The panda and the koala depend on a type of bamboo and on eucalyptus leaves respectively. Their habitats are shrinking due to human activity. Populations of pandas and koalas have dropped, and the panda is at risk of extinction.

If fitness is based on reproductive success, then to maximise this, animals need to act in such a way as to secure essential resources. Thus although much competition is in relation to food, animals also compete for resources such as shelter, nesting sites and mates.

Intra-specific competition

As you will remember, this refers to conflict between members of the same species. It may involve aggression, although those animals which avoid aggression are usually at an evolutionary advantage as they escape damage to their reproductive capabilities.

■ Ritualised aggression

Many animals have evolved forms of conflict behaviour in which fighting between members of the same species is restrained, greatly reducing the risk of serious injury. Such fighting may include the use of ritualised signalling.

Such ritualisation has been observed in red deer. The conflict begins in the autumn and goes through three stages (see figure 8.5). First, two males roar at each other. Second, they walk alongside each other in a pattern described as the 'parallel walk'. Third, they confront each other:

they lock antlers and push. The fight may end at any stage when one of the contestants retreats. They are likely to suffer minor injuries, occasionally serious ones, but the level of aggression shown is well below what it could be. Less than one in four of the fights reach the third stage (Clutton-Brock and Albon, 1979).

Rattlesnakes have also developed a ritualised form of conflict. These snakes possess a strong poison which is used against prey and dangerous enemies. However, when two rattlesnakes fight, each exerts pressure on the other to push it to the ground. The loser, once floored in this way, retreats and both contestants survive relatively uninjured (Ridley, 1995).

Tinbergen (1965) pointed out that it is relatively rare to see two animals locked 'in mortal combat' and wounding each other. The majority of fights take the form of bluff or threat. Many fish fight by sending a strong water-jet towards their opponent by means of strong sideways tail beats. Although they do not actually touch each other, the movement of water produced by these tail beats sends a powerful stimulus to the opponent's sensitive lateral-line organs (Tinbergen, 1965).

Thus the high costs of aggression favour compromise behaviour. Codes of conduct have evolved which set limits as to how far aggression can go. Lorenz (1966) suggested that animals can enjoy the benefits of aggression because they have evolved mechanisms that are ritualised into threat displays and bluff which inhibit them from all-out aggression which may result in serious injury or death. For example, chimpanzees will stare, raise an arm, shake branches or shout loudly. Some species, such as lizards, will make their bodies appear larger than they actually are, others will display their armouries, teeth for instance. Maynard-Smith (1991) explained such behaviour by suggesting that although an animal which fights fiercely would beat restrained opponents, these animals would increase in number. As their numbers grow, they would increasingly have to fight other fierce rather than restrained fighters. They would be likely to injure one another seriously. This might eventually benefit the restrained fighters which run away and never get hurt. Thus fierce fighting is a good strategy only when such fighters are few in number. This approach is based on game theory (see figure 8.6).

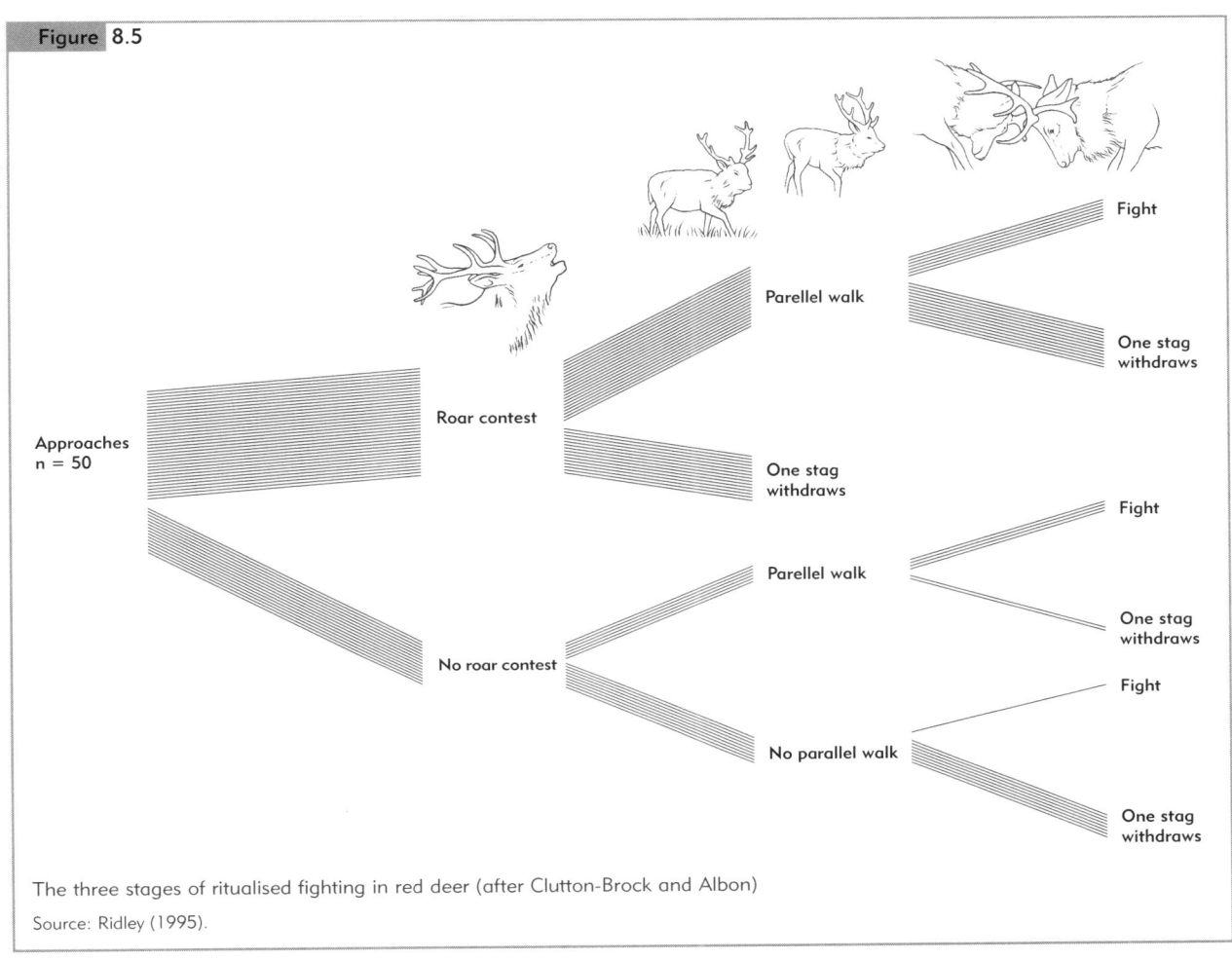

Figure 8.5

The three stages of ritualised fighting in red deer (after Clutton-Brock and Albon)

Source: Ridley (1995).

8.6 Evolutionarily stable strategies and fighting behaviour

■ The hawk–dove strategy

The approach is to specify two or more tactics, then to set values for these, indicating cost or benefit (payoff). In the hawk–dove model, for instance, it is postulated that the animal can adopt one of three possible tactics:

■ *escalate* – it can attack its opponent aggressively
■ *display* – it neither escalates nor retreats
■ *retreat* – it leaves the contest.

These three behaviours are combined into two strategies:

■ hawk – escalate: retreat only if injured
■ dove – retreat at once if opponent escalates, otherwise display.

The strategy is evolutionarily stable in that no other strategy considered does better. The hawk–dove strategy is known as a *mixed* strategy as it contains two strategies, the hawk and the dove. An evolutionarily stable strategy (ESS) with only one strategy – doves, say – would be a *pure* ESS.

(Evolutionarily stable strategies are also discussed in Units 9 and 10.)

Maynard-Smith and Price (1973) applied the analytical technique of game theory to the fighting behaviour of animals. They invented the term 'evolutionarily stable strategy' (ESS). Maynard-Smith (1982) defined an ESS as a strategy '. . . which if adopted by most individuals of a population cannot be invaded by another strategy that is initially rare'.

Game theory is particularly appropriate for the analysis of social situations where the consequences for one animal depend on the behaviour of another. Although it was originally used to provide a model of restraint in fighting it can be applied to other social situations. The aim is to identify a strategy which, if widely adopted, cannot be improved on. The strategy is stable, hence the term evolutionarily stable strategy.

■ Appeasement behaviour

Appeasement behaviour also reduces the occurrence of outright aggression. Both Darwin (1872) and Lorenz (1967) described appeasement responses. The function of such behaviour is to inhibit aggression in another member of the same species. An appeasement gesture tends to be the opposite of the response which elicits aggression.

A cichlid fish, for example, 'elicits aggression in another by displaying its colours, unfolding its fins or spreading its gill covers to exhibit its body contours as fully as possible, and by moving in strong jerks'. The appeasement response is exactly the opposite: 'It grows pale, draws in its fins, displays the narrow side of its body and moves slowly, stealthily . . .' (Lorenz, 1966). Similarly, the appeasement display in the lesser black-backed gull is almost the exact opposite of the threat posture (Manning and Stamp-Dawkins, 1992).

Darwin (1872) had observed the same contrast between submissive and threatening behaviour in dogs. He called this the **principle of antithesis**. What he meant can be seen in the drawings of a domestic dog taken from his book *The Expression of the Emotions in Man and Animals* (see figure 8.7).

Activity 9

Compare the two drawings in figure 8.7. How many instances can you find where signals of threat seem to be the opposite of appeasement?

(Suggested answer on page 276.)

The above examples suggest that Lorenz is perhaps correct in his view that appeasement responses evolved through an animal doing

Figure 8.7

The dog on the left is approaching another dog with hostile intentions; the same dog on the right in a humble and affectionate frame of mind

Source: Darwin (1872).

everything to avoid stimulating aggression. What selection pressure might cause this to evolve?

■ Dominance and territoriality

Dominance hierarchies and territorial behaviour also reduce the extent to which outright aggression occurs within a species. Ritualised fighting occurs in dominance and territorial contests. Dominance is a common but not universal kind of relationship between members of a group in which some animals (the dominant ones) have precedence over others (the subordinate animals). Precedence concerns access to such resources as food, mates and resting places. Schelderup-Ebbe (1935) was the first to study dominance. He studied domestic hens. Many studies have been done since and a great deal is known, therefore, about dominance in these birds.

When hens are put together they at first fight among themselves. They gradually learn to recognise each other, and know which are the stronger and weaker individuals in the flock. Each hen learns to give way to individuals stronger than herself, thus avoiding fights she would probably lose. Dominant hens assert their superiority by pecking subordinates; pecked subordinates give way to the dominant hen. The exact form of dominance within a group of hens depends on the size of the group. In groups of less than, say, ten hens, a simple linear hierarchy will form. Thus the alpha hen is dominant over the rest. In larger groups, the hierarchy can become more complex. 'Loops' may form in which, for example, one bird (A) dominates another (B) which dominates (C) which itself dominates (A) (see figure 8.8). Dominant hens take the best food and roost sites.

Dominance hierarchies are found in many species. They are established in stable groups where individuals learn to recognise each other. In some species one or two males become leaders (the dominant males) and the rest show varying degrees of subordination. Dominant males gain priority access to resources, for example the first choice of food and mates. Cox and LeBoeuf (1977) found that the most dominant 6 per cent of bull elephant seals inseminated 88 per cent of the females. High ranking red deer and kangaroos both have priority at feeding places.

There are several forms of dominance hierarchy. In some species males are dominant over females. In others the sexes may form separate hierarchies or, as in hyenas, females dominate males. In some species hierarchies are difficult to detect, and it may be that one animal is dominant and the rest subordinate to that animal. Dominance reduces aggression since subordinate animals learn to avoid fights that would be damaging to them.

Thus dominance brings several advantages. Since it involves ritualisation and convention, it reduces aggression between competing individuals.

A territory is an area defended by an animal or a group of animals in order to secure access to limited resources, such as food or mates. Territorial behaviour involves the same patterns of ritualised fighting as seen in dominance interactions. Also, dominance and territoriality may occur in the same population, with territorial behaviour merging into dominance and vice versa depending on circumstances. Thus Odell (1977) found that dominant male northern elephant seals defend areas containing approximately 50 females. However, one larger group was controlled by males in a dominance hierarchy. Odell suggested that when space is limited, females may aggregate in one large group; the same males are then forced to coexist in an area larger than one from which any one of them could exclude all the others. Thus instead of being territorial, they form a dominance hierarchy. Male hedge sparrows defend territories when food is plentiful, but when less abundant the territorial boundaries break down, with one male becoming dominant over the others (Davies, 1983; 1985). The males of some dragonfly species defend a territory when numbers are low, but develop dominance hierarchies when numbers are high (Ueda, 1979).

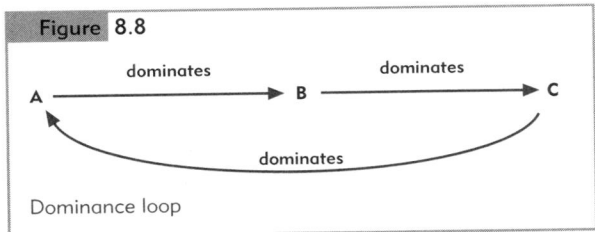

Figure 8.8

A —dominates→ B —dominates→ C

A ←dominates— C

Dominance loop

Territories have evolved for different reasons. They enable an animal or group of animals to retain an optimum share of resources, particularly food, nesting sites, hiding places and potential mates, their precise function varying between species. They are biologically adaptive in that they are an effective way of spacing out animals. They also ensure the procreation of the strongest males which ward off competitors without expending too much energy in fighting. Territoriality serves to minimise aggression, so it is both an aspect of aggression and a check upon it. Strategies for advertising territories include vocalisation (bird song) and using scent marking or special visual displays around the territory perimeter. Such strategies intimidate intruders without the need to resort to aggression.

Territorial conflicts are typically few, taking the form of border skirmishes when a same-sex intruder ignores signs of ownership and invades a resident's territory. Territorial aggression is often displayed in a similar way to that occurring in dominance disputes, so single encounters may be enough to demarcate a territorial boundary. When a territory holder meets an intruder within the territorial boundary, the holder is likely to win in any contest. If this occurs at the territorial boundary, the outcome is less certain.

Since territoriality and dominance are closely related to reproductive and social behaviours, they are discussed further in Units 9 and 10.

Perhaps one of the most important areas of within-species conflict involves competition for mates. This is examined in Unit 9.

Inter-specific competition

■ Competition and niche differentiation

Competition between species occurs when two populations require the same resources, that is, when they share the same **ecological niche**. This term refers to the precise requirements of a species in terms of food and shelter. The competition between them is described as niche overlap. The more overlap, the greater the competition. Such competition may result in the exclusion or

extinction of one species, but not necessarily. Over many generations the requirements of one species may change, so that overlap and, therefore, competition are reduced. This is known as **niche differentiation** and is an important evolutionary process.

Cormorants and shags provide an example of niche differentiation. They are both marine diving birds, both feed on fish and they share the same hunting ground. However, the cormorant feeds on sea-bottom dwelling fish such as prawns and flounders, whereas the shag feeds on fish which live in the upper waters. Since niche overlap has been reduced there is less competition.

Fighting may occur between related species which depend on the same prey. Several examples of this occur in Africa. Jackals will struggle with a hyena over a kill. Different species of vulture will descend onto the remains of a dead animal, and will squabble as each tries to get a share of the food.

Competition for food does not only take place between related species. For instance, it occurs between birds and squirrels; between lions and crocodiles over a kill. Competition takes place between different species of birds at bird feeders. Species such as house sparrows or grosbeaks establish dominance over other species. It is possible that such competition may have contributed to the evolution of taking food away to eat it hidden, or burying and hiding it. Squirrels bury nuts, leopards carry their food into trees. Competition for nest sites has been observed between hole nesting birds and small mammals.

Activity 10

Scan the TV programme schedules for details of wildlife programmes. Many of these include examples of different species competing or squabbling over food, and provide good examples of inter-specific competition. Or, as suggested in Activity 8 (see page 260), watch the birds in your garden. Whether you see them in the garden or on television, write down instances of competition between species.

Predator–prey and cooperative relationships

The predator–prey relationship

Most competition between species, however, occurs in the predator–prey relationship. This is sometimes said to confer some benefit since predation may improve the genetic composition of the prey population by removing the less fit animals. However, this is by no means always the case, since young, immature and inexperienced animals are often those taken. Predation also has consequences for the evolution of behaviour in both predator and prey.

Predators need to find, catch and eat prey; prey species need to avoid being eaten. The never-ending struggle to eat and to avoid being eaten has evolutionary consequences. Those characteristics which enable an organism to obtain prey will be favoured by natural selection. Similarly, natural selection will favour characteristics which reduce an animal's chance of being taken by a predator.

Both predator and prey need acute senses, well-developed nervous systems, and muscular coordination. Predation will lead to predator and prey gradually improving in their abilities. Those which do not are less likely to survive or reproduce. Thus where predator and prey are characterised by speed and alertness, these are likely to be a direct evolutionary consequence of predation.

Predators use a wide variety of hunting methods. These include ambush, stalking, pursuit, tools and traps, also group hunting. For example, several members of the cat family (the *felidae*) stalk and ambush their prey; this allows them to approach closer and thus reduce the length of the pursuit. Some species such as the octopus move through the water, feeling for possible prey. Some birds and mammals move through undergrowth, disturbing prey, which are then pursued. Chimpanzees use sticks to obtain termites. Woodpecker finches are also tool users, digging out food from crevices with sticks or plant stems. Several species prepare traps of one kind or another. Spiders' webs are an example of this.

In response to the innumerable methods used for catching prey, animals have evolved a wide variety of anti-predator adaptations. Many species use flight to escape predation. The defence tactic here is to run, fly or swim faster than the predator. The prey may zigzag, change direction, or jump. Such unpredictable movements make it difficult for the predator to follow. Such tactics have certainly contributed to the speed and agility of many animals.

A cheetah uses stealth so as to be able to approach its prey such as a gazelle. The gazelle is alert and on the lookout for danger. Competition between predator and prey has shaped the behaviour and capacities of both animals: the ability of the cheetah to approach unseen, the tendency of gazelles to move about in groups, to remain alert and react swiftly, and the speed of both animals. Dawkins (1986) pointed out that as the generations go by gazelles will tend to run faster, react more swiftly, therefore becoming progressively more difficult to catch; the cheetah will chase more effectively. The high speed of the cheetah has a cost, however: it can only chase at speed for a relatively short time. This has contributed to the evolution of the stealthy approach which allows it to come close to the prey, thus increasing its chance of a catch. Dawkins and Krebs (1979) compared the predator–prey evolutionary phenomenon to the human arms race between military powers. An advance on one side results in pressure for counter measures on the other, and the weaponry becomes ever more powerful and sophisticated.

■ Endler's five stages

Endler (1991) suggests that selection pressure acts at several stages in the predator–prey relationship. These are:

1 encounter
2 detection
3 identification
4 approach
5 consumption.

Let us look at some of the forms of behaviour that evolve in predator and prey in relation to these stages:

1 *Encounter.* Prey animals need to behave in such a way as to reduce the likelihood of meeting a predator. Chimpanzees and monkeys reduce the risk of predation by sleeping in trees. Ground squirrels seek safety in their burrows. Some animals form large aggregations where the risk of encountering a predator is greatly reduced. Some potential prey animals move about cautiously, alert for danger, ready to freeze or run if they sense a predator is near. Some are active only at night. Some prey species develop acute senses which allow them to detect predators from a distance and thus avoid them. Similarly, the predators need to maximise their opportunities of encountering prey. Some will hunt at night as it reduces the likelihood of their being spotted. Some lie in ambush for prey in likely places such as a waterhole, or where previous experience indicates prey are

likely to be found. Some species develop acute senses which enable them to locate prey at a distance.

2 *Detection.* Prey animals have developed a variety of methods of reducing detection by predators. Some have achieved this through camouflage which makes a prey animal difficult to see against the background. The colouring of plover chicks makes them almost impossible to see against their background, especially as they remain motionless. Protective mimicry is a form of camouflage seen in species which resemble specific things in the environment such as leaves and sticks. Stick insects are an example of this, or a butterfly with closed wings resembling a dead leaf. Species living in northern latitudes such as the stoat and ptarmigan develop white colouration in winter rendering them less conspicuous against a snow-covered landscape. Similarly, predators have developed adaptations which help them to detect prey. Some nocturnal species have eyes adapted to seeing in low levels of light. Bats and dolphins use echo-location to detect prey. Some animals have acute hearing which enables them to detect movements of prey; arctic foxes can hear lemmings under the snow. The visual acuity of birds of prey is much greater than that of human beings and allows them to see prey from high in the sky.

3 *Identification.* Some species have evolved adaptations which make them look much larger than they are; some species of butterfly have evolved wing markings which resemble eyes which reduce their likelihood of being identified as prey. Some insects mimic the colouration of an unpalatable or poisonous species. Thus hover flies mimic the yellow and black colouring of wasps. However, some birds which prey on insects are able to detect the difference between genuinely distasteful prey and the mimics. Many species use the sense of smell to identify prey. The echo-location used by bats and dolphins to detect prey also enables them to identify prey species.

4 *Approach.* Some predators have developed the ability to approach their prey closely, either through stealth or ambush. Birds of prey swoop

down on their prey, fast and sudden; the owl does so silently, thus giving the prey animal little chance of escape. In turn, prey species have evolved acute senses and rapid reactions. Some birds and mammals have eyes placed so as to increase their field of vision. This helps them to avoid predators. Social animals such as prairie dogs have sentries which remain on the alert and warn of danger. The skunk stops predators from approaching by emitting a foul smelling spray. It also warns with a 'keep off' display.

Activity 11

Do some research with animals around you. Compare the position of the eyes in prey animals (rabbits for instance, and birds) and in predators (such as dogs and cats).

5 *Consumption*. Predators need the equipment and digestive systems to deal with prey. A snake can swallow prey whole; a lion has teeth and jaws which enable it to consume flesh, hide and bone. Predators may need to break through protective shells. Thrushes hammer snails on a hard surface; sea otters break open shells by battering them with both front paws on a stone held on their chests. Prey species have developed a wide variety of defence mechanisms. Many of these are chemical. The great crane toad has glands which secrete poison. If the toad is picked up, the poison acts on the mucous membranes of the predator's mouth and the prey is dropped almost at once. Several insects also emit irritating or toxic chemicals. Some lizards are able to shed part of the tail. This continues to move and may distract the predator, allowing the lizard to escape. The hairstreak butterfly has false antennae. Instead of attacking the true head of the butterfly (from which there would be no escape), the bird is deceived into attacking the tail end, and the butterfly may be able to escape. Many species have evolved hard shells into which they retreat; the hedgehog has spines, and rolls up into a ball.

Activity 12

Several examples have been given above of predator–prey encounters at each of Endler's (1991) stages. Do some research of your own, and find further examples in the following pages. (Examples of animals cooperating in hunting and defence can be found in Unit 10.)

Many animals escape predation through flight. Some escape into an alternative habitat by, for instance, diving into water or climbing a tree.

Dolphins and bats both hunt using echo-location, and their hearing is acute. However, as you will realise, their prey develop adaptations which help them to escape. An example of this is the noctuid moth which has evolved ears which warn it of an approaching bat. The moth is sensitive to the high pitched sounds used by the bat to locate prey. Since the moth has an ear on each side of the thorax, it can determine from which side the bat is approaching. Further, the moth can detect the bat from a distance considerably greater than that at which the bat can pick up the echo from the moth. Therefore, if a moth hears a bat approaching (the bat's calls become louder as it gets nearer), the moth can avoid the bat by flying in the opposite direction.

If the moth fails to detect the bat until it is nearby, the moth gains nothing by flight, and has developed a second strategy. It descends to the ground in loops and spirals which confuse the bat, making it difficult to catch.

Many species have developed defences in the form of spines (hedgehogs and porcupines for example) or a hard outer covering. A widespread defence adaption is for an animal to freeze, thus rendering itself difficult to detect against the background. *Cavia aperea* (a relative of the guinea pig) will freeze when alarmed (Rood, 1972).

Some defence adaptations involve attack. Thus some species fight back with unpleasant sprays or odours. Although the skunk is perhaps the most notorious example, it is not the only one. The Bombardier beetle emits a jet of irritant chemicals from the tip of the abdomen (Eisner and Aneshansley, 1982). Some species of ants and termites emit an unpleasant chemical substance when defending their nest.

Many prey species are aggressive themselves, and may turn and attack the predator. Prey that are as large as or larger than the attacker have similar strength, and are usually able to fight back.

Many prey which are poisonous or with chemical defences have evolved conspicuous warning signals. Thus the skunk is black and white, the Monarch butterfly orange and black. That such conspicuous colouring deters predators has been demonstrated by Brower (1958) and Roper and Redston (1987). Brower found that Florida scrub jays will learn to avoid Monarch butterflies. This butterfly is poisonous, and birds are ill after eating one. Roper and Redston investigated the importance of the conspicuous colouring in avoidance behaviour. Their results indicate that conspicuous colouring is effective in enabling birds to learn what food to avoid.

Some species mimic inedible prey. The example of the hover fly was mentioned earlier. Some edible insects mimic the yellow and black colouring of the unpleasant-tasting Cinnabar moth caterpillar. Such a tactic is likely to protect due to learned taste aversions: from eating one prey, the predator learns to leave similar looking prey animals alone. This is known as **Batesian mimicry**. But if the first animal eaten with such colouring is an edible mimic, the predator will not develop an aversion, and will be likely to continue to eat similar looking prey until it encounters a distasteful or poisonous form. Thus for Batesian mimicry to be successful, predators should encounter at least *some* of the genuine version. Generally speaking, if such mimicry is to function as a protection, the number of mimics should not exceed the inedible forms.

There is much evidence to suggest that the relationship between predator and prey has led some species to seek safety in numbers. Thus several species feed and move about in groups. With a number of animals on the alert, the approach of a predator is more likely to be detected. The gazelle that grazes in a herd of many animals has a much better chance of survival. Any

sign of danger will be signalled immediately, and one signal is enough for all; the whole herd will flee before the predator has been able to draw close.

Many species benefit from living in groups. For example, Powell (1974) found that starlings react more swiftly to a model of a hawk when in groups than when alone. Kenward (1978) revealed that larger flocks of wood pigeons take off sooner in response to a bird of prey than do smaller groups. They are also less likely to lose a member of the group to the predator.

There are additional safety advantages of living in a group, apart from detecting predators. The group can take evasive action, and confuse the predator by scattering. The fact that another member of the group may be taken also contributes to the safety of the individual. Hamilton (1971) showed that an individual has a greater chance of survival the closer it is to the centre of a group. This is known as the *selfish herd principle*.

Activity 13

Write down some mammalian species where there is 'safety in numbers'.

While many animals live permanently in groups or herds, some solitary animals adapt their behaviour when this has survival value. Puffins spend most of their lives at sea fishing, but come ashore to breed. They nest in holes and burrows on cliff tops. Here they are preyed on by black-headed gulls, who also nest on the cliffs and have young to feed. The puffins are safe while in their burrows but, of course, they need to fish, and are at risk as they move between their nests and the sea. They counter this by flying in large numbers in a circular pattern all through the day. They become part of this pattern when they fly to the sea and return to their nests. This makes it difficult for the gulls to attack them, and puffins likely to be caught are those which fail to gain the safety of the flight.

Pressures of obtaining prey and avoiding predation have resulted in the coevolution of predatory and defence behaviours. As the prey species gains a fractional advantage in avoiding predation, this is matched by an adaptation in the predator, improving the ability to obtain prey.

Exploitation

Another way in which one species may prey on another is through exploitation. They do so by exploiting the normal feeding or reproductive behaviour of that species. The angler fish is a good example. The fish is well camouflaged so is not readily seen by its prey. A lure dangles in front of its mouth which resembles a live worm, the food of smaller fish, shrimps and so on. When the prey fish see the lure, they dart at it, and are at once snapped up by the angler fish (Pietsch and Grobecker, 1978).

The Australian death adder has a similar way of obtaining food and, like the angler fish, is difficult to see against the (desert) background. The end of its tail is thin and pink, and moves, so that it resembles a worm. Any bird that attempts to feed on this 'worm' will be killed and eaten by the snake.

One species of firefly exploits the courtship behaviour of another. Male fireflies seek to attract a receptive female by signalling in a particular pattern of flashes. Females reply with a signal of their own. The females of the carnivorous species mimic the signalling pattern of other species, and give the signal that they are ready to mate; the males of the other species are deceived, alight beside the female, and are eaten.

The cuckoo is notorious for the way in which it exploits other birds. The female lays her egg directly in the nest of the foster species: a robin, hedge sparrow, reed warbler and so on. She may remove one of the host's eggs to make room for hers. She will choose a nest of newly laid eggs so that the young cuckoo will hatch at about the same time as the host bird's own eggs. When the cuckoo hatches, it pushes out the other eggs or nestlings.

The advantages of such behaviour to the angler fish and cuckoo (for example) are obvious, but it is more difficult to appreciate how the behaviour of the prey fish and cuckoo hosts would evolve.

Signalling is involved in all of the above instances, and this is clearly an important factor in exploitation. The snake and the angler fish provide lures to obtain their prey; the wide gape of the nestling cuckoo signals 'feed me' to the foster parents.

The gape of the cuckoo acts as a supernormal stimulus to the parent birds, that is it induces a feeding response even stronger than the response to the natural stimulus (the wide gape of the young cuckoo may well attract strange birds to feed it). But one might expect selection pressure to improve discriminative ability in both the angler fish and birds chosen as hosts by the cuckoo.

Why are the prey fish deceived by the lure of the angler fish? Natural selection will have acted on their ancestors, favouring the tendency to approach small wriggling objects, the worms on which they feed. How much survival value would there be in the prey fish developing caution, and the ability to discriminate between the lure and the real thing? If a fish were to be overcautious, it might miss out on real worms as well as avoiding the lure, and thus not find enough to eat. At the same time selection has acted on the angler fish. Those which best mimic worms are those most likely to obtain prey and survive. As the prey fish improve their powers of discrimination so, in order to survive, must the angler fish improve its mimicry.

In the case of the cuckoo, why has selection pressure not evolved the ability in the host birds to discriminate between the cuckoo nestling and their own? It would seem most advantageous that they should discriminate early on, and reject the cuckoo's egg. This would make sense in evolutionary terms since they would still be able to breed that season. It is in part explained by the fact that in many cases cuckoos' eggs mimic those of the host species. Further, it has been found that the cuckoo chicks themselves contribute to their foster parents' willingness to feed them. Working with reed warblers, Davies *et al.* (1998) demonstrated that the begging call of the cuckoo chick sounds very similar to a brood of reed warbler chicks. Thus mimicry occurs at the nestling stage as well as at the egg stage.

Commensalism and symbiotic relationships

There are many forms of cooperative behaviour between different species of animal. Many species have developed signals which warn of approaching danger. The alarm call of song birds such as the blackbird is an example. Most song birds make such calls, and since these calls resemble one another, other species respond to them. The similarity of alarm calls is perhaps due to the need for them to be difficult for a predator to localise, but several species benefit from this fact. On the plains of Africa different species (impala, wildebeest, zebra and gazelles) graze in mixed groups. This gives the benefit of additional security from predators since each will respond to the alarm signals of at least one of the other species. Each species benefits from the association, but each is able to live independently.

Commensalism is often used to refer to a one-sided relationship where one animal benefits and the other is not affected. For example, hyenas will take the remains of a kill left by lions. If the lions have abandoned the kill, the hyenas benefit and the lions are unaffected.

Activity 14

Try to think of an example of commensalism between humans and another species. In this case, the benefit is to the other species, not the humans!

(Suggested answer on page 276.)

Mixed species groupings are seen in fish, foraging and migrating birds, roosting bats, some mixed troops of primates, some dolphins, some open plains ungulates, also monkeys and birds. In some instances the relationship will be of benefit to one animal with little effect on the other. Where both animals benefit, the term **symbiosis** is generally used (an alternative term is *mutualism*). The word 'symbiosis' comes from the Greek and literally means 'living together'.

It is probable that the main benefits of such relationships are reduced predation and improved foraging efficiency. Evidence suggests that when food is in short supply, some species of birds forage in mixed flocks. Individuals which might fail to find food on their own may be able to take advantage of the foraging experience and success of the others. More eyes may make it more likely that food which can be used by all will be discovered.

Among mixed herds of ungulates individuals of different species may facilitate the feeding of others. Thus animals of one species may remove those parts of a plant which are obstacles or are indigestible to animals of another species. Also, as they feed, ungulates disturb insects which are then caught and eaten by birds such as cattle egrets and brown-headed cowbirds.

Munn (1984) studied mixed flocks in South America, where up to 70 species may forage together in a single flock. Some birds spend their entire lives in the same flock, while other species join the flock on a less permanent basis. A few species within the flock maintain a territory. One species in the flock acts as a sentinel, sounding an alarm at the appearance of a predator. The sentinels also benefit; they catch insects which are disturbed by other foragers. When sentinels are not present, other birds are less likely to forage in exposed positions.

Activity 15

Using this text write down examples of (a) commensal, and (b) symbiotic relationships.

(Suggested answers on page 276.)

The grouper or Parrot fish is an example of a symbiotic relationship. This fish floats in the water with mouth and gill covers open. Small fish swim in and out of these areas, removing fungus, dead skin and parasites. Both species benefit: one has its parasites removed, the other gains a food supply. Another species of fish, the Opal eye, gathers in groups, and waits to be cleaned. Most species of cleaner fish have evolved tapered snouts and teeth which enable them to pick off the parasites; they tend to be highly coloured, and predatory fish ignore them.

In Africa large grazing animals have a similar relationship with ox-pecker birds. The birds pick off ticks, lice, fleas and maggots. Through many generations the ox-pecker bird has adapted to its way of life; its beak is flattened which enables it to push through the animal's hair and take firm hold of tick or maggot. The ox-pecker has long claws which enable it to hold on when the host is moving, and a short tail which provides support when it is on a vertical surface such as the flank or neck of an animal (a giraffe, for instance!). The host animals have adapted by showing complete tolerance of the ox-pecker birds. Both species appear to benefit from the relationship; the birds obtain food and the hosts are relieved of health-threatening parasites in inaccessible parts of the body. The animals also gain from the early warning of predators provided by the birds which fly off at the approach of a predator.

Giant tortoises in the Galápagos are cleaned by small finches. In response to the birds the tortoise raises itself on its legs in a position which lifts its shell clear of the ground. In so doing it exposes parts of its body which are normally hidden. The finches immediately fly onto the tortoise and remove the parasites.

Some species of aphid have no defence mechanisms of their own, but are protected by ant caretakers. Their life cycles are synchronised. Ants transport aphids to new plants, and take them underground in winter. The benefit to the ants is that they milk the aphids for the honeydew which is excreted by aphids and similar insects which feed on plant juices.

▨ Human beings and symbiosis

An example of mutualism involving humans exists between people and a species of bird, the greater honeyguide. The honeyguides lead people (the Boran people of Kenya, for example) to bee hives. These are found in rocks, trees, crevices and termite mounds, and are not easy to find. The humans break into the hives to extract the honey, leaving bee larvae and wax for the birds.

Either through evolution or learning the humans and honeyguides have developed complex interspecific communication. The Borans produce a loud whistle to attract the birds. In response the birds fly close to them, emitting a call. Through a combination of flight, calls and perching patterns, the birds lead the people to the area where the hive is located. The birds signal when they have reached the location of the hive. This is necessary as the hive may not be immediately obvious.

When guided by the birds it took an average of about three hours to find the hive. Without the honeyguides people required nearly nine hours. The honeyguides benefit because human help gives them much greater access to the hives. The majority of hives are unavailable without human help. The birds also benefit from the smoke used to clear out the bees since this reduces the likelihood of their being stung. This remarkable relationship has been thoroughly investigated (Isack and Reyer, 1989) and indeed ancient rock paintings suggest that this interaction may have been going on for at least 20 000 years!

The relationships between species do not fall neatly into categories. They range from loose relationships where both organisms benefit, but are not dependent on one another, to true symbiotic relationships where the partners depend on one another. These relationships develop because the behaviours of the species concerned have evolved on a mutually adaptive basis.

An essential factor which contributes to coevolution of behaviour, whether cooperative or involving predator–prey relationships, is frequent and reliable encounters between the species concerned. These may begin on a casual or on a chance basis.

Animals adapt to the environment in many ways. The environment is complex, including the weather (subject to change) and interactions with other animals. This all contributes to selection pressure.

Adaptationism

Evolution helps us to understand why humans and other animals behave in the way they do. However, it is necessary to be careful, and not to assume that because a structure or pattern of behaviour has evolved that it has a function, or that it represents the most adaptive solution to a particular problem. It is easy to assume that because an organism has evolved a certain pattern of behaviour, it is adaptive, and to consider this as an adequate explanation of such behaviour.

Adaptationism refers to the view that structures and behaviour shaped by evolution are adaptive and therefore contribute to the fitness of an organism. Those that argue against this might point to the hedgehog: the hedgehog has evolved a defence response of rolling up into a ball. This is not appropriate behaviour in the face of an oncoming car and would not, therefore, seem to be adaptive. However, the behaviour evolved as an anti-predator response, and has been inherited from ancestors living in an environment where there were no cars or roads. Environments change, and many organisms alive today have inherited adaptations appropriate to the environment of their ancestors, but not to their own.

Activity 16

Moths fly towards light, and into candle flames. Is this adaptive behaviour? Can you

Activity 16 *cont'd*

suggest why this behaviour evolved? In what way might it have been adaptive?

(Suggested answer on page 276.)

The advantage of the adaptationist approach is that it can lead to research and discovery as Dawkins (1982) pointed out. Von Frisch (1967) refused to believe that flowers varied in colour for no reason than to delight the eye (this was commonly believed). He took the adaptationist view that since different colours had evolved, this must be adaptive. He set out to investigate this empirically and, through a series of experiments, demonstrated that bees have colour vision. We now know that the colour of flowers is an important factor in the relationship between bees and flowers.

Adaptationists do not hold the view that natural selection results in perfect organisms with optimal functioning. That this is not so is demonstrated by the eye, since the retina seems to be built back to front. Light has to pass through layers of retinal cells and blood vessels before reaching the light sensitive cells at the back of the retina, resulting in some loss in quality of vision.

Nor does adaptationism imply that all characteristics which evolve are adaptive. Some might evolve because they are linked to an adaptation. Thus blood is red because natural selection has produced a fluid able to carry oxygen round the body. Red blood cells contain haemoglobin which combines with oxygen. Haemoglobin gives blood its colour.

In contrast to the adaptationist approach which uses objective methods to determine whether a trait is adaptive or not, an **armchair adaptationist** would give an evolutionary explanation of behaviour without testing this empirically. Unless there is supporting evidence, the evolution of a particular structure or pattern of behaviour should not be assumed to be adaptive.

Evolution now

Evolution is taking place today. Evolutionary biologists are studying the process of evolution in the wild. This requires an isolated population, since such a population cannot easily interbreed with others, nor is it likely to move away.

Peter and Rosemary Grant have been studying finches on islands in the Galápagos since 1973. This seems particularly appropriate as the finches Darwin saw in the Galápagos played an important part in his theory of natural selection. The Grants and their fellow workers have concentrated mainly on the finches on one island, Daphne Major. Detailed records of family trees, breeding success and breeding failure have been kept, together with details of weather conditions and type and availability of food. The birds have been trapped, photographed and measured, then released.

Fortunately, it was found easy to measure their beaks accurately; this is important as length and type of beak is closely related to the food on which they rely.

Over the years the weather has varied. In times of drought the struggle for existence has been intense. On Daphne Major when food was scarce, it was found that the Medium Ground Finches with the very longest beaks *or* the very shortest were favoured. Those with the biggest beaks were favoured because they could handle large seeds, those with the smallest because they could take the tiniest seeds.

In severe conditions on another island (Genovesa) two finches survived, the Large Cactus Finch and the Large Ground Finch. In the Large Ground Finch beaks increased in length and depth; in the Large Cactus Finch they decreased. All finches with beak measurements in between died.

A change of less than a millimetre in the length of a beak significantly affects whether or not that bird will thrive and leave offspring, or die before it is able to reproduce. Thus when times are hard, certain forms of beak are favoured by natural selection because they have great adaptive value.

This is a brief mention only of the many findings obtained. The work going on in the Galápagos is revealing that evolution is taking place, and that it occurs as Darwin surmised. The work is described by Weiner, 1995.

Self-assessment questions

11 a Outline the term exploitation.
   b Using an example, indicate how exploitation may evolve.

12 Explain the difference between commensalism and symbiosis. Give an example of each.

13 Explain why the strong colouring of the cleaner fish might have evolved. Why do the grouper and Opal eye not cheat and eat the cleaner fish?

14 a Give a definition of the term adaptationism.
   b Indicate in what way adaptationism may lead to a greater understanding of evolution.
   c What is wrong with being an armchair adaptationist?

(Suggested answers on page 279.)

Unit summary

- All species alive today have evolved through a process of *natural selection* which has shaped both form and behaviour. *Evolution* has been studied by looking at fossilised animals, comparing the behaviour of related species, and by experiment. *Natural selection* takes place because animals which are poorly adapted to their environments are less likely to survive and to reproduce than well-adapted animals.
- *Genetic variation, inheritance* and *overproduction* of young are necessary conditions for evolution.
- *Fitness* refers to the ability to survive and to reproduce. The fittest are those which leave most offspring.
- Environments change; in order to survive, organisms need to adapt. Evolution may not be a gradual process but involve periods of little change punctuated by periods of rapid change.
- New species occur through *phyletic transformation* and *speciation*. Sudden environmental change may lead to a species becoming extinct.
- *Artificial selection* resembles natural selection in that it determines which animals are able to breed.
- *Ontogeny* refers to behaviour which develops within an *individual's* lifetime. *Phylogeny* refers to behaviour which has evolved in a *species* over countless generations. Both phylogeny and ontogeny contribute to behaviour.
- The tendency of animals to overproduce leads to competition for resources. Competition may be *within* or *between species*.
- Much *intra-specific competition* involves *ritualised aggression*. Ritualised aggression, dominance and territoriality reduce the risk of serious injury. *Dominance hierarchies* occur in many species. High ranking animals have priority of access to resources. *Territories* enable an animal or group of animals to secure access to limited resources.
- Competition between species occurs when they share the same ecological *niche*. Most competition between species occurs in the *predator–prey relationship*. This leads to predators developing a variety of hunting methods, and to prey developing anti-predator adaptations. Endler suggests there are five stages in the predator-prey relationship.
- Some species exploit the feeding or reproductive behaviour of others. Other species cooperate in *commensal* or *symbiotic relationships*. In a symbiotic relationship both species benefit.
- *Adaptationists* believe that form and behaviour shaped by evolution are adaptive.
- Evolution is still taking place in the Galápagos.

Terms to define

armchair adaptationist
artificial selection
Batesian mimicry
conspecific
ecological niche
fitness
genetic variation
inter-specific aggression

intra-specific aggression
mutation
natural selection
niche differentiation
principle of antithesis
punctuated equilibria
symbiosis

Further reading

Krebs, J R and Davies, N B (1993) *An Introduction to Behavioural Ecology*, Blackwell, Oxford.

A clear and readable approach to work in this area.

Ridley, M (1993) *Evolution*, Blackwell Scientific Publications, Boston, MA and Oxford.

A very accessible account of evolutionary theory and research.

Weiner, J (1995) *The Beak of the Finch: Evolution in Real Time*, Vintage, London.

A gripping tale of ongoing research in the Galápagos.

White, M and Gribbin, J (1995) *Darwin, A Life in Science*, Simon and Schuster, London.

An enjoyable account of Darwin's work.

Answers

■ Suggested answers to activities

1

Evolution is studied by examining and comparing fossil remains. Conclusions are drawn about the life style and behaviour of the organism on the basis of its structure.

The evolution of behaviour is studied by comparing the behaviour of related species alive today. According to the traits which are common to several of these species, it is possible to draw conclusions as to the behaviour of their probable ancestor.

Evolution is also investigated by experiments in natural and artificial conditions. (Methods of studying evolution are considered in more detail on pages 249–50.)

3

The wolves would vary in several ways, including body build, length of legs, musculature, lung capacity and in their ability to cooperate over hunting. Those wolves with a slim body and long legs would be able to run fast, so these features would be well adapted to chasing deer. The ability to hunt cooperatively would also improve their chances of success.

4

The English Fantail pigeon appears to have considerably more elaborate ornaments than its ancestor, and the Pouter pigeon also looks very different. The show racer's differences are less visually obvious.

The pigeons in these drawings vary most in regard to their tails, shape and colour. The main variation in the finches is in terms of the length and shape of their beaks.

The varieties of domestic pigeon have come about as a result of *artificial selection* where the pigeon breeder only allows pairs with desired characteristics to mate. The differently shaped beaks of the finches have evolved through *natural selection*. The different forms of beak are specialised for the different types of food they eat. Strong beaks are needed to deal with large, tough seeds; small beaks are best for very small seeds. A long thin beak enables birds to eat cactus seeds (see page 273).

Both the effects of artificial selection in pigeons and of natural selection in finches demonstrate the importance of genetic variation in the evolution of new forms and species.

5

You would select the males and females which you have found to be the most docile and friendly. You would breed from these, and then from the most docile and friendly of their descendants. You would not allow dogs which did not have these characteristics to breed.

6

There are several reflexes present in the human newborn; 12 or more. These include the Moro (or startle reflex), the stepping reflex, the grasping (or palmar) reflex, the plantar reflex, the rooting reflex and the sucking reflex. These disappear after a few months.

■ The Moro reflex: this occurs when the newborn infant is startled by a noise or if it is dropped a few inches. First the infant stretches out its arms and spreads its fingers, then brings its arms back to its body, and clenches its fingers.

- The grasping reflex: when a pencil or finger is placed in the infant's palm, the infant will grasp it tightly. Strength of the grasp is increased if the object is pulled away.
- The plantar reflex: if a pencil is placed on the soles of an infant's feet near to the toes, the infant responds by trying to flex its feet.
- The stepping reflex: if it is held up with its feet on a flat surface and moved forwards, the infant will make stepping movements.
- The rooting reflex: if its cheek is touched, the baby will turn its head towards the stimulus and open its mouth.
- Sucking reflex: if a finger or teat is put into a neonate's mouth, it will respond by sucking.

The rooting reflex would certainly seem to have survival value in that it helps the infant to find the nipple. The sucking reflex is vital to survival: without it the neonate will not feed. With regard to the other reflexes mentioned above, their survival value is less obvious. Some think the Moro reflex is a remnant of our ape-like ancestry. Should an infant fall, the infant which quickly grasps its mother's hair would be the most likely to survive. A similar explanation might apply to the grasping reflex. If an infant's mother failed to maintain her hold on her newborn, the infant's tight grasp would prevent it from falling. This theory is supported by the fact that the strength of the grasp in the human neonate is increased if the object is pulled away; further, some infants can support their whole weight for up to a minute.

9

The appearance of the ears, tail and the hair on the back of the dog with 'hostile intentions' is the opposite of these in the other. Thus the tail is up, ears are pricked and the hair is standing on end in the one dog; all are down in the other. The stance is also different with the hostile dog standing upright, while the other has lowered the front of its body almost to the ground.

14

Cockroaches, house mice and house spiders all benefit from living close to humans.

15

Commensal relationships are likely to be found in species which forage or move around in mixed groupings. These are found in many species including some birds, roosting bats, fish and primates. In some instances the benefit to one species may be the alarm signals given by another. Commensal relationships are also found between such species as lions which may leave part of their kill and others (such as hyenas and vultures) which feed on the remains.

Examples of a symbiotic relationship are those found between large grazing animals and ox-pecker birds. Further instances include the relationship of ants with aphids, and the relationship between cleaner fish and Opal eye and Parrot fish (see pages 270–71).

16

It is possible that a point of light represented the exit from a confined area, in which case flying towards it would make sense.

If moths navigate (as do many insects) by using the moon or stars then, again, the behaviour would have adaptive value. The confusion between navigating by a celestial body and responding to a candle (or lamp) as though it were in the sky would explain why the moth flies into the flame. When the behaviour evolved candles did not exist.

In either case, flying towards the light almost certainly had adaptive value at one time. In much of the world, thanks to our lighting systems, this is no longer always the case.

■ Suggested answers to self-assessment questions

1

a Fossils are the remains of animals long dead and do not, therefore, behave. By studying the anatomy of fossil remains and comparing them with species alive today, it is possible to infer how the fossil species behaved. For example, the teeth of a fossilised animal would indicate the nature of its food. If it was a grazing animal, this might mean that it moved about in herds, since grazing species tend to do this. However, although this is plausible, it is an inference and not fact. It could be incorrect.

b Kettlewell released equal numbers of light and dark forms of the peppered moth in polluted and unpolluted areas. When he recaptured samples of these moths he caught twice as many dark forms as light in the polluted area. In the unpolluted area the number of light moths caught was double that of the dark. This suggests that the dark forms were favoured by natural selection in the polluted area because they were hard to see when they settled on the darkened trees. In the unpolluted area light forms were favoured because they were less visible against the lighter lichen-covered trees.

An alternative experiment you could describe is that of Benkman and Lindholm (1991) on crossbills (see page 252).

c The fact that animals overproduce themselves results in competition for food and other scarce resources. Competition may be among members of the same species, or between different species. Natural selection acts by favouring traits which help animals to compete successfully, whether for food, mates or shelter.

Animals which compete successfully are more likely to survive long enough to reproduce. The traits which enabled them to do so are passed on to their offspring.

2

a i Adaptive behaviour is behaviour which enables an animal to survive in its environment and which therefore contributes to its reproductive success. This applies to all aspects of behaviour including, for instance, efficient foraging, parental care and effective defence.

ii A mutation is a small change in the genes; mutations can be inherited and can be beneficial, as in the case of the lungfish where the mutation enables it to survive when its environment dries up, or harmful, as in haemophilia. Many mutations have no effect.

iii Environments change, and this may put animals under selection pressure. In a time of drought, for instance, food will be sparse and this will lead to intense competition. If the competition is between two species, it may lead to one of them becoming extinct. Within-species competition for scarce resources may lead to a population diverging into two forms, each of which is adapted to a different food source. Thus birds with long beaks suitable for digging food out of crevices and birds with short beaks efficient at cracking open tough seeds may survive. All those with intermediate beaks would die. If only one source of food was available, only those best able to obtain this would survive. Thus selection pressure reduces variation (see pages 253–4).

iv Fitness refers to the ability to survive and to leave offspring. The fittest animals leave most offspring. Fitness in this sense is *not* the same as you spending time in the gym to get fit.

b The mutation of a dark form of the peppered moth confers an advantage to moths in a polluted environment; it would be a disadvantage to moths inhabiting a clean environment (see page 252).

3

In artificial selection the human breeder decides which animals are able to breed. Thus if docile animals are wanted, the breeder will select the most docile males and females and breed from them only. The principle is the same in natural selection except that environmental factors determine which animals breed. Because of competition only individuals best suited to their environment survive long enough to breed.

4

a Where a whole population gradually changes over the generations until it becomes a new species, this is known as phyletic transformation. Speciation refers to when a new species branches off from a continuing population: where one species existed, there are now two. This occurs when two parts of a population cease breeding together.

b Where a population is divided physically by, say, a landslide or a river changing course, the two parts of the population are no longer able to interbreed. When they share the same area, but do not breed together, some degree of interbreeding is still possible. Physical separation, therefore, is more likely to result in speciation because there is no possibility of interbreeding.

5

a Phylogeny: the evolution of behaviour within a species over very many generations.
Ontogeny: the development of behaviour during the lifetime of an individual.

b i The behaviour of solitary wasps in providing for their offspring is largely phylogenetic. Thus the mason wasp builds cells for her young, supplies them with food, deposits an egg in each, then seals the cell. All members of the species show the same pattern of behaviour, it appears fully formed, and there is no opportunity for it to be learned. It has evolved over many generations and is inherited.

ii Tool using behaviour in chimpanzees, such as using a stone to break open a nut, is acquired during the lifetime of the individual. It is passed on culturally from one animal to another. It is not present in all chimpanzees, being seen in chimpanzees living in some locations only. This behaviour is therefore ontogenetic in origin.

iii The ability of the blue tit to open milk bottles is clearly an example of learning; milk bottles were not around during the millenia when blue tits were evolving. However, the way in which the bottle is opened closely resembles tits' innate behaviour in stripping bark from trees to obtain the insects underneath. Thus both heredity and learning ability enable the blue tit to find an alternative source of food. Genes predispose animals to behave in certain ways and influence learning.

6

a Ritualised aggression refers to aggression which involves ritual behaviour rather than all-out fighting. Such aggression is found in red deer stags. Their fights involve three stages: roaring, parallel walks and antler pushing. Each stage gives the animals the opportunity to assess the strength and stamina of the other. Roaring, for instance, requires effort, and the stag able to roar longest is likely to be the stronger. Either animal may retreat at any stage.

b Ritualised fighting reduces the risk of serious injury, or damage to the reproductive organs of the individual. Although an animal which fights fiercely is likely to win if it encounters less aggressive individuals, the benefit of such all-out fighting is unlikely to last. This is because over time these aggressive fighters would increase in number so that eventually they would encounter animals which fight as fiercely as themselves. This would result in serious injury. Animals which avoid fighting now have an advantage. Thus in the longer term fierce fighting does not benefit the individual.

7

a i Resource defence refers to the guarding and protection of food, mates, nest area and so on against others, usually of the same species.

ii The term dominance hierarchy was first used by Schelderup-Ebbe (1992) who first observed the behaviour in a flock of hens. There is one individual (the alpha) which is dominant over all the others, one below (the beta) which is dominant over the remainder, but who defers to the alpha individual and so on, down the line to the last who is subordinate to all the others. Such a hierarchy (or pecking order) is known as a linear hierarchy, but there are many kinds of dominance hierarachy, and not all are as clearly defined as the linear hierarchy. Dominance is found in both male and female animals.

iii A territory is an area defended by an animal or group of animals against others of the same species. Territories vary greatly in size, and range from very large to the area around a bird's nest.

b Dominant individuals gain priority of access to resources. Thus dominant males have greater reproductive success than subordinates. High ranking animals have priority at feeding sites. This has been observed in many species including kangaroos and red deer. Dominance also reduces aggression between competing animals due to the fact that it involves ritualisation and convention. Territoriality enables animals to protect and retain valuable resources such as food, nesting sites and mates. In many species possession of a territory is necessary for a male to obtain a mate. As with dominance, territoriality helps to reduce aggression. Evidence suggests that territories are an effective means of distributing animals.

8

a Ecological niche: the exact resources needed by an animal to feed, protect itself and breed successfully.

b Niche overlap refers to the extent to which the requirements of two species are the same.

c The predator–prey relationship is the term given to the interaction between two populations – the predator and the prey. The predator attacks and kills the prey, the prey resists this through speed (escape), alertness, defensive aggression and moving about in groups (see pages 265–9 for more information).

9

a We are all familiar with the arms race whereby, as one country perfects weapons of attack or defence, another creates something with which to counter these. The first country improves its weapons yet again . . . and so it goes on. In the predator–prey relationship the prey species, say, improves in its ability to escape the predator. As a result of this, the predator species evolves more efficient means of obtaining prey, since only the predator which succeeds in catching prey survives to reproduce. Over time the prey species develops greater ability to avoid predation, and the predator to obtain prey. Thus the speed of both cheetah and gazelle, for instance, increases over the generations.

b Coevolution refers to the fact that the techniques of predators in catching prey, and tactics of the prey in avoiding capture, evolve together. The adaptations in each develop as a result of the evolutionary conflict between the two. If a prey species did not gradually improve its ability to avoid capture, there would be no pressure on the predator to develop improved hunting abilities. Improved hunting abilities in the predator result in the prey species evolving better avoidance mechanisms.

10

a i Hover flies are an example of Batesian mimicry. They possess yellow and black colouring, similar to that of wasps. Some insects mimic the yellow and black colouring of the caterpillar of the Cinnabar moth. Birds find the caterpillar distasteful and, once they have tried them, tend to avoid similar prey (including the mimic) in future.

ii The chick of the plover has plumage which closely resembles the pebble background and is virtually impossible to see. Stick insects provide further examples of effective camouflage.

b If taking a form of prey results in an unpleasant or painful consequence a learned aversion develops. Similar but edible prey are also avoided. For this avoidance to develop it is necessary that the prey species encounters a proportion of the real thing. If only mimics were encountered, the aversion would not develop. Camouflage is successful providing the camouflaged animal or insect remains motionless against the background.

11

a Exploitation involves making use of another animal or species and giving nothing in return. The other species may be disadvantaged as a result of exploitation. The cuckoo exploits other bird species.

b The behaviour of the angler fish and its prey will have coevolved gradually over many generations. The two species would need to inhabit the same area so that contact is possible. An ancestor of today's angler fish may have had a movable appendage which had some resemblance to a worm. If this attracted some prey fish (with relatively poor discriminative ability) which mistook it for a worm, the angler fish would benefit from prey coming within reach. The ancestors of the prey fish benefited if they approached small wriggling objects since these were likely to be worms on which they fed. Those with the ability to discriminate between real and false worms will benefit since they are more likely to survive. There is, therefore, pressure on the prey fish to improve its powers of discrimination, and so reduce the chance of approaching the predator. In turn the angler fish must improve its mimicry if it is to continue to lure prey fish.

12

Commensalism is generally used to refer to a relationship where one animal benefits and the other is not affected. An example of commensalism is the relationship between humans and urban foxes. The foxes benefit from the food left by humans. This has little effect on the humans who may be unaware of the foxes.

In symbiosis both animals benefit from the relationship. Examples include the Parrot fish and the ox-pecker birds (see pages 270 and 271).

13

The strong colours of the cleaner fish render them easily recognisable. This is a necessary quality if the grouper and Opal eye are to distinguish them from the fish which they do eat. Evolution has resulted in the grouper and Opal eye not cheating, as if they ate the cleaner fish, they would lose the service provided by these fish. This is necessary if they are to survive and reproduce. Research has revealed that they deteriorate rapidly when cleaner fish are removed from their environment.

14

a Adaptationism refers to the belief that because a structure or pattern of behaviour has evolved, then it is adaptive.

b Most adaptationists carry out appropriate research to determine whether or not this is the case. Thus von Frisch (1967) did research to determine whether the fact that flowers have evolved bright colours is adaptive. Adaptationism in this sense, therefore, leads to discovery and to greater understanding (see page 272).

c An armchair adaptationist assumes that just because a structure has evolved, then it *must* be adaptive. However, unless this is confirmed by research, it may be inaccurate and misleading.

Unit 9

Reproductive Strategies

Gillian Lang

This unit covers:

Sexual selection

Mating strategies, availability of resources and social structure

Parental care

Parent-offspring conflict

Evolutionarily stable strategies: mating systems and parental care

By the end of this unit, you should be able to:

- show understanding of the nature of sexual selection in relation to mate choice and competition for mates

- demonstrate awareness of the relationship between mating strategies, social organisation and availability of resources

- show knowledge of those factors which determine the nature and extent of parental care

- provide evolutionary explanations of conflict between parents and young.

Unit 9 Contents

Sexual selection

Sexual versus asexual reproduction

Biologists define fitness in terms of reproductive success, that is, the number of surviving offspring produced by an organism (see Unit 8 page 253). A species which fails to reproduce becomes extinct. An evolutionary psychologist or biologist is therefore interested in the behaviours involved in reproduction, especially so since animals devote considerable resources to the production of offspring.

Although most species reproduce sexually, it is not known why. Sexual reproduction takes up large amounts of time and energy; it may make participants conspicuous and at risk of predation. Nor is it the most efficient means for an individual to pass on its genes. Asexual reproduction results in offspring with exactly the same genes as the parent. In sexual reproduction each parent contributes just half of the genetic make-up of the offspring: thus only half of each parent's genes are passed on.

Since sexual reproduction is widespread it is assumed that it has evolutionary advantage. Several biologists have attempted to explain what this might be. Williams (1996) pointed out that all plants and animals reproduce sexually at least occasionally but some, such as aphids, also reproduce asexually. They do so at the beginning of the season, reproducing sexually later on.

■ Advantages of sexual reproduction

Sexual reproduction results in diversification of the offspring since sex is a process which creates new genetic mixes (combinations). When eggs and sperm combine, new combinations of chromosomes come together in the zygote. Each offspring in a sexual species therefore has a new genetic configuration, different from its parents and siblings, and from all other members of the species. Thus offspring produced sexually have different **genotypes**. The term genotype refers to those characteristics of an animal which are determined by its genes. An animal's **phenotype** depends on the interaction of its genes with the environment (food, habitat, social conditions, etc.).

Williams (1996) suggested that it is this which makes sexual reproduction a better strategy than asexual reproduction. Thus, when aphids reproduce sexually their offspring vary, and in a changing environment some are likely to be better adapted than others.

Similarly, where animals live in an environment where future conditions are unpredictable, there is a greater chance that one of the genetically diverse offspring produced sexually will have a genotype suited to whatever the conditions turn out to be.

Hamilton (1980) explained that the environment of an animal does not consist merely of physical factors such as ecology and weather, but includes other living organisms. Such organisms include parasites and predators which also evolve through natural selection, and may therefore develop new genotypes better suited to overcoming the existing defences of prey or host species. Thus sexual reproduction may be favoured because diversification in offspring might result in some genotypes evolving improved defences against predators and parasites.

The question of why sexual reproduction is so widespread has not been resolved however, and remains an area of debate and research.

Sexual reproduction

Reproductive behaviour in animals has the function of bringing together two opposite sex gametes at fertilisation. The gametes are produced by meiosis, a form of cell division which takes place in the reproductive organs under the control of sex hormones. Gametes contain half the chromosomes of normal body cells.

At fertilisation each gamete contributes to the fertilised egg (zygote), thus restoring the full number of chromosomes, half from each parent. The zygote divides many times to become a new individual. The contribution made by each parent is very different. The female produces large, non-motile gametes (eggs) which contain material needed for the offspring's early growth as well as genetic information (DNA). Males produce small, motile gametes (sperm) which contribute DNA only. This imbalance between male and female gametes is known as **anisogamy**, and has important consequences in relation to the behaviour of male and female animals. (This is discussed in detail on pages 287–8, 302–3.)

■ External fertilisation

How do gametes find each other so as to achieve fertilisation? The gametes of most aquatic animals are shed straight into the water where they survive independently of the parent. The movement of the water facilitates fertilisation. However, as water movement may also carry gametes away from each other, aquatic animals must produce vast numbers of them to compensate for wastage.

The process of shedding gametes is not random; individuals within a group normally come to reproductive maturity at the same time. This phenomenon is synchronised by lunar cycles or pheromones (pheromones are based on chemical stimuli – see Unit 10, page 345) which keep members at similar stages of development. An example of this can be seen in palolo worms which live among the coral reefs of Samoa and Fiji and breed only in November. Spawning occurs when the rear parts of the worms become packed with gametes. The pressure of water at high tide causes the rear parts to become detached, rise to the surface, and burst open. Thus fertilisation is opportune and subsequent development occurs without any parental involvement.

Tinbergen (1953) described the mating behaviour of the three-spined stickleback. In the breeding season the male defends a territory and constructs a nest. He attracts a female with his zig-zag dance and leads her to the nest. She enters and he trembles his snout against the base of her tail.

She spawns and leaves the nest, whereupon the male enters and fertilises the eggs. (The reproductive behaviour of the stickleback is considered further on page 286.)

■ Internal fertilisation

Some species have evolved a process of internal fertilisation and development, thus improving the success rate of fertilisation, and providing protection against loss of young. For aquatic species, such as the dogfish, this is advantageous because all the sperm can be deposited and retained near the ova to facilitate fertilisation. For land animals, internal fertilisation is always necessary as gametes cannot survive outside a fluid environment. Sperm are deposited within females in seminal fluid, a process which requires different sexual structures for males and females.

Before internal fertilisation can occur, a female must be sufficiently receptive to and attracted by a male, so that he can transfer his sperm during copulation. Receptivity is linked to hormones in a reproductive cycle, and usually is greatest at oestrus, when the ova are shed from the ovary and the chances of fertilisation are highest. Oestrus has the effect of making a female attractive to the male, and produces receptive behaviour which facilitates copulation. However, in some species such as orang utans and some monkeys, also human beings, ovulation is concealed, that is, there are no overt signs that ovulation is taking place. In such instances copulation is not confined to a period of oestrus. Ovulation is concealed in most species of bird.

Activity 1

Write down some of the differences you might expect to find in human societies if human beings only mated during a time of oestrus.

(Suggested answers on page 311.)

Internal fertilisation does not always involve an intromittent organ such as a penis. The majority of birds do not have a penis. They mate through the male depositing sperm from his cloaca at the opening of the female's cloaca. The sperm are drawn up into the female's reproductive tract for storage where they wait until the female is ready to release the eggs, whereupon they are fertilised by the stored sperm.

Courtship

Before mating can occur, the sexes must be attracted to each other. In many species this is accomplished through ritualistic interactions of the male and female. Visual or aural signalling is likely to be involved, and there may be a change in appearance. In many species of bird, for example, the males develop bright plumage during the mating season.

Patterns of courtship vary enormously between species. Courtship itself may last for a few minutes, or continue for many weeks. Albatrosses, for instance, tend to court one another intermittently for several months. There is no courtship at all in some species.

Courtship has several functions, one of which is to ensure that animals mate with individuals of the correct species, appropriate sex and condition.

Matings between different species happen only rarely in nature. Where it does happen, the offspring (known as hybrids) tend to be sterile. The offspring of a male donkey and a mare is known as a mule. A hinney is the result of a mating between a female donkey and a stallion. Both are sterile. (There are exceptions to this however, see figure 9.1; see also figure 9.2 for an example of cross-breeding in captivity.) Natural selection, therefore, favours animals which mate with their own species, thus producing fertile offspring.

9.1 What is a species?

Species is a difficult concept to define. Most biologists define a species as reproductively isolated organisms which mate naturally in the wild and produce viable offspring. This is known as the biological species concept, or BSC (Brookes, 1998). There are several well-known examples of between-species breeding resulting in sterile offspring, such as the mule and the hinney, which lend support to this definition.

It has long been thought that the 14 species of finch indigenous to the Galapagos Islands were distinct species. Each has a differently shaped beak adapted to a particular type of seed (see Unit 8 page 255). However, recent research has shown that some of these species interbreed, producing healthy, hybrid offspring. Between-species breeding has also been recorded in other organisms. A notable example of this is the blue whale which has bred with the fin whale. The resulting offspring are fertile (Brookes, 1998).

Thus, although the BSC approach to distinguishing one species from another is generally useful, its limitations need to be recognised. As yet there seems to be no means of determining between species which is 100 per cent reliable.

9.2 Cross-breeding in captivity

In the summer of 1997 there were reports in the press of a black swan causing some nuisance to villagers in Berkshire. When the bird was removed to a nearby sanctuary, it was noticed that the so-called swan had legs and beak resembling those of a goose. It also looked like a goose. Experts concluded that the bird was a cross between a goose and a swan. This would be unlikely to happen in nature, but cross-breeding can occur with birds in captivity. One of the parents of the hybrid (a swan perhaps) might have been incubated in a clutch of goose eggs, and imprinted on the goose, also on the goslings hatched at the same time, perceiving itself, therefore, as a goose.

Male crickets have evolved a distinctive song which they sing during courtship which ensures that they breed with their own species. Experimental research involving the playing of cricket songs through a loudspeaker has revealed that a female will only approach a loudspeaker playing the song of her own species (reported in Ridley, 1995).

Tinbergen (1951) demonstrated that the zig-zag movement of the male three-spined stickleback is necessary for the female to be attracted to the nest.

Courtship allows synchronisation of mating and parental behaviour (figure 9.3). In many species of bird, for example, courtship results in appropriate motivational states so that the partners cooperate effectively, building the nest, incubating the eggs and feeding the young. Similarly, when the female stickleback spawns, it is essential that the male immediately fertilises the eggs.

Courtship also overcomes aggression. In solitary species males and females tend to be aggressive to one another except when the female is in oestrus. The appropriate courtship behaviour helps prevent attacks on the female, and allows copulation to take place. In some species of spider, the male is at risk of being killed by the female, and it is essential that the courtship ritual is followed with precision. The signalling may involve visual, tactile or sound stimuli.

9.3 Synchrony in seahorses

Seahorses are monogamous. Once a male and female have formed a pair, they are faithful to each other. The courtship ritual is complex, including quivering, tail-wrapping, and circling. They face each other, interlink their tails and rise upwards. This elaborate courtship ritual, which is repeated again and again, ensures that their reproductive states are fully synchronised. This is essential since the female's eggs need to be ready at the exact moment when the male's pouch is ready to receive them (Masonjones, 1997).

The need for perfect synchronisation also contributes to the fact that they are monogamous, with neither cheating on the other.

■ Courtship and male quality

Semler (cited in Ridley, 1995) looked at mating preferences in female sticklebacks, comparing a red-bellied male with a male of a non-breeding colour. Females generally choose to spawn with the red-bellied male. It would seem that female choice is involved in the development of the elaborate courtship patterns found in sticklebacks. If a male fails to produce part of the display typical of his species, the female will not mate with him.

Courtship allows the female to compare males in terms of the resources they can provide. This may be demonstrated through nuptial gifts. This is seen in some species of bird where the male provides food. A male tern, whilst courting, will offer fish to the female. The fish are quite small, and since they are held crossways in his beak, are visible to the female. Such courtship feeding may be indicative of the male's willingness and ability to contribute to the feeding of the young.

Many male insects and spiders also provide nourishment for the female. This may be in the form of captured prey. Male hanging flies catch a fly, and offer this to the female. She is more likely to mate with him if the prey is large. This makes good sense as the male who provides the better nourishment enables the female to produce a greater number of eggs.

The courtship display may indicate whether the male has good genes; whether he is strong, dominant and vigorous. The female stickleback is more likely to mate with a male who performs the zig-zag dance at a high rate. This may indicate strength and vigour; good genes to pass onto her offspring.

In solitary species, or where males and females live separately, there may be little or no courtship. Signalling is very important however, since it brings male and female together. Solitary species communicate over long distances on the basis of sound or pheromones. Thus the female Emperor moth attracts males on the basis of odour. (Pheromones are discussed in Unit 10, pages 344–5.)

The Siberian dwarf hamster also attracts a male through pheromones. She spreads her scent which will attract males, around the entrance to her burrow. Female elephants live in matrilineal groups of related adults and young. Females come into oestrus for a period of six days about every four years and broadcast their sexual readiness by emitting a call of low frequency which can be heard over several miles. Bulls are sexually active (when they are described as being in *musth*) for part of the year only. It is therefore essential that male and female come together at the appropriate times. If a bull is in musth when he hears a female call, he will respond by making his way to her.

Activity 2

Carry out some research of your own and look for examples of behaviour involved in courtship. Spring is a good time to see such behaviour in birds. Alternatively, watch some wildlife programmes on television. Write down any examples you find, giving details of the species and the behaviour.

(Suggested answers on page 311.)

■ Sexual selection

Much courtship behaviour involves flamboyant colouration or behaviour. It is frequently very complex. It may include considerable levels of aggression. Male red deer engage in ferocious fighting using horns or antlers, which uses up valuable energy and may result in injury or even death. The decorative plumage of such birds as peacocks and birds of paradise also require energy. They are also likely to make their possessors conspicuous to predators and less able to escape a predator. Animals are also vulnerable to predation whilst they fight.

Why have such exaggerated traits evolved? Since they appear to have obvious disadvantages there must, surely, be some benefit which makes up for these. The fighting and the displays go beyond what is required to ensure that mating is with the same species.

Why do males fight so fiercely? Why are the males of so many species larger than the females? Why do males display so conspicuously?

Darwin (1871) set out to account for these traits by postulating an additional evolutionary process which he termed *sexual selection*. He defined this as 'the advantage which certain individuals have over others of the same sex and species solely in respect of reproduction'.

What Darwin's theory suggests is that males compete with each other to determine which males will gain access to females. This, argued Darwin, has led to the evolution of greater aggression in males, their larger size, and their possession of weapons (such as antlers and horns), since these factors would be important in combat with rivals.

Females, on the other hand, *choose* which males they mate with. If, suggested Darwin, males possessing colourful plumage or elaborate mating displays were more favoured by female choice, then such traits would remain despite their negative effects on survival; their advantage in relation to sexual success (obtaining a mate) would counterbalance the reduced level of individual survival.

Darwin's theory of sexual selection goes a long way towards explaining the problem posed by the conspicuous and seemingly detrimental traits found in many species. However, it is not a sufficient explanation of why evolution favours size and aggression in males, and mate choice (discrimination) in females. Trivers (1972) developed a theory which succeeds in explaining this. He suggested that the difference in form and behaviour between male and female is due to anisogamy.

■ Anisogamy and male competition

Anisogamy refers to the fact that the female produces a much larger gamete than the male. Each offspring is the result of a joining of one egg and of one sperm cell. The disparity between the two is considerable; the sperm may be less than a millionth the size of an egg cell. A male with the same food supply as the female, and converting energy into gametes at the same rate, can produce many more gametes than a female. A male therefore has the ability to fertilise numerous females, providing he can mate with them. The consequence of this is that a male who copulates with numerous females has a great advantage in terms of progeny over a male who mates with one or two females only.

Compared to the vast numbers of sperm produced by male animals, the female eggs are in short supply. In her lifetime, a woman grows a mere few hundred eggs. A man may make 100 million sperm each day. Thus natural selection will favour any adaptation in a male which enables him to compete successfully with other males in the contest for females, and to fertilise as many eggs as possible. This then, according to Trivers, is the theoretical basis of the evolution of competition between males.

In general, females do not benefit from copulating with many males (although there are exceptions to this as considered on page 299). Rather than additional sperm, females require resources that can be used to produce eggs, or which increase the survival rate of eggs and young. The rate of reproduction in females is influenced by the rate at which they can produce eggs, not by the number of males with whom they copulate. Competition between females then is likely to occur in relation to resources such as food, nest sites, help in rearing young, or territory.

■ Anisogamy and female choice

If males vary in quality, it would make sense for females to be choosy as to which male she will mate with. For example, if one male has a better territory than another, it would pay the female to choose the male with the better territory since this will increase the chance of successfully raising young. Thus selection would favour the female who chooses the male with a good territory. In mammalian species, production of the egg is only the beginning of the female's investment into her offspring; further options are closed, so a female mammal needs to be careful in her choice of mate.

As described on page 286, a female may choose a male who feeds her during courtship, as this may indicate his ability to provide for her and their offspring. Similarly, the ability of a red deer stag to roar for a prolonged period is indicative of his strength and quality. Selection will favour a female

who chooses the strong male, or the male who is able to provide for her offspring.

Thus Trivers's theory explains the evolution of female choice. Males are not choosy as to which female they will mate with. In general, males are selected to mate with as many females as possible.

Natural selection then will favour adaptations in males which contribute to additional copulations. It will favour those females which choose to mate with higher quality males. Thus the theory of sexual selection, originally proposed by Darwin and modified by Trivers, provides a convincing explanation of the differences found in the sexual behaviour of male and female animals: the critical factor in the difference found between form and behaviour of male and female animals is the contribution made by each sex to the production of young. Trivers (1972) used the term **parental investment** (PI) to refer to the resources devoted to reproduction by each parent. He defined this as investment by the parent which contributes to the offspring's chance of success but reduces the parent's ability to invest in further offspring.

Greater PI reduces the opportunities for producing more progeny. The number of eggs produced by a female will be smaller if more nutrient is provided in the eggs; retaining young in the body and feeding young through a placenta, building nests or providing shelter, incubating eggs, feeding young and guarding them from predators, are all forms of parental investment which affect the total number of offspring produced. Sexual selection therefore involves two mechanisms, male competition and female choice.

Male competition occurs between males fighting for possession of one or several females. This is known as **intra-sexual selection** and is clearly described by Halliday (1994). Intra-sexual selection refers to selection resulting from fighting between individuals of one sex, usually males, which leads to the evolution of fighting ability, large body size and weapons such as antlers and horns (figure 9.4).

Inter-sexual selection refers to selection resulting from males competing to attract females. It leads to the evolution of conspicuous colours,

Figure 9.4

Fighting in red deer (Cronin, 1991)

Competition between males: fighting and territoriality

Males of many species fight for possession of females. Red deer fight using their antlers in aggressive contests. Although much fighting involves ritual and may be restrained (see Unit 8 page 260), real injuries may be inflicted, injuring or even killing an animal (Clutton-Brock *et al.*, 1982). Male lions fight to take over a group of lionesses, a new male challenging and trying to usurp the resident male. Stallions fight for possession of a group or *harem* of females. The winner of the contest will remain with the mares until he is defeated and ousted by a younger, stronger stallion.

displays, structures and odours which attract females. Inter-sexual selection (female choice) involves choosing a male on the basis of his quality. Either system is likely to result in the female mating with the 'best' male.

Halliday (1994) commented that the distinction between intra-sexual and inter-sexual selection is not altogether a valid one. As Brown (1983) pointed out, both forms of selection involve competition between male genotypes. In evolutionary terms, therefore, they are equivalent. Males displaying to a female are competing with one another just as much as if they were fighting.

In some of the examples cited above (such as horses and lions) the females are aggregated. In such instances, the females are the resource being defended. The male elephant seal defends his harem of females from other males. Fighting may be very fierce, and may inflict serious injuries on the contestants, but if the male can maintain exclusive access to the harem, he can mate with many females (Cox and Le Boeuf, 1977).

Territoriality involves defending a resource such as food or shelter. (A territory refers to an area defended against other animals of the same species.) The defended area is used exclusively by the territory holder or holders. The area within which an animal carries out its normal activities is a home range. In some species, the entire home range is defended by an individual, a pair or a group. The size and function of a territory varies greatly (see Unit 8 pages 263–4).

> ## Activity 3
>
> Try to think of examples of competition between human beings where fighting is not involved, but where successful gain and status are perceived as attractive.
>
> *(Suggested answers on page 312.)*

Sexual selection theory recognises that the goal of an animal is not merely to survive but to produce offspring.

Natural selection has resulted in numerous adaptations by which males seek to increase their chances of mating. There are many ways in which males compete for females, or for the opportunity to fertilise their eggs. These include fighting, territoriality, sperm competition and infanticide. They can be divided broadly into pre- and post-copulatory conflict.

Territories are advantageous for the rearing of offspring since there is a better or more reliable food source, decreased risk of predation or cannibalism, good shelter, and so on. In many species, males (females in some instances) obtain a territory before seeking a mate. Male pied fly-catchers arrive in northern Europe several days ahead of the females and set up large territories. Alatalo *et al.* (1986) demonstrated that male success in obtaining a mate matched the quality of the territory in terms of food supply and cover. This suggests that females may choose a male on the basis of the quality of the territory he is defending. This is not surprising since the survival of her offspring may depend on good cover and a plentiful supply of food.

The male willow warbler defends an area which will include food for himself and eventually for his mate and their young. Male red-winged blackbirds set up territories which will enable them to mate with those females which are attracted to the territory. During the breeding season, great tits are strongly territorial and defend their supply of insects. In winter, however, they join large flocks consisting of several species, indicating that their territoriality is linked to the rearing of young.

Lekking

A form of territoriality where males of some species defend territories with no resources is known as lekking. This occurs when females from a large area are attracted to many males displaying together. The males aggregate and defend small areas within which each male displays. One of the most studied species is the sage grouse. The male is considerably larger than the female. In spring, males gather early in the day and for three to four hours each defends his small territory and displays to females with his colourful tail and expanding throat pouch. The female moves among the territories, usually mating with one male only. She then leaves and lays her eggs. She rears the young with no help from the male (Gibson and Bradbury, 1986). Gibson and Bradbury (1985) demonstrated that the females choose males which display the longest and the most vigorously.

Lekking has been observed mainly in birds but also occurs in mammals, insects and fish. Uganda kob males, for instance, form leks to which females are attracted. The benefit of the lekking system to

---

Activity 4

Write down three differences between lekking and other forms of territorial behaviour described above.

(Suggested answer on page 312.)

---

the female seems to be in the quality of the male: his ability to defend a small territory and the quality of his display.

Dominance

Where a food supply is scattered and not easily defended, territorial behaviour is unlikely to develop. This applies to ungulates such as eland, buffalo and wildebeest. Where animals do not defend a territory, reproductive success may be achieved through dominance. Jarman (1974) reported that this may occur in eland and buffalo. McCann (1981) recorded that the highest ranked animal in a herd of bison was responsible for 33 per cent of all recorded matings, with the top five bulls accounting for 85 per cent in total. Dominant male red deer have greater reproductive success than subordinates (Clutton-Brock *et al.*, 1982).

Research also suggests that, in general, dominant male and female primates have greater reproductive success than subordinates. Harcourt (1989) found that of 14 dominant males, 13 were more successful in obtaining copulations than subordinates.

In some species males are dominant over females, in others females are dominant over males. In many cases, separate male and female hierarchies develop. Under certain conditions species which tend to be territorial develop *dominance hierarchies* instead. This is clearly illustrated in the dunnock (see pages 300–1). Territorial behaviour and dominance are discussed in more detail in Unit 8.

Post-copulatory conflict

Sperm competition

Male damselflies defend territories on the banks of ponds and streams where the females come to lay their eggs. The female must mate with the territory holder before he will allow her to deposit her eggs. The female therefore mates several times, usually each time she lays eggs. However, before the male releases his own sperm, he removes any sperm already inside the female from a previous mating. Barbs on part of his intromittent organ enable him to do this. Waage (1964, 1986) found that such sperm competition occurs in several species of damselfly.

However, this is not the end of the matter! It is not in the reproductive interests of those males who have already mated with the female damselfly that their sperm is subsequently removed. They have evolved adaptive behaviour which makes this less likely to happen, such as guarding the female. This is known as *post-copulatory guarding,* and the male stays with the female until she has finished laying her eggs. In some species of damselfly the male retains his hold on the female as she lays her eggs. This is termed *contact guarding.*

There are several forms of mate guarding behaviour. Contact guarding makes it virtually impossible for another male to copulate with the female, whilst the male has the option of leaving if further opportunities for mating present themselves. When there are many competitors nearby, contact guarding is likely to develop. Where additional females are likely to enter a male's territory, non-contact guarding is the more adaptive behaviour.

The sexual competition between males as to whose sperm fertilises a female's eggs involves no direct conflict, but is competition nonetheless. It is common in animals with external fertilisation and is found in many species of fish. In the bluegill sunfish, the male clears a nest area and after mating looks after the young. However, the young may not all be his since a small male known as a 'sneaker' may remain nearby until the female spawns, whereupon he darts in, very rapidly, and releases sperm.

In animals with internal fertilisation the evolution of sperm competition is dependent on certain characteristics of female physiology. A delay between mating and actual fertilisation is necessary, and sperm is stored in the female's reproductive tract. An additional requirement, of course, is that the female mates with more than one male.

Removal of sperm occurs in some bird species. Davies (1983) observed that, prior to mating, the male dunnock (hedge sparrow) pecks at the cloaca of the female. This causes sperm from previous matings to be ejected, whereupon the male mounts and copulation occurs.

In most species of bird, the female is the main caregiver to the young. Her reproductive success is likely to be enhanced if the male also cares for the young. What factors increase the probability that he will do so? If two males inseminate the same female, each will father, on average, half of her offspring. However, the structure of the female's reproductive tract ensures that sperm from the last male with whom she copulates will fertilise most or all of her eggs. This 'last male paternity' means that it is adaptive for males to remain with the female with whom they have mated, and to guard her from other males. This makes it more likely that he will contribute to care of the young.

Additional adaptations involved in sperm competition include increased production of sperm, and the use of a copulation plug. This last involves the male sealing the female's genital opening with a gelatinous substance which prevents further mating, for the time being at least. The plug dissolves in time, but by then the female may no longer be receptive.

Another form of sperm competition is thought to be connected with the relatively high weight of the testes in some species, for example chimpanzees. This is linked to promiscuous mating systems and is discussed on page 300.

■ Infanticide

Infanticide is an extreme form of post-copulatory conflict. It was first observed by Schaller (1972) in lion prides. When a new male takes over a harem of females, he kills all the young lion cubs. The female no longer has young to suckle and in consequence comes into oestrus and is receptive. Thus, by killing the cubs, the male brings forward the time when he can begin fathering his own young. Similar behaviour has been reported in rodents, horses and primates. Hrdy's work with langurs (1977) clearly demonstrates the value of infanticide to an individual's reproductive success and, therefore, why it has evolved. Hanuman langur monkeys live in groups consisting of related females and their offspring. There will usually be one male who will mate with all the females when they come into oestrus. He will continually have to defend his position against bands of males. When such a band forces the resident male to leave, they fight between themselves. This results in the winning male seeing off the others, and becoming the resident male.

Hrdy (1977) reported that most such takeovers resulted in infanticide. The reason for this is linked to the fact that the new resident male is only likely to remain in position for a relatively short period of time, about 27 months.

Female langurs, like many mammals, delay ovulation while lactating. A female who is feeding her young will not become fertile for many months. The new male will therefore have a long wait before he can mate with her, and father his own offspring. This is then followed by a long gestation period. If a male waits for a young infant to be weaned before he impregnates the female, his own infant will be born at the same time as he himself is likely to be expelled by another male.

The male therefore kills the unweaned infants causing the mother to ovulate, and to become receptive. If he does not do so, his own infants will be killed by his successor. This pattern of infanticide has reproductive advantage because of a combination of factors: the high rate of male takeover, and the long interval before oestrus (due to lactation).

Whilst infanticide makes sense in terms of mate competition, it is not in the reproductive interest of females. Some female langurs attempt to protect their infants from the male, some leave the group until their infants are weaned. However, a mistake or brief moment of carelessness will result in the infant being killed.

An alternative strategy observed in some pregnant females is *pseudo*-oestrus, where they copulate repeatedly with the male. It is possible that this may confuse paternity of the infant when it is born, making it unclear as to whether an infant born several months after the male takeover was fathered by the previous or by the new resident. It is probable, therefore, that the new male will not kill the new infant when the possibility exists that it could be his own. (See figure 9.5 for a discussion of faked sexual signals.)

9.5 Can signals be faked?

Zinner (1997) has suggested that female baboons may be able to fake sexual interest. Females of many primate species advertise receptivity by developing bright pink ano-genital swellings. This usually coincides with ovulation and encourages the males to copulate. Zinner observed that the females sometimes produced the swelling when they were pregnant or lactating, and therefore not ovulating. This occurred within two weeks of a new male taking over a group. Since these females did not conceive despite their apparent fertility, Zinner suggested that the sexual swelling functions to deceive the males, and to prevent the males from killing the females' infants to hasten ovulation.

However, others believe that such signals evolve in such a way that they *cannot be faked*. If signals can be faked, and are no longer honest, they lose their significance, and animals will no longer respond to them.

Source: Zinner, cited by Motluk (1997)

In some species the females also practise infanticide. For instance, when the female jaçana establishes a new territory, she kills young that are already there, and so brings forward the time when the male incubates her own eggs, rather than those of other females (Emlen *et al.*, 1989). The jaçana is an example of 'sex-role reversal' which is discussed on page 299.

The peacock's tail

The preceding pages have considered aspects of conflict involved in reproductive behaviour, including fighting, sperm competition and infanticide. In some of the instances discussed there is an element of female choice. Thus courtship displays and lekking provide females with important information about a potential mate. Or a female may choose a male on the basis of the quality of his territory.

Fighting between males would seem to have selective advantage in that the strongest male will win and his strength and fighting ability will confer benefit on his mate or mates, and/or his offspring. It is less obvious why males with the most extravagant displays should be more successful in obtaining mates than those with a lesser display.

What has led to the evolution of the bizarre and highly exaggerated displays of such species as the peacock and birds of paradise, or the evolution of the complex songs of the wren and the nightingale? The following pages consider attempts to answer this question.

Activity 5

Sexual selection involves competition for mates. Draw up a table listing the types of pre-copulatory and post-copulatory competition.

(Suggested answer on page 312.)

Darwin (1871) proposed that the exaggerated male ornaments of the peacock (figure 9.6) evolved to attract females, despite their possible harmful effects on the males. Even if the possession of such colourful traits resulted in a male not living for long, if he lived long enough to mate and to leave numerous offspring, his traits would be passed onto the next generation.

Figure 9.6

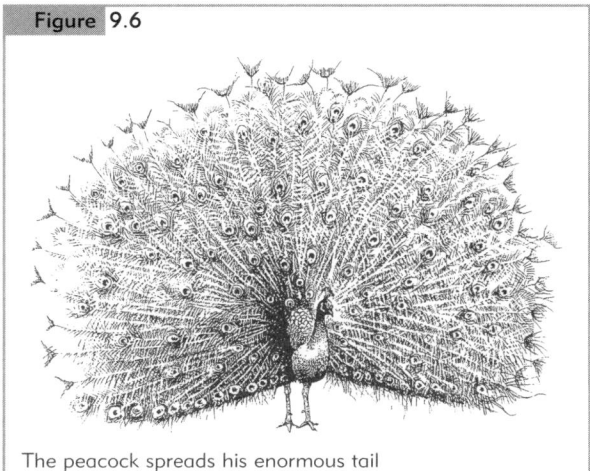

The peacock spreads his enormous tail

Since Darwin proposed this theory, others who work in this area have modified or extended his ideas. Additional theories have been suggested. Fisher (1930) suggested that exaggerated traits could evolve on the basis of female choice. He argued that an attractive mate is adaptive for a female because she will have attractive sons. This benefits her in terms of their reproductive success because the next generation of females will inherit their mother's preference whilst her sons will inherit their father's 'attractive feature'. Thus the more a preference for, say, long tails is successful, the more males there will be in successive generations with long tails, and the females will prefer even longer tails. The genes for choosing long tails and for growing long tails become involved in a linked process of positive feedback: thus the female preference and long tails evolve together in a runaway process. Fisher's theory is often referred to as the *sexy son theory* (or *good taste theory*).

Tails could increase in length until they begin to have detrimental effects and reduce the survival of males which possess them. If so, why has natural selection not eliminated such traits? Surely natural selection would favour females who produced sons with (for example) shorter tails?

Suppose a female chose a mate with a shorter tail. She may well produce sons with higher levels of survival, but they would also be 'unsexy' shorter-tailed sons. Furthermore, they will exist in a population in which most females prefer males with long tails. Females will not therefore choose to mate with them. The female who chooses the shorter-tailed male will consequently have no grandchildren, and the preference for a shorter-tailed male will not spread in the population. In order to have 'sexy sons', females have to choose as mates those males with the longest tails (or the gaudiest tail, most flamboyant display, etc.).

The advantage to the females of sharing the majority preference is that they produce sons who are likely to be successful. Once such a preference spreads in a population therefore, it would be self-sustaining. Thus in the sexy son theory, females prefer males with exaggerated ornaments because such traits are passed onto their sons who, in turn, succeed in attracting mates. This is consistent with Fisher's suggestion that a balance would develop between the positive and negative effects of the trait: mating success and reduced survival respectively.

Is Fisher right? Several questions need to be considered. Firstly, do females actually prefer males with exaggerated traits? Research suggests that they do. For example, Andersson (1982), in an ingenious investigation, demonstrated that female widow birds prefer males with the longest tails. Male widow birds have a thick black tail, much longer than their body. When their tails were artificially shortened or lengthened, Andersson found that the number of nests increased on the territories of the birds with the extra long tails. This indicates that the males with longest tails gained more mates than those with normal or shorter-length tails (figure 9.7).

Møller (1988) obtained similar results with swallows. Male swallows with artificially lengthened tail streamers attracted females earlier and were more likely to father a second brood. They also produced more fledglings in a season.

Not all birds have eye-catching feathers. Instead, several species gather brightly coloured objects, stones, snail-shells, and so on. There are several species of bowerbird which do this: the male with the best decorated nest is the most likely to attract a female.

Wallace (1889, 1891) suggested that courtship displays provide the female with information on the quality of the male's genes. A male who can sing loudly or grow a magnificent or long tail implies that he can father healthy and vigorous offspring. This is known as the *good genes theory*.

Wallace suggested that females select qualities such as vigour, disease resistance, health and stamina. It may appear that females choose on the basis of beauty because beauty and quality tend to coincide. Thus health and vigour are reflected in bright colours and elaborate structures. However, this theory does not adequately explain the extravagance of the gaudy plumage and long tail. It underestimates the possible costs of such extreme characteristics.

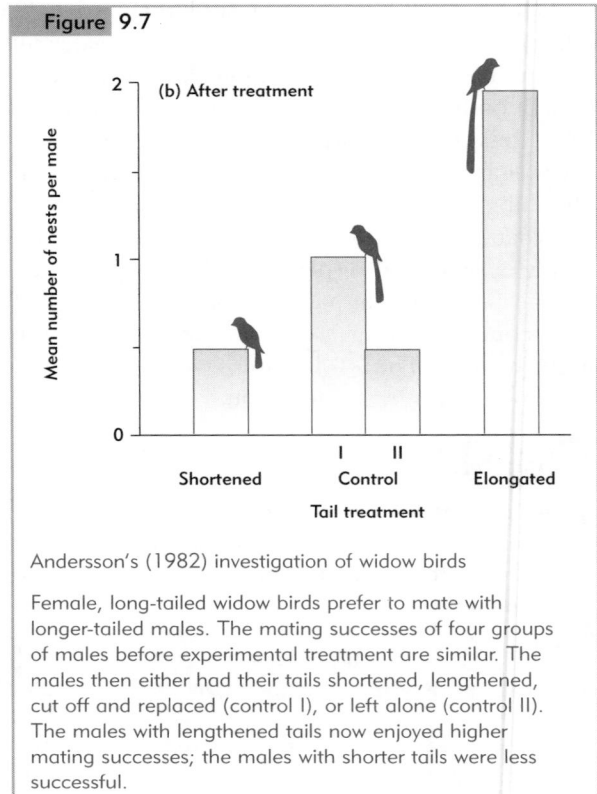

Figure 9.7

Andersson's (1982) investigation of widow birds

Female, long-tailed widow birds prefer to mate with longer-tailed males. The mating successes of four groups of males before experimental treatment are similar. The males then either had their tails shortened, lengthened, cut off and replaced (control I), or left alone (control II). The males with lengthened tails now enjoyed higher mating successes; the males with shorter tails were less successful.

Source: Ridley (1995).

Hamilton and Zuk (1982) suggested that a male with plumage in good condition or with bright colours, might indicate superior genes for resistance to disease and parasites. Similarly, the ability of an animal to grow and maintain a long tail, or to produce a complex and prolonged courtship display, indicates superior genes, since both require energy and vigour. Therefore, by choosing such a male, the female will produce sons with these good genes.

Handicap theories of female choice propose that by succeeding, despite the handicap of excessive ornament, the male is demonstrating his superiority. Zahavi (1975), for example, suggested that the more a bird such as the widow bird is handicapped by its plumage, the more honest is the signal which is conveyed to the female: the fact that he has survived, despite the handicap of his plumage, is a sign of his genetic quality.

There is some support for Zahavi's theory. Mathematical models indicate that such a handicap might influence survival and reflect quality. Thus the weaker the male, the harder it would be to produce and to maintain a tail of a given length. Research into swallows indicates that possession of an extra long tail is indeed detrimental to the male. Male swallows were artificially given extra long streamers. The following season these males were unable to grow a tail as long as their natural tail of the previous year. Carrying the additional weight of the extended tail streamers had a detrimental effect on the birds (Møller, 1989).

Such findings suggest that Zahavi (1975) may have been right; that the elaborate ornaments signal good genes, since their possessors survive despite their detrimental effects. Zahavi (1975, 1987) and Grafen (1990) believed that such signals are honest. Zahavi pointed out that loud calls and energetic displays are costly for the signaller. They are therefore a means whereby a signaller can demonstrate his quality (vigour, for instance). An example of this is the roaring of red deer stags which is demanding in terms of energy and stamina. Prolonged roaring during courtship indicates the quality of the stag.

Females of many primate species advertise that they are receptive by developing bright pink swellings. These signal that the female is fertile and encourage the male to copulate. It is believed that such signals have evolved in such a way that they cannot be faked since faking would cease to invest them with any meaning (see figure 9.5 on page 292). Not all signalling is honest however. For instance, female fireflies flash in two ways. One pattern attracts males of their own species, the other mimics the pattern of a smaller species of firefly. When the males of this smaller species respond to the signal and arrive ready and willing to copulate, the female eats them! (Loyd, 1965, 1975).

It is possible, therefore, that the elaborate plumage and displays are not honest and do not indicate good genes. However, it is also possible

that such traits evolve because in the first instance they were correlated with a positive characteristic such as strength. Thus a male who can sing loudly or grow a magnificent or a long tail can father healthy and vigorous offspring.

Activity 6

Write down as many examples as you can think of where birds or animals become more colourful during courtship, and/or compete on the basis of display or vocalisation.

(Suggested answers on page 312.)

■ Evaluation

Darwin's theory, and the others described here, do provide convincing explanations of why males have evolved such exaggerated plumage and displays. Questions remain however. The theories do not altogether explain why natural selection has not discriminated against these exaggerated traits when they are harmful to their possessor.

Halliday (1978) suggested that there is a problem with the above models, whether of a runaway or good gene type. This is the problem of genetic depletion. When choice evolved, females which chose males with certain genes were favoured. However, the consequence of this would be that all males would become genetically similar, possessing the chosen genes. When this point is reached, it no longer makes any difference whether the females choose or not. Because all males have the same genes for length of tail, any differences between males would be due to environmental rather than genetic factors and would not, therefore, be passed onto the female's offspring.

The theories do not seem to take into account the effects of coevolution between prey and predator. If long tails, or the elaborate plumage of the peacock, are likely to make their possessors more vulnerable to predation, fewer would survive to pass on their genes. The same applies to prolonged displays.

It is possible that the female's preference for an extravagant display developed from courtship behaviour. Thus the display may have evolved from signalling which developed to provide unambiguous information as to species and gender. Over many generations the stronger form of the signal might have become more attractive to the female. This preference for the stronger signals would give reproductive advantage to those males with stronger, more dramatic feathers or displays. In time this could lead to exaggerated traits or displays. The male silver-washed fritillary butterfly, for instance, is attracted to a flashing wing pattern produced by the female. Magnus (1958) demonstrated that males prefer an artificially speeded up rate of flashing to the real thing.

A study carried out by Burley (1981) demonstrated the importance of the size of the signal. Burley was studying zebra finches in the laboratory. All the birds were identified by coloured rings placed on their legs. Burley noticed that the females seemed to have a strong preference for the males with the red rings on their legs. This led to a series of experiments which revealed that the more red a male has on his body, the more attractive he is to the female. Thus female zebra finches have a preference for red on the male; the more red, the stronger the preference. If females (whatever the species) have a preference, then the evolutionary effect of sexual selection will be the enhancement of the preferred characteristic.

Clearly, more research needs to be done. In attempting to provide answers, theories of sexual selection have posed further questions. However, in promoting research they have increased our knowledge and understanding. It seems that Darwin was right in his view that the concept of sexual selection is needed to account for such phenomena as the peacock's tail.

Self-assessment questions

1 a Explain the difference between asexual and sexual reproduction.
   b Sexual reproduction is widespread. Outline one reason why evolutionary biologists find this surprising.
   c Suggest one possible reason for the fact that sexual reproduction is widespread.

2 a Write down three functions served by courtship.
   b Suggest why a swan is unlikely to mate with a goose in natural surroundings. (If you need more information consult Unit 10.)

3 a Outline the following terms: (i) gamete; (ii) anisogamy.
   b Explain why a male benefits from mating with many females.
   c Explain why a female is more likely to seek resources rather than numerous mates.

4 a Outline with examples: (i) sperm competition; (ii) mate guarding.
   b When are the following most likely to occur?
      (i) contact guarding; (ii) non-contact guarding; (iii) infanticide.

5 a Summarise the following theories: (i) handicap theory; (ii) Wallace's good genes theory; (iii) Fisher's sexy son theory.
   b Outline two criticisms of these theories.

(Suggested answers on pages 313–14.)

Mating strategies, availability of resources and social structure

Animals display a bewildering variety of mating systems and parental behaviours which serve to maximise reproductive success. The way in which male and female sexual and parental behaviours evolve in a species is influenced by factors such as parental investment, the distribution of resources and population density.

There are many forms of mating strategy. These can be broadly divided into four main types:

- **Polygyny**: in a polygynous mating system one male has exclusive access to a group or harem of females. In some instances a small group of males will share access to a larger group of females.
- **Monogamy**: this refers to the situation where males and females usually mate with just one member of the opposite sex. Where a male and female mate only with each other, this is known as pair bonding. A pair bond may be formed for life, or for a single season (when it is described as serial monogamy).
- **Polyandry**: in a polyandrous mating system females mate with several males whilst males, in general, have but one mate.
- **Promiscuity**: the system is described as promiscuous when both males and females have several mates.

Polygyny

Emlen and Oring (1977) suggested that polygyny is likely to occur in relation to:
- defending a harem
- defending a resource such as food and shelter
- where access to females depends on the male being dominant over conspecifics.

Where females group together, the male is able to mate with many females, providing he prevents other males from mating with them. The bull northern elephant seal fights other males to prevent them from mating with females in his harem. Red deer stags guard their harem of females. These are examples of harem polygyny. Since red deer stags and bull elephant seals spend a considerable amount of time in fighting, the females are wholly responsible for the care of the young. The males offer no paternal care or resources such as provided by a territory. The benefit to the female and her young is that the intense inter-male rivalry ensures that the father is of good quality. Her sons will win fights and gain females and her daughters will be strong. Only very strong males can control a large area for a whole season.

Harem polygyny develops where females are aggregated and resources are dispersed over a wide area, so making it too costly for a male to defend an area from intrusion by others. A territory would need to be so large as to be virtually undefendable.

Harem polygyny provides a male with exclusive mating rights to a considerable number of females. A variation of this is where several males form a group; in this situation the reproductive success of the individual is determined by his position in a dominance hierarchy. Several types of grouping occurs in hamadryas baboons. A small group of up to ten females, say, will include a single male. The male will fight off rival males.

Resource polygyny occurs where resources required by the females are clumped together, and can therefore be defended by males. An example of this is the red-winged blackbird. A male that can defend a territory can mate with those females which are attracted to the territory. Parental care is given mainly by the females, although the males guard the nest from predators, and have been observed to help in feeding the young. The better the territory, the more females will be attracted to it, and the greater the reproductive success of the male. Depending on the size of his territory, the number of females nesting in it varies from none to as many as 15. Thus a male with a poor territory may not breed at all. In some species of bird, where the male has a small number of females in his territory, he may offer some care to the offspring. The extent of care will depend on how many females are nesting in his territory. Thus the quality of resources influences the amount of parental care offered by the male in a polygynous system.

In a polygynous mating system, the care of the young usually lies with the females. However, the male is present and in many cases offers protection to the female and her young. The red-winged blackbird is an example of this, as is the silverback male gorilla who protects the female and her young from bachelor males seeking a female. This is essential since the bachelor males will kill a female's young in order to obtain her as a mate. It is in the interest of the male to protect the young in his group since they are likely to be his.

Lekking is a form of dominance polygyny. The males defend neither resource nor females, but each sexually displays and defends a small area to which females are attracted. The male therefore mates with a series of females, who then depart. The female builds the nest, incubates and rears the young, whereas the male contributes nothing to his offspring but his sperm.

Thus distribution of resources influences the mating system. The distribution of resources first influences the behaviour of the females, which in turn determines the mating system. Safety is also a factor since some species such as deer clump together to avoid predators. Since males aim to obtain as many matings as possible, they guard a group of females, or defend a territory in which females live. Where females are solitary and widely dispersed, they are monopolised by one male in a monogamous system.

Monogamy

Monogamy is relatively rare. The swan and the albatross are examples of monogamous species which pair for life. Some species pair for the season. Monogamy evolves where a higher survival rate of offspring from one mating outweighs the advantage of the male seeking additional matings.

Thus monogamy tends to evolve where both parents are needed for the care of the young. Where one parent can rear a brood alone, the other is likely to gain by deserting and seeking additional mating opportunities.

In mammals, the retention of young in the female's body, plus the fact that she provides milk for the young, means that often the male is unable to improve the survival chances of his progeny. Since it is not certain that the young are his, and he is unable to feed them in the early stages of growth, his parental investment is small. Consequently, it is in his best interests to desert the female after fertilisation and to seek more mates. Thus polygyny or promiscuity tend to be the most common mating systems in mammals. However, where the male provides a significant contribution to care of the young, then monogamy may occur in mammals. For example, males in several canid species such as African hunting dogs, jackals and wolves feed regurgitated food to the pups. All the adult Cape hunting dogs share in rearing the young in a communal burrow. In some primate species males contribute to care of the young. The male marmoset carries the infant through a long period of dependency; the white-handed gibbon lives in monogamous family groups, male and female, with four to five offspring.

Where breeding conditions are unfavourable, it may not be possible for one parent to raise the brood alone. Thus cooperation between parents is essential. The female Emperor penguin lays one egg in the depth of winter. This is a large investment and takes a great deal of energy. After laying therefore she leaves in order to feed and to renew her resources. The male incubates the egg in a pouch, and nurtures the newly hatched chick. After several weeks the female returns and takes over the care of the chick, feeding it regurgitated fish. After his long period without food the male needs to feed, and leaves for the sea. Without such cooperation the species would become extinct. If the male deserted the female in such conditions in order to gain additional matings, there would be no progeny from the first mating.

Bi-parental care in birds is the rule rather than the exception. The feeding of nestlings involves the strenuous collection of food. Since this can be carried out equally well by both male and female, and since chicks have high demands for food, this may be why so many species of bird are monogamous.

Small forest antelopes are selective feeders, taking the young shoots of a variety of plants. The male defends a territory sufficient to provide food for himself, his mate and his offspring. In this instance it is the distribution of resources that produces a monogamous system.

Reproductive synchrony also tends to result in a monogamous system where both parents care for the young. Where birds nest in colonies, as in many species of seabird, females may mate and begin to lay eggs on or about the same day. This has an important consequence for the male. If he were to seek an additional mate, he would be unlikely to find an unmated female! If he were to leave the first female, this could result in a poor survival rate of his first set of nestlings. His level of reproductive success is likely to be greatest therefore by staying with his first mate and helping her to rear their offspring.

Both male and female herring gulls incubate and feed the young. This is advantageous for their reproductive success because, not only can the young be guarded continuously against attack by cannibalistic conspecifics or other predators, but each parent can take turns in foraging for food. Many studies have revealed that protection of eggs and young by one or both parents makes eggs significantly less liable to predation.

Sperm competition may also lead to the male remaining to help rear the young. If a male deserts a female, she may mate with another male. In numerous species the anatomy of the female's reproductive tract is such that most of her eggs are fertilised by the last male to inseminate her. This 'last male paternity' means that if the male deserts, few of her young will be his. It is to his reproductive advantage, therefore, that he stay with the female to prevent her from copulating with additional males rather than seeking further matings himself. This also tends to lead to both parents caring for the offspring.

Activity 7

Carry out some research on birds and animals you are familiar with. What is their mating system? Try to find examples not included here.

Polyandry

The jaçana has a polyandrous mating system. The female is considerably larger than the male, and holds a good-sized territory. She has exclusive access to a number of mates. Within her territory males defend smaller territories against each other, in which they construct nests. The female lays her eggs in the nest, leaving the males to incubate the eggs and to feed the young. This is an example of sex-role reversal. Like polygyny, polyandry may arise where one sex controls resources required by the other.

Polyandry tends to result in the type of social organisation found in the spotted sandpiper. The females, which are significantly larger than the males, precede the males to the breeding areas where they establish territories. When the males arrive, the females compete using agonistic displays and fighting. The successful females pair with the males, but when they have laid their eggs, they desert, and leave the male to incubate the eggs and to care for the young.

The female repeats the process, establishing another territory, pairing with another male. She may mate with as many as four males, but will only help with incubation and care with her final mate. Her likelihood of attracting a mate is related to the size of the territory she is able to establish.

There is a form of polyandry where several males cooperate in breeding with one female. The males tend to be siblings. All cooperate in defending the territory and in feeding the nestlings. Oring (1986) suggested that this may evolve when conditions are severe and two parents are not able alone to rear a brood successfully.

Where the breeding season is short, in the Arctic for instance, the female can improve her reproductive success by mating with one male, leaving him and mating with another. The first male will incubate her first clutch of eggs, the subsequent male the second. This system is dependent on the abundant supply of food which is available during the short, Arctic summer.

Promiscuity

In a promiscuous mating system, both males and females seek to mate with several members of the opposite sex. Again, many factors are involved. The weight of the testes in relation to male overall body weight seems to be related to mating strategy. Chimpanzees are promiscuous, and the males have a relatively high testes weight. Species with low testes weight are monogamous, for example gibbons. Or they may be polygynous, as where one male gorilla monopolises several females (Stewart and Harcourt, 1987).

The explanation for this seems to be that when females mate with many different males, a male can enhance his reproductive success by producing large quantities of semen for transporting the gene-carrying sperm. The male that produces a greater volume may be more likely to have his sperm fertilise the female's ovum. Hence the larger weight of testes in animals where females mate promiscuously (Harcourt *et al.*, 1987).

Chimpanzees live in communities broken down into temporary sub-groups, or *parties*. They share a communal range which they defend. Males live in the groups in which they were born, whilst females move to neighbouring groups at adolescence, thus avoiding inbreeding. *Dominance hierarchies* form in both male and female groupings, with males dominant over females. The males are closely bonded.

When a female chimpanzee comes into oestrus, almost all the group (with the exception of her sons) will try to mate with her. In such mating systems, care of the young is usually carried out by the females.

There is, however, considerable variation of mating behaviour found in chimpanzees, nor are common chimpanzees as promiscuous as the pygmy chimpanzee (the bonobo). Common chimpanzees show three mating types: possessiveness, consortship and opportunistic mating.

In consortships male and female form a temporary exclusive pair bond, whilst a possessive relationship is one in which a male forms a short-term relationship with an oestrus female. He is likely to be an alpha male and will try to prevent lower ranking males from copulating with the female. (Takahata *et al.*, 1996)

A factor which is thought to contribute to promiscuity in some species is the practice of infanticide. The female chimpanzee mates with many males. If males have mated with a female, they are less likely to kill her infant; it could be his own. Possessiveness and consortships observed in some chimpanzee groups are a means whereby a male seeks to ensure that he is the father of the young.

Hasegawa (1992) suggested that promiscuous mating may promote sperm competition. Thus the females who mate frequently are likely to be impregnated by the good genes of the male who wins out in sperm competition.

Activity 8

Choose an example of each of the four mating systems, then draw up and fill in a simple chart similar to the one below.

Mating system	Male	Female
Monogamous		
Polygamous		
Polyandrous		
Promiscuous		

Summarise the benefits of each system to the male and female in terms of reproductive success. Review your findings. Do both genders benefit equally?

(Suggested answers on page 312.)

The dunnock shows promiscuous mating behaviour. However, the behaviour is influenced by the availability of food, and monogamous, polygynous, polyandrous and promiscuous relationships may all be found in a single population of dunnocks (Davies, 1983, 1985; Davies and Lundberg, 1984). The dunnock is a fascinating example of how mating behaviour may be influenced by the availability of resources.

Both males and females establish territories, some of which are better supplied with food than others. Male and female territories overlap. Where a male's territory exclusively overlaps two, smaller, female territories he mates with both, thus achieving polygyny.

When food supply is poor, females establish larger territories, and these may overlap two male territories. In consequence, both males associate with the female, and their territorial boundaries break down, with the males forming a dominance hierarchy. The alpha male follows the female around and tries to prevent her from mating with the beta male, but she will mate with the beta male whenever she is out of sight of the alpha male. The advantage of this system is that both males feed the young since they assume they are their own. This gives the young a much better chance of survival when food is sparse.

A promiscuous mating system develops when the boundaries between male territories disappear; the large, fused territory which results is likely to overlap with the territories of single females (females maintain exclusive territories). Davies and Lundberg (1984) observed that this produced groups varying from three males and two females, to two males with four females. In the promiscuous as in the polyandrous grouping, the alpha male tries to stay with the female and to drive away the persistent beta males. Alpha males tend to achieve about 60 per cent of the copulations, the beta males about 40 per cent.

These different systems arise from differences in food distribution and abundance. A good supply of food results in small female territories, and leads to monogamy and polygyny. Where food is sparse, female territories are larger, leading to polyandry and promiscuity. The females build the nests and incubate the eggs. Females in the polyandrous and promiscuous groups try to avoid the alpha males, and actively seek out beta males. Why do they do this? There are three possible reasons:

■ Males will help to feed the nestlings only if they have copulated with the female. Thus if she copulates with both the alpha and beta males, both help to feed the young. The female is able to lay more eggs, and her nestlings will be fed at a higher rate than if she had help from only one male. This also gives the young a much better chance of survival if the food supply is scarce.

■ There is some evidence that beta males peck and destroy eggs of females they have not mated with. Female dunnocks lay several clutches per season. Destruction of a female's eggs (infanticide) would cause her to lay a new clutch, and provide the beta male with another chance to fertilise her eggs.

■ Mating with the beta male will reduce sexual harassment. This is important since if a female is constantly chased during the prelaying stage, she is more likely to produce eggs which do not hatch.

Males gain most success in a polygynous system, whilst females are likely to be more successful in a polyandrous trio where the beta male also contributes to the care of the young.

The meticulous research into the mating behaviour of the dunnock reveals the relationship between a mating system and availability and distribution of resources. The relative abundance of food determines territory size: this determines the mating system.

Fighting between males is common in many mating systems. This may be associated with territorial defence. However, not all species defend territories: the distribution of resources may be such that they are not defendable. The large antelope species which live in open grassland move about in great herds of males and females. The males do not defend a territory and the mating system is promiscuous (Jarman, 1974). Males achieve mating rights on the basis of dominance.

There is also a relationship between the type of mating system and the amount of care given by the parents. In monogamous species both parents are likely to participate in care of the young, in polyandrous systems the male tends to provide most of the care, whilst in polygynous and promiscuous systems, the female is generally the parent which provides care. There are other important variables which influence parental care. These are considered in the next section.

Activity 9

Think for a few minutes and write down which mating system applies to human beings.

(Suggested answer on page 312.)

Parental care

Having read the previous section on mating systems, you will be aware that there is considerable variation in the extent of care provided by parents. In some species there is no parental care at all. In others both sexes, to a greater or lesser extent, care for the young, whilst in many instances care of the young is left entirely to the female.

The greatest level of parental care is found in birds, mammals and eusocial insects. The mating system in insect societies exists in relation to a complex society with division of labour. In many such species, ants and honeybees for example, the queen lays the eggs which are cared for by workers. The workers are very closely related. This offers, perhaps, a partial explanation of why they devote their lives to the reproductive activity of others (for more on this see Unit 10 page 322).

Marine invertebrates such as the palolo worm provide no parental care, and their contribution to their offspring is complete once fertilisation has taken place. Most other species, including most insects, provide at least a minimum of parental care. This may consist solely of laying eggs in favourable surroundings and, in some instances, guarding them until they hatch. Parental care may include nest construction, incubation, feeding and defence from predators. In those species where parents care for their young for lengthy periods of time, care will include instruction and socialisation.

Activity 10

Turn to page 308 and read 'ESSs and parental care'. The concept of evolutionarily stable strategies (ESS) helps explain why species have evolved different forms of mating and parental behaviour.

Oystercatchers have a highly specialised diet of shellfish and the young learn this through interactions with their parents. In primate societies, the young need to learn the social structure of the group in which they live, and how to interact with other animals.

Why is there such variation in parental care? Why does the male of many species desert, leaving the female to care for the young? Why do some species show maternal care, others paternal, yet others bi-parental? To some extent, these questions have been considered in relation to mating behaviour. This section focuses on four factors which have been suggested as being important factors in the evolution of parental care:

- Anisogamy.
- The association hypothesis (Williams, 1975).
- The order of gamete release hypothesis (Dawkins and Carlisle, 1976).
- The paternity certainty hypothesis (Ridley, 1978).

Trivers (1971) suggested that parental investment (PI) is a critical factor in the evolution of parental behaviour. He argued that the sex which has the smaller gametic investment (see pages 287–8) is under selective pressure to desert his progeny since such behaviour allows him to fertilise more eggs. Further, the costs of nurturing the embryo involve a high level of PI, greater than that of the male.

The consequence of this difference in PI is that the sex with the lower PI can increase its reproductive success (the number of surviving offspring) by mating as often as possible. Thus the male can increase his reproductive success by deserting his mate after fertilisation, and leaving her to care for the young; where the male is not involved in the care of the young, his reproductive success is limited by the number of females he is able to fertilise. Trivers pointed out that the sex which invests most in the production of offspring will have least to gain from seeking additional mates.

In contrast, the sex with the greater PI is *not* likely to increase reproductive success through additional matings. Trivers made it clear that the sex which invests most in the production of offspring will gain least benefit from seeking additional mates. Their reproductive success is limited by the resources which they can devote to reproduction. This sex therefore becomes a resource for which the other sex competes.

If a male contributes a greater PI than the female, Trivers's theory would predict a reversal of sex role, where females compete for access to males. Examples include the jaçana (see page 299) and the spotted sandpiper (Oring, 1986). The females are larger than the males and establish territories through fighting. They compete for males on the basis of physical combat and displays. The successful female pairs with the males, but after mating and laying eggs she deserts, leaving the male to incubate the eggs and care for the chicks.

The females endeavour to establish additional territories and mates. These may number as many as four. The female helps her last mate with incubation and care of the offspring. Although such sex reversal is rare, the fact that it occurs confirms the applicability of Trivers's theory.

Trivers's theory concerning the relationship between anisogamy (gamete dimorphism), parental investment and sexual selection is a significant contribution to understanding the evolution of parental behaviours.

Activity 11

Rate the following species on the basis of the care they provide on a scale of, say, 1 to 5. A score of 1 might indicate laying eggs in favourable surroundings, or guarding the eggs until they hatch. A 5 on this scale would indicate a high level of care, where the parent or parents look after the offspring until they are mature. (You might prefer to rank order the species on the basis of parental care.) Rank the sexes separately.

humans, oystercatchers, domestic dogs, sticklebacks, seahorses, elephants, palolo worms, domestic cats, rats, spotted sandpipers, bluetits (or other species of bird), guinea pigs, horses, lions, aphids, butterflies, bees.

Alternatively, select species yourself on the basis of your own experience, wildlife programmes, or material contained in this unit. Exclude any about which you are uncertain.

Williams (1975) proposed the *association hypothesis* which states that the parent which cares for the young is likely to be the parent which remains in close proximity to the embryos. After fertilisation, members of one sex find themselves in closer proximity to the embryos than the other, and are therefore predisposed to care for the young when environmental factors favour the evolution of parental care. In species with internal fertilisation, the parent in close proximity to the young is generally the female. The fact that a correlation has been found in many fish species between maternal care and internal fertilisation, and the predominance of maternal care in mammals, supports Williams's hypothesis. It also succeeds in explaining why maternal care is predominant in animals and insects.

In what situations do males remain close to eggs they have fertilised? In many species the males are territorial, and defend an area to which females are attracted for mating. If a female lays eggs in a male's territory (the three-spined stickleback for example), a male who remains may still attempt to attract females. Such a polygynous system gives a male reproductive advantage in that he has the benefits provided by parental care, but retains additional mating advantages.

The *order of gamete release hypothesis* attempts to account for the differences in parental care by stating that if caring for offspring reduces the total number of progeny an animal can produce, it would result in each sexual partner attempting to desert after mating, leaving the other to care. Which sex gives care therefore depends on the sex left with the eggs and sperm after fertilisation. Where fertilisation is internal (the male usually deposits sperm within the female), the female is left with the eggs and sperm. There is a time between fertilisation and egg laying when desertion by the female is physically impossible. The male, however, can desert. With external fertilisation the female spawns first, and can leave before the male deposits his sperm.

Thus the order of gamete release hypothesis predicts a correlation between internal fertilisation and maternal care; external fertilisation and paternal care.

This hypothesis succeeds in explaining many examples of parental care, although not all. Nor does it explain why the carer is usually the male rather than either care by male or female being on a chance basis in cases where eggs and sperm are released simultaneously (Gross and Shine, 1981).

Ridley's *paternity certainty hypothesis* proposes that a parent would be more likely to care for offspring that are really its own. This suggests that males are more likely to care for young when fertilisation is external, since this increase the likelihood that the offspring are his own. Fertilisation occurs in his presence. With internal fertilisation, the male cannot know what is happening inside the female's reproductive tract, since she may mate with more than one male. There is no doubt that the eggs are the female's own however. Thus the difference in the certainty of paternity for males should favour care by males where fertilisation is external, and care by females where it is internal.

Does the available evidence support this? Evidence obtained with fish does tend to support the hypothesis, since where parental care exists in aquatic species, it is generally carried out by the male. The male stickleback, for instance, protects the eggs and young from predators, and removes parasites from the nest. In this instance, the male may have a higher PI than the female because all of the eggs will have been fertilised by his sperm, but possibly not all of them will have come from one female.

Since it is difficult to determine paternity with internal fertilisation, the male has no certainty that the young are his own. To achieve reproductive success, therefore, he should desert the female and seek additional matings. This seems to be the case in that there is a relationship between the form of fertilisation and the sex which cares for the young: paternal care tends to occur when fertilisation is external, maternal care when fertilisation is internal.

Where fertilisation is internal, care may be provided by one or both parents or by non-parents in a social group. In precocial birds (which walk and feed themselves soon after hatching, such as chickens and ducks single parents are usually female. They have the higher investment in that they are always present at laying, and there is no proof that any one male contributed to fertilisation.

Ridley (1995) commented that paternal care usually corresponds with external fertilisation. The certainty of paternity hypothesis and the order of gamete release hypothesis both aim to explain this. In mammals, if one parent provides the care, it tends to be the female since she is present at the birth, and her gene contribution is indisputable.

Ridley (1978) suggested that territoriality has had an important influence on the evolution of parental care. He pointed out that a relevant factor in understanding the role of territoriality is the tendency for males to be territorial rather than the females. He suggested that sexual selection is the most satisfactory explanation of this, since most species only defend their territory in the breeding season. He added that territoriality stablises the evolutionarily stable strategy (ESS) of paternal care once this has evolved (see pages 307–9). It would be sensible for females to choose territorial males since males with a territory have demonstrated their ability to defend an area, and so are the most likely to be able to defend eggs and young.

Trivers (1972) also stressed the importance of territoriality or nest construction in the evolution of PI. He suggested that if a sex defends a territory before mating, then the sex might be selected to care for the young.

It would seem that the following factors are involved in determining which parent is selected to care for the young:

- The ability of one rather than two parents to care for the young.
- The likelihood that the parent which deserts can mate again.
- The mode of fertilisation – internal or external.
- The certainty a male has that the young are his.
- The female's ability to protect her offspring.

What does a male gain by sharing the caregiving? Where two adults are required to provide for the young then it is likely to evolve that the male will share the caregiving. The male in such instances is likely to gain greater reproductive success by remaining with the female, and helping to ensure all progeny reach adulthood. If he were to desert, he may fertilise more eggs, but if the first offspring do not survive, his reproductive success is reduced.

Bi-parental care is most common in birds, but also occurs in mammals and fish. It is probable that bi-parental care in mammals has evolved from maternal care, whilst in fish it began with paternal care (Gross and Sargent, 1985). In mammals it seems to evolve when males can contribute meaningfully to care of the young. Thus canids regurgitate food for their offspring; some primates, such as marmosets, carry the young. Bi-parental care in birds is very likely due to their high demands for food. Care in fish is usually limited to protection.

Activity 12

Match each of the summaries below to the following hypotheses:
association hypothesis; paternity certainty hypothesis; order of gamete release hypothesis.

a   ____ states that males are more likely to care for young when fertilisation is external, and care is by females when it is internal. When fertilisation is external, males are more likely to care for the young since they are likely to be his own. Where fertilisation is internal, the male cannot be sure that they are his own.

b   ____ predicts a relationship between internal fertilisation and maternal care; external fertilisation and paternal care. This is because where fertilisation is internal, there is a time between egg laying or giving birth when desertion by the female is impossible. Where fertilisation is external (as in fish), the female spawns first, and is able to leave before the male fertilises the eggs.

c   ____ states that the parent which remains in closer proximity to the young after fertilisation is likely to be the parent which cares for the young.

(Suggested answers on page 312.)

Self-assessment questions

6   a   Outline examples where the availability of food and social structure influences the mating system adopted by a species.
    b   Indicate which other factors may influence mating systems.

7   a   Which species provide the greatest levels of care?
    b   Explain why the sex with the smaller parental investment is under selective pressure to desert its progeny.
    c   Outline the benefits gained by a male who shares in caring for his offspring.

(Suggested answers on page 314.)

Parent-offspring conflict

Conflict between parents and their young is found in many species. Parents often risk injury, even death, for their young. Such altruistic behaviour may be selected if it results in the survival to adulthood of sufficient young to ensure that the tendency to behave in this way is passed on.

However, parents are not genetically identical to their offspring, and, on occasion, the long-term interests of the parents may be better served by withholding care from offspring and allowing them to die; in some cases, actually killing them. Such behaviour may increase the parents' reproductive success if it allows them to produce a greater number of offspring in the future.

Several species of birds, particularly such birds of prey as hawks and owls, routinely lay more eggs than they are likely to be able to rear (Stinson, 1979). Incubation begins with the laying of the first egg. Further eggs are laid at intervals, the later eggs serving as insurance should the first egg fail to hatch, or the first chick die through disease or predation. The parents have a replacement to which they can turn their attention. Thus chicks hatch at different times and vary in size, with the eldest being the largest and strongest. This chick is given most of the food by the parents. In a year when food is less than plentiful the smaller chick will starve. The benefit to the parents is that at least one chick is likely to survive to adulthood, and pass on the parent's genes.

Mock *et al.* (1987) studied siblicide in great egrets and great blue herons. Both species are monogamous and both lay three to four eggs. The older egret chicks frequently attack and kill younger siblings (although this was less common in the heron chicks). The parents are present during the attacks but do not intervene. In some species the dead chick is fed to the survivor. Similar behaviour has been observed in owls and eagles. Again, such behaviour ensures that at least some nestlings receive adequate food, and have a good chance of reaching adulthood.

In those species where nestlings do not commit siblicide, in a good year the parents may be able to rear all nestlings, thus increasing their reproductive success. But unless it is abundant, these birds withhold food from the smallest or weakest offspring. The larger, stronger chicks will be most successful in obtaining food from their parents.

If, by withholding care from some offspring, the parents succeed in raising at least *one*, this is clearly a good strategy. If they were to attempt to rear all their young, none might survive.

Trivers (1974) suggested that conflict between parents and offspring is likely to evolve because of the genetic imbalance (asymmetry) between them. Offspring have only 50 per cent of the same genes as their siblings and are likely to demand more than their fair share of parental investment. Parents, who are equally related to all offspring, will tend to distribute parental care evenly. Offspring may not all be present at the same time: thus a parent may want to conserve resources for future offspring, even though the existing offspring may want these resources now.

Much of the conflict between parents and young occurs at weaning. Trivers's theory is particularly appropriate to the weaning conflict in mammals. The lactating mother seal, for instance, attempts to wean her young off milk whilst the young seal attempts to extend the period of suckling. Studies have revealed that lactation is extremely physiologically demanding on the females: a female will not be able to conserve body reserves for more offspring until she has weaned the current one (Clutton-Brock *et al.*, 1989).

To deter her young from suckling, a female becomes gradually more aggressive towards her young. For example, the female macaque monkey removes her offspring from her nipple by pushing the infant away, and placing it on the ground. The infant protests, and tries to return to the nipple, but is pushed away more and more frequently. Eventually all its attempts to suckle are rejected.

A yearling horse is driven away by its mother when she has a new foal. For a while it will try to return, but the mother will continue to chase it away.

It would seem that maternal aggression which occurs at weaning is due to a conflict of interests. Trivers (1974) argued that it is due to natural selection acting in opposing ways in parents and offspring. Early in life the offspring benefits from maximum care (lactation for instance) to such an extent that the greatest benefit to the parent is achieved by giving such care rather than withholding it. However, the offspring reaches a stage of development where it is capable of doing almost as well without care as with it. It may now be in the parent's best interests to invest in new offspring rather than continue to care for the current ones.

Thus weaning represents a time when it is more profitable for the mother to pass on her genes to new offspring, rather than to invest further resources in offspring which are mature enough to have a good chance of survival without her. Yet the interests of the young are still best served by retaining parental care for as long as possible. Hence the conflict between the two!

Infanticide as observed in lions, gorillas, langurs and chimpanzees appears to resemble parent-offspring conflict. However, it is in fact different. It involves the killing of another male's young (or the young of another female in the case of the jaçana) to hasten the time when he can sire his own offspring and increase his own reproductive success. (This was discussed on pages 291–2.)

Activity 13

Try to observe conflict between parents and offspring for yourself. Your best opportunity to do this will be through watching animals that people often have as pets, such as dogs, cats, rabbits, guinea pigs, and so on. If you are walking in the countryside at the right time of year, you may be able to observe such conflict in sheep. Since the conflict takes place over a limited period of time, shortly before the young are fully weaned, you may need to do some research on when to look out for the behaviour. Write down details of what you observe.

Self-assessment questions

8 a Explain why it may be in parents' best interest to withhold care from their offspring.
   b Indicate how natural selection may affect parents and offspring differently.
   c Explain why infanticide is not a form of parent-offspring conflict.

(Suggested answers on pages 314–15.)

Evolutionarily stable strategies: mating systems and parental care

This section looks at the application of evolutionarily stable strategies (ESSs) to mating systems, and to the parental care of young.

ESSs and mating systems

Male bullfrogs defend territories along the edges of ponds, from where they call to attract mates (Howard, 1978). The large males fight with competing males. The larger males win the fight in the majority of contests.

Male size in bullfrogs increases with age, and in contests between males of different ages, the older males almost always win. These large males have the greatest reproductive success. They mate with the larger and more fertile females, and eggs laid in their territories have a higher rate of survival than eggs laid in territories of smaller males.

Small and medium-sized bullfrogs mate as opportunity presents itself. They also call, but do not defend a territory. When challenged, they do not fight, and move to another area.

The youngest and smallest males are termed parasitic or satellite males. They position themselves near the larger males, but do not call. When females come in response to the calls of the large males, the satellite males try to intercept and to mate with them. Their success is very limited.

The mating success of the medium-sized males is intermediate between that of the large territorial and the satellite males.

There appear, therefore, to be three tactics available to the bullfrog which produce different levels of success. Apply the games theory model to this and the ESS would seem to be:

■ if small, be a parasite
■ if medium-sized, be a non-territorial calling male
■ if large, call and defend a territory.

In the *conditional* ESS outlined above, the payoffs for each strategy are not equal. In a *mixed* ESS the payoffs for each component must be equal. The Coho salmon (Gross, 1985) seems to be an example of a mixed ESS. After hatching, the young salmon swim out to sea where they feed and grow. When mature, they return to the waters in which they hatched in order to breed, following which they die. Females are mature at three years, but alternative life histories have evolved in the males. Some males mature and return at the age of three, developing exaggerated hooked jaws which are used in fighting. These are known as hooknose males. In contrast, other males – jacks – mature and return at the younger age of two when they are considerably smaller than the hooknose males. The hooknose males fight to establish dominance and access to spawning females. The jacks, on the other hand, hide in rocks, debris and so on, from where they dart out to deposit sperm over eggs as opportunity arises.

Gross (1985) reported that jack fertilisation was less successful than hooknose fertilisation. However, this is based on a short-term measure of mating success and is not, therefore, a sufficient measure of fitness. It does not allow for the difference between the breeding lifespan of hooknose and jack males: the genes for the jack strategy are passed on every *two* years, while genes for the hooknose strategy are passed on every *three* years!

When this is taken into account, the reproductive success of the jack and hooknose males is very similar. Overall, the two strategies are equally successful ways of passing on genes. This can therefore be considered as an example of a mixed ESS where the payoffs for different strategies are equal.

ESSs and parental care

The *games theory* model is helpful in understanding the evolution of parental care. There is great variation between species in this respect. Nevertheless, Harvey (1994) suggested that it is reasonable to assume that, in general, one parent is better than none, and two parents are better than one.

However, the improvement in survival of young is likely to be much smaller with an increase from one to two parents, than from none to one. This may lead to conflict between the sexes as to which should carry out parental care: the carer cannot breed whilst caring for young, whilst the deserter can mate again and produce more offspring.

To create an ESS model of parental care it is helpful to begin with two strategies, both of which are possible for either sex:
1 Guard (G).
2 Desert (D).

If ecological conditions favour uni-parental care, it is better for an individual to be the sex which deserts, as long as the other sex does not desert also.

Maynard Smith's (1977) games theory model for the evolution of parental care indicates how different patterns might evolve. The model assumes that the success of a breeding pair depends on:
■ parental care after the eggs are laid
■ the investment put by the female into the eggs. (This will vary according to whether she guards or deserts. A female that guards will produce fewer eggs than one who deserts. A male that deserts has a certain probability of finding another mate.)

Payoffs can be calculated based on the average female and the average male in four possible populations:
1 Both sexes desert.
2 Both sexes guard.
3 Male guards alone.
4 Female guards alone.

What are the advantages and disadvantages of each strategy? Take 1, for instance, where both sexes desert. The female produces more eggs than if she were guarding, but each egg is less likely to survive since it has no parent to feed it once hatched, or to fend off predators. The payoff for the male when both desert is the same as for the female *plus* the chance of having more offspring. What are the ESSs for this model, and under what conditions would they evolve? For both sexes to desert, it must pay better *for each sex* to desert rather than to guard, even though the other sex also deserts. Firstly, there must be a better reproductive payoff for the female to lay a large number of eggs which neither parent stays to care for, than it would be if she laid a smaller number and stayed to look after them as a single parent (it would have to be a smaller number of eggs if she stays because she diverts energy from egg production into care). Otherwise she will guard. Secondly, the male must get a better payoff from leaving the offspring of his first mating with no parent to care for them, than he would by staying to care for them as a single parent, in which case he would not have the time and energy to mate again. Otherwise *he* will guard.

Conditions for the other three possible ESSs (2–4) can be worked out in the same way.

When this is done, the model indicates, for example, that care by one parent is likely to evolve when care by one parent makes a *large* difference to the young, but when care from two parents adds *little* extra benefit.

The stickleback ESS (female deserts, male guards) will be favoured if the number of eggs laid by a deserting female is sufficiently greater than the number laid by a guarding female.

In birds such as the duck, the ESS of female guards, male deserts, is stable, providing that the probability of the male mating again is sufficiently large.

Maynard Smith's model involves each sex either guarding or deserting. In the real world the situation is likely to be more complex: not an all-or-none situation, but rather one of how an animal might respond to changes in allocation of resources to offspring by a partner. An individual which puts less effort into feeding young, for instance, is more likely to survive to the next breeding attempt.

So, if one parent reduces its rate of feeding young, how should the other parent respond? It could pay it to increase the feeding rate since this would make the brood more likely to survive. Or it could pay the parent to reduce its feeding rate, thus improving its chance of surviving to breed again.

Research in this area has produced different results. These vary from reduced effort by the partner, no change in effort, to increased effort (Clutton-Brock and Godfrey, 1991).

The ESS model can help explain why mating and parenting have developed dissimilarly in different species. It depends on the balance between the ability to secure a mate and the likelihood of losing parental investment. For example, desertion by female mammals is unlikely to be an ESS because the infant carried during gestation would probably die. The mother's parental investment from courtship to birth would be lost.

Activity 14

It is often difficult to determine to what extent human behaviour is determined by culture or by evolution. On the basis of what ESSs can tell us about the evolution of parental care, consider whether evolution would favour the evolution of bi-parental or uni-parental care in humans.

A wide range of behaviours have evolved in relation to maximising reproductive success. Research is revealing many of the variables concerned, and the application of games theory model provides a theoretical approach to the evolution of reproductive strategies.

Sexual and parental behaviour involves social interactions between individuals, although the extent of such interactions varies widely. Further aspects of sociality, including altruism, bonding and systems of communication are examined in Unit 10.

Self-assessment questions

9 a Explain, with examples, the difference between conditional and mixed ESSs.
  b What does Maynard Smith's (1977) games theory model on the evolution of parental care assume is necessary for breeding success?
  c On the basis of the games theory model, explain when the following ESS would be likely to evolve:
    i   Both sexes guard.   iii Male guards alone.
    ii Both sexes desert.   iv Female guards alone.

(Suggested answers on page 315.)

Unit summary

- Since fitness is linked to reproductive success, evolutionary theorists are interested in the behaviour involved in reproduction.
- Because most species reproduce sexually it is thought that this provides an evolutionary advantage.
- *Courtship* involves signalling between male and female. It varies greatly between species and serves several functions, one of which is to ensure that mating occurs between appropriate individuals.
- Courtship may involve flamboyant *display* and/or high levels of aggression. Research suggests that courtship displays allow the female to choose a male on the basis of the resources he can provide, or the quality of his genes.
- *Darwin's theory of sexual selection* suggests that males fight to gain access to females. This has led to their larger size and possession of horns. It also suggests that females choose which male to mate with on the basis of his display, plumage, etc. Whilst helpful, Darwin's theory does not altogether explain why evolution favours size and aggression in males and mate choice in females.
- Trivers (1972) suggested that the difference in form and behaviour between males and females is due to *anisogamy*. The consequence of anisogamy is that males are selected to mate with as many females as possible. Anisogamy results in females being selected to choose to mate with males of high quality who can contribute most benefit to the young.
- Competition between males for females includes *fighting*, *territoriality* and *dominance*; also *sperm competition* and *infanticide*.
- Since long tails or exaggerated plumage could be detrimental to their possessor, several theories have been developed to account for these: These include Fisher's *sexy son theory*, Wallace's *good genes theory*, and *handicap theory*. These theories are helpful but are not wholly successful in explaining why natural selection has not discriminated against such exaggerated traits when they are detrimental to their possessor.
- Organisms have evolved a wide variety of *mating strategies* which maximise their reproductive success. These strategies can be divided into four main types: *polygamous, monogamous, polyandrous* and *promiscuous*.
- Mating strategy is influenced by several factors including food distribution and abundance, availability of resources, parental investment and social organisation.
- Trivers (1971) suggested that *parental investment* is a critical factor in the evolution of parental care.
- The *association hypothesis, order of gamete release hypothesis,* and the *paternity certainty hypothesis* offer alternative explanations for the different forms of parental care.
- *Bi-parental care* is most common in birds.
- Evidence suggests that which parent cares for the young is determined by whether one or both parents are needed, the mode of fertilisation, the opportunity of a parent which deserts to mate again and the certainty of the male that the young are his.
- When food is scarce, it may be in the parents' best interest not to attempt to rear all their young, thus increasing their chances of raising at least one.
- Much conflict occurs at weaning. This would seem to be due to a conflict of interests between parent and young.
- Evolutionarily stable strategies provide insight into mating strategies and parental behaviour, and contribute to research in this area.

Terms to define

anisogamy
genotype
inter-sexual selection
intra-sexual selection
monogamy

parental investment
phenotype
polyandry
polygyny
promiscuity

Further reading

Cartwright, J (1996) 'The mating game', *Psychology Review*, 2(3), pp. 6–10.

A very readable account of mating behaviour and reproductive success.

Dawkins, R (1989) *The Selfish Gene*, Oxford University Press, Oxford.

In this deservedly famous book, Dawkins argues that it is the gene not the organism that is the true unit of natural selection.

Ridley, M (1995) *Animal Behavior*, Blackwell Scientific, Boston.

A concise and accessible approach to animal behaviour containing many useful examples.

Ridley, M (1993) *The Red Queen*, Penguin, Harmondsworth.

A thought-provoking and entertaining discussion of sex and evolution.

Answers

■ Suggested answers to activities

1

It is possible that the family as we know it would not exist. Anthropologists believe that the fact that human females are sexually attractive and enjoy sexual activity all the year round strengthens the bond between men and women, and encourages them to stay together. If sexual activity took place solely at a time of 'oestrus', a man might only be with his partner during her fertile time. The man could spend long periods away without any fear of her being unfaithful.

Another consequence might be that a man and wife would prefer to stay close together when the woman is fertile. The man could then be sure that he is the father of any offspring subsequently born. Perhaps men and women would take their annual holidays together at this time.

Men might be more likely to be unfaithful, preferring to be with a receptive partner. This might lead to much changing of partners.

On the other hand, none of these might happen: the prolonged dependence of the human infant might result in men and women staying together to cooperate in raising their offspring.

How do your ideas compare with these? As you can see, there are several possible differences.

2

The following suggestions should give you some ideas of what to look out for. Since courtship is often ritualised and complex, it really is worthwhile to try to observe and describe it in detail yourself, even if only in a few species. Pigeons and doves fan their tails and bow. Herring gulls show head bobbing, and the male feeds the female. Snails press their 'feet' together and touch one another with their tentacles. The male mallard raises his head, then plunges it into water; the female holds her head low on the water. The male bullfinch spreads his wings and tail, and displays his pink breast to the female. Male and female great-crested grebes perform the 'weed dance', which includes head shaking and presenting each other with strands of weed. Courtship in the male pheasant includes erecting his ear tufts, swelling of the wattles round his eyes, spreading his wings and tail. The male guinea pig purrs, sways his rump, and treads the ground. In many species courtship is accompanied by vocalisations.

3

Humans compete for such things as qualifications, high income, high-status jobs, possessions, and so on. Research suggests that such success contributes to the sexual attractiveness of people. This is discussed in Unit 11 in relation to evolution and human behaviour.

4

- Unlike other forms of territorial behaviour, the males defend a small area which contains no resources.
- The males are clustered together in large aggregations.
- The males display within their territory. The females choose between the males on the basis of the display. It seems that the females are attracted to so many males displaying together.

5

Table 5	
Pre-copulatory	Post-copulatory
Fighting	Sperm competition
Territoriality	Mate guarding
Lekking	Infanticide
Displaying to attract female	

6

Many species of duck develop colourful plumage during the breeding season; breeding condition is signalled by colouration in male sticklebacks and guppies. The plumage of the male chaffinch becomes brighter in the spring (compare the head of the male chaffinch in spring and winter). Puffins are brightly coloured in the breeding season, and instantly recognisable. The male cuckoo will often combine his spread tail display with the 'cuckoo' call (only the male calls in this way). The male bluetit

puffs out his yellow chest. The male nightingale and sedgewarbler both sing: this seems to be to attract a female since once they have paired and eggs are laid they cease to sing. Frogs croak in competition for mates. Many species compete by displaying their plumage; peacocks and pheasants for example.
Try to find your own examples when you are in the appropriate environment, or by watching wildlife programmes.

8

You should include the following considerations when setting out the chart:
Monogamy: both sexes benefit equally since both contribute to the care of the young; in long-term pair bonding the longer a pair stays together, the greater their breeding success.
Polygyny: the male benefits because he has exclusive mating rights and can pass on his genes to very large numbers of offspring. However, in some species some males may be unable to obtain a mate. The female and her young may benefit from protection given by the male.
Polyandry: in this rare system the female benefits since she gains additional matings and produces several clutches of eggs. The males help with care of the young. This system may also reduce sexual harassment of females by males and, through sperm competition, ensure the most vigorous sperm fertilises the eggs. Some males may benefit from the system in that without it they may not mate at all.
Promiscuity: the female may benefit since sperm competition may ensure that her egg is fertilised by the most vigorous sperm. The system may reduce infanticide. The males gain additional matings.
Examples of the different mating systems can be found on pages 297–301.

9

This question is not as easy to answer as it might seem. Human beings are generally described as monogamous although, if you think about it, not all humans are monogamous in the strict sense of pairing for life. Perhaps the term *serial monogamy* is more appropriate, referring to the fact that many humans have more than one partner, but not all at the same time.

12
a   paternity certainty hypothesis
b   order of gamete release hypothesis
c   association hypothesis

Suggested answers to self-assessment questions

1

a   Asexual reproduction refers to reproduction where offspring have *exactly* the same genes as the parent. In sexual reproduction both the male and female contribute to the genetic make-up of the offspring: the resulting individual will be different from both parents and from its siblings; different from all other members of the species.

b   Sexual behaviour involves considerable time and energy. During sexual activity participants are conspicuous, and at increased risk of predation. Also, it is a less efficient means for an individual to pass on its genes. Half the offspring's genes come from one parent and half from the other.

c   Evolutionary biologists believe that sexual reproduction is widespread because it has an evolutionary advantage. The advantage might be due to the fact that it results in offspring with different genetic combinations (see page 283). A female who produces genetically varied offspring is more likely to produce at least one which is able to survive in a given environment. It is possible that sexual reproduction confers other benefits. Research continues.

2

a   ■ Courtship ensures that individuals mate with others of the same species, and of the appropriate sex and condition (fertile and ready to mate).

   ■ Courtship ensures that mating and parental behaviour are sychronised. Thus it encourages bird pairs to cooperate in building the nest, incubating the eggs and feeding the brood.

   ■ It serves to overcome aggression in those species where this might be a problem. For instance, the male of some spider species is at risk of being killed by the female. Signalling involved during courtship prevents this.

b   A swan is unlikely to mate with a goose in natural surroundings because each bird will have been reared by parents of the same species, and with siblings of the same species. Research shows that early experience influence behaviour and sexual preference in some birds (this is discussed in more detail in Unit 10).

3

a   i   In sexual reproduction females produce eggs, males sperm. Each of these are known as gametes.

   ii Anisogamy refers to the fact that females produce *much* larger gametes than males. Furthermore, the number of female gametes (eggs) is limited. In human beings, for instance, a woman produces about 400 ripe eggs during her reproductive lifetime. There are about 500 million sperm in a single ejaculation.

b   Because of the vast numbers of sperm he produces, the male has the ability to fertilise as many females as he is able to mate with. Thus a male who copulates with numerous females has reproductive advantage over a male who mates with one or two females only.

c   In general, a female does not benefit from copulating with numerous males. This is because her reproductive success is limited by the rate at which she can produce eggs. It is also affected by the extent of her parental investment. A female mammal, for example, carries the young within her body for a considerable length of time. To maximise her reproductive success she therefore seeks resources rather than additional mates (see page 288 and Trivers, 1972).

4

a   i   Sperm competition is a form of sexual competition between males which involves no direct conflict. The element of competition is concerned with which male's sperm actually fertilises a female's egg. It occurs after mating has taken place. Example: before releasing his own sperm, the male damselfly removes any sperm deposited in the female by a male with whom she has mated previously. Davies (1983) reported sperm competition in the dunnock. Before mating the male pecks at the cloaca of the female which results in the ejection of sperm from previous matings (see page 291).

   ii When sperm from a previous male has been removed, the male mates with the female. So as to prevent another male from removing *his* sperm, he remains with the female. Thus the male damselfly stays with the female until her eggs are laid, thus ensuring they are fertilised by his sperm.

b   i   In some species of damselfly the male maintains his grip on the female while she lays her eggs. This is most likely to occur when male competitors are nearby.

   ii When it is probable that additional females are likely to enter his territory, the male is more likely to release the female but stay with her. He is thus able to reduce the chance of his own sperm being removed whilst increasing his opportunities of further matings.

iii   Infanticide is a form of post-copulatory conflict. It was first observed in lions where a new lion taking over a group of females kills the young lion cubs (Schaller, 1972). This results in the female coming into oestrus and being willing to mate.

It is likely to occur in those species which delay ovulation during lactation, and which have a long gestation period. A female with young to feed will not be fertile for a considerable time, therefore the male will have a long wait before he can mate with her and father his own young. By killing the existing young, the new male begins a process which allows him to father his own young much sooner than if he waited.

5

a   i   The fact that a male can survive despite having excessive ornamentation. A long tail is a handicap in the sense that it is more weight to carry around, and its possessor is more likely to be taken by a predator. The very fact that he has survived despite this indicates his quality.

ii   Courtship displays enable the female to determine the quality of the male's genes. A male who can roar loudly for a long time, or who can grow a magnificent tail, is demonstrably strong and will father healthy and vigorous offspring.

iii   The advantage to a female of an attractive mate is that she will have attractive sons. Because this preference for attractive males will be passed onto the next generation of females, her sons will be more likely to obtain a mate and produce offspring.

b   ▤   One criticism is that the theories do not really explain why elaborate plumage or prolonged displays are not selected against. They do not take into account the influence of coevolution on prey and predator (see Unit 8). It would be expected that if possession of a long tail made its possessor more vulnerable to a predator, fewer would survive to pass on their genes.

▤   Another criticism is related to genetic depletion. As Halliday (1978) pointed out, if females continually favour males with certain genes, only these males will breed. In time, these males would become genetically similar. At this point any differences between the males would be due to environmental rather than genetic factors: the differences would not, therefore, be passed on to the female's offspring (see pages 293–5 for more detail and further criticisms).

6

a   Where food is scarce, monogamy tends to develop. This is thought to be because two parents are needed to care for the young. Birds which nest in colonies are monogamous. This may be due to the need for both parents to care for the young, also to protect them from cannibalism. Territorial behaviour develops when resources are defendable. Animals which need to defend large territories to ensure sufficient resources tend to be monogamous. However, some territorial animals are polygynous. Thus when the red-winged blackbird establishes a territory with good resources, he may have several females nesting there. The number of females depends on the quality of his territory. Polyandry and polygyny are found where one sex controls resources required by the other. Polyandry may develop when conditions are harsh. By mating with additional males, the female ensures several males are available to help in the care of young.

Where food is widely distributed and it would be costly to defend an area, animals tend to move about in groups. This leads to harem polygyny. A polygynous system is also likely to evolve where males defend a group of females and the resources they need.

Where animals feed on open grassland, they form great herds. The mating system is promiscuous, with access to mates on the basis of dominance.

All mating systems have been observed in the dunnock. Both male and female have territories. Availability of food determines the size of the territory. This in turn influences the mating system.

b   Safety (against predators); parental investment; reproductive synchrony; sperm competition.

7

a   Mammals, birds and eusocial insects.

b   The sex with the lower parental investment can gain greater reproductive success by seeking as many matings as possible. If the female can rear the young without the male, the male's reproductive success is dependent on the number of females he is able to fertilise.

c   In some species, the demands of the young are such that two parents are required to care for them. If the male deserted to seek additional matings, the young would be unlikely to survive and his reproductive success would be less. His reproductive success is therefore increased by staying to help the female, and thus improving the likelihood that his progeny will reach adulthood.

8

a   Unless food is plentiful, it may not be possible for parents to rear all their offspring to adulthood. By withholding food from some and feeding only the strongest, the parents are more likely to raise one than none. If they tried to raise all, then none might survive.

b Young benefit most by obtaining as much parental investment as possible, and for as long as possible. When offspring are immature, parents gain most reproductive success by providing care. But once the offspring are sufficiently mature to be able to do almost as well without care as with it, the parents' long-term interest is best served by withdrawing care and investing in new offspring.

c Infanticide involves killing the young of *another* parent to bring forward the time when the individual can sire his own young, and further his own reproductive success. Infanticide occurs between unrelated animals, parent-offspring conflict between (of course!) related individuals.

9

a A conditional ESS is one in which the payoffs for each strategy are not equivalent. An example of this is found when games theory model is applied to the mating behaviour of the bullfrog. This results in three possible strategies with different payoffs in terms of mating success (see page 307).

A mixed ESS is one where the payoff for each component is equal. The coho salmon has two mating strategies involving mature males mating at the age of three, and smaller males (jacks) mating at the age of two. Since jacks mate sooner than mature males, but are less successful in fertilising eggs, the overall reproductive success of mature males and jacks is much the same. Overall, therefore, the two strategies are equally successful.

b This model assumes that the reproductive success of a breeding pair depends on the parental care given after the eggs are laid, and the female's investment in the eggs.

c i For this to evolve, firstly the female must get a better payoff by laying a smaller number of eggs which both she and the male look after, than she would if she laid a larger number of eggs and left only the male to look after them. Secondly, it must pay the male better in terms of survival of the offspring if *both* parents look after the eggs than if he left the female to do so whilst he moved onto a second mate.

ii See page 308.

iii The female stickleback deserts, and the male guards. For this to evolve, the females must first receive a better payoff by laying a greater number of eggs which are looked after by the other parent, than she would by laying a smaller number of eggs which both parents look after (the number of eggs will be smaller if she stays because she has to put some energy into care instead of egg production). Secondly, it must pay the male better to stay as the single parent rather than putting his energy into a second mating and a second clutch of eggs in the same year, but leaving his offspring unguarded.

iv This strategy is found in ducks. For it to evolve, firstly the female must get a better payoff by laying a smaller number of eggs which she then stays to look after alone, than she would by laying a larger number of eggs which neither she nor the male stays to look after. Secondly, the payoff for the male must be greater by leaving his first mate to look after her smaller number of eggs and by mating with another female, than by helping his first mate and not mating a second time.

Unit 10

Kinship and Social Behaviour

Gillian Lang

This unit covers:

Altruism

Social behaviour

Imprinting and bonding

Signalling systems

By the end of this unit, you should be able to:

- describe altruism and discuss explanations of altruistic and apparently altruistic behaviour
- demonstrate awareness of the range of social groupings, and evaluate their advantages and disadvantages
- appreciate the nature and consequences of imprinting and bonding in precocial and altricial species
- explain and evaluate the different systems of signalling and communication in non-human animals.

Unit 10 Contents

Altruism

In everyday life the term altruism refers to behaviour which serves to benefit others; that is, unselfish behaviour. Dawkins (1989) defined altruism as the behaviour of an animal which increases another's benefit at the expense of its own. Such behaviour appears to make the altruist more likely (however slightly) to die, and the recipient more likely to survive. Thus the recipient benefits with some cost to the altruist. Ridley (1995) described altruism as '. . . the transfer of some benefit from the altruist to the recipient, at some cost to the altruist'. An example of altruistic behaviour would be the onlooker who jumps into the sea to save a drowning child. The onlooker risks his or her own life.

Activity 1

Write down examples of altruism in humans that you have encountered. These may be real or fictional. If you have read Charles Dickens's *A Tale of Two Cities* (for instance), a striking example of altruism may be found in the behaviour of Sydney Carton.

When describing altruistic behaviour in humans, intentionality is implied on the part of the individual. Thus the traveller who gives up a seat on the train to someone on crutches does so with the intention of helping that individual. However, when discussing altruism in relation to animal behaviour, it is necessary to define it objectively, by focusing on the behaviour itself, not on any real or seeming intentionality. Whether behaviour is interpreted as selfish or altruistic depends on the consequences of that behaviour. If it lowers the likely survival of the altruist whilst raising it for the recipient, it is defined as altruistic. When an animal behaves towards another in such a way as to benefit itself at the expense of the recipient, the behaviour is defined as selfish. The subjective intentions (if any) of the organism are ignored.

Thus altruism and selfishness are defined objectively, based on behaviour and its consequences.

Many parents demonstrate altruism in the care they devote to their offspring. They feed them, often at considerable cost to themselves, and may risk their lives in defending them.

Examples of altruistic behaviour are to be seen in the **cooperation** of eusocial insects such as termites and honeybees. They work for the benefit of others, do not reproduce, and bees may die defending the hive.

Jarvis (1981) described the social system of mole rats, which resembles that of the eusocial insects. There is likely to be just one breeding female, plus the workers which obtain food and look after the colony.

The alarm call emitted by many species is thought to be a form of altruism since it is likely to draw attention to the caller. An example of this occurs in Belding's ground squirrels which sound an alarm call at the approach of a predator. Ground squirrels are preyed on by several species such as coyotes and badgers and, since the warning call is conspicuous and easily located, the risk to the caller is considerable. Several species of birds and mammals give warning signals in response to danger. This benefits the majority but, as with Belding's ground squirrels, at some risk to the individual which emits the warning.

Altruistic behaviour is found in group-living animals where one female may feed the young of another. Such behaviour has been observed in several species including guinea pigs (Fullerton *et al.*, 1974). Male canids such as wolves and hyenas who have not mated will regurgitate food for the cubs. In some species of birds, the young are fed by one or more others in addition to the parents. This occurs in Florida scrub jays and in many cases the helpers are the offspring from previous years.

There seem to be many instances of apparently unselfish behaviour such as sharing food, warning of predators and grooming others to remove parasites.

The problem with altruism (Darwin's paradox)

Altruistic behaviour is of particular importance to Darwin's theory of natural selection. This is because the concept of altruism appears to run contrary to the theory. Natural selection favours behaviour which will increase the survival and reproductive success of the individual. We would therefore expect organisms to pursue their own interests, regardless of others: to be selfish, in fact.

Darwin's theory of natural selection states that natural selection acts on the individual on the basis of three principles:

■ Organisms overproduce themselves.
■ Individuals vary according to their ability to survive and reproduce.
■ These abilities are heritable: thus traits which contribute to fitness of parents (ability to survive and reproduce) are likely to be inherited by their offspring.

Thus individuals are selected to produce as many offspring as possible. Altruistic behaviour, however, is likely to reduce the reproductive success of the altruist, whilst increasing the ability of the recipient to reproduce.

If Darwin's theory is correct and natural selection acts in such a way as to increase the reproductive success of the individual, the evolution of altruistic behaviour is something of a paradox. The theory seems to predict that animals would behave selfishly so as to maximise their ability to reproduce. How can altruism be explained? In *The Descent of Man* (1871) considered how natural selection might favour the evolution of Darwin moral behaviour in humans.

Evolution and group selection

One attempt to explain altruism in the context of natural selection is group selection. Wynne Edwards (1961) suggested that natural selection favoured the group or species. Thus in group selection altruistic behaviour evolves because it benefits the group. Wynne Edwards offered several examples of behaviour of individual animals: these he described as adaptations which protect resources for the group as a whole.

One example concerns the winter flocking of starlings. This is known as **epideictic** behaviour, a term coined by Wynne Edwards (1962) to describe behaviour where birds deliberately mass in crowds to facilitate population estimation. Many organisms aggregate in large flocks, herds, shoals, and so on. By gathering in large groups, animals are able to carry out a census of their population. Thus when huge flocks of starlings gather together on telegraph wires this gives the flock an idea of whether there are too many of them in relation to weather conditions and availability of resources, and they can respond by some going elsewhere or by some of the birds limiting their clutch size. The size of the population is therefore adjusted according to the availability of resources within the foraging area. In a severe winter and when numbers are large, the birds cut back their rate of breeding so that the number of birds does not exceed available resources. When numbers are few and the winter mild, then breeding will be increased, since resources to support increased numbers are available.

Wynne Edwards did not suggest that the birds make conscious decisions, but that stress responses to cold weather and crowding results in lower levels of breeding. He suggested that this benefits the group rather than the individual. The group selectionist argument also seems to explain such forms of altruistic behaviour shown by social insects where sterile workers serve the community and do not breed, or where birds give warning signals. Such behaviour benefits others rather than the individual.

If Wynne Edwards is correct, then selection may be thought to act at group level. Thus the more successful groups of animals would be those in which animals behave altruistically to one another; groups which lack altruism would be less successful. However, trying to explain altruism in terms of group or species selection leads to problems. Let us examine these.

Groups tend to be relatively stable in comparison with the rate at which individuals reproduce and die, and it would be expected that selection at the level of the individual would outweigh selection at group level. Individual animals vary in their ability to survive and reproduce. Selection, therefore, is more likely to act on the individual.

To explain the evolution of a moral sense, Darwin (1871) proposed a form of group selection where a tribe which had many members ready to help one another and to sacrifice themselves for the good of all would defeat most other tribes. This sounds plausible, but how likely is it to happen? Darwin himself pointed out that it was doubtful if benevolent parents, loyal to others, would rear greater numbers of offspring than selfish and treacherous parents of the same tribe. More of the self-sacrificing individuals would die.

It is difficult to understand how a tribe of selfless (altruistic) people would develop in the first place. The demands of the environment would be more likely to favour the genes of people who hoarded food rather than shared it, or who leave neighbours to defend their own young rather than risk injury themselves through helping them.

This demonstrates the problem with group selectionist theory: it is difficult to imagine group selection selecting a trait that would not be favoured by individual selection. Dawkins (1989) demonstrated this clearly: take a group of altruistic animals. Within such a group there will be some who act selfishly rather than show altruism. A selfish individual will be able to exploit the altruism of the unselfish animals. This animal therefore is more likely to survive and to have children. These will inherit the selfish characteristics. With each succeeding generation, the ratio of altruistic to selfish animals will change: there will be more selfish and fewer altruistic animals. As Dawkins pointed out, even in the unlikely event of a group consisting entirely of unselfish individuals, it is likely that selfish individuals would migrate from selfish groups. In time the selfish animals would overwhelm the altruistic ones.

This reasoning can be applied to Wynne Edwards's (1986) example of flocking behaviour in starlings. In time, a mutation would occur which did not produce the stress-mediated inhibition of breeding response. What would be the consequence of this?

Activity 2

Write down what would happen if such a mutation appeared, then read the following paragraph. Were you right?

Over time, a bird with this mutation would produce more offspring than other members of the flock. If the mutation were heritable, then more and more birds would breed without restraint; these birds would eventually form the majority of the population.

Kin selection and inclusive fitness

Animals behave altruistically. How can this be explained if natural selection acts on the individual? As discussed earlier, parental behaviour involves altruism. Parents devote time and energy to tending their offspring, at considerable cost to themselves. This does not contradict the theory that natural selection acts on individuals since the more children and grandchildren produced, the greater the advantage in terms of natural selection. Biological fitness refers to the ability to survive and to reproduce. Parents and their offspring are closely related, therefore parental altruism towards their young is not surprising.

Take the example of the ground-nesting lapwing where the parent bird 'pretends' to be injured, thus luring the predator away from the nest. By putting itself in danger it saves its offspring. Parents share half their genes with their offspring. If the display leads to the parent being killed by the predator, the offspring may survive. Since they share many of the parent's genes, the parent's genes survive. The altruistic behaviour therefore is explained as an adaptation which is good for the parent's genes, not the good for the parent as an individual.

Hamilton (1964) pointed out that this also applies to other close relatives. How closely related are you, for example, to your parents, your brothers and sisters, your cousins? How many genes do you have in common?

Hamilton focused on the extent of the relationship, pointing out that on average an animal shares half of its genes with its siblings, an eighth of its genes with its first cousins; the less closely related, the smaller the proportion of shared genes. Tending its own offspring, therefore, contributes to the spread of an animal's genes. So too does helping less close relatives, although not to the same extent.

Thus an animal can maximise its opportunities of passing on its genes in two ways: firstly, by reproducing itself (Darwinian fitness); secondly, by helping relatives. Hamilton (1964) subsumed these two strategies under the term *inclusive fitness*.

Altruistic behaviour towards a relative may help the relative to reproduce, whilst reducing the ability of the altruistic individual to reproduce (cost). Such behaviour will only be favoured by natural selection if the benefit outweighs the cost to the altruist. If the altruism does not enable the recipient to produce a greater number of offspring, then genes for such behaviour will not spread in a population.

Maynard Smith (1964) suggested the term **kin selection** to describe selection that takes account of other relatives as well as immediate descendants.

If this approach is correct, then altruistic behaviour would be found where animals are related, not merely where the relationship is parent to offspring. Does the evidence support this?

Belding's ground squirrels are a social species subject to considerable predation. At the approach of a predator an animal sounds the alarm at considerable risk to itself. The theory of kin selection, or inclusive fitness, would predict that the squirrels are related. Young female ground squirrels tend to stay in the group in which they are born and are, therefore, likely to be surrounded by animals to whom they are related. These females call more than females who do not stay in groups of close relatives; males move to other groups and call less than females. Thus a Belding's ground squirrel

calls more when in a group of close relatives (Sherman, 1977, 1980). This is strong evidence for kin selection theory.

Florida scrub jays (as their name indicates) are found in Florida, where they inhabit areas of oak scrubland. Woolfenden and Fitzpatrick (1984) have studied them for many years. Breeding birds are helped by non-breeding birds. Helpers feed the young, protect them, and help to defend the territory of the breeding pair.

Not all breeding pairs have helpers, but for those that do the number of helpers ranges from one to six. Although helpers vary in age, 90 per cent are the offspring of at least one of the pair. The majority of helpers (over 60 per cent) are, in fact, helping their own parent. Both sexes act as helpers, but older helpers (up to seven years of age) tend to be male.

Most lionesses spend their lives in the pride into which they were born. A pride will consist of related animals – mothers, daughters, sisters, aunts, cousins, and so on. Lionesses in the pride cooperate with each other: they hunt together, defend their area together. The birth of cubs tends to be synchronous, and cubs are reared and defended by all the mothers. Cubs may even be suckled on a communal basis (Packer *et al.*, 1988).

Altruistic behaviour is likely to be found in such groups since the animals are related, and individual recognition is not required.

The eusocial insects are highly cooperative and show extreme levels of altruism. They cooperate in nest building, care of young, foraging and defending the nest. Some individuals are sterile but cooperate to ensure the survival of the brood produced by the queen.

Selection at gene level

Both Williams (1966) and Dawkins (1989) hold the view that altruistic behaviour has evolved for the benefit of the genes: that altruistic behaviour of parent to young is an adaptation which is good for the parent's genes, not simply for the good of the parent. Thus the parent's genes survive in the offspring. Such altruistic behaviour benefits the genes rather than the offspring as individual organisms. The same explanation holds good for the altruism exhibited by social insects and social mammals.

Kin selection, then, is based on the principle that natural selection can favour an animal acting in such a way as to help its relatives, even though this action is costly to the animal itself. If natural selection takes place at the level of the gene, the problem of altruism disappears.

If altruistic behaviour has evolved for the benefit of the genes, then it seems likely that other adaptations have evolved for the good of the genes. This is suggested by Williams (1966) and argued by Dawkins (1989) in his book *The Selfish Gene*: the unit of selection is at the level of the gene, not the individual. Thus individuals do not replicate themselves: genes do.

The genes we and other organisms inherit from our parents produce individuals with certain physical and behavioural traits. If these traits ultimately lead to successful reproduction and rearing of young, then the genes themselves are perpetuated. Individuals which fail to reproduce and to rear young die out, so do their genes. Thus genes which contribute to reproductive success survive in that they are replicated in subsequent generations.

What the theory is asking you to do is to imagine a gene which has the effect of causing the organism of which it is a part of behave so as to help copies of itself survive in other organisms.

Dawkins (1989) writes: '... any gene that behaves in such a way as to increase its own survival chances in the gene pool at the expense of its alleles will survive. The gene is the basic unit of selfishness.' (An allele is any one of two or more possible forms of a gene.)

Animals and people do not spread their genes. **Selfish genes** spread themselves by causing organisms to behave in certain ways: to seek food, a mate, to rear young. Thus humans gain pleasure from eating, love, sexual activity, children. In this way genes are passed on.

Thus altruism has not evolved through group selection. If an animal does not reproduce, its genes are not passed on. However, if this same animal enables one of its relatives to reproduce by showing altruism, then some of its genes are replicated in the offspring of the relative. By this means, the selfish genes succeed in being replicated. The selfish gene does not necessarily lead to selfish behaviour on the part of the individual, it can result in altruistic behaviour. The selfishness is at the level of the genes, not the individual.

Thus kin selection is a means by which a gene for altruism could practise discrimination. The rules can be simple: in a species where relatives live close together the rule might be 'help those near at hand' or 'help those reared in the same burrow (or nest) as myself'. Thus altruism is shown to relatives.

Activity 3

Imagine two situations:
a   You have the chance to save your own life, or those of two brothers, *or* eight cousins.
b   You have the chance to save your own life *or* three brothers *or* nine cousins.

On the basis that full siblings have 1/2 chance of having the same gene (allele) for altruism, and first cousins a 1/8 chance of sharing the same gene, in which of these two options would natural selection favour your self-sacrifice? Why?

(Suggested answer on page 348.)

Altruistic behaviour can therefore be explained on the basis of inclusive fitness (Hamilton) or kin selection (Maynard Smith). Such behaviour ensures the survival of an individual sharing some of the genes of the altruist.

Apparently altruistic behaviour

Apparently altruistic behaviour is that which appears, at first sight, to be of benefit to other individuals. On closer examination, however, it may be shown to have a greater benefit for the individual displaying the behaviour. This possibility is considered below in relation to alarm calls, epideictic behaviour and reciprocal altruism.

As mentioned above, Wynne Edwards suggested that epideictic behaviour serves to adjust the population of, for instance, a flock of starlings to the available resources. However, he pointed out that it would be to the selfish advantage of the individual to pretend that the population is large, whether or not this is, in fact, the case. Thus if starlings are estimating population size by how much noise is produced in the roost, it would be to the benefit of the individual to call extra loudly, so as to sound like two starlings rather than one. Thus, rather than limit their own clutch size, they call extra loudly to encourage *other* starlings to limit *their* clutch size, whilst reproducing their own genes as vigorously as possible. The starling who succeeds in doing this gains selective advantage since it is reducing the number of individuals who do not carry the same genes.

Dawkins (1989) used the term *Beau Geste* effect to describe this possible deception about numbers. Animals may use this deception when a predator is nearby as it would be to their advantage to be considered numerous, and therefore more difficult to attack.

Alarm calls may draw a predator's attention to the caller as well as alerting other members of the prey species to the presence of a predator. Alarm calls may not be altruistic however. For example, when one member of a group of ground feeding birds spots a predator, what should this bird do? If silence is maintained, all the birds are vulnerable to attack. The individual might fly up into a tree but would then be on his own, and vulnerable. It is far better to fly up into the tree and sound an alarm, thus encouraging the rest of the birds to do so at the same time. This behaviour allows the bird both to

escape from the predator and to become hidden in among the others. Charnov and Krebs (1975) suggested that the bird sounding the alarm call is manipulating the rest of the flock. Since this is in the interests of the caller, it is not altruistic behaviour.

Thompson's gazelles have developed a behaviour called stotting which is a way of jumping high in the air when threatened by a predator. Dawkins (1989) pointed out that the gazelles appear to be deliberately seeking the predator's attention. Ardrey (1970) believed that the behaviour is altruistic, and best explained by group selection. Zahavi (1977) proposed that stotting is a signal to the predator, not to the other gazelles. Dawkins suggested it means something like 'See, I'm young and healthy and hard to catch. You'll stand a better chance of a meal with one of those old wrecks over there'. If Zahavi is right, far from being altruistic, stotting is an example of selfish behaviour.

Such examples reveal how difficult it is to determine whether behaviour is or is not altruistic. This is why it is often referred to as *apparently altruistic* behaviour.

Reciprocal altruism

Altruism shown to related animals can be considered as not truly altruistic since it benefits individuals which share the same genes. But suppose those who benefit from altruism are *not* related. If all individuals cooperated then all would be better off but, as discussed on page 323, the best strategy for an individual is to behave selfishly. However, if the cost of an altruistic act is compensated by altruism in return, the situation looks rather different. How might such cooperation evolve?

Trivers (1971) suggested that altruism which takes place between unrelated animals should be termed *reciprocal altruism*. The idea of reciprocity seeks to explain altruism between unrelated animals. The concept includes the notion that rather than two animals each gaining immediate benefit, the first benefits on one occasion, the

Activity 4

Write down examples of *apparently* altruistic behaviour which may be altruistic or selfish. Include reasons for your choice.

(Suggested answers on page 348.)

second on another. Williams (1966) concluded that such delayed reciprocal altruism can evolve in a species where individuals are capable of recognising and remembering each other.

Slater (1994) pointed out that certain conditions must be met before reciprocal altruism can develop:

- Animals must have a sufficiently long life span and live in stable groups so that the same individuals encounter each other repeatedly in situations where altruism can be shown.

- Animals must be able to recognise one another as individuals, and detect when an individual 'cheats', that is, accepts altruism without offering it. If cheaters are not detected and discriminated against, genes for cheating will spread in the population at the expense of the altruist. Dawkins (1989) suggested that this can be explained using Maynard Smith's concept of the *evolutionarily stable strategy (ESS)*. Dawkins proposed a hypothetical population of birds parasitised by a tick which carries a dangerous disease. Whilst preening removes the majority of ticks, mutual grooming is needed to remove them from birds' heads. Thus bird A removes ticks from B; later, when A has ticks, B can return the favour. Such mutual grooming is widespread in both birds and mammals.

But suppose B cheats? He has benefited from A's altruism, but does not return it. It would seem that cheating has selective advantage. Has it? Suppose, suggested Dawkins, that the bird population consists of suckers and cheats. *Suckers* groom anybody who needs it; *cheats* accept altruism but never groom anyone else. The cheat genes would spread through the population and suckers would become extinct. However, what happens to the cheats when there are no more suckers? They would be likely to die out also. This would not be an ESS.

The situation would change if, in addition to suckers and cheats, the population also includes grudgers. *Grudgers* groom both a stranger and an individual who has groomed them previously, but not an individual who has refused to groom them (a cheat). Once there are sufficient grudgers in a population, their chances of meeting each other are sufficiently great to offset their wasted effort in grooming cheats. They now do better than cheats in terms of having ticks removed, and the cheats are driven towards extinction. This is a plausible theory of how reciprocal altruism might evolve.

- The cost of the altruistic act must be low in relation to the benefit the recipient receives from it. The higher the cost, the more certainty there must be that there will be an opportunity for the act to be reciprocated.

The Prisoner's Dilemma

When unrelated animals meet for the first time how should they behave in order to allow the development of reciprocal altruism? The situation resembles that found in the games theory problem known as the 'Prisoner's Dilemma'.

Imagine two prisoners charged with a crime. Each has two options:

1   Cooperate with the other and refuse to confess.
2   Defect (from their alliance) and confess.

If both cooperate, then each will get a very light sentence since nothing can be proved against either of them (R). If one defects and gives evidence whilst the other refuses to talk, the defector gets an even lighter sentence than by cooperating (T), but the other will now get a stiff sentence (S). If both give evidence against the other, then each gets a lighter sentence than by being the one who stayed silent, but heavier than that resulting from mutual cooperation (P). There is thus a scale of outcomes, T-R-P-S:

T - temptation to defect
R - reward for mutual cooperation
P - punishment for defection
S - sucker's payoff

T is the best, S the worst outcome for the individual. The prisoners have to make their decisions without knowing what the other will do.

What would you do in such a situation? What will the prisoner do? He is likely to defect since defection pays better than cooperation. Yet if both defect, each does less well than if both had cooperated.

This is summarised in table 10.1, with numerical values representing the different outcomes.

The defector gains the higest payoff. When the two cooperate, the payoff for each is smaller than for that of the defector. What is best for the individual leads to *mutual* defection where neither benefit. Both would do better if *both* cooperated (see also figure 10.2 on non-zero-sumness).

But the Prisoner's Dilemma is a one-off situation. Suppose those involved play the game repeatedly. In such a situation cooperation can develop.

Activity 5

You will need fellow students or friends and relations willing to play the Prisoner's Dilemma. Ask a number of them to play it just the once, and record numbers of those which cooperate and those which defect. Secondly, ask a few to play the game several times. Record how many trials are needed before players begin to cooperate. You will need to provide a payoff for the various tactics. (A method of investigating the Prisoner's Dilemma is described in Beer, 1982.)

Research has been carried out into how cooperation might develop. Dawkins (1989) referred to the work of Axelrod and Hamilton (1981) who ran competitions based on games theory for computer simulations. Fourteen strategies were submitted. The winning strategy was called *tit-for-tat* and resembles Dawkins's population of suckers, cheats and grudgers: the fact that the strategy proved so successful lends further support to the theory that reciprocal altruism would be an ESS. Where animals meet each other repeatedly, then it seems likely that cooperation and reciprocal altruism would evolve.

Wilkinson (1984, 1985) carried out detailed studies of vampire bats which fly from their roosts at night to feed on blood. Wilkinson established that the bats are able to recognise each other, an essential condition if reciprocal altruism is to take place. Unsuccessful feeding trips are common. Wilkinson found that an animal which had fed one night would share its blood meal with one that had not been successful in obtaining food. The favour was returned when the situation was reversed. The sharing sometimes took place between related animals, but not invariably. The more closely any two bats associate, the more likely they were to share a meal with the other. Out of 13 examples of sharing blood, only one involved a stranger.

Arak (1984) reported that reciprocal altruism has been observed in baboons where males often form partnerships to obtain females. Subordinate males have few chances to challenge the dominant male and to mate, but they help each other. Whilst one keeps the dominant male occupied, the other male copulates with the female. Next time they reverse roles. This form of reciprocal altruism enables both males to achieve more matings (and therefore more offspring) than they could achieve alone.

Table 10.1

		PLAYER B	
		Cooperate	Defect
PLAYER A	Cooperate	R = 3 Reward for mutual cooperation	S = 0 Sucker's payoff
	Defect	T = 5 Temptation to defect	P = 1 Punishment for mutual defection

Summary of the Prisoner's Dilemma (based on Axelrod and Hamilton, 1981)

10.2 Non-zero-sumness

The Prisoner's Dilemma is a non-zero-sum game, a game where one player's gain is not cancelled out by the other player's loss. Either by cooperating or reciprocating, *both* players can be better off. In a zero-sum game one player's gain is the other player's loss, as though a fixed amount was being divided betwen the two. In a game of squash or table tennis there is only one winner. But in a non-zero-sum game one can benefit without the other losing; both players can win if they work together.

How might this be relevant to, say, a chimpanzee? Imagine that you are a chimp who has just found some food, and you give some to another who has not had much to eat lately. You might give him, say, 140 g; consider this as a 5-point loss for you. In a sense, his gain is greater than your loss because he was really hungry and needed the food. So consider his gain as worth 6 points. It is possible that on some future occasion he will repay you by giving you 140 g of similar food. This is an example of non-zero-sumness. One player's gain is not cancelled out by another's loss. *Both* players can be better off. If the other chimp were to repay you when *you* were hungry, then it is now his turn to lose 5 points and for you to gain 6.

The importance of the concept of non-zero-sumness is that it helps us to understand how reciprocal altruism might evolve. It is not, however, a sufficient explanation, since even in a non-zero-sum game a player can still gain by cheating.

Source: based on Wright (1994)

What prevents them from cheating? As discussed earlier, there seems to be an obvious advantage in receiving altruism but not returning it. Thus in the above example one baboon could get the best of both worlds if he accepted the help but did not return it.

Reciprocal altruism is most likely to evolve in species which form stable groups and where individuals recognise each other. If baboons can recognise each other individually, the altruist could bear a grudge against the cheat and refuse to cooperate with him in future. Thus in the longer term cheating will not pay.

Seyfarth and Cheney (1984) reported reciprocal altruism in the vervet monkey. Whilst a considerable proportion of grooming is between related animals, this is not always the case. Some grooming occurs between non-related animals. These monkeys produce a call to solicit aid in disputes. This call was recorded by Seyfarth and Cheney and played back to the monkeys. Non-related individuals were more likely to respond to these calls if that individual had recently been groomed by the caller.

More studies are needed before it can be concluded with certainty that reciprocal altruism does indeed exist. Because it requires the ability of animals to recognise one another as individuals and to be able to defect cheats, reciprocal altruism may be relatively rare.

Kin selection theory has proved invaluable in increasing our understanding of altruistic behaviour. It is less certain that reciprocal altruism takes place, especially as many animals live in related groups, and it is difficult to be certain that animals are not related.

Altruism takes place between individuals during social interactions. The following pages look at the variety of social groupings, and consider their advantages and disadvantages.

Activity 6

Is reciprocal altruism found in humans? Try to think of some examples, and write them down.

Social behaviour

This is a very broad term since nearly all animals exist in pairs or groups for at least part of their lives. Sociality is difficult to define.

Eusocial insects form highly structured societies. In many instances they are divided into castes such as soldiers, workers and reproductives which are morphologically distinct (that is, they have different forms) from each other, and each has a different role in the colony. Caste depends largely on what the insects are fed when young.

Social organisation in vertebrates is much more variable. Some species are social in that they form distinct and enduring groupings that are easily distinguished from other such groupings. A troop of baboons is an example of this. They move around and forage together, sleep close to one another, mate and rear offspring within the group. Interactions within the group are friendly; interactions with non-group members may be hostile. Female elephants may live in the same family grouping for 40 or 50 years. They clearly know and react to each other as individuals (Manning and Stamp Dawkins, 1992).

What of those birds which nest in colonies? They are not social to the same extent as the baboons, but aggregations of large numbers within a small space form a cohesive body. Each pair of birds will defend its nest and the immediate area round it, but all colony members may cooperate in noticing and possibly driving away a predator (Birkhead, 1977).

With the exception of the mother-young relationship, orang utans are described as solitary see figure 10.3. Yet each male's home range covers the foraging areas of two or three females (a home range is the area in which an animal moves about and feeds). Stranger males are evicted from his home range by the resident male, females resist the advances of a stranger. This suggests that some basis exists for the detection of strangers, and suggests a degree of sociality.

Sloths lead independent lives and come together for mating. Contact at other times appears to be mutually antagonistic, and the young disperse early. Syrian hamsters show similar behaviour, with the non-oestrus female antagonistic towards the male.

Thus there are degrees of **sociality**. Sociality can be defined as some degree of interaction between

10.3 Diversity in primate social systems

Chimpanzees live in communities of groups of closely related males and unrelated females. A community includes all those individuals regularly seen in temporary groups known as parties (Boesch, 1996). Males remain in the groups in which they were born, whilst females migrate to other groups. Males defend the group territory. They also fight to establish dominance hierarchies, and for the position of alpha male. Females also form hierarchies but compete less aggressively. Male chimpanzees are dominant over females: if a mixed-sex party finds a prized food, this is certain to end up in the possession of a male! Both sexes use same-sex coalitions to achieve a goal. Chimpanzee parties tend to be unstable, although in some populations females form stable groupings which are mutually supportive. In other populations females spend much of their time alone.

Gorillas live in stable family troops consisting of one mature male, the silverback, and three to four adult females and their young. The females are subordinate to the silverback. He suppresses quarrels between the females in his harem and protects the troop from bachelor silverbacks seeking a mate. Such a male will attempt to kill a female's infant: if he succeeds, she will leave her mate and go with him. Apart from this there is little aggression among gorillas, and some troops include more than one silverback. Little competition takes place between them.

Orang utans are essentially solitary. This is probably due to the fact that they are selective feeders, preferring fruit and requiring large amounts of food. There is little interaction between adults, and the only stable social groupings are mother-infant pairs, or mother with infant plus juvenile. Infants are dependent on their mothers until they reach adolescence at about ten years. Births occur at eight-year intervals. There are two types of male orang utan: large males which are aggressive towards each other, and possessing striking facial ornaments, and males which are very much smaller. Females appear to prefer to mate with a large male, and may travel with him in a consortship.

White handed gibbons are monogamous, living in family groups of male and female and up to four offspring. They are not aggressive, and one is not dominant over another. They defend a territory. Spider monkeys also live in family groups consisting of a breeding pair and their offspring.

Grooming is an important social activity in primates. It is involved in bonding, and is seen most between allies and friends; also in chimpanzee coalitions where two or three form a mutually cooperative alliance.

associating animals. Anything, therefore, that occurs between two or more animals could be called social behaviour. Interactions vary from temporary associations and aggregations, to stable units, and to interactions between several such units within communities.

Hinde (1983) identified several types of social relationship: sexual, affiliative, reconciliatory and competitive. Broadly speaking, interactions between individuals can be divided into those which are cooperative and those which are competitive.

It is helpful to distinguish between those instances where animals form temporary aggregations linked to external factors such as predation seasonal variations in food supply, and interactions based on social attraction or social exchange. Unstructured and temporary aggregations are not considered as truly social, even though animals within them associate. Social behaviour involves the transformation of transient interactions and associations into repeated systems of interaction. It is reasonable to propose that this involves a higher level of society than an aggregation (Lee, 1994).

Whilst some species such as the sloth and hamster are solitary for all activities (save those involved in reproduction), others tend to form unstable aggregations for sleeping, mating and infant rearing. Some species may or may not form aggregations depending on the distribution of food. Thus when food is dispersed, they do not aggregate, but when it is confined to a small area, then aggregations occur. This seasonal variation has been observed in several species including sparrows (Elgar, 1987), minnows (Freeman and Grossman, 1992) and hares (Monaghan and Metcalfe, 1985). Thus an important variable in determining whether a species is solitary or social is the availability and distribution of the resources necessary for it to survive (see also Unit 9 page 297).

Group living confers both advantages and disadvantages. Advantages include:

- Foraging and hunting.
- Protection from predation.
- Communication; exchange of information.

Activity 7

If you get the opportunity, sprinkle the appropriate food onto the surface of a fishpond or tank and watch to see what happens. It is probable that several fish will arrive and eat the food. Consider whether such behaviour is social or not. Compare it with the behaviour of a flock of chickens if you were to scatter grain for them. Compare both fish and chickens with humans at, say, a football match or in a queue at a supermarket checkout.

Foraging and feeding

An animal in a group may obtain information about the location of current feeding sites from other members of the group. For example, Greene (1987) found that ospreys (which nest in colonies) forage more successfully when they receive information concerning the position of a school of fish from another osprey. After catching a fish, an osprey returns to the colony with the fish held in its feet. This is easily visible to other birds, and the information is enhanced by the calling and undulatory flight display of the returning bird, which only occurs when it has caught a fish of the appropriate species. Other birds in the colony respond quickly by setting off in the appropriate direction.

Brown (1986) found that cliff swallows who had not succeeded in finding food tend to follow birds which had been successful, and thus find their way to the food source. Brown commented that the food source was so plentiful that the successful birds were not disadvantaged by being followed.

Many social carnivores hunt socially. Examples include wolves and other canids, killer whales, brown pelicans and group-living spiders. In some species the number of successful hunts increases in proportion to the number of hunters (Packer and Ruttan, 1988). Kuuk (1972) reported that spotted hyenas hunting alone succeeded in catching wildebeest calves in 15 per cent of attempts, whilst pairs succeeded on 74 per cent of occasions.

Ridley (1995) writes that lionesses hunting in groups are more successful than lionesses hunting alone, who are successful on about 15 per cent of such hunts. Thus carnivores such as lions benefit by hunting in groups since they catch more food than when hunting alone. A group is also able to take larger prey such as buffalo. Hunters are also able to adjust the size of the hunting party according to the size of prey being sought. Hyenas, for instance, hunt singly for Thomson's gazelle, but in groups for the larger zebra.

Wolves, wild dogs, and Cape hunting dogs hunt together. Wolves hunting moose, or dogs hunting wildebeest, start by charging several prey in the group or herd. The prey flee, but the predators have a chance to select a vulnerable individual. They pay particular attention to prey that straggle and separate an individual from the herd. It can then be attacked by the pack as a whole.

Activity 8

The hunting techniques of wolves and African hunting dogs are made use of in herding sheep. When you are in sheep country, or when relevant programmes are broadcast on television, watch the tactics employed by the sheepdogs as they herd the sheep. They are essentially the same as those in the wolf and hunting dog, and have been retained over many years of selective breeding.

Bednarz (1988) studied Harris hawks (which feed on jackrabbits). They hunt in family units of the male and female, plus up to four non-breeding helpers. The number of kills per individual was found to be greater for the large groups. Their tactics include several birds pouncing on the prey, with individuals taking turns to lead the pursuit.

Chimpanzees in Tai on the Ivory Coast of West Africa hunt cooperatively. They hunt in teams, with individual members having specialised roles. They prey mainly on two species of colobus monkey. These are about half the weight of an adult chimpanzee and therefore are able to move onto branches which would not support a chimp. They can also leap from tree to tree whereas the chimp is more likely to swing from one tree to another. It is therefore difficult for a lone chimp to catch a colobus monkey.

Some members of the chimpanzee hunting group or *party* keep a troop of colobus moving through the trees, but do not actually chase them. Others prevent the monkeys from breaking away, whilst others quickly climb up into the trees as the monkeys are driven into them. These individuals usually make the kill (Boesch, 1994). Group hunting in chimpanzees is clearly cooperative, and the benefit obvious: without cooperation it is very unlikely that a colobus monkey would be caught, and colobus flesh is highly prized.

Whilst hunting by wolves and chimps involves real cooperation it is often difficult to determine where behaviour is truly cooperative, or just several animals simultaneously running down prey. There is also disagreement about the extent to which carnivores benefit from group hunting. Packer (1986) suggested that the benefit to lions of group hunting may not be in a higher rate of kill, but in that the presence of additional animals helps to keep other carnivores from the kill. Gittleman (1989) observed that black-backed jackals lose 30 per cent of their kills to spotted hyenas. Lions may also lose a kill to hyenas, or even to crocodiles. Larger groups than are needed for killing are better able to defend discovered carcasses from hyenas and other lions, and Packer (1986) suggested that scavenging may be more profitable than hunting for lions. The benefit of numbers in

retaining a kill or carcass may have contributed to lions living in prides containing several animals.

In trying to assess the benefit of hunting as a group rather than as an individual, it needs to be remembered that for the individual to benefit, hunting in pairs (for instance) must be twice as successful as hunting alone; hunting in a group even more so since there are more animals feeding on the prey. The relationship between foraging success and group size can be considered in the context of optimal foraging theory (OFT) discussed in Unit 11. This requires balancing the costs and benefits associated with different strategies. A large herd of grazing animals, for example, will require a rich source of food if all animals in the group are to feed sufficiently. It might benefit a hungry animal when food availability is poor to accept the increased risk of foraging with a smaller group, where smaller numbers means fewer eyes and ears to look out for predators. Animals which forage in groups have more time available for feeding since they share costs or vigilance in looking out for predators. There are many eyes, ears and noses on the alert for danger. Predators are less likely to attack successfully, and in some instances do not attack if discovered. Elgar (1989) reviewed over 50 studies which show that birds and mammals spend less time in vigilance and more time in feeding the larger the group they are in. Thus, in a time of plenty, the same animal is likely to benefit most by feeding in a larger group where there is less risk of being caught by a predator (Pulliam and Caraco, 1984). However, since there are more advantages to be gained from group living than those associated with feeding behaviour, OFT models are perhaps not generally appropriate in evaluating group hunting and foraging (Packer *et al.*, 1990).

In summary, group hunting and foraging involves cooperation to defend food, and to transmit to others the location of food. Animals may be more successful in killing prey if they hunt with others, rather than singly, whether or not cooperation is involved. Foraging animals gain protection from predators, and are able to spend more time feeding when in larger groups.

Protection from predation

Where animals group, each is less likely to be taken by a predator. Hamilton (1971) described this as the selfish herd principle (see Unit 8). The selfish herd effect predicts that individuals within the centre of a group will be less likely to be taken by a predator than animals on the periphery. Experiments carried out by Andersson and Wicklund (1978) with fieldfare indicated that the nearer a nest is to the centre of a colony, the less likely is the nest to suffer predation.

Not all members of a group have an equal chance of being taken, since predators may choose the young, or animals weakened by age or injury. Even without considering the vulnerable, the chance of an individual being taken is decreased by dilution. For example, the majority of wildebeest calves are typically born during a two-week period at the start of the rainy season. Calves born at this time are less frequently captured by predators than calves born before or after this period.

Animals which live in groups or herds tend to move together: this makes it difficult for a predator to select and keep up with a single target. A group can take evasive action by scattering in all directions, giving an appearance of chaos. Animals escaping all at once may also signal to the predator that it has been spotted and that further pursuit is a waste of time and energy.

These benefits of grouping do not necessarily apply only to members of the same species. African ungulates respond to predation by forming mixed groups of territorial males (Gosling, 1986).

Activity 9

Carry out a simple experiment. Find someone who can catch, and throw balls at him or her. Begin throwing one ball at a time, then throw several at once. What happens? It is unlikely that even one will be caught. Why?

(Suggested answer on page 348.)

Grouping may also aid in a more active form of defence, as shown by several species of bird.

Tinbergen (1953) described the behaviour of wagtails in response to a sparrow hawk. They cluster above the hawk as it flies, now and then swooping down on it. Birds which nest in colonies deter a predator by mobbing it. Chaffinches will mob a predator such as an owl or hawk. Puffins fly to and from the sea in a pattern which makes them less vulnerable to predation (these defence patterns are described in more detail in Unit 8).

The bluegill sunfish reduces predation through group living. Male bluegill sunfish guard their eggs from predators such as snails and other fish. The sunfish nest in colonies. When a predatory fish approaches a nest, the resident male drives it away. When the nest is in the centre of the colony, other males from nearby nests also attack the predator, thus providing a more effective defence. This is not the case in relation to solitary nests, or nests on the edge of a colony.

A larger colony of cliff swallows detects a predator sooner than a smaller one. Thus a predator can approach nearer to a small colony than a larger before being detected (Brown and Brown, 1987). Large flocks of birds take off sooner in response to a bird of prey than smaller flocks, and an individual is less likely to be taken. An individual in a larger group also benefits in that it is required to spend less time looking out for predators. Bertram (1980) reported that the larger the group, the less time the individual spends looking out for predators. Many animals are on the lookout for danger.

Another advantage in relation to predation, closely related to the notion of many eyes and ears alert for predators, is the emitting of alarm calls. Thus when one individual spots a predator, all members of the group are warned. Many species of birds sound warning calls, rabbits signal alarm by thumping the ground and by revealing white tails as they escape. In some species such as prairie dogs, meerkats and ground squirrels, individuals take turns to watch out for possible predators, and warn the colony of danger. In socially living meerkats (mongooses), vigilance is undertaken by specific individuals which take turns to go to a high look-out point such as a tree. They keep watch for predators whilst others feed (Macdonald, 1986).

Animals may cooperate in deterring the predator, or in defence. A zebra stallion will defend his group of mares and young from such predators as hyenas and wild dogs. Several groups may join together, until as many as 200 zebra form one large group. A number of zebra stallions stay in the rear, kicking and biting at the predators. Musk oxen form defensive circles around the young. Their heads, armed with horns, are on the outside, providing a defence against the predator. Lionesses cooperate in defence of their area (Packer and Pusey, 1983).

Social insects benefit from the colony being defended on a collective basis. Thus honeybees have workers which guard the hive, and will sting potential invaders.

Costs of group living

The evidence reveals many advantages of group living in relation to feeding behaviour and predation. There are costs however. Thus whilst individuals may benefit from gaining information concerning a food source, the food must be shared. This may lead to competition, with some animals obtaining more food at the expense of others. Such competition has been observed in hyenas (Frank, 1986). (Direct competition is discussed in more detail in Unit 8.)

Indirect competition may be a consequence of group living. A colony of 20 million Mexican free-tailed bats inhabit a cave in Texas. The large numbers of bats searching for food may result in some members of the colony having to travel 200 kilometres in order to obtain food (Tuttle, 1988).

Thus animals may be forced to forage over large areas to fulfill the food requirements of all. Animals within a group may feed at different rates and have different requirements. Animals on the periphery of a group may have reduced intake due to greater exposure to predators, and more time needed to watch out for predators.

The African social spider is a rare example of group-living spiders. Reichert (1985) found that the quantity of food consumed by an individual correlated negatively with the size of the feeding group. Thus the larger the group, the less food obtained by the individual.

Animals feeding as a group are more visible and may, therefore, attract predators. They create more noise, and occupy a larger area.

Despite some of the disadvantages outlined above, many ethologists believe that the main benefits provided by group living are in relation to foraging and antipredation.

The wide variety of groupings which exist reflect the fact that each has evolved as a compromise between the costs and benefits of group living. Once a grouping has developed, whether or not it lasts will depend on the balance between these costs and benefits for each participating individual. These are affected by such factors as body size and energy requirements; predators and competitors; the nature of the food supply and its availability. Thus large patches of food encourage grouping, whilst solitary feeding is likely to occur when food patches are too small for more than one animal to exploit at any one time (this is likely to occur with selective feeding where certain foods are preferred).

The behaviour that will be favoured by natural selection, whether social, solitary, territorial and so on, will be that which favours the long-term reproductive success of the animal.

One of the consequences of group living is competition and conflict but (as discussed in Unit 8) animals tend to avoid fighting when possible. Different forms of social behaviour such as territoriality and dominance reduce the amount of direct fighting.

Social structure

■ Territoriality
A territory is usually defined as a defended area and is also considered in more detail in Units 8 and 9. There are many forms of territorial behaviour and many species which have territories. Tinbergen (1953) demonstrated that the territory holder is likely to win a contest between two male sticklebacks; it is common in contests between a territory holder and an intruder for the territory holder to win.

In many cases, a territory is defended in order to exploit the food resources in it as efficiently as possible. This is exemplified by the golden-winged sunbird which feeds on nectar. By defending their territory, the birds ensure that a better supply of nectar is available. Although defending the territory involves expending energy, this is more than compensated by the increased levels of nectar available (Gill and Wolf, 1975).

Although territorial behaviour serves different functions in different animals, in all cases the space will be defended to secure access to some limited resources or to protect young. Territorial behaviour, like ritualised fighting and dominance, has the consequence of reducing aggression.

Another form of territory is seen in those ground-nesting seabirds such as gulls, terns and gannets. These territories are about one metre across, and contain no food. They consist of a small defended area round the nest. They serve to protect the eggs and young from the cannibalistic nature of others in the colony.

Conflict may occur between groups of animals over group territories. Groups may defend territories. In general, larger groups tend to defeat smaller groups when they come into conflict. This is another factor resulting in animals evolving to live in large groups.

■ Dominance

Dominance hierarchies (Unit 9 page 290) serve to minimise aggression since subordinates avoid fights with dominant individuals.

In some animals the social structure varies according to the season. Male chaffinches tend to dominate females in winter flocks and displace them at feeding sites. This is reversed in spring when females tend to displace the males. Clutton-Brock and Albon (1989) studied red deer on the Island of Rum in the Hebrides. Outside the breeding season males and females live apart, the

males in bachelor herds, females in herds containing young of both sexes. In the rutting season males gather females into groups which they defend from other males. Once the rutting season is over both sexes return to their respective herds for the winter.

In some species the social structure is less changeable. Wolves maintain a stable family structure based on an extended family unit. There is usually one dominant male leader, but several adult males may form part of the family. Many primates also tend to retain a uniform social structure throughout the year (see Figure 10.3 page 329). As pointed out in Unit 9, an advantage of being dominant is greater reproductive success. Also, low-ranking animals will have to forage where food is less abundant or where there is most danger. In some species they will wait until others have fed. Thus low-ranking chimpanzees will have to wait, and will only get what remains when others have had their fill.

Activity 10

Imagine you have been given the opportunity of becoming a non-human primate for a year. Think carefully and decide which you would prefer to be. Give reasons for your choice. Alternatively, you might prefer to be another species altogether. Why?

What happens to individuals early in life may have consequences for later social behaviour. The importance of such experience is considered next.

Self-assessment questions

5 a Explain why the term 'sociality' is difficult to define.
   b Give an example of: (i) cooperative interaction; (ii) competitive interaction.
   c Explain the difference between temporary groupings and truly social behaviour.

6 a Outline, with examples, the benefits of group living in relation to: (i) obtaining food; (ii) protection from predation.
   b Outline some of the costs of group living.
   c Which of the following are possible influences on the development of social systems in animals: (i) availability of food; (ii) risk of predation; (iii) food requirements and patterns of foraging; (iv) ability to catch prey.

(Suggested answers on pages 349–50.)

Imprinting and bonding

Ethologists and psychologists have long been aware of a process where the newly hatched young of **precocial** birds (able to feed and move about immediately after hatching) follow the first moving object they see. Lorenz studied this behaviour in goslings, observing that their social behaviour was determined by this early experience. He termed it 'imprinting'. It is often described as a form of learning since it enables the young to learn the characteristics of the species.

A characteristic of the imprinting process is that the young birds pass through a sensitive period when this learning takes place. There is some debate as to whether this time should be described as a critical period or a sensitive period, but many psychologists believe that it does not apply only to precocial species, but to **altricial** species also. (Altricial species are immature at birth. Examples include dogs, monkeys and ourselves.) Thus many species pass through a time when they are particularly susceptible to environmental influences, where their early experiences are of particular importance to their long-term social development.

The following pages examine the concepts of **imprinting** and bonding, also the importance of critical periods in relation to normal development. You will find that the original meaning of the term imprinting has broadened and may, for instance, be used to refer to the way in which attachment bonds develop between parent and young.

Lorenz (1937) was the first to describe in detail how young goslings will follow the first moving object they see after hatching. This behaviour, known as filial imprinting, is a special form of learning in which baby animals rapidly learn to recognise and follow a moving object soon after birth. A newly hatched duckling or gosling will follow virtually any object it sees.

Lorenz's work began as a result of a chance finding at his estate near Vienna. He noticed that several young greylag geese were following him, at the same time making the same sounds that goslings emit when following their parent. Lorenz realised that some part of their normal development had gone wrong. It seemed clear that they had a built-in tendency to follow: normally this would be the parent but on this occasion, for some reason, it was Lorenz. Why?

The fact that some goslings followed Lorenz suggested that it was unlikely that goslings inherit information about what their parents should look like, and that the action of following was learned. Lorenz, therefore, decided to investigate the factors involved. He divided a clutch of eggs laid by a greylag goose into two groups. One group he left to be hatched by the mother, the remaining eggs were put in an incubator. Lorenz made sure that he was the first moving object the incubator goslings saw when they hatched.

The goslings hatched by the goose followed her, those hatched by the incubator in the presence of Lorenz, followed him. To ensure this was not a chance happening, Lorenz marked the goslings to distinguish the goose-hatched from the incubator-hatched and, when the groups had mingled, put them all under a large box. When the box was raised the goslings separated: those hatched by the goose went to the mother, the others to Lorenz.

Lorenz carried out several more studies. He found that there is a period soon after hatching when goslings will follow a moving object. This process, which is known as imprinting, causes a bond of attachment to develop, and enables the gosling to recognise other members of its species. Lorenz also found that when goslings were imprinted on a human, they would ignore other adult geese when the time came to pair and to mate. Lorenz concluded that imprinting influences the choice of sexual partner. He believed that once imprinting has occurred it is irreversible, and that the individual imprints on a species or class of objects rather than on an individual; also that it only occurs in those birds which are precocial and ground nesting, such as geese, ducks and chickens. A similar process has been observed in other precocial species such as sheep and guinea pigs.

Sensitive periods

Lorenz believed that imprinting can only occur within a strictly limited period of time – a critical period – which takes place shortly after birth.

Hess (1958) investigated this critical period and also the length of time birds must be exposed to an imprinting object before they become capable of discriminating it. Mallard ducklings were isolated straight after hatching from incubated eggs and were deprived of daylight, food and water. Figure 10.4 shows the apparatus, which consisted of male mallard models containing loudspeakers through which a tape recorder played a human voice calling 'gock, gock, gock'. The ducklings were placed on an illuminated circular runway surrounding this, and the rest of the room was in darkness.

There were two conditions. In one, ducklings were placed with the model, which was kept in motion for ten minutes. In the other, the ducklings were placed with the model for 30 minutes. The model moved a short distance every five minutes.

All the ducklings were tested for following behaviour 5 to 70 hours after the experiment. A female model with an authentic call was used to test whether the duckling preferred the male model they had been exposed to or the more natural-sounding female model. The ducklings' call note (distress or pleasure) was noted. All the ducklings were subjected to four tests:

■ Both models silent and stationary.
■ Both models motionless and both calling, with the duckling 0.3 metres away from each.
■ The male stationary, the female moving, both calling.
■ The female model calling and moving; the male silent and stationary.

The strength of imprinting was based on the number of times a duckling moved towards the male model. The strongest imprinting occurred 13 to 16 hours after hatching, although it occasionally

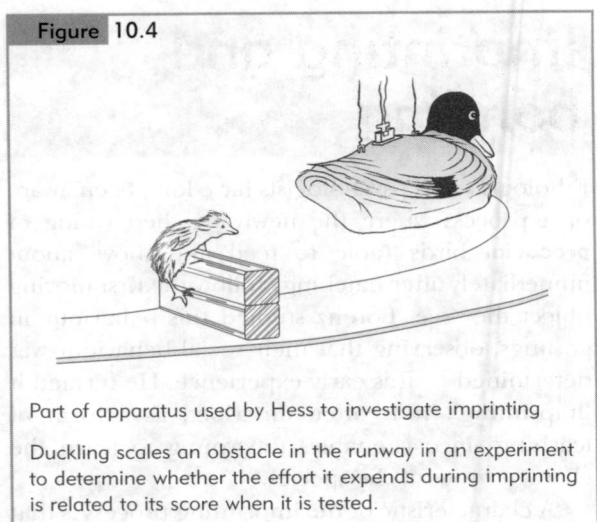

Figure 10.4

Part of apparatus used by Hess to investigate imprinting

Duckling scales an obstacle in the runway in an experiment to determine whether the effort it expends during imprinting is related to its score when it is tested.

Source: Hess (1958)

took place outside this time. Beyond 28 hours no imprinting occurred.

Additional experiments showed that the strength of imprinting increased with the distance travelled and seemed to be dependent on the effort exerted by the duckling in following the imprinting object rather than the duration of the imprinting period. This was confirmed by two supplementary experiments involving 10-centimetre hurdles placed on the runway which the ducklings had to scale, or having the decoy ascend an incline. In each case, imprinting was found to be stronger.

Several factors are important if imprinting is to occur. To begin with the imprinting object must be capable of detection. This is dependent on the visual, auditory and possibly other sensory systems of the youngster (Halliday and Slater, 1983); a relatively conspicuous object facilitates imprinting. In some species auditory interactions are important. Thus Hess found that in mallards, calling between mother and ducklings both before and after hatching contributes to imprinting. Although visual and auditory stimuli are particularly important in birds, olfactory stimuli are important for imprinting in mammals. If infant guinea pigs are raised in the presence of a particular odour, when adult they are more attracted to other guinea pigs which share that odour than those which do not (Carter and Marr, 1970). Sheep and goats need to smell and see their offspring shortly after birth. Failing this, they will reject them. There is a considerable amount of evidence which suggests that the smell of the lambs promotes the ewe's special attachment to them and maintains her maternal behaviour. Thus in maternal imprinting parents learn to recognise their own offspring. It is just as important for parents to do this as it is for offspring to recognise their own parents. This has survival value in that parents know which young to protect, and ensures that the offspring are not rejected.

Critical or sensitive?

Research has shown that if young birds are kept in isolation, the imprinting period can be extended beyond the length of the normal critical period. For this reason, Sluckin (1965) suggested that the term *sensitive* period be used rather than *critical*. Thus the length of the critical period varies according to the conditions in which the young are reared. As Hinde (1966) pointed out, the time during which a specified type of learning most readily occurs is not rigidly determined, and can be modified by environmental factors. The length of the sensitive period also varies, of course, according to species.

The end of the sensitive period is influenced by experience; it comes to an end because of the learning process itself. The learning involved in imprinting involves developing a schema of what is familiar; unfamiliar objects elicit fear and avoidance behaviour.

Activity 11

Write down those factors which contribute to imprinting.

(Suggested answer on page 348.)

Short- and long-term consequences of imprinting

Lorenz believed that imprinting occurred only in precocial birds. The biological importance of imprinting to such species is considerable. Initially, it ensures that the young follow the appropriate parent and that they stay together as a group: ducklings, for example, which do not imprint on a parent imprint on each other. Once birds have formed an attachment, they lose the tendency to follow a new moving object, reacting (as stated above) with fear. This has survival value in that a novel moving object at this stage might well be a predator.

Lorenz believed that imprinting also determines sexual preference in adulthood. The goslings which imprinted on him tried to mate with him when sexually mature. This raises two questions. Was Lorenz right, or does sexual preference develop over a longer period of time? In other words, is there a distinction to be made between *filial* and *sexual* imprinting? The second question is whether or not sexual imprinting is permanent or reversible. If imprinting is irreversible, then sexual imprinting on an appropriate adult is vital for the survival of the species.

When a newborn lamb is reared by a human foster parent, the lamb follows the human and shows little interest in its own species. The same has been found in some species of zoo animal, and hand rearing is therefore used only when there is no alternative. However, the effects of such early experience do not seem to be permanent in guinea pigs. Beauchamp and Hess (1971) reared some newborn guinea pigs with a chick and some with guinea pigs. At three weeks the young animals preferred the species with which they were reared, but eventually all preferred their own species.

Guiton (1966) investigated that irreversibility of imprinting by rearing domestic cocks in isolation for the first 47 days of life. He compared their development with communally reared cocks. The isolated cocks were fed during the imprinting period by an assistant who wore yellow rubber gloves. When tested for sexual preference, these birds would try to copulate with a stuffed yellow rubber glove, suggesting that sexual imprinting had taken place. Both groups were then reared in pens with females until they were adult, when they were tested again. Now both groups only copulated with hens. These results seem to refute Lorenz's view that imprinting is irreversible.

However, sexual imprinting has been demonstrated in numerous bird species: early experience *does* influence choice of sexual partner at maturity. A notable example of this has been demonstrated by Immelmann (1972) working with Estrildine finches, both the zebra and Bengalese varieties. When these birds were cross-fostered (zebra males raised by a Bengalese female), the zebra males preferred to court Bengalese females. Others repeated this work with female zebra finches raised by a Bengalese: the females showed a clear preference for males of the foster species. Subsequent contact with their own species did not alter this preference for the foster species.

However, the situation is complex: it is influenced by the species the bird is reared with. Where a single zebra finch is reared in a Bengalese brood (by a Bengalese female), the preference for the foster species is very strong. If the brood contains both Bengalese and zebra finches, the preference is considerably weaker.

Harris (1971) swapped herring gull eggs with those of black-headed gulls in their nesting sites. This resulted in 407 herring gull chicks being reared by black-headed gull foster parents, and 335 black-headed gull chicks being reared by herring gull foster parents. When old enough, the young herring gulls migrated with their foster parents, and Harris later found 29 mixed pairs of gulls in the colonies where he had switched the eggs, suggesting that the young birds had imprinted on the foster species.

The apparent contradictions in the evidence can be resolved. It seems that the initial following response of imprinting in young animals does not necessarily lead to a sexual preference, although it might influence it. Experience during adolescence is more important, as demonstrated by Guiton. In the natural world, sexual behaviour develops following a period of adolescence where the individual interacts socially with other members of the species.

If a bullfinch is reared in isolation, it responds to the human as to a parent, later on as to a mate. However, if the bullfinch is given the opportunity prior to its first breeding season to socialise with its own species, the preference for humans gradually disappears. But without this opportunity, the preference for humans remains (Nicolai, 1956). Thus it seems that the sensitive period for sexual imprinting is longer than for filial imprinting, and that sexual imprinting requires social interaction with conspecifics during adolescence.

Another relevant factor, as Bateson (1979) pointed out, is that it makes sense for sexual imprinting not to occur until young birds begin to develop adult plumage. Thus the characteristics of both mother and siblings contribute to sexual imprinting and the choice of sexual partner.

Activity 12

Write down some species which are precocial, and some which are altricial.

(Suggested answers on page 348.)

Attachment bonds

The bonds between female primates and their young are strong and last for a considerable time. The bond of attachment between a bonobo son and his mother are particularly strong. He grooms with her more than anyone else. His social success, and ability to compete with other males, is much influenced by his relationship with his mother, and her position in the hierarchy.

The relationship between mother and young is important for normal social development. This has been demonstrated experimentally by Harlow *et al.* (1965). Rhesus monkeys brought up in isolation developed abnormal social behaviour and rejected their young. However, when these monkeys were kept with female monkeys younger than themselves, their behaviour returned to normal.

Hinde (1974) studied the development of group-living rhesus monkeys. At first the young are very dependent, but as the infant grows, it begins to explore the world around it, with its mother providing a secure base. If the mother is removed for a time, the infant becomes distressed, although other females in the group give it attention. When its mother returns, the infant clings to her much more than before the separation. Hinde found that the effects of this separation were long lasting. Several years later these monkeys were more fearful in strange situations than those which had experienced no separation.

Bowlby (1969), influenced by the work with animals, suggested that there is a critical period in human beings from about 18 months to three years of age, when a bond of attachment is formed. Bowlby suggested that failure to form an attachment bond during this time would be likely to result in psychological difficulties in adolescence and adulthood. Bowlby was much influenced by work on imprinting and believed that in many cases the effects he described were irreversible.

Many psychologists have investigated the effects of lack of bonding in infancy on later development, and findings often seem contradictory.

It is an area where so many factors are involved that it is difficult to disentangle them. The notion of a critical period as used by Bowlby is not supported by the evidence. The situation is not as straightforward as work with other species may suggest. Early life experiences are important and may have long-term consequences. These are not necessarily irreversible however, and more research is needed in this area.

The development of a bond of attachment in human beings does not seem to meet Lorenz's criteria for imprinting: that it can take place only in a critical period, is irreversible, and affects behaviour which has yet to develop such as sexual choice. However, the concept of imprinting has become more flexible. It is no longer used solely to refer to a rapid and unique learning process which occurs in precocial birds. The way bonding develops between parent and young, with attachment behaviour directed towards a particular person (or people) resembles imprinting sufficiently to be included in the wider use of the term (see Unit 20 page 722–5).

The distinction between filial and sexual imprinting is a useful one, with the term 'filial' referring to a young animal becoming attached to the parent. Sexual imprinting can be better understood as a process extending throughout adolescence and requiring social interaction with conspecifics.

Imprinting, both filial and sexual, can be considered as taking place during a sensitive period varying considerably in length. The term 'critical' is best used when referring to physical or embryonic development.

Early experience clearly has long-term consequences in many species, although the extent to which it can be modified by later experience varies considerably. A vast amount of evidence points to the importance of critical or sensitive periods where input from the environment is needed at a certain time if a given behaviour is to develop normally. During maturation there are times when the brain is particularly sensitive to certain stimuli. These periods vary in onset and length, but seem to be genetically determined. Such critical periods occur during embryonic development, also in relation to the continuing development of the brain after birth.

For example, if sensory experience is interrupted for long enough, then there is a permanent deficit. In both young animals and human children, if one eye is not used for a significant length of time, the sight in that eye is impaired. Normal development of vision requires input from each eye reaching the cells in the visual cortex. If a child has a squint or a bandaged eye early in life, input from the other eye may come to dominate the visual cortex. If this lack of input to one eye happens during the critical period, the child may grow up with little sight in the eye, although there is nothing wrong with the eye itself. By the age of five years, the problem cannot be reversed even if the initial problem has been cured.

In the instances outlined above it seems justifiable to refer to those times when input from the outside world is so vital as *critical*.

Thus there are many forms of behaviour where a critical or sensitive period is involved, and where normal development is dependent on a combination of heredity and environment. The influence on social behaviour may be direct. Thus imprinting influences the social interactions of the

organism, first with its parent, and later with regard to sexual preference.

Activity 13

There is much evidence which suggests that both animals and humans are influenced by early life experiences. Carry out a small survey among friends and relatives into whether they feel this applies to them. Consider preferences for such things as music, hobbies, sport, food, art, books, etc.

Self-assessment questions

7　a　Define the term 'imprinting'.
　　b　Outline the advantages of imprinting.
　　c　Discuss whether sexual preference is determined by imprinting.
　　d　Indicate the effects on rhesus monkeys of separation from the mother.

8　a　Explain why the term 'sensitive' period is appropriate when referring to imprinting or attachment. Indicate when the term 'critical' is appropriate.
　　b　Discuss why we would expect imprinting in precocial species to differ from imprinting in altricial species.

(Suggested answers on pages 351.)

Signalling systems

Social interactions and social structure depend on the ability of organisms to communicate with one another. In response to this, a wide variety of signalling systems have evolved. Signals are used as a form of communication.

Activity 14

Imagine how it would be if you had no visual sense, no ability to hear, to smell, or to touch. How would you communicate?

Communication

Communication is surprisingly difficult to define. In everyday life, the term is used to refer to the

sharing of information between two or more individuals through coded signals. Attempts to define communication include: the transfer of information from one individual to another, or the process whereby one animal responds to a signal produced by another. Altmann (1962) defined communication as '. . . a process by which the behaviour of an individual affects the behaviour of another'.

Many biologists define the term as the transfer of information between animals. However, this definition is rather too broad. For instance, it does not make it clear whether communication is confined to transfer within a species or between species – and communication does seem to occur between species. For example, the alarm call of one species of bird may warn another species that a predator is approaching. Similarly, grazing animals may be warned of a predator by the behaviour of other species grazing in the same herd.

Foraging ants leave scent trails which allow other members of the colony to find the food supply. However, a predator such as snake may use the scent trails to locate the nest. The former is a straightforward example of communication within a species, but the latter? Is this an example of communication?

Should communication be defined so that it is limited to the evolution of signals within a species, where signaller and receiver are mutually adapted to communicate with one another? It removes the problem of trying to decide whether the fact that scent trails may lead a predator to the nest is a form of communication. What is certain, however, is that organisms do receive a considerable amount of information from other species.

Would you consider that plants in flower are communicating with bees? The plants have no nervous system and are unable to modulate a the signal, yet they communicate with bees in that the nectar guide patterns on flowers enable bees to locate the nectar. Both species benefit (Elsner, 1981).

Perhaps a more useful definition would be: communication has taken place when the behaviour or signalling from one individual changes the behaviour of another.

Although it is difficult to produce a concise definition of communication there are several defining characteristics:

- There is a signal, a sender and a receiver.
- The sender and the receiver possess appropriate structures to send and to receive signals.
- In general, the sender and the receiver are of the same species, but this is not always the case, as mentioned earlier.
- The communication has adaptive advantage to the sender, but it may or may not be of benefit to the receiver.

Activity 15

Write down some examples of communication in animals. To how many of them do the defining characteristics given in the preceding paragraph apply?

In general, the evidence suggests that a relationship has evolved between communicating animals to their mutual benefit. Take the ants for example. Their scent trails enable others from the nest to find food. This is an advantage that outweighs the penalty that the scent trails might lead a predatory snake to the nest.

The evolution of communication within a species depends on several things: what is to be communicated; how well the sensory systems (modalities) are developed; whether the signal has to travel short or long distances; and the habitat. Thus information which has to travel a long distance through dense vegetation will not be based on vision. Nor is a nocturnal species likely to use vision. There is an interaction between the type of signal used, the evolution of different sensory systems, and the function the signal has to perform.

Sense modalities

■ Touch

Sense modalities include touch, vision, hearing and smell. Touch is limited in scope for obvious reasons, yet it is one of the most basic forms of communication as virtually all living organisms respond to touch. It is an important form of communication for many invertebrates. Cockroaches and lobsters communicate through touch. They have long antennae for feelers which they use to explore about a body length ahead of them. In some termite colonies touch dominates the social interactions of blind workers.

Touch is also used by primates. Harlow and Zimmerman (1959) showed that touch (as contact) is important in young monkeys in the forming of an attachment bond. Grooming plays a vital role in maintaining social structure in primate societies.

The disadvantage of touch as a form of communication is that the animals need to be in close proximity, and it cannot be used to communicate over distance.

■ Vision

The senses of vision, hearing and smell permit communication over much greater distances. Sound and smell have advantages over vision. They can (to some extent) travel through and round obstacles such as trees and vegetation. Visual communication allows a great deal of information to be transmitted, and has the advantage in that it is directional, permitting the source of the signal to be located. However, visual signals only function over relatively short distances.

Vision is involved in alarm signals: the flashes of white, for example, seen in such species as rabbits and antelope when they flee a predator.

Visual communication is seen widely in vertebrates and in cephalopod molluscs with good eyes. These include cuttlefish, which use colour displays to convey signals to conspecifics. Also, at least 35 different communication patterns have been observed in squids and octopuses. They have flexible bodies and the ability to change colour. They are able, therefore, to change shape, position and colouration (Moynihan and Rodaniche, 1977). As you would expect, these cephalopods have good vision. Visual communication will not develop in species with poor vision.

Some birds use colour displays as a means of defining their territories. The humming bird is a good example of this. Where it is only the male who defends a territory, he is brilliantly coloured, iridescent, but the female relatively plain. Where both birds defend the territory, both are brilliantly coloured. Where only the female defends, she is the coloured one of the pair.

Colour is also used to signal breeding state, as in the red underparts of the male stickleback (see also figure 10.5). Vision is also involved in identifying the breeding state of the female.

Visual communication occurs in a great many courtship displays. The peacock is an example of this, also the lekking behaviour of grouse and the collecting of bright objects by male bower birds to attract a female. In greylag geese much is communicated through posture; posture is involved in courtship, aggression, defence and submission. Aggressive intentions are signalled visually by many species, including tigers and canids. Canids snarl, show their teeth, flatten their ears, and so on. Tigers position their ears revealing a white dot; this signals threat or aggression. Primates too have evolved various gestures and facial expressions which communicate at close quarters.

Social status may also be communicated visually. Thus rank in wolves is indicated by the position of the tail, head and ears, and general body posture. A low-ranking animal will carry its tail down, pressed between its legs. It will show

10.5 Innate releasing mechanisms

Earlier in the 20th century ethologists studying the ability of organisms to respond selectively to certain stimuli suggested that there is a relationship between a particular stimulus and a particular response. Tinbergen (1951) described this as an innate releasing mechanism (IRM).

Tinbergen himself studied this behaviour and his work is very well known. In the breeding season, the male three-spined stickleback will attack another male in breeding condition which approaches his territory. By using models, Tinbergen demonstrated that the colour red was the crucial factor in eliciting the aggression. A realistic model lacking the red colour produced little effect, but as Tinbergen (1965) wrote: 'A cigar-shaped model with just an eye and a red underside releases much more

intense attack than a perfectly shaped model which is not red.'

IRMs are not confined to aggressive behaviour however. Tinbergen and Perdeck (1950) investigated the begging response in newly hatched herring gull chicks. A series of experiments with models revealed that the most effective stimulus to elicit the chick's begging response (pecking at the parent's beak) was a red spot on a yellow beak.

The concept of innate releasing mechanisms is useful in that it has contributed to the study of the ability of organisms to respond selectively to stimuli. However, it can be criticised in that it suggests that this ability is innate. The ability to respond selectively is likely to be influenced by learning or to be acquired through learning.

flattened ears, and carry its head low. A high-ranking animal will carry its head and tail high and have pricked ears.

Visual communication is limited by the visual acuity of the observer, and by the need for sender and receiver to be within sight of each other, since vision is blocked by vegetation and other obstacles. Visual communication also requires light, or the ability to manufacture light. Fireflies have overcome the problem of light by manufacturing their own and can signal at night over long distances.

Visual signalling may be combined with a second modality, sound for example. Greylag geese signal with a combination of posture and sound. Similar postures signal greeting or aggression: the correct meaning is determined on the basis of the accompanying vocalisation.

■ Sound

Sound has the advantage in that, to a certain extent, it can go round obstacles, can be used in the dark and is easily modulated. It is very effective in that it attracts attention and is, therefore, very efficient as an alarm signal. Sound signals and the way they are delivered are closely adapted to their function. For species which live in dense vegetation, evolution will have selected for low-frequency calls as these carry best through jungle and tropical forests.

Habitat also influences calling behaviour since the higher the point from which a signal is delivered, the further it carries. Some birds sing their territorial songs from the topmost branches of trees; larks sing as they fly high over their territory.

Bird vocalisations include songs and calls. Calls are usually short and simple, and have many signalling functions for birds. Alarm calls, for example, need to travel, and evolution has shaped similar calls in several species, such as chaffinches and blackbirds. Such calls are difficult to locate. Songs tend to be more complex. In most cases it is the males which sing and this occurs mostly, but not exclusively, during the breeding season. It is likely that sexual selection has contributed to the complexity of bird song (see Unit 9). Two of its main functions seem to be to attract females and to denote a holder's territory.

Auditory signalling may enable individuals to keep in touch with each other. The young of such precocial species as sheep and guinea pigs call frequently when moving about. Such calling maintains contact and ensures that the young do not stray too far.

Some species have evolved different vocalisations in response to different types of predator. The California ground squirrel has two basic alarm calls, a chatter and a whistle. A chatter generally indicates the presence of a ground predator, a whistle a bird of prey (Owings and Leger, 1980).

Vervet monkeys (Seyfarth and Cheney, 1980) use four different alarm calls in the presence of four main predators – leopards, eagles, pythons and baboons. Research findings reveal that the monkeys distinguish between the different predators on the basis of the calls.

Similarly complex signals have been observed in whale and dolphin vocalisations (Payne, 1983). Sound allows much greater flexibility than sight for underwater communication, and it would be expected that those animals which need to communicate over distance in water would evolve sound. Sound travels considerably further and faster in water than on land. Sight is not nearly as useful under water as it is confined to those animals in close contact with each other. Marine mammals such as dolphins and whales communicate mainly on the basis of sound. Dolphins also communicate through touch, nudging, slapping and stroking one another. Taste is also involved in finding mates and obtaining food. Their main sense, however, is hearing. Sight and smell are relatively unimportant.

Activity 16

In spring or early summer, listen out for birds singing and try to locate the singer. It will often be perched on a high branch or the top of a tree; a lark will be flying high, probably above a meadow.

Dolphins are vocal animals which use a wide range of sound for communication and navigation. They have adapted to life in water by developing sound-producing and sound-detecting systems. Through sound, dolphins recognise one another – mate, young, friend, enemy, prey and predator. They are capable of about 30 different sounds, each animal producing a characteristic call which enables one dolphin to recognise another dolphin at a distance, and to keep in touch with others which are out of sight (Janik, 1997).

Dolphins also produce ultrasonic sounds which they use as a form of *sonar* or echo-location system. The sonar clicks are achieved by air being pushed forcibly through passages and sinuses in the dolphin's head. An oval-shaped bulge on the forehead of the dolphin reveals the presence of the melon, the organ which focuses the sounds into a beam. The animal is able to use the beam of sound to scan the water ahead. Since the dolphin uses sound to sense its underwater surroundings, it needs to detect the returning echoes. In its lower jaw is the 'acoustic window', from where the echo is transmitted to the inner ear.

All the cetaceans (marine mammals) navigate and communicate in this way. The great whales produce a variety of sounds. The blue and humpback whales for example, sing *songs* that can be heard over great distances. The blue whale is very large and produces very low notes which travel as far as 2000 kilometres.

Such large animals require vast amounts of food. This makes it difficult for them to move about and feed in groups. They remain within hearing of each other, using sound to maintain sociality. Thus the grouping of these great animals is based on sound rather than vision.

The smaller cetaceans such as dolphins, porpoises and killer whales can swim very fast. This necessitates accurate navigation. The ultrasounds emitted by these animals permit both the detection of obstacles ahead and the nature of such obstacles: dolphins can distinguish not only the distance of an object but also its shape, texture and flexibility.

■ Smell (chemical communication)

Organisms also communicate with one another on the basis of chemical stimuli, usually on the basis of smelling or tasting such substances. The substances involved are usually referred to as *pheromones*. These are substances which, when received by an individual of the same species, release a specific reaction, a definite behaviour or developmental process. Rogel (1978) pointed out that a stimulus need not be olfactory (based on scent) in order to be a pheromone; it may be ingested or absorbed.

Chemical forms of communication are used by most animals, including those that use other forms of communication. They are probably the most widely used form of communication, and have numerous advantages. They can travel long distances, they can diffuse round objects, and can be used in the dark. They are relatively stable and can be used to communicate without the need for the signaller to be present, as in territorial marking behaviour. Several members of the cat family, including the cheetah, have ranges which overlap. Since they prefer to avoid each other, the age of a scent mark provides useful information. An animal or group is able to avoid meeting others of the same species by keeping away from an area where the signals are fresh.

Chemical signals can be detected over considerable distances. The male silkworm moth can detect the scent of a female from over two kilometres away, and is able to use it to guide him to her. However, chemical signals are considerably attenuated (weakened) with distance, and for this reason only simple messages can be transmitted. Chemical signals are also limited in that they cannot be changed quickly. Nor can they be used to provide a pattern of communication, as can be done with sound and vision. For this reason they are often used to leave a relatively simple but stable message. Thus many animals, including canids, lemurs, deer, etc, use chemical signals to mark their territory. Chemical signals are also used to convey information about the condition of breeding females. They are also important in maintaining the social structure of eusocial insects such as the honeybee.

Pheromones (figure 10.6) can be divided into two classes: primer and releaser pheromones. Releaser pheromones produce an immediate change in the behaviour of the recipient. For example, the mongoose reacts to the scent of a strange animal with aggression. Rasa (1973) therefore suggested that the scent of the mongoose acts as a threat. Several species scent mark in response to existing scent marks. These include animals such as guinea pigs and dogs.

Activity 17

If you have the opportunity to take a male dog for a walk, observe where it urinates. This will be at frequent intervals, and likely to occur after the dog has been sniffing the scent of a dog which scent marked the tree or lamp-post previously. The behaviour is essentially the same as that of a wolf patrolling the boundaries of its territory, and marking whenever it encounters the scent of another wolf. Wolves also visit scent posts which they mark regularly.

10.6 Cupid's darts?

Snails are hermaphrodites (each has both male and female reproductive organs). They exchange sperm by, in effect, each partner harpooning the other with a dart which allows the transfer of sperm. Working with the common garden snail, Koene and Chase (1998) have found that these darts are coated with a pheromone. This pheromone contributes to the success of the sperm by increasing the accessibility of the female copulatory canal, and by closing off an organ which digests sperm.

Primer pheromones, in contrast, are slow to act, and prolonged stimulation is required. The maintenance of social structure in eusocial insects is due to the action of primer pheromones. For instance, the queen honeybee secretes a pheromone which prevents the workers from rearing queens. The effect of primer pheromones can also be seen in the oestrus cycle of some species. Bruce (1970) wrote that in some species the male exerts a controlling influence over oestrus. When female mice are grouped and no male is present, oestrus is suppressed. The introduction of a male results in the start of a new cycle, with the oestrus cycle of the group becoming synchronised (Whitten, 1966; Bruce, 1970). Similar effects have been observed in other species. It has frequently been observed that the menstrual cycles of women who live together often become sychronised. Recent research has revealed that this is due to pheromones secreted by the women (Stern and McClintock, 1998). Despite this finding, evidence tends to suggest that pheromones are of relatively little importance in human behaviour, and it is unlikely that research chemists will succeed in producing a substance that will act as an attractant of one sex to the other (figure 10.7).

Communication is not always honest. There are several examples of this, a notable one being the female firefly, which attracts males of another species by sending a signal indicating willingness to mate. She eats the male when he arrives. Mimicry is another example of deceit (see Unit 8).

Humans are highly efficient communicators. We communicate by sound, vision, touch and, perhaps, pheromones. We communicate non-verbally and through language. Is language unique to us? This is an area of much discussion and controversy. It is considered in Unit 11.

10.7 Love chemicals?

Biochemists are still trying to identify the pheromones which act as sexual attractants in humans. Some companies have claimed to have done so, and market perfumes accordingly. One such perfume contained a pig pheromone. Since pheromones (unlike hormones which have similar effects in different species) are species-specific, the effect of the pig pheromone is likely to attract pigs rather than humans!

Activity 18

You can investigate the calling behaviour which keeps the young of some precocial species in contact with the mother. When sheep have lambs, or shortly after ducklings have hatched, stand and listen for the calls of the young when they become separated. You may also hear the mother respond. Guinea pigs show similar behaviour and are well worth watching if you have access to a mother with young living in an area large enough for such behaviour to be shown.

Self-assessment questions

9   Explain why the term 'communication' is difficult to define.

10 a   Outline some examples of signalling systems in relation to sociality.
    b   Briefly explain the difference between releaser pheromones and primer pheromones.

11 Compare the advantages and disadvantages of at least two forms of communication.

(Suggested answers on page 351–2.)

Unit summary

- *Altruism* (or apparent altruism) has been observed in many species. Altruistic behaviour is behaviour which benefits another. Although some behaviour appears to be altruistic, it may have greater benefit for the individual displaying it than for the recipient.
- On the basis of Darwin's *theory of natural selection* we would expect animals to be selfish rather than altruistic.
- *Group selection theory* suggests that altruism has evolved because altruistic behaviour favours the group. This theory is unsatisfactory because a few selfish animals in a group of altruistic individuals would survive and reproduce at the expense of the unselfish ones.
- *Kin selection* explains altruism on the grounds that altruism towards relatives benefits the individual's genes although it is costly to the individual.
- *Gene selection theory* states that selection occurs at the level of the genes, not the individual.
- Research suggests that some animals may show altruism towards non-related individuals; this

is known as *reciprocal altruism*. Reciprocal altruism is explained on the basis of reciprocity, with one animal benefiting on one occasion, the other on a later occasion (also known as tit-for-tat). For reciprocal altruism to occur, animals need to be able to recognise each other.
- The *Prisoner's Dilemma* is a problem based on games theory which examines when cooperation is or is not likely to occur.
- There are many forms of *social interaction*, ranging from highly structured societies to species whose only social contact is for reproductive purposes. Social interactions can be categorised as *cooperative* or *competitive*.
- Group living confers advantages and disadvantages. Benefits of group living include less risk of predation and greater success in hunting. Disadvantages include competition for food; increased predation in some instances.
- *Territoriality* and *dominance* are forms of sociality which minimise aggression.
- *Early experience* has consequences for later social development.

Summary cont'd.

- *Imprinting* refers to a process whereby young precocial animals follow their parent soon after birth or hatching. Lorenz believed that imprinting can only occur within a strict time limit which he described as *critical.* Subsequent research suggests that the time for imprinting is *sensitive* rather than critical as it can be extended in certain conditions.
- *Filial imprinting* refers to the attachment of young birds or animals to the parent.
- *Sexual imprinting* is a slower process where interactions with parent and siblings determine sexual preference.
- The attachment between mother and young is important for normal social development in rhesus monkeys.
- Bowlby suggested that there is a critical period in human development where a bond of attachment between infant and mother figure is formed.
- *Communication* plays an important role in social interactions.
- The evolution of communication systems within a species depends on several factors.
- Some information transmitted during intra-specific communication may benefit another species.
- *Sensory modalities* are tactile, auditory, visual and chemical. Animals possess signalling systems based on more than one sense modality.
- Communications are not invariably honest.
- Some species, such as vervet monkeys, dolphins and whales, have evolved complex vocalisations.

Terms to define

altricial
cooperation
epideictic
imprinting

kin selection
precocial
selfish gene
sociality

Further reading

Dunbar, R I M (1988) *Primate Social Systems*, Cornell University Press, Ithaca, NY and Croom Helm, London.

An absorbing account of the complex social lives of primates.

Lorenz, K (1952) *King Solomon's Ring*, University Paperbacks, Methuen.

A non-technical approach to animal behaviour which is often amusing and always interesting.

Tinbergen, N (1965) *Social Behaviour in Animals*, Methuen, London.

This very readable book includes details of Tinbergen's remarkable studies of animal behaviour.

Answers

Suggested answers to activities

3

Natural selection would favour your sacrifice in option b. This is due to the fact that if you sacrificed yourself in this instance, the likelihood is that more copies of the gene would be passed on than if you saved yourself. In option a, you, two brothers or eight cousins are equivalent in terms of passing on the gene. There is no difference between you and your two brothers or two cousins on which natural selection could operate.

4

(You may have chosen different examples, including epideictic behaviour.)

- *Signalling the approach of a predator.* Altruistic interpretation: benefits others, but may draw attention of the predator to the caller. Selfish interpretation: if the individual sounded no alarm but flew into a tree, it would be alone and vulnerable; by sounding the alarm it causes others to fly into the tree also. It is now one of many.
- *Stotting behaviour in Thompson's gazelle.* Altruistic interpretation: the behaviour of jumping into the air suggests the gazelles are trying to attract the predator's attention to itself and away from others. Selfish interpretation: the behaviour is informing the predator that the individual is young and hard to catch; the predator would have a better chance with another gazelle.

9

This resembles the escape behaviour found in some group-living animals where individuals scatter to avoid a predator, moving rapidly in all directions. It is difficult to focus on one out of so many, and the predator becomes confused. The problem in trying to catch one of several objects moving fast towards you is very similar.

11

Factors which influence imprinting include: effort involved in following imprinting object; strongest imprinting most likely to occur within a limited time span; detectable or conspicuous imprinting object; auditory interactions between mother and young; olfactory stimuli. (Not all of these apply to all species; the type of imprinting to which these apply is filial imprinting.)

12

Precocial: ducks, geese, chickens, guinea pigs, sheep, goats, etc.
Altricial: blackbirds, dogs, bullfinches, dogs, cats, monkeys, human beings, etc.

Suggested answers to self-assessment questions

1

a   Both altruism and selfish behaviour are defined on the basis of the consequences of the behaviour, not on the subjective intentions of the individual. Behaviour of an animal which benefits another at some cost to itself is described as altruistic: such behaviour may reduce the likelihood of the survival of the altruist, whilst improving the chances of the other. When an organism acts in such a way as to benefit itself at the expense of another, the behaviour is described as selfish.

b
- Giving an alarm call which warns others of danger is thought to be altruistic because it may draw the attention of the predator to the caller.
- Eusocial insects such as bees and termites provide examples of altruistic behaviour. Many in the colony carry out the various tasks for maintaining the colony, forgoing the opportunity to reproduce.
- Parents are altruistic in that they devote considerable resources to their offspring at a cost to themselves.

(You may, of course, have chosen different examples.)

c   Natural selection is ruthless and favours those qualities which enable an organism to (i) survive and (ii) reproduce. An organism which behaves altruistically is less likely to survive, whilst the recipient's chance of survival is increased. On the basis of Darwin's theory of natural selection, therefore, we would expect selfish rather than unselfish behaviour to evolve, with organisms putting their own interests first, regardless of those of others.

2

a   Wynne Edwards suggested that natural selection acts on the group or species. Thus if a group benefits through individuals being altruistic to one another, then this behaviour is favoured by natural selection.
One of Wynne Edwards's examples is based on the behaviour of birds where they flock together to facilitate population estimation (known as epideictic behaviour). In a severe winter and when numbers are large, the birds reduce their rate of breeding, so that the number of birds in the flock is not too large for the resources available. This benefits the group rather than the individual (for more detail see page 320).
Alternative examples of behaviour benefiting the group rather than the individual may be found in eusocial insects; examples also include the warning signals given by some social-living organisms.

b The problem with group or species selection theory is that it seems very unlikely that group selection would select a trait which would *not* be favoured by individual selection. It is easy to imagine the benefits to a group if all behave altruistically to one another. However, migration from outside the group might result in a selfish individual joining the group (a genetic mutation could have the same effect). This individual would take the best food, best breeding site and behave in such a way as to further its own interest. It would survive at the expense of the altruistic animals. Its genes would be passed onto its offspring and gradually more and more of the group would consist of selfish individuals. The unselfish individuals would be overwhelmed by selfish ones. Thus traits which benefit a group are unlikely to last: they are likely to lose out in competition with traits which benefit the individual.

3
a These terms are based on the principle that natural selection may favour behaviour where an organism gives help to individuals which share some of the same genes, even though giving such help is costly to the individual. Thus natural selection would favour altruistic behaviour towards other individuals which share the same genes, for example parents towards offspring.
b The theories predict that altruism would be found between related animals, not merely from parents towards young. An example is that of Belding's ground squirrels, a social species liable to predation. If a predator approaches, one of the colony will sound the alarm. This is altruistic since this increases the risk of the caller being taken. Research has shown that most calling takes place between female animals which are closely related.
c i This is because if the behaviour helped animals which do not show similar behaviour then natural selection will not favour those that do.

4
a Some forms of behaviour appear at first sight to be altruistic. However, when investigated more closely such behaviour may be found to benefit the animal displaying the behaviour rather than the recipient.
b The theories which seek to explain altruistic behaviour in terms of natural selection state that it benefits individuals which share the same genes: the closer the relationship, the more likely the occurrence of altruistic behaviour, since selection occurs at gene level, and the more closely any two individuals are related, the more likely they are to share the same gene for altruism. Thus altruism between close relations contributes to the survival of these genes. If animals are not related, this is not the case; helping an unrelated individual will not contribute to the survival of the altruist's genes.

c Reciprocal altruism seeks to explain such behaviour on the basis that animals which show such behaviour both benefit: thus animal A benefits on one occasion; animal B benefits on another.
d Animals need to be able to recognise each other as individuals, and be able to refuse altruism to an individual who accepts it but does not return it. Also, animals need to live long enough, and in stable groupings. This allows them to encounter each other on repeated occasions where they can recognise one another and show altruism to one another.
e ■ An example of such behaviour has been reported in vampire bats. They fly out at night to find a meal of blood, and it is common for an individual to fail to obtain a meal. However, bats which have fed will share their meal with an individual that has not. The favour is returned when the situation is reversed. The more any two bats associate with one another, the greater the likelihood that each will favour the other over sharing a meal (Wilkinson, 1984; 1985).
■ Reciprocal altruism has also been observed in vervet monkeys (Seyfarth and Cheney, 1984). Grooming takes place between related and unrelated animals. Vervet monkeys emit a call to obtain help in a dispute. The likelihood of a non-related animal responding was greater when that individual had recently been groomed by the monkey calling for help. There is a further example of reciprocal altruism on pages 326–7, but it is important to remember that it has not been established for certain that it does take place. Further, because of the conditions necessary for it to occur, it is likely to be rare.

5
a Although this is a term familiar to all of us, it is difficult to define because almost all organisms interact to some extent during some part of their lives. Social interactions vary from the brief coming together of male and female during mating, to the highly structured societies of the social insects. The wide variations in sociality found in different species contribute to the difficulty in defining what is meant by the term.
Great diversity in social behaviour is found among the vertebrates. In some social groupings individuals forage and sleep close to one another, they mate and rear their young within the group, they recognise one another. Examples include baboons and elephants. Other species are essentially solitary, such as the orang utan and Syrian hamster. Yet even here some social interaction takes place in the context of reproduction and care of young.
Some species of insect are clearly solitary, the mason wasp for example, while eusocial insects are *highly* social. The term 'social' refers to interactions of many kinds. The difficulty arises because anything occuring between two or

more individuals may be termed social, whether temporary or long term; nor are *all* interactions necessarily social.

b i Cooperative interactions include those found in eusocial insects such as ants and bees, where high levels of organisation and cooperation result in an efficient and structured society. Males and females of many species cooperate in the production and care of young. In birds this is likely to include nest building, incubation and feeding of young. Female elephants cooperate in protecting infants. Some species cooperate in hunting prey, for example wolves. Grooming is an important social activity, and involves cooperation.

ii Examples of competitive interactions include fighting for possession of a mate, for position in a dominance hierarchy, in defence of a territory and for access to food. Competitive interactions also occur between parent and offspring when the young are sufficiently mature to require less care, and the parent's interests are better served by conserving resources for future offspring.

c Social groupings may vary on a continuum from a brief and temporary aggregation based on external factors such as food, to long-term interactions based on attraction, social exchange and kinship (as found in some primates, including baboons). For example, many birds descending onto a loaded birdtable is a temporary aggregation based on a food supply and is not considered as truly social, although there may be interactions between them. Thus some species of bird may become dominant over others. Animals may also cluster together to reduce risks of predation. Truly social behaviour involves individuals reacting to each other (rather than to external factors) on the basis of attraction, cooperation or hostility.

6

a i Animals which hunt in groups may have greater success in obtaining food. Many social-living carnivores, ranging from spiders to wolves to whales, cooperate in hunting. Spotted hyenas hunting wildebeest calves in pairs are more successful than when hunting alone (Kuuk, 1972). In some species, success in hunting increases in relation to the number of hunters (Packer and Ruttan, 1988). Packer (1980, 1986) questions whether lionesses do cooperate during the kill, and whether groups of lions are more successful than when hunting alone. Harris hawks hunt for prey in family groups (Bednarz, 1988); group fishing in blackheaded gulls provides each with a better return than fishing alone (Gottmark *et al.*, 1980).

Group living also enables group members to learn of the whereabouts of food (see page 330).

Cooperation is essential in the pursuit and capture of the colobus monkey by chimpanzees. A lone chimpanzee could not succeed.

Group hunting can benefit those involved even when they are merely hunting together, rather than cooperating. Several animals attacking can bring down larger prey than a single animal. Group hunting also reduces the likelihood of the kill being taken by other animals.

ii Animals which live in groups are less likely to be taken by a predator. This is partly on the basis of relatively large numbers (dilution), also the nearer an individual is to the centre of a herd or colony, the less likely it is to be taken (the selfish herd principle – Hamilton, 1971). This would seem to apply to the fieldfare: Andersson and Wiklund (1978) found that the nearer a nest is to the centre of a colony, the lower the risk of predation. Puffins reduce predation by flying together between their nests and the sea. In addition, other individuals may attack a predator which enters the colony. Male bluegill sunfish guard their eggs. When the nest is in the centre of the colony, males from other nests also attack a predator. Many species cooperate in deterring predators; birds such as chaffinches and wagtails will mob a predator. Musk oxen form protective circles round the young. Group living also makes it more likely that a predator will be detected since there are many eyes and ears alert for danger. A large colony of cliff swallows detects the threat sooner than a small colony (Brown and Brown, 1989). Mongooses, rabbits, prairie dogs and many species of bird, emit warning signals.

Animals which live in groups can evade predation by all moving together, or scattering in several directions, thus confusing the predator.

As part of a group of adults and their offspring, young animals are less at risk of predation due to relatively large numbers (dilution) and to the fact that in such species as zebra and musk oxen, the males aid in defending the young against predators.

b Group living is likely to result in increased competition for food, with some individuals obtaining more at the expense of others. Such direct competition occurs in many species, including hyenas.

Competition may be indirect. If a colony is very large, some individuals will have to travel further afield to obtain food. Some members of a colony of Mexican free-tailed bats may have to travel 200 kilometres (Tuttle, 1988). Animals feeding as a group make more noise and are more visible, therefore may attract predators.

c   All are considered to have implications for the evolution of social systems. (If your answer was different, read the relevant pages through again. These variables are likely to interact.)

7

a   Find 'imprinting' in the Glossary.

b   Imprinting in precocial species such as ducks and goslings ensures that the newly hatched young follow the appropriate parent and stay together as a group: ducklings which do not imprint on the parent do so on each other. Further, once imprinting has taken place, large moving objects elicit fear rather than a tendency to follow, thus reducing the risk of predation. Imprinting also enables the young to learn the characteristics of the species; sexual imprinting ensures they prefer to mate with their own species. Maternal imprinting enables the mother to recognise her own offspring, and which to protect. It also ensures that she does not reject them.

c   First, it is useful to distinguish between filial and sexual imprinting. Filial imprinting refers to the response of young animals to follow and become attached to their parents. Sexual imprinting refers to the development of a sexual preference; both occur early in life. Cross-fostering in finches strongly suggests that sexual preference in zebra finch males is influenced by sexual imprinting. Work also suggests that both parent *and* siblings have an influence on sexual preference (Guiton, 1966; Nicolai, 1956). This helps to explain the seemingly contradictory evidence regarding the permanence or otherwise of sexual imprinting. Many studies have failed to distinguish between imprinting in, say, newly hatched young (filial imprinting) and the slower process which takes place during social interactions prior to full sexual maturity. Thus filial imprinting probably influences sexual preference, but in natural conditions sexual preference would be based on a longer period of social interaction with conspecifics.

    d   Harlow *et al.*'s (1965) work suggested that monkeys brought up in isolation did not develop normal social behaviour. However, subsequent research where the monkeys experienced the company of younger females indicates that these effects are not permanent. In contrast to this, Hinde (1974) showed that the effects of separation from its mother on an infant rhesus monkey may indeed have long term consequences.

8

a   Research has shown that even when a particular time has been identified, imprinting occasionally takes place outside it. For example, Hess (1958) found that most imprinting in mallard ducklings occurred 13–16 hours after hatching, but that some took place beyond this period. Several studies have shown that when young birds are kept in isolation, the length of the imprinting period can be extended. The end of the imprinting period is influenced by the process itself: once the individual has imprinted on the imprinting object, unfamiliar objects are avoided. The term 'sensitive' is appropriate therefore, since although research suggests there is a period of time when imprinting is most likely to happen, the timing is *not* critical: if imprinting does not occur in this time, it will occur outside it.

The term 'critical' is appropriate in reference to embryonic development, or to when the brain is still developing and needs sensory input at certain times if it is to develop normally. If the sensory input is not available at the right time, the brain's development is affected. The effects are permanent; the timing is *critical*.

b   Precocial young are relatively mature at birth or hatching, and able to move around very soon afterwards. Their perceptual systems are well-developed, and the young are very soon able to follow the mother around. Because of their mobility and relative independence, such young might easily become separated from the mother, and lost. Rapid imprinting, where the young learn to follow the mother, is therefore both possible and necessary. Altricial young are helpless at birth, highly dependent and, in many species, blind and unable to move. The young are therefore confined to the den or nest in which they were born or hatched; the parent or parents can leave them to search for food and return to feed them. In some species the mother stays with the young; in others the young cling to the mother and are carried around by her. Because of their immobility they are not able to actively follow the mother. Also, their sensory systems tend to be insufficiently developed to allow for rapidly learning the characteristics of the mother. Since the young are immature and do not move around, rapid imprinting is not necessary. They learn the characteristics of the parent and the species gradually.

9

One reason why it is difficult to define communication concerns whether or not it should be confined to communication *within* a species, where the signaller and receiver are mutually adapted to send and receive signals. This limitation on the use of the term would exclude the information provided by prey to predator, for example when scent trails left by ants lead a predator to the nest. An alternative attempt to define communication defines it as a process where the behaviour of one animal affects the behaviour of another. In this case, communication both within and between species fits the definition. Thus a warning signal given by one species also alerts another species to the danger and affects its behaviour. But are the ants communicating to the predator?

Flowers do not behave, yet flowers in bloom provide foraging bees with valuable information regarding the availability of pollen and nectar. This seems to be a form of communication in that the behaviour of the bees changes: they react to the information presented by the flower.

10

a   Touch is important in the formation of attachment bonds between mother and young in primates, and grooming plays an important role in forming alliances and maintaining social structure. Touch is essential for the social interaction of blind workers in termite colonies. Visual signalling is involved in many aspects of social behaviour. Thus many species use visual displays to attract a mate during courtship. Many species, including dogs and wolves, tigers and geese, use visual signalling to indicate threat and submission. Visual displays are used by hummingbirds to define territorial boundaries; the colour red signals readiness to breed in a male stickleback and elicits aggression in other breeding males.

Vocalisation in the form of song is used by many bird species to mark out territory, and to attract a female or females. Several social-living species call at the approach of a predator, thus enabling conspecifics to avoid danger. Cetaceans use sound to recognise individuals and maintain contact with each other. Auditory signalling between a mallard female and her young contributes to the imprinting process, and the parents and young of some precocial species such as sheep and guinea pigs maintain contact through calling.

Pheromones are essential in maintaining the structure of eusocial insect colonies, ensuring that each group of individuals carries out appropriate tasks. Pheromones or chemical stimuli have an essential role in attracting a male to a female in breeding condition. This is true of a wide range of species including moths and hamsters. Pheromones also regulate the breeding cycles of social species such as mice. Chemical stimuli also function to demarcate territorial boundaries, and may elicit aggression. (Additional information concerning signalling systems, sexual behaviour and aggression can be found in Unit 9.)

b   Releaser pheromones produce an immediate change in the behaviour of the recipient. Thus the scent of an oestrus female will produce sexual behaviour in a male; the scent of a strange animal will produce aggression in some species. for example the mongoose.

Primer pheromones act slowly. In mice a primer pheromone secreted by the male synchronises oestrus in the females; the social structure of eusocial insects is maintained by primer pheromones.

11

One of the main advantages of touch as a form of communication is that most organisms respond to it. It is a useful means of communication in species which live in close contact with one another. However, it is very limited because, of course, it is only available to organisms in close proximity. In contrast, chemical signalling can be used to communicate over long distances, and can transmit information when the signaller is no longer present, as in territorial scent marking. Such a signal can last for a long time. The disadvantages of this form of signalling is that the signal weakens considerably over distance; further, only simple messages can be transmitted. Unlike sound and vision, chemical signalling cannot be used to transmit patterns of information. It is, however, well suited to providing stable messages and in maintaining social structure in social-living species. Chemical signalling has the advantage over vision in that it is not impeded by obstacles such as trees because it can diffuse round them.

Vision, however, is more flexible. It can alter in response to change, and can transmit detailed patterns of information. It also allows the source of the signal to be located. However, unlike chemical communication, it can only communicate over relatively short distances, where sender and receiver are in view of each other. It is blocked by undergrowth, and requires light (except for those species which manufacture their own light source, such as fireflies). It is effective in providing alarm signals, but is less effective than sound, which attracts attention.

Attracting attention is one of the advantages of signalling with sound, which is why it is particularly suitable as a warning signal. Sound can be used to communicate over much greater distances than vision, and is not impeded where obstacles such as trees intervene between signaller and receiver. Sound can be used day or night, and enables individuals not in visual contact to keep in touch with one another. It is far more useful underwater than vision because it can be used to communicate over great distances, whereas to communicate visually, underwater animals need to be close together. Sound is similar to vision in that a sound signal can be changed quickly to adapt to a changing situation; it allows for complex communication as shown by vervet monkeys, dolphins and whales.

Unit 11

The Analysis of Behaviour

Gillian Lang

This unit covers:

Analysis of behaviour

Foraging and homing

Animal language

Evolutionary explanations of behaviour

By the end of this unit, you should be able to:

- describe and evaluate classical and operant conditioning
- discuss the application of the principles of learning to behaviour in the natural environment, including foraging and homing
- show knowledge of animal language and critical awareness of attempts to teach human language to non-human animals
- show understanding of evolutionary explanations of human behaviour, and of their strengths and limitations.

Unit 11   Contents

Analysis of behaviour

Comparative psychology

The evolutionary approach in psychology holds the view that the behaviour of humans and other animals is the result of evolution through natural selection. Behaviour in this sense includes the ability to learn, as shown to its greatest extent by human beings, and the innate, stereotyped behaviour patterns found, for example, in some insects.

Comparative psychologists of behaviourist investigations study animal behaviour with the aim of increasing our understanding of human behaviour. The comparative psychologist seeks to extrapolate from the behaviour of animals and animal societies to human behaviour.

Ethologists seek to determine and understand the behaviour of a species as it occurs in its natural environment. The ethologist will often begin by working in the field, but it is legitimate to transfer the species being studied to the laboratory, providing conditions are kept as natural as possible (see Tinbergen's research on IRMs, Unit 10).

It is also possible, of course, to carry out experimental studies of animals in the field.

Some comparative psychologists and ethologists do, in fact, generalise from the findings obtained by ethologists to increase our understanding of human behaviour. However, this is not the *purpose* of ethological study.

Learning theory

Behaviourists are comparative psychologists who study non-human animals under laboratory conditions. This means that they study a narrower range of behaviour than ethologists – who are also interested in the learning abilities of the animals they observe. The key features of behaviourist investigations are as follows:

- Investigations are carried out in laboratories.
- The animals used are usually bred for the purpose and have never experienced life in the wild.
- The range of species studied is narrow. Rats and pigeons are popular because they have a reasonably developed cortex and are easy to maintain. Behaviourists who have the necessary resources and facilities have studied more advanced species such as primates and dolphins.

Activity 1

Contrast the key features of behaviourist investigations outlined above and the ethological approach.

(Suggested answer on page 384.)

Learning is the process where behaviour and understanding are modified as a result of experience. There are several definitions of learning, for instance 'learning refers to a more or less permanent change in behaviour which occurs as a result of practice' (Kimble, 1964, p. 2) or 'we can define learning as that process which manifests itself by adaptive changes in individual behaviour as a result of experience' (Thorpe, 1956, cited in Kimble, 1964, p. 2).

Behaviourists stress the importance of the environment in the development of behaviour. They are concerned with objective, measurable responses, with identifying a predictable relationship between a specific response and a given environmental stimulus. They do not seek causes within the organism. This is known as the **stimulus-response** (S-R) approach.

A **stimulus** can be defined as any event which has an effect on an organism; a **response** as an action or a physiological reaction. Early **behaviourism** held that all behaviour from the simple to the complex could be explained in terms of rewards and punishments, and on the formation of associations between stimuli and responses. However, as you read the following pages you will find that the idea of automatic associations is an oversimplification of what happens during learning.

In 1913, Watson defined psychology as the Science of Behaviour. In his book *Behaviorism* (1913) he stressed the importance of studying observable, measurable behaviour. His main thesis was that psychology should be objective.

The Russian physiologist Pavlov was one of the first to take an objective approach to learning. He studied the conditioned reflex in dogs. This area of psychology is now referred to as classical or respondent (sometimes Pavlovian) conditioning.

Activity 2

Do you rely on an alarm clock to wake you in the mornings? Have you found yourself waking before the alarm goes off? If so, why do you think this is?

(Suggested answer on page 384.)

Classical conditioning

Pavlov was a Nobel prize-winning physiologist studying digestion in dogs. He had experienced problems with some of his experiments because the dogs would salivate before they were given food. They salivated, for instance, when they saw or heard the assistant who normally gave them their food. Pavlov (1927) wrote '... the secretion may be provoked even by the sight of the person who brought (the food), or by the sound of his footsteps' (p. 13).

Pavlov realised that an association was being formed between the salivary reflex and stimuli such as food containers and footsteps. This so interested him that he redirected his research to study it. A small opening made in the dog's cheek allowed saliva to be collected and precisely measured, thus indicating the strength of a response.

He carried out detailed investigations into the salivation reflex and discovered that any stimulus or change which directly preceded the food could itself produce salivation. He established that at the start of the experiments the dogs salivated only when meat powder was placed on the tongue, and not to a neutral stimulus such as a tone. No stimulus, of course, is entirely neutral; the auditory stimuli used by Pavlov produced an attention or orienting response in the dogs, but were neutral in that they did not elicit salivation.

In a typical experiment the hungry dog was placed on a stand and restrained in a harness. A ticking metronome or tone was sounded, followed about two seconds later by the meat powder. Initially, the dog salivated to the powder. After several such pairings the dog would salivate to the sound of the tone (or metronome) alone. The dog had been conditioned to respond to a neutral stimulus (the tone) with salivation. Before conditioning, salivation occurred only in response to the food.

Thus Pavlov demonstrated that the dog had learned to respond to a neutral stimulus with a reflex response.

Prior to conditioning, the original response was salivation and the original stimulus was food, so the food is known as the unconditioned stimulus (UCS) and salivation as the unconditioned response (UCR) (figure 11.1). After pairing the food (UCS) with the tone, the dog now salivates to the tone. Pavlov therefore called this the conditioned response (CR) and the tone the conditioned stimulus (CS).

The example of conditioning described above involves what is called an *appetitive* response, since food is the UCS. Other reflex responses can be

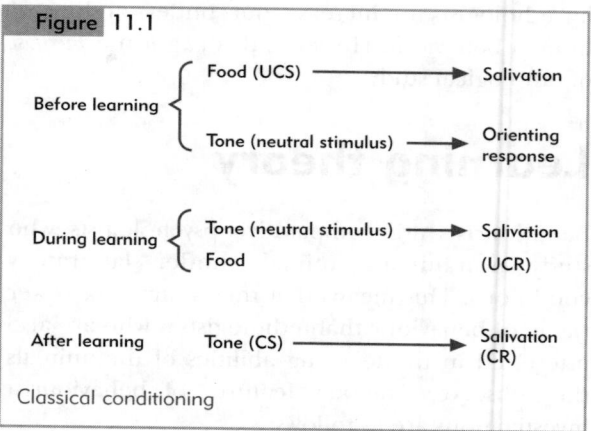

Figure 11.1

Before learning
{
Food (UCS) ⟶ Salivation
Tone (neutral stimulus) ⟶ Orienting response
}

During learning
{
Tone (neutral stimulus) ⟶ Salivation
Food (UCR)
}

After learning
Tone (CS) ⟶ Salivation (CR)

Classical conditioning

conditioned, fear for example. If a flashing light is paired with a brief electric shock to the feet of a rat, the rat will learn to respond with a fear response to the light alone. Few such pairings are needed and the conditioned response (fear of the light) may develop after a single pairing (Le Doux, 1997).

If a response such as fear of a light can be acquired through classical conditioning, might this be how some people develop a phobia?

Watson and Rayner's (1920) study of Little Albert suggested that this is possible. Watson and Rayner used Albert, an 11-month-old baby in an institution, to demonstrate that Pavlovian conditioning applied to human beings. They first established that Albert was not frightened of certain things including a white rat and a Father Christmas mask.

At the start of the conditioning procedure, the white rat was presented to Albert who reached towards it. As he did so, a loud noise was sounded behind him. Albert began to cry, apparently frightened by the noise. This procedure was repeated on a further six occasions. The rat was then presented alone. When Albert saw the white rat, he was frightened and pulled away from it.

Watson and Rayner had conditioned Albert to respond with fear to something he had previously found attractive.

Activity 3

Write down the UCS, UCR, CS and CR in the case of Little Albert.

(Suggested answers on page 384.)

Pavlov carried out extensive studies of the variables which affect conditioning. He found that when a conditioned response has been acquired, similar, but not identical, stimuli will elicit the response. Thus if a dog has been conditioned to salivate to a tone of a particular frequency (the CS), it will also salivate to tones of higher and lower frequencies. The greater the similarity between the new stimuli and the CS, the stronger the conditioned response. This is known as stimulus *generalisation* (figure 11.2).

In Watson and Rayner's study, Little Albert responded with fear to objects that resembled the white rat, for example the Father Christmas mask. The child's fear generalised to similar stimuli. Further, not only will a dog salivate to a tone of a different frequency than the CS but also to an alternative sound such as a bell or a buzzer. Thus a response is elicited not only by the conditioned stimulus but by stimuli that share some of its characteristics.

Generalisation is adaptive. If we had to learn a new response to every new situation, we would spend all our time learning! We would need to test all fires to see if they burned us. We need to transfer our learning from one situation to another. If a certain type of cheese makes someone ill, it is sensible to avoid cheese with similar characteristics in future.

Too much generalisation, however, is not adaptive. It is essential for their survival that birds discriminate between edible and poisonous berries; if they were to avoid all berries because one sort made them ill, they might not find enough to eat. Humans need to discriminate between edible and poisonous fungi; it is not necessary to avoid all fungi because some are poisonous.

Discrimination involves learning to make one response to one stimulus and no response, or an alternative response, to a different stimulus.

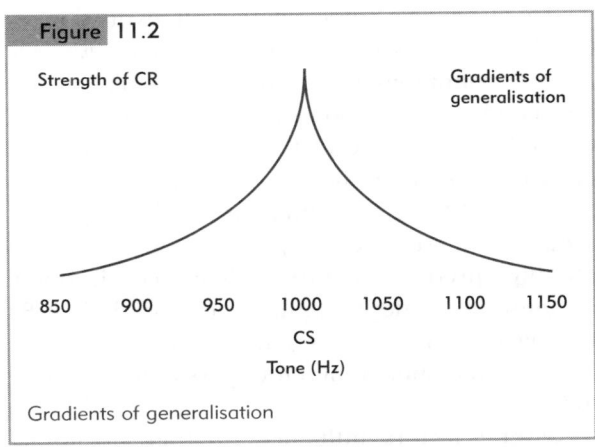

Figure 11.2

Strength of CR

Gradients of generalisation

850   900   950   1000   1050   1100   1150

CS

Tone (Hz)

Gradients of generalisation

If the CS (a tone, say) continues to be presented with the UCS (food), the UCR (salivation) is strengthened. However, if the CS is no longer paired with the UCS (food), the CR (salivation) weakens, and finally dies. The conditioned response is said to have extinguished. *Extinction* resembles forgetting, but in fact it is an example of an adaptive response: an organism needs to react to changes in the environment. When the CS is no longer a signal for the UCS, there is no benefit in responding.

That extinction is not forgetting can be seen in the phenomenon known as *spontaneous recovery*. If an animal is removed from the experimental situation for a period of time following extinction, is then returned and the CS presented, the conditioned response will return. In the case of Pavlov's dogs, salivation to the tone had extinguished. When returned to the experimental situation after a rest period, they would salivate when the tone (CS) was sounded. The response had recovered spontaneously with no further pairing of the CS and UCS. The response, however, was weaker than before.

Further, if the CS and UCS are again paired after extinction has occurred, the CR will return quickly, needing fewer pairings than before, indicating that the original learning had not been forgotten.

Pavlov interpreted the phenomena of extinction, spontaneous recovery and reconditioning by suggesting that during extinction animals actively inhibit learned responses rather than forget them.

An alternative interpretation of extinction is based on what is known as the *information-expectancy theory* of conditioning (Rescorla, 1988). This holds that conditioned responses are not automatically formed through CS-UCS pairings, but are behaviours emitted in anticipation of a future event. The CS acts as a signal for the UCS. Animals acquire a conditioned response when one event reliably predicts another. The conditioned response is made in anticipation of the UCS. During extinction, the CS no longer signals the UCS and the animal therefore pays little attention to it.

Several factors influence whether or not a conditioned response is learned. One of these involves the law of **contiguity** which states that in order to become associated stimuli need to occur close together in time. Thus the strongest learning occurs when the interval between presentation of the CS precedes the UCS by about half a second.

In the natural environment, signals indicating the presence of food, predators or other significant events are likely to be followed closely by the event or predator itself. However, taste aversion studies demonstrate that the law of contiguity does not apply in all cases. Garcia and Koelling (1966) gave rats sweet-tasting water. The water produced nausea an hour after ingestion. The rats learned to avoid the sweet water in just one trial, despite the considerable time lapse between the UCS (sweet water) and the UCR (nausea). Rats rapidly learn to avoid poisonous substances. They take only small quantities of any new food they encounter. If this is poisonous and they survive, they avoid it completely in the future although such poisoning does not produce illness until a considerable time after the food was taken (Barnett, 1963). Yet timing is relevant even in this context: Mackintosh (1984) pointed out that a short time lapse produces a stronger aversion response than a considerably longer interval.

Classical conditioning is involved in a great deal of human and animal behaviour, although real-life situations tend to be more complex than conditioning in the laboratory. However, the laboratory study of higher order conditioning does seem to suggest the sort of processes which might occur in the real world.

Pavlov investigated *higher order conditioning* in dogs by first establishing a strong salivation response to the sound of a metronome (figure 11.3). He then paired a second neutral stimulus, a black square, with the metronome. After repeated pairings the black square alone produced salivation, even though it had never been paired with food. The response (CR2) to the black square, however, was not as strong as to the first conditioned stimulus (CS1).

In real life someone may receive exciting and good news when listening to a particular song. Afterwards this song elicits a feeling of happiness because of its association with good news. It may then happen that the individual hears this song

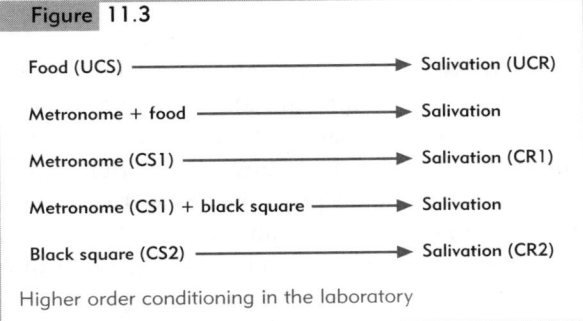

Higher order conditioning in the laboratory

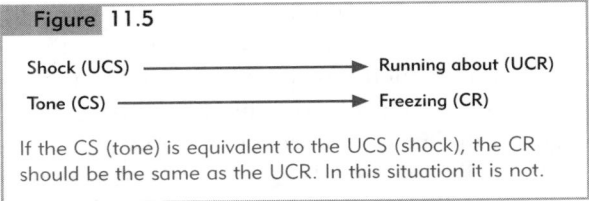

If the CS (tone) is equivalent to the UCS (shock), the CR should be the same as the UCR. In this situation it is not.

when in a particular wine bar. If this happens a few times, the wine bar may become associated with the song, and therefore produces the feeling of happiness. This may happen even though the individual was somewhere else when the good news came. It is thought that many of our emotional reactions have developed through a process similar to higher order conditioning (figure 11.4).

Pavlov believed that pairing the UCS with CS allows the CS to substitute for the UCS in evoking a reflexive response. Thus the CS becomes equivalent to the UCS in eliciting a response. Is Pavlov right? Can the UCS and CS be considered as equivalent after conditioning?

If they are equivalent, then the CR should be essentially the same as the UCR: the only change is in the stimulus which elicits it. However, the CR is often quite different from the UCR. For example, in many animals a mild shock (UCS) produces a UCR of activity (running), while the CR to the CS (tone) is freezing or curling up (figure 11.5).

Thus the evidence suggests that Pavlov was mistaken in his view that pairing allows the CS to substitute for the UCS. An alternative approach to understanding when and how organisms acquire conditioned responses is Rescorla's (1988) information expectation theory of conditioning which suggests that the CS acts as a signal for the UCS.

Pavlov believed that any stimulus that an organism is able to perceive can elicit a conditioned response, and that any reflex can be conditioned. However, many animals are unable to acquire an avoidance response to electric shock since their natural response to an alarming stimulus is to freeze or to curl up. If hedgehogs learned to avoid alarming stimuli (such as car headlights, noise, etc.) rather than curl up, there would be fewer hedgehogs killed on the roads.

Evolution seems to have selected rats which learn aversions very rapidly when taste is paired with stomach illness, but not to associate visual stimuli with sickness. However, if delayed sickness occurs in birds, they will associate the *appearance* of the food with the illness, and develop a conditioned avoidance response. This makes good sense in terms of the natural environment since birds use vision in their search for food (Martin and Lett, 1985). In the wild, birds rapidly learn to avoid poisonous foods. Rhesus monkeys also learn more readily in response to visual than to auditory cues (Warren, 1973).

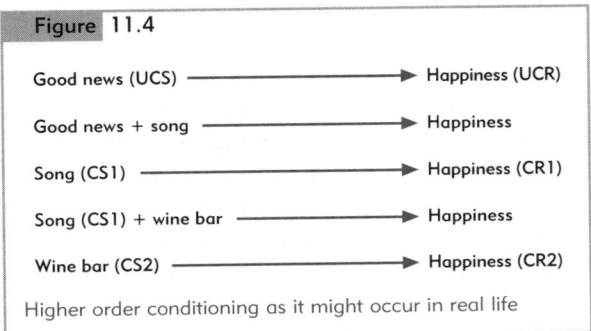

Higher order conditioning as it might occur in real life

Activity 4

Ask some friends if they have ever developed a dislike or an aversion to a particular substance when they have become ill after eating or drinking it. Are they likely to find the appearance or the smell of it off-putting? Did they develop an aversion to other stimuli present at the time? The colour of the tablecloth, for example?

Thus some stimuli are more naturally connected with some responses than others. Conditioning therefore is more complex than a simple association of two stimuli occurring close together in time. There seem to be biological limits on the ability of animals to develop a conditioned response. This is revealed in the fact that it is very difficult to condition fear in humans to such objects as flowers and houses. Ohman *et al.* (1976) carried out several experiments in which it was attempted to condition fear in student volunteers to a variety of stimuli. These were categorised as *prepared* CSs (pictures of snakes, spiders) or *unprepared* CSs (faces, flowers, houses). Ohman *et al.* found that fear conditioned much more readily to prepared stimuli than to unprepared.

Seligman (1970) developed the theory of *biological preparedness* which explains this. The theory suggests that our ability to acquire fear of such creatures as snakes and spiders has a biological rather than a cultural origin. Those of our ancestors who readily learned that certain things were dangerous would have had a clear survival and reproductive advantage over others who learned such protective fear less rapidly. Thus evolution seems to have selected for an ability to learn rapidly fear of certain categories of objects or situations. This ability does not extend to objects associated with modern living such as electric points and cars because they are of recent origin and not, therefore, subject to natural selection.

Activity 5

List some potentially dangerous objects or situations, then divide them into those for which, according to Seligman's theory, you would expect to be biologically prepared and unprepared.

(Suggested answer on page 384.)

Thus the situation with regard to conditioning is clearly much more complex than Pavlov's original theory of the automatic association of two stimuli occurring close together in time.

The laboratory studies do suggest that in natural conditions animals learn to make associations between food and other biologically important items with naturally occurring stimuli. However, in the natural world there are vast numbers of stimuli, many more than in a laboratory, with many potential CSs and a variety of UCSs. Animals do not wait for stimuli to occur together, but actively search for the situation which leads to benefits or escape from danger.

Natural selection has shaped the way in which animals are able to learn most effectively according to their needs. These vary greatly between animals, and the basic principles of classical conditioning do not seem to apply equally to all species in all situations.

Operant conditioning

At about the time Pavlov was studying the conditioned reflex in dogs, Thorndike was studying animal learning. He devised standardised problems for them to solve, and meticulously recorded their responses to these tasks. His best-known investigations concerned hungry cats in a puzzle box. To escape, the cat had to open the door by pulling a loop of string.

Thorndike found that at first a cat would show a variety of seemingly random responses such as walking round the box, clawing the sides, meowing, and so on. Over a series of trials the cats required less and less time to produce the correct response to escape, while the inappropriate responses were discarded. The improvement was very gradual. Although the animals eventually solved the puzzle, they did not appear to understand the situation, or gain insight into the problem (Thorndike, 1898).

Thorndike concluded that the cat's ability to solve the problem involved no understanding of the relationship between pulling the string and the door opening, but a process of trial and error learning where responses which lead to success are *stamped in* by the positive consequence. He suggested that a response which does not result in a positive consequence gradually becomes weaker. A response which produces a satisfying effect gradually becomes stronger. Thorndike called this the Law of Effect. This law states that if a response made in the presence of a given stimulus is followed by a satisfying effect, it is more likely to be repeated when the stimulus is again encountered. Similarly, responses which produce discomfort are weakened.

Activity 6

Take 16 matches and arrange them as shown below. Then ask a friend to change the five squares into four by moving only two matches. All 16 matches must be included. Observe the methods used to solve this problem. Would you describe them as 'trial and error'?

(Suggested answer on page 384.)

Whilst Skinner extended many of Thorndike's ideas he was particularly concerned with determining *how* behaviour is influenced by its consequences. He also felt it important to distinguish between two forms of learning: respondent (or classical) conditioning and operant (or instrumental) conditioning.

In respondent conditioning, behaviour is *elicited* by a specific stimulus, while in operant learning, the response is *emitted*. There is no particular stimulus that will consistently elicit an operant response. The behaviour is emitted by the organism. Elicited behaviour is seen as involuntary, emitted behaviour as voluntary. Skinner called this operant conditioning since the animal *operates* on the environment.

Skinner accepted that many stimuli determine whether or not an operant is emitted, but he believed that, in general, it is possible to ignore them. He stressed that actions, *operants*, are emitted

and controlled by their consequence. If a response is emitted and followed by a reinforcing stimulus, the probability that it will occur again is increased. Thus the key concept in operant conditioning is *reinforcement*.

A reinforcer is defined as any event which increases the probability of occurrence of a response. For a hungry animal, food would act as a reinforcer, for a human being, money perhaps, or social approval.

It is important to distinguish between reward and reinforcement. Behaviour which is reinforced is strengthened. Rewards such as money, prizes and so on frequently do strengthen behaviour but not always. Only when something strengthens behaviour is it acting as a reinforcer. It is not always apparent what will and what will not strengthen a response in a particular organism or a particular situation.

Skinner developed the Skinner box, a form of apparatus which permits precise control and measurement of behaviour (figure 11.6). The box contains a lever which a rat can press, or a disc which a pigeon can peck. It also contains a food tray into which a pellet of food can be delivered as reinforcement. Pressing the bar or pecking the disc is the response to be learned: the operant response. A correct response is followed by a pellet of food (reinforcement) being delivered into the food tray.

Figure 11.6

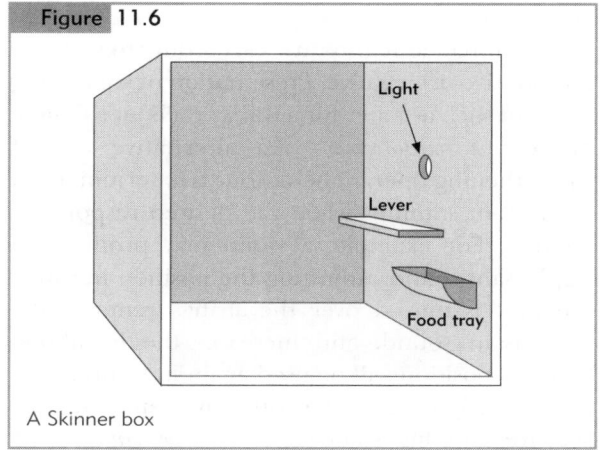

A Skinner box

There are several kinds of reinforcement. One distinction is between primary and secondary reinforcement. Primary reinforcers are naturally reinforcing in their own right, for example food, water or sex.

Secondary reinforcers acquire their reinforcing properties through being associated with a primary reinforcer. For example, when you reinforce a dog for good behaviour, you give it a food reward (primary reinforcement) and at the same time say 'Good boy/girl!' After several pairings, the words alone will be sufficient to reinforce good behaviour. Secondary reinforcers have the great advantage in that they can be used when it is not practicable to reinforce immediately with primary reinforcement.

Or imagine that a rat has been trained to press a lever for a reinforcement of food. Immediately before a pellet is delivered, a distinct tone is sounded. After a number of trials, the tone alone has reinforcing properties. Providing it is still occasionally paired with food, it can be used to condition another response. Secondary reinforcers are often referred to as 'conditioned reinforcers'.

Activity 7

Write down two examples of secondary reinforcement in humans, explaining how they become reinforcing.

(Suggested answers on page 384.)

Reinforcement also varies according to whether it is positive or negative. Presentation of something pleasant such as water for a thirsty rat is an example of *positive reinforcement*. An alternative way of strengthening operant behaviour is to terminate an unpleasant stimulus when the desired response is emitted. For example, a violin may produce an unpleasant sound. Adjusting the position in which the bow is moved over the strings removes the unpleasant sound, and increases the likelihood that this position will be used again in future. Strengthening behaviour by removing an aversive stimulus is known as *negative reinforcement*.

In the laboratory, it is investigated through escape or avoidance learning.

Escape learning requires an animal to make a response which terminates an aversive stimulus. It is often investigated using a shuttlebox, an oblong piece of apparatus with two compartments. The rat receives mild electric shocks in one compartment. It learns to jump the barrier into the other compartment and escape the shock. Escape learning can also be studied in the Skinner box. If the rat presses the lever, the shock is turned off for a given length of time. The rat soon learns to press the lever!

Avoidance learning is more complicated. It requires a stimulus which reliably predicts the arrival of the electric shock. Thus a tone might be sounded a few seconds before the shock arrives. If the rat in the shuttlebox learns to jump the barrier before the shock is delivered, it can avoid it rather than escape it. This can also be studied in a Skinner box with a grid floor. A warning is sounded before the floor is electrified and the rat is able to avoid the shock by pressing the lever before the shock is delivered. This is often referred to as signalled avoidance.

Activity 8

Can you think of an example of signalled avoidance in everyday life?

Escape and avoidance learning both involve aversive stimuli. Responses are reinforced by cessation or removal of an unpleasant or painful stimulus.

It is easy to confuse negative reinforcement with punishment since aversive stimuli are involved in both. Both positive and negative reinforcement make it more likely that a given response will be emitted. *Punishment* weakens a response, reduces the likelihood of it occurring again. The term punishment refers to an unpleasant stimulus or event which, when contingent upon a response, weakens it. Thus if a rat has been trained to press a lever through the use of positive reinforcement, but now each time it presses the lever it receives a shock, the rate of lever pressing will drop, then end.

However, there is evidence that punishment is less efficient in weakening behaviour than reinforcement is in strengthening it. In many instances punishment seems merely to suppress a response. An experiment carried out with rats by Estes (1970) suggested that punishment suppresses behaviour rather than weakens it. Children tend to repeat things for which they have been punished when they believe they are unobserved.

Punishment has other disadvantages. It can produce undesirable side-effects such as aggression. Thus Miller (1941) found that electric shock punishment resulted in one rat attacking another in the same cage.

Skinner believed that reinforcement has a much stronger influence on behaviour than punishment. Reinforcement has the advantage in that it indicates which behaviour is correct or desirable. Punishment does not indicate the correct response.

When used correctly, punishment can be effective in that it suppresses an incorrect response long enough for the organism to try an alternative response which can then be reinforced. This indicates which is the correct response to make. Punishment, therefore, is likely to be most useful when it is accompanied by reinforcement of the desired behaviour (Holz and Azrin, 1966).

The third way in which reinforcement varies is according to whether it is partial or continuous. A rat given a food pellet for every lever press is on a continuous reinforcement schedule, but animals receiving food reinforcement satiate and cease responding. Continuous reinforcement therefore is generally only used during training. Usually, reinforcement is given only for some of the time, on an intermittent or partial basis.

▪ Schedules of reinforcement

Skinner (1938) and Ferster and Skinner (1957) examined the effect of varying the frequency and timing of reinforcement by devising partial systems. It has been found that different patterns of reinforcement have very different effects on responding.

There are four basic patterns of reinforcement used by psychologists, although these can be combined in a variety of ways. The patterns are known as Schedules of Reinforcement (figure 11.7). Some schedules are based on the number of responses emitted (ratio schedules), others on the basis of time between responses (interval schedules). In an interval schedule, a response is reinforced after a specified length of time since the last reinforcement.

1   *Fixed interval schedule (FI)* – the animal is reinforced for the first response made after a fixed time interval has passed. Thus on a FI 60 schedule, the first response made after 60 seconds is reinforced. However often the rat presses the lever, it will not be reinforced until the 60-second interval has passed. How does this affect responding? Overall, the rate of responding is slow, but speeds up as the end of the time interval approaches. Immediately after reinforcement responding is slowed. This produces an effect known as 'scallops' (see figure 11.7).

2   *Variable interval schedule (VI)* – the first response after a period of time is reinforced, but the length of time varies. On a VI 60 schedule, the first response emitted after an *average* of one minute is reinforced. The actual time between reinforcements will vary. For example, reinforcement may be given for the first response emitted after 15 seconds, 20 seconds, 75 seconds, 80 seconds, 30 seconds, and so on. On a VI schedule the response rate is slow but steady. The shorter the average interval, the faster the rate of responding.

3   *Fixed ratio schedule (FR)* – reinforcement is given after a predetermined number of responses. On an FR 15 schedule, reinforcement is delivered after every 15 responses. This schedule produces a high rate of responding, with a brief pause after each reinforcement.

4   *Variable ratio schedule (VR)* – reinforcement is given after a specified number of responses, but the number of responses between

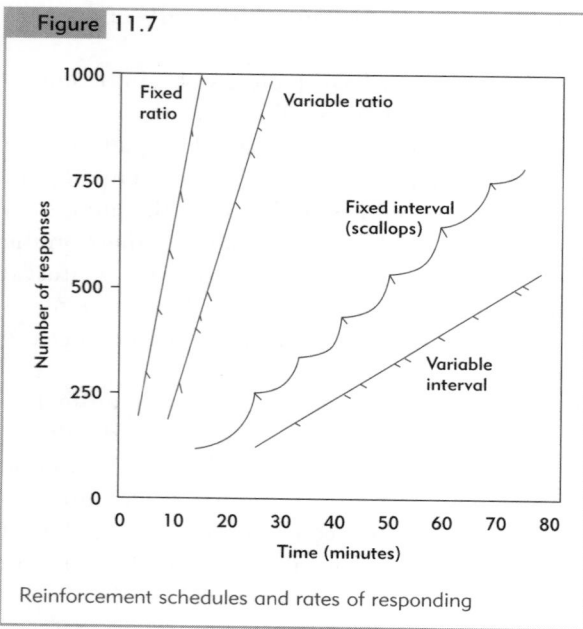

Figure 11.7

Reinforcement schedules and rates of responding

reinforcements varies. On a VR 20 schedule, the number of responses emitted before reinforcement is given varies around an average of 20. This might be 25 responses for the first reinforcement, 10 for the second, 30 for the third, and so on. This schedule produces a very high and stable rate of responding.

Activity 9

Try to think of real-life examples of the four schedules, FI, VI, FR and VR. Write down your ideas.

(Suggested answers on page 384.)

■ Intermittent reinforcement and extinction

It has also been demonstrated that extinction following a partial reinforcement schedule occurs more slowly than following continuous reinforcement. It is known as the partial reinforcement effect and is well illustrated in the resistance of gambling to extinction. Why is behaviour which has been partially reinforced more difficult to extinguish than continuously reinforced behaviour?

One suggestion is that during partial reinforcement the organism has already learned *not* to expect reinforcement after each response. It is therefore more difficult to discriminate between partial reinforcement and no reinforcement than between continuous and no reinforcement. Such discrimination is necessary if the animal is to change its behaviour. An alternative approach is that suggested by Amsel (1962). Amsel hypothesised that lack of reinforcement leads to frustration. The frustration inhibits responding. In an animal which has experienced partial reinforcement, the frustration response has become associated with occasional reinforcement. The animal is therefore more able to tolerate the frustration without a fall in responding.

■ Superstitious behaviour

In one experiment Skinner (1948) studied the behaviour of food-deprived pigeons. Reinforcement was given at random intervals. A pigeon tended to repeat whatever it was doing just prior to the reinforcement. If this happened more than once, this particular behaviour came to dominate the pigeon's activity.

Skinner termed this superstitious behaviour, since it resembled the superstitious behaviour shown by people due to a chance occurrence of an act and reinforcement. For instance, if a student sits an examination whilst wearing (say) something red and achieves success, then that student may believe that the red brought luck, and will wear red again on the next comparable occasion. The behaviour is likely to be maintained although wearing red may only occasionally be linked to success. This chance reinforcement resembles partial reinforcement, and helps explain why superstitious behaviour is resistant to extinction.

Activity 10

Do you think Skinner is right? Can you think of examples of superstitious or ritualistic behaviour in people you know?

■ Shaping

When a rat is first put into a Skinner box, it may accidentally press the lever and obtain reinforcement. However, it is very likely that the rat will not press the lever and it may be necessary to use a procedure known as **shaping**. The rat is reinforced each time it makes a response which comes closer to the desired response. The rat might be reinforced when facing the lever, next when it sniffs it, and so on. Thus through a series of stages known as successive approximations, the rat learns to press the lever to obtain reinforcement.

Shaping is an extremely powerful procedure and can be used to train animals to perform complex behaviours, and to help human beings overcome a variety of psychological problems. It is also necessary in operant conditioning procedures since one cannot reinforce a response until it has been emitted.

Activity 11

Write down how you would train a dog to shake a paw, then ask friends how they would go about this. Compare their approach with yours.

(Suggested answer on page 384.)

■ The discriminative stimulus

This is another very important aspect of operant conditioning. Once a rat is emitting the desired operant response, a discriminative stimulus can be introduced. Thus if a light comes on, this signals that reinforcement will follow the bar press. If the rat is only reinforced in the presence of the light, this becomes a discriminative stimulus.

Similarly, a pigeon has to peck at a disc in order to obtain reinforcement. An illuminated disc may be used as a discriminative stimulus (or SD).

When the disc is illuminated, pecking will be reinforced, when not illuminated, pecking is not reinforced.

When shopping, you are unlikely to enter a shop where no lights are on, and there are no other signs of activity. These are the sort of discriminative stimuli that indicate to you whether or not it is worth entering a shop. What discriminative stimuli indicate whether it is worth attempting to obtain a drink from a drinks machine?

Organisms learn from the stimuli available in their environment when a given response is likely to result in a favourable consequence. Generalisation and discrimination are important parts of this process.

If shaping is combined with a process known as chaining, long strings of responses can be conditioned. The resulting behaviour can appear complex. Chaining involves a series of operant responses and discriminative stimuli.

Evaluation

Much of the evidence obtained in operant research suggests that in order to be effective reinforcement must occur immediately after the response. This is not necessarily so, however. Rats are able to learn which of two pathways in a maze leads to reinforcement, even when an interval of several seconds elapses between the path chosen and the outcome of that choice. This has been studied by removing the rats from the maze immediately following their choice of pathway, regardless of whether this was correct or incorrect. If their choice was correct, they were returned to the maze several minutes later to receive food. They are able to learn successfully even with delays of at least five minutes between correct choice and reinforcement (Mackintosh, 1984).

Behaviourists believe that it is not necessary to consider cognitive activity within the organism during learning. Observational learning studied by Bandura and others revealed that cognitive factors should not be ignored if learning is to be understood; operant theory also stresses the importance of reinforcement, yet learning through imitation can occur in its absence. Bandura (1977) proposed that the importance of reinforcement and punishment is in the information that they provide as to the likely consequences of certain behaviour under certain conditions. Learning through imitation is not confined to human beings as shown by examples of cultural transmission (see box 11.8).

Further evidence that reinforcement is not always necessary was obtained by Tolman and Honzik (1930) in their investigation of maze learning in rats. This work also revealed a distinction between learning and performance: such learning is known as *latent learning*. Everyday life would seem to include many instances of concealed learning, and learning taking place in the absence of reinforcement. Many television programmes provide information on how to do certain things, how to treat someone who is choking, for instance. Several months later a situation may arise where the knowledge is needed: the individual is able to apply it, and a life is saved.

Insight learning also reveals the importance of cognition. Köhler (1925) gave chimpanzees problems to solve in relation to obtaining fruit. After unsuccessfully trying to reach the fruit, the chimps would be quiet, apparently doing nothing, then would carry out the appropriate actions to obtain the fruit. They arrived at the solution quite suddenly, showing no evidence of trial and error. Köhler criticised Thorndike's puzzle boxes on the grounds that they did not allow the cats to show insight. Insight is likely to be shown when the animal is familiar with the individual components of the situation since insight involves reorganising them so as to produce a solution.

Experiments with animals and humans using operant conditioning procedures reveal principles which apply in the natural world as well as in the laboratory. However, the real world is considerably more complex, and learning involves considerably more than the automatic strengthening of behaviour as proposed by Skinner. Rather than stressing the importance of contiguity and predictability, it might be more helpful to consider how animals balance the two and distinguish between chance and causal relationships. Mackintosh (1984) wrote:

> *'The process of conditioning is one which enables animals to establish a subtle and accurate picture of the causal sequence of events in their environment, to predict where and when food or danger can be expected, and to modify their behaviour accordingly' (p. 33).*

Although many forms of learning are not satisfactorily explained by classical and operant conditioning, much of the current understanding of learning in both laboratory and natural conditions has been gained using techniques devised by the learning theorists.

The role of learning in relation to foraging and migratory behaviour is considered in the following pages.

11.8 Imitation and cultural transmission

Is imitation found in animals? The term *cultural transmission* is used where one animal acquires a form of behaviour through imitating another. Tits learn to remove freshly delivered milk-bottle tops which allows them to drink the cream. Fisher and Hinde (1949) suggested the spread of the behaviour was due to imitation. Sherry and Galef (1984) found the black-backed chickadee can learn through imitation.

The animal most often cited as imitating is the Japanese macaque. Ethologists have been studying these monkeys since 1950. When observers left sweet potatoes on the beach, a young female, Imo, began to take the potatoes into the sea to wash off the sand. Within five years, 80 per cent of the macaques were washing the potatoes.

Matsuzawa (1996) reported that chimpanzees may acquire the skill of using stone tools for cracking nuts through observing other group members. Field experiments also revealed transmission of knowledge from one generation to another. The younger chimps learned to crack nuts by watching an adult female.

Self-assessment questions

1 a Explain the importance of learning in relation to adaptive behaviour.
  b Outline generalisation and discrimination, and explain why they are adaptive.

2 a Explain the law of contiguity. Give an example of when it does not apply.
  b Discuss Pavlov's view of how organisms acquire conditioned responses, and suggest an alternative explanation.
  c Using examples, indicate some of the biological limitations on conditioning.

3 a Explain, with examples, the difference between: (i) primary and secondary reinforcement; (ii) positive and negative reinforcement.
  b Explain: (i) why punishment may not be effective; (ii) what conditions are needed for it to be effective.
  c Outline some of the similarities between classical and operant conditioning.

4 a Behaviour is more resistant to extinction following partial rather than continuous reinforcement. Outline *one* reason which is thought to explain this.
  b Briefly explain: (i) superstitious behaviour; (ii) discriminative stimulus.
  c Identify two kinds of learning where cognitive factors seem to be involved.

(Suggested answers on pages 385–6.)

Foraging and homing

Foraging refers to the methods organisms employ to obtain food. It is therefore a very important aspect of an animal's behaviour. An animal which is less than efficient at this has a reduced chance of survival. The ability to learn and to react to changes in the environment are vital to an animal's ability to forage successfully.

Foraging takes many forms and can be classified in different ways. Thus some animals search for their food, whilst some sit and wait for it to come within striking distance. Searchers include the grazers and the hunters. Foraging can also be classified on the basis of the food taken. Classes include carnivores, insectivores, herbivores and frugivores. There are also omnivores (which take a varied diet).

Food must be recognised and caught or obtained in some way. Each species must recognise its own kind of food. The behavioural adaptations of different foragers will differ: thus a searcher will need sense organs able to locate food, equipment to deal with it once obtained, stealth to allow close approach to prey and speed to chase fleeing prey. A herbivore will need to be able to find suitable grazing, and possess teeth able to graze efficiently.

Efficient 'sit and wait' foragers require the ability to identify patches where food is to be found, to build traps, webs and so on. Animals also vary in that some are specialists, feeding on only one or two types of food, and some are generalists. A generalist (also known as an omnivore) eats many kinds of things. Rats will eat almost anything: they are generalists. Worms too eat almost anything that they can take in. The toad is a **specialist feeder**, taking small arthropods such as beetles and earthworms.

Some species are highly specialised, for example the koala of Australia which feeds on a species of eucalyptus, and the panda which in its natural environment confines itself to bamboo shoots. The panda has a sixth finger which enables it to hold bamboo; this is an example of a specialist adaptation.

The extent to which the ability to learn enables organisms to obtain food varies according to species, and whether an animal is a specialist or a generalist. Learning seems to be particularly important for a generalist. An animal which takes a variety of food will need to identify what food is edible, what is not. Learning will involve perception, the development of a **search image**. Forming a search image means learning to see something that had not previously been seen: learning from experience.

Animals learn which food is palatable. The caterpillars of the cinnabar moth taste unpleasant to birds. The birds rapidly learn to associate the taste with the black and yellow colouring, and once tried, these caterpillars are not taken again. Other insects with similar colouring will be avoided. Rats avoid food which makes them ill.

The toad, a passive forager, does not recognise its prey in detail, but snaps at small, dark, moving objects. Learning does not seem to play a large part in its response to such stimuli (Ewert, 1987). However, even sit-and-wait hunters need some ability to learn if they are to be successful in obtaining food. A frog, for example, needs to position itself in a place where food is available, and frogs quickly learn where this is likely to be.

Activity 12

Write down the names of about 20 species, including mammals, birds, amphibians, insects and so on. Then divide them into specialist and generalist feeders.

(Suggested answers on page 384.)

Learning is important in the foraging behaviour of bees. Foraging bees make repeated journeys to collect pollen and nectar from flowers. They land spontaneously on objects which have flower-like characteristics. Gould and Marler (1987) pointed out that although they recognise flower-like objects innately, bees have to learn which of these are likely to hold food. The first things bees learn about a flower is its odour. This is revealed by the fact that amongst hundreds of flowers, they select the ones with strong odours. The odour becomes a conditioned stimulus. That bees are able to modify their behaviour during foraging was demonstrated by Schmid-Hempel (1986) who attached small weights to foraging worker bees. Would they compensate for this extra weight by gathering less nectar? The bees were found to adjust the weight of nectar collected thus compensating for the weights attached to them.

The amount of nectar collected also varied according to the distance over which it had to be carried.

Activity 13

Carry out a study into which flowers are most visited by bees. Keep a record of the colour and shape of the flowers visited. Did the bees show any preference?

Optimal foraging behaviour

Since successful foraging is essential for survival, it would be expected that natural selection would result in animals possessing effective strategies for obtaining food. Several theorists have suggested that there may be general rules for effective foraging, whether this concerns a lion preying on a zebra, a bird feeding on nuts, or bees foraging for nectar and pollen. **Optimal foraging theory (OFT)** attempts to determine whether general rules can be usefully applied to foraging behaviour, and looks at feeding from a cost-benefit point of view. It is largely concerned with the optimal food or food type for an animal to eat, where to find it, and the most efficient ways in which to search for it. According to OFT, animals should feed in such a way as to maximise benefits and minimise costs. The efficiency of foraging behaviour is based on the relationship between energy intake over a given period minus the energy expended during that period.

Individuals which forage efficiently would be expected to have a selective advantage over less efficient foragers. OFT aims to demonstrate mathematically how an individual should behave if it is to maximise its fitness. Two models which attempt to do this are the prey model and the patch model. The prey model is concerned with the types of prey for which the organism can search at the same time: the prey differ according to the energy they contain and in the time needed to handle them. The patch model is concerned with food which is not evenly distributed, that is, it occurs in patches.

The prey model assumes that the animal aims to maximise its energy intake. It takes into account the types of prey available, how much energy the prey provides, and how much time and energy the animal requires to take and consume the prey.

If an animal obtains a higher energy intake by concentrating on one type of prey, then according to OFT, it should do so. The model also takes into account certain physical constraints of the predator in relation to the speed at which it can run, consume food and so on.

For oystercatchers, the optimal choice of which mussels to take depends on several factors – the overall size, the thickness of the shell and whether the shells are covered in barnacles (Meire and Eroynck, 1986). There is a cost-benefit balance in the size of the mussels and the time spent opening them.

There is a cost-benefit effect according to whether an animal is a generalist or a specialist feeder. There is a wider variety of food available to generalist feeders, therefore they are likely to spend less time searching for food. However, they are likely to take longer when dealing with the food.

A specialist feeder will require a longer search time, but will benefit in that less time is needed to deal with the prey: a specialist feeder is well adapted to feeding on the particular species. Some bumblebees are specialist feeders, some generalist. Laverty and Plowright (1988) compared a specialist with two generalist bumblebees. When presented with their particular plant, the specialist bees found the nectar quickly and efficiently. The generalist species tended to search in the wrong part of the flower. Thus whilst generalists tend to spend less time seeking food, they require longer in which to manage and consume it.

The patch model has a more general application than the prey model. It is used to predict the behaviour of animals feeding in patches. OFT implies that:

- an efficient predator should focus only on areas which provide an optimal return of resources in relation to effort expended

- should the return provided by resources drop in a particular patch, the animal should move and look elsewhere
- the predator should concentrate on the most productive patches rather than search an area at random. This will increase the likelihood of finding food.

Krebs *et al.* (1978) investigated foraging behaviour in birds. They were interested in how the forager would behave when confronted with two food patches in its environment. The forager recognises both patches as areas where food is available, but does not know the concentration of food in the patches. Krebs *et al.* used an operant conditioning procedure to investigate this. Great tits were able to obtain food by hopping onto either of two perches. One perch was more likely to provide food than the other. At first, the great tits hopped onto both perches, but by the end of a session hopped consistently onto the perch most likely to yield food. They discriminated between them on the basis of the quantity of food available.

This is what OFT would predict, that the birds first sample the alternative sources of food, then remain where most is provided.

Bumblebees travel about and spend time in the most profitable patches. Heinrich (1979) found that they would spend a considerable amount of time within one patch, then fly directly and quickly to the next.

Cost is not only found in foraging methods, but in distance travelled. Kramer and Nowell (1980) reported that chipmunks adjust the amount of food in their pouches according to their travel time from the home area. The amount of food loaded into their pouches and choice of feeding site are both chosen on an optimal basis according to the time needed for travel.

Learning contributes to the ability to forage optimally. Learning is likely to be of less significance to a specialist feeder such as the toad or cabbage butterfly than to generalist feeders such as rats. The importance of learning is shown in the behaviour of those birds and mammals which collect more food than they require, and hide it. This is likely to give them an advantage over foragers which are less able to learn, and are therefore less flexible. They have access to a rich source of food, and they do not have to share it. Some animals store the food in one place which they visit regularly, whilst others disperse the food around their territory. Marsh tits store hundreds of seeds during winter. Whilst they do not recover all the seeds, they are able to recall numerous hiding places with great accuracy (Shettleworth, 1983). Scrub jays, for instance, are able to adjust their hiding and recovery strategies according to the rate at which the food perishes. This reveals that they remember 'where and when particular food items were cached'. (Clayton and Dickinson, 1998, p. 272). Such behaviour is indicative of efficient foraging.

Although OFT provides a framework for investigating foraging behaviour, it does have limitations. These include the following:

1 OFT models do not consider the forager in the context of other competing foragers, but focus on the individual and its food. For instance, they do not allow for the fact that whilst dominant individuals may be able to forage optimally, subordinate animals may be unable to do so. They may need to be on the alert for harassment from dominant animals, or for possible predators.

2 To assume that the maximum gain is based on energy intake may be wrong for many animals.

3 OFT tends to oversimplify foraging behaviour. The motivational and physiological state of the animal is ignored. Foraging behaviour may vary according to the time of day, time of year, hunger, presence of hungry offspring, competitors, and so on (see 1 above).

4 OFT is difficult to follow in detail for those who have no background in economics and mathematics.

However, OFT does encourage those who study foraging to investigate the costs and benefits of different types of food, and different foraging strategies.

There are examples all around us of the ability of animals to make good use of a food source: the bluetits which peck through milk-bottle tops, the birds which descend onto a loaded birdtable and the seabirds which follow fishing boats. Clearly such behaviour is learned. Fishing boats and milk bottles were not part of the evolutionary environment. Selective pressure has resulted in the ability to respond quickly to changes in the distribution and availability of food. Not all species are flexible however, and for this reason their future is at risk. The panda and koala are examples.

Many animals which forage return with food to a den or nest. To do so, they need to be able to find their way home, and have evolved several systems which enable them to do this. The ability of homing and migrating animals to find their way is examined next.

Homing and migration

Homing refers to the process by which an animal finds its way back to its home site. It may have left in order to forage, to breed or to migrate.

Migration refers to long-distance travel from one location to another, with subsequent return to the first. Migration may involve thousands of miles of travel each year. Examples include the seasonal travel of birds and insects, the mass movements of grazing animals across the African grasslands and the return of mature salmon to the waters in which they hatched.

One method of investigating the ability to home involves releasing the animal at some distance from its home site and recording its behaviour. Many birds have the ability to find their way home over considerable distances. Manx shearwater, for example, when taken from their nest sites in Wales and released as far away as Venice in Italy, have returned to their nests after 14 days. Albatrosses have been removed from their nests and transported by air over considerable distances: 14 out of 18 birds returned to their nests, one making a journey of over 6400 kilometres in 32 days. The monarch butterfly migrates over considerable distances, covering as much as 2000 kilometres. It is found mainly in North America and surrounding regions. As temperatures begin to fall in the autumn they migrate south. In the spring they travel north again (Baker, 1978; Urquhart, 1987).

Many researchers have studied the homing pigeon since it is tame and easy to study. Pigeons taken from the home-loft to some unfamiliar place, then released, can find their way home. When released, a pigeon circles for a few minutes, then sets off, usually in the direction of its home-loft. Many investigators believe that the pigeons use the position of the sun to navigate. However, they can navigate when the sky is overcast and it is possible that a magnetic sense acts as a backup system. This seems likely in that when magnets are attached to their heads the ability of the pigeons to navigate is impaired, but only when the sun is not visible (Baker, 1982). They also navigate less accurately when the earth's magnetic field is disturbed.

There is also evidence that pigeons use olfactory cues. Experiments have included interfering with the ability to smell. If the olfactory nerves in a homing pigeon are cut so that it is unable to smell, it has difficulty in finding its way to its loft from an unfamiliar location (Pool, 1996).

Activity 14

Try to obtain an inexpensive compass, and use it to determine direction.

The wide range of results concerning navigation in pigeons suggests that they use a number of cues. The ones which are used in any one situation will depend on the conditions prevailing at the time.

Garden warblers require information from both the stars and the earth's magnetic field if they are to fly off on the right heading at migration time (Weindler et al., 1996). Weindler el al. concluded that the interaction between celestial and magnetic information is very complex.

Findings indicate that birds cannot navigate by the stars alone; that the stars provide general directional cues, but that the earth's magnetic field is essential if the birds are to fly on exactly the right heading.

Activity 15

Take an atlas of the world and trace the migratory route of the eels (see figure 11.9).

Researchers in bird navigation such as Baker (1984) suggest that birds develop a mental map during their first migration. This may be composed of landmarks, geographical features such as coastlines and mountain ranges, olfactory cues, and local variations in the magnetic field. This is then used for the return trip and subsequent journeys.

Pool (1996) suggested that only use of visual landmarks can explain some aspects of homing, for example '. . . the same swallows find their way back to a small mission in San Juan Capistrano in California' (p. 30).

A species which is known to use olfactory cues is the salmon. Salmon migrate to the sea, but when fully grown return to the very same stretch of water in which they hatched in order to spawn. It seems that young salmon become conditioned to the smell of the river where they hatched before the migration to the sea. Ants are able to find their way back to the nest by following the scent trails left by the foragers.

Honeybees make orientation flights when they leave the hive or food source. This enables foragers to learn how the characteristics of the feeding area fit in with the surroundings; also to learn those objects which will act as landmarks for when they return.

The bee-killing digger wasp makes an orientation flight which allows it to learn the landmarks around its burrow before leaving in search of prey, as demonstrated by Tinbergen (1958) in his ingenious investigation. Much of its behaviour is innate, but learning is necessary if it is to find its way back to its burrow.

Navigation seems to include an inherited component. In some instances, the ability to

Activity 16

Imagine yourself in a city which you do not know, apart from the route from your hotel to a shopping area. How would you find your way back to your hotel if you were transported blindfold in a car to an area of the city unknown to you?

(Suggested answer on page 385.)

migrate seems to be largely innate since adults leave before the departure of the young of that year. The young, however, travel successfully to the same area. Examples of this include some species of bird, also eels (figure 11.9) and the Bogong moth.

In addition to landmarks, bees also use the sun to determine direction. Using the position of the sun, a worker bee can fly back to the hive without any need to use landmarks on the ground. When the sky is overcast, the bees deduce the position of the sun from the pattern of polarised light (figure 11.10).

Thus animals are able to use a variety of cues to find their way home. They have the ability to memorise landmarks, to create a mental map of an area and to carry out complex calculations based on the sun, the stars and the earth's magnetic field.

Many approaches are being used to unravel the complexities of homing behaviour. It has proved a very difficult area to investigate due, in part, to the fact that animals tend to have more than one system; if one system cannot be used, another can substitute. Research also suggests that there is a complex interaction between genetically coded information and learning.

Why do animals migrate? They do so for several reasons. Grazing animals follow the rainfall across

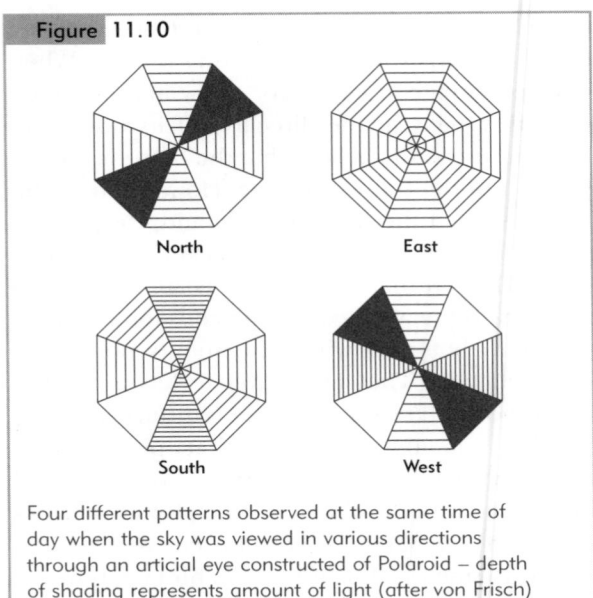

Figure 11.10

North

East

South

West

Four different patterns observed at the same time of day when the sky was viewed in various directions through an articial eye constructed of Polaroid – depth of shading represents amount of light (after von Frisch)

the plains of Africa. This provides them with a better source of food. Others move from an area which becomes too cold, or provides insufficient food. Increased day length in northern latitudes enables birds to obtain more food since they do not forage at night: this is particularly important if they have young to feed. The blue whale migrates from the Antarctic feeding grounds. Although food is plentiful here, the cold water is hazardous to the newborn. Where an environment is constant with regard to food and temperature, an animal does not need to migrate. Nor do those species migrate which are able to adapt to such changes, such as bears and hedgehogs which both hibernate. The reasons for the migration of some species are not well understood.

11.9 The mystery of the eels

Deep in the warm waters of the Sargasso Sea between Bermuda and the West Indies, eels lay their eggs. These hatch into tiny young which are carried eastwards by the Gulf Stream. Many reach Britain and western Europe where they swim into the rivers and then remain for several years. When mature, they swim south-westwards, back to the Sargasso Sea. Here they spawn and die.

It is not known how they achieve this epic journey, although research suggests that for part of the way they use the stars. The mystery has yet to be solved.

Activity 17

Over the year sample the outside temperature on, say, a weekly or fortnightly basis. How much temperature variation is there between winter and summer?

(Suggested answers on pages 386–7.)

Self-assessment questions

5 a In relation to foraging behaviour, explain the difference between a generalist and a specialist, and consider the costs and benefits associated with each.
  b Outline one investigation into foraging behaviour.
  c Discuss the importance of learning in relation to foraging behaviour.

6 a Explain what is meant by the term 'optimal foraging'.
  b What prediction does OFT make in relation to the feeding behaviour of animals?
  c Explain the following: (i) prey model; (ii) patch model.
  d Discuss the usefulness of OFT in the study of foraging behaviour.

7 a Explain why animals migrate.
  b Outline some of the ways in which homing is investigated.
  c Discuss some of the navigational cues used by organisms which fly.

8 a Outline examples of homing based on olfactory cues.
  b Discuss the role of learning in homing and migratory behaviour.
  c Explain why navigation is difficult to investigate.

Animal language

Foraging bees communicate the location of a food source to other foragers. Communication is an essential component of sociality in animals. That animals have complex communication systems is not in doubt. Such systems are often referred to as animal language. They seem to differ from human language, however. Human language uses symbols; symbols can be put together to give new meanings. Human language is productive: that is, a limited number of signs can be combined and recombined into an infinite number of sentences. Human language enables us to communicate about the past and the future; of possibilities, abstract ideas, truths and falsehoods. Human language is learned and passed on by tradition.

Hockett (1959, 1960) set out to identify those characteristics which typify language. He proposed that there are certain features of language which he called **design features**. These are widely accepted as criteria against which attempts to demonstrate language in animals may be assessed. These include:

- *Discreteness* – language is organised into discrete units; the meaning of a communication is based on the position of these units (phonemes) within the utterance.
- *Displacement* – the ability to refer to things which are not present in time or place (not in view; are in the past or future).
- *Interchangeability* – language is a two-way process: senders can both receive and transmit information.
- *Learnability* – language can be learned.
- *Prevarication* – language can be used to refer to things which are not true.
- ***Productivity*** – the sounds of language can be combined into an infinite number of meanings and novel utterances.
- *Reflexiveness* – enables users to refer to themselves.
- *Specialisation* – language has the specific function of communication; it is not a by-product of another form of behaviour.
- *Traditional transmission* – language may be passed on from generation to generation.

Additional characteristics of language include: (a) language is spontaneous; (b) language is a two-way process involving turn taking; (c) language is arbitrary, meaning that there is no relationship between a symbol and what it represents (Aitchison, 1983).

The waggle dance

The waggle dance of the honeybee is a fascinating example of animal language. It was unravelled by von Frisch (1967) during years of meticulous observation and experiment.

When a forager bee has found a food source, it returns to the hive and, after giving up the food it has obtained, begins to dance on the vertical surface of the comb. The waggle dance conveys information concerning the direction and distance of the food source.

The direction of the waggle dance indicates the direction in which the food supply can be found. The distance to the food source is conveyed by the speed of the waggle dance. If the dancer moves rapidly, this means that the distance is short. Longer distances are indicated by a progressively slower waggle dance.

Language in mammals

Guinea pigs have evolved three systems of communication: postures, vocalisations and olfactory stimuli (communicating with pheromones). Several people have studied the vocalisations of guinea pigs including Coulon (1973) and Berryman (1974). Guinea pigs make up to 13 different calls of which some occur during sexual and aggressive encounters. Calls are also involved in greeting and in signalling alarm and distress.

Marine animals need to evolve a communication system appropriate to living under water. Cetaceans, including the humpback whale, communicate by sound. The whale orders these sounds into songs. A song will include sequences of sounds which known as themes. A song may last for ten minutes or longer, and is repeated over and over again. The songs change gradually over time (see Unit 10).

Unlike the waggle dance of the honeybee, the function of the song of the humpback whale is not yet understood. However, since human beings can identify an individual whale by his song, it seems likely that the songs are associated with identification and location of individuals, thus maintaining social contact. It is also possible that they have some sexual significance.

> ## Activity 18
>
> **Look up the term 'language' in a dictionary. What does this suggest to you?**
>
> *(Suggested answer on page 385.)*

Language in primates

Whilst the ability to acquire and use human language has been investigated in some of the larger primates, their 'natural' language has not yet received so much attention. However, this has been studied in the vervet monkey and, to a lesser extent, the bonobo (pygmy chimpanzee).

Vervets are social animals which live in groups. They are efficient communicators. Their calls have been investigated in relation to social interactions and to predators by Cheney and Seyfarth (1990).

These monkeys make at least ten sounds with which they communicate information to one another. They respond differently to a considerable number of individual monkeys, and alarm calls vary according to whether the danger is a leopard, a snake or a bird of prey.

The alarm call might represent no more than an involuntary alarm reaction. However, research findings suggest the call may be voluntary, made with the intention of communicating the presence of danger. For instance, vervets have been heard to emit the call indicating 'leopard' when no leopard is present, but when their own troop is doing badly in a fight with another troop of monkeys. Further, a lone vervet when chased by a leopard made *no* alarm call. Such observations suggest that at least some of the communications made by vervets may be voluntary.

Savage-Rumbaugh *et al.* (1996) investigated communication in wild-living bonobos. When feeding, bonobo groups split into parties, moving from one feeding area to another in single file. Observers noted that separate parties seemed to know the exact direction taken by other parties. Observers were able to follow signs left by the chimps such as firmly flattened leaves, bent leaves, a broken branch lying or stuck into the ground. Since the human trackers lost the apes in the absence of these signs, and since bonobos are able to travel without disturbing vegetation, it seemed possible that the signs served to signal a direction at an intersection. It is therefore possible that the bonobos were using vegetation in a symbolic manner, indicating where they were going next. Before any firm conclusion can be drawn, however, more research is needed.

■ Teaching language to primates

Much of the work in determining whether primates are capable of language has concentrated on their ability to acquire *human* language.

Attempts to teach language to animals have been taking place for over 60 years. Psychologists and linguists still argue as to whether language as defined by Hockett (1960) and Aitchison (1983) is confined to humans.

Early attempts at teaching language to primates focused on trying to teach chimpanzees to talk. These showed that chimpanzees lack the vocal apparatus necessary for human speech sounds. However, psychologists realised that chimpanzees might be able to learn a form of language not based on sound, and research efforts were directed towards teaching primates a non-spoken language.

Gardner and Gardner (1969) taught American sign language (ASL) to Washoe, a female chimp. Chimps have good manual dexterity, and are physically capable of making the signs of ASL. Many deaf people in America use ASL (or Ameslan) which is based on a number of gestures and signs which can be combined on the same basis as spoken language.

At 11 months old Washoe was removed from other chimpanzees and placed in an environment that was as human as possible. From the outset, the Gardners communicated with Washoe (and with each other in her presence) only by signing. They used operant conditioning techniques during her training, rewarding Washoe for using correct signs. If a sign was nearly right, it was perfected by shaping and moulding her fingers into the correct position.

For the first time it appeared that a primate had mastered a language with which it could talk to humans. After four years of training, Washoe used about 130 signs. The Gardners reported that some of these could be generalised to new situations. Thus she might sign 'more' for more food, or 'more' for more tickling. Once the first signs had been learned, Washoe began to combine them, for example 'gimme sweet' and 'Washoe sorry'. Later she developed three-word sentences, and invented some novel phrases. For example, when taken out in a rowing boat by her trainer she called a swan a 'water bird'.

By the age of five years her linguistic abilities were reported as similar to those of a three-year-old child. However, Washoe was not exposed to ASL until she was 11 months old, whilst human children are exposed to language from the moment they are born.

It had been hoped that Washoe would teach ASL to her offspring. Sadly, her two babies died soon after birth. She adopted a slightly older infant chimpanzee, Loulis, 11 months old. Washoe used signs to Loulis, and he has imitated several of these.

A chimpanzee called Lana was taught to operate a keyboard controlled by a computer (Rumbaugh, 1977). Each of the 50 keys displayed a symbol representing a word in a specially created language called 'Yerkish'. When Lana typed a symbol, it was be displayed on the screen and, by using correct grammar, she was able to obtain rewards. She learned to correct mistakes by checking the sequence of symbols on the screen, indicating some ability to read.

This method had the advantage of being available 24 hours a day. Lana was able to communicate via her computer and even initiated some conversations. She also invented new words when confronted with a new object for which she knew no name. For example, when she saw a ring for the first time, she typed 'finger bracelet'. She showed some knowledge of syntax, since she could discriminate between 'Lana groom Tim' and 'Tim groom Lana'.

Koko is a gorilla. Patterson (1978, 1980) taught her to use ASL. After seven years of training Koko had mastered some 400 signs, and was able to understand many equivalent English words for them. Koko, it is claimed, developed the ability to use syntax and has created several novel sentences and sign combinations such as 'bottle match' for a cigarette lighter. She is also reported as using sign language to convey anger, use metaphor and even to tell lies. Koko is able to converse about past events, also to refer to an emotional event that she is not experiencing at the time. She has also developed her own form of abuse in the phrase 'you big dirty toilet'. Koko's use of language seems to be more advanced than that of the chimpanzees.

Evidence from the above studies suggests that primates have some capacity to acquire language. They can use symbols meaningfully and spontaneously; they can acquire relatively large vocabularies, string 'words' together into meaningful sequences, and even create novel sentences. There is some evidence that chimpanzees will use sign language amongst themselves. As mentioned earlier, Washoe signed to Loulis, and Fouts (1972) observed that the chimps in the colony he set up would sign to each other, even when no humans were present.

Many psychologists and psycholinguists remain doubtful. One of these is Terrace (1979). Terrace trained his chimpanzee Nim Chimpsky (named after linguist Noam Chomsky) to use ASL. Nim was kept in a home environment, with surrogate human parents and teachers. In a carefully controlled study they communicated with Nim and amongst themselves in ASL, keeping transcripts of all signs and sign combinations that Nim produced. At nearly four years old he had acquired 125 signs, some being given in linear sequences. Nim could name things spontaneously, for example signing 'dog' when hearing a dog bark. However, Terrace became sceptical of primate capabilities when he re-examined his own videotapes of Nim.

Nim's utterances seemed very similar to those of young children when they start to produce two-word sentences such as 'juice Tommy' or 'me up'. However, Terrace noted that Nim's utterances did not increase in length as do those of children, and were not used in progressively longer sentences over time. Most phrases were apparently random combinations often involving 'me', 'hug' or 'Nim'. Only 12 per cent of his signings were spontaneous; the rest were responses to gestures from his teachers. He never asked for anything that he could not see, never signed unless expecting a reward, and would not sign to another chimp who knew ASL unless his teacher was present to coax him.

Terrace (1979) concluded that there is no evidence for grammatical competence in non-human species, and that chimpanzee language also lacks the spontaneity of human languages. Is a chimpanzee stringing signs together any different from a pigeon trained to peck at different coloured discs in a particular sequence regardless of their arrangement? If these were marked in sequence 'please give me food', would this be considered language?

Terrace examined the work of the other researchers, and is as doubtful about the abilities of the other primates to use language as he is about Nim's. For example, he found that films on public release consistently had initial promptings from Washoe's trainers edited out. When uncut versions were examined, every one of Washoe's multi-sign utterances followed similar signs made by her trainer.

Terrace suggested that the primates have been operantly conditioned to make certain signs in order to get what they want, and that they are often inadvertently cued by their trainers to produce these signs in sequence: the apes are not really aware of what the signs mean.

Is Terrace right? It is difficult to interpret the use of novel utterances such as Washoe's 'water bird' or Lana's 'finger bracelet'. Both Terrace and Sebeok and Umiker-Sebeok (1980) suggested an alternative explanation of such signings. Perhaps Washoe signed water and then noticed the swan and signed 'bird'. It is doubtful whether her trainer could have concealed his delight at this. This would act as social reward (reinforcement) and from then onwards Washoe would associate the double sign with a swan.

Sebeok and Umiker-Sebeok (1980) pointed out that there are probably many uncontrollable experimenter effects. The best ape trainers could be particularly effective at unconscious cueing, and their facial movements and expressions could influence the performance of the apes.

Terrace's (1979) paper criticising the research into ape language raised issues, and revealed many problems. Unfortunately, some psychologists interpreted it as meaning that apes have no ability to acquire language. Others realised that a more careful approach was needed. Research is still going on, but steps have been taken to avoid some of the problems identified by Terrace and Umiker-Sebeok.

Savage-Rumbaugh (1990; Savage-Rumbaugh *et al.*, 1993) has taken a different approach, and is enabling chimpanzees to acquire language in the same way as human children. Instead of teaching symbols to the chimpanzees and gradually building up a vocabulary, she has used a large vocabulary of symbols right from the start, using them in the presence of the chimps as language is used round human children. Savage-Rumbaugh concentrated first on enabling the chimps to understand language since human children understand language before they speak it.

Savage-Rumbaugh used a device known as a 'lexigram'. This is a board with a matrix of 256 geometrical shapes. The symbols represent words and nouns. The instructor can produce simple requests or commands by touching the appropriate shapes. The sentence is said aloud at the same time to encourage and test the development and understanding of spoken English.

The early results with a bonobo named Matata were not encouraging. However, Matata had taken (kidnapped might be a better term) a newborn infant from his mother, Lorel, whom she treated as her own. The infant Kanzi would run round the test room, jump on Matata's head, push her hand away from the keyboard as she tried to choose the correct symbol, and steal the food she earned as a reward. He seemed to be fascinated by the keyboard. As was subsequently discovered, Kanzi

learned to communicate by listening and watching while Matata was being taught. He then used what he had learned to communicate with her trainers. Kanzi appeared to know all the things Savage-Rumbaugh had been trying to teach Matata.

Kanzi's ability with language is impressive. His ability has been tested with care, avoiding the sort of problem identified by Terrace. He is given verbal requests to carry out actions by someone he cannot see. Savage-Rumbaugh's assistant in the same room with Kanzi wears earphones so that she is unable to indavertently give help or cues to Kanzi. He is asked such questions as 'Can you put the raisins in the bowl?' or 'Can you give the cereal to Karen?' If instructed 'Go to the group room and get the ball' and there was a ball where he was sitting, Kanzi would glance at it, go towards the group room, perhaps touch the ball and on 50 per cent of occasions would hand it to the experimenter. A linguistically more complex version, however, proved easier for Kanzi. When instructed 'Get the ball that's in the group room' he would rarely look at the ball in front of him, and responded correctly to 77 per cent of such requests.

Savage-Rumbaugh concluded that chimpanzees can acquire language skills spontaneously through being socially exposed to a language-rich environment as human children are. Also, like human children, early exposure is critical. On the basis of her research, Savage-Rumbaugh commented that 'these results indicate that the propensity of the pygmy bonobo for the acquisition of primitive language skills is considerably in advance of that reported for other apes' (Savage-Rumbaugh and Lewin, 1994, p. 151). (See figure 11.11.)

As yet not enough is known. It may be that some primates are capable of some aspects of language, but not others. However, it is true to say that language research has revealed primates to have hitherto unsuspected cognitive abilities. The number of studies is relatively small, and more research is needed. Perhaps the difference between primates and humans in relation to language is that whilst apes can acquire some competence in language, they are not predisposed to use language.

Activity 19

True or false? Are any of the following statements true?

a   Only humans can lie.
b   Language is unique to humans.
c   Communication in non-human animals is innate.
d   All human communication is learned.

(Suggested answers on page 385.)

Language in dolphins

Whilst most attempts to teach language to animals have involved primates (our closest relations), Herman *et al.* (1984) investigated language ability in dolphins. The research focused on the ability of dolphins to understand rather than produce language, and suggested that dolphins are able to understand both the semantic and syntactic elements of language.

11.11 Conversational chimps?

Research findings indicate that, in most people, the left hemisphere of the brain is responsible for language.

Brain studies have revealed that an area of the brain, the *planum temporale* or *PT*, is larger in the left hemisphere in human beings. Because of this and since it overlaps Wernicke's area (known to be important for language comprehension), the PT is thought to be essential for understanding language.

It was thought that this asymmetry occurred only in human beings. However, Gannon *et al.* (1998) examined 18 chimpanzee brains and found that in 17 the PT was larger on the left side. Thus a characteristic thought to be linked to language and present only in humans has been found in chimpanzees!

Does this means that chimpanzees have the necessary brain structure for language? In which case, why have they not evolved language? Perhaps attempting to investigate linguistic abilities in chimps by teaching them human language is not the most appropriate method to investigate whether or not they have the capacity. Perhaps we should carry out more studies on communication in wild-living chimpanzees.

Or perhaps neurologists are mistaken and the PT is not essential for human language. What do *you* think?

Self-assessment questions

9   a   On the basis of Hockett's design features, outline whether the waggle dance of the bee is a form of language.
    b   With reference to the following design features, indicate whether primates can acquire language:
        (i) discreteness; (ii) displacement; (iii) interchangeability; (iv) prevarication; (v) productivity;
        (vi) traditional transmission.
    c   Discuss the difficulty in defining language.

10 a   Outline some of the criticisms of research into the ability of primates to acquire human language.
    b   Explain in what way Savage-Rumbaugh's approach to language acquisition in chimpanzees differs from that of earlier researchers.
    c   Describe one study of primate language or communication in the natural environment.

(Suggested answers on pages 387–8.)

Evolutionary explanations of behaviour

Darwin has had a great influence on psychology. By revealing the relationship between humans and other animals, Darwin contributed to the development of comparative psychology.

Evolutionary psychology aims to make sense of human behaviour patterns by understanding how and why they evolved. It takes the view that it is impossible to understand human nature without awareness of how it evolved. Whilst evolutionary psychology promises to explain a great deal, it is also promoting much argument. In the following pages evolutionary explanations of some features of human behaviour are considered and you will be able to decide for yourself how convincing they are.

Ourselves and altruism

One aspect of human and animal behaviour which has been much examined by evolutionary biologists is altruism (see Unit 10). Research has revealed that amongst animals, most altruism benefits the kin of the altruist. Is this true of ourselves? Do we love relatives more than non-relatives? It would seem that we do. Nepotism is widespread, and the care given by parents to their children shows high levels of altruism. Is this affected by relatedness? Although there are many caring step-parents, a step-parent is much more likely than a biological parent to harm a young child (Pinker, 1997).

We are also altruistic to non-relatives, friends for instance. Attempts to explain this have concentrated on the concept of reciprocity where favours are given on a tit-for-tat basis. Trivers (1971) suggested that reciprocal altruism is a beneficial strategy when each individual gains more than he or she loses by the favour.

Activity 20

Can you think of everyday examples of such reciprocity in human beings?

(Suggested answers on page 385.)

The principal requirement for reciprocal altruism to evolve is a stable relationship between individuals, and the capacity to recognise each other so as to detect cheats. How many individuals would our ancestors need to be able to recognise? It is thought that our ancestors lived in hunter-gatherer bands numbering about 150. This is the number found in the average address book!

Activity 21

How many names do you have in your address book? Your friends in theirs? Your parents? Calculate the average number of names.

Our ancestors would, therefore, have been able to practise reciprocal altruism, returning favours but refusing them to those who accepted but did not return them. The concept of reciprocity is evident in many aspects of human relationships and is reflected in our language, for example 'One good turn deserves another', 'I owe you one' and so on. Further, we are very well able to remember faces, which is precisely what is necessary for reciprocal altruism.

Murder in the forest

It is rare in most species for adults to kill adults. Even in those species where such killing does occur, the odds in favour of the killer have to be very good indeed. In practice, this means several individuals against one or two.

There are many instances where humans show extreme hostility to others in the form of torture, rape and killing. Diamond (1991) reported that tribespeople in Western New Guinea take it for granted that strangers will be killed if they enter one another's territory. Numerous anthropological studies reveal that humans have been aggressive throughout recorded history. War is waged against other groups. Wars in pre-Christian Samoa, for example, were frequent and bloody. Constant raids and retaliations took place. When the Spanish invaded the New World, they treated the indigenous Indian population with appalling cruelty and killed many of them. The Holocaust is yet another example, and that such behaviour still takes place is only too evident in Bosnia and Rwanda. It is common in such conflict for women to be raped or abducted.

Why did such behaviour evolve? The answer can perhaps be found in our closest relative, the chimpanzee.

Chimpanzees are what Wrangham and Peterson (1997) call a party-gang species, which means that due to the kinds of food they eat, members of a group are sometimes found alone or in very small parties. This makes them vulnerable since party-gangs of males chimps from one group raid neighbouring territory and kill single adults from other groups. Of two communities studied at Gombe, one group wiped out another group by killing individuals over a period of just under four years (Goodall, 1986). Young females are likely to be abducted. What is the advantage to the chimpanzees of behaving in this way? The raids are low risk, the raiders gain extra food from an extended territory, additional females and the weakening or elimination of their neighbours – potential threats and rivals for resources. The critical factor in this behaviour is party size. It is possible that the advantages of this between-group hostility selected for the evolution of the ingroup/outgroup bias observed in humans. The Robber's Cave study (Sherif *et al.,* 1961) (see Unit 4 pages 125–6) demonstrated the readiness with which ingroup loyalty and outgroup hostility develops.

The talking primate

Many psychologists agree with Chomsky that humans have an innate ability for language. Evolutionary explanations of language consider why selective pressure favoured its development. What contributions might language have made to fitness? Information exchange about flora and fauna, or other people, or both, would certainly have had survival value (Pinker, 1994). It would have contributed to the formation of alliances through exchange of information (gossip). Enquist and Lemar (1993) suggested that gossip may have evolved as a mechanism for monitoring and controlling the activities of cheats.

Activity 22

Try telling someone where the widest selection of magazines is to be found without using language. Or where one can buy the best bread . . .

The ideal partner

If males and females were not sexually attracted to one another, the human species would become extinct. Can the evolutionary approach help us to understand what attracts one person to another? Because the human female's parental investment (PI – see Unit 9) is vastly greater than that of the male, and the human child is dependent for a long time, she is likely to seek a partner who can help her to make the most of her investment and help in the care of any children.

Although the human male can increase his reproductive success by seeking several sexual partners, it may be in his best interests to stay with his partner, have several children with her, and help to rear them.

The above factors suggest that women are likely to be attracted to males who can provide support, and that men are likely to be attracted to women young enough to produce several children. Research based on lonely hearts advertisements in the UK and the USA suggests that this is so. Regardless of culture, men are likely to seek a youthful partner (Dunbar, 1995). Males were more likely to request youth or physical attraction in a partner, and were also less likely to refer to their own appearance, and level of attractiveness. In contrast, women were four times as likely as men to seek characteristics associated with income and status such as 'college educated, professional, home owner'. The male advertisers were correspondingly likely to advertise such attributes!

> ## Activity 23
>
> Study the lonely hearts columns in a magazines or national newspaper. Is there a tendency for the male advertisers seeking a woman partner to ask for younger or physically attractive women? And for women to ask for men with status or earning potential?

You may wonder if this is a cultural effect confined to western cultures. Buss (1989) analysed questionnaires completed by over 100 000 people in 37 different countries. Regardless of culture, women consistently rated the status and earning potential of a partner as important, whilst men focused on youth and physical appearance.

The significance of men requesting attractiveness (smooth skin, shiny hair, slimness) is that it is linked to youth and fertility. Thus it would seem that what men and women find attractive in a potential partner is related to the ability to produce and care for children. It is accepted of course that our preferences are also influenced by cultural factors.

Art and the ancestral savannah

Appreciation of art and music seems to be something that is uniquely human. Yet Diamond (1991) argued that art is not unique to humans, and that it could have its origins in our evolutionary past. There is more than one approach to the evolutionary origins of our aesthetic sense, one of which is based on the environment in which we evolved. This approach investigates our habitat preference. Human beings are thought to have evolved in the African savannah. When American children and adults are shown slides of landscapes and asked how much they would like to visit or live in them, results

suggest that both children and adults like savannah-type landscapes, whilst adults also tend to like the landscapes they grew up in. Pinker (1997) wrote that 'our sense of natural beauty is the mechanism that drove our ancestors into suitable habitats. We innately find savannahs beautiful, but we also like a landscape that is easy to explore and remember, and that we have lived in long enough to know its ins and outs' (p. 376). A survey of gardeners yielded similar results (Orians and Heerwagen, 1992). The landscapes perceived as loveliest are indistinguishable from optimal savannah: semi-open, but not overgrown, with large trees, changes in elevation, and water.

> ## Activity 24
>
> Find some pictures, postcards will do, of different landscapes, for example savannah type, a built-up area, a seascape. Ask family and friends to rate them on a scale indicating how much they like each one.

The value of a house today depends partly on its situation, whether it is near grassland, or water, whether or not it has a view. Thus perhaps our sense of what is beautiful does depend in part on our evolutionary past.

Some have attacked evolutionary explanations of behaviour as involving a misunderstanding of the human mind. Such critics point out that not every characteristic is adaptive; that human intelligence and consciousness make us qualitatively different from all other species. Critics of evolutionary theory suggest that human behaviour is shaped by culture rather than genetic past.

Evolutionary theorists do not claim that every trait is adaptive. Some traits will be the by-products of selective pressure for other things. Moreover, many now live in an environment that is radically different from that in which we evolved. Human behaviour evolved over millions of years in the African savannah during the Pleistocene. Behaviour that was adaptive millions of years ago may no longer be so. Thus whilst some of our behavioural tendencies are appropriate to the modern world, others are not, and may even be **maladaptive**. Further, because we live in such a different world, the interests of the individual may no longer coincide with those of their genes. Certainly, environmental factors, both social and individual, strongly affect the ways in which our evolutionary heritage is expressed, but to claim that everything is due to culture fails to answer the question of why, for example, most emotions and many values are found in all societies so far studied.

One of the strengths of the evolutionary approach is that it provides a coherent theoretical basis to understanding human behaviour. On the basis of theory hypotheses are formulated and tested. If a hypothesis cannot be refuted, then it can be accepted, and we have gained further knowledge about ourselves. It is now generally accepted that some emotions have evolved in both animals and humans, since emotion can contribute to survival: fear motivates avoidance of danger; love ensures care of young; anger contributes to defence.

Evolutionary explanations of behaviour are neutral in that they make no judgement as to whether behaviour is morally good or reprehensible. Where an evolutionary explanation is offered for an undesirable form of behaviour, this in no way justifies such behaviour.

When Darwin published his theory of natural selection in *The Origin of Species* (1859) he believed that he was explaining the evolution of the minds as well as the bodies of animals and humans. Although we must not assume without adequate reason that an evolutionary explanation is correct, we are learning a great deal about ourselves through this approach. In view of the importance of Darwin's theory of natural selection to comparative psychology, it seems appropriate to end with his words: 'much light will be shed on the origin of man and his history' (Darwin, 1859). Many psychologists would agree and indeed, if we really want to change the less desirable aspects of human behaviour, the first essential is to understand them.

Self-assessment questions

11 a Suggest some benefits to humans of reciprocal altruism.
   b Discuss the usefulness of evolutionary explanations of behaviour.

(Suggested answers on page 388.)

Unit summary

- *Comparative psychologists* study animal behaviour with the aim of increasing our understanding of human behaviour. Findings may be obtained through experimental work in laboratories or through studying the behaviour of animals in their natural environment.
- *Behaviourists* focus on directly observable behaviour and on identifying the relationship between a stimulus and the response to the stimulus.
- Pavlov studied the *conditioned reflex* and demonstrated that through association a previously neutral stimulus can come to elicit a *reflex response*.

- Although the principles of *classical conditioning* are thought to apply to all species, they do not apply equally to all species in all situations.
- *Operant conditioning* was developed by Skinner who distinguished between operant conditioning and classical conditioning, pointing out that in operant conditioning the organism *operates* on the environment. Operant conditioning has many applications, although evidence suggests that learning is more complex than operant theory suggests.
- *Foraging* organisms use a variety of methods to obtain food. Some search for food (grazers and hunters), others sit and wait for prey.
- The ability to learn in relation to foraging varies according to species, and is particularly important for *generalist feeders*.

Summary cont'd.

- *Optimal foraging theory (OFT)* looks at feeding on a cost-benefit basis, according to the principle that efficient foragers should feed so as to maximise benefits and minimise costs.
- Evidence reveals that many organisms use more than one system of *navigation*. Pigeons are thought to use several cues for navigation such as the position of the sun, the earth's magnetic field, olfactory and visual cues. Several species of bird navigate using a combination of the earth's magnetic field and the stars.
- Several species have evolved complex *communication* systems including cetaceans, vervet monkeys and bees.
- Psychologists have been trying to teach language to animals for over 60 years in order to discover if *language* is unique to humans.
- Several chimps and a gorilla have mastered some aspects of human language.
- Attempts to teach primates human language have been criticised on the grounds that the animals have been operantly conditioned and that trainers inadvertently cue them to produce signs in sequence.
- *Evolutionary theory* assumes that since humans are similar to other animals in many ways, we can seek to explain much human behaviour by studying the evolution and function of behaviour in other species. Evolutionary theory has been criticised on the grounds that human beings are qualitatively different from all other species.
- Evolutionary theorists do not claim that every trait is *adaptive*; some traits are by-products of selective pressure for other things. Behaviour which was adaptive for our hunter-gatherer ancestors may no longer be so, and may now be *maladaptive* in terms of fitness.
- We should not conclude that a trait has an evolutionary basis unless the hypothesis that it is has been thoroughly tested.
- *Social* and *cultural* factors are also important determinants of human behaviour.
- Evolutionary explanations do not justify unacceptable behaviour, but may enable us to change it by increasing our understanding.

Terms to define

behaviourism
contiguity
design features
maladaptive (behaviour)
migration
optimal foraging theory (OFT)
productivity (of language)

response
search image
shaping
specialist feeder
stimulus
stimulus-response

Further reading

Cartwright, J (1996) 'Human mating behaviour', *Psychology Review*, 3, 22–6. 'Choosing a mate', *Psychology Review*, 3, 8–13.

Two very readable articles written primarily for A-level students.

Davies, R (1995) 'Selfish altruism', *Psychology Review*, 1, 2–9.

An illuminating and clearly argued discussion of altruism in human beings.

Dunbar, R (1995) 'Are you lonesome tonight?', *New Scientist*, 145, 26–31.

An accessible and thought-provoking account of human sexual behaviour.

Ridley, M (1993) *The Red Queen*, Penguin, Harmondsworth.

An entertaining and clearly written book on sex and the evolution of human nature.

Savage-Rumbaugh, S and Lewin, R (1994) *Kanzi*, Doubleday, New York.

The exciting and heart-warming story of Kanzi, a bonobo chimpanzee.

Answers

■ Suggested answers to activities

1

The ethological approach is suitable for studying any species including insects, arthropods, invertebrates, birds and mammals. Studies are carried out in the field, occasionally in the laboratory where naturalistic conditions are recreated (in a fish tank, for instance). The animals studied are wild, and only captured when it is necessary to remove them to a laboratory: they are not bred for the purpose. Ethologists aim to study natural behaviour in the natural habitat.

2

This is probably due to classical conditioning where a stimulus associated with the alarm is waking you up. This might be increased daylight coming through the curtains or a sound produced by the clock mechanism before the alarm goes off.

3

UCS – loud noise
UCR – crying (fear response)
CS – white rat
CR – fear of white rat

5

Prepared	*Unprepared*
precipice, deep water, snake, darkness, confined space	power drill, travel by car, electric point, knife, gun

6

7

a   Money. It satisfies no physical requirements but can be used to obtain food, shelter, etc.

b   A pat on the back. Many secondary reinforcers depend on interests. Thus a ticket to a football match is reinforcing for someone keen on football.

9

FI :   if you give yourself a small treat at regular intervals whilst you are studying (say every 90 minutes), you would be using an FI schedule. Another example is the pay-packet at the end of every week or month.

VI :   someone who fishes is likely to experience VI reinforcement since the intervals between catching fish are likely to vary.

FR :   this is experienced by factory workers who get paid on the basis of the number of items produced, or units assembled. Thus they will receive a certain amount for, say, every ten items produced.

VR :   gambling is a form of variable ratio reinforcement. Slot machines are programmed on this basis.

11

Select a suitable reinforcer – a piece of biscuit perhaps. Reinforce the dog when he is sitting. Then only reinforce when he is sitting and looking at you. Then withhold reinforcement until he moves a paw; this may occur naturally or you may have to move it yourself a few times. When he lifts his paw, withhold reinforcement until he holds the paw out long enough for you to take it.

12

Specialist feeders	Generalist feeders
toads, panda, koalas, vampire bats, humming birds, tiger moth caterpillars, etc.	bluetits, rats, herring gulls, dog, foxes, worms, etc.

16

You would need a map which would function in the same way as a *cognitive map*. This enables you to find your way home from any point.

18

Unless it is a particularly concise dictionary, you will find several definitions. This indicates that the term is used to mean different things.

19

a   False.

b   Depends on how language is defined.

c   Much communication in non-human animals is innate, but not all.

d   False. We also communicate non-verbally. Some of this is learned, some is innate (pupil size and blushing, for example).

20

If A goes to B's party, it is likely that B will be asked to A's party. If a friend buys you coffee one day, you are likely to buy that friend coffee on another. At Christmas people tend to send cards and give presents to those from whom they receive them. One person buys a round of drinks in a bar; next round someone else buys the drinks, and so on.

■ Suggested answers to self-assessment questions.

1

a   This concerns an organism's ability to change its behaviour so as to adapt to altered circumstances. An organism which depends on inherited behaviour patterns rather than the ability to learn is unable to adapt, whereas an organism which can learn is able to alter its behaviour in response to environmental change.

b   Generalisation: when a particular response is conditioned to one stimulus, similar stimuli will elicit that response. It is adaptive in that it enables an organism to transfer learning gained in one situation to other similar, but not identical situations.
Discrimination: the ability to distinguish between different stimuli and respond appropriately to them. It is adaptive since failure to discriminate between different stimuli might, for example, impair the ability to find food (see pages 357–8).

2

a   The law of contiguity states that events or stimuli need to happen close together in time if they are to become associated. For examples see pages 358–9.

b   See pages 358–9 for Pavlov's view and that of Rescorla.

c   Rats seem unable to learn to associate sickness with visual stimuli. Many animals are unable to learn to avoid electric shock because their natural response to an alarming stimulus is to freeze or curl up. It is difficult to condition humans to fear unprepared stimuli (see page 360).

3

a   i   Primary reinforcement is based on the needs of the organism and is reinforcing in its own right. Examples include food, water and sex. Secondary reinforcers acquire their capacity to reinforce through association with a primary reinforcer. In humans, money is a powerful secondary reinforcer (see page 361).

   ii   A positive reinforcer is something pleasant such as food for a hungry animal. Negative reinforcement strengthens a response by ending or taking away an unpleasant stimulus (see pages 362–3). It is important not to confuse negative reinforcement with punishment.

b   i   Punishment aims to weaken a response by an unpleasant stimulus resulting when a response is emitted. It is not always effective, and may suppress a response rather than weaken it. It may also produce undesirable side-effects such as aggression or anxiety (see page 363).

   ii   When used alone punishment does not indicate the alternative, desired response.
It can be effective if it is used in such a way that the organism can attempt an alternative response which can then be reinforced. Combining punishment with reinforcement indicates which behaviour is desirable whilst weakening undesirable behaviour.

c   Similarities between the two forms of conditioning include the following:

■   A learning period is involved in both, with reinforcement strengthening the response. Thus in classical conditioning a period of pairing the CS and UCS is necessary, and a period of responding plus reinforcement in the Skinner box.

■   Contiguity applies to both. If a response is to be conditioned to a CS in classical conditioning, or a new response is to be associated with reinforcement, the UCS or reinforcement must occur close in time to the response. In classical conditioning this refers to the UCS closely following the neutral stimulus; in operant conditioning reinforcement follows immediately after the response is emitted. (There are a few exceptions.)

- The phenomena of extinction, spontaneous recovery, generalisation and discrimination occur in both forms of conditioning.
- Secondary reinforcement in operant conditioning resembles higher order conditioning.

Differences include the following:

- In classical conditioning the response is elicited by the UCS; the response is reflexively 'forced' by the UCS. The UCS has to be presented before the response until conditioning has taken place. In operant conditioning reinforcement is given after the response is made and strengthens it.
- In classical conditioning the UCS occurs without regard to the subject's behaviour, whereas in operant conditioning the reinforcement is contingent on the subject's response.
- In classical conditioning a UCS can only trigger one type of reflex response. Thus food triggers salivation. In operant conditioning reinforcement can be used to strengthen many different responses using shaping procedures.
- One of the main differences seems to be that operant conditioning involves voluntary responses whilst classical conditioning involves involuntary responses. (There is some work, however, which suggests that involuntary behaviour can be conditioned using operant teachniques.)

4
a   You could give either of the reasons outlined on pages 364–5.
b   i   Behaviour based on a chance relationship between a response and reinforcement.
    ii A discriminative stimulus enables us and the animal in the Skinner box to determine whether or not it is worthwhile carrying out a particular action (see page 365).
c   Two such forms of learning include latent and insight learning (see pages 365–6).

5
a   Generalist foragers such as rats take a wide range of food. This has the advantage of greater variety of food: generalists therefore are likely to spend less time in searching for food. However, they are likely to need more time in which to deal with it. They also benefit in that if one source of food becomes unavailable, others are available to them. Generalists are also known as omnivores.
    Specialists feed on one or two types of food only. The toad and panda are examples of this. The advantage is that they require less time to deal with the food, the disadvantage is that they will require a longer search time and, if the food source is scarce, a specialist may starve. Laverty and Plowright's (1988) work on generalist and

specialist bumblebees demonstrates the cost and benefits of specialist and generalist feeding.
b   The investigations of Laverty and Plowright (1988) and Krebs *et al.* (1978) (page 369) are suitable examples.
c   Foragers need to be able to search for, recognise and obtain their food. The extent of learning required varies according to the type of foraging involved. Even passive foragers require some learning ability in order to identify patches in which food is to be found, for example, frogs (see page 368). The ability to learn does not seem to be so important for specialist feeders as for generalists. Specialist feeders need only to recognise their food, whilst generalists need to identify suitable food, and to avoid food which is unpleasant or poisonous (see pages 367–8). Also, generalists need to learn how to deal most effectively with their food.
    Learning is an essential aspect of the foraging behaviour of bees. Although bees have the innate ability to recognise flower-like objects, they need to learn which flowers provide most food. Learning is also involved where animals collect more food than they require, and hide it. Research suggests that later retrieval is on the basis of memory rather than trial and error.

6
a   Optimal foraging refers to the searching and obtaining of food in the most efficient way possible.
b   OFT predicts that animals will feed in such a way as to maximise benefits and minimise costs.
c   i   The prey model is based on types of prey available in the environment. The organism can search for these at the same time. However, prey differ in the energy they contain, and in the time needed to handle them. According to OFT, if the individual gains greater energy by concentrating on one type of prey, then this is what it will do.
    ii The patch model refers to food which is not evenly distributed, and which occurs in patches. OFT predicts that an efficient predator would concentrate on areas which provide an optimal return in relation to effort expended.
d   OFT is useful in that it provides a framework for investigating foraging behaviour, particularly with reference to the costs and benefits of alternative foraging strategies, and different types of food. It has enabled researchers to design investigations which have yielded information about how animals forage, for example see pages 368–9. However, OFT can be criticised in that it does not consider the forager in relation to other competing foragers, but focuses on the individual and its food. Further, to assume that maximum gain is based on energy gain may not apply to all animals. These factors, plus the fact that OFT ignores the motivational and physiological state of the animal, suggests that OFT takes

an over-simplistic approach to foraging behaviour. In addition, it is difficult to follow in detail for people who have no background in mathematics or economics.

7

a   There are several ways in which animals benefit from migration (see page 372).

b   Methods of investigation are described on pages 370–2.

c   Bees use the position of the sun to determine direction; if the sun is obscured by cloud, they use the pattern of polarised light. Many researchers believe that pigeons use the position of the sun in the sky to find their way home. However, since they are able to navigate successfully when the sky is overcast, it seems that they are able to use alternative cues. Interfering with their ability to detect the earth's magnetic field affects their ability to navigate when the sky is overcast suggesting that they use this sense when the sun is obscured. There is some evidence that they may be able to use olfactory cues, and recent evidence suggests that one pigeon may follow another. It may be that they use the sun and the earth's magnetic field to head in the right direction, or follow another pigeon for the same reason. Some birds follow geographical features such as coastlines or mountain ranges. Visual cues seem to be important in the precise location of the home site – a particular building for instance. It is also likely that they develop a mental map of the area around the home site based on visual cues, variations in the magnetic field and smell. Baker (1984) suggested that birds acquire such a map during their first migration.

8

a   Examples include homing in salmon, ants and pigeons.

b   Baker (1984) suggested that birds learn the details of the route home on the outward journey. Thus details such as visual landmarks, olfactory cues, and variations in the magnetic field form the basis of a mental map which enables birds to find their way home. This would apply to both foraging and migratory flights. Wiltschko *et al.* (1985) pointed out that inexperienced young pigeons require cues obtained during the outward journey in order to find the way home. In many species navigation includes an inherited component. Thus the migrating young do not travel with the adults but migrate successfully. The Bogong moth dies when the eggs are laid, so the basis of the migration is inherited. Much research indicates an interaction between learned and innate components. Honeybees make orientation flights when they leave the hive or food source: they thus learn how the characteristics of the area fit in with their surroundings. The bee-killing digger wasp studied by Tinbergen also learns. As it makes her orientation flight, she learns the landmarks round her nest.

c   Homing and navigation have been studied for many years, but much remains to be discovered. The behaviour is difficult to investigate largely because of the great variety of navigation systems involved, and the fact that most animals have more than one system of navigation. An additional factor is the vast distance covered by some migrating animals. This creates particular difficulties when studying marine animals such as whales and eels.

9

a   The waggle dance of the honeybee meets some of Hockett's criteria for language. The dance serves to transmit information to other foragers about the location of a distant food source, thus it seems to satisfy Hockett's criterion of displacement. It is also interchangeable since individuals are able to both transmit and receive information. It also shows specialisation: it specifically functions to communicate, not as a by-product of some other behaviour. However, the dance follows a set pattern and does not therefore meet the criteria for productivity or discreteness. Nor does it meet the criteria for learnability and prevarication. The ability is innate, and it is not used to convey information of where food is not to be found.

b   i   Discreteness: there is some evidence for this. Lana was able to correct syntactically incorrect sentences, and could discriminate between 'Lana groom Tim' and 'Tim groom Lana'. More recently, Kanzi, a bonobo, has demonstrated that he can react to meaning denoted by syntax.

   ii   Displacement: Koko is described as being able to refer to past events, and to refer to an emotional state that she is not experiencing at the time.

   iii Interchangeability: Fouts (1972) observed that chimpanzees in a colony he set up signed to each other even when no humans were present.

   iv   Prevarication: Koko used language to convey an untruth.

   v   Productivity: it was claimed that Lana's 'finger bracelet' the first time she saw a ring, and Washoe signing 'water bird' when she saw a swan when on a lake are examples of novel combinations. Koko is reported as making new sign combinations such as 'bottle match' for a cigarette lighter.

   vi   Traditional transmission: Washoe used signs to communicate with her adopted infant Loulis, which he imitated. Kanzi learned to communicate with lexigrams by observing his mother.

c   Language is not easy to define largely because it has many characteristics. Part of the problem is concerned with whether or not human language is the only form of communication which we should refer to as language. However, several forms of animal communication are often referred to as language. Is any transmission of information a form of language, a signal for instance, such as an alarm call or colouring indicative of breeding readiness? It seems reasonable to conclude that signalling does not constitute language, but at what level does communication involve more than signalling and become language? Does the definition of language depend on how much information is communicated? Is language wholly different from other forms of communication? It is because of these difficulties that linguists and psychologists have proposed certain criteria for defining language. These are based on human language and provide a means against which communication systems can be assessed. One of the problems in defining language is that the term is often used interchangeably with communication.

10

a   Much of the criticism has come from Terrace (1979) and Sebeok and Umiker-Sebeok (1980). This is described on pages 376–7.

b   Savage-Rumbaugh set out to enable chimpanzees to acquire language in the same way that human children do, rather than to teach them gradually to build up a vocabulary of signs or symbols. She exposed the chimpanzees to a large vocabulary of symbols, using them around the chimps, just as language surrounds children.

c   Savage-Rumbaugh *et al.* (1996) investigated the way in which wild-living bonobos follow the direction taken by other groups (parties). Evidence suggests that bonobos deliberately leave signals which indicate the direction taken (see page 375). (Another study you could describe is that with vervet monkeys, page 374.)

11

a   If one person helps another, and the help is returned on a later occasion, both individuals benefit, providing the cost of doing the favour is smaller than the cost of receiving it. Thus on one occasion an individual may have no food while another has plenty and can share it. This situation may later be reversed. In modern life the help may be in the form of helping out with childcare, money, helping someone who is ill, etc. In our ancestral environment if a hunter kills a large prey animal and shares it, many will benefit. He will not lose as the meat does not keep. He (and everyone else) benefits if all behave in this way, sharing meat and receiving meat in return.

b   The evolutionary approach in psychology aims to increase our understanding of human behaviour by considering how and why it evolved. It can help us to understand behaviour which does not seem appropriate or useful. Such behaviour may have contributed to fitness in the very different environment in which we evolved. It is important to bear in mind, however, that some behaviour might be the by-product of selective pressure for other traits. On the basis of evolutionary theory, hypotheses can be formulated and attempts made to refute them. If an evolutionary explanation is offered in relation to an aspect of human behaviour, it should not be accepted until it is clear that it cannot be refuted. Then and then only should it be accepted as a legitimate explanation of human behaviour. Evolutionary explanations of behaviour do not justify undesirable human behaviour. It should not be assumed that evolutionary theory can explain everything. Not all behaviour is adaptive, and does not always provide the optimum solution to a problem. Further, due emphasis must be given to the important effects of culture and experience on behaviour, and the interaction between innate predispositions and experience. Human beings have evolved the ability to respond flexibly, to choose and to make their own decisions.

Biopsychology

Unit | 12

Nervous Systems and Behaviour

Lorna Jones, Darrell de Souza and Irene Taylor

This unit covers:

Neural transmission

Effects of psychoactive drugs on behaviour

The central and autonomic nervous systems

Control systems and behaviour

By the end of this unit, you should be able to:

- show awareness of how behaviour can be explained in terms of activity in the nervous system (neural and synaptic activity)

- demonstrate an awareness of the effects of drugs on behaviour

- describe the position, structure and function of the central nervous system, autonomic nervous system and endocrine system and how they interact during behaviour

- understand how sensory, cognitive, affective and homeostatic mechanisms are involved in normal and abnormal functions.

Unit 12 Contents

Introduction

Imagine you are alone one night and have been awoken from a deep sleep by the phone ringing. It takes a moment for you to realise what has happened. You feel cross at being woken up and don't want to leave your warm bed. However, you are anxious about bad news, and so spur yourself to do so. As you make your way to the telephone, you are bringing to mind all the people who might be ringing you – and why – and you pick the receiver up with very mixed feelings. These 'unmix' very quickly when the voice from the other end sweetly apologises for dialling the wrong number.

Your actions in climbing out of bed and reaching the phone, your thoughts and words were all controlled by neural activity in your central nervous system. Your feelings resulted from neural activity in your autonomic nervous system and chemical activity in your endocrine system.

Explaining how behaviour can be understood in terms of neural and chemical activity is a *reductionist approach* (see pages 24–7). This seeks to describe behaviour in simple, mechanical terms. It reduces the nervous system to its biological structures and what these do, concentrating on what can be seen and measured, rather than on psychological processes. This is a key issue for debate in psychology. It can be argued that fully understanding the mind's complexities needs more knowledge than can be gained by studying only anatomy and biochemistry. On the other hand, it is argued that no behaviour can be understood without such knowledge, even though this brings with it a danger of 'not being able to see the wood for the trees'.

The nervous and endocrine systems are structured so that information from many sources can be relayed to central processing areas in the brain where it is interpreted, a suitable response generated and an appropriate emotion experienced. This is fine, if the information is complete – but what if it is not? Look at Activity 1, then read on.

You might have said the picture is a geometrical figure. In fact it is reputed to be a Mexican riding a bicycle, seen from above. You may have experienced this kind of deception in real life, seeing something which you know is familiar but

Activity 1

There is a game which consists of cards, each with a different picture on it which has been drawn from an unfamiliar angle. The game requires participants to identify the objects depicted. One of the pictures looks like —O—. What do you think it depicts?

cannot quite make out – like something on your bedside table when you first wake up. A normal reaction is to imagine all sorts of possibilities until you move your angle of vision. You then perceive clearly what the object is – and experience a feeling of relief as the mystery is revealed. Unfamiliar or incomplete information does not stop our brain from functioning but it does modify both interpretation and response.

Activity 2

Draw some common objects from uncommon angles and ask friends to guess what the objects are. You will probably find that their suggestions get more accurate with practice. This shows how adaptive our brains can be in learning new 'tricks'.

This kind of experience is normal for people who can see and hear, but what if a person is born blind or profoundly deaf? Can information ever be complete and perfect?

Much of our behaviour is driven by the results of previous experiences. Our responses are related to the inherited pattern and nature of our brain's physiological structure. This means that everything we experience is interpreted as a best guess from the information available – and our response is the best one we can make in the circumstances.

Consider the wide variety of functions for which our brains are responsible. Sensation and movement, language and memories, personality and intelligent thinking, consciousness and our ability for self-reflection to name but a few. It is fascinating to think that ultimately all of these can be traced to the interrelated action of microscopic cells from which the structures of our nervous and endocrine systems are made.

This unit covers the anatomy (structure) of these systems; and how their physiology (functioning) governs and coordinates our behaviour by their interrelated activities. It also discusses how their functioning can be affected by psychoactive drugs.

Neural transmission

'The brain is the organ that moves the muscles. That may sound a bit simplistic but ultimately, movement – or more accurately, behaviour – is the primary function of the nervous system' (Carlson, 1994, p. 20).

For the brain to be able to organise appropriate movements it needs information on what is happening in the environment. To this end the body contains cells specialised for the tasks of receiving, processing and transmitting information. As humans we are complex animals that do not react automatically to environmental changes; our brains are flexible and able to behave in accordance, not only to present conditions, but also to those encountered previously. These abilities are all made possible by the billions of cells in the nervous system.

The basic units of the body are *cells*. There are many different kinds. Each kind is similar to all others by having the same components, but each is different to others by having a specialised shape and function. One of the components of cells is a semi-fluid, jelly-like substance called *cytoplasm*, surrounded by a cell membrane. Embedded in the cytoplasm of most cells is another, denser component composed of *nuclearplasm*, called the *nucleus*. This controls the activity of the cytoplasm where the specialised functions take place, for instance the manufacture of secretions in glandular cells. Cytoplasm and nuclearplasm together constitute *protoplasm*, 'the stuff of life', in which the processes associated with life are carried out. In the nervous system there are a number of specialised cells called glial cells and neurons.

Glial cells

Glial cells outnumber neurons by 10:1 (Groves and Rebec, 1992). The term 'glia', meaning glue, stems from the original (false) belief that these cells cement the neurons together. They form a substantial portion of brain tissue and lie between neurons and blood vessels. They function as supporting cells and probably play a role in neural development. Unlike most neurons, glial cells can divide and reproduce. It is thought that in doing so they may provide nerve fibres with an opportunity to make connections with other neurons. They may therefore be important as part of the learning and memory processes.

Glial cells provide physical and functional support for neurons in the central nervous system (CNS) and peripheral nervous system (PNS). This support comes from *satellite cells*. This physical matrix holds the neural circuits together and absorbs dead cells and debris:

- The largest glial cells are *astroglia/astrocytes* (star-shaped). They cover the outer surface of blood vessels in the brain and also contact neuron cell bodies. In this way they are thought to be involved in the passage of chemicals from the blood into neurons. (Chan-Ling and Stone, 1991).

- Glial cells that wrap around the axons of some neurons in the CNS are called *oligodendroglia/ oligodendrocytes* and are rich in *myelin*, a fatty insulating substance which helps speed up the conduction in the axons around which they sheath.

- *Schwann cells* are satellite cells which perform a similar function to oligodendroglia in the PNS.

Schwann cells and oligodendroglia are illustrated in figure 12.1. Note that each Schwann cell constitutes one myelin segment, whereas each oligodendroglia cell covers several. Only Schwann cells can help in regrowth after damage so there is very little axonal regeneration in the CNS.

In myelinated axons ions pass through the axonal membrane only at the gaps between the adjoining myelin segments. These gaps are known as the **nodes of Ranvier**. Myelination increases the

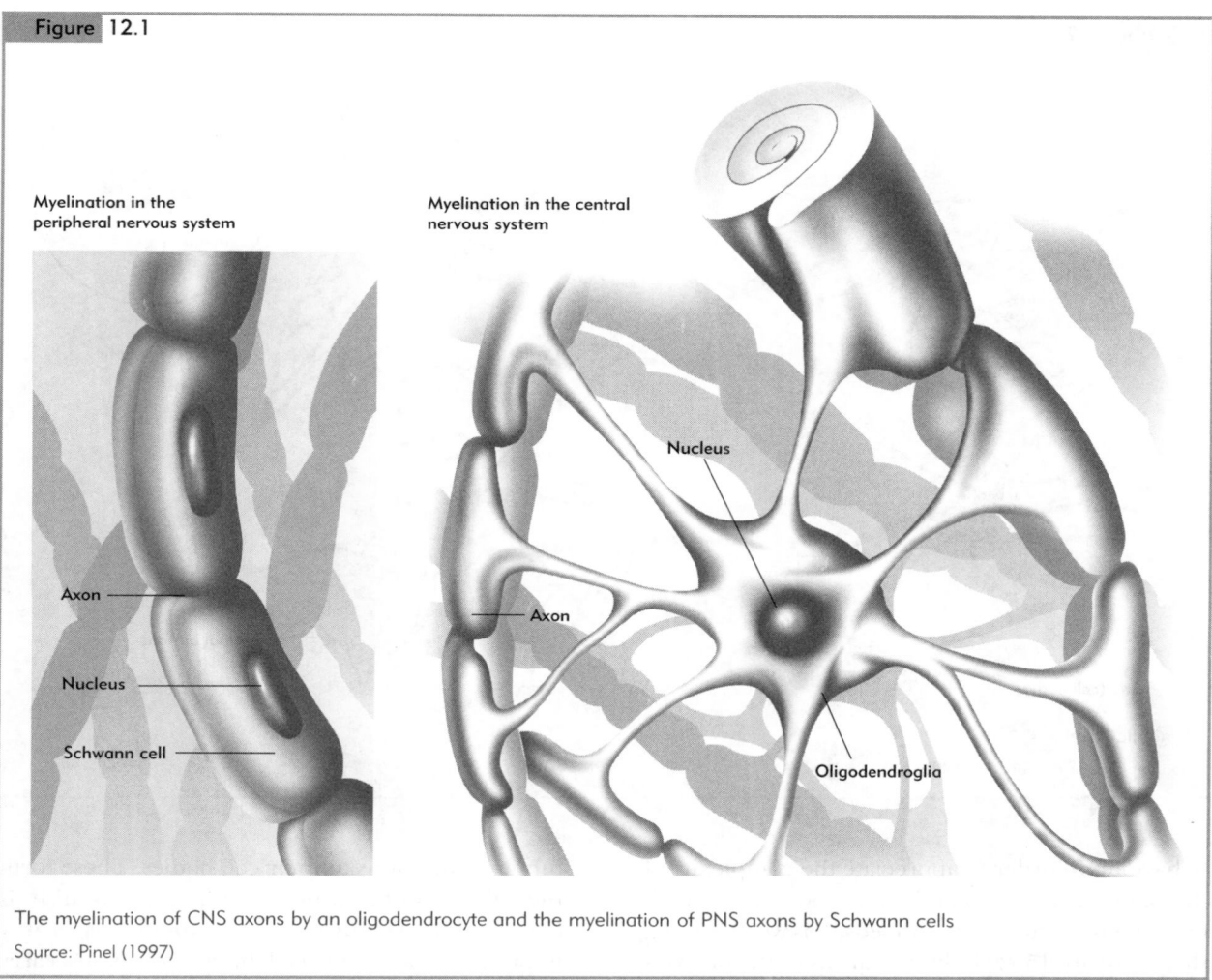

Figure 12.1

Myelination in the peripheral nervous system

Myelination in the central nervous system

Nucleus

Axon

Axon

Nucleus

Schwann cell

Oligodendroglia

The myelination of CNS axons by an oligodendrocyte and the myelination of PNS axons by Schwann cells

Source: Pinel (1997)

speed of transmission of the impulse as the signal 'jumps' down the axon from node to node, known as **saltatory conduction**. Conduction is quicker in myelinated large-diameter motor neurons which can conduct up to speeds of 100 metres per second. Unmyelinated axons conduct at about 1 metre per second.

Neurons

Neurons are specialised for initiating and conducting electro-chemical impulses, a function which forms the basis of all brain activity and

Activity 3

See if you can fill in the blanks in the following sentences describing the different types of cells. The basic units of the body are cells of which there are many different kinds. One of the components of cells is a semi-fluid, jelly-like substance called _____. Embedded in the _____ of most cells is another, denser component composed of _____ called the _____. Cytoplasm and _____ together constitute _____, 'the stuff of life'.

(Suggested answers on page 428.)

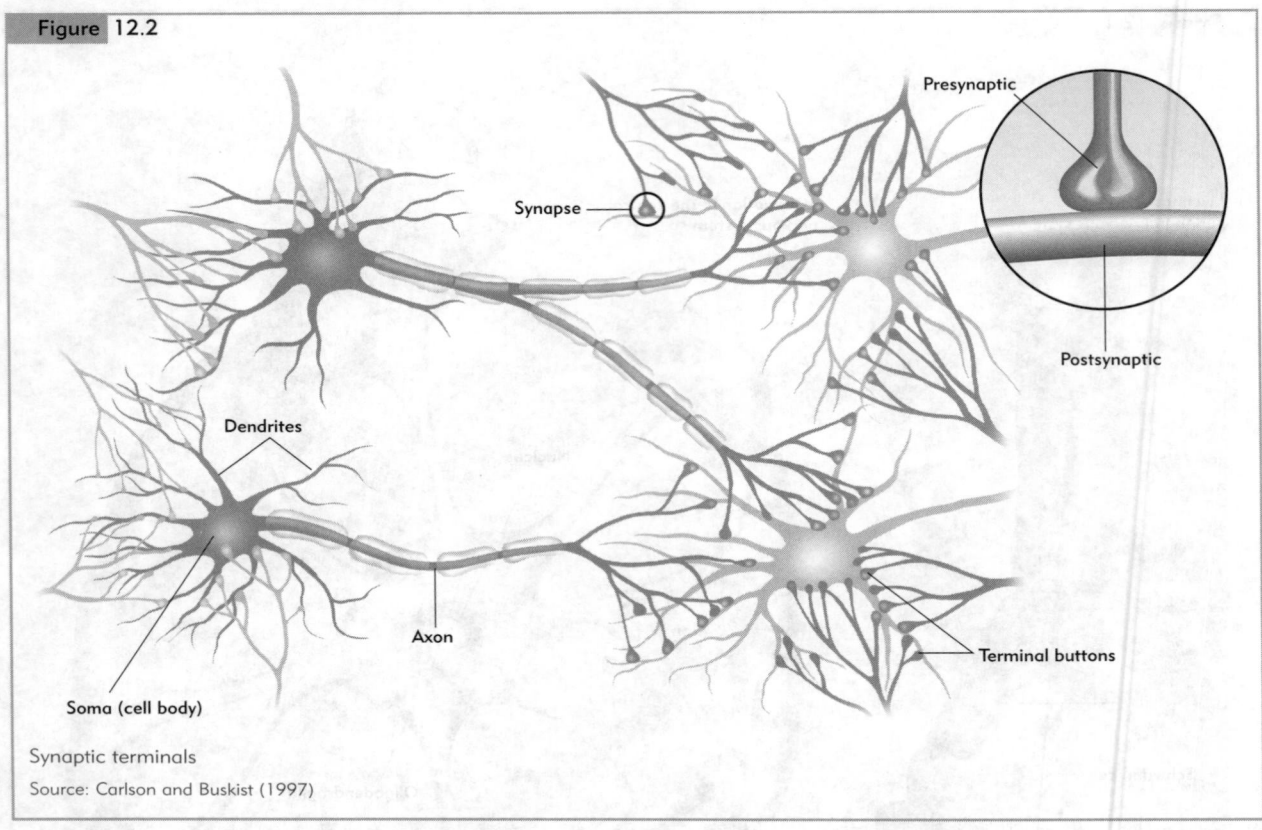

Figure 12.2

Presynaptic

Synapse

Postsynaptic

Dendrites

Axon

Terminal buttons

Soma (cell body)

Synaptic terminals

Source: Carlson and Buskist (1997)

behaviour. In order to appreciate the complexity of the brain, its function and its vast potential (much of which is apparently untapped), it is worth noting that there are 15–20 billion neurons in the nervous system. Some 10 billion of these are located in the brain and most connect with several hundreds, sometimes thousands, of other neurons. Thus the influences on a single neuron are many, and the number of different interconnections and neural pathways is truly mindboggling! Figure 12.2 shows an example of these interconnections.

Although it is believed that most neurons in the brain cannot regenerate – and that they may degenerate at a rate of a thousand a day – this represents a gradual loss of a mere 1 per cent of the total over a whole lifetime. However, it is possible for interconnections between neurons to go on increasing for most of the lifetime of an active brain. Figure 12.3 illustrates some of the different kinds of neurons.

You can see from figure 12.3 that neurons have

tubular extensions to their cell bodies. These form the fibres along which the nerve impulse is conducted. Dendrons and **dendrites** carry impulses towards the cell body and axons carry them away from the cell body towards the dendrites of another cell. Axons terminate in fine branches having swollen endings called *synaptic terminals*, which lie close to receptor sites on the cell body or dendrites of another neuron. The tiny gap between the synaptic terminal of one neuron and the cell body or dendrites of the adjacent neuron is known as a *synaptic cleft*. The synaptic cleft, together with the membranes of the pre-synaptic terminal and the post-synaptic receptor sites, constitute a **synapse**. *Sensory neurons* are concerned with information arriving from the environment.

Consider all the things that you are currently registering through your senses. You probably included things relating to the senses of vision, hearing, touch, taste and smell. All such sensory information is detected by specialised receptors in

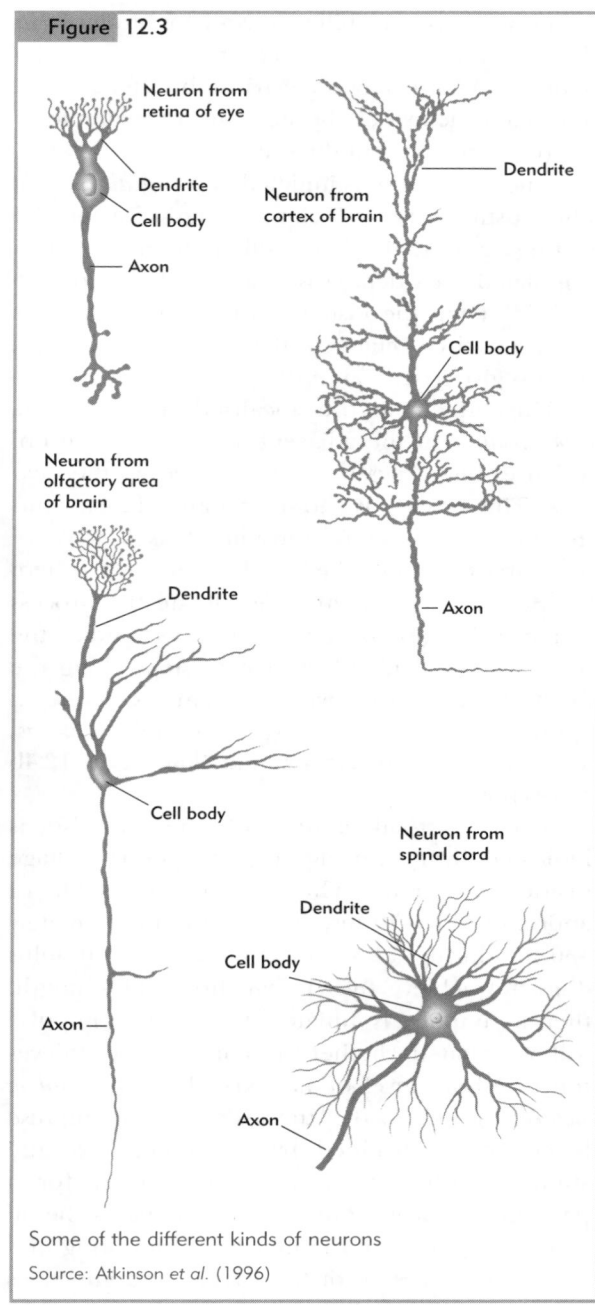

Figure 12.3

Neuron from retina of eye

Dendrite

Cell body

Axon

Neuron from cortex of brain

Dendrite

Cell body

Axon

Neuron from olfactory area of brain

Dendrite

Cell body

Axon

Neuron from spinal cord

Dendrite

Cell body

Axon

Some of the different kinds of neurons

Source: Atkinson et al. (1996)

our sense organs. When these are stimulated, they initiate impulses which are then transmitted along peripheral neurons to a nerve centre. Do activity 4, then read on.

Your participant will probably ask you to stop at a point quite distant from the elbow. This is

Activity 4

How close together do you think touch receptors in the skin are? Ask someone to help you find out. Ask the person to hold one arm out, palm upwards having rolled the sleeve up. With your finger, gently trace a small circle on the person's wrist – and then another just below the elbow. Now tell the person that you are going to trace a spiral up his or her arm, and to tell you when you have reached the point, below the elbow, where you traced the second circle. Ask the person to shut his or her eyes while you do this. Can you explain the results?

because the sensory receptors for touch are further apart in some places than others and do not discriminate between stimuli so well. In our fingers, hands and lips, where we do most of our feeling, the sensory receptors are closer together than in our arms, back and feet.

However, we are often aware of more about the nature of a stimulus than our senses tell us. We are able to compare different stimuli, for example relative temperatures of water. We can also interpret information such as the meaning of particular sounds when someone is talking to us.

We also receive information from the internal environment, which we are not necessarily aware of, such as the position of our limbs and the activities of our internal organs. Internal receptors are called *proprioreceptors* and provide continual feedback about the state of tension (contraction) in both skeletal muscles and the walls of internal organs – information vital for the accurate coordination of body functioning.

Motor neurons transmit impulses which produce muscular contractions.

Activity 5

Think about what happens when your eyes scan this text or your hand prepares to turn the page.

Both these actions involve muscle contractions which occur when motor nerve impulses, initiated in the brain, are transmitted along motor axons to a muscle, causing it to contract.

Secretory neurons are similar to motor neurons but stimulate activity in glands, rather than muscles. For example, the gland known as the adrenal medulla is controlled by secretory nerves from a part of the brain called the hypothalamus. This stimulates it to secrete adrenaline, a hormone active during intense emotional experiences (see page 421).

Association neurons (sometimes called connector neurons) exist in various forms and provide interconnections within the brain and spinal cord. Their many fine dendrites and terminal branches form dense networks of communication between sensory and motor neurons, sensory and secretory neurons and between association neurons.

The nerve impulse

Neurons function in two basic ways. Firstly, by transmitting electro-chemical impulses along the length of the axon; secondly, by secreting a chemical neurotransmitter from the synaptic terminals.

The ability of neurons to transmit electro-chemical impulses from a cell body along an axon to synaptic terminals, rests with the nature of the nerve cell membrane. The membrane actively secretes sodium ions (Na^+) out of the axoplasm by a mechanism known as the 'sodium pump'. This maintains a higher concentration of potassium ions (K^+) and chloride ions (Cl^-) inside a neuron relative to the outside and a higher concentration of Na^+ ions outside relative to the inside. The result is that, in relative terms, the inside of a neuron is more negatively charged than the outside.

The difference in charge across the nerve cell membrane exists in all inactive neurons. This is known as the *resting potential*. Stimuli which alter the resting potential may cause a nerve to initiate (fire) a nerve impulse in one of three ways. One way is mechanical, by distorting the neuron, for example in the auditory apparatus of the ear. A second way is chemical, by affecting the membrane's permeability to Na^+, for example in the olfactory organ of the nose and between neurons. A third way is electrical, by affecting the internal structure of the neuron, for example in the rods and cones of the eye.

A nerve impulse is initiated at a *critical threshold* when a stimulus of sufficient strength disrupts the resting potential. The cell membrane at a stimulated area depolarises, allowing Na^+ ions to rush in. Then the inside of the neuron becomes more positively charged than the outside. This process gives rise to an *action potential*.

The effect in the localised area triggers *depolarisation* in the adjacent area of the neuron, which in turn triggers a similar effect in the next area. This process is shown in figure 12.4a. Thus the nerve impulse is transmitted as a wave of depolarisation along the length of the axon. Where the Schwann cells help to accelerate the process (ionic exchanges taking place in leaps between the nodes of Ranvier, rather than in steps along the axon length) the whole event is over in approximately 4 milliseconds in myelinated axons. This is known as **saltatory conduction**. Figure 12.4b shows how it happens.

The electrical nature of the impulse is indicated by measuring the changes in voltage inside the axon. The resting potential, of approximately –70 mv, changes to approximately +30 mv during an action potential. If a stimulus does not achieve the critical threshold strength, then no impulse is initiated. However, an impulse will be initiated whether the stimulus just achieves the threshold level or far exceeds it. This *all or nothing effect* shows that the strength of an impulse is neither determined by the strength of the stimulus initiating it, nor will it differ for a particular neuron. Pinel (1997) compares the all or nothing firing of the neuron to the firing of a gun. The squeezing of the trigger of a gun does not make the bullet travel faster or further anymore than does the speed or amplitude of the action potential.

The 'sodium pump' restores the resting potential to the axon, making it possible for another nerve impulse to be transmitted. This *refractory period* (the duration of recovery time) varies according to the neuron. No impulse is

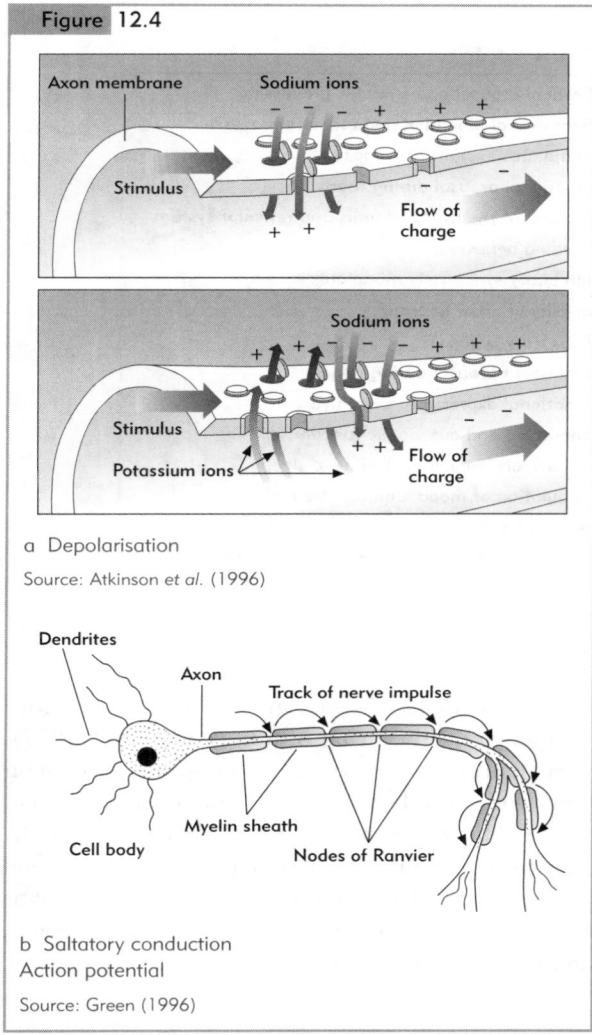

Figure 12.4

Axon membrane   Sodium ions

Stimulus

Flow of charge

Sodium ions

Stimulus

Potassium ions

Flow of charge

a Depolarisation

Source: Atkinson et al. (1996)

Dendrites

Axon

Track of nerve impulse

Myelin sheath

Cell body

Nodes of Ranvier

b Saltatory conduction
Action potential

Source: Green (1996)

Synaptic transmission

Synaptic clefts constitute actual physical gaps of about 0.005 millimetres between neurons. Waves of depolarisation are unable to cross them. Communication between neurons is attained by chemical **neurotransmitters** secreted from the synaptic terminals of the pre-synaptic neurons when a nerve impulse reaches them. Neurotransmitters diffuse across the synaptic cleft and bind to specific post-synaptic receptor sites on an adjacent neuron. The effect produced depends on the nature of the synapse into which they are secreted. Figure 12.5 shows a synapse; table 12.6 lists some of the more common neurotransmitters, their location and action.

At *excitatory synapses*, neurotransmitters decrease the post-synaptic membrane potentials, i.e. lower the threshold. Thus depolarisation and initiation of nerve impulses in the post-synaptic neuron become more likely. At *inhibitory synapses*, the reverse is true. Post-synaptic membrane potentials are increased, heightening the threshold level and making initiation of a nerve impulse less likely. This effect builds up over a short period of time. If sufficient excitatory synapses are activated, the membrane potential will be reduced enough to generate a nerve impulse. However, activation of inhibitory synapses will counteract this. Remember that any one neuron may synapse with thousands of others.

possible during the initial **absolute refractory period**, regardless of stimulus strength. However, during the later **relative refractory period** a nerve impulse can be initiated by a sufficiently strong stimulus. Thus stimulus strength is coded by the number of impulses per second passing along the neuron, known as **temporal summation**.

Activity 6

Make labelled drawings of the different kinds of neurons. On each, indicate its origin and termination, and state its functions. (If you have any difficulty, turn back to page 397.)

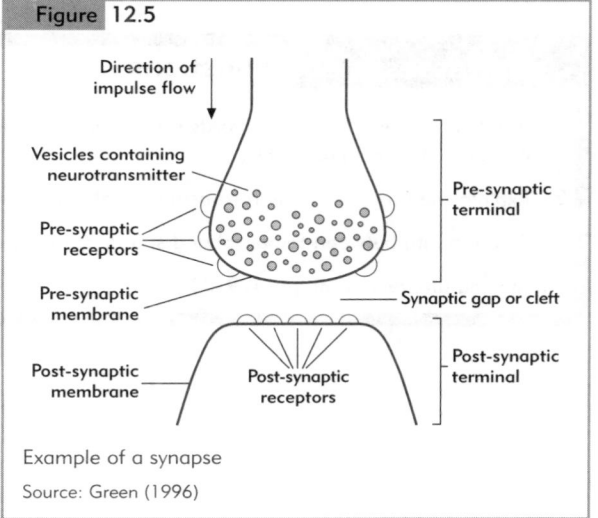

Figure 12.5

Direction of impulse flow

Vesicles containing neurotransmitter

Pre-synaptic receptors

Pre-synaptic membrane

Post-synaptic membrane

Post-synaptic receptors

Pre-synaptic terminal

Synaptic gap or cleft

Post-synaptic terminal

Example of a synapse

Source: Green (1996)

Table 12.6

Neurotransmitter	Place of secretion	Effects
Acetylcholine	Hind brain	Cortical arousal and stimulus processing
	Mid brain (hippocampus)	Behavioural inhibition and memory processes
	CNS	Stimulates excitatory synapses
Adrenaline	Adrenal medulla	Emotional arousal during fear
Dopamine	Mid brain	Arousal of the hypothalamus and reticular system
	Pituitary gland	Feeding behaviour
Gamma-amino butyric acid (GABA)	CNS	Inhibitory synapses – modulates activity in other neurons
Glutamate	CNS	Excitatory synapses
Noradrenaline	Adrenal medulla	Emotional arousal during anger
	Hind brain (pons and medulla)	Emotional expression. Cognitive, endocrine and autonomic functions
Serotonin	Mid brain	Behavioural inhibition and deep sleep
		Regulation of mood, control of eating and regulation of pain

Some neurotransmitters and their effects

Some of these will be excitatory, others inhibitory and many may be active at any particular moment. Thus, whether a neuron fires an impulse or not depends on the summed effect of excitatory and inhibitory activity, known as **spatial summation**.

Each neuron continuously integrates signals over both time and space as it is continually bombarded with stimuli through the thousands of synapses covering its dendrites and cell body.

Synapses near the axon hillock have more influence on the firing of a neuron (Pinel, 1997). Any neurotransmitters left in the synapse are taken back for re-use by the axon terminals that released them, known as *re-uptake*, or are deactivated by enzymes present at the synapses. It is the total pattern of activity in the nervous system that is crucial and it is this neural excitation which generates our conscious experience.

Self-assessment questions

1 Briefly describe in your own words the meaning of the 'all or nothing' response, and explain how impulse strength can be coded in spite of this.

2 Explain the function of neurotransmitters at excitatory and inhibitory synapses.

3 Differentiate between temporal and spatial summation.

(Suggested answers on pages 429–30.)

The effects of psychoactive drugs on behaviour

As noted above, neurotransmitters are released at the synapse, where in many cases they travel a very short distance to the post-synaptic membrane receptors. However, some neurons release chemicals which circulate in the brain and act on receptors of many thousands of neurons, some of which are a considerable distance apart. These chemicals are known as **neuromodulators** because they modify the activity of certain neurons throughout the brain (Carlson and Buskist, 1997). These can be seen as the brain's own 'drugs'. They can excite or inhibit many different groups of neurons and result in several physiological and behavioural effects. A neuromodulator 'adjusts the sensitivity of populations of cells to the excitatory and inhibitory signals at fast-acting directed synapses' (Pinel, 1997, p. 99).

One of the best known groups of neuromodulators are the *endorphins*, or *opioids* ('opium-like'). Endorphins stimulate receptors in certain parts of the brain and their behavioural effects include decreased sensitivity to pain, thus enabling the individual to continue in ongoing activity. One such endorphin is *enkephalin*. Endorphins were first reported by Hughes *et al.* in 1975 when several researchers studying the effects of morphine and other opiates discovered there were special receptor sites for such drugs within the brain. It was found that brain chemicals exist with a similar structure to opiates. These substances seem to act as neuromodulators stimulating certain receptor sites. Researchers tried to explain why the brain would produce such neurotransmitters. It has been suggested that endorphins are released in response to pain or vigorous exercise and so help reduce the pain which might interfere with ongoing behaviour. Additionally, it is thought that opioids intensify positive sensations, for example 'jogger's high'. It would appear the brain possesses an internal mechanism for reducing negative or painful sensations and magnifying pleasant sensations, and morphine and other opiates stimulate this naturally occurring system. Understanding synaptic transmission is thought to be the first step towards understanding how certain disorders can be treated and the key to successful treatment for drug addiction.

Today drugs and their effects on human life are central to discussion and the focus of media interest. The desire to experience some altered state of consciousness seems to be an intrinsic part of the human condition (Gossop, 1987). **Psychoactive drugs** do this. The chemicals they contain interfere with the normal functioning of the nervous systems, thus affecting behaviour. Some, like caffeine, nicotine and alcohol, are socially tolerated in many cultures. Others, like morphine and some codeine preparations, are obtainable only by prescription. A few, like LSD, are legally banned and are obtained illegally – often in impure form.

Addiction, tolerance and withdrawal

Recreational drug use (and abuse) has had devastating effects on the lives of many people, both socially and economically. Traditional methods used to control drug abuse and treat addictions have been only marginally successful. This has led researchers to develop effective drug therapies using knowledge of how drugs exert their effects on the nervous system. We, as humans, are able to tolerate and eliminate small quantities of almost any substance or drug without permanent harmful effects. However, if large doses are taken or a small amount is used frequently, then physical or mental health may be affected. When the use of a drug adversely affects health, or the individual's ability to function in society, it is defined as *drug abuse*. In drug abuse there are three related phenomena as follows:

- **Addiction**, which is really a behavioural term, refers to how the user seeks out and uses the drug with increasing frequency.

- **Tolerance** means that increasing amounts of the drug are needed to obtain the same effect.
- **Withdrawal** refers to the feeling and symptoms that develop when the user stops taking the drug.

Two types of dependence exist. *Physiological dependence*, or neurological adaptation, occurs when the need is based on organic factors, such as changes in the body chemistry, and is what most people see as dependence. However, *psychological dependence*, or habituation, is equally important. This relates to the strong desire for the drug even when the user's body no longer needs it. Drug users get into the drug habit as a way of coping and feeling good. As we will see, several psychological mechanisms probably encourage such dependence, although neurological adaptation does not always lead to psychological dependence or habituation. Both physiological and psychological dependence often occur together and enhance the user's need and dependence on the drug.

Tolerance and dependence are independent properties. Most drugs lead to marked tolerance, especially the addictive drugs. However, some drugs do not appear very addictive, although great tolerance builds up (LSD is one such example). Tolerance and dependence are not inevitable, for example not everyone who drinks alcohol drinks frequently enough and in sufficient quantity to develop a tolerance, and many drinkers do not become dependent.

The severity of withdrawal symptoms varies a great deal with different addictive substances. Heroin, despite the publicity it receives, almost never directly causes death, whereas withdrawal from barbiturates and alcohol can. Nicotine withdrawal is less obvious, but as any heavy smoker, trying to kick the habit, will tell you, it is subtle and persistent. Most of the symptoms of withdrawal can be predicted quite accurately from the effects of the drug itself. Usually, the effects of withdrawal are the opposite of the drug's effects, for example heroin slows down stomach contractions and withdrawal brings on stomach cramps, whereas nicotine causes an increased heart rate and withdrawal slows it down. Severity of withdrawal is closely related to the course of action of the drug itself. Heroin, a fast-acting drug, has a fast-acting, severe withdrawal. Some of the psychoactive drugs

---

Activity 7

Choose the word(s) which best defines the sentence:

a The user seeks out and uses the drug with increasing frequency. (addiction/tolerance)

b Feelings and symptoms that develop when the user stops taking the drug. (tolerance/withdrawal)

c A strong desire for the drug even when the user's body no longer needs it. (physiological dependence/psychological dependence)

d Almost never causes death, whereas withdrawal from barbiturates and alcohol can. (heroin/nicotine)

(Suggested answers on page 428.)

---

and their possible levels of addiction can be seen in table 12.7.

During the last 20 years knowledge of the functioning of neurotransmitters and receptors has enabled the development of research in the field of *molecular psychology* (Franklin, 1987), which investigates and analyses the molecular interplay between neurons. Thousands of different molecules appear to be involved, not just the transmitters and receptors but also enzymes which manufacture and synthesise neurotransmitters and other molecules that modulate their action (Groves and Rebec, 1992).

Synaptic transmission involves a 'lock and key' action of the neurotransmission molecules which change the electrical properties of the target cell, either causing it to fire or preventing this action. Drugs are themselves chemicals and can be seen affecting our feelings and behaviour by interfering with this system. They produce their effects by changing the biochemical events which occur when neurons connect at the synapse. Drugs can be defined in terms of their effects in neurotransmission:

- *Agonists* are drugs that increase the actions of neurotransmitters, often by mimicking their actions.
- *Antagonists*, or blockers, inhibit or interfere with the impact of neurotransmission at the receptor.

Table 12.7

Drug category	Acute toxicity	Chronic toxicity	Relative risk of addiction
Alcohol	Psychomotor impairment, impaired thinking and judgement, reckless or violent behaviour. Lowering of body temperature, respiratory depression	Hypertension, stroke, hepatitis, cirrhosis, gastritis, pancreatitis. Organic brain damage, cognitive deficits. Foetal alcohol syndrome. Withdrawal effects: shakes, seizures, delirium tremens	3
Cocaine, amphetamine	Sympathetic overactive: hypertension, cardiac arrhythmias, hyperthermia. Acute toxic psychosis: delusions, hallucinations, paranoia, violence. Anorexia	Unpleasant tactile sensations. Stereotyped movements. Seizures, withdrawal depression. Chronic rhinitis, perforation of nasal septum	1
Caffeine	Cardiac arrhythmias. Insomnia, restlessness, excitement. Muscle tension, jitteriness. Gastric discomfort	Hypertension. Anxiety, depression. Withdrawal headaches	5
Cannabis (marijuana, hashish)	Psychomotor impairment. Additive effect with alcohol and sedative	Apathy and mental slowing, impaired memory and learning (brain damage?). Impaired immune response?	4
Nicotine	Nausea, tremor, tachycardia. High doses: hypertension, bradycardia, diarrhoea, muscle twitching, respiratory paralysis	Coronary, cerebral, and peripheral vascular disease, gangrene. Gastric acidity, peptic ulcer. Withdrawal irritability, impaired attention and concentration. Retarded foetal growth, spontaneous abortion. Other substances in tobacco smoke: bronchitis, emphysema, lung cancer	2
Opiates	Sedation, analgesia, emotional blunting, dream state. Nausea, vomiting, spasm of ureter and bile duct. Respiratory depression, coma, additive effects with alcohol and sedatives. Impaired thermo-regulation. Suppression of sex hormones	Disorders of hypothalamic and pituitary hormone secretion. Constipation. Withdrawal cramps, diarrhoea, vomiting, gooseflesh, lacrimation	2
Hallucinogen (LSD, PCP)	Sympathetic overactivity. Visual and auditory illusions, hallucinations, depersonalisation. PCP: muscle rigidity, elevated body temperature, staggering gait, agitation, violence, stereotyped movements, convulsions	Flashbacks. Depression, prolonged psychotic episodes	5

Some of the toxic effects of and the risk of addiction to psychoactive drugs.

Source: Goldstein and Kalant (1990)

Note: Listed here are effects due to the drugs themselves. The effects are dose-related and subject to individual variation in sensitivity, so not all are expected to be seen in every user. Approximate rankings for relative risk of addiction are on a 5-point scale, where 1 is most severe.

The various ways in which drugs can influence synaptic transmission are summarised in figure 12.8a.

Many drugs exert their effects on behaviour by one or more of these mechanisms. Direct-acting drugs have a chemical structure very similar to the neurotransmitters so they can combine with the receptors in an agonistic or antagonistic manner. Using the 'lock and key' analogy, agonists can act as a master key, turning on the receptor molecules

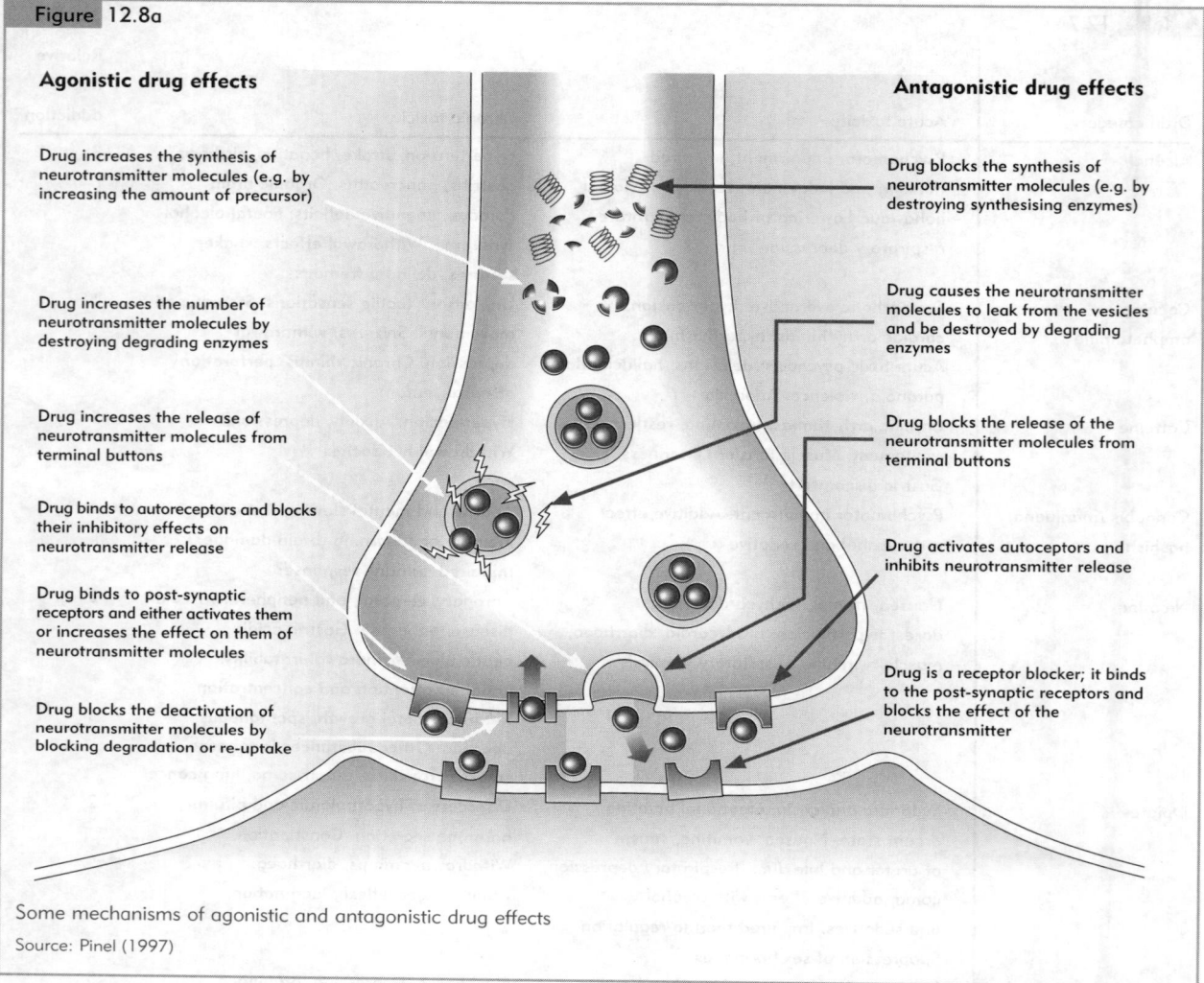

Figure 12.8a

Agonistic drug effects

Drug increases the synthesis of neurotransmitter molecules (e.g. by increasing the amount of precursor)

Drug increases the number of neurotransmitter molecules by destroying degrading enzymes

Drug increases the release of neurotransmitter molecules from terminal buttons

Drug binds to autoreceptors and blocks their inhibitory effects on neurotransmitter release

Drug binds to post-synaptic receptors and either activates them or increases the effect on them of neurotransmitter molecules

Drug blocks the deactivation of neurotransmitter molecules by blocking degradation or re-uptake

Antagonistic drug effects

Drug blocks the synthesis of neurotransmitter molecules (e.g. by destroying synthesising enzymes)

Drug causes the neurotransmitter molecules to leak from the vesicles and be destroyed by degrading enzymes

Drug blocks the release of the neurotransmitter molecules from terminal buttons

Drug activates autoceptors and inhibits neurotransmitter release

Drug is a receptor blocker; it binds to the post-synaptic receptors and blocks the effect of the neurotransmitter

Some mechanisms of agonistic and antagonistic drug effects

Source: Pinel (1997)

even when the neurotransmitter is not present. For example, nicotine stimulates acetylcholine receptors on neurons in certain parts of the brain. Alternatively, antagonists block the lock so the key will no longer fit into it. For example, curare, once used by South American Indians on darts in their blowguns, blocks the acetylcholine receptors located on muscle fibres and prevents synaptic transmission. The victim is paralysed, unable to breathe and suffocates (see figure 12.8b). Some psychotherapeutic drugs operate in this way. For example, anti-psychotic drugs alleviate the symptoms of schizophrenia by blocking receptor molecules responsive to the transmitter *dopamine* thought to be malfunctioning in schizophrenics

(see Unit 25 pages 944–5) for further discussion of the dopamine hypothesis).

Indirect-acting agonists and antagonists alter the functioning of neurotransmitters by interfering with the mechanisms of synthesis, transport, release or deactivation of particular neurotransmitters. Some drugs stimulate certain terminal buttons to release their neurotransmitters even when the axon is not firing, others prevent the release even when the axon fires. Often such drugs are more or less specific to one transmitter and thus affect selected synapses which release these neurotransmitters.

Some drugs inhibit re-uptake so that molecules of the transmitter continue to stimulate the post-

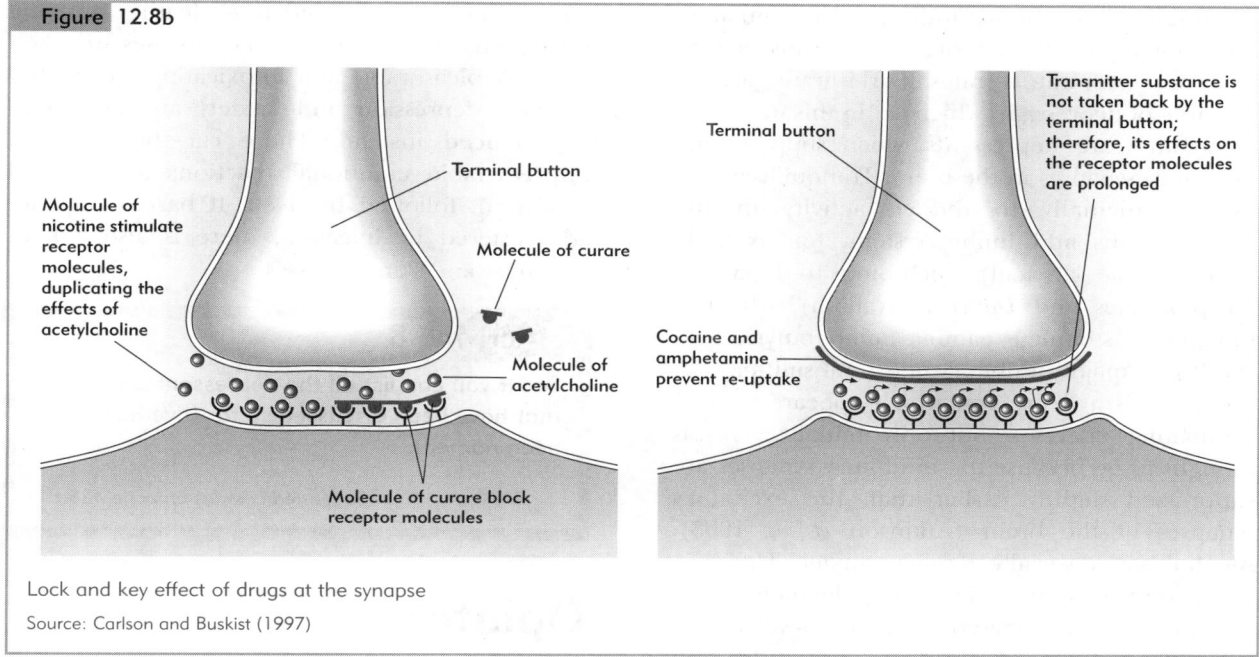

Figure 12.8b

Molucule of nicotine stimulate receptor molecules, duplicating the effects of acetylcholine

Terminal button

Molecule of curare

Molecule of acetylcholine

Molecule of curare block receptor molecules

Terminal button

Transmitter substance is not taken back by the terminal button; therefore, its effects on the receptor molecules are prolonged

Cocaine and amphetamine prevent re-uptake

Lock and key effect of drugs at the synapse

Source: Carlson and Buskist (1997)

synaptic receptor for a longer time, thus prolonging the effects of the transmitter. The excitatory effects of cocaine and amphetamines are produced partly by their inhibiting the re-uptake of certain transmitters, including dopamine.

Many drugs act as re-uptake inhibitors. They act by blocking the re-uptake from the synapse into the pre-synaptic button. This can increase the effects of the neurotransmitter as it continues to activate the post-synaptic receptors. For example, serotonin has been found to be a powerful mood enhancer. 'A person's mood is like a symphony, and serotonin is like the conductor's baton' (Stockard, 1997, p. 56). Stockard suggests that other neurotransmitters might tells us that our stomach is full, whereas serotonin tell us whether we feel satisfied. He uses the analogy of a glass of water which other neurotransmitters help us to see, with serotonin helping us to think of the glass as half-full or half-empty. Selective-serotonin-re-uptake inhibitors (SSRIs) such as Prozac block serotonin re-uptake (see Unit 26 page 975).

The behavioural effect of drugs can usually be linked to changes in the functioning of brain transmitters. The following section looks at a few examples. Most of us have experienced the psychoactive effect of such chemicals taken in coffee, tea, alcohol and cigarettes. Drugs can be seen as 'chemical compounds with selective biological activity on the cells of the body, and psychoactive drugs as those which act on brain cells, i.e. neurons' (Green, 1994, p. 24).

Classification of psychoactive drugs is not rigid; different behavioural responses are observed at different doses. For example, alcohol is a depressant but at low doses excitation is observed.

There are four main groups of psychoactive drugs: depressants, which decrease synaptic activity; stimulants, which increase it; opiates, which have both excitatory and inhibitory effects; and hallucinogens, which distort our sense of reality. The next section discusses some examples from each of these groups.

Depressants

Depressants may act directly on the nervous system by filtering out sensory stimulation to cortical areas. Pain killers, such as *aspirin*, work in this way, blocking receptor sites of neurotransmitters so that nerve impulses cannot reach the sensory cortex.

Depressants may also act indirectly by stimulating the parasympathetic nervous system, thus slowing heart and respiratory rates. Barbiturates are an example of depressants which act in this way.

Sedatives are depressants which suppress the excitatory synapses in the brain. Tranquillisers are used medicinally to reduce activity in the hypothalamus and limbic system, for example *chlorpromazine* (largactil) which binds to dopamine receptor sites and *Diazepam* (valium), which is thought to stimulate gamma-amino butyric acid (GABA), a major inhibitory neurotransmitter.

Alcohol is a depressant which appears to have stimulating effects – but only initially. This is thought to be because the inhibitory synapses are suppressed slightly earlier than the excitatory synapses in the brain (Atkinson *et al.*, 1993). Alcohol is used socially to relieve anxiety. However, it can reduce both anxiety *and* judgement. This, together with an increased confidence level, results in many accidents – the leading cause of death in 15–24-year-olds.

Alcohol attacks almost every tissue in the body (Anderson *et al.* 1993). Chronic alcoholism results in chronic brain damage and *Korsakoff's syndrome* – causing memory loss, and sensory and motor impairment. It erodes the muscles of the heart, increasing the likelihood of a heart attack. It penetrates the placental membrane and affects the foetus, sometimes resulting in *foetal alcohol syndrome (FAS)*. The FAS child suffers some or all of the following symptoms: mental retardation, poor coordination, poor muscle tone, low birth weight, retarded growth and physical deformity (Mattson *et al.*, 1988). In rats a single day of alcohol exposure during the foetal growth period reduced the adult brain weight (Goodlett *et al.*, 1990). Alcohol has both excitatory and anti-anxiety effects, thus producing positive and negative reinforcement. Reinforcement appears to be the result of the release of dopamine in the nucleus accumbens, but how this occurs is unknown.

Barbiturates produce the same effects as alcohol by depressing the CNS and stimulating the parasympathetic nervous system, thus slowing heart and respiratory rates. Low doses produce a relaxed state, with feelings of sociability and good humour. When misused, or taken with alcohol,

their effects can be lethal – death occurring through respiratory failure. Larger doses are taken for their pleasurable and intoxicating effects, but hostility, depression and anxiety are sometimes experienced instead. There can be extreme, unpredictable emotional reactions and mental confusion, followed by sleep. If barbiturates are administered by injection, there is also risk of gangrene and skin abscesses.

Activity 8

See if you can list all the depressant drugs that have been discussed so far (five have been named).

(Suggested answers on page 428.)

Opiates

Opiates have both excitatory and inhibitory effects on behaviour and are derived from the opium poppy. They are prescribed medically for pain relief, cough suppressants and diarrhoea. They are chemically similar, to and mimic the action of, endorphins – natural brain neuromodulators which bind to post-synaptic receptor sites producing feelings of pleasure and reducing discomfort (Julien, 1992). They are used extensively after surgery and in terminal illness because they depress reflex functions such as coughing, respiration and heart rate. Like sedatives, they block impulses and prevent them reaching the sensory cortex. They also depress bowel activity and dilate blood vessels, giving a feeling of warmth. Unlike barbiturates, there is little interference with sensation, motor skills or intellect – even with high doses which produce drowsiness, contentment and euphoria. However, excessive doses produce stupor and coma.

Morphine is a commonly used opiate – and is often abused. Intense euphoria and feelings of well being are experienced on first taking it (new users may also experience nausea and vomiting), but as receptor sites become blocked, new ones are produced so that the next time the drug is taken, more is needed to attain the same state as before.

Heroin, another commonly abused opiate, breaks down to *morphine* in the body. *Codeine* is the least powerful of the opiates and is widely used medically.

Tolerance for opiates such as heroin increases rapidly with use so physical addiction can occur quickly and withdrawal symptoms are equally rapid. Evidence suggests that opiates exert their reinforcing effects by activating dopaminergic neurons especially in the nucleus accumbens (DiChiara and Imperato, 1987). It is this reinforcing effect which makes them so addictive (Carlson, 1994).

Stimulants

Stimulants are physical energisers which act by stimulating neuronal firing rates, especially in the sympathetic nervous system. They act in a manner similar to adrenaline, increasing heart and respiratory rates and giving a feeling of well-being to users. However, tolerance to the stimulant effects develops so users are tempted to increase the dose to toxic proportions. The mood-elevating effects can lead to psychological dependence. Long-term, regular use can lead to depression, lethargy and hunger.

Amphetamines are synthetic stimulants, used medically to treat mental and physical fatigue and, at one time, in weight control programmes. With low doses, users feel more alert, energetic, confident and cheerful than before and less bored or tired. With higher doses, intense exhilaration, rapid flow of ideas and feelings of greatly increased physical and mental capacity are common (Institute for the Study of Drug Dependence, 1991). Repeated high doses over a few days can produce schizophrenia-like symptoms of delirium, panic, hallucinations and feelings of persecution (amphetamine psychosis). There is also the risk of heart failure and damage to blood vessels because of the rise in blood pressure.

Cocaine is a stimulant derived from the leaves of the Andean coca shrub. It has powerful stimulant properties similar to those of amphetamines. Coca leaf chewing may have been practised among South American Indians as long ago as 2500 BC. Natives still use it as an aid to arduous or extended work.

Research indicates that cocaine blocks the re-uptake of the neurotransmitters dopamine, serotonin and noradrenaline (Atkinson *et al.*, 1993). It produces physiological arousal accompanied by exhilaration, feelings of well-being, decreased hunger, indifference to pain and fatigue, and feelings of great physical strength and mental capacity. Sometimes these desired effects are replaced by anxiety or panic. Large doses or a 'spree' of quickly repeated doses over a period of hours can lead to an extreme state of agitation, anxiety, paranoia and perhaps hallucination.

After-effects of cocaine include fatigue and depression, but are not as strong as for amphetamines. Neither tolerance nor withdrawal symptoms occur with repeated use of cocaine, but strong psychological dependence may result from the grandiose feelings of physical and mental well-being it gives users. However, with frequent use, experiences of euphoria are replaced by a restlessness, hyperexcitability, nausea, insomnia and weight loss. With continued use a state of mind similar to paranoid psychosis may develop (Institute for the Study of Drug Dependence, 1991).

If drugs of different types are taken together, to counter the effects of each other, a dangerous cycle can be established which is difficult to break. For example, the comedian John Belushi died in 1982 from combining cocaine and heroin.

Ecstasy is an hallucinogenic amphetamine (Methylene-dioxymethamphetamine – *MDMA*), also known as '*E*'. It produces feelings of empathy with others at low doses, and restlessness and anxiety similar to the effects of amphetamines at higher doses. The long-term biological effects are the focus of research due to the unexpected deaths of several healthy young people. All of these collapsed at 'raves' or shortly afterwards and exhibited symptoms associated with severe heatstroke. The cause of many of the deaths is a surge in 5-HT which raises the body temperature and this rises even higher after dancing in a hot nightclub. Overheating can lead to convulsions, coma and/or death. A few deaths have been due to drinking too much water. Under the influence of MDMA some people have drunk 20 litres of fluid. Pure water does not put back the blood sodium and this dilutes the blood. Cells in the body swell and this can be particularly dangerous in the brain due to the restriction of the skull, and brain damage occurs. MDMA also triggers the release of anti-diuretic hormone which prevents the kidneys getting rid of excess water. Some long-term users have reported increased ailments such as colds and flu, and it is thought that MDMA may adversely affect the immune system.

Tobacco, next to caffeine, is one of the most widely used psychoactive drugs in society. When smoked, the psychoactive compound of tobacco is *nicotine* and about 4000 other chemicals referred to as *tar*. These are absorbed through the lungs. Acetylcholine receptors are stimulated, as are the dopaminergic neurons containing these receptors. Dopamine is also released at the nucleus accumbens (Damsma *et al.*, 1989). Tolerance develops to the negative effects and smokers report feeling more relaxed, alert and less hungry after a cigarette. Withdrawal symptoms include depression, anxiety, irritability, constipation and problems sleeping and concentrating. Long-term use results in *smoker's syndrome* (Pinel, 1997), characterised by chest pain, difficulty breathing, coughing and a susceptibility to lung disorders such as pneumonia, bronchitis, emphysema and lung cancer. There is also an increased risk of cancer of the throat, mouth, kidneys, bladder and stomach. Smokers are also likely to suffer cardiovascular diseases.

Ill effects are not restricted to smokers. People who live or work with them may also suffer heart disease and cancer. As with alcohol, the effects are also critical for the unborn child. Women who smoke give birth to smaller, less mature babies and this can cause problems after birth. There is also an increased risk of miscarriage, stillbirth or the early death of the child. It is thought that nicotine is particularly deadly due to *free radicals*, chemicals which can break down many biological molecules, including DNA (Fischer-Nielson *et al.*, 1993).

Hallucinogens

Hallucinogens act to distort reality in some way. Perception of both internal and external environments may change and stimuli may also be experienced in different modalities (for example, sounds may be perceived as colours) or on different scales (for example, hours may seem like minutes and centimetres like metres).

Marijuana, derived from the cannabis plant, is probably the most commonly used hallucinogen. The active ingredient in marijuana (or *cannabis*) is THC (delta-9-tetrahydrocannabinol and other THC chemicals). This stimulates specific neuromodulator receptors for THC in the brain. When taken, users experience an initial feeling of stimulation and euphoria followed by a feeling of tranquillity and sleep. Some users undergo distortions of place and time, changes in social perception and 'out-of-body' experiences (Tarb, 1971), others feel anxiety and depression. This may depend on the initial state of the user, euphoria being experienced when users are happy and depression when sad. Marijuana affects memory such that users may lose the thread of a conversation, or forget what they are saying. Learning is disrupted during the transference of new information from short- to long-term memory (Darley *et al.*, 1985). The performance of complex tasks is impaired, especially those involving motor coordination and tracking a moving object. Research in America suggests that a quarter of all drivers of vehicles in accidents are under the influence of marijuana alone, or marijuana in combination with alcohol (Jones and Lovinger, 1985).

Lysergic acid diethylamide (LSD) is derived from ergot, a fungus found growing on grasses. It acts by replacing the neurotransmitter serotonin in the brain and therefore affects awareness. LSD users experience vivid, emotional and perceptual distortions which may be intensely beautiful (a good trip), or literally terrifying (a bad trip), depending on the mood of the drug-taker (Barron *et al.*, 1972). The same person may have good and bad trips, either on different occasions, or within the same occasion. Loss of feelings of reality may lead to irrational and disorientated behaviour, or to panic. Some users experience 'flashbacks' (illusions or hallucinations similar to those at the time of taking the drug) days, weeks or months afterwards.

Drugs such as LSD suppress the activity of serotonin-secreting neurons which permit dream mechanisms to become active. Serotonin plays an important role in dreaming, which usually occurs when we are asleep. During daytime, when we are awake, the serotonin-secreting neurons inhibit the mechanisms responsible for dreaming. Not all hallucinogens interfere with serotonin synapses. For example, cocaine and amphetamine also produce hallucinations but they affect the dopamine-secreting synapses. Such hallucinations are usually auditory whereas LSD hallucinations are usually visual and more immediate.

Phencyclidine (PCP) is a chemically synthesised hallucinogen which was originally used as an anaesthetic because of its ability to relieve pain without producing deep coma. PCP prevents sensory filtering so that, although users experience feelings of dissociation from the environment, they may also simultaneously experience heightened sensory input and feel bombarded by an overload of stimuli – made worse if someone tries to help.

Activity 9

Devise a table listing all the drugs discussed, indicating which group they belong to and their affect on human behaviour.

(Suggested answers on pages 428–9.)

In conclusion, it is worth noting that drugs do not always produce the specific effects as noted above. Generally, they can produce the effects noted, but their impact may vary dependent on other factors as follows:

- The *expectations* of the user often determines the drug's effects.
- The user's *physical state* can determine the drug's effects. Some people are more tolerant than others. Whether the person is tired or rested, whether he or she has eaten recently, all make a difference to its effect.
- *Previous experience* also alters the effect. First-time users often report different reactions.
- The influence of the drug is often affected by *other drugs* used by the individual, with some combinations being deadly.

Why do people take psychoactive drugs?

Most adults in the UK and the USA use psychoactive drugs such as caffeine, alcohol and tobacco daily. Despite laws and the police, illicit drugs are available to those who want them. The peak age of drug use is between 18 and 21 years with a steady decline thereafter (Robson, 1994).

When asked, most teenagers will say they take the drugs because they like the experience, and it helps take away shyness, anxiety and lack of confidence. Recreational drug use carries a considerable risk which can affect the physical and mental health of the user. Research suggests several contrasting explanations.

■ The biological perspective

Some research suggests that there is a generic predisposition in certain people which may lead to addiction. Most of the research has been on alcoholism with most people exposed to alcohol at some point in their life as it is legally and readily available in the shops. Such research has found steady drinking to be influenced by heredity. Cloniger *et al.* (1985), in a Swedish Adoption study, found males were more at risk and sons of heavy drinkers were more likely to become steady drinkers themselves even when their adopted families did not drink. It is thought that they have underactive serotonin and dopamine neurons and it is suggested that this results in differences in the sensitivity of neural mechanisms involved in reinforcement, exploration, and punishment (Cloniger, 1987).

This vulnerability may be linked to the efficiency of metabolism of drugs – the way in which the body transports and breaks down drugs. Enzyme systems that drive these processes are genetically determined. If a user is efficient in producing acetaldehyde, an unpleasant metabolite of alcohol, but less efficient at moving it on to the next stage of metabolism, this would act as a deterrent (the user would feel sick and more prone to a hangover). An efficient metabolism would encourage the user to drink more.

Recent research in animals suggests there is a brain pathway concerned with the experience of pleasure. The mesotelecephalic-dopamine system mediates the rewarding effects of drugs (Chen, 1993). The theory suggests that anything stimulating this system will result in drug-seeking behaviour. Recent work suggests that this can be induced by environmental cues associated in the user's memory with previous drug use (White and Hiroi, 1993). Such behavioural triggers are discussed further below. Some psychoactive drugs are not included in this reward system. A separate system may be linked with mechanisms which can neutralise punishment, such as depression, fear and anxiety, and may be just as addictive as those enhancing pleasure (Robson, 1994).

The role of this pathway offers some explanation of addictive behaviour in humans, but as people have more cortical control over innate mechanisms than laboratory rats, it does not explain why we choose to take drugs in the first place.

■ The psychodynamic perspective

Human behaviour can be seen to be affected by unconscious conflicts, and drugs are used to reduce or conceal the anxiety generated by such inner turmoil. This idea is difficult to test empirically and is not seen as a valid explanation for the use of pyschoactive drugs by many psychologists. Drugs are seen as one of the palliative measures used by people coping with stress. This is discussed in Unit 15 pages 557–60).

■ The behavioural and social learning perspectives

The basic principles of social learning theory suggest that drugs are taken because the effects are rewarding. Such circuits, as described above, are evident in the brain, and animals will self-administer many of the drugs that people abuse because they find the effects rewarding (Chen, 1993). Tiffany (1990) also suggests that people take drugs to reduce negative feelings rather than generate positive ones. This explanation may be applicable to withdrawal.

Social learning can offer a useful explanation as to why people begin to use alcohol, tobacco and other psychoactive substances.

Such explanations involve:

- the positive reinforcement as noted by the Behaviourists
- cognitive mediation, whereby such use is consistent with personal decisions
- vicarious learning through contemplating the behaviour of others.

This modelling can occur after observing family, friends or the media. Association learning has been shown to occur through advertising or films, linking an attractive model or actor to the alcohol or tobacco they imbibe.

Conditioning has been found to be important during the developments of tolerance. Siegel and his colleagues (1982) propose that addicts become tolerant when they self-administer the drug in the same or similar environments and consequently take larger doses to counteract the diminishing effects of the drug. If a large dose of the drug is given in a new or strange situation, this anticipatory tolerance effect is not present and there is a greater risk of death by overdose. This theory assumes that the conditioned stimuli associated with administering the drug elicit conditioned responses opposite to the unconditional effects of the drug – known as *conditioned compensatory responses*. These responses increasingly counteract the effect of the drug and produce situational tolerance. These studies suggest that what the animal has learned to expect shapes its behaviour.

■ The cognitive perspective

Drug abuse can also be seen as automatic processing on the part of those involved (Tiffany, 1990). Cognitive systems and expectancy control many aspects of obtaining drugs and using them. Tiffany suggests these soon become automatic and without conscious awareness. Once a drug has been used on a number of occasions individuals may find themselves responding, almost automatically, to external cue such as the environment or sound and smells associated with the drug use. They may also react to internal cues or emotions such as wanting to celebrate or 'drown their sorrows'. Self-efficacy, whether individuals believe they have the skills necessary to achieve a desired outcome, such as 'kicking the habit', have become central to therapies for addiction. Useful interventions have been directed towards the development of social skills in high drinking situations, perceived control and enhanced self-efficacy.

■ The socio-cultural perspective

How the individual's family and the society in which he or she lives shapes attitudes and behaviour is central to both starting and maintaining a 'drug career'. Usually, the source of supply is from the immediate social circle. Drug use is more common among the poor and deprived, many of whom have a disrupted family life with few educational prospects. Although important in relation to dependency and drug-related problems, this approach seems to offer few explanations on the initial experimentation and subsequent use. Although drugs are more accessible in urban areas, it has not been shown to have a great effect on the frequency of experimentation in different schools (Robson, 1994).

■ The biopsychosocial perspective

The three important theoretical models which try to explain drug use are the biological, psychological and socio-cultural. All three are likely to play a part in the reasons why people use drugs and become addicted. Contemporary theories tend to see them as complementary, with one or two seen more dominant in any one individual (Schwartz, 1982). Within this perspective, psychologists focus on the behaviour of the individual rather than the biological abnormality, which is the focus of biomedical perspective. An individual's behaviour is maintained by the balance of drives, stemming from the genes, biochemistry and patterns of learned behaviours in the social and physical environment. The addictive behaviour is maintained by many sources which are multidimensional in nature. The biopsychosocial model has provided a bridge between the various perspectives and has proved fruitful in areas of health psychology and behavioural medicine, especially in the area of drug addiction.

Activity 10

Choose the appropriate perspective describing drug use for the following. Select from:
(i) behavioural/social learning, (ii) biological, (iii) cognitive, (iv) psychodynamic, (v) socio-cultural.

a   There is a genetic predisposition which may lead to addiction.

b   Drugs are taken because the effects are rewarding and after observing others.

c   Human behaviour is affected by unconscious conflicts and drugs are used to reduce or conceal the anxiety generated by the turmoil.

d   Drug abuse can be seen as automatic mental processing and expectancy without conscious awareness.

e   The individual's family and the society in which he or she lives shapes attitudes to drugs and maintains their usage.

(Suggested answers on page 429.)

Is there an addictive personality?

Apparently not! Some people, for both internal and external reasons, appear to be more vulnerable to addiction than others, but it has been found to be difficult to predict with any accuracy who will be at risk. Many researchers tend to minimise the causal role of personality factors in substance abuse.

For what it is worth, the typical drug-user-to-be is likely to possess at least some of the following characteristics: rebelliousness, nonconformity to conventional values, and a tolerant attitude towards unusual or deviant behaviour; a relative lack of ambition and commitment to school work or career building; independent mindedness, self-reliance, and a reluctance to abide by the rules; impulsivity; preoccupation with pleasure-seeking and risk-taking;

a history of physical or mental illness, impaired emotional well-being, or consistently low self-esteem.' (Robson, 1994, p. 8)

In general, addictive populations tend to show more deviancy than non-addictive, but addictive sub-groups hardly vary from one another (Lowe, 1995). Generally, most adolescents and students try a drug for three main reasons:

■ Fun and curiosity (50 per cent).
■ To feel more socially comfortable – peer pressure (30 per cent).
■ To forget their troubles or moderate unpleasant emotions (20 per cent) (Robson, 1994). Figure 12.9 gives more information.

Figure 12.9

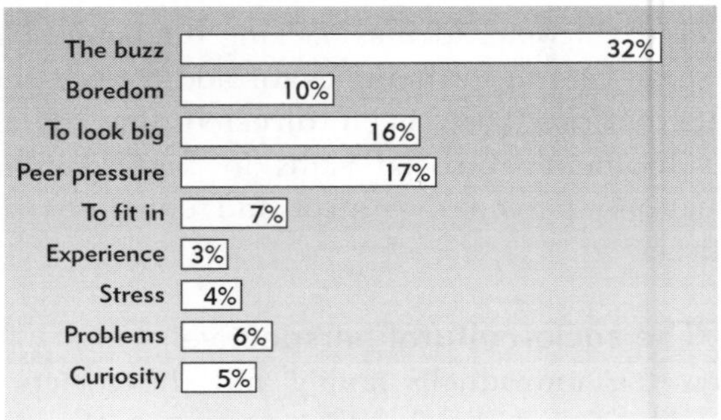

The buzz 32%
Boredom 10%
To look big 16%
Peer pressure 17%
To fit in 7%
Experience 3%
Stress 4%
Problems 6%
Curiosity 5%

The reasons young people use drugs
Source: Parents Against Drug Abuse in *Guardian Education* (1996)

Self-assessment questions

4 Differentiate between addiction, tolerance and withdrawal.

5 What are agonists and antagonists, and how can they influence synaptic transmission?

6 Choose *one* psychoactive stimulant and summarise its behavioural effects.

7 Note some of the individual characteristics associated with a drug user and suggest *two* reasons why psychoactive drugs are used.

(Suggested answers on page 430.)

The central and peripheral nervous systems

The central and peripheral nervous systems form a network for communication throughout the body and are responsible for coordinating all our behaviour, whether we feel in control of that behaviour or not. Activity 11 shows in part how the network is organised in terms of position and function.

Positionally the network forms both a *central nervous system (CNS)* found in the nerve centres of the brain, brain stem, spinal cord and related groups of nerve cells called *ganglia*; and a *peripheral nervous system (PNS)*, found in sensory receptors and nerve fibres connecting them to the nerve centres.

Functionally, the *somatic nervous system* relays impulses from sense organs, via the PNS, to the CNS and from the CNS to the muscles attached to the skeleton. It governs all the movements we perform voluntarily, as well as our higher cognitive functions such as thinking and language. The *autonomic nervous system (ANS)* controls bodily functions over which we have no concious control such as stomach contractions and glandular secretions. It relays impulses from internal organs, via the PNS, to the CNS. It also relays impulses from the CNS to glands and the muscular walls of internal organs. Autonomic actions are mainly involuntary.

Activity 11

Use the figure below and the previous text to see if you can fill in (a), (b) and (c) in the diagram of the structure of the nervous system below.

(Suggested answer on page 429.)

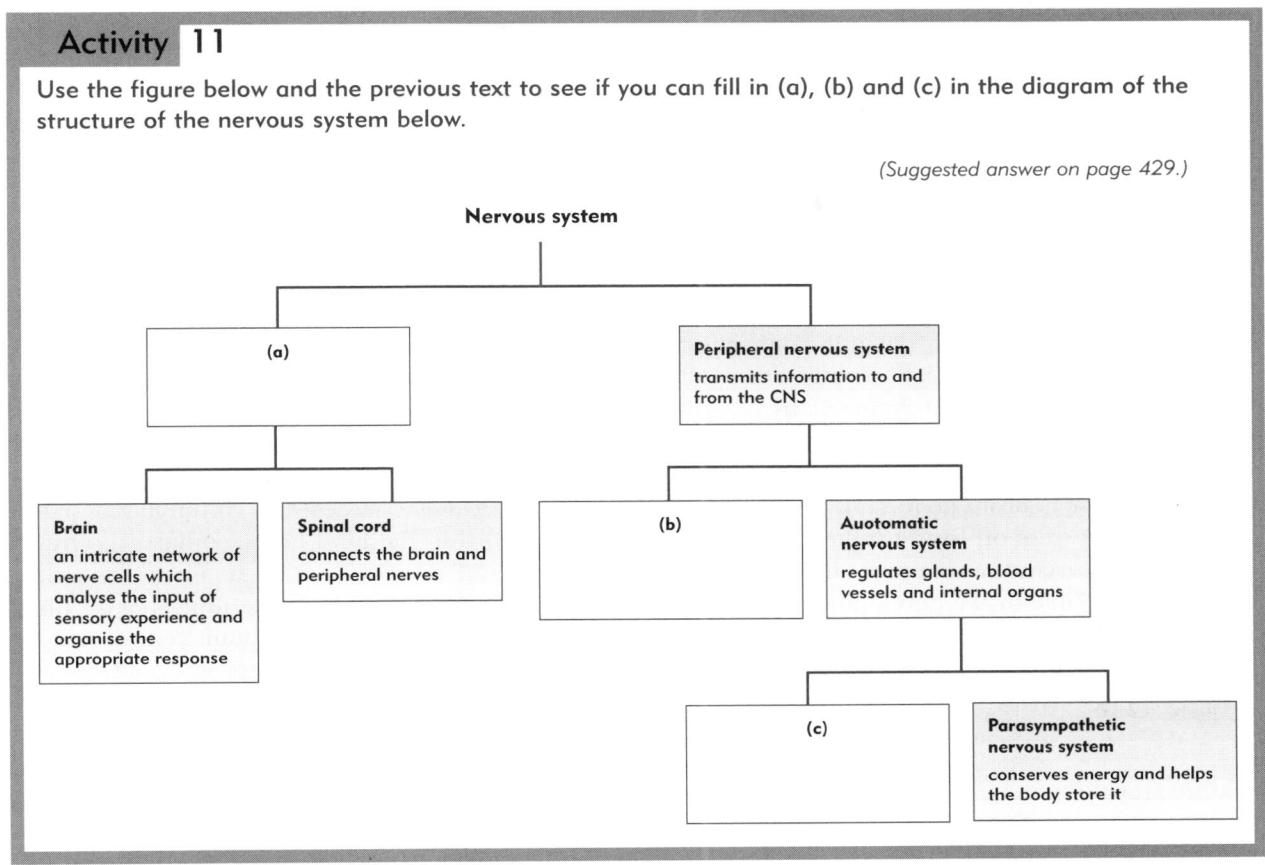

The central nervous system: brain and spinal cord

In primitive organisms, the CNS is composed of peripheral nerves and a central, longitudinal tube of concentrated nerve cells. Information from the environment is fed by the peripheral nerves to some of these central nerve cells, where it is interpreted. Other nerve cells instigate response activities such as movement, feeding and excretion.

In higher animals, sensory information is more comprehensive and specific. Through evolution, the central tube of nerve cells has developed into the *spinal cord*. Its front end, where most of the information is received and interpreted, has developed into the *brain*.

Nerve tracts of the PNS carry sensory information from different parts of the body, along the spinal cord, to the brain in the form of coded patterns of impulses. Motor responses are carried from the brain to specific body muscles or glands.

The brain and spinal cord are well protected by three layers of membrane, called *meninges*, and by the bones of the head and the spinal column. *Cerebro-spinal fluid*, which provides nutrients and removes waste products, is found in four ventricules (cavities) in the brain and the central canal of the spinal cord.

The brain is a highly specialised organ able not only to instigate immediate actions in response to present information, but also to compare new information with old, thus allowing an adaptive and beneficial response. It can also use information from past and present experiences to predict the possible future consequences of an action – and to conjure up ideas about abstract concepts. For ease of understanding, the brain may be described in three concentric layers – the central core, limbic system and cerebrum (see figure 12.10). The layers do not act in isolation, however, and are interconnected by nerve tracts.

Nerve tracts are the axons of neurons. As the brain evolves in the foetus, synaptic connections are formed. The chemical signals the cells exchange to establish these connections are still not understood. It appears that more neurons exist than will eventually be needed. Approximately 50 per cent of these neurons do not form connections and eventually die off during the individual's lifetime. This survival mechanism allows for extra cells to be available in the developmental process, if needed (Carlson, 1994).

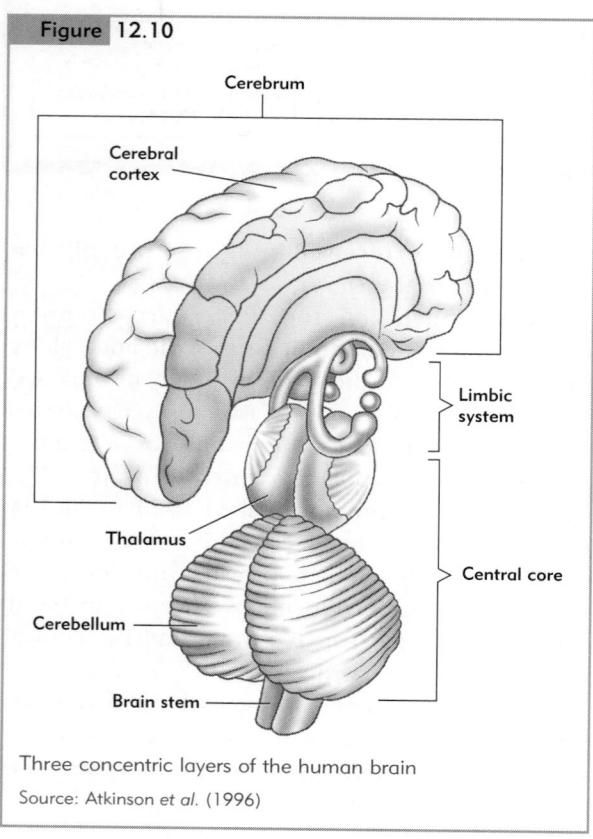

Figure 12.10

Cerebrum

Cerebral cortex

Limbic system

Thalamus

Central core

Cerebellum

Brain stem

Three concentric layers of the human brain

Source: Atkinson et al. (1996)

Thousands of pathways of groups of axons develop in the brain during maturation to connect one brain area to another and appear to be genetically specified. Connections are orderly and systematic so that the surface of the body is 'mapped' onto the surface of the brain.

■ The central core of the brain

The central core is the innermost concentric layer. It includes parts of the hind brain and the mid brain, thalamus and hypothalamus (see figure 12.10). Many basic survival mechanisms, such as metabolic control, endocrine activity (see page 419) and homeostatic regulation are located in these structures.

The *medulla oblongata*, a continuation of the spinal cord in the hind brain, contains a series of columns of neurons, known as nuclei, as well as both ascending and descending nerve fibres passing between the higher brain centres and the spinal cord. These fibres cross sides here so that those entering the medulla on the left-hand side will leave from the right-hand side, and vice versa. The medulla contains reflex centres controlling respiration, cardiac function, swallowing, vomiting and sneezing. Many of the nerves which serve the body organs enter or leave the brain at the medulla.

The *pons* (meaning bridge) is a mid brain structure located in front of the medulla at its upper end. Nerve fibres over its lower surface relay information to the cerebellum, other fibres pass between the cerebrum and spinal cord. It also contains centres influencing feeding and facial expression.

The *reticular formation* of the mid brain is a complex network of nuclei, cell bodies and nerve fibres passing up the brain stem behind the pons. Moruzzi and Magoun (1949) found that stimulating this area with a small electric current would awaken a sleeping cat. They concluded that it has a function in consciousness and called it the *reticular activating system (RAS)*. The RAS acts like an alarm system. All sensory inputs are relayed here, as well as to the cerebral cortex. When stimulated it sends a general signal round the entire cortex so that the stimulus can be identified by the appropriate centre. The RAS can be selectively sensitive to different stimuli, for example a sleeping mother may waken at the slightest cry from her baby, but sleep through a thunderstorm. Damage to the RAS causes permanent coma (e.g. Lindsley *et al.*, 1957) but if uninjured it can maintain a wakeful state, as in a newborn baby whose cerebral cortex has not yet begun to function.

General anaesthesia of descending fibres results in the deactivation of skeletal muscles. These fibres refine motor activities by modifying muscle movements which would otherwise be jerky and uncontrolled. This is true for both voluntary and reflex movements – even those reflexes centred in the spinal cord. Muscle movements involved in the knee jerk in monkeys are enhanced by stimulating the upper part of the RAS, whereas stimulating lower centres causes inhibition of movement (Magoun *et al.*, 1947).

The *cerebellum*, part of the hind brain, receives sensory information about our spatial position both from our muscles and the organs of balance in our inner ears. It also receives information from the *somatomotor cortex* (see page 417). This information enables it to control balance and muscle tone, and also to coordinate the voluntary movements needed for skilled activities such as walking, cycling and playing the piano. Marr (1967) likens the cerebellar cortex to a simple memorising device. Although the cerebellum can memorise the stretch of muscle at any one point, the other senses (usually sight) are used to make fine adjustments.

If the cerebellum is damaged, there is a delay in the initiation and termination of movements (Holmes, 1917). Also, when trying to flex one finger in apposition to the thumb, cerebellar patients frequently flex all four. It has been suggested by Marr (1971) that it may be that the initial command is to flex all four, and then to suppress flexion on the unwanted ones – in this case the other three.

The *thalamus* lies above the brain stem towards the front of the brain. It is shaped 'somewhat like two small footballs, one within each cerebral hemisphere' (Thompson, 1975). The thalamus is important in relaying information from the brain stem to specific cortical areas and contains interconnecting centres which also link the brain stem and limbic system located in the second concentric layer of the brain. These centres, for example the lateral geneculate body which relays optic signals, appear to be significant in regulating spontaneous electrical activity within the cortex and are also involved in levels of awareness by influencing the pons. The thalamus is also associated with a pain centre. Lesioning the thalamus where fibres from the spino-thalamic tract synapse gives cancer patients relief from unbearable pain. If the lesion is made a few millimetres in front of this area, no such relief is gained.

The *hypothalamus* lies between the mid brain and thalamus in close connection with the pituitary gland. Centres in the hypothalamus are sensitive to changes in blood temperature and content and help to maintain homeostasis (see page 425). The hypothalamus also influences motivation and emotion through connections with the ANS. Olds (1953) found that a rat, stimulated in a region near the anterior hypothalamus, behaved as if 'coming back for more' by returning to the one corner of a large enclosure where the stimulus was applied. Later experiments supported the existence of a 'reward centre' in the brain which was found to be focused in the medial fore brain bundle. Although small in size, the hypothalamus is an important part of the brain involved in important complex behaviours such as regulating the sympathetic branch of the ANS and the control of the pituitary gland (the 'master' gland).

■ The limbic system

The limbic system forms the second concentric layer of the brain. It is located around the central core of the fore brain and consists of a group of interconnecting structures and regions. All authors include the amygdala and hippocampus in the limbic system; some (e.g. Green, 1987) also include the thalamus and hypothalamus below it. One of its functions is to integrate information both from the cortex, about our external world, and from the brain stem, about our internal world. It then feeds this integrated information back to both areas.

At the base of the temporal lobe lies the amygdala. It apparently plays important roles in motivational and emotional behaviour (e.g. Green *et al.*, 1957); psychomotor epilepsy (e.g. Gloor, 1960); learned avoidance behaviour (e.g. Robinson, 1963); social dominance (e.g. Rosvold *et al.*, 1964); and autonomic reactions such as feeding and attention (e.g. Goddard, 1964). However, although the amygdala is implicated in all these functions, it is not essential for any of them.

The *hippocampus* lies under the lateral ventricle and is involved with short-term memory and sequential actions. Hippocampal lesions appear to affect the concentration necessary for these functions (e.g. Thomas and Otis, 1958). However, Green (1960) advises caution, pointing out that lesions may induce seizure, which could create disturbances in concentration on its own.

Activity 12

Which area of the brain is referred to in each of the following sentences? Choose from: thalamus; hypothalamus; limbic system; hippocampus.

a _____ is involved in short-term memory and sequential actions.

b _____ influences motivations and emotion through connections with the ANS.

c The _____ is important in relaying information from the brain stem to specific cortical areas.

d _____ is located around the central core of the fore brain and consists of a group of interconnecting structures and regions.

(Suggested answers on page 429.)

■ The cerebrum

The cerebrum forms the outermost concentric layer of the brain and is composed of nine million neurons collected into two *cerebral hemispheres*. Similar regions within the two hemispheres are connected by the corpus callosum – a bridge of about 250 million axons. In humans it is also connected by two commisural pathways, each containing a few million axons.

The cerebrum's surface is characteristically convoluted to give an extremely large surface area, known as the cortex, which varies between 1.5 and 4.5mm in depth. It is composed of regular columns of cells, and specialised functions are catered for in specific regions (see figure 12.11).

The *somatic cortex* contains a region which receives information from the sense organs via the brain stem and limbic system; and a region which instigates motor activity. Visual and auditory regions coordinate these senses; the association cortex contains areas where higher cognitive processes such as thought, language and memory occur.

The *somatosensory cortex* lies just behind the central fissure. Electrically stimulating neurons in this region of the right hemisphere gives rise to sensory experience in different parts of the left side of the body – and vice versa. In each hemisphere, body parts are represented in the sensory cortex in an upside-down way with an area of tissue proportional to their use. For instance, the parts which receive information about our tongue are towards the bottom and occupy quite a large space – while information from our feet is received in relatively small spaces towards the top. Penfield and Rasmussen (1950) describe humans, in terms

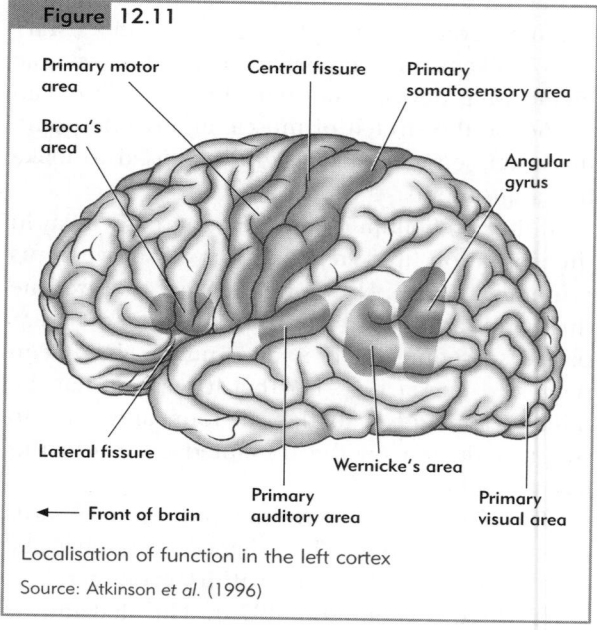

Figure 12.11

Localisation of function in the left cortex

Source: Atkinson *et al.* (1996)

of the sensory cortex, as mostly fingers, lips and tongue.

The *somatomotor cortex* lies just in front of the central fissure. Electrically stimulating neurons in this region of either hemisphere causes skeletal muscles to contract. Movements on the left side of the body are controlled by areas in the right hemisphere – and vice versa. As in the sensory regions, the body is represented in an upside-down way with an area of tissue proportional to its use. Damage in these regions leads to a corresponding paralysis in the muscles controlled.

The *visual cortex* receives impulses relayed from the *lateral geniculate bodies (LGB)* to which visual information is carried by the optic nerves. These join at the optic chiasma, where half the fibres cross over to the opposite hemisphere (see figure 13.9). This arrangement allows both hemispheres to receive information from the whole visual field.

Within the visual cortex, the columns of cells are very highly organised. For example, Hubel and Wiesel (1965) demonstrated by using microelectrodes that certain cells respond only to bars of light orientated at specific angles and moving in specific directions. Other cells respond to bars of light at different orientations, or to more complicated shapes – or movements. (See Unit 13 p. 445.)

The *auditory cortex* is located on the surface of the temporal lobes. It is involved in the analysis of complex auditory signals and is particularly concerned with human speech patterns (Atkinson *et al.*, 1996). Nerve fibres from both ears pass into the auditory cortex of both hemispheres. Thus, if damage occurs to either hemisphere, or ear, hearing loss will not necessarily be total. Also the difference in time for an impulse to reach the two hemispheres allows perception of the direction from which a sound has come.

The *association areas* of the cortex are similar in structure to other cortical areas (Rockel *et al.*, 1980), although the volume of these regions varies from virtually none in rats, to nearly three-quarters of the cerebral cortex in humans. Association areas function by monitoring and integrating information from more than one sense or process, for example thought processes involving delayed

responses. French and Harlow (1962) allowed monkeys to watch food being placed into one of two cups, which were then covered and hidden from view for between 5 and 60 seconds. When a screen (used to hide the cups) was removed, normal monkeys were able to choose the cup containing food, while those with lesioned association areas could not solve the problem if the delay exceeded one second. Milner (1964) found similar ability loss in humans with frontal lesions when attempting to solve problems involving frequent shifts of thought.

Electrically stimulating the temporal lobes appears to activate long-forgotten memories. Penfield and Roberts (1959) reported that stimulation of this area in patients undergoing brain surgery produced vivid memories of long-forgotten events. If this part of the brain is surgically removed, these vivid memories no longer occur, although patients are still able to describe them. However, less than 8 per cent of patients experienced such vivid memories so it is impossible to attribute all memory functions to this area.

Activity 13

Six areas of the cortex have been described. Try to name them. (If you have difficulty re-read the section 'The cerebrum'.)

(Suggested answer on page 429.)

■ The spinal cord

The spinal cord is a nerve centre for both the somatic and autonomic nervous systems. Afferent nerves, carrying impulses from body organs, skin and skeletal muscles, are composed of sensory axons and enter the spinal cord dorsally (from behind). The cell bodies of the afferent neurons form ganglia just outside the spinal cord where each peripheral nerve enters. The cell bodies of efferent nerves are located within the spinal cord which their axons leave ventrally (from the front), carrying impulses to muscles or glands. Association neurons, forming an H-shaped mass of grey matter around the central canal (see figure 12.12) lie between the afferent nerve endings and the dendrites of efferent cell bodies. Longitudinal tracts of nerve fibres relay information along the spinal cord and also to and from the brain.

Simple *reflex actions* have survival value by saving us from dangerous situations and are controlled from the spinal cord. Imagine, for example, your dinner has been left in the oven for you. You take it out but the heat penetrates the cloth you are using. What is your immediate reaction? Your immediate reaction was probably to avoid pain by dropping the plate (a reflex action), but your thoughts told you that you would lose your dinner if you did, so you would first put your plate down and then react to the heat. Thus reflexes may be overridden by brain mechanisms after information has been passed to the cortex via longitudinal nerve tracts.

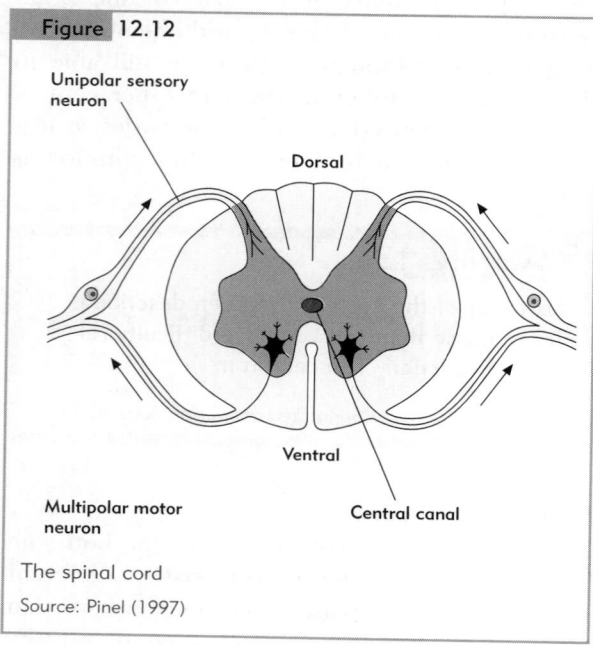

Figure 12.12

Unipolar sensory neuron

Dorsal

Ventral

Multipolar motor neuron

Central canal

The spinal cord

Source: Pinel (1997)

The peripheral nervous system

This system which operates outside the brain and spinal cord includes:

- The *somatic nervous system (SNS)* which interacts with the external environment via nerves from the sensory system (skin, muscles, joints, sense organs, etc.).
- The *autonomic nervous system (ANS)* which participates in the regulation of the internal environment of the body via nerves from the internal organs to the CNS and nerves carrying messages from the CNS to the internal organs. The ANS also stimulates the release of *hormones* from the *endocrine glands*.

■ The somatic nervous system

This system, which connects the CNS to the sensory receptors and skeletal muscles, allows us to have control over body movements. Sensory and motor neurones, in tracts and bundles, inform the brain on the external environment and allow for the brain's responses via the skeletal muscles.

■ The autonomic nervous system

The ANS is concerned with controlling involuntary actions, for example heart beat and glandular activity. Like the somatic nervous system, it is composed of nerve centres and peripheral nerves, although there are fewer receptors. These are usually embedded in the walls of internal organs and give feedback about their state and activity. Secretory neurons carry impulses from nerve centres to glands and motor neurons carry impulses to muscles in the walls of internal organs. Secretory responses are always involuntary, whereas motor responses may be either involuntary or voluntary. The ANS functions through two sections, sympathetic or parasympathetic systems. These work in opposition to each other because normally we have no conscious control over our glands and internal organs.

The *sympathetic nervous system* stimulates activity in the organs and glands involved in arousal states using energy and is particularly active in the 'fight or flight' response (see page 422). Its nerve centres are found in ganglia beside the spinal cord; nerves connect these both with each other and with the spinal cord – and hence the brain. Nerves from these centres synapse with nerves in the walls of organs. The *parasympathetic nervous system* helps to conserve body energy, promoting digestion and facilitating elimination of waste. Its nerve centres are located at the base of both the brain and spinal cord and nerves from these synapse outside the organs they control.

Activity 14

Imagine you are sitting quietly working in class, when someone comes in to talk to the teacher. You think you hear your name mentioned (this works well if you have a guilty conscience)! What are your immediate reactions? What is your heart doing; how is your breathing; and what about your hands, mouth and stomach? (Now read on.)

These questions are directed towards making you aware of reactions which occur during a strong emotion. You probably felt your heart and breathing rates increase. Your mouth may have felt dry, your palms sweaty and you had 'butterflies' in your stomach. These are all involuntary responses. You would probably lift your head as well and try to hear what the visitor was telling the teacher (these are voluntary responses).

When the visitor entered the classroom, your sympathetic nervous system became dominant and all your responses prepared your body for instant action, should it be needed. Your faster heart beat increased the rate of blood flow in your blood vessels. Your deeper and faster breathing supplied the blood with extra oxygen and removed greater amounts of carbon dioxide. Your sweaty palms resulted from surface blood vessels dilating, so that more blood could reach your voluntary muscles – bringing vital supplies of glucose (from the liver) and oxygen, for the energy you would need during a quick getaway. Among the responses you would have been unaware of were increased liver activity, to supply the blood with extra glucose, and your pupils dilating to give you added visual sensitivity. What about inhibitory responses? These also occurred – in your digestive system. As digestive secretions are reduced, your mouth becomes dry and you experience stomach 'butterflies'.

If the visitor left without looking at you and the teacher remained silent, you may think you had been mistaken about hearing your name. Soon you may notice that your heart and breathing rates have decreased, your 'butterflies' have gone and your hands are less sweaty. Your parasympathetic nervous system has now become dominant and reversed the effects of the sympathetic nervous system. Where strong emotions are aroused, ANS activity is exaggerated by endocrinal activity, which is discussed in the next section.

Usually, the two systems work in opposition to each other: the sympathetic nervous system being active during times of high energy, for example during emotions like fear and anger; the parasympathetic nervous system being active during times of low energy, for example during emotions like sadness and depression. However, there are exceptions to this. When experiencing extreme fear and excitement, although the sympathetic nervous system is dominant, parasympathetic responses of bladder or bowel voiding may occur. Sometimes, the two systems cooperate – for example, in males during sexual intercourse, the parasympathetic nervous system controls erection but the sympathetic nervous system controls ejaculation.

The endocrine system

The endocrine system consists of ductless glands which secrete complex chemical substances called *hormones*. This system is not only controlled by ANS activity but also plays a large part in its functioning. Like the ANS, it is concerned with involuntary body processes and in maintaining homeostasis, although the hormones take longer to exert their effects than those produced by the neural activity of the ANS.

The endocrine glands (see figure 12.13), located in different parts of the body, are well supplied with blood vessels. They secrete hormones which pass from the glands into the blood stream, exerting a chemical control in organs remote from the glands. Hormones may be highly specific in their action by influencing only one target organ. For example, follicle stimulating hormone (FSH), secreted by the pituitary gland, stimulates only the sex organs. Alternatively, they may have general effects by influencing a body process, for example insulin, secreted by the pancreas, facilitates glucose uptake by all active cells.

■ The pituitary gland

The pituitary gland is sometimes called the master gland because it influences most of the others. It is found at the base of the brain in close contact with the hypothalamus – this influences its activity through hormones known as releasing factors. Each of these stimulates the pituitary gland to secrete one of its own hormones (see table 12.14).

Most pituitary hormones exert their control through a homeostatic mechanism called *negative feedback*. This keeps blood hormone levels constant. Low circulating hormone levels cause the hypothalamus and pituitary gland to release hormones which stimulate non-active glands to begin secreting their hormones. As blood levels of these rise, the pituitary and hypothalamic hormones which stimulated them are inhibited. Subsequently, circulating hormone levels fall and the whole process is repeated. An analogy might be to a thermostat on a central heating system.

■ The thyroid gland

The thyroid gland, located in the neck, secretes the hormone *thyroxine* in response to thyroid stimulating hormone from the pituitary gland. Thyroxine effects tissue growth by controlling *metabolism*. If the thyroid gland is removed in young animals, their growth is stunted and they fail to develop sexually. For example, thyroid deficiency in tadpoles prevents metamorphosis into frogs, and in human infants, low thyroxine levels cause cretinism, a kind of 'incomplete' growth. Cretins remain small, do not mature sexually, are mentally subnormal and often obese (Clegg and Clegg, 1979). However, if thyroid deficiency is treated early enough, the effects can be reversed.

Damage or tumour in an adult thyroid gland results in myxoedema, a condition in which the face becomes puffy and thick skinned. Sufferers also lose interest in things around them, become slow-witted and, because metabolism is reduced, they become very sensitive to cold.

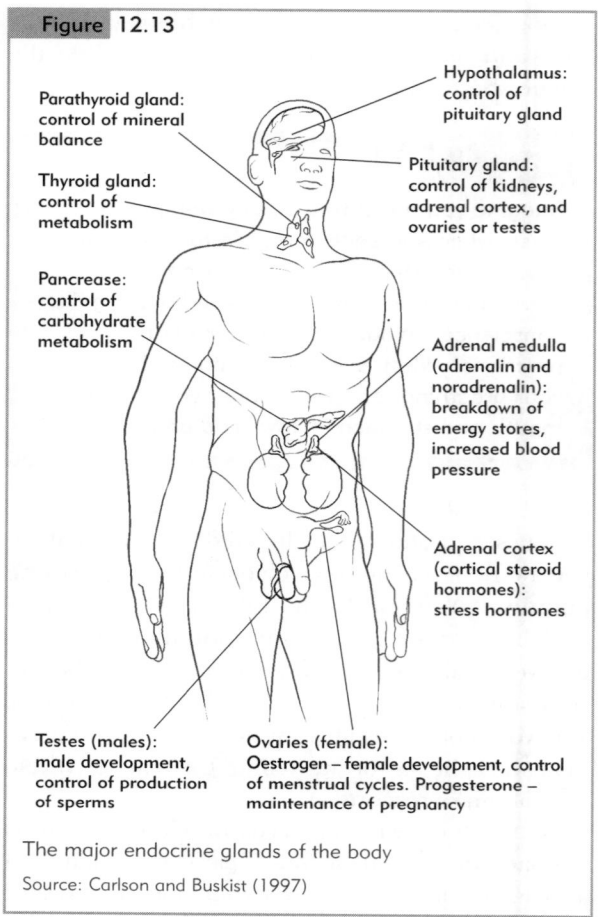

Figure 12.13

Parathyroid gland: control of mineral balance

Thyroid gland: control of metabolism

Pancrease: control of carbohydrate metabolism

Hypothalamus: control of pituitary gland

Pituitary gland: control of kidneys, adrenal cortex, and ovaries or testes

Adrenal medulla (adrenalin and noradrenalin): breakdown of energy stores, increased blood pressure

Adrenal cortex (cortical steroid hormones): stress hormones

Testes (males): male development, control of production of sperms

Ovaries (female): Oestrogen – female development, control of menstrual cycles. Progesterone – maintenance of pregnancy

The major endocrine glands of the body

Source: Carlson and Buskist (1997)

Over-activity of the thyroid results in thyrotoxicosis, which causes swelling in the neck, bulging eyes, increased metabolism, weight loss and insensitivity to cold. Thyroid activity increases in low temperatures. This is why slimming diets seem to work better in the winter when the thyroid is more active. It also helps to explain why we feel less energetic when it is hot.

■ The adrenal gland

An adrenal gland is located above each kidney and their secretions help to prepare organisms for resistance to damage and danger. Each has two separate parts, specialised for different functions. The *adrenal cortex* secretes a group of hormones called corticoids (see figure 12.15). Corticoids, active during times of high activity in the

Table 12.14

Hormone	Chief function
Thyroid stimulating hormone (TSH)	Stimulates thryoid to secrete thyroxine
Follicle stimulating hormone (FSH)	Stimulates the ovaries and testes to produce the sex hormones oestrogen and testosterone
Leutinising hormone (LH)	Stimulates development of the mammary glands – brings about ovulation
Leuteotrophic (LTH) Lactogenic hormone or Prolactin	Stimulates milk secretion
Adreno-cortico-trophic hormone	Stimulates the adrenal cortex to secrete cortisone
Growth hormone (somatotrophin)	Promotes growth
Intermedin – Melanin stimulating hormone (MSH)	Controls skin pigment cells
Anti-diuretic hormone (ADH)	Controls body water level, blood pressure, kidney function and smooth muscle action
Oxytocin	Stimulates contraction in pregnant uterus and milk ejection

Pituitary hormones and their functions

sympathetic nervous system, are controlled by *adreno-cortico-trophic hormone* from the pituitary gland. This in turn is controlled by a hypothalamic

12.15 Corticoids and their functions

Glucocorticoids operate during prolonged arousal of the ANS, and in extreme hunger by conserving blood glucose levels. They also operate during times of stress, for example from muscular exercise, injuries, exposure and psychological trauma. Their beneficial effects in suppressing inflammation are used medicinally, but these benefits are sometimes outweighed by disadvantages which include bones becoming brittle and the digestive lining breaking down.

Mineralocorticoids help to maintain a constant body weight by regulating the salt and water content of the body (aldosterone is one of these).

Sexcorticoids control our secondary sexual characteristics after puberty. Tumours in the adrenal cortex may affect these, for example by development of a beard in women, or breasts in men.

releasing factor (CRF). It is important to remember this when considering the overall reaction to stressful stimuli because negative feedback prevents a prolonged high level of hormone after a stressor has been removed. Remember the example of the visitor to the classroom on page 419? Individuals may survive without corticoids, but they would need to include plenty of salt in their diets and to remain in a constant warm temperature in order to do so.

The *adrenal medulla* secretes two hormones – adrenaline and noradrenaline – which both prepare us for an emergency by enhancing the effects of the sympathetic nervous system. It is interesting to note, however, that it is the sympathetic nervous system which influences the adrenal medulla to secrete its hormones in the first place, and it does this in response to a stressor, for example the visitor in the classroom. Adrenaline and noradrenaline stimulate the hypothalamus, maintaining its activity in this kind of situation. This is one reason why it takes a little while for a strong emotion to subside after a stressor has been removed. As adrenaline and noradrenaline give us an increased preparedness for action, they are often called the 'fight or flight' hormones (see page 540).

▨ The ovaries and testes

The ovaries in females and testes in males produce sex hormones in response to FSH from the pituitary gland. Cells in the ovaries are the major source of *oestrogen* and *progesterone*, female sex hormones which control the onset of menstruation and foetal development if fertilisation occurs. Cells in the testes are the major source of the male sex hormone, *testosterone*, which controls development of spermatozoa.

Both males and females produce oestrogen and progesterone and the balance between them influences gender behaviour. If a mother receives testosterone when pregnant, a female foetus may develop male sex organs but retain female genes, causing problems – especially at puberty. Testosterone is also implicated in aggression and dominance, and imbalance of oestrogen and progesterone associated with feelings of irritability and fatigue during pre-menstrual tension.

Self-assessment questions

8 Note the functions of *two* structures in the central core of the brain.

9 Outline the structures in the peripheral nervous system.

10 Compare and contrast the roles of the sympathetic and parasympathetic sections of the autonomic nervous system.

11 Briefly outline the negative feedback mechanism operating in the pituitary gland.

(Suggested answers on pages 430–1.)

Control systems and behaviour

From studying the nervous and endocrine systems, we can understand more about how they integrate to control complex behaviour. This section introduces how these systems control sensory and cognitive functions, affective behaviour and homeostasis.

Sensory functions

Sense organs are highly specialised to respond to fine details regarding our environment. This information from the sense organs is interpreted by the brain and assimilated into an internal representation which we call our perception of the world. This representation is based on, and related to, everything that has happened to a person in the past.

Sensory processing allows us to ignore irrelevant detail. For example, you are now concentrating on reading this page and may even be trying to relate it to previous ones, or information gained elsewhere. Environmental stimuli, such as the feel of your clothes, the state of your hair and peripheral noises are less important to you. Although your senses are receiving them and you may be aware that they are there, they remain in the background of your attention.

When new and changing events occur, we orientate to them. If the change is large and sudden, we may react initially with a reflex action called a *startle response*, as in the classroom situation (see page 419). The startle response involves the rapid arousal of the sympathetic nervous system.

If a sudden loud noise is repeated, we *habituate* to it – our startle reflex diminishes as our responses reduce with successive presentations. Habituation may be useful to filter uninteresting or non-threatening stimuli from consciousness. Green (1987) views it as a simple form of learning, since it involves attention as well as the storage of information in memory and a change in response level on the basis of experience. The process can be explained by the somatic nervous system alerting the ANS, which becomes aroused and implicates the endocrine system. The results of ANS and endocrinal activity alert the CNS, which interprets the situation and instigates a behavioural response – in this case a return to pre-existing internal conditions.

Our internal environment is monitored by proprioceptors which pass information about the state of our body organs, for example our spatial position (see page 397). Other sensory monitors are located in brain centres, for example the hypothalamus monitors the blood for hormone levels, nutrient content and temperature. If body temperature is low, both voluntary and involuntary homeostatic responses are instigated.

A voluntary response occurs when ANS activity is interpreted as a feeling of cold – you may look for extra clothes to put on, or light the fire. If body temperature rises, you may take off a layer of clothes, or take a cold shower!

An involuntary response occurs when the surface blood vessels constrict, reducing the amount of blood in them. Less sweat is produced and in consequence heat loss through the skin is reduced. Shivering may also occur, which is an autonomic mechanism to generate heat through muscular activity.

Our choice of which stimulus to attend to is often related to our motivational and emotional state. For example, if beginning to feel hungry, you may switch your attention increasingly from the printed word to thoughts of food. Eventually, you may temporarily abandon studying in order to satisfy your body's demands for refreshment. Your studying is controlled by a combination of somatic nervous system and CNS activity, the hunger sensations by your ANS and endocrine system. Thus attention to sensory information can direct behaviour from both voluntary and involuntary sources – or redirect it to take account of new information from either.

Sensory functions are affected by damage or disease to body organs. For example, in the somatic nervous system damage to the optic nerve may cause blindness; in the ANS, damage to the thyroid may alter our sensitivity to body temperature (see page 420).

Cognitive functions

Sensory information is processed in the cerebral hemispheres of the brain and stored in memory. You would probably answer the question 'What is this object?' far more quickly if the object is familiar, than if it is not. Although the physiology of memory is poorly understood, the *interneuronal theory* of memory suggests that new relationships are formed between neurons during learning (Russel, 1975). Frequently used synapses become smaller as the terminals of one neuron grow closer to the dendrites of another. This results in a facilitated pathway which will cause the post-synaptic neuron to fire more readily to neurotransmitters at this synapse than at less frequently used ones. A familiar object is often seen and therefore has a *facilitated pathway*; an object which is less familiar does not have a facilitated pathway, therefore the response takes longer to generate. This is why learning a new concept is easier if some of the terms used to teach it are already known. The new terms can be added to our perceptual world in conjunction with existing facilitated pathways. The same is also true for words; however, objects and words are processed in different parts of the brain.

A split-brain patient is someone who has had his or her corpus callosum (see page 464) severed to prevent epileptic seizures spreading from one hemisphere to the other. Studying such patients has shown that the sequential functions of speech and other verbal abilities are processed in the left hemisphere, whereas spatial processing of images, mathematics and music occurs in the right hemisphere (see figure 12.16).

Kimura (1963) used a dichotic listening task (a different message played to each ear) to demonstrate lateralisation of functions within the two hemispheres of the brain. The left hemisphere interprets speech sounds generated by the human voice, while the right hemisphere interprets non-speech sounds such as coughing,

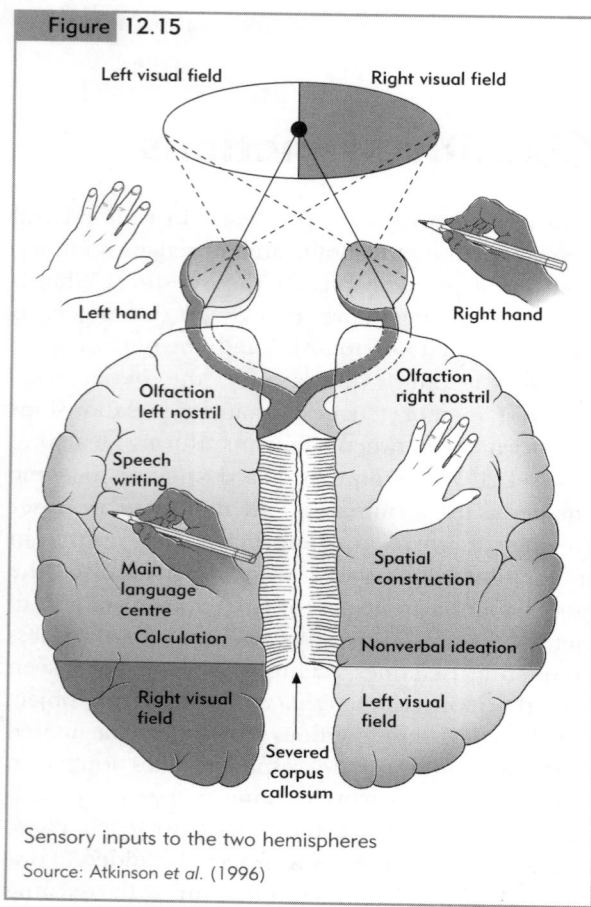

Figure 12.15

Left visual field

Right visual field

Left hand

Right hand

Olfaction left nostril

Olfaction right nostril

Speech writing

Main language centre

Spatial construction

Calculation

Nonverbal ideation

Right visual field

Left visual field

Severed corpus callosum

Sensory inputs to the two hemispheres

Source: Atkinson *et al.* (1996)

laughing and crying. Further discussion on lateralisation of brain functions can be found in Unit 13 page 456.

Affective behaviour

Have you ever said something which has been taken the wrong way, then realised its double meaning – and blushed? In a situation like this, you know you have said something emotive and can understand why your friends are laughing and you feel embarrassed. In this case, your thoughts are produced in your CNS, although the actual words used rely on motor activity from the somatic nervous system for their expression. Your feelings result from ANS activity, which is enhanced by adrenaline secretion.

The memory of a happy experience involves using your CNS to imagine the scene and your ANS to experience the emotion. Your CNS then interprets this feeling as one of pleasure. When thinking of something tasty, your CNS governs the anticipation and your ANS the salivation response. Most cognitive behaviours are, in fact, accompanied by some sort of feelings which are normally appropriate to the particular situation and according to cognitive theory, strongly influenced by it. However, sometimes it works the other way round and the cognitive interpretation of an activity is based on our affective state (emotional level of arousal).

Schachter and Singer (1962) induced an aroused state in participants by injecting them with adrenaline (falsely telling them it was a vitamin compound). They were then placed in an environment in which a stooge was behaving either euphorically or angrily. The participants interpreted their own emotion according to the emotion expressed by the stooge.

Sometimes we misinterpret our ability to cope with our emotional state. Stress relates to constant demands which keep arousal of the sympathetic nervous system above a normal and optimal level – resulting in prolonged increased ANS activity and high levels of adrenaline or noradrenaline. In the long term this may lead to physical illness as the emotional energy builds up and remains in the body, causing dis-ease. People most at risk are those who experience strong emotions without feeling able to vent them, or who repress their emotions because they feel they cannot control the situation. This might occur through a perceived inability to make a good decision, or through a lack of status (employees cannot control their bosses).

Cognitive psychologists seek to reduce the latent energy of emotional states by changing the attitude of their clients from one of subjective resignation, anger or frustration, to an objective understanding of the situation and confidence to cope. In other words, they try to change their focus of personal control from the ANS (which controls our behaviour involuntarily) to the CNS (which is under voluntary control) See Unit 15 for a further discussion of stress.

Homeostasis

Homeostasis maintains the body's internal state within fairly narrow limits. We have already seen how the ANS and endocrine system interrelate to prepare the body for action in cases of crisis, such as that in the classroom situation, and after the event to return the internal environment to 'normal' (see page 419). We have also discussed the role of homeostasis in the endocrine system. If homeostatic mechanisms are affected by, for example, disease or dietary deficiency, body functioning breaks down. For instance, if the diet lacks iodine, the thyroid gland cannot produce thyroxine. This causes the gland to swell and myxoedema results (see page 420). In this section we discuss how homeostasis works in more detail.

Sugar is the major source of all our energy and is therefore an important nutrient in our diet. Sugar is converted to glucose within the body. If the amount of glucose in the blood is too low, we suffer from *hypoglycaemia* which results in lethargy and eventual coma. Too much glucose in the blood produces hyperglycaemia which causes excitability – and eventual coma. Blood glucose levels are controlled by the hormones *insulin* and *glucogon* secreted by the pancreas. After a meal, digested nutrients are carried in the blood stream to the liver. Here glucose is converted into glycogen which forms an energy store. As we use energy in our daily activities, the glycogen is reconverted into glucose and passes into the blood for use by the active cells. Insulin is necessary for cells to absorb glucose; glucogon is necessary for them to release it. If insulin is unavailable, the homeostatic mechanism breaks down, and glucose is neither absorbed into the liver cells – leaving us without an energy store of glycogen, nor into the active cells – which consequently cannot function, causing the lethargy.

Homeostasis breaks down when diabetes, diagnosed by dangerously high levels of glucose in the urine, results from an inability of the pancreas to produce insulin. The treatment for this condition is to re-establish the homeostatic mechanism by regularly administering insulin and adjusting the diet, so that only enough sugar is eaten for the insulin to process. If an overdose of insulin is given, too much glucose is absorbed by the cells resulting in hypoglycaemia. If too much sugar is eaten, it cannot be absorbed and hyperglycaemia results. Thus it can be seen that homeostatic mechanisms not only play a large part in physiological processes but also have psychological and behavioural effects.

Another example of homeostasis is provided by the maintenance of a constant body weight through mechanisms which control salt and water levels in blood plasma.

Psychotherapeutic drugs

Some of the psychoactive drugs noted on page 405–9 have been found helpful in controlling some serious mental disorders. Drugs that block dopamine receptors, such as anti-psychotic drugs (e.g. Chlorpromazine and Clozapine), have made it possible for some people to live outside a mental hospital. Similarly, anti-depressant drugs such as fluoxetine (Prozac) which stimulate synapses using serotonin by inhibiting serotonin re-uptake, have saved lives which may have been lost through suicide. Bio-polar depression, sometimes known as manic-depression, in which moods alternate between severe depression and a period of exited, unrealistic elation, have been controlled by a simple inorganic compound – lithium carbonate. The biochemical therapeutic effect of lithium on the brain is still unknown and medication has to be carefully monitored as too much can be toxic.

Although in both the UK and the USA cannabis is a controlled drug and is not available for medical use, it has been found to help reduce the nausea caused by drugs used in the treatment of cancer, relieve asthma attacks, decrease the pressure within the eyes of people suffering glaucoma and reduce the symptoms of certain motor disorders. Devane *et al.* (1992) discovered the brain produced a neuromodulator which stimulates the THC receptor so it is hoped that drugs may be developed that have the therapeutic qualities of THC without the adverse effects on cognition.

Therapeutic intervention in psychopathology is discussed in Unit 26 page 974.

Unit summary

- *Neurons* are specialised cells in the nervous system, found especially in the brain, which initiate and conduct electro-chemical impulses enabling us to behave, not only in accordance with current conditions but also to those encountered previously.

- *Dendrites* receive impulses from the terminal buttons of other neurons and carry them towards the cell body, and *axons* carry them away from the cell body towards the synapse.

- The *synapse* is the area where the synaptic terminals of one neuron lie close to the receptor sites of another neuron, with a gap between the two known as the synaptic cleft.

- Neurons transmit electro-chemical impulses along the axon, which trigger the secretion of chemical *neurotransmitters* across the synapse.

- A sufficiently strong stimulus during the *relative refractory period* (at the end of the cell's recovery time) can initiate a nerve impulse. The number of impulses passing along the neuron per second is coded, and is known as *temporal summation*.

- The neurotransmitters secreted by the synaptic terminals diffuse across the synaptic gap and bind to the post-synaptic receptor sites on the adjacent neuron. Some *excitatory* neurotransmitters decrease the post-synaptic membrane potentials and the initiation of nerve impulses in the post-synaptic neuron becomes more likely. At *inhibitory* synapses the

opposite occurs. Post-synaptic membrane potentials are increased, making the initiation of a nerve impulse less likely.

- The *summation* of all incoming excitatory and inhibitory activity will determine whether the neuron will fire or not. This is known as *spatial summation*.

- *Neuromodulators* modify the activity of certain neurons throughout the brain, exciting or inhibiting many groups of neurons. A well-known group of neuromodulators is *endorphins/opioids*, including enkephalin, which helps reduce pain and intensify positive sensations.

- *Psychoactive drugs* effect behaviour due to the chemicals they contain interfering with the normal functioning of the nervous system.

- Recreational drug use and abuse can have a devastating effect on the lives of many people, involving *addiction* (when the user seeks out and uses the drug with increasing frequency), *tolerance* (increasing amounts are needed to obtain the same effect) and *withdrawal* (the feelings and symptoms which develop when the user stops taking the drugs).

- Physiological and psychological dependence occur and enhance the user's need for the drugs.

- Drugs can be defined in relation to their effects in neurotransmission, where they can act as *agonists* (which increase the action of neurotransmitters) or *antagonists* (which block or inhibit the impact of neurotransmission at the receptor).

Summary cont'd.

■ There are *four* main groups of psychoactive drugs: *depressants* (which decrease synaptic activity), *stimulants* (which increase activity), *opiates* (which have both excitatory and inhibitory effects) and *hallucinogens* (which distort our sense of reality).

■ Drugs do not always produce the expected effects as a result of several factors, including the expectations of the user, the influence of other drugs taken and the effect of previous experiences.

■ Several conflicting explanations are given about drug use: *biological* (including genetic explanations), *psychodynamic* (the use of drugs to reduce anxiety and palliative measures used in times of stress), *behavioural/social learning* (drugs are taken because they are rewarding and vicarious learning occurs from observing others), *cognitive* (routine use can result in automatic cognitive responses), *socio-cultural* (the role of family and society in maintaining a 'drug career'), *biopsychosocial* (behaviour is maintained in the social world by sources which are multi-dimensional).

■ Generally, most adolescents and students try drugs due to curiosity, peer pressure and to moderate unpleasant emotions.

■ The central nervous system *(CNS)* includes activity in the brain and spinal cord. Nerve tracts of the peripheral nervous system carry the sensory information from different parts of the body along the spinal cord to the brain, and motor responses from the brain to the muscles and glands.

■ The brain not only instigates immediate actions but also compares new information with old.

■ The peripheral nervous system *(PNS)* includes the *somatic nervous system* (interactions of the external environment with nerves in the sensory system) and the *autonomic nervous system (ANS)*, which regulates the internal environment and stimulates the release of hormones from the endocrine glands.

■ The ANS functions through two systems: *sympathetic* (stimulates activity in organs and glands, and is active in the '*fight or flight*' response) and *parasympathetic* (helps conserve body energy and promotes digestion).

■ The *endocrine system* secretes hormones and is not only controlled by the ANS activity but also plays a part in its functioning. The pituitary gland, found at the base of the brain, close to the hypothalamus, influences most of the other glands.

■ The nervous and endocrine systems integrate to control complex behaviour, such as sensory and cognitive functions, affective behaviour and *homeostasis*. Homeostasis maintains the body's internal state within fairly narrow limits.

■ Psychoactive drugs can sometimes be helpful in controlling serious mental disorders.

Terms to define

absolute refractory period
addiction
dendrites
homeostasis
neuromodulators
neuron
neurotransmitters
nodes of Ranvier

psychoactive drugs
relative refractory period
saltatory conduction
spatial summation
synapse
temporal summation
tolerance
withdrawal

Further reading

Carlson, N R (1998) *Physiology of Behaviour,* 6th edn, Allyn & Bacon, Boston.

Excellent sections on psychoactive drugs and more background for those interested in the physiology of behaviour.

Green, S (1994) *Principles of Biopsychology,* Laurence Erlbaum, Hove.

British text covering the chapter content in a reader-friendly format.

Green, S (1996) 'Drugs and behaviour', *Psychology Review, 3(1)*, 14–17.

Reviews drug effects on behaviour and suggests that the attitude of users is not always consistent with those of society.

Pinel, J P J (1997) *Biopsychology,* 3rd edn, Allyn & Bacon, Boston.

For the dedicated biopsychologist. More detailed information on neural transmission, drugs and the brain.

Robson, P (1994) *Forbidden Drugs,* Oxford University Press, Oxford.

Detailed information on 'recreational' drugs, including side-effects. Also includes possible reasons why people use these drugs, addiction and treatments. The writer discusses the facts in an accessible, psychosocial manner, avoiding jargon and assuming no prior knowledge.

Answers

■ Suggested answers to activities

3

cytoplasm; cytoplasm; nuclearplasm; nucleus; nuclearplasm; protoplasm.

7

a addiction
b withdrawal
c psychological dependence
d heroin

8

aspirin; barbiturates; chlorpromazine (largactil); Diazepam (valium); alcohol

9

Table 9

Drug	Type	Effect
Painkillers (aspirin)	Depressant	Filter out sensory information to cortical areas; therefore don't feel pain
Sedatives (valium, largactil)	Depressant	Suppress excitatory synapses in brain; therefore have calming effect
Alcohol	Depressant with some stimulatory effects	Initially stimulating, then depressing. Can reduce anxiety and judgement
Barbiturates	Depressant	Slow heart and respiratory rates; therefore produce relaxed state
Opiates (morphine)	Depressant and stimulant	Mimic action of endorphins, therefore produce feeling of pleasure and reduces discomfort

Table 9 Cont'd		
Drug	Type	Effect
Heroin	Depressant and stimulant	Similar to above
Codeine	Depressant and stimulant	Similar to above but less powerful
Amphetamines	Synthetic stimulant	Stimulate neuronal firing rates in sympathetic nervous system, increasing heart and respiratory rates; therefore give feeling of well-being
Cocaine	Synthetic stimulant	Blocks re-uptake of neurotransmitters dopamine, serotonin and noradrenaline. Produces exhilaration, decreased hunger, indifference to pain. Feeling of great physical strength and mental ability
Ecstasy	Sympathetic stimulant with hallocinogen effects	Surge in 5-HT raises blood temperature and overheating results in increased water intake. Similar effects to amphetamines at high doses. Low doses produce empathy with others
Tobacco (nicotine)	Stimulant	Stimulates acetylcholine receptor and dopaminergic neurons containing these. Relaxation, feelings of alertness and reduction of appetite
Marijuana	Hallucinogen	Distorts reality. Stimuli experienced in different modalities
LSD	Hallucinogen	Suppresses the activity of serotonic-secreting neurons in brain and affects visual awareness. Produces a dream-like state

Table 9 Cont'd		
Drug	Type	Effect
PCP	Hallucinogen (chemically based)	Prevents sensory filtering. Produces feelings of dissociation but also heightened sensory output

10

a biological
b behavioural/social learning
c psychodynamic
d cognitive
e socio-cultural

11

a **Central nervous system** processes, interprets, stores and transmits information between the brain and nerve cells in the spinal cord linking with muscles, glands and organs
b **Somatic nervous system** controls the skeletal muscles
c **Sympathetic nervous system** mobilises the body for action, by organising and mobilising energy resources to deal with threatening situations

12

a hippocampus
b hypothalamus
c thalamus
d limbic system

13

somatic; somatosensory; somatomotor; visual; auditory; association areas.

■ Suggested answers to self-assessment questions

1

A nerve impulse is generated by depolarisation across the membrane of a neuron. This will only happen when a specific threshold stimulus is applied, however far above the threshold this stimulus strength reaches. This means that there are only two conditions with regard to an impulse; either it does not occur, or it does occur, regardless of the stimulus strength above threshold. These circumstances have led to the term '*all or nothing*' *response*. An impulse in any nerve fibre always travels at the same speed, therefore this cannot code for stimulus strength. Strength is coded for by the number of impulses per second which pass along the fibre (the stronger the stimulus, the greater the number of impulses passing along the fibre per second).

2

Excitatory synapses increase the possibility that an impulse will be initiated in the post-synaptic neuron. Inhibitory synapses decrease this possibility. The combined action of the two kinds of synapse functions to facilitate the perception of important stimuli such as beneficial or threatening ones, and filtering out the perception of unimportant stimuli such as neutral or non-threatening ones.

3

Temporal summation is the integration of post-synaptic potentials/impulses produced in rapid succession at the same synapse to produce a stronger signal. When a neuron is stimulated in its relative refractory period, the second impulse is superimposed on the first, making it more likely to fire (if an excitatory synapse) or less likely to fire (if an inhibitory synapse).
Spatial summation relates to how the number of separate impulses arriving simultaneously on different parts of the receptor sum to form a stronger impulse (if excitatory) or weaker impulse (if inhibitory). Simultaneous excitatory and inhibitory impulses can cancel each other out. It is the sum of total impulses arriving at any one time that determines the strength of the impulse.

4

Addiction refers to how the user seeks out and uses the drug with greater frequency.
Tolerance means that increasing amounts of the drug are needed to obtain the same effect.
Withdrawal refers to the feeling and symptoms that develop when the user stops taking the drug.

5

Agonists are drugs that increase the actions of neurotransmitters whereas *antagonists* block or inhibit neurotransmission at the receptor.
Some of the following are ways in which they can influence synaptic transmission:
- increasing the release of a neurotransmitter, e.g. L Dopa is an agonist for dopamine
- inactivating an enzyme, e.g. PCPA is a serotonic antagonist
- encouraging the vesicles to leak the transmitter substance
- inhibiting the release of the transmitter substance
- stimulating the post-synaptic receptors
- blocking the post-synaptic receptors
- blocking the re-uptake, e.g. cocaine acts as an agonist by blocking the re-uptake of dopamine.

6

Choice would probably be from: amphetamines, cocaine, ecstasy, tobacco/nicotine. Behavioural effects are described on pages 407–8.

7

Characteristics include: rebellious, lack of conformity to conventional values, tolerance towards unusual/deviant behaviour, relative lack of ambition and commitment to school work, rather independent and self-reliant, reluctance to abide by the rules, impulsive, pleasure-seeking and risk-taking, history of physical or mental illness, emotionally unstable, low self-esteem. Reasons for drug use include: curiosity and pleasure, peer pressure, palliative (to moderate unpleasant emotions and control stress).

8

Structures in the central core of the brain:
- *Medulla oblongata* controls respiration, cardiac, function, swallowing, vomiting and sneezing.
- *Pons* influences feeding and facial expression.
- *Reticular formation* is involved in consciousness, refines motor activities by modifying muscle movements, both voluntary and reflex movements.
- *Cerebellum* controls balance, muscle tone and coordinates voluntary movements such as walking, cycling and playing the piano.
- *Thalamus* regulates activity in the cortex and is involved in levels of awareness by influencing the pons. Also associated with the pain centre.
- *Hypothalamus* helps maintain homeostasis, and influences motivation and emotion. It regulates the sympathetic branch of the ANS and the control of the pituitary gland.

9

- *Somatic nervous system* connects the CNS to the sensory systems and controls the skeletal muscles.
- *Autonomic nervous system* regulates the internal environment of the body via nerves from the CNS to the internal organs.

10

A table may be a useful way to do this:

Table 10

Sympathetic system	Parasympathetic system
Prepares an organism for activity, therefore: heart rate increases; breathing rate increases; conversion of glycogen to glucose increases; pupils dilate; arteries to muscles and brain dilate	Conserves and restores body energy resources, therefore: heart rate decreases; breathing rate decreases; conversion of glucose to glycogen increases; pupils constrict; arteries to digestive system and bladder dilate

11
     See page 420 for a description of this mechanism which keeps blood hormone levels constant, similar to a room thermostat in a heating system.

12   Some of the ways the nervous systems control these behaviours could be put into a table:

Table 12	
Sensory control	Affective control
Sensory processing allows us to ignore irrelevant detail.	Thoughts are produced by the CNS.
When new stimuli are picked up, we orientate to them. If the stimulation continues, we may stop responding (habituate). The somatic nervous system alerts the ANS and, via endocrinal activity, this alerts the CNS.	Feelings result from the ANS enhanced by adrenaline secretion, e.g. memory involves using the CNS to imagine the scene and the ANS to experience the emotion.
A behavioural response is made to return to pre-existing internal conditions.	The CNS interprets the feeling.

13
     Malnutrition is linked with *microcephaly* – if in the last three months of pregnancy, the cerebellum suffers most due to depletion of glial cells, also affects cortical areas. This results in clumsiness, lack of coordination. Production of fats is also affected at this time (affecting myelination), and results in fewer inter-neural connections being made.

14
     You may have included:
- *Anti-psychotic drugs* such as chlorpromazine and clozapine.
- *Antidepressant drugs* such as fluoxetine (Prozac).
- *Bi-polar depression* controlled by lithium carbonate.
- *Side effects for cancer treatment* controlled with cannabis.

Unit 13

Cortical Functions

Graham Davies and Irene Taylor

This unit covers:

Techniques for studying brain structure and activity

Sensory perception

Lateralisation (or assymetry) of function

Split-brain studies

By the end of this unit, you should be able to:

- understand the methods and techniques used to investigate cortical functions
- understand the structure of the visual system and the processes involved in visual perception
- be aware of the organisation of sensory and motor functions of the brain and the localisation of functions such as language across the cerebral hemispheres including knowledge gained from split-brain studies.

Unit 13   Contents

Introduction

'A disembodied brain is not very exciting to look at. Stored in a formaldehyde-filled container, it is merely a putty-colored, wrinkled glob of tissue that looks a little like a walnut, whose growth has gotten out of hand. It takes an act of imagination to envision this modest looking organ writing Hamlet, *discovering radium, painting 'The Last Supper', or inventing French cuisine. Obviously, you can't judge a book, or a brain, by its cover.' (Wade and Tavris, 1993, p. 89)*

The human brain is encased in the protective bone skull, so how do scientists study it? In this unit we look at the various methods which have been developed to investigate the workings of the brain, both invasive and non-invasive techniques.

The brain performs two major functions: it controls the movement of the muscles and regulates the body's internal environment. In order to perform such tasks the brain must be informed about what is happening in both internal and external environments. This information is received by the sensory systems including the five main senses: sight, hearing, smell, taste and touch. Others would suggest other senses should be considered, such as the vestibular senses in the inner ear which provide us with information on head orientation and movement. In this unit we consider vision, the sensory modality studied most by psychologists and other scientists. It is not surprising that vision is the most studied as more information about the external environment comes to us through our eyes than other sense organs. We are most active during the hours of daylight and are 'wired' to take advantage of this illumination from the sun. Animals active at night usually have a more sensitive sense of hearing.

If there is an 'executive' organ in the body, it must be the brain. In about 1.5 kilograms are packed functions and processes that the most sophisticated computer cannot mimic. So far, no computer can store and rewrite its programmes in response to experience, simultaneously controlling complex internal processes, as does the brain. So far, no computer has been able to reproduce emotional experiences or the creativity of the human brain. Most of the complicated 'wiring' of the brain occurs in the uppermost part of the cerebrum, the **cortex**, where higher forms of thinking take place which enable us to control our environment.

We have two of almost everything, one on the left and one on the right. This is reflected in the two cerebral hemispheres of the brain. These are separate except for the fibres connecting them. Although similar in appearance, there are differences in function, referred to as **lateralisation of function**, such as language. In this unit we consider how the right and left hemispheres have different abilities with the capacity to function independently with different thoughts, memories and emotions. This is a rather challenging concept if you are to think of yourself as a 'unitary being'.

Techniques for studying brain structure and activity

To understand how the brain works we need to know about its anatomy and its chemistry. Its anatomy has been known for some time and many of the names of structures come from the shape or function of the structure such as amygdala (almond shaped) and pons (a bridge). As we saw in Unit 12, the brain consists of many billions of neurons and pathways. These structures cannot be seen in great detail without specialised neuroanatomical techniques including staining and microscopy.

Neuroanatomical techniques

It is difficult to see neural connections as axons and dendrites are closely intertwined on a minute scale. Neural tissue has to be prepared to obtain a clear view of neural structure. Initially, brain tissue undergoes fixation to preserve the tissue from decomposition. This hardens the soft and fragile brain and kills micro-organisms which might destroy it. Sections of the brain are then prepared for examination under a microscope. This preparation entails staining to allow the outline of the neurological structures to be seen in detail. At the end of the nineteenth century an Italian physician, Golgi, discovered that silver chromate stained neurons black (the *Golgi stain*). Individual neurons including axons, dendrites and synaptic connections, could then be seen for the first time. A few years later a German psychiatrist, Nissl, developed a staining procedure to enable cell bodies to be distinguished. The *Nissl stain* is not selective for neurons; it also stains all nerve cells, including glia. Because the staining binds only to structures in the cell bodies, the estimated number of cells in an area can be counted. Only areas composed of mainly cell bodies are densely stained.

Myelin stains colour the myelin sheaths making it possible to study the sheaths of myelinated axons. These are useful for visualising the myelinated areas of the central nervous system (CNS). Staining procedures do not allow the pathways of single fibres to be distinguished; it is the neuroanatomical tracing techniques which allow this. Anterograde labelling methods use chemicals which are taken up by dendrites or cell bodies and transported towards the terminal buttons. After a few days the brain is removed and sliced to reveal the locations of the injected chemicals. When a researcher wishes to know which parts of the brain synapse with a particular nucleus, retrograde labelling methods are used. Chemicals are injected and taken up by terminal buttons and transported towards the cell bodies. When, after a few days, the brain is sliced, the locations of the injected chemicals can be seen. These tracing techniques require chemicals to be injected into a living brain and until recently were not possible on a living human brain. More recently, a fluorescent carboncyanine dye (*DiI*) has been used after death. Crystals of DiI are placed in the fibre being investigated. These dissolve in the lipid membranes of the remains of axons and travel to the end of the axons. When examined under ultraviolet light, the chemical shows as a fluorescent red revealing the location of the axons.

Another neuroanatomical technique providing information on the detail of the neuronal structure is electron microscopy. Thin slices of neural tissue are coated with an electron-absorbing substance taken up by different parts of the neurons to different degrees, then a beam of electrons is passed through the tissue onto a photographic film. This results in an electron micrograph showing neuronal structure in detail.

Visualising the living brain

Conventional X-rays give little information on the living brain. Only the shapes of general structures can be seen. Contrast X-ray techniques can be used, during which a substance is injected into either the ventricular system or the circulatory system of the brain which absorbs the X-rays. This heightens the contrast between the compartments and surrounding tissue.

In the 1970s X-ray technology advanced and several methods of studying the living brain developed. First of all came computerised axial tomography, or **computed tomography**, (figure 13.1) referred to as a **CT** (*or CAT*) *scan*, a computer-assisted procedure in which the patient lies with his or her head in a large cylinder as shown in figure 13.2. On one side an X-ray tube projects an X-ray beam to a detector on the other side. The X-ray tube and detector automatically rotate around the head taking a range of X-ray photographs. The information from each X-ray photograph is computerised to generate a CT scan of one horizontal section of the brain. As seen in figure 13.2, the X-ray tube and detector then move along to photograph another section of the brain.

Scans are usually obtained of eight or nine horizontal brain sections. These scans are useful in the diagnosis of pathological conditions such as tumours and degenerative diseases. This enables physicians to see if surgery is necessary and also enables neuropsychologists to infer brain functions by studying behaviour of individuals who have

13.1 Computer-based techniques for monitoring brain activity

Computed tomography (computerised axial tomography or CAT, sometimes abbreviated to CT) combines the principles of X-rays and computer technology. A patient is placed on a radiolucent (allows the passage of X-rays) couch which is then moved into position within a central aperture of the machine. X-rays, emitted from a continually rotating source, pass through a cross-section of the patient's head, emerging in a range of different intensities depending on the volume and density of brain structures within the cross-section. X-ray sensitive detectors situated around the scanner convert these into electrical signals and feed them to the computer. This produces a television picture, which can be displayed on a monitor for examination. CAT scans are particularly useful for showing up tumours.

Positron emission tomography (PET) is a scanning technique which provides information about neural activity in the brain. Patients are injected with the radioactive tracer 2-deoxyglucose (2-DG) which is used by brain cells in the same way that normal glucose is – the more active the cell, the more 2-DG is used. 2-DG emits positrons (positively charged particles) which are detected by the scanner and fed to the computer. This converts the information to a PET scan which shows on a monitor, each level of activity showing up as a different colour. PET scans are used to identify epilepsy, blood clots and brain tumours. They have also been used to compare the brains of schizophrenics to those of non-schizophrenics (Andreasen, 1988) and to investigate the functional centres of higher mental processes (Posner *et al.*, 1988).

Magnetic resonance imaging (MRI) is a diagnostic technique using magnetism and radio waves to generate images. It therefore has no risk from X-rays. Certain atomic nuclei, found in all body cells, undergo changes when they are placed in a strong magnetic field and then subjected to a particular radio frequency pulse. The changes cause the nuclei to emit small, but measurable radio signals, which are fed into a computer and converted into a television picture. MRI is more sensitive than CAT and is used to locate tumours, cysts and lesions in the blood supply throughout the nervous system.

Figure 13.2

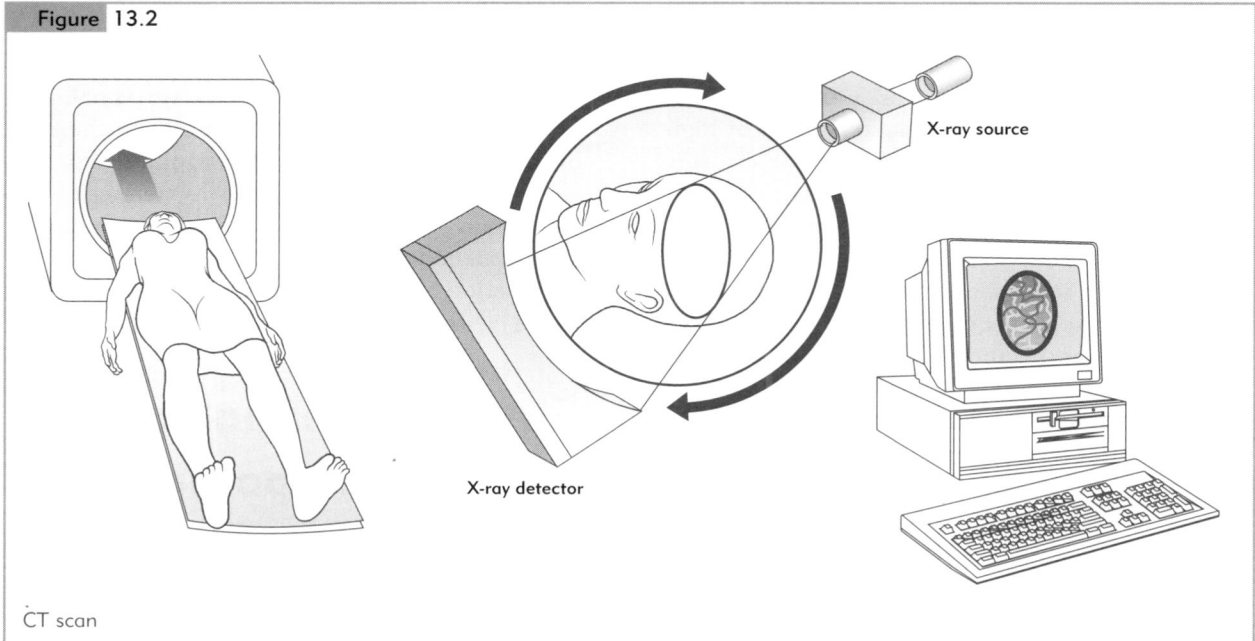

X-ray source

X-ray detector

CT scan

brain damage and injury. The CT scan enables the determination of the approximate location of the damage.

Even clearer images can be seen using **magnetic resonance imaging (MRI)** in which high resolution images are constructed from the measurement of waves that hydrogen atoms emit when activated by radio-frequency waves in a magnetic field. Belliveau *et al.* (1991) found they could use MRI technology to measure brain activity. Known as *functional MRI*, this process provides a 3D image of the brain with areas of activity indicated in colour, produced through the increase of oxygen (in blood) flowing to active areas of the brain.

Another brain-imaging technique which provides images of brain activity rather than structure is **positron emission tomography (PET)**, in which radioactive 2-deoxyglucose (2-DG) is injected. This is in the form of sugar which is harmless. It enters and accumulates in active cells. Eventually it breaks down and leaves the cell and as these radioactive isotopes decay, they emit particles called positrons which are picked up by the PET scan, showing the activity levels of that section. Tadecola (1993) found areas of activity in the brain increase the blood flow which results in active neurons releasing nitric oxide, so if radioactive water is injected into the circulation system of the brain, when the individual engages in some activity the PET scan will indicate the areas in which blood flow is increased during the action. Areas of high activity show up as red and yellow. The visual cortex can be seen to have a high level of activity in the first scan during which the individual was scanning a visual display.

The PET scan is a sensitive detector of radioactivity like a Geiger counter which measures radioactivity and sends the information to a computer. This draws a colour cross-sectional picture of the brain unlike an X-ray which emits X-rays. Psychologists such as Posner (1993) investigated brain areas activated during various mental functions such as listening to music and working out problems. Others have looked at the differences in PET scans between people suffering neurological disorders and those from normal

brains. Andreasen (1988) found the PET scans of schizophrenics revealed differences in metabolic function to those who did not have this condition.

Pinel (1997) noted four advantages in using functional MRI rather than PET:
- No injections are needed into the brain.
- It provides both structured and functional information in the same picture.
- Spatial resolution is better.
- It can monitor changes at the time they occur rather than having to wait for the chemicals to break down.

Activity 1

Describe briefly these three non-invasive techniques for studying the brain:
a   computerised axial tomography
b   positron emission tomography
c   magnetic resonance imaging
(If you have any difficulty, re-read pages 436 and 437.)

Even more advanced techniques of imaging are under development. SQUID and SPET sound more like animals than scanning devices. Super-conducting Quantum Imaging Device and Single Positron Emission Tomography are able to visualise the active brain when the individual is performing some task. These machines enable very small areas of the brain to be examined. Currently, there are only a few of them in use due to their high cost. Scanning procedures are seen as non-invasive as they do not harm the living brain. Other such non-invasive techniques which have been used over a long period of time are recording techniques such as the electroencephalogram (EEG).

Electroencephalogram and evoked potentials

Gross electrical activity of the brain can be monitored using electroencephalograms. Electrodes are placed on the scalp and information about different brain areas is recorded on an *electroencephalograph (EEG)* in the form of brain waves. EEGs are used during investigations of sleep and dreaming. They are also used to locate gross abnormalities in electrical functioning such as those caused by epilepsy, tumour and haemorrhage.

Using EEG, Kosslyn (1988) found hemispheric differences in brain patterns when someone is undertaking a language-based task compared to when the person is undertaking a spatial task. The scalp EEG signal reflects the sum of electrical events throughout the head. The activity is recorded between disc-shaped electrodes taped to the scalp.

A related method known as evoked potentials is when a stimulus is presented several times and the EEG recordings are averaged to separate the effects of stimulation from the background brain activity. The EEG can provide a detailed moment-to-moment record of brain activity when a stimulus is being processed (but with less precision than some of the scanning techniques noted above). The changes in rhythm have been clinically used to detect pathological states and diagnose the site and extent of tumours and other brain damage such as epilepsy.

Invasive physiological research methods

More invasive physiological methods have been used on animals and sometimes humans during neurosurgery. These include:
- lesions
- electrical stimulation and recording techniques.

Stereotaxic surgery is often used when a researcher needs to place a particular part of the brain with as little damage as possible to the surrounding tissue. A stereotaxic apparatus allows the investigator to locate the brain structures precisely and hold the animal's head in the proper orientation and also hold the electrode or cannula. Once the stereotaxic coordinates are calculated, the animal is anaesthetised and the scalp is cut to

expose the skull so the exact point for the lesion or electrode is determined.

Lesion methods involve part of the brain being removed, damaged or destroyed and the behaviour of the animal (or human) is carefully assessed to determine the functions of the lesioned structure. You will find an account of behaviour change in Phineus Gage after brain damage reported in Unit 15 page 532. There are several problems interpreting lesion effects as follows:
- The structures of the brain are small, convoluted and tightly packed so even a skilled surgeon cannot destroy a structure without damage to adjoining structures. Thus the associated behaviour may be accredited to the wrong area.
- The lesion procedure may leave post-operative effects.
- Subtle changes (such as personality changes in humans) may not be recorded.
- Records or memory of the patient's family are often used with the associated problems of such data collection (see Unit 27 page 1005).

Electrical stimulation and recording of the brain is possible using *microelectrodes*. These are very fine needles which can be precisely located onto or into specific nerve cells or axons. They can be used either as sources of stimulation or for recording neural activity – which can then be displayed visually on an oscilloscope. They are sometimes used as a screening process to mimic neural activity before major brain surgery. Electrical stimulation should produce behaviour and feelings lost through injury or illness but which are normal for that brain area (see page 445 for further discussion of single-cell recording).

Using microelectrodes to study behaviour opens up similar problems to those experienced by psychologists using anatomical techniques. Electrical stimulation is not always specific and cells near to the target cell may be affected, thus distorting interpretation.

Pinel (1997) notes that electrical stimulation of a brain structure usually has behavioural effects opposite to those produced by lesions to the same structure. It is a flexible and painless procedure used by many researchers, including Penfield and

Delgado, but, like any method, it is subject to problems:

- The artificial stimulation does not resemble the more intricate electrical potentials of neuronal and synaptic activity. It is more likely to be powerful and result in more extreme reactions (researchers continue to refine these techniques to make them more similar to neural stimulation).
- The stimulation may affect surrounding areas.

Psychopharmacological methods

Psychopharmacology is the study of how chemicals affect the nervous systems. Neurotransmitters are necessary for neural function and researchers may seek either to mimic the effect of a particular transmitter, or block it. Chemicals affect only those cells which are receptive to them, so behaviour changes are less open to misinterpretation than when using microelectrical techniques. For instance, Grossman (1960) showed that the neurotransmitter noradrenalin stimulates the specific nerve pathways controlling eating, whereas acetylcholine stimulates those controlling drinking.

The major purpose of psychopharmacology is to administer drugs (chemicals) which either increase or decrease the effects of neurotransmitters. They can be:

- fed to the participant
- injected into the stomach abdomen muscles, into the fatty tissue under the skin or into a vein.

One problem is that many drugs do not cross the blood–brain barrier so drugs are sometimes injected in small quantities through a fine hollow needle (a cannula) stereotaxically implanted in the brain.

Many procedures are used for measuring this chemical activity in the brains of laboratory animals. One such is the *2-deoxyglucose (2-DG)* technique which involves injecting radioactive 2-DG into the animal. Because it is similar to glucose the neurons active during the test situation absorb it, but do not metabolise it. The animal is killed, the brain removed, sliced and then subjected to autoradiography (coated with photographic emulsion, stored in the dark and then developed in a similar way to photographic film). Areas of the brain that absorbed the high levels of 2-DG appear as black spots and the density of spots in various regions is colour coded.

Using the psychopharmacological approach, Sokolov (1975) confirmed the columnar arrangement of cells in the visual cortex by injecting radioactive glucose, which is absorbed by most cells, into animals' brains. Slices of brain tissue from the sacrificed animals were then developed on photographic plates. The most active areas showed up where the glucose had accumulated.

Chemical stimulation is more specific than electrical as it activates the cell bodies rather than the axons so the stimulation is usually more localised. As we saw in Unit 12, pharmacologists have discovered many drugs that have an effect on synaptic transmission. These drugs can be injected directly into the brain where they affect synaptic transmission in localised regions.

The structure of the brain is covered in Unit 12. In this unit we look in more detail at the cerebral cortex, the thin, but important, layer of neural tissue covering the cerebrum. In Activity 2 you can review your knowledge of the structure of the cortex.

Activity 2

Complete the following sentences:

a The _____ cortex receives information from the sense organs.

b The visual cortex receives information relayed from the _____ _____ _____.

c Electrically stimulating neurons in the _____ _____ causes the skeletal muscles to contract.

d The _____ _____ of the cortex cover three-quarters of the cerebral cortex in humans.

(If you had difficulty answering any of the above, look back to Unit 12 before proceeding.)

(Answers on page 469.)

The cerebral cortex surrounds the cerebral hemispheres like the bark of a tree (cortex means 'bark'). In the human brain the cortex is convoluted with small grooves known as *sulci*, larger grooves known as *fissures*, and *gyri* which are the bulges between the sulci and fissures. This convolution enlarges the surface area of the brain with two-thirds of the surface hidden in the grooves. The thickness is about 3 mm and consists of mostly glia and cell bodies, dendrites and interconnecting axons which give it a greyish-brown colour, leading to it being called 'grey matter'. Beneath the cortex are the millions of axons connecting the cortex with other regions of the brain. The white of the myelin leads to the name 'white matter'. The cerebral cortex is seen to be the part of the brain responsible for our ability to reason, plan, remember and imagine. At this moment, your sensory and perceptual processes are demonstrating their incredible skills. Your eyes are moving along the page identifying letters and words at a rapid speed. When you glance up you perceive a world of colour and motion.

Self-assessment questions

1 Briefly outline *two* neuroanatomical staining techniques.

2 Note some of the advantages of using functional MRI rather than PET.

3 When are EEG recordings useful?

4 Summarise *one* invasive technique used to study the brain.

5 Outline *one* of the techniques used in psychopharmacology to understand the nervous system.

(Suggested answers on page 470.)

Sensory perception

The process of becoming aware of something through our senses has two stages. **Sensation** is the registering of stimuli by our sense organs; **perception** involves their interpretation so that they become meaningful to us. Humans carry out complex perceptual tasks unconsciously, effortlessly and quickly. We take many of these so much for granted that we have difficulty in realising their existence. For example, when you look at this page, your visual sense registers the image produced by the words. Your brain then interprets these in the light of past experience.

You are probably familiar with the senses of vision, hearing, smell, taste and touch. These are not the only senses; others include kinaesthesis and balance. Each of these gives us information about our environment, contributing to our overall state of knowledge about what really is 'out there'.

In this section we concentrate on the visual sense, which is the most researched of the senses, reflecting its importance to human beings. Visual perception is discussed in detail in Unit 16.

The sensory basis of visual perception

The visual sense involves the ability of the eyes to distinguish environmental stimuli. The term *visual acuity* refers to the ability to differentiate separate points of light projected onto the retina. The minimum level of light intensity that the visual system is capable of recognising is known as the *absolute threshold* of vision.

Both of these concepts relate to the ability of receptors in the eye to be stimulated by light which Forms a small part of the electromagnetic spectrum. The visible spectrum ranges from about

380 to 760 nanometers (nm). We are blind to all other wavelengths. The electromagnetic spectrum extends beyond this, from X-rays and ultra-violet rays at lower wavelengths, to infra-red and radio waves at higher wavelengths.

The human eye

The human eye (figure 13.3) is able to focus light waves from both near and distant objects onto cells located within a thin receptive layer called the **retina** which lies on the inside of the back of the eyeball. Image formation is achieved through the refraction of light rays by the imaging mechanisms of cornea, pupil and lens.

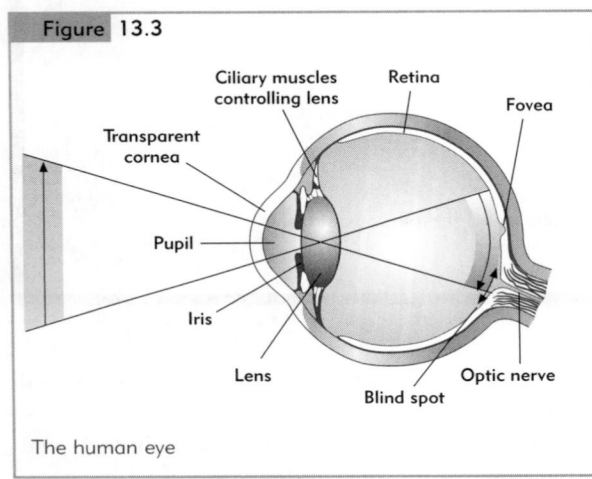

Figure 13.3

The human eye

Imaging mechanisms

Light from an object first passes through the transparent cornea, which has fixed convexity and refracts the light rays inwards to begin the process of image formation.

From the cornea, light passes through the pupil. This is an adjustable, circular aperture in the iris, which forms a ring of muscles controlling the pupil size. When fully open (in dim light), it can admit about 16 times more light than when fully contracted (in bright light). The pupil helps to maintain image quality in different light levels. However, this is insufficient to deal with the full range of light intensities to which the eye can be exposed. As a result, the eye has alternative strategies to deal with changes in light intensity (see page 443). Pupil size is also sensitive to mental

effort and emotions, for example our pupils dilate when we see someone we are attracted to.

The lens, which is convex in shape, has an adjustable curvature which permits light from objects at different distances to be focused onto the retina. Lens curvature is adjusted by the action of the ciliary muscles. It increases when we fixate a near object and decreases when we fixate a distant one. The term *accommodation* is used to describe the change in curvature of the lens.

The retinal cells

As shown in figure 13.4, there are five different layers of cells at the retina:

- receptors
- horizontal cells
- bipolar cells
- amacrine cells
- retinal ganglion cells.

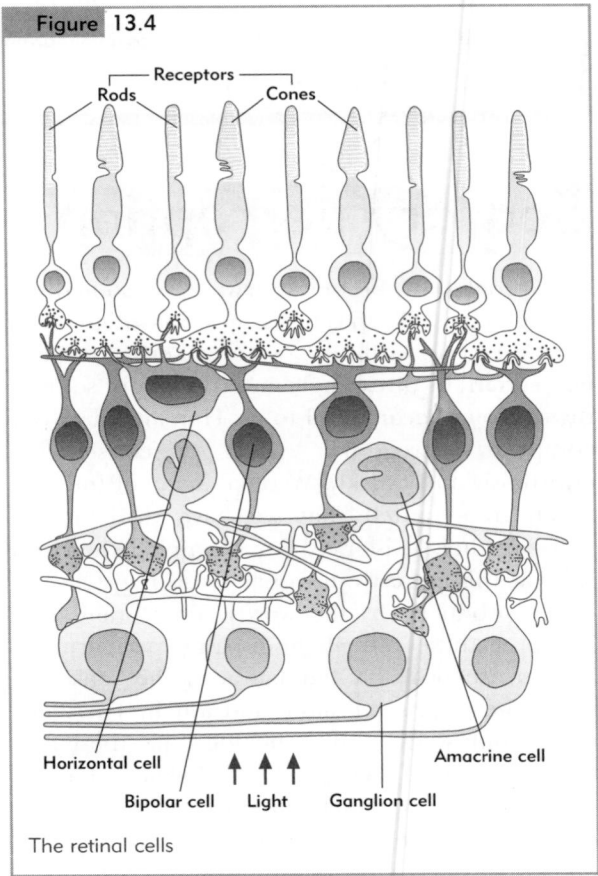

Figure 13.4

The retinal cells

The amacrine and horizontal cells are specialised for communication across the various channels known as *lateral communication*. Barnstable in 1993 noted that amacrine and bipolar cells release the inhibitory neurotransmitter GABA, whereas the receptors and bipolar cells release the excitatory neurotransmitter glutamate. Somewhat surprisingly, light has to pass through bipolar cells, ganglion cells and blood vessels to reach the receptors, which lie at the back of the retina.

> ## Activity 3
> What do you think happens to your vision when you leave a dark room and go outside into bright sunlight? The answer is in the next paragraph.

Such a situation will strongly activate all the light receptors in the eye, so that you will appear to be dazzled. However, after a few seconds *light adaptation* occurs as the eye can register the intensity of light falling on the retina. In order to do this, each receptor cell contains photopigment which bleaches when light falls upon it. Through this process, the strength of signal produced by a given quantity of light is lessened, the receptors becoming increasingly sensitive to differences in bright light. At the same time, they become decreasingly sensitive to changes in low light.

Although light adaptation is rapid, the reverse process (dark adaptation) is much slower, *taking* about 30 minutes to complete. This is because the photopigment in the eyes needs to regenerate.

Due to the fact that the receptor cells adapt to different light intensities, we are unable to maintain vision for more than a few seconds without eye movements. Physiological nystagmus is the term given to a continuous, tremor-like movement of the eyes which we are unconscious of making. This serves to keep the image always in motion upon the eye, thus ensuring that the receptors are freshly stimulated and hence maintaining vision.

There are two types of receptor cell in each human retina, which absorb light and respond electrically. Cones are ideally suited for receiving bright light. They number about 6 million and are markedly concentrated in the fovea, a broadly circular area in the central part of the retina. They decrease rapidly in number in all directions from the fovea.

Rods are capable of registering low light intensities and are significantly more numerous than the cones, with about 120 million in each eye. They are absent from the fovea and are found principally around the periphery of the retina.

Axons from both rods and cones synapse onto neurons known as bipolar cells. These in turn synapse onto further neurons known as ganglion cells, which number about 1 million. At the margin of the retina, several hundred rods pool their information and serve each ganglion cell. Thus, very low levels of light can be registered here. In the fovea, however, only a few cones serve each ganglion cell. The result of this is that the margin of the retina is highly sensitive to faint objects, but lacks the ability to detect fine detail. The fovea is the best area for visual acuity and can recognise fine detail but lacks the sensitivity of the retinal margin.

> ## Activity 4
> Next time you are outside in bright light, fix your gaze on an object in front of you. How much detail can you see from the margins of your visual field?
> Can you explain the difference between the view straight ahead, and what you can see at the margins?

The axons from the ganglion cells form the *optic nerve* which leaves the retina at the *blind spot* (figure 13.5), an area of the retina without receptor cells and therefore unable to respond to light.

> ## Activity 5
> Find your blind spot using figure 13.5.

Figure 13.5

The optic disk, where the fibres of the optic nerve leave the eye, has no visual receptors and is therefore a blind spot. To find the blind spot in your left eye, close your right eye and look at the magician. Then slowly move the book towards and away from yourself. The rabbit should disappear when the book is between 22 and 30cm from your eye.

The blind spot

Source: Wade and Tarvis (1993)

The visual pathways and the brain

The optic nerve conveys visual information to the dorsal *lateral geniculate nucleus* in a region of the brain known as the thalamus. From here, axons link to the primary visual cortex at the rear of the brain. Half of the information from each eye is sent to the left visual cortex, and half to the right. This makes good sense because it is helpful to perception to combine information received by the two eyes. It also serves to reduce the impact of any damage caused to one eye or to one brain hemisphere.

When you look at an object, your visual system does not conduct an image of the object from the retina to the cortex, rather it decodes key information about the object, especially its edges and location, and conducts the information to the cortex. It is the cortex that reconstructs the image from the various pieces of information given. (You will find further discussion of this reconstruction process and the role of top-down processing in Unit 16 and on page 453.)

Thousands of pathways develop in the brain connecting one brain region to another. These connections are orderly and systematic and seem to be specified genetically. The surface of the retina of the eye is 'mapped' onto an area of the cortex. Kandel and O'Dell (1993) found the orderly synaptic connections in the sensory system of the brain are controlled by neural activity. There appear to be critical periods during which some synapses in the retina connect with a target region, stabilise and become permanent whilst others are 'weeded out'. The terminal buttons which disappear are replaced by others, and the remaining axons sprout new branches that grow new terminal buttons. The synapses which remain are those whose activity is correlated with that of

Activity 6

Below is an unlabelled diagram of the eye. Label the diagram and add the function of each of its parts.

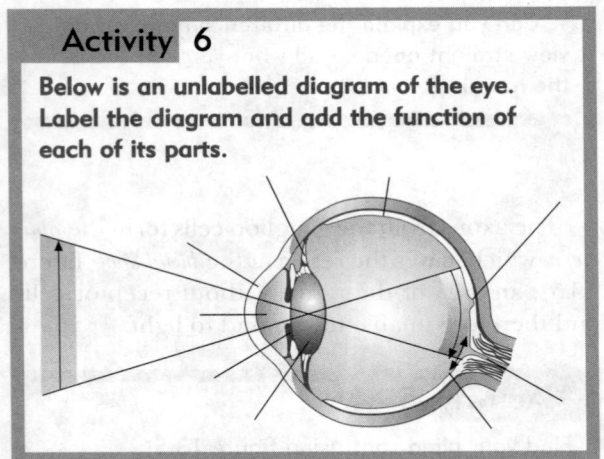

their neighbours. In the visual system, as can be seen in figure 13.6, it is the relative location on the retina of the cell body from which they originate. Adjoining terminal buttons are likely to fire at the same time, as they will both be located in a region of light or shadow, whereas distant neurons may sometimes be disparate with one in light and the other one in shadow on some occasions.

Thus terminal buttons located on the same cell as those from neighbouring retinal cells are the ones to survive. Carlson (1994) notes that if action potentials in the axons of optic nerves are blocked during the critical period, this weeding out does not take place and the connections remain haphazard. This has the same effect as raising the animal in the dark.

■ Receptive fields

As noted on page 439, microelectrodes are used to record brain activity. *Single-cell recording* measures the activity of a single neuron. For example, to study ganglion cells a microelectrode can be positioned in the optic nerve after it has left the eye. Small spots of light are then presented on a screen to an animal whose head movements have been restrained and the ganglion cell's responses to the stimuli are recorded. The part of the retina which produces a change in the activity of the ganglion cell is called the ganglion cell's **receptive field**. The process of single cell recording is very complex and painstaking. Apparently David Hubel (1989) compared the process to mowing a lawn with nail scissors. Hubel and Wiesel (1979) won the Nobel Prize in 1981 for their work on the retina-geniculate-striate system which is reported in more detail in Unit 16 page 579. Hubel and Wiesel concluded that the functions of many of the neurons in this system were to respond to the degree of brightness contrast between the two areas of their receptive fields.

In mammals, receptive fields are circles or ovals and in the main are of two types with antagonistic surrounds which respond to light in an opposite way to that of the centre:

■ On centre, off surround receptive fields will produce a burst of activity when light shines on the centre but will not respond (show

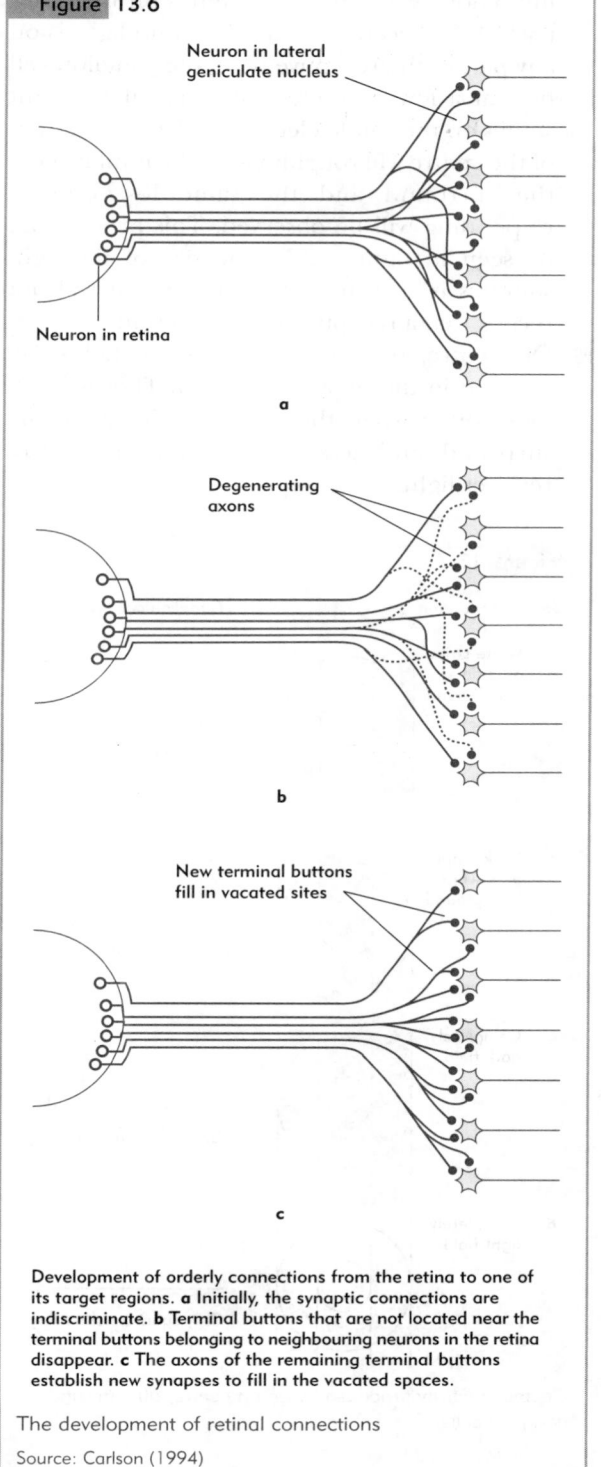

Figure 13.6

Development of orderly connections from the retina to one of its target regions. **a** Initially, the synaptic connections are indiscriminate. **b** Terminal buttons that are not located near the terminal buttons belonging to neighbouring neurons in the retina disappear. **c** The axons of the remaining terminal buttons establish new synapses to fill in the vacated spaces.

The development of retinal connections

Source: Carlson (1994)

inhibition) when the light shines on the outer part of the receptive field. When no light is on any part of the receptive field, the ganglion cell fires at a low rate and conversely, if the light shines on the whole electric field, the activation of the centre will roughly equal the inhibition of the surround and the same low rate of responding will be observed. This process can be seen in figure 13.7. The size of the light stimulus is crucial: if it is too large it will not record that a receptive field is present.

■ Off centre, on surround receptive fields will respond in the opposite manner. They will fire more often when the light stimulus is on the surround and less often when the centre receives light.

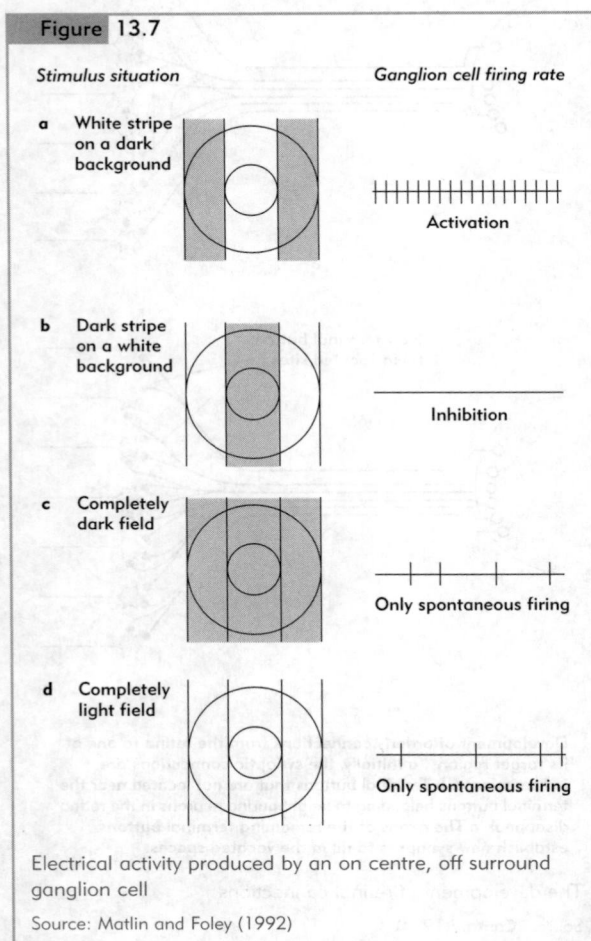

Figure 13.7

Stimulus situation — *Ganglion cell firing rate*

a White stripe on a dark background — Activation

b Dark stripe on a white background — Inhibition

c Completely dark field — Only spontaneous firing

d Completely light field — Only spontaneous firing

Electrical activity produced by an on centre, off surround ganglion cell

Source: Matlin and Foley (1992)

Activity 7

Re-label figure 13.7 to show how an off centre, on surround would react to the stimulus presented.

(Answer on page 469.)

Research on retinal ganglion cells by Lennie (1980) and Schiller (1986) revealed three structurally different ganglion cells referred to as X, Y and W cells.

■ X cells are most common and respond steadily during stimulation with small receptive fields. They are useful for picking up precise details about the visual stimulus and are thought to be important in perceiving visual pattern or detail in a non-moving stimulus.

■ Y cells respond in quick bursts when stimulated and then return to the previous firing rate. They have a large receptive field thought to be involved in perception of movement and stereoscopic depth. They are thought to be insensitive to colour.

■ W cells seem to respond to more homogeneous, evenly distributed stimulation unlike the X and Y cells which show the characteristic on/off centre receptive fields. W cells are the slowest conducting of the three types and seem to respond best to moving stimuli.

Far more is known about the X and Y cells, and their characteristics are summarised in table 13.8.

■ **The primary visual pathway**

After leaving the eye the optic nerves come together and cross over at the optic chiasma (or chiasm). Axons from the ganglion cells of the inner half of each retina cross and ascend to the opposite side of the brain to the lateral geniculate nucleus. The axons from the ganglion cells of the outer part of the retina ascend to the lateral geniculate nucleus on the same side of the brain to the primary visual cortex. After the ganglion cells forming the optic nerve cross over at the optic chiasma, they are regrouped and known as the *optic tract*. The lens inverts the image projected onto the

Characteristic	Type of Ganglion Cell	
	X	Y
Nature of receptive field	Centre-surround	Centre-surround
Cell size	Small	Large
Size of receptive field	Small	Large
Kind of response	Sustained	Quick bursts
Speed of conduction	Slow	Fast
Kind of stimulus responded to	Precise details	Movement
Area of brain where ganglion terminates	Lateral geniculate nucleus	Lateral geniculate nucleus and superior colliculus

Table 13.8

A summary of the characteristics of X and Y cells

Source: Matlin and Foley (1992)

retina and reverses left and right. Due to the crossing over of the axons from the nasal halves of retinas at the optic chiasma, each hemisphere of the brain receives information from the opposite side of the visual picture. Figure 13.9 shows how, when the individual is looking straight ahead, the right hemisphere receives information from the left half of the visual field and the left hemisphere receives information from the right half of the visual field. Because there are no synapses at the optic chiasma, the information from each retina remains intact and unchanged. It is the slight differences in images

Figure 13.9

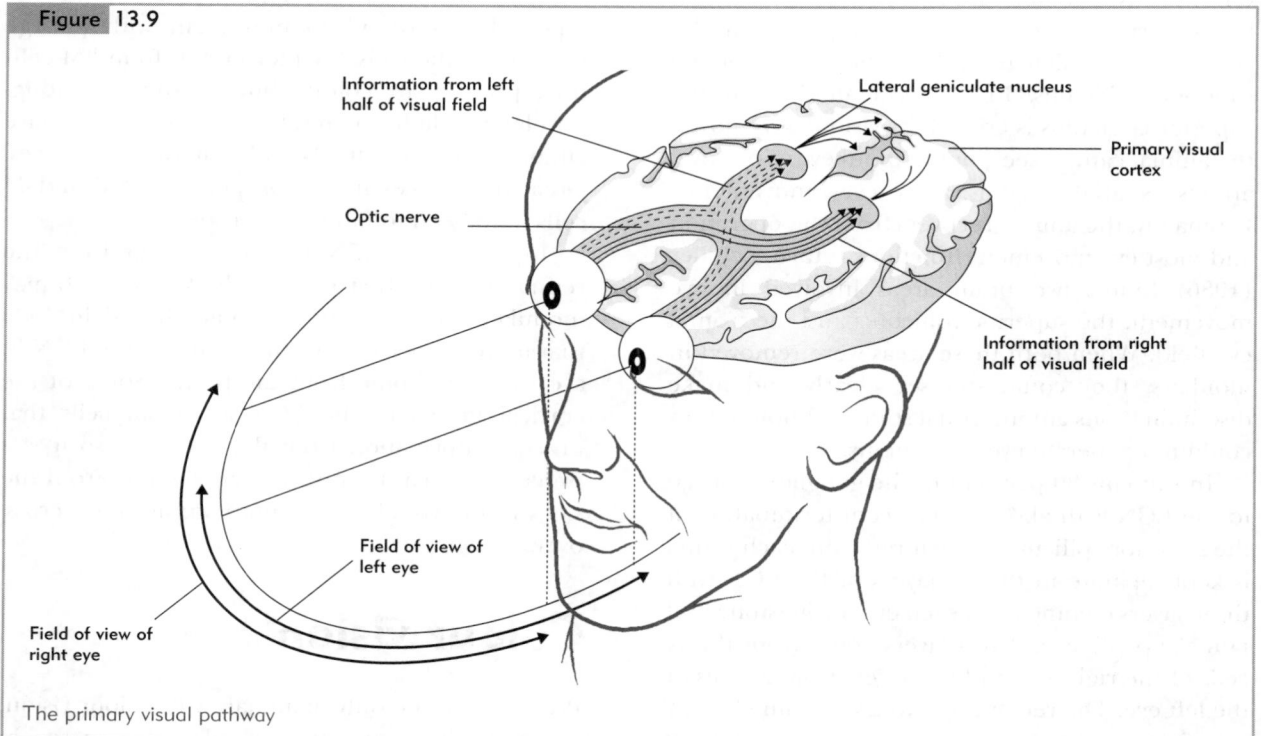

The primary visual pathway

formed at the two retinas which helps us see the world as three dimensional. The crossover at the optic chiasma brings information from each retina to the same region of the visual cortex.

Activity 8

Look straight ahead and notice some object in the left visual field. This object is being registered on both right and left retinas, but the information will end up on the right side of the visual cortex.

The information from each eye remains separate in the optic tract. The optic tract fibres travel to two areas: the *superior colliculus* and the lateral geniculate nucleus (LGN). In humans some of the Y and all of the W ganglion cells go to the superior colliculus and then onto Areas 18 and 19 of the visual cortex. Information from the auditory and skin senses also goes to the superior colliculus which probably integrates information from the various senses. Matlin and Foley (1992) noted that the superior colliculus receives input from the visual cortex which modulates the activity of the superior colliculus. In fish and amphibians the superior colliculus is critical for vision (if removed the animal cannot see), but in monkeys its removal affects spatial vision and eye movements. Ultimately, the animal recovers from the operation and most eye movement functions return. Schiller (1986) found two brain areas involved in eye movement: the superior colliculus and the frontal eye field. When both these areas were removed in monkeys, they could still see clearly and make discriminations among visual stimuli although they could not generate eye movements.

In humans 80 per cent of the ganglion cells go to the LGN with about 20 per cent terminating at the superior colliculus. The input from each retina is kept separate in the six layers of the LGN with three layers coming from each eye. Livingstone and Hubel (1988) found two layers come from the X cells of the right eye and two layers from X cells of the left eye. The remaining two layers come from Y cells from each eye. In the two inner layers the cell bodies are larger than those on the outer four layers. It is for this reason that the former are called magnocellular (M) layers and the latter parvocellular (P) layers. These two sets of layers belong to different systems responsible for the analysis of different types of retinal ganglion cells. The primary visual cortex is often called the *striate* cortex because it contains a dark staining layer of cells where the neurons from the lateral geniculate nucleus terminate in the lower part of layer IV, giving it a striped effect.

The primary visual pathway is composed of these two relatively independent channels of communication: the M and P layers. The outer P pathway is composed of the parvocellular neurons of the lateral geniculate nuclei and retinal ganglion cells that synapse on them and receives information from the X cells. The more numerous P neurons receive input mainly from cones and are particularly sensitive to colour, fine detail and stationary or slow-moving objects. Conversely, the inner M pathway is composed of the magnocellular neurons of the lateral geniculate nuclei and the retinal cells that synapse on them and receives information from the Y cells. The M neurons are especially responsive to movement with a large input from the rods. Shapley (1990) found M cells unresponsive to colour but sensitive to long-wavelength light. Lateral geniculate cells have circular receptive fields with on or off centres. Great differences in the proportion of P and M cells have been found between species.

Input to the LGN not only comes from the retina but also other parts of the brain which may modulate its functioning. Schiller found in 1986 that up to 80 per cent of the inputs to the LGN in a cat did not come from the retina. Some of the cortical inputs to the LGN are from cells that process information from the two eyes, so it is a processing area not only a relay station. From the LGN to the visual cortex there are no other cross-overs or synapses.

Colour vision

Primates are the only mammals with colour vision, but many birds and fish are also able to see in colour.

Activity 9

Consider for a few minutes how different your life would be without colour. Perhaps you are one of the small percentage of people (mostly male) who do not have full colour vision? Draw up a list of problems you would encounter in a world without colour.

(Suggested answer on page 470)

Some people do suffer colour deficiencies. Nathans (1989) found about 8 per cent of males and about 0.4 per cent of females to be less sensitive to red and green or blue and yellow. Some people are completely colour blind (about one in a million), experiencing only shades of black, white and grey.

So far we have considered the properties of ganglion cells in response to light and dark. However, some objects selectively absorb some wavelengths of light and reflect others giving them different colours. Colour mixing of lights is different from pigment mixing such as mixing of yellow and blue paints which results in green, whereas a beam of red light and a beam of bluish-green light will result in yellow light. If we mix yellow and blue lights, we will get white light, so the white we see on a television screen actually consists of tiny dots of red, blue and green light.

■ Theories of colour vision

Two early theories of colour vision have both been found applicable to different levels of visual processing. In 1802 Thomas Young, a British physicist and physician, noted how the human visual system can synthesise any colour from various amounts of any set of three colours of different wavelengths. This became known as trichromatic theory. He hypothesised that the eye contains three types of colour receptor cones each sensitive to a different hue. The brain synthesises colours by combing the information from each receptor. He suggested the receptors were sensitive to blue, green and red. This theory was further developed by Hermann von Helmholtz in 1852, so you will sometimes see this theory referred to as the Young–Helmholtz theory.

More recent research has shown that cones in the human eye do contain three types of photopigment, each of which absorbs light of a particular wavelength: 420, 530 and 560 nm. These, overlapping wavelengths actually correspond to blue-violet, green and yellow-green but most researchers refer to them as blue, green and red cones so we shall do likewise. Red and green are present in about equal proportions with fewer blue cones. White light stimulates all three cones equally and yellow light stimulates red and green cones equally well with no effect on the blue cones. The colour of a particular stimulus is presumed to be encoded by the ratio of activity in the three different receptors. Genetic defects in colour vision appear to be due to problems with one or more of these cones.

Trichromatic theory cannot explain all colour phenomena. It became apparent that another mechanism must be involved beyond the receptor level which combines this information from the cones in a more complex manner. An opponent-process theory was suggested by a German physician, Hering, at the end of the nineteenth century. He noted that some colour mixtures seemed impossible, for example greenish-red or yellowish-blue.

Hering incorrectly assumed that the opponent-processes occurred at the receptor cell level rather than at higher levels so initially the opponent-process theory was incompatible with the trichromatic theory.

Cells respond to stimulation with an increase in activity when one colour is present and a decrease in activity when another colour is present. When a region of the receptive field is illuminated with a colour, the cell rate of firing increases and when a complementary colour illuminates the area, firing of the cells decreases. He suggested two different classes of cell in the visual system for encoding colour and another for encoding brightness. Hering suggested each of the three classes of cell encoded two complementary colour perceptions. One set of cells signals red in one direction and green in the opposite direction. Another set was hypothesised to signal blue in one direction and yellow in the opposite direction. A final set of brightness cells signalled black and white.

The first direct evidence of these opponent-process cells came from Svaetichin (1956) studying carp fish which have excellent colour vision. He was recording responses at the level of the horizontal cells at the retina (see figure 13.4 on page 442 to refresh your memory of these if you need to). The horizontal cells receive information from the photoreceptors and it was found that the wavelength of light presented to the cones influenced how the horizontal cells responded with red-on/green-off, yellow-on/blue-off and another cell responding to light intensity similar to the white-black receptor suggested by Hering. DeValois and DeValois (1975) found that in humans this opponent process might operate at ganglion level. They proposed six kinds of higher level cells, as can be seen in figure 13.10, linking with the three cones: one responsive to short wavelengths (S), one to medium wavelengths (M) and one to long wavelengths (L).

When light from a particular wavelength reaches a cone, the cone passes this information to at least two of the six kinds of higher level cell, with S cones only passing information onto two levels, whereas L cones pass onto all six. You will note that the +Wh and −Bl receive only stimulation, whereas

the +Bl and −Wh receive only inhibition, and the other two sets work in opposing ways.

The LGN also encodes colour in a similar opponent-process fashion with little or no reorganisation in the LGN. In the primary visual cortex many cells still operate in the opponent-process manner, but Mollon found in 1982 that this was not as common as in the LGN. The cortex seems to contain a number of cells which process colour in a more complex manner.

Trichromatic and opponent-process theories competed for many years as a single explanation of colour vision. Scientists now know that *both* are needed to explain our ability to respond to colour. Trichromatic theory explains how colour coding occurs at receptor level in the cones, whereas opponent-process theory accounts for processing at a higher level such as ganglion cells.

◼ The structure of the visual cortex

When Hubel and Wiesel (1982) were exploring the properties of individual cells, they found the layers of the visual cortex (see Area 17 in figure 13.11) had a certain structure. Vertical cells were in a *column*, which had a high response rate to a line of certain orientation. When recordings were taken a

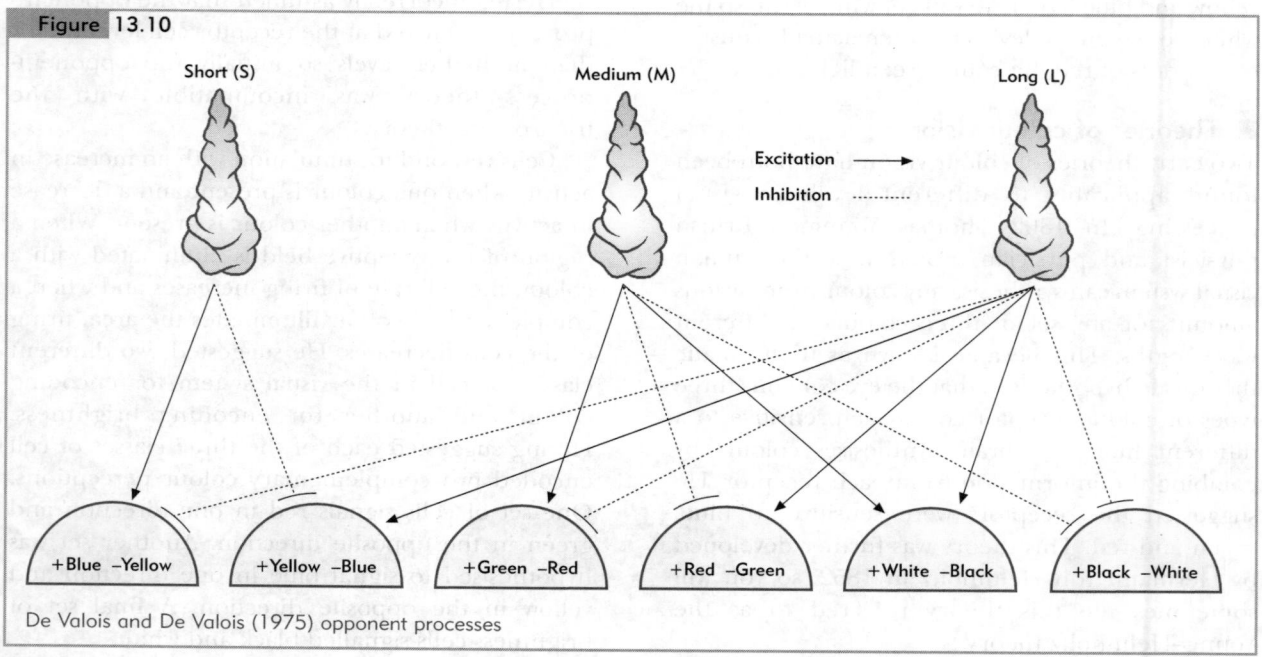

Figure 13.10

Short (S)   Medium (M)   Long (L)

Excitation ———▶
Inhibition ·············

+Blue −Yellow   +Yellow −Blue   +Green −Red   +Red −Green   +White −Black   +Black −White

De Valois and De Valois (1975) opponent processes

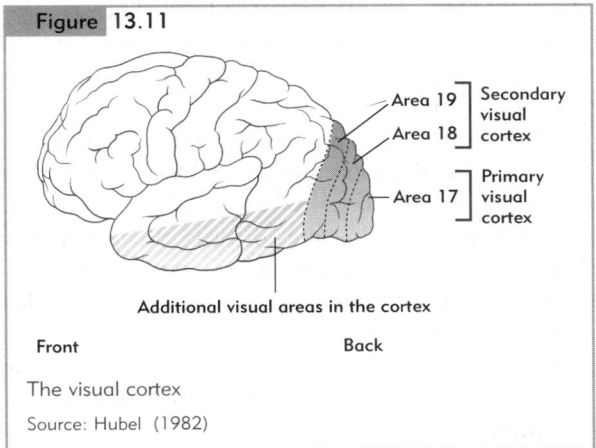

Figure 13.11

The visual cortex

Source: Hubel (1982)

Labels in figure: Area 19, Area 18 — Secondary visual cortex; Area 17 — Primary visual cortex; Additional visual areas in the cortex; Front; Back

fraction of a millimetre (0.05 mm) away, a new column of cells had a preferred orientation that had rotated by about 10° so if the previous column produced the highest response rate at a 45° angle, the cells in the column 0.05 mm away would produce the highest response rate at a line at a 55° angle.

Figure 13.12 illustrates the series of columns noted by Hubel and Wiesel when they moved the electrodes a distance of 1 mm along the cortex. The preferred stimulus changed from a horizontal line to a vertical line and completed the cycle by returning to a horizontal line. A black space is found in layer IVc as these cells have centre-surround preferences, not an orientation preference. Hubel and Wiesel named this sequence of columns a hypercolumn. Figure 13.12 shows a 3D diagram as the cells in the cortex receive information from both eyes, usually with a preference for one eye which has a higher response rate. This is known as ocular dominance. Each patch, no bigger than 1 mm and 2 mm deep, is encoded by the visual system for stimulus-orientation, the two kinds of ocular dominance and a variety of locations. The 2-DG technique noted on page 438 has been used with autoradiography to confirm Hubel and Wiesel's findings with virtually all cells in layer IVc activated by the stimulus, not just at 1 mm intervals.

Later researchers have extended our knowledge of the primary (striate) cortex. DeValois and DeValois and their colleagues suggested that the visual cortex operates on a code of spatial frequency, not a code of straight lines and edges hypothesised by Hubel and Wiesel. Support for spatial frequency theory has been shown by neurons in the visual cortex responding more robustly to sine-wave gratings. These are a set of equally spaced, parallel alternating light and dark stripes created by varying the light across the grating. The variation in brightness is measured in cycles per degree of visual angle.

Most neurons in the primary visual cortex (Area 17) respond best when a sine-wave grating of a particular frequency is presented at a particular angle in a particular location of the visual field. Pinel (1997) suggested that spatial-frequency detection by visual neurons extends and complements previous research rather than refutes it. Many experiments have confirmed that spatial frequency plays a central part in visual perception.

A polka dot pattern of neurons, known as **blobs**, appear at regular intervals in Area 17. Livingstone in 1987 postulated three systems of information in the visual system, the M and P layers noted earlier and the blobs forming the third system thought to be crucial for conveying colour information. Albright *et al.* (1984) suggested that this organisation in columns may not be restricted to the primary visual cortex only; it may well be a feature of most of the visual cortex.

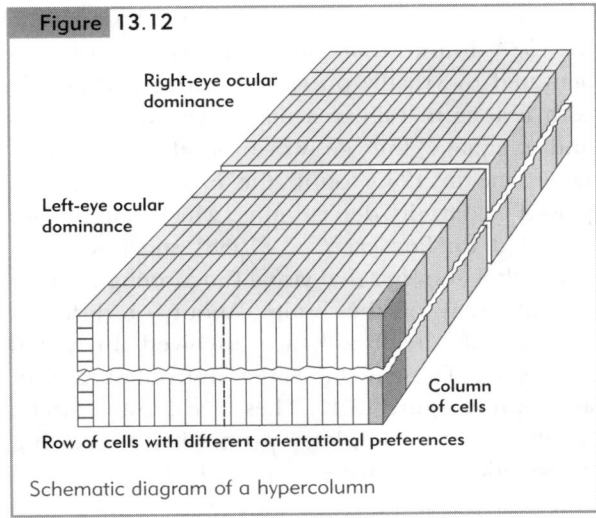

Figure 13.12

Schematic diagram of a hypercolumn

Labels in figure: Right-eye ocular dominance; Left-eye ocular dominance; Column of cells; Row of cells with different orientational preferences

Most investigators believe the brain is organised in modules ranging in size from a hundred thousand to a few million neurons. Each module receives information from other modules, decodes and passes information to other modules. The striate cortex is divided into approximately 2500 modules containing approximately 150 000 neurons. Neurons in each module are devoted to the analysis of various features contained in one very small part of the visual field. The individual modules are likened to tiles in a mosaic with inputs from the P and M layers of the LGN via different sub-layers of the striate cortex.

The modules consist of two colour-sensitive segments, each surrounding a blob. Their structure can be seen in figure 13.13. The neurons outside the blob are sensitive to orientation, movement, spatial frequency and binocular

disparity, but not to colour. Each half of the module receives inputs from only one eye, but the circuitry within the module combines the information from both eyes.

The modules in the striate cortex are organised in a regular manner. Blasdel (1992) found that neurons in a region are in a sequence corresponding to the hues in the visual spectrum. It was found that changes in orientation sensitivity run at right angles to changes in ocular dominance. The blobs, located at regular intervals along these lines, receive information from only one eye and contain cells not sensitive to orientation.

Most of the research on vision has concentrated on the primary visual cortex, but, as can be seen in figure 13.11, there are at least two other areas at the back of the brain involved in processing vision:

- Area 18: the secondary visual cortex
- Area 19: the extrastriate cortex.

These two areas were noted earlier in discussion of the superior colliculus which sends information to the secondary visual cortex rather than the primary visual cortex. The secondary visual cortex also receives information from the primary visual cortex, so much of the information coming into this area has already been processed. Many cells in Areas 18 and 19 respond to input from both eyes, so apparently binocular information may be processed in this area.

The extrastriate cortex has been found to be involved in complex visual processing. Posner *et al.* in 1988 found that the extrastriate cortex is activated by visually presented words, and people with lesions in this area may have normal vision and language but be word blind. Moran and Desimone in 1985 found the extrastriate cortex played a part in determining which stimuli are attended to. Posner *et al.* (1988) suggested that research is showing that visual functioning involves several areas of the brain. About 15 different regions of the brain are involved in visual processing. These include areas in front of Area 19 as shown in figure 13.11. These areas appear to be involved in complex processing receiving information from Areas 18 and 19.

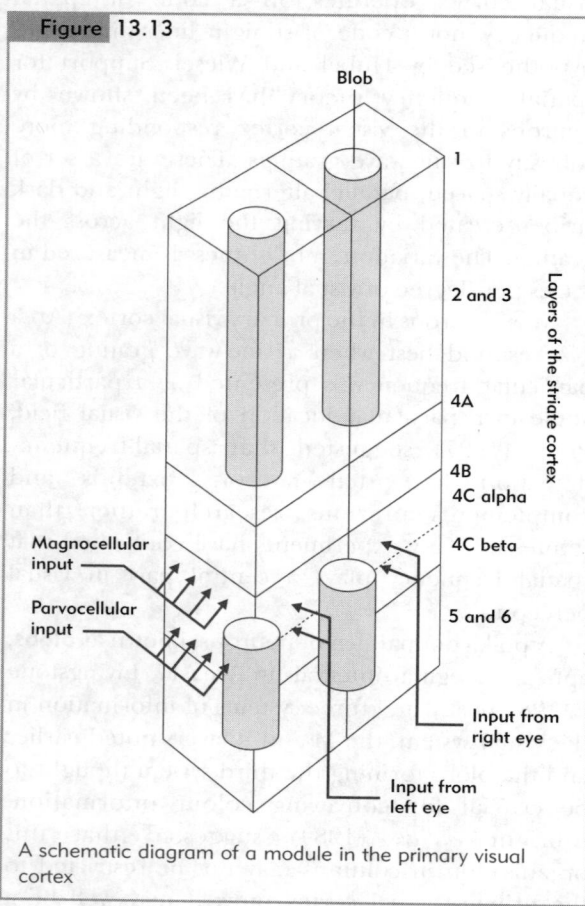

Figure 13.13

A schematic diagram of a module in the primary visual cortex

Activity 10

Are the following sentences true or false?

a The eye contains three types of colour receptor cone each receptive to a different hue: blue, green and red.

b Opponent-process theory is incompatible with trichromatic theory.

c Layers of cells in the striate cortex are arranged in circles, as noted by Hubel and Wiesel.

d DeValois and DeValois suggested that the primary visual cortex operates on a code of spatial frequency.

e Livingstone (1987) noted three systems of information in the visual system: M layers, P layers and blobs.

(Answers on page 470.)

So far we have looked at the bottom-up, data driven, approach to visual processing showing how the visual system passes information through increasingly sophisticated levels of processing. However, Matlin and Foley (1992) noted that top-down processing, showing the influence of prior knowledge and experience, has been demonstrated in several areas of visual perception.

Top-down visual processing

Many tasks depend on the association between visual qualities and experience, and part of the visual cortex is known as the *association cortex.* Matlin and Foley (1992) cited how Gross *et al.* were recording activity of cells in the association cortex of monkeys, presenting the usual stimuli of lines and spots of light. Having studied a cell for a considerable time and finding very little response, they were about to move on to look at another cell. One of the team decided to wave goodbye to the cell by raising his hand in front of the monkey's eye. At this point the cell started to fire rapidly. The team found that hand-shaped stimuli produced the most vigorous responses from this cell, showing that cells in this part of the visual cortex respond to specific complex shapes.

Colour constancy refers to the fact that the perceived colour of an object is not a simple function of the wavelengths reflected by it. A blue jacket hanging on the back of a chair looks the same colour in direct sunlight at midday as it does later in the evening by the light of a desk lamp, although the wavelengths reflected by it have changed. Objects tend to stay the same colour despite major changes in the wavelengths of light they reflect. Colour constancy means we can tell objects apart and respond appropriately to them. Bron *et al.* in 1986 noted how the ability to distinguish between objects would diminish without colour constancy.

Edwin Land, who invented the Polaroid camera, illustrated in 1977 how participants viewing displays of coloured rectangular shapes named Mondrians (after the Dutch painter Mondrian who used them in his work) retained colour constancy even when he manipulated the wavelengths of light to make each appear white. However, when he blocked out the surrounding areas without changing the lighting conditions, the participants saw the Mondrians as white. These demonstrations suggested:

- Colour of objects is not simply related to the wavelengths they reflect.
- Colour of objects depends to some extent on the light reflected by the surrounding areas.

Land's theory of colour constancy became known as *retinex theory* due to the explanation involving the interaction of the retina with the cortex. He pointed out that, although the wavelengths of light reflected by an area change with changes of illumination, the efficiency by which the surface absorbs each wavelength and reflects the unabsorbed light does not change. According to retinex theory, the visual system calculates the reflection of surfaces and perceives their colour by comparing the ability of adjoining surfaces to absorb light in the three wavelengths (short, medium and long) corresponding to the three classes of cone.

Colour constancy depends on contrast between adjacent areas of the visual field so a good strong red will not be seen if the objects around do not reflect the blue and green part of the spectrum. Dual-opponent colour cells, which have been found in the monkey's visual cortex, respond with vigorous 'on' firing when the centre of their circular receptive field is illuminated with one wavelength such as green and the surround is simultaneously illuminated with another wavelength such as red. These same cells display vigorous 'off' firing when this is reversed. These dual-opponent colour cells respond to the contrast between wavelengths reflected by adjacent areas of their receptive field. These dual-opponent colour cells have been found by researchers such as Zeki (1993) in the blobs discussed on pages 451–2.

Sensory system organisation in the cortex

There are three different sensory systems in the cerebral cortex:

- The *primary sensory cortex* receives most of its input from the thalamic relay nuclei, for example the primary visual cortex receives most of its input from the LGN of the thalamus.

- The *secondary sensory cortex* receives information from the primary sensory cortex of that system or from other areas of the secondary sensory cortex.
- The *association cortex* is any area of the cortex receiving information from more than one sensory system, most of the input coming from areas of the secondary sensory cortex.

Pinel (1997) noted that the three major properties which characterise these systems are the following:

- hierarchical organisation
- functional segregation
- parallel processing.

Hierarchical organisation can be seen with the movement in the visual system from receptors to the LGN and from there onto the primary sensory cortex, the secondary sensory cortex and then the association cortex. Each level sees neurons responding to stimuli of greater specificity and complexity. Each level receives inputs from lower levels and decodes and analyses further before passing on up the hierarchy. This hierarchical structure can be seen when damage occurs. The higher the level of damage, the more specific and complex the deficit, so damage of the visual receptors produce an inability to see, whereas damage to the secondary visual cortex or visual association cortex will produce complex sensory deficits which can be quite specific. Such a deficit was recorded by Sacks (1985) for Dr P., part of which can be seen in the case study below.

Case Study from *The Man Who Mistook His Wife For a Hat and Other Clinical Tales*

Dr P. was a musician of distinction, well-known for many years as a singer . . . and as a teacher . . . . It was obvious within a few seconds of meeting him that there was no trace of dementia [intellectual deterioration] . . . . He was a man of great cultivation and charm who talked well and fluently, with imagination and humour. . . .

'What seems to be the matter?' I asked him at length.

'Nothing that I know of,' he replied with a smile, 'but people seem to think that there's something wrong with my eyes.'

'But *you* don't recognise any visual problems?'

Case study cont'd

'No, not directly, but I occasionally make mistakes.'. . .

It was while examining his reflexes . . . that the first bizarre experience occurred. I had taken off his left shoe and scratched the sole of his foot with a key – a frivolous-seeming but essential test of a reflex – and then, excusing myself to screw my ophthalmoscope together, left him to put on the shoe himself. To my surprise, a minute later, he had not done this.

'Can I help?' I asked.

'Help what? Help whom?'. . .

'Your shoe,' I repeated. 'Perhaps you'd put it on.'

He continued to look downwards, though not at the shoe, with an intense but misplaced concentration. Finally his gaze settled on his foot.

'That is my shoe, yes?' Did I mis-hear? Did he mis-see?

'My eyes,' he explained, and put his hand to his foot. 'This is my shoe, no?'

'No, it is not. That is your foot. *There* is your shoe.'

Was he joking? Was he mad? Was he blind? If this was one of his 'strange mistakes,' it was the strangest mistake I had ever come across.

I helped him on with his shoe (his foot), to avoid further complication. . . . I resumed my examination. His visual acuity was good; he had no difficulty seeing a pin on the floor. . . .

He saw all right, but what did he see?. . .

'What is this?' I asked, holding up a glove.

'May I examine it?' he asked, taking it from me.

'A continuous surface,' he announced at last, 'infolded on itself. It appears to have' – he hesitated – 'five out-pouchings, if this is the word.'

'Yes,' I said cautiously. 'You have given me a description. Now tell me what it is.'

'A container of some sort?'

'Yes,' I said, 'and what would it contain?'

'It would contain its contents!' said Dr P., with a laugh. 'There are many possibilities. It could be a change purse, for example, for coins of five sizes. It could . . .'

'Does it not look familiar? Do you think it might contain, might fit, a part of the body?'

No light of recognition dawned on his face . . .

I must have looked aghast, but he seemed to think he had done rather well. There was a hint of a smile on his face. He also appeared to have decided the examination was over and started to look around for his hat. He reached out his hand and took hold of his wife's head, tried to lift it off, to put it on. He had apparently mistaken his wife for a hat! His wife looked as if she was used to such things. (Sacks, 1985, pp 7–13)

It was originally assumed that the primary, secondary and association areas of a sensory system were functionally homogenous in that they acted together to perform the same function. Recent research has shown *functional segregation* occurs whereby each level (primary, secondary and association) have different areas which specialise in different types of analysis.

The early research, such as that by Hubel and Wiesel, suggested the different levels were connected in a serial manner with information flowing along one pathway. More recent evidence suggests sensory systems are parallel systems, with information flowing over multiple pathways. *Parallel processing* shows the simultaneous analysis of a signal in different ways by multiple parallel pathways of a neural network.

Zeki (1993) is one of many recent researchers to establish that sensory systems are hierarchical, functionally segregated and parallel. There appear to be many specialist areas at multiple levels, interconnected by multiple parallel pathways. Complex stimuli are seen as integrated wholes, not combinations of independent aspects. Perceptions appear to be the product of combined activity of many cortical areas. There are not only messages passing up the system but also coming down in descending pathways and moving laterally via a web of connections at each level of the hierarchy. Space does not allow for further discussion of this new and fascinating area of research in sensory perception. The interested reader can follow the references given at the end of the unit.

■ Blindsight

One interesting phenomenon on which highlights how the visual information can control behaviour without conscious awareness is known as **blindsight**. Patients who have lost all of their primary visual cortex are not surprisingly reported as being totally blind. However, it has been demonstrated that these cortically blind people can perform tasks such as grabbing a moving object, while claiming they can see nothing! This ability is known as blindsight.

How can patients note the location of objects, their orientation and movement if they cannot consciously see them? This is seen to occur because not all visual signals are transmitted via the primary visual cortex; some parallel tracts ascend from the subcortical structures into the prestrite area. Zeki (1993) suggested that the integration of primary visual cortex is needed for conscious perception whereas the visual association cortex receives information via the superior colliculus and the dorsal lateral geniculate nucleus. As Carlson (1994) noted, the superior colliculus sends visual information to the areas of the brain that guide hand movements, but they do not seem to send them to the part of the brain responsible for conscious thought.

Self-assessment questions

6 Define the terms *sensation* and *perception*. If you are not sure of your definitions, read page 441 again.

7 Summarise the primary visual pathway from the retina to the visual cortex.

8 How does retinex theory explain colour constancy?

9 Briefly note the major properties characterising sensory system organisation.

10 How can 'blindsight' be explained?

(Suggested answers on page 470.)

Lateralisation (or asymmetry) of function

We have two of almost everything, one on each side of the body. Similarly, in the brain there are two hemispheres which are entirely separate except for the fibres connecting them, known as the *corpus callosum*.

The sensori-motor system

Pinel (1997) noted three principles of the sensori-motor system:

- It is hierarchically organised.
- Motor output is guided by sensory input.
- Learning and experience changes the nature and the locus of sensori-motor control.

Hierarchical organisation

Pinel likens the sensori-motor system to a large efficient company directed by commands 'cascading' down through the hierarchy from the association cortex (the company president) to the muscles (the workers). The president specifies specific goals and leaves the plan of action to the lower levels. Fetz (1993) is one of the recent researchers who emphasised the role of parallel systems in this process. This allows the association cortex to exert control over the lower levels in more than one way, for example when inserting a contact lens, the association cortex can inhibit an eye blink (usually under autonomic control). As with the sensory systems noted above, functional segregation is a characteristic of the different levels, with different units (neural structures) performing different functions. The main difference between the sensori-motor system and the sensory systems presented earlier is the direction of the information flow. In sensory systems the information flows upwards through the hierarchy, whereas in the sensori-motor system the information mainly flows down.

Sensory feedback

The eyes, organs of balance and the receptors of the skin, muscles and joints all monitor responses and feed the information back into the sensori-motor circuits. This sensory feedback plays a part in directing the continuation of the responses. Lacquaniti in 1992 found that many of these adjustments are controlled by the lower levels without involving the higher levels. Pinel (1997) compared this to the efficiency of some large companies where clerks do not have to check with the managing director when they encounter a problem.

Sensori-motor learning and control

Halsband and Freund (1993) noted how initially the responses are made under conscious control. Then with practice these actions become organised and integrated sequences that flow smoothly, adjusted by sensory feedback without conscious regulation. The organisation of individual responses into continuous motor programmes, and the transfer of control to lower levels of the nervous system, can be seen in swimming, dancing and sporting activities.

If we stay with the analogy of a large efficient company, we can see the following:

- The executives (specific areas of the cortex) issue commands based on information given to them by the posterior parietal cortex.
- These commands are forwarded to the managing director (the primary motor cortex) for distribution to the office managers of the sensori-motor hierarchy (the spinal sensori-motor circuits).
- The sensori-motor circuits direct the actions of the workers (the muscles) with sensory feedback playing an important role at each level of the hierarchy.

Georgopoulos (1991) suggests there is a hierarchy of *central sensori-motor programmes* that have certain patterns of activity programmed in at most levels except for the very highest levels. These programmes are triggered by the association cortex initially which activate certain sequences at lower levels. For example, turning the pages of this book could be executed by specific spinal programmes that control the various actions needed. Once activated, each level can operate on the basis of sensory feedback without cortical involvement and you may well not be aware of them. So just as office workers in a company know how to complete many different tasks and execute them in the light of the current conditions when required to do so, the mechanisms in the human brain responsible for this smooth-running are the cerebellum and the basal ganglia.

It has been suggested by Fentress (1973) that some fundamental central motor programmes are not learned. Two influential processes are as follows:

- *Response chunking* is thought to occur whereby chunks can become combined into higher-order chunks.
- *Changing the level of control* and shifting to lower levels can sometimes free up the system at a higher level and allow it to operate on more esoteric aspects of performance. This can be seen in skilled musicians who can concentrate on interpreting a piece of music as they no longer need to focus consciously on striking the correct notes (figure 13.14). It is thought that typing can be performed at speed because different circuits at lower levels can act simultaneously without interfering with one another (parallel processing).

■ The primary motor cortex

The primary motor cortex is located in the precentral gyrus on the frontal lobe. It is the major point at which cortical sensori-motor signals converge and where these sensori-motor signals leave the cerebral cortex. Penfield and Boldrey mapped out the primary motor cortex of conscious human patients in 1937 using electrical stimulation during neurosurgery. The motor cortex in each hemisphere is responsible for movement on the opposite side of the body, so stimulation of the right motor cortex moves parts of the left side of the body and stimulation of the left motor cortex moves the right side.

The primary motor cortex is organised as a motor homunculus (homunculus means 'little man') with most of it devoted to controlling the parts of the body capable of intricate movements, such as the hands and mouth (see figure 13.15). More recent research, including that of Strick and Preston (1983), has revealed that in monkeys, and perhaps humans, there are two different areas in the primary motor cortex of each hemisphere that control the contralateral hand. Single electrode recordings made by Schieber and Hibbard (1993) found that most primary cortex finger neurons are involved in the movement of more than one finger. There is considerable overlap in the locations of neurons so the control of individual finger movement depends

Figure 13.14 Skilled performance

Figure 13.15

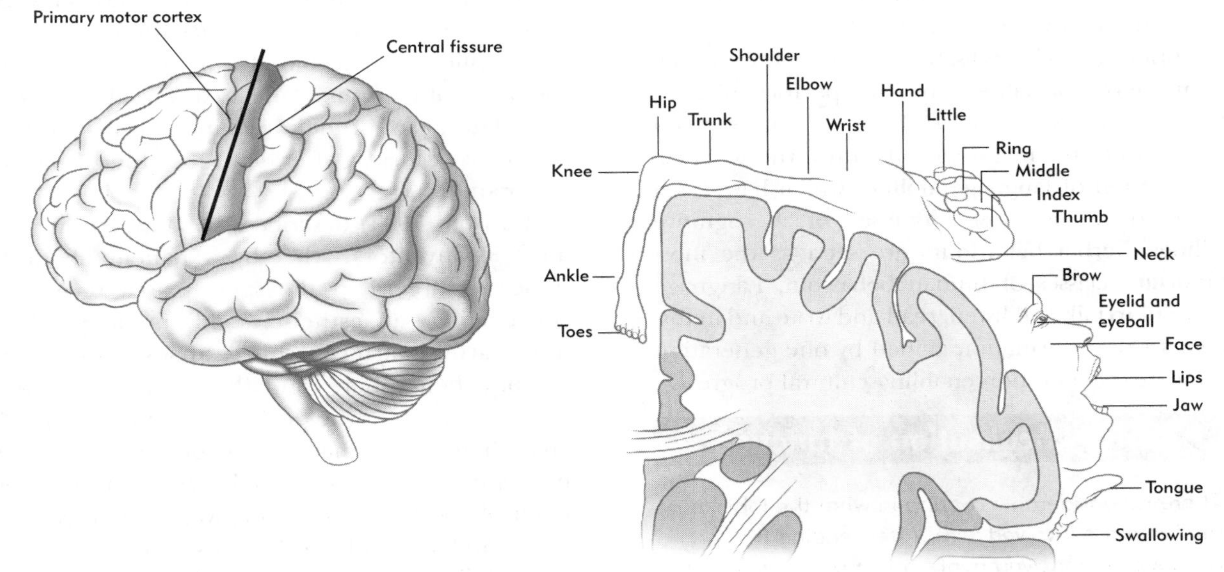

The motor homunculus

Source: Pinel (1997)

on a network of neurons distributed throughout the primary motor cortex.

Each site in the primary motor cortex controls the movement of a particular group of muscles, receiving somatosensory feedback, with one notable exception. One of the hand areas in the primary motor cortex of each hemisphere receives inputs from receptors in the skin rather than from the muscles and joints. This helps to explain the sensitivity of touch reception and sterognosis (the process of identifying objects by touch).

Damage to the human primary motor cortex has less effect than might be expected. It disrupts the ability to move one body part, such as a finger, independently of others, affects sterognosis and reduces speed and accuracy, but does not produce paralysis. Damage to the corpus callosum, frontal or parietal lobes produces deficits known as apraxia (the inability to perform learned, skilled movement). A person with apraxia finds it difficult to make controlled movements of a limb in response to verbal requests. Most apraxias are due to lesions of the left parietal lobe (the majority of the population being right-handed and right-footed). The left parietal lobe sends information

about the requested information to the left frontal association cortex which directly controls the movement of the right limb by activating neurons in the left primary motor cortex. This indirectly controls the movement of the left limb by sending information to the right frontal association cortex. Apraxia is also caused by damage to the left frontal association cortex or its connections with the right hemisphere.

Activity 11

Match each of the descriptions on the left with one of the terms on the right:

a Consists of two hemispheres.
b Site of the primary visual cortex.
c Wrinkled outer covering of the cerebrum.
d Site of the primary motor cortex.

i   frontal lobes
ii   cortex
iii occipital lobes
iv   cerebrum

(Answers on page 470.)

The two halves of the brain look identical but there is a growing body of evidence which suggests that the hemispheres are functionally different. The brain shows lateralisation of function with each hemisphere specialised for the performance of different tasks. Such differences have been highlighted by investigations into the cortical organisation of language abilities which have been found to be the most lateralised of all cognitive abilities. Verbal behaviours are seen as the most important classes of human behaviour. Language allows us to talk and listen, read and write and in this way pass on information gained by one generation to the next generation enabling cultural progress.

13.16 Localisation of function

There is considerable overlap in what the lobes of the brain are involved with. After reading the previous sections you might assume that different parts of the brain do different jobs (*localisation of function*). However, as you will see in the concluding sections of this unit, objective research finds that although certain areas of the cortex appear to be closely involved in specific functions, many perceptual, learning and memory functions are distributed across large areas of the brain.

Karl Lashley was an early researcher who set out to find where memories are stored in the rat's brain. He trained rats to run a complex maze to find food and then he destroyed part of their cortex. Destroying any part of the cortex led to the loss of some functions, but the size of the lesion was found to be more important than the location. Even when 90 per cent of the rat's visual cortex was removed, the rat could still find its way around the maze. He gave up trying to find the site (or *engram*) in 1950 and concluded that all parts of the cortex must be involved in learning.

Language and the cerebral cortex

Our knowledge of the physiology of language has been gained by observing the effects of brain damage on people's verbal behaviour. Most of this knowledge comes from people who have suffered strokes or cerebrovascular accidents whereby interruptions to the blood flow have resulted in the death of neurons in the area. Verbal behaviour is a lateralised function with most language problems occurring after damage to the left side of the brain.

Carlson (1994) described the *Wada test* (named after its inventor), whereby a patient about to undergo surgery in the speech area receives a short-acting anaesthetic (sodium amytal) in one carotid artery which anaesthetises one cerebral hemisphere, and then when the effects have worn off the other carotid artery is anaesthetised so that the involvement of each hemisphere in speech can be assessed. The left hemisphere is dominant in over 95 per cent of right-handed people, so for most people they lose their ability to speak when the left hemisphere is anaesthetised, but when the right hemisphere is anaesthetised, they can still talk and carry on a conversation. About 70 per cent of left-handed people also have left-hemisphere dominance, so for the majority of people most of the brain damage noted in the following studies will be in the left (speech-dominant) hemisphere.

Less invasive techniques are sometimes used to check on language lateralisation on people not awaiting surgery. *Dichotic-listening tests* can be used in which, for example, three pairs of spoken digits are presented through earphones. The participants may hear the sequence 5, 8, 3 in one ear and simultaneously 4, 9, 1 in the other. They are then asked to report all of the digits. Kimura found in 1961 that most people report more of the digits presented to their right ear than the left, thus supporting the left-hemisphere dominance of language. She also found that people identified as right-hemisphere dominant by the Wada test performed better with their left ear than the right in dichotic-listening tasks. She suggested that although sounds from each ear are sent to both hemispheres, the contralateral connections are stronger and take precedence when both are competing for access. Kimura also found in 1973 that the gestures accompanying speech tend to be made with the hands contralateral to the dominant hemisphere. PET and MRI images undertaken by Roland in 1993, when participants are engaged in reading and language tasks, found greater activity in the left hemisphere.

It appears that the left hemisphere is more specialised for the analysis of sequences of stimuli, with the right hemisphere more specialised for the analysis of space and geometric shapes which are presented at the same time. As the left (dominant) hemisphere is involved in the control of sequences of voluntary movements, it seems logical that the left hemisphere should also house the localisation of neural circuits involved in speech perception.

Although the primary circuits involved in speech comprehension and production are located in the left hemisphere, research shows that the right hemisphere plays an important part in organising a narrative by selecting and assembling the things we want to say. The right hemisphere is involved in the expression and recognition of emotion in the tone of voice and in the control of prosody (the rhythm and stress in speech) so both hemispheres make a contribution to our language ability. We discuss this below. First, we provide you with an early model of language and then look at the modifications made to this by recent research.

■ The Wernicke–Geschwind model of language

Paul Broca, in the middle of the nineteenth century, suggested that an area of the left frontal lobe played an important role in the language process. *Broca's area* in the left frontal lobe is involved specifically with speech production (Broca, 1861). *Wernicke's area*, in the left temporal lobe, is concerned with making sense of words (Wernicke, 1874). Since then other speech areas have been identified in the left hemisphere.

The Wernicke–Geschwind model of language (Geschwind, 1975) proposes that auditory codes and word meanings are stored in Wernicke's area. When a phrase is spoken, appropriate auditory

codes are activated, then transmitted via the arcuate fasciculus to Broca's area, where they stimulate activation of corresponding articulatory codes. These codes are transmitted to the motor cortex, which instigates the specific sequence of movements needed for the speech organs to say the phrase.

Within the brain, spoken words are first perceived in Heschle's gyrus and then transmitted to Wernicke's area where they are translated for meaning. Written words are first perceived in the primary visual cortex, transmitted to the visual association area, then to the angular gyrus where visual and auditory information is integrated, and finally to Wernicke's area.

When spelling a word, it must be activated in the auditory area and transmitted to the angular gyrus via Wernicke's area, before the letters can be obtained. If you read the words on this page to someone else, information would be passed from the visual cortex, where the written words are perceived, to the visual association area, through the angular gyrus, to Wernicke's area, across to Broca's area, and finally to the motor cortex before you could speak them (see figure 13.17).

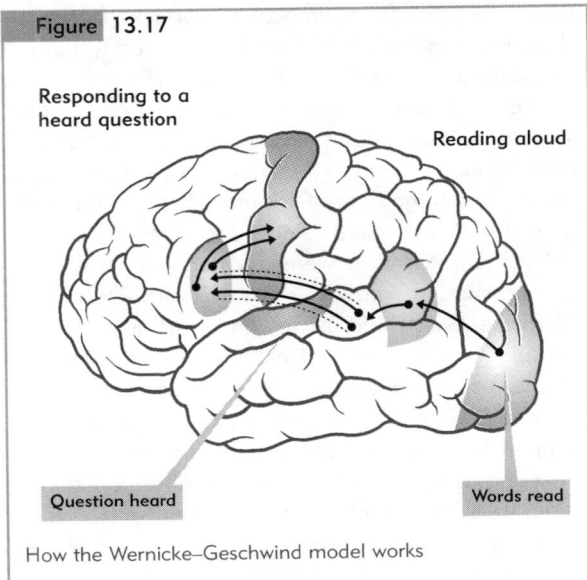

Figure 13.17

Responding to a heard question

Reading aloud

Question heard

Words read

How the Wernicke–Geschwind model works

Activity 12

Fill in the blanks.
The Wernicke–Geschwind model of language proposes that auditory _____ and word _____ are stored in Wernicke's area. When a _____ is spoken appropriate _____ codes are activated then transmitted via the arcuate fasciculus to _____ area where they stimulate activation of corresponding _____ codes. These codes are transmitted to the motor cortex which instigates the specific _____ of movements needed for the _____ organs to say the phrase.

(Answers on page 470.)

Critics of the model noted the following:

■ The model was based on evidence from aphasic patients with brain damage such as strokes and tumours, and such damage often spreads to other areas of the brain.

■ Broca and Wernicke's aphasias do not exist in the pure form described by Wernicke and Geschwind. Benson (1985) notes that aphasia nearly always involves both expression and reception, so they are usually described as *Broca's aphasia* for the former and *Wernicke's aphasia* for the latter.

■ Broca's aphasia and Wernicke's aphasia do not necessarily result from damage of these areas as more recent research shows (see figure 13.18).

13.18 Research that challenges the Wernicke–Geschwind model

Surgical removal of language areas identified in the Wernicke–Geschwind model have not confirmed the predictions of the model. Lesions which destroy all of Broca's area but not the surrounding tissue have been found to have no long-lasting effects on speech by Penfield and Roberts in 1959. Some speech problems exist after the initial lesion but this is thought to be due to post-operative swelling, and as this subsides so do the speech problems. Consequences of the removal of Wernicke's area show that a good portion can be removed without long-lasting effects (see Ojemann, 1979).

Accident or disease-related brain damage studied by Hecaen and Angelergues in 1964 in 215 right-handed patients with small, medium and large areas of damage in the left hemisphere found small lesions in Broca's area seldom produced lasting deficits. Some deficits were reported when the damage was in Wernicke's area. Contrary to the Wernicke–Geschwind model, problems of articulation were just as likely to occur following medium-sized parietal or temporal lesions as they were following lesions in Broca's area. The only support for the model came from large lesions involving three lobes. Large lesions of the anterior brain were more likely to be associated with articulation problems than equivalent lesions of the posterior brain. None of the 215 patients displayed specific syndromes such as Broca's aphasia and Wernicke's aphasia predicted by the Wernicke–Geschwind model.

CT and MRI scans of aphasic patients allow the brain damage of living aphasic patients to be observed. CT studies by Mazzocchi and Vignolo (1979) and Naeser *et al.* (1981) confirmed that large anterior lesions of the left hemisphere were more likely to produce language expression deficits than large posterior lesions. Large posterior lesions were more likely to produce deficits in language comprehension than large anterior lesions. These findings have been supported by MRI studies undertaken by Damasio in 1989. Damasio also found a few aphasic patients with damage restricted to the medial frontal lobes in the supplemental motor area and anterior angulate cortex.

Cortical stimulation using microelectrodes has been found useful in testing predictions of the Wernicke–Geschwind model. Penfield and Roberts in 1959 found sites which blocked or disrupted speech in conscious neurosurgical patients scattered throughout a large cortical area (frontal, temporal and parietal cortex), rather than the areas predicted by Wernicke–Geschwind. Right-hemisphere stimulation almost never disrupted speech. Ojemann in 1983 assessed tasks such as naming, reading simple sentences, short-term verbal memory and ability to recognise phonemes

13.18 Research that challenges the Wernicke–Geschwind model *cont'd*

during stimulation. Contrary to the predictions of the model, he found:

- the areas of the cortex at which the stimulation could disrupt language extend beyond the boundaries of the Wernicke–Geschwind model
- all of the specific language abilities were represented at both anterior and posterior sites
- there were major differences among the patients in the organisation of language abilities. The disruptive effects of stimulation at a particular site were frequently quite specific, which

led Ojemann to suggest that the language cortex is like a mosaic with columns of tissue performing a particular function widely distributed throughout the language area of the cortex. Mateer and Cameron, in another stimulation study undertaken in 1989, found the cortex around the lateral fissure to be specialised for *phonological analysis* (sounds of language) and the other speech areas to deal with *grammatical analysis* (structure of language) and *semantic analysis* (meaning of language).

Parallel-processing of language

The Wernicke–Geschwind model is a *serial model* in that each process mediated involves a chain of responses in a linear sequence. A dual-route parallel model of language has been developed from cognitive neuroscience research. In this model, Coltheart in 1985 suggested that two types of processing of the same input occur simultaneously over two different neural pathways. For example, reading aloud is mediated by two procedures:

- the *lexical procedure* based on specific stored information we have acquired about written words in our vocabulary
- the *non-lexical procedure* based on general rules of pronunciation which allows us to pronounce unfamiliar words.

Evidence supporting this dual-route comes from Hinton *et al.* (1993) in cases of dyslexia (pathological reading difficulty) in which either one or other procedure is impaired but not both. Dyslexics in whom the lexical route appears dysfunctional are said to suffer *surface dyslexia*, whereas dyslexics in which the non-lexical route is dysfunctional while the lexical route remains functional are said to suffer *deep dyslexia*.

In cases of surface dyslexia, patients lose their ability to pronounce words based on their specific memories of the words but can still use rules of pronunciation in their reading. This means they can read words that follow the common rules and the errors made are usually by the misapplication

of common rules. For example, 'lose' is pronounced as if it rhymed with 'hose'.

In deep dyslexia, they lose the ability to apply rules of pronunciation in their reading, but can pronounce familiar concrete words based on memory. Therefore they are incapable of pronouncing new words and have difficulty pronouncing uncommon or abstract words. Someone with deep dyslexia might say 'hen' for 'chicken'. (See Unit 19 page 688).

The mechanisms for mediating deep dyslexia are thought by Coltheart (1980) to be lateralised in the left hemisphere. Patterson *et al.* in 1989 were able to support this hypothesis by a study of a dyslexic who had had the left cerebral hemisphere removed at the age of 14 years. She was capable of processing familiar concrete words but not non-words using her right hemisphere. She appeared to be reading on the basis of meaning and appearance of words rather than translating letters into sounds.

The Wernicke–Geschwind model does not have to be correct to be useful. This model is clear and testable and has produced a great deal of research in the field. From the early work of Broca, Wernicke and Geschwind, potential language sites in the cortex were identified. With improved technology, more recent researchers have extended this knowledge which has not confirmed the strict localisation previously suggested. Pinel (1997) suggested that the mass of research generated 'will stand as the ultimate testimonial to its worth' (p. 436).

Split-brain studies

In a normal brain the two hemispheres communicate with one another by the corpus callosum, the bridge of fibres connecting them (some 200 million axons). Sometimes surgery is needed, often for intractable epilepsy to prevent a seizure spreading from one hemisphere to the other. Many patients seemed to behave no differently after surgery than before. Roger Sperry and his colleagues decided to investigate this paradox.

Split-brain animal studies

Myers and Sperry, in 1953, undertook early studies on cats which had the corpus callosum severed and found:

■ each hemisphere of a **split-brain** cat could function independently
■ one function of the corpus callosum was to transfer learned information from one hemisphere to the other.

The cats were trained to perform a simple visual discrimination task. They were presented with two panels, one with a circle on it and one with a square. The position of these varied randomly from trial to trial (either right or left) and the cat had to learn which symbol to press to gain a food reward. The cats not only had the corpus callosum severed but also the optic chiasma to prevent visual information crossing to the ipsilateral hemisphere.

In figure 13.19 you can see how they isolated the visual discrimination learning in one hemisphere:

■ The corpus callosum was cut.
■ The optic chiasma was cut.
■ One eye was blindfolded.

This restricted all incoming visual information to the hemisphere ipsilateral to the uncovered eye. The cats learned the discrimination task with a patch on one eye in the same length of time as cats whose corpus callosum and optic chiasma had not been cut. This showed that one hemisphere working alone can learn simple tasks as quickly as two hemispheres working together. When the blindfold was transferred to the other eye, the experimental cats (with their corpus callosum and optic chiasma severed) were unable to do the task. Myers and Sperry concluded that cutting the corpus callosum prevented the information going into one hemisphere from reaching the other. This is summarised in figure 13.20a.

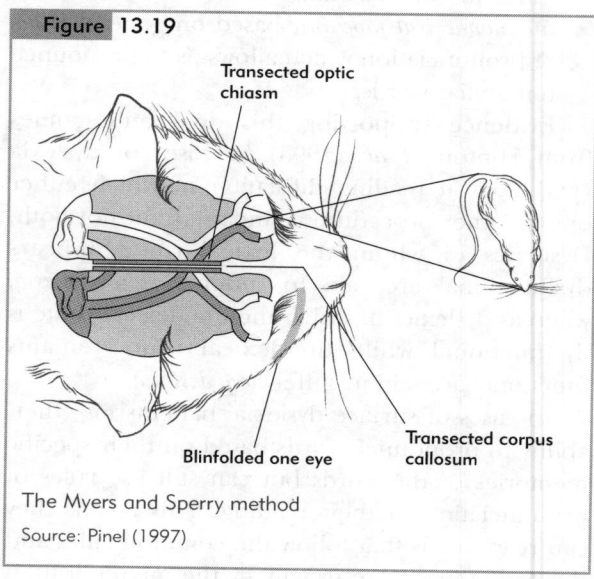

Figure 13.19

Transected optic chiasm

Blinfolded one eye

Transected corpus callosum

The Myers and Sperry method
Source: Pinel (1997)

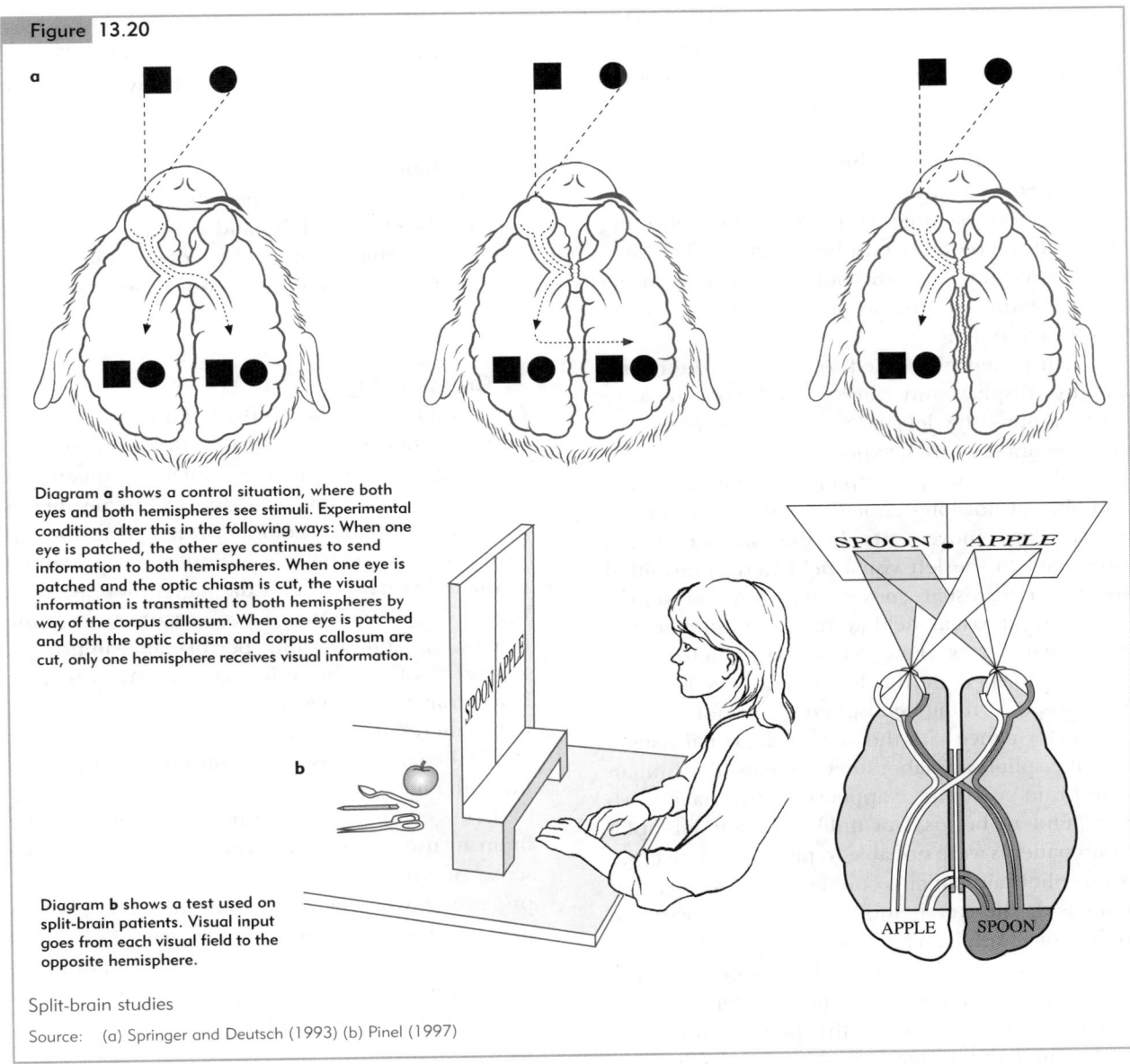

Figure 13.20

a

Diagram **a** shows a control situation, where both eyes and both hemispheres see stimuli. Experimental conditions alter this in the following ways: When one eye is patched, the other eye continues to send information to both hemispheres. When one eye is patched and the optic chiasm is cut, the visual information is transmitted to both hemispheres by way of the corpus callosum. When one eye is patched and both the optic chiasm and corpus callosum are cut, only one hemisphere receives visual information.

b

Diagram **b** shows a test used on split-brain patients. Visual input goes from each visual field to the opposite hemisphere.

Split-brain studies

Source: (a) Springer and Deutsch (1993) (b) Pinel (1997)

Each cat brain had the capacity to act as two separate brains with the corpus callosum acting to transmit information between them. Their findings have been confirmed by many researchers, with a number of species and various tasks. For example, split-brain monkeys cannot perform tasks requiring fine tactual discrimination (such as distinguishing rough and smooth) with one hand if it was learned with the other, provided they are not allowed to watch their hands.

Split-brain human studies

Two neurosurgeons, Vogel and Bogen decided to use the split-brain technique to help patients with intractable epilepsy to reduce the discharges to the hemisphere in which they originate. Therapeutic benefits were found to be better than expected with many patients not suffering another convulsion. The patient was unchanged in personality, intelligence and behaviour generally. Only under experimental conditions could the neuropsychological status be examined.

Sperry and one of his colleagues Gazzaniga developed a battery of tests with the same technique as was used with animals for delivering information to one hemisphere and not the other. They could not sever the optic chiasma, as in the animal studies, so instead they used the technique illustrated in figure 13.20b.

Each patient was asked to fixate on the centre of the display and then visual stimuli were flashed onto the left or right of the screen for 0.1 seconds. This exposure time was long enough for the participants to perceive the stimuli, but not long enough for the confounding effect of eye movements. In this way the stimuli presented to the left visual field were transmitted to the right visual cortex and those presented to the right visual field were transmitted to the left visual cortex. Fine tactual and motor tasks were performed by the hands under a ledge so the non-performing hemisphere could not monitor the performance with the help of the visual system.

Like split-brain laboratory animals, the human split-brain patients appeared to have two independent brains, but unlike the animals split-brain patients were not able to perform some tasks. Most split-brain patients could perform speech not tasks with the left hemisphere but not with the right. For example, if a picture of a spoon is flashed to the right visual field of the patient, the left hemisphere can tell the experimenter that the spoon has been seen, or the patient can reach under the ledge to feel the objects and select the spoon. Similarly, if the spoon is presented to the left hemisphere by being placed in the right hand, the left hemisphere can indicate this in speech or by choosing another spoon with the right hand under the ledge. However, if the non-speaking right hemisphere is asked to indicate the identity of the object presented to the left hemisphere, it cannot do so. The objects can be identified with the right hand but not the left hand.

When test objects are presented to the right hemisphere, either visually (in the left visual field) or tactually (in the left hand), the responses are totally different. Asked to name the object flashed in the left field the patient is likely to say that nothing appeared on the screen. Similarly, although, the patient can report an object is in his or her hand, he or she cannot say what it is. Imagine how confusing it must be for the patient to feel an object in the left hand and choose another like it from objects under the ledge, while the left hemisphere is claiming it does not know its identity!

■ Cross-cueing

Communication between the hemispheres of split-brain patients can occur by cross-cueing. Gazzaniga, in 1967, described such cross-cueing in a series of tasks looking at the left hemisphere's ability to respond to colours presented in the left visual field. A green or red stimulus was presented in the left visual field and the patient was asked to report the colour. At first performance was at the chance level, but over time performance improved, suggesting that the information was somehow being transferred over neural pathways across the hemispheres. However, as can be seen in figure 10.21, the patient was using a variety of strategies to make the judgement.

Cross-cueing is a natural tendency of the brain to use whatever information it has to make sense of what is going on. This shows top-down processing whereby the brain 'fills the gap' to make sense of incoming information. This probably accounts for the normal behaviour of split-brain patients who appear unaffected by surgery in their normal life.

■ Z lens studies and lateralisation of function

Eran Zaidel, who was aware of the restrictions of the brief presentation time needed to ensure stimuli reaches only one hemisphere, developed a new method of restricting visual stimuli to one hemisphere. This became known as the Z lens, a contact lens that permits patients to move their eyes freely, with no time limits, but ensuring the information goes only to one hemisphere. Using this Z lens, Zaidel in 1978 was able to reveal a range

13.21 Cross-cueing in a split-brain patient

'We soon caught on to the strategy the patient used. If a red light was flashed and the patient by chance guessed red, he would stick with that answer. If the flashed light was red, and the patient by chance guessed green, he would frown, shake his head and then say, "Oh no, I meant red." What was happening was that the right hemisphere saw the red light and heard the left hemisphere make the guess "green". Knowing that the answer was wrong, the right hemisphere precipitated a frown and a shake of the head, which in turn cued in the left hemisphere to the fact that the answer was wrong and that it had better correct itself! . . . The realization that the neurological patient has various strategies at his command emphasizes how difficult it is to obtain a clear neurological description of a human being with brain damage.' (Gazzaniga, 1967, p. 27)

of comprehension abilities in the right hemisphere. Vocabulary tests were performed by the right hemisphere, at least as well as by a normal 10 year old. However, following verbal instructions, the 'token test' (a type of discrimination learning task) was undertaken less proficiently and often characteristics of aphasia were displayed.

Zaidel has continued to provide evidence of right hemisphere language although he admits that there is still much to learn about language abilities in the disconnected hemisphere. He noted in 1994 that the two hemispheres of the brain show striking differences. Some of these differences in lateralisation can be seen in table 13.22.

Recent investigations suggest that the cooperation between the two hemispheres may be based on the relative costs and benefits, such as the difficulty of the task. Banich and Belger (1990) noted that cognitively difficult tasks appear to be aided by cooperation between the hemispheres, whereas simple tasks are often undertaken by one hemisphere. It was also found by Boles and Law in 1992 that each side of the brain contains multiple cognitive resources. A decrease in efficiency, shown by increased reaction times, was shown when a task demanded the same cognitive resource. Baron (1996) gave an example of how, when driving, one can listen to the emotional voice of a distraught friend in the passenger seat, because although these are both right-hemisphere tasks, they are using very different resources (spatial position and emotion). He compares this with steering the car and scanning a road map, which can prove dangerous as they are putting demands on the same resource.

In the research with split-brain patients, language has been shown to be the most profound difference between left and right brain. It is worth considering how brains differ in their organisation and bear in mind that different experiences and environments may have a part to play in human

Left-Hemisphere Dominance	GENERAL FUNCTION	Right-Hemisphere Dominance
Words Letters	VISION	Geometric patterns Faces Emotional expression
Language sounds	AUDITION	Non-language sounds. Music
	TOUCH	Tactual patterns Braille
Complex movement	MOVEMENT	Movement in spatial patterns
Verbal memory	MEMORY	Nonverbal memory
Speech Reading Writing Arithmetic	LANGUAGE	Emotional content
	SPATIAL ABILITY	Geometry Direction Distance Mental rotation of shapes

Table 13.22

Cerebral lateralisation of function

Source: Pinel (1993)

development. Biopsychology can be illuminated by integration of cultural explanations. 'Analyzing a human being in terms of physiology alone is like analyzing the Taj Mahal solely in terms of the materials used to build it' (Wade and Tavris, 1993, p. 107).

Self-assessment questions

14 Outline a procedure used to investigate the hemispheric differences of human split-brain patients.

15 If each side of the brain can operate independently of the other, what can be seen to be the benefits of an integrated brain?

(Suggested answers on page 471.)

Unit summary

- *Neuroanatomical techniques* have been developed to study the brain, including staining and microscopy.
- Researchers can now study the living brain with *CT*, *PET scans* and *MRI*.
- Invasive techniques such as *stereotaxic surgery*, *lesions* and *microelectrode stimulation and recordings* have furthered our knowledge on brain function, although they are subject to confounding due to the artificiality and interference of the procedure on the nervous system.
- *Psychopharmacology* has proved useful in mapping out neural networks and looking at specific behavioural changes.
- Visual information proceeds from the retina of the eye to the thalamus, and from there to the primary cortex.
- Single cell recordings have identified the neural system involved in the *receptive fields* of the retina via the ganglion cells.
- The primary visual pathway includes both *magnocellular (M) layers* and the *parvocellular (P) layers* analysing information from different types of retinal ganglion cells.
- Colour vision allows for fine discrimination. Both *trichromatic theory* and *opponent-process theory* help explain our ability to see colour.
- The structure of the visual cortex is seen to have a system for stimulus orientation based on spatial frequency, with neuron *blobs* organised in thousands of modules.

- Areas outside the primary visual cortex, such as the estrastriate cortex, have been found to be involved in complex visual processing.
- The influence of *top-down processing* can be seen in many cortical activities including colour constancy, whereby the interaction of the retina with the cortex is explained by *retinex theory*.
- The sensory system is seen to be hierarchically organised with *functional segregation* and *parallel processing*.
- *Blindsight* shows how the visual information can control behaviour without conscious awareness.
- The sensori-motor system is also *hierarchically organised*, with motor input guided by *sensori-motor control, modified by learning and experience*.
- The organisation of the motor cortex as a *motor homunculus* helps to explain the sensitivity of touch perception.
- *Lateralisation of function* has shown how each hemisphere is specialised for the performance of certain tasks.
- *Language* has been found to be more specialised in the left hemisphere, with the right hemisphere more specialised for *spatial* analysis.
- *Parallel models of language* now suggest that types of processing occur simultaneously over different neural pathways, as shown in *dyslexia* research.
- *Split-brain* studies have highlighted the lateralisation of the two hemispheres and the possible relative costs and benefits of cooperation between the two.

Terms to define

blindsight
blob
cortex
CT (computed tomography)
lateralisation of function
MRI (magnetic resonance imaging)
perception

PET (positron emission tomography)
psychopharmacology
receptive field
retina
sensation
split-brain

Further reading

Green, S (1994) *Principles of Biopsychology*, Laurence Erlbaum, Hove.

A student-friendly British text written with lucidity and more detail than is presented in the current text on cortical functions.

Matlin, M W and Foley H J (1996) *Sensation and Perception*, 4th edn, Allyn & Bacon, Boston.

A must for anyone interested in the psychology of perception. The authors address both the physiological and psychological aspects of perception in an organised, up-to-date framework. Useful also for Unit 26.

Pinel, J P J (1997) *Biopsychology*, 3rd edn, Allyn & Bacon, Boston.

An excellent American text for the potential biopsychologist. Superb colour illustrations which bring the brain to life.

Springer, S P and Deutsch G (1998) *Left Brain, Right Brain*: Perspectives from Cognitive Neuroscience, 5th edn, New York, Freeman.

American text which focuses on the area of hemispheric differences. 'Jargonfree' and written in an inviting style, which explains why the authors received the American Psychological Foundation Distinguished Contribution Award.

Answers

■ Suggested answers to activities

1
    Answer in text.

2
a   somatic
b   lateral geniculate bodies (LGB)
c   somatomotor cortex
d   association areas.

6
    Check your diagram against figure 13.3. Did you have the following functions? The transparent cornea, pupil and lens all allow light to enter the eye. As the light passes through them it is refracted and objects are focused onto the retina. The iris controls the amount of light entering the eye. The ciliary muscles control the shape of the lens to allow accommodation of light. The retina is the layer of the eye which contains the nerve receptors for sight. The fovea is the place on the retina where cones are most numerous. The fovea is the most light sensitive region of the eye. The blind spot is the place where the axons of the retinal nerves leave the eye. There are no receptors here. The optic nerve carries impulses from the retinal receptors to the brain.

7
a   inhibition
b   activation
c   and
d   only spontaneous firing

9

You could have noted some of the following:

- Driving or flying an aircraft would be difficult or impossible as you would not be able to distinguish signals.
- You would not be able to distinguish between ripe and unripe fruit and other foods.
- Some games such as snooker would lose their meaning.
- Searching out objects would be more difficult especially among the flora and fauna of the natural world.
- Some careers would be impossible, for example pharmacist, market gardener, butcher, laboratory technician, pilot.

10

a   True
b   False
c   False
d   True
e   True.

11

a   iv
b   iii
c   ii
d   i

12

If you have difficulty, turn back to page 461, where you will find the paragraph

■ Suggested answers to self-assessment questions

1

Golgi, Nissl or myelin stains could have been described (see page 436 for full details).

2

You could have noted some of Pinel's points:

- No injections are needed into the brain.
- It provides both structured and functional information in the same picture.
- Spatial resolution is better.
- It can monitor changes at the time they occur rather than having to wait for the chemicals to break down.

3

They can provide a detailed record of ongoing activity and this can help diagnose the site and extent of tumours.

4

You could choose from microelectrode recording and stimulation, stereotaxic surgery, lesions (see page 439 for full details).

5

Techniques include 2-deoxyglucose (2-DG) (more detail can be found on page 438).

6

Answer in text.

7

After leaving the eye the optic nerves come together and cross over at the *optic chiasma* (or chiasm). Axons from the ganglion cells of the inner half of each retina cross and ascend to the opposite side of the brain to the lateral geniculate nucleus. The axons from the ganglion cells of the outer part of the retina ascend to the lateral geniculate nucleus on the same side of the brain to the primary visual cortex. After the ganglion cells forming the optic nerve cross over at the optic chiasma, they are regrouped and known as the *optic tract*. The lens inverts the image projected onto the retina and reverses left and right. Due to the crossing over of the axons from the nasal halves of retinas at the optic chiasma, each hemisphere of the brain receives information from the opposite side of the visual picture and because there are no synapses at the optic chiasma, the information from each retina remains intact and unchanged. It is the slight differences in images formed at the two retinas which helps us see the world as three dimensional. The cross over at the optic chiasma brings information from each retina to the same region of the visual cortex.

8

Retinex theory notes the interaction of the retina with the cortex whereby the visual system calculates the reflection of surfaces and compares their colour with the ability of the adjoining surfaces to absorb the three wavelengths of light.

9

The three main properties are:

- hierarchical organisation
- functional segregation
- parallel processing.

10

Not all visual signals are transmitted via the primary visual cortex. Parallel tracts carry information from the subcortical structures, such as the superior colliculus, into the prestriate cortex (see page 456 for further details).

11

The main principles are:
- hierarchical organisation
- motor output is guided by sensory output
- sensori-motor control is modified by learning and experience.

12

These include:
- microelectrode stimulation
- dichotic–listening tasks (see page 460 for further details).

13

Positive evaluation includes the following:
- It is a clear and testable model.
- It has stimulated a great deal of research.
- It has helped identify potential language sites in the brain such as Broca's area and Wernicke's area.

Criticisms include the following:
- Localisation is not as specific as first suggested.
- Much of the evidence comes from brain-damaged patients.
- Aphasias are not as specific as originally described. (See also table 13.18 on pages 462–3.)

14

The patient is asked to fixate on the centre of a display and visual stimuli are flashed on the screen for 0.1 seconds, either on the left or the right, so that the information is transmitted to either the right or the left hemisphere. The participant's hands are hidden by a ledge so that the non-performing hemisphere cannot use the visual system to help.

15

You could have included:
- The brain can work efficiently by using both hemispheres when the task is difficult and only one when the task is simple.
- It allows for the transfer of abilities by rerouting information if an area is damaged.
- It allows for more high-order skills characteristic of human behaviour.

Unit 14

Awareness

Lorna Jones and Irene Taylor

This unit covers:

Awareness

Bodily rhythms

The physiology of awareness

Altered states of awareness including sleep and dreams

Other altered states of awareness including hypnosis

By the end of this unit, you should be able to:

■ demonstrate awareness of the research into the physiological and psychological factors involved with bodily rhythms and states of awareness

■ understand sleep and dream states

■ explain and discuss the nature and function of sleep and dreams

■ show a critical awareness of theories and research on hypnosis.

Unit 14   Contents

Introduction

Much of our behaviour follows regular rhythms:
- We sleep in cycles.
- Our patterns of sleep and waking follow a daily cycle.
- Individual performance on tasks varies over the course of the day with shifts in our alertness or energy.

'To everything there is a season, and a time for every purpose under heaven' (Ecclesiastes, cited in Wade and Tavris, 1993, p. 117). This unit looks at bodily rhythms, especially circadian rhythms.

We spend at least a third of our life in a state during which we have little awareness and few fleeting memories – the dream-like world of sleep. This unit looks at sleep and dream states and the factors affecting the length and quality of sleep. Theories of sleep are also discussed.

Another more controversial state of awareness is that of hypnosis. Does it exist? This unit looks at the dispute concerning the nature of this special state of awareness, and briefly covers meditation and psychoactive drug states of awareness.

Imagine that you are sitting in a classroom. It is 2 o'clock in the afternoon and you are gazing out of the window, watching clouds drift across the sky. One looks like a woolly sheep and you see it gradually change shape into a dolphin. Suddenly you hear your name called rather sharply and you come to with a start, realising that your thoughts had drifted gently away from the lesson. All the time you had been aware of your school friends, the desks and your teacher talking, but you had altered the focus of your attention from the information which you were being given, to the cloud formations which caught your eye and imagination. You were unaware, however, that this had happened until you were recalled to reality by the teacher (who was well aware that it had!).

Activity 1

What do you think awareness is. Jot down on paper a definition and then read on.

Awareness

The word *awareness* has been linked to such a wide range of meanings and implications that psychologists prefer to consider it as a continuum, ranging from a total lack of it to a finely tuned sensitivity to the environment.

Consciousness

Consciousness is a state of awareness towards the sensitive end of this continuum. It is

> 'one of the fundamental defining features of our species . . . to be human is to possess not only self-awareness but also the even more remarkable capacity to scan and review mentally that which we are aware of' (Reber, 1985).

The terms 'consciousness' and 'awareness' are often used interchangeably, although each psychological approach views them slightly differently.

The *behaviourist approach* disregards consciousness completely, viewing it as a side-effect of body functioning or 'epiphenomenal flotsam' (Reber, 1985); whereas *cognitive psychologists* believe that it is important because it influences behaviour. Both these approaches prefer to work with objective measurements such as responses to conditioning and neurochemical activity. *Physiological psychologists* see consciousness in terms of brain activity and arousal, studying both the nervous and chemical activity of the brain. *Freudian psychoanalysts* believe there are different dimensions of consciousness, including the *conscious*, comprising all we are fully aware of at any one time; the *pre-conscious*, which is at the fringe of consciousness – easily attainable when desired; and the *unconscious*, containing repressed memories and desires about which we are unaware. *Humanistic psychologists* think that consciousness is important for the feelings of control it gives us over ourselves and our actions. They assess brain activity through the subjective feelings of awareness described by individuals at any one time.

Activity 2

Can you apply any of these views to the classroom experience described on page 475?

Attention

It is difficult to be fully conscious of something you are not attending to. *Attention* is the experimental psychologist's code name for consciousness (Allport, 1980). *Focal attention* is the centre of our conscious awareness, consisting of everything we deliberately attend to. *Peripheral attention* concerns everything around us that we are vaguely aware of, including our thoughts and feelings. Focal attention can be likened to Freud's 'conscious' and peripheral attention to his 'pre-conscious' (see page 475).

Activity 3

Are both kinds of attention necessary? Try estimating how many noises there are around you. Now sit still for a minute and count the different noises as you become aware of them. Do your guess and your count tally? If not, can you explain why they don't?

If you attended to all stimuli impinging on you at any one time you might be unable to respond adaptively to those most important to you, so it makes sense for the unimportant stimuli to be filtered out of your focal attention.

Activity 4

Try the senses of sight, touch and smell to see if you get similar results.

Dissociation

If you have played games which involve running, you were probably unaware of what your legs and arms were doing at the time, yet running is a very skilled and complex form of behaviour. One way to describe the situation is through the divided consciousness of focal and peripheral attention. When first learning a skill, we need focal attention to ensure everything is done correctly. Once proficient, we can turn our attention to something else while performing the skill automatically (Lloyd *et al.*, 1984). Another way to describe the situation is to say that the control of running is still there but is *dissociated* from consciousness, thus allowing a person to concentrate on the game. Janet (1899) proposed that some thoughts and actions become dissociated from the rest and function without our awareness or control.

Hilgard (1977) identified dissociation during hypnosis. Participants, apparently unaware of what was happening to them, could, under certain conditions, describe their situation very clearly. Hilgard called the part of the mind outside awareness the **hidden observer**, suggesting that it exists to monitor everything that happens (see page 501 for further details).

Extreme cases of dissociated memories or divided consciousness occur in people who have multiple personalities; for example, the case of Jonah, who had four distinct personalities (Ludwig *et al.*, 1972). Frischholtz (1985) suggested that multiple personalities develop between ages four and six in response to dangerous or threatening situations. Patients are usually highly susceptible to hypnosis and some become so used to creating new personalities to 'escape' from difficult situations that they may end up with many more – 16 in the case of Sybil (Schreiber, 1974).

The function of consciousness

Humphrey (1982) thought consciousness gave flexibility to behaviour and this had survival value for our ancestors. Ruch (1984) believed it evolved to guide and integrate non-conscious problem-solving systems. Gross (1987) argued that consciousness is incidental to information processing, since we are unaware of the processes we use for problem solving but very much aware of the solution, within focal attention.

Atkinson *et al.* (1993) described the functions of consciousness as:

- giving awareness of external and internal events
- reflecting on past experience

- engaging in problem-solving
- selectively attending to some stimuli in preference to others and deliberately choosing and executing actions in response to environmental conditions and personal goals.

These functions give consciousness quite a responsibility. They also give it an evolutionary advantage by allowing:

- increased knowledge of events within and around us
- a greater ability to control those events and initiate future ones
- a release from the physiological world to the freedom permitted through thoughts and emotions.

Bodily rhythms

The natural world is full of cycles and rhythms, in which events re-occur in ordered sequences. Some last only fractions of a second, like the release of energy from glucose in our body cells. Others work on longer timescales, like the 200-million-year rotation of the Milky Way. Between these extremes are many others, for example seasonal patterns and the daily sleep-wake cycle.

Have you ever seen advertisements for biorhythm charting? These systems are purported to identify the times of day and times of your life which are positive or negative. They cite 'studies' showing accidents and deaths which often occur on these negative 'critical' days. Research, however, has not supported these claims. Critics point out that studies:

- have not reported the majority of people who were not in a critical period when they had accidents or died
- did not include control groups for comparison
- ignore the other variables such as illness, fatigue, stress, emotion and drugs.

Studies such as that undertaken by Wheeler in 1990 have found little support for biorhythm theory. As noted above, humans are, however, affected by biological rhythms, some of which are triggered by external, or *exogenous* events such as

daylight and some of which are internal, or *endogenous*. Basically, endogenous bodily rhythms fall into three categories:

- **Circadian rhythms** occur approximately every 24 hours. Examples, are the sleep-wake cycle and body temperature, which changes by about 1 degree over 24 hours, peaking usually in the late afternoon and dropping to a low in the early hours of the morning.
- **Infradian rhythms** occur less frequently than once a day. These are seen more in animals and birds with such activity as migration and hibernation. In humans, the female menstrual cycle is an example of an infradian rhythm.
- **Ultradian rhythms** occur more frequently than once a day. Wade and Tavris (1993) noted that many physiological changes often follow a 90-minute schedule when uninterrupted by cultural customs. Such things as hormone levels, food appetite, performance on spatial and verbal tasks display ultradian rhythms. The most studied ultradian rhythm occurs during sleep.

The circadian rhythm

Many people have preferred times to go to bed and get up. When prevented from keeping to these times, they cannot sleep – so get irritable. Others are unable to establish a regular bedtime because of family, social or work expectations.

Activity 5

Where do you fit in? Suppose you have regular sleep times, would you keep to the same hours if you were isolated in a cave for several months without any idea of time? (Now read on.)

Siffre (1972) thought he would – and, on coming out of the cave, he was surprised to learn that he had been there for five months instead of the three months he had calculated. When organisms live in isolation like this, their daily rhythms normally deviate slightly from the 24-hour day-night cycle produced by the Earth's rotation. Electroencephalogram (EEG) patterns provide a particularly good indicator of this regular daily cycle, known as the *circadian rhythm* from the latin circa (about) and dies (day).

Cues from the environment, especially the daily cycle of light and dark, control circadian rhythms. These are called **zeitgebers**, from the German Zeit (time) and Geber (giver). Circadian cycles have been modified in the laboratory by regulating light artificially to ten hours of daylight and ten hours of darkness, resulting in participants operating in a 20-hour day.

Studies have been undertaken in an environment devoid of zeitgebers, and circadian (*free-running*) behaviour has been recorded.

Aschoff and Wever (1979) investigated circadian rhythms in time-free environments by isolating participants in a bunker, screened from outside noise and night, but in contact with the world through a dumb-waiter (pulley hatch). All 200-plus participants had body temperature and motor activity monitored. Volunteers were asked to try to keep to their normal day and night times, but apart from that they could do what they liked. The first three days were spent with time-awareness, the remaining 12 without. The great majority of participants were surprised when told the time was up. They regarded the experience as very positive and were keen to participate in further experiments. Regular hours were kept, with time asleep remaining about one third of each 'day'. In the absence of time-awareness, however, the days 'slipped' an hour.

Aschoff and Wever (1979) found a similar trend for body temperature – and although the rhythms varied slightly between individuals, they all lasted about 25 hours, each maintaining an accurate, regular pattern over time. These rhythm times were different for each participant – and all were different from the 24-hour environmental rhythm.

Researchers originally suggested *one* biological 'clock' or pacemaker in the brain might control these various rhythms but now it is thought there are several, interrelated clocks. Folkard, at the Association for the Teaching of Psychology Annual Conference in 1995, noted several of these:

- A strong, endogenous body clock controlling body temperature and other physiological measures which is relatively unaffected by external factors.
- A somewhat weaker process, more exogenous in nature (more affected by external factors), controlling among other things the sleep-wake cycle.

These processes can run at different periods in some individuals, who are known as 'internally synchronised', and it is possible to make separate estimates of them.

These cyclic fluctuations in body temperature are reflected in performance on simple tasks usually at their best when body temperature and other processes are at their peak. Daniel and Potasova in 1989 asked chemical workers to perform several different tasks:

- A tapping task requiring rapid hand movements.
- A simple, visual search task where participants searched for a target letter and pushed a button when it had been found.
- A more complex task, involving grammatical transformations in a series of sentences.

Their body temperature was recorded at various times of the day. As can be seen in figure 14.1, there was a clear relationship between tapping and body temperature. This relationship was also found for the visual search task. This relationship was not found for the more complex task, suggesting fluctuations in body temperature may have greater impact on simple tasks than on more complex ones.

Folkard and his colleagues in 1992 and 1993 discovered that some rhythms such as pulse rate are entirely due to variations in activity level and are exogenous in origin, whereas others such as body temperature and subjectively-rated alertness are partly controlled by the endogenous body clock. Folkard and Akerstedt (1992) developed a mathematical model capable of predicting, with some accuracy, an individual's alertness level. They

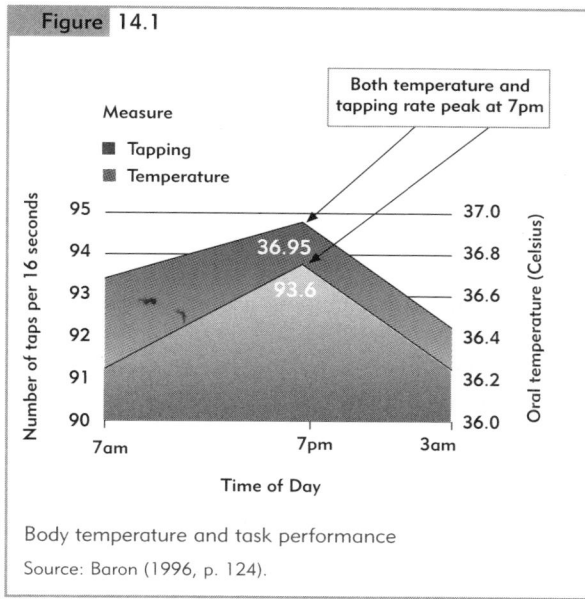

Figure 14.1

Measure
■ Tapping
■ Temperature

Both temperature and tapping rate peak at 7pm

36.95
93.6

Number of taps per 16 seconds
Oral temperature (Celsius)

Time of Day
7am 7pm 3am

Body temperature and task performance
Source: Baron (1996, p. 124).

extended the model (Akerstedt and Folkard, 1995) to include the prediction of sleepiness. Some behaviours are outside the range of the model, for example cheerfulness and performance on tasks entailing choice reaction time. Folkard suggested that in these cases the critical factor is not the phase of the endogenous body clock or how long an individual has been awake, but rather the phase of the body clock when his or her last sleep occurred. Sleeping in the 'wrong' phase decreased cheerfulness and produced 'lapses' of attention during the following wakeful period. This research may have implications for shift work which forces an individual to sleep at the wrong phase of his or her endogenous body clock.

Activity 6

Are you an owl or a lark? In the following list complete each sentence with either 'Day' or 'Evening/Night'.
a I feel most alert during the
b I have most energy during the
c I prefer to have classes during the
d I prefer to study during the
e I get my best ideas during the

Activity 6 cont'd

f When I finish my education, I would prefer to find a job during the
g I am most productive during the
h I feel most intelligent during the
i I enjoy leisure activities most during the
j I prefer to work during the

Source: Baron (1996) adapted from Wallace, 1993
(Read on to find out what this means.)

If you answered 'Day' to eight or more of the questions in Activity 6 you are probably a morning person, a 'lark', whereas if you answered 'Evening/Night' to eight or more you are probably a night person, an 'owl'. Larks are usually most alert and active early in the day whereas owls are normally at their best in the afternoon or evening. Studies such as those undertaken by Akerstedt and Froberg (1976) and Wallace (1993) found higher levels of adrenaline in larks and body temperature peaking earlier in the day (usually before noon) whereas owls often peak much later in the day, often after 6 pm. Wallace also found that susceptibility to hypnosis correlated with these peak times for owls and larks.

Under normal cues, we are not aware of these circadian rhythms, but when our normal routine changes such as in shift work these rhythms are disrupted. This also happens with 'jet lag' when we fly across several time zones. Zeitgebers controlling circadian rhythms are accelerated on eastern flights (*phase advances*) and decelerated on western flights (*phase delays*). Hobson (1989) suggested that in the days prior to flying people should gradually adjust their sleep cycle. Exposure to intense light early in the morning has been found, by Czeisler *et al.* (1989), to promote phase advances after eastern flights where adjustments are more difficult. Sleep patterns often adjust reasonably quickly over a number of days but temperature and hormone cycles can take longer. Physical and mental performance is affected. A similar but less dramatic effect can be found when the clocks are adjusted forward for one hour in the spring. Monk and Aplin (1980) found that people slept less well in the week following the spring clock adjustment and suffered a general malaise and tiredness. Such effects are not as strong in the autumn when the clock 'falls back' one hour and people gain an extra hour in sleep.

This internal desynchronisation occurs for shift workers whose zeitgebers remain the same but who have to adjust their natural sleep-wake cycles to meet the demands of changing work schedules. This can result in a drop in efficiency, tiredness, and the likelihood of more accidents. Digestive upsets often accompany sleep disturbances.

The consequences of shift work for people in many occupations, including air personnel, health professionals, police officers and long-distance drivers, are critical. Many major disasters have been attributed to human error, often lack of alertness. Working at night is not a problem. Many workers with a regular schedule find they can adapt. The problems tend to affect those people who have to switch shifts, sometimes on a rotating basis, so circadian rhythms never have chance to re-synchronise. These people frequently work a shift for a few days and then, after a two-day break, change to a different shift. Shift workers constantly re-setting their biological clocks suffer the worst effects, with fatigue and serious sleep disorders. Other adverse affects include increased risk of heart attacks and ulcers and a higher rate of accidents. Research has shown that employers scheduling phase delays rather than phase advances for their shift workers can improve efficiency and job satisfaction. Coleman (1986) found that shift workers who transfer onto a shift beginning later are much happier and efficient. It is easier to go to sleep four hours later and get up four hours later (a phase delay) than go to sleep four hours earlier and get up four hours earlier (a phase advance). Czeisler et al. (1990) found that night workers are much more alert if they work under bright lights and sleep in a completely dark room.

The circadian clocks

The consistency of circadian rhythms within individuals suggests that the internal mechanism controlling them is in the form of a biological clock. Circadian cycles occurring in the absence of environmental influences were first described in plants. De Mairan (1729) reported how sunflower leaves and stems contract and close towards sunset, whether the plant is exposed to light or kept in complete darkness. Other descriptions were not forthcoming until the 20th century, when much research was directed not only to identifying rhythms in all forms of life but also to the physiological structures and biological processes responsible.

Fulton and Bailey (1929) reported sleep-wake disorders in humans with brain tumours in the *suprachiasmatic nuclei (SCN)*, a region of the hypothalamus. Moore and Eichler (1972) and Stephan and Zucker (1972) destroyed the SCN in rats, causing motor activity and drinking behaviour to become randomly distributed throughout the day – although the amount of each was unaffected. This could mean that the biological clock itself is located in the SCN, or the SCN coordinates centres in a larger system. To investigate this, Inouye and Kawamura (1979) disrupted the circadian rhythms of a rat by severing all nerve fibre connections to the SCN. They reported a discharge pattern from implanted electrodes inside the SCN which exhibited a circadian rhythm. It appeared the SCN was indeed the source of the clock.

Carlson (1994) noted how the SCN of a rat consists of about ten thousand small neurons, the dendrites form synapses with one another, a characteristic of this part of the hypothalamus considered to be related to the specialised function of these nuclei. It is considered that the control the SCN has over the other parts of the brain may be due to the secretion of neuromodulators (see Unit 12 page 399 for more information on synaptic transmission).

By the late 1970s the SCN had been shown to control all kinds of circadian rhythms, including the sleep-wake cycle. In 1990, Ralph et al. removed the SCN from the foetuses of a strain of mutant hamsters that had an abnormally short (20-hour) free-running sleep-wake cycle and transplanted them into normal adult hamsters whose free-running sleep-wake cycle of 25 hours had been destroyed by SCN lesions. The transplants restored sleep-wake cycles in the normal adults, but these were now 20 hours in length rather than the original 25 hours. Transplants from normal rats into SCN-mutant adult male rats had the complementary effect of restoring sleep-wake cycles that were 25 hours in length rather than the original 20 hours.

Because light is the primary zeitgeber for the activity cycles of most mammals it is no surprise to find that the SCN receives fibres from the visual system. From the retina, visual axons branch off from the optic nerve in the area of the optic chiasma and form the *retinohypothalamic tracts* which leave the optic chiasma and project into the SCN. As well as this direct pathway from the retina to the SCN, there is also an indirect pathway from the retina through the thalamus. Both pathways mediate the effects of light as a zeitgeber. The differences in their function have not yet been discovered.

Rusak *et al.* (1990) found that 30 minutes of intense artificial light during the night initiated a phase advance in the circadian sleep-wake cycle of rats and hamsters. Ginty *et al.* (1993) suggested that activation of the retinohypothalamic tract influences circadian rhythms by controlling gene expression in the SCN.

Several studies in the 1990s have indicated that the SCN contains all that is necessary for generating the mechanisms of entrainment of the daily clock. The 'ticking' of the clock in the SCN is thought to be at individual neuron level rather than through interactions. Michel *et al.* (1993) found individual neurons separated from the eye of a mollusc and kept alive in tissue culture maintained their own circadian rhythm of neural activity, suggesting that circadian time may be mediated by molecular mechanisms within individual neurons.

Circadian rhythms are thought to be at the basis of several affective disorders. *Seasonal Affective Disorder (SAD)* is a type of depression which affects some people during the winter months. This is far more serious than the general dissatisfaction many feel with the cold and dark winter months. Wehr *et al.* (1991) found SAD sufferers were fundamentally different from other depressed clients. The winter depressives slept more and showed an increase in appetite whereas the reverse is usually shown in unipolar depression. *Phototherapy* has been found to be helpful for SAD sufferers. Stinson and Thompson (1990) are some of many researchers who have found that clients have improved when exposed to extremely bright lights for a certain period of the day. Perhaps this acts as a zeitgeber and helps re-set the biological clock to the day-night cycle.

Pinel (1997) pointed out that although the SCN appears to be the site of the major circadian clocks, it is not the only one. He noted the following evidence:

- Under certain conditions, bilateral SCN lesions have been shown to leave some circadian rhythms unaffected while abolishing others.
- Bilateral SCN lesions do not eliminate the ability of all environmental stimuli to entrain circadian rhythms.

Animals fed on a daily schedule, whose SCN had been destroyed, still show conditioned anticipation of food at the appropriate time, thus demonstrating the existence of another clock.

SCN is also involved in rhythms longer than 24 hours as shown in male hamsters who show annual rhythms of testosterone secretion, which seem to be affected by the length of the day: if the day is less than 12 hours they operate as if it is winter and if the day is longer than 12 hours they operate as if it is summer.

The control of seasonal rhythms involves another part of the brain: the pineal gland situated on top of the mid brain in front of the cerebellum. This gland secretes *melatonin*, which controls seasonal rhythms in mammals. In response to input from the SCN, the pineal gland secretes melatonin during the night. This acts on several brain structures, including the SCN, and controls hormones and physiological processes controlling seasonal variations. Ralph and Lehman (1991) found that transplants of SCN do not restore seasonal rhythms.

Although great progress has been made into the neural mechanisms of biological clocks, there are still questions unanswered:

- What is the nature of the physiological processes providing the underlying rhythms?

■ Where are the circadian clocks other than in the SCN?

■ By what means do such clocks influence cyclic behaviours, such as sleep and waking?

Self-assessment questions

1 Note two definitions of consciousness.

2 What are the three main categories of bodily rhythms?

3 What is the relationship between cyclic fluctuations, body temperature and task performance?

4 Note some of the problems experienced by individuals who work rotating shifts.

5 Summarise some of the research which suggests that the SCN controls different circadian rhythms.

(Suggested answers on pages 508–9.)

The physiology of awareness

The degree to which we are consciously aware of the environment should correspond to the degree of physiological *arousal* experienced. This arousal can be measured by monitoring both brain activity and the changes in other bodily systems.

The measurement of brain activity

An electroencephalogram (EEG) is a measure of electrical brain activity, recorded by an oscilloscope through electrodes placed on the scalp. It gives a visual presentation of the amplitude and frequency of brain waves (sometimes called spikes or spindles). Brain waves are the spontaneous electrical discharges of the brain, the summed post-synaptic activity of cerebral neurons, especially in the cortex. They are measured in Hertz (Hz), units representing the number of cycles per second.

When fully alert and active, the EEG shows an irregular pattern of *beta waves* (13–30 Hz). This is the frequency of our everyday mind, associated with thinking, doing, focal attention and problem-solving. Insomniacs show this EEG pattern, as do people under stress. The greater the stress, the higher the beta frequency become (Proto, 1989).

The *alpha* pattern is composed mainly of waves between 8 and 12 Hz, obtained when awake and relaxed. If you are normally calm and unflappable you will probably exhibit much alpha activity. Alpha waves also appear during *rapid eye movement (REM) sleep*, so called because of continual muscle movements around the eyes.

A low-frequency, high-voltage alpha rhythm can be seen as reflecting neural *synchrony*. This is the regular, synchronised pattern of activity of a number of neurons. Conversely, beta activity is referred to as *desynchrony*, as individual neurons are transmitting different messages, with much information-processing going on. Carlson (1994) used the analogy of a large group of people singing the same words (representing alpha and beta) corresponding to a number of groups, each carrying on separate conversations.

In a state of deep sleep, the EEG contains slow *delta waves* (1–3.5 Hz). EEGs of young babies show predominantly delta wave activity.

Figure 14.2 shows examples of these brain waves.

Brain activity is also measured using computers, in conjunction with radioactive tracers (normal body chemicals which have been made

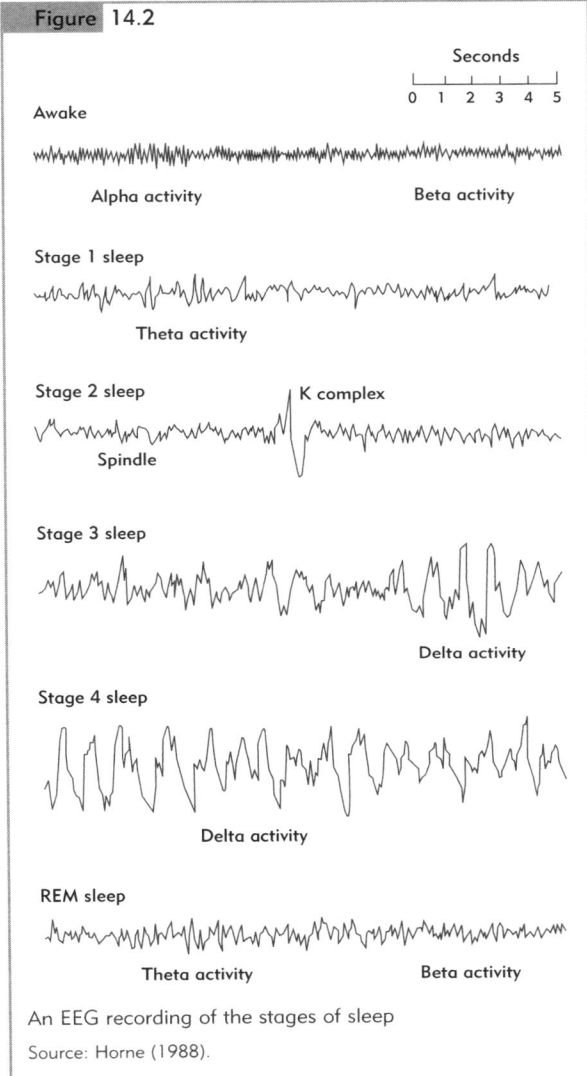

Figure 14.2

Awake

Alpha activity · Beta activity

Stage 1 sleep

Theta activity

Stage 2 sleep · K complex

Spindle

Stage 3 sleep

Delta activity

Stage 4 sleep

Delta activity

REM sleep

Theta activity · Beta activity

An EEG recording of the stages of sleep

Source: Horne (1988).

room where the experimenter spends the night awake. The participant is prepared for electrophysiological measurements before sleep. Electrodes are attached to the scalp and connected to the EEG to monitor brain activities, and to the chin to monitor muscle activity on the *electro-myogram (EMG)*. Electrodes attached around the eyes monitor the eye movements on the *electro-oculogram (EOG)*. Other measuring devices are sometimes used to monitor heart rate, respiration and skin conductance, some of which are described in figure 14.3.

All these wires are bundled together and plugged into a junction box at the head of the bed. The changes that occur as the participant falls asleep are then recorded, as are the responses during sleep. In this way, the changes occurring during normal sleep are recorded and the factors affecting these can be investigated. The participant usually spends several nights in the sleep laboratory before commencing the study so that he or she can adjust to the new conditions.

One of the best ways to explain what sleep research has revealed is to describe the changes in brain activity and other processes that occur during a single night of sleep.

14.3 Physiological measurements which increase with arousal

Measurements of the circulatory system
   Heart rate can be measured either directly through a stethoscope or indirectly by counting pulse rates.
   Blood pressure is measured at the brachial artery in the upper arm using an instrument called a sphygmomanometer.
   Galvanic skin response (GSR), a measure of the skin's electrical resistance (related to the circulatory system through sweating), can be monitored using a galvanometer.

Measurements of the respiratory system
Respiratory volume can be measured by using a spirometer.
   Respiratory rate is measured by counting the number of breaths per minute.

radioactive). These react in a similar way to their non-radioactive counterparts and can be traced by means of X-rays. These techniques are discussed in Unit 13 page 438–40.

■ Monitoring physiological responses in sleep research

Most of our knowledge on human sleep has come from research conducted in sleep laboratories. A sleep laboratory is normally located at a university or hospital and includes one or several small bedrooms adjacent to an observation

Stages of sleep

From EEG recordings, the time we are asleep can be shown to contain different stages which recur regularly as *ultradian cycles* – each showing a characteristic pattern of brain activity. During the prodromal period we are quite easily woken, but as we sink into sleep proper, our brain waves become slower and it becomes increasingly difficult for someone to wake us. Aserinsky and Kleitman (1953) revealed a pattern of sleep stages, related to the difficulty of waking. Spectral analyses of EEGs provide information about the predominant waves at any one moment and confirm these stages. Sleepers experience these approximately every 90 minutes throughout the course of the night, although this differs with age. These stages are summarised in figure 14.4.

During **REM sleep**, eye movements appear in rapid bursts lasting between 100 and 200 microseconds. There are also jerks and twitches of muscles in the face, larynx, hands and feet, and sometimes penile erection in males. In spite of these activities, however, muscle tone is reduced and the body deeply relaxed.

If you have observed REM sleep in a dog you may have thought it was dreaming about 'chasing rabbits'. This may be a valid suggestion. About 80 per cent of people report dreaming when woken during REM sleep as opposed to 7 per cent woken during non-REM sleep. Later studies suggest, however, that this figure could be as high as 74 per cent (e.g. Borbély, 1986).

Madsen *et al.* (1991) found that during REM the blood flow in the human brain was high in the visual association cortex. This is consistent with reported dreams often being characterised by good visual images. Figure 14.5 summarises some of the terminology associated with sleep.

14.4 Stages of sleep

When awake, the EEG of a normal person shows two basic patterns of activity: alpha and beta activity. The typical sleep pattern of a participant follows the same pattern:

- *Stage 1 sleep* is marked by *theta* activity which is between 3.5 and 7.5 Hz, a transition stage between sleep and wakefulness. It has a low-voltage, high-frequency signal similar to, but slower than, active wakefulness.
- *Stage 2 sleep* occurs about ten minutes later. This stage is generally irregular but contains some theta activity and also *sleep spindles* and *K complexes*. Sleep spindles are short bursts of 12–14 Hz waves that occur between two and five times per minute during stages 1–4 of sleep. Bower et al. (1985) suggested that these spindles represent the mechanism that decreases the brain's sensitivity to sensory input, thus keeping the person asleep. Older people have fewer sleep spindles and wake up more often during the night. K complexes are sudden, sharp wave-forms which, unlike spindles, occur only during stage 2 sleep. They occur about one per minute but can be triggered by noises. The participant is now sleeping soundly, but if woken might report that he or she had not been asleep.
- *Stage 3 sleep* appears about 15 minutes later, signalled by the occurrence of high-amplitude *delta* activity which is less than 3.5 Hz.
- *Stage 4 sleep* is not easily distinguished from stage 3. Delta activity increases from 20 to 50 per cent in stage 3 to over 50 per cent in stage 4.
- The participant stays in stage 4 for a time and then retreats back through the cycle to stage 1, where activity is now different and characterised by rapid eye movements (REM sleep).
- *REM sleep* is recorded by the EOG from the muscles near the eyes. The EMG becomes silent, with less muscle tone, almost like paralysis although males may experience erections and females may have vaginal secretions. This stage is also known as *paradoxical sleep* because of the presence of beta activity (which is usually present when the participant is alert and attentive). The brain is also shown to be active by increased blood flow and accelerated oxygen consumption.

14.5 Sleep terminology

Alpha activity	Regular, medium-frequency waves of 8–12 Hz occurring when resting quietly, often just before sleep.		Characterised by rapid eye movements, loss of muscle tone, and low-amplitude, high-frequency waves.
Beta activity	Irregular, mostly low-amplitude waves of 13–30 Hz occurring when alert and attentive to environmental events.	*Non-REM*	Sleep stages 1–4 are usually called non-REM sleep, although some dreams have been reported outside emergent sleep stage 1.
Theta activity	The transition stage between sleep and wakefulness, characterised by waves of 3.5–7.5 Hz in sleep stage 1.	*Slow-wave sleep*	This refers to sleep stages 3 and 4 because of presence of delta activity.
Delta activity	High-amplitude (less than 3.5 Hz) waves characteristic of sleep stages 3 and 4, the largest and slowest waves.	*Sleep spindles*	Short bursts of waves of 10–14 Hz which occur between two and five times per minute during sleep stages 1–4, especially stage 2.
Initial stage 1	The period of stage 1 occurring at the onset of sleep, not associated with dreaming.	*K complexes*	Sudden, sharp waves, which, unlike sleep spindles, are usually found only in sleep stage 2.
REM sleep	Also known as *emergent stage 1* or *paradoxical sleep* because the EEG and autonomic changes are similar to wakefulness.		They occur spontaneously at the rate of approximately one per minute but can be triggered by noises.

After the first cycle of sleep, from stage 1 to stage 4 and back to emergent stage 1/REM sleep, the rest of the night is spent going back and forwards through these stages, as displayed in figure 14.6.

Each cycle is about 90 minutes long and as the night progresses more time is spent in emergent stage 1 and less time in the other stages, especially stage 4. There are often brief periods when the participant is awake, although these are not usually remembered next morning. Most research has focused on the role of REM sleep and **slow-wave sleep**, with most researchers suggesting that the non-REM stages 1 and 2 are less important than the others. Stage 4 sleep seems to be the deepest sleep, in that only loud noise will wake up the participant, who will be groggy and confused on waking. If, in REM sleep, the participant is woken by something meaningful, such as his or her name, he or she will be alert and attentive. When woken during REM sleep the participant will almost certainly report

dreams, which are narrative, story-type, whereas if woken during slow-wave sleep he or she is unlikely to report dreams. If pushed, he or she might report

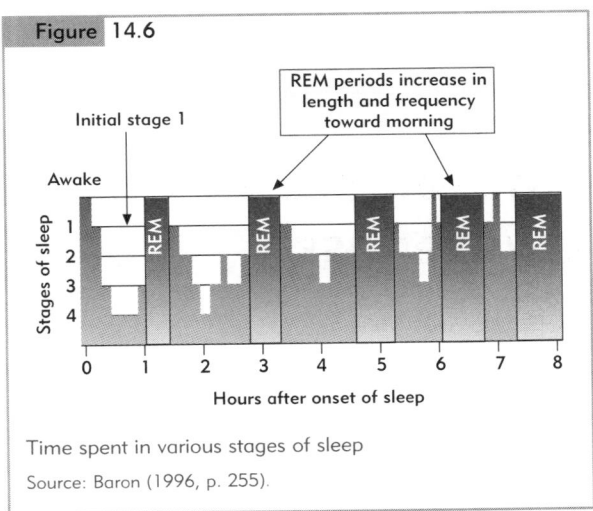

Figure 14.6

Time spent in various stages of sleep

Source: Baron (1996, p. 255).

a situation in which he or she is suffocating, or being crushed, or just simply a feeling of dread.

By the time you are 72, you will probably have spent five years dreaming. **Dreams** provide a succession of images, primarily visual and often in colour, with some auditory and tactile sensations. They resemble a motion picture in which the dreamer is both actor and viewer at the same time.

Activity 7

Match the following statements with the appropriate sleep stage. Choose from: stage 1; stage 2; stage 3; stage 4; REM/paradoxical sleep.

a Blood flow in the visual association cortex is high.

b Characterised by a low-voltage, high-frequency signal, slower than active wakefulness.

c Delta activity increases to more than 50 per cent.

d The participant is now sleeping soundly with recorded sleep spindles and K complexes.

(Suggested answers on page 507.)

Although sleep is often reported as a 'state of unconsciousness', Carlson (1994) suggested this is incorrect. Although sleep is different from consciousness whilst awake, participants woken from REM sleep have shown that they are conscious, so sleep is perhaps better described as an *altered state of awareness*.

Altered states of awareness

James (1902) wrote:

'Our normal waking consciousness, rational consciousness as we call it, is but one especial type of consciousness . . . parted from it by the filmiest of screens, there are potential forms of consciousness entirely different. We may go through life without suspecting their existence; but . . . at a touch they are there in all their completeness . . . they may determine attitudes though they cannot fashion formulas, and open a region, though they fail to give a map . . . they forbid a premature closing of our accounts with reality!'

Here James is referring to what psychologists refer to as 'altered states of awareness'. These occur during sleep, dreaming, hypnosis, meditation and as a result of the effects of psychoactive drugs.

Sleep

When we go to bed each night, we expect to experience an altered state of awareness which lasts for a number of hours and in which we cease to see, hear and feel what is going on around us.

If animals, including humans, are left alone in a non-stimulating environment, they usually fall asleep – so it would seem that sleep is the natural state, interrupted by active, waking periods. Sometimes we feel it necessary to prolong these periods voluntarily, for example students during a boring lecture may try to remain awake by doodling, chewing pens and so on. If waking periods are prolonged involuntarily, we may be able to catch up with brief 'cat-naps' (so-called microsleeps) (Roediger *et al.*, 1984). These usually go undetected because the eyes remain open. You may have experienced them yourself after all-night parties or long journeys.

Have you ever been quietly drifting into sleep when your muscles suddenly 'jump' and you wake up? The sudden, convulsive spasm which caused this is called a mycolonic jerk. It is quite normal, if not very pleasant. It is only one of a number of incidents which may occur in the *prodromal period* on the threshold of sleep. For example, you may experience imaginary and creative ideas which carry you along in a dreamlike way similar to the day-dream on page 475. These twilight dreams, or hypnogogic visions, are characterised by beta waves and are quite easily followed with the conscious mind. Authors, artists and poets quite often experience their most creative ideas at these times and so, probably, will you. However, unless you capture them immediately in words or pictures, you will have forgotten them by morning. Tolstoy, Wagner and Einstein all experienced hypnogogic visions – and all kept paper and pencil at the bedside.

■ Deprivation and disruption of sleep and dreaming

Sleep is seen to be as necessary as food or water. Sleep deprivation in laboratory rats results in death in about 21 days, only about three days longer than it might have been without food or water. However, the procedure used to keep the rat awake involves the rat walking on a turntable to avoid either bumping into a wall or falling into water if brain waves indicative of sleep occur. Other variables, including stress, could be equally important in the resultant death.

Human studies are even more confusing. A few people get by with very little sleep. Holmes (1997) reported a Canadian man, aged 57 years, who slept less than two hours per night for more than 25 years. Apparently, he overslept one night in the sleep laboratory, sleeping 2 1/2 hours. The next day he was groggy and performed poorly!

Before we look at the various theories of sleep we will look at the amount of sleep needed. Are we 'gluttons, anorexics, or fast-food junkies?' (Spinney, 1997, p. 18). These three alternatives are provided by three experts in sleep research:

■ Michael Bonnet (1997), in the USA, suggested we need about 8 1/2 hours of sleep per night and he believes that our 'workaholic' culture is resulting in sleep deprivation, causing accidents on motorways.

■ Jim Horne (1997), in the UK, believes we can manage with less sleep without damaging our health. Perhaps more accidents are reported on motorways due to more people using motorways and such driving being dull and boring. He believes that excess sleep can be just as dangerous as excess body weight. We become sleep gluttons. He believes slow-wave sleep, which is more dominant in the first six hours of sleep, to be biologically essential, with lighter forms of sleep more optional. He found in sleep-laboratories that when participants are

sleep-deprived for 72 hours they need only eight hours of sleep to recover most of their concentration powers. Most of this 8-hour period is spent in slow-wave sleep. He also noted how people adapt to less sleep by sleeping more efficiently – falling asleep more quickly, spending less time in light sleep, and waking less often during the night.

■ Diane Boivin (1997) and her colleagues in the USA, and Simon Folkard in the UK, suggest that rather than amount of sleep it is waking at the wrong time for our body clock which is more critical (see page 479). Research demonstrated how our body clocks directly affect our moods. Normally there is a sharp drop in body temperature about 5 am and a longer-lasting rise in body temperature some eight hours later. If an individual wakes during the dip in the cycles he or she is more likely to feel irritable (even after eight hours sleep). Wakefulness needs to be centred around the peak in body temperature between 2–4 pm to have optimal effects on mood (which is normal for most people). If it is centred around the dip in body temperature early in the day it is found to be linked with bad temper.

Thompson (1975) reported going without sleep for 60 hours. He had difficulty in staying awake the first night, and after 48 hours experienced mild perceptual distortions, illusions and hallucinations. However, there was no apparent decrease in performance of skilled and perceptual tasks. After one night's sleep, normal health was restored.

In 1959, the disc jockey Peter Tripp stayed awake for 200 hours. His experiences are described in figure 14.7.

Throughout the ordeal, Tripp was able to give perfectly sensible three-hour programmes each night and only a few of his listeners were aware of his condition. After a 13-hour sleep, the terrors, illusions and mental agony disappeared, but strain and depression remained for about three months.

Gardner (1965) wanted to break the world record for remaining awake. For 11 days, he kept active by talking and playing games with his family and friends. Although tired, sometimes confused and occasionally feeling pressure around his head

14.7 The effects of staying awake on Peter Tripp

- After two days he saw 'cobwebs' in his shoes, and specks on the table appeared as 'bugs'. Memory was difficult.
- After five days he needed a stimulant to keep going for the walks, talks and broadcasts he made.
- After 100 hours he could perform only one or two of the daily monitoring tasks.
- After 170 hours the tests were 'torture': a simple algebraic problem needed such a superhuman effort that he was frightened.
- After 110 hours there were signs of delirium.

- At about 120 hours he opened a drawer and saw 'flames' spurting out. He thought he was being tested when he 'saw' a tweed suit of 'furry worms', a jumping tie and a salivating nurse.
- He concocted rationalisations like a psychotic patient.
- Symptoms were worst when body temperature was lowest.
- On the final morning he thought the neurologist was an undertaker who had come to bury him alive.
- The last day was a nightmare.

(the hatband effect), he appeared before the cameras after the 11 days and behaved perfectly normally, having experienced few of Tripp's symptoms.

Why the difference? There is no certain answer, but Tripp was in a highly charged, emotional atmosphere – tested and checked regularly with many people watching. Gardner was at home with family and friends, insulated from public interest. He was also younger and probably in better physical condition.

Tripp's experience seems to be unique, since participants kept awake for over 200 hours by Dement (1974) and Webb (1975) showed similar effects to Gardner's (sleepiness, itchy eyelids which tend to droop, and trouble with dull routine tasks; when interested, however, performance efficiency increased to near-normal). Also, feelings of sleepiness followed a circadian cycle, reaching a maximum at about 4 am. When participants finally slept, they made up only about 15 hours of their lost sleep, after which they felt fine.

Gardner's record was broke by Maureen Weston in 1977 who, in a rocking chair marathon, stayed awake for 449 hours (18 days and 17 hours). Most researchers have found very little physiological alterations in behaviour attributed to lack of sleep (Horne, 1983; Martin, 1986). Boring, passive, easy cognitive tasks, especially those demanding long periods of attentiveness such as that used in a study by Brendel *et al.* (1990), have been found

susceptible to sleep deprivation. After two or three days of sleep deprivation it becomes difficult for participants to avoid microsleeps.

Activity 8

Complete the following sentences:

a _____ refers to a sudden convulsive spasm which occurs as you are drifting off to sleep.

b A _____ or 'cat-nap' may occur when we are tired or bored.

c Bonnet believes our 'workaholic' culture is resulting in _____.

d Peter Tripp found after no sleep for _____ there were signs of delirium.

e _____ tasks have been found susceptible to sleep deprivation.

(Suggested answers on page 507.)

Both REM and non-REM sleep were affected in the studies described above, but what if dreaming is disrupted by disturbing only REM sleep? Dement (1960) deprived people of REM sleep for six nights by waking them each time they showed signs of entering it. Participants in a control group were also woken, but not during REM sleep. On nights seven and eight, all participants were allowed to sleep normally. Dement found that those deprived of REM sleep had to be woken more and more often over the six experimental nights. They also complained of psychological discomfort (one participant left the experiment because of anxiety). When allowed to sleep they spent 60 per cent more time in REM sleep than normal. The control group experienced no such increase, nor did they report any psychological distress.

Care must be taken, when considering the above findings, not to interpret REM sleep as dreaming. Not everyone woken during this stage reports having been dreaming, and dreams also occur during non-REM sleep (see page 484).

Two consistent effects have been noted when participants are deprived of REM sleep:

- With each successive night of REM deprivation there is a tendency for participants to initiate REM sleep, so researchers have to wake them more frequently.
- Following REM sleep deprivation participants spend more time in REM sleep. This is known as the *rebound phenomenon*. Brunner *et al.* (1990) found this to occur for two or three nights and suggested that REM sleep is regulated separately from slow-wave sleep, and that perhaps it serves a different function.

The calming effect of REM sleep appears to be contradicted by studies of severely depressed people who find deprivation of REM to have an anti-depressant effect. *Total* sleep deprivation has an anti-depressant effect for such participants but the effects are different. Total sleep deprivation produces immediate effects which are short-lived. Wu and Bunney (1990) cited several such studies showing that such antidepressant effects would last until the next night when normal sleeping was reinstated. The following morning the depression had returned. At present, total sleep deprivation is not a practical treatment for depression as clients cannot stay awake indefinitely.

Partial sleep deprivation, even if only for a few hours, has been found to be beneficial. Many anti-depressant drugs are found to suppress REM sleep.

Pinel (1997) noted that the compensatory increase in the proportion of slow-wave sleep following total sleep deprivation suggests that the regulation of slow-wave sleep takes precedence over the regulation of REM sleep and can thus be seen to be more important. REM sleep is seen by many to have a memory consolidation function and is discussed further on pages 492–3.

Sleep disorders

Do you ever have trouble getting off to sleep or staying asleep? If you do, you may be in the group of about 30 per cent of adults suffering from **insomnia**. This is one of two complementary categories noted by Pinel (1997):

- *Insomnia* Disorders of initiating and maintaining sleep (DIMS).
- *Hypersomnia* Disorders of excessive sleep or sleepiness.

He noted a third class, specifically related to *REM-sleep dysfunction*. We shall look only at insomnia. Hypersomnia and REM-sleep-related disorders are noted briefly in figure 14.8.

There is no agreed definition of **insomnia**. The amount of sleep required varies from individual to individual, with some people feeling fine on five hours of sleep whereas others feel unrefreshed after ten hours. It is ironic that the most important cause of insomnia is *iatrogenic* (physician created). Sleeping pills such as benzodiazepines are initially effective in increasing sleep, but the patient is soon trapped in a rising spiral of drug use as tolerance develops and progressively more of the drug needs to be taken to produce the original, sleep-inducing effects.

If the patients tries to sleep without medication he or she may suffer rebound symptoms and *drug dependency insomnia*. Drugs also interfere with REM sleep and lead to other sleep disturbances.

Sleep apnea is another common type of insomnia, found especially in older people. The individual cannot sleep and breathe at the same time. He or she momentarily stops breathing many times a night. He or she awakens and begins to breathe again and then drifts back to sleep. Sleep apnea usually leads to a sense of having slept poorly and often is diagnosed as insomnia. It is thought to be of two types:

- That resulting from obstruction of the respiratory passage by muscle spasm or *atonia* (lack of muscle tone), most common in overweight people.

14.8 Hypersomnia and REM-sleep-dysfunction

Hypersomnias

By far the most well known of these is *narcolepsy*, a sleep disorder in which individuals are overcome by uncontrollable periods of sleep, lasting about 10–15 minutes, during waking hours. It is the inappropriateness of the sleep pattern that distinguishes this condition, as narcoleptics fall asleep at any time, for example in the middle of a conversation, while eating, or while making love! Narcolepsy is also classified as a REM-sleep-related disorder because, unlike other people, they go straight into REM sleep when they fall asleep. This suggests that REM sleep phenomena encroach on wakefulness.

REM-sleep-dysfunction

The two important characteristics of REM sleep are dreaming and paralysis. The paralysis results from a brain mechanism which prevents us from acting out our dreams. *REM-sleep-behaviour disorder* was reported by Schenck *et al.* (1986) when such paralysis does not occur. Perhaps, as suggested by Culebras and Moore (1989) this is produced by damage to the pons area of the brain. It can also involve abnormalities in the brain, sometimes genetic.

Cataplexy is often associated with narcolepsy, and is characterised by recurring loss of muscle tone, often triggered by emotional experiences, and can even occur while making love! In a mild form, this will require the patient to sit down for a few minutes. In its extreme form, the patient falls to the ground, paralysed, but fully conscious. These attacks usually last for less than one minute. Brain mechanisms responsible for REM sleep are normally inhibited by serotonin-secreting neurons, so treatment usually involves drugs which increase such inhibition.

■ That resulting from the failure of the CNS in stimulating respiration, which Mendelson (1987) found to increase with age.

Two other types of insomnia both involve legs:

■ *Nocturnal myclonus* results in periodic and repeated episodes of body twitching throughout the night, especially legs, which can result in individuals complaining of poor sleep and daytime sleepiness.

■ *Restless legs* results in tension or uneasiness in the legs, which individuals find difficult to describe and which prevents them falling asleep.

Somnambulism (sleep-walking) is quite a dramatic problem, usually associated with childhood. Empson (1984) found about 25 per cent of children experience at least one sleep-walking episode. Sleep-walkers are often difficult to wake up but, contrary to opinion, it is not dangerous to wake them.

Sleep-talking usually occurs during non-REM sleep, and only sometimes as part of REM-sleep dreaming. Often a conversation can be held with the sleep-talker, indicating it occurs near to the boundary of sleeping and waking.

Night terrors, again usually associated with children, refers to the child awakening from deep sleep with signs of intense arousal, racing pulse, and a powerful feeling of fear. The child seldom has any memory of a dream related to this and after calming usually goes straight back to sleep. These night terrors seem to appear during stage 4 slow-wave sleep. In contrast, *nightmares*, which more of us have experienced, occur during REM sleep and can often be vividly recalled.

Both somnambulism and night terrors seem to be related to disturbances in the autonomic nervous system, which plays a key role in regular brain activity in sleep. Both of these conditions tend to cure themselves as the child gets older and there is no evidence that they are related to mental disorders or personality.

Insomnia cannot kill or disable. It is often not a problem of too little sleep but more often a problem of too little undisturbed sleep. For some people, insomnia seems to involve disturbances in the internal mechanisms that regulate body temperature. You will remember from the earlier discussion of circadian rhythms (page 477) that core temperature drops during sleep. This conserves energy and permits many body functions to operate on reduced rates. Sewitch (1987) found that the body temperature of insomniacs remains relatively high.

Many of the other sleep disorders are thought to involve disturbances of the body clock within the SCN in the hypothalamus. This clock interacts with other structures in the brain such as the serotonin-producing parts of the reticular activating system and sections of the fore brain just in front of the hypothalamus. These structures are involved in regulating the circadian rhythms, including the sleep-wake cycle. The disturbance of these delicately balanced mechanisms can result in sleep disorders.

■ Theories and functions of sleep

Activity 9

Why do you think we need to sleep? Jot down some ideas and then read on to see if you were correct.

Several theories of sleep and dreams have been suggested, over many years, to try and explain their function. Currently, most of the research is divided between two main groups of researchers:

■ Sleep is a tactic for conserving energy and recharging energy stores.

■ Sleep is when the brain goes 'off-line' to do the jobs it cannot do when we are fully conscious.

These two approaches are discussed after summarising the main early theories.

■ Sleep as an adaptive response

Evolutionary theory proposes that sleep evolved as an instinctive, behavioural response to keep us quiet at night when predators abounded (Meddis, 1975, 1977; Webb, 1975, 1982). Carlson (1994) suggested this theory makes sense in terms of ecological niches (living spaces). Short-tailed shrews, although having safe burrows, sleep little because of their continuous need to eat. Ground squirrels also have safe burrows, although they do not need to eat constantly and sleep for 14 hours a day. Prey animals such as sheep, zebra and deer, sleep for two

hours a day and then only in brief naps. Most primates are diurnal, being awake and active during daylight. During the hours of darkness, when food is difficult to obtain and predators are harder to see, energy could be wasted through maladaptive activity. It is therefore more adaptive to remain inactive, despite being vulnerable to predators. *Hibernation theory* (Rogers, 1981) also proposed that sleep has evolved to keep us quiet in the dark, to conserve energy and keep animals out of possible danger in the cold, short, winter days.

Several researchers noted criticisms of theories suggesting that sleep is an adaptive response. Holmes (1997) reminded us that rodents warm their bodies back to normal temperature several times during hibernation in the winter and then sleep through these 'active' periods. Rather an inefficient system.

Sleep is found in some mammals who might be better without it. Carlson (1994) gave the example of the Indus dolphin living in the muddy waters of the Indus estuary in Pakistan. This dolphin has become blind, presumably because vision is not helpful in this environment, and it has developed a sonar system for navigation and to help locate prey. These dolphins still sleep for the equivalent of seven hours a day taken in naps of between 4 and 60 seconds each. If sleep were adaptive, then it should have been eliminated by the process of natural selection. The unique sleep behaviour of some other marine mammals can be found in figure 14.9.

It does appear that sleep is physiologically necessary, although not simply as a response to physiological need.

Sleep as an adaptive response is also named *circadian theory* by Pinel (1997). He sees the explanation of between-species differences in sleep-time to be central to any successful theory of sleep. He referred to the research on circadian rhythms and sleep deprivation (see pages 477–80) and stressed the importance of circadian theory *and* recuperation/restoration theory in explaining sleep function.

■ Sleep as a restorative process

Most researchers feel that sleep fulfills some kind of restorative process, enabling us to recover from the effects of wear and tear which occur when we

14.9 Sleeping with half a brain

Some marine mammals have evolved an unusual sleep pattern whereby the cerebral hemispheres take turns at sleeping. Mukhametov (1984) reported dolphins having one hemisphere always alert while the other is in deep, slow-wave sleep. When the right or left brain of the dolphin is prevented from taking its turn then only that side builds up a sleep *'debt'*. This pattern has also been reported in several dolphin and whale species and also some seals. It may have evolved to ensure part of the brain is always alert to control breathing in the water. Support for this comes from research showing that when dolphins are given drugs to put both sides of the brain to sleep they stop breathing entirely.

are awake. What exactly sleep restores is debatable. The simple explanation is that the brain 'tires itself out' and needs to 'recover'. Some support for this view comes from Horne who found the most complex thought processes are the first to suffer after sleep deprivation. This correlates with frontal lobes which are the most active part of the brain when we are awake.

Slow-wave sleep appears to be necessary for the restoration of the brain. The secretion of growth hormone occurs during sleep, shortly after the first occurrence of delta activity in slow-wave sleep. Obal *et al.* (1991) found that a drug inhibiting the release of growth hormone also suppressed sleep in rats. Growth hormone increases the ability of amino acids to enter cells. These are the constituents of proteins and protein synthesis is an important aspect of the restoration of body tissue, as proteins are relatively fragile and need to be renewed and replaced constantly. Horne (1988) pointed out that growth hormone only facilitates protein synthesis if the amino acids are readily available in the period up to five hours after a meal. After this time they are coverted into fats and stored in the adipose tissue. For most people this means the pool of amino acids is low for most of the night as they have eaten several hours before going to sleep. Ramm and Smith (1990) found the

rate of protein synthesis in the brains of rats increased during slow-wave sleep. This suggests the brain is restoring itself as well as resting.

Holmes (1997) noted some research pointing to the role of a molecule called *adenosine* in this process. Adenosine is an energy molecule that cells use for a readily available supply of energy. It is also a molecular messenger, acting on receptors to inhibit nerve cell activity, especially in the 'arousal centres' found in the brain stem, which keeps us awake. Caffeine seems to work by blocking adenosine receptors.

So far we have not really distinguished between the different types of sleep. Research into slow-wave sleep and REM sleep emphasises their importance over other types. Benington and Heller, reported in Holmes (1997), suggested that the brain needs time to replenish emergency stores of energy and looked to glucose as an explanation. Glucose is the brain's staple fuel. It is carried in the blood stream and a small reserve is kept locked up as glycogen. Benington and Heller looked at the link between slow-wave sleep and REM sleep and suggested that this supply may need recharging during sleep. Adenosine may trigger and control this charging. REM activity is seen as the brain trying to recover from the biochemical rigours of slow-wave sleep. The brain's need for REM sleep appears to build up during slow-wave sleep. Benington and Heller noted that potassium ions leak out of brain cells during slow-wave sleep in rats and the cells become unresponsive to normal electrical inputs. REM sleep is thus seen as a chance to recover these potassium ions before the deficit causes a metabolic upset. When this leak was blocked, the rats lost their need for REM sleep.

This *glycogen hypothesis* is still relatively untested and some researchers have rejected it in favour of a link between sleep and memory. Smith (1997) and his colleagues found laboratory rats spend more time in REM sleep after training to avoid a shock. Similar effects have been found in human studies of college students who usually have more REM activity in the week after 'cramming' for exams. Depriving either rats or students of REM sleep after a period of learning hinders them from remembering what they have learned.

Smith (1997) saw REM sleep as helping prepare memories for long-term storage in the brain. He found this preparation occurred at precise intervals after the learning period, a type of REM sleep 'window', which varies with the complexity of the task, the more complex the task, the sooner the REM sleep was needed, as if the brain were in a hurry to process the information before it forgot it. Smith (1997) suggested humans also have REM sleep windows, which are needed for *procedural memory* (remembering 'how'), not for *declarative memory* (remembering 'what'). These types of memory are discussed in Unit 18. People who missed REM sleep remembered less about puzzles requiring manipulation of symbols but the sleep loss did not interfere with simple, paired-learning tasks. This was taken to suggest that simple tasks require less processing during REM sleep.

■ The brain is 'off-line' in sleep

Krueger (1997) suggested that the brain takes itself off-line during sleep, so it can exercise infrequently-used neural pathways. Synapses are thought to be maintained by frequent usage, so pathways not used frequently are at risk of degeneration.

Krueger, cited by Holmes (1997), suggested that these circuits can be exercised in the confines of sleep without the individual acting out the behaviour. This theory also explains why we need to be unconscious in sleep. So far there is little evidence to support Krueger's theory, other than that the messenger molecule *interleukin-1* which accumulates during waking and encourages sleep to begin, is involved in the formation of synapses. Kreuger is researching insects to track individual nerve cell's reaction to interleukin-1 and other synapse-shaping molecules.

Carlson (1994) summarised four functions of REM sleep:

- Vigilance.
- Learning.
- Species-typical reprogramming.
- Brain development.

So far none has been supported unanimously nor proved wrong. Conflicting evidence on the importance of REM sleep comes from studies such as those reported by Lavie *et al.* (1984). These show people who have almost no REM sleep but who appear to suffer no ill effects.

Although REM sleep has been identified as one of the important stages of sleep, we have not, so far, singled out one of the most researched aspects of this stage – *dreaming*.

Why dream?

> ### Activity 10
>
> Do you dream? Have you ever tried to understand the purpose of any dreams you remember? Do you have recurring dreams or nightmares?
> Get together with a partner and discuss any dreams you can remember. Make a list of what you see to be the purpose of dreaming. (Read on to see the various explanations of dreaming.)

Pinel (1997) summarised some of the commonly held beliefs on dreaming which have found empirical support:

- External stimuli can become incorporated into a dream, so if the roof starts leaking onto you in your sleep you may well include water in your dream.
- Dreams run on 'real time' so that if participants are awoken during REM sleep they are often reasonably accurate as to the length of the dream period.
- Most people dream, even those who report they do not dream. If they are woken during REM sleep they would usually report a dream.
- Penile erections during sleep do not correlate with 'sexy' dreams and even babies have REM-related penile erections.
- Sleep-walking and sleep-talking do not usually occur during REM sleep, they are more likely to occur during stage 4 sleep (see page 490).

Explanations of the purpose of dreaming come from three main areas of research:

- Psychoanalytic view.
- Physiological view.
- Cognitive view.

Dreams: Psychoanalytic view

Sigmund Freud believed that dreams provide an important way of accessing the unconscious mind. Dreams were seen as disguised messages, of unacceptable, repressed wishes, many of which were of a sexual nature. Jung, a follower of Freud, also considered dreams to have significance. These two theories are summarised in figure 14.10.

Freud proposed that no matter how strange the dreams, they contain important messages, often disguised, and the help of an analyst is needed for interpretation. However, he left no clear-cut rules for dream analysis, and later research has not supported his theory.

Dreams: Physiological view

The modern alternative to Freudian theory is Hobson's *activation-synthesis theory*, which proposes that the brain is active during REM sleep (*activation*) and that dreams are the conscious interpretation of this activity (*synthesis*). This theory gives a physiological explanation of dreams. According to this perspective, dreams are simply the subjective experience of random, neural activity in the brain. The brain is trying to make a coherent story out of the random brain stem signals produced during REM sleep. Cut off from signals of the outside world, once every 90 minutes (during REM sleep), the primitive brain–stem sends electrical and chemical messages to parts of the cortex, especially parts that process visual information. These are known as *PGO waves* and are similar to those produced during an epileptic seizure.

Crick and Mitchison (1983, 1986) argued that the purpose of REM sleep was to eliminate patterns of spurious or harmful neural connections which build up in the brain during the day. These networks, like spider's webs, malfunction when overloaded. A mechanism is needed to 'de-bug' the system – hence the need for REM sleep during which the 'network' is isolated from inputs. They believed that association networks, within the

14.10 Psychoanalytic approaches to dreams

Freud (1856–1939) believed that the unconscious mind powerfully influences the conscious mind (see above). Fundamental instinctive urges, with socially unacceptable motives, are repressed in waking life but may find expression in dreams. His *psychoanalytic theory* (Freud, 1902) describes dreams as having two elements: a *manifest* (seen) content, which disguises and dramatises the repressed urges which are hidden in the second element; the *latent* content (the real meaning of the dream). The manifest content derives from thoughts of the previous day, combined with past thoughts and emotions, and is constructed in three ways. *Condensation* combines several ideas into abbreviated form, so that a single word or figure may have multiple meanings in the dream. *Displacement* occurs when one thing represents another, for example one part of the body may represent a different part. *Symbolisation* is where objects or events signify something else, for example the male sex organ is symbolised by any long, pointed object, while the female organ is symbolised by boxes or baskets. However, the fact that young infants and animals low in the phylogenic scale exhibit REM sleep, argues against this theory being completely credible.

Jung (1875–1961) was student of Freud who adopted a more religious, philosophical and mystical approach to personality. He extended the concept of consciousness to include a *collective unconscious*, consisting of everything ever known to humanity, including archetypes (universal images) and fundamental concepts such as 'mother', 'wise old man' and 'God'. Jung believed that dreams incorporate some of these universal concepts and that they are psychic products obeying 'psychic laws, which must therefore be treated as psychic phenomena' until 'experience teaches us a better way'. Dreams are where the conscious and unconscious meet and interact.

cortex, become overloaded by incoming information, causing bizarre connections to occur – perceived as fantasies. Hallucinations or obsessions may also occur when nerve firing is indiscriminate. The 'clean-up' is carried out by neural activity between the RAS and cortex during REM sleep. By trying to remember dreams we are focusing on material we are 'turning out'. So dreams are seen by Crick and Mitchison as little more than random noise with no real content.

Hobson, cited in Mestel (1997), did not see dreams as spurious, unwanted rubbish, even though, unlike Freud, he did not see the content to be of hidden significance. He saw the REM period itself to be valuable rather than the dreaming by-product. He suggested the PGO waves have nothing to do with reality. The cortex, not realising this, tries to make sense of the input resulting in the weird dreams we remember.

Hobson and his colleagues have also identified nerve cells in the brain stem which control the 'switch' from REM to deeper sleep. One set (they called these the 'REM-on' neurons) secrete acetylcholine and the others ('REM-off') secrete norepinephrine and serotonin. They suggested these turn the 90-minute cycle on and off. The absense of norepinephrine and serotonin are seen as the reason why cortical thinking, insight and memory are absent from dreams. Many neurophysiologists have linked low serotonin levels to lack of judgement and thought, and low norepinephrine to poor concentration.

Critics of Hobson such as Foulkes and Antrobus, reported by Holmes (1997), suggested the following:

- There is no evidence to suppose the PGO waves introduce bizarreness into dreams.
- Most dreams reported by participants in sleep laboratories are not bizarre when reported.
- The link between REM and dreaming is not as clear-cut as first thought, with dreaming now reported in stage 4 sleep (see page 490).

Night-dreaming was seen by Antrobus to be no different from day-dreaming. He saw dreaming to be more cognitive in function. His view is discussed in more detail below.

■ Dreams: Cognitive view

Evans's (1984) *cognitive* approach extends a physiological reason for dreams. During REM sleep, sensory and motor pathways disengage and the brain can review the day's experiences, updating, reorganising and programming memory in the light of new information. During dreams, the connections are briefly reinstated and the conscious mind becomes aware of the activity. The brain, however, tries to interpret dreams like normal sensory inputs and this tends to give them bizarre qualities.

Antrobus, in a review of sleep and dreaming in 1991, concluded that during REM sleep, just as during wakefulness, the areas of the cortex involved in perceptual and cognitive processes are highly active. However, when we are asleep we are isolated from sensory input and feedback from movement, so the only input is from internal processes. He argued that this forms the basis of the imagery and ideas in dreams. Rather than being meaningless, dreams represent the brain's interpretation of this neural activity and reflect aspects of our memories and waking experience. Supporting evidence comes from people who are attempting to make important changes in their lives, who often report having *dreams of absent-minded transgressions (DAMIT dreams)*. Gill (1985) reported on people who, trying to stop smoking or drinking, notice they have slipped back into this behaviour in a dream and this leads to a feeling of panic or guilt in the dream. This often awakens them, feeling upset. Hajek and Belcher (1991) studied several hundred people enrolled on a programme to help them stop smoking. They found about 33 per cent reported DAMIT dreams while trying to stop, never having had such dreams previously. More importantly, such dreams were positively related to their success in stopping smoking. A higher proportion of participants with DAMIT dreams were still not smoking a year after the programme finished. Hajek and Belcher (1991) suggested that the guilt and panic produced by the dream was a type of negative reinforcement which helped the people break the habit.

A clear link in this research can be seen between what is happening in people's daily lives and the content of their dreams. Dreams can therefore be seen to have meaning. Contradicting Freud, the dreams are not hidden desires causing anxiety but rather conscious anxieties. Cartwright (1989, 1991) also saw dreams as a means of dealing with emotional issues. She found that, during a crisis, the brain's dreaming mechanism moves into 'high gear'. For example, depressed people going through a divorce were found to dream more, earlier in the night. Their dreams lasted longer and were more emotional than usual. When people were coping well, their dreams often suggested strategies and the mood of the individual was better in the morning. Poor copers often just reiterated their problems in their dreams and came to no resolutions. They often felt much worse the next morning, having spent less time in REM sleep. Cartwright considered dreaming to provide a very useful cognitive function.

Some researchers have tried to manipulate the dream period to become 'expert' dreamers. LaBerge (1986) reported on *lucid dreams*, where the dreamer is aware of the dream and able to influence the course of the dream. This lucid dreaming is found to be a positive experience and several techniques have been devised to train people to intervene during REM sleep.

The lack of consensus about the function sleep and dreaming leads many researchers, including Horne, to suggest that they have a variety of functions, rather than a single, universal function common to all mammals.

Hobson (1995) proposed the function of sleep operates at different levels:

- Sleep suppresses activity at times when it is inefficient, so at a *behavioural level* it is not only efficient but also useful in the social/family situation.
- Sleep can be seen operating at a *developmental level*, a type of behavioural rehearsal for neural circuits.
- The major changes between the cycle of non-REM and REM sleep involve all the body's physiological systems at a *metabolic level*.

In conclusion, sleep and dreaming appear to have both physiological and psychological functions. Sleep helps an organism avoid external dangers and adapt internally by recuperating body tissues and energy. It is also useful as a vessel through which dreams can work, perhaps as organiser, self-analyser and therapist, an expansion of wakeful life, or even prophetically. Without sleeping and dreaming, our wakeful hours become disorientated and disrupted.

Self-assessment questions

6 Differentiate between alpha and beta waves shown on the EEG.

7 Note *two* alternative suggestions about the amount of sleep needed for healthy individuals.

8 Discuss evidence showing REM sleep to be important for psychological well-being.

9 Summarise *two* alternative theories about the purpose of sleep.

10 Outline *two* explanations of why we dream.

(Suggested answers on page 509.)

Other altered states of awareness

Sleep and dreaming are not the only altered states of awareness. Others include those produced by hypnosis, meditation and psychoactive drugs.

Hypnosis

Many people have misconceptions about **hypnosis**, much of which can be traced to unfortunate use of demonstrations of hypnosis as a form of entertainment on stage and television. Much of this, especially in the early days, was ethically suspect.

Activity 11

From your knowledge or experiences of hypnosis shown on television or in the theatre, make a list of any ethical guidelines such as those of the BPS or APA which may have been disregarded. (see Unit 3 page 90).
You may wish to do this as a group activity.

Psychologists cannot agree on a definition of hypnosis as they suggest more needs to be known before it can be adequately defined. Heap (1996) suggested that this is a fallacy as most psychologists have no difficulty in discussing, demonstrating and conducting experiments on hypnosis, in various clinical settings. He bypassed the general definition by describing what takes place when hypnosis is demonstrated and noting the common properties.

Hypnosis involves the interaction between two or more people, one of whom is the *hypnotist* and the other(s) the hypnotic participant(s). Heap (1996) suggested that there are two central processes:

■ Trance.
■ Suggestion.

Trance refers to a waking stage during which the participant's attention is detached from the immediate environment and absorbed by inner experiences, such as feeling, cognition, and imagery. This is seen to be similar to day-dreaming or absorption in a book or music.

Suggestion is a communication usually given verbally by the hypnotist to direct the participant's imagination so as to elicit alternatives in the way he or she is behaving, thinking or feeling. Suggestion is often used to refer to the process by which the participant responds to the request. This behaviour has an automatic quality whereby the hypnotist may request the participant to concentrate on something. For example, the hypnotist may ask the participant about his or her hand, the suggestion may be made that the hand is cold and insensitive. Imagery may be used, such as dipping the hand into cold, icy water and the participant often reports the effects of this cold felt in the numbness of the hand. *Ideosensory* suggestions are those which

elicit somatosensory experience, such as arms feeling lighter or visual and auditory experiences. A special type of suggestion used is known as the *post-hypnotic suggestion*, whereby the response is intended to take place some time later. Heap (1996) gave the example: 'Each and every time you experience these anxious feelings, this relaxing scene will come immediately to mind.' (Heap, 1996, p. 499)

Trance and suggestion are seen to interact, with the suggestion leading the participant's attention away from external circumstances and towards the physical experience. Encouraging the participant to assume the trance state has been shown by Hilgard (1965) to increase responsibility to suggestion. Hypnotists often precede hypnotic suggestions with a series of suggestions, aimed at encouraging the trance state. This is known as *hypnotic induction*, and often involves relaxation methods and guided imagery. These traditional induction methods are not essential but do enhance the expectation and motivation of the participant. They also provide a relaxation routine of *self-hypnosis* which can often be used after the session to control anxiety.

Hypnosis can be seen as a state of intense relaxation and concentration, in which the mind becomes detached from everyday worries. In this relaxed state, the subconscious part of the mind can respond creatively to suggestion. Brain waves during hypnosis show a similar pattern to wakefulness, indicating that the hypnotised participant is not asleep. Usually the participant remains fully aware of what is happening and remembers later, unless explicitly instructed to forget. Even then the memory can be restored by a pre-arranged signal. The participant is in an alternative state of awareness where he or she often reports the focus of attention as being outward, for example on the hypnotist's voice. This state is sometimes compared to complete absorption in a book or music. Hilgard (1967) found people who can become absorbed in such activities often make good participants in hypnosis.

■ Hypnotic susceptibility

Bates (1993) found great individual differences in susceptibility to hypnosis. Baron (1996) noted:

- About 15 per cent of adults are highly susceptible (as measured by responses to a graded series of suggestions by the hypnotist).
- About 10 per cent are highly resistant.

The remaining 75 per cent are somewhere inbetween. Little evidence shows a reliable relationship between traditional measures of personality or intelligence with hypnotisability, nor are there reliable sex differences. However, Gibson and Heap (1991) found females to be slightly higher in susceptibility. There is a strong relationship between age and susceptibility, with the peak occurring between the age of nine and twelve years. Research has looked at the neuropsycho-physiological characteristics of participants who are highly hypnotisable. For example, Crawford *et al.* (1993) supported the view that such individuals have more efficient frontolimbic sustained attentional and disattentional systems. Subjective evidence from participants, on the shift from a non-hypnotised to the hypnotised state, describes a shift away from more analytical and sequential modes of processing to a more imaginative and holistic processing. This is consistent with the neuropsycho-physiological evidence of a more frontal, possibly left-based, hemispheric activation prior to hypnosis followed by a more posterior hemispheric, possibly right-based involvement with hypnosis. Crawford (1994) suggested these shifts, which are seen more in the highly hypnotised participants, may reflect their greater cognitive flexibility.

There is some evidence from Covino *et al.* (1994) that hypnotic susceptibility and dissociative tendencies are higher in bulimic women, whereas anorexics are generally found to have lower levels of hypnotisability. Everill and Waller (1995) suggested that hypnotic susceptibility may be a risk factor in the development of eating disorders such as bulimia, especially where there is a history of abuse. Oakley *et al.* (1997) suggested that the hypnotic approach may be particularly effective in bulimia and perhaps with survivors of childhood abuse.

Baron (1996) summarised the characteristics of those susceptible to hypnotism as follows:

- High on visual imagery.
- Frequently have vivid fantasies.
- A tendency to become involved in sensory and imaginative experiences and become absorbed in such.

- Dependency on others from which they seek direction.
- Positive expectations of the influence of hypnotic suggestions and their effects.
- Experience *dissociation*, whereby they have some portion of the self split from the rest.

Hypnosis is usually induced through relaxation techniques, and may produce the altered states of awareness show in figure 14.11.

■ Induction of hypnosis

Induction techniques used in therapy are given in more detail below, as these become specialised dependent on the age, cognitive and social development of the participant. The basic requirements appear to be that the participant is willing and cooperative. Despite common myths:

- hypnosis cannot be used to coerce the participant into criminal and deviant behaviour, as he or she cannot be hypnotised against his or her will
- the hypnotist is not a magician, merely an assistant or facilitator to the central performer – the participant.

As noted above, susceptibility is a central factor. The person wishing to be hypnotised relinquishes some control over behaviour to the hypnotist and is willing to accept some reality distortion. A variety of methods are used, but basically the participant is given the suggestion of drowsiness and relaxation (perhaps being told they are slipping further and

---

14.11 Changes characteristic of hypnosis

Initiative for planning actions decreases and participants wait to be told what to do and to be asked how they feel.

Attention becomes more selective and participants concentrate only on what they are told to, e.g. the hypnotist's voice.

Imagery is enhanced and participants can experience displacement of time and space.

Reality becomes distorted, e.g. if asked to wash socks, participants will accept that the tub and soapy water are already present.

Suggestibility increases slightly.

Post-hypnotic amnesia can be induced.

further away from voluntary control). Various techniques are used to aid this trance condition, for example the participant may be asked to concentrate on a small object, or to imagine certain bodily sensations.

Banyai and Hilgard (1976) demonstrated that relaxation is not critical to induction of hypnosis and that in some cases the trance induction could be quite active. This was shown by participants riding a stationery laboratory bicycle whilst receiving suggestions of strength and alertness. Atkinson *et al.* (1996) compared this with the trance induction used by the whirling dervishes of some Muslim religious orders.

With very little training, *self-hypnosis* is possible. This is important in the participant gaining a sense of mastery and control, which can reinforce therapeutic suggestions. Hart and Hart (1996) promoted its use with children, especially with frequently occurring disorders such as migraines and stuttering.

Therapists have provided children with audio tapes of therapy sessions, or provided techniques such as fixation on a special coin, followed by relaxing imagery, to encourage continuation of self-hypnosis outside therapy. They note that children will often discontinue self-hypnosis after about six weeks, due to boredom, or forgetting to practice. Psychotic and mentally unstable people should not attempt self-hypnosis.

■ Properties of hypnosis

Some of the properties of hypnosis which have clinical relevance are summarised by Heap and Oakley *et al.* (1996) in figure 14.12.

These properties have been determined by empirical research, have been shown to have an increased probability of occurring during hypnosis, and can be exploited both formally and informally for the benefit of the participant.

Many hypnotic phenomena appear to be impossible to achieve without hypnosis, but some

---

14.12 Properties of hypnosis

Some properties of hypnosis which are of clinical relevance are:

(a)
- Increased suggestibility, or at least an increased willingness to accept suggestions less critically.
- Enhanced capacity for imagery and role enactment, so that imagined events are experienced as 'real'.
- Greater accessto childhood memories, though not a literal return to an earlier stage of cognitive development.
- Reduced reality testing. A greater tolerance of logical incongruities – so-called 'trance logic'.
- Enhanced relaxation responses, which can be learned and applied in everyday situations.
- Increased rapport (Sheehan, 1992).
- Increased expectancy of positive outcome of therapy (Coe, 1993).
- More focused attention and enhanced ability to disattend to extraneous thoughts or feelings.
- An opportunity to create, develop and control dissociative experiences.

Source: Oakley *et al.*, 1996, p. 504.

(b)
- With regular pratice, the alleviation of the effects of everyday stress (Benson, 1975);
- Alteration in the experience of the passage of time, usually leading to underestimation (Von Kirchenheim and Persinger, 1991);
- Some amnesia for events which clearly registered because the subject responded overtly to them (Cooper, 1972);
- Attenuation of the experience and increased tolerance of ongoing discomfort and pain (Hilgard *et al.* 1975);
- An enhanced predisposition to go to sleep (Anderson *et al.* 1979).

Source: Heap, 1996, p. 499.

have been demonstrated in the absence of hypnosis. The 'human plank' demonstration falls in this category. A participant is suspended horizontally between two chairs, one under the head and the other under the feet, whilst another person stands on the stomach or chest, supported only by the rigidity of the participant's body. Normal, healthy people have been shown performing this task without hypnosis, but under carefully worded instructions to cooperate with the experimenter. Activities such as learning to ignore painful stimuli, acting as if a child, imagining non-existent objects and failure to remember suggested words, have all been performed by people knowing they are pretending. Hypnotised people usually believe their behaviour is involuntary, and report different, subjective experiences to non-hypnotised people.

Another controversial property of hypnosis involves *hypnotic memory enhancement*. Police departments, especially in the USA, originally used such techniques to enable witnesses to remember details of a crime. Witnesses under hypnosis are told to 'zoom in' to details they may have forgotten (for example, car licence plates or a criminal's face). Reiser and Nielson (1980) used a 'freeze frame' technique to examine fleeting details at leisure.

However, hypnosis can only help if the information has been perceived and has left a memory trace. It cannot enhance the memory, it can only enhance its recollection. Orne *et al.* (1988) pointed out that hypnosis can not only help people recollect memories but also *modify* their memories. They reported on a hypnotised rape victim who was asked to mentally 'take off' the attacker's mask and report what the face looked like. On the basis of this face that the victim had never seen, a man was convicted on her 'eyewitness identification'. Because many witnesses are eager to help the police they are more susceptible in hypnosis, and several studies have demonstrated that this can lead to false memories. Laurence and Perry, reviewing a number of studies in 1988, suggested that testimony from hypnotised participants is not always reliable. Subtle hints made by the person asking the questions can inadvertently change the way participants remember events.

The eyewitness testimony of someone who believes sincerely in what they are saying can have a powerful effect on a jury, especially when the witness is remembering precise details about an episode. Due to the many studies showing no beneficial effects of hypnosis on the accuracy of memory, such as Kihlstrom in 1985 and McMaster in 1990, most courts in the USA and the UK do not allow witnesses to testify once hypnotised. Methods not involving hypnosis have been developed by cognitive psychologists to help elicit enhanced memory. Malpass and Devine (1981) developed a guided memory method, whereby the participant visualises the original environment, mood, thoughts and feelings. State-dependent memory cues often help the participant remember details he or she had forgotten.

Hypnotic coercion has also caused concern, with some reports of the unethical use of hypnosis outside the laboratory. For example, Kline (1972) reported a physician who used hypnosis to seduce female patients. Orne and Evans (1965) highlighted the role of *demand characteristics*, in that participants assume safety precautions are operating as part of the experiment or treatment.

As noted in Unit 28 pages 1031–2, participants are not passive, they often behave according to how they interpret the situation. Carlson and Buskist (1997) concluded:

- The context of the setting is seen as a guarantee that the participant will be protected from harm and from harming another person.
- It is difficult to determine an individual's moral code and it is surprising how some people are quite willing to perform antisocial acts.
- Even if the act is harmful to someone else or would violate a moral code, participants may, through *diffusion of responsibility*, see this to be the experimenter's problem.

Another, even more debatable, property of hypnosis, is that it enhances *access to unconscious material*, normally below the level of conscious awareness, which may influence the participant's behaviour, thoughts and emotions. Lynn and Nash (1994) noted the difficulty of demonstrating this empirically, with more of the information coming from case studies.

A related property of hypnosis is the *suppression of experience from conscious awareness*. Hilgard (1986) was one of many researchers who demonstrated that an unconscious part of the mind still has access to the suppressed experience. He named this the **hidden observer**, which refers to a mental structure that monitors everything that happens, including events that the hypnotised participant is not consciously aware of perceiving. Many practitioners, especially in the USA, believe that the process of suppressing conscious experience and gaining access to the unconscious (known as *dissociation*) is central to the concept of hypnosis. Critics of the hidden observer experiments such as Spanos (1986) noted that suggestibility may have produced the results.

Activity 12

Are the following statements true or false?

a   The 'human plank' demonstration can only be undertaken by a hypnotised participant.

b   Hypnotised participants have greater tolerance of logical incongruities.

c   Hypnosis leads to an underestimation of the passage of time.

d   The 'hidden observer' is seen to monitor all that is happening, except for events that the participant is not aware of perceiving.

e   Most courts in the USA and the UK do not allow hypnotised participants to testify.

(Suggested answers on page 508.)

■ Historical antecedents of hypnosis

Modern hypnosis can be traced back to Paris in the 18th century and the work of Anton Mesmer, who developed a theory of healing based on a vital fluid, which he called 'animal magnetism'. Blockage of this fluid resulted in illness and he devised a technique whereby this could be released. He thus gave his name to *mesmerise* ('hold spellbound'). Fancher (1990) noted that, despite Mesmer's treatment having recognition as a therapy by many, he was driven out of Paris by the French government after an investigation disclaimed animal magnetism.

In the middle of the 19th century, James Braid, who practised in Manchester, renamed mesmerism, and the term *hypnosis* was used for the first time. This was not only a change in name, but also involved a 'paradigm shift' based on a physiological theory of visual fatigue and fixed attention on the words of the hypnotist. This elevated the status of psychological factors and verbal suggestion.

Although making little impact in the UK, Braid did influence developments in Europe at the end of the 19th century, where a controversy developed between Charcot and Bernheim in France. Charcot believed hypnosis was a psychopathological state related to hysteria, whereas Bernheim felt there was no special 'state' of hypnosis and that the procedure enhanced the participant's responsiveness to suggestion. This debate was the precursor to today's *state* versus *non-state* controversy which is discussed below.

For many reasons, including the rise of behaviourism and psychoanalysis at the beginning of the 20th century, interest in hypnotism waned. Freud originally included hypnosis in therapy but later considered it to have limited value by comparison with other psychoanalytical techniques.

In the 1950s, both the British and American Medical Associations issued statements supporting the usefulness of hypnosis in therapy. Over the next 40 years several British and American societies and institutions linked to hypnosis were founded, including the British Society of Experimental and Clinical Hypnosis and The Institute of Hypnosis and Parapsychology which were founded in the UK and the USA in 1977. There has since been a rekindling of interest in hypnosis amongst applied psychologists, who together with academic, medical and dental colleagues, have been responsible for research papers on theoretical and clinical issues. In 1997 '*Hypnosis UK*' appeared on the Internet, established by Dr Charles Barr, to promote a wider understanding and acceptance of hypnosis.

■ Modern theoretical controversies

Two theories have dominated explanations of hypnosis, commonly called the state or non-state controversy.

■ *State* theories are dominated by the *neo-dissociation theory*, which suggests that hypnosis operates by inducing dissociations in consciousness. This is supported by Hilgard (1986) and Bowers (1990). Hilgard proposed a hierarchy of cognitive systems under the control of an 'executive ego', each of which is able to become dissociated from the others and from consciousness. Hypnosis can influence the executive ego and alter this arrangement, so experiences normally available to consciousness may be rendered inaccessible, and those repressed in the unconscious may become accessible. This can be demonstrated by the 'hidden observer' effect (see page 501). According to this view, participants who are hypnotised are in an altered state of awareness in which one part of the mind accepts suggestions made by the hypnotist, while the other part (the hidden observer) observes this without participating.

Barber (1989) challenged the view that hypnosis is an altered state of awareness, since hypnotists could not identify genuine hypnotised participants from a control group who were pretending. Also, there is no test which can demonstrate scientifically the existence of such a state. Despite this controversy, increasing numbers of doctors and dentists find hypnosis valuable when anaesthetic is ill-advised because of a patient's medical condition (Whaddon and Anderton, 1982).

■ *Non-state* theories include the *socio-cognitive* or *role-playing view*, which looks at the relationship between the hypnotist and the participant or client. The hypnotised person is seen to play a *social role*. Having seen television programmes on hypnosis or read about it, most people have a reasonable understanding of what it involves. Lynn *et al.* (1990) and Spanos (1991) reported how participants give statements about changes in perception and feelings which they *expect* to experience. This is seen *not* to be an example of the participant lying but rather that they sincerely believe they are experiencing an altered state of awareness and have no choice but to act as they feel or as suggested.

Kinnunen *et al.* (1994) thus felt that the behaviour of participants and their reports of experiences whilst hypnotised are genuine but reflect their beliefs about hypnosis. A cognitive psychological concept named 'strategic enactment' (Spanos, 1991) proposed that the participant is actively endeavouring to create the experiences described by the hypnotist (for example, amnesia) by adopting some appropriate cognitive strategy which, if used successfully, may be attributed to 'being hypnotized'. Wagstaff (1991) contended that when the participant is unable to develop an appropriate strategy to create the effect desired by the hypnotist, he or she will in many cases feel obliged to report or consciously act out the intended response.

Theoretical explanations of hypnosis do not affect the way hypnosis is used in practice but clinicians tend to veer towards the 'state' end of the continuum. The distinction made by Heap (1996) between trance and suggestion is seen to be more helpful in clinical applications (see page 497).

■ Clinical applications of hypnosis

Heap (1996) felt there can be no doubt that cognitive and social factors are important determinants of the responses of the participants, often dependent on the context in which hypnosis is taking place. He argued that debate on the 'state' or 'non-state' nature of hypnosis can be compared to the analogy of the blind man feeling the different parts of the elephant. Everyone is correct, in some way, but without general agreement. He believed the debate stems from a failure to agree on a definition of hypnosis independent of any theory. Oakley *et al.* (1996) noted that the state and non-state debate is now blurred with the realisation that these are not mutually exclusive forms of explanation – both are possible, as different parts of the process.

All clinicians emphasise that hypnosis is *not* a therapy in its own right, it is seen to be an adjunct, enabling context for the delivery of therapy. Many such as Vingoe (1987) suggest that labels such as 'hypnotherapy' and 'hypnotherapist' are misleading and should be abandoned, even though widely used in psychology.

14.13 Clinical applications of hypnosis with adults

Stress management
May be approached using deep relaxation produced by hypnotic suggestion, sometimes with the addition of 'special place' imagery, and the use of a keyword or object to elicit the relaxed response by post-hypnotic suggestion at a later time (Stein, 1963).

Insomnia
The deep relaxation associated with hypnosis, although not resulting in the participant falling asleep, can be used to help insomnia (Gibson and Heap, 1991).

Pain relief
Hypnosis has been widely and effectively used to counteract both acute and protracted pain. Established cognitive-behavioural methods of pain control involving imagery, relaxation, dissociation and distraction are enhanced when delivered in a hypnotic context (Hart and Alden, 1994).

Phobias
The cognitive-behavioural approach used with phobias, involving hierarchy-based covert desensitisation techniques, are particularly effective in combination with hypnosis (Crawford and Barabasz, 1993).

Regression
There are many 'uncovering' or 'exploratory' techniques used. Resolution of traumatic experiences exposed via exploratory techniques is frequently achieved in hypnosis (Watkins, 1993). Case study A in figure 14.14 is an example of a safe remembering technique used with a survivor of childhood abuse.

Depression
With the advent of effective cognitive-behavioural methods for treating depression, the use of hypnosis is becoming more widely accepted (Alladin and Heap, 1991).

The use of hypnosis in therapy is dependent on the background of the therapist and the therapy used. The importance of this is emphasised by both the American and British Medical Associations, who run recognised, accredited courses on clinical and applied hypnosis. A number of clinical applications are summarised in box 14.13.

Children respond readily to hypnosis due to their capacity to become involved in fantasy. Many childhood disorders are amenable to hypnosis, although Hart and Hart (1996) noted that it is underused, and often only as a last resort when more traditional methods have failed. Due to misconceptions of hypnosis, mainly a result of stage hypnotism, many parents may refuse the use of hypnosis on their child. Olness and Gardner (1988) discussed the use of hypnosis for the following childhood conditions:

- Acute and chronic pain.
- Anxiety disorders, such as phobias and exam anxiety.
- Sleep disorders.
- Habit disorders such as speech problems, enuresis and tics.
- Medical problems including asthma, dermatological problems, headaches and migraine (see Case study B in figure 14.14).

Hart and Hart (1996) reaffirmed that the important variable is that the therapist is trained firstly to work with children and only secondly in the use of hypnosis. Using self-hypnosis, children have been shown able to control physiological processes such as peripheral blood flow and bronchial dilation.

The use of hypnosis by specialists can be seen to be beneficial across a wide range of disorders and for a wide age range of clients, from childhood to adulthood. The success is seen to be due to the appropriate adaptation of the method to the personality, capabilities and motivation of the client. Oakley *et al.* (1996) saw it increasing the effectiveness of therapy, expanding clinical horizons and facilitating rapport with clients. In figure 14.14, two case studies demonstrate the usefulness of hypnosis in therapy.

(Suggested answers on page 508.)

Activity 13

Make a table showing the different states of awareness. Try to give a psychological benefit for each.

Meditation

Meditation is a form of mental relaxation which helps to produce a state of personal well-being and peace of mind that is in harmony with the world. Traditional techniques are devices from Zen buddhism. For example, *transcendental meditation*, a form of oncentrative meditation made popular in the 1960s by Maharishi Mahesh Yogi, involves concentrating the mind on repeating words or syllables called mantras.

During meditation, physiological arousal is reduced, blood flow stabilises and blood lactate levels fall (Benson and Friedman, 1985; Shapiro, 1985). Electroencephalograms show high levels of alpha activity (Proto, 1989).

Meditation may not produce a unique state of awareness. Roediger *et al.* (1984) found that people report similar states after jogging, chopping wood, climbing mountains and sexual intercourse. However, Harre and Lamb (1983) were convinced that meditation is more than this. Its true potential can only be realised when used as a means to personal development, insight and autonomy.

Delmonte (1990; 1995) described how the mind, in certain respects, observes itself observing the outside world.

Outcomes of meditation include expanded awareness, perceptual alteration, loss of orientation in time and space. The experiences can be negative as well as positive. The highest level consciousness reported is blissful and subtle, an almost sensationless state. Many years of meditation are needed to reach such states.

Many sports psychologists such as Cox *et al.* (1993) found meditation useful in achieving maximum performance from athletes. It helps to reduce stress before an event and also helps athletes relax different muscle groups and appreciate differences in muscle tension.

14.14 Case studies demonstrating use of hypnosis in therapy

Case study A

A sexually abused *adult* client, who needed to revisit and resolve some early experiences, was helped by Oakley, and reported by Oakley *et al.* (1996). A 'special place' had been established. This was a roof fortress, with a roof garden. The client chose a helicopter as a means of transport and the roof garden acquired a helipad. This enabled the client to fly back to a 'happy time' in her childhood, landing in a barn. Imagery was used extensively and she reported wearing a dress with blue and yellow flowers as a six-year-old. She was able to describe the surroundings in detail, along with the sounds and smells of the farm. The client found the helicopter very useful, as it could land and take off quickly if the memories became traumatic. It could also hover at a distance, representing safety and control.

Case study B

A thirteen-year-old *boy* was reported by Hart and Alden (1994). He had suffered frequent tension headaches for a period of three years, not responding to analgesic medication, although coolness applied to his head gave some relief. He enjoyed flying so he was asked to imagine being on a plane. Imagery was used to enhance this, such as reminding him of the 'no smoking' seats on the plane. He was asked to walk around the plane and find the 'no headache' seats and ask the flight assistant for help if required. Once seated in the 'no headache' seat he was asked to reach up and turn on the air-conditioning by twisting the appropriate knob. It was suggested that this would result in cool air blowing across his forehead, removing discomfort. This technique proved useful and he was asked to practise it daily. One week later he reported it had helped relieve the headache. Over a period of three months he found it helpful in reducing the number of headaches and in controlling the headache if one arose.

Psychoactive drugs

Psychoactive drugs alter states of awareness by affecting the functioning of the nervous system either by inhibition (with depressants), increased excitation (with stimulants) or distortion (with hallucinogens). Some have been used for thousands of years to achieve altered states of awareness (for example cocaine) and many are used in medicine (for example morphine). They can also be abused, with devastating consequences. (Psychoactive drugs and their effect on the nervous system are discussed further in Unit 12 pages 401–2.)

Self-assessment questions

11 Differentiate between *trance* and *suggestion* and describe how these are seen to interact during hypnosis.

12 Note some of the physiological and psychological characteristics of those people found susceptible to hypnosis.

13 Outline *two* properties of hypnosis which have been supported empirically, and *two* properties which have caused concern and are of questionable use.

14 Discuss the 'state' and 'non-state' controversy on hypnosis.

15 Why might the term 'hypnotherapy' be seen as misleading?

(Suggested answers on page 509.)

Unit summary

- *Awareness* can be seen as a continuum, from zero to a finely tuned sensitivity to the environment.
- *Consciousness* is seen as being towards the sensitive end of this continuum, often used interchangeably with awareness, although psychological approaches view them differently. Several *functions* of consciousness have been identified, including the evolutionary advantages.
- *Bodily rhythms* fall into three main categories: circadian, infradian and ultradian.
- The *zeitgebers* (daily cycles of light and dark) have been modified in the laboratory and also in free-running (time-free) behaviour to show that in the absence of time-awareness, an hour a day is 'lost'.
- Several interrelated *body clocks* have been noted by researchers, including a body clock that is relatively unaffected by external factors which controls body temperature, and a weaker process affected by external factors which controls the sleep-wake cycle amongst others.
- *Jet lag and shift work* can have a disruptive effect on the zeitgebers controlling circadian rhythms, resulting in tiredness, a drop in efficiency and the likelihood of more accidents, along with sleep disturbances.
- The *suprachiasmatic nuclei* (SCN) in the hypothalamus has been found to be central to the working of the circadian clock, thought to be at individual neuron level.
- Control of seasonal rhythms in mammals involves *melatonin*, secreted by the pineal gland.
- The measurement of brain activity by EEG shows different *brain waves*, including alpha, beta, theta and delta, operating during different stages of sleep.
- Sleep progresses through *stages* approximately 90 minutes in length.
- *Rapid eye movement (REM) sleep*, also known as 'paradoxical sleep', occurs during emergent stage 1, with more time spent in this stage as the night progresses, and less time spent in stage 4.
- Sleep is one of many *altered states of awareness*. These also include dreaming, hypnosis, meditation and the effects of psychoactive drugs.

Summary cont'd.

- Human studies of *sleep deprivation* show a great diversity in the amount of sleep needed before performance and behaviour are affected, with researchers disagreeing on the optimum amount of sleep needed.
- REM sleep deprivation causes more discomfort and a compensatory *rebound phenomenon* occurring for several nights following deprivation.
- *Slow-wave sleep* increases following total sleep deprivation, taking precedence over the regulation of REM sleep, thus suggesting it to be more important.
- *Sleep disorders*, including insomnia, hypersomnia and REM-sleep dysfunction, are thought to involve disturbance of the body clock in the SCN.
- *Sleep theories* include sleep as an adaptive response, sleep as a restorative process and sleep as time when the brain is 'off-line'.
- Alternative *theories of dreams* include psychoanalytic, physiological and cognitive views, with a lack of consensus, leading some researchers to suggest that dreaming serves a variety of functions.
- Definitions of hypnosis have proved controversial, but *trance* and *suggestion* are seen to interact, with suggestion leading the participant's attention away from external circumstances and towards the physical experience.
- There are great individual differences in *hypnotic suggestibility*, but if the participant is willing to hand over some control to the hypnotist, self-hypnosis is possible. This is the first step in reinforcing therapeutic suggestions.
- Accepted *properties of hypnosis* include increased suggestibility and enhanced capacity for imagery which can have several therapeutic effects, including reduction of stress and pain relief.
- Several of the *unsubstantiated properties* of hypnosis include memory enhancement, coercion and access to unconscious material.
- *'State' and 'non-state' theories of hypnosis* are now not seen to be mutually exclusive, so both may play a part in the process of hypnosis.
- Hypnosis is not a therapy but has been found to be an *aid to therapy*, when used by trained therapists and with established therapies.
- *Meditation* can expand awareness and result in both positive and negative experiences, more recently used by sports psychologists to improve an athlete's performance.
- The effects of *psychoactive drugs* on the nervous system, through excitation and inhibition, can alter states of awareness.

Terms to define

circadian rhythms
consciousness
dreams
hidden observer
hypnosis
infradian rhythms
insomnia

meditation
REM sleep
slow-wave sleep
suggestion
trance
ultradian rhythms
zeitgebers

Further reading

Association for the Study of Dreams, PO Box 1600, Vienna, Virginia, VA 22183, USA. Publication *Dreaming*.

A peer-reviewed academic interdisciplinary journal. An annual conference is held which attracts hundreds of participants.

Baron, R A (1996) *Essentials of Psychology*, Allyn & Bacon, Boston, MA.

Covers the many areas discussed in Unit 14 on awareness, presented in Baron's usual, interesting written style.

Carlson, N R (1998) *Physiology of Behaviour*, 6th edn, Allyn & Bacon, Boston, MA.

A source book for those wishing to follow up the physiological aspects of awareness in more detail (especially Chapter 9 'Sleep').

Mind Travellers, *New Scientist* supplement, 26 April 1997.

Interesting variety of articles on sleep and dreaming including:
Concar, D 'Calling all insomniacs', pp. 2–3
Holmes, B 'Night moves', pp. 8–13
Mestel, R (A) 'Noises from the cellar', pp. 14–17
Mestel, R (B) 'Get real, Siggi', pp. 21–3
Spinney, L 'Dinning out at the Shuteye Cafe', pp. 18–20

Pinel, J P J (1997) *Biopsychology*, 3rd edn, Allyn & Bacon, Boston, MA.

Well-illustrated introduction to the fundamentals of sleep, dreaming and circadian rhythms in Chapter 12, giving detailed description and discussion of neural mechanisms involved in the circadian clock(s).

Prentice, P (1995) 'Dream analysis', *Psychology Review*, 2(1), 12–15.

Discussion of the nature and role of dreams and dreaming.

The Psychologist (1996) 9(11).

The following articles in this special edition on hypnosis try to represent a summary of research and practice in hypnosis by recognised BPS clinical psychologists:
Hart, C and Hart, B 'The use of hypnosis with children and adolescents', pp. 506–9
Heap, M 'The nature of hypnosis', pp. 498–501
Oakley, D, Alden, P and Mather, M D 'The use of hypnosis in therapy with adults', pp. 502–5

website: *http://www.hypnosis.org.uk*

Website set up by Dr Charles Barr PhD in 1997 to promote a wider understanding and acceptance of hypnosis. Known as 'Hypnosis UK'.

Answers

▰ Suggested answers to activities

7
a   REM/paradoxical sleep
b   stage 1
c   stage 4
d   stage 2

8
a   mycolonic jerk
b   microsleep
c   sleep deprivation
d   110 hours
e   boring, passive, easy cognitive tasks

12

a F
b T
c T
d F
e T

13

Table 13

State of awareness	Psychological benefit
Natural states:	
Fully conscious	Total awareness of everything which has happened, is happening and may happen in, to and around us. It gives us some control over – and flexibility to – our behaviour, adding to our chances of survival
Tonic alertness	By being aware of natural rhythms and daily bodily cycles, we can order our lives to make the best use of our time and abilities
Phasic alertness	Through physiological arousal, our ability to cope with unexpected or novel situations increases
Focal attention	Enables us to concentrate on important or novel stimuli without interference from other stimuli
Peripheral attention	Enables us to dissociate actions, memories or events which are not immediately necessary to our situation, but which may at any moment be needed
Sleep	Enables us to conserve energy, replenish body chemicals, relax tired bodies and minds – and dream
Dreaming	Gives us connections with our unconscious, enables us to reorganise events of the past day, helps in decision making, creating new ideas and possibly predicting future events

Table 13 Cont'd

State of awareness	Psychological benefit
Artificial states:	
Meditation	Although placed under the 'artificial' heading, we are in control of this state and can decide if and when to induce it. It enables conscious relaxation of body and mind, give us feelings of well-being and harmony with the world, and an insight into our thoughts and motives
Hypnosis	Enables us to become susceptible to someone else controlling our thoughts and actions – which may be of benefit when we want to give up an unwanted habit.
Psychoactive drugs	When used in moderation, may free us from pain, tension or lethargy. However, there is a danger that because of their initial effects, we may overuse (abuse) them

■ Suggested answers to self-assessment questions

1

There are several definitions including behavioural, physiological, psychoanalytical and humanistic (see page 475).

2

Circadian, infradian, ultradian (see page 477)

3

Fluctuations in body temperature may have greater impact on simple tasks than more complex ones (see pages 478–9).

4

Problems include fatigue, sleep disorders, increased chance of heart attacks and ulcers, higher rate of accidents.

5

Research could include:

■ Ralph *et al.* (1990) – change in sleep-wake cycles of rats.

■ Ginty *et al.* (1993) – activation of the retinohypothalamic tract controls gene expression.

■ Michel *et al.* (1993) – molecular mechanisms in individual cells.

6

See page 482 and box 14.5 on page 485.

7

You may have suggested:

■ Minimum of $8^1/_2$ hours (Bonnet, 1997).

■ Minimum of 6 hours (Horne, 1997).

■ Amount of time irrelevant – correlation with body temperature (Boivin, 1997).
(See page 487 for further discussion.)

8

Points which could have been included:

■ Deprivation of REM results in a rebound phenomenon.

■ Brain recovery from biochemical rigours of slow-wave sleep – glycogen hypothesis (Benington and Heller, reported in Holmes, 1997).

■ Consolidation of memory (Smith, 1997, p. 27).
Conversely:

■ Antidepressant effect.

■ Theta rhythm is not consistent in humans.

■ Dolphins have no REM but are intelligent mammals.
(See pages 489–92 for further discussion of these topics.)

9

You could have chosen from:

■ Sleep as an adaptive response (Webb 1975, 1982; Meddis 1975; 1977).

■ Sleep as a restorative process (Horne).

■ Brain is 'off-line' to exercise infrequent circuits (Kreuger, 1997).
(See pages 491–3 for further discussion of these topics.)

10 There are three main views to choose from:

■ Psychoanalytic (Freud) – repressed desires.

■ Physiological (Crick and Mitchison 1983, 1986; Hobson, cited in Mestel, 1997) – activation-synthesis.

■ Cognitive (Evans, 1984; Antrobus, 1991) – brain reviewing, updating, reprogramming.
(See pages 494–6 for further discussion on these topics.)

11

Trance and suggestion are explained on page 497. Suggestion leads the participant's attention away from external circumstances towards more physical experiences, whereas trance leads the participant to concentrate on inner experiences.

12

Physiological

■ Females slightly more susceptible (Gibson and Heap, 1991).

■ Children are more susceptible than adults.
Psychological

■ More efficient frontolimbic attention system (Crawford *et al.*, 1993).

■ More posterior left hemisphere involvement (Crawford *et al.*, 1994).

■ Bulimics more susceptible than anorexics (Covina *et al.*, 1994).
A summary of characteristics taken from Baron (1996) can be found on page 498.

13

Summary of properties which have been empirically supported can be found in figure 14.12 on page 499. Those properties of questionable use include:

■ Memory enhancement.

■ Hypnotic coercion.

■ Access to unconscious material.

■ Suppression of experience from conscious awareness.
(See pages 500–1 for further details.)

14

Review of 'state' and 'non-state' theories can be found on page 502.

■ *State* – neo-dissociation theory suggests hypnosis operates by the dissociation in consciousness.

■ *Non-state* – include the socio-cognitive/role-playing view which focuses on the relationship between the hypnotist and the participant.
Evaluation could include Heap (1996) – problems of definition and Oakley *et al.* (1996) – theories are not mutually exclusive.

15

Hypnosis is *not* a therapy. It can be seen as a very important *aid* to therapy dependent on the expertise and background knowledge of the therapist using recognised therapies.

Unit 15

Motivation, Emotion and Stress

Graham Davies, Lorna Jones and Irene Taylor

This unit covers:

Motivation

Emotion

Stress

By the end of this unit, you should be able to:

- discuss brain activities related to motivation, emotion and stress
- understand physiological and alternative explanations of motivation, emotion and stress
- discuss the effects of stress, including the relationship between stress and illness
- demonstrate awareness of strategies which may be used to reduce stress.

Unit 15 Contents

Introduction

If a friend invited you to the Bahamas for a holiday next month how would your react?

Think 'Ooh, the Bahamas – sun, sea and romance – great'! Say 'yes please' and feel excited?

Think 'I'd love to go, but my exams are next month'. Say 'no thank you' and feel disappointed?

Think 'That's marvellous, but I can't afford it'. Say 'yes please' (in spite of this) because you feel you need a holiday and start planning how you will manage; or 'no thanks' (because of it) and feel envious of people with money?

You may have no enthusiasm for anything because you have a headache (or have just eaten a large meal) and say 'no' initially, but later regret this decision. You may even say 'no' because you do not want to go, and would prefer to climb a mountain! All these choices probably caused you some anxiety and may have made demands on you that you felt difficult to meet.

In fact, many considerations need to be taken into account for any course of action. The final choice depends on how much we want to do that particular thing, the factors we perceive to motivate us to do it and how we are feeling (our emotions) at the time. Feeling pressured into doing things we feel unable or unwilling to do is an aspect of stress. It is these phenomena – motivation, emotion and stress – which are discussed in this unit.

Motivation

Physiological mechanisms of motivation

Motivation is concerned with wants and needs. It refers to the processes of arousing, maintaining and regulating specific patterns of behaviour. It impels, or pushes, organisms into activity, giving them direction. The words 'motivation' and 'emotion' come from the Latin meaning 'to move'

and the psychology of motivation indeed aims to explain what moves us, and why we do what we do. Motivation often accounts for why different people, with equal abilities, do not achieve similarly. Figure 15.1 shows examples of different kinds of motivators. It seems obvious why the donkey is motivated in each case. What do you think is motivating the farmer?

Much of our behaviour is motivated towards pleasurable consequences, away from pain and hurt. Some behaviour, however, seems motivated by forces over which we apparently have no control, or which have survival value. In this section, we look at some examples of physiological motivators, seen as *primary* motivators.

■ Hunger and eating

Food provides us with nutrients and energy to stay active and alive. Some nutrients, for example glucose, can be stored when first eaten and

Figure 15.1

Some different kinds of motivators

released later as blood glucose levels drop. The liver and adipose (fat) tissue are involved with storage, but both have limited capacities. If we avoided eating for about six weeks, we would not only exhaust our spare supplies but would also become fatally ill (body tissues break down in order to provide the blood with nutrients). Hunger prevents this happening by motivating us to eat when falling blood nutrient levels cause a physiological imbalance. The greater the imbalance, the stronger the hunger and the more we are motivated to eat, even to the extent of dreaming about food if we are unable to obtain it. This relationship between physiological need and eating seems simple, but is it?

You can probably identify several reasons for eating: boredom, the food looks (or smells) attractive, you are given it, or it is part of a meal. We often eat meals because it is a mealtime, not always because we are hungry. Mealtimes become learned habits, differing widely between individuals in terms of the number of meals eaten each day, and also what and how much is eaten and when. For example, some European cultures eat five meals a day and consume a high proportion of meat; whereas some African cultures eat only one meal a day, with very little meat. However, unless we are still growing, we tend to maintain a constant personal weight, unless conditions such as anorexia nervosa or obesity intervene.

Some people eat everything put in front of them, perhaps because this is what they were taught in childhood, or because they like the taste.

Most people, however, stop because they are satiated (have eaten enough). Cannon (1929) used the term **homeostasis**, which means self-regulating, to refer to the body's ability to maintain a relatively constant internal state. Maintaining blood nutrients – and a constant body-weight – requires a control system capable of initiating eating through hunger and stopping eating when satiated. Pinel (1997) referred to this set-point assumption whereby any such system has three components:
- a set-point mechanism which defines the set-point
- a detector mechanism which detects deviations from the set-point

- an effector mechanism which acts to eliminate the deviations.

Such systems are **negative-feedback systems** in which changes in one direction elicit compensatory effects in the opposite direction.

What makes us hungry?

We have already identified boredom, and the sight and smell of appetising food as reasons for eating, but these may be socially learned and related to hunger, or to homeostasis. So how do we know when we are hungry? Stomach contractions may be one factor. Cannon and Washburn (1912) found a significant positive correlation (relationship) between hunger pangs and stomach contractions after subjects had a balloon inflated in their stomachs. However, Wangensten and Carlson (1931) reported a normal desire for food in a patient whose stomach could not contract because it had been surgically removed! Thus, hunger pangs cannot fully answer the question.

Blood glucose level was originally seen to be the most important factor. Homeostatic mechanisms were seen as keeping this relatively constant by causing excess glucose (for example after a meal) to be stored as glycogen in the liver and muscles, then reconverting it to glucose as blood levels fall (for example after exercise, or before a meal). Cells obtain glucose from the blood and utilise it during metabolic (chemical) reactions. However, glucose can only cross cell membranes when the hormone insulin is present. It is therefore not available to cells in its absence. (Hormones are chemicals which control a specific target organ or body process.) According to the various versions of glucostatic theory, we become hungry when blood glucose levels drop below their set-point and we become satiated when the glucose levels reach their set-point again. This is a logical theory as glucose is the brain's primary fuel.

Another set-point theory is lipostatic theory related to body fat. Lipids (fats) are stored in *adipocytes* and these make up the fatty tissue of the body (known as *adipose* tissue). As the level of fats in the adipocytes drops, compensatory eating occurs to adjust the level. Nisbett (1972) suggested we have body-weight stabilisers around this point which can be modified by damage to the hypothalamus (see pages 517–18). Support for this theory comes from the fact that the weight of most adults remains relatively constant.

Glucostatic theory and lipostatic theory were viewed as complementary not mutually exclusive. Glucostatic theory was considered to account for initiating eating and termination once satiated, whereas long-term regulation was covered by lipostatic theory. These set-point theories do have several weaknesses, as noted by Pinel (1997):

- For any warm-blooded species to survive, a hunger/food system which prevents energy deficits is needed, rather than a system which stops as soon as immediate needs are met (Weingarten, 1985).

- Early studies found that a large reduction in body fat or blood glucose induced eating in laboratory animals, but no such effects seem to occur in normal humans. Efforts to reduce the size of a meal by asking participants to consume a high-calorie drink before eating have not been successful. Lowe (1993) found that *beliefs* about the calorific content of the drink seem to influence the size of the subsequent meal rather than the actual calorific content.

- Set-point theories fail to recognise the influence of factors such as taste, learning and social influences on hunger and eating.

Activity 1

Imagine your favourite food in front of you.
Perhaps a bowl of strawberries, a plate of fish and chips or a curry?
Are you beginning to feel hungry?

The sudden desire for a food is not always related to hunger pangs. When we have already eaten a large meal we may often be tempted by the sight or smell of a dessert or cake. This seems to contradict set-point theories and has led to the development of positive-incentive theory. This focuses on the *anticipated* pleasure of eating and its *positive-incentive value* (Bolles, 1980; Booth, 1981).

This theory proposes that the degree of hunger depends on the positive-incentive value of the food at that particular time. This can be affected by several factors such as the anticipated taste of the food to be consumed, time of day in relation to meal times, blood glucose levels, and social factors such as the presence of others who might be eating (Pinel, 1997).

Unlike the set-point theories, positive-incentive theory sees the major determinant of hunger to be due to the interaction of several factors (Cabanac, 1971). So, returning to our example, if you have just eaten a large meal the positive-incentive value of eating more food is low, but if your friends are all having a delicious ice-cream dessert your anticipation of the taste may induce you to have one also.

Several researchers have suggested that body-weight drifts around a *settling-point*, the equilibrium level achieved by the various factors influencing body-weight (Wirtshafter and Davis, 1977; Booth *et al.*, 1981). This is based on the idea that as the body fat levels increase, changes occur to inhibit further increases until a balance is achieved between all the factors encouraging weight gain and loss. This provides a loose kind of homeostatic regulation without returning the body to a set-point. In this way the body-weight remains stable only as long as there are no changes in the contributory factors. If there are changes, the input is limited by negative feedback which prevents further change in that direction. In the set-point model, the negative feedback would have triggered a return to the set-point. Pinel (1997) likened the settling-point theory to a 'leaky-barrel model' (figure 15.2):

- The amount of water entering the hose is the equivalent of food available.
- Water pressure at the nozzle can be seen as the positive-incentive value of the available food.
- The amount of water entering the barrel can be seen as the amount of energy consumed.
- The water level in the barrel is equivalent to the body-fat level.
- The amount of water leaking out of the barrel can be seen as the energy expended.

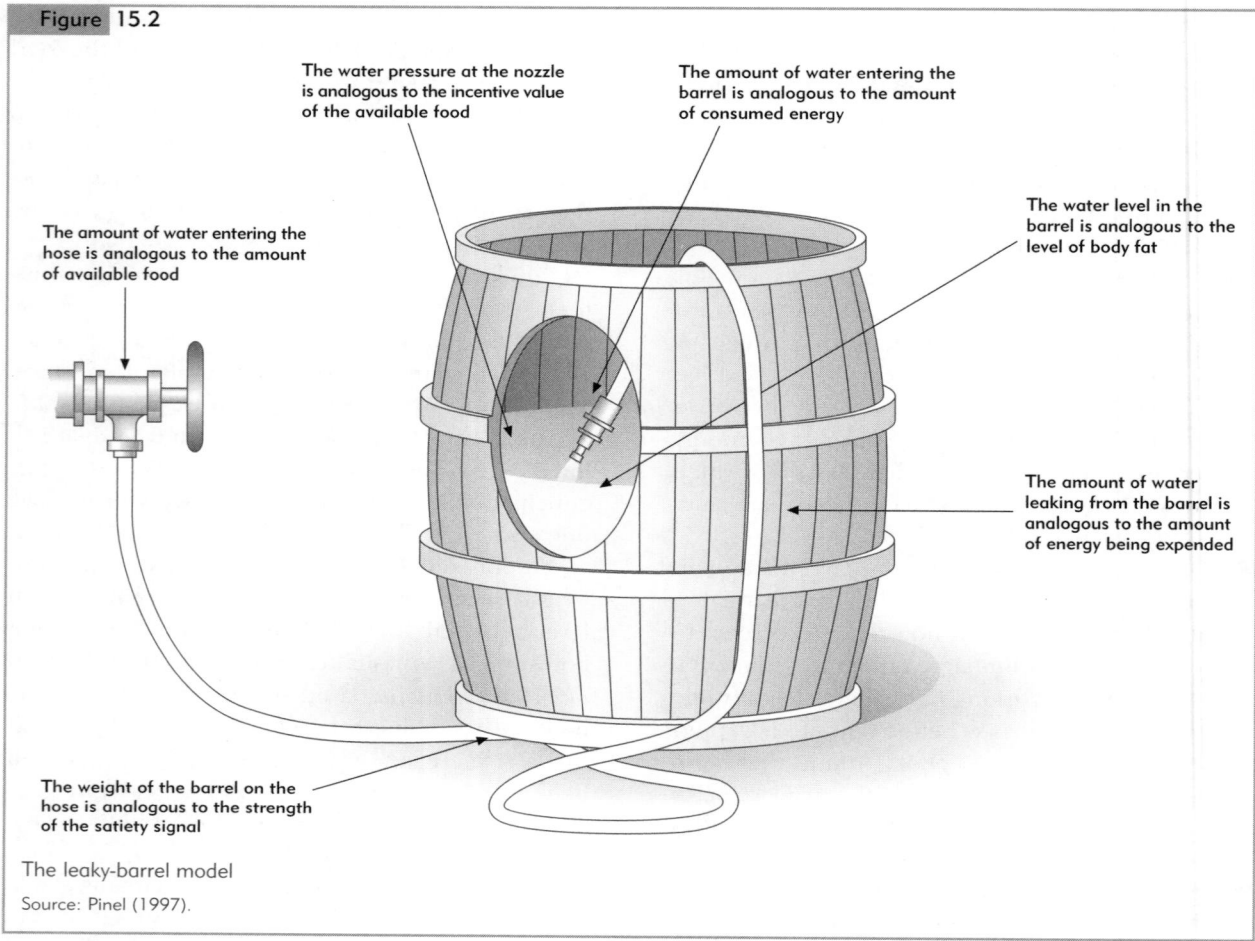

Figure 15.2

The water pressure at the nozzle is analogous to the incentive value of the available food

The amount of water entering the barrel is analogous to the amount of consumed energy

The amount of water entering the hose is analogous to the amount of available food

The water level in the barrel is analogous to the level of body fat

The amount of water leaking from the barrel is analogous to the amount of energy being expended

The weight of the barrel on the hose is analogous to the strength of the satiety signal

The leaky-barrel model

Source: Pinel (1997).

■ The weight of the barrel on the hose can be seen as the strength of the satiety signal.

Pinel (1997) suggested that the leaky-barrel model is more consistent with the research data and makes fewer assumptions. The model helps understand and predict changes in body-weight in various situations and the psychological mechanisms likely to mediate such changes. Unlike set-point theories, it also allows a more positive approach towards changing body-weight by changing factors which influence energy intake and output. Although an interesting novel suggestion, the leaky-barrel model needs to be more specific about the contributory factors if it is to be seen as an explanation of body-weight homeostasis.

Activity 2

Choose the most appropriate word to complete the following sentences:
a   Absorption of nutrients in the body takes place through the _____ or upper intestine.
b   The components of a set-point system are a set-point mechanism, a _____ and an effector.
c   _____ theory suggests that hunger and satiety are regulated by a blood glucose set-point.
d   Evidence suggests that hunger is a function of the _____ value of food.

(Suggested answers on page 564.)

Satiety and cessation of eating

Booth (1981) thought that learning plays an important role in satiety. We learn what foods we enjoy eating, how much of them we can eat and when, so that we meet our body's nutritional requirements. In other words, we monitor and regulate our food intake by experience. This regulation is most effective when we eat familiar foods because we can predict their effect.

Stomach receptors appear to monitor both quantity and quality of food. However, severing the gastric branch of the vagus nerve does not inhibit eating. So, although neural receptors may be responsible for monitoring stomach volume, the food content must be monitored by another kind of receptor. Koopmans (1981) transplanted an extra stomach and intestine into rats and joined the major arteries and veins of the implants into the animal's circulatory system. When food was injected into the implanted stomach and kept there, the animal ate less in proportion to its volume and calorific content. The transplanted system had no nerves suggesting that the satiety signal reached the brain via the blood. Nutrients are not absorbed from the stomach so the source of the satiety signal was seen to be a chemical released from the stomach in response to calorific value and volume of food. These gastrointestinal satiety chemicals are known as peptides, a type of hormone, and are released when ingested food interacts with receptors in the gastrointestinal tract.

Gibbs *et al.* (1973) injected one of these peptides (cholecystokinin (CCK)), which is released in the duodenum, into hungry rats and found they ate smaller meals. This suggested that circulating gut peptides provide the brain with information about the quantity and nature of food in the gastrointestinal tract, affecting satiety. Several gut peptides have been found to bind to receptors in the brain and several have been found to reduce food intake, including CCK (Woods and Gibbs, 1989). Part of this inhibitory effect of peptides is thought to be indirect. Researchers still disagree about whether CCK serves as an intestinal satiety signal, although presence of food in the intestine does inhibit eating. Research suggests that nutrient detectors are located inside the duodenum before digestion has taken place (Greenberg *et al.*, 1991).

The liver is the first organ to learn that food has been received from the intestines. Research has found the liver to have detectors sensitive to glucose (Russek, 1971; Novin *et al.*, 1983). These signals are thought to consolidate the signals coming from the stomach and the duodenum.

Long-term satiety factors may be provided from the adipose (fat) tissue or from increased levels of insulin, some of which travels to the hypothalamus, part of the brain found to be highly involved in the control of hunger and satiety.

Control centres for hunger

Magender (1826) proposed hunger centres within the brain, which control both the onset and cessation of eating. Mohr (1840) reported hyperphagia (overeating) in patients with lesions in the hypothalamus, at the top of the brainstem (see figure 15.3).

Lesioning the ventromedial hypothalamus (VMH) causes hyperphagia in rats (Hetherington

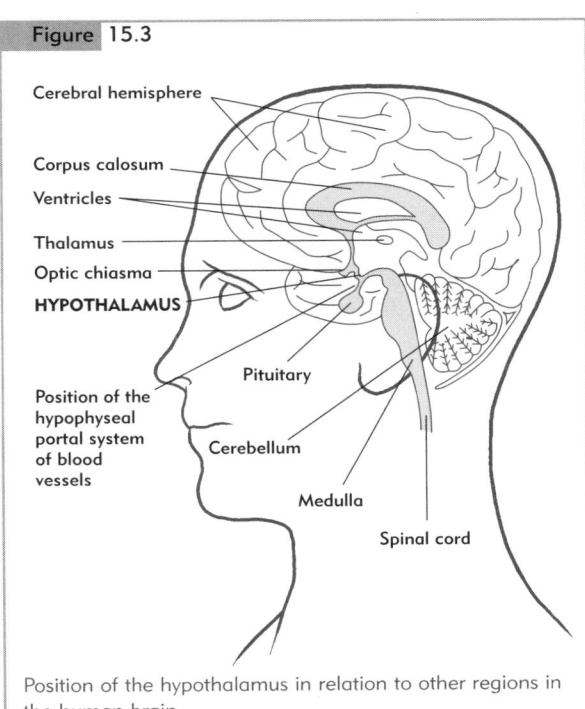

Figure 15.3

Cerebral hemisphere
Corpus calosum
Ventricles
Thalamus
Optic chiasma
HYPOTHALAMUS
Position of the hypophyseal portal system of blood vessels
Pituitary
Cerebellum
Medulla
Spinal cord

Position of the hypothalamus in relation to other regions in the human brain and Ranson, 1940). However, Hoebel and Teitelbaum (1966) found that the hyperphagia only lasted a few days, after which food intake returned to near normal levels, enough to maintain a new, higher weight at an obese level. Obese rats, injected with insulin and force-fed to super-obese weights, reduced their intake until their post-operational, obese weights were regained. Also, when the same animals were starved until they returned to pre-operational weights, they became hyperphagic until they reached their obese weights once more. Non-obese rats given the same treatment return to normal weight.

Nerve tracts passing through the hypothalamus are often destroyed during operations. It is possible that feeding anomalies may be due to loss of nerve impulses through these tracts, rather than to destroying control centres themselves. Three tracts which may be involved are the noradrinergic bundle, which relays impulses from sense organs to the sensory cortex; the trigeminal system carrying impulses to and from the thalamus and facial muscles of chewing, and the nigrostriatal bundle which initiates motor activity.

Subsequent research has found that lateral hypothalamus (LH) lesions produce a wide range of motor disturbances in addition to the effects on feeding and drinking, suggesting that the LH is not only a satiety or feeding centre. Although not a feeding centre, the LH has neurons that respond to the positive-incentive properties of food rather than the food itself (Rolls and Rolls, 1982). When monkeys were allowed to eat a palatable food there was a decline in the response of LH neurons to that food but their response to other palatable foods

did not decline. Satiety seems to be somewhat taste-specific, with appetite for different food unaffected, known as sensory-specific satiety.

The effects of ventromedial hypothalamus (VMH) lesions on eating seem to be partially attributable to the destruction of fibres connected to the paraventricular nucleus, focusing attention on the role of eating. Increased eating occurs when there are injections of noradrenaline, GABA, neuropeptide Y, galanin peptide and opioid peptides in certain conditions (Leibowitz, 1992). Noradrenaline, GABA and neuropeptide Y increase the consumption of carbohydrates by increasing the size of carbohydrate meals. It is unclear whether noradrenaline stimulates eating directly, or indirectly by increasing the secretion of insulin by the pancreas. Galanin peptide alters the secretion of insulin and corticosterone which indicates metabolic as well as behavioural effects (Tempel and Leibowitz, 1990).

The mechanisms by which eating is influenced by these chemicals is still unknown. However, cutting the branch of the vagus nerve serving the pancreas significantly reduces such eating and suggests the effects on eating may be secondary to the metabolic effects of the chemical injections. The neurochemical effects on the hypothalamus can be seen in table 15.4.

■ Obesity and eating disorders

Obesity is found in animals which store body fat in excessive quantities. It can be defined as having 30 per cent or more in excess of appropriate weight. Obesity has been identified as a major health problem for humans. There has been a rapid

Table 15.4

Neurochemical	Site of action	Effect
Norepinephrine (NE)	Paraventricular nucleus	Stimulates carbohydrate intake
Serotonin (5-HT)	Paraventricular nucleus	Inhibits carbohydrate intake
Galanin peptide	Lateral hypothalamus	Stimulates fat intake
Neuropeptide Y	Lateral hypothalamus	Stimulates ravenous eating; effect suppressed by α_2 blockers

Neurochemicals that affect eating when injected into the hypothalamus
Source: Carlson (1994).

increase in obesity, especially in the USA where it has doubled in the twentieth century (Kuczmarski, 1992). This rapid increase suggests environmental rather than genetic factors are responsible. Set-point theories cannot explain this increase; they support that permanent weight gain should not occur in normal adults.

In evolutionary terms we now live in an environment very different from that of our ancestors. In many cultures foods of high positive-incentive value are now readily available, leading to a high level of consumption. Almost all excess body-weight is carried in the form of fat. A certain amount is necessary to allow for daily fluctuation; obesity occurs when deposits exceed withdrawals. We expend energy through muscular activity (exercise) and the production of heat. Heat, made through the resting metabolism and digesting and assimilating food, accounts for most of our energy expenditure (Calles-Escandon and Horton, 1992). Physical activity accounts for only a small part of energy expenditure. Many weight-loss programmes emphasise the role of exercise but most studies have found that exercise does not facilitate weight loss (Sweeney et al., 1993). Exercise does have many other benefits such as cardiovascular fitness and a sense of wellbeing so it can be seen as beneficial to people of all weights.

The mechanisms that control eating usually work well in most people so what can the research on the normal regulation of food intake tell us about eating disorders?

Variables such as lack of impulse control, poor ability to defer gratification and maladaptive eating styles have been suggested as possible causes of obesity. Rodin et al. (1989) reviewed the research evidence and found little support for any of these factors. They also found depression and unhappiness to be the *effect* of obesity rather than its cause, with dieting making the situation worse. There have been many interlinked variables which do appear to play an important role in obesity and these are noted in figure 15.5. Metabolic factors also play an important role in obesity.

Carlson (1994) suggested obesity is not an *eating* disorder but rather a *metabolic* disorder. An efficient metabolism results in an excess of calories which are stored as fat, whereas an inefficient metabolism

15.5 Factors linked with obesity

■ Habit
The effect of learning in the early active years of life may influence the amount we eat. We are often encouraged to eat everything we are given. Later in life, when we are less active, we are conditioned to eat in a similar manner, perhaps eating more than we need.

■ Metabolism
The internal, physiological processes, which include the production of energy from nutrients, vary greatly between individuals and may be genetic.

■ 'Yo-yo' effect
The effects of dieting and relapse can result in a change of metabolism. Steen et al. (1988) measured the metabolic rate in two groups of high-school wrestlers, one which fasted before a match and binged after (to qualify for a lower-weight group) and a control group which did not. The experimental group developed a more efficient metabolism and thus became fat more quickly and lost weight more slowly when fasting again. Carlson and Buskist (1997) suggested such people have difficulty maintaining normal body-weight as they become older.

■ Stress
Stress may also cause excessive eating, due to an increased arousal of motor activity, which may result in becoming overweight. Carlson (1977) suggested that social pressures may then cause enough stress to stimulate the nigrostriatal bundle to increase eating, so causing a vicious circle in which excess weight leads to stress, which leads to eating, and thus to further weight increase.

results in no excess calories. A fuel-efficient person therefore runs the risk of obesity (Carlson, 1994). Metabolic rate has been found to have a strong genetic basis (Bouchard, 1989, 1991; Price and Gottesman, 1991). Stunkard *et al.* (1986) found the body-weight of adults who had been adopted as infants to correlate with their *biological* parents more than their adopted parents. Similar findings come from Sorensen *et al.* (1989) when comparing full and half siblings.

Obese strains of rats and mice have provided insight into the biological factors related to obesity. The Zucker rats possess a pair of defective genes which lead to obesity. They have chemically high levels of insulin in their blood and exhibit other endocrinal differences. Brain abnormalities have been suggested for the obesity. Sanacora *et al.* (1992) found Neuropeptide Y in these rats to be extremely high. It is not known if this is also related to human obesity.

Genetically obese (Ob) mice have a low metabolism, overeat and get extremely fat. They often develop diabetes in adulthood, as do obese people. The protein *leptin* is normally secreted in fat cells but not in the Ob mice due to a genetic mutation. Leptin affects the metabolism and acts as an anti-obesity hormone. Research found Ob mice given daily injections of leptin develop an increase in body temperature and metabolic rate, become more active and eat less. Weight eventually returns to normal. This also occurs when the leptin is injected directly into the brain, indicating that the chemical acts on the neural circuits controlling eating and metabolism (Carlson and Buskist, 1997). Tartaglia *et al.* (1995), using molecular genetic techniques, discovered the leptin receptor in the brain. In order for leptin to reduce weight it must have functioning receptors in the brain. It is thought that some people have leptin receptors that do not respond to the leptin in the blood.

Obesity is the greatest eating problem in humans today but anorexia nervosa and bulimia nervosa affect some people, especially adolescent women. The factors involved in these disorders are discussed in Unit 25 on page 928. The effects of bulimia nervosa, as with anorexia nervosa, cause severe health problems for the sufferer, most of which can be reversed once normal eating habits are reinstated (Cooper, 1995). Unfortunately, this option is not chosen by many anorexics or bulimics.

Figure 15.6 contains a report of Pinel's (1997) discussion with an anorexic student which highlights the serious problem there is with this terrible disorder and the practical value of research in this area.

■ Thirst and drinking

As in the control of eating and satiety, the hypothalamus is thought to be centrally involved in thirst and drinking (Epstein, 1982; Grossman, 1990).

Most drinking, like eating, occurs in the absence of deficits and as such is known as spontaneous drinking. This is thought to be motivated by positive-incentive properties of the liquid involved, the anticipated pleasurable effects of the beverage. This includes the flavour, pharmacological and social factors. Water deprivation increases the positive-incentive value of virtually all salt-free drinks. Rolls *et al.* (1980) found that after 24 hours of deprivation water itself was found to have a pleasant taste. Water is also needed for the digestion and metabolism of food, so drinking often occurs in association with eating.

Set-point theories suggest that drinking terminates when satiated, but this model cannot explain the spontaneous drinking noted above nor the fact that drinking usually stops before the water has been absorbed into the body. Also, all animals tend to drink more than they need when water is readily available. Sham drinking has been found to be proportional to the length of the preceding period of water deprivation (Blass and Hall, 1976), despite the water leaving via a fistula before it can be absorbed. Longer periods of water deprivation produce greater increases in the positive-incentive value of water. Even total replenishment of an animal's water resources has only a small inhibitory effect on deprivation-induced drinking. These findings cannot be explained by set-point theories. Sensory-specific satiety affects drinking as it does eating. Animals drink more when there are a

15.6 A conversation with an anorexic student (Pinel, 1997)

She began by telling me how much she had been enjoying the course and how sorry she was to be dropping out of the university. She was articulate and personable, and her grades were first-class. Her problem was anorexia; she weighed only 82 pounds, and she was about to be hospitalised.

'But don't you want to eat?' I asked naively. 'Don't you see that your plan to go to medical school will go up in smoke if you don't eat?'

'Of course I want to eat. I know I am terribly thin – my friends tell me I am. Believe me, I know this is wrecking my life. I try to eat, but I just can't force myself. In a strange way, I am pleased with my thinness.'

She was upset, and I was embarrassed by my insensitivity. 'It's too bad you're dropping out of the course before we cover the chapter on eating,' I said, groping for safer ground.

'Oh, I've read it already,' she responded. 'It's the first chapter I looked at. It had quite an effect on me; a lot of things started to make more sense. The bit about positive incentives and learning was really good. I think my problem began when food started

to lose its positive-incentive value for me – in my mind, I kind of associated food with being fat and all the boyfriend problems I was having. This made it easy to diet, but every once in a while I would get so hungry that I would lose control and eat all of the things that I shouldn't. I would eat so much that I would feel ill. So I would put my finger down my throat and make myself throw up. This made me feel a bit better, and it kept me from gaining weight, but I think it taught my body to associate my favourite foods with illness – kind of a conditioned taste aversion. Now, food has no incentive value for me whatsoever. What do you think of my theory?'

Her insightfulness impressed me; it made me feel all the more sorry that she was going to discontinue her studies.

After a lengthy chat, she got up to leave, and I walked her to the door of my office. I wished her luck and made her promise to come back for a visit. The image of her emaciated body walking down the hallway from my office has stayed with me.

variety of beverages available and also when a drink is reintroduced after several days of non-availability (Pinel and Rovner, 1977). De Bold *et al.* (1981; De Bold, 1985) discovered that a hormone atrial natriuretic peptide (ANP) secreted by the atria of the heart appears to be an emergency back-up system that helps prevent high volumes of blood plasma by promoting the excretion of sodium. ANP is secreted when the atria are stretched more than usual. Blood plasma is controlled mainly by sodium concentration but ANP also increases the excretion of water, inhibits the secretion of renin, vasopressin, and aldersterone. It also inhibits both drinking and sodium appetite. ANP receptors are found in the adrenal medulla, the pituitary, and the brain (Quirion, 1989). At least some of the effects of ANP are exerted in the subfornical organ (SFO), part of the circumventricular system near the thalamus in the brain.

Social motives (non-homeostatic drives)

Several researchers have noted the importance of including non-homeostatic drives such as social motives. These are known as secondary drives. People set goals for themselves and then go about achieving them (Bandura, 1990; Dweck, 1990). Social motives can often be important in influencing people's actions and these develop in the context of family, friends and culture.

Wade and Tavris (1993) referred to humans as 'the curious animal'. In many ways we are governed by cognitive motives to understand and organise our experiences. We are also known as *social* animals with a need for affiliation (nAff), the desire to be with others, make friends and cooperate.

Individuals vary in their need for affiliation, some people like to be surrounded by friends, whereas others like having 'some space'. Cultures vary on the value they place on affiliation. American culture emphasises independence whereas the Japanese culture emphasises family links and group interdependence (Pascale and Athos, 1981). Most people depend on one another for different things at different times. Both sexes depend on each other, although for different reasons (Brehm, 1992). True isolates are difficult to find.

Bandura (1990) noted a need of self-efficacy, the belief that a person will succeed in what he or she sets out to do. This can come from several sources such as vicarious learning, learning experiences and psychological state at the time (see Unit 22 page 828 for more information on the development of self-efficacy). Self-efficacy affects how well someone completes a task, the commitment to the goal, and even how he or she responds to criticism. People with high self-efficacy try harder whereas those low on self-efficacy are more likely to give up. Ozer and Bandura (1990) have shown how self-efficacy can be acquired by training and by experiences that provide skills and a sense of control.

Murray (1938) first identified the need to achieve (nAch) as one of 20 human motives. This is the need to tackle and solve challenging problems. It involves a positive self-feeling associated with successful performance judged against perfection. Ausubel (1968) suggested that nAch has three components: a cognitive drive to understand, a feeling of self-enhancement and a need for approval.

Activity 3

Can you relate any of the three components of nAch to your own experience? Think of some of your achievements.

a   How strong was your wish to understand the situation?
b   How much did you gain from your success?
c   How much did you want the approval you got?

Now think of your psychology studies – how much are you motivated to achieve?

McClelland *et al.* (1953) investigated the relationship between nAch, as measured by the Thematic Apperception Test (TAT), and other characteristics of male students. The TAT involves participants studying two sets of stimulus pictures. Participants creatively describe events leading up to the scene depicted, the scene itself, and what is going to happen in the future – dramatically for the first set of pictures and imaginatively for the second. From the descriptions, scores can be assigned to several characteristics, nAch is only one of these.

Activity 4

Look at figure 15.7 and write about it in not more than 300 words. (Now read on.)

High-ranking scores are gained when the description includes working persistently and energetically in order to achieve something credible – get ahead in business or lead a group to create something. Did you write about any of these things in your own description? McClelland *et al.* (1953) found high positive correlations between nAch and course grades, maintenance of effort, aspiration and independent behaviour.

Later research found the need for achievement as shown by the TAT not to be related to an individual's conscious, self-reported need for

Figure 15.7 Example of a stimulus photo from the Thematic Apperception Test. Source: Atkinson *et al.* (1993)

achievement. Achievement motives seem to come either as an *implicit* (unconscious) motive or an *explicit* (self-aware) motive (McClelland *et al.*, 1989). An individual may express a desire to succeed at something but never appear motivated towards achieving the goal. The two types of achievement motivation respond to different incentives and have different stress and arousal correlates. Implicit motivation predicts sustained achievement motivation due to the pleasure derived from the task whereas explicit achievement motivation is more dependent on the immediate incentive rewards so will vary from situation to situation.

Some researchers have focused on *why* an individual needs to achieve. Dweck (1990) found people motivated by *performance* goals are concerned with doing well and avoiding criticism. Those motivated by *learning* goals are more concerned with increasing their competence and skills. Whether the individuals will master the task or give up appears *not to be related to ability*. However, when people are focused on how well they are performing they will often stop trying when they temporarily fail. Failure is seen as a personal fault. Conversely, those whose goal is learning regard failure as a source of useful information which will help them succeed. Failure does not discourage them, they will persevere (Elliott and Dweck, 1988) (see also Unit 2 page 66).

McClelland (1975) also found that some people are motivated by a need for power (nPower), a learned motive to dominate or control others. People who have high power motivation seek prestige and visibility. They choose powerful careers. This desire for power drives many to become leaders, but the type of power distinguishes the effective leaders from the others. Spangler and House (1991) studied the speeches, letters and biographies of 39 US presidents and found they had a lower need for affiliation and achievement but a higher need for power. The presidents also displayed a high need to use power for social rather than personal objectives.

Theories of motivation

Early theories of motivation focused on the appearance of certain kinds of behaviour at certain times, and fluctuations in responses. More recent theories have incorporated anatomical structures, physiological measurements and cognition to account for why we do things, and when.

■ Instinct theory

Imagine someone behind you trips and falls over. Would you help them, as if by instinct? Darwin (1859) believed instincts to be innate, unlearned tendencies to behave in specific ways in response to various biological and social needs.

The concept of accounting for behaviour through instincts caught on and eventually over 5000 were suggested – virtually every kind of behaviour being described as the result of an instinct. You can probably think of some original ones for yourself, for example you carry a case to college because you have a case-carrying instinct. As we rarely display stereotyped patterns of unlearned behaviour the credibility of instincts as an explanation for behaviour disappeared.

Psychoanalytic theory, however, still maintains that instincts exist. Freud accepted that physical energy is needed to drive the homeostatic functions of the body. He proposed a corresponding psychic energy which drives the functions of the mind. Through instincts, these two energies are interchangeable, thus linking the body's needs to the mind's wishes.

Freud grouped instincts into two categories: eros (life instincts) and thanatos (death instincts). The most important life instinct, according to Freud, is sex. He described our sex drive as our main motivator. Death instincts, by comparison, are destructive, working internally and silently. Freud had difficulty in studying them, and aggression is the only one he positively identified.

Freud believed that instincts motivate all our behaviour through the id, an unconscious level of our personality in which instincts are stored, together with our libido (the energy which drives the eros). The id works on the 'pleasure principle', striving for immediate gratification of its (selfish) desires. It is rare, however, for these 'primitive, amoral and rash' desires to be accepted in society. Very early in life, therefore, a second part of our personality develops to constrain the id's impulses, whilst seeking to satisfy its demands. Freud called this the ego. He thought that one of the ways it functions is by defence mechanisms (unconscious strategies to reduce anxiety), through which (unacceptable) desires are, for example, repressed. However, motivating libidinal energy remains and must be redirected into more socially acceptable outlets, for example when a frustrated student reduces anger against teachers by playing tennis aggressively. Repressed desires influence our behaviour from the unconscious, where they remain, together with our instincts. Thus, although our behaviour is goal directed, both ego control and defence mechanisms obscure the real motives, unless they are revealed through slips of the tongue, dreams, the use of hypnotism, or drugs.

Psychoanalytic theory of motivation is based on the unconscious and can only be exposed through, for example, test assessment and dream analysis. These rely heavily on the subjective judgment of analysts who may themselves be responding to hidden motives from their own unconscious!

■ Drive or drive-reduction theory

Woodworth (1918) suggested that human behaviour is like the operation of a machine, in which the passive mechanism is made to 'go' by giving it drive. Drives are internal states of arousal caused by bodily or tissue needs. Arousal motivates an animal to initiate behaviour which will fulfil the need; the intensity of behaviour being related to the strength of the need.

Homeostatic drive theory can explain, for example, how our body temperature normally remains fairly steady at 37°C. Sensors in the hypothalamus monitor blood temperature and stimulate mechanisms which cause body heat to be conserved, or lost, whenever the temperature goes beyond its normal range. For example, when the body produces excess heat during exercise, blood temperature rises above normal, resulting in a homeostatic drive to reduce body temperature. Peripheral blood vessels in the skin dilate, allowing more blood to flow through them. This, in turn, causes sweat glands to increase their rate of secretion and heat is lost when this evaporates from the skin surface. Normal temperature is thus restored, without conscious effort.

Hunger and thirst (see pages 513–21) are homeostatic drives over which we have far more conscious control. Homeostatic drive theory explains our desire to eat by the fact that lowered levels of nutrients and water, required by the body during metabolism, cause a tissue need. This produces a hunger or thirst drive which causes a desire for food or water, with consequent restoration of the internal balance.

Hull (1943) also believed that behaviour can be described in terms of primary homeostatic drives. His drive-reduction theory explains activity as being directed towards reducing these drives. Hull considered that the source of all behaviour could be traced to the satisfaction of primary biological needs. The motivating power to do this is expressed through primary drives which provide the energy.

Hull thought that there could be no activity if there was no drive, and that we only act in ways we have learned. This means that even if an animal is motivated to act, it may not do so unless it has learned how. From laboratory studies on non-human animals, Hull developed a formula for the relationship between behaviour and motivation:

Behaviour (probability of response)	=	drive strength (need)	x	habit strength (learned behaviour)

Hull also added the concept of secondary drives which are learned through generalisation and substitution of primary homeostatic needs. They allow an increase in the number of goals towards which behaviour is directed. For example, money is the source of our ability to buy food (so becomes associated with reduction of a primary need). However, money also enables us to buy shelter and comfort (generalisation) and in turn may come to have reinforcing properties for itself (substitution).

Mowrer (1950) identified anxiety reduction as being one of the main secondary drives and instigators of behaviour. This has survival value in motivating behaviour away from traumatic events, and diminishing their harmful effects.

The drive-reduction theory has been disputed on several points:

- Drive is almost impossible to measure and therefore cannot be experimentally tested.
- Most events we experience are drive-*increasing* rather than reducing, for example fairground rides, sports activities and conversation.
- Electrical stimulation of the brain reported by Olds and Milner (1954) showed reinforcement does not result in drive reduction but that it produces an increase in drive (figure 15.8).

Incentive (expectancy) theory

Secondary goals can be thought of as incentives, defined as objects in the environment important in arousing behaviour. Lorenz (1950) developed a hydraulic model to explain how incentives and drive-reduction may work together.

Numerous studies have shown that incentives can act as great motivators. This theory has been applied in occupational psychology and the area of work. Mitchell and Lawson (1987) noted that work output increases if:

- we believe hard work will improve performance
- good performance will result in rewards such as increased pay
- the rewards gained are those we value.

This theory can be related to nAch (see page 522) and the role of *intrinsic* and *extrinsic* motives, rather a complex interaction which demonstrates how giving rewards for something already found intrinsically motivating may reduce the pleasure and hence the motivation.

Neither external incentives nor drive-reduction theory fully explain motivation. They cannot account for the fact that stimulation appears to be an important motivational goal on its own. There are theories, however, which *do* account for internal feelings. Some of these are discussed now.

Theory of needs

Murray (1938) believed that our internal needs provide powerful motivators for behaviour. His theory of needs suggests we have viscerogenic (survival) needs, for example for food and water. These are stronger than psychogenic (psychological) needs, for example for achievement and affiliation.

15.8 Reward circuits in the brain

Intracranial self-stimulation (ICSS) has been demonstrated in rats (Olds and Milner, 1954) and humans (Bishop *et al.*, 1963). Rats will perform a response such as pressing a lever to administer brief bursts of electrical stimulation to specific sites in the brain. Most early studies involved *septal* or *lateral hypothalamic stimulation*. Rats would press a lever several thousand times an hour to stimulate these sites, stopping only when exhausted. The *mesotelencephalic dopamine system*, a system of dopaminergic neurons projecting from the mid-brain (mesencephalon) into various regions of the telencephalon play an important role, especially the *nucleus acumbens*. The nucleus acumbens is seen to play an important role in mediating the effects of natural motivated behaviours but not in the incentive motivation to engage in them.

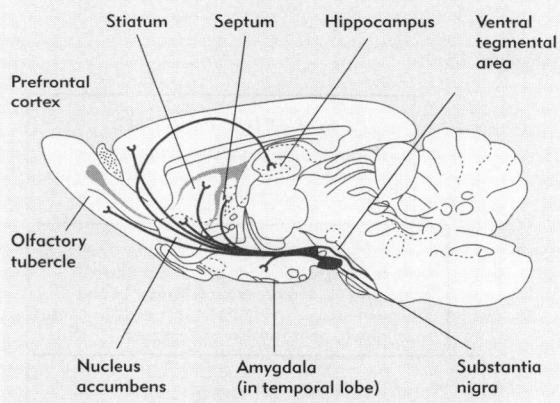

This system is seen mediating the effects of psychoactive drugs (Chen, 1993). Dopamine and the nucleus acumbens are seen to be part of a *reward circuit* and the ICSS may be part of a 'fast-forward' system which eliminates the need for drives and reinforcement. It is such a powerful system that it is seen to have some biological significance. What exactly this is awaits research and demonstrates that there are many aspects of motivation still to be discovered.

When two conflicting needs arise simultaneously, the stronger one will be satisfied first. For instance, if a friend rings up just before a meal, to invite you to come round and revise for an exam you are taking next day, your viscerogenic hunger will probably have priority over your psychogenic need for achievement. Murray also recognised that motivation results from a combination of personal needs and press (environmental factors). Press arouses particular personal needs, for example hunger when you see a picture of your favourite food, or the need to achieve success after watching a person you admire being successful (see also nAch, page 522).

Like Murray, Maslow (1943) thought that motivational needs are innate and instinctive. In addition, he considered that failure to learn how to satisfy them inhibits individual development and full functioning. Maslow described hierarchies of growth needs and knowing needs. Figure 15.9 depicts the strength of these needs in relation to others, by the area they cover, and also by their position in the hierarchy.

Maslow (1943) argued that in the hierarchy of growth needs, physiological needs are stronger than all other needs and must be satisfied first:

'It is quite true that man lives by bread alone – where there is no bread. But what happens to man's desire when there is plenty of bread and when his belly is chronically filled? At once other (and higher) needs emerge and these, rather than physiological hunger, dominate the organism – and when these in turn are satisfied again new (and still higher) needs emerge – and so on.'

There is no all-or-nothing effect. In Maslow's hierarchy of growth needs they emerge or recede depending on the situation. Higher level growth needs tend to become 'hidden' beneath cultural and parental dictates, and some people do not develop above the second level. Others, however, overcome these social restraints and become so absorbed by high-level needs, that physical ones go largely unnoticed.

Maslow's second hierarchy has only two levels: knowing needs and understanding needs. The former is stronger than the latter and occurs overtly (openly) as curiosity. Maslow thought we have conflicting motives for behaviour which can be directed towards either self-development or safety.

Motivation towards safety occurs when we are unsure of ourselves, anxious about what others think of us, or unwilling to try new ways of doing things. Motivation towards growth takes place when we are interested in and aware of ourselves within a universal dimension. Maslow thought that if we let others dictate our choice of direction, for example enhancing the attraction of safety needs by promising approval, or emphasising the danger of growth needs by threatening disaster, we lose self-trust and the ability to feel delight in the experience. If we *do* make a growth decision, however, we gain in self-confidence and lose our fear of others.

Maslow's hierarchy of needs and motives has not been supported by evidence (Smither, 1988; Inglehart and Hildebrandt, 1990):

Figure 15.9

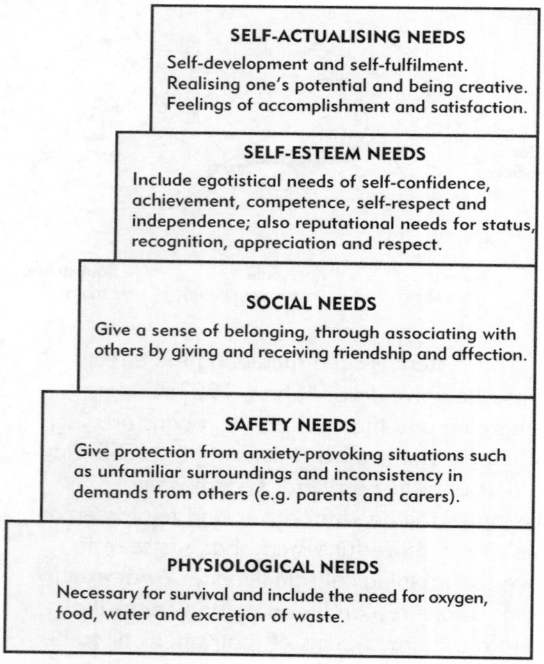

SELF-ACTUALISING NEEDS
Self-development and self-fulfilment. Realising one's potential and being creative. Feelings of accomplishment and satisfaction.

SELF-ESTEEM NEEDS
Include egotistical needs of self-confidence, achievement, competence, self-respect and independence; also reputational needs for status, recognition, appreciation and respect.

SOCIAL NEEDS
Give a sense of belonging, through associating with others by giving and receiving friendship and affection.

SAFETY NEEDS
Give protection from anxiety-provoking situations such as unfamiliar surroundings and inconsistency in demands from others (e.g. parents and carers).

PHYSIOLOGICAL NEEDS
Necessary for survival and include the need for oxygen, food, water and excretion of waste.

Hierarchy of growth needs

Source: adapted from Maslow (1943).

- Human needs can be organised vertically as well as horizontally and perhaps people have simultaneous needs for different levels of need such as security and self-esteem. A person seeking love may be strongly motivated by social conviction or a sense of beauty (Neher, 1991).
- People do not necessarily progress onto 'higher' motives such as **self-actualisation** when 'lower' needs such as safety and love are met; there is great individual variation.
- Higher needs may outweigh lower needs, for

example to die of torture rather than give up convictions.
- Conditions in society promote some motives such as safety and physical security more than others (Inglehart and Hildebrandt, 1990).
- The difficulty of operationally defining terms such as **self-actualisation** means it cannot be tested experimentally. (See Unit 2.)

Perhaps we all develop our own individual hierarchy of motives as we develop from childhood to late adulthood?

Self-assessment questions

1 Outline physiological factors that tell us when we are hungry.

2 What is meant by the positive-incentive value of eating?

3 Summarise the set-point model of body-weight.

4 List some of the social motives.

5 Describe and discuss three theories of motivation.

(Suggested answers on page 565.)

Emotion

Physiological mechanisms of emotion

Since the **autonomic nervous system (ANS)** is linked with functions in other bodily processes, we are cognitively aware of many of the fluctuations which occur. We experience different arousal levels as different feelings, discriminating between these by interpreting them as **emotions**. Our behaviour differs according to which emotion we have identified, and how strongly we are aroused. Emotions thus have three components:
- *physiological changes* within the body
- a *subjective experience* by which we interpret them
- a *behavioural response* associated with these feelings.

In this section we explore the physiological mechanisms of emotion. Without emotion, life

would be 'bland and empty' (Carlson and Buskist, 1997, p. 432). Emotions are relatively brief and occur as a consequence of events which motivate us.

Have you ever felt really happy, that it is good to be alive, and all is well with the world? Then felt guilt as you remember those who cannot be happy because of the effects of illness, disasters, war or crime? Happiness and guilt are both emotions.

Activity 5

How many emotions do you think there are? Write down those you remember having experienced. Do you think there are some which you may not have experienced? Look at your list and see if you can classify the emotions into groups. (Now read on.)

Psychologists have classified emotions in several ways. Did your system compare with any of those in figure 15.10?

15.10 Psychologists have classified emotions in several ways (adapted from Gross, 1987)

Wundt (1986)
Based his system of three dimensions on introspection. The first dimension lay between pleasant and unpleasant feelings, the second between calmness and excitement, the third between relaxation and tension.

Schlosberg (1941)
Identified three dimensions of emotion from photographs of posed facial expressions. The pleasant – unpleasant and sleep – tension dimensions correspond to Wundt's ideas. The third is different, lying between acceptance and rejection.

Osgood (1966)
Observed live emotional displays to classify emotions according to pleasantness, activity and potency.

Ekman et al. (1972), and Ekman and Friesen (1975)
Compared photographs of posed facial expressions to arrive at their classification of six universal primary emotions: surprise, fear, disgust, anger, happiness and sadness.

Plutchick (1986)
Identified eight primary emotions: surprise, fear, disgust, anger, joy, sorrow, acceptance and expectancy.

A 'prototype' approach has been used to examine cultural universals of emotion from which a set of primary emotions have been classified. The more culture-specific emotions are described as secondary emotions. As can be seen in table 15.11, there are several primary emotions which appear in most studies, such as fear, anger, sadness, joy, surprise and disgust.

Table 15.11

Tomkins	Ekman	Izard	Plutchik	Shaver et al.	Storm and Storm	Weiner and Graham	Oatley and Johnson–Laird
Fear	Fear	Fear	Fear	Fear	Fear		Fear
Anger	Anger	Anger	Anger	Anger	Anger		Anger
Enjoyment	Happiness	Joy	Joy	Joy	Happiness	Happiness	Happiness
Distress	Sadness	Sadness	Sadness	Sadness	Sadness[a]	Sadness	Sadness
Disgust	Disgust	Disgust	Disgust				Disgust
Interest		Interest	Anticipation				
Surprise	Surprise	Surprise	Surprise	Surprise[b]			
Contempt	Contempt	Contempt					
Shame		Shame		Shame[c]			
			Acceptance	Love	Love/liking		

Primary emotions as seen by leading theorists

[a] Includes shame and pain.

[b] This category was marginal to the others and not really considered an emotion by subjects.

[c] This was a basic-level category only among the Chinese.

Source: Ekman et al., 1987; Ekman and Heider, 1988; Izard, 1971, 1990; Oatley and Johnson-Laird, 1987; Plutchik, 1984; Shaver et al., 1987, 1992; Storm and Storm, 1987; Tomkins, 1981; Weiner and Graham, 1984; Wade and Tavris (1993).

However, there are areas of disagreement with several emotions such as shame, guilt and pride which prove difficult to measure in the brain or identify in the face. Ortany and Turner (1990) suggested that although it is useful to classify emotions for research it should not lead to some emotions being seen to be more fundamental than others.

Cultures determine the reasons for the display of various emotions, with display rules governing how and when they may be expressed. Cultures also dictate how and when we should show an emotion we do *not* feel. This has been called 'emotion work' and can be seen in sad behaviour shown at funerals and happiness shown at weddings. Job training often includes the emotion work and can be seen in the display of cheerfulness seen in some shop assistants, flight attendants and others in the service industries. This effort can sometimes make social relations more pleasurable and ensure positive emotions are likely in clients (Wade and Tavris, 1993).

Activity 6

From the list you compiled in Activity 5 identify a strong emotion you have recently felt. Close your eyes, take a long, slow, deep breath and imagine yourself re-experiencing this feeling. Jot down what is happening inside your body during this imaginary experience. If you find this difficult, focus on your stomach, mouth, heart and hands. (Now read on.)

Did you experience 'butterflies in the stomach', dry mouth, rapid heartbeat and sweaty palms? These all indicate high levels of sympathetic arousal. The 'butterflies' and dry mouth are due to inhibition of the digestive system, the rapid heartbeat and sweaty palms result from an increased heart rate and dilation of peripheral blood vessels. The physiological mechanisms involved in this process include the interaction of the ANS, the endocrine glands and the central nervous system (CNS).

■ The role of the autonomic nervous system

The sympathetic and parasympathetic systems are separate sections of the ANS. Figure 15.12 shows the effect each has on the sensation and control of glands and internal organs.

The ANS consists of nerve centres and nerves which act rapidly. It governs bodily processes not normally under voluntary control. Two systems of nerves are involved, each having opposing effects on the internal organs. Stimulation of the sympathetic nervous system sets the body up for activity, directing the blood flow to peripheral muscles and increasing heart and breathing rates. Stimulation of the parasympathetic nervous system supports activities involved with building up the body's supply of stored energy, including salivation, digestion and blood flow to the gastrointestinal system and prepares the body for relaxation. These two systems act in complex ways not fully understood.

■ The role of the endocrine glands

The **endocrine glands** secrete complex chemicals, known as hormones, into the bloodstream. Hormones reach every cell because every cell in the body is in contact with the blood system, either directly or indirectly. Hormones act more slowly than nerve impulses, as they are carried in the blood rather than in the nerves, which act more quickly. Hormones fall into two groups. Specific hormones influence only one organ, but general hormones affect all cells. For example, thyrotrophic hormone is a specific hormone secreted by the pituitary. The pituitary is an endocrine gland that plays a major part in the arousal and stress response and is known as the 'master gland'. It influences only the thyroid gland, stimulating it to secrete thyroxine, a general hormone which affects all cells by regulating their glucose uptake and respiratory activity. The pituitary is connected by many nerve pathways to the hypothalamus thus linking the ANS and CNS and allowing the close interaction they need to be in control of the body.

Both the ANS and the endocrine glands work towards maintaining stability in the internal environment of an organism, a state which Cannon

Figure 15.12

SYMPATHETIC NERVOUS SYSTEM		PARASYMPATHETIC NERVOUS SYSTEM
Glycogen converted to glucose – energy released	**Liver**	Glucose converted to glycogen – energy conserved
Blood vessels dilate – activity increases	**Blood vessels**	Blood vessels constrict – activity decreases
Blood vessels dilate – sweating increases	**Sweat glands**	Blood vessels constrict – sweating decreases
Passages dilate – rate and depth of breathing increases	**Lungs**	Passages constrict – rate and depth of breathing decreases
Muscle stimulated – rate and volume increase	**Heart**	Muscle inhibited – rate and volume decrease
Secretions inhibited – butterflies may be felt	**Stomach**	Secretions stimulated – food digested
Adrenalin secreted – body prepared for action	**Adrenal glands**	Adrenalin inhibited – body relaxes
Pupil dilates – visual field increases	**Pupil**	Pupils constrict – visual field decreases

Divisions of the autonomic nervous system and their effects on some internal organs

(1927) described as homeostasis. Homeostasis refers to maintaining the balance of body temperature, body fluids and the nutrients stored in the body, many of which need to operate within narrow limits. Many of the body's systems, such as eating, were thought to be included in this set-point system (see page 514), but are now considered to be under more flexible control. Cannon (1927) referred to the ANS as 'interofective' since it affects the internal environment, and the CNS as 'exterofective' since it provides a direct relationship with the external environment.

It is conceivable that a person could survive without an ANS, but to make up for the lack of internal, homeostatic mechanisms a constant and very favourable, external environment would be required – one free from threat.

The autonomic responses facilitate the emotional behaviour and provide quick mobilisation of energy.

Hormonal responses reinforce the autonomic responses and the *endocrine system* is also implicated in emotional arousal (figure 15.13). Each endocrine gland shown in figure 15.13 secretes one or more hormones and is well supplied with blood vessels. The hormones pass into the blood within the glands, before being transported around the body in the circulatory system to the target organs

Figure 15.13

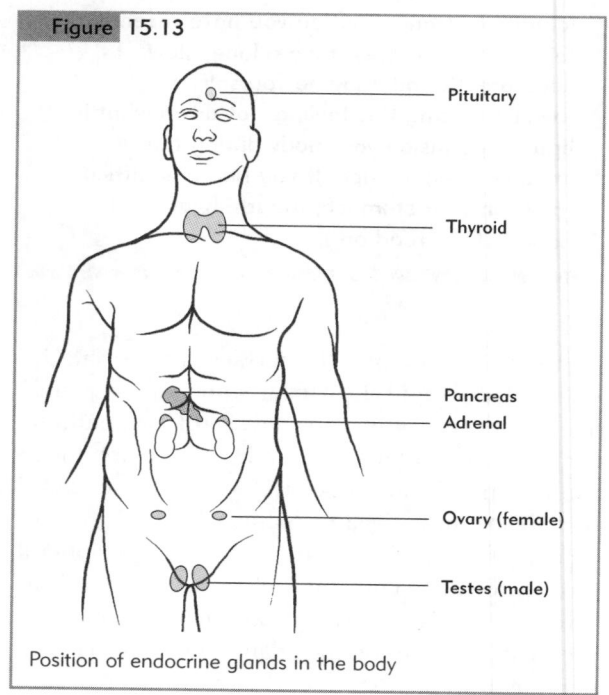

- Pituitary
- Thyroid
- Pancreas
- Adrenal
- Ovary (female)
- Testes (male)

Position of endocrine glands in the body

where they exert their control. For instance, antidiuretic hormone (ADH) secreted by the pituitary and aldosterone by the adrenal, both exert their effect on the kidneys (their target organ). The glands most concerned with emotional arousal are the adrenal medulla, pituitary, thyroid and adrenal cortex. The adrenal medulla secretes the hormones adrenaline and noradrenaline. It is activated by sympathetic nerves when we are alerted to environmental changes, especially major or sudden ones. These hormones act as neurotransmitters for the sympathetic nervous system and increase the flow of blood to the muscles keeping the body alert and prepared for action, i.e. motivated for 'fight or flight' (see page 540). The strength of the emotional arousal depends on the volume of hormone secreted. Adrenaline and noradrenaline secretion continues until the need for vigilance passes and their blood levels return to normal.

The pituitary, thyroid and adrenal cortex interact in complex feedback systems, originating from the hypothalamus, when the arousal syndrome is initiated. Releaser hormones from the hypothalamus stimulate the pituitary to secrete hormones controlling the activity of other glands. Thyroid-stimulating hormone (TSH) stimulates the thyroid to secrete thyroxine which controls the body's rate of metabolism and oxygen utilisation. Adreno-cortico-trophic hormone (ACTH) stimulates the adrenal cortex to secrete a group of hormones called corticoids, which help to sustain arousal. Corticoids increase blood glucose levels (needed for energy) in two ways. They promote the conversion of cellular proteins to glucose; and inhibit the conversion of glucose to glycogen in the liver (for storage). Water and salts are conserved under the influence of corticoids.

Elevated thyroxine and corticoid levels in blood, passing through the hypothalamus and pituitary, inhibit the secretion of releaser hormones TSH and ACTH so that blood levels of thyroxine and corticoids revert to normal. Also, sympathetic influence on the hypothalamus decreases as the environmental changes become familiar, or incongruencies are solved.

The role of the brain and the central nervous system

Stimulation of parts of the brain can cause an animal to attack or try to escape (anger and fear). As these responses are the result of central nervous system (CNS) activity, the hormonal and autonomic responses noted above are *controlled* by the brain, particularly the limbic system. The limbic system is a collection of nuclei circling the thalamus, including the amygdala and the hypothalamus (figure 15.14).

The amygdala appears to control the integration of the autonomic, hormonal and neural responses to a number of situations, especially those involving fear, anger and disgust (Carlson, 1994). It receives inputs from the olfactory system, the association cortex of the temporal lobe, the frontal cortex and the remaining limbic system. It sends information to the frontal cortex, hypothalamus, hippocampal formation and the brainstem controlling autonomic functions and species-specific behaviours. Damage

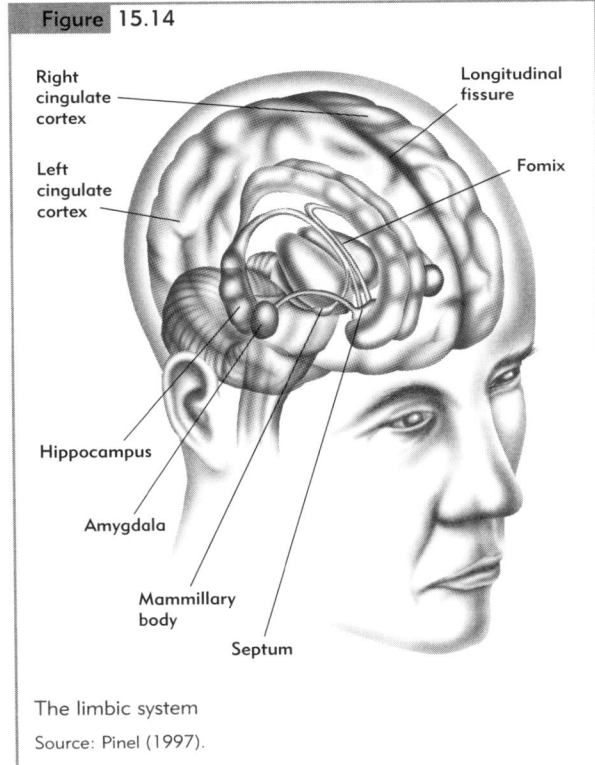

Figure 15.14

Right cingulate cortex

Left cingulate cortex

Longitudinal fissure

Fomix

Hippocampus

Amygdala

Mammillary body

Septum

The limbic system
Source: Pinel (1997).

to any of these areas will interfere with emotional response patterns, so just as stimulation of the amygdala leads to emotional reactions so its destruction disrupts them. Recordings of single neurons in the amygdala indicate that some respond when the animal perceives particular stimuli which have emotional significance.

The effects of anxiety-reducing (*anxiolytic*) drugs appear to be produced partly through the central nucleus of the amygdala but Yadin *et al.* (1991) found that benzodiazepines still had an anxiolytic effect after the amygdala was destroyed. The amygdala cannot therefore be responsible for all the effects of these drugs.

Carlson (1994) described the amygdala as the 'push button' for emotional responses rather than the control centre. The activation of the amygdala occurs when a threatening stimulus is detected. This detection is thought to involve several neural mechanisms, especially those in the thalamus, sensory association cortex and the orbitofrontal cortex. The thalamus can detect simple auditory and visual stimuli that warn of danger and passes these on to the amygdala directly thus bypassing the cortex (Rosen *et al.*, 1992). Perhaps, as suggested by LeDoux (1989) this acts as an 'early warning system' and then the cortex assesses the situation to see if the action is appropriate (figure 15.15).

Have you ever entered your bedroom late in the evening without switching on the lights and thought there was someone sitting in the chair only to discover, when your eyes adjusted to the dark, that it was a pile of clothes you had not tidied away!

Emotional reactions to more complex situations require input from the neocortex and this is provided by the temporal lobe receiving information from the visual, auditory and somatosensory association cortex. The amygdala is thus informed about everything happening to the individual.

Perceiving the meaning of social situations is a very complex activity which involves more than just sensory analysis. It involves experiences, memories, inferences and judgments. These skills come from a number of cortical areas with the orbitofrontal cortex, at the base of the frontal lobes, playing an important part. The importance of this region can be seen by the effects of damage to this region.

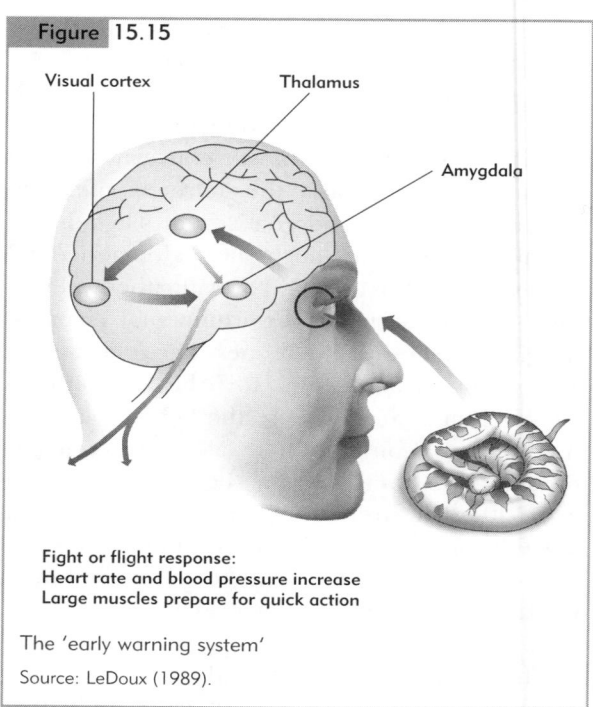

Figure 15.15

Visual cortex   Thalamus

Amygdala

Fight or flight response:
Heart rate and blood pressure increase
Large muscles prepare for quick action

The 'early warning system'

Source: LeDoux (1989).

The most famous case study of damage to the orbitofrontal cortex is that of Phineas Gage who, due to an accident at work, ended up with a rod going through his left cheek, brain, and out of his left forehead. Before the accident he was a serious, industrious and energetic man. After the accident he became irresponsible and thoughtless. He was unable to make plans or carry them out. Most of the damage was to the orbitofrontal cortex. Further studies on other people with damage to this region noted similar effects.

The orbitofrontal cortex is involved in translating judgments into appropriate feeling and behaviours. Unit 26 page 973 looks at *psychosurgery* involving pre-frontal lobotomies to relieve emotional suffering such as anxiety, obsession and compulsions. Most of these operations disrupt the functions of the frontal lobes (particularly the orbitofrontal cortex) by severing the connections between this area and the rest of the brain. However, the procedure also makes people indifferent to the social consequences of their behaviour and the feelings of others. It also interferes with their ability to make and execute plans.

Expression and comprehension of emotion involve the *right hemisphere* of the brain more than the left. Kolb and Taylor (1988) found that frontal lesions also disrupted the perception of facial expressions. They suggested the location of the lesions within the hemisphere is important. However, damage to the right hemisphere is more likely to produce deficits in expression and understanding the emotions displayed by tone of voice or facial expression than damage to the left hemisphere. Fewer facial expressions of emotion are shown by people with right-hemisphere lesions. The left hemisphere appears to be more active during *positive* emotions. PET scans have shown that when people are asked to think of 'happy' events or choose happy faces from a selection the left hemisphere is more active (Gur *et al.*, 1994). Conversely, the right hemisphere is more active when *negative* events are evoked.

Activity 7

Which physiological structures are involved in the following reactions to events?

a John is watching *Murder after Midnight*. Which hormones are making his heart beat fast and his palms feel sweaty while he watches the victim waiting for the murderer to climb the stairs?

b Francesca is running away from her brother who is wearing a werewolf mask. Which limbic structure is probably responsible for her reaction?

c Anna is enjoying watching a video of her daughter's wedding. Which brain hemisphere is likely to be activated?

(Suggested answers on page 564.)

Theories of emotion

Physiological signs of emotional arousal are fairly easy to assess, by measuring heart and respiratory rates, blood pressure and sweat production. However, there are also behavioural and psychological aspects of emotional arousal. Behavioural changes show not only in our actions but also in our facial expressions and body posture. Some of these (for example happiness, sadness and anger) are universally exhibited from babyhood. We can understand the kind and strength of emotion being experienced by a person even if we cannot speak the same language (Ekman, 1982). Others, for example fear and surprise, are harder to interpret.

Behavioural gestures are often culturally specific and may be misinterpreted by other cultures. For example, clapping hands is a sign of worry or disappointment to the Chinese but a sign of pleasure to the English.

Trying to understand the psychological perception of emotion is harder than identifying the physiological changes which occur during arousal. There are several different theoretical approaches: five are introduced in this section.

■ James–Lange theory

Have you ever been going upstairs and slipped; or been confronted by a snarling dog? You would probably explain your subsequent actions by saying you had been frightened, and so you reached for the banister or ran. The James–Lange theory of emotion would disagree.

Independently, James and Lange (1884) suggested that we *act* first, *then* experience an emotion. We become afraid *because* we run away from an angry bull, or we feel sad *because* we are crying. The running and crying occur in response to physiological changes, the emotion felt is the cognitive sensation of these changes (figure 15.16).

The James–Lange theory implies that a different set of physiological changes exists for each emotion. Cannon (1927) criticised the theory on four grounds.

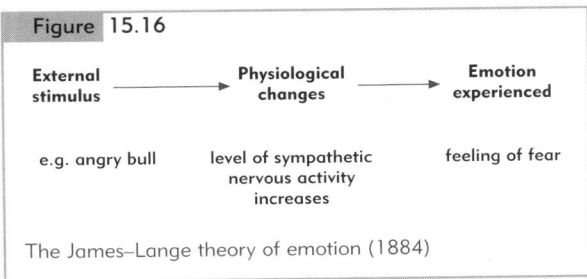

Figure 15.16

The James–Lange theory of emotion (1884)

■ The internal organs are poorly supplied with nerves, therefore visceral (bodily) changes occur too slowly to provide a source of emotional feeling. However, James and Lange were probably more concerned with expressive behaviour, than with internal changes which we cannot feel (Gross, 1987).

■ If adrenaline is injected artificially, a true emotion is not experienced, even though the same bodily changes occur. Marañon (1924) injected 210 subjects with adrenaline. Seventy-one per cent said they experienced only physiological symptoms, others described their feelings 'as if' they were experiencing an emotion, a few imagined their emotions. Also, 25 adult males with spinal cord and ANS damage reported changes in emotional feelings, especially fear, anger and sexual feelings. They also described 'as if' emotions, suggesting that they understood the emotion but did not *feel* it. The higher the damage in the spinal cord, the more disruption occurred (Hohmann, 1966).

■ Cannon argued about the necessity of physiological changes to the experience of emotion. Sherrington (1900) severed the spinal cords and vagus nerves (supplying the internal organs) in dogs; Cannon (1927) removed the sympathetic nervous systems of cats. In both experiments, the animals showed normal emotional reactions after recovery. However this may have been due to experience (Lloyd *et al.*, 1984).

■ Cannon's fourth criticism refers to the belief that the pattern of autonomic arousal differs very little from one emotional state to another; for example, both anger and the sight of a loved one cause the heart to beat faster. Physiological studies contradict each other here. Early studies demonstrated physiological similarities in most emotions, except fear and anger. Ax (1953) found that during fear, adrenaline seems to dominate the hormonal response, whereas during anger, both adrenaline and noradrenaline are involved. However, with increasing accuracy of physiological measurements, evidence is revealing distinct patterns for different emotions. Ekman and his colleagues (Ekman *et al.*, 1983; Levenson *et al.*, 1990) studied the effect of emotional expressions on physiological performance. The subjects, mainly actors, were coached to hold expressions of surprise, disgust, sadness, anger, fear and happiness for ten seconds. Differences in their heart rate and temperature can be seen in figure 15.17.

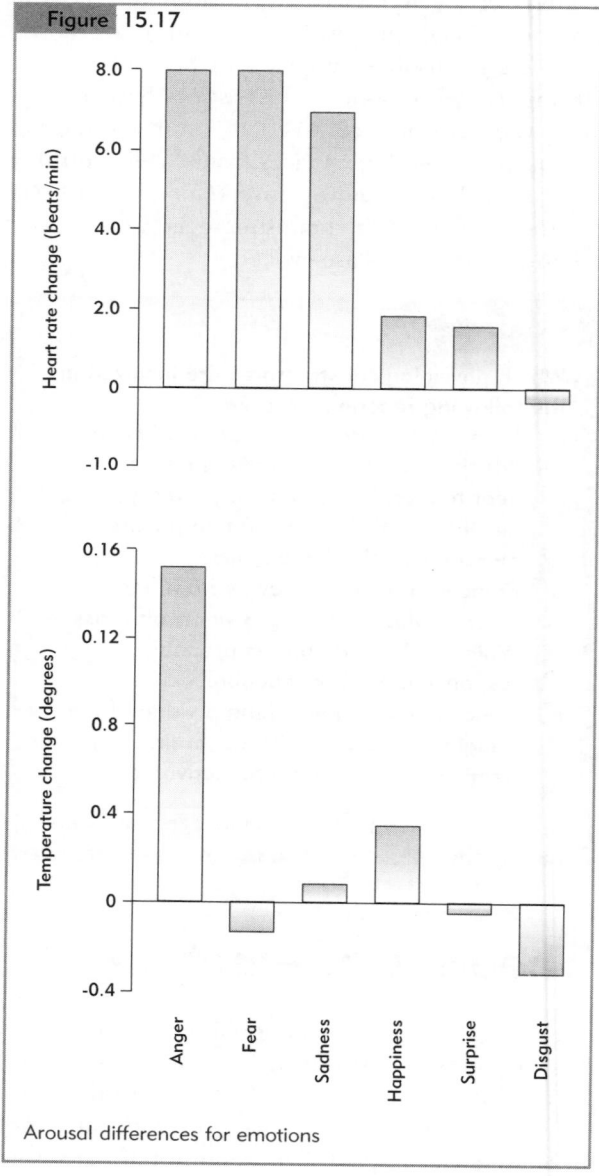

Figure 15.17

Arousal differences for emotions

Different facial expressions did alter responses in the ANS:

- Anger was found to increase heart rate and skin temperature.
- Fear increased heart rate but decreased skin temperature.
- Happiness decreased heart rate without affecting skin temperature.

Carlson (1994) suggested the role of experience as a possible reason for the way facial muscles cause changes in mood or activity of the ANS. Some of these responses may have been classically conditioned so that feedback from the facial muscles may elicit an autonomic response and a change in perceived emotion. Alternatively, responses could be innate. There is adaptive value in emotional expressions which communicate feelings and intentions to others. These differences in response to various emotions have been found consistently across populations of different ages and cultures.

Perhaps imitation is involved. Early imitation of facial expressions has been observed in the newborn (Field, 1982). This early response is unlikely to be learned. Look at the photographs in figure 15.18. Did you find you also felt inclined to change your expression a little?

Cannon–Bard theory

Cannon and Bard (1931) independently put forward an alternative theory, now known as the Cannon–Bard theory of emotion. When external changes stimulate the hypothalamus, impulses are sent simultaneously both to start the arousal response and to alert the cerebral cortex. Here the emotion is experienced in relation to the level of arousal. The higher this is, the more intense the emotion. Figure 15.19 shows this diagramatically.

James–Lange and Cannon–Bard made different predictions on the role of feedback from the autonomic and somatic nervous systems. The James–Lange theory sees emotion dependent on feedback from the autonomic and somatic systems whereas the Cannon–Bard theory sees emotion as completely independent of this

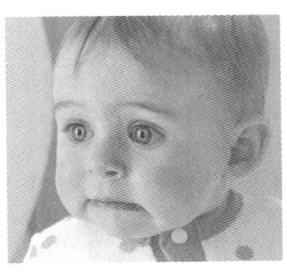

Figure 15.18 Pictures of happy, sad and surprised faces posed by an adult and the responses made by an infant
Source: Field, T. (1982).

feedback, taking them to be parallel processes with no direct causal relationship. Both of these theories have been found to be incorrect. People with spinal damage at the neck who have virtually no autonomic and somatic feedback still are capable of emotion (Lowe and Carroll, 1985) and, as noted above, in the facial expression studies autonomic and somatic responses can influence

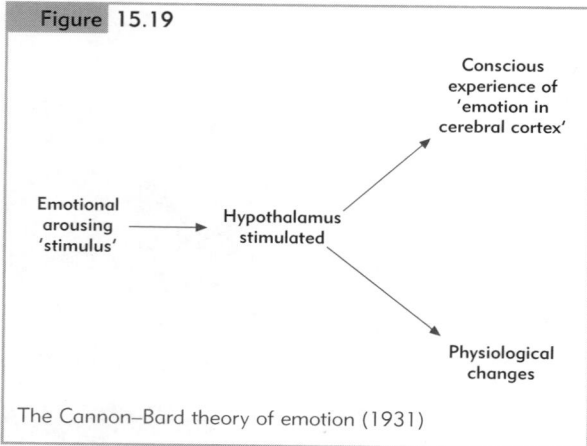

The Cannon–Bard theory of emotion (1931)

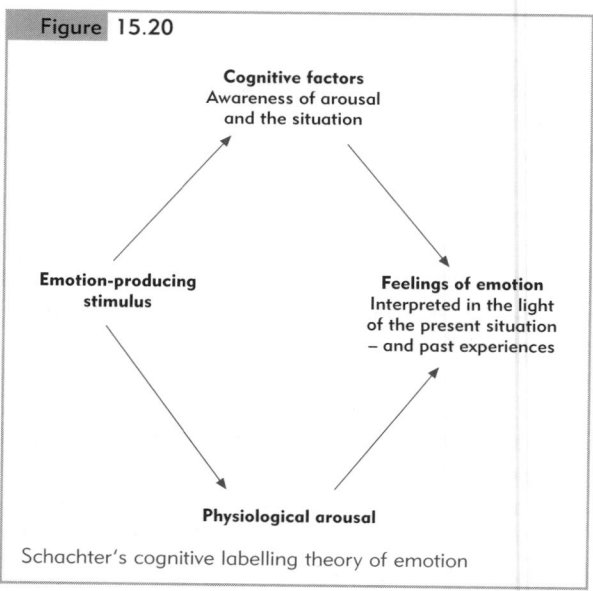

Schachter's cognitive labelling theory of emotion

emotion. Current research suggests that the *interaction* of three important factors results in the emotional perception and includes the role of cognition:

- perception of the emotion-producing stimulus
- autonomic and somatic responses to the stimulus
- the experience or feelings of emotion.

Cognitive labelling theory

Schachter's cognitive labelling theory disagrees both with James's idea that physiological changes cause an emotional experience and with Cannon's idea that they are separate. Also, neither the James–Lange theory nor the Cannon–Bard theory provides for cognitive processes. Like James, Schachter believed that physiological arousal precedes the experience of emotion but differs in that he believed we have to decide which emotion we are experiencing by assessing the information around us. In other words, emotion results from an interaction between our state of arousal and our cognition of the situation. For example, if we are at a party and everyone else is laughing or looking happy, we will probably interpret our own feeling of arousal as happiness. If others are being serious, or crying, we would interpret our feelings differently (see figure 15.20).

Schachter's theory is a theory of attribution. He suggested that the emotion we experience is dependent on the attributions made by people about what is going on. Schachter's theory encouraged the study of attribution (see Unit 4 pages 120–5).

Evidence for this theory comes from Schachter and Singer (1962). Volunteer participants were misinformed into thinking an investigation concerned the effect on vision of 'suproxin' (a drug containing vitamin C). The 'drug' was, in fact, adrenaline, which has no direct effects on vision.

- Group A participants were informed correctly of the side effects (for example palpitations, sweaty palms).
- Group B was misinformed – participants being told they would probably experience numbness, itchy sensations and a slight headache.
- Group C was uninformed (told nothing about side effects).
- Participants in group D, the control group, were not given adrenaline, but a saline placebo which has a neutral effect.

After injection of the drug, participants were shown to a waiting room where a stooge (confederate of the experimenter) was already waiting. For half the subjects in each group, the stooge behaved in a euphoric way, for example doodling on a notepad, or making and flying a paper aeroplane. For the other half, the stooge behaved angrily about a questionnaire participants were given to complete. The questions asked for very personal information and the stooge became progressively more annoyed and agitated, eventually tearing up the questionnaire, flinging the pieces on the floor and saying 'I'm not wasting any more time. I'm getting my books and leaving.'

Participants' emotional experiences were assessed by the degree to which they joined in with the stooge's behaviour and by their own rating of how euphoric or angry they felt. Pulse rates, taken before and after the experiment, decreased slightly for the placebo group, but increased for all subjects given adrenaline. However, although groups A, B and C experienced the same level of arousal, they all behaved very differently. Most participants reacted predictably, those in group B showing the greatest similarity of behaviour and feelings to the stooge, followed closely by those in group C. Group A participants were little affected.

Schachter and Singer suggested that participants in groups A and D had feelings they were expecting, but those in groups B and C were not expecting their feelings of arousal and consequently had to find a reason for them. The only information available was the behaviour of the stooge, so they interpreted their arousal accordingly. Cognitive factors, as well as physiological arousal, therefore appear to be important determinants of the way emotion is labelled, and of the resulting behaviour.

Green (1996) noted some of the problems of this study:

- The only significant differences noted were observer rating of emotional *behaviour* and not self-reports of emotional *feelings*.
- Adrenaline may have cause the participants to imitate the stooge's behaviour without changing the emotional state.
- The participants' emotional state prior to the study had not been controlled so it was a confounding variable.
- The artificiality of the situation reduces its validity.

- Attempts to replicate this ethically dubious study have proved unsuccessful (see below).

Despite the methodological criticisms which have been levelled against Schachter and Singer's original study, it does highlight that the *cognitive* interpretation of the situation needs to be taken into account when considering the perception of emotion.

Some participants, however, did not act predictably, especially those in the placebo group who experienced a fairly high level of emotion even though they were supposedly unaroused. Was this due to the experimental situation, which produced it own arousal? Also, having an injection creates arousal through anxiety. Would it have made a difference if the control group had been given a drug like chlorpromazine which *reduces* arousal? Schachter and Wheeler (1962) injected subjects with either adrenaline, saline or chlorpromazine, telling them all it was suproxin. After the injection, participants watched an excerpt from a comedy film.

Participants were expected to relate their feelings of arousal to this film. Reactions were assessed by observing the number of smiles, grins, laughs and belly-laughs during the film and by asking participants how enjoyable and funny they found it. As predicted, those injected with adrenaline found and showed most amusement while those injected with chlorpromazine showed least.

Marshall and Zimbardo (1979) repeated Schachter and Singer's (1962) experiment using only the euphoric condition (they thought it unethical to induce anger in unsuspecting people). Results were disappointing, so they repeated it using larger doses of adrenaline. Unexpectedly, these participants reported feeling unhappier than other subjects, the opposite of Schachter and Singer's prediction. This may be because unexplained arousal is normally regarded as unpleasant and the experimental situation was a manufactured one.

A more realistic investigation, which confirmed Schachter's prediction, was carried out by Dutton and Aron (1974). Unsuspecting male visitors to the Capilano Canyon in Canada, aged between 18 and 35, were approached by an attractive female experimenter pretending to carry out a survey on people's reactions to scenic attractions. Participants were asked to invent a short story about an ambiguous picture of a woman. These were later scored for sexual content, assumed to reflect sexual attraction towards the interviewer. Stories related by participants interviewed on an unstable suspension bridge, 71 metres above the canyon (high arousal condition), contained significantly more sexual content than stories of subjects interviewed on a solid wooden bridge (low arousal condition). The experimenters concluded that although similar autonomic arousal occurs for all emotions, it is the interpretation of the arousal which is important.

As shown by the Dutton and Aron experiments, people make mistakes in how they attribute their arousal. This has been called the misattribution effect (Ross and Nisbett, 1991).

The role of cognition in attribution and appraisal has been extended in other theories, two of which are outlined below.

■ Lazarus's appraisal theory
Lazarus (1980) suggested a three-stage response in emotion:
- The individual makes an initial and sometimes unconscious cognitive appraisal of the situation (*primitive evaluative perception*) to decide if there is a threat.
- Coping action is taken if necessary.
- The individual takes a closer look and identifies the emotions he or she is feeling.

This initial *cognitive* reaction has been disputed by Zajonc (1980) who argued that cognition and emotion are independent systems with the emotional response preceding cognition in some circumstances. The 'early warning system' of emotion suggested by LeDoux (1989) (see page 532) could support Lazarus's theory.

Scherer (1994) noted that this debate revolved around the *level* of cognitive processing involved, not whether processing took place. Cognition is usually seen to involve the neocortex. Most researchers acknowledge that emotion can be evoked in the absence of conscious cognitive mediation but would also agree that some cognitive processing is required for most emotion.

■ Weiner's attribution theory
Weiner (1986, 1992) found certain attributions produced specific emotions. Once the initial evaluation has been made he suggested the individual looks at what caused the event. These attributions of *causality* can modify the emotion felt. It is the interaction of the perceived internal and external causes, controllability and outcome which will determine the emotional responses (figure 15.21).

Emotions are central to human life so it is not surprising that they are influenced by, and in turn have an influence on, many variables. Emotions are responses to events seen to be important to us. The reasons for the importance of some events are often complicated and the emotional reactions produced involve complex cognitive processes. Other events are quite simple and so simple brain processes can produce the emotional reactions.

Although no single, comprehensive theory of emotion has been supported, cognitive factors have been found important.

The cognitive approach to emotion may help to explain clinical reports of patients who react emotionally without feeling the appropriate emotion, for example acting in a hostile manner but not feeling angry. Cognitive theory links emotional feelings to associations with particular situations. Past experience influences our beliefs about the present situation, and these beliefs then influence our interpretation of the emotion we are experiencing.

As you can see below and in Unit 26 page 970, cognitive therapy can help people learn how their thinking affects their emotions and they can be helped to change their thinking accordingly (Beck, 1991).

'They can ask themselves what the evidence is for their beliefs that the world will collapse if they get a C in biology, that no one loves them, or that they will be lonely forever. In such cases, it is not only that emotional reasoning prevents critical thinking; the failure to think critically also creates the emotion' (Wade and Tavris, 1993, p. 323).

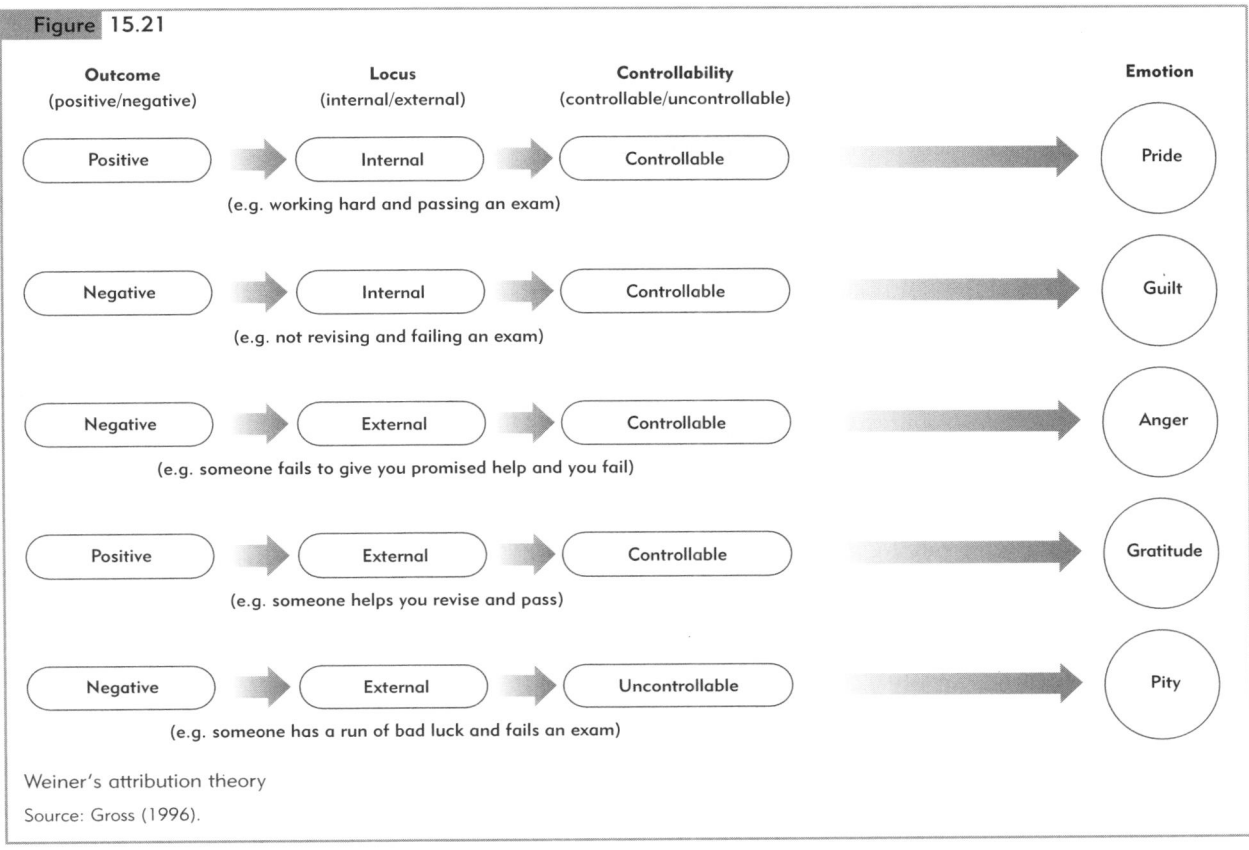

Weiner's attribution theory
Source: Gross (1996).

Self-assessment questions

6 Distinguish between *primary* and *secondary* emotions.

7 Explain what is meant by *display rules* and *emotion work*.

8 Summarise the action of the amygdala in emotion.

9 What criticisms have been made about the James–Lange theory?

10 What reasons have been suggested for the changes in mood apparently caused by modelled facial expressions?

11 Outline one theory of emotion based on attribution.

(Suggested answers on page 565)

Stress

Most of the research on emotion has concentrated on negative emotions such as fear and anxiety because of the major impact of these states on our health and wellbeing. The consequence of these emotions and resultant **stress** is the focus of the last part of this unit.

> 'Stress is a pattern of physiological, behavioural, emotional and cognitive responses to real or imagined stimuli that are perceived as blocking a goal or endangering or otherwise threatening our wellbeing.' (Carlson and Buskist, 1997, p. 539)

These stimuli, whether physiological (for example loud noise) or psychological (for example death of a close relative), are called stressors. The body's reaction to all stressors is the same, with great individual differences. This pattern of physiological responses is a behavioural adaptation which helped our ancestors fight or run away from the wild animal or enemy and has become known as the 'fight or flight' response. McEwen (1994) found that stressors are varied as is the magnitude of the stress response, individual differences in response and the strategies adopted by the individual to cope with the stress.

Stress has been used to describe the cause or the effect of an emotion, as well as the state of the person experiencing it. The word also has a wide range of meanings in everyday language, from a mild problem that is easily overcome, to overwhelming pressure from which it seems difficult or impossible to escape.

Some consider stress to be exhilarating, whilst others run before the danger it poses to their wellbeing and sense of stability. Circumstances can also affect stress and the same person can perceive a similar situation as stressful one day, but pleasurable the next. Cox (1978) believed that

> 'stress can only be sensibly defined as a perceptual phenomenon arising from a comparison between the demands on the person and his [or her] ability to cope.

An imbalance in this mechanism, when coping is important, gives rise to the experience of stress, and to the stress response'.

Looker and Gregson (1990) agreed with Cox in thinking that stress results from an imbalance between the demands we perceive ourselves to be under, and the coping resources we think we have. The difference relates to how much stress we feel. They differentiate between distress, normal stress and eustress. Distress is caused by too much or too little demand for our coping ability, so we feel pressured or bored. Normal stress fluctuates constantly as different demands are made upon us, but we perceive ourselves able to cope with them. *Eustress* gives the experience of exhilaration when we feel we have plenty of ability to deal with an elevated level of stimulation.

Looker and Gregson (1990) used the analogy of a pair of scales to illustrate this (figure 15.22). The pointer moves through four zones according to the balance between perceived demands and perceived ability to cope.

Activity 8

For a week, using the analogy of scales in figure 15.22 record the demands you feel are being made upon you – and how well you feel able to cope with them. Record also what you actually did each time. Examine your responses in relation to the Yerkes–Dodson curve (figure 15.23). Keep this record, you will need it later (see page 545).

Physiological mechanisms of stress

As noted above, emotions include behavioural, autonomic and endocrine responses. Stress is a biological response experienced as emotion and our physical response to stressors is governed by the ANS and controlled by the hypothalamus.

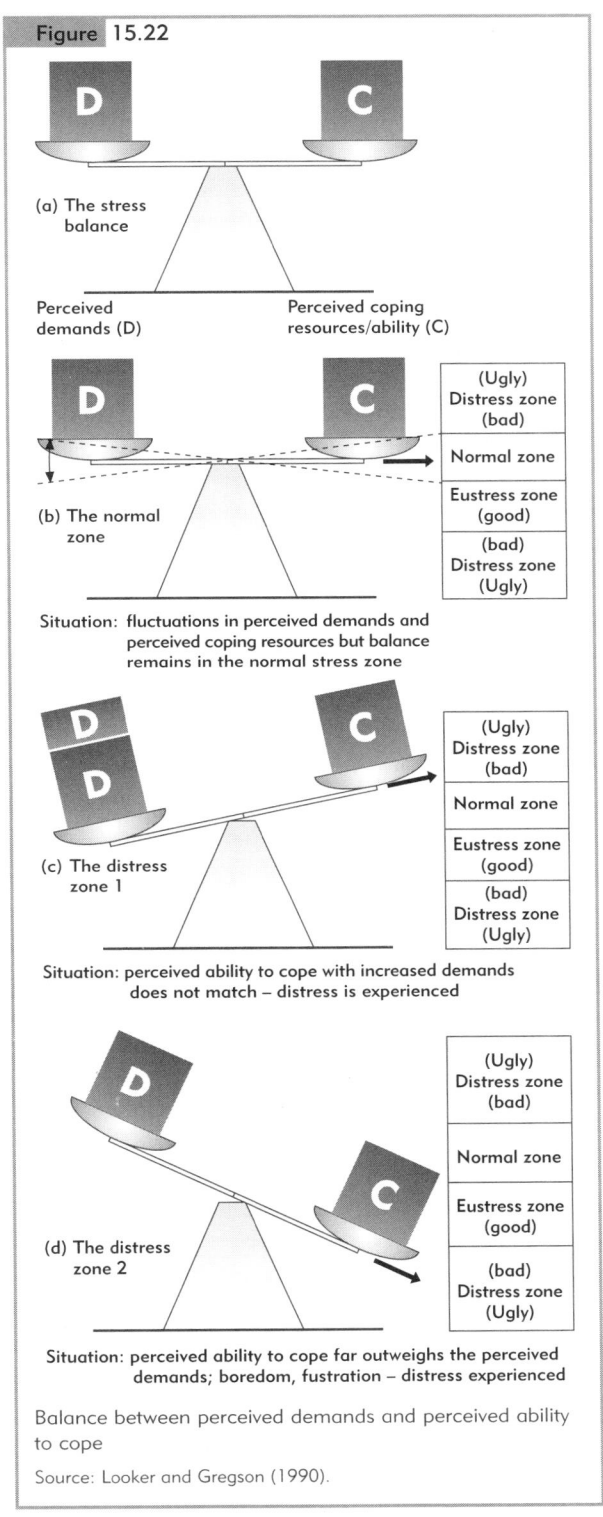

Figure 15.22

(a) The stress
balance

Perceived demands (D)

Perceived coping resources/ability (C)

(Ugly)
Distress zone (bad)

Normal zone

Eustress zone (good)

(bad)
Distress zone (Ugly)

(b) The normal zone

Situation: fluctuations in perceived demands and perceived coping resources but balance remains in the normal stress zone

(Ugly)
Distress zone (bad)

Normal zone

Eustress zone (good)

(bad)
Distress zone (Ugly)

(c) The distress zone 1

Situation: perceived ability to cope with increased demands does not match – distress is experienced

(Ugly)
Distress zone (bad)

Normal zone

Eustress zone (good)

(bad)
Distress zone (Ugly)

(d) The distress zone 2

Situation: perceived ability to cope far outweighs the perceived demands; boredom, fustration – distress experienced

Balance between perceived demands and perceived ability to cope

Source: Looker and Gregson (1990).

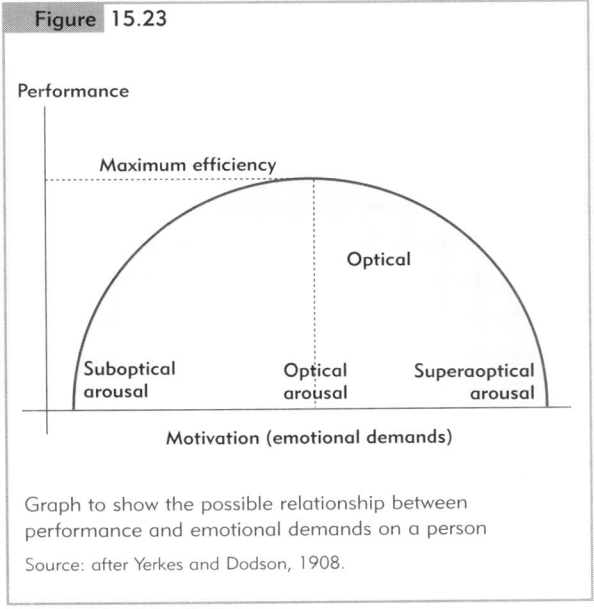

Figure 15.23

Performance

Maximum efficiency

Optical

Suboptical arousal

Optical arousal

Superaoptical arousal

Motivation (emotional demands)

Graph to show the possible relationship between performance and emotional demands on a person

Source: after Yerkes and Dodson, 1908.

■ The hypothalamic-pituitary-adrenal stress syndrome

The stress response occurs when a perceived threat to comfort initiates a series of autonomic and glandular activities within an organism. The organs most directly concerned with the response are the hypothalamus and the pituitary and adrenal glands. Each is linked to one or both of the others by nervous and hormonal pathways, and the effect they have on the body during arousal is the hypothalamic-pituitary-adrenal stress syndrome.

The hypothalamus lies in the brain above the pituitary and below the thalamus (see figure 15.3 on page 517). It is the centre of several homeostatic systems as well as being the monitor and controller of many hormone levels in the blood. The circadian clock (which controls our natural waking and sleeping rhythms) is located in or near it; thirst responses are directly mediated by it; it plays a critical role in the relationship between hormones and female sexual behaviour.

The pituitary is located on the lower surface of the hypothalamus, to which it is connected by the hypophyseal portal system of blood vessels. This carries two groups of hormones from the hypothalamus: those which are secreted directly from the pituitary in the form in which they were produced by the hypothalamus; and those which stimulate the secretion of hormones produced in the pituitary. Thus it is entirely under the control of the hypothalamus.

This is both neural and neurochemical. Figure 15.24 lists the pituitary hormones and their range of effects.

An adrenal gland is located above each kidney. The inner part, the adrenal medulla, secretes the hormones adrenaline and noradrenaline in response to impulses in autonomic nerve pathways from the hypothalamus. These act to release energy stores, increase metabolism and provide an efficient mechanism for response to a crisis by increasing sympathetic nervous system activity, thus causing arousal. Noradrenaline is also a neurotransmitter (see Unit 12 page 399). Some physiological and behavioural stress responses appear to be mediated by noradrenergic neurones. Stressful situations increase the release of noradrenaline in the hypothalamus, frontal cortex and lateral basal forebrain (Yokoo *et al.*, 1990;

Cenci *et al.*, 1992). The release of noradrenaline in the brain appears to be produced by a pathway from the central nucleus of the amygdala to the noradrenergic regions of the brainstem (Wallace *et al.*, 1992). The outer part, the adrenal cortex, secretes over 30 hormones, known collectively as corticoids, in response to adreno-cortico-trophic hormone (ACTH) from the pituitary. Corticoids are classified according to their action:

- Glucocorticoids help to increase blood sugar and protein breakdown. Excess secretion results in growth retardation, muscle wastage, thinning of the skin and suppression of the immune system.
- Mineralocorticoids help to control the salt balance in the body and through this the water balance. Excess secretion leads to oedema (retention of fluid in the tissues) and high blood pressure.
- Sex corticoids govern secondary sexual characteristics. High levels give feelings of elation, security and support (Looker and Gregson, 1989).

During the normal response to a short-lived threat such as electric shock, the hypothalamus is stimulated by both pain and nervous disruption. Impulses pass to the adrenal medulla. Large amounts of adrenaline are secreted which

15.24 Hormones released from the pituitary (Green, 1994)

- **Anterior lobe (adenohypophysis)**
  Growth hormone: promotes growth by stimulating protein synthesis in all cells of the body.
  Thyroid-stimulating hormone (thyrotropin): stimulates thyroid gland to release thyroxin, which helps regulate the body's metabolic rate.
  Adrenocorticotrophic hormone (ACTH): stimulates adrenal cortex to release corticosteroids in states of arousal and stress.
  Follicle-stimulating hormone and luteinising hormone: act together to promote testosterone release and sperm cell growth in males and oestrogen release and egg cell production in females.
  Prolactin: promotes milk production by action on female mammary glands.

- **Posterior lobe (neurohypophysis)**
  Vasopressin (antidiuretic hormone): promotes water retention by direct action on kidney tubules.
  Oxytocin: stimulates uterine contractions during labour.

stimulate the hypothalamus to secrete cortico-releasing factor (CRF). CRF in turn stimulates the flow of ACTH which causes the release of corticoids into the bloodstream. Corticoids inhibit the action of the hypothalamus and pituitary with the result that all systems return to normal, a negative feedback system. Figure 15.25 shows the reaction in diagrammatic form.

CRF is also secreted within the brain where it acts as a neuromodulator, especially in the limbic system involved in emotional responses (Carlson, 1994).

These physiological changes are adaptive, producing a psychological and physical state of readiness for action. However, such responses can be maladaptive in producing anxiety which may interfere with performance of a task. Prolonged and severe stress, which are often part of many people's life style, also creates an increased risk of illness. Hans Selye (1956) suggested that prolonged secretion of glucocorticoids were most damaging. The short-term effects of glucocorticoids are essential to life but the long-term effects include increased blood pressure, damage to muscle tissue, infertility and suppression of the immune system making the individual vulnerable to infections and perhaps cancer. Stunted growth in children is another damaging effect and the body also finds it difficult to heal itself after injury. The long-term effects of stress on health are discussed on page 552–5.

Sources of stress

Stressors have been identified from a variety of sources, including environmental stress, work-related stress, life events and daily hassles.

■ Environmental stress
Early research focused on the physical aspects of the environment such as extremes of temperature, lighting and noise. There are great individual differences in tolerance to these.

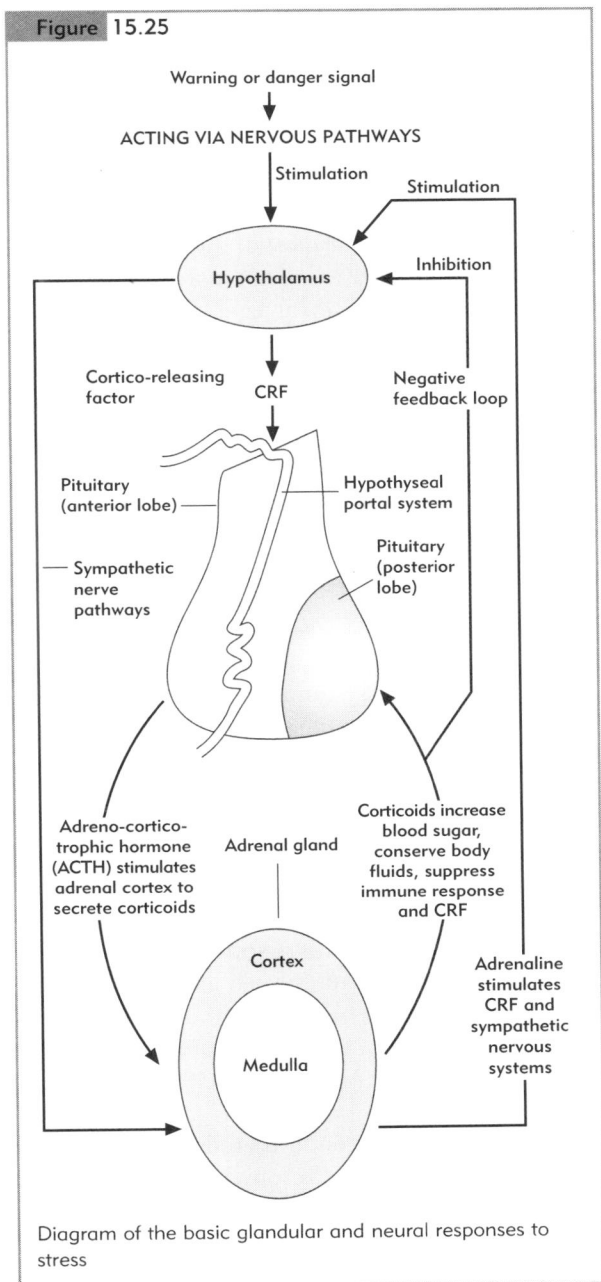

Figure 15.25

Warning or danger signal

ACTING VIA NERVOUS PATHWAYS

Stimulation

Stimulation

Hypothalamus

Inhibition

Cortico-releasing factor

CRF

Negative feedback loop

Pituitary (anterior lobe)

Hypothyseal portal system

Pituitary (posterior lobe)

Sympathetic nerve pathways

Adreno-cortico-trophic hormone (ACTH) stimulates adrenal cortex to secrete corticoids

Adrenal gland

Corticoids increase blood sugar, conserve body fluids, suppress immune response and CRF

Adrenaline stimulates CRF and sympathetic nervous systems

Cortex

Medulla

Diagram of the basic glandular and neural responses to stress

At one time *overcrowding* was linked to crime, however, this has not been supported by subsequent research which controlled for age, class and ethnocentricity. Some cultures live in denser population conditions with no related increase in crime. For example, Tokyo is far more crowded than many cities in the USA but has a lower incidence of crime. Crowds can be stressful or they can be fun. New Year's Eve in Prince's Street Gardens, Edinburgh, Cup Final day at Wembley, Pavarotti in the Park are all large-crowd occasions which are enjoyable for most of the people present. Of course, put the Pavarotti fan in a crowd listening to a popular music group at a gig which may not be to his or her liking and he or she may feel uncomfortable and have a stressful experience as a result. As with noise, crowding becomes stressful when it impinges on your sense of freedom and control, not stressful when you *are* crowded but rather when you *feel* crowded. Health and mental performance suffer when people feel trapped (Taylor, 1991). These effects can last long after the event.

Until recently, the stress associated with major disasters such as explosions, fires and earthquakes was not studied systematically. However, the condition post-traumatic stress disorder has now been studied (see Unit 25 page 926). Psychological problems following large-scale disasters include nightmares and flashbacks, irritability and difficulty in concentrating, general unresponsiveness and distress at reminders of the event (Lindy *et al.*, 1987). Whether such events leave long-term psychological problems is a source of controversy with some research finding such effects and others showing them to be minimal. Most distress eventually subsides, perhaps dependent on the social support available from family, friends and community (Kaniasty and Norris, 1993). When a whole community is affected, as with an earthquake, then such resources are not always available.

In the short term, reaction to human-made disasters such as bombs and nuclear accidents seem to produce more psychological trauma than natural disasters such as floods (Baum and Fleming, 1993). This may be linked to violation of our expectations in that we do not expect to have control over earthquakes, hurricanes and other natural disasters whereas what is seen to be human

error or deliberate intent to kill is difficult to accept (Baron, 1996).

It has also been pointed out that human-made disasters can have long-term stress implications. People continuing to live in an area of contamination by toxic chemicals or radiation can have chronic long-term stress effect (Baum and Fleming, 1993).

Children seem to suffer post-traumatic stress disorder second-hand from observing frightening television programmes. Simons and Silveira (1994) reported two case studies of children who were traumatised after watching a television programme *Ghostwatch* in the UK. The children were helped by behavioural and cognitive strategies including relaxation techniques and anxiety management (see Unit 25 page 926).

■ Work-related stress

Most adults spend more time at work than in any other activity so it is not surprising that the area of work is a source of stress. Most people would associate *overload* as the major cause, being asked to do too much in a short period of time, but being asked to do too little can result in boredom which is also stressful. Cartwright (1994) noted that stress resulted in the loss of about 120 million working days in 1993 in the UK, and this is thought to be the 'tip of the iceberg', with many such absences not reported.

Work-related stress caused by environmental factors such as noise and temperature is tolerable within a given range, outside which physiological and psychological disturbance can be caused. In fact, more working days are lost each year due to occupational stressors than to accidents. This is something to think about! If you then consider that accidents themselves are often the indirect result of stress, you have even more food for thought!

Work-related stress may be experienced by those who travel abroad extensively, for example pilots and executives. Travel disrupts circadian rhythms which, if upset or interfered with, can result in the breakdown of homeostatic mechanisms within an individual and performance deterioration.

Cox *et al.* (1978) proposed that in work-related stress the perceived demand covers both external environmental aspects as well as internal ones such as needs, values, motivation and job satisfaction. Perceived coping ability lies in the confidence of the individual to carry out work to the satisfaction of an employer. Cox and Mackay's transactional model of stress illustrates their theory (figure 15.26).

Activity 9

Re-examine the record you made of your perceived demands and responses in Activity 8 (page 540). Are there any elements in common with the transactional model in figure 15.26?

All jobs involve certain stress which some people manage to cope with effectively. Some are not as fortunate and over a period of time become worn out. Such people are described as suffering 'burnout' (Pines and Aronson, 1988; Lee and Ashforth, 1990). The characteristics of burnout are summarised in figure 15.27.

Melamid *et al.* (1992) found burnout could increase the risk of coronary heart disease (CHD).

Several factors have been linked with burnout such as poor opportunities for promotion and the presence of inflexible rules and procedures which make the individual feel trapped and develop negative views on his or her job. Satisfying social life outside the work setting can act as a buffer to burnout. With appropriate help, an individual suffering burnout can recover, especially if co-workers are involved in providing help and support.

■ Stressful life events and daily hassles

Activity 10

Can you think of some of your own life changes when you have felt under pressure? Write these down, remembering to include both positive and negative events. (Compare your list to the research which follows.)

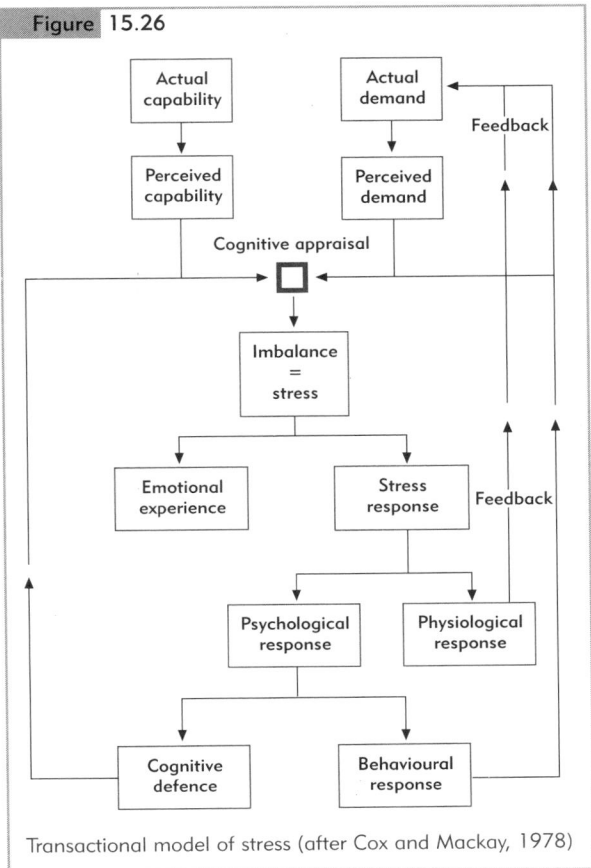

Figure 15.26

Transactional model of stress (after Cox and Mackay, 1978)

Any change in an individual's life, whether pleasant or unpleasant, requires some re-adjustment. Studies of personal histories suggest that physical and emotional disorders tend to cluster around periods of major change in an individual's life. The social re-adjustment rating scale (see table 15.28) marks an attempt by Holmes and Rahé (1967) to measure stress in terms of life changes. Life events are ranked in order, from most stressful (death of a spouse) to least stressful (minor violations of the law).

Thousands of interviews and medical histories were used to identify stressful events. As marriage appeared to be a critical event for most people, it was placed in the middle of the scale with an arbitrary value of 50. Some 400 men and women of varying ages, backgrounds and marital status were

Figure 15.27

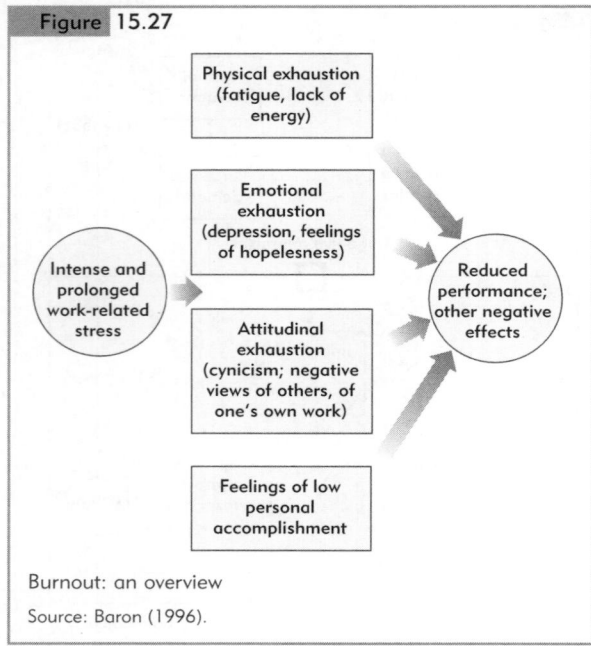

Burnout: an overview

Source: Baron (1996).

Table 15.28

Rank	life event	Mean value
1	Death of spouse	100
2	Divorce	73
3	Marital separation	65
4	Jail term	63
5	Death of close family member	63
6	Personal injury or illness	53
7	Marriage	50[a]
8	Dismissal from work	47
9	Marital reconciliation	45
10	Retirement	45
11	Change in health of family member	44
12	Pregnancy	40
13	Sex difficulties	39
14	Gain of new family member	39
15	Business re-adjustment	39
16	Change in financial state	38
17	Death of a close friend	37
18	Change to different line of work	36

Table 15.28 *cont'd*

Rank	life event	Mean value
19	Change in number of arguments with spouse	35
20	Mortgage over £10 000	31
21	Foreclosure of mortgage or loan	30
22	Change in responsibilities at work	29
23	Son or daughter leaving home	29
24	Trouble with in-laws	29
25	Outstanding personal achievement	28
26	Wife begins or stops work	26
27	Begin or end school	26
28	Change in living conditions	25
29	Revision of personal habits	24
30	Trouble with boss	23
31	Change in work hours or conditions	20
32	Change in residence	20
33	Change in schools	20
34	Change in recreation	19
35	Change in church activities	19
36	Change in social activities	18
37	Mortgage or loan less than £10 000	17
38	Change in sleeping habits	16
39	Change in number of family gatherings	15
40	Change in eating habits	15
41	Holiday	13
42	Christmas	12
43	Minor violations to the law	11

Social re-adjustment rating scale (Holmes and Rahé)

[a] Marriage was arbitrarily assigned a stress value of 50. No event was found to be any more than twice as stressful. Here the values are reduced proportionally and range up to 100.

An individual's level of stress is calculated in the following way:
1 The participant is asked to describe specific life-events experienced during a particular period of time, for example the past two years.
2 The appropriate stress value for each life event is assigned to the individual and a total stress index is arrived at by adding together all the stress values the individual has received.

Source: Taylor and Hayes (1990).

then asked to compare marriage with other life events. They were asked such questions as: 'Does the event call for more or less re-adjustment than marriage?', 'Would the re-adjustment take shorter or longer to accomplish?' They then rated each event on the basis of its severity and the time required for adjustment.

Early studies using the scale showed it to have wide application. Minority groups in the USA and people in both underdeveloped and highly developed countries tended to rate events similarly. However, later studies have found significant differences in perceptions of life events.

Studies using the social re-adjustment rating scale have found, however, a consistent relationship between the number of stressful events in an individual's life and his or her emotional and physical health. People whose life-change units summed to more than 300 over a period of a year are more susceptible to health problems than those with lower scores (see also Unit 23 page 872).

Holmes and Rahé (1967) accounted for the findings relating life changes to illness by postulating that the more critical the changes experienced by an individual, the greater the effort required to adapt. This effort is presumed to lower the body's natural resistance to disease. For example, Cohen et al. (1993) in a study on the common cold, asked 420 volunteers to record all significant stressful events which had affected them over the previous 12 months. An experimental group was given nose drops containing a virus known to cause the common cold and a control group was given uncontaminated nose drops. Both groups were then put into quarantine for seven days. Results found those in the experimental group who had reported two or more negative life events during the previous year were more likely to develop a cold than less-stressed volunteers.

■ Johnson and McCutchen (1980) used a modified form of the scale to show that older children and adolescents who experienced life changes as negative, and who perceived themselves as having less control over the environment, were more likely to become ill than those who experienced the changes as

positive and perceived themselves to have more control over the environment.

■ Brown (1986) suggested that some life events may be consequent upon illness rather than the other way round (for example depression may result in being fired from work or in changed sleeping habits).

■ Some events become stressful once a person is ill or depressed.

■ All life events are not stressful to everyone. Cognitive appraisal of the events is important. Even the death of a partner may not be as stressful for someone locked into an unhappy relationship and retirement is often a relief to many highly stressed employees.

■ Counting the number of stressful events is not sufficient as a measure unless the individual's appraisal of the events is considered (Cohen et al., 1983).

Lazarus and his colleagues (Kanner et al., 1981; Lazarus et al., 1985) devised a hassles and uplifts scale to assess the daily and cumulative impact of everyday demands. This scale incorporates both negative and positive aspects of events. They found it a better predictor of psychological symptoms than the social re-adjustment rating scale. Among the hassles they include personal worries such as weight, health and appearance; family worries such as rising food prices, domestic bills and property investments; and community worries such as vandalism, theft and other crimes. Uplifts are given by feelings of wellbeing and satisfaction, good relations and friendly communications as well as nice surprises such as being invited out for a meal.

Williams (1992) found that an increase in major life events and daily hassles or an increase in hassles compared with uplifts was associated with increased risks of hospitalisation for American participants over a two-year period. Participants' daily hassle scales also predicted how frequently they used the out-patient department of the hospital.

Perhaps the repetitive, frequent nature of daily hassles can exert a more adverse effect on health than major life events. Reporting of daily hassles and negative life events is very subjective, with some being stressful to one individual but not to another. Some people for whom daily hassles have been found to be a health hazard are those identified as very anxious and quick to overreact (Kohn *et al.*, 1991). For such people, a small hassle can be 'the last straw'.

It is difficult to separate the effects of stress from factors such as diet, smoking, drinking and other general health habits. An individual trying to cope with the demands of a new and more difficult job might increase his or her alcohol intake, eat too much snack food, get less sleep and fail to exercise. An increased susceptibility to illness in such a case is more likely to stem from the changes in health habits than from the direct action of stress on resistance to disease.

People differ in their tendency to focus on physical symptoms and in their inclination to seek medical help. A respiratory infection or stomachache that one person ignores may send another to a doctor. People who are unhappy and discontented tend to focus on body symptoms and seek medical advice more often than people busily involved in activities they enjoy. Since the data for many life change studies come from medical reports, it could be that it is biased in this direction.

Individual differences in seeking help are even more pronounced when the discomfort is psychological, rather than clearly physical.

Life events often involve social stressors such as conflicts with people, for example at home or at work. A conflict is experienced as a difficult or impossible choice to make or carry out. For example, if a young couple finds that one of them has contracted a long-term and painful illness which requires much nursing, does the healthy partner continue to work to provide the essentials of living, or does he or she leave work to provide the nursing and attention required at home? This situation faces many homes and the answer is so difficult to find that both physiological and psychological distress can result.

To sum up, stressful life events clearly play a role in illness, but they do so in interaction with biological factors (pre-existing susceptibilities toward certain disorders), life habits and the psychological characteristics of the individual.

Activity 11

Select three items from the social re-adjustment rating scale in table 15.28 (page 546) which would be judged differently by:
- different age
- male and female
- different cultures and sub-cultures.

If you were drawing up a new scale today what new stressors might you include?

(Suggested answers on page 564.)

Responses to stressors

The body's immediate reaction to a stressor is one of arousal brought about by the hypothalamic-pituitary-adrenal stress syndrome (see page 541). This arousal may have physiological, psychological or psychosomatic effects.

■ Physiological responses to stressors

Some of the physiological responses to stressors are shown in figure 15.29.

Selye (1956) considered stress to be a 'non-specific (physiological) response of the body to any demand made upon it'; that is, a response to the demands of the environment. As a medical student, Selye noted a general malaise among patients, irrespective of the specific nature of their illnesses. This was characterised by reduced appetite causing loss of weight, strength and ambition together with an associated facial expression. From his observations, he described the **general adaptation syndrome** (GAS), a universal stress response which serves both to protect the organism and to preserve its sense of being. With continuous or repeated exposure to a stressor, the response progresses through three identifiable stages:

15.29 Physiological responses to stress

Rapid heartbeat
Breathlessness
'Butterflies in the stomach'
Dry mouth
Sweaty palms
Weak knees
Loss of appetite
Feeling shaky or jittery
Flushed skin
Incontinence
Pilo-erection (hair raising)
Feeling hot
Feeling sick or 'knotted inside'
Feeling withdrawn
Inability to relax
Clenched hands and teeth
Pupil dilation
Release of stress hormones (e.g. adrenaline)
Release of glucose from the liver
Increased blood supply to the brain/skeletal muscles

- alarm
- resistance
- exhaustion.

When confronted with a stressor there is an *alarm* reaction by the ANS resulting in the production of adrenaline and other adrenal hormones such as steroids (the 'fight or flight response'). During the alarm stage resistance to the stressor temporarily drops below normal and a shock reaction may occur, resulting in impairment of normal physiological responses. This occasionally results in death.

With continued exposure to the stressor (or another stressor) the *stage of resistance* begins during which the ANS returns to normal. This reflects the individual's adaptation to environmental stressors.

Extended exposure will result in the *stage of exhaustion* during which the energy and ability to adapt is lost and resistance drops below normal

levels, leaving the individual susceptible to illness and even death. Animal research showed the adrenal glands to be enlarged, with their store of steroids depleted. The level of salt in the blood fell dramatically and the kidneys were damaged due to receiving excess hormones. Selye (1956) also found if a second source of stress was introduced during the resistance stage the animals died quickly, unable to draw on any other resources.

Why do these mechanisms which were devised to help us have such a devastating effect? The answer could be that they are meant to be temporary and only when responses become continuous rather than episodic do the effects become dangerous.

Although Selye (1956) believed this syndrome of sickness was imposed on all diseases, it appears that he overstated the case. Mason (1971) noted that exercise, fasting and heat do not produce the syndrome. Further, the response is different if the organism perceives the stressor as grounds for anger, since there is evidence to suggest that anxiety is associated with the release of adrenaline and anger with the release of noradrenaline.

Many of the harmful effects of long-term stress are caused by our own reactions and Selye's (1956) model, although helpful for understanding the physiological reaction of the body, does not explain the psychological components of stress. As noted above, many of the reactions to stressors are dependent on the people's *cognition* and individual differences in temperament or experience.

The role of cognition on stress

Stress occurs when an individual perceives the situation to be threatening (primary appraisal) and considers that he or she will not be able to cope with the danger or demands (secondary appraisal) (Croyle, 1992).

Tomako *et al.* (1993) asked people to give primary and secondary appraisals before starting a counting task. They were asked 'How threatening do you think the task will be?' (primary appraisal) and 'How able are you to cope with the task?' (secondary appraisal). Researchers predicted that those who felt they could not successfully complete the task would suffer more stress whereas those who were more confident would perceive the task as a challenge and exhibit greater physiological arousal. These predictions were confirmed. Greater stress was indicated by the former group and higher arousal by the latter group, which also scored more highly on both the perceived and actual measures of performance (see figure 15.30).

Perception of the ability to exert some *control* over the stressful situation seems to be a critical factor. Earlier work with monkeys and rats highlighted this important variable.

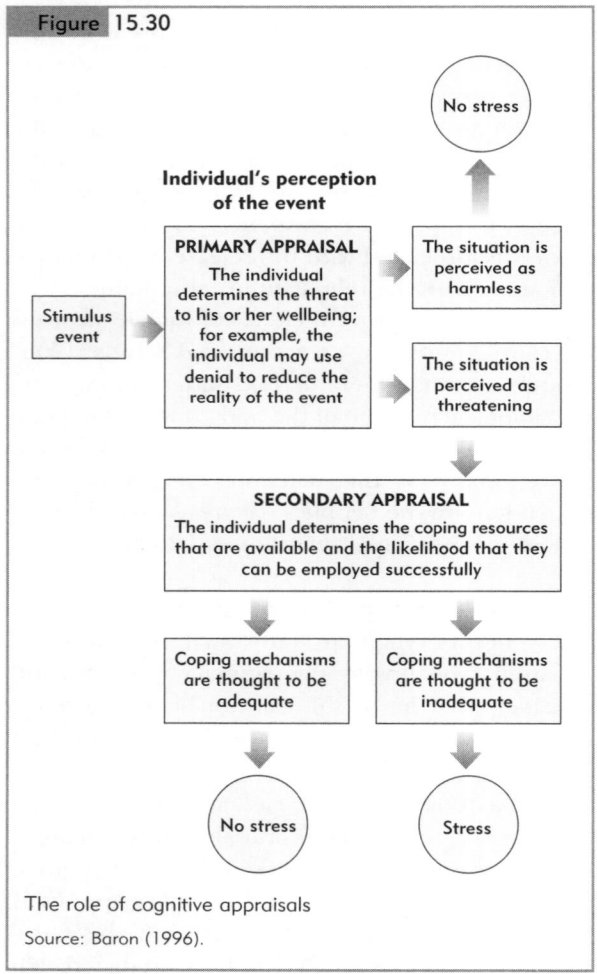

Figure 15.30

The role of cognitive appraisals

Source: Baron (1996).

Brady *et al.* (1968) claimed to show the kind of stress that can produce ulcers. Two monkeys, seated side by side in restraining chairs for many hours at a time, were subjected to a device which could deliver electric shocks. One monkey, known as the 'executive monkey', had access to a lever. When pressed, the lever would de-activate the shocking device for 20 seconds and both monkeys would avoid shocks. When the 'executive monkey' failed to respond in time because of inattention or fatigue, both monkeys received a shock. As they received identical shocks throughout the experiment, any physiological damage due to the shocks would have affected them equally. Only the 'executive monkey', however, developed ulcers. The conclusion reached was that the constant alertness required to respond at appropriate intervals produced a continuing state of tension that resulted in ulcers. The control monkey, which had no contingency (control) over the avoidance of shock, was somehow less reactive and less disturbed.

It should be pointed out that Brady *et al.*'s study is flawed methodologically as the monkeys were not randomly allocated to conditions – the 'fastest learners' were always assigned the executive role. Later research has shown that such participants tend to be the most emotional. It is also dangerous to generalise from other species to humans since humans have different life styles and cognitions about decision making and environmental situations.

A later investigation (Weiss, 1972) achieved very different results, and seems to indicate that Brady *et al.*'s conclusion was too simplistic. A rat that could avoid shock by turning a wheel in response to a warning signal, developed less ulceration than a yoked companion, which was unable to avoid the shocks. Weiss suggested several reasons for the difference between his results and those obtained in the studies with monkeys. The 'executive monkey' was responding at a very fast rate, without immediate feedback to indicate that its response was successful, until some time later when it received, or failed to receive, the shock. The stress for the 'executive monkey' was evidently much greater than for the 'executive rat', which was required to make an avoidance response at well-spaced intervals and knew that the response would prevent shock until the next warning signal. So having some *control* over the aversive situation was found to reduce the stress level. There have been similar findings involving humans in which situations that permit some control are less likely to produce signs of stress (Gatchel *et al.*, 1989). Perhaps the 'illusion of control' is sufficient (Carlson and Buskist, 1997)? Rotter (1966) originally identified people who believed they had control over a situation to be exhibiting 'internal locus of control' and those who believed the outcome was outside their control to have 'external locus of control'. Some cultures place different emphasis on who is responsible for success or failure. A study of 194 Anglo-American teenagers and 194 Taiwanese teenagers undertaken by Lian-Hwang Chiu in 1988 found the Anglo-Americans to be more internal in assuming responsibility for their success whereas the Chinese were more internal in assuming responsibility for their failures.

Rotter (1966) and later Seligman (1975) believed this internal control was a learned behaviour. Seligman (1975) identified **learned helplessness** which can develop in animals and humans when the earlier learning suggests the individual will not be able to control the stimulus, for example a loud noise (Hiroto and Seligman, 1975). Such perception can result in the development of depression (see Unit 25 page 931).

Different styles of thinking which distinguish between pessimists and optimists have been termed 'explanatory style' by Seligman (1991). An optimistic explanatory style is related to high self-esteem, achievement, physical health and long life expectancy (Scherer and Carver, 1988). Carver *et al.* (1993) suggested that optimists are more stress-resistant because they adopt strategies for dealing with stress, such as problem-focused coping and seeking social support. Conversely, pessimists tend to use strategies such as denial or giving up on the goal producing the stress. The various strategies used by pessimists and optimists can be found listed in table 15.31. Some evidence suggests that males use the strategies identified as used by optimists more than females (Ptacek *et al.*, 1994).

Pessimism may lead to depression or stress progressing to illness as suggested by a longitudinal study of Harvard University graduates undertaken by Peterson *et al.* (1988). They followed a group of males who were all in good health at the beginning of the study. Thirty-five years later they found those who had a pessimistic explanatory style were in worse health than the optimists.

Taking a problem-focused approach rather than an emotion-focused one may be an important factor, a focus more on what you *do* rather than what you *feel*. The higher expectation of success and refusal to give up when things go wrong, combined with a sense of humour and reinterpreting the situation in a positive light, has been found important (Carver *et al.*, 1989).

Table 15.31

Strategies preferred by	Description
Optimists	
Problem-focused coping	Making specific plans for dealing with the source of stress; implementing such plans
Suppressing competing activities	Refraining from other activities until the problem is solved and stress is reduced
Seeking social support	Obtaining the advice of others; talking the problem over with others
Pessimists	
Denial/distancing	Ignoring the problem or source of stress; refusing to believe that it exists or is important
Disengagement from the goal	Giving up on reaching the goal that is being blocked by stress
Focusing on the expression of feelings	Letting off steam instead of working on the problem directly

Source: Baron (1996).

Optimists do not repress anxiety, rather do they acknowledge problems and illness and have confidence in their *control* to overcome them (Schwartz, 1990). Cognitive therapy has been used successfully to teach depressed people new explanatory styles.

Some people have been found more resistant to the effects of stress. The cluster of characteristics which identifies this group has been named 'hardiness' by Kobasa (1979). Kobasa found hardy individuals differ from others in three ways:

- High levels of *commitment* with involvement in current activity and a value of its worth.
- Change is seen as a *challenge*, an opportunity for growth and development, rather than a threat.
- A stronger sense of *control* over the events in their lives.

Kobasa's findings support those of Lazarus (see page 538) in highlighting how cognitive appraisal of the situation and the extent to which an individual thinks he or she can control the stressor play an important part in the effects of stress. Kobasa and Maddi (1991) saw early family home life to be strongly linked with hardiness. They found parental warmth, a stimulating home environment and family support in solving problems to be positively correlated with hardiness.

Stress and ill-health

The link of stress with ill-health is strong (Kiecolt-Glaser and Glaser, 1992). It has been linked with the occurrence of heart disease, high blood pressure, hardening of the arteries, gastric ulcers, diabetes and cancer (figure 15.32).

Early in the twentieth century psychosomatic medicine developed, referring to the interaction of mind (*psyche*) and body (*soma*). Freud proposed that many illnesses were the result of unconscious conflicts. Unfortunately, much of the early research led to the view that psychosomatic illness was 'all in the mind' whereas the psychosomatic approach stresses the interaction of mind and body and how the body can also affect the mind. This interaction can be seen in the link between stress and gastric ulcers. The Brady and Weiss studies (see pages 550–1) found increased ulceration when animals were under stress.

Gastric ulcers are painful lesions in the lining of the stomach and duodenum. In humans they are prevalent in people who live under stressful conditions. Each day the average human adult secretes several litres of gastric chemicals, including hydrochloric acid, which breaks down

15.32 Some conditions in which stress has been implicated

- **Cardiovascular disorders**
high blood pressure
heart attack
angina
stroke
auto-immune disease

- **Digestive disorders**
peptic ulcers
mouth ulcers
intestinal inflammation
constipation
diarrhoea

- **Respiratory disorders**
asthma
giddiness

- **Allergies**
eczema

- **Muscle tensions**
backache
migraine
neck and shoulder pain
menstrual change

- **Mental disorders**
depression
nervous breakdown

- **Other conditions**
poor sleeping habits
accidents
cancer

food during digestion. Some cases of gastric ulcers are associated with high levels of hydrochloric acid, but this is not the only factor as many sufferers do not show such high concentration. Stress has been found to increase hydrochloric acid secretion and weaken the gastrointestinal tract's defences against this. The activity of the sympathetic system of the ANS in stress moves blood away from the gastrointestinal tract towards the skeletal muscles reducing the efficiency of the mucous barrier they supply. In the parasympathetic rebound there is a surge of hydrochloric acid which can then more readily penetrate the walls of the gastrointestinal tract (Pinel, 1997).

The amygdala has been found to play an important role in this process (Henke, 1992). Stimulation of certain parts of the amygdala increases the release of hydrochloric acid and decreases blood flow in the gastric mucous. This can produce gastric ulcers within a few hours.

One of the leading causes of death in western society is coronary heart disease (CHD) which can result in heart attacks, when the blood vessels serving the heart become blocked, and strokes, which involve blood vessels in the brain.

Type A behaviour
There are great individual variations in emotional reactivity to stress which affect blood pressure and have detrimental effects on health. An early attempt to link a behavioural pattern in certain people to CHD was identified by Friedman and Rosenman (1959). As can be seen in figure 15.33

they distinguished between a **Type A behaviour** pattern which seemed to increase the risk of CHD and Type B, calmer and less intense and less likely to suffer heart disease.

Lyness (1993) noted the emotional reaction of Type A individuals may result in constriction of peripheral blood flow, higher blood pressure and increased pulse rate. Such changes may result in excessive wear and tear on the arteries of the heart and lead to CHD (Contrada, 1989). Dembrowski and Williams (1989) found the emotional responses of Type A individuals accompanied by increased adrenaline and noradrenaline which may lead to greater fatty deposits on the walls of the blood vessels.

The early enthusiasm on Type A behaviour has now been moderated by several contradictory findings. For example, Ragland and Brand (1988) found that although Type A individuals were more likely to have heart attacks they had a better survival rate than Type B personalities. The personality that led to a heart attack may in itself be more likely to work hard in recovery! Other studies have failed to find any difference in CHD between Type A and Type B personalities (Dimsdale, 1988).

Some aspects of the Type A personality have been suggested as being of particular importance in CHD. A high risk factor was found to be *hostility*. Williams (1985) noted that men who were chronically angry and resentful, with a hostile attitude towards others, were found more prone to heart disease even when other risk factors such as smoking were controlled. *Antagonistic* or *cynical*

15.33 Type A and Type B

Some people have a greater autonomic reactivity than others, and in challenging situations are competitive, impatient and hostile (Cooper et al., 1981). This tends to elevate blood cholesterol levels, increase blood clotting time and put great strain on the heart. This is known as **Type A behaviour** and those who exhibit it are susceptible to coronary heart disease. Glass (1977) proposed that Type A individuals use this particular behaviour

pattern as an attempt to maintain a sense of control over environmental stressors – a style of coping which brings heavy health penalties.

People displaying less autonomic reactivity are said to display **Type B behaviour**. They speak more slowly, are more relaxed and content, and less competitive and hostile when responding to environmental stress. Neither do they suffer from the same health problems as Type A individuals.

hostility was found to be particularly dangerous. Such men are aggressive, suspicious, confrontational, rude, cynical, uncooperative, with a lack of trust in others. The link between hostility and heart disease in women is less clear (Smith *et al.*, 1990). Not all Type Bs are as relaxed as previously suggested. Friedman (1991) identified 'phoney Type Bs' who, although stating they were unaffected by pressure and lacking aggression, were really competitive, angry and tense and more prone to heart disease.

Although personality factors do appear to be involved in illness their precise nature is uncertain. Negative emotions or personality traits may be involved in illness but they are not the major cause.

■ The immune system

Long-term stress can be harmful to health and even result in brain damage often due to the increased level of glucocorticoids, adrenaline and noradrenaline. Stress can also lower resistance to infection. The immune system which protects the body from foreign micro-organisms can also be impaired. In the 1980s a new field of biopsychological research was set up to study the interaction of the psychological factors, the nervous system and the immune system. This field is known as **psychoneuroimmunology** and has focused on three main areas:

■ How does stress disrupt the immune function?
■ Does the link between stress and decreases in the immune function have any clinical significance?
■ Which physiological and psychological mechanisms are involved?

The immune system can malfunction and allergic reactions sometimes occur. When an antigen causes cells in the immune system to overreact, a particular immunoglobulin produces an inflammatory response. The chemicals produced can enter the general circulation and cause life-threatening complications. The reasons why these occur is still unknown.

The immune system can also attack its own cells. Such **auto-immune diseases** occur when the immune system becomes sensitised to a protein in the body and the system then attacks the tissue containing this protein. The reason for this malfunction is not known but it often follows viral or bacterial infections. Such auto-immune diseases include rheumatoid arthritis, diabetes and multiple sclerosis.

Although several human studies have shown positive correlations between stress and ill-health, such studies alone cannot determine causality. Stressed people may report more illness during times of stress because they expect to be more ill or because the stress results in changes in diet, drug use or sleep. However, 'human correlational studies and the controlled animal experiments leave little doubt that stress does increase our susceptibility to infectious diseases' (Pinel, 1997, p. 453).

There are numerous mechanisms by which stress could influence the immune system. Hypothalamic lesions not only disrupt the visceral responses to fear but also disrupt the immune system. The bone marrow, thymus gland and lymph nodes all receive neural input so it would not be suprising to find these have an effect on the immune system (so far the precise mechanisms are unknown).

The immune system is also sensitive to the chemicals produced in the nervous system. Inescapable, intermittent shock produced decreased sensitivity to pain (analgesia) and the suppression of natural killer cells (Shavit *et al.*, 1984). Both were seen to be mediated by the body's own opioids as these effects disappeared when a drug blocking the opiate receptors was administered. Shavit *et al.* (1986) also found natural killer-cell activity was suppressed when morphine was injected directly into the brain. The precise mechanism involved in the brain has not yet been identified.

■ Type C personality

Researchers have suggested a 'cancer-prone personality' which can be a risk factor for the disease. Morris (1980) was one of the researchers to suggest a **Type C** (cancer-prone) **personality**. This was described by Temoshok *et al.* (1985) as an individual who is cooperative, unassertive and patient. Perhaps this type of individual suppresses negative emotions such as anger and complies with those in authority. Temoshok (1987) suggested such blocked emotions result in the release of neuropeptides in the brain which disrupt homeostatic mechanisms and impair the body's ability to defend itself from cancer cells.

Most of the studies investigating the personal characteristics associated with cancer have been on people already suffering cancer. They have looked at the relationship of personality to the severity of the disease or made comparisons with those not suffering cancer. Such correlations are open to alternative explanations of causality as it is difficult to determine cause and effect.

Grossarth-Maticek *et al.* (1985) carried out a longitudinal study in former Yugoslavia which started in 1966 and ran for ten years. The found people identified as having Type C personality most likely to suffer cancer (especially lung cancer). This has been supported by more recent research by Grossarth-Maticek and Eysenck (1990).

The Grossarth-Maticek studies, although useful in demonstrating a personality link, cannot distinguish if the potential for cancer is due to the suppression of the immune system by the personality type or whether it is due to the associated behavioural characteristics. For example, a passive personality is less likely to take responsibility for their own health, they may be less alert to the warning signals of cancer or disregard these until it is too late.

Most investigators believe that if the immune system plays a role in the link between personality and cancer it affects the *growth* of the tumours and not the *formation* (Carlson and Buskist, 1997). Personality variables may affect the individual *directly* by altering the immune system or *indirectly* by affecting the health-related behaviour. So far researchers have not been able to distinguish between these. Some clinicians are concerned that there is an emphasis on the belief that thinking negatively causes illnesses and thinking positively cures them. They are concerned that this may tempt people to forego medical treatment.

Heredity and exposure to carcinogens are far more important risk factors in tumour formation and so far standard medical treatments provide the most effective form of therapy. Early medical treatment is essential so there is cause for concern that any delay might be fatal. Clinicians are also concerned for the effects on patients who might feel responsible for not being able to cure themselves.

Activity 12

Trust this task is not a source of stress for you. Complete the following sentences:

a Type _____ personality is thought to increase the risk of CHD.

b Psychoneuroimmunology is the study of _____ .

c _____ occur when the immune system malfunctions and begins to attack itself.

d A person who is cooperative, unassertive, patient, suppresses anger and is compliant may be a _____ personality.

(Suggested answers on page 564.)

Stress management

So far we have concentrated on the negative aspects of stress, but not all stress is harmful. Some stress is positive and feels good such as falling in love, competing in a sports event or even completing some project that you enjoy. This was named 'eustress' by Selye (1956). He believed that all stress cannot be avoided and people aiming for a stress-free life are setting themselves an impossible goal. We should try and minimise the wear and tear of stress rather than eliminate it completely. The good news is that we can learn to control stress and mitigate the damaging effects by developing *coping* strategies. People cope differently with all the challenges, hassles, disappointments and dangers they meet in life. It is advantageous to have a variety of strategies available to manage stress. We consider below some of these stress management techniques, both individual and social, that help us deal more effectively with stressors. Lazarus (1991) and Folkman (1984) suggested there are two types of coping responses:

- *Problem-focused* coping is directed towards the source of stress.
- *Emotion-focused* coping is directed towards the individual's personal reaction to the stressor.

The following classification breaks down coping strategies into:

- *Individual strategies* such as direct, indirect, compensatory and palliative strategies.
- *Social support and social interest* such as the benefits and costs of friends and family and also the strength gained by helping others.
- *Psychological techniques* such as the recommendations of Kobasa in relation to hardiness and Meichenbaum's stress-inoculation training.

Individual strategies

1 *Direct coping/problem-focused coping*

This involves some kind of action which will affect the demand in some way. Sometimes the way forward is relatively obvious and can be clearly defined and acted upon. However, people often define a problem incorrectly and this will affect the coping strategy used. Problem-focused coping can be psychologically beneficial in improving self-esteem and control. This approach is used more by those with optimistic explanatory style.

Skills training can prove useful, including time management (learning how to make time work for rather than against us). Environmental change such as changing the work environment or ending a relationship can also help.

Direct coping strategies boost feelings of personal control but rely heavily on altering the demand which is not always possible. Sometimes emotions come in the way of assessing the problem accurately. Most people use a combination of emotion-focused and problem-focused coping. Fontenot and Brannon (1991) found that at work problem-focused coping was used when the stress was a job-related crisis whereas emotion-focused coping, such as anger, was likely to be used when the stress was initiated by an annoying colleague.

2 *Indirect coping/behavioural coping*

This includes strategies which do not alter demand but alter the way the individual *experiences* the demand. Indirect coping helps the adjustment responses in situations which cannot be changed and where direct coping is inappropriate or impossible. **Cognitive restructuring**/'rethinking strategies' (Taylor, 1989) can help the individual find meaning from the stressful experience ('Why did it happen?' 'What does it mean in my life now?'). Such techniques can help the individual gain control of the situation and help restore self-esteem (see figure 15.34 for information on three such strategies: reappraisal, social comparison and avoidance). There is a change in the *perception* of the demand.

There are also methods of changing bodily experiences when confronted with unalterable demands. For example, relaxation training such as learning how to tense and relax muscles and meditation can have beneficial effects on health and stress reduction. Progressive relaxtion techniques involve recognising the body's stress signals and using this as a cue to relax by focusing on the various groups of muscles involved. Learning to tense and relax muscles, lie or sit quietly, put aside worries, 'chill out' can have beneficial effects on the immune system. Relaxation training can be part of biofeedback which is based on operant conditioning whereby an individual can learn to control autonomic responses such as heart rate and blood pressure. These techniques allow control of the ANS which reduces the possibility of stress-linked disorders.

Behaviour therapy/modification programmes have also proved successful in coping with stress. These involve learning programmes which attempt to change an individual's behaviour by classical and operant conditioning (this is covered in more detail in Unit 26 page 964). These therapies involve systems of reward/reinforcement of new and appropriate behaviour.

15.34 Cognitive coping strategies

■ Reappraisal/restructuring

If the cognitive appraisal of the situation is resulting in stress, reappraising can sometimes make the stressor less threatening. Sometimes just replacing a negative statement with a more positive one can reduce stress (Meichenbaum, 1997; Lazarus, 1991). Problems can be changed into challenges, losses into gains so that, for example losing a job can be seen as an escape from a 'dead end' and the chance for a change in direction. This approach can help teach the individual that control over a stressful situation is possible.

■ Social comparison

It can sometimes be helpful to find that others are less fortunate, so the individual can appreciate the positive aspects of his or her position.

■ Avoidance

This can be a useful strategy when a decision is out of your hands, vigilance is needed when action is possible and necessary. Both strategies are necessary. For example, dwelling on everything that could go wrong when in hospital is not an effective strategy whereas avoidance (choosing distracting activities) is more helpful. Vigilance is needed in recovery to ensure the best treatment and care is made available. Avoidance can sometimes lead to *denial* which is discussed further below.

3 *Compensatory coping*

This involves strategies that can lessen the effects of stress, such as hobbies which can be absorbing but not be too demanding (unless they are planned to cope with under-stimulation stress). Exercise can be a useful outlet for tension or stress but health checks are needed before strenuous exercise is taken. Physical exercise has been found beneficial in relieving not only stress but also anxiety and depression (Plante and Rodin, 1990). However, exercising to *avoid* problems does not reduce stress unless the individual also focuses more directly on the problem. Compensatory strategies cannot help people avoid the problems producing stress rather they can be seen as complementary to direct and indirect coping strategies.

4 *Palliative coping*

Palliative coping involves methods of indirect coping which can give *temporary* relief from stress but are harmful when used long term. Alcohol/drugs/eating can sometimes help people escape from the immediate effects of stress and give them time to adjust and think. Because stress raises blood pressure and heart rate, clinicians sometimes recommend drugs such as betablockers

which act directly on the nervous system to reduce physiological arousal and alleviate the initial stress. Such treatments are often intended to be short term until the alternative coping strategies have developed.

Ego-defence mechanisms are mental strategies noted by Freud for short-term relief from anxiety and are summarised in figure 15.35. They include denial and displacement. The individual will often not show the usual indications of stress and when reality finally penetrates, the individual often suffers severe stress or breakdown (these strategies are covered in more detail in Unit 24 page 898).

Palliation wears off and leaves the demand unchanged but it allows *time* for the person to re-assess the situation.

■ Social support and social interest

Social support refers to the help we receive from others in times of stress. We can benefit from others in times of stress, from their experience in dealing with similar stressors and the encouragement and support provided in helping overcome the stressor. Social support appears to affect the immune system. Baron *et al.* (1990) noted that the partners of cancer patients,

15.35 Freudian defence mechanisms

The most primitive defence mechanism is *denial*, where the individual blocks out a situation by refusing to acknowledge that it exists.

Rationalisation translates a situation into a logically or socially desirable one. It serves to ease disappointment, for example 'I didn't really want it anyway', and it gives acceptable motives for socially unacceptable behaviour, for example 'I told a lie because I thought it would be harmful to tell the truth'.

When individuals see their own faults to exaggerated degrees in other people, *projection* occurs. Thus their own faults do not seem so bad in comparison, for example 'Everyone in the department is cruel and unkind so I have to treat them harshly'.

The expression of opposite feelings is called *reaction formation*. An example can be seen where a parent lavishes protection and indulgence on an unwanted child – compensating for lack of love by being a 'good parent'.

Intellectualisation involves detachment from an emotionally threatening situation, by explaining it in abstract or intellectual terms, for example 'My sister died because the car hit her'.

Undoing is seen in an action designed to prevent or atone for unacceptable thoughts or impulses, as when Lady Macbeth kept washing her hands in an unconscious desire to cleanse the blood of murder from her soul.

When an event or situation is entirely wiped from the memory giving rise to amnesia, *repression* occurs, for example, when someone acts 'out of character' by doing something he or she is ashamed of, then he or she completely forgets about it.

Displacement is a channelling of stress energy into a new 'acceptable' outlet. For example, if an employee is 'ticked off' by the boss, kicking back (as he or she would like to) is impossible, so the cat suffers instead! A more productive example can be seen when a childless couple displace their love for the children they cannot have into the sphere of animals by adopting stray cats and dogs.

---

although under terrible stress, do not show a drop in immune functioning if they have high levels of social support.

Friends also help by providing emotional support such as concern and affection. It is perhaps this attachment which people need throughout their lives (Hobfoll and Stephens, 1990). Even pets such as cats and dogs have been found to provide such companionship and help relieve stress (Siegal, 1990). Such help from friends is most beneficial at times of high-level stress and less so for mild stressors (Rook, 1987).

Cultures differ in the support they give and in the value they place on friends and family. The more mobile western cultures value more short-lived friendships and sociability whereas in more settled communities friendship develops slowly but becomes very strong.

Activity 13

The exam is close. You cannot complete your revision programme and are under stress. Read the different ways of responding to stress again and select which one(s) you would be likely to give in this situation. Which method of stress management described would be most suitable for you? Explain your answer.

The social support from friends and family can be a double-edged sword. Friends and family sometimes can become a *source* of conflict and stress. Relationships can impose 'burdens of care' (Wade and Tavris, 1993). Shumaker and Hill found in 1991 that many women in mid-life can find themselves exhausted by caring for a chronically sick relative.

These are the factors found to be related to how helpful social support can be:

- *Amount of support* – with too much creating dependency and taking away the individual's sense of control.
- *Timing* – after a major event such as the death of someone close it can be a time when support and understanding is needed. Later it is the friends who try to re-introduce the individual to a social life.
- *Type of support* is critical – friends at work can often help more than family if the stress is work related.
- *Density of support* – in dense social networks all friends know one another and everyone becomes involved. Women particularly benefit from such networks (Shumaker and Hill, 1991). Dense networks can sometimes be a problem when the individual needs to move into areas outside the group which is often reluctant to 'let go' (Wade and Tavris, 1993).

Activity 14

a Green (1994) summarised many of the methods of coping with stress in figure 15.36. Classify each one under the following headings:
- Direct/problem-focused.
- Indirect/behavioural.
- Compensatory.
- Palliative.

b Make a table showing the ways in which we can manage stress. Suggest some advantages and disadvantages for each.

(Suggested answers on page 564.)

15.36 Summary of coping strategies (Green, 1994)

Psychotherapy
More useful when the stress is chronic (long lasting) and part of an individual's personality, i.e. their 'normal' way of perceiving the world around them. Attempts to identify the conflicts underlying this irrational view.

Cognitive and behavioural therapies
Help subjects to restructure their cognitions and to gain a more realistic view of their coping abilities and the demands on them. May involve teaching them new skills and procedures to deal with the world. Examples of this approach include Beck's cognitive therapy and Meichenbaum's stress-inoculation training.

Skills training
Closely related to the last approach. Particularly useful where the stress is highly specific, for example fear of examinations could be reduced by training in time management and revision techniques, plus relaxation and desensitisation therapy for the examination itself.

Relaxation
As relaxation is the polar opposite of a stress response, the subject is trained in relaxation or meditation techniques to reduce the arousal response in reaction to stressors. Unless regularly incorporated into the life style, relaxation techniques tend to have short-lived effectiveness.

Environmental change
Where the source of stress is clearly external, the environment can sometimes be altered to reduce it. This can involve such things as changes in work patterns, or perhaps ending a relationship.

Biofeedback
Useful in the control of physical signs of stress such as raised blood pressure and headaches. Electronic detectors give feedback on blood pressure or muscle tension, and the subject is trained in techniques such as relaxation to reduce these indicators of stress.

cont'd

15.36 Summary of coping strategies (Green, 1994) cont'd

■ Drugs

The two most commonly prescribed groups are the benzodiazepines, such as librium and valium, and the betablockers such as propranolol. Both groups have a mild tranquillising action with betablockers having more of an effect on peripheral arousal systems. In general, drugs should be used only in the short term, perhaps to cover a period of acute stress.

The most effective programmes for coping with stress will usually involve a combination of methods and are called multimodal approaches.

Adler (1938, 1964) believed that people involved with others are better able to cope with problems, have higher self-esteem and are psychologically stronger than those who do not get involved. Crandall (1984) supported this view that people who score high on *social interest*, who show more compassion and cooperate had fewer stressful experiences and were better able to cope when they had them. This ability to look outside oneself seems to link many of the coping strategies noted above.

■ Psychological techniques

Based on the characteristics of the hardy personality, Kobasa (1986) suggested that stressed individuals needed to *focus* on the physical signs of stress to isolate the source(s) (as undertaken in relaxation training). The individual is then helped to analyse the stressful situation to seek out other ways in which it could have been handled. This reappraisal can help in suggesting alternative stategies. The individual is also encouraged to take on other challenges to help develop their self-efficacy and give them a feeling of control. This prevents the development of **learned helplessness**. Although this technique has not been fully evaluated, it does combine many of the coping strategies which have been found successful. It is a cognitive-behavioural approach as is the stress-inoculation training of Meichenbaum (1985) (see Unit 26 page 969 for discussion of other cognitive-behavioural therapies used in mental health treatment).

Meichenbaum (1985) believed in a preventative approach towards stress. He suggested we develop a coping plan to help deal with specific stressors. This training programme has a problem-focused approach designed to build up coping skills and strengthen resistance by exposure to the real and imagined stress stimuli in a clinical setting with support from a therapist. This programme has been found effective by a number of people from different backgrounds, including teachers, nurses, police trainees (Bishop, 1994) and professional athletes (Cox, 1991). A summary of the procedure can be found in figure 15.37.

The effects of stress can be mediated by cognitive appraisal, good health procedures and the use of effective coping strategies. As humans we have evolved our own particular approach to dealing with stressors in our life which are often well learned and difficult to change. The cognitive-behavioural approach is not always applicable and a multimodal coping approach may be undertaken in therapy. It is reassuring to see that the autonomic stress response, the 'fight or flight' response, can be moderated by higher cognitive processes to lessen its potentially harmful long-term effects.

There is substantial evidence that only when stressful events and a pre-existing biological vulnerability interact does illness develop. This interactive model is known as a vulnerability-stress/*diathesis-stress* model (a diathesis is a predisposition to a disorder). The vulnerability makes the individual susceptible, but only when stress is encountered does the disorder actually develop. This is discussed further in Unit 26 page 978.

15.37 Summary of Meichenbaum's (1985) stress-inoculation training programme (Carlson and Buskist, 1997)

Conceptualisation phase

Goal 1: Learning the transactional nature of stress and coping.

Goal 2: Learning to become better at realistically appraising stressful situations by learning self-monitoring skills with respect to negative or maladaptive thoughts, emotions, and behaviours.

Skills acquisition and rehearsal phase

Goal 3: Learning problem-solving skills specific to the stressor.

Goal 4: Learning and rehearsing emotion-regulation and self-control skills.

Goal 5: Learning how to use maladaptive responses as cues to implement the new coping strategy.

Application and follow-through phase

Goal 6: Learning to practice imagery rehearsal using progressively more difficult or stressful situations.

Goal 7: Learning to apply new coping skills to other, perhaps unexpected, stressors.

Activity 15

As psychologists, how would you interpret the causes of stress in the individuals reported below? What suggestions would you recommend for their treatment?

a   Jenny is 25 years old. At school she was a good student passing her O Levels with good grades. She left school before her A Levels when she became pregnant. She married the father of the child and had another baby a year later. The marriage has now ended with her husband leaving her for someone else. She is working as a wages clerk which she finds very boring and finds herself clock-watching. Although hating the job she has not considered looking for another one because she doesn't feel she could cope with any more responsibility. She came to the doctor for help with her sleeping. She reported feeling tired all the time and not wanting

Activity 15 cont'd

to eat. She was forcing herself to do so for the sake of her children.

b   Jeffrey is 34 years old, married with three children. He is a sales executive with a large international company. He travels extensively. His day usually starts about 6 am and involves a minimum of two hours travelling to reach his venue. His job is very competitive involving weekly sales promotions, monthly area meetings and prizes. He seldom arrives home before 8 pm and he often brings work home. He frequently works Saturday and invariably works at home part of Sunday. He collapsed at work and was taken to hospital where he was diagnosed as having had a minor heart attack. Fortunately this would leave no after effects. His doctor reports him being very tense and impatient.

Self-assessment questions

12 Outline the role of the physical structures involved in the hypothalamic-pituitary-adrenal stress syndrome.

13 a   Which hormones are released by the adrenal medulla?
    b   What are the effects of these on behaviour?

14 Summarise the general adaptation syndrome.

15 Outline the physiological reaction of the body to stress which could lead to the development of gastric ulcers.

(Suggested answers on page 565.)

Unit summary

- Physiological (*primary*) motivators include food and water. Hunger motivates us to eat when falling blood nutrient levels cause a physiological imbalance. Similarly, thirst ensures we replenish the two-thirds of our body weight composed of water. Hunger is also affected by taste, learning, and social influences, a focus on *positive-incentive* value.

- A settling-point theory/'leaky-barrel' model in which body-weight drifts around an equilibrium level is consistent with the research data but needs to be more specific about contributory factors. The hypothalamus is central to understanding hunger, especially in relation to the role of brain chemicals, such as noradrenaline, GABA and neuropeptide Y.

- *Obesity* is a major health hazard in humans. The rapid increase in obesity during the twentieth century, in the western world, suggests environment rather than genetic factors are involved. Habit and metabolism are regarded as important variables, also stress and a change in metabolism due to the effects of dieting. Leptin, a protein normally secreted by fat cells, is thought to play an important role.

  Most drinking, like eating, occurs in the absence of deficits. The positive-incentive value of liquid is thought to initiate spontaneous drinking.

- Non-homeostatic drives include *social motives*, known as secondary drives. These include the need for affiliation (nAff), need for self-efficacy, need for achievement (nAch), and need for power (nPower).

- Early theories of motivation focused on instincts, and drive reduction. More recent theories include the role of incentives and higher-level needs (including self-development and fulfilment).

- We experience different arousal levels as different feelings and interpret them as emotions. This involves the interaction of the autonomic nervous system (ANS), the endocrine glands and the central nervous system (CNS). The pituitary gland links the ANS and CNS, allowing this close interaction. The hormonal and autonomic responses of the body are controlled by the brain, especially the *limbic system*, including the amygdala, described as the 'push button' for emotional responses. Perhaps this acts as an 'early warning system'?

- The James–Lange theory of emotion suggests we *act* first and *then* experience emotion, whereas the Cannon–Bard theory suggests impulses are sent at the *same time* to start the arousal response and alert the cerebral cortex. More recent theories consider the *role of cognition and attribution*.

- Stress is a biological response experienced as emotion, with our physical response to stressors being governed by the hypothalamus. Stressful situations increase the release of adrenaline and noradrenaline. Stressors can be environmental, work-related, life-events and daily hassles. *Cox and Mackay's transactional model* (1978) of stress integrates both external aspects as well as internal ones such as needs, values, motivation and job satisfaction.

- Selye (1956) noted a universal stress response (*general adaptation syndrome*) which seems to protect the individual through three stages: alarm, resistance and exhaustion. Such mechanisms become dangerous when continued stress results in responses becoming continuous. Cognition plays an important role in the perception of stress, especially the control over the situation. Perceived control over a situation reduces stress. *Learned helplessness* can develop when earlier learning suggests the individual will not be able to control the situation.

- The link between stress and ill-health is strong, especially heart disease, gastric ulcers, diabetes and cancer. A *Type A behaviour* is suggested to be linked with coronary heart disease, and *psychoneuroimmunology* studies the interaction of psychological factors, the nervous system, and the immune system. A *Type C (cancer-prone) personality* is an individual seen to be

Summary cont'd.

unassertive, cooperative and patient. He or she perhaps represses negative emotions, such as anger, and may be more likely to suffer cancer. It is thought this may affect the growth of tumours rather than their formation.

■ Coping responses can be problem-focused or emotion-focused. Strategies can be classified as individual or as involving social support. Psychological techniques may also be employed.

Terms to define

auto-immune diseases
autonomic nervous system (ANS)
cognitive restructuring
emotions
endocrine glands
general adaptation syndrome
homeostasis
learned helplessness

motivation
negative-feedback systems
psychoneuroimmunology
self-actualisation
stress
Type A behaviour
Type B behaviour
Type C personality

Further reading

Carlson, N R (1998) *Physiology of Behavior* (6th edn), Allyn & Bacon, Boston, MA.

More detailed information on all physiological aspects of motivation, emotion and stress.

Goleman, D (1996) *Emotional Intelligence*, Bloomsbury.

Well-written text which argues that our emotions play a more important role in thought, decision making and individual success than is commonly acknowledged.

Green, S (1994) 'Stress: what is it?', *Psychology Review, 1(1)*, 23–7.

Student magazine article which examines the various definitions of stress, the physiology of stress and sources of stress in an interesting, readable review.

Parkinson, B (1996) 'What makes emotions emotional', *Psychology Review, 3(2)*, 2–5.

Student magazine article which covers the various explanations of emotion in an interesting manner.

Pinel, J P J (1997) *Biopsychology*, 3rd edn, Allyn & Bacon, Boston, MA.

For the biopsychologists who want more detail on the areas covered in this chapter.

Answers

■ Suggested answers to activities

2
a   duodenum
b   detector
c   glucostatic
d   positive-incentive

7
a   adrenaline
b   amygdala
c   left

11

Could include the following:
■ age:
death of a family member (5) not only differences in the other family members dependent on age but also the age of the person who died; *marriage (7)* would the marriage of a teenager be judged differently than that of a person over 80?; *dismissal from work (8)* could be different for a 50-year-old employee after 30 years with a company rather than a 20-year-old student on a holiday job?
■ male and female:
pregnancy (12) might be judged differently by the woman who is more directly affected; *son or daughter leaving home (23)* might be judged differently by the mother or father, dependent also on the gender of the child leaving; *wife begins or stops work (26)* will probably be judged differently by the wife or husband.
■ culture or sub-culture:
marriage (7) may be judged differently if arranged by the family rather than the couple; *begin or end school (27)* many cultural and sub-cultural differences here.

A new SRRS could include numerous individual choices. Perhaps failing exams and unemployment might be among yours?

12
a   A
b   the immune system and behaviour mediated by the nervous system
c   auto-immune diseases
d   Type C (cancer-prone)

14
a   ■   Direct/problem-focused.
          Skills training.
          Environmental change.

■   Indirect/behavioural.
      Psychotherapy treatment includes indirect coping often involving the client's understanding of the unconscious reasons for his or her behaviour. Cognitive and behavioural therapies.
      Relaxation.
      Biofeedback.
■   Compensatory.
      Hobbies.
      Exercise.
■   Palliative.
      Psychotherapy. Many of the ego-defence mechanisms are palliative.
      Drugs, including alchohol, are usually seen as short term and palliative.

b

Table b

Activity	Advantages	Disadvantages
Unwinding activities (e.g. bath/shower, gardening, playing squash, etc.)	Releases tension in muscles; redirects anger; feel 'better after'	Doesn't tackle the underlying problem
Removing self from the situation	Solves immediate problem	May cause other problems
Therapy (counselling)	Helps client adjust to situation	Could be expensive; success depends on rapport with therapist
Medication	Will relieve symptoms	Doesn't solve underlying problem

15

You may have suggested some of the following:
a   Jenny could be suffering from learned helplessness. She might benefit from a cognitive-behavioural programme and some of the cognitive restructuring programmes as outlined on pages 556–7.
b   Jeffrey has the characteristics of a Type A personality. A multimodal approach might prove beneficial including relaxation training and perhaps the psychological techniques of Kobasa and Meichenbaum.

Suggested answers to self-assessment questions

1

Stomach contractions, drop in blood glucose levels, drop in level of fats in the adipocytes.

2

The degree of hunger depends on the anticipated pleasure of eating at that time.

3

As body fat levels increase modifications are made to prevent further increases until a balance is achieved between all the factors encouraging weight gain and loss.

4

Need for affiliation (nAff)
Need for self-efficacy
Need for achievement (nAcn)
Need for power (nPower)

5

You could have included:
- Instinct theory (page 523).
- Drive or drive-reduction theory (page 524).
- Incentive (expectancy) theory (page 525).
- Theory of needs (page 525).

6

Primary: emotions seen displayed across cultures and recognised universally.
Secondary: culture-specific emotions.

7

Display rules: cultural norms which govern when and how emotions are expressed.
Emotion work: cultural rules which tell us when and how to show emotions we actually do not feel.

8

The amygdala appears to control the integration of the autonomic, hormonal and neural responses to situations involving fear, anger and disgust. It receives inputs from the olfactory system, association cortex, frontal cortex and the limbic system and has been described as a 'push button' for emotional responses, perhaps a pre-cortex *early warning system*.

9
- Visceral changes occur too slowly to be a source of emotional feeling.
- If adrenaline is injected artificially then true emotion is not felt.
- Emotion can be shown without emotional physiological changes.

10

The role of experience – classical conditioning of responses. Also possible that these are innate due to their adaptive value.

11

Theories of attribution include Schachter and Singer (pages 536–7) and Weiner (page 538).

12

Main structures include the hypothalamus, and the pituitary and adrenal glands:
- Hypothalamus is the centre of several homeostatic mechanisms. It also monitors and controls many hormone levels in the blood.
- The pituitary is connected to the hypothalamus, carries hormones, with a range of effects, both neural and neurochemical, from the hypothalamus.
- The adrenal glands, one above each kidney, secrete adrenaline and noradrenaline from the internal medulla to increase metabolism and provide an efficient mechanism for reaction to a crisis. The outer part, the adrenal cortex, secretes corticoids (see pages 541–3 for further details).

13
a   Adrenaline and noradrenaline.
b   See page 542.

14

A universal stress response which occurs irrespective of the specific nature of the stress. See pages 548–9 for full description of this syndrome.

15

Gastric ulcers are painful lesions in the lining the stomach and duodenum. They are prevalent in people suffering stress, which has been found to increase the secretion of hydrochloric acid and to weaken the gastrointestinal tract's defences against this (see pages 552–3).

Cognitive Psychology

Unit 16

Perceptual Processes

Sharon Cheyne and Graham Davies

This unit covers:

Perceptual organisation

Theories of perception

Individual, social and cultural variations in perceptual organisation

The development of perceptual processes

By the end of this unit, you should be able to:

- recognise how perception is organised
- evaluate the major theories of perception
- discuss individual, social and cultural variations in perceptual organisation
- explain the development of perceptual processes.

Unit 16 Contents

Perceptual organisation

The process of becoming aware of something through our senses is a two-stage one. *Sensation* is the registering of stimuli by our sense organs; perception involves their interpretation so that they become meaningful to us. Humans carry out complex perceptual tasks unconsciously, effortlessly and quickly. We take many of these so much for granted that we have difficulty in realising their existence. For example, when you look at this page, your visual sense registers the images produced by the words. Your brain then interprets these in the light of past experience. Perception brings together what we see and what we already know.

You are probably familiar with the sense of vision, hearing, smell, taste and touch. These are not the only senses; others include *kinaesthesis* and balance. Each of these gives us information about our environment, contributing to our overall state of knowledge about what really is 'out there'.

This unit concentrates on the visual sense, which is the most researched of the senses, reflecting its importance to human beings. Our capability for visual perception allows us both to manipulate and to interpret our personal world, and to find our way around it. To do this, we need to be able to judge the direction, distance, size and shape of objects so that we can recognise them.

Perhaps the main task of visual perception can be seen as constructing an *internal representation* of the world. Once this has been achieved, it can be compared with material stored in the memory and then subjected to the recognition process.

The sensory basis of visual perception

A detailed description of the sensory basis of visual perception can be found in Unit 13. Here a brief reminder will be sufficient. When we see something, our eyes receive information in the form of light waves reaching the retina. The light sensitive cells of the retina, called the rods and cones, convert the light waves into electrical impulses which are sent to the visual cortex of the brain via the optic nerve. When the electrical signals, which represent the light waves arrive in the visual cortex, they are organised and interpreted, so perception occurs.

Activity 1

There are four statements below. Two describe sensation, two describe perception. Which are which?

a   It is a purely physical experience.
b   It involves the brain interpreting the information.
c   It happens automatically, with no conscious thought.
d   It is an active process, where the brain seeks to understand the information it receives.

(Suggested answers on page 606.)

The process of perceiving

Making sense of the world, or perception, involves two sources of information:
- the sensations from the environment which arrive at our senses
- our past experiences and expectations which affect what is perceived.

Give a brief and spontaneous description of the sketch shown in figure 16.1. What do you actually see? What do you perceive? Eye and brain can tell different stories!

There are three processes involved in perception, although theories differ in how much emphasis they place on these processes:

1   *Selection.* From every sensation received, certain things are selected for focus. For example, hunger will cause us to pay attention to any

Figure 16.1

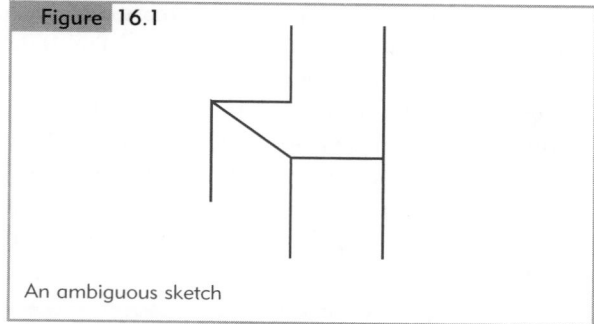

An ambiguous sketch

sensation to do with food. A group of people walking in the Lake District could go on the same walk, but see the same things differently: a geologist would focus on the rocks, a botanist would select the plants, an ornithologist would notice the birds. Think about a football crowd and how opposing supporters view the referee's decisions.

2 *Inference*. This involves going beyond the information given to the eye. The retina is a two-dimensional curved surface, yet the world is perceived in three dimensions, so the brain must go beyond the information received by the eye. Hold out a finger, horizontally, at arm's length. Place your pen vertically behind it. When you look at the pen, you infer the invisible part is actually there. You rely on your past experience to fill in the gap, just as you did when you saw the 'chair' earlier in figure 16.1.

Activity 2

Psychologists are interested in explaining how the perceptual processes work. Put the following four processes into the order in which they occur:
Selection of stimuli, inferences; receiving sensations; organisation.

a

b

c

d

(Suggested answer on page 606.)

3 *Organisation*. The brain assembles sensations into mental pictures of the world. It creates objects out of the patterns of light waves received. Our brains like the sensations we receive to be meaningful. Why is it frustrating yet fascinating to look at figure 16.2?

Perceptual organisation is concerned with the questions asked when we look at the world. These concern what and where objects are, and what they are doing. This section looks at the perception of movement, space (depth and distance), pattern recognition, perceptual constancies, visual illusions and the Gestalt theory of perceptual organisation.

The perception of movement

The perception of movement allows us to work out what objects in our visual field are doing. It also helps us to separate objects from their backgrounds and to recognise individual objects. Points which are close together and moving at the same speed across a stationary image are very likely to be perceived as parts of the same object. Perception of movement also assists us to judge depth and distance (this is dealt with in a later section, see page 574). Such an ability has great

Figure 16.2

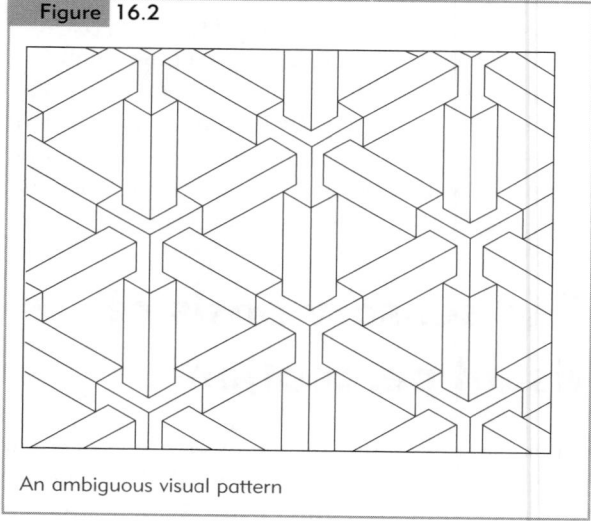

An ambiguous visual pattern

biological value, for example helping us to avoid danger.

In order to perceive movement successfully, the visual system must be capable of distinguishing between objects *moving* in our visual field (with our eyes stationary or moving), and *stationary* objects in our visual field (with our eyes moving).

Activity 3

Look at a stationary scene in front of you and slowly move your head from side to side. Your visual field will appear stationary. If, however, you keep your head still and move your eyes by placing a finger on the top of each eyelid and gently pressing your eyeball, the whole field appears to move. Why is this? (The answer is in the next paragraph.)

It seems, therefore, that when the brain sends a signal for the eyes to move (as it does with voluntary eye movements), this information is stored by the brain and used to compute the retinal motion that will occur as a result of the eye movement. If actual and predicted motion correspond, this is attributed to the fact that the eyes have moved. When moving your eyes physically with your fingers, no such signal for voluntary eye movement is sent by the brain, so the motion of the visual field is not cancelled.

◼ Systems used in the perception of movement

Gregory (1977) distinguishes between two interdependent systems in the perception of movement: the image–retina movement system and the eye–head movement system.

In the *image–retina movement system* (figure 16.3a) the eye remains stationary. As a particular stimulus moves across the visual field, a succession of neighbouring retinal locations are stimulated. It is likely that this form of motion is perceived as a direct result of firing by a succession of receptors in the retina, corresponding to the movement of the image across it (Schouten, 1967).

The *eye-head movement system* (figure 16.3b) is employed when a moving stimulus is tracked by a moving eye, with the result that the image of the object concerned remains stationary on the retina. In this case, the movement of the background across the retina provides the motion information. However, movement of the background is unnecessary for the perception of movement, as this will still be perceived when a spot of light is moved in a room that is darkened so that no background is visible.

In such situations, the interpretation of movement apparently comes from a neural mechanism, operated by the turning of the eyes in their sockets, which is the related to the retinal image.

◼ Optical stimulation patterns and movement perception

Optical stimulation patterns also provide us with information on movement (see figure 16.4). As an object moves towards us, its retinal image expands (this is known as *looming*). The reverse happens when an object is moved directly away from us. Also, as an object moves, it systematically covers and then uncovers the view of anything which lies behind it. Gibson (1966) describes this as a rupturing of the continuity of texture.

Flow patterns also help us to detect motion. (These are discussed on page 576 and pages 588–9.)

Finally, Johansson (1973, 1975) has demonstrated that motion can be perceived without knowledge of the shape of the moving form. An actor's movements were filmed and presented to participants in a form that eliminated all of the background and the outline of the actor's body. This was achieved by providing a total of 10 dots of light at the major body joints, which were insufficient on their own to suggest a human figure. Accurate perceptions of a human figure walking or running were produced after only a couple of steps had been taken. Later studies have shown that recognition of our own and friends' movements is possible using this method, as is recognition of the mover's sex (Cutting and Kozlowski, 1977; Cutting *et al.*, 1978).

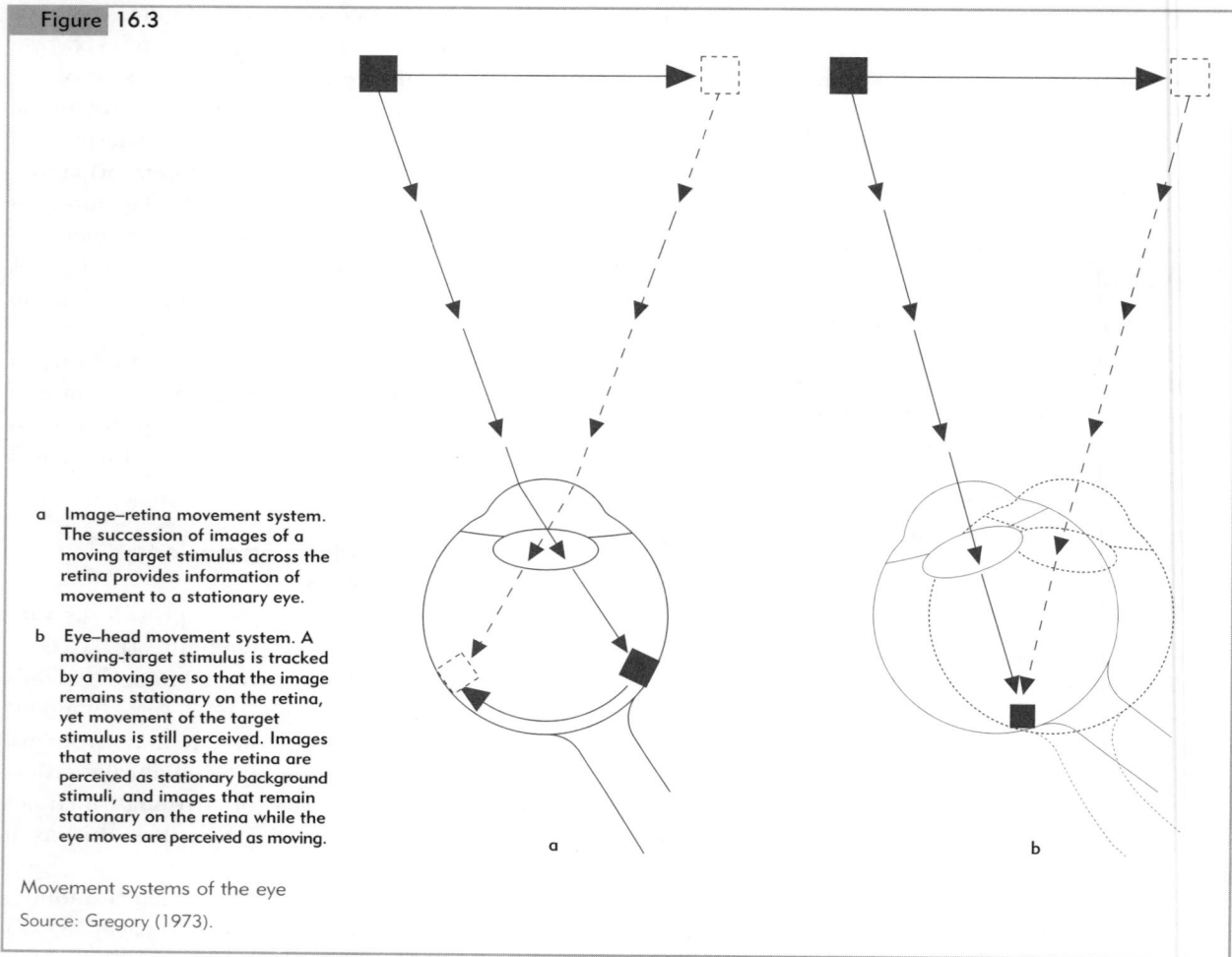

Figure 16.3

a Image–retina movement system.
The succession of images of a
moving target stimulus across the
retina provides information of
movement to a stationary eye.

b Eye–head movement system. A
moving-target stimulus is tracked
by a moving eye so that the image
remains stationary on the retina,
yet movement of the target
stimulus is still perceived. Images
that move across the retina are
perceived as stationary background
stimuli, and images that remain
stationary on the retina while the
eye moves are perceived as moving.

Movement systems of the eye

Source: Gregory (1973).

The perception of space (depth and distance)

The image formed upon the retina is two-dimensional, yet humans can accurately perceive both the distance of objects from the observer and their three-dimensional nature. This is achieved through the action of *depth cues*. Accommodation, convergence and stereopsis give *binocular* cues to depth that rely on both eyes for their effect. The remainder provide *monocular* cues, needing vision from only one eye.

■ Accommodation

The process of accommodation, which results in a change of curvature in the lens of the eye, depends on distance from the object. The lens flattens for distance objects and thickens for close objects. Theoretically, it should be possible for the visual system to record the extent of accommodation of the lens and thus gauge distance to the fixation point. There is, however, no firm evidence to suggest that this happens. This could be because such a method would be of value only at distances of less than about 6 metres, as the lens curvature does not alter for distances beyond this. Also, such a method would allow us to judge only the distance of a single fixation point and could offer no

Figure 16.4

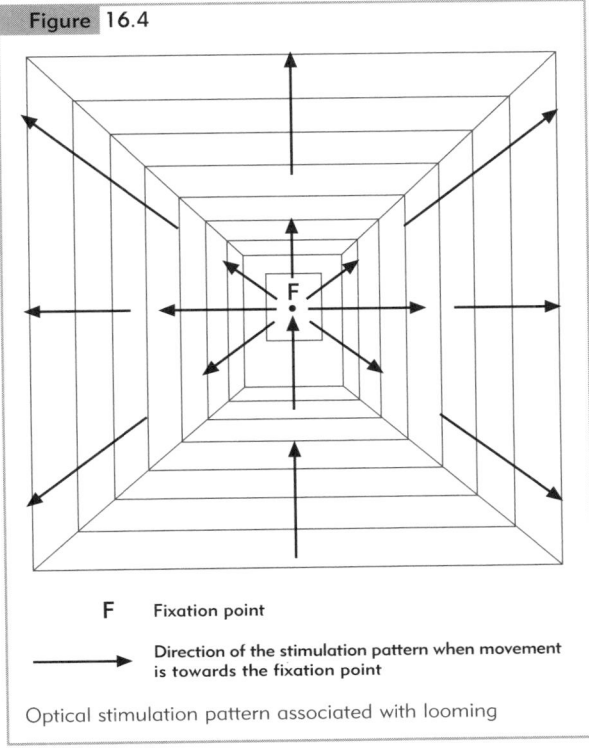

F   Fixation point

→   Direction of the stimulation pattern when movement
is towards the fixation point

Optical stimulation pattern associated with looming

information about the distance of other points within the visual field.

■ Convergence

The term convergence refers to the angle of the eyes when an object is centred on the retina. Thus, it might be theoretically possible for the visual system to read off and interpret this angle. It seems that convergence may be able to help us to judge depth when used in association with **stereopsis** (see below), but the limitations of convergence as a depth cue are the same as those for accommodation.

■ Stereopsis

Activity 4

Open and close each of your eyes alternately. What happens to the objects you are looking at? (The answer is in the next paragraph.)

You should have found that the scene before you appears to shift laterally. This is because, due to its different location, each eye sees a slightly different view of the world.

Stereopsis provides an important means of perceiving distance. Foley has compared the ability to judge distance accurately using binocular and monocular vision. Binocular vision is significantly more accurate, though near objects are estimated slightly further away. Distant objects are estimated slightly nearer (Foley, 1980, 1985).

Activity 5

Hold two objects (pens or pencils are ideal) in front of you, one a few centimetres behind the other. Close your left eye and fixate on the nearer object. What happens to the further object if you open and close your left eye? Repeat the above procedure, this time fixating on the further object. What differences do you notice? Try to predict what will happen if you repeat the above procedure with your right eye first closed, then opening and shutting it. (The explanation is in the following paragraph.)

What actually happens is illustrated in figure 16.5. When both eyes fixate on an object, the images that are cast in the two eyes by the object lie on corresponding points of the two retinae. However, the images cast on the retinae by objects that are nearer or further than the fixation point will be at disparate points. This *binocular disparity* will increase as the distance between the object and the fixation point increases.

Our visual system is capable of combining the two images produced by our two eyes so that we perceive a single object. However, it is also apparently capable of the complex task of registering the degree of disparity, thus yielding an impression of depth. The visual cortex has disparity selective cells (Ohzawa *et al.*, 1990) which have high rates of electrical discharge when the stimuli registers on different (disparate) areas of the two retinas. Some cells respond to low, others to high levels of disparity. The response rate is low in

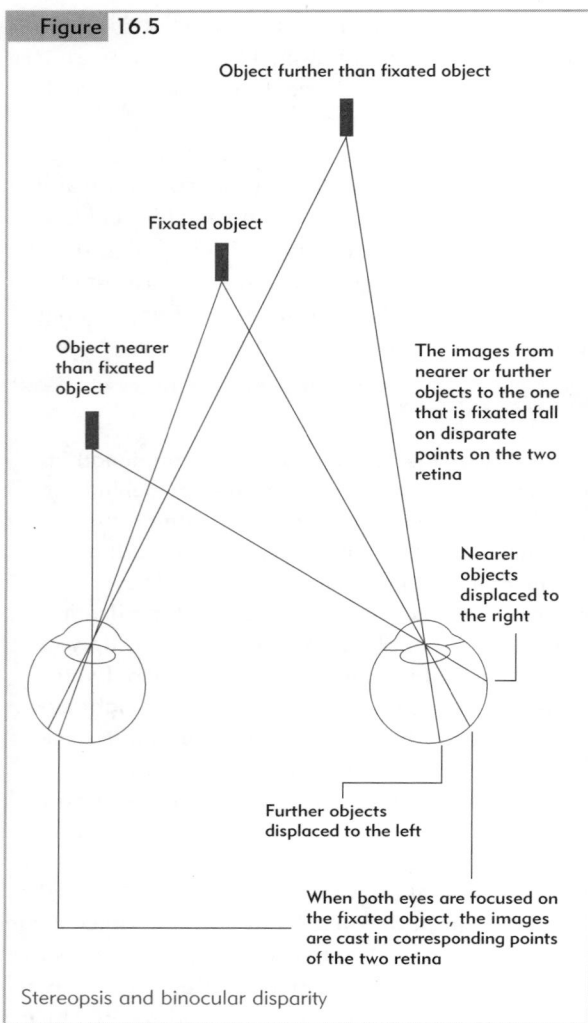

Figure 16.5

Object further than fixated object

Fixated object

Object nearer than fixated object

The images from nearer or further objects to the one that is fixated fall on disparate points on the two retina

Nearer objects displaced to the right

Further objects displaced to the left

When both eyes are focused on the fixated object, the images are cast in corresponding points of the two retina

Stereopsis and binocular disparity

disparity selective cells when there is input from only one eye (Bruce and Green, 1985).

The role of motion

Activity 6

Fixate your gaze on objects in the middle distance, then move your head from side to side. How do objects that are nearer to you and those that are further from the chosen objects appear to move? Is there a difference? (Read on for an explanation.)

The motion of objects in our visual field helps us to perceive depth. **Motion parallax** is the term given to the movement of the image of an object across the retina. It is able to provide cues to depth because a scene is viewed from different directions.

You should have noticed that nearer objects appear to move in the opposite direction to the head – the nearer they are, the further and faster they move. More distant objects move in the same direction as the head – moving further and faster with increasing distance. Motion parallax is helpful in judging the shape of a three-dimensional object, as nearer parts of it will be swept across the eyes when the head is moved. It also provides information on a point to which someone is heading. This will stay stationary on the retina whilst other points around it expand radially (see figure 16.6).

Looming (see page 573) also provides a cue to depth, as do the relative rates of motion by parts of a three-dimensional image which is being rotated. For instance, when a cube is rotated, its centre moves more slowly relative to the corners.

Pictorial cues

Pictorial cues (figure 16.7) enable us to judge depth even from a two-dimensional image. The most important of these is *perspective*, which operates because the closer something is to us, the larger its retinal image. Thus, parallel railway lines receding into the distance show convergence, and the same-sized objects produce smaller retinal images the further away from the observer they are.

Another depth cue which depends on the concept of perspective is *height in the visual field*. Objects that are resting on the ground's surface further away from the observer, appear higher in the visual field than those nearer to the observer. Perspective is also instrumental in the interpretation of texture gradients. As a surface recedes from the observer, its texture density increases.

Interposition works as a depth cue when one object obscures part of another. The visual system interprets the partially obscured object as further away.

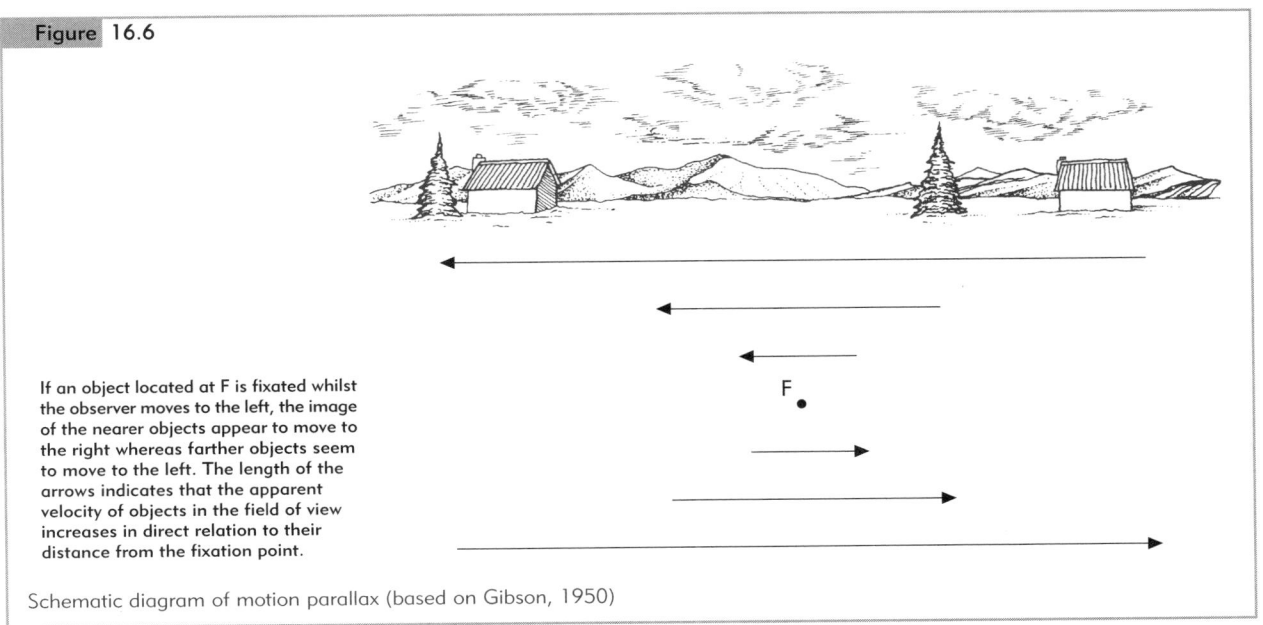

Figure 16.6

If an object located at F is fixated whilst the observer moves to the left, the image of the nearer objects appear to move to the right whereas farther objects seem to move to the left. The length of the arrows indicates that the apparent velocity of objects in the field of view increases in direct relation to their distance from the fixation point.

Schematic diagram of motion parallax (based on Gibson, 1950)

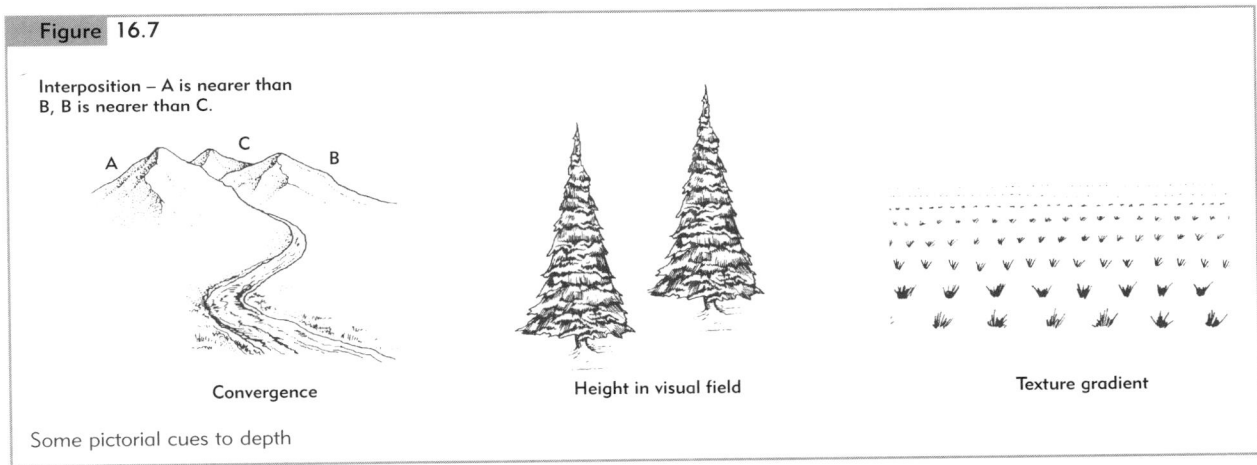

Figure 16.7

Interposition – A is nearer than B, B is nearer than C.

Convergence   Height in visual field   Texture gradient

Some pictorial cues to depth

Further information about distance comes from the *amount of light reflected* from a surface. Less light is reflected from an oblique surface and this helps to provide information about the three-dimensional shape of an object. Similarly, *shadows* can also provide information, as it is always assumed that illumination comes from above.

The atmosphere scatters blue light more readily than red light. One result of this is that the sky appears to be blue. A second result is that, over very long distances, more light is scattered between the observer and distant objects which appear to take on a bluish tinge. You may have noticed how a distant line of hills appears bluish.

Finally, the known size of objects gives us a powerful cue to depth. Even if other cues are absent, we can still judge distances fairly accurately as the brain can compute this from information on the known size of the object and the size of its current retinal image.

Pattern recognition

If we are to be able to perceive and recognise objects, we need to be able to distinguish both their edges and their internal features from the retinal image. To achieve this successfully, we need to go through a **pattern recognition** process (we must be able to recognise the *contours* within the image). Such contours are formed principally by changes in light intensity. These changes in brightness may be defined sharply, as at the edges of objects, or may be gradual when they occur at the edge of a shadow.

Having recognised the contours, the visual system is faced with the highly complex task of *object recognition*. We have to be able to recognise objects at different distances, from different viewing angles and in different lighting conditions. Animate objects provide additional dimensions which also need to be considered, for example their expressions.

A *structural description* is an abstract description of all things which could loosely belong to a particular class. For example, we would recognise all the objects in figure 16.8 as the letter 'T' – and would manage to do this very quickly. It seems that we first locate the edges and lines forming the T. It also seems that the visual system actually constructs abstract descriptions of objects. This information is then broken down into descriptions of its component parts (a horizontal and a vertical bar) and how these are linked together. These are then matched with abstract representations which we have stored in our memories, of all letters Ts, i.e. the properties that all letter Ts share in common. This process is highly flexible as we would still recognise an image as the letter T even if it was composed of a series of disconnected dots.

The orientation of the stimulus is also important in pattern recognition. Rock (1988) demonstrated that when known text is inverted, it is difficult to detect any disparity. Rock demonstrates the effect: 'Psychology' and ʎƃolohɔʎsԀ may not appear very different until the page is turned upside down when the disparity will be evident (after Rock, 1998). Past experience of the word psychology seems to permit flexibility in recognising the word in one orientation.

■ Pattern recognition theories

Two pattern recognition theories will be discussed here. These are the template matching and feature detection models, both of which tend to be bottom-up in nature.

■ Template matching models

The term template refers to a pattern used to ensure that something is made to a correct size. The *template matching hypothesis* (for example, Selfridge and Neisser, 1960; Uhr, 1963) suggest that information on shape or patterns entering the sensory memory is compared with that contained in our long-term store. If there is sufficient overlap between the template and the stimulus, the shape or pattern would be classified as belonging to the class represented by the template. This theory implies that we have vast numbers of individual templates which we have acquired as a result of our previous experiences.

■ Feature detection models

Feature detection models were developed to avoid the difficulties faced by the template matching approach (above). They operate by analysing

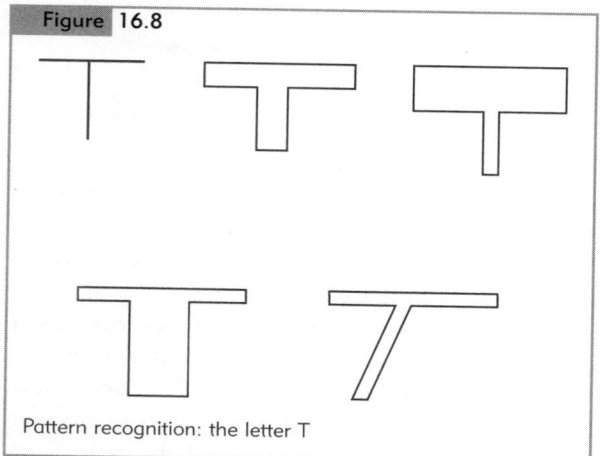

Figure 16.8

Pattern recognition: the letter T

shapes into features (i.e. their component parts). For example, the features of an upper-case (capital) T would be a horizontal bar at the top, a vertical bar and a junction between these bars in the top centre of the character.

These models developed from neurophysiological studies carried out on non-human animals in the 1950s and 1960s. These examined the responses of individual cells in the visual systems to simple stimuli. By using this technique, it was possible to find out the kinds of stimuli that would activate different types of cell. For example, Hubel and Wiesel (1959) found cortical cells in cats which responded to lines or edges in a particular orientation. Other cells were found to respond to more complex features, such as right angles.

This kind of information can be interpreted in two ways. Firstly, it has been suggested that each single cell extracts unambiguous information about features of objects in the visual field. These form the basic units of analysis from which the visual system constructs perceptions. The second possibility is that feature detectors are organised into a hierarchy, with the output at one level forming the input at the next.

Direct testing of humans is not possible with this approach but some indirect evidence has been obtained. For example, Gibson (1969) asked participants to identify individual letters presented for a fraction of a second using a *tachistoscope,* and recorded the number of times each letter was confused with others in the alphabet. It was found that letters with many features in common (for example, b and p) were frequently confused, whereas letters with few features in common (such as x and b) were not.

■ Evaluation of pattern recognition theories

A general criticism of both theories presented here is that the processes involved are significantly more complex than feature detection theories suggest. The template matching hypothesis has considerable problems associated with it. For example, if there is more than one way of perceiving a stimulus, a separate template would be needed for each of these. Such an inability to recognise even slight deviations from the original makes this hypothesis exceptionally inefficient. This model also makes it difficult to explain how we recognise letters in unusual typefaces.

Some problems also occur with feature detection models. The lack of direct evidence from human neurophysiological studies has already been mentioned; the assumption is that the visual systems of humans and other mammals are sufficiently similar for this not to be an issue.

An objection to the view that single cells form the basic units of analysis is that, in practice, most individual cells respond to a range of stimuli, which means that it is difficult to say precisely what activates each cell. Similarly, there is an objection to the view that feature detectors are hierarchically organised – the neural circuitry involved is far more complex than a simple hierarchy would suggest. The models also fail to take into account top-down aspects of processing such as the context within which perception takes place.

The perceptual constancies

Constancy can be defined as the tendency to perceive objects or their qualities in the same or similar ways, despite differences in their retinal images. Size, shape, lightness and colour constancy will be discussed here.

■ Size constancy

As an object of known size is moved away from us, the size of its retinal image decreases. Despite this, we still tend to estimate its size correctly. Size constancy may, however, break down when there is an absence of distance cues. For example, errors are more likely to be made when the distances involved are very great.

Size constancy appears to work as a result of a combination of recognition of the object involved and the ability to judge distance. Remove one of these and size constancy may fail. For example,

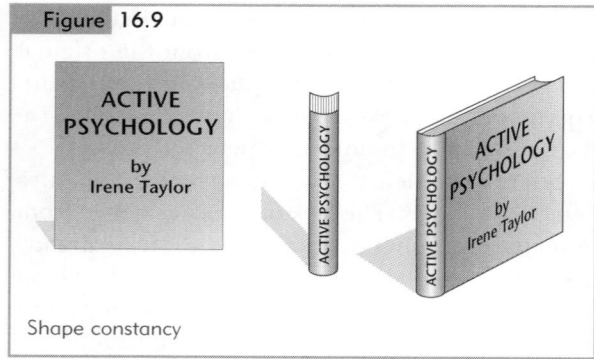

Figure 16.9

Shape constancy

when participants were asked to look at double-sized and half-sized playing cards through a pinhole (which removed all cues to distance), they perceived them to be normal size, but the large one appeared to be at half its real distance and the small one at twice its real distance (Sutherland, undated).

■ Shape constancy

Activity 7

Look at the pictures of a book in figure 16.9 and decide what shape you think the book is in each case.

You probably said that the book was rectangular in each case. When an observer sees a surface that is tilted with regard to their own position, the image on the retina will be a different shape to that of the original surface. However, despite this, shape constancy will be maintained and the original shape perceived. The necessary calculations that the visual system has to make in calculating constancy are highly complex and vital to the accurate construction of our perceptual world.

■ Lightness constancy

Activity 8

Place a piece of white paper and a piece of coal (or some other black, shiny object) in a darkened room. Shine a torch at each item in

Activity 8 *cont'd*

turn (this works best with a weak beam of light). What do you notice about their relative lightness? (Read the next paragraph for an explanation.)

The amount of light received by the eyes from a sheet of white paper (which has low reflectance) in poorly lit conditions is less than that received from a black object such as a piece of coal (which has high reflectance) in brightly lit conditions. Despite this, we still perceive the paper as white and the coal as black. The key factor which affects lightness constancy is therefore *reflectance* which remains a constant factor. The amount of light reflected from a white surface can be nine times that from a black one. However, the amount of light falling on a surface may vary by a factor of several thousand.

Therefore, the visual system apparently has the ability to calculate the reflectance of surfaces.

■ Colour constancy

Colour constancy operates through our tendency to interpret colours of familiar objects as the same even when changes in the colour of their illuminating light give them a different hue. As the colour of a surface depends on the proportion of light of different wavelengths reflected back to the eyes, the visual system must be capable of taking into account changes in the wavelengths received by the eye and correcting for this. You will always recognise your own clothes as being the same colour, whatever the level of illumination. Have you ever misjudged colour when buying clothes in an artificially lit shop environment, or misjudged the colour of a friend's clothes in environments such as a disco?

Visual illusions

Although we are usually unaware of what is happening to our perceptual systems, they often ignore some of the information that is presented and misinterpret other information received. The result will be an **illusion**, which is caused by discrepancy in perception which cannot be predicted from the actual stimuli concerned. An illusion may be experienced by any of our senses and can be regarded as a hypothesis formed as a result of incomplete perceptual data. Illusions are consistent phenomena, often being experienced in different individuals in the same way. They are subject, therefore, to regular rules, which make them useful research tools for investigating the workings of the perceptual system. Below we look at some examples of visual illusions, some of which result from physiological adaptation and others from cognitive processes.

Illusions of perceived size and distance

Have you ever looked at the moon when it is very low in the sky and wondered why it looks so much larger than when it is high in the sky? The *moon illusion* is one of size and distance, the actual image cast on the retina is the same size in both cases. Kaufman and Rock (1962) suggest that when we look at a horizon moon, the depth cues, such as interposition and perspective, indicate that it is a long way away (see figure 16.10). However, when the moon is high in the sky, the distance to it appears shorter – we do tend to perceive the sky above as being nearer to us than the sky at the horizon. Unconsciously, the observer knows that this is not true and therefore reinterprets the apparent size difference to mean that the moon is further away when it is high in the sky.

Kaufman and Rock (1962) have tested this hypothesis experimentally, using an apparatus which permitted participants to view an artificial moon of standard size in the sky and to adjust the size of another artificial moon at the horizon. It was found that when participants view artificial moons, they experience greater illusions when the visible horizon appears to be further away. Kaufman and Rock updated their theory to suggest the terrain below the horizon moon in the main source of the illusion. On the horizon the moon looks large compared with small land objects. In a vast uncluttered sky the moon looks smaller. Baird's theory (1982) is also supportive. Baird suggests a comparison line exists between the moon and

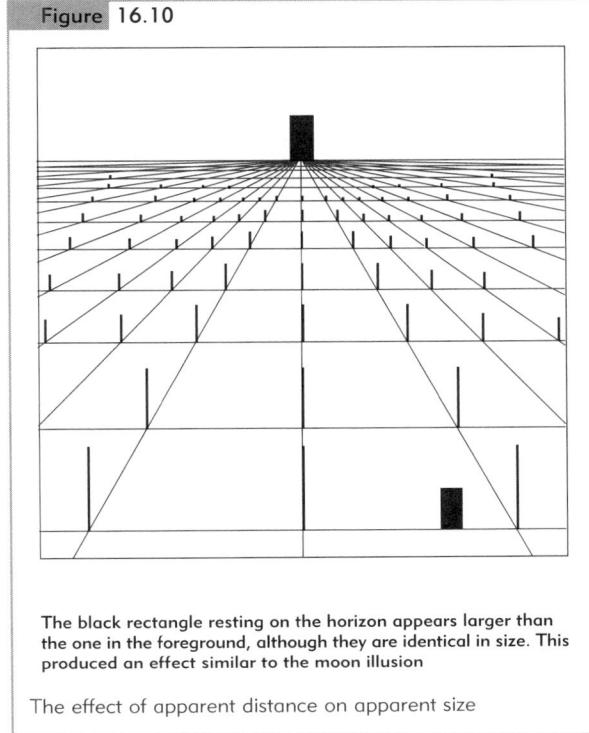

Figure 16.10

The black rectangle resting on the horizon appears larger than the one in the foreground, although they are identical in size. This produced an effect similar to the moon illusion

The effect of apparent distance on apparent size

objects on the ground below. As the moon rises in the sky, the empty sky becomes its reference point and comparison with the earth is less important. Another important theory is Reed's terrestrial passage theory (1989). Reed suggests observers treat the moon as if it was passing through the earth's (terrestrial) atmosphere. In the earth's atmosphere an object passing overhead, for example a plane, would appear to grow larger. It would cease to grow larger as it moves further away. The moon overhead fails to grow larger and so is seen as very distant and small.

The moon illusion has proved difficult to explain. Its distance creates problems of size perception, methods of investigation used have not always been comparable and as Coren (1989) suggests, the moon illusion is complex and probably arises from several sources.

Contrast effects

Contrast effects are powerful illusions which demonstrate that the visual system deals with the contrast between adjacent areas in the visual field, not just the light intensities of individual areas. Therefore, surroundings are taken into account when reaching conclusions which result from perceptual adaptations. Figure 16.11 shows two such illusions.

In the first of these, called *simultaneous brightness contrast*, the two central squares are the same shade of grey. It is the effect of the surrounding light and dark areas which affects their perceived appearance. If you look at the *Hermann grid*, you will see that there appear to be dark spots at the intersections of the lines (which disappear if you look directly at them). This illusion seems to be produced by the different amounts of light at the intersections.

■ Illusions of misalignment

Two examples of illusions of misalignment of line orientation are shown in figure 16.12.

In the case of the Zöllner illusion (Zöllner, 1860) a set of parallel diagonal lines apparently cease to be parallel when short horizontal and

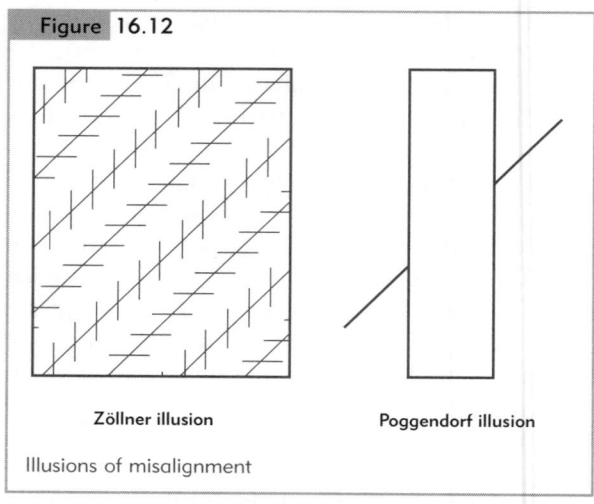

Figure 16.12

Zöllner illusion   Poggendorf illusion

Illusions of misalignment

vertical lines are superimposed upon them. This is thought to be due to interactions between the brain cells which signal line orientation. The Poggendorf illusion was developed from the Zöllner illusion; indeed Poggendorf was the editor of the journal to which Zöllner sent his research paper. One suggestion for this illusion is that the diagonal distance between the points where the line intersects the rectangle may be underestimated, and that the illusion results from this underestimation. The Müller-Lyer illusion (Müller-Lyer, 1889) is a powerful and consistent illusion in which the length of a line between two outward-pointing arrowheads is overestimated compared to a line of the same length between two inward-pointing arrowheads (figure 16.13a). Several researchers have interpreted this illusion in terms of apparent distance. Among them are Thiery (1896), Tausch (1954) and Gregory (1963). Gregory's *perspective-constancy theory* (figure 16.13b) suggests that false distance cues are provided by the arrowheads and, as a result, parts of the illustration are perceived as being further away. A size constancy mechanism then comes into operation and the illusion is produced. This explanation has been criticised by several researchers. For example, Fisher (1970) has suggested that the illusion may result from the convergence of lines without any need for recourse to an explanation involving depth cues. Also, if the arrowheads are replaced by

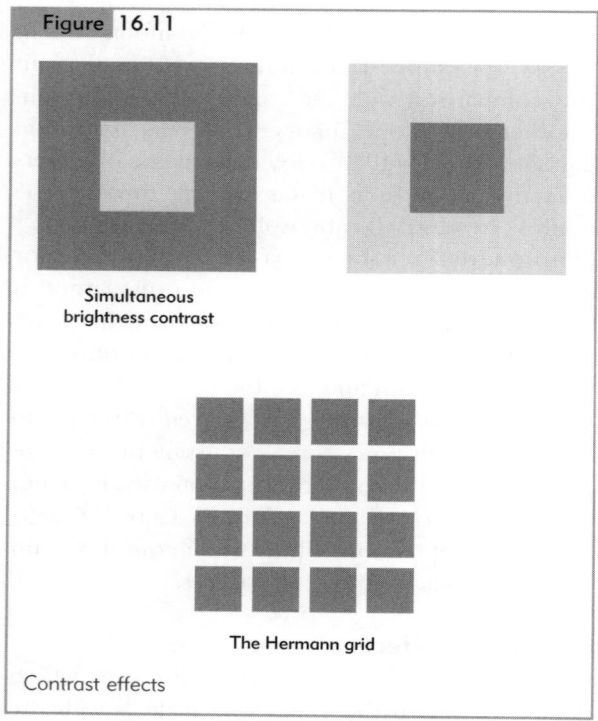

Figure 16.11

Simultaneous
brightness contrast

The Hermann grid

Contrast effects

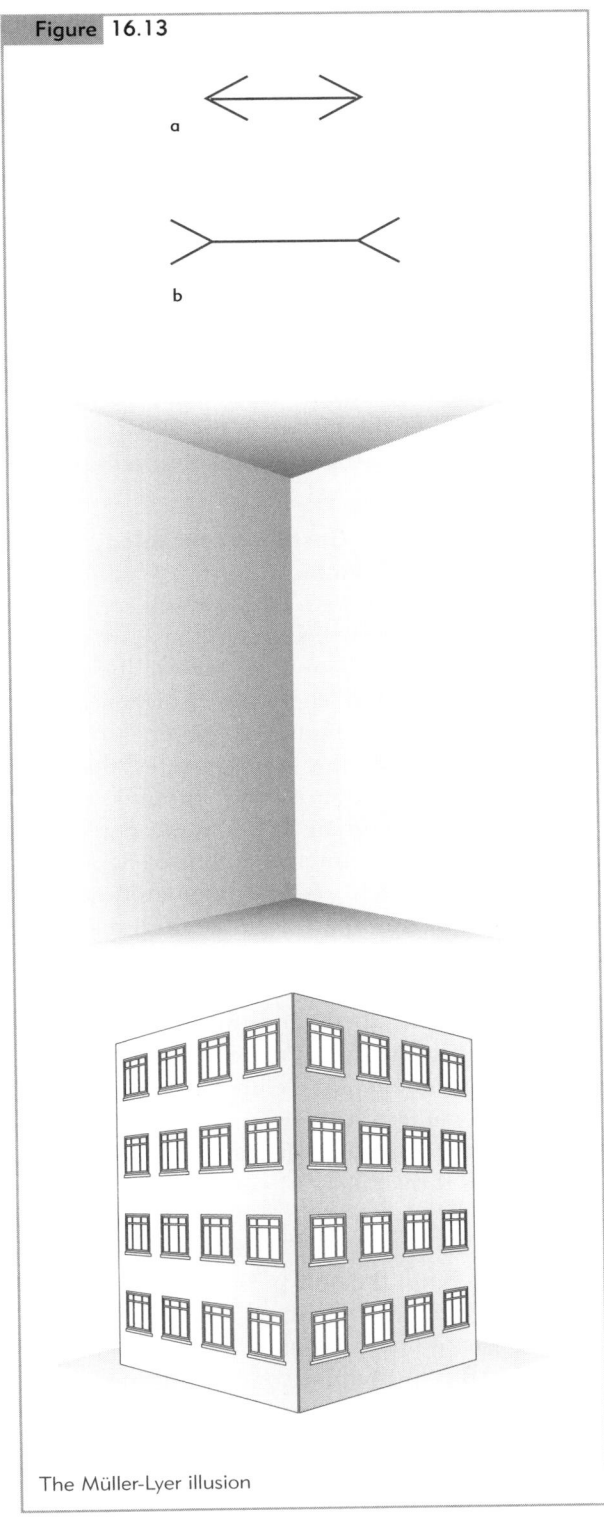

Figure 16.13

The Müller-Lyer illusion

circles (which are difficult to see three dimensionally), the illusion remains (figure 16.14). A tactile version of the illusion has been reported in blind and normally sighted, blindfolded persons, a situation in which depth cues are absent (Patterson and Deffenbacher, 1972).

■ Illusory figures

Sometimes we may make an inference of an illusory figure in the presence of a few cues only. Figure 16.15 shows the *Kanizsa triangle*.

Activity 9

What cues do you have to the perception of triangles in figure 16.15?

In this illusion, there are cues suggesting the presence of triangles in the lines and segments of the circles, but no triangles are actually outlined. Despite this, they are almost invariably perceived; sometimes people will even describe the central

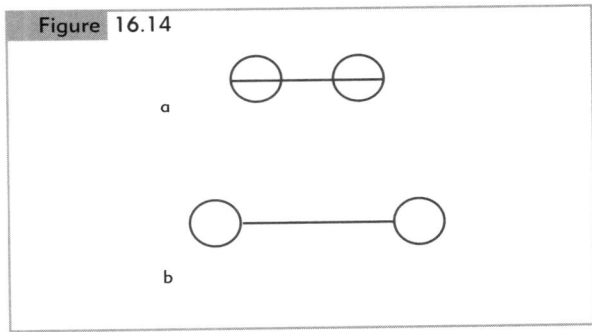

Figure 16.14

Figure 16.15

Kanizsa traingle

triangle as being lighter than its surrounding area! This must be closely linked to the normal perception of objects – a simplified example of the kind of challenge that nature continually presents (Gregory, 1987).

■ Ambiguous figures

When only one perception of an object is possible, our perception tends to remain stable. However, in an ambiguous figure, when more than one interpretation is feasible, then each possibility will be entertained in turn. Perception is an active process, seeking the most likely explanations of our environment. It is only when we look at such ambiguous figures as the Rubin vase and the Necker cube (figure 16.16) that we realise how perception continually searches for solutions to problems.

The Gestalt theory of perceptual organisation

Gestalt theory tries to explain the relationship between the world and everyday experience through (hypothetical) brain processes. The approach began in Germany, being developed by Wertheimer (1880–1943), Koffka (1886–1941) and Kohler (1887–1964). Their key beliefs are that there are certain phenomena which reveal the basic laws of perception, perceptual processes are dynamic and the perceptual world is organised into patterns.

The Gestalt theorists stressed the importance of perceiving whole objects rather than their independent components, believing that perception was organised according to a number of principles. These can all be accommodated within the *law of Prägnanz* which states that perceptual organisation will always be as good as conditions allow.

> ### Activity 10
>
> Look back at the Rubin vase in figure 16.16. Why do we see this picture in two ways?

According to **Gestalt psychology**, this demonstrates the simplest form of perceptual organisation. When we look at stimuli containing at least two regions, such as Rubin's vase, we usually interpret them as *figure and ground*, the figure appearing in front of the ground. As we are capable of interpreting this figure as either two facial profiles or a vase, this demonstrates that our interpretation of figure and ground is not generated by the figure itself but by our perceptual system. If one of the interpretations of figure and ground is more likely to occur than another, then we are more likely to perceive that interpretation.

Several of the Gestalt principles concern the *grouping* of objects. We tend to group stimuli when trying to interpret them, and this is achieved in a variety of ways. The first of these is *proximity*, which refers to the tendency for elements of a figure to be perceived together if they lie near each other. This is demonstrated in figure 16.17a, which is normally perceived as three pairs of lines with an extra line to the right.

If you study figure 16.17a carefully, you should see that this is not the only possible interpretation. You probably noticed that it can also be interpreted as three sets of lines with an extra line to the left. However, the principle concerning proximity suggests that most people will tend not to interpret it in this way.

Figure 16.17b demonstrates *closure*. When we see incomplete figures such as this, we tend to interpret

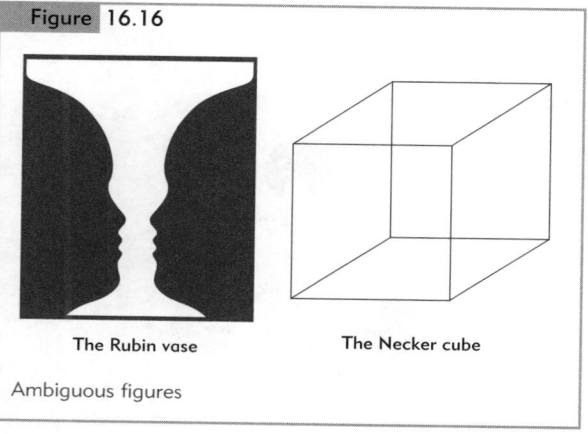

Figure 16.16

The Rubin vase   The Necker cube

Ambiguous figures

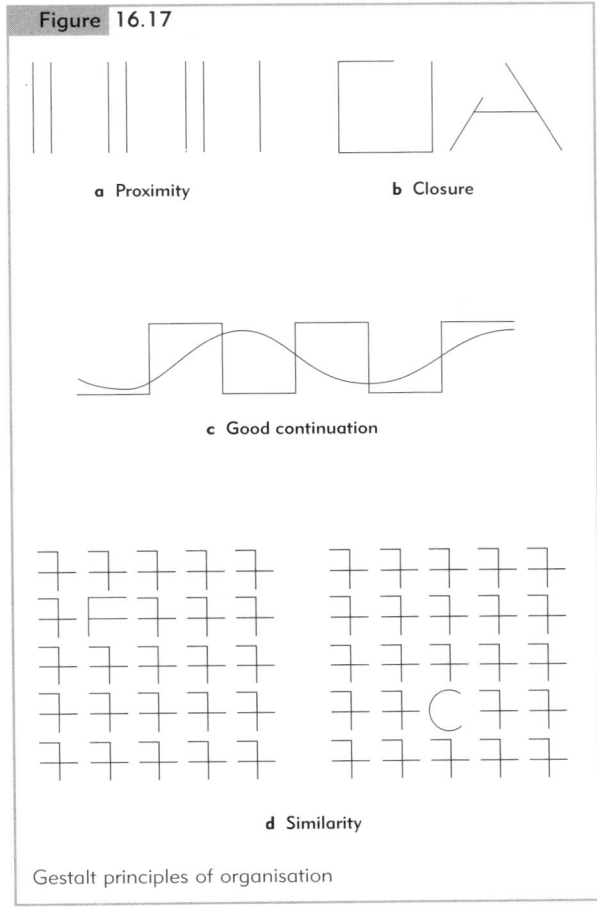

Figure 16.17

a Proximity   b Closure

c Good continuation

d Similarity

Gestalt principles of organisation

stimuli that we view into patterns, and to do this consistently.

There is some empirical support for Gestalt theory. For example, Banks and Prinzmetal (1976) demonstrated the role of proximity by presenting participants with a stimulus array that consisted of the target letter T and some non-target characters that were broadly similar (figure 16.18). Participants found the target letter more quickly in the display in which this letter was further away from the non-targets.

Gestalt theory may apply less successfully to the perception of complex objects. The objects that we come into contact with in everyday life tend to be much more complex than the simple patterns we have described in this section, and the Gestalt laws stand up less well to scrutiny when we consider three-dimensional objects.

Also, the laws can be regarded as being subjective and may sometimes conflict. For example, look at figure 16.19. This will usually be perceived as three squares with an extra line to the right. This demonstrates the principle of closure yet, at the same time, violates the principle governing

them as being complete. Another determinant of grouping is the law of *good continuation*, which states that we tend to perceive the organisation which interrupts the fewest lines. Hence we interpret figure 16.17c as a curved line intersecting a line resembling castle battlements, rather than as a loosely connected set of truncated rectangles. *Similarity* (figure 16.17d) refers to our tendency to group together similar objects. Thus it is harder to recognise the letter F in the top part of this figure than it is to recognise the C in the lower part.

■ Evaluation of Gestalt theory

There is some agreement about certain aspects of Gestalt theory but less evidence for others. It is certainly true to say that wholes are more than the sum of their parts. Also, we do tend to organise the

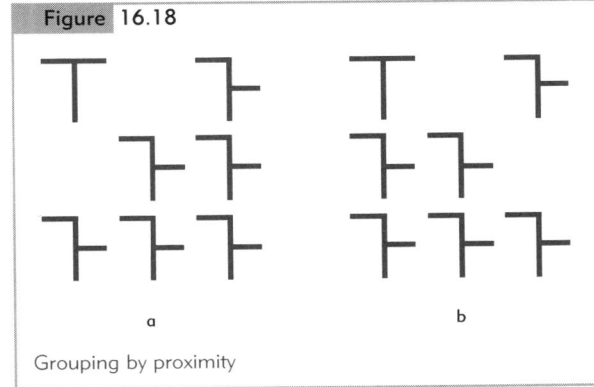

Figure 16.18

a   b

Grouping by proximity

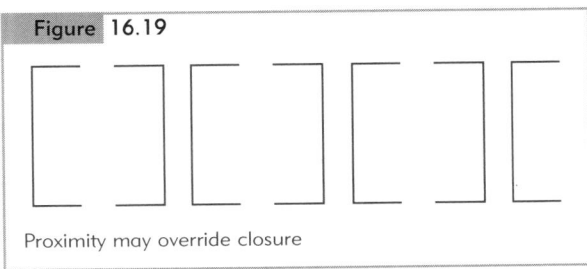

Figure 16.19

Proximity may override closure

proximity. It seems that, in this case, closure acts as a stronger principle and overrides proximity.

Some of the arguments put forward by the Gestalt theorists appear to be circular. For example, Gordon (1989) suggests that descriptions of the phenomena have too often become explanations. One example is Pragnanz. Perception has a tendency to be as good as conditions allow, and this is Pragnanz. Why is this the case? Because of Pragnanz.

However, whatever the problems, Gestalt theory has been responsible for the generation of

much research and has had a permanent and profound influence on the psychology of perception.

Activity 11

There are three basic key beliefs which underlie Gestalt theory. Jot down on a piece of paper what these are. (If you have difficulty remembering, turn back to page 584 and re-read the first paragraph.)

Self-assessment questions

1 What is the difference between sensation and perception?
2 Distinguish between monocular and binocular cues in the perception of space?
3 In pattern recognition what is the essential difference between template matching and feature detection models?
4 Why do psychologists study illusions?
5 In Gestalt psychology what is meant by the following:
   a the law of Pragnanz
   b figure ground perception
   c grouping by proximity
   d closure
   e good continuation
   f similarity?

(Suggested answers on page 606.)

Theories of perception

This section looks at theories and explanations of perception. Gregory's constructivist theory, Gibson's direct theory, Marr's computational theory and Neisser's cyclic theory are all considered.

Gregory's constructivist theory of perception

Gregory's **constructivist theory** of perception (for example, Gregory 1966, 1980) takes the view

that perception is a constructive sequence of events which resembles the formation and testing of hypotheses. He suggests that signals received by the sensory receptors trigger neural inputs. These interact with the knowledge stored in our memories to produce data of a psychological nature.

These data are then used to suggest hypothese by which we make sense of our world and predict events in it. Therefore, perception involves searching for the best available interpretation of the data which are presented. The theory is *top-down* in nature as inferences are made about the nature of stimuli, which are then tested by hypotheses. Top-down theories emphasise the role of the cognitive system in interpreting incoming sensory data. Gregory has supported this interpretation of the nature of perception by some powerful arguments, and it is to these that we now turn.

Perceiving through hypothesis generation permits behaviour to be appropriate in circumstances in which all object characteristics are not sensed. For example, it allows us to interpret the book in figure 16.9 as a book, even though the book in this case is not rectangular, which we might regard as being an essential characteristic.

When we are in familiar situations, we are able to anticipate something without any time delay. For example, if we are asked to maintain the alignment between a pointer and a regularly moving object on a screen, we can do this without any time delay. If this is achievable, then a degree of anticipation must be entering into perception.

Perception is not linked to one specific interpretation of a stimulus pattern. For example, when we examine ambiguous figures (such as the Rubin vase and Necker cube in figure 16.18) we do not consistently maintain one interpretation of the figure concerned.

We also tend to misinterpret objects which are unlikely to occur, preferring, instead, to interpret them as ones which are more likely to occur. For example, figure 16.20 shows the inside of a hollow mask, illuminated from behind. It is almost impossible not to interpret this as a normal face, with the eyes further from us than the nose. The unfamiliar interpretation is simply rejected.

Perception may be paradoxical in nature, as in the case of the 'Penrose figure' in figure 16.21.

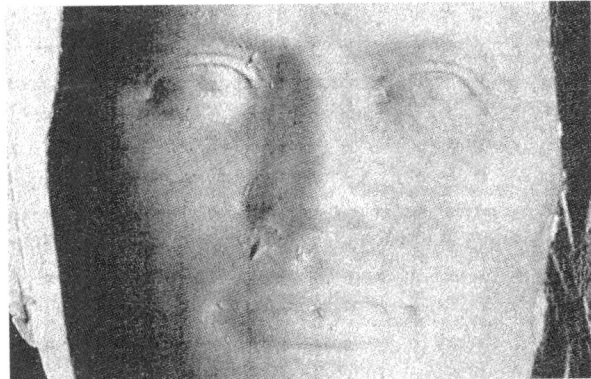

Figure 16.20   Picture of a hollow mask

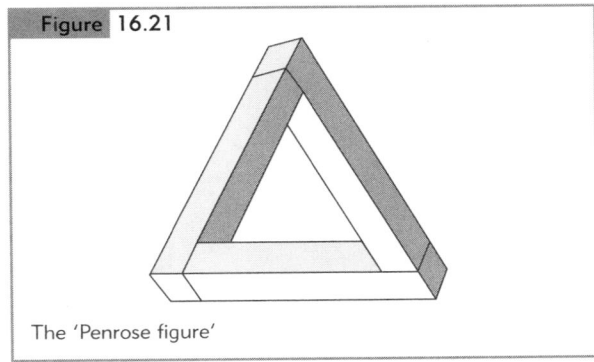

Figure 16.21

The 'Penrose figure'

Although we are able to interpret any one region of this figure as three dimensional, it is impossible to see the whole figure as such.

A considerable cognitive component is involved in the interpretation of pictures. Thus, these may be presented in a stylised way or at a markedly different size from reality. Despite this, we normally have no trouble in identifying them in terms of what they represent.

Perception may take place in the absence of conscious experience. For example, we may perceive a photograph of someone as being more attractive if their pupils are enlarged, yet be unaware of why we have made that decision.

Finally, we may experience hallucinations. It is possible to have perceptual experiences even in the absence of any direct stimuli as in the Kanizsa triangle. Gregory has applied his theory of perception to the interpretation of visual illusions (see page 582). A famous example is his three-dimensional interpretation of the Müller-Lyer figure that is discussed briefly on page 582. Gregory interprets this as being due to misapplied size constancy.

■ Evaluation of Gregory's constructivist theory

Gregory's constructivist theory explains how, through perceptual constancy, perceptual set (a preparedness for a particular type of experience) and stored schema, the experience of new perceptual stimuli is subjected to hypothesis testing. The Ames Room illusion provides a good example (figure 16.22).

Figure **16.22**

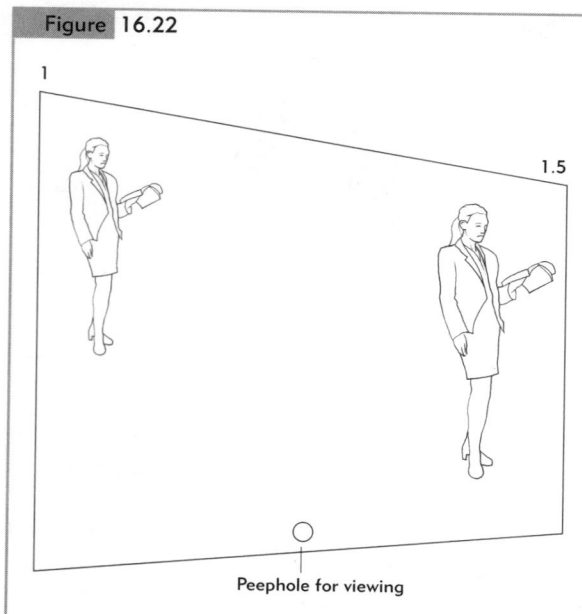

Peephole for viewing

In this illusion a room is constructed which, when viewed from a particular viewing point, seems to be a normal room. This is not really the case as one corner is actually much further away from the viewer than the other corner. The floor and ceiling levels are also sloping. The effect of the illusion is that people of the same size appear to be a different size if they move about the room.

The Ames Room illusion

Illusions are misplaced hypotheses. According to Gregory, predicting from hypotheses based on meagre sensory data is an indication of intelligent behaviour. If the brain were not able to fill in the gaps, the perceptual world would come to a standstill. Using hypotheses testing as a basis for perception may result in some mistakes, but, according to Gregory, it is a small price to pay for freedom from total reliance on sensory stimulus behaviour. It is an adaptive behaviour, enabling us to cope in less familiar surroundings.

Although Gregory proposes some ingenious explanations for perceptual phenomena, there are certain questions which remain unanswered. For example, there is a serious problem concerning the relationship between perception and actual knowledge. If Gregory's theory is correct, then why do illusions persist even when we are fully aware of them (looking at the horizon moon – see page 581 – is a good example of this). Why are we unable to

adapt our hypotheses once they have been demonstrated to be false?

If we are to accept that perception is governed by hypotheses, another question arises: how do we test these? This problem is not made any easier by the fact that we are so often unaware of the hypotheses concerned.

As with the Gestalt theory, it appears likely that Gregory's theory applies best with simple stimuli rather than with the complex stimuli so often encountered in the real world. However, he has provided a wealth of carefully conducted research that is a major contribution to visual perception.

Gibson's direct or ecological theory of perception

Gibson's **ecological theory** of perception is often referred to as the 'direct perception' theory. The inclusion of the term 'ecological' stresses the importance Gibson placed on the need to consider perception under real-life conditions as opposed to the unnatural conditions of the laboratory.

Gibson believed that retinal images are usually highly complex in nature and are rarely of single objects. Therefore, studying simple stimuli experimentally is not a fruitful approach to the study of perception; rather, we should be considering complete arrays of stimuli studied under natural conditions. According to Gibson, perception involves the 'picking up' of information from this array in a direct way. He did not distinguish between sensation and perception, seeing the former as being more useful than the latter. So there is no room for complex hypothesis testing procedures. This is a *bottom-up* approach, with little room for unconscious information processing. Bottom-up theories emphasise the importance of data-driven information in perceptual processing.

The key feature of the ecological theory is that we are aware of the world in an indirect way – sensory inputs need to be elaborated upon before perception is completed. Gibson suggested that human beings cannot be directly aware of their physical worlds. For example, perception of colours lies not in the objects concerned but in our heads. The actual sensory inputs are often far too degraded to be able to specify external scenes and objects. These inputs often contain insufficient detail to enable perceptions to be made. Therefore, we need to add further information to them and this is achieved by involving processes such as the memory system. Usually the inferences made as a result of this additional process are correct, but incorrect inferences do sometimes occur and, as a result, we make a perceptual error or experience an illusion. We also need to integrate our visual inputs over time if we are to unify our perceptions because visual perception occurs in the form of a sequence of fixations.

Gibson developed a school of psychology which he termed *ecological optics*. This considered the environment, in which the visual system has evolved, to be fundamentally important. Objects do not occur in isolation from each other, and properties such as depth cues and motion are regarded as being vitally important to our perception. Ecological optics largely ignores concepts such as 'retinal images' in favour of picking up information from the patterns of light which arrive at the eye from the environment, together with the information that these patterns carry.

Gibson's work was inspired by working with pilots during the Second World War when he became particularly interested in the *optic flow* of motion experienced, for example when a pilot landed an aircraft (flow patterns have already been discussed on page 573). Gibson believes that, as an object moves, it covers and uncovers parts of the background. We use this information to perceive motion of an object relative to its background. He noted the invariance of this phenomenon and others which help us to perceive motion and distance. Among the others are motion parallax, linear perspective (see page 576) and texture gradient. Gibson noted that textures always expand as you move towards them, and always contract as you move away. The retinal image of an object will interrupt the texture gradient at a specific point and we can work out how far away the object is by the position of the interruption.

■ Evaluation of Gibson's ecological theory

Gibson equates sensation closely with perception. Gibson (1988) has argued that the sensory information provided from the whole environment together (especially size, shape, distance and movement cues) provide the information necessary for individuals to cope with their perceptual experiences. His theory particularly fits with the explanation of the movement of animals in their environment.

In this context sensations need not be interpreted by hypothesis testing and inputs need not be matched against mental representations. Light rays from the environment provide sufficient information for the animal to interact directly with the environment. Gibson points out that animals use the ambient optic array (all the transmitted and reflected light rays) which provide dynamic information enabling the animal to move around in its environment. Perception occurs in the context of direct contact with the environment.

Gibson's theory is important in the stress it lays on the function of perception to provide the necessary information for interacting with the environment. It emphasises the role of sensation and environmental clues in perception. Gibson's theory supports the distinctive features model of pattern recognition. It suggests size constancy and depth perception are closely based on sensory experience. The theory provides only a weak account of illusions as the latter often depend on inferences beyond the sensory data. Gibson however criticises illusions as lacking in ecological validity, but naturally occurring illusions (such as the moon illusion) lack an explanation in his theory.

Gibson's theory does not however, really explain the activity of the visual system in perception. It does not develop explanations of the process of the transmission of retinal activity to the brain, hence perception is seen as a rather passive process. Another limitation of the theory is that it best explains innately programmed reactions to the natural environment, for example birds migrating for the first time, using the stars in the southern hemisphere to guide them. It does not however explain why birds may repeatedly fly into transparent window panes, failing to learn from earlier experiences. Gibson has perhaps underestimated how difficult a process perception actually is. His theory also ignores the possible role of culture in perception.

Marr's computational theory of visual perception

Marr's computational theory of visual perception owes its origin to his belief that we cannot understand the properties of individual cells in the visual pathway without a computational theory of vision. His effort at providing such a theory was published posthumously after his untimely death in 1980.

Marr suggested that we need to understand what perception accomplishes before we can actually examine the mechanisms involved. His approach is concerned principally with how the visual system recovers lines and edges from the images formed by light falling on the retina, a highly complex process. He was also interested in how the brain matches a point in one retinal image with a corresponding point in the other retinal image, and how objects are represented in the brain in order to facilitate their recognition. In this short account we focus on how Marr suggests that we compute shape.

According to Marr, the key requirement for his theory is an ability to account for the shape of objects. Other aspects of vision, such as texture and brightness, were considered secondary to this. The starting point for seeing is the retinal image itself – consisting of a distribution of light intensities across the retina. The task of visual processing is to describe the object viewed from the image being presented.

Marr proposed that, during perception, we form three successive visual representations of

increasing complexity. The *primal sketch* is the first of these to be formed. This aims to extract explicit information from the pattern of light on the retina, and consists of edges, contours and blobs. The second representation to be formed is the $2\frac{1}{2}D$ *sketch*. This is more detailed and contains some information on depth as well as on the orientation of surfaces. The $2\frac{1}{2}D$ sketch, however, is still organised only with reference to the viewer and is not yet linked to the external environment.

The final stage is the *3D model representation*, in which shapes and their orientation explicitly refer to three-dimensional objects in a way that exists independently of the observer's retinal image. The viewer has now obtained a model of the external world. Recognition takes place.

Marr and Nishihara (1978) consider that the three-dimensional shape representation scheme outlined above was formed from a hierarchy of generalised shapes. Figure 16.23 shows how this works for a description of the human form.

First of all, the body is given an axis. This can then be used to specify the position of the head, torso, arms and legs. Each of these has an axis of its own, which, in turn, serves to specify the position of further subsidiary parts. Once a generalised representation of a person has been computed in this way, it can be compared with standard representations stored by the individual concerned.

■ Evaluation of Marr's computational theory

Marr managed to integrate computational, physiological and psychological knowledge into his computational approach, a contribution that would probably have been far greater but for his death at the age of 35. He brought home to researchers the need to recognise just how important it is to study the nature and function of the task under investigation, and set very high standards of scientific rigour.

His suggestion that different levels of explanation exist for visual processes is a good idea. However, the concept of representing shapes through a hierarchy of cylindrical (or other) shapes is likely to be oversimplified, and it

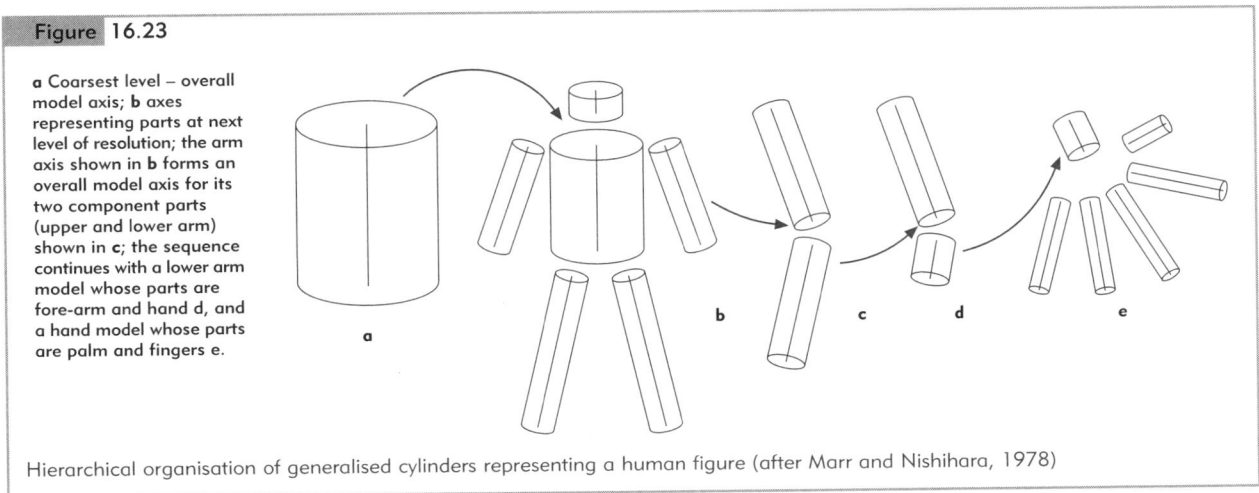

Figure 16.23

a Coarsest level – overall model axis; **b** axes representing parts at next level of resolution; the arm axis shown in **b** forms an overall model axis for its two component parts (upper and lower arm) shown in **c**; the sequence continues with a lower arm model whose parts are fore-arm and hand **d**, and a hand model whose parts are palm and fingers **e**.

Hierarchical organisation of generalised cylinders representing a human figure (after Marr and Nishihara, 1978)

is unclear how objects are perceived that do not break down into their component parts in this way.

Neisser's cyclic model of perception

Neisser (1976) proposed that the process of perception involves expectations being tested against sensory cues. Feature detection occurs as a matching process against stored mental representations. When features are matched against a higher level representation realisation of the nature of the object in view occurs. Neisser starts with the belief that people have expectations about objects they are likely to meet in a given context. Initially in perception, the automatic process of sampling occurs whereby, using bottom-up processing, a representation of the object in view is formed. The process is pre-attentive. Then an interaction of top-down processing can occur to construct a possible model of the object. Attention is now directed to the stimulus if it is perceived as of possible interest. A perceptual model is tested against the sensory cues available in the environment. Perceptual models search for the cues available to confirm, or disconfirm the

hypothesis being suggested. Neisser's model is called a cyclic model because it involves a continuous process of checking and rechecking the sensory cues to confirm the perceptual model being presented. Thus there is interaction between perceptual constructs and sensory data. Finally, a top-down model becomes a perception which is confirmed (figure 16.24).

Neisser referred to his model as analysis-by-synthesis because a perceptual model (synthesis) selects information about features from the environment (analysis). This synthesis–analysis process continuously monitors the environment using past experiences to generate hypotheses. An

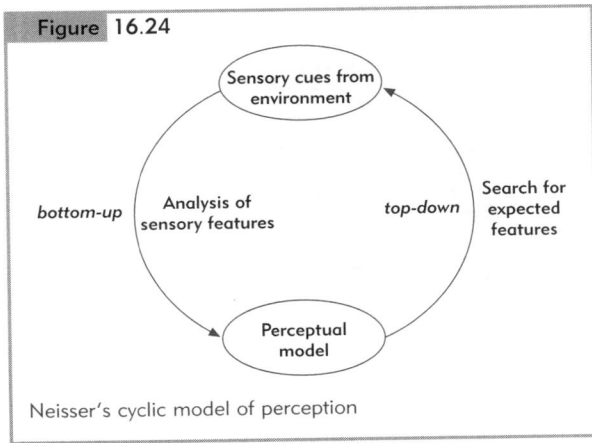

Figure 16.24

Neisser's cyclic model of perception

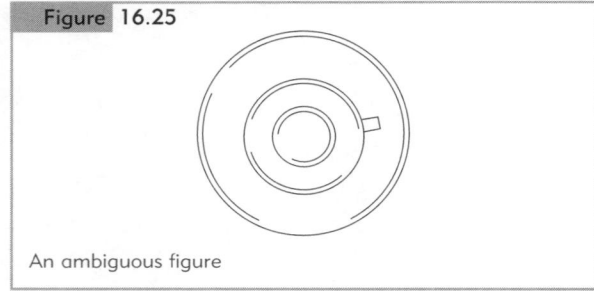

Figure 16.25

An ambiguous figure

example of analysis-by-synthesis can be seen in figure 16.25. What perceptual models can be generated based on the sensory information provided here?

Now look at figure 16.26 over the page which creates the perceptual hypothesis for figure 16.25. Once the figure has been provided with a suitable perceptual context, a hypothesis can be generated. Without the perceptual model (the synthesis), it is difficult to carry out the analysis of the object.

■ Evaluation of Neisser's cyclic model

By way of evaluation of Neisser's theory it must be stated that there is a difficulty in defining the point at which perception actually occurs. It would seem likely that it is at the point at which the perceptual model is confirmed, but this does not explain how humans cope with totally unexpected perceptions. Neisser's theory fits in well with Gregory's ideas about hypothesis testing, though perhaps Neisser's hypotheses are more general interpretations of the changing visual field. Both Neisser and Gregory emphasise the part played by the concept driven nature of perception.

Self-assessment questions

6 What does Richard Gregory suggest when he says perception is hypothesis testing?

7 Why is Gibson's theory of perception called an ecological theory?

8 How does David Marr use the idea that the task of visual processing is to describe the object viewed from the image being presented?

9 What does Neisser mean when he says perception is the process of analysis through synthesis?

10 List the four main theories of perception in the order top-down to bottom-up theories.

(Suggested answers on page 606.)

Individual, social and cultural variations in perceptual organisation

It is possible that as people experience different environments and as perception is partly a mental construction, the way people see the world will differ. There are a number of reasons why the world you see may be different from the world which other people see. Some of these reasons may be to do with individual factors affecting physiology, sex differences and/or cultural differences.

Physiological factors

One cause of differences in visual perception is colour blindness. Another variable in perceptual experience is caused by drugs, such as barbiturates, tranquilisers and alcohol which decrease sensory awareness. For example, alcohol depresses visual functioning by having a direct effect on the retina. Excessive alcohol has been linked to defects in red-

Figure 16.26

The hypothesis for figure 16.25

green colour vision (Granger and Ikeda, 1968). Stimulants can increase visual responsiveness. Coren, Porac and Ward (1979), writing about individual differences in perception, suggest the activity outlined below.

Activity 12

Test the effect of a caffeine stimulant on figure reversal.

Look at the Necker cube in figure 16.27 and observe that sometimes the face with the corner labelled A seems closer than the face with the corner labelled B. Sometimes B seems closer and A further away. Ask a friend to count how many times the figure is reversed for you in one minute. As the friend times you, call out each time the figure is reversed. Then drink a cup of coffee (not decaffeinated!). The caffeine is a stimulant and should increase your visual responsiveness although the effect will take about 10–15 minutes to appear. So, after 15 minutes repeat the cube viewing

Activity 12 cont'd

process. The stimulant could well have increased the number of perceptual shifts which you experience.

Hallucinogenic and psychoactive drugs, for example LSD and marijuana, have strong perceptual effects, yet even everyday drugs such as aspirin may cause dimness of vision or ringing in the ears (Goodman and Gilman, 1965).

Another physiological factor which results in variation in perception is damage to the nervous system. Patients with certain types of damage may fail to recognise objects, or may not be able place objects in space. These problems are termed *agnosias*, from the Greek *a* meaning not and *gnosis* meaning intuitive knowledge. People suffering agnosias perceive but do not seem able to understand the information presented to them. An example of this can be seen in figure 16.28.

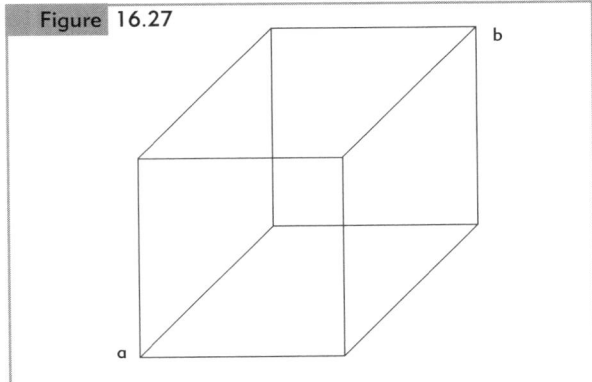

Figure 16.27

Sex differences in vision

For a long time there has been thought to be a difference in male/female visuo-spatial abilities. Tasks which require the use of spatial abilities generally produce sex differences favouring males. In embedded figure tests, such as that shown in Figure 16.29, the target is embedded in the more complex figure beside it. Try not to be put off by the shading and see if you can identify the target in the complex figure.

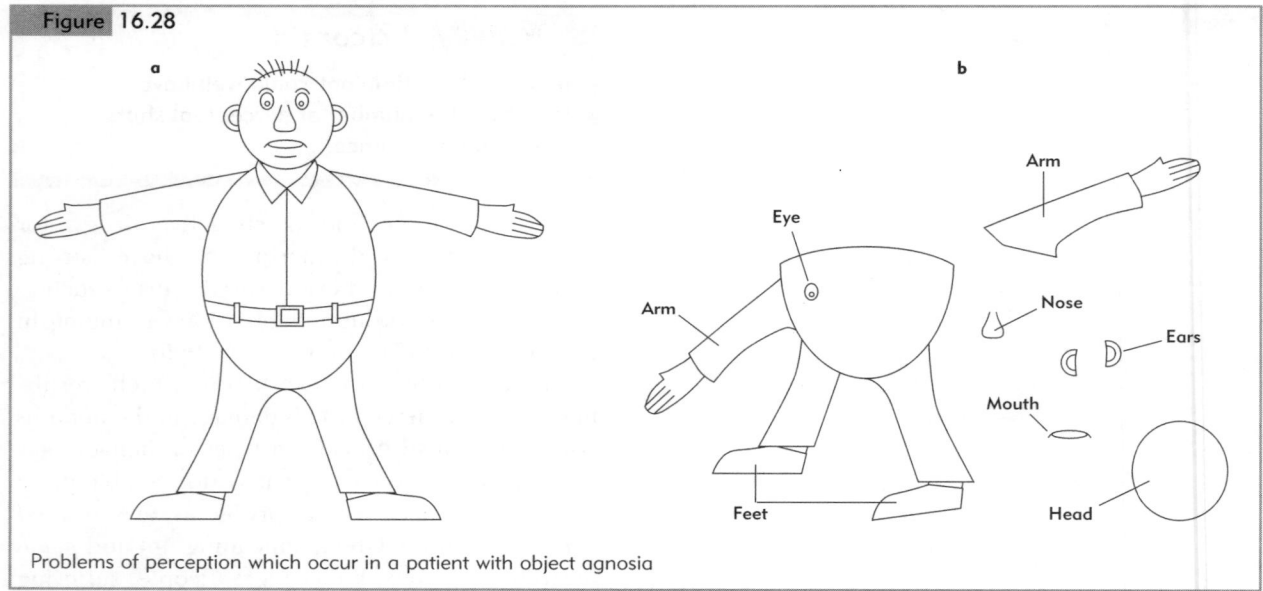

Figure 16.28

a

b

Arm

Eye

Arm

Nose

Ears

Mouth

Feet

Head

Problems of perception which occur in a patient with object agnosia

In figure 16.30 the task is to identify the target which has been rotated.

The tasks shown in these figures produce sex differences which favour males. To some extent the differences could be the result of learned experiences, but there is some evidence to suggest physiological factors could partly be responsible. Dawson (1969) found that West African males who suffered from a disease that resulted in high oestrogen levels (associated with females), showed reduced spatial ability. Further, males who are insensitive to androgens show reduced spatial abilities, whilst females with high androgen levels (associated with males) show stronger spatial abilities (Masica *et al.*, 1969; Peterson, 1976).

Cultural differences in perception

There have been a large number of studies demonstrating cultural differences in perception.

Figure 16.29

Target

Complex figure in which target is embedded

An embedded figure test

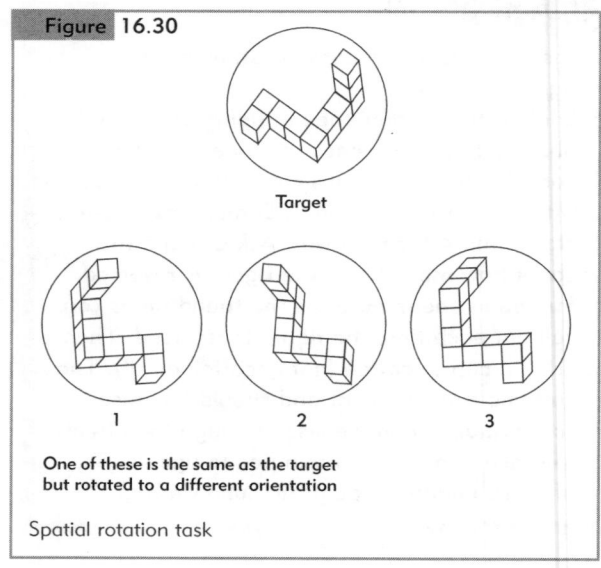

Figure 16.30

Target

1   2   3

One of these is the same as the target but rotated to a different orientation

Spatial rotation task

Different environments produce different visual stimuli. People are thus exposed to different visual patterns and this may alter their perceptual experiences. In a number of studies of cultural differences in perception, Hudson (1960, 1962) examined cultural factors connected with interpreting pictorial depth information. Figure 16.31 shows a picture of the type used by Hudson depicting a hunting scene in which two types of depth cues can be used. The first is interposition, where objects closer to the observer block out parts of objects which are more distant, hence the antelope blocks out part of the rock. The second pictorial cue is that of familiar size. People are aware of the relative size of objects, so if an object is depicted as small or large, it will be judged in distance in line with expectations, based on known size. For example, in figure 16.31 if the elephant is shown as a small item, and in the picture it casts a smaller image than the antelope, it must be further away, since people know, in real life, an elephant is larger than an antelope.

Hudson used picture stimuli, such as the one shown in figure 16.31, because it allows for two- and three-dimensional responses, hence he could see whether there was any cultural variation in this. For example, a three-dimensional response to the picture would indicate the hunter was trying to spear the antelope. A two-dimensional response would say the hunter was trying to spear the elephant which is closer to the tip of the spear in the picture. Using stimuli such as these pictures, a number of studies have been carried out in Africa testing people from different tribal groups and environments (Deregowski, 1972). Results indicate relatively isolated and uneducated African adults and children have difficulty perceiving pictorial depth. It may be, however, that the inability to perceive depth also arises from a number of other factors. As Gross (1996) suggests, the picture studies may be an unusual medium for people of other cultures, the depth cues presented in these pictures may not be the ones typically used by people of other cultures and the western artistic convention depicted in Hudson's work may be unfamiliar and confusing to people of other cultures. Thus the measuring tool may simply not be adequate to assess depth perception in a culture fair way.

One explanation of cross-cultural differences is the **carpentered world hypothesis** (Gregory, 1966; Segall *et al.*, 1966; Davidoff, 1975) which suggests the western view of the world is constructed based on the rectangular environment and many linear depth cues. It was observed that Zulus living in

Figure 16.31

A figure used to test the ability to respond to pictorial depth cues (based on Hudson, 1962)

round huts with round doors did not rely much on linear perspective. In 1966 Segall, Campbell and Herskovits reported a series of studies that compared the perceptual response of people from a carpentered and non-carpentered world. Comparisons were made, based on visual illusions, for example the Müller-Lyer illusion (see page 582). It was found that size distortion in this illusion depended on the three-dimensional interpretation of the figure, and that the distortion was greater for urban groups who were more likely to experience a carpentered environment. Killbride and Liebowitz (1975) studying the Ponzo illusion (see figure 16.32), found that people in Uganda who responded in three dimensions to the depth cues in pictures, demonstrated the distortion shown in illusions, whilst those who did not see depth showed little distortion in illusions. There is evidence to suggest that the experience of education and the availability of graphic and pictorial representations are important in the development of three-dimensional representations.

Lack of experience involving distance perception has also been shown to hamper size

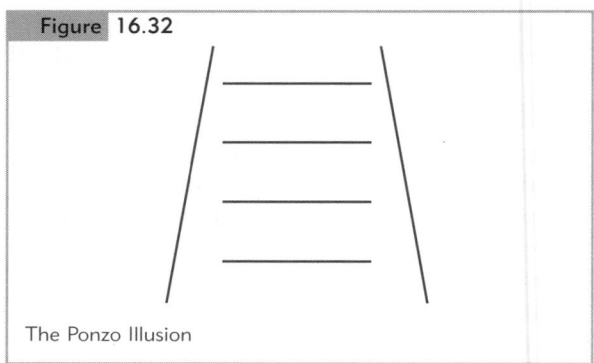

Figure 16.32

The Ponzo Illusion

constancy. Turnbull (1961) observed the behaviour of Bambuti Pygmies in Zaire, in an African forest region. The significance of their environment lies in the fact that their viewing range is limited to about 30 metres. Turnbull took his Bambuti guide, Kenge, out of the forest and across the plain to where a herd of buffalo could be seen in the distance. Kenge saw the buffalo as 'insects' which appeared to grow larger as they were approached. Kenge was convinced that some sort of trickery was being mounted.

Self-assessment questions

11 Give three reasons why there may be variations in visual perception.

12 What sort of problem might an agnosic person have?

13 What difference in perception is persistently found between males and females and how can the difference be accounted for?

14 Give three examples of cross-cultural differences in perception.

15 Suggest why cross-cultural pictorial studies may be flawed.

(Suggested answers on pages 606–7.)

The development of perceptual processes

The question of how perceptual processes develop has long been part of the so-called **nature–nurture**

debate, which is concerned with whether different capabilities are innate or learned. With a few exceptions, these standpoints have now been integrated as it is no longer believed that one or the other of these viewpoints is able to explain perception completely. The questions now have become:

■ What perceptual abilities do newborn infants have?

■ What are the contributions of learning and maturation to the acquisition of perceptual abilities?

Research techniques

A major problem when conducting research on the development of perceptual processes is establishing what the capacities of newborn infants are.

Perhaps the most serious problem for researchers is that newborn infants cannot talk or respond to instructions. They also have only a limited repertoire of behaviours which a researcher might study to try and establish whether an infant is responding to a particular stimulus. A further important set of issues concerns the ethical problems associated with studying human infants. For example, it is impossible to gain their consent to take part in investigations and there is a need to avoid situations which might cause them distress.

As a consequence of the research difficulties, psychologists have adopted some ingenious strategies. These include a series of techniques for studying perception in human infants, examining how well adults read when their perception has been limited or altered artificially in some way, and the study of perceptual processes in non-human animals.

One of the more ingenious techniques to be used when studying human infants is the **preferential looking method**, originally introduced by Fantz (1961) (see page 599). This works best with infants up to six months old and involves an infant being placed, face-up, in crib which forms part of an apparatus often referred to as a *looking chamber* (figure 16.33). The infant is then presented with two stimuli on the ceiling of the apparatus. The

experimenter, who cannot be seen by the infant, records the amount of time that the infant spends looking at each stimulus. This is achieved either directly (preferably with the experimenter unaware of which pattern has been presented to which side of the visual field) or by using a video camera. The stimuli are presented on the ceiling of the chamber in different positions in order to control for the possibility that infants prefer looking in a certain direction. If infants spend longer looking at one stimulus than another, then it is possible to draw the conclusion that the infant can tell them apart. Here a problem lies in interpreting the situations in which no preference is shown – it is impossible to tell whether this is due to an inability to discriminate or to a lack of preference. Other methods of studying infant perception include measuring changes in heart or breathing rate (for example Campos *et al.*, 1970). A change is taken to indicate that the infant can discriminate between stimuli. Measuring changes in electrical activity in the brain, by the use of electrodes attached to the scalp, is also assumed to indicate an infant's ability to discriminate between stimuli.

Figure 16.33

This apparatus was used to test the visual interest of chimpanzee and human infants. Here a human infant lies on a crib in the chamber, looking at objects hung from the ceiling. The observer, watching through a peephole, records the attention each object is given.

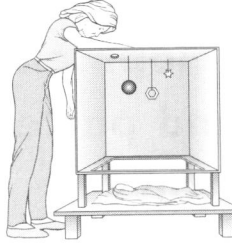

The visual depth apparatus consists of a board laid across a sheet of heavy glass, with patterned material directly beneath the glass on one side and several metres below it on the other. Placed on the centre board (left), the child crawls to its mother across the 'shallow' side. When called from the 'deep' side, the baby pats the glass but despite the tactual evidence that the 'cliff' is in fact a solid surface the child refuses to cross over to the mother.

The looking chamber

Studies of altered perception in adults are able to tell us something about the nature of perception. There are two main types of such studies. In *distortion studies* adult perceptual abilities are deliberately masked or altered in some way (for example, through the wearing of prismatic lenses) and the effects examined, such as the time taken to adjust to the modified visual experiences. In the second approach – *restored vision* studies – individuals with a perceptual deficiency, such as congenital cataracts, may have that problem corrected. It then becomes possible to examine how their new-found visual ability is put to use.

With the ethical limitations on the use of humans in research, many investigators have turned to the use of non-human animals in order to investigate systematically how their visual experiences (or lack of them) influence perception. Although such studies can be useful, we must always be mindful of the problems which occur when generalising results from such studies on to humans. Problems of interpretation may also occur. For example, a schedule of visual deprivation may alter the course of normal perceptual development in unpredictable ways, introducing confounding variables such as excessive arousal to novel stimulation (Schiffman, 1982). This last problem is also likely to occur in restored-vision studies with human participants.

The development of object and pattern recognition

Do we need visual experience if we are to perceive objects and patterns? Before looking at how children acquire the ability to recognise objects and patterns, we shall examine what happens if there is a total absence of visual stimulation. This can provide important information on whether experience is necessary for these abilities to develop.

■ The effects of deprivation of visual stimulation

Can visual deprivation affect the brain structures involved in perception? The answer to this question appears to be 'yes'. In one *perceptual deprivation* study, Hubel and Wiesel (1962) deprived cats of visual stimulation by blindfolding them and found that their receptive fields did not develop normally. In another study, Hubel (1979) sewed up the left or right eyelids of two-week-old monkeys. When the monkeys were 18 months old, the closed eye was opened and a radioactive tracer was injected into the good eye. Hubel found that the cortical cells serving the good eye had expanded in number, while those serving the closed eye had diminished. This suggests that there is a critical period for the development of the visual cortex.

Riesen (1947) studied the total absence of visual stimulation on chimpanzees who were kept in total darkness until the age of 16 months. When tested for their visual abilities, they showed a papillary reflex and were therefore able to detect light. However, they were unable to discriminate patterns. It is difficult to conclude from this that pattern recognition requires experience to develop. It remains possible that this result occurred because the chimpanzees' visual cortex had deteriorated or because their retinal system had not developed properly due to the lack of visual stimulation.

Riesen (1965) overcame this difficulty by fitting monkeys, chimps and kittens with translucent goggles that admitted only unpatterned light. When the goggles were removed, certain visual abilities (such as the ability to discriminate colour, size and brightness) proved to be unaffected, but it was shown that patterned light was necessary for the development of more complex visual abilities. Thus, the animals had problems with following a moving object, distinguishing between shapes, with depth perception and in distinguishing between stationary and moving objects.

It appears that the longer the period of deprivation in infant animals, the greater the deficit in their perceptual abilities. Adult cats can, however, have an eye patched for a long period without losing visual ability in the eye concerned. This has led to the suggestion of a *critical period* for the development of perceptual abilities early in life.

The development of visual acuity

It seems, therefore, that some of the less complex perceptual abilities are present without experience being needed, although evidence suggests that their quality may not be as good as that in adults. Newborn human infants certainly have rather poor visual acuity (see below). This is a prerequisite for object and pattern recognition, and poor acuity may be compounded by the high levels of astigmatism in infants compared to adults. Preference techniques have been applied to the study of this area. For example, infants were presented with a uniform grey field and then striped patterns of decreasing width until they could no longer identify the stripes. Using this technique, it was shown that, at one month, visual acuity is very low. It increases very quickly over the first six months, then progress slows, with capabilities comparable to adults being achieved between the ages of one and five (Teller *et al.*, 1974; Pirchio *et al.*, 1978), although it continues to improve until about the age of ten to twelve years old (Weymouth, 1963).

What implications does poor visual acuity have for object perception? In another experiment using preference techniques, Goldstein (1989) has shown that, at one month old, visual acuity is so poor that only the outside contours of a face tend to be examined. However, this is probably adequate for an infant's needs. It is also difficult for infants of this age to perceive facial expressions, but by three months old an infant has acquired this capability.

The improvement in acuity that takes place is apparently maturational. The eye, retina and visual cortex, as well as their neural connections, all continue to develop over the first six months of life.

Away *et al.* (1973) have shown that if eye surgery is carried out in an infant's first year, then the acuity of the patched eye decreases. This provides some further evidence for the existence of a critical period in this stage of life (Aslin and Banks, 1978).

Recognising objects and people

At one month old, infants cannot distinguish the fine details of objects and only large objects are discriminated. Salapatek (1975) among others, has suggested that for the first six to eight weeks of life infants' attention is focused on where things are in the world, searching particularly for clearly defined edges rather than looking randomly over a form. This has been studied by photographing the corneas of infants. It has also been shown that infants of this age can follow moving objects with their eyes and, as we shall see below, may be better at recognising faces than other objects.

At about eight weeks, the emphasis changes markedly; the infant becomes more interested in what an object is and scans *across* objects rather than along their edges. This may reflect the maturation of brain structures.

Olson (1981) has shown that babies can discriminate between objects by three months old, and possibly earlier, with recognition of their mothers developing earlier than most recognition abilities. By two months, babies can distinguish their mothers from strangers when they can combine vision with voice, touch and smell. A purely visual discrimination can usually be achieved by three months (Hayes and Watson, 1981). Also by three months old, Barrera and Maurer (1981) have shown that infants prefer to look at photos of their own mothers rather than at the photo of another woman who is unfamiliar to them.

Some important work on form perception has been carried out by Fantz using the preference technique (see figure 16.33). Fantz (1961, 1970) has shown that infants aged between four days and six months prefer curves to straight lines, and prefer forms resembling a face to others.

Studies of object perception in human adults have been substantially limited to natural experiments involving those who have been accident victims or who have received operations for conditions such as cataracts. Evidence comparable to that obtained from the deprivation studies using animals can be acquired from studying restored vision and the visual experiences of people who were previously unable to see. Von

Senden (1932) reported cases of patients who had been blind since birth with cataracts, and who were then operated on and given their sight. Some of their visual abilities were normal, while others were seriously impaired. Patients could distinguish figure-ground relationships (see page 584), discriminate objects by size or colour and follow moving objects, but they had trouble distinguishing a triangle from a circle by using sight alone.

Gregory and Wallace (1963) reported the case study of SB. He was aged 52 when he was operated on to restore sight. He could recognise objects visually if he was already familiar with them through touch; otherwise he had problems. He was unable to judge distance by sight alone or to interpret facial expressions.

Activity 14

Why do you think this was? (Some ideas are given in the next paragraph.)

The results from such studies do not provide convincing evidence for the role of learning as it is possible that the patients' vision may have been affected by post-operative disturbances. Also, their pre-operative visual experiences were variable: some had no vision at all, others had limited but seriously impaired vision. In general, a lengthy period of learning has been needed after restored vision before object recognition functions effectively but this may be a result of neural regeneration, so conclusions are not straightforward.

In an introspective study, Stratton (1896) covered one of his eyes and wore a lens which inverted the image received by the other. He wore this lens for most of his waking time over an eight-day period, wearing a blindfold at other times. Initially, he experienced some difficulties but he adapted quickly. He did not experience any after effects when he removed the glasses after eight days, which indicates that he had adapted to the changing conditions by learning the appropriate motor responses rather than by learning to see the world in an upside-down way. This suggests that the visual system is extremely flexible and that adaptation can take place as a result of learning.

Further evidence that contributes to our understanding of object perception and pattern recognition comes from studies of non-human animals. Blakemore and Cooper (1970) studied cats whose only visual stimulation was to see either vertical or horizontal stripes – they were even prevented from seeing their own bodies by the fitting of large collars. They found that kittens became blind to stripes in the direction that was not experienced. It was suggested that they had developed few cells which were responsive to stripes in the other direction.

In conclusion, it seems that although some of our less complex object recognition abilities are likely to be innate, some degree of environmental stimulation is needed for both the maintenance and the development of perceptual capacities.

The development of constancy

The complex responses involved in constancy (see page 579) have appeared by an early age. Bower (1966) *conditioned* two-month-old infants to turn their heads towards a 30-cm cube at a distance of 1 metre – conditioning was achieved by reinforcing the infants by an adult suddenly appearing in front of the baby and playing 'peekaboo' (which involves the adult smiling, nodding and speaking to the child), then quickly disappearing from view. Once conditioned, the infants were able to distinguish a 30-cm cube at 1 metre from a 90-cm cube at 3 metres. As these stimuli would have produced exactly the same-sized retinal image, it was concluded that at least some size constancy was present at this age.

Other researchers have confirmed the early appearance of constancy. Bornstein *et al.* (1976) showed that the majority of infants have at least some colour constancy by four months old, and Zeigler and Leibowitz (1957) demonstrated that six-month-olds have some size constancy, but the role of experience in perfecting this ability is shown by the fact that even eight-year-olds show less size constancy than adults.

Further evidence for the influence of experience comes from Turnbull's (1961) account of size constancy in the Bambuti pygmies in Zaire (see page 596).

The development of depth perception

The brain has a formidable capacity for interpreting depth. Although experience plays a part, it seems likely that much of this capacity is innate. Evidence for this comes from the fact that a capacity for stereoscopic vision is inbuilt in the nervous system, and Fox (1981) demonstrated that stereoscopic vision is present by four months of age.

Gibson and Walk (1960) devised an apparatus called the *visual cliff* consisting of a tilted surface, made safe by a low barrier surrounding it. In using this apparatus, the assumption was that if babies placed on a board in the centre possessed depth perception, they would avoid the 'deep' side. Babies capable of crawling were used (aged six months plus), and the majority did avoid the 'deep' side, but were perfectly willing to crawl out on the 'shallow' side. Thus, it can be concluded that babies of six months old have depth perception. It does not establish that this behaviour is innate as it could have been learned by this age. However, kids, lambs and chicks less than 24 hours old also avoided the 'drop'. It may be that this ability develops as soon as mobility is achieved.

Campos *et al.* (1970) took this research a stage further. Younger babies, not yet capable of crawling, were studied by recording their heart rates while they were on the visual cliff apparatus. The heart rates of infants as young as two months decreased when they were placed on the 'deep' side, but did not change when placed on the 'shallow' side. There was no such difference in the responses of one-month-old infants. This does not establish that infants of this age lack depth

perception, however, as this result could be due to their poorly developed visual acuity.

As already explained, when an object moves towards us, the size of retinal image thus produced magnifies quickly. This is termed *looming*, and has been the focus of much research in this area. Bower and his research associates demonstrated that infants will withdraw their heads when a large cube is moved towards them.

If a shadow is placed on a screen and rapidly magnified, avoidance reactions are generated. These do not occur when looming simulates an object that is not going to collide with the viewer. Looming reactions occur in infants as young as two weeks (Ball and Tronick, 1971), and this provides further evidence for the view that this is an inbuilt characteristic of the visual system. However, this evidence and that from Bower's study are not conclusive as it is difficult to tell if infants are responding to the approaching object or fixating on its top edge. We can be sure that such an ability is present by four to five months old as by then infants both blink and show head withdrawal – the normal adult reactions to a looming stimulus. We may also note that infants respond to perspective depth cues by 26–30 weeks old (Yonas *et al.*, 1978).

The development of motion perception and coordination

Some of the abilities associated with motion perception are present at a very young age. For example, the ability to track a moving stimulus is present within 48 hours of birth. This should not be surprising as an awareness of motion is very important to an understanding of objects. As an example, Slater (1989) used a preference technique to establish that infants prefer moving stimuli to stationary ones.

It appears that learning plays a key role in the coordination of perception and movement. Some key studies have been carried out here by Held and his research associates (1967). They kept kittens in a dark room except for a period of six hours per day when they were placed, singly, in an illuminated patterned environment. They could move about freely but were collared in such a way that they could not see their bodies. When they were presented with a horizontal stimulus, they failed to show eye-paw coordination. They did, however, learn this within hours once the collar was removed.

Held and Hein (1963) showed that active movements are needed for such coordination to develop. They used a *carousel* apparatus (figure 16.34) in which two kittens were placed in such a way that they were unable to see each other. One kitten was free to walk and, as it did so, it moved the second kitten which was carried around the apparatus in a gondola. Both kittens received identical visual stimulation, but only the active kitten developed eye-paw coordination.

Held (1965) carried out an experiment with human participants who were given prism goggles to wear which distorted the directions of objects within their visual fields. Participants were initially very clumsy, but soon adapted. If, however, participants wore these goggles whilst being transported around in a wheelchair, they failed to adapt.

Figure 16.34

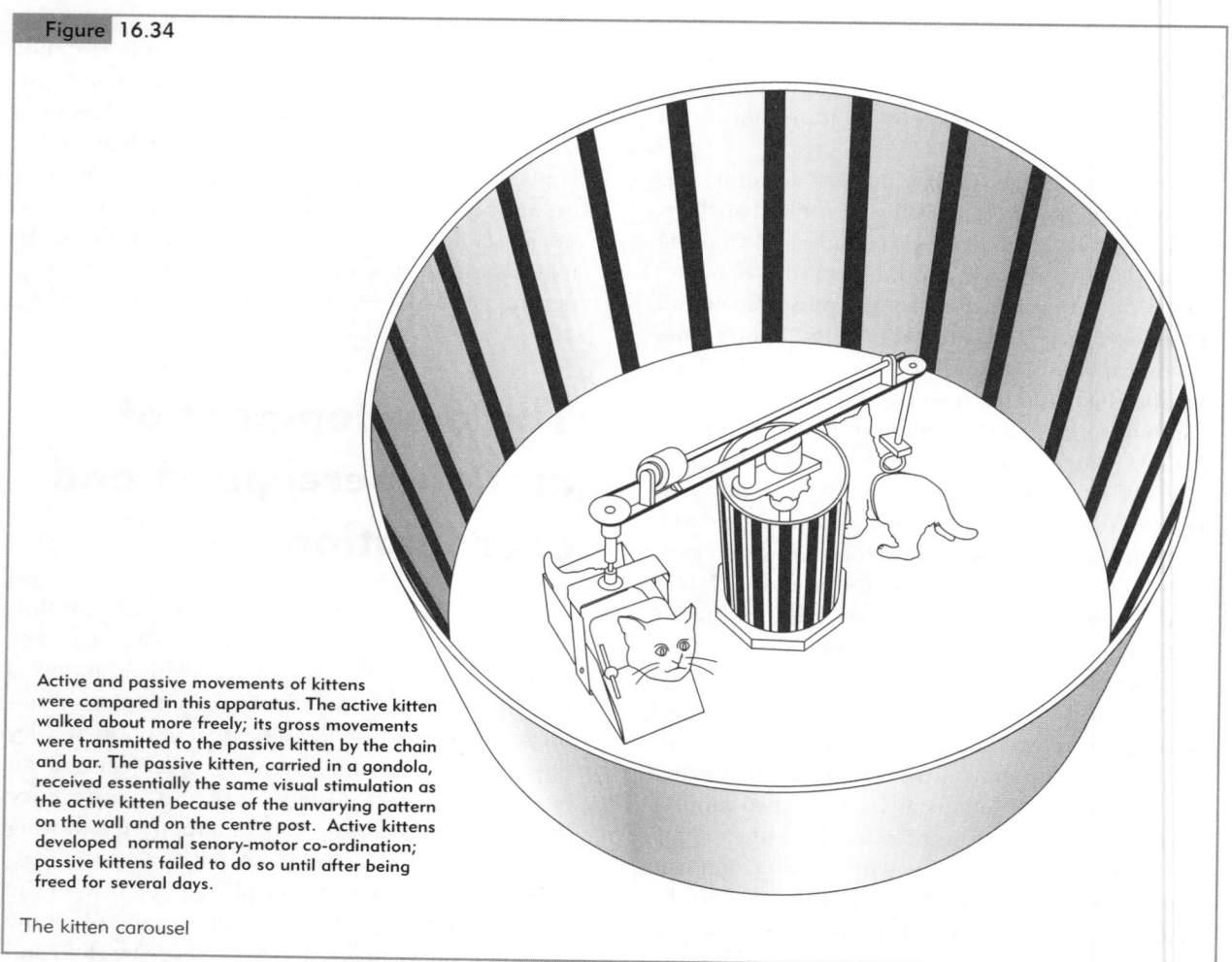

Active and passive movements of kittens were compared in this apparatus. The active kitten walked about more freely; its gross movements were transmitted to the passive kitten by the chain and bar. The passive kitten, carried in a gondola, received essentially the same visual stimulation as the active kitten because of the unvarying pattern on the wall and on the centre post. Active kittens developed normal senory-motor co-ordination; passive kittens failed to do so until after being freed for several days.

The kitten carousel

Evaluation

So how can perceptual development in children be explained? Michael W Eysenck summarises the approaches to answering this question:

'According to Eleanor and James Gibson, the major process is one of perceptual differentiation. They argued that the stimuli presented to our sense organs contain all the information we need for accurate perception. What happens during the course of perceptual development is that children gradually learn to identify the crucial features of any stimulus.

A very different view of perceptual development is the perceptual enrichment hypothesis. According to this hypothesis, the stimuli presented to our senses are often rather impoverished in terms of the information they provide. Accurate perception develops as children learn to supplement sensory information with their increasing body of relevant knowledge and experience . . .

It is entirely possible, of course, that perceptual development involves both differentiation and enrichment. Which process is used presumably depends on the quality of the stimulus information. Complex visual stimuli presented for a long period of time in bright light require perceptual differentiation for accurate perception, whereas visual stimuli presented very briefly in dim light need perceptual enrichment.' (Eysenck, 1993, p. 25)

Self-assessment questions

16 Suggest three approaches which psychologists have used to assess the role of innate factors in perception.

17 What can neonate (newborn) humans see?

18 What evidence is there that some perceptual abilities are learned?

19 What other factor in addition to innate ability and learned experiences improves visual perception?

20 Explain the contribution of the terms 'perceptual differentiation' and 'perceptual enrichment' to an understanding of the development of perception.

(Suggested answers on page 607.)

Unit summary

- Sensation is the registering of stimuli by the sense organs, whilst perception involves the interpretation of those stimuli so they become meaningful.
- Perception involves the processes of selection, inference and organisation of the sensations which are registered. Theories vary in the emphasis they place on these processes.
- The perception of movement results from information from the eye-head movement system and the image-retina movement system.

The process of looming and flow patterns also help in the detection of movement. The perception of space (depth and distance) is achieved through the use of binocular and monocular depth cues.
- Pattern recognition theories such as template matching and feature detection suggest how objects may be recognised.
- Perceptual constancy refers to the tendency to perceive objects or their qualities in the same or similar ways, despite differences in their retinal images. Explanations of size, shape, lightness and colour constancy have been suggested.

Summary cont'd.

- Illusions demonstrate discrepancy in our perceptual system. Examples of illusions of perceived size and distance, contrast effects, misalignment, illusory figures and ambiguous figures have been given.

- The Gestalt theory of perceptual organisation suggests there are basic laws of perception. Gestalt theorists stress the importance of perceiving whole objects rather than independent components. The principles of perception are accommodated within the Law of Pragnanz. Gestalt organisation includes the use of figure and ground, grouping, proximity, closure, good continuation and similarity. There is some empirical evidence to support Gestalt theory, but it is more difficult to apply the theory to the perception of complex objects.

- The four theories of perception which have been discussed are Richard Gregory's constructivist theory, Gibson's direct theory, Marr's computational theory and Neisser's cyclic theory.

- *Perception for Gregory* is hypothesis testing of sensory data, albeit often unconsciously. Gregory's theory is a top-down explanation. The processes involved are those of selection, inference and organisation which aid the testing of hypotheses. Innate ability and past experience provide the basis for the hypotheses. Gregory argues that intellectual ability enabling conceptual models to be formed, frees people from the limitation of judgement based on sensory data alone.

- *Gibson's theory of direct perception* almost equates sensation with perception. It is a bottom-up explanation. For Gibson, there is little need to explain mental representations, as sensory processing from the optic array explains most of perceptual organisation. Gibson's theory is most effective where an explanation of an organism moving around its environment is required. Gibson's theory is weak in the explanation of illusions and the conceptual basis of constancy and perceptual set.

- *Marr's computational theory* uses a computer analogy whereby the task of perception is explained as the function of vision. He believes perception is the result of processing involved in a sequence of representations, each one building on the information gleaned from the last. Thus the model is built up by three stages of processing the representations. Marr's theory emphasises bottom-up processing, although top-down processing based on stored knowledge occurs in the final stage of constructing a perception. The interaction between top-down and bottom-up processing is not really spelt out.

- *Neisser's cyclic model* combines feature detection with the conceptual basis of perception. Models which people store provide the basis for the search for sensory cues. Perception is an interaction between conceptual models (synthesis) and sensory cues (analysis). It is however hard to explain, using Neisser's model, how people become interested in novel features of their environment.

- There are a number of genetic and environmental influences which operate on the perceptual system which lead people to see the world in different ways.

- These influences can be physiological, as in the case of colour blindness, drugs or damage to the nervous system.

- They can be sex linked resulting in differences in visuo-spatial perception.

- They can be cross-cultural differences. It would appear that some cross-cultural differences in perception may be the result of people learning to use cues that are common to a particular environment, whilst failing to use cues that are rare in that environment.

- A number of sophisticated research techniques have developed to assess the perceptual abilities of infants. These include studying infants' preferential looking choices, measuring changes in heart or breathing rates and measuring changes in electrical activity in the brain. These methods are assumed to indicate visual discrimination on the part of the infant.

Summary cont'd.

- There are both practical and ethical problems in the study of infants, though infants are an important source of information for assessing the role of neonate perceptual ability.
- Perceptual deprivation studies have been carried out on cats and chimpanzees and it has been found that the longer the period of visual deprivation in infant animals, the greater the deficit in their perceptual abilities.
- It has been established that infants have poor visual acuity and that improvement is maturational. Object recognition in infants at first depends on defining edges and later surfaces. Evidence suggests that by three months face recognition is well established.
- Studies of patients who have had their sight restored must be treated with caution, but they do show a period of learning is usually required before object recognition is achieved. Studies of human perceptual distortion indicate the visual system is flexible and perceptual adaptation can be learnt. In cats, perceptual deprivation, then restoration of the full visual field shows physical limitation in the nervous system due to lack of stimulation in deprivation conditions.
- Bower has demonstrated the development of some shape and size constancy in young infants. Size constancy improves with age and is affected by cultural experience. Visual cliff studies on animals and human infants show the early existence of depth perception. Slater's work has demonstrated visual tracking ability in young infants. The necessity of learning in the coordination of perception and movement has been demonstrated in studies with cats and humans.

Terms to define

carpentered world hypothesis
constancy
constructivist theory
ecological theory
Gestalt psychology
illusion

motion parallax
nature–nurture debate
pattern recognition
preferential looking method
stereopsis

Further reading

Eysenck, M W (1993) *Principles of Cognitive Psychology*, Laurence Erlbaum, Hillsdale NJ.

Contains a chapter for students who wish to extend their understanding of this topic. It is very accessible and covers a number of sections dealt with in this chapter.

Greene, J (1990) 'Perception' (Chapter 10), in I Roth (ed.) *Introduction to Psychology*, vol. 2, The Open University, Laurence Erlbaum, Hove.

A very accessible chapter covering physiology, psychophysics, Gestalt theories, perceptual organisation, theories of perception and the development of perception. There are some very clear illustrations.

Gregory, R L (1977) *Eye and Brain*, 2nd edn, Weidenfeld and Nicolson, London.

Covers all aspects of visual perception. It contains many illustrations and it is particularly useful for physiology, illusions and perception as hypothesis testing.

Answers

■ Suggested answers to activities

1
a   sensation   c   sensation
b   perception   d   perception

2
a   receiving sensations   c   inferences
b   selecting stimuli   d   organisation

■ Suggested answers to self-assessment questions

1

Sensation is a biological experience. Perception includes sensation but also involves the interpretation of sensory information. This interpretation involves the processes of selection, inference and organisation.

2

Monocular cues work when one eye only is used; binocular cues require the use of two eyes.

3

The main difference between template matching and feature detection is that template matching stores the shape of the object whilst feature detection operates by analysing the shape into features and from the features the visual system creates percepts.

4

Psychologists study illusions because they suggest something about the role of cognitive functions in perception. Illusions cannot be explained by physical stimuli presented. A cognitive process takes place resulting in a misperception.

5
a   The law of Pragnanz is the principle by which the meaningful organisation of stimuli occurs. It states perceptual organisation will always be as good as conditions allow.
b   Figure ground suggests meaningful figures appear in front of the background.
c   Grouping by proximity refers to elements which lie close to each other being perceived together.
d   Closure is when incomplete figures are interpreted as complete.
e   Good continuation is where the organisation of objects is perceived as continuous rather than broken into smaller sections wherever possible.

f   Similarity is the tendency to group similar objects together.

6

Richard Gregory states perception is hypothesis testing. He thus suggests perception involves searching for the best possible interpretation for the data presented. Inferences are constructed about the stimuli and they are then tested by hypotheses.

7

Gibson's ecological theory looks at perception in a real-world setting, as opposed to laboratory or illusion-based explanations.

8

Marr argues that during perception we form three successive visual representations of increasing complexity; the primal sketch, the $2\frac{1}{2}$D sketch and the 3D representation, after which recognition takes place.

9

People have conceptual models (synthesis) which provide the basis for analysing new stimuli (analysis).

10

Gregory's constructivist theory; Neisser's cyclic model; Marr's computational theory; Gibson's direct theory.

11

Physiological reasons for example the effect of drugs, colour blindness, damage to the nervous system, sex differences in spatial abilities, cultural variations.

12

He or she may not be able to interpret what he or she sees.

13

Visuo-spatial perceptual superiority in males may be the result of hormone influences and/or may result from learned experiences.

14

Any two of the following: the ability to use depth perception may vary (Hudson's figures); Deregowski, Segall, Campbell and Hersgovits – people in a non-carpentered world do not see the Müller-Lyer illusion; Killbride and Liebowitz – some Ugandans do not see the Ponzo illusion; Turnbull – the Bambuti pygmies do not use size constancy.

15   Gross (1996) has suggested other cultures may not be used to seeing pictorial representations on paper, they may use different depth cues to those presented in the Hudson-type pictures and the artistic conventions may be different from the western type of pictures they are shown.

16   Studies of neonates, studies of people immediately after they have had sight restored, for example Von Sendon's review, Gregory and Wallace's 'SB'. When sight is restored to visually deprived animals who have had no visual learning opportunity, they can be compared with animals who have had a visual learning opportunity and the differences noted, for example Held and Hein, Blakemore and Cooper, Riesen.

17   Some amount of object and pattern recognition, but limited acuity. Can recognise faces by three months. Tracking of objects. By two months some shape and size constancy. From two months some understanding of depth. By about four–five months a baby responds to a looming object as an adult would.

18   Riesen's chimpanzee who saw the world through translucent goggles needed patterned light to develop complex visual abilities. Gregory and Wallace's 'SB' case study suggested (but did not necessarily prove) learning is essential in perception. Stratton's studies of visual distortion show appropriate perceptual motor responses can be learnt. Blakemore and Cooper's cats needed to explore the full visual field to produce full operation of the visual cortex. Held and Hein showed active movements in cats were necessary for paw-eye coordination to develop. Size constancy in humans improves with age, right up to adulthood.

19   Maturation of the visual nervous system.

20   Perceptual differentiation refers to the ability of a person to pick on the crucial features of a stimulus from the sense organs. Perceptual enrichment suggests the need to supplement the sense organs with a relevant body of knowledge and experience.

Unit 17

Attention and Performance Limitations

Tony Malim and Sharon Cheyne

This unit covers:

The nature of attention

Focused auditory attention

Theories and evidence relating to focused visual attention

Theories and evidence relating to divided attention

Research into automatic processing

Theories of and research into performance deficits

By the end of this unit, you should be able to:

- discuss theories and evidence relating to focused auditory attention and focused visual attention

- discuss theories and evidence related to divided attention

- consider research into automatic processing

- discuss theories of and research into performance deficits including action slips and dual task limitations.

Unit 17 Contents

Introduction

Attention is an area of cognitive psychology that has generated both theoretical and applied interest over many years. As early as 1890, William James discussed the selective nature of attention. He suggested: 'It is the taking possession of the mind, in clear and vivid form, of one out of what seem several simultaneously possible objects or trains of thought.' Such theorising based on introspective reporting went out of fashion with the advent of the behaviourist dominance in the early twentieth century. Theoretical developments in internal processes such as attention underwent little further progress until the middle of the twentieth century.

The impetus to reawaken interest in attention arose in the applied field. It was important, for example, to know about the efficient focus of attention on a radar screen. During the Second World War, radar operators needed to attend to monotonous displays over an extended period of time and respond accurately. Selective attention became important in the training of airline pilots who, faced with a vast amount of information in the cockpit, had to select what was relevant in order to make the appropriate response. Demand for answers to practical problems encouraged research and by the 1950s attention had become a focus of academic study. Using the then modern technology of the tape recorder, Colin Cherry (1953) at Massachusetts Institute of Technology, began studies of attention using dichotic listening tasks. In Britain, Donald Broadbent (1958) published findings from split span studies. Both drew attention to the nature of focused auditory attention. Studies of visual search by Neisser (1960s) led to further work on focused and divided visual attention. The 1970s brought a change in the direction of research as **divided attention** became the focus with its implication that several tasks could be attended to at any one time. Allport (1989) suggested attention was specialised in several modular processors. Eysenck (1982) suggested a central processor would control these specific processing mechanisms.

The shift to explaining parallel processing was refined with the development of theories (for example Schneider and Shiffrin, 1977), to explain that attention could be automatic (i.e. not conscious) or controlled (i.e. conscious). More recently interest has focused on what happens when attention fails either as a result of overload or **performance deficit** when slips and mistakes are made (Reason, 1984).

The nature of attention

Early explanations of attention focused on its selective nature among sensory stimuli experienced. William James (1890) had assumed that focused attention involved a conscious process of selection, or a directed focus of awareness. According to Baars (1988), it is attention which controls access to people's conscious experience. Theories of automaticity, however, suggest that attention can be paid to some stimuli without the process involving conscious experience.

Methods used to study attention

Psychologists have used a number of methods when studying focused and divided attention. The laboratory study of focused attention involves selection between two stimuli being presented at the same time. The methods by which this has been carried out involve dichotic listening tasks and shadowing or split span studies. Dichotic listening tasks involve different auditory information being presented to each ear simultaneously. Usually participants are asked to shadow, or speak out loud, one source of information. Shadowing ensures that the selected input is being attended to. In split span studies, participants are asked to attend to and report the differing information presented to each ear.

Studies of visual attention present a different challenge as it is not possible to attend to two visual stimuli simultaneously. Studies have therefore focused on how many stimuli, or how wide an area of stimuli, can be viewed simultaneously. Divided attention has been researched by dual task studies. These involve participants being required to carry out two tasks at the same time. These tasks can involve using the same, or different, sense modalities.

Most studies of attention, although not the diary studies used in attention deficits, are based on laboratory methods. Whilst these permit high levels of control and manipulation, there is a consequent loss of validity as the many and varied stimuli of the real world are not represented and the stimuli presented lack a meaningful context for the participants.

The information processing approach

When psychologists have sought to explain attention, they have frequently done so by using the **information processing approach** as an analogy, although neurological studies are also beginning to reveal data against which to test out the theoretical models in existence.

The term *information processing* refers to the use of modelling to describe the way in which information from the world around us is dealt with in the human brain. It involves investigating the ways in which information is received by our senses, sifted and selected, stored and used. It operates on the basis that there is an input through the senses, a processor that interprets the incoming data and an output, for example in the form of attention.

One way to examine how we come to terms with the environment around us is to view it as a process, or series of processes, similar to that which occurs when a computer deals with information that has been fed into it. By using these elements we are able to process the data provided by the

environment in order to make an appropriate response to it.

> ## Activity 1
> Jot down on a piece of paper a definition of what information processing is. When you have done this, compare your answer with the definition given above.

Analogies are ways of explaining phenomena using the reasoning of parallel examples. Using the analogy of computers makes it possible to devise *models* of information processing which stimulate how the brain processes information. These models can be tested experimentally. From the results obtained it may become possible to understand how the brain deals with the information continually presented to it through the senses. Models of information processing are imperfect, however, because the brain is an immensely complex and sophisticated organ while the models are, of necessity, very simple.

The organisation of information processing

Information processing is a highly organised form of behaviour. Psychologists have suggested a variety of ways in which information may be processed. These can be used as tools when developing models of information processing systems.

■ Bottom-up and top-down processing

In *bottom-up processing* the interpretation of information is driven solely by independent stimulus inputs. For example, understanding speech may be considered a bottom-up process – first we have to recognise the individual speech sounds, then merge them to form syllables, words, phrases and, eventually, meaningful sentences.

Top-down processing, on the other hand, is driven by an individual's prior knowledge and experience.

Thus it starts with a meaningful hypothesis which is then analysed into its component parts. For example, when speaking we start with the information that we wish to convey and then break it down into the necessary speech sounds. Context is a key element in top-down processing. For example, when we are reading someone's poor handwriting, it is much easier to decipher the words when we are already familiar with the subject matter that the person is writing about.

What usually seems to happen is that individuals use both top-down and bottom-up processing simultaneously. One kind of processing will prove more important for one type of task and with one individual; the other will be used for different tasks by other individuals. Perception is greatly influenced by the expectations a person has about what is going to be perceived. Remembering depends quite heavily upon cues provided by the environment.

■ Serial and parallel processing

> #### Activity 2
>
> Try patting your head with one hand and rubbing your stomach with the other. What happens? Can you do both at once or do you find yourself doing one activity after the other?

Serial processing assumes that where more than one task is involved, one task is completed before another is commenced. For instance, if four separate tasks are involved, task number two will be processed only when task number one has been completed, and so on, in serial order.

> #### Activity 3
>
> Now try patting your head while reciting the days of the week backwards. Would you say that both tasks are being processed simultaneously?

Parallel processing occurs when more than one task is being processed simultaneously – in parallel.

Would you agree that this happened in the patting and reciting exercise?

There is some dispute about the relative importance of serial and parallel processing. Indeed, for any particular task, it is hard to decide which kind of processing is involved. The brain's processing mechanisms are so powerful and sophisticated that it seems likely that parallel processing is the norm. However, the chaos that might result from several independent processes going on at the same time seems to suggest the existence of a central control system of some kind. Sometimes, later stages may not be processed until the results from earlier ones are available. The control system would need to regulate this.

> ### Self-assessment questions
>
> 1 In your own words explain what is meant by selective and divided attention.
>
> 2 In what ways is the information processing approach similar to the operations carried out by a computer?
>
> 3 Explain the idea that bottom-up processing is data driven and top-down processing is concept driven.
>
> (Suggested answers on page 633.)

Focused auditory attention

As human beings we are constantly surrounded by an environment which demands our conscious attention. At the same time, our consciousness has a limited capacity. For this reason, we need to select which of the many demands being made upon our attention will enter our consciousness. This section examines some of the factors which determine focused or *selective attention* – in other words, how we select what we will pay attention to.

Some of the characteristics which determine whether we pay attention to a stimulus are shown in table 17.1.

All of these characteristics are used by advertisers who wish to catch our attention.

Table 17.1

intensity

size

duration

emotional content or tone

repetition of the stimulus

suddenness

novelty

movement

Characteristics determining whether we pay attention to a stimulus

Activity 4

Next time you watch television concentrate on three different commercials. Consider how effective you think each is: very effective, fairly effective or not at all effective. Then reread table 17.1 and consider how many of the listed characteristics applied to the three commercials and whether they affected your judgement of them.

A lack of these characteristics may means that the viewer's attention is not attracted – a rabbit wishing to avoid a predator's attention reduces the number of attention-grabbing stimuli it puts out by freezing. The camouflage employed by a chameleon works in a similar way by changing the colour of the chameleon's skin to help it to blend in with its environment.

Theories and evidence relating to focused auditory attention

The cognitive approach to psychology involves setting up models of how the brain operates, testing these by means of experiment and then modifying them in the light of the results of the experiment. When investigating selective attention, cognitive psychologists have focused on how we select one auditory message to attend to, disregarding others.

Activity 5

Imagine you are talking to a friend in a crowded place such as a restaurant or a lecture room. How much notice do you take of the conversations of those around you? What happens if someone mentions your name? Read on to find out.

Colin Cherry (1953) described what became known as the 'cocktail party phenomenon'. When we are in a crowded room, at a party perhaps, and several people are talking at once, we can focus our attention on a single conversation to the exclusion of the rest. However, if someone on the other side of the room mentions our name, we may instantly refocus our attention to try to hear if anything is being said about us. Cherry conducted experiments using a shadowing technique in an attempt to throw light on this. These involved two messages being presented to participants, one to each ear. They were then asked to shadow one of these messages by repeating it out loud. Cherry found that very little information could be extracted from an *unshadowed* message except for the physical attributes of the speaker, such as sex and loudness or softness of the voice. Participants also noticed if a tone replaced speech. With regard to content, very little was picked up and participants did not even notice if the speaker was using a foreign language or if the speech was reversed. It seems that the unattended message received almost no processing.

Moray (1959) corroborated this in a similar experiment by testing participants' memories of material presented to their unshadowed ear. There was virtually no correct recall even when words were presented 35 times.

The experience of the participants in shadowing tasks seems to make a difference to their performance. Underwood (1974) compared the ability of those who had never experienced this kind of task before with that of Moray, a researcher who was experienced in detecting digits presented to the unshadowed ear. The former were able to detect only 8 per cent; Moray managed 67 per cent.

Table 17.2	
Digits presented to:	
left ear	right ear
7	6
3	8
2	9

Example of digit pairs presented in a dichotic listening task

■ Broadbent's filter model of focused attention

In an experiment using the split span approach, Broadbent (1958) presented three pairs of digits to each participant dichotically; one of each pair to the left ear and one of each pair simultaneously to the right ear (table 17.2).

Participants found it much easier to recall all the digits presented to one ear, then all of the digits presented to the other, rather than to recall them in the order in which they were heard. So, in the example in table 17.2 it was easier to remember 732, 689, than 76, 38, 29. In fact, when asked to recall the digits in pairs, participants were able to achieve only 20 per cent correct responses. Broadbent explained this by suggesting that when two messages are relayed to the brain together, they reach a *sensory buffer* which allows only one of them to go through. The other remains at the buffer for later processing, thus avoiding overloading the limited processing capacity.

Switching from one ear to the other in the **dichotic listening task** caused the digits to remain in the short-term memory store (see Unit 18 page 640) for longer, and this meant that they were

more likely to be forgotten, due to the time-limited nature of the short-term memory. Which message receives preference is determined by either the physical characteristics of the message itself or the way in which it is received by the individual's ear on arrival.

Broadbent's *filter model* proposes a selective filter which operates while the sensory information is retained in the short-term memory store. Only a limited amount of this information then receives processing. Past events held in the long-term memory store (see page 617) provide some basis for this selection, determining the probability of future outcomes (figure 17.3).

Physical characteristics determine the selection of material for processing, together, to some extent, with the emotional and motivational state of the individual. This idea is based upon the factors which cause us to pay attention to one thing and ignore another (see table 17.1 on page 614).

Broadbent's own experiments provide evidence for this model. The basis for selection is physical, i.e. which ear is approached. Cherry also

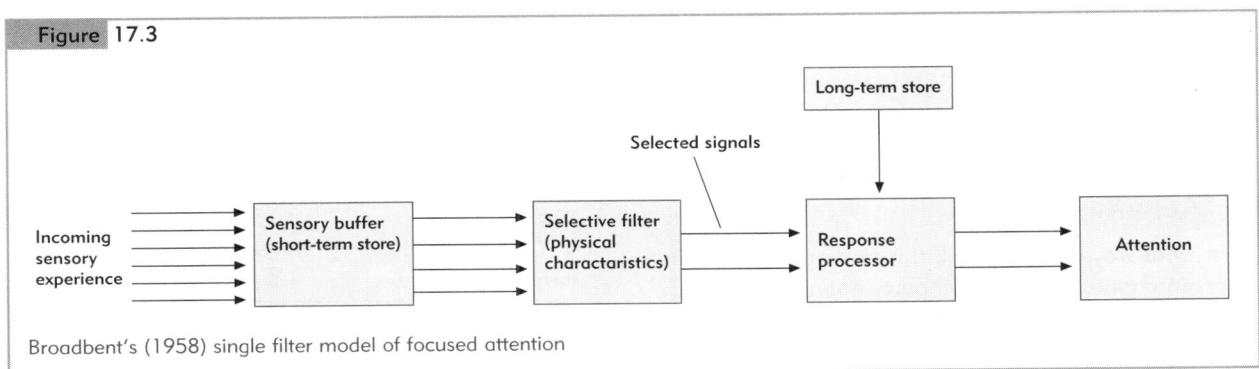

Figure 17.3

Broadbent's (1958) single filter model of focused attention

concluded that messages were selected on the basis of physical properties. This is an all-or-nothing process without any provision for processing unselected material. However, Broadbent's model cannot explain the 'cocktail party phenomenon' because filtering of the information so early in the processing implies that most of the material being received by our senses remains unprocessed.

There might, however, be other physical characteristics to take into account. In Broadbent's experiments, similar material was presented to each ear. Allport *et al.* (1972) combined the shadowing of passages from Orwell's *Selected Essays* with the learning of words presented to the other ear. Very few words were remembered, which might have been expected from Broadbent's filter theory. However, when the same shadowing task was coupled with pictorial learning, there was reasonably good retention of the pictorial information. Thus the physical dissimilarity of the two inputs – that is, being presented to eye and ear rather than to two ears – seems to make a difference.

There is a suggestion that the inability of participants to recall consciously the meaning of the unshadowed, unattended message did not mean that the message remained unprocessed. It might be that meaning can be processed without conscious awareness.

Von Wright *et al.* (1975) set out to examine this. First, participants attended to a long list of words and sometimes received an electric shock when the Finnish word meaning 'suitable' was presented. Then participants shadowed one list of words and ignored a second list that was presented simultaneously. When the previously 'shocked' word, or its synonym (a word with the same meaning), or a homonym (a word which has the same sound), was presented among the non-attended words, there was a noticeable change in *galvanic skin response* in a small number of the trials.

Activity 6

In what ways do you think this finding parallels research into the 'cocktail party phenomenon', i.e. ignoring peripheral conversation until one's name is mentioned?

In both cases there is a response to stimuli which are not being attended to nor consciously processed. This indicates an emotional response to a word which, apparently, had not been processed. This evidence fits in with the 'cocktail party' finding that you can identify your own name from across the room, even when you are listening attentively to a different conversation. You have, after all, an emotional involvement with it. Moray (1959) presented participants' own names to the unattended ear and found that they registered this about one-third of the time in a shadowing task. In short, there seems to be far more processing of the unattended message than Broadbent allowed for.

Gray and Wedderburn (1960) varied Broadbent's digit experiment to show that it was not just the physical characteristics of the unattended message which were retained. Digits were interspersed with a coherent message (see table 17.4 for an example).

Whereas Broadbent found participants had difficulty in switching attention from ear to ear (see page 615), Gray and Wedderburn found a different result in that participants produced a message based on meaning. For example, in table 17.4, a participant might produce 'Who goes there' or '765'. The implication of this is that the selection of which message to attend to can occur either before or after some processing has taken place. Selection in this case was based upon semantic characteristics (i.e. those based on meaning), not just physical ones. This is contrary to Broadbent's filter theory. Broadbent later (1977) incorporated a general executive controller for higher level operations to address this problem, such as time sharing between tasks, to account for it.

Table 17.4	
Information presented to:	
left ear	**right ear**
Who	7
6	goes
there	5

Example of dichotic messages similar to those used by Gray and Wedderburn

■ Treisman's attenuator model of focused attention

Treisman's **attenuator model** (1964) provides for two modifications to Broadbent's model. Firstly, processing is not 'all or nothing' – some of the unselected information is also processed but in an attenuated *(reduced)* form (figure 17.5).

Secondly, Treisman's theory is more flexible, using a hierarchy of criteria to establish priorities for processing. Instead of the single threshold Broadbent envisaged, Treisman proposed a hierarchy of varying thresholds, from physical properties at one extreme to meaning at the other. Where there is a shortage of processing capacity, there is progressive failure to process messages towards the top of the hierarchy.

This means that full analysis of the stimulus is available only where resources permit. Moreover, there are two levels of selection. At the first level, a set of analysers attenuate some messages so that they are of weaker strength. At a higher level, there are what she calls 'dictionary units' or word analysers. The strength of a signal and its perceptual threshold will determine whether attention is triggered or not. Familiar words, for instance one's own name, need only a weak signal to trigger attention. Unfamiliar words need a much stronger one.

Treisman found much less interference from the unattended channel when this was used for a technical discussion than when it was used for easy prose. Also, a bilingual participant, who had more difficulty in rejecting a message in a known foreign language, was able to report whether the two messages had the same (or different) meanings.

In another experiment, the messages were switched halfway through – the message to the right ear was presented to the left and vice versa. This time the participant shadowed just one or two words from the new message and then went back to the original message, even though it was now coming into the other ear. Treisman seems to provide answers to the weaknesses of Broadbent's model, although early selection may not serve a useful purpose if there are limitations on the degree of selection at this stage. Also, Treisman does not say how the executive decisions are made. Solso (1979) queried whether a simple attenuator has the capacity to analyse the intricate features of a message, compare them with a master control and decide what should and should not pass through the filter – and do this as quickly as is necessary.

■ Deutsch and Deutsch and Norman's pertinence model of focused attention

The fairly extensive processing of unattended messages can also be explained by the pertinence model. This could be referred to as a late filter model, in contrast to Treisman's and Broadbent's early filter models. In an early filter model some material is filtered out before it is analysed for meaning. In a late filter model all material is analysed for meaning before any is filtered out. The pertinence model argument is that all incoming stimuli are fully analysed but that the relevance and importance of one particular stimulus in a particular situation will cause a response to it in preference to any other stimulus. Although all theories accept the existence of a

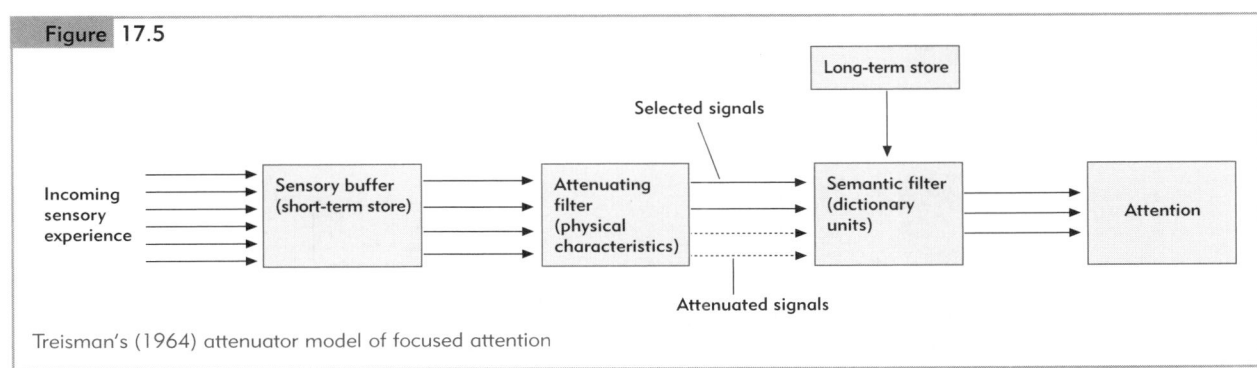

Figure 17.5

Treisman's (1964) attenuator model of focused attention

bottleneck in the processing of information, it is much nearer to the response end of the system in Deutsch and Deutsch (1963) and Norman's (1969, 1976) models where selection occurs only after all the incoming information has been analysed. Each word activates a representation in the memory store and only those which are most pertinent (or relevant) to the activity in hand receive attention (figure 17.6). The pertinence model is closer to a top-down, or concept-driven explanation than the early selection models of Broadbent and Treisman are.

A comparison of the attenuator and pertinence models

Treisman and Geffen (1967) attempted to compare the attenuator and pertinence models. Participants shadowed one of the two concurrent auditory messages. At the same time, monitoring was done by asking participants to tap when target words were detected.

According to Treisman's model, there should be an attenuated analysis of the non-shadowed message. Participants should therefore detect fewer target words on that message than on the other one. Deutsch and Deutsch and Norman claim that both messages are analysed and that it is at the response end of the process that the difference comes. There should, therefore, be no

difference in the detection rate of the target words in the two messages. In fact, the detection rates were:

- shadowed message – 87 per cent
- non-shadowed message – 8 per cent.

Some argument followed this. Deutsch and Deutsch (1963) and Norman (1969, 1976) pointed out that their model assumed that only important inputs led to responses. Participants in the experiment had to make two responses (first to shadow, then to tap) for the shadowed words, but only one response (tap) for the non-shadowed words. Therefore the shadowed words were clearly likely to be regarded as more important.

Treisman and Riley (1969) tried to ensure that exactly the same responses were expected of shadowed and non-shadowed target words. Participants were told to stop shadowing and tap as soon as they detected a target word in either message. Whilst the results turned out to be less dramatic than those of the earlier study, there were still many more target words detected in the shadowed than in the non-shadowed message.

Treisman's model seems to be more plausible than Deutsch and Deutsch and Norman's. It is surely an uneconomical use of brain capacity to process inputs fully and then completely ignore most of the analysed information. The biggest problem with Deutsch and Deutsch and Norman's

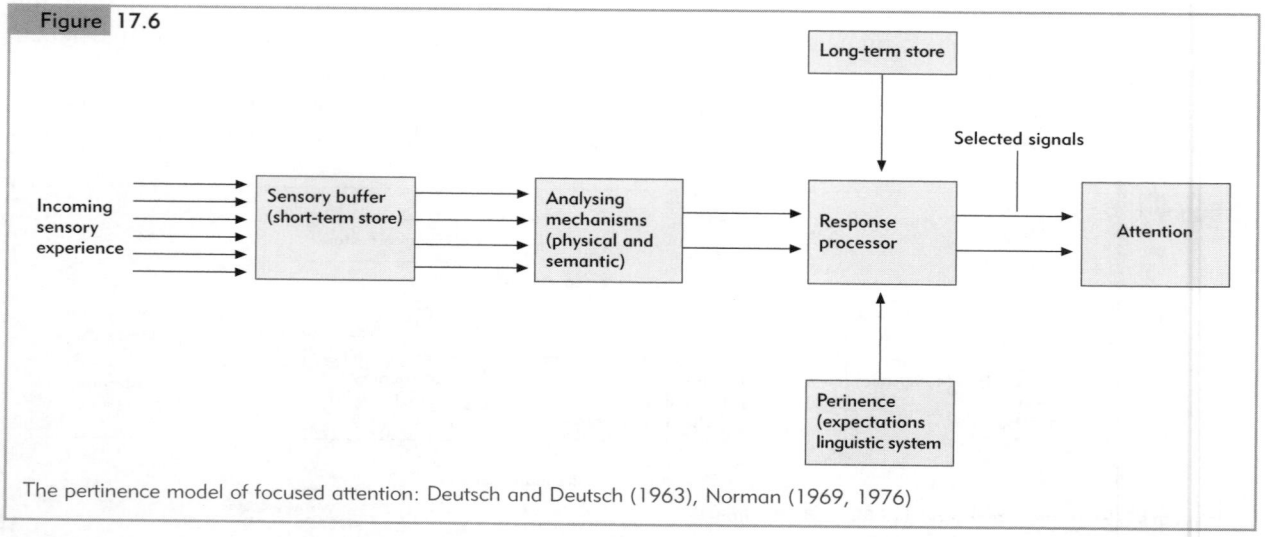

Figure 17.6

The pertinence model of focused attention: Deutsch and Deutsch (1963), Norman (1969, 1976)

model is therefore its perceived wastefulness in terms of processing space as a lot of redundant material is processed in a late selection model. However, although Treisman and Geffen's (1967) experiment (see page 618) seems to lend support to a filter early in processing, a late filter model is better able to explain the retention of information that is not immediately attended to. Interference resulting from shadowing one message weakens the unattended message.

Johnston and Heinz's model of focused attention

Johnston and Heinz's model (1978) is more flexible as it proposes that selection might take place at several different stages of processing. More processing resources are taken up when more stages of processing are passed through before selection (i.e. when this occurs closer to the response). Consequently, there would be a tendency for selection to occur as early as possible in the prevailing circumstances.

Johnston and Heinz tested their model by presenting target and non-target words to both ears simultaneously. Target words were shadowed. There were two conditions: a low sensory discrimination condition, where all the words were spoken by the same male voice, and a high sensory discrimination condition, in which target words were spoken by a male voice and non-target words by a female voice.

In the high sensory discrimination condition, sensory information based upon the voices can be used; in the low discrimination condition only semantic information is available on which to base the selection. Johnston and Heinz therefore predicted that non-target words would be more thoroughly processed in the low sensory discrimination condition and this would use more processing resources. If Deutsch and Deutsch and Norman were right, then there would be complete analysis of the non-target words in both conditions. In the event, recall of words was better in the low sensory discrimination condition. This finding is more in line with Treisman's approach than that of Deutsch and Deutsch and Norman.

Johnston and Wilson (1980) found further evidence of flexibility. Participants were presented with pairs of words, one to each ear, and were asked to identify target words from a particular category which had at least two distinct meanings. For example, 'bears' might be a target word under the category of 'wild animals'. Each such target was accompanied by another word which biased its meaning appropriately, say, 'brown'; one that biased it inappropriately, for example 'suffers', or a neutral control word, for instance 'vehicle'.

In the divided attention condition, where participants did not know which ear the target would be presented to, detection of target words was easier when accompanied by an appropriate word (brown) than by a neutral word (vehicle). An inappropriate accompaniment (suffers) made detection of the target more difficult than in the neutral or appropriate conditions.

When attention was divided between the two ears, it seemed that there was processing of the non-target words according to their meaning. However, when all the target words were presented to the left ear, and all the non-target words to the right, the type of non-target words made no difference to the detection rate. It would seem that the processing that was done was not according to meaning but according to which ear it was expected the target would be presented to (see figure 17.7). This suggests that the amount of processing received by the non-target words is only that which is necessary to perform the task. This supports the concept of flexibility suggested by the Johnston and Heinz model.

Evaluation of theories of focused auditory attention

- Broadbent believed a limited amount of information could be attended to and the choice of what to attend to was carried out early in the process by filtering based on the physical characteristics of the stimuli. However, when Gray and Wedderburn explained the cocktail party effect experimentally, Broadbent's single filter model proved to be too simplistic. Treisman's attenuator model containing two filter processes, one based on physical

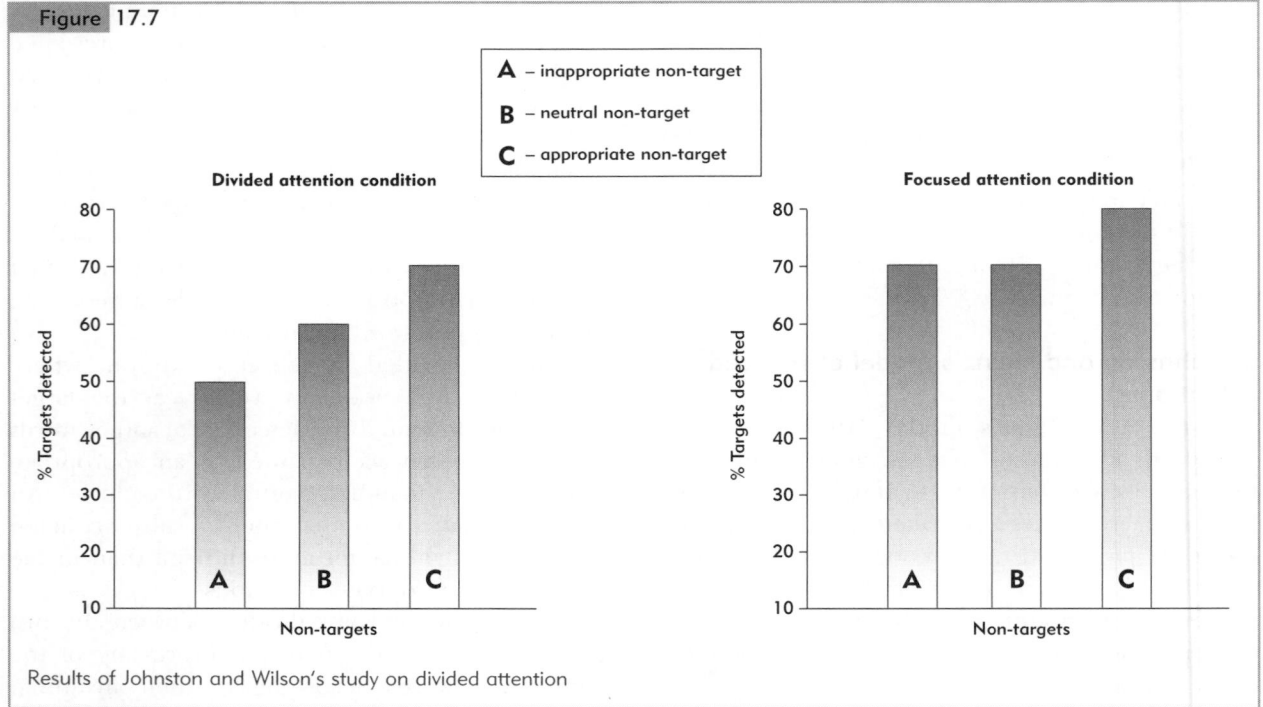

Figure 17.7

A – inappropriate non-target
B – neutral non-target
C – appropriate non-target

Results of Johnston and Wilson's study on divided attention

characteristics and one on semantic characteristics, provided a more appropriate explanation.

■ There are disadvantages to Treisman's model. It involves some processing of redundant material. More importantly, it is complex in its operation and cumbersome, requiring processing in two filters. Further, the model does not specify how the process of attenuation takes place, nor how the semantic analyser operates.

■ A less complex model is the pertinence model, but the gain made on complexity is offset by the loss in terms of greater redundancy. In this single filter late selection model, a lot of information is carried through the processing to the stimulus analysing mechanism. It is unlikely that, in an organ so advanced as the human brain, so much redundancy would be built into the processing. Comparison of evidence supporting the early selection Treisman and late selection pertinence model (for example Treisman and Geffen, 1967;

Treisman and Riley, 1969) tend to support the Treisman view of earlier selection than the pertinence model suggests.

■ Johnston and Heinz's model suggests a flexible compromise whereby the amount of processing required by the task determines the extent to which information is processed.

■ On balance, the evidence suggests, more is known about non-attended messages than Broadbent's model implies, but not so much is known as the late selection models indicate. Treisman's model is most strongly supported, although parts of it remain only partially explained. Johnston and Heinz's more flexible model of a number of stages of processing suggests an efficient system, where there is little processing of unwanted inputs.

■ All of the models of focused, or selective auditory attention imply a serial process at work, whereby a sequential operation results in selection for attention. This analogy of a serial processing mechanism was comparable to the processes used in computers at the same time.

From the late 1960s onwards, researchers came to question whether 'finding the filter' was the only approach required to understanding attention. A different question was being asked about attention. Explanations of the complexity and variety of tasks which people can attend to at one time were sought. Interest focused on multi-processor, or divided attention models. These are considered later in the unit.

Self-assessment questions

4   What is meant by focused attention?

5   Which of the descriptions below fits which model?
   a   There is too much redundancy of processing in the system.
   b   Selection can take place at different stages of processing depending on the demands of the task.
   c   This theory cannot explain the cocktail party effect.
   d   It is rather cumbersome for a process we experience instantly.

6   Name one piece of evidence to support the theories of:
   a   Broadbent
   b   Treisman
   c   Johnston and Heinz.

7   Why are the filter models of attention called serial models?

8   What is the difference between early and late selection models of attention?

(Suggested answers on pages 633–4.)

Theories and evidence relating to focused visual attention

Much of the research in this area of psychology is of recent origin. One explanation of how visual attention is focused is the **zoom lens model** (Eriksen, 1990).

The zoom lens model

According to this model, everything in a relatively small area of the visual field (the spotlight) is judged to be seen clearly, but it is thought to be more difficult to see anything not falling within the attentional beam. Eriksen suggests the spotlight has an adjustable beam, whereby the area covered by the beam can be varied in size. Evidence in support of Eriksen came from a study by LaBerge (1983). He presented participants with five-letter words and a probe task requiring them to respond as quickly as possible. The probe could appear in the position of any of the five letters of the word. In one condition participants were asked to respond to the whole word by categorising it. In another condition they were asked to respond to the middle letter only by categorising it. It was expected that, when being asked to respond to the middle letter, a narrow attentional beam would be employed and when asked to respond to the word, a broader beam would be used. The results of the study indicated that where participants were asked to respond to the word and their attentional beam was broad, it did not matter at which point on the display the visual probe occurred, response times were equally fast. However, when participants focused on the middle letter, the position of the probe was critical. Responses were significantly slower where the probe had not been presented in the centre of the five-letter display. LaBerge demonstrated the probe would be responded to more quickly when it fell within the central attentional beam than when it did not. He also demonstrated the attentional spotlight can have a narrow beam (letter task) or broad beam (word task).

A theory of focused visual attention would also suggest there would be minimal processing of visual stimuli falling outside the zoom lens spotlight. Studies have confirmed this prediction. For example, Johnston and Dark (1986) investigated the time taken by participants to identify words which were at first out of focus, but gradually became clearer. They discovered that presenting the same word, or word of similar meaning, to an unattended part of the visual field, immediately prior to the test word, usually had no positive effect in identifying the test word. This suggests, in line with the zoom lens theory, no semantic processing of the unattended words.

However, the analogy of a zoom lens has proved to be oversimplified. Other research has shown that unattended visual stimuli can be processed. In a study by Driver and Tipper (1989), participants were presented with a circular arrangement of red and black numbers or letters. The task involved counting the red items and ignoring the black items. Speed of response was slower where participants were counting numbers rather than letters. Counting red numbers proved a harder task than counting red letters, due to task similarity, i.e. counting and numbers. There was, however, no distraction effect from the black letters or numbers. In the second part of the study, red and black numbers were presented again and it was found that numbers presented in different quantities in the second trial slowed reaction time compared with the first.

Importantly, this applied to both the red and the black numbers. Although originally it may have been assumed that the black numbers had no effect as a distractor in trial one, the second part to the study shows they were processed to some extent in trial one in order to have an effect in the second part of the study. This is known as the negative priming effect. It suggests unattended visual stimuli

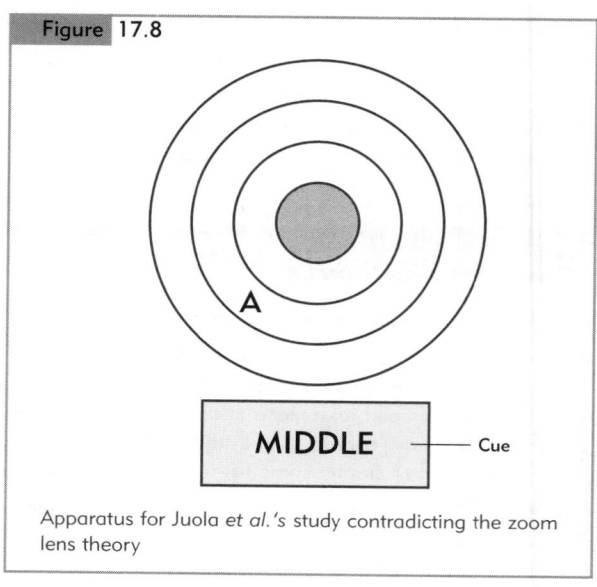

Figure 17.8

MIDDLE — Cue

Apparatus for Juola et al.'s study contradicting the zoom lens theory

are processed. This is contrary to the zoom lens theory.

Another study which casts doubt on the zoom lens theory is that of Juola et al. (1991). The study involved a target letter being presented in one of three concentric circles: the inner, middle or outer ring (figure 17.8).

The participants fixated on the centre of the display and were given a cue which gave information about which ring the target letter would appear in. If the zoom lens theory is correct, speed and accuracy of response would be greatest for targets presented in the inner circle rather than in the outer rings. However, performance was best when the target was presented in the ring which had been cued, regardless of whether it was the inner or outer rings. Hence the centre of the visual display had no advantage in terms of speed and accuracy of target spotting. This is not supportive of zoom lens theory which suggests a strong centre spotlight.

■ Evaluation of the zoom lens model

Focused visual attention appears to be more flexible than the zoom lens model suggests as attention can be directed to items within the visual field which are not the centre of the visual field. Further, unattended visual information can have a negative priming effect on later visual judgement.

Figure 17.9

A	C	M	J
X	S	D	R
L	7	Q	E
B	H	F	T

Visual search task in which the number is being sought

The process of visual search

Another approach to understanding how visual attention is achieved is to look at the very early attentional processes of **visual search**. An example of a visual search task can be found in figure 17.9.

Neisser (1964) carried out a number of visual search studies and more recently they have been the method used by Anne Treisman in the development of her **feature integration theory** (1986). In this theory Treisman argues there are two types of visual processing: pre-attentive processing involving automatic, rapid, parallel processing and focused attention involving slower, serial processing where objects are identified one at a time, requiring more conscious effort. Focused attention is more demanding and is the 'glue' that brings together the features of a stimulus, for example the colour and the shape that make up an object. Activity 7 involves the use of pre-attentive and focused attention.

Activity 7

Find two marker pens of different, bright colours, for example red and blue. Follow the instructions below for A and B.

A   On a plain sheet of white paper mark one red X, one blue X and one red O at random. On a second sheet randomly mark one blue X, 9 red Os and 10 red Xs. Ask a friend to find the blue figure on each sheet and notice whether the two

Activity 7 cont'd

tasks take about the same time. In both tasks, regardless of the distractor items, the blue figure seems to 'pop out' of the page.

B   Keep the sheet of paper from part A with the 20 figures on it. Take another sheet of white paper and randomly mark on it one blue X, five red Xs, seven blue Os and seven red Os. Ask a friend to locate the blue X on each sheet and notice whether the second task, which requires focused attention, takes much longer.

Task A only requires visual processing of one feature, 'blueness', in order to get the right answer. Task B requires a conjunction (or combination) of features in order to get the right answer. Features of 'blue' and 'cross' have to be 'glued' together visually to achieve the correct answer. This is what Treisman means by focused attention.

As a development of the theory, Treisman and Sato (1990) have argued that the amount of similarity between the target letters and the distractors is a factor influencing search time. If distractor items have at least one feature of the target, they are scanned; if they have no features of the target, they are ignored. So if the target was a red X, distractors such as a blue X or a red circle would be scanned, but a green circle would be ignored. Duncan and Humphreys (1989, 1992) have further contributed to visual search by suggesting that the similarity between targets and non-targets slows down search time and the similarity between non-target items speeds up search time. They argued that the slowest search times occur when non-target items are dissimilar to each other but similar to the target.

Visual search studies have contributed to understanding the processing involved in the early stages of focused visual attention. Research into this whole area still continues.

Theories and evidence relating to divided attention

By the 1970s studies of attention had switched from locating a filter to trying to judge whether there was a finite capacity to attentional processes and to investigating multiprocessing models. Ulric Neisser (1976) had demonstrated the ability to process in parallel, at least in visual search tasks. Neisser believed there was no known mathematical or physiological limit to processing ability and that the extent to which information could be processed in parallel depended upon such things as the mental effort required for the task and prior experience of the task. Practice may well develop the processing capacity which people have. So a person can make a cup of tea, listen to conversation and listen to the radio all at the same time if they are familiar tasks which do not place too high a demand on the processing channels. However, reading a difficult psychology textbook, for the first time, reduces the capacity to attend to other things which are happening around us. Studies began to demonstrate the ability which people have to process in parallel. In 1972 Allport *et al.* had shown that pictorial information could be combined with shadowing George Orwell's essays (see page 616). Dissimilar tasks seemed to be able to be performed in parallel. A further study showed participants who were skilled pianists could shadow a speech message, whilst playing music they did not know from a score previously unseen. Provided the tasks did not require the same processing channel, a number of tasks could be attended to at the same time without their performance being impaired.

One of the early theoretical models of divided attention within a limited capacity was that of Kahneman's resource allocation model (1973).

Kahneman's resource allocation model of attention

Kahneman's model is interesting in that it connects individuals' capacity to process information with both their arousal levels and the external demands upon them (see figure 17.10).

Arousal refers to an individual's state of alertness and, by implication, to his or her capacity to deal with the demands of the world. The total available processing capacity will be affected by the level of arousal. It is possible to identify both internal and external factors which determine arousal, and it is worthwhile describing some of these.

Internal factors include personality differences between individuals. Among other factors, Eysenck differentiated between individuals on the basis of their *stability* or *neuroticism*. Biologically, he saw the limbic system (located in the lower brain and closely linked to the autonomic nervous system) as the mediator of a person's neuroticism. In neurotic

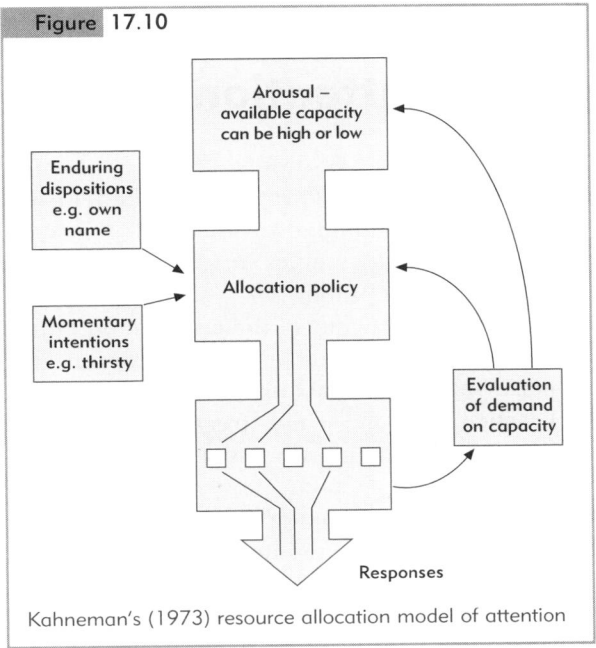

Kahneman's (1973) resource allocation model of attention

individuals the sympathetic nervous system tends to have a lower stimulation threshold than in stable individuals. For this reason, emotional responses occur more easily.

Other internal factors which relate to arousal include *circadian rhythms*. Individuals vary in their basic arousal level through 24 hours, often reaching a low point in the middle of the night and high points during the day. However, timing of these cycles varies among individuals.

External factors which determine arousal levels include noise, drugs and specific stimulation from events happening in our environment. Conversely, arousal levels will be lowered by lack of stimulation. Mackworth (1950) gave participants vigilance tasks requiring sustained attention (for example watching a radar screen) and found that attention deteriorated as the task time increased. Factors which reduced this deterioration involved external stimulation, for example a telephone ringing intermittently, being told how well the task was progressing and having others in the room, especially if they were seen by the participant as having a high status.

Kahneman's capacity model works on the assumption that selection of what we pay attention to is, in part, determined by the available processing capacity. This is governed by our natural disposition or personality, our immediate intentions and any other demands being made on our attention. Selection of information thus depends upon our enduring disposition, our immediate concerns and any resources available to us. Several attentional responses can be made at the same time, provided their total effort does not exceed the available capacity.

The central processor assesses the demands made by each task and allocates attention. If the supply of attention does not meet the demand, performance is adversely affected.

Kahneman's model assumes that processing makes constant demands at the point of allocation, yet people would not report being aware of this process going on. The model also assumes an upper limit to attentional processes, which is something which has never been proven.

Allport's modular theory of divided attention

Allport is one theorist who rejects the idea of a central processor, or controller of attention. He believes such an approach fitted an analogy of a serial processing computer and now the more modern parallel processors make a more appropriate analogy (**modular theory of attention** – see figure 17.11).

There is some support for Allport's view of differentiated structures being involved in attention in cognitive neurological studies. Directing attention to a task causes extra mental work for which there should be evidence in brain

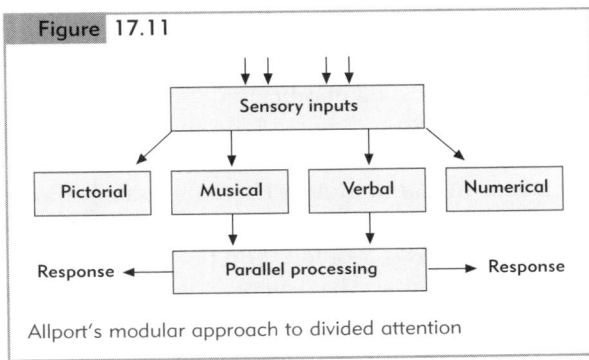

Allport's modular approach to divided attention

activity. Posner and Peterson (1990), using PET (positron emission tomography) data have shown that a number of areas of the brain are separately employed in engaging and disengaging attention. PET scans show increased blood flow in areas of the brain associated with mental processing. An area in the posterior parietal lobe appears to be responsible for disengaging attention from its present focus. Part of the midbrain's superior colliculus is involved in shifting the focus of attention (this region is also involved in eye movements). An area in the thalamus called the *pulvinar* focuses attention on a new location. There is also evidence that the right cerebral hemisphere, more than the left, is responsible for sustaining or concentrating attention on a particular task (Pardo *et al.*, 1991). There does not appear to be an overall controlling system operating in attention.

Allport (1989) has argued that successful dual task performance can be explained in terms of different sensory modules operating on a task. As Eysenck and Keane (1995) pointed out, there are problems with this approach:

- There is no consensus about the nature and number of processing modules.
- Modular theories cannot be falsified, because it is always possible to account for findings by suggesting modules exist to explain performance on a task.
- If a number of modules operate in parallel, there would be problems of coordinating their outputs in order to produce coherent behaviour.

Synthesis theories of processing information

Eysenck (1982), within the field of attention, and Baddeley (1986), within the field of memory, have suggested processing may be mode specific but that a central processor (Eysenck), or central executive (Baddeley), coordinates and directs the processing behaviour in the modules. The latter all act more or less independently, but due to the central processor, chaos is avoided. The problem with this elegant solution is that there does not, as yet, appear to be much psychological evidence for such a unitary system of attention.

Empirical studies of divided attention

Whatever the model of divided attention which is favoured in the long term, Eysenck and Keane (1995) made a number of valuable points in relation to dual task studies which investigate the ability to divide attention:

- The level of difficulty of the task is important – the harder one task is, the poorer the performance on dual tasks.
- Practice in one task frees attention to concentrate on the other task in a dual task situation.
- Task similarity in input or response will result in poor attention, due to interference.
  Empirical investigations of the factors outlined by Eysenck and Keane are as follows:
- Dual tasks which are both easy tasks can be performed well together; dual tasks which are difficult result in poor performance on one or both tasks. Sullivan (1976) demonstrated that when participants were asked to detect target words in a non-shadowed message, it was much easier to do this when shadowing a second message that was simple than one which was complex.

Activity 8

Try out the study outlined above. Find a passage of a book and identify three target words, for example 'the' would occur a number of times. Vary the passage to be used for shadowing. A complex textbook and a children's story, or an easy-to-read novel would be suitable. Participants should detect more target words where the shadowing task is easy than where it is difficult.

- Practice frees attention in a dual task study. The well-practised driver can converse or listen to the radio at the same time as driving, unlike the learner driver. An experimental study of the value of practice was demonstrated by Spelke *et al.* (1976). Their subjects, Diane and John, were given 90 hours' training on a variety of tasks. Firstly, they were asked to read and understand short stories, whilst at the same time writing down words which were being dictated. At first they performed poorly on both tasks. After 30 hours' practice, however, their performance on both tasks had improved considerably.

■ Why is it difficult for you to rub your stomach and pat your head at the same time (see Activity 2, page 613)? The similarity of the tasks create interference in performance. Allport *et al.* (1972) asked their participants to shadow auditorily presented prose passages, whilst learning auditorily presented words. The similarity of the tasks resulted in very poor performance in a memory recognition task for the words. The tasks were then made dissimilar by using the prose shadowing task alongside learning pictorial information. This time recognition memory resulted in 90 per cent of the pictures being recognised. Similarity of the task can affect the stimuli, the processing requirement and/or the required response. All these types of similarity can affect performance.

Activity 9

With the help of two other people, try the Allport *et al.* similarity of tasks study. One person can be the participant, whilst the other person helps you to present the material dichotically.

Self-assessment questions

14 In Kahneman's model of attention, which part of the model divides attention?

15 Identify one main difference between Allport's modular theory and Eysenck's **synthesis theory** of divided attention.

16 What three factors do Eysenck and Keane identify which affect people's ability to carry out dual task studies?

17 Under what conditions is it most difficult to carry out dual tasks?

(Suggested answers on page 634.)

Research into automatic processing

One question which psychologists have begun to investigate is the likelihood that some of the processing carried out when attention is paid to something may well be automatic. Eysenck (1995) pointed out that automatic processes have a number of characteristics which have generally been agreed upon. **Automatic processing** is fast and makes no demands on attentional capacity. It is not a conscious process, but it is a process which occurs automatically in response to the appropriate stimuli. Few, if any tasks, meet all the criteria for fully automatic attention.

The work of Schneider and Shiffrin

Empirical studies into **automaticity** have been carried out by Schneider and Shiffrin (1977) and Shiffrin and Schneider (1977). They make a theoretical distinction between automatic and controlled processing. The latter is of limited capacity, requires a focus of awareness and can be used flexibly in changing circumstances. Automatic processes, on the other hand, are not of limited capacity, require no attention and are difficult to modify once learned.

In Schneider and Shiffrin's basic experiment (1977) (figure 17.12) participants were asked to memorise one, two, three or four items (consonants or numbers). This was the memory

Figure 17.12

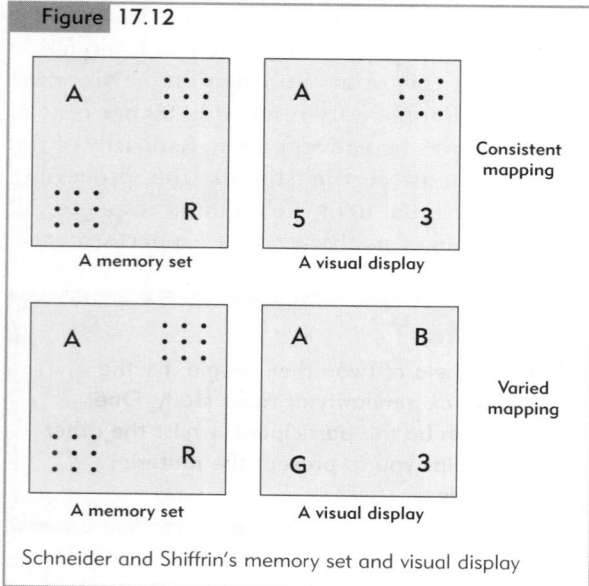

A memory set   A visual display   Consistent mapping

A memory set   A visual display   Varied mapping

Schneider and Shiffrin's memory set and visual display

set. They were then asked to look at a visual display containing one, two, three or four items (consonants or numbers).

The visual display required either consistent or varied mapping. In the consistent mapping condition consonants were used in the memory set and numbers were used as distractors in the visual display (or vice versa). The consistent mapping task was carried out automatically according to Schneider and Shiffrin, as participants in this condition have so much practice in distinguishing letters and numbers. In the varied mapping condition the memory set consisted of a mixture of consonants and numbers and so did the visual display. Controlled processing was required for this task. Results, not surprisingly, showed a considerable difference in reaction time between consistent and varied mapping. The controlled attention required for varied mapping produced a considerably slower reaction time than the automatic processing required for consistent mapping. Further, the number of items in the memory set and the visual display hardly affected decision time in the consistent mapping condition, but increased numbers of items slowed down decision time in varied mapping where automatic processing was not possible.

In a second study, Shiffrin and Schneider (1977) tested the effect of practice on processing.

The experimental arrangement was much the same as in the first experiment but consistent mapping was always used. The memory set items were initially drawn from consonants B to L and the distractors were always drawn from consonants Q to Z. The participants took part in 2100 trials and decision time got much faster as the process became increasingly automatic. Using the same participants, a further 2400 trials took place, but this time using reverse consistent mapping: the memory set items were now drawn from the second set of consonants (Q to Z) in the alphabet and the visual distractors were drawn from the first set of consonants (B to L). This reversal of consistent mapping produced serious interference in the performance of the task and it took 1000 trials to recover the performance which participants had showed at the beginning of the experiment. One can therefore conclude that it is very difficult to abandon outlived, automatic processes.

By way of evaluation, Eysenck points out that Schneider and Shiffrin's experiment is not truly automatic processing as the number of items in the memory set and visual display does affect the speed of the decision in the varied mapping condition. If automatic processing is parallel, the number of items to be found should not affect decision time. Further, to say that a process becomes automatic with practice does not explain how this happens. It is not clear whether it is the speed of performing the task which alters, or the nature of the processing.

Norman and Shallice's theory of automaticity

Norman and Shallice's theory (1986) which incorporates automaticity identifies three levels of attentional functioning. They are: fully automatic processes, partially automatic processes and fully conscious processes. Fully automatic processes require little conscious awareness, but a small amount is needed to regulate and avoid processing problems. Selection of schema for attention takes place on the basis of environmental demands and internal priorities. Regulation is carried out by a process known as contention scheduling. Partially automatic processes require some attentional awareness and more contention scheduling. Fully conscious processes of attention need a high level control mechanism, which Norman and Shallice call the supervisory attentional system. Thus their approach to understanding attention suggests more of a continuum of conscious to automatic processing than is suggested by Schneider and Shiffrin. The Norman and Shallice model also suggests two control mechanisms for attention, that of contention scheduling and that of a supervisory attentional system.

Although models of automatic attention may describe different levels of attention processing, they do not really explain how automatic attention develops. Logan (1988) does try to provide an explanation of how attention becomes an automatic process. He believes that prolonged practice leads to the storage in memory of responses to certain stimuli. Thus he argues, 'Automaticity is memory retrieval: performance is automatic when it is based on a single step direct access retrieval of past solutions from memory.'

Activity 10

An experimental method of demonstrating the power of routine, or automatic cognitive processing is the Stroop Effect (Stroop, 1935). In this example, past habits and learned experiences interfere with a response which participants are asked to give.

Write down, on pieces of card, ten nouns which have a colour association, for example bluebell, strawberry. Write the words with a colour association in any colour, except the

Activity 10 cont'd

colour which is associated with the word, for example bluebell could be written in red. Now write down any ten nouns with a similar number of syllables but without a colour association, for example, gate, building, on pieces of card. Use the same variety of colours you have used for the colour association words. It does not matter which word is written in which colour. Write the sets of words the same size and style of print. Shuffle the pieces of card on which the words are written. Ask your friends and family to help you. Instruct them that they will see a word written on a card and they are to say out loud, what colour the word is printed in. Turn over the cards one at a time and if the participants say the wrong colour of print, or hesitate unduly, place the card concerned in a separate pile. At the end of the exercise count up the cards on the separate pile with a conflicting colour association and count up the cards with a neutral colour association. You should have more cards on the conflicting colour association pile. Why do you think that is?

If the automatic process of reading operates when we look at words, then reading the words with a colour association, written in a conflicting colour ink, for example strawberry written in green, causes a cognitive conflict. What we do automatically, i.e. read, interferes with what we are asked to do, i.e. name the colour of print, thus slowing down reaction time to colour naming.

Self-assessment questions

18 Give two characteristics of automatic and two characteristics of controlled processing.

19 Give an illustration, from real life, of how practice produces automatic processing and makes flexible behaviour difficult to achieve.

20 Explain Logan's point of view that automaticity can be explained as memory retreival.

(Suggested answers on page 634.)

Theories of and research into performance deficits

Psychologists have spent a lot of time considering how attention is paid to tasks. Another approach, and one that is relevant to everyday life, is when adequate attention is not paid to tasks and human error, or absentminded mistakes or slips, occur. These have come to be known as **performance deficits**. (Of course another area of performance deficit which has already been considered is that of failure in dual task performance (pages 626–7)).

Performance deficit was investigated by Reason (1984). He identified two major types of errors. The first type are mistakes which are errors in planned actions. They involve miscalculations when a person is not paying attention, for example pulling out of a road junction whilst failing to observe approaching traffic. The second type are slips. These are lapses in functioning, for example forgetting a name. Often these latter go largely unnoticed publicly.

Reason (1979) investigated performance deficits in a set of diary studies. He asked 35 people to keep diaries of their action slips over a two-week period. During this time, over 400 entries were made and Reason classified most behaviour into one of five types of slips:

1 Storage failures accounted for 40 per cent of the errors. Here, intentions or actions were forgotten or were incorrectly recalled. For example, someone may stir the sugar in the tea twice.

2 Test failures made up 20 per cent of errors. Here the participant failed to monitor and carry through a sequence of actions. For example, someone may intend to make a cup of tea but the water intended for the teapot may end up being poured into the washing up bowl for the dishes. At the critical point of pouring the water, the action was not monitored and the wrong sequence of action was set in train.

3 Subroutine failures made up 18 per cent of errors. In this case problems occurred through inserting, omitting or reordering a sequence of actions. For example, standing at the door calling the cat to come in when you had forgotten to put the cat out an hour earlier!

4 Discrimination failures made up 11 per cent of errors. Such errors involved mistaking one object for another, for example putting bubble bath onto your hair instead of shampoo.

5 Programme assembly failures made up 5 per cent of errors. This involved displaying an inappropriate sequence of actions. For example, someone might throw away the potatoes and keep the potato peelings.

Reason has provided an interesting set of categories in which to describe errors of performance. In practice, it is sometimes difficult to work out which category an error fits into, as sometimes the categories seem to overlap. Also, as Eysenck and Keane pointed out, his record only shows what people said they did. Some errors may have gone unrecalled, and it is difficult to interpret the percentages of errors unless the frequency of occasions on which a particular sort of error could have occurred, but did not, is known. Diary studies do not really explain the underlying cognitive processes involved in the production of these slips and mistakes.

Activity 11

Try out Reason's diary investigation. In your class ask the students to keep a diary of slips and mistakes they make for a day, or a week. See if the reported behaviour is similar to the results obtained by Reason. You could display the class results in a pie chart. Alternatively, design a questionnaire to investigate slips of absentmindedness. Students may wish to ask family or friends to answer the questions. Again, the results could be compared to Reason's findings.

Some explanations have been put forward to try and explain why these errors occur (Reason, 1992; Sellen and Norman, 1992). Starting with the theoretical assumption that there are two modes of attention control – automatic and conscious (for example as suggested by Schneider and Shiffrin, pages 627–8) – errors can occur in the automatic mode when well-practised actions are carried out with the minimum of attention. Conscious attention is less prone to performance deficit errors. A more hierarchical explanation has also been offered (Norman, 1981; Sellen and Norman, 1992) in the form of schema theory. At the highest level a schema represents the goal of the actions. Lower-level schemas correspond to the actions involved in achieving the goals.

Schemas are activated by intentions and environmental conditions. Slips can occur in the formation of an intention, with the faulty activation of a schema or with the faulty triggering of an active schema, leading to action being determined by the wrong schema. Many of Reason's action slips would fit into this theoretical framework.

Caution must, however, be applied. There may not be a unitary system of conscious and automatic attention: it has always proved difficult to locate a control processor in such a system, and presumably it would be the control processor which would identify the overall goal or intention. Broadbent's (1982) work, using questionnaires to investigate action slips, showed people who scored high on one sort of action slip tended to score high on other types as well. This suggests (in support of the above ideas) a problem in an overall control system. It has also been shown that people who make a lot of errors have difficulty doing two tasks at once (Martin and Jones, 1983), suggesting individual differences in control systems for attention. This problem of making errors when doing several tasks may also explain why people's everyday functioning may be affected when their cognitive capacity is overloaded.

Self-assessment questions

21 Outline two areas where psychologists have studied attention deficits.

22 Give examples of the five types of errors indicated by Reason to show people's slips and mistakes. Try to give examples from your own experience, or that of your friends and family. The categories are as follows: storage failures, test failures, subroutine failures, discrimination failures and programme assembly failures.

23 Explain why errors occur in well-practised actions.

24 Demonstrate from the evidence that some people are more prone to errors than others.

(Suggested answers on page 634.)

Unit summary

- Broadbent's theory of focused auditory attention demonstrated *selective attention* operated by filtering based on the physical characteristics of the stimuli. Treisman suggested there were two filters and that incoming material could be attended to for meaning, if it was important.
- The *pertinence model* suggests all information is processed for meaning before anything is filtered out. Johnston and Heinz's model is more flexible. It takes into account the nature of the processing task.
- The zoom lens model of *focused visual attention* suggests focused visual attention is achieved by an adjustable beam. There is minimal processing of the visual stimuli which fall outside the beam. Evidence to support the model comes from La Berge (1983) and Johnston and Dark (1986).
- Studies demonstrating a *negative priming effect* (Driver and Tipper, 1989) provide contrary evidence to the zoom lens model

Summary cont'd.

along with studies which demonstrate that focus on the centre of a display produces equal accuracy on the central and peripheral items (Juola *et al.*, 1991).

■ Work done on *divided attention* has helped to provide a more complete understanding of the information processing involved in attention. The theoretical explanations of how attention is paid to more than one task are still varied.

■ Kahneman suggested the *amount of mental effort* required determines the division of attention.

■ Allport suggested attention is modularised along different channels for different sense modalities. Eysenck postulated that such a form of processing as this would require a controlling central processor to coordinate the system. Evidence to support divided attention does not clearly weigh in favour of one model.

■ Eysenck and Keane provided evidence to show that the difficulty of the task, the amount of previous practice and the similarity of the tasks all affect the ability to attend to and perform tasks effectively.

■ In 1935 J Ridley Stroop demonstrated the power of *automatic processing* in colour naming. Studies by Schneider and Shiffrin (1977) demonstrated automatic processing and its development with practice.

■ Norman and Shallice (1986) described three levels of attentional functioning: fully automatic, partially automatic and fully conscious processes. These levels are governed by control mechanisms of contention scheduling and a supervisory attentional system.

■ Logan suggested automatic processing is a change in the way information is processed; it is direct memory retrieval.

■ *Performance deficits* can be studied by assessing failure in dual task studies. Where the tasks are similar, difficult and have not previously been practised, performance deficit is likely to be high (Eysenck and Keane's approach).

■ The study of performance deficits, resulting from the failure of attention, is providing an alternative slant on cognitive processes involved in attention. It has become apparent that the majority of slips occur in highly practised activities. This may seem rather strange, but it is in this condition that attention is most automatic and least conscious.

■ Taking a real world approach to this topic, Reason used *diary studies* to provide detailed descriptions of the mistakes and slips that people make. Reason also looked at disasters resulting from human error.

■ Theoretical explanations of the underlying cognitive processes suggest action slips are closely allied to *automatic processing* and slips may occur within a set of schema activated to achieve a goal. Some explanations emphasise individual processing differences making some people more prone to action slips (Broadbent, 1982). It is highly probable that *cognitive overload* increases the likelihood of performance deficits. All of these explanations tend to assume a unitary attention control system which is by no means proven.

■ Overall there are a number of common characteristics of *absentminded* behaviour. Slips are more likely in highly familiar surroundings, when tasks are being performed automatically. Slips are more likely to occur if people are feeling preoccupied, distracted or feeling under time pressure. Errors are also more likely to occur when people change well-established routines.

Terms to define

attenuator model
automatic processing or automaticity
dichotic listening task
divided attention
feature integration theory (Anne Treisman)
information processing approach
modular theory of attention

parallel processing
performance deficit
serial processing
synthesis theory
visual search
zoom lens model

Further reading

Eysenck, M W (1993) *Principles of Cognitive Psychology*, Laurence Erlbaum, Hove.

An approachable book for A-level work on attention. It contains up-to-date relevant material.

Eysenck, M W and Keane, M T (1995) *Cognitive Psychology: A Student's Handbook*, 3rd edn, Psychology Press, Hove.

Excellent material for students who wish to explore this topic in considerable depth.

Reason, J and Mycielska, K (1982) *Absent Minded? The Psychology of Mental Lapses and Everyday Errors*, Prentice Hall, Englewood Cliffs, NJ.

The material covered here is not usually covered in detail in A-level texts.

Eysenck, M W (1997) 'Doing two things at once', *Psychology Review, 4(1)* September.

An interesting article relating divided attention to the real world.

Answers

■ Suggested answers to activities
Answers to activities are to be found in the text.

■ Suggested answers to self-assessment questions

1

Selective attention is when you focus on one aspect of a situation. Divided attention refers to simultaneous focus on more than one aspect of a situation.

2

In information processing, inputting information is like keying data into a computer. Processing is like the manipulation of the data in the computer processor. Output of information in a computer would be, for example, to the screen or to a printer, whilst output of information in a human would be a behavioural output.

3

Bottom-up processing is data driven when the processing is carried out on the basis of the incoming stimuli. Top-down processing is concept driven when past experience is used to interpret the incoming data.

4

The selection of some stimuli for focused awareness.

5
a   The pertinence model.
b   Johnston and Heinz.
c   Broadbent.
d   Treisman.

6

a   Broadbent's own split span studies with pairs of digits.

b   Any one of: Treisman's own studies, Gray and Wedderburn (1960), Von Wright *et al.* (1975), Moray (1969), Treisman and Geffen (1967), Treisman and Riley (1969).

c   Johnston and Wilson (1980).

7

A sequence of operations which results in only certain material being selected for attention.

8

In early selection models, selection takes place before everything has been analysed for meaning. In late selection models, everything is analysed for meaning before selection takes place.

9

Attention is focused on what falls in the spotlight, but not what is outside the spotlight. The spotlight can be varied in size.

10

We can only look at one thing at once, but we can hear several sources of information at once. So, if we only look at one thing at once, selection (the direction of our gaze), occurs before internal processing.

11

Experiments have demonstrated a negative priming effect, showing there is some unconscious recall of material from outside the area of the zoom (for example Driver and Tipper (1989); Joula *et al.* (1991)).

12

Visual search involves looking for a number, letter or figure in a visual array.

13

Pre-attentive processing involves lower-level tasks where the visual requirement is to find one feature. Focused attention requires a conjunction (or joining) of features. Focusing attention provides the 'glue' that creates an object out of different features.

14

The central processor.

15

In Eysenck's view there is a controller to coordinate and plan attention.

16

The similarity of the tasks, the amount of practice in the tasks and the difficulty of the tasks.

17

Dual tasks are most difficult where the tasks are similar, there has been no practice in the tasks and the tasks in themselves are difficult.

18

Characteristics of automatic behaviour: fast, not conscious, memory retrieval, not flexible.
Characteristics of controlled attention: limited capacity, requires a focus of awareness, flexible, takes longer than automatic responses.

19

Learning to drive a car with an indicator switch on the right-hand stem, then switching to driving a different car with the light switch on the left-hand stem. There is a tendency still to try to indicate using the stem on the right.

20

When a well-practised stimulus is presented, an automatic response gets stored in the memory and is accessed without conscious thought.

21

■ Dual task problems, particularly when the same processing channel is required to carry out the tasks.

■ Absentmindedness, mistakes and slips.

22

Give your own examples. If you get really stuck thinking of these, use the examples in the text on page 630.

23

Well-practised actions require little if any conscious processing, so we can make slips because little attention is being paid to what we are doing.

24

Broadbent (1982): people who score high on one sort of action slip, tend to score high on others as well. Martin and Jones (1983): people who make a lot of errors have difficulty carrying out two tasks at once.

Unit 18

Memory

Lorna Jones, Graham Davies and Sharon Cheyne

This unit covers:

Models of memory

Organisation of memory

Forgetting

Practical applications of memory research

By the end of this unit, you should be able to:

- discuss theories and research studies relating to the nature of memory
- explain the organisation of information in memory
- offer explanations of forgetting
- understand the practical applications of research into memory and forgetting.

Unit 18 Contents

Introduction

Memory is the term given to the structures and processes involved in the storage and subsequent retrieval of information. Throughout the history of psychology the topics of remembering and forgetting have been studied. Why should memory be such an important topic? You can start to discover this for yourself by answering the questions in Activity 1.

Activity 1

a   Write down on a piece of paper all the things you use your memory for.

b   Write down the problems you have had when your memory has let you down.

Did you find that in order to make sense of your past, in order to function in the present and in order to plan the future, your memory has a role to play. Imagine never being able to recall where you have met people before, or your own telephone number, or the names of your family and friends. Imagine never being able to put together your own life history. You would never make sense of how past experiences have influenced you.

Read the case study of Clive Wearing on page 638. It provides a graphic account of the devastating effects that the failure of memory had upon a man.

This unit is concerned with exploring theories and research studies relating to the nature of memory. Theories have considered the structure of memory and the processes that operate within the structures, as well as the different types of memories that are stored and retrieved. Explanations of the organisation of information in memory are considered, followed by psychological explanations of forgetting. The practical applications of memory research are also looked at.

Models of memory

Memory can be considered to involve three processes: encoding, storage and retrieval. *Encoding* transforms sensory input into storable form. *Storage* retains encoded material in the brain, the stored material being called the trace or engram. *Retrieval* is the process of recovering the memory trace from storage. Different approaches have developed, both experimental and non-experimental, to try to clarify our understanding of how these processes work.

The phenomenological approach

The *phenomenological* or episodic approach to memory focuses on real-life experiences, describing these from an individual's unique perspective. The development of this approach was associated with Bartlett (1932) who believed that memory is dynamic and active and more than just a passive store of material. Reading an old diary will often reveal this – we may be surprised at the differences between our present memory of an event and what was written at the time.

Activity 2

Read the story 'The war of the ghosts' below. After reading it, do something else for half an hour and then write it down from memory. Then try writing down what you remember after one week. Compare all three versions and note the differences.

'The war of the ghosts': One night two young men from Egulac went down to the river to hunt seals, and while they were there it became foggy and calm. Then they heard war-cries and they thought 'Maybe this is a war party.' They escaped to the shore ...
(Cont'd page 639).

Case study – Clive Wearing

Clive Wearing is a particularly dramatic example of the terrible after effects of encephalitis. He is so impaired that he cannot remember what happened more than minutes before, with the result that he is convinced that he has only just recovered consciousness. He keeps a diary which records this obsession – page upon page of records indicating the date, the time and the fact that consciousness has just been regained. When confronted with evidence of earlier apparent conscious awareness, by being shown a video of himself, for example, he becomes upset and denies the evidence, even after many years of being in this condition. It is as if, faced with the enormity of a life limited to a horizon of a few seconds, he clings to the view that he has just recovered consciousness, with the implication that in the future all will be well.

Whenever his wife appears, Clive greets her with the joy appropriate to someone who has not seen a loved one for many months. She has only to leave the room for two or three minutes and return for the joy to be repeated, a process that is always full of emotion, and always expressed in the same way. Clive lives in a permanent present, unable to register change or to use the past to anticipate the future, a situation he once described as 'Hell on earth. It's like being dead — all the bloody time!'

Clive's memory for his past is less dramatically impaired than his ongoing memory. Nevertheless it is severely disrupted — he knows who he is, and can give you a broad outline of his earlier life, but with very little accurate detail. He was not certain, for instance, whether his current, second, wife and he were married or not. He could remember, given appropriate prompts, certain highlights of his life, such as singing for the Pope during a papal visit to London or directing the first performance of Messiah in London with authentic instruments and décor. He had written a book on the early composer Lassus, but could remember virtually nothing about him. His visual memory was also impaired — he had spent four years in Cambridge, but did not recognize a photograph of his old college. His general knowledge was similarly reduced — he had no idea, for example, who was the author of *Romeo and Juliet*.

There was, however, one area that was remarkably preserved, namely his musical skills. On one occasion his wife returned home to discover that his old choir was visiting him, and that he was conducting them just as he did in the old days. He could sight-read music and was able to accompany himself on the harpsichord, playing quite complex music and singing with great skill and feeling. Alas, he appears to find the transition from music back to his desolate state of amnesia particularly disturbing, with the result that music does not seem to provide the kind of solace that one might have hoped.

Clive has been in this state since 1985. He is still convinced that he has just woken up. He still lives in a desolate, eternal present. He cannot enjoy books because he cannot follow their plots, and takes no interest in current affairs because, likewise, they are meaningless because he does not remember their context. If he goes out, he immediately becomes lost. He is indeed a prisoner limited to a brief island of consciousness in a sea of amnesia.

Source: Baddeley (1993).

and hid behind a log. Now canoes came up and they heard the noise of paddles, and saw one canoe coming up to them. There were five men in the canoe, and they said 'What do you think? We wish to take you along. We are going up the river to make war on the people.'

One of the young men said 'I have no arrows.'

'Arrows are in the canoe,' they said.

'I will not go along. I might be killed. My relatives do not know where I have gone. But you,' he said, turning to the other, 'may go with them.'

So one of the young men went, but the other returned home.

The warriors went on up the river to a town on the other side of Kalama. The people came down to the water. They began to fight and many were killed. Presently the young man heard one of the warriors say 'Quick, let us go home: that Indian has been hit.' Now he thought: 'Oh, they are ghosts.' He did not feel sick, but they said he had been shot.

So the canoes went back to Egulac, and the young man went ashore to his house, and made a fire. And he told everybody and said 'Behold I accompanied the ghosts, and we went to fight. Many of our fellows were killed, and many of those who attacked us were killed. They said I was hit, and I did not feel sick.'

He told it all, and then he became quiet.

When the sun rose he fell down. Something black came out of his mouth. His face became contorted. The people jumped up and cried.

He was dead.

By carrying out *longitudinal studies* using stories such as 'The war of the ghosts', Bartlett demonstrated three ways in which our memory changes over time. *Simplification* of memory occurs by dropping details such as names. Did you remember the names Egulac and Kalama? *Transformation* may turn unfamiliar events into ones which are more familiar (for example, hunting seals may be changed to fishing). *Rationalisation* makes

the original material more easily understandable by substituting unfamiliar elements with more familiar ones and by incorporating the attitudes, interests and cultural expectations of the reader.

From his work, Bartlett also found that parts of a picture are more likely to be remembered in the future if attention is drawn to them, or if they are bizarre (e.g. a dog in an underwater scene). The strength of the phenomenological approach is its emphasis on natural situations. Bartlett criticised the experimental approach as lacking validity, for instance in Ebbinghaus's research the use of nonsense syllables bears little relationship to everyday experiences. However, the phenomenological approach also has its drawbacks – objective measurement of the phenomena that Bartlett described is difficult. Baddeley (1976) pointed out that specific predictions cannot be made from his work with any degree of certainty.

Structural models

As an alternative to Bartlett, the experimental approach has advanced our knowledge of memory by creating models which attempt to unite theory and fact and thus improve understanding. When a model is proposed, experiments can be devised to test it. In consequence, the model may or may not be modified to meet the new findings. Structural models have memory stores with defined characteristics, for example their capacity, and fixed routes of information flow.

The models described here accept the existence of separate short-term and long-term memory stores. The limited capacity short-term store (STS) contains highly accessible information underlying our conscious processing abilities, while the long-term store (LTS) refers to the huge repository of information needed for cognitive functioning.

The multi-store model

Structural models of memory assume information is stored and rehearsed in specific places in the brain. These specific places are the memory stores where information can be both held and subject to retrieval. A number of theorists have described features of this model. This section will focus on the Atkinson Shiffrin approach. Atkinson and Shiffrin (1968) described the memory as specific stores of information. The **multi-store model** can be seen in figure 18.1.

In their multi-store approach information is received first by the modal-specific sensory stores. Some of the information briefly held in the sensory stores is attended to and passes to the STS. Once there, information can be displaced or lost, or it can be rehearsed and passed into the LTS. Atkinson and Shiffrin (1968) believed the greater the rehearsal in the STS the greater the likelihood of retaining the memory trace. The multi-store approach incorporates the structures of memory and the processes of attention and rehearsal which explain the development of a memory trace passing through the structural model.

In the multi-store model the sensory registers briefly analyse and store information. The sensory register for vision, termed *ionic memory*, was investigated by Sperling (1960) using a *tachistoscope*. Different displays were presented at 50 centimetres; for example, three rows of four letters. Pointers shown immediately afterwards indicated to participants whether to recall a particular row or the whole display. Results showed that participants only remembered four or five letters from a complete display of 12 items, but remembered at least three correctly if asked for any particular row. Thus the whole array must have been available for retrieval since participants did not know which row would be asked for until it had disappeared from view. Ionic

memory is highly transient, as Sperling found that no retrieval occurred if intervals between stimulus and report signal exceeded one second. Sensory registers have also been demonstrated for other senses, for example audition (termed *echoic memory*). Eysenck and Keane (1995) pointed to an example of transient auditory store of information, the echoic store. They argued that if someone is reading a book or a newspaper and is asked a question, he or she may respond with the question 'What did you say?', and at the same time realise what has been said. This storage of auditory information depends on an echoic memory working.

As well as containing storage space, Atkinson and Shiffrin (1968) believed that the STS contains the memory's control processes. These can select information from the sensory registers for further analysis, direct material into a more or less permanent LTS, permit it to be forgotten, or initiate a response. Short-term store can be seen as containing a buffer, its capacity being shared among its functions so that when demands are high in one area, there is a reduction in the capacity available for others. Where rehearsal capacity demands are small, more items can be retained, but this is a slow way to transfer to LTS. Imagery is a faster but more space-demanding transfer method.

Short-term store capacity has been shown to be seven plus or minus two 'chunks' of information, each 'chunk' containing one or more items (see page 659). Miller (1956), experimenting with random digits, called this the 'magic number 7'. We need STS to understand long sentences, do complex calculations and retain information required briefly (for example, a telephone number needed only once). Non-verbal forms of storage are possible in STS. To the auditory-verbal-linguistic component suggested by Atkinson and Shiffrin (1968) can be added others for vision (Posner *et al.*, 1969), smell (Engen *et al.*, 1973) and touch (Gilson and Baddeley, 1969).

■ Evidence for the multi-store model

Some of the strongest evidence for the multi-store model comes from **serial position effect** studies and studies of brain-damaged patients. In serial position effect studies participants are given a list of words and then asked to recall the words in any

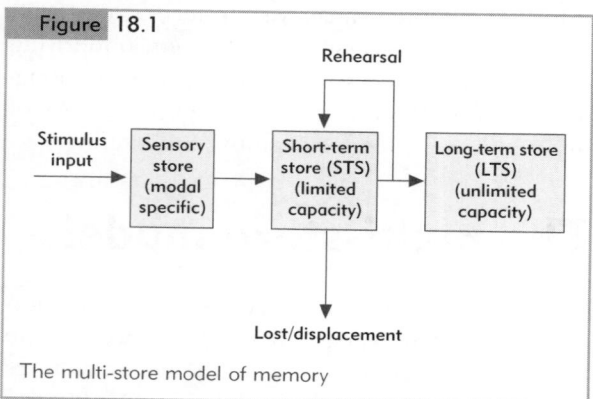

Figure 18.1

The multi-store model of memory

order. The likelihood of recalling any word depends on its position in the list, that is, its serial position. Words from the beginning and the end of the list are better recalled than those in the middle of the list. Better recall of the words early in the list results from a primacy effect, whilst better recall at the end of the list results from a recency effect. The primacy effect results from words having been rehearsed and stored in the LTS, whilst the recency effect results from words still consciously present in the STS. Poorest recall is of words in the middle of the list, as these are lost whilst rehearsal of the early items takes place. This effect is shown in figure 18.2.

Glanzer and Cunitz (1966) demonstrated the serial position effect and further that a distractor task presented immediately after the list can substantially reduce recall of the words at the end of the list, whilst better recall for words at the beginning of the list remains. The Brown–Peterson technique (Brown, 1958; Peterson and Peterson, 1959) demonstrated independently by John Brown, a British psychologist, and the Petersons, two American psychologists, showed the greater the length of the distractor task the greater the damage to recall in the recency effect. Peterson and Peterson (1959) asked participants to learn three nonsense letters, or trigrams. The participants then counted backwards for a short period of time, after which they tried to recall the letters they had originally seen in the trigram. Typical results are shown in figure 18.3. Recall of trigrams decreased as the delay before recall increased. Participants forgot more than 50 per cent of what they had studied after a five-second delay. After an 18-second delay 80 per cent of the material to be recalled had been lost. The Brown–Peterson technique demonstrated the fragility of memory after a delay of a few seconds. Studies of primacy and recency effects and the effect of delay on recall support the Atkinson Shiffrin multi-store model.

The study of people with brain damage provides further evidence in favour of the multi-store model. One of the early neurological cases which supports the multi-store model is that of HM (Milner, 1966). HM had surgery to the temporal lobes and the hippocampus in order to cure epilepsy, but was left with an unusual type of memory loss. He had a normal short-term memory and could recall his distant past but he could not retain any new information. He appeared to lack the ability to transfer information from the STS to the LTS. Patients suffering from Korsakoff's Syndrome (a condition which can affect long-term alcoholics and in which memory is irreversibly damaged) have poor long-term memories but fairly normal short-term memories when assessed by digit-span tasks and recency-effect tasks (Baddeley and Warrington, 1970; Butters and Cermak, 1980).

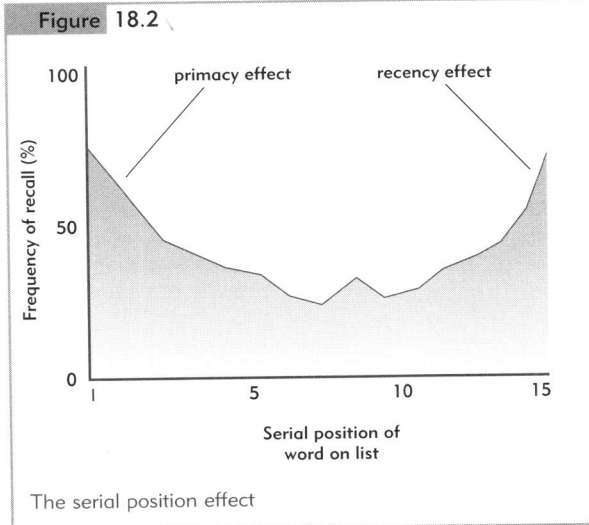

Figure 18.2

The serial position effect

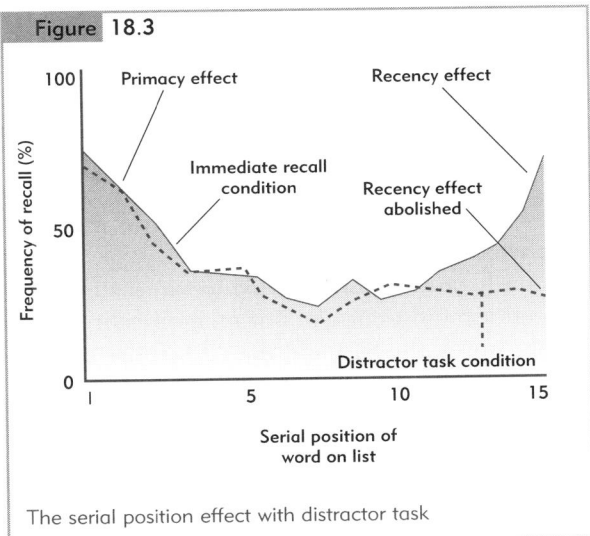

Figure 18.3

The serial position effect with distractor task

Activity 3

A variation of the Brown–Peterson technique: take five index cards, or small pieces of card. Write three words, of two syllables each, in a list on one side of each card. On the opposite side of the card write a three-digit number. For example:

SIDE 1	SIDE 2
butcher	576
content	
record	

When you have made the five cards leave them for a while, then shuffle them, take one card, show yourself Side 1 for two seconds. Turn over the card and count backwards from the number given, in threes, for 18 seconds. How many words can you recall? Repeat the exercise with the other cards. Compare your results with those in figure 18.3.

Fewer brain-damaged patients have the problem of poor short-term memory and normal long-term memory. One such patient, KF, was reported by Shallice and Warrington (1970). As a result of a motorcycle accident, KF had suffered damage to the left parieto-occipital region of the brain. He had no difficulty with long-term memory recall, but he could only recall one or two items in digit-span tasks, and in recency-effect tasks his free recall could be as poor as one item. He did perform better in some other STS tasks. These differences in STS and LTS tasks are best explained by the theory that there are different memory stores.

■ Evaluation of the Atkinson Shiffrin multi-store model

The multi-store model provides a distinction between the different types of memory stores; the sensory stores, the STS and the LTS. It has proved a useful starting point from which other theorists have been able to expand and refine the nature of these memory stores. For example, the STS proved a useful starting point for the working memory model (see next page) and the LTS has been expanded upon by the concepts of episodic, semantic and procedural memories (see below).

By way of criticism, it can be said that the multi-store model is too simplistic in the way it treats the STS and LTS as unitary items, where the division of functions within the store is not explained. Warrington and Shallice (1972), who carried out further investigations of KF, the brain-damaged patient, demonstrated this. They discovered his memory deficit was limited to verbal material such as letters, words and digits, but did not extend to sounds such as a telephone ringing. It would thus appear that the STS is not unitary. The rather passive view of the STS processes suggested by the Atkinson Shiffrin model does not grasp the complexity of conscious mental processing involved in this stage of memory. The working memory model does provide a more comprehensive explanation of the active processing involved.

Explanations of the organisation and division in the LTS have been suggested by, for example Tulving (1972, 1985), and can be seen in figure 18.4.

Episodic memory recalls events in our lives. It is a qualitatively distinct conscious awareness and it is this which fails in a free recall task. **Semantic memory** contains information about ourselves, concepts, rules and language. It can be accessed without reference to the events accounting for its

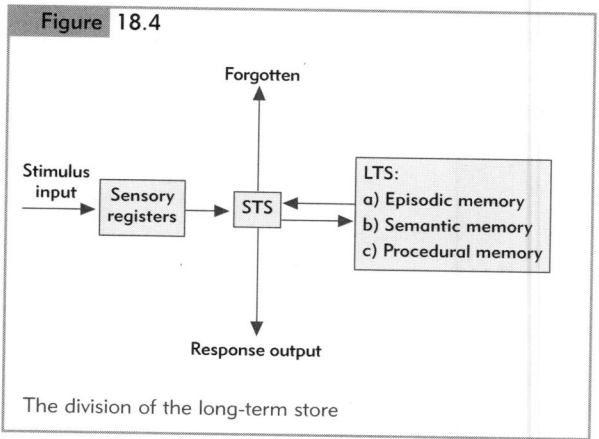

Figure 18.4

The division of the long-term store

formation. It is open to conscious examination and can be altered by experience. **Procedural memory** consists of information that we are not consciously aware of, for example the ability to ride a bicycle. This is the most primitive form of memory, present in all organisms capable of learning.

A further criticism of the Atkinson Shiffrin multi-store model lies in the over-simplicity of the concept of rehearsal to explain how all information becomes established in the LTS. Repetitive rehearsal is not the only, or most effective, way of establishing LTS traces. Craik (1983) pointed out that rehearsal itself differs in quality. For example, semantic rehearsal which involves understanding the meaning of the material to be remembered is more effective than mere repetition of the material.

Working memory model

Baddeley (1993) referred to the **working memory** as a system that permits several pieces of information to be held in the mind, at the same time, and to be related to each other. For example, in problem-solving tasks, components of the problem need to be processed and held in the memory until they can be combined to solve the problem. It is the working memory that is engaged in this process.

Baddeley and Hitch (1974) tried to tease out the components which made up the working memory. Initially they reasoned that if short-term memory functions as a working memory, people should have difficulty when engaged in dual tasks which both involved the same sort of information processing. In a study of divers (Baddeley and Hitch, 1974), the ability to reason was measured when divers were breathing air at pressures experienced at over 100 feet underwater. Participants were presented with a series of sentences describing the order of presentation of two letters A and B. The sentences were followed by the pair of letters AB and BA. The participants had to decide whether the sentences were correctly described in the letter pair. For example,

B is followed by A.　　BA　True/False

The answer of course is 'True'.

Divers worked at the task for three minutes and their performance at depth was measured. Baddeley and Hitch decided that if the sentence-checking task needed reasoning skill it would be difficult to recall digit spans at the same time, so participants were given six digits to say aloud, for example 731928, whilst completing the sentence-checking task. The results showed a tendency for reasoning to be slowed down, although both tasks could be carried out. Baddeley and Hitch suggested that the two tasks could not be dependent on the same limited capacity system and that a number of processing components could be involved. They assumed there was a control system operating, which they called the central executive. They suggested there could be a number of 'slave' systems to which the central executive could delegate some short-term storage functions, thus freeing some of its own capacity for information-processing tasks.

As the working memory model has evolved, three slave systems have been identified; the articulatory or phonological loop, the primary acoustic store and the visuo-spatial scratch pad.

■ The articulatory or phonological loop

Other models of short-term memory had suggested verbal rehearsal processing and, in keeping with this, Baddeley and Hitch (1974) suggested that a sub-vocal speech system could be one of the 'slave' systems of the central executive. They named this the *articulatory loop* now more often referred to as the phonological loop. Among the evidence used to support the phonological loop is the *phonological similarity* effect whereby recall errors tend to be phonologically similar to correct items which participants recall, suggesting that items for recall are sounded out. For example, participants recall F for S or B for G. Another piece of evidence for the existence of the phonological loop comes from studies by Baddeley and Hitch into the effect of word length on memory span. Try out Activity 4, which is an adaptation of Baddeley and Hitch's work.

Activity 4

Read down each column silently then look away. Write down the words you can recall.

some	association	twice	opportunity
harm	considerable	worst	immediately
bond	representative	wit	organisation
yield	individual	come	university
hate	suspicious	fair	miserable

Source: Adapted from A D Baddeley (1993).

Generally, results from tests such as that shown in Activity 4 show the greater the length of the word the longer the rehearsal time, the more time there is for the memory trace of early words to fade away. Preventing the rehearsal of the words by *articulatory suppression* (e.g. saying 'the' outloud whilst learning the words) overcomes the difference in recall between long and short words as sub-vocal rehearsal ceases to be important. Articulatory suppression also diminishes the phonological similarity effect for the same reason.

■ The primary acoustic store

As the working memory model developed, the primary acoustic store was added (Salame and Baddeley, 1982) to explain the role of auditory imagery in processing.

Humans are able to recollect tunes or recall the sounds of nature. Auditory input can be received directly by the primary acoustic store. Without an acoustic processor, such an ability would be difficult to imagine. The acoustic store also receives information indirectly from the phonological loop, in the sense that you can hear your own voice. Baddeley and Hitch (1974) tested whether this 'inner ear' has a role to play in reading. Do people need to sub-vocalise in order to create sounds which the primary acoustic store processes? Baddeley and Hitch gave participants words which were similar in sound, but spelt differently, for example doe and dough. Participants were required to respond to these words by saying the sound was the same. They had to respond 'not same' to words

such as dough and rough. Judgments about the words were made equally well with and without suppressing articulation, suggesting it is not necessary to vocalise the sound of the word in order to understand the word. Instead, in certain circumstances, a non-verbal auditory system seems to operate to help in the processing of the written word.

■ The visuo-spatial scratch pad

Baddeley and Hitch (1974) explored the role of a visual and spatial processor in the working memory. Quoting the work of Roger Shepard (1978) of Stanford University in California, they demonstrated that spatial processing operates in our memory. Try out the task (designed by Roger Shepard, 1978) in Activity 5.

Activity 5

If the shapes below were made out of paper they could be folded to make a solid with the shaded area being the base. Imagine folding the shapes and work out whether the arrows will meet head on.

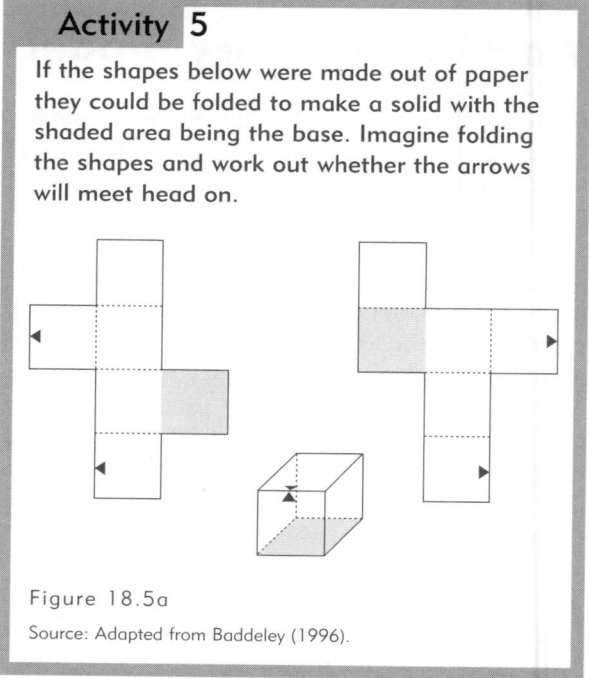

Figure 18.5a

Source: Adapted from Baddeley (1996).

In Shepard's shape-folding tasks the time taken to solve the problem was related to the number of folds required. Participants were 'folding' the cube in their heads! Baddeley and Hitch (1974) suggested there is a relationship between visual imagery and working memory. They believed spatial information to be stored in an abstract code in the memory and that a spatial slave system enables information to be displayed and manipulated. Following on from the work of Brooks (1968), Baddeley and Hitch (1974) showed that in dual task studies, a visuo-spatial task (such as taking a mental imaging walk around a letter 'F') was interfered with by having to point to 'Y' (for yes) when the corner reached was at a top or bottom line and 'N' (for no) when the corner reached was not at a top or bottom line. There was no interference when the imaging task was paired with a verbal response rather than a pointing response.

Two tasks using visual and spatial processing interfere in working memory, whilst one visual and one verbal task operating on differing 'slave' systems can be carried out more effectively. In a similar experiment by Baddeley (1973), participants had to carry out a tracking task, keeping a pointer on a moving spot of light. They were then given blocked letters, as shown in figure 18.5b, and had to say 'yes' or 'no' depending on whether they were at a top, bottom or inner corner. Participants had great difficulty tracking the light spot whilst visualising letters. As both tasks required visualising, disruption of performance occurred.

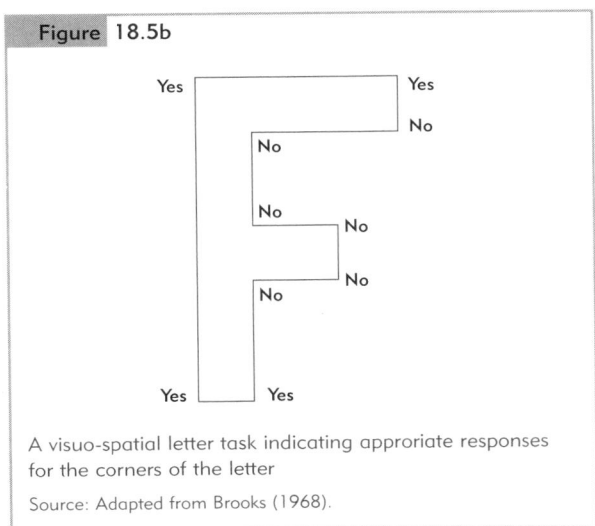

Figure 18.5b

A visuo-spatial letter task indicating appropriate responses for the corners of the letter

Source: Adapted from Brooks (1968).

■ The central executive

The central executive is the controller of the working memory. It is believed to be a limited capacity attention system which controls the phonological loop, the primary acoustic store and the visuo-spatial scratch pad and relates them to long-term memory. It is the most complex part of the working memory and almost certainly involves memory and processing.

Knowledge of how the central executive functions is limited. One of its functions is as a supervisory attention channel used for a variety of purposes, helping when lower processing channels are inadequate. It is thought to be involved in planning, decision making and where poorly mastered sequences of activity need extra processing. Patients with neurological frontal lobe damage seem to suffer problems associated with central executive impairment.

■ Evaluation of the working memory model

Eysenck and Keane (1995) pointed to the following positive aspects of the working memory model.

- It provides an explanation for the active processing of information.
- It helps to explain partial deficits in the STS in brain-damaged patients. If there are three components in the working memory then selective deficits in one area can be expected (see KF, Shallice and Warrington's patient, on page 642).
- The working memory model is more wide ranging than the Atkinson Shiffrin multi-store model which only covers verbal rehearsal. The working memory model covers verbal, acoustic and visuo-spatial rehearsal.

By way of criticism, Eysenck and Keane (1995) pointed out that the exact nature of the central executive is not clear. In terms of capacity and functioning, it is thought to be 'modality free' (i.e. can process information from any sense mode). There is, however, no conclusive evidence that it is a unitary system at all.

Levels of processing theory

The **levels of processing** theory was developed by Craik and Lockhart (1972), who considered that the structural models had outlived their usefulness as a research tool. Their alternative approach investigated the way new information is processed, rather than the memory structure involved. They suggested that a new stimulus can be processed at different levels, which become more complex as depth of processing increases; as it does, for instance, with a word's shape, sound and meaning (see figure 18.6).

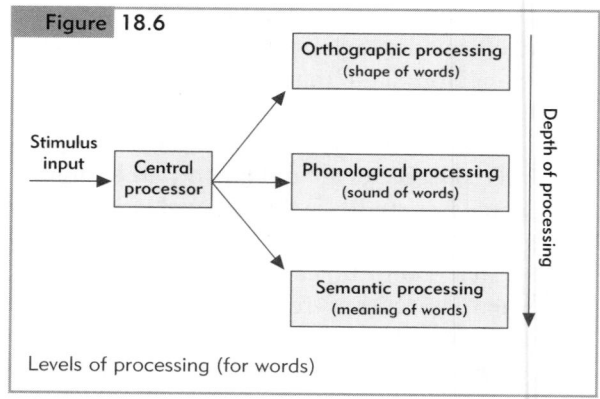

Figure 18.6

Levels of processing (for words)

Activity 6

Which level – that is, shape, sound or meaning – requires the deepest processing and which the shallowest? Compare your ideas to the findings described in the following paragraphs.

The central processor controls conscious mental activity and is therefore analogous to STS. Craik and Tulving (1975) investigated levels of processing for words. Participants were induced to process a series of words at particular levels by being given a question immediately before presentation of each word. For example, 'Is the word printed in capital letters?' (orthographic level) 'Does the word rhyme with weight?' (phonological level) 'Is the word a type of fish?' (semantic level). Given an unexpected memory test, the results showed that the likelihood of retrieval was a direct function of depth of processing (see figure 18.7).

Craik and Lockhart (1972) concentrated on the nature of rehearsal and suggested that the length of memory is directly related to the level of processing and not just the amount of processing (as Atkinson and Shiffrin (1968) had suggested). Their viewpoint was demonstrated in a study by Craik and Watkins (1973) in which participants

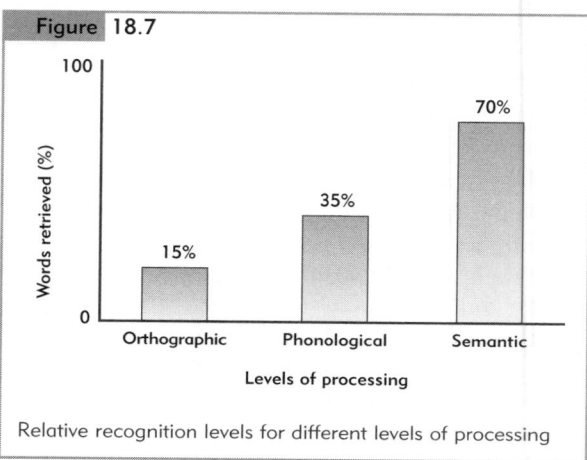

Figure 18.7

Relative recognition levels for different levels of processing

listened to a list of words and were asked to remember the last word beginning with an identified letter. For example, if in the list the target letter was 'l' the word 'lurid' should be easily recalled.

List to be recalled:

grass, level, rejoin, potato, wolf, carpet, lady, launderette, legal, aim, stable, bungle, lurid, tadpole.

Lurid was well remembered. Participants were then asked to recall from the list as many other words as they could beginning with 'l'. The Atkinson Shiffrin multi-store model would predict that 'lady', and 'launderette' would be least frequently recalled, due to the brief time available for rehearsal before the word legal is listed. In fact, all the target 'l' words were equally likely to be recalled, suggesting the amount of rehearsal alone does not explain the nature of recall.

■ Evaluation of the levels of processing theory

Craik and Lockhart (1972) have made an important contribution in drawing attention to the effects of different types of processing. They suggested that variations in how well material is rehearsed can affect how well it is remembered. They focused on memory traces being formed as a result of perceptual and attentional processes, thus linking them together.

A number of criticisms have, however, been made of their theory. Alternative suggestions have been put forward.

■ The most important criticism is that there is no way of independently assessing how processing takes place. The theory predicts, without really proving, that deeply processed words are best remembered and best remembered words are deeply processed. Thus the model contains an element of circularity.

■ It is difficult to control the level of processing which participants actually use in levels-of-processing tasks. They may be using extra processing to that which is asked of them.

■ Eysenck (1984, 1986) believed that the levels of processing focus too narrowly on the processing activities occurring when memory is acquired. He believed there are a number of other determinants of acquiring long-term memories. They include: the nature of the task; the kind of stimulus used; the individual characteristics of the subject; and the type of retention task used to measure memory. For example, Morris et al. (1977) showed that on a standard levels-of-processing task, if recognition is requested by finding a rhyming word, then the original 'find the rhyme' words are the ones best remembered in a rhyming-recognition task. So, a form of coding (rhyme) which might be shallow for one task might be deep and meaningful for another. They argued that their findings support a transfer-appropriate processing theory, whereby different kinds of processing enable learners to store different kinds of information with regard to the stimulus. The stored information is thus more likely to be retained if the memory test relates directly to the processing task used.

■ Craik and Tulving (1975) demonstrated that elaboration of material, as well as depth of processing, is important in recall. Elaboration was varied by manipulating the complexity of the sentences presented. Cued recall was twice as high where words had come from complex sentences, thus suggesting that elaboration aids memory. The type of elaboration also is important. For example, participants were much more likely to recall:
'A mosquito is like a doctor because they both draw blood.'
'A mosquito is like a raccoon because they both have heads, legs, jaws.'
(Bransford et al., 1979).

■ Eysenck (1979) argued that people remember distinctive material which differs from other memory traces. In a study by Eysenck and Eysenck (1980), participants were asked to remember, amongst other things, nouns which are not pronounced phonetically, for example comb with a silent 'b'. Participants were asked to sound every letter in the words. Other nouns, for example 'knee', were pronounced normally and others were processed in line with their meaning. In an unexpected recognition memory test, distinctive words such as 'comb' were better remembered than words such as 'knee', which sounded normally. Also, there was little difference in recall between the distinctive non-semantic words such as 'comb' and other words processed semantically.
The study illustrates the importance of distinctiveness in memory-recall tasks. Where letters were sounded phonetically, the word was made distinct. Recall was not significantly different from when words were processed semantically, which is not what the levels of processing theory would predict.

Self-assessment questions

1 What three processes are involved in the operation of memory?

2 What are the two main sources of evidence on which the Atkinson Shiffrin multi-store model is based?

3 What evidence exists to support the working memory model?

4 What is meant by the term 'levels of processing'?

5 Suggest two ways in which the multi-store model differs from the levels of processing model.

(Suggested answers on pages 668–9.)

Organisation of memory

Finding things stored away neatly in their proper places is much easier than when they are jumbled up. It is the same with memory, retrieval is much easier from an organised memory than from a disorganised one. In this section we look at some of the ways that we can organise our memory stores.

By category and hierarchy

Access to information can be facilitated if organised by *category* and *hierarchy* (as in figure 18.8).

Bower *et al.* (1969) presented participants with word lists arranged either hierarchically or randomly. When participants were tested for recall, results were two to three times better with the hierarchical lists. This is easy to understand using an analogy with a library. If books are kept in sections depending on subject or category, the search for a particular title can be speeded up by going first to the relevant bookcase, then to the correct shelf and finally to the appropriate book. It seems that memory can be scanned similarly to retrieve information more efficiently.

The limited capacity of the STS can be assisted by the organisational device of chunking, so information such as telephone numbers can be grouped to aid storage and recall.

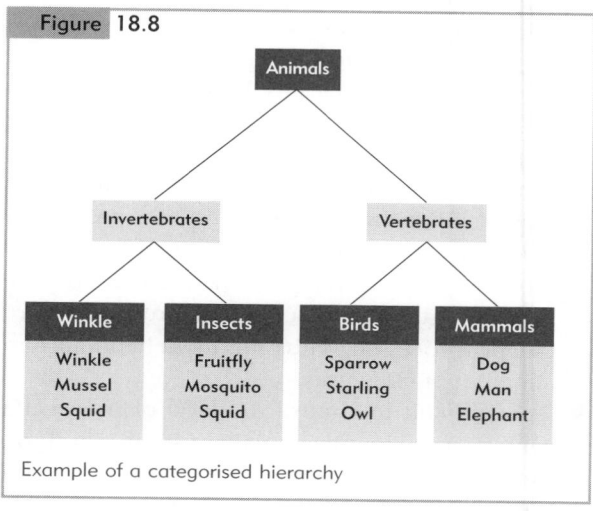

Figure 18.8

Example of a categorised hierarchy

Activity 7

Look at each word in List A for about two seconds, then turn your book over and write down those you can remember.

List A: words to memorise

Primrose	Concrete
Bull	Curtains
Caterpillar	Tile
Eiderdown	Daisy
Steel	Turbot
Velvet	Carnation
Rubber	Tortoise
Flute	Lilac
Cream	Sparrow
Rose	Spade

Activity **7 cont'd**

Now look at List B and categorise each word as follows: LA if it represents a living animal, LP if a living plant, IH if inanimate (not living) and hard, IS if inanimate and soft.

List B: words to classify

Word	Category	Word	Category
Elderberry		Amoeba	
Recorder		Lichen	
Aster		Foxglove	
Brontosaurus		Sponge	
Jumper		Alsatian	
Cushion		Teapot	
Toy		Pig	
Window		Duster	
Rhinoceros		Lupin	
Monkey		Brick	

Now turn your book over and try to write down all the words. How did you get on this time? Were you surprised at the number you remembered? You probably recalled more words from List B because you were actively employed in associating these words with categories of information stored in LTS, whereas List A has no such associations.

By imagery

'One picture is worth 50 words'; 'Use diagrams to illustrate your answer.' How often have you found that illustrations help your understanding? *Imagery* can be defined as the creation of a mental picture. It is quite different to verbal memory. After studying patients with damage to one of their temporal lobes, Paivio (1971) proposed that the processing of words and images occurs separately. According to Paivio (1971), concrete words, which can be images, are encoded twice in memory, once in verbal symbols and once as image-based symbols. This increases the likelihood that they will be remembered. Paivio called this the **dual coding hypothesis**. It has parallels with the processing involved in the working memory model by the mode-specific processors of the phonological loop acoustic store and the visuo-spatial scratch pad (see pages 644–5).

A rare but different kind of visual imagery to that described by Paivio is *eidetic imagery*. Haber (1969) demonstrated it by using a scene from *Alice in Wonderland* where Alice is talking to the Cheshire Cat on the branch of a tree. Eidetic imagers could look briefly at the picture, store it almost perfectly and later 'read off' great detail from their image such as the number of stripes on the cat's tail. Such images are not quite like photographs, as details are sometimes added, altered or deleted. Evidence suggests that they only occur when picture content is interesting.

Stromeyer and Psotka (1970) investigated the eidetic powers of a young teacher called Elizebeth. She was presented with a 10 000 dot pattern for one minute to her right eye, and after 10 seconds another was presented to her left eye. When asked to superimpose the two images she exclaimed that she saw the letter 'T' coming towards her. Elizebeth could see such images even with 24 hours between the two presentations.

By context

It is easier to retrieve a particular episode if you are in the same *context* as that in which the episode occurred (Estes, 1972). Storing an image of the context in which an event takes place can generate a memory trace which can be scanned for information retrieval. For example, when mentally retracing steps to remember where you put something, you may use images to take you back to the original context.

Context has been shown to affect our memory in several ways. Godden and Baddeley (1975) presented divers with material to learn, either on dry land or underwater. Subsequent retrieval was best when the recall environment matched that of the original learning.

In *state-dependent learning* the internal state of the organism provides the contextual cue for retrieval. Such learning can be defined as that occurring during a particular psychophysiological state of an organism. Recall is most effective when the organism is placed in the same state again. It has been demonstrated for a wide range of altered states of awareness, including those due to depressants (Goodwin *et al.*, 1969, alcohol), stimulant drugs (Bustamante *et al.*, 1970, amphetamines), hallucinogenic drugs (Eich *et al.*, 1975, marijuana), hypnosis (Bower *et al.*, 1978), mood states (Weingartner, 1978, depression) and stages of sleep (Bonnet, 1983).

State-dependent effects seem to occur only when other retrieval cues are absent, as in free recall situations (Eich, 1980). They may be explained in terms of Tulving's encoding specificity principle. Perhaps the 'invisible' cue of psychophysiological states is a low-level one, only called upon when higher-level cues are absent.

Tulving and Thomson (1973) developed the **encoding specificity principle**. They considered recall and recognition to be parts of a single retrieval process in which currently available material interrelates with memory contents. Thus recall and recognition differ only in the efficiency of the retrieval cues provided. These cues need to be incorporated into the episodic memory trace where material is encoded if it is to be used to help retrieval in the future. Tulving and Thomson saw both recall and recognition as involving the retrieval of information only from episodic memory, using temporal and contextual information implicit in retrieval cues. These are matched to the episodic trace, a process which Tulving called *ecphory* and which produces a conscious memory of the original event. Success of retrieval depends on an overlap between stored information and that currently available, the superiority of recognition over recall being explained by greater information overlap. The strength of this approach is that it stresses the importance of context in recognition.

By semantic memory

Memory for meaning is, in a way, our encyclopaedia of understanding. How is the meaning of the world represented and organised inside our heads? How is this meaning retrieved from our memories? In an attempt to answer these questions, Collins and Quillian (1969) created a computer program, the Teachable Language Comprehender (TLC), to explain the structure and processes of semantic memory. From this, the Collins and Quillian (1972) model of semantic memory developed. Collins and Quillian described semantic memory as a network, or an interrelated body of knowledge, in which each concept is a node in the network. Thus through pathways the concepts are interrelated. Information is retrieved and accessed from the network by the process of 'spreading activation.' The spread of activation corresponds to a search through memory. An example is given in figure 18.9.

In the example given, the word 'robin' can activate the other words in the network. Can you activate the pathway between 'robin' and 'breathes'? Between 'animal' and 'red breast'?

Empirical testing of semantic models has been carried out via reaction-time testing. Collins and Quillian (1969) predicted that two concepts that are closer together in a network should need less time for verification that two that are further apart. For example, it should be faster to verify 'a robin is a bird' (as it takes less time for the spread of activation) than 'a robin is an animal', which requires a greater spread of activation. Results indicated reaction increased as the semantic distance between the two concepts increased, thus supporting the idea that semantic information is organised in a hierarchical nature.

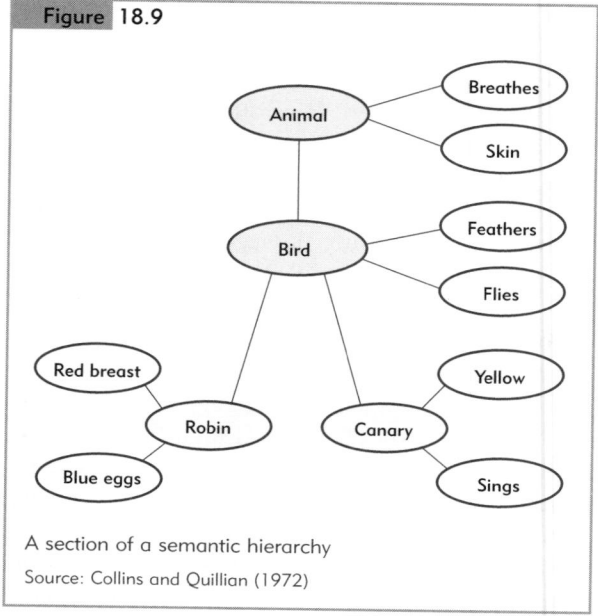

Figure 18.9

A section of a semantic hierarchy

Source: Collins and Quillian (1972)

Following further empirical work (e.g. Rosch, 1973) it became apparent that typical members of a category are more rapidly judged than atypical members. This typicality effect now suggests that the hierarchy is such that the typical members of a category are structurally closer to the category name and thus can be retrieved more quickly than less typical members. This can be seen in figure 18.10 where the short pathways indicate strongly related semantic concepts and the long pathways denote a lesser degree of semantic relatedness.

In 1975, Collins and Loftus revised the spreading activation model, suggesting that the network is not hierarchically organised and that semantic distances reflect how related the concepts are, in typicality. For example, a robin would be recognised faster as a bird than a turkey would. A turkey is a less typical bird example. Individual personal experiences were also recognised to play a part in the relationship between the concepts.

By schemas and scripts

The idea of a memory schema implies a large unit of organisation for storage. Bartlett's (1932) pioneering work on memory (see page 637) makes use of this concept. More recent work has focused on *scripts* as the unit of organisation. Scripts are a development of schema theory and are favoured by computer scientists to explain the concept of 'driven', or 'top down', structure which helps people to interpret information from the senses. Representations of entire episodes or events are

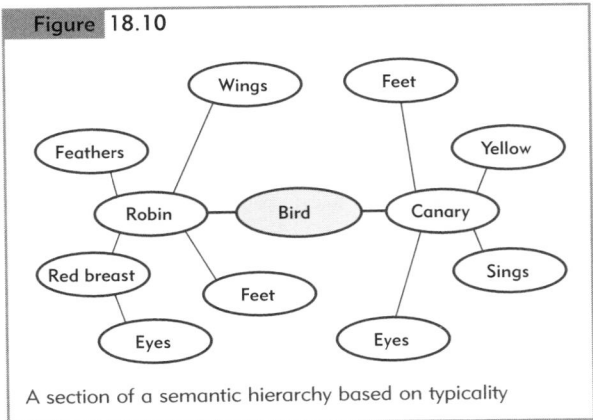

Figure 18.10

A section of a semantic hierarchy based on typicality

called scripts. They provide general knowledge about the structure of events and situations. Scripts which we develop guide our interpretation and understanding of daily experiences. They provide a set of expectations about what usually happens. Scripts are in one respect a 'shorthand' for the whole event. According to Schank and Abelson (1977), our understanding is guided by the scripts we know. Consider the script behind this story:

'John went to restaurant. He asked the waiter for a hamburger. He paid by cheque and then left.'

The two headers (phrases or words that activate the script), are 'restaurant' and 'hamburger'. These 'primes' create activation of the whole restaurant script. Scripts have frames which are details of events which would normally occur. If details to fill the frames are not provided, then the 'default' will fill in the details. The default value is the typical value that occupies a frame. A simplified example of Schank and Abelson's restaurant schema can be seen in figure 18.11.

■ Evidence for scripts

A number of laboratory studies by Graesser (1981) and a field experiment by Nakemura *et al.* (1985) demonstrated that scripts of stories are stored in generic memory traces and that atypical events are stored specifically during comprehension. In Nakemura *et al.*'s (1985) study, a classroom lecture was given and a memory test for the event followed. It was found that memory was better for atypical information such as sipping coffee, than for typical information such as writing on the blackboard. It is thought that typical information was being stored in the script rather than in the memory trace during that particular study. Galambos and Rips (1982) showed that when people make a quick judgment about whether an action is part of a script, they answer more rapidly when the action is typical in that script, thus suggesting direct accessing of the script speeds up recall. The availability of scripts and schema reduces the amount of processing required to identify and memorise events.

By way of evaluation of schema theory, the following criticisms have been made by Cohen (1993):

■ The concept of schema is too vague to be useful.

18.11 A simplified version of Schank and Abelson's (1977) restaurant script

Name:	Restaurant
Props:	Tables
	Menu
	Food
	Bill
	Money
	Tip
Entry conditions:	Customer is hungry
	Customer has money

Roles:	Customer
	Waiter
	Cook
	Cashier
	Owner
Results:	Customer has less money
	Owner has more money
	Customer is not hungry

Scene 1: Entering
Customer enters restaurant
Customer looks for table
Customer decides where to sit
Customer goes to table
Customer sits down

Scene 2: Ordering
Customer picks up menu
Customer looks at menu
Customer decides on food
Customer signals waitress
Waitress goes to cook
Waitress gives food order to cook
Cook prepares food

Scene 3: Eating
Cook gives food to customer
Customer eats food

Scene 4: Exiting
Waitress writes bill
Waitress goes over to customer
Waitress gives bill to customer
Customer gives tip to waitress
Customer goes to cashier
Customer gives money to cashier
Customer leaves restaurant

Source: Bower et al. (1979)

- Things which are unexpected and unusual are often well remembered and they are not part of the script.
- The schema theory does not show how schemas are acquired. It is not clear which develops first, the schema to interpret the experiences, or vice versa.

By types of memories

Organisation in memory can be explored by consideration of different memory types. Tulving (1975) drew a distinction between *episodic* and *semantic* memories. Episodic memories mainly account for our personal experiences, in other words, our own life history. Semantic memories refer to our knowledge about the world, rules and language. Of course, there is some overlap because our knowledge about the world in general is not totally divorced from our understanding gained from our own (episodic) memories. The two are not quite as separate as Tulving originally implied. Cohen and Squire (1980) made a distinction between procedural and declarative memories. Procedural memories correspond to knowing how to do things such as ride a bicycle or get dressed. They do not involve conscious recollection. Tulving later added this memory type to his classification (see figure 18.12).

Flashbulb memories are a special type of episodic memory involving a vivid recollection of some important event such as the news of the Dunblane massacre or the Manchester bombing. Are you able to recall exactly what you were doing when the news broke? Where were you, who were you with? How did you hear the news? According to Brown and Kulik (1982), a neural mechanism, triggered

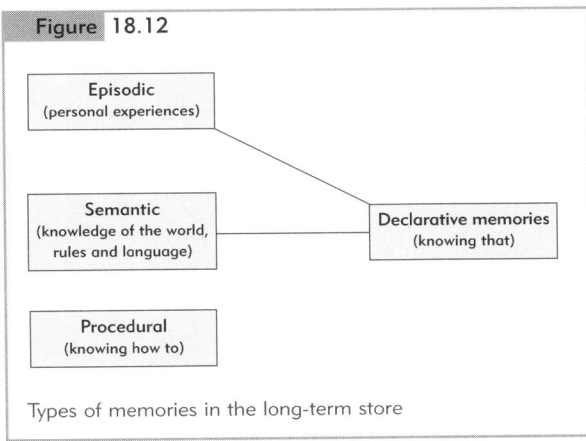

Figure 18.12

Types of memories in the long-term store

by events which are emotionally arousing, imprint a memory trace. In addition, it must be said, flashbulb memories may remain due to frequent rehearsal after the event.

By explicit and implicit memories

The distinction between **explicit memory** and **implicit memory** is a recent classification showing division of memory types in the LTS. Memory tasks involving free recall, cued recall or recognition require the use of explicit memory when, 'performance on a task requires conscious recollection of previous experiences' (Graf and Schacter, 1985, p. 501). Perhaps (if you are female), you choose a dress which you recall looks good on someone else. Recently, great interest has been shown in implicit memory, 'when performance on a task is facilitated in the absence of conscious recollection' (Graf and Schacter, 1985, p. 501). In this instance you may choose a dress which you have seen on someone else but you are not consciously aware of this affecting your choice. Testing implicit memory might involve the completion of a word-fragment test as in Activity 8.

Writing GREAT instead of GREEN demonstrates an implicit memory effect as 'great' occurs five times more frequently than 'green' in the English language. 'Good' occurs sixteen times more frequently than 'gold'. The term used for this implicit memory result is repetition priming, where a previous encounter with information facilitates later performance on the same information, albeit unconsciously (Ashcraft, 1994, pp. 353–4). Interestingly, in amnesiacs, where explicit memory tasks result in poor performance, implicit memory tasks often result in normal levels of performance (Nissen and Bullemer, 1987). It is likely that there are various kinds of implicit memory which do not involve conscious recollection.

Self-assessment questions

6 Why might categories and hierarchies aid storage and retrieval of information?

7 According to Paivio (1971) why should words which can be imaged be recalled more easily than words which can not be imaged?

8 What is meant by state- and context-dependent memory and how do they link to the encoding specificity principle?

9 Schemas and scripts can be used to explain 'top down' processing. Why is this so?

10 Define explicit and implicit memories.

(Suggested answers on page **669**.)

Forgetting

Forgetting, like retrieval, can occur at any stage of the memory process. As mentioned on page 640, it is a very important part of our memory system, although it may be viewed as both a weakness and a strength. It may prove a severe handicap, as so much human activity depends upon knowledge accumulated over time. Alternatively, it may be advantageous. Old information may be no longer needed (for example, what we had for dinner last week) or we may need to 'update' information, (such as when a friend changes address – forgetting the old address helps us to remember the new more effectively. Forgetting also has advantages where memories are stressful, painful or embarrassing.

Encoding failure

The idea that material in STS may be forgotten because it is displaced by new items has already been discussed (see page 640). Material is lost through an encoding failure – it is not transferred from STS to LTS as the limited capacity of STS is exceeded.

Storage failure

Storage failure appears to be fundamental to forgetting, causing permanent unavailability of an item in STS or LTS. Loss of material from STS was investigated by Brown (1958) and Peterson and Peterson (1959). Participants had to recall verbal items after varying lengths of time, during which they counted backwards to prevent rehearsal. From the results they suggested that trace decay eroded the proportion of remembered items over time, in a way similar to figure 18.13. They assumed that the remembered items had been coded in LTS.

In LTS, it is difficult to test for storage failure; one cannot separate the situation where something is forgotten from one in which memory fails due to the use of inappropriate cues. Storage failure can thus arise from the unavailability of material or

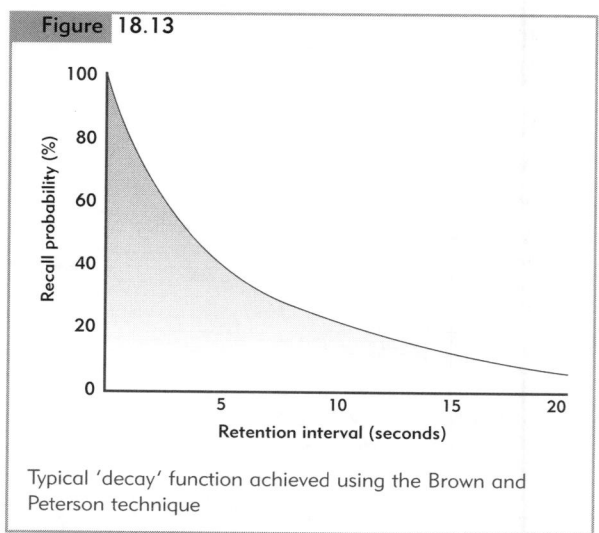

Figure 18.13

Typical 'decay' function achieved using the Brown and Peterson technique

from inaccessibility whereby stored material can not be accessed. Therefore, storage failure often becomes a 'default' explanation for forgetting when retrieval failure cannot explain it.

Do we forget simply because material is no longer used? Thorndike (1936) proposed the Law of Disuse, which states that memories deteriorate with time if they are not used. Ebbinghaus (1885) demonstrated this deterioration in an introspective study (using self as the subject) when he learned lists of nonsense syllables such as 'JEK'. After periods ranging from minutes to 31 days, he measured the number of trials required to relearn these. He presented his results as the percentage 'savings' made in the number of trials needed to do this. 'Savings' were greatest in the first hour after initial learning but then decreased, resulting in a concave curve now known to be typical of forgetting in general.

Disuse has weaknesses as an explanation for forgetting. Although forgetting and disuse may be related, we cannot state that memories deteriorate because of disuse over time, as this tells us nothing about what actually happens to the memory concerned. McGeoch (1932) used an analogy to a parallel line of argument: 'in time iron, when unused, may rust but oxidation, not time, is responsible'. Similarly with memory it must be factors, which occur over time, that cause it to break down.

Retrieval failure

Retrieval failure is also fundamental to forgetting, and can be demonstrated when subjects can retrieve information under one condition, but not under another. *Context* is central to this concept. For example, disguises can affect facial memory (Patterson and Baddeley, 1977), a change in clothing can adversely affect memory (Thompson *et al.*, 1982) and even a change in expression (Parkin and Goodwin, 1983). A change in verbal context produces similar results – retrieval may fail when recognition is attempted, if the target word is processed in a context different from the original one. For example, Light and Carter-Sobell (1970) showed that 'jam' was retrieved less often when paired with traffic, if it had been originally presented in the context of food. As Zechmeister and Nyberg (1982) put it: 'a (movie) star is not a (twinkling) star is not a (sheriff's) star is not a (Christmas) star'. The influence of context is also shown by Godden and Baddeley's (1975) study of divers and in *state-dependent forgetting* (see page 649).

Penfield (1958) described surgery he carried out in the 1940s to relieve epileptic seizures. As few neurons register pain in the human brain, the operations were partially conducted under local anaesthetic. Some patients reported vivid, often trivial recollections when their temporal lobes were electrically stimulated. This led Penfield to believe that nothing was ever actually lost from memory; what was lost was *access* to this information.

Loftus and Loftus (1980) criticised Penfield's data by showing that less than eight per cent of his patients had these vivid recollections – and less than a third of these showed genuine recall. Despite this, Penfield's views on the permanence of memories are still widely held, for example by hypnotists.

There are also practical difficulties in using retrieval failure to explain forgetting. It is harder to establish if information is lost from LTS, than it is from STS. Also, the explanation allows no role for motivation in forgetting.

Retrieval failure assumes that forgetting is unconscious, yet sometimes we have a conscious 'feeling of knowing' when we cannot remember something. Have you ever met someone whose face is familiar but whose name eludes you? Maddening, isn't it? Perhaps instead you find it difficult to remember the name of a book you once borrowed and would like to consult again. You know its size and colour but both title and author escape you. This experience, where you feel that you know the answer but cannot access it, is known as the *tip-of-the-tongue* (TOT) phenomenon.

Brown and McNeill (1966) read to their participants definitions of low-frequency target words such as sextant (a navigational instrument), questioning them about their thoughts if TOT states occurred. Results showed that they could often specify accurately the number of syllables in the target word, and its initial letter. Final letters, suffixes and stressed syllables were other associations quoted by some participants.

Activity 9

Why do we forget? Three factors have been discussed in the text. Try to list them.

(Suggested answers on page 668.)

Interference theory

Interference theory is based upon associations made during learning. When new associations have elements in common with old ones, they may interfere with each other causing loss of information. For example, McGeoch and MacDonald (1931) asked participants to learn a list of adjectives until they could repeat it correctly. They then either rested or performed one of a variety of tasks such as learning numbers, nonsense syllables or synonyms of the original adjectives. Results showed that the degree of forgetting increased as the interfering material became more like the original.

Two forms of interference have been recognised subsequently.

Retro-active interference occurs when new learning impairs old memories, for example when a biology lesson comes straight after psychology the biological perspective may interfere with memory of the psychological one. *Pro-active interference* takes place when old memories interfere with new learning. For example, it may take longer to learn how to change gear on a motorbike if you have previously learned how to do this on a pedal cycle.

Interference can be tested experimentally by using the arrangements shown in figure 18.14, or variations of them. This approach has been widely used (e.g. Underwood, 1957) but this explanation for forgetting lacks validity. Such experimental tasks are uncharacteristic of most everyday situations and interference effects are much less striking in everyday situations.

Activity 10

Read through List A. Try to remember the adjective associated with each noun. When you have done this, cover up the list and try to remember the adjective associated with each of the nouns listed again underneath. Repeat the procedure until you get all five adjectives right and note the number of learning trials required. Then go to List B and repeat the procedure.

List A	List B
sailor–tipsy	vicar–cheery
actor–pompous	curate–merry
politician–crafty	parson–happy
lawyer–noisy	rector–jovial
singer–doleful	priest–jaunty

Test	Test
politician?	parson?
sailor?	priest?
singer?	vicar?
lawyer?	curate?
actor?	rector?

Did you find it easier to learn List A where the nouns and adjectives are dissimilar than List B where they are similar (similarity causes more interference)?

Source: A D Baddeley (1996).

Amnesias

The term **amnesia** refers to any loss of memory. Amnesias have been classified according to duration and the nature of their effects. *Transient amnesias* are temporary inabilities to remember. They can result from carbon monoxide poisoning (e.g. from car exhausts), epileptic fits, hypoglycaemia (low blood sugar levels) or electro-convulsive therapy (using electric shock treatment deliberately to produce seizures in the hope of bringing relief to the mentally ill). Transient amnesias may also occur after 'closed head injuries' involving loss of conciousness and brain movement within the skull.

Organic amnesias are permanent, resulting from serious brain damage. They may originate from disorders like Alzheimer's Disease or Korsakoff's Syndrome, tumours, vascular defects, surgery, viral infections or injuries such as gunshot wounds.

Generally, severity of amnesia is directly related to that of the trauma concerned. Memory may fail for events occurring before the amnesia-producing trauma, a condition called *retrograde* amnesia (for subsequent events – *anterograde* amnesia). Patients with retrograde amnesia tend to recover memories for earlier events before later ones, demonstrating failure to access memory. Permanent amnesias often remain for the period immediately prior to trauma, perhaps a natural defence mechanism whereby an individual can avoid remembering something particularly unpleasant.

■ Psychopathological amnesias and emotional forgetting

These may result from anxiety-provoking or very painful memories, for example in traumatic or highly embarrassing situations, or during moral conflict. Freud (1915) used the term *repression* to describe how some patients could not consciously make memories available due to their distressing nature. It was as if a protective shell had been constructed by the person concerned. Repressed information might become accessible in certain situations, such as under hypnosis.

Freud refers to a universal tendency to forget the disagreeable. Investigations testing this have

Figure 18.14

Type of interference	Condition	Sequence of events in experiment			Outcome
		1	2	3	
Retroactive	Experimental	Learn List 1	Learn List 2	Recall List 1	Recall phase; experimental group perform significantly more poorly than control group.
	Control		Unrelated activity/rest		
Proactive	Experimental	Learn List 1	Learn List 2	Recall List 2	
	Control		Unrelated activity/rest		

Experimental arrangements for testing interference

tried to show that unpleasant memories are harder to remember than pleasant ones. There are difficulties with this as patient situations are hard to mimic. Consequently, severe interpretative and methodological problems arise. For example, participants may show response bias, being unwilling to report unpleasant memories even if they can remember them. Also, level of arousal is an uncontrolled variable (Parkin *et al.*, 1982).

Emotion can exert state-dependent effects on forgetting. Recall is more likely if it is attempted in the same emotional state as the original learning (see page 649). Bower (1981) instructed participants to keep diaries of their emotional lives for one week, later hypnotising them into pleasant or unpleasant moods. Those hypnotised into pleasant moods forgot more unpleasant events; those in unpleasant moods forgot more pleasant ones. Clark and Teasdale (1981) showed that patients with low levels of depression tend to have more pleasant memories and those with high levels of depression less pleasant memories.

Profound psychopathological amnesias can be displayed in several ways; the best known of which are fugue states, the adoption of multiple personalities and hysterical amnesias. Fugue states can occur after personal crisis, an individual failing

to cope with reality and taking flight from it. The affected person is unaware of the symptoms which may involve total forgetfulness of past events, taking on a new identity and wandering away from familiar surroundings. Such a state would be unrecognisable to someone unknown to the person affected. Little or no organic damage is suffered. Although these states are normally of short duration, Pratt (1977) recorded a case lasting 15 years.

Multiple personality states are rare, occurring where a person adopts two or more personalities – 16 in the case of 'Sybil' (Schreiber, 1974). In such states, one personality (A) may be known to another (B) but B is not known to A and the 'controlling' personality may vary. They are apparently a response to traumatic personal events, for example Sybil was a victim of abuse by her mother. The existence of multiple personality states is open to question. In the case of the Hillside Strangler, Kenneth Bianchi, the prosecution called Martin Orne as an expert witness. Orne demonstrated that Bianchi's multiple personalities were a faked attempt to avoid the death penalty (Orne *et al.*, 1984).

Hysterical amnesias are more common and are associated with specific traumas. They are characterised by events resembling fits, during which contact is lost with reality and some re-enactment of the 'forgotten' event takes place. Recall of the traumatic incident is only possible under exceptional circumstances.

■ Theoretical implications of amnesia

Studying amnesiacs helps to provide evidence for the separate existence of STS and LTS. Amnesiacs typically have a seriously damaged LTS, yet intact linguistic abilities and STS. For example, in a classic case study reported by Milner (1968, 1971) the patient, HM, underwent surgery for the relief of severe epilepsy. Tissue removal from both temporal lobes of his brain left him with a severe anterograde amnesia. After the operation he could not learn an address or where he had put things and repeatedly asked the same questions. However, his IQ had not deteriorated, he could converse, perform everyday tasks and had a normal short-term memory span.

It appears that LTS is selectively damaged. For example, on a range of tests involving the retention of new material such as free recall tasks, Baddeley and Warrington (1970) showed a difference in the strength of primacy effects between amnesiacs and controls; both showed similar recency effects, yet primacy effects were markedly weaker for amnesiacs – evidence for the separate existence of short-term and long-term memory stores.

In Atkinson and Shiffrin's multi-store model, information must pass through STS, which acts as the memory's control centre, to get to LTS. A totally defective STS should therefore be impossible (a person would be unconscious). However, KF, a patient described by Shallice and Warrington (1970) had an auditory digit span of only one. Baddeley and Hitch's (1974) working memory model can perhaps account for this unusual pattern of recall, if the deficit was not in KF's 'central executive' but in one of its slave systems, perhaps the articulatory loop.

The extent of LTS impairment in amnesiacs is debatable but consistent trends emerge which provide some support for Tulving's (1985) division of the LTS into episodic, procedural and semantic components. Procedural memory is apparently preserved, as is shown by the ability to use previously acquired motor skills. Semantic memory can be substantially spared, as demonstrated, for example, by normal reading abilities, being able to understand conversation, and normal intelligence test performance. However, some impairment in semantic memory is indicated by Korsakoff's Syndrome, patients who cannot define new words from their immediate pre-trauma period (Nyssen, 1956) and by amnesiacs failing to acquire new general knowledge. Indeed, it is worth pointing out that semantic memory tasks which can be performed by amnesiacs are those acquired early in life – perhaps amnesia should be regarded as a failure of more recent memories.

The major difficulties experienced by a typical amnesiac concern failure of episodic memory; amnesiacs cannot easily remember personal events, either from after the amnesia (including trauma) or the more recent period before it. However, it remains possible that the episodic and semantic memory systems are interrelated – semantic memory may depend on episodic function. Cohen and Squire (1980) suggested the term declarative memory as incorporation of both episodic and semantic memory, amnesia being a deficit in this. Amnesiacs may be able to learn new things, although they have no conscious awareness of when or where the original learning took place, or what they learned. More often, the tasks which indicate that memory is unimpaired involve dealing with a situation that incidentally allows some previous experience to help the amnesiac to cope.

Craik and Lockhart's (1972) levels of processing approach, in which semantically processed material is better retained, may be used to discuss the idea that amnesia is a specific deficit in the encoding procedure. If this is so, retrograde amnesia is hard to explain. However, retrograde amnesia is less evident when patients are concentrating on a cognitively demanding task. Therefore the deeper the level of processing taking place at the time of trauma, the less extensive is the retrograde amnesia. It is possible that consolidation or integration of traces may be more rapid with deeper processing. Butters and Cermak (1980) showed that amnesiac patients sometimes fail to encode material semantically. However, forcing amnesiacs to process items deeply (semantically) does not greatly affect their memory loss. It must also be pointed out that amnesiacs need semantic processing in order both to read and understand conversation. It appears on the face of it to be an artificial distinction to separate these two types of semantic processing.

Our knowledge of amnesia, as with that of memory processes in general, is far from complete. Controversy remains over whether there is one or more forms of amnesia. Detailed knowledge of the brain damage involved is rare. Researchers are also faced with small samples from which it is difficult to generalise. It should not be surprising, therefore, that no one approach to memory is able to accommodate all the available information.

Self-assessment questions

11 Explain what is meant by the idea that problems of forgetting arise due to difficulties in the availability of material.

12 What evidence is there to support the interference theory of forgetting?

13 Outline three types of amnesia.

14 Discuss the Freudian idea that repression explains forgetting.

15 Give one reason why it is useful to study amnesiacs.

(Suggested answers on page 699.)

Practical applications of memory research

This section examines three areas in which memory research has practical benefits. It considers ways in which memory can be improved, memory for medical information and the implications of work in eye-witness testimony.

Improving memory

The answer to 'Can I improve my memory?' is 'yes' but this depends on using active techniques and persevering with them. Organisation helps; the use of context and categorised systems has been discussed on pages 648–53. Techniques used for committing material to memory or improving it are known as **mnemonics**, from the Greek 'mneme' meaning 'memory'.

The first mnemonic based on visual imagery was devised by the Greek poet Simonides in about 500 BC. He was invited to attend a banquet following a wrestling victory at the Olympic Games. He was called away from the banquet and soon after the floor of the banqueting hall collapsed, killing and mutilating the guests. Simonides had such a good visual memory he could remember where most of the guests had been sitting when he had left, so he was able to identify the bodies for family burials. He went on to devise a visual mnemonic system which involved visualising a room in detail and placing various items around the room. When he wanted to remember the items he scanned the room in his mind's eye.

Chunking during encoding

On page 640 you read about the number of items which can be held in STS. Ericsson et al. (1980) were interested in magic number 7 and worked with a participant (SE, a long-distance runner), who had a normal memory span and average intelligence for an undergraduate. For 20 months he spent three to five hours a week on memory-span tasks involving digits. By devising a strategy of recoding these into running times, he could store lists of 12 digits as *chunks* of four digits each (for example, 3:49.2 'near world record mile time'). He supplemented this with ages (89.3 'very old man') and dates (1944 'near the end of World War II'). Using this system, his memory span increased from seven to 28 digits. Then he organised the chunks into a hierarchy of 'groups' and 'supergroups', until eventually he could retrieve an average of almost 80 digits.

However, when tested on consonants, SF's memory span reverted to 'about six' items. It seems he was unable to increase his STS capacity through practice; his increase in digit span was due to the use of mnemonic associations in LTS. Chunking is helpful, though, when you need to store large amounts of information. Take, as an example, learning a poem. You first look through the words, then 'chunk' them into lines, verses and finally the whole poem. Thus, at recall, one word may evoke the complete work. However, it is necessary to make the chunks meaningful, possibly through other associations in LTS.

Activity in acquisition

Suppose you put aside two hours each day to study. When you have read all your notes once, you read them again . . . and again, hoping that you will remember more each time. You may do but far more people find they know just as much – or little – however many times they read something.

Gates (1917) found that subjects reading continuously remembered less than if they *actively* asked themselves questions as they read. Ideas like this have led to memory improvement techniques, for example the *PQRST method* of Thomas and Robinson (1982) who wanted to help students remember textbook material. The letters refer to its stages of preview, question, read, self-recitation and test. The preview stage helps to organise the material by rapidly scanning it, to get an idea of the major topics and sections. After the preview, questions are asked, derived from the headings of each section. The 'read' stage tries to answer these questions. Self-recitation encourages retrieval practice by involving vocal or sub-vocal recall at the end of a section. The test phase, at the end of a chapter, helps learning by recalling facts and seeing how these relate to one another. PQRST thus involves three basic principles beneficial to memory organisation, elaboration and practice.

You may like to try this method to help you understand this unit.

Feedback

Feedback is 'learning about how you did'. It can help to reinforce a memory trace. The closer it is to the

act of learning and the more detailed, the stronger the trace becomes. The latter stages of the PQRST technique can be thought of as using feedback to reinforce verbal traces.

Activity 11

Feedback may also be applied to motor tasks. Collect together a blindfold, paper, pencil and ruler. Sit at a table with the pencil, paper and ruler in convenient positions in front of you and blindfold yourself. Try to draw ten lines on the paper, each 10 cm in length (condition 1) and then remove the blindfold. Measure each line and record your results.

For the next two conditions you will need help. First draw another ten lines wearing the blindfold but this time ask your helper to say if the line is too long or too short each time you draw one.

Then repeat with ten more lines but this time ask your helper to tell you exactly how much longer or shorter your lines are.

Finally, repeat condition 1.

Tabulate the error sizes for each condition. Find the mean error by adding all errors in that condition and dividing by ten, ignoring minus signs. Did your error decrease as feedback became more specific? What about the last condition? Did you maintain the improvement or did your mean error increase again?

Quality of feedback helps confidence grow. In turn, this both increases the enjoyment of the task and the motivation to improve. You may already have discovered this, for example when you have homework or coursework returned to you. Practice creates well-worn pathways of associations in the brain which in turn increase retrieval abilities.

Imagery and encoding

Imagery (discussed on page 649) can help the organisation of memory. The more bizarre the image, the better able you are to remember it. If you find it difficult to learn new concepts because you cannot remember the new words, images may help by making comparisons with something familiar. Such a technique could help you with revision. For instance, it may be helpful to compare the nervous system with an image of a telephone switchboard. The neural connections linking all parts of the body to the brain could be imagined as 'wires' from a switchboard connecting many different locations.

When learning languages it can be useful to connect corresponding words with images linking them. Pressley *et al.* (1982) showed that this *mnemonic keyword method* of learning works well. It aims to identify part of a foreign word that sounds familiar and then form an image connecting it with the English word. The French word for umbrella is 'parapluie'. Parachute could be the key word and the image connecting them could be like that in figure 18.15.

Suppose you wanted to learn about memory so that you could tell your friends about it without referring to any notes. You could divide the subject into small areas such as 'approaches' and 'remembering', then imagine each in a different room in your house. When you give your talk, walk through your house in your imagination, 'reading off' topics from each room in turn. You could also sub-divide each room by using the furniture. For instance, take the area 'approaches'. If you put that in the hallway you could imagine floor tiles representing 'structural models' and the stair carpet as 'levels of processing'. In ways like this, ancient scholars and bards stored knowledge and relayed it to their disciples, a technique now called the *method of loci*.

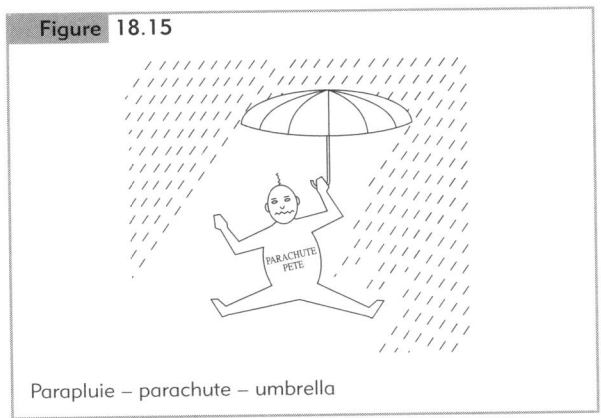

Figure 18.15

Parapluie – parachute – umbrella

Mnemonics

Verbal mnemonics try to improve organisation when encoding takes place, for example PQRST is an easy way to remember Thomas and Robinson's (1982) memory improvement technique. Perhaps you have used 'every good boy deserves favour' for remembering the line notes on a music score or 'Richard of York gave battle in vain' for the colours of the spectrum. These verbal mnemonics are, in fact, a combination of loci, associations and imagery. They work best if you need to remember several items together, such as the music notes on a score or the items on shopping lists. Unlike music notes which remain the same, shopping lists alter each time you go shopping, so a *peg-word* system is needed where each peg-word is associated with a particular list position. One set of these enables you to remember an infinite number of difference lists.

Miller *et al.* (1960) looked to rhyming for their peg-words. For example, 'two is a shoe', 'nine is a line'. Using this system, list items are associated with peg-words and imagined in improbable ways. Associations are easier to remember if unusual or bizarre. For instance, if milk was the second item on your shopping list you might imagine a shoe spilling over with milk. The peg-words must be learned first in order to use the system, but once learned they are there for any list you need to remember.

Other examples of mnemonics using rhyming include 'I before E except after C' and '30 days hath September, April, June and November'. It seems that the rhythmic pattern helps us to remember, as do the rhymes, by reducing the number of retrieval possibilities.

Chaining material to be learned into narrative stories can also help remembering. Bower and Clark (1969) asked participants to make stories from lists of ten unrelated nouns. Subsequently, 93 per cent showed correct recall, compared to only 13 per cent for control participants who were not asked to create stories but who had spent the time studying the lists. You might like to try this using your own lists of words.

Memory improvement techniques can be used to help boost the quality of life for people suffering memory loss, such as those with Alzheimer's

Disease and stroke victims. Relatives, too, benefit from any improvement. Diaries and daily timetables may act as prompts for routine activities and the use of cueing devices such as alarm clocks may help improve their success. Use of mnemonic aids, such as those based on rhymes, initial letters or imagery, may also be of benefit.

Whatever approach is used, verbal mnemonics help memory by shortening the sequence to be learned or elaborating it, and giving it meaning.

Activity 12

THE PEG-WORD SYSTEM
Learn the following set of peg-words that rhyme with the numbers one to ten.

one	bun
two	shoe
three	knee
four	door
five	hive
six	sticks
seven	heaven
eight	gate
nine	vine
ten	hen

Write down ten nouns, which can be visualised, and which you would like to learn. Learn each word on your list by combining it with images in the peg-word list above. For example, if your first word is mouth you might imagine a mouth with a bun sticking out of it. If your second word is tree you might imagine a shoe growing on a tree and so on. Using this method it is easy to answer questions like 'What is the seventh item on the list'?

Remembering to do things: prospective memory

Memory is often thought of as recalling things from the past, but there is another angle to memory, and that is our ability to carry out our intentions, for example to remember to switch the video on to record at a certain time, to take some tablets, or telephone someone at a certain time. When we forget to carry out our intentions, the consequences can be embarrassing or occasionally disastrous.

Wilkins and Baddeley (1978) investigated taking tablets as a task that is dependent on **prospective memory**. They simulated a tablet-taking routine by asking 31 participants to press a button on a small box at 8.30 am, 1 pm, 5.30 pm and 10 pm each day for one week. If they were for any reason late they still had to press the button. The box device recorded the time the button was pressed.

The results showed most responses to be within five minutes of the target time. Towards the end of the week there were more late responses. Late responses were most likely at 1.00 pm and 5.30 pm. There was no relationship between the activities the participants were engaged in and late responses. As it was not possible to control the activities participants engaged in whilst taking part in this study, it was not really possible to indicate the factors involved in prospective memory accuracy or lateness. The study involved a simulation of a real-world situation, but the lack of control or description of the conditions when recall occurs, or fails to occur, impeded the identification of factors which are important in prospective memory. Identifying what happens in memory to allow recall to occur is an important research area.

Another area of research in prospective long-term memory has been people's memory to comply with appointments. Failure to keep appointments with dentists or at hospitals can be costly in terms of time and resources. Some studies have involved manipulating reminders to effect attendance. Gates and Colborn (1976) compared letter reminder, which produced 84 per cent attendance, with telephone reminders, which produced 80 per cent attendance. A control group with no reminder produced 55 per cent attendance. The difference between non-attendance and attendance prompted by a reminder is greater when the time between appointments is a long one.

Prospective memory needs links with the usage of memory aids to cue recall. Surveys of the use of memory aids (e.g. Harris, 1980) identify diaries, shopping lists and notes as important. In order to provide practical advice on how to improve prospective memory, more work needs to be done on the factors involved in accurate prospective memory, the use of appropriate external memory aids and mnemonic techniques. One encouraging factor for people (though not for researchers) in studies of prospective memory is that errors are fairly rare. In a study by James (1990) only nine out of 140 participants forgot to change the clock for British Summer Time. The small number involved makes the identification of important factors difficult. As yet, there is little practical advice on improving prospective memory that has the support of empirical studies. The use of external retrieval aids can be helpful provided they are part of a regular routine. Mnemonic devices can be useful provided the initial effort of investment in them is not too great.

Memory for medical information

Ley (1978) researched recall of medical information. Surprisingly, despite the importance of the doctor's advice and information, Ley found that recall was estimated at 43–63 per cent. Elderly people recalled less than younger people and those with some medical knowledge recalled more than those with little medical knowledge. Levels of anxiety in patients seemed to matter. Those with low or high levels of anxiety forgot most, whilst those with moderate levels had better recall. The amount of information given to patients was inversely related to the amount of information recalled. Probably due to the primacy effect, patients recalled diagnosis better than advice or information given. From his work, Ley produced six suggestions for doctors:

- Give instructions and advice first.

- Stress the importance of instructions and advice.
- Use short words and short sentences.
- Use explicit categories such as; this is the treatment you will need, this is what you must do to help yourself. The doctor should announce the category then supply the information.
- Repeat the information.
- Be specific. For example, say 'You must lose seven pounds', rather than 'You must lose some weight'.

Eye-witness testimony

One of the most fruitful applications of psychological research since the 1970s has been in the understanding and assistance psychologists have provided in the area of the reliability of eye-witness testimony. It is vital to be able to judge whether eye-witness testimonies are reliable. Though mistaken identity is difficult to estimate, it has been suggested that false convictions based on this may be as high as 5 per cent in the USA (Radin 1964). In the UK, the Devlin Committee (1976) analysed over 2000 identification parades held in England and Wales in 1973 and discovered that in 350 cases eye-witness identification was the only evidence of guilt and in 74 per cent of cases resulted in conviction (Taylor, 1994).

Psychologists have identified factors which may lead to inaccurate recall and identification and have suggested techniques which may facilitate more accurate recall. A framework for consideration of eye-witness testimony has been put forward by Fruzzetti et al. (1992). This involves thinking about what happens in:

- the perception of events
- the retention of information about the event
- the retrieval of the memories.

The perception of events
Perception factors relate to the witness and the event itself. Age is one witness factor. Adults provide more information about an event than

children, though children can show adult levels of accuracy on topics of particular interest to them (King and Yuille, 1987). There is evidence that children are susceptible to leading questions (Goodman and Read, 1986), though this is a controversial point. From a review of literature discussing children used as witnesses, Davies (1989) concluded that children aged between six and seven and ten and eleven years are not inaccurate in their memories of an event, they are not given to invention, they do not deliberately lie in testimonies and their memory for important details is not significantly altered by adult suggestion after the event. The differences between child and adult recall may have been overstated. Recall from older people is not as detailed as that of young or middle-aged adults (List, 1986).

Do the police give more accurate eye-witness testimonies than people in other occupations? Yuille (1984) showed they gave more details at a greater level of accuracy and were less influenced by post-event questioning, but other studies (Tickner and Poulton, 1975) showed no difference between police and civilian recall. Whatever the evidence, it is seems likely that courts expect the police to have better recall and that this may weight the influence of evidence by the police.

Do people who feel stressed at an event they have witnessed suffer poorer recall? Applying the Yerkes–Dodson Law (1908), performance relates to stress in a curvilinear fashion. Low and high stress should produce a poorer performance than moderate stress which facilitates performance. Naturalistic studies do not always back up this prediction. In one study carried out between four and five months after a shooting in which one person had been killed and another person injured, 13 witnesses were interviewed (Yuille and Cutshall, 1986). Although the event had been very stressful, recall was accurate and the level of stress reported at the time of the crime was not significantly related to subsequent recall. However, one confounding variable may have been that the higher stressed witnesses were standing closer to the crime and may simply have got a better view, aiding later recall.

It has also been shown that expectations are an important witness factor in the perception of an event. There may be as many biases in perception as there are witnesses where expectations differ. Certainly at any football match perceptions of the same game and of the referee's performance will differ with the expectations of opposing fans.

Perception factors relating to the event itself may also affect testimonies. Longer exposure time to events increases accuracy, although people do overestimate the duration of events they observe. Loftus *et al.* (1987b) showed participants a 30-second tape of a simulated bank robbery. When participants were asked how long the robbery had lasted, the average estimate was two-and-a-half minutes. Details of size, clothing and face were lost when there was a weapon focus. Loftus *et al.* (1987a) monitored eye movements in participants shown one of two films of an encounter in restaurant, one with and one without weapon. Participants in the weapon version fixated on the gun and were subsequently less able to identify the robber from photographs. The violence of an event has also been investigated. In one study (Clifford and Hollin, 1981), participants were shown the same film except that a violent scene was included for half the participants in the experimental group. In the violent scene, a woman was stopped by a man and forced backwards into a wall, at which point her handbag was taken. The woman was left crying. In the film without the violent scene, the man merely asked the woman for directions. Participants who saw the violent scene were less accurate in their answers to subsequent questions. The mental shock associated with violence apparently disrupted the memory processes.

■ The retention of information about the event

Does information change whilst it is being retained? Can memories change in storage? That information is forgotten with the passage of time was shown by Ebbinghaus (1885) at the end of the nineteenth century. More recently, Wagenaar and Groeneweg (1990) compared testimonies and documentary evidence from 78 concentration camp victims. Witnesses agreed on basic facts, but many details were forgotten. Out of 36 witnesses tortured by Marinus De Rijke at a concentration camp, 35 remembered his name after 40 years, although the names of guards, which had been reported at early interviews were largely forgotten. There is evidence to suggest that memories can be augmented once the original trace has been stored. Overhearing other witnesses increases the likelihood of recall of something not originally noticed. Participants may compromise memories they have with later details they acquire. Loftus (1975) showed 40 witnesses a three-minute video of a lecture that was disrupted by eight demonstrators. Half the participants were later given a questionnaire suggesting there were four demonstrators, others had it suggested that there were 12 demonstrators. A week later those told there had been 12 demonstrators reported an average of 8.9. Those told there were four demonstrators reported an average of 6.4. In this instance a compromise seemed to arise between the actual and the post-event information. Another area of investigation of stored memories is whether people, under certain circumstances, actually report non-existent objects. Loftus *et al.* (1978) showed participants slides involving an accident between a car and a pedestrian. Half the participants were shown a slide of a red car turning a corner near a stop sign, the other half were shown a slide of the car passing a give way sign. Once round the corner, the car was seen to hit a pedestrian. Following the slide sequence, participants were immediately asked questions, including one which mentioned a give way or stop sign. For half the participants, the question matched the actual scene presented, for the other half the question mentioned the existence of a sign they had not seen. Later the participants were asked to identify the slides they had seen. For those who had received consistent information, 75 per cent picked the slide they had actually been shown. Only 41 per cent of those who had been given inconsistent information chose the correct slide. (If they had simply guessed they should have been right 50 per cent of the time.) Thus it can be seen that post-event information has a powerful influence.

Central details of an event are thought to be less malleable to change. In a 1979 study, Loftus demonstrated that if misleading information is central to what happened, participants are not misled. Participants were shown slides of a man stealing a red purse. They were later read a narrative account of the theft in which it was suggested that the purse was brown. Participants were not, however, misled and reported the purse was red. It would appear it is difficult to mislead people, post event, on central information, but much easier to mislead on peripheral information. Whether misinformation replaces the original memory or whether the two memories coexist has proved difficult to establish conclusively. In a number of studies Loftus has demonstrated the 'misinformation effect' whereby original memories are changed by subsequent information, but it is possible that the two memories coexist as Christiaansen and Ochalek (1983) suggested. They showed participants slides depicting a crime. Two days later, participants read a narrative story of the slide sequence. For one group the narrative was accurate; for the other group the narrative contained some inaccurate details. Forty-five minutes after the misleading narrative the misled participants were informed there had been some discrepancies between the narrative and the slide sequence. Those who were told this recalled the information from the original sequence accurately despite having been misled by the narrative. The original memory had not been altered by the misleading facts supplied afterwards. Research in this area has not yet provided a definitive conclusion.

■ The retrieval of memories

Does the manner in which memories are retrieved affect the accuracy or the amount of information retrieved? Does the answer received depend on the question asked? It is well established that police and lawyers should take care to avoid asking leading questions. Multiple-choice questions can produce erroneous answers. Open-ended questions produce least complete answers. Specific questions with open-ended answers allow the police to probe for what might otherwise not be recalled. Combinations of open-ended description by the witness and specific questioning by the interviewer to probe into the 'gaps' produces the greatest detail whilst minimising bias. Further details of information from other witnesses should not be given in order to minimise post-event changes. Non-verbal cues from the interviewer, for example nodding in agreement, may reinforce errors and encourage guessing. Even single words used in a question can influence memory. For example, Harris (1973) asked 'How tall was the basketball player?' as opposed to 'How short was the basketball player?' A 26 cm mean difference was produced by this one word change. This finding is in line with much of Loftus's early work which shows a single word change can influence memory recall dramatically. How then can recall be aided? The use of a cognitive interview seems to be promising method for improving recall. Geiselman *et al.* (1985) described the cognitive interview method. Four techniques are placed in front of the witness as a guide during the interview. The techniques are read by the interviewer at the start of the interview. They are:

- Reinstate the context surrounding the incident and how you were thinking and feeling at the time.
- Report everything you can remember, whether or not you think it is important.
- Report things in a different order, for example

from end to beginning as well as from beginning to end.

- Try to recall the incident from different perspectives, as if you were standing somewhere else, or were one of other people at the scene.

These techniques are designed to create as many recall cues as possible in the hope of triggering otherwise unrecalled details. It has been shown that the cognitive interview produces greater accuracy than hypnosis or the standard police interview. Nor does it lead to the generation of incorrect information. It thus demonstrates a significant contribution of applied psychology.

Psychologists have also contributed to the effective use of identity parades. It has been shown that identity parades are more successful at picking a suspect where witnesses do not feel nervous (Ainsworth and King, 1988). Reducing the level of stress by the use of one-way mirrors and familiarisation with the procedure should therefore also help. Where photographs have been shown to witnesses prior to an identification parade, suspects seen in the photographs are more likely to be picked out of a parade, even when they were not involved in the original crime. It has been further demonstrated that the confidence of witnesses affects the judgment of judges and juries. Yet, those who are confident are not significantly more reliable. Judges and juries need to be warned about this.

Self-assessment questions

16 Describe the PQRST method of learning.

17 Name two visual mnemonic methods and suggest where they may be used.

18 What is prospective memory? Why has it proved difficult to investigate so far?

19 State three factors which have been identified in helping memory of medical information.

20 Suggest three areas which have been identified as possible sources of bias or unreliability in eye-witness testimony studies.

(Suggested answers on page 669.)

Unit summary

- The *phenomenological* approach to the processing of memory is associated with Bartlett (1932) and *structural models* such as the *multi-store* model consider the whole memory framework whereas the *working memory* model focuses on processing in the early stages of memory. *Levels of processing* are linked to perception, attention and ability to recall.

- Evidence to support these approaches has been difficult to demonstrate without considering the effect of other factors on levels of processing.

- It is possible to identify different variables which may be important in memory retention. Psychologists have tried to explain the *organisation* that occurs in memory, especially in the LTS. The use of categories, hierarchies and imagery as organisational devices facilitates recall.

- The *context* in which a memory was coded or the *internal state* that an individual experienced at the time of coding seems to be important in the way a memory is organised and accessed.

- The *encoding specificity principle* in which the material available at recall links to the specific memory trace coded supports the notion of *state-* and *context-dependent* memory.

- *Semantic* memory has been thought to be hierarchically arranged, although the structural basis of the hierarchy has been variously described.

- Recent approaches to organisation such as Schank and Abelson's (1977), have stressed that *schemas* and *scripts* are important as units of organisation.

- Distinctions have been drawn between *declarative (episodic and semantic)* memories and *procedural* memories.

- *Explicit* memories require conscious effort whilst *implicit* memories resulting from priming and experience are not conscious.

- *Forgetting* can occur during the encoding, storage or retrieval of information. It occurs due to unavailability arising from problems in encoding or storage, or inaccessibility which is associated with difficulties in retrieval. Forgetting can also occur due to amnesia of a transient, organic or psychopathological type.

- Problems of encoding and storage can be due to displacement, trace decay or interference.

- Retrieval failure can occur when the memory trace is not cued.

- Experiments have shown memory to be context- and state-dependent.

- The *TOT phenomenon* suggests that though we 'forget' we have a 'feeling of knowing' and that the problem lies in retrieval.

- *Interference* affecting recall can be pro-active, or retro-active.

- Similarity between material usually creates interference, though this effect is much more marked in the laboratory than in real life.

- Studies to *amnesic* patients have theoretical implications linking types of forgetting to models of memory and types of memory.

- The practical applications of memory research are numerous.

- A number of factors have been suggested for improving memory: chunking, active acquisition of a trace, feedback to strengthen a trace, imagery and *mnemonics*.

- *Prospective memory*, or remembering to do things, has also been considered as well as research into memory for medical information.

- A large number of factors have been investigated, relating to the question of *reliability of eye witnesses*. These factors focus on accuracy in perception of the event, ability to store a memory accurately and the ability to retrieve a memory completely and without bias.

- Psychologists have been able to contribute a number of insights to the legal profession to assist in producing accurate evidence and identification of suspects.

Terms to define

amnesia
dual coding hypothesis
encoding specificity principle
episodic memory
explicit memory
implicit memory
levels of processing
memory

mnemonics
multi-store model
procedural memory
prospective memory
semantic memory
serial position effect
working memory

Further reading

Baddeley, A D (1993) *Your Memory. A User's Guide*, Prion, London.

An accessible book full of useful activities which demonstrate the theoretical points being made.

Cohen, G (1996) *Memory in the Real World*, 2nd edn, Psychology Press, Hove.

Links experimental studies with the everyday use of memory.

Eysenck, M W and Keane, M T (1995) *Cognitive Psychology: A Student's Handbook*, 3rd edn, Psychology Press, Hove.

An up-to-date, in-depth approach.

Gruneberg, M and Morris, P (1992) *Aspects of Memory: The Practical Aspects*, vol. 1, 2nd edn, Routledge, London.

Contains particularly useful chapters on eye witness testimony and memory aids.

Answers

■ Suggested answers to activities

9

■ Material is not transferred from STS to LTS (encoding failure).

■ Material is not stored (storage failure).

■ Material cannot be accessed (retrieval failure).

■ Suggested answers to self-assessment questions

1

Encoding, storage and retrieval.

2

Serial position effect studies and neurological case studies.

3

Evidence supporting the working memory model includes phonological loop, studies of phonological similarity effect, acoustic store, studies of similar sounding words, with the suppression of articulation visuo-spatial scratch pad, Shepard's folding tasks and Brooks and Baddeley's letter tasks.

4

Levels of processing: different depths of processing identified by Craik and Lockhart (1972). The levels, or depths are: the appearance of the material (orthographic processing), the sound of the words in the material (phonological processing) and the meaning of the words in the material (semantic processing). According to Craik and Lockhart (1972), the greater the depth of processing the stronger the memory trace.

5

The multi-store model suggests two processes, in the STS and LTS. Levels of processing do not suggest separate stores, but that the depth of processing determines the trace strength. Multi-store suggests the amount of rehearsal determines the storage of a trace, whilst levels of processing suggest the type of rehearsal is critical in determining whether the memory is stored.

6

Categories and hierarchies group and structure the material in a meaningful way, producing chunks of meaningful material rather than a random arrangement of many disjointed words.

7

Words which can be imaged can be dual coded, once visually, once verbally, double the memory trace to be used for retrieval purposes. Words which cannot be imaged are only coded once.

8

State refers to the internal emotional state in which the learning took place. Context refers to the external environment in which the learning took place. Encoding specificity principle refers to the conditions under which the trace was encoded. Reproducing the state or context connects with the way the trace was encoded and hence is likely to aid recall.

9

Schemas and scripts are both based on the idea that the brain stores concepts or ideas in an organised way and uses these to interpret new information. In other words, the stored past experiences influence the data which arrive from the senses.

10

Explicit memory is the process of performing a task which uses conscious recollection of past experiences. Implicit memory is the process of performing a task in the absence of conscious recollection of past experiences.

11

Problems of availability refer to the difficulty of accessing material which has not been encoded and/or stored adequately in memory. These problems can occur in the STS and LTS. It is most likely that material in the STS has not adequately been coded and thus does not reach the LTS. Hence the desired material is not stored and is unavailable for recall. Problems of accessibility refer to the difficulty of accessing material which is stored. For example, we know an old school friend, but cannot remember their name (which we know perfectly well) yet we are sure that we know their name. The name is stored, but cannot be accessed.

12

Evidence to support the interference theory of forgetting: McGeogh and McDonald (1931) and studies of pro-active and retro-active interference such as Underwood (1957).

13

Transient amnesia: temporary inability to remember. Organic amnesia: permanent inability to remember resulting from brain damage. Psychopathological amnesia: inability to remember resulting from emotional trauma.

14

People bury emotional, traumatic experiences by choosing to 'forget' them. Repression cannot explain why people forget desirable or emotionally neutral experiences. People do forget things they really want to remember, and this does not fit the repression model.

15

Amnesiacs can provide empirical evidence to support theoretical models. They provide information about the physical functioning of the brain.

16

It creates an active process of studying, using preview, question, read, self-recitation and test.

17

Choose from:
- Method of loci for remembering a list of items, or key ideas.
- Peg-word system for remembering items in a fixed order, useful when delivering a speech, or trying to recall an agenda when the order of delivery matters.
- Key-word system, making visual connections between English and foreign language vocabulary. Useful for learning vocabulary in foreign languages.

18

Prospective memory refers to the ability to carry out intentions, to remember to do things in the time ahead. It can be difficult to investigate because it is often difficult to control the activities participants are engaged in whilst taking part in the studies, thus the factors involved in prospective memory are hard to identify.

19

Choose three from:
- Having some medical knowledge;
- Being younger;
- Moderate levels of anxiety;
- The primacy effect operates so the diagnosis which is given first is better recalled than advice and information given later.

20

Three sources of bias or unreliability in eye-witness testimonies: in the perception of the event; in the storage of the memory; and in the retrieval of the memory. Examples could be weapons or violence or age of witnesses in the perception of the event. The impact of leading questions or later information added could change the memory. The type of questioning used to retrieve the event could influence the memory.

Unit 19

Language and Thought

Sharon Cheyne, Tony Malim and Graham Davies

This unit covers:

Language acquisition

Language production and comprehension

Models and explanations of human thought

The relationship between language and thought, including social and cultural variations

By the end of this unit, you should be able to:

■ understand theories and research findings in the process of language acquisition

■ discuss explanations and research findings in language production and comprehension

■ discuss models and explanations of human thought

■ assess theories and evidence relating to the relationship between language and thought, including social and cultural variations.

Unit 19   Contents

Introduction

Most species of animals have communications system. For example, Van Frisch (1955) has shown that bees convey information about food sources through dance-like movements. Animal communication systems, however, lack the flexibility of human language.

Language acquisition

Brown (1986) saw human language as an arbitrary system of symbols, which can be combined to transmit an unlimited variety of messages through a system of rules called grammar. Traditionally, transmission of language is primarily via speech, but we should not forget that it can also be signed or written down. In this section we discuss the stages that children go through to reach adult linguistic competence.

Attaining linguistic competence

As long as children have language spoken to them, linguistic competence develops along a similar timescale in all cultures and is therefore substantially maturationally determined. Psychologists have explored this universal timetable using several different research methods. The diary approach, used by Piaget to study the development of his own children, has many advantages. It is longitudinal, the researcher is familiar with the participant and can thus interpret the child's attempts at language, and the child will behave normally. However, results cannot be taken as representative and recording may also be patchy and biased. Audio- and video-tape recordings can also be used to capture the full quality of children's communication and the context in which it takes place. Higgins (1988) has produced an audio-tape of the language development of her daughter, Josephine. This illustrates the acquisition process and could profitably be listened to in conjunction with this section (see further reading on page 710). Several stages of language development have been described.

■ Prelinguistic stage: the first year
During the prelinguistic stage, most mothers quickly learn to distinguish the different cries their babies make and know whether they are, for example, hungry or simply wanting attention. From about eight weeks babies make 'cooing' sounds which associate with the baby being in a pleasurable state. By about five months old, babies enter the babbling stage when all sorts of **phonemes** (or sounds), are tried out, though 'ma' and 'da' sounds are very common. The babbling has speech-like rhythms and inflections. The number of phonemes used increases until about nine months, when phonemic contraction occurs whereby babies begin to drop sounds that are not spoken to them. During the babbling stage, sounds are often repeated, 'dadadadadadada' for example, and this is called *echolalia*.

■ One-word stage: twelve to eighteen months
At approximately one year old, infants produce their first word and enter the one-word stage. At this point words are consistently matched with objects. Babbling will continue for some time after this and is called *scribble talk*. Words are used only as labels at first, but more complex messages can be conveyed by *holophrases* – when the meaning of a single word utterance is indicated by the context in which it is used, for example 'coat' might mean 'I want to put on my coat' or 'I want to take off my coat'.

Activity 1

A child may use the word 'juice'. List how many meanings this one word may have. (Some possibilities are listed on page 710.)

Vocabulary growth is at first quite slow. Nelson (1973) found it took several months to reach the stage where ten words are used. This may be because more energy and concentration at this time is invested in learning to walk. Later, words are added more quickly. Nelson found that 50 words are typically used by 20 months, mostly relating to things children can do, touch and play with. Gesture, tone and situation add meaning to the words used.

■ Two-word stage: from 18 months

This stage subdivides into stage one grammar (18–30 months) and stage two grammar (30 months–5 years). Around 18 months to 2 years old, children start the two word stage, by putting two words together, for example 'daddy cup' and 'mummy cup'. As with many actions at this stage, words may be constantly repeated. Vocabulary now increases very rapidly, so that for example, Josephine Higgins went from about 70 words at 18 months to 529 words at 2 years (Higgins, 1988). Bee and Mitchell (1980) referred to the period 18 months to 30 months as a time of stage one grammar, where speech is typically telegraphic, where a lot of information is conveyed in a few words. This speech is a little like the language once used in telegrams, where the sender paid by the word and words were left out if meaning could be retained without them. Thus a telegram might read 'arriving 5.30 train' and similarly a child's comment on a parent asleep on the sofa might be 'daddy sleep'.

Activity 2

Look at table 19.1 which gives examples of telegraphic speech. Which words had been omitted by the child? To what extent is the meaning of the sentences clear?

The meaning of these two-word utterances is still dependant on context. The word order is also kept to a rigid sequence which aids meaning. 'Mummy cup' can mean both 'this is mummy's cup' or 'mummy is drinking from a cup'.

In stage two grammar, from about 30 months, **syntax** (rules for combining words) develops

Table 19.1

A bottle
Broke-it
Here (the) bottle
Hi daddy
Horse doggie
Broke it
It a bottle
Kitty cat
Oh a doggie
Poor daddy
Thank you
That hat?
That monkey
Want a bottle
Want bottle
What that?

Examples of telegraphic speech used by Daniel, aged 21 months (after Ingram, 1981)

rapidly and vocabulary grows so fast that it is hard to keep track of it. The mean length of utterances increases as words, omitted earlier, are included. Berko (1958) invented an animal called a 'wug' to demonstrate that 3 and 4-year-old children gradually learn to apply rules. He showed a picture of one to a child and then pointed to a picture of two of them and asked the child to complete the sentence: "Here is a wug, here are two ___.' Most children said 'wugs', thus showing that they were using a rule about plurals. In fact, all sorts of syntactic rules seem to be extracted by children from speech around them. We can see the process going on by the sometimes amusing misapplications which are made. 'We wented to the farm and sawed the sheeps', for example, contains overgeneralised rules about tense and plurals. It is important to note that these rules are not taught but extracted by the child, a point we shall return to later.

What implications does this have for any theory that language is learned? Word meanings are also overgeneralised. For example, Clark and Clark (1977) reported how the word 'ticktock' was first used by a child for a watch and later extended to refer to all clocks and watches, bathroom scales, a reel of hose and a gas meter. They suggested that children gradually narrow down the appropriate referents for words by a sort of hypothesis testing process. De Villiers and De Villiers (1979) said that children may be able to distinguish a dog from a sheep, providing that the features which distinguish them are pointed out and, more importantly, alternative words are available. Two-year-olds can tell a watch from a gas meter and will do so if they have the words. Children at this stage may also show *underextensions*, using a word more narrowly than adults do. They may, for example, use the word 'doggie' for their own family pet but not for other dogs.

By about age five, language remarkably close to that of an adult has been acquired. However, there are still some items, such as irregular words and passive sentence forms, which may present sources of difficulty. Nonetheless, children's achievement in language is spectacular. By the age of six children have mastered about 14 000 words. Contrast this with adults' difficulty in learning 1000 words in a foreign language, and children's achievement is plain.

Activity 3

Try to gain access to some books produced for use with infants who are just beginning to learn how to read. Do the number of words and sentence construction suit the stages of language acquisition of the children for whom the books are designed?

Theories of language acquisition

The acquisition of language in such a short time is a tremendous achievement for any child, but the question 'how does it happen?' was left for a long time to linguists to answer. Psychological attempts to answer it came later, following three major schools of thought: behaviourist, rationalist and cognitive. This section discusses these approaches, focusing on the theories of Skinner, Chomsky and Piaget respectively. In addition, the cognitive

approach has been extended to consider the social context of linguistic development (for example by Bruner). The cognitive approach and the social context of language development have come to be known as the interactionist approach as language development is dependent upon the child having some interaction with its physical and social world.

The behaviourist approach to language acquisition

The behaviourist approach developed early in the twentieth century as a protest against introspection, in which individuals examined and reported their own thought processes when subjected to some kind of stimulus. Behaviourists (for example Watson and Skinner) felt that the process of introspection itself could alter what was going on in the mind. They thought it was too subjective and that there was a need to investigate psychological phenomena more scientifically and objectively. They were not interested, therefore, in what went on inside the 'black box' that was the mind, but only in the stimuli which went into the mind and the scientifically observable and measurable responses that resulted.

It is important to know that the behaviourists subscribed to the view, originally put forward by the philosopher Locke in the eighteenth century, that we are born with a mind like a 'tabula rasa' (a clean sheet). This suggests that everything which we are eventually capable of doing is learned, nothing is innate. Much is learned through conditioning – the association in the mind of stimuli that occur frequently together.

Skinner's theory of language acquisition
Skinner (1957) attempted to explain language acquisition in terms of operant conditioning which proposes that behaviour is learned through the process of reinforcement. He argued that children's speech is shaped by carers selectively rewarding, both consciously and unconsciously, their children's words. Children's vocabulary thus

increases through trial and error, correct words being reinforced by getting what they asked for. Saying 'more juice' is likely to be more effective than simply crying. Receiving attention and praise for speaking could also act as reinforcers. Similarly, incorrect words are not reinforced and are subjected to the process of extinction.

Skinner perceived a basic desire for humans to communicate their needs. Hungry children, attempting to communicate hunger, might produce utterances which in the loving ears of their carers are heard as 'milk'. These might be very far away from the word as it is normally spoken. The children would then be reinforced by being offered milk and this offering might be paired with something like 'milk, darling'. Acceptance of the milk would, in turn, reinforce the carers. In this way, children's utterances gradually approximate more and more to the desired speech, a process known as shaping. Skinner called this kind of utterance a *mand,* that is one which results from the *demand* of the child for milk.

Alternatively, a stimulus might be an object or a person. A child might see, for example, a car and indicate it by making an utterance which, again, in the carer's ears is interpreted as 'car'. Reinforcement comes by the carer saying 'That's right, darling, that's a car.' Again, a shaping process leads eventually to the child producing something which is recognisable as 'car' and associating it with the object concerned. Skinner refers to an utterance of this kind as a *tact,* referring to the relationship built up between the word and the object.

Skinner also referred to echoic responses. These occur when children imitate sounds heard from others and get immediate approval. This increases the probability of the utterance occurring again in similar circumstances. Past reinforcements lead to language generalisations in other situations. Skinner also believed accents and dialects were unconsciously modelled.

■ Evaluation of Skinner's theory of language learning

There is much that is admirable and sensible in what Skinner said; learning in behaviourist terms clearly has some role to play. Can Skinner's theory fully explain language acquisition? Skinner only used very simple cases to illustrate this theory. Most of our natural verbal behaviour is not in the form of mands or tacts at all, but rather in the form of inter-verbal responses – that is, when *you* say something and *I* reply.

None of these mands or tacts get sufficient use to be conditioned reliably. For instance, a question such as 'Are you feeling well?' might elicit the responses 'yes' or 'no'. Operant conditioning theory does not allow these answers to be reinforcers for the same response. For conditioning to occur, a reinforcer cannot vary in this way.

Perhaps, most importantly, it would take several lifetimes to condition the large number of words and phrases that even a small child might use. It would be impossible, in this way, to develop the range of vocabulary that almost every adult achieves.

Skinner's theory does not take into account the fact that children frequently make creative and novel utterances, which they have never heard. They might say 'mouses', for instance, or 'he seed', or 'he goed' – all quite common amongst children. Skinner's conditioning model also depends very much on the role of parents (or carers) acting as models for their children's speech.

The problem with a conditioning approach is that it does not explain more than a very small part of the very complex process of language learning.

It is questionable whether parents shape their children's speech by selective reinforcement. Brown *et al.* (1969) tape-recorded mothers talking to their young children. They found little evidence of mothers shaping their children's grammar. Mothers responded to content rather than grammatical structure. Further, as M Eysenck (1993) points out reinforcement theory would predict children would grow up speaking truthfully but ungrammatically, when in fact the opposite is closer to what really happens.

Imitation and reinforcement do not explain the role of parents in language learning. Adults talking to young children talk differently from the way they speak to adults. This simple speech style used with young children has been called *'motherese'*, or, using less sexist terms, parentese or **baby talk register (BTR)**. Studies have shown that in, BTR, sentences are shorter, spoken in a high-pitched voice and emphasise key words. (Gelman and Shatz, 1977). For purposes of communication adults adjust the level of language to what the child can cope with. Even 4-year-olds have the capacity to simplify their language for younger children (Shatz and Gelman, 1973). So children do not directly imitate adult language, rather adults and children use BTR adapted to the child's level. Adults also extend and recast sentences in an accessible way to the child to encourage language development.

The rationalist approach to language acquisition

The rationalist approach is an opposing view to behaviourism. It starts from the premise that language is a species-specific capacity in humans. This means that just as birds fly and fishes swim the ability to learn and use language is genetically endowed, helping humans to adapt and survive.

The approach goes back to Plato's 'theory of ideas' in the fourth century BC which maintains that we have an innate idea of what constitutes a concept, for example, 'a man', 'a dog', 'a chair'. We can identify them when we meet them in real life by relating what we see to the innate idea we have.

The leading proponent of the rationalist view of language is Chomsky. His theory of language development will now be discussed.

■ Chomsky's theory of language acquisition (1957; 1965)

In contrast to Skinner, Chomsky adopted a view of language acquisition which emphasised the fact that children have an innate ability to acquire and use language. His approach incorporates the suggestion that to do this children use an inherited hypothetical blueprint called the **language acquisition device (LAD)**, which is species-specific to humans.

The theory focuses attention not on word meanings, but on syntax. It distinguishes between language performance and linguistic competence in terms of understanding and an ability to apply rules to create new sentences. Chomsky's theory attempts to explain the competence acquired in language.

Chomsky used this idea of a species-specific capacity to explain how children have an innate knowledge that there are rules governing the language they are learning – this is where the LAD comes in. It provides an ability to recognise and use the rules. Phonological rules govern the common sounds that make up words, semantic rules govern word meanings and syntactic rules control how words are strung together to form sentences. These rules are common to the underlying structures of many thousands of languages.

Chomsky's theory suggests that children are born with *transformational grammar* – an ability to translate the *surface structure* of a sentence into a deep structure of meaning and vice versa. The surface structure refers to the arrangement of words in the sentence, whilst the *deep structure* refers to the logical, grammatical relationship between the words. This is supported by certain features being common to all spoken languages, known as linguistic universals, including the existence of nouns, verbs, consonants and vowels. It is as if children are electric wordprocessors; the words stored and used depend on the language they hear spoken to them, but the machine arrives already preprogrammed to deal with language (Thomas, 1985).

The deep structure of the LAD enables humans to generate syntactically and semantically correct language through the operation of generative rewriting rules. By means of pencil and paper exercises Chomsky illustrated the existence of language structures. For example, people would recognise that the two following sentences, which look different, mean the same thing:

Joan likes James.

James is liked by Joan.

The deep structure analyses the sentences for meaning. Sentences with different surface structure can have the same deep structure meaning. For example,

They are cooking apples.

The rules of transformation help people to understand whether the apples are being described or heated.

Evidence for the existence of a LAD comes from the speed with which language is learned. Without a LAD, children would be unable to learn a language as quickly as they do. With it, language can develop naturally under the fine tuning of the environment, (i.e. through speech which the child hears). Also, nearly all children manage to learn language, even though the environments in which they are brought up vary enormously. Whatever the environment, there seems to be a similar order for the acquisition of language skills by children.

We saw on page 676 that it is very hard to explain, by learning theory alone, how children are able to break down the stream of sounds they hear into words and sentences. Children may frequently produce language which they are most unlikely to have heard from adults, for instance 'wented' or 'goed'. They create these novel forms themselves by applying linguistic rules and principles, and ungrammatical utterances such as 'me runned home' may result.

Heriot (1971) suggested that such utterances result from children attempting to apply rules of grammar and syntax, without having sufficient experience to know the irregularities. Children's speech errors tend to suggest some analysis of what they hear and generalisation from that analysis. They try to work it out and sometimes get it wrong.

It is not usually the grammar of the wrong utterances which their adult carers attend to and correct, but the content. 'Us goed to the zoo yesterday' is more likely to meet with the response 'No, you didn't, you went with me to uncle Joe's' than 'We went to the zoo'.

Support for Chomsky comes from Lenneberg (1967) who proposed that a specific biological mechanism underpins language development and that there is a *critical period* for language learning. Physical control of the speech organs would be the lower limit and puberty, according to Lenneberg, is the upper limit. Studies of children who have suffered severe language deprivation show some support for Lenneberg, at least to the extent that language is difficult to achieve after a certain period of deprivation, suggesting that there is a sensitive period within which language is most easily learned. One such case study is Genie (Curtiss, 1977). In 1970 social workers found a 13-year-old girl whose parents had locked her up in a small room since the age of 20 months. During the day they had strapped her to a potty seat and at night they confined her to a straitjacket type of sleeping bag. Genie was barely cared for, physically abused and kept in an environment with almost no language stimulation from humans, television or radio. When Genie made sounds she was beaten into silence to ensure the secrecy of her existence. After Genie's discovery her physical, social, educational and language rehabilitation was undertaken. With regard to language, she did make some progress. She used both gestures and words to convey meaning. Gradually, she used words to describe her needs and moods and she even learned to lie. Despite this progress, her grammar and pronunciation of words remained abnormal. The case study is confounded by the possibility that Genie may also have had impaired mental functioning, which itself could have affected her language development. Generally, this case study would support the sensitive period idea of language development. Lenneberg (1967) has studied normal and Down's syndrome children in language development. He found a positive correlation between motor milestones and language development. This holds for Down's syndrome children as well as normal children, suggesting a maturational process is unfolding. Also deaf children babble and develop sign language on their own without training, suggesting the maturation process is in operation.

Chomsky's theory is supported by Brown *et al.* (1969) who found that mothers responded to children by extracting meaning from relatively crude communications. Nelson (1973) found that mothers who systematically corrected poor pronunciation had children who learned more slowly. Following on from this, children seem to acquire principles of syntax so that their speech is creative.

Although Chomsky's research was limited to pencil and paper exercises, there are studies which support Chomsky's theory. For example, McNeill (1966) observed the grammatical relationships in the telegraphic speech of young children. Children might say, 'Me want that coat' but not' Want that coat me'. Brown and Bellugi (1964), analysing the speech of two children Adam and Eve, noted the use of overgeneralisation. For example, the use of 's' to form plurals was observed in 'sheeps' and 'tooths'. The use of 'ed' to form the past tense was observed in 'comed' 'doed' and 'growed'. From these errors the linguist can infer that rules are being overgeneralised. Hence children, from an early age behave as if they expect language to be governed by rules.

However well Chomsky's theory is supported by research findings, it has been criticised on the grounds that language is not just a set of grammatical rules. Some psychologists have suggested that children's speech arises not so much from an innate LAD, but from the child's prelinguistic knowledge. Specifically, this refers to the child's ability to categorise the world prior to communicating about it. This approach suggests understanding and communication underpin children's language, rather than grammatical competence. This approach has been called the interactionist approach and is considered in the subsequent section.

The cognitive approach to language acquisition

The cognitive approach suggests that language, in common with much of learning, is a process of gradually building new on old. At birth a child has some limited intellectual abilities, which are subsequently enlarged and developed by contact with the environment. The most influential theorist of this approach has been Piaget, who felt the development of language depended on other cognitive processes that occurred during a child's development. Thus language is part of a child's maturational development.

■ Piaget's theory of language acquisition

The first two years of life are rooted in sensory motor experiences, symbolic actions do not appear until towards the end of this period. Children, during this period, do develop object permanence and this is possibly a prerequisite of understanding that words represent objects. Children's first words focus on familiar objects or action, not on random things. Children use words to express what they already understand.

Piaget saw language simply as a means of representing the environment, which did not need to be explained in any special way. Language develops as intellectual abilities mature, and is dependent upon this maturity. We have already discussed how Piaget believed that the maturing of intellectual abilities involves the development of schemas. He applied the same principles to language acquisition. New words are *assimilated* into existing schemata which are subsequently changed by *accommodation* to take account of the new stimulus. A process of building takes place, in which language is simply seen as one form of representing the environment. Piaget saw two stages in language acquisition, which he called egocentric speech and social speech.

Egocentric speech is used extensively in the pre-conceptual period between two and four (see pages 674–5) as children learn an increasing number of words. Sometimes there is social communication when children ask for something, for example a toy or drink, but more often it involves a running commentary by the child on what is occurring at the time and is not intended to communicate anything to anyone else. When this happens in a social setting, it may be mistaken at first for social speech, but soon becomes apparent that the child is talking without any desire to communicate. Piaget called this kind of speech collective monologue believing that it reflected children's egocentrism. Children at this stage are unable to explain something to another child from the perspective of that child (Piaget and Inhelder, 1969). *Social speech* becomes more dominant between five and seven as intuitive thinking increases and children are able to communicate both desires (asking for something) and thoughts.

Language, according to Piaget, performs three functions. The first of these is to communicate with other people opening social channels. The second is to enable children to internalise words in the form of thoughts and as a system of signs. The third, and most important, is to internalise action so children do not have to depend on manipulating things physically to solve problems. This is where formal operational thinking fits in.

■ Evaluation of Piaget's theory of language acquisition

It has been argued that Piaget underestimated children's linguistic achievements, which in some ways are more remarkable than the intellectual growth that occurs simultaneously. Language was seen by Piaget as having a secondary status, subordinate to intellectual development. This ignores the possibility that language may be a factor in intellectual development itself. Observations which have been made of children suggest that their use of linguistic skills can extend their intellectual ability. Children work at acquiring and using language, so the actual learning of language can be seen as an intellectual activity.

The social context in which learning occurs has been underestimated by Piaget. Within it, language is crucial as a medium of communication. Like Chomsky, Piaget paid too little attention to the social and cultural aspects of language and too much to its structure.

The social-interactionist approach to language acquisition

This approach emphasises the child's social communication experience. Communication is an enjoyable means of entering a social community.

Communication starts for children well before they learn to talk. Schaffer (1977) wrote about **interactional synchrony**, the development of a meshing between children's and their carers, responses to each other's stimulation. There is already, during babyhood, a dialogue developing between carer and child. Kaye (1977) illustrated this by describing how a mother may influence her child's patterns of bursts and pauses in sucking, by jiggling, stroking and talking to the baby. Linguistic competence is preceded by communicative competence. Language, when it happens, increases the flexibility of the communication which has already been established.

Ryan (1974) observed that children experience verbal exchanges with their mothers where the mother interprets, extends, comments on and repeats what the child has 'said'. Through these interactions the child and adult create a range of formats, or habitual exchanges, which become the basis for interpreting what both parent and child mean. In addition to these pre-speech conversations, games such as peek-a-boo and joint picture book reading extend the formats. Bruner (1983) referred to these interactions as the *language acquisition support system (LASS)*. He feels they are most important for language development. Eye contact, reciprocity between speakers and early interactions help the infant to combine an interest in objects with social communication. These social formats provide the environmental context which helps to structure the child's understanding of the world and early language utterances. It is in this social context that the distinction between the subject and the object and the noun and the verb is developed. So, in other words, the child recognises that language is about saying something meaningful about the environment to other people. If the social interactionist approach and cognitive approach are combined, they become a powerful theory to explain the child's meaningful use of language and communication skill.

Self-assessment questions

1 Make a flow chart to summarise the sequence of the acquisition of language in children.

2 Skinner believes language is learned through the expression of mands, tacts and echoic responses. Explain what each of these refers to.

3 Explain the following terms, used by Chomsky, to explain his model of language acquisition: (a) language acquisition device, (b) transformational grammar, (c) deep structure, (d) surface structure, (e) linguistic universals, (f) semantic rules and (g) syntactic rules.

4 As far as Piaget is concerned is language mainly a cause, or a consequence of cognitive development? Explain your answer.

Self-assessment questions cont'd

5 Outline three examples in which child/parent social interaction is thought to develop communication formats which assist language acquisition.

6 Write a paragraph to outline to what extent theories of language acquisition support the idea that environmental and social factors play a part in the development of children's language.

(Suggested answers on pages 710–11.)

Language production and comprehension

Language production theory is concerned with explaining how different types of knowledge work together to produce meaningful utterances that are appropriate to particular contexts. This may be regarded as largely a top-down process – starting with an idea to be expressed, which then has to be converted into individual speech sounds. Research into language comprehension is mainly a bottom-up process. It deals with how language is understood: deducing meaning from the combination of individual speech sounds called **morphemes**. See figure 19.2 for the hierarchical structure of language.

Language production

The production of language can be achieved in spoken or written form. Research into language production has concentrated more on the processes involved in the former than the latter. The aim has been to find out how the elements of the production process fit together. Controlled experiments have been used as well as studies of speech disruptions such as hesitations and speech errors. Simulating language production using computer programs is also proving fruitful.

Activity 4

Listen to someone speaking, or tape a short conversation. Write down some of the kinds of speech error or interruptions to speech fluency that are made.

When you have done this, compare your list with the one below.

pauses	repetitions
hesitations	interjections
ums and ahs	stuttering
corrections	slips of the tongue
false starts	

Speech production has been studied by tape recording speech and analysing it or by collecting

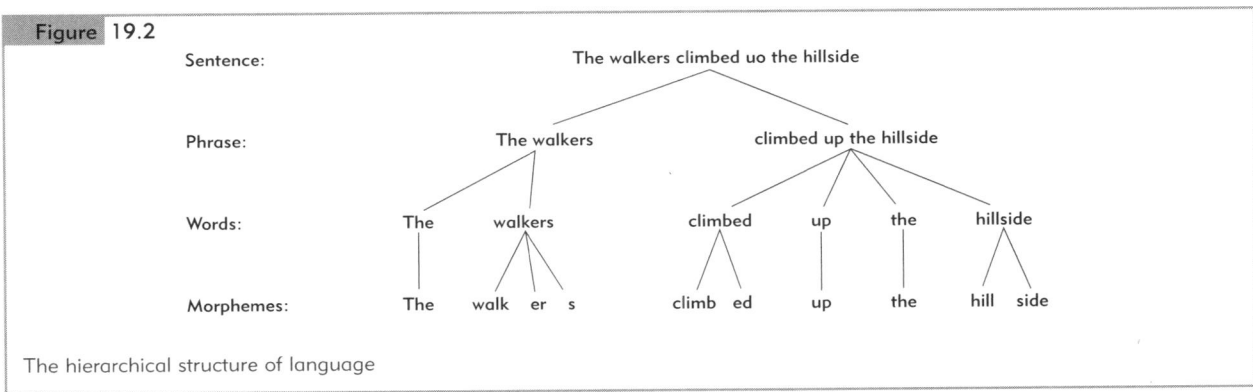

Figure 19.2

Sentence: The walkers climbed uo the hillside

Phrase: The walkers   climbed up the hillside

Words: The   walkers   climbed   up   the   hillside

Morphemes: The   walk   er   s   climb   ed   up   the   hill   side

The hierarchical structure of language

speech errors, thus seeking to understand the workings of the system from the way the system breaks down. At the theoretical level major contributions have been made by Garrett (1976; 1984) and Dell (1986).

Garrett's model of speech production

In Garrett's theoretical model of speech production five levels of representation are involved in speaking a sentence and they occur in the following sequence:

1 The *message level* representation – this is a pre-linguistic representation of the idea which the speaker wishes to communicate.
2 The *functional level* representation – this is the structural grammatical outline for the utterance, although at this stage no words have been fitted into the slots in the outline.
3 The *positional level* representation – this involves the words of the sentence that will be produced.
4 The *phonetic level* representation – this indicates information about the pronounciation of words in the intended sentence.
5 The *articulatory level* representation – this contains sets of instructions for speaking the words in the sentence in the correct order.

Garrett's theory has not been fully tested, but there is some support for the major ideas, especially that speakers use planning and use pauses as a way of aiding planning. Analysis of involuntary and unintentional speech errors also lends some support to Garrett's model. Speech errors often involve words from the end of a sentence intruding into the beginning of a sentence demonstrating the sort of forward planning which Garrett's model suggests.

Studies of pausing in speech show that pauses occur between speech clauses, which seems to suggest a decision is being taken about what to say next. When Garrett encourage people to speak without pausing, they were able to do this, but produced more repetition of words and phrases. This would suggest that pauses are important in planning in spontaneous speech and if they are not

used, then repetition becomes a mechanism for having time for planning. Speakers also look at their listeners less frequently during pauses than when speaking. This suggests the complex processes involved in planning require concentration. Greene and Cappella (1986) recorded monologues from people who had been asked to argue in favour of a new law on drugs. All monologues were at least 45 seconds long and when speakers made a move from one major part of their argument to another, there was a decreased fluency in speech at the transition point. Greene and Cappella repeated the study but provided speakers with a structure for organising their argument. Here the tendency for dysfluency at the 'move' boundaries disappeared. This is consistent with the idea that increasing the cognitive demands of planning the spoken word produces increases in pauses in speech. Studies of the distribution of pauses in spontaneous speech, for example Ford and Holmes (1978), have found pauses tend to cluster between one sentence and the next, suggesting the sentence is a unit of planning. Pause analysis has also shown that a smaller grammatical unit, the clause, is important (Garrett, 1982). Building on Goldman-Eisler's (1968) work showing that the complexity of the structure of the sentence has little impact on the length of pauses, Levelt (1989) concluded that although the clause is a planning unit, pauses between clauses reflects semantic processes rather than being related to processes involving the construction of the sentence. This further suggests that syntactic processes are more automatic and

Activity 5

Tape record someone speaking freely about a topic of his or her choice or of your choice. Make a tally of the number of pauses that occur between sentences. Listen again to the recording and tally the pauses that occur between clauses. (A clause is a grammatically complete part of a sentence.) Listen once more to see whether pauses occur anywhere other than between sentences or clauses. Do your results support the research carried out?

make fewer demands on processing than do semantic processes.

Another way of identifying the importance of clauses comes from identifying speech errors and slips. In a detailed look at slips of speech, Garrett (1975; 1976) reported and analysed around 3400 slips of speech. Ninety-seven of these involved word exchanges, for example 'One spoon of sugar' became 'One sugar of spoon'. Eighty-five per cent of the word exchanges reported came from within the same clause. Another fairly frequent exchange error involved parts of words (root **morphemes**) becoming detached and exchanging positions. For example, 'The hills are snowy' could be verbalised as 'The snows are hilly'. The 's' and 'y' have remained in their original position, whilst snow and hill have changed places. Another forward planning error is anticipation error, when a word is spoken earlier in the clause than it should be, for example 'Please pencil the pencil' instead of 'Please sharpen the pencil'. Spoonerisms provide another case of errors involving material from the later part of a sentence appearing early in the sentence. The Reverend Archibald William Spooner (1844–1930), an Oxford don, from whom the terms originates, was said to have remarked to one of his students: 'You have hissed all my mystery lectures.' The student would have realised he was being challenged about his absence from history lectures, despite the confused consonant exchange. The pattern of pauses in speech and the evidence that misordering errors involve parts of the same sentence, or clause, suggest that clauses are planning units in the production of speech. Word exchanges indicate that when people speak, several units of stored representations of knowledge are active at the same time, (Garrett, 1982, Dell, 1986). Between these active units exchanges can occur. The advantage of parallel action in speech planning probably helps to ensure fluency within speech clauses. Pauses between speech clauses may represent the time needed to build up activation in the representations needed for the coming clause.

Another researched area of speech production problems are those where the speakers struggle to find the right word, yet know that they know the word. These **tip of the tongue (TOT) phenomena**

suggest that phonological information, i.e. getting the correct sound for the word, is accessed along a different route from the meaning of the word, as meaning can be recalled but the sound of the word cannot. William James (1890) captured the agony of the TOT state in the following passage:

> 'Suppose we try to recall a forgotten name. The state of our consciousness is peculiar. There is a gap therein: but no mere gap. It is a gap that is intensely active. A sort of wraith of the name is in it, beckoning us in a given direction, making us at moments tingle with the sense of our closeness, and then letting us sink back without the longed for term. If wronged names are proposed to us, this singularly defined gap acts immediately so as to negate them. They do not fit its mould . . . The rhythm of a lost word may be there without a sound to clothe it: or the evanescent sense of something which is the initial vowel or consonant may mock us fitfully, without growing more distinct.' (Quoted in Smyth et al., 1994, p. 190.)

TOT states reflect the failure to retrieve a word that matches a concept. In a TOT state it feels as if the meaning of the word has been accessed perfectly but what is missing is the sound form. Jones and Langford (1987) gave participants definitions of a word, then a word related in meaning (for example compass) or in sound (for example sextet) to a target word (for example sextant). They called the word they provided the blocker. They found that the chance of a TOT state being induced increased when the blocker was a word similar in sound to the target. They concluded that semantic access to the desired word had been achieved, hence the semantic blocker had no effect, but the sound blocker had an interference effect which got in the way of finding the target word. Burke *et al.* (1991) created a model which demonstrates how semantic nodes, or connections, are activated when phonological ones are not. This could underlie the TOT phenomena. In their model, the strength of links between semantic and phonological nodes builds up with use, so TOT phenomena should be more common with less frequently used words, which is the case.

Dell's model of speech production

Another model of speech production that accounts for errors or slips is Dell's (1986) model. Dell's model is not a complete explanation of speech production, but it does show how a computer model of a cognitive process can explain word finding and can produce speech errors common to everyday life. Dell's model consists of simple units which can be activated and can transmit this activation to other units which builds up a network of connections ending up as speech production. For example, a speaker wishes to produce the word 'net'. 'Net' exists in the word node. Through node connections 'net' is linked to the sounds, or phoneme nodes, that make up the word. The node connections are bidirectional (i.e. work both ways) in their activation. The word node and phoneme nodes also link to the syllable nodes ensuring that the syllables appear in the right order in the word. This process is illustrated in the simplified model of Dell's lexical network of speech production in figure 19.3.

In the model shown in figure 19.3, the required word 'net' is divided into sounds at the phonemic nodes and reconstructed into an appropriate syllable order in the wordshape network. In addition to the spread of activation through the lexical (or word) network, there is also a spread of activation through a tactic frame which provides a syntactic structure for the appropriate use of nouns, verbs, adverbs, etc. Insertion rules operate to select the most activated lexical node compatible with the slot in the tactic frame. As activation spreads down a network, the most active elements are selected and placed in the appropriate slots. As activation spreads down, it also sends activation back up to the connected nodes so, in the example in figure 19.3 'net' is the activated node but 'not' will receive some activation. Once a word has been selected, the activation level of the node is reduced to the starting level. An advantage of Dell's model (1988), which mimics real-life speech, is its ability to make speech errors. Dell points out that there are three ways in which this can be achieved:

- There can be interference from a node which has received activation, other than the intended one.
- Words just spoken or about to be spoken will be active to some extent. This fits with the idea that the clause is the planning unit.
- There is activation from other cognitive and perceptual processes which might not directly be linked to speech.

In real life these interference problems produce the following errors. Word substitutions occur when there is activation of a word similar in meaning or sound. For example, whilst 'net' is the target word, 'not' has received quite a lot of activation. Where word substitution errors are made, they are between words of the same syntactic

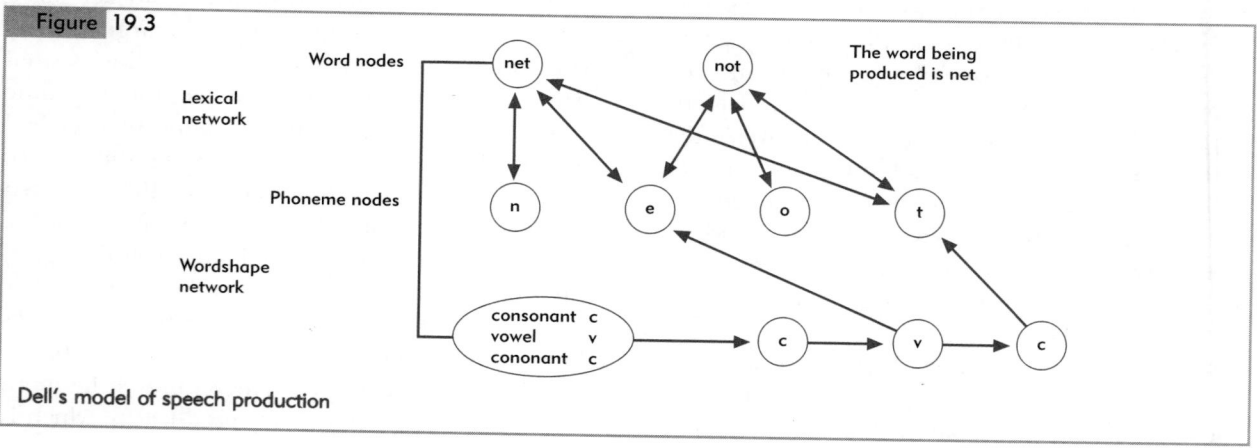

Figure 19.3

Word nodes — net · not — The word being produced is net

Lexical network

Phoneme nodes — n · e · o · t

Wordshape network — consonant c / vowel v / conomant c — c · c · v · c

Dell's model of speech production

class (Dell, 1988). How frequently and how recently a word has been used affects its resting activation level, making some words more likely to be substituted than others. In the example of spoonerisms and word exchanges, the right components of words have been selected but the sequencing of the components goes wrong. In the example 'You have hissed all my mystery lectures' a later component 'h' has received more activation than 'm'. It thus occurs too early, leaving the active 'm' for a later slot.

Brain injury and speech production problems

Garrett's model (1975; 1982) is helpful in explaining some of the speech production problems which occur in brain-injured patients. Here is a recap of the model which has been described earlier. The model (see page 682) begins with a conceptual plan which represents the speaker's intentions. This plan then encourages processes of word retrieval and syntactic procedures to commence. These sets of information are integrated at the functional level of the model, as yet the precise form of the sentence and the phonemic form of the words has not been produced. In due course the sound form of the words and the position of the words are arranged. Finally articulation occurs. According to Garrett's model, patients who have damage in syntactic processing alone, should know the message they would like to communicate, be able to retrieve the appropriate words and be able to articulate them. They would however have a problem in assembling the syntactic framework so sentences would be produced in a jumbled order. People suffering from *anomia*, or word finding difficulty, have other processing problems involving the difficulty of finding the appropriate lexical form (words) at the functional level. The following illustrates the difficulty a patient had in accessing content words, (Allport and Funnell, 1981; quoted in Smyth *et al.*, 1994). The patient is asked to draw a picture of a kitchen scene. The words in square brackets are the researcher's attempt to guess what the patient is trying to say.

Well it's a . . . [kitchen], it's a place, and it's a girl and boy, and they've got obviously something which is made . . . some . . . [biscuits], some . . . made . . . Well . . . [the stool] it's just beginning to . . . [fall] go and be rather unpleasant . . . And . . . this is the . . . [mother?] the woman, and she is [pouring?] putting some . . . [water] stuff . . .

The production of written language

There are differences between the production of spoken and written language. The errors and pauses which are evident in spoken language are not found in written language. An important theory which looks at the writing process is that of Hayes and Flower (1986). They identified three interrelated processes involved in writing:

- The planning process – involves the production and arrangement of ideas in a way that will achieve the writer's goals.
- The sentence generation process – converts the plan into the written word.
- The revision process – involves evaluating what has been written. This could involve single words, or the whole structure.

These processes indicate the general order involved in writing, although there can be recapping to an earlier stage at any point.

Writing plans can be based on different strategies. In knowledge-telling strategies, the writer tries to write down all he or she knows. In strategic knowledge processes the methods to be used in constructing the writing plan are also explored. Expert writers possess the latter and are able to transform knowledge into a coherent and logical text. Expert writers take longer than non-expert writers on revision of their work. This is partly because they are more skilled at detecting errors which need revision and also because experts focus more on overall coherence whilst non-experts limit their revision to individual words and phrases and the former takes longer. Hayes and Flower identified strategy differences between experts and non-experts and the application of their ideas could be of assistance to poor writers. However, their method of getting people to report the strategies they used does not allow for the possibility that people use strategies unconsciously or intuitively which may also affect the process of expert writing.

Michael W. Eysenck (1993) has drawn attention to the similarities and differences between the production of speech and the production of written material. He pointed out that both forms of expression involve deciding what message is to be communicated and how this is to be done. There is evidence that people who are good at spoken language are also good at written language. Gould (1978; 1980) compared written and spoken language, via written versus dictated letters. Dictation is at best 35 per cent faster than writing. The proportion of time spent on language processes is about the same for dictated and written letters. People who were good at speaking or dictating also tended to be good at writing. It would appear that the planning processes involved in both forms of communication may be the same whilst the physical form of the communication, that is speech or writing, is of less importance.

There are however differences in the speech and writing processes. First, speech is six times faster than writing. Some studies of brain-damaged patients have shown that either speech or writing can be impaired, but not necessarily both, suggesting different processes may be involved. Michael W. Eysenck quoted the example of an engineer, EB who suffered a stroke that prevented him from using inner speech or overt speech, but his written language was quite good. His first memories after his stroke were as follows:

'Gradually after what seemed days and days, I got back enough strength to pull myself up and sit if I held on. I tilted off to the right and and had a hard time maintaining my balance. The nurse and doctor and an orderly helped me up then . . . I got to another part of the hospital where there were two doctors asking me questions I couldn't answer.' (Levine, Calvanio and Popovics, 1982; quoted in Michael W. Eysenck, p. 124.)

There are also reported cases where patients can speak fluently, but are not able to write. These examples suggest that spoken and written information is stored separately and brain damage may selectively disrupt either speaking or writing. It is possible that speaking and writing depend on the same knowledge base and planning process but that there are differences as the processes get closer to the written or spoken word.

Activity 6

When you write an essay discuss the amount of planning you have carried out. How do you think planning has helped you to write a better essay? How long was your plan compared with your essay? Generally it has been found that plans are one-sixth the length of essays. Discuss whether you would write a better essay if you spent more time planning. To what extent do you use planning and revision processes? Do you think you can improve the coherence and logical presentation of your work? If you use a wordprocessor, do you use less planning and more revision? If you use a computer-based speech dictation program, how do you plan what you are going to say?

Language comprehension

Cognitive psychologists are interested in the processes involved in the comprehension of written and spoken text. This section considers language comprehension from a cognitive point of view.

■ Reading comprehension

Explaining reading initially involves the understanding of eye movements. When someone reads a text, they make rapid eye movements, known as *saccades* (lasting about 25–30 milliseconds) and between these lie fixation periods which last about 250 milliseconds. The amount of information extracted from a fixation period has been studied by Rayner and Pollatsek (1987). They measured perceptual span, which is the range of letters from which information is extracted. This can vary depending on such factors as the size of print and the complexity of the text. Typically, the perceptual span includes three to four letters to the left of the fixation and about fifteen letters to the right (figure 19.4). (This applies to people who read from left to right.) Fixations take up 90 per cent of reading time. Thus it seems to be of greater value to look ahead in a text, although 10–20 per cent of eye movements involve regressions, or looking back. A greater quantity of regression occurs in poor readers.

The fixation of letters is the first stage of explaining reading, but it is not yet adequately clear how people move from this initial stage to activating meaning and sound which accompany the fixation of letters. Early theories which tried to explain letter recognition suggested that people stored internal letter templates with which stimuli could be compared. A vast number of templates would, however, be needed to cope with the variety of letter scripts and handwriting which would be encountered. An alternative to template matching is the recognition of distinctive features – **feature detection theory** (Oden, 1979). This model suggests combinations of curves and lines would make configurations which would be recognisable as letters. Once again, the variability of handwriting would present a problem. There is some evidence that the variety of forms that letters take may be focused on 'abstract letter identities' before being compiled into words (Evett and Humphreys, 1981). These abstract identities would serve to standardise varied letter formations for each letter into a standard abstract identity for each letter.

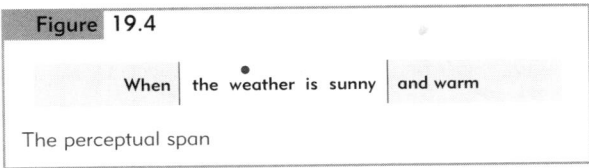

Figure 19.4

When | the weather is sunny | and warm

The perceptual span

It is by no means certain whether it is necessary to recognise each letter, prior to word recognition. McClelland and Rummelhart's (1981) model of reading comprehension suggests processing of letters and words can occur simultaneously. Their model is based on a computer simulation mimicking word recognition. The simulation only works with letters written in capitals and can only deal with words of up to four letters. In their model, feature information begins the activation of letter units. Activation is then transferred to connected word units. Word units transmit activation back to letter units. Each unit is capable of two types of connections, activating connections which increase excitation and inhibitory connections which suppress excitation. For example, if the word CAP was presented, the curved C would set off the appropriate feature detectors. The letter recognition unit would activate perhaps C, G, O and Q. All the letters except C would send inhibitory signals back to the feature detection level. The word level would activate perhaps, CAP CAN and CAT. The latter two words would send inhibitory messages to the letter detectors, leaving CAP as the most likely match. The advantage of this feature detection (bottom-up) and word recognition (top-down) processing operating at the same time is that the speed of word recognition is increased. The comparison with human wordprocessing is limited as this computer simulation is not based on processing of the size and flexibility which really simulates human, everyday, word recognition.

There is evidence to support the McClelland and Rummelhart (1981) model in that humans are faster at recognising letters from real words than non-words. This is called the 'word superiority effect' (Reicher, 1969). McClelland and Rummelhart's model would suggest this occurs because of the faster processing where real words are suggested by the word recognition units, whereas non-words are not helped by this process. In other words, the top-down processing is greater for words than for non-words. For non-words processing is dependent on slower, data-driven processing.

It is not always necessary to have all the letters of a word to activate the word units. So, for example, the word CARAVN will activate the word to describe a mobile home, despite the missing A. Word recognition occurs because the missing letter is inserted from within the word unit system, as the best guess. Context is another factor which also increases the likelihood of a word being recognised, so, in the sentence 'They went on holiday and stayed in the caravn' the context further increases the likelihood of the last word being recognised.

The McClelland and Rummelhart (1981) model with simultaneous bottom-up and top down-processing explains speedy letter and word recognition. Stored knowledge interacts with incoming stimuli to speed up the perception of words.

Michael W Eysenck (1993) describes Ellis and Young's (1988) three route model of reading words. According to this model, route one is taken when unfamiliar words, or non-words are recognised by converting the written letters to sounds (called *grapheme-phoneme conversion*), or by creating an analogy between the letter pattern and the pronunciation of known words. This phonic mediation route (figure 19.5) could explain reading comprehension where words can be sounded out, but this would not help comprehension of some words in the English language, for example yacht.

Evidence for the use of different reading routes has been drawn from studies of brain-injured patients. Patient WB (Funnell, 1983) had acquired phonological **dyslexia** and could read only one of 30 non-words for example cobe, nust. These latter words could not be accessed by meaning but could be sounded out. Yet WB was able to read 75 out of 80 words on a graded reading test. What had been lost in WB's case was the ability to use a phonic mediation route to sound out new words.

Route two is taken by accessing the meaning of the written word from information available in the long-term memory store. This works well with familiar words. McClelland and Rummelhart's (1981) model proposes a direct access route to reading where word units are activated which are then thought to activate the meaning of the word. This route is the semantic route to reading (figure 19.6).

Loss of the semantic route to reading, but with phonic mediation preserved, is known as *surface dyslexia* (Patterson *et al.*, 1985). In this condition words previously recognised from visual appearance appear unfamiliar. Irregular words are more difficult to read than more regular phonically matching words (see Unit 13 page 463).

So both direct semantic and phonic mediation routes are available for reading. It seems likely that the direct semantic route is used but with unfamiliar words and with non-words, people switch to the phonic route (Ellis, 1984).

Route three involves accessing the pronunciation of written words from the long-term memory, although the words pronounced are not understood. Evidence for the existence of this third route to accessing the written word comes from the case of WT (Coslett, 1991). WT had left temporal lobe damage and could accurately read aloud regular and irregular words, but only 25 per cent of non-words, hence the phonic route of sounding words was not being used effectively. It appeared that WT was using the direct semantic access route, yet when tested for understanding of the words being read WT showed significant impairment for words of low imageability (the ease with which a mental picture can be created). If WT could not access the meaning of the words, then the semantic route could not be being used. There is therefore a third route to reading comprehension which involves not accessing the

---

Figure 19.5

Written word → IDENTIFY LETTERS → CONVERT LETTER STRINGS TO SOUNDS → IDENTIFY SPOKEN FORM → ACCESS MEANING

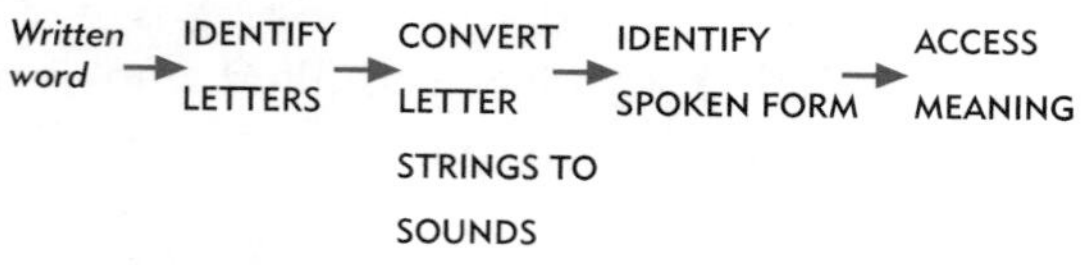

The phonic mediation route to meaning

Source: Smyth *et al.* (1994), p. 47.

Figure 19.6

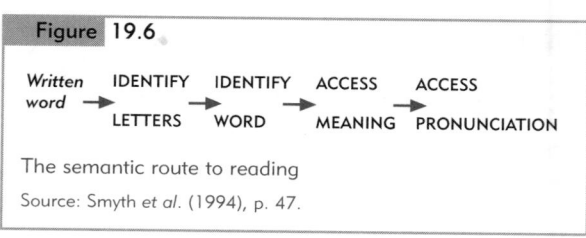

Written word → IDENTIFY LETTERS → IDENTIFY WORD → ACCESS MEANING → ACCESS PRONUNCIATION

The semantic route to reading

Source: Smyth *et al.* (1994), p. 47.

meaning of the words and not using phonics (figure 19.7).

In this model there is some sort of link between word recognition and pronounciation, without accessing sound or meaning.

There is still important work proceeding in the field of reading comprehension. A connectionist model of word recognition and naming has been developed (Seidenberg and McClelland, 1989). This model learns pronounciation and does not rely upon word recognition units. It operates by converting words into sounds, involving a single route of processing. There is still potential for more computer simulation and analogy in this area of study.

Speech perception

To process speech efficiently it is necessary to take advantage of as many cues as possible. Noise, distraction and incoherent verbalisation have also to be dealt with in the process of speech perception.

The context of speech provides a useful cue. Marslen-Wilson and Tyler (1980) asked participants to listen for a target word in three types of two-sentence passages. Examples of the three types with the word *lead* in italics are as follows:

1 Normal prose:
    The church was broken in last week. Some thieves stole most of the *lead* off the roof.

2 Anomalous but grammatically correct prose:
    The power was located in great water. No buns puzzle some in the *lead* off the text.

3 Scrambled prose:
    It was great power water the located. Some the no puzzle buns in *lead* text the off.

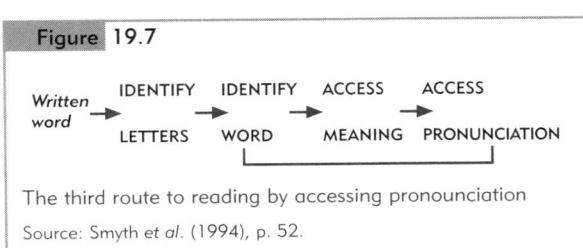

Figure 19.7

The third route to reading by accessing pronounciation

Source: Smyth *et al.* (1994), p. 52.

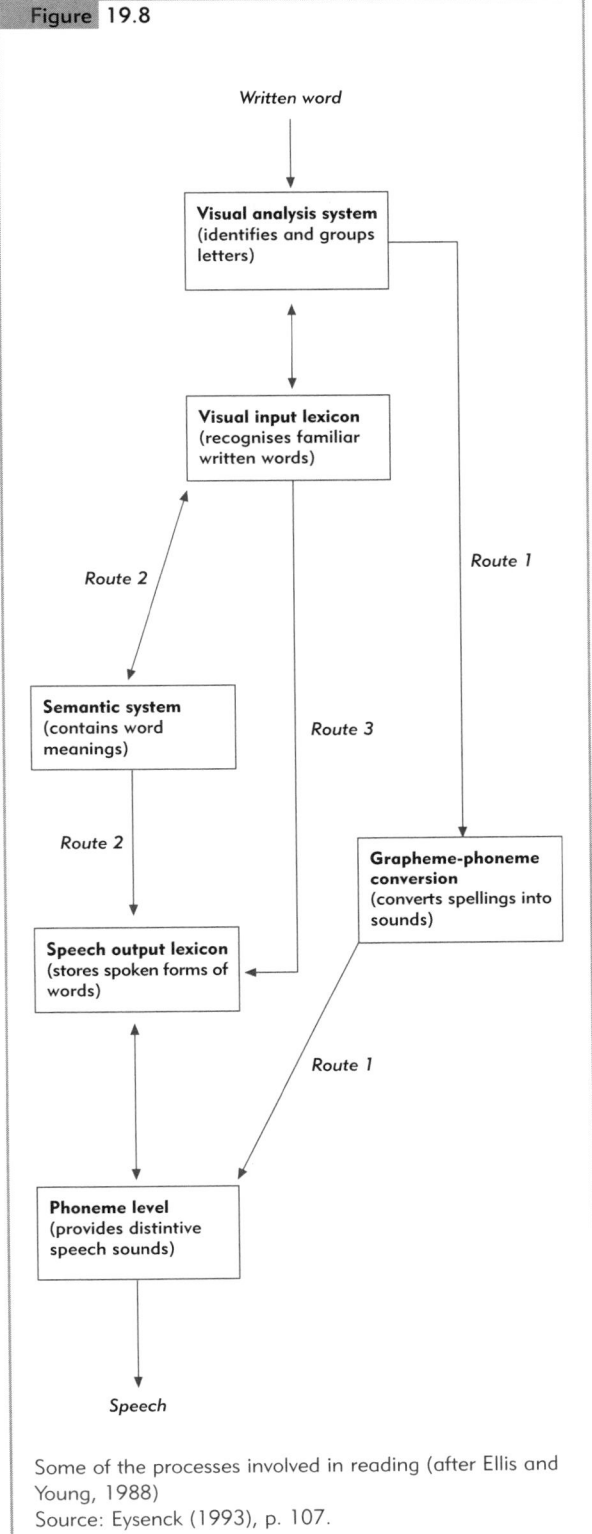

Figure 19.8

Some of the processes involved in reading (after Ellis and Young, 1988)
Source: Eysenck (1993), p. 107.

Participants had to press a button when they heard the target word *lead*. Reaction times were faster in the normal prose condition (305 milliseconds) than in either the anomalous (373 milliseconds) or the scrambled (364 milliseconds) conditions. This shows the beneficial effects of context on speech perception (Smyth *et al.*, 1994, p. 212).

The ability to segment speech signals is also of importance. This is only too evident when we try to listen to a foreign-language radio station. Segmenting is aided by the rhythm of speech. In English words can have strong and weak syllables. The syllables in capital letters in the following words are strong syllables, BRACElet, deMAND. In English 90 per cent of words start with a strong syllable. Listeners make use of this information when segmenting words (Cutler and Butterfield, 1992). Perhaps lack of knowledge of stress patterns in foreign languages is part of our difficulty in knowing where one word ends and another begins in foreign radio stations. An important model of auditory word recognition is the cohort model (Marslen-Wilson and Welsh 1978; Marslen-Wilson, 1987). According to this model, early word sounds activate recognition units of words, known to the listener, which begin in the same way as the new word. The 'word initial cohort' is activated with sounds compatible with the new sound. More frequently used words become more activated. Sounds which increasingly differ from the word being activated decline in activation. Eventually, the most activated word is left for recognition. At this stage context does not play a part in word recognition, although context will for other reasons, have an effect on word perception speed.

There is a problem with this theory and that is why do we ignore mispronunciations? If someone says 'bank' for 'dank', surely a different cohort of words would be activated? Marslen-Wilson suggested that as similar physical signals are activated by the confused words, there will be some activation for both words and we may override the mispronunciation with the context cues. Visual aspects of speech comprehension are also helpful. It is well known that many people lip read and there have been a number of experimental demonstrations. McGurk and MacDonald (1976) suggested visual and auditory signals are combined early on in processing the signals. They video-taped

someone saying 'ba-ba-ba' repeatedly. They then replaced the sound with someone saying 'ga-ga-ga'. With eyes closed 'ga-ga' was heard, but people looking at the face reported hearing 'da-da'. When presented with conflicting signals, the perceptual system resolved this by compromising. In normal circumstances or particularly where there is a lot of background noise visual information is used to supplement auditory stimuli.

Activity 7

Find a television programme where you can clearly see the faces of the people who are speaking. Turn off the volume on the television. Watch the lip movements of the speakers. Are you able to work out what the speakers are saying? If you also video the programme, you can check how much of the spoken content you were able to decipher.

Understanding speech is not simply a matter of understanding words, sentence structure is also processed. Listeners do not wait until someone has reached the end of a sentence before they begin to process it. People use information in the early context cues of a sentence to help them understand later parts of the sentence. An example of how efforts to make sense of sentences is continuous can be seen in what is known as 'garden-path' sentences. In these, if we try to process the sentence word by word, we are led 'down the garden-path' and confused. For example:

The old dog the footsteps of the young.
I told the girl the cat scratched Bill would help her.

(Smyth *et al.*, 1994, p. 217.)

There would not be a problem with these sentences if the interpretation was deferred until the end of the sentence, but because interpretation is placed on the words as we read them it is possible to mislead people with these sentences. In everyday spoken language there are strong cues in the patterns and pauses of speech which work against us being confused by 'garden-path' sentences. We also make use of word arrangements or grammar to help us decode speech. When we parse speech (assign a structured, syntactic description to speech), we use strategies based on knowledge of sentence structure. Neurophysiological studies of language disorder have demonstrated that sentence structure is processed separately from word or sentence meaning. In patients suffering from Broca's **aphasia** the ability to process sentence structure is lost, whilst words can still be understood for meaning. Caramazza and Zurif (1976) asked patients to match sentences to a choice of two pictures. One sentence used was 'The apple that the boy was eating was red'. If the content words were understood – apple, boy, eat, red – but the word order, or function words – the, that, was – were not understood, patients still arrived at the correct interpretation, as other interpretions, based on meaning were not plausible, for example the apple eating the boy. Where sentences depended on syntax for interpretation, these patients had problems. For example, there were problems interpreting the sentence 'The cow that the monkey is scaring is yellow'. With only meanings to help them and without any syntactic skill, patients did not know whether the sentence was about a yellow monkey scaring a cow, being scared by a cow, etc. Broca's aphasics could not select the correct picture in this type of sentence because of impairment to their syntactic parsing mechanisms. This supports the idea that syntactic parsing is a separate process to handling meaning in speech comprehension.

Context effects also help understanding. This occurs where use is made of information which is not directly included in the material we are trying to understand. Context effects can be general, based on our knowledge of the world, or specific, based on the particular material being considered. Bransford and Johnson (1972) illustrated the importance of specific context effects to great advantage. They gave participants the following passage:

'The procedure is actually quite simple. First you arrange items into different groups. Of course one pile may be sufficient depending on how much there is to do. If you have to go somewhere else due to lack of facilities, that is the next step; otherwise you are pretty well set. It is important not to overdo things. That is, it is better to do too few things at once rather than too many. In the short run this may not seem important but complications can easily arise. A mistake can be expensive as well. At first, the whole procedure will seem complicated. Soon, however, it will become just another facet of life. It is difficult to forsee any end to the necessity for this task in the immediate future, but then one never can tell. After the procedure is completed one arranges the materials into their appropriate places. Eventually, they will be used once more and the whole cycle will then have to be repeated. However that is part of life' (p. 722).

Participants given the passage with no extra information found it difficult to understand. Those provided with the title 'Washing Clothes' found the passage reasonably easy to understand. It helps to have an appropriate context. We draw on background knowledge to help our understanding of new material. Memory and language are linked. Interpretations of what people say go beyond the words uttered. Mental models are used to aid perception. We use inference in understanding, without it conversation would be laborious, although occasionally any of us can draw the wrong inference from what is being said.

Self-assessment questions

7 Name three methods psychologists have used when trying to study language production.

8 Why do pauses occur in speech?

9 In the speech error known as a 'spoonerism' what is actually happening in speech processing?

10 In the production of written language suggest two ways in which expert writers differ from non-expert writers.

11 Explain how McClelland and Rummelhart's (1981) model of reading comprehension uses top-down and bottom-up processing simultaneously.

12 Outline the three routes to reading suggested by Ellis (1984). Explain when each might be used.

13 What cues do people use to help them decipher speech?

(Suggested answers on pages 711–12.)

Models and explanations of human thought

Human thought is a wide-ranging topic which has been studied from a number of angles. Thinking encompasses such areas as concept formation, the development of schema and scripts, the use of cognitive maps, insight, mental models, the role of algorithmic and heuristic processing and the use of logic in thinking, to name but a few. In addition, the computer analogy has made important contributions and developments to the understanding of human thought processes. This section focuses on three important areas of human thinking: reasoning, problem solving and decision making.

Human reasoning

One of the main questions which psychologists have tried to answer is whether humans reason logically. Logical reasoning involves following a set of rigorous procedures for researching whether valid conclusions have been reached. Sometimes this involves using formulas, which are means of **algorithmic thinking**. In algorithmic thinking systematic methods will always bring about a correct result. So logic is a set of mental procedures which are a general algorithm for drawing valid conclusions about the world. The rules of logic are applied to statements known as premises. From premises a conclusion is drawn. This sort of reasoning is called a syllogism, i.e. it is an inference based on the premises. For example: A is equal to B, B is equal to C (these are two premises), therefore A is equal to C (conclusion).

The Greek philosopher, Aristotle, was the first person to study syllogism 2300 years ago. The syllogism has been used by psychologists to see whether people reason in a logical way. On the whole, people are not good at detecting logically valid or invalid arguments. People are affected by the truth of the statements involved and their own personal beliefs which get in the way of 'pure logic'. Even professional logicians take time to learn the formal rules of logic, so it is not surprising that ordinary people struggle with logical reasoning. Johnson-Laird (1983) explained the difficulties people have by drawing attention to the point that abstract logic is difficult to follow as people need to develop a mental representation of the premises in order to understand them. They must then integrate the premises and look at the implications. Giving some sort of meaning to the premises helps, for example A for actor, B for best, C for character. It helps by providing some sort of concrete representation of the premises. Incorrect responses in syllogisms relate to the number of alternative conclusions which can be reached. People find it difficult to consider a number of integrated possibilities between the premises (Johnson-Laird, 1983).

Another difficulty people have with formal reasoning is that the use of words like if/then, and, or, which link sentences together also act as logic reasoning tools (Rips, 1983). In the abstract argument: if p then q, p therefore q, it helps if the argument is put into an example. Byrne (1989) used the following example:

If she has an essay to write (p) then she will study late in the library (q). She has an essay to write.

The conclusion that she will study late in the library is easy to reach.

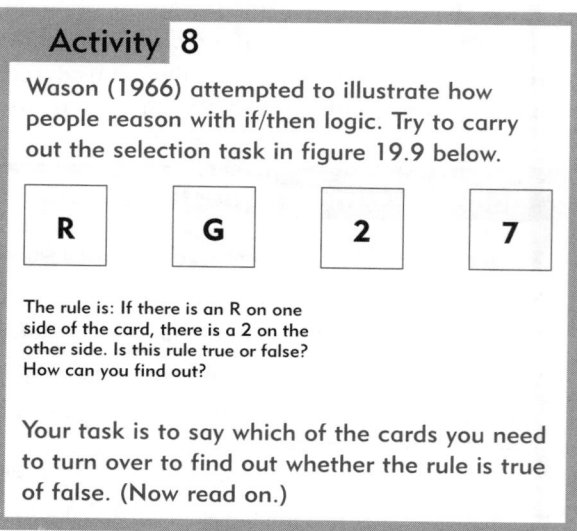

Activity 8

Wason (1966) attempted to illustrate how people reason with if/then logic. Try to carry out the selection task in figure 19.9 below.

| R | G | 2 | 7 |

The rule is: If there is an R on one side of the card, there is a 2 on the other side. Is this rule true or false? How can you find out?

Your task is to say which of the cards you need to turn over to find out whether the rule is true of false. (Now read on.)

In answer to this problem, most people select the R or the R and 2 card. This is not correct. The starting point is to see whether any of the cards fail to obey the rule. The correct cards to select are the R and the 7. These were chosen by only 5 per cent of university students. The card with 7 on it would disprove the rule if it had an R on the other side. The R card would have a 2 on the other side to prove the rule. This task is easier to solve if it is less abstract.

Activity 9

Try the more concrete version of Wason's selection task as shown in figure 19.10 below Wason and Shapiro, 1971).

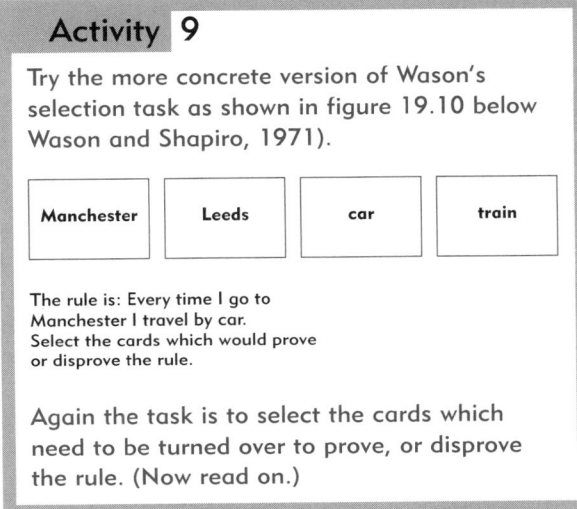

The rule is: Every time I go to Manchester I travel by car.
Select the cards which would prove or disprove the rule.

Again the task is to select the cards which need to be turned over to prove, or disprove the rule. (Now read on.)

The cards which need to be turned over are the Manchester and train cards. Sixty-two per cent of participants obtained the correct result. In the more abstract Wason task only 12 per cent gave the correct answer. It would appear that concrete and meaningful material is easier to manipulate, but Griggs and Cox (1982) failed to replicate the study in Florida. This led Griggs and Cox to suggest that people need specific, familiar, prior experiences as the basis on which to reason. Further insight into reasoning logic has developed from the work of Cheng and Holyoak (1985). Cheng has argued that people do develop reasoning rules, at a pragmatic level from their own experiences, rather than at a logical or syntactic level. Where people have been exposed to rules involving permissions and obligations they are able to abstract rules from this. For example, if someone is voting, they must be 18. The permission schema (simplified) acts as follows:

1 If action A is taken (voting), precondition P (age 18) must be satisfied.

2 If precondition P (age 18) is not satisfied, action A (voting) must not be taken.

Checking these rules will indicate whether the permission schema has been followed. They are abstract in that any item can stand for action A and permission P. Cheng *et al.* (1986) suggested people possess these abstract schema in a pragmatic reasoning way, not as rules of formal logic. This represents a new approach in a field where it has been demonstrated that people are not very good at using formal, abstract, reasoning rules.

A different approach to **deductive reasoning** has been developed in Johnson-Laird's (1983) 'mental models' approach. This approach stresses that the meaning of the ideas we are trying to reason with is what is important. It is argued that reasoning is a semantic process, based on the operation of mental models, rather than a set of rule-based abstract or pragmatic operations. Johnson-Laird suggested that when people reason out a problem they construct one or more mental models. Eysenck and Keane (1995) gave the example shown in figure 19.11.

From the premises given, both mental models are possible. In Johnson-Laird's theory, comprehension of the premises leads to the construction of one or more mental models. The models can produce novel conclusions not specified in the premises. The novel conclusions

---

Table 19.11

Premises

The lamp is on the right of the pad.

The book is on the left of the lamp.

The clock is in front of the book.

The vase is in front of the pad.

Conclusion

The clock is to the left of the vase.

Mental model one

book	pad	lamp
clock	vase	

Mental model two

pad	book	lamp
vase	clock	

Example of mental models

Source: Eysenck and Keane (1995), p. 416.

can be checked against the premises. Errors are likely to occur where there are several models that have to be held in working memory as processing capacity may become overloaded (Johnson-Laird, 1983). Using the mental models approach, Johnson-Laird has tried to explain why people find it difficult reasoning with negatives. 'Seven is not an even number' is harder to understand than 'seven is an odd number'. It is suggested that the difficulty with negatives lies in understanding the negative statement rather than in carrying out any reasoning which may be required.

Work on human reasoning has shown that abstract logic, pragmatic schemas and mental models are three accounts of how people reason. Sometimes people use abstract reasoning, usually where the premises are straightforward. Pragmatic schemas are used in reasoning out some problems where specific past experiences help. Mental models focus on human understanding of the problems in premises, rather than the rules for manipulating the premises. There is however, still much to be explained about human deductive reasoning.

The formation of concepts is probably one of the most important functions of the thinking process. A concept makes it possible to think in terms of categories rather than of particulars – of 'dog' as an idea rather than a specific 'Fido'. To do this we need to focus on particular features. If we regularly see an object which has the same set of features, we associate these in our minds and make a similar response every time we meet this particular collection of features together. For example, when we come across a dog (whether it happens to be a pekinese or an Irish wolfhound), we know it is a dog because all members of the category 'dog' have certain features in common, which we have abstracted and stored.

This process provides us with great economy of thinking, which becomes greater when we add language. Also, most importantly, we make responses not to individual representatives of a category but to the category itself. This means we can deal with the world around us more efficiently than if our responses were all made to particular individuals.

Bruner's view of concept formation

Bruner *et al.* (1956) made a major contribution to research on the learning of concepts, identifying several types using the procedure outlined in figure 19.12.

A conjunctive concept needs all of a set of characteristics to be included. For example, a cricket ball needs to be round, hard, made of leather and possess a seam. If it lacks any of these attributes, it is not a cricket ball.

A disjunctive concept needs one or more of a number of characteristics, but not necessarily all. For example, being 'out' in cricket can involve a number of alternatives: the ball has been bowled and has hit the stumps; the ball hit the batter's pads when they are in front of the stumps; the batter has hit the ball and a fielder has caught it before it touches the ground; and so on.

A relations concept relates two or more attributes to each other: 'more than. . .' or 'less than. . .', for instance.

According to Bruner and his colleagues, participants use four main strategies in learning concepts. Conservative focusing appeared to be the most efficient. This consisted of focusing on the first positive instance (i.e. the first card where the experimenter responded 'Yes, this is one of them') and selecting another card which differed from it in only one attribute. If the new card was another positive instance of the concept, then the changed attribute must be irrelevant to it. For example, if the concept consisted of those cards which had two borders and a cross or crosses and the first positive instance was a card with two borders and two green crosses, and the second positive instance was a card with two border and two black crosses, then the colour of the symbol must be irrelevant. In this way, it was possible progressively to eliminate the irrelevant attributes.

A related but riskier strategy was that of focus gambling. Here, instead of focusing upon one attribute at a time and so eliminating irrelevancies, the participants attempted to change two or more

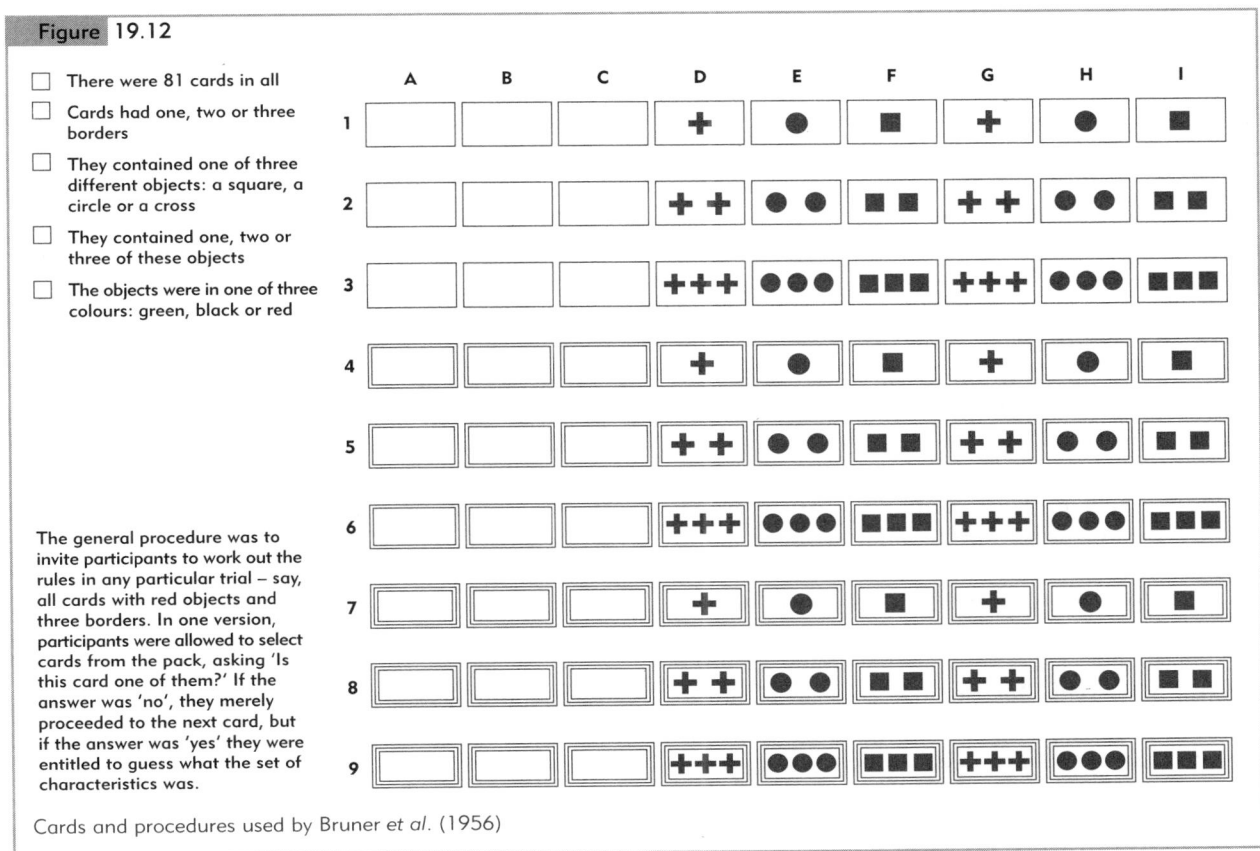

☐ There were 81 cards in all

☐ Cards had one, two or three borders

☐ They contained one of three different objects: a square, a circle or a cross

☐ They contained one, two or three of these objects

☐ The objects were in one of three colours: green, black or red

The general procedure was to invite participants to work out the rules in any particular trial – say, all cards with red objects and three borders. In one version, participants were allowed to select cards from the pack, asking 'Is this card one of them?' If the answer was 'no', they merely proceeded to the next card, but if the answer was 'yes' they were entitled to guess what the set of characteristics was.

Cards and procedures used by Bruner et al. (1956)

attributes when selecting the second card. If that card also turned out to be a positive instance, then a great deal of information had been obtained, but if the instance was a negative one, there was no way of telling which of the different attributes was responsible for the error.

A third strategy identified was successive scanning. This involved starting with a hypothesis and selecting cards that provided information relevant to it. The participant scanned for, and remembered, only those attributes that were relevant to the hypothesis formed.

The fourth and least effective strategy was simultaneous scanning, which was similar to successive scanning, except that the participant attempted to scan for, and remember, all the attributes at once, instead of concentrating on one at a time and disposing of each in succession.

Activity 10

It will help you to understand what Bruner was trying to do if you attempt the following exercise.

Take an ordinary pack of playing cards, which have attributes such as suits, colours and numbers, and ask a friend to select a concept. For example, the concept might be one or more court cards, odd or even numbers or perhaps numbers that are greater or smaller than, say, five.

Then, to find the concept, deliberately adopt each of the strategies discussed above in turn, and test its difficulty by counting the number of guesses of positive examples needed to identify it.

(Explanation on page 694.)

Did your results fit with Bruner's findings? Which strategy suited you best? Which was easier, conjunctive or disjunctive concepts? Did it make much difference how many attributes there were?

You probably found that conjunctive concepts are easier to deal with than disjunctive ones, and that the more attributes a concept has, the harder it becomes to identify it.

■ Evaluation of Bruner's research on concept formation

The fact that scanning strategies were less successful than focusing ones was due mainly to what Bruner *et al.* termed cognitive strain – the memory loading that was involved. This was particularly true with simultaneous scanning where participants were attempting to hold several hypotheses in their minds at once, as well as all the information from the cards that related to each.

A difficulty of this study is that it may lack the realism of everyday life situations. A participant in a laboratory situation can suspend judgement about the nature of a concept while focusing upon one attribute after another. In real life an immediate judgement is required. For instance, it may be useful to form a concept of 'dangerous dog' in order to decide whether to approach or avoid a particular dog. In this situation individuals will act on the best available hypothesis. The strategy they adopt will be a scanning one.

Recent work on concept formation in everyday life has focused on theories of prototypes as a way of storing information. Mervis and Rosch (1981) suggested that many concepts are rather 'fuzzy'. They suggest prototypes are organised around a set of characteristics. Any particular instance of the concept will have a number of features, but not all of them. So, for example, some birds, like blackbirds will have more typical features then say ostriches. So, according to prototype theory, concepts do not have to have exactly the same features. Prototypes are better able to account for concrete concepts, for example ball, than for abstract concepts, for example belief. This may be because the range of characteristics in an abstract concept is considerable.

Problem solving

When you want to achieve something, but there are obstacles in the way, there is a problem to be solved. The most efficient way to solve the problem would be to diagnose the problem, formulate a plan for solving it, carry out the plan, then evaluate the result to see whether the problem remains. (Bransford and Stein, 1993). If the problem is complicated, it may be necessary to break it down into smaller sub-problems to deal with it. Another approach is to work backwards, where the end goal is known, for example a holiday, then it is necessary to work out what steps are needed to achieve that goal. A third approach is to use knowledge and past experience to see if there are analogies to the problem to be resolved. A solution which has worked before may be helpful with a similar problem. With a difficult problem it is sometimes helpful to incubate the problem, after which the solution may suddenly appear. It may be that whilst incubating the problem incorrect ideas, which are blocking the path to a correct solution may be forgotten (Best 1995).

One of the first explanations of problem solving was Thorndike's (1898) demonstration of a cat finding its way out of a puzzle box by using trial and error. In the 1920s the Gestalt psychologists (for example Kohler, 1925) demonstrated insight as a method when apes solved problems reaching bananas by regrouping objects available to them in their cages. M Eysenck (1993) pointed out that there are limitations to both these approaches. Thinking and problem solving have more purpose than Thorndike suggested and **insight** does not occur as often as the Gestalt psychologists suggest. A good illustration of the usefulness of incubation is provided with Silveira's (1971) necklace problem (figure 19.13). In the necklace problem, there are four separate pieces of chain, each of three links. All the links are closed. It costs two cents to open a link and three cents to close one. The 12 links must be joined together to make a single necklace chain at a cost of 15 cents.

The problem was solved within 30 minutes by only 55 per cent of those who worked continuously

Figure 19.13

The necklace problem (Silveira, 1971)

at it; 64 per cent of those who took a 30-minute break during the task solved it and 85 per cent of those who had a four-hour break solved it (cited in M Eysenck, 1993, pp. 133–4).

A number of obstacles to problem solving do seem to exist. If there are a number of possible solutions to a problem, for example where something which is lost has been placed, people may not consider all the possibilities. This may be due to limited capacity of working memory. The hypotheses which people consider may be the ones which most easily come to mind rather than the ones which are most likely to be correct (Tversky and Kahneman, 1974).

Sometimes people are blinded by one hypothesis and they continue to use it when a better alternative is readily available. In Luchins's (1942) water jar problem participants were asked to imagine they had three jars A, B and C (figure 19.14). They were given seven problems to solve where the capacity of the jar was listed and the final quantity of liquid required in the jars. All three jars had to be used to obtain the amount of liquid specified as the goal.

Imagine that you have three jars, A, B, and C. In each of seven problems the capacity of the three jars is listed. You must use the three jars in order to obtain the amount of liquid specified in the Goal column. You may obtain the goal amount by adding or subtracting the quantities listed in A, B, and C.

Problem one can be best solved by filling up jar B, removing one jar full with jar A and two jars full with jar C. Problems one to five can all be solved in this fashion and they create a 'mental set' for the problem solver. Most participants will continue to use this method when they reach problems six and seven. Here past learning will be at a disadvantage, because there are easier ways of solving the later problems. Control groups who began by solving problems six and seven almost always used the easier method.

Another example of blindness to hypotheses, or mental set is **functional fixedness**, demonstrated by Maier (1930; 1931). He showed participants into a room with two strings hanging from the ceiling. The task was to tie the strings together, but when the participant held onto one of the strings, the other could not be reached. The solution is to tie an object of weight to one of the strings so it can be swung backwards and forwards like a pendulum. Then, holding the second string, the first one can be caught when the swing approaches. Maier tried to give hints to people who failed to solve the problem. He brushed past the string to set it in motion, he told participants that with the aid of a pair of pliers and nothing else they would be able to solve the problem.

Functional fixedness and mental set involve the misdirection of past experiences to the problem. In these situations there is a negative transfer from past experiences, although with practice and hints, this negative transfer can be overcome. One approach to building problem solving skills is to try to understand the processes used by expert problem solvers compared with novices. Psychologists have sought to understand what skills experts bring to problem solving that novices do not. Knowledge based on past experiences seems to be important, as experts look for analogies between the present and past problems. Experts

Table 19.14

Problem	A	B	C	Goal
1	24	130	3	100
2	9	44	7	21
3	21	58	4	29
4	12	160	25	98
5	19	75	5	46
6	23	49	3	20
7	18	48	4	22

Luchin's Water Jar Problem

Source: Matlin (1989), p. 330.

are better at seeing the link between present and past problems. Experts use existing knowledge to organise new information into chunks, which makes the problem to be solved more manageable and it can be visualised more clearly. In one study expert and novice physicists sorted physics problem into groups. The novices grouped together problems which looked similar (such problems involving blocks lying on an inclined plane), whilst the experts grouped problems together that could be solved by the same principle (such as Newton's second law of motion), (Chi *et al.*, 1981). Experience also gives experts a broad perspective so they perceive the whole problem and do not have to work slowly backwards to identify the parts of the problem which will arise (Medin and Ross, 1992). Also, successful problem solvers can explain each step in the solution and are aware of what they precisely can and cannot understand as they go along (Medin and Ross, 1992). There is however a fine line between using past experience and being trapped by it. Top-down, conceptual processes can create a bias towards certain approaches, preventing experts from seeing the problem in a new way.

Algorithmic problem solving will ensure a solution to a problem, but it would be a slow, inefficient approach in many human situations. In many instances, therefore, humans use **heuristics** strategies, involving a selective search of part of a problem, in order to move closer to an answer. Newell and Simon (1972) studied people solving problems and produced a computer simulation called the **General Problem Solver (GPS)**. The researchers had asked people to think out loud when solving problems. From these verbal reports general strategies were abstracted. From this they developed a computer program to solve different sorts of problems, although the program did not always use the same strategies which humans used. Newell and Simon suggested that the problems people solve can be understood by looking at the initial state of the problem, the goal state and all the mental operators, or moves, that can be applied to one state to change into a different state. Using this approach, problem solving can be seen as a set of sub-goals that intervene between the initial state and the goal state, with moves, or mental operators, producing a move from one state to the next.

Newell and Simon found that when people tried to solve problems they proceeded by heuristic methods, using rules of thumb to set sub-goals to reduce the difference between the current state and the end state. This approach is called means-end analysis. Sub-goals are used to approximate to the end state, although sometimes it may be necessary to increase the difference between the initial state and the end state to move towards the goal. In practice people find this difficult. This is evident in problems such as missionaries and cannibals in Activity 11.

Activity 11

Three missionaries and three cannibals need to be transported across a river in a boat which only holds two people. If the cannibals outnumber the missionaries, the missionaries will be attacked and eaten. Try to get all the missionaries and cannibals across the river without anyone being eaten.

(Suggested answer on page 710.)

Newell and Simon's GPS worked well with 'transportation problems' such as missionaries and cannibals and the Tower of Hanoi (see Activity 12), solving letter code problems, proofs in logic, trigonometry and grammatical analysis of sentences, but it did not have the wide application they hoped it would have and it was taken no further (Gardner, 1985). The GPS was important in demonstrating how solutions can be reached with well-defined problems where there is a specified initial state and a goal state and a number of possible moves in moving from one to the other. There have been a number of successful computer programs which simulate human problem solving in fields such as chess, chemistry and medicine. It is beyond the scope of this unit to discuss these in detail.

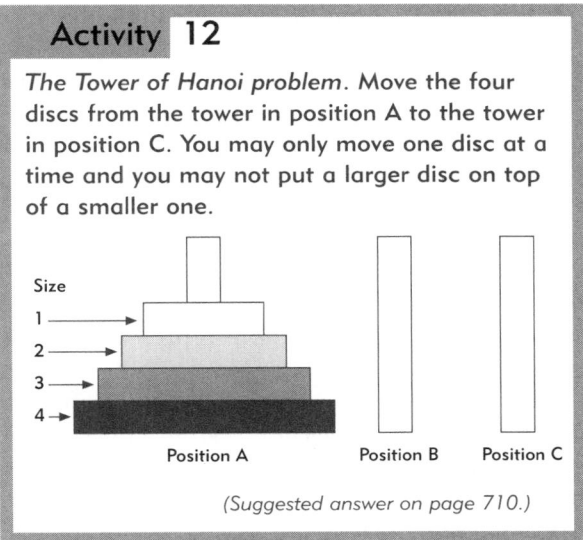
Decision making

In real life people spend a lot of time thinking about decisions they intend to make. Important matters such as what sort of career to follow, whether to marry or whether to move house, occupy a lot of time and thought. Even small decisions such as what to wear can be time consuming. Decisions usually involve comparison of the positive and negative characteristics of the choice or of alternative choices that could be made. In theoretical terms this has been described in Wright's (1984) normative, multi-attribute utility approach. Here the expected value of a number of choices is usually measured and the object with the highest weighted total (or greatest expected value) is usually chosen. In practice, decision making is not a totally rational affair. People show 'bounded rationality' (Simon, 1955), that is they are rational and sensible only to a certain point. Limited time and processing capacity leads people to make decisions they are satisfied with, though the choice may not be ideal.

Decision making as a heuristic process has been put forward by Kahneman and Tversky. They suggest a number of heuristics, or rules of thumb, guide human decision making. They also point out the biases and errors that can occur in the process where the strategies which people use can be applied beyond the range of their usefulness. One of the most important heuristics used in decision making is representativeness. If you have a coin and you toss it six times, what will be the pattern of heads and tails as it lands? H H H T T T or T H H T H T? The second outcome looks more random and is what most people would choose. It seems more representative of the outcome you would expect. Kahneman and Tversky (1972) believed that when people make decisions about the representativeness of samples, for example tossing coins, they do not use true probability as a basis for judgement, they use a representative heuristic of what they think the sample will produce. In fact, the true probability of six coin tosses would just as likely be H H H H H H. Representativeness is normally a useful heuristic, but if it is overused, it can lead to incorrect decisions. This explains the gamblers' fallacy that a certain fruit machine jackpot is 'due' because it has not been paid out recently. In one study by Kahneman and Tversky (1972), people were asked to make judgements about families with six children. People judged families as more likely to be arranged in the sequence G B B G B G than B B B G G G. They used representativeness rather than true probability.

Another factor which should be used in rational decision making, but which is often ignored, is sample size. Kahneman and Tversky (1972) asked college students to respond to the following question:

'A nearby town is served by two hospitals. About 45 babies are born each day in the larger hospital. About 15 babies are born each day in the smaller hospital. Approximately 50 per cent of all babies are boys, as you know. However, the exact percentage of babies who are boys will vary from day to day. Some days it may be higher than 50 per cent, some days it may be lower. For a period of one year, both the larger hospital and the smaller hospital recorded the number of days on which more than 60 per cent of the babies born were boys. Which hospital do you think recorded more such days?*

– *The larger hospital*
– *The smaller hospital*
– *About the same (say, within 5 per cent of each other)'*
(*Quoted in Matlin, 1989, p. 420.*)

Most students answered 'About the same'. The sample size was ignored. A large sample is statistically more likely to reflect the characteristics of the population. The larger hospital is more likely to have the sample closer to 50 per cent baby boys. Large numbers give more accurate representativeness than small numbers. In real life, very often people stereotype others on the basis of small numbers.

Another bias in decision making involves people using a past performance measure as *representative,* to predict future behaviour when this is not valid. Statistically when two measures of behaviour are correlated, if the score on the first measure is extreme, the score on the second measure is likely to regress towards the mean. The mean is the average of the scores when their values are added together and divided by the number of scores. When people make judgements, they tend to rely on the representativeness of the first behaviour and use it to predict the second behaviour, ignoring the statistical tendency for regression towards the mean. Representativeness is such an important heuristic, however, that people do ignore sample size and knowledge about regression towards the mean when they make predictions. Another problem which people have is ignoring the base rate, or the proportion of the categories they are judging, in the population as a whole. Kahneman and Tversky (1973) used the following demonstration to illustrate their point:

'Imagine that some psychologists have administered personality tests to 30 engineers and 70 lawyers, all people who are successful in their fields. Brief descriptions were written for each of the 30 engineers and the 70 lawyers. A sample description follows. Judge that description by indicating the probability that the person described is an engineer. Use a scale from 0 to 100. Jack is a 45 year old man. He is married and has four children. He is generally conservative, careful and ambitious. He shows no interest in political and social issues and spends most of his free time on his many hobbies which include home carpentry, sailing and mathematical puzzles. The probability that the man is one of the 30 engineers in the sample of 100 is ____ %.' (*Quoted in Matlin, 1989, p. 425.*)

In the example above, it is more likely that Jack is a lawyer. Most people ignored this base-rate information and judged on representativeness suggesting Jack was an engineer.

Another heuristic which people use in making decisions is the *availability heuristic,* where they estimate probability in terms of how easy it is to think of examples of something (Kahneman and Tversky, 1973). Errors can occur because people are influenced by what is most familiar and by most recent occurrences. For example, people who are acquainted with a lot of divorce provide higher estimates of divorce rates than people who rarely meet divorce (Kozielecki, 1981). Another example of availability heuristic is people's tendency to use causal scenarios. A causal scenario is the explanation of how one event causes another. When an event is judged, the ease with which a causal scenario comes to mind affects the judgement.

Yet another heuristic which people use is the *anchoring and adjustment heuristic.* This is used when people make estimates. First, an approximation is guessed, the anchor, then adjustments are made on the basis of additional information (Tversky and Kahneman, 1982). Answers are often reasonable, but people rely too heavily on the anchor and make small adjustments. In real life this happens when people are asked to estimate sweets in a jar. They are unduly influenced by previous estimates given and merely make small adjustments to those.

In sum, in the early 1970s Kahneman and Tversky described how heuristics affecting representativeness, availability and anchoring and adjustment are important when people make decisions. In the late 1970s/1980s they explained another potential source of bias, decision frames (Kahneman and Tversky, 1979; 1984; Tversky and

Kahneman, 1981). Here they suggested the way in which a question is asked, or framed, and the background context can affect the decision made. The background to this approach lies in the development of *prospect theory* (Kahneman and Tversky, 1979). The theory has two important concepts, risk aversion and risk seeking. People generally avoid taking risks if the alternative is positive and likely. Kahneman and Tversky (1979) gave the following example.

People were given the choice of the following lotteries:

1   90 out of 100 tickets win £3000; 10 out of 100 tickets win £0, *or*

2   45 out of 100 tickets win £6000; 55 out of 100 win £0.

Eighty-six per cent of people opted for choice one, which is consistent with loss aversion. With losses, however, people tend to be risk seeking. Kahneman and Tversky (1979) gave people the following choice.

3   90 out of 100 tickets lose £3000; 10 out of 100 tickets lose £0 *or*

4   45 out of 100 tickets lose £6000; 55 out of 100 tickets lose £0.

In this case 92 per cent of people opted for choice four. They chose the riskier option, though the overall outcome is the same in both cases. This switch from risk aversion to risk seeking is called the reflection effect. Kahneman and Tversky also proposed that there are two key stages in decision making. The first stage is the *editing stage* where the prospects available are altered to simplify their mental representation and the choices that have to be made. The second stage involves *evaluating* the edited prospects and choosing the prospect with the most personal appeal. During editing there is a coding operation where possible outcomes are measured against what is desired (the aspiration level), so choices are gains or losses measured against this. The coding of choices as gains or losses occurs in a context. This is known as the *framing effect*. Editing is now referred to as framing (Tversky and Kahneman, 1981). There have been many studies to support the framing effect. In one study, Neale and Northcraft (1986) asked professional salespeople and students to simulate buying a large quantity of refrigerators. Both groups sold more when the problem was phrased in a positive frame, in terms of profit, rather than in a negative frame, in terms of expenses.

Decision taking has been shown to involve *bounded rationality*. Up to a point, rational, normative judgement is employed, but heuristics are also usually applied, or sometimes overapplied, leading to biases and errors. More recently, prospect theory and framing theory have developed decision making, so more is understood about the context in which people take decisions about the risks and gains involved.

Self-assessment questions

14   Does research suggest that people try to use logical reasoning?

15   Explain the difference between algorithmic and heuristic thinking.

16   Outline four ways in which people try to solve problems.

17   Outline three problems which people may experience when they try to solve problems.

18   Outline the three main sources of bias that can affect heuristic decision making. They were identified by Kahneman and Tversky in the 1970s.

(Suggested answers on page 712.)

The relationship between language and thought, including social and cultural variations

A number of proposals have been put forward to explain the relationship between language and thought. They can be grouped into three main viewpoints: that language determines thought; that thought determines language; that thought and language have different origins but come together as children develop.

The view that language determines thought

The view that there is no thought without language was shared by the supporters of the linguistic relativity hypothesis and the behaviourists. These views are discussed in the sections which follow.

■ The linguistic relativity hypothesis

Whorf (1941) was an adherent of the view that language determines thought. He was a linguist whose particular area of expertise was Indian languages. His theory has become known as the *linguistic relativity hypothesis* or the Whorfian hypothesis. Whorf noticed that the Hanuxoo people of the Philippines had 92 names for rice, the Inuit people had more than 20 words for snow, and that there are many words in Arabic which relate to camels. He felt that these differences in terminology between languages must influence thought and how the world is perceived. For example, he considered that the Inuit Eskimos have different thought patterns from the British because of the many names in their language for snow, whereas we have just a few words for it.

Whorf also used linguistic evidence to suggest that Hopi Indians think differently to English speakers because they have just one word for the English words insect, aeroplane and pilot, make no distinctions between past, present and future tenses, and some words which are nouns in English are treated by them as verbs. For example, lightning in English is represented by the Hopi verb 'rehpi', which means to lighten. Whorf also noticed that the Zuni Indians do not distinguish verbally between yellow and orange – he suggested that they cannot perceive the difference between these colours.

Evidence for the linguistic relativity hypothesis comes from a study of Navaho Indians by Carroll and Casogrande (1958) who compared form perception and recognition in Navaho-speaking and English-speaking children. The Navaho language has words which are capable of distinguishing objects that are long and flexible, long and rigid, and flat and flexible – words absent in English. Carroll and Casogrande contended that Navaho speakers should be superior to English speakers in this aspect of their cognitive development and this was, indeed, found to be the case. Support for the Whorfian hypothesis was however undermined when a control group of Anglo American children showed an even stronger tendency to classify by form.

Research by Ervin-Tripp (1964) support the Whorfian hypothesis. He gave bilingual Japanese-Americans a series of sentence completion and word association tests. They performed like Japanese when they were asked to answer in Japanese, and like Americans when they were asked to answer in English. Their thought was apparently influenced by the language in which they responded.

Language is dynamic rather than static and therefore has the capacity to adapt to environmental differences as and when required. For example, it is not entirely true to say that English has only a single word for snow. English-speaking glaciologists use the terms 'neve' and 'firn' to refer to soft, powdery snow and compacted snow, respectively, and American skiers distinguish between 'powder' and 'corn'.

Whorf's conclusions concerning the research with the Hopi Indians may be criticised on the grounds that the mere fact that the Hopi do not have different words for insect and aeroplane does not mean that they are perceived as the same thing. Greene (1975) pointed out (among other examples) that the English word 'drive' can mean the route leading to a house, a shot in golf, achieving a hard bargain and what you do to a car. Would it be reasonable to suppose, however, that the English speaker cannot recognise these different interpretations of the word drive? A similar overreliance on literal meanings may mean that there is no significant difference in the perceptions of 'lightning' (English) and 'it lightened' (Hopi), or in the interpretation of tenses – although the Hopi have no means of distinguishing tenses, they do have a concept of time. In the end there is very little difference between the English 'I will leave in eight days' and the Hopi 'I go on the eight day'.

The suggestion that Zuni Indians cannot perceive the difference between yellow and orange can be contradicted by findings from a study by Lenneberg and Roberts (1956). They studied three groups of participants in terms of their linguistic abilities to distinguish yellow and orange. These were Zuni speakers, English speakers and a group bilingual in both languages. The bilingual participants achieved results that were intermediate between the other two groups, which suggests that the different cultures have alternative sets of labels for these colours rather than fundamentally different perceptions. This could indicate that thought influences language rather than the other way round.

Similarly, other research using colours (for example, Berlin and Kay, 1969; Rosch, 1973) seems to suggest that although colour terminology may vary across languages, this is a result of the way information is coded and stored rather than the direct influence of language on colour perception.

If you travel in a European train and read the notices, you might see:
- 'Do not lean out of the window' (English)
- 'Nicht hinauslehnen' (German)
- 'E pericoloso sporgersi' (Italian)

Activity 13

Does the very peremptory sound of the German reflect the way Germans think, or does it determine it? Does the fact that the literal translation of the Italian is: 'It is dangerous to poke your head out' influence the way that Italians think about it?
This is very difficult to test.

If Whorf is right, you would suppose that any group of people whose language development is retarded – the deaf for example – would also show impaired thought.

Furth (1966) concluded that whilst the deaf did show retardation in those areas of cognition which involve language, there was no such effect on intellectual functions that were independent of language. Other studies, however, have shown that deaf people do show inferior performance on tasks that are not language-dependent. However, deaf children often suffer in other ways as well, for example cultural deprivation, poor education and emotional disturbance.

More recently, work by Bloom (1981) has focused on language differences between English and Chinese, in particular the English language construction that can indicate that a statement is counterfactual. For example, 'If I could drive a car, I would take you home'. The sentence implies the speaker cannot drive and what is said is hypothetical. In the Chinese language there is no direct equivalent and in studies carried out Bloom found Chinese speakers were less likely to give hypothetical interpretations to a hypothetical story, although responses varied according to the wording of stories and the level of education of the participants. Bloom concluded that differences in linguistic form may well be responsible for differences in the way English and Chinese people categorise and think about the world. Au (1983) conducted similar experiments with English and Chinese people and found little difference in hypothetical responses. Bloom's study is still, however, recognised as important for showing there is a link between language, grammar and human cognition.

In sum then, does the evidence suggest that language determines thought? Differences in words, for example relating to colour, snow or camels does not support the idea that different words lead to different patterns of thought. Syntactic and grammatical differences between languages, such as hypothetical thought, provide stronger evidence for the notion that language affects cognition. An interesting new source of evidence comes from bilingual studies. Early work in the field by Ervin-Tripp (1964) has been described. People who are bilingual are often associated with two different cultural systems, so how does this affect their pattern of thought and their personality? Studies reported about bilingual people (Hull, 1987; Dinges and Hull, 1992) suggest the existence of cultural and personality differences depending on the language being used (Chinese-English and Korean-English bilinguals were tested). There is also evidence to suggest that our perceptions of other people depend on the language spoken. Matsumoto and Assar (1992) asked bilingual observers in India to look at 40 different facial expressions of emotion. They were to report how emotion was being portrayed in the faces and how intensely. Judgements were made one week apart, first in English and second in Hindi. Judgements of the emotion being portrayed were made more accurately in English, but the emotions were perceived as more intense when the ratings were made in Hindi. It may be concluded that language and culture are intertwined with environmental conditions and demands shaping attention to and understanding of the world, with language evolving to describe, in detail, aspects of the world especially important in one's own culture.

As Reber (1985) points out:

'It is likely that the complex interweaving between culture, social values, language and thought produces a rich representation of one's world knowledge which one's language can stretch or expand as necessary to encompass the perceptions and cognitions needed for effective verbal communication. From this view,

language is an attempt to "map" thought rather than its controller.'

Such a view should be borne out from our own experiences. After all, we are all familiar with the use of carefully selected phrasing by politicians. In the end, there may be very little difference, in reality, between 'cutting excessive spending' and 'cutting services'!

The *behaviourist* view of the relationship between language and thought is a deterministic theory. The father of behaviourism, Watson (1912), took the view that thought and language were essentially the same thing; thought was merely sub-vocal speech.

A dangerous study carried out by Smith *et al.* (1947) refuted Watson's position. Smith was kept alive on a respirator after taking a curare derivative which completely paralysed him. He was unable to engage in speech, sub-vocal activity or any other bodily movement. He should, therefore, have been incapable of thought but reported that he was quite capable of understanding what people were saying and could think about what was going on. (You may care to consider the ethical implications of such research.)

Bernstein (1961) proposed some evidence which could be used to support the behaviourist view when he investigated social class differences in language use and how these affected intellectual abilities. In a study comparing the intellectual performance of boys from lower-working-class homes with boys from public schools, he concluded that working-class and middle-class children speak two different forms of language, which he termed *restricted and elaborated codes* (figure 19.15).

As a result of using these codes, Bernstein thought that working-class children are prevented from developing their intellectual potential fully – the codes have a profound influence on their thinking and learning, therefore language determines level of thinking.

Evidence against this view comes from Labov (1970) who suggested that such apparent differences in the ability to think and use language were merely artefacts of the research situation. Labov compared speakers of 'standard English'

Table 19.15

Restricted code	Elaborate code
Simplistic grammar	More complex grammar
Repetitive	Less repetitive
Rigid	Flexible
Limited use of adjectives and adverbs	Wider use of adjectives and adverbs
Uses more pronouns than nouns	Uses more nouns than pronouns
Short, incomplete sentences	Longer, complete and more complex sentences
Assumes listener knows what the conversation is about	Makes meaning explicit
Heavy reliance on non-verbal communication	Less reliance on non-verbal communication
Emphasises the present	Emphasises the past and future
Does not permit abstract thought	Allows expression of abstract thought

Characteristics of the restricted and elaborated codes

with those who use 'Black English' dialects. These two forms of English differ grammatically, so it would follow that black children who were tested for their intelligence using a test phrased in standard English would be at a disadvantage when compared to speakers of standard English.

Labov's findings led him to believe that speakers of both forms of English are equally capable of understanding each other and expressing the same ideas. This belief was borne out by research using the BITCH test (Black Intelligence Test of Cultural Homogeneity, devised by Williams in 1972). The test was written in Black English, and when white children were tested using it, they performed very poorly (Genshaft and Hirt, 1974).

The view that thought determines language

Much of the evidence against the view that language comes before thought supports the alternative view that thought comes before language. The most influential proponent of this view was Piaget who was interested in children's cognitive development and how the relationship between 'the knower and the known changes over time'. Piaget described thought not only as determining language, but also as preceding it.

In Piaget's view, children form an internal representation of the world by thinking. He describes imitation, for example, as thinking. When children see someone doing something and later copy it, thinking takes place. This does not have to involve language. In fact, much of the thought described by Piaget is pre-linguistic.

Piaget believed that language is just one of several vehicles for thinking. As actions become internalised, language may affect children's range of symbolic thinking but is not necessary for its original development. He also believed that although children can be taught a language, they cannot understand the words without a knowledge of the underlying concepts. They would be no better than a talking bird!

Thought is necessary if language is to be understood. Sinclair-De-Zwart (1969) found support for Piaget here. Children who could conserve volume could also understand comparative concepts, such as 'bigger', 'more' and 'some', whereas children without conservation could not, even if given training.

Although Piaget went into great detail in describing the development of intellectual capacity in children, he largely overlooked the influence of language in the developing thought processes.

The view that thought and language have different origins

Vygotsky believed that thought and language have different origins and remain separate entities, developing in stages along parallel lines, although their functions may overlap.

The stages of thought begin with unorganised ways of grouping things into *congeries* or heaps by their common links – which are made in the child's perception and may not be logical. Thinking in *complexes* comes next, where children perceive unchangeable concrete and factual bonds between the individual components of objects. The final stage is *conceptual thinking* where children are able to make abstract links between components and also to analyse them. This allows flexibility for incorporating new information, unlike the inflexible way of thinking in terms of complexes.

Vygotsky described four stages of speech development: *non-intellectual* or *thoughtless* speech develops into a *naïve* stage in which the symbolic function of words is acquired. *Egocentric* language comes next and this develops into *inner speech* where children are able to manipulate thoughts by using soundless speech. Speech, for Vygotsky, begins on the social plane of interactions with others and gradually becomes internalised into the psychological plane of inner speech with social speech just becoming a means of communication.

Vygotsky proposed that three processes occur as children move from stage to stage. Destruction of the original structures is followed by reconstruction and transition of new structures as the next stage emerges. He also stressed that conceptual thinking is very much dependent on the quality of language a person possesses, and vice versa.

Thought is used without language when the vehicle of thinking is non-verbal, for example visual or movement, as when tracing a spiral. Language is used without thought when expressing feelings or trying to attract attention – a 'How are you?' 'Very well, thank you, and you?' kind of exchange.

When the two functions overlap, they can be used together to produce verbal thought and rational speech. At this point, language has the dual function of internally monitoring and directing thought, as well as externally communicating the results of thinking to other people. As adults, we generally restrict the use of overt speech to communication with others (after all, talking to yourself raises eyebrows) but we do use inner language to think aloud, for example in moments of stress when we are trying to solve a difficult problem.

Vygotsky was convinced that *inner speech served to provide a mental orientation,* to overcome difficulties and to gain conscious understanding of a problem. He saw this inner speech as the natural successor to the egocentric speech of infants. When you go into an infant classroom, what strikes you is the buzz of language, not of children talking to one another, but talking to themselves about what they are doing.

Vygotsky used the analogy of two circles to represent the two functions of non-verbal thought and non-conceptual speech, i.e. thought without language, and language without thought (figure 19.16). As children's cognitive abilities develop, the two circles meet and overlap, but never completely. This shows that children acquire verbal thought, in which concepts can be given word labels, whilst still being capable of the non-rational verbal exchanges and thinking aloud already described.

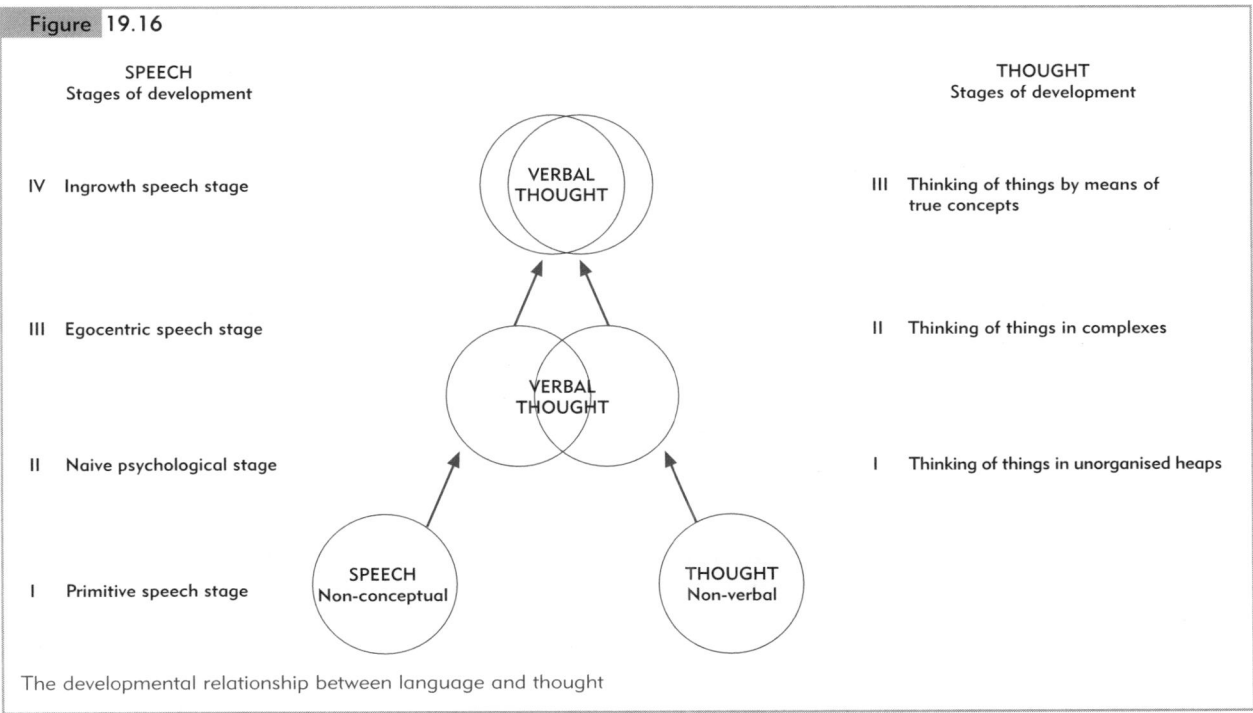

Figure 19.16

SPEECH
Stages of development

THOUGHT
Stages of development

IV   Ingrowth speech stage

III   Thinking of things by means of true concepts

III   Egocentric speech stage

II   Thinking of things in complexes

II   Naive psychological stage

I   Thinking of things in unorganised heaps

I   Primitive speech stage

VERBAL THOUGHT

VERBAL THOUGHT

SPEECH Non-conceptual

THOUGHT Non-verbal

The developmental relationship between language and thought

Self-assessment questions

19   Why did Whorf suggest that language precedes thought?

20   A number of studies (for example Lenneberg and Roberts, 1956) have been carried out on colour naming to test the Whorfian hypothesis. What do they generally show?

21   Give an example of how bilingual evidence suggests culture affects language and thought.

22   Is there a social class difference in thought?

23   In Piaget's view does thought or language develop first?

24   Outline the relationship between language and thought in Vygotsky's theory.

(Suggested answers on page 712.)

Unit summary

- The *behaviourist* (Skinner), *rationalist* (Chomsky) and *cognitive* (Piaget/social interactionist) theories of language have been put forward to explain the development of language acquisition. Whilst Skinner and Chomsky take extreme positions on language being *learned* or *innate*, the cognitive/social-interactionist approach emphasises the *maturational* basis of language within cognitive development and within a social context.

- Garrett's theoretical model of speech production discusses *five levels of representation* which are sequentially involved in speaking a sentence.

- Pauses are used to aid sentence and clause planning and errors in speech are usually a misapplication of the words or structure in a planned clause.

- Dell's model of *word retrieval in speech production* provides a detailed computer simulation explanation and also seems able to explain many of the errors that are common in speech production.

- Garrett's model has been used to illustrate the impact that brain damage can have on speech production.

- Reading comprehension initially involves the fixation of letters within the perceptual span.

- It has been suggested that letter recognition could be achieved by *template matching, feature detection* or converting the varied forms of written letters into *abstract letter identities*.

- McClelland and Rummelhart's (1981) model of reading comprehension suggests simultaneous bottom up and top down processing of letters and words.

- Ellis and Young's (1984) *three route model of reading comprehension* suggests different processes operating when written material is accessed.

- *Speech perception* involves the utilisation of many cues both visual and auditory. Context cues in a sentence are important.

- The segmentation of speech and stress patterns in speech are used in perception.

- The *Cohort model of auditory word recognition* suggests speech perception operates when an internal representation of sound is comparable with the sound being heard.

- Visual aspects of speech comprehension are used especially in adverse noise conditions.

- Psychologists have investigated whether people use *algorithmic thinking* and have found that humans sometimes find the use of abstract logic and formal reasoning difficult.

- Cheng and Holyoak (1985) have suggested humans use reasoning at a more *pragmatic* level, based on their own experiences. Johnson-Laird (1983) suggested humans use mental models, or semantic processes as a basis for reasoning.

- *Inductive reasoning* involves concept formation which provides a grouping for thought, leading to economy of processing.

- Approaches to *problem solving* include breaking down the problem into sub-goals, working backwards from the solution, using past experiences to develop analogies, incubating the problem, trial and error and regrouping information to develop insight.

- Problem solving can be limited by available working memory capacity and the negative transfer of past experience in *mental set* and *functional fixedness*.

- Experts are better than novices at problem solving because they use past experience to see connections in underlying structures, they have a wider overview and know exactly where they are within a problem.

- Newell and Simon (1972) used the GPS to illustrate how many problems could be solved using *means-ends analysis*.

- Decision making involves considering the benefits and costs of choices. People are, however, only rational to a point.

- Kahneman and Tversky (1973) demonstrated the use of *heuristics* in decision making and the biases and errors that occur.

Summary cont'd.

- In the 1980s Kahneman and Tversky developed *prospect theory* to show how people avoid and seek risks in decisions and how they frame issues.
- The view that language determines thought was expressed by the *Whorfian hypothesis* (1941). Supporting evidence comes from studies of the Hopi Indians and the Navaho Indians.
- Research studies using colour perception to explore language and thought have not supported Whorf. They have found that colour differences are perceived even where there is not a specific colour word to describe the colour hue.
- Studies of deaf children with language retardation have proved controversial to interpret in terms of the effect of language on intellectual functioning.
- Studies of bilingual people suggest language and culture are intertwined. Language has evolved as a way of mapping thought rather than controlling it.

- Watson's behaviourist view considers thought to be merely sub-vocal speech, although this was not supported by the Smith *et al.* (1947) curare study.
- Bernstein's (1961) evidence on *social class differences* and language does suggest that patterns of speech affect the intellectual performance of boys. A different view taken by Labov's work on 'Black English' which suggests the structure of this language is different from, but not inferior to, standard English.
- Evidence supporting the view that thought determines language comes from Piaget's theory that conceptual understanding precedes meaningful language. Training in language does not develop conceptual thought (Sinclair-de-Zwart, 1969).
- Vygotsky held the view that language and thought have different origins which come together as the child develops so that much of verbal thought and rational speech overlap.

Terms to define

algorithmic thinking
aphasia
baby talk register (BTR)
deductive reasoning
dyslexia
feature detection theory
functional fixedness
general problem solver (GPS)

heuristics
insight
interactional synchrony
language acquisition device (LAD)
morpheme
phoneme
syntax
tip of the tongue (TOT) phenomena

Further reading

Eysenck, M W (1993) *Principles of Cognitive Psychology*, Laurence Erlbaum, Hove.

This provides a very detailed account of much of the material covered in this unit.

Matlin, M W (1994) *Cognition*, 3rd edn, Harcourt Brace, Orlando, FL.

This book covers most of the material in this unit in a detailed and accessible way. There are many demonstrations and examples to clarify and support points being made.

Matsumoto, D (1994) *People, Psychology from a Cultural Perspective*, Brooks/Cole, Pacific Grove, CA.

Chapter 6 on language and language acquisition approaches the topic area from a cross-cultural angle.

Developmental Psychology, *Language Development*, Psychology Live Series Videos, Uniview Productions, Hoylake.

A 40-minute video which illustrates the developmental stages of children's language. It also contains suggestions for practical work and references.

Answers

◼ Suggested answers to activities

1

> There is the juice.
> I want some juice.
> Where is the juice.
> I have spilt some juice.
> Can we buy some juice?

11

> Missionaries = M; cannibals = C; right = R; left = L.
> Steps to the solution:
> 1   Move 2 M, R to L bank of river
> 2   Move 1 M, L to R
> 3   Move 2 M, R to L
> 4   Move 1 M, L to R
> 5   Move 2 C, R to L
> 6   Move 1 M, 1 C L to R
> 7   Move 2 C, R to L
> 8   Move 1 M, L to R
> 9   Move 2 M, R to L
> 10   Move 1 M, L to R
> 11   Move 2 M, R to L

12

> 1   Move size 1 to position B
> 2   Move size 2 to position C
> 3   Move size 1 to position C
> 4   Move size 3 to position B
> 5   Move size 1 to position B
> 6   Move size 2 to position A

> 7   Move size 1 to position C
> 8   Move size 2 to position B
> 9   Move size 1 to position B
> 10   Move size 4 to position C
> 11   Move size 1 to position C
> 12   Move size 2 to position A
> 13   Move size 1 to position A
> 14   Move size 3 to position C
> 15   Move size 1 to position B
> 16   Move size 2 to position C
> 17   Move size 1 to position C

◼ Suggested answers to self-assessment questions

1

> **Pre-linguistic stage: 0–12 months**
> ↓
> Variety of cries
> ↓
> Cooing
> ↓
> Babbling – phonemes
> ↓
> Phonemic contraction – echolalia

One-word stage – consistent match between symbol and sound; 12–18 months

Word labels

Holophrase

↓

Vocabulary growth (approx. 50 words at 20 months)

Two-word stage

Stage one grammar (18–30 months)

Linking two words

Telegraphic speech

Vocabulary increases to around 500 words

Stage two grammar (30 months to 5 years)

Development of syntax

Overgeneralisation and underextension

Vocabulary growth

Rapid increase in mean length of utterance

By age 5, language use similar to that of an adult

2

Mands refer to the process of shaping children's language resulting from children asking for things which they then receive. Thus children's demands are met through using language.

Tacts are the connections between the utterance made by the child and the object the child is attempting to name. These are developed through behaviour shaping techniques. Thus a child gets reinforced for naming objects.

Echoic responses are the responses made by a child imitating others. They are usually reinforced.

3

a Language acquisition device refers to an innate language ability enabling children to extract the basic rules of grammar from the speech they hear. This is a fairly automatic process dependent upon children experiencing speech.

b Transformational grammar are the rules which determine how sentences can be transformed in a language, particularly from deep to surface structure.

c Deep structure of language describes the grammar, common to all languages. This enables a child anywhere in the world to acquire any language.

d Surface structure is the pattern of grammar and sentence structure which is found in one particular language and which distinguishes it from other languages.

e Linguistic universals are the common structural features of language, for example the existence of nouns, verbs, consonants and vowels.

f Semantic rules are the rules that govern word meanings.

g Syntactic rules are the rules combining how words are put together in meaningful and correct sentences.

4

Language, for Piaget, is mainly a consequence of cognitive development. Children carry out actions, develop thoughts and then use language expressions for these thoughts. Language develops with intellectual maturity and is an expression of it. Language develops through egocentric, then social speech. It subsequently enables a child to use signs for thoughts and eventually frees a child from having to manipulate things physically in order to solve problems.

5

a Interactional synchrony refers to the coordination of communication between young babies and adults. It takes place through such things as turn taking, use of gaze, pre-verbal conversations.

b Stroking and talking to the baby.

c Verbal exchanges where the mother interprets, extends, comments on and 'repeats' what the child has said.

d Use of parentese (BTR or motherese), repeated, simple sentences, clear pitch to simplify language for the child's level of understanding.

6

Skinner's theory suggests environmental and social factors are the explanation of language acquisition. Reinforcement and modelling shape language once sounds are produced. Chomsky only requires some experience of language to shape the surface structure. The linguistic universals, transformational grammar and deep structure are innate factors. The cognitive/social-interactionist approach emphasises the maturational basis of language and the influence of the social context. The latter is important in developing pre-linguistic communication, the social format of the LASS and an interest in social communication.

7

The methods used are controlled experiments, studies of speech disruption and computer modelling.

8

Pauses allow time to plan the next clause or sentence. This seems to be more important for semantic planning than for syntactic structuring.

9

A spoonerism involves mixing up phonemes when a clause is activated. A phoneme from late in the clause is activated too early and exchanged with a phoneme from early in the clause.

10

In the production of written language expert writers use strategic knowledge processes such as revising the structure and logical coherence of the text. Non-expert writers use knowledge-telling strategies which extend no further than concentrating on revision of words and phrases.

11

In McClelland and Rummelhart's model top-down processing operates when the stored knowledge of words is activated and fed back to the letter recognition units. Meanwhile bottom-up processing occurs as a response to the stimuli where letter units respond to the feature detectors.

12

The three routes to reading are phonemic mediation, semantic matching and accessing pronounciation. Phonemic mediation is likely to be used with difficult or unfamiliar words or with non-words. Semantic matching is likely to be used for reading of familiar words. Accessing pronounciation without accessing sound or meaning is only likely to occur where there is damage to other processing routes as it does not involve reading with understanding.

13

People use a number of cues to help them decipher speech: the meaning of the words, the context of the sentence, the passage or their wider knowledge; the stress patterns of words, pauses, syntax of the sentence; visual cues of gesture, lip reading and facial expression.

14

Sometimes people use abstract logical reasoning, particularly when the conclusion they draw from the premises is fairly straightforward. People also use pragmatic logic, based on past experiences of similar reasoning rules. It has also been suggested that people use semantic mental models by converting premises into meaningful mental representations. Human beings do not find the use of abstract mental reasoning easy.

15

Algorithmic thinking is a way of solving problems that will lead to a correct solution if it is undertaken systematically. It can be a long and inefficient process, but a solution is gauranteed. Heuristic thinking, on the other hand, involves using past experience from which strategies, or rules of thumb are developed. A solution is not guaranteed, but the task is more manageable.

16

Methods by which people try to solve problems could include: trial and error, insight, incubating the problem, working backwards from the solution, means-ends analysis, breaking the problem down into sub-goals, use of analogies.

17

Three reasons people might have difficulties solving problems are limited capacity of working memory, mental set arising from past experiences and functional fixedness, or not being able to see familiar objects in a new use.

18

The three main sources of bias affecting heuristic decision making are overuse of representativeness, availability of subjective experiences to draw on and the tendency to anchor a heuristic too narrowly and adjust too closely to it (Kahneman and Tversky).

19

When Whorf studied Indian languages he found that the vocabulary used differed from European languages. He believed the different vocabulary structured thought and the way that the world was perceived.

20

Cross-cultural studies of colour naming show that although colour naming may vary with cultures, colour perception is similar regardless of the extent of the vocabulary of colour terms.

21

Description of studies by Ervin-Tripp, Bloom, Hull, Dinges and Hull or Matsumoto and Assar would answer this question. These studies variously suggest different languages produce different structures of thought, personality or response to emotions.

22

Bernstein (1961) suggested that there is. He hypothesised that the elaborate code of the middle class produces certain advantages in the structure of thought and expression compared with the restricted code of the lower working class.

23

According to Piaget, conceptual thinking develops before language can be used meaningfully.

24

Vygotsky suggests language and thought have separate origins and as children develop, language and thought come to overlap so that verbal thought and rational speech come together. Speech comes to monitor and direct thought as well as being a social tool for communication.

Developmental Psychology

Unit 20

Early Socialisation

Liz Conroy, Graham Davies, Peter Reddy and
Irene Taylor

This unit covers:

The development of sociability

Attachments

The effects of early experience

Social and cultural variations in child rearing

By the end of this unit, you should be able to:

- understand the process of social development in the early years of life
- explain the development of attachments and mutual demand systems
- consider how enrichment, deprivation and separation affect the child
- understand the effects of cross-cultural differences and culturally specific aspects of child rearing.

Unit 20   Contents

Introduction

Socialisation is 'the process by which a society's behaviour patterns, standards and beliefs are transmitted from one individual to another' (Schaffer, 1995). This unit looks at how the child's early social behaviour develops. Initially, maturation puts the child in a state of readiness and socialisation provides the content.

Hartup (1989) suggests that the child needs to develop **vertical** and **horizontal relationships**. Vertical relationships involve an attachment to someone who is in a more powerful position such as a parent, teacher or someone older than the child. The bond is powerful with different behaviours expected of each partner. Horizontal relationships are more egalitarian and include same age peers who have equal power. Hartup sees these two kinds of relationship serving different functions for the child and both essential for the child to acquire the necessary social skills. In vertical relationships the child learns the fundamental social skills required by society and in horizontal relationships the child may try out these skills and learn new skills of cooperation, competition and intimacy.

When does socialisation begin? Most psychologists believe that early experience can have profound effects throughout life. Just as malnutrition may lead to permanent physical handicap, so a lack of appropriate emotional experience may cause psychological repercussions throughout an individual's life. Such apparent common sense is now widely accepted, although it is only a few generations old and draws on Freud's pioneering work in the field of psychoanalysis at the start of the twentieth century. However, despite its apparent relevance, this had little impact on developmental psychology until the 1940s.

From his work treating emotionally disturbed adults, Freud produced a profoundly influential theory which suggested that children are born with powerful instinctual needs and drives. Each society places constraints on the gratification of these needs and drives and the social constraints are transmitted through parental child rearing practices. These constraints come into conflict with the child's drives. Freud thought that the resolution of these conflicts, especially in the first five years of life, formed the basis not only of such adult disturbance as may occur, but of personality in general. It becomes necessary, therefore, to look at children's social and emotional development in order to understand adult feelings and behaviours. We begin this unit by considering the development of sociability.

The development of sociability

Humans are a social species. The communication we have with others and the relationships that are formed through that communication are important elements in our lives – and a life without other people is almost inconceivable. Babies may be born with a tendency to be interested in people around them, but how do babies develop a growing social orientation? In this section we consider the development of *sociability* – defined by Schaffer (1989) as 'the child's willingness to engage others in social interaction, and to seek their attention or approval'.

Activity 1

Write down what babies can do in their first few weeks of life and consider how they help the baby to communicate. (Some ideas follow.)

One way in which babies develop social communication is through their enjoyment of *contingent stimulation* by others, or by events in their environments. This is a kind of mutual reward or reinforcement system which follows on appropriately from a baby's action, rather like a reply (see figure 20.1 for an example of contingent stimulation). We often provide contingent response when we react to a baby smiling, waving an arm in the air or cooing. These encourage the baby into reciprocal interaction (turn taking) and we take turns in responding contingently to an action by the

20.1 An example of contingent stimulation

Watson and Ramey (1972) showed how attractive contingent stimulation could be to 8-week-old babies in an experiment using electric motor powered mobiles which were suspended above babies' cots. In the experimental condition the mobile was connected to a pressure switch in the baby's pillow, so that a small head movement would cause it to rotate for one second through 90 degrees. The number of times the pillow switch was activated was recorded and compared with control conditions in which either the mobile was switched off and did not move at all, or the pressure switch was disconnected and the mobile moved automatically every few seconds, quite regardless of what the baby was doing. The mobiles were given to families to use at home and they were asked to use them for 10 minutes a day for a fortnight. The results showed a substantial and highly significant increase in the number of activations of the mobile in the experimental condition and little change in the control conditions. Clearly the babies had learned to move their heads for the reward of seeing the mobile move.

Interestingly, when the researchers went to collect the equipment, they found that most of the mothers of babies in the experimental condition had been using the mobiles more than they had been asked to because their babies had developed a strong response to them. For example, they would smile and coo at the mobile and it would be hard to distract them from it. Although this finding was incidental to the study and so not very systematic, it illustrates how interesting contingent stimulation is to babies.

other. These actions acquire meanings and the turn taking becomes reciprocal communication – the bedrock of sociability, of attachments and ultimately of social existence and civilisation.

Kaye (1984) argues that the baby is not as social from birth as some have suggested; rather that adults interpret almost any part of the baby's behaviour which could be considered as social and treat it as intentionally social. At first, the baby's part in social communication is purely automatic and all the work towards it is done by adults, who create a framework or scaffold for the child to make use of as development takes place.

Whether turn taking is initiated by the adult or not there is a body of evidence showing that this *contingent responsiveness* of the parents to the child is linked to more secure attachment in the child (Sroufe and Fleeson, 1986; Isabella Belsky and von Eye, 1989; Pederson *et al.*, 1990). The parents need to be sensitive to the child's cues. When mothers are '*psychologically unavailable*' (coined by Sroufe) and do not have contingent responsiveness, it appears to result in attachment insecurity.

Very young infants, however, can make use of their senses to their own advantage and we shall now consider how they do this when developing sociability.

Vision and sociability

Vision is the primary sense of humans and therefore has great importance to the development of sociability. It allows meaningful eye contact to be established, initially with cares, and helps infants to coordinate signals with others, thus helping to form the foundation for social interactions. When cares reinforce signals, such as smiles, infants develop confidence, thus facilitating further social contact.

However, it must be pointed out that vision is not essential to the development of sociability, since blind children are capable of forming social interactions successfully. Other senses may therefore be as, or more, important.

■ Looking

At birth, babies have limited visual abilities. For example, focusing is initially limited to about 21–23 centimetres (the approximate distance of a mother's eyes from those of her infant during breast feeding and cuddling). Adults will often place their faces at about this distance for babies to focus on, although *looking* is directed to all sorts of objects as well, for example rattles, bottles, mobiles and cuddly toys. Infants, however, do not look indiscriminately at everything. In the first months of life, they increasingly prefer to look at complex objects, especially if these have distinct contours and strong contrasts. For example, early studies of face perception in babies (Fantz, 1961) suggested that newborns have an innate preference for faces (see figure 20.2). By age three months an infant can recognise something about the mother's face, even in a photograph. This was shown by a preference of time spent looking at a photo of the mother's face rather than one of unfamiliar women (Barrera and Maurer, 1981).

The early research focused on the possibility of an innate, unlearned preference for faces, but later research found infants to be attracted to curved lines, high contrast, interesting edges and complexity, which faces possess (Banks and Salapatek, 1983; Aslin, 1987). This early research has been criticised as lacking ecological validity in that the artificial, two-dimensional stimuli of face-like pictures are not what the infant is likely to see in real life.

More recent research has studied real faces, especially of the mother, and the coordination of the sight and sound of the mother (see Unit 19 page 680 for further discussion of this in relation to language development).

Some research suggests there may be a sensitive period just after birth when the newborn is ready to learn the specific features/contours of the mother's face. Walton and Bower (1991) found seven-hour old babies preferred a coloured image of their mother on the screen to that of a stranger with similar hair colour. The preference appeared to be for the face itself rather than the hair colour.

Butterworth and Harris (1994) suggest that early learning may depend on sight and sound with special reference to social '*objects*' in the natural environment. It is possible that babies rapidly learn what their mother looks like from the acquired knowledge of what she sounds like. By the age of four months babies appear to have detailed knowledge of their mother's face and voice.

Figure 20.2

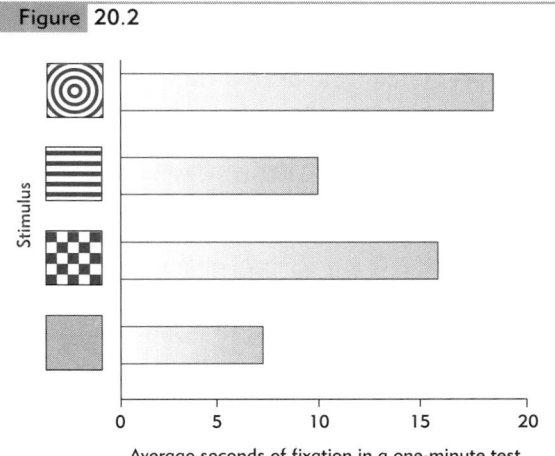

Fantz measured the time that babies would spend looking at stimulus patterns presented in pairs. At all ages between 1 and 15 weeks infants preferred to look at a bullseye rather than stripes and at a chequeboard rather than a plain square. He concluded that infants show a very early preference for more complex stimuli.

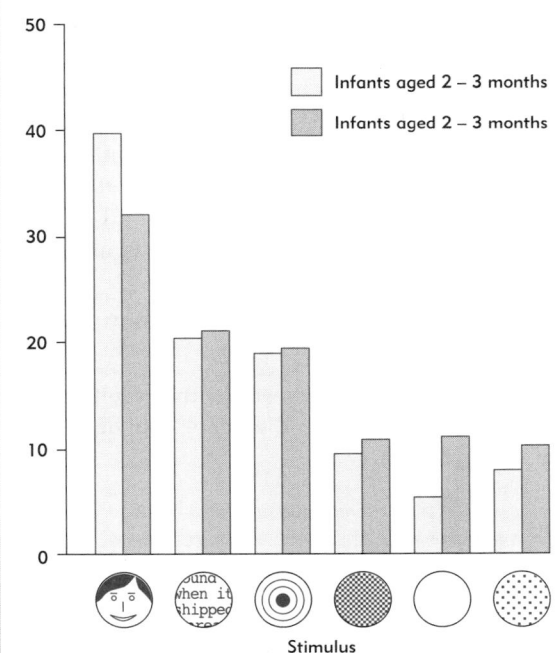

In a second experiment, Fantz showed that infants between 2 and 4 months of age prefer a stylised face to other circular patterns of varying colour or brightness. Thus 2 month-old babies can differentiate faces.

Some of the research by Fantz (1961) on looking

Video and film recordings of mother–baby interactions have shown split-second timing in mutual eye contact and head turning (Stern, 1977). He calls both mothers and babies virtuoso performers in their moment-by-moment interactions, noting how expert babies were at regulating the stimulation they received. He emphasised how active babies are in their communication and how the intricate patterns of interactions he observed took both participants to create them. Stern goes on to suggest that what we call mothering is really this natural, seemingly almost effortless interaction and has nothing to do with simpler caretaking tasks such as feeding and changing. It is the quality of interaction which lays the foundation for love and friendship, essential aspects of sociability and the forming of attachments.

■ Smiling

Smiling is a powerful visual signal that is present in babies' social repertoire. It is present at birth and occurs about 11 times per 100 minutes at this time. Smiling is associated with a change in EEG (brain activity) during certain states of arousal and can be elicited by a high-pitched voice at birth, a human voice in the third week and eye-to-eye contact from the fourth week. Babies who are blind or deaf smile at about the same age as sighted and hearing infants – this indicates that smiling is an innate response (Eibl-Eibesfeldt, 1970).

> ### Activity 2
> Write down, in your own words, the results of Fantz's experiments on the perceptual abilities of young babies.
>
> *(Suggested answer is on page 746.)*

Adults typically find babies' smiles deeply rewarding and respond readily to a smiling child, for example by speech, tactile contact or even a smile in return. This reinforcement, in turn, encourages further smiling by the infant. Smiling soon becomes linked to familiar social stimuli and through social interaction is readily elicited by specific people. By about three months smiling is truly social and reciprocal, much to the delight of

the carers. The baby discriminates between familiar and unfamiliar people, although no fear of strangers is shown at this stage (Camras *et al.*, 1991). Infants show laughter by the age of three or four months (Sroufe and Waters 1977).

Sound and sociability

The benefit of *sound* is that it can be used in the absence of eye contact. Thus communication can be established by people out of sight of each other. Sounds form the basis of early vocalisations. Crying is present from birth and carers soon discriminate between different kinds. Babbling forms the foundation for speech. However, although all babies babble, only those who can hear verbal responses from their carers will go on to develop speech. Thus, although hearing, like vision, is important to the development of sociability, it is not paramount, since deaf children can form successful social relationships with others.

Research has shown how mothering is closely related to sensitivity and contingent stimulation; also how commonplace these are in adult–baby communication and games and how caretaker sensitivity is correlated with social development and attachment later on. Richards (1972) filmed babies from birth to 6 months while their mothers were complying with a request to 'chat' with them. He found complex and sophisticated interactions in which mother and baby influenced each other and sustained conversation-like exchanges. Indeed he concluded that babies no more than a few weeks old showed signs of intentions to speak.

■ Crying

One of the most striking behaviours of newborn babies is their ability to cry. This is a very powerful, perhaps inbuilt, signal for an adult. Just think how hard it is to ignore – and how disturbing it can be to listen to. Babies cannot take themselves to adults, at least not at first, but crying is a very good way of bringing adults to them. Initially, babies will cry when in physical discomfort. However, adults usually respond to crying by social activity – for example, feeding, talking to or picking up babies. This is likely to result in crying stopping and this is reinforced by other people's nurturant actions. Thus babies gradually come to realise the consequences of their crying and become able to use it to help their development of sociability in a more sophisticated way.

That sociability is influenced by crying can be demonstrated by the fact that 3-month-old children show social discrimination for familiar people and often stop crying more quickly when picked up by their mothers than when picked up by others. This is also shown when children cry on separation from their carer (see page 725).

The role of smell, taste and the feeding situation in sociability

Chemical stimuli are provided by aromatic molecules in the substances which pervade the receptors of the nerves of taste and smell. Babies quickly learn to discriminate the taste of familiar milk, and the smell of their carers as they are nursed and fed. This was demonstrated in an investigation by McFarlane (1977) who introduced babies to two breastpads simultaneously and found that at two days they would turn to any breastpad, but by ten days they would only turn to those of their mothers. This showed they were able to discriminate between them by this time, although the mothers judged this did not happen until two weeks. Breastpads are used by mothers who are breastfeeding their infants to mop up any leakages between feeds. They therefore hold both the taste and smell of the mother's milk.

Feeding was once considered to be crucial to the formation of sociability and the bond between mother and child. Prolactin is the hormone that governs milk production. Its secretion is triggered by babies stimulating their mother's nipples while suckling. Therefore both mother and baby are dependent on each other. However, precocious animals which are self-feeding from the outset (for example chicks and goslings) still develop sociable behaviour. Harlow's research (see page 722) has shown it to be less important than tactile contact,

although we must be wary of generalising the fundings from such research to humans.

In humans, tactile contact occurs during feeding. Babies normally produce a burst-pause cycle where 5–20 sucks are followed by a 4–15 second pause. Mothers stroke or jiggle their babies during these pauses and this both stimulates the babies to resume sucking and promotes mother–infant contact (Schaffer, 1977).

Whether children are breast-fed or bottle-fed appears to have little relevance to their psychological development. What does seem to be essential is a close relationship with the person doing the feeding. So, although feeding on its own is not essential to the development of sociability, it is important for secondary reasons because it provides an opportunity for carers to have close contact and communication with their infants. The ability to recognise the taste of milk from their carers, and their smell, allows infants to reciprocate this attention and strengthen the relationship between them. Bremmer (1994) also found that babies may recognise the characteristic way they are picked up by their mother.

Mussen et al. (1974) describe how, before a feed, hungry babies become agitated and may cry. As their internal discomfort decreases during feeding, they gradually become calm and less active. They study the faces of their carers in whose arms they are resting. When their carers also talk to them and stroke them, they learn to associate feeding times with comfortable, pleasant sensations which come from the sight, sound, touch and smell of their carers. It is these forms of pleasurable contact which stimulate interaction and make feeding time important for sociability, as can be seen in figure 20.3.

Tactile contact and security

The comfort derived from *tactile touch contact* is now known to be a key factor in the development of sociability, an idea first put forward by Blatz *et al.* (1935). Certainly an infant's clinging, nuzzling and sucking help to activate maternal responsiveness.

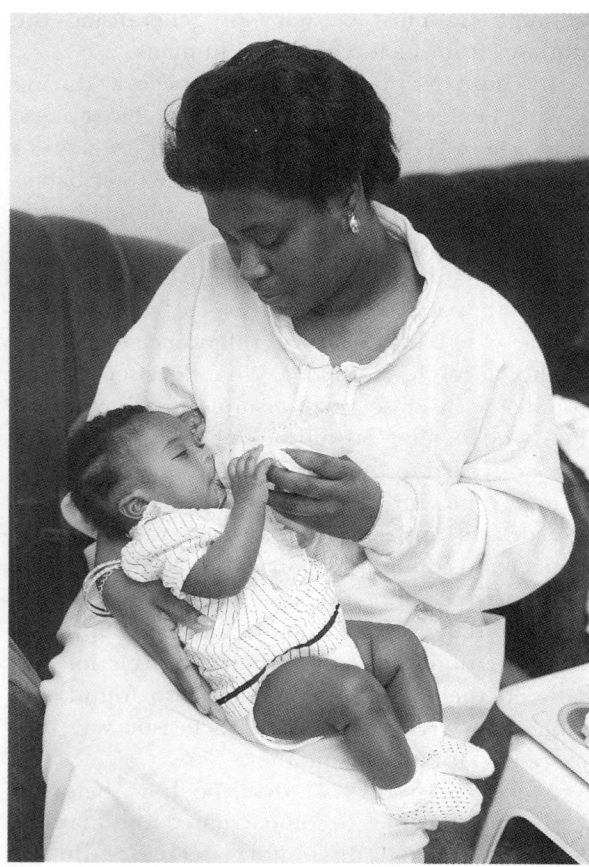

Figure 20.3

Activity 3

Jot down answers to these questions:

a Do deaf children babble?

b At what age can a baby distinguish between its mother's milk and that from another source?

c Do children who are breast-fed establish a closer bond with their mothers than those who are bottle-fed?

(Answers are on page 746.)

Evidence for this comes from three main areas, the first two of which derive from research with non–human animals. Do not forget that these bring with them the inevitable problems of generalisation to human infants.

Animals which are self–feeding from birth (for example ducklings) still seek close contact with their mothers. This indicates that feeding cannot be the key factor in the development of their sociability (see also Unit 10 pages 335–40).

A second area of research is based on studying primates – used due to the ethical constraints on using human participants in such research. What do you think these ethical constraints are?

Harlow and Harlow (1965, 1969) separated infant rhesus monkeys from their mothers and reared them with pairs of artificial surrogate mothers. Figure 20.4 illustrates the main points from this research which demonstrated the fundamental importance of tactile contact.

Although generalisation of such animal studies to human children is problematic, there are so many similarities to the contact comfort children receive from soft toys or blankets. Because so many children show such behaviour it seem likely that physical contact such as hugging, cuddling and kissing is important in human attachment. Passman and Weinberg (1975) found that two and three year olds placed in a strange room play for longer periods of time without distress when a security blanket is present. These findings suggest that the presence of this object provide the same comfort and reassurance as provided by their mothers.

A third area of study – observational work using human participants – shows that swaddling infants will calm them. When infants cling to someone, rocking and cuddling is of crucial importance if sociability is to develop.

A **critical period** is a biologically predetermined time during which if specific responses are not acquired they never will be. Klaus and Kennell (1976) suggested that there is a critical period following birth when it is important for mother and child to have close bodily contact. Although the idea of a critical period remains controversial, they did find that extended tactile contact (extra skin-to-skin contact between mother and child) led to the mothers giving their infants more attention, showing them more affection and establishing

20.4 Harlow and Harlow's (1965, 1969) research into infant monkeys

The two surrogate mothers provided were of the approximate size of a monkey mother, but were formed from wire mesh, with stylised wooden heads and faces.

On one the wire mesh remained uncovered, on the other it was covered with a soft towelling material. Given a choice of surrogate mothers to cling to, the infant monkeys showed a strong preference for the soft towelling covered 'mother'. They would cling to it when frightened (for example when a toy bear beating a drum was introduced into the cage) and use it as a base from which to

explore their environment. If deprived of the towelling 'mother', they would show classic primate signs of distress such as rocking themselves rhythmically.

When the wire surrogate mother was fitted with an artificial nipple through which the infants were fed, they showed a strong preference to remain clinging to the towelling mother and would leave it only for short periods while feeding. Infants sought the greatest contact when the towelling 'mother' was fitted with a nipple and also supplied food.

higher levels of eye contact. However, babies may be separated at birth due to problems such as illness, yet still develop sociability successfully. Such an effect as Klaus and Kennell describe may therefore be relatively short-lived.

Schaffer and Emerson (1964) and Schaffer (1971) have noted that certain children resist cuddling. These may be those who are exceptionally active, slow to develop attachments

and who establish lower amounts of bodily contact. For example, Maccoby (1980) reports that deaf children develop attachments more slowly, as do Down's Syndrome children (Jones, 1977). It seems that such children are less likely to initiate contact and take the opportunity do develop sociability. However, in the absence of comfort derived from tactile contact, infants may rely more on the sense of sight, hearing and smell.

Self-assessment questions

1 From memory, list the key factors which contribute to the development of sociability in infants.

2 In what ways might parents foster the development of sociability in children.

3 Discuss Harlow and Harlow's (1965, 1969) studies demonstrating the importance of contact comfort in rhesus monkeys.

(Suggested answers on page 748.)

Attachments

Babies are helpless at birth and rely on carers, typically their mothers, for basic life support needs. It is to the baby's advantage, therefore, if the carer can be induced to feel attracted to the baby. As the carer responds to the baby's signals, the baby

reciprocates, such that a two-way bond, or attachment, develops between them. An **attachment** can therefore be defined as an affectional bond that is formed between infants and their carers. We can infer the existence of an attachment from the baby's behaviour, which serves the function of creating or maintaining contact with, or proximity to, the object of the attachment. Attachments therefore have survival value and may function to offer the baby security and physical protection. They can also be thought of as a readiness to learn as the part of the infant.

Attachment behaviours may include following with the eyes, following in person, showing pleasure on seeing a known person, showing distress when that person leaves, seeking attention, or being more confident and less anxious when that person is present. As you can see, attachment behaviour includes a wide range of behaviours, even more so if we think of other less obvious behaviour such as tantrums, which are likely to occur with an attachment figure but not with a relative stranger. Also, if we define an attachment behaviour as one likely to bring baby and mother together, then we must consider the mother's behaviour as well as the baby's. Unfortunately, it has proved impossible to weld these differing behaviours together to create a unitary measure of attachment strength as the behaviours vary from time to time and place to place.

It might appear that the concept of attachment is therefore of limited value. However, Ainsworth (1982) suggested that it is patterns of behaviour rather than individual behaviours that we should focus on because they are more stable. Certainly attachment follows a predictable developmental course that is consistent among each species, humans included.

Activity 4

Note some of the ways that a child demonstrates they are attached to their carer. (Check above to see if you are correct.)

In the 1940s, psychoanalysis in Britain developed away from Freud's early ideas. Increasing attention came to be paid to children's object relations and their relationships with significant other people, especially in early childhood. In 1951, one British psychoanalyst, Bowlby, produced an influential report for the World Health Organisation which was prompted by the needs of large numbers of parentless refugee children at the end of the Second World War. Entitled *Maternal Care and Mental Health*, it inspired a widely read paperback published in 1953 (see 'further reading' on page 746). Bowlby's report reflects psychoanalytic theory in its emphasis on the importance of children's early relationships with their mothers as a prototype for all future relationships. Bowlby concluded that children need to form an attachment, an emotional bond, if they are to grow up to become happy, stable and normal adults.

The development of attachments

Bowlby's attention was drawn to *ethological* research (that on animals in their natural habitat) in his attempt to discover how attachments form. One ethologist, Lorenz, hand-reared greylag goslings in order to observe their behaviour just after hatching. He found that the goslings quickly formed an apparently permanent attachment to him rather than a mother goose. Lorenz suggested that this occurred in a critical period, but subsequent research clarified that goslings passed through a **sensitive period** (an optimal time for this behaviour to become established). A sensitive period differs from a critical period in that if specific responses are not acquired by a certain time, then it will be much more difficult for them to be acquired subsequently. This sensitive period occurs in goslings soon after hatching, when they will form an attachment to any moving object (normally this would be the mother goose). Lorenz called this process *imprinting*. It seemed to offer support to the Freudian notion that early experience profoundly affects later development.

Imprinting is, however, confined to fowl and some other precociously mature species, for example sheep. There is little or no evidence for imprinting occurring in human infants; trying to apply it to human infants therefore appears ill-founded (see Unit 10 pages 335–7).

Bowlby, however, was interested in how imprinting could contribute to our understanding of attachment in human babies, who cannot physically follow their mothers for several months after birth. He knew that babies and young children are highly attractive to adults. In fact, babies are a very strong stimulus in general. You probably find it difficult to ignore a baby's cries, this is especially so for parents. Babies have bright, large eyes, smell attractive and have uncoordinated movements which, in our species as in many others, elicit automatic tender and nurturant responses.

On an evolutionary scale, it seems logical to suggest that babies who were always with their mothers were protected from dangers of environmental changes and predators. These children would then survive and produce offspring of their own. Natural selection would thus favour parents and offspring who remained together. Bowlby thought that both infants and mothers would have evolved a biological need to stay in constant contact with each other. He also believed there was a sensitive period for this behaviour to become established.

Although babies cannot physically follow mothers just after birth, they can – and do – follow them with their eyes, smile, cry and instigate sociability. The mother's need to stay in contact induces them to respond and so the attachment forms, gradually becoming strengthened with reciprocal responses. Indeed, coordinated biological systems predispose both infant and carer to be responsive to one another. However, the quality of the attachment is related to the quality of the mother's responses.

Additionally, play is a factor in attachment – adults have entertainment value! The preferred playmate is often the father and play may help to form the different relationships that develop with each parent.

Humans also have certain factors, unavailable to other animals, which help to sustain and deepen their attachments. Language is one of these. As the medium of communication, language forms the basis of expression for feelings and emotions.

The attachment figure

An attachment figure refers to any familiar person with whom a baby forms an emotional bond. This has traditionally been regarded as the biological mother, although research has shown that this need not always be the case.

■ Mothers as attachment figures

Bowlby at first assumed, in line with earlier Freudian theory and with learning theory, that the first attachment was based on the mother feeding her baby. He suggested that a single intense attachment is formed with a single, ever-present adult – normally the child's mother (or a permanent substitute). Bowlby called this *monotropy*. Should such an attachment be unavailable, then the child's social, emotional and even intellectual development could be impaired. This might occur if the child is raised outside a

Figure 20.5

family (for example in a residential nursery), an attachment figure is partially unavailable (for example if a mother works) or if a relationship is broken temporarily (for example by hospitalisation) or permanently (by death or separation).

Bowlby's ideas had an immediate impact in the political and social climate at the end of the Second World War. Families who had been separated by evacuation and military service were now reunited; many women, more or less willingly, gave up their jobs to returning servicemen, stayed at home and had children: the post-war baby boom.

■ Attachment to persons other than the mother

Bowlby's suggestion that only one attachment is made and that is to the mother was challenged by Schaffer and Emerson (1964) who found *multiple attachments* in 90 per cent of their sample of Scottish babies at 18 months old. These were often in a hierarchy, for example a distressed baby might be comforted by an older brother but would prefer to go to mother if she was there. The primary attachment is most frequently with the mother, but in about a third of cases it is with someone else. An interesting example comes from Schlesinger (1980) who noted that sign language trainers often found their deaf infant charges attached to them.

Activity 5

Try to sum up, in your own words, Bowlby's ideas on attachment. (If you have any difficulty, reread the section on pages 724–5.)

Attachment to persons other than a mother figure was also demonstrated in a case study of six orphaned three year olds at a children's home at Bulldogs Bank in Cumbria. Freud and Dann (1951) described these children who had been rescued from a concentration camp at the end of the Second World War, having been inmates since the age of 6–12 months. They had limited opportunities to establish attachments with adults and as a result had formed intense attachments to

each other. They would become highly distressed even when briefly separated.

Attachment figures may perform different functions; fathers and mothers, for example, typically interact differently with children. A father's style is more likely to be vigorous in play, more adult in language and more distant physically relative to a mother's style. Belsky (1979) suggests that such gender differences go beyond style to embrace roles.

Considering the mother–child dyad in isolation is artificial. Even in a small nuclear family other people such as family members, friends and neighbours play important key roles in the life of the child. As noted above, fathers are important attachment figures in many children's lives. For some children they are the most preferred person even though they spend less time than mother with them (Kotelchuk, 1976). Fathers are more likely to play a game of some kind, often 'rough-housing' (Parke and Tinsley, 1987) so their attachment behaviour appears different to that of mother. This enjoyment can be seen in figure 20.6.

Bowlby's prescription of a full-time mother permanently at home with her baby is frequently atypical. However, we now think that attachments are formed in a similar way to any other relationship, by interaction and communication. A sensitive, responsive person who interacts with a baby (for example, by playing), will be someone who the baby will be attracted to and will form a relationship with. Do not forget though that the sensitivity of the person will be paramount.

As long as a person is available to a child consistently for part of the time, it is the quality of interaction that counts. It seems unlikely that a child will be harmed, all other factors being equal, simply by the absence of a major attachment figure, typically the mother, at work each weekday. Other factors, however, may not be equal, for example substitute care needs to be of an equally good quality.

Thus Bowlby's ideas are now of mostly historic interest but he began research into attachment and his ideas profoundly influenced public policy and the received wisdom or common sense of childcare.

Problems are likely to arise if the quality of substitute care lacks the sensitive and responsive

Figure 20.6

interactions that we have identified as important, or if frequency of staff changes prevents consistent care. Infants need to become attached to their substitute carers and, implicit in the idea of sensitive and responsive interaction, infants need to be adequately stimulated. In Britain there remains a shortage of day-care places, but a few children can attend education oriented, and therefore stimulating, nursery schools or pre-school playgroups for part of the day. A few others may be able to attend workplace nurseries or social services day nurseries, but the most likely source of day care is a private child-minder.

Research into the effectiveness of nursery care and child-minding

Low staff turnover, good staff–child ratios and a stimulating environment have been identified as important for success. Generally, American studies have seen child–minding as neutral in effect, certainly not harmful. However, Ainsworth and her colleagues still argue that attachments for children in day care are likely to be insecure. A review of US studies by Belsky (1988) concluded that more than 20 hours of non-parental day care per week during the first year of life could result in insecure attachment. However, the method of testing attachment security, the strange situation test, may not be as stressful for children of working mothers who are familiar with being left with strangers in a strange room. Ignoring their mother may reflect this familiarity with the situation and their independence, rather than show signs of maladaptiveness (Clarke-Stewart, 1988).

Early studies in Britain were less positive. Mayall and Patrie (1977, 1983) studied registered child-minders in inner London and found under-stimulated, insecure children who scored poorly on tests of cognitive and linguistic ability. These results may be unrepresentative because of the fairly poor socio-economic health of inner London. The children may have simply bought their existing home problems into the nursery. On the other hand, it might be reasonable to expect registered minders to be better than the large numbers of unregistered minders who were not investigated.

Child-minding provision has expanded considerably in the 1980s and 1990s. There is now more training and support for minders, more are registered and the implementation of the 1988 Children's Act may have helped to eliminate really poor practice.

More recent studies in Europe and the UK have supported the view that many of the problems exhibited by children who had received day care in infancy were due to problems in the family rather than day care *per se*. In the UK priority for day care in nurseries is given to families with serious psychosocial problems so it is not surprising to find such children have behavioural difficulties (McGuire and Richman, 1986). When this factor is controlled, infants who have been in day care are seen to score as high as other children on tests of intelligence, personality, self-confidence and emotional adjustment. Melhuish (1990) studied a large sample of children whose mothers returned to full-time employment from mainly professional and managerial jobs after maternity leave. Day care involved a mixture of child-minders, relations and private nurseries. At the age of three years the only difference between these children and those cared for at home was that they were more sociable and willing to share, especially the group who had been in nurseries. No 'problem' behaviour was distinguishable between day care and other children.

On the other hand, Bowlby's ideal of full-time mothering at home has not always worked well. Pugh and Harlow (1962) found that children can be seriously understimulated at home and not form an attachment to someone physically present because little interaction takes place. Full-time child care can be extremely stressful and demanding, especially if the carer has little support, so it is not surprising that research into depression has found that single mothers with three or more children under 14 and no confiding relationship are most at risk (Brown and Prudo, 1981). Depressed carers are unlikely to provide stimulating companionship for children at home and in some circumstances it is reasonable to conclude that quality and quantity of care for children is negatively correlated.

When viewed cross-culturally day care is shown to play an important role in child rearing; the quality and stability of the care appear to be important factors. Child care can be enjoyable but too much can overburden the carer to the disadvantage of both parent and child. Not all parents have the skills and resources to spread the burden of care and avoid becoming overloaded. Day care should be accessible to all because for some children it is the best form of available care. In fact arguments are presented later for seeing nursery education as a positive source of enrichment for children (see pages 737–8). Clarke-Stewart (1989) notes that maternal employment is a reality and therefore the issue is not whether children should be in day care but rather how we can ensure that this experience is supportive and beneficial to their development.

Activity 6

Make a list of the qualities a working mother should look for in a child-minder if she wants the arrangement to be successful.

(Suggested answers are on page 746.)

The timing of attachment behaviour

Attachment begins to develop from the reciprocal interaction of carer and child and takes over a year to develop fully. From about 18 months of age, children's horizons wide and attachment becomes less based on maintaining proximity and more on creating an adult-like bond of affection and trust.

■ The growth of attachment behaviours

The attachment process is generally regarded as starting when babies can tell one person from another, although both object relations theory and cultural expectation suggest that the mother is naturally or instinctively prepared to fall in love with her baby. The (object relations school) psychoanalyst Winnicott (1958) thought that mothers are in a state of extra sensitivity in which they identify with babies so as to be prepared to meet their needs.

Recognition of parents does not come in the first two months of life. By three months old, some infants frown when approached by strangers and stop crying more quickly when picked up by their mothers. At four months there is clear preference for their own household. By six months, crying and smiling are replaced as the primary means of contact by calling out and crawling. By seven months, children typically show distress at separation from familiar carers and by eight months they use mother as a haven and can be considered truly attached.

The strange situation (see page 730) has been used to investigate the importance of adults to children and at what age – the development of stranger wariness is strongly correlated with the onset of attachment. Cohen and Campos (1974) investigated children's preference for mother, father or a stranger when present together. They found that children usually stayed closer to the mother than the father, and to the father than the stranger.

Attachment usually reaches its peak intensity (as measured by protest and distress over separation) at about 12–18 months of age, peaking at 13 months (Kagan, 1976). This appears to occur irrespective of culture and differences in child-rearing practices.

Bowlby (1969) recognises four phases of attachment (see table 20.7). The last phases here demonstrate the decreasing of attachment behaviours as the child continues to develop and it is to this process that we now turn.

Detachment

Detachment is the name given to the waning of attachment behaviours as the child gradually ventures further away from the attachment figure and distress at brief separations lessens. This reflects the child's growing familiarity with a range of different situations, thus the environment comes to be perceived as less fear provoking. Language development also widens the scope for children's communication and they become increasingly able to control everyday tasks themselves, such as eating and going to the toilet. However, although children's need for intense contact diminishes, it

Activity 7

Without looking back, define the following terms in your own words, stating the relevance of each to attachment: ethology, sensitive period, imprinting, monotropy, multiple attachments, detachment.

(Suggested answer on pages 746–7.)

does not disappear entirely – rather it changes its nature. Other people are still important, but they gradually become considered as independent persons in their own right and relations are modified to take other people's perspectives into account. Detachment occurs over time and children gradually play comfortably at greater and greater distances from their mothers.

During the time of detachment, children will revert to attachment behaviour if they are tired, ill or emotionally upset as they would be, for instance, during a period of separation (Heinicke and Westheimer, 1966). This shows how tenuous their self-confidence is at this time and indicates a need for encouragement and a feeling of security.

Table 20.7

Phase	Age (months)	Characteristic behaviour of the child
1	2–3	Responds socially to any person who approaches
2	3–6	Responses increase in intensity and become more oriented towards the attachment figure
3	6–30	Maintains proximity to the attachment figure; subsidiary attachment figures develop; wary of strangers
4	30+	Conceives the attachment figure as a separate person who can be influenced by own actions

Phases of attachment (Bowlby, 1969)

Self-assessment questions

4   According to Bowlby, what would happen to the child if monotropy did not occur?

5   Note the different interaction styles exhibited by mothers and fathers.

6   Outline what are seen to be the advantages and disadvantages of day care for the infant.

(Suggested answers on page 748.)

The effects of early experience

Freud, Lorenz and Bowlby all supported the view that early experiences shaped later behaviour and such results were permanent. More recent evidence questions this view and demonstrates that, given the right conditions, effects can be reversed.

Having examined sociability and attachment, we now turn to what happens when early experiences differ substantially from the norm. In this section we will examine the effects of separation, deprivation and enrichment upon the child.

The effects of separation

Separation of carers and infants occurs when a disruption in normal routine is caused by temporary absence of one of them. Research into the effects of separation of infants from their carers has revealed that children's distress is related to their age and experiences, and includes both physiological and behavioural elements.

■ The 'strange situation' studies

Ainsworth (1967, 1971) investigated the effects of separation by creating an artificial laboratory setting called the **strange situation**. Mothers would take their infants to play in an unfamiliar room. During their playtime the children experienced a standardised pattern of arrivals and departures of both mother and a stranger (see figure 20.8). She identified three behaviour patterns.

Ainsworth categorised the most common pattern as *securely attached*. Children were distressed when their mothers left, but wholeheartedly welcomed her return. They also confidently explored the new environment using her as a base when she was present. A second pattern, *anxious–resistant (insecure–ambivalent) attachment*, occurred in a group of children who were

20.8 Sequence of events in the 'strange situation'

1 Mother and child enter the experimental room. The child is placed on a small chair surrounded by toys and the mother goes to sit at the opposite end of the room.
2 A stranger enters the room, sits quietly for a while, then approaches the child and attempts to engage with the child in play.
3 Mother leaves the room.
4 Mother returns and engages the child in play while the stranger slips out.
5 Mother leaves. The child is left alone for three minutes.
6 Stranger returns.
7 Mother returns.

ambivalent towards their mothers when they returned, anxious beforehand and very distressed without them. The third pattern of separation behaviour classified by Ainsworth was *anxious–avoidant (insecure–avoidant) attachment* in which the children showed distress at separation and either ignored of avoided their mothers when they returned (see box 20.9).

These differences may well represent differences in the way the social relationships are first established. Many psychologists feel that the security of the first attachment relationship(s) is influential in preparing the way for future relationships. Ainsworth saw the cause to lie with the responsiveness of the mother, and especially in the first few months of life. This was seen as helping to build up the child's trust in the mother and leading to a sense of security in the child. Conversely, mothers who are not psychologically 'in tune' or are inconsistent in their behaviour are seen to be related to insecure–avoidant and insecure–ambivalent children.

A fourth category, called *insecure–disorganised*, has been added by Main and Solomon (1990) to account for some of the children who do not fit into the other categories. These children show mixed behaviour, for example they may approach the mother without looking at her. Some such

20.9 Strength of attachment (Ainsworth, 1979)

Secure attachment (65% of children)
With mothers present, babies played comfortably with toys and were friendly to the stranger. When their mother left, they showed signs of distress, visually searched for her and cried loudly. When she returned, they went to her immediately, but calmed down after being held or hugged, then resumed playing.

Anxious–avoidant (insecure–avoidant) attachment (25% of children)
Babies paid little attention to the mother when present and they did not seem distressed when she

left. Some showed distress, but were as easily comforted by the stranger as the mother. On her return the mother was ignored or approached tentatively, the baby turning or looking away.

Anxious–resistant (insecure–ambivalent) attachment (10% of children)
Babies stayed close to their mothers and showed anxiety when she was not nearby. They were very upset on her return, simultaneously seeking and resisting physical contact (for example crying to be picked up, then crying to be put down). They kept a wary eye on the mother and did not resume playing.

children seem disoriented, emotionless or depressed. This group accounts for about 10–15 per cent of American babies and the percentages are higher in children from homes where they are ill-treated or where parents suffer from mental abnormalities (see pages 734–6 for studies which link such styles of parenting with later behaviour problems).

Attachment behaviours have been found to remain stable unless there are major life changes for the child (Main and Cassidy, 1988). Family stress is likely to affect the parents' responsiveness to the baby and in turn this will affect the child's security. Securely attached children have been found to be more sociable, confident, independent, have higher self-esteem and show fewer behavioural problems later.

■ Early attachments and later relationships
The correlation of early attachment behaviour and the nature of romantic relationships later in life have been studied. Early secure attachment has been found to be positively related to adults who find it easy to develop trusting relationships (Simpson 1990, Vormbrock 1993). Hazan and Shaver (1987) found that the insecurely attached in childhood had problems in developing later relationships, the insecure–ambivalent group continued to have anxious relationships and expectations of rejection (see Unit 2). Some

psychologists suggest that long-term effects of early security on adult personality and relationships is speculative and still open for future research to refine (Woodhouse *et al.*, 1991).

Ainsworth's three categories appear valid in that they are thought to persist and relate to patterns of behaviour during the early years of life and, as noted above, may persist into adulthood. However, the sample Ainsworth first used was small and the proportions of children in each category have not always been the same in studies of other cultures, for example in Japan (Uliyalle *et al.*, 1985). Cultural values can influence attachment. Butterworth and Harris (1994) report how German babies may be socialised for independence whereas Japanese babies rarely leave their mother in the early months of life. This is seen to influence their behaviour in the 'strange situation'. It does not necessarily mean that Japanese babies are more anxious/insecure; attachment must be seen in the appropriate socio-cultural context (see pages 740–1 for further discussion of cross-cultural differences).

Children who are with their carers most of the day will suffer more from separation fear. Ainsworth (1967) showed this in a study of Ugandan and American babies. Ugandan babies are nursed until they are two years old, being carried most of the time. American babies spend most of the first six months in a crib or playpen alone. Ugandan children show separation fear when about six months old; American children two to four months later.

Separation is often unpredictable, such as during illness of either carer or child. Distress shows up in the child as a sequence of recognisable stages. Robertson and Robertson (1971) filmed the behaviour of 17-month-old John when he was placed temporarily in a residential nursery. John passed through a sequence of what Schaffer (1995) identified as protest, despair and detachment (see page 737). They went on to show how a substitute foster mother, rather than a residential nursery, might make an inevitable brief separation less traumatic if well prepared for.

Rutter (1971) showed that material of family separation need not necessarily lead to emotional problems, but the circumstances of separation are important. An extended holiday taken by the mother in a harmonious family may provide no difficulty, but a separation of similar length in a context of family conflict and emotional blackmail was likely to be related to later behavioural problems.

It may also be inappropriate to blame mothers as insensitive, cold and rejecting if their babies are not relaxed and happy. Innate differences in temperament may account for the differences in behaviour. We now consider the role of temperament on attachment behaviour.

The role of temperament on attachment behaviour

Some researchers have drawn attention to the role of the baby's own innate temperament on attachment behaviours (Kagan 1984, Campos *et al.*, 1983). Perhaps 'easy' babies might become more securely attached than 'difficult' babies? Recently, research has focused on how temperament can predict the baby's distress when the mother leaves rather than the reaction when re-united (Vaughn, Lefever, Seifer and Barglow, 1989). Babies with an 'easy' temperament are not as distressed when mother leaves, whereas those with a 'difficult' temperament are typically distressed.

Both temperaments can behave as securely attached on being reunited or as insecure–avoidant (for the 'easy' group) and insecure–ambivalent (for the 'difficult' group). Thus the overall

Activity 8

Use the table below to chart the findings of the 'strange situation'. (If you have any difficulty re-read box 20.9.)

Type of attachment	Behaviour displayed by child when			
	mother present	mother leaves	stranger enters	mother returns
Secure				
Anxious–avoidant (insecure–avoidant)				
Anxious–resistant (insecure–ambivalent)				

reaction of a child to the departure and return of the carer appears to depend on both the carer's responsiveness to the child *and* the temperament of the child (Belsky and Rovine, 1987).

The effects of deprivation and privation

What happens to infants when they are deprived of normal levels of care? The effects of a lack of warmth in upbringing can be severe. Two terms which have been coined here are:

- **maternal deprivation** – the loss of the principle carer through separation.
- **maternal privation** – the absence of any opportunity to form an attachment.

Bowlby and subsequent researchers have proposed that a wide range of conditions might be laid at the door of an absent mother figure, including delinquency, mental illness and intellectual retardation. Bowlby used the term **affectionless psychopathy** to refer to a lack of meaningful relationships caused by an inability to have emotional feelings for other people. Just as a malnourished child might be physically stunted or worse, a maternally deprived child might be emotionally stunted and might even become a psychopathic criminal.

The effects of deprivation and privation are difficult areas to research. Ethical constraints have limited research with human infants to case studies of severely deprived children and investigations based on institutions where the level of care has been inadequate. More strictly controlled research has been conducted on non-human animals, principally primates.

▨ Research on institutionalised children
Institutions may avoid the extremes of poor quality child care, but may still provide unstimulating environments for children to develop in. This was particularly true until the 1940s. Institutional practice at this time often reflected priorities of cleanliness, control of infection and adequate nutrition, rather than intellectual, social or emotional development. Babies might be left unstimulated and isolated for lengthy parts of the day, and contact with adult carers might occur only when it was their turn on the production line of feeding and changing. Toddlers might be in large groups supervised by a single nurse and would rarely be played with or receive individual attention. It is not surprising that children in such situations might suffer physical and mental retardation. Sadly, such institutions are not entirely a thing of the past – recently we have become aware of very poor institutional care in Romania, for example. Early institution studies by Goldfarb (1943) and Spitz (1946) were used by Bowlby to support his *maternal deprivation hypothesis.*

Goldfarb (1943) compared 15 children who were institutionalised between six months and $3\frac{1}{2}$ years of age to another group of 15 who were placed into foster homes during their first year. The institutional environment provided basic needs but lacked social stimulation. The institutionalised children performed more poorly on tests of intelligence, social maturity, speech and the ability to form relationships. Goldfarb attributed this to the role of institutional rearing, although the selection of children for fostering was not a random process. Pre-existing differences between the two groups may have confounded the results as it is possible that the more able children were fostered, being more attractive to potential foster parents.

Spitz (1946) studied human infants aged between 6 and 12 months who were in inadequately run institutions while their mothers were in prison. Fifteen per cent of the children developed unusual behaviours, crying continually and showing an indifference to the presence of adults. This took place despite the fact that physical care was adequate. The effects were put down to a combination of separation and an emotionally sterile environment. Spitz did not, however, examine other potential causes of retardation.

Activity 9

Can you suggest how the institutions could
have improved the psychological care of
children?

*(Read the following text and then see
page 747 for suggested answers.)*

Difficulties in using these early institutions as
examples of deprived environments include the
inadequacy of interaction between staff and
children, a problem exacerbated by the
discontinuity of care caused by shift work and
staffing changes. More recent studies have looked
at these issues in relation to developmental
progress.

Barbara Tizard (1974) studied three groups of
children aged four years who had spent most of
their lives in residential nurseries/institutions. One
group was still in the institution, one group had
been adopted and the third group restored to their
mothers. Intelligence tests found all the children to
be functioning normally. Children still in the
institution (and adopted) were found to be
marginally higher than those restored to their
parents. This was attributed to the amount of adult
attention given in the three settings. The
institution had a 1:1 staff ratio and good provision
of toys, books and outings. Children who had
returned to their mothers often were given less
attention due to the considerable problems and
stress in their mother's life. In this respect good
institutions can be seen to be better than some
parental homes.

Tizard followed up the children at the ages of
eight and sixteen. She was particularly interested in
children who had been adopted. All the adoptions
had taken place when the children were above the
upper limit of attachment according to the '*critical
period*' hypothesis (most were aged three to four
years and some were aged seven years when
adopted). All the children had formed a close
attachment to their adopted parents, even those
who had been older at adoption. These findings

suggest that the '*critical period*' hypothesis needs to
be modified.

Similar support comes from Dennis (1973)
working in an institution in the Lebanon. Children
were raised in a deprived environment in infancy
until the age of three. At the age of six most of
the children had been transferred to other
institutions (one for boys and one for girls); a few
had been adopted. Dennis did a follow-up when
they were in their teens. Intelligence tests found
little difference between the institutionalised boys
and those adopted (IQs ranged from 80–85, below
average but within the normal range), whereas the
girls scored lower and had severe learning
difficulties (IQ average was 53). Dennis found a
great difference to exist between the boys' and
girls' institutions. The former was better staffed
with the boys given more individual attention,
whereas the latter was similar to the deprived
institutions from which the girls had come. It
would appear that the *quality* of the environmental
care was the determining factor. Although the
change in regime did not take place until age six,
there was no indication that earlier effects could
not be reversed. These latter studies suggest that
early experience need not leave permanent effects
– early deprivation can be reversed by better care
and stimulation.

Research indicates practical implications for
children in care and/or hospital:
- Children should not be removed from home
  unless it is the last resort.
- When separated, contact with parents should be
  maintained.
- Substitute care should be stable and personal.
  Such conditions can be seen operating in
  modern nurseries.

The above recommendations can be seen
operating currently with some hospitals providing
overnight accommodation for parents and nearly
all having flexible, liberal visiting hours. Social
workers try to maintain contact between parents
and children. If residential care is needed then
fostering is preferred and residential homes are
small and intimate.

Figure 20.10   Good modern childcare.

■ Case studies of children suffering deprivation/privation

Do you remember the distinction made between deprivation and privation? (Refer to page 733 to check if you are correct.) Case studies of deprived children have yielded conflicting results about the lasting effects of maternal deprivation.

Activity 10

Read the case studies overleaf which outline the cases of two such children, Anna and Isabelle. Why do you think the two case studies had different outcomes?

(Suggested answers are in the text below and following the case studies.)

More recent case studies have provided further evidence of the resilience of children suffering such early (de)privation. Koluchova (1976) reported on twin boys who were discovered at the age of seven in Czechoslovakia. After a childhood of severe neglect and abuse mainly from their stepmother, and spending most of their time in either a dark cellar or a closet, they made a

remarkable recovery. Much of this was attributed to their relationship not only with one another but also with their foster mother and her sister. Intelligence testing found an increase in an IQ in the range of 40–50 at the age of seven to the normal range of 100–101 by the age of 14. They had also developed good relationships with their foster parents. By the age of 18 they were reported as having '*normal*' heterosexual relationships (Skuse, 1984a, 1984b). The two sisters also had success with another deprived child, '*LH*', who had been diagnosed as mentally deficient and suffering behavioural problems. Her intelligence level improved as did her social behaviour, although not to the high level of the twins.

A further case study on the language development of '*Genie*', discovered at the age of 13 having suffered a lifetime of isolation and abuse, appears in Unit 22. Although the focus of the research was more on language progress, there was no doubt that her social skills improved for a few years when she made good progress on all fronts. Unfortunately, after a few years she entered another unsettled period in her life. During this period she spent time in a number of foster homes and a legal injunction prevented any further reporting on her case. By this time she had apparently returned to her previous '*silent world*'.

Case studies can be useful in giving insight into events not possible to study experimentally but one major problem, as noted above, is often the lack of information on the psychological condition of the child at birth. Looking at the intelligence level later in life does not allow for a baseline comparison, so there is always the possibility that findings might be due (at least partly) to innate factors. The twins reported by Koluchova (1976) had been in hospital as babies so records did show them to be performing as normal at that time. Such studies do show that early privation can be mitigated to a greater or lesser extent by a warm, loving relationship with another person and this need not necessarily be the mother.

In the case of Anna it is impossible to tell whether isolation was the sole cause of her failure

Case study – Anna (based on Davis, 1947)

Anna (Davis, 1940, 1947) was deprived of normal contacts with others and received only minimal human care until she was discovered at age six. Her mother lived with the child's grandfather, who strongly disapproved of the fact that Anna was illegitimate. Anna was therefore born at a friend's house and her early life was marked by several changes of 'home', which included children's homes and those of potential adopters (one couple rejected on grounds of suitability were still given Anna by her mother). As early as three weeks old, Anna was described as being in very poor condition. Later one of the homes catalogued her condition as including impetigo, vaginitis, an umbilical hernia and a skin rash.

At $5\frac{1}{2}$ months old she was brought home to her grandfather's house and kept in the attic, as the mother did not want to incur the grandfather's wrath. Anna was given minimal care and kept barely alive, was fed on virtually nothing but cow's milk and received no friendly attention or instruction.

When found at age six she was emaciated, apathetic and could not walk, talk or 'do anything that showed intelligence'. She then made limited progress. At age seven she could walk, understand simple commands, feed herself and show some neatness and evidence of memory. She still could not speak. By age nine she had begun to develop speech, was toilet trained and had become socialised into a group. She died at age ten.

Case study – Isabelle (based on Mason, 1942)

Isabelle (Mason, 1942) was another illegitimate girl, the daughter of a deaf mute who kept her in seclusion in a dark room to age $6\frac{1}{2}$. When found, her communication was limited to croaks and gestures as no speech had been used to her. She also showed a strong fear of strangers. She was assessed as being wholly uneducable. However, careful training yielded rapid results and Isabelle learned very quickly. For example, she vocalised one week after training began, used sentences within two months, could write well after 11 months and after 18 months possessed a vocabulary of 1500–2000 words. At age eight she was described as bright, cheerful, energetic and having normal intelligence.

to make progress. It is possible that she had some kind of congenital mental deficiency as her mother had a measured IQ of only 50 – this might have limited Anna's potential. Careful training did, however, yield impressive results with Isabelle. This leaves us with two hypotheses, without conclusive support for either: maternal deprivation has severe lasting effects or, alternatively, these damaging effects are recoverable.

■ The effects of duration of deprivation

Duration of deprivation can cause marked differences in its effects. Rutter (1972) divided the consequences of deprivation into short term (months) and long term (years). It should be remembered that there is a continuum between these.

Short-term deprivations might occur when, for example, a child enters hospital or a residential nursery. Typically a child will pass through three stages noted by Schaffer (1995):

- The *protest* phase is characterised by crying and acute distress.
- This is followed by *despair*, when the child becomes utterly miserable and apathetic.
- Eventually *detachment* occurs, in which everyone is treated remotely.

Such deprivations may have no lasting effects, although positive correlations have been established with short-term disturbance.

Fifty years ago, it was commonplace for hospitals to restrict visiting times to children and even discourage parental visits entirely as they seemed to disturb the children. Spitz described a syndrome of physical and mental deterioration resulting from prolonged hospitalisation in children which he called hospitalism.

When parents are in hospital, however, the effects on children may not be negative. Many children have been utterly spoiled and given more attention than normal by relatives when this happens.

Long-term deprivations, as we have already seen, may have lasting effects. However, Rutter points out that there are many factors influencing the extent to which children are affected. These include the age at which deprivation occurs. Children aged between six months and four years seem to be the most vulnerable to emotional distress (prior to six months they show little distress at separation and after four years old they seem able to cope with it better). Also, males seem to be slightly more vulnerable, as are children with socially inhibited or aggressive temperaments. Other factors are the previous relationship between carer and child and the circumstances of any previous separation experiences.

Activity 11

Make a comparison of the effects of short-term and long-term separations of children and their carers.

(Suggested answers are on page 747.)

The enrichment of early experience

Enrichment of the environment through the provision of increased stimulation can lead to accelerated development, as long as an infant is maturationally ready for it. Evidence for this comes from studies with both non-human animals and human infants. We shall look only at human studies.

Skeels and Dye (1939) studied orphaned children who were regarded as being so retarded that adoption was out of the question. A group of 13 children, aged seven months to 2½ years, was transferred to a mental institution. Here, each was placed in the care of a trusted inmate who acted as a mother substitute in many respects, for example, handling the children, playing with them, talking to them and supervising their toilet training. The children had plenty of space and were well equipped with toys. The results of this enriched environment were dramatic – the children showed an average gain of 27.5 IQ points – compared to an average loss of 26.2 IQ points by a contrast group of 12 children who remained behind in the orphanage.

As a follow-up, Skeels (1966) studied the same children 21 years later and found those from the enriched environment superior to the contrast group in many respects, for example high-school achievement record and proportion who were self-supporting.

Although this research has severe methodological weaknesses, not least the fact that the two groups of children were not selected in any scientific manner, the results do show what is achievable. They have encouraged deliberate enrichment programmes for disadvantaged children.

One such programme is *Project Head Start*, first funded in the US in 1965 in an effort to stimulate the cognitive development of pre-school children from poor backgrounds. The project children attended special classes in which they engaged in play learning activities involving techniques such as the use of building blocks and concept learning. An alternative approach involved teachers visiting the children in their own homes. Sometimes the parents or carers were also taught how to provide this extra stimulation. Darlington (1986) has shown that programmes are more successful when this happens.

Generally, Head Start programmes have produced mixed results, children being more confident on entering school and showing higher IQ levels although these have not been found to be long lasting (Haskins, 1989). The advantages have been found to be long lasting in other ways with previous Head Start children performing better academically as teenagers. Their behaviour at that time was also better than controls, they had better linguistic skills and better job prospects. They also appear to exhibit more positive self-esteem than non-participants (McKey *et al.*, 1985). The Head Start project was criticised as an intervention programme and more recent programmes try to involve parents and families so that they can impact more directly on the deprivation of the home (see Unit 21) for further research on environmental influences on intellectual ability).

Evaluation of the maternal deprivation hypothesis

Current research indicates that it is the *total* of the child's experiences rather than single events that influence behaviour. Factors such as disturbed and distorted family relationships are more likely to influence long-term behaviour because they impact on the whole of childhood rather than one particular period (as can be seen in box 20.11).

Studies looking at the parental competence of women who have been separated from their parents as children found that separation alone is not sufficient to explain parenting difficulties as an adult; other factors are also involved (Wolkind and Kruk, 1985; Dowdney *et al.*, 1985). From such research it is becoming apparent that separation alone is rarely associated with long-term consequences. Schaffer (1995), summarising several of these studies, concluded that often it is the family situation which may have given rise to the need for separation and it is to this situation

20.11 Adverse factors affecting separation (Woodhead *et al.*, 1991)

Research since Bowlby's early studies has shown that delinquency and an inability to care for others does not result from early separation *per se*, but may develop in association with a variety of adverse factors. Separation *per se*, whether it lasts a month, a year, or is permanent, has not been found to have any direct long-term effects on development. It seems rather that any apparent adverse effects on the child are due to the train of adverse experiences that may follow separation, e.g. being taken into care, or the pattern of chronic adverse experiences that may have preceded it, e.g. abuse or marital discord (Rutter 1981).

Bowlby's claim that even transient separations of a day or a week are in themselves inevitably distressing and damaging has also not been substantiated. Of course, these separations may

cause intense distress, but the evidence suggests that this is only the case when separation from the mother occurs in combination with one or more of the following adverse factors: the absence of other people to whom the child is attached; the child is in a strange environment; the child is passed from one person to another, and no one person takes over the 'mothering' role, that is gives particular attention, comfort and affection to the child (Robertson and Robertson 1971). When these conditions prevail, distress is likely to follow, and repeated total separations, as when a child has frequent changes of foster homes, may well be damaging, although research evidence on this point is limited. There is certainly reason to believe that familiarity and continuity play an important role in early development (Tizard 1986).

that the child may return. Only when the separation is part of the long sequence of adversity are the children likely to be affected.

Activity 12

Make a table of the main points of Bowlby's ideas on attachment and deprivation. Critically evaluate each point, remembering to include positive as well as negative comments.

(Suggested answers are on page 747.)

Some children appear to have considerable resilience in the face of stress and later experiences can mitigate the effect of earlier deprivation or privation. Ongoing research may determine factors such as positive school experiences and good relationships with parent substitutes which can help mitigate adverse early experiences. Schaffer (1995) suggests that such relationships are essential even if the children will eventually have to be separated again. 'Better the grief of yet another separation than a period of emotional solitude' (p. 129).

Recent research suggests that early years are important but so are the later ones. The eventual outcome is determined not only by early experience but also by subsequent experience. Fortunately children appear to have some resilience and if conditions improve they appear to be able to recover.

Self-assessment questions

7 Summarise briefly the timing of attachment behaviours.

8 Describe the behaviour of children identified as being 'insecurely disorganised' (Main and Solomon, 1986).

9 Discuss some of the behaviours in later life which have been found to correlate with early attachment behaviour.

10 What relationship has been found between the baby's temperament and attachment behaviours?

11 Note the problems of accepting case study information as evidence for the effects of deprivation and privation.

(Suggested answers on page 748.)

Social and cultural variations in child rearing

This section looks at the culturally specific aspects of child rearing and the cross–cultural effects of such differences. There is no commonly agreed definition of **culture**. Bee (1995) defines it as: 'some system of meanings and customs, including values, attitudes, goals, laws, beliefs, morals . . . [which] . . . must be shared by some identifiable group . . . and transmitted from one generation of that group to the next' (p. 12).

Reasons why studying culture is important for understanding child development can be presented. These include:
- to discover whether the relationship of the environment and the outcome for the child is the same in all cultures
- to understand the environmental/'nurture' effects we need to understand the culture of the child growing up.

This research is in its infancy but similarities and differences are becoming apparent. Research by Wachs *et al.* (1993) found Egyptian children with families who talked a lot to them as infants were later rated as more competent, which parallels findings from American studies. Conversely, Lambert (1993) found that high mortality was linked with availability of pre-natal care in poor African–Americans but not amongst Mexican–Americans.

A socio-cultural approach to development

Socialisation involves the child learning how to look at social reality through the 'lenses' of the culture in which the child lives (Bem, 1993). According to Bem, we are not aware of using such lenses which she sees as transparent. The child looks through the lens and the view is biased by this (see Unit 22 for discussion of this in relation to gender schema). Early cross-cultural studies were **ethnocentric** in that researchers viewed other cultures through their own **cultural lenses**. There is now an awareness of this bias in more recent studies and more cross-cultural research can be seen. There is now a desire to try to understand the behaviour within the context of the culture in which the child lives.

Mothers were videotaped interacting with five-month-old infants in Japan, France and the US (Bornstein, Tal and Tamis-Le Monda, 1991; Bornstein *et al.*, 1992). They noted the similarity of the babies' behaviour in the levels of nurturance and imitation. Subtle differences were found:

- American mothers stimulated babies more than Japanese and French (they pointed, named, described, touched and positioned babies more).
- American and French mothers were more likely to encourage the babies to interact with objects more than with them.
- American mothers were more likely to use 'motherese' (see Unit 19 page 676 for more on the language often used by adults when talking to children). Both Japanese and French mothers used this occasionally but used more normal adult tones and language generally.

Cultural differences in parenting

Historically, cultural arrangements in western societies have been generalised as the norm for child rearing and a necessary condition for mental health. However, Weisner and Gallimore (1977) indicated that mothers were the primary carers in only 46 per cent of the sampled societies. In many societies older siblings and other children had that responsibility. Historically, older siblings were often the carers in Britain until education became compulsory. Even today most children have wide-ranging family arrangements for caring. Woods (1995) reports that early responsibility for the care of others is related to more concern about others. This is true for both boys and girls. Older children can often be seen modelling the behaviour of adults towards younger children.

Different styles of parenting affect the biology, growth, health and survival of infants. Such research is known as ethnopaediatrics. Small (1995) points out that one-third of the world's population is under the age of 15 years so such research is essential. Worthman reported by Small (1995) believes there is a need to identify parental practices that conflict with the needs of infants and not presume that western beliefs are valid world-wide.

Activity 13

What parenting practices might seem to be 'right' for western carers?

(Read on to note research on some of these and then to page 747 for suggested answers.)

World-wide differences are found in the ways that babies' needs are met. Child care in each society tries to socialise the infant into the type of child and eventually adult that is valued in that culture. Different societies have differing expectations and these change within a society over time so what is seen as good for one generation may not be accepted by the next.

■ Feeding practices

One area of controversy is feeding practices. This has sometimes resulted in bottle feeding being imposed on Third World populations where inadequate sanitation and medical care result in an increase in mortality. Infants have been shown to be sensitive to different feeding methods. Barr (1995) compared western babies who are usually fed every few hours with babies in Botswana who are fed more regularly (every fifteen minutes). He found the latter did not cry for as long as western babies. When he gave western newborns an extra feed of either milk or sugar water between feeds, they stopped crying and seemed happier. He suggests that neither method is 'correct' but it shows how sensitive the newborn is to the feeding routine.

■ Sleeping patterns

Harkness and Super (1995) studied sleeping patterns in a cross-cultural study of infants from Kenya and the US. They found the Kenyan infants wake up several times a night whereas the Americans start to sleep through the night after a few months, conforming to their parents' expectations. In a second study, they found Dutch children go to bed earlier and sleep for an average of two hours longer than Americans. The Dutch parents saw regularity at bedtime to be important in child rearing, whereas the Americans stressed the importance of maximising the relationship between the parent and the child in the early evening. Harkness and Super suggest that the organisation reflects the different cultural expectations.

Small (1995) reports on McKenna and Mosko's Californian research on infants in a sleep laboratory where babies were filmed by video and had heart rate and breathing monitored when sleeping next to their parent in the night. This is often seen to be dangerous and/or unhealthy by western cultures. This showed mothers and babies sharing breaths, with sleeping mothers unconsciously reaching out to comfort the baby when necessary. They contend that the babies 'learn to breathe' as they are aroused by their mother in the night. The research suggests that isolating babies at night is wrong. The babies' heart rate and breathing are shown to be positively affected by hearing the mother speak, laugh or sing. Family noise appears to promote healthy infant sleep! Cultural variations in sleeping arrangements can be seen in figure 20.12.

Cultural variety in close contact is noted by LeVine. He found Kenyan babies were carried around by the mother from birth, fed on demand and slept with the mother until about 17 months, at which time the mother returned to work leaving the toddler in the care of older sisters and brothers, some as young as five years. Mothers were found to respond quickly to the distress of the child and soothe him/her physically. They hardly spoke to the child and did not encourage them to express emotions. Conversely, American mothers constantly interact both verbally and visually with the child, with the parent encouraging social interaction and exploration. Each culture is socialising the child for life in their society. Each culture was found to have a 'righteous' attitude about the parenting they used, for example the

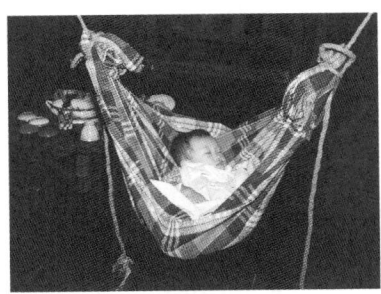
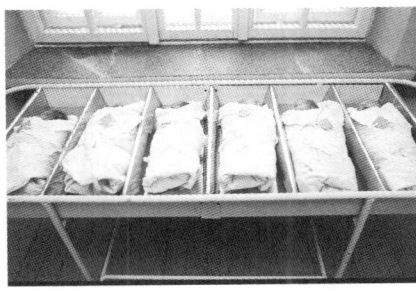

Figure 20.12   Sweet dreams

American mothers were horrified at leaving a baby with a five year old and the Kenyan mothers were shocked at how long the American mothers took to respond to comfort their babies (Small, 1995).

Activity 14

Copy and complete the following:

a   American mothers _____ their babies more than Japanese and French.

b   Mothers are the primary carers in _____ per cent of societies studied.

c   American mothers interact _____ whereas Kenyan mothers _____.

(Re-read pages 740–1 and then look at the suggested answers on page 747.)

■ Attachment

Ainsworth's *strange situation* test (1967, 1971) was used by Sagi *et al.* (1991) to investigate cross-cultural differences in types of attachment (see pages 730–1 for discussion of the original studies). They looked at infants from the US, Israel, Japan and Germany. American findings replicated the early studies in finding 71 per cent to be securely attached, 12 per cent were insecure–ambivalent and 17 per cent were insecure–avoidant. Differences were apparent for the other cultures. The Israeli group, who lived on a kibbutz and were looked after by many others most of the time, had a strong relationship with their mothers and were found not to be insecure–avoidant (5 per cent). The Japanese, who spent most of the time with their mothers, showed similar attachment styles to the Israeli group with no insecure–avoidant characteristics. The German group were very different from the others in that there were fewer secure–attached (40 per cent). Even more of the German group were found to be insecure–avoidant (49 per cent) and 11 per cent were insecure–ambivalent. This difference was attributed to the detached manner of the German mothers who showed less outward affection than the mothers from the other cultures. This study shows that despite different child rearing styles, about a third of the children in the non-German groups were securely attached. More research is needed to discover why differences exist in the other third.

Activity 15

Draw up a table of studies comparing western child-rearing practices with other cultures, including feeding, sleeping and attachment.

(Suggested answers are on page 747.)

Styles of child rearing

The interaction of different styles of child rearing was studied by Baumrind (1972) who identified several interactions with distinctly different outcomes. She looked at the interaction of warmth and nurturance, level of parental expectation (known as *maturity demands*) and the clarity and consistency of rules and communication between the parent and child. Three main styles emerged:

■   **permissive parenting**–high in nurturance, low in maturity demands, control and communication

■   **authoritarian parenting**–high in control and maturity but low in nurturance and communication

■   **authoritative parenting**–high on all four characteristics.

Maccoby and Martin (1983) modified these categories (see figure 20.13) which were used by Steinberg and Dornbusch *et al.*

Steinberg and Dornbusch *et al.* (1987, 1989, 1991, 1992), in a longitudinal study of high school children in the US, looked at these parenting styles. Questionnaire findings on relationships with parents found children with authoritative parents replied positively on many features viewed favourably by American culture:

■   look at both sides of any issue

■   joint decision making in the family

■   school progress praised and teenagers encouraged to try harder.

School grades as a function of parenting style can be seen in figure 20.13.

■ Relationship to school performance

Parenting styles were then looked at in relation to school performance and it was found that the

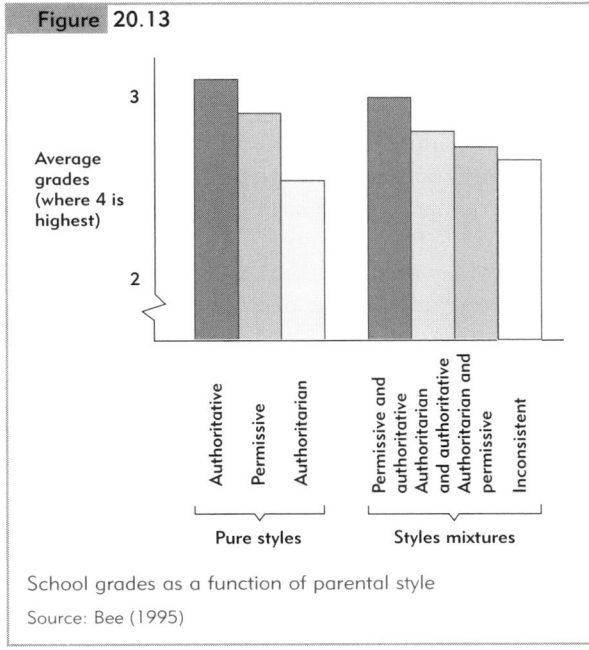

Figure 20.13

Average grades (where 4 is highest)

Pure styles: Authoritative, Permissive, Authoritarian

Styles mixtures: Permissive and authoritative, Authoritarian and authoritative, Authoritarian and permissive, Inconsistent

School grades as a function of parental style

Source: Bee (1995)

teenagers with authoritative parents had the highest grades. As this was a longitudinal study the school performance could be monitored over the two-year period of the study. The difference in success of the children of the authoritative parents was found to be maintained. They also noticed that such parents behaved differently towards the school – they were more likely to get involved with the school, attend school functions and talk to teachers. When the authoritative parents did not have this involvement, the student outcomes were not as positive. Conversely, a teenager whose parents were highly involved with the school but not authoritative did not have the same positive outcomes. It therefore appears that the combination of authoritative parents with school involvement is associated with the best results (Steinberg et al., 1992).

Ethnic differences were looked at separately and authoritative parenting was found to be related to positive outcomes for all groups studied (white, African–American, Hispanic–American, Asian–American) and these teenagers were found to be more self-reliant and less delinquent than those from non-authoritative families. However, school performance varied between the ethnic groups. Good grades were linked with such parenting for

whites and Hispanic–Americans but only weakly for the other two groups. Asian–Americans do well in school even though their parents are the least authoritative, so parenting alone cannot explain ethnic group differences in academic achievement.

■ Peer group influence

Steinberg and Dornbusch (1992) have tried to explain these differences by looking at other aspects of the family and cultural systems. The belief in the importance of education for later success has been found important. All four groups seemed to believe that doing well at school improved their career chances later but the groups disagreed on the consequences of doing badly at school. Asian students were more pessimistic about the prospects of a good job if they performed badly and they spent more time on homework, whereas both Hispanic and blacks were less concerned. White and Asian students also seemed to have more peer support for academic success. Black students found it more difficult to get peer group support. The choice for academic black Americans appears to be between popularity with their peer group *or* achieving good results. It would appear that peer influence can be more important than parental style when correlated with achievement.

Steinberg and Dornbusch (1992) concluded:

■ Children are affected by parental style and this may persist into adulthood.
■ Children respond positively to parents who are both affectionate and firm (authoritative).
■ Parental styles interact with the dominant culture to which the child is expected including peer groups.

Activity 16

Each definition below is followed by a pair of words. Which word best fits the definition?
a Baumrind's (1972) authoritarian style parent was high on (nurturance/control).
b Baumrind's permissive style parent was low on (nurturance/communication).
c Steinberg and Dornbusch (1992) found that teenagers with authoritative parents obtained (higher/lower) grades at school.

We need to know far more about whether the relationship between environmental events and characteristics of the child is the same in every culture. Sternberg and Dornbusch were able to demonstrate within-cultural differences of authoritative parents in relation to ethnic differences in the US. It is likely that with different cultural lenses certain characteristics valued by western societies may be found unimportant in some non-western cultures. Despite cultural variations, children grow up and show great flexibility in new situations. Small (1995) notes that American children raised to be independent often return home as adults to live with their family, whereas Kenyan children who are not verbally prompted by parents still achieve highly in western style classrooms.

On a wider front, several aspects of child rearing and parenting may be found valid only for one particular culture and they better prepare children of that society for adult life. These methods may be inappropriate for other cultures. Future research is needed to understand this cultural diversity and how best to improve child rearing world-wide.

Self-assessment questions

12 Why are cultural variations important in understanding child development?

13 Why might early cross-cultural studies be seen to be ethnocentric?

14 Note some cross-cultural differences found in types of attachment.

15 Distinguish between authoritarian, authoritative, and permissive styles of parenting and the relationship found between these and academic performance and behaviour.

(Suggested answers on page 748–9.)

Unit summary

- Babies develop *social communication* by contingent stimulation by others or events in the environment. The contingent responsiveness by parents to the child is linked to more secure attachment in the child.
- *Sociability* is developed through the senses. Looking, smiling, crying, feeding and tactile contact are some of the factors shown to be used.
- Affectional bonds between babies and their carers, known as *attachment*, have survival value and offer the infant security and protection. Several attachment behaviours have been identified, demonstrating how the child is attached to the carer.
- *Bowlby's research*, based on psychoanalytic theory, emphasised the importance of children's early relationships with their mothers. He concluded that such attachments were critical to normal development in the child.
- Research on *imprinting*, in animals and birds, attempted to look at how attachments form. *Critical* and *sensitive* periods were identified. Bowlby tried to use this research to understand attachment in human babies.
- The attachment figure has traditionally been seen to be the biological mother but research has demonstrated that children form *multiple attachments*.
- Contrary to Bowlby's findings, high quality day care has not been found necessarily detrimental.

Summary cont'd.

- Attachment develops from the reciprocal interaction of carer and child, taking a year to develop fully and reaching its peak intensity at about 12–18 months.
- *Detachment*, the waning of attachment behaviours, reflects the child's growing familiarity with a range of different situations. Although the need for intense contact diminishes, it does not disappear completely. Attachment behaviour reappears when the child is tired, ill or emotionally upset.
- The effects of separation have been studied by Ainsworth in the '*strange situation*' studies. Research identified common patterns of attachment such as *securely attached, anxious–resistant* and *anxious–avoidant* behaviours. Later research added *insecure disorganised* behaviour as a further category. Such behaviours need to be considered in the appropriate socio-cultural context.
- Maternal or family separation need not lead to emotional problems – the *quality of the relationships* and the emotional contact surrounding this are relevant factors, as is the role of the infant's own innate temperament.
- Maternal deprivation and privation were seen by Bowlby to lead to *affectionless psychopathy*, but further research on institutionalised children, children in care or hospital, and isolation studies have found the child to be more resilient than was originally thought.

- *Enrichment* of the environment can aid the child's development. Projects such as Headstart and later intervention projects, involving parents and families, have been found beneficial.
- Positive school experiences and good relationships with parent substitutes can help negate adverse early experiences. Not only early experience but also subsequent experience determine the eventual outcome. Familiarity and continuity play an important role in early development.
- Studies on *cross-cultural aspects* of child rearing have often been *ethnocentric*. '*Cultural lenses*' identified by Bem, can result in unconscious bias. More recent research tries to understand the behaviour within the culture in which the child lives.
- Different *styles of parenting* affect the biology, growth, health and survival of infants. Child care in each society tries to socialise the infant into the type of child, and eventually adult, that is valued in that culture. Different societies have different expectations and these change within society over time.
- Cross-cultural differences in feeding practices, sleeping patterns and types of attachment are some of the areas studied.
- Different styles of child rearing, including permissive, authoritarian, authoritative, have been found to have different outcomes. These have been found to be related to within-cultural differences in school performance.

Terms to define

affectionless psychopathy
attachment
authoritarian parenting
authoritative parenting
critical period
cultural 'lenses'
culture
ethnocentric

horizontal relationships
maternal deprivation
maternal privation
permissive parenting
sensitive period
socialisation
'strange situation'
vertical relationships

Further reading

Bee, H (1995) *The Developing Child*, 7th edn, Harper Collins, London.

Extremely accessible and well-written chapters on socialisation and attachment.

Bowlby, J (1953) *Child Care and the Growth of Love*, Penguin, Harmondsworth.

The classic text which stimulated research into maternal deprivation.

Clarke, A M and Clarke, A D B (1976) *Early Experience: Myth & Evidence*, Free Press, New York.

Includes readings from a wide range of relevant research. A classic text.

Rutter, M (1981) *Maternal Deprivation: Reassessed*, 2nd edn, Penguin, Harmondsworth.

Useful review and critique of Bowlby's early research.

Schaffer, R (1995) *Early Socialisation*, BPS Open Learning Units.

Comprehensive review of socialisation, including attachments by one of the researchers in the field.

Stern, D N (1977) *The First Relationship: Infant and Mother*, Fontana, London.

An interesting account of the establishment of mother–infant synchrony.

Woodhead *et al.* (1991) *Growing up in a Changing Society*, Routledge, London.

Includes relevant chapters by researchers in the field, including Tizard, Clarke-Stewart and Hetherington.

Answers

Suggested answers to activities

2

Babies prefer complex patterns to simple ones. They prefer a face-patterned, oval shape to an oval with the features randomly distributed. As they mature, they prefer a familiar face to an unfamiliar one.

3

a Yes

b Two days

c There is no evidence of this – the important factor is the sensitivity to the baby's needs from the primary carer.

6

A good child-minder should offer:
- a safe and secure environment
- a stimulating environment, with lots of toys and activities for the child
- time to talk and play with the child
- a willingness to work in concert with the mother with regard to discipline and the structuring of the child's day.

7

You may have said something similar to:
- Ehology is the study of animals in their natural environment and allows a comparison to be made between human attachment and that in non-human animals.
- Sensitive period is a period during development in which a specific behaviour develops more easily. It allows for differences in individual growth and environment, unlike a critical period. There may be a sensitive period for attachment during the first three years of life.
- Imprinting is a process during which offspring learn to recognise and follow their parents. It occurs mainly in precocious birds and may be the evolutionary basis of attachment. There is therefore little evidence for imprinting taking place in human infants.

- Monotropy is an intense attachment to a carer who is always there. If attacement does occur, a child may suffer social, emotional and intellectual impairment.
- Multiple attachments are formations of attachment bonds to more than one person. Different kinds of attachment figures, thus enriching social development.
- Detachment is the process ofo becoming independent. During it, the child's 'world' increases and other people's perspectives are taken into account.

9

a good staff-child ratio

b good provision of toys, books, outings etc.

c more individual attention

11

Did you include the following:

- In the short term, children may be distressed, but the effects are not lasting ones.
- In the long term, separation can disrupt the attachment process and consequences such as insecurity may result, but this can be mitigated by school experience and good parent substitutes.

12

Bowlby's main points include:

- monotropy
  - importance of bonding in first few hours
  - over 20 hours/week day care in first year results in insecurity
  - importance of bonding with at least one person
- critical period hypothesis
  - imprinting
  - babies are attractive to adults
- 'affectionless psychopaths'
  - insecure attachment

  - later romantic attachments affected

  - isolation of child in residential care

but
- multiple attachments

- success of kibbutzim

- role of father, siblings, friends but not necessarily mother

- modified to sensitive period
- late adoptions successful

- responsiveness of mother
- cross-cultural differences
- family conflict more of a problem
- length of separation and/or distress important
- role of innate temperament
- more likely to be due to lack of stimulation
- discontinuity of care
- case studies – reversal

- early effects are irreversible
  - inadequacy of much day care

- problems in family, more long-lasting than day care
- some parents ill-equipped for child care
- cultural and cross-cultural differences
- limited success of intervention

13

Western *cultural lenses* might focus on the following 'right' behaviour:

- Mother is the best carer.
- Only adults should have the responsibility for child care.
- Babies should feed every few hours.
- Babies should sleep in a separate room as soon as possible.
- Bedtime should be regular and early in the evening.
- Mothers should interact with babies as much as possible.
- Day care may result in the child becoming insecure.

14

a stimulated

b 46

c verbally and visually/hardly spoke to the child

15

Western practices:
- fed every few hours

- sleep separate from the mother
- sleep through the night after a few months
- adults are the primary carers

- adults provide stimulating experiences for the child
- American and French encourage the children to interact with objects
- motherese used by adults with children

Other cultures:
- Botswana – 'drip-feed' every 15 minutes
- Kenyan babies wake up several times a night

- Kenyan babies are left with older children/siblings
- less stimulation from Japanese and French parents

- Kenyans speak little to babies
- Japanese and French make less use of 'motherese'

16
a   control
b   communication
c   higher

■ Suggested answers to self-assessment questions

1

The factors in the development of sociability in infants are:

a   vision – eye contact with carers leading ultimately to social interaction

b   smiling – when babies smile they elicit a response from the carer

c   sound – crying from a baby produces a response from the carer

d   smell and taste – important in feeding (a contentedly sucking infant is rewarded with smiles and cuddling)

e   tactile contact – remember the experiences of Harlow and his monkeys? If not, re-read pages 722–3.

2

Did you include the following points?
Contingent stimulation to encourage reciprocal communication; holding babies at 21–23 cm (their focusing distance) to foster eye contact; provision of an interesting environment to stimulate the baby; talking to the baby to encourage verbal skills; plenty of tactile stimulation to give the baby feelings of reassurance and security.

3

See pages 722–3 for details of the study.
Evaluation points might include:
■   generalisation of animal studies to humans is problematic
■   contact comfort from soft toys and blankets is seen universally and thus likely to be important in human attachment
■   swaddling infants will calm them
■   holding, rocking and cuddling are seen to be important in the development of sociability.

4   The child's social, emotional and intellectual development could be impaired.

5   Father seen to be more vigorous in play (rough-housing), more adult in language and more distant physically relative to the mother.

6
Negative points include:
■   if not of a high quality, day care can result in insecurity in the child
■   especially if more than 20 hrs/week during the first year of life
Positive points include:
■   full-time child care can be stressful and some mothers become depressed and unlikely to provide stimulating companionship at home
■   not all parents have the skills and resources to spread the burden of care so day care can be seen as a positive source of enrichment for children

7
See pages 728–9 and table 20.7 for a more detailed review:
■   by eight months the child uses mother/carer as a haven and can be seen to be truly attached
■   usually reaches peak intensity by 12–18 months, peaking at about 13 months

8
■   behaviour rather mixed e.g. may approach the mother without looking at her
■   children appear disoriented, emotionless or depressed
■   higher incidence in children from homes where they are ill-treated or with parents suffering mental abnormalities

9
■   early secure attachment is found positively correlated with adults who find it easy to develop trusting relationships
■   insecure–avoidant children found it difficult to develop intimate relationships
■   insecure–ambivalent children continued to have anxious relationships and have expectations of rejection

10
Babies with an 'easy' temperament are not as distressed when mother leaves, whereas those with a 'difficult' temperament are typically distressed.

11
■   often lack of information in the psychological condition of the child at birth means there is no baseline comparison. Findings may thus be due to innate factors
■   it is not possible to isolate confounding variables for examination

12
■   to understand the relationship of the environment and possible outcome for the child in different cultures
■   need to understand the culture in which the child develops to understand the influence of environmental factors

13 Ethnocentricity likely due to cultural 'lenses' of the viewer biasing findings (see page 740).

14

Sagi *et al.* (1991) found when compared with an American sample:

- Israeli and Japanese children were not found to be insecure–avoidant
- the German group had fewer secure–attached children and were found to have higher percentages of insecure–ambivalent children

15

Styles of parenting	Academic performance and behaviour
Authoritarian high in control/maturity low in nurturance/ communication	■ children perform less well but Asian-Americans still do well in school
Permissive high in nurturance low in maturity/control/ communication	■ less well than other groups
Authoritative high on control/ communication/ nurturance/maturity	■ teenagers highest grades especially whites and Hispanic–Americans ■ parents often interested in school (an important factor) ■ self-reliant ■ less delinquency ■ importance of peer support

Unit 21

Cognitive Development

David Bosworth, Graham Davies, Lorna Jones,
Peter Reddy and Irene Taylor

This unit covers:

Piaget's theory of cognitive development

Other theories of cognitive development

Recent research into cognitive development

The integration of more recent theories of cognitive development into classroom practice

The development of measured intelligence

By the end of this unit, you should be able to:

■ demonstrate knowledge of the patterns and processes of cognitive development

■ be able to evaluate theories of cognitive development in terms of empirical evidence, and show an awareness of their practical application, for example to education

■ demonstrate an understanding of the factors associated with the development of measured intelligence including genetic and environmental influences

■ consider the factors influencing performance in intelligence tests and the controversies surrounding their use.

Unit 21   Contents

Introduction

It takes the best part of 20 years for newborn babies to become adults. Psychologists are interested in all aspects of this developmental process which involves the changes in thinking and reasoning which lead to adult understanding. In the 1930s, psychologists such as Piaget and Vygotsky began to find that children's thinking and reasoning were often quite unlike adult's abilities and that they gradually became more like those of adults as they got older.

This unit is concerned with what psychologists have found out about cognitive development – how thinking and reasoning in children develop into adult abilities. Theories of Piaget, Bruner and Vygotsky are considered, as well as some of the controversies and practical applications of research in cognitive development. We then look at innate and environmental influences on intelligence test performance.

Piaget's theory of cognitive development

Piaget, born in Neuchâtel in a French-speaking part of Switzerland, was trained in zoology. He added to this an interest in epistemology (the nature, limits and origins of knowledge). His approach to the development of logical thinking is sometimes known as genetic epistemology.

Piaget's work was unfashionable in psychology for many years. For one thing, he did not write in English; more importantly, the behaviourist approach dominated psychology until the 1950s. This approach was not interested in the study of thinking or the mind, but only in observable behaviour. As this view changed, Piaget's work became widely read and influenced others to continue research into cognitive development. It has also had a practical influence on education.

We will deal with Piaget's theory of cognitive development in two parts: firstly, the mechanisms by which Piaget claimed that children's thinking is caused to change; secondly, the sequence of stages which Piaget claimed that children's thinking goes through as a consequence of these causes.

Mechanisms of change in children's thinking

According to Piaget, cognitive development is complete when we are able to think, or reason logically, in an adult way. Newborn children are not only physically immature and lacking in knowledge of the world, but also think or reason differently from adults. In fact, as we see later (see pages 755–9), one of the features of Piaget's work is the way he helps us to see just how different young children's reasoning and problem solving are.

■ Adaptation

Children achieve adult logical thinking by actively trying to make sense of the environment they are born into. This adaptation to environment is something that all organisms do, for example plants grow towards the light. Their growth is due to maturation – but plants also adapt to environmental conditions of light, soil and moisture. At a general level, all life on Earth is moulded by, or has adapted to, the environment by the process of evolution.

What then are the mechanisms which cause adaptation to come about? Part of the answer is maturation, thus humans will mature – for example acquire the ability to walk on two legs – and use one or more languages, but this is not the whole story. Experience is also needed. Piaget said that experiences of the physical world (for example the sight, sound and touch of objects) and of the social world (for example learning the distinction between self and others, making relationships, experiencing praise and disapproval) are needed for logical thinking to develop.

■ Equilibration

Although the mental activities of babies and adults differ, they are linked. A child initially has a very limited set of mental representations linking sensory input (for example the sensation provided by a nipple in the mouth) and behaviour or motor output (for example sucking response). Piaget used the term **scheme** (sometimes termed **schema**) to refer to a sequence of mental activities which routinely connect sensations and behaviour.

During infancy, the limited number of schemes grows rapidly, becoming more complex and forming the basis of thinking. Thus a scheme for a bottle might develop from something which provides food when sucked to a much more complex mental representation (for example a type of container, made of plastic or glass). The process by which this happens, by which schemes grow and branch out, is explained by **equilibration**.

Equilibration is the process by which a state of equilibrium or balance is achieved between the external world and our thought processes. Piaget believed that we all have a drive to achieve such consistency in our thinking. However, such a cognitive balance is difficult for children to achieve, because they are continually faced both with their own development through maturation and with new and unfamiliar objects or social situations.

Activity 1

Read the following passage about a child making sense of Christmas:

'One morning, shortly before Christmas, a psychologist visited a playgroup and asked each of the ten children present to make up a recipe for Christmas dinner. A four-year-old, Penny, offered the following :

"You need one big bag of turkey meat (buy one dead with no feathers. The turkey don't mind being eaten but it don't say so). One ball of cabbage (nasty, nobody likes it). Twenty potatoes (round ones, not smashed). A lump of stuffing (make sure it can't drop out – use a nail). A fancy bowl of apple sauce (the apples don't mind going into the sauce). Twenty bags

---

Activity 1 cont'd

of sweets for after dinner. When the alarm goes off, get up and rush around a lot. Tell people Happy Christmas, but not to get in the way. Unfold the turkey and open the holes and push the stuffing up. Get the kitchen really hot and then cook the food. Then open presents. When the food is ready, put on your apron and your hat and eat the food. Everybody likes the sweets best."'

Can you identify the statements which show that Penny's scheme for Christmas is inconsistent with knowledge which she will acquire in the future?

(Suggested answer on page 799.)

We can easily see that Penny's construction of her understanding of Christmas has inconsistencies. For example, if the cabbage really is 'nasty' and 'nobody likes it', why is it served? As she develops, Penny will be thrown out of equilibrium by this inconsistency and through the process of equilibration will construct a more sophisticated and elaborate understanding of Christmas which resolves this inconsistency and restores balance. This temporary restoration of equilibrium, Piaget claims, happens through **assimilation** and **accommodation**.

■ Assimilation and accommodation

Assimilation is coming to terms with new information by relating it to existing schemes. For example, a child used to sucking from a bottle will adapt to a new object by dealing with it in the same way; in other words, by using the same scheme.

Accommodation is the developing of new schemes from old ones when faced with new information or an unfamiliar object. For example, children used to adapting to new objects by picking them up with a whole-hand grasping movement (assimilation) will eventually find that it is difficult to pick up very small objects. They therefore develop a new scheme, picking them up with a thumb and opposed finger (which is much easier).

Similarly, Penny will adapt to the inconsistencies in her understanding of Christmas and cabbages by accommodation. She will conclude that some people really do enjoy boiled cabbage even though she finds it nasty. Piaget in fact suggests that we are all more or less continually adapting to new information. This involves combining the processes of assimilation and accommodation. For example, despite the similarities between a teat on a bottle and a dummy, babies soon learn to suck at them differently – thus using both processes. Adaptation through assimilation and accommodation continues throughout childhood.

Activity 2

Try picking up three objects of differing size, for example a large ball, an orange and then a pin. How does your technique differ?

Piaget's stages of cognitive development

As well as the factors consistent throughout development outlined above, Piaget thought that children pass through four distinct stages of cognitive development. Each of these stages needs to be completed successfully before the next one is commenced. The ages at which stages are started and completed should be regarded as approximate.

■ The sensorimotor stage

The first of Piaget's stages is the sensorimotor stage which lasts until a child is about two years old. In the first few weeks of life, much of a baby's behaviour consists simply of reflex responses. For example, when a baby's fist is clenched, a touch on the back of the hand will result in the hand opening, and if the palm is touched with a finger, the baby will grasp the finger. Later the reflex disappears and the baby chooses what and when to grasp. The first action schemes develop and rapidly increase in number as babies begin to coordinate input and motor output. Through applying action schemes, the baby builds up a mental picture and finds out about surrounding objects, for example what can be grasped, picked up or sucked.

During the first year of life, infants discover two important natural features of the world which we, as adults, take for granted. Firstly, they are profoundly egocentric, being unable to distinguish between self and non-self. Nothing can be perceived as existing independently until this difference is discovered. Secondly, consequent to realising this distinction, a baby learns that objects continue to exist even when they are not being perceived or acted upon. Until an infant achieves an understanding of **object permanence** (an important milestone in cognitive development), out of sight literally means out of mind and therefore non-existent.

Piaget suggested that although three-month-old babies may attempt to grasp an object which is waved within range and follow it with their eyes, they will not attempt to search for the object when it is moved out of sight. Furthermore, the whole object must be visible before a baby will reach for it. Piaget suggested that at about six months, infants will reach for familiar, but partially hidden objects, and at about eight months will search for objects that they have observed being completely covered (for example by a cushion).

Another development at this stage is general symbolic function. By this, Piaget means the ability to think using symbols and signs. Symbols are things that represent something or someone else, for example a doll may symbolise a baby, child or an adult. It is fascinating to watch a child move from dealing with a doll as just another object to be shaken, thrown or chewed on, to dealing with it more meaningfully in a symbolic way.

Unlike symbols, signs do not resemble the things they represent. Spoken language is a sign system and develops considerably in the sensorimotor stage. Piaget sees language as reflecting thought, which has its origins in actions. An alternative view might suggest that thought could be conceived of, to some degree, as internal speech. The ability to use language would thus give a very powerful boost to cognitive development in general. This is a topic which is discussed in Unit 19 pages 679–80.

The pre-operational stage

The pre-operational stage is divided into two sub-stages:

- the pre-conceptual period (ages two to four approximately)
- the intuitive period (ages four to seven approximately).

The pre-operational stage ends with the child starting to think operationally. **Operational thinking** is the basis of adult logical reasoning. It is a special kind of mental routine that is capable of both transformation for some purpose and reversibility. In the meantime, although symbolic thinking and the use of language continue to develop impressively, children's thinking is dominated by what is seen rather than by logical principles.

The factor which lies behind this is **egocentrism**. Pre-operational children are egocentric in their inability to take anyone else's point of view into consideration. This is a rather different meaning from the inability to distinguish self from non-self when a very young baby (see page 755). Piaget claims that children literally cannot see another's point of view. They understand neither that objects will be seen differently from other viewpoints, nor that other people might feel or think differently from themselves. Penny's account of Christmas (page 754) illustrates this. Her assertion that cabbage is 'nasty, nobody likes it' is derived from her personal view, regardless of whether or not others agree with her.

Two other factors relate closely to egocentrism. One is children's general difficulty in seeing more than one dimension or aspect of a situation, notably in the pre-conceptual period of this stage. Thus a task requiring more than one feature of an object to be attended to at the same time will not be successfully completed. A child will focus or centre on a single element. Thus children will have difficulty in decentring, both from their own egocentric viewpoint to take other people's points of view into account, and from a single, dominant characteristic of a problem to become aware of other less obvious features.

The second factor is **animism**, by which Piaget meant that children tend to refer to inanimate objects as if they are alive. Thus all kinds of objects are attributed emotions, motives, intentions, thoughts and desires. Animism may be seen as a product of egocentrism, as children imagine everything, and everyone, to think like themselves.

Activity 3

List examples of animism and egocentric thinking in Penny's account of Christmas (see page 754).

(Suggested answer on page 799.)

Piaget and Inhelder (1956) demonstrated egocentrism using a table-top model of a mountain scene (figure 21.1). After an opportunity to familiarise themselves with the model, children were asked to choose the picture (from a selection provided) which showed the view seen by a doll placed before the model at a different angle to the child. In order to select the correct view, the child had to take the doll's perspective into account. Although each mountain was painted a different colour and topped with either a house, cross or snow for clarity, only children of eight or over consistently selected the correct view. Six-year-olds achieved some success, and four-year-olds typically chose their own viewpoint.

Pre-operational children also have difficulty in dealing with other tasks logically, for example classifying things, putting things into logical series or sequences and understanding the relationships between categories (such as grapes) and sub-categories (such as black grapes and green grapes).

In classifying things, children centre on one particular characteristic. They are unable to classify effectively if required to take more than this one characteristic into account.

If shown a garage with yellow cars and blue cars, a five-year-old is likely to agree that the yellow ones are cars and the blue ones are cars. However, if then asked, 'If all the yellow cars drive away, will there be any cars left?' the child is quite likely to say that there will not be. Piaget believed that such an incorrect answer reflects not merely a confusion over verbal labels, but a deeper inability to decentre and consider more than one element or characteristic at the same time.

Figure 21.1

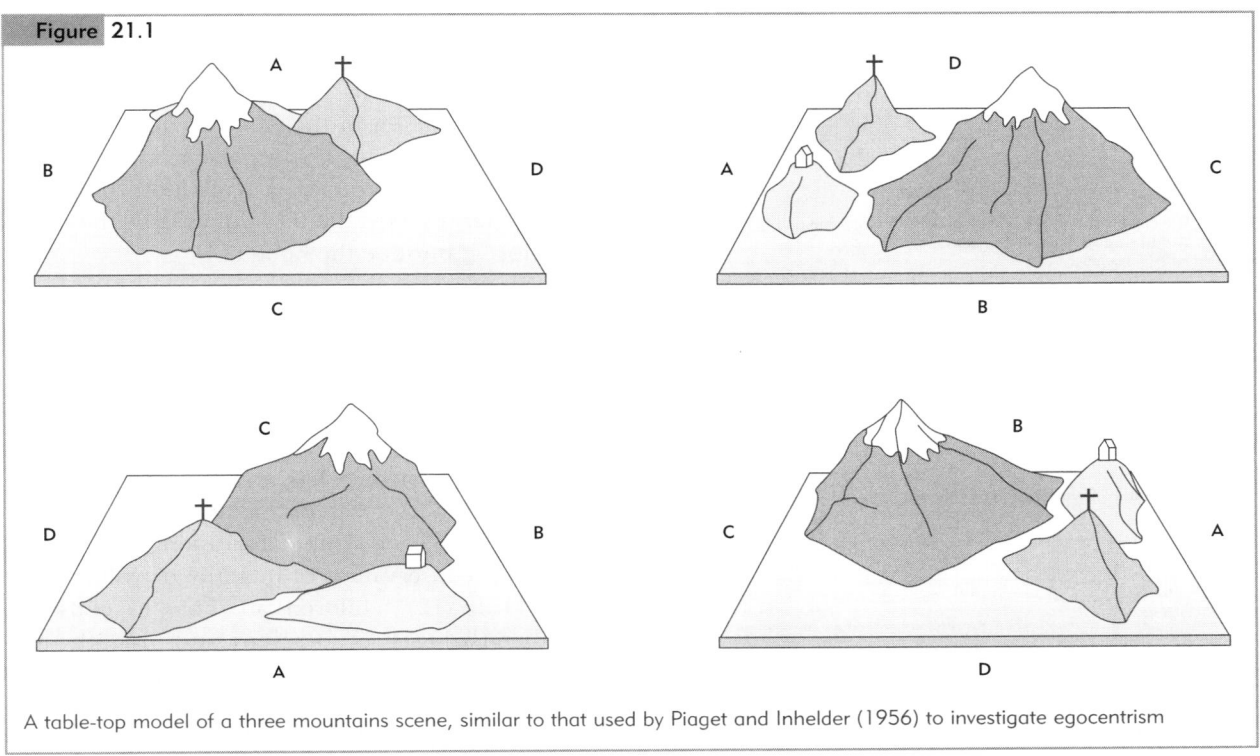

A table-top model of a three mountains scene, similar to that used by Piaget and Inhelder (1956) to investigate egocentrism

Activity 4

Test yourself on your knowledge of the pre-operational stage by completing the following:

a   In the pre-operational stage children's thinking is dominated by what is _____ rather than _____.

b   Pre-operational children are _____ in their inability to take anyone else's view into consideration.

c   _____ means that children tend to refer to inanimate objects as if they are alive.

(Suggested answers on page 799.)

Conservation is probably the most widely investigated area of pre-operational children's thinking. By this, Piaget meant the ability to understand that certain properties of an object remain the same despite a transformation in appearance. Piaget considered that children were capable of conservation when they could make correct judgements about such transformations and give satisfactory reasons for this. An example is conservation of volume. A quantity of juice remains the same when poured from a short, fat glass into a tall, thin glass. Pre-operational children centre on the appearance of the glasses and are likely to judge the volume of juice in the tall, thin one as greater (because the level is higher), than in the short, fat one. Figure 21.2 shows the procedures used in experiments demonstrating conservation of substance, volume and number.

The reasons for this transformation in appearance are firstly compensation – the height in the tall glass is compensated for by the width in the fat glass. Secondly, reversibility takes place – if the operation or transformation was reversed, the quantities would be seen to be the same. The third reason is identity – nothing has been added or taken away so it must be the same.

Children not yet able to conserve are likely to make a fake judgement despite seeing the transformation for themselves (for example pouring the water from one glass to another) or

Figure 21.2

Experiment 1   Conservation of substance

1   The child is shown two identical balls of plasticine and is asked 'Are these two "cakes" the same?'.

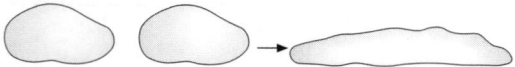

2   The experimenter rolls out one ball of plasticine into a sausage shape. The child is asked 'Does the sausage have the same amount of plasticine as the "cake"?'.

Experiment 2   Conservation of volume

(a)   (b)

1   The child is shown a short, 'fat' beaker (a) containing milk and is asked to pour milk from a jug into a second identical beaker (b) until it has the same amount of milk as the first beaker. The child agrees that the amount of milk in each beaker is identical.

(a)   (b)   (c)

2   The child is then shown a tall, 'thin' beaker and is asked to pour the contents of one of the original beakers into it. The child is then asked 'Is there the same in (c) as there is in (a)?'.

Experiment 3   Conservation of number

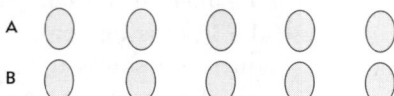

1   The child is shown counters placed in two identical rows (A and B). The child agrees that the two rows have the same number of counters.

2   The experimenter 'bunches up' the counters in row B. The child is asked 'Do the two rows still contain the same number of counters?'.

Experiments demonstrating conservation of substance, volume and number

Source: Taylor and Hayes, (1990)

even carrying out the transformation themselves. Once children have achieved operational thinking, they are able to do a 'what if' mental reversing of the transformation in their heads and realise that the water is the same. This represents the 'triumph of logic over appearance', a realisation that if the process was reversed then it would still be the same, therefore it must be the same now.

■ The concrete operational stage

By the end of the concrete operational stage (approximately 7 to 11 years) operational thinking is consolidated and conservation fully attained. Children become so practised in mental reversal that mistakes become less and less likely. Twelve-year-olds find reversal problems so obvious that they will think you stupid for asking. As well as achieving conservation of quantity or volume (by ages 11 to 12), children are able to conserve number (by ages six to seven) and mass (by age nine). Although thinking becomes operational in nature it is limited to things concretely or physically present. For example, if given the problem, 'Jo is taller than Lucy. Jo is shorter than Maria. Who is the tallest?' children in the concrete-operational stage will have difficulty. If, however, the three people were physically present, children could easily order them by height.

■ The formal operational stage

In the formal operational stage (approximately 11 to 15 years), Piaget claimed that logical adult thinking and reasoning emerge. Thus abstract notions such as democracy or justice can be thought through for the first time. Other adult cognitive attainments are the ability to think about hypothetical possibilities and to solve problems through logical deduction. These can be illustrated by Piaget's pendulum task (figure 21.3).

Children who are still in the concrete operational stage will experiment by changing the variables – but not in the *systematic* way required for formal operational thought. Piaget carried out this original work in schools in Geneva and this led him to suggest that formal operational thinking was characteristic of young people aged 11–15 years.

Figure 21.3

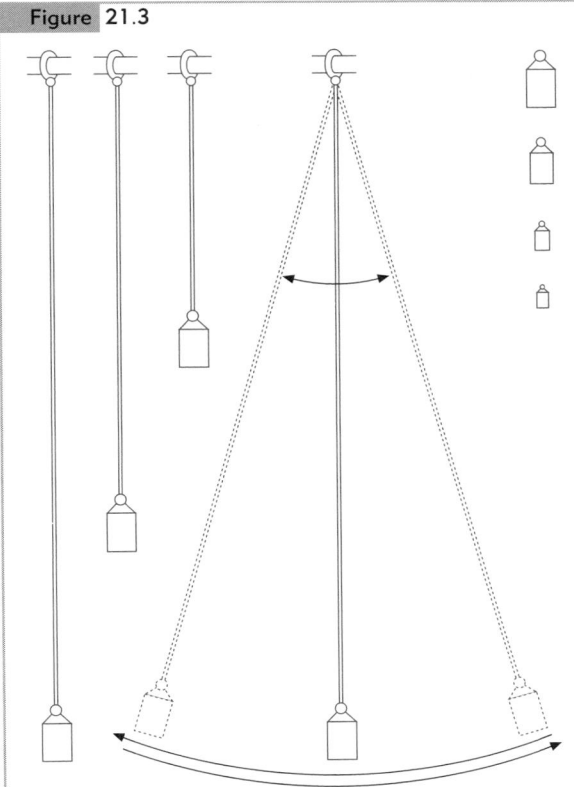

The task is to discover what determines the amount of time a pendulum will take to swing back and forth

The apparatus includes a length of string attached to a hook at one end and several weights which can be attached to its other end.

The method involves manipulating the following variables: the length of the string, the weight of the pendulum, the height of the initial swing and the force of the push.

Results – formal operational thought will be demonstrated only if hypotheses are formulated and tested systematically – manipulating one variable at a time while holding others constant and making logical deductions from the results of each trial.

Piaget's pendulum task – used to test for formal operational thought

Source: Inhelder and Piaget (1958)

Implications of Piaget's work

Initially, Piaget had little impact on the English-speaking psychological world. His writing was complex, difficult to understand and in French. Then, as now, psychology was dominated by English-speaking north Americans. His ideas were way outside mainstream learning theory both in terms of method and choice of subject. Psychology has been defined as the 'science of behaviour' and Piaget's work was seen by critics as being marginal to both parts of the definition. Only when the study of mind began to return into psychology in the 1980s – the so-called cognitive revolution – did Piaget's work become widely influential.

Piaget gave a new perspective to the declining field of developmental psychology. Some 50 years of scholarship had produced an extensive and detailed literature describing children's development, but it was like a disappearing seam of coal – there was little left to mine. Piaget put the study of children back to the top of the agenda by opening up the completely new field of children's thinking.

■ Implications for educational theory and practice

Piaget's view of children as active constructors of their own cognitive world had considerable educational implications. Piaget saw 'making sense' as highly personal and in line with a child's age, and therefore level of maturation. It follows from this that knowledge can be transferred directly to a child only in part. Children construct an understanding of something for themselves. We can see this mixture of learned knowledge and constructed meaning clearly in Penny's account of Christmas (see page 754). She has actually made sense of the experience of Christmas in a unique way, but this is also related to the way other children of similar age see it. She resolves possible difficulties about eating the turkey by telling us that it has given its permission, although she is aware that it has not actually said so.

The precariousness of Penny's reference system is clear to an adult and is continually changing. For Piaget, children's logical difficulties cannot be overcome by feeding them indigestible chunks of adult logic. Whatever new information of this type children are given will be understood by them in a way that is only partially predictable and will not be entirely absorbed. For Piaget, there is no shortcutting the four stages and very little point in even trying to speed them up as the sequence of stages is invariant. Whatever experiences children have will be understood in relation to their level of maturation.

One implication of this for education is that teachers can encourage cognitive growth in children by providing experiences they can actively engage in and make sense of. Thus a function of schooling should be to promote the development of appropriate thinking skills as children pass through the different stages. This has implications for curriculum planning, since no matter how intelligent children in a particular stage are, there is no point in presenting them with problems involving levels of thought which are beyond their capabilities. For example, presenting pre-operational children with problems containing more than one dimension, or concrete operational children those with three dimensions would prove counter-productive. Similarly, it would be a waste of time to present simple problems involving only one or two dimensions to children capable of abstract thinking.

Educators need also to be aware of when children's conservational abilities are acquired (see page 757–8). Tasks which are too difficult may inhibit a child from trying, tasks too simple may elicit boredom, both are detrimental to learning. An awareness of this is not always the case. Children can be seen actively learning in figure 21.4.

Cognitive development comes about by engaging in a programme of stimulating activities which motivate assimilation and accommodation in children. A teacher's job is to provide a satisfactory environment for this to occur, promoting the development of thinking skills which are appropriate to each child's stage of cognitive development. Piaget believed that children's cognitive growth can be facilitated, but not taught. The implications of Piaget's work can be seen in figure 21.5.

This approach to children's development is striking and immediately appealing. In particular, it reinforces the importance of play as an active process in which children directly act on their world to *construct* an understanding of it. Play is therefore the principle way in which children

Figure 21.4 Children involved in active learning

learn. Children are not passive; they actively seek to understand. From these points it can be seen that Piaget's approach did not contribute much (new) to the idea of progressive education, but he produced a vast body of data and theory which provides a sound basis for this, and many developmental psychologists have accepted Piaget's theory as a starting point (Flavell, 1992).

Activity 5

See if you can name Piaget's four stages of cognitive development giving the approximate ages of the children at each stage.

(Suggested answers on page 799.)

Piaget saw the principle goal of education as being 'to create adults who are capable of doing new things'. This did not mean repeating what other generations had done, but creating, inventing and discovering. How far have Piaget's ideas had an impact on educational practice? There is no doubt that greater emphasis has been placed on **discovery learning** and activity-based work in nursery and primary schools than previously and that this takes into account children's likely readiness to learn. With older children, material such as that in Nuffield science programmes is designed to take into account the transition into concrete operational and formal operational thought, giving practical hands-on experience of conservation-like tasks. Some

21.5 Implications of Piaget's work for education

- Children's language and thought are different from an adult's. Teachers should recognise this and attempt to discover each child's unique perspectives.
- Children need to manipulate things in order to learn and formal verbal instruction is generally ineffective, especially for the young child. This type of activity will constitute a major portion of the acquisition of genuine knowledge, as formal instruction must be preceded by direct experience.
- Children are most interested and learn best when an experience is fairly novel (needs to be both familiar enough to be assimilated into existing cognitive structures and unfamiliar enough to produce some degree of conflict). This helps accommodation.

- Children should prefer to work as individuals, as cognitive structures differ from child to child and all children will not find the same event interesting, but they can be encouraged to work together in pairs and small groups to learn from observation and competition.
- Children's thought progresses through a series of stages, each with distinctive strengths and weaknesses. Teachers should respect this and not force the use of material for which the child is not ready.
- Intellectual growth is promoted by arguing and debate.
- The teacher's monitoring of the child's intellectual level/stages allows for the provision of alternative strategies if the method is not leading to success so the child can gain knowledge from solving the problem.

supporters of Piaget's ideas would take these applications much further. However much face validity his ideas on education would seem to have, it is important to know if they work in practice.

Brainerd (1985) reviewed the evidence concerning how modifiable cognitive development is and the value of Piagetian curricula. The major problem with the systematic use of Piagetian concepts in early education is the difficulty in knowing the point which children have reached in their cognitive development. To overcome this, extensive diagnostic and testing procedures are necessary. Children, however, do not conveniently 'pop' from one stage to the next in a few days.

Criticisms and reformulations of Piaget's work

Few parts of Piaget's work have not been re-examined, criticised and in some cases reformulated. In many ways Piaget emerges

triumphant – Flavell (1985) referred to his contribution as '. . . nothing short of stupendous, both quantitatively and qualitatively'. Research, however, has now moved on, although still broadly in the same framework, and Piaget is starting to become more of historical than of immediate relevance.

In general, Piaget has been criticised as underestimating the abilities of sensorimotor and pre-operational children and overestimating the capabilities of formal operational children. He has also been criticised for neglecting the importance of language and social factors.

■ Object permanence

Piaget's account of the development of object permanence (see page 755) stimulated considerable research in the field. A number of critics consider that he underestimated the age at which children achieve it. Bower (1974) used a variety of imaginative research designs to claim that babies may acquire object permanence substantially earlier than Piaget suggested. For example, using four- to six-month-old babies as participants, he made an object disappear by bringing a screen down in front of it. When the screen was lifted and the object was not there, Bower looked for evidence, such as a raised pulse, which would indicate surprise in the baby. Bower found surprise when the object was missing rather than when it was present, suggesting that the babies understood object permanence.

So it would appear that out of sight is *not* out of mind as Piaget had originally suggested. Bower argued that different conditions differentiate between something that is temporarily hidden (occluded) and something that disappears instantly (as if 'annihilated'). Bower suggested the babies' perceptual systems are capable of distinguishing between temporary occlusion and annihilation.

Baillargeon (1991) studied five-month-old babies' ability to understand occlusion by presenting two groups with rabbits moving behind a horizontal screen and reappearing at the far end (figure 21.6). The rabbits were either tall or small and after introductory trials a central portion was removed and the tall and small rabbit disappeared and reappeared without appearing at the central window. Babies attended longer to trials when the tall rabbit failed to show at the window than when the small rabbit passed by (he was smaller than the height of the window). Baillargeon suggested that not only does the baby perceive that the rabbit continues to exist but also retains its original size when occluded. Further studies with younger babies aged three months using long and short carrots found similar results.

These studies do not explain why the babies in Piaget's studies did not reach for the toys behind the cushion/covers. If they understand object permanence why did they not search? Immaturity of the nervous system has been suggested as an important variable. Perhaps the babies' limited ability to hold things in mind may be a determining factor (Wellman *et al.*, 1986). Another important variable is the child's ability to reach and grasp. Evidence suggests that babies require several months to master such skills. Problems of integrating vision, action and memory could be a contributory factor. Piaget is supported in that babies pass through a stage where they are prone to error in visible displacement. For example, a small

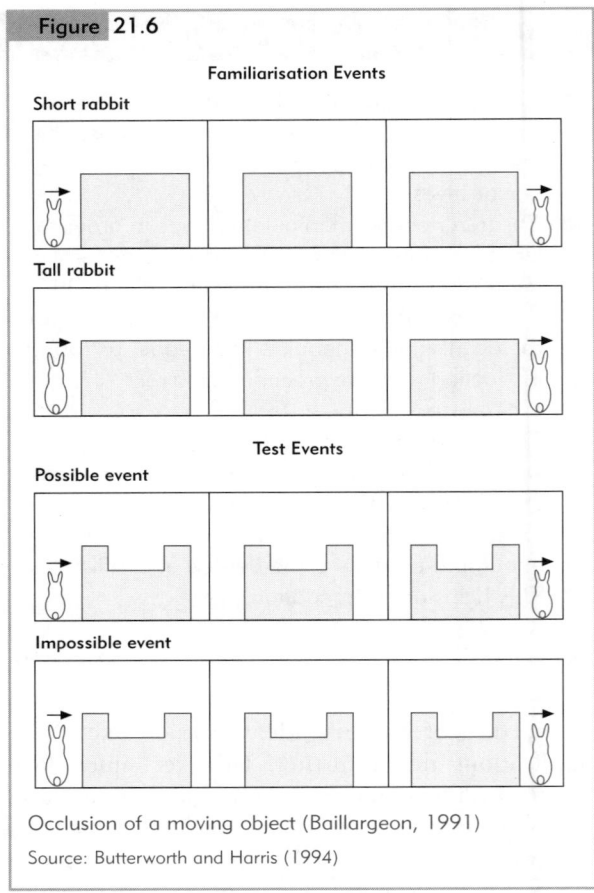

Figure 21.6

Familiarisation Events

Short rabbit

Tall rabbit

Test Events

Possible event

Impossible event

Occlusion of a moving object (Baillargeon, 1991)

Source: Butterworth and Harris (1994)

child, Sarah, searching for Teddy hidden behind a cushion must hold the Teddy in her mind, reach and grasp the cushion, before reaching and grasping Teddy. Quite a complex hierarchically integrated sequence of events! So even when babies understand object permanence, there will still be times when their inability to hold things in memory leads to error. Such errors can still be seen in adults' *absent-minded* moments.

■ Ability to decentre

Piaget thought that children in the pre-operational stage were unable to decentre and take other viewpoints into account (as shown, for example, by the three mountains task described on page 757). Much research has been focused on this aspect of the pre-occupational period. For example, Hughes (1979) devised an apparatus involving a cross-shaped arrangement of walls (figure 21.7). Participants were asked to hide a child doll from a policeman doll. To do this successfully, a child has to take the policeman–doll's point of view into account. Many more children (88 per cent of three and a half to four year-olds) were successful at this task than at the three mountains task. We may conclude that Piaget's task underestimated children's ability to decentre. Children who failed the task did so because they could not understand another's point of view. All research designs require children to do more than the task set. They must also, for example, understand it, pay attention and overcome anxiety at the strangeness of the situation. Piaget's participants may not have understood the task, or they may have given the answer which they thought Piaget wanted. It remains possible that they may have shown the ability to decentre under more favourable circumstances.

Similarly in America, Borke (1975) found that the task itself had an effect on the children's performance. She questioned the aaropriateness of the mountains task and also the interpretation of photographs. She used a practice display and three experimental displays, two familiar to the child and including a mountains display (see figure 21.8).

Two identical models were presented one for the child to look at, the other for Grover to drive around. Children were tested individually. The practice session showed the fire engine on the two tables next to one another, one of which was a moveable turntable. The children were aged between three and four years attending a day nursery. A character from the children's television programme *Sesame Street* (Grover), well known to the children, was used. The following instructions were given:

'He will drive his car along the road. Sometimes Grover likes to stop and look out of his car. Now the turntable on this other table turns so you can look at it from any side. When Grover stops to look out of his car, I want you to turn the scene that moves so you are looking at it in the same way Grover is.'

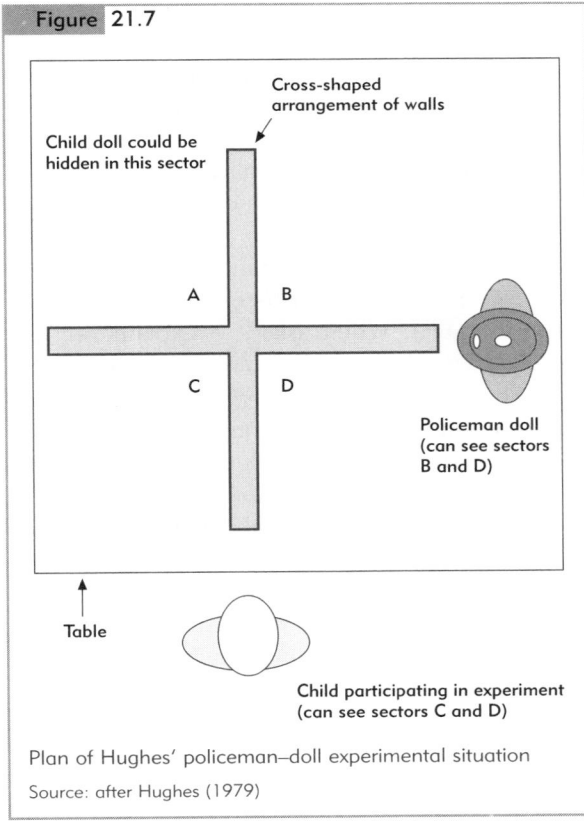

Figure 21.7

Plan of Hughes' policeman–doll experimental situation

Source: after Hughes (1979)

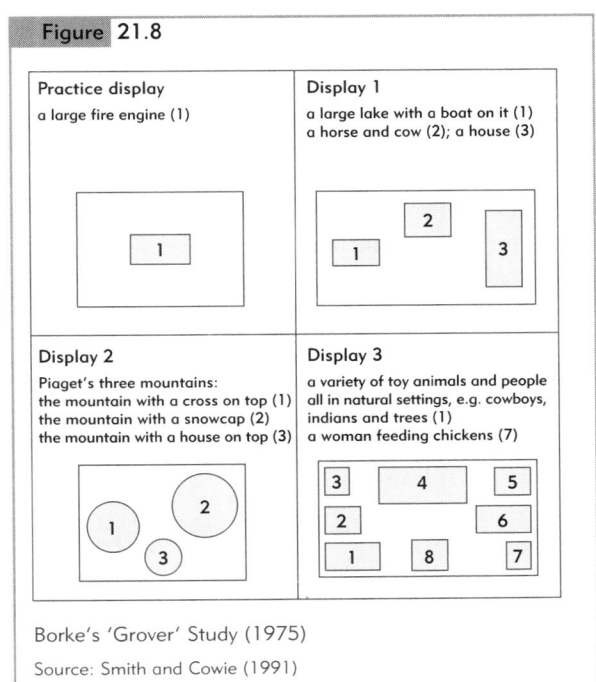

Figure 21.8

Borke's 'Grover' Study (1975)

Source: Smith and Cowie (1991)

Grover was then parked at each of the three sides presenting a different view to the child. If necessary the child was helped to put the turntable into the correct position and was allowed to walk around to the same position as Grover.

After this practice session the child progressed to the experiment itself in which the other three displays were presented one at a time. The experimental displays were as follows:

1 A boat on a lake, a horse, a cow and a house.
2 Piaget's three mountains task.
3 A variety of toy animals and people in a natural setting e.g. cowboys, Indians, tree and a woman feeding chickens.

They were asked to rotate their replica display to the same view as Grover. She found that revolving the turntable seemed easier to the child than picking out photographs (as previously asked by Piaget).

The results showed significant differences between the displays. As seen from table 21.9 participants found Display 1 easy to copy, even Display 3 which was more complex was not found difficult. However the Piagetian Display (2) provided more problems for the children.

Borke found that the incorrect responses did not differ significantly between displays, with thirty one per cent egocentric answers (the same view as the child) and sixty nine per cent random answers. Borke concluded that the task was a critical influence and when the child was familiar with this they were able to take the perspective of the other person at the young age of three or four, thus challenging Piaget's concept of egocentrism. As

Table 21.9

Display	Age	
	3 years	4 years
1	80	80
2	42	67
3	79	93

The percentage of correct responses in Borke's *Grover* experiment

with the Hughes' (1978) policeman–doll study, the task *'made more sense'* to them than did the mountains task.

■ Conservation

Piaget also appeared to have underestimated children's abilities with regard to conservation, which is apparently achieved successfully at a rather younger age than he suggested.

McGarrigle and Donaldson (1975) devised a more child-centred way of investigating conservation of number. Using two rows of equally spaced counters, which a child has agreed are identical, they used an accidental transformation condition in which a 'naughty teddy' (produced by the experimenter) 'messes up' one row so as to space it out. Compared with an intentional transformation condition in which the experimenter spaces out one row of counters, 50 out of 80 four- to six-year-old children gave the correct answer – that there are still the same number of counters in each row. McGarrigle and Donaldson argued that this showed that Piaget had underestimated children's ability to conserve. However, they did not ask their participants to explain why the two rows were the same.

Neilson *et al.* (1983) replicated the 'naughty teddy' research and found that far more children gave a conserving answer in the accidental transformation condition (naughty teddy) than in the intentional transformation condition (experimenter). When asked to explain why the two rows were the same, however, there was no difference between the two transformation conditions in terms of the numbers able to give an acceptable argument. It seems that children simply disregarded the transformation made by 'naughty teddy' as irrelevant, whilst taking that performed by the experimenter seriously. Thus they are likely to give a superficially correct answer which overestimates their ability to conserve. McGarrigle and Donaldson's study shows that for children aged up to about seven or eight, the meaning of a change in the appearance of something is embedded in the social context in which it takes place. They have great difficulty in disembedding questions from their contexts. This shows how easy it is to misinterpret research findings to give the answers we expect or want to hear.

Flavell (1985) pointed out that false positives and false negatives are both possible. Children may give correct answers without having the cognitive skill under investigation, or fail to give a correct answer despite possessing the skill. The question may be misunderstood, an alternative or inappropriate cognitive strategy used, or skill may be available only in relation to certain problems – but not necessarily the one set.

Research has now moved on, partly because of the futility of simply confirming or disconfirming the age at which a concept, like conservation, is acquired. Piaget was interested in the sequence of stages rather than the age that each appeared. Cross-cultural research does appear to support such sequences. What we now have is detailed research into children's cognitive growth, still inspired by Piaget, but moving into new areas, such as children's awareness of their own cognitive processes, and also the role of social factors.

Equilibration

Piaget's equilibration model of how cognitive growth occurs has also been criticised. Flavell (1985) pointed out that for equilibration to happen, children must notice that there is a conflict between two factors and respond to it by going forward constructively, rather than retreating defensively to an entrenched way of thinking, or simply avoiding the problem. Also, they must actually come up with a new and better understanding which resolves the problem.

This is a tall order, and Flavell thought it unlikely that very much cognitive growth can be explained solely by the equilibration mechanism. Other processes may be involved.

Is formal operational thought universal?

It would appear that Piaget overestimated the universality of formal operational thinking. Shayer et al. (1976, 1978) gave young British students, aged between 15 and 16, tasks such as the pendulum problem and found only 30 per cent were using the

formal operational thought as identified by Piaget. They found many young people were still consolidating concrete operations at this age. Similar findings were obtained in an American sample of 20 young females by Martorano (1977). They were aged between 12 and 18 and by the age of 18 only two of the girls were successful on all ten tasks presented. There was a range of 15–95 per cent success among the remaining girls.

In both the US and Britain the tasks were similar to those presented in schools. In non-literate societies formal operational thinking is found delayed or non-existent. This questions whether it is a developmental stage. In 1972 Piaget considered this question and suggested three options:

- different rates of progress depending on environmental/cognitive stimulation so in some 'deprived' conditions it may never be achieved
- more diversity with increasing age means the later period can no longer be considered a 'stage'
- a combination of the previous two views whereby most 'normal' people achieve this stage by the end of their teenage period, but they reach it in different areas dependent on their experience in areas of study, or vocational training.

Piaget favoured the last option which is consistent with cross-cultural research showing that non-literate cultures become proficient in logical reasoning related to their culture. Blurton Jones and Konner (1976) found the Kalahari bush people used such reasoning in their tracking and hunting of animals. More recent theories on the structure and measurement of intelligence by Sternberg (1988) support the existence of such multiple intelligences (see page 785–6).

Several aspects of Piaget's theory have been questioned but other aspects remain influential. His emphasis on qualitative change has been supported by other developmentalists such as Vygotsky and Bruner who are discussed in the next section. Even though his stage concept has not been supported by more recent research, we find most educationalists and developmentalists operate within this four-part division of infants, nursery/pre-school, primary/schoolchildren and secondary/adolescent. Piaget's neglect of social context is considered an important reason why his research tends to underestimate children's ability. Piaget was testing the children's *individual* competence on tasks often taken in a social situation. Margaret Donaldson and her co-workers made us aware of context in the task situation which enables children to make sense of what they are being asked to do. Such research demonstrates that the children's responses are often influenced by their interpretation (or cognition) of the adult's meaning and intentions. This research highlights the social nature of the processes by which children's understanding develops.

Later researchers such as Vygotsky and Bruner considered such **social cognition** to be far more important, especially in relation to teaching and education. We shall now look at these two developmentalists in more detail.

Self-assessment questions

1　Explain the relationship of assimilation, accommodation and equilibration in the adaptation process.

2　Would you advise a student teacher to abandon formal instruction entirely with the under fives? List the evidence for and against formal instruction.

3　Compare Piaget's findings with those of Hughes, McGarrigle and Borke.

4　Note at least *three* aspects of Piaget's theory which have been modified by later research.

(Suggested answers on page 801.)

Other theories of cognitive development

Piaget is not the only researcher who has produced theories of cognitive development in children. In this section, we examine the theories proposed by two other theorists, Vygotsky and Bruner. We then consider some of the recent research on the information-processing approach and the theory of mind.

The cognitive theory of Vygotsky

Vygotsky investigated conscious thought processes, memory and perception, but in particular, was interested in thought and language. He was interested in how thought and language, which he saw initially separate, later interact and influence one another. The behaviourists had previously considered thought to be the same as language whereas these were seen to be independentp rocesses by the introspectionists. Vygotsky disagreed with both these earlier approaches. He thought that the behaviourists' emphasis on studying stimulus–response associations blocked them from considering more complex human behaviours and that the introspectionists were unscientific in their approach. He therefore set out to investigate the interaction of thinking and language.

Vygotsky analysed many studies from different countries and devised his own methods of investigating thought and speech among children, adolescents and adults in the Soviet Union. Among these are what have subsequently become known as Vygotsky's blocks, a testing instrument for children which measures whether they have mastered a concept, rather than memorised a word for it (figure 21.10).

Vygotsky concluded from his investigations that at an early age the child makes short-term links rather than higher level discriminations, for example the child might put together blocks with common property (or properties) such as all

21.10 Vygotsky's blocks (after Vygotsky, 1962)

A set of 22 wooden blocks is used, which differ in their size, shape, colour and height such that no two blocks are totally alike. One of four nonsense words is written on the base of each block. 'Lag' is written on all tall, large blocks; 'bik' on all flat, large ones; 'mur' on tall, small ones; 'cev' on short, small ones.

The tester spreads the blocks in front of the child and turns one up to show the nonsense word on its base. The child is then asked to pick up all the blocks which are the same, i.e. which have the same nonsense word on the bottom. After this is done, the examiner turns up a 'wrong' block and shows the child the different name.

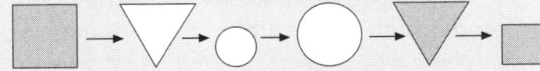

The process is repeated until the child solves the problem. Since the concept tested using this technique applies to both vertical and horizontal components of the blocks, and there is no single word to represent this, the child cannot have known or rote memorised the concept prior to the testing session.

triangles or all red ones. He discovered a type of thinking common to pre-school children, an example of which is chain complexes, as shown in figure 21.10. Vygotsky noted four developmental stages of concept formation which can be seen in table 21.11. He suggested that children's thought and speech begin as separate functions without there necessarily being any connection between them. Neither is there parallel progress in thought and speech development. Each goes through a series of developmental stages in which 'their two growth curves cross and recross' (Vygotsky, 1962) so that, although language development may boost and transform thinking, the two always remain separate.

Vygotsky thought that between the ages of two and seven, children's language performed two functions. One function was to monitor and direct internal thoughts, the second was to communicate these thoughts to others. He saw egocentric speech as a mixture of these two functions, i.e. as 'inner speech' or 'verbal thought', which a child has not yet learned to distinguish between. So, for example, children will talk out a thought or explain something aloud to themselves. He noticed that this kind of speech begins to disappear as social speech develops, but may reappear as 'thinking aloud' if a child is faced with difficult problem.

Vygotsky saw thought and language as tools for planning and carrying out actions. Using language, people can organise thinking and perception, acting in a self-regulatory manner.

Activity 6

Have you been aware of 'thinking aloud' yourself? Try to remember the reason(s) for doing so. Do you agree with Vygotsky? Is it accompanying what you are doing (Piaget) or guiding you in what you do (Vygotsky)?

Table 21.11	
1 *Vague syncretic stage*	Largely trial and error without understanding.
2 *Complexes stage*	Some appropriate strategies are used but the main attributes are not identified.
3 *Potential concept stage*	One attribute only (e.g. tall) can be dealt with at a time.
4 *Mature concept stage*	The child is able to deal with several attributes simultaneously (e.g. tall and square).

Vygotsky's stages of concept formation

Vygotsky's theory can explain the past and predict the future of verbal–thought development for children in general (Thomas, 1985). However, it was still only in skeleton form when he died. Thus it may lack the completeness of detail that he envisaged. It does not allow for influences on development such as child-rearing practices, although recent researchers (noted below) have investigated this (Dunn, 1988).

Thomas also believed that Vygotsky did not account for the results of the blocks experiments in sufficient detail, suggesting that more elements and a better explanation of their interaction are needed. However, Vygotsky's theory can be tested experimentally and has been highly regarded in Russia (Luria, 1976) and more recently in the west.

Vygotsky did not wait for the child to be 'ready', but suggested the child could learn from people more knowledgeable. His theory stresses on the role of interpersonal processes and the role of society in providing a framework within which the child's understanding develops. This coordinated framework of the child's experiences and the socio-cultural interaction with teachers and parents helps to develop understanding defined by the culture. Herein lies a distinction between Piaget and Vygotsky: Piaget believed in biological maturation; Vygotsky, however, suggested this is necessary but not sufficient to explain intellectual development fully. Vygotsky suggested that the cultural context and social interaction are critical.

■ Zone of Proximal Development

A central concept of Vygotsky's theory is the **Zone of Proximal Development (ZPD)**, which provides an explanation of how the child develops with the help of others. The ZPD is the distance between what the child can achieve on his or her own by maturation and what the child will achieve with the help of others, who are more experienced adults or more competent peers. Vygotsky sees the child being initiated into the intellectual life of the community and thus socially constructing his or her understanding of the world. This 'expert' intervention needs to be at a level beyond the child's existing knowledge to provide a challenge, but not too distant from the child's current understanding

so it can be understood. If the new challenge is in the ZPD then the child can understand something not understood alone and learn from the experience. In an individual test situation the full potential of the child may not be demonstrated; competence may only be demonstrated when the child collaborates with someone else. This intervention is most effective when it is contingent on existing skills and knowledge but still within the ZPD. This allows the child's understanding to be challenged but he or she can still learn new things without experiencing failure.

Vygotsky's theory does not contradict Piaget's theory, rather it reflects their different cultural backgrounds. Piaget was originally a biologist and his theory reflects this, whereas Vygotsky's theory reflects his socialist background. He stressed the sociability of interaction and implied that the child is not egocentric if he or she can interpret the social cues of others. Wertsch *et al.* (1980) noted the progress of the child in various tasks, with the help and support of others moving from a joint or social regulation to a more self-regulated approach. Language is seen as central to this process, with the mother or caretaker talking the child through the task in the early stages, then gradually saying less and allowing the child to take over more during the later stages until the child is in control of the task and the adult only makes the occasional comment or suggestion if necessary. At this point Wertsch *et al.* noted the child using speech to regulate actions, with overt speech becoming inner speech.

Activity 7

You might find it useful to observe young children interacting with adults. Make sure you are quiet so you do not disturb them. Do the adults 'talk them through' the tasks they are doing? Can you see a difference between the younger and the older children, with the adults giving less support/help to the older group? Note examples to compare with other members of your class group. (See Unit 19 for discussion of such motherese.)

■ Joint Involvement Episodes

Schaffer (1996) also noted the importance of these Joint Involvement Episodes (JIEs) and defined them as 'social interactions that appear to play a particularly important role in influencing development' (Schaffer, 1996, p. 252). He cited a study by Freund (1990) of three- and five-year-old children working with their mothers on a sorting task. The children's performance on the task was measured before and after an interactive session. When compared with a group of children who did not experience interaction (although they were given feedback on completion of the errors made), it was found that there were more significant gains for the mother–interaction children. The joint involvement with the adult appears to be directly responsible for improved performance. Children whose mothers gave verbal help in goal direction, monitoring, strategy and planning during the joint session improved most on independent problem solving. This suggests that the mothers' active involvement with their children's attempts on the task was the crucial factor.

However, support for the value of JIEs is not unanimous. There are so many differences between participants, tasks, conditions and measures in the various studies that it is difficult to know why there is a disparity in findings. It would appear that the weight of evidence suggests that joint problem solving does lead to improved independent problem solving at least in the short-term.

A number of studies have investigated the different strategies adopted by adults and the ways these are manifested in the interaction with the child, rather than the 'child-alone' versus 'child-with-adult' type. The age and ability of the child play an important part in this interaction, with the mother providing more complex types of information, increasing demands and handing over more responsibility as the children get older. The adults appear to be responding to the child's developmental behaviour and competence as perceived in the situation. There is now awareness of the importance of the social context which may have different meanings for different children, according to the predisposition they bring with them. This means for some children the adult's presence may have an inhibitory rather than a facilitative effect.

The socio-cognitive view can be seen in the more recent research of Dunn (1988) in the UK. She used an ethological approach in Cambridge investigating family life with pre-school children from a range of backgrounds. At the start of the study none of the mothers were working full-time. Researchers entered into the family setting but tried not to join in activities. If children spoke to them they answered but they did not enter into any of the activities. Dunn's findings challenge the earlier views in finding that the youngsters *had* tuned in to others, described as affective tuning, and this highlights the social understanding of the pre-school child. Dunn's findings showed:

- early *understanding of others' feelings*, sometimes as young as 18 months, with interest shown in the affective states of another; by 36 months they were likely to comfort another when needed
- an *understanding of goals of others* was revealed in play, especially those involving turn-taking, with sustained coordination by the age of 12 months; they could demonstrate the intention of others by about 18 months
- an understanding of *which rules apply* in various contexts and what is acceptable in the family was shown to be well developed by the third year
- they also demonstrated an awareness of the thinking of others, *the theory of mind*, which is discussed below (see page 774).

Dunn thus supports Vygotsky in moving away from a single cause of behaviour and highlights the social learning of context-specific behaviour. When the situation is *socially real*, understanding can be displayed.

Schaffer (1996) noted that there is still much to be learned about socially mediated versus independent problem solving. It is not just Piaget versus Vygotsky but rather a matter of defining the conditions under which independent or joint functioning is the most effective way of promoting cognition. Both Piaget and Vygotsky stressed the importance of *action*. Piaget saw this as individual and constructive, whereas Vygotsky saw it beginning in the external social world and gradually becoming internalised and a central feature of the child's intellectual processes which allow for the opportunity to 'try things out' in the mind. Piaget saw the child's deeper knowledge coming from the children finding out for themselves, whereas Vygotsky suggested culture demands that the immature learn and the mature teach. In this way the capacity to learn from the instruction can be seen as a 'fundamental feature of human intelligence' (Lloyd, 1995).

Even in young children there are circumstances where self-directed activity even in the early stages of acquiring task competence enhances problem solving and where adults hinder rather than help. Schaffer (1996) noted the dangers of over-emphasising the part played by social context. It is unlikely that all skill acquired at all stages of development originate in social interactions. There is a need to establish 'what kind of social interactions promote what kind of cognitive achievement at what age and in what manner' (Schaffer, 1996).

Another researcher who has developed and applied Vygotsky's ideas in an educational setting is the American psychologist Jerome Bruner.

The socio-cognitive theory of Bruner

Bruner (1966) saw cognitive development in terms of different ways of representing the world known as **modes of internal representation** rather than in terms of stages as Vygotsky did – although the modes appear at different times.

■ Modes of representation

The first of these to appear is the *enactive mode*. Using this, children represent objects and actions through motor behaviours.

Activity 8

Ask a friend to describe how to crack an egg, or try to describe it for yourself. Can you manage to do so without using your hands?

It is very difficult to describe an action like this without demonstrating it with your hands – which is using the enactive mode to describe the actions involved. The enactive mode of representation does not disappear with age. Adults may still best represent some routine behaviour, for example cracking eggs, putting on make-up or shaving, in terms of actions.

The second mode of representation to emerge is the *iconic mode* – from the Greek word for image. Children of approximately the same age as those in Piaget's pre-operational stage (ages two to seven) deal with the world in terms of images. This is illustrated by children's failure at conservation tasks.

Both Bruner and Piaget agreed that a change of major importance occurs at around six to seven years old. For Piaget it was the shift into operational thinking and for Bruner it was the ability to use the *symbolic mode* of representation. Bruner believed this happens as a result of language. The power of symbolic reasoning is neatly demonstrated by Bruner and Kenney's (1966) study requiring children to reorder a disturbed array of glasses (figure 21.12). This showed that six-year-olds could recreate the required pattern easily enough, but were unable to transform the pattern into its mirror image. In other words, they could return the glasses to their original largest to smallest order, but could not create a mirror image order of smallest to largest. However, according to Bruner, seven-year-olds can think symbolically (represent the world internally) and are no longer tied to an image. As a result, they can successfully complete the transformation task.

Activity 9

Try to determine which of Bruner's modes are involved in the following tasks (note if more than one mode is involved):

a   an architect planning a shopping complex

b   playing a video gameb

c   skiing

d   presenting information on cognitive development to a group of students

e   analysing data using statistics.

(Suggested answers on page 799.)

Figure 21.12

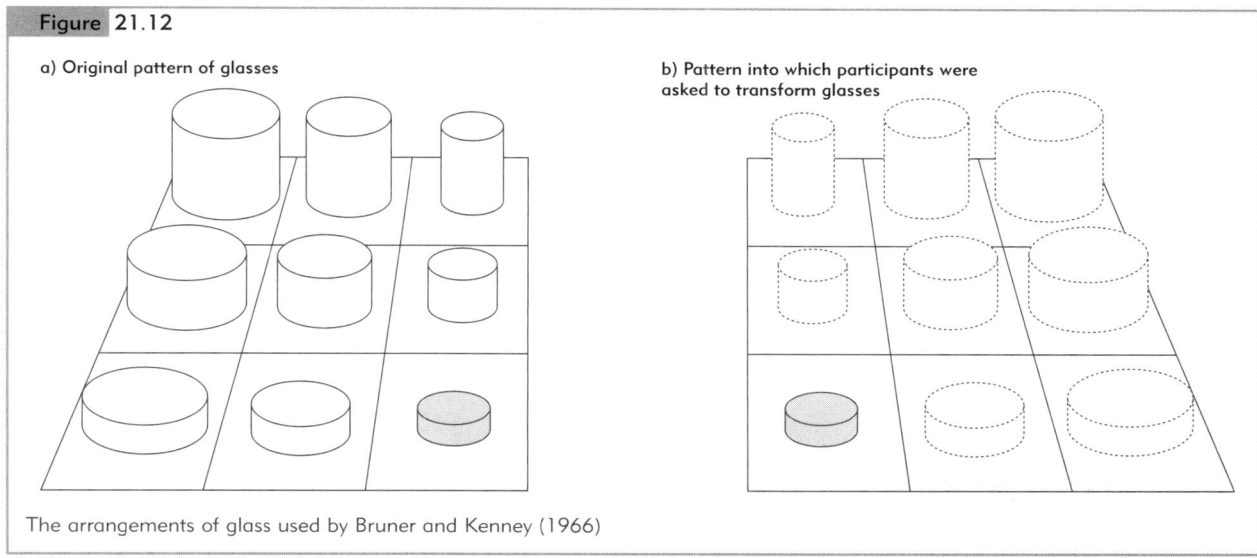

a) Original pattern of glasses

b) Pattern into which participants were asked to transform glasses

The arrangements of glass used by Bruner and Kenney (1966)

■ The role of instruction in education

Bruner was responsible for introducing Vygotsky's ideas to researchers outside Russia and this influence can be seen in his work especially in relation to language development and cognitive growth. Bruner argued that children learn language in the familiar context of social exchanges with mothers and other carers. Like Vygotsky, Bruner valued the role of instruction and social interaction in cognitive growth. He stressed the close relationship between perception and cognition which creates hypothesis testing of what is seen. This is based on schemes developed and Bruner noted the role of others in the process. He used the term **scaffolding** to explain the support given to the child by adults and others, especially linguistic support. He suggested that without instruction the child's spontaneous activities cannot be transformed into rational thought. Studies highlight the scaffolding processes at work when the mother or carer builds on the infant's capacity to adjust his or her line of gaze to that of the mother by commenting on the object of joint attention.

Bruner was concerned with structuring teaching to create self-motivated learners. He suggested that the social relationships a child develops at school are likely to be influential in terms of readiness or capacity to learn at school. Teachers should try to present information at the level appropriate for the child and have awareness of all three modes of representation. All the modes should be used when appropriate for the child in an *effective sequence* based upon the learner's own experiences and interests. Reinforcement should move from extrinsic to intrinsic during learning with the corrective feedback of information.

He suggested that the curriculum should incorporate a number of different *pathways* to the same ends so that learners can benefit from a variety of learning experiences. In this way the principles of the subject area come to be understood by the person at increasingly sophisticated levels. This is known as the spiral curriculum. So like Vygotsky, Bruner argued that instruction is an essential part of learning.

Activity 10

Draw up a revision table of similarities and differences between Piaget, Bruner and Vygotsky.

(Suggested answers on page 800.)

These later researchers have sought to extend the early work of Piaget to explain how the child develops understanding of the social world and how the child's thinking and reasoning about the world depends on the very subtle processes of this social interpretation. For Bruner and Vygotsky, the teaching–learning situation is seen as a social exchange involving joint activity. Adults play an important role in the process (remember contingency, scaffolding and 'stand alone competence'). This has become known as **social cognition**, 'how the social environment influences thoughts, perceptions and beliefs' (Fiske and Taylor, 1991).

Many of the experiments that challenged Piaget's view evolved through research which views cognitive development as the acquisition of several separate information-processing skills.

Recent research into cognitive development

The information-processing approach to cognitive development

Information processing is based on the metaphor of the human mind as an information processor with a limited capacity (such as a computer as displayed in figure 21.13).

Information processing extends Piaget's theory in trying to provide a more detailed account of how the intellectual processes change with age. For example, we know that digit span increases with age from about two or three items at the age of two to about seven by adolescence and adulthood (Lloyd, 1995). This approach is more specific on what information is relevant to performance on a task, so the focus is to understand the child's capacity to process, store, retrieve and actively manipulate information (including perception, attention and memory) and how this changes with age.

Information-processing theorists disagree about how they challenge Piaget. They believe the

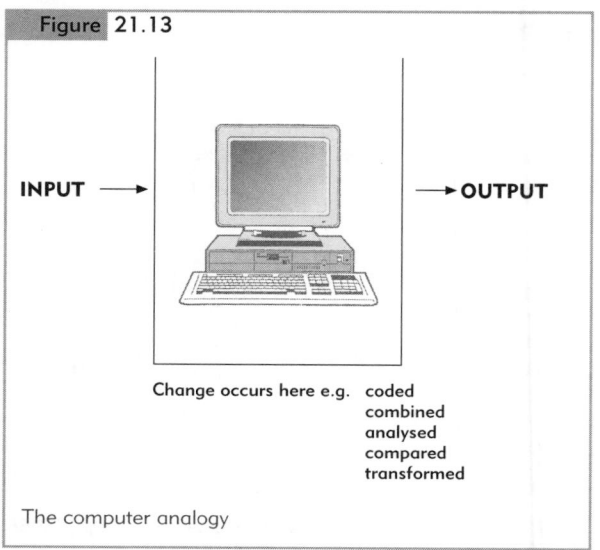

Figure 21.13

INPUT ⟶   ⟶ OUTPUT

Change occurs here e.g. coded
                         combined
                         analysed
                         compared
                         transformed

The computer analogy

Piagetian tasks fail to separate the various information-processing skills, but they disagree on whether development is best seen as a series of qualitatively distinct stages or as a continuous process of change. Some, such as Klahr (1982), suggest that the concept of stages is misplaced and should be abandoned because the discontinuity is due to methodological problems in assessment. We return to this issue below (see page 790) when we look at tests which have been developed to measure intellectual development.

- Researchers such as Case (1985) have tried to modify and extend Piaget's stage model and believe that gradual changes in information-processing skills do lead to discontinuous stage-like thinking processes in the child.

- Other researchers believe, like Piaget, that there are stages but that these are in separate domains such as language, mathematical understanding and social reasoning, and that these stages all develop separately at their own pace, relatively independently of the others (Mandler, 1983).

The information-processing approach assumes that the child has limited ability to process the information and, lacking experience, is not skilled at using the techniques or strategies to help improve performance.

We look initially at the development of the 'basic capacities' (Meadows, 1993) of information processing:

- sensory processing and recognition
- attention and scanning for information
- categorisation and strategies in memory used for improving performance
- learning and coordinating different modalities (such as sound, touch and vision) to integrate the information.

Sensory processing and recognition

Newborns have been shown to have considerable perceptual abilities to perceive the world around them (see Unit 16 page 601). These skills improve rapidly over the early years. Information-processing approaches suggest that this is due to development of cognitive schemes. Several researchers have provided evidence that newborns possess ability to form such schemes. Walton and Bower (1992) found newborns look longer at a face they have seen before than that at one which is unfamiliar, suggesting that they have formed a mental representation of the facial features with which they compare the new face. Such evidence runs contrary to Piaget's understanding of much later development of object permanence.

Attention

In early childhood attention can be seen to progress from 'unfocused scanning to focused planfulness' (Baron, 1996). Young children are easily distracted; they do not appear to focus attention fully on what they are doing. By the age of seven, they seem to be able to filter out distracting stimuli (Higgins and Turnure, 1984). For a small percentage of children (around 5 per cent) this ability does not develop and they have been identified as suffering from Attention-Deficit Hyperactivity Disorder (ADHD). These children are unable to concentrate on any task for longer than a few minutes.

As they grow older, children seem to acquire greater skills in planfulness, which can be seen in their decisions about where and how to direct their attention. By the age of nine, they can plan activities in detail, often searching for various kinds of shortcuts (Gauvain and Rogoff, 1989).

Memory

Storage capacities and ways of handling information improve with age. The basic strategy of *rehearsal* appears not to be used consistently until nine to ten years. *Organisation* of such information into larger *chunks* can be seen about the age of ten (Kunzinger, 1985). Elaboration, the shared meaning in things to be remembered, is an extension of organisation and can be seen to develop later with increasing age. Children seem to acquire increasingly sophisticated scripts (mental representations of expected sequences of events for various situations). Simple scripts are described by children as young as three years and some would suggest that children as young as one or two years can act out rudimentary scripts using toys before they have the verbal skills to describe them (Bauer and Mandler, 1992).

Coordinating different modalities

Search strategies to aid retrieval appear to be quite late developing. Keniston & Flavell (1979) gave 6–18 year olds a task involving writing down letters of the alphabet read out to them. Older children used a search strategy, such as going through the alphabet systematically to decide if the letter was present. With development comes the ability to apply strategies to more and more domains with increasing flexibility.

Robert Siegler (1976) was interested in these rule-based strategies. Building on Piaget's work he saw encoding as central to cognitive development. If crucial features are not adequately represented, then other strategies cannot develop. Several tasks he gave children led him to conclude that behaviour of children under five years is not rule-based. He suggested the following pattern linked with Piaget's stages:

- pre-operational – one dimensional
- transitional – beginning to see in more than one dimension
- concrete operational – beginning to make judgements with the objects present

- formal operational – uses plans to help solve a problem.

He noted that, when encountering new problems, children often fall back on lower levels ('fall back rules'). Competence is seen to increase with experience which he sees to be critical.

Research suggests that the rudiments of these processes can be seen in very young children but there are experience-related and age-related changes. Researchers disagree as to whether these changes are related to:

- increases in the size of the information-processing capacity such as an increase in digit span
- changes in the strategic use of this capacity (unrelated to the size) with information handling techniques developing and the ability to apply the strategies with flexibility to more domains.

For example, pre-school children rarely show deliberate efforts to remember information and they may not allocate their resources efficiently, whereas over the primary school years children's memorising strategies improve.

One late developing accomplishment is the ability to master one's actions and demonstrate knowledge about one's cognitive strategies, known as **metacognition**. 'Metacognition is knowing about cognition: knowing about thinking, knowing about memory, knowing about how we use language and ideas – in short, knowing about knowing.' (Hayes, 1994, p. 662)

Metacognition

This metacognitive growth is seen to include:

- the development of understanding and knowledge of one's own cognitive capacity
- the development of the ability to regulate one's mental world, an executive function which monitors and controls ongoing cognitive performance and thereby the ability to detect problems at input and output and modify performance accordingly.

Metacognition is necessary for effective learning and is more noticeable during and after adolescence. Lloyd (1995) noted that the awareness of good students as to what they can do

and how they monitor their performance distinguishes them from the average student. Such able students, using metacognition, can distribute effort on the basis of this self-knowledge. An example of this would be the way in which thoughts are generated such as, 'I need to remember this so I must make a note of it'.

As this awareness develops, new and more sophisticated strategies develop. Strategies for enhancing attention and memory combine so that young people are able to monitor progress toward chosen goals and examine the feedback when it is received. In this way they are capable of *self-regulation* of their cognitive processes along with other aspects of their behaviour.

Metacognition, with a strong social component, has become known as the child's theory of mind, when the child realises that another's state of mind may or may not be the same as his or her own.

The theory of mind

By gaining a theory of mind children become capable of distinguishing between their real worlds and representations of them.

Understanding the concept of 'pretend' appears to be one of the first steps towards acquiring a theory of mind. Leslie (1987) reported examples from the early development of pretend play. In one example, a two year old picks up a banana and holds it to his ear, pretending that it is a telephone. The child's mother might respond by joining in the pretence. This involves the child becoming capable of decoupling – disconnecting representations of objects (the banana as the telephone) from the objects that they are representations of (the real telephone). The willingness with which such young children enter into and use pretence shows that they are capable of considering and understanding the different realities involved.

At around four years of age, children become capable of understanding a false belief in others (Wimmer and Perner, 1983). The basic method used in false belief experiments employs a story in which the participants have to predict where a story character will look for an object after it has been moved unexpectedly from where this character had put it. An example of such a story is shown in figure 21.14.

Another ability acquired at around this age is the appearance–reality distinction, the ability to distinguish between what something looks like and what it really is (Flavell *et al.*, 1983). Participants were presented with various objects that apparently resembled something else, for example an imitation rock made from sponge and an imitation pencil made from rubber. Eighty-five per cent of four year-olds (but only 47.5 per cent of three year-olds) could successfully answer questions aimed to test whether they could conceive that, although the objects looked like a piece of rock and a pencil, they were in fact something else in reality.

The abilities to understand false belief and the appearance–reality distinction are not the only ones which help to demonstrate the development of a theory of mind in young children. Other abilities acquired during the pre-school years include distinguishing between present and prior beliefs, intentions and actions, utterances and actual beliefs held, and facial expressions and actual feelings. The rapid and consistent emergence of these abilities between two and four years old suggests that at least some of the development is maturational (Astington *et al.*, 1988). Rapidly developing language skills also almost certainly play a part.

Chandler *et al.* (1989) were interested in the significance of language use in their examination of false belief. Beal (1988) also took the view that communication (the translation of thoughts into messages) is a 'bridge between the "mental worlds" of different people' (Forrester, 1992, p. 26). However, Forrester (1992) expressed concern that despite much research in the area we still await evidence that the possession of a 'theory of mind' will aid the child's acquisition of social cognitive skills and a more critical level of theorising.

However, it is still not possible to state categorically when a theory of mind first emerges, not least because of the difficulty of designing experimental techniques suitable for assessing the conceptual knowledge held by very young children. Also, we still do not know the full extent to which development of a theory of mind is affected by cultural variations.

Research in this area is continuing and interesting spin-offs are resulting, for example shedding light on cognition and autism. Autism can be partly explained by the failure to develop an adequate theory of mind (Baron-Cohen *et al.*, 1985). Ultimately, a new grand theory may emerge, but the complexity and sheer volume of material being produced makes this unlikely at present. We know vastly more about cognitive development than we did even ten years ago, and we can think of

21.14 Example of the experimental testing of false belief

Equipment: Three dolls (to represent Mary, Peter and Mummy)
Toy ball
Two pieces of doll's furniture (cupboard and chest of drawers)
All are on a table in front of the participant.

Procedure: The experimenter introduces Mary and Peter, who are outside playing with the ball. Mummy calls them in because it's bedtime. On the way in, Mary watches Peter put the ball in the cupboard.

In the morning Mary gets up early, takes the ball out of the cupboard and goes outside to play. When she comes in for breakfast Peter is still in bed, and she puts the ball in the chest of drawers. Later on, Peter gets up and decides he wants to play with the ball.

The participant is asked, 'Where will Peter think the ball is'? A participant answering 'in the cupboard' demonstrates an understanding of the fact that Peter holds a false belief about the location of the ball.

this as a painting-in of Piaget's already drawn sketch. Detail is added and sometimes the composition is changed, but the basic picture is recognisably the same. We gain enormously in richness and detail, but sometimes the outlines get a little hazy.

Activity 11

Fill in the blanks in the paragraph below:
Understanding the concept of _____ appears to be one the first steps towards _____ theory of mind. Leslie (1987) reported examples of the early _____ of pretend play. In one example, a two year old picks up a banana and holds it to his ear, pretending that it is a _____. The child's mother might respond by joining in the _____. This involves the child becoming capable of _____ – disconnecting representations of objects (the banana as the telephone) from the objects that they are _____ of (the real telephone). The _____ with which such young children enter into and use pretence shows that they are capable of _____ and _____ the different realities involved.

(Answers in the text, page 774.)

Developmental models of information processing

There have been several developmental models of information processing including Case (1974, 1984, 1985, 1992) and Sternberg (1984, 1985). Despite differences among them, they are united by the assumption that humans, like computers, have limited information-processing capacities. Children have difficulty caused by uneven attention, limited memory, and limited strategies for acquiring and using information. As they mature and develop, such limitations are reduced. Many of these limitations have been documented above and suggest cognitive performance will improve when:

■ they are interested in a task
■ information is presented slowly
■ they have good background knowledge.
(Cole and Cole, 1993.)

It is worth noting that these are the characteristics of experiments in which children were able to demonstrate competence on Piagetian-type tasks. Information-processing theorists believe the focus should move from universal stages of development to an assessment of a given task's demands on the processing of information.

Robert Case has tried to develop a general theory of intellectual development rooted in Piagetian theory. He tried to integrate cognitive, linguistic and social development and still allow for and explain development specific to different domains. This theory looks at children's thinking in successive stages. Case's account is more mechanistic than the biological theory of Piaget. Like Piaget, he suggested the child develops schemes which are coordinated and form four major structured stages. Case saw executive schemes developing. These can coordinate the many schemes needed to perform a task. He also acknowledged an affective component with the child motivated to solve problems and be pleased with success and conversely unhappy with failure. He saw even infants having some control over these cognitive and affective aspects with the nature of such control changing with age. The Piagetian influence can be seen in Case's theory as outlined in table 21.15. Within each stage there are sequences, with a number of simple schemes being put together.

Case suggested four regulatory processes:
■ problem solving
■ exploration
■ imitation
■ mutual regulation.

Table 21.15	
Stage	Characteristics
Sensory operations	Child using sensory representations and motor responses. Meadows (1993) gave an example of the sensory representation of a frightening face and the child running away or hiding his or her face.
Representational operations	Durable internal concrete images which can be reproduced, e.g. the child remembers the 'scary' face and uses this to draw a monster.
Logical operations	More abstract and more open to transformation abstractly on a simple level.
Formal operations	Complex representation and complex transformations of abstract information.

An outline of Case's theory (taken from Meadows (1993))

In some ways Case can be seen to embrace some of the concepts of Vygotsky and Bruner. The first two processes have a Piagetian 'flavour'. Problem solving and exploration seem to link in with the Piagetian functional invariants of assimilation, accommodation and equilibration. The last two processes of imitation and mutual regulation can be seen to adopt more of the concepts supported by Vygotsky and Bruner, an explicit recognition of social facilitation in development. In this way the child inherits the tools used by adults, at first by mutual regulation and then, in more internalised ways, uses them as independent strategies and skills.

Case suggested that the child is constrained by a limited *short-term storage space (STSS)* with little available for information processing. There are great similarities here with the concept of a 'working memory' which is active but limited in size. He believed the capacity of STSS increases with age, but only slowly so it restricts the overall rate of cognitive development. With practice this STSS begins to operate more efficiently and automatically thus releasing more attentional resources.

This implies that the major difference between adults and children is the amount of practice they have had on basic cognitive operations. Adults will have had more practice on general basic operations but the child may have had more practice in some domains, for example using computers in school.

Meadows (1993) suggested that developmental changes in absolute amount of processing space (if they exist) are less important than changes in how cognitive operations are used. She suggested that more important are the changes in what information is stored, how it is accessed and the development of a range of processing skills which can gather and act on information. Case suggested that these changes, which could be domain specific, are combined so that cognitive development is homogeneous across domains. This is due to maturational limits imposed by the development of the child's nervous system where nerve cells are not fully developed in early childhood. Development allows for complex and more hierarchically integrated cognition.

Sternberg's model (1984, 1985) is 'an information-processing analysis of intelligence with developmental implications' (Meadows, 1993, p. 229). He suggested a main developmental mechanism of strategy construction based on:

■ the use of knowledge acquisition components
■ performance components such as the processes of encoding, drawing inferences and mapping relations between similar components
■ metacomponents which select and monitor performance seen by Sternberg (1984) as the foundations for the development of intelligence.

Meadows (1993) noted great overlap in the various theories with a frequent emphasis on self-monitoring and processes for automatisation and the detection of consistencies and inconsistencies. But Case and Sternberg take different positions on the role of the knowledge base with Case seeing this as playing only a small part in processing. Similarly, there are disagreements on how far development is influenced by the outside world, particularly by interaction with other people. Case included the role of others in his theory with imitation and mutual regulation aiding cognitive development. All models centre on a similar range of tasks, problems derived from cognitive psychology. Case did try to extend these to include social and affective areas.

Activity 12

Choose the correct sentence associated with each of these three theorists:

- Case
- Siegler
- Sternberg.

a   Encoding is central to cognitive development and children often fall back on lower levels when problem solving.

b   The child has limited short-term storage space (STSS) with little available for information-processing and this increases with age.

c   A developmental analysis on intelligence is based on knowledge acquisition components, performance components and metacomponents which select and monitor performance.

(Suggested answers on page 800.)

Flavell (1984) found the models to be interesting but not convincing: 'there is more variety in *what* gets developed, and also more variety in *how* these varied developments get accomplished' (p. 206). Different learners may have different sorts of cognitive processes available to them depending on the developmentally early ways they have processed information. He compared this to current technological advances, which make things possible that were impossible or difficult before. Changes in information-processing mechanisms may be one of the sources of differences between novices and experts. Meadows (1993) drew attention here to the role of the knowledge base which she considered to be far more important than Flavell.

Another criticism of the information-processing models is that they ignore the role of biological evidence. Information-processing models are mechanistic. Even if the machine is active, constructive and self-modifying, it does not allow for tasks which humans perform without conscious or strategic effort such as recognising an object in the environment. Perhaps the newer models of information processing which are based on the ways nerve cells (neurones) work may provide a better account of such cognition. These are referred to in different ways, for example 'neural networks', 'connectionism' and 'parallel distributed processing'. What is proposed varies from model to model but they all see information processing involving a large number of units working in parallel. Like neurones, they stimulate and inhibit each other through networks of connections. Information is not stored in any one place but rather exists as a pattern between connections. So the information about Piaget would not be stored in one place but only come together when particular sets of units/neurounes are active in a certain pattern.

Units which are active together have their excitatory connections strengthened so that over a time a network that repeatedly receives the same input will develop a strong set of connections. In this way, even if only some of the connections are stimulated the whole configuration will come into play. There is no information store, no knowledge of rules and no metacognition independent of these active units. This seems compatible with what we know about the nervous system, where neurones excite and inhibit each other in complex networks, carrying out the processing so fast that parallel processing must be involved. Connectionist networks can learn from experience by changing the weights of the connections and thus the strength of the excitatory or inhibitory links between units. Research into these newer models may lead to understanding a more specific account of assimilation and accommodation than outlined by Piaget. They may also clarify whether development is 'stage-like', or whether there is continuity.

The integration of more recent theories of cognitive development into classroom practice

Education in a school system has developed over the last two centuries and consequently promoted a great deal of research into the methods used. Originally, only the children of a small elite were offered private tuition to enable them to gain a degree in Higher Education as seen appropriate for their status. The education of children of the 'masses' enabled them to recite from their religious texts and calculate simple sums. It was not the general education that we see today. The educators of today have two main problems:

- knowledge is accumulating rapidly
- the mode of representing knowledge has undergone fundamental changes.

Most western societies today expect all their children to attain the level reserved for the small elite of yesterday. However, it is now achieved in large classes where child-initiated encounters with the teacher are difficult to maintain. The teacher needs to interact with the child to understand the individual level of competence. Wood (1988) suggested that this classroom setting can be counterproductive in highlighting the child's *lack* of knowledge in front of his or her peers.

Instruction has focused on the mastery of two basic symbol systems:

- written language
- mathematics.

These form the basis of the National Curriculum operating in schools in the UK in the late 1990s.

Piaget's view of the active child constructing his or her own cognitive world changed the overall pattern of delivery of such skills, especially in mathematics (see pages 759–61). The later theorists (Vygotsky, Bruner and the information-

processing group) have also influenced classroom practice. Some of these will be discussed below in relation to reading and mathematics.

The teaching of reading

Experts now agree that reading requires the coordination of information on the actual letters and words in text and the 'higher order' understanding of the meaning of the topics being referred to.

Earlier in the twentieth century the focus was on the 'bottom-up' processing of the words, and the sounds of the letters that compose the words, known as the phonetic approach. In this way the child would be given access to the meaning of the words. More recently, researchers focused more on the 'top-down' processing of reading comprehension believing that reading cannot progress without this. The reading in figure 21.16 demonstrates the importance of comprehension in the reading task.

The evidence suggests that teachers should use a strategy which integrates the use of interesting literature with specialised training in decoding (Stahl and Miller, 1989). The mixture will vary from one child to another, often as Piaget suggested, dependent on innate ability and environmental experiences.

■ Reciprocal teaching

Reciprocal teaching (Palincsar and Brown, 1984) is one teaching method based on Vygotsky's Zone of Proximal Development (ZPD). This allows the children to participate in the act of reading for meaning before they have acquired the reading skills needed for independent reading. In reciprocal teaching, the teacher and a small group of students read a passage of text silently and then take turns to discuss its meaning. The leader, either the teacher or another student, begins by *asking a question* about the general meaning and then *summarises* the content in his or her own words. Members of the group, with the summary, re-read the passage and discuss the content to *clarify* its meaning. Finally, the leader asks for *predictions* on what will come next. The key elements are:

21.16 Top-down processing in reading

The kind of top-down information needed for meaningful reading can be seen in the following two passages. Although the words in each are of roughly equivalent difficulty (that is, the 'bottom' components are similar), note how much more difficult it is to understand the second passage:

PASSAGE 1
When Mary arrived at the restaurant, the woman at the door greeted her and checked for her name. A few minutes later, Mary was escorted to her chair and was shown the day's menu. The attendant was helpful but brusque, almost to the point of being rude. However, her meal was excellent, especially the main course. Later she paid the woman at the door and left.

PASSAGE 2
The procedure is really quite simple. First you arrange items into different groups. Of course, one pile may be sufficient depending on how much there is to do. If you have to go somewhere else due to lack of facilities that is the next step, otherwise you are pretty well set. It is important not to overdo things. That is, it is better to do too few things at once than too many. In the short run this may not seem important but complications can easily arise. A mistake can be expensive as well. . . . After the procedure is completed, one arranges the materials into different groups again.

Then they can be put into their appropriate places. Eventually they will be used once more and the whole cycle will then have to be repeated. (Bransford, 1979, p. 135)

The first passage is easy to comprehend because we realise right away that it is about a restaurant. We have well-worked-out scripts for restaurants that allow us to anticipate what will happen, thereby providing top-down constraints on our reading of the passage. The second passage is harder to comprehend because it fails to provide a top-down indication of what it is about. You can verify this difference by trying to remember, without looking back, what the second passage says. As soon as you are told that the passage is about washing clothes, however, the separate sentences fall into place as you read, and the passage is easily interpreted. If readers cannot imagine what a passage is about, even if they can decode all of the words, the interpretation that is crucial to true reading does not occur.

Source: Cole and Cole (1993).

- asking about content
- summarising
- clarifying
- predicting.

These elements all focus on the meaning of the text and allow the children to see and hear the teacher and other students modelling the behaviour needed for comprehension. A number of studies have found reciprocal teaching to be effective, not only in improving reading generally but also improving reading of social studies and science texts (Brown *et al.*, 1982).

Peer tutoring

The socio-cognitive conflict brought about by reciprocal teaching is also the basis of peer tutoring. Foot *et al.* (1990) also related to the Vygotskyian model in explaining how peer tutoring works. The tutor (child) is more knowledgeable than the tutee and the aim is for this expertise to be shared between the children. Because the 'expert' is only just ahead of the 'novice' the tutor can appreciate the difficulties and use **scaffolding** within the tutee's ZPD. This interaction is seen as necessary for cognitive growth. It is not simply the joint encounter that promotes such development but also communication and instruction from the 'expert' peer. Such joint intellectual activity becomes internalised.

Computer-based tutoring systems

Computer-based tutoring systems can provide a branching programme suited to the child's ability. They also provide opportunities for socially interactive learning whereby 'experts' in this area are a valuable resource in the classroom (Blaye *et al.*, 1991; Crooke, 1992).

Cooperative group work

The social process of negotiating with other students provides a 'scaffold' when needed. Doise and Mugny (1984) saw this as aiding the child to reconstruct his or her ideas when suitable motivated: 'peers can and, more important, will provide explanations in one another's proximal zones of development and will engage in the kind of cognitive conflict needed for disequilibration and cognitive growth' (Slavin, 1987, p. 1166).

Slavin noted the importance of motivation and intergroup competition in learning and also the structure of the group learning environment. This will encourage questioning, evaluating and constructive criticism.

Brown and Palincsar (1989) suggested this cooperative learning will be most helpful to the student with only a partial grasp of the topic who will be cognitively stimulated by the conflicting views from the more 'expert' student whose views he or she trusts.

Children spend a large part of their time outside the classroom so it is logical to extend the learning process, especially with very young children, to the home situation. Parents and family members can continue the process as shown by Hewison and Tizard (1980) where children reading to their parents for an extra ten minutes each day made better progress than those given extra instruction from another teacher.

The teaching of mathematics

The information-processing approach lends itself readily to the teaching of formal mathematics. This approach shifts the focus from a universal stage theory, as developed by the Piagetians, to assessment of given tasks in terms of their information-processing demands.

Gelman *et al.* (1986) outlined three kinds of knowledge which they saw as essential pre-requisites for more advanced forms of mathematics:

1 *Conceptual knowledge* – the knowledge needed to understand the underlying principles of the problem. This knowledge is seen to improve during middle childhood speeding up mathematical calculations. Bisanz and Lefèvre (1990) found that many 11-year-old children along with most adults indicated they had mastered such principles.

2 *Procedural knowledge* – includes the strategies essential to mastering mathematical operations such as adding and subtracting. Siegler and his colleagues (1984, 1991) have documented the development of procedural knowledge. They noted how children of about seven years of age, when asked to add numbers such as 2+8, may start with 2 and then use their fingers to add 8 more. A couple of years later, they would be more likely to reverse this to 8+2 which is easier, as they realise that order is not important in an addition task. Later still, this task became more automatic as the children became more knowledgeable, using direct recall and/or 'paper and pencil' techniques replacing fingers.

3 *Utilisation knowledge* – the knowledge of procedures to use to help solve a problem, increases with age and instruction. Carraher *et al.* (1985) studied mathematical problem solving in young children selling products on the streets in Brazil. They asked the children mathematical problems related to the goods they were selling. The children were correct about 98 per cent of the time. When they were asked to write down answers to similar written problems, this percentage dropped to 74 per cent and 37 per cent when the problems had no real-life relevance.

Just as there was disagreement about whether the emphasis should be on phonetic or semantic rules in teaching reading, so has there been discussion on the effective way to teach mathematics:

- drill and practice on small parts of the process
- understanding first and then move on to practice later.

Brownell's (1928) approach focused on the latter suggestion which builds on the three kinds of knowledge noted above (conceptual, procedural and utilisation). McConnell (1934, 1958) compared both approaches and found drill was efficient for acquiring rapid and automatic responses to the training material but when the children were tested on novel combinations the meaning approach led to better results.

Both approaches are seen as necessary for sound mathematical understanding. A variety of effective procedures have been worked out relating to specific content domains (Rasmussen *et al.*, 1964; Dienes, 1966; Resnick and Ford, 1981).

Information-processing theorists suggest that adolescents do not have *qualitatively* different ways of thinking and problem solving. They suggest that such differences are due to their increasing capacity to process information. Siegler (1983) noted adolescents used more efficient strategies for solving problems. They became better at holding information in memory whilst relating one component of a task to another. Such evidence suggests that adolescents acquire powerful rules which are then applied to particular problem-solving situations with increasing consistency.

Information-processing theorists thus believe that humans, like computers, have limited information-processing capacities. Young children can be seen to have difficulties caused by:

■ attention which is easily distracted
■ incomplete and unsystematic search strategies
■ difficulty in focusing on the most relevant features of the task.

Chi and Klahr (1976) found five-year-old children could perceive no more than three objects presented on a screen briefly whereas adults could take in six or seven. Several studies have demonstrated that metacognition (see page 774) allows older children and adults to work through various steps in complex problems without losing track of what they are doing. They have accumulated more knowledge, can process information more rapidly and use more effective strategies for dealing with problems (Chi and Koeske, 1983; Siegler, 1991).

The implications of the information-processing approach in education were noted by Cardwell *et al.* (1996) (figure 21.17).

In the real world of today people must have basic reading, numeracy and writing skills if they are to function well in society. Unfortunately, many children leave school without acquiring them. Kozol (1985) found 25 per cent of adults in the US read so poorly that they cannot cope adequately with the demands of everyday life. Similar findings exist in the UK.

The research into reasons why some children may not succeed in the school system in the western world has been influenced by the variation in aptitude known as 'intelligence', which has been suggested as an explanation for such differences in school performance. The concept of intelligence is universally accepted. In most cultures there are terms that describe such individual differences as the way people solve problems and the type of problem they are good at solving (Nerlove *et al.*, 1974; Segall *et al.*, 1990). However, the precise meaning differs between cultures thus making it difficult (some would say impossible!) to measure precisely. We now conclude this unit by looking at the development of measured intelligence.

21.17 Implications of the information-processing approach in education

■ Know what information is needed and what has to be done with it to be successful.
■ Do not overload short-term memory.
■ Try to find out what rule the child is using if consistent errors are being made.

■ Encourage 'meta cognitive' knowledge about strategies and their usefulness (e.g. 'Why does summarising in your own words help?').
(Source: Cardwell *et al.*, 1996.)

The development of measured intelligence

Few concepts in psychology have received more devoted attention than *intelligence* and few have resisted clarification so thoroughly (Reber, 1985). Intelligence is another psychological term with many meanings and considerable problems of definition. In this section we look at it in more detail.

Activity 13

Write down what you understand by 'intelligence'.

Whilst it is common to consider intelligence as something quite separate from personality, Cattell thought differently, and linked them by describing intelligence as a factor of personality. Did you consider it as part of personality, like Cattell? It is a factor, however we choose to describe it, that is part of a person's make-up. Whether it is used to describe the ability to remember things, work out problems, get along well in life or even to answer questions in intelligence tests, it describes some form of behaviour.

A wide range of definitions of intelligence have been offered and some of these are outlined in table 21.18.

In their simplest form, definitions regard intelligence as the ability to adapt to environmental requirements, or the capacity for learning or abstract thinking. Most children in western cultures today can expect to complete attainment and/or intelligence tests to decide the type of education they receive and the work they will undertake as adults. To enable you to understand the nature of intelligence testing we must look at the theoretical background on intelligence as a factor in children's development.

Early theories of intelligence

Early theories focused on intelligence as an inherited attribute which could not be altered. Spearman (1904), Thurstone (1938) and Burt (1955) saw intelligence as a *general* characteristic which can be seen as a component in most tasks, so someone who scores high on one task will also score highly on another. Some theorists, such as Hebb (1949) and Cattell (1963), debated the role of environmental factors.

Psychologist	Definition
Binet	To judge well, to comprehend well, to reason well.
Spearman	General intelligence which involves mainly the education of relations and correlates.
Terman	The capacity to form concepts and to group their significance.
Vernon	All-round thinking capacity or mental efficiency.
Burt	Innate, general, cognitive ability.
Heim	Intelligent activity consists in grasping the essentials in a situation and responding appropriately to them.
Wechsler	The aggregate or global capacity of the individual to act purposefully, to think rationally and to deal effectively with the environment.
Piaget	Adaptation to the physical and social environment.

Table 21.18

The variety of ways in which early psychologists defined 'intelligence' (after Pyle, 1979)

■ Intelligence 'A', 'B' and 'C'

Hebb (1949) used the term intelligence 'A' to refer to our genetically determined intellectual potential. This has been linked to brain structure, indicating what can be achieved if all possible neural pathways are fully utilised. Intelligence 'B' describes actual behaviour and results from an interaction between intelligence 'A' and the environment – therefore it cannot be greater than 'A'. We can measure intelligence 'B' if we devise the right sort of test for observational procedure, but 'A' could only be measured through complex neurological techniques (as yet unavailable) so it is impossible to determine.

Intelligence tests only measure a sample of behaviour, so they cannot measure the whole of intelligence 'B'. This is where intelligence 'C' comes in. Vernon (1955) introduced the term to explain the intelligence measured by intelligence tests.

Another approach has described intelligence as being one of three possibilities (Heim, 1970):

1 how well someone can perform on an intelligence test (which simply tells us how good he or she is at answering intelligence test questions)
2 how individuals organise their life – how well they cope with particular situations and with other people (probably as assessed by an observer)
3 an inherited ability to be able to learn in a particular situation.

Pause to consider: are you more (or less) able to work things out now than you were, say, five years ago? Does this mean that you are more (less) intelligent than you were then? Do you deal with situations differently now than five years ago? How does this link with our discussion on change in personality? How are personality and intelligence similar, and how do they interact with each other?

■ Cattell's two-factor theory

Cattell (1963) proposed that the general factor of intelligence can be divided into two distinct intelligence factors with a degree of correlation between them. Crystallised intelligence accumulates throughout life and is the ability to learn skills and habits which can be used in familiar situations. These skills and habits would not, by definition, be much good in new and unique situations, unless there is some common ground with previously met conditions. Is this, too, an element of intelligence – the ability to recognise when an apparently new problem actually has many of the elements of a previously met one?

Cattell said that we would need fluid intelligence for a completely new situation to be handled correctly or for solving abstract problems. With high levels of it we can cope with new problems and situations, but with low levels we would be at a loss. It is possible that someone will not appreciate the fact that he or she is in a new situation and deal with it inappropriately. Seeing some similarities with previously met conditions the person reacts as if all the conditions are the same. From this it can be seen that crystallised and fluid intelligence normally have to overlap when recognising and solving new problems.

The early theories were based on the role of high-level cognitive processes identified by Binet and Simon (1916, pp. 42–3):

> 'To judge well, to comprehend well, to reason well, these are the essential activities of intelligence. A person may be a moron or an imbecile if he is lacking in judgement; but with good judgement he can never be either.'

These were factor theories in which the theorists tried to isolate the number of factors that make up intelligence. Theorists have not reached agreement on the number or nature of these factors, so perhaps we should see factor analysis as a tool offering guidelines about intellectual abilities which are seen to be part of intelligence (Eysenck, 1994). These theories are useful in giving insight into the *structure* of intelligence including the general factor identified by Spearman, other group or primary mental abilities identified by Thurstone (1938) and specific factors associated with one test or a small group of tests as proposed by Spearman.

One problem of these factor theories is that they *describe* the structure but do not try to *explain* the processes or mechanisms involved in intelligent behaviour. Eysenck (1994) noted another problem for factor theories in relation to Idiot Savants, mentally handicapped individuals who are highly accomplished in certain areas. The factor theorists predict that such individuals should score highly on tests related to the *general* factor to intelligence. This is not the case, as Idiot Savants will show a large discrepancy between their special skills and their apparent low general intelligence level.

Howe (1989) suggested that all different skills are to a large extent autonomous or separate, although in relation to Idiot Savants he pointed out that anyone who spent several hours a day concentrating on one area of interest could retain a lot of information about that topic. Eysenck (1994) suggested that research on Idiot Savants, although interesting, does not have serious implications for factor theories.

Contemporary theories of intelligence

More recent theorists have recognised that intelligence consists of more than the processes identified by the factor theorists. There is now a focus on the processes involved in thinking, problem solving and other mental activities and also the type of intelligence displayed when solving problems in everyday life. Two recent theories which try to include for such activities are those of Gardner (1983) and Sternberg (1985, 1986).

■ Multiple intelligences

Howard Gardner (1983) attacked the idea of intelligence as a single component and replaced this with a theory of several intelligences, multiple intelligences. He argued that several independent intelligences exist and can be identified each using separate parts of the brain. He has attacked the genetic views of theorists such as Herrnstein and Murray (1994) who saw intelligence as relatively fixed at birth and not subject to later change. The relative contribution of nature and nurture in relationship to intelligence is discussed on pages 792–6.

Gardner soon moved away from seeing intelligence in a unitary way to the search for the different intelligences. He studied diverse samples, from those who were brain-damaged to those who were seen to be operating at the highest 'genius' level, along with traditional developmental evidence of how skills were developing at different ages. He also used evolutionary evidence to try and explain how a certain skill may have evolved. From his studies he identified seven intelligences: linguistic, musical, spatial, logical-mathematical, bodily-kinaesthetic, personal and social understanding (as can be seen in table 21.19). He did not see this as a final list and was open to more being identified.

Table 21.19

Kind of intelligence	Characteristics
Linguistic	Special sensitivity to language, which allows one to choose precisely the right word or turn of phrase and to grasp new meanings easily
Musical	Sensitivity to pitch and tone, which allows one to detect and produce musical structure
Logical-mathematical	Ability to engage in abstract reasoning and manipulate symbols
Spatial	Ability to perceive relations among objects, to transform mentally what one sees, and to recreate visual images from memory
Bodily-kinaesthetic	Ability to represent ideas in movement; characteristic of great dancers and mimes
Personal	Ability to gain access to one's own feelings and to understand the motivations of others
Social	Ability to understand the motives, feelings, and behaviours of other people.

Howard Gardner's idea of multiple intelligences
Source: from Cole and Cole (1993).

He noted they all develop at different times and at different rates with language developing quickly at an early age and personal and social intelligence, such as understanding others and oneself, developing later. People who do well in any area use combinations of these different intelligences.

Many schools in the US have tried to implement Gardner's ideas in order to develop all aspects of children's performance. He sees good observation and assessment as the key tool for teachers. Early work in schools using such techniques have found considerable variation in the different intelligences at the age of three or four. Schools have found his techniques useful, especially for those children lacking interest and motivation. Gardner's techniques involve the students thinking about how to approach their work and demonstrate understanding of what they have learned. Such schools put the student's interests and strengths central in the equation.

Gardner recognised the danger of labelling the child in this approach ('he's musical', 'she's linguistic'), and suggested that tutors be aware of this danger and recognise and be prepared for the fact that children's interests develop with age.

Hayes (1994) noted several criticisms of Gardner's theory including the lack of inclusion of socio-cultural context apart from in social

Activity 14

Ask a few of your friends and family to describe someone they think of as being of high intelligence, if possible from a range of different backgrounds. Sort their answers into the categories used by Gardner for multiple intelligences. Which factors may have influenced their understanding of intelligence?

(Suggested answers on page 800.)

understanding, which is seen as a separate intelligence. Gardner did not consider the way that social cognition can affect the other skills. Eysenck (1994) also questioned whether all the intelligences identified are central and should be included in a theory of intelligence, in other words some are seen as more important in everyday life.

Gardner also can be criticised for not having identified the processes involved in each type and as several people can score highly on all types, this tends to suggest that they are not completely independent of each another. However, it is to Gardner's credit that he has tried to explain, genius skills and also those of the Idiot Savant, as well as how people differ from the norm.

Sternberg's triarchic theory

According to the information-processing approach we need to understand the cognitive strategies used by children who score high or low on this dimension. One theory which looks at the role of information processing in intelligence is Sternberg's triarchic theory (1985, 1986) figure 21.19. He distinguished academic and practical intelligence and a third type he calls 'wisdom'. The three types are as follows:

- *Componential* – the cognitive mechanisms which underlie the ability to think critically and analytically, so people high on this usually make excellent students.
- *Contextual* – intelligence within the socio-cultural setting. Some would call this 'streetwise' intelligence, so people high on this aspect are competent at adapting to and shaping the environment in everyday encounters. This aspect distinguishes Sternberg's theory from other theories of intelligence by dealing with cultural diversity and acknowledging this in aspects of intelligence.
- *Experiential* – includes the influences on intelligence of past experiences and the way we build up skills and knowledge from these. This includes the ability to deal with situational demands and also the development of automatic information-processing skills. Sternberg's distinction between the ability to

adapt to novelty and automatic processing can be seen to resemble the fluid and crystallised intelligence suggested by Cattell (1963) described on page 784.

Sternberg also extended his theory to include personality (1988). He included intellectual styles or different ways in which people use the original three types in problem solving during everyday life, for example several people with 'streetwise' intelligence also appear to share similar personality characteristics such as confidence and sociability. Eysenck (1994) felt that this produces a confusing mixture of intelligence and personality not helping to identify the various sub-groups of intelligence.

Sternberg's theory is the most comprehensive theory of intelligence to date, including links between areas of cognitive psychology and intelligence and also allowing for interaction of internal and external factors like thinking and problem solving in the real world. As noted above, both Sternberg and Cattell (1963) also considered the relationship of experience and practice on intelligent performance. Sternberg's theory allows for cultural diversity but also recognises the similarities we all share as human beings.

None of the theories noted above include details of the role of biological factors in intelligence. Hebb (1949), as discussed on page 784, included the genetic component in

21.20 Sternberg's triarchic theory of intelligence (from Baron, 1996)

Componential intelligence
- Ability to think abstractly and process information
- Tasks that can be used to measure the elements of componential intelligence are analogies, vocabulary, and syllogisms

Experiential intelligence
- Ability to formulate new ideas and combine unrelated facts
- Examples include scientific creativity and diagnosing a problem with an automobile engine

Contextual intelligence
- Ability to adapt to a changing environment and to shape one's world to optimise opportunities
- Contextual intelligence deals with an individual's ability to prepare for problem solving in specific situations; for example, a Lapp herder in northern Scandinavia stuffs his boots with dried grasses for warmth

intelligence 'A' but did not expand on this. Recent research in neuropsychology has looked at the role of biological factors in intelligence.

■ Recent research on the role of biological factors in intelligence

Matarazzo (1992) suggested that intelligence is closely linked to the physiological processes in the brain, especially how efficient these are. This is confirmed by Reed and Jenson (1993) who found the speed of male participants responding to visual stimuli correlated to scores on an intelligence test (Raven's Matrices). The higher the measure of neural speed, the higher the score on the intelligence test.

Andreason *et al.* (1993) found a link between certain parts of the brain and scores on the Wechsler Adult Intelligence Scale (WAIS). Biological differences between male and female brains have been found by Berenbaum and Hines (1992) and Law *et al.* (1993). There is some evidence that the corpus collosum, which is the neuronal band joining the two hemispheres of the brain, may differ between the two sexes. This could have a subtle effect on cognitive abilities such as higher levels of verbal fluency in females.

Some of the differences noted in table 21.21 could be due to biological factors which tend to predispose females and males towards different patterns of cognitive functioning in some situations.

Additional evidence comes from studies of people who have experienced brain damage to one side of the brain. Males and females react differently to such damage. This research indicates that damage to the left cerebral hemisphere produces deficits in verbal intelligence for both sexes but reductions in other aspects such as non-verbal aspects is larger for females. For most people the left hemisphere plays a more important role in verbal abilities and the right hemisphere a more dominant role in non-verbal abilities. Damage to the right hemisphere produces larger deficits in verbal intelligence among females suggesting that females show higher levels of processing in both hemispheres, known as bilateral processing (Turkheimer and Farace, 1992). Females appear to process more information than males in both hemispheres of the brain (figure 21.22).

So biological factors can be seen to be important in determining intelligence, but it is important to bear in mind that biological predisposition is one of many factors that can be influenced by social and environmental variables and this is discussed on pages 790–2.

Intelligence was originally seen as a property which could be measured in the same way as height or weight. It was seen possible to measure this mental capacity by administering a series of tests.

Intelligence testing

Since it is unclear what we mean by intelligence there are inevitable problems in devising tests to

Table 21.21	
Cognitive ability	Gender differences
Vocabulary	No appreciable difference
Reading	Girls score higher than boys, but this difference disappears in adolescence
Spelling	Girls score higher than boys
General information	Males score higher at all ages
Mathematics	Girls outperform boys in the first two years of high school; this difference disappears by the time they are seniors
Spatial visualisation	Boys score slightly higher than girls, and this difference persists through adolescence
Perceptual speed	Females score higher than males at all ages
Memory	No difference between males and females

Gender differences in cognitive abilities

Source: Baron (1996).

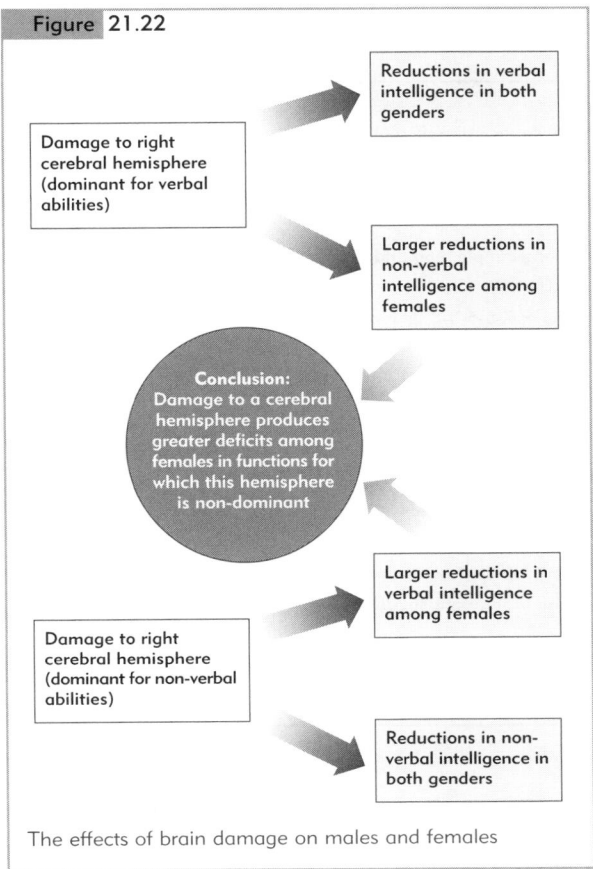

Figure 21.22

Damage to right cerebral hemisphere (dominant for verbal abilities)

Reductions in verbal intelligence in both genders

Larger reductions in non-verbal intelligence among females

Conclusion: Damage to a cerebral hemisphere produces greater deficits among females in functions for which this hemisphere is non-dominant

Larger reductions in verbal intelligence among females

Damage to right cerebral hemisphere (dominant for non-verbal abilities)

Reductions in non-verbal intelligence in both genders

The effects of brain damage on males and females

measure it! Tests of achievement attempt to measure the level of mastery that has been gained in a particular subject and tests of aptitude are used to predict future performance. Intelligence tests are essentially aptitude tests which try to predict performance over a range of abilities.

■ Tests of general intelligence

In 1904, Binet and Simon were asked by the French government to devise a test which would discriminate between children who would benefit from education and those who would not. Their first step was to decide on tasks which people of particular ages might be expected to accomplish. In this way a range of activities and scholastic problems was built up. If a person has the mental capacity of a ten year-old, then that person has a mental age of ten, regardless of chronological age (i.e. their actual age in years). The Simon–Binet

test was soon adapted for use in the US where it became known as the Stanford–Binet test (a term still used even though the test has been revised several times). Binet's test was successful in identifying children in need of special help and so the test was extended to measure variations in the intelligence among children of the normal range of intelligence.

This concept is the basis of the tests more often used now. For example, Wechsler proposed a range of mental abilities that can be individually measured, and developed tests over a long period, culminating in the Wechsler Adult Intelligence Scale, or WAIS, first published in 1939 and subsequently revised. Modifications to this provide the Wechsler Intelligence Scale for Children, or WISC (1948, 1974, 1991). The WAIS is the most widely used test of general intelligence (the current version is a revision known as the WAIS–R1974). Table 21.23 shows tests items included in the WAIS.

The Wechsler Scales are seen as an improvement on the Stanford–Binet test as they include non-verbal or *performance* items in addition to the verbal items.

The idea of an intelligence quotient (IQ) which refers to a measurement of intelligence was also introduced (Stern, 1912). The calculation used is:

$$IQ = \frac{\text{mental age}}{\text{chronological age}} \times 100$$

If an individual's mental age and chronological age are equal then an IQ of 100 is obtained, for example $8/8 \times 100 = 100$. IQs over 100 indicate that intellectual age is higher than average ($9/8 \times 100 = 112.5$) and conversely IQs below 100 indicate that the individual is scoring less than average ($7/8 \times 100 = 87.5$). However, at some point mental growth levels off and chronological growth continues so IQ scores can be seen to reflect the individual's performance on the test relative to people of the same age.

Producing an intelligence test is a time-consuming process. Suitable questions need to be selected and the test standardised. The standardisation process involves testing large numbers of people and establishing norms, i.e.

Table 21.23

Test	Description
Verbal scale	
Information	Questions tap a general range, for example 'How many nickels make a dime?'
Comprehension	Tests practical information and ability to evaluate past experience; for example 'What is the advantage of keeping money in a bank?'
Arithmetic	Verbal problems testing arithmetic reasoning
Similarities	Asks in what way certain objects or concepts (for example, egg and seed) are similar; measures abstract thinking
Digit span	A series of digits presented auditorily (for example, 7-5-6-3-8) is repeated in a forward or backward direction; tests attention and rote memory
Vocabulary	Tests word knowledge
Performance scale	
Digit symbol	A timed coding task in which numbers must be associated with marks of various shapes; tests speed of learning and writing
Picture completion	The missing part of an incompletely drawn picture must be discovered and named; tests visual alertness and visual memory
Block design	Pictured designs must be copied with blocks; tests ability to perceive and analyse patterns
Picture arrangement	A series of comic-strip pictures must be arranged in the right sequence to tell a story; tests understanding of social situations
Object assembly	Puzzle pieces must be assembled to form a complete object; tests ability to deal with part-whole relationships

Test items included in the Wechsler Adult Intelligence Scale
Source: Atkinson et al. (1996).

finding what most people of a given age can achieve (a similar process to that involved in standardising type or trait personality tests).

It is assumed that intelligence is normally distributed within the population. There will be a small number of people with a low IQ, many having values around the average score of 100 and a few with high scores.

The Stanford–Binet test, Wechsler Scales, and more recently the British Ability Scales (BAS, Elliot *et al.*, 1979) are *individual* tests designed to be used with one person at a time. Tests were also developed for group use and became very popular in the 1940s and 1950s in schools. These tests soon became subject to criticism, especially in relations to cultural bias. Several of the questions were seen to favour children living in more middle-class populations who were more familiar with the questions asked, for example 'Was the Emperor Concerto written by Beethoven, Mozart, Bach, Brahms, or Mahler?' (answer is Beethoven). This

socio-cultural perspective focuses on several important issues including:

- Is it possible to design a test of intelligence that applies to all people across cultures?
- If there are many kinds of intelligence, should we use intelligence tests that measure only one type of intelligence, usually that valued by the dominant culture?

We now look more carefully at these issues.

Factors influencing intelligence test performance

There are many IQ tests using different styles of questioning. Some are restricted to specific organisations such as education authorities, and most are restricted to registered, trained users.

The norms established for IQ tests must be based on a sample representing the population being tested. If you test another population – Asian or West Indian, for example, when the norms are

European, or secretaries when the norms are for doctors – the results will be invalidated because the test is not culture fair.

In 1960, when the Stanford–Binet IQ test was revised, many migrant workers and unemployed were excluded from the group the test was standardised on. However, it was used to test both black and white children, thus giving an unfair comparison between cultures (Ryan, 1972) as it looked at how black children performed on tests of white people's intelligence. A further revision was therefore made in 1973 which attempted to address this problem.

Despite revisions, problems still remain with IQ tests. For example, a difference in average IQ has been reported by Ogbu (1986) between two groups of equally bright African-American students. One group did well at their studies and went on to obtain high-status jobs. The other group regarded doing well and obtaining a high-status job as 'acting white', i.e. betraying their racial identity. This group was unsuccessful in their studies. Cultural expectations may also be responsible for a similar difference in IQ scores between the low caste and high caste populations in India, Japan and New Zealand (Ogbu, 1986).

Some tests are designed to be culture fair. These are usually non-verbal, for example Raven's Progressive Matrices – a test based on spatial abilities. However, given the key role of language to human thinking, this kind of test may be criticised. Also, culture fair tests must be perceived to be desirable by those undertaking them. Anastasi (1988) and Lopez (1995) note several cultural values related to test performance including familiarity with the testing situation, rapport with the tester and experience of solving problems alone rather than with others.

Fairness of tests is not only an issue when applying them to different cultural groups, but also when it comes to testing different social classes. Intelligence test questions should accommodate this sort of problem. Allowances should also be made for people who are brought up in one environment and then asked to cope with questions from another way of life.

In the film *Crocodile Dundee*, Dundee, who hails from the Australian outback, finds dealing with pedestrian crossings difficult when he comes across them for the first time. Is he less intelligent than the New Yorkers he meets? Are New Yorkers who get attacked by crocodiles in Australia less intelligent than outbackers?

We can easily give people a low IQ falsely if they cannot answer questions beyond their realm of experience. Another problem occurs when someone can deal with verbal material well but not other kinds of material. Is this person less intelligent?

This is where validity and reliability come in. Tests must measure what they set out to measure, although Kline (1982) regarded most well-known intelligence tests to be valid since there is much agreement relating to evidence of this issue. Tests are considered to be reliable if they produce consistent results, which are reproducible. (See Unit 28 for more on reliability.)

Intelligence tests do put some children at a disadvantage but they can be good predictors of classroom performance by measuring the knowledge and skills useful at school.

How can educationalists accept cultural differences in intelligence and at the same time help those from minority cultures master the skills they need to succeed in school and society? Both of these aspects are important (Lopez, 1995).

Anne Anastasi (1988), a test specialist, found tests are still useful and can help identify those students who need help. However, many socio-cultural researchers suggest we abandon the 'deficit model' of intelligence testing and recognise that a cultural group can be *different* without being *deficient*. Many people, usually of the dominant culture, see intelligence and success at school as an innate factor rather than environmentally determined.

Helms (1992) noted that intelligence tests are often Eurocentric in that they accept European standards as the norm. Answers are often seen as right or wrong valuing only logical thinking. Many children from other cultures may accept this to some degree or accept other values, which may affect their test performance. These subtle cultural factors may affect the way the child approaches that test and thus influence test scores. Heath (1989) found mothers of black American children asked them questions requiring more than one answer which helped develop their verbal skills but did not help them succeed in intelligence tests.

Do IQ test scores really mean anything? The answer to this question has to be 'yes'. The main point concerns what they mean. We have already seen that different things can be called intelligence and that different tests measure different aspects of it. Ideally, an IQ score should be accompanied by additional information, for example that it applies to a verbal, spatial or divergent ability. Some tests are timed and some are not – can they possibly be measuring the same thing? This brings us back to the somewhat cynical question, 'Is IQ simply a measure of how well IQ test questions can be answered'?

Intelligence: innate or learned?

The debate as to whether intelligence is innate or learned has aroused fierce passions. It has often become politicised, and is notable for the dogmatic nature of the opinions expressed.

The quest to discover the inherited level of intelligence and the amount that can be attributed to the environment or upbringing continues. Many studies have compared the intelligence of family members using correlation coefficients. These are statistical techniques measuring the degree of relationship between sets of variables, in these cases intelligence test scores. A correlation coefficient always has a value between +1 and −1 with a value of +1 indicating a positive relationship in which the highest values from one set of data are paired with the highest values from another. A value of 0 can indicate no relationship.

Although the debate gets fresh life from time to time, many psychologists think that the nature–nurture argument is a sterile one, since it is virtually impossible to apportion abilities to either element.

In a number of publications, Hans Eysenck has suggested that a definite portion of intelligence can be attributed to inherited qualities with the rest

being formed by the nurturing process (for example Eysenck, 1971). Even here there is considerable argument.

Perhaps, since we cannot alter the hereditary element, we should work with what we have and make the most of it, encouraging people to act to the highest level of their abilities.

◼ Twin studies and kinship studies

Evidence for the nature side of the debate comes particularly from twin studies. Monozygotic (MZ or identical) twins result from a single ovum being fertilised by a single sperm and they are genetically identical. Any differences in intelligence between them must therefore be due to non-genetic factors in their pre-natal, natal and/or post-natal environments. Dizygotic (DZ or fraternal) *twins* result from the fertilisation of two separate ova, and are no more alike genetically than any other sibling pair.

On rare occasions, for reasons like maternal death or illness, MZ twins are reared apart. These particularly interest researchers because they provide the conditions for a natural experiment in which heredity is a controlled variable. Such research cannot, for both practical and ethical reasons, be undertaken in any other way with human participants.

We might expect a correlation coefficient of +1 between MZ twin pairs if intelligence is inherited, or a coefficient of 0 if it is a function of the environment. We could also propose that any reductions in a correlation value below +1 can be attributed to pre- and post-natal environments or imperfections in the methods used.

Table 21.23 shows four early twin studies which have reported significant positive correlations as evidence for the heritability of IQ.

Burt's research has been substantially discredited and so cannot be considered in scientific terms (Kamin, 1974). This leaves us with just 68 cases of MZ twins reared apart (MZAs) from three studies.

Shields's correlations for MZAs (+0.77) and MZ twins reared together (+0.76) were higher than those for DZ twins (+0.51). He suggested that this is evidence for separation having no effect on the IQs of genetically identical individuals. Kamin

Table 21.24

Study	Year	Country	Correlation obtained for MZ twins reared apart
Newman *et al.*	1937	US	+0.67 (19 pairs)
Shields	1962	England	+0.77 (37 pairs)
Juel-Neilsen	1965	Denmark	+0.62 (12 pairs)
Burt	1966	England	+0.86 (53 pairs)

Correlation values obtained from early twin studies

(1974), however criticised this conclusion on several grounds (see figure 21.25).

Some of these points warrant further comment. Shields defined separation as being 'at least five years during childhood'. Age of separation in his sample of MZAs ranged from birth to 9.5 years, and separation experiences varied widely. Many had regularly contacted each other, some had lived in the same community (even next door), and 75 per cent had attended the same school. One pair, separated at birth, were reunited at age five and tested at age 40! Twenty-seven out of 40 pairs were

21.25 Kamin's criticisms of Shields's (1974) study

- Shields pooled his results for DZ twins reared separately and together.
- The sample size for DZ twins was only seven.
- The two IQ tests used were standardised entirely on males, but the twin pairs were of both sexes.
- One IQ test was standardised on army personnel, yet two-thirds of the sample were female civilians.
- IQ tests were not standardised for age.
- There were differences between the researchers carrying out the IQ tests (experimenter bias).
- Participants were not assigned randomly to different environments.
- The twin pairs studied had a wide range of ages (8–59).
- The twin pairs studied had very different separation experiences.

brought up by relatives, and many of the others by acquaintances of equal socio-cultural level or by foster homes matched by adoption agencies.

Kamin criticised both the other studies in table 21.25 for confounding age and sex. The ages of participants in the study by Newman *et al.* ranged from 11 to 59 (12 female pairs, seven male), and in Juel-Neilsen's from 22 to 77 (nine female, three male pairs). Although this criticism seems reasonable, Kamin's recalculations have themselves met with criticism. Scarr-Salapatek (1976) described Kamin's statistical manipulations as 'breakdowns with minute and often arbitrary subgroups carried to extreme lengths' – in one case, a correlation is based on just three twin pairs. Also, Fulker (1975) reported that of the eight correlations used by Kamin as evidence for age–sex confounding, there is a highly significant relationship (+0.75) between the obtained correlations and their sample sizes!

The Newman *et al.* and Juel-Neilsen studies used volunteer participants responding to media requests. Kamin legitimately criticised both because the intelligence tests used were standardised on different populations to those from which the twins were drawn. The twins also differed in terms of amount of contact during separation, age at separation, and time between the ending of separation and testing. He also criticised Newman *et al.* for their definition of MZ ('so strikingly alike that even your friends and relatives have confused you'), their reliance on the verbal reporting of experiences and the 'carrot' of a free visit to Chicago to participate.

Bouchard and McGue (1981) gathered data from several kinship studies. Kamin argued that the higher correlations for MZs compared to DZs result from their more similar environments (for example, because of their similar appearances there is increased likelihood of being treated similarly). However, it is difficult to accept that MZs have much more similar environments than DZs, without making a case for DZs having much more similar environments than siblings.

More recently Bouchard and colleagues (1987, 1990), looking at separated twins, some of whom had been separated very early in life, found great similarity in intelligence, personality and mannerisms in identical twins when they were located later in life. Many had lived in different environmental conditions. Their IQs correlated as closely as twins reared together.

Certain questions remain substantially unanswered if an environmental hypothesis is to explain IQ. In particular, why are DZ correlations nearer to those for siblings than to those for MZs, and why should the correlations for DZ twins reared together and siblings be more alike than MZAs are with either? Kamin has made a major contribution in drawing attention to data weaknesses, but he has not succeeded in establishing a purely environmental basis for intelligence either. As Dobzhansky (1973) pointed out, 'MZ twins are treated more alike because they are!' Lytton et al. (1977) suggested that this could result from genetic similarity affecting the environment rather than the other way round. Observations like this suggest we should place less confidence in twins as an outstanding source for demonstrating the heritability of intelligence.

Activity 15

Are the following statements True (T) or False (F)?

a A correlation coefficient has a value between +2 and −2.
b MZ twins are seen to be genetically identical.
c Shields's correlation for MZ twins reared together was lower than that for DZ twins.
d Bouchard et al. (1987, 1990) found great differences in intelligence and personality in separated identical twins when they were located later in life.

Brain efficiency

Another line of research linked to the role of heredity in intelligence is looking at the efficiency of neural functioning which is found related to scores on intelligence tests (Reed and Jensen, 1993; Haier et al., 1996). Intelligent people have efficient brains; they can complete mental tasks with less physical effort. However, as Baron (1996) pointed out, this research is still speculative; additional experimental evidence is needed before such a positive correlation can be seen to be causal.

Adoption studies

There is considerable disagreement over the role of environment in intelligence. Extensive use has been made of adoption studies, in which children's intelligence levels can be compared to both their biological and their adoptive mothers (although it must be remembered that adoptive parents are often selected carefully). For example, McGurk (1975) reported that the IQ of adopted children tends to move towards that of their adoptive parents. On average, this is significantly higher than the IQ of their biological parents. However, the view of the Assistant Director of the British Agengies for Adoption and Fostering, reported by Ballantyne (1989), states that 'Most research shows that children do reflect their adoptive parents' IQ to an extent, but it is much more closely related to the IQ of their biological parents'.

Generally it seems that the presence of adoptive parents of higher IQ level will raise a disadvantaged child's IQ.

There is also evidence that deprived environments may result in lowering of IQ scores (for example Scarr-Salapatek, 1971). Bayley (1970) has shown that the IQs of children from homes of high and low socio-economic status widen in the pre-school years, the environmental conditions thus accentuating any differences in intelligence present at birth.

Adoption studies such as those reported by Locurto (1990) have shown that average IQ levels of adopted children can be about 20 points higher than those of their biological parents and siblings.

Enrichment programmes

Human intelligence appears to be the product of a complex interaction of genetic factors and environmental conditions (Plomin, 1989; Weinberg, 1989). Several enrichment programmes have found children to benefit from extra help and also increase their IQ scores. Project Headstart, an American programme, provided educational and social skills training for young children from disadvantaged environments. Results have been mixed. Haskins (1989) found no long-lasting gains in IQ scores but the children who participated in the programme were less likely to fail in school or need remedial help in school. They were also found to have higher self-esteem than non-participants (McKey *et al.*, 1985). At the other end of the educational spectrum, there is growing concern about children who are intellectually gifted who might not be reaching their potential in school (Resnick, 1993). In some areas special schools for the gifted have been set up.

A range of other environmental factors has been found related to IQ scores, including nutrition, family background and the quality of the education (Bouchard and Segal, 1985). Brown and Pollitt (1996) supported the notion that malnutrition affects intellectual development by compromising many aspects of the child's development. Their research provides insight into how poor diet and economic adversity in childhood impede intellectual functioning later in life. In a longitudinal study carried out in Guatemala, children and young adults from a poor background who were given a highly nutritious supplement (Atole) from before the age of two years were found to perform at the same level on performance tests as those from a better environment (figure 21.26).

The strongest effect of Atole was observed for those in the worst poverty who preformed as well as the most privileged in the village. The nutrient also showed increased achievement in education over several years for those on Atole. Intelligence can be seen to be influenced by nature and nurture.

Overall, evidence favours an integrated effect of both genes and environment – neither alone can fully explain the origin of intelligence. The two are inextricably linked: 'the contribution of nature is a

21.26 Poverty and malnutrition: the Guatemalan Project (Brown and Pollitt, 1996)

In a project carried out by the Institute of Nutrition of Central America and Panama, children and young adults in Guatemala who had received nutritional supplements in infancy were studied to assess the influence of early diet and poverty on later intellectual development. Subjects were given a battery of cognitive tests. Individuals who regularly consumed a highly nutritious supplement called Atole before the age of two performed at about the same level on most tests, such as tests of vocabulary skills, regardless of economic status (graph a). But the performance of those given a less nutritious supplement called Fresco varied with poverty level. Evidently, good nutrition early in life can help counteract the destructive effects of poverty on intellectual development. Among individuals who had more than two years of formal education, those who consumed Atole scored significantly higher than those who received Fresco (graph b)—an indication that poor nutrition in infancy can subsequently undermine the benefits of schooling.

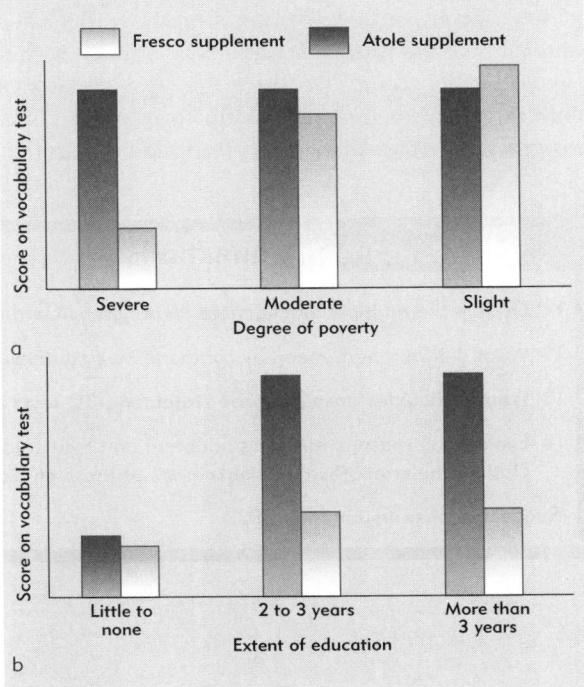

function of nurture and nurture a function of nature' (Medawar, 1977). Evidence for a genetic component in IQ remains, if a less influential one than that suggested by the MZA studies. However, the available literature is riddled with inadequate sample sizes, biased subjective judgements, selective adoption, failure to separate so-called 'separated' twins, unrepresentative samples, gratuitous and untested assumptions about environmental similarity, inappropriate statistical manipulation and even scientific fraud. 'The fact is . . . that there just are not enough good data, especially on rather rare, but interesting groups like identical twins or siblings reared in different families . . . we should be prepared to admit that any calculations based on them are liable to a good deal of uncertainty' (Vernon, 1979). On top of this 'nothing demonstrates more clearly how scientific methodology and conclusions are shaped to fit ideological ends than the sorry story of the heritability of IQ' (Rose, 1984).

Perhaps test-users should 'learn to use intelligence tests more intelligently – by keeping a person's background in mind, interpreting the results cautiously, and using results to benefit individual children' (Tavris and Wade, 1995, p. 409). Tavris and Wade noted that the underlying neutrality of the Binet test was lost in 'transit' across the Atlantic. Binet produced a test to select children who needed extra help to improve their progress, whereas Americans often see intelligence tests as revealing permanent inherited traits: 'the IQ controversy might never have occurred if the United States had imported Binet's cultural values along with his test of intelligence' (Tavris and Wade, 1995, p. 409).

Psychologists feel uncomfortable in finding behavioural genetics supporting the stronger role of heredity. Herrnstein and Murray (1994, 1996) and Rushton (1996) are seen as racist and sexist in highlighting a growing division between the cognitive elite and an underclass which could lead to an increasingly genetically determined society.

Perhaps it is worth pointing out that genetic factors establish *a range of possible responses* to a given environment, called malleability by Weinberg (1989). Such malleability can be seen operating positively in enrichment programmes, malnutrition research and studies investigating the quality of the child's home (Bradley and Caldwell, 1984). The challenge for any society would appear to be how to promote the potential of *all* citizens. Howe, in 1998, noted that IQ is more malleable than the pessimistic forecasts given by Herrnstein and Murray (1996). Howe stated that the empirical findings provide no support for the conclusions that intelligence is unalterable. 'We must never lose sight of the fact that what really matters in the world is not the level of our intelligence but what we achieve with this intelligence' (Sternberg, 1986, cited in Wade and Tavris, 1993, p. 410).

Self-assessment questions

11 Outline the multiple intelligences identified by Gardner (1983).

12 What did Sternberg mean by *componential, contextual* and *experiential?*

13 What difficulties arise from the statement, 'IQ tests measure intelligence'?

14 Explain the reasons for using adoption and twin studies to investigate the nature–nurture debate on intelligence. Outline the strengths and weaknesses of these studies.

(Suggested answers on page 802.)

Unit summary

- According to Piaget, children think and reason differently from adults, using *adaptation* to the environment.
- Maturation and experience help the child develop *schemes*, which grow and extend through *equilibration* and the complementary processes of *assimilation and accommodation*.
- Piaget thought children progress through four sequential *stages of development:* sensorimotor, pre-operational, concrete operational and formal operational. These stages are distinguished by the changing understanding of the child as shown by *object permanence, egocentrism, animism,* and the growth of *operational thinking*.
- Piaget's view of children as *active constructors* of their own cognitive world had educational implications, including the promotion of *discovery learning*, whereby the child's cognitive growth is facilitated, taking into account the child's readiness to learn.
- In general Piaget has been criticised as underestimating the abilities of sensorimotor and pre-operational children and over-estimating the capabilities of formal operational children, and for neglecting the role of language and social factors.
- Vygotsky was interested in how thought and language later interact and influence one another. He saw these as tools for planning and carrying out actions.
- Vygotsky suggested the child can learn from others who are more knowledgeable, and stressed the role of interpersonal processes and the role of society in providing a framework in which the child's understanding can develop. He believed that biological maturation is necessary but not sufficient to explain intellectual development. Cultural and social interaction is seen to be critical for development.
- The *Zone of Proximal Development (ZPD)* is central to Vygotsky's theory. This refers to the distance between what the child can achieve on his or her own by maturation and what the child will achieve with the help of others who are competent.
- Schaffer also noted the importance of *Joint Involvement Episodes (JIEs)* and Dunn, using an ethological approach, referred to social understanding of the pre-school child. This supports Vygotsky in highlighting the social learning of the context-specific behaviour – *social cognition*.
- Bruner was responsible for introducing Vygotsky's ideas to the western world. Like Vygotsly, Bruner valued the role of instruction and social interaction in cognitive growth. He moved away from the idea of stages of development, instead introducing different *modes of internal representation* of the world (*enactive, iconic, and symbolic*).
- Bruner used *scaffolding* to explain the support given to the child by others, especially linguistic support. Bruner suggested the curriculum should incorporate a number of different pathways, using all modes, so the principles of the subject area come to be understood by the learner at increasingly sophisticated levels – the *spiral curriculum*.
- The *information-processing approach* to cognitive development is based on the metaphor of the human mind as an information processor with limited capacity similar to a computer. This extends Piaget's theory by trying to provide a more detailed account of how the intellectual processes change with age. Information-processing theorists disagree on whether development is seen as a series of qualitatively different stages or as a continuous process of change.
- *Metacognition* is necessary for effective learning and more noticeable during and after adolescence, enabling more sophisticated strategies to develop.
- The *theory of mind* refers to when the child realises another's state of mind may or may not be the same as his or her own.
- Case's model of information processing is more mechanistic than Piaget's biological

Summary cont'd.

theory. It sees *executive schemes* developing. These can coordinate the many schemes needed to perform a task. Case adopted some of the concepts of Vygotsky and Bruner and recognised social facilitation in development by which the child inherits the tools used by adults.

■ Information-processing models ignore the role of biological evidence and are mechanistic so more recent models of information processing, such as *neural networks, connectionism* and *parallel-distributed processing*, provide a more plausible account of cognition.

■ Various teaching methods involving social interactions, such as *reciprocal teaching* and *peer-tutoring*, provide a scaffold when needed. Parents, peers and family members can continue the process.

■ The information-processing approach lends itself readily to the teaching of formal mathematics, with metacognition allowing other children and adults to work through various steps in complex problems without losing track of what they are doing.

■ Early factor theories of intelligence were useful in isolating a number of factors that make up intelligence (the *structure*), but they did not explain the *processes* or mechanisms involved in intelligent behaviour.

■ Contemporary theories of intelligence focus on the processes involved in thinking and problem solving in everyday life. Such theories include *Gardner's theory of multiple intelligences* and *Sternberg's triarchic theory*.

■ Intelligence testing was first introduced by Binet and Simon in France, to discriminate between those who would benefit from state education and those who might need extra support and help. Intelligence is seen to be normally distributed within the population, with a small number of people with a low IQ and a few with high IQ. Most people score around the average of 100.

■ Several factors influence test performance, including cultural values such as familiarity with the testing situation, rapport with the tester and experience of solving problems alone rather than with others. Social class differences also create bias, whereby questions can be outside the experience of the participants. Tests can often be *Eurocentric*, accepting European standards as the norm, and disadvantaging children from other cultures.

■ The nature–nurture debate on intelligence can be seen as sterile, in that it is virtually impossible to separate the relative variables. Early twin studies have been discredited but more recent studies have found great similarity in intelligence for separated twins when they are reunited later in life.

■ The role of environment on measured intelligence has been investigated and enrichment studies and adoption studies demonstrate how human intelligence appears to be the product of a complex interaction of genetic factors and environmental conditions (including nutrition).

Terms to define

accommodation
animism
assimilation
conservation
discovery learning
egocentrism
equilibration
metacognition

modes of (internal) representation
object permanence
operational thinking
scaffolding
scheme/schema
social cognition
Zone of Proximal Development (ZPD)

Further reading

Butterworth, G and Harris, M (1994) *Principles of Developmental Psychology,* Laurence Erlbaum, Hove.

Good sections on Vygotsky and Bruner by writers who are also researchers in child development.

Cole, M and Cole, S R (1993) *The Development of Children,* 2nd edn, Freeman, New York.

Generally a good text on child development but especially useful sections on the information-processing approach and the applications of theories in education.

Daniels, H (1996) *An Introduction to Vygotsky,* Routledge, London.

For anyone wanting more background on Vygotsky's view of cognitive development.

Eysenck, M (1994) *Individual Differences: Normal and Abnormal,* Laurence Erlbaum, Hove.

Student friendly text with excellent chapters on intelligence.

Howe, M J A (1998) 'Can IQ change?', *The Psychologist, 11,* 69–72.

Useful short paper which summarises the core theoretical perspectives on this topic.

Lloyd, P (1995) *Cognitive and Language Development,* BPS Books, Leicester.

Open Learning text which guides the reader through these areas of developmental psychology using activities and questions, with more detail than space would allow in the current unit.

Answers

Suggested answers to activities

1

Here are some examples (you may have found others):
- bags of sweets for after dinner
- a lump of stuffing . . . (make sure it can't drop out – use a nail)
- tell people Happy Christmas, but not to get in the way
- get the kitchen really hot and then cook the food
- everybody likes the sweets best.

3

Examples of egocentric thinking are the ball of cabbage ('Nasty, nobody likes it') and the sweets ('Everybody likes the sweets best').
Some examples of animism are: the 'dead' turkey not minding being eaten and the apples 'not minding' going into the sauce.

4
a   seen, logical principles
b   egocentric
c   animism

5
i   sensorimotor added (0–2)
ii   pre-operational – pre-conceptual (2–4) and intuitive (4–7)
iii   concrete operational (7–11)
iv   formal operational (11–15)

9
a   iconic/symbolic
b   enactive/iconic/symbolic
c   mostly enactive but probably all modes involved
d   mainly symbolic but presentation may involve enactive and iconic skills
e   strong use of symbolic mode, some may more use of iconic images in analysis

10

Similarities:

Piaget, Bruner and Vygotsky see the child's understanding moving from a simple to a more complex cognitive level with age.

All see the child as an *active* learner:

- learning by doing, rather than just listening
- role of experience.

Piaget – an individual activity.

Vygotsky – beginning in the social world and then becoming internalised.

Bruner and Piaget see major changes occurring at age 6–7.

Piaget – shift to operational thinking.

Bruner – ability to use symbolic mode.

Vygotsky and Bruner see instruction as important in the learning process.

Both see the social aspects to be important:

Bruner – '*scaffolding*'.

Vygotsky – '*Zone of Proximal Development*'.

Both see the importance of language in the development of cognition.

Differences:

Piaget stresses biological maturation whereas Vygotsky sees this as necessary but not sufficient to explain intellectual development – cultural context and social interaction are critical.

Piaget described schemes, which increase and change through assimilation and accommodation, whereas Bruner described different ways of representing the world.

Piaget's stages must be passed through in order, one stage superseding the previous, whereas Bruner's modes, although in sequence are not superseded and remain throughout life.

Piaget practically ignores the social aspects of the situation.

Piaget saw language as a tool to be used in operational thought, whereas Bruner and Vygotsky saw language playing a more important role in logical thinking.

12

Information processing theorists:

Siegler   (a)
Case   (b)
Sternberg   (c)

14

You will need to consider:

Table 14	
Multiple intelligence	Examples
linguistic aspects	good in discussion, can talk to anyone, writes well
musical	a wizard on a guitar/keyboards/can sing or hum most tunes
logical-mathematical	good at puzzles, can work things out easily in the head
bodily-kinaesthetic	good dancer, mimics, good control seen in sporting activities
personal	empathic, can relate well to others, easy to talk to, good negotiator
social	well developed social skills, good to have around when there is discord

In our society we tend to give more credit to verbal and mathematical abilities (note the importance of these in the National Curriculum in British schools in the 1990s), so it is likely that descriptions will include these factors rather than more practical skills.

Historically, the rich were educated in the former skills, whereas the labouring classes developed more practical skills. It would appear that this prejudice is still with us. Was this shown in the definitions you collected?

15

a   False
b   True
c   False
d   True

Suggested answers to self-assessment questions

1

Becoming knowledgeable can be seen as an evolutionary process in that knowledge is adaptive. It involves the interaction of the individual and the environment, so just as the internal organs of the body ensure an equilibrium between the individual and environment, so can the process of gaining knowledge be seen as assimilation and accommodation. Knowledge is assimilated into the scheme and accommodation occurs when such knowledge requires adaptation or integration. In this way equilibration is achieved – there is balance.

2

Make your decision on the merits of your thoughts on the evidence.

Evidence *for* may include:

- Children of similar maturation see things in a related way.
- The stages of cognitive development are invariable and therefore predictable.
- Curricula can be planned in a way which stimulates children's development in the stages as they go through them.

Evidence *against* may include:

- 'Making sense' is highly personal to children, in line with maturation.
- Knowledge can be transferred directly only in part.
- Children's reference systems are always changing.
- New information will not be absorbed entirely – and will be understood in a way that is only partially predictable.
- Can take into account when individual children are ready to move on to problems of the next stage.

3

Piaget underestimated children's ability. Egocentrism develops by 12 months. Operational thinking depends on the ability to decentre by age seven. Conservation of number appears by age six to seven, mass by age nine and volume by age 11 to 12. Formal operational thinking is achieved by age 15.

Hughes found decentring in children of three to four years using the policeman doll experiment.

McGarrigle and Donaldson found conservation of number in four to six year olds. They also found that children link changes in to the social context in which they can take place.

Borke found children of three and four years able to decentre (80%) when familiar objects/toys were used, such as children's TV character (Grover). But when shown Piaget's mountain problem, only 42% of three year olds could do this.

4

You could have included:

i   Object permanence has been found to occur substantially earlier than first suggested by Piaget. Research by Bower, Baillargeon is discussed on pages 761–2.

ii Ability to decentre has been found to occur earlier than suggested by Piaget when the task is more familiar to the child (see discussion of Hughes, Borke on pages 762–3).

iii Conservation also has been shown at earlier ages than suggested by Piaget (see pages 764–5).

iv Formal operational thought appears to occur later than suggested by Piaget or not at all! (see pages 765–6).

v   Lack of support for the stage concept (see Bruner and Vygotsky on page 765).

vi Neglect *social cognition* (see Vygotsky and Bruner page 766).

5

Modes are seen as different ways of making internal representations of the external world. They develop sequentially, but unlike stages we do not move from one into another, leaving the earlier stage behind. Rather, we make use of all three modes throughout life. The earlier modes may not be used as much in later life due to the dominance of symbolic mode. There are great individual differences in the use of the different modes.

6

E.g. Freund (1996). JIEs are social interactions, usually between children and adults, which play an important role in developing cognition.

7

- understanding feelings of others by about 18 months
- comfort another when needed by 36 months
- turn taking and sustained coordination by about 18 months
- understanding of rules in various contexts (what is acceptable in the family) by the third year
- awareness of the thinking of others (theory of mind)

8

- sensory processing and recognition
- attention and scanning for information
- categorisation and strategies in memory used for improving performance
- learning and coordinating different modalities (such as sound, touch and vision) to integrate the information

9

- reciprocal teaching (see pages 779–80)
- peer tutoring (see page 780).

10

- conceptual knowledge to understand the underlying principles of the problem
- procedural knowledge including strategies such as adding and subtracting
- utilisation knowledge of procedures to help solve the problem (best when presented in context)

11

- *linguistic* – sensitivity to language (ability to choose the correct word/phrase and grasp new meanings easily)
- *musical* – sensitivity to pitch and tone which allows the detection of music
- *logico-mathematical* – ability to engage in abstract reasoning and manipulate symbols
- *bodily kinaesthetic* – ability to represent ideas in movement such as dance, mime, and sports
- *personal* – ability to access one's feelings and understand the motivations of others
- *social* – ability to understand motives, feelings and behaviour of others and display good social skills

12

- *componential* – the cognitive mechanisms which underlie the ability to think critically and analytically, so people high on this usually make excellent students
- *contextual* – intelligence within the socio-cultural setting, some would call this 'streetwise' intelligence. People high on this aspect are competent at adapting to and shaping the environment in everyday encounters. This aspect distinguishes Sternberg's theory from other theories of intelligence in dealing with cultural diversity and acknowledging this in aspects of intelligence
- *experiential* – includes the influences on intelligence from past experiences and the way we build up skills and knowledge from these. This includes the ability to deal

with situational demands and also the development of automatic information-processing skills. Sternberg's distinction between the ability to adapt to novelty and automatic processing can be seen to resemble the fluid and crytallised intelligence suggested by Cattell (1963) (described on page 784)

13

You may have included:

Confidence of validity – it is difficult to prove validity of intelligence tests.

Tests may ask questions outside the experience of the testee – this would influence the score. Misinterpretation of intelligence may result.

Questions may not allow for differences in culture or social class.

Questions may not reflect the full range of intellectual abilities. Some intelligence concepts may not be tested for, for example, creativity.

Tests may be taken under adverse conditions giving a low assessment of intelligence.

14

Adoption studies allow comparisons between natural origins of intelligence (from the biological parents) and nurtural effects on intelligence (from the adoptive parents).

Twin studies allow comparisons between natural origins of intelligence (from monozygotic twins) and nurtural effects on intelligence (from dizygotic twins).

Strengths include:

It is the only way of knowing how much nature and how much nurture is responsible for our intelligence.

Weaknesses include:

Poor sample sizes; difficulty in identifying monozygotic and dizygotic twins correctly; most studies use correlational analysis which does not allow for cause and effect to be identified; different separation experiences of monozygotic twins.

Unit 22

Social Behaviour and Diversity in Development

Graham Davies, Lorna Jones and Irene Taylor

This unit covers:

Moral development

The development of the self concept

The development of gender

By the end of this unit, you should be able to:

- compare, contrast and evaluate theories of moral development
- understand the development of self
- discuss psychological theories of the development of gender identification and gender role.

Unit 22 Contents

Introduction

In this unit we look at:

■ three key areas of development: morality, the self concept and gender
■ some of the characteristics that distinguish individuals, and how these characteristics emerge or change over time.

Moral development

As children grow up, their internalised conceptions of right and wrong gradually change. Moral development is concerned with how we acquire the rules and principles of social behaviour which distinguish right from wrong. There are three components to morality.

■ A *cognitive* component is concerned with our state of knowledge about morality and our understanding of what is right or wrong.
■ The *behavioural* component concerns how we actually behave.
■ An *affective* component concerns how we feel about morality (e.g. shame, pride).

Each of the different theories of moral development tends to focus of one of these components.

We first briefly examine Freud's psychoanalytic theory, before moving on to examine how cognitive and social learning theories have explained moral development.

Freud's psychoanalytic theory of moral development

Freud's *psychoanalytic theory of moral development* concentrates on the affective component of moral development. It is particularly concerned with feelings of guilt (and the anxiety that is associated with it) on the one hand, and of pride and self-esteem on the other.

Freud considered that moral behaviour is controlled by the component of our personality known as the **superego**. This consists of two parts: the **ego-ideal** and the conscience. The ego-ideal involves the internalisation of parental moral standards and promises the ego rewards, such as pride and elevated self-esteem, for acting in a moral way. The conscience is the way in which we remain faithful to the standards of the ego-ideal. It threatens the ego with punishment for immoral behaviour. As a consequence, we renounce instinctual desires, particularly these concerning sexual drives and aggression. This frees aggression that might have been directed outwards towards others and instead directs it inwards towards the self. This punishment of the self is experienced as guilt. A strong conscience is therefore associated with enough energy to keep these impulses in check, so the more guilt we feel, the stronger our conscience – and the more moral our behaviour will be.

The superego emerges as a result of normal development at the end of the phallic stage (see figure 22.1).

■ Evaluation of Freud's psychoanalytic theory of moral development

There has been much debate over Freud's work on the superego, particularly with regard to its supposed origin within the family, the age at which the superego emerges, the nature of conscience and gender differences.

It is not surprising that Freud's theory has been attacked. Tyson and Tyson (1990) noted how his views are heavily dependent on the time in which he lived and the family framework in which he grew up. Penis envy has been questioned by many and also the conclusion that female identity is weaker than male, hence a weaker superego. Chodorow (1974) reinterpreted Freud's description of sex-role development and saw identification as a two-way process involving the parents and the child. Just as the daughter identifies with the mother, so the mother sees characteristics in her daughters like herself and sees sons to be the male opposite. Boys reinforce this differentiation by taking on the masculine role, whereas girls evoke further feelings

22.1 The phallic stage – resolving a Greek tragedy

Between the ages of three to six years, Freud saw children trying to resolve a sexual family problem. He saw this as having similarities with a Greek tragedy in which the king of Thebes, Oedipus, unknowingly kills his father and marries his mother. Freud called this conflict the *Oedipal complex*, during which boys do not repeat this tragedy but rather, as they leave infancy, they must distance themselves from their mother and become closer to their father.

Initially boys become jealous of the intimate relationship they see between their father and mother. The boy wishes to possess his mother and feelings for his father become ambivalent. He lives in fear of being punished (by castration) and feels guilty about his thoughts. Eventually he resolves this, according to Freud, towards the end of the pre-school period. Two defence mechanisms help:

- **identification** with his father, whereby the boy develops a strong desire to look, act and feel like his father, and in this way banish his feelings of hostility and fear; now he is a powerful figure also
- repression of his feelings for his mother gives him control over his infantile desire and thus stops him from desiring total possession of her – this removes the original source of guilty feelings.

Resolving the Oedipal complex not only results in the development of the boy's gender identity but is also seen by Freud as the emerging of the superego. Now the boy can see what is expected of him for being male. He is acting in a gender appropriate way in society and society's values are accepted.

What about girls? According to Freud, female identification is triggered by the girl's discovery that she does not have a penis – 'penis envy'. She blames her mother for this 'deficiency' and transfers her love to her father. Now she feels guilty and fears she will be punished by loss of her mother's love. This is named the *Electra complex*. She overcomes the fear and guilt by

- repressing feelings of love for her father
- identification with her mother.

Freud believed that female identification could never be as complete as male because the object of the primary identification and the secondary identification are the same person: the mother. Not only does this affect gender identity but also the development of the superego. He concluded that women show less sense of justice and their judgements are often influenced by feelings of affection or hostility (Freud, 1925).

of similarity by defining themselves as feminine, with the basis of empathy built into their self concept, unlike the boys. This affiliation with the mother gives girls a built-in basis of understanding the needs of others. In Chodorow's account she sees the two sexes having different pathways, each with its strengths and weaknesses. Males achieve identity from separation and may see themselves threatened by intimacy, conversely females achieve identity by attachment and are threatened by separation.

Others disagreed totally with Freud's account :

- a rejection of Freud's belief that female development is secondary to males, as all human embryos initially follow the female pattern, modified later by male hormones (Emde, 1992)

- sexual identity cannot be the consequence of resolving the Oedipal conflict as many aspects of gender and moral development can be seen before the age at which Freud assumed it to be resolved (Stoller, 1980)
- currently disturbances in identity formation are thought to be caused by psychological traumas often resulting from parents who are sexually abusive, not from the child's inability to resolve infantile sexual desires (Cichetti and Carlson, 1989).

There is no evidence that females have a weaker morality than males, with little difference shown in terms of morality. Where such differences exist, it is often shown that females are more likely to resist temptation (Hoffman, 1975).

One criticism of Freud's theory in terms of its present-day relevance is that it fails to take into account influences such as the media (particularly television) and the role of peers (for example, in playschools). This is, of course, a reflection of changing times rather than a criticism of Freud's theory itself. At the time he was writing (in the late nineteenth and early twentieth centuries) such influences either did not exist or were less influential, and the family was a stronger unit.

There has been doubt expressed by some psychologists that the superego really emerges at ages five or six. For example, Kohlberg (1969) saw moral development as occurring in stages which extend from childhood into adulthood (see page 809).

If, as Freud suggested, we possess a conscience that is internalised within us, then we might expect it to act consistently when we are faced with different situations.

Early studies involving moral knowledge tests (Hartshorne and May, 1928–30) found that there was little evidence of consistency in moral behaviour, as children tended to act morally in one situation but not in another. For example, Hartshorne and May in 1928 and 1930 concluded that honesty was situation specific, which fails to support Freud's view of an internalised conscience.

However, studies such as these provide only a measure of attitudes towards wrong acts and do not measure those components of morality concerned with moral judgements or reasoning. Also, they may be criticised for their lack of validity. For example, children's test scores for moral knowledge may decrease as they get older (Turiel, 1976). This apparent decline in their moral knowledge is more likely to be due to different ways of thinking about the moral issues involved rather than any actual decline. One example of how this might happen is the fact that older children tend to

give more importance to extenuating circumstances than younger children do. They are therefore less likely to make a judgement that an action is wrong when such circumstances exist.

Cognitive theories of moral development

The cognitive-developmentalists view the child's own understanding as central to the socialisation process: the ability to think, understand and know the world and operate successfully in it. Piaget's stage theory of intellectual development, in which the child actively structures experiences, is seen as the cornerstone of moral development. The link of the theory to morals was first proposed by Jean Piaget; Lawrence Kohlberg later developed and extended this.

Some of the basic rules of morality are acquired relatively early in childhood, such as knowing that it is wrong to steal. However, the understanding of such beliefs changes over childhood and adolescence as children become more and more capable of moral reasoning. The cognitive theories of moral development focus on the acquisition of moral knowledge, considering that this occurs in distinct stages which begin in early childhood and continue through adolescence and into adulthood.

■ Piaget's theory of moral development

Modern cognitive developmental theory concerned with morality dates back to Piaget, whose influential book *The moral judgement of the child* was published in 1932. Piaget believed that the key concepts involved in mature morality are a sense of justice and a respect for the rules of the social order. In order to study how children's knowledge and understanding of morals develops with age, Piaget studied different moral concepts, including the nature of rules, justice, moral responsibility and the legitimate basis of authority.

Piaget studied children aged between six and twelve and identified two types of morality which formed a developmental sequence. Between ages three and eight, Piaget suggested that children show a *heteronomous orientation*. This is characterised by a unilateral respect for adults, who are perceived as being the sources of rules and prohibitions – that is, rules are perceived as being externally determined and absolute.

The second type of morality is known as the *autonomous orientation*. This is a more mature form of morality characterised by reason, justice and mutual respect.

Why is there this shift from the heteronomous orientation to the autonomous? Piaget linked both orientations to his theory of cognitive development. Young children show high levels of egocentric thought and adults are likely to coerce them into action in particular ways by imposing

their own rules. Egocentrism also leads to the respect that children show for authority figures. As children's egocentrism wanes and children increasingly see others' points of view, more cooperative social relationships develop. There is then a shift away from the heteronomous orientation to the autonomous.

Piaget studied the rules which related to the game of marbles in an attempt to access children's moral rules. He found marked differences in conceptions of the rules between children at the two orientations. Children at the heteronomous orientation have no understanding of the rationale behind rules. They see them as external, fixed and absolute and held by everyone – notice how a failure to see another's point of view is shown here. Their source is external to the child (i.e. adults) and obeying rules (or commands) coming from an adult is good; disobedience is bad, whatever the quality of the rule concerned. As children have a unilateral respect for adults, rules are perceived as unchangeable. It is their letter rather than their spirit that is all important; acts are evaluated in terms of exactly how well they conform to rules. Even altering a rule will be regarded as a transgression. Moral reasoning is absent; instead the children believe rules are imposed from outside and are not negotiable.

As the children begin to decentre they realise that rules can be changed and punishment does not always follow some behaviour. This is the autonomous level, at which obedience to rules is no longer the criterion by which being good is assessed and the moral judgements underpinning rules become the basis for evaluating them. Thus a conclusion on the fairness of a rule may conflict with the views of those who made the rule. The child now sees rules as deriving from cooperation between people. He or she can conceive that they can be altered if everyone agrees. Rules will vary according to the nature of the situation.

Piaget studied children's views of responsibility for their actions by means of assessing situations involving the intentions and consequences of the actions of characters in pairs of stories. These described characters who stole, lied or acted clumsily, and participants were asked who the naughtier character was. Again, Piaget found major differences between children at the two orientations in terms of their conception of responsibility. Children at the heteronomous orientation tended to judge the situations on a 'bigger is worse' criterion and did not take intention into account. The opposite was true of children with an autonomous orientation.

Piaget also considered children's conceptions of justice. He showed that children at the heteronomous orientation believe that transgressions require punishments, and that these will result in future obedience. The more severe the punishment, the better. They also see nothing wrong with a group being punished for the misdeeds of an individual. They also believe in imminent justice – that unpleasant accidents which follow a transgression are a form of punishment for it.

At the autonomous orientation, children believe that punishment should 'fit the crime' and motivation is taken into account. Punishing a group for the misdeeds of an individual is no longer seen as appropriate; belief in imminent justice diminishes.

■ Evaluation of Piaget's theory of moral development

Piaget's theory was a pioneer in its field. Unlike his theory of cognitive development, Piaget did not revise it. Extensive revision was to wait for the work of Kohlberg, which is outlined in the next section.

Research findings on heteronomous and autonomous orientations do not entirely support Piaget's views. For example, Weston and Turiel (1980) have shown that young children do not always view conformity to authority as right – they may be critical of adults who contradict their own judgements concerning an act.

Piaget's use of game rules as a way of studying moral rules has also been criticised, as young children seem capable of distinguishing between these. Therefore there may be no case for suggesting that game rules form part of morality. Later researchers, such as Weston and Turiel (1980) and Smetana (1981), have shown that all rules are not treated alike by children, even

children as young as three. Some rules may be changed if all agree, others may not. It seems that Piaget underestimated children's capabilities in this respect.

Young children with a heteronomous moral orientation also seem able to have a greater understanding of punishment than Piaget suggested. Irwin and Moore (1971) have shown that three to five year olds can distinguish between deserved and undeserved punishments. Also, Weston and Turiel (1980) have shown that five to seven year olds can conceptualise the appropriateness of punishment. Their participants distinguished between a story of a child who had made a social transgression (where a punishment was considered appropriate) and one who had made an arithmetical error (who should not be punished).

However, Piaget's theory provided a very powerful boost to research in the area of moral development. The techniques which he introduced (particularly the use of moral dilemma stories) have stood the test of time and have been used widely by other researchers. An important example is provided by Kohlberg's theory which we consider next. This both extends and elaborates on Piaget's work.

Activity 3

Describe, in your own words, the characteristics of the two types of morality which Piaget thought formed a developmental sequence in children, namely heteronomous orientation and autonomous orientation. (If you have any difficulty, turn back to page 808 and re-read the section.)

■ Kohlberg's theory of moral development

Kohlberg (e.g. 1958, 1976) produced a theory of moral development which was strongly influenced both by Piaget's work on morality and by his stages of cognitive development. He set out to determine whether the development of moral judgement can be divided into stages, studying children, adolescents and young adults in order to do this.

As with Piaget, Kohlberg used a technique involving the analysis of test questions relating to moral dilemma stories recounted to participants (figure 22.2 contains an example).

The child or young person who had been told the story would then be asked questions such as 'Should Heinz have stolen the drug?' 'What if the person dying was a stranger?'

Activity 4

How do you think children of different ages would answer these questions?

There are no single correct or incorrect answers to these questions. Although dilemmas such as this are hardly the kind of everyday moral dilemmas faced by children, most understand the problem well enough to discuss it. Their moral reasoning clearly changes over time. Some of Kohlberg's data comes from longitudinal studies. Examples of some of the responses given by one participant to the question 'Why shouldn't you steal from a store?' are shown in figure 22.3.

22.2 Example of a moral dilemma story (Kohlberg and Elfenbein, 1975)

'In Europe, a woman was near death from a special kind of cancer. There was one drug that the doctors thought might save her. It was a form of radium that a druggist in the same town had recently discovered. The drug was expensive to make, but the druggist was charging ten times what the drug had cost him to make. He paid $200 for the radium and charged $2000 for a small dose of the drug. The sick woman's husband, Heinz, went to everyone he knew to borrow the money, but he could only get together about $1000 which is half of what it cost. He told the druggist that his wife was dying and asked him to sell it cheaper or let him pay later. But the druggist said, 'No, I discovered the drug and I'm going to make money from it.' So Heinz got desperate and broke into the man's store to steal the drug for his wife.'

22.3 Responses of one participant to the question 'Why shouldn't you steal from a store?'

Age 10: 'It's not good to steal from a store. It's against the law. Someone could see you and call the police.'

Age 17: 'It is a matter of law. It's one of our rules that we are trying to help protect everyone, protect property, not just to protect a store. It's something that's needed in our society. If we didn't have these laws, people would steal, they wouldn't have to work for a living, and our whole society would get out of kilter.'

Age 24: 'It's violating another person's rights, in this case, to property.'

From analysis of the reasons given for the responses to moral dilemma questions, Kohlberg devised a stage model of moral development. Individuals would go through these stages in sequence, stages could not be missed, nor could they move back to a previous stage. This developmental model was divided into three levels, each level containing two stages (see table 22.4).

Kohlberg's principal findings were that most children aged seven and younger resolve moral dilemmas at Level 1. By age 13, most have progressed to Level 2. This, for many, is as far as they progress. Level 3 stage 6 is reached only by 10 per cent of adults. To achieve this, a high level of formal operational thinking is needed – the individual must be capable of abstract thought. Kohlberg's levels correspond to the levels of cognitive development suggested by Piaget (see figure 22.5).

Although Kohlberg's work parallels that of Piaget in many ways, there are important differences. The first key difference is that at the earliest levels moral judgements are based on orientation towards power and punishment rather than to respect for authority and rules. Secondly, Kohlberg proposed that an autonomous morality emerges later than Piaget suggests, not emerging (if at all) until late adolescence or early adulthood.

Table 22.4

Level/Stage	Description
1 Preconventional level	
Stage 1: Punishment-and-obedience orientation	Morality judged in terms of consequences.
Stage 2: Naive hedonistic orientation	Morality judged in terms of what satisfies own needs or those of others.
2 Conventional level	
Stage 3: Good boy–good girl orientation	Morality judged in terms of adherence to social rules or norms with respect to personal acquaintances.
Stage 4: Social-order–maintaining orientation	Morality judged in terms of social rules or laws applied universally, not just to acquaintances.
3 Postconventional level	
Stage 5: Legalistic orientation	Morality judged in terms of human rights, which may transcend laws.
Stage 6: Universal ethical principle orientation	Morality judged in terms of self-chosen ethical principles.

Description of Kohlberg's levels and stages of moral development (taken from Baron, 1996) (According to Kohlberg, we move through three distinct levels of moral development.)

22.5 Parallel stages of cognitive and moral development

Cognitive Stage

Preoperations
The 'symbolic function' appears but thinking is marked by centration and irreversibility.

Concrete operations
The objective characteristics of an object are separated from action related to it; classification, seriation, and conservation skills develop.

Beginning formal operations
The ability to use propositional logic develops.

Early basic formal operations
The hypothetico-deductive approach emerges, involving the ability to develop possible relations among variables and to organise experimental analyses.

Consolidated basic formal operations
Operations are now completely exhaustive and systematic.

Source: Walker (1980)

Moral Stage

Stage 1. Heteronomy
The physical consequences of an action and the dictates of authorities define right and wrong.

Stage 2. Exchange
Right is defined as serving one's own interests and desires, and cooperative interaction is based on terms of simple exchange.

Stage 3. Expectations
Emphasis is on good-person stereotypes and concern for approval.

Stage 4. Social system and conscience
Focus is on maintaining the social order by obeying the law and doing one's duty.

Stage 5. Prior rights and social contract
Right is defined by standards that have been agreed upon by the whole society.

Kohlberg (1984) believed that moral thinking in stages 3 and 4 depends on partial ability to engage in formal operational thought, in particular the ability to consider all possible known factors relevant to the choice. Such children are still reasoning concretely because they are not considering possible factors and they do not hypothesise abstractly. Stage 5 reasoning does not appear until early adulthood (in some cases not at all!). The highest stage 6 is achieved by very few individuals, but as history has shown, some people will put their own lives at risk because of the belief in principles seen to apply to all of humanity. Altruistic behaviour, such as that of the European Gentiles who rescued Jews during the Second World War and of people such as Gandhi in India, Martin Luther King in the US and Nelson Mandela in South Africa, who practised civil disobedience for the common good, is an example of stage 6 reasoning.

■ Evaluation of Kohlberg's theory of moral development

Kohlberg's work has been a major contribution to our understanding of moral development and has shown that moral development tends to follow a sequence of stages. It has stimulated a great deal of research, for example Snarey (1985) listed studies carried out in 27 different cultural areas. Almost all of these show a broadly similar progression from stages 1 to 4, but there was much less evidence for stage 5 reasoning in these studies, which has led to the suggestion that Kohlberg's work is culturally biased.

■ *Is morality sequential?* – Kohlberg did not suggest that everyone reaches stage 6 but he did see the order of progression to be invariant and universal. Individuals move 'up' but do not move 'down'. There is a consensus from researchers that stage 2 reasoning dominates at age ten years and stage 3 reasoning is common at about age 16 (Colby *et al.*, 1983; Walker *et al.*, 1987). However, very little evidence exists for post-conventional reasoning. Gibson (1990) found only 13 per cent of men aged 40–60 years were rated as using stage 5.

Fairly strong evidence exists that the stages are sequential as suggested by many studies (Colby *et al.*, 1983 in the US; Snarey, Reimer and Kohlberg, 1985,

in Israel). Very little evidence (about 5–7 per cent) exists of regression, which can be accounted for by the less than precise measurement techniques used.

Others (for example Gilligan, 1977) have been concerned that Kohlberg has stressed justice as the major theme in moral development. Cases could also be made for aspects of morality such as empathy, caring for others and sympathy.

■ *Is moral development universal?* – Variations of Kohlberg's dilemmas have been presented to children and adults in different cultures (both western and non-western, industrialised and non-industrialised). John Snarey (1985) reviewed and analysed several of these and found supporting evidence for:

– the increase of reasoning with age
– similar findings from many longitudinal studies
– cultural differences in levels reached with stage 5 typical of the highest level in both western and non-western complex urban societies, whereas stage 4 is most typical of peasants and tribal communities (Boyes and Walker, 1988).

It would appear that Kohlberg's theory does seem to cover universal dimensions of moral reasoning in all cultures, but this reasoning occurs in a cultural context so culture-based factors must not be ignored.

■ *Are there sex-differences in moral reasoning?* – Gilligan (1982) has also pointed out the important fact that Kohlberg's work is male biased – all the original participants used by Kohlberg were male. She pointed out that the concept of morality is different between the sexes. She made the case for the alternative ethic of care and responsibility as being more appropriate when studying the development of moral reasoning in women. Gilligan and Ward (1990) suggested that inadequate measures of moral development can perpetuate cultural biases against different groups in our society. Gilligan argued that because of socialisation, boys are more likely to value abstract notions of justice and fairness whereas girls are more likely to value relations with people. The differences found earlier between boys and girls were still found to exist. Younger girls were concerned with caring for others and dilemmas concerning friends were discussed in terms of loyalties, whereas boys spoke more about peer pressure. However, older boys were found more likely to discuss caring and helping. Gilligan and Ward are critical of many of the narrow measures of morality which may miss many of the strengths in different communities.

Empirical studies have not found overall support for the gender differences noted by Gilligan. In a review of 80 studies, Walker and de Vries (1985) found that only 22 showed sex differences and in 9 of these, females scored higher on Kohlberg's scale than males. Bee (1995) noted that although no differences in justice and care orientation are found between boys and girls, it does not necessarily mean there are no differences in the assumptions males and females bring to relationships or moral judgements.

■ *Does moral judgement match moral behaviour?* – Kohlberg never stated there would be a one-to-one correspondence between behaviour and reasoning but he did suggest there was some connection. In 1984 Kohlberg and Candee studied students involved in the 'free speech' movement at Berkeley University and found the higher the stage of reasoning, the more consistent the behaviour was with the reasoning. Eisenberg *et al.* (1987, 1991) also found certain types of pro-social reasoning correlated with the child's level of reasoning. Schroeder *et al.* (1995) found cultural effects on the types of actions seen as good or bad, but universal patterns and reasoning in what motivates helping.

Bee (1995) suggested several factors other than level of reasoning that have a bearing on moral behaviour:

■ habits in moral situations may result in people performing at a lower lever

■ whether individuals see the situation as demanding their individual participation

■ the costs and benefits to the individual of helping or refraining from behaving in a morally 'wrong' way

■ competing motives or ethics such as pressure from a peer group, motives for self protection or self reward.

Moral behaviour can be seen to result from many influences of which moral reasoning is only one factor. Social aspects also need to be considered.

Social learning theory of moral development

Social learning theory of moral development is concerned with the influence of modelling by others, the result being **vicarious learning** by the child. This may be expanded by the twin influences of reinforcement and punishment. Behaviour is more likely to be imitated if a role model is observed being rewarded than if punished.

Do role models need to be known personally to the child before they influence moral behaviour? The answer to this is 'no'. Parents and other family members are the most important influence, but the influence of models may go far beyond these to media personalities or top sports performers. Although a child may learn from observing any model, imitation of behaviour is more likely to happen if the model displays behaviour which is considered appropriate to the child concerned (Bandura *et al.*, 1961). Figure 22.6 shows some of the factors which help to dictate whether a particular model is copied.

Activity 5

Write down the names of some people who you consider to be powerful role models for young people. Work through the factors in figure 22.6 to see if you can identify the reasons why they are imitated.

In a series of laboratory experiments carried out in the 1960s, Bandura and his research associates showed that aggressive behaviour can be acquired from the vicarious observation of an aggressive role model, especially when the aggressive behaviour was reinforced (or at least not punished). Bandura *et al.* (1965) were able to distinguish between competence and performance by demonstrating that imitated behaviour is not always shown immediately. Latent learning occurs, whereby behaviour observed may not be displayed until much later. Although such experiments are artificial, they throw some light on how moral behaviour may be acquired through modelling.

22.6 Characteristics of role models that increase the likelihood of imitation

- Perceived relevance to the individual
- Perceived similarity between the model and child
- Friendly models are more likely to be copied
- Powerful models are imitated more quickly
- Models who behave consistently are more likely to be copied

Moral development, according to the social learning theorists, may be perceived as a development from extrinsic sources of reinforcement and punishment to intrinsic sources. The shift from extrinsic to intrinsic reinforcement results from observation and imitation of an individual model's behaviour. Initially, reinforcers are extrinsic and can be either directly applied rewards and punishments or vicarious in their nature (the child observes someone else being rewarded or punished). Eventually, reinforcers become intrinsic and the child develops the self-regulatory mechanisms of self-satisfaction and self-criticism.

■ Evaluation of social learning theory of moral behaviour

Social learning theory has been criticised on the grounds that the laboratory studies carried out in this area (such as Bandura's) are artificial in nature and focus on children's responses to a single adult model, which is an over-simplification of reality (Bronfenbrenner, 1973). Such role models are not known to the child concerned, which is a departure from the normal situation children find themselves in when acquiring moral knowledge. It is worth noting that many adolescents can be seen modelling behaviour of popular singers and actors who are not personally known to them.

Cognitive factors are recognised in social learning theory. Mischel (1973) identified several 'person variables' which affect the way individuals process information received when viewing models; for example, social approval is only effective if it is behaviour valued by the child. Such cognitive factors are seen as one of many factors involved in development with behaviour seen to be the most important variable.

Another criticism of social learning theory is that, unlike cognitive theory, it tells us little about how development actually progresses. Despite these limitations, however, social learning theory has made a valuable contribution to our knowledge of moral development.

Activity 6

a Make a table comparing Piaget's and Kohlberg's theories of moral development.
b Draw flow charts illustrating how moral behaviour is acquired according to both Freudian psychoanalytic theory and social learning theory.

(Suggested answers on pages 844–5.)

Research in developmental psychology has moved away from looking for single causes to explain behaviour; as discussed in Unit 21 on Cognitive Development (pages 762–6), when tasks given to the child are socially real, findings differ from those of earlier research. Social cognition has been found important:

'Increasingly, we are becoming aware that the child develops its own, very sophisticated social understanding, which it applies to the situations within which it finds itself.' (Hayes 1994, p. 724)

The role of social cognition

We noted earlier the possible connections between cognitive structure and social-cognitive reasoning. Kohlberg hypothesised that the child first moves to a new level of logical thought and then applies this to relationships as well as objects, and then applies this reasoning to moral problems. He suggested that some formal operational thinking and mutual perspective taking in relationships are necessary (but not sufficient) for conventional moral reasoning to emerge. Further development is needed, especially more abstract thinking, for postconventional reasoning to occur.

Lawrence Walker (1980) gave some support for Kohlberg in finding that among a group of young adolescents tested on formal operations, social understanding and moral reasoning, over half were reasoning at the same level across the domains. When they were ahead in one domain, it was usually logical thinking followed by social understanding and then moral judgements. Bee (1995) noted that although cognitive understanding makes advances in social and moral reasoning possible, it is not guaranteed; the necessary experience in relationships and moral problems is essential also.

The cultural context and social interaction noted earlier by Vygotsky in the *Zone of Proximal Development* and Bruner by scaffolding (see Unit 21) have demonstrated the importance of interaction in sociability. This was found by Judy Dunn (1988) in the UK in her ethological studies of family life. The findings challenge the earlier theories of moral development by showing moral awareness to be present at the age of 18 months. This research highlights the social learning of context-specific behaviour. She found:

- highly developed understanding of others' feelings sometimes shown by 18 months, and the likelihood of comforting others by 36 months
- revealed in play was an understanding of the goals of others with sustained coordination often by 12 months, with the demonstration of understanding the intentions of others by 18 months
- an understanding of social rules and which apply with different family members devolving in the third year
- a steadily developing awareness of understanding others' minds which is quite sophisticated by four years. This was also supported by Paul Harris (1988).

Several researchers have shown the increasing sophistication of the child's social understanding with increasing age. A good summary of related studies can be found in Hayes (1994).

Self-assessment questions

1 What is meant by moral development?

2 Explain why Freud proposes that females have weaker superegos than males.

3 Note two criticisms of Piaget's theory of moral development.

4 What are the problems of accepting Kohlberg's final stages of development?

5 Give one explanation other than level of reasoning why behaviour is not always related to moral development.

(Suggested answers on page 845.)

The development of the self concept

The process of social development continues throughout life. However, bearing in mind our genetic potential, the effects of our early experiences have a tremendous influence on the way we develop socially. The role we play in society depends to a large extent on how our self concept develops. This section addresses the effects which early experiences have on our self concept and our self-esteem.

There is no agreement about the definition of 'self'. Often the terms *self* and *self concept* are used to refer to an individual's awareness of self. The self is often seen to include at least three components: self-image, self-esteem and the ideal self.

- *Self-image* is the way we describe ourselves – our body image – the cognitive aspect.
- *Self-esteem* refers to the extent to which we like or accept ourselves – the affective aspect.
- *Ideal self* is the kind of person we would like to be and often affects our behaviour.

Self can also be seen to have many facets: it can be private (within us), it can be shown to others and can also be part of what we use to view and monitor the process itself (Jackson and Humphreys, 1995). Bee (1995) suggested that the self acts as a 'filter for experience, shaping our choices and affecting our responses to others' (Bee, 1995, p. 289).

By the time they are three, children begin to get an understanding that they have a separate psychological identity, a private, thinking self, distinguishable from the bodily self that others can see.

The development of self in infancy

The first part of development of self occurs when the child realises that he or she is separate from others and has an understanding of himself or herself as a 'stable, continuing entity' (Bee, 1995). Both psychoanalytic theory and cognitive developmental theory see the changes in the child's understanding of self in the first two years to be extremely important.

Freud noted how the mother and child are initially together as one. At this point the infant has no understanding of being separate from the mother. Some of this understanding of the distinction between self and others he saw developing in the first two or three months of life.

Piaget saw the first major 'landmark' in the child's cognitive life to be the basic concept of object permanence, which he saw to be a necessary precursor for the child achieving self-permanence.

Michael Lewis (1990, 1991) saw the early development of self as occurring in two steps:

- The **existential self** ('I exist') develops during the first two or three months of life. Lewis sees this understanding developing from the early interaction of the infant with objects and carers. Examples would be when the child hits a hanging toy to make it swing or a cry brings help from a carer. So a sense of 'I' begins. It will be 9 to 12 months before the child fully understands object permanence and a more subjective self emerges.
- The **categorical self** (sometimes equated with the self-image) demands a self-awareness whereby the child defines the self by placing himself or herself in a number of categories.

Flavell (1978) preferred to think that the emergence of private self has something to do with children's ideas on their own face and eyes. From remarks such as 'Look at me when I speak to you' and 'I saw you reading but you didn't see me', Flavell thought that children learn to believe that the pronouns 'I' and 'me' refer to their faces; the pronoun 'you' refers to the whole body.

One way to tell if children have developed an understanding of themselves as separate from others is to see if they can recognise themselves.

Using a technique first used by Gallup (1977) with chimpanzees, Lewis and Brooks-Gunn (1979) found with human infants that when a baby is placed in front of a mirror, by 9 to 12 months they will look at their reflection and try to interact in some way. While pretending to wipe the child's face the mother put a little rouge on the baby's nose. When the infant looks in the mirror again the researchers were interested in noting whether she reaches for the rouge spot on her own nose (not the reflected nose). This is thought to show self recognition and awareness of the self. At 9 to 12 months very few infants can do this, whereas by 21 months about 75 per cent can do it. The researchers found a similar pattern in the age at which children refer to themselves by name when they are shown a photograph of themselves.

Susan Harter (1983) saw five steps in the infant's emerging understanding of the existential self (see figure 22.7).

22.7 Some steps in the infant's emerging sense of the existential self

Age	Step
The self as subject, as an active, independent causal agent	
5–8 months	Interested in mirror image, but shows no indication that she sees herself as a causal agent.
9–12 months	Understands the relationship between his own movement and the movement in the mirror (e.g., he may wave at the mirror). Seems clear that the infant sees himself as an active agent in space, able to cause things to happen by his own movement.
12–15 months	Can use a mirror to locate people or objects in space; she reaches for the object, not the mirrored version of it. Grasps the fact that other people cause their movements just as she causes hers.
The self as an object of one's knowledge	
15–18 months	In mirror studies, this is the age at which the child reaches for the rouge spot on his own nose. Also will point to himself. If shown pictures, can distinguish between self and others; thus has some kind of schema of his own face.
18–24 months	Infant can state her own name; may give her name to the figure in the mirror. Can distinguish between a picture of herself and one of another girl her age.

Source: Harter (1983)

From this research, infants of 18 months seem not only to see themselves as separate, but also have some understanding of their own appearance. Before the age of two years, when confronted with a photograph of themselves they may use their own name, and by the age of three years, almost all children can refer to themselves in the pictures using their own names and the correct personal pronouns. These reactions suggest that an awareness of self emerges during the second year of life (see figure 22.7).

The question arises as to whether the emergence of a psychological, private self is linked to children's ability to see things from other peoples' perspectives. Vygotsky (1934) thought that between three and a half and four years of age, children gradually change their use of speech. At first they use speech for thinking aloud, then for talking to themselves, thinking silently and finally, for communicating with others.

Whether the self concept is linked to egocentrism, language or thinking, it is evident that by three and a half to four years old children do have such a concept. This confers on them a position in relation to other people within a social world. Bannister and Agnew (1977) found the ability to do this does not happen in an instant and believe there is a developmental progression. Focusing in terms of external appearance and activities develops first, then a gender identity, which includes their likes and dislikes, and finally thinking in terms of more abstract qualities occurs – in a social context.

The development of self in middle childhood

Over the primary school years of middle childhood the child's self concept becomes more abstract. Children's self descriptions become more comparative. They see themselves as 'better at Maths than my friends' or 'not as good at games as others'. The self concept becomes more complex, less focused on external characteristics and more on internal qualities. This can be seen by completion of the Twenty Statements Test (TST), (Kuhn and McPartland, 1954). Before reading any further perhaps you may like to complete Activity 7 now.

Activity 7

Ask yourself the question 'Who am I?' and write down as many answers as you can up to 20 starting with 'I am . . .'
You could investigate this further by giving the task to people of different ages.

Increasingly, children define themselves, not only in terms of their own qualities, but also in terms of other people with whom they are involved, both singly and in groups. Kuhn (1960) demonstrated this by asking many hundreds of individuals between 7 and 24 years of age to make 20 statements in answer to the question 'Who am I?' On average the youngest participants referred to themselves in terms of groups less than six times, whereas the oldest did so 11 times.

Kuhn showed that as the child develops, the sense of self becomes less physically oriented and increasingly influenced by social factors. Only 25 per cent of statements made by seven year olds related to social roles such as 'I am a daughter' compared to 50 per cent of such statements made by 24 year olds.

Montemayor and Eisen (1977) examined the self concept of 9 to 18 year olds. They found the younger children described themselves in more physical terms. As they progressed through the concrete operational stage, their descriptions became more focused on internal qualities such as feelings and ideas. The school-age child begins to see his or her own characteristics (and those of others) as relatively stable. The older group answers were even more abstract and referred to ideologies and beliefs. This would seem appropriate for the formal operational stage identified by Piaget.

Did any of your responses in Activity 7 tally with the findings presented in figure 22.8? Would your answers differ if you wrote them for a different audience such as a stranger, a friend or just for yourself?

William Damon and Daniel Hart (1988), in an extensive study of changes in the child's self concept, found that children of all ages, in descriptions of themselves, refer to their appearance, activities, their relations with others and their psychological characteristics, but the weighting of the various characteristics changes with age. As can be seen in table 22.9, children of six to seven years are more likely to describe themselves in a categorical way ('I am six years old') and sometimes in terms of others ('I am better at games than John'). Between 8 and 11

22.8 Describing the self

When asked to write twenty statements in answer to the question, 'who am I?' most people give more than half of their answers in role terms (e.g. male, married) and the rest in terms of personality traits or evaluations (e.g. sad, outgoing, good at sport). In one experiment using this test (Mulford and Salisbury, 1964), over one thousand adults were tested and their responses were analysed to discover the roles which people most frequently used to describe themselves. The four commonest types of description were in terms of:

Role	Responses falling in this category
1 Family relationships (e.g. brother, mother)	70%
2 Occupation (e.g. nurse, clerk)	68%
3 Marital status (e.g. divorced, single)	34%
4 Religious identity (e.g. Christian, Hindu)	30%

Women used family categories more than men, who mentioned their occupation and sex more often. Age was mentioned most by the youngest (under-30s) and oldest (over-70s) in the sample.

Source: Roth (1990).

Table 22.9

Level	Physical	Activity-based	Social	Psychological
1 Categorical identification (4–7 years)	I have blue eyes. I'm 6 years old.	I play baseball. I play and read a lot.	I'm Catholic. I'm Sarah's friend.	I get funny ideas sometimes. I'm happy.
2 Comparative assessments (8–11 years)	I'm bigger than most kids. I have really light skin because I'm Scandinavian.	I'm not very good at school. I'm good at math, but I'm not so good at art.	I like it when my mom and dad watch me play baseball. I do well in school because my parents respect me for it.	I'm not as smart as most kids. I get upset more easily than other kids.
3 Interpersonal implications (12–15 years)	I am a four-eyed person. Everyone makes fun of me. I have blonde hair, which is good because boys like blondes.	I play sports, which is important because all the kids like athletes. I treat people well so I'll have friends when I need them.	I am an honest person, so people trust me. I am very shy, so I don't have many friends.	I understand people, so they come to me with their problems. I'm the kind of person who loves being with my friends; they make me feel good about being me.

Damon and Hart's developmental model of self-concept
Source: After Damon and Hart, 1988.

these descriptions are likely to be supplemented by perceptions of the self which include the implications of these characteristics ('I am richer than Lisa so she doesn't play with me any more').

Activity 8

The following answers were given to the TST in the Montemayor and Eisen study (1977). The answers belong to respondents aged 9, 11 and 17.

(A)

My name is A. I'm a human being. I'm a girl. I'm a truthful person. I'm not very pretty. I do so-so in my studies. I'm a very good cellist. I'm a very good pianist. I'm a little bit tall for my age. I like several boys. I like several girls. I'm old-fashioned. I play tennis. I am a very good swimmer. I try to be helpful. I'm always ready to be friends with anybody. Mostly I'm good, but I lose my temper. I'm not well-liked by

Activity 8 cont'd

some girls and boys. I don't know if I'm liked by boys or not. (Montemayor and Eisen, 1977, pp. 317–318)

(B)

I am a human being. I am a girl. I am an individual. I don't know who I am. I am a Pisces. I am a moody person. I am an indecisive person. I am an ambitious person. I am a very curious person. I am not an individual. I am a loner. I am an American (God help me). I am a Democrat. I am a liberal person. I am a radical. I am a conservative. I am a pseudoliberal. I am an atheist. I am not a classifiable person (i.e. I don't want to be). (Montemayor and Eisen, p. 318)

(C)

My name is Bruce C. I have brown eyes. I have brown hair. I have brown eyebrows. I am — years old. I LOVE! Sports. I have seven

Activity 8 cont'd

people in my family. I have great! eye site. I have lots! of friends. I live on 1923 Pinecrest Dr. I am going on — in September. I'm a boy. I have a uncle that is almost 7 feet tall. My school is Pinecrest. My teacher is Mrs. V. I play Hockey! I'm almost the smartest boy in the class. I LOVE! food. I love fresh air. I LOVE school. (Montemayor and Eisen, 1977, pp. 317–318)

a   Which answers belong to each participant?
b   Can you link the increasing sophistication in the three examples with Piagetian stages?

(Suggested answers on page 845.)

Ziller (1973) was interested in the development of *self-other orientation*, where coalitions are formed to resolve conflict between the interests of self and those of others. When individual and group interests and values are similar, there is little conflict between them and a trusting relationship builds up with shared goals and values. Predictions of others' behaviour are fulfilled, expectations can be trusted and a stable social sub-system develops. However, this can only happen if children themselves are willing to reveal their personal intentions, to be predictable and to live up to others' expectations. Ziller found that, with increasing age, children feel more and more bound up in a social network and also feel more an individual within that network.

Social groups may be discriminated against by other social groups. When this happens drawbacks occur.

Activity 9

Jot down groups which you think are discriminated against. What are the drawbacks attached to belonging to these groups? Are there any advantages?

We cannot always opt out of our social world, but we do have some control over the extent to which we enter into social closeness with or isolation from other people. Most people find a balance between their private selves and their social selves which allows them to support others and be supported by them without necessarily being physically or emotionally involved in a personal way. However, in order to enter into a cooperative, mutually trusting relationship with others, children must learn not only to monitor their own behaviour but also to understand how their behaviour appears to others.

The outcome of this process will depend on a negotiated working consensus of what is expected and what is projected (Goffman, 1959). Thus a different role will develop for each group to which an individual belongs, giving foundation to H G Well's statement, 'I am not a man I am a mob'.

Activity 10

Write down the roles you hold in the groups to which you belong. What impression do you project in each? Is this the impression you want to project?

Did you put that the impression you project is different both between groups and also between members of those groups? Do you sometimes exaggerate or hide things to strengthen the impression, for example when you want sympathy or when you want to keep something secret that you are ashamed of having done?

■ The influence of social factors on the developing self

Cooley (1902), Mead (1934), Argyle (1969) and Goffman (1971) have all highlighted the influence of social interactions on the developing self. One of the earliest psychologists to note the multi-faceted social self was William James in 1890. He saw the self developing from social comparisons. We compare ourselves with others, especially 'significant others', and use this to develop our understanding of what we are like.

Argyle (1969, 1983) includes social comparisons in the four important social factors influencing the self concept. Many self concepts are comparative such as 'small' or 'clever'. The other three factors noted are:

- reaction of others
- identification
- social roles.

The reaction of others provides the 'looking-glass self' described by Cooley (1902). We begin to see ourselves through the expectations of others. Children also imitate and identify with people who they see to be important to them – the significant others. In this way the child moves from an egocentric world to one where he or she tries to act out the role from another's view. This imitating and acting out of a variety of roles increases with age.

Goffman (1961) claimed that the roles we play are important to the self concept. He suggested we choose roles which reflect how we see ourselves. When we are playing the role it can be seen as a mask concealing our true self, but rather showing who we are and how we wish to be treated. These roles are incorporated into the self concept.

George H Mead (1934) saw the social construction of the self as a fundamental building block of human development. We gain an awareness of the social world by participating in language and play. In this way we begin to take on the perspective of another and in this way become able to reflect on ourselves. Mead saw society resting on these shared meanings and shared understanding about each other's intentions. We have to be able to take on the role symbolically, to imagine how they might react to us and acquire a sense of self by being able to see ourselves from the view point of another, known as *symbolic interactionism*. Part of this social self is evaluative and concerned with whether people like us, trust us, admire us and so on.

Mead's theory has been criticised in that it was never systematically written up; it was more a collection of notes from his lectures and notes which resulted in many inconsistencies and contradictions. The theory has been examined and reformulated by other researchers working within his framework. For example, Selman (1980) presented research on friendship development in terms of a broader model of social perspective taking. He was conscious that the symbolic interactionists do not see chronological ages to be appropriate to the study of social processes. He was influenced by Piaget and the cognitive-developmental view and also Mead and the symbolic-interactionists. He took a position midway between both views and noted general age trends in the development of self-awareness as shown through the answers of schoolchildren aged between 7 and 11 years to dilemmas about typical problems and conflicts encountered by friends. This allowed the researcher to ask children their views on the formation of their own friendships in a fairly natural way.

Selman identified five stages in the development of self, three of which occur in middle childhood. These show the changes from the infant's physical orientation to when the young person appreciates and can 'reflect upon; monitor and even control his actions and his thoughts' (Gardner 1982, p. 490). Selman was able to demonstrate that friendship reflects an individual's developing ability to take the perspective of the other. He was seeking to establish the child's own perspective on his or her social world as advocated by the symbolic interactionists. He was able to demonstrate that the child's perspective is a different one from that held by adults observing children.

However much your surface behaviour might change between groups or people, you probably found that everything you do conforms to a stable set of standards and values which you have acquired and in which you believe. This set of stable values belongs to your **ego-ideal**, a concept of your *ideal self*, the self which you want to be like. An ego ideal is constructed from the behaviour of admired others through modelling and identification and it may or may not be realistic in terms of the real self.

Clinical psychologists (especially Rogers, 1951) regard a large discrepancy between the real and ideal selves as an unhealthy sign, but Katz, Zigler and Zelk (1975) saw it more as a sign of maturity. They found that when schoolchildren rated statements for their real selves and for their ideal selves, the discrepancy was greater for the older participants and lower for children who were psychologically disturbed. Leahy and Huard (1976) found that children with high discrepancies between ideal and real selves were more perceptive about others' perspectives. They suggested that role-taking skill is related to the ability to develop different concepts of an actual and ideal self. With increasing age, children try to shape their own behaviour towards their ideal self which helps them develop control over impulses. Children who have an ideal self which is no better or mature than their real self remain impulsive longer than normal developing children.

Self-esteem and identity in adolescence

Self-esteem is the value we place on ourselves relative to the roles we play and with regard to our ideal self – an evaluation of how we measure up to ourselves in the light of our own standards and values. By age ten, children have built up their self concept – of how they appear to others. They know that they have an internal, private self inaccessible to others, and have assumed social roles by becoming integral members of a number of social groups through interacting with other members of those groups.

If children's evaluations of their own behaviour against their self-set standards is favourable and they are satisfied with themselves, they have a positive self-esteem. James (1896) referred to this as self-satisfaction, which is a ratio between what we accomplish and what we set out to accomplish. However, this is not as straightforward as it sounds. Paradoxically, people who accomplish much may feel poor self-worth because they have not achieved the perfection they set out to achieve, while those who set out to do nothing may have high self-worth because they have failed nothing. There is some risk that children who aspire to do well may lose self-esteem through failure, yet risk is needed in order to enhance the ego-ideal. It is only when self-definition contains these risks, that success or failure can be linked to self-esteem.

Erik Erikson (1968) had a psychoanalytic background and saw development progressing through stages of conflict as did Freud, but unlike Freud he saw the conflict to be psychosocial in origin (see figure 22.10).

In middle childhood he saw children resolving the conflict of industry versus inferiority. This inferiority challenges the self-esteem.

Self-esteem is often seen as a measure of mental health (Jahoda 1958). High self-esteem in childhood has been linked to satisfaction and happiness in later life (Crandall, 1973; Bachman, 1970). Low self-esteem has been linked with depression, and maladjustment in school and in social relationships (Damon, 1963).

Coopersmith (1967) found that people assess their own success in four ways (see figure 22.11).

Coopersmith (1967) administered a battery of tests to 10- to 12-year-old boys and found that self-esteem is very stable at this age. Even three years later children held the same position relative to other children. Coopersmith(1968) asked teachers to rate the children for reactions to failure, self-confidence in new situations, sociability with peers and need for encouragement and reassurance. He chose five groups of 17 white, middle-class boys, of equal intelligence and social standing without obvious emotional disturbances from high–high self-esteem (high in both their own self-esteem and on the teacher's rating), to low–low self-esteem (low on both their own self-esteem and on the teacher's rating). Boys in the high–high group tended to rate themselves as more independent and creative than the other groups. Figure 22.12 gives their results in greater detail.

Low self-esteem boys were reluctant to take an active part in activities and constantly underrated themselves. They were self-conscious and found it hard to make friendships. Boys in the middle groups scored in between – and also for confidence – and needed some reassurance of social acceptance. As adults, boys in the high self-esteem groups did better educationally than boys in other groups and were more successful in their careers.

The self-esteem of the boys was found correlated with the style of parenting. Three parental characteristics appeared to produce high self-esteem in middle childhood were:
- close, affectionate relations with mothers
- clearly defined limits on the children's activities
- respect for individuality and self-expression within the limits set, with parents showing respect by reasoning and taking the children's points of view into account.

Coopersmith argued that a well-structured, demanding environment encouraged the development of self-reliance and independence

22.10 Erikson's psychosocial stages of development

In Erikson's theory, the individual's psychological development is assumed to occur through the resolution of basic psychological conflicts, which form the foundation for later development. The psychosocial conflicts which the individual must face at different ages are as follows:

Early infancy
Trust versus mistrust

To gain a balance between trusting people and risking being let down, or being suspicious and mistrustful and therefore being unable to relate to others fully

Later infancy
Autonomy versus shame and doubt

To develop a sense of personal agency and control over behaviour and actions, or to mistrust one's personal abilities and anticipate failures

Early childhood
Initiative versus guilt

To develop an increasing sense of personal responsibility and initiative, or to develop increased feelings of guilt and doubt

Middle childhood
Industry versus inferiority

To learn to overcome challenges through systematic effort, or to accept failure and avoid challenges, leading to an increasing sense of inferiority

Puberty and adolescence
Identity versus role confusion

To develop a consistent sense of personal identity faced with the changes in social role and expectations of adolescence, or simply to become overwhelmed by choices and expectations and to fail to develop a sense of a consistent inner self

Young adulthood
Intimacy versus isolation

To develop intimate and trusting relationships with others, or to avoid relationships as threatening and painful

Mature adulthood
Generativity versus stagnation

To develop a productive and positive life incorporating recognition of personal achievements, or to stagnate and fail to develop or grow psychologically

Late adulthood
Integrity versus despair

To become able to look back on one's life in a positive fashion and to evaluate one's achievements, or to feel that life has been meaningless and futile

Source: Adapted from Erikson (1968).

22.11 Ways in which we assess success (Coopersmith, 1967)

- By the power we have to influence and control other people.
- By the significance of what we have done: how acceptable it is to others, how much attention they give it and how affectionately they respond to it.
- By virtue of how we adhere to our moral and ethical standards.
- By our competence to meet the demands for achievement: success helps us to direct risk areas for self-investment.

22.12 Characteristics of boys with high self-esteem (Coopersmith, 1968)

- They had expectations of being well received and successful.
- They had confidence and trust in their own judgements.
- They had the courage to express opinions on new ideas (even when they knew these might meet with a hostile reaction).

- They were assertive and socially active.
- They took an active part in group discussions.
- They had little difficulty in forming friendships.
- They were unselfconscious and unpreoccupied with personal problems.

more than a permissive one. However, we must be careful not to infer that certain types of parenting result in different levels of self-esteem. The studies only show relationships between the two; there may be other variables involved.

It is fair to note that the Coopersmith study was taken from a small biased sample, not representative of the general (American) population.

Children who come from working-class homes tend to have lower self-esteem than others, and girls in general have lower self-esteem than boys (Gordon 1981). Self-esteem is also difficult to measure as questionnaires are always open to participant bias and children do not willingly admit to undesirable characteristics. Also, self-esteem in not uniform. Harter (1982) found that children rate themselves differently in cognitive, social and physical domains and that their feelings of self-worth in one aspect of a domain may differ from other aspects.

Susan Harter and Robin Pike (1984) studied self-evaluations in four domains seen related to self-esteem: cognitive competence, physical competence, peer acceptance and maternal acceptance. The children who were aged between four and seven years showed in their responses that they evaluated themselves in terms of competence and acceptance, but they combined physical and cognitive competence and also peer and maternal acceptance. Working with older children, Harter (1982, 1987) found children made more differentiated self-evaluation (including cognitive, social and physical competence) at this time. These older children were able to evaluate their overall self-worth, whereas the younger children only evaluated themselves in specific domains. An

overall sense of oneself in relation to others seems to arise at about the age of eight years.

Susan Harter's research highlighted the importance for the self-esteem of the difference between the value an individual places on some skill or quality and the amount of skill or quality the individual sees himself or herself as having. It is this discrepancy that is reflected in the self-esteem. Children with high self-esteem can be seen as satisfied with meeting their own standards, whereas those with low self-esteem see a discrepancy between what they would like to be (or what they think they ought to be) and what they are. Being good at something won't raise the child's self-esteem unless the particular skill or quality is valued by the individual. We see here again the role of social cognition.

Harter's research showed that the self-esteem is clearly not fixed, although the tendency towards low or high self-esteem is a relatively stable personal characteristic, at least after the age of about eight years (Bee, 1993).

Cole and Cole (1993) suggested that the key to self-esteem seems to be the feeling, largely transmitted by the family, that one has some ability to control both oneself and one's environment. This strong and positive sense of self within the family context cannot completely protect the children from outside sources, but it can provide a secure foundation for trials when they are alone.

The psychological effects of puberty

In a longitudinal American study, Peterson (1989) followed over 300 adolescents and their parents, from 12 to 14 years, assessing by interview and psychological tests twice a year. They were also assessed again in their last year of high school. Puberty was shown to have significant effects on body-image, self-esteem, moods, relationships with parents and members of the opposite sex. Many of these seem related to the personal and social effects of the body's physical changes.

The timing of these changes has been found critical to their self-concept. Early or late maturation, which is determined by maturing one year earlier or later than average, can affect the satisfaction of the adolescent with his or her appearance. This is particularly noticed in boys in western society where physical prowess is valued highly. Those who have reached puberty by about 13 or 14 years are found to have a more positive self-esteem than similar-aged boys who have not reached puberty. However, such early maturing boys experience more negative effects in that they are often more likely to smoke, drink, use drugs and be in trouble with the police (Duncan *et al.*, 1985). Peterson (1989) found the late maturing boys often end up as the most psychologically healthy group by the time they reach their final year.

Conversely, early maturing girls express more depression and anxiety and have lower self-esteem (Brooks-Gunn, 1983; Simmons and Blyth, 1988). They are also more likely to have conflict at home, drop out of school and have psychological problems (Caspi and Moffitt, 1991; Stattin and Magnusson, 1990).

Girls in western society are exposed to female models in books and the media who are extremely thin. This may have a bearing on the dissatisfaction with their appearance combined with a decline in self-esteem found in adolescent girls by Crawford and Ungar (1995). Girls gain more body fat in adolescence whereas boys develop muscle. Comparisons between early and late maturing girls find the former girls to have a less positive body image. The onset of menstruation is associated with discomfort and although early maturing girls often date earlier and more often than their later maturing counterparts they appear to suffer more from societal expectations and double standards associated with female sexuality and pregnancy (Gross, 1996).

A study of 3000 children aged 8 to 16 years by the American Association of University Women (1991) found that there was little difference between self-esteem of boys and girls at age eight, with both sexes being quite confident and assertive. This was found to drop considerably over the next eight years, as can be seen in figure 22.13.

The researchers found that 50 per cent of black girls did not have this 'dip' in self-esteem and this ethnic difference has also been supported in other studies (Bush and Simmons, 1987; Martinez and Dukes, 1987).

Carol Gilligan and her colleagues (1990) have tried to explain the loss of self-esteem in terms of a conflict between their own self-confidence and the realisation of how others in the culture see women. They can solve the problem by either standing up for themselves or discrediting their feelings. Gilligan suggested that black girls get more support from parents and relatives in being assertive and independent. By rejecting authority they can sometimes jeopardise their chances of academic success, whereas those who suffer self doubt have lowered self-esteem.

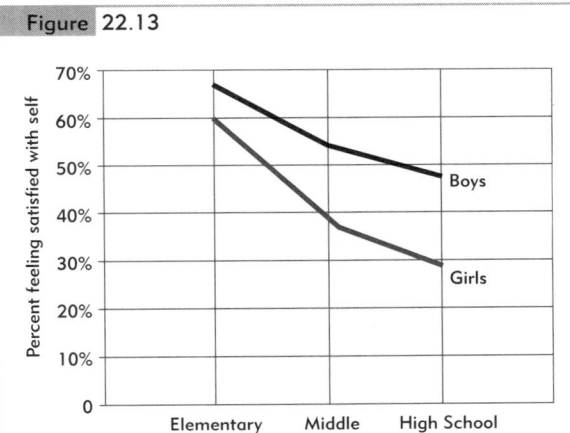

Figure 22.13

Gender differences in adolescent self-esteem
This graph shows the percentage of children in elementary school, junior high, and high school who agree with the statement, 'I'm happy the way I am.' White boys and girls do not differ much in childhood, but by high school there is a big gap between them on this question and on four others that reflect self-esteem (American Association of University Women, 1991).

The Peterson (1989) study did, however, find that early adolescence was trouble free for over half of those studied, with only 30 per cent having intermittent problems. Only 15 per cent were found to have ongoing problems which were still evident at the end of their school life.

■ Achieving identity in adolescence

As shown in figure 22.10, Erikson believed the most important task for the adolescent is to develop a consistent sense of personal identity when faced with the changes in social role and expectations of that time. Erikson's description of the kind of thinking required corresponds to Piaget's description of formal operational thinking. Support for this can also be seen in the descriptions given by adolescents in Damon and Hart's (1988) study (see pages 818–19 above).

The process of identity formation was seen by Erikson to be difficult not only for the adolescent but also for his or her family and friends, as the young person often takes out mixed feelings on others. Sometimes this can also be self-destructive.

> 'In general it is primarily the inability to settle on an occupational identity which disturbs young people. To keep themselves together they temporarily over identify, to the point of apparent complete loss of identity, with the heroes of cliques and crowds . . . . They become remarkably clannish, intolerant, and cruel in their exclusion of others who are 'different' in skin color or cultural background . . . and often in entirely petty aspects of dress and gesture arbitrarily selected as the signs of an in-grouper or out-grouper. It is important to understand . . . such intolerance as the necessary defense against a sense of identity confusion, which is unavoidable at [this] time of life.' (Erikson, 1980, pp. 97–8)

Erikson defined this period as an **identity crisis**, but he believed it to be part of healthy psychosocial development. Many roles need to be tried, modified and sometimes discarded in order to shape the integrated concept of self. In a complex society such as today, the adolescent has an almost infinite choice of how to behave and what to do in life. This identity may also be at different stages of development in various sexual, occupational and ideological areas of life. He saw this crisis to be resolved ideally in early or mid-twenties so that young adults have a coherent sexual identity and vocational choices. Until this conflict is resolved, Erikson saw the adolescent as having identity confusion.

Erikson's theory was very difficult to test empirically but it has been tested and extended by James Marcia (1966, 1980). Using semi-structured, open-ended interviews, he identified four patterns of coping with the task of identity formation:

- *Identity achievement* includes those who have passed through the period of identity crisis and are now actively pursuing their own goals.
- *Moratorium* includes the group still undergoing the identity crisis, actively seeking answers but still in conflict with others, such as parents or teachers; at best they can be seen as sensitive and open-minded, at worst self-righteous, indecisive and anxious.
- *Foreclosure* refers to those who have made a commitment but show no signs of having had an identity crisis; they give the impression that they would have problems if anything cropped up that may challenge their beliefs.
- *Identity diffusion* relates to Erikson's identity confusion category; they may have had an identity crisis or not but they still have no integrated sense of self; they cannot reach decisions and make a commitment.

Research supports both Erikson and Marcia in finding a consistent shift away from identity diffusion towards identity achievement with increasing age (see table 22.14). Alan Waterman (1985) summarised a number of studies and found the level of identity achievement to vary depending on the domain in question (lower for political ideology than for occupational choice). Extended education can extend foreclosure. Teenagers and young adults who are in identity achievement or moratorium rather than diffusion or foreclosure are:

- more independent and autonomous
- likely to gain higher grades in college
- more likely to reason at the level of formal operations

Table 22.14				
Age group	Identity achievement	Moratorium	Foreclosure	Identity diffusion
Primary school	5.2%	11.7%	36.6%	46.4%
Middle school	9.0	14.6	37.1	39.3
Secondary school	21.3	13.5	36.0	29.2
University	22.8	28.3	25.7	23.2
Postgraduate	39.7	15.5	31.3	13.5

The patterns of coping with identity formation identified by Waterman, 1985

Source: Waterman, 1985.

■ more successful in establishing satisfying intimate relationships.

La Voie (1976) found these groups to have higher self-esteem also. It is worth noting that all the participants in the studies Waterman analysed were in college or about to enter. Perhaps young people who go into work immediately will be able to form occupational identity earlier. They may have to work out some kind of personal identity sooner. It is possible that the whole conception of adolescent identity crisis is strongly influenced by the cultural assumptions in western societies where full adult status is postponed for almost a decade after puberty. The diversity which exists in our western culture may promote the identity crisis Erikson described.

The cultural context of self

Psychological research on the self has been criticised as being *ethnocentric* in being only relevant for cultures in which the focus is on the individual. Moscovici (1985) noted how the idea of an autonomous, free-standing, self-regulating 'individual' is a fairly recent western concept. Many cultural assumptions are made including the emphasis on 'survival of the fittest' which encompasses individuality and independence (Nobles, 1976). In cultures with a different historical background the idea of the self is very different.

Smith and Bond (1993) saw the need to distinguish between the independent and interdependent self. Many cultures, especially those characteristic of many Asian, Chinese and Japanese populations, can be seen to hold a collectivist perspective. This can be seen by looking at the Chinese word *ren* (meaning person) which refers to the way the person's behaviour corresponds (or not) to group standards. Similarly, Japanese children are taught early to think about how their behaviour will affect others, so the Japanese notion of self relates more to social interaction and social relationships. The African perspective promotes the '*survival of the tribe*' and encourages cooperation and collective responsibility, which leads to the development of an extended, collective self.

Recent western research acknowledges that members of family, neighbourhood or social class are a very important part of the self concept. Nicky Hayes (1993) suggested that the growth of many religious cults may be linked to an unconscious search for belonging, to help handle the psychological pressures of anonymity and alienation imposed by western industrial culture.

'Belonging to a religious organisation or to a cult, or even to a voluntary organisation, provides a substitute for the human contexts emphasised so much in other societies.' (Hayes, 1993, p. 17)

Johnston (1985) argued that the self is no longer seen as a 'unitary' phenomenon but rather as an interpersonal unit. Who we are and how we wish to be seen is seen linked to the culture into which we are socialised. The self concept appears to be an important influence on the individual's behaviour and how others respond. One of the elements is the confidence in our ability to think, choose and make appropriate decisions. Bandura (1977) labelled this component of the self concept as **self-efficacy**. When self-efficacy is low, there is likelihood of depression, helplessness and lower self-esteem. Helen Bee (1993) reminded us of the importance of such social cognition on the choices made by the child. A child who believes he or she cannot read will behave differently from a child who reads fluently. He may not try to improve for fear of failure. The child may result in later choices of activities which do not demand reading and later still may affect occupational choice. These beliefs can develop early in life and act as *self-fulfilling prophecies* – the expectations of success are of greater importance than the ability itself and the cycle of success or failure is begun. It is self perpetuating. We tend to live up to the expectations of others. Our expectations influence the way we behave towards people and this can lead them to behave in such a way that our original expectations are confirmed.

Selman (1980) suggested that the development of the self concept depends on experiences that occur in a social context. Self-efficacy can be a significant mediating concept on behaviour. The understanding of how well we perform in skills which we value develops in a social context often by comparison of our performance with others'. Social cognition can thus shape our choices and our responses to others.

Self-assessment questions

6   List the 'landmarks' which have been identified in the development of the self concept.

7   In your own words, define self–other orientation.

8   Distinguish between self concept and self-esteem.

9   Explain what is meant by acquiring a sense of self from symbolic interactionalism.

10 Outline the four patterns of coping with the task of identity formation suggested by Marcia.

(Suggested answers on page 845.)

The development of gender

Fundamental to our self concept is an awareness of being male or female. Developmental psychologists are concerned about how we come to achieve this awareness, what effect it has on others and how it influences our adult behaviour.

Sex and gender are terms which are often used interchangeably although sex is correctly limited to biological characteristics, whereas gender refers to attitudes and behaviours relating to maleness and femaleness, and which will be tolerated by the culture and society in which we live.

The extent to which biology and environment interact when we develop a **gender identity** in childhood, and later adopt a **gender role**, puts the issue of gender development firmly in the region of interaction between nature and nurture.

Gender identity

The term gender identity refers to the degree to which we perceive ourselves to be male or female. One of the first things to be determined about us is our sex. We become biologically male or female at conception, when a sperm from the male parent fertilises an ovum in the female parent. All normal ova and half of all sperm carry an X chromosome.

The other half of all normal sperm carry a Y chromosome. Inheriting a Y chromosome confers maleness on a future child. The Y chromosome controls supplies of androgens, which affect the development of primary sex organs and the brain in the male foetus. In the absence of androgens a female child will develop.

How soon do we become aware of our sex and develop a gender identity? If asked whether they are a boy or girl, most young children will understand the question and respond correctly, but they do not understand that their sex will not change as they grow older. Only those who have developed **gender constancy** will do this (Kohlberg, 1966). Gender constancy is described as the ability to know that sex is a biological characteristic which does not change with age or experience no matter what the person is wearing or however the person behaves.

Thompson (1975) demonstrated that children learn gender identity before gender constancy. Children of two years were able to separate pictures of men and women if these were stereotypically dressed, but they could not do the same for pictures of children – or predict their toy preferences. Three year olds could separate pictures of boys and girls, but did not know whether they would be a mother or father when they grew up. Lloyd and Duveen (1990) found that infants as young as 18 months could understand gender words such as 'mummy', 'daddy', 'girl' and 'boy' and pick out an appropriate photograph from a pair of male and female photographs.

Kohlberg showed a doll to children and asked them if it was possible for the doll to change sex. Children of four years said 'yes', the sex of the doll could change; children of six years said it could not. Kohlberg thought that this ability in the six year olds was comparable to their ability to conserve in other cognitive tasks.

Bem (1989) criticised Kohlberg's findings on the grounds that the children may not have understood that the experimenter wanted them to pretend that the doll is a stand-in for a real person. Support for gender constancy being achieved at an earlier age comes from a study carried out by Martin and Halverson (1983). They asked children 'If you wore (opposite-sex) clothes, what would you really be – a boy or girl?' Over 90 per cent of four to six year olds gave the correct answer. Also, Miller (1984) showed pictures of school children dressed in opposite-sex clothes, then asked classmates if the children were boys or girls. Virtually all the children between three and five years responded correctly. So it seems that gender identity is achieved early on in life, but the knowledge that gender remains constant only comes later.

Sex typing

Closely related to gender identity and gender constancy is the concept of **sex typing**. This refers to the acquisition of behaviours and characteristics that a culture considers sex-appropriate (Atkinson *et al.*, 1993).

When do you think sex typing begins? Does sex typing arise because girls and boys are innately different in their behaviour, or because they are taught to be different? Sex typing in children may begin soon after they are born. Right from the beginning, girls and boys are dressed differently and given different toys (Rheingold and Cook, 1975). This may be because parents are reacting to innate sex differences in behaviour (Maccoby, 1980). Luria and Rubin (1974) asked parents of new born babies, similar in weight and health, to describe their offspring as they would to a close friend. They described boys as being more alert, coordinated and stronger than girls, who they described as being smaller, softer and less attentive than boys. It seems, therefore, that adults have sex-typical expectations in their attitude to children.

Not only are boys perceived as being different to girls, but they are also treated differently. For example, Martyna and Watson (1976) found that participants treated a baby more roughly when they thought it was called David, than when they thought it was called Lisa.

Sex-typed interests are encouraged by parents, who are likely to give their children sex-typed toys to play with (Maccoby and Jacklin, 1974). Most psychologists believe differences arise from the different socialisation practices for girls and boys, and from the influence of gender stereotypes and gender roles. The power of such influences can be seen in research conducted by Etaugh and Liss (1992). Children of various ages from pre-school up to mid-teens were asked about choice of toys, identity of friends, jobs performed around the house and career choices. Sex-typing was shown in the boys' choice of male toys and girls' choice of female toys. Parents and friends more or less went along with their choices and these were the toys they received. Most of the children had same-sex friends. Household chores also were sex-typed with only 29 per cent of the boys having kitchen-related tasks. They were more likely to do clearing up tasks or have no household tasks at all! Career choices were also linked, with children who did more active work outside in the garden being more likely to show interest in occupations seen to be more 'male' oriented. Such evidence highlights the role of social and cultural factors in gender differences.

Children are also treated differently during play. For instance, Fagot (1978) demonstrated that fathers engage in rough and tumble play with boys but not with girls. They praise both boys and girls for taking part in sex-related activities and respond negatively to sex-inappropriate behaviour. Fathers are harder on boys to maintain sex-appropriate behaviour (Campbell, 1996).

Activity 11

So what are the characteristics that the sexes possess, and how do they differ? Write down your own feelings about what is right for each sex.

Maccoby and Jacklin (1974) carried out an ambitious review of over 2000 studies of sex differences in personality or cognitive abilities. By comparing studies with significant sex-related characteristics to those with non-significant findings, Maccoby and Jacklin identified only four areas where sex differences are significant. These are outlined in figure 22.15.

Although there was cross-cultural evidence in the literature which supported the findings of sex differences, there were criticisms. Some studies used smaller sample sizes and weaker statistical tests, yet Maccoby and Jacklin gave equal weight to all of them. This may have confounded the interpretation by under-representation of the truth. Also, studies which detect differences are more likely to be published than those which do not. This may confound the results by over-representation of the truth.

Another form of confounding may have been introduced by placing behaviours into broad behaviour categories, showing no sex differences. These may have masked more sensitive behaviours, for example, which did. The broad category of social sensitivity showed no sex differences, but the finer categories of nurturance and empathy may have done so. Few strong sex differences were reported by later studies which tried to avoid these problems (Eisenbert and Lennon, 1983).

Durkin (1995) found the literature on sex differences to be far from conclusive on aggressive and verbal ability. There is evidence of some superiority in males on spatial tasks but these differences are small and within-sex differences are quite large, with some boys scoring quite low and some girls scoring highly. Durkin cited Hyde et al.'s

22.15 Sex differences in intellectual abilities and personality identified by Maccoby and Jacklin (1974)

Aggression	– from age two boys are more physically aggressive than girls.	Mathematics	– from 10–11 boys perform better than girls on maths tests.
Verbal ability	– from 10–11 girls perform better than boys on tests of verbal ability.	Spatial abilities	– from 10–11 boys perform better than girls on tests of spatial abilities.

meta-analysis based on participants sampled from the general population rather than students. This analysis found mathematical differences between the sexes to be quite small and often in the opposite direction to the stereotype in that females scored higher. It was also found that mathematical differences are only noted in adolescence, suggesting the role of factors other than biological/genetic.

Bem (1974) thought that gender identity and sex typing should not be viewed as bipolar, that is, as exclusively male or female. She claimed that individuals may develop both masculine and feminine characteristics, such as toughness and warmth, yet still function effectively. Bem described such people as **androgynous** and showed them to be more psychologically healthy and well adjusted, with a higher self-esteem, than individuals rigidly typed as masculine or feminine (Bem, 1975, 1983).

Are mothers or fathers more involved in sex typing? Most people would probably say that mothers were more involved, since they normally have more contact with their children. However, Langlois and Downs (1980) found that fathers showed more disapproval and interfered more than mothers when their sons played with 'feminine' toys. They were less bothered when their daughters played with 'masculine' toys, but they still interfered more than mothers did. Langlois and Downs also found a similar kind of behaviour in boys, who will call other boys 'cissy' if they see them playing with girls' toys, crying or showing concern towards another person. Girls do not exhibit this kind of behaviour.

Being a cissy is perceived to be much worse than being a tomboy. Boys are frowned upon for playing 'like a girl', but girls are shown approval when playing 'like a boy'. This does not stop boys from playing with lipstick and dolls, but it does affect where and when they play with them. In an observational study, Kobasigawa *et al.* (1966) found that boys do play with 'taboo' toys but only when no one is watching, whereas girls play with what they want to, regardless of who is watching.

Ethological studies of children in their own homes, such as those of Judy Dunn (1988), show that at about the age of three years children begin to develop an understanding of many attributes of sex roles. Dunn reports on a three-year-old girl arguing with an older brother about who can play with a vacuum cleaner belonging to the girl. The boy has just repaired it. When asked by her mother if she will let her brother have a turn she replies, '*I have to do it*. Ladies *do it*' (Dunn, 1988, p. 57).

Paley (1984) noted a change in children's sex-typed behaviour and conceptions of sex roles in the years from three to six. At the age of four, boys seem less comfortable playing in the doll corner whereas girls spend more and more time in this area. By the age of five the girls often have to protect their domain from raids by the boys. The children now subscribe to the cultural definitions of male and female behaviour.

The naturalistic studies noted above are good at showing *what* develops but are less able to explain *how* the changes come about. To this end several experimental studies have tried to tease out cause and effect. Beverly Fagot and her colleagues (1986) presented children between 21 and 40 months of age with pairs of photographs of males and females. Children aged over 36 months were more likely to be able to identify males and females. More importantly, those of any age who could do this were more likely to play with children of their own sex.

In a follow-up study, Fagot and Leinbach (1991) found that mothers of children who could label pictures correctly were more likely to give them sex-related toys and express more traditional beliefs about sex roles. This was seen by Fagot and Leinbach as evidence of parental behaviour shaping their children's understanding. However, Fagot *et al.* (1986) found such children did not always choose **sex-stereotyped** toys when playing freely on their own. By four years children are aware of what are seen to be 'boys' things' and 'girls' things' and their choice becomes more sex-stereotyped (Leinbach and Fagot, 1989).

Gender role

Just as there are distinct sex-typed differences at ages two to three in the way boys engage in rough and tumble play and girls play with dolls, by adolescence there are distinct sex-stereotyped differences in the **gender roles** they adopt. These differences are reflected both in the way they behave and also in their interests and occupational choices.

In school, girls are encouraged to be 'nice', 'kind' and 'helpful' and follow the rules rather than being academic, achieving and successful (Walkerdine, 1990). Girls who challenge this are devalued, 'lacking femininity'. Dweck *et al.* (1978) found girls are led to believe that poor performance is due to lack of ability (an *internal* attribution) whereas it is seen to be due to *external* attribution in the boys ('not doing their homework').

Alice Eagly (1987) suggested that membership of sex groups creates role expectations with different occupational experiences and this is reflected in different skills and expectations about behaviour. Russo (1979) referred to the 'motherhood mandate', in that a woman not wanting children is seen as abnormal. Lee and Cowie (1986) found that most adolescent girls wish to marry and have children. Ussher (1989) also noted how many women suffering from post-natal depression feel they are not good enough mothers. Many researchers are now concerned that in many modern families the women are trying to run dual careers and dual lives, resulting in great costs and expectations – the 'Superwoman' syndrome.

Activity 12

Write down what you expect from typical males in the way of behaviour and occupational choices. Do the same for typical females.

Attitudes to gender role are changing, but traditionally typical males have been described as being assertive, independent, relatively aggressive and good at maths and sciences. Typical females have been described as dependent, relatively passive, emotional and good at verbal tasks (Ruble, 1983). This agrees with Maccoby and Jacklin's 1974 review findings (see page 830) and underlines just how pervasive the differentiation between the

sexes is. Occupational choices are expected to reflect these qualities, for instance boys are expected to become scientists or medical practitioners and girls to become secretaries or nurses. By studying developmental processes from different approaches, we stand to gain a better understanding of why this happens. It may also help us to understand atypical development such as transsexualism.

■ The biological approach to the development of gender role

The biological approach to the development of gender role regards people as the product of their genetic inheritance. It suggests that if genes can control prenatal differences in anatomy such as facial features and sex, they may also control psychological differences such as dominance, aggression and interest in infants.

Evidence does suggest that males and females do differ in brain structure. Several studies have shown gender differences in the corpus callosum (Clarke *et al.*, 1989). The corpus callosum refers to the 200 million nerve fibres which link the two hemispheres of the brain. Hinse *et al.* (1992), using the brain-imaging technique of Magnetic Resonance Imaging (MRI), looked at the correlation of the size of certain part of the corpus callosum and cognitive abilities of the 28 women involved. They found a significant positive relationship between the size of the parts of a corpus callosum region and the women's score on a verbal test; conversely the score of the language lateralisation measure was negatively correlated to an area found to be larger in men. These findings need to be treated cautiously as correlational findings cannot specify causality, but they are interesting in demonstrating the relationship of brain structure and sex differences in cognitive processes and behaviour.

Animal studies have demonstrated that exposure of a developing brain to male sex hormones has long-term effects. Carlson (1995) found such hormones altered the development of the brain and later behaviour. It has been suggested that exposure to different patterns of hormones during development may result in differences in the human brain (Hofman and Swaab, 1991). There is little evidence so far on the effects of such brain differences on gender behaviour. Typically, animal experiments use rats to investigate the influence of hormones appropriate for the opposite sex. The hormones are injected at a sensitive developmental period and most animals later exhibit behaviour characteristics of the opposite sex with regard to aggression, parenting, rough and tumble play, and mating. We cannot be sure, however, that what applies to one species also applies to another and ethical considerations prevent similar experimentation in humans.

There is, however, some support for these findings from reports of naturalistic studies. For example, Money and Erhardt (1972) and Hines (1982) studied children with congenital adrenogenital syndrome (CAS). They had been exposed to hormones appropriate to the opposite sex when their mothers received hormonal treatment during pregnancy. Females exposed to male hormones *in utero* later exhibited more masculine gender role behaviour than a control group who were not exposed to opposite-sexed hormones. Interpretation of these findings is not as straightforward as you might think. For instance, the children were often born with gonadal abnormalities and the exhibited behaviour may have arisen from the child's own, her parents', and even possibly the investigators' reactions to the more masculine appearance.

Previously, Money *et al.* (1975) had reported that sex typing was important to the way individuals viewed themselves. They studied pairs of individuals with CAS who had been brought up as different sexes, but were matched for external genital appearance.

Diamond (1965, 1968) criticised these studies on the grounds that

■ Money and Erhardt had not sufficiently taken into account the extent to which innate differences have to be overcome.

■ Also, their participants were atypical and results may not necessarily apply to the general population.

Requests for sex changes among those with adrenogenital syndrome are, however, very rare (Money, 1971). This is probably due to the fact that the human nervous system is so flexible that it can adjust to environmental influences in early childhood (Money and Erhardt, 1972), i.e., the effects of biological sex differentiation can be overridden by the effects of learning.

Berenbaum and Hines (1992) assessed differences in children's preferences for toys: traditional male toys, traditional female toys and toys seen to be gender neutral. Children were aged between three and eight years and included girls with CAS. The researchers were interested in which toys would be chosen with open access to all toys. CAS girls were found to choose more traditional boys' toys than girls who did not have CAS. It is

Case study – a normal twin boy raised as a girl

Money (1974) reported the case of normal monozygotic twin boys. One of the boys had his penis burned off in a circumcision accident. His parents decided to raise him as a girl and accordingly dressed him in girls' clothes and treated him as if he was female. At 17 months he went through an operation for sex-change and at puberty underwent hormonal treatment. In his early years, he responded to this treatment by showing interest in clothes, cleanliness and housework. In fact, apart from some tendency towards becoming a tomboy at the age of five, he behaved very much like a girl is 'expected' to do. The 'normal' twin developed as a boy is 'expected' to do, adopting a rough and tumble approach to play and showing no interest in clothes, housework and washing. Relationships between the twins were such that the normal one took on a protective role and the damaged one the role of a 'fussy little mother'.

possible that the CAS girls had been encouraged to play more with these toys by parents because of their more 'masculine' characteristics. However, the researchers found no such differential treatment to exist in this study. The evidence is seen to support the finding that biological processes play a significant role in development.

In the above case study it is impossible to separate out the extent to which the physical appearance of the children influenced their sex-typing, and how much of it was influenced by their hormones. Also, biological intervention was not totally responsible for the girlish behaviour of the damaged twin; sex-typed learning played a part as well. The same problems of interpretation underlie most of the studies using this approach. Biosocial theory tries to address these problems.

■ Biosocial theory of the development of gender role

Biosocial theory of the development of gender role seeks explanations from an interactionist point of view. The belief is that individuals develop a gender role which is consistent with the way their carers brought them up. At the same time, it suggests that carers are influenced by the children, both by the way they look and in the way that they behave.

What are the things you find attractive in a baby? Does the sex of the baby make any difference? It is perhaps easier to feel attracted towards a baby who is cooing and chuckling than towards a baby who is yelling, or even perhaps towards one who is always asleep. It is possible to agree then that we treat babies who attract us in a different way from those who do not. Thus, in a general way, children influence their own development. Sex-related differences are just as important as other characteristics in this respect. For instance, at three weeks, boys are more irritable than girls (Moss, 1967). A biosocialist might interpret this as an example of sex-typing brought about by the interaction of the baby's and mother's responses to each other. Mother may not respond immediately to a baby's cries (boys don't cry!) and the baby becomes irritable because his needs are not met.

According to Money and Erhardt, there is considerable flexibility in the way children categorise themselves in their early years, but these years also constitute a sensitive period, since reassigning sex after gender identity has been established (see page 829) can result in extreme psychological disturbance.

Diamond (1982) followed up the 'girl' twin reported by Money (1974) in the study on page 833 and found that she was an unhappy adolescent, uncertain about her gender. She looked rather masculine and envied the boys' type of life. This was seen by Diamond to demonstrate the strength of biological factors.

More recently, evolutionary psychologists have suggested that it is the adaptive processes males and females have undergone in the course of evolution that have led to gender differences, especially in relation to reproduction. Buss (1995) suggested that women need to identify and attract a male to invest his resources in her and her children. Men need to identify and attract a fertile female willing to give birth to his child. Kimura (1987) also suggested that brain differences have resulted from the evolution of the hunter-gatherer male and the female working nearer to home due to child-bearing restrictions. This could explain the improved spatial abilities of males who had to learn to keep track of where they were when hunting so they could return home. They also had to develop coordination of body movements to aim and throw in hunting.

However speculative Kimura's and Buss' accounts can be seen to be, they do provide a biological, evolutionary approach to understanding gender differences.

■ The psychoanalytic theory of the development of gender role

The psychoanalytic theory of the development of gender role argues that children learn about their gender in the phallic stage of psychosexual development, when pleasure is derived from stimulation of the sex organs. Children learn that not everyone is like themselves in body outline. They also begin to have sexual desires for the opposite-sexed parent. This forms the basis of the Oedipus and Electra complexes and the beginning of **identification** with the same-sexed parent. Gender role develops from the resolution of this inner conflict at this stage.

Sex-appropriate behaviours are produced as children identify with the same-sex parent. Fathers may have an important role to play in this process. Fathers pay special attention to sons when they are about two years old and interaction increases between them. This results in the boys channelling their attention towards their father's behaviour. The same does not happen with daughters. Fathers are more likely to withdraw their attention from girls, who subsequently channel their attention towards their mother's behaviour (Lamb, 1979).

What do you think happens if the father is absent? If the father is present for the first four years, there is no adverse effect on gender role. However, if the father is absent in the first four years, boys become more dependent on peers, less assertive and less interested in physical activities. Girls find it difficult to make heterosexual relationships when they reach puberty (Hetherington, 1972). Research on alternative family life-styles shows that children of homosexual single mothers develop gender roles just as normally as do children of heterosexual single mothers (Green, 1978). Also, children reared by lesbian parents do not differ from those reared in homes with a heterosexual single parent when it comes to gender role and sexual orientation (Golombok *et al.*, 1983). In fact, poor relationships are much more likely to affect gender role than sexual orientation (West, 1977).

Many children today will experience their parents going through a divorce before they are 16. Some researchers have looked at this in relation to psychoanalytic theory. If Freud is correct, the impact of divorce should be greatest if the divorce occurred before or during the phallic stage when the identification process requires the presence of both parents (see page 806 for information on the Oedipal complex). If the children stay with the mother after the divorce then this should be worse for the boys as they no longer have a male role model and may end up with a confused identity. This latter hypothesis gains support from studies such as Hetherington (1989) and Kline *et al.* (1989), who show boys having increased behaviour and study problems. Pre-school children, however, are generally shown to have no more lasting negative effects than children from other ages, thus challenging Freudian theory. Wallerstein (1984,

1989), in a longitudinal study, found that although children under the age of five were most overtly upset at the time, they showed the best long-term adjustment.

Freud's theory assumes that gender role identification occurs indirectly in that the children have unconscious conflict between their desires and fears and try to resolve these by identification. The social-learning theorists see the process of identification to be simply a matter of observation and imitation.

■ Social learning theory of the development of gender role

Social learning theory of the development of gender role seeks description through reinforcement, modelling and observation. The belief is that they are no special phychological processes or principles needed to explain gender development (Mischel, 1966; Bandura *et al.*, 1986). By observation, children develop hypotheses about what is appropriate for themselves (Perry and Bussey, 1984). Gender role is seen to be achieved by shaping towards male or female gender appropriate behaviours, for example boys are reinforced for aggression and punished for dependency, whereas girls are punished for aggression and rewarded for dependency.

Sex-appropriate behaviour can also be learned from observing and imitating same sex models. Turner (1995) noted such direct tuition whereby sex-appropriate behaviour is reinforced or rewarded and sex-inappropriate behaviour is punished. Hoyenga and Hoyenga (1993) suggested that such practice and training in gender-appropriate tasks will improve performance on them.

Albert Bandura (1969, 1986) noted that the ability to learn from observation is dependent on several factors:

- *availability* – the behaviour to be observed must be available either directly in the environment or indirectly through books, magazines or televisions
- *attention* – children can only learn if they pay attention to the model and understand the main features of the behaviour; often children need to see complex behaviour more than once to determine its significant features

- *memory* – only when the observation is labelled will the behaviour be effective and memorable; this is seen by Bandura to increase with the acquisition of language and knowledge of the basic social categories
- *motor reproduction process* – only if the behaviour observed is possible in the child's repertoire will it be copied; sometimes the child has not developed the skills required and will not attempt to copy the behaviour
- *motivation* – something must be motivating the child, so imitation will only occur if it is seen to be important or rewarding to the child.

Research has shown that parents do seem to reinforce sex-typed activities very early in the child's life. Fagot and Hagan (1991) and Lytton and Romney (1991) found that at as early as 18 months parents buy different toys and respond more positively when their sons and daughters play with sex-appropriate toys. This can be seen particularly with boys. Fathers and other males seem more disturbed by 'girlish' behaviour shown by boys (Siegal, 1987). This is not seen as clearly in the mother's behaviour. Women appear to be more tolerant of cross-sex behaviour. This may explain why the male stereotype develops earlier than the female stereotype.

Fagot and Leinbach (1989) carried out a longitudinal study into sex-typed behaviour in relation to parent's behaviour. They looked at five behaviour patterns seen to distinguish between boys and girls:

- rough physical play
- male-typed toy play
- female-typed toy play
- communication
- aggression

They found that before children could label properly (18 months) the children did not differ in the noted categories, but both fathers and mothers of the children who were to become early labellers responded to sex-appropriate behaviour more positively. Fathers of the potential early labellers were found to have more traditional attitudes towards the role of women and child-rearing. By 27 months, when about half the children could label correctly, the early labelling children of both sexes played with more sex-appropriate toys.

Turner and Gervai (1995), in studies of older pre-school children and children who have entered school in Hungary and the UK, have found that boys who had parents with more traditional attitudes to sex-typed behaviour behaved in a more gender-typical way. Their findings showed more consistency of such effects on boys than girls. Fathers who were more 'feminine' (expressive) in personality had children who showed less self-assertion, showing off and play-fighting characteristic of 'male' behaviour. Also, fathers who were more involved in child-care and shared domestic chores had children who were less stereotypical and sons who were more likely to play with dolls and do more art work. Turner (1995) suggested that the findings demonstrate that parents who are gender-typed may teach gender identity by labelling and reinforcement more consistently than less gender-typed parents. Once this gender identity is achieved by the child, self-socialisation will influence their gender-typed preferences and behaviour with increasing pressure from peers.

Social learning theories emphasise the influence of the situation and circumstances in shaping and maintaining behaviour. They support the view that as situations and circumstances change, so do the behaviours in question. Eleanor Maccoby (1990), reviewing many studies, found that boys and girls do vary in gender-appropriate behaviour, often depending on the gender of the child they are playing with. Pre-school girls are very seldom passive when playing with other girls – such behaviour is reserved for play with boys. Maccoby suggested this is because the boy usually dominates in this situation unless there is an adult to intervene. Social learning theorists distinguish between acquisition of the behaviour in childhood and its maintenance in adult life (Lott and Moluso, 1993). This allows for flexibility in behaviour and can explain why a child who is strongly sex-typed in behaviour in childhood may become less so in adulthood, due to careers or relationships which allow for such. The transition can sometimes be seen to be quite painful as the growing adolescent or adult becomes torn between the expected behaviour of the family or culture and the gender rules of the larger society. If you have ever been the only female or male in a group of the opposite sex you may have felt that your sex, because of your singularity, is often what is noticed by everyone and used to explain your behaviour (Geis, 1993; Kantor, 1977, 1993).

Activity 13

Either in small groups or alone, consider the following:

a   How might parents encourage sex-appropriate behaviour and discourage sex-inappropriate behaviour?

b   Who, other than parents, are the role models for boys and girls?

c   Can you name any current 'stars' (sports, film, TV or others) who may be chosen as models by young children?

(Suggested answers on page 845.)

Cross-cultural evidence from Whiting and Edwards (1988) also supported a social-learning view in finding that in most cultures girls and boys early in life choose to play and interact more with their own sex. This would provide more opportunities for reinforcement of same-sex behaviour. By age five this choice is very marked. It is shown only to break down in adolescence, led by the girls (Campbell, 1996). This behaviour is very resistant to intervention by adults and scientific manipulation (for example, token economy experiments). The social world of boys and girls is very different with:

■ boys meeting in larger groups, involved more in rough and tumble play, leaders issuing commands, rules binding (not to be broken), competitive

■ girls playing more in dyads and triads, having more friendship networks with grooming contact (e.g. stroking), leader makes suggestions, criticise in more constructive ways, more 'turn-taking' in speech, cooperative rather than competitive, rules are arbitrary with appeals for reciprocity and a striving for equality.

Another cross-culture study by John Williams and Deborah Best (1990) found how widely these stereotypes exist. In all the 24 countries in the study

the children aged between five and eight years had less strong gender stereotypes than the older people in the society, but in every country the qualities associated with men were stronger than those associated with women, and this was characteristic of adults *and* children. In virtually all countries the male stereotype was stronger than the female. Some differences did emerge, showing that some children learn stereotypes earlier in some countries than others, but the patterns were found to increase with age in all cultures.

Many researchers see such effects demonstrating more of a biological influence because they occur so early, before verbal and cultural stereotypes could have had that effect. Campbell (1996) noted robust evidence of babies as young as seven months preferring their own sex, even before adults can note the difference!

Boys are encouraged more in physical activities than girls and adults offer sex-linked toys to children (Smith and Lloyd, 1978). When it comes to schoolwork, parents also have different expectations of achievement from children. For example, they are likely to offer girls help with maths but encourage boys to do it themselves.

■ The role of the media

Much research has been devoted to the role of television on the development of gender role behaviour. Eysenck (1996) noted that children between the ages of four and 11 watch an average of about three hours a day, with some children watching considerably more. It would certainly be surprising if this did not have some affect on the way they viewed sex-typed behaviour. Research in the area is mainly correlational due to the difficulties in performing controlled experimental research and the question of ecological validity of such. One natural experiment which looked at sex-role stereotypes was undertaken by Williams (1986) in Canada. He was able to compare television viewing in three different areas:

■ *Notel* had no TV channels available
■ *Unitel* had one TV channel available
■ *Multitel* had four TV channels available.

Sex-role stereotyping was found to be greater in the areas receiving TV channels than in the Notel area. Notel started to receive access to one TV channel during the two-year study and the sex-role stereotyping was found to increase in the Notel area.

Several studies have noted similar effects related to television viewing. Manstead and McCulloch (1981) found that stereotypes on television often do not reflect reality. In their study of TV advertisements they found men and women to be presented in their traditional role:

- Males were portrayed as powerful, dominant, rational, interested in DIY, more likely to be the central character and be the 'voice-over'.
- Women were portrayed as mothers and housewives, users of products rather than sources of information about them.

These stereotypes are found in all programmes, even in children's programmes such as *Sesame Street* and *Mr. Roger's Neighbourhood*, with males being seen as more dynamic and women as of higher socio-intellectual status. Wober *et al.* (1997), in a UK study of children aged between five and 12, found that when children were asked which jobs they had seen characters undertaking on television, they noted men in more occupational roles and women more in service industries or taking care of infants. Their own choices of careers seemed to be along the lines of those they had noted observed.

Content analysis on obituaries of women in senior management in Australia and Germany from the years 1974, 1980, 1986 was undertaken by Kirchler (1992). Words describing male and female managers were placed into 53 gender-related categories and sexual stereotyping was found to differentiate the male and female managers. Males were described as intelligent, experienced and unselfish opinion-leaders. Conversely, the female managers were described as adorable and likeable in the earlier texts. By 1986 females were described as more courageous and more highly committed than their male counterparts, but the males were still reported as more knowledgeable and expert in their field. Many studies have shown little difference to exist between female and male managers, so Kirchler concluded that these differences are the result of gender stereotyping. Although perceptions of female managers are changing, Kirchler noted that their success is often

attributed to unstable factors such as effort or motivation, whereas the success of male managers is attributed to more stable characteristics such as expertise or knowledge. This covert stereotyping may be acting to undermine women managers' chances of success.

Many children's programmes on television project sex-stereotyped behaviour: boys being portrayed in active, problem-solving roles, showing courage and daring, girls typically portrayed as more passive, avoiding danger and watching someone else (a male) achieve (Sternglanz and Serbin, 1974). Book characters show similar qualities.

Weitzman(1972), a prize-winning author, noted that males outnumber females 11–1 in books and more recent research notes that this discrepancy still exists (Huston, 1983; Huston *et al.*, 1990). Huston *et al.* found that males outnumber females by two to one or three to one on most programmes except commercials, but in the latter case they were usually the 'voice-over'. Women are more often shown in home settings or romantic situations whereas men are more often found in work settings, with cars or playing sports. Similarly, men are depicted as problem-solvers, aggressive, active and independent compared with the more emotional, passive and deferential women. Women were more likely to be seen as the sex object or the handmaiden.

Activity 14

There are several activities involving content analysis of the media and books/newspapers similar to some noted above that you might find interesting. These can be undertaken alone, but as a great deal of data is available for analysis you might like to undertake the research in a group. A couple of ideas are suggested below:

1 Videotape a number of TV advertisements (or a range of programmes). Watch those shown before 9 pm which are more likely to be watched by children. Choose the categories which distinguish between the characteristics of males and females (see research noted above for ideas).

Activity 14 cont'd

2   Obtain copies of children's comics and magazines. How are the males and females portrayed? Choose the characteristics noted in previous research above. In this case you may find the activities and interests seen to be gender-appropriate interesting.

You will need to think carefully about your sampling here. Rather than sampling participants, you are sampling programmes, books and magazines. You will still need to obtain a representative sample.

If you are undertaking this activity with others, you will also need to carry out a pilot study to check inter-rater reliability.

Showing children television programmes in which gender-role stereotypes have been reversed, such as a girl being elected president, has been successful to some extent in changing conventional sex-stereotyping expectations (Davidson *et al.*, 1979). However, real-life experiences have more influence. Cordua *et al.* (1979) produced films which depicted characters in unconventional sex-stereotyped occupations. The part of doctors were taken by women and the part of nurses by men. Afterwards, the children were shown pictures of the actors and questioned about the part they played in the film. Children said what they expected to see. Only those who had experienced women doctors and male nurses in their own lives were likely to respond correctly; the other children tended to reassign the sexes to their traditional roles.

Turner (1995) pointed out that children of both sexes are exposed to more female models in their early years, and yet boys obtain strong sex-types at a very early age. Turner and other researchers feel that although children will imitate a model if they see the behaviour to be appropriate, social learning theory alone cannot explain gender role development. It is necessary but not sufficient to explain the behaviour. There is less sex-typed reinforcement than some of the research leads one to expect and probably not enough to explain the very early discrimination that children appear to make based on gender characteristics. Even when children have parents who treat sons and daughters very similarly, the gender labels and same-sex playmates are noticeable. Even if we have evidence that parents treat their sons and daughters differently, we cannot be sure of the *direction* of such behaviour. Most of the studies are correlational and as such cannot determine cause and effect. It is always possible that the children's gender-typed behaviour is causing the parents to respond differently (Turner, 1995). It is known that boys play with dolls less than girls and it may well be that the parents are reinforcing preferences rather than (or as well as) creating them. Turner reports evidence showing such effects to occur in that fathers of girls score higher on feminine scales than do fathers of boys and this correlated with their attitudes to child-rearing. Perhaps, as Lytton and Romney (1991) suggested, the adults' expectations and reinforcement builds on the children's own preferences in a cummulative way. In this way the effects are amplified.

Social learning theory may have something to offer in the way of explaining the development of gender role, but it also has drawbacks. A serious problem is that it cannot define one of its central concepts – reward or reinforcement. What is reinforcing for one two-year-old girl is often different from another. Bandura's factors (see page 835) help explain this to some extent in allowing for the role of cognitive variables, but these are seen to be of secondary importance. They do not explain where these concepts come from. Social learning theory assumes that children are passive recipients of their environmental forces. Parents, relatives, peers and society, as well as books and the media, all 'do it' to them. This does not agree with the belief that children form their own hypotheses about what is, and is not, appropriate for themselves in the way of gender role (see next page). What does uphold this belief is the fact that the majority of four and five year olds believe there should be no sex-typed restrictions of choice of occupation, whereas six to seven year olds believe there should be (Damon, 1977). Cognitive-developmental theory may be able to explain this.

Cognitive-developmental theory of the development of gender role

Cognitive-development theory sees the child to be actively trying to make sense of the social world. The development of gender role was described by Kohlberg (1966), who thought that the most important factor in the development of gender is the child's level of cognitive understanding. Between two and seven years children learn gender constancy (see page 829). Early on in life, children are labelled as 'boy' or 'girl' and this leads to the child's perception of self as masculine or feminine. This perception adds to their self concept. Together with a growing knowledge and understanding of gender, it is critical to sex-typing by directing and organising thoughts and activities. A girl might say (at two and a half years) 'I am a girl and therefore I must behave like a girl.' What is important here is the motivation to behave consistently with one's own gender identity. This is not done to achieve rewards, as the social learning theorists suggest. Children willingly take on the task of sex-typing both themselves and their peers.

Kohlberg saw children developing gender identity over a number of years. This then leads them to imitate same-sex models and undergo 'self-socialisation' (Turner, 1993), so they find it rewarding to behave in line with their gender identity. This gender concept means we classify ourselves as male or female and realise our gender is constant over time. Many studies have supported Kohlberg in finding that children do seem to be more aware of same-sex models after they understand constancy (Frey and Ruble, 1992). However, sex-typed behaviour is displayed by most children before they reach their second birthday, many years earlier than the cognitive-developmentalists believe they have gender constancy. As was seen in criticisms of Piaget's theory of cognitive development, Kohlberg's theory underestimates the pre-operational child's potential level of understanding.

Kohlberg believes that gender development is linked to children's moral realism. They see themselves as having a moral obligation to adapt to the physical realities of their identity. They see this as a 'divine or moral law'.

Activity 15

Look back to Kohlberg's theory of moral development and use it to explain why children of six to seven believe that people should take up sex-typical occupations.

(Suggested answers on page 845.)

At this age Kohlberg describes children's understanding of right as 'people behaving in ways which uphold the views of society'. Sex-stereotypical occupations are accepted through observational learning and these are incorporated into children's cognitive understanding of what is appropriate for each.

The cognitive-developmental theory is currently the most influential theory of gender identity and sex-typing (Atkinson *et al.*, 1993), but there are limitations. For example:

- It cannot explain individual differences in gender role development, such as all the variations in gender role between extreme feminism and extreme masculinism.
- It can explain how we come to have an understanding of gender, but it does not explain how we come to do so.
- It fails to explain why children organise their concepts around being male or female in the first place. Why is sex chosen rather than other potential categories in defining self?

Sandra Bem (1985) and others suggested that gender is seen to be central to our understanding of ourselves and becomes on 'organising principle' for the child trying to look at reality through the 'lenses of that culture' (Atkinson *et al.*, 1996).

Gender schema theory of the development of gender role

Gender schema theory of the development of gender role was developed by Bem (1981, 1985, 1993) as a socio-cultural approach to psychological development. Bem believes that children are active agents in their own socialisation. She noted that most cultures elaborate sex differences and these infiltrate into practically every aspect of life. Children need to learn the rules and norms of their own culture. In fact, the distinction between the sexes is so important that it should become a 'set of lenses for looking at everything'. Of all the possible choices children have for behaviour (for example, which toy to play with, who to play with), culture emphasises the rule to consider 'first and foremost whether the toy or activity is appropriate to your sex'. By looking through the lenses in this way, children build up a set of *gender schema* against which they evaluate their behavioural alternatives.

Bem believes that we are typically unaware of these schema (in the same way that we look through glasses, not at them). They are not taught directly; the lesson is embedded in the cultural practices of daily life. For instance, those who prefer to change traditional sex stereotypes and advocate sex equality still focus on sex. Children still build their gender role round maleness or femaleness. They still judge their self-worth in terms of 'Am I masculine or feminine enough?'

As in social learning theory, gender schema theory views sex-typing as neither inevitable nor unmodifiable. Children become sex-typed because sex happens to be a major focus around which their culture chooses to organise its view of reality. If the culture alters in this respect, so will the children (Atkinson *et al.*, 1996).

Gender schemas change as they accommodate new experiences but continue to influence actions and beliefs. Situational experiences can also explain why even gender schema will not stop someone behaving in a way seen appropriate for that occasion. For example, a male may behave in a 'caring' manner with an elderly relative and a female may take over a meeting in a more 'masculine' way if the situation demanded this. Many researchers have found the situation can predict the behaviour more consistently than knowing the gender of the people concerned (Eagly and Wood, 1991; Lott and Maluso, 1993).

Many psychologists feel that the social worlds of boys and girls are so very different. The amount of time spent within the peer groups makes this a strong influence on gender-typing. As noted elsewhere, children choose to spend a great deal of time playing with children of the same sex. Girls tend to form close intimate friendships whereas boys play in more hierarchically organised groups, the former more concerned with sharing confidences and the latter with status and dominance. This segregation of play may result in different interaction skills developing for boys and girls. Figure 22.16 shows such gender differences in terms of different social worlds.

22.16 Gender differences in communication patterns

Maltz and Borker (1982) studied gender differences in communication patterns. In friendly conversations, men were more likely to interrupt, challenge, ignore, respond unethusiastically and make declarations of fact or opinion. Women were more likely to ask questions, maintain the flow of the conversation, use more personal pronouns and show silent forms of protest when interrupted.

Maltz and Borker argue that these differences are not simply an expression of male power, but that men and women differ in their ideas of what a friendly conversation entails. They propose that such differences can be understood by thinking of men and women as occupying separate sub-cultures, and that such differences arise because of skills learnt during interactions with peers in childhood when children spend the vast majority of their time in single-sex groups.

To summarise: boys in all-boy groups, compared with girls in all-girl groups, are more likely to interrupt one another, use commands, threats, boasts, refuse to comply with another child's demand, more often give information, heckle a speaker, tell jokes or stories, 'top' someone else's story.

Girls in all-girl groups are more likely than boys to express agreement with what the speaker has just said, pause to give another girl a chance to speak, or, when starting to speak, acknowledge a point previously made by another speaker.

Thus, amongst boys, speech serves largely egotistic functions – to assert status and to attract and keep an audience – whereas, amongst girls, it serves more socially-binding functions – to negotiate and maintain relationships.

Source: Turner (1995, p. 44).

Turner (1993) suggests that social categorisation helps the children make sense of their social world. Gender schema demonstrates how one of the first distinctions made by children is male versus female, and the social relations between boys and girls can be seen in terms of in-group and out-group relations. Individuals see themselves in terms of their own sex group and favour the group. They exaggerate the differences between the groups and the status of someone in the group could be enhanced by discriminating against members of the other out-group. This can often be seen in young boys and girls insulting the opposite sex. In this way social stereotypes can be seen to amplify and distort such differences and form the basis of gender differences observed in adults.

The processes of gender development can be seen to require the integration of biological factors, socialisation, and the more active role of the child's own cognitive processes concerning sex-appropriate behaviour. Sex hormones predispose boys and girls to behave in certain ways and these are 'honed' by the socio-cultural expectations of parents and others seen to be important by the child.

'In order to understand gender identity more fully scientists will need to integrate findings from diverse fields of research not only within psychology, but also from biology, anthropology and sociology.' (Turner, 1995, p. 46)

Self-assessment questions

11 Note two possible factors which may help maintain sex stereotyping in female occupational choice.

12 Outline the principal characteristics of the various theories of gender role development.

13 Identify what constitutes your own gender role, and that of friends. Which theory (or theories) can explain the information best?

14 What contribution have cross-cultural studies made to our understanding of gender stereotyping?

15 According to Bem, how do children build up their gender schema?

(Suggested answers on page 846.)

Unit summary

- Moral development is concerned with how we acquire the rules and principles of social behaviour, which distinguish right from wrong, including *affective, cognitive* and *behavioural* components.

- Freud saw moral behaviour to be controlled by the superego, part of the personality, including the ego ideal and the conscience. The superego is seen to develop normally at the end of the phallic stage when the child identifies with the same-sex parent.

- *Cognitive-developments* emphasise the role of the child's changing understanding with age. Piaget's stage theory of intellectual development is seen as the cornerstone of moral development. Kohlberg later developed and extended this theory.

- Several studies support broadly similar progression through the early stages but less evidence exists for the later stages of Kohlberg's theory, perhaps reflecting cultural and gender bias.

- *Social learning theorists* note the influence of vicarious learning of morals from role models.

- The role of social cognition challenges the early theories by highlighting the social learning of context-specific behaviour, involving experience in relationships and moral problems.

Summary cont'd.

- Although there is no consensus about the definition of self, it is seen to include the affective, cognitive and behavioural components seen in the development of morals.

- Studies show an awareness of self emerges during the infant's second year. Children's self descriptions become more comparative during middle childhood, less focused on external characteristics and more on internal qualities (as shown by the Twenty Statements Test).

- The influence of social factors on the developing self have been highlighted, such as social comparisons and social roles. The social construction of self was seen by Mead to be a fundamental building block in human development. We take on the role symbolically, to imagine how others will react to us, and in this way learn the perspective of another in symbolic interactionism.

- Development in puberty has been shown to have long-lasting effects for early and late-maturing boys.

- The psychosocial conflict of identity crisis is seen by Erikson to be a healthy stage of normal development in adolescence, and the pattern of coping with the task of identity formation has been outlined by Marcia.

- Psychological research on the self has been criticised as being ethnocentric, in only being relevant for cultures in which the focus is on the individual. Many cultures, such as some of the Asian, Chinese and Japanese, can be seen to have a collectivist perspective.

- Self-efficacy can also be seen as a significant mediating concept on behaviour, demonstrating how social cognition can shape our choices and responses to others.

- Fundamental to our self concept is an awareness of being male or female. Gender identity is achieved early in life, but knowledge that gender remains constant comes later.

- Sex-typing, the acquisition of behaviours and characteristics seen to be sex-appropriate in a culture, begins early in life and is reinforced by parents and society. By adolescence there are distinct sex-stereotyped differences in the gender roles adopted.

- The *biological approach* tries to explain gender differences by showing differences in brain structures and sex hormones. Biosocial theory extends this view to include the interaction of social factors on an underlying biological predisposition.

- *Psychoanalytic theory* sees gender role developing during the phallic stage through identification with the same-sex parent. Freud's theory assumes that gender role identification occurs indirectly through the unconscious conflicts of children between their desires and fears which they try to resolve by identification.

- *Social learning theorists* see the process of identification to be simply a matter of observation and imitation. Sex-appropriate behaviour can be learned from observing and imitating same-sex models. The role of cognition is seen as a contributing factor.

- The role of the media has been highlighted with support from correlational studies which cannot determine cause and effect.

- *Cognitive-developmental theory* sees the child to be actively trying to make sense of his or her world. This suggests we classify ourselves as male or female and realise our gender is constant over time. However, this fails to explain why children organise their concepts around being male or female in the first place.

- Sandra Bem is one of many who suggest that gender is so central to our understanding of ourselves that it becomes an organising principle.

- Children see their culture through the transparent lenses of that culture. *Gender schema theory* is a socio-cultural view of how children view their world and learn to behave appropriately, involving social categorisation.

- Explaining gender development requires the integration of biological factors, socialisation, and the more active role of the child's own cognitive processes concerning sex-appropriate behaviour.

Terms to define

androgynous
categorical self
ego-ideal
existential self
gender constancy
gender identity
gender roles

identification
identity crisis
self-efficacy
sex-stereotyped
sex typing
superego
vicarious learning

Further reading

Bee, H (1995) *The Developing Child*, 7th edn, Harper Collins, New York.

An excellent text covering the topics of the current unit in more detail than space allows here.

Cole, M and Cole, S R (1993) *The Development of Children*, 2nd edn, Freeman, New York.

See especially chapter 10, 'Social Development in Early Childhood', and chapter 14, 'The Social Relations of Middle Childhood'.

Turner, P (1995) *Sex, Gender and Identity*, BPS Books, Leicester.

Comprehensive cover of this section of the current unit.

Answers

■ Suggested answers to activities

Activities 1, 3–5, 7, 9–12, 14: answers in text.

2

a   The superego consists of the **ego-ideal** and the **conscience**.

b   The ego-ideal involves the intervention of **parents' moral standards**.

c   The conscience threatens the **ego** with punishment for immoral behaviour.

d   The more guilt we feel the **stronger** the conscience and the more moral our behaviour will be.

e   Boys resolve the Oedipal complex by **identification**.

f   Girls undergo **penis envy** in the Electra complex.

g   **Girls** identify less strongly than **boys** and thus have a weaker superego.

h   Hoffman (1975) found females are more likely to **resist temptation**.

6

a   Did you include the following comparisons?
   ■   both are stage models, cognitive in nature and see morality as developing over time

   ■   Kohlberg's theory is an enlargement and revision of Piaget's
   ■   both used stories based on moral dilemmas
   ■   there are similarities between Piaget's heteronomous and autonomous orientations and Kohlberg's levels 1 and 2 respectively
   ■   both theorists proposed that someone cannot move back to a previous stage and both failed to account for any sex differences in morality

Key differences between the theories are:
   ■   Kohlberg stresses the importance of power and punishment, whereas Piaget stresses the importance respect for authority and rules.
   ■   Kohlberg's participants were drawn from a wider age range (and some were studied longitudinally)
   ■   Kohlberg believed that an autonomous morality emerges later (if at all).

b   Did you suggest the following sequences?
   Freudian psychoanalytic theory:
   resolution of Oedipus conflict ⟶ identification with same-sex parent ⟶ superego formation (conscience + ego-ideal) ⟶ internalised control of behaviour

Social learning theory:

role model $\longrightarrow$ observation $\longrightarrow$ vicarious learning $\longrightarrow$ moral behaviour $\longrightarrow$ reinforcement $\longrightarrow$ repetition of moral behaviour. Also, immoral behaviour may be discouraged by punishment, resulting in the immoral behaviour falling into disuse.

latent learning $\longrightarrow$ observed behaviour may not be displayed for some time $\longrightarrow$ may emerge when environmental factors reinforce the behaviour.

8

a A: 11 B: 17 C: 9

b Note the move away from the description of external characteristics towards more internal qualities, the signs of the formal operational thinker.

13

a ■ use of the positive and negative reinforcement when sex-appropriate behaviour is exhibited
  ■ buying sex-appropriate toys, games and clothes
  ■ decorating the child's room in sex-appropriate colours

b ■ music, sports, TV and film stars
  ■ peer group

c ■ current popular singers, musicians, TV and sports personalities, and film stars.

15

Six to seven year olds display moral realism and display a moral obligation to adopt the characteristics seen to be appropriate by their parents and adults – they respect the rules, which are seen as unchangeable. So, for example, if few women are engineers then this must have been externally determined and be non-negotiable.

■ Suggested answers to self-assessment questions

1

How children develop their internalised conception of right and wrong, how we acquire the rules and principles of social behaviour which distinguishes right from wrong.

2

The superego develops at the end of the phallic stage when the boy strongly identifies with his father, thus taking on society's values associated with male behaviour – the stronger the identification the stronger the superego. Girls do not identify as strongly with their mothers at this time so their superego will be weaker.

3

■ research does not fully support heteronomous and autonomous orientations
■ use of game rules in his research may not reflect real-life morality

■ underestimates the morality of young children, who can distinguish between deserved and undeserved punishments – can distinguish between social transgressions and others
■ does not include social considerations – social cognition.

4

■ little evidence of postconventional reasoning
■ not universal, may be culturally determined – typical of urban societies.

5

Habits, need for individual participation, costs and benefits, pressure from peer group, self protection and self-reward (see page 813).

6

Did you remember that:
■ at six months infants reach out and touch their own reflection in a mirror
■ at 18 months children discriminate themselves from their reflection in a mirror
■ between three and a half and four years children change speech patterns from being self-oriented to communicating with others
■ at seven years children view themselves more as individuals than group members
■ from seven, individuals increasingly perceive themselves in relation to other people, and develop an ego-ideal?

7

Self–other orientation is the way we relate to others in a group. When interests and values are shared, a trusting relationship builds up. Trust grows from predictability and this requires a willingness from group members to reveal their intentions.

8

Briefly, the self concept refers to all the ideas, feelings and attitudes individuals have about themselves. Self-esteem is the extent to which they value these things in themselves.

9

Mead saw children becoming aware of their social world through language and role play. In this way they begin to take on others' perspectives and reflect on themselves. This symbolic role-taking allows the individual to imagine how others might react towards them (see page 821).

10

See page 826 for a description of
■ identity achievement
■ moratorium
■ foreclosure
■ identity diffusion.

11

- girls are encouraged to be 'kind' and 'helpful' rather than becoming academic, achieving and successful
- internal attribution of poor performance in girls – lack of ability
  external attribution of poor performance in boys – not working hard enough
- role expectations differ – motherhood mandate.

12

Key concepts you may have identified include:
- the biological theory of gender role – genes are responsible for our gender identity; gender roles adopted according to sex hormones; support from individuals with adrenogenital syndrome and Testicular Feminising Syndrome; can be criticised from cross-cultural studies and case studies of atypical individuals
- biosocial theory of gender role – uses an interactionist approach; children influence their own development; adults respond to children and input their own expectations; there is a sensitive period during which children categorise themselves as male or female
- psychoanalytic theory of gender role – gender identity forms in phallic stage of psychosexual development through successful resolution of the Oedipus and Electra complexes; sex-appropriate behaviours are learned through identification with the same-sex parent; fathers pay special attention to boys at two and withdraw from daughters – this helps channelling during identification; the first four years are critical in developing gender identity; if father is absent in these years, gender roles are affected; parental sex practices do not affect normal gender identity; poor relationships between parents and children does affect normal gender identity
- social learning theory – explains gender role through reinforcement, modelling and observation; children form hypotheses about sex-appropriate behaviour from observation; no special processes needed; children are encouraged to perform sex-appropriate behaviours and are given sex-appropriate toys to play with; theory suggests children are passive receptors of their environment; this is too simplistic to explain hypothesis testing
- cognitive-developmental theory – devised by Kohlberg; children learn gender constancy between two and seven years; self concept plus knowledge of gender directs thought and activities towards sex-

typing; this is not done for reinforcement; closely related to moral development in perception of 'right' and 'wrong' sex-appropriate behaviours; the theory can explain how we come to have an understanding of gender but cannot explain how we come to do so
- gender schema theory – developed by Bem as a socio-cultural approach; children are active agents in their own socialisation; cultures elaborate sex differences which can be found in all aspects of life; children learn rules and norms of their society; sex differences are so important that children should see them through a set of lenses; culture rules gender appropriate roles; children build up a set of gender schema from looking through the lenses; we are unconscious of these lenses; children judge their own self-worth in terms of their gender schema (am I masculine or feminine enough?); sex-typing is neither inevitable nor unmodifiable; children become sex-typed because that is what their culture chooses.

13

Answer will vary dependent on gender identity expressed. May choose to include:
- biological factors such as hormones
- social learning by imitation
- cognition, especially social cognition
- may be eclectic, including all theories.

14

- Social learning view supported in that in most cultures girls and boys, early in life, choose to play and interact with their own sex, where there are more opportunities for reinforcement of same-sex behaviour (Campbell, 1996).
- Williams and Best (1990) found sex-stereotyping widespread in 24 countries, with the qualities of men stronger and characteristic of adults and children.

15

Gender is so central to our understanding of ourselves. It becomes an 'organising principal'. We develop 'gender lenses' – activities and toys are chosen if appropriate for our sex. Gender schema change to accommodate new experiences and sometimes allow for someone behaving in a generally gender inappropriate manner if the situation demands it. These gender schema are not taught directly, rather are they embedded in the cultural

Unit 23

Adolescence, Adulthood and the Ageing Years

Peter Hull and Irene Taylor

This unit covers:

Adolescence

Theories of adult development

The ageing years

Critical life-events

By the end of this unit, you should be able to:

- identify and discuss social, cultural and individual factors affecting development in adolescence, adulthood and senescence

- understand theories and research into personality change in adulthood

- discuss the impact of particular life-events in adulthood, for example marriage, parenting, divorce, loss and bereavement, unemployment and retirement.

Unit 23   Contents

Introduction

In this unit we look at the following issue:
■ When do we stop developing as individuals? Is it when we reach our teens, our middle age or when we die?

We begin with some anecdotal evidence – a personal mini-autobiography by one of the co-authors:

'When I left school at 16 I had achieved three 'O' levels (the predecessors of GCSEs). I must have disappointed a lot of people at the time. Like many young men of my era, who lived in 'centres of engineering' such as Coventry, I was persuaded to serve an apprenticeship in engineering. So I spent the next five years of my life learning the skill of toolmaking, and attended the local technical college to study for a National Certificate in Engineering.

After completing my apprenticeship, my life began to change drastically. Within two years I was married and the first of three children had arrived. Life had taken on new meaning, greater responsibility, more sharing and new kinds of activities, gardening and DIY gradually replacing cycling and model aircraft building. During this period, a succession of career moves took me away from toolmaking towards other ways of using my engineering knowledge in order to earn my living. I progressed from engineering to sales management and then to marketing management.

After this came a complete career change from engineering to construction. Meanwhile, the children were growing up, sorting out their subject choices at school and gradually becoming more independent. Then came a turning point which, at the time, seemed to have no particular significance or likely consequence. My wife and I visited the Ideal Home Exhibition in London and while there we spent some time visiting the Open University stand.

One year later, I was working through my first Open University foundation course, in which I was introduced to psychology – and became 'hooked'. So, during my children's final years at school and college, I was working towards my BA degree. Ultimately, in
the year that my daughter was awarded her degree at college, I was awarded my degree from the Open University. In that same year, when 47 years old, I was made redundant from the construction company where I had worked as marketing manager for the past eight years.

There followed a period of reassessment and another complete career change. I completed my honours degree with the OU, joined a teacher training course, became a part-time – then a full-time – teacher of psychology (at the same college from which, many years earlier, I had obtained my certificate in engineering). Now, I find myself writing this chapter for you. My life continues towards further inevitable changes in the future . . .' (Peter Hull)

A great deal of detail, drama and emotions have been omitted from this potted autobiography, but we hope that sufficient information is given to illustrate the point that there is much developmental change during adulthood. Looked at from a psychological point of view, you should be able to recognise certain trends which are common to many people. Stages of stability and growth are followed by events which cause sudden change, for example, marriage, family, redundancy and career change. Some of the events are unique to the writer's experience; some were critical to the subsequent pattern of his life.

So, during our adult development most of us go through a series of experiences that may be common to others, or unique. These involve scheduled (normative) changes, such as leaving school, going to college or starting work. Additionally, there may be unscheduled (non-normative) changes, equally critical to your development, such as redundancy and change events. Both types of change are determinants of our psychological development and behaviour and they are therefore of interest to psychologists.

In the rest of this unit we examine psychological theories which seek to explain how development and change can affect an individual's life during adulthood.

Erikson's theory of psychosocial development

Erikson (1950), a psychoanalyst, proposed a *lifespan* theory of **psychosocial development**, believing that it is the way in which we resolve these inner conflicts that determines the development of personal characteristics. He adopted the view that we pass through eight stages of *psychosocial development* during our lifetime. Each stage involves the resolution of a different conflict between opposing forces (see table 23.1).

Erikson was interested in children's development and the effects of society on it. Differences in development may be explained by diversity in cultural background. We return to this idea later in the unit when we consider adolescence. Above all, Erikson extended Freud's view of psychosexual development, believing that ego development played a major part in a person's total development and fulfilment in life directed by psychological and *social* forces not just by sexual motives.

It is important to understand the idea of critical conflict which is basic to each stage of Erikson's theory. This conflict lies between the opposite polarities of a series of continua; the favourable outcome is to take up a balanced position between

Table 23.1

Critical conflict	Stage	Ego quality (favourable outcome)
	DEATH	
Ego-integrity versus despair/disgust	8 Old age	Wisdom
Generativity versus self-absorption	7 Maturity	Care
Intimacy versus isolation	6 Young adulthood	Love
Identity versus role confusion	5 Adolescence	Fidelity

Table 23.1 *cont'd*		
Competence (previously industry) versus inferiority	4 School age	Competence
Initiative versus guilt	3 Play age	Purpose
Autonomy (independence) versus shame/doubt	2 Early childhood	Will
Trust versus mistrust	1 Infancy	Hope
	BIRTH	

Erikson's eight stages of psychosocial development

the two extremes. Figure 23.2 illustrates stage 5 in Erikson's theory, in which the opposite polarities are identity and role confusion. People who have a good idea of their identity would come nearer to the desirable outcome of self-awareness and would have more confidence to make commitments. People with less self-awareness may have a poorer sense of identity and come nearer to the undesirable outcome of the continuum – less able to make commitments.

Stages 1–3 concern early childhood and are therefore beyond the remit of the unit. Stage 4 occurs during the later primary school years. At this stage, the critical conflict is between the forces of competence or industry (the ability and motivation to tackle tasks that need to be achieved at school and at play, for example) and having a sense of

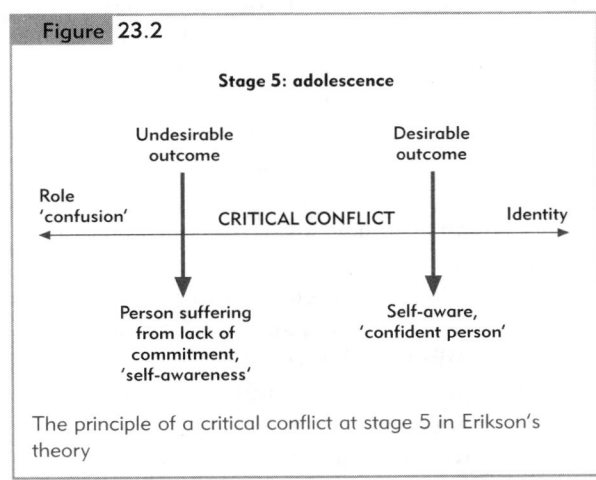

Figure 23.2

Stage 5: adolescence

The principle of a critical conflict at stage 5 in Erikson's theory

inferiority which prevents task achievement and reduces motivation. At this stage, children become aware of their own abilities. They understand that they are judged in comparison to their peers. During this period of development a sense of inferiority can develop. Alternatively, a child that is encouraged and given confidence will develop the ego quality of competence. Erikson argued that a sense of balance is required. Too much emphasis placed on competence at this stage will result in a person later becoming a slave to work, with achievement suffering from restricted horizons.

Erikson regarded stage 5 as critically important for adolescents (see table 23.1). Without a sense of identity it is difficult to cope with life in an adult world. In addition to radical biological changes and the need to develop social roles, adolescents face confusing arrays of choices as they become more independent and free from previous restrictions. What career to follow, which friendship groups to join, what dress style to select, which attitudes to hold, are all choices facing young people at this stage. Many of these choices are related to a striving to develop a sense of identity. Erikson argued, for example, that young people's first relationships with the opposite sex are a means of overcoming self-consciousness. They enable them to acquire knowledge of how they appear to others, because this is reflected in the eyes of intimate and trusted partners.

The desirable outcome of the identify conflict in stage 5 is a sense of identity and self-awareness with confidence to make commitments, and when this is achieved an ego quality of fidelity can emerge, with the ability to sustain loyalty to others, ideas and values. An undesirable outcome may give rise a lack of fidelity, resulting in poor relationships with others.

In Erikson's sixth stage of young adulthood, the critical conflict is between intimacy and isolation, out of which arises the capacity for love. So, at this stage a person faces the choice between forming an intimate and lasting relationship or, at the opposite extreme, increasing isolation and absorption with the self. This is often the stage of life during which marriages are undertaken and families conceived. It involves individuals sacrificing their own needs to benefit others dependent on them.

During maturity, Erikson's seventh stage, the critical conflict involves a choice between the polarities of generativity or self-absorption. The essential element of generativity is concern at guiding the next generation. Often this is achieved through parenthood, but not necessarily so. Adults may also achieve it by passing on their skills and knowledge, or by production and creativity. Erikson argues that those unable to achieve generativity, become stagnated and preoccupied with self-indulgence and this cuts them off from an important source of satisfaction and personal growth. The desirable ego quality that can develop at this stage is that of care. This involvement allows adults to discover new meanings in life.

Finally, in old age it is natural for people to look back and reflect. The conflict lies between **ego-integrity** and despair. Erikson's definition of ego integrity is not specific, but it clearly involves acceptance of one's own mortality and the consequences of the way one has conducted the affairs of life, including acknowledging the fact that there have been opportunities both missed and taken. Integrity develops from a feeling of confidence in one's own ego and a lack of any desperate need to 'put things right'. Despair involves a concern that impending death will leave unfulfilled goals and unrealised potential. It may be expressed in disgust with life and other people, or as a feeling of helplessness as death approaches, similar to the helplessness faced by infants at birth. Erikson (1964) argued that '*only integrity can balance the despair of the knowledge that a limited life is coming*

to its conclusion'. Wisdom marks the ego quality of a person at the stage of old age who has overcome the polarity of despair.

Evaluation of Erikson's theory

Erikson has provided an explanation of development through life in terms of the relationship between the inevitability of biological maturation and social expectations. The theory takes the whole life-span into account describing both the problems to be overcome at each stage and the ideal outcome, thus emphasising the healthy personality.

Bond *et al.* (1993) noted the implications of the life-span approach:
- the situations of older people will vary and result in greater variety with increasing age
- development occurs on a number of fronts with social, emotional and physical development varying at each stage of life
- a recognition of the interaction of the individual person and the environment.

Erikson was able to show development as an ongoing process throughout life.

Critics have distinguished between stages of child development, governed by maturational and biological changes, and stage theories of adult development which highlight the increasing impact of environmental change (Baltes, 1983). Because these events are different for each individual, the adult 'stages' cannnot be as universal or inevitable as the stages in childhood. Erikson is also criticised for generalising from a very limited sample, for example his early work did not include women.

There is a great deal of support for adolescence being seen to be a time of identity confusion for many and this will be discussed further below (see page 857 and also Unit 22, page 826). However, this identity crisis is not restricted to the adolescent period; many adults in today's society find themselves in a similar position as one career ends and decisions have to be made for the future (Holstein, 1983). Competence can also be seen to be gained over the life-span and not restricted to childhood (Wade and Tavris, 1993).

Although the theory is difficult to test and the details are arguable (Gross, 1993), increasingly the concepts are being taught in psychological, social and educational fields. Erikson developed his theory from his work in many parts of Europe and the US, and there are socio-cultural differences between groups which may not be clear from the description above. These should become apparent, however, as we examine some alternative theories of development.

Adolescence

Adolescence can be defined as the transitional period in a person's life between childhood and adulthood. Hall (1904) regarded it as a time of **storm and stress**. It is certainly a period of dramatic personal change – both biological and psychological, the outcome of which can have important consequences for a young person's life. In this section we examine development in adolescence and show how this period can vary between individuals and cultures.

Physiological development in adolescence

Puberty is the term given to the period of rapid physiological changes in adolescence which culminates in the attainment of reproductive capacity. Profound changes occur which affect almost all of the body, resulting in increasing sexual dimorphism as adult physique matures. Girls consistently reach puberty about two years before

boys (Kulin, 1972), although there is a wide range of individual differences.

The adolescent *growth spurt* is the most rapid period of height gain after infancy. There are few differences between pre-adolescents in terms of their height, weight or strength. Adolescence introduces a marked change to this pattern. Figure 23.3 shows how the timing of the growth spurt varies between the sexes.

The sex hormones are oestrogens and progestins in females and androgens in males (the key one being testosterone). Females also secrete androgens and males progestins and oestrogens in smaller proportions. These sex hormones are, in turn, responsible for the production of the *primary and secondary sexual characteristics* (see table 23.4).

Some questions immediately spring to mind when considering the psychological effect of physical changes that occur during adolescence. For example, what effects do the timing of these developments have on young people? Do late developers feel inferior in any way to earlier

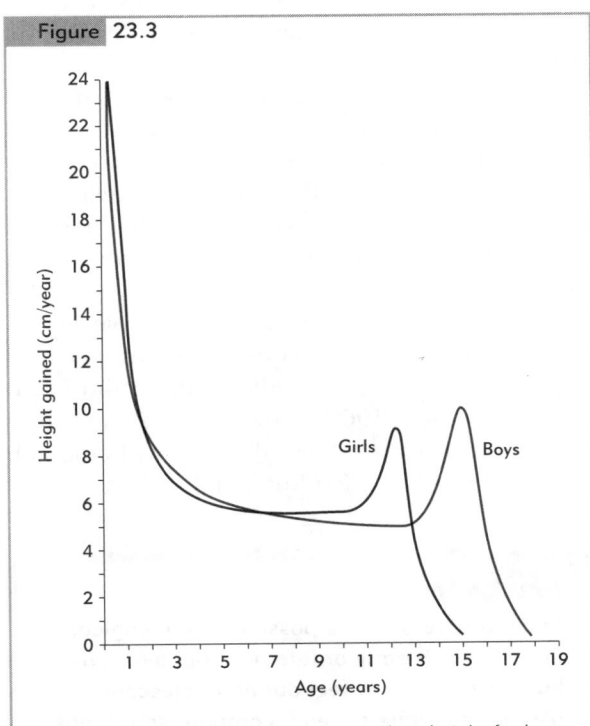

Figure 23.3

Typical individual curves showing growth in height for boys and girls

Table 23.4	
Primary sexual characteristics	
Girls	Boys
Maturation of ovaries	Maturation of seminal vesicles
Onset of menstruation	Sperm production
Enlargement of vagina	Enlargement of penis
Enlargement of clitoris	Enlargement of testes
Enlargement of uterus	Enlargement of prostate gland
Secondary sexual characteristics	
Girls	Boys
Breast development	Voices break
Fat deposition (breasts, buttocks, upper thighs, back of arms)	Facial hair

Both sexes
Changes in body shape
Growth spurt
Growth of pubic hair
Growth of axillary (armpit) hair

Primary and secondary sexual characteristics

developers? What is the effect that these changes have on 'body image' and future psychological development?

While changes are occurring in body shape and an increasing awareness of the opposite sex is developing, adolescents become increasingly concerned about how they look. Body image can have long-term effects on the feelings of confidence of young people in interactions with both sexes.

Studies have shown that young people have a greater awareness and concern about personal appearance than the middle-aged. Arnhoff and Damianopoulos (1962) showed that 20 year olds were more likely to select their own photograph from a series of body photographs, than 40 year olds were. Also, Kuhn (1960) has shown that self-image becomes less physically oriented as people grow older. (See Unit 22, page 818 for further details on the self concept in adolescence.)

Social and cultural influences on adolescent development

The uniformity of dress and style among groups of young people clearly indicates that *peer groups* can exert considerable pressure to conform to social expectations. In addition, the media provide a continuous stream of idealised body images which young people strive to emulate. It is argued that anorexia nervosa may be at least partly due to pressure to conform to a perceived ideal body type.

Adolescents may feel it necessary to conform to a number of social pressures, for example to make adequate career choices, meet the norms of peer groups and live up to idealised media images. Such social pressures may vary between cultural groups.

Activity 4

Make a note of some possible psychological effects which early or late development may have. How did *you* feel during adolescence? (As you continue to read, compare your ideas with the research discussed in the following section and Unit 22, pages 824–6).

In some cultures the transition from childhood to adulthood can be smooth and continual, whereas in other cultures the transition between childhood and adulthood is sudden, being marked by an initiation ceremony which clearly defines the change in status. You could suggest that in less complex societies the future role of adolescents is clearly defined by the society in which they live. Thus, role confusion is less likely to exist. Rituals which mark the change from adolescence to adulthood, and encouragement to take part in adult activities, both serve to enable the change of role to be adopted in a clearly defined way. The problem in complex western societies is the confusion of roles available to adolescents. Coming at a time of so many physical changes, the numerous choices facing adolescents and the expectations of others tend to create the role confusion identified by Erikson.

Differences in identity formation between different cultures have been reviewed by Markus and Kitayama (1991) who noted a distinction between cultures which promote an independent sense of self, such as many western cultures, and those which adhere to an interdependent sense of self, such as the Japanese (see table 23.5) (see Unit 22 page 827 for further discussion on the 'cultural context of self').

Markus and Kitayama noted that western cultures emphasise an individual identity which creates more pressure on adolescents to make decisions and choices in order to resolve their identity. Unfortunately very little evidence exists from modern technological collectivist societies; most of our knowledge comes from more hunter gatherer or agricultural societies (Condon, 1987; Schlegel and Barry, 1991). Such evidence discussed by Markus and Kitayama suggests that adolescents have fewer independent decisions to make, with fewer distinct adult roles in such societies.

In some cultures the time span between puberty and adulthood is only a few months and then the adolescent is involved in adult tasks. In western societies this period is now extended and:

'begins with a biological marker (puberty) but ends with a social marker (the society's definition of adulthood, such as the legal age to vote, marry . . .' (Tavris and Wade, 1993, pp. 509–10)

We do not need to look further than the society in which we live to see *within-cultural* ethnic differences in identity during adolescence (Phinney, 1990; Spencer and Dornbusch, 1990). Many adolescents have a conflict between *ethnic identity* (seen as identifying with an ethnic, racial or religious group) and *acculturation* (seen as

---

Table 23.5

Feature compared	Independent	Interdependent
Definition	Separate from social context	Connected with social context
Structure	Bounded, unitary, stable	Flexible, variable
Important features	Internal, private (abilities, thoughts, feelings)	External, public (statuses, roles, relationships)
Tasks	Be unique	Belong, fit-in
	Express self	Occupy one's proper place
	Realise internal attributes	Engage in appropriate action
	Promote own goals	Promote others' goals
	Be direct; 'say what's on your mind'	Be indirect; 'read other's mind'
Role of others	*Self-evaluation*: others important for social comparison, reflected appraisal	*Self-definition*: relationships with others in specific contexts define the self
Basis of self-esteem*	Ability to express self, validate internal attributes	Ability to adjust, restrain self, maintain harmony with social context

Differences between independent and interdependent views of self (Markus and Kitayama, 1991)

*Esteeming the self may be primarily a western phenomenon, and the concept of self-esteem should perhaps be replaced by self-satisfaction, or by a term that reflects the realisation that one is fulfilling the culturally mandated task.

Source: Cole and Cole (1993)

identifying with and feeling part of the dominant culture). Wade and Tavris (1993) noted that research suggests these are combined in many varied patterns (see figure 23.6), and can account for many conflicts in the US, both between and within groups. This can be seen as due to different ideas on the balance between ethnic identity and acculturation. They refer to the ongoing debate on group names such as 'black', 'Negro' and 'African Americans'.

However, the biological aspects of adolescence cannot be ignored. The work of Jones, Clausen and others tends to confirm that both the timing and outcome of the changes taking place can affect the psychological development of adolescents.

Theories of adolescence

Erikson's theory of psychosocial stages of development has already been described (pages 850–2,) and there is particular reference to adolescence on pages 850–1 (see also Unit 22 pages 822–7 on achieving identity in adolescence). A previous psychoanalytic theory is that of Freud who, in the early 1900s, described stages of *psychosexual development*, with adolescence occurring at the genital stage.

According to Freud, the balance within the personality becomes disturbed at adolescence, and Oedipal feelings for the opposite-sex parent re-emerge. Freud thought that the task of adolescents is to restore their psychic balance so that they will be able to loosen their dependence on parents and become interested in members of the opposite sex.

Anna Freud (1937) thought that her father put too much importance on sexuality in childhood and not enough on it in adolescence. She described two defence mechanisms, which arise at adolescence, to deal with an upsurge of anxiety-provoking id instincts. *Asceticism* defends adolescents against having to take an active part in id-driven desires and activities by abstaining from them – particularly sexual ones. *Intellectualisation* helps adolescents come to terms with these anxiety-provoking situations through reading about them, or discussing them. This works in a similar way to children coming to terms with situations causing anxiety through roleplay.

Blos in 1967 suggested that family ties are weakened by the process of *individuation*, during which adolescents *disengage* from the family as their main source of emotional support. This disengagement produces regression, manifested in hero worship, for example of pop stars and television idols as a means of finding substitute parents. Blos also described *ambivalence*, which he explains as necessary in order to prevent adolescents becoming dependent on their carers again. Ambivalence refers to the unpredictable mood swings which adolescents experience – a reflection of the early childhood conflict between dependence and independence.

The theory of *cultural relativism* is concerned with the societal expectations of adolescents as they pass from childhood to adulthood. Behaviours expected from youngsters, and applauded, are unacceptable in adults. We have already mentioned some of the different kinds and lengths of transition from childhood to adulthood (see page 853).

23.6 Ethnic identity and acculturation (Wade and Tavris, 1993, p. 513)

Patterns of Ethnic Identity and Acculturation

A person who belongs to an ethnic minority often faces conflict between identifying with his or her ethnic group and with the majority culture. There are several ways of resolving it:

Biculturalism: Strong feelings of ethnicity and acculturation ('I am just as loyal to my nation as to my ethnic group')

Assimilation: Weak feelings of ethnicity, strong sense of acculturation ('My ethnicity isn't important; my nationality is all that counts')

Ethnic separatism: Strong sense of ethnic identity, weak feelings of acculturation ('My ethnicity comes first; if I join the mainstream, I'm betraying my origins')

Marginality: Weak feelings of ethnicity and acculturation ('I'm an individual and don't identify with any group'; 'I don't belong anywhere')

In western cultures the transition contains three changes in expectation, or *discontinuity* from immature to mature behaviour:

■ Firstly, in the area of responsibility, whereas children are expected to live in a play world, adults must take responsibility for their lives in the world of work.

■ Secondly, society expects adults to assume authority – as opposed to the submissiveness expected of children.

■ Thirdly, there is a taboo on children having sexual relationships. Adults, on the other hand, are expected to form such relationships – and forget the taboo 'overnight'.

Mead (1961) thought, like Erikson, that adolescent problems are caused mainly by social problems such as those outlined above. The welter of choices open to teenagers sets up obstacles to establishing a meaningful identity. This is made more difficult because there is no enduring frame of reference and no single set of values for them to relate to, for example in politics and religion.

Marcia (1966, 1980) identified the four patterns of coping with identity formation:

■ identity achievement
■ moratorium
■ foreclosure
■ identity diffusion.

(See Unit 22 pages 826–7 above for further discussion). He was able to show a move away from identity diffusion to achievement with increasing age (see figure 22.14).

Both psychoanalytical, psychosocial theories and relativism describe adolescence as inevitably being a period of **storm and stress**, during which an identity crisis is experienced and there is conflict with the older generation.

Activity 5

Jot down your own adolescent experiences of stress, self-image and conflict with carers.

Coleman, through **focal theory**, painted a picture which may not be as bad as that depicted by the theories described so far. For instance, psychiatric disorders indicative of stress do not escalate during adolescence. Many of those that are present are, in fact, continuations of childhood problems. Only 20 per cent of teenagers agree that they often feel miserable or depressed and, where problems have arisen during adolescence, these can be traced more often to a particular situation, such as parental discord, than to difficulties of transition (Rutter *et al.*, 1976). Offer (1969) believes that most teenagers are able to adjust to adult life and make meaningful heterosexual relationships because they have strong egos.

Siddique and D'arcy (1984) also found that distress in adolescence was the exception, rather than the rule. The majority have good relationships with both adults and peers, and enough personal resources to make adjustments to environmental stressors. Destruction and aggression, dishonesty and anxiety provoked conditions such as nail biting and headaches only 15 per cent or less of the time (Fogelman, 1976).

In fact, a study of 14 000 British 16 year olds showed that it is parents who experience more difficulty at this time – describing their children as solitary, irritable and 'fussy or overparticular' (National Children's Bureau, 1976). Do your own experiences agree with these findings?

An identity crisis may be indicated by a poor self-image or low self-esteem. In a sample of nearly 2000 (Simmons and Rosenberg, 1975), poor self-image was more often found in early adolescence than in either childhood or late adolescence, and was commoner in girls than boys. A later study by Coleman and Hendry (1990) concluded that although early adolescents may suffer from low self-esteem, it occurs in only a relatively small proportion of all teenagers. Does this agree with your own experience?

The term **generation gap** was a phrase coined to describe the conflict occurring between generations when adolescents try to break away from family ties and become independent.

Activity 6

What problems are faced by parents/adolescents at this time? Does a generation gap exist?

As in the National Children's Bureau study outlined above, Bandura (1972) found that where problems occur, it is more likely to be parents who experienced them. More often, however, parents become less restrictive and controlling as children become more autonomous and mutual trust and confidence develop between adolescents and their parents. Also, Offer and Offer (1957) found little evidence for peer pressure at that time. Most adolescents were selective in their choice of reference groups, which were not necessarily in opposition to parental values and most likely extensions of them.

Coleman used the evidence that adolescence is not in fact as black a picture as previous theorists had described it to develop his **focal theory** (1974–80). He based this on bi-yearly test results from 800 adolescents between 11 and 17, which showed that attitudes towards different issues, such as self-image, being alone and relationships, peaked for both sexes, but at different ages. For boys, anxiety about heterosexual relationships peaked at 11, fears of peer rejection at 15 and conflict with parents at 17.

The theory explains these findings by suggesting that adolescents confront, and come to terms with, only one critical conflict at a time. In this way they adjust to potential stressful events relatively easily – spreading the process of adapting to adulthood over a span of years. Problems are most likely to occur in those who try to cope with two or more problems at a time (Coleman and Hendry, 1990).

■ Evaluation of theories of adolescence
While psychoanalytic and psychosocial theory suggest that adolescents inevitably experience storm and stress, identity crises and conflict with the older generation, there is little evidence to support this. Also, it is based on clinical evidence, which in itself provides a distorted picture. Coleman and Hendry (1990) summarised the situation:

■ While acknowledging that there is some change in self concept, only a small minority experience an identity crisis.

■ Relationships between adolescents and their parents are mostly positive and constructive, promiscuity and anti-social behaviour are less common than many might think.

■ Young people do not usually reject adult values and there is no evidence for a higher incidence of psychopathology during adolescence than at other times.

So, although a small minority may show disturbances, the vast majority of teenagers cope well and show no undue signs of turmoil and stress.

The cultural relativism concept looks at the transition between childhood and adulthood in different cultures and outlines the differences in societal expectations as this happens. Gross (1993) suggested that confusion between youth and youth movement (seen as the innovator of change) arises by misinterpretation of the data. Distortion may occur where adolescent behaviours are quite threatening to adults, and the fact that adolescents may be unable to give a true picture of what is happening may be neglected.

Focal theory acknowledges that adolescence may be a difficult time, but focuses on normal development rather than the problems. It is based on empirical evidence and gains support from Kroger (1985), who found identical patterns of development in the US and New Zealand – despite cultural differences. Simmons and Blyth (1987) also found support for the hypothesis that teenagers adjust less well when coping with more than one interpersonal issue at a time. Porteus (1984) showed that problems of early adolescence, for example rules, permissiveness and bullying, decline in later years to be replaced by concerns of employment and self-evaluation.

For normal adolescents extreme turmoil is the exception not the rule (Offer and Sabshin, 1984). They studied more than 20 000 adolescents and found they could identify three groups differentiated by their temperament, childhood experiences, opportunities, coping skills and social life:

■ About half suffered no emotional upsets, most had good family relationships and appeared to have the skills, self-confidence and good friends needed to help with any problems.

■ Those who suffered more family problems such as divorce, death of a close relative or illness and depended more on the positive evaluation of peers and parents often felt discouraged.

■ About 20 per cent were found to fit into the 'storm and stress' pattern with behavioural problems at home and school and reported more difficulty than satisfaction in their lives. Backgrounds tended to be unstable, with more conflicts and problems.

The traditional theories of adolescence appear to overestimate the 'generation gap'. Most adolescents report good relationships with parents (Galambos, 1992). Terri Apter (1990) studied 65 diverse mother–daughter pairs in Britain and the US and found adolescent girls stated the person they felt closest to was their mother. They had disputes over the usual domestic issues – household jobs, clothes, school – but these were not seen as serious. Perhaps such disputes more likely reflect the change towards a more reciprocal adult relationship (Paikoff and Brooks-Gunn, 1991).

Apter (1990) also noted a distinction between meanings of *separation*. Adolescents are traditionally seen to be maturing, breaking the bonds and separating from parents. However, Apter makes a distinction between '*individuation*, the process of becoming a distinct individual with your own values and needs, and a complete *rift*, a severing of affection and an effort to replace the parent with other mentors and influences' (Wade and Tavris, 1993, p. 110). Apter points out it is possible adolescents can become individuals not by rejecting their parents but by developing a new balanced relationship with them.

Individual variations in adolescence

We must be careful not to undervalue the problems which some adolescents face. Some may experience depression, sometimes combined with fears about their future. It is possible that hormonal changes may make some more vulnerable than others. Likewise, schizophrenic breakdown can affect a few adolescents. The reason for this adolescent timing as yet unknown. Awareness of special provision for adolescents has been acknowledged by many schools and colleges, with the availability of a counsellor or personal tutor should they wish to talk to someone outside the family. At the extreme level an unhappy adolescent may attempt suicide. Rutter and Rutter, in 1992, noted that although numbers of suicides in this age group are small, it is increasing in the population aged 10–20.

Different combinations of both personal and social factors mean that the classification of a 'typical' adolescent is false. Tucker, in 1996, noted several individual variations which, when combined, determine stress in adolescence:

■ temperament
■ family history
■ physique
■ aptitude and ability
■ socioeconomic background
■ locality
■ friends
■ life-events.

Activity 7

Either alone or in a group, choose three of the individual variations noted by Tucker (1996) and suggest how these could affect adolescent development.

(Suggested answers on page 883.)

Coleman has given us the comforting picture that, although teenagers may be confronted with problems of adjustment, they have ample resources to be able to cope with them and emerge into adulthood as well-balanced, responsible citizens.

In summary, the historical and cross-cultural evidence, in combination with what we know about the transition from childhood to adulthood in our own society, suggests the following formulation: the transition to adulthood universally engenders conflict as young people come to terms with sexual maturity and the need to adopt adult roles. As a recognised stage of development during which the young person becomes prepared for adult roles, however, adolescence is not universal. Consequently, the way one experiences the transition to adulthood depends on one's cultural circumstances. (Cole and Cole, 1993, p. 649)

Theories of adult development

Activity 8

Becoming adult
Note some of the characteristics, events or particular ages at which you see the adolescent becoming an adult.
Can you identify any possible cultural or gender variations?
Some of these can be seen as 'rites of passage'. Can you think of any? Do you think they help the transition?

(Suggested answers on page 883.)

Erikson (see figure 23.1) described two stages of adulthood prior to old age, namely young adulthood and maturity. These periods have not been clearly defined, although the conflicts facing a person at these stages have. An alternative view is to consider adult development in terms of phases which broadly compare with the patterns of biological change.

You may recall that on page 850 we discussed both the scheduled and unscheduled changes that occur in a person's life. The outcome in terms of our psychological development is determined by the way that these changes are accommodated.

The following theories of development during adulthood attempt to explain psychological development in relation to the biological changes taking place during the ageing process.

Neugarten's theory of adult development

Neugarten *et al.* (1964) studied the biographies of 700 participants during the 1950s, focusing on the mid-life period of their lives. They also gave them Thematic Apperception Tests. Their research reaffirmed Buhler's early evidence for a major shift of emphasis at mid-life, from the attainment of goals to achieving fulfilment. There is some non-psychological research evidence to support this too. For example, a recent popular survey reported that walking, gardening and creative pursuits tend to replace career-enhancing activities during a person's forties.

Levinson's theory of male adult development

Levinson (1978) studied the adult development of men. He took a structural view, that male adult life is a series of building periods interspersed with transitional periods. The theory only concerns adulthood and assumes that men go through structural changes, determined by age, which have psychological consequences.

Adulthood is regarded as containing two eras: early adulthood and middle adulthood, with three

Era	Age (in years)	Development	Key task
	65		
	60	LATE ADULT TRANSITION	
Middle adulthood	55	Culmination of middle adulthood	Coming to terms with retirement
		Age 50 transition	Adjustments to lifestyle changes made in the mid-life transition may be needed
	50		
		Entering middle adulthood	Revised life structure begins to be established. Can be a period of creativity or decline. May be new job or separation.
	45		
		MID-LIFE TRANSITION	
	40		
		Settling down	To create a niche in society. To 'make it'.
	33		
		Age 30 transition	Time for reflection. May be a crisis if early goals unsatisfactory.
Early adulthood	28		
		Entering the adult adult world	The 'novice phase'. Following a 'dream'. In career, discover a 'mentor figure'. Develop a job. Form a loving partnership.
	22		
		EARLY ADULT TRANSITION	
	17		

Table 23.7

Levinson's developmental periods of early and middle adulthood

major transitions at the beginning, middle and end (see table 23.7). He saw these as 'seasons' rather than stages, rejecting the stage concept of continual improvement.

The primary source of data was a series of five to ten unstructured biographical interviews with each of the 40 male participants. Additional secondary data was obtained from varied sources, for example

through interviewing the men's wives, visiting their place of work, and administering Thematic Apperception Tests. They even used evidence from novels about ambition and 'success' to obtain further evidence about their social expectations.

Like Erikson, Levinson sees adult development in terms of periods of growth and transition, with critical tasks that have to be resolved in order to achieve satisfactory progress. The concept of *life structure* is central to the theory. This refers to the underlying pattern of life at a particular time. There are several important components including

- work and family
- racial and ethnic background
- the interaction of life-events.

According to Levinson, there are several different life structures reflecting people's cognitive understanding about the meaning of life as they move from one transition period to another. These transition periods last for about five years.

Scheduled changes occur during, and arising out of, the biological maturation process. During the critical transitional periods, Levinson believes that we face a number of crises. He lays particular emphasis on the **mid-life transition** phase during which we have to face up to, and come to terms with, a number of opposing polarities. One example is the young versus old polarity that faces people at this age. Waning physical power, for example in sports, increases a person's feeling of vulnerability. So a person becomes increasingly aware of limited physical abilities, while at the same time experiencing the feelings of being young. It is also during this time that we may become aware of our own mortality through the death of a parent, colleague or friend. One outcome which often occurs from the resolution of this polarity is the need to leave a legacy, something by which we wish to be remembered. Another polarity that has to be faced during the mid-life transition is masculinity versus feminity, in which we become less impressed with the social expectation of a sexual stereotype. Men, using Levinson's participants as an example, are better able and willing to express the feminine side of their character.

Levinson also argues that men have to come to terms with the consequences of their own destructive impulses. Finally, the polarity attachment versus separateness requires a need to balance involvement with others because of our dependency, sexuality, aggression, ambition and affection against separateness, in which we become concerned with our inner experiences. The balance of importance given to these polarities changes over time and during the mid-life transition it becomes possible to accept a need for some separation to enable creativity to develop. Creativity is seen as arising out of being able to take time for reflection, which only becomes possible by disengagement from the world.

Levinson also discovered and defined key tasks that have to be completed during growth periods (see figure 23.7). In early adulthood, one of these is the *dream*, which is an overriding vision of a possible future that directs our actions in the world but may not directly influence our immediate goals. We may see ourselves in one of a range of goals, for example business tycoon or pop star. A second is a *mentor*, a respected older adult – a sponsor, host and guide, or someone who sets an example – who helps a young adult cope with new work experiences and who provides moral support. However, mentors can also be resented for having greater experience.

Levinson's work can be criticised from a number of points of view:

- Methodologically, it relies heavily on introspective and anecdotal evidence from a small group of men.
- It also assumes that marriage will take place in adult life rather than late teens or early twenties.
- It suffers from gender bias, since it does not address the question of adult development of women at all, and seems to assume that they will continue to take a subservient role, whereas for women who have children early in life the period of age 33–40, far from 'settling down', is often a time of return to work or college.
- Culturally the research suffers from western male bias in its orientation, describing the life of Americans in the middle of the 20th century.

Gender differences differentiate between the 'dream' of men and often a 'split dream' involving career *and* family which is typical of many women (Roberts and Newton, 1987). This suggests men and women experience differing patterns of change and growth in adulthood.

Levinson (1986) decided to investigate women's views in a longitudinal study. These summarised by Craig (1992), showed 'gender splitting' by women between careers and marriage.

Only the 'homemakers' had a unified dream – to be full-time wives and mothers. The age 30 transition is seen to be important to women also and this transitory period can last longer than for men, with many women finding it difficult to integrate careers and families. Women, unlike men, often interrupt their careers for child-care (Nicholson, 1993) for an average of about seven years. In most dual-income families the women increase their share of the work load in the home. Barush (1984) and Barush *et al.* (1983) sampled married women aged 35–55, with and without children. Their interview data indicated that employed married women, both with and without children, reported the highest psychological well-being. Divorced women were found to be less satisfied. The lowest level was reported by married women without children who were not employed outside the home.

Support for the existence of crises in development, identity crisis and *mid-life crisis* gain little support from empirical evidence. Although Levinson did not invent the idea of a mid-life crisis, he did highlight this period as one typical of all men. However, as noted by Tucker in 1996, in both adolescence and mid-life ony a minority have a difficult time. Most adults find mid-life a good period in their life. Positive factors include:

- job satisfaction
- more money as children leave home
- enjoyment of social status, stable marriage etc.

However, if there are problems at work, redundancy or unemployment, this causes problems. Similarly, marital problems and/or failing health can result in increased stress. It is the balance of positive and negative factors which determine satisfaction. These will vary between individuals.

Despite the criticisms, the above description of Levinson's work should enable you to note the structural nature of male adult development in which schedules of changes have to be accommodated. These scheduled changes are accompanied by transitional periods in which critical dilemmas have to be addressed. In this respect, all life-span theories of adult development tend to be similar. However, these theories only address the question of scheduled changes, whereas adult development is often accompanied by unscheduled changes – remember the autobiographical introduction to this unit (page 849).

■ Evaluation of theories of adult development

Many theorists do not see development to be 'stage-like' and prefer to see development as a more gradual process. Rutter and Rutter (1992) noted that stage theories suggest everyone takes the same route, thus underestimating the effects of life-events on the individual.

The life-span approach

Research has moved away from the theories of adult development. Development can be seen to be more complex and subject to several determinants of change. Baltes and Schaie (1973) were some of the early pioneers heralding this change. Two factors have been undervalued. Development is for life, not just a feature of childhood, and as such is both biologically and culturally determined.

Baltes, cited in Lewis (1996), noted three main influences (see figure 23.8):

- *normative age-graded influences* which refers to experiences due to biological maturation (such as puberty) or cultural norms (such as age of starting school)

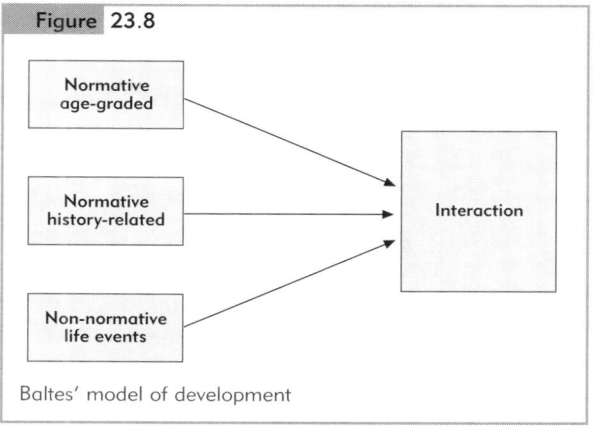

Figure 23.8

Baltes' model of development

- *normative history-related influences* which demonstrate the effects of generational changes; for example, the lower age of puberty over the last century (biological), and the raising of the school leaving age from 14 years to 16 years (and later for many), since the Second World War
- *non-normative life-events* are such critical life-events which do not necessarily affect everyone, such as a motor accident or divorce, which nevertheless influence the course of development.

These non-normative life-events are seen to be important in shaping development and are discussed in more detail on pages 871–80 below.

Although not strictly part of the adult developmental cycle, the way people respond to stressful events can have a major impact on their developmental experience and progress through life. Bee and Mitchell (1980) argued that these provide an explanation of individual differences in development which the stage theories do not adequately explain.

Self-assessment questions

5 Outline the characteristics of the early and middle adulthood eras identified by Levinson and the critical transitions men may have to resolve in mid-life.

6 Contrast the theories of Erikson and Levinson in terms of biological and social effects in adult development.

7 Outline, in your own words, the *three* main influences on life-span development noted by Baltes.

(Suggested answers on page 884.)

The ageing years (senescence)

Activity 9

How would you define ageing? Is it a positive or negative process? What is the view held in our society? How old do you feel? Answer the following questions on 'The Ages of Me' taken from Kastenbaum (1979):

1 In other people's eyes, I *look* as though I am about _____ years of age.

2 In my own eyes, I judge my *body* to be like that of a person of about _____ years of age.

3 My *thoughts and interests* are like those of a person about _____ years of age.

4 My *position in society* is like that of a person about _____ years of age.

5 Deep down inside, I really *feel* like a person about _____ years of age.

and just one more question:

Activity 9 cont'd

6 I would honestly *prefer* to be about _____ years of age.

You might find it interesting to try this quiz with your parents or a member of an older generation such as a grandparent.

Kastenbaum (1979) in his research found that:
- very few people are consistent in putting the same age for all questions
- one of the differences in people over the age of thirty years is that they 'feel' younger than their chronological age
- often those over the age of thirty preferred to be younger (some were content)
- it was rare to find anyone preferring to be older.

Some of the different 'kinds of age' defined by Kastenbaum in figure 23.9 can be seen to be open to more negative or 'value-laden' interpretation than others.

Senescence is the period of old age. The popular view is that it is a time for withdrawal, reducing roles and declining mental and physical abilities. This ageist approach reflects the low status sometimes

23.9 Kastenbaum's 'Kinds of Age'

Chronological age is the exact number of years that someone has lived

Biological age is concerned with the state of the body

Subjective age is how old a person feels to themselves

Functional age refers to the kind of life that someone leads, the job that they do, their family responsibilities, and the like

Social age refers to how we are accepted by others, and the age-group with whom we mix

Source: Adapted from Kastenbaum (1979)

given to the elderly in our society. Old people may be unable to obtain new jobs, and in many cases must retire at or near retirement age. They may be discouraged socially and tend to become separated from family life. Indeed, one of the biggest growth areas in housing construction has been the development of purpose-built homes for the elderly, to cater for elderly people at various levels of fitness.

There appears to be an aversion to growing old and many examples of discrimination based on age can be seen. Butler (1975) found many examples of **ageism** (negative discrimination against the elderly):

■ people denied opportunities on the basis of age

■ examples of 'playing the young against the old' not based on the abilities of the individual involved

■ many developed societies give priorities to resources for the young rather than the old

■ unemployment and redundancy are greater for people over 45 years.

Unfortunately ageism can be seen today in the attitudes, descriptions and jokes about the elderly. There are also seen to be 'double standards' in relation to gender, with women affected by ageist stereotyping more than men:

AGEISM.

Figure 23.10 Source: *Sunday Observer Magazine.*

- Physical attractiveness is seen more important to women in our society.
- Men tend to marry younger women whereas the reverse is less frequent.
- Men are seen to benefit from the power, prestige and career associated with maturity, unlike women.

However, as a consequence of advances in, for example nutrition and medicine, life expectancy has increased considerably. The result has been a major demographic trend towards an increasing proportion of elderly people in the population. Ageism is an attitude and belief system that will need to change. To reflect this, there has been increasing research into the effects of ageing and their psychological consequences.

The aim of this section is to look at ageing in terms of the consequences of biological and cognitive changes, and social effects. All of these perspectives provide different theoretical assumptions and we use different methods of investigation. One of the major methodological divisions is the choice made between *cross-sectional* and *longitudinal* studies:

- Cross-sectional studies measure *cohorts* of *different* age groups (a cohort is a group of people born during the same period of time, thus sharing similar life-events, schooling, health factors).
- Longitudinal studies follow the *same* group of people and assess them at intervals over time.

Cross-sectional studies cannot separate the cohort influences and are unable to detect possible causal changes (for example, a cross-sectional study of retirement effects would find it difficult to differentiate between changes which could be the cause or the consequence of retirement). Conversely longitudinal studies are costly in time and money, and continuity of research personnel is a problem. Testing instruments also become dated and group behaviour can be affected by historical and social changes. Efforts to record change, especially cognitive change, are complicated by problems of measurement. Longitudinal designs often do not confirm the decline in performance suggested by cross-sectional designs.

A combination of cross-sectional and longitudinal studies referred to as a *cross-sequential* design, in which cohorts of different ages are simultaneously followed over time, can perhaps help sort out the relative influence of social and historical factors. Some of the problems inherent in the hybrid design unfortunately still remain (see Unit 28 page 1027 for further discussion of these designs).

Physical changes during senescence

Biologically, the ageing process has been defined by Bee and Mitchell (1980) under five categories:

- smaller
- slower
- weaker
- lesser
- fewer.

Old people become smaller, due to compression of the connective tissues between bones and increased curvature of the spine. Calcium deficiency, particularly in women, where it is linked to hormonal changes following the menopause, can lead to a loss of bone mass and bones may become more brittle. The result can be osteoporosis, an unpleasant condition in which bone tissue is lost and the risk of fractures is significantly increased. Fortunately, better dietary knowledge, improved surgical techniques for such operations as hip and knee replacements and hormone replacement therapy are all now making inroads into this condition.

Some muscle mass is lost too, and this is replaced by scar tissue. Reaction time and reflexes may become slower and bladder control may be lost. Muscles become weaker and have less capacity for sustained effort. A loss of elasticity causes wrinkling of the skin and eyesight and hearing may become impaired. Taste buds and teeth may be lost, so that the differences between the tastes of food may get less distinct. Body hair may also be lost. Brain weight reduces as brain cells die, affecting cognitive abilities. Dementia may affect a significant proportion of the elderly, but it is not an inevitable consequence of ageing. The best known form of dementia, **Alzheimer's disease**, is described in figure 23.11.

A major difference during the ageing process concerns reproductive capacity. Whereas women lose reproductive capacity at the menopause during middle age, men can usually continue to produce sperm until death.

The gradual processes of ageing categorised by Bee and Mitchell commence at about the age of 30, but we are likely to remain unaware of them until our sixties. Also, there is great variation between individual experiences of the ageing process, which is usually gradual rather than a sudden decline. There is some evidence that lifestyle affects the ageing process. Research on communities with longer life expectancies in different parts of the world has revealed a number of common factors. These are:

- clean, bracing air
- outdoor work
- no forced retirement but work continuing on the basis of fitness
- extended family ties and support
- high social respect for the elderly
- possibly a genetic disposition to longevity
- a vegetarian diet
- an unpolluted water supply.

Finally, it is argued that we possess a genetically inherited biological clock that, given no intervening pathological cause, predetermines our life-span. Aschoff (1938) argued that people very rarely, if ever, reach a natural death, because it is usually caused by some pathological intervention such as disease. Many gerontologists argue that we are capable of intervening in the biological clock, and that in the future it will be possible to extend the average human life-span, assuming that we are capable of ridding human life of disease and organ failure.

The benefits of ageing are now being identified by researchers – wisdom, experience, a sense of humour (Erikson and Kivnick, 1986; Helson and Wink, 1987). Lewinsohn (1990), studying people aged between 14–70 years, noted a *lower* incidence of depression and stress in the older group.

'In a society that values youth and the new, it is easy to overlook the values of experience and the old.' (Wade and Tavris, 1993, p. 502)

23.11 Alzheimer's disease

Alzheimer's disease is a form of dementia which affects some three per cent of the population over the age of 65 and about ten per cent over the age of 85 (Pinel, 1997). It is becoming increasingly common as cures are found for other illnesses, thus allowing more people to survive into old age. The disease involves progressive damage to the brain, with significant damage to neural tissue and a developing deficit in the neurotransmitter acetylcholine, which is known to have an important function in memory. The course of the disease usually lasts for a period between a few and ten years. It usually starts gradually, with symptoms such as loss of memory and confusion. As the condition worsens and brain damage becomes more extensive, more and more abilities are lost until death inevitably results. At the moment there is no known treatment.

Alzheimer's disease sometimes appears in people as young as 40 years but the likelihood becomes greater with increasing age. Recent research has focused on a genetic link as findings suggest that anyone who has a family member suffering from Alzheimer's has a 50 per cent chance of contracting the disease if they live past 80 years (Breitner, 1990). A gene mutation on chromosome 21 has been found associated with the early onset of Alzheimer's in several families (Goate et al., 1991). Other chromosomal abnormalities have been found on chromosome 14 (Schellenberg et al., 1992) and chromosome 19 (Corder et al., 1993). These results suggest that Alzheimer's disease is not a unitary disorder with a single genetic cause.

The effects of ageing on cognitive processes

Psychologists have examined the effects of ageing on a number of cognitive processes. Memory is implicated in most of these, for instance problem solving, and tasks involving rehearsal in short-term memory. I recall how my mother lost the ability to follow a knitting pattern even though she had previously been expert at it. This kind of task requires holding information in short-term memory long enough to be able to carry it out in practice. You can probably think of other examples where elderly people you know have similar difficulties. This section will focus on how ageing affects memory.

Some degree of memory loss in the elderly can be regarded as normal. At least some of this loss may be related to unfortunate events accumulated throughout life, such as head injury or minor brain damage resulting from alcoholism or electrochemical therapy. The elderly are more vulnerable to memory loss that occurs in this way simply because they have lived longer – and such factors need to be considered if the co-effects of ageing and memory are to be studied effectively.

This is not the only methodological problem which researchers face. Others include difficulties with all longitudinal studies, for instance the time scale, and it is often the least able or motivated who drop out. Parkin (1993) pointed out that when undertaking age-related studies of memory, researchers must ensure that elderly participants are not underperforming through lack of confidence or motivation.

Although short-term memory abilities may decrease in the elderly, short-term memory capacity does not seem to diminish. For example, Botwinick and Storandt (1974) found that performance in a digit span task decreased by only about eight per cent. However, older participants perform consistently less well than younger ones on free-recall experiments involving a distractor task (Parkin and Walter, 1991). Recognition abilities involving familiarity do not deteriorate

significantly (Craik and McDonald, 1987) although those involving context do (for example, Micco and Masson, 1992). There may also be age-related impairments on episodic memory, but it seems that semantic memory is relatively unaffected (Salthouse, 1982).

Most memory tests assess *explicit* memory (asking people to remember something learned prior to the test) and this type of memory does appear to decline with age (Morris *et al.*, 1990). *Implicit* memory (which tests more general learning) shows no such decline so the elderly do not lose their ability to learn and remember (Graf, 1990). More on explicit and implicit memory can be found in Unit 18.

Activity 10

How vital to survival are the different kinds of memory? Does deterioration affect the most – or least – vital of these?

(Suggested answer on page 883.)

More recently there has been a move away from judging memory deficits in terms of acquisition, storage and retrieval. It is now considered to be a decline in information-processing resources which affects accuracy at both recognition and recall (Craik and McDowd, 1987; Stuart-Hamilton, 1991). Older people have difficulty processing novel information, especially if they are dealing with other problems and distractions at the same time. They do not appear to encode the material deeply, rather they code it more generally, taking in less of the specific unique features of the item or its context. This occurs at both acquisition and retrieval. They seem to lack the mental 'energy' to take in more than the basic features of their environment.

An elderly individual's performance is determined to a great extent by the testing conditions and the materials used. Poor performance does not always reflect low ability. Research now focuses on more natural studies. When more meaningful material is used the older people often perform as well as the young (May *et al.*, 1993; Sinott, 1986). Schaie (1977) argued that the elderly have progressed to a final *reintegrative* stage which is not usually examined by most intelligence tests, so the qualitatively different ways of thinking in later life are not displayed in the tests (Bond *et al.*, 1993). Older people who have particular skills can often make use of experience to develop efficient ways of doing a job and modify their behaviour to outweigh the detriments of ageing (Twining, 1988). Marion Diamond (1984, 1988), from her studies of active people over the age of 88 years, subscribed to the 'use it or lose it' philosophy and argues that brain function does not decay 'naturally'. Not all subscribe to this view and point out that you have to have it to use it!

Social aspects of senescence

Deterioration in cognitive performance may be linked with lifestyle. Rubin (1973) found that institutionalised elderly participants were more egocentric and performed less well on conservation tasks than those who led independent lives.

Kuypers and Bengtson (1973) saw this to be caused by 'social breakdown', due to role loss as the result of retirement with no guidelines on how to spend their time. In this way the elderly become receptive to ageist attitudes and begin to see themselves as incompetent. They begin to see themselves as 'old'. Improvements in mental alertness and increased activity is reported when people in residential care have been encouraged to take the initiative for themselves (Langer, 1983).

There are two major conflicting theories relating to the social effects of old age: **social disengagement theory** (the decrement model) and **activity theory** (the personal growth model).

Cumming and Henry (1961) argued that gradual *social disengagement* leads to psychological well-being, but if it occurs suddenly through, say,

illness or retirement, problems of psychological adjustment may be caused. Neugarten (1973, 1977) found that older people reduce commitments to their families and community activities. However, while agreeing that social disengagement takes place, Lowenthal and Boler (1965) question whether this is a voluntary aspect of the ageing process.

Activity theory, on the other hand, suggests that continuous social interaction is necessary for the ageing process to be negotiated satisfactorily. Havinghurst (1964) argued that the needs of the elderly in this respect are the same as those of middle age. Neugarten and Havinghurst (1969) supported this in research which indicated that socially active elderly people are more satisfied with their lives than those who are socially disengaged. Many elderly people become active in the community, or develop new hobbies and interests. In this respect and for 'fit' members of the community, it may be that personality determines whether social disengagement or increased social activity takes place.

Neither of these theories on social adjustment in ageing have been widely accepted. Neugarten (1972) stressed the importance of personality in choosing this lifestyle, perhaps continuing a lifestyle already undertaken. Wadeley (1996) suggested that the 'disengagement' effect may be a 'cohort' effect which may disappear as later generations, who are healthier and more financially secure, enjoy themselves in old age.

Theories of senescence

All theories depend very much upon the experience and understanding of the theorist concerned. It may be easier to explain the psychology of phenomena within experience, since personal experiences can be related to these. This provides a difficulty for theorists of senescence, as they are trying to explain something which lies 'in the future' for them. Researchers have tried to understand, and account for, the physical and social changes which take place as a person ages, and how these changes are related to the pressures and expectations society puts upon senior citizens. However, these senior citizens may see the picture – from first-hand experience – in a very different light!

Activity 11

Without looking back, describe briefly the difference between social disengagement and activity theory.

(Suggested answer on page 883.)

■ Erikson's theory of senescence

Erikson (see page 852) regarded the last stage in life as a conflict between **ego-integrity** and despair and disgust, the desired outcome of which is the development of the ego quality of wisdom. This arises by coming to terms with mortality and accepting the limitations of life.

The key to understanding the polarities of the psychodynamic forces on an elderly person is defining Erikson's term ego-integrity.

Activity 12

Re-read the definition of ego-integrity on pages 852. Try to list some of the psychological aspects of an elderly person's life that support this definition. Then compare it with the list in figure 23.12.

The opposite polarity of despair and disgust arises from an inability to accept these inevitable consequences of life. This inability leads to a fear of death, efforts to change the consequences of the past, to complete things not completed and to 'put things right'. Butler (1963), Neugarten (1976) and Boylin *et al.* (1976) have all argued that the increased reminiscing and introspection of the elderly is a means of adjusting to these consequences, thus avoiding the despair polarity. So, much of the activity during Erikson's eighth stage can be seen as preparation for death.

■ Peck's theory of senescence

Peck (1968) argued that elderly people have to face three major tasks in order to achieve satisfactory psychological growth during their final years:

- coming to terms with retirement from work, through focusing on an alternative source of satisfaction that provides self-esteem
- reducing reliance on physical powers and becoming more aware of the satisfaction to be gained from relationships with others and mental creativity
- realising, and coming to terms with, their own mortality.

■ Evaluation of theories of senescence

Both Erikson and Peck seek to provide an explanation of the psychological adjustments during the process of development in old age.

23.12 The features of life that have to be accepted by an elderly person to achieve Erikson's state of ego-integrity

- The elderly person has to be able to look at life from a long-term view and to recognise that it has meaning and purpose.
- It is necessary to recognise that all people, of whatever economic, cultural or social status, follow the same progression from birth, through growth to an inevitable death. Death becomes more acceptable as a result.

- The elderly person has to accept that the events of his or her life were bound to happen when they did and in the way they did.
- The person has to realise that all these happenings, good or bad, are experiences from which we achieve psychological growth and obtain some value as a result.

Therefore, they explain how personality differences are reflected in the way individuals have differing experiences of the ageing process. However, they both focus on the need for people to face up to their own mortality and prepare for death.

Activity 13

Using the headings *physical*, *cognitive* and *social*, list the adjustments which people may have to make as a result of the ageing process.

(Suggested answers on pages 883–4.)

Self-assessment questions

8 What *double standards* are seen in gender stereotypes of the elderly.

9 Note some of the universal factors which are found linked with life expectancy.

10 Referring to the work of Peck, how might satisfactory psychological growth be achieved during a person's final years?

(Suggested answers on pages 884–5.)

Critical life-events

Theories of childhood, adolescence and ageing are all linked with physiological change. More recently there has been more interest in how *critical life-events* shape development. Many changes are not age-linked, unless culturally imposed (such as retirement), and adult development has been shown to be more under the control of the environment than biology. Instead of focusing on stages, this approach has concentrated on transitions or milestones marking adult life resulting in personal adjustment and change. These transitions in life can result in marked changes in behaviour, resulting in personal adjustment and change (Baltes, 1983; Schlossberg, 1984, 1989).

Neugarten (1987) distinguished between:
- *normative* changes such as leaving school, marriage, parenting, retirement
- *non-normative* changed such as divorce, sudden death, unemployment.

These have been further defined by Schlossberg (1984, 1989) who noted *four* kinds of transition:
- *Anticipated transitions* which are events planned for and rehearsed, such as going to school, starting a job, getting married, having a child.

- *Unanticipated transitions* which are unexpected events not allowing for preparation, such as losing a job, failing an exam, enforced retirement.
- *Non-event transitions* which are expected changes which do not occur, such as not getting married, not being able to have children, an expected promotion which doesn't occur, retirement not being possible because the income is needed.
- *Chronic hassle transitions* in which situations can result in a long drawn-out period before action can be taken, such as marriage breakdown, terminal illness in someone close, problems in the workplace.

This approach recognises that adaptation is necessary for all these transitions, that what is an expected event for one person may be unexpected by another, and that not all transitions create a crisis. Schlossberg (1989) believed that life-events, not age, determine the issues seen to be important (see figure 23.13). She saw these events uniting men and women, young and old, in that someone entering college may feel the same sense of disorientation as someone entering retirement. Similarly an adolescent and her grandmother may be both feeling lonely without close friends.

23.13 Coping with life's ups and downs (taken from Schlossberg, 1989)

Adult *themes* identified include:

belonging
Are you central to your social world?

mattering
Do you feel that you matter to others?

autonomy
Do you have reasonable control over your life, in love, work and play?

competence
Do you feel able to do what you need and want to do?

renewal
Do you have energy and enthusiasm for what you do?

identity
Do you have a strong sense of yourself, of who you are?

intimacy
Do you have important, close attachments?

commitments
Are there activities, people or values to which you are committed, giving meaning to your life?

When does a transition turn into a crisis?

A crisis can be seen as a sudden severely upsetting situation resulting in rapid readjustment. Schlossberg notes important factors:

- Unanticipated events or *non-normative* events can result in major stress, such as the death of a parent earlier than anticipated or unexpected unemployment.
- *Too many changes* all at the same time, such as moving away from home and friends, taking on new responsibilities and having to support yourself.
- 'Locus of control' as identified by Rotter (1966): if you feel you have *internal control of the situation* rather than seeing it as *external* and therefore uncontrollable, this can help reduce stress.
- *Coping skills*, such as seeing the changes as a challenge rather than a situation which has no solution, are necessary.
- *Social support* available from friends, family and associates can also help alleviate the stress of change.

'*Adult life is full of transitions, problems, fun, choices, worries, chances, and unexpected curves. Having them is what it means to live. Meeting them is what it means to be adult.*' (Wade and Tavris, 1993, p. 526)

Holmes and Rahe (1967) produced a **social readjustment rating scale** (SRRS) which considers critical life-events in terms of their impact as stressors. Stressors such as the death of a spouse, moving house, redundancy, having a mortgage and even organising for Christmas were given rating values on a scale from 0–100. The scale enables the comparative value of stressful events to be assessed and predicts the level of this stress on mental and physical health (see table 23.14 and Unit 15 pages 546–7).

Holmes and Rahe considered that an accumulation of rating values totalling about 400 in a period of two years would be likely to result in physical or psychological illness. However, although major events in life may require considerable readjustment of lifestyle, most people make the changes without too much difficulty. Not all life-events occur without

prior knowledge, for example marriage and retirement, and this gives an opportunity to adjust before they happen, thus reducing their stressful effects and allowing a smooth transition period. With unplanned events such as unemployment or bereavement, there are usually support agencies to help with the adjustment.

There is also a problem of interpretation of the SRRS in that *association does not imply causation*, for example a high score for someone suffering a serious illness may be caused by the illness itself and the loss of paid employment may be the result of the illness. Nevertheless the idea of critical life

Activity 14

If you were drawing up the SRRS today, what would you see to be the key items?
Rank what you see to be the ten most stressful events. Now ask a group of friends to put them in rank order. How do they compare?

Table 23.14

Rank	Life-Event	Mean value	Rank	Life-Event	Mean value
1	Death of spouse	100	23	Son or daughter leaving home	29
2	Divorce	73	24	Trouble with in-laws	29
3	Marital separation	65	25	Outstanding personal achievement	28
4	Jail term	63	26	Wife begins or stops work	26
5	Death of close family member	63	27	Begin or end school	26
6	Personal injury or illness	53	28	Change in living conditions	25
7	Marriage	50*	29	Revision of personal habits	24
8	Dismissal from work	47	30	Trouble with boss	23
9	Marital reconciliation	45	31	Change in work hours or conditions	20
10	Retirement	45	32	Change in residence	20
11	Change in health of family member	44	33	Change in schools	20
12	Pregnancy	40	34	Change in recreation	19
13	Sex difficulties	39	35	Change in church activities	19
14	Gain of new family member	39	36	Change in social activities	18
15	Business re-adjustment	39	37	Mortgage or loan less than £10 000	17
16	Change in financial state	38	38	Change in sleeping habits	16
17	Death of a close friend	37	39	Change in number of family gatherings	15
18	Change to different line of work	36	40	Change in eating habits	15
19	Change in number of arguments with spouse	35	41	Holiday	13
20	Mortgage over £10 000	31	42	Christmas	12
21	Foreclosure of mortgage or loan	30	43	Minor violations to the law	11
22	Change in responsibilities at work	29			

Social re-adjustment scale (Holmes and Rahe, 1967)
* Marriage was arbitrarily assigned a stress value of 50. No event was found to be any more than twice as stressful. Here the values are reduced proportionally and range up to 100.
An individual's level of stress is calculated in the following way: 1 The subject is asked to describe specific life-events experienced during a particular period of time, for example the past two years. 2 The appropriate stress value for each life-event is assigned to the person and a total stress index is arrived at by adding together all the stress values the person has received.

events is valuable because it moves away from theories which presume chronological age is as meaningful in adulthood as in childhood.

Marriage or living alone

Marriage is the baseline critical life-event used by Holmes and Rahe in the development of their social readjustment rating scale. Both Erikson and Buhler saw establishing a satisfactory relationship with a member of the opposite sex as crucial to development. Several factors have been identified as being influential in the quality of marriage and its stability. Figure 23.15 identifies some of these.

Some of the factors in figure 23.15 may now appear dated as work and family patterns have undergone considerable change. The diversity of life cycle transitions in modern life mean great individual differences exist and multiple life courses are followed. The 'typical traditional' family consisting of a housewife and 'bread-winning' father with a couple of children exists only for about 15 per cent of the population. Families now also consist of a single parent and children; adult(s) who adopt children; extended families; couples who are childless by choice; individuals of different ages who live together; gay and lesbian couples, many of whom are parents (Wade and Tavris, 1993). Marriage rates in the UK and the US have dropped considerably in recent years.

23.15 Factors influencing marital quality and stability (based on Lewis and Spanier, 1979)

Marriages are more successful if:
- partners have similar education, religion, age or social class
- partners are better educated, older and more skilled in social relationships before they marry
- parents have had lasting and satisfying marriages
- parents and friends support the marriage
- the bride is not pregnant at the time of marriage
- the husband has a higher-status job and stable income
- both partners are satisfied with the wife's work status
- there is similarity of interests and personal qualities
- there is a high ratio of positive and negative interactions
- there is greater self-disclosure and communication between partners
- each partner fulfils the role expectations of the other.

The association of marriage and health, both physical and mental, has been reported by several researchers (Baruch, 1984; Cochrane, 1996). Baruch and colleagues (1983, 1984) studied women, married and divorced, aged between 35–55 years, both with and without children. They found the highest level of psychological well-being reported was amongst married women who were in paid employment. Divorced working women reported a lower level, and the lowest level reported were the married women without children who were not in paid employment outside the home.

It should be remembered that these factors are all overall trends – you can probably think of several examples of successful marriages which do not meet the criteria outlined in figure 23.15. The overall pattern of marriage seems to be that there is less satisfaction in it for partners over time. One reason for this could be the sheer number of different roles a parent has to occupy (Rollins and Galligan, 1978). However, if couples remain together, there is evidence to suggest that an increase in satisfaction in marriage occurs after the last child leaves home (Rollins and Feldman, 1970).

Cochrane (1996) cited UK data showing 22 per cent of single people more likely to die than married; 30 per cent more if divorced, and the mortality rate is more than 45 per cent if widowed. He points out that the relationship of marital status and risk of hospitalisation for mental illness is even stronger:
- single people are three times more likely to be admitted to a mental hospital in any one year than married people
- widowed people are four times more likely to be admitted
- divorced people have five and a half times relative risk compared to married.

This relationship between marriage and mental health has also been found in the US, Finland and Norway. The stress link with transitional changes associated with bereavement and divorce are well known, and will be discussed further on the pages which follow, but there are thought to be factors associated with marriage which 'protect' the individual from ill health, one of which has been found to be higher levels of self-esteem (Kessler and Essex, 1982). Much of the satisfaction and fulfilment linked with marriage are seen to come from the intimacy and security of the relationship, sexual satisfaction and procreation, and the pleasure of seeing children develop. Although these factors may relate also to those not married, they are seen to be normal expectations for most married couples.

Of course it is possible that the association between marriage and mental health could be in the opposite direction – mental health status causes marital status – known as the *selection for marriage hypothesis*. This assumes that marriage is desirable and to some extent competitive. Predisposition to ill-health could reduce the likelihood of a person marrying. This could be gender-related in that the qualities seen associated with the masculine stereotype would result in an emotionally unstable man not appealing to a future wife, whereas the same characteristics in a woman would not prejudice her chances to the same extent. If this selection for marriage is based on mental health amongst men more than woman, then it could partly explain lower rates of mental illness found in married men than in married women (Cochrane, 1996).

Parenting

Parenting is seen by most developmental psychologists as part of a young adult's commitment to life goals, which also include career establishment and the stabilisation of beliefs. Erikson argues that the ego quality which develops through parenting is the ability to care for others. The commitment and love resulting from the establishment of a family culminate in later maturity as the ego quality of generativity – a person who is outgoing rather than isolated.

Parenting has a significant effect on the partners concerned. For a start, it introduces new roles of mother and father, who are then less able to spend uninterrupted time together. This means that activities which have previously been undertaken may have to change in order to include the children. There is a reduction in marital satisfaction as a result of this, particularly if there are children at different stages of development.

Whether the arrival of a child is perceived as stressful or difficult often depends on other factors. For example, Estes and Wilensky (1978), in a study of couples with young children, found that family morale after the arrival of children was significantly higher among employed professionals than unemployed professionals.

The majority of parents, however, derive considerable satisfaction from parenting. For example, Hoffman and Manis (1978) found that over 80 per cent of their sample of parents reported that their lives had changed in ways that were neutral or positive after their first child was born. Feshbach (1985), however, noted the small daily 'hassles' of parenting young children (such as discipline problems, demands on time, and interruptions) which can cause more stress to be reported.

Increasing numbers of single men and women, both heterosexual and homosexual, are deciding to become parents, sometimes by artificial insemination and adoption, with a 'baby boom' amongst lesbians in the 1980s (Slater and Mencher, 1991). Despite concern over the psychological well-being of such children, research finds children of gay and lesbian parents do not differ from others on general adjustment or their own sexual orientation (Wade and Cerise, 1991).

Parenthood appears to impact more on mothers than fathers as females still have most of the responsibility for child-rearing. More men are involved in child-care but the average father leaves the child-care to his wife (Pleck, 1987). Jump and Haas (1987), in a study of married couples in full-time employment, found the wives spend 42.5 hours per week on child-care compared to 26.7 hours by husbands.

Research also shows that women and men who have custody of children develop nurturant skills, and display more responsibility and self-control. Some new mothers, especially those who may have been given little support, become less self-confident, self-accepting and less happy (Helson *et al.*, 1984).

Activity 15

How do you think parenting roles differ between
a   parenting a three-year-old infant
b   parenting a 12-year-old entering adolescence?

(Suggested answers on page 884.)

Divorce

Some would argue that divorce is all too prevalent in modern society, with about 30–50 per cent of marriages ending this way. It could perhaps be argued by psychologists that this is due to people enjoying more free will with increased social leniency – they need no longer feel trapped in unsatisfactory relationships. Levinson (1978) noted that the mid-life transition is a period of reassessment during which separation and divorce tend to take place.

Marriages made at a very young age are more likely to end in divorce. For example, American research (National Center for Health Statistics, 1977) has shown that men marrying in their teens are three times more likely to divorce than those marrying in their late twenties; girls aged 14–17 four times more likely to divorce than those marrying in their late twenties.

Couples who divorce report high levels of boredom in the relationship, and indicate that their partner no longer fulfills needs for affection, esteem or approval (Bradbury and Fincham, 1990; Cottrell *et al.*, 1992).

Other factors related to divorce include a low income, unrealistic expectations about the relationship, and pregnancy at the time of marriage (Kurdek, 1993). Genetic factors have also been found linked with divorce. McGue and Lykken (1992) suggest that inherited personal characteristics may make it difficult for some people to maintain a long-term relationship. Such characteristics have yet to be identified.

Judith Wallerstein, who has studied divorce for about 20 years, noted great individual differences in reaction to divorce. It may be beneficial to parents leaving an unhappy relationship but sometimes less so for children who may lose contact with one parent. Single parents are more often women and the standard of living for many drops after a divorce (Weitzman, 1985). Being an absentee parent can also be difficult, especially for men trying to maintain a relationship without the day-to-day contact.

The effects of the divorce on parents can be seen similar to those of children, made worse by prolonged bitterness and custody disputes. It can also be seen to be positive in allowing a new beginning after a difficult, damaging marriage (Wallerstein and Blakeslee, 1989).

Unemployment

The 'work ethic' is still strong in our society. Greenberg and Baron (1995) found that a large percentage of employed adults, when asked 'Who are you?' replied in terms of their job or occupation, so it is not surprising that losing one's job can be stressful.

An eight-year longitudinal study of Australian school leavers was undertaken by Winefield and Tiggemann (1991). This showed unemployed individuals reported lower self-esteem, feelings of depression and poor general health when compared with the employed. Similar findings are reported by Argyle (1989) who identified five major causes of distress in the unemployed (other than financial):

- length of unemployment following a similar pattern to the bereaved
- commitment to work, with the more commitment to the job lost the greater the distress experienced
- social support from the family which can act as a 'buffer' against the stress of unemployment
- the level of activity in the unemployed period such as hobbies, interests and unpaid work
- perceived cause of unemployment.

To be out of work is often seen as a sign of failure but the mass unemployment of recent years, affecting people in all occupations, can help people accept the situation and feel less responsibility for the loss. Argyle cited evidence from Warr (1984) showing higher self-esteem in the unemployed in areas where the local level of unemployment is high.

New patterns of employment are now emerging in the highly technological society in which we live. There are now more people working on short-term contracts with periods of unemployment in-between and also more people working part-time or from home. The cohorts of future workers may be better prepared for the more diverse work and non-work patterns of the millennium.

Any person who has experienced unemployment will be aware of the stress that goes with it. However, it can also provide an opportunity for change and reassessment. Reigal (1975), Ferguson (1980) and Gilligan (1982) have argued that crises can provide a stimulus for growth. Fryer and Payne (1984) have shown that the personality of the person facing unemployment affects their approach to the problem. The unemployed person needs the ability to use an autonomous approach and perceive the situation in such a way that new opportunities are revealed. They found that the coping strategy used by the unemployed was important. Some were able to use unemployment as an opportunity for development and change. Pearlin (1980), in a study of 2 000 participants, found that the way people interpreted the meaning of stressful events had an impact on their ability to cope. For example, some were able to reduce the value of the stressful role in their lives and raise the value of the role that gave them satisfaction. However, they also found that both stressors, and the means of coping with them, were unequally distributed in our society.

Retirement

Retirement strictly relates to the cessation of employment. However, not everyone is employed – housewives, for instance, and the unemployed. For these people the state recognises a retirement age. Although retirement often involves a sudden change of role, it is usually expected (apart from when it is early and compulsory) so does not always result in a reduction in health or lessening of psychological well-being. However, some researchers, for example Atchley (1977), argue that a number of stages are involved (see figure 23.16).

Through middle adulthood there are two pre-retirement phases. During the first, thoughts of retirement are subordinated to work and little preparation is made for it. In the second, as retirement draws closer, much preparation and planning occurs. Some preliminary disengagement may take place from responsibilities at work.

Following retirement, five phases take place. In the first, the honeymoon phase, activities planned prior to retirement are undertaken. Feelings during this phase are of optimism and pleasure. This is followed by depression and a feeling of being 'let down' in the disenchantment phase, when retirement activities are found to be unsatisfactory. The third reorientation phase involves facing the realities of retirement through contemplation. In the fourth, the stability phase, people become fully adjusted to retirement and engage in routines

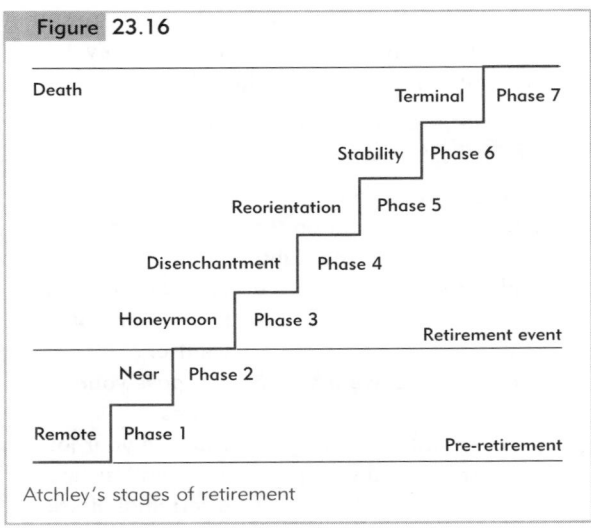

Figure 23.16

Atchley's stages of retirement

which are within their limitations and capabilities. Finally, in the terminal phase, people disengage entirely from retirement activities for a number of reasons, such as illness or disablement.

Individual differences have a major impact on the way these phases are negotiated. Personality differences, social differences and age of retirement may all be involved. Atchley's model has helped understanding of the developmental nature of the retirement process and the preparation for this period in our lives, but this model can now be seen to be rather rigid and dated in relation to the latest generations taking up retirement. This group are rather diverse, with some having taken early retirement due to 'downsizing' by companies, or leaving a stressful position early. Many have more money and better health to enjoy it. The majority who retire are satisfied with their retirement (Crowley, 1986; Newton et al., 1984). Well-being in retirement has been found linked to:

- having sound financial and psychological resources
- choice of when to retire
- good health
- close relationships
- interesting activities to follow.

There are many healthy elderly people who have chosen not to retire at the statutory age. They challenge the notion that mandatory retirement should be age-linked and demand to be evaluated in terms of competence on the job.

Activity 16

Life-event transitions
Match the transition on the left with the correct choice on the right:

1	chronic hassle	a	you don't have a baby when you want one
2	anticipated event	b	you pass your exams
3	non-event	c	you lose your job
4	unanticipated event	d	your mother has a terminal illness

(Suggested answers on page 884.)

Death and dying

Death is an event and a word that tends to be avoided in western society. It is often spoken of metaphorically with such terms as 'passed away', 'taken away', or 'no longer with us'. However, people are increasingly encouraged to see death as a normal and natural ending to life.

People are also increasingly being made aware of terminal illness, for example cancer. The terminally ill are often cared for in hospices which provide specially trained nurses and doctors who can give understanding, sensitive and considerate care.

Kübler-Ross (1969) studied 200 terminally ill patients and identified five stages through which a dying person passes:

- *Denial* is the first reaction to knowledge of being terminally ill. It may involve believing that doctors are incompetent and have made an error of diagnosis. Kübler-Ross believes that denial is a beneficial way of coming to terms with the shock of the situation.
- When denial ceases to be available to a person, through realisation that medical diagnosis is correct, it is replaced with *anger*. At this stage, the dying person needs an understanding carer who is aware of the source of the anger.

- During the third stage, a terminally ill person tries *bargaining* with his or her God for an extension of life or a lessening of pain.
- The onset of critical physical conditions, which may result in hospitalisation, causes a sense of loss and depression in the fourth stage which may take two forms.
  Reactive depression results in a patient becoming depressed at physical or social losses already suffered. People suffering from this should be given reassurance and encouragement.
  Preparatory depression relates to the imminent loss of loved ones. Sufferers should be allowed to express their emotions and prepare themselves for this impending loss.
- In the final stage, *acceptance,* terminally ill patients can appear to become emotionless and detached. Kübler-Ross argued that if patients are given help and understanding through the former stages of anger and depression, these feelings will be lost. Gentle support through this stage is required.

People unable to negotiate the anger stage, or who die through accident, suicide or a short illness, either do not go through these stages of dying or go through them very rapidly. These findings have not been confirmed by all researchers. Arnoff and Spilka (1985) videotaped the terminally ill to look for visual evidence of the five stages presented by Kübler-Ross and found no evidence of them becoming happier with approaching death. Other patterns have been found, including hope being present in the terminally ill (Metzger, 1980). Perhaps we should not expect that a single pattern should emerge at the end of life for the diverse individuals working through the final period of their life. After death, the bereaved have to pick up the pieces of their own lives. The final section of this unit considers psychological theories dealing with bereavement.

Bereavement

Bereavement is usually regarded as any loss. It is experienced in the death of a person close to us, but can also apply in situations such as divorce or robbery. Recent research has indicated that hormonal changes during bereavement can cause a weakening of the immune system and can result in mental and physical illness. Therefore, it is important to understand responses to bereavement.

Bowlby (1980) identified five stages of bereavement following the death of a person close to us. These are:

■ concentration on the deceased person
■ appeals to others for help
■ despair
■ withdrawal and disorganisation
■ reorganisation and focus on a new object of interest.

This process takes about two years and is helped by sensitive support from someone who can listen to the emotional feelings expressed by the grieving person. During this period the bereaved often suffer physical ailments and diseases as well as the psychological feelings of hopelessness and despair. The unexpected and non-normative death of a young person can be particularly traumatic, for example the loss of a young partner in an accident or from a terminal illness.

Figure 23.17 illustrates how Kübler-Ross views the process through which a bereaved person must pass following the death of a spouse. It shows how over the years of partnership two people become moulded and feel as one. When separation occurs, there are 'jagged edges' which gradually heal on the outside, but remain as small 'gaps' internally.

Norris and Murrell (1990) noted the following reactions when grieving for a loved one:

■ *shock* – a numbness and sense of unreality which can last for hours or days

■ *protest and yearning* for the deceased which may include hallucinations
■ *disorganisation and despair* can last for a year or more during which the bereaved may be apathetic and depressed
■ in most cases this is followed by *detachment, reorganisation and recovery* as the bereaved establishes new roles, regains a sense of purpose and begins to pick up the pieces.

Even in the final stage of bereavement there will be painful bouts of remission, often on birthdays and anniversaries. A minority continue to show signs of depression two years later, often in those for whom the loss was unexpected and who believe they will never be happy again (Stroebe *et al.*, 1988).

Developmental psychology today has become increasingly aware of the complexity of possible influences. Models looking for a single determinant of change are no longer popular. Research now tries to untangle the combination of factors which distinguish the difference between individuals sharing the same genetic or social background. We all share certain characteristics with others, such as experiencing universal normative change like puberty; some characteristics are common to our generation or culture, like leaving school at a time of high unemployment; some characteristics are unique to our individual circumstances. It is the relative contribution of all these components that life-span developmental psychologists investigate.

We have tried to show how ageist attitudes will have to change to accommodate the increasing length of a person's life expectancy. Education can

---

Figure 23.17

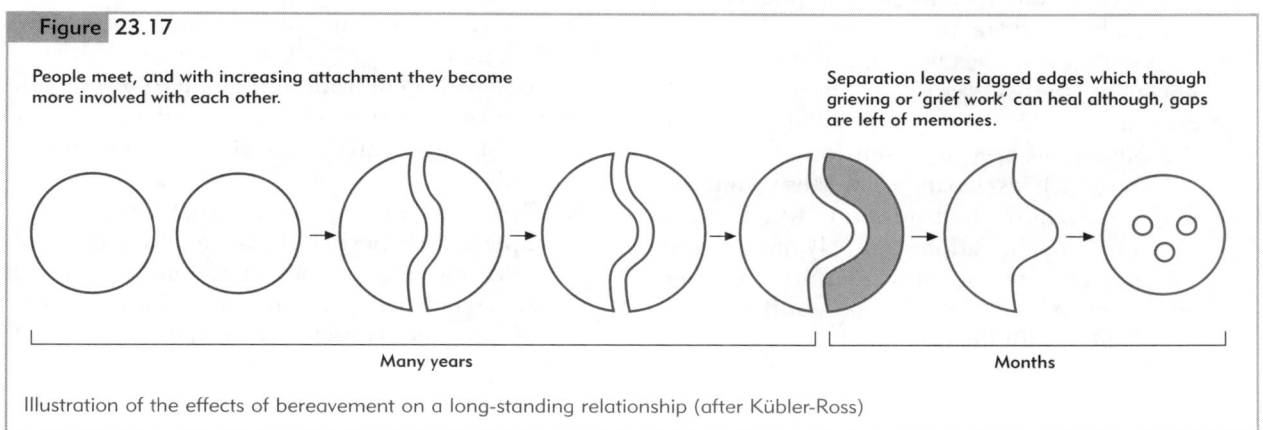

People meet, and with increasing attachment they become more involved with each other.

Separation leaves jagged edges which through grieving or 'grief work' can heal although, gaps are left of memories.

Many years   Months

Illustration of the effects of bereavement on a long-standing relationship (after Kübler-Ross)

help this process. Many universities have run adult courses under the title of the 'Third Age' that are designed to prepare people positively for retirement and make this period of their lives as fruitful and creative as possible. An understanding of adult development which this unit seeks to generate will, we hope, make some contribution towards this.

Self-assessment questions

11 Note the type of transitions marking adult life, identified by Schlossberg.

12 Marriage and parenting are two of life's critical life-events. Note factors which have been shown to alleviate stress at these times.

13 Summarise factors which will influence the effects of retirement on an individual.

14 In what ways are the five stages of dying defined by Kübler-Ross similar or different to the five stages of bereavement identified by Bowlby?

(Suggested answers on page 885.)

Unit summary

- Erikson proposed a life-span theory of *psychosocial* development involving eight stages from birth to death. He modified Freud's theory by including psychological and social influences. *Critical conflict* occurs between the two opposite polarities in each stage, involving biological maturation and social expectations.

- Adolescence can be seen as the transitional period in an individual's life between childhood and adulthood. Rapid physiological changes occur during *puberty*, reached approximately two years earlier in girls than boys. The timing of maturation in adolescence has been found to have long-lasting effects, especially for late-maturing boys.

- Cross-cultural studies highlight the difference between the *independent* sense of self encountered in many western cultures, and the *interdependent sense* of self found in other cultures, such as Japanese. Western cultures emphasise individual identity which puts pressure on the adolescent. *Within-cultural ethnic* differences in identity during adolescence can result in conflict and *acculturation* with the dominant culture.

- Theories of adolescence include the psychoanalytic view of both Sigmund and Anna Freud who see the task of the adolescent as being to loosen their dependence on parents and become interested in members of the opposite sex. Anna Freud notes *ego-defence* mechanisms such as *asceticism* and *intellectualisation* which help the adolescent to deal with anxiety-provoking id instincts.

- *Cultural relativism* is concerned with societal expectation of adolescents passing from childhood to adulthood. In western cultures this transition includes *discontinuity* in responsibility, authority and sexual relations.

- Erikson suggests adolescence to be a stage of identity confusion and Marcia has noted patterns of coping with identity formation. Coleman's *focal theory* suggested that adolescents confront and come to terms with only one conflict at a time, and in this way adjust to potentially stressful events relatively easily.

- There is little evidence that adolescents experience a period of 'storm and stress' and conflict with the older generation. For normal adolescents extreme turmoil is the exception not the rule. However, a small number suffer

Summary cont'd.

depression and other psychological disturbance. The effects of adolescent stress can be moderated by factors such as temperament, aptitude and ability, socio-economic background and life-events.

■ Theories of development during adulthood attempt to explain psychological development in relation to the biological changes taking place during the ageing process. Both Neugarten and Levinson note a major shift of emphasis at mid-life, from an attainment of goals, to achieving fulfilment. The existence of crises in development gains little support from empirical evidence. Most adults find mid-life to be a good period in their life.

■ Stage theories suggest everyone takes the same route, thus underestimating the effects of life-events on the individual. Research has moved away from theories of adult development towards a *life-span approach*. Baltes noted three main influences which are both *normative* and *non-normative*. Non-normative life-events are seen to be important in shaping development.

■ The period of late adulthood is known as *senescence* and seen by some to be a time of withdrawal, reducing roles and declining mental abilities. This has led to low status often being given to the elderly in society. *Ageism* (negative discrimination towards the elderly) exists and can be seen in attitudes, descriptions and jokes about the elderly. 'Double standards' can be seen in ageist stereotyping of women.

■ Biologically the ageing process results in loss of, for example, muscle tone and body hair. Dementia (especially Alzheimer's disease) may affect a significant proportion of the very old. Gradual ageing starts from about the age of 30 but we are unlikely to notice until at least the age of 60. There are great differences in the ageing process which are shown to be affected by lifestyle. The benefits of ageing, such as wisdom, experience and a sense of humour, have been identified by researchers.

■ Memory loss occurs in the elderly, especially *explicit memory*. On the other hand *implicit memory* shows no decline, in that the elderly do not lose their ability to learn and remember. Negative results from early studies have been partially explained by the artificiality of such experiments. Research focusing on more natural studies, using meaningful material, find older people often perform as well as the young.

■ Two conflicting theories on the social effects of ageing are *social disengagement theory* (the decrement model) and *activity theory* (the personal growth model). Neither of these theories has been widely accepted. Disengagement may be a 'cohort' effect specific to the generation studied and may disappear in later generations, who are healthier and more financially secure in late adulthood.

■ Erikson regarded the last stage in life as a conflict between *ego-integrity* and *despair*, with the desired outcome being the ego quality of wisdom. Peck focuses on the three tasks of coming to terms with retirement; adjusting to reduced physical powers and becoming aware of mental creativity, gaining satisfaction from relationships; coming to terms with their own mortality. Both theories focus on the need for people to face up to their own mortality and prepare for death.

■ Schlossberg identified several adult 'themes' which help us cope with life's ups and downs. Several factors, such as coping skills and social support, will also determine how we react to critical life-events. Holmes and Rahe's scale (SRRS) enables the comparative value of stressful events to be assessed and predicts the level of this stress on mental and physical health. However, in interpreting the SRRS it is worth noting that an association does not imply causation, but considering life-events moves away from seeing chronological age as being as meaningful in adulthood as it was in childhood.

■ Life-events such as marriage, parenting and divorce highlight the social significance of such events with both positive and negative psychological effects. The 'work ethic' in our

Summary cont'd.

society determines the importance of unemployment and retirement as critical life-events. Coping with both of these events demonstrates how best we come to terms with life-event transitions. Even in death, dying and bereavement, patterns of coping emerge. Such knowledge can help us develop understanding of the 'Third Age' and help us prepare positively for retirement and make this period satisfying and fruitful.

Terms to define

activity theory
adolescence
ageism
Alzheimer's disease
ego-integrity
focal theory
generation gap

mid-life crisis/transition
psychosocial development
puberty
senescence
social disengagement theory
social readjustment rating scale (SRRS)
storm and stress

Further reading

Cochrane (1996) 'Marriage and madness', *Psychology Review, 3(1)*, 2–5.

Student magazine article examining the links between marital status and mental health.

Cole, M and Cole, S R (1993) *The Development of Children*, 2nd edn, Freeman, New York.

Chapter 15 on adolescence and beyond, chapter 16 on the psychological achievements of adolescence (especially the sections on the self, and the transition to adulthood), and chapter 17 on development and later life, are particularly relevant to the current unit.

Stevens, R (1983) *Erik Erikson: An Introduction*, The Open University Press, Milton Keynes.

For the reader interested in finding out more about Erikson's psychosocial theory.

Tucker, N (1996) *Adolescence, Adulthood and Ageing*, BPS Open Learning Books, Leicester.

Open-learning text including tasks and SAQs, carefully structured, appropiate for self-study. A good revision guide.

Answers

▦ Suggested answers to activities

1 Answers in text.

2 Answers in text.

3
Turn back to figure 23.1. You also need a column including the following:

Stage 4 – motivation to tackle tasks which need to be achieved at school and having a sense of inferiority which prevents this achievement

Stage 5 – adolescents have to make choices, about career, friends, attitudes etc. while striving for a sense of identity

Stage 6 – conflict between isolation and intimacy, marriage may take place

Stage 7 – can stagnate, stand still or concern self with next generation (children) or with passing on skills to others or being creative etc.

Stage 8 – accepting that one's life has not been as one might have liked it to be. Feeling confident in what one has become or degenerating into despair.

4 Answers in text.

5 Answers in text.

6 Answers in text.

7
You could have included
temperament
some people are more anxious and irritable
family history
some families are more supportive; there are also differences *within* families, due to temperament and relationships
physique
self-confidence is more likely in those who like their self image. Those with physical disabilities may have particular problems in becoming accepted by their peer group
abilities/aptitude
some find schoolwork easier than others, while some develop talents (for example sports, arts, music)
socioeconomic background
those from settled and supportive background benefit from stability. If parents are educated they can help with homework. Those from a deprived background have a struggle – those in institutional care especially.
locality
life in a suburban area differs greatly from an inner city,

as does rural life. Social, economic and geographic differences affect the social life of adolescents
friends
can help to have supportive friends but they could encourage anti-social behaviour such as alcohol/drug abuse
life-events
death of a parent, friend, or serious illness or accident, bitter divorce or unemployment are just some of the critical life-events which can have a devastating effect. The effect will vary dependent on social support, inside and outside the family, and also factors such as those noted above.

8
Events could include:
■ leaving school and taking a job
■ 18th or 21st birthday
■ leaving home and setting up house with friends
■ driving a car
■ getting married
Cultural differences:
■ rites of passage such as initiation ceremonies
■ an arranged marriage
Gender differences:
■ voice change in boys/change in body shape for girls
■ a girl having her first child (impacts on the female more)

10
Might include:
■ differentiate between explicit and implicit memory – implicit more important in everyday life and less likely to be affected
■ methodological flaws in lab studies – elderly perform as well as younger people when the information is meaningful
■ use of experience moderates any reduction in efficiency.

11
Social disengagement theory is when old people reduce their commitments to their families and society. Activity theory maintains that continuous social interaction is necessary.

12 Answers in text.

13
Physical adjustments should refer to changes in muscle, connective (including bones) and nervous tissue – which

includes the brain. *Cognitive* adjustments should include changes to short-term memory, episodic memory and semantic memory. *Social* adjustments should include changes outlined in social disengagement and activity theories.

14 Answers in text.

15

You may include:
- three year old – more physically demanding of attention and routine chores
- 12 year old – psychologically more demanding, may argue and discuss problems, child no longer within parent's view most of the time.

16

1d, 2b, 3a, 4c.

Suggested answers to self-assessment questions

1
- situations of older people vary and result in greater variety with increasing age, more than allowed for in a stage model
- environmental changes impact more than allowed for in Erikson's theory
- sampling problems in that Erikson's early research did not include women
- western cultural bias

2

You could include the following points:
- Many tribes have initiation ceremonies which precipitate adolescents into adulthood.
- We have a protracted adolescence, particularly for those in higher education, which makes it unclear when maturity is expected.

3

The three social pressures you could have identified are:
- a person's social role involving career choices and relationships
- concern about body image due to rapidly changing body shape
- peer pressure from others of the same age and belief system.

The first of these was identified by Erikson in the dimension of role confusion versus identity. Erikson argues that a person's self-awareness is dependent upon the resolution of this conflict. You should have noted too that this is dependent upon the cultural norms of the society in which the adolescent has been raised. The

second is concern about the body image due to the idealised images produced by society and the media. An idealised body image may not be achievable due to the physical structure of the body inherited from parents and this may affect self-esteem. Finally, first relationships and friendships play an important part in developing an identity.

4

Coleman suggests adolescents do not have one crisis, rather do they have a number of conflicts at different times during adolescence which they come to terms with as they occur. Only when more than one occurs at the same time might problems arise

5

Might include:

early adulthood	–	starting a job
		forming a loving relationship
middle adulthood	–	reassessing life, perhaps changing jobs
		changing lifestyle
		preparing for retirement
mid-life transition	–	adjusting to a reduction in physical prowess but still feeling young
		becoming aware of our mortality, maybe by the death of someone close
		may become less gender-stereotyped
		attachment versus separateness (need for space in one's life as well as needing others socially)

6 See table 6 over the page.

7

Baltes suggested three main influences on life-span development:
- normative age-graded influences
- normative history related influences
- non-normative life-events (see pages 863–4 for further details).

8

Double standards in gender stereotyping are shown in that women are affected more than men:
- physical attractiveness is seen to be more important to women in our society
- vmen tend to marry younger women whereas the reverse is less frequent
- men are seen to benefit from the power, prestige and career associated with maturity unlike women.

Table 6

	Erikson	Levinson
Physical	maturational psycho-social stages of development in which critical tasks must be resolved	structural changes determined by age but have psychological consequences – periods of growth and transition
Social	intimacy vs isolation: sacrificing one's own needs for those of someone else generativity vs self-absorption: concern for the next generation, developing care and nurturance	critical transition periods: early adult transition (similar to Erikson) – 'dream' or vision of the future which directs actions mid-life transition with several difficult choices to be made

9

Could include: clean air, outdoor work, choice of retirement time, extended family network and good social support, genetic predisposition, vegetarian diet.

10

Peck argues that there are three essential tasks faced by a person during senescence:

■ There is a need to find an alternative to work on which to focus attention. This could be a retirement interest or hobby.

■ As physical powers are waning there is a need to realise that satisfaction can be gained from mental creativity and relationships with others. Many people, for example, take up painting or writing as an activity in retirement.

■ The final task of senescence is to come to terms with mortality and accept that life has a limited span. As an example of this, I once heard a radio interview with the late Harold Macmillan who was the British Prime Minister from 1956 to 1962. Then approaching his nineties he was still actively fulfilling speaking engagements. The former Prime Minister explained that it was difficult to know how to reply to the many invitations he received, some as many as 12 months ahead. 'How can you say to someone,' he said, '"Yes, I would love to come and speak at your dinner but I should warn you that I might be dead."'

11

Schlossberg (1984, 1989) who notes *four* kinds of transition:

■ Anticipated transitions
■ Unanticipated transitions
■ Non-event transitions
■ Chronic hassle transitions
(See page 871 for further detail.)

12

Could include:
Marriage
■ similarity of partners in age, interests, education
■ older when they marry
■ financial stability
■ men appear to benefit more than women
Parenting
■ financial stability
■ joint involvement in parenting
■ older parents

13

Well-being in retirement has been found linked to:
■ having sound financial and psychological resources
■ choice of when to retire
■ good health
■ close relationships
■ interesting activities to follow.

14

Stage 1 – very different; Kübler-Ross concentrates on denial whereas Bowlby focuses on the deceased.

Stage 2 – both theories have anger but against different subjects: Kübler-Ross against doctors etc., Bowlby against the deceased.

Stage 3 – similar: Kübler-Ross has bargaining with God, Bowlby has appeals for help from other people.

Stage 4 – similar: Kübler-Ross has depression, Bowlby has despair.

Stage 5 – very similar: Kübler-Ross has acceptance, Bowlby refocusing.

Abnormal Behaviour

Unit 24

Models of Abnormality

Chris Henney

This unit covers:

Defining abnormality

Approaches to abnormal behaviour

Diagnostic classification systems

Methods used in diagnosis

By the end of this unit, you should be able to:

- understand some of the problems involved in defining abnormality
- discuss practical and ethical issues relating to labelling behaviour as abnormal
- understand the following models of abnormality – psychodynamic, behaviourist, humanistic, cognitive and biomedical
- describe the following two classification systems – ICD 10 and DSM IV
- have insight into the following methods of diagnosis – interviews, psychometric tests, neurological tests and observation.

Unit 24 Contents

Introduction

In this unit, we look at the following issues:
- the difficulties and complexities of making a definition of abnormality
- models of classification for abnormality
- the methods and uses of **diagnosis**
- how interpersonal and cultural factors can affect the reliability of diagnosis.

Defining abnormality

What is meant by 'abnormality'? How do we know whether a person is abnormal? Rosenham and Seligman (1989) defined abnormality as the absence of normality. The problem with this definition is that we have to decide what we mean by normality. It is a hotly debated issue on which even the professionals disagree.

Consider the case study below. (Joyce Brown is a fictitious name used to protect the identity of the person whose case was reported by the American media.)

This case highlights several points for discussion. Arguably, the most important is the implication that if a person is labelled 'abnormal',

he or she may be viewed as being mentally ill and in need of treatment. As a result, some people believe that labelling behaviour serves no useful purpose, and only succeeds in raising many difficult issues relating to civil rights.

Thomas Szasz is one particular critic of the role of psychiatry in labelling behaviour. He points out that, as there is no generally accepted criteria for identifying mental illness, any type of unusual behaviour may potentially be perceived as a symptom of mental illness. As a result, psychiatry has a great potential for social abuse. Political deviants and eccentrics can all too easily be labelled and committed to psychiatric units for involuntary treatment.

There is some evidence to support Szasz. The psychiatrists involved in Joyce Brown's case clearly disagreed about her diagnosis. It could be argued that the interpretations of the psychiatrists were influenced by the groups for which they were working. Judgements of this sort are often not clear cut. Consider the imaginary case studies of 'Bill' and 'Jane' on page 892.

The two investigations described in the case study on page 893 were carried out by Rosenhan (1973). They provide evidence in support of Szasz. In the first study, the voices were immediately taken to be symptoms of schizophrenia, even in the absence of other symptoms. The person making the diagnosis was 'set to perceive' a mental illness.

Case study – Joyce Brown

In 1987 the Mayor of New York initiated a programme to help the homeless. Teams of social workers and medical experts were sent onto the streets to find the homeless, attend to their medical problems and, if necessary, take them to a hospital for treatment.

Joyce Brown was homeless and living on the street in a wealthy area of the city, by a restaurant and a bank. She smelled and sometimes soiled herself. She frequently abused passers-by and burned any money that was given to her.

Joyce was taken to a psychiatric clinic against her will and diagnosed as suffering from schizophrenia. Her case went to court because she claimed that she was not mentally ill but chose to live that way. Psychiatrists working for the American Civil Liberties Union supported her claim. She burned money rather than spending it because it was too dangerous to carry at night, and her filthy condition was because she sometimes could not gain access to public toilets. She was not malnourished or suicidal and posed no threat to herself or others.

Case studies – Bill and Jane

Bill has recently retired after a long and successful career. His wife died many years ago and his children are leading independent, happy lives. He chooses to live alone in an isolated cottage near the sea. He reads, listens to music and goes for solitary walks, never engaging in conversation with passers-by. His daily help attends to his needs including his shopping. He watches no TV, buys no newspapers and only listens to music on the radio. He refuses visitors except for the weekly visits from his children. They are the only people who are able to contact him using his ex-directory telephone number.

Jane is a member of a small religious group which does not permit the use of alcohol or stimulants including caffeine. Trendy clothes and the use of make-up are unacceptable. The group members do not visit night-clubs, discos, cinemas, or watch popular TV programmes. Jane goes to a college where all of the other students do these things. She travels to and from college alone and eats alone. She enjoys the company of the other students in classes, but spends all of her free time either reading alone in the corner of the common room or reading journals in the library.

Once the pseudo-patients were admitted, everything they did was interpreted in the context of the diagnosis. The second study demonstrates again how easily people's perceptions can be influenced by information. Once the professionals knew about the pseudo-patients, they began to see them 'everywhere'.

Is there any evidence of Szasz's final allegation that the system has potential for social abuse? Sadly, there are many examples of such abuse from both the past and the present. Involuntary confinement and drug treatment have been forced upon people in many countries. For instance, in Russia the biologist Zhores Medvedev was confined to a mental hospital where his reformist ideas resulted in a diagnosis which included a personality disorder.

Activity 1

In the cases of Bill and Jane, do you think either of them is abnormal? Discuss these case studies with members of your group. What do you think influenced people's decisions? What conclusions did you come to about Bill and Jane?
Your decision may have been different from other members of the group because everyone approaches ambiguous situations with their own values and prejudices.

Concepts of abnormality depend on the individual making the judgement, the culture and the historical context. The treatment of homosexuals is a vivid illustration of the latter. In 1973, homosexuality was removed from the list of classified psychiatric conditions in the UK . From 1973 onwards, people involved in homosexual relationships were no longer considered mentally ill and in need of treatment.

Statistical criterion

How do we decide whether behaviour is abnormal or not? One suggestion is that behaviour which does not occur frequently, i.e. unusual behaviour, is classified as abnormal. This means of classification is known as the statistical criterion.

Activity 2

Can you think of any problems relating to using statistical criteria for defining abnormality? (Now read on.)

Such classifications have many problems. How many gifted composers like Elgar do you know? Such talent is very unusual, but we would not

Case study – pseudo-patient studies carried out by Rosenhan (1973)

Eight volunteers presented themselves at different psychiatric hospitals in the USA complaining to staff that they heard a voice that said 'dull', 'empty' and 'thud'. These were the only symptoms they complained about and, in fact, none of the volunteers heard voices. The voices were part of a deliberate deception. All of the volunteers were admitted to the hospital and diagnosed as suffering from schizophrenia. Once admitted to the hospital the volunteers, or pseudo-patients, began to observe their surroundings and take notes.

The staff viewed the note taking as another example of abnormal behaviour to be recorded in the case notes. It was the genuine patients who concluded that the pseudo-patients were not real patients but were in fact researchers. All of the pseudo-patients were discharged between 7 and 52 days later with the diagnosis of schizophrenia in remission.

In a second investigation, staff at another hospital were told about the study and informed that during the following three months one or more pseudo-patients would appear at admissions. During this time, staff were asked to rate how likely it was that each patient admitted was a genuine patient or a pseudo-patient.

More than 20 per cent of the patients who were admitted for treatment were judged to be pseudo-patients by one member of staff and 10 per cent were judged to be pseudo-patients by two members of staff. In fact, no pseudo-patients were admitted during this period.

classify Elgar as abnormal. How many people do you know who are suffering from or have suffered from the effects of stress? Probably quite a few and many of them sought treatment. In our society, stress-related conditions are not unusual, but they do qualify for diagnosis and treatment.

Elements of abnormality

Clearly, the statistical model is too simple. It lacks an essential element – value judgment. Unusual gifts that give enjoyment are valued; the negative effects of stress are not. It seems that several factors need to be taken into consideration before a person's behaviour can be judged to be abnormal. Rosenhan and Seligman (1989) suggested seven factors or elements that should be taken into consideration when deciding whether or not behaviour is abnormal (figure 24.1).

Not all of these elements will be present in any one case and different combinations of factors will occur in different people. Sometimes the criteria outlined in figure 24.1 are difficult to apply. The following are examples which help to highlight the difficulties:

- *Suffering and observer discomfort.* Consider, for example, a grieving widow. There is no doubt that she is suffering, but this is normal; in fact it would be abnormal if she showed no emotion. Suffering does not always imply abnormality. But what happens if she is still deeply distressed several months later? Is her emotion too intense? Is it going on for too long? Once more we are faced with the question of individual judgement.
- *Maladaptiveness and incomprehensibility.* Joyce Brown's case (see page 891) draws attention to the difficulties involved in assessing mal adaptiveness and incomprehensibility. She claimed that she was not hurting herself, whilst others would argue that her life on the streets was damaging her health. Her decision to live on the streets and burn money rather than bank it is difficult to understand, but many would recognise an unwillingness to be tied to the financial worries of owning property and possessions.
- *Unpredictability and loss of control.* In many instances these would not be enough to justify a label of abnormality. The usually obliging employee who hands in his or her notice following a sudden blazing row with a very

24.1 Elements of abnormality (after Rosenhan and Seligman)

■ Suffering

Abnormality is a painful experience. For example, a person suffering from depression is suffering psychologically.

■ Maladaptiveness

Behaviour is adaptive if it promotes the well-being of the individual and society. Self-destructive behaviour or people who physically or mentally harm others are not viewed as being well adapted to society.

■ Irrationality and incomprehensibility

This is behaviour which makes no sense to the observer. The person who spends several hours a day washing his or her hands for fear of contamination from germs appears irrational because this behaviour is not logical. The observer cannot comprehend it.

■ Unpredictability and loss of control

A person does something which is completely out of

character, for example a normally quiet, courteous student who has a sudden outburst of aggression.

■ Vividness and unconventionality

Such behaviour is vivid because it stands out. It is unusual. Exotic forms of dress, for instance 'Elvis look-alikes' or excessively loud, extrovert behaviour in public places, may be seen as unconventional or abnormal.

■ Observer discomfort

Unusual behaviour or socially unacceptable behaviour embarrasses observers. For example, people feel uncomfortable when another person stands too close or avoids eye contact.

■ Violation of moral and ideal standards

This involves judging behaviour against society's norms, for example to kill someone is wrong.

---

demanding boss may well be acting out of character and be temporarily out of control. Such an action, however, is unlikely to justify a label of abnormality.

- *Unconventionality*. This depends on what is viewed to be normal in the society in which we live. What is acceptable at one time in history is not acceptable at another. A woman who painted her face with wax and sat behind a fire screen in the drawing room to avoid melting her make-up would be considered odd by today's standards. It was considered desirable behaviour for gentlewomen in the eighteenth century.

- *Violation of moral and ideal standards*. This depends on the norms of the group. The moderate consumption of alcohol, which is an acceptable part of social relaxation in most western communities, would be considered unacceptable in Islamic communities.

The seven elements of abnormality proposed by Rosenhan and Seligman help to clarify some of the issues involved in judging behaviour, but the decisions are still open to discussion.

Activity 3

Below are two imaginary case studies for you to consider and discuss with your group. Is the behaviour abnormal? Should it be treated? Remember you are not being asked to diagnose the behaviour, that is for the experts. (Ethical guidelines recommended by the British Psychological Society.)

Labelling

Rosenhan and Seligman make the point that it is very easy to generalise from the actions and thoughts of a person and to assign to that individual assumed characteristics of behaviour. This leads us to see the person as being 'odd' or 'abnormal' rather than to consider separately certain aspects of the individual's behaviour. This process is known as labelling.

Case studies – Fred and Ushma

1   Fred is middle-aged. He has a demanding job with a high salary which provides a comfortable life style for his family. During his last health check he was told that he was gaining weight and his blood pressure was slightly higher than usual. Fred, keen to remain healthy, has changed his diet and started taking regular exercise. He refuses, however, to take the doctor's advice and give up smoking 20 cigarettes a day. He says that he enjoys smoking and that it helps him to relax. The 'no smoking policy' at work means that he has to stand outside the building whatever the weather to enjoy his smoke. At home, his family is becoming increasingly concerned. His younger daughter is becoming agitated because she is afraid that he will die if he does not give up the habit, and his wife cannot sit in the same room with him when he is smoking because it causes her to suffer an asthma attack.

2   Whilst Ushma was shopping, she experienced some alarming physical symptoms, fainted in the shop and was taken to the local hospital by concerned neighbours. She was examined and told that there was nothing seriously wrong with her.

Following this incident, Ushma went out once more, but began to feel faint as she was walking along the road. She was afraid that the same thing would happen again and went home. After that she has refused to go out alone. She has taken sick leave from work, given up her social activities and insists that her husband or one of the children accompanies her to the shops. She now avoids going out whenever possible, claiming that she is perfectly content to be at home.

Labelling has various disadvantages, and has been criticised, most notably by Szasz as follows:

- Labels may be accompanied by social stigma. A family may lose friends, the sufferer may lose a job or find it difficult to obtain employment as expectations of bizarre behaviour may be assumed.

- Labelling can lead to self-fulfilling prophecy. Many studies have been carried out in schools which demonstrate that when teachers expect children to succeed they will, whereas if children are expected to fail, they will (Elliott and Dweck, 1988). Similarly, a person who has been labelled as abnormal behaves as expected.

Despite the difficulties involved in identifying abnormal behaviour and the ethical implications of using psychiatric labels, there are several justifications for making a psychiatric diagnosis. These, together with an overview of the two main classification systems, are considered later in the unit. First, we briefly review the five main approaches to abnormality.

Self-assessment questions

1   List Szasz's arguments against classifying mental illness.

2   With reference to pages 893–4 state in your own words two reasons why the statistical criterion for judging abnormality is too simple.

3   List the seven criteria, suggested by Rosenham and Seligman, for judging whether or not behaviour is abnormal.

(Suggested answers on page 919.)

Approaches to abnormal behaviour

Throughout history there have been a variety of attempts to understand abnormal behaviour. Many different approaches have been adopted; each approach has produced a different explanation or model of abnormality. In this section we examine:

- psychodynamic models
- behaviourist models
- humanistic models
- cognitive models
- biomedical models.

The psychodynamic approach

Psychodynamic theories subscribe to the idea that active forces within the person's mind, such as instincts and conflicts, direct behaviour. The psychodynamic approach is concerned with how both conscious and unconscious psychological forces influence both the mind and behaviour. Freud (1856–1939), the founder of this approach, was a doctor who specialised in diseases of the nervous system. The type of illness that Freud treated is illustrated in the case study below.

Freud worked closely with Dr Breuer at the beginning of his career. Dr Breuer's patient 'Anna O', who is described in the case study below, was suffering from a condition called *conversion hysteria*, a condition that has been recognised for centuries. The patient suffers from physical symptoms which appear to have no physical cause.

Breuer used hypnosis to help treat the patient, but found that eventually he was able to help her simply by allowing her to talk about her problems. This was referred to as the 'talking cure' and was later developed by Freud into a therapy called psychoanalysis. Freud noticed that in all cases of conversion hysteria, the symptoms began with a traumatic event in which the patient was unable to express the appropriate emotions. The events and the emotions had been forgotten, or repressed, i.e. pushed into the deep parts of the mind because they were too painful for the person to face. Freud thought that the energy from the unexpressed emotions had been converted into physical energy and was being expressed as physical symptoms. If the patient uncovered the memory and was able to express the appropriate emotion, then he or she could be cured. Freud publicly challenged the prevailing view that such patients deserved little time from the doctor because they exaggerated and malingered. He said that their suffering was real and they needed help.

Freud's work led to the development of a theory of personality, which he used to explain both normal and abnormal behaviour. Freud claimed that the processes underlying normal and abnormal behaviour are the same. This is considered to be one of his many contributions to psychology because it helped to change attitudes

Case study – Dr Breuer's illustration of conversion hysteria: 'Anna O'.

The patient was an intelligent girl who was 21 years old and nicknamed 'Anna O'. Her illness lasted for two years. During this time she suffered from a series of physical and psychological disturbances. She suffered paralysis and loss of sensation in her right arm and leg. Her eye movements were disturbed and her vision restricted. She had difficulties with the posture of her head and had a severe nervous cough. These were just some of her symptoms, for which a medical examination revealed that there was no physical reason. Her symptoms had started at a time when she was nursing her father through a serious illness from which he eventually died.

and contributed to a more humane treatment of the mentally ill. The theory of personality can be considered in two parts:

- the structure of personality
- the development of personality.

The structure of personality

Freud distinguished between conscious, subconscious and unconscious thought processes:

- Conscious thoughts are those we are aware of.
- Subconscious thoughts are those memories which are easily accessible with a little prompting.
- **Unconscious** thoughts are deeply processed memories that are not readily accessible.

He claimed that the personality has three parts:

- The *id* is present from birth and contains basic drives and instincts. Sex and aggression were recognised by Freud to be the two most powerful driving forces, but he considered sex to be the most dominant. He claimed that our id behaviour is directed at obtaining pleasure and that the satisfaction of our basic needs is pleasurable and so we are governed by our attempts to satisfy these needs.
- The *ego* functions as the reality principle. As the child grows, he or she becomes more aware of the constraints of his or her environment. The ego harnesses the id, delaying the satisfaction of drives and channelling them into socially accepted forms of behaviour by means of defence mechanisms. There is constant tension between the powerful forces of the id and the ego.
- The *superego* represents conscience. It develops as a result of the resolution of the Oedipus complex in boys and the Electra complex in girls. The superego internalises society's views of what is permissible or forbidden.

The superego reinforces the ego's attempts to harness the id. Conflict between opposing forces results in anxiety.

The development of personality

Another of Freud's major contributions was his emphasis on the importance of childhood on the development of personality. Freud said that personality developed through four stages from infancy to adulthood. Each stage related to the physical development of the child and was associated with the area of the body which was particularly sensitive at that time. The sensitive areas were called **erogenous zones**.

If the child experiences a trauma at a particular stage, especially a trauma related to the erogenous zone, fixation occurred. Fixation was when behaviour from one stage was fixed into the personality and became an integral part of the personality throughout life. Table 24.2 shows the progression though the stages of development and some of the possible behaviour relating to fixation in each stage.

Latency marks a period of rest when social factors play an important part in ego development. The child is exposed to the world outside the family; this is the time when **defence mechanisms** are developed. Defence mechanisms are unconscious ways of resolving the conflicts between the id, ego and superego, hence reducing tension. Freud claimed that these defence mechanisms were used by everyone, but were exaggerated in people suffering from psychological disturbance. In some cases, the defence mechanisms became so exaggerated that they caused problems. Figure 24.3 outlines Freud's defence mechanisms (see also figure 15.35).

Post Freudians

More recent psychodynamic theorists, whilst agreeing with many aspects of Freud's theory, have broadened the base of the theory:

- *Adler* (1870) stressed the role of society and the need to compensate for feelings of inadequacy.
- *Jung* (1875–1961) believed that we have a **collective unconscious**, containing memories from past generations. He also recognised another major drive, the spiritual drive, which became the dominant drive in mid-life.
- *Horney* (1945) saw anxiety as a social rather than biological experience. This could result in a child developing social coping strategies, for example becoming submissive to regain lost love.

Table 24.2

Stage	Erogenous zone	Pleasurable behaviour	Some results of fixation
0–1 year			
Early oral	Mouth	Sucking	Self-centred, dependent, greedy, glutinous, smoker
Late oral	Mouth	Biting	Cynical, verbally 'biting', nail biting
1–3 years			
Anal	Anus	Retaining or expelling faeces	Obsessive compulsive, very orderly, punctual, obstinate, miserly
3–5/6 years			
Phallic	Genitals	Genital stimulation	Homesexuality, exhibitionism, excessive ambition
6–puberty			
Latency	None		Development of defence mechanisms
Puberty			
Genital	Genitals	Genital stimulation	Discomfort with the opposite sex; sexually related problems

The effects of fixation in psychosexual stages of development

24.3 Freud's defence mechanisms

Repression: the person forgets what he or she does not wish to remember by pushing unwanted thoughts into the unconscious mind.

Reaction formation: the person believes that his or her motive for doing something is the exact opposite from what it really is.

Projection: the person does not recognise his or her own motives – these are ascribed to someone else.

Displacement: this is when the object or person on the receiving end of behaviour is disguised by substituting a different one.

Rationalisation: the person explains his or her behaviour in a way that hides the individual's true motive, substituting another motive instead.

Sublimation: this is when a substitute activity is used to gratify needs. It is generally associated with the sex drive.

Denial: refusing to accept reality.

Identification: incorporating another person into our personality. Thinking, feeling, and acting as if we were that person.

Isolation: separating contradictory thoughts and feelings into different compartments.

Regression: reverting to an earlier stage of development.

■ *Erikson* (1902) agreed with Jung that personality continues to develop throughout adult life, but he thinks that social influences play an essential part in development (see pages 850–3).

■ **Evaluation of the psychodynamic approach**

Freud was a pioneer in the treatment of psychological distress. He helped to demystify psychopathological conditions, making them more understandable to the world at large. He drew attention to the role of unconscious thought processes in behaviour and the effects of childhood experiences on later life. He demonstrated the role of conflict in relation to anxiety and he identified defence mechanisms which are now widely acknowledge in psychiatry and counselling. His methods for helping patients by encouraging them to talk out their problems have been widely adopted and adapted by a variety of therapists.

The psychodynamic approach remains controversial and has been criticised on several counts, particularly relating to the difficulties of scientific evaluation. Up to the present, no one has demonstrated the existence of the id, ego and superego. Similarly, it is difficult to demonstrate that fixation at different stages of development results in the development of particular personality and behavioural characteristics. Evidence is often conflicting. Fisher and Greenberg (1977) found some studies that demonstrated a correlation between oral personality characteristics and the length of time the child was breastfed. Other studies have found no such relationship.

The difficulty with these studies and many other attempts to support Freud's theory is that the studies are often based on retrospective evidence which may be unreliable. They are correlation studies, thus eliminating the possibility of establishing cause and effect. There may also be many other factors in the relationship between the mother and child which could contribute towards the development of personality characteristics.

Activity 4

Below are some examples of defence mechanisms. Match the examples to Freud's defence mechanisms which are described in figure 24.3.

a Elvis 'look-alikes'.

b A child starts bed wetting when her mother goes into hospital.

c Forgetting a dental appointment.

Activity 4 cont'd

d A vain person will not recognise that he or she is vain but will see vanity in everyone else.

e A man who cannot satisfy his sexual needs will embark on energetic physical activity to release tension.

f A preacher who, subscribes to the Christian ethic that it is wrong to kill, ministers to a murderer.

g A student with a poor exam result who says she was badly taught rather than admit the real motive that she did not want to try too hard in case she failed.

h People with serious illnesses sometimes will not accept that that there is anything wrong with them.

i The boss makes an employee angry, but he cannot shout at the boss because he will lose his job, so he goes home and shouts at the family cat instead.

j A daughter who really hates her mother is very solicitous of her mother's health and comfort.

(Suggested answers on page 918.)

The behaviourist approach

This dominated psychology between the 1920s and 1960s, and was the main challenge to Freud. Unlike the psychodynamic approach, the behavioural approach focuses on behaviour, not unconscious mental processes. We learn about the future by association with the past. According to behaviourists, all behaviour is shaped by the environment through processes of reward and punishment. A change in the environment will lead to a change in behaviour and it is possible to use experiments to determine which aspect of the environment caused the behaviour.

Abnormal behaviour is seen to be a result of faulty learning, which can be unlearned.

Case study – Watson and Rayner's study of 'Little Albert' (1920)

Albert was a young boy of 11 months old when he was rendered fearful of white furry objects after a series of trials in an experiment in which a loud, unpleasant noise was paired with a white laboratory rat. Before the pairings, Albert showed no fear of the rat, but after only a few trials he showed signs of distress and withdrew whenever he saw the rat, even though there was no further noise. He showed distress at objects resembling the rat, including fur coats and a mask of Santa Claus with a long white beard.

Treatment based on the **behaviourist model** aims at changing a person's response to the environment.

The two main behaviourist approaches are:
- classical conditioning
- operant conditioning.

Classical conditioning

This explains how we can learn through association and it is based on reflex reactions (see Unit 11 pages 356–60 for a review of the principles of classical conditioning). It was first demonstrated by Pavlov (1849–1936) in his experiments to investigate the salivary reflex in dogs. The case study of Little Albert, described above, demonstrates how the principles of classical conditioning can be applied to the acquisition of fear.

Activity 5

Try to explain Little Albert's behaviour in the following terms:
conditioned stimulus (cs), conditioned response (cr), unconditioned stimulus (ucs), unconditioned response (ucr).

(Suggested answers on page 918.)

The Little Albert study has been criticised for ethical reasons. Albert had been subjected to a very distressing situation. The psychologists attempted to restore Albert to his previous condition by using extinction. They presented the rat without the noise expecting the behaviour to diminish. The experiment was never concluded because Albert's mother withdrew him from the study.

Operant conditioning

This relies on voluntary behaviour rather than reflexes. The first experiments were carried out by Thorndike who proposed the Law of Effect. This, simply stated, says that any action that is followed by a pleasant reward will be repeated; actions that are not followed by a reward or are associated with unpleasant experiences will not be repeated. Using white rats and pigeons in a laboratory, Skinner demonstrated that it was possible to develop new behaviour by a process of behaviour shaping, i.e. leading the organism to the desired behaviour through a series of simple stages. Figure 24.4 outlines some of the principles of operant conditioning; figure 24.5 describes Skinner's five schedules of reinforcement.

Activity 6

Using figure 24.4, try to explain the following situations in terms of operant conditioning:

a Joanne is 3, and her behaviour is causing problems. Each time she goes into the supermarket, she has tantrums. She demands sweets and screams and kicks until her mother finally gives in to her demands.

b Tariq is not working well at school. When he first started school he was very enthusiastic, but his teacher had to spend most of her time helping other children, so she rarely had time for Tariq. When he took his work home, his parents pointed out his mistakes in an effort to help him. Eventually, he stopped working and began to find naughty things to do. The teacher is now spending much more time with Tariq.

(Suggested answers on page 918.)

24.4 The principles of operant conditioning

Positive reinforcer: an item or event that the organism likes, needs, or desires, that is closely associated with a particular response, increasing the likelihood of that response occurring again.

Primary reinforcer: this occurs naturally, like food or sleep. It satisfies some physical need.

Secondary reinforcer: this can be exchanged for a primary reinforcer, for example money. Money is of no use unless it can be used to obtain something that satisfies our needs.

Negative reinforcer: an event which, by its removal, increases the likelihood of a response occurring.

Punishment: an unpleasant experience which is associated with a response, making the response less likely to occur.

Schedules of reinforcement: this refers to the relationship between the stimulus and the response (see figure 24.5).

24.5 Skinner's schedules of reinforcement

There are five schedules of reinforcement :
- *Continuous reinforcement* – behaviour is reinforced each time it occurs.
- *Fixed ratio reinforcement* – behaviour is reinforced every third, eighth or tenth time it occurs.
- *Variable ratio reinforcement* – behaviour is rewarded intermittently, not according to a fixed number of responses.

- *Fixed interval reinforcement* – behaviour is rewarded at regular time intervals.
- *Variable interval reinforcement* – behaviour is rewarded at irregular time intervals.

Variable patterns of reinforcement result in faster learning, which is harder to extinguish than learning from continuous reinforcement or fixed patterns of reinforcement.

■ Evaluation of the behaviourist approach

- The main advantage of behaviourism is that it is scientifically based and the theories can be tested.
- Historically, it offered a practical alternative to the psychodynamic approach.
- Treatments based on behaviourist principles are still used and have the advantage of being relatively quick and cheap to administer.
- The approach has been criticised for being too simplistic, on the basis that behaviourists ignore the role of thinking, making the assumption that all behaviour is a result of associations being made between stimulus and response.

The humanistic approach

The humanistic approach was developed in the 1950s in the United States as a reaction against the psychodynamic and behavioural approaches that were dominating psychology at that time. For this reason it is called the *third force*. Humanistic psychologists believe in free will and reject the deterministic views of the psychodynamic and behaviourist psychologists. Psychodynamic psychologists believe that behaviour is determined by unconscious thought processes, whereas behaviourists believe that behaviour is determined by the environment.

The **humanistic model** focuses on the *whole person*, believing that people are capable of self awareness and have the power to choose and direct their own actions. When trying to understand people, humanistic psychologists explore the content of a person's conscious awareness, attempting to understand how each individual experiences the world and himself or herself. They reject the scientific approach because they do not think that there are a common set of laws that can be applied to all people. Humanistic psychologists are interested in helping people to use their awareness to understand themselves and take responsibility for their lives. The main goal is to help their clients become *self-actualised*, i.e. to develop their full potential as human beings.

Several humanistic psychologists, for example Laing, began their careers as psychoanalysts. Jung was recognised as a psychoanalyst, but many of his views were compatible with the humanistic approach. One of the important aspects of Jung's therapy was his focus on the growth of the individual. When asked about his methods, he replied that he treated each patient as individually as possible because 'the solution to the problem is an individual one. Universal rules can be postulated only with a grain of salt' (Jung, 1961).

■ Carl Rogers's theory

The best known humanistic psychologist is Carl Rogers, who developed client-centred therapy. The concept of *self* is central to Roger's theory. Self is the perceptions, attitudes and values that define who we are. Another important concept is *ideal self*, which is the person we would like to be. In a well-adjusted individual, there is a close correspondence between the self and the ideal self.

We live our lives in the knowledge of our self concept and change our self concept if our experiences show inconsistencies. For example, a person may see himself or herself as a caring person, but change his or her self concept after refusing to give up his or her job in order to care for an elderly relative.

Sometimes patients will ignore the inconsistencies and operate defence mechanisms. Excessive use of the mechanisms results in anxiety and the rigid adherence to the self concept. The more the person denies the inconsistencies, the more maladjusted the behaviour.

According to this approach, the aim of the therapy is to help the person come to terms with his or her self concept, to find out who they are, and to become self-actualised. This is done by developing a trusting relationship with the therapist, who attempts to see the world through the eyes of the client and, in a non-judgemental way, aims to help the client to solve his or her own problems (see Unit 26 page 962 for a further discussion of Rogers's client-centred therapy).

■ Evaluation of the humanistic approach

- The humanistic approach has been criticised for being non-scientific and therefore difficult to evaluate.
- The approach to counselling developed by Rogers in widely used, but there is little evidence to support the view that individuals are striving for actualisation.
- The therapy is restricted to reasonably intelligent, articulate people. It is not helpful to confused individuals.
- Psychoanalysts would argue that individuals do not always know themselves and that humanistic psychologists pay too little attention to unconscious thought processes.

The cognitive approach

The humanistic psychologists rebelled against the mechanistic view of people proposed by the behaviourists. People are not mindless machines connecting stimulus to response like rats in a laboratory. Human beings have a unique capacity to think.

Cognitive psychologists also reacted against the simplistic views of the behaviourists, but their approach was more scientific. Cognitive psychologists believe that abnormal behaviour is a result of distorted thinking, or cognitions. If the thoughts, or cognitions, are changed, this will lead to a change in behaviour.

In the 1970s, the cognitive approach to abnormal behaviour came to the forefront as a result of separate contributions from several psychologists, the most notable being Bandura, Beck and Ellis, but Kelly is credited with being the first person to describe a cognitive approach to treating clients. Many different cognitive approaches are now widely used: all of them involve making certain assumptions, which are outlined below.

- The behaviourist view that a person responds passively to a stimulus is too simplistic.

- The psychodynamic view that a person is driven passively by unconscious internal processes ignores the fact that the person is thinking.
- Humanistic psychologists focus on feelings at the expense of cognitions.
- Cognitive therapies focus on the present. Unlike behaviourists and psychodynamic psychologists, they concentrate on what is happening now rather than unravelling the past.
- Changing the way a person thinks will help to change feelings and behaviour.
- Cognitive psychologists acknowledge that cognitions may not be the only factor involved. Some responses are not cognitive but automatic, and emotions and actions affect cognitions.

Bandura's social learning theory

Bandura says that behaviour is learned by copying models. He draws attention to the effects of vicarious reinforcement, whereby the person develops expectations about the consequences of behaving in a particular way. For example, if a child sees his friend being punished for not doing her homework, he would expect to be punished for not completing his own work.

Individuals have two types of expectancy:
- outcome expectancy, which is the person's estimate that a given behaviour will lead to a particular outcome
- efficacy expectancy, which is the person's belief that he or she can successfully carry out behaviour that leads to a desired outcome.

Activity 7

How would Bandura explain the following? Anne-Marie is afraid of dogs. Her mother is also afraid of dogs. Anne-Marie's fear is causing a problem because her fiancé has a small friendly dog which he is attached to. She wants to live with her fiancé, but will not share the house with the dog.

(Suggested answer on page 918.)

Beck's attribution theory

Several cognitive theorists, for example Beck, base their treatments on changing attributions. Attributions are the way people explain causes of their own and other people's behaviour (figure 24.6).

The aim of cognitive therapists is to identify attribution styles and change thought processes. Figure 24.6 demonstrates how depression could result from adopting a particular cognitive style. Therapy would involve changing the style of thinking.

24.6 Different types of attributions

- *Internal* is when behaviour is attributed to the person.
  Example: 'I obtained a low mark because I am not good at maths.'
- *External* is when behaviour is attributed to the environment.
  Example: 'I obtained a bad mark because I have a poor maths teacher.'
- *Stable* is when the cause of behaviour is seen to be unchangeable.
  Example: 'I will never be good at maths.'
- *Unstable* is when the cause of behaviour is seen to be changeable.
  Example: 'I will be better at maths when I move to another class.'
- *Global* is when the cause seems to occur in more than one aspect of the person's life.
  Example: 'I am poor at maths because I am not clever. I am not good at anything.'
- *Specific* is when the behaviour applies to a particular situation.
  Example: 'I am poor at maths but quite good at everything else. I have a mental block when it comes to numbers.'

Martin (1981) demonstrated how a person's attribution style could be related to depression. He showed how a student could develop depression after failing an important exam:

Internal attribution: *'It's my fault. I answered the questions incorrectly.' This results in lowered self-esteem.*

Stable attribution: *'If I resit the exam, the same thing will happen again.' This results in losing the motivation to change.*

Global attribution: *'I make a mess of everything I do. I will never succeed at anything.' This results in a lack of motivation to change or try something new.*

This kind of attribution style for a negative event means that the person has low self-esteem, feels that the future is bleak and that he or she has no control to change anything. All are features of depression.

Activity 8

A student has passed some of his exams but is depressed. What sort of attributions is this depressed student making to positive events? 'I passed that because it was an easy exam. Anyone could pass that. It was just a fluke. If I sat it again, I would probably fail. I can only do exams in that subject. I'm no good at anything else.'

(Suggested answer on page 918.)

■ Ellis's rational–emotive approach

Some therapists, such as Beck, concentrate on cognitive distortion. Ellis focuses on the fact that some people try to live up to unrealistic ideas. Some of Ellis's assumptions are shown in figure 24.7. Ellis attempts to uncover unrealistic cognitions. His patients are often surprised when they realise that they believe such ideas and as a result have been trying to live in an impossible way.

■ Evaluation of the cognitive approach

■ The cognitive behavioural approach is being widely used and is proving to be effective in a number of situations, for example in the treatment of mild depression. It is also being

24.7 Examples of false assumptions listed by Ellis

■ It is necessary for every adult to be loved and approved of by every significant person in their lives.

■ We should all be thoroughly competent, adequate and achieve in all respects if we are to be considered worthwhile.

■ We should be upset and disturbed by other people's problems.

■ A person's past history is the thing that determines present behaviour. An event that has strongly affected us will always have the same effect.

used in conjunction with other approaches. More details of this can be found in Unit 26.

■ It has been criticised by some for being superficial in that it can be regarded as focusing on symptoms of abnormal behaviour and ignoring causes.

■ By ignoring possible medical and historical factors and by suggesting that abnormality results from distorted thinking, the blame for the behaviour is placed on the shoulders of the individual. Some people question the ethics of this kind of approach.

Gerard Egan (1994) applies the principles of problem solving and learning to counselling and psychotherapy, claiming that these principles underlie every approach to helping. His problem management approach to therapy has been widely accepted internationally.

The biomedical model

The study of abnormal behaviour is historically linked with medicine. Abnormality is approached as an illness with biological causes in the **biomedical model**. Symptoms are grouped into patterns to form a syndrome which can be labelled and classified. Once the condition has been identified, there is a search for an **aetiology**, or cause, which should lead to treatment. The most widely used biological treatment is the administration of drugs, although sometimes electrical therapy or brain surgery is used.

The biomedical model suggests four possible causes of mental illness:

- germs
- genetics
- brain biochemistry
- neuroanatomy.

The role of germs in psychopathology

The effects of some germs have been well documented for some time. For example, if a pregnant woman contracts rubella in the early stages of her pregnancy, the developing nervous system of the foetus is damaged, causing the child possibly to be born with visual and/or auditory defects.

The search for viral causes for mental illness is still active. Liv Bode (1995) has found traces of a virus called **Borna Disease Virus (BDV)** in the blood cells of people with mood disorders. The disease is normally found in horses, making them hyperactive. Kathryn Carbone has also found antibodies against BDV in patients suffering from depression and other mood-related disorders, but researchers claim that much more research is required before proving that the person has been in contact with the virus, or that the virus does cause the abnormal behaviour.

The role of genetics in psychopathology

Since the technology has been available to identify individual genes, research in this field has expanded rapidly. Some conditions have been known to have genetic origins for many years. Consider the case study below.

Huntington's Chorea is a result of a steady loss of nerve cells and is controlled by a dominant gene on chromosome 4. Anyone who has the gene will develop the disease. In 1993 researchers finally developed a genetic screening test which could identify whether someone will get Huntington's Chorea.

Activity 9

Discuss with your group the ethical dilemmas faced by people who have relatives with Huntington's Chorea. For instance, if your parent had the disease, would you want to be screened? What about your children, or an unborn child?

Brain biochemistry

Major progress has been made in the understanding of brain chemistry in the last few years. The best documented has been the discovery of the role of neurotransmitters in the brain. For example, a link has been established between dopamine and schizophrenia (see Unit 26 for a detailed discussion of this). More recently, interest has been shown in the role played by serotonin. Serotonin is a naturally occurring chemical which acts as a neurotransmitter and a local hormone. It affects temperature regulation, sleep and wakefulness, sexual behaviour and psychotic behaviour. It works by locking onto nerve receptors called 5-HT receptors. There is some evidence that arsonists and people who have killed themselves by violent means have low levels of 5-HT receptors in the brain. It is also implicated in addictive behaviour. Studies have shown that rats addicted to alcohol reduce their intake after being given drugs

Case study—Huntington's Chorea

The face begins to twitch. Later, tremors spread to other parts of the body. At first walking and speech become slow and clumsy, later becoming impossible. There are also psychological symptoms: depression, memory impairment, anxiety, poor judgement, possibly alcohol or drug abuse and changes in sexual behaviour, varying from lack of sexual response to promiscuity. The condition starts between the ages of 30 and 50, sometimes earlier. The symptoms get progressively worse for 15 years until the sufferer dies.

that block the 5-HT receptors. Other conditions, such as migraine and depression, also seem to be connected to serotonin. Depression has been linked to a reduction of brain neurotransmitters, including serotonin.

■ Neuroanatomy

There are many conditions that result from damage to the brain. The symptoms depend on which part of the brain has been damaged, but all cases of organic brain disease exhibit some of the following:

■ loss of memory and other intellectual functions
■ a lack of awareness of the body and surroundings
■ swift changes in emotion
■ often a loss of emotional resilience, in that the person's emotions are easily aroused and easily affect the ability to make decisions and learn.

Damage to the brain is caused in many ways. The most common is a result of head injury, either through an accident or fighting. Misuse of alcohol is implicated in a large number of accidents and incidents of violence. Sometimes viruses or bacteria cause damage, for example meningitis is a result of a viral infection of the meninges (a membrane covering the brain and spinal cord). It can cause motor and sensory impairments and cause mental retardation in young children. Strokes are another common cause of brain injury. They are a result of the blood supply to an area of the brain being impeded, causing destruction of the brain cells.

■ Evaluation of the biomedical model

■ One of the strengths of the biomedical model is that its basic concepts are objective and measurable. However, it does not provide all the answers. The relationship between physical and psychological causes and effects is complex. Organic illnesses give rise to psychological conditions, and it is not easy to establish whether a psychological event causes changes in the physical condition or the physical condition causes changes in the psychology.

■ What comes first, the depression or the change in brain chemistry? If it is possible to correct the brain chemistry by psychological intervention, it may be preferable to medical treatments such

as drug administration, the side-effects of which can be very unpleasant.

■ One of the main contributions of the biomedical approach is the development of diagnostic classification systems, which are discussed later in the unit.

The consequences of adopting a model

The implications of each model for treatment, together with practical and ethical issues relating to the use of different therapies, is discussed in Unit 26.

Anyone adopting a particular model or explanation of abnormality is making a decision in advance about the kind of data he or she will collect and how the information will be interpreted. Some possibilities will be ignored and some data will be overlooked when decisions have to be made. For example, behaviourists ignore biochemistry in their view of schizophrenia, pointing out that it is prevalent in lower-class groups living in poor social conditions. This is because they begin with the assumption that behaviour is a result of response to the environment. Biomedical psychologists would point out that there are a large number of socially deprived people who do not have schizophrenia. The behaviourists may then reply that those who do not have schizophrenia were subjected to different reinforcement histories. The biomedical model would suggest that biochemical factors predispose individuals to schizophrenia and the condition means that they are unable to function well in society and look after themselves and will therefore end in the lower social class. The behaviourists would say that the biologists were so intent on looking for chemical causes, they were ignoring social factors. The biologists would claim that the behaviourists were so keen to find social causes that they overlooked the biological factors.

To an objective observer, it may seem that there could be some truth in both points of view. Certainly, the current view is that abnormality is too diverse and too complex to be explained by a single model, and that an *eclectic* approach may be the best way forward. An article by Meise and Fleischhacker (1996) drew attention to the need to treat people suffering from schizophrenia by two methods. One is the administration of drugs, such as clozapine, to alleviate the debilitating symptoms. The second is a psychosocial rehabilitation programme to help sufferers deal with the debilitating effects of the illness, so that they can fulfil some social roles and learn to cope with the problems of unemployment and possible homelessness which results from the illness. The researchers point out that at the moment in the UK the patient receives medical treatment from one agency and rehabilitation from social services. This often results in piecemeal treatment, because of the lack of integration of the two systems. An eclectic approach may be desirable, but the implementation of the approach will depend on local authority planning, which focuses on political issues and costs.

Whatever the contributions different groups make to understanding abnormal behaviour, sufferers will not benefit from the research unless there is a concerted effort to integrate the knowledge and provide the facilities for treatment.

Self-assessment questions

4 Explain in your own words the following terms:
   a psychoanalysis
   b repression.

5 State one way in which each of the following disagreed with Freud:
   a Jung
   b Adler
   c Erikson.

6 List the difference between:
   a the psychodynamic approach and
   b the behaviourist approach to behaviour.

7 Define the following terms:
   a self
   b ideal self
   c self-actualisation.

8 Complete the following sentences:
   a Cognitive therapies concentrate on the present; behaviourists concentrate on the _____.
   b Cognitive therapies concentrate on conscious thought processes; psychodynamic therapies concentrate on _____.
   c Cognitive therapists focus on cognition; humanistic therapists focus on _____.

9 Give an example of the role of each of the following in the explanation of abnormal behaviour:
   a germs
   b genetics
   c brain biochemistry
   d neuroanatomy.
(Suggested answers on page 919.)

Diagnostic classification systems

We have already seen that the biomedical model has given rise to the development of systems for classifying abnormal behaviour.

Throughout history, there has been a search for the causes of deviant behaviour. Many civilisations in the past – for example the Chinese, Egyptians and Ancient Greeks – thought that afflicted people were being controlled by evil spirits. This idea was also prevalent in the Middle Ages. Treatment was in the hands of the priests who attempted to exorcise the evil spirits. During the seventeenth century mentally disturbed men, women and children were hunted down, accused and tortured because they were thought to be witches.

Whilst such views of mental illness dominated thinking at various points in history, there was another view which from time to time gained precedence. The view was that abnormal or deviant behaviour was a result of biological causes. This medical view led to attempts to classify abnormal behaviour according to the symptoms the person displayed. Hippocrates the Greek, who is recognised as the father of modern medicine, classified mental disorders into three categories: mania, melancholia (depression) and phrenitis (brain fever). He thought that mental health depended on the balance of the four 'humors' or body fluids – blood, black bile, yellow bile and phlegm – and that an imbalance produced disorders. For example, he thought that melancholia was caused by too much black bile. His treatments were gentle. For melancholia, he prescribed careful diet, tranquillity, sobriety and an abstinence from sexual activities. Our current knowledge of anatomy makes his explanations seem bizzare, but it is interesting to reflect that today's health experts frequently put forward the view that a balanced life style is essential to maintaining good physical and mental health.

The medical view prevailed throughout history gaining dominance at different points in time. In 1913, Emil Kraepelin laid the foundations of the current systems used to classify mental disorders. He thought that mental illness was like physical illness because certain signs and symptoms occurred together with sufficient regularity to merit the condition being called a disease. Several classification systems have been attempted since Kraepelin's system and a number of revisions have been made. One of the difficulties is that the diagnoses were *unreliable*, i.e. different physicians examining the same patient arrived at different conclusions about what the patient was suffering from. Some conditions are easier to identify than others, for example phobias are easily identified, but there is much less agreement about personality disorders.

Attempts to revise the system have improved their reliability, but there are still areas of disagreement, partly because a **diagnosis** ultimately depends on the judgement of individual practitioners, and the amount of information available to them. (See Unit 26 page 955.)

The two most widely used classification systems are:

- the International Classification of Diseases (ICD)
- the Diagnostic and Statistical Manual of Mental Disorders (DSM).

ICD 10

The International Classification of Diseases is a classification of all medical diseases. It was developed by the World Health Organisation and lis currently in its tenth edition (ICD 10). Part of the manual is devoted to mental disorders. Figure 24.8 shows the main categories and some of the disorders identified in this section of the manual.

There are many similarities between the ICD 10 and the DSM IV, which is outlined below, and attempts are being made to bring the two systems closer together.

DSM IV

The DSM was first established by the American Psychiatric Association in 1952. Since then there have been a number of revisions. The revised edition that is in use at the moment is the DSM IV (figure 24.9). The DSM IV has been developed by a team of psychologists, psychiatrists and other professionals who have redefined descriptions of the disorders by drawing on published studies and research analysing existing information.

The manual describes hundreds of disorders focusing on the following:

- *diagnostic features*, i.e. symptoms that must be present for a person to be said to be suffering from the disorder
- *associated features*, i.e. clinical symptoms that are usually present, but not essential for a diagnosis to be made
- *associated laboratory findings and physical signs*, i.e. biological factors associated with the condition
- *age-related, culture-related and gender-related features*, i.e. variations in each disorder that may relate to age, culture and gender.

24.8 Examples of the classification of disorders according to ICD 10

Psychoses

Senile and presenile organic psychotic conditions
Senile dementia, Alzheimer's disease, Huntington's disease, Brain infection

Schizophrenia and related disorders
Paranoid, Hebephrenic [disorganised], Catatonic

Psychoactive substance disorders
States relating to: intoxication, abuse, dependence and withdrawal with reference to the following substances: alcohol, amphetamines, caffeine, cocaine, hallucinogens, inhalants, nicotine, cannabis, opioids

Affective [mood] disorders
Depressive disorder, Bipolar disorder, Seasonal

affective disorder [SAD]

Neurotic disorders
Generalised anxiety

Phobias
Obsessive compulsive disorder Post-traumatic stress reaction

Disorders specific to childhood and adolescence
Dyslexia, autism, hyperkinetic disorder, conduct disorder

Mental retardation
Mild, severe, profound

Personality disorders
Psychopathic disorder

24.9 Examples of the classification of disorders according to DSM IV

■ **Disorders first diagnosed in infancy, childhood or adolescence**
Mental retardation (Axis II)
Learning disorders
Reading disorder, Mathematics disorder
Pervasive developmental disorders
Autism
Attention deficit and disruptive behaviour disorders
Attention-deficit/Hyperactivity disorder, conduct disorder
■ **Delirium, dementia, amnesia and other cognitive disorders**
Dementia
Dementia of Alzheimer's type with early onset, Dementia of Alzheimer's type with late onset, Dementia due to HIV disease, dementia due to head trauma, Dementia due to Huntington's Disease, Dementia due to Creutsfeld-Jakob disease
■ **Substance-related disorders**
Alcohol-related disorders
Alcohol use disorders, Alcohol-induced disorders
Amphetamine-related disorders
Amphetamine use disorders, Amphetamine-induced disorders

Caffeine-related disorders
Cannabis-related disorders
Cocaine-related disorders
Hallucinogen-related disorders
Inhalant-related disorders
Nicotine-related disorders
Opioid-related disorders
Other (or unknown) substance-related disorders
■ **Schizophrenic and other psychotic disorders**
Schizophrenia, Paranoid type, Disorganised type, Catatonic type, Undifferentiated type, Residual type
■ **Mood disorders**
Depressive disorders
Major depressive disorder, Dysthymic disorder
Bipolar disorders
Bipolar disorder, Cyclothymic disorder
Other mood disorders
Mood disorders due to general medical condition, Substance-induced mood disorders
■ **Anxiety Disorders**
Panic disorder without agoraphobia, Panic disorder with agoraphobia, Specific phobia, Social phobia, Obsessive-compulsive disorder, Post-traumatic stress disorder

24.9 Examples of the classification of disorder according to DSM IV cont'd

- **Somatoform disorder**
Conversion disorder (Conversion hysteria), Hypochondrias
- **Sexual and gender-related disorders**
- **Eating disorders**
Anorexia nervosa, Bulimia nervosa
- **Sleep disorders**
- **Impulse disorders**

Kleptomania
- **Personality disorders**
- **Other conditions that may be a focus of clinical attention**
- **Problems related to abuse or neglect**
Sexual abuse of a child, Neglect of a child
- **Relational problems**

24.10 Diagnostic axes of the DSM IV

Axis I   The actual disorder, i.e. the diagnostic label.

Axis II   Personality disorders, i.e. maladaptive aspects of the personality that affect the person's life.

Axis III   Medical conditions relevant to the disorder.

Axis IV   Psychosocial and environmental problems that could affect the diagnosis and treatment, for example divorce, retirement, pregnancy.

Axis V   Assessment of functioning on a scale of 1–90. Examples are adjustment to work and social relationships over the past year.

The diagnostician requires information from several sources because the disorder is classified along five axes (see figure 24.10).

Cultural factors in diagnostic classification

One of the major changes made on the DSM IV is the attempt to take account of the role of cultural factors in the development of the conditions and in the diagnostic processes. It is hoped that the inclusion of sections focusing on cultural factors will alert the diagnostician to the possibility of unintended bias in diagnosis as a result of their own cultural background (see page 911).

The DSM IV contains a new section in the description of each disorder which includes culturally related features. Cultures have different ways of describing distress and there are some symptoms that are specific to particular cultures. There is a new appendix that describes culture-bound disorders and there has been an attempt to fit culturally specific disorders into defined categories. For example, in some rural areas of Japan some people hold the belief that they are possessed by foxes. The condition is called *kitsunetsuki*.

Evaluation of classification systems

- Two major criticisms are that the systems do not identify causes nor do they fit in with the theories proposed by the alternative models discussed earlier in the unit.
- Currently, the systems are used by some, but not all, psychologists. In the next section we consider some of the arguments for and against the use of diagnostic systems.

- Jung (1961) said:

    'Clinical diagnoses are important since they give the doctor a certain orientation, but they do not help the patient. The crucial thing is the story. For it alone shows the human background and the human suffering, and only at that point can the doctor's therapy begin to operate.' (Figure 24.11.)

Activity 10

Can you think of any good reasons for a clinician to make a diagnosis? Discuss them with your group before reading on.

The following reasons are usually given for making a *diagnosis*:

- It assists communication between professionals since it is easier to use one word than a lengthy description of each patient.
- It leads to possible treatment plans.
- If the condition is classified, it is easier to start researching the aetiology.
- It enables research into the causes. One could start by asking what do all the cases have in common? Identifying common factors could lead to identification of possible causes.

Figure 24.11   Carl Jung

- The DSM IV also helps to identify other factors relevant to treatment such as the mental condition of the patient, and social, environmental and cultural factors relevant to further treatment.
- The DSM IV also attempts to determine the patient's willingness to cooperate with the treatment plan.

Inter-rater reliability between diagnosticians

However, if the diagnosis is to be useful it must be reliable. There should be inter-rater reliability between the diagnosticians.

Activity 11

What is meant by inter-rater reliability when referring to diagnosis?

(Suggested answer on page 918.)

The role of expectancy in diagnosis

Several factors influence diagnosis. We have already seen that individual judgements play an important part. The case study on page 912 (Langer and Abelson, 1974) demonstrates the effect of preconceptions on interpersonal perception. In this case, the professionals were being influenced by information they had been given.

The role of interpersonal factors in diagnosis

Sometimes the characteristics of the patient can affect the judgement of the person making the diagnosis. The relative ages, sexes ad cultures of the

Case study – the effect of expectation on diagnosis (Langer and Abelson's study, 1974)

Professionals watched a video of a young man being interviewed. One group was told that he was a job applicant, the other group was told that he was a patient in a psychiatric clinic.

The group who thought he was a job applicant described him as attractive, conventional and innovative. A panel of independent judges who looked at the group's descriptions said the members of the group were describing a well-adjusted person.

The second group who thought he was a patient described him as uptight, defensive, passive and aggressive. The independent panel of judges said that members of this group had described a very disturbed person.

patient and clinician are factors which can affect judgement. The DSM IV has attempted to address the considerable concern about the influence of cultural factors on diagnosis. The case study below highlights some of the cultural issues relating to diagnosis.

The main question arising from this study is: how have these ethnic differences arisen? Is it because the black patients are perceived to be in more need of compulsory care or are there other factors? The researchers suggested that the reasons are complex. Black patients see the mental health service as inaccessible and not appropriate to their requirements. Because they are out of contact with the services, they may delay seeking treatment until the condition is so bad that treatment becomes compulsory.

This interpretation is reinforced by other research findings. For example, there is little evidence to suggest that women, black people or other disadvantaged groups are more likely to be diagnosed as suffering from a psychopathological condition (Abramowitz and Murray, 1983). However, there is some evidence for an opposite bias (Lopez, 1989). There seems to be a tendency to diagnose non-male, non-white groups as showing *less* disturbance than they actually have and for assuming that conditions like depression are more 'normal' for women than men, just as substance abuse is seen to be more normal among black people than white people. The result is that these disorders are perceived to be less serious than they actually are. They could therefore go unrecognised and untreated until the condition has reached a serious stage.

Davies's study raises several other issues related to diagnosis. One key point is that a person will not be diagnosed if he or she fails to see a doctor. The decision to seek help will vary from person to person. A study by Salmon and May (1995) demonstrates how the way in which a patient presents symptoms affects the doctor's decisions.

Case study – a study investigating the risk of compulsory psychiatric admission in London

The researchers (Davies et al., 1996) investigated the risk of begin detained for compulsory treatment under the Mental Health Act 1983 in a group of people with psychotic disorders (serious mental illnesses) from different ethnic groups. Of the 439 patients diagnosed as psychotic, nearly 50 per cent of the white population had been detained compared to 70 per cent of the black Caribbean and 69 per cent of the black African patients. The conclusion was that black Caribbeans and black Africans were more likely to be detained than white people.

Cultural and linguistic constraints may prevent a patient expressing emotional distress. A doctor's insensitivity to psychological concerns may lead to misinterpretation of a patient's complaints. The doctor may assume a complaint is physical rather than emotional.

Activity 12

Discuss with your group factors that may encourage or discourage a person from going to a doctor or psychologist for help.

Self-assessment questions

10 Draw up a table indicating points for and against the diagnostic labelling of behaviour.

11 Draw up a table to show the advantages amd disadvantages of systems for classifying psychopathological conditions.
(Suggested answers on page 919.)

Methods used in diagnosis

The clinical interview

The best tool for diagnosis is considered to be the face-to-face interview. Open-ended interviews in which the interviewer shows empathy towards the patient is considered the best way to encourage the patient to discuss his or her problems. Empathy is the ability to see things in a sympathetic way from the point of view of the patient without making judgements about the patient. However, structured interviews are considered better for obtaining information about traumatic events and substance abuse (American Psychiatric Association, 1996).

Interview techniques are not without their problems. Many practical and ethical considerations need to be made. For example, children must be accompanied by a parent or another adult. Some elderly patients may be confused or slightly deaf. They may need someone to help with the communication. Similarly, there may be a language problem if the interviewer does not speak the same language as the patient. An interpreter who can be relied upon for confidentiality and to give direct translations, not interpretations, is essential.

Activity 13

Interviews are interpersonal situations. What is meant by an interpersonal situation?

(Suggested answer on page 918.)

Psychometric tests

Interviews are not the only methods used for obtaining information. Sometimes psychometric tests or neurological tests may be used to support information gained in the interview. These can be divided into three broad categories:

■ intelligence tests
■ personality inventories
■ projective tests.

Intelligence tests

The *Wechsler Adult Intelligence Scale* (WAIS) is one of the most widely used tests. It provides an intelligence quotient (IQ) which is made up from two subscores, verbal IQ and a performance IQ. The verbal IQ is made up from general knowledge, vocabulary and various reasoning tests. The performance score is gained from more practical tests such as the ability to do puzzles and copy designs. They play a large part in assessing brain damage and mental retardation and are widely used in schools when educational assessments are required.

■ Personality inventories

There are a wide range of inventories in use, usually they take the form of questionnaires. The *Minnesota Multiphasic Personality Inventory* (MMPI) is one example. It consists of 550 questions relating to behaviours, thoughts and feelings. Patterns of scores have been found by looking at the scores obtained by people who suffer from identified conditions such as depression. A person's score pattern can then be compared to other known scores. The MMPI is the same as any other questionnaire because it is subject to distortions. It is easy to lie, be evasive and there is a tendency to present oneself in the best possible light.

■ Projective tests

These tests were developed by psychodynamic psychologists. The general principle is that the person is presented with an ambiguous picture or pattern and asked to write or talk about it. The idea is that individuals will put their own interpretation on the image and consequently project their attitudes and motives into the picture.

The most widely used tests are the *Rorschach Test*, which is a set of symmetrical patterns made from ink blots, and the *Thematic Apperception Test* (TAT), which is a series of ambiguous pictures (see figure 15.7). Scoring these tests requires a considerable amount of skill and the inter-rater reliability is very low. For this reason, many professionals do not use them, though they can be helpful for identifying underlying tendencies. For example, if a person sees aggression as a underlying theme, it could alert the tester to an aggressive personality trait that has been overlooked.

Neurological tests

These tests use brain *x-ray techniques* and *electroencephalographs* (EEGs) to investigate the way

that the brain is working. EEGs measure electrical discharges from the brain. Both techniques are useful for diagnosing abnormal brain functions, for example epilepsy. The tests require skilled operators and are costly. (See Unit 13 for a further discussion on brain x-ray techniques).

Whenever tests are used the assumption is that the condition is present at the time of testing and that the test will correctly determine whether or not the condition is present. The clinician is always working within the probability levels that the tests will give the correct results.

Observation

During an interview the clinician gains valuable information by observing the behaviour and non-verbal communications of the patient. Information from observations can also come from a variety of other sources, for example nursing staff if the patient is in hospital, social workers or teachers.

Activity 14

Identify the practical and ethical considerations that need to be taken into account when obtaining information by observation.

(Suggested answer on page 918.)

A useful source of information is self observation. In this situation, the person is asked to keep records of his or her own behaviour. This overcomes some of the ethical difficulties identified in Activity 14. It is, however, only suitable for some conditions. For example, Mischel (1976) asked a patient to record her asthma attacks. The records showed that 9 out of 15 of the attacks happened when she had been in contact with her mother. On 80 per cent of the days when she had not seen her mother, she suffered no attacks. Mother seemed to be a key contributor to the onset of the attacks. This had not been revealed in interviews with the patient and was not suspected because talking about her mother did not provoke an attack.

Observation is very useful, particularly when investigating difficult behaviour in children, but it is time consuming and costly. It can also be unreliable.

Activity 15

Jane's primary school teacher is concerned about her behaviour. How would you observe Jane's behaviour in order to make a diagnosis? What difficulties do you think you may encounter when attempting to carry out the observation?

(Suggested answer on page 918.)

Comorbidity

This section has explored the uses of diagnosis, and some of the methods used for diagnosis together with difficulties involved in arriving at an accurate assessment. There are critics of the diagnostic process because diagnosis is essentially labelling behaviour and there are objections to this. Nevertheless, many clinicians feel that diagnosis is useful and the recent ICD 10 and DSM IV systems have drawn attention to an important phenomenon that has been given little attention until recently: this is *comorbidity*. Comorbidity is the presence of more than one disorder at the same time (Wittchen and Esan, 1993). In fact, at least one-third of cases in general practice fulfil the criteria for more than one disorder, for example anxiety and depression often appear at the same time. Comorbidity presents a complex pattern which the classification systems are helping to unravel. This may provide useful information in the future because body chemicals have a variety of roles and the imbalance of one of them could easily produce a variety of conditions. The better the understanding of biochemistry and the clearer the clinical picture, the easier it will be to clarify the relative roles of biological and social processes in psychopathology.

Self-assessment question

12 List the methods used by clinicians to obtain information which is used for the diagnosis of psychopathological conditions.

(Suggested answer on page 919.)

Unit summary

- Defining 'normality' and 'abnormality' are problematic and the *labelling* of an individual as 'abnormal' often results in the person being seen to be mentally ill and in need of treatment. *Szasz* highlights how such labelling has the potential for *social abuse*, such as involuntary confinement and drug treatment. Labelling can lead to a *self-fulfilling prophecy* and be accompanied by *social stigma*.

- *Statistical criteria* are used in classification, thus defining unusual behaviour as abnormal. However some unusual behaviour is valued by society and not seen as abnormal. *Elements of abnormality* outlined by Rosenhan and Seligman consider seven factors which need to be taken into account when defining behaviour as abnormal:

- Different approaches/models have been adopted to try and explain abnormality. These include *psychodynamic, behaviourist, humanistic, cognitive* and *biomedical* models. *Psychodynamic* approaches emphasise the mental role of *instincts* and *conflicts* and how they direct behaviour. This approach is concerned with

Summary cont'd.

conscious and *unconscious* behaviour. Freud suggested we use *defence mechanisms,* unconscious ways of resolving conflicts, which are universal but exaggerated in people suffering mental disturbance. Post-Freudians such as *Adler, Jung, Horney and Erikson* have extended his theory.

■ The *behaviourist* approach was the main challenge to Freud. Abnormal behaviour is seen as *faulty learning* which can be unlearned. Two main behavioural techniques involve *classical and operant conditioning.*

■ The *humanistic* approach, sometimes named *'the third force',* believes in free will and rejects the deterministic views of both the psychodynamic and behaviourist models. *Carl Rogers* developed *client-centred therapy* which aimed to help the clients reach their full potential *self-actualisation.*

■ The *cognitive* approach sees abnormality as *distorted thinking.* If these cognitions are changed it will lead to a change in behaviour. *Bandura, Beck, Ellis & Kelly* developed cognitive techniques focussing on what is happening *now* rather than unravelling the past.

■ The *biomedical* model is the historic link with medicine and the *aetiology* of the abnormality is identified. Usually this is seen to originate from germs, genetic, brain chemistry and neuroanatomy. Currently the biomedical and cognitive approaches are dominating psychology but many clinicians now subscribe to an *eclectic* approach.

■ *Diagnostic classification systems* have been developed from the early work of *Kraepelin.* The two most widely used systems today are *ICD10* and *DSMIV.* The role of interpersonal factors and cultural issues are now considered.

■ For a diagnosis to be useful there must be good *inter-rater reliability* between diagnosticians. Interpersonal factors, culture and race can influence the reliability of the diagnosis and although these are now considered in the DSM, they can still influence the clinician's decision.

■ Several methods are used in diagnosis. These include the *Clinical interview, psychometric tests, neurological tests and observation* which help gain information needed for an accurate diagnosis. *Comorbidity,* the presence of more than one disorder at the same time, also must be considered.

■ Even so, diagnostic labels facilitate communication between clinicians and may provide avenues for understanding the causes of psychopathological conditions. Many psychologists maintain that making an accurate diagnosis is essential if appropriate treatment is to be administered.

Terms to define

aetiology
behaviourist model
biomedical model
Borna Disease Virus (BDV)
collective unconscious
defence mechanisms
diagnosis

erogenous zones
genital stage
humanistic model
psychodynamic
unconscious

Further reading

Green, S (1994) *Individual Differences: Normal and Abnormal*, Laurence Erlbaum, Hove.

Chapter 5 covers the behavioural, biomedical and psychoanalytic models of abnormality and suggests they can only be understood in terms of an eclectic (diathesis-stress) approach.

Humphreys, P (1997) 'Social, cutural and subcultural differences in the determination of (ab)normality', *Psychology Review, 3(4)*, 10–15.

An exploration of social and cultural diversity in relation to sexuality. 'One society's normality is another's abnormality' on p. 13 is a thought provoking article.

Kline, P (1994), 'Some psychoanalytic perspectives', *Psychology Review, 1(2)*, 7–9.

Although Freudian theory is over 100 years old it is shown to be relevant to many contemporary issues in psychology.

Prentice, P (1995) 'Dream analysis', *Psychology Review, 2(1)*, 12–15.

Freud, Adler, Erikson and Jung are discussed along with neuro-chemical explanations of dreams and dreaming. This article also links with Unit 14 on awareness.

Answers

▪ Suggested answers to activities

4

a	identification	f	isolation
b	regression	g	rationalisation
c	repression	h	denial
d	projection	i	displacement
e	sublimation	j	reaction formation

5

Before learning

Rat ————————→ neutral response

Loud noise (ucs) ———→ Fear (ucr): a reflex response

During learning

Rat (cs) + noise (ucs) —————————→ Fear (ucr)

After learning

Rat (cs) —————————————→ Fear (cr)

The fear reaction generalised to objects which resembled the white rat.

6

a   It seems that Joanne's mother is encouraging her behaviour by rewarding her tantrums. The sweets always follow the tantrum. She is inadvertently using a variable reinforcement schedule. Joanne never knows how long her behaviour is going to have to last before the reward arrives.

b   Tariq started so well, but received no reward for his efforts, as the teacher's attention was always focused on other children. His parents were inadvertently punishing his efforts by making critical remarks about his work. There was no incentive to carry on with his work. He gained the teacher's attention (his reward) by being naughty. The desired behaviour, i.e. working, was ignored; the undesired behaviour was rewarded.

7

Anne-Marie has learned her fear from her mother. Her mother was an influential role model whom Anne-Marie observed and copied. The outcome expectancy is that the dog will harm her. The efficacy expectancy is that she will not be able to overcome her fear in order to live with her fiancé's dog.

8

For positive events, the student was making external, unstable, specific attributions.

External: 'It was an easy exam.'
Unstable: 'It was a fluke.'
Specific: 'I can only do exams in that subject.'

11

Different clinicians will arrive at the same conclusion about what is wrong with the person.

13

In a clinical interview there are usually two people relating to each other: the patient and the clinician. They are both bringing perceptions, stereotypes, emotions, past experiences and personalities into the situation. These factors will affect the way each relates to the other.

14

Observation of body language is a necessary part of the diagnostic process. However, if the person is being observed in hospital, at home or at school, the main ethical consideration is the invasion of the person's privacy. People should be told that they are being observed and informed consent should be given. However, if a person knows that he or she is being watched, the behaviour is likely to change, and this in turn could affect the diagnosis.

15

First, it would be necessary to identify which behaviour was being observed. A method of recording would have to be established. The times and lengths of the recordings would also need to be established. Trial runs would be necessary and some method arranged for checking the reliability of the recordings. This could involve the use of two observers or videoing behaviour so that it could be viewed on more than one occasion, possibly by more than one observer.

The process will be time consuming and could present practical difficulties if the teacher is attempting to make observations in a classroom with other children needing to be taught. It would also be necessary to make observations in situations other than the classroom, such as at home. This requires the cooperation of the parents and also presents the practical problem of who is to do the observation. It also raises ethical issues relating to the invasion of privacy.

Suggested answers to self-assessment questions

1
- Labelling serves no purpose.
- Labelling can lead to social or political abuse.
- There is no accepted criteria for mental illness.
- Different people perceive and interpret behaviour in different ways.

2

Some talents are unusual but desirable, so they are not classed as abnormal. Some characteristics are common, but because they are not desirable they are classed as abnormal.

3

Rosenham and Selgman's seven criteria for judging abnormal behaviour are listed in figure 24.1 on page 894.

4
a Psychoanalysis – method used by Freud to obtain information about a person's unconscious thoughts and feelings.
b Repression – defence mechanism by means of which thoughts or memories that give rise to anxiety are pushed into the unconscious mind.

5
a (i) Jung believed there was a collective unconscious, i.e. thoughts passed down from generation to generation. (ii) Personality development continued into adult life. Freud said it stopped when the person was sexually mature, i.e. in the genital phase. (iii) Jung recognised a 'spiritual' drive.
b (i) Social issues were important to personality development. (ii) There is a drive to overcome feelings of inferiority.
c (i) Personality development continues throughout life. (ii) Socio-cultural influences play an important part in personality development.

6
a Psychodynamic approach: (i) Behaviour determined by unconscious thought process. (ii) Abnormal behaviour is a result of conflict in the unconscious. (iii) Behaviour can only be changed by understanding and resolving conflicts.
b Behaviourist approach: (i) Behaviour determined by the environment. (ii) Abnormal behaviour is a result of faulty learning. (iii) Behaviour can be changed by changing the environment.

7
a Self is the perception, attitudes and values that define who we are.
b Ideal self is the person that we would like to be, or that we are striving to be.
c Self-actualisation is the process of fulfilling one's potential.

8
a past
b unconscious thought processes
c thinking
d emotions

9
a Borna Disease Virus; meningitis virus leads to brain damage
b Huntington's Chorea
c Dopamine in schizophrenia; serotonin in depression
d Stroke leads to brain damage which leads to behaviour impairment which can lead to emotional reactions such as depression.

10 See table 10 over the page.

11 See table 11 over the page.

12

Clinical interview: structured; unstructured.
Psychometic methods: intelligence tests; inventories.
Projective tests: Rorschach blot tests; Thematic Apperception Test.
Neurological tests; EEG.
Observation by the clinician; self observation.

Table 10

For labelling	Against labelling
The person is comforted by knowing what is wrong.	Labelling can lead to social political abuse.
The person feels less isolated if he or she knows others have the same condition.	Labels are accompanied by social stigma.
Labelling (diagnosis) leads to treatment.	Labelling can lead to self-fulfilling prophecy.
Labelling may help to find a cause.	

Table 11

Advantages	Disadvantages
Aids to diagnosis	Differences between classification schemes can confuse
Enable description of syndromes	Labels patients
Actions communication shorthand	Reliability and validity not good in places
	Time consuming

Unit 25

Psychopathology

Chris Henney

This unit covers:

Anxiety disorders

Eating disorders

Depression

Schizophrenia

By the end of this unit, you should be able to:

- understand the main symptoms of schizophrenia; depression; anxiety disorders including phobias and post-traumatic stress disorder, and the eating disorders anorexia nervosa and bulimia

- understand the explanations of each of the conditions based on the following models: psychodynamic, behaviourist, cognitive, humanistic and biomedical

- note the possible contributions of genetic/neurological and social/psychological factors

- compare and evaluate the explanations.

Unit 25 Contents

Introduction

Psychopathology means diseases or disorders of the mind. The aim of this unit is to describe and consider explanations of abnormalities and psychological disorders.

Anxiety disorders

There are several disorders in which fear or **anxiety** play a major role. In this section we discuss phobias and post-traumatic stress disorder.

Phobias

Phobias are persistent and irrational fears of objects or situations. For example, the case of Little Albert's phobia of white furry animals is described in Unit 24 page 900. Another famous case study is described below.

In both of these cases the child developed an intense fear of animals. There are many different phobias some of which are shown in figure 25.1.

Simple specific phobias usually start in children between the ages of 3 and 8 years. They may continue for many years. Others may start early in adulthood. They are more common in women than men. *Complex phobias* start in later life, between the ages of 18 and 28. Social phobias usually start between the ages of 11 and 16. Agoraphobia is more common in women, social phobia more common in men. There has been a considerable amount of research into phobias, and different models offer different explanations.

25.1 Classification of phobias

■ Specific phobias
The fear is directed at a limited set of stimuli which elicit intense fear which is so unrealistic that it interferes with daily life. There are five groups:
- animal type, for example fear of spiders or dogs
- natural environment type, for example fear of heights
- blood injury type, for example fear of dentists or injections
- situational type, for example claustrophobia
- miscellaneous type, for example choking.

■ Complex phobias
Agoraphobia – a fear of open spaces or crowds. Social phobia – a fear of situations in which the person is being observed, such as public transport, or social events.

■ The psychodynamic approach
Freud's interpretation is related to the resolution of the Oedipus complex in the phallic stage of development. The young boy is in love with his mother and wishes to seduce her. He is jealous of his father and wishes to kill him. He is also afraid that his father might punish him with the ultimate sanction, castration. Usually, this conflict is resolved by the young boy taking on the identity of his father. This represents the superego or conscience, the parent within. A similar, but more complex, situation was proposed for girls who need to resolve the Electra complex.

In Hans's case above he is struggling unconsciously with the Oedipus complex. The conflict creates so much anxiety that the anxiety is displaced onto another object, in Hans's case

Case study – Little Hans (Freud, 1909)

When he was 4 years old, a boy called Hans saw a horse fall down in the street. The huge animal thrashed its legs violently in an attempt to get up. When Little Hans was 5 years old, his father consulted Freud because Hans had developed a fear of horses that was so intense he refused to go out of doors because he was afraid that a horse would bite him.

horses. The phobia is cured when the person gains insight into the unconscious conflict. Freud produced evidence that Hans's father was perceived by Hans to be like a horse. He used to play at being carried on his father's back; his father was the horse. His father wore glasses similar to horses' blinkers and he had a white moustache, which Hans thought made his father look like a horse.

The evidence for the Oedipus complex is controversial because it comes from case studies. In fact, the Little Hans study was one of Freud's main sources. Other interpretations have been made. Wolpe and Rachman (1960) criticised Freud's interpretation. They could find no evidence that Hans wished to sleep with his mother or that he hated or feared his father. They could find no evidence for the supposed relationship between Hans's father and horses. They proposed a different explanation, based on association learning.

Activity 1

Discuss Freud's possible reply to Wolpe and Rachman's criticism.

■ The behaviourist approach

Wolpe and Rachman (1960) suggested a Pavlovian explanation.

Activity 2

Try to explain Hans's fear of horses using the following concepts: conditioned stimulus (cs), conditioned response (cr), unconditioned stimulus (ucs), unconditioned response (ucr). (See Unit 11 page 356 for a review of these terms.)

(Suggested answer on page 950.)

There is evidence from several sources that fears can arise in this way, for example Little Albert (see Unit 24 page 900). There are, however, some difficulties with this explanation. For instance, why does the fear not extinguish when the person has had no contact with the feared object because he or she has been avoiding it? Mowrer (1939) proposed that operant conditioning played a part in the preservation of phobias. He suggested two stages: firstly, a neutral stimulus is paired with an unpleasant stimulus as a result of classical conditioning; secondly, the person avoids the conditioned stimulus and the avoidance results in a relief from anxiety (negative reinforcement). The avoidance response through operant conditioning becomes habitual. For example, a person with a social phobia no longer goes to parties because he vomited at the last party and was humiliated. His fear does not extinguish because he will not allow himself to be subjected to extinction trials, i.e. go to parties when he does not vomit, thereby losing the association between fear of humiliation and parties. Not attending parties is also reducing anxiety, reinforcing the avoidance behaviour.

Cognitive psychologists would argue that this view is simplistic and that cognitions play a part. According to Bandura (1986), the best predictor of avoidance behaviour is not the amount of anxiety the person is experiencing but *efficacy expectations*, i.e. a person's expectation based on past performance about how well the individual thinks he or she will cope.

■ The cognitive approach

There are several sources of evidence to suggest that cognitions, or thoughts, play a significant part in phobias. There is evidence that phobia sufferers tend to show cognitive biases. For example, they are hyperattentive to threatening material. Someone with a wasp phobia focuses on a wasp in the room to the exclusion of everything else. The fears are also accompanied by perceptual distortions. Rachman and Cul (1992) found that people who were afraid of spiders were more inclined to think that the spider in a bowl was jumping towards them compared to people who had no fear of spiders.

People with phobias are also prone to judgemental biases; they tend to overestimate the threat. Rosenhan and Seligman (1989) reported a person who suffered from lift phobias, who believed that the probability of the cable snapping was very small when she was a long way from the lift but as she approached the probability of disaster grew to 1/100 and then 1/2.

Another cognitive approach is a development of Bandura's theory. Rachman (1991) suggested that modelling and negative information are involved in fear acquisition. A study by Mineka and Cook (1993) demonstrated the role of modelling in the acquisition of phobias. Monkeys reared in a laboratory were conditioned to fear snakes by looking at a split video screen showing a scared monkey on one side and a snake on the other. Modelling theory would suggest that the monkeys were anticipating something unpleasant when seeing a snake because they had witnessed other monkeys being afraid of them, i.e. vicarious reinforcement.

Negative information is verbal information from significant others, books or the media. Rachman suggested that, together with modelling, it can give rise to fears or reinforce fears. Health initiatives like AIDS prevention advertising rely on this. Social psychology experiments demonstrate that people assign more value to negative information than to positive information. Rachman's theory receives some support from a study by Merckelbach and Meesters (1996). They found that fears reported by children are related to the extent to which the mothers expressed their own fears in the presence of their children.

The cognitive perspective has contributed to the understanding of phobias and has led to some effective therapies. More details about these can be found in Unit 24. There are however some unanswered questions:

- Why do some people develop phobias and others do not?
- Why are females more susceptible than males to most phobias?
- Why are some objects more likely to be the focus of phobias than others?

As early as 1930, Valentine reported observations of his own children in which he was able to condition them to a fear of a caterpillar by pairing the caterpillar with a loud whistle but could not condition them to a fear of opera glasses. It is also interesting to note that a fear response did not occur when model monkeys were shown to be fearful of flowers. This could suggest an evolutionary readiness to be fearful of some stimuli.

The biomedical model focuses on some of these questions.

The biomedical approach

Valentine's observation has been highlighted by Seligman (1971) in his famous quote:

'Agoraphobia, specific fear of animals, insect phobias, fear of heights . . . are relatively common phobias. And only rarely, if ever, do we have pyjama phobias, grass phobias, electric outlet phobias, hammer phobias, even though these are likely to be associated with danger in our world.'

Seligman attempts to explain this observation using a theory based on Darwin's theory of natural selection. In past generations, individuals who learned quickly to avoid dangers were more likely to survive. They would then pass on the genetic information which enabled them to pass the learned fear response to their offspring. The result is that present generations have a nervous system that is physically prepared for being conditioned to avoid particular stimuli. This compliments conditioning approaches, but evidence in favour of the theory is mixed.

A recent line of enquiry focused on the role of the brain hemispheres (figure 25.2. See also figure 13.22). Tucjker and Newman (1991) have proposed a theory based on the information that the left hemisphere is responsible for logical thinking and the right hemisphere is responsible for controlling emotional reactions. They suggested that specific phobias stimulate the right hemisphere which in turn causes people to be overattentive to the threat and overestimate the negative outcome.

Several questions remain unanswered. There is still no explanation for the fact that females are more prone to phobias than males. One possibility is that sex hormones interact with conditioning processes. Another problem is that some specific fears seem to arise in children without any environmental antecedents (Menzies and Clarke, 1995). One possibility is that the fears are a result of developmental processes and are made worse by conditioning, modelling and information processing. Longitudinal studies are needed to evaluate these ideas.

Activity 3

Design an experiment to test Seligman's theory that some objects are more likely to be associated with anxiety than others. Discuss the ethical implications of actually carrying out the experiment.

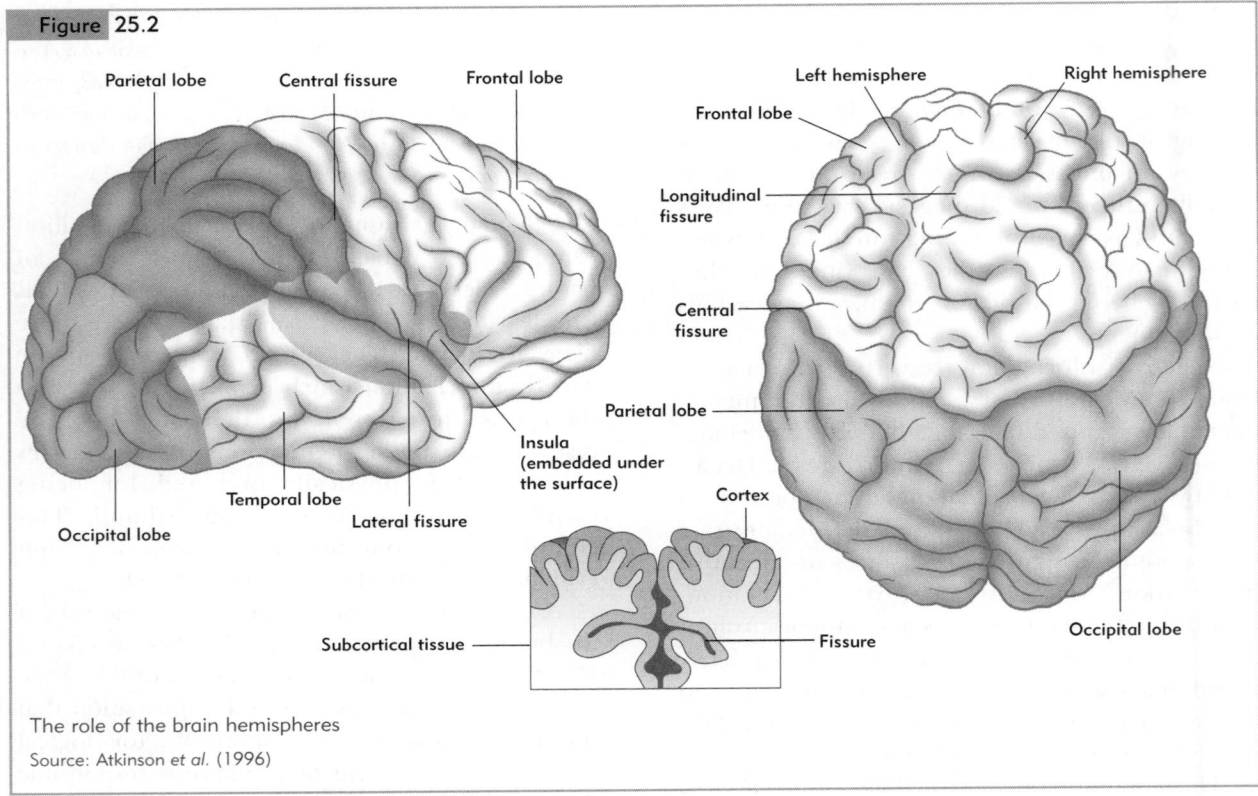

Figure 25.2

The role of the brain hemispheres

Source: Atkinson et al. (1996)

Post-traumatic stress disorder (PTSD)

Imaginary case study

Emma is 30 years old. She is single and has a responsible job in a large company. Whilst she was shopping, a terrorist bomb exploded, causing widespread damage and seriously injuring several people. Emma received cuts from flying glass but was otherwise physically unharmed. However, soon after the trauma she experienced nightmares in which she relived the incident. She was unable to sleep and was tense and restless during the day. She avoided the town centre and found it difficult to concentrate at work. Sometimes she found herself daydreaming and reliving the event.

Emma was suffering from *post-traumatic stress disorder*. The common symptoms are vivid recollections or re-experiences of the trauma. The person may develop deep anxiety, depression or exceptionally aggressive behaviour. They may also avoid situations reminding them of the event. These behaviours interfere with daily life, upsetting relationships and health.

Post-traumatic stress disorder (PTSD) is described in the DSM IV (see Unit 24 page 908) as a reaction to a catastrophic event outside the range of normal human suffering, for example earthquakes, war, rape, violent crime, air crashes. Three symptoms define the disorder:

- The person relives the trauma in dreams, or flashbacks or daydreams.
- The person becomes numb to the world and avoids anything that reminds him or her of the event.

■ The person experiences symptoms of anxiety that were not there before the trauma.

The disorder was first recognised on the DSM 1980, though descriptions of people suffering from the disorder have been available for many years. The disorder was referred to as 'shell shock' during the two world wars and victims often received little sympathy. In fact, it was frequently seen as a weakness and sufferers were told to 'snap out of it'. Recent research has focused on victims of war and natural disasters. The two most promising lines of research are the biomedical and cognitive-behavioural approaches.

The biomedical approach

Research by Pitman *et al.* (1990) suggests that hormones and neurotransmitters which are involved in memory may be responsible for the intrusive memories in PTSD. The trauma may overstimulate these hormones and neurotransmitters which results in the memory becoming overconsolidated so it will not fade.

The cognitive-behavioural approach

Several psychologists think that Mowrer's two-factory theory (see page 924) is useful for the understanding of some of the symptoms of PTSD, and there have been some successful attempts at therapy based on this model.

However, in a review Joseph *et al.* (1995) suggested that several factors were involved in the development of PTSD. These included:

■ stimulus factors, i.e. factors in the environment that were likely to trigger avoidance responses.

■ personality factors such as self-esteem, which is thought to be important in integrating the traumatic information.

■ state factors.

■ appraisal factors.

McFarlane (1989) studied Australian fire-fighters following bush fires. He found that the development of PTSD did not depend on the intensity of exposure to the fire, the degree of perceived threat or the extent of the personal loss. It depended on the psychological state of the person at the time. People who had been chronically distressed in personal relationships were more likely to develop the disorder. Another interpretation of this could be that these people do not receive the social support that may help them to overcome the trauma because their relationships are poor.

There is some empirical support for the role of appraisal factors. A study by Solomon *et al.* (1988) examined Israeli soldiers who had fought in the Lebanon War. They found that attribution and coping styles played an important role in the development of PTSD. Coping strategies which involved identifying and analysing problems with a view to getting help were better than emotional focusing, such as wishful thinking, denial and emotional venting (see Unit 15 page 544).

Evaluation

Post-traumatic stress disorder appears to be a complex syndrome, the understanding of which needs input from several models. The two main difficulties faced by the researchers are that:

■ it is usually impossible to know what the sufferer was like before the trauma

■ because the condition is now defined as a psychiatric condition in the DSM classification, sufferers can claim compensation. In some cases this could lead to an exaggeration of and/or prolonging of the symptoms.

Self-assessment questions

1 What is meant by a phobia? Give an example of a simple phobia.

2 Make a table to compare the approaches of the following models to the development of phobias: psychodynamic; behaviourist; cognitive; humanistic; biomedical.

3 List the symptoms of post-traumatic stress disorder.

4 List the factors suggested by the biomedical and cognitive theories which could be involved in the development of post-traumatic stress disorder.

(Suggested answers on page 950.)

Eating disorders

In this section the following two eating disorders are considered: *anorexia nervosa* and *bulimia nervosa*.

Anorexia nervosa and bulimia nervosa

> ### Activity 4
>
> Read the two case studies below and then decide which is anorexia and which is bulimia.
>
> (a) Meg is a shy, sensitive, intelligent girl who does well at school. When she was 16 years old, she gained a little weight and was teased by her family. She began to diet and several people congratulated her on her 'new look'. However, the dieting continued and soon her mother realised that all was not well. Meal times became a battle. Meg ate very little, often saying she preferred to eat in her room. Her mother found uneaten food hidden in cupboards. Meg was finally taken to the doctor, who was not fooled by the baggy clothes she was wearing. He gave her a thorough physical examination and found that she was seriously underweight, her periods had stopped several months ago and he discovered that occasionally she made herself sick to avoid assimilating food.
>
> (b) Linda is a student who finally took herself to the doctor after talking to her personal tutor. Her lecturers described Linda as an able student who was a perfectionist with low self-esteem. She told the doctor that she was unhappy with her body shape and weight but that food was controlling her life. She was constantly thinking about dieting. She felt guilty when she ate and on these occasions her mood was low. She said she did not know how to eat normally,

> ### Activity 4 *cont'd*
>
> sometimes she would go without food for stretches and then would binge until she was sick. The bingeing was worse in times of stress.
>
> *(Answer is in the next paragraph.)*

Meg is suffering from anorexia nervosa and Linda is suffering from bulimia nervosa. The conditions share some common features: the sufferers are usually young women who are preoccupied with food and are concerned with their body image. The conditions are not however confined to women.

■ Diagnostic criteria for anorexia nervosa

Despite the similarities, anorexia and bulimia are different. The DSM IV outlines three criteria for anorexia nervosa:

- a refusal to eat food to maintain the body weight over a minimum for the age and height
- an intense fear of weight gain or becoming fat
- a disturbance in the way body weight, size and shape is perceived. For example, an anorexia sufferer often perceives herself to be fat when she is emaciated.

The low food intake causes medical complications including malnutrition, and the absence of menstrual cycles.

■ Distinctions between anorexia nervosa and bulimia

Bulimia nervosa is more common than anorexia, and sufferers, unlike anorexics, recognise that their eating behaviour is abnormal. Most bulimia sufferers are within a normal weight range, though their weight may fluctuate. They are less able to control their food than anorexics, for example one small taste of a forbidden food like cake can trigger a bingeing session that will only stop when the person has stomach pains and/or vomits. They experience feelings of guilt following the binges and may purge, usually by self-induced vomiting. The purging causes medical complications such as gastrointestinal difficulties and eroded teeth, but menstruation usually continues.

Attempts to understand these eating disorders have combined information from several models.

The biomedical approach

There have been suggestions that the hypothalamus is involved in weight control. Each person is thought to have a weight range which is normal for that individual. The range is set partly by genetics and partly by early eating habits. If the weight falls below a certain level, the hypothalamus will alter thinking and behaviour to restore the correct weight, i.e. the person will become preoccupied with food and eat more.

Diets move the body below the set point causing the hypothalamus to alter behaviour in order to restore the weight. The person becomes preoccupied with food and may wish to binge. The dieter starts on a psychological battle to retain the lowered set weight. Some dieters succeed and overcontrol the intake becoming anorexic, others do not gain control and move into a bulimic pattern of binge–purge. It is not clear why some gain excessive control and others do not. It has been suggested that they are different psychological types.

Hormonal disturbances are also thought to be contributory factors. A study by Weltzin *et al.* (1995) (figure 25.3) investigated the role of serotonin in bulimia nervosa.

The study suggests that serotonin is involved in bulimia, but it does not identify what causes the change in serotonin levels. One interesting observation is that serotonin is also implicated in depression, and bulimia sufferers do suffer from symptoms of depression – they also respond to anti-depressive drugs. This suggests that bulimia may be connected in some way to mood disorders.

■ Evaluation

The medical model makes a contribution to the understanding of eating disorders but other factors are involved. Several questions are left unanswered:

- Why are some personality characteristics found to be associated with the conditions?
- Why are young women the most susceptible group?
- Why are eating disorders on the increase?

The psychodynamic approach

Freud viewed eating disorders as personality problems resulting from an oral fixation. Although there is no direct evidence for this, some of

25.3 The role of serotonin in bulimia nervosa (Weltzin et al., 1995)

Observations on animals and humans revealed that reduced serotonin levels are associated with decreased satiety and increased food intake. Weltzin investigated the role of serotonin by comparing ten women who suffered from bulimia with a control group of ten healthy women who were matched for age and weight. The participants were given tryptophan, a drug which alters the serotonin levels. The participants had been free from medication for a month and were studied during the first ten days of the menstrual cycle in a double blind experiment, i.e. neither the participants nor the psychiatrists making the assessments knew how much tryptophan had been administered.

The drug levels were checked using blood samples and the participants were rated using self report and by observations from two psychiatrists.

The results showed that the manipulation of serotonin levels in the bulimia sufferers produced marked overeating and mood changes which were not observed in the control group. This suggests that a disturbance in serotonin levels is involved in bulimia and it may also relate to the accompanying feelings of depression and bingeing sessions. It is possible that binge eating elevates moods by increasing serotonin activity. Studies on animals and humans show that relative proportions of carbohydrates and protein can effect serotonin release.

the facts fit the theory. Sufferers are concerned about the way they are perceived by others, seeking approval which is characteristic of an oral fixation.

Hilda Bruch (1996) proposed a different psychodynamic approach which focuses on ego development. She suggested that parents respond either effectively or ineffectively to children. Effective parents are sensitive to the child's needs; when the child cries they know whether it is hungry or afraid and behave appropriately by feeding or comforting the child. These children develop a sense of control (autonomy) and learn to differentiate different body states.

Ineffective parents are less sensitive, they misinterpret the child's needs and feed or comfort inappropriately, for example the hungry child would not be fed. These children grow up unable to distinguish body states and do not feel in control. They rely on external cues from parents and others to determine their behaviour and when they are adolescent they try to gain control over their body size and shape. Some are successful and may become anorexic; others are unsuccessful and spiral into a binge–purge pattern.

■ Evaluation

There is some support for this theory:

- Steiner *et al.* (1991) noticed that parents of adolescents with eating disorders did not allow their children to define their own needs; they did it for them.
- Rebert *et al.* (1991) noticed that when sufferers were anxious or upset they mistakenly thought they were hungry and responded by eating.
- Vitousek and Manke (1994) demonstrated that people with eating disorders are more concerned than normal controls about how others view them and they also feel they have less control over their lives.

■ The cognitive-behavioural approach

This approach focuses on the effect of the environment and social factors stressing the role of cognition and understanding. Eagles *et al.* found that there had been an increase in anorexia sufferers in Scotland over the past 27 years and

Hock *et al.* identified a similar increase in bulimia in the Netherlands over a five-year period in the 1980s.

Activity 5

Discuss with your group possible reasons for the increases in anorexia and bulimia described above.

(Suggested answer on page 950.)

Some psychiatrists have become increasingly concerned about the effect of publicising successful, attractive, public figures who have suffered from eating disorders since this might glamorise the disorder and is unlikely to deter young vulnerable adolescents from dieting – it could even encourage it. The media also reflect and reinforce society's view that 'thin is beautiful'. Several studies have shown that attractive actresses in both adverts and drama tend to be judged as thin.

Braun *et al.* (1994) have shown that suggestibility is a personality factor that is comorbid with eating disorders. It follows that highly suggestible people could be more influenced by the media and therefore more susceptible to the images portrayed (figure 25.4) and be more concerned about their own image (see also suggestibility to hypnosis Unit 14 page 497).

Activity 6

Undertake a practical investigation. Choose from the following:

a   Design a questionnaire to investigate people's attitudes to body types.

b   Do a content analysis of journals or TV programmes to investigate the relative proportions of different male and female body types.

c   Design a questionnaire to investigate whether or not there is a difference between the attitude of teenage boys and girls to eating and dieting?

Before using your questionnaires to obtain data remember to discuss your plans and the ethical issues with your tutor.

Figure 25.4 Highly suggestible people may be influenced by images in the media

Self-assessment questions

5 Make a table to illustrate the differences between anorexia nervosa and bulimia nervosa.

6 Phillip Cohen (*New Scientist*, 22 November 1997) drew attention to a condition referred to as muscle dysmorphia. The sufferers have an unhealthy preoccupation with their muscles. They recognise muscularity in others but not in themselves. They see themselves as puny. They give up jobs to spend more time in the gym, they experiment with elaborate body-building diets and use steroids to develop their muscles even when they are affecting their health. Parallels have been drawn between this condition and anorexia nervosa. Can you identify the similarities?

(Answers on page 951.)

Depression

Everyone feels 'depressed' at times. The case study below describes a period of normal depression. It is a response to external factors.

Case study: Jane is blue

It is a dark grey day in winter. Jane's boyfriend, John, has just ended their two-year relationship and Jane's mock examination marks are so poor that she thinks she will fail to get into university. She stays in bed, does not want to eat, cries intermittently, snaps at her mother and her sister when they try and coax her into the family circle. Unwashed hair, creased clothes, no make-up, swollen eyed, Jane is a picture of misery. The following day her friend Shamala rings and eventually persuades her to go to a party with her. Lloyd invites her out on a date now John has left her. She discovers that as all her friends did badly in the exam, the teacher is giving them a second chance to improve next week. Life is not so bad after all.

Most people can identify with Jane. The depression is short-lived and life returns to normal. For the person suffering from clinical depression, the picture is much worse. There are several kinds of clinical depression which are considered below. One theory known as the *continuity hypothesis* (figure 25.5) argues that clinical depression is an exaggerated form of everyday blues (Coyne, 1994). This theory also suggests that there is a continuum from everyday blues, to mild depression (dysthymiia), to more severe depression, sometimes referred to as neurotic depression, which can cause

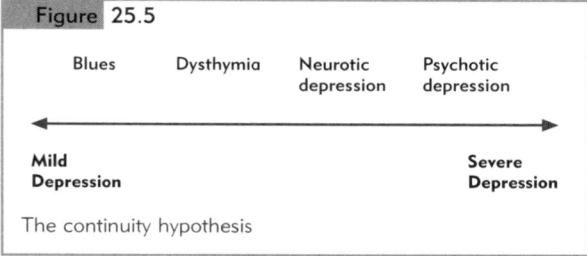

Figure 25.5

Blues — Dysthymia — Neurotic depression — Psychotic depression

Mild Depression — Severe Depression

The continuity hypothesis

havoc in people's lives although sufferers still remain in touch with reality. The final point on the continuum is psychotic depression which is very severe and the person loses touch with reality.

Some people, however, disagree with the continuity theory. They argue that neurotic and psychotic depression are two entirely different illnesses.

In the past a distinction has been made between *reactive depression* and *endogenous depression*:

- Reactive depression is depression that is linked to an uncontrollable loss, such as the death of a close relative or unemployment.
- Endogenous depression seems to come from inside the person, possibly due to biological factors.

In practice these distinctions are difficult to make so this distinction is no longer used for the classification of depression.

Symptoms of depression

Figure 25.6 outlines the symptoms of clinical depression.

■ Who suffers from depression?

Depression affects all age groups, but symptoms differ depending on the age of the sufferer. People born after 1960 are ten times more likely to become depressed than their grandparents.

Activity 7

There was an increase in depression during the twentieth century. Can you suggest any reasons for this?

(Suggested answer on page 950.)

Types of depression

The DSM IV (see Unit 24 page 908) distinguishes between several types of depression.

25.6 Symptoms of depression

■ External symptoms
The person feels sad, miserable, hopeless, lonely, worried, useless, guilty.

■ Cognitive symptoms
Depressed people have low self-esteem and believe in a hopeless future.

■ Motivational symptoms
The depressed person finds it difficult to get going, for example they often find it difficult to get up in the morning. This undermines work and social behaviour.

■ Physical symptoms
In moderate and severe depression, there is loss of appetite. In mild depression, there is a tendency to eat excessive amounts of carbohydrate; sleep disturbances are also common and the person may become preoccupied with health and sometimes loses interest in sex.

■ Major depressive disorder (unipolar depression)

Unipolar depression is one of society's major health problems. A recent American study indicated that 17 per cent of the population will experience major depression at some time in their lives (Blazer *et al.*, 1994). Women are more susceptible than men. Fifty per cent of sufferers only experience one episode. Some experience several episodes, which may come in blocks or be separated by years. Some people recover fully; others may find it difficult to resume relationships or continue employment.

■ Dysthymic disorder

This is mild persistent depression. The person becomes morose, inverted, overconscientious and incapable of having fun. There are often low energy levels, low self-esteem, disturbances of eating, sleeping and thinking. The person may also have suicidal thoughts. The disorder is more common in women.

■ Bipolar depression

In this condition the person suffers both manic and depressive moods. The symptoms of mania are shown in figure 25.7. Bipolar depression occurs in similar frequency in men and women. Several features distinguish bipolar depression from major depression (figure 25.8).

25.7 The symptoms of mania

The person has an elevated mood; he or she sees the world as a wonderful place and has endless enthusiasm.

The individual has inflated self-esteem, seeing himself or herself as attractive, important and powerful, capable of achieving things he or she knows nothing about. The person has little sleep, is very talkative and highly active. His or her thoughts race from one idea to another and the individual's behaviour becomes impulsive. For example, he or she may embark on buying sprees, careless business investments or reckless driving.

25.8 Distinctions between bipolar and major depression

- Bipolar depression is less common than major depression.
- Bipolar depression occurs with equal frequency in both sexes, whereas major depression is more prevalent in women.
- People who are married or have close relationships are less likely to suffer from major depression. These factors make no difference to bipolar depression.
- People with major depression have histories of low self-esteem; those with bipolar depression have histories of hyperactivity.
- In bipolar depression, the depressive episodes are more likely to be associated with slowing down and/or excessive sleep.
- Bipolar depression is more likely to run in families than major depression, i.e. there seems to be a genetic link.

The disorder usually starts in late adolescence with a manic episode. Following this a variety of patterns can occur. The person may return to normal, then dip into depression, then return to normal and then back to mania and so on. The length of cycle varies from person to person. Some people experience mood changes without returning to normal states. This rare condition is called rapid cycling type.

On the surface, mania seems to be the opposite from depression, but closer examination shows that it is in fact very similar.

■ Cyclothymic disorder

This is rather like bipolar disorder. For several years the sufferer never goes longer than a few months without either hypomanic or depressive behaviour. Both males and females are equally at risk. In hypomanic phases sufferers can work for long hours without fatigue – the mental powers are sharpened before they lapse into a depressive state. If the depressive episodes are not too severe, people with this form of depression can achieve great things. Many famous people, for example Abraham Lincoln, Winston Churchill, and around one-third of British writers and artists suffer mood swings. There seems to be a link with creativity. Close relatives of manic depressives are often very creative.

The following section considers different explanations of depressive disorders. The focus is on an explanation of unipolar depression rather than on mania or manic depressive conditons.

The psychodynamic approach

The psychodynamic approach considers long-term vulnerability to depression to be more important than precipitating events in the immediate past. Two explanations are mentioned here.

Firstly, depression may be seen as resulting from anger turned upon the self (Abraham, 1911). Depressed individuals, outwardly at least, often seem drained of anger, and the suggestion is that their anger may be bound up inside them. Freud (1917) considered that this was demonstrated by the differences in reactions between depressives and those experiencing normal bereavement to the loss of persons they love. The world now seems empty for the mourner, but self-esteem is not threatened. In contrast, depressives feel a powerful sense of worthlessness and guilt, and judge themselves to be failures, even though there is no justification for this.

According to Freud, this form of depression originates from events in a depressive's childhood, where an intense love has been undermined by disappointment with another person.

Evidence from more recent research tends not to support this view. For example, Weissman *et al.* (1971) showed that depressed individuals often demonstrate intense anger towards those around them, whereas if depression resulted from anger turned inward on the self, it might be expected that depressed people would show little anger towards others.

A second psychodynamic approach (for example Rado, 1928) sees depressives as *'love addicts'* who need to be showered with love and who excessively depend on others for their self-esteem. They insist on a constant flow of love and become very skilled at extracting demonstrations of it from others. However, depressives care little for the actual personality of the person they love.

▪ Evaluation

Psychodynamic theories are difficult to test, but two claims have been supported by empirical evidence:

- Neitzel and Harris (1990) demonstrated that a high level of dependence is a characteristic of depressed people and that dependent people are more prone to depression.
- Kendler (1992) demonstrated that depressed people are not more likely to have suffered a parental death in childhood, but they are more likely to have suffered separation through family conflict. It appears that poor parenting is more important than the death of a parent at placing a child at risk from depression.

The humanistic approach

Depression is a response to a feeling of *'nonbeing'* because the person fails to live competently. If a depressed person says he or she feels guilty, humanistic therapists would say the person is guilty because he or she is failing to make choices, to fulfil his or her potential and to take responsibility for his or her life. One aspect of the depressive's experience is the fear of aloneness. Depressives are dependent, and depression is precipitated by loss. Loneliness is an important constituent of depression.

Humanistic psychologists argue that loneliness is not something to be avoided or treated. It is a human condition and should be used as a means of personal growth. Loneliness is hard for people to accept. They become anxious and react to their solitary state by engaging in wasteful superficial social activities which do not allay their fears. This futile struggle adds to the depression.

The behaviourist approach

The behaviourist approach is a collection of theories. There are two major approaches:

- those focusing on external reinforcers
- those focusing on interpersonal processes.

Many behaviourists see depression as *extinction*. Once behaviours are no longer rewarded, people cease to perform them. They become inactive and withdrawn, i.e. depressed. Lewinson (1974) suggested the following causes for the reduction in reinforcement. He claimed that positive reinforcement of a person depended on three broad factors:

- the number and range of stimuli reinforcing that person
- the availability of the reinforcers in the environment
- the person's skill in obtaining the reinforcement.

Changes in the environment can affect any one of these. There is evidence in support of Lewinson's point about social reinforcement. Studies have shown that depressives are much less adept than controls of interacting with others.

Depressives are more likely than non-depressives to elicit negative reactions from people. This forms the basis of interpersonal theories of depression. Depressives have an *aversive behavioural style* which involves trying to elicit caring behaviour from people whom they think no longer care enough. Instead of love, the depressive gets shallow reassurance or even withdrawal from put-upon family and friends. These responses from family and friends often make the depression worse.

There is some evidence that the depression gives rise to the style of behaviour which changes when the person recovers. However, interpersonal factors do contribute to maintaining the depression.

The cognitive approach

Cognitive psychologists claim that depression is a result of the way people think. There are several cognitive theories, including:

■ *Aaron Beck's theory* that depression is caused by negative thoughts about the self about ongoing experience and the future
■ *Martin Seligman's theory* that a depressed person expects bad events to occur and believes that there is nothing that can be done to prevent them
■ *Abramson's attribution theory* that depression is related to a person's *attribution style* (attribution theory is discussed in Unit 24 page 903).

■ Beck's theory of depression
Beck claims that two cognitive mechanisms are involved in the production of depression:
■ cognitive triads
■ errors in logic.

The **cognitive triad** involves negative thoughts about the self, ongoing experiences and the future. Sufferers have negative thoughts about themselves, for example 'I am worthless, defective,

inadequate'. They interpret their experiences as bad, and small obstacles become impassable barriers. For instance, an invitation to a dance may be seen as an inconvenience and the fact that the individual's best shoes need repairing would be a reason not to go. Sufferers' thoughts about the future are that negative experiences will continue, for example 'I will never find a job that I like'.

Beck suggests five different *errors in logic*. They are outlined in figure 25.9.

■ Seligman's learned helplessness theory
Learned helplessness was discovered by Seligman in the laboratory by accident (figure 25.10).

Further experiments using human participants have produced broadly similar results and clarified the nature of learned helplessness. For example, Hiroto (1974) induced learned helplessness in humans using inescapable loud noise as the unpleasant stimulus. Abramson *et al.* (1978) demonstrated that learned helplessness in humans is most apparent when we blame ourselves for the ineffectiveness of a response, perceive the problem as being likely to persist in the long term and believe that failure will occur in a wide variety of circumstances.

Seligman believed that learned helplessness could provide a model for at least some forms of human depression. Humans often become passive when depressed, and fail to initiate behaviours which might help them to cope. The approach has been useful in generating further research, although problems remain, not the least being whether helplessness (or hopelessness in some more recent studies) is a cause or an effect of depression.

■ Abramson's attribution theory
Abramson said that when people blame themselves for being ineffective, they think they have no control over what happens to them and this is related to the person's attribution style. Details of this approach have been discussed in Unit 24 page 904 where we have shown the importance of attributions to the person's depressive state and self-esteem.

25.9 Beck's five errors in logic

1 *Arbitrary inference*: A person draws the wrong conclusions when there is no evidence to support them. For example, a trainee accountant may draw the wrong conclusion when his supervisor says she will check all his work. The student may conclude wrongly that the supervisor thinks he is incompetent.

2 *Selective abstraction*: A person focuses on small negative details and ignores the important features. For example, the teacher praises the student's work and suggests one minor amendment. The student's selective abstraction is, 'The teacher thinks my work is hopeless'. In spite of all the good comments, only the mistake was remembered.

3 *Overgeneralisation*: A person draws global conclusions about himself or herself based on a single event. For example, 'I didn't iron his shirt, therefore I am a bad wife'.

4 *Magnification/minimisation*: This is when small bad events become magnified and large good events become minimised. For example, a student ignores the fact that he has just been offered a well-paid job and thinks that not having a new shirt to go out in is a major disaster.

5 *Personalisation*: A person feels personally responsible for events. For example, he or she blames himself or herself for not taking more care of an elderly neighbour who slipped on wet leaves.

25.10 Seligman's experiment to demonstrate learned helplessness

Seligman was interested in conditioning and was studying avoidance learning. The apparatus used was a shuttle box. This is a box which is divided into two compartments. An electric shock can be delivered through the floor of either compartment. Only one side is electrified at any one time. A warning signal is given before the floor is electrified and the animal can escape to the other compartment.

In the learned helplessness experiments, dogs were strapped into a harness so that they could not escape the electric shocks. Later they were put into

the shuttle box where they had to learn to escape the shock by jumping a barrier into the neighbouring compartment. The control dogs that had not received the shocks learned to avoid the shocks very quickly. Only two-thirds of the experimental dogs were able to do so. The dogs seemed passively resigned to suffering the shock and even if they successfully avoided the shock on one occasion, they did not do so on the next. Some dogs had to be pushed over the barrier 200 times before the learned helplessness wore off.

■ **Evaluation of the cognitive approach**

On the positive side, the theory makes clear suggestions for therapy which does help some people who suffer from depression. However, the treatment does not work for everyone, especially those who have bipolar or severe depression. These people can often be helped by prescribing drugs. This suggests that there are biological factors involved in depression.

The biomedical approach

This approach focuses on physical causes of depression. There are several reasons for supposing that biological processes are involved:

- It sometimes occurs after natural physiological changes in women, for example following childbirth, menopause or menstruation.
- There is a similarity of symptoms across cultures, races and ages.
- Drugs such as tricyclic antidepressants and Mao inhibitors help major depression, and lithium is used to treat bipolar depression.
- Depression can be induced in 'normal' people as a side-effect of medication. For example, resperine given to reduce blood pressure can cause depression.

Biopsychologists focus on several areas of research, including *genetics* and *biochemistry*.

Genetic studies

Evidence demonstrating that genetics play an important part in the development of both major depression and bipolar depression comes from three sources.

- *Family studies.* Strober *et al.* (1988) demonstrated that first-degree relatives of people with major depression are between one and three times more likely to develop the disorder than relatives of people without the disorder. For bipolar depression there is ten times more likelihood of developing the disorder if a close relative has it.
- *Twin studies.* In the past, research has indicated that the **concordance** rate for bipolar depression was higher than the concordance rate for major depression, suggesting that genetic factors were more important for bipolar depression. However, a study by Kendler *et al.* (1992, 1993) suggested that genes play an important part in both major and bipolar depression.
- *Adoption studies.* Wender *et al.* (1986) compared biological and adopted parents, siblings and half-siblings of adoptees. They found that major depression was eight times greater in biological relatives of people suffering from mood disorder than in the biological relatives of normal adoptees.

Biochemical research

There are two major biochemical theories – one is that depression is due to a hormonal disorder; the other that it is due to an imbalance of neurotransmitters in the brain:

1 *Hormone research.* One suggestion is that depression is a result of the malfunction of the hypothalamus because this part of the brain is known to control mood and other bodily functions that are often disrupted during periods of depression, for example sexual behaviour and appetite. One view is that the hypothalamus regulates the pituitary gland which in turn produces hormones that control the gonads, thyroid glands and adrenal glands. There is evidence that this system is disrupted during depression:

   - People suffering from depression show abnormal hormone levels.
   - People with abnormal hormone levels show depression as a side-effect.
   - Tests have shown that many depressives have enlarged adrenal glands.
   - People suffering from depression can be treated by altering hormone levels. For example, changes in thyroid output have helped recovery from depression.
   - Hormone imbalances are implicated in both bipolar and major depression. However, there is some debate as to whether or not this is the major cause of the depression in both cases.

2 *Neurotransmitter imbalance.* Attention has focused on a group of neurotransmitters called catecholamines, in particular norepinephrine and serotonin. One theory is called the **catecholamine hypothesis**. This theory suggests that increased levels of norepinephrine produce mania whilst decreased levels cause depression. The only way to test this theory, however, without damaging the brain tissue of people suffering from mania and depression is to rely on animal studies and research on the effects of drugs. Tricyclic drugs that are used for the treatment of depression work by blocking the re-uptake of norepinephrine by the pre-synaptic neurone. This suggests that the depression is due to too little norepinephrine. However, more recently developed tricyclic drugs do not work by blocking the re-uptake of

norepinephrine (McNeal and Cimbolic, 1986), suggesting that the picture is more complicated than originally thought. There is also some evidence that the problem is not that there is not enough norepinephrine, but that the post-synaptic neurones are undersensitive to it (Charney and Price, 1988).

A further problem with this theory is that tricyclic drugs take two weeks to work, suggesting that they are readjusting a mechanism rather than having an immediate effect on the synapses (Delgado *et al.*, 1992).

Another complication is that the neurotransmitter, serotonin, seems to be involved, because L-tryptophan, which increases serotonin levels, is used to treat *both* mania and depression. Prange *et al.* (1974) suggested a combined norepinephrine-serotonin hypothesis: a deficiency of serotonin gives rise to a predisposition to mood disorder; if a person has a deficiency of serotonin too much norepinephrine will produce mania and too little norepinephrine will produce depression (see Unit 26 pages 975–6).

Self-assessment questions

8   Identify the correct description below for each of the following terms:
    (i) endogenous depression, (ii) major depressive disorder (unipolar depression), (iii) bipolar depression, (iv) reactive depression.
    a   The person suffers a severe bout of depression at some time in their lives.
    b   Depression that seems to come from inside the person.
    c   Depression that is caused by an unpleasant event in the person's life.
    d   The person suffers from alternating manic and depressive episodes.

9   One theory of depression is that the neurotransmitters norepinephrine and serotonin are involved. List the arguments for and against the catecholamine hypothesis.

(Suggested answers on page 951.)

Schizophrenia

Schizophrenia is one of the most severe and debilitating psychiatric disorders. It affects 0.4–0.8 per cent of the population. It interferes with daily functions in all areas of life: social relationships, work and self care. It is devastating for the sufferers and their families and costly to society accounting for 20–25 per cent of hospital beds in psychiatric units (Meisse and Fleischhacker, 1996).

Symptoms of schizophrenia

Figure 25.11 outlines the main symptoms of schizophrenia.

On the DSM IV, in order to be diagnosed as schizophrenia, the disorder must start before the age of 45 years and the symptoms last for at least 6 months, producing a deterioration in the person's level of functioning. The following two factors should also be present:

■ There must be a gross impairment of reality testing, i.e. the person makes seriously incorrect inferences about reality. This may, for example, take the form of delusions or hallucinations.

■ The disturbance must affect psychological processes including thought, perception, emotion, communication and psychomotor behaviour.

Public attention is often drawn towards schizophrenia by the media. A typical example is shown in figure 25.12. In fact, *very few schizophrenia sufferers behave in the way described.*

25.11 Some of the main symptoms occurring in schizophrenia

■ Thought disorders

Thought processes are very disturbed and the person is out of touch with reality. Sometimes there are **delusions**, for example the person imagines he or she is someone else like Jesus or the person may think he or she is being controlled by outside forces such as laser beams or aliens.

The train of thought frequently seems illogical. For example, the person might say, 'The grass is glass, the moon is full, Merry Christmas'.

■ Perceptual disorders

The most dramatic of these are **hallucinations**; the most common is hearing voices. Sometimes the person sees things that do not exist, for example, worms crawling from power sockets. Many sufferers do not experience these symptoms but they do report altered perceptions: human voices may slow down, colours may change and they may lose the ability to judge object size and distances.

■ Emotional disorders

Fear is common. The sufferers are frightened of what is happening to them; hallucinations can be terrifying. One sufferer said, 'It is like being awake in the middle of a nightmare from which you cannot escape.' Sometimes emotions are flattened or inappropriate; the latter is often because the sufferer is living in a different reality from everyone else.

■ Communication

Some sufferers are poor communicators; they are not good at small talk, giving one word in reply to questions. Conversation is also difficult because the person is out of touch with reality. One of Bleuler's patients wrote: 'I wish you a good, happy, joyful, blessed and fruitful new year and many good wine years to come, as well as a healthy and good apple year and sauerkraut and cabbage and squash and seed year' (Bleuler, 1950; cited in Rosenhan and Seligman, 1984).

■ Psychomotor dysfunctions

The person may exhibit odd movements, for example frequent grimacing. A rare but dramatic state is *catatonia* when the person 'freezes' into a statue-like position for several hours.

Figure 25.12

Horror Stabbing in The Park

A mother of two young children was stabbed to death today whilst walking her dog in the local park. In an unprovoked attack she received 15 stab wounds and later died in hospital. A man is helping police with their enquiries. He is said to be suffering from schizophrenia.

Subtypes of schizophrenia

We speak of schizophrenia as though it is one disorder. The DSM IV identifies several subtypes, some of which are described in figure 25.13.

Type 1 and Type 2 schizophrenia

Many professionals argue that the criteria for schizophrenia is overinclusive. Any two people suffering from it have completely different patterns of symptoms. In the same way that people suffering

25.13 Characteristics of subtypes of schizophrenia according to DSM IV

■ Disorganised schizophrenia (hebephrenic schizophrenia)

Speech is incoherent. There are mood disturbances, for example the person may be emotionally flat or extremely silly. The behaviour is disorganised, for example the person may refuse to wash or dress. Sometimes there are delusions.

■ Catatonic schizophrenia

This is relatively rare. There is serious disturbance of motor behaviour. Usually, the person becomes immobile and sometimes mute. The body is flexible and will stay in any position it is moved into for several hours. The condition can last for weeks.

■ Paranoid schizophrenia

Sufferers have delusions of persecution. Sometimes they are vague, sometimes they are more specific, for example sufferers think that friends are plotting against them. Sometimes the delusions are fantastic, for example sufferers think they are being controlled by radio waves. Hallucinations which are usually auditory occur – sufferers hear voices that may be taunting, jeering, accusing or threatening. Emotional attitudes change. There are feelings of grandeur – sufferers may think they are powerful or immortal, they may think they are Christ or Napoleon or any other famous powerful figure.

from headaches have different intensities of pain in different parts of their head for different reasons, so it is argued that schizophrenia could be several different conditions grouped under the same heading. For this reason there have been other attempts to distinguish between sufferers in different ways.

One method which is considered helpful is to distinguish between *Type 1* and *Type 2* schizophrenia. Table 25.14 gives a summary of the differences.

- Type 1 sufferers show *positive symptoms* such as delusions, hallucinations and serious thought disorder. These symptoms can be treated using drugs.

- Type 2 sufferers show *negative symptoms* such as flat emotion, poverty of speech, loss of interest in everyday functions like self care. These symptoms are much more difficult to treat because they do not respond to drugs and are associated with changes in the brain structure.

Table 25.14

	Type 1	Type 2
Symptoms	**Positive**	**Negative**
	Delusions	Poor speech
	Hallucinations	Flat emotions
	Incoherence	Social withdrawal
	Bizarre behaviour	Poor motivation
Onset	Later	Earlier (late teens/early twenties)
Prognosis (predicted outcome)	Good	Poor
Abnormalities of brain structure	Absent	May be present
Response to drugs	Good	Poor
Sex of sufferer	More likely to be female	More likely to be male

A summary of the differences between Type 1 and Type 2 schizophrenia

In the following section the models described in Unit 24 are used to illustrate research into the origins of schizophrenia.

Activity 8

People who suffer from schizophrenia have many problems to cope with as a result of their condition.

'A general negative attitude of society towards the mentally ill also represents an impediment to progress and a problem' (Meisse and Fleischhaker, 1996).

Discuss with your group the practical problems faced by schizophrenia sufferers and their families, taking into account the comment of Meisse and Fleischhaker.

The psychodynamic approach

- According to Freud, schizophrenia was a form of regression. Sufferers are overwhelmed by anxiety because their egos are not strong enough to cope with id impulses.
- Later psychodynamic theorists believe that there are several kinds of schizophrenia, some biological.
- They also stress the role of interpersonal factors more than Freud.

The behaviourist approach

- The behaviourists claim that people with schizophrenia have inadequate coping skills.
- Ullman and Krasner (1975) suggested that schizophrenia is a learned behaviour consisting primarily of attention problems.
- Sufferers are seen as people who have received little or no reinforcement for socially acceptable responses and who are receiving powerful rewards for bizarre responses.

■ The contribution of genetic factors

The simplistic view of the S-R associations proposed by the behaviourists has added little to the understanding of schizophrenia, but the behaviourist approach has drawn attention to the role of environmental factors in schizophrenia. Some of the early evidence that supported the idea that environment played an important role in the development of schizophrenia came from twin studies and family concordance studies. The studies were originally designed to try to establish whether schizophrenia had genetic origins. The evidence in figure 25.15 demonstrates that there appears to be a genetic factor involved but the environment still plays a part.

Other studies have focused on families and investigated the likelihood of a person developing schizophrenia if a relative has it. Table 25.16 shows that a person is more likely to get schizophrenia if a close relative has it than if a distant relative has it. Nicol and Gottesman's data supports the findings of the twin studies that there seems to be a genetic factors involved in schizophrenia but the other factors also contribute.

■ Family theories

Many researchers have focused their attention on the role of the family in the development of schizophrenia.

Some families seem to foster schizophrenia in one or more family members; these families are known as *schizophrenogenic families*. Two theories relating to family influences are of particular interest:

- those that focus on parent–child communication
- those that consider the amount of **expressed emotion (EE)** within a family.

■ Communication theories

Many researchers believe that the parents of people suffering from schizophrenia distort their

25.15 Gottesman and Shields's study to identify the relative contributions of genetics and environment to the development of schizophrenia

In 1972 Gottesman and Shields carried out a longitudinal study at the Maudsley and Bethlem Royal psychiatric unit. Between 1948 and 1964 every patient admitted to the unit was asked whether he or she had a twin. Altogether they found 55 patients were twins. The other twin was located and agreed to take part in the study. There were 22 pairs of monozygotic twins (genetically identical) and 33 pairs of dizygotic twins (not genetically identical). The age range was between 19 and 64 years.

There were two findings relevant to schizophrenia:

■ 50 per cent of the monozygotic twins and 9 per cent of the dizygotic twins were concordant for schizophrenia (both twins suffered from it).

■ Using the length of hospitalisation to indicate the severity of the schizophrenia (two years counted as chronic; less than two years is acute), further assessment was made: for monozygotic twins there was 77 per cent concordance for chronic schizophrenia and 27 per cent concordance for acute schizophrenia. These rates were higher than for dizygotic twins. The findings suggest that genetics do play a part in schizophrenia but because there is not 100 per cent concordance rate for monozygotic twins, it appears that environmental factors also make a contribution.

Table 25.16

Relationship	Genetic relatedness	Risk of developing schizophrenia
Identical twin (monozygotic)	100%	46%
Offspring of two schizophrenic parents	–	46%
Fraternal twin (dizygotic)	50%	14%
Offspring of one schizophrenic parent	50%	13%
Sibling	50%	10%
Niece or nephew	25%	3%
Spouse	0%	2%
Unrelated person	0%	1%

Likelihood of a person developing schizophrenia if a member of the family has it

Source: data from Nicol and Gottesman (1983)

children's perceptions in two ways: firstly, by encouraging them to doubt their own feelings, perceptions and experiences; and secondly, by catching the child in *double binds* (Bateson, 1956; Laing and Esteerson, 1964). Figure 25.17 shows an example of a **double-bind communication**.

The double bind has been a popular view of schizophrenia, but it is now receiving less support. In fact, the ethical implications of blaming families for this illness are becoming increasingly recognised.

■ Expressed emotion

In recent years research has focused more positively on the kind of family environment that gives the patient the best chance of recovery. Expressed Emotion (EE) is a key factor.

Expressed emotion refers to the way that emotions are communicated in families. Brown *et al.* (1972) noticed that patients who had been discharged from hospital and returned to close family were more likely to be readmitted to the hospital, and it only happened to sufferers of schizophrenia. It was

25.17 An example of a double-bind communication

A mother visits her son who is recovering well from an acute schizophrenic episode. He is pleased to see her and puts his arms round her. She stiffens and freezes. He removes his arm and she immediately asks, 'Don't you love me any more?'.

He blushes and she tells him that he should not be so embarrassed and afraid of his feelings.

The mother is giving two conflicting messages: she discourages him from showing his feelings and then tells him he should not be embarrassed to show them. He is in a no-win situation.

almost as if the family caused an emotional change and that schizophrenia sufferers were more susceptible to it.

Brown interviewed relatives to find an index of the level of expressed emotion. Three kinds of emotional comments were found to be important:

- emotional overinvolvement
- critical comments
- hostility (comments rejecting the person rather than the person's behaviour).

Camberwell (1989) performed a study in which families were interviewed and the level of expressed emotion was assessed. When the patients were discharged, they were followed up nine months later. The relapse rates were: 59 per cent for those from high EE families and 20 per cent for those from low E families.

Tarrier (1988) followed this up by measuring the physiological responses of patients when high EE relatives were present. The arousal levels of the schizophrenia sufferers was higher than that of normal controls. This led to the suggestion that living with high EE relatives tips the patient over a threshold level causing a recurrence of the condition. Findings such as these also led to the speculation that drugs used to treat schizophrenia simply dampen down the system so that the threshold is not reached.

A study by Scazufca and Knipers (1996) suggested that the picture is complex. They showed that the level of EE is related to the family's estimation of the burden of care placed on them by their relative's illness. The higher the perceived burden of care, the higher the level of EE. It is the way the relative sees the patient as affecting his or her social life, employment prospects, household affairs, finances and the patient's ability to care for himself or herself that gives rise to the burden of care. Clearly, environmental and psychosocial factors play a part in the condition of the patient.

Activity 9

Discuss with your group the possible effects on individual members of a family of being told that they are largely responsible for their relative developing schizophrenia.

The humanistic approach

Humanistic psychologists have also added to the debate by highlighting social factors. Laing is the most outspoken of the humanistic psychologists. Societies' values are contradictory and many people find the contradictions difficult to live with. In fact, it has been suggested that it is the people who are well integrated into modern society who are truly mad, whilst those who are alienated are sane. Some people find a way of living with the contradictions, some are just too sensitive, many of these are especially vulnerable to the meaninglessness of our world and these people are likely to develop schizophrenia.

Laing (1964) argued that schizophrenia is a response to a stressful environment. He said it arises from a sense that a situation cannot be lived with or avoided. The escape route is withdrawal into schizophrenia. The question arising from the humanistic approach is: 'Does the structure of society relate to schizophrenia?'

- **Society and schizophrenia**
- The lower the social class, the higher the rate of schizophrenia.

- The larger the city, the more powerful the relationship.
- In a low social class schizophrenia is eight times more likely to develop compared to higher social classes.

By examining the occupations (social class) of the fathers of schizophrenics and looking to see whether offspring have changed their social class, it may be possible to establish whether schizophrenia results in a downward move or whether social class contributes to schizophrenia.

A survey of one county in New York State found support for both views. Incidence of schizophrenia was remarkably high for people in the lowest social class confirming the class relationship. However, data on fathers' occupation was ambiguous because it was equally high for fathers in 'high' and 'low' occupation groups.

Kohn (1973) suggested that low-class people attach greater value to conformity to authority than middle class. They are less likely to be able to cope in a crisis because they are accustomed to conforming, not to being self directed. The defensive posture of a conforming person invites attack, thus conforming does not alleviate tension. The stress remains, so the conforming person is more vulnerable to schizophrenia.

These studies highlight one of the problems of the humanistic view, namely that it is difficult to research scientifically. The cognitive approach, however, is more successful in producing objective data.

The cognitive approach

The cognitive approach sees the problem of schizophrenia as a biologically based attention deficit with other symptoms developing as part of the problem. Attention deficit causes the person to become more susceptible to stress and, given enough stress, schizophrenia develops.

Some researchers think that the basic problem is overattention to environmental stimuli. This seems to be related to Type 1 schizophrenia (see pages 939–940). Type 2 seems to be related to underattention to environmental stimuli. This approach links in with evidence from biological research.

The biomedical approach

The biomedical approach to schizophrenia has been conducted along three lines:
- the study of genetic factors
- investigation of the biochemistry of schizophrenia
- comparison of the brain structures of schizophrenic brains and 'normal' brains.

■ Genetic research and adoption studies

Evidence for the role of genes in the development of schizophrenia has come from twin studies and family *concordance* studies. Evidence has also come from adoption studies. Figure 25.18 shows examples of some of the studies.

More recent research has used technology to attempt to identify the gene responsible for schizophrenia. So far results from this research have been disappointing, but more recently it has been suggested that several genes located at different points on the same chromosome could jointly contribute to the development of schizophrenia. (When several genes contribute towards a single characteristic, it is referred to as **polygenic inheritance**.)

One suggestion arising from this is that the severity of the condition could depend on the number or pattern of genes contributing. However, whatever the results of genetic research, it does not explain *how* the genes affect the biology of the individual.

■ The biochemical approach

Current research is focusing on the neurotransmitters in the brain. Much evidence has been put forward to show that schizophrenia results from a neurotransmitter imbalance. The **dopamine hypothesis** suggests that schizophrenia is correlated with an excess availability of the neurotransmitter dopamine. Figure 25.19 summarises evidence in favour of the dopamine hypothesis.

The dopamine hypothesis has excited considerable interest, but even though dopamine appears to play some part in schizophrenia, the picture is more complicated:

25.18 Adoption studies

Study 1

Heston (1966) studied 47 children of schizophrenic mothers placed in adoptive or foster homes less than one month after birth.

The control group was 50 offspring raised in the same homes as the schizophrenic offspring. They were given IQ Tests, psychological tests, and two psychiatric interviews from two independent assessors who knew nothing about the child's background or the child's mother.

Five of the schizophrentic offspring were diagnosed as schizophrenic. None of the non-schizophrenic offspring was diagnosed as schizophrenic. Thirty-seven of the offspring of people suffering from schizophrenia were given a psychiatric diagnosis. Nine of the offspring of people not suffering from schizophrenia were given a psychiatric diagnosis.

Study 2

Kety *et al.* have done a series of studies (1968, 1975, 1994; cited in Kety, 1998) using Danish records of adopted children. They investigated 5500 children and 10 000 of their biological parents.

Thirty-three children were diagnosed as schizophrenic. Relatives of the children and relatives of a control group (biological and adoptive parents, siblings, half-siblings) were interviewed. The rate of schizophrenia in the biological relatives of schizophrenia sufferers was double that (21.4 per cent) of the biological relatives of the control group (10.9 per cent). The rates of schizophrenia for the adoptive relatives was similar for both groups (5.4 per cent; 7.7 per cent).

Adopted children who developed schizophrenia in later life were more likely to have biological than adoptive parents suffering from schizophrenia. These studies together with the twin studies and family concordance studies mentioned earlier suggest both genetic and environmental components in schizophrenia.

25.19 Evidence in favour of the dopamine hypothesis

- Amphetamine facilitates the effects of dopamine. Amphetamine addicts display symptoms indistinguishable from those seen in schizophrenia.
- Drugs which alleviate the symptoms of schizophrenia, for example chlorpromazine, are known to work by blocking dopamine receptors.
- Post-mortems on the brains of schizophrenia sufferers show an increase in dopamine receptor sites (Owen *et al.*, 1978).

Activity 10

Draw a table showing the points for and against the dopamine hypothesis.

(Suggested answer on page 950.)

- Chlorpromazine drugs do not work on the negative symptoms of schizophrenia, they only damp down the positive symptoms like hallucinations and delusions.

- About 30 per cent of acute cases show little improvement when given dopamine blockers and 7 per cent of these patients show no improvement at all (Johnston and Sandle, 1996).
- In 1988 Kane demonstrated that the drug chozapine was effective in the treatment of schizophrenia, but currently no one is sure how it works. It is known to be only a weak dopamine blocker and it affects other neurotransmitters, for example serotonin.

■ Evidence from post-mortems is conflicting. Some researchers have found an increase in receptor sites thought to inhibit dopamine production (Cross *et al.*, 1981).

■ Neuropsychological evidence

Research in this area offers some promising lines of enquiry. Computerised tomography (CT) scans have shown that the lateral ventricles in the schizophrenic brain are bigger than in the healthy brain, and magnetic resonance imaging has revealed less tissue in the temporal lobes of schizophrenia sufferers. (See also Unit 13.)

Frith's studies using PET (positron emission tomography) scans (1987) have shown reduced brain activity in the prefrontal cortex (figure 25.20) of schizophrenia sufferers. There are also abnormalities in other brain structure, for example the hippocampus (figure 25.21), but researchers believe that no single brain mechanism is at fault.

McGuire (1993) demonstrated that when the patients were hearing voices, there was increased activity in Broca's area not present when the voices were silent. The advantage of the scans is that they can be used to study living, working brains without damaging them. They enable us to identify which areas of the brain are malfunctioning, but they are limited because they do not explain how different parts of the brain are interacting, what is

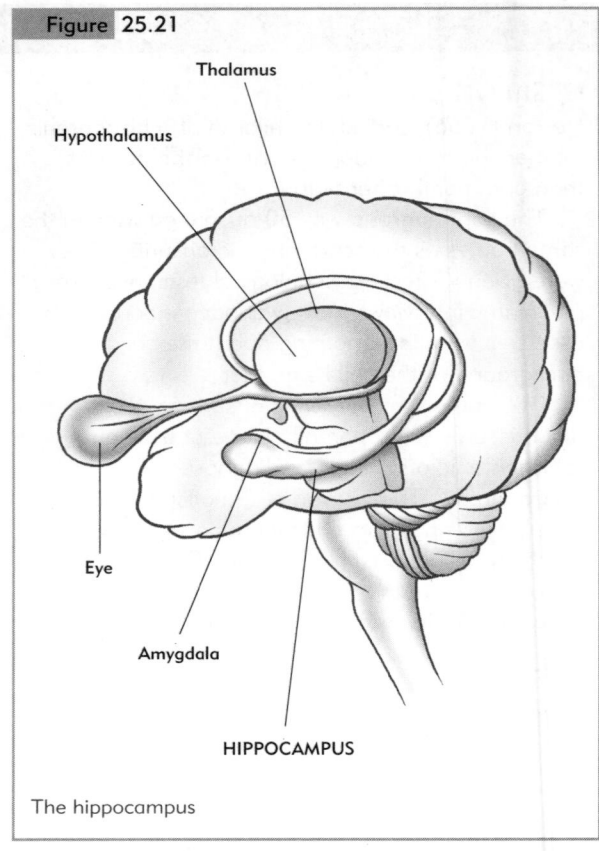

Figure 25.21

Thalamus

Hypothalamus

Eye

Amygdala

HIPPOCAMPUS

The hippocampus

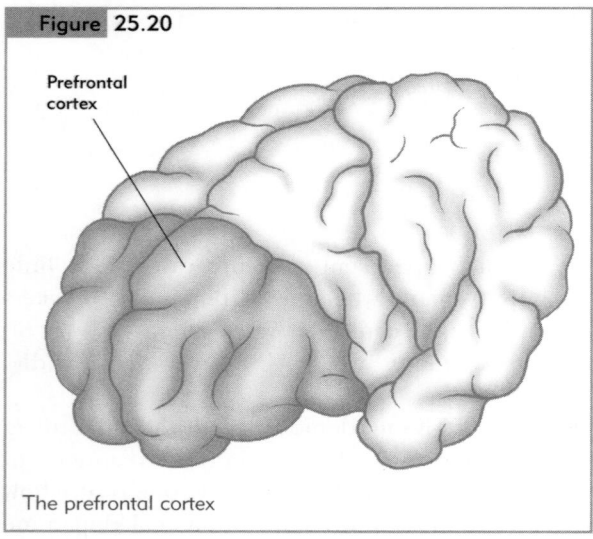

Figure 25.20

Prefrontal cortex

The prefrontal cortex

stimulating them and how the chemical changes are working.

Despite all the evidence, it is still not clear what is causing schizophrenia. Evidence is leading to the idea that there are several different conditions all under the label of schizophrenia. Each may have different biological components and possibly different causes. Weinberger (1996) proposed one theory which argued that the disease begins in the early development of the brain, either because of genetic defects or environmental triggers, possibly even a virus.

It is possible that this leads to faulty brain development which may lead to symptoms in young adults if these connections are triggered by environmental stress.

There are other ideas, but for the sufferer the theories are only useful if they improve the treatment.

Self-assessment questions

10 List the symptoms of schizophrenia.

11 Which of the following types of schizophrenia is described below:
disorganised schizophrenia; catatonic schizophrenia; paranoid schizophrenia?
He believes that he is the only human left on earth. Aliens have inhabited the bodies of everyone he sees and they are plotting to kill him. He thinks he is the only person who can save the world.

12 Put the following symptoms under the correct headings: Type 1 Schizophrenia; Type 2 schizophrenia.
a delusions, b hallucinations, c loss of interest in everyday functions, d poverty of speech, e serious thought disorder, f flat emotion, g bizarre behaviour, h social withdrawal.

13 What is expressed emotion? How does it affect the person suffering from schizophrenia?

14 Explain the role of the drugs chlorpromazine and clozapine in the evidence for and against the dopamine hypothesis.

(Suggested answers on page 951.)

Unit summary

- *Psychopathology* (diseases or disorders of the mind) includes anxiety disorders, eating disorders, depression and schizophrenia.
- *Anxiety disorders* include phobias and post-traumatic stress disorder. *Phobias* are persistent and irrational fears of objects or situations seen by the *psychodynamic* theorists as unconscious anxieties which can be *displaced* on other objects. However the *behaviourist* approach has provided evidence from several sources that irrational fears can develop from association learning (*classical conditioning*) and negative reinforcement of avoidance behaviour (*operant conditioning*).
- *Cognitive* psychologists would argue that thoughts play an important part in phobias. *Cognitive bias* is shown with the phobic hyperattentive to threatening material. They also acknowledge the role of *modelling*. The *biomedical* approach has focussed on the role of genetics and neuroanatomy.
- *Post-traumatic stress disorder* is a reaction to a catastrophic event outside the range of normal human suffering. The *biomedical* approach supports the view that hormones and neurotransmitters may be involved with intrusive memories and the *cognitive-behavioural approach* has highlighted the role of environmental triggers and attribution & coping styles.

- *Eating disorders* include anorexia nervosa and bulimia nervosa with *bulimia nervosa* is more common than *anorexia nervosa*. Genetics and hormonal disturbances are thought to be contributory factors by the *biomedical* model. *Psychodynamic* theorists see eating disorders as personality problems resulting from *oral fixation* and ineffective early parenting. The *cognitive-behavioral* approach focusses on the effect of the environment and social factors stressing the role of cognition and understanding with the media reflecting and reinforcing that '*thin is beautiful*'.

- Several types of *depression* have been distinguished including *unipolar depression* and *bi-polar depression*. The *psychodynamic* approach considers long-term vulnerability to depression to be important, such as anger turned upon the self. Conversely depressives could be seen as '*love addicts*' depending on others for their self-esteem. The *humanistic* approach sees depression as a response to the

Summary cont'd.

individual's failure to live competently, a failure to make choices and *realise potential*. *Behaviourists* may focus on external reinforcers or interpersonal processes such as *aversive behavioural styles*.

■ *Cognitive* psychologists have focussed on the cognitive mechanisms involved in depression such as *cognitive triads* (Beck), *learned helplessness* (Seligman) and *attributional style* (Abramson). The physical causes such as genetics and biochemistry are considered by the *biomedical* approach.

■ *Schizophrenia* is one of the most severe and debilitating psychiatric disorders. The main symptoms include delusions, hallucinations and disturbance of the psychological processes of thought, perception and emotion. Several different types have been distinguished including *Type 1 & Type 2*.

■ Freud saw schizophrenia as *regression* when the ego is not strong enough to cope with id urges whereas post-Freudians stress the role of interpersonal factors. *Behaviourists* have raised awareness of related environmental factors including the *family*. Researchers have shown that *double-bind communication* and *expressed emotion* in families can trigger the occurrence or reoccurrence of schizophrenia.

■ Social factors have also been highlighted by the *humanists* such as Laing, who believes that schizophrenia is the natural response to a stressful environment.

■ The *cognitive* approach sees the problem of schizophrenia as a biologically based *attention deficit* with other symptoms developing as part of the problem. This approach links very closely with the *biomedical* approach focussing on the role of genetic factors, biochemistry and neurophysical evidence.

■ It is still not clear what is causing schizophrenia. It appears there are several different conditions under the label which may have different biological components and different *aetiology*. Some models can be applied more readily to some conditions than others but no single model can provide an explanation for all conditions.

■ It appears that some models can be applied more readily to some conditions than to others, although no single model can provide an explanation for all of the conditions. In fact, in many cases it seems that for a full understanding of the condition a combination of several approaches may be needed.

■ Some may argue that applying models to each psychopathological conditions leads only to academic debate. The models can however provide a platform for research into the causes of the conditions and this understanding, together with adequate financial support, should lead to treatments which could change the lives of many sufferers and their carers.

Terms to define

agoraphobia
anxiety
catecholamine hypothesis
cognitive triad
concordance
delusions
dopamine hypothesis

double-bind communication
expressed emotion (EE)
hallucinations
polygenic inheritance
schizophrenia
unipolar depression

Further reading

Cochrane, R (1995) 'Women and depression', *Psychology Review, 2 (1)*, pp. 20–24.

Possible explanations and discussion of the sensitive issue of the high incidence of depression in women, dealing especially with socio-psychological lifestyle considerations.

Green, S (1994) *Individual Differences: Normal and Abnormal*, Laurence Erlbaum, Hove, chapter 6.

Includes many of the major forms of psychopathology and discusses general problems in determining actiology.

James, O (1997) 'Serotonin – a chemical feel-good factor', *Psychology Review, 4 (1)*, p. 34.

Short article previously published in *The Observer* 'Review' outlining serotonin's role in the brain.

Petkova, B (1997) 'Understanding eating disorders', *Psychology Review, e (1)*, pp. 2–7.

A feminist perspective which suggests that there is a need to define female identity in its own terms to overcome eating disorders.

Prince P, 'Schizophrenia: the viral connection', *Psychology Review, 2 (2)*, p. 34.

A useful short article.

Answers

■ Suggested answers to activities

2

Before learning

Horse ———————————→ Neutral response

Frightening experience (cs) ——→ Fear response (cr)

During learning

Horse (ucs) + Frightening experience (cs) —→ Fear (cr)

Horse (ucr) ———————————→ Fear (cr)

5

One suggestion that you may have discussed is the role of the media. There have been many studies based on Bandura's social learning theory which demonstrate the potential the media has for presenting models. The media provide role models who may be contributing to the increase in eating disorders.

7

Suggested discussion points:

(i) Doctors may be more alert to symptoms of depression and hence are likely to diagnose it.

(ii) The social climate has changed, people are more tolerant towards depression, hence a person may be more likely to talk about their symptoms and go to a doctor.

(iii) Social conditions have changed. There are fewer extended families and local communities. There is less social support for vulnerable people which could lead to an increase in depression.

10

Refer to pages 944–5 to check your answers against the points made in the text.

■ Suggested answers to self-assessment questions

1

A phobia is a persistent irrational fear of an object or a situation. See figure 25.1 for examples of simple phobias.

2

See below.

Table 2

Types of model	Types of approaches			
	Environmental factors	Biological factors	Insight	Unconscious
Psychodynamic	Interaction between child and mother	–	–	Unresolved conflicts
Behaviourist	Response to environment	–	–	–
Cognitive	Response to environment	–	Irrational thought processes	–
Humanistic	Interactionist / Failure to receive unconditional self regard when a child	–	Incongruity between real self and ideal self	–
Biomedical	–	Genetic tendencies / Brain function	–	–

3

Vivid recollections or re-experiences of the trauma.
Deep anxiety; depression or exceptional aggression or both.
Avoiding situations reminiscent of the event.
Problems with relationships.
Sleep disturbances.

4

Biomedical: hormones and neurotransmitters.
Cognitive: personality factors such as self-esteem; the psychological state of the person at the time of the trauma; attributional and coping styles.

5

Table 5	
Anorexia	Bulimia
Refusal to maintain body weight	Can be underweight, normal or overweight
Hunger denied	Intense hunger and binge eating
Fear of putting on weight	Guilt about eating

6

Two similarities are:

- body perceptions are changed
- the person is controlling his or her body size and shape.

7

Psychodynamic:
Origin in childhood conflict. May result in anger turned upon self, excessive dependence on others for self-esteem or unattainably high aspirations.
Cognitive:
Beck's theory based on cognitive distortions.
Seligman's theory based on learned helplessness.
Abramson's theory based on attributional biases.

8

(i) b, (ii) a, (iii) d, (iv) c.

9

Table 9	
For the hypothesis	Against the hypothesis
Drugs used for the treatment of depression block the re-uptake of norepinephrine by the pre-synaptic nerve.	Some tricyclics do not block the re-uptake of norepinephrine by the pre-synaptic nerve.
L-tryptophan increases serotonin levels and is used to treat mania and depression.	Tricyclics take two weeks to work, suggesting that a system is readjusting.

10

See pages 938–9.

11

Paranoid schizophrenia.

12.

Type 1: a, b, e, g.
Type 2: c, d, f, h.

13

Expressed emotion (EE) is a highly charged emotional atmosphere created by the sufferer's relatives who are emotionally overinvolved with the patient, make critical remarks and demonstrate hostility toward the patient. The person suffering from schizophrenia is more likely to suffer a relapse if he or she returns home to a family with a high level of expressed emotion.

14

In support of the hypothesis:
Chlorpromazine alleviates the symptoms of schizophrenia. It works by blocking dopamine receptors suggesting that too much dopamine is responsible for schizophrenia.
Against the hypothesis:
Clozapine, on the other hand, is effective in the treatment of schizophrenia, but it is only a weak dopamine blocker.

Unit 26

Therapeutic Approaches

Chris Henney

This unit covers:

Therapies and therapists

Therapies based on the psychodynamic approach

Humanistic therapies

Group therapy

Behaviour therapies

Cognitive and cognitive-behaviourial therapies

Psychophysical therapies

Recent issues related to therapy

By the end of this unit, you should be able to:

- describe therapies based on the following models of behaviour – psychodynamic, humanistic, cognitive, behaviourist and medical

- compare and evaluate the therapies and understand the problems involved in comparing and evaluating therapies

- recognise some of the practical and ethical issues relating to the use of each therapy

- understand some of the cultural and political issues relating to the treatment of pychopathological conditions.

Unit 26 Contents

Introduction

In this unit we look at:
- the role and approach of therapists
- various models of therapy and evaluations of these
- cultural and political issues relating to therapy.

Therapies and therapists

In recent years there has been an increased interest in and understanding of the brain functions and behaviour, and this has led to the development of a bewildering array of therapies.

Therapies can be divided into two basic types:
- *Psychotherapy*, which is the treatment of emotional and behavioural disorders using methods based on psychological theories and principles.
- *Psychophysical therapy*, which is the treatment of emotional and behavioural disorders using methods which involve altering the function of the brain by using physical means such as drugs.

When a person needs help, the therapy used depends on the individual's problem and the approach or model favoured by the therapist.

Figure 26.1 gives an idea of the range of people who give therapeutic help.

Choice of therapist

The choice of therapy depends on making an accurate *diagnosis*. This often presents difficulties. Sometimes the diagnosis changes as the therapy progresses, suggesting that a different approach is required. This can cause problems for less-qualified helpers because specialised help may be needed which they are not qualified to give. For example, a counsellor may start advising a client with marital difficulties and discover, during the course of the counselling, that one partner has an alcohol problem. In this situation, the counsellor might feel it appropriate to refer the client to a psychologist or psychiatrist.

Activity 1

What might happen in a situation where a friend, relative or counsellor is helping a bereaved person? What do you think would be a sensible course of action? Explain your reasons.

(Suggested answer on page 982.)

26.1 Some of the people who give therapeutic help

A close friend, teacher, or family member: provides sympathetic listening to problems.

A trained counsellor, GP, vicar, teacher, nurse: listens, provides support and discusses problems without making judgements.

A psychologist: has qualifications in psychology, usually a degree, and may have additional training in techniques such as behaviour shaping or counselling. Some become psychoanalysts.

A psychiatrist: is a qualified doctor who can administer physiological methods of treatment. A psychiatrist may also specialise in behavioural techniques, psychoanalysis or counselling.

A psychoanalyst: has been trained to perform in-depth analyses of clients and give interpretations based on the school of analysis they trained in. During training, psychoanalysts have to undergo personal analysis.

Problems relating to diagnosis

One difficulty relating to diagnosis is that similar symptoms presented by patients may have different causes. For example, identifying the form of depression a client is suffering from can be tricky because the distinctions between types of depression are not always clear. Sometimes, a person suffering from depression also has life problems (for example, bereavement) which could contribute to the condition. Alternatively, the condition may appear to be related to life problems, but a full case history will show the therapist otherwise. Usually a diagnosis is possible but the cause of the problem remains unknown. Thus a person suffering from phobia may be given different treatments depending on what is seen to be the cause by the therapist.

If the therapist thinks the fear results from a problem with learning, the person would be given behaviour therapy, but if the therapist considers that the phobia indicated an anxious personality, other forms of psychotherapy might be considered more appropriate.

Evaluation of therapies

Despite the difficulties associated with diagnosis, therapists are able to help people with varying degrees of success. Some of the therapies derived from the models discussed in Unit 24 are reviewed in this unit and evaluations given. There are factors which make evaluation of any therapy difficult:

- *Spontaneous remission* occurs when a person recovers without therapy. Many people improve within two years after the onset of the condition, whether or not they are receiving therapy. It is therefore difficult to determine whether or not treatment has effected the improvement.
- *Sampling methods* – the sample of patients being evaluated is biased, because most therapists only treat people they think they can help. Those they think they cannot help do not

receive therapy and some therapists have more stringent criteria than others. This makes comparison between the effectiveness of different therapies unreliable.

Whichever therapy is used it should be remembered that the condition and treatment involve the patient, the therapist, and family, friends and other significant people such as employers. When making decisions about treatment the therapist is faced with a number of practical and ethical issues which need to be resolved.

Self-assessment questions

1 Compare psychotherapies and pyschophysical therapies.

2 Effective treatment depends on making an accurate diagnosis. List three factors which could make diagnosis difficult.

3 State two factors which make evaluation of any therapy difficult.

(Suggested answers on page 982.)

Therapies based on the psychodynamic approach

The psychodynamic approach rests on two basic assumptions:

- Firstly, becoming aware of our basic motivations helps us to change and become more adaptable.
- Secondly, the causes of mental disturbances are unresolved conflicts which the person is not aware of and is therefore unable to deal with.

Psychodynamic therapists help patients by encouraging them to talk out their problems with the analyst who offers interpretations of the symptoms and the causes of behaviour. The approach originated with the work of Freud.

Freudian psychoanalysis

Freudian therapy is referred to as psychoanalysis Freud (figure 26.2) originally developed psychoanalysis to help patients suffering from conversion hysteria.

Activity 2

Refer back to the case of Anna O in Unit 24 page 896.
Explain what is meant by conversion hysteria.

(Suggested answer on page 982.)

Freud developed a technique used by Breuer to try to help these patients. He asked them to talk about their past, sometimes under hypnosis. Freud noticed that some of the patients who came to see him had experienced traumatic events in situations where appropriate emotions could not be

Figure 26.2 Sigmund Freud

expressed. He suggested that conversion hysteria was the result of displacement, in which the energy from the repressed emotion was redirected to physiological processes, causing physical symptoms like apparent paralysis.

Freud found that patients could be helped by reliving their bad experiences and giving vent to their emotions. Catharsis, i.e. reliving the past experiences, is an important part of the therapy. Often, this was achieved by transference of feelings to the therapist who sympathetically worked through their bad experiences with them. Transference is when the patients act and feel toward the therapist in the same way as they acted and felt towards key people in their childhood such as parents and siblings. Figure 26.3 shows an example of catharsis and transference.

Freud thought that maladjustment was caused by conflict between the forces of the id and the restraints of the ego and superego. These unresolved conflicts are pushed into the unconscious part of the mind, where they stay, but sometimes surface in unconscious ways affecting the behaviour of the person even when adult.

Freud thought that phobias were the displacement of anxiety generated by conflict onto an innocent object. For example, Freud's interpretation of Little Hans's fear of horses (reported in Unit 25) was that Hans was in the process of trying to resolve his Oedipus complex. He was strongly attached to his mother and felt intensely hostile towards his father because his father possessed his mother. The hostility was accompanied by anxiety because he thought his father might retaliate and castrate him. He used the unconscious defence mechanism, displacement, and displaced his fear and hostility onto horses.

Activity 3

The case of Little Hans highlights practical and ethical issues relating to working with children. Can you identify them?

(Suggested answer on page 982.)

Through psychoanalysis, Freud helped patients to uncover the source of conflict which had caused their phobia and to gain insight into the repressed anxiety.

Except for Little Hans all of Freud's patients were adults. He employed several techniques to probe the unconscious mind in order to lift the repressed experiences. One technique is **free association**. Patients are encouraged to give free rein to thoughts, saying whatever comes to mind without the censorship which can happen in everyday life. Eventually, the patients learn to bypass defences built up over the years and reach the root of the problem. In order to facilitate this process Freud asked his patients to lie on a couch with their eyes closed.

Another technique used by Freud is *dream analysis*. He believed that dreams are windows into the unconscious mind, and that by interpreting dream content unconscious wishes and conflicts can be revealed. A demonstration of his technique is illustrated in the case study below.

During psychoanalysis, Freud uncovered the source of conflicts and interpreted events to patients in the light of his theory. In this way, patients were helped both to put their conflicts into historical context and to understand themselves better. Freud's work has led to the development of projective tests which were discussed in Unit 24.

26.3 An example of transference from the case of Anna O

Freud reported an incident which occurred when Dr Breuer was treating Anna O. She had refused to drink despite a severe thirst, and had survived for six weeks by living on fruit. During a therapy session, she revealed that she had seen her lady companion's dog drinking from a glass. The patient had been disgusted and angry but had repressed her feelings because she was in a conflict situation in which it would have been impolite to criticise. She said nothing, repressing the incident by pushing it and her feelings into her unconscious mind.

During therapy, Anna related the story, this time giving vent to her anger. After this she was able to drink. The unconscious conflict had been resolved and the anxiety about drinking had gone.

Case study – Freudian dream analysis

A young woman who had been married for several years had the following dream: she was at the theatre with her husband, and on one side of the theatre the stall seats were empty. Her husband said that her friend Elise and her fiancé had wanted to come but had decided not to because they could only get bad seats, three for one and a half florins, which of course they could not take. The patient replied that in her opinion they did not lose much by that.

During therapy the woman made the following associations: Elise was a friend of her own age who had just become engaged; during a recent theatre outing she had booked seats too early and had to pay too much for them; the money in the dream reminded her of 150 florins her sister-in-law had rushed out and spent on jewellery.

Freud drew attention to the fact that 'too early' and 'in too great a hurry' were the themes of associations. He combined this with the view that the theatre symbolised marriage, and the number three represents man. He uncovered the woman's repressed thoughts that she had been foolish to marry in such haste and wished she had followed Elise's example because she was unhappy with her husband and regretted the early marriage.

Post-Freudian psychoanalytic therapies

Freud's techniques have been used by later psychoanalysts, who have sometimes disagreed with the details of his theory.

▦ Adler's theory

Adler disagreed with Freud's emphasis on sex. He thought that the main motivating force was a striving to overcome handicaps to compensate for feelings of inferiority. He explained neurosis as a drive for power which has arisen as an attempt to compensate for feelings of inferiority. His main contribution, however, was his emphasis on the social context of the person and the person's relationships with others. He thought that psychological disturbance was a result of the person's present circumstances rather than childhood experiences, and that mature people had overcome their inferiority complexes, resolved their struggle for power and devoted themselves selflessly to the well-being of others.

▦ Jung's analytical psychology

Jung aimed at uncovering aspects of the personality which would help a person to develop as a complete individual. He considered Freudian dream symbolism to be too rigid, introducing a more flexible approach to dream analysis. He also maintained that not all neurosis had its origins in the past, neither should it be regarded as something entirely negative, although he accepted that aggressive and sexual urges and willpower were contributory factors. He thought neurosis was functional, attempting to compensate for a one-sided attitude to life by drawing attention to a side of personality which had previously been neglected or repressed.

Jung drew attention to the development of neurosis in people around 40 years old. At this age, he claimed that sexual urges and power drives were not responsible for the neurosis, and that people developing neurosis at this stage of their lives needed a different kind of help. Jung recognised another important drive, the cultural or spiritual drive which becomes dominant at this time. In fact, one third of Jung's clients were not considered neurotic: they were intelligent, successful middle-aged people who found life empty and meaningless. They had consciously explored all possibilities and had turned to the therapist asking 'What do you advise?' or 'What shall I do?'.

Jung said that when conscious thought processes were no longer helpful a person should examine unconscious processes. His therapy helped patients to explore latent possibilities in themselves, thus discovering what sort of people they really were. By developing an appropriate life style, they could integrate all aspects of their personalities.

▦ Modern psychodynamic therapy

Most present-day psychodynamic therapists use Freudian vocabulary but they practise a modified form of analysis based on Freud's theory, together with those of his successors (figure 26.4). They are concerned with the unconscious but they differ from Freud in a number of ways:

- They prefer to sit facing the client rather than use a couch and they take a more active role in the therapy, offering more direct advice than Freud.
- Past history is taken into consideration, but the main focus is on the present situation.
- Therapy sessions tend to be briefer and less intense than Freud's, the therapist and patient meet once or twice a week for a period of months or years.

Evaluation of psychodynamic therapies

- One of the major criticisms of **psychodynamic therapies** is that interpretations given to patients are based on a theory which is difficult to support scientifically.

  The case of Anna O, which is at the root of psychotherapy, has been investigated by

26.4 An example of the modern psychodynamic approach to the treatment of depression

When treating depression, psychodynamic therapy stresses that changing the long-term factors which cause vulnerability to the condition is more important than the short-term improvement of the symptoms. Therapists may try to make patients conscious of any relevant early conflicts resulting from, in particular, anger at rejection by another or greed for love and self-esteem from others. Once the conflicts have been identified, patients can work through them to gain control of their feelings. It may also be necessary to try to get depressives to modify their goals so that these are realistic and achievable; as a result, the depressives will no longer feel helpless.

The concept of anger causing rejection by another is of Freudian origin. Greed for love and esteem from others, together with the need for depressives to modify their goals, are post-Freudian concepts.

Ellenberger (1970). He succeeded in tracking down the records of Anna (Bertha Pappenheim) and found a previously unknown, detailed report by Breuer, together with reports from the doctor at the sanatorium where Anna was treated. There was no mention of a talking cure but there were details of drug treatment. It appears that Anna was not suffering from conversion hysteria but from an organic illness. If Ellenberger has located the correct report it could be argued that the foundation of Freudian therapy is based on flawed evidence. However, as analysts point out, it does not detract from the benefits that many have received from psychodynamic therapies.

■ Another methodological problem is that the different psychodynamic therapists give different interpretations to patients, depending on the theory they subscribe to.

■ More recently the problem of *false memories* has been identified. Several of Freud's patients claimed to have been involved in sexual relationships with a parent at an early age, but they later retracted their statements, claiming to have invented the stories. Freud wondered why the patients had invented these stories; he finally concluded that they were a result of wishful thinking. This line of thinking led to his psychosexual theory of personality. Present-day therapists have been faced with similar situations in which patients have claimed to have been sexually assaulted by a parent during their childhood. Sometimes the accused parent has attempted to sue the therapist, saying that the stories were untrue and that therapists were putting ideas into the patient's mind.

■ Many attempts to compare psychoanalytic therapies with other therapies have suggested that other therapies may be equally effective. Figure 26.5 provides a summary of some of Eysenck's criticisms of Freudian therapy. This classic study highlights difficulties involved in evaluating therapies.

Other psychologists have, however, produced evidence supporting psychodynamic therapies:

■ For example, Meltzoff and Kornreich (1970) found that 84 per cent of the studies reviewed indicated positive effects from the psychoanalysis.

■ A well controlled study from Sloane *et al.* (1975) used 90 outpatients with neurosis or personality disorders (those suffering from severe depression requiring medication were excluded). Treatment was given in equal amounts by experienced therapists, several outcome measures were employed and groups were matched. Some patients received psychoanalytic therapy, but whichever therapy was used 80 per cent improved compared to 48 per cent of the controls who received no therapy.

■ Psychodynamic therapists argue that successful therapy depends on the patient gaining insight into the situation and recent research has shown that psychodynamic methods do help people to

26.5 Eysenck's criticism of Freudian therapy

Eysenck (1952) reported that two-thirds of all neurotics who enter psychotherapy, regardless of whether it is all psychoanalysis or any other kind, improve substantially within two years. However, an equal proportion of neurotics who never undergo psychotherapy also improve within two years. Eysenck's findings, based on 8053 cases from 24 studies, caused considerable controversy and have been criticised on the following grounds:

■ The cases could not be directly compared because of the differences of technique between studies.

■ The criteria chosen to assess improvement in each study were different.
■ There were variations in the way the disturbance had started and in the length of time patients had been suffering.
■ The diagnosis of neurotic was considered inaccurate in many cases.
■ There were variations in the amount of therapy received and in its quality.
■ There were differences in the duration and thoroughness of the follow-up.
■ There were errors in the computation of the data.

discover important things about themselves (Luborsky *et al.*, 1986) and the more accurate the therapist's interpretation the more likely the person is to improve (Piper *et al.*, 1993).

■ There is however evidence that long-term benefits can be gained from the therapy even if incomplete interpretations are given. Wallerstein (1989) did a follow-up study of 42 people who had received psychodynamic therapy. He found that even after 30 years, regardless of whether or not complete interpretations had been given, the patients were more able to make positive changes in their lives as a result of being in therapy. Psychodynamic therapy seems to work best on articulate, well-educated people (Luborsky *et al.*, 1988). Most people agree that psychodynamic therapy is only useful for people able to sustain an intensive therapeutic relationship and that it is not suitable for serious disturbances or major personality disorders. With regard to therapy for phobias (as in the case of Little Hans) prognosis is poor with the psychodynamic therapies. Treatment is lengthy, and behaviour therapy (see pages 965–970) is generally more successful.

Studies supporting the use of psychodynamic therapies generate optimism, but it is still generally accepted that evidence for or against the effectiveness of any therapy is inconclusive. The main predictors of therapy outcome are the skill of the therapist and the attitudes of the patients, with those who are motivated to change doing better. The type of therapy comes a distant third (Bergen and Lambert, 1978).

Self-assessment questions

4 What are the two basic assumptions made by psychodynamic therapists?

5 Explain the following terms: catharsis and transference.

6 State two techniques used by Freud to explore the unconscious mind.

7 Adler and Jung thought that Freud put too much emphasis on the sex drive. Each of them identified other drives which they considered to be important. State which these are.

8 The phenomenon of false memories raises practical and ethical issues. Try to identify them.

(Suggested answers on pages 982–3.)

Humanistic therapies

Before reading this section, you may find it useful to refer back to Unit 24 to review the key concepts relating to the humanistic model of behaviour.

Humanistic therapists aim to help clients fulfil their potential by 'finding themselves' and making deliberate choices so that they can live more meaningful lives. Unlike psychoanalysts, humanistic therapists believe that the person who understands the client best is the client not the therapist. The therapist does not try to interpret what is said, but encourages clients to do this themselves. The best-known humanistic therapist is Carl Rogers, who developed **client-centred therapy**.

Carl Rogers's client-centred therapy

Client-centred therapy is based on humanistic principles in which patients talk out their problems. Rogers's therapy centres on the person's own viewpoint and focuses on the individual's subjective experiences of the world. This makes it necessary to study conscious awareness, i.e. how a person experiences the world and makes sense of life.

Rogers linked client-centred therapy to his theory that individuals have a concept of self perception, i.e. an individual has an awareness of personal characteristics, relationships with others, and the values attached to these perceptions. This conscious scheme of self has a regularity and guiding influence on behaviour. The person also has a concept of *ideal self,* that is the person they would most like to be. Anxiety and maladjustment occur either when the concept of self is threatened by a dim awareness of experiences which contradict it, or when there are large discrepancies between the concept of the real self and the ideal self.

Therapists can make suggestions which help clients recognise hidden aspects of their problems. This results in a change in *self concept.* The clients are then encouraged to make decisions on how to overcome their problems from the viewpoint of their altered self concepts. This decreases the discrepancies which are causing the maladjustment.

In order to do this successfully the therapist needs to display three qualities:

- *Unconditional positive self-regard.* The therapist adopts a non-judgemental attitude, warmly accepting the person no matter what he or she says or feels.
- *Empathy.* This involves accurately hearing what the client is saying. The therapist tries to see the world through the eyes of clients and is then able to help the clients listen to themselves and consequently gain insight into themselves.
- *Genuineness or congruence.* The therapist's communications have to be honest and sincere and not hidden behind a professional mask.

■ Evaluation of client-centred therapy

Unlike Freud, Rogers made efforts to provide scientific evaluations of his therapy. One technique he used was to tape the therapy sessions for later analysis, thus removing some of the mystique surrounding them.

Butler and Haigh (1954) tried to evaluate client-centred therapy using a Q sort of technique. This involves 100 cards covering whole ranges of attitudes towards the self, each showing a self-descriptive statement (for example 'I often feel guilty', 'I am likeable'). First, the cards were sorted into nine piles arranged according to how closely they described the client now, then according to how the client would like to be. This enabled the researcher to work out discrepancies between actual self image and ideal self. Clients asked to do this both before and after therapy showed a reduced discrepancy between real and ideal self after therapy. A control group which had not received therapy retained the discrepancy.

This is just one example of how Rogers's work has been evaluated. Many other research studies have been carried out and the main conclusions are summarised in figure 26.6.

26.6 Evaluation of research on client-centred therapy

- When self-esteem improves, the personality becomes better integrated, less anxious, more tolerant of stress and more objective when dealing with reality.
- In many cases attitudes towards the self become more positive during therapy.
- Communicating with an understanding, accepting therapist is an essential ingredient in successful therapy.

Criticisms of client-centred therapy:
- The only evidence we have that therapy is effective is what the client says. Few have observed the client's behaviour in social situations before or after therapy.
- Not all problems stem from difficulties in resolving self-image. Some problems have biological origins, others could stem from faulty learning.
- Not everyone agrees that we are striving to become self-actualised.
- Psychoanalysts would argue that no one ever understands their problems as clearly as the humanists suggest.

Group therapy

Group therapy is based on the idea that people with problems can be helped by talking out problems in a group. For the therapy to be successful, everyone participating has to make a serious commitment to the group and respect each others' confidentiality. Groups vary in their size and composition depending on their function. For example, a family group would consist of members of the same family. A support group would be larger and consist of people from varying backgrounds who share the same problem. For example, members of Alcoholics Anonymous are all trying to overcome problems related to the use of alcohol.

Therapists can be viewed as group conductors, guiding the proceedings and creating an atmosphere in which everyone can interact openly and honestly. During therapy sessions they remain unobtrusive, observing not only what group members are saying but also their interactions and individual roles.

The part that the therapists play depends on the nature of the group. For example, in psychodynamic groups, therapists may take the initiative and assume the role of interpreting what their patients say. In family groups, different therapists function in different ways depending on the nature of the problem. All family therapists, however, share one common assumption, which is, that although only one member of the family has a problem, the root of the disturbance lies in the family relationships. Some therapists focus on the communications between family members, others draw attention to the roles each person is playing so that the family members can gain insight into this and how they contribute to the problem. In some situations, such as treating a child with behaviour problems, the role of the therapist is to teach parents a more effective way of dealing with the child's behaviour.

One recent finding is that depression is often associated with marital conflict and some therapists have used marriage therapy in cases where the husband or wife is suffering from depression. A comparison between this approach and cognitive-behavioural therapy suggests that it is equally as effective at reducing depression and more effective at reducing marital discord (Beach *et al.*, 1994).

Evaluation of group therapy
There are many different kinds of groups. We have focused on **family therapy** and support groups.
- In the case of support groups patients benefit from group therapy by learning from each other, and often come to realise that their thoughts and feelings are not unusual. Also, they may find that they are not as isolated from other people as they thought.

Activity 4

Consider the case of Meg. Her family group consists of her mother and father, a younger brother and an older sister. Her mother has a part-time job and her father has a demanding job which involves working long hours, frequently away from home. Her brother is at school studying for important exams and her sister has a job with fixed holidays.

The therapist thinks that **family therapy** will help Meg because part of her problem is her need for gaining approval from her family. The therapist wants to set up family group sessions for one afternoon a week over a period of eight weeks. What are the practical problems involved in setting up these sessions?

(Suggested answer on page 982.)

- Studies on family therapy have shown that it is useful in the treatment of schizophrenia and eating disorders.
- Therapists may find that working in groups is less emotionally draining than when working with only one patient, because they are not the only recipient of every patient's feelings. In psychodynamic groups transference is often dissipated throughout the group.
- A disadvantage of group therapy is that some people cannot benefit from it. For example, some patients are too disturbed to participate, or are unable to understand what is happening in the group. Others might feel threatened in group situations.

It is difficult to evaluate group therapy as a whole for the following reasons:

- There are a wide variety of the group structures, organisations and objectives.
- Group interactions are complex, making it difficult to assess which factors are responsible for behavioural changes.
- Comparisons between groups are difficult because individual investigators use different criteria for assessment.

In a review of group research, Bednar and Kaul (1994) concluded that group treatments are as helpful as individual therapy. Some people, however, have been distressed by some types of group therapy. It is, therefore, important that group leaders are able to screen out the vulnerable who need individual attention (Sadock, 1989).

Self-assessment questions

9 State two differences between the assumptions of humanistic psychologists and psychodynamic psychologists.

10 Refer back to Unit 25 and consider the symptoms of schizophrenia. Do you think that client-centred therapy would be an appropriate treatment for schizophrenia? What are the implications of your answer?

11 State three reasons why it is difficult to evaluate group therapy.

(Suggested answers on pages 982–3.)

Behaviour therapies

The therapies that we have talked about so far have been based on the idea that the sufferers gain insight into their conditions. Patients talk out their problems with the therapist, thus gaining help by discovering the cause of their problems and coming to terms with them.

Behaviour therapy is based on the idea that behavioural problems result from faulty learning; the therapist therefore aims to change patients' behaviour by re-learning. The theory is that if clients can be taught to respond more appropriately to situations their problems will be solved. The behaviourist approaches to therapy stress the importance of the environment to psychopathological behaviour. We first examine behaviour therapies based on conditioning and then consider therapy based on social learning theory.

Behaviour therapy based on classical conditioning

Classical conditioning involves learning the association between stimuli without any conscious action on the part of the person concerned. The responses are reflex responses. Therapies based on classical conditioning include **aversion therapy, systematic desensitisation, implosion** and **flooding** (the last three are also known as exposure therapies). The idea behind these therapies is to replace the maladaptive response with a more appropriate response.

■ Systematic desensitisation

Systematic desensitisation is a therapy based on the principle of counter-conditioning. Developed by Wolpe (1958) to relieve fears or phobias, it involves elimination of the fear response in a given situation by replacing it with the incompatible response of relaxation.

A phobia can be treated using systematic desensitisation. Wolpe describes systematic desensitisation as a three-stage process.

■ First, the patient is trained to relax deeply and completely.

■ Next the patient is asked to identify the cause of the fear and propose a hierarchy of frightening situations.

■ Counter-conditioning is then put into practice by encouraging the patient to relax in progressively more frightening situations. Sometimes they are asked to imagine the situations but the therapy is considered to be more effective if the person can experience the real-life situations. For example, in the case of the spider phobia the patient is asked to hold a dead spider rather than imagine holding one.

■ Flooding and implosion

Flooding and implosion are also used to help patients overcome fears and phobias. *Flooding* is used to refer to real situations, whereas *implosion* refers to imaginary situations. The therapies are based on the idea the person is put into the frightening situation and not allowed to escape for several hours, until eventually the fear diminishes (Marks, 1969). The assumption is that patients find the reality of the situation less daunting than their expectations of it.

Flooding, for example, has been used to help people with obsessive compulsive behaviour in which they have a fear of being contaminated by germs and will not touch anything, often spending the whole day washing their hands or cleaning. The clients actually contaminate themselves by touching or handling dirt until they realise that nothing has happened to them and that there is no real threat.

A more recent flooding approach is the use of virtual reality. Lamson treated acrophobics (those with a fear of heights) by putting them into a virtual reality situation in which they found themselves in a café which opened onto a high terrace. A plank led from the terrace to a bridge. During the 50-minute treatment session they had to walk onto the terrace and cross the plank to explore the bridge; 33 out of the 36 volunteer patients were able to achieve their own targets such as climbing a ladder at the end of the treatment. The virtual reality provided the patients with a sense of achievement, giving them more the confidence to tackle their own goals (reported in *New Scientist*, 11/6/94).

If implosion therapy is being used, a therapist might construct stories and scenes of terror about a patient's phobia which the patient is forced to listen to. For example, a therapist may re-tell tales of plane crashes to a client who has a fear of flying.

Activity 5

Can you identify a problem with flooding therapy?

(Suggested answer on page 982.)

26.7 The use of classical conditioning techniques in the treatment of post-traumatic stress disorder

There is evidence to suggest that exposure therapy (implosion, flooding or systematic desensitisation) can be used to alleviate some of the symptoms of post-traumatic stress disorder (PTSD) (Keane and Kalonpet, 1992). Studies have been done on combat-related PTSD using Vietnam War veterans. It is difficult to create war situations so stimuli associated with the trauma such as helicopter sounds and gunfire were used, together with imaginary scripts. The treatment does benefit the patients but some symptoms such as withdrawal and emotional numbing were not eased and need a different approach.

Richard and Rose (1991) also used exposure therapy to help the survivors of the *Jupiter* and *Marchioness* sinkings. Sufferers were given up to eight 1$\frac{1}{2}$ hour sessions of imagined and real life exposure. There was more than an 80 per cent reduction in severity of persistent symptoms after 6- and 12-month follow-ups.

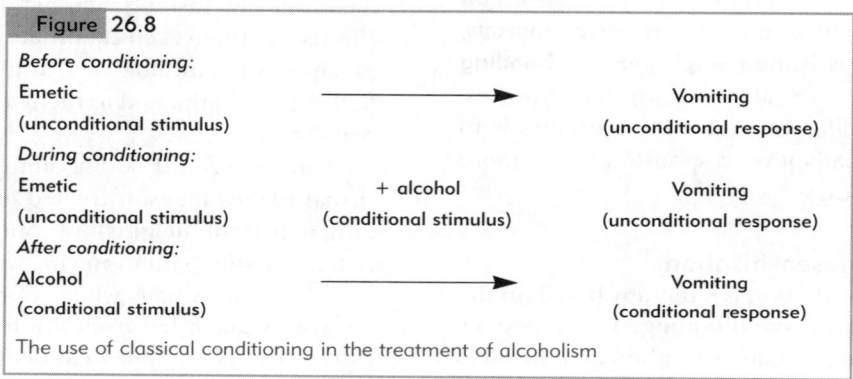

Figure 26.8

Before conditioning:

Emetic ⟶ Vomiting
(unconditional stimulus) (unconditional response)

During conditioning:

Emetic + alcohol Vomiting
(unconditional stimulus) (conditional stimulus) (unconditional response)

After conditioning:

Alcohol ⟶ Vomiting
(conditional stimulus) (conditional response)

The use of classical conditioning in the treatment of alcoholism

(See figure 26.7 for a discussion of the use of exposure therapy in the treatment of post-traumatic stress disorder.)

Aversion therapy

Aversion therapy is used to break habits like fetishes, alcoholism, overeating, and smoking. Therapy is based on the principle that if the undesirable habit is associated with punishment it will be extinguished. For example, alcoholics may be treated by being given emetics (substances which make you sick) when alcohol is consumed. Thus drinking alcohol is associated with vomiting and abstinence results (see figure 26.8).

Evaluation of therapies based on classical conditioning

■ Aversion therapy has been the subject of ethical controversy because of its deliberate use of unpleasant stimuli. Aversions may also generalise to unintended things, for example an aversion to alcohol may generalise to unintended hotels and restaurants where alcohol is sold.

■ Yates (1971) suggested that although problem behaviour disappears for a while, follow-up studies show that patients tend to relapse into their bad habits. This is due to stopping the reinforcement of newly learned behaviour when the patient returns home to a familiar environment. Old and undesirable behaviour will be strongly rewarded.

■ Many psychologists consider the idea that a stimulus can provoke a response without conscious thinking is too simplistic. Franks and Wilson (1973) suggested that the success of the aversion therapy was a result of the relationship between the patient and the therapist, not the result of classical conditioning.

- Systematic desensitisation works and can be short term and cheap. It has been used to treat phobias and other problems involving anxiety, such as fear of social disapproval (Kazdin and Wilson, 1978).
- Flooding and implosion have also been used to help in the treatment of obsessive-compulsive disorder and post-traumatic stress disorder.
- The main difficulty with the techniques are ethical considerations relating to exposing patients to distressing situations.

Systematic desensitisation, implosion and flooding have been assessed by many different researchers. The conclusions reached are that patient's improvements are not the result of simple conditioning but cognitions are also involved.

Three processes are taking place:

- The patient expects to be helped.
- The patient learns during desensitisation that the situation can be controlled.
- The patient may begin to use relaxation consciously and actively to help cope with a situation that he or she feels more confident of controlling.

Behaviour therapy based on operant conditioning

Operant conditioning involves learning the association between an action and its consequences. Therapists who use operant conditioning think that problem behaviour is the result of faulty learning because unacceptable behaviour has been reinforced. Operant conditioning therapies are different from therapies based on classical conditioning because the responses are not reflex behaviour.

Activity 6

Skinner (1938, 1953) recognised different forms of reinforcement: positive reinforcement, negative reinforcement and punishment. Try to describe them.

(Suggested answer on page 982.)

■ Behaviour shaping

Therapy based on operant conditioning uses a technique known as behaviour shaping. This is a process of reinforcing responses which progressively resemble the desired behaviour. Desired responses are positively reinforced, and any undesired responses are punished or negatively reinforced.

One behaviour-shaping technique involves the use of **token economies**. This method has been used in psychiatric hospitals and in schools for children with behaviour problems. In the hospitals patients are given tokens or points in exchange for performing specific tasks such as cleaning teeth or bed-making. They can then exchange the tokens for special privileges: new clothes, snacks, television time, overnight passes or telephone time. Some hospitals have a board displaying the number of tokens that can be obtained for different tasks and the number that can be removed as penalties for undesirable behaviour.

Systems such as these have been used successfully with disturbed patients (Paul and Lentz, 1977) and in institutions for delinquent children (Braukmann and Fixen, 1975). One advantage of the system is that it can be operated by the staff on an individual basis, thus catering for individual needs. The disadvantages are that some investigators claim that if the tokens are removed the behaviour reverts back: 'token economy, token behaviour'. Unfortunately, the system can be open to abuse, and in some cases civil rights groups have complained about the ethics, particularly when meals have been contingent on tokens or when patients are performing ward duties for tokens rather than being paid a wage for tasks like cleaning.

■ Biofeedback

Normally, operant conditioning is concerned with voluntary responses whereas classical conditioning is concerned with involuntary ones. There are, however, some internal physiological responses such as heart rate, blood pressure and contraction of smooth muscles, stomach excitations, brain waves and penal erection which do not fall into either category because, although they are controlled involuntarily, they can be modified using an operant conditioning technique called biofeedback. Biofeedback is a method by which people with the help of various machines are able to control their physiological responses. Blancard and Epstein (1978) identified three steps involved in biofeedback:

- Signals showing an undesired response from the target organ (for example muscular tension) are electronically detected and amplified.
- The signals are converted to a visual or auditory signal which is fed back to the patient.
- Using this immediate feedback, the patients learn to control internal systems by changing their behaviour. For example, the patient may learn to relax in such a way as to reduce heart rate and blood pressure.

Biofeedback has been used successfully to treat headaches, pain of muscular origin and stress-related conditions like high blood pressure where the symptoms have physiobiological origins. Biofeedback of internal states is used effectively in stress management programmes. An example of the use of biofeedback is shown in the case study below.

The main disadvantage of biofeedback is the high cost, which is partly due to the amount of equipment required for physiological measures such as pulse rate, muscle tension or breathing. Simple relaxation techniques which do not require equipment are equally effective. From a review of clinical case studies, Gatchel (1988) concluded that biofeedback as a sole form of treatment is no more effective than muscle relaxation techniques. In fact, many Eastern cultures claim that for hundreds of years they have successfully used relaxation techniques such as Tai Chi and yoga to control psychological responses.

■ Evaluation of therapies based on operant conditioning

- Like classical conditioning, operant conditioning is based on the idea that learning is automatic and that no conscious thinking is involved. Investigations into the benefits of behaviour shaping indicate that when reinforcement stops improvements do not persist.
- When behaviour changes seemed permanent it has been suggested that it is the relationship between the therapist and patient and changes in the patient's thinking that are the crucial therapeutic factors.
- However, this kind of therapy is effective in a number of disorders.
- It is brief and can be carried out with a minimum of training.

Behaviour therapy based on social learning theory

Therapy based on social learning theory involves patients learning an appropriate response by copying a model who is performing acceptable behaviour (figure 26.9). The therapy can be used in three situations:

- When patients do not have the required behaviour in their repertoire because it has never been learned. For example, an extremely shy person may never have made social contacts and may not know how to behave.

Case study: the use of biofeedback for the treatment of back pain

Budzynski et al. (1973) described a patient who had been suffering from severe back pains for three and a half years because of a high level of muscular tension in his forehead and neck. With the patient in a comfortable position, the therapist placed electrodes on the relevant muscles in the forehead and neck. When the tension in these muscles dropped below a curtain level, a tone sounded; when the tension exceeded the level, the tone ceased. After several training sessions the patient was able to keep the tone on and the headaches disappeared. Booster sessions together with relaxation practised at home have kept the patient free of headaches.

26.9 Examples of the use of modelling to treat maladaptive behaviour

- Lovaas *et al.* (1966) used modelling to teach speech to autistic children.
- The techniques have also helped to reduce fears of surgical and dental work (Melamed and Siegel, 1975; Melamed *et al.*, 1975).
- Bandura and Menlove (1968) used modelling to reduce fear of dogs in children. The children watched fearless models engage in various interactions with a dog. The children later showed an increased willingness to approach dogs.

- When patients have forgotten a form of behaviour and need to relearn it.
- When patients behave inappropriately because of anxiety or some other psychological dysfunction.

Evaluation of therapy based on social learning theory

- Therapies based on modelling have been used successfully to treat a number of psychopathological conditions.
- Research has shown them to be equally as effective as systematic desensitisation and flooding for the treatment of phobias (Rachmen, 1976).
- They have also been used to teach new, socially approved behaviour to disturbed schizophrenic patients (Bellack *et al.*, 1976).

Cognitive and cognitive-behavioural therapies

Cognitive therapy is based on the idea that problems arise from faulty thinking and aims to change the ways clients perceive their situations. Cognitive therapy, like behaviour therapy, attributes inappropriate behaviour patterns to environmental influences. However, unlike behaviour therapy, cognitive therapists believe that the root of the problems lies in faulty thinking and the role of the therapist is to help patients to understand their thinking patterns and change them. Cognitive-behavioural therapies incorporate both the behaviourist and cognitive approaches.

There are now many different forms of cognitive-behavioural therapy that have become a leading force in psychotherapeutic practice. They are linked together because they all share the same basic assumptions. Figure 26.10 outlines the basic assumptions of cognitive therapies.

In the 1970s, cognitive approaches came to the forefront of therapy as a result of the separate contributions of several eminent psychologists such Bandura, Kelly, Beck and Ellis. Many psychologists see Bandura as the link between behaviourist and cognitive theorists. Bandura influenced the development of cognitive-behavioural therapy by

26.10 Assumptions made by cognitive psychologists

- The behaviourist view that people respond passively to environmental stimuli is too simplistic.
- The psychodynamic view that people are driven by unconscious internal processes ignores the fact that people think.
- Humanistic therapies ignore cognition and focus on feelings.
- Past events do influence behaviour but it is more appropriate to focus therapies on the present.
- Cognitive psychologists believe that changing the way the person thinks will help to change feelings and behaviour.
- Cognitions may not be the only factor involved in behaviour, some responses are not cognitive but automatic.
- Emotions and actions can affect cognitions.

drawing attention to the effects of vicarious reinforcement discussed in Unit 21.

Kelly's cognitive therapy

Kelly (1955) is often credited with being the first person to describe a cognitive approach to therapy. He began his career as a psychoanalyst but gradually developed his own personality therapy because he noticed that his patients were trying to make sense of their world and make predictions about it. He suggested that people behave like scientists, developing their own theories and evaluating them, using evidence gained from experience. Everyone constructs an individual internal model based on pairs of opposing concepts called *personal constructions*. These may include, for example, warm/cold, intelligent/dull, old/young.

Everyone's model is unique and based on personal experiences, so musical/non-musical may be included in the constructs of a musician whereas an athlete may include fit/unfit. When we meet people, we evaluate them using a construct model, but this evaluation model may change as we get to know the people better. Education and life experiences often cause us to change our construct systems, for example when adolescents learn about politics they may develop a construct of left-wing or right-wing.

Kelly claimed that patients requiring therapy can be helped by gaining insight into the way they use their construct systems. For example, a woman who has an unsatisfactory relationship with her daughter may have a construct critical/understanding. She indicates to the therapist that she sees herself as critical when dealing with her daughter and understanding when relating to others. This insight might encourage the woman to consider supportive ways of relating to her daughter.

Beck's cognitive therapy

Beck (1967) noted that depressed patients had negative views about themselves, the world and the future. They saw themselves as deficient, inadequate, deserted and lacking qualities to cope with a situation. They thought that there were insurmountable obstacles preventing them from achieving goals. Their view of the future was that their troubles would go on indefinitely and get worse. Beck claimed that *cognitive distortions* were at the root of the depression. He suggested that some people learn to think negatively because of childhood experiences. The therapist helps the depressed person by first identifying the *attributional style* and then confronting the patient with different interpretations of events or by pointing out exaggerations or inconsistencies.

Beck extended his ideas to other psychopathological conditions. For example, he considered that someone with a phobia had similar fears of a situation to everyone else, but the phobic person exaggerated both the likelihood of an event occurring and also its consequences. An example is given in figure 26.11.

Beck's therapeutic approach involves helping patients to recognise distortions in their thinking and to change them. A simple example (Beck and Young, 1984) is the female patient who said 'No one will find me attractive unless I lose weight'. This was contradicted by the therapist who reminded her of a number of satisfying love affairs she had experienced at her present weight.

Other methods used by Beck and his followers when changing perceptions include interrupting unpleasant thoughts by turning them off, and imagining a particular event six months, a year or several years later. Also, a patient may be helped to become more detached, and positive images can be used to provide a substitute for negative images or to promote relaxation.

Ellis's rational-emotive therapy

Whilst Beck concentrated on cognitive disorders, Ellis (1955) developed a technique called **rational-emotive therapy**, based on the notion that some people try to live up to unrealistic ideas. Rational emotive therapy helps to uncover unrealistic cognitions and allows people to reassess their beliefs and goals. Ellis's patients were often surprised when they realised that they had been trying to live in an impossible way.

26.11 An example of the role of cognitions in phobias

An example of the effect of cognitions on phobias was identified by White and Sellwood (1995). They were studying people with injection phobia. These people display an unusual physiological response which results in 50–60 per cent of these people fainting when exposed to injections. The authors demonstrated that cognitive factors prevented them from getting treatment for the phobia. They attempted to treat a patient using systematic desensitisation, but she was unable to make the correct response in all but the least threatening of the graded situations because her cognitions were causing too much anxiety. One problem was that she thought there was a 49 per cent chance of the needle snapping when injected into someone.

This was challenged by asking the patient to break the needle, which she could not do. Her estimate of the breaking needle went down to 3 per cent.

Her assumption that the entire length of the needle would be inserted into her arm was tackled by showing her a video of a patient having a blood sample taken. She then realised that the needle did not go in all the way. The patient also overestimated the amount of time the injection would take. This was overcome by asking her to time the sequence shown on the video. The cognitive therapy together with the desensitisation procedure following the cognitive intervention helped the patient to overcome her problem.

■ Evaluation of cognitive and cognitive-behavioural therapies

- Cognitive-behavioural therapy is gaining support and becoming more diverse, but at the moment it is unclear which of the therapies is most effective.
- It has been criticised as treating the symptoms, rather than the cause, but therapists do not claim that cognitive therapy will always cure a person, only that it may help bring relief through greater understanding.
- White and Sellwood (1995) have demonstrated how it can be used to treat phobias and there is evidence that it helps with some of the effects of post-traumatic stress disorder. It has been used to help in the treatment of eating disorders, seen in the case study shown below.
- Some severe conditions such as schizophrenia, and some major depressions, however, require alternative methods of treatment because the sufferer is too confused or disturbed to relate to the therapist in an insightful way.
- Beck's cognitive therapy has been shown to be successful at relieving depression (for example Shaw, 1977).

Haaga and Davison (1989) provided the following evaluation of Ellis's rational-emotive therapy:

- It reduces reports of different kinds of anxiety.
- It is less effective than behavioural therapy for the treatment of agoraphobia (although combining the two approaches may be advantageous).
- It may be useful in treating antisocial behaviour, depression and excessive anger.
- It may help healthy people to cope better with everyday stress.
- It may achieve therapeutic success, not so much through a reduction in irrational thinking, but rather through supporting patients to confront their fears and take up new, more adaptive behaviour.

Case study – the use of cognitive therapy in the treatment of bulimia nervosa (Vittus, 1996)

Jill was 25 years old and single. She worked as a flight attendant for a large airline company. Her job was demanding and the airline insisted on high standards of personal presentation. One of their requirements related to the weight of the flight attendants – if they exceeded a specified weight they lost their jobs.

Case study *cont'd*

On her way home after a particularly demanding day, Jill bought half a gallon of ice cream, a pound box of biscuits, a medium-sized frozen pizza, a loaf of French bread and a quart of milk. When the pizza was barely cooked she ate it along with everything else, cramming food into her mouth and dribbling over her blouse. When she had finished eating she knelt in front of the toilet, pushed her fingers down her throat and vomited back everything she had eaten.

The next day she went to see a doctor about feeling weak and dizzy. She was acutely embarrassed when he asked about her eating patterns, but because she wanted to get well she told him about the binge/vomit pattern that had been going on for years. She said that she felt disgusted by her behaviour and also admitted to periods of mild depression. The binge/vomit pattern had started in her early teens: she had tried to diet but had discovered that vomiting back food was a more effective way to lose weight. She had also used laxatives to purge food from her system.

The doctor assured her that she was not disgusting and that she was suffering from a condition called bulimia nervosa. Jill was relieved to know that she was suffering from a recognised condition and went to an outpatient clinic for treatment.

The first priority was to focus on her eating problems. The following goals were set:
- Identify the circumstances that surrounded the bingeing.
- Restructure her thoughts about herself and her eating.
- Educate her about the health risks involved in bulimic behaviour.
- Outline the need for meal planning.
- Make her aware of cultural standards that were contributing to her bulimic behaviour.

Jill kept a detailed record of her eating and noted her moods to see how they related to bulimic behaviour. She found that she frequently binged in the late afternoon or early evening, especially after a long, stressful flight. She experienced a sense of relief after binge/purge episodes because she was using them to cope with stressful events.

Jill had distorted, illogical self cognitions regarding her body image and self-worth. The therapist used dialogue to review her thoughts.

For example:

Jill   'I felt miserable all day because I put on a pair of trousers that were too tight.'
Therapist 'Have you thought of any other possibilities?'
Jill   'Like what?'
Therapist 'They might have shrunk in the wash; it was a hot clammy day, they might have just been sticking to you; they might not have fitted in the first place.'

Jill's education involved planning meals, looking at health risks and learning to identify contributory cultural factors. In her case it was easy to identify the pressures being placed on her by her employers, but for many bulimia sufferers the pressures are more subtle – coming from the media and advertisers. In our culture, for example, women receive some conflicting messages. One only has to reflect on the differences between very thin supermodels and well endowed topless models to see the very contrasting ideal-body types that the more susceptible may compare themselves to.

The therapy helped Jill. Six months afterwards she was sticking to a regular eating pattern and had only had two binge sessions.

The therapy may or may not provide a lasting cure, there are many complicating factors (which were identified in Unit 25), such as the role of serotonin which is currently not fully understood.

Self-assessment questions

12 What is the basic assumption of behaviour therapy?

13 Fill in the missing gaps.

Theory	Therapy
Classical conditioning	A
	Aversion therapy
	Flooding/implosion
B	Behaviour shaping
	Biofeedback
C	Modelling

14 What is the basic assumption of cognitive therapy?

(Suggested answers on page 983.)

Psychophysical therapies

Psychophysical therapies are sometimes referred to as *psychosomatic* therapies. These therapies are based on the medical model. Therapists seek to help patients by altering the brain function using physical methods such as brain surgery, **electro-convulsive therapy (ECT)**, or drugs. These approaches are often used in conjunction with psychotherapy for conditions with a medical origin or conditions that do not respond to psychotherapy.

■ Psychosurgery

The best results obtained from psychosurgery have been in the treatment of mood disorders, particularly prolonged major depression which cannot be treated any other way. The surgeon aims to interrupt brain circuits involved in emotional responses by making tiny lesions to destroy some of the nerve cells.

All psychophysical therapies involve ethical dilemmas. In the case of surgery the effects are irreversible and there are some risks to the patient, so further medical opinions have to be obtained before proceeding. Surgery may be suggested if the patient has been suffering for many years and all other methods have failed. However, as other treatments have improved, the use of surgery has declined and is now only occasionally required.

■ Electro-convulsive therapy (ECT)

ECT involves placing two electrodes on the patient's forehead, usually on the right-hand side of the brain. A short electric current is passed through the electrodes causing convulsions rather like fits. Before beginning treatment the patients are given a general anaesthetic and muscle relaxant to prevent bones breaking during the convulsions. A typical course of treatment might be six–eight treatments at twice weekly intervals.

ECT is useful for treating severe depression which might result in suicide or in cases where depression has developed later in life, for no apparent reason. Unfortunately, it is not known precisely how ECT works as the whole brain is subjected to shock, not just those areas which provide the beneficial effects. It probably works by increasing the availability of the neurotransmitter noradrenaline. There may be side-effects which could include memory loss, usually temporary, or motivational changes.

ECT is usually only given when the patient has not responded to any other treatment. When doctors decide whether or not to give ECT they have to balance the possibility of three to four deaths per 100 000 treatments against the death rate from untreated depression.

Drug treatments

Drugs used for psychological disturbances are called psychotherapeutic drugs. (See also Unit 12.) Three categories are discussed here: sedatives or anti-anxiety drugs, anti-depressants and anti-psychotics.

■ Anti-anxiety drug treatments

There are three groups of anti-anxiety drugs: barbiturates, benzodiazepine derivatives and beta-blockers.

- *Barbiturates* work by depressing the nervous system, especially in the reticular activating system (a part of the brain concerned with sleep arousal). These drugs are rarely used therapeutically because they are addictive and cause serious withdrawal symptoms like sleep disorders or fits.

- *Benzodiazepine* derivatives such as valium have replaced barbiturates because they cause less dependence. They are used to treat anxiety on its own or when it accompanies another condition like schizophrenia or depression. They can be combined successfully with other drugs. They are also used to help people suffering from sleep problems caused by anxiety. Benzodiazepines work by attaching to neurones in the brain that receive the neurotransmitter GABA. This prevents the cell from firing. When the benzodiazepines bind to the neurones they increase the ability of GABA to bind to them.

This slows down physical arousal throughout the body, thus reducing anxiety (Lloyd *et al.*, 1992). Figure 26.12 provides an evaluation of benzodiazepines.

- *Beta-blockers* suppress physical symptoms of anxiety such as palpitations and 'butterflies in the stomach', producing a mild improvement for general anxiety disorders. They work by preventing norepinephrine from activating the sympathetic nervous system (Tyrer, 1992).

■ Anti-depressant drug treatments

In recent years three groups of anti-depressant drugs have been isolated: tricyclics; MAO inhibitors; second-generation drugs.

- *Tricyclic anti-depressants.* Imipramine is only one of a group of drugs which are thought to work by inhibiting the re-uptake of the neurotransmitters, noradrenaline and serotonin (Goodwin 1992). In depressed people noradrenaline and serotonin are removed too quickly after the nerve cell has fired. If the re-uptake is blocked by tricyclics, noradrenaline and serotonin can increase their activity on the neurones, thus reducing the depression (Goodwin, 1992).

There have, however been problems with this explanation because the beneficial effects of the drugs do not begin for 7–14 days. Some researchers believe that the drugs act by increasing the sensitivity of the neurones to noradrenaline and serotonin (Singh and Licki, 1993).

26.12 An evaluation of benzodiazepines

Benzodiazepines are useful for general anxiety conditions and they have been used to reduce tension in war veterans suffering from post-traumatic stress disorder (Marmar *et al.*, 1993). They are not, however, used for specific phobias.

There are several problems related to the use of benzodiazepines:

- They are not a long-term solution to anxiety because when the drugs are stopped the anxiety returns (Rickel and Schweizer, 1992).

- People can become physically dependent on the drugs if they are used for long periods.
- There are side-effects, for example, drowsiness, lack of coordination, impaired memory, depression, aggressive behaviour (Apter, 1993).
- The drugs can cause serious problems if taken with other substances; even combined with small amounts of alcohol they can cause serious respiratory problems.

Drugs such as *imipramine* have been used widely to treat depression but side-effects including dryness of mouth and constipation may be experienced; these vary depending upon both patient and dosage. The side-effects, however, are fewer with more recently developed drugs. Imipramine has a wide range of uses. For example, it has been used to treat phobias, some of the symptoms of post-traumatic stress disorder and the depressive symptoms of bulimia nervosa and anorexia nervosa.

■ *Monoamine oxidase inhibitors (MAOIs)*. These have a narrower range of usefulness than tricyclics. They are thought to act by inhibiting the enzyme monoamine oxidase from breaking down neurotransmitters, hence increasing their available levels. They are thought to be most useful for helping atypical depressions. Unfortunately, they can cause unpleasant side-effects, sometimes lethal, especially if foods containing the chemical tyramine are eaten when the drug is being used. Tyramine is found in a variety of food and drinks, such as cheese, chocolate, red wine, beer and yoghurt.

■ *Second-generation drugs*. These are chemically different from tricyclics and MAOIs. An example is fluoxetine hydrochloride *(Prozac)*. They work by altering the sensitivity of norepinephrine and serotonin receptors (Richelson, 1989). Some, called selective *serotonin re-uptake inhibitors (SSRIs)* are thought to alter only serotonin re-uptake without affecting anything else. Side-effects associated with tricyclics do not occur but some people experience nausea and headaches (Goodwin, 1992). Recently there have been concerns about the long-term side-effects of Prozac.

It is generally acknowledged that anti-depressant drugs help by relieving the symptoms of depression and need to be taken until the underlying depressive state is resolved. In resistant cases, various combinations of treatment may be necessary. Figure 26.13 outlines a study which compares the effectiveness of different treatments for depression.

The anti-depressant drugs described above are useful for the treatment of unipolar depression but they are not effective in the treatment of bipolar depression. For preventing mood swings in bipolar depression *lithium carbonate* is used. Figure 26.14 summarises studies investigating its effectiveness.

26.13 Comparing different treatments for depression by the National Institute of Mental Health, USA (1994)

There were 239 moderately to severely depressed people taking part in the study. They were assigned to one of four different treatment groups:

■ Beck's cognitive therapy.

■ Interpersonal therapy, which involves developing insight into relationships which are thought to cause depression.

■ Treatment using the anti-depressant drug imipramine.

■ A control group, which was given a placebo instead of drugs.

The treatment, which lasted for 16 weeks, was carried out by 28 carefully selected and trained therapists. The Hamilton Rating Scale for Depression was used to test for the level of depression.

Results: 50–60 per cent of those who completed their treatment were almost free from depression at the end of the treatment compared to 29 per cent of the placebo group. Drug therapy reduced symptoms more quickly than the other treatments, but they had caught up by 14 weeks.

These results are consistent with findings from other studies which have shown that cognitive and interpersonal therapies are more effective than behaviour therapy and psychodynamic therapies and that the combination of psychotherapy and drugs is the most helpful in the treatment of depression (Kleman et al., 1994).

26.14 The effectiveness of lithium carbonate in the treatment of bipolar depression

- Kerman *et al.*, 1994 studied the effect of lithium carbonate on manic symptoms. Patients were assigned to a treatment group where they were given lithium carbonate or a placebo by a doctor. Different doctors were then asked to assess the patients. These doctors did not know which patients had received the treatment or what the nature of the study was. Lithium was found to be more effective than the placebo in reducing the symptoms of mania. The problem with this study is that there were different patients in each group and some people who were given the lithium (40 per cent) did not improve.

- Abou-Saleh (1992) used an ABAB experimental design to test the effectiveness of lithium on individuals. Each patient was given lithium for a while, then a placebo, then lithium, and changes in their behaviour were noted. The manic symptoms decreased when lithium was given and reappeared when the placebos were substituted.
- There is also evidence from similar studies that depressive symptoms are also decreased. Lithium carbonate seems to act as a mood stabiliser.

At the moment no one is sure how lithium carbonate works. It is thought to alter synaptic activity in nerve cells that use noradrenaline and serotonin, but it does not work in the same way as other anti-depressants. One theory is based on the fact that when the neurone fires, the neurotransmitter causes a series of cellular changes in the receiving nerve cell transmitter. These cellular changes then cause the cell to fire. Lithium may affect the process involved in the cellular changes. Another theory is that lithium alters the sodium ion activity in the neurones.

Evaluation of lithium therapy

- Lithium helps around 50 per cent of the people suffering from bipolar depression. The correct dosage can only be found by trial and error. Too little has no effect and too much can result in unpleasant side-effects.
- Bipolar depression is a severe illness which causes problems in all areas of the person's life so the drug therapy is used in conjunction with psychotherapy to help patients and their families come to terms with the illness. Psychotherapy involves educating patients and their families so that they have a better understanding of the illness and helping patients to manage family and social relationships. There are also problem-solving sessions which help them to come to terms

with the problems they encounter as a result of their condition, such as how to look after children or hold down a job when symptoms reappear.

- Studies suggest that psychotherapy together with drug treatment result in patients spending less time in hospital and more time in work (Clarkin *et al.*, 1990).

Anti-psychotic drugs

In 1952 anti-psychotic drugs revolutionised the treatment of schizophrenia. The drugs can be grouped according to their chemical structures. One of the most extensively used drugs is *chlorpromazine* which belongs to a group called the phenothiazines. These act by reducing the activity of the neurotransmitter *dopamine*. It is thought that people with Type 1 schizophrenia have large numbers of receptors on the neurones that receive dopamine, and the drugs act by simply blocking the receptor sites on the post-synaptic membrane. Several studies have been performed to test the effectiveness of anti-psychotic drugs. Examples are shown in figure 26.15.

Chlorpromazine only treats the positive symptoms of schizophrenia and there can be unpleasant side-effects which are similar to the symptoms of Parkinson's disease, i.e. continuous muscle tremors and shaking, and slow shuffling movements.

26.15 Studies showing the effectiveness of anti-psychotic drugs in the treatment of schizophrenia

In Cole *et al.*'s 1964 study 344 patients from 9 hospitals were involved. They were randomly assigned to one of four treatment groups: three groups used different anti-psychotic drugs, the fourth was a placebo group.

A double-blind experimental design was used. Neither the patients nor the hospital staff knew which treatment the patients had been given. After six weeks the staff evaluated the patients: 75 per cent of the patients in the anti-psychotic drug groups were judged to be much improved compared to 25 per cent of the placebo patients.

May, *et al.* (1981) used a total of 28 hospitalised patients and compared the following five treatments:

- anti-psychotic drugs only
- psychodynamic therapy only
- anti-psychotic drugs plus psychotherapy
- milieu therapy (a form of humanistic therapy)
- ECT.

Patients treated with only drugs or drugs plus psychotherapy showed most improvement. Psychodynamic and milieu therapy were not effective and ECT fell between the two.

It is now generally accepted that drugs are necessary for the treatment of schizophrenia, but it is important that patients continue medication because symptoms return if drugs are stopped (Davies *et al.*, 1993).

More recently a new drug, *clozapine* has been used and found to be effective for 80–85 per cent of schizophrenia sufferers who have been treated with it. Clozapine produces fewer side effects than chlorpromazine because it blocks fewer receptors (Chengappa *et al.*, 1994) and it has sometimes effectively treated some of the negative symptoms (Breier *et al.*, 1994). There are, however, some side-effects such as drowsiness, dizziness and possible weight gain and on some rare occasions it can cause agranulocytosis which is a serious reduction in white blood cells. Patients using this drug have to have regular blood tests.

■ Evaluation of drug therapies

Drugs have revolutionised the treatment of some psychopathological conditions but there are problems involved in administering and evaluating drug therapies. Figure 26.16 summarises some of these difficulties.

Self-assessment questions

15 Put the following groups of drugs in category A, B or C: (A) anti-anxiety, (B) anti-depressants, (C) anti-psychotic. (i) phenathiazines, (ii) barbiturates, (iii) tricyclics, (iv) MAO inhibitors, (v) benzodiazepine derivatives, (vi) beta-blockers, (vii) second-generation drug such as Prozac.

(Suggested answers on page 983.)

26.16 Problems involved in administering and evaluating drug therapies

- An accurate diagnosis is required in order to administer appropriate treatment.
- It is difficult to supervise treatment and make sure that patients are taking the drugs when they should be.
- There is the possibility of side-effects which can be unpleasant or very occasionally fatal. These effects have to be balanced against the consequences of not giving treatment.
- Physical treatments rarely offer a complete cure; they usually need to be combined with other forms of treatment.

- When evaluating drug therapies patient compliance with the treatment programmes is a factor which has to be considered (Guenther and Meise, 1990). Many patients fail to complete their courses of treatment or stop taking the drugs when they feel better. In some cases, for example, schizophrenia, if they do this the symptoms reappear and it often takes longer to return the patient to their previous level of functioning (Wyatt, 1991).

Recent issues related to therapy

In the last few years a number of issues relating to the treatment of mental disorders have arisen, some as a result of political changes. The following three issues are discussed briefly: culture and treatment; multi-disciplinary approaches; **community care** programmes.

Cultural issues

The aims of some forms of psychotherapy are in conflict with the basic beliefs of some cultures. Many western therapies are based on the idea of the person developing as an individual. In some cultures, identification with the family is very important and a family member who tried to assert his or her own individuality would be viewed as deviant and would be condemned. Western psychotherapy aims at self-expression, assertiveness and, in the case of humanistic therapies, self-actualisation. Many non-western cultures condemn such characteristics because they are seen as selfish.

There are also cultural barriers to the psychotherapy process:

- In societies where family loyalty is highly valued, it may be considered unreasonable to expect a patient to discuss feelings about family issues with a stranger.
- Many groups will not accept that talking will help a problem; they expect to be treated with medicine or herbal remedies (Kleinman and Kleinman, 1985).
- Some non-western groups encourage obedience rather than independent thinking, so people learn to avoid their own thoughts, and are not prepared for the self exploration required in western psychotherapy; the therapist is expected to be directive.

Multi-disciplinary approaches

Many treatments are used in conjunction with each other. In fact, one advantage of physical treatment is that the patient's mood and behaviour can be stabilised enough for them to respond to psychotherapies. This leads to a multi-disiplinary approach in which several specialists team together to deal with a different aspect of the person's condition. This combination of treatments links into the *diathesis-stress model* of abnormality which says that the development of a particular condition is a result of genetic and environmental factors.

Community care programmes

In recent years there has been a move towards closing large residential hospitals and treating patients in the community, focusing on the development of coping strategies. Originally the reason for moving patients into the community was to encourage the patients to live independent lives where they had self-respect and personal dignity. They ate, slept, washed, and dressed according to the hospital's rota, having no choice about what they ate, what they wore or even how they spent their time. There was no privacy – they slept in large dormitories and lived and ate in communal rooms. However, in sheltered accommodation in the community, with support, these patients could make their own decisions and live their own lives. In some situations this has worked well. In many cases the housing and support have not been adequate, leading to social problems of a different sort, for example homelessness.

Other consequences of the care in the community programme are the effects on the carers and their families. In many cases sufferers who would once have been helped in hospital when a condition such as bipolar depression was causing serious distress are now being looked after at home. Currently, there appears to be little research on the effects of such situations on the children in these families.

Self-assessment questions

16 List the problems involved in evaluating drug therapies.

(Suggested answers on page 983.)

Unit summary

- Therapies can be divided into two basic types: *psychotherapy* and *psychophysical therapy* (also known as *biomedical* or *somatic* therapy). Choice of therapy is dependant on accurate diagnosis which can be problematic. *Evaluation* of the therapy is made difficult by factors such as *spontaneous remission* and *sampling methods*.

- *Psychodynamic* therapies help patients by encouraging them to talk through problems with an analyst who offers interpretations of the symptoms. Freudian analysis is referred to as *psychoanalysis* and involves *transference* using techniques such as *free association* and *dream analysis*. Post-Freudians such as Adler, Jung and modern psychodynamic therapists prefer to take a more *active role* in therapy than Freud.

- *Humanistic* therapies aim to help clients fulfil their potential making meaningful choices. Carl Rogers developed *client-centred therapy* in which therapists make suggestions to help clients recognise hidden aspects of their problems. Therapists need to display *unconditional positive self-regard, empathy, honesty and sincerity*.

- *Group* therapy is based on people with problems being helped by the group. *Family* therapy assumes that the whole family plays a part in the problems of the individual member. Group treatments can be as helpful as individual therapy but some people find group sessions stressful so therapists need to screen out the vulnerable.

Summary cont'd.

- *Behaviour* therapy is based on the concept that behavioural problems are the result of *faulty learning*. They stress the importance of the environment. Behaviour therapy based on classical conditioning includes *systematic desensitisation, flooding and implosion* and *aversion therapy* whereas therapy based on *operant conditioning* includes *behaviour shaping, token economies* and *biofeedback* which includes both classical and operant conditioning. Behaviour therapy can also be based on *social learning theory* involving *modelling*.

- *Cognitive* therapy is based on the concept of problems arising from *faulty thinking* and aims to change the ways clients perceive their situations. *Cognitive-behaviourist* therapists incorporate both the behaviourist and cognitive approaches. Therapists such as Kelly (*personal constructs*), Beck (*attributional styles*), and Ellis (*rational-emotive therapy*) have gained support but at the moment it is unclear which of the therapies is most successful.

- *Psychophysical therapies* are based on the *biomedical model*. Therapists try to help patients by altering brain functions with physical treatments such as *psychosurgery*, *electroconvulsive therapy (ECT)* and *drug treatments* including *anti-anxiety, anti-depressant and antipsychotic treatments*.

- Recent issues have arisen including *cultural barriers* to the therapeutic procress. Also many treatments are used in conjunction with one another. This *multi-disciplinary approach* links to the *diathesis-stress* model of abnormality which emphasises the interaction of genetic and environmental factors.

- *Community-care programmes* have sometimes been successful in allowing people to live more normal lives outside a closed hospital. However in some cases housing and support have not been adequate resulting in homelessness an/or undue stress on the family.

- Central to the success of any therapy is the client's *motivation* and *relationship with the therapist*.

- Whichever therapy is selected, the patient's motivation and the patient's relationship with the therapist appear to be key factors which contribute to a successful outcome of the treatment.

Terms to define

aversion therapy
behaviour therapy
client-centred therapy
cognitive therapy
community care
electro-convulsive therapy (ECT)
family therapy
flooding

free association
implosion therapy
psychodynamic therapies
rational-emotive therapy
systematic densensitisation
token economies

Further reading

Aponte, J F, Rivers, R Y and Wohl, J (1995) *Psychological Interventions and Cultural Diversity*, Allyn & Bacon, Boston, MA.

General issues faced by practitioners are addressed, including diverse ethnic and racial populations. Although this is an American text it is still relevant in the UK, demonstrating how specific types of interventions can prove helpful for certain minority groups.

Green, S (1994) *Individual Differences: Normal and Abnormal*, Laurence Erlbaum, Hove.

Chapter 7 describes and evaluates behaviour therapy, psychotherapy, cognitive therapy and somatic (biomedical) therapy, and discusses the problems associated with evaluating the effectiveness of therapy.

Green, S (1996) 'Drugs and psychological disorders', *Psychology Review, 3(2)*, 25–8.

A discussion of some of the problems associated with drug therapy as recommended by the biomedical approach, including side-effects and the effectiveness of treatment.

Prentice, P (1995) 'From theory to therapist', *Psychology Review, 2(1)*, 5–7.

An overview of psychological therapy discussing the different therapies and the 'pathways' for prospective therapists.

Answers

Suggested answers to activities

1

The bereaved person may become depressed and the helper may find himself or herself in a situation where he or she is being of no help to the sufferer. The sensible course of action would be to seek help from a doctor. It may not be easy to perusade a depressed person to go to a doctor; it may be necessary to ask the doctor to call on them. Depressed people sometimes commit suicide, so it is important to ask about suicidal feelings.

2

Conversion hysteria is a condition in which physical symptoms are experienced, like paralysis of an arm, without medical reasons to explain them (i.e. there is no damage to the nervous system or muscles).

3

When working with children, parents or guardians must be kept informed throughout the treatment. Hans was very young and probably not able to understand the interpretations given to him, nor would he be old enough to communicate his own thoughts. Communicating information in this kind of therapeutic situation presents practical problems.

4

How many complications have you identified?
Mother   The sessions may suit her if they are timed for when she is not working.
Father   It may be very difficult for father to come to an arrangement with his employer, particularly if the sessions coincide with times when he is meant to be working away from home; in fact, an unsympathetic employer may find someone else to do the job, threatening father's promotion opportunities or even his job. How might father feel?
The brother   His examination results will determine whether or not he gains a university place. Missing classes on a regular basis could jeopardise this. How might the brother feel?
The older sister   Her employer may be sympathetic and give her time off, possibly deducting it from her annual leave, or the employer may give her unpaid leave. The employer may simply say no. How might the sister feel?

5

There are ethical problems – the therapy is very intense and some people find it hard to tolerate. For this reason some therapists say it should only be used as a last resort.

Even though it is hard to tolerate, flooding can change behaviour faster than systematic desensitisation (Gelder, 1991).

6

Positive reinforcement occurs when behaviour is encouraged by a reward being given, and negative reinforcement occurs when a reward is gained by the removal of an unpleasant stimulus. Note that negative reinforcement is not the same as punishment which takes place when an unpleasant stimulus is applied in order to reduce undesirable behaviour. Skinner noticed that, as in classical conditioning, if a reinforcer is removed, extinction of the behaviour concerned gradually takes place.

Suggested answers to self-assessment questions

1

Both groups of therapies are used to treat people with psychopathological conditions. Psychotherapies use methods based on psychological theories, whereas psychophysical therapies use methods which involve alteration of the brain functions by physical means.

2
- The diagnosis may alter as the therapy proceeds because more information becomes available.
- Some people are better able to communicate their feelings and problems than others.
- Similar symptoms may have different causes.

3
- Spontaneous remission.
- Methods for sampling treatment groups and control groups vary between studies, making comparison difficult.

4
- Being aware of our basic motivations helps us to change and become more adaptable.
- The causes of mental disturbances are unresolved conflicts in the unconscious mind.

5

Catharsis is reliving past experiences together with the accompanying emotions.
Transference is when feelings linked to past events are projected onto the therapist.

6

Free association and dream analysis.

7

Adler thought the motivating force was to overcome handicap in order to compensate for feelings of inferiority.
Jung thought the spiritual drive was important.

8

It is difficult to know whether or not patients are telling the truth, as often they cannot distinguish between fact and fiction themselves. Implying that patients are not being truthful could result in them losing trust, consequently damaging the therapeutic relationship. Sometimes accusations of abuse are made; such accusations need to be taken seriously but if they are false they seriously affect innocent people. If the accusations are false we are left with the same question that Freud contemplated – why are these stories invented?

9

Humanistic psychologists think that clients have the best understanding of themselves, not the psychologist. Psychodynamic psychologists think that the therapist understands patients best, and that most anxieties are unconscious.

10

Client-centred therapy is unlikely to be successful because people suffering from schizophrenia are out of touch with reality and have limited self-insight. Their communication skills are also impaired, making any form of talking therapy difficult if not impossible. The implication of this is that humanistic therapy is only suitable for a limited number of articulate people. It has limited value for conditions where the client does not have a grasp of reality.

11

See page 964.

12

The environment is of paramount importance in the development of psychological conditions and that psychological problems are a result of faulty learning. The problems can be remedied by relearning.

13

A desensitisation; B operant conditioning; C social learning theory.

14

Problems arise as a result of faulty thinking. The person can be treated by changing his or her thought processes.

15

(i) C   (ii) A   (iii) B   (iv) B   (v) A   (vi) A   (vii) B

16

See figure 26.16, page 978.

Research Methods

Unit 27

The Nature of Psychological Enquiry

Sara Nadin

This unit covers:

Key issues: ethics in psychological research; quantitative and qualitative approaches

Experimental approaches

Alternatives to the experiment

By the end of this unit, you should be able to:

- appreciate the central role of ethical issues in the adoption of different research approaches

- describe the different research methods available to psychologists, both quantitative and qualitative

- critically assess the advantages and disadvantages of different research strategies

- make an informed choice about the most appropriate methods to adopt for a given topic of study.

Unit 27 Contents

Introduction

The future of psychology is dependent upon the conduct of good quality research employing sound methodological techniques. Research provides the foundation for the knowledge and theories which we have come to accept as psychology. Whilst 'armchair' theorising may produce some interesting ideas about people and behaviour, such ideas are largely worthless unless they are linked to actual research. Psychologists have a variety of methods available to them in order to do this research. The aim of this unit is to explore that range, discussing the merits and disadvantages of different methodological approaches, imparting an understanding of why, in certain situations, a particular method is adopted in favour of another.

Before discussing specific methods, there are two issues which the student of psychology should be aware of. The first concerns the importance of *ethics* in methodological practice; the second concerns the debate about *quantitative and qualitative approaches* to research.

Key issues

Ethics in psychological research

Ethical considerations should be central to any research conducted, from the planning stage through to the completion. Such awareness is essential and needs to be instilled in all of those carrying out psychological research, from the new student to the accomplished academic. Ignoring ethical considerations, no matter how trivial the research may appear, can never be justified. The well-being of those involved in research, whether they are aware of this involvement or not, must be protected. Researchers should also consider the potential impact any outcomes of their research may have both upon those directly involved in the research and upon groups the sample may represent.

These issues have already been explored in greater detail in Unit 3. Students new to psychology are strongly advised to familiarise themselves with the ethical guidelines and issues covered in that unit before commencing with any research ideas. Too often, ethical considerations are brought in as an afterthought. They need to be central to the initial ideas and planning stage of research, forming an integral part of the research process.

Whilst there is a general set of ethical guidelines produced by the British Psychological Society (BPS), researchers should be aware of ethical issues associated with particular methods. Different methods give rise to specific ethical concerns, an awareness of which will help in the selection of appropriate methods and, ultimately, in the design and conduct of ethically sound research. The various issues associated with particular methods are discussed in the relevant sections which follow. As is mentioned below, there is an ethical dimension to the quantitative/qualitative debate on research methods.

Quantitative and qualitative approaches – the debate

Traditionally, psychology has been dominated by quantitative approaches associated with the **positivist tradition** with its emphasis upon the empirical observation of the objective world. Based upon the model of the natural sciences, the aim has been upon developing *objective knowledge* through the establishment of *cause and effect* relationships, ideally pursued using the *experimental method*. Such an approach enables the quantification of results, a process which renders theoretical concepts observable, manipulable and testable (Henwood and Pidgeon, 1995).

Whilst the experimental method is still popular and remains the preferred method of many psychologists, its dominance has been questioned with the rise of alternative qualitative techniques. Such techniques have arisen out of the recognition of the limitations of the experimental approach, both of the phenomenon under study and the level of understanding generated. Influenced by disciplines such as sociology and anthropology, the qualitative movement gathered pace in the 1970s. Labelled as **new paradigm research**, it emerged in the wake of the 'crisis' of the 1960s where the problems of interpretation associated with traditional quantitative approaches (**old paradigm research**) could no longer be ignored.

For new paradigm researchers, the experimental situation is seen to restrict what can actually be studied, with the artificial setting bearing little resemblance to real life. The reduction to quantifiable data negates the importance of contextual factors in the generation of understanding, ultimately failing to do justice to the richness and complexity of reality. From an *ethical* point of view, the experimental situation is regarded as dehumanising, treating 'subjects' as objects. Qualitative approaches highlight the importance of ethical considerations, with the experience of those participating being of central importance. The power bias inherent in the researcher–participant relationship should be openly recognised and the moral position of the researcher made explicit (Foster and Parker, 1995). The experimental method is regarded as representing an abuse of that power, imposing its own definition of what is worthy of being studied upon the subjects, in the name of good scientific practice.

With qualitative approaches the emphasis is on meaning and how meaning is constructed through social activities and systems, rather than upon the generation of abstract universal laws. Non-numerical data are considered desirable as they free the researcher to be sensitive to multiple interpretations, which may be represented in a variety of ways. Typical qualitative data are thus language based, be it an observer's records of observations made, verbatim transcripts from an interview, or historical records of past events.

Critics of the qualitative school suggest that such an approach is of little value in terms of furthering psychological knowledge. Qualitative research is regarded as **relativist**, which means that in effect 'anything goes', with qualitative techniques lacking in the standards and rigour traditionally associated with the experimental method. This has led to the distinction often made between 'hard' quantitative research and 'soft' qualitative research. Others suggest that scientific rigour is not the preserve of the experimental approach, and the focus of qualitative researchers should be on developing rigorous qualitative methods.

This brief outline of the 'quantitative/qualitative' debate represents the extreme views, the two research paradigms considered incommensurable and irreconcilable. Such an extreme position is not necessary, with contemporary opinion suggesting that both quantitative and qualitative methods can and should coexist within the same research framework. In this way, the strengths of each approach can be realised, the researcher selecting the method(s) considered most appropriate to advance the study of the subject under examination. Two advocates of this position, Foster and Parker (1995), make the following useful suggestion: 'You should try to be open to the promise and limitations of all the alternatives'. It is with this piece of guidance in mind that we now explore those alternatives.

Activity 1

Complete the following comparison table adding all the characteristics, strengths and weaknesses of old and new paradigm research. The 'solution' section is for you to say which choice you would make.

	Old paradigm	New paradigm
Characteristics	Traditional positivist approach	Emerged in response to criticisms of old paradigm
Strengths	High degree of rigour	Enables multiple interpretations to be considered
Weaknesses	Dehumanising – treats subjects as objects	It is relativist
Solution		

(Suggested answer on page 1014.)

Experimental approaches

The experimental method has been used extensively throughout the history of psychology. Its use has complemented commonsense and accepted notions of appropriate methods for scientific disciplines, replicating the example traditionally set by physics. So what is it about the experiment which affords it its continued popularity within psychology?

Characteristics of the experiment

The experiment as used in psychology is a research strategy which involves the manipulation of certain specified variables (independent variables). The effects of this manipulation are measured on certain other variables (dependent variables), whilst all other variables are controlled and remain constant. In this way, the experiment allows the identification of *causal relationships* between different factors, relationships which are more problematic to establish using alternative methods.

The control necessary for the exploration of such causal relationships is best established within a laboratory setting, using the individual as the unit of analysis, who is *randomly assigned* to the different treatments under manipulation. **Randomisation** is used to ensure there are no systematic patterns in the allocation of participants to experimental conditions which may account for any differences found between the conditions. The adoption of this method, which essentially follows that of the

natural sciences, is consistent with the accepted wisdom of what science is about. Some, critical of this model of research, suggest that the popularity of the experiment lies in the accessibility it grants to this 'science game' (Pyke and Agnew, 1991). It is the high value afforded to scientifically validated findings which are assumed to generate relevant, practical and useful knowledge, rather than the merits of the method *per se*, which make the experiment such an attractive option. (This debate is explored further in Unit 2 pages 54–61.)

Perhaps the biggest issue calling into question the value of the laboratory-based experiment is that of **ecological validity** – do people behave the same in the laboratory as they do in the real world? The artificiality of the laboratory-based experiment gives rise to a range of problems (such as *demand characteristics* and *experimenter expectancy* effects – see figure 27.1) which ultimately question the outcomes of experimental research as valid representations of real-life behaviour. This is not to say that the laboratory-based experiment is of no value. Laboratories can be disguised to resemble more natural settings, thus increasing the ecological validity without losing control over *extraneous variables* (figure 27.1). Experimenter expectancy effects and demand characteristics can also be reduced by the use of deception, making it more unlikely that participants will guess the true aim of the experiment. The use of deception, however, does give rise to obvious ethical issues concerning the rights of participants (see Unit 3 pages 84–86).

Examples of laboratory-based experiments

Behaviourism provides us with a clear example of early laboratory-based experimental research in psychology. Concerned with the identification of stimulus–response relationships, the laboratory

27.1 Sources of bias in experimental settings

■ **Extraneous variables**

Variables which are not controlled in a study but may still interfere and affect the results. The more naturalistic a study becomes, the higher the potential influence of extraneous variables.

■ **Demand characteristics**

Where the experimental situation biases the participants to behave in certain ways. Cues in the experimental situation may give participants an idea of what the experiment is about, causing them to behave in a particular way.

■ **Experimenter expectancy**

Where the experimenter gives away the aim of the experiment influencing participants to respond in a particular way, usually by doing what they think is 'right'.

---

offered the control needed to isolate different variables and their effect on each other (see Unit 11 for examples of behaviourist research).

Continuing in the experimental tradition is cognitive psychology. Research in the fields of perception, memory and attention are rich with examples of laboratory-based experimental research (see the studies on memory by Ebbinghaus, 1885, Peterson, 1959, Craik and Lockhart, 1972; the studies on attention by Allport *et al.*, 1972, Shaffer, 1975; the studies on visual processing by the Gestalt psychologists, for example Garner and Clement, 1963, Pomerantz, 1981). Using the control afforded by the laboratory setting, much has been learnt about the processes underlying many cognitive functions.

Both behaviourism and cognitive psychology have focused largely upon behaviours which can be broken down into simplified operations with law-like qualities. The outcomes have usually been expressed as rational 'models' indicating the relationships between different factors. Whilst the experiment may be considered the most appropriate method for such research, some question its relevance for the exploration of more complex socially meaningful behaviour.

Field experiments

As an alternative to the laboratory-based experiment, many advocate the use of the **field experiment**. A field experiment is an experiment carried out in the natural setting of those being studied. The experimenter still manipulates the independent variable and participants are randomly assigned to the different experimental groups. This increases the *ecological validity* of the findings, with results generalisable to natural settings similar to those studied in the field experiment. There is also less potential for demand characteristics and experimenter expectancy effects as participants are less aware of their behaviour being measured than when in a laboratory setting. This increased ecological validity, however, is achieved at the expense of control over extraneous variables, which is the main disadvantage of the field experiment. As such, direct causal inferences are more difficult to make. Another possible disadvantage of the field experiment is that it can be more expensive and time consuming than the laboratory-based experiment.

■ **Examples of field experiments**

Good examples are often found in social psychology where the artificiality of a laboratory setting would have an obvious effect. Field experiments into altruism provide us with obvious examples of behaviour which would be very difficult to investigate in formal laboratory settings.

Darley and Batson (1973) investigated the helping behaviour of students subject to varying time constraints. Those with the least time to complete a given task were less likely to help a stranger in need compared to those given more time. This was a field experiment because the experimenters varied the independent variable of time constraints with students randomly allocated to different groups, and it was carried out in the natural setting of the student university campus.

Quasi experimental designs

Often, although an experimental procedure may be desired/followed, it may be impossible to ensure the random allocation of participants to treatment and control groups. The consequence of this is that any differences found may be due to differences between the two groups at the outset rather than the result of any independent variable. This is known as a **quasi experimental design**. An example of quasi experimental design is a study to measure the perceptions of anti-smoking literature by a group of smokers and a group of non-smokers. These groups would be predetermined by whether they smoked or not. Whilst quasi experimentation is often discussed negatively in terms of what is lacking as compared to the *true* experiment, some are keen to emphasise the value of such an approach. Early advocates Campbell and Stanley (1963, cited in Robson, 1993) suggested that flexibility in the design and interpretation of experiments allows for the consideration of the circumstances under which the study took place and how this may have affected the outcomes. Cook and Campbell (1979) warned against assuming the superiority of randomised (i.e. 'true' experimental) designs. They suggested that if a randomised design is going to be used, then it should be planned to be interpreted as a quasi experimental design, just in case something goes wrong with the randomised design, as it may well do in the real world (cited in Robson, 1993).

The natural experiment

In the **natural experiment** the experimental conditions occur naturally and are measured/observed for research purposes. The researcher does not intervene at all. There is no manipulation of the independent variable, with control and experimental groups occurring naturally. Participants are not randomly allocated to the different treatment groups. Ecological validity is enhanced due to the reality of the situation and because participants are less likely to be affected by demand characteristics or experimenter expectancy effects (although this is still a possibility). As with the quasi experimental design, the lack of random allocation to different groups introduces the possibility that any differences found may be attributable to differences between the groups rather than the independent variable.

■ Examples of natural experiments

The natural experiment offers a way of studying issues of social concern which it would be unethical to study using *true* experiments. A good example of such research is that relating to the impact of disasters and the effect of extreme stress and trauma. Robson (1993) cited a few examples:

- Green *et al.* (1990) compared survivors from the Buffalo Creek dam disaster with other non-equivalent groups.
- Verplanken (1989), in a study of attitudes towards nuclear energy, was able to compare views of such groups both before and after the Chernobyl disaster.
- Caetano *et al.* (1983) was able to investigate the effect of the sudden disruption caused to remote Shetland communities by the discovery of oil.

Ethical questions arising from the use of the experiment

A range of experimental procedures utilised in psychology has given rise to much criticism. Examples of dubious practice here include the use of deception. It is largely in response to the practices used in experimental procedures that the BPS ethical guidelines were initially proposed (see page 81). Whilst these principles are an essential guide to good practice in psychological research, they do not offer definitive solutions to all ethical issues associated with the experiment. Two such issues are:

- *Use of placebo/control group.* Experimental designs often depend upon the use of a control group. Where new treatments are being tested, placebos will be given to the control group, i.e. those who do not receive any treatment. Is it right to withhold potentially useful interventions from participants, and on what basis are the experimental and control groups selected?

- *Devalues the person.* A more general ethical criticism is to do with the way the experimental approach defines the individual. It is regarded by some as dehumanising, treating the participants as objects and exploiting the power bias inherent in the experimenter/subject relationship. As such, an alternative approach to the study of people should be adopted, placing more value upon the participants' experience in the research situation.

In deciding upon the most appropriate experimental approach, the advantages and disadvantages of each should be carefully considered. Obviously a lot will depend upon *what* is being studied, which may actually limit the options available if the study is to be ethically viable. Table 27.2 compares the three different types of experiment discussed across a number of dimensions, which may help inform decisions about which strategy to adopt.

Activity 2

State whether the following examples are laboratory, field or natural experiments:

a Researchers go into a school in order to compare the conservation abilities of a group of 5 year olds with a group of 7 year olds.

b In a study to investigate the effect of categorisation on word recall, one group is given a list of words organised into categories to remember, another group is given the same list not organised into categories. The number of words recalled by each group is compared.

c In a study of the effects of gender on giving behaviour, a female and a male homeless person are observed and the number of donations they each elicit is recorded and compared.

d In a study similar to that above, two researchers, one male and one female, pose as homeless people requesting donations.

e A manufacturing company is about to introduce new production equipment into one of its departments. Levels of job satisfaction are measured before and after the introduction of the new equipment to see if it has been affected.

(Suggested answers on page 1015.)

Self-assessment questions

4 What are the characteristics of the laboratory-based experiment which make it a popular choice in psychology?

5 Explain why you might use a field experiment instead of a laboratory-based experiment. Illustrate your answer with an example.

6 a What is a quasi experiment?
  b When are such designs most likely to be used?

(Suggested answers on page 1016.)

Table 27.2

Type of experiment	Control	Ecological validity	Bias (demand characteristics; experimenter expectancy)	Subject availability	Ethics
Laboratory-based	High degree of control. Random allocation possible. Control over extraneous variables enabling identification of cause and effect.	Low ecological validity due to artificiality of setting. Generalisations therefore questionable.	Potential for these effects high due to artificiality of setting. Can be reduced through disguise of setting and use of deception.	Can be difficult to get participants to agree to take part and to turn up. Often based solely on student populations at universities making generalisations questionable.	Use of placebo or control: is it fair to withhold treatment from some and administer it to others? Deception: is it fair to deceive participants as to aims of experiment?
Field	Less control than laboratory-based experiment. Some control assured by random allocation of participants, but extraneous variables may affect results.	Higher ecological validity due to natural setting with results more generalisable to similar settings.	Potential for these effects reduced as participants less likely to be aware that they are being observed.	Sample is more likely to be representative of general population, but it still may be difficult to get people to agree to participate.	Same as above.
Natural	Lack of control over extraneous variables makes cause and effect problematic. Lack of random allocation means any differences could be result of differences in the groups initially.	Ecological validity high due to naturalistic setting, therefore results are more generalisable.	Bias from these effects reduced as experimental conditions would occur naturally, therefore participants less likely to be aware that they are being observed.	Participants usually more readily available and representative of general population.	Ethical obligations blurred: should people be studied without their consent and how can they be debriefed?

Comparison of laboratory-based, field and natural experiments across five factors

Alternatives to the experiment

Correlational studies

One alternative to the experiment is the correlational study. This is where relationships between different factors or variables are measured to see if changes in one variable are related to changes in another variable. If, as one variable changes, then so does another in a consistent manner (i.e. not just a one-off), then the two factors may be co-related. Such studies are useful where direct manipulation of the variables would be undesirable (unethical) or impossible. One obvious example here is the relationship between smoking and cancer. This cannot possibly be examined experimentally by forcing some people to smoke, comparing them with a group prevented from smoking. However, looking at the relationship between smoking and the probability of getting cancer allows us possible insights into this relationship.

The principle disadvantage of the correlation as compared to the experiment is that *correlations do not necessarily mean causality*. Two variables might indeed be co-related – but this does not mean to say that changes in one variable have *caused* the changes in the other. So, there may exist a correlation between layers of clothing worn and number of ice-creams sold. It would be wrong to conclude that wearing fewer clothes causes people to eat more ice-cream. A **third variable explanation** is more likely – being in the sun causes people to wear fewer layers of clothing and to eat more ice-cream. It may also be difficult to ascertain the direction of any causal relationship in correlational studies – which variable is prompting the changes? So, if a relationship is found between the amount of violence watched on TV and levels of aggression, is it that watching the TV violence is more likely to lead to aggressive behaviour, or that people who are more aggressive are more likely to watch violent programmes?

■ Different types of correlation

There are three different types of correlational relationship. These are described below along with a scattergram. Scattergrams (also called scattergraphs) are the usual way of representing a correlation in picture form. The values of one variable are plotted against the values of another along two axes.

1   A **positive correlation** – as one variable *increases*, then the other also *increases*. Example: the more sweets that are eaten the more tooth decay experienced; the less sweets that are eaten, the less amount of tooth decay experienced. So the changes in the two variables are in the *same direction*. Using a scattergram, a positive correlation will look like the example shown in figure 27.3.

2   A **negative correlation** – as one variable *increases*, then the other *decreases*. Example: as visits to the dentist increase, then levels of tooth decay decrease *or* as visits to the dentist decrease, then levels of tooth decay increase. The changes in the two variables go in *opposite directions*. On a scattergram, a negative correlation will look like the example shown in figure 27.4.

3   **No correlation** (or zero correlation) – this is where no correlation exists between two variables. Example: the amount paid for a tube of toothpaste bears no relation to levels of tooth decay. These variables are said to be uncorrelated. On a scattergram, a zero correlation will look like the example shown in figure 27.5.

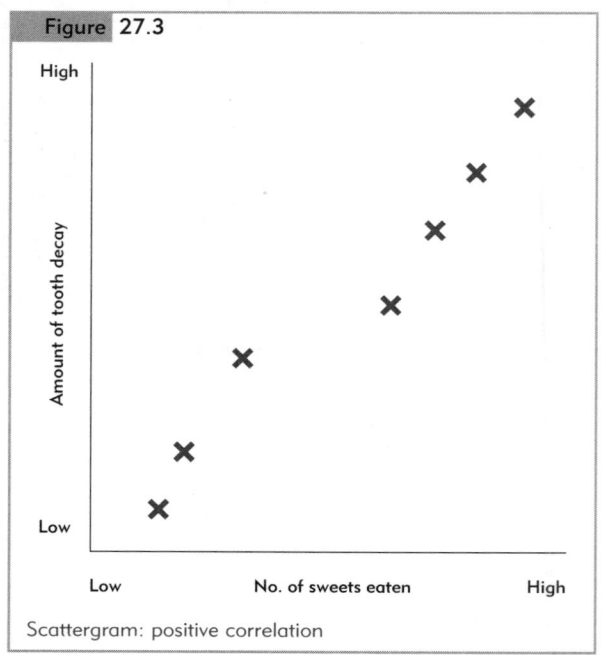

Figure 27.3

Scattergram: positive correlation

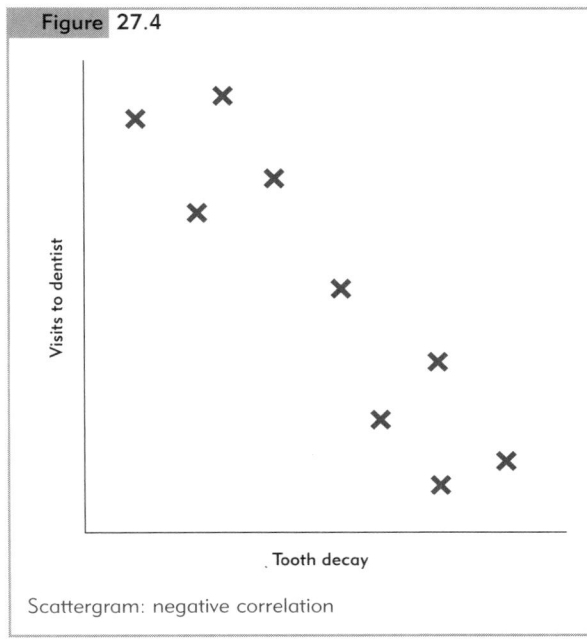

Figure 27.4

Visits to dentist (y-axis)

Tooth decay (x-axis)

Scattergram: negative correlation

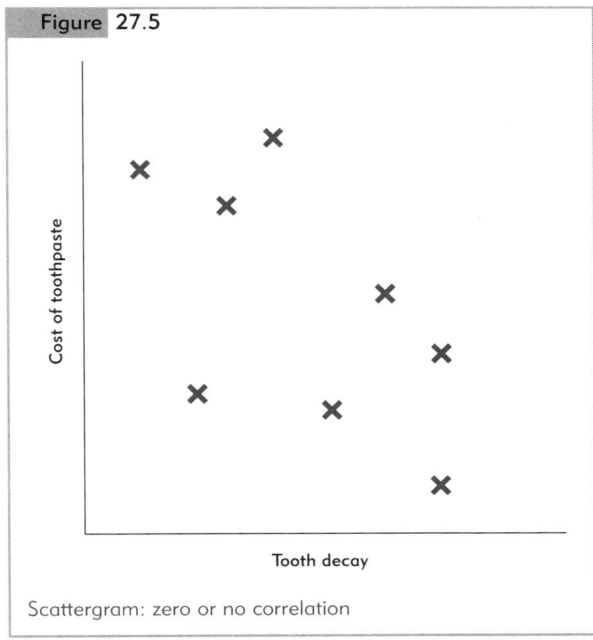

Figure 27.5

Cost of toothpaste (y-axis)

Tooth decay (x-axis)

Scattergram: zero or no correlation

Be careful not to confuse negative correlations with no correlation. With negative correlations there is an association between the different variables, just as in positive correlations – it is just the direction of that relationship which is different. With no correlation, there is no relationship between the different variables.

Activity 3

Collect shoe sizes and heights from ten or more different people. (Try to ensure that the same measurement scales are used so that all the measurements are consistent and do not need converting.) Plot these measurements on a scattergram using one axis for height and the other for shoe size.

Looking at the scattergram, does there appear to be a relationship between these two variables? If so, is the relationship positive or negative?

(Suggested answer on page 1015.)

As well as being represented in the form of a scattergram, correlations are also represented by a **correlation co-efficient**. This is a figure ranging between −1 and +1 which is calculated using an appropriate statistical test. A score of −1 indicates a *perfect negative correlation* – as one variable increases, then the other decreases in exactly the same magnitude. A score of +1 indicates a *perfect positive correlation* – as one variable increases, then so does the other, again in exactly the same proportions. The closer the figure is to either −1 or +1, then the stronger the relationship. This range of scores is indicated on the scale in figure 27.6.

Perfect correlations are extremely rare in psychological research, with reports of correlations which appear too near to perfect often giving rise to suspicion concerning the validity of the data. (One infamous example here is the work of Cyril Burt who reported consistently high correlations in the IQ scores of identical twins. This, and other anomalies in his work, aroused suspicion leading to his work being uncovered as fraudulent (see figure 21.24, Unit 21, page 793).

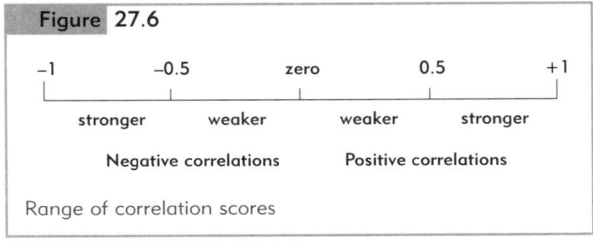

Figure 27.6

−1	−0.5	zero	0.5	+1
stronger	weaker		weaker	stronger
Negative correlations			Positive correlations	

Range of correlation scores

Examples of correlational research in psychology

In twin studies, the psychological attributes of twins are measured and compared to see if the scores are correlated. Often high correlations are taken as an indicator of the genetic determination of the attribute measured. Perhaps the most famous examples of such research are the twin studies on intelligence where identical twins were reported to show higher correlations in IQ (intelligence quotient) scores compared to non-identical twins or siblings (for example Shields, 1962; Juel-Nielsen, 1965). Results from these studies offered the strongest support for the genetic determination of IQ and had a direct impact on social and educational policy. They indicate how correlational data can be misused to great effect to imply causality. Subsequent critiques of this research have outlined numerous flaws in the studies cited, including 'third variable' explanations of the correlations, i.e. the twins were often found to have shared very similar environments which may actually account for the similarities in IQ scores found.

Another well-known example of correlational research is the study on maternal deprivation conducted by Rutter *et al.* (cited in Rutter, 1972). This study explored the possible relationship between separations from the mother in early childhood and anti-social behaviour in adolescent boys. The correlation between these two factors was low, revealing little association between the two. Had the correlation been high, this *might* have been indicative of a relationship, although both factors might have been caused by a third variable, for example family discord resulted both in separations at birth and in later anti-social behaviour.

Advantages and disadvantages of correlational research

Summarised in figure 27.7 are the advantages and disadvantages associated with correlational research.

27.7 Advantages and disadvantages of correlational research

Advantages

1 The technique allows an investigator to identify the direction and strength of relationships between two or more variables. This is done by measuring naturally occurring variables without manipulating or controlling them, giving the added advantage of increased ecological validity as well as enabling the measurement of many variables which cannot be measured experimentally.

2 Zero correlations are very useful for asserting that two things are not related. So, if watching violence on TV has no association with levels of aggression, then we could conclude that watching violence on TV does not appear related to aggressive behaviour. Similarly, it is sometimes important to demonstrate the independence of different measures in psychology in order to prove that they are measuring different things. A good example here is in the design of psychometric tests such as IQ tests. If two items on a questionnaire are very strongly correlated, this may indicate that they are actually measuring the same thing – in which case, why have both items? If two items are unrelated, however, this suggests that they are both measuring different things.

3 Correlation allows prediction: if an association exists between two variables, and we know the strength of that relationship, then this allows us to predict the value of one variable as the other changes. Thus we know the probable magnitude of change in one variable given changes in another related variable.

4 For practical reasons, it is often much easier to collect sufficient correlational data on a number of variables for research purposes (for example, by using a questionnaire on which responses to different scales can be correlated) than when using the experimental method.

Disadvantages

1 Correlations and cause: a correlational relationship is not an indication of cause. Simply because two variables are related to each other does not mean to say one causes the other – changes in both may be caused by a third variable which has not been measured.

2 Potential misuse of correlational research as support for causal explanations: this is quite often done in the media or by politicians where correlations are used to imply/infer cause.

27.7 Advantages and disadvantages of correlational research *cont.*

3   There is a danger in assuming that all correlations are linear. It is therefore important to plot all results on a scattergram as this may reveal relationships not revealed by the calculation of the correlation co-efficient alone. One example here is a **curvi-linear** relationship which when plotted would look like this:

Expressed as a correlation co-efficient, the figure would be close to zero, indicating no relationship.

Examples of such relationships include health and vitamin C intake – no vitamin C may be associated with bad health; a moderate intake may be associated with good health, but health does not go on improving as vitamin C intake goes on increasing. Too much vitamin C will actually result in a reduction in healthiness. A similar relationship may exist between stress and performance. Little or no stress may not be good for performance as there is little incentive or motivation. Moderate levels of stress may increase performance as it may be motivating, whereas too much stress will result in a deterioration of performance. (You may be able to relate to this if you think about how you perform when completing work for deadlines or when preparing for exams!)

▓ Ethical issues associated with correlational research

As with all research strategies, the BPS guidelines for the conduct of research should always be followed when conducting correlational research. Of particular concern when doing correlational research is the way in which research results may be interpreted and used. Correlations will often be used instead of experimental designs in research of a socially sensitive nature, and is thus quite likely to have a direct impact upon people's lives and the way they are treated in society. The existence of relationships between variables may be wrongly used to infer causality providing justification for a range of possible actions. An example here is the early research measuring the correlations between the IQ scores of twins (see page 998).

Activity 4

Is there a relationship between number of hours spent studying and exam scores? The data below show the number of hours 15 students spent studying for an exam and the exam score they obtained.

Student	A	B	C	D	E	F	G	H	I	J	K	L	M	N	P
Hours	14	5	15	15	7	3	6	1	12	4	11	3	0	10	11
Percentage score	73	48	14	71	60	28	58	66	72	41	65	35	12	70	74

a   Plot the data on a scattergram.
b   Is there a relationship between the two variables?
c   If so, in what direction is that relationship?
d   Is the relationship strong or weak? Explain your answer.
e   Is there an optimum number of hours studied? Explain your answer.
f   What possible explanations could there be for the scores of student H and student C?

(Suggested answers on page 1015.)

Self-assessment questions

7   What is the principle disadvantage of the correlational study compared to the experiment?

8   Explain the relationship between variables in:
    a   a positive correlation
    b   a negative correlation.

9   Correlations can be expressed statistically with scores ranging from −1 to +1. Explain what these scores represent.

(Suggested answers on page 1016.)

Observational methods

All psychological research involves some element of observation. Interest in and decisions about what to study and how are usually based upon the initial observation of behaviour or events. Whether conducting a formal experiment or a field study, good observational skills are needed if important factors are not to be missed. Even when the results are expected, researchers should always remain alert to the potentially unexpected, which, as well as providing useful feedback for the present study, would give valuable guidance in the planning of future research.

Observational techniques can be used both in controlled laboratory settings and in the field. Coolican (1994) makes the distinction between observation as a specific technique and observation as an overall research design:

■ *Observation as a technique*: where observation is employed as a specific method or tool to measure a certain aspect of behaviour, often within an overall experimental approach. Within this context, observations are more likely to be laboratory based. Examples here include Milgram's (1974) studies on obedience and Bandura's (1965) studies of aggression.

■ *Observation as an overall research design*: where observation is chosen to contrast it with other designs, such as the experiment, reflecting the decision to observe naturally occurring behaviour and not to intervene directly and manipulate variables. Such designs are likely to be naturalistic observations utilising varying degrees of participation.

A similar distinction is made by Banister *et al.* (1994) who also link the differences to the distinctions made between quantitative and qualitative approaches to research. Experimental observation, which usually involves the manipulation of variables, is set firmly within traditional empirical approaches to psychological research where the emphasis is on quantitative data gathering. Alternatively, observation can be adopted within a qualitative framework where the emphasis is upon naturally occurring behaviour and understanding real people in everyday situations.

Recent trends in psychology have seen a shift to the adoption of observation as on overall research design. This complements the increasing popularity of *new paradigm research* adopting a more holistic approach to research, utilising qualitative techniques.

It would be a mistake to assume the distinctions made above are hard and fast. Some of the techniques of observation discussed below will be ideally suited to both experimental and non-experimental contexts. Even where such techniques generate numerical data, the overarching context may be qualitative.

■ Participation and disclosure

Before choosing the most appropriate observational techniques, decisions must first be made as to:

■ the extent of participation desired, and

■ the degree of disclosure between the observer and those being observed, i.e. how overt the observer's role is.

With non-participant observation, the observer observes from a distance and should exert minimal impact upon the behaviour being observed. With participant observation, the observer becomes involved in the group being observed, although the extent of this involvement can vary. Patton (1980, cited in Coolican, 1994) distinguished four roles an observer may adopt depending upon the desired levels of participation and disclosure (figure 27.8).

▣ Techniques of data collection available to the observer

Most observational studies involve the recording of behaviour in a relatively systematic fashion. The specific techniques adopted, however, can vary enormously. Banister *et al.* (1994) suggested seven dimensions along which observations will usually vary:

1   *Structure of the observation*: this can range from highly structured, detailed observation to very diffuse, unstructured description.
2   *Focus of the observation*: this can range from a very narrow concentration on specific aspects (such as a non-verbal cue) to a broad focus.
3   *Knowledge of those being observed about the process*: this can vary from being known by all (for instance, in the observations of a teacher's classroom techniques) to being known by none (for instance, secretly observing people in a public setting).
4   *Explanations given to those being observed*: these can vary from full explanations to no explana-

tions at all. This may involve giving highly ethically dubious false explanations where participants are told the observer is watching something different from that which is really of interest.
5   *The time scale of what is being observed*: this can vary from one-off observations to extended observations over time.
6   *The methods used*: these can vary from simple note-taking to the use of video/audio equipment, and from checklists to the use of stopwatches.
7   *Feedback given to those observed*: this can range from a full sharing of observations and interpretations to no further contact at all with the participants.

Whilst researchers may wish to devise their own observational strategy when considering the above factors, there is a range of set techniques available, usually resembling a coding or categorisation system. Bales' 'Interaction Process Analysis' (1950) is one example of a well-known coding scheme designed for the observation of small group interactions. Another well-used coding scheme is that designed by Flanders (1970), designed for analysing teacher and pupil behaviour in the classroom (for more detail about this scheme and how to develop your own scheme, see Robson, 1993, pp. 210–13).

The advantage of these techniques and structured observation generally is increased *consistency* and reliability in the observations made. In this way different observers, once trained in the

---

27.8 Different roles an observer may adopt

1   *Full participant*: the observer's true research role is hidden or *undisclosed* and members take the researcher as an authentic member of the group.
2   *Participant as observer*: the participant's observational role is not hidden but kept discreet – *partial disclosure*. It is not seen to be the main reason for the participant's presence, with group members relating to the observer principally through the group's normal range of activities.

3   *Observer as participant*: the participant's role of observer is *disclosed* with this being accepted as the main role of the researcher by the group being studied.
4   *Full observer*: this is the non-participant observer who has no involvement in the group being studied and should have no effect upon the behaviour being observed. This is the role usually adopted in experimental settings. Participants may or may not be aware that they are being observed.

technique to be used, are more likely to produce *standardised accounts* of the behaviour observed. This is known as *inter-rater reliability* and any good coding or categorisation system should result in high levels of inter-rater reliability. If designing your own categorisation system, it is essential first to test it out on a sample of the type of behaviour to be observed. Known as a **pilot test**, this will provide essential feedback as to how well the coding system works and what modifications are needed.

The actual recording of observations may be done with a camcorder, a stills camera, a tape recorder or through handwritten notes taken on the spot. These may be positioned discretely, or one-way mirrors can be used in order to prevent awareness of the observer's presence.

Activity 5

Working in small groups, devise a categorisation system for the coding of aggressive acts. Apply this to a short piece of video-taped material – a children's cartoon would be ideal. Discuss the following:
- How well did it work?
- Was inter-rater reliability high?
- What problems did you encounter?

(Suggested answer on page 1015.)

■ Sampling of behaviour to be observed

As it is often impossible to observe and record all behaviour in the research situation, a sample of behaviour is usually selected. Again this selection should be systematic in order to ensure it is representative of the range of behaviours under study. Various different sampling techniques exist to ensure this representativeness:

- *Time interval sampling*: behaviour is observed across a series of short intervals within a given period, for example in a two-hour session six consecutive periods each of 20 seconds may be recorded and will constitute the data.
- *Time-point sampling*: this is where the sample of behaviour is taken at a predetermined point in time, say every fifth minute, a 30-second period of behaviour is recorded.

- *Event sampling*: this is where only behaviour meeting a pre-specified definition is recorded. This is often useful for behaviour which is infrequent.
- *Situation sampling*: when behaviour is observed in a number of different situations.

The aim of these sampling techniques is to increase the representativeness of the findings and to help ensure that observations are not simply restricted to very specific times and specific situations.

For those more concerned with a qualitative approach to observational research, high levels of structure are to be avoided. Categorisation and coding schemes break down behaviour into its simplest components. This fails to acknowledge the social meaning of behaviour which is essential if the interpretation is to be of any value.

Whilst the qualitative researcher may use the same tools to gather the observational data (for example camcorder, tape recorder, field notes), their approach to the extent of information gathered and to the interpretation/analysis of this information may depart radically from the structured sampling and categorisation techniques referred to above. The focus is on a more *holistic* analysis where whole patterns of behaviour are recorded in detail and interpreted against a given context, instead of breaking down behaviour into discrete components and 'pigeon holing' it into an externally imposed categorisation system.

■ Examples of observational studies in psychology

As mentioned earlier, the classic studies on obedience and aggression by Milgram and Bandura are good examples of laboratory-based observational studies. The field of child development is rich with examples, as often observation is the only technique suitable for the study of young children (it would be difficult to give a child a questionnaire or a set of instructions). These are often conducted in naturalistic settings (or in laboratories disguised to look natural) so as to minimise the effect of the research situation on the child's behaviour. Examples here include the study of play where we have Piaget's (1951) detailed observations of his own children. Sylva *et al.* (1980) also conducted detailed observational studies of children at play which emphasised the value of structured play as an aid to childhood development.

Social psychology is rich with examples of observational studies conducted in the field. The subject of 'personal space' is an area in which observational studies dominate (for example Felipe and Sommer, 1966; Watson and Graves 1966; Sommer, 1969). Argyle (for example, 1988) has published a range of studies on non-verbal behaviour revealing important insights about the nature of non-verbal communication.

Another area of psychology making extensive use of observational techniques is ethology, where the emphasis is on the study of animals in their natural environments. The early studies of Lorenz (1935) and Tinbergen (1951) are examples here, as are the observations of chimps made by Goodall (1978).

◼ Advantages and disadvantages of observational studies

On the whole, observational studies are less intrusive and less likely to create artificial behaviour, especially where people do not know they, or an aspect of their behaviour, is being observed. Whilst this may be more difficult to achieve in *laboratory observations* as compared to naturalistic observations, questioning the ecological validity of such studies, the laboratory does give greater control over extraneous variables, as well as reducing observer variation and bias.

Naturalistic observations enable the study of behaviours and participants which could not be done experimentally. Thus, social situations can be studied which would be impossible to replicate in the laboratory (such as football crowd behaviour). This enables the context to be taken into consideration, arguably generating more socially meaningful explanations of behaviour. Naturalistic observations are also ideal for the study of children and animals where other techniques simply would not work (for example techniques dependent upon language comprehension such as questionnaires, or the understanding of instructions as in many experimental procedures).

The cost of greater ecological validity is lack of control over extraneous variables. *Observer bias* is also more easily introduced with such studies harder to replicate. It may also be difficult to remain discrete, especially if camcorders are being used. The use of such equipment, however, does enable the accurate recording of behaviours and situations which can later be analysed independently, providing some reliability in interpretation. The strengths of *participant observation* lie in the richness of the 'data' generated and the increased ecological validity, focusing upon the wider social context in the production of meaningful accounts of behaviour. If observers are accepted and are able to gain the trust of those being observed, they are likely to gain access to information which they would otherwise be denied.

As with naturalistic observations, with participant observation there may be difficulties in replicating and verifying the accounts produced by the observer. Without the ability to independently check the interpretations generated, there is greater potential for observer bias to be introduced and a distorted picture generated. There is also the danger of researchers becoming too emotionally involved with those they are observing which may also cloud their objectivity. Where observers disclose their role, then the behaviour of those being observed will inevitably be affected in some way. The greater the level of involvement, then the greater this affect will be.

Observational studies can be very time consuming and labour intensive. There is a danger of amassing great quantities of data, especially with less structured observations, which then takes a great deal of time and effort to interpret. Compounding this, particularly in naturalistic observations, is the lack of control such that the researcher cannot tell or predict when an 'event' will occur. This may be especially problematic where event sampling is used.

◼ Ethical issues associated with observational techniques

A number of ethical concerns are raised by the adoption of covert roles in observational studies and in relation to interpretations of the behaviour observed. Is it right to observe and record the behaviour of others without their knowledge? What about the principle of obtaining informed consent and the right to withdraw from a study? Often covert roles may be adopted in order to study behaviour of a socially sensitive nature. This raises questions about the protection of those being observed – can anonymity be guaranteed, especially where a very specific subsection of the population is being studied? Where socially undesirable behaviour is studied by a single observer in a covert role, how can we be sure that the observations recorded are representative and unbiased? If people do not know they are being studied, it denies them the right to question any assumptions made.

Figure 27.9 summarises the key terms used in observational research.

Activity 6

Draw a table summarising the advantages and disadvantages associated with the different types of observational studies.

(Suggested answer on page 1015.)

■ Content analysis: an alternative observational technique

Content analysis is an indirect observational technique used to analyse the content of 'documents'. It is known as *indirect* observation because it does not involve the direct observation of people, but of the communications that they produce (Coolican, 1994). It is thus based upon the analysis of documentary representations of a particular behaviour, event or issue, representations which have been produced for another purpose. Common examples of such documents include newspapers, magazines, books and archival records. It also includes non-written documents such as films, television programmes and adverts. The fact that the documents have been produced for another purpose is important. Understanding the motives of why a document was produced and the target audience is essential in generating a full and accurate interpretation of the content of that message.

First used at the beginning of the 20th century in the analysis of the US press, content analysis became a popular tool of social psychologists. Used in the analysis of pre- and post-war propaganda, it has since become a popular technique for the analysis of all mass communications, from advertising to political speeches.

Robson (1993) suggested content analysis is akin to structured observations. The actual analysis involves the systematic categorisation and coding of the chosen communication, resulting ultimately in a quantifiable description of it. Whilst commonly used with existing documents, content analysis can also be applied to qualitative interview and questionnaire data. (More detail on how to carry out a content analysis is given on page 1054.)

27.9 Summary of key terms associated with observations

Participation: the extent to which observers become involved or remain apart from the activities of those being observed.

Disclosure: the extent to which observers reveal their true role to those being observed.

Structure: the degree of formality or tightness of the procedure followed in the observation process or the extent (specificness) to which the observational procedure is defined.

Inter-rater reliability: the extent to which different observers will produce similar accounts of those observed.

Observer bias: where the values/beliefs of observers or their relationship with those being observed influences the observations made. This is more likely when there is only one observer who becomes closely involved with those being observed.

Self-assessment questions

10 Explain the variations in disclosure and participation open to the observer to adopt.

11 What is 'inter-rater reliability'?

12 What sampling techniques are available and why might they be used?

13 Why is content analysis called an indirect observational technique?

(Suggested answers on pages 1016–7.)

The case study approach

An alternative research strategy is that of the *case study*. This is where an individual or small group of people such as a family are taken as the unit of analysis. The case study has been used in a range of disciplines, from industrial relations and management to clinical medicine and criminology.

Robson (1993) suggested that the case study represents a *research strategy* rather than a specific method. The focus is upon the *individual case* recognising the need to understand the *context* of the phenomenon under study. This is done using a range of specific methods such as interviews, observations and survey techniques. The case study is thus an example of a *multi-method* approach to psychological research. This allows the consideration of a range of perspectives, something which Robson (1993) suggested other approaches may benefit from.

As when these specific techniques are used individually, within the context of the case study the emphasis upon *rigour* and the importance of gathering *empirical data* remains.

It is often assumed that the case study utilises qualitative methods and itself represents a 'softer' approach. Whilst it may be useful as an exploratory precursor to the more rigorous approach of the experiment, it is seen by some to have little value as a method in its own right. Others argue that the case study is not a flawed experimental design, or a poor second choice. It represents a valuable research strategy in its own right. Whilst the rigours

of the experimental method may be more widely established, attention needs to focus upon establishing similar qualities, for example relating to reliability and validity, within the context of the case study. Neither does the use of the case study rule out quantitative techniques, but again these need further development – quantitative techniques used in the experiment will not be automatically appropriate to the case study setting.

Typically, case studies may focus upon the impact of a particular intervention introduced. In contrast to the experiment, though, this is usually as part of the 'real life' of those being studied, and not set up as part of an artificial experimental procedure. Usually, little control is exerted over exposure to the intervention. For some this questions the representativeness of any findings and the validity of conclusions reached, given the potential for extraneous variables to influence the outcomes. For others, it is precisely this 'reality factor' which gives the case study its strength and relevance.

■ Examples of case study research in psychology

Case studies have informed theory and practice in many areas of psychology. Below are some examples from different areas.

Cognitive psychology. Gregory and Wallace (1963) reported the famous case of SB, who, blind from birth, had his sight restored at the age of 52. Using a variety of techniques to assess the physiological and the psychological impact of regaining his sight, the research provided extremely valuable insights into issues such as the role of learning in visual perception. The research also questioned the assumption that in regaining his sight, SB's life would necessarily be enhanced. (See Roth (1990), for more details of this case study.) Other case studies in cognitive psychology can be found in the study of exceptional memory abilities. Luria (1968) reported the case of S, a mnemonist with exceptional memory abilities. Similarly, Hunt and Love (1972) reported the case of VP, whose performance on commonly used memory tests was far superior to that of the average person. Whilst some may argue that such research is not that relevant because it only applies to very few exceptional individuals, Cohen (1990) argued that such cases show what the human memory *can* do, questioning the limits and constraints upon memory suggested by current models. The implication for memory training is that we all have the ability to use our memory more effectively.

Child development. Research into the effects of extreme privation are largely based upon case studies. For obvious ethical reasons, adopting an experimental approach to study privation effects would be impossible. Freud and Dann (1951) reported the case of six orphans rescued from a concentration camp at the end of the Second World War and brought to Britain. By assessing the children and reporting upon their developmental progress, much was learned about attachment processes and the potential for long-term adjustment. Koluchova (1972, 1976) reported the case study of the Czech twins who were subjected to extreme physical and psychological cruelty until found at the age of seven. Again, by assessing the children and following their intellectual and social progress into adulthood, important knowledge was gained about the effects of such treatment and how best to counter its effects.

Clinical psychology. Probably the most obvious example of case study research in this area is Freud's work. Much of Freud's theory is based upon his analysis of his patients in which he identified common patterns of meaning in the hysterical symptoms they each exhibited. One famous case study is that of Anna O who displayed a range of physical symptoms for which there was no apparent physical cause. By tracing back the case history of Anna, Freud was able to link the physical symptoms to psychologically traumatic experiences she had had earlier on in life. Therapy then focused upon working through the repressed emotions associated with these earlier events (see pages 896 and 958 for more details about Anna O).

Freud's use of the case study approach shows how general theory can be generated from the study of the specific case. The logic Freud adopted was that followed in the medical sciences – to trace the course of 'normal' functioning by the examination of abnormal cases. The mental anomalies Freud observed in his own patients were merely exaggerations or distortions of normal mental functioning. Contemporary clinical settings provide a clear example of the case study approach in practice. Clients must be assessed individually utilising techniques appropriate to them, drawing upon information from a variety of sources.

■ Advantages and disadvantages of the case study

Summarised below are a range of strengths and weaknesses associated with the case study approach. These are adapted from Coolican (1994).

Strengths include the following:

- *Outstanding cases*: dramatic occurrences may happen which could not be studied in any other way. This is true of the examples of case studies from cognitive psychology and child development outlined above. Such cases, in dealing with the extremes of the human condition, serve to highlight potentials which may have previously been regarded as unrealistic.

- *Contradicting a theory*: one contrary case is enough to challenge seriously an assumed trend or theory or cause–effect relationship. Again, the cases outlined above relating to the effects of childhood privation questioned the widely held wisdom concerning the permanence of such effects, leading to new directions in theory and research.

- *Data pool*: the results of a number of case studies into the same topic area can be pooled, sorted and analysed, and any common threads identified. This may then form the basis of further quantitative research which may explore further the common links.

■ *Insight*: the unique richness of the case study is a great strength providing insights which would not be realised by any other approach. This is particularly valuable when attempting to understand issues of a socially sensitive nature. A case study enables questions to be generated as the research progresses and for the relevant information to be gathered in an appropriate manner. This is not possible with other more structured approaches.

■ *Reality with rigour*: as a method which acknowledges the importance of the context, the ecological validity of the case study is high, assuming a high degree of rigour is maintained in the specific research tactics/methods adopted. One way of introducing more rigour is to cross-check accounts produced in the case study with other sources of information such as diaries, accounts of close relatives and any other independent sources of information.

Weaknesses include the following:

■ *Lack of generalisability*: each case is unique, and checking the reliability and validity of the data is problematic. Whilst a very rich picture of a particular case may be generated, these findings are specific to that case and cannot be assumed to be representative of any general patterns.

■ *Interviewer–interviewee interaction*: some have questioned the ability of the researcher to obtain objective data when conducting case study research because of the often close relationship which evolves between the researcher and the subject(s). Again, it is difficult to cross-check the objectivity of data obtained, although as suggested above, it may be possible to cross-reference the data with other information from other sources.

■ *Subjective selection*: the researcher also introduces other aspects of subjectivity in deciding what to select to tell the case study story. It is the limited opportunity to check such interpretations which makes this problematic, again emphasising the need for methodological rigour in case study research.

■ Ethical issues associated with case study research

Obviously, whatever research tactics are adopted within the context of a case study, the ethical guidelines for their use must always be observed. There is also an extra responsibility to protect case study participants. Researchers will be party to detailed personal information from a variety of sources about specific individuals or groups. Thus, protecting the identity of those participating is of paramount importance. Researchers should also prepare themselves for the possible disclosure of personal difficulties or problems. It is important in such situations for researchers to recognise when they are not qualified to deal with such problems, but instead to provide the participant with a possible source of support should he or she so desire it.

Activity 7

It is your job to follow the progress of a pupil who has just started at the school where you work. Not knowing much about the pupil you decide to build up a case history of her. What methods would you use to get your information and how would you assess her progress? What problems might you encounter?

(Suggested answer on page 1015.)

Self-assessment questions

14 'The case study should be regarded as a research strategy rather than a specific method.' Explain why.

15 What are the advantages and disadvantages of adopting a case study approach?

16 Find an example of case study research (try to choose one not given in this chapter). Assess the contribution that the chosen case study has made to relevant psychological theory.

(Suggested answers on pages 1017–8.)

Self-report techniques

Whereas the experiment and the observation are dependent upon what people do, another important source of data is what people say about themselves. Interviews and questionnaires are common **self-report techniques** used in psychology in which people are asked a range of questions and their responses are recorded.

The interview or questionnaire can be used as a stand-alone technique, for example to conduct a survey. Alternatively, it can be used in combination with other techniques as part of a **multi-method approach**. (For example, interview data may be used to complement observational data within the overall research framework of a case study.) With interviews the questions are asked by an interviewer who also records the interviewees' responses. Questionnaires, on the other hand, are usually given to respondents to complete themselves. Consequently, questionnaires tend to be based on very structured questions presented in a particular order. By contrast, interviews offer much more scope for varying the degree of structure contained within them. Other self-report techniques include rating scales, psychometric tests and diary techniques.

■ Varying degrees of structure in interviews and questionnaires

A highly structured questionnaire or interview schedule will contain predetermined questions in a predetermined order, often offering a choice of responses for the respondent to select. These are known as **closed questions**. Often, where such questions are used there is no need for the researcher to be present and the questionnaires can be administered by post.

Alternatively, at the other end of the scale is the *open-ended interview* which has very little structure and is flexible so can be adapted according to the context of the interview, with the content very much under the control of the respondent. Often a common mid-ground is used, i.e. the semi-structured interview, where the interviewer has clearly defined purposes but is flexible in terms of wording and order of presentation of the questions. Coolican (1994) distinguished between five degrees of structure characterising different types of interview (figure 27.10).

27.10 Variations in structure characterising different types of interview

1 *Non-directive*: interviewee talks about anything he or she likes and the psychologist gives no directing influence to the topics but helps and guides the discussion. Would be useful in the early exploratory stages of a case study where the area of interest still remains undefined. This technique of interviewing is often used by counsellors or psychotherapists and not always within a research context.

2 *Informal interviews*: the aim is to gather data, but in a non-structured way. The interview content is determined by the interviewee. There are no pre-set questions which he or she has to answer or fixed responses which the interviewee has to select from.

3 *Informal but guided*: here the informality is retained but the interviewee is provided with a guide which is an outline of the topics to be covered and the questions to be asked. The interviewer is still free to vary the order of topics and the wording of questions as he or she sees appropriate in each interview situation.

4 *Structured but open-ended*: here a standardised procedure is followed where each interviewer asks a set of predetermined questions in a predetermined order, ensuring greater consistency in the data gathered. Respondents are still free to answer as they choose.

5 *Fully structured*: as with the last, questions are predetermined in a pre-set order and respondents have to select a predetermined response. This may be administered as a questionnaire with no actual interviewing involved.

The more structure in an interview schedule, then the more the series of questions resembles a questionnaire, and hence the quality of the data generated is more heavily dependent upon the design of the questionnaire. Where there is less structure, the skills of the interviewer and the dynamics of the interview situation will play a much greater role in determining the quality of the data generated.

Figure 27.11 summarises the advantages and disadvantages associated with varying degrees of structure.

Practical advice on carrying out interviews and questionnaire design

Robson (1993) suggested a few practical hints worth considering when conducting interviews and designing questionnaires.

When interviewing:

- avoid talking too much – let the respondent do the talking
- ensure that questions are not too long or too complicated and are worded simply – avoid jargon

- put questions in a clear and non-threatening way
- eliminate cues which lead interviewees to respond in a particular way – avoid leading questions and present questions neutrally
- enjoy it – don't give the message that you are bored or scared. The dynamics of the situation will affect the quality of the data gathered.

When designing self-completed questionnaires:

- make questions specific rather than general – general questions are open to wider interpretations
- use closed rather than open questions – closed questions are less open to varied interpretations and the data generated is easier to code and analyse
- offer a 'no opinion' option rather than assuming/imposing a level of agreement or disagreement upon respondents
- avoid agree/disagree responses – respondents have a tendency to agree irrespective of the item content
- avoid leading questions which imply which response is wanted
- do not use jargon and keep the response system simple.

27.11 Advantages and disadvantages of more/less structure

Advantages of more structure
- Responses can be more easily compared and are more easily analysed.
- Ensures all predetermined topics are covered.
- Can be used by several interviewers.
- More easily replicable and less prone to bias from interpersonal variables.

Disadvantages of more structure
- Information gained is narrow – important issues not thought of may be missed by constraining the respondent.
- The ability to respond flexibly to the individual and the context is lost, reducing the richness of the picture generated.
- Wording of questions may introduce bias or may be too complex/inappropriate for some respondents.

Advantages of less structure
- Interview can be moulded to the individual, situation and context.
- A fuller, richer picture is generated in the interviewee's own terms.
- This technique is more likely to leave interviewee at ease.

Disadvantages of less structure
- Because it is unique, different interviewers would generate different information. It is thus relatively unreliable and of limited representativeness.
- The information gathered is more difficult to analyse.
- The whole interaction is strongly influenced by interpersonal variables.

Activity 8

You want to assess attitudes towards the use of animals in experiments.

a   Design a short questionnaire (with five to ten questions) for this purpose. Try out the questionnaire on a colleague.

b   Now design an interview schedule for the same purpose (again include five to ten questions). Conduct the interview with another colleague.

Remember to use the guidelines above. (It may help to look at Unit 3 page 89 if you need help with your questions.)

Now consider the following:

i   How well did each work? What problems did you encounter?

ii   How does the type of information generated differ?

iii   How could you use the 'data' to best effect?

It would be useful to get feedback from the person who did the questionnaire and the interview when considering the above questions.

(Suggested answer on page 1015.)

Whether using an interview or a questionnaire, it is advisable first to do a **pilot test** or **study**, i.e. to test it out on a small set of your sample population. This will be the best feedback you can get on the quality of the questions you have designed, allowing you to make appropriate modifications. It also allows a realistic assessment of how long the interview/questionnaire is going to take – an important practical consideration which often gets overlooked. If major modifications are needed, then a second piloting stage is advisable.

■ Advantages and disadvantages of interviews and questionnaires

Robson (1993) outlined the advantages and disadvantages common to both interviews and questionnaires as well as those specific to each method. These are outlined in figure 27.12.

■ Ethical issues associated with interview and questionnaire techniques

Honest and open responses in interview and questionnaire situations are often dependent upon a guarantee of complete confidentiality. Researchers should thus be aware of potentially awkward situations where such guarantees could be compromised. One example here is workplace surveys, the use of which is on the increase. Those who have commissioned the survey may feel they have a right to know exactly who has said what. Therefore it is important that the issue of confidentiality is discussed and agreed upon before the survey commences. Researchers also need to be careful to protect the identity of participants in any feedback process. So, for example, if there is only one employee in a particular department, feedback on a departmental basis should be avoided. Similarly, any quotes extracted from interview transcripts should be general enough to protect the respondent's identity.

■ Examples of studies using interview and questionnaire methods

We have probably, at some point in our lives, all either taken part or been asked to take part in a survey of some sort. Market research surveys are the obvious examples where we may be approached on the street, or contacted through the post or by telephone and requested to answer a few questions.

It is not difficult to find examples of psychological research utilising interview and questionnaire techniques. Wober *et al.* (1987) conducted a large-scale British survey into the relationship between TV viewing and sex-role stereotyping. This was based on a cross-section of 344 children aged between 5 and 12. The study illustrated the strength of the survey method in providing large amounts of data.

The influential work of Adorno *et al.* (1950) which resulted in the theory of 'The Authoritarian Personality' (see pages 130–132 for details of this theory) utilised both interview and questionnaire techniques (as well as using thematic apperception tests – see Unit 15 pages 522–3). A total of 2099

27.12 Advantages and disadvantages of interviews and questionnaires, common to both and specific to each method

■ Disadvantages

Common to both:

1 Data are affected by the characteristics of the respondents (for example their memory, knowledge, experience, motivation and personality).
2 Respondents will not necessarily report their beliefs accurately – there is likely to be a *social desirability* bias where people respond in a way that reflects them in a good light.
3 Response set: a tendency among respondents to agree with items/questions rather than disagree. Questions should therefore be mixed, prompting both agreement and disagreement, hopefully ensuring some validity in the responses generated.

Specific to interviews:

3 Data may be affected by the characteristics of the interviewers (for example their motivation, personality, skills and experience).
4 Data may be affected by the *interaction* of interviewer/respondent characteristics (for example, whether they are of the same or different class or ethnic background).
5 Respondents may feel their answers are not anonymous and be less forthcoming or open.

Specific to questionnaires:

6 Typically have a low response rate. Those who do respond constitute a self-selected sample which as a group may share certain characteristics making generalisations problematic.

7 Ambiguities in, and misunderstandings of, the survey questions may not be detected.
8 Respondents may not treat the exercise seriously which may not be detected.

■ Advantages

Common to both:

1 They provide a relatively simple and straightforward approach to the study of attitudes, beliefs and motives.
2 They may be adapted to collect representative information from almost any human population enabling generalisations to be made.
3 Highly structured interviews and questionnaires have high amounts of data standardisation.

Specific to interviews:

4 The interviewer can clarify the questions.
5 The presence of the interviewer encourages participation and involvement and the interviewer can judge the extent to which the exercise is taken seriously.

Specific to questionnaires:

6 Often this is the only way of retrieving information about the history of a large set of people.
7 They can be extremely efficient at providing large amounts of data, at a relatively low cost, in a short period of time.
8 They allow anonymity, which can encourage frankness when sensitive areas are involved.

Source: adapted from Robson (1993) pp. 128–9.

people completed questionnaires. The questions were of three types: those requesting factual information; opinion-attitude scales; and open-ended projective questions. On the basis of responses to these questions, a subsample was then selected – the highest and lowest 25 per cent scorers on the opinion-attitude questions. These were then interviewed in a semi-structured manner exploring the themes of religion, politics and minority groups.

Herzberg *et al.*'s study into work motivation (1959) was based upon the use of structured interviews with a sample of 203 participants. A set of 14 questions was introduced using a standardised paragraph requesting participants to think of a time when they felt extremely good or extremely bad about their job. The research made a significant contribution to theories of work motivation and concepts of job satisfaction.

Self-assessment questions

17 Describe how interviews and questionnaires may vary in terms of structure.

18 What are the advantages and disadvantages associated with varying degrees of structure?

19 What is a pilot study and why is it advisable to do one when using questionnaires or interviews?

20 From any area of psychology, give details of one piece of research based upon interview techniques and one based upon questionnaire methods.

(Suggested answers on page 1018.)

Conclusions

At this stage you will have gained an appreciation of the wide variety of methods available to psychologists. As has been illustrated, there are advantages and disadvantages associated with every approach. It is up to the researcher to decide which method or methods to select, a decision which will be affected by a number of factors including: what is being studied; the ethical viability of different methods; the preferences of the researcher; and the availability of resources such as time, money and participants. Before deciding upon a research strategy, it is useful to be reminded of Foster and Parker (1995): 'You should try to be open to the promise and limitations of all the alternatives.'

Unit summary

- A range of methods is available to the psychologist for the conduct of research. *Ethical considerations* must be central when considering the most appropriate research methods.

- Traditionally, *quantitative* methods have dominated psychology, borrowing the experimental technique as modelled in the natural sciences. More recent developments have challenged the central role of the experiment, with *new paradigm research* advocating a more realistic, qualitative approach to the study of human behaviour and processes.

- Ideally, the method(s) selected should be that which is most appropriate for the topic under study.

- The *experiment* is valued for the control and rigour it affords as well as the status of being labelled scientific. There are different types of experiment: laboratory-based, field experiments and naturalistic experiments.

- Critics point to the limitations of the experimental situation which is unrealistic and serves only to break down behaviour into its simplest components. The experiment is a popular choice among behaviourists and cognitive psychologists.

- *Correlational* techniques assess the strength of a relationship between two or more variables. Useful where direct manipulation of variables is not possible (for example the study of childhood privation), but causality cannot be inferred. Correlations can be either *positive* or *negative* (expressed as a correlation co-efficient between -1 and $+1$), although other more complex relations may exist, for example bimodal. The main danger of correlations is when they are used to imply causality providing justification for actions which may have a direct impact upon society.

Summary cont.

■ Good *observation* is the cornerstone to all research. Specific observational techniques or tools can be used within an overall experimental approach or they can be adopted as a research strategy in their own right with the emphasis upon naturalistic, qualitative observation.

■ The observer's role can vary in terms of degree of disclosure and extent of participation. Observational studies vary along a range of dimensions including structure. There is a range of structured coding systems readily available. High degrees of structure are associated with increased levels of *inter-rater reliability*.

■ Observational techniques are commonly used to study children and social behaviour which could not be studied experimentally. They are also used extensively by ethologists for studying animals in their natural environments.

■ As observational techniques often grant access to information of a highly sensitive nature, there are special ethical responsibilities upon the researcher to protect the confidentiality of those observed. This is particularly apparent when adopting a covert role and when using participant observation (whether overt or covert).

■ *Content analysis* is an indirect observational technique. Rather than observing people directly, it is the communications they produce, for example newspapers, speeches, TV adverts, which are analysed. It is important to understand the context surrounding the production of the documents analysed.

■ The *case study* represents a research strategy in which other techniques are used to study the individual case. This can be as rigorous as the experiment whilst dealing with reality, but has been criticised for being unrepresentative. Strengths include high ecological validity and the richness of the data generated due to the multi-method approach. It is used in many areas including cognitive, child development and clinical psychology.

■ *Self-report techniques* (questionnaires and interviews) can be used as stand-alone techniques or as part of wider research strategy with other methods. Interviews vary in amount of structure – the more structured they are, the more they resemble a questionnaire.

■ Highly structured interviews/questionnaires are easier to administer and are useful for generating large amounts of standardised data quickly (for example by post). Less structured approaches can provide a richer, more realistic picture. They are commonly used within many areas of psychology, for example attitude measurement and clinical interviews.

Terms to define

closed questions
content analysis
correlation co-efficient
correlations (positive, negative, curvi-linear)
ecological validity
field experiment
multi-method approach
natural experiment
new paradigm research

old paradigm research
pilot test/study
positivist tradition
quasi experimental design
randomisation
relativist
self-report techniques
third variable explanation

Further reading

Coolican, H (1994) *Research Methods and Statistics in Psychology*, 2nd edn, Hodder & Stoughton, London.

A comprehensive and readable account of different research methods from both quantitative and qualitative traditions. Contains useful learning exercises and summaries of information.

Robson, C (1993) *Real World Research: A Resource for Social Scientists and Practitioner-Researchers*, Blackwell, Oxford.

An excellent guide to different methods available and what to consider before selecting a method. The emphasis is upon the practical realities of conducting research, highlighting issues and pitfalls which often go unacknowledged in many methodology texts which seek only to describe the different methods.

Answers

■ **Suggested answers to activities**

1

	Old paradigm	New paradigm
Characteristics	Traditional positivist approach – the development of objective knowledge using empirical observation and the experiment; enables concepts to be observed, manipulated and tested; favours quantitative data; labelled 'hard' research	Emerged in response to criticisms of old paradigm; influenced by sociology and anthropology; emphasis is on importance of contextual factor; favours non-numerical, or qualitative data; labelled 'soft' research
Strengths	High degree of rigour; enables identification of cause and effect relationships; use of 'hard' data results in hard knowledge which is not open to interpretation	Enables multiple interpretations to be considered; does not treat participants as objects and does not impose definitions of what is worth studying; the methods can be as rigorous as the experiment; attempts to present realistic, rather than artificial, representations
Weaknesses	Dehumanising – treats subjects as objects; reduction to quantifiable data gives limited picture – takes no account of contextual factors; limited as to what can be studied and the level of understanding generated; exploits the power bias inherent in the researcher/participant relationship	It is relativist – which means 'anything goes'; methods used are not rigorous
Solution	The two approaches should coexist allowing the strengths of each to be realised	

2

a field;　b laboratory;　c natural;　d field;　e natural.

3

Should produce a scattergram which is likely to indicate a positive correlation, i.e. as shoe size increases then so does height.

4

a Scattergram: axes should be drawn to a similar scale; ensure each axis is labelled; it should be large enough to be read clearly.

b Yes.

c The direction is positive – exam scores increase as the number of hours spent studying increases.

d Appears to be fairly strong – the more the data points fall in a straight line, then generally speaking, the stronger the relationship. The more scattered the data points are, then the weaker the relationship.

e Yes – about 11. Few extra marks are gained by studying for longer than 11 hours.

f Student C: studied for so long, he fell asleep in the exam. Student H: one of those few lucky students who can do very well with very little effort (either that, or the student cheated!)

5

Whilst each coding system will vary, consideration of the following points may help:

■ What counts as an aggressive act, for example a kick, punch, throwing something?

■ Does verbal aggression, such as shouting, count?

■ Does there have to be a victim?

■ Is it important to differentiate between characters?

■ Is it necessary to record the time and sequence of the aggressive acts?

This may result in a coding chart similar to the one below:

	Kick	Punch	Shout	Victim	Time
Character A					
Character B					
Character C					

6

The table should include the following points:

Observations generally:

■ Advantages: observations are less intrusive than experimental situations and are therefore less likely to affect behaviour.

■ Disadvantages: can be time consuming and labour intensive; danger of amassing a lot of data which is then difficult to analyse (especially in less structured observations).

Laboratory-based observations:

■ Advantages: give greater control over extraneous variables; standardised procedures adopted reduce variations between observers and the potential for observer bias.

■ Disadvantages: difficult to achieve ecological validity.

Naturalistic observations:

■ Advantages: can study situations which cannot be studied experimentally. Many situations cannot be replicated in the laboratory with much behaviour dependent upon the social context. Ideal for studying animals and children in their natural environments. Result in higher ecological validity.

■ Disadvantages: studying in the field gives less control over extraneous variables; observer bias is more likely to be introduced; it may be difficult to remain discrete if wanting to observe unobtrusively.

Participant observations:

■ Advantages: produces a rich picture which takes account of the social context when generating meaningful accounts of behaviour – therefore more ecologically valid. The close relationship between the observer and those observed may give access to information which may not be obtained otherwise.

■ Disadvantages: observer bias more likely with accounts more difficult to replicate or verify. Observers may become too involved which may cloud their objectivity. Special ethical responsibility to protect participants if given access to sensitive information, especially where a covert role has been adopted.

7

■ *Possible sources of information:* previous school records; interviews with parents; interview with the new pupil; assess her abilities on arrival using ability tests.

■ *Monitoring her progress:* could be done by teachers' assessments; direct observation of the pupil; interview with the pupil and parents; use of test/exam results.

■ *Problems:* the more methods used, the more time consuming, but only a partial picture will be generated if too little information is gathered. May have difficulty getting access to previous records. People may not agree to be interviewed.

8

The questionnaire and interview schedule should be cross-checked against the guidelines suggested by Robson on page 1009. Examples of possible problems include: ambiguities in the questions; with closed questions responses may be limited; if asked to choose from a range of possible answers, this may force a choice on respondents; questions may be too narrow and issues which are important to the respondent may be ignored. For the interview schedule, there may be problems concerning how best to record responses. Open-ended questions may result in answers to one question providing answers to others.

The interview data are likely to be much more in-depth and qualitative compared to the questionnaire data. The former are therefore likely to be much more informative. Whilst it may be easy to summarise the questionnaire responses, the interview responses may require a qualitative analysis in order to categorise the information and identify relevant themes.

■ Suggested answers to self-assessment questions

1

Ethical concerns should be central when planning research and selecting appropriate methods in order to ensure maximum protection of participants and those whom the research may represent. Different methods give rise to different ethical concerns. These must be considered to ensure that the design and conduct of research is ethically sound.

2

Old paradigm research refers to the traditional 'mind set' in psychology which advocated quantitative approaches utilising the experimental method. The emphasis is upon objectivity and the establishment of cause and effect relationships.

New paradigm research rejects the traditionally quantitative approaches and puts the emphasis upon objectivity. The focus is upon interpretative processes involved in the establishment of knowledge with qualitative techniques used to explore these processes.

3

The division between quantitative and qualitative research represents two extremes which are often considered incompatible. This denies the possibility of considering both quantitative and qualitative approaches within the same research framework and realising the strengths of both. It would be preferable to remain open to the promise and limitations of all the methods regardless of whether they are 'quantitative' or 'qualitative'.

4

The laboratory-based experiment allows greater control

and the manipulation of specific variables. This enables the establishment of cause and effect relationships which would be more difficult to establish using different methods. There is also the higher value which is afforded to findings which have been 'scientifically' validated by using a controlled experiment.

5

Field experiments may be used where the laboratory setting is considered to be too artificial, affecting the behaviour to be studied. Carrying out a study in the field reduces the potential bias caused by demand characteristics and experimenter expectancy (although there is less control over extraneous variables).

6

a A quasi experiment is one in which the experimenter has no control over the allocation of participants to conditions.

b This type of design is used in situations where it would be impossible to intervene or where membership of the control or experimental group is predetermined, for example by being male or female if exploring gender differences; by being a smoker or a non-smoker if comparing these groups.

7

The principle disadvantage is that causality cannot be inferred. Even where two variables appear to be strongly related, it does not mean one has caused the other. An equally plausible explanation is that both may have been caused by a third variable.

8

a Positive correlation: as one variable increases then so does the other

b Negative correlation: as one variable increases then the other decreases.

9

A minus score indicates a negative correlation. The nearer the figure is to −1, then the stronger the relationship, for example −7 or above would be considered strong relationships. A plus score indicates a positive correlation. Again, the nearer the figure is to +1, then the stronger the relationship. A score of zero indicates no relationship, a score of +1 or −1 indicates a *perfect* positive/negative relationship.

10

Variations in disclosure and participation:
■ *Full participant*: research role is completely hidden or undisclosed.

- *Participant as observer*: research role is disclosed but kept discrete; the researcher's role as participant is foremost.
- *Observer as participant*: research role is disclosed and is main role of researchers, although they also participate in the group's activities.
- *Full observer*: non-participating observer who has no involvement in the activities of the group being studied. Role is usually undisclosed to avoid affecting behaviour studied.

11

Inter-rater reliability is the level of consistency between the observations made by different observers of the same event. High levels of inter-rater reliability are associated with good coding/categorisation systems.

12

Sampling techniques available:

- *Time interval sampling*: behaviour is observed across a series of short intervals within a given period, for example in a two-hour session six consecutive periods each of 20 seconds may be recorded and will constitute the data.
- *Time-point sampling*: this is where the sample of behaviour is taken at a predetermined point in time, say every fifth minute, a 30-second period of behaviour is recorded.
- *Event sampling*: this is where only behaviour meeting a prespecified definition is recorded. This is often useful for behaviour which is infrequent.
- *Situation sampling*: when behaviour is observed in a number of different situations.
  The aim of these sampling techniques is to increase the representativeness of the findings and to help ensure that observations are not simply restricted to very specific times and specific situations, and that valid generalisations can be made.

13

Content analysis is known as an indirect observational technique because it does not involve the direct observation of people, but the communications they have produced, for example newspapers, magazines, books, films, TV adverts, speeches.

14

Adopting the case study as a research strategy requires the researcher to take account of the context of the phenomenon under study. It necessitates adopting a multi-method approach such that a variety of research tactics/methods are used to generate as rich a picture as possible. Whilst still maintaining methodological rigour, this allows a variety of perspectives to be considered.

15

Summarised below are a range of strengths and weaknesses associated with the case study approach. These are adapted from Coolican (1994, pp. 124–5).
Strengths of the case study

- *Outstanding cases*: dramatic occurrences may happen which could not be studied in any other way. Such cases, in dealing with the extremes of the human condition, serve to highlight potentials which may have previously been regarded as unrealistic.
- *Contradicting a theory*: one contrary case is enough to seriously challenge an assumed trend or theory or cause–effect relationship.
- *Data pool*: the results of a number of case studies into the same topic area can be pooled, sorted and analysed and any common threads identified.
- *Insight*: the unique richness of the case study is a great strength providing insights which would not be realised by any other approach – valuable when attempting to understand issues of a socially sensitive nature; it enables questions to be generated as the research progresses and for the relevant information to be gathered in an appropriate manner. This is not possible with other more structured approaches.
- *Reality with rigour*: ecological validity is high, assuming a high degree of rigour is maintained in the specific research tactics/methods adopted.

Weaknesses of the case study

- *Lack of representativeness*: difficult to make generalisations from each unique case. Checking the reliability and validity of the data is problematic.
- *Interviewer–interviewee interaction*: some have questioned the ability of the researcher to obtain objective data when conducting case study research because of the often close relationship which evolves between the researcher and the subject(s).
- *Subjective selection*: the researcher also introduces subjectivity in deciding what to select to tell the case study story with limited opportunity to check such interpretations.

16

The aim of this question is for you to consider the value of case studies in relation to wider psychological theory. This will obviously vary according to the case study selected. For the cases cited in this chapter:

- Gregory and Wallace's study of SB (1963) gave important insights into the role of learning in visual perception. The cases of exceptional memory illustrate what is actually possible as well as giving insights into effective mnemonic strategies.

■ Studies of child privation (for example Freud and Dann (1951); Koluchova (1972, 1976)) did much to question assumptions concerning the permanance of these effects as well as questioning assumptions related to the prime importance of the biological mother in the formation of attachments.

■ Freud's study of Anna O and others provided specific illustrations of Freud's ideas giving greater credibility to his theories. Just as he had identified common patterns of meaning in the specific symptoms of his patients, so similar patterns could be identified in others, resulting in the explanations of personality development proposed by Freud.

17

See figure 27.10 on page 1008.

18 See figure 27.11.

19

A pilot study is an exploratory testing of a research procedure to see how effective it is and what, if any, modifications are necessary. It should be conducted with a subset of the sample population to be studied. Pilot tests are useful for checking the wording of questions as well as giving an indication of the likely responses. They also give an idea as to how long the interview/questionnaire will take.

20 Whilst the examples given in this section can be used, it would obviously be more beneficial for you to find your own. (This may involve you looking more closely at the methods employed in different studies using journals of psychological research.)

The Design and Implementation of Experimental and Non-experimental Research

Sara Nadin

This unit covers:

The stages involved in the research process

Hypotheses and variables

Design issues

Sampling

Final stages of research preparation

Essential good practice when conducting research

By the end of this unit, you should be able to:

- plan and implement a psychological investigation
- distinguish between different types of hypotheses and variables
- understand ways of controlling extraneous variables
- select appropriate experimental designs
- understand how to generate a representative sample
- identify biases introduced by participants and researchers
- establish the validity and reliability of different measures.

Unit 28 Contents

Introduction

As a student of psychology it is highly likely that you will be required to conduct psychological investigations. The aim of this unit is to explain the stages usually involved in conducting research and the decisions which have to be made along the way.

The stages involved in the research process

Summarised in figure 28.1 is a stage model of the research process. This is not to say that all research passes through all of these stages in this sequence. Real research is usually not that neat or predictable! The model does however represent a useful guiding framework, especially for the novice researcher.

Deciding on the focus

The first stage of any research is to decide upon the focus of the research. What is it that you want to investigate? There may be a specific topic in

28.1 Stages involved in the research process

1 Decide on the focus of the study.
2 Become familiar with background research.
3 Specify the aim.
4 Decide on the methodology.
5 State hypothesis or expected outcomes.
6 Design the study.
7 Decide on analysis of outcomes.
8 Determine sample and prepare necessary equipment/materials.
9 Pilot study (*essential in surveys*).
10 Conduct main study.
11 Collate and analyse data.
12 Write report and submit.

psychology which is of particular interest to you. Alternatively, you may be instructed to conduct a study in a particular area. Only once you have decided upon the focus of your study can you undertake further planning.

Familiarisation with background research

Having decided on a focus, it is then necessary to familiarise yourself with relevant theory and research. This serves two important functions:

- It will enable you to identify more specifically what you want to investigate – a honing down process which is essential for the generation of clear research aims.
- It will enable you to get a grasp of the range of methods already used in that particular field, giving you some ideas as to what works best. The danger here is of limiting yourself to the methods and designs already used, discouraging a more creative approach to the research. Students should not be discouraged from trying out new ideas.

If a popular topic area is chosen, then there will be no difficulty in finding relevant research. In such cases, the most likely difficulty will come from having too much background research available, and deciding just how to cut it down. For other less popular areas, more time and effort may have to be spent in actually locating relevant background materials, although it is most unlikely that there will be nothing available.

Generating research aims and selecting the method(s)

Familiarisation with background research should enable the generation of your own research aims. As Robson (1993) pointed out, the generation of clear research aims provides a useful bridge between the research question and the design of the enquiry. With some research questions the most appropriate method and research design will be obvious. With others, there may be more options available, the selection of which will depend upon consideration of a number of factors, some of which are explored below.

Fundamental to the choice of methodology is its *ethical* and *practical feasibility*. Researchers at all levels will probably find they are under a range of very real practical constraints. Obvious ones here are time and resources (for example equipment, number of researchers, research deadlines), as well as availability and willingness of participants. The ethical viability of any study must be considered through consultation with the BPS (1996) *Code of Conduct and Ethical Guidelines for Research* (see Unit 3 pages 79–82). Often, students new to psychology will, in their enthusiasm, come up with grand research ideas. Unfortunately, these may lie beyond your capabilities as a student, requiring a level of professional competence. Examples here include research in the field of clinical psychology and in areas of educational psychology. For practical and ethical ease, the novice researcher is advised to keep it simple and clear.

Hypotheses and variables

Having defined the aims of the research, which state in broad terms what it is you expect to find, you should be able to generate specific hypotheses. A **hypothesis** is a testable statement predicting the precise relationship between different factors known as variables (see below). In experimental designs this usually suggests there will be a difference between two or more groups as a result of manipulation of one of the variables. This is known as the **experimental hypothesis** or **alternative hypothesis**. In correlational designs the hypothesis to be tested usually suggests there is a relationship between the different variables measured. This is known as the **research hypothesis**, as it is not an experiment (also known as the alternative hypothesis).

As well as the experimental hypothesis, there is also the **null hypothesis**. The null hypothesis predicts that there will be no difference between the variables identified in the experimental hypothesis. In cases where the experimental hypothesis is supported, we can *accept* the experimental hypothesis and *reject* the null hypothesis. Where the experimental hypothesis is not supported, we cannot reject the null hypothesis and accept that there is no difference between the hypothesised variables.

Making hypotheses testable

It is important that the terms used in the hypothesis are specific enough to be 'operationalised' or actually measured. So, for example, in a study investigating the effects of repetition on memory it would not be enough simply to state that repetition improves memory. Exactly how this improvement is to be measured needs to be stated:

> *Participants instructed to repeat the list of words will recall more words than those not instructed to repeat the list of words.*

Similarly, if exploring the relationship between intelligence and academic achievement, it would not be enough to say that higher intelligence is related to higher academic achievement. Specifically how the two variables of intelligence and academic achievement are to be measured needs stating:

> *There will be a positive correlation between scores obtained on an IQ test and number of GCSEs gained.*

Quite often, **operationalising** variables is more difficult than it may first appear. Often the psychological attributes which people choose to measure do not have an unambiguous behavioural correlate or representation which simply needs counting up.

These attributes are all open to interpretation and may mean different things to different people. Attributes such as a person's height, or time taken

Activity 1

Think about the following attributes:
- intelligence
- attitudes to authority
- attractiveness
- stress
- personality

How would you operationalise these in order to measure them?

(Suggested answers on page 1036.)

to do something are much simpler because the units of measurement are clear and universally defined. Where particular attributes are open to interpretation, it is important to state clearly what is actually going to be taken as an indicator of that attribute. Intelligence may be represented in the form of a score on a particular intelligence test; stress levels could be measured using a pencil and paper anxiety scale or a physiological indicator could be used, for example heart rate or blood pressure. (This issue is linked to the issues of validity discussed on pages 1033–4.)

Directional and non-directional hypotheses

Another characteristic of a hypothesis is its 'tailedness'. This relates to the direction of the expected affect or relationship. A hypothesis can be one- or two-tailed. **One-tailed** hypotheses (also known as **directional** hypotheses) are more specific in that they state the direction of the relationship or affect. So, for the example used earlier, repetition is expected to produce an *increase* in word recall. If we expected that repetition affected recall, but were not sure whether it led to an increase or a decrease, then this would result in a **two-tailed** hypothesis, such as:

There will be a difference in the number of words recalled between those who are asked to repeat the word list and those who are not.

(Two-tailed hypotheses are also known as **non-directional** hypotheses.) In order to support this hypothesis the result can go in one of *two* directions – an increase or a decrease. In order to support the one-tailed hypothesis the result must go in the *one* specified direction.

Similarly, correlational hypotheses can be one- or two-tailed. If we are not sure how intelligence is related to academic performance, we would generate a two-tailed hypothesis such as:

There is a correlation between scores obtained on an IQ test and number of GCSEs gained.

If, however, we suspect *higher* IQ scores are related to *higher* numbers of GCSEs obtained, we would generate a one-tailed hypothesis such as:

There is a positive correlation between scores obtained on an IQ test and number of GCSEs gained.

Alternatively, we may have reason to believe that the opposite is true, which would again lead us to a one-tailed hypothesis:

There is a negative correlation between scores obtained on an IQ test and number of GCSEs gained.

Activity 2

State whether the following research ideas would generate one- or two-tailed hypotheses:
a   Diet affects health.
b   Sleep deprivation causes a deterioration in spelling ability.
c   Eating carrots affects vision at night.
d   Number of siblings is related to ability to socialise.
e   Having a dog promotes positive psychological well-being.
f   Stress affects performance in sporting activities.
g   The teacher/pupil ratio affects academic performance.
h   Alcohol leads to a deterioration in visual acuity.

(Suggested answers on page 1036.)

All about variables

As stated earlier, the hypothesis predicts a relationship or affect between different factors, known as variables. The experimental or alternative hypothesis in an experiment contains two types of variable:

■ The **independent variable** is the variable which is altered or manipulated by the experimenter. This is commonly referred to as the **IV**.

■ The **dependent variable** is the variable which is measured to see if the alteration in the independent variable has had an effect. This is commonly referred to as the **DV**.

If the independent variable is found to affect the dependent variable, this indicates a *cause and effect* relationship (assuming other variables are kept under control). For example, in a study to test the effects of categorisation on memory, the following hypothesis was generated:

Participants presented with words listed in categories will recall more words than those presented with words not listed in categories.

The independent variable is whether the words are listed in categories or not, because that is what is being manipulated. The dependent variable is the number of words recalled – that is what is being measured.

Activity 3

Which are the independent and dependent variables in the following examples?

a In a study to explore age differences in conservation abilities a group of 5-year-olds was given a conservation task and the responses were recorded. The same task was then given to a group of 7-year-olds and the responses were recorded.

b The possibility that group decision making leads to riskier decisions was investigated. Participants were first presented with a number of situations individually. They had to decide how they would act in each situation. Participants were then brought together as a group and told to come to a decision upon which they were all agreed.

Activity 3 *cont*.

The responses that participants generated individually were then compared with the responses from the group.

c In a study to explore the visual preferences of babies, babies were presented with stimuli of varying complexity. The length of time the babies spent gazing at each stimulus was measured and compared.

d In a study to explore the visual preference of babies at different ages, three groups of babies aged one month, three months and six months were presented with stimuli of varying complexity. The length of time the babies spent staring at each stimulus was measured and compared.

e The effect of the presence of others upon performance was studied by having participants complete a task in a room on their own and then again in a room where others were present. Performance on the two tasks was compared.

(Suggested answers on page 1036.)

Controlling other variables

As mentioned above, establishing that the IV has affected the DV is dependent upon the control of other variables, ensuring that they are not responsible for the change in the DV.

Variables other than the independent variable which can affect the dependent variable are known as **extraneous variables**. If the potential effect of extraneous variables is not controlled, they have a confounding effect on the results. The extraneous variable thus becomes a **confounding variable**. It is the task of the researcher to ensure that extraneous variables do not become confounding variables.

■ **Controlling extraneous variables**

Good design will help to keep the range of extraneous variables to a minimum (for example by using good sampling techniques and standardising

Activity 4

In the following examples, explain why we cannot be sure that any changes in the DV are a result of the manipulation of the IV:

a   Volunteers suffering from depression take part in trials to assess the effectiveness of a new drug treatment for depression.

b   In an experiment to measure the effect of categorisation on word recall, participants are first given a list of words grouped in categories to memorise. After a short interval they are asked to recall as many words as possible. Participants are then required to do the same, this time with a list of words which are not grouped in categories. Their performance in the two conditions is compared.

c   In a study examining age differences in a visual recognition task, it happens that all those in one age group happen to be men and all those in the other age group happen to be women.

d   In a comparison of leadership abilities between senior management and shop-floor staff, the majority of those who constitute the group of senior managers are men whilst the majority of shop-floor staff are women.

e   You and four colleagues run an experiment to determine the effects of different levels of background noise upon concentration levels. You are allowed to use five rooms in the college to which you each take your group of participants. Each group is then exposed to a different level of noise and concentration ability is measured.

(Suggested answers on page 1036.)

their effect. One such technique is **counterbalancing**. This attempts to spread the effect of any confounding variables across all experimental conditions or groups. So in the example described in Activity 4b, the fact that the participants have already memorised a categorised list before being given the uncategorised list may affect their performance in the second condition. This is known as an **order effect** as it is a consequence of the order in which participants are exposed to the two conditions. This order effect could be cancelled out by having one group of subjects complete task A first then task B, and the other group of subjects complete task B first followed by task A.

Another technique for controlling the effects of confounding variables is through **randomisation**. So, in the example of the drug trial (Activity 4a), participants would not volunteer themselves to either the experimental (drug) or the control (non-drug) condition. Instead they would be randomly assigned to either of the two conditions. For the example of possible order effects on task completion (Activity 4b), participants could be randomly assigned to complete either task A first followed by task B, or vice versa. By randomly assigning participants to the different experimental groups or conditions, this eliminates the potential for systematic differences between the groups to account for any observed differences.

Another way of reducing the impact of confounding variables is to use **standardised procedures**. This helps to ensure that all participants are treated in exactly the same way ruling out the possibility that changes in the DV are due to differences in experimental procedures rather than the IV. Standardised procedures also help to control the potential impact of using different experimenters or researchers whose own expectations may affect the way they conduct an experiment unless procedures are standardised (see section on experimenter effects, page 1032). So, in Activity 4e, it is more than exposure to the IV which differentiates between the groups. Each group has a different experimenter conducting the experiment in different rooms. The best way of reducing the potential bias differences, such as these introduce, is to have the same experimenter using the same standardised instructions and

all procedures). Where extraneous variables cannot be eliminated, one way of controlling their impact is to keep them constant in both the experimental and control conditions. By keeping them constant, any effect they may have will be the same across both conditions and will therefore not be responsible for any difference observed.

As well as keeping potentially confounding variables constant, there are other ways to control procedures in the same setting with all groups. Once again, the underlying principle is to minimise the differences between groups, attempting to ensure that as far as possible the only thing which distinguishes between them is exposure to the IV.

Self-assessment questions

1 What is meant by 'operationalising variables'?

2 Explain the difference between a one-tailed and a two-tailed hypothesis.

3 Distinguish between extraneous and confounding variables.

4 How can extraneous variables be controlled?

(Suggested answers on page 1037.)

Design issues

Whichever method(s) you use, a range of design issues will need considering. Such issues concern the most effective ways to gather data for the purposes of your research. So, if conducting an experiment, which experimental design should you adopt? If using a questionnaire, how do you ensure it includes all the right questions? If doing an observational study, do you know exactly what you are looking for and how to record what you see? For a case study, what information do you want and how will you gather it? These issues are explored in each of the relevant sections in Unit 27, pages 1005–1007. Below is a more detailed look at design options for the experimental method. This is followed by a consideration of issues related to non-experimental quantitative research and qualitative research.

Different experimental designs

Assessing the impact of an independent variable experimentally necessitates a comparison with the control condition which has not been exposed to the IV. This then provides the 'base line' from which changes are measured. Exactly how this base line comparison is obtained depends upon the experimental design adopted. The three most common designs are described in figure 28.2 along with their advantages and disadvantages.

The advantages and disadvantages outlined in figure 28.2 give some idea of what to take into consideration when selecting the most appropriate experimental design. Sometimes this will be dictated by the nature of the investigation. Choice will also be dictated by practical considerations: such as the number of participants required and their availability; the amount of time available; access to resources such as materials, equipment or rooms. If there are no such practical constraints, then it is a matter of deciding what is of greatest advantage: to rule out the possibility of person variables confounding the results, or to eliminate the potential for bias caused by order effects or fatigue.

Alternative research designs

There is a range of research designs in which the basic principle is the comparison of different groups. The comparison measures used may be obtained using a variety of experimental, non-experimental and qualititative methods.

28.2 The three most common experimental designs

■ Between groups design: comparisons are between different groups of participants

1 **Independent groups design.** This is where there are two groups of independent participants. One group is assigned to the control condition, the other to the experimental condition. The two groups are then compared to see if there are any differences in the dependent variable.
Advantages: no order effects as in the repeated measures design.
Disadvantages: because different people are in the two groups, personal differences, known as *participant variables*, are more likely to confound the results.

2 **Matched pairs design.** Similar to the independent measures design as again there are two separate groups of participants: one group is assigned to the control condition, the other to the experimental condition. The difference is that the groups are matched in an attempt to make them as similar as possible in terms of relevant participant characteristics. If differences in the DV are still found between the control and the experimental groups, then these are more likely to be a result of the IV rather than as a result of having different people in the control and experimental conditions—as in the independent measures design above. The ideal participants for a matched pairs design would be identical twins, with one twin being placed in each condition (but then they would not be representative of the target population).
Advantages: matching process means results are less likely to be confounded by participant variables. No order effects as in the repeated measures design.
Disadvantages: Matching participants can be time consuming. Loss of one participant means loss of a pair.

■ Within groups design: comparisons are within the same group of participants

3 **Repeated measures design.** One group of participants is exposed to both the experimental and the control conditions. Performance between the two conditions is then compared.
Advantages: this design eliminates potentially confounding person variables because the same people take part in both conditions. Also, half as many participants are needed as in the other two designs.
Disadvantages: being exposed to two conditions may lead to fatigue or may produce *order effects* where exposure to one condition affects performance in the other condition. Participants are more likely to guess the aim of the experiment as they can compare the two conditions. This design may take more preparation in terms of materials, for example in a memory experiment, the same stimulus lists of words cannot be used for the two conditions as in the other two designs. Different lists will have to be generated for both the experimental and control conditions, although these will have to be standardised and considered equivalent.

■ Longitudinal studies

Longitudinal studies involve the comparison of the same group of people over a long period of time. This is in effect a repeated measures design. Such studies enable the following of developmental and life changes, especially useful in the study of children. They are also useful for studying the effects of an intervention or treatment programme. The main disadvantage of this type of study is the time needed. It may also be difficult to ensure continued involvement from participants.

■ Cross-sectional studies

Cross-sectional studies are an alternative to the longitudinal study, which instead of following the same group for a length of time, compares different groups at the same time. It is therefore less time consuming than the longitudinal study and more economical. Any applications the research may have are also more immediate than in longitudinal studies. However, the fact that the groups are made up of different people may confound comparisons.

Qualitative studies

Whilst a qualitative study will start with a clear definition of the scope of the research, the precise focus may only emerge as the research progresses. As such, there are no set hypotheses to test. This does not mean that anything will do. Foster and Parker (1995) stressed that with such research it is important to: (a) set an initial research question, and (b) to narrow this question down as the research proceeds. Setting the initial research question involves defining the following:

- The precise boundaries of the question.
- Which participants, or group of participants, are needed.

- The intended research process: what it is you are intending to do.
- What it is you expect to find.

Once the research is underway, you are likely to find that adaptations are needed. Some of your interview questions may not make sense or may be irrelevant to a particular group; you may learn something new which challenges the assumptions made at the outset of the research. This process of reflection and adaptation is an integral part of the research process and not a mark of bad design or planning. It provides an opportunity for discussion and learning which more restrictive procedures or techniques may inhibit.

Self-assessment questions

5 Explain the different ways of obtaining a control comparison group in experimental designs.

6 Compare and contrast longitudinal and cross-sectional studies.

7 What steps can be taken to ensure methodological rigour in qualitative studies?

(Suggested answers on page 1037.)

Sampling

One aim of conducting psychological research is to generate explanations of behaviour, explanations which can be applied beyond the research setting itself and to those not necessarily involved in the research. We take the research situation as *representative* of people and behaviours, from which we make *generalisations*. In order to ensure that the generalisations we make are valid, the sample we select must be representative of the population about whom we wish to make such generalisations. The population from which we select our sample is known as the *target population*. So, if we wanted to conduct a survey into political awareness of 15-year-olds in the UK, our target population would be all 15-year-olds in the UK. A study to explore the impact of company size upon stress levels of senior managers would have as its target population senior mangers from companies of a range of sizes.

When the sample we select is not representative of our target population, the result is *sampling bias*. Sampling bias undermines the applicability of research findings. A common source of sampling bias in psychological research lies in the fact that studies often use volunteers who themselves cannot be considered representative – what is it that makes them volunteer distinguishing them from those who do not volunteer? Also, much research is carried out in universities based solely upon student participants. This limited representativeness is the basis of more fundamental criticisms suggesting that psychology is both gender and culturally biased (see Unit 2 page 62–9). Much psychological theory is based on studies using white, middle-class, western males, yet the resulting theory is often presented and interpreted as being applicable to all, regardless of culture or gender. Whilst this is an example on a grand scale it illustrates the point.

It is important therefore to:

- ensure your sample is representative of the target population and free from bias; and
- not make generalisations beyond the target population you have identified.

There are a number of techniques to help ensure that the sample of participants you select is representative. The first step in any sampling procedure is to identify your target population. You can then decide on what basis you will select participants from this population.

Different sampling techniques

In random sampling every member of the target population has an equal chance of being selected. There is absolutely no relationship between those selected and it is impossible to predict who will be selected. This can be done manually by assigning all members of the target population with a number. All numbers are then placed in a box and shuffled, from which the desired number of participants is selected. Alternatively, this can be done using a computer which will generate series of random numbers. The sample would constitute those who corresponded to the numbers generated. Similarly, random number tables can be used. Working through the table either horizontally or vertically, these provide the numbers of those who will constitute the sample.

Getting a true random sample is not as easy as it may first appear. Often practicalities mean it is impossible for all members of the target population to be available for selection. Also, the random sample will have to be sufficiently large to represent the population you are interested in. The larger this target population, then the larger the required sample, which can again create practical difficulties. Often students will mistakenly report that they used a 'random sample', taking random to mean that they did not use any systematic method of selection – it was simply a matter of who they could get hold of. This is in fact an opportunity sample (see figure 28.3). *Remember: to be random, all members of the target population must* *have an equal chance of being selected.* The reality of the research situation, i.e. small scale, with limited resources such as time and available participants, means that often alternatives to random sampling (figure 28.3) are used in an attempt to ensure representativeness.

Sample size

Having decided upon the sampling procedure, you then have to decide on sample size. Generally speaking, the greater the variability in your target population, then the larger your required sample in order to ensure an accurate representation. The impact of this variability will depend upon the type of research. So, in an experimental situation where high levels of control attempt to minimise the effect of 'participant variables', one suggested optimum sample size is 25–30 (Coolican, 1994). For survey research, Foster and Parker (1995) cite Reaves's (1992) recommendations for sample sizes (table 28.4).

Activity 5

Define the target population for the following research ideas:

a A study to explore regional differences in voting behaviour.

b A comparison of the psychological well-being of elderly people cared for in their own homes and those cared for in nursing homes.

c A study to investigate gender differences in TV viewing among school children.

d An experiment to explore the impact of background noise on reaction times.

e A survey to assess if attitudes towards nuclear power vary according to how close people live to a nuclear power station.

f An investigation to see if attitudes about conservation differ between those who do not own cars and those who do.

g A local GP introduces a computerised information system. The impact this has upon patients' perceptions of the care they receive is assessed.

(Suggested answers on page 1036.)

28.3 Alternatives to random sampling

■ Stratified sampling

This is when the different groups in the target population are reflected in the sample in the same proportions. So, if your study focused upon a college in which 70 per cent of the students were studying for A-levels and 30 per cent were attending vocational courses, then 70 per cent of the sample would be A-level students and 30 per cent would be vocational students. It is possible to be even more specific and break down the sample by subject being studied. It will depend upon what is relevant for your study. Once you have defined the different groups or strata for your sample along with the number of participants required from each group, the sample is then selected randomly.

■ Quota sampling

This is like stratified sampling in that the sample is chosen to reflect the different strata of the target population in the same proportions. The actual selection process however is not random, with the researcher selecting whomever may be available until the desired quota for that particular group has been reached.

■ Systematic sampling

Selection is on the basis of, say, every third or every tenth person in the target population. So, for example, you may systematically work through a class register selecting every sixth pupil.

■ Snowball sampling

This is where the sample is generated as the research progresses. You may start with one or two key individuals who then put you in touch with other people, and so on. Like a snowball rolling down a hill, the sample gradually gets larger. This is more often used in qualitative research.

■ Self-selecting samples

This is a sample made up of those who volunteer themselves to take part in research, for example in response to an advertisement. It can also be those who happen to be in the research situation at the appropriate time with no intervention from the researcher. So, a naturalistic observational study of gender differences in public greeting behaviour would be based on a self-selected sample.

■ Opportunity sample

This is when the sample is made up of those who fit the sample criteria, who happen to be there and who are willing to take part in the study. University and college students are often selected on this basis.

Table 28.4	
Size of population	Size of sample
50	46
100	79
500	219
1000	279

Reaves's (1992) recommendations for sample sizes

Sampling of behaviours

The concept of sampling is also important in the context of observational studies. Often, it would be impractical to observe behaviour continously, thus a selection of behaviour is chosen. As when selecting a sample of participants, it is important that the behaviours or situations observed are representative. As explained on page 1029, there are a number of techniques available for behaviour sampling in observational studies. These include:

■ time interval sampling
■ time point sampling
■ event sampling
■ situation sampling.
   (See page 1002 for further details.)

Final stages of research preparation

What type of analysis?

Good research preparation includes consideration of how the data gathered are to be analysed. This will help structure the way the data are actually gathered making the actual task of data analysis a whole lot easier and not nearly as psychologically daunting. All too often students do not do this, launching themselves into their research, ending up buried under seemingly unfathomable piles of data. It is especially important to consider data analysis in qualitative studies where often method and analysis are interdependent. The type of analysis used will almost certainly influence what and how the data are collected. (See Unit 29 for detail on techniques of data analysis.)

Pilot studies

Good preparation involves, where possible, conducting a *pilot study*. This is an exploratory study which enables the testing out of your proposed research procedures. This could be anything from running a practical experiment to testing the items on a questionnaire you have designed. Whilst carrying out a pilot study is highly recommended for all methods, it is *essential* when conducting a survey. The pilot study should be conducted on a subset of your population in order to ensure the feedback obtained is relevant. Any modifications in procedure can thus be made *before* the main study, avoiding the horror of discovering too late that your procedures are flawed.

Self-assessment questions

8 Why is sampling used in psychological research?

9 Define 'random sampling'.

10 What kind of sampling is most often used in psychological research and what problems does this create?

11 Explain the relevance sampling has in observational research.

(Suggested answers on page 1037.)

Essential good practice when conducting research

The aim of this final section is to illustrate ways in which the research situation can introduce bias, and the procedures available to psychologists in order to keep such bias to a minimum. Also essential for good practice is the need to establish the validity and reliability of the measures psychologists use. Procedures to achieve this are explained below.

Biases inherent in the research situation

Most research situations involve some kind of interaction between the researcher(s) and those participating, over and above the actual behaviour being measured/investigated. The most obvious example of this is in the formal experiment with its procedures and setting making participating an experience in itself for those involved. This can be contrasted to covert naturalistic observations where the behaviour of people is observed in natural settings without their knowledge. The dynamics associated with being human are still present, however, in the form of the experimenter or researcher. The fact that the research situation is a social situation means that the behaviour of those involved will be affected.

Summarised in figure 28.5 are common effects created by the research situation. Certain effects are associated with the experimenter, others with the participants.

One source of bias which the experimenter may introduce is **experimenter expectancy**. This is where the experimenter unintentionally gives away the aim of the experiment through verbal and non-verbal cues, 'leading' participants to behave in the way the experimenter expects them to. This effect was shown by Rosenthal (1966) who gave his students a group of 'maze dull' and 'maze bright' rats. The 'maze bright' rats showed superior maze learning than the 'maze dull' rats, despite the fact that the rats had actually been randomly assigned to each group.

■ Controlling participant and experimenter effects

Since the source of much bias is the expectations of both the experimenter and the participants in terms of how they are supposed to behave, one way of controlling this is to keep them in the dark so they do not know what to expect. This process is known as 'blinding'. There are two types of blind:

- the **single blind**, where participants are not told the aims of the investigation
- the **double blind**, where both the participants and the experimenter do not know the aims of the investigation. In practice, this usually means ensuring that the experimenters do not know which participants are in the control condition and which are in the experimental condition. This practice is commonly used in medical procedures for trialling new drugs.

Whilst these procedures may help, they do not prevent participants hazarding a guess at the aims of the study, nor do they control other experimenter effects such as the personal attributes of the experimenter.

Remember: whilst these effects are generally greater in more artificial situations, it would be wrong to assume that they are present only in experimental research. All research situations depend upon human interpretation at some level and as such they are all open to bias. The best we can do as psychologists is to try and keep these biases to a minimum and openly acknowledge the assumptions and values we bring to the research situation.

28.5 Effects introduced by participants and researchers

■ Participant effects

Studies in which the behaviour of participants is affected by the research procedure itself are known as *reactive studies* and the associated behaviour **participant reactivity**. So what is it participants are reacting to? Participants react to what are called the demand characteristics of the research situation. These are cues in the research procedure or environment which reveal the aims of the study. People tend to react by behaving in a way which they think makes them look good. This is known as the **social desirability effect**. Alternatively, participants may feel anxious at the thought of having their behaviour measured or assessed which may also affect their responses. This is known as *evaluation apprehension*.

■ Experimenter effects

The researcher or experimenter can influence research outcomes in a number of ways. Coolican (1994) identified a few:

- the fudging of results
- failure to follow procedures because they are too loosely defined
- personal attributes of the experimenter such as attractiveness, sex
- the psychological paradigm of the researcher which may blind him or her to alternative ideas.

Establishing the validity and reliability of measures used

An important way of controlling potential bias in the observation and measurement of behaviours and psychological attributes is to establish the validity and reliability of the measures we use. This is especially true of abstract concepts which do not necessarily have an obvious meaning or behavioural correlate. Examples here include intelligence, attitudes and personality. The common way of measuring such attributes is by using psychometric tests. Thus, whenever psychometric tests are developed it is essential that their validity and reliability is demonstrated.

■ Psychometric tests

For abstract constructs such as intelligence or attitudes, we need to ensure that we are measuring what we say we are measuring – this is the *validity* of the measure. We also need to ensure that the measure we use is *reliable* and will produce the same results consistently at different times. An intelligence quotient (IQ) test which one day gave you an IQ of 120 and the next day an IQ of 70 would not be reliable. We may also question the validity of an IQ test of all the items related to scores of football matches played by the premier division in 1998. Whilst such a test may be measuring something, it is not intelligence.

There are a number of ways in which to establish the validity and reliability of psychological tests. These are explained in figure 28.6.

28.6 Ways of establishing validity and reliability of psychometric tests

■ Test reliability: ensuring test scores are consistent

Test-retest reliability: when the same test is repeated at a different time. If the test is reliable, there should be a high correlation between the two scores.

Split half reliability: measures the internal consistency of test items to ensure that different test items produce similar results. The items on the test are divided into two sets, half in each set. The scores from each set are then correlated. A high correlation indicates good internal consistency.

Equivalent forms: where the scores from one test are correlated with scores from a different test measuring the same attribute.

■ Test validity: ensuring the test is measuring what it claims to be measuring

Face validity: the crudest measure of validity, where the items are inspected to assess their appropriateness. It is an eyeball measure to check if, on the face of it, the test appears valid. So, in a test of verbal ability you would not expect to find mathematical problems.

Content validity: the test is assessed to ensure it includes all the areas it is intended to cover. This usually involves giving the test to experts in that area who can tell whether the test misses essential components or gives undue weighting to certain factors. It is a more sophisticated version of face validity.

Predicitive validity: where a prediction is made on the basis of a test score. If this prediction is borne out, the test is said to have high predicitive validity.

Construct validity: where test results should be consistent with other psychological constructs or behaviours. So, if scores on a personality test define an individual as extrovert, we would expect this individual to behave differently in social settings to someone defined as introvert by the same test. Because we are often trying to measure abstract constructs such as attitudes, motivation and personality, links with related concrete concepts are important in establishing the validity of such measures.

Activity 6

In attempting to assert the reliability of an attitude scale you use the test-retest method. You are disappointed to find a low correlation between the two sets of scores. Does this necessarily mean your scale is not reliable? (Now read on.)

If we find a low correlation between the test and the retest scores, this does not necessarily indicate low reliability. The attribute we are measuring, be it an attitude or personality, may have actually changed between the two testing periods. Obviously, the longer the delay between the test and the retest then the higher the possibility of this happening. Also, with ability tests, completing the test once may lead to a practice effect where performance the second time around improves.

Whilst a test may be reliable, this does not mean that it is valid. Obtaining the same scores consistently on an IQ test does not mean that the test is measuring intelligence. It could well be measuring something else, such as memory ability.

■ Observational studies

Validity and reliability are important when assessing behaviours using observational techniques. We need to define (or operationalise) attributes in terms of particular actions or behaviours. So, if we are measuring aggressiveness, what are we taking as valid indicators of aggression? Are we to include verbal behaviour? Are we to consider intentionality or the consequences of different actions? Do we take account of the context, for example, for acts of retaliation?

Having agreed upon what it is that constitutes aggression, we need then to ensure that our observations are reliable. So, if we were to rate the same episode of behaviour at different times, the ratings produced should be very similar. Also, different people rating the same episode of behaviour should also produce consistent ratings (known as *inter-rater reliability* – see Unit 27 page 1004). The need to establish validity and reliability in observations highlights the importance of preparation and training *before* any actual research commences.

Self-assessment questions

12 Why is it difficult to eliminate all potential experimenter and participant effects?

13 Describe biases which may be introduced to the research situation by: (a) the participants, and (b) the researcher.

14 How can participant and experimenter effects be controlled?

15 Define reliability and validity.

16 Explain the importance of reliability and validity in relation to psychometric tests and observational studies.

(Suggested answers on page 1038.)

Conclusions

The aim of this unit has been to provide practical guidance enabling you to work through the research process. This is not intended to be prescriptive. Often the various stages of the research process will need tailoring to fit the specifics of the chosen research situation. Regardless of methodology, you should be left with an appreciation of how essential good preparation is in the production of high quality research. Remember, all of the issues covered in this unit are those which should be considered *before* any research actually commences.

Unit summary

- The research process can be usefully broken down into a number of stages.
- Most research is based upon the testing of specific *hypotheses*. Making hypotheses testable depends upon successfully 'operationalising' variables.
- An experiment involves the manipulation of the *independent variable* to see if it affects the *dependent variable*. Establishing this cause and effect relationship is dependent on the control of *extraneous variables* ensuring they do not turn into *confounding variables*. Ways to control extraneous variables include: keeping them constant across all conditions; counterbalancing; randomisation; and standardising procedures.
- *Design issues* concern the specifics of how data are to be gathered. Common designs in experimental research are: the independent groups design; matched pairs design; and the repeated measures design. Other designs which may incorporate the experimental method include cross-sectional and longitudinal studies.
- Good *sampling* is essential in establishing the representativeness of findings. The sample is selected from the target population using a variety of sampling techniques: random; stratified; quota; systematic; snowball; self-selecting; and opportunity. Sampling is also important in observational studies.
- Wherever possible it is advisable to conduct a *pilot study*. It is also useful to decide upon the desired technique of analysis before any data are actually gathered.
- The research situation is open to various sorts of bias simply because it is a social situation. The *demand characteristics* of the research situation cause participant reactivity. This could result in a social desirability effect or may cause evaluation apprehension.
- Researchers may introduce bias, for example by not following procedures. One demonstrated effect is *experimenter expectancy* where the researcher unintentionally gives cues and influences behaviour in the desired way. Participant and experimenter effects may be reduced by using single and double blinds.
- It is important to establish the *validity and reliability* of the measures psychologists use – for which there are a number of techniques available.
- In observational research it must be established which behaviours are valid representations of what we want to study, and to ensure that *inter-rater reliability* is high.
- Good preparation is the key to producing high quality psychological research.

Terms to define

alternative hypothesis
confounding variable
counterbalancing
cross-sectional studies
dependent variable (DV)
double blind
experimental hypothesis
experimenter expectancy
extraneous variable
hypothesis
independent groups design
independent variable (IV)
longitudinal studies

matched pairs design
null hypothesis
one-tailed/directional
operationalising
order effect
participant reactivity
randomisation
repeated measures design
research hypothesis
single blind
social desirability effect
standardised procedure
two-tailed/non-directional

Further reading

Coolican, H (1994) *Research Methods and Statistics in Psychology*, 2nd edn, Hodder & Stoughton, London.

An excellent and essential source, providing detailed explanations of different methods, their implementation, as well as the analysis of research outcomes.

Clegg, F (1982) *Simple Statistics: A Course Book for the Social Sciences*, Cambridge University Press, Cambridge.

A very accessible book covering the essentials of research design and data analysis.

Answers

■ Suggested answers to activities

1

There are no right or wrong answers in this activity. Ideas may centre upon the relevant theories which define what it is to be intelligent or attractive. The point is to appreciate that such abstract constructs are open to interpretation highlighting the need to assess critically the validity of what is actually going to be measured as an indicator of a particular attribute.

2
a   Two-tailed
b   One-tailed
c   Two-tailed
d   Two-tailed
e   One-tailed
f   Two-tailed
g   Two-tailed
h   One-tailed

3
a   IV = age; DV = ability to conserve.
b   IV = being alone and then in groups; DV = the riskiness of the decisions reached.
c   IV = the varying complexity of the stimuli; DV = length of time spent staring at each stimulus.
d   IV = age of the babies and the varying complexity of the stimuli; DV = length of time spent staring at each stimulus.
e   IV = whether others are present or not; DV = task performance.

4
a   Those who volunteer may want to make a recovery. It would thus be difficult to separate out the real effects of the drugs from any 'placebo' effect, where the participants' belief that they are getting an effective treatment actually produces an improvement in their condition.
b   Memorising the categorised list may affect the way participants memorise a subsequent list, for example they may seek to group the items into categories.
c   Any differences found may be due to gender differences rather than the effect of the IV.
d   Again, differences found may be due to gender rather than seniority. This highlights the circularity of definitions of leadership behaviour – by defining leadership in terms of typically male characteristics, those most likely to fit the definition of good leaders are men.
e   Variations in the different experimenters and in the different settings may confound the results.

5
a   Target population is those who are eligible to vote in the relevant regions identified.
b   Target populations are those cared for in nursing homes and those cared for in their own homes. It would be ideal to select the sample from populations in similar areas who have been receiving the different types of care for similar periods of time.
c   The target population would be all school children.
d   The target population would be the general public.
e   The target populations would be defined by geographical proximity to nuclear power stations and would include all those able to complete the survey within each of the pre-specified areas.
f   Target populations would be those who do not own cars and those who do.
g   The target population would be all those who have *visited* the GP since the computerised information system was installed.

◼ Suggested answers to self-assessment questions

1

Operationalising variables means to define the variables specifically enough to say how they will actually be measured, i.e. in terms of the concrete operations which correspond to their meaning.

2

A one-tailed (directional) hypothesis will state the expected direction of the outcome, for example greater, more than, less than; whereas a two-tailed (non-directional) hypothesis will not state the direction and simply state there will be an effect.

3

Extraneous variables are all variables other than the IV which may potentially affect the DV. Confounding variables are those extraneous variables which *do* affect the DV and thus confound the results. The aim is to prevent extraneous variables becoming confounding ones.

4

Extraneous variables can be controlled by:
- ensuring they remain constant across all conditions (an aspect of standardisation)
- using counterbalancing – where half of participants take part in condition A followed by condition B and the other half take part in condition B followed by condition A (this cancels out any potential order effects)
- randomisation – randomly assigning participants to the control and experimental conditions eliminating any systematic differences between the two groups
- standardisation – keeping all aspects of the research situation as constant as possible, for example the same experimenter giving the same instructions in the same setting, such that the only thing which distinguishes between the groups is exposure to the IV.

5

There are three designs commonly adopted to obtain a control condition in experiments:
i   Independent groups design – where there are two groups of independent participants, one group is assigned to the control condition, the other to the experimental condition.
ii   Matched pairs design – as above, only participants in the two groups are matched along relevant variables.
iii Repeated measures design – where the same group of participants is exposed to both the experimental and the control conditions.

6

Longitudinal and cross-sectional studies are similar in that they involve the comparison of various groups, usually at different stages in a 'process'. With longitudinal studies, this involves following the same group of people over a long period, whereas in cross-sectional studies, different groups are compared at the same point in time. Cross-sectional studies have the advantage of being quicker, producing more immediate results; longitudinal studies have the advantage of following the same people, controlling for the effect of participant variables which are not controlled for in cross-sectional studies.

7

Methodological rigour can be ensured in qualitative studies by setting an initial research question and narrowing this down as the research proceeds. Setting the initial research question involves defining: (i) the boundaries of the research; (ii) the participants; (iii) the intended research process; and (iv) what you expect to find. These may be modified and adapted through reflection which should be an integral part of the research process.

8

Sampling is used because it is usually practically impossible to involve all members of the target population. The aim of sampling is to obtain a subsection of the target population which is representative of that population, thus enabling generalisations to be made about the target population from the sample.

9

Random sampling is when every member of the target population has an equal chance of being selected.

10

The most common types of samples used in psychological research are opportunity samples and self-selected samples. This usually means that the typical research participant is a student who cannot be considered representative of the general population. Also, those who volunteer themselves to take part in research cannot be considered representative – what is it about them which distinguishes them from those who do not volunteer?

11

Sampling in observational studies is necessary as it is usually impossible to observe behaviour continuously. As with selecting a sample of participants, the sample of behaviour should be representative of the phenomenon under study so that generalisations can be made. There is a variety of observational sampling techniques available to help ensure representativeness.

12

However much control a researcher may have over a research situation, it is still a social situation dependent upon human interaction and interpretation. There is thus room for variations to be introduced.

13

a   Biases are introduced by participants who react to the research situation (known as participant reactivity). These reactions include acting in a socially desirable way to make themselves look good, and feelings of apprehension at the thought of being assessed/measured (known as evaluation apprehension).

b   Biases are introduced by the researcher in a variety of ways: fudging results; not following procedures; the researcher's personal attributes; the psychological paradigm or mind set of the researcher; also through his or her own expectations when they unknowingly give cues which influence the participant's behaviour in the expected direction (experimenter expectancy effect).

14

The impact of the expectations of the participants and the researchers can be controlled by using single and double blinds; also using standardised procedures minimises the effects of different experimenters who may have different expectations using different procedures.

15

Reliability refers to the consistency of a particular measure – will it generate the same outcome regardless of where and when it is used and who uses it? Validity refers to the content of the measure – is it measuring what it claims to be measuring?

16

Validity is important in psychometric tests as they are often used to measure abstract constructs such as intelligence, personality or motivation. It is thus necessary to define what is meant by the different constructs and exactly what will be taken as an indicator of them. Tests should also generate consistent results if they claim to be measuring a stable characteristic.

In observational studies it is important to be sure that the behaviour measured is a valid indicator of the phenomenon under study, for example by defining clearly and precisely what constitutes an aggressive act. It is also important that different observers will rate behaviour in the same manner – this is known as inter-rater reliability.

Unit 29

Quantitative and Qualitative Approaches to Data Analysis

Sara Nadin

This unit covers:

Quantitative data analysis

Using statistical tests

Qualitative data analysis

Producing the written report

Procedures for statistical tests

By the end of this unit, you should be able to:

- choose appropriate ways of summarising data in order to describe it

- present data in the appropriate picture form, for example bar chart, histogram, etc.

- select the right statistical test for data

- assess the significance of your results using a statistical test

- consider approaches to the analysis of qualitative data including content analysis

- follow the conventions for writing up research into a report.

Unit 29 Contents

Introduction

The type of data you have will determine the type of analysis to be used. Quantitative data (i.e. numbers) require the use of quantitative analysis; qualitative data (for example, observations of behaviour) require qualitative analysis.

As well as explaining the various possible ways of conducting quantitative and qualitative analysis, this unit also aims to impart the following understanding: analysing data statistically is not as difficult as you might believe; analysing data qualitatively is not easy as you might believe. If you are considering doing a qualitative study because you would prefer to avoid working with statistics, then think again! This unit has been designed to assist all students to undertake statistical analysis with confidence.

Quantitative data analysis

Quantitative data is used in two ways:
- descriptively – to provide relevant summaries of the data
- inferentially – where statistical tests are used to determine the strength of any relationship or effect between the different variables measured.

Usually, both levels of analysis are employed. In the next two sections the various descriptive statistics are explained together with the different statistical tests available. It is up to the researcher to decide which descriptive statistics are most appropriate and which statistical test(s) to use.

Descriptive statistics

Descriptive statistics, as the term suggests, simply offer the researcher ways of describing and summarising data. It may be largely meaningless and confusing to present raw data. We therefore need to present the material in a way which is digestable and informative.

◼ Measures of central tendency and measures of dispersion

Two popular types of descriptive statistics used are **measures of central tendency** and **measures of dispersion**. **Measures of central tendency** provide values which are typical of the set of data. For example, we may say that on average it takes us 15 minutes to walk to college. Some days it may take slightly less, some days slightly more, but 15 minutes is representative. There are three measures of central tendency commonly used: the **mean**, the **median** and the **mode**. These are explained in figure 29.1.

Activity 1

Find the mean, median and mode for the following sets of scores:
Set 1: 8, 5, 16, 12, 7
Set 2: 16, 11, 3, 21, 2, 7, 3, 22
Set 3: 12, 5, 4, 6, 14, 17, 6, 14, 8, 13
(Use the step-by-step procedure for the ranking on page 1062 if needed.)

(Answers on page 1060.)

Measures of dispersion tell us about the spread of scores around the mean indicating how much they vary from this 'typical' value. The most popular measures of dispersion used are: the **range**, the **variance** and the **standard deviation (SD)**. These are explained in figure 29.2.

◼ Standard deviation and the normal distribution

The explanatory power of the standard deviation can only be fully appreciated by understanding its relationship to the normal distribution. The normal distribution refers to the pattern in which traits and characteristics are usually spread amongst the population. For example, most people are of 'average' height and fewer people are at the extremes of either being very tall or very small. Similarly, with intelligence, most people are of average intelligence with the number of people decreasing as the scores shift away from this average, be it higher or lower.

29.1 Measures of central tendency

■ Mean

Commonly known as the average. Calculated by adding up all of the values in a group and dividing the total by the number of values we have.

For example, six people take an intelligence quotient (IQ) test and get the following scores: 112, 118, 97, 132, 101 and 105. The mean IQ score is:

$$112 + 118 + 97 + 132 + 101 + 105 = \frac{665}{6}$$
$$= 110.8$$

■ Median

The score or value which is in the middle of the set of data. The scores are first put in numerical order – this is known as ranking – and then the central score is selected. For example, for the above scores – 97, 101, 105, 112, 118, 132 – we would need to find the mean of 105 and 112 because both scores fall in the middle of the set of data. The median IQ score is:

$$\frac{105 + 112}{2} = 108.5$$

If the person who scored 132 had not taken part, leaving five scores, the median would be 105. (Ranking can get confusing when dealing with a large set of numbers – see page 1062 for a step-by-step procedure.)

■ Mode

This is the most frequent occurring score in the data set. For the above IQ scores there is no mode as each of the scores occurs only once. For the following set of scores: 10, 10, 13, 14, 14, 14, 17, 19, 20, 20 the mode is 14. For the set of scores: 10, 11, 11, 13, 14, 15, 15, 18, 19, 20, there are two modes, 11 and 15, which is known as *bi-modal*.

This pattern of distribution is most commonly represented in the form of the **normal distribution curve** (figure 29.3).

The area under the curve represents the population. The vertical axis represents the frequency of people. Fewer people fall into the tail-end areas of the curve with the curve reaching its peak in the middle. This indicates that most people fall around the average, with the numbers decreasing the further away we move from the centre of the curve.

The normal distribution curve has certain mathematical properties:

■ the mean, median and mode are exactly the same and fall at the mid point of the curve

■ the curve is symmetrical around its mid point with 50 per cent of the population falling on one side and the other 50 per cent falling on the other side.

The standard deviation indicates exactly what proportion of the population falls within the different areas under the curve. This is illustrated in figure 29.4.

From this we can see that the majority of the population (68.26 per cent) falls within minus one and plus 1 standard deviation of the mean; 95.44 per cent of the population fall within plus and minus 2 standard deviations; 99.74 per cent fall within plus and minus 3 standard deviations from the mean. By using two scores, the mean and the standard deviation, a variety of conclusions about the spread of scores may be reached.

Therefore, if the average height of population is 200 centimetres and the standard deviation is 20, we are able to conclude:

■ 34.13 per cent of the population will be between 200 and 220 centimetres in height and another 34.13 per cent of the population will be between 180 and 200 centimetres in height, such that 68.26 per cent of the population will be between 180 and 220 centimetres in height

■ 95.44 per cent of the population will be between 160 and 240 centimetres in height (i.e. plus and minus 2 standard deviations from the mean)

29.2 Measure of dispersion

The range

This indicates the range of scores in a data set telling us how spread out or close together they are. It is calculated by finding the lowest value in the data and subtracting this from the highest value in the data. Although the two sets of scores below may have the same mean, the range indicates that the scores in Set A are much more spread out or dispersed than the scores in Set B.

$$\text{Set A mean:} \quad \frac{2 + 2 + 3 + 5 + 6 + 6 + 8 + 9 + 9 + 10}{10} = 6; \text{ range} = 10 - 2 = 8$$

$$\text{Set B mean:} \quad \frac{5 + 5 + 5 + 6 + 6 + 6 + 6 + 7 + 7 + 7}{10} = 6; \text{ range} = 7 - 5 = 2$$

Interquartile range

The interquatile range is similar to the range but concentrates on the middle 50 per cent of the scores by ignoring the top and bottom quarters (or 25 per cent) of the scores. The score which has one-quarter of the scores below it is taken as the lowest value and is then subtracted from the score which has three-quarters of the scores below it. This eliminates the possibility of extreme scores presenting an unrepresentative picture, as can happen using the range.

The semi-interquartile range

This is the value of the interquartile range halved.

The variance

This is a measure of the variation in a set of scores which takes into account *each* individual score. This gives a more precise indication of the variance than when using the range, which only takes account of two extreme scores. The amount by which each individual score differs or deviates from the mean is calculated and squared. To find the mean of these squared deviations, they are added together and the total is divided by the number of scores. The result is the variance.

The standard deviation (SD)

Whilst the variance indicates extent of variability in the scores, the fact that the deviations have been squared means that the variance score obtained bears little relation to actual scores. The scores need to be scaled back down for them to be meaningful. This is done by finding the square root of the variance (thus cancelling out the squaring procedure). The result is the standard deviation. A small standard deviation indicates that scores are grouped closely around the mean (scores on average do not deviate or differ much from the mean); a large standard deviation indicates that the scores are more spread out (scores on a average do deviate or differ a lot from the mean).

Activity 2

a   Using the explanation given in figure 29.2 write out a step-by-step procedure for calculating the standard deviation, i.e. Step 1: calculate the mean of the set of scores; Step 2 etc.

Activity 2 *cont.*

b   Using this procedure find the standard deviation of the following set of scores: 11, 16, 4, 7, 21, 13, 17, 6, 15, 12.

(Suggested answers on page 1060.)

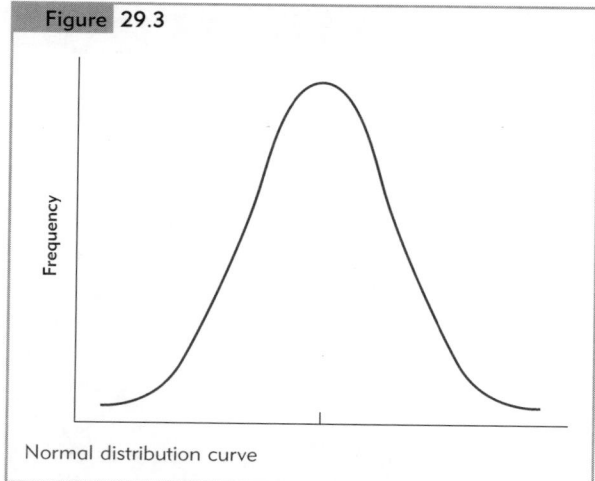

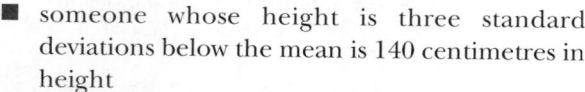

Normal distribution curve

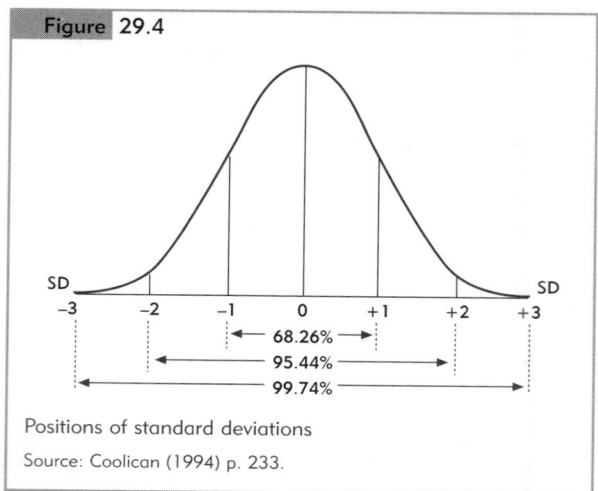

Positions of standard deviations

Source: Coolican (1994) p. 233.

- someone whose height is three standard deviations below the mean is 140 centimetres in height
- 48.87 per cent of the population are between 140 and 200 centimetres in height and another 48.87 per cent are between 200 and 260 centimetres in height.

By calculating the standard deviation we know roughly what the spread of scores looks like and the scores of different portions of the population may be calculated.

Using graphs and charts

As well as describing data using measures of central tendency and dispersion, a useful way of summarising and presenting data is using graphs and charts. When used appropriately they are an effective and appealing way of illustrating the data. The different types of graphs and charts most frequently used are explained below.

Whatever way you choose to display your data there are certain practical points you should follow:

- *Labels* – ensure the graph/chart has a *full* title and that all axes are labelled.
- *Key* – where keys are necessary, those should be presented with the graph/chart, enabling an immediate interpretation.
- *Size* – ensure the graph/chart is large enough to be clear and appropriately positioned.

Remember, the aim of using graphs and charts is to increase clarity in the presentation of data, making it more accessible.

Histograms

Histograms are used to display the distribution of values or scores in a set of data. All of the scores are displayed against the intervals or categories along which data was collected – this is called the continuous variable. Even if there are no cases in a particular category or interval, this category will still be represented on the histograms. In this way it is possible to gain at a glance an overview of how the scores are distributed. Frequency is shown on the vertical axis, and the category or interval on the horizontal axis. The number of cases in each category or interval is represented as a vertical bar. An example of a histogram is shown in figure 29.5.

Bar charts

Bar charts may look similar to histograms. They do however differ in several ways. Bar charts do not aim to show the frequency of distributions across a continuous variable. The data can be used more selectively, simply to compare the scores obtained in different groups or conditions. It is also possible to use summary scores such as the mean. Because the bar chart does not aim to show the whole pattern of scores, the bars should have a gap between them to show they are not related to each other in a continuous manner. An example of a bar chart is shown in figure 29.6.

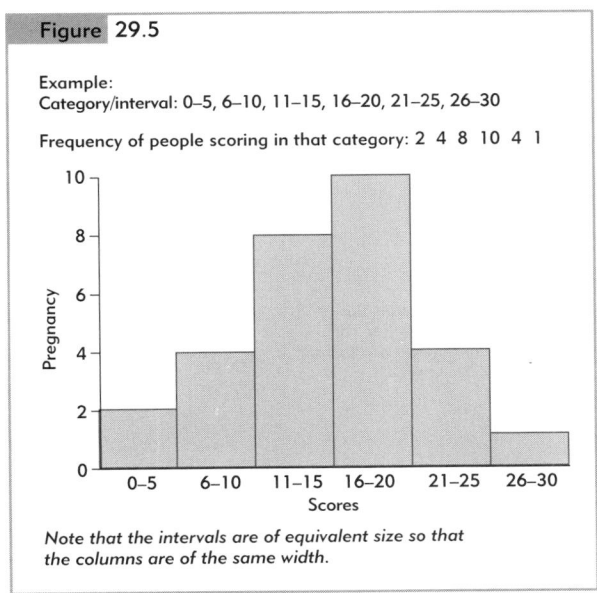

Figure 29.5

Example:
Category/interval: 0–5, 6–10, 11–15, 16–20, 21–25, 26–30

Frequency of people scoring in that category: 2 4 8 10 4 1

Note that the intervals are of equivalent size so that
the columns are of the same width.

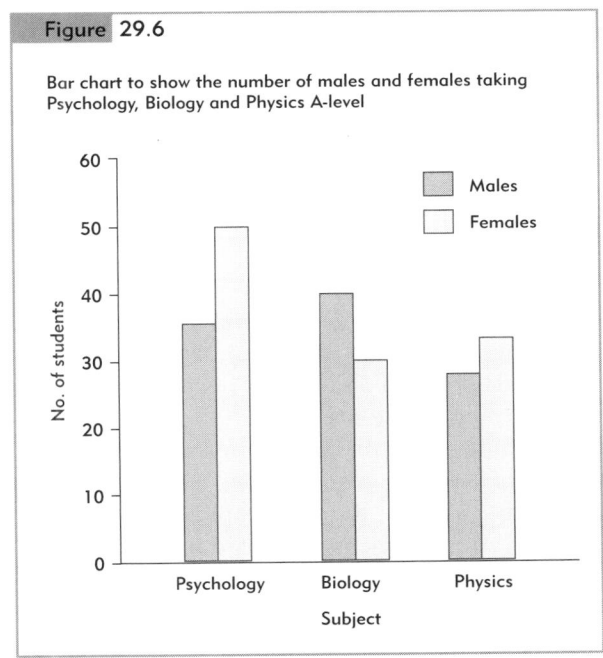

Figure 29.6

Bar chart to show the number of males and females taking
Psychology, Biology and Physics A-level

It is essential when using bar charts not to
present the data in a misleading way. You should
not attempt to exaggerate any differences between
groups by selecting a large scale for the vertical axis
and not giving an indication of the whole range of
scores (figure 29.7).

■ Frequency polygons

Frequency polygons are very similar to histograms
showing the distribution of scores of a continuous
variable. Instead of using columns, however, a dot
is placed at the centre of the top of each column

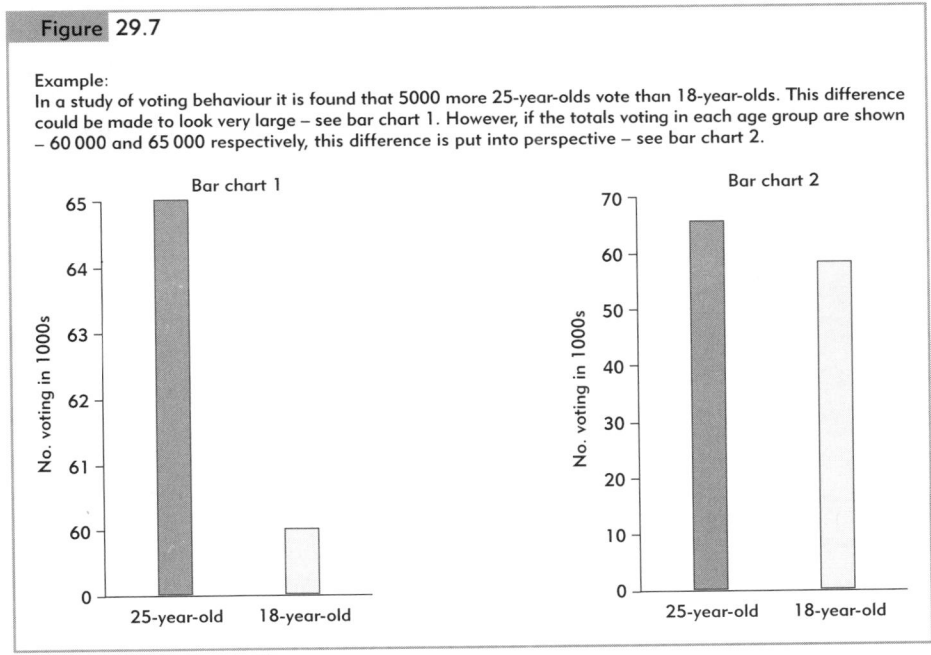

Figure 29.7

Example:
In a study of voting behaviour it is found that 5000 more 25-year-olds vote than 18-year-olds. This difference
could be made to look very large – see bar chart 1. However, if the totals voting in each age group are shown
– 60 000 and 65 000 respectively, this difference is put into perspective – see bar chart 2.

(i.e. at the mid point of that category or interval), and the dots are then joined together (figure 29.8). Frequency polygons are very useful for displaying the distribution of scores when comparing two or more conditions or groups.

◼ Pie charts

Pie charts are a useful way of showing how the data are subdivided between different groups. A pie chart takes the form of a circle which represents the whole sample. This is then divided up according to the proportions of the sample or data falling into the different categories. For example, if four categories each contain 25 per cent of the sample, the circle will be divided into quarters. An example is illustrated in figure 29.9.

Whilst pie charts provide an appealing way of presenting data, they can lose their impact when there are lots of different categories. Labelling the different segments can get messy and it may be difficult to determine the size or value of the different sections.

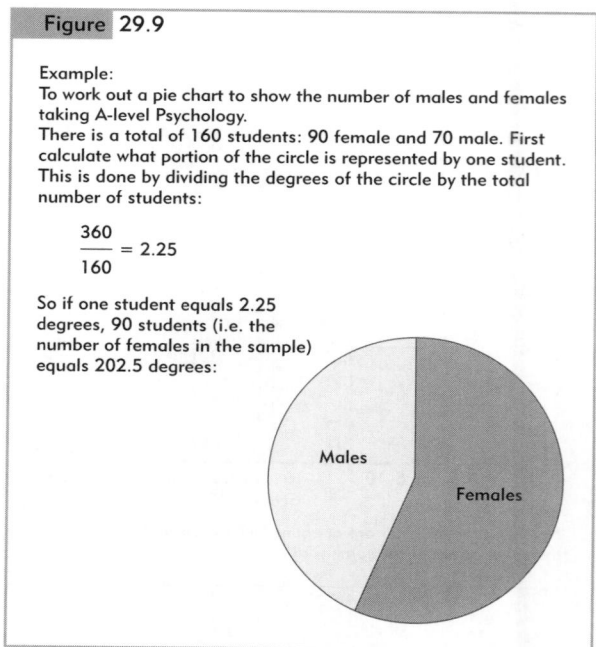

Figure 29.9

Example:
To work out a pie chart to show the number of males and females taking A-level Psychology.
There is a total of 160 students: 90 female and 70 male. First calculate what portion of the circle is represented by one student. This is done by dividing the degrees of the circle by the total number of students:

$$\frac{360}{160} = 2.25$$

So if one student equals 2.25 degrees, 90 students (i.e. the number of females in the sample) equals 202.5 degrees:

◼ Scattergraphs/scattergrams

Scattergraphs or *scattergrams* are used to show the relationship between two sets of scores in correlational studies. One variable is represented along one axis and the other variable along the other. The scattergraph is a very useful way of illustrating the strength and direction of any relationship. It is also very useful for revealing relationships which may otherwise go unnoticed, such as curvilinear relationships. For this reason, a scattergraph should always be used to display correlational data (figure 29.10).

Scattergraphs and their use is explored in greater detail on page 996.

Conclusion

This section has covered a variety of ways in which data can be described. This does not mean that students should use all of them. Ask yourself, is this measure of central tendency or dispersion relevant? You must be prepared to explain

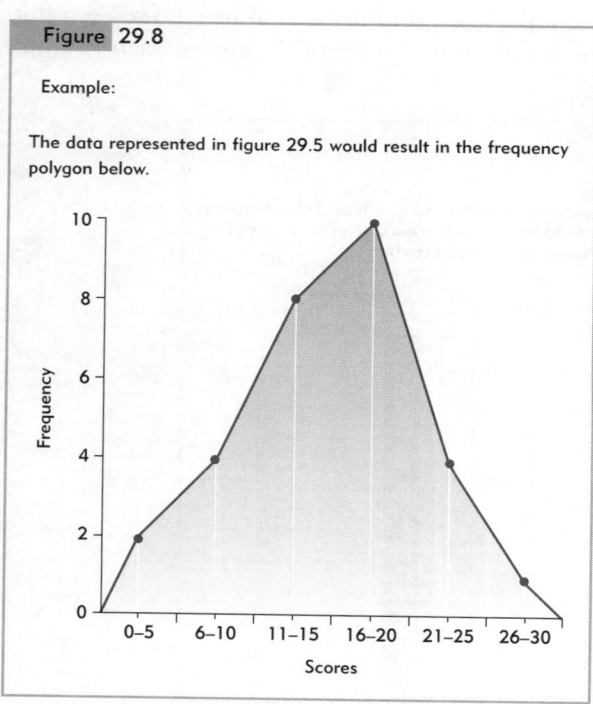

Figure 29.8

Example:

The data represented in figure 29.5 would result in the frequency polygon below.

Figure 29.10

Example:
Data were gathered exploring the relationship between hours spent revising and exam marks obtained:

Hours: 10 6 8 4 12 7 11 2
Marks: 77 58 70 43 80 68 69 40

This data are represented in the following scattergraph:

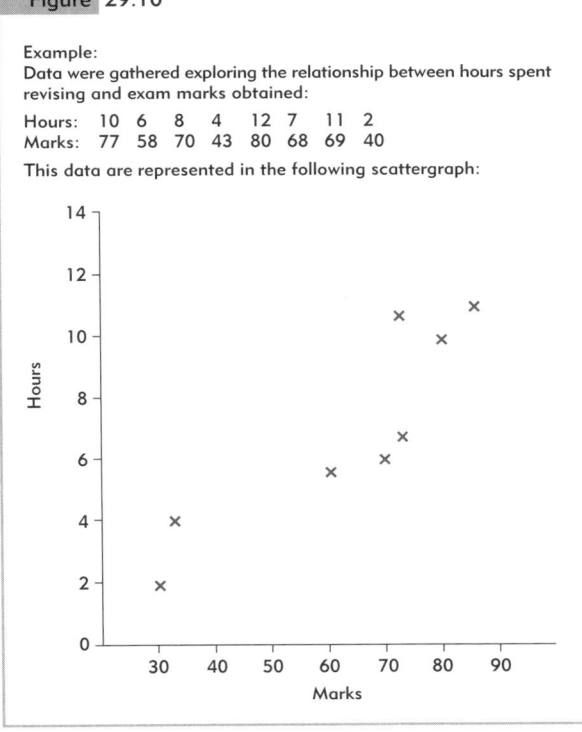

the explanatory value of the measure you use. Do not just present the mean, median, mode, range, variance and standard deviation without first considering how much value they add. Similarly, with bar charts and graphs, be selective in their use. Remember: the ultimate aim of summarising and describing data is to aid clarity.

Self-assessment questions

1 Why are the mean, median and mode known as measures of central tendency and how are they determined?

2 Why, in statistical terms, is the variance a more accurate representation of the spread of scores than the range?

3 What does a large standard deviation indicate about the spread of scores?

4 What is the difference between a histogram and a bar chart?

(Suggested answers on page 1060.)

Using statistical tests

The aim of statistical analysis of the data is to determine the strength of any effect or relationship between the different variables measured. If an effect or relationship is strong enough it is said to be significant and that the experimental or research hypothesis has been supported. If an effect or relationship is weak and therefore nothing of significance has been found, then the null hypothesis is supported and the experimental or research hypothesis is rejected. This is what the statistical test indicates.

The use of statistical tests is very simple. There are two basic things you need to know:

- how to select the appropriate test, and
- how to tell when an effect is strong enough to be called significant.

At this level you do not need to know the various steps involved in the different tests, nor the mathematical logic underlying them. If you can add up, subtract, divide and multiply (all these may be done on a calculator), and follow instructions, then you can carry out statistical tests with accuracy.

Selecting the appropriate test

The type of test selected depends upon three factors:

1 whether you are looking for a *difference* between scores (as in experimental designs) or a *relationship* between scores (as in correlational designs)

2 what type of data you have

3 what experimental design you have used (i.e. whether independent or related – see page 1027).

■ Factor 1: are you looking for a difference or a correlation?

Hopefully, the answer to this question is obvious. If not, then you should go back to your hypotheses.

What is it you are predicting? (Hint: experimental designs generally predict a difference, correlational designs predict a correlation.)

■ Factor 2: what type of data do you have?

There are three types of data:

- **Nominal data** – when the figures represent the number in a particular category and all those within a category are indistinguishable from each other. There is no individual score for each participant. Examples include the classification on the basis of sex (male or female) or the number of 7-year-olds who can conserve and those who cannot conserve.

- **Ordinal data** – where the data indicates the position in a group enabling the values to be ranked from highest to lowest, or first to last; for example, scores on an agility task taken by ten participants. Their scores can then be ranked. Rankings indicate nothing about the size of the difference between the scores. Whilst we may know who came first, second or third, it is not known by how much those in the various positions beat each other.

- **Interval data** – the most detailed form of data where the size of the difference between scores is given. The size of the intervals between scores is standardised such that the difference between a score of two and of six is exactly the same as the difference between a score of 23 and 27. Examples of interval data include the number of words recalled in a memory test (given that the words are of equal difficulty), and standardised measures such as time and distance. (Measures such as time and distance are also known as ratio scales because they have a true zero point – it is not possible to get negative measures of time and distance, or indeed, number of words recalled. The lowest possible score on these scales is zero.)

Establishing that the measures used by psychologists produce interval data has been an area of controversy. This is because many measures are designed to measure abstract constructs such as attitudes or intelligence where it is very difficult to establish that the units of measurement are equivalent along the whole of the scale. So, can it be said on an IQ test that the difference between a score of 90 and 110 is equivalent to the difference between a score of 130 and 150 or 60 and 80?

Each level of data provides us with more information, with nominal data being the simplest and interval data the most complex. The more information you have about something, then the more indepth and informed your analysis can be. The more sensitive tests designed for interval data do this by highlighting relationships which cruder forms of tests and data would be insensitive to detect.

It is possible to reduce data to a lower level of complexity. Interval data can be treated as ordinal. Ordinal data can be reduced to nominal data by grouping together scores and detailing how many scores fall within the upper and lower limits of that group.

■ Factor 3: What design have you used?

Again, hopefully this is obvious. If you have done a correlational study, then it is by definition a related design. If you have done an experiment in which the same group of participants took part in both the experimental and the control conditions, then you have a related design.

If you have two separate groups, one of which is exposed to the experimental condition, the other to the control, then you have an unrelated or independent design. A matched pairs design is treated as a related design because each of the scores is related to the score of the equivalent pair.

Activity 3

Fill in the table putting each of the designs outlined above in the appropriate column.

Related designs	Unrelated designs

This table will provide you with a useful, quick reference guide. To recap on the different experimental designs, see page 1027.

(Suggested answer on page 1060.)

Now you should be ready to select the appropriate test. This is best illustrated using the decision tree shown in figure 29.11 which combines the three factors above.

■ Criteria for using parametric tests

Additional criteria must be satisfied before using t tests and the Pearson's correlation coefficient. These are known as *parametric tests* (the others as non-parametric tests) which refers to the greater power they have in picking up significant differences where they exist. This power is however dependent upon a number of assumptions about the data. These include:

■ that the data are of interval level
■ that the sample data are drawn from a normally distributed *population*
■ that the variances between the two sets of scores are similar – this is known as **homogeneity of variance**.

The first point concerning type of data has been discussed above.

Establishing that the data you have gathered comes from a normally distributed population can usually be assumed from what you know about the variable measured, i.e. that it is normally distributed. For example, we know that height is normally distributed, and the standardisation of IQ scores means they too are normally distributed (see page 1042 for an explanation of the normal distribution).

Establishing that the variances between the two sets of scores is similar is easily done by comparing the ranges of the two sets. Homogeneity of variance can usually be assumed in related designs where the similarities in the sample mean that variances are unlikely to differ markedly. (Complications may arise when the sizes of the samples differ greatly where more complex procedures may be needed to establish the homogeneity of the variance. These are most unlikely to be needed at this level.)

Having selected the appropriate test using the decision tree (figure 29.11) follow the step-by-step procedures for your chosen test. These are explained at the end of this section on pages 1062–1087.

Once you have carried out the appropriate test using your data, the next step is to interpret the test

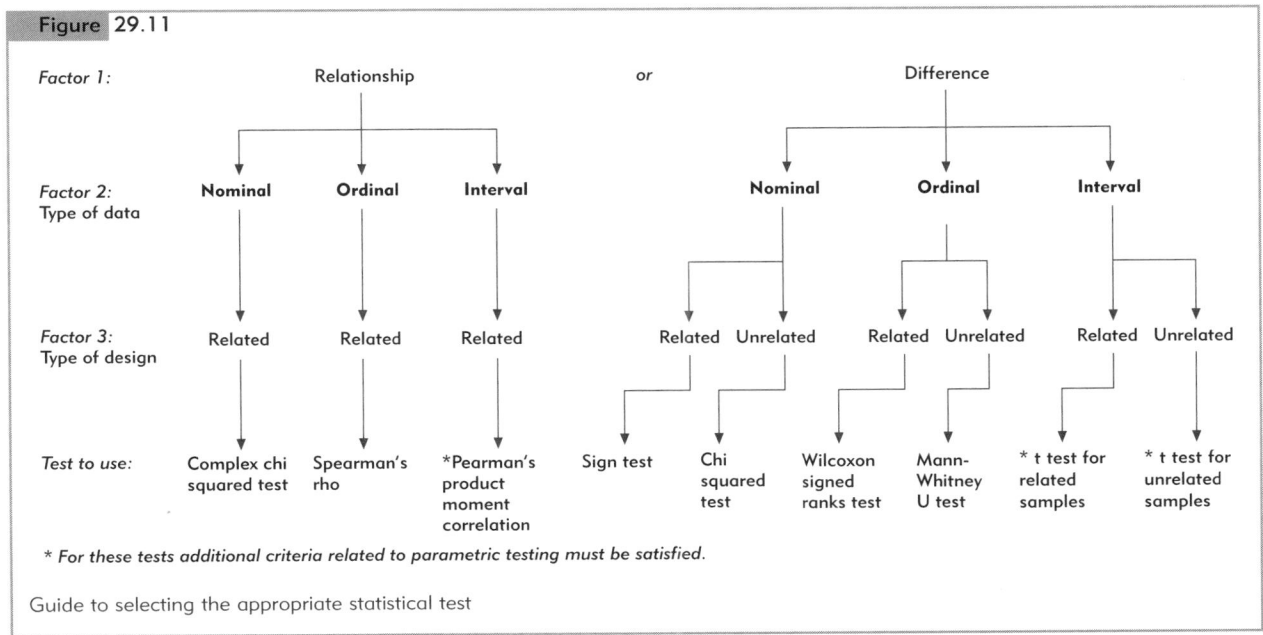

Figure 29.11

| *Factor 1:* | Relationship | | | *or* | Difference | | |

| *Factor 2:* Type of data | **Nominal** | **Ordinal** | **Interval** | | **Nominal** | **Ordinal** | **Interval** |

| *Factor 3:* Type of design | Related | Related | Related | | Related Unrelated | Related Unrelated | Related Unrelated |

| *Test to use:* | Complex chi squared test | Spearman's rho | *Pearman's product moment correlation | Sign test | Chi squared test | Wilcoxon signed ranks test / Mann-Whitney U test | * t test for related samples / * t test for unrelated samples |

* For these tests additional criteria related to parametric testing must be satisfied.

Guide to selecting the appropriate statistical test

result. This relates to the second point you need to know about statistical testing: how to tell when an effect is strong enough to be called significant.

Probability and levels of significance

It should make common sense that if you expect a difference between groups, then the bigger that difference is the more sure you can be that there has been an effect. But, how big is big enough? It is necessary to try and rule out the possibility that the result which has been obtained occurred by chance. Thus if things have a very low likelihood or probability of occurring by chance and they do occur it is likely or probable that they have resulted from something the researcher has done. For example, I tell you I have developed a coin-flipping technique which guarantees the coin will land on a side of my choosing. I flip the coin and it lands on heads just as I predicted. Are you likely to be impressed? Why not?

Your answer should have been something like 'Well it had a one in two (or 50 per cent) chance of landing on heads anyway'. What you are saying is that it had a very high probability of occurring by chance and it is therefore not of any significance that it happened. Now, suppose I had a 20-sided coin and I tell you I have developed a coin-flipping technique which will make the coin land on any side of my choosing. I flip the coin and it lands on the side I selected, or even you selected. Are you likely to be impressed? Why?

You probably said 'yes' simply because it is unlikely to have landed on the side I selected purely by chance, after all there were 19 other sides it could have landed on. In the case of the 20-sided coin you are more likely to believe that it was my flipping technique which obtained the result than with the two-sided coin. Similarly, if I had a 100-sided coin and succeeded, you would be even more impressed and more convinced that it was my flipping techniques which caused the result.

What this illustrates is that the more the possibility of chance factors accounting for the result can be reduced, then the more likely it is that the researcher has caused the result.

Chance factors can never be completely ruled out, the success of the national lottery testifies to our commonsense belief in this. Even though the odds of winning the lottery are millions to one, people do win. What we have to decide is what level of chance we are prepared to accept in order to conclude that an outcome is of significance.

The usual minimum level used in psychology is 1 in 20 or 5 per cent, i.e. the chance of obtaining a particular result by chance is one in 20 – it is thus significant when it does occur. Put another way, it is 95 per cent certain that there has been a significant effect.

Where you need to be more sure that your results have not occurred by chance then the chance factors could be set at one in 100 or 1% (0.01), i.e. the likelihood of a result occurring by chance, is one in 100 – it is thus of great significance when it does occur. In other words, it is 99 per cent certain that there has been a significant effect. This is the level usually used in medical research where it is important to be as certain as possible that any effects are the result of the drug/treatments being tested.

■ Type 1 and type 2 errors
The lower you set your significance levels, then the easier you make it to accept your experimental or research hypothesis. Making it easier to accept your experimental hypothesis means you are more prone to accepting it when there has actually been no effect and what you have observed is the chance factor. When this happens, this is termed a **type 1 error**.

The higher you set your significance levels, i.e. 1 per cent (0.01), then the harder you make it to accept the research or experimental hypothesis. Whilst this will make you more sure of an effect should a significant result be obtained, the danger here is of missing a significant effect because you have set your levels too high. When this happens the experimental hypothesis may be mistakenly rejected assuming there has been no effect when actually there has. This is known as a **type 2 error**.

The chances of making a type 1 error depend upon the significance level that has been set. With a 5 per cent level this means that five times in every hundred you will reach the wrong conclusion in accepting the experimental hypothesis. With a 1 per cent level you are accepting that one time in every hundred you will reach the wrong conclusion in accepting the experimental hypothesis. This means that you are more likely to make a *type 1 error with a significance level of 5 per cent* than to make a *type 2 error with a significance level of 1 per cent*.

Rejecting and accepting hypotheses

Now, let's go back to that test result. You will need to compare your result with what is called the *critical value* which is a figure taken from the relevant significance table. The critical value selected is determined by the level of significance required and whether the hypothesis is one- or two-tailed. At the end of the testing procedure there is an instruction such as 'If the obtained result exceeds the critical value, then the result is significant' (each instruction will vary according to the particular test you are using). A significant result means you can accept the experimental hypothesis: a non-significant result means you must reject the experimental hypothesis and accept the null, i.e. that there is no difference or association. When reporting upon the significance of our findings it is essential that you state the level of significance used. *For the purposes of your research you are advised to use the 5 per cent level of significance.*

Obtaining a non-significant result does not mean that your research has failed and that it is not worth writing up. This should be seen as an opportunity to explore *why* you did not get the outcome you expected and potentially gives us a lot to consider in the discussion (see page 1057). Were there methodological flaws for which you can suggest modifications? Do you need to reassess your predictions by going back to previous research? What is the potential importance of not finding a significant difference or association?

Data analysis concludes with a statement about which of your hypotheses are supported and retained. All that is left to do now is to discuss what you have found and the implications your results may have.

Self-assessment questions

5   What three things do researchers need to know in order to select an appropriate statistical test?

6   Explain the criteria which need to be satisfied in order to conduct a parametric test.

7   Explain the difference between type 1 and type 2 errors.

8   With a significance level of 10 per cent are researchers more likely to make a type 1 or a type 2 error?

(Suggested answers on pages 1060–1.)

Qualitative data analysis

Qualitative data can come from a variety of sources, can take a variety of forms and can be dealt with in a variety of ways. Much will depend upon 'how' the data are actually used. Coolican (1994) distinguishes between two main uses of qualitative data:

■ As a supplement to quantitative data – provide further illumination of what the statistical analyses reveal. For example, scores on a job satisfaction questionnaire may mean much more if supplemented by actual comments from employees.

■ As meaningful in their own right.

Where the overarching paradigm is that of quantification, the qualitative data may be reduced to statistical representations or frequencies. Content analysis is an example of one approach to qualitative data analyses which does this. Alternatively, qualitative researchers may aim to produce qualitative analyses in order to represent the meaning contained in such data. This approach to qualitative data analysis sits firmly within the 'new paradigm' school of thought (see page 990), which is critical of the prescriptive, reductionist tools of analysis used by those of the 'old paradigm' (see page 990).

Consistent with this lack of prescription is a more open-ended approach to data analysis. As such it is difficult and, for many, undesirable, to describe step-by-step procedures for the qualitative analysis of qualitative data. Even when a clearly identified technique is selected (for example discourse analysis), there is flexibility in how such techniques can be applied, according to the demands of the research situation.

It would be impossible here to explain the different analytical techniques simply because there are so many and because they rarely follow clearly defined procedures. Despite the range of techniques available, similarities can be identified in the way they deal with data which principally focus upon the meaningful categorisation of information. Generic approaches to categorisation are explained. The general procedures involved in content analysis are also explained. You are advised to consult more specific texts if intending to use qualitative techniques of analysis.

Sources of qualitative data

Qualitative data can be the product of a variety of research methods and tools. These include:
- case studies
- interviews
- observations
- open-ended questionnaires.

The data produced can also take a variety of forms including: transcripts of interviews; detailed observational notes of the researcher; video-recorded material and tape-recorded material: archival records and the participants' own diaries. Whatever form the data may take, the main objective of analysis is categorisation. As suggested in Unit 28, you are strongly advised to consider precisely what data you are going to end up with and what you intend to do with it *before* you actually carry out the research. This is especially relevant in qualitative research where such considerations may help structure the way the data are gathered, making the job of analysis a lot easier.

Analysing the data

The approach to the analysis of qualitative data will vary according to how well defined the aims and expectations of the study are. If you are clear about the ideas you are testing, then the analysis is more likely to proceed along traditional lines, *after* the data has been collected. It is still important to remain open to new ideas which may emerge from the data however.

If you are not sure of what the clear expectations are, then the data analysis and method will be more interdependent, where early examination of the initial data gathered will guide the research expectations and the collection of subsequent data. In this way, methodology and analysis is an iterative process where one feeds into the other.

Robson (1993) suggested some useful basic rules for the analysis of qualitative data, and these are outlined in figure 29.12.

Categorising qualitative data

The main emphasis in qualitative analysis is upon the systematic reduction of data by categorising or coding it in some way. These categories may actually be predetermined if you are setting out to explore clear theoretical ideas. For example, if you

29.12 Basic rules for dealing with qualitative data

1 Analysis of some form should start as soon as data are collected. Do not allow data to accumulate without preliminary analysis.

2 Make sure you keep tabs on what you have collected (literally – get it indexed).

3 Generate themes, categories, codes, etc. as you go along. Start by including rather than excluding; you can combine and modify as you go along.

4 Dealing with the data should not be a routine or mechanical task; think, reflect! Use analytical notes to help get from the data to a conceptual level.

5 Use some form of filing system to sort your data. Be prepared to re-sort. Play with the data.

6 There is no one 'right' way of analysing this kind of data – which places even more emphasis on being systematic, organised and persevering.

7 You are seeking to take apart your data in various ways and then trying to put them together again to form some consolidated picture. Your main tool is comparison.

Source: Robson (1993) p. 377.

---

are analysing data from a structured interview, the interview questions and the ideas under investigation may provide an initial interpretive framework for the categorisation of the data. Where the research aims are not so clearly defined,

the categories and coding will emerge as the analysis progresses.

Coolican (1994, p. 386) suggests a number of categorisation processes typical of qualitative approaches to data analysis (figure 29.13).

29.13 Categorisation processes (Coolican, 1994)

▪ Initial categorising

The researcher will begin with a large quantity of written notes. As the notes are read and re-read it should be possible to group different items together. Items may fall into more than one category, so it is advisable to have several copies of the data which can be cut and pasted, or to use a computer package which will do the same.

▪ Indigenous categories

Before the researcher develops his or her own categories, the ones used by the participants themselves are considered. For example, if looking at football crowd behaviour it may be useful to explore how the various groups of fans describe themselves in order to understand their actions fully.

▪ Researcher's categories

These may emerge clearly on data analysis or during data collection. It may be possible to identify different dimensions along which people vary, for example the extent to which students agree with animal experimentation.

▪ Typologies

The different dimensions identified, when combined may produce different 'types'. For example, a student who agrees with animal experimentation, viewing such research to have a high benefit (benefit dimension), may be considered a 'pragmatist'. Those who reject animal experimentation regardless of the benefit may be considered 'egalitarianist'. Types are not a definition of what something actually is – they are simply a descriptive tool offering a greater degree of complexity than a straightforward category label.

▪ Quotations

Using verbatim quotations from participants is a powerful way of 'telling it like it is'. Often quotations summarise and typify perfectly a particular view or perspective identified in the data. It is important to obtain consent from the original speaker(s) before publishing any quotations.

Content analysis

Content analysis is a technique designed for the analysis of qualitative data which reduces it to a quantitative representation. The 'meaningfulness' of the data is retained in the definition of the categories to be used, which seek to represent the meaning behind the message.

As outlined on page 1004, content analysis is used to analyse documentary representations of a particular behaviour, event or issue. Typical examples of 'documents' include newspapers, magazines, television programmes and advertisements, radio programmes and archival records. The aim of content analysis is to go beyond the actual message identifying the meaning behind their construction. So, in a TV commercial advertising washing powder, what else might the commercial be saying, for example in relation to who does the laundry? The actual analysis involves the systematic categorisation and coding of the chosen communication, resulting ultimately in a quantifiable description of it.

■ **How to conduct a content analysis**

1 Define a research question – what it is you want to examine, for example stereotyping in TV advertisements; the political biases of different newspapers.
2 Select a sample – decide how you will select the material for analysis. This may be predetermined, for example a particular political speech, or transcripts from interviews you have conducted. Where it is not, the sample should be representative of the chosen target material, for example a random selection of ten copies of a particular newspaper from a given time period; advertisements from every other advertising slot during a week of children's TV. The basic principles of sampling discussed on page 1028 apply here.
3 Define the coding unit – the units into which the material is going to be categorised. This can be done at a variety of levels. Common units of analysis include: each word; each theme; each paragraph; or the whole item.
4 The categories into which the units of information can be coded then need defining.

These will be determined largely by the research question. For example, in an analysis of the political content of newspapers, if themes are chosen as the unit of analysis, each theme could be put into any one of the following categories: pro-Conservative Party; pro-Labour Party; pro-Liberal Democrat Party; etc. Alternatively, categories may be defined by 'issues' such as environmental issues, health issues, education issues, defence issues, etc.

5 Test the clarity and reliability of your categorisation system – ensure that your category definitions are unambiguous enabling coding at the defined unit. This is best checked for by having someone else use the system who should be able to generate the same codings as you given the same piece of material.
6 Carry out the analysis – categorise the selected communications by checking off each unit of material into one of the categories. Ideally, this should involve another person ensuring that your expectations do not bias the interpretation of the communication. This will generate statistical data, for example a tally of the number of units of material which fall into each category, which can then be subjected to statistical analysis if required.

Robson (1993) identified a number of advantages and disadvantages associated with content analysis. These are summarised in figure 29.14.

Conclusions

There is a danger in assuming that qualitative analysis represents an easy option, especially for those 'number phobics' who decide they will do a qualitative study simply because they cannot bear the thought of 'doing statistics'. Choosing qualitative research and analysis for such reasons is a very big mistake – good qualitative research is not easy. It is labour intensive, often frustrating, requiring a high degree of autonomy and insight, as often you will be the only one steering yourself through analytical processes which are not very well specified. Although, the open-endedness of qualitative analysis may make it the attractive option, it also makes it a very demanding one.

29.14 Advantages and disadvantages of content analysis

■ Advantages

1 It is an unobtrusive measure allowing you to observe without being observed.
2 The data are in permanent form allowing them to be subjected to re-analysis and reliability checks.
3 It may provide a low-cost form of longitudinal analysis where a series or a run of particular document types are available.

■ Disadvantages

1 The documents available may be limited or partial.
2 The documents have been written for some other purpose and it is difficult to allow for the biases this introduces.
3 It is difficult to assess causal relationship. For example, is sex stereotyping in advertisements a cause of, or a reflection of, sexual inequality in our society?
4 It can be extremely time consuming.
Source: adapted from Robson (1993) p. 280.

Self-assessment questions

9 Explain the two ways in which qualitative data can be used.
10 Which methods are most likely to produce qualitative data?
11 What is the main aim of qualitative analysis of qualitative data?
12 What is the aim of content analysis?

(Suggest answers on page 1061.)

Producing the written report

Reports of psychological research follow a common general structure, and there are a number of conventions guiding the way the information should be presented. These conventions apply predominantly to experimental designs, and the student new to psychology is advised to follow them. With non-experimental and qualitative designs the conventions for reporting research are less restrictive.

The fundamental aim of the research report is to enable a reader to replicate the study. The psychological report is broken down into a number of sections. These are explained in sequential order below.

One way to familiarise yourself with the structure of a report is to look at a research article published in a psychological journal such as the *British Journal of Psychology*.

Sections in an experimental research report

The title: this should be brief and informative giving the reader an idea of the aim of the research and, if possible, an indication of the methods used.

Abstract: this is a summary of the research which goes at the beginning of the report (although it is usually written last). The abstract should contain four or five sentences summarising: (a) the topic of the study; (b) the participants and the procedure; (c) the outcome (results); (d) some interpretation of the results (Foster and Parker, 1995, p. 186). The aim of the abstract is to enable readers to determine if the research is relevant without having to read the whole report. The abstract is usually indented to make it stand out at the beginning of the report.

Introduction: this should contain a summary of background literature, followed by an explanation of how the current research develops from that. The introduction may begin at a general level and become more and more specific, narrowing down the focus of the research to a few key studies. These should then provide the basis for developing the *aims* of the research which is followed by more specific statements of what the researcher expects to find in the form of the *hypotheses.*

Method: this should summarise

- *the design of the study* – to include the type of design used (for example repeated measures design); the number of groups being used; a description of the IV (independent variable) and DV (dependent variable); an outline of any control measures used such as randomisation or counterbalancing
- *the participants* – detailing how many took part and how they were selected (i.e. which sampling technique was used); any other relevant information such as the number of males and females, or whether they were all students
- *details of any materials or apparatus* – these should be described in sufficient detail to enable replication (lengthy copies of standardised instruction or other written materials such as word lists should be put in the appendices)
- *the procedures* – what happened in the study, which should be described in enough detail to enable someone unfamiliar with the study to be able to replicate it; any instructions given to participants should be included word for word (lengthy standardised instructions can be put in the appendices).

Results: first, these are summarised in a descriptive way. Raw data appear in the appendix at the back of the report. Data should not be presented just for the sake of it – before working out and presenting the mean, median and mode, consideration should be given to whether they are all relevant. Tables and graphs are often used, these should be appropriately labelled. A brief explanation of what the summary descriptive statistics show follows.

Then the results of the statistical analysis should be stated. This should include:

- an explanation of which test(s) is being used and why
- details of the level of significance and the corresponding critical value including any N values or degrees of freedom and whether the hypothesis was one- or two-tailed
- the outcome in relation to the hypotheses stating whether results were significant and which hypothesis was supported.

(Where there is more than one experimental or research hypothesis, this needs to be done for each hypothesis in turn.)

Discussion: this should begin with a brief explanation of what the researcher has found, stating the implications for the proposed hypotheses. The results should then be discussed in the light of the background research where any peculiarities in results may be explored. The study should then be evaluated, which means considering in full any flaws which may have emerged with either the procedures or the apparatus/materials. The impact these may have had upon the results should be explored.

Any implications the research may have should then be considered. What does the research say (if anything) about the theory underlying the study?

The discussion should conclude with suggestions for further research. These may be modifications suggested to the present study in the light of limitations identified (for example a restricted sample), or it may be that the research has given rise to new ideas requiring further investigation.

References: a full list of all references used must be included. Where the researcher has referred to a particular study which has been cited in a textbook (but where he or she has not actually read the original report for that study), then this should be acknowledged, stating the book in which the study was cited. References should be listed in alphabetical order and contain the author(s), title, year, publisher and, if a journal article, the name of the journal, the volume and page numbers.

Appendices: these should contain all of the raw data and calculations for any statistical analysis. They should also include copies of materials used, such as standardised instructions or letters sent to participants.

For you to test the clarity of your own report, ask a non-psychologist who is unaware of your research interests to read it. Ask this person whether there is enough information contained for him or her to be able to repeat the study.

Writing up a report for non-experimental quantitative research

Common examples of this research include surveys and correlation research. Be clear about stating this, preferably in the title. If it is not an experiment, then do not say that it is. The format used when writing up such research is very similar to the format of the experiment. Appropriate modifications will be needed however, as suggested by Foster and Parker (1995). These include:

- defining the variables in the research – there is not an IV and a DV as in experimental research and they should not be described as such; simply refer to them as the 'research variables'
- defining the design – experimental designs (such as repeated measures) are not used, therefore do not describe your study as if they were used.

Writing up qualitative research

Foster and Parker (1995, pp. 203–4) provided some useful guidelines for producing a qualitative research report. These are summarised below. Again, the format is similar to that of the experimental research report, with changes mainly affecting the content of the different sections.

Abstract: this should specify the focus of the research, what was done to explore it further, what happened and what conclusions were drawn.

Introduction: this should include background research including that from quantitative studies. This is often relevant in terms of explaining the

researcher's preference for a qualitative approach. Where relevant research does not exist, this absence should be identified – but be sure that you have looked thoroughly. More time should be spent on reviewing the methodology to be used than in an experiment. This is because:

- qualitative approaches are relatively new and less is known about them
- it ensures that the researcher has thought through why a quantitative approach is not appropriate
- reflection upon methodology is crucial to the qualitative researcher and an integral part of the generation of meaning.

The method: as with experimental research the method should be explained in sufficient detail to enable replication. Not that results should be replicable, but that by employing the same methods additional information could be gained. The number of participants involved should be detailed, along with any other relevant information about the sample, including how it was selected.

Analysis: this section should be referred to as the analysis rather than the results to avoid giving the impression that the outcomes are an inevitable and immutable fact given the data. This acknowledges the role of the researcher in constructing interpretations of the data.

Where a structured analytical technique is used, the steps involved in this should be explained. Exactly how the researcher got from the raw data to the codes, categories or quotes you present should be detailed. Each stage of the analysis should be explained to enable the reader to understand how the ultimate interpretation of the data has been generated.

Discussion: two main tasks should be carried out here: (a) to link the research to the material presented in the introduction explaining how the research is similar to or departs from existing research; (b) to reflect upon the methodology, reviewing the processes engaged in in order to produce the report. This is a useful way of showing how the position of the researcher (for example his or her beliefs and expectations) played a part in the generation of the categories used. Reflecting upon the methodology is also a useful way of identifying gaps in the research which can be picked up in further studies.

Concluding comments

Regardless of the type of study conducted, there are a few practical points relevant to the writing up of all research:

- It is advisable to write up the research as soon as possible after data collection. This helps enormously with the discussion, where reflecting upon the research process is important. There is nothing worse than coming back to a set of data a few months later trying to remember exactly what the data represent and exactly what went on in the study.

- It is essential to respect the confidentiality of participants and make sure their identities are kept anonymous. If pupils from a school have taken part in your research for example, do not disclose the name of the school. If you have assessed job satisfaction of employees, do not disclose the name of the company or companies involved. If you are using quotations, ensure that the person saying them cannot be identified from what is said.

- Where possible try and use a wordprocessor. This makes inevitable corrections and revisions to the report a lot easier and is an essential tool of the qualitative researcher, due to the repetition of data involved. It also helps ensure that the final report is well presented and legible.

Unit summary

- *Quantitative data* can be analysed descriptively and inferentially. Often both are used.

- Two types of descriptive statistics often used are *measures of central tendency* (mean, median and the mode), and *measures of dispersion* (the range, variance and standard deviation).

- Statistics can also be described in picture form using histograms, bar charts, frequency polygons and scattergraphs.

- *Inferential statistics* involve the use of statistical tests to determine the strength of any relationships. Selecting the appropriate test depends upon whether the study is a correlation or an experiment; the type of data we have and the type of experimental design used.

- Additional criteria must be satisfied if a *parametric test* is used.

- The result of the statistical test must be interpreted to ascertain *significance*. A significant result means that it is unlikely that the results would have occurred by chance. The usual significance level of 5% means that we can be 95% sure that our results have not occurred by chance.

- A *type 1 error* is when we mistakenly accept the experimental hypothesis when what we have actually observed is the chance factor. These are more likely when we have a low significance level. A *type 2 error* is where we mistakenly reject the experimental hypothesis when there actually has been an effect. This is more likely when we set a high significance level (e.g. 1%).

- The analysis of *qualitative data* is used either as a supplement to quantitative data or as meaningful in its own right. The analysis of qualitative data may produce quantitative or qualitative representations of the data depending upon the approach of the researchers.

- Qualitative data is produced using a variety of methods and can take a variety of forms. Qualitative approaches to the analysis of qualitative data are often open ended, the main emphasis of which is the categorisation and coding of data. *Content analysis* is one technique which is used in reducing quantitative data to statistical representations.

Summary cont.

■ Contrary to popular belief the statistical analysis of data is not as difficult as it may first appear and the qualitative analysis of data is not as simple as it may first appear. Choosing qualitative analysis in order to avoid statistics is a mistake!

■ When writing up research it is advisable to use the *structured framework* commonly adopted in psychology journals. This framework will need adapting if the research is qualitative.

Terms to define

descriptive statistics
homogeneity of variance
interval data
mean
measures of central tendency
measures of dispersion
median
mode

nominal data
normal distribution curve
ordinal data
range
standard deviation (SD)
type 1 error
type 2 error
variance

Further reading

Clegg, F (1982) *Simple Statistics: A Course Book for the Social Sciences*, Cambridge University Press, Cambridge.

This is a simpler explanation of statistical analysis with the emphasis on 'user friendliness'.

Coolican, H (1994) *Research Methods and Statistics in Psychology*, 2nd edn, Hodder & Stoughton, London.

This text covers all you need to know and more about the statistical analysis of data. It provides detailed explanations of the concepts explained in this unit. Ideal for the student wanting to know more.

Foster, J J and Parker, I (1995) *Carrying Out Investigations in Psychology: Methods and Statistics*, BPS Books, Leicester.

This book provides good practical advice for conducting and writing up research. It is thorough and also accessible.

For conducting qualitative analyses students are advised to consult:

Banister, P, Burman, E, Parker, I, Taylor, N, Tindall, C (1994) *Qualitative methods in Psychology – A Research Guide*, Open University Press, Buckingham, Philadelphia.

Whilst the emphasis in this book is on qualitative methods rather than analysis, the inter-dependence of the two makes it a very useful guide to the conduct of qualitative research, as well as providing good references for qualitative analysis.

Denzin, N K and Lincoln, Y S (eds) (1998) *Strategies of Qualitative Enquiry*, Sage, London.

A very useful book containing chapters on different qualitative approaches from a variety of experts in the field.

Answers

■ Suggested answers to activities

1

    Set 1: mean = 9.6; median = 8; mode = none (all figures occur only once).

    Set 2: mean = 10.62; median = 9; mode = 3.

    Set 3: mean = 9.9; median = 10; mode = 14 and 6 (known as bi-modal).

2

a   Step 1: calculate the mean of the set of scores.

    Step 2: subtract each score from the mean to find the difference.

    Step 3: square each difference score obtained in step 2.

    Step 4: add the values from step 3 together and divide by the number of scores.

    Step 5: find the square root of step 4 – this is the standard deviation.

b   Step 1: 11 + 16 + 4 + 7 + 21 + 13 + 17 + 6 + 15 + 12

$$= \frac{122}{10} = 12.2$$

Step 2:		Step 3		
12.2 – 11	=	1.2 × 1.2	=	1.44
12.2 – 16	=	–3.8 × –3.8	=	14.44
12.2 – 4	=	8.2 × 8.2	=	67.24
12.2 – 7	=	5.2 × 5.2	=	27.04
12.2 – 21	=	–8.8 × –8.8	=	77.44
12.2 – 13	=	–0.8 × –0.8	=	0.64
12.2 – 17	=	–4.8 × –4.8	=	23.04
12.2 – 6	=	6.2 × 6.2	=	38.44
12.2 – 15	=	–3.2 × –3.2	=	10.24
12.2 – 12	=	0.2 × 0.2	=	0.04

    Step 4: total of step 3 = 260

    Step 5: square root of 260 = 16.125

    SD = 16.125

3

Table	
Related designs	**Unrelated designs**
Repeated measures	Independent groups
Matched pairs	
Correlations	

■ Suggested answers to self-assessment questions

1

The mean, median and mode relate to the typical scores in a data set.

The mean is found by totalling all the scores and dividing the total by the number of scores.

The median is found by ranking the scores and selecting that which falls in the middle of the data set.

The mode is the most frequent occurring score.

2

The variance takes account of each individual score, whereas the range only takes the two most extreme scores into consideration.

3

A large standard deviation indicates that the scores are spread out rather than being bunched closely around the mean.

4

A histogram displays the frequencies of a whole set of scores representing the pattern of distributions. Each column on a histogram is related to the one next to it as they represent measures along a continuous variable.

A bar chart can be used to represent selections of data and the columns are not related to each other in a continuous manner.

5

In order to select an appropriate statistical test, researchers should know whether they are looking for a difference or a correlation, the type of data they have, and whether the design is related or unrelated.

6

Data must be interval; sample must be selected from a normally distributed population; the sets of scores must have similar variances (known as homogeneity of variance).

7

A type 1 error is when the experimental hypothesis is accepted by mistake, i.e. there has not actually been an effect. A type 2 error is when the experimental hypothesis is rejected by mistake, i.e. when there has actually been an effect.

8

A type 1 error is more likely to be made because a lower significance level makes it easier to accept an experimental/research hypothesis.

9

Qualitative data can be used to either supplement quantitative data, or as meaningful in its own right.

10

The methods most likely to result in qualitative data include case studies, observations, interviews and questionnaires using open-ended questions.

11

The main aim of qualitative analysis is to reduce the data through the use of categorisation or coding.

12

Content analysis seeks to break down and represent data quantitatively in meaningful categories. The categories represent the meaning behind the message.

Procedures for statistical tests

On the following pages are step-by-step procedures for all of the statistical tests referred to on page 1049. An example is worked through to make it easier to follow. You are advised to write out your analysis in a similar step-by-step manner in order to avoid unnecessary confusion. The first process explained is how to rank numbers.

Ranking sets of scores

Ranking is necessary in order to find the median in a set of figures (see page 1041). It is also a necessary step in several of the statistical tests which follow. Whilst putting numbers in size order is relatively simple, if the set of numbers is large, then it can get confusing.

Example:

Rank the following set of figures: 13, 4, 9, 11, 15, 13, 5, 19, 13, 6, 19, 2, 24.

Step 1: count up the number of scores in the data set. These are the ranks the scores will have. Write the ranks out.

Number of scores = 13

Ranks: 1   2   3   4   5   6   7   8   9   10   11   12   13

Step 2: take the lowest number from the set of data and write it under rank 1. It will help to cross through the figure in the data set with a pencil. Then take the next lowest score putting this below rank 2.

Data: 13, 4, 9, 11, 15, 13, 5, 19, 13, 6, 19, 2, 24

1	2	3	4	5	6	7	8	9	10	11	12	13
2	4											

Step 3: continue this process until all the figures in the data set are listed under the appropriate ranked score.

1	2	3	4	5	6	7	8	9	10	11	12	13
2	4	5	6	9	11	13	13	13	15	15	19	24

This gives the appropriate rank for each score in the data. Where there are equal scores in the data, these share the same rank. The rank they are given is half-way between the scores that are the same.

1	2	3	4	5	6	7	8	9	10	11	12	13
2	4	5	6	9	11	13	13	13	15	15	19	24

There are three scores of 13. Each is given the rank score of 8. There are two scores of 15. These are each given the rank of 10.5. The final ranks given are shown opposite:

Rank:	1	2	3	4	5	6	8	8	8	10.5	10.5	12	13
Score:	2	4	5	6	9	11	13	13	13	15	15	19	24

The sign test

Used when:
- looking for a difference
- data are nominal
- design is related.

Example:

A study was conducted to assess the effect of playing classical music on anagram solving ability. It is expected that more anagrams will be solved whilst classical music is playing than when it is not playing.

Step 1: arrange the data in two columns next to each other. It does not matter which column of scores comes first. Then subtract each score in the second column from each score in the first column – record whether the answer is positive or negative in the sign column. (There is no need to record the actual figure.) If the two figures are equal, record a zero.

Participant	No music score	With music score	Sign
1	11	16	−
2	9	14	−
3	14	14	0
4	12	13	−
5	10	12	−
6	10	11	−
7	14	13	+
8	11	15	−

Step 2: count the number of times the less frequent sign occurs. This is known as S.

The plus signs are less frequent and occur once, so $S = 1$.

Step 3: count the total number of pluses and minuses to obtain N (ignore any zero scores).

There are seven signs in total, so $N = 7$.

Step 4: decide whether the hypothesis is one- or two-tailed and what level of significance is required.

Here the hypothesis is *one-tailed* and a *5 per cent level (0.05)* of significance is required.

Step 5: using the significance table (figure 29.15 overleaf), find the N figure in the first column. Then work across to the column which corresponds to the level of significance that has been selected – note that they differ for one- and two-tailed hypotheses. This gives the critical S value.

With an N of 7, and 0.05 level of significance for a one-tailed test, the *critical S value is 0.*

Step 6: state whether the S value is equal to or less than the critical S value obtained. If it is, then the result is significant. If it is not, then the result is not significant.

Here the S value obtained (1) is not equal to or less than the critical S value (0). Therefore, the result is not significant.

Step 7: state the conclusion in relation to the hypothesis.

In this example, the result of the analysis was non-significant. Therefore, the null hypothesis cannot be rejected. It is concluded that the playing of classical music has no effect on anagram solving ability.

Table 29.15

N	Level of significance for one-tailed test				
	0.05	0.025	0.01	0.005	0.0005
	Level of significance for two-tailed test				
	0.10	0.05	0.02	0.01	0.001
5	0	–	–	–	–
6	0	0	–	–	–
7	0	0	0	–	–
8	1	0	0	0	–
9	1	1	0	0	–
10	1	1	0	0	–
11	2	1	1	0	0
12	2	2	1	1	0
13	3	2	1	1	0
14	3	2	2	1	0
15	3	3	2	2	1
16	4	3	2	2	1
17	4	4	3	2	1
18	5	4	3	3	1
19	5	4	4	3	2
20	5	5	4	3	2
25	7	7	6	5	4
30	10	9	8	7	5
35	12	11	10	9	7

Critical values of S for the sign test (S must be *equal to or less than* the stated value to be significant)
Source: Clegg (1982).

Wilcoxon signed ranks test

Used when:
- looking for a difference
- data are ordinal
- design is related.

Example:

A study was conducted to see if playing classical music affected anagram solving ability. It is expected that more anagrams will be solved when classical music is played than when it isn't. (Note that the same data are used here as in the preceding sign test. Remember, data can be reduced to a simpler level – so, for the sign test the ordinal data was treated as nominal. When possible, it is preferable not to reduce the data to a simpler level. This enables more sensitive tests to be used which take account of all the information provided in the data.)

Step 1: arrange the data in two columns next to each other. It does not matter which column of scores comes first. Then subtract each score in the second column from each score in the first column – record your answer being careful to note the sign.

Participant	Control score	Research condition score	Difference	Rank
1	11	16	−5	6.5
2	9	14	−5	6.5
3	14	14	0	
4	12	13	−1	2
5	10	12	−2	4
6	10	11	−1	2
7	14	13	+1	2
8	11	15	−4	5

Step 2: rank the differences, ignoring the signs, giving the smallest difference rank 1. Do not rank any zeros. For clarity it may help to add the rank scores to the table as above.

Difference:	1	1	1	2	4	5	5
Rank:	1	2	3	4	5	6	7
Shared rank:		2				6.5	

Step 3: add the ranks for all the differences that are negative and all the differences that are positive.

Ranks for negative differences: 6.5 + 6.5 + 2 + 4 + 2 + 5 = 26
Ranks for positive differences: 2

Whichever of these totals is the smaller is known as T.

So, $T = 2$.

Step 4: count up the number of pairs of scores, ignoring any which had a difference score of 0. This is known as N.

There are eight pairs of scores but participant 3 had a difference score of 0.
Therefore, $N = 7$.

Step 5: decide whether the hypothesis is one- or two-tailed and what level of significance is required.

The hypothesis in this example is one-tailed and a 0.05 (5 per cent) level of significance is required.

Step 6: using the significance table (29.16 opposite), find the N figure in the first column. Then work across to the column which corresponds to the level of significance that has been selected – note that they differ for one- and two-tailed hypotheses. This gives the critical T value.

With an N of 7 and a 0.05 level of significance for a one-tailed test, this gives a *critical T value of 4.*

Step 7: is the T value obtained from the data equal to or less than the critical T value. If it is, then the result is significant; if it is not, then the result is not significant. State what this means in relation to the hypothesis.

In this example the obtained value of T = 2, which is less than the critical value of T which is 4. This means that the results are significant. The experimental hypothesis therefore is accepted and it can be concluded that anagram solving ability improves if classical music is played.

(Contrast this with the results obtained using the sign test on the same set of data. Whereas the results of the sign test were not significant, the results of the Wilcoxon test are significant. This is because the Wilcoxon test is more sensitive to any differences in the data and the fact that ordinal data provide us with more information to be able to pick up such differences.)

Mann-Whitney U test

Used when:
■ looking for a difference
■ data are ordinal
■ design is unrelated.

Example:

An experiment is conducted to assess the effects of categorisation on word recall. One group is given a list of words grouped in categories, the other group is given an uncategorised list. It is expected that categorisation will aid recall. Word recall in the two conditions is compared.

Step 1: put data in two columns with a gap between them.

Condition a	Condition b
categorised	*uncategorised*
18	13
22	17
23	20
27	14
28	11
23	10
20	16
17	9

Table 29.16

N	Level of significance for one-tailed test				N	Level of significance for one-tailed test			
	0.05	0.025	0.01	0.005		0.05	0.025	0.01	0.005
	Level of significance for two-tailed test					Level of significance for two-tailed test			
	0.10	0.05	0.02	0.01		0.10	0.05	0.02	0.01
5	1	–	–	–	28	130	117	101	92
6	2	1	–	–	29	141	127	111	100
7	4	2	0	–	30	152	137	120	109
8	6	4	2	0	31	163	148	130	118
9	8	6	3	2	32	175	159	141	128
10	11	8	5	3	33	188	171	151	138
11	14	11	7	5	34	201	183	162	149
12	17	14	10	7	35	214	195	174	160
13	21	17	13	10	36	228	208	186	171
14	26	21	16	13	37	242	222	198	183
15	30	25	20	16	38	256	235	211	195
16	36	30	24	19	39	271	250	224	208
17	41	35	28	23	40	287	264	238	221
18	47	40	33	28	41	303	279	252	234
19	54	46	38	32	42	319	295	267	248
20	60	52	43	37	43	336	311	281	262
21	68	59	49	43	44	353	327	297	277
22	75	66	56	49	45	371	343	313	292
23	83	73	62	55	46	389	361	329	307
24	92	81	69	61	47	408	379	345	323
25	101	90	77	68	48	427	397	362	339
26	110	98	85	76	49	446	415	380	356
27	120	107	93	84	50	466	434	398	373

Critical values of T for the Wilcoxon signed ranks test. (T must be *equal to or less than* the stated value to be significant)

Source: Wilcoxon and Wilcox (1964), p. 28, table 2.

Step 2: count the number of scores in each column to give Na and Nb. Then multiply these together – this gives NaNb.

Na = 8, Nb = 8; NaNb = $8 \times 8 = 64$

Step 3: take the number of scores in condition a and add 1.

$8 + 1 = 9$

Step 4: multiply the answer found in step 3 by the number of scores in condition a. Then divide by 2.

$9 \times 8 = 72$

$$\frac{72}{2} = 36$$

Step 5: rank all the numbers in both groups taking all the numbers together, giving the smallest score rank 1. Put the rank scores into the table on page 1067 next to the corresponding values.

Score:	9	10	11	13	14	16	17	17	18	20	20
Rank:	1	2	3	4	5	6	7	8	9	10	11

Score:	22	23	23	27	28
Rank:	12	13	14	15	16

Condition a	Rank	Condition b	Rank
18	9	13	4
22	12	17	7.5
23	13.5	20	10.5
27	15	14	5
28	16	11	3
23	13.5	10	2
20	10.5	16	6
17	7.5	9	1

Step 6: add all the ranks given to the items in condition a.

$9 + 12 + 13.5 + 15 + 16 + 13.5 + 10.5 + 7.5 = 97$

Step 7: add the value found in step 2 to the value found in step 4, and subtract the value found in step 6.

$64 + 36 = 100 - 97 = 3$.

Step 8: subtract the value of step 7 from the value of step 2.

$36 - 3 = 33$

Step 9: take the result of step 7 and the result of step 8. Whichever of these is smaller is known as U.

Result of step 7 = 3; result of step 8 = 33; therefore $U = 3$.

Step 10: find the critical value of U using the Mann-Whitney test tables (figures 29.17 and 29.18) and the Na and Nb figures from step 2. Where the Na and Nb columns intersect are the critical values. There are two values which relate to different levels of significance. In this example the value which is positioned lower will be the one that is required (this represents a 0.025 level for a one-tailed test and a .05 level for a two-tailed test).

Na = 8, Nb = 8 which generates a critical value of 13 (0.025 level for one-tailed hypothesis)

Step 11: state whether the result is significant. The obtained U must be equal to or less than the critical U. What does this mean in relation to the hypothesis?

Obtained U = 3; critical U = 13; therefore result is significant at 0.025 level.

The experimental hypothesis is therefore accepted and it can be concluded that recall of words when categorised is significantly better than when words are not categorised.

Table 29.17

Nb	1	2	3	4	5	6	7	8	9	10	11	12	13	14	15	16	17	18	19	20
Na																				
2	–	–	–	–	–	–	–	–	–	–	–	–	–	–	–	–	–	–	0	0
	–	–	–	–	–	–	–	0	0	0	0	1	1	1	1	1	2	2	2	2
3	–	–	–	–	–	–	–	–	0	0	0	1	1	1	2	2	2	2	3	3
	–	–	–	–	0	1	1	2	2	3	3	4	4	5	5	6	6	7	7	8
4	–	–	–	–	–	0	0	1	1	2	2	3	3	4	5	5	6	6	7	8
	–	–	–	0	1	2	3	4	4	5	6	7	8	9	10	11	11	12	13	14
5	–	–	–	–	0	1	1	2	3	4	5	6	7	7	8	9	10	11	12	13
	–	–	0	1	2	3	5	6	7	8	9	11	12	13	14	15	17	18	19	20
6	–	–	–	0	1	2	3	4	5	6	7	8	10	11	12	13	15	16	17	18
	–	–	1	2	3	5	6	8	10	11	13	14	16	17	19	21	22	24	25	27
7	–	–	–	0	1	3	4	6	7	9	10	12	13	15	16	18	19	21	22	24
	–	–	1	3	5	6	8	10	12	14	16	18	20	22	24	26	28	30	32	34
8	–	–	–	1	2	4	6	7	9	11	13	15	17	18	20	22	24	26	28	30
	–	0	2	4	6	8	10	13	15	17	19	22	24	26	29	31	34	36	38	41
9	–	–	0	1	3	5	7	9	11	13	16	18	20	22	24	27	29	31	33	36
	–	0	2	4	7	10	12	15	17	20	23	26	28	31	34	37	39	42	45	48
10	–	–	0	2	4	6	9	11	13	16	18	21	24	26	29	31	34	37	39	42
	–	0	3	5	8	11	14	17	20	23	26	29	33	36	39	42	45	48	52	55
11	–	–	0	2	5	7	10	13	16	18	21	24	27	30	33	36	39	42	45	48
	–	0	3	6	9	13	16	19	23	26	30	33	37	40	44	47	51	55	58	62
12	–	–	1	3	6	9	12	15	18	21	24	27	31	34	37	41	44	47	51	54
	–	1	4	7	11	14	18	22	26	29	33	37	41	45	49	53	57	61	65	69
13	–	–	1	3	7	10	13	17	20	24	27	31	34	38	42	45	49	53	57	60
	–	1	4	8	12	16	20	24	28	33	37	41	45	50	54	59	63	67	72	76
14	–	–	1	4	7	11	15	18	22	26	30	34	38	42	46	50	54	58	63	67
	–	1	5	9	13	17	22	26	31	36	40	45	50	55	59	64	69	74	78	83
15	–	–	2	5	8	12	16	20	24	29	33	37	42	46	51	55	60	64	69	73
	–	1	5	10	14	19	24	29	34	39	44	49	54	59	64	70	75	80	85	90
16	–	–	2	5	9	13	18	22	27	31	36	41	45	50	55	60	65	70	74	79
	–	1	6	11	15	21	26	31	37	42	47	53	59	64	70	75	81	86	92	98
17	–	–	2	6	10	15	19	24	29	34	39	44	49	54	60	65	70	75	81	86
	–	2	6	11	17	22	28	34	39	45	51	57	63	69	75	81	87	93	99	105
18	–	–	2	6	11	16	21	26	31	37	42	47	53	58	64	70	75	81	87	92
	–	2	7	12	18	24	30	36	42	48	55	61	67	74	80	86	93	99	106	112
19	–	0	3	7	12	17	22	28	33	39	45	51	57	63	69	74	81	87	93	99
	–	2	7	13	19	25	32	38	45	52	58	65	72	78	85	92	99	106	113	119
20	–	0	3	8	13	18	24	30	36	42	48	54	60	67	73	79	86	92	99	105
	–	2	8	14	20	27	34	41	48	55	62	69	76	83	90	98	105	112	119	127

Critical values of U for the Mann-Whitney test. For each value of Na and Nb there are two numbers. The top one is the value of U which *must not be exceeded* for significance at the 0.005 level for a one-tailed test (0.01, two-tailed test); the lower one gives the value for the 0.025 level for a one-tailed test (0.05, two-tailed)

Source: Snodgrass (1978), table C.7.

Table 29.18

N₁	1	2	3	4	5	6	7	8	9	10	11	12	13	14	15	16	17	18	19	20
N₂																				
1	–	–	–	–	–	–	–	–	–	–	–	–	–	–	–	–	–	–	0	0
2	–	–	–	–	0	0	0	1	1	1	1	2	2	2	3	3	3	4	4	4
3	–	–	0	0	1	2	2	3	3	4	5	5	6	7	7	8	9	9	10	11
4	–	–	0	1	2	3	4	5	6	7	8	9	10	11	12	14	15	16	17	18
5	–	0	1	2	4	5	6	8	9	11	12	13	15	16	18	19	20	22	23	25
6	–	0	2	3	5	7	8	10	12	14	16	17	19	21	23	25	26	28	30	32
7	–	0	2	4	6	8	11	13	15	17	19	21	24	26	28	30	33	35	37	39
8	–	1	3	5	8	10	13	15	18	20	23	26	28	31	33	36	39	41	44	47
9	–	1	3	6	9	12	15	18	21	24	27	30	33	36	39	42	45	48	51	54
10	–	1	4	7	11	14	17	20	24	27	31	34	37	41	44	48	51	55	58	62
11	–	1	5	8	12	16	19	23	27	31	34	38	42	46	50	54	57	61	65	69
12	–	2	5	9	13	17	21	26	30	34	38	42	47	51	55	60	64	68	72	77
13	–	2	6	10	15	19	24	28	33	37	42	47	51	56	61	65	70	75	80	84
14	–	2	7	11	16	21	26	31	36	41	46	51	56	61	66	71	77	82	87	92
15	–	3	7	12	18	23	28	33	39	44	50	55	61	66	72	77	83	88	94	100
16	–	3	8	14	19	25	30	36	42	48	54	60	65	71	77	83	89	95	101	107
17	–	3	9	15	20	26	33	39	45	51	57	64	70	77	83	89	96	102	109	115
18	–	4	9	16	22	28	35	41	48	55	61	68	75	82	88	95	102	109	116	123
19	0	4	10	17	23	30	37	44	51	58	65	72	80	87	94	101	109	116	123	130
20	0	4	11	18	25	32	39	47	54	62	69	77	84	92	100	107	115	123	130	138

Critical values of the Mann-Whitney U for a one-tailed test at .05 or a two-tailed test at .10
(Dashes indicate that no decision is possible at the stated level of significance.)

Source: Mann and Whitney (1947); and Auble (1953).

t test for related samples

Used when:
- looking for a difference
- design is related
- data are interval
- where sample is drawn from normally distributed population
- where there is homogeneity of variance between the sets of scores.

(These last two are necessary requirements for conducting a parametric test – see page 1049.)

Example:

An experiment investigates the effect of noise upon typing speed. Researchers do not know whether noise will improve typing speed or reduce it. Participants are matched in pairs for typing ability, and one of each pair is placed in each group. Both groups are asked to type a piece of text. The control group does this under quiet conditions, the experimental group under noisy conditions. The time it takes to complete the task is recorded below.

Pair no.	No noise	Noise
1	17	23
2	14	26
3	19	20
4	12	18
5	9	12
6	10	10
7	20	29
8	26	38

Step 1: count the number of scores involved. This value is called N.

There are 8 pairs of scores, so $N = 8$.

Step 2: subtract 1 from the value of N. This gives the degrees of freedom (df).

Degrees of freedom $= N - 1 = 8 - 1 = 7df$

Step 3: multiply the values of step 1 and step 2 together.

$8 \times 7 = 56$

Step 4: find the mean for each set of scores.

No noise: $17 + 14 + 19 + 12 + 9 + 10 + 20 + 26 \quad = \dfrac{127}{8} = 15.9$

Noise: $23 + 26 + 20 + 18 + 12 + 10 + 29 + 38 = \dfrac{176}{8} = 22$

Step 5: subtract the smaller of the two values found in step 4 from the larger.

$22 - 15.9 = 6.1$

Step 6: subtract each score in the second column from its partner in the first. Note the sign (+ or −).

17	−	23	=	−6
14	−	26	=	−12
19	−	20	=	−1
12	−	18	=	−6
9	−	12	=	−3
10	−	10	=	0
20	−	29	=	−9
26	−	38	=	−12

Step 7: square each difference found in step 6 and total the values.

$(-6)^2 + (-12)^2 + (-1)^2 + (-6)^2 + (-3)^2 + 0 + (-9)^2 + (-12)^2 = 36 + 144 + 1 + 36 + 9 + 81 + 144$
$= 451$

Step 8: add up the differences found in step 6, taking the sign into account.

$(-6) + (-12) + (-1) + (-6) + (-3) + 0 + (-9) + (-12) = -49$

Step 9: square the value found in step 8 and divide by N (step 1).

$$(-49) \times (-49) = \frac{2401}{8} = 300$$

Step 10: subtract the value found in step 9 from that found in step 7 and divide by the value found in step 3.

$$451 - 300 = \frac{151}{56} = 2.696$$

Step 11: take the square root of the value obtained in step 10.

$$\sqrt{2.697} = 1.641$$

Step 12: divide the value of step 5 by that found in step 11. This is known as t.

$$\frac{6.1}{1.641} = 3.72; \; t = 3.72$$

Step 13: find the significance using the table in figure 29.19 and the degrees freedom obtained in step 2. You must know whether the hypothesis is one- or two-tailed and the level of significance required. The obtained t value from the data must be greater than *the critical value of t given in the table in order for the result to be significant.*

With 7 degrees of freedom, the critical value of t for a two-tailed test at a 5 per cent level of significance = 2.365

Step 14: state the conclusion.

The obtained value of t is greater than the critical value, therefore results are significant. The experimental hypothesis can be accepted which states that noise has a significant effect upon typing speed.

t test for unrelated samples

Used when:
- looking for a difference
- design is unrelated
- data are interval
- the population from which the sample is drawn is normally distributed
- the two sets of scores have similar variances.

(These last two are the criteria for conducting a parametric test – see page 1049.)

Table 29.19

| | Level of significance for one-tailed test | | | | |
	0.05	0.025	0.01	0.005	0.0005
	Level of significance for two-tailed test				
df	0.10	0.05	0.02	0.01	0.001
1	6.314	12.71	31.82	63.66	636.6
2	2.920	4.303	6.969	9.925	31.6
3	2.353	3.182	4.541	5.841	12.92
4	2.132	2.776	3.747	4.604	8.610
5	2.015	2.571	3.365	4.032	6.869
6	1.943	2.447	3.143	3.707	5.959
7	1.895	2.365	2.998	3.499	5.408
8	1.860	2.306	2.896	3.355	5.041
9	1.833	2.262	2.821	3.250	4.781
10	1.812	2.228	2.764	3.169	4.587
11	1.796	2.201	2.718	3.106	4.437
12	1.782	2.179	2.681	3.055	4.318
13	1.771	2.160	2.650	3.012	4.221
14	1.761	2.145	2.624	2.977	4.140
15	1.753	2.131	2.602	2.947	4.073
16	1.746	2.120	2.583	2.921	4.015
17	1.740	2.110	2.567	2.898	3.965
18	1.734	2.101	2.552	2.878	3.922
19	1.729	2.093	2.539	2.861	3.883
20	1.725	2.086	2.528	2.845	3.850
21	1.721	2.080	2.518	2.831	3.819
22	1.717	2.074	2.508	2.819	3.792
23	1.714	2.069	2.500	2.807	3.767
24	1.711	2.064	2.492	2.797	3.745
25	1.708	2.060	2.485	2.787	3.725
26	1.706	2.056	2.479	2.779	3.707
27	1.703	2.052	2.473	2.771	3.690
28	1.701	2.048	2.467	2.763	3.674
29	1.699	2.045	2.462	2.756	3.659
30	1.697	2.042	2.457	2.750	3.646
40	1.684	2.021	2.423	2.704	3.551
60	1.671	2.000	2.390	2.660	3.460
120	1.658	1.980	2.358	2.617	3.372
240	1.645	1.960	2.326	2.576	3.291

Critical values of t. t must be *equal to or more than* the stated value to be significant

Source: Powell (1976), page 72.

Example:

Effect of presence of others on ability test performance was assessed. One group of participants completed the tests in a group setting, the other group of participants completed the tests alone. It is expected that performance will be better in the group condition than in the alone condition. The number of mistakes made by participants in each group was recorded.

Others present	Alone condition
3	4
5	2
2	7
2	8
6	7
1	3
4	5
2	6

Step 1: count the number of scores obtained in each set to obtain Na and Nb, then add the two together.

Na = 8; Nb = 8; 8 + 8 = 16

Step 2: multiply Na and Nb together. Then divide the value found in step 1 by this figure.

$8 \times 8 = 64; \dfrac{16}{64} = 0.15$

Step 3: add the scores in list a.

3 + 5 + 2 + 2 + 6 + 1 + 4 + 2 = 25

Step 4: square every score in Na and total all the squares.

$(3)^2 + (5)^2 + (2)^2 + (2)^2 + (6)^2 + (1)^2 + (4)^2 + (2)^2 = 9 + 25 + 4 + 4 + 36 + 1 + 16 + 4 = 99$

Step 5: square the value obtained in step 3 and then divide the result by the value of Na.

$\dfrac{(25)^2}{8} = \dfrac{625}{8} = 78.125$

Step 6: subtract the value found in step 5 from that of step 4.

99 – 78.125 = 20.875

Step 7: add the scores in list b.

4 + 2 + 7 + 8 + 7 + 3 + 5 + 6 = 42

Step 8: square each of the scores in list b and total them.

$(4)^2 + (2)^2 + (7)^2 + (8)^2 + (7)^2 + (3)^2 + (5)^2 + (6)^2 = 16 + 4 + 49 + 64 + 49 + 9 + 25 + 36 = 252$

Step 9: square the value obtained in step 7, then divide the result by the value of Nb (see step 1).

$$\frac{(42)}{8} = \frac{1764}{8} = 220.5$$

Step 10: subtract the value found in step 9 from that found in step 8.

$$252 - 220.5 = 31.5$$

Step 11: add together the values of step 6 and step 10.

$$20.875 + 31.5 = 52.375$$

Step 12: subtract 2 from the value of step 1. This gives the degrees of freedom (df).

$$16 - 2 = 14$$

Step 13: divide the value of step 11 by step 12. Then multiply the result by the value of step 2.

$$\frac{52.375}{14} = 3.74 \times 0.15 = 0.561$$

Step 14: take the square root of the value obtained in step 13.

$$\sqrt{0.561} = 0.748$$

Step 15: obtain the mean of list a (step 3 divided by Na), and the mean of list b (step 7 divided by Nb). Then subtract the smaller from the larger.

$$\frac{25}{8} = 3.15; \quad \frac{42}{8} = 5.25; \; 5.25 - 3.15 = 2.10$$

Step 16: divide the value of step 15 by that of step 14 to obtain t.

$$\frac{2.13}{0.748} = 2.85$$

Step 17: evaluate the significance of t using the table in figure 29.19 (page 1073) and the degrees of freedom obtained in step 12. The obtained t value must be greater than the critical value in the table to obtain significance. State the conclusions in relation to the hypothesis.

With 14 degrees of freedom, with a one-tailed test the critical value for 5 per cent level of significance is 1.761. The obtained t value of 2.85 is greater than the critical value, therefore the result is significant. The experimental hypothesis can be accepted and it may be concluded that completing ability tests whilst others are present significantly improves performance than when completing the tests alone.

Chi squared test

Used when:

■ data are nominal (i.e. numbers of people in different categories)
■ the entries in each cell are independent
■ the expected frequencies for each cell are not less than five.

Example:

A study was conducted to see if there was an association between age and whether people voted at the last election. Fifty people aged 30–35 and 50 people aged 25–30 were asked whether they did or did not vote at the last election. Responses are recorded below:

Step 1: plot the data into a large 2 × 2 table. The number in each cell is called the observed frequency. Obtain row and column totals and a grand total (N).

Table

	Column 1 did vote	Column 2 did not vote	Total
	cell a	cell b	
Row 1 30–35 years olds	28	22	50
	cell c	cell d	
Row 2 25–30 year olds	10	40	50
Total	38	62	100

Step 2: multiply the row 1 total with the column 1 total, and divide the answer by the overall total, (N). This gives the expected frequency for cell a. Do this for the remaining three cells.

Cell a: $\dfrac{50 \times 38}{100} = \dfrac{1900}{100} = 19$

Cell b: $\dfrac{50 \times 62}{100} = \dfrac{3100}{100} = 31$

Cell c: $\dfrac{50 \times 38}{100} = \dfrac{3100}{100} = 19$

Cell d: $\dfrac{50 \times 62}{100} = \dfrac{3100}{100} = 31$

Step 3: find the difference between each observed frequency and each expected frequency for each cell, always taking the smaller from the larger. Then for each cell value, subtract 0.5.

Cell a: 28 – 19 = 9 – 0.5 = 8.5
Cell b: 31 – 22 = 9 – 0.5 = 8.5
Cell c: 19 – 10 = 9 – 0.5 = 8.5
Cell d: 40 – 31 = 9 – 0.5 = 8.5

Step 4: square each of the cell values obtained in step 3 and divide the answer for the expected frequency for that particular cell.

Cell a: $\dfrac{(8.5)}{19}$ = 3.80

Cell b: $\dfrac{(8.5)}{31}$ = 2.33

Cell c: $\dfrac{(8.5)}{19}$ = 3.80

Cell d: $\dfrac{(8.5)}{31}$ = 2.33

Step 5: add together the four values obtained in step 4 to get chi squared.

3.8 + 2.33 + 3.8 + 2.33 = 12.26

Step 6: evaluate the value of chi squared using the table in figure 29.20 using the required level of significance depending on whether your hypothesis is one- or two-tailed. In a simple chi squared test the degrees of freedom (df) will always be 1.

Critical value at 0.05 level for one-tailed test is 2.706. The value obtained from the data must be *equal to or greater than* the critical value. The obtained chi squared is 12.26, therefore results are significant.

Step 7: state conclusion in relation to the hypothesis.

Results are significant at 0.05 level. The experimental hypothesis is accepted and it can be concluded that there is a significant association between age and whether people voted at the last election.

Complex chi squared test

Used when:
- looking for an association when there are more than two categories for the variables measured
- data are nominal (number of people falling in a particular category)
- entries in each cell must be independent
- expected frequencies for each cell must not be less than 5.

Table 29.20

df	Level of significance for one-tailed test			
	0.05	0.025	0.005	0.0005
	Level of significance for two-tailed test			
	0.1	0.05	0.01	0.001
1	2.706	3.841	6.635	10.83
2	4.605	5.991	9.210	13.82
3	6.251	7.815	11.34	16.27
4	7.779	9.488	13.28	18.47
5	9.236	11.07	15.09	20.52
6	10.64	12.59	16.81	22.46
7	12.02	14.07	18.48	24.32
8	13.36	15.51	20.09	26.12
9	14.68	16.92	21.67	27.88
10	15.99	18.31	23.21	29.59
11	17.28	19.68	24.73	31.26
12	18.55	21.03	26.22	32.91
13	19.81	22.36	27.69	34.53
14	21.06	23.68	29.14	36.12
15	22.31	25.00	30.58	37.70
16	23.54	26.30	32.00	39.25
17	24.77	27.59	33.41	40.79
18	25.99	28.87	34.81	42.31
19	27.20	30.14	36.19	43.82
20	28.41	31.41	37.57	45.31

Critical values of X^2. X^2 must be *equal to or more than* the stated value to be significant

Source: Powell (1976), p. 72.

Example:

Television viewing preferences of males and females were assessed. Participants had to indicate which category of TV programme they watched the most. The categories available were: sport; soaps; comedies; thrillers; documentaries. 50 girls took part and 170 boys. The results are recorded in the table below.

Table

	Sport	Soaps	Comedies	Thrillers	Documentaries	Totals
Boys	64	29	32	36	9	170
Girls	12	92	18	21	7	150
Totals	76	121	50	57	16	320

Step 1: put data into a table like that above. The figures in each cell are the observed frequencies. Add the totals for each row and each column as well as the grand total (i.e. 320 above). Be sure to leave enough space so that another number can be added to each cell later on.

Step 2: calculate the expected frequencies for each cell by taking the row total and the column total for each cell and multiplying them. This answer is then divided by the grand total, N.

row 1 × column 1: $\dfrac{170 \times 76}{320} = 40.375$

row 2 × column 1: $\dfrac{150 \times 76}{320} = 35.625$

row 1 × column 2: $\dfrac{170 \times 121}{320} = 64.281$

row 2 × column 2: $\dfrac{150 \times 121}{320} = 56.718$

row 1 × column 3: $\dfrac{170 \times 50}{320} = 26.562$

row 2 × column 3: $\dfrac{150 \times 50}{320} = 23.437$

row 1 × column 4: $\dfrac{170 \times 57}{320} = 30.281$

row 2 × column 4: $\dfrac{150 \times 57}{320} = 26.718$

row 1 × column 5: $\dfrac{170 \times 16}{320} = 8.5$

row 2 × column 5: $\dfrac{150 \times 16}{320} = 7.5$

Step 3: put each expected value from step 2 into the table below the appropriate obtained frequency. Check that they all exceed 4.

Table

	Sport	Soaps	Comedies	Thrillers	Documentaries	Total
Boys	64	29	32	36	9	170
	40.375	64.281	26.562	30.261	8.5	
Girls	12	92	18	21	7	150
	35.625	56.718	23.437	26.718	7.5	
Total	76	121	50	57	16	320

Step 4: for each cell find the difference between the obtained and the expected frequency by subtracting the smaller figure from the larger. This value is then squared and then divided by the expected frequency for that cell.

row 1, column 1: $\dfrac{(64 - 40.375)^2}{40.375} = \dfrac{558.14}{40.375} = 13.824$

row 2, column 1: $\dfrac{(35.625 - 12)^2}{35.625} = \dfrac{558.14}{35.625} = 15.667$

row 1, column 2: $\dfrac{(64.282 - 29)^2}{64.282} = \dfrac{1244.819}{64.282} = 19.365$

row 2, column 2: $\dfrac{(92 - 56.718)^2}{56.718} = \dfrac{1244.819}{56.718} = 21.948$

row 1, column 3: $\dfrac{(32 - 26.562)^2}{26.562} = \dfrac{29.572}{26.562} = 1.113$

row 2, column 3: $\dfrac{(23.437 - 18)^2}{23.437} = \dfrac{29.560}{23.437} = 1.261$

row 1, column 4: $\dfrac{(36 - 30.261)^2}{30.261} = \dfrac{32.936}{30.261} = 1.088$

row 2, column 4: $\dfrac{(26.718 - 21)^2}{26.718} = \dfrac{32.695}{26.718} = 1.224$

row 1, column 5: $\dfrac{(9 - 8.5)^2}{8.5} = \dfrac{0.25}{8.5} = 0.029$

row 2, column 5: $\dfrac{(7.5 - 7)^2}{7.5} = \dfrac{0.25}{7.5} = 0.033$

Step 5: add up all the values found in step 4. This gives you the value of chi squared.

13.824 + 15.667 (etc.) + 0.029 + 0.033 = 75.552

Step 6: obtain the degrees of freedom (df) needed to evaluate chi squared. It will always be the number of rows minus 1 multiplied by the number of columns minus 1.

$(2 - 1) \times (5 - 1) = 1 \times 4 = 4$, so *df = 4*

Step 7: use the table in figure 29.20 (page 1078) to evaluate the significance of the chi squared value obtained. The value obtained must be equal to or exceed the critical value in the table for the required level of significance.

For a two-tailed test the critical value is 9.488 (0.05 level at 4 df). The obtained value (75.552) exceeds this. The result is therefore significant.

Step 8: state the conclusion.

Television viewing preferences were assessed according to gender and analysed using a chi squared test. The value of chi squared was found to be significant at 0.05 level for a two-tailed test. It can be concluded therefore that males and females prefer to watch different types of TV programmes.

   Note: this test only indicates that the distributions of the groups have different shapes. The researcher has to decide how the shapes differ and where the most substantial discrepancies lie by inspecting the data.

Spearman's Rho

Used when:
- looking for a correlation
- data are ordinal.

Example:

Number or hours spent revising and exam marks obtained. A positive correlation is expected. Results for ten students were taken and are recorded below:

Student	Hours revising	Exam mark
1	16	81
2	4	54
3	14	79
4	10	59
5	3	32
6	12	73
7	13	76
8	9	42
9	10	67
10	8	64

Step 1: draw a scattergraph for the two sets of scores, the vertical axis measuring one variable, the horizontal axis measuring the other.

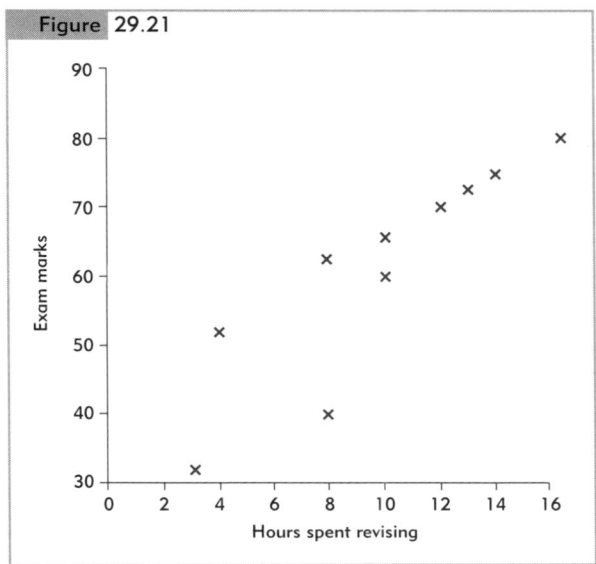

Figure 29.21

Step 2: now cast the data into a table with seven columns. These will be:

P   the label for each participant or source of paired scores
A   the scores on one variable
B   the scores on the other variable

Ra   the scores from a given ranks
Rb   the scores from b given ranks
D   each value in list Rb subtracted from its partner in Ra
D^2 each value in D squared.

Table 29.22

P	A	B	Ra	Rb	D	D^2
1	16	81	10	10	0	0
2	4	54	2	3	−1	1
3	14	79	9	9	0	0
4	10	59	5.5	4	1.5	2.25
5	3	32	1	1	0	0
6	12	73	7	7	0	0
7	13	76	8	8	0	0
8	9	42	4	2	2	4
9	10	67	5.5	6	−0.5	0.25
10	8	64	3	5	−2	4

Step 3: count the number of paired scores in the sample to obtain N.

There are ten pairs of scores. N = 10

Step 4:   multiply N by its own value twice, then subtract its own value.

$(10 \times 10 \times 10) - 10 = 1000 - 10 = 990$

Step 5: total the values in column D^2.

Total = 11.5

Step 6: multiply the value found in step 5 by the number 6. Then divide the result by the value found in step 4.

$$\frac{11.5 \times 6}{990} = \frac{69}{990} = 0.069$$

Step 7: subtract the value of step 6 from the number 1. Retain the sign. The result should always lie between −1 and +1. This is known as rho. A positive sign indicates a positive correlation, a negative sign a negative correlation.

$1 - 0.069 = 0.931$

Step 8: evaluate the significance of rho using the table in figure 29.23. Find the critical value of rho using the N value and the desired level of significance. The obtained value of rho must be equal to or more than the critical value.

With a N of 10, the critical value of rho for a one-tailed test at 0.05 level of significance is 0.564. The obtained value is more than the critical value, therefore the result is significant (p = 0.05) and the experimental hypothesis can be accepted.

Step 9: state the conclusion.

Results were significant at 0.05 level for a one-tailed test showing that there was a significant positive association between the number of hours spent studying and exam marks obtained.

Table 29.23

	Level of significance for one-tailed test			
	0.05	0.025	0.01	0.005
	Level of significance for a two-tailed test			
N	0.1	0.05	0.02	0.01
5	0.900	1.000	1.000	–
6	0.829	0.886	0.943	1.000
7	0.714	0.786	0.893	0.929
8	0.643	0.738	0.833	0.881
9	0.600	0.683	0.783	0.833
10	0.564	0.648	0.746	0.794
12	0.506	0.591	0.712	0.777
14	0.456	0.544	0.645	0.715
16	0.425	0.506	0.601	0.665
18	0.399	0.475	0.564	0.625
20	0.377	0.450	0.534	0.591
22	0.359	0.428	0.508	0.562
24	0.343	0.409	0.485	0.537
26	0.329	0.392	0.465	0.515
28	0.317	0.377	0.448	0.496
30	0.306	0.364	0.432	0.478

Critical values of Spearman's rho. Rho must be *equal to or more than* the stated value to be significant. (Treat a negative value of rho as if it were positive, when using the table, but when interpreting it, do not forget that it will indicate an *inverse* relationship.)

Source: Snodgrass (1978), table C.6.

Pearson's product moment correlation

Used when:
- looking for a correlation
- data are interval
- the relationship is linear, shown by a scattergram
- scores are from a normally distributed population
- scores have similar variances.

Example:

It is expected that time taken to consume a meal varies according to how long it is since the last meal was eaten. A negative correlation is predicted – the longer it has been since the last meal was eaten, then the quicker the 'test meal' will be consumed.

Participant	Time since last meal (hrs)	Time taken to eat test meal (mins)
1	1	19
2	16	3
3	4	10
4	3	20
5	10	4
6	8	6
7	12	4
8	6	7

Step 1: draw a scattergram for the two sets of data, the vertical axis measuring one variable, the horizontal axis measuring the other. Check that the relationship is linear.

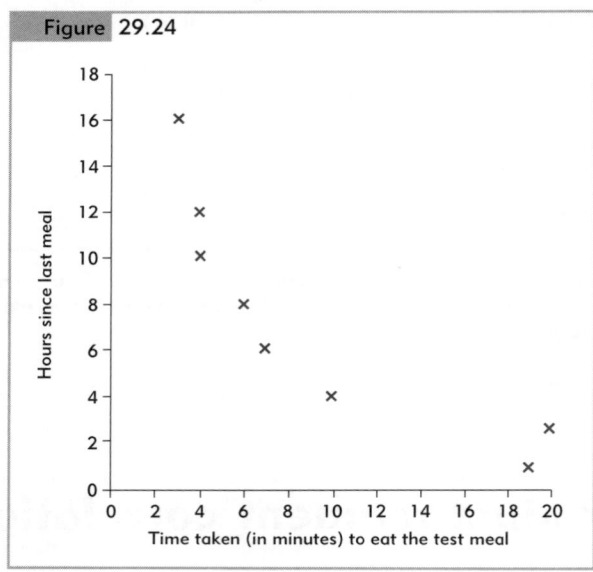

Figure 29.24

Step 2: put the data into a table with six columns where:

P   the participants or the source of each pair of scores
A   the scores on one variable
A^2 each A score squared
B   the scores on the second variable
B^2 each B score squared
AB   each A score multiplied by its matching B score.

Table 29.25

Participant	A	A²	B	B²	AB
1	1	1	19	361	19
2	16	256	3	9	48
3	4	16	10	100	40
4	3	9	20	400	60
5	10	100	4	16	40
6	8	64	6	36	48
7	12	144	4	16	48
8	6	36	7	49	42
Total	60	626	73	987	345

Step 3: count the number of scores which are paired off to get N.

There are ten pairs of scores. N = 10

Step 4: multiply the total of the column for A² by N.

$626 \times 10 = 6260$

Step 5: square the total of column A.

$(60)^2 = 3600$

Step 6: subtract the value of step 5 from that found in step 4.

$6260 - 3600 = 2660$

Step 7: multiply the total of column B² by N.

$987 \times 10 = 9870$

Step 8: square the total of column B.

$(73)^2 = 5329$

Step 9: subtract the value of step 8 from the value found in step 7.

$9870 - 5329 = 4541$

Step 10: multiply together the values obtained in step 6 and step 9.

$2660 \times 4541 = 12\ 079\ 060$

Step 11: take the square root of the value in step 10.

$\sqrt{12\ 079\ 060} = 3475.49$

Step 12: multiply the total of column AB by N.

$345 \times 10 = 3450$

Step 13: multiply together the totals for the columns A and B.

$60 \times 73 = 4380$

Step 14: subtract the value of step 13 from that of step 12 making sure the appropriate sign is retained.

$3450 - 4380 = -930$

Step 15: divide the value of step 14 by the value of step 11. This is known as r.

$$\frac{-930}{3475.49} = -0.26758$$

Step 16: evaluate the significance of r. First obtain the value of N – 2, then obtain the critical value for the required level of significance (figure 29.26) and whether your hypothesis is one- or two-tailed. The obtained value must be equal to or more than the critical value. (Ignore the sign.)

$N - 2 = 10 - 2 = 8$

Critical value of one-tailed test at 0.05 level = 0.549.

Obtained value r = −0.26758.

Results are therefore not significant and the null hypothesis cannot be rejected.

Step 17: state the conclusion.

No significant relationship was found between the time taken to consume a meal and the length of time since participants consumed their last meal. (The sign indicates the direction of any relationship, which in this case was negative, although the relationship was not strong enough to be significant.)

Table 29.26

	Level of significance for one-tailed test			
	0.05	0.025	0.005	0.0005
	Level of significance for two-tailed test			
N − 2	0.10	0.05	0.01	0.001
2	0.9000	0.9500	0.9900	0.9999
3	0.805	0.878	0.9587	0.9911
4	0.729	0.811	0.9172	0.9741
5	0.669	0.754	0.875	0.9509
6	0.621	0.707	0.834	0.9241
7	0.582	0.666	0.798	0.898
8	0.549	0.632	0.765	0.872
9	0.521	0.602	0.735	0.847
10	0.497	0.576	0.708	0.823
11	0.476	0.553	0.684	0.801
12	0.457	0.532	0.661	0.780
13	0.441	0.514	0.641	0.760
14	0.426	0.497	0.623	0.742
15	0.412	0.482	0.606	0.725
16	0.400	0.468	0.590	0.708
17	0.389	0.456	0.575	0.693
18	0.378	0.444	0.561	0.679
19	0.369	0.433	0.549	0.665
20	0.360	0.423	0.537	0.652
25	0.323	0.381	0.487	0.597
30	0.296	0.349	0.449	0.554
35	0.275	0.325	0.418	0.519
40	0.257	0.304	0.393	0.490
45	0.243	0.288	0.372	0.465
50	0.231	0.273	0.354	0.443
60	0.211	0.250	0.325	0.408
70	0.195	0.232	0.302	0.380
80	0.183	0.217	0.283	0.357
90	0.173	0.205	0.267	0.338
100	0.164	0.195	0.254	0.321

Critical values of Pearson's r. r must be *equal to or more than* the stated value to be significant

Source: Powell (1976), p. 72.

Glossary

absolute refractory period period immediately after the cell fires during which no impulse is possible, regardless of stimulus strength

accommodation according to Piaget it is that part of the adaptation process by which an idividual modifies an existing scheme to incorporate or adapt to new experiences; may involve the creation of new schemes if the old one cannot handle the new information

activity theory also known as the *personal growth model*, first proposed by Havighurst, whose research supported the view that the needs of the elderly are the same as those of middle age – more satisfaction with social activity

actor-observer effect attribution of our own behaviour to situational causes but others' behaviour to internal causes

addiction the user seeks out and uses the drug with increasing frequency

adolescence period between childhood and adulthood when a number of important physical, social, intellectual and emotional changes take place

aetiology the cause of a disorder

affectionless psychopathy term coined by Bowlby to describe later behaviour of the child (including delinquency, mental illness and intellectual retardation), seen to be caused by the lack of early bonding with the mother figure

affiliation always has positive connotations; involves associations or relationships bringing usually cooperative contact between people

ageism negative discrimination against the elderly

agentic state in this state people see themselves acting as agents on behalf of another

aggression action where the direct purpose is to cause injury, damage or harm to another person

agoraphobia anxiety disorder characterised by a fear of being in situations from which it is impossible to escape, for example agoraphobics avoid crowds, enclosed spaces or open spaces

algorithmic thinking systematic method of solving problems that will lead to a correct solution; algorithms reduce error until the desired goal is reached, but they are not always the most efficient way of problem solving

alternative hypothesis hypothesis which predicts there will be an effect on a relationship between different variables

altricial immature and dependent at birth

altruism acting in the interests of others at some (or all) cost to oneself

Alzheimer's disease form of dementia affecting about three per cent of the population over the age of 65, and about ten per cent over the age of 85, distinguished by symptoms such as loss of memory and confusion. Resulting from progressive damage to neural tissue and deficit in the neurotransmitter acetylcholine

amnesia loss of memory, or forgetfulness, usually as the result of a physical cause, for example as in Korsakoff's syndrome which is caused by long-term alcoholism

anchoring the way in which we use one item of information to compare with other judgements

androgynous term used by Bem (1975, 1983) to describe individuals who develop both masculine and feminine characteristics, such as toughness and warmth, yet still function effectively, and seem to be psychologically well adjusted, with higher self-esteem, than individuals rigidly typed as masculine or feminine

animism referring to inanimate objects as if they are alive

anisogamy where one sex produces a much larger gamete than the other (thus the female egg contains the essentials for early growth and development, and the male sperm, DNA only)

anthropocentric assumption that humans are at the centre of things and are the standard against which non-humans are compared

anthropomorphism attributing animals with characteristics which may be specific to humans

anti-conformity occurs when an individual opposes the group majority on all occasions without any sense of independence

anti-social behaviour a generic term for any behaviour that harms or offends another person, e.g. aggression

anxiety feeling of fear that may be related to a specified object, accompanied by increased physiological arousal

aphasia disorder of speech; people have difficulty articulating speech, although they can understand language; associated with problems in Broca's area of the cortex

armchair adaptationist someone who explains behaviour in terms of evolution without testing this objectively

artificial selection where human beings breed only from animals with desired traits

assimilation that part of the adaptation process, according to Piaget, which involves incorporating new experiences into the existing scheme

assumed university assumption that psychology and the scientific method is relevant to and should be accepted universally by all

attachment an enduring emotional bond infants form with specific people such as mother or carer

attenuator model Anne Treisman's model of focused attention, by which a signal can be weakened as it is being processed

attraction tendency to be drawn towards a person that we find pleasing or interesting – someone that induces positive affect

attribution process whereby we make judgements of others based on our perception of their actions

authoritarian parenting child rearing distinguished by a high level of control and parental expectations, but low on nurturance and communication

authoritative parenting style of child rearing distinguished by a high level of control, parental expectation, and also high on nurturance and communication

autocratic leader gives orders, discourages communication or participation of group

auto-immune diseases the immune system becomes sensitised to a protein in the body and the system attacks the tissue containing this protein (it attacks its own cells)

automatic processing or automaticity processing which does not require conscious effort or attention; usually develops as a result of practice

autonomic nervous system (ANS) the part of the peripheral nervous system controlling the bodily processes not normally under voluntary control. Two sub-systems are involved: the sympathetic nervous system and the parasympathetic nervous system

autonomous state in this state individuals act according to their own values and ideals

aversion therapy form of behaviour therapy which aims to remove undesired behaviours by pairing them with unpleasant stimuli, such as electric shocks or nausea

baby talk register (BTR) style of speech adopted by adults when talking to a baby, characterised by simple, short sentences and repetition

Batesian mimicry where edible insects mimic the colour of a poisonous or unpleasant tasting insect (and so avoid being eaten)

behaviour therapies group of therapies based on behaviourist principles that abnormal behaviour is learned and can be treated by changing the learned responses

behaviourism approach to psychology which focuses on the study of directly observable behaviour

behaviourist model theoretical approach which emphasises the effect of the environment on behaviour

biomedical model theoretical approach which claims that mental disorders are illnesses caused by germs, genetics, faulty biochemistry or faulty brain anatomy

blindsight the ability of people who are cortically blind to perform visually mediated tasks without conscious awareness

blobs neurons in peg-like, dual-opponent colour columns in the primary visual cortex, except for lower layer IV

Borna Disease Virus (BDV) virus that may be implicated in depression

British Psychological Society (BPS) professional body representing psychologists in the UK which appropriately qualified psychologists can join

buffering effect/hypothesis social network/support/relationships are used to protect a person from ill mental health when stressful experiences arise

bystander behaviour also known as bystander effect or apathy – the unwillingness of people witnessing an emergency to become involved in events

carpentered world hypothesis an environment of many straight lines and right angles, characteristic of the buildings of modern society. Such an environment may be responsible for some differences in visual perception, according to theorists such as Richard Gregory

catecholamine hypothesis theory that increased levels of the neurotransmitter epinephrine (adrenaline) produce mania and decreased levels cause depression

categorical self sometimes equated with the self-image, whereby the child defines the self by placing herself in a number of categories

catharsis the indirect release of aggression

circadian rhythms diurnal (daily) cycles of body function

client-centred therapy form of positive therapy developed by Carl Rogers whereby clients talk through their problems with a non-directive and reflective therapist. The client is seen to be the expert on his or her problems and can work them out in a non-judgemental atmosphere

closed questions used in self-report techniques; involve a high degree of structure, usually requesting the respondent to select an answer from a predetermined set which can then be easily coded

cognitive restructuring reducing stress by cognitive coping, such as changing problems into challenges

cognitive therapies group of psychotherapies which are based on the idea that abnormal behaviour is a result of distorted thinking. The aim of the therapies is to change patterns of thought

cognitive triad Beck's theory of depression – a set of negative thoughts that characterise depressives

collective unconscious term used by Jung to describe the memory traces from past generations

community care providing care for the mentally ill in the local community as opposed to large psychiatric hospitals

comparative psychology a branch of psychology based upon the study of different species for the purpose of drawing comparisons with humans

compliance involves giving in to another person but private views are still held; seldom results in permanent behavioural change

concordance when both twins have the same disorder, they are said to be concordant for that disorder

conformity tendency to yield to other or group pressure

confounding variable variable, other than the independent variable, which actually *does affect* the dependent variable

consciousness the way we monitor ourselves and our environment and accurately represent these in awareness

conservation the Piagetian concept that objects remain the same even though the appearance may have changed

conspecific another member of the same species

constancy perception of the world as constant, despite changes to the retinal image

constructivist theory this theory suggests knowledge we already have affects our perception of what we expect things to look like. This top-down processing happens as expectations we have about the world, work downwards to influence the sensory input. Constructivist theory is also referred to as top-down, or concept driven processing

content analysis an indirect observational technique for analysing the content of documents

contiguity view that if two stimuli are to become associated, they need to occur close together in time

contingency model (of leadership) links factors relating to the situation with the leader's and the followers' personalities

cooperation behaviour where animals collaborate to achieve an end, such as obtaining food or rearing young

correlation co-efficient the statistical representation of the strength of a correlational relationship; can range from −1, (indicating a negative correlation) to +1 (indicating a positive correlation) − the closer the figure is to 1 (plus or minus), then the stronger the relationship (a value of zero indicates no relationship)

correlations (positive, negative, curvi-linear) existence of a relationship (not necessarily causal) between two or more variable: positive correlation − as one variable increases, then so does the other; negative correlation − as one variable increases, the other decreases; curvi-linear correlation − where one variable increases in relation to another variable *up to a certain point*, after which that variable *decreases* in relation to the other

correspondent inference theory an attribution theory which attempts to explain how we use others' behaviour as a basis for inferring their established dispositions

cortex the thin (*c.*3mm) outer layer of neural tissue covering the cerebrum

counterbalancing attempt to control order effects where half of the participants are exposed to condition A followed by condition B, and the other half are exposed to condition B followed by condition A, thus controlling any unwanted effect

covariation if two events occur together repeatedly, then cause is more likely to be inferred than if they occur together rarely

critical period a biologically predetermined time during which, if no specific responses are acquired, they never will be

cross-sectional studies comparison study comparing different groups at the same point in time

CT (computed tomography) computerised X-ray procedures used to visualize the brain and other parts of the living body

cults quasi-religious organisations using devious psychological techniques to gain and control followers

cultural identity seeks to explain how membership of one's culture affects how one behaves towards and perceives one's own cultural group members and those of other cultures

cultural 'lenses' a term coined by Sandra Bem to describe how we are biased by the culture in which we live − these are used unconsciously and we view social reality through these transparent, invisible lenses

culture there is no commonly agreed definition but it can be seen as a system of meanings and customs shared by an identifiable group, and transmitted from one generation to the next. Socially transmitted knowledge

data mining sifting through existing mountains of data to come up with relevant new findings

deductive reasoning form of reasoning where conclusions can be drawn from statements that are made, assuming the statements are true; syllogistic reasoning where conclusions are drawn from premises is based on deductive reasoning

defense mechanisms techniques identified by Freud by which the ego keeps threatening material out of the conscious mind

delusion a false belief that a person refuses to relinquish despite evidence to the contrary

democratic leader helps group to plan, concerned with welfare and participation of group members

dendrites receive impulses from the terminal buttons of other neurons

dependent variable (DV) variable which is measured in experimental designs to see if the IV has had an effect

descriptive norms describe how most people behave in a given situation

descriptive statistics statistical representations of data which provide summary descriptions of the data, e.g. graphs, tables

design features features identified by Hockett as typifying language

determinism view that behaviour is caused and occurs in a predictable sequence − it is not a result of individual choice

diagnosis classifying and labelling a person's problem using a specified classification scheme

dichotic listening task task used in attention where one message is presented to one ear and another massage is presented to the other ear

discovery learning Piagetian emphasis on children learning from their own experiences (active learning) rather than being given information directly from others, this takes into account the child's readiness to learn

discrimination negative behaviour expressed from the basis of a prejudice

divided attention task where participants are asked to perform two or more tasks at the same time

dopamine hypothesis theory that schizophrenia is the result of excessive amounts of the neurotransmitter dopamine

double blind neither the participants nor the experimenter know who is exposed to the experimental condition

double-bind communication a situation in which a parent gives contradictory messages to the child (it was thought to be a cause of schizophrenia)

dreams images, thoughts and feelings experienced during sleep, mostly in REM sleep

dual coding hypothesis a memory trace is encoded twice, once verbally and once visually. The hypothesis was put forward by Paivio (1971)

dyslexia special difficulties in interpreting words, letters or in learning to read; can be a developmental disorder or acquired as a result of brain trauma

ecological niche the precise requirements of a species in terms of food and shelter

ecological theory this requires organisms to be considered within their ecological setting. In Gibson's direct theory of perception, the emphasis is on direct contact between an animal's senses and the important features of its environment. Perception occurs as a result of the animal's registration of the sensory features of its environment

ecological validity extent to which a study situation is representative of reality

egocentrism being in a cognitive state, described by Piaget, in which the child sees the world only from his/her own perspective, without awareness of other perspectives

ego-ideal Freudian term describing part of the superego, this is seen as the internalisation of parental moral standards and promises ego rewards, such as pride and self-esteem for acting in a moral way

ego-integrity last stage of life, regarded by Erikson to be a conflict between ego-integrity and despair. Integrity is seen as the recognition by the elderly person that life has had meaning and purpose and acceptance of their own mortality. An acceptance of the good and bad experiences in life from which we achieve psychological growth and value

electro convulsive therapy (ECT) brief electrical shock applied to the head/brain, resulting in an electrical seizure. Used therapeutically for severe depression

emotions different arousal levels experienced as different feelings

empathy an understanding and awareness of the emotions and feelings of other

empiricist view that abilities and psychological attributes are the result of experience (equivalent to 'nurture')

encoding specificity principle a memory trace is stored in an episodic context, hence using context cues helps to retrieve the trace

endocrine glands glands which secrete chemicals known as hormones into the bloodstream, so they reach every cell in the body

epideictic term used for behaviour where birds mass together in flocks to facilitate population estimation

epiphenomenalism consciousness is merely a by-product of a complex neurological system

episodic memory memory for events in our own lives, for example our own birthday

equilibration part of the adaptation process, described by Piaget, whereby a state of equilibrium or balance is achieved through assimilation and accommodation, and the individual incorporates the effects of the external world and thinking processes. This is essential for cognitive development, and is based on the notion of a natural balance between the individual and the world

erogenous zones according to Freud's theory these pleasure centres become the focus of the child's attention during various stages of development

ethics concerned with the acceptability of human behaviour, with right and wrong, with what is good and bad behaviour

ethnocentric inability to imagine or understand the social beliefs, ideas or the world from any viewpoint other than one's own culture or social group

ethology influenced by zoology, biology and comparative psychology, it is the study of animals in their natural environments in an attempt to establish the genetic and environmental influences on behaviour

eurocentric view that Europe is at the centre of psychological theory and sets the standard against which others are measured

existential self understanding of one's existence ('I exist') which develops during the first few months of life, from the early interaction of the infant with objects and carers, a more subjective self emerges later (c. 9–12 months)

existentialist the individual operates on the basis of free will unconstrained by society or social groups

experimental hypothesis hypothesis which predicts there will be a difference between the experimental and the control conditions caused by the manipulation of the independent variable (also known as the alternative hypothesis)

experimenter expectancy the expectations of the experimenter influence the outcomes in the expected direction

explicit memory memory where there is awareness of remembering

expressed emotion (EE) a measure of close relatives' criticism and emotional over-involvement when relating to schizophrenics

extraneous variable variable, other than the independent variable, which can potentially affect the dependent variable

extrapolation assumption that patterns of behaviour observed in animals can be generalised to humans

falsificationist theory theory proposed by Karl Popper suggesting that the hallmark of good science is that it is open to being proved wrong – when this happens, the theory is rejected and another, with greater explanatory power, is proposed

family therapy form of group therapy in which members of the same family make up group rather than treatment of the individual alone

faulty heuristics heuristics provide simple cues to help us deal with too much information; advertisers exploit this by suggesting products have qualities which they actually do not – these qualities become the heuristic cue to selection of a product

feature detection theory theory of pattern recognition in which it is suggested the distinctive parts of the object are extracted at an early stage in perception

feature integration theory (Anne Treisman) where visual perception requires focused attention to combine features of the object

field experiment experiment conducted in the natural setting, rather than in the laboratory – intervention and control are still exerted through randomisation

fitness capacity to survive and reproduce

flooding therapy based on classical conditioning in which the patient is exposed to the feared stimulus or situation

focal theory Coleman's research found that adolescents confront and come to terms with only one conflict at a time and in this way adjust to potentially stressful events relatively easily

free association psychoanalytic technique of recovering unconscious conflicts in which the patient is encouraged to say whatever comes into his or her mind

free will behaviour is under the control of the individual who has the freedom to choose how to behave

functional fixedness difficulty people have in problem solving when they focus on the usual uses for objects and ignore more unusual possibilities which provide the solution

fundamental attribution error tendency to overestimate the attribution of others' behaviour to dispositional causes (personal characteristics)

gender constancy the knowledge that we have our gender identity for life, it will not change (the final step in developing a gender concept)

gender identity involves labelling oneself as male or female and categorizing others in the same way (the first step in gender concept development)

gender roles the lifestyle adopted by adolescence, including attitudes, behaviours, interests, and occupational choices related to our gender

general adaptation syndrome (GAS) universal stress response involving three stages: alarm, resistance and exhaustion

general problem solver (GPS) computer program, devised by Newell and Simon (1972), which uses heuristics to tackle specific problems

generation gap phrase coined to describe the conflict occurring between generations, when adolescents try to break away from family ties and become independent, seen to be overestimated by traditional theorists

generational effects impact any treatment or behaviour may have upon members of the next generation of that species

genetic variation individual members of a species vary slightly in their genetic composition and thus have slightly different physical or behavioural traits

genital stage in Freudian theory it is the fifth stage in development when he adolescent finds pleasure in heterosexual relationships

genotype genes that an organism inherits (the 'recipe' for development – see also phenotype)

Gestalt psychology was popular in the first half of the twentieth century in Europe. It emphasises the holistic nature of people's experience. The theory suggests there are parts of perception, memory and learning that can only be understood by following the principle that 'the whole is greater than the parts'

goals when associated with relationships: the objectives to be met from a relationship

group polarisation group members become more biased towards one extreme when making a decision

groupthink tendency for a group to over-conform when making a decision

hallucinations perceptions that occur in the absence of sensory stimuli, for example seeing something that does not exist

hermeneutics analysis of interpretive procedures employed by a particular method/discipline; the emphasis is on how meaning is socially constructed, rejecting notions of 'absolute truth'

heuristics problem solving strategies in which 'rules of thumb', or past experiences are used to narrow down the options of ways of dealing with the problem; more manageable than algorithmic approaches, but a solution is not guaranteed

hidden observer a metaphor used by Hilgard (1986) to describe a mental structure which monitors everything, including events of which the hypnotised participant is not consciously aware

homeostasis process by which the body's internal environment (e.g. temperature and glucose level) are maintained at optimal level

homogeneity of variance the spread or range of two sets of scores is similar

horizontal relationships attachment of the child to people who have equal power, such as peers

hostile attributional bias tendency to perceive others' actions as being intentionally antagonistic even when the situation is ambiguous

humanistic model theoretical approach emphasising the individual's capacity for insight and self-development

hypnosis one person responds to the suggestions made by another and experiences alterations in perception, memory, and voluntary actions

hypothesis testable statement concerning the relationship between different variables

identification process of incorporating into oneself the qualities and ideas of another person, seen by Freud to resolve the Oedipal complex, whereby the child tries to identify with the same-sex parent

identity crisis period of adolescence, seen by Erikson to be a conflict between identity and role confusion, with the desirable outcome being a sense of identity and self-awareness with confidence to make commitments

idiographic focuses upon the distinctiveness of the individual

illusion a trick played on the senses to give a false interpretation of incoming sensory data

implicit memory memory where there is no awareness of remembering the original trace

implosion therapy therapy based on classical conditioning which is like flooding. Patients imagine themselves to be in the feared situation

imprinting a special form of learning in which baby animals rapidly learn to recognise and follow a moving object soon after birth

independence maintenance of expressions of behaviour without regard to group norms

independent groups design experimental design with different participants in the experimental and control conditions

independent variable (IV) variable which is manipulated in experimental designs

indigenous psychology a psychology where the native culture of those being studied is given primacy in the understanding and interpretation of behaviour

inductivism popular scientific philosophy of the seventeenth century which advocated the progression of science through the empirical observation of objective phenomena

information processing approach model which analyses cognitive processes in terms of the manipulation of information which is involved; in the model, information is received and manipulated so it can be interpreted and a response provided

informed consent decision of a participant to take part in a study once they have been provided with all details about the study

infradian rhythms biological cycles which occur less frequently than once a day

injunctive norms behaviour that ought to be followed in a given situation

insight involves reaching a sudden conclusion or solution as a result of a restructuring of the available information

insomnia disorders of initiating and maintaining sleep

interactional synchrony the process of the baby moving its face and body in time with the speaker; used to describe a baby's early attempts at pre-linguistic communication with parents/carers

interpersonal relationship a long-term relationship, between two or more persons, based upon strong emotional ties involving commitment and mutual reciprocity

inter-sexual selection selection resulting from males competing to attract females

inter-specific aggression aggression between members of different species

interval data most complex level of data; the size of difference between scores is shown because scores are standardised on a scale ensuring that individual scores are of equivalent intervals on the scale, e.g. time

intra-sexual selection fighting between members of one sex (usually males) for one or more females

intra-specific aggression aggression between members of the same species

kin selection selection which favours relatives as well as direct descendants

labelling effects application of a label on the basis of tests result which may set in motion a self-fulfilling

prophecy where the individual increasingly behaves in a way consistent with that label

language acquisition device (LAD) Chomsky's name for the innate device which, he believes, facilitates language comprehension and production in the human species

lateralisation of function specialisation of each brain hemisphere for the performance of different tasks

learned helplessness can develop when earlier learning suggests that the individual will not be able to control a situation. Resembles depression in that bad events are expected and cannot be controlled

levels of processing theory which states information can be processed at different levels. Shallow-processed information will not be remembered as well as deeply processed information. The theory is associated with Craik and Lockhart (1972)

longitudinal studies comparison study of the same group of people over a long period of time

maladaptive (behaviour) behaviour which does not contribute to fitness

matched pairs design experimental design with different participants in the control and experimental groups, with participants matched along relevant criteria

matching hypothesis people who are attracted to each other and form relationships do so according to matched similarities such as physical attractiveness, attitudes and so on

maternal deprivation loss of the principle carer early in the child's life

maternal privation absence of any opportunity for the child to form an attachment to the principle carer

mean commonly referred to as the average; calculated by adding up a set of scores and dividing the total by the number of scores in the data set

measures of central tendency summary statistics which are typical of the set of data (mean, median and mode)

measures of dispersion summary statistics which describe the spread or variability of scores in a set of data

mechanistic explanations of behaviour in mechanical terms, which

is the dominant model of explanation in western science

median the scores which falls in the middle of the data set

meditation awareness in which the individual is relaxed, separate from the outside world and can gain a wider consciousness

memory the structures and processes involved in the storage and retrieval of information. Memory can also refers to the content of what is stored

mere exposure hypothesis the premise that a person will be drawn to another merely because he or she has been exposed to that person on a number of occasions

metacognition an individual's knowledge of his/her own thinking processes – knowing about the operation of one's abilities such as thinking, memory and how we use language and ideas

mid-life crisis early developmental psychologists, such as Neugarten and Levinson, emphasised a mid-life transition period during which adults (especially males) come to terms with a number of polarities

migration long-distance travel from one location to another with eventual return to the first

minimal group paradigm refers to studies based on social identification which seek to create artificial groups by spurious characteristics (e.g. tossing a coin) and then analysing the resultant outcomes of in-group out-group effects

mnemonics memory aids. These devices tend to be visual, for example the method of loci, or verbal mnemonics, for example the use of meaningful abbreviations for unconnected items in a list

mode most frequently occurring score in the data set

modes of (internal) representation different ways by which we cognitively represent the world, according to Bruner – the three modes by which we do this are *enactive, iconic* and *symbolic*, which Bruner sees as following in sequence, but they are not stages as they can act in parallel, and are available throughout life

modular theory of attention theory which assumes different processing channels for different sense modalities, for example Allport's theory

monogamy system where male and female stay together and (in most species) share care of young

morpheme smallest unit of speech to have meaning

motion parallax when an observer moves, distant objects appear to move more slowly than closer objects. The visual system can use this information to help estimate how far away objects are

motivation the processes of arousing, maintaining and regulating specific patterns of behaviour (it impels, or pushes, the organism into activity)

MRI (magnetic resonance imaging) procedure in which high resolution images of the structure of the living brain are constructed by measuring waves emitted by hydrogen atoms when they are activated by radio-frequency waves in a magnetic field

multi-method approach research strategy which adopts a range of specific techniques (for example observational methods and self-report measures) in order to build up as rich a picture as possible combining a variety of perspectives; case study research is commonly multi-method in its approach

multi-store model models of memory which suggest memory traces are processed or stored in different structures, such as the short term store (STS) or long term store (LTS)

mutation a small change in a gene or genes

narrative tradition focuses upon the unfolding of stories surrounding the phenomena under study – in this way, a contextualised understanding is generated through the analysis of the discourse of a particular culture

nativist view that abilities and psychological attributes are inborn (equivalent to 'nature')

natural experiment where experimental conditions occur naturally without any intervention (randomisation of participant groups therefore not possible)

natural selection certain traits are selected or favoured by the environment

nature–nurture debate refers to two differing theoretical viewpoints: nature emphasises inherited characteristics, whilst nurture emphasises the effect of learning and the environment

negative-feedback systems function to maintain stability in the neuroendocrine system, for example a signal of change in one direction results in a compensatory effect in the other direction

neuromodulators naturally secreted substance acting like a neurotransmitter but not restricted to the synaptic cleft/gap, it adjusts the sensitivity of populations of cells to the excitatory and inhibitory signals at fast-acting synapses

neuron a nerve cell, seen as the basic building blocks of the nervous system, specialised for the conduction of information via nerve impulses

neurotransmitters chemical messengers released by the pre-synaptic terminals which bind with the post-synaptic neurons, enabling the action potential to cross the synapse

new paradigm research increasingly popular approach which emerged in the 1960s in reaction to the old paradigm; the emphasis is upon the understanding of the context of situations adopting a holistic approach through the use of qualitative techniques

niche differentiation when the requirements of two organisms competing for the same resources diverge, so that they no longer compete within the same ecological niche

nodes of Ranvier an unmyelinated gap of the axon between adjacent oligodendroglia or Schwann cells allowing the impulse to jump from node to node, thus speeding up conduction

nominal data simplest form of data where scores are grouped into categories and there is nothing to distinguish between those in the same category

nomothetic concerned with the generation of universal or general laws

normal distribution curve graphical representation of a normally distributed population in which the mean, median and mode are the

same, with 50 per cent of the population falling above this mid point and 50 per cent of the population falling below it

normative theory decision-based theory of how leaders should adapt to a given situation and take into account how much participation should be allowed by followers

norms typical behaviour that might be representative of a group

null hypothesis hypothesis which predicts there will be no difference between variables nor relationship between them

obedience complying to the rules set by a recognised authority, which may impose sanctions for disobedience

objectifying using an objective piece of information in order to make sense of the world and facilitate communication

object permanence understanding that objects exist, have substance, and continue to exist when out of sight

old paradigm research dominant approach to research prior to the 1960s based upon the scientific approach and quantitative methods

one-tailed/directional when the alternative hypothesis states the expected direction of the outcome, for example bigger, greater, more than, etc.

operational thinking seen by Piaget to be the basis of adult, logical reasoning, it is a mental structure enabling both transformation and reversibility, and includes general mental actions, such as mental addition and subtraction – hence the stage changes named *pre-operational*, *concrete operational* and *formal operational*

operationalising defining variables specifically enough to be actually measured

optimal foraging theory (OFT) an approach to the study of feeding on a cost-benefit basis

order effects the order in which the participants are exposed to the different experimental conditions has an effect upon the outcomes

ordinal data there is a score for each individual, allowing the scores to be placed in rank order

parallel processing two or more cognitive processes or operations occur at the same time

parental investment (PI) amount of energy expended in producing and rearing offspring

participant reactivity the behaviour of participants is affected by aspects of the research procedure and setting

pattern recognition recognition of objects or shapes as unitary, rather than as separate perceptual features

perception how the brain interprets sensory information to help make sense of the physical world

performance deficit the inability to carry out a task, or tasks effectively; this may result from dual task limitation or from mistakes or slips in processing

permissive parenting style of child rearing distinguished by a high level of nurturance, low levels of control, parental demands and communication

PET (positron emission tomography) technique used for visualising the activity of the brain by measuring radioactive 2-DG or radioactive water in the various parts of the brain

phenomenological focuses upon the study of immediate experience and the individual's perceptions of those experiences

phenotype physical and behavioural characteristics of an organism (phenotypes and genotypes differ, largely due to the effects of the environment)

phoneme smallest unit of sound in a spoken language

physics envy used to describe the state of other subjects which seek to be like physics, which is regarded as the role model of scientific theory and practice

pilot test/study exploratory testing of a research procedure designed to see how effective it is and what, if any, modifications are necessary before commencing in full with the study; useful for experimental, observational and self-report procedures

polyandry mating system where one female has more or less exclusive access to a number of males (rare)

polygenic inheritance when more than one gene is implicated in a particular characteristic

polygyny mating system where the male has more or less exclusive access to a number of females

positivist tradition approach which states that the development of knowledge should be based on empirical observation of the objective world forming the basis of ideas about what constitutes good scientific practice

precocial birds or animals which are mobile and relatively mature soon after birth or hatching

preferential looking method method of studying infant perception whereby two stimuli are presented simultaneously and the time spent looking at each one is recorded. It is assumed the infant can discriminate between the two stimuli and looks longer at the one he or she prefers

prejudice negative attitude towards a group or individual based on preformulated generalisations

presumptive consent a sample of the population to be involved in a study agrees that the deception to be used is considered acceptable

principle of antithesis Darwin's term for the fact that the appeasement posture is virtually the opposite to that of threat (for example, tail and ears down as opposed to up)

prior general consent potential participants are asked if they would take part in a study involving deception – the sample is selected from only those who agree

procedural memory memory for how to do things such as riding a bike, or walking. We are not usually aware of these memory traces

productivity (of language) refers to the fact that the sounds of human language can be combined into an infinite number of utterances and meanings

promiscuity where reproductive interactions are short, and where males and females mate with many of the opposite sex

propaganda advancement of a view in an attempt to persuade rather than present a balanced overview – this is done by presenting false information or omitting accurate information; often contrasted with education which seeks to communicate knowledge rather than persuade

pro-social behaviour behaviour that benefits others

prospective memory remembering to carry out intentions, or remembering to do things at the appropriate time

protocol changes changing the procedures of experiments (for example to reduce the required number of animals upon which a drug has to be tested)

proximity closeness or nearness, sometimes also termed propinquity

psychoactive drugs chemicals which affect behaviour and thinking by interfering with the normal functioning of the nervous system

psychodynamic theoretical position based on Freud's theory which claims that behaviour is driven by unconscious thought processes

psychodynamic therapy treatment based on psychodynamic theory in which patients are encouraged to uncover conflicts in the unconscious which are causing their problems

psychological operations used by the US military in situations of conflict; refers to the control of information in order to influence the emotions, motives, reasoning and behaviour of foreign governments, organisations, groups and individuals

psychometric tests tests (usually pencil and paper ones) designed to measure psychological attributes such as intelligence and personality

psychoneuroimmunology the study of interactions amongst psychological factors, the nervous system, and the immune system

psychopharmacology the administration of chemicals (drugs) into the brain to increase or decrease the effects of neurotransmitters

psychosocial development Erikson's theory of life-span development suggests we pass through eight stages, each of which involves the resolution of psychological and social conflicts

puberty period of rapid physiological changes in adolescence which culminates in the attainment of reproductive capacity, often reached by girls about two years before boys

punctuated equilibria where periods of little evolutionary change in the fossil record are interrupted by periods of rapid change

quasi experimental design study which basically follows the principles of the experiment but where conditions occur naturally (randomisation of participants is not possible)

randomisation used to ensure there are no systematic patterns in the allocation of participants to experimental conditions, helping to ensure any differences found are due to the effects of experimental variables

range indicates how scores are spread out or close together in a data set. Calculated by finding the lowest value in the data and subtracting this from the highest value in the data

rational-emotive therapy cognitive therapy used by Ellis which aims at identifying and changing irrational thought patterns

receptive field the part of the retina which, when stimulated, produces a change in the activity of a connected ganglion cell

reciprocal altruism a term from the socio-biological perspective involving a person helping another in the expectation that someone will help that person if in need

reductionism breaks down behaviour into its separate component parts attempting to generate explanations at the most basic level

relative refractory period period following the cell's absolute refractory period – at this time an impulse may be initiated by a strong stimulus

relativist often used to criticise the 'new paradigm' approaches; if all understanding is relative, then anything can be classed as knowledge – this devalues what actually comes to constitute knowledge

REM sleep stage of sleep characterised by rapid eye movements, lack of muscle tone and emergent stage 1 sleep

repeated measures design experimental design where the same group of participants is exposed to both the control and experimental conditions

research hypothesis hypothesis predicting there will be a relationship between different variables as in correlational designs (also known as the alternative hypothesis)

response any behaviour which results from a stimulus

response sets tendency of people to respond to test items in a certain way

retina the thin neural receptor layer at the back of the eye

role playing people are asked to behave in a certain situation in a way which they would naturally do were they not being observed

rules shared opinions and beliefs about what should and should not be done; rules are developed in order that goals may be attained; rules can be based on social norms or legal sanctions

saltatory conduction rapid transmission of the nerve impulse along myelinated neurons whereby the impulse jumps from one node of Ranvier to the next

scaffolding Bruner's term used to describe the support given to the child by adults and others, especially linguistic support

scheme/schema mental structure that provides the individual with a model for action in similar circumstances, described by Piaget. Includes both physical actions and mental actions – an experience is assimilated into a scheme and then the scheme is modified or created through accommodation

schizophrenia a group of severe mental disorders characterised by disturbances in thought, perception and emotion

scientific method based on the objective observation of phenomena under controlled conditions, usually experimental, which seeks to highlight cause and effect relationships

scientific paradigms theoretical assumptions, laws and methodological techniques associated with a particular world view or body of thought held by a scientific community

search image a mental representation of appropriate food

self-actualisation self-development and self-fulfilment needs, realising one's potential with feelings of accomplishment and satisfaction, seen by humanists such as Maslow to be fundamental to healthy human behaviour

self-disclosure information revealed about oneself to another person

self-efficacy part of the self-concept labelled by Bandura (1977), as our ability to think, choose, and make appropriate decisions – linked very closely to the self-esteem – our sense of our ability to accomplish things

selfish gene theory that natural selection acts not on the species, not on the individual, but on the gene

self-report techniques methods of data collection which rely upon what the participants say about themselves; includes questionnaires and interviews, diary reports, psychometric tests, measurement scales

self-serving bias the way in which we attribute our own positive outcomes to internal causes (within our control) and negative outcomes to external causes (out of our control)

semantic memory knowledge and understanding of the world, for example knowing who is the prime minister

senescence period of late adulthood – old age

sensation the detection of stimuli by the sense organs

sensitive period an optimal time for a behaviour to become established; if specific responses are not acquired by a certain time, then it will be more difficult (but not impossible) for them to be acquired subsequently

sentient having the capacity to suffer or experience enjoyment or happiness

serial position effect the tendency better to recall items presented at the beginning or the end of a list. Serial position effect has been used to validate the existence of a STS and LTS in memory

serial processing one cognitive process is completed before the next process begins

sex-stereotyping a narrow set of qualities associated with a given gender role, defining the qualities of male behaviour and female behaviour in any given culture

sex typing set of attitudes and behaviours we learn to adopt in relation to gender identity

shaping process in operant conditioning which develops behaviour in gradual steps

single blind participants do not know the aims of the study or which condition they are in

slow-wave sleep (SWS) sleep stages 2, 3 and 4

social categorisation means of classifying people into groups within society

social cognition how the social environment can influence an individual's thoughts, perceptions and beliefs – this theory of development sees social interaction to be the most important factor in children's cognitive development

social constructionsim view that there are no universal truths about human nature because people construct reality differently

social desirability effect participants behave in a way which makes them look good

social disengagement theory also known as the decrement model, in which Cumming and Henry argued that gradual social disengagement leads to psychological well being

social exchange exchanges within a relationship are based on rewards, costs and profits gained in terms of socially-based attributes, such as physical attractiveness and status, and concrete rewards, such as flowers and chocolates

social identity theory helps to explain how membership of social groups influences our own self-identity and our perceptions and reactions to others

social readjustment rating scale (SRRS) scale developed by Holmes and Rahe which considers critical life events in terms of their impact as stressors, such as the death of a spouse, moving house and redundancy. The scale enables the comparative value of stressful events to be assessed and predicts the level of stress on mental and physical health

social representations a shared meaning or belief of the social group to which one belongs that helps to explain out own social reality and the context in which we live

socialisation process by which a society's behaviour patterns, standards and beliefs are transmitted from one individual to another

sociality refers to social interactions between two or more individuals

socially sensitive research research with potential social consequences or implications for those involved in the study or the groups they represent

sociobiology study of the biology basis of social behaviour strongly influenced by the ideas of evolutionary biology

socio-cultural perspective approach in psychology which explores the impact of cultural diversity upon psychological theory and practice, often highlighting the inappropriateness of western psychological theory when applied to other cultures

soft determinism a less extreme form of determinism which accepts that although behaviour may follow predictable sequences, the individual still has the freedom to choose which of those sequences to follow

spatial summation summed effect of excitatory and inhibitory activity by the neuron which determines whether the neuron will fire or not

specialist feeder an organism which eats one or two types of food only

speciesism discrimination and exploitation based upon a difference in species

split-brain the functioning of the brain when fibres between the two hemispheres (corpus callosum) are severed

standard deviation (SD) average variability of scores in relation to the mean of that set of scores (it is also the square root of the variance)

standardised procedures as many different aspects of the research setting as possible are held consistent, for example instructions given, the setting and the experimenters used

stereopsis aids visual perception of a three-dimensional image. It is the result of integrating information about the visual field, from both eyes. Stereoscopic vision is constructed in the cortex

stereotype set of widely shared generalisations about the characteristics of a group or class of people

stimulus an internal or external event which produces a response or sensory experience

stimulus-response an attempt to interpret behaviour in terms of stimulus-response units without considering the role of cognitive factors within the organism

storm and stress period of adolescence, identified by Hall at the beginning of the twentieth century. Seen to be a period of dramatic personal change, both biological and psychological, the outcome of which can have important consequences on a young person's life

'strange situation' method of investigating the effects of separation on the child, developed by Ainsworth, taking place in the laboratory: mothers would take the infant to play in an unfamiliar room; during playtime the child's behaviour would be monitored during a standardised pattern of arrivals and departures of both the mother and a stranger

stress a biological response experienced as emotion, can refer to a stress response or to a stressor

subliminal advertising message or image presented below our threshold of recognition in an attempt to influence our behaviour

suggestion a communication, usually given verbally by the hypnotist, to direct the participant's imagination, so as to elicit different behaviour, thinking or feeling

superego Freudian concept, the part of the personality which acts as a 'conscience' and develops as part of the identification process – contains the parental and societal values and attitudes incorporated by the child

symbiosis relationship between different species where both benefit

synapse area where the synaptic terminals of one neuron lie close to the receptor sites of another neuron, with a gap between the two known as the synaptic cleft/gap

syntax rules for combining words and creating the structure of a sentence, or phrase

synthesis theory theory assumes a central processor of some type coordinates the attentional processing occurring in the sense modules

systematic desensitisation therapy based on classical conditioning in which the patient is taught to relax in situations that get progressively closer to the feared object so that eventually a relaxation response replaces fear when the feared object is encountered

temporal summation when sufficient action potentials arrive at the pre-synaptic terminal within a short space of time to release enough neurotransmitter to depolarise the post-synaptic membrane and initiate an action potential

third variable explanation when a relationship between two variables is actually caused by a third unmeasured variable

tip of the tongue (TOT) phenomena memory state in which individuals feel they know the desired information, but are unable to bring it into their conscious memory

token economy system based on conditioning aimed at modifying behaviour. The person is given tokens as rewards for desired behaviour. These tokens can be exchanged for special privileges or desired items

tolerance increasing amounts of the drug/chemical are needed to obtain the same effect

trance a waking state in which the participant's attention is detached from ongoing environmental stimulation towards absorption with inner experiences

two-tailed/non-directional the alternative hypothesis does not state the expected direction of the relationship between the different variables

type 1 error making the mistake of accepting the experimental or research hypothesis when there has been no effect

type 2 error making the mistake of rejecting the experimental hypothesis when there has actually been an effect

Type A behaviour behaviour characterised by competitive drive, impatience, hostility, overcommitment to achievement. It is seen to be related to higher incidence of cardiovascular disease (e.g. coronary heart disease)

Type C (cancer-prone) personality personality in which the individual is seen to be unassertive, cooperative and patient, perhaps repressing negative emotions such as anger. Such a personality may be more likely to encourage the growth of tumours (not their formation)

ultradian rhythms biological cycles that occur more frequently than once a day

unconscious in Freudian theory it is the part of the mind the contains hidden memories, thoughts and desires

unipolar depression (major depressive disorder) a mood disorder characterised by the existence of depression without mania, i.e. only one mood (negative) state

variance measure of the variability in a set of scores taking account of each individual score

vertical relationships attachment made to someone in a more powerful position to the child, such as a parent or teacher

vicarious learning learning from observing the actions of others

vicarious reinforcement reinforcement contingencies that affect the likelihood of a behaviour or action based on watching a model receive reinforcement

visual search task involving looking for a target, or targets, in a visual array

withdrawal feelings and symptoms which develop when the user stops taking the drug

working memory conscious immediate memory. A model of its functioning is the Baddeley and Hitch (1974) working memory model

zeitgebers environmental cues, such as the light/dark cycle which programme circadian rhythms

Zone of Proximal Development (ZPD) Vygotsky's description of the distance between what children can achieve on their own and what they will achieve with the help of others, such as adults or more experienced peers; this helps the initiation of the child into the intellectual life of the community and thus *socially constructs* his/her understanding of the world

zoom lens model model of focused visual attention which assumes people attend to a visual field that lies within an attentional spotlight; this spotlight is adjustable

References

Abou-Saleh, M T (1992) Lithium, in E S Paykel (ed) *Handbook of Affective Disorders*, Guilford.

Abramson, L V and Martin, D J (1981) Depression and the casual inference process, in J M Harvey, W Ickes and R F Kidd (eds) *New Directions in Attribution Research*, 3rd edn, Erlbaum, Hillsdale, NJ.

Adler, A. (1927) *The Practice and Theory of Individual Psychology*, Harcourt Brace Jovanovich, New York.

Adler, A (1938/1964) *Social Interest: A Challenge to Mankind*, Capricorn, New York.

Adorno, T W, Frenle-Brunswick, D J, Levinson, D J and Sanford, R N (1950) *The Authoritarian Personality*, Harper and Brothers, New York.

Ainsworth, M D S (1967) *Infancy in Uganda: Infant Care and the Growth of Love*, John Hopkins Press, Baltimore.

Ainsworth, M D S, Bell, S M and Stayton, D J (1971) Individual differences in strange-situation behaviour of one-year-olds, in H R Schaffer (ed.), *The Origins of Human Social Relations*, Academic Press, New York.

Ainsworth, M D S, Blehar, M C, Waters, E and Wall, S (1978) *Patterns of attachment: A Psychological Study of the Strange Situation*, Erlbaum, Hillsdale, NJ.

Ainsworth, P B and King, E (1988) Witnesses' perceptions of identification parades, in M M Gruneberg, P E Morris and R N Sykes (eds) *Practical Aspects of Memory: Current Research and Issues* vol. 1, Wiley, Chichester.

Aitchison, J (1983) *The Articulate Mammal*, Hutchinson, London.

Akerstedt, T and Folkard, S (1995) Validation of the S and C components of the three-process model of alertness regulation, *Sleep*, 1-6.

Alatalo, R V, Lundberg, A and Glynn, C (1986) Female pied flycatchers choose territory quality not male characteristics, *Nature*, 323, 152-153.

Albright, T D, Desimone, R and Gross, C G (1984) Columnar organization of directionally selective cells in visual area MT of the macaque, *Journal of Neurophysiology*, 51, 16-31.

Alladin, A and Heap, M (1991) Hypnosis and depression, in M Heap and W Dryden (eds) *Hypnotherapy: A Handbook*, Open University Press, Milton Keynes.

Alliger, G M and Williams, K J (1991) Affective congruence and the employment interview, *Advances in Information Processing in Organizations*, 4, 31-43, in R A Baron and D Byrne (1997), *Social Psychology*, Allyn & Bacon, Boston.

Alloy, L B, Kelly, Minetia *et al.* (1990) in L B Alloy, J R Acocella and Brotzi (1996) *Abnormal Psychology Current Perspectives*, 7th edn, McGraw Hill.

Allport, D A (1989) Visual attention, in M I Posner (ed) *Foundations of Cognitive Science*, MIT Press, Cambridge, MA.

Allport, D A, Antonis, B and Reynolds, P (1972) On the division of attention: A disproof of the single channel hypothesis, *Quarterly Journal of Experimental Psychology*, 24, 225-35.

Allport, D A and Funnell, E (1981) Components of the mental lexicon, *Philosophical Transactions of the Royal Society*, London, B295, 397-410.

Altmann, S A (1962) A field study of the sociobiology of rhesus monkeys, *Macaca mulatta*, *Annals of the New York Academy of Science*, 102, 338-435.

Amato, P R (1983) Helping behaviour in urban and rural environments: Field studies based on a taxonomic organisation of helping episodes, *Journal of Personality and Social Psychology*, 45, 571-586.

Amato, P R (1986) Arousal and helping behaviour in a real-life emergency, *Journal of Applied Social Psychology*, 16, 633-641, in A R Baron and D Byrne (1997) *Social Psychology*, 8th edn, Allyn & Bacon, Boston, MA.

American Association of University Women (1991) *Shortchanging Girls, Shortchanging America*, Report prepared by Greenberg-Lake: The Analysis Group Inc. for the AAUW, Washington, DC.

American Psychiatric Association (1995) Practice Guideline for Psychiatric Evaluation of Adults, *American Journal of Psychiatry*, November supplement, 152.

Anastasi, A (1988) in C Tavris and C Wade (1995) *Pschology in Perspective*, Harper Collins, New York.

Anderson, C A, Deuser, W E and DeNeve, K M (1995) Hot temperatures, hostile affect, hostile cognition and arousal: Tests of a general model of affective aggression, *Personality and Social Psychology Bulletin*, 21, 434-448, in R A Baron and D Byrne (1997) *Social Psychology*, 8th edn, Allyn & Bacon, Boston, MA.

Anderson, P, Cremona, A, Paton, A *et al.* (1993) The risk of alcohol, *Addiction*, 88, 1493-1508.

Andersson, M (1982) Female choice selects for extreme tail length in a widow bird, *Nature*, 299, 818-20.

Andersson, M and Wicklund, C G (1978) Clumping v spacing out: Experiments on nest predation in fieldfares (*Turdis pilaris*), *Animal Behaviour*, 26, 1207-1212.

Andreasen, N C (1988) Brain imaging: Applications in psychiatry, *Science* 239, 1381-1388.

Andreason, N C, Flaum, M, Swayze, V *et al.* (1993) in R A Baron (1996) *Essentials in Pschology*, Allyn & Bacon, Boston, MA.

Antrobus, J (1991) Dreaming: Cognitive processes in during cortical activation and high afferent thresholds, *Psychological Review* 96–121, 98

Aponte, J F, Rivers, R Y and Wohl, J (1995) *Psychological Interventions and Cultural Diversity*, Allyn & Bacon, Boston, MA.

Appleby, M (1985) Hawks, Doves and Chickens, *New Scientist*, 10th January, 16-18, in N Hayes (1995) *Psychology in Perspective*, Macmillan, Basingstoke.

Apter, J T (1993) Frontiers in biological psychiatry new drug development, *New Jersey Medicine*, 90 (2), 144-146.

Apter, T (1990) *Altered Loves: Mothers and Daughters During Adolescence*, St Martin's Press, New York.

Arak, A (1984) Playing games is a serious business, *New Scientist*, 31-34.

Ardrey, R (1970) *The Social Contract*, Collins, London.

Argyle, M (1983) *The Psychology of Interpersonal Behaviour*, 4th edn, Penguin, Harmondsworth.

Argyle, M (1988) *Bodily Communication*, 2nd edn, Methuen, London.

Argyle, M (1989) *The Social Psychology of Work*, 2nd edn, Penguin, Harmondsworth.

Argyle, M (1992) *The Social Psychology of Everyday Life*, Routledge, London.

Argyle, M (1998) *Psychology: Social Influence*, BPS Open Learning Units, Leicester.

Argyle, M and Furnham (1983)

Argyle, M and Henderson, M (1985) *The Anatomy of Relationships*, Penguin, Harmondsworth.

Aronson, E (1992) *The Social Animal*, 6th edn, W H Freeman, New York.

Artmann, H, Grau, H, Adelman, M and Schleiffer, R (1985) Reversible and non-reversible enlargement of cerebrospinal fluid spaces in anorexia nervosa, *Neuroradiology*, 27, 103-112.

Asch, S E (1951) Effects of group pressure upon the modification and distortion of judgements, in H Guetzkow (ed) *Groups, Leadership and Men*, Carnegie Press, Pittsburg PA.

Asch, S E (1956) Studies of independence and conformity: A minority of one against a unanimous majority, *Psychological Monographs*, 70 (9).

Ashcraft, M (1994) *Human Memory and Cognition*, 2nd edn, Harper Collins, London.

Aslin, R N (1987) Visual and auditory development in infancy, in J D Osofky (ed.) *Handbook of Infant Development*, 2nd edn, Wiley, New York.

Asner, J (1990) Reworking the myth of personal incompetence: Group psychotherapy for bulimia nervosa, *Psychiatry. Ann.*, 20 (7), 395-397.

Atkinson, R C and Shiffin, R M (1971) The control of short-term memory, *Scientific American*, 224, 82-90.

Atkinson, R C and Shiffin, R M (1968) Human memory: A proposed system and its control processes, in W K Spence and J T Spence (eds) *The Psychology of Learning and*

Motivation: Advances in Research and Theory vol. 2, Academic Press, London.

Atkinson, R L, Atkinson, R C, Bem, D J and Hoeksema, S (1996) *Introduction to Psychology*, 12th edn, Harcourt Brace, New York.

Atkinson, R L, Atkinson, R C, Smith, E E and Hilyard, E R (1983) *Introduction to Psychology*, 8th edn, Harcourt Brace Jovanovich, New York.

Au, T K (1983) Chinese and English counterfactuals: The Sapir-Whorf hypothesis revisited, *Cognition* 15, 155-187.

Aune, R K and Basil, M C (1994) A relational obligations approach to the foot-in-the-mouth effect, *Journal of Applied Social Psychology*, 24, 546-556, in R A Baron and D Byrne (1997) *Social Psychology*, 8th edn, Allyn & Bacon, Boston, MA.

Ax, A F (1953) The physiological differentiation of fear and anger in humans, *Psychomatic Medicine*, 15, 422-433.

Axelrod, R and Hamilton, W D (1981) The evolution of cooperation, *Science*, 211, 1390-1396.

Ayres, J (1983) Strategies to maintain relationships: their identification and perceived usage, *Communication Quarterly*, 31, 207-225, in N Hayes (1994) *Foundations of Psychology: An Introductory Text*, Routledge, London.

Azrin, N H and Holz, W C (1966) Punishment, in W K Honig (ed) *Operant Behaviour: Areas of Research and Application*, Appleton-Century Crofts, New York.

Baars, B J (1988) *A Cognitive Theory of Consciousness*, Cambridge University Press, New York.

Bachman, J G (1970) *The impact of family background and intelligence on tenth grade boys: Vol 2 Youth in transition*, MI Survey Research Center, Institute for Social Research, Ann Arbor, MI.

Baddeley, A D (1986) *Working Memory*, Oxford University Press, Oxford.

Baddeley, A D (1993) *Your Memory: A User's Guide*, Prion, London.

Baddeley, A D, Grant, S, Wright, E and Thomson, N (1973) Imagery and working memory, in P M A Rabbit and S Dornic (eds) *Attention and Performance V*, Academic Press, London.

Baddeley, A D and Hitch, G J (1974) Working memory, in G H Bower (ed) *The Psychology of Learning and Motivation* vol. 8, Academic Press, London.

Baddeley, A D and Warrington, E K (1970) Amnesia and the distinction between long- and short-term memory, *Journal of Verbal Learning and Verbal Behaviour*, 9, 176-189.

Baillargeon, R (1991) The object concept revisited: New directions in the investigation of the infant's physical knowledge, in C E Granrud (ed), *Visual Perception and Cognition in Infancy*, Carnegie-Mellon Symposia on Cognition, vol 23, Erlbaum, Hillsdale NJ.

Baird, J C (1982) The moon illusion: II A reference theory, *Journal of Experimental Psychology* General III, 304-315.

Baker, R R (1978) *The Evolutionary Ecology of Animal Migration*, Holmes & Meier, New York.

Baker, R R (1982) *Migration, Paths through Time and Space*, Hodder & Stoughton, London.

Baker, R R (1984) *Bird Navigation. The solution of a Mystery?*, Hodder & Stoughton, London.

Baker, S M and Petty, R E (1994) Majority and minority influence: Source-position imbalance as a determinant of message scrutiny, *Journal of Personality and Social Psychology*, 67, 5-19, in R A Baron and D Byrne (1997) *Social Psychology*, 8th edn, Allyn & Bacon, Boston, MA.

Bales, R F (1950) *Interaction Process Analysis: A Method for the Study of Small Groups*, Addison-Wesley, Reading, MA.

Baltes, P B (1983) Life-span developmental psychology: Observations on history and theory revisited, in R M Lerner (ed) *Developmental Psychology: Historical and Philosophical Perspectives*, Erlbaum, Hillsdale, NJ.

Baltes, P B and Schaie, L (1973) *Lifespan Developmental Psychology*. Academic Press, London.

Bandura, A (1965) Influence of models reinforcement contingencies on the acquisition of initiative responses, *Journal of Personality and Social Psychology*, 1, 589-595.

Bandura, A (1977) Self-efficacy: Toward a unifying theory of behavioural change, *Psychological Review*, 84, 191-215.

Bandura, A (1986) *Social Foundations of Thought and Action: A Social Cognitive*

Theory, Prentice-Hall, Englewood Cliffs, NJ.

Bandura, A (1990) Some reflections on reflections, *Psychological Inquiry*, 1, 101-105.

Banich, M T and Belger, A (1990) Inter-hemispheric interaction: How do the hemispheres divide and conquer a task?, *Cortex*, 26, 77-94.

Banister, P, Burman, E, Parker, I, Taylor, M and Tindall, C (1994) *Qualitative Methods in Psychology: A Research Guide*, Open University Press, Milton Keynes.

Bannister, D and Fransella, F (1986) *Inquiring Man: The Psychology of Personal Constructs*, 3rd edn, Groom Helm, London.

Banyai, E A and Hilgard, E R (1976) A comparison of active-alert hypnotic induction with traditional relaxation induction, *Journal of Abnormal Psychology*, 85, 218-224.

Banyard, P (1996) Psychology and Advertising, *Psychology Review*, 3(1), 24-27.

Barnard, N D and Kaufman, S R (1997) Animal research is wasteful and misleading, *Scientific American*, 276 (2), 64-66.

Barnstable, C J (1993) Glutamate and GABA in retinal circuitry, *Current Opinion in Neurobiology*, 3, 520-525.

Baron, R A (1989) Personality and organizational conflict: The type A behaviour pattern and self-monitoring, *Organizational Behaviour and Human Decision Processes*, 44, 281-297, in R A Baron and D Byrne (1997) *Social Psychology*, 8th edn, Allyn & Bacon, Boston, MA.

Baron, R A (1994) The physical environment of work settings: Effects on task performance, interpersonal relations and job satisfaction, in B M Straw and L L Cummings (eds), *Research in organisational behaviour*, 16, 1-46, JAI Press, Greenwich, CT.

Baron, R A (1995) The sweet smell of ... helping: Effects of pleasant ambient odours on prosocial behaviour in shopping malls, Manuscript submitted for publication in R A Baron and D Byrne (1997) *Social Psychology*, 8th edn, Allyn & Bacon, Boston, MA.

Baron, R A (1996) *Essentials of Psychology*, Allyn & Bacon, Boston, MA.

Baron, R A and Byrne, D

(1997) *Social Psychology*, 8th edn, Allyn & Bacon, Boston, MA.

Baron, R A, Fortin, S P, Frei, R L *et al.* (1990) Reducing organisational conflict. The potential role of socially induced positive affect, *International Journal of Conflict Management*, 1, 133-152, in R A Baron (1996) *Essentials of Psychology*, Allyn & Bacon, Boston, MA.

Baron, R A and Greenberg, J (1990) *Behaviour in Organizations*, 3rd edn, Allyn & Bacon, Boston, MA.

Baron, R A, Rea, M S and Daniels, S G (1992) Effects of indoor lighting (illuminance and spectral distribution) on the performance of cognitive tasks and interpersonal behaviour: The potential mediating role of positive affect, *Motivation and Emotion*, 16, 1-33.

Baron, R A and Richardson, D R (1994) *Human Aggression*, 2nd edn, Plenum, New York.

Baron, R A and Thornley, J E (1992) Positive affect as a potential mediator of the effects of pleasant fragrances on task performance and helping, *Environment and Behaviour*, 26, 766-784, in R A Baron and D Byrne (1997) *Social Psychology*, 8th edn, Allyn & Bacon, Boston, MA.

Baron, R S, Vandello, J A and Brunsman, B (1996) The forgotten variable in conformity research: Impact of task importance on social influence, *Journal of Personality and Social Psychology* 71(5) 915-927.

Baron-Cohen, S, Leslie, A M and Frith, U (1985) Does the autistic child have a theory of mind?, *Cognition* 21, 37-46.

Barr, R (1995) in M F Small (1995) Bringing up baby, *New Scientist*, 146, 36-39.

Barrera, M E and Maurer, D (1981) Recognition of mother's photographed face by the three-month-old infant, *Child Development* 52, 714-16.

Bartlett, F C (1932) *Remembering: A Study in Experimental and Social Psychology*, Cambridge University Press, London.

Bartram, D (1995) The development of standards for the use of psychological tests in occupational settings: The competence approach, *The Psychologist* 8, 219-23.

Bates, B L (1993) Individual differences in response to hypnosis, in J W Rhue, S J Lynn and I Kirsch (eds)

Handbook of Clinical Hypnosis, Washington, DC.

Bateson, P (1986) When to experiment on animals, *New Scientist*, 109 (1496), 30-32.

Bateson, P P G (1979) How do sensitive periods arise and what are they for? *Animal Behaviour*, 27, 470-486.

Batson, C D (1987) Prosocial motivation: Is it ever truly altruistic?, in C D Batson, K C Oleson (1991) Current status of the empathy-altruism hypothesis in M S Clark (ed) *Prosocial Behaviour*, Sage, Newbury Park, CA.

Batson, C D (1997) Self-other merging and the empathy-altruism hypothesis: Reply to Neuberg et al (1997), *Journal of Personality and Social Psychology*, 73(3), 517-522.

Batson, C D and Oleson, K C (1991) Current status of the empathy-altruism hypothesis, in M S Clark (ed) *Prosocial Behaviour*, Sage, Newbury Park, CA.

Batson, C D, O'Quin, K, Fultz, J, Vanderplas, M and Isen, A (1983) Self-reported distress and empathy and egoistic versus altruistic motivation for helping, *Journal of Personality and Social Psychology*, 45, 706-718.

Batson, C D, Sager, K, Garst, E, Kang, M, Rubchinsky, K and Dawson, K (1997) Is empathy-induced helping due to self-other merging? *Journal of Personality and Social Psychology*, 73(3), 495-509.

Bauer, P J and Mandler, J M (1992) Putting the horse before the cart: The use of temporal order in recall of events by one-year-old children, *Developmental Psychology*, 28 441-452, in R A Baron (1996) *Essentials of Psychology*, Allyn & Bacon, Boston, MA.

Baum, A and Flemming, I (1993) Implications of phychological research on stress and technological accidents, *American Psychologist*, 48, 665-672.

Baumrind, D (1972) Socialization and instrumental competence in young children, in W W Hartup (ed.) The young child: Reviews of research, vol 2, 202-224, *National Association for the Education of Young Children*, Washington, DC

Beach, S R H, Whisman, M A and O'Leary, K P (1990) Marital therapy for depression: Theoretical foundation current status, future directions, *Behaviour*

Therapy, 25, 345-371.

Beal, C R (1988) Children's knowledge about representations of intended meaning, in J W Astington, P L Harris and D Olsen (eds.) *Developing Theories of Mind*, Cambridge University Press, Cambridge.

Beauchamp, G K and Hess, E H (1971) The effects of cross-species rearing on the social and sexual preference of guinea pigs, *Zeitschrift für Tierpsychologie*, 128, 69-76.

Beck, A T (1991) Cognitive therapy, *American Psychologist*, 46, 368-375.

Bednar, R H and Kaul, T S (1994) Experimental group research: Can the cannon fire?, in A E Bergin and S L Garfiel (eds) *Handbook of Psychotherapy and Behaviour Change*, 4th edn, Wiley.

Bednarz, J C (1988) Cooperative hunting in Harris' hawks (*Parabuteo unicinctus*), *Science*, 239, 1525-1527.

Bee, H (1995) *The Developing Child*, 7th edn, Harper Collins, New York.

Bee, H and Mitchell, S K (1980) *The Developing Person: A Life Span Approach*, Harper and Row, New York.

Beer, J (1982) *Experiments in Psychology*, Weidenfeld and Nicolson, London.

Bell, S T, Kuriloff, P J and Lottes, I (1994) Understanding attributions of blame in stranger rape and date rape situations: An examination of gender, race, identification, and students' social perceptions of rape victims, *Journal of Applied Social Psychology* 24, 1719-1734.

Belliveau, J W, Kennedy, D N, McKinstry, R C and Bushbinder, B R (1991) Functional mapping of the human visual cortex by magnetic resonance imaging, *Science*, 254, 621-768.

Belsky, I and Von Eye (1989) in H Bee (1995) *The Developing Child*, 7th ed, Harper Collins, New York.

Belsky, J and Rovine, M (1987) Temperament and attachment security in the strange situation: An empirical rapprochement, *Child Development*, 58, 787-795.

Bem, S (1985) Androgyny and gender schema theory: A conceptual and empirical integration, in T B Sonderegger (ed.) *Nebraska Symposium on Motivation: Psychology and Gender, 1984*, Vol 32, University of Nebraska Press, Lincoln.

Benbow, C P and Stanley, J C (1980) Sex Differences in Mathematical Ability: Fact or Artifact? *Science*, 210, 1262-1264.

Benington and Heller (1997) in Mind Travellers, *New Scientist* supplement, 26 April 1997, 10-11.

Benkman, C W and Lindholm, A K (1991) The advantages and evolution of morphological novelty, *Nature*, 349, 519-520.

Benson, D F (1985) Aphasia, in K M Heilman and E Valenstein (eds) *Clinical Neuropsychology*, Oxford University Press, New York.

Benson, D F (1985) Aphasia, in K M Heilman and E Valenstein (eds) *Clinical Neuropsychology*, Oxford University Press, New York.

Berenbaum, S A and Hines, M (1992) Early androgens are related to childhood sex-typed toy preferences, *Psychological Science*, 3, 203-206, in R A Baron (1996) *Essentials of Pschology*, Allyn & Bacon, Boston, MA.

Berko, J (1958) The child's learning of English morphology, *Word*, 14, 150-177.

Berkowitz, L (1993) *Aggression: Its Causes, Consequences and Control*, McGraw-Hill, New York.

Berlin, B and Kay, P (1969) *Basic Colour Terms: Their Universality and Evolution*, University of California Press, Berkeley, CA.

Berman, M, Gladue, B and Taylor, S (1993) The effects of hormones, type A behaviour pattern and provocation on aggression, in *Men, Motivation and Emotion*, 17, 182-199, in R A Baron and D Byrne (1997) *Social Psychology*, 8th edn, Allyn & Bacon, Boston, MA.

Bernstein, B (1961) Social class and linguistic development: A theory of social learning, in A H Halsey, J Floyd and C A Anderson (eds) *Education, Economy and Society*, Collier-Macmillan, London.

Berryman, J C (1974) *A Study of Guinea Pig Vocalizations: With Particular Reference to Mother-Infant Interactions*, Ph.D. thesis, University of Leicester, Leicester.

Berscheid, E, Dion, K, Hatfield, E and Walster, G W (1971) Physical attractiveness and dating choice: A test of the matching hypothesis, *Journal of Experimental and Social Psychology*, 7, 173-189.

Bertram, B C R (1980)

Vigilance and group size in ostriches, *Animal Behaviour*, 28, 278-286.

Best, J B (1995) *Cognitive Psychology*, 4th edn, West Publishing, Minneapolis, MN.

Bierhoff, H W, Klein, R and Kramp, P (1991) Evidence for the altruistic personality from data on accident research, *Journal of Personality*, 59, 263-280.

Binet, A and Simon, T (1905) cited by A M Colman in "Aspects of Intelligence", in I Roth (ed) (1990) *Introduction to Psychology*, vol 1, Oxford University Press, Oxford.

Binet, A and Simon, T (1916) *The Development of Intelligence in Children*, Publications of the Training School at Vineland, Vineland NJ, (reprinted 1980 by Williams Publishing Co, Nashville TN.

Birkhead, T R (1977) The effect of habitat on breeding success in common guillemots (*Uria aalgae*), *Journal of Animal Ecology*, 46, 751-764.

Bisanz, J and Lefevre, J (1990) Mathematical cognition: Strategic processing as interactions among sources of knowledge, in D P Bjorkland (ed) *Children's Strategies: Contemporary Views of Cognitive Development*, Erlbaum, Hillsdale, NJ.

Bishop, G D (1994) *Health Psychology: Integrating Mind and Body*, Allyn & Bacon, Boston, MA.

Bishop, M P, Elder, S T and Heath, R G (1963) Intracranial self-stimulation in man, *Science* 140, 394-396.

Blakemore, C and Cooper, F W (1970) Development of the brain depends on the visual environment, *Nature*, 228, 477-8.

Blasdel, G G (1992) Orientation selectivity, preference and continuity in monkey striate cortex, *Journal of Neuroscience*, 12, 3139-3161.

Blass, E M and Hall, W G (1976) Drinking termination: Interactions between hydrational, orogastric and behavioural controls in rats, *Psychological Review*, 183, 356-374.

Blaye, A, Light, P, Joiner, R, et al (1991) Collaboration as a facilitator of planning and problem solving on a computer based task, *British Journal of Educational Psychology*, 61, 471-483.

Bloom, A (1981) *The Linguistic Shaping of Thought: A Study on the Impact of Language on*

Thinking in China and the West, Erlbaum, Hillsdale, NJ.

Bode, (1995) in R Mostel (1995) Horse killing virus may cause mental illness! *New Scientist* 11 March 1995.

Bodenhausen, G V, Kramer, G P and Susser, K (1994) Happiness and stereotypic thinking in social judgement, *Journal of Personality and Social Psychology*, 66, 621-632, in R A Baron and D Byrne (1997) *Social Psychology*, 8th edn, Allyn & Bacon, Boston, MA.

Boesch, C (1994) Cooperative hunting in wild chimpanzees, *Animal Behaviour*, 48, 653-667.

Boesch, C (1996) Social Grouping in Tai Chimpanzees, in W C McGrew, L F Marchant and T Nishida (eds) *Great Ape Societies*, Cambridge University Press, Cambridge.

Boles, D B and Law, M B (1992) Orthogonal lateralized processes have orthogonal attentional resources, Paper presented at the annual meeting of the Psychonomic Society, St Louis, MO, in R A Baron (1996) *Essentials of Psychology*, Allyn & Bacon, Boston, MA.

Bolles, R C (1980) Some functionalist thought about regulation, in F M Toates and T R Halliday (eds) *Analysis of Motivational Processes*, Academic Press, London.

Bond, J, Coleman, P and Pearce, S (1993) *Ageing in Society*, Sage, London.

Bond, M H, Chiu, C K and Wan, K C (1984) When modesty fails: The social impact of group-effacing attributions following success or failure, *European Journal of Social Psychology*, 14, 335-8.

Bonnet, M (1997) in Mind Travellers, *New Scientist* supplement, 26 April 1997, 18-19.

Booth, D A (1981) The physiology of appetite, *British Medical Journal*, 37, 135-140.

Booth, D A, Fuller, J and Lewis, V (1981) Human control of body weight: Cognitive or physiological? Some energy-related perceptions and misperceptions, in L A Cioffi (ed) *The Body Weight Regulatory System: Normal and Disturbed Systems*, Raven Press, New York.

Bootzin, R R, Acocella, J R, Alloy, L B (1993) *Abnormal Psychology: Current Perspectives*, 6th edn, McGraw Hill, New York.

Bootzin, R R, Acocella, J R, Alloy, L B (1996) *Abnormal Psychology: Current Perspectives*,

7th edn, McGraw-Hill, New York.

Bornstein, M H and Lamb, M E (1992) *Development in Infancy: An Introduction*, 3rd ed., Random House, New York.

Botting, J H and Morrison, A R (1997) Animal research is vital to medicine, *Scientific American*, 276 (2), 67-69.

Bouchard, C (1989) Genetic factors in obesity, *Medical Clinics of North America*, 73, 67-81.

Bouchard, C. (1991) Heredity and the path to overweight and obesity, *Medicine and Science of Sports Exercise*, 23, 285-291.

Bouchard, T J, Jr, Lykken, D T, McGue, M *et al.* (1990) Sources of human psychological differences: The Minnesota study of twins reared apart, *Science*, 250, 223-228.

Bouchard, T J, Jr and Segal, N L (1985) Environment and IQ, in B B Wolman (ed) *Handbook of Intelligence: Theories, Measurements and Applications*, Wiley, New York.

Bower, G H, Black, J B and Turner, T J (1979) Scripts in memory for text, *Cognitive Psychology*, 11, 177-220.

Bowers, K S (1990) Unconscious influences and hypnosis, in J L Singer (ed) *Repression and Dissociation: Implications for Personality Theory, Psychopathology and Health*, University of Chacago Press, Chicago.

Bowlby, J (1953) *Child Care and the Growth of Love*, Penguin, Harmondsworth.

Bowlby, J (1969) *Attachment and Loss, I Attachment*, Hogarth Press, London.

Bowlby, J (1980) *Attachment and Loss, III: Loss, Sadness and Depression*, Basic Books, New York.

Bradbury, T N and Fincham, F D (1990) Attributions in marriage: Review and critique, *Psychological Bulletin*, 107, 3-33.

Bradley, R H and Caldwell, B M (1984) 174 Children: A study of the relationships between the home environment and cognitive development during the first five years, in A W Gottfried (ed) *Home Environment and Early Cognitive Development: Longitudinal Research*, Academic Press, New York.

Brady, J V (1958) Ulcers in "Executive Monkeys", *Scientific American*, 199, 95-100.

Brady, J V, Porter, R W, Conrad, D G and Mason, J W (1958) Avoidance behaviour and the

development of gastroduodenal ulcers, *Journal of the Experimental Analysis of Behaviour*, 1, 69-72.

Bransford, J D and Johnson, M K (1972) Contextual prerequisites for understanding: Some investigations of comprehension and recall, *Journal of Verbal Learning and Verbal Behaviour*, 11, 717-726.

Bransford, J D, Morris, J J, Morris, C D and Stein, B S (1979) Some general constraints on learning and memory research, in L S Cermack and F I M Craik (eds) *Levels of processing in human memory*, Erlbaum, Hillsdale, NJ.

Bransford, J D and Stein, B S (1993) *The Ideal Problem Solver*, 2nd edn, W H Freeman, New York.

Braun, D L, Sunday, S P and Halmi, K S (1994) Psychiatric comorbidity in patients with eating disorders, *Psychology Medicine* 24, 859-867.

Bray, G A (1992) Pathophysiology of obesity, *American Journal of Clinical Nutrition*, 55, 488-494.

Brehm, S S (1992) *Intimate Relationships*, 2nd edn, McGraw Hill, New York.

Breier, A, Buchanan, R W, Kirkpatrick, B *et al.* (1994) Effects of dozapine on positive and negative symptoms in outpatients with schizophrenia, *American Journal of Psychiatry*, 151 (1) 20-26.

Brendel, D H, Reynolds, C F, Jennings, J R, Hoch, C C (1990) Sleep stage physiology, mood and vigilance responses to sleep deprivation in healthy 80-year-olds and 20-year-olds, *Psychophysiology*, 27, 677-685.

British Psychological Society (1996) *Code of Conduct, Ethical Principles and Guidelines*, BPS, Leicester.

Broadbent, D E (1958) *Perception and Communication*, Pergamon, Oxford.

Broadbent, D E (1982) Task combination and selective intake of information, *Acta Psychologica*, 50, 253-90.

Brookes, M (1998) The species enigma, *New Scientist*, 158, 2138.

Brooks, L R (1968) Spatial and verbal components of the act of recall, *Canadian Journal of Experimental Psychology*, 22, 349-368.

Brower, L. (1958) New perspectives on the migration biology of the monarch butterfly, in J W Grier and T

Burk (1992) *Biology of Animal Behaviour*, Wm C Brown.

Brown, A L and Palinscar, A S (1989) Guided, cooperative learning and individual knowledge acquisition, in L B Resnick (ed), *Knowing, Learning and Instruction*, Erlbaum, Hillsdale, NJ.

Brown, C R (1986) Cliff swallow colonies as information centers, *Science*, 234, 83-85.

Brown, C R and Brown, M B (1987) Group living in cliff swallows as an advantage in avoiding predators, *Behavioural Ecology and Sociobioloby*, 21, 97-107.

Brown, J A (1958) Some tests of the decay theory of immediate memory, *Quarterly Journal of Experimental Psychology*, 10, 12-21.

Brown, J L (1983) Intersexual selection, *Nature* 302, 472

Brown, J L and Pollitt, E (1996) Malnutrition, poverty and intellectual development, *Scientific American*, February, 26-31.

Brown, R (1986) *Social Psychology: The Second Edition*. Free Press, New York.

Brown, R. (1988) Intergroup relations, in M Hewstone, W Stroebe, J P Codol and G M Stephenson (eds) *Introduction to Social Psychology*, Blackwell, London.

Brown, R and Bellugi, U (1964) Three processes in the child's acquisition of syntax, in P K Smith and H Cowie (1988) *Understanding Children's Development*, Basil Blackwell, Oxford.

Brown, R, Cazden, C B and Bellugi, U (1969) The child's grammar from 1 to 3, in J P Hill (ed) *Minnesota Symposium on Child Psychology, 2*, University of Minnesota Press, Minneapolis, MN.

Brown, R *et al.* (1982) in P K Smith and H Cowie (1991) *Understanding Children's Understanding*, 2nd edn, Blackwell, Oxford.

Brown, R I F (1989) Gaming, gambling, risk taking, addictions and a developmental model of a pathology of man-machine relationships, in T Charlton and K David (eds) *Elusive Links: Television, Video Games and Children's Behaviour*, Park Published Papers.

Brown, R. and Kulik, J (1982) Flashbulb memory, in U Neisser (ed) *Memory Observed: Remembering in Natural Contexts*, W H Freeman, San Francisco.

Browne, K and Pennell, A. The effects of video violence on

young offenders, *Research Findings* (65), Home Office Research and Statistics Directorate.

Brownell, W A (1928) *The Development of Children's Number Ideas in the Primary Grades*, University of Chicago Press, Chicago.

Bruce, H M (1970) Pheromones, *British Medical Bulletin*, 26, 10-13.

Bruce, V and Green, P (1985) in M W Matlin and H J Foley (eds) *Sensation and Perception*, 3rd edn, Allyn & Bacon, Boston, MA.

Bruch, H (1986) Anorexia nervosa: The therapeutic task, in K D Brownell and J P Foreyt (eds) *Handbook of Eating Disorders: Physiology, Psychology and Treatment of Obesity, Anorexia and Bulimia*, Basic Books, New York.

Bruner, J S (1983) *Child's Talk: Learning to Use Language*, Oxford University Press, Oxford.

Bruner, J S, Goodnow, J J and Austin, G A (1956) *A Study of Thinking*, Wiley, New York.

Brunner, D P, Dijk, D J, Tobler, I and Borbely, A A (1990) Effect of partial sleep deprivation on sleep stages and EEG power spectra: Evidence for non-REM and REM sleep homeostasis, *Electroencephalography and Clinical Neurophysiology*, 75, 492-499.

Burke, D M, MacKay, D G, Worthley, J S and Wade, E (1991) On the tip of the tongue: What causes word finding failures in young and older adults?, *Journal of Memory and Language*, 30, 542-579.

Burke, M. (1995) Identities and disclosure: The case of lesbian and gay police officers, *The Psychologist*, 8, 543-547.

Burley, N (1981) Sex ratio manipulation and selection for attractiveness, *Science*, 211, 721-2.

Burt, C (1955) The evidence for the concept of intelligence, *British Journal of Educational Psychology*, 25, 158-177.

Bush, D M and Simmons, R (1987) Gender and coping with the entry into early adolescence, in R C Barnett, L Biener and G K Baruch (eds) *Gender and Stress*, Free Press, New York.

Buss, D M (1987) Sex differences in human mate selection criteria: An evolutionary perspective, in C Crawford, M Smith and D Krebs (eds) *Sociobiology and Psychology: Ideas, Issues and*

Applications, Erlbaum, Hillsdale, NJ.

Buss, D M (1989) Sex differences in human mate preferences: Evolutionary hypotheses tested in 37 cultures, *Behavioural and Brain Sciences*, 12, 1-49.

Buss, D M (1994) Mate preference in 37 cultures, in W J Lowner and R S Malpass (eds) *Psychology and Culture*, Allyn & Bacon, Boston, MA.

Butler, R (1963) The life review: An interpretation of reminiscence in the aged, *Psychiatry*, 26, 65-76.

Butters, N and Cermak, L S (1980) *Alcoholic Korsakoff's Syndrome: An Information Processing Approach*, Academic Press, London.

Butterworth, G and Harris, M (1994) *Principles of Developmental Psychology*, Lawrence Erlbaum, Hove.

Byrne, D (1971) *The Attraction Paradigm*, Academic Press, New York.

Byrne, D (1992) The transition from controlled laboratory experimentation to less controlled settings: Surprise! Additional variables are operative, *Communication Monographs*, 59, 190-198.

Byrne, D and Clore, G L (1970) A reinforcement-affect model of evaluative responses, *Personality: An International Journal*, 1, 103-128.

Byrne, R M J (1989) Suppressing valid inferences with conditionals, *Cognition* 31, 61–83

Cabanac, M (1971) Physiological role of pleasure, *Science*, 173, 1103-1107.

Calles-Escandon, J and Horton, E S (1992) The thermogenic role of exercise in the treatment of morbid obesity: A critical evaluation, *American Journal of Clinical Nutrition*, 55, 533S-537S.

Campbell, A (1996) Sex differences and social behaviour in children and adults, Paper presented at the *ATP Annual Conference*, University of Durham, July 1996.

Campos, J J, Barrett, K C, Lamb M E, et al (1983) Socioemotional development, in P Mussen (ed.) *Handbook of Child Psychology*, vol 2, Wiley, New York.

Campos, J J, Langer A and Krowitz, A (1970) Cardiac responses on the cliff in pre-locomotor human infants, *Science*, 170, 196-197.

Camras, L A, Malatesta, C and Izard, C (1991) in R Feldman

and B Rime (eds) *Fundamentals of Non-verbal Behavior*, Cambridge University Press, Cambridge.

Cann, A, Calhoun, L G and Banks, J S (1995) On the role of humour appreciation in interpersonal attraction: It's no joking matter, *Humour: International Journal of Humour Research*, R A Baron and D Byrne (1997) *Social Psychology*, 8th edn, Allyn & Bacon, Boston, MA.

Caprara, G V, Barbaranelli, C, Pastorelli, C and Perugini, M (1994) Individual differences in the study of human aggression, *Aggressive Behaviour* 20, 291-303, in R A Baron and D Byrne (1997) *Social Psychology*, 8th edn, Allyn & Bacon, Boston, MA.

Caramazza, A and Zurif, E B (1976) Dissociation of algorithmic and heuristic processes in language comprehension: Evidence from aphasia, *Brain and Language*, 3, 572-582.

Carlson, N R (1994) *Physiology of Behaviour*, 5th edn, Allyn & Bacon, Boston.

Carlson, N R (1998), *Physiology of Behaviour*, 6th edn, Allyn & Bacon, Boston, MA.

Carlson, N R and Buskist, W (1997) *Psychology: The Science of Behaviour*, 5th edn, Allyn & Bacon, Boston, MA.

Carraher, T N, Carraher, D W and Schliemann A D (1985) Mathematics in the streets and in the schools, *British Journal of Developmental Psychology*, 3, 21-29.

Carroll, J B and Casagrande, J B (1958) The function of language classifications in behaviour, in E E Maccoby, T M Newcombe and E L Hartley (eds) *Readings in Social Psychology*, 3rd edn, Holt, Rinehart & Winston, New York.

Carter, C S and Marr, J N (1970) Olfactory imprinting and age variables in the guinea pig (*Cavia porcellus*), *Animal Behaviour*, 18, 238-244.

Carthy, J D (1963) *Animal Navigation*, George Allen & Unwin Ltd, London.

Cartwright, J (1996) Human mating behaviour, *Psychology Review*, 3, 22-6.

Cartwright, J (1996) The mating game, *Psychology Review*, 2(3), 6-10.

Cartwright, R D (1989) in R A Baron (1996) *Essentials of Psychology*, Allyn & Bacon, Boston, MA.

Cartwright, R D (1990) in R A Baron (1996) *Essentials of Psychology*, Allyn & Bacon,

Boston, MA.

Cartwright, S (1994) Paper presented at ATP Association for the Teaching of Psychology conference, Manchester, January 1994.

Carver, C S and Glass, D C (1978) Coronary-prone behaviour pattern and interpersonal aggression, *Journal of Personality and Social Psychology*, 36, 361-366.

Carver, C S, Pozo, C, Harris, S D *et al.* (1993) How coping mediates the effect of optimism on distress: A study of women with early stage breast cancer, *Journal of Personality and Social Psychology*, 65, 735-390.

Case, R, (1974) Structures and structures, some functional limitations on the course of cognitive growth, *Cognitive Psychology*, 6, 544-573.

Case, R, (1984) The process of stage-transition: A neo-Piagetian view, in R J Sternberg (ed.) *Mechanisms of Cognitive Development*, Freeman, New York.

Case, R, (1985) *Intellectual Development: A Systematic Reinterpretation*, Academic Press, New York.

Case, R, (1992) Neo-Piagetian theories of intellectual development, in H Bellin and P B Pufall (eds) *Piaget's Theory: Prospects and Possibilities*, Erlbaum, Hillsdale NJ.

Cassell, C and Walsh, S (1993) Being seen but not heard: Barriers to women's equality in the workplace, *The Psychologist*, vol 6.

Cattell, R B (1963) Theory of fluid and crystallized intelligence: A critical experiment, *Journal of Educational Psychology*, 54, 1-22.

Cenci, M A Kalen, P, Mandel, R J and Bjoerklund, A (1992) Regional differences in the regulation of dopamine and noradrenaline release in medial frontal cortex, nucleus acumbens and caudate-putamen: A microdialysis study in the rat, *Brain Research*, 581, 217-228.

Chalmers, A F (1982) *What Is This Thing Called Science?*, 2nd edn, Open University Press, Milton Keynes.

Chan-Ling, T and Stone, J (1991) Factors determining the morphology and distribution of astrocytes in the cat retina: A "contact spacing" model of astrocyte interaction, *The Journal of*

Comparative Neurology, 303, 387-399.

Chandler, M, Fritz, A S, and Hala, S (1989) Small scale deceit: Deception as a marker of two, three and four year olds' early theory of mind, *Child development*, 60, 1263-1277.

Charlton, T (1997) The inception of broadcast television: A naturalistic study of television's effects in St. Helena, South Atlantic, in T Charlton and K David (eds) *Elusive Links: Television, Video Games and Children's Behaviour*, Park Published Papers.

Charlton, T and David, K (1997) *Elusive Links: Television, Video Games and Children's Behaviour*, Park Published Papers.

Charnov, E L and Krebs, J R (1975) The evolution of alarm calls: Altruism or manipulation?, *American Naturalist*, 109, 107-112.

Chen, J (1993) Dopaminergic mechanisms and brain reward, *Seminars in the Neurosciences*, 5, 315-320.

Cheney, D L and Seyfarth, R M (1990) *How Monkeys See The World*, University of Chicago Press, Chicago.

Cheng, P N and Holyoak K J (1985) Pragmatic reasoning schemes, *Cognitive Psychology*, 17, 391-416.

Cheng, P N, Holyoak, K J, Nisbett, R E and Oliver, L M (1986) Pragmatic versus syntactic approaches to training deductive reasoning, *Cognitive Psychology*, 18, 293-328.

Chengappa, K N Z, Sheltou, M D, Baker, R U *et al.* (1994) The prevalence of akathisia in patients receiving stable doses of clozapine, *Journal of Clinical Psychiatry*, 55 (4), 142-145.

Cherry, E C (1953) Some experiments on the recognition of speech with one and two ears, *Journal of the Acoustical Society of America*, 25, 975-79.

Chi, M T H, Feltovich, P J and Glaser, R (1981) Categorisation and representation of physics problems by experts and novices, *Cognitive Science*, 5, 121-152.

Chi, M T H and Klahr, D (1975) Span and rate of apprehension in children and adults, *Journal of Experimental Child Psychology*, 19, 434-439.

Chi, M T H and Koeske, R D (1983) Network representation of a child's dinosaur knowledge,

Developmental Psychology, 19, 434-439.

Chiu, Lian-Hwang (1988) Locus of control differences between American and Chinese adolescents, *Journal of Social Psychology*, 128, 411-413.

Choderow, N (1974) Family structure and feminine personality, in M Z Rosaldo and L Lamphere (eds) *Women, Culture and Society*, Stanford University Press, Stanford, CA.

Chomsky, N (1957) *Syntactic Structures*, Mouton, The Hague, Netherlands.

Chomsky, N (1965) *Aspects of the Theory of Syntax*, MIT Press, Cambridge, MA.

Christiaanson, R E and Ochalek, K (1983) Editing misleading information from memory: Evidence for the co-existence of original and post-event information, *Memory and Cognition*, 11, 467-475.

Cialdini, R B (1994) Interpersonal influence, in S Shavitt and T C Brock (eds) *Persuasion*, 195-218, Allyn & Bacon, Boston, in R A Baron and D Byrne (1997) *Social Psychology*, 8th edn, Allyn & Bacon, Boston, MA.

Cialdini, R B, Brown, S L, Lewis, B P, Luce, C and Neuberg, S L (1997) Reinterpreting the empathy-altruism relationship: When one into one equals oneness, *Journal of Personality and Social Psychology*, 73(3) 481-494.

Cialdini, R B, Kallgran, C A and Reno, R R (1991) A focus theory of normative conduct, *Advances in Experimental Social Psychology*, 24, 201-234, in R A Baron and D Byrne (1997) *Social Psychology*, 8th edn, Allyn & Bacon, Boston.

Cialdini, R B, Kenrick, D T and Baumann, D J (1982) Effects of mood on prosocial behaviour in children and adults, in N Eisenberg-Berg (ed) *Development of Prosocial Behaviour*, Academic Press, New York.

Clark, M S (1991) *Prosocial Behaviour*, Sage, Newbury Park.

Clarke, A M and Clarke, A D B (1976) *Early Experience: Myth and Evidence*, Free Press, New York.

Clarke, M S, Mills, J and Corcoran, D (1989) Keeping track of needs and inputs of friends and strangers, *Journal of Personality and Social Psychology*, 15, 533-542.

Clarke-Stewart, K A, (1988) The "effects" of infant day care

reconsidered, *Early Childhood Research Quarterly*, 3, 293-318.

Clarke-Stewart, K A, (1989) Infant day care: Maligned or malignant?, *American Psychologist*, 44, 266-273.

Clarkin, J F, Click, I D, Haas, G L, Spencer, J H *et al.* (1990) A randomised clinical trial of impatient family intervention V results for affective disorders, *Journal of Affective Disorders*, 18, 17-28.

Clayton, N S and Dickinson, A (1998) Episodic-like memory during cache recovery by scrub-jays, *Nature*, 395, 272-274.

Clegg, F (1982) *Simple Statistics: A Course Book for the Social Sciences*, Cambridge University Press, Cambridge.

Clifford, B R and Hollin, C (1981) Effects of type of incident and the number of perpetrators on eyewitness memory, *Journal of Applied Psychology*, 66, 364-370.

Cloniger, C R (1987) Neurogenetic adaptive mechanisms in alcoholism, *Science*, 236, 410-416.

Cloniger, C R, Bohmann, M, Sigvardsson, S and von Knorring, A-L (1985) Psychopathology in adopted-out children of alcoholics (1985): The Stockholm Adoption Study, *Recent Developments in Alcoholism*, 3, 37-51.

Clutton-Brock, T H and Albon, S D (1979) The roaring of red deer and the evolution of honest advertisement, *Behaviour*, 69, 145-70.

Clutton-Brock, T H and Albon, S D (1989) *Red Deer in the Highlands*, BSP Professional Books, Oxford.

Clutton-Brock, T H, Albon, S D and Guinness, F E (1989) Fitness costs of gestation and lactation in wild mammals, *Nature*, 337, 260-262.

Clutton-Brock, T H and Godfrey, C (1991) Parental investment, in J R Krebs and N B Davies (eds) *Ecology: An Evolutionary Approach* (1981), Blackwell Scientific, Oxford.

Clutton-Brock, T H, Guinness, F E and Albon, S D (1982) *Red Deer: Behaviour and Ecology of Two Sexes*, Edinburgh University Press, Edinburgh.

Cochrane, R (1995) Women and Depression, *Psychology Review*, 2(1), 20-24.

Cochrane, R (1996) Marriage and madness, *Psychology Review*, 3(1), 2-5.

Cohen, G (1990) Memory, in I Roth (ed) *The Open University's Introduction to*

Psychology, vol 2, Psychology Press, Hove.

Cohen, G (1993) Everyday memory and memory systems: The experimental approach, in G Cohen, G Kill and M LeVoi, *Memory: Current Issues*, 2nd edn, Open University Press, Buckingham.

Cohen, G (1996) *Memory in the Real World*, 2nd edn, Psychology Press, Hove.

Cohen, J M and Cohen, M J (1971) *Penguin Dictionary of Modern Quotations* 2nd edn, Penguin, Harmondsworth.

Cohen, N J and Squire, L R (1980) Preserved learning and retention of pattern analysing skills in amnesia: Dissociation of knowing how from knowing that, *Science*, 210, 207-210.

Colby, A, Kohlberg, L and Lieberman, M (1983) A longitudinal study of moral judgment, *Monographs of the Society for Research in Child Development*, 48, 1-2.

Cole, J O, Klerman, G L, Goldberg, S C *et al.* (1964) Phenothiazine treatment in acute schizophrenia, *Archives of General Psychiatry*, 10, 246-261.

Cole, M and Cole, S R (1993) *The Development of Children*, 2nd edn, Freeman, New York.

Coleman, J C and Henry, L (1990) *The Nature of Adolescence*, 2nd edn, Routledge, London.

Coleman, R M (1986) *Wide Awake at 3 am*, W H Freeman, New York.

Collins, A M and Quillian, M R (1969) Retrieval time from semantic memory, *Journal of Verbal Learning and Verbal Behaviour*, 8, 240-247.

Collins, A M and Quillian, M R (1972) How to make a language user, in E Tulving and W Donaldson (eds) *Organization of Memory*, Academic Press, New York.

Coltheart, M (1980) Deep Dyslexia: A right hemisphere hypothesis, in M Coltheart, K Patterson and J C Marshall (eds) *Deep Dyslexia*, Routledge, London.

Coltheart, M (1985) Cognitive neuropsychology and the study of reading, in M I Posner and O S M Marin (eds) *Attention and Performance*, vol 11, 3-37, Erlbaum, Hillsdale, NJ.

Coltheart, M (1985) Cognitive neuropsychology and the study of reading, in M I Posner and O S M Marin (eds) *Attention and Performance, Vol. 11*, 3-37, Erlbaum, Hillsdale, NJ.

Condon, R G (1987) *Inuit Youth*, Rutgers University Press, New Brunswick, NJ.

Contrada, R J (1989) Type A behaviour, personality hardiness and cardiovascular responses to stress, *Journal of Personality and Social Psychology*, 57, 895-905.

Cook, T D and Campbell, D T (1979) *Quasi Experimentation: Design and Analysis Issues for Field Settings*, Rand McNally, Chicago.

Cooley, C H (1902) *Human Nature and the Social Order*, Charles Scribner's Sons, New York.

Coolican, H (1994) *Research Methods and Statistics in Psychology* 2nd edn, Hodder & Stoughton, London.

Cooper, P J (1995) Eating disorders, in A A Lazarus and A M Colman (eds) *Abnormal Psychology*, Longman, London.

Corder, E H, Saunders, A M, Strittmatter, W J *et al.* (1993) Gene dose of apolipoprotein E type 4 allele and the risk of Alzheimer's disease in late onset families, *Science*, 261, 921-923.

Coren, S, Porac, C and Ward, L M (1979) Activity on caffeine stimulant and figure reversal, in M W Matlin and H J Foley (eds) *Sensation and Perception*, international edn (1979), Academic Press.

Coren, S and Ward, L M (1989) in M W Matlin and H J Foley (eds) *Sensation and Perception*, 3rd edn, Harcourt Brace Jovanovich, San Diego.

Coslett, H B (1991) Read but not write "idea". Evidence for a third reading mechanism, *Brain and Language*, 40, 425-443.

Costa, P T Jr and McCrae, R R (1994) The revised NEO personality inventory, in R Briggs and J M Cheek (eds) *Personality Measures: Development and Evaluation*, JAI Press, Greenwich, CT.

Cota, A A, Evans, C R, Dion, K L, Kilik, L and Longman, R S (1995) The structure of group cohesion, *Personality and Social Psychology Bulletin*, 21, 572-580, in R A Baron and D Byrne (1997) *Social Psychology*, 8th edn, Allyn & Bacon, Boston, MA.

Coulon, J (1973) Le repertoire sonores du cobaye domestique et sa signification comportmentale, *Rev. Comp. Animal.*, 7(2), 121-132.

Covina, N A, Jimerson, D C, Wolfe, B E, Franko, D L and Frankel, F H (1994) Hypnotizability, dissociation and bulimia, *Journal of Abnormal Psychology*, 103, 455-459.

Cox, C R and LeBoeuf, B J (1977) Female incitation of mate competition: a mechanism of mate selection, *American Naturalist*, III, 317-335.

Cox, R H (1991) Intervention strategies, in A Monat and R S Lazarus (eds) *Stress and Coping: An Anthology*, Colombia University Press, New York.

Cox, R H (1993) in R L Atkinson, R C Atkinson, D J Bem and S Hoeksema (1996) *Introduction to Psychology*, 12th edn, Harcourt Brace. Fort Worth, TX.

Cox, R H, Qiu, Y and Liu, Z (1993) *Overview of Sports Psychology*, Harcourt Brace, Fort Worth.

Craig, G J (1992) *Human Development*, 6th edn, Prentice-Hall, Englewood Cliffs, NJ.

Craig, J A, Koestner, R and Zuroff, D C (1994) Implicit and self-attributed intimacy motivation, *Journal of Social and Personal Relationships*, 11, 491-507.

Craik, F I M and Lockhart, R S (1972) Levels of processing: A framework for memory research, *Journal of Verbal Learning and Verbal Behavior*, 11, 671-684.

Craik, F I M and Tulving, E (1975) Depth of processing and retention of words in episodic memory, *Journal of Experimental Psychology*, 104, 268-294.

Craik, F I M and Watkins, M J (1973) The role of rehearsal in short-term memory, *Journal of Verbal Learning and Verbal Behavior*, 12, 599-607.

Crandall, C S (1988) Social contagion of binge eating, *Journal of Personality and Social Psychology*, 55, 588-598, in M Argyle (1998) *Psychology: Social Influence*, BPS Open Learning Units, Leicester.

Crandall, J E (1984) Social interest as a moderator of life stress, *Journal of Personality and Social Psychology*, 47, 164-174.

Crawford, H J (1994) Brain dynamics and hypnosis: Attentional and disattentional processes, *International Journal of Clinical and Experimental Hypnosis*, 42, 204-231.

Crawford, H J and Barabasz, A E (1993) Phobias and intense fears: Facilitating their treatment with hypnosis, in J W Rhue, S J Lynn and I Kirsch (eds) *Handbook of Clinical Hypnosis*, American Psychological Association, Washington, DC.

Crawford, H J, Brown, A M and Moon, C E (1993) Sustained attentional and disattentional abilities: Differences between low and highly hypnotisable persons, *Journal of Abnormal Psychology*, 102, 534-543.

Crawford, M and Unger, R K (1995) Gender issues in psychology, in A M Colman (ed) *Controversies in Psychology*, Longman, London.

Creasey, G L and Myers, B J (1986) Video games and children: Effects in leisure activities, schoolwork and peer involvement, in T Charlton and K David (eds) *Elusive Links: Television, Video Games and Children's Behaviour*, Park Published Papers.

Crook, C (1992) Cultural artifacts in social development: The case of computers, in H McGurk (ed.) *Childhood Social Development: Contemporary Perspectives*, Lawrence Erlbaum, Hove.

Crowley, J (1986) Longitudinal effects of retirement on men's well-being and health, *Journal of Business and Psychology*, 1, 95-113.

Croyle, R T (1992) Appraisal of health threats: Cognition, motivation and social comparison, *Cognitive Therapy and Research*, 16, 165-182.

Culebras, A and Moore, J T (1989) Magnetic resonance findings in REM sleep behaviour disorder, *Neurology*, 39, 1519-1523.

Cumberbatch, G (1987) *The Portrayal of Violence on British Television*, BBC Publications, London, in R Gross (1996) *Psychology: The Science of Mind and Behaviour*, 3rd edn, Hodder and Stoughton, London.

Cumberbatch, G (1997) Media violence: Science and common sense, *Psychology Review*, 3(4), 2-7.

Cunningham, M R (1989) Reactions of heterosexual opening gambits; female selectivity and male responsiveness, *Personality and Social Psychology Bulletin*, 15, 27-41.

Cunningham, M R (1989) Reactions to heterosexual opening gambits; female selectivity and male responsiveness, *Personality and Social Psychology Bulletin*, 15, 27-41.

Curtiss, S (1977) *Genie: A Psycholinguistic Study of a Modern Day "Wild Child"*, Academic Press, London.

Cutler, A and Butterfield, S (1992) Rhythmic cues to speech segmentation. Evidence from juncture misperception, *Journal of Memory and Language*, 31, 218-236.

Czeisler, C A, Johnson, M P, Duffy, J F, Brown, E N (1990) Exposure to bright light and darkness to treat physiological maladaption to night work, *New England Journal of Medicine*, 322, 1254-1259.

Czeisler, C A, Kronhauer, R E, Allan, J S, Duffy, F J (1989) Bright light induction of strong (Type O) resetting of the human circadian pacemaker, *Science*, 244, 1328-1333.

Damasio, H (1989) Neuroimaging contributions to the understanding of aphasia, in F Boller and J Grafman (eds) *Handbook of Neuropsychology*, vol 2, Elsevier.

Damon, W (1983) *Social and Personality Development*, W W Norton, New York.

Damon, W and Hart, D (1988) *Self-Understanding in Childhood and Adolescence*, Cambridge University Press, Cambridge.

Damsma, G, Day, J and Fibiger, H (1989) Lack of tolerance to nicotine-induced dopamine release in the nucleus accumbens, *European Journal of Pharmacology*, 168, 363-368.

Damsma, G, Pfaus, J G, Wenkstern, C et al. (1992) Sexual behaviour increases in the nucleus accumbens and striatum of male rats: Comparison with novelty and locomotion, *Behavioural Neuroscience*, 106, 181-91.

Daniels, H (1996) *An Introduction to Vygotsky*, Routledge, London.

Darley, J M and Bateson, C D (1973) From Jerusalem to Jerico: A study of situational and dispositional variables in helping behaviour, *Journal of Personality and Social Psychology*, 27, 100-108.

Darley, J M and Latane, B (1968) Bystander intervention in emergencies: Diffusion of responsibility, *Journal of Personality and Social Psychology*, 8, 377-383.

Darley, J M, Teger, I and Lewis, L D (1973) Do groups always inhibit individuals' responses to potential emergencies? *Journal of Personality and Social Psychology*, 26, 395-399.

Darwin, C R (1859) *The Origin of Species by Means of Natural Selection*, John Murray, London.

Darwin, C R (1871) *The Descent of Man and Selection in Relation to Sex*, John Murray, London.

Darwin, C R (1872) *The Expression of the Emotions in Man and Animals*, University of Chicago Press, London.

Davidoff, (1975) in S Coren, C Porac and L M Ward (eds) *Sensation and Perception*, international edn (1979), Academic Press, San Diego, CA.

Davies, G (1989) Children as witnesses, in A M Colman and J G Beaumont (eds) *Psychological Survey*, no 7, BPS/Routledge, Leicester.

Davies, N B (1983) Polyandry, cloaca-pecking and sperm competition in dunnocks, *Nature*, 302, 334-336.

Davies, N B and Lundberg, A (1984) Food distribution and a variable mating system in the dunnock, *Prunella modularis*, *Journal of Animal Ecology*, 53, 895-913.

Davies, N, Kilner, R and Noble, D (1998) Proceedings of the Royal Society, series B, 265, reported in *New Scientist* 158, 15.

Davies, R (1995) Selfish altruism: A problem in dialectics, *Psychology Review*, 1(4), 2-9.

Davies, S, Thornicroft, G, Leese, M, Higginbotham, A and Phelan, M (1996) Ethnic differences in risk of compulsory psychiatric admission among representative cases of psychosis in London, *British Journal of Medicine*, 2 March 312.

Davison, G C and Neale, J M (1994) *Abnormal Psychology*, 6th edn, John Wiley, New York.

Dawkins, R (1982) *The Extended Phenotype*, Oxford University Press, Oxford.

Dawkins, R (1986) *The Blind Watchmaker*, Penguin, Harmondsworth.

Dawkins, R (1989) *The Selfish Gene*, Oxford University Press, Oxford.

Dawkins, R and Krebs, J R (1978) Animal signals: Information or manipulation?, in J R Krebs and N B Davies (eds) *Behavioural Exology: An Evolutionary Approach*, Blackwell Scientific, Oxford.

Dawson, (1966) In S Coren, C Porac and L M Ward (eds) *Sensation and Perception*, international edn (1979), Academic Press, San Diego, CA.

de Alberdi, L (1990) *People, Psychology and Business*, Cambridge University Press, Cambridge.

De Bold, A J (1985) Atrial natriuretic factor: A hormone produced by the heart, *Science*, 230, 767-770.

De Bold, A J, Borenstein, H B, Veres, A T and Sonnenberg, H (1981) A rapid and potent natriuretic response to intravenous injection of atrial myocardial extracts in rats, *Life Science*, 28, 89-94.

de Villiers, P A and de Villiers, J G (1979) *Early Language*, Harvard University Press, Cambridge, MA.

Dean, A L, Malik, M M, Richards, W and Stringer, S A (1986) Effects of parental maltreatment on children's conceptions of interpersonal relationships, *Developmental Psychology*, 22, 617-626.

Delemonte, M M (1990) in D Fernald (1997) *Psychology*, Prentice Hall, Englewood Cliffs, NJ.

Delemonte, N M (1995) in D Fernald (1997) *Psychology*, Prentice Hall, Englewood Cliffs, NJ.

Dell, G S (1986) A spreading-activation theory of retrieval in sentence production, *Pschological Review*, 93, 283-321.

Dell, G S (1988) The retrieval of phonological forms in production: Tests of predictions from a connectionist model, *Journal of Memory and Language*, 27, 124-142.

Dembrowski, T M and Williams, R B (1989) Definition and assessment of coronary-prone behaviour, in N Schneiderman, P Kaufmann and S M Weiss (eds) *Handbook of Research Methods in Cardiovascular Behavioral Medicine*, Plenum, New York.

Denmark, F, Russo, N F, Frieze, I H and Sechzer, J A (1988) Guidelines for avoiding sexism in psychological research, *American Psychologist*, 43(7), 582-585.

Dennis, W (1973) *Children of the Creche*, Appleton-Century-Crofts, New York.

Denzin, N K and Lincoln, Y S (1998) *Strategies of Qualitative Enquiry*, Sage, London.

Deregowski, J B (1972) Pictorial perception and culture, *Scientific American*, 227, 82-88.

Deutsch, J A and Deutsch, D (1963) Attention: Some theoretical considerations, *Psychological Review*, 70, 80-90.

Deux, K, Dane, F C and Wrightsman, L S (1993) *Social Psychology in the '90s*, 6th edn, Brooks Cole, Belmont, CA.

Deux, K and Wrightsman, L S (1988) *Social Psychology*, (5th edn), Brooks Cole, Belmont, CA.

Devalle, D (1996) Da Capo: Science and social psychology, in R Spasford (ed), *Issues for Social Psychology*, Open University, Milton Keynes.

DeValois, R L and DeValois, K K (1975) Neural coding of color, in E C Carterette and M P Friedman (eds) *Handbook of Perception, vol 5*, Academic Press, New York.

Devane, W A, Hanus, L, Breuer, A et al. (1992) Isolation and structure of a brain constituent that binds to the cannabinoid receptor, *Science*, 258, 1946-1049.

Diamond, J (1991) *The Rise and Fall of the Third Chimpanzee*, Vintage, London.

Diamond, M (1982) Sexual identity, monozygotic twins reared in discordant sex roles and a BBC follow-up, *Archives of Sexual Behaviour*, 11, 181-186.

Diamond, M (1984) A love affair with the brain (a conversation), *Psychology Today*, 18(11), 62-73.

Diamond, M (1988) *Enriching Heredity: The Impact of Environment on the Anatomy of the Brain*, Free Press, New York.

DiChiara, G and Imperato, A (1987) Preferential simulation of dopamine release in the nucleus acumbens by opiates, alcohol and barbiturates: studies with transcerebral dialysis in freely moving rats, *Annals of the New York Academy of Sciences*, 473, 367-381.

Dienes, Z P (1966) *Mathematics in the Primary School*, Macmillan, London.

Dimsdale, J E (1988) A perspective on Type A behaviour and coronary disease, *The New England Journal of Medicine*, 318, 110-112.

Dindia, K and Baxter, L A (1987) Maintenance and repair strategies in marital relationships, *Journal of Social and Personal Relationships*, 4, 143-158, in N Hayes (1994) *Foundations of Psychology: An Introductory Text*, Routledge, London.

Dinges, N G and Hull, P (1992) Personality, culture and international studies, in D Lieberman (ed.), *Revealing the world: An interdisciplinary reader for international studies*,

Kendall-Hunt, Dubuque, IA.

Doise, W and Mugny, G (1984) *The Social Development of the Intellect*, Pergamon, Oxford

Dovidio, J F, Piliavin, J A, Gaertner, S L, Schroeder, D A and Clark, R D III (1991) The arousal: Cost-reward model and the process of intervention: a review of the evidence in M S Clark (ed) (1991) *Prosocial Behaviour*, Sage, Newbury Park CA.

Dowdney, et al (1985) in R A Baron (1996) *Essentials of Psychology*, Allyn & Bacon, Boston, MA.

Downey, J L and Damhave, K W (1991) The effects of place, type of comment and effort expended on the perception of flirtation, *Journal of Social Behaviour and Personality*, 6, 35-43, in R A Baron and D Byrne (1997) *Social Psychology*, 8th edn, Allyn & Bacon, Boston, MA.

Driver, J and Tipper, S P (1989) On the nonselectivity of "selective seeing": Contrasts between interference and priming in selective attention, *Journal of Experimental Psychology: Human Perception and Performance*, 15, 304-14.

Duck, S (1988) *Relating to Others*, Open University Press, Milton Keynes.

Duck, S (1992) *Human Relationships*, Sage, London.

Dunbar, R (1995) Are you lonesome tonight?, *New Scientist*, 145, 26-31.

Dunbar, R I M (1988) *Primate Social Systems*, Cornell University Press, Ithaca, NY and Croom Helm, London.

Dunbar, R I M (1993) Co-evolution of neocortex size, group size and language in humans, *Behavioural and Brain Sciences*.

Duncan, J and Humphreys, G W (1989) A resemblance theory of visual search, *Psychological Review*, 96, 433-458.

Duncan, J and Humphreys, G W (1992) Beyond the search surface: Visual search and attentional engagement, *Journal of Experimental Psychology: Human Perception and Performance*, 18, 578-88.

Duncan, P, Ritter, P L, Dornbusch, S M, Gross, R T and Carlsmith, J M (1985) The effects of pubertal timing on body image, school behavior and deviance, *Journal of Youth and Adolescence*, 14, 227-235.

Dunn, J (1988) *The Beginnings of Social Understanding*, Harvard University Press, Cambridge, MA.

Durkin, K (1995) *Developmental Social Psychology: From Infancy to Old Age*, Blackwell, Oxford.

Dwair, M and Van Sickle, T D, Western psychotherapy in traditional Arabic societies, *Clinical Review*, 16(3), 231-249.

Dweck, C (1990) Towards a theory of goals: Their role in motivation and personality, in R A Dienstbier (ed) *Nebraska Symposium Motivation*, vol 38, University of Nebraska Press, Lincoln.

Dweck, C S, Davidson, W, Nelson, S and Enna, B (1978) Sex differences in learned helplessness: II. The contingencies of evaluative feedback in the classroom. III. An experimental analysis, *Developmental Psychology*, 14, 268-276.

Eagly, A H (1987) *Sex Differences in Social Behaviour: A Social-Role Interpretation*, Lawrence Erlbaum Associates, London.

Eagly, A H (1994) On comparing women and men, *Feminism & Psychology*, 4 (4), 513-522.

Eagly, A H, Makhijani, M G and Klonsky, B G (1992) Gender and the evaluation of leaders: a meta-analysis, *Psychological Bulletin*, 111, 3-22, in R A Baron and D Byrne (1997) *Social Psychology*, 8th edn, Allyn & Bacon, Boston, MA.

Eagly, A H and Wood (1991) in P Turner (1995) *Sex, Gender and Identity*, BPS Books, Leicester.

Eaton and Weil (1955) in A Bandura and R Waites (1963), *Social Learning and Personality Development*, Holt, Rhinehart and Winston, New York.

Eibl-Eibesfeld, I (1951) Beobachtungen zur Fortpflanzungsbiologie und Jungendentwicklung des Eichhornchens, in J W Grier and T Burk (1992) *Biology of Animal Behaviour*, Wm C Brown.

Eisenberg, N, Miller, P, Shell, R *et al.* (1991) Prosocial development in adolescence: A longitudinal study, *Developmental Psychology*, 27, 849-857.

Eisenberg, N, Shell, R, Pasternack, J *et al.* (1987) Prosocial development in middle childhood: A longitudinal study, *Developmental Psychology*, 23, 712-718.

Eisenman, R (1985) Marijuana use and attraction: Support for Byrne's similarity attraction concept, *Perceptual and Motor Skills*, 61, 582, in R A Baron and D Byrne (1997)

Social Psychology, 8th edn, Allyn & Bacon, Boston, MA.

Eisner, T and Aneshansley, D J (1982) Spray aiming in bombadier beetles: Jet deflection by the coanda effect, *Science*, 215, 83-5.

Elgar, M (1987) Food intake rate and resource availability: flocking decisions in house sparrows, *Animal Behaviour*, 35, 1168-1176.

Elgar, M (1989) Predator vigilance and group size among mammals and birds: a critical review of the evidence, *Biological Review*, 64, 13-34.

Ellenberger, H F (1970) *The Discovery of the Unconscious*, Basic Books, New York.

Elliot, R (1988) Test abilities race and conflict, *Intelligence*, 12, 333-350.

Elliott, C D, Murray, D J and Pearson, L S (1979) *British Ability Scales*, National Foundation for Educational Research, Slough, in R A Baron (1996) *Essentials of Psychology*, Allyn & Bacon, Boston, MA.

Elliott, E S and Dweck, C S (1988) Goals: An approach to motivation and achievement, *Journal of Personality and Social Psychology*, 54, 5-12.

Ellis, A W (1984) *Reading, Writing and Dyslexia: A Cognitive Analysis*, Lawrence Erlbaum, Hove.

Ellis, A W and Young, A W (1988) *Human Cognitive Neuropsychology*, Lawrence Erlbaum, Hove.

Elsner, N (1981) Developmental aspects of insect neuroethology, in K Immelmann, G W Barlow, L Petrinovitch and M Main (eds) *Behavioural Development*, Cambridge University Press, Cambridge.

Emde, R N (1992) Individual meaning and increasing complexity: Contributions of Sigmund Freud and René Spitz to developmental psychology, *Developmental Psychology*, 28, 347-359.

Emlen, S T, Demong, N I and Emlen, D J (1989) Experimental induction of infanticide in female wattled jacanas, *Auk*, 106, 1-7.

Emlen, S T and Oring, L W (1977) Ecology, sexual selection, and the evolution of mating systems, *Science*, 197, 215-33.

Endler, J A (1991) Interactions between predators and prey, in J R Krebs and Davies, N (eds) *Behavioural Ecology: An Evolutionary Approach*, Blackwell, Oxford.

Enquist, M and Lemar, O (1993)

The evolution of cooperation in mobile organisms, *Animal Behaviour*, 45, 747-757.

Epstein, A N (1982) The physiology of thirst, in D W Pfaff (ed) *The Physiological Mechanisms of Motivation*, pp 165-214, Birkhauser, Boston, MA.

Epstein, A N (1987) Drinking behaviour, in G Adelman (ed) *Encyclopedia of Neuroscience*, Birkhauser, Boston, MA. p 340

Eriksen, C W (1990) Attentional search of the visual field, in D Brogan (ed) *Visual Search*, Taylor and Francis, London.

Erikson, E H (1965) *Childhood and Society*, Penguin, Harmodsworth.

Erikson, E H (1968) *Identity: Youth and Crisis*, W W Norton, New York.

Erikson, E H (1980) *Identity and the Life Cycle*, International University Press, New York.

Erikson, E H, Erikson, J M and Kivnick, H Q (1986) *Involvement in Old Age*, W W Norton, New York.

Erikson, M F, Sroufe, L A and Egeland, B (1985) The relationship between quality of attachment and behaviour problems in preschool in a high-risk sample, *Monographs of the Society for Research in Child Development*, 50, 147-166, in P Erwin (1993), *Friendship and Peer Relations in Children*, Wiley, Chichester.

Ervin-Tripp, S (1964) Imitation and structural change in children's language, in E H Lenneberg (ed) *New Directions in the Study of Language*, MIT Press, Cambridge, MA.

Erwin, P. (1993) *Friendship and Peer Relations in Children*, Wiley, Chichester.

Estes, W K (1970) *Learning Theory and Mental Development*, Academic Press, New York.

Everill, J T and Waller, G (1995) Dissociation and bulimia: Research and theory, *European Eating Disorders Review*, 3, 129-147.

Evett, L J and Humphreys, G W (1981) The use of abstract graphemic information in lexical access, *Quarterly Journal of Experimental Psychology*, 33a, 325-350.

Ewert, J P (1987) Neuroethology of releasing mechanisms: Prey catching in toads, *Behavioural and Brain Sciences*, 10, 337-403.

Eysenck, H J (1971) *Race, Intelligence and Education*, Temple-Smith, London.

Eysenck, M W (1979) Depth, elaboration and distinctiveness, in L S Cermak and F I M Craik (eds) *Levels of*

Processing in Human Memory, Erlbaum, Hillsdale, NJ.

Eysenck, M W (1982) *Attention and Arousal: Cognition and Performance*, Springer-Verlag, Berlin.

Eysenck, M W (1984) *A Handbook of Cognitive Psychology*, Lawrence Erlbaum, Hove.

Eysenck, M W (1993) *Principles of Cognitive Psychology*, Erlbaum, Hillsdale, NJ.

Eysenck, M W (1994) *Individual Differences*, Lawrence Erlbaum, Hove UK.

Eysenck, M W (1994) *Perspectives on Psychology*, Lawrence Erlbaum, Hove.

Eysenck, M W (1996) *Simply Psychology*, Lawrence Erlbaum, Hove.

Eysenck, M W and Eysenck, M C (1980) Effect of processing depth, distinctiveness and word frequency on retention, *British Journal of Psychology*, 71, 263-74.

Eysenck, M W and Keane, M T (1995) *Cognitive Psychology: A Student's Handbook*, 3rd edn, Lawrence Erlbaum, Hove.

Fagot, B and Leinbach, M D (1989) The young child's gender schema: Environmental input, internal organisation, *Child Development*, 60, 603-672.

Fagot, B and Leinbach, M D (1991) in P Turner (1995) *Sex, Gender and Identity*, BPS Books, Leicester.

Fagot, B, Leinbach, M D and Hagen, R (1986) Gender labeling and adoption of sex-typed behaviours, *Developmental Psychology*, 22, 440-443.

Fancher, R E (1990) *Pioneers of Psychology*, 2nd edn, Norton, New York

Fantz, R L (1961) The origins of form perception, *Scientific American*, 204, 66-72.

Fantz, R L (1961) The origins of form perception *Scientific American*. 204. 66-72.

Felipe, N J and Sommer, R (1966) Invasion of personal space, *Social Problems*, 14, 206-14.

Fentress, J C (1973) Development of grooming in mice with amputated forelimbs, *Science*, 179, 704-705.

Ferster, C B and Skinner, B F (1957) *Schedules of Reinforcement*, Appleton-Century-Crofts, New York.

Feshback, N (1985) Chronic maternal stress and its assessment, in J N Butcher and C D Speilberger (eds) *Advances in Personality*

Assessment, vol 5, Erlbaum, Hillsdale, NJ.

Festinger, L (1957) *A Theory of Cognitive Dissonance*, Harper Row, New York.

Festinger, L., Schachter, S and Black, K (1950) *Social Pressures in Informal Groups: A Study of Human Factors in Housing*, Stanford University Press, Stanford, CA.

Fetz, E E (1993) Cortical mechanisms controlling limb movement, *Current Opinion in Neurobiology*, 3, 932-939.

Field, T (1982) Individual differences in the expressivity of neonates and yourn infants, in R S Feldman (ed) *Development of Nonverbal Behaviour in Children*, Springer-Verlag, New York.

Fischer-Nielson, S, Loft, S and Gjervig Jensen, K (1993) Effect of ascorbate and 5-aminosalicyclic acid on light-induced 8 hydroxydeoxyguanosine formation in V79 Chinese hamster cells, *Carcinogenesis*, 14, 2431-2433.

Fisher, J and Hinde, R A (1949) The opening of milk bottles by birds, *British Birds*, 42, 347-357.

Fisher, R A (1930) *The Genetical Theory of Natural Selection*, Clarendon Press, Oxford.

Fisher, S and Greenberg, R P (1977) *The Scientific Credibility of Freud's Theories and Therapy*, Basic Books, New York.

Fiske, S T and Taylor, S E (1991) *Social Cognition* 2nd ed., McGraw Hill, New York.

Flanders, N (1970) *Analysing Teaching Behaviour*, Wiley, New York.

Flavell, J H (1984) Discussion, in R J Sternberg (ed.) *Mechanisms of Cognitive Development*, Freeman, New York.

Folkard, S (1995) in D Hatcher (ed) *Proceedings of the ATP Conference, Swansea, July 1995*, The Association for the Teaching of Psychology.

Folkard, S and Akerstedt, T (1992) A three-process model of the regulation of alertness-sleepiness, in R J Broughton and B D Ogilvie (eds) *Sleep, Arousal and Performance*, Birkhauser, Boston, MA.

Fontenot, K and Brannon, L (1991) Gender differences in coping with job stress, Paper presented at the annual conference of the American Psychological Association, San Francisco, 1994.

Foot, Morgan and Shute (1990) in P K Smith and H Cowie (1991) *Understanding Children's*

Understanding, 2nd edn, Blackwell, Oxford.

Ford, M and Holmes, V (1978) Planning units and syntax in sentence production, *Cognition*, 6, 35-53.

Forge, K L and Phemister, S (1987) The effect of prosocial cartoons on preschool children, *Child Study Journal*, 17, 83-88 in R A Baron and D Byrne (1997) *Social Psychology*, 8th edn, Allyn & Bacon, Boston, MA.

Forrester, M A (1992) *The Development of Young Children's Socio-Cognitive Skills*, Lawrence Erlbaum, Hove.

Foster, J J and Parker, I (1995) *Carrying Out Investigations in Psychology: Methods and Statistics*, BPS Books, Leicester.

Fouts, R S (1972) The use of guidance in teaching sign language to a chimpanzee, *Journal of Comparative and Physiological Psychology*, 80, 515-522.

Frank, L G (1986) Social organisation of the spotted hyena (*Crocuta crocuta*): Dominance and reproduction, *Animal Behaviour*, 34, 1500-1509.

Franklin, J (1987) *Molecules of the Mind*, Atheneum, New York.

Freedman, J L and Fraser, S C (1996) Compliance without pressure: The foot-in-the-door technique, *Journal of Personality and Social Psychology*, 4, 195-202.

Freeman, M C and Grossman, G D (1992) Group foraging by a stream minnow: shoals or aggregations? *Animal Behaviour*, 33, 993-999.

Freud, A and Dann, S (1951) *An Experiment in Group Upbringing: Psychoanalytic Study of the Child*, vol 6, 127-168.

Freud, S (1900/1953) *The Interpretation of Dreams*, Hogarth Press, London.

Freud, S (1963) *Two Short Accounts of Psychoanalysis*, Pelican, Harmondsworth.

Freund, L S (1990) Maternal regulation of children's problem-solving behavior and its impact on children's performance, *Child Development*, 61, 113-126.

Frey, K S and Rubl, D N (1992) Gender constancy and the "cost" of sex-typed behaviour: A test of the conflict hypothesis, *Developmental Psychology*, 28, 714-721.

Friedman, H S, Tucker, J S, Schwartz, J E, Martin, L R, Tomlinson-Keasey, C, Wingard, D L and Criqui, M H (1995) Childhood conscientiousness and longevity: Health behaviours

and cause of death, *Journal of Personality and Social Psychology*, 68, 696-703, in Baron, R A and Byrne, D (1997) *Social Psychology*, 8th edn, Allyn & Bacon, Boston, MA.

Friedman, M and Rosenman, R H (1959) Association of specific overt behaviour patterns with blood and cardiovascular findings - blood cholesterol level, blood clotting time, incidence of arcus senilis and clinical coronary artery disease, *Journal of the American Medical Association*, 162, 1286-1296.

Friend, R, Rafferty, Y and Bramel, D (1990) A puzzling misinterpretation of the Asch "Conformity" study, *European Journal of Social Psychology*, 20, 29-44 in P B Smith and M H Bond (1993) *Social Psychology Across Cultures: Analysis and Perspectives*, Harvester Wheatsheaf, Trowbridge.

Frisch, K von (1955) *The Dancing Bees*, Harcourt Brace, New York.

Frisch, K von (1967) *The Dance Language and Orientation of Bees*, Belknap Press, Cambridge, MA.

Fruzzetti, A E, Toland, K, Teller, S A and Loftus, E F (1992) Memory and eyewitness testimony, in M M Gruneberg and P E Morris (eds) *Aspects of Memory, The Practical Aspects*, vol. 1, 2nd edn, Routledge, London.

Fullerton, C, Berryman, J C and Porter, R H (1974) On the nature of mother-infant interaction in the guinea pig, *Cavia porcellus*, *Behaviour*, 48, 145-156.

Fultz, J, Batson, D D, Fortenbach, V A, McCarthy, P M and Varney, L L (1986) Social evaluation and the empathy-altruism hypothesis, *Journal of Personality and Social Psychology*, 50, 761-769.

Funder, D C and Colvin, C R (1991) Explorations in behaviour consistency: Properties of persons, situations, and behaviour, *Journal of Personality and Social Psychology*, 59, 149-158.

Funnell, E (1983) Phonological processes in reading: New evidence from acquired dyslexia, *British Journal of Psychology*, 74, 159-180.

Furth, H G (1966) *Thinking without Language: Psychological Implications of Deafness*, Free Press, New York.

Gaertner, S L, Mann, J, Murrell, A and Dovidio, J F (1989) Reducing intergroup bias: The benefits of

recategorization, *Journal of Personality and Social Psychology*, 57, 239-249, in R A Baron and D Byrne (1997) *Social Psychology*, 8th edn, Allyn & Bacon, Boston, MA.

Gaertner, S L, Rust, M C, Dovidio, J F, Bachman, B A and Anastasio, P A (1993) The contact hypothesis: The role of a common ingroup identity on reducing intergroup bias, *Small Groups Research*, 25 (2) 224-249, in R A Baron and D Byrne (1997) *Social Psychology*, 8th edn, Allyn & Bacon, Boston, MA.

Galambos, J A and Rips, L J (1982) Memory for routines, *Journal of Verbal Learning*, 21, 260-281.

Gale, A (1994) Ethical issues in psychological research, in A Coleman (ed) *Companion Encyclopedia of Psychology*, vol 2, Routledge, London.

Galli, I and Nigro, G (1987) The social representation of radioactivity among Italian children, *Social Science Information*, 26, 535-549, in N Hayes (1997) Social representations: A European theory, *Psychology Review*, September, 13-16.

Gallup, G (1977) Self-recognition in primates: A comparative approach to the bi-directional properties of consciousness, *American Psychologist*, 32, 329-338.

Gamson, W B, Fireman, B and Rytina, S (1982) *Encounters with Unjust Authority*, Dorsey Press, Homewood.

Gardner, H (1983) *Frames of Mind: The Theory of Multiple Intelligences*, Basic Books, New York.

Gardner, H (1985) *The Mind's New Science: A History of the Cognitive Revolution*, Basic Books, New York.

Gardner, R A and Gardner, B T (1969) Teaching sign language to a chimpanzee, *Science*, 165, 664-672.

Garrett, M F (1975) The analysis of sentence production, in M M Smyth et al (1994), *Cognition in Action*, Lawrence Erlbaum, Hove.

Garrett, M F (1976) Syntactic processes in sentence production, in M M Smyth et al (1994), *Cognition in Action*, Lawrence Erlbaum, Hove.

Garrett, M F (1982) Production of speech: Observations from normal and pathological language use, in M M Smyth et al (1994), *Cognition in Action*, Lawrence Erlbaum, Hove

Garrett, M F (1984) The organisation of processing

structures for language production: Applications to aphasic speech, M W Eysenck and M T Keane (1995) *Cognitive Psychology: A Student's Handbook*, 3rd edn, Lawrence Erlbaum, Hove.

Gatchel, R J, Baum, A and Krantz, D S (1989) *An Introduction to Health Psychology*, 2nd edn, Newbery Award Records, New York.

Gates, S J and Colborn, D K (1976) Lowering appointment failures in a neighbourhood health center, *Medical Care*, 14, 263-267.

Gauntlett, D (1997) Introduction: Why no clear answers on media effects? in T Charlton and K David (eds) (1997) *Elusive Links: Television, Video Games and Children's Behaviour*, Park Published Papers.

Gazzaniga, M S (1967) The split-brain in man, *Scientific American*, 217, 24-29.

Geis (1993) in P Turner (1995) *Sex, Gender and Identity*, BPS Books, Leicester.

Geiselman, R E, Fisher, R P, MacKinnon, D P and Holland, H L (1985) Eyewitness enhancement in the police interview: Cognitive retrieval mnemonics versus hypnosis, *Journal of Applied Psychology*, 70, 401-412.

Gelder, M (1991) Psychological treatment for anxiety disorders: Adjustment disorder with anxious mood, generalised anxiety disorders, panic disorder, agoraphobia and accident personality disorder?, in C Coryell and G Winokur (eds) *The Clinical Management of Anxiety Disorders*, Oxford University Press, Oxford.

Gelman, R, Meck, E and Merkin, S (1986) Young children's mathematical competence, *Cognitive Development*, 1, 1-29.

Gelman, R and Shatz, M (1977) Appropriate speech adjustments: The operation of conversational constraints on talk to two year olds, in P K Smith and H Cowie (eds) *Understanding Children's Development*, Basil Blackwell, Oxford.

Georgopoulos, A P (1991) Higher order motor control, *Annual Review of Neuroscience*, 14, 361-377.

Gergen, K J, Gulerce, A, Lock, A and Misra, G (1996) Psychological science in cultural context, *American Psychologist*, 51(5), 496-503.

Gergen, K J and Gergen, M M

(1981) *Social Psychology*, Harcourt Brace Jovanovich, New York.

Gibbs, J, Young, R C and Smith, G P (1973) Cholecystokinin decreases food intake in rats, *Journal of Comparative and Physiological Psychology*, 84, 488-495.

Gibson, D R (1990) Relations of socioeconomic status to logical and sociomoral judgment of middle-aged men, *Psychology and Aging*, 5, 510-513.

Gibson, E J and Walk, R D (1960) The "visual cliff"", *Scientific American*, 202, 64-71.

Gibson, H B and Heap, M (1991) *Hypnosis in Therapy*, Lawrence Erlbaum Associates, London.

Gibson, J J (1966) *The Senses Considered as Perceptual Systems*, George Allen & Unwin, London.

Gibson, J J (1986) *The Ecological Approach to Visual Perception* (reprint of 1979 edn), Erlbaum, Hillsdale, NJ.

Gibson, R M and Bradbury, J W (1985) Sexual selection in lekking sage grouse: phenotypic correlates of male mating success, *Behav. Ecol. Sociobiol.* 18, 117-23.

Gibson, R M and Bradbury, J W (1986) Male and female strategies on sage grouse leks, in D I Robenstein and R W Wrangham (eds) *Ecological aspects of social evolution*, Princeton Press, Princeton, NJ.

Gilbert, D and Jones, E E (1986) Perceiver-induced restraint: interpretations of self-generated reality, *Journal of Personality and Social Psychology*, 50, 269-280, in R A Baron and D Byrne (1997) *Social Psychology*, 8th edn, Allyn & Bacon, Boston, MA.

Gill, F B and Wolf, L L (1975) Economics of feeding territoriality in the golden-winged sunbird, *Ecology*, 56, 333-345.

Gill, J (1985) Czechpoints, *Time Out*, p 15, 22 August 1985.

Gilligan, C (1982) *In a Different Voice: Psychological Theory and Women's Development*, Harvard University Press, Cambridge, MA.

Gilligan, C, Lyons, N P and Hammer, T J (eds) (1990) *Making Connections: The Relational Worlds of Adolescent Girls at Emma Willard School*, Harvard University Press, Cambridge, MA.

Gilligan, C and Ward, J (1990) *Mapping the Moral Domain*, Harvard University Press, Cambridge, MA.

Gittleman, J L (1989) Carnivore group living: comparative trends, in J L Gittleman (ed) *Carnivore behaviour, ecology and evolution*, Cormstock, Ithaca, NY.

Glanzer, M and Cunitz, A R (1966) Two storage mechanisms in free recall, *Journal of Verbal Learning and Verbal Behavior*, 5, 351-360.

Gleitman, H (1986) *Psychology*, 2nd edn, Norton, New York.

Goate, A, Chartier-Harlin, M C, Mullan, M *et al.* (1991) Segregation of a missence mutation in the amyloid precursor protein gene with familial Alzheimer's disease, *Nature*, 349, 704-706.

Goffman, E (1968) *Asylums*, Penguin, Harmondsworth.

Goffman, E (1971) *The Presentation of Self in Everyday Life*, Penguin, Harmondsworth.

Goldman-Eisler, F (1968) *Psycholinguistics: Experiments in Spontaneous Speech*, Academic Press, London.

Goldstein, A and Kalant, H (1990) Drug policy: Striking the right balance, *Science*, 249, 1513-1521.

Goleman, D (1996) *Emotional Intelligence*, Bloomsbury, London.

Goodall, J (1978) Chimp killings: Is it the man in them?, *Science News*, 113, 276.

Goodall, J (1986) *The Chimpanzees of Gombe: Patterns of behaviour*, Harvard University Press, Cambridge, MA.

Goodlett, C R, Marcussen, B L and West, J R (1990) A single day of alcohol exposure during the brain growth spurt induces brain weight restriction and cerebellar Purkinje cell loss, *Alcohol* 7, 107-114.

Goodman, G S and Reed, R S (1986) Age differences in eyewitness testimony, *Law and Human Behavior*, 10, 317-332.

Goodman and Gilman (1965) in S Coren, C Porac and L M Ward (eds) *Sensation and Perception*, international edn (1979), Academic Press.

Goodwin, G M (1992) Tricyclic and newer anti-depressants, in E S Paykel (ed) *Handbook of Affective Disorders*, Guilford, New York.

Gosling, L M (1986) The evolution of male mating strategies in antelopes, in D I Rubenstein and R W Wrangham (eds) *Ecological Aspects of Social Evolution*, Princeton University Press, Princeton, NJ.

Gould, J D (1978) An

experimental study of writing, dictating and speaking, in M W Eysenck and M T Keane (1995), *Cognitive Psychology: A Student's Handbook*, Lawrence Erlbaum, Hove.

Gould, J D (1980) Experiments in composing letters: Some facts, some myths and some observations, in M W Eysenck and M T Keane (1995), *Cognitive Pschology: A Student's Handbook*, Lawrence Erlbaum, Hove.

Gould, J L and Marler, P (1987) Learning by instinct, *Scientific American*, 256 (1), 62-73.

Gover, G (1968) Man has no `killer' instinct, in M F A Montague (ed) *Man and Aggression*, Oxford University Press, New York.

Graesser, A C (1981) *Prose Comprehension Beyond the Word*, Springer-Verlag, New York.

Graf, P (1990) Life-span changes in implicit and explicit memory, *Bulletin of the Psychonomic Society*, 28, 353-358.

Graf, P and Schacter, D L (1985) Implicit and explicit memory for new associations in normal and amnesic subjects, *Journal of Experimental Psychology: Learning, Memory and Cognition*, 11, 501-518.

Grafen, A (1990) Sexual selection unhandicapped by the Fisher process, *Journal of Theoretical Biology*, 53, 205-214.

Granger and Ikeda (1968) in S Coren, C Porac and L M Ward (eds) *Sensation and Perception*, international edn (1979), Academic Press.

Gray, J A (1987) The ethics and politics of animal experimentation, in H Beloff and A M Coleman (eds) *Psychology Survey*, no 6, BPS, Leicester.

Gray, J A and Wedderburn, A A (1960) Grouping strategies with simultaneous stimuli, *Quarterly Journal of Experimental Psychology*, 12, 180-184.

Gray, J D and Silver, R C (1990) Opposite sides of the same coin: Former spouses' divergent perspectives in coping with their divorce, *Journal of Personality and Social Psychology*, 59, 1180-1191, in K Deaux, FC Dane and L S Wrightsman (1993) *Social Psychology in the '90s*, 6th edn, Brooks Cole, Belmont, CA.

Green, S (1994) Drugs and behaviour, *Psychology Review*, 3(1), 14-17.

Green, S (1994) *Individual Differences. Normal and Abnormal*, Lawrence Erlbaum, Hove.

Green, S (1994) *Principles of Biopsychology*, Lawrence Erlbaum, Hove.

Green, S (1994) Stress: What is it?, *Psychology Review*, 1(1) 23-27.

Green, S (1996) Drugs and psychological disorders, *Psychology Review*, 3(2), 25-28.

Green, S (1996) in M Cardwell, L Clark and C Heldrum, *Psychology for A Level*, Collins, London.

Greenberg, J and Baron, R A (1995) *Behaviour in Organisations*, Prentice-Hall, London.

Greene, E (1987) Individuals in an osprey colony discriminate between high and low quality information, *Nature*, 329, 239-241.

Greene, J (1975) *Thinking and Language*, Methuen, London.

Greene, J (1990) Perception (ch 10) in I Roth (ed) *Introduction to Psychology*, vol 2, Open University/Lawrence Erlbaum, Hove and Milton Keynes.

Greene, J O and Cappella, J N (1986) Cognition and talk: The relationship of semantic units to temporal patterns of fluency in spontaneous speech, *Language and Speech* 29, 141-57

Gregory, R L (1973) The confounded eye, in R L Gregory and E H Gombrich (eds) *Illusion in Nature and Art*, Duckworth, London.

Gregory, R L (1977) *Eye and Brain*, Weidenfeld and Nicolson, London.

Gregory, R L and Wallace, J G (1963) Recovery from early blindness, *Experimental Psychology Society*, monograph no 2.

Grier, J W and Burk, T (1992) *Biology of Animal Behaviour*, Wm C. Brown.

Griffin, D and Bartholomew, K (1994) Models of the self and other: Fundamental dimensions underlying measures of adult attachment, *Journal of Personality and Social Psychology*, 67, 430-445, in R A Baron and D Byrne (1997) *Social Psychology*, 8th edn, Allyn & Bacon, Boston, MA.

Griggs, R A and Cox, J R (1982) The elusive thematic materials effect in Wason's selection task, *British Journal of Psychology*, 92, 407-420.

Grogan, S (1998) *Body Image: Understanding Body Dissatisfaction in Men, Women and Children*, Routledge, London.

Gross, M R (1985) Disruptive selection for alternative life histories in salmon, *Nature*, 313, 47-48.

Gross, M R and Sargent, R C (1985) The evolution of male and female parental care in fishes, *American Zoologist*, 25, 817-822.

Gross, M R and Shine, R (1981) Parental care and mode of fertilization in ectothermic vertebrates, *Evolution*, 35, 775-793.

Gross, R (1996) *Psychology: The Science of Mind and Behavior*, 3rd edn, Hodder & Stoughton, London.

Grossarth-Maticek, R, Bastiaans, J and Kanazir, D T (1985) Psychosocial factors as strong predictors of mortality from cancer, ischaemic heart disease and stroke: The Yugoslav prospective study, *Journal of Psychosomatic Research*, 29, 167-176.

Grossarth-Maticek, R and Eysenck, H J (1990) Personality, stress and disease: Description and validation of a new inventory, *Psychological Reports*, 66, 355-373.

Groves, P M and Rebec, C V (1992) *Introduction to Biological Psychology*, 4th edn, J A Brown, Dubuque, IA.

Gruneberg, M and Morris, P (1992) *Aspects of Memory: The Practical Aspects*, vol 1, 2nd edn, Routledge, London.

Guiton, P (1966) Early experience and sexual object choice in the brown leghorn, *Animal Behaviour*, 14, 534-538.

Gunter, B and Harrison, J (1995) Violence on television in Britain, BBC and ITV: London, in T Charlton and K David (eds) (1997) *Elusive Links: Television, Video Games and Children's Behaviour*, Park Published Papers.

Gur, R C, Skolnick, B E and Gur, R E (1994) Effects of emotional discrimination tasks on cerebral blood flow: Regional activation and its relation to performance, *Brain and Cognition*, 25, 271-286.

Hagell, A and Newburn, T (1994) Young offenders and the media, in G Cumberbatch (1997) Media violence: science and common sense, *Psychology Review*, 3(4) 2-7.

Haier et al (1996) in R A Baron (1996) *Essentials of Psychology*, Allyn & Bacon, Boston, MA.

Hajek, P and Belcher, M (1991) Dream of absent-minded transgression: An empirical study of a cognitive withdrawal symptom, *Journal of Abnormal Psychology*, 100, 487-491.

Halliday, T R (1978) Sexual selection and mate choice, in J R Krebs and N B Davies (eds) (1981) *Behavioural Ecology: An Evolutionary Approach*, Blackwell Scientific, Oxford.

Halliday, T R (1994) Sex and evolution, in P J R Slater and T R Halliday (eds) *Behaviour and Evolution*, Cambridge University Press, Cambridge.

Halliday, T R and Slater, P J B (eds) (1983) Genes, development and learning, *Animal Behaviour*, 3.

Halmi, K A (1995) Changing rates of eating disorders: What does it mean? *American Journal of Psychiatry* 152(9).

Halsband, U and Freund, H (1993) Motor learning, *Current Opinion in Neurobiology*, 3, 940-949.

Hamer, D *et al.* (1993) Androgen involvement in homosexuality, *American Journal of Human Genetics*, 53, 844-852.

Hamilton, W D (1964) The genetical evolution of social behaviour (I and II), *Journal of Theoretical Biology*, 7, 1-16; 17-52.

Hamilton, W D (1971) Geometry for the selfish herd, *Journal of Theoretical Biology*, 31, 295-311.

Hamilton, W D (1964) The genetical evolution of social behaviour, I and II, *Journal of Theoretical Biology*, 7, 1-16; 17-52.

Hamilton, W D (1980) Sex v. non-sex v. parasite, *Oikos*, 35, 282-290.

Hamilton, W D and Zuk, M (1982) Heritable true fitness and bright birds: a role for parasites, *Science*, 218, 384-387.

Harcourt, A H (1989) Environment, competition and reproductive performance of female monkeys, *Trends in Ecology and Evolution*, 4, 101-105.

Harcourt, A H, Harvey, P H, Larson, S G and Short, R V (1981) Testis weight, body weight and breeding systems in primates, *Nature*, 293, 55-57.

Hare-Mustin, R T and Marecek, J (1994) Asking the right questions: Feminist psychology and sex differences, *Feminism & Psychology*, 4(4) 531-537.

Harkness and Super in M F Small (1995) Bringing up baby, *New Scientist*, 24th June, pp 36-39.

Harlow, H F (1959) Love in infant monkeys, *Scientific American*, 200(6), 68-74.

Harlow, H F and Harlow, M K (1965) The affectional systems, in A M Schrier, H F

Harlow and F Stollnitz (eds) *Behaviour of Non-human Primates*, Academic Press, New York.

Harlow, H F and Zimmerman, R R (1959) Affectional responses in the infant monkey, *Science*, 130, 421-432.

Harris, J E (1980) Memory aids people use: Two interview studies, *Memory and Cognition*, 8, 31-38.

Harris, M P (1971) Species separation in gulls, in R Hoste (ed) *Modern Biology: Selected Readings*, Penguin, Harmondsworth.

Harris, P L *Children and Emotion: The Development of Psychological Understanding*, Blackwell, Oxford.

Harris, R J (1973) Answering questions containing marked and unmarked adjectives and adverbs, *Journal of Experimental Psychology*, 97, 399-402.

Hart, B B and Alden, P (1994) Hypnotic techniques in the control of pain, in H B Gibson (ed) *Psychology, Pain and Anaesthesia*, Chapman & Hall, London.

Hart, C and Hart, B (1996) The use of hypnosis with children and adolescents, *The Psychologist*, 9, 506-509.

Harter, S (1983) Developmental perspectives on the self-system, in P M Mussen (ed) *Handbook of Child Psychology: Vol 4. Socialization, Personality and Social Development*, Wiley, New York.

Hartup, W W (1989) Social relationships and their developmental significance, *American Psychologist*, 44, 120-126.

Hasegawa, T (1992) The evolution of female promiscuity: chimpanzees and Japanese macaques, in Y Ito (ed) *Aggression and cooperation among animal societies*, Tokaidaigaku-Shuppankai, Tokyo.

Haskins, R (1989) Beyond Metaphor: the efficacy of early childhood education, *American Psychologist*, 44, 274-282.

Hatfield, E (1988) Passionate and companionate love, in R J Sternberg and M L Barnes (eds) *The Psychology of Love*, Yale University Press, New Haven.

Hauffe, H C and Searle, J B (1992) Letter to *Nature*, 357, 26.

Hayes, J R and Flower, L S (1986) Writing research and the writer, *American Psychologist*, 41, 1106-1113.

Hayes, N (1993) *Principles of Social Psychology*, Lawrence Erlbaum, Hove.

Hayes, N (1994) *Foundations of Psychology: An Introductory Text*, Routledge, London.

Hayes, N (1995) *Psychology in Perspective*, Macmillan, Basingstoke.

Hayes, N (1998) Spreading the word: How social representations happen, *Psychology Review*, 4 (3).

Hazan, C and Shaver, P (1987) Romantic love conceptualized as an attachment process, *Journal of Personality and Social psychology*, 52, 511-524.

Heap, M (1996) The nature of hypnosis, *The Psychologist*, 9, 498-501.

Heap, M and Dryden, W (1991) *Hypnotherapy A Handbook*, Open University Press, Milton Keynes.

Heath, S B (1989) The learner as cultural member in M L Rice and R L Schiefelbusch (eds) *Teachability of Language*, Brookes, Baltimore, MD.

Hebb, D O (1949) *The Organisation of Behavior*, Wiley, New York.

Heilman, M E, Block, C J and Lucas, J A (1992) Presumed incompetent? Stigmatization and affirmative action efforts, *Journal of Applied Psychology*, 77, 536-544, in R A Baron and D Byrne (1997) *Social Psychology*, 8th edn, Allyn & Bacon, Boston, MA.

Heinrich, B (1979) *Bumblebee economics*, Harvard University Press, Cambridge, MA.

Heller, F (1986) *The Use and Abuse of Social Science*, Sage, London.

Helms, J E (1992) Why is there no study of cultural equivalence in standardized cognitive ability testing? *American Psychologist*, 47, 1083-1101.

Helson, R, Mitchell, V and Moane, G (1984) Personality and patterns of adherence and nonadherence to the social clock, *Journal of Personality and Social Psychology*, 46, 1079-1097.

Helson, R and Wink, P (1987) Two conceptions of maturity examined in the findings of a longitudinal study, *Journal of Personality and Social Psychology*, 53, 531-541.

Henke, P G (1992) Stomach pathology and the amygdala, in J P Aggleton (ed) *The Amygdala: Neurobiological Aspects of Emotion, Memory and Mental Dysfunction*, Wiley-Liss, New York.

Henwood, K and Pidgeon, N (1995) Grounded theory and psychological research, 6*he Psychologist*, March 1995, 115-118.

Herman, L, Richards, D G and Wolz, J P (1984) Comprehension of sentences by bottle-nosed dolphins, *Cognition*, 16, 129-219.

Hernstein, R J and Murray, C, (1994) *The Bell Curve: Intelligence and Class Structure in American Life*, with a new afterword by Charles Murray, Free Press, New York.

Herzberg, F, Mausner, B and Snyderman, B (1959) *The Motivation to Work*, Wiley, New York.

Hess, E H (1958) "Imprinting" in animals, *Scientific American*, March, 71-80, in *Psychobiology* (1966), W H Freeman and Company, San Francisco and London.

Hess, E H (1966) *Psychobiology: The Biological Bases of Behaviour (Readings from Scientific American)*, W H Freeman and Co., San Francisco and London.

Heston, L L (1966) Psychiatric disorders in foster home reared children of schizophrenic mothers, *British Journal of Psychiatry*, 122, 819-825.

Hetherington, E M (1989) Coping with family transitions: Winners, losers and survivors, *Child Development*, 60, 1-14.

Hewison, T and Tizard, J (1980) Parental involvement in reading attainment, *British Journal of Educational Psychology*, 50, 209-215.

Higgins, A T and Turnure, J E (1984) Distractibility and concentration of attention in children's development, *Child Development*, 55, 1799-1810.

Higgins, L T (1988) *Learning to Talk*, BPS Books, Leicester.

Hilgard, E R (1965) in *Hypnotic Suggestibility*, Harcourt Brace Jovanovich, New York.

Hilgard, E R (1967) in R L Atkinson, R C Atkinson, D J Bem and S Hoeksema (1996) *Introduction to Psychology*, 12th edn, Harcourt Brace Jovanovich, New York.

Hilgard, E R (1986) *Divided Consciousness: Multiple Controls in Human Thought and Action*, Wiley, New York.

Hinde, R A (1966) *Animal Behaviour: A Synthesis of Ethology and Comparative Psychology*, McGraw-Hill, New York.

Hinde, R A (1974) *Biological Bases of Human Social Behaviour*, McGraw-Hill, New York.

Hinde, R A (1983) *Primate Social Relationships. An Integrated Approach*, Blackwell Scientific, Oxford.

Hines, M, Allen, L S and Gorski, R A (1992) Sex differences in subregions of the medial nucleus of the amygdala and the bed nucleus of the stria terminalis of the rat, *Brain Research*, 579, 321-326.

Hinton, G E, Plaut, D C and Shallice, T (1993) Simulating brain damage, *Scientific American*, 269, 76-82.

Hobfoll, S E and Stephens, M A P (1990) Social support during extreme stress: Consequences and intervention, in I G Sarason, B R Sarason and G R Pierce (eds) *Support: An Interactional view - Issues in Social Support Research*, Wiley, New York.

Hobson, J A (1989) *Sleep*, Scientific American Library.

Hockett, C F (1959) Animal languages and human language, *Human Biology*, 31, 32-29.

Hockett, C F (1960) The origin of speech, *Scientific American*, 203, 89-96.

Hoffman, M A and Swaab, D F (1989) The sexually dimorphic nucleus of the preoptic area in the human brain: A comparative morphometric study, *Journal of Anatomy*, 164, 55-72.

Hoffman, M L (1975) Altruistic behaviour and the parent child relationship, *Journal of Personality and Social Psychology*, 31, 937-943.

Hoffman, M L (1976) Empathy, role-taking, guilt and development of altruistic motives, in T Lickona (ed) *Moral Development and Behaviour*, Holt, Rhinehart and Winston, New York.

Hogg, M A and Hains, S C (1996) Intergroup relations and group solidarity: Effects of group identification and social beliefs on depersonalised attraction, in R A Baron and D Byrne (1997) *Social Psychology*, 8th edn, Allyn & Bacon, Boston, MA.

Hogg, M A and Vaughan, G M (1995) *Social Psychology: An Introduction*, Prentice Hall/Harvester Wheatsheaf, Hemel Hempstead.

Holmes, B (1997) Night moves, in Mind Travellers, *New Scientist* supplement, 26 April 1997, 8-13.

Holmes, T H and Rahé, R H (1967) The social readjustment rating scale, *Journal of Psychosomatic Research*, 11, 213-218.

Holstein, K A (1983) Identity development: A comparison of adults and adolescents, Paper presented at the annual meeting of the American Psychological Association, Anaheim, CA.

Horne, J A (1983) Mammalian sleep function with particular reference to man, in A R Mayes (ed) *Sleep Mechanisms and Functions in Humans and Animals*, Van Nostrand Reinhold, New York.

Horne, J A (1988) *Why We Sleep: The Functions of Sleep in Humans and Other Mammals*, Oxford University Press, Oxford.

Horney, K (1945) *Our Inner Conflicts: A Constructive Theory of Neurosis*, Norton, New York.

Hovaas, O I, Schaffer, B and Simmons, J Q (1965) Building social behaviour in autistic children by use of electric shock, *Journal of Experimental Research in Personality*, 1, 99-109.

Howard, R D (1978) The evolution of mating strategies in bullfrogs, *Rana catesbiana*, *Evolution*, 32, 850-871.

Howe, M J A,(1998) Can IQ change? *The Psychologist*, 11, 69-72.

Howe, M J A, (1989) The strange achievements of idiot savants, in A M Colman and J G Beaumont (ed.) *Psychology Survey*, No 7, BPS, Leicester.

Howlett, R (1998) Behaviour Ecology: Cuckoos beg the answer, *Nature*, 393, 213-215.

Hrdy, S B (1977a) Infanticide as a primate reproductive strategy, *American Scientist*, 65, 40-9.

Hrdy, S B (1977b) *The Langurs of Abu: Female and Male Strategies of Reproduction*, Harvard University Press, Cambridge, MA.

Hubel, D H (1982) Explorations of the primary visual cortex, 1955-78, *Nature*, 299, 515-524.

Hubel, D H and Wiesel, T N (1962) Receptive fields, binocular interaction and functional architecture in the cat's visual cortex, *Journal of Physiology*, 195, 106-154.

Hubel, D H and Wiesel, T N (1968) Receptive fields and functional architecture of monkey striate cortex, *Journal of Physiology*, 195, 215-243.

Hubel, D H and Wiesel, T N (1979) Brain mechanisms and vision, *Scientific American*, 241(3), 150-162.

Hudson, W (1960) Pictorial depth perception in sub-cultural groups in Africa, *Journal of Social Psychology*, 52, 183-208.

Hudson, W (1962) Pictorial perception and educational adaptation in Africa, *Psychologica Africana*, 9, 226-239.

Huesmann, L R (1988) An information processing model for the development of aggression, *Aggression Behaviour*, 14, 13-24, in R A Baron and K Byrne (1997) *Social Psychology*, 8th edn, Allyn & Bacon, Boston, MA.

Huesmann, L R (1994) *Aggressive Behaviour: Current Perspectives*, Plenum, New York.

Huesmann, L R and Eron, L D (1986) *Television and the aggressive child: A cross national comparison*, Erlbaum, Hillsdale, NJ

Hughes, J, Smith, T W, Kosterlitz, H W *et al.* (1975) Identification of two related pentapeptides from the brain with potent opiate agonist activity, *Nature*, 258, 577-581.

Hull, P V (1987) *Bilingualism: Two Languages, Two Personalities?*, Resources in Education, Educational Resources Clearing House on Education, University of Michigan Press, Ann Arbor, MI.

Humphreys, P (1997) Social, cultural and subcultural differences in the determination of (ab)normality, *Psychology Review*, 3(4), 10-15.

Humphreys, P W (1994) Obedience: After Milgram, *Psychology Review*, 1, 2-5.

Hunt, E and Love, T (1972) How good can memory be?, in A W Melton and E Martin (eds) *Coding Process in Human Memory*, Winston/Wiley, Washington, DC.

Huston, A C (1983) in P Turner (1995) *Sex, Gender and Identity*, BPS Books, Leicester.

Huston, T L, Ruggiero, M, Conner, R and Geis, G (1981) Bystander intervention into crime: A study based on naturally-occurring episodes, *Social Psychology Quarterly*, 44, 14-23.

Hyde, J S (1994) Should psychologists study gender differences? Yes, with some guidelines, *Feminism & Psychology*, 4(4) 507-512.

Immelmann, K (1972) Sexual and other long term aspects of imprinting in birds and other species, *Adv. Study Behaviour*, 4, 147-174.

Inglehart, R and Hildebrandt, K (1990) `Cultural change and changing world views', Paper presented at the annual meeting of the American Psychological Association, Boston, MA.

Isack, H A and Reyer, H U (1989) Honeyguides and honey gatherer: Interspecific communication in a symbiotic relationship, *Science*, 243, 1343-1346.

Jacobs, J and Eccles, J S (1985) Science and the media: Benbow & Stanley revisited, *Educational Researcher*, 14, 20-25.

Jaffe, Y and Yinon, Y (1983) Collective aggression: The group-individual paradigm in the study of collective antisocial behavior, in A Blumberg, P Hare, V Kent and M F Davies (eds) *Small Groups and Social Interaction*, Wiley, Chichester.

Jahoda, M (1958) *Current Concepts of Positive Mental Health*, Basic Books, New York.

James, I (1990) Prospective memory in the real world: Practical considerations for effective recall of future intentions, unpublished PhD thesis, Lancaster University, Lancaster.

James, O (1997) Serotonin - a chemical feel-good factor, *Psychology Review*, 4(1) 34.

James, W (1890) *The Principles of Pschology*, Holt, New York.

Janik, V (1977) Signature tune, *New Scientist*, 155 (2090), 23.

Janis, I L (1972) *Victims of Groupthink: A Psychological Study of Foreign-policy Decisions and Fiascoes*, Houghton-Mifflin, Boston, MA.

Jarman, P J (1974) The social organisation of antelope in relation to ecology, *Behaviour*, 48, 215-255.

Jarvis, J U M (1981) Eusociality in a mammal: Cooperative breeding in naked mole rat colonies, *Science*, 212, 571-573.

Jasper, A. (1998) Sugar and spice and all things nice...? *Manchester Evening News*, 29 January 1998, p.8.

Jensen, A R (1969) How much can we boost IQ and scholastic achievement?, *Harvard Educational Review*, 39, 1-123.

Johnson-Laird, P N (1983) *Mental Models: Towards a Cognitive Science of Language, Inference, and Consciousness*, Harvard University Press, Cambridge MA.

Johnston, E C and Sandle, R (1996) Treatment resistance in schizophrenia, *British Medical Journal*, 312, 325-326.

Johnston, E C and Sandle, R (1996) Treatment resistance in schizophrenia, *British Medical Journal* 312, 325-326.

Johnston, W A and Dark, V J (1986) Selective attention, *Annual Review of Psychology*, 37, 43-75.

Johnston, W A and Heinz, S P (1978) Flexibility and capacity demands of attention, *Journal of Experimental Psychology: General*, 107, 420-35.

Johnston, W A and Wilson, J (1980) Perceptual processing of non-targets in an attention task, *Memory and Cognition*, 8, 372-377.

Joiner, T E, Jr (1994) The interplay of similarity and self-verification in relationship formation, *Social Behaviour and Personality*, 22, 195-200, in R A Baron and D Byrne (1997), *Social Psychology*, 8th edn, Allyn & Bacon, Boston, MA.

Jones, G V and Langford, S (1987) Phonological blocking in the tip of the tongue state, *Cognition*, 26, 115-122.

Jones, J L (1995) *Understanding Psychological Science*, Harper Collins, New York.

Joseph, S, Williams, R and Yule, W, (1945) Psychosocial perspectives in post-traumatic stress syndrome, *American Journal of Psychiatry* 15(6) 515-544.

Juel-Nielson, N (1965) Individual and environment: A psychiatric-psychological investigation of monozygotic twins reared apart, *Acta Psychiatrica et Neurologica Scandinavica*, monograph supplement 183.

Jump, T L and Haas, L (1987) Fathers in transition: Dual-career fathers participating in child care, in M S Kummel (ed) *Changing Men: New Directions in Research on Men and Masculinity*, Sage, Beverly Hills, CA.

Jung, C G (1963) *Memories, Dreams, Reflections*, Collins Routledge & Kegan Paul, London.

Juola, J F, Bowhuis, D G, Cooper, E E and Warner, C B (1991) Control of attention around the fovea, *Journal of Experimental Psychology: Human Perception and Performance*, 15, 315-330.

Jussim, L, Nelson, T E, Manis, M and Soffin, S (1995) Prejudice, stereotypes and labelling effects: Sources of bias in person perception, *Journal of Personality and Social Psychology*, 68, 228-246, in R A Baron and D Byrne (1997) *Social Psychology*, 8th edn, Allyn & Bacon, Boston, MA.

Kagan, J (1984) *The Nature of the Child*, Basic Books, New York.

Kahneman, D (1973) *Attention and Effort*, Prentice Hall, Englewood Cliffs, NJ.

Kahneman, D and Tversky, A (1972) Subjective probability: A judgement of representativeness, *Cognitive Psychology*, 3, 430-454.

Kahneman, D and Tversky, A (1973) On the psychology of prediction, *Pschological Review*, 80, 237-251.

Kahneman, D and Tversky, A (1979) Prospect theory: An analysis of decision under risk, *Econometrica*, 47, 263-291.

Kahneman, D and Tversky, A (1984) Choices, values and frames, *American Psychologist*, 39, 341-350.

Kamin, L J (1974) *The Science and Politics of IQ*, Penguin, Harmondsworth.

Kaniasty, F and Norris, F H (1993) A test of the social support deterioration model in the context of natural disaster, *Journal of Personality and Social Psychology* 64, 395-408.

Kanner, A D, Coyne, J C, Schaefer, C and Lazarus, R S (1981) Comparison of two modes of stress management: Daily hassles and uplifts versus major life events, *Journal of Behavioral Medicine*, 4, 1-39.

Kanter, R (1977) *Men and Women of the Corporation*, Basic Books, New York.

Kantor (1993) in P Turner (1995) *Sex, Gender and Identity*, BPS Books, Leicester.

Kastenbaum, R (1979) *Growing Old: Years of Fulfillment*, Harper & Row, New York.

Kaufman, L and Rock, I (1989) The moon illusion 30 years later, in M Hershenson (ed) *The Moon Illusion*, Erlbaum, Hillsdale, NJ.

Kelley, H H (1967) Attribution theory in social psychology, in D Levine (ed) *Nebraska Symposium on Motivation*, vol 15, Nebraska University Press, Lincoln, NE.

Kelly, G A (1955) *The Psychology of Personal Constructs*, Norton, New York.

Kendler, K S, Neale, M C, Kessler, R C, Heath, A C and Eaves, L J (1992) A population based twin study of major depression in women: the impact of varying definitions of the illness, *Archives of General Psychiatry*, 49, 275-276.

Kendler, K S, Neale, M C, Kessler, R C, Heath, A C and Eaves, L J (1993) A longitudinal twin study of one year prevalence of major depression in women, *Archives of General Psychiatry*, 50, 843-852.

Kenrick, D T, Neuberg, S L, Zierk, K L and Krones, J M (1994) Evolution and social cognition: contrast effects as a function of sex, dominance and physical attractiveness, *Personality and Social Psychology Bulletin*, 20, 210-217.

Kenward, R E (1978) Hawks and doves: Factors affecting success and selection in goshawk attacks on wood pigeons, *Journal of Animal Ecology*, 47, 449-460.

Kessler, R C and Essex, M (1982) Marital status and depression: the importance of coping resources, *Social Forces*, 61, 484-507.

Kettlewell, H B D (1965) Insect survival and selection for pattern, *Science*, 148, 1290-1296.

Kety, S S, Rosenthal, D, Wender, P H, Schulsinger, F and Jacobsen, B (1975) Mental illness in the biological and adoptive families of adopted individuals who have become schizophrenic: a preliminary report based on psychiatric interviews, *Genetic Research in Psychiatry*.

Kety, S S, Wender, P H, Jacobsen, B, Ingraham, H J, Sanssoun, L, Faber, B and Kenney, D K (1994) Mental illness in the biological and adoptive relatives of schizophrenic adoptees: Replication of the Copenhagen study in the rest of Denmark, *Archives of General Psychiatry*, 51, 442-455.

Kiecolt-Glaser, K J and Glaser, R (1992) Psychoneuroimmunology: Can psychological interventions modulate immunity?, *Journal of Consulting and Clinical Psychology*, 60, 569-575.

Kihlstrom, J F (1985) Hypnosis, *Annual Review of Psychology*, 36, 385-418.

Killbride and Liebowitz (1975) in S Coren, C Porac and L M Ward (eds) *Sensation and Perception*, international edn (1979), Academic Press.

Kimple, G A (1964) *Conditioning and Learning*, Methuen and Co Ltd, London.

Kimura, D (1961) Some effects of temporal-lobe damage on auditory perception, *Canadian Journal of Psychology*, 15, 156-165.

Kimura, D (1973) The asymmetry of the human brain, *Scientific American*, 228, 70-78.

Kimura, D (1987) Sex differences, human brain organization, in G Adelman (ed) *Encyclopedia of Neurosciences*, *Vol II*, Birkhauser, Boston, MA.

King, M S and Yuille, J C (1987) Suggestibility and the child witness, in S J Ceci, M P

Toglia and D F Ross (eds) *Children's Eye-Witness Memory*, Springer-Verlag, New York.

Kinnunen, T, Zamansky, T and Block, M (1994) Is the hypnotized subject lying?, *Journal of Abnormal Psychology*, 103, 184-191.

Kirchler, E (1992) Adorable women, expert man: changing gender images of women and men in management, *European Journal of Social Psychology*, 22, 363-373.

Kirkpatrick, S A and Locke, E A (1991) Leadership: do traits matter?, *Academy of Management Executive*, 5(2), 48-60, in R A Baron and D Byrne (1997) *Social Psychology*, 8th edn, Allyn & Bacon, Boston, MA.

Kitchell, J A (1986) The evolution of predator-prey behaviour: Naticid gastropods and their molluscan prey, in M H Nitecki and J A Kitchell (eds) *Evolution of Animal Behaviour, Paleontological and Field Approaches*, Oxford University Press, New York.

Kitzinger, C (1994) Should psychologists study sex differences, *Feminism and Psychology* 4(4).

Kitzinger, C and Coyle, A (1995) Lesbian and gay couples: Speaking of diffrence, *The Psychologist*, 8, 64-69.

Klahr, D (1982) Nonmonotone assessment of monotone development: An information processing analysis, in S Strauss (ed.) *U-shaped Behavioral Growth*, Academic Press, New York.

Kleinke, C L, Meeker, F B and Staneski, R A (1986) Preference for opening lines: comparing ratings by men and women, *Sex Roles*, 15, 585-600 in R A Baron and D Byrne (1997) *Social Psychology*, Allyn & Bacon, Boston, MA.

Klerman, G L, Weissmann, M M, Markowitz, J *et al.* (1994) Medication and Psychotherapy, in A E Bergin and S L Gargiel (eds) *Handbook of Psychotherapy and Behaviour Change*, Wiley, New York.

Kline, M, Tschann, J M, Johnston, J R *et al.* (1989) Children's adjustments in joint and sole custody families, *Developmental Psychology*, 25, 430-438.

Kline, P (1972) *Fact and Fancy in Freudian Theory*, Methuen, London.

Kline, P (1993) *The Handbook of Psychological Testing*, Routledge, London.

Kline, P (1994) Some psychoanalytic perspectives, *Psychology Review*, 1(2), 7-9.

Kobasa, S C (1979) Stressful life-events, personality and health: An inquiry into hardiness, *Journal of Personality and Social Psychology*, 37, 1-11.

Kobasa, S C (1986) in R A Baron (1996) *Essentials of Psychology*, Allyn & Bacon, Boston, MA.

Koene, J and Chase, R (1998) Cupid's arrow is tipped with love potion, *New Scientist* (In Brief) 159, 27.

Kohler, W (1925) *The Mentality of Apes*, Harcourt Brace & World, New York.

Kohn, P M, Lafreniere, K and Gurevich, M (1991) Hassles, health and personality, *Journal of Personality and Social Psychology*, 61, 478-482.

Kohnberg, L and Candee, D (1984) The relationship of moral judgment to moral action, in W M Kurtines and J L Gewirtz (eds) *Morality, Moral Behaviour and Moral Development*, Wiley, New York.

Koluchova, J (1972) Severe deprivation in twins: A case study, *Journal of Child Psychology and Psychiatry*, 13, 107-114.

Koluchova, J (1976) The further development of twins after severe and prolonged deprivation: A second report, *Journal of Child Psychology and Psychiatry*, 17, 181-188.

Koopmans, H S (1981) The role of the gastrointestinal tract in the satiation of hunger, in L A Cioffi, W B T James and T B Van Italie (eds) *The Body-Weight Regulatory System: Normal and Disturbed Mechanisms*, Raven Press, New York.

Korte, C, Ypma, I and Toppen, A (1975) Helpfulness in Dutch society as a function of urbanization and environmental input level, *Journal of Personality and Social Psychology*, 4, 572-577.

Kotelchuk, M (1976) The infant;s relationship to the father: experimental evidence, in M E Lamb (ed.) *The Role of the Father in Child Development*, Wiley, New York.

Kozielecki, J (1981) *Psychological Decision Theory*, Polish Scientific, Warsaw, Poland.

Kozol, J (1985) *Illiterate America*, Doubleday, Garden City, NY.

Kral, J G (1989) Surgical treatment of obesity, *Medical Clinics of North America*, 73, 251-264.

Kramer, D L and Nowell, W (1980) Central place foraging in the eastern chipmunk, *Tamias striatus*, *Animal Behaviour*, 28, 772-8.

Kramer, F M, Jeffery, R W, Forster, J L and Snell, M K (1989) Long-term follow-up of

behavioural treatment for obesity: Patterns of weight regain among men and women, *International Journal of Obesity*, 13, 123-136.

Krebs, J R and Davies, N B (1993) *An Introduction to Behavioural Ecology*, Blackwell, Oxford.

Krebs, J R, Kacelnik, A and Taylor, P (1978) Optimal sampling by birds: An experiment with great tits, *Parus major*, *Nature*, 27-31.

Kreuger, J (1997) in Mind Travellers, *New Scientist* supplement, 26 April 1997.

Krosnick, J A, Betz, A L, Jussim, L J and Lynn, A R (1992) Subliminal conditioning of attitudes, *Personality and Social Psychology Bulletin* 18, 152-162 in R A Baron and D Byrne (1997) *Social Psychology*, Allyn & Bacon, Boston, MA.

Kruuk, H (1972) *The Spotted Hyena*, University of Chicago Press, Chicago.

Kübler-Ross, E (1969) *On Death and Dying*, Macmillan, New York.

Kuczmarski, R J (1992) Prevalence of overweight and weight gain in the United States, *American Journal of Clinical Nutrition*, 55, 495S-502S.

Kuhn, M H and McPartland, T S (1954) An empirical investigation of self attitudes, *American Sociological Review*, 19, 68-76.

Kuhn, T S (1970) *The Structure of Scientific Revolutions*, University of Chicago Press, Chicago.

Kunzinger (1985) in R A Baron (1996) *Essentials of Psychology*, Allyn & Bacon, Boston, MA.

Kuypers and Bengtson (1973) in J Bond, P Coleman and S Pearce (1993) *Ageing in Society*, Sage, London.

LaBerge, D (1983) Spatial extent of attention to letters and words, *Journal of Experimental Psychology: Human Perception and Performance*, 9, 371-379.

LaBerge, S (1986) *Lucid Dreaming*, Ballatine Books.

Labov, W (1970) The logic of non-standard English, in F Williams (ed) *Language and Poverty*, Markham, Chicago.

Lacquaniti, F (1992) Automatic control of limb movement and posture, *Current Opinion in Neurobiology*, 2, 807-814.

Ladd, G W (1991) Family-peer relations during childhood: pathways to competence and pathology? *Journal of Social and Personal Relationships*, 8, 307-314.

LaFreniere, P J and Sroufe, L A (1985) Profiles of peer competence in the preschool: interrelations between measures, influence or social ecology, and relation to attachment theory, *Developmental Psychology*, 21, 56-69, in P Erwin (1993) *Friendship and Peer Relations in Children*, Wiley, Chichester.

Laing, R D (1964) Is schizophrenia a disease? *International Journal of Social Psychiatry*, 10, 184-195.

Laing, R D (1967) *The Politics of Experience and the Bird of Paradise*, Penguin, Harmondsworth.

Land, E H (1977) The retinex theory of colour vision, *Scientific American*, 237, 108-128.

Landau, S F (1984) Trends in violence and aggression: A cross-cultural analysis, *International Journal of Comparative Sociology*, 24, 133-158.

Langer, E J (1983) *The Psychology of Control*, Sage, Beverly Hills, CA.

Langer, E J and Abelson, R P (1974) A patient by any other name... clinical group differences in labelling bias, *Journal of Consulting and Clinical Psychology*, 42, 4-9.

Langlois, J H, Roggman, L A and Rieser-Danner, L A (1990) Infant's differential social responses to attractive and unattractive faces, *Developmental Psychology*, 26, 153-159.

Lankenau, H, Swigar, M E, Bhimani, S (1985) Cranial CT scans in eating disorder patients and controls, *Comprehensive Psychiatry*, 26, 136-147.

LaPrelle, J, Hoyle, R H, Insko, C A and Bernthal, P (1990) Interpersonal attraction and descriptions of the traits of others: Ideal similarity, self similarity and liking, *Journal of Research on Personality*, 24, 216-240, in R A Baron and D Byrne (1997) *Social Psychology*, Allyn & Bacon, Boston, MA.

Larsen, S F and Laszlo, J (1990) Current historical knowledge and personal experience in appreciation of literature, *European Journal of Social Psychology*, 20, 425-440, in N Hayes (1998) Spreading the word: How social representations happen, *Psychology Review*, 4 (3).

Latane, B and Darley, J M (1968) Group inhibitions of bystander intervention in emergencies, *Journal of Personality and Social Psychology*,

10, 215-221.

Latane, B and Darley, J M (1970) *The Unresponsive Bystander: Why Doesn't He Help?* Appleton-Century-Crofts, New York.

Latane, B and Nida, S (1981) Ten years of research on group size and helping, *Psychological Bulletin*, 89, 308-324.

Latane, B and Rodin, J (1969) A lady in distress: Inhibiting effects of friends and strangers on bystander intervention, *Journal of Experimental Social Psychology*, 5, 189-202.

Laurence, J R and Perry, C (1988) *Hypnosis, Will and Memory: A Psycho-Legal History*, Guilford Press, New York.

Laverty, T M and Plowright, R C (1988) Flower handling by bumblebees: a comparison of specialists and generalists, *Animal Behaviour*, 36, 733-740.

Lavie, P, Pratt, H, Scharf, B, Peled, R and Brown, J (1984) Localized pontine lesion: Nearly total absence of REM sleep, *Neurology*, 34, 1118-1120.

LaVoie, J C (1976) Ego identity formation in middle adolescence, *Journal of Youth and Adolescence*, 5, 371-385.

Lavrakas, P J (1982) Fear of crime and behaviour restrictions in urban and suburban neighbourhoods, *Population and Environment*, 5, 242-264.

Law, D J, Pellegrino, J W and Hunt, E B (1993) Comparing the tortoise and the hare: Gender differences and experience in dynamic spatial reasoning tasks, *Psychological Science*, 4, 35-40, in R A Baron (1996) *Essentials of Psychology*, Allyn & Bacon, Boston, MA.

Lawson, R (1994) in Goddard (1994) Virtual therapy reaches new heights, *New Socialist*, 11 June 1994.

Lazarus, R S (1980) in R A Baron (1996) *Essentials of Psychology*, Allyn & Bacon, Boston, MA.

Lazarus, R S (1991) Progress on a cognitive-motivational-relational theory of emotion, *American Psychologist*, 46, 819-834.

Lazarus, R S and Folkman, S (1984) *Stress, Appraisal, and Coping*, Springer, New York.

Lazarus, R S, Opton, E M, Nomikos, M S and Rankin, N O (1985) The principle of short-circuiting of threat: Further evidence, *Journal of Personality*, 33, 622-635.

Le Doux, J E (1997) Emotion, memory and the brain, in

Mysteries of the Mind, Scientific American special issue, March 1997, 68-73.

LeDoux, J (1989) in D Goleman (1995) *Emotional Intelligence: Why It Can Matter*, Bloomsbury, London.

Lee, P C (1994) Social structure and evolution, in P J B Slater and T R Halliday (eds) *Behaviour and Evolution*, Cambridge University Press, Cambridge.

Lee, R T and Ashforth, B E (1990) On the meaning of Maslach's three dimensions of burnout, *Journal of Applied Psychology*, 75, 743-747.

Left et al (1989-90) The Camberwell study, in M Birchwood and N Tarrier (1992) *Innovations in the Psychological Management of Schizophrenia Assessment, Treatment and Services*, Wiley, London.

Leibowitz, S F (1992) Neurochemical-neuroendocrine systems in the brain controlling macronutrient intake and metabolism, *Trends in Neurosciences*, 15, 491-497.

Leinbach and Fagot (1989) in P Turner (1995) *Sex, Gender and Identity*, BPS Books, Leicester.

Lenneberg, E H (1967) *Biological Foundations of Language*, Wiley, New York.

Lennie, P (1980) Parallel visual pathways: A review, *Vision Research*, 20, 561-594.

Lerner, M J (1980) *The Belief in a Just World: A Fundamental Delusion* Plenum Levine, New York.

LeVay, S (1993) *The Sexual Brain*, MIT Press, Cambridge, MA.

LeVay, S (1996) Queer in the head, *Guardian, The Week*, 7 December 1996, pp 1-2.

Levelt, W J M (1989) *Speaking: From Intention to Articulation*, MIT Press, Cambridge, MA.

Levine, D N, Calvanio, R and Popovics, A (1982) Language in the absence of inner speech, *Word*, 15, 19-44.

Levine, R V, Martinex, T S, Brase, G and Sorenson, K (1994) Helping in 36 US cities, *Journal of Personality and Social Psychology*, 67, 69-92, in R A Baron and D Byrne (1997) *Social Psychology*, 8th edn, Allyn & Bacon, Boston, MA.

Levinson, D J (1986) A conception of adult development, *American Psychologist*, 41, 3-13.

Levy, B and Langer, E (1994) Aging free from negative stereotypes: Successful memory in China and among the American deaf, *Journal of Personality and Social Psychology*,

66, 989-997, in R A Baron and D Byrne (1997) *Social Psychology*, 8th edn, Allyn & Bacon, Boston, MA.

Lewin, K, Lippitt, R and White, R K (1939) Patterns of aggressive behaviour in experimentally created "social climates", *Journal of Social Psychology*, 10, 271-299.

Lewinsohn, P (1990) Depression across the age span, paper presented at the annual meeting of the Western Psychological Association, Los Angeles.

Lewis, C (1996) *Aspects of Human Development*, BPS Open Learning Units, Leicester.

Lewis, M (1990) Social knowledge and social development, *Merrill-Palmer Quarterly*, 36, 93-116.

Lewis, M (1991) Ways of knowing: Objective self-awareness of consciousness, *Developmental Review*, 11, 231-243.

Ley, P. (1978) Memory for medical information, in M M Gruneberg, P E Morris and R N Sykes (eds) *Practical Aspects of Memory*, Academic Press, London.

Leyens, J -P and Fraczek, A (1984) Aggression as an interpersonal phenomenon, in H Taifel *The Social Dimension*, vol 1, Cambridge University Press, Cambridge.

Lindy, J D, Green, B L and Grace, M L (1987) Commentary: The stressor criterion and post-traumatic stress disorder, *Journal of Nervous and Mental Disease*, 175, 269-272.

List, J (1986) Age and schematic differences in the reliability of eye-witness testimony, *Developmental Psychology*, 22, 50-57.

Livingstone, M S (1987) Art, illusion and the visual system, *Scientific American*, 258(I), 78-85.

Livingstone, M S and Hubel, D H (1988) Segregation of form, color, movement and depth: Anatomy, physiology and perception, *Science*, 240, 740-749.

Lloyd, B and Duveen, G (1990) A semiotic analysis of the development of the social representation of gender, in G Duveen and E Lloyd (eds) *Social Representation and the Development of Knowledge*, Cambridge University Press, Cambridge.

Lloyd, G K, Fletcher, A and Minchin, M C W (1992) GABA agonists as potential antiolytics, in G D Burrows, S M Rohm and R Noyes

Handbook of Anxiety, vol 5, Elsevier, Tokyo.

Lloyd, J E (1975) Aggressive mimicry in Photuris fireflies: Signal repertoires by femmes fatales, *Science*, 187, 452-453.

Lloyd, P (1995) *Cognitive and Language Development*, BPS Books, Leicester.

Locurto, C (1990) The malleability of IQ as judged from adoption studies, *Intelligence*, 15, 295-312.

Loftus, E F (1975) Leading questions and the eye-witness report, *Cognitive Psychology*, 7, 560-572.

Loftus, E F (1979) *Eye-witness Testimony*, Harvard University Press, Cambridge, MA.

Loftus, E F, Loftus, G R and Messo, J (1987) Some facts about weapon focus, *Law and Human Behavior*, 11, 55-62.

Loftus, E F, Miller, D G and Burns, H J (1978) Semantic integration of verbal information into visual memory, *Journal of Experimental Psychology: Human Learning and Memory*, 4, 19-31.

Loftus, E F, Schooler, J W, Boone, S M and Kline, D (1987) Time went by so slowly: Overestimation of event duration by males and females, *Applied Cognitive Psychology*, 1, 3-13.

Logan, G D (1988) Toward an instance theory of automatisation, *Psychological Review*, 95, 492-527.

Lopez (1995) in C Tavris and C Wade (1995) *Psychology in Perspective*, Harper Collins, New York.

Lorenz, K (1941) Vergleichende Bewegungsstudien bei Anatiden, *J. Ornithol.*, 89, 194-294.

Lorenz, K (1952) *King Solomon's Ring*, University Paperbacks, Methuen, London.

Lorenz, K (1966) *On Aggression*, Methuen & Co Ltd., London.

Lorenz, K (1993) The companion in the birds' world, *Auk*, 54, 245-273.

Lott, A J and Lott, B E (1974) The role of reward in the formation of positive interpersonal attitudes, in T Huston (ed) *Foundations of Interpersonal Attraction*, Academic Press, New York.

Lott and Moluso (1993) in P Turner (1995) *Sex, Gender and Identity*, BPS Books, Leicester.

Lowe (1995) in R A Baron (1996) *Essentials of Psychology*, Allyn & Bacon, Boston, MA.

Lowe, J and Carroll, D (1985) The effects of spinal injury on the intensity of emotional experience, *British Journal of Clinical Psychology*, 24, 135-136.

Lowe, M R (1993) The effects of dieting on eating behaviour: A three-factor model, *Psychological Bulletin*, 114 100-121.

Luborsky, L, Crits-Christoph, P and Mellou, J (1986) Advent of objective measures of transference concept, *Journal of Consulting and Clinical Psychology*, 54, 39.

Luborsky, L, Crits-Christoph, P, Mintz, J and Auerbach, A (1988) *Who Will Benefit from Psychotherpay? Predicting therapeutic outcomes*, Basic Books, New York.

Luchins, A S (1942) Mechanisation in problem solving, *Psychological Monographs*, 54 (whole no 248).

Luria, A R (1968) *The Mind of a Mnemonist*, Basic Books, New York.

Lynn, R (1996) *Dysgenics: Genetic Deterioration in Modern Populations*, London Praeger, Westport, CT.

Lynn, S J and Nash, M R (1994) Truth in memory: Ramifications for psychotherapy and hypnotherapy, *American Journal of Clinical Hypnosis*, 36, 194-208.

Lynn, S J, Rhue, J W and Weekes, J R (1990) Hypnotic involuntariness: A social cognitive analysis, *Psychological Review*, 974, 169-184.

Lytton, H and Romney, D M (1991) Parents' different socialization of boys and girls: A meta-analysis, *Psychological Bulletin*, 109, 267-296.

McCann, T S (1981) Aggression and sexual activity of male southern elephant seals, *Mirounga leonina, Journal of Zoology*, 195, 295-310.

McClelland, J L and Rummelhart, D E (1981) An interactive activation model of context effects in letter perception. Part 1: An account of basic findings, *Psychological Review*, 88, 375-407.

Maccoby, E E (1990) Gender and relationships: A developmental account, *American Psychologist*, 45, 513-520.

Maccoby, E E and Martin, J A (1983) Socialization in the context of the family: parent-child interaction, in E M Hetherington (ed.) *Handbook of Child Psychology: Vol 4. Socialization, Personality and Social Development*, Wiley, New York.

McConnell, T M (1934/1958) Discover or be told? in C W

Hunnicutt and W J Iverson (eds) *Research in the Three R's*, Harper & Row, New York.

Macdonald, D W (1986) A meerkat volunteers for guard duty so its comrades can live in peace, *Smithsonian*, April, 55-64.

McFarland, D J (1987) *Animal Behaviour*, Addison Wesley Longman.

McGuffin, P, Katz, and Rutherford, J (1991) Nature, nurture and depression: A twin study, *Journal of Comparative Psychological Medicine*, 329-335.

McGuire, J and Richman, N (1986) The prevalence of behaviour problems in three types of preschool children, *Journal of Child Psychology and Psychiatry*, 27, 455-472.

McGurk, H and MacDonald, J (1976) Hearing lips and seeing voices, *Nature*, 264, 746-748.

McKey, R H, Condelli, L, Granson, H *et al.* (1985) *The Impact of Head Start on Children, Families and Communities* (final report of the Head Start Evaluation Syllabus and Evaluation Project), Washington, DC.

Mackintosh, N (1984) The Mind in the Skinner, *New Scientist*, 2, 30-33.

Mackintosh, N J (1983) *Conditioning and Associative Learning*, Oxford University Press, Oxford.

McMaster, N L (1990) The courts and hypnotically refreshed memory: A review of the literature, *Australian Journal of Clinical Hypnotherapy and Hypnosis*, 11, 1-9.

McNeal, T and Cimbolic P. (1986) Antidepressants and biochemical theories of depression, *Psychological Bulletin*, 99, 361-374.

McNeill, D (1966) The creation of language, in P K Smith and H Cowie (1991) *Understanding Children's Development*, Basil Blackwell, Oxford.

Macrae, C N, Milne, A B and Bodenhausen, G V (1994) Stereotypes as energy saving devices: A peek inside the cognitive toolbox, *Journal of Personality and Social Psychology*, 66, 37-47, in R A Baron and D Byrne (1997) *Social Psychology*, 8th edn, Allyn & Bacon, Boston, MA.

Madson, P I, Holm, S, Vorstrup, S, Freiberg, I (1991) Human regional cerebral blood flow during rapid-eye-movement sleep, *Journal of Cerebral Blood Flow and Metabolism*, 11, 502-507.

Maffei, M, Halaas, J, Ravussin, E (1991) Leptin levels in human

and rodent: Measurement of plasma leptin and ob RNA in obese and weight-reduced subjects, *Nature Medicine*, 11, 1155-1161.

Magnus, D B E (1958) Experimentelle Untersuchungen zür Bionomie und Ethologie des Kaisermantels (*Argynnis paphia L*), *Zeitschrift für Tierpsychologie*, 15, 307-426.

Maier, N R F (1930) Reasoning in humans, I: On direction, *Journal of Comparative Psychology*, 10, 115-43.

Maier, N R F (1931) Reasoning in humans, II: The solution of a problem and its appearance in consciousness, *Journal of Comparative Psychology*, 12, 181-194.

Main, M and Cassidy, J (1988) Categories of response to reunion with the parent at age 6: Predictable from infant attachment classifications and stable over a 1-month period, *Developmental Psychology*, 24, 415-426.

Main, M and Solomon, J (1990) Procedures for identifying infants as disorganized/disoriented during the Ainsworth Strange Situation, in M T Greenberg, D Cicchetti and E M Cummings (eds), *Attachment in the preschool years: Theory, research and intervention*, University of Chicago Press, Chicago.

Malpass, R S and Devine, P G (1981) Guided memory in eyewitness identification, *Journal of Applied Psychology*, 66, 343-350.

Malthus, T (1798) *Essay on the principle of population*, in M White and J Gribbin (eds) (1996) *Darwin: A Life in Science*, Simon & Schuster, New York.

Malum, T, Birch, A and Wadeley, A (1992) *Perspectives in Psychology*, Macmillan, London.

Mandler, J (1983) Representation, in P H Mussen (ed), *Handbook of Child Psychology: vol 3. Cognitive Development*, Wiley, New York.

Manning, A and Stamp Dawkins, M (1992) *Animal Behaviour*, Cambridge University Press, Cambridge.

Manstead, A S R and McCulloch, C (1981) Sex-role stereotyping in British television advertisements, *British Journal of Social Psychology*, 20, 171-180.

Marcia, J E (1966) Development and the

validation of ego identity status, *Journal of Personality and Social Psychology*, 3, 551-558.

Marcia, J E (1980) Identity in adolescence, in J Adelson (ed) *Handbook of Adolescent Psychology*, Wiley, New York.

Marks, I M (1969) *Fears and Phobias*, Academic Press, New York.

Markus, H R and Kitayama, S (1991) Culture and the self: Implications for cognition, emotion and motivation, *Psychological Review*, 98, 224-253.

Marslen-Wilson, W D (1987) Functional parallelism in spoken word recognition, *Cognition*, 25, 71-102.

Marslen-Wilson, W D and Tyler, L K (1980) The temporal structure of spoken language understanding, *Cognition*, 8, 1-71.

Marslen-Wilson, W D and Welsh, A (1978) Processing interactions and lexical access during word recognition in continuous speech, *Cognitive Psychology*, 10, 29-63.

Martin, B J (1986) Sleep deprivation and exercise, in K B Pandolf (ed) *Exercise and Sport Science Review*, 213-229.

Martin, C L and Parker, S (1995) Folk theories about sex and race differences, *Personality and Social Psychology Bulletin*, 21, 45-57, in R A Baron and D Byrne (1997) *Social Psychology*, 8th edn, Allyn & Bacon, Boston, MA.

Martin, G M and Lett, B T (1985) Formation of associations of coloured and flavoured food with induced sickness in five main species, *Behav. & Neural Biology*, 43, 223-237.

Martin, G M and Lett, B T (1985) Formation of associations of coloured and flavoured food with induced sickness in five main species, *Behavioral and Neural Biology*, 43, 223-237.

Martin, M and Jones, G V (1983) Distribution of attention in cognitive failure, *Human Learning*, 2, 221-226.

Martinez, R and Dukes, R L (1987) Race, gender and self-esteem among youth, *Hispanic Journal of Behavioural Sciences*, 9, 427-443.

Masica, Money, Ehrhardt and Lewis (1969) in S Coren, C Porac and L M Ward *Sensation and Perception*, international edn (1979), Academic Press, San Diego, CA.

Maslach, C and Jackson, S E (1984) Burnout in organizational settings, in S Oskamp (ed) *Applied Social Psychology Annual*, vol 5, pp

135-154, Sage, Beverly Hills, CA.

Masson, G and McCarthy, S (1994) *When Elephants Weep: The Emotional Lives of Animals*, Jonathan Cape, London.

Matarazzo, J D (1992) Biological and physiological correlates of intelligence, *Intelligence*, 16, 257-258.

Mateer, C A and Cameron, P A (1989) Electrophysiological correlates of language: Stimulation mapping and evoked potential studies, in F Boller and J Grafman (eds) *Handbook of Neuropsychology*, vol 2, 91-116, Elsevier.

Matlin, M W (1989) *Cognition*, 2nd edn, Holt, Rinehart and Winston International Edition, Dryden Press, Fort Worth, TX.

Matlin, M W (1994) *Cognition*, 3rd edn, Harcourt Brace, Orlando, FL.

Matlin, M W and Foley, H J (1992) *Sensation and Perception*, 3rd edn, Allyn & Bacon, Boston, MA.

Matlin, M W and Foley, H J (1996) *Sensation and Perception*, 4th edn, Allyn & Bacon, Boston, MA.

Matsumoto, D (1994) *People, Psychology from a Cultural Perspective*, Cole, Pacific Grove, CA.

Matsumoto, D and Assar, M (1992) The effects of language on judgements of universal facial expressions of emotion, *Journal of Nonverbal Behavior*, 16, 85-99.

Matsuzawa, T (1996) Chimpanzee intelligence in nature and in captivity: Isomorphism of symbol use and tool use, in W C McGrew, L F Marchant and T Nishida (eds) *Great Ape Societies* (1996), Cambridge University Press, Cambridge.

Matthews, K A (1982) Psychological perspectives on the type A behaviour pattern, *Psychological Bulletin*, 91, 293-323.

Mattson, S N, Barron, S and Riley, E P (1988) The behavioural effects of prenatal alcohol exposure, in K Kuriyama, A Takada and H Ishii (eds) *Biomedical and Social Aspects of Alcohol and Alcoholism*, Elsevier, Tokyo.

May, P R, Tuma, A and Dixon, W J (1981) Schizophrenia: A follow-up study of the results of five years of treatment, *Archives of General Psychiatry*, 38, 776-784.

Maynard Smith, J (1958) *The Theory of Evolution*, Penguin, Harmondsworth.

Maynard Smith, J (1964) Group

selection and kin selection, *Nature*, 201, 1145-1147.

Maynard Smith, J (1977) Parental investment: A prospective analysis, *Animal Behaviour*, 23, 1-9.

Maynard Smith, J (1982) *Evolution and the Theory of Games*, Cambridge University Press, Cambridge.

Maynard Smith, J and Price, G R (1973) The logic of animal conflict, *Nature*, 246, 15-18.

Mays, V.M., Rubin, J., Sabourin, M. & Walker, L. (1996) Moving towards a global psychology: Changing theory and practice to meet the needs of a changing world, *American Psychologist*, 51(5), 485-487.

Mazzocchi, F and Vignola, L A (1979) Localisation of lesions in aphasia: Clinical-CT scan correlations in stroke patients, *Cortex*, 15, 627-654.

Mead, G H (1934) *Mind, Self and Society*, University of Chicago Press, Chicago.

Meadows, S (1993) *The Child as Thinker*, Routledge, London.

Medin, D L and Ross, B H (1992) *Cognitive Psychology*, Harcourt Brace Jovanovich, Fort Worth, TX.

Meeus, W H J and Raajmakers, Q A W (1986) Administrative obedience: carrying out orders to use psychological-administrative violence, *European Journal of Social Psychology*, 16, 311-324, in P B Smith and M H Bond (1993) *Social Psychology Across Cultures: Analysis and Perspectives*, Harvester Wheatsheaf, Trowbridge.

Meichenbaum, D (1985) *Stress Inoculation Training*, Pergamon Press, New York.

Meichenbaum, D H (1977) *Cognitive-Behaviour Modification: An Integrative Approach*, Plenum Press, New York.

Meire, P M and Eroynck, A (1986) Are oyster-catchers (*Haematopus ostralegus*) selecting the most profitable mussels (*Mytilis edulis*) *Animal Behaviour*, 43, 1427-1435.

Meise, U and Fleishhacker, W W (1996) Perspectives on treatment needs in schizophrenia, *British Journal of Psychiatry*, 168(29), 9-16.

Melamed, S, Kushnir, T and Shirom, A (1992) Burnout risk factors for cardiovascular diseases, *Behavioural Medicine*, 18, 53-60.

Melhuish, E C (1990) Research on day care for young children in the United Kingdom, in E C Melhuish and P Moss (eds) *Day Care for*

Young Children: International Perspectives, Routledge, London.

Melton, G B and Gray, J N (1988) Ethical dilemmas in AIDS research: Individual privacy and public health, *American Psychologist*, 43 (1), 60-64.

Menzies, R G and Clarke, J C (1995) The etiology of phobias: A non-ascriptive account, *Clinical Psychology Review*, 15(21), 23-48.

Merckelbach, H, de Jong, P J, Muns, P and Van den Hart, M A (1996) The etiology of specific phobias: A review, *Clinical Psychology Review*, 16 (4) 361-377.

Mervis, C B and Rosch, E (1981) Categorisation of natural objects, *Annual Review of Psychology*, 32, 89-115.

Mestel, R (1997) Noises from the cellar, Mind Travellers, *New Scientist* suppplement, 26 April 1997, 14-17.

Mewstel, R, (1995) Horse-killing virus may cause mental illness, *New Scientist*, 11 March 1995.

Michel, S (1993) Circadian rhythms in membrane conduction expressed in isolated neurons, *Science*, 259, 239-24.

Milgram, S (1974) *Obedience to Authority*, Harper and Row, New York.

Milgram, S. (1970) The experience of living in cities, *Science*, 167, 1461-1468.

Milgram, S and Toch, H (1969) Collective behaviour: Crowds and social movements, in G Lindzey and E Aronson (eds) *Handbook of Social Psychology*, 2nd edn, vol 4, Addison Wesley, Reading, MA.

Miller, N E (1941) The frustration-aggression hypothesis, *Psychological Review*, 48, 337-342.

Miller, D R and Swanson, G E (1960) The changing American parent: A study in the Detroit area, in D Krech, R S Critchfield and E L Ballachey (1962) *Individual in Society*, McGraw-Hill, New York.

Miller, N E (1985) The value of behavioral research on animals, *American Psychologist*, 40, 423-440.

Milner, B R (1966) Amnesia following operation on temporal lobes, in C W N Whitty and O L Zangwill (eds) *Amnesia*, Butterworth Press, London.

Mischel, W (1968) *Personality and Assessment*, Wiley, New York.

Mischel, W (1971) *Introduction to Personality*, 2nd ed, Holt

Rinehart and Winston, New York.

Mischel, W (1973) Towards a cognitive social learning reconceptualization of personality, *Psychological Review*, 80, 252-283.

Mitchell, - (1983) in Griffiths, M (1997) Video games and childrens' behaviour, in T Charlton and K David (1997) (eds) *Elusive Links: Television, Video Games and Children's Behaviour*, Park Published Papers.

Mitchell, T R and Larson, J R, Jr (1987) *People in Organizations: An Introduction to Organizational Behaviour*, 3rd edn, McGraw Hill, New York.

Mock, D W, Lamey, T C, Williams, C F and Pelletier, A (1987) Flexibility in the development of heron sibling aggression: An intraspecific test of the prey-size hypothesis, *Animal Behaviour*, 35, 1386-1393.

Moehlman, P D (1979) Jackal helpers and pup survival, *Nature*, 277, 382-383.

Mo[/]ler, A P (1988) Female choice selects for male sexual tail ornaments in the monogamous swallow, *Nature*, 332, 640-2.

Mo[/]ler, A P (1989) Viability costs of male tail ornaments in a swallow, *Nature*, 339, 132-134.

Molnar, R E (1977) Analogies in the evolution of combat and display structures in ornithopods and ungulates, *Evolutionary Theory*, 3, 165-190.

Monaghan, P and Metcalfe, N B (1985) Group foraging in wild brown hares: Effects of resource distribution and social status, *Animal Behaviour*, 33, 993-999.

Money, J (1974) Prenatal hormones and postnatal socialisation in gender identity differentiation, in J K Cole and R Dienstbier (eds) *Nebraska Symposium on Motivation*, University of Nebraska Press, Lincoln.

Monk, T H and Aplin, L C (1980) Spring and autumn daylight saving times changes: Studies of adjustment in sleep timings, mood and efficiency, *Ergonomics*, 23, 167-178.

Montemayor and Eisen (1977) in P K Smith and H Cowie (1991) *Understanding Children's Understanding*, 2nd edn, Blackwell, Oxford.

Moran, J and Desimone, R (1985) Selective attention gates visual processing in the extrastriate cortex, *Science*, 229, 782-784.

Moray, N (1959) *Attention:*

Selective Processes in Vision and Hearing, Hutchinson, London.

Moreland, R L. and Beach, S R (1992) Exposure effects in the classroom: the development of affinity among students, *Journal of Experimental Social Psychology* 28, 255-276.

Morgan, D L (186) Personal relationships as an interface between social networks and social cognitions, *Journal of Social and Personal Relationships*, 3, 403-422 in N Hayes (1994) *Foundations of Psychology: An Introductory Text*, Routledge, London.

Moriarty, T (1975) Crime, commitment, and the responsive bystander: Two field experiments, *Journal of Personality and Social Psychology*, 31, 370-376.

Morris, C D, Bransford, J D and Franks, J J (1977) Levels of processing versus transfer appropriate processing, *Journal of Verbal Learning and Verbal Behavior*, 16, 519-533.

Morris, R G, Craik, F I and Gick, M L (1990) Age differences in working memory tasks: The role of secondary memory and the central executive system, *Quarterly Journal of Experimental Psychology: Human Experimental Psychology*, 42, 676-686.

Morris, T A (1980) "Type C" for cancer? Low trait anxiety in the pathogenesis of breast cancer, *Cancer Detection and Prevention*, 3, 102.

Moscovici, S (1976) *Social Influence and Social Change*, Academic Press, London.

Moscovici, S (1985) Social influence and conformity, in Lindzey and Aronson (eds) *Handbook of Social Psychology*, 3rd edn, Random House, New York.

Moscovici, S and Zavalleroni, M (1969) The group as polariser of attitudes, *Journal of Personality and Social Psychology*, 12, 125-135.

Moynihan, M H and Rodaniche, A F (1977) Communication, crypsis and mimicry among cephalopods, in T A Sebeok (Ed) *How Animals Communicate*, Indiana University Press, Bloomington, Indiana.

Moynihan, M H and Rodaniche, A F (1977) Communication, crypsis and mimicry among cephalopods, in T A Sebeok (Ed) *How Animals Communicate*, Indiana University Press, Bloomington, Indianna.

Muczyk, J P and Reimann, B C (1987) The case for directive leadership, *Academy of*

Management Review, 12, 647-687, in R A Baron and D Byrne (1997) *Social Psychology*, 8th edn, Allyn & Bacon, Boston, MA.

Muehlenhard, C and Cook, S (1988) Men's self-reports of unwanted sexual activity, *Journal of Sex Research*, 24, 58-72.

Mukerjee, M (1997) Trends in animal research, *Scientific American*, 276(2), 70-77.

Mukhametov, L (1984) in Mind Travellers, *New Scientist* supplement, 26 April 1997, 13.

Munday, P (1998) reported by A Motluk, *New Scientist*, 158, 22.

Munn, C A (1984) Birds of a different feather also flock together, *Natural History*, 93(II), 34-42.

Murphy, K R and Davidshofer, C O (1991) *Psychological Testing: Principles and Applications*, 2nd edn, Prentice Hall, Englewood Cliffs, NJ.

Myers, R E and Sperry, R W (1953) Interocular transfer of a visual form discrimination habit in cats after section of the optic chiasma and corpus callosum, *American Association of Anatomists: Abstracts of Papers from Platform*, p.351.

Myerscough, R and Taylor, S (1985) The effects of marijuana on human physical aggression, *Journal of Personality and Social Psychology*, 49, 1541-1546, in K Deaux, F C Dane and L S Wrightsman (1993) *Social Psychology in the 90s*, Brooks Cole, Pacific Grove, CA.

Nadler, A (1991) Help-seeking behaviour: Psychological costs and instrumental benefits, in M S Clard (ed) (1991) *Prosocial Behaviour*, Sage, Newbury Park, CA.

Naeser, M A, Hayward, R W, Laughlin, S A et al. (1981) Quantitative CT scan studies in aphasia, *Brain and Language*, 12, 140-164.

Nakamura, G V, Graesser, A C, Zimmerman, J A and Riha, J (1985) Script processing in a natural situation, *Memory and Cognition*, 13, 140-144.

Nathans, J (1989) The genes for colour vision, *Scientific American*, 260 (2), 42-49.

Neale, M A. and Northcraft, G B (1986) Experts, amateurs and refrigerators: comparing expert and amateur negotiators in a novel task, *Organizational Behavior and Human Decision Processes*, 38, 305-317.

Neher, A (1991) Maslow's theory of motivation: A critique, *Journal of Humanistic*

Psychology, 31, 89-112.

Neisser, U (1964) Visual search, *Scientific American*, 210, 94-102.

Neisser, U (1967) *Cognitive Psychology*, Appleton-Century-Crofts, New York.

Neisser, U (1976) *Cognition and Reality*, W H Freeman, San Francisco.

Nelkin, D and Lindee, M S (1995) *The DNA Mystique: The Gene as Cultural Icon*, W H Freeman, New York.

Nelson, K (1973) Structure and strategy in learning to talk, *Monographs of the Society for Research in Child Development*, 38, 149.

Nemeth, C J (1986) Differential contributions of majority and minority influence, *Psychological Review*, 93, 23-32, in R R Reno, R B Ciladini and C A Kallgren (1993) The transsitutional influence of social norms, *Journal of Personality and Social Psychology*, 64, 104-112, in R A Baron and D Byrne (1997) *Social Psychology*, 8th edn, Allyn & Bacon, Boston, MA.

Nerlove, S B, Roberts, J M, Klein, R E et al. (1974) Natural indictors of cognitive ability, *Ethos*, 2, 265-295.

Neuberg, S L (1989) The goal of forming accurate impressions during social interaction: attenuating the impact of negative expectancies, *Journal of Personality and Social Psychology*, 56, 374-386, in R A Baron and D Byrne (1997) *Social Psychology*, 8th edn, Allyn & Bacon, Boston, MA.

Neuberg, S L, Cialdini, R B, Brown, S L, Luce, C, Sagarin, B J and Lewis, B P (1997) Does empathy lead to anything more than superficial helping? Comment on Batson et al (1997), *Journal of Personality and Social Psychology* 73 (3), 510-516.

Newell, A and Simon, H A (1972) *Human Problem Solving*, Prentice Hall, Englewood Cliffs, NJ.

Newman, J and McCauley, C (1977) Eye contact with strangers in city, suburbia and small town, *Environment and Behaviour*, 9, 547-558.

Newson, E (1994) Video violence and the protection of children, *Psychology Review*, 1(2), 2-5.

Newson, J and Newson, E. (1965) Patterns of infant care in an urban community, in M Hardy and S Heyes (1987) *Beginning Psychology*, 3rd edn, Weidenfeld & Nicolson, London.

Newton, N A, Lazarus, L W and Weinberg, J (1984) Aging: Biopsychosocial perspectives, in D Offer and M Sabshin (eds) *Normality and the Life Cycle*, Basic Books, New York.

Nicholson, J (1993) *Men and Women: How Different are They?*, Oxford University Press, Oxford.

Nicolai, J (1956) in R A Hinde (1966) *Animal Behaviour*, McGraw Hill, New York.

Nisbett, R E (1972) Humger–obesity and the ventromedial hypothalamus, *Psychological Review*, 79, 433-453.

Nissen, M J and Bullemer, P (1987) Attentional requirements of learning: Evidence from performance measures, *Cognitive Psychology*, 19, 1-32.

Nobles, W W (1976) Extended self: Rethinking the so-called Negro self-concept, *Journal of Black Psychology*, 2, 99-105.

Norman, D A (1969) Memory while shadowing, *Quarterly Journal of Experimental Psychology*, 21, 85-93.

Norman, D A (1976) *Memory and Attention*, 2nd edn, Wiley, Chichester.

Norman, D A (1981) Categorisation of action slips, *Psychological Review*, 88, 1-15.

Norman, D A and Shallice, T (1986) Attention to action: Willed and automatic control of behaviour, in R J Davidson, G E Schwartz and D Shapiro (eds), *The Design of Everyday Things*, Doubleday, New York.

Novin, D, Robinson, B A, Culbreth, L A and Tordoff, M G (1983) Is there a role for the liver in the control of food intake? *American Journal of Clinical Nutrition*, 9, 233-246.

Oakley, D, Alden, P, Mather, M D (1996) *The Psychologist*, 9(11), 502-505.

Obal, F, Payne, L, Kapas, L, Opp, M and Krueger, J M (1991) Inhibition of growth hormone-releasing factor suppresses both sleep and growth hormone secretion in the rat, *Brain Research*, 557, 149-153.

Odell, D K (1977) Structure of northern elephant seal population breeding on San Nicolas Island, California, in 1971, *Animal Behaviour*, 25, 208-214.

Oden, G C (1979) A fuzzy logic model of letter identification, *Journal of Experimental Psychology: Human Perception and Performance*, 18, 185-197.

Offer, D and Sabshin, M (1984) Adolescence: Empirical

perspectives, in D Offer and M Sabshin (eds) *Normality and the Life Cycle*, Basic Books, New York.

Ogbu, J U (1981) Origins of human competence: A cultural-ecological perspective, *Child Development*, 52, 413-429 in P Erwin (1993) *Friendship and Peer Relations in Children*, Wiley, Chichester.

Ohlott, P J, Ruderman, M N and McCauley, C D (1994) Gender differences in managers' developmental job experiences, *Academy of Management Journal*, 37, 46-67, in R A Baron and D Byrne (1997) *Social Psychology*, 8th edn, Allyn & Bacon, Boston, MA.

Öhman, A, Frederickson, M, Hugdahl, K and Rimmo, D (1976) The premise of equipotentiality in human classical conditioning. Conditioned electrodermal responses to potentially phobic stimuli, *Journal of Experimental Psychology*, 105 (4), 313-337.

Ohzawa, I, DeAngelia, G C and Freeman, R D (1990) Stereoscopic depth discrimination in the visual cortex: Neurons ideally suited as disparity detectors, *Science* 249, 1037-1041.

Ojemann, G A (1979) Individual variability in cortical localization of language, *Journal of Neurosurgery*, 50, 164-169.

Ojemann, G A (1983) Brain organization for language from the perspective of electrical stimulation mapping, *Behavioural and Brain Sciences*, 2, 189-230.

Olds, J and Milner, P (1954) Positive reinforcement produced by electrical stimulation of septal area and other regions of rat brain, *Journal of Comparative and Physiological Psychology*, 47, 419-427.

Oliner, S P and Oliner, P M (1988) *The Altruistic Personality: Rescuers of Jews in Nazi Germany*, Free Press, New York.

Olivardia, Harrison, Pope, Mangeveh (1995) Eating disorders in college men, *Journal of American Psychiatry*, 152(9), 1279-1285.

Olness, K and Gardner, G (1988) *Hypnosis and Hypnotherapy with Children*, Grune and Stratton, New York.

Orbach, S and Schwartz, J (1997) Why are boys slugs and snails and little girls all things nice?: Playing the

Gender Game, *The Guardian - The Week*, 14 June, 1-2.

Orians, G H and Heerwagen, J H (1992) Evolved responses to landscapes, in J H Barkow, L Cosmides and J Tooby (eds) (1992) *The Adapted Mind: Evolutionary Psychology and the Generation of Culture*, Oxford University Press, New York.

Oring, L W (1986) Avian polyandry, *Current Ornithology*, 3, 309-351.

Orne, M T, Dinges, D F and Orne, E C (1984) On the differential diagnosis of multiple personality in the forensic case, *International Journal of Clinical and Experimental Hypnosis*, 32, 118-169.

Orne, M T and Evans, F J (1965) Social control in the psychological experiment: Antisocial behaviour and hypnosis, *Journal of Personality and Social Psychology*, 1, 189-200.

Orne, M T, Whitehouse, W G, Dinges, D F and Orne, E C (1988) Reconstructing memory through hypnosis, in Pettinati(ed) *Hypnosis and Memory*, Guilford, New York.

Ortany, A and Turner, T J (1990) What's basic about basic emotions?, *Psychological Review*, 97, 315-331.

Osterman, K, Bjorkqvist, K, Lagerspetz, K M J, Kaukianainen, A, Juesmann, L W and Fraczek, A (1994) Peer and self-estimated aggression and victimization in 8-year-old children from five ethnic groups, *Aggressive Behaviour*, 20, 411-428, in R A Baron and D Byrne (1997) *Social Psychology*, 8th edn, Allyn & Bacon, Boston, MA.

Owings, D H and Leger, D W (1980) Chatter vocalizations of California ground squirrels: predator and social-role specificity, *Zeitschrift für Tierpsychologie*, 54, 135-184.

Owusu-Bempah, J and Howitt, D (1995) How Eurocentric psychology damages Africa, *The Psychologist*, October, 462-465.

Ozer, E M and Bandura, A (1990) Mechanisms governing empowerment effects: A self-efficacy analysis, *Journal of Personality and Social Psychology*, 58, 472-486.

Packer, C (1986) The ecology of sociality in felids, in D I Rubenstein and R W Wrangham (eds) *Ecological aspects of social evolution*, Princeton University Press, Princeton, NJ.

Packer, C, Herbst, L, Pusey, A E,

Bygott, J D, Cairns, S J, and Mulder, M B (1988) Reproductive success in lions, in T H Clutton-Brock (ed), *Reproductive Success: Studies of Individual Variation in Contrasting Breeding Systems*, University of Chicago Press, Chicago.

Packer, C and Pusey, A E (1983) Male takeovers and female reproductive parameters: A simulation of oestrous synchrony in lions (*Panthera leo*), *Animal Behaviour*, 31, 334-340.

Packer, C and Ruttan, L (1988) The evolution of cooperative hunting, *American Naturalist*, 132, 159-198.

Packer, C, Scheel, D and Pusey, A E (1990) Why lions form groups: Food is not enough, *American Naturalist*, 136, 1-19.

Paikoff, R L and Brooks-Gunn, T (1991) Do parent-child relationships change during puberty?, *Psychological Bulletin*, 110, 47-66.

Pain, S (1998) Darwin's paradise awash, *New Scientist*, 157, 4.

Paivio, A (1971) *Imagery and Verbal Processes*, Holt, New York.

Paley, V G (1984) *Boys and Girls*, University of Chicago Press, Chicago.

Palincsar, A S and Brown, A L (1984) Reciprocal teaching of comprehension fostering monitoring activities, *Cognition and Instruction*, 1, 117-175.

Pantin, H M and Carver, C S (1982) Induced competence and the bystander effect. *Journal of Applied Social Psychology*, 12, 100-111.

Pardo, J V, Fox P T and Raichle, M E (1991) Localization of a human system for sustained attention by positron emission tomography, *Nature*, 349, 61-64.

Parents against Drug Abuse (1996) *Guardian Education*, 23 April 1996.

Park, K A and Waters, E (1989) Security of attachment and preschool friendships, *Child Development*, 60, 1076-1081, in P Erwin (1993) *Friendship and Peer Relations in Children*, Wiley, Chichester.

Parkin, A J (1987) *Memory and Amnesia: An Introduction*, Blackwell, Oxford.

Parkin, A J, Lewinson, J and Folkard, S (1982) The influence of emotion on immediate and delayed retention: Levinger and Clark reconsidered, *British Journal of Psychology*, 73, 389-393.

Parkinson, B (1996) What makes emotions emotional, *Psychology Review*, 3(2), 2-5.

Pascale, R and Athos, A G (1981) *The Art of Japanese Management*, Simon & Schuster, New York.

Passman, R H and Weisberg, P (1975) Mothers and blankets as agents for promoting play and exploration by young children in a novel environment: The effects of social and nonsocial attachment objects, *Developmental Psychology*, 11, 170-177, in R A Baron (1996) *Essentials of Psychology*, Allyn & Bacon, Boston, MA.

Pastor, D L (1981) The quality of mother-infant attachment and its relationship to toddlers' initial sociability with peers, *Developmental Psychology*, 17, 326-335, in P Erwin (1993) *Friendship and Peer Relations in Children*, Wiley, Chichester.

Pastor, D L (1981) The quality of mother-infant attachment and its relationship to toddlers' initial sociability with peers, *Developmental Psychology*, 17, 326-335, in P Erwin (1993) *Friendship and Peer Relations in Chilren*, Wiley, Chichester.

Patterson, F G (1978) The gestures of a gorilla: Language acquisition in another pongid, *Brain and Language*, 3, 72-97.

Patterson, F G (1980) Innovative uses of language by a gorilla: a case study, in K Nelson (ed) *Children's Language*, vol. 2, Gardner Press, New York.

Patterson, K E, Marshall, J C and Coulthart, M (eds) (1985) *Surface Dyslexia: Neuropsychological and Cognitive Analyses of Phonological Reading*, Lawrence Erlbaum, London.

Patterson, K, Vargha-Khadem, F and Polkey, C E (1989) Reading with one hemisphere, *Brain*, 112, 39-63.

Paul, G H and Lentz, R (1997) *Psychosocial treatment of the chronic mental patient*, Harvard University Press, Harvard, MA.

Paulson, F L (1974) Teaching co-operation on television: An evaluation of Sesame Street social goals programs, *AV Communication Review*, 22, 229-246.

Pavlov, I P (1927) *Conditioned Reflexes*, Oxford University Press, London.

Payne, R (1983) *Communication and Behaviour of Whales*, Westview Press, Boulder, Colo.

Pedersen, D M (1994) Privacy preferences and classroom seat selection, *Social Behaviour and Personality*, 22, 393-398.

Pederson, D R, Moran, G, Sitko, C *et al.* (1990) Maternal sensitivity and the security of infant-mother attachment: A Q-sort study, *Child Development*, 61, 1974-1983.

Penfield, W and Boldrey, E (1937) Somatic motor and sensory representations in cerebral cortex of man as studied by electrical stimulation, *Brain*, 60, 389-443.

Penfield, W and Roberts, L (1959) *Speech and Brain Mechanisms*, Princeton University Press, Princeton, NJ.

Peplau, L A (1984) Power in dating relationships, in J Freedman (ed) *Women: A Feminist Perspective*, 3rd edn, Mayfield, Palo Alto.

Peterson, (1976) in S Coren, C Porac and L M Ward (eds) *Sensation and Perception*, international edn, Academic Press, San Diego, CA.

Peterson, A C (1989) Developmental transitions and their role in influencing life trajectories, Paper presented at the Annual Meeting of the American Psychological Association, New Orleans.

Peterson, C, Seligman, M E and Vaillant, G (1988) Pessimistic explanatory style is a risk factor for physical illness: A thirty-five year longitudinal study, *Journal of Personality and Social Psychology*, 55, 23-27.

Peterson, L and Brown, D (1994) Integrating child injury and abuse-neglect research: Common histories, etiologies and solutions, *Psychological Bulletin*, 116, 293-315.

Peterson, L R and Peterson, M J (1959) Short-term retention of individual items, *Journal of Experimental Psychology*, 58, 193-198.

Petkova, B (1997) Understanding eating disorders, *Psychology Review*, 1, 2-7.

Petkova, B and James, O (1997) Serotonin - A chemical feel-good factor, *Psychology Review*, 4(1), 34.

Phinney, J (1990) Ethnic identity in adolescents and adults: Review of research, *Psychological Bulletin*, 108, 499-514.

Piaget, J (1951) *Play, Dreams and Imitation in Childhood*, Routledge, London.

Piaget, J and Inhelder, B (1969) *The Psychology of the Child*, Routledge & Kegan Paul, London.

Pietsch, T W and Grobecker, D B (1978) The compleat angler: Aggressive mimicry in antennarid anglefish, *Science*,

201, 369-370.

Piliavin, J A, Dovidio, J F, Gaertner, S L and Clard, R D III (1981) *Emergency Intervention*, Academic Press, New York.

Piliavin, J A and Piliavin, I M (1973) The good Samaritan: Why does he help? Unpublished manuscript, University of Wisconsin.

Pilliavin, I M, Rodin, J and Pilliavin, J A (1969) Good Samaritanism: An underground phenomenon?, *Journal of Personality and Social Psychology*, 13, 289-299.

Pinel, J P J (1997) *Biopsychology*, 3rd edn, Allyn & Bacon, Boston, MA.

Pinel, J P J and Rovner, L I (1977) Saccharin elation effect, *Bulletin of the Psychonomic Society*, 9, 275-278.

Pinker, S (1994) *The Language Instinct*, Harper Collins, New York.

Pinker, S (1997) *How the Mind Works*, Allen Lane, Penguin, Harmondsworth.

Piper, W E, Joyce, A S, McCallum, M and Asium, H F (1993) Concentration and correspondence of transference interpretation in short-term psychotherapy, *Journal of Consulting and Clinical Psychology*, 6, 586-596.

Pitman, R K, Orr, S P, Forgue, D F, Altman, B, Jong, J B and Hertz, L R (1990) Psychophysiological responses to combat imagery of Vietnam veterans with post-traumatic stress disorders versus other anxiety disorders, *Journal of Abnormal Psychology*, 99, 49-54.

Plante, T G and Rodin, J (1990) Physical fitness and enhanced psychological health, *Current Psychology: Research and Reviews*, 9, 3-24.

Pleck, J H (1987) American fathering in historical perspective, in M S Kimmel (ed) *Changing Men: New Directions in Research on Men and Masculinity*, Sage, Beverly Hills, CA.

Plomin, R (1989) Environment and genes: determinants of behaviour, *American Psychologist*, 44, 105-111.

Pool, R (1996) Is it a plane? Is it a bird? *New Scientist*, 152 (2055), 29-32.

Posner, M I and Petersen, S E (1990) The attention system of the human brain, *Annual Review of Neuroscience*, 13, 25-42.

Posner, M I, Petersen, S E, Fox, P T et al. (1988) Localization of cognitive operations in the human brain, *Science*, 240, 1627-1631.

Powell, G V N (1974) Experimental analysis of the social value of clocking by starlings (*Sturnus vulgaris*) in relation to predation and foraging, *Animal Behaviour*, 22, 501-505.

Prange, A J Jr, Lynn, C W, Lacoe, B A, Wilson, J C and Stukeleather, R A (1974) L-tryptophan in mania contribution to a permissive hypothesis of affective disorders, *Archives of General Psychiatry*, 30, 56-62.

Pratkanis, A R and Aronson, E (1992) *Age of Propaganda: The Everyday Use and Abuse of Persuasion*, W H Freeman, New York.

Prentice, P (1995) Dream analysis, *Psychology Review*, 2(1), 12-15.

Prentice, P (1995) From theory to therapist, *Psychology Review*, 2(1), 5-7.

Prentice-Dunn, S and Rogers, R W (1982) Effects of public and private self-awareness on deindividuation and aggression, *Journal of Personality and Social Psychology*, 43, 503-513.

Price, R A and Gottesman, I I (1991) Body fat in identical twins reared apart: Roles for genes and environment reviewed, *Behavioural Genetics*, 21, 1-7.

Price, R A and Vandenberg, S G (1979) Matching for physical attractiveness in married couples, *Personality and Social Psychology Bulletin*, 5, 398-400.

Prince P, Schizophrenia: The viral connection, *Psychology Review* 2, 34

Ptacek, J T, Smith, R E and Dodge, K L (1994) Gener differences in coping with stress: When stressor and appraisals do not differ, *Personality and Social Psychology Bulletin*, 20, 421-430.

Pullium, H R and Caraco, T (1984) Living in groups: Is there an optimal group size? in J R Krebs and N B Davies (eds) *An Introduction to Behavioural Ecology*, Blackwell, London.

Pyke, S W and Agnew, N (1991) *The Science Game: An Introduction to Research in the Social Sciences*, 5th edn, Prentice Hall, Englewood Cliffs, NJ.

Quirion, R (1989) Receptor sites for atrial natriuretic factors in brain and associated structures: An overview, *Cellular and Molecular Neurobiology*, 9, 45-55.

Rabbie, J. (1982) Are groups more aggressive than individuals? in P B Smith and M H Bond (1993) *Social Psychology Across Cultures*, Harvester Wheatsheaf, Hemel Hempstead.

Rachman (1991) in H Merckelbach, P J de Jong *et al.* The Etiology of specific phobias: A review, *Clinical Psychology Review*, 16 (4), 337-361.

Radin, E D (1964) *The Innocents*, William Morrow, New York.

Ragland, D R and Brand, R J (1988) Type A behaviour and mortality from coronary heart disease, *New England Journal of Medicine*, 318, 65-69.

Ralph, M R, Foster, T G, Davis, F C and Meneker, M (1990) Transplanted suprachiasmatic nucleus determines circadian period, *Science*, 247, 975-978.

Ralph, M R and Lehman, M N (1991) Transplantation: A new tool in the analysis of the mammalian hypothalamic circadian pacemaker, *Trends in Neuroscience*, 14, 362-366.

Ramm, P and Smith, C T (1990) Rates of cerebral protein synthesis are linked to slow wave sleep in the rat, *Physiology and Behaviour*, 48, 749-753.

Rasa, O A E (1973) Marking behaviour and its social significance in the African dwarf mongoose, *Helogale undulata rufula*, *Zeitschrift für Tierpsychologie*, 32, 293-318.

Rasmussen, I., Hightower, R and Rasmussen, P (1964) *Mathematics for the Primary School Teacher*, Learning Materials, Chicago.

Ratnasuriya, R H, Eisler, I, Szmukler, G I and Russell, G F M (1991) Anorexia nervosa: Outcome and prognostic factors after 20 years, *British Journal of Psychiatry*, 158, 495-502.

Rayner, K and Pollatsek, A (1987) Eye movements in reading: A tutorial review, in M W Eysenck (1993) *Principles of Cognitive Psychology*, Lawrence Erlbaum, Hove.

Reason, J and Mycielska, K (1982) *Absent Minded? The Psychology of Mental Lapses and Everyday Errors*, Prentice Hall, Englewood Cliffs, NJ.

Reason, J T (1979) Actions not as planned: The price of automatisation, in G Underwood and R Stevens (eds) *Aspects of Consciousness*, vol 1, Academic Press, London.

Reason, J T (1984) Absentmindedness and cognitive control, in J E Harris and P E Morris (eds) *Everyday Memory, Actions and Absentmindedness*, Academic Press, London.

Reason, J T (1992) Cognitive underspecification: Its variety and consequences, in B J Baars (ed) *Experimental Slips and Human Error: Exploring the Architecture of Volition*, Plenum Press, New York.

Rebert, W M, Stanton, A L and Schwarz, R M (1991) Influence of personality attributes and daily moods on bulimic eating patterns, *Addictive Behaviours*, 16(6), 497-505.

Reed, C F (1989) Terrestrial passage theory, in M W Matlin and H J Foley (eds) *Sensation and Perception*, 3rd edn, Academic Press.

Reed and Jenson (1993) in R A Baron (1996) *Essentials of Psychology*, Allyn & Bacon, Boston, MA.

Reicher, G M (1969) Perceptual recognition as a function of meaningfulness of stimulus material, *Journal of Experimental Psychology*, 81, 274-280.

Reichert, S E (1985) Why do some spiders cooperate? *Agelena consociata*, a case study, *Florida Entomologist*, 68, 105-116.

Reiser, M and Nielson, M (1980) in N R Carlson and W Buskist (1997) *Psychology: The Science of Behaviour*, 5th edn, Allyn & Bacon, Boston, MA.

Reno, R R, Cialdini, R B and Kallgren, C A (1993) The transsituational influence of social norms, *Journal of Personality and Social Psychology*, 64, 104-112, in R A Baron and D Byrne (1997) *Social Psychology*, 8th edn, Allyn & Bacon, Boston, MA.

Rescorla, R A (1988) Pavlovian conditioning: It's not what you think, *American Psychologist*, 43, 151-159.

Rescorla, R A (1990) Associative structures in instrumental learning. Eighteenth Sir Frederic Bartlett lecture, Experimental Psychology Society, Oxford.

Resnick, L B and Ford, W W (1981) *The Psychology of Mathematics Instruction*, Erlbaum, Hillsdale, NJ.

Rhue, J W, Lynn, S J and Kirsch, I (1993) *Handbook of Clinical Hypnosis*, American Psychological Association, Washington, DC.

Rice, R W (1978) Construct validity of the least preferred co-worker score, *Psychological Bulletin*, 85, 1199-1273, in M A Hogg and G M Vaughan (1995) *Social Psychology: An Introduction*, Prentice Hall/Harvester Wheatsheaf, Hemel Hempstead.

Richardson, D R, Hammock, G S, Smith, S M, Gardner, W and Signo, M (1994) Empathy as a cognitive inhibitor of interpersonal aggression, *Aggressive Behaviour*, 20, 275-289 in R A Baron and D Byrne (1997) *Social Psychology*, 8th ed, Allyn & Bacon, Boston, MA.

Richebon, E (1989) Antidepressants, in J Hoborn *Abnormal States of Brain and Mind*, Birhawer.

Rickels, K and Schweizer, F (1990) The clinical and long term management of generalised anxiety disorders, *Journal of Clinical Psychopharmacology*, 10 (suppl. 33), 101-110.

Ridley, M (1978) Paternal care, *Animal Behaviour*, 26, 904-932.

Ridley, M (1993) *Evolution*, Blackwell Scientific, Boston, MA and Oxford.

Ridley, M (1993) *The Red Queen*, Penguin, Harmondsworth.

Ridley, M (1995) *Animal Behaviour*, Blackwell Scientific, Boston, MA.

Rips, L J (1983) Cognitive processes in propositional reasoning, *Psychological Review*, 90, 38-71.

Robert W M, Stanton A L and Schwarz, R M (1991) Influence of personality attributes and daily moods on bulimic eating patterns, *Addictive Behaviours* 16(6), 497-505.

Roberts, R and Newton, P M (1987) Levinsonian studies of women's adult development, *Psychology and Ageing*, 39, 165-174.

Robson, C (1993) *Real World Research: A Resource for Social Scientists and Practitioner Researchers*, Blackwell, Oxford.

Robson, P (1994) *Forbidden Drugs*, Oxford University Press, Oxford.

Rock, (1988) in M W Matlin and H J Foley (eds) *Sensation and Perception*, 3rd edn (1992), Academic Press, San Diego, CA.

Rodgers, S (1997) Psychological Operations, *Psychology Review*, April 1997, 26-29.

Rodin, J, Schank, D and Striegel-Moore, R (1989) Psychological features of obesity, *Medical Clinics of North America*, 73, 47-66.

Roeder, K D (1965) Moths and ultrasound, *Scientific American*, 212 (4), 94-102.

Rogel, M J (1978) Pheromones in primates, *Psychological Bulletin*, 85(4), 810-830.

Rogers, C R (1959) A theory of therapy, personality and interpersonal relationships as developed in the client centred framework, in Koch (ed) *Psychology: A Study of Science*, vol 3, McGraw-Hill, New York.

Rogers, M, Miller, N, Mayer, F S and Duvall, S (1982) Personal responsibility and salience of the request for help: Determinants of the relations between negative affect and helping behaviour, *Journal of Personality and Social Psychology*, 43, 956-970 in R A Baron and D Byrne (1997) *Social Psychology*, 8th edn, Allyn & Bacon, Boston, MA.

Roggenbuck, M E and Jenssen, T A (1986) The ontogeny of display behaviour in *Sceloporus undulatus (Sauria: Iguanidae)*, *Ethology*, 71, 153-165.

Rokeach, M (1960) *The Open and Closed Mind*, Basic Books, New York.

Roland, P E (1993) *Brain Activation*, Wiley-Liss, New York.

Rolls, B J, Wood, R, Rolls, E T (1980) Thirst following water deprivation in humans, *American Journal of Physiology*, 239.

Rolls, E T and Rolls B J (1982) Brain mechanisms involved in feeding, in L M Barker (ed) *The Psychobiology of Human Food Selection*, AVI Publishing Company, Westport, CT.

Rood, J P (1972) Ecological and behavioural comparisons of three genera of argentine cavies, *Animal Behaviour Monographs* 5 (1).

Rook, K S (1987) Social support versus companionship: Effects of life stress, loneliness and evaluations by others, *Journal of Personality and Social Psychology*, 52, 1132-1147.

Roopnarine, J L (1987) Social interaction in the peer group: Relationship to perceptions of parenting and to children's interpersonal awareness and problem solving ability, *Journal of Applied Psychology* 8, 351-362.

Roper, T J and Redston, S (1987) Conspicuousness of distasteful prey affects the strength and durability of one-trial avoidance learning, *Animal Behaviour*, 35, 739-747.

Rosch, E (1973) Natural categories, *Cognitive Psychology*, 4, 328-350.

Rose, S, Lewontin, R C and Kamin L J (1984) *Not in Our Genes*, Penguin, Harmondsworth.

Rosen, J B, Unpublished results cited by M Davis (1992) The role of the amygdala in fear-potentiated startle:

Implications for animal models of anxiety, *Trends in Pharmacological Sciences*, 13, 35-41.

Rosenbaum, D L (1973) On being sane in insane places, *Science* 179, 250-258.

Rosenbaum, M E (1986) The repulsion hypothesis: On the nondevelopment of relationships, *Journal of Personality and Social Psychology*, 51, 1156-1166.

Rosenhan, D L and Seligman, M E (1984) *Abnormal Behaviour*, W W Norton, New York.

Rosenthal, R (1966) *Experimenter Effects in Behavioural Research*, Appleton-Century-Crofts, New York.

Rosenthal, R and Jacobson, L (1968) *Pygmalion in the Classroom*, Holt, Rhinehart & Winston, New York.

Ross, L (1977) The intuitive psychologist and his shortcomings, in L Berkowitz (ed) *Advances in Experimental Social Psychology*, vol 10, Academic Press, New York.

Ross, L and Nisbett, R E (1991) *The Person and the Situation: Perspectives of Social Psychology*, McGraw Hill, New York.

Roth, I (1990) *Introduction to Psychology*, vol 2, Lawrence Erlbaum/Open University, Hove and Milton Keynes.

Rotter, J B (1966) Generalised expectancies for internal versus external control of reinforcement, *Psychological Monographs*, 30(1) 1-26.

Rozin, P, Millman, L and Nemeroff, C (1986) Operation of the laws of sympathetic magic in disgust and other domains, *Journal of Personality and Social Psychology*, 50, 703-712, in R A Baron and D Byrne (1997) *Social Psychology*, Allyn & Bacon, Boston, MA.

Rumbaugh, D M *et al.* (1977) The LANA Project: Origin and Tactics, in D M Rumbaugh (ed) *Language learning by a Chimpanzee* 1977, Academic Press, New York.

Rusak, B, Robertson, H A, Wisden, W and Hunt, S P (1990) Light pulses that shift rhythms induce gene expression in the suprachiasmatic nucleus, *Science*, 248, 1237-1240.

Rusbult, C E and Zembrodt, I M (1983) Responses to dissatisfaction in romantic involvements: A multidimensional scaling analysis, *Journal of Experimental Social Psychology*, 19, 274-293.

Rushton, J P (1989) Genetic similarity in male friendships, *Ethology and Sociobiology*, 10, 361-373, in R A Baron and D Byrne (1997) *Social Psychology*, Allyn & Bacon, Boston, MA.

Rushton, J P (1990) Sir Francis Galton, epigenetic rules, genetic similarity theory, and human life-history analysis, *Journal of Personality*, 58, 117-140 in R A Baron and D Byrne (1997) *Social Psychology*, Allyn & Bacon, Boston, MA.

Rushton, J P (1996) in R McKie, An insult to intelligence, *The Guardian*, 12 February 1996.

Russek, M (1971) Hepatic receptors and the neurophysiological mechanisms controlling feeding behaviour, in S Ehrenpreis (ed) *Neurosciences Research*, vol 4, Academic Press, New York.

Russell G F M (1994) Anorexia through time, in C Szmukler, Dare and J Treasure (eds) *Eating Disorders: Handbook of theory, Treatment and Research*, Wiley, New York.

Russell, M S and Burch, R L (1959) *The Principles of Humane Experimental Technique*, Methuen, London.

Rutter, M (1972) *Maternal Deprivation Reassessed*, Penguin, Harmondsworth.

Rutter, M (1981) *Maternal Deprivation Reassessed*, 2nd edn, Penguin, Harmondsworth.

Rutter, M and the English Romanian Adoptees (ERA) Study Team (1998) Developmental catch-up and deficit, following adoption after severe global early privation, *Journal of Child Psychology and Psychiatry*, 39, 465-476.

Rutter, M and Rutter, M (1992) *Developing Minds: Challenge and Continuity Across the Lifespan*, Penguin, Harmondsworth.

Ryan, J (1974) Early language development, in P K Smith and H Cowie (1991) *Understanding Children's Development*, Basil Blackwell, Oxford.

Ryder, R (1991) Sentientism: A comment on Gray and Singer, *The Psychologist*, May 1991.

Sadock, B J (1989) Group psychotherapy, combined individual group psychotherapy and psychodrama, in H I Kaplan and B J Sadock (eds) *Comprehensive Textbook of Psychiatry*, vol 1, 5th edn, Williams and Wilkins, Baltimore, MD.

Saks, M J and Krupat, E (1988) *Social Psychology and its Applications*, Harper & Row, New York.

Salame, P and Baddeley, A D (1982) Disruption of short-term memory by unattended speech: Implications for the structure of working memory, *Journal of Verbal Learning and Verbal Behavior*, 21, 150-164.

Samuels, C and Ewy, R (1985) Aesthetic perception of faces during infancy, *British Journal of Developmental Psychology*, 3, 221-228, in P Erwin (1993) *Friendship and Peer Relations in Children*, Wiley, Chichester.

Sanacora, G, Finkelstein, J A and White, J D (1992) Developmental aspect of differences in hypothalamic preproneuropeptide Y messenger ribonucleic acid content in lean and genetically obese Zucker rats, *Journal of Neuorendocrinology*, 4, 353-357.

Sanl, H (1993) Phobias: is there a way out? *New Scientist*, 18 December 1993.

Savage-Rumbaugh, E S (1990) Language acquisition in a non-human species. Implications for the innateness debate, *Developmental Psychobiology*, 23, 599-620.

Savage-Rumbaugh, E S and Lewin, R (1994) *Kanzi*, Doubleday, New York.

Savage-Rumbaugh, E S, Murphy, J, Sevcik, R A, Brakke, K E, Williams, S L and Rumbaugh, D M (1993) Language comprehension in ape and child, *Monographs of the Society for Research in Child Development*, 58, 3-4.

Savage-Rumbaugh, E S, Williams, S L, Furuichi, T and Kano, T (1996) Language perceived, Paniscus branches out, in W C McGrew, L F Marchant and T Nishida (eds) *Great Ape Societies*, 1996, Cambridge University Press, Cambridge.

Scarr, S Race and gender as psychological variables: Social and ethical issues, *American Psychologist*, 43 (1), 56-60.

Scazufca, M and Kuipers, E (1996) Links between expressed emotion are burden of care in relatives of patients with schizophrenia, *British Journal of Psychiatry*, 168, 580-587.

Schachter, S (1959) *The Psychology of Affiliation*, Stanford University Press, Stanford, CA.

Schachter, S and Singer, J E (1962) Cognitive, social and physiological determinants of emotional state, *Physiological Review*, 69, 379-99.

Schaffer, R (1977) *Mothering*, Fontana, London.

Schaffer, R (1995) *Early Socialization*, BPS Open Learning Units, Leicester.

Schaffer, R (1996) in H Daniels (1996) *An Introduction to Vygostky*, Routledge, London.

Schaie, K W (1993) The Seattle longitudinal sudies of adult intelligence, *Current Directions in Psychological Science*, 2, 171-175.

Schaller, G B (1972) *The Serengeti Lion*, University of Chicago Press, Chicago.

Schank, R C and Abelson, R P (1977) *Scripts, Plans and Understanding*, Erlbaum, Hillsdale, NJ.

Schelderup-Ebbe, T (1935) Social behaviour of birds, in C Murchison (ed) *Handbook of Social Psychology*, Clark University Press, Worcester, MA.

Schellenberg, G D, Bird, T D, Wijsman, E M *et al.* (1992) Genetic linkage evidence for a familial Alzheimer's disease locus on chromosome 14, *Science*, 258, 668-672.

Schenck, C H, Bundlie, S R, Ettinger, M G and Mahowald, M W (1986) Chronic behavioral disorders of human REM sleep: A new category of parasomnia, *Sleep*, 9, 293-308.

Scherer, K R (1994) Toward a concept of "Modal emotions", in P Ekman and R J Davidson (eds) *The Nature of Emotion: Fundamental Questions*, Oxford University Press, New York.

Scherer, K R and Carver (1988) in R A Baron (1996) *Essentials of Psychology*, Allyn & Bacon, Boston, MA.

Schieber, M H and Hibbard, L S (1993) How somatotopic is the motor cortex hand area?, *Science* 261, 489-492.

Schlegel, A and Barry, H (1991) *Adolescence: An Anthropological Inquiry*, Free Press, New York.

Schlossberg, N K (1984) Exploring the adult years, in A M Rogers and C J Scheirer (eds), *The Stanley Hall lecture series*, Vol 4, American Psychological Association, Washington, DC.

Schmid-Hempel, P (1986) The influence of reward sequence on flight directionality in bees, *Animal Behaviour*, 34, 831-837.

Schneider, B H (1991) A comparison of skill-building and densensitization strategies for intervention with aggressive children, *Aggressive Behaviour*, 17, 301-311, in R A Baron and D Byrne (1997) *Social Psychology*, 8th edn, Allyn & Bacon, Boston, MA.

Schneider, W and Shiffrin, R M (1977) Controlled and automatic human information processing: I. Detection, search and attention, *Psychological Review*, 92, 424-428.

Schroeder, D A, Penner, L, Dovidio, J F and Piliavin, J A (1995) *The Psychology of Helping and Altruism: Problems and Puzzles*, McGraw-Hill, New York.

Schumacher, S A and Hill, D R (1991) Gender differences in social support and physical health, *Health Psychology*, 10, 102-111.

Schurz, G (1985) Experimentelle Überprufung des Zusammenhangs zwischen Persönlichkeitsmerkmalen und der Bereitschaft zum destruktiven Gehorsam gegenüber Autoritäten, *Zeitschrift für Experimentelle und Angewandte Psychologie*, 32, 160-177, in P B Smith and M H Bond (1993) *Social Psychology Across Cultures: Analysis and Perspectives*, Harvester Wheatsheaf, Trowbridge.

Schwartz, A E (1994) Americans online seldom fond of disagreement, *Albany Times Union*, 20 December 1994, in R A Baron and D Byrne (1997) *Social Psychology*, Allyn & Bacon, Boston, MA.

Schwartz, G E (1990) The data are always friendly: A new look at repression and health? Paper presented at the annual meeting of the Western Psychological Association, Los Angeles, 1990.

Scott, W D (1917) *The Psychology of Advertising*, Small Maynard Boston, MA in Pratkanis and Aronson (1992) *Age of Propaganda: the Everyday Use and Abuse of Persuasion*, W H Freeman, New York.

Sebeok, T and Umiker-Sebeck, J. (1980) Does man alone have language? *Science*, 208, 1349-1351.

Segall, M H, Campbell, D T and Herskovits, M J (1966) *The Influence of Culture on Visual Perception*, Bobbs-Merrill, Indianapolis.

Segall, M H, Dasen, P R, Berry J W *et al.* (1990) *Human Behaviour in Global Perspective: An Introduction to Cross-Cultural Psychology*, Pergamon Press, New York.

Seiber, Stanley, *American Psychologist*, 43, No 1.

Seidenberg, M S and McClelland, J L (1989) A distributed, developmental model of word recognition and naming, *Psychological Review*, 96, 523-568.

Seligman, M E P (1991) *Learned optimism*, Knopf, New York.

Seligmen, M E P (1975) *Helplessness: On Depression, Development and Death*, W H Freeman, San Francisco.

Sellen, A J and Norman, D A (1992) The psychology of slips, in B J Baars (ed) *Experimental Slips and Human Error: Exploring the Architecture of Volition*, Plenum Press, New York.

Selman, R L (1980) *The Growth of Interpersonal Understanding: Development and Clinical Analysis*, Academic Press, New York.

Selye, H (1950) *The Physiology and Pathology of Exposure to Stress*, Acta, Montreal.

Selye, H (1976) *The Stress of Life*, McGraw-Hill, New York.

Seyfarth, R M and Cheney, D L (1984) Grooming, alliances and reciprocal altruism in vervet monkeys.

Shakoor, B and Chalmers, D (1991) Co-victimization of African, American children who witness violence: Effects on cognitive, emotional and behavioural development, *Journal of the National Medical Association*, 83, 233-237, in R A Baron and D Byrne (1997) *Social Psychology*, 8th edn, Allyn & Bacon, Boston, MA.

Shallice, T and Warrington, E K (1970) Independent functioning of the verbal memory stores: A neuropsychological study, *Quarterly Journal of Experimental Psychology*, 22, 261-273.

Shapley, R. (1990) Visual sensitivity and parallel retinocortical channels, *Annual Review of Psychology*, 41, 635-658.

Shatz, M and Gelman, R (1973) The development of communication skills: Modification in the speech of young children as a function of the listener, *Monographs of the Society for Research in Child Development*, 38, 152.

Shavit, Y, Depaulis, A, Martin, F C (1986) Involvement of brain opiate receptors in the immune-suppressive effect of morphine, *Proceedings of the National Academy of Sciences*, 83, 7114-7117.

Shavit, Y, Lewis, J W, Terman, G W (1984) Opioid peptides mediate the suppressive effect of stress on natural killer cell cytotoxicity, *Science*, 223, 188-190.

Shaw, J L, Borough, H W and Fink, M I (1994) Perceived sexual orientation and helping behaviour by males and females: The wrong number

technique, *Journal of Psychology and Human Sexuality*, 6, 73-81 in R A Baron and D Byrne (1997) *Social Psychology*, 8th edn, Allyn & Bacon, Boston, MA.

Shea, B C and Pearson, J C (1986) The effects of relationship type, partner intent and gender on the selection of relationship maintenance strategies, *Communication Monographs* 53, 352-364, in N Hayes (1994) *Foundations of Psychology: An Introductory Text*, Routledge, London.

Shepard, R N (1978) The mental image, *The American Psychologist*, 33, 125-137.

Sherif, M et al. (1961) *Intergroup conflict and cooperation: The robber's cave experiment*, University of Oklahoma Press, Norman.

Sherman, P W (1977) Neoptism and the evolution of alarm calls, *Science* 197, 1246-1253.

Sherman, P W (1980) The limits of ground squirrel nepotism, in G W Barlow and J Silverberg (eds) *Sociobiology: beyond nature-nurture*, Westview Press, Boulder, Colo.

Sherry, D and Galef, B G (1984) Cultural transmission without imitation: milk bottle opening by birds, *Animal Behaviour*, 32, 937-938.

Shettleworth, S J (1983) Memory in food-hoarding birds, *Scientific American*, 248(3), 102-110.

Shields, J (1962) *Monozygotic Twins Brought Up Apart and Brought Up Together*, Oxford University Press, Oxford.

Shiffrin, R M and Schneider, W (1977) Controlled and automatic human information processing: II. Perceptual learning, automatic attending and a general theory, *Psychological Review*, 84, 127-190.

Shotland, R L and Stebbins, C A (1980) Bystander response to rape: Can a victim attract help? *Journal of Applied Social Psychology*, 10, 510-527.

Sieber, J E and Stanley, B (1988) Ethical and professional dimensions of socially sensitive research, *American Psychologist*, 43(1), 49-55.

Siegal, M (1987) Are sons and daughters treated more differently by fathers than by mothers?, *Developmental Review*, 7, 185-209.

Siegel, J M (1990) Stressful life events and the use of physician services among the elderly: The moderating role of pet ownership, *Journal of Personality and Social*

Psychology, 58, 1081-1086.

Siegel, S, Hinson, R E, Krank, M D and McCully, J (1982) Heroin "overdose" death: Contribution of drug-associated environmental cues, *Science*, 216, 436-437.

Siegler, R S (1976) Three aspects of cognitive development, *Cognitive Psychology*, 8, 481-520.

Siegler, R S (1983) Information processing approaches to development, in P H Mussen (ed) *Handbook of Child Psychology: Vol 1. History, Theory and Methods*, Wiley, New York.

Siegler, R S (1991) *Children's Thinking*, 2nd edn, Prentice Hall, Englewood Cliffs, NJ.

Siegler, R S and Shrager, J (1984) Strategy choices in addition and subtraction: How do children know what to do?, in C Sophian (ed) *Origins of Cognitive Skills*, Erlbaum, Hillsdale, NJ.

Silveira, J (1971) Incubation: The effect of interruption timing and length on problem solution and quality of problem processing, unpublished PhD thesis, University of Oregon.

Silvern, S B (1986) Classroom use of video games, *Education Research Quarterly*, 10, 10-16 in T Charlton and K David (eds) (1997) *Elusive Links: Television, Video Games and Children's Behaviour*, Park Published Papers.

Simmons, R and Blyth, D A (1987) *Moving into Adolescence*, Aldine de Gruyter, New York.

Simon, H A (1955) A behavioral model of rational choice, *Quarterly Journal of Economics*, 69, 118.

Simpson, J A (1990) Influence of attachment styles on romantic relationships, *J. of Personality & Social Psychology*, 59, 971-980, in R A Baron (1996) *Essentials of Psychology*, Allyn & Bacon, Boston, MA.

Sims, A C P and Gray, P (1993) The media, violence and vulnerable viewers, Document presented to the Broadcasting Group, House of Lords, in Newson, E (1994) Video Violence and the Protection of Children, *Psychology Review*, 1(2), 2-5.

Singer, B and Toates, F (1987) Sexual motivation, *Journal of Sex Research*, 23, 481-501.

Singer, P (1991) Speciesism, morality and biology: A response to Jeffrey Gray, *The Psychologist*, May 1991, BPS, Leicester.

Singer, P (1993) *Practical Ethics*, 2nd edn, Cambridge University Press, Cambridge.

Singh, A and Lucki, I (1993) Anti-depressant-like activity of compounds with varying efficacy at S-HT receptors, *Neuropharmacology*, 32(4), 331-340.

Singh, D (1993) Adaptive significance of female physical attractiveness: Role of waist to hip ratio, *Journal of Personality and Social Psychology*, 65, 293-307.

Skinner, B F (1938) *The behaviour of organisms*, Appleton-Century-Crofts, New York.

Skinner, B F (1948) Superstition in the pigeon, *Journal of Experimental Psychology*, 38, 168-172.

Skinner, B F (1957) *Verbal Behaviour*, Appleton-Century-Crofts, New York.

Skuse, D (1984a) Extreme deprivation in early childhood - I. Diverse outcomes for three siblings from an extraordinary family, *Journal of Child Psychology and Psychiatry*, 25, 523-541.

Skuse, D (1984b) Extreme deprivation in early childhood - II. Theoretical issues and a comparative review, *Journal of Child Psychology and Psychiatry*, 25, 543-572.

Slater, P J B (1994) Kinship and altruism, in P J B Slater and T R Halliday (eds) *Behaviour and Evolution* (1994), Cambridge University Press, Cambridge.

Slater, P J B and Halliday, T R (eds) (1994) *Behaviour and Evolution*, Cambridge University Press, Cambridge.

Slater, S and Mencher, J (1991) The lesbian family life cycle: A contextual approach, *American Journal of Orthopsychiatry*, 61, 372-382.

Slife, B D and Williams, R N (1995) *What's Behind the Research? Discovering Hidden Assumptions in the Behavioural Sciences*, Sage, Beverly Hills, CA.

Small, M F (1995) Bringing up baby, *New Scientist*, 24 June 1995, pp. 36-39.

Smeaton, G, Byrne, D and Murner, S K (1989) The repulsion hypothesis revisited: Similarity irrelevance or dissimilarity bias?, *Journal of Personality and Social Psychology*, 56, 54-59.

Smith, C (1997) in Mind Travellers, *New Scientist* supplement, 26 April 1997, 11-13.

Smith, E R, Byrne, D and Fielding, P J (1995) Interpersonal attraction as a function of extreme gender role adherence, *Personal Relationships*, 2, 161-172 in R A Baron and D Byrne (1997) *Social Psychology*, Allyn & Bacon, Boston, MA.

Smith, P B and Bond, M H (1993) *Social Psychology Across Cultures: Analysis and Perspectives*, Harvester Wheatsheaf, Trowbridge.

Smith, T W, Sanders, J D and Alexander, J F (1990) What does the Cook and Medley Hostility Scale Measure? Affect, behavior and attributions in the marital context, *Journal of Personality and Social Psychology*, 58, 699-708.

Smither, R D (1988) *The Psychology of Work and Human Performance*, Harper & Row, New York.

Smyth, M M, Collins, A F, Morris, P E and Levy, P (1994) *Cognition in Action*, 2nd edn, Lawrence Erlbaum, Hove.

Snarey, J R (1985) Cross-cultural universality of social moral development: A critical review of Kohlbergian research, *Psychological Bulletin*, 97, 202-232.

Snarey, J R, Reimer, J and Kohlberg, L (1985) Development of social-moral reasoning among kibbutz adolescents: A longitudinal cross-sectional study, *Developmental Psychology*, 21, 3-17.

Snyder, C R and Fromkin, H L (1980) *Uniqueness: The Human Pursuit of Difference*, Plenum, New York.

Snyder, M (1979) Self-monitoring processes, in L Berkowitz (ed) *Advances in Experimental Social Psychology*, 12, 85-128.

Solso, R L (1979) *Cognitive Psychology*, Harcourt, Brace, Jovanovich, New York.

Sommer, R (1969) *Personal Space: The Behavioral Basis of Design*, Prentice Hall, Englewood Cliffs, NJ.

Sorenson, K A, Russell, S M, Harkness, D J and Harvey, J H (1993) Account making, confiding and coping with ending of a close relationship, *Journal of Social Behaviour and Personality*, 8, 73-86 in R A Baron and D Byrne (1997) *Social Psychology*, Allyn & Bacon, Boston, MA.

Spangler, W D and House, R J (1991) Presidential effectiveness and leadership motive profile, *Journal of Personality and Social Psychology*, 60, 439-455.

Spanos, N P (1986) Hypnotic behaviour: A social-psychological interpretation of amnesia, analgesia and "trance logic", *Behavioural and Brain Sciences*, 9, 449-467.

Spanos, N P (1991) A sociocognitive approach to hypnosis, in R A Baron (1996) *Essentials of Psychology*, Allyn & Bacon, Boston, MA.

Spearman, C (1904) General intelligence, objectively determined and measured, *American Journal of Psychology*, 15, 201-293.

Spelke, E S, Hirst, W C and Neisser, U (1976) Skills of divided attention, *Cognition*, 4, 215-230.

Spencer, M B and Dornbusch, S M (1990) Ethnicity, in S S Feldman and R Elliott (eds) *At the Threshold: The Developing Adolescent*, Harvard University Press, Cambridge, MA.

Spinney, L (1997) Dining out at the Shuteye Café, in Mind Travellers, *New Scientist* supplement, 26 April 1997, 18-20.

Springer, S P and Deutsch, G (1993) *Left Brain, Right Brain*, 4th edn, Freeman, New York.

Springer, S P and Deutsch, G (1998) *Left Brain, Right Brain: Perspectives from Cognitive Neuroscience*, 5th edn, Freeman, New York.

Sroufe, L A and Fleeson, J (1986) Attachment and the construction of relationships, in W W Hartup and Z Rubin (eds) *Relationships and Development*, Erlbaum, Hillsdale, NJ.

Stahl, S A and Miller, P A (1989) Whole language and language experience approaches for beginning readers: A quantitative research synthesis, *Review of Educational Research*, 59, 87-116.

Stampfl, T G and Lewis, D J (1967) Essentials of implosive therapy: A learning based psychodynamic behavioural therapy, *Journal of Abnormal Psychiatry*, 72, 496-503.

Stattin, H and Magnusson, D (1990) *Pubertal maturation in female development*, Erlbaum, Hillsdale, NJ.

Staub, E (1992) *The Roots of Evil: The Origins of Genocide and Other Group Violence*, Cambridge University Press, Cambridge, in P Humphreys (1994) Obedience: after Milgram, *Psychology Review*, 1, 2-5.

Steel, C M, Critchlow, B and Liu, T J (1985) Alcohol and social behaviour: The helpful drunkard, *Journal of Personality and Social Psychology*, 48, 35-46.

Steen, S N, Oppliger, R A and Brownell, K D (1988) Metabolic effects of repeated weight loss and regain in adolescent wrestlers, *Journal of the American Medical Association*, 260, 47-50.

Stein, C (1963) The clenched fist technique as a hypnotic procedure in clinical psychotherapy, *American Journal of Clinical Hypnosis*, 6, 113-119.

Steinberg, L, Dornbusch, S M and Brown, B B (1992) Ethnic differences in adolescent achievement: An ecological perspective, *American Psychologist*, 47, 723-729.

Steinberg, L, Dornbusch, S M et al. (1987) in H Bee (1995) *The Developing Child* (7th edn), Harper Collins, New York.

Steiner, H, Smith, C, Rozenkranz, R T and Litt, I (1991) The early care and feeding of anorexics, *Child Psychiatry Human Development* 21(3), 163-167.

Stern, D N (1977) *The First Relationship: Infant and Mother*, Fontana, London.

Stern, D N (1977) *The First Relationship: Infant and Mother*, Harvard University Press, Cambridge, MA.

Stern, K and McClintock, M K (1998) Regulation of ovulation by human pheromones, Letter to *Nature*, 392, 177-178.

Sternberg, R J (1985) *Beyond IQ: A Triarchic Theory of Human Intelligence*, Cambridge University Press, New York.

Sternberg, R J (1988) What theorists of intellectual development among children can learn from their counterparts studying adults, in E M Hetherington, R Lerner and M Perlmutter (eds) *Child Development in Life-Span Perspective*, Erlbaum, Hillsdale, NJ.

Sternberg, R J and Detterman, D K (1986) *What is Intelligence?*, Cambridge University Press, New York.

Sternberg, R J (ed) (1984) *Mechanisms of Cognitive Development*, Freeman, New York.

Stevens, R (1983) *Erik Erikson: An Introduction*, Open University Press, Milton Keynes.

Stewart, K J and Harcourt, A H (1987) *Primate Societies*, University of Chicago Press, Chicago.

Stinson, C H (1979) On the selective advantage of fratricide in raptors, *Evolution*, 33, 1219-1225.

Stinson, D and Thompson, C (1990) Clinical experience with phototherapy, *Journal of Affective Disorders*, 18, 129-135.

Stockard, J. (1997) The mood molecule, in *Time*, Canadian edition, 29 September 1997, 56-57.

Stoller, R J (1980) A different view of the Oedipal conflict, in S I Greenspan and G H Pollack (eds) *The Course of Life, I: Infancy and Early Childhood*, Mental Health Study Center, Adelphi, MD.

Strick, P L and Preston, J B (1983) Input-output organization of the primate motor cortex, in J E Desimone (ed) *Motor Control Mechanisms in Health and Disease*, 321-327, Raven Press, New York.

Strober, M, Morrell, W, Burroughs, J, Lampert, C, Danfork, H and Freeman, R (1988) A family study of bipolar 1 disorder in adolescence, early onset of symptoms linked to increased familiar loading and lithium resistance, *Journal of Affective Disorders*, 15, 255-268.

Stroebe, W, Stroebe, M S and Domittner, G (1988) Individual and situational differences in recovery from bereavement: A risk group identified, *Journal of Social Issues*, 44(3), 143-158.

Strube, M J (1989) Evidence for the type in Type A behaviour: A taxonometric analysis, *Journal of Personality and Social Psychology*, 56, 972-987.

Strube, M J, Turner, C W, Cerro, D, Stevens, J and Hinchey, F (1984) Interpersonal aggression and the type A coronary-prone behaviour pattern: A theoretical distinction and practical implications, *Journal of Personality and Social Psychology*, 47, 839-847.

Stuart-Hamilton (1991) in J Bond, P Coleman and S Pearce (1993) *Ageing in Society*, Sage, London.

Stunkard, A J, Sorensen, T I A, Harris C (1986) An adoption study of human obesity, *New England Journal of Medicine*, 314, 193-198.

Summers, R J (1991) The influence of affirmative action on perceptions of a beneficiary's qualifications, *Journal of Applied Social Psychology*, 21, 1265-1276, in R A Baron and D Byrne (1997) *Social Psychology*, 8th edn, Allyn & Bacon, Boston, MA.

Surrey, D (1982) It's like good training for life, *Natural History*, 91, 71-83 in T Charlton and K David (eds) (1997) *Elusive Links: Television, Video Games and Children's Behaviour*, Park Published Papers.

Sutherland, V J and Cooper, C L (1990) *Understanding Stress: A Psychological Perspective for Health Professionals*, Chapman & Hall, London.

Sutherland, V J and Davidson, M J (1989) Stress among construction site managers: A preliminary study, *Stress Medicine*, 5, 221-235, in V J Sutherland and C L Cooper (1990) *Understanding Stress: A Psychological Perspective for Health Professionals*, Chapman & Hall, London.

Svaetichin, G (1956) Spectral response curves from single cones, *Acta Physiologica Scandinavica Supplementum*, 134, 7-46.

Swain, J, Finkelstein, V, French, S and Oliver, M (eds) (1993) *Disabling Barriers - Enabling Environments*, Sage, London.

Sweeney, M E, Hill, P A, Baney, R and DiGirolamo, M (1993) Severe vs moderate energy restriction with and without exercise in the treatment of obesity: Efficiency of weight loss, *American Journal of Clinical Nutrition*, 57, 127-134.

Swim, J K, Aikin, K J, Hall, W S and Hunter, B A (1995) Sexism and racism: old-fashioned and modern prejudices, *Journal of Personality and Social Psychology*, 68, 199-214, in R A Baron and D Byrne (1997) *Social Psychology*, 8th edn, Allyn & Bacon, Boston, MA.

Sylva, K D, Roy, C and Painter, M (1980) *Childwatching at Playgroup and Nursery School*, Grant McIntyre, London.

Szaz, T S (1961) *The Myth of Mental Illness*, Harper and Row, New York.

Szaz, T S (1977) *Psychiatric Slavery*, Free Press, New York.

Tajfel, H and Wilkes, A L (1963) Classification and quantitative judgement, *British Journal of Psychology*, 54, 101-114, in N Hayes (1994) *Foundations of Psychology: An Introductory Text*, Routledge, London.

Tartaglia, L A, Dembski, M, Weng, X (1995) Identification and expression cloning of a leptin receptor, OB-R, *Cell*, 83, 1263-1271.

Tavris, C (1992) *The Mismeasure of Woman*, Simon & Schuster, New York.

Tavris, C and Wade, C (1995) *Psychology in Perspective*, Harper Collins, New York.

Taylor, J (1992) A questionable treatment, *Nursing Times*, 88(40), 41-43.

Taylor, P M (1992) *War and the Media: Propaganda and Persuasion in the Gulf War*, Manchester University Press, Manchester.

Taylor, S (1994) The current status of eye-witness research in psychology and law, *Psychology Teaching*, 1994.

Taylor, S E (1989) *Positive Illusions: Creative Self-deception and the Healthy Mind*, Basic Books, New York.

Taylor, S E (1991) *Introduction to Health Psychology*, McGraw Hill, New York.

Taylor, S P, Gammon, C B and Capasso, D R (1976) Aggression as a function of the interaction of alcohol and threat, *Journal of Personality and Social Psychology*, 34, 938-941, in K Deaux, F C Dane and L S Wrightsman (1993) *Psychology in the 90s*, Brooks Cole, Pacific Grove CA.

Temoshok, L (1987) Personality, coping style, emotion and cancer: Towards an integrative model, *Cancer Surveys*, 6, 545-567.

Temoshok, L, Heller, B W, Sagebiel, R W (1985) The relationship of psychosocial factors to prognostic indicators in cutaneous malignant melanoma, *Journal of Psychosomatic Research*, 20, 139-153.

Tempel, D L and Liebowitz, S F (1990) Galanin inhibits insulin and corticosterone release after injection into the PVN, *Brain Research*, 536, 353-357.

Terman, L M (1916) *The Measurement of Intelligence*, Houghton Mifflin, Boston, MA, MA.

Terrace, H S (1979) *Nim*, Knopf, New York.

Thomas, G V and Blackman, D (1991) Are animal experiments on the way out?, *The Psychologist*, May 1991.

Thorndike, E L (1898) Animal intelligence: An experimental study of the associative processes in animals, *The Psychological Review Monograph Supplements*, 2(4) (Whole no. 8).

Thorpe, W H (1961) *Bird Song*, Cambridge University Press, Cambridge.

Thurstone, L L (1938) Primary mental abilities, *Psychological Monographs*, 1, 1.

Tickner, A H and Poulton, E C (1975) Watching for people and actions, *Ergonomics*, 18, 35-51.

Tiefer, L (1978) The kiss, *Human Nature*, 1, 28-37.

Tiffany, S T (1990) A cognitive model of drug urges and drug-use behaviour: Role of automatic and nonautomatic processes, *Psychological Review*, 97, 147-168.

Tillett, R (1996) Psychotherapy assessment and treatment (selections), *British Journal of Psychiatry*, 168, 10-15.

Tinbergen, N (1951) *The Study of Instinct*, Clarendon Press, Oxford.

Tinbergen, N (1953) *The Herring Gull's World*, William Collins, London.

Tinbergen, N (1965) *Social Behaviour in Animals*, Methuen, London.

Tinbergen, N and Perdeck, A C (1950) On the stimulus situation releasing the begging response in the newly hatched herring gull chick, *Behaviour*, 3, 1-39.

Tizard, B (1991) in Woodhead *et al.* (1991) *Growing up in a Changing Society*, Routledge, London.

Tizard, B and Rees, J (1974) A comparison of the effects of adoption, restoration to the natural mother and continued institutionalization on the cognitive development of four-year-old children, *Child Development*, 45, 92-99.

Tolman, E C and Honzik, C N (1930) Introduction and removal of reward and maze learning in rats, *University of California publications in Psychology*, 4, 257-275.

Tomaka, J, Blascovich, J, Kelsey, R M and Leitten, C L (1993) Subjective, physiological and behavioural effects of threat and challenge appraisal, *Journal of Personality and Social Psychology*, 65, 248-260.

Townsend, P, Davidson, N and Whitehead, M (1992) *Inequalities in Health: The Black Report and the Health Divide*, Penguin, Harmondsworth.

Treisman, A M (1964) Verbal cues, language and meaning in selective attention, *American Journal of Psychology*, 77, 206-19.

Treisman, A M (1986) Features and objects in visual processing, *Scientific American*, 255(5), 114B-125.

Treisman, A M and Riley, J G A (1969) Is selective attention selective perception or selective response?: A further test, *Journal of Experimental Psychology*, 79, 23-34.

Treisman, A M and Sato, S (1990) Conjunction search revisited, *Journal of Experimental Psychology: Human Perception and Performance*, 16, 459-478.

Triesman, A M and Geffen, G (1967) Selective attention: Perception or response?, *Quarterly Journal of Experimental Psychology*, 19, 1-18.

Trivers, R L (1971) The evolution of reciprocal altruism, *Quarterly Review of Biology*, 46, 35-57.

Trivers, R L (1972) Parental investment and sexual selection, in B Campbell (ed) *Sexual Selection and the Descent of Man*, Aldine, Chicago.

Trivers, R L (1974) Parent-offspring conflict, *American Zoologist*, 14, 249-264.

Tucker, N (1996) *Adolescence, Adulthood and Ageing*, BPS Open Learning Units, Leicester.

Tulving, E (1975) Episodic and semantic memory, in E Tulving and W Donaldson (eds) *Organisation of Memory*, Academic Press, London.

Tulving, E (1985) How many memory systems are there? *American Psychologist*, 40, 385-398.

Turkheimer, E and Farace, A (1992) A reanalysis of gender differences in IQ scores following unilateral brain lesions, *Psychological Assessment*, 4, 498-501, in R A Baron (1996) *Essentials of Psychology*, Allyn & Bacon, Boston, MA.

Turnbull, C M (1961) *The Forest People*, Simon and Schuster, New York.

Turner (1993) in P Turner (1995) *Sex, Gender and Identity*, BPS Books, Leicester.

Turner, P (1995) *Sex, Gender and Identity*, BPS Books, Leicester.

Tuttle M D (1988) *America's neighbourhood bats*, University of Texas Press, Austin, TX.

Tversky, A and Kahneman, D (1974) Judgements under uncertainty: Heuristics and biases, *Science*, 185, 1124-1131.

Tversky, A and Kahneman, D (1981) The framing of decisions and the psychology of choice, *Science*, 211, 453-458.

Tversky, A and Kahneman, D (1982) Judgements under uncertainty; heuristics and biases, in D Kahneman, P Slovic and A Tversky (eds) *Judgements Under Uncertainty; Heuristics and biases*, Cambridge University Press, New York.

Twining (1988) in J Bond, P Coleman and S Pearce (1993) *Ageing in Society*, Sage/Open University, London and Milton Keynes.

Tyrer, P (1992) Anxiolytics not acting at the benzodiazepine receptor: Beta blocker, *Progress in Neuro Psychopharmacology and Biological Psychiatry*, 16(1), 17-26.

Tysoe, M (1988) *All This and Work Too. The Psychology of Office Life*, Fontana, London, in L de Alberdi (1990) *People, Psychology and Business*, Cambridge University Press, Cambridge.

Tyson, P and Tyson, R L (1990) *Psychoanalytic Theories of Development: A Integration*, Yale University Press, New Haven.

Ueda, T (1979) Plasticity of the reproductive behaviour of a dragonfly with reference to the social relationship of males and the density of territories, *Research on Population Ecology*, 21, 135-152.

Ullman, L P and Krasner, L (1975) *A Psychological Approach to Abnormal Behaviour*, Prentice Hall, Englewood Cliffs, NJ.

Underwood, G (1974) Moray vs the rest: The effects of extended shadowing practice, *Quarterly Journal of Experimental Psychology*, 26, 368-372.

Van Lear, C A, Jr and Trujillo, N (1986) On becoming acquainted: A longitudinal study of social judgement processes, *Journal of Social and Personal Relationships*, 3, 375-392, in S Duck (1992) *Human Relationships*, 2nd edn, Sage, London.

Vaughan, K, Doyle, M, McConaghy, N Blaszcznski, F (1992) The relationship between relative's expressed emotion and schizophrenia relapse: An Australian replication, *Social Psychiatry and Psychiatric Epidemiology*, 27(1), 10-15.

Vaughn, B E, Lefever, G B, Seifer, R *et al*. (1989) Attachment behaviour, attachment security and temperament during infancy, *Child Development*, 60, 728-737.

Vingoe, F (1987) When is a placebo not a placebo? That is the question, *British Journal of Experimental and Clinical Hypnosis*, 4, 165-167.

Vitkus, J A (1996) *A Casebook in Abnormal Psychology*, 3rd edn, McGraw Hill.

Vitousek, K and Manke, F (1994) Personality variables and disorders in anorexia nervosa and bulimia nervosa, *Journal of Abnormal Psychology*, 103 (1), 137-147.

Von Wright, J M, Anderson, K and Stenman, U (1975) Generalisation of conditioned GSR's in dichotic listening, in P M A Rabbit and S Dornic (eds) *Attention and Performance*, vol V, Academic Press, London.

Vormbrock, J K (1993) Attachment theory as applied to wartime and job-related marital separation, *Psychological Bulletin*, 114, 122-144 in R A Baron (1996) *Essentials of Psychology*, Allyn & Bacon, Boston, MA.

Vroom, V H (1984) Leadership and decision-making, cited in N Hayes (1994) *Foundations of Psychology: An Introductory Text*, Routledge, London.

Vroom, V H and Yetton, P N (1973) *Leadership and Decision Making*, University of Pittsburgh Press, Pittsburgh, PA.

Vygotsky, L S (1962) *Thought and Language*, MIT Press, Cambridge, MA.

Waage, J K (1984) *Sperm Competition and the Evolution of Animal Mating Systems*, Academic Press, New York.

Waage, J K (1986) Evidence for widespread sperm displacement ability among *Zygoptera (Odonata)* and the means for predicting its presence, *Journal of the Linnean Society of London, Biology*, 28, 285-330.

Wade, C and Cerise, S (1991) *Human Sexuality*, 2nd edn, Harcourt Brace Jovanovich, San Diego.

Wade, C and Tavris, C (1993) *Psychology*, 3rd edn, Harper Collins, New York.

Wadeley, A (1996) Persuasion and propaganda, *Psychology Review*, November, 17-19.

Wagenaar, W A and Groeneweg, J (1990) The memory of concentration camp survivors, *Applied Cognitive Psychology*, 4, 77-87.

Wagner, Elejabarrieta and Lahnsteiner (1995) How the sperm dominates the ovum - objectification by metaphor in the social representation of conception, *European Journal of Social Psychology*, 25, 671-688, in N Hayes (1998) Spreading the word: How social representations happen, *Psychology Review*, 4 (3).

Wagstaff, G F (1991) Compliance, belief and semantics in hypnosis: A non-state sociocognitive perspective, in S J Lynn and J W Rhue (eds) *Theories of Hypnosis: Current Models and Perspectives*, Guilford Press, New York.

Walker, L J (1980) Sex differences in moral reasoning, in W M Kurtines and J L Gerwirtz (eds) *Handbook of Moral Behaviour and Development*, Vol 2, Erlbaum, Hillsdale, NJ.

Walker, L J and De Vries, B (1985) Moral stages/moral orientations: Do the sexes really differ? in C Black (ed) *Gender Differences in Research in Moral Development*, Symposium conducted at the meeting of the American Psychological Association, Los Angeles.

Walker, I J, De Vries, B and Trevarthan, S D (1987) Moral stages and moral orientations in real-life and hypothetical dilemmas, *Child Development*, 58, 842-858.

Wallace, A R (1889) *Darwinism*, Macmillan, London.

Wallace, A R (1891) *Natural Selection and Tropical Nature: Essays on descriptive and theoretical biology*, Macmillan, London.

Wallace, D M, Magnuson, D J and Gray, T S (1992) Organization of amygdaloid projections to brainstem dopaminergic, noradrenergic cell groups in the rat, *Brain Research Bulletin*, 28, 447-454.

Waller, D, Fairburn, C G, McPherson, A, Kay, R, Lee, A and Norwell, T (1976) Treating bulimia nervosa in primary care: A pilot study, *International Journal of Eating Disorders*, 19(1) 99-103.

Wallerstein, J (1989) Children after divorce: Wounds that don't heal, *The New York Times Magazine*, 22 January 1989.

Wallerstein, J and Blakeslee, S (1989) *Second Chances: Men, Women and Children a Decade after Divorce*, Ticknor & Fields, New York.

Wallerstein, J S (1984) Parent-child relations following divorce, in J Anthony and C Chiland (eds) *Clinical Parenthood*, Vol 8, The Yearbook of the International Association of Child and Adolescent Psychiatry, Wiley, New York.

Wallerstein, R S (1989) The psychotherapy research project of the Menninger Foundation: An overview, *Journal of Consulting and Clinical Psychology*, 57, 195-200.

Walster, E, Aronson, E, Abrahams, D and Rottman, L (1966) Importance of physical attractiveness in dating behaviour, *Journal of Personality and Social Psychology*, 4, 508-516.

Walster, E H, Walster, G W and Berscheid, E (1978) *Equity Theory and Research*, Allyn & Bacon, Boston, MA.

Walton, G E, Bower, N J A and Bower, T G R (1992) Recognition of familiar faces by newborns, *Infant Behaviour and Development*, 15, 265-269.

Walton, G E and Bower, T G R (1991) Newborn preferences

for familiar faces, Paper presented at a *Meeting of the Society for Research in Child Development*, Seattle, WA.

Warr, P B (1984) Work and unemployment, in P J D Drench (ed) *Handbook of Work and Organisational Psychology*, Wiley, Chichester.

Warren, J M (1973) Learning in vertebrates, in D A Dewsbury and D A Rethlingshafen (eds) *Comparative Psychology*, McGraw-Hill, New York.

Warrington, E K and Shallice, T (1972) Neuropsychological evidence of visual storage in short-term memory tasks, *Quarterly Journal of Experimental Psychology*, 24, 30-40.

Wason, P C (1966) *Reasoning*, in M W Eysenck (1993) *Principles of Cognitive Psychology*, Lawrence Erlbaum, Hove.

Wason, P C and Shapiro, D (1971) Natural and contrived experience in reasoning problems, *Quarterly Journal of Experimental Psychology*, 23, 63-71.

Waterman, A S (1985) Identity in the context of adolescent psychology, *New Directions for Child Development*, 30, 5-24.

Watkins, H H (1993) Ego-state therapy: An overview, *American Journal of Clinical Hypnosis*, 35, 232-240.

Watson, J B (1913) Psychology as the behaviourist views it, *Psychological Review*, 20, 158-177.

Watson, J B and Rayner, R (1920) Conditioned emotional reactions, *Journal of Experimental Psychology*, 3, 1-14.

Watson, O N and Graves, T D (1966) Quantitative research in proxemic behaviour, *American Anthropologist*, 68, 971-85.

Wehr, T A, Gieson, H A, Schultz, P M, Anderson, J L (1991) Contrasts between symptoms of summer depression and winter depression, *Journal of Affective Disorders*, 23, 173-183.

Weinberg, R A (1989) Intelligence and IQ: Landmark issues and great debates, *American Psychologist*, 44, 98-104.

Weindler, P, Wiltschko, R and Wiltschko, W (1996) *Nature* 383, 158-60.

Weiner, B (1986) *An Attributional Theory of Motivation and Emotion*, Springer-Verlag, New York.

Weiner, B (1992) *Human Motivation: Metaphors, Theories and Research*, Sage, Newbury Park.

Weiner, B, Amirkhan, J, Folkes, V S and Verette, J A (1987) An attributional analysis of excuse giving: Studies of a naive theory of emotion, *Journal of Personality and Social Psychology*, 52, 316-324 in R A Baron and D Byrne (1997) *Social Psychology*, 8th edn, Allyn & Bacon, Boston, MA.

Weiner, J (1995) *The Beak of the Finch*, Vintage, London.

Weingarten, H P (1985) Stimulus control of eating: Implications for a two-factor theory of hunger, *Appetite*, 6, 387-401.

Weiss, J M (1972) Influence of psychological variables on stress-induced pathology, in J Knight and R Porter (eds) *Physiology, Emotion and Psychosomatic Illness*, Elsevier, Amsterdam.

Weitzman, L J (1985) *The Divorce Revolution*, Free Press, New York.

Weltzin, M, Fernstrom, J D, Neuberger, S *et al.* (1995) Acute tryptophan depletion 2nd increased food intake and irritability in bulimia nervosa, *American Journal of Psychiatry* 1668-1671.

Wertsch, J V, McNamee, G D, McLane, J B *et al.* (1980) The adult child dyad as a problem-solving system, *Child Development*, 50, 1215-1221.

Wheeler, A (1990) Biological cycles and rhythms vs biorhythms *Skeptical Inquirer*, 75-82.

White, C and Sellwood, W (1995) Cognitive factors in the maintenance of injection phobia, *Journal of Behavioural and Cognitive Psychotherapy*, 23, 57-61.

White, M and Gribbin, J (1966) *Darwin: A Life in Science*, Simon & Schuster, London.

White, N M and Hiroi, N (1993) Amphetamine conditioned cue preference and the neurobiology of drug seeking, *Seminars in the Neurosciences*, 5, 329-336.

Whiting, B B and Edwards, C P (1988) *Children of Different Worlds: The Formation of Social Behaviour*, Harvard University Press, Cambridge, MA.

Whitten, W K (1966) Pheromones and mammalian reproduction, in A Mclaren (ed) *Advances in Reproductive Biology*, Academic Press, New York.

Whorf, B L (1956) *Language, Thought and Reality*, Wiley, New York.

Wilkins, A J and Baddeley, A D (1978) Remembering to recall in everyday life: An approach to absentmindedness, in M M Gruneberg, P E Morris, R N Sykes (eds) *Practical Aspects of Memory*, Academic Press, London.

Wilkinson, G S (1985) The social organization of the common vampire bat. *Behavioural Ecology and Sociobiology*, 17, 111-121.

Williams, G C (1966) *Adaptation and Natural Selection*, Princeton University Press, Princeton, NJ.

Williams, G C (1975) *Sex and Evolution*. Princeton University Press, Princeton, NJ.

Williams, G C (1996) *Plan and Purpose in Nature*, Weidenfeld & Nicolson, London.

Williams, J E and Best, D L (1990) *Measuring Sex Stereotypes: A Multination Study* (rvsd), Sage, Newbury Park, CA.

Williams, R (1972) The BITCH-100: A culture specific test, Paper presented at the annual convention of the American Psychological Association, Honolulu, HI.

Williams, R B Jnr, Barefoot, J C and Shekelle, R B (1985) The health consequences of hostility, in M A Chesney and R H Rosenman (eds), *Anger and Hostility in Cardiovascular and Behavioural Disorders*, Hemisphere, New York.

Williams, R, Zyzanski, S J and Wright, A L (1992) Life events and daily hassles and uplifts as predictors of hospitalization and outpatient visitation, *Social Science Medicine*, 34, 763-768.

Williams, T M (1986) (ed) *The Impact of Television: A Natural Experiment in Three Settings*, Academic Press, New York, in T Charlton and K David (eds) (1997) *Elusive Links: Television, Video Games and Children's Behaviour*, Park Published Papers.

Williams, T M (ed) (1986) *The Impact of Television: A National Experiment in Three Communities*, Academic Press, New York.

Wilson, E O (1975) *Sociobiology: The New Synthesis*, Harvard University Press, Cambridge, MA.

Wilson, E O (1978) *On Human Nature*, Harvard University Press, Cambridge, MA.

Wilson, F M (1995) *Organizational Behaviour and Gender*, McGraw Hill, Maidenhead.

Winick, C (1994) Propaganda, in R J Corsini *Encyclopedia of Psychology*, vol 3, 2nd edn, Wiley, New York.

Wirtshafter, D and Davis, J D (1977) Set points, settling points and the control of body weight, *Physiology and Behaviour*, 19, 75-78.

Wober, J M, Reardon, G and Fazel, S (1987) *Personality, Character Aspirations and Patterns of Viewing Among Children*, IBA Research Papers, London.

Wolfe, J (1958) *Psychotherapy by Reciprocal Inhibition*, Stamford University Press, Stamford, CA.

Wolpe, J and Rachman, S. (1960) Psychoanalytic "evidence": A critique based on Frend's case of Little Hans, *Journal of Nervous and Mental Disease*, 131, 135-147.

Wood, D J (1988) *How Children Think and Learn*, Blackwell, Oxford.

Woodhead *et al.* (1991) *Growing up in a Changing Society*, Routledge, London.

Woods, B (1995) *Basics in Psychology*, Hodder & Stoughton, London.

Woods, S C and Gibbs, J (1989) The regulation of food intake by peptides. The physiology of human eating disorders: Pre-clinical and clinical perspectives, *Annals of the New York Academy of Sciences*, 75, 236-242.

Woolfenden, G E and Fitzpatrick, J W (1984) *The Florida Scrub Jay: Demography of a cooperative breeding bird*, Princeton University Press, Princeton, NJ.

Wrangham, R and Peterson, D (1997) *Demonic Males*, Bloomsbury, London.

Wright, G (1984) *Behavioural Decision Theory: an Introduction*, Penguin, Harmondsworth.

Wright, R (1994) *The Moral Animal*, Abacus, London.

Wynne-Edwards, V C (1986) *Evolution through group selection*, Blackwell Scientific, Oxford.

Wynne-Jones, R (1996) "Stupid Blacks" book row, *Independent on Sunday*, 14 April 1996.

Yadin, E, Thomas, E, Strickland, C E and Grishkat, H L (1991) Anxiolytic effects of benzodiazepines in amygdala-lesioned rats, *Psychopharmacology*, 103, 473-479.

Yerkes, R M and Dodson, J D (1908) The relation of strength of stimulus to rapidity of habit formation, *Journal of Comparative and Neurological Psychology*, 18, 459-482.

Yokoo, H, Tanaka, M, Yoshida, M (1990) Direct evidence of conditioned fear-elicited enhancement of noradrenaline release in the rat hypothalamus assessed by intracranial microdialysis, *Brain Research*, 536, 305-308.

Yuille, J C (1984) Research and teaching with police: A Canadian example, *International Review of Applied Psychology*, 33, 5-24.

Yuille, J C and Cutshall, J L (1986) A case of eye-witness memory of a crime, *Journal of Applied Psychology*, 71, 291-301.

Zahavi, A (1975) Mate selection - a selection for handicap, *Journal of Theoretical Biology*, 53, 205-214.

Zahavi, A (1977) Reliability in communication systems and the evolution of altruism, in B. Stonehouse and C M Perrins (eds), *Evolutionary Ecology*, Macmillan, London.

Zaidel, E (1975) A technique for presenting lateralized visual input with prolonged exposure, *Vision Research*, 15, 283-289.

Zajonc, R B (1968) Attitudinal effects of mere exposure, *Journal of Personality and Social Psychology*, Monograph Supplement 9(2) 1-27.

Zajonc, R B (1980) Compresence, in P B Paulus (ed) *Psychology of Group Influence*, Erlbaum, Hillsdale, NJ.

Zeki, S. (1993) The visual association cortex, *Current Opinions in Neurobiology*, 3, 155-190.

Zillman, D (1993) Mental control of angry aggression, in D M Wegner and Pennebaker (eds) *The Dynamics of Aggression*, Erlbaum, Hillsdale NJ in R A Baron and D Byrne (1997) *Social Psychology*, 8th edn, Allyn & Bacon, Boston, MA.

Zimbardo, P G (1973) On the effects of intervention in human psychological research: With special reference to the Stanford prison experiment, *Cognition*, 2, 243-256.

Zindi, F (1994) Differences in psychometric performance, *The Psychologist*, December 1994, 549-550.

Zinner, D (1997) Reported in A Motluk, Wise mothers fake it, *New Scientist*, 156, 10.

Index

CW00924150

ILKLEY
PUBLIC LIBRARIES

REFERENCE DEPARTMENT

Book No. 143939 *Ref.*

Reference Books must not be taken away from the library,
except by special permission of the librarian.

Date due for return

17. OCT. 1970
10. NOV. 1970

23. NOV. 1970

WITHDRAWN FROM BRADFORD LIBRARIES

Trees and Shrubs

HARDY IN THE BRITISH ISLES

Volume I

A - C

Trees and Shrubs

HARDY IN THE BRITISH ISLES

W. J. BEAN
C.V.O., I.S.O., V.M.H.

Eighth Edition fully revised

GENERAL EDITOR
SIR GEORGE TAYLOR
D.Sc., F.R.S., V.M.H.
Director of the Royal Botanic Gardens, Kew

Volume I

A–C

JOHN MURRAY

First Edition (Vols I & II) 1914
First Edition (Vol. III) 1933
Seventh Edition 1950

Eighth Edition fully revised (Vol. I) 1970
Published in collaboration with
The Royal Horticultural Society
Revisions and additions for Eighth Edition
© *M. Bean and John Murray (Publishers) Ltd 1970*

Printed in Great Britain by
Butler & Tanner Ltd, Frome and London

0 7195 1790 7

CONTENTS

PREFACE TO EIGHTH EDITION

William Jackson Bean was born in Yorkshire in 1863, the son of a tree nurseryman. His first appointment was to the garden staff at Belvoir Castle, Leicester. In 1883 he was accepted at Kew as a student-gardener, and there he remained. Eventually he became Curator of the Royal Botanic Gardens and in all he served for forty-six years. During this long period he acquired an exceptionally wide experience of living plants, travelling extensively to increase his knowledge. For some forty years he made a particular study of woody plants in cultivation and became the foremost specialist whose advice was constantly sought. He was caught up in the prolific tide of plant exploration in the first half of this century, when new material of unusual horticultural merit poured into the country, particularly from S.W. China, due to the unrelenting labours of collectors such as Farrer, Forrest, Rock, Kingdon Ward and Wilson. Bean was admirably equipped to keep abreast of these introductions and he was in close touch with the collectors, the botanists and the growers to ensure that his records were as complete as possible. His great work, *Trees and Shrubs Hardy in the British Isles*, was a labour of love; having worked in the Gardens all day he would settle to his writing in the evenings, going out from time to time to check whether his descriptions were accurate. The First Edition was published in the autumn of 1914 in two volumes. It was an event of outstanding importance in the chronology of horticultural literature. The volumes in their original form were the product of constant observation, massive correspondence and immense industry and bore a more personal imprint than is usual in a comprehensive manual of reference. In addition to the botanical descriptions and other basic information of the kind to be expected in works of this nature, there are the personal assessments of the plants, the references to particular specimens, the reminiscing and all the other enlivening touches that give to the book its highly individual character. It soon acquired an enduring popularity and five further editions were issued in Bean's lifetime; the seventh edition, in three volumes, appeared in 1950, three years after Bean's death, but nearly all the preparatory work for the revision had been done by him. The many changes of recent years, both from new introductions

vii

and from research into taxonomy and nomenclature, have at last made a full and thorough revision necessary. The task of editing the book would clearly be a formidable one: how were the spirit and intention of Bean to be preserved and the individual quality of the book retained while bringing it fully in line with modern knowledge and practice? There was also the matter of finance. The work would inevitably take many years and involve many people; the book would have to be entirely reset and many of the illustrations replaced. Apart from the great strain this would place upon the capital resources of John Murray, the price might have to be raised to a level unacceptable to students. After some preliminary discussion approaches were made in various quarters to try to obtain a grant towards the capital outlay. Happily, the Royal Horticultural Society agreed to invest substantially in the new edition and the Nuffield Foundation agreed that the importance of the work to scholars was such that they would be prepared to offer a guarantee against loss. With these two assurances work could be set in hand.

At a meeting between members of the R.H.S. Council and John Murray on 31st July 1963, a planning committee had been drafted and I was now invited to lead the team of editors; the members of this team, experienced and fully competent to advise on all matters concerning this somewhat encyclopaedic venture, were selected to represent the widest possible experience. Those who agreed to act were: Mr Harold Hillier, Mr F. P. Knight, Mr S. A. Pearce and Mr J. R. Sealy. The moment we started examining the task in detail our sense of temerity increased. We realised most forcibly perhaps for the first time what a truly great book it was. The first question was whether any substantial alteration by other hands was really appropriate however much the book needed revision. Previous revisions had been greatly restricted in scope by the impracticability of completely resetting the work and hence of making any substantial alterations to the existing text. Another partial revision, confined to nomenclatural changes and the addition of further species, but leaving the original matter more or less intact, would have condemned the work to becoming with the lapse of time more and more a fossilised horticultural classic and less and less a practical guide for everyday reference. The loss would have been all the more lamentable in that by far the greater part of the Seventh Edition is just as valid today as it was when first written. It would have been a great waste to compromise, as it were, this very considerable mass of valuable information by retaining those passages which were for one reason or another by then inaccurate, inadequate or outdated. It was therefore decided—whether correctly or not the reader must judge by the result—to reset the whole work and embark on a thorough revision while scrupulously trying to preserve the character of the original.

The work started. Every member of the team had a full-time job to maintain at the same time as this editorial work. From the start we were beset by a succession of severe illnesses which greatly reduced our total working capacity. After two years, at a stage when most of those engaged in the work had begun to despair of a timely and worthy completion of the task and we were looking around urgently for further help, I remembered Mr Desmond Clarke and asked him to join us. He agreed, to our immense relief. But we had no idea at the time how crucial his help was to prove. Ever since that time he has never spared himself, bringing to the work an informed and inspired application and shouldering an ever larger proportion of the load. His correspondence has been vast; his enquiries at Kew have had an uncanny knack of picking on sensitive and debatable botanical points which need elucidating. Praise for his persistence and energy cannot be too high; it is no exaggeration to say that without him the work would have foundered.

I must turn to the principles upon which we have worked. The twin aims that have guided us throughout—to conserve and yet to modernise—have not always been easy to reconcile. For instance the new typography has in it an element of compromise: we wanted to keep the 'feel' of Bean while using a fresher typeface; we have used italics in the way now customary, that is, for synonyms and for generic and specific names mentioned in the running text; we have retained the majority of the line drawings but have included several replacements and new drawings by Miss Mary Grierson of the Royal Botanic Gardens, Kew. The requirements of the Botanical Code in the matter of author citations and the application of the new *Code of Nomenclature for Cultivated Plants* have led to changes in presentation which are explained in Chapter IX, 'Taxonomy and Nomenclature' (pp. 99–100), and in Chapter X, 'Cultivars and their Nomenclature' (pp. 101–2). Authors' names are abbreviated in accordance with modern practice and a 'List of Authors', with a key to the abbreviations, will appear at the end of Volume IV together with the main index. Volumes I–III will contain short indices of synonyms and of those plants which are described out of alphabetical order, partly to give essential guidance while Volume IV is still unpublished but also to make each volume self-contained and cut down the need to consult the main index. All the introductory chapters in the Seventh Edition are being retained and fully revised, but in order to make room for the large number of additional species that have been included in Volume I the chapters on the choice of tree and shrub species for various purposes and situations have been relegated to Volume IV. One caution: the work consists fundamentally of descriptive accounts of the individual plants. Although care has been taken to ensure botanical accuracy as far as that is possible, the work is not to be regarded as giving a monographic coverage to the various genera.

Something must be said about the treatment of the original text. Great care has been taken to alter it only where necessary. New matter is, as far as is practicable, added at the end of each entry; where this has not proved possible much of the original wording has been retained. The necessity of rewriting Bean's text is nearly always attributable to one of three causes. First, many of the descriptions were written so soon after the introduction of the species concerned that the accompanying judgements as to their hardiness and worth could only be provisional. It is now usually possible to give a firmer verdict (though it remains exceedingly difficult to make any useful generalisation about certain borderline species). Secondly, every change in the taxonomic status of a plant inevitably demands some alteration of the text in which it was described and discussed. Thirdly, many of the references to particular specimens of trees and shrubs are by now out of date—some by half a century or more. Their correction or replacement has necessitated some rewording in the surrounding text to avoid confusion. In particular, Bean's use of the first person has often had to be relinquished at such times. The use of the pronoun 'I' always indicates Bean's views or experiences: where revised judgements or comments have been made by the present editors it has been dropped.

Now I must try to give credit to all those who have shared in the work. Their ungrudging help has been an immense encouragement to Mr Desmond Clarke and myself. Miss Margaret Bean has shown the closest interest in progress at all stages and we are indebted to her both for her assistance in preparing the complicated master copy for the printer and for later help in reading the proofs. We are particularly grateful to Mr Harold Hillier for so generously giving us the benefit of his great knowledge and experience. The time he has spent in answering a host of questions from Mr Desmond Clarke, either personally or by letter, is very considerable. Mr F. P. Knight and Mr S. A. Pearce put in much work in the early stages, sharing between them the task of revising the introductory chapters; they were both compelled to withdraw from full involvement because of illness and other heavy commitments but have continued to make themselves available for discussion and advice. Mr J. Robert Sealy has given the most painstaking scrutiny to the entire botanical content, with the assistance of colleagues at Kew, especially Mr Martin Sands and Mr David Hunt. Mr Hunt has also contributed the chapter, 'Taxonomy and Nomenclature'. (The chapter on 'Cultivars and their Nomenclature' was written by Mr Desmond Clarke). Mr C. D. Brickell has read the proofs and provided much useful comment and further information. Dr Charles Hubbard has generously provided the revised treatment of the various bamboos. Mr Alan Mitchell of the Forestry Commission has made special expeditions and has freely provided the results of his studies on the trees in gardens and collections of the British Isles. Mr David Wright has supplied a great deal of information on the whereabouts of notable trees and shrubs. Special acknowledgement must also be made to Dr Harold Fletcher and the staff of the Royal Botanic Garden, Edinburgh; and to the Royal Horticultural Society, whose staff at Vincent Square (in particular, Mr P. F. M. Stageman) and Wisley have given the utmost assistance. My position has been that of General Editor; apart from the revision of the historical introduction my main function has been as a co-ordinator.

Finally I hope that the others who have helped in various ways and to varying extents with Volume I will not take exception to a briefer mention. In listing their names we offer them our sincere thanks. They are:

Dr Giovanni Abrami
Mr R. F. Adam
Mr E. B. Anderson
Major P. L. Barber
Dr G. Barker
Mr R. C. Barnard
Mr K. E. Beckett

The Hon. Mrs Bell
Major Simon Bolitho
Mr Albert Burkwood
Sir Ilay Campbell, Bart.
Mr J. M. Colledge
Mr Geoffrey Collins
Mr E. H. M. Cox

Mr P. A. Cox

Mr H. S. J. Crane

The late Miss H. Davenport Jones

Mr F. R. Daw

Mr Jack Drake

Mr T. H. Findlay

Mr Basil Fox

Mr P. H. Gardner

Mr David Gilliland

Mr J. S. L. Gilmour

Mr N. Hadden

Mr Eliot Hodgkin

Mr A. J. Huxley

Captain Collingwood Ingram

Mr Will Ingwersen

Mrs Johnstone

Mr Roy Lancaster

Sir Giles Loder, Bart.

Mr C. Marchant

Mr Maurice Mason

Lady Mersey

The Earl of Morton

Mr Brian Mulligan

Mr C. G. Nice

Mr T. G. Nitzelius

The Hon. Mrs O'Neill

Mr Geoffrey Pilkington

Mr Oleg Polunin

Mr Charles Puddle

The Earl of Rosse

Mr R. Shaw

Mr Leslie S. Slinger

Mr B. N. Starling

Dr W. T. Stearn

The late Sir Frederick Stern

Mr Patrick Synge

Lord Talbot de Malahide

Mr H. Taylor

Mr Graham S. Thomas

Mr Neil Treseder

Mr Vyvian Tylor

Mr V. R. Waldron

Mr R. J. Walker

Mr Robert Walpole

Dr T. J. Walsh

Mr Donald Waterer

Prof. D. A. Webb

Commander A. M. Williams

Mr Julian Williams

Dr P. F. Yeo

GEORGE TAYLOR

PREFACE TO SEVENTH EDITION

Living things are always changing, and something new could always be added to a book which deals with so wide a field as *Trees and Shrubs Hardy in the British Isles*. My father finished writing the first edition in 1913, and it was published in the autumn of the following year. By 1933 so many new species had been introduced, and so much knowledge has been gained about plants new to cultivation in this country when the book first appeared, that a third volume was published to deal with this new material. In response to numerous requests, the scope of the third volume was also widened to include many species which can only be satisfactorily grown in the milder parts of the British Isles.

To preparing the present edition my father devoted the last years of his long life. It again brings the information up to date, while the additional genera and species which appeared in Volume III are now placed in their proper alphabetical order. He finished reading the galley proofs shortly before his death. The final proofs have been corrected by Mr H. S. Marshall, the Librarian at Kew Gardens, who also compiled the index, and a great debt of gratitude is owed to him for the care he has devoted to this task.

My father would certainly have wished to thank by name all those who helped in the preparation of this edition. Unfortunately I only know the names of those who have helped us since his death; sincere thanks are due to my father's old friend, Dr Wilfrid Fox, whose expert advice has been invaluable, to Sir Edward Salisbury, the Director of Kew Gardens, who enabled us to make use of facilities only available at Kew, and to Mr G. Atkinson, the artist and photographer at Kew, for his help with the additional photographs which appear in this edition.

G. E. BEAN

1949

PREFACE TO FIRST EDITION

Since Loudon published his great work, about seventy-five years ago, no book in English dealing comprehensively with the trees and shrubs hardy and cultivated in Britain has been published. During that period an enormous number of new species have become available for cultivation through the labours of collectors like William Lobb in Chile and California, Hartweg and Jeffrey in western N. America, J. G. Veitch and Maries in Japan, Fortune and Wilson in China. The present work is an attempt to bring together brief descriptions of all the species and more important varieties of hardy woody plants established in cultivation, with notes on their distinctive characters, garden value, and culture. It is hoped that it may prove of use to the numerous amateurs, country gentlemen, and landowners who are interested in shrubs and trees, also to nurserymen, park superintendents, and to professional gardeners.

The great accession of Chinese plants during the last fourteen years has made the task a much more difficult one. Many of the plants introduced by Wilson are as yet unidentified, and the hardiness and garden value also of a great number have not yet been definitely ascertained. Still, most of the earlier introduced ones have been dealt with, also those of later introduction that have flowered and been identified.

The question of nomenclature is always a vexed one. The only thing certain is, that it is impossible to please everyone. With regard to generic names, I have endeavoured to be as conservative as possible. When botany was largely under the influence of the Hookers and Bentham in England, and of Asa Gray in America, the tendency was towards the reduction of genera and species. There is no doubt the process was carried too far. The merging, for instance, of *Mespilus* with *Pyrus*, *Pterostyrax* with *Halesia*, *Maackia* with *Cladrastis* was not justifiable. In these and a few similar cases the older generic names have been revived. But there has lately risen a school of workers, with a strong following on the Continent and in the United States, whose aim is to subdivide species, genera, and Natural Orders to the fullest extent. Whilst much of this is, no doubt, the result of a closer study and a more critical insight than the older men practised, some of it seems to represent a desire of change for change's sake. At any rate, if adopted in its entirety, it would involve such confusion and readjustment of nomenclature as to render its acceptance by cultivators in the last degree unlikely in this country.

In the case of nomenclature of species, I have with few exceptions clung to what is known as the Kew Rule of giving a plant the specific name first published in conjunction with the proper genus.

In the preparation of this work I have had the enormous advantage of being able to make full use, not only of the magnificent collections of living plants at Kew, but also of the herbarium of trees and shrubs which has been in course of formation there for thirty years, at first by the late Mr Geo. Nicholson, and during the last thirteen years by myself. There are very few of the descriptions that have not been made from authentic material—living or dried.

Some explanation of the term 'hardy' as used in the following pages is perhaps needed. There is a great variety of climate in the British Isles, and the word 'hardy' has a very different significance, say, in eastern Northumberland from what it has at Falmouth or Cork. Although we are apt, almost instinctively, to regard the softness of the climate as progressing from north to south, it is, in Great Britain, rather from east to west. Thus, plants can be grown on the west coast of Scotland as far to the north as Ross-shire, such as *Desfontainea*, *Tricuspidaria* and Himalayan rhododendrons, which are absolutely hopeless in the open air at Kew. To have included a consideration of all the shrubs and trees that can be grown outside in the mildest corners of Great Britain and Ireland would have inconveniently and unduly extended the limits of this work. A considerable proportion of them can only be regarded as greenhouse plants in most parts of Great Britain. The word 'hardy' may be taken generally as applicable to Kew. This district is fairly average in regard to temperature, although, being flat and low-lying, plants are particularly liable there to injury by spring frosts. With comparatively few exceptions, the trees and shrubs dealt with here may be grown at Kew, either fully in the open or against walls.

I have to express my thanks to Sir David Prain, the Director of Kew, for permission to borrow books belonging to the Kew library; also to Messrs Elwes and Henry for the privilege of seeing proof-sheets of the *Trees of Great Britain and Ireland*, and to the editors of the *Gardeners' Chronicle* for permission to adapt some articles of mine which appeared in that journal a few years ago on transplanting, pruning, and one or two other subjects. To my colleague, Mr W.

Dallimore of Kew, I owe a debt of gratitude for assistance in reading the proofs.

The illustrations in the text have been drawn by Miss E. Goldring from photographs made by Mr E. J. Wallis. For some of the subjects illustrated I am indebted to Sir Frederick W. Moore, of the Royal Botanic Gardens, Glasnevin, Dublin.

W. J. B.

KEW, *April* 1914

SOURCES OF PLATES

LIST OF DRAWINGS IN TEXT

Those marked with an asterisk were drawn by Miss E. Goldring; the remainder are by Miss Mary Grierson.

PART ONE

INTRODUCTION

HISTORICAL NOTES

It has long been the custom to attribute to the Romans the introduction to Britain of certain common trees and shrubs. From the fact that remains of the seeds of *Pinus pinea*, the stone pine of Italy, have been found in the refuse heaps of Roman encampments in Britain, it is evident that edible seeds and possibly fruits were imported from Italy for the soldiers' use, and in that way the sweet chestnut, the walnut, the mulberry, and other trees with edible fruits or seeds may, as has often been stated, have been first brought to this country. Possibly, also, some of the most popular ornamental exotic trees and shrubs, like the common lime, were brought over by them too. As for the common elm and box, often attributed to the Romans, there appears no reason for disputing their genuineness as natives of southern England.

After the withdrawal of the Roman legions in the fourth and fifth centuries, the country relapsed into comparative barbarism, but subsequent to the establishment of Christianity the introduction of plants from the Continent was, no doubt, carried on by religious houses, especially after the Norman Conquest. Most attention was given to the scented and medicinal plants, like rosemary and thyme, and to fruit-trees. It is also likely that a number of ornamental as well as useful trees, shrubs, and herbs were first introduced during the Dark Ages by mariners and others touching at continental and Mediterranean ports, or by travellers inland. But the fact is, what they, the Romans, or the monks accomplished, must to us remain largely mere guesswork.

We only touch certain ground in this matter in the year 1548, when **Wm Turner** published his *Names of Herbes*. Turner, sometimes called the 'Father of English Botany', was born at Morpeth early in the sixteenth century and, after becoming Dean of Wells, died in 1568. At one time he lived and had a garden at Kew, and his *Names of Herbes* was dated from the neighbouring Syon House, then the residence of the Duke of Somerset, Lord Protector, to whom Turner was physician. In this and his other works, the number of foreign trees and shrubs enumerated barely amount to thirty. But it is quite probable, with the lack of intercommunication then prevailing, that others were in cultivation in the country unknown to him.

3

In 1597, nearly fifty years after the appearance of Turner's first work, a famous *Herbal* was published by **John Gerard**. Gerard was born at Nantwich in 1545, and was trained as a surgeon, which profession, as well as that of apothecary, he practised in London. For the purpose probably of supplying his own simples, he established a physic, or botanic garden at Holborn. From his *Herbal* and other sources of information, it appears that by the end of the sixteenth century about one hundred foreign trees and shrubs were in cultivation in England. Of big trees, there were the Oriental plane, holm oak, common spruce, *Pinus pinaster*, *Cupressus sempervirens*, as well as the walnut, stone pine, and sweet chestnut previously mentioned. It is interesting to note also, as recorded by Gerard, the cultivation in 1596 of two woody plants of American origin, *Yucca gloriosa* and *Thuja occidentalis*, the first apparently of their country.

Gerard died about 1607, and after him the next great herbalist was **John Parkinson** (1567–1650), a London apothecary in the service of James I, and the author of a herbal and other works. He was one of the most noteworthy cultivators in the early seventeenth century who interested themselves in the introduction of new plants. By Aiton he is credited with introducing, or it is perhaps more correct to say, being the first to cultivate, about forty kinds of trees and shrubs, all from N. America or Europe. The influx of new trees and shrubs from N. America proceeded slowly during the seventeenth century, but about fifty species appear to have become established in Britain.

Two names which frequently occur in connection with the introduction of new woody plants about the middle of the seventeenth century are those of the two Tradescants, who, between 1640 and 1656, have attributed to them about twenty species. The elder **John Tradescant** was a Dutchman who came to England about the end of the sixteenth century. He is said to have been a considerable traveller in Europe, N. Africa, and the Orient. About 1629 he was appointed gardener to Charles I. He had a garden and museum at Lambeth, and died about 1652. His son, **John Tradescant the younger,** was a man of similar tastes and carried on the museum and garden at Lambeth. In 1656 he published a catalogue of the plants grown in the latter. He travelled in N. America, especially Virginia, whence he introduced the locust tree (*Robinia pseudoacacia*), *Juglans cinerea*, *Acer rubrum*, *Celtis occidentalis*, and the American plane, *Platanus occidentalis*. These and others he propagated for sale. He died in 1662.

In the latter part of the seventeenth century and the early years of the following one, the most notable name in connection with hardy trees and shrubs is that of **Henry Compton,** Bishop of London from 1675 to 1713. In his garden at Fulham he got together the most extensive collection that had hitherto been seen in the British Isles. By 1713, when Compton died, probably 400 species of foreign trees and shrubs were in cultivation in England. Of especial interest at that time were the American introductions, such as the spruces, red oaks, hickories, walnuts, magnolias, thorns, maples, and the tulip tree. Many of these had been sent home to Bishop Compton by **John Banister,** a missionary in Virginia, who was the author of the first catalogue of American plants. He was killed in 1692 by falling from a rock whilst collecting.

Another person interested largely in this branch of horticulture, and contemporary with Compton, was the **Duchess of Beaufort,** who planted extensively in the gardens at Badminton.

The foundation of the Oxford Botanic Garden in 1621, of Chelsea Physic Garden about 1674, and that of the Edinburgh Botanic Garden in 1680, must have had a stimulating effect on the cultivation of exotic trees and shrubs, as well as of other plants. At this period the site now covered by the Botanic Gardens of Kew was owned by **Sir Henry** (afterwards Lord) **Capel,** in whose hands it became one of the finest private gardens in the kingdom.

Among trees introduced in the seventeenth century, the one destined to play the most important part in the sylva of Great Britain and Ireland was the common larch (*Larix decidua*), said to have been first brought to Britain, under the auspices of Parkinson, in 1629. It was not, however, until a century later, namely in 1738, that it first began to be planted as a forest tree. The pioneer in this work was the 2nd **Duke of Atholl,** and it was his son, the 3rd Duke, whose planting (it is said) of 27 millions of larch trees gained him the sobriquet of 'the planter'.

Next in importance to the larch, and introduced the same year, was the horse-chestnut. It reached Western Europe by way of Constantinople through the agency of the botanist Clusius, but its true native home, which is northern Greece, long remained a mystery. The common silver fir was introduced by **Sarjeant Newdigate** from Central Europe in 1603. The well-known tulip tree first reached this country in 1663; whilst the cedar of Lebanon, than which no tree ever introduced has made a finer or more conspicuous feature in our gardens and parks, came a few years later.

The eighteenth century witnessed a remarkable increase in the interest taken in hardy trees and shrubs by planters in the British Isles, both amateur and professional, and in the number of exotic species cultivated. One of the most notable amateurs was the **Duke of Argyll** (1680–1761), who planted largely at Whitton, near Hounslow. He has been described indeed as the most assiduous collector and planter of his time in England, and was by Pope nicknamed 'the tree-monger'. Although the Whitton property has latterly been cut up into lots for building, there were in 1903 many fine trees planted by the Duke still thriving, notably the grove of cedars of Lebanon said to have been raised from seed in 1725, a group of magnificent deciduous cypresses, red maple, etc. After his death, in 1761, many of the smaller trees were removed to the then newly formed arboretum at Kew, but it is doubtful whether any now survive.

A name which will be found to occur frequently in the body of this work is that of **Peter Collinson** (1694–1768), an amateur who certainly stands out as one of the chief patrons of arboriculture in the eighteenth century. Collinson was a linen-draper in London, in which business he appears to have amassed a considerable fortune. In his later years he planted largely in his garden at Mill Hill, near Hendon. The site is now occupied by the Mill Hill School and its grounds. Collinson was instrumental in introducing many new plants, more especially N. American ones.

Among botanical cultivators of the eighteenth century two names are conspicuous: **Philip Miller** (1691–1771) and **William Aiton**. Miller, so well known by his *Dictionary*, which passed into eight editions in his lifetime, was curator of the Physic Garden at Chelsea, an institution he is said to have raised to the first position among all botanic gardens of the time. Aiton (1731–93) was his pupil, and by him was recommended to the Dowager Princess of Wales, in 1759, to take charge of the botanic garden at Kew, founded that year, an event destined to have so important an influence on horticulture and botany in the English-speaking world. Aiton died in 1793, and his memory lives chiefly as the author of the *Hortus Kewensis*, a work which enumerates and gives a brief description of 5,500 species of plants with their date of introduction. This work is, in fact, the chief source of information in regard to the introduction of exotic plants up to the time of its publication.

A cultivator of whom Collinson and others wrote in eulogistic terms was **Lord Petre** (1713–42), who planted extensively at Thorndon Hall, in Essex. Writing in lament of his early death, Collinson calls him the 'worthiest of men', and his loss the 'greatest that botany or gardening ever felt in this island'.

The introduction of trees and shrubs from N. America in the latter half of the eighteenth century owes much to the two Bartrams —John (1699–1777) and his son William (1729–1823). **John Bartram** is famous as the first American-born botanist, and the founder of the first American botanic garden. This garden, situated in Philadelphia, is still in existence. He and his son collected chiefly on the mountains of the S.E. United States.

Contemporary with the Bartrams was **André Michaux** (1746–1803), a Frenchman who resided in America from 1785 to 1796. He travelled much in eastern N. America, and was the first to introduce many of the trees and shrubs of that region to Europe. They were sent to France, and some of the trees raised from his seed may still be seen in the gardens of the Petit Trianon, and at Balaines.

The foundation of the *Botanical Magazine* by **William Curtis** (1746–99) in 1787 is an event that merits a passing notice. It has appeared in parts each year from that date up to the present time. Each number now contains eleven coloured plates of plants accompanied by text figures and descriptions in English with a Latin diagnosis. Over 10,000 plates have appeared in 176 volumes and a considerable proportion of the plants figured are of hardy trees and shrubs, as may be judged from the frequent quotation of plates in this work.

Among nurserymen of the eighteenth century, those whose fame persists in connection with our present subject are: **James Gordon,** who was at one time gardener to the Lord Petre aforementioned. About 1750 he established a nursery at Mile End. He introduced *Ulmus americana, Sophora japonica* (one of his original trees, introduced in 1753, is still alive at Kew), and the maidenhair tree. **James Lee** (1715–95), in partnership with one Kennedy, founded a nursery at Hammersmith (Olympia now partly covers the site), which ultimately became the finest in the kingdom. The firm did not finally disappear until about the beginning of the twentieth century.

A German named **Conrad Loddiges** started as a nurseryman at Hackney in 1771 and established a business which, so far as hardy trees and shrubs are concerned, became by far the most important in the British Isles. It was on the collections maintained by this firm more than any other that **J. C. Loudon** relied for living material in the preparation of his great work in 1835–7: *Arboretum et Frutice-tum Britannicum*, the four volumes of text containing 2,694 pages with 2,546 figures, and another four volumes containing 412 plates. The firm of Loddiges, equally famous as cultivators and introducers of orchids and greenhouse plants, continued to exist until the middle of the nineteenth century.

In 1772 the first of professional plant collectors, **Francis Masson,** was sent out from Kew to the Cape of Good Hope. From that time until 1862 a succession, sometimes interrupted, of plant collectors went out from Kew to many parts of the world. But it must be admitted that their work, largely guided and fostered in those early days by **Sir Joseph Banks** (1743–1820), went on more in tropical and subtropical countries than in those whence plants hardy in this country come. Altogether about 500 new hardy trees and shrubs were introduced in the eighteenth century, three-fifths of them from N. America.

In the early years of the nineteenth century the most important collector of woody plants was **John Fraser** (1752–1811). Born at Tomnacloich, Inverness, he came to London as a young man and ultimately started in business at Chelsea as a hosier and linen-draper. Living near the famous Chelsea Physic Garden, he appears to have acquired a love for plants that soon set him longing for travel in search of new ones. With the assistance of **Sir James Smith,** first President of the Linnean Society and authority on willows, and that of Aiton of Kew, he went to N. America about 1780. During the next twenty years he crossed the Atlantic ten or twelve times (latterly in company with his son of the same name), and introduced many of the trees and shrubs now most cherished in our gardens, amongst them magnolias—*M. fraseri* was named after him—azaleas, *Pieris floribunda*, and *Rhododendron catawbiense*, the chief parent of the garden race of rhododendrons. His most success-ful work was done in the S.E. United States. His later years were clouded by ill-health and financial embarrassment, and he died at Sloane Square in 1811, when only sixty years of age. Loudon describes him as one of the most enterprising, indefatigable, and persevering men who ever devoted themselves to botany and plant discovery.

No single event up to the time of its occurrence can be said to have exerted so stimulating an influence on the cultivation of hardy trees and shrubs in our islands as the foundation of the **Horticultural Society** in 1804. In 1824 they initiated one of the most famous of plant-collecting expeditions; they sent **David Douglas** to western N. America, a region which hitherto had only been touched at, thirty years before, by Archibald Menzies, when he accompanied Vancouver on his voyage of discovery. Douglas (1798–1834), like nearly all these early collectors, was of Scottish descent. Born at Scone, near Perth, he went as a youth to the Botanic Garden at Glasgow, where his botanical tastes gained for him the patronage of Sir Wm Hooker, by whom he was recommended to the Horticultural Society as a plant collector. He reached British Columbia in April 1825, and sent home the seeds of many species during that and the two following years. In 1829 he again left England and reached the mouth of the Columbia River in June 1830. In this region and in California he worked during the succeeding two or three years. Among the most notable additions Douglas made to cultivated trees were the Douglas fir, *Pinus radiata, P. lambertiana, P. monticola, P. sabiniana, P. ponderosa*, and *P. coulteri; Abies amabilis, A. grandis*, and *A. procera* (syn. *A. nobilis*); *Picea sitchensis; Acer macrophyllum* and *A. circinatum; Arbutus menziesii*. Among shrubs whose first sending we owe to him are *Garrya elliptica, Ribes aureum, R. sanguineum* and *R. speciosum, Rubus parviflorus* and *R. spectabilis, Gaultheria shallon*. Douglas came to a horribly tragic end on 12th July 1834. He was collecting plants alone in the Sandwich Islands when he fell into one of the pit-traps constructed by the natives to catch wild bulls, in which an animal was already entrapped. He was found terribly gored and mangled and quite dead a few hours later.

Hitherto the foreign hardy trees and shrubs introduced had been almost wholly obtained from Europe and N. America. We have now briefly to notice a man who devoted much of his life to the introduction of plants from Japan. **Philipp F. von Siebold** (1796–1866) was born at Wurzburg in Bavaria and went to Japan in 1823. In 1830 he returned to Europe, and in collaboration with Zuccarini published his fine illustrated work, the *Flora Japonica* (1835–42). In 1850 he founded a nursery at Leyden to which he successfully introduced many trees and shrubs from Japan and China. After his death many of his original trees were secured by the firm of Simon-Louis of Plantières near Metz.

As regards Chinese plants, not much had yet been done. Some plants had been introduced during the famous embassy of **Lord Macartney** to the Chinese court in 1792–3, and a young man named **William Kerr** had been sent out from Kew to China in 1803. He introduced the double-flowered *Kerria japonica* and the Chinese juniper, but appears to have done little among hardy trees and shrubs. Soon, however, the vast increase of shipping, and the greatly augmented intercourse between various parts of the world, began to render the introduction of plants easy by means of seeds sent by amateurs resident in foreign ports. Especially was this the case when the disturbing and retrogressive influences of the Napoleonic wars ceased with Waterloo.

In N. America the work of the Frasers was carried on by **John Lyon,** commemorated by the genus *Lyonia*, who filled in the period between the Frasers and Douglas. Like the former, he worked chiefly on the wonderful flora of the S.E. United States. He introduced many trees and shrubs in large quantities (although not for the first time) between 1806 and 1818, and thus did much to add to the beauty and interest of gardens. Many of the fine old N. American trees still adorning our gardens were brought over by Lyon. He was of Scottish parentage, but the place and date of his birth are not known, nor very certainly that of his death. According to Nuttall, the botanist, he 'fell a victim to a dangerous epidemic amidst those savage and romantic mountains which had so often been the scene of his labours'.

During the second and third decades of the nineteenth century a few Himalayan trees and shrubs had been sent to England, chiefly by **Buchanan-Hamilton** and **Wallich,** successive directors of the Botanic Garden at Calcutta; but the first genuine revelation of the riches of that region was reserved for **Joseph Dalton Hooker** (1817–1911). This famous botanist and traveller was sent from Kew to collect in India between 1847 and 1851, and, among other things, introduced the splendid Sikkim rhododendrons, which became the glory of many gardens in the milder parts of the kingdom.

No name in the annals of horticulture holds a more honoured place than that of **Veitch.** The enterprise of this well-known firm, Messrs James Veitch & Sons (which was founded near Exeter in 1808 and removed to Chelsea in 1853), was the means of introducing more ornamental exotic plants to this country than any other single agency up to the present time. They were the first to exploit systematically the riches of Chile in the interests of English gardens and parks. To that country in 1840 they sent one of the most famous of collectors, **William Lobb** (1809–63), a Cornishman. During that journey he introduced *Araucaria araucana* in quantity. He returned to England in 1844, but left for S. America again the following year, and during the next two or three years introduced many valuable shrubs, such as *Berberis darwinii*, the *Lapageria*, *Embothrium*, *Desfontainea*, and many of the Chilean conifers. In 1849 he was sent by Messrs Veitch to California and Oregon, and, as the pages of this work will show, introduced a wealth of fine trees and shrubs from that region, the most wonderful for its sylva of all the regions of the globe. One of Lobb's greatest achievements was the introduction of the Wellingtonia (*Sequoiadendron giganteum*), then but newly discovered, in quantity to Britain in 1853. He also introduced in quantity many of the trees discovered by Douglas. After his engagement with Messrs Veitch terminated, he returned to California, where he died of paralysis in 1863.

The collections in the noted tree and shrub nursery of Messrs Veitch at Coombe Wood, near Kingston-on-Thames, owing to the expiration of the lease, were dispersed in 1913. The firm no longer exists, but the Exeter branch, which became a separate concern in 1863, is still in business as Messrs Robert Veitch & Sons.

In 1836 the Horticultural Society sent **K. T. Hartweg** (1812–71), a native of Carlsruhe in Germany, to Mexico. He remained there seven years and introduced many plants, but mostly tender ones. The trees are only suitable for the warmer parts of Britain. Among them were several curious oaks, still to be found in old gardens, several of the remarkable Mexican pines and *Abies religiosa.* He went to California in 1846–7 and worked at Monterey and in the upper valley of the Sacramento River.

One of the greatest of all plant collectors was **Robert Fortune** (1812–80), a native of Berwickshire. After spending some time in the Botanic Garden at Edinburgh, he went, in 1841, to the Horticultural Society's gardens at Chiswick. Two years later the Society selected him to collect for them in China. In 1844 he visited the tea-growing district of Ningpo, and after introducing many beautiful plants, both hardy and tender—a goodly proportion of which were subjects that had long been cultivated by the Chinese—he returned to

England in 1846. He was appointed curator of the Chelsea Physic Garden, but in 1848 resigned this post and went again to China for the purpose of transmitting the tea plant to the hill countries of India. By means of seeds and plants he succeeded in doing this, and thus laid the foundation of the great tea industry of India. In 1852, and again in 1858, he went to China, collecting and studying Chinese horticulture—on the latter occasion in the interests of the United States Government. In 1860 he worked in Japan. Fortune's name will be found frequently to occur in the following pages in connection with the introduction of E. Asiatic plants.

An association of mostly Scottish gentlemen was formed about the middle of the nineteenth century in Edinburgh to exploit the natural products of western N. America. It was called the **Oregon Association.** In 1850 the Association engaged **John Jeffrey** to collect for them in western N. America. Jeffrey was a native of Fifeshire, and as a young man entered the Edinburgh Botanic Garden. He adopted what was then the most convenient method of crossing the N. American continent, which was by way of the Hudson Bay Company's posts, and reached his collecting ground in 1851. In 1852 he worked in California. Jeffrey explored and collected with great zeal during these two years, but by the third year his engagement appears to have become irksome to him, the roving passion seized him, and he joined an expedition to explore the Colorado and Gila Rivers in Arizona, and was never heard of again. He introduced, among other things, *Abies magnifica, Tsuga heterophylla,* and *Pinus jeffreyi.*

After W. Lobb, the next Chilean collector was **Richard Pearce,** who worked for Messrs Veitch from 1859 to 1866. He reintroduced many of the plants sent home by his predecessor, and British gardens owed to his labours new stocks of *Eucryphia glutinosa,* the *Embothrium,* and *Desfontainea.* Among conifers, *Araucaria araucana* was again introduced, *Podocarpus nubigenus,* and for the first time, *Podocarpus andinus.* Pearce died in Panama in July 1867.

Since the labours of Siebold in Japan, earlier in the century, the beautiful flora of that country had yielded little for the gardens of Europe. The opening of the ports to foreigners afforded an opportunity for renewed discovery, and in 1860 **John Gould Veitch** (1839–70) reached Japan, and initiated in the interests of his firm one of the most successful of all plant-collecting enterprises. He was especially fortunate in the number of new conifers he introduced, amongst which were *Abies veitchii*, *A. firma*, *Picea jezoënsis* var. *hondoënsis*, *P. polita*, several pines, and, for the first time in quantity, the umbrella pine (*Sciadopitys verticillata*).

The foundation, in 1872, of the Arnold Arboretum at Jamaica Plain, in the environs of Boston, Mass., under the auspices of Harvard University and the late **Charles Sprague Sargent,** must be accounted one of the most pregnant events in regard to the discovery, introduction, and cultivation of hardy trees and shrubs during the last century. This institution, conducted with admirable skill and energy, has exerted an influence on the gardens of Europe hardly less beneficent than on those of its own country. The exploitation of the N. American sylva, more especially on the eastern side, had been comparatively neglected since the departure of the earlier collectors like Fraser and Lyon. Some of the interesting plants they found had disappeared from cultivation. The work was revived by Professor Sargent and a renewed interest has sprung up, especially in the United States, in that most beautiful flora of the Alleghenies and other parts of the south-east. Sargent travelled not only all over N. America but also in Japan, whence he introduced to cultivation a large number of beautiful trees and shrubs. He remained director until his death in 1927 at the age of eighty-six. It was due to the enterprise of a more recent director, **Elmer Drew Merrill,** in encouraging native Chinese collectors that *Metasequoia glyptostroboides* was discovered in Hupeh, introduced into the Arnold Arboretum and thence generously distributed.

Charles Maries, a native of Stratford-on-Avon, collected in Japan and China for Messrs Veitch between 1877 and 1879. His name will be found frequently mentioned in the body of this work as the introducer of plants from those countries, but more especially Japan. He first brought *Hamamelis mollis*, *Styrax obassia*, and *Abies mariesii* under cultivation, also numerous forms of Japanese maples. In 1882 Maries entered the service of one of the native princes of India, and died at Gwalior in 1902.

A great impetus to the interest taken in hardy trees and shrubs has been given by the discovery and introduction of new species from central and western China. The work was initiated in the first place by the Jesuit missionaries of France, among whom **David, Delavay,** and **Farges** were most prominent. These men, stationed in districts new·to Europeans, spent their leisure time in botanising and collecting seeds, which were first sent to the Jardin des Plantes at Paris and to **Maurice L. de Vilmorin,** in whose grounds at Les Barres a vast collection was got together. M. de Vilmorin died 22nd April 1918. The collection still exists and is now the property of the State.

So far as Great Britain is concerned, the introduction of the plants of central and western China had its beginning in the work of **Augustine Henry.** This famous traveller and collector was born in Co. Derry, Ireland, in 1857, and was educated at Queen's Colleges, Galway and Belfast. After studying medicine he, in June 1881, entered the Chinese Imperial Maritime Customs Service at Shanghai. The following year he was transferred to Ichang, a port on the Yangtze Kiang, 1,000 miles from the sea. A few miles above the town the great river finds its exit from the mountains into the great plain by way of wonderful gorges. It was in these mountains that Henry commenced to collect plants in 1885. The flora proved to be of extraordinary richness, and during the next four years he sent an enormous number of dried plants to Kew. Henry remained in various posts in China until 1900, spending most of his leave in exploration and botanical collecting, travelling much over the provinces of Hupeh, Szechwan, and Yunnan. He also travelled and collected in Hainan and Formosa. After his return home he studied forestry in France, and soon after, in association with H. J. Elwes, commenced the great work, *The Trees of Great Britain and Ireland*. He ultimately became Professor of Forestry in the Royal College of Science, Dublin, and died in 1930. **Henry John Elwes** (1846–1922), of Colesbourne, Gloucestershire, was a wealthy landowner who devoted his leisure and outstanding talents to forestry, horticulture, botany and natural history. He travelled widely, and some of the most interesting passages in *The Trees of Great Britain and Ireland* were contributed by him from personal knowledge of the temperate forests of both hemispheres. This work was conceived, financed and partly written by him and he was also the author of the original volume of *Monograph of the Genus Lilium* (1877–80) which, with its supplements, is one of the classics of horticultural and botanical illustration.

The amazing richness of the vegetation of the far provinces of China, as revealed by Henry's dried plants, and the wonderful beauty many of the trees and shrubs were seen to possess, induced Messrs Veitch to send out a collector to obtain in a living state such as were likely to be of horticultural value. On the recommendation of Sir Wm Thiselton-Dyer, then director of Kew, **Ernest Henry Wilson** was dispatched to China in 1899. Wilson was born at

Chipping Campden, Gloucestershire, in 1876; after working as a young man in the Botanic Gardens, Birmingham, he went in 1897 to Kew. He possessed a combination of mental and physical qualities which made him one of the greatest of plant collectors. Of athletic build, and endowed with an indomitable courage and perseverance —attributes of the highest necessity to the plant collector in untrodden wilds—he had also that deep love of science, especially of botany, without which the man who adopts this work is but poorly equipped. To these qualities Wilson joined a business aptitude and an adaptability to new circumstances which led to his dealings with the Chinaman being invariably successful. In all, he visited China four times, twice in the interests of Messrs Veitch (1899–1902 and 1903–5), and twice under the auspices of Harvard University and a number of subscribers (1907–9 and 1910–11). Wilson's services to horticulture and his contributions to botany have not probably been equalled by those of any other collector. To give some idea of the magnitude of his labours, it may be mentioned that he introduced some 1,200 species of trees and shrubs, amongst which have been found about 400 new species and 4 new genera; and he collected over 65,000 sheets of herbarium specimens.

Wilson had a serious accident in western China in 1910. When crossing a steep mountain slope his party became involved in a stone avalanche and Wilson was struck by a stone, which broke his right leg in two places. He had to be carried to Chengtu, a three days' journey, before medical help was available. It was three months before he was able to get about on crutches and during that period his leg had narrowly escaped amputation. It was during the autumn of this year that he collected (or his men for him) the seeds of the conifers of western China which are now in cultivation. When he arrived back at Boston, Mass., his leg was reset, but it always remained somewhat shorter than the left one. After working at the Arnold Arboretum for between two and three years he was sent by Professor Sargent to Japan, a fruitful journey to which we owe his volumes, *The Cherries of Japan* and *The Conifers and Taxads of Japan*. Early in 1917 he started on his sixth journey to the Far East and visited the Liukiu and Bonin Islands, Korea, Japan, and Formosa. It was during this expedition that he visited Kurume on the island of Kyushu in South Japan for the purpose of seeing a collection of some 250 varieties of azalea raised by Japanese gardeners from *Rhododendron obtusum*. He secured a selection of fifty sorts which he landed safely in the United States. The 'Wilson 50' and later additions are now known as 'Kurume' azaleas.

On his return in 1919 he was appointed assistant director of the Arnold Arboretum under Professor Sargent and in July of the following year started on a world-wide tour in the interests of that institution to England, France, Australia, New Zealand, Singapore, India, Ceylon, E. and S. Africa. On the death of Professor Sargent in 1927 he was appointed to the charge of the Arnold Arboretum under the title of 'Keeper'. This title struck American people as quaint and more suggestive of golf courses, but I believe Wilson chose it because of its English associations. His love for the country of his birth was deep and unfailing, its citizenship he never relinquished, and to it I know he had hoped eventually to return. He and his wife were both killed in a motor accident near Worcester, Mass., on 5th October 1930, a pathetic end to the career of one of the greatest of plant collectors. Of trees and shrubs adapted for the average climate of Great Britain he has introduced far more than any other collector, chiefly because it was his fortune to work in areas cooler and considerably farther to the north than those traversed by the more notable of his contemporaries.

Reginald Farrer will live in horticultural history more as a writer than as a collector. He went to Kansu, a province in N. China, in 1914–15, accompanied by W. Purdom, who had already visited the same province in 1909 in the interests of Messrs Veitch and the Arnold Arboretum. Kansu is a poor field for the plant collector compared with the provinces of Hupeh, Szechwan, or Yunnan, and Farrer found very little that was new and of garden value to add to our tree and shrub collections. But *Buddleia alternifolia* alone should keep its introducer's memory alive; and *Viburnum farreri* (*fragrans*), the winter-flowering shrub, although previously introduced by Purdom, owes its present popularity to Farrer's abundant seed and to his praise of its beauty. *Potentilla fruticosa* var. *farreri*, with its finely cut foliage and abundance of small, deep golden-yellow blossom, is a distinct and charming addition to the several forms of this shrub.

In 1919 he went to Upper Burma accompanied by **E. H. M. Cox,** and entered, broadly speaking, the same field in which, before and after him, Forrest and Kingdon Ward worked. He introduced seeds of various barberries, *Magnolia rostrata* and numerous rhododendrons, but his outstanding introduction was the 'coffin' juniper,

Juniperus recurva var. *coxii*. Farrer succumbed to an illness of a diphtheritic nature in Upper Burma on 17th October 1920. His work as a collector was not equal to that of most of his contemporaries, but as a versatile, picturesque, and descriptive writer with an inexhaustible supply of adjectives at his command, always apt and vivid, he was unrivalled and will long be remembered. His home was at Ingleborough in west Yorkshire.

William Purdom, Farrer's friend and companion in Kansu, was born at Heversham in Westmorland on 10th April 1880. He trained at Kew, and went to Kansu, Shensi and Shansi in 1909, collecting for Messrs Veitch and the Arnold Arboretum. He apparently struck a poor section of that region and the results of the journey were meagre. He introduced *Viburnum farreri*, but in the absence of any special praise of it by him it remained practically unknown and not even named until Farrer appeared on the scene. As already stated, he accompanied Farrer on the 1914–15 expedition to Kansu. Their relations appear to have been of the happiest, and Farrer, in dedicating his *Eaves of the World* to 'My dear Bill', describes him as 'an absolutely perfect friend and helper, through whom alone these odysseys were made possible and pleasant'. Purdom died at Peking, 7th November 1921.

Frank N. Meyer, for nearly ten years collector and explorer for the United States Department of Agriculture in China, Siberia, and Turkestan, was primarily concerned with the introduction of trees, shrubs, and herbs of economic value, rather than with purely ornamental plants. Nevertheless he collected large numbers of the latter, but few new species were among them. He introduced to America many varieties of the Citrus tribe, kakees and other fruit-trees suitable for the southern United States and California. A spruce and a rhamnus are named after him, also the dwarf lilac, *Syringa meyeri*, described in the following pages, a very interesting and ornamental shrub. He died in China in 1918, his body being found in the river Yangtse Kiang bearing no indication of the cause of his death.

George Forrest was born at Falkirk in March 1873. He died of heart failure at Tengyueh on 5th January 1932, just as he had, practically, completed his seventh and what he had intended should be his last journey. His name will long live as one of the greatest of plant collectors, co-equal with such men as Wilson, Fortune, and Douglas. As a discoverer and introducer of rhododendrons he

stands supreme, making even the work of such pioneers as J. D.
Hooker and Wilson appear comparatively insignificant in regard to
that particular genus. There is no doubt that too many species have
been made out of his collections, but with even the most drastic
reduction they will still be numbered by hundreds. His work enlarged our conception of the genus *Rhododendron* to an amazing
degree, bringing as it did into the ken of botanical science such
extreme types as R. *giganteum*, a tree 80 ft high, R. *forrestii* var.
repens, a creeping plant a few inches high, R. *sinogrande*, with leaves
over 2 ft long and over 1 ft wide, and R. *radicans,* with leaves ½ in.
or less in length. He collected generally in regions considerably
warmer and to the south of Wilson's country, and the greater proportion of his introductions will only be seen at their best in the
south and west.

Unlike Wilson, Farrer, and Kingdon Ward, Forrest never wrote
much. Words perhaps did not come easily to him, but I think he
looked forward after his explorations were over to writing up some
of his experiences. Of pure adventure, especially in his early journeys,
he had his share, as anyone may judge who reads his two articles in
the *Gardeners' Chronicle* for 21st and 28th May 1910. There he gives
an account of how, on the borders of Tibet and China, he was
hunted for eight days by bloodthirsty bands of Lamas, hiding by
day and trying to find a way out of the toils by night. Eventually,
after some hairbreadth escapes, he won free to the Chinese city of
Talifu. Two French missionaries with whom he had set out were
caught, and after being horribly mutilated were disembowelled and
beheaded.

The dates of Forrest's expeditions were as follows: 1904–7,
1910–11, 1912–14, 1917–19, 1921–2, 1924–5, 1930–2. The first of
these was undertaken in the interests of Mr A. K. Bulley; the remainder chiefly organised and financed by amateurs and the Royal
Horticultural Society.

Frank Kingdon Ward, the most notable and experienced of more
recent collectors, was born at Manchester in 1885 and educated at
St Paul's School and Christ's College, Cambridge, where he gradu-
ated in 1907. In 1909–10 he commenced his travels in the Far
East by accompanying the Bedford (Natural History Museum)
expedition across China. During the years 1911 and 1913 he collected
for Mr A. K. Bulley in Szechwan and Yunnan, and during 1914 in
Upper Burma. From 1914 to 1919 he was in the army, attaining there

the rank of captain. After his demobilisation and up to 1932 he was almost continuously engaged in exploring and collecting in Upper Burma, S.W. China, and Tibet, or writing accounts of his adventures and discoveries. The latter are embodied in a series of fascinating volumes—the first, *The Land of the Blue Poppy*, published in 1913; the last, *Pilgrimage for Plants*, published posthumously in 1960. As a purely geographical explorer and apart from his work as a plant collector, Kingdon Ward holds an honoured place. His books, *In Farthest Burma* (1921), *From China to Hkamti Long* (1924), *The Mystery Rivers of Tibet* (1923), and *The Riddle of the Tsangpo Gorges* (1926) deal more especially with this phase of his career. In recognition of his contributions to geographical knowledge he was awarded the Founder's Medal by the Royal Geographical Society in 1930. For over fifty years Kingdon Ward was a vigorous and indomitable collector mostly in the Sino-Himalayan regions. In all he undertook about twenty-five expeditions and introduced many first-class plants into cultivation. He was particularly interested in *Rhododendron* and some of his more notable introductions are R. *magnificum*, R. *pemakoense*, R. *rex*, and R. *wardii*. As a plant collector he was much esteemed for the fine germinating quality of the seeds he sent home, his care in selecting the best forms, and for the admirable field notes he made, notes which not only indicate the probable garden value of the plants but are also of great assistance to the botanist. He died in 1958.

Harold F. Comber, who has provided some relief from the monotony of Chinese expeditions during the present century by making two journeys to the southern hemisphere, was born in 1897 at Nymans, Sussex, where his father was head gardener. After a training in private gardens and in the Botanic Garden, Edinburgh, he was engaged in 1925 by a syndicate organised by the **Hon. H. D. Mc-Laren** (the late **Lord Aberconway**) to visit the Andes of Chile and the Argentine. He returned in 1927 after successfully carrying on the work of Lobb and Pearce. Chile does not provide an abounding field for the collector of trees and shrubs hardy enough to succeed in our average climate, but Comber found a number of valuable plants not previously established in cultivation. Amongst them are a beautiful *Fabiana* and some fine barberries, such as *Berberis comberi*, *linearifolia*, × *lologensis*, *chillanensis*, and *montana*. In 1929–30 he visited Tasmania in the interests of a body of subscribers. Of course, the climate of this island is too mild for it to be expected that many plants genuinely hardy in the British Isles are likely thence to come. But there are many that would succeed in the southern and western counties, and to these Comber has made many valuable additions. He appears always to have collected at as high altitudes as possible, an important factor in regard to hardiness which collectors in mountainous countries have often ignored. Amongst the most notable of his introductions are the coloured forms of *Olearia phlogopappa* (syn. *O. gunniana*). Comber died in the U.S.A. in 1969.

Joseph Francis Charles Rock, whose name as a prolific collector of rhododendron seed has been prominent in this country for many years, was a native of Vienna, where he was born January 1884. From 1908 to 1919 he lived in Hawaii, first as a botanist to the Hawaiian Board of Agriculture and Forestry, later to the University of Hawaii. In 1920 he became agricultural explorer to the U.S. Department of Agriculture; in 1923–4 and again in 1927–30 he led the Chinese-Tibetan expeditions of the National Geographic Society of the United States, and in 1924–7 a botanical and zoological expedition organised by Harvard University to the same regions. For the next thirty years he was active under various auspices in exploration in western China, amassing large collections of herbarium specimens and seeds of ornamental plants for introduction into the Western World. He was forced to leave China where he had settled and in 1955 returned to Hawaii, where he died in December 1962. Rock was an outstanding linguist. Besides his native German he was fluent in English, Italian, French, Spanish, Tibetan, Greek, and various indigenous languages of western China. He had also a working knowledge of Arabic which he acquired during travels in Egypt as a boy in company with his father.

R. E. Cooper, a native of Kingston-on-Thames, where he was born in 1890, was notable for his work in north-eastern India and especially in Bhutan. In the latter country no one had worked so systematically or for so long since the memorable journeys of Thomas J. Booth in 1852, which resulted in the introduction to our gardens of *Rhododendron hookeri* and *R. nuttallii* and other notable plants. Cooper commenced his career as a collector in 1913 when he was sent to the Eastern Himalaya by A. K. Bulley. His first year was spent in Sikkim; the two following years—1914 and 1915—in Bhutan. The year 1916 was occupied in exploring the Kulu Valley north of Simla and farther northwards in Lahoul and Ladak. He then joined the army and remained in war service until 1919. In 1921 he was appointed superintendent of the Botanic Garden at Maymyo, Burma; in 1930 he joined the staff of the Edinburgh Botanic Garden and, on the death of L. B. Stewart in 1934, was appointed curator, a post which he held until 1950. In recognition of his purely geographical work he was awarded the Diploma of Fellowship by the Royal Scottish Geographical Society in December 1931 and in 1942 he was elected to the Fellowship of the Royal Society of Edinburgh. He died in 1962.

Cooper found altogether over forty species of rhododendron on his journeys, the majority of which had originally been discovered by Hooker and other travellers. Several of them, however, had dropped out of cultivation and their re-introduction was greatly appreciated. Of many other species, he discovered variations hitherto unknown, notable amongst them being a yellow-flowered *Rhododendron cinnabarinum*. Of quite new species, science owes to his labours the following: *argipeplum, brachysiphon, epapillatum, papillatum, polyandrum*, and *rhabdotum*. R. *cooperi*, named in his honour by Sir Isaac Bayley Balfour, has since been sunk under *camelliaeflorum*. Amongst other valuable plants he introduced, both woody and herbaceous, was *Viburnum grandiflorum*, the Himalayan ally of the popular *V. farreri* from N.W. China, also a cotoneaster which bears his name.

Notable recent collectors who have enriched our gardens from the Sino-Himalaya are **F. Ludlow** and **George Sherriff**, who in 1933 undertook the first of a series of expeditions in the Himalaya including south-eastern Tibet. They were accompanied in 1938 by **George Taylor**, in 1946–7 by **Henry Elliot**, and in 1949 by **J. H. Hicks**. On these journeys over a thousand gatherings of rhododendron, including a number of new species, were made, besides other woody plants, and many have become established in this country. Sherriff died in 1967.

A few new species of woody plants have been introduced by expeditions to the Himalaya since 1949, but unfortunately the main collecting grounds in the Sino-Himalayan region are now closed to plant hunters from the West.

PART TWO

CULTIVATION

CHAPTER I

PROPAGATION

The raising of new stocks of plants, especially trees and shrubs, is one of the most fascinating and satisfying of the gardening arts. With scientific aids and modern techniques, scope has widened considerably. There is increased interest and generally there are few subjects which cannot be propagated vegetatively. Even so, seeds where obtainable, remain the chief means of raising in quantity stocks of a species having fixed hereditary characters, and also certain forms of them which are known to breed true to type.

There are really three methods by which trees and shrubs may be increased: 1, by seeds, which is Nature's way; 2, by taking away part of a plant and enabling it to exist separately, i.e. by division, layers, and cuttings of either stem or root; 3, by taking part of one plant and joining it to another already possessing a root system of its own, i.e. by grafting or budding.

The raising of new healthy trees is undoubtedly best accomplished with but few exceptions by means of seeds, and especially is this the case for conifers, timber trees, and long-lived trees generally. For shrubs that have a low-branching system and renew themselves continually by new basal growth, cuttings and layers in most instances are quite as good. Seeds cannot be relied on to perpetuate varieties that have originated from branch sports, such as those with coloured or abnormally shaped leaves; and only partially can they be relied on to reproduce aberrant forms of seedling origin like fastigiate or weeping trees, dwarfs, and such-like. Seeds from such trees usually reproduce few or perhaps none of the abnormal form that bore them, the majority reverting wholly or in part to the normal type. Thus very few weeping or fastigiate varieties of trees are found in Nature. Excepting those like Lombardy poplars and willows, which may increase by pieces of branch broken off by wind, etc., and take root on the ground, they exist only as individuals. Civilised man propagates them artificially for his use and pleasure, otherwise they would disappear. On the whole, if fine, clean-grown, healthy, long-lived trees are desired they should be raised from seed. Still, there are other factors to be considered. Many foreign trees do not bear seed in this country until they are old, often not then, so other means must be employed. Plants raised from seed do not as a rule flower so soon as those which originate from cuttings or grafts. Occasionally, too, as with desert shrubs like *Calophaca wolgarica*, the root system is ill-adapted for our climate, and they are much longer-lived when grafted on plants with more adaptable roots; in the case of *Calophaca*, which belongs to the Leguminosae, use is made of *Caragana* or *Laburnum* as a stock.

SEEDS

Except where large quantities of plants are required, as is usual with forest trees, hawthorn, holly, and such-like, it is not advisable to sow seeds of trees and shrubs in the open ground. They are much more under control, germination is quicker and more certain, if they are sown in boxes or pots in a cold frame or slightly heated house. If the quantity justifies it, they may be sown in prepared soil on the floor of a frame. Where no convenience of this sort exists the protection afforded by a cloche, or handlight, in the open ground is a considerable advantage.

Soil and Drainage. The soil in which seeds are sown should be fine where it is in contact with the seed, and it should be thoroughly well drained. If a pot is used, at least one-third of its depth should be filled with crocks or other coarse material as drainage. For fine seeds like rhododendron, the pot may be at least half filled. Above the crocks leaves or loam fibre is placed to prevent the fine particles of soil running amongst them. Finally, the pot is nearly filled with a light compost of sifted loam, peat or leafsoil, and sand and made moderately firm. In the case of peat-loving plants like the heath family, loam is not required. For shallow pans or boxes less drainage is of course required, but except for large seeds a depth of 2 to 3 in. of soil will suffice.

A common mistake is that of sowing seed too thickly. Small seeds of dust-like nature, such as *Rhododendron,* should be sown on the surface of the soil. A little fine sand or soil mixed with the seeds will aid even distribution. Young seedlings standing too closely together are apt to become drawn up and weakly, and there is a tendency for them to damp-off and decay. Another frequent mistake is that of sowing seeds too deeply. A good old gardeners' rule is that a seed should *not be buried more than its own depth*. Thus a walnut should be buried an inch deep, whilst minute seeds must not be covered at all, or only receive a sprinkling of fine sand.

Moisture. A most important requisite for the perfect germination of seeds is the provision of a uniform and proper degree of moisture in the soil and in the atmosphere. There is nothing more harmful to minute seedlings than rapid fluctuations between dryness and saturation. Large robust seeds like acorns or most of the pea family are not so susceptible as the more minute and delicate ones. The ingenuity of the cultivator may be exercised to secure as uniform a condition of moisture as possible. Thus newly sown seeds should be heavily shaded to prevent rapid drying out of the soil under the influence of hot sun. Fresh supplies of water must be given, but for minute seeds it should be applied almost in the form of spray, or by partly immersing the receptacle in a container of water and allowing moisture to rise by capillary attraction. The slight disturbance of the minute plant by careless watering, repeatedly done, before the radicle (or primary root) has had time to fix itself firmly, causes many to perish. In the case of minute seeds it is best to water the soil thoroughly before sowing. If they are placed in a close atmosphere and shaded, germination may take place before watering becomes again necessary. It need scarcely be said that as soon as germination takes place light becomes essential.

Whilst the majority of seeds do not, perhaps, require the amount of care indicated above, I have thought it worth while to mention the conditions most favourable to germination. For new and valuable plants any amount of attention will be repaid, and it will not be thrown away on commoner subjects.

It should be mentioned that a gentle moist heat will often stimulate seeds of even very hardy plants into germination that might otherwise fail. This has repeatedly been seen in the case of seeds that have been sent long distances, and become dried by exposure to various influences *en route*. Old seeds, except those of an oily nature, can benefit in the same way.

The length of time it takes a seed to germinate is dependent on many circumstances. Newly gathered seed germinates more quickly than old, and, as has just been intimated, warmth accelerates that process.

Storage of Seeds. Correct storage of seeds following harvesting or purchase is most essential, and this is very important if they cannot be sown immediately, or if time and conditions are unsuitable.

Although it may vary with different genera and species, the viability of seeds is often influenced by storage, and with many, storage for any length of time in a dry state can be definitely harmful. The dormant state of a ripe seed is a resting stage in the life history of the plant. It is a living organism which, in most instances, is capable of immediate response and will commence to germinate when afforded suitable conditions, i.e. moisture, warmth, and suitable temperature.

It is a great mistake to subject seeds, particularly those of a fleshy or mucilaginous nature, to hot, dry storage, which is not only unsuitable but also very harmful. It should be remembered that under natural conditions, seeds as they are shed fall to the ground beneath the parent plant, or they are carried by some agency farther away, where they may commence to germinate almost at once amongst loose soil and decaying leaves. This happens with 'conkers', acorns and winged seeds of maples (*Acer*). With other seeds a period of rest is spent amongst the decaying leaves and soil, usually in a low temperature but not a dry one. With the advent of spring, increased heat and moisture, germination starts without difficulty or delay, provided the seeds are undisturbed.

A study of the behaviour of seeds under natural conditions clearly illustrates the need to avoid storage in a dry condition and high temperature. Under such conditions they lose their viability because they become too dry and shrivel. A cool airy place where there is an even temperature warm enough to dispel damp, but not to cause excessive dryness, will be found suitable.

The usual paper packet and also the air-tight tin is not conducive to the best results, especially for seeds of many of our trees and shrubs, and in particular, larger seeds of fleshy nature. These, like the acorns and chestnuts, should be sown as soon as possible after collection. If this is not possible or there is some reason for keeping them in a dormant state, storage in pans or trays of damp peat-moss or sand in a temperature of 35–37°F is advisable.

The storage of seeds and its effect on germination has been the subject of a good deal of research and much written matter has been published. The book *Twenty Years of Seed Research* by Lela V. Barton and William Crocker(Faber & Faber) provides much information on the importance of seed storage.

Stratification. Seeds with a hard outer covering such as holly, thorn, plum, and peach can lie dormant for twelve to eighteen months or longer. To save time, space, and trouble, such seeds will germinate more freely if given pre-sowing treatment or stratification at a low temperature. The process is quite simple and consists of mixing the seeds immediately after collection with moist sand or sandy soil in pots or boxes and standing them out-of-doors for a year or longer. Usually a position in the lee of a hedge or wall, preferably the north side, is chosen and where the receptacles will be subjected to frost and snow; the more severe the effects of such treatment the better.

After this treatment, the outer bony covering of the seeds is softened and they will germinate quite readily when sown. The usual procedure is to separate the seeds from the sand or soil by sifting, if they are to be sown in receptacles, but if sown out-of-doors in prepared seed-beds, they may be sown with the sand direct into the drills. With small seeds, it is better to separate them from the sand by washing in a fine-mesh sieve, otherwise they may be sown too deeply. Generally it is better to sow small quantities of seeds under glass in frames or a greenhouse, rather than risk complications that can occur with outdoor sowing.

All soft, fleshy seeds, like acorns and chestnuts, need to be sown as soon as they fall, or at any rate kept moist until they are sown. But as a general rule it is best to sow seeds of trees and shrubs about mid-February. By the time they have germinated the sun has acquired considerable power, and they are not likely to suffer from the effects of damp and lack of light. This applies particularly to seeds obtained from abroad in autumn; still, where doubts exist as to their vitality, a proportion may be sown as soon as received and the remainder in February.

DIVISION

This is the simplest mode of propagation, for it consists merely in separating an old plant into a number of pieces, each with more or less root attached. It is best done just as growth is recommencing in spring, and if the pieces can be separated with plenty of root attached they may be planted straight away in permanent quarters. Such shrubs as the dwarf spiraeas, *Kerria*, *Mahonia aquifolium*, *Euonymus fortunei* and all with a similar method of renewing themselves by fresh growths from the ground may be treated in this way. Bamboos are increased by division, but in their case it is best deferred until mid-May; even then they are liable to suffer and become unsightly, especially those of a close-growing habit that form hard, matted masses of root which can only be divided by chopping. In the case of valuable plants, or pieces with poor roots, a gentle bottom heat is a very useful aid. The pieces should be potted and the pots plunged in a propagating bed with gentle bottom heat in a greenhouse. Heated frames, or ordinary cold frames fitted with electric soil heating cables, can also be used.

LAYERING

Shrubs and trees with branches near the ground can almost always be increased by this method. Nature herself frequently adopts it. It consists in burying a portion of a shoot or branchlet without severing it wholly from the tree. The process is as follows: a shoot is brought to the ground and is pegged down to it at a point 6 to 18 in. from the end. The pegged part should be notched or slit lengthwise so as partially to sever it, and then be covered with sufficient earth to keep it moist. The free end of the shoot can be staked partially upright to keep it fixed. Brittle wood sometimes cannot be cut at the buried part without breaking, but some method of interrupting the flow of sap should be adopted, such as twisting the stem to damage the bark and check the flow of sap, which causes the formation of callus or healing tissue from which roots will emerge. The essentials to secure in layering are, a state of permanent moistness at the buried part, and secure fixing. Whilst the time at which layering is best done is spring, it may be performed at almost any time, but the incision of the buried part needs more care, or perhaps omitting altogether, if the plants are in full leafage. One summer is usually required for the new root system to have become sufficiently developed for the layer to be removed. It may require two for some plants, as, for instance, rhododendrons.

In establishments where little convenience for striking cuttings in heat is available, layering is a very useful and very certain means of increase. Provided the earth and the branchlet can be brought together, very few plants indeed refuse to take root. But, of course, this is often difficult or impossible.

In nurseries, where large stocks are required for sale, plants known as stools are devoted entirely to the production of shoots for layering. Dwarf shrubs, like heaths and daphnes, are often layered by merely weighting a branch to the ground by placing a stone on it.

Air Layering with Polythene. The practice of air layering is an old one; in fact it was used by the Chinese for centuries before it was introduced to Europe and also America. For many years the method was used for the propagation of certain warm greenhouse plants, where its success depended not only on the moist atmospheric conditions, but also on the rooting medium, which was generally sphagnum moss or peat, being kept constantly moist; this involved watering of the rooting medium daily and during warm weather, several times a day. The method thus became laborious and quite often ineffective, in spite of the constant attention.

With the introduction of plastic or polythene film the limitations of this form of propagation have been overcome, and today the method can be successfully employed for the propagation of certain hardy trees and shrubs out-of-doors which are not easy to propagate by usual methods. Obviously there is no point in air layering subjects which can be easily propagated by other vegetative methods.

By using polythene tubing to surround the layer and its rooting medium the need for constantly moistening the rooting media is no longer necessary, provided it is effectively sealed both above and below the layer with adhesive tape, and made air-tight. This prevents the evaporation of moisture from the moss, which will remain damp indefinitely even when the layer is exposed to the drying conditions of sun and wind.

Air layering, even with the aid of polythene, is not in the majority of instances a quick method, but it does allow shrubs and trees to be propagated without the aid of a greenhouse or propagating frame.

The best time for air layering is during April, when in most seasons the sap is flowing freely and growth is active. The actual preparation of the layer is quite simple, and with most subjects a mature one-year-old twig or shoot is selected and should, for preference, be about the thickness of an ordinary pencil. Much does, however, depend on the species or variety of shrub or tree, and subjects having firm wood are more easily worked than those with pithy wood.

The actual operation is not difficult and the making of the air layer is quite simple. With a sharp knife a longitudinal cut is made about 9 in. below the tip of the growth and starting just below a node; it should extend upwards for about 2 in. and penetrate nearly to the centre of the wood, forming a tongue. The cut surfaces are then treated with a hormone rooting powder as an inducement to quicker rooting, and the tongue of the cut should be wedged open by a small piece of wood or a twist of moss. This prevents it growing together and ensures a maximum area for callus formation. The polythene tube, which should be about 8 in. long and 4 in. wide (when flat), is then passed over the branch to extend about 3 in. below the prepared cut and the end folded and bound securely with adhesive tape, which should run on to the bare bark. Sphagnum moss, which has been moistened and chopped fairly fine, is then packed into the tube to surround the entire cut area and should extend to within 3 in. of the top. The tube is then closed by folding and binding with adhesive tape, in a similar way as the base. If correctly and carefully done, all air will be excluded and the moss will remain constantly moist.

With most trees and shrubs it is necessary to support the layer by tying it to a stake or to another nearby branch. If this is not done, there is the possibility of the layered branch being broken off during a storm or high winds.

After-treatment is practically nil, but an occasional inspection of the layer is wise in order to make sure the polythene film is unbroken and that the sealed ends are secure. Provided all is well, the moss will remain moist and roots will form from the callused cut and grow out into the moss, but the time involved will vary with the type of subject and also the season. With most trees and shrubs which respond to this form of propagation, the roots should be clearly seen through the polythene when they have penetrated the moss.

At this stage the layer can be cut from the parent plant, and the polythene tube and the moss carefully removed, and the new plant potted up in the usual way. It is wise, and usually necessary, to place it in a close frame or greenhouse to become established. When the roots are freely encircling the pot, the plant should be removed to cooler conditions in a cold frame, but planting out into the nursery or other selected position should not take place until the following spring.

Although other rooting media can be used, sphagnum moss is generally accepted as being the most suitable. Vermiculite and fibrous peat have been used but they have not proved very successful. It is essential to avoid bulky packing of the polythene tube, because it serves no purpose, and if it is too wet and heavy there is always a danger of the polythene splitting, especially during a wet season.

CUTTINGS

Next to seeds, cuttings afford the best and most important means of propagation. Although trees are, no doubt, on the whole best raised from seeds, shrubs raised from cuttings are in most cases apparently quite as healthy and long-lived as seedlings. As compared with grafting, the method has the advantage of putting them on their own roots, which obviates the sucker nuisance.

Many more trees and shrubs can be increased by cuttings than is generally supposed; for instance, elms, birches, hornbeams, apples, and cherries are amongst those that can be rooted from hard-wood cuttings. The process is with them not always a certain one, but it is still a possible one. It would, indeed, be rash to say of any exogenous tree that its increase by means of cuttings is absolutely impossible. The best, or perhaps the only possible way, must be found by experience, although old and professional propagators seem to know by intuition when is the best time, and what are the best methods of rooting cuttings of plants they have not even seen before.

A cutting differs from a layer chiefly in the fact that it is completely severed from the parent plant from the first. Theoretically the propagator's work is to keep the piece of shoot alive and fresh until it is able, by the production of its own roots, to live independently. His chief aim is to prevent undue transpiration, i.e. the loss of more moisture from its tissues than it can reabsorb. It follows, therefore, that cuttings of succulent leafy young growth, which transpire freely and are subject to early decay, must take root soon, if they are to survive. A close atmosphere for all, and a brisk bottom heat for many, is needed. But for cuttings in a leafless state, made during late autumn from ripe wood where transpiration has practically ceased, no heat at all is needed; cuttings of such subjects as willows, tamarisk, poplars, and currants, as well as very many more, take root in the open ground. As a general principle it may be stated that the younger and softer cuttings of hardy trees and shrubs are, the more essential a close atmosphere and bottom heat become. As the growths from which cuttings are made harden and become more woody with the advancing season, the emission of roots becomes, in general, slower. Whether it is best to take cuttings young, medium, or old, in the case of any given plant, depends on its nature. It is a matter on which experience is the only sure guide, and is dealt with in the descriptive part of this work, usually under the notice of the genus.

For the vast majority of the plants dealt with in the present work that are habitually increased by cuttings, it will be found that the most suitable time to make them is from mid-July to the end of August. That is the busy time of the hardy tree and shrub propagator who relies on cuttings. The growths of the year have by then become moderately firm and woody; they are old enough and solid enough to retain their vitality sufficiently, and yet not so old as to have become hard and hide-bound. The character of the wood at a given date varies of course with the season; in hot summers it is ready sooner.

With shrubs and trees which are known to be difficult to root, it is wise to experiment with cuttings in various stages of development. It must be remembered that the stages of growth and its development will vary from year to year, and therefore hard and fast rules regarding the actual time of insertion of soft-wood or semi-ripe cuttings cannot be made. Experience must be the deciding factor.

Selection. The importance of propagating cuttings from single plant selections (*clones*) cannot be emphasised too strongly. It is only by rigid control of selected or known stocks and propagating from them, that the best form of a plant is perpetuated. This applies particularly to cultivars, or any plant of outstanding form or habit.

Making the Cutting. The expert propagator is very careful in selecting the growths from which he proposes to make his cuttings, especially leaf-bearing ones. He avoids very strong, vigorous, leading or 'sappy' shoots, but usually prefers the short side twigs, a few inches long, which he can remove with a slight 'heel' of the previous year's wood attached at the base. This 'heel' of older wood is a valuable factor, particularly for subjects with hollow or pithy stems, and cuttings possessing it will root when those without it fail. Its firmer tissues prevent decay at the base. In its absence the base of a cutting should be just below a joint. The average leafy cutting is from 2 to 4 in. long, about one-third of which is inserted in the soil. Cuttings of heaths and such-like shrubs with very fine branchlets are made 1 to 1½ in. long. If the cutting be too long, the succulent top rather than the heel should be cut away. With cuttings that have inconveniently large leaves, it is a good plan to clip off

half each leaf, and of course the whole of the leaves at the base of the
cutting must be cut cleanly away. A sharp knife is an absolute necessity for making cuttings; it should be of almost razor-like keenness,
so that all the material can be cut cleanly away and not bruised. For
making small cuttings a safety-razor blade can be conveniently used.

In preparing a compost for cuttings it is just as necessary as it is
with seeds to secure good drainage; therefore, if pots, pans or boxes
are used, they should be drained as advised for seeds. All the soil as
far as the cuttings descend (and if pots are used it need not go very
much deeper) should be finely sifted. For most shrubs two parts
clean silver sand to one of sifted loam will be suitable. If the plants
are peat-lovers, the sand may be increased to a proportion of three
parts to one of peat. Other rooting media can be used and these
include various grades of sands, particularly Cornish sand, Bedfordshire silver sand, and also vermiculite and powdered volcanic rock.
Most cuttings will root freely in these substances, but they must be
removed as soon as they are well rooted and potted or boxed into a
compost containing ample nourishment. When placing the cutting
in the soil the base of the cutting must settle firmly on the bottom of
the hole made for it. It should not be suspended so that a hollow
exists beneath its base. When the cuttings are firmly inserted they
should be well watered and then, if in receptacles, put in the propagating case.

Bell-glasses, cloches, and handlights are extremely useful for
placing over cuttings, either under glass or in open beds. By their
aid much valuable propagating may be done in the open. For this
work a sheltered shady spot should be selected; the soil should be
prepared in the proportions advised, rather deeper than the cuttings
descend, and when inserted the cuttings should be covered by the
glass, the chief use of which is to keep a permanently moist, still air
and prevent undue loss of moisture. Where no other convenience
exists this method may be tried for any hardy shrub. For many it may
fail, but for the various heaths, brooms, double-flowered gorse,
rosemary, lavender, and numerous others, it is the best method
available. Cuttings made in September and October usually form a
callus during the winter, and take root the following spring.

Most species of *Ampelopsis* and *Vitis*, including the common
grape-vine, can be propagated in spring by single buds, or 'eyes', as
they are usually termed. Healthy buds from the most vigorous part
of the previous year's shoot are selected, and are cut with about half

an inch of wood each side of the bud. The pieces are usually made boat-shaped, i.e. with a sloping cut at each side, the cuts approaching each other on the under side. They are best placed singly in 3-in. pots and pressed into soil and left with only the tip of the bud exposed. Bottom heat is needed.

Root-cuttings. A considerable number of hardy trees and shrubs can be increased by cutting up the root into pieces and planting them in soil. They usually produce leafy shoots more quickly and surely when given bottom heat. The sumachs (*Rhus*), *Xanthoceras sorbifolia*, mulberry, and all those that naturally produce root-suckers like elms, *Robinia*, etc., may be propagated in this way. When other means fail, it is worth trying for any plant that produces fairly thick fleshy roots. The pieces are usually made about 3 in. long and should be inserted with that part of the root uppermost which was nearest the stem. They ought not to be less than $\frac{1}{6}$ in. thick.

The Paris Frame. There is a once-favoured system of propagation without heat which may still prove useful in gardens too small to justify the erection of the ordinary outfit of the propagator (bottom heat, etc.). This is known as the 'Paris frame', the method having come to us from France. An ordinary one- or two-light frame is placed in an open spot and filled to within 9 to 12 in. of the glass with drainage and a mixture of very sandy soil. In this the cuttings are inserted on the ordinary plan after being made in the usual way. But their after-treatment is radically different. The frame is never shaded, no matter how hot the sun may be, and it is never ventilated except when watered, which it must be once every hour during hot sunshine or even oftener during the fiercest heat. These are the three essentials: no shade, no ventilation, continual watering during bright sunshine. The last, of course, implies the need of drainage. Some striking successes have been achieved by this system, especially among those plants ordinarily needing fire-heat to increase by cuttings. Although the watering demands constant attention in hot sunny weather, the plan on the whole is very cheap, convenient and useful. Some practitioners use pure sand for a rooting medium.

Mist Propagation. A moist atmosphere within a propagation house or frame has always been recognised as essential to keep young leafy soft-wood cuttings fresh and in a turgid condition.

To maintain such a condition in the past it was necessary to syringe frequently and damp over the cuttings and the rooting media in which they were inserted. To reduce transpiration, heavy shading of the glass was adopted, also double glass lights, or one frame within another with an air space between them. Bell-jars or cloches were used to cover completely small batches of cuttings.

These aids are now something of the past, because with the aid of modern techniques, the laborious part of maintaining the correct environment has been removed, and with the installation of electrical equipment, automatic and controlled spraying, known as 'intermittent mist', can be maintained and will operate throughout the day and night. The need for the closed frame and its attendant glass lights is no longer necessary because under mist conditions the cuttings are inserted in open beds or cases in a greenhouse or frame. Although cuttings, particularly small batches, can be inserted in receptacles (boxes, pans, or pots) there is really no need for them and generally it is the practice to insert them direct into the propagating bed.

It is not intended nor considered necessary to discuss at length the actual layout and installation of a mist unit, because information on the various systems is available in leaflet and book form and readily obtainable. A unit may consist of a number of vertical or horizontal spray nozzles or jets, arranged over an open propagating bench having a brick or wooden surround 8 in. deep, to contain the drainage material and propagating media. The unit or system is wired and connected to the electric supply and also to a water supply. Alternatively a rainwater supply can be used, but an auxiliary electric pump is necessary to supply water at the required pressure. Control of the mist can be achieved by a number of devices, but the one most generally in use is known as an 'artificial leaf' or 'hydrostat'. This in no way resembles a plant leaf, and in its various forms consists of two electrodes set a short distance apart in an ebonite block having a flat surface.

The 'leaf' is placed in an upright position amongst the cuttings and in a convenient spot between the spray nozzles. Its purpose is to control the frequency of the intermittent mist spray and it does so in the following way:

When sufficient moisture has collected on the flat surface of the 'leaf' to form an electrical contact between the two electrodes, a switch is operated to close a solenoid valve, which shuts off the mist spray from the nozzles. As the moisture evaporates from the surface of the artificial leaf, contact is broken between the electrodes and this causes a relay valve to open, and the mist is turned on and will continue to operate until sufficient moisture is collected on the 'leaf' and contact between the electrodes is again established to close the relay valve and turn off the supply of water to the mist-spray nozzles. Thus the cuttings are kept constantly moist and the conditions within the house are never dry.

Good drainage is essential and it is most important that the rooting medium should not become water-logged. To prevent this, benches or beds should have drainage holes, and the base should be covered with a 3–4 in. layer of coarse material, such as washed shingle. Above this a layer of porous rooting medium, 3–4 in. thick, is provided in which the cuttings are inserted.

Although quite a variety of materials have been tried and used as rooting media, equal parts sharp sand and granulated peat have been found suitable, and most cuttings of trees and shrubs will root freely in it. Various grades of clean sand have been used with good results, including ordinary sharp river sand, Cornish sand, and Bedfordshire silver sand. Vermiculite, ground pumice, and also Perlite, are other materials which have been used either alone or mixed with sand or peat.

The water supply is important and it is essential that it should be clean, because sediment or other foreign matter will not allow correct seating of the solenoid valve, and will block the spray nozzles and generally clog the entire system.

Hard water will also cause trouble, and can cover the leaves of the cuttings with a calcareous deposit, which prevents the normal functions of the leaves. Such a condition is particularly harmful to many of our choice shrubs and, in particular, to members of the Ericaceae. For these and most other subjects, rainwater is preferable, and it does give better results. The use of rainwater from storage supply tanks does, however, involve the installation of an electric pressure pump to supply the mist unit and provide adequate spray from the nozzles.

In addition to normal heating of the house or frame, bottom heat supplied by low-voltage soil-warming cables, placed below the rooting medium, is generally considered essential and particularly for certain types and varieties of cuttings, also for winter propagation. Slow rooting and poor results may be attributed to the temperature of the rooting medium being too low. This has been noticeable with cuttings of the Ericaceae and in particular certain rhododendrons. Generally a soil temperature of 70–75°F is to be recommended. Overheating is avoided by the use of rod-type thermostatic control.

Although the rooting of cuttings under mist is much quicker and easier, the establishment of the rooted cuttings after they are potted can be a problem. It is the interim period of gradual inurement to drier and more airy conditions that is difficult. To overcome this, there is a system of controlled intermittent mist provided by a weaning unit, which can be set to reduce the frequency of the mist, and also to have the nozzles operating only during the day. By gradually lengthening the time between the 'on' mist periods, young plants are accustomed to drier and cooler conditions.

Use of polythene-covered frames or tents is also adopted to inure newly potted cuttings gradually to normal conditions. These structures can easily be made and they need not be large. It is obvious that the period of treatment depends largely on the subject and can vary considerably. Soft cuttings need more careful handling than do woody cuttings; also the time of year and the length of day are influencing factors.

As a general rule, young plants raised from cuttings under mist are established singly in pots, and grown on in them for some months in frames, or they are plunged in sheltered outdoor beds prior to planting out into nursery quarters. With most subjects propagated during the spring and summer, transplanting to outdoor beds should be delayed until the following spring.

Growth Substance Preparations. Scientific research has shown that plant growth and development is partly controlled by hormones. They are very active substances produced in the plant itself.

Research on the subject of plant hormones has resulted in the discovery of chemically related substances which have a similar influence on plant growth and development. These substances can be produced synthetically and they are widely used to stimulate root production and to promote more rapid and easier rooting of cuttings.

In addition to their use for the treatment of cuttings, such synthetic growth substances are also used for treating the partially cut stems of woody plants during the process of layering, particularly the method known as air layering.

Plant growth substances

The chemicals mainly used for the treatment of cuttings to promote root development are: gamma (indole 3-) butyric acid, indole-3-

acetic acid, and 2-naphthoxyacetic acid. Generally, the first two are used for the treatment of soft-wood and half-ripe-wood cuttings at strengths from 10 to 25 parts per million and 30 to 60 parts per million. For ripe-wood cuttings (hard-wood cuttings) 60 to 200 parts per million can be used. 2-Naphthoxyacetic acid is used in lower concentrations—from 2 to 25 parts per million according to the texture of the wood; the lowest concentration being for soft-wood cuttings.

Hormone-type growth substances under proprietary names are available in liquid or powder form and may be obtained from horticultural sundriesmen. They are available in three grades (Nos. 1, 2, and 3) for use on soft-wood, half-ripe, and ripe-wood cuttings respectively. They should be used strictly in accordance with the manufacturer's directions.

The pure growth substances mentioned above may be obtained from firms which supply chemicals for laboratory use, if it is desired to make up one's own solutions of a given strength.

Treatment of cuttings

After preparing in the usual way by trimming with a sharp knife or razor blade, the cuttings are treated by dipping the cut ends into a powder (pharmaceutical talc) containing the growth substances, after which they are immediately inserted in the propagating medium.

If treated with a growth substance in solution the cut ends and the lower part of the stems are immersed in the liquid for a period of 12 to 24 hours. After treatment the cuttings are washed in clean water before inserting them in the propagating bed or receptacles.

Generally the results obtained by the treatment of cuttings of all types with growth substances are good, but they may vary according to the subject. With certain trees and shrubs, and in particular magnolias and rhododendrons, the results, although interesting, can be disappointing. Much depends on conditions, and the temperature in particular should not be allowed to fluctuate. Bottom heat or bed temperatures are most important and the optimum should be 70–72°F. A higher temperature is not necessarily conducive to quicker rooting or better results; in fact it can be responsible for excessive callus formation and failure to produce active roots.

Growth-substance–Fungicide Treatment. Mixing an organic fungicide with a growth substance has been successfully used as a form of sterilisation of soft or semi-ripe cuttings to eliminate the danger of base-rotting of the cutting. Several proprietary fungicides have been used. In recent years 'Captan' and a growth substance used in equal parts have given good results with some types of cutting which have not previously responded to 'hormone' treatment alone, or which have proved to be shy or slow in rooting. The fungicide can be used in powder form and mixed with the growth substance. Alternatively, the cuttings can be treated by the growth-substance solution for 12–24 hours, then washed in clean water and finally dipped in the 'Captan' powder.

The combined growth substance and fungicide treatment of cuttings is particularly helpful with cuttings which have a susceptibility to damping-off or rotting at the base. With certain evergreen shrubs and trees, and in particular conifers and rhododendrons, the sterilisation with a fungicide in addition to growth-substance treatment has shown some spectacular results.

GRAFTING

Natural grafting or the growing together of stems or branches, is a common occurrence with quite a number of our native trees, shrubs, and climbers. It is frequently found on such trees as the common elm, beech, ash, and maples, also various conifers. It is common in the ivy, where the union or fusion is brought about by compression, when one branch grows over another. Similar examples can be found amongst cultivated trees and shrubs, and the growing together of the stems of the climbing hydrangea is an example.

The practice or art of grafting is therefore not necessarily a means of propagation created by man, although the various methods by which the operation can be achieved demand considerable skill and practice. Undoubtedly some of the methods have been made more elaborate than is really necessary. Grafting as a gardening art has in the past been somewhat of a jealously guarded secret amongst professional propagators; there being a reluctance to divulge the finer principles of the practice.

In medieval times it was the most venerated of all the operations common to horticulture and the most cherished of the mysteries of the craft. The late Mr F. W. Burbidge made the famous observation that it is 'always a makeshift, very often a fraud'. A certain latitude must be accorded to coiners of epigrams, but there is no doubt grafting has been much too commonly practised by nurserymen. The latter part of Mr Burbidge's statement no one can dispute. The grafting of cotoneasters on common hawthorn, of phillyreas on privet, and of choice willows on common sallow, can only fittingly be described as a 'fraud'. It is unnecessary, because in each case the plants are easily obtained from cuttings; it weakens rather than improves their vigour, and suckers from the stock are an endless bother and worry. Numerous other instances might be given.

Not always, however, is grafting a 'makeshift'. I have already instanced *Calophaca wolgarica* as a shrub difficult to keep alive on its own roots; to it may be added *Caragana jubata* and *Halimodendron argenteum*. These shrubs inhabit dry regions with great winter cold, and their roots appear unable to thrive under the wet, comparatively warm conditions of our winters, at least in ordinary positions. Consequently they are grafted on laburnum or *Caragana arborescens*, which labour under no such disability. *Cytisus scoparius* 'Andreanus' again, and other varieties of common broom that do not come true from seed, are often short-lived when raised from cuttings, due to the formation of an imperfect callus at the base, which leaves the centre of the stem not entirely sealed over and subject to decay. In their case, grafting low down on young seedling laburnums has no disadvantages that I am aware of. In the case of trees and shrubs which do not produce seed in this country and cannot readily be increased by cuttings or layers, grafting has to be resorted to. In very many instances grafted trees thrive well and are long-lived, although not so much so as seedlings. I know grafted oaks, for instance, that must be 100 years old, in perfect health and vigour. There is nothing to be said against the grafting of such trees as weeping beech, weeping ash, fastigiate oaks, or, indeed, any garden form that does not reproduce itself by seed, if it be done on their respective types. The identical nature of stock and scion makes a perfect union possible. On the whole, it may be said that grafting, with the allied processes of inarching and budding, is often a valuable, sometimes an indispensable, resource. Attempts should always be made to get a tree or shrub on its own roots first; it is when those fail that grafting should be resorted to.

There are various modes of grafting, but they all have one principle in common. This is that the inner bark (or cambium) of stock and that of scion should be placed in contact. Roughly speaking, the stem of an exogenous plant consists of four parts: in the centre is the pith, then comes the wood, then the cambium, lastly the true bark. So far as grafting (also the formation of roots in cuttings) is concerned, the whole matter centres in the cambium, which is composed of active growing or formative cells. The most perfect grafting is where the cut surfaces of stock and scion are so arranged that the greatest amount of each set of cambium is brought in contact with the other, and kept there until a union is formed. The other parts do not matter.

It is not appropriate here to discuss the various methods of grafting. When once the underlying principle is understood the success of the operation is dependent as much on practice and deftness of hand as anything. Professional propagators in nurseries have a very small percentage of failures compared with the fumbling beginner. The operation is really delicate joinery. What is termed 'whip-grafting' is the simplest and commonest method; in this a long slanting cut is made on the stock, a similar one is then made on the scion; the two cut surfaces are then placed together, taking care that the inner barks, on both sides if possible, but certainly on one, are coincident. In this position the two are firmly tied together with bast and the whole is covered with a grafting wax or bitumen seal to keep the uniting parts air-tight. Scions are normally 2 to 6 in. long, and the chances of success are naturally greatest when they and the stock are of the same diameter.

The propagating case, mildly heated, is of great assistance in grafting. The most convenient method and the surest with rare or delicate trees and shrubs is to have the stocks brought into a moist house and grafted there. Such shrubs as *Hamamelis*, rhododendrons, and brooms are always treated that way. The stocks may be potted, or their roots laid in earth. Robust common trees like oaks, maples, and the ordinary fruit-trees can be done out-of-doors. For deciduous trees and shrubs, and, indeed, for most things, spring is the best time, usually April out-of-doors, earlier under glass. But many evergreens and some deciduous things are successfully grafted under glass in late summer and early autumn. As a general rule, for spring grafting, propagators like to have the stock slightly more forward in growth than the scions; the latter are often cut some time beforehand and laid in the ground to keep them back, and for indoor grafting the stocks are usually taken under glass some time before the operation.

On the whole, in private establishments, propagation by grafting is of much less importance and general practicability than that by cuttings or layers. There is, however, one mode of grafting that might be more generally practised and has no objections to be urged against it. This is grafting the twigs of a plant on pieces of its own root. When all other attempts at propagation have failed this has been known to succeed. Pieces of root about the thickness of the proposed scion should be selected. After the two are fitted and tied together in the ordinary way the root should be potted, leaving only that part of the scion which is above the cut exposed, then placed in gentle bottom heat. Wistarias are very readily propagated in this way.

INARCHING, OR GRAFTING BY APPROACH

This process bears the same relation to grafting that layering does to propagation by cuttings. The scion is not separated from the mother-plant until a new union has taken place with the stock or foster-mother. The essential principle is exactly the same as in grafting. The two plants are brought together—one at least has usually to be in a pot—the branches selected for union are then fitted together by taking a slice off one and a corresponding slice off the other. The inner barks have to be placed in contact, and the two tied together and finally covered with wax or bitumen just as for grafting. As already mentioned, inarching or growing together often occurs in Nature, especially in trees with crowded branches like limes. The method is too inconvenient to be generally adopted, but a quaint use is sometimes made of it to unite the tops of two young trees of the same sort at the entrance to a garden or summer-house so that they ultimately form a gothic arch.

BUDDING

Largely practised for the propagation of roses, flowering cherries, peaches, red chestnuts, etc., this process possesses the same merits and demerits as grafting. It only differs from grafting in that the scion is a single bud with a little bark attached, instead of a piece of branchlet. Budding can only be done in summer when the bark parts freely from the wood, usually in July and August. The buds selected are generally those near the base of the current year's shoot. They are cut out with a sharp knife, leaving about $\frac{1}{2}$ in. of bark above and below the bud and a narrow strip at each side of it. A little wood is usually cut out with the bud, and this must be carefully removed. The process consists in making a T-shaped incision in the year-old (or may be older) bark of the stock, lifting up the pieces at the angles of the cut with the handle of the budding knife and then pushing the newly made bud-scion under the lifted pieces. The latter are then to be laid back over the scion and the whole bound up in worsted or bast, leaving only the bud exposed. The scion-buds should lie dormant until the following spring.

The principle of budding is exactly the same as in grafting: the cambium of the bud and its attendant bark is laid flat on that of the stock. On this account the chances of union taking place are increased; but budding is the more delicate operation because of the softness and tenderness of the material dealt with. Dull days should, if possible, be selected for the work, and the quicker it is accomplished the greater success is gained.

For further detailed information on the principles and practice of grafting and budding, reference should be made to books which deal specifically with propagation.

BIBLIOGRAPHY

ADRIANCE, G. W. and BRISON, F. G., *Propagation of Horticultural Plants*. McGraw-Hill, New York and London, 1939.

GARNER, R. J., *The Grafter's Handbook*. Faber, London, revised ed. 1958.

KEMP, E. E., 'Notes on Mist-spraying Propagation Equipment', *Journal Royal Hort. Soc.* (1958), Vol. 83, pp. 427–9.

KING, E. J., *The Propagation of Plants*. Hutchinson, 4th imp. 1950.

KNIGHT, F. P., BEAN, A. G. M., and HANGER, F. E. W., 'Mist Technique Propagation', *Journal Royal Hort. Soc.* (1957), Vol. 82, pp. 458–74.

LOWNDES, D., 'Progress Report on Mist Propagation', *Gardeners' Chronicle* (1958), Vol. 143, pp. 151–60.

MAHLSTEDE, J. P. and HABER, E. S., *Plant Propagation*. John Wiley, New York and London, 3rd imp. 1962.

PROCKTER, NOËL, J., *Simple Propagation*. Collingridge, London and New York, 1960.

ROWE-DUTTON, PATRICIA, *Mist Propagation of Cuttings*. Commonwealth Agricultural Bureau, Farnham Royal, Bucks, England, 1959.

SHEAT, W. G., *Propagation of Trees, Shrubs and Conifers*. Macmillan, London and New York, 3rd imp. 1963.

SHEPHERD, F. W., *Plant Propagation*. Annual Report Rosewarne Experimental Stn (1957), pp. 56–60.

TAYLOR, G. C. and KNIGHT, F. P., *The Propagation of Trees and Shrubs*. Dulau, London, 1927.

WELLS, JAMES S., *Plant Propagation Practices*. Macmillan, New York, 1955.

WRIGHT, R. C. M., *Plant Propagation*. Ward Lock, London, 1955.

CHAPTER II

HYBRIDISING AND SELECTION

Perhaps the most fascinating of all branches of plant cultivation is the production of new forms in the garden itself. New plants of garden origin, as distinct from those newly introduced from other countries, are obtained in three ways: by branch 'sports', by selection among seed-raised plants, and by hybridisation. So far as trees and shrubs are concerned, the first process is purely accidental, the second frequently so.

(1) Branch sports are abnormal shoots that occasionally appear on adult trees or shrubs and are taken off and propagated by cuttings, buds, or grafts, or by air layering suitable shoots on the parent plants. Many of them preserve their abnormality indefinitely, but others have a strong tendency to revert to the normal type. Nearly all variegated shrubs and trees, those with deeply cut leaves, and those with double flowers originated as branch sports.

(2) The production of new forms under cultivation by selection from seed has given to gardens some of their most beautiful plants; but in regard to trees and shrubs (trees especially), the intervals between the generations are too long for the work to attract the ordinary man as a set purpose. Most new forms of seedling origin in gardens have originated as chance breaks, noticed by nurserymen or others among batches of plants raised to furnish ordinary stock. Most weeping, fastigiate, and dwarf trees have originated in this way; also purple-leaved, large- or small-leaved varieties, and forms with richer-coloured or larger flowers. Like branch sports, they must be increased by vegetative parts—cuttings, grafts, etc.—and propagated in this way they show little or no tendency to revert back to the normal type. Raised from seed they show a strong but not a uniform tendency to revert to the parent type; thus often a small proportion come true or even show the peculiarity of the form to an increased extent; a larger proportion are more or less inter-mediate; the remainder will be indistinguishable from the type. The purple beech is an illustration; comparatively few of its seedlings come quite true, they are mostly of an ineffective purplish green or coppery hue, but a number of purple beeches have been raised from

47

seed, such as 'River's Purple' or 'Swat Magret', whose purple is of a deeper shade than that of the original tree. André's broom, *Cytisus scoparius* 'Andreanus', with its maroon wing petals, is a similar instance; most of its seedling progeny are more or less reversions towards the common broom.

(3) The hybridisation of two plants of varying character is the quickest and surest means of producing new forms under cultivation. One is certain of getting something new, even if it be something in no way superior to either parent, and often the breeder can form some idea of what he is likely to obtain. We undoubtedly owe our most valuable garden shrubs to hybridisation, sometimes by human, sometimes by insect agency. The garden races of rhododendron and azalea, roses and clematis, and such beautiful plants as *Berberis* × *stenophylla, Magnolia* × *soulangiana, Ceanothus* × *burkwoodii, Cytisus* × *kewensis* and *C.* × *dallimorei, Spiraea* × *arguta, Hypericum* × *moserianum,* are a few examples of those which had their origin in the intentional or sometimes accidental crossing of species. Hybrid trees and shrubs have usually a vigour superior to that of either of their parents. As this is work which any amateur may do, it will be worth while to devote a few words to the operation of hybridising itself.

The first equipment of the operator is a true understanding of the structure of the flowers to be operated on. Ordinarily, a flower consists of sepals, petals, stamens, and pistil, which may be regarded as of two sections: first, the protective or ornamental; second, the essential or sexual parts. The first or outer section consists of calyx (or sepals) and corolla (or petals), sometimes calyx alone. They play no part in the production of seed; their purpose is to protect the sexual parts when young, and later, by displaying bright colour, to help to advertise the flower and attract the notice of insects to fertilise it. That function performed, their work is done, and they usually fall away. The real reproduction of the plant by seed is accomplished by the stamens (male) and the pistil (female). The process of fertilisation or impregnation is brought about by the transference of pollen (usually a minute yellow powder borne in sacs called anthers at the top of the stamen) to the summit of the pistil. The pistil has three parts; at the base is the ovary, a swollen body which contains the incipient seeds, or ovules; above that is a stalk of varying length called the style, bearing at the top a knob (ultimately viscid), called the stigma. It is upon the stigma that the pollen must lodge and germinate so that the male gametes travel down the pollen tube through the stigma, style and ovary to enter the ovules and so ensure fertilisation and the production of seeds.

Whilst Nature adopts various methods to prevent the fertilisation of a flower by its own pollen (often by the non-synchronous ripening of the pollen and receptivity of the stigma; often by separating the sexes on different plants), her intention is that the impregnation should be done by pollen from a flower of the same species. Thus whilst, in the higher groups, she abhors in-breeding, she also objects to mules. The hybridiser, on the other hand, has to bring about the fertilisation of the flower of one species or variety by the pollen of another of his own choosing. His aim is usually to unite in the progeny qualities in the parents severally possessed, such as hardiness or better habit with greater flower beauty. There are limits, of course, to the choice of parents, just as there are in the animal world. Species of the same genus are capable as a rule of being hybridised, although sometimes physical divergences prevent it. Occasionally, too, species of different but closely allied genera will cross-breed, e.g. × *Osmarea burkwoodii* (*Osmanthus delavayi* × *Phillyrea decora*). Progeny of the more distantly related parents are generally barren.

To secure hybridisation two essential points must be borne in mind: viz., the stigma should be in a receptive condition, and the impregnation of the flower by pollen from any other flower than the one selected by the operator must be prevented.

The stigma usually indicates its readiness to receive the pollen by becoming sticky, but it is often desirable to dust it over afresh with pollen every day for a few days after the viscidity appears.

The first thing to do in regard to the other point is to protect it from its own pollen. With plants left to themselves, Nature often secures this herself, but not always. The hybridiser leaves as little as possible to chance, and so the careful operator commences by removing the stamens from the flower he wishes to cross-fertilise, and to do this effectually he breaks open the flower before it expands naturally, and cuts away the anthers before the pollen has become ripe (i.e. dust-like). If it be a small shrub, it is often advisable to take it up and keep it in a cool airy glass-house until the impregnating process is over. The only danger then is that a stray bee or other insect may enter and deposit foreign pollen on the stigma; but if the petals be removed as well as the stamens the danger is a very remote one. All flowers other than those impregnated must be removed.

Out-of-doors, owing to wind, insects, and other disturbing agencies, the process is not so much under control. The removal of the stamens from the flower to be impregnated is again necessary before the petals expand; and to prevent a fertilisation other than the desired one, it is usual to enclose that part of the branchlet bearing the flower with white gauze or transparent paper, unless the shrub or tree is in a well-isolated position. The removal of the stamens is best accomplished by the aid of a pair of finely pointed scissors, and it is scarcely needful to say that all bruising and scratching of the pistil is to be avoided. The fertilised flower should be ticketed with a number corresponding to one in a notebook, under which particulars as to parentage, dates, etc., are entered. As soon as the flowering season is past, and consequently all danger of chance impregnation over, the gauze or paper guards must be removed.

Pollen may be kept in a viable condition for a considerable period by storing this in suitable containers in which calcium chloride is placed as a drying agent and preservative. This enables desirable crosses to be made between early and late-flowering plants of the same genus, and also allows for the pollen to be packed and despatched for use elsewhere.

The Act of Parliament passed in 1964, giving Plant Variety Rights to raisers of new plants, should provide an incentive for more planned hybridisation to be carried out.

Where trees and shrubs are raised from seeds it is important to keep a close watch on the resultant plants so that any which show characteristics superior to or different from the parents may be segregated and kept under observation. Any considered worthy of retention may then be increased by vegetative propagation.

Vegetative propagating material should always be used to perpetuate superior forms of species, as seeds cannot be relied upon to come true, particularly if these are gathered from a plant growing in close proximity to others of the same genus.

If it is decided to give selected plants a clonal name the International Code of Nomenclature for Cultivated Plants should be followed. It is published by the International Bureau for Plant Taxomony and Nomenclature, of 106 Lange Nieuwstraat, Utrecht, and is distributed in Great Britain by the Royal Horticultural

Society, Vincent Square, London S.W.1; and in the U.S.A. by the
Arnold Arboretum, Jamaica Plain 30, Mass. Names, however,
should not be applied to any plant for which a registration authority
has been established without first of all submitting the proposed
name to the registrar for approval. Particularly important to note
is the use of 'fancy' and not latinised epithets for clones. Thus, a
variant with variegated leaves noted in a batch of seedlings should
not be called 'Variegata' but given a clonal name such as 'Gold
Edge'. If, however, a latinised epithet of this kind was validly
published prior to January 1st 1959 it should be retained.

CHAPTER III

NURSERY WORK AND METHODS

Assuming that the young plant has been raised by one or other of the methods just described, a few words may be devoted to its treatment afterwards. Whether raised from seed or from cuttings, the newly rooted plants stand much too closely together to remain long without mutually damaging each other. Cuttings put in at the most usual time, i.e. July and August, do not grow much that year after the roots have formed. They are, as a rule, most conveniently rooted in pots, and in these they may usually remain undisturbed until the following spring, when they are separated and planted in rows in prepared nursery ground. Plants raised earlier in the season from seeds or soft cuttings, having a growing season in front of them, cannot be wintered in the seed- or cutting-pots. If of vigorous constitution and quick growth, they may be planted out in the nursery ground as soon as well rooted. But as by that time the season is well advanced and hot dry days occur, it is usually necessary to give them shading and special attention in watering for a week or two. With delicate, very small or particularly important plants it is better, especially in the case of seedlings, to transplant them ('prick them off' is the common term) into shallow wooden boxes of fine soil, although not so fine as for the seeds themselves. These boxes, 2 or 3 in. deep, may be purchased cheaply at most horticultural providers. Treated in this way, the baby plants may be kept in frames or even given a mild heat to ensure their quick attachment to the new soil, and loss is reduced to a minimum. Choice rhododendrons and others of the heath family can only be treated satisfactorily in this way. In taking the plants from the seed- or cutting-pots reasonable care should be taken to preserve the roots as much as possible, and, if practicable, to take a little ball of soil as well. As the plants are transferred from the seed-pot to the shallow box, they should be set regularly in rows, so that when again removed from the boxes into the open ground a square block of soil may be cut out and taken with each plant.

The ground or nursery into which young trees and shrubs are planted should be sheltered naturally or artificially. Clipped ever-

52

green hedges are frequently planted to secure this end, such as holly, privet, or *Chamaecyparis lawsoniana*. But in most gardens some nook large enough and sheltered enough can be found. The soil should be of a light rather than a heavy nature, for it induces a more fibrous root system, and the necessary space allotted for peat-loving things should have peat mixed with the ordinary soil.

The chief use of a nursery ground is to enable one to watch over and encourage the growth of trees and shrubs from their babyhood until they are big enough to fight their own battles along with the other occupants of the garden, park, or street to which they may be consigned. A nursery is also very useful, even if only of small size, as it affords material for making good losses by death, or for extending existing plantations at the least expense. There is always as well the peculiar satisfaction of raising one's own plants.

When once the plants are safely established in the nursery their after-care consists chiefly in transplanting, pruning, and training, all of which questions it will be convenient to deal with as affecting hardy trees and shrubs in general, whether in nursery quarters or not.

It should be clear that the foregoing account deals with the raising of small quantities of plants by the amateur gardener.

Commercial nursery practice has undergone major changes in recent years, mainly because of the invention of special machines or the adaptation of existing equipment for ground preparation, planting, irrigation, lifting for dispatch, and spraying for chemical control of weeds, pests, and diseases. The use of mist has also speeded up plant propagation.

The necessity for handling large quantities of young plants quickly has become vital, and the practice of 'bedding-in' has become well established. This means simply providing an efficient intermediate treatment for young plants between the established, hardened-off rooted-cutting and seedling stage and lining out in nursery rows. Beds about 4 ft wide separated by suitable paths are to be seen in most tree and shrub nurseries in which the new plants are arranged thickly across the beds in rows about 1 ft apart, where they remain for about six to nine months before being transplanted.

It should be remembered that many shrubs such as *Cytisus, Cistus,* evergreen *Ceanothus* and *Romneya* which resent root disturbance must be grown on in pots before they can be given permanent quarters.

The vogue for Garden Centres, in which a wide range of woody plants is grown in easily portable containers so that they may be sold throughout the year, calls for special equipment for the preparation of large quantities of soil and the movement of numerous heavy containers. This ever-increasing practice is now so important that it has its own specialised literature.

GLOSSARY

The craft of growing trees has its own language and among the terms in use are the following:

ROOT-STOCK	The young tree on which buds or grafts of another kind are inserted.
WORKED TREE	This means the tree has been propagated by being grafted or budded (i.e. worked) on to a root-stock.
BOTTOM WORKED	Grafted or budded on a root-stock at or about ground level.
TOP WORKED	Grafted or budded on the top of a specially grown stem. This method is used particularly for propagating weeping trees.
MAIDEN TREE	A tree of one year's growth, usually from a bud or graft.
BUSH TREE	This may branch into two or more main stems from near ground level, or may have a short clean trunk of about 2 ft before branching. In the latter case it is sometimes referred to as a 'bush tree on a leg'.
FEATHERED TREE	A young tree with a single main stem on which the side branches are still growing.
HALF-STANDARD TREE	With a stem clear of side branches up to about 4 ft from ground level.
STANDARD TREE	With a clean stem measuring at least $5\frac{1}{2}$ ft from ground level to the first branch.
BALLED TREE	One which has a ball of soil adhering to its roots, and is usually dispatched by nurserymen with sacking or other suitable material wrapped around the ball. This method is used mostly for evergreen trees.
BARE-ROOTED TREE	A tree which has practically no soil adhering to its roots when dispatched from a nursery. Most deciduous trees are handled as bare-rooted specimens.
HEADING BACK	This means the cutting back of that portion of the

stem of a root-stock to within about 6 in. above the point where the bud was inserted. This work is done in early spring before the leaves unfold and after it has been ascertained that the bud is alive or has 'taken', to use a nurseryman's term.

SNAG The portion of stem of the root-stock left above the bud after heading back and which is used as a support to 'tie in' the new young growth which develops from the bud.

SNAGGING The action of cutting away the snag when the new stem from the bud has developed and the support is no longer necessary. This operation requires the skilful use of a pruning knife, and nothing is easier to the unskilled worker than cutting away the snag and the new young tree as well. It is a delight to see skilled craftsmen carrying out this operation, and the production of trees with straight stems is largely dependent on this initial work.

LEGGING-UP This means the removal of the side branches on a feathered tree in order to produce a half or full standard. Expert judgement is required regarding the extent of the removal of the side branches in one year. It is a mistake to cut away too many side branches at one time as this results in the production of a thin whippy stem, which cannot support a top-heavy head of branches.

HEAD This refers to the collection of branches at the top of the stem of a half or full standard tree. The 'diameter of head' means the distance through the head of branches and is sometimes given in price quotations for trees. Where large specimens are involved this measurement is taken in two directions. It is perhaps important to record that the intending purchaser of a tree can reasonably ask for particulars of the height of stem, the overall height of the tree and the diameter of the head of branches.

LEADER This is the leading branch of a tree and in a well-grown specimen there should be no difficulty in tracing this as a direct continuation of the trunk from ground level.

DOUBLE-
LEADER   Where two competing leaders have developed, one of
          which must be shortened or removed.

LATERAL   A branch which grows sideways from the trunk or a
          secondary branch growing from a main one.

POLLARDING Means the cutting back of the natural head of branches
            of trees to form a basic framework and to which the
            subsequent new branches which develop are cut back
            at intervals.

CHAPTER IV

TRANSPLANTING

There is no operation connected with the cultivation of trees and shrubs upon whose proper performance more depends than transplanting. To its successful accomplishment not only the health, the proper placing, but the very presence of a plant in a garden are due. It may be said, indeed, that it is only the art of transplanting that makes a garden possible. In itself, however, it is an evil, although so necessary a one. With few exceptions, a tree that is rightly placed and in proper soil is better left undisturbed at the root.

To understand the importance of transplanting it is well to consider the typical root system of a plant. If a tree old enough to have formed a woody stem be carefully taken out of the ground and examined, it will be found to have a root system somewhat as follows: Proceeding directly from the stem there will be three, four, or more radiating main roots similar to the stem in character; these are, of course, developed from the first roots emitted by the seedling and have become woody with age. Issuing from them are other ramifications, becoming smaller at each subdivision, till at last they cease to be woody and are invested merely by hair-like organs. It is important to remember that the nutrition of the plant is entirely dependent on these hair-like roots. All the other portions serve merely as conduits from them to the stem, and as supports and hold-fasts for the plant. In transplanting it will thus be seen how important it is that as many as possible of the finest rootlets should be preserved. A plant bears transplanting well or badly according to its power of renewing these rootlets quickly, or to its capability of existing with little loss of vitality until they are renewed. The finer and less woody portions of the root system send out these fine fibres more freely and quickly than the older parts do, which is why young plants, even tiny seedlings are transplanted with less risk than old ones.

Plants like rhododendrons and others of the heath family are easily transplanted because they produce an enormous quantity of fibrous roots close to the stem, enabling a much larger proportion of working roots to be removed with it than is possible with the majority of trees and shrubs.

The occasional transplanting that young trees undergo in well-managed nurseries is practised for the same reason. The shortening of the roots involved by removal induces the production of a large quantity of fibrous roots close to the stem, which are thus easily removed with the plant. The tendency of the active fibrous roots is to spread out farther and farther away from the stem, and thus enlarge the feeding-ground of the tree. Consequently the longer the tree remains undisturbed, the greater the proportion of them that have perforce to be sacrificed in transplanting, and the greater is the risk involved in its ultimate removal. In selecting trees and shrubs, but more especially trees, the experienced purchaser looks askance at the plants with long clean leads and an aspect of lush vigour. These things are too suggestive of undisturbed roots. He prefers the short-jointed, comparatively stunted growth indicative of judicious transplanting.

Methods of Transplanting. The commonest and most simple method of transplanting is to take a plant out of the soil, with as many of its roots as can conveniently be saved, and to transfer it to its new quarters nearly or quite free from soil. Trees and shrubs to be sent long distances have necessarily to be dispatched in this state. For the great majority of young trees and shrubs with deciduous foliage the plan is perfectly safe. For evergreen shrubs that do not form close masses of roots, as rhododendrons do, it is risky. And with both deciduous and evergreen plants, the risk is increased the older they become and the longer they remain undisturbed.

Seedlings and cuttings removed from seed-beds, boxes, etc., to more roomy quarters rarely fail if care be taken; but it has to be remembered that the younger and more succulent they are, the less able are they to withstand dryness, exposure, and delay. It is therefore essential to inure tender seedlings and also rooted cuttings to cooler conditions prior to transplanting. Such treatment, referred to by gardeners as 'hardening off', is usually carried out by an interim period in cold frames. Seedlings of important kinds have sometimes to be transplanted whilst they are growing, and in that case it is a good plan to lay them on damp moss or canvas as they are taken up. After they are replanted they should be watered thoroughly, and occasionally sprinkled afterwards if they show signs of drooping. But with the seedlings of most deciduous hardy trees and shrubs it is best, and usually most convenient, to transplant them in open weather sometime between the fall of the leaf and the renewal of growth. (See notes on time for transplanting.)

When the removal of a plant has been decided on, it will be incumbent to decide also whether a proportion of the soil in which it is growing shall be carried with it, or whether it shall be taken with naked roots only. Several circumstances will have to be considered, such as the nature of the plant, the distance it has to be taken, the labour and cost involved, etc. But, generally, it may be said that old plants, plants that have long been undisturbed, and most evergreens should be transplanted with balls of earth. On the other hand, young plants and most deciduous ones may be moved with naked roots.

Transplanting without Soil attached to the Roots. In transplanting a tree or shrub without soil, it has always to be borne in mind that the greater the proportion of fibrous roots that are retained the greater will be the degree of success. With small plants up to two or three years old it is, as a rule, sufficient to push the spade or fork beneath them and raise them bodily from the ground, and then carefully shake the roots free from soil. But with older specimens greater care is needed, such as those whose roots have spread 3 ft or more from the stem. With such specimens it is necessary to commence operations at a sufficient distance from the stem—proportionate, of course, to the size of the tree, but always far enough away to preserve a considerable proportion of the fibrous roots—by digging a trench; then, by working inwards, chiefly with a fork, the roots should be carefully shaken free from the soil. In the case of large and important specimens this work must not be hurried.

In replanting a tree that has been taken up in the way described, the first consideration should be to provide a hole wide enough to allow the roots to be spread out to fullest extent. This applies to plants of any size, but it is more important the larger they are. Roots should never be doubled back or made to fit the circumference of a hole. They should be placed in the earth as nearly as possible in the same relative positions as they were when taken out. With regard to the depth at which trees should be planted, it may be said that the thickened base of the stem, where it begins to divide into the several main roots, should always be above ground. A guide to the depth of planting can usually be ascertained from the soil mark on the stem which will clearly show the previous soil level at which the tree or shrub was growing in the nursery. The mistake of too deep planting is nearly always made, especially where the holes have been deeply dug, because insufficient allowance is made for settling. To obviate deep planting and to determine the correct depth at which to place the shrub or tree, a planting board should be used. This can be made from a piece of wood 5 or 6 ft long, 3 in. wide and 1 in. thick. Graduate the board at intervals of 6 and 12 in. and at the centre, cut a V-shaped notch. When the board is placed across the planting hole the central position and the level of planting is readily ascertained.

A convincing lesson may be learnt in connection with this question of depth from naturally sown trees. It will be noticed that there is always some tendency—and often it is a very marked one—for the base of the stem to be elevated above the surrounding ground. When this part is buried the stem is much predisposed to decay at the 'collar'. The bark of the stem or trunk, which Nature intended to be exposed to the atmosphere only, is kept permanently dark and moist. This renders it, no doubt, peculiarly susceptible to cell-rupture by alternate freezing and thawing, and to the attacks of fungi. Plants that die from this cause usually die quite suddenly, causing much wonder. Still, some trees, such as poplars and elms, do not seem to mind deep planting.

When rearranging the roots in their new quarters, the aim should be to spread them out evenly in all directions. The soil in immedate contact with them should be fine and worked well in amongst the fibres. It is advantageous to have at hand some friable soil, such as old potting soil, to place over and around the roots before filling in with the ordinary soil. When once the roots are well covered the soil may be trodden or rammed firmly about them, but the planter should bear in mind that the moister and heavier the soil the less of this consolidating process will be needed. Where the soil is light and free, or even moderately so, a thorough watering has the mechanical effect of settling the soil about the roots thoroughly.

Transplanting with Soil attached to the Roots. Whilst the removal of trees and shrubs with a mass of earth about the roots is the most troublesome and costly method, it is the safest, and should always be adopted for large or particularly valuable examples. So far as the physiology of the plant is concerned, the operation presents no problems, for the aim is to transfer the plant with its root-environment practically undisturbed. Such difficulties as arise are chiefly mechanical. With the necessary appliances and mechanical skill, trees hundreds of years old can be transferred to new quarters. But in the ordinary routine of garden work one has rarely to deal with masses of soil weighing more than one ton. Below that there is every gradation down to seedlings with an ounce or two of soil attached. Whatever the size may be the chief object is the same, viz., to transfer *intact* the 'ball' of earth with the roots that permeate it. With small plants the task is easy. The 'ball' may be kept together with the hands; often it may be carried from one place to another on a spade or fork, or on a wheelbarrow or truck. But the larger the ball and the less matted the roots, the more careful has the planter to be. Still, the main object is always the same, and that is, to keep the 'ball' from breaking. With rhododendrons and such-like plants with dense masses of fibrous roots, it is often self-supporting, but usually artificial support is necessary. This is best afforded by shaping the ball to a cylindrical form and binding it together with two cords, one near the top, the other near the bottom. The 'ball' should first be wrapped round in stout canvas or matting, and a number of thin boards (staves of a barrel are the ideal) should be inserted between it and the cords, so as to prevent the latter cutting into the soil. It is very important that the cords should be made as tight as possible. This is done by making a noose at one end, and, after threading the other end through the noose, pulling each cord as tight as it can be made. A tourniquet is sometimes used for tightening the cords.

After the soil has been supported by some such means as these, the ball has to be partially undermined, first on one side and then on the other, and a pair of stout lifting-boards inserted. The plant is then ready to be lifted out of the hole and carried away to its new position. When the weight is greater than can be managed by a few men, mechanical appliances have to be used. Transplanting machines of various sizes, made to lift from $\frac{1}{2}$ to 8 or 10 tons, were once popular for moving sizeable specimens. Today, the tractor with its power-lift can be quickly and effectively used to lift and transport trees and shrubs with a large 'ball' of soil. There are, too, mobile cranes which can be used with excellent results. In the absence of mechanical equipment, much can be done with a lifting jack, rollers, and planks, the plant being rolled up an inclined plane out of its hole on to a low trolley to be taken to its destination.

Preparation of Large Trees for Removal. Where it is desired to transplant particularly valuable or important trees, especially trees that have long been undisturbed, and are known to have their feeding roots so far spread out from the stem as to make it impossible to take a necessary proportion of them with the tree, it is often desirable to prepare the 'ball' six months, a year, or even two years before-

hand. It is done in this way. The dimensions of the 'ball' to be removed are fixed on and marked out. A trench is dug out rather nearer
the stem than the marked lines, and as deep as the roots go. All the
roots, of course, are roughly severed in the process, and these should
be cut cleanly back. It is important that tap roots, if they exist,
should be severed also, and to do this half the 'ball' or less should be
undermined, and then filled in again before another section is dealt
with. After all this is done, the trench should be filled in again, the
soil rammed firmly and watered.

The object of this process is to provide the tree with a stock of
fibrous roots so near to the stem that they, or most of them, can be
taken away with it at the time of transplanting, and thereby enable it
to take hold of the soil at once in its new quarters. One growing season at least must elapse between the preparation of the tree and its
ultimate removal. Some trees may be prepared in the early spring
and removed in the autumn of the same year. With most a full year
should be allowed. In some cases it may be well to prepare half the
'ball' one year and the other half the next. This is to avoid the check
caused by severing all the roots at one time.

Time for Transplanting. The most convenient time for the
removal of trees and shrubs is during the winter months, say from
the middle of October to the middle of March. With very few exceptions, all deciduous trees and shrubs may be transplanted with
safety during that period. Still, the earlier part of the time is better
than the latter part. As far as possible all deciduous plants should be
planted after the leaves have changed colour, but just before they
fall. The roots are not yet inactive, and they get a grip of the new
soil before winter sets in. The period, however, is so short that this
must be regarded rather as counsel of perfection than as being always
practicable. The worst time for the work is during the period of dry
east winds in March and early April. But after that again there frequently comes a time when, if the work has not been done before, it
may still be safely accomplished. This is during soft or showery
weather, when the buds are bursting. The roots have by now become
active again, and if the plants can be kept moist for a few days
(natural rain showers, of course, are best, but watering and spraying
are a great help), they start growing again immediately. The deciduous magnolias can be shifted best at this time, usually mid-May
with them. In trade nurseries much transplanting has perforce to be
deferred until the end of the selling season.

Evergreens. These are much more difficult to transplant safely than deciduous plants are. The reason of this is that the leaf-bearing part of the plant is never so independent of the root system. Even in midwinter the leaves both breathe and transpire, so that a cessation in the supply of moisture from the root, however partial, is felt much more than it is by a leafless plant.

In the case of rhododendrons and many other evergreen members of the heath family, the fine roots are so numerous, and get so complete a grip of the soil, that the whole root system can be removed practically intact. But in their case the problems of transplanting scarcely arise; with ordinary care it can be done at almost any season of the year. It is with such evergreens as hollies, evergreen oaks, cherry laurels and Portugal laurels, arbutuses, and all those with a more or less rambling root system that difficulties appear. They can, of course, be moved with safety if the 'balls' of earth in which they grow are taken with them, but that cannot always be done, as in the case of plants that have to be sent long distances, or those growing close together, as in a holly hedge. Consequently, they have to be removed with little or no soil attached to the roots. It is in such cases that it becomes very important that the right time be chosen.

It is essential with such evergreens as those just named that the plants, although not in the full vigour of their growth, should nevertheless not be in their most inactive state. The best times, therefore, are autumn before growth ceases, or in late spring after growth commences. With regard to planting, warm moist days in late September and early October are particularly advantageous in the south of England. In the cooler, moister north a few weeks earlier are better. Spring planting should be deferred till the drying east winds are over. Showery, warm days in May are best.

Many discussions have been held as to whether the autumn or the spring planting of evergreens is preferable. With suitable weather and smart workmanship at the time, and with due attention to watering the following summer, success, I think, is about equally probable at either season. Just as a hard winter setting in very early might prejudice one against autumn planting, so might a long dry time in May and June prejudice another against spring planting. This much, however, is certain, from midwinter onward to early April is the most dangerous time. In the case of the most susceptible of these evergreens it is better to be earlier in autumn or later in spring than the reverse. Evergreen oaks transplant better in early

June than in April. Bamboos, if planted in autumn, should be moved early; but in their case experience proves that mid-May is equally good.

Experience has shown that it contributes considerably towards the recovery of evergreens whose roots have been damaged by transplanting, to remove a proportion of the leaf growth, or even leaves alone, from the branches. By reducing the leaf surface the amount of transpiration is correspondingly reduced, and the demand for moisture is brought nearer to the amount the damaged and reduced root-system is able to supply. In the case of evergreen oaks and vigorous hollies, quite half the leafy part of the plant may often be removed with advantage. In N. America, where the summer is more trying than ours for newly planted hollies, they make a practice of almost denuding them of leaves in these circumstances.

Aids to Transplanting. Mulching with a loose covering of straw, bracken, leaves, peat, or if available, well-rotted farmyard manure, has long been practised to conserve moisture and also prevent fluctuations in soil temperature. It is very essential for trees and shrubs transplanted during the spring, possibly at a time when periods of drying winds may be experienced, to have a safeguard against drying out of the soil, and for this nothing equals a good mulch.

A study of any area of natural woodland, with its annual mulch of fallen leaves, will clearly illustrate the value of providing a surface layer of loose material to the roots. The ultra-tidiness of gardeners in forking through shrubberies can be detrimental, and generally for most shrubs and trees it is better to be less tidy and leave the surface covered with a good layer of decaying material. It will prove far more beneficial to the plants and particularly their feeding roots. The present-day success of growing mixed collections of plants in what is termed woodland gardens, is in the main due to the more natural condition and also generous mulching.

Protection of the main trunk and branches of transplanted trees by wrapping with bands of hessian or paper (tough crepe paper) is a method practised where there is danger of sunscorch or suncrack to the bark. It can also greatly help the tree to re-establish itself and create a fresh rooting system. It applies particularly to trees placed in isolated positions and especially street and avenue trees, which can be subjected to the effects of hot sun on one side of the main trunk or to reflected heat from road or paving surfaces.

Generally the wrapping is used for the first year or two, after which it can be removed when the tree has become established and acclimatised.

In recent years, plastic transplanting sprays have been introduced for the treatment of trees and shrubs, especially evergreens, to reduce wilting, shock, and plant mortality due to the effects of transplanting. The plastic spray diluted with water at the rate of 1 part spray to 4 parts water, is applied to the foliage and stems to provide a seal against rapid transpiration or the loss of moisture through the stomata. The treatment is best when the spray is applied with a syringe or solo-type sprayer, using a fine nozzle. To ensure satisfactory results and also quick drying of the film on the foliage, a fairly high temperature is required; 70°F being the optimum.

The plastic spray provides a thin protective film-like covering to the leaves and stems, which is practically invisible provided the tree or shrub has been correctly treated. It not only retards transpiration, but also assists more rapid recovery of the rooting system. Another advantage which is claimed for the use of a transplanting spray is that the planting of trees, especially evergreens, can be carried out over a longer period and also during unfavourable weather.

In addition to plastic sprays, wax emulsions and rubber compounds have been developed. They all serve the same purpose; the reduction of transpiration and the prevention of drying up of the bark following root disturbance due to transplanting. Use of these substances is not necessarily limited to the treatment of large or established trees or shrubs. Young nursery stock, where there is the likelihood of the foliage flagging and becoming limp following transplanting, can be treated by spraying with or dipping into a solution of the compound, and excellent results have been achieved.

Watering has always been necessary for the successful establishment of newly planted trees and shrubs and it must be liberal, not only to ensure sufficient moisture to the roots, but also to settle the soil. With modern irrigation equipment, the provision of adequate supplies of moisture is not the problem it was years ago. With the aid of misting sprayers, effective watering can be provided without flooding or excessive washing of the soil. Also there is no damage to the foliage or growth.

Other means of watering is by punctured plastic tubing laid amongst the shrubs or trees. The supply of water can be adjusted to provide a drenching spray or it can be just a trickle, allowed to continue over a period of a day or night or longer. Use has also been made of punctured polythene or plastic tubing to provide moisture to the trunk and branching systems of newly transplanted specimen trees. The tubing fixed to the trunk and main branches supplies a fine spray of water to keep the bark continually moist, and thus prevent rapid transpiration. It will keep trees in a turgid condition and greatly assist them to overcome the shock of transplanting. The method is particularly useful where large specimen trees, both deciduous and evergreen, are transplanted to provide immediate features, but its use must be judiciously exploited; the supply of water being controlled according to weather conditions and requirements.

CHAPTER V

SOIL AND TOPDRESSING

If one could choose one's own soil for the cultivation of trees and shrubs generally, it would be a deep loam of a light rather than a heavy nature, and free from all calcareous substances. Such a soil is easily worked and would support the most varied collection of species, including the great family of Ericaceae, whose members give so much beauty to gardens. The species found on limestone are numerous, but to very few of them is lime absolutely essential. For some, such as certain species of clematis and juniper, and such conifers as *Abies pinsapo,* it is advisable to add lime to soil deficient in it; but generally one is led to the belief that trees and shrubs inhabit limestone regions not so much from choice as from necessity. The beech, for instance, or the whitebeam, commonly found wild on the limestone, thrive just as well apparently where it is absent. Peat-lovers, again, are by no means incapable of thriving on a loamy soil. The heath family, including such genera as *Calluna, Erica, Rhododendron, Daboecia,* and *Pieris,* are usually found wild on peaty soil, but every one of them will succeed in loam of a sandy nature and free from lime, especially if decayed leaf-mould or peat be added to it.

The great value of decayed leaves—the leaf-mould or leaf-soil as it is termed by gardeners—cannot be over-estimated. In recent years it has become in some districts a scarce commodity and one not readily purchased in quantity. For this reason peat-moss and bracken peat have been widely used to improve soils, particularly those of a sandy or gravelly nature, where trees and shrubs are to be planted.

Leaf-mould, where it is available, is a most valuable commodity, and an essential one to incorporate with the soil for most shrubs and trees, and in particular the various members of the Ericaceae.

The composting of leaves and other suitable materials is one of the essentials of present-day gardening, and the greater the quantity which can be produced the better, because all soils, whatever their type and nature, can be improved both in texture and fertility by incorporating well-decayed leaves and compost.

As a topdressing for evergreens, a layer of leaves has much to recommend it, and in the case of those with low branches like rhododendrons, which prevent the leaves being blown away, it is a good plan in autumn to cover the ground, say from 6 to 9 in. deep, with a layer of newly fallen leaves. In the event of a hard winter they keep the soil comparatively warm, gradually decaying and settling down to a shallow covering, which keeps the soil cool and moist during the following summer. The surface roots of rhododendrons and most shrubs thrust themselves greedily into this humus; being light and easily permeated by air, it has not the evil results that sometimes follow heavy topdressings of some other materials such as spent hops or grass mowings, which, too frequently and heavily applied, are apt to bury the plant unduly and set up decay at the collar, just as deep planting does.

Topdressing. This term is applied to the practice of placing material, usually of a feeding nature, on the surface of the soil permeated by roots of trees and shrubs, as distinct from burying it in the ground. It has two allied purposes: that of nourishing the plant, and improving soil fertility.

In the case of old and failing trees, or starved and weakly ones, especially those of a surface-rooting nature like beech, elm, lime, maples, and numerous others, no treatment aiming at their renovation is more efficacious than a topdressing of well-rotted manure, compost, or leaf-mould, from 3 to 6 in. in thickness. The ground should be lightly pricked over before it is applied. If the tree is standing on a lawn the grass should be taken off in turves and replaced after the topdressing is done. In this case leaves are unsuitable as part of the compost, because they decay into such small compass that the ground settles much and unevenly; loam and manure should be used, or even loam by itself. If possible, it is best to topdress lawn trees in early October, and leave the ground open through the ensuing winter and early spring, re-turfing or sowing with grass seed the following April.

The commonest form of topdressing, especially of shrubs, is the summer one, designed to keep the soil and roots moist and cool in the broiling heats of July and August, especially after transplanting. The material should be of an open nature, and perhaps, for general use, the best of all is a mixture of short rotted manure and leaf-soil, or pulverised compost. For rhododendrons and the heath family generally, a 4-in. layer of decayed leaves is very good, although a mixture of peat and spent hops can be equally good. Such a topdressing is remarkably effective in keeping the ground moist—better, indeed, than many waterings. Newly planted shrubs and trees, and all those liable to suffer more than ordinarily from drought. should always have this treatment.

CHAPTER VI

STAKING OR OTHER MEANS
OF SUPPORT

The artificial support of trees is mainly a concomitant of transplanting. Trees grown on without removal from the spot where the seed was sown, or even those given permanent places when quite young, rarely need support. It is the tree that has attained a considerable size and then lifted from its anchorage that requires artificial assistance to withstand storms. The sooner a tree, and to a less extent a shrub, is given its permanent place the better, consistent with its safety and capability of holding its own among other plants.

A tree, say 6 ft or more high, planted in an exposed position, must be given support, unless it has been shifted with a heavy mass of soil attached to its roots; even so, it is wise to provide support at least until the tree is re-established. If the plant has been removed without soil, the usual support is afforded by a stake proportionate in length and thickness to the main stem of the tree, and driven firmly into the ground. Some regard must be paid to the avoidance of injury to the roots in driving in the stake. It must be well sharpened, so that it forces its way between the roots a little distance from the stem, rather than crushes through them. It is an excellent plan to drive in the stake *before* the tree is planted and arrange the roots around it. It is only necessary, especially if the soil has been trenched deeply, to see that in the inevitable settling of the soil the ties do not cause the tree to be suspended rather than settle naturally with the soil.

A stake should not go any higher than necessary. It is by no means an object of beauty, and should be as unobtrusive as possible. The chief aim is to keep the stem perfectly steady at the base until the roots themselves are capable of doing it. If a newly planted tree is allowed to sway about so that the base of its stem forms a socket in the soil, its progress will be slow and its appearance ungainly. A short, stout stake standing 3 ft out of the ground will prevent this better than a longer thin one. (The use of a stake for straightening the crooked stem of a young tree by bracing the two together is a quite different object.) Some soft or elastic substance should be inserted between the tying material and the stem, and between the stem and the stake, to prevent the ties cutting in and chafing.

A useful temporary support for newly planted trees of goodly size is afforded by affixing three pieces of cord, or, still better, three wires, to the stem well up the tree, and then fastening the lower end of each to a stout stake driven in the ground at equal distances round the tree. Transplanted trees with low branches can also be well supported without any risk of injury by securing three or four of the branches to stout stakes at intervals round the tree near its circumference. Any form of artificial support should be removed as soon as possible; it can be unsightly, and if neglected can cause damage by chafing or the cutting in of the ties, and, once firmly established, the tree is better without it.

Use of the patent rubber or plastic tree-ties provides excellent support and what is very important, they will, if correctly attached, eliminate the danger of chafing or cutting into the bark—a common cause of irreparable damage.

Although there are several proprietary makes of tree-ties on the market, they are somewhat similar in design and have a block or distance piece to fit between the stem of the tree and the stake. They are adjustable and attachment is by nailing to the stake or by a buckle.

For trees growing in roads, in playing fields, and other places where they are exposed to the possibility of mechanical or malicious damage, the provision of a steel-mesh tree guard to protect the main stem or trunk is essential, at least for the early years and until the tree is well established. To ensure firm fixing of the guard, a good stout stake is required, to which the guard can be secured with staples.

Under TRANSPLANTING, I have advised the reduction of the top-growth with the object of partially restoring the balance between branch and root that must nearly always be more or less disturbed by that operation. It has the further advantage of reducing the power of wind on newly planted trees, and thus rendering staking or other means of support for them less needed.

CHAPTER VII

PRUNING TREES AND SHRUBS

The art of pruning as applied to ornamental trees and shrubs may be said to serve one or more of the following purposes: To improve or alter the shape and appearance of the plant; to increase the quantity and improve the quality of the blossom; to bring about an improvement in health. Of all the arts that go to make up horticulture, pruning is the one most frequently misapplied. Its proper practice necessitates an intimate acquaintance with the habit and nature of the subject operated on. For instance, a collection of flowering shrubs, in so far as they need pruning at all, cannot be pruned properly unless the workman knows the time of flowering of each one. Again, the aim in pruning a large-growing tree is to make it as perfect a specimen of its kind as possible; contrary to the ideas of many, it is not intended to bring it to some arbitrary, more or less formal, outline. Therefore a knowledge of its size and habit is essential. Unless the operator possesses such knowledge the plants are best left alone, for bad pruning or pruning without a definite aim is worse than none.

Pruning for Shape. Pruning for the purpose of regulating the shape and size of a tree or shrub is usually practised in order to maintain it in some conventional form, such as is seen in topiary work, clipped hedges, rounded or pyramidal bushes, etc. This kind of pruning is of the simplest, being, as a rule, merely a process of clipping. Such matters as time of flowering and habit are of no moment. The chief question is, when is the best time of prune?

Fully grown hedges or bushes of yew, holly, and box are usually clipped in July or August. During these months work in the garden is often less pressing than at other times, and they are as suitable as any other. The plants, moreover, retain their neat appearance throughout the autumn, winter, and spring months. With young hedges more careful procedure is necessary. The clipping should be done earlier, say in June, and a second shortening back of the stronger growths takes place in September. This more frequent pruning is necessary to give a thick base to the hedge or bush. When old hedges need cutting back to the bare wood, as they occasionally do, the work should certainly be undertaken in spring so as to allow the longest possible period for the naked places to become furnished with growth again. The inside branches of a hedge or clipped bush are necessarily stunted and gnarled, and do not break readily into new growth. The same rules as to time of pruning apply also to those level banks of cherry laurel and rhododendron, so often employed to furnish shady places in gardens. The ordinary annual pruning may be done between July and September, but the occasional hard cutting back must be done, say, in March or April.

Pruning large-growing Trees. This branch of pruning is not generally understood nor practised as frequently as it should be. The great majority of trees are planted and left to assume such forms as conditions and circumstances permit. This is mainly due to the fact that the work is specialised and necessitates the use of ladders and ropes, also skill on the part of the worker; this adding up to an expensive operation. It is the pruning of ornamental trees only that is in question. Forestry, or the growing of trees for profit, is a thing quite apart from ornamental arboriculture in park and garden. The forester aims solely at building up a trunk which will yield the maximum amount of useful timber, whilst the tree occupies the least possible space. The main object of the arboriculturist is so to control the growth of his trees as to produce individually beautiful specimens. He may desire a noble contour of branch and foliage, or a lofty tree showing a fine trunk, or one with its leafy canopy reaching to the ground; but the production of cubic feet of timber is, in itself, a secondary matter.

In pruning such trees as I am now considering—the oaks, elms, ashes, maples, chestnuts, and others of a similar type—it is rarely necessary to give any consideration to the production of flowers and fruit. The flowers are frequently of little beauty, and even in the case of beautiful flowering trees, like the horse-chestnut, such pruning as is required should be done before the trees reach their adult stage. It may be said of all trees that the earlier their training is commenced the less of it will be needed.

Formation of the Tree Trunk. In the great forest areas of the globe trees are generally found growing in masses and as close together as their minimum requirements of light and space permit. The trunks which the forester loves to obtain are straight, erect, and naked, the branches being killed off by want of light as the tree increases in height, leaving only the canopy of leafy growth at the top. Only occasionally are there found wild specimens well filled out on every side, evenly balanced, and furnished almost to the ground with foliage, such as it is generally the planter's aim to obtain in pleasure-grounds and gardens. In these latter places, however, where often trees from many different parts of the world are congregated on a few acres of ground, and planted singly or in small groups, many species, especially those of exotic origin, have a tendency to become unduly bushy-headed and dumpy in appearance, and to lose that stateliness which properly proportioned height and breadth give. The first aim in pruning is to prevent this deformity and to obtain a straight strong trunk or central axis of sufficient height.

There is also another consideration. No danger to big trees is so common as that which arises from the forking of the trunk. This divides the tree into two, three, or more parts, which do not always sway in unison during high winds, in consequence of which a crack starts sooner or later at the fork. Damp enters, fungoid parasites follow, and finally a storm comes which rends the tree in twain. In sheltered places and in plantations the danger from winds is not great; but the majority of our specimen trees are given space for their fullest development and need a strong single bole. Most people admire loftiness in trees, but height in isolated specimens adds to the risk of damage by wind. It will nearly always be found that trees of great age and size are comparatively low and spreading, or, if they are lofty, their trunks are undivided for the greater part of their length. All the lofty trees of the earth—the gum trees of Australia, the pines, firs and sequoias of North America, and the palms of the tropics—are of this type.

The Leading Shoot. To secure the development of a trunk of this character, it is necessary to keep a watch on it when it is young. The first and most important point is that it should always be kept to a single leading shoot. As long as the top of the tree remains accessible to the pruner, rival leaders should be shortened back or removed; and if the original leader by accident gets broken, it should be replaced by another shoot. In most of our deciduous trees a suitable side shoot near the top can usually be selected to replace the broken leader. It should, if necessary, be brought into position by tying to a stake, and may be encouraged to make headway by pruning back other shoots near that might otherwise assume the lead.

But many conifers, especially those of the spruce and fir tribes, produce their branches in regular tiers or whorls, and such branches are of no use for replacing a lost leading shoot. They are not capable of transforming themselves into erect-growing shoots, and if one is tied up it always tries to regain its original horizontal or drooping position. Propagators of these conifers experience the same difficulty when they attempt to increase their stock by grafting, or rooting, side branches. To obtain a new leader for these trees, the broken one should be cut off close to the uppermost tier of branches, and this tier and, in cases, the one below must also be very much shortened back. This will cause the cut-back leader to push out one or more shoots of the erect-growing kind, the most vigorous of which must be selected as the new leading shoot and the others removed.

When a tree has reached, say, half its natural height, and often much less, it may be left to itself, for it will nearly always be found that once a strong leading shoot has developed it will retain its predominance, provided no accident occurs, for as long as the natural form and habit of the tree allow.

Side-pruning. The greater proportion of the trees used for furnishing our gardens are of exotic origin. Species from all the cool temperate regions of the globe, inhabiting, in their native state, every variety of position and climate those latitudes afford, are brought under practically uniform conditions in the few acres of a British garden. It happens, therefore, in even the most favoured places, that some of the trees are not given the conditions most suitable for them. The effect (especially on species from somewhat warmer countries) is often shown in a tree assuming a stunted, bushy habit under cultivation, whereas in its own home it is lofty and graceful. In such cases it is the work of the pruner to aid the tree in assuming its natural form.

This can be done by two methods. The horizontal development of such trees, as opposed to their vertical development, should (1) be checked by pruning back the side branches. The cut should, as often as possible, be made at a fork, so as to leave a smaller branch with its twigs, rather than a stump. The operator's judgement should also be exercised as to whether (2) a proportion of the branches should not be entirely removed. A comparison of the number of branches on a young tree with those of a fully grown example of the same species shows how drastically Nature thins the branches. The pruner should be guided by this fact in such cases as those under discussion and remove too crowded branches. As a matter of fact, experience has proved conclusively, over and over again, that a tree may be brought out of its stunted state and made to grow again in height by this process alone. The importance of shaping a tree into its proper form whilst it is still young cannot be too strongly insisted on. Much trouble may be saved by removing superfluous and wrongly placed growths whilst they are still young and succulent. Without developing a rigid formality of outline, a young tree should, nevertheless, be kept in the main to a pyramidal shape. This is, in fact, involved in the maintenance of a due balance and symmetry of the branches and the predominance of the leader. Moreover, it is the natural shape of nearly all young trees of the type now under discussion—the larger growing trees of our gardens and parks— as may be noticed from any healthy, uninjured, self-sown young tree. But provided the main fact is recognised, this question as to where symmetry and balance merge into mere formality may very well be left to individual taste and judgement.

The pruning of specimen trees may be summarised thus: keep them to a single leading shoot; thin out and shorten back the branches of stunted or unduly spreading specimens; preserve, in the main, a conical or pyramidal shape whilst they are young. When once the basis of a trunk has been developed sufficiently, the tree may be left to assume that natural shape and outline characteristic of the species to which it belongs.

Removing Large Limbs of Trees. The question is frequently asked, what is the best season of the year at which to remove limbs of trees? For such dry woods as oaks, beeches, hornbeams, etc., experience proves that the season does not matter at all, providing the wound is immediately coated with a bituminous dressing. But it is different with the more sappy woods like birch, horse-chestnut, many maples and conifers. The 'bleeding' of such trees is often long-continued, and causes much debility if branches are removed in spring; whilst in the case of some conifers it has been known to cause death. The best time for removing branches from such trees, and indeed the safest generally, is November. At this time there is no active flow of sap and the wound can be treated with a bituminous dressing to provide complete protection. There is also ample time for the wound to harden and commence to heal before active growth recommences. The removal of big limbs should be resorted to only when absolutely necessary. It is always dangerous in the case of soft woods like birch, lime, and horse-chestnut, and except in the case of neglected trees, it constitutes no part in the routine of any proper system of pruning. But where limbs have been partially wrenched off by storms, or where questions of safety or other considerations necessitate their removal, it should be done preferably at the time of year recommended above, and in the manner now to be described.

Large branches should always be removed in at least two pieces. Usually they should be cut off in several; but this is a matter to be decided on the spot. One thing, however, is necessary for the proper finishing of the work and that is, the *last* piece to be sawn off should be light in weight, and only from 6 to 12 in. long. If an attempt is made to remove a big, heavy branch close to the trunk in one cut, it nearly always results in an unsightly wound, owing to the branch breaking away when the saw is about half-way through the cut, and tearing away part of the bark of the trunk.

A limb or branch must always be *cut off so close to the trunk or larger branch from which it springs that no stump at all remains.* The old, but very pernicious, practice of leaving a stump a few inches long is still too often adopted. It is curious how such a practice lingers in spite of endless examples of its evil results. The stump is sometimes left, I believe, with a view to its ultimate removal, the idea being that this is not such a shock to the tree as close amputation at once. Another advocate of the practice will tell you the stump 'draws the sap'—a phrase of obscure meaning, but intended, I believe, to convey the idea that the sap flows more freely to the wound, and heals it more quickly than when the branch has been sawn close off. Although one may still find stumps or 'snags' left by amateur pruners of trees, the general position is much improved. Today it is the practice of tree surgeons and also the employees of government and local authorities to accept 'flush cutting' as it is termed. When carefully and correctly carried out and the wound 'cleaned up' by trimming the bark, not only is the formation of healing callus encouraged, but the possibility of die-back due to wound infection greatly reduced.

Dressing a Wound. After trimming the bark and wood around the wound it should be covered with a waterproof, antiseptic dressing. For this, there is none better than a bituminous compound containing a copper fungicide. The coating should be renewed as often as is necessary till the wound is covered with new bark. The best armour that a tree can have to protect it against fungoid enemies is that with which Nature has provided it, viz., its bark. But when accident has caused a flaw in the armour, the most efficient substitute is one of the proprietary bituminous or rubberised compounds made and sold specially for the treatment and protection of wounds. The practice of nailing lead or zinc over wounds is a mistaken one. It affords no genuine protection against fungoid parasites, and hides whatever mischief may be going on underneath.

Pruning of Flowering Shrubs. As a general rule, evergreen shrubs do not need pruning at all in a systematic way. Such plants as rhododendrons, arbutuses, kalmias, and others of the heath family, evergreen barberries, *Osmanthus delavayi, Garrya elliptica*, etc., if they need pruning at all, require it only to improve or alter their shape, or to prevent their becoming too large for their quarters. In such cases pruning should be performed as soon as the flowering season is over. Sometimes evergreen shrubs become thin and lanky in growth, and can only be brought back to a sturdy vigour by pretty hard pruning. This should be done in spring just before the recommencement of growth, so as to allow as long a season as possible for them to become leafy again. This is all the more necessary because one may have to cut back to oldish wood, which does not break so freely. A season's flower must be sacrificed unless the plant is a very early flowering one.

Autumn-flowering heaths, such as *Calluna vulgaris, Erica tetralix, E. vagans, E. ciliaris, E. cinerea,* etc., can be improved by being cut back to some extent in spring before new growth starts. This removes the old flowering twigs of the previous season, and helps to keep the plants dwarf. It is the more necessary because of the long, lank growth these heaths make in garden soils, as compared with the hard, dense growth of the wild moorland plants. They should not be clipped back farther than the wood of the previous season.

Deciduous Shrubs. The pruning of this class of plants, where it is necessary at all, has to be regulated in accordance with the flowering season of each species. For the present purpose they may be roughly divided into two groups, viz.: (1) Those that flower on the current season's growth; and (2) those that flower from the wood of the previous year. The first group is much the smaller. It comprises *Ceanothus* 'Gloire de Versailles' and the other deciduous hybrids; *Spiraea japonica* and its allies, *Buddleia davidii* and its varieties, *Hydrangea* *paniculata, Genista tinctoria, Cystisus nigricans,* etc. All these shrubs blossom in the latter part of the season; their flowering is, indeed, the culmination of the season's growth. In the second group the flower-buds are formed during the summer and autumn, and remain dormant throughout the winter. To it belong the cherries, spring-flowering spiraeas, wild roses, barberries, and, in fact, all the earlier flowering trees and shrubs, which, of course, constitute the great majority.

Briefly stated, the rule which indicates the time to prune all flowering trees and shrubs is this: *Prune at such a season as will allow of the fullest possible period of growth before the next flowering season comes round.*

The first group—those whose flowers are borne on the growths of the current year—should be pruned during winter or early spring; at any rate before growth recommences. The previous year's wood may, if necessary, be cut back 'hard', that is, to within a few buds of its base. Such hard pruning, however, is only desirable where the shrub is already as large as is required. Small specimens need only the ends of the shoots removed. It must here be mentioned that a small proportion of our second group have to be pruned in the same manner as that just described. These are the very earliest flowering trees and shrubs, such as forsythias, peaches, almonds, *Prunus triloba, Erica carnea.* Although they blossom on the wood of the previous year, they do so before new growth has started, and if they are cut back as soon as the flowers are past, it is only the old flower-bearing wood that is removed. The entire growing season still remains for the development of the new wood.

Thinning. I now turn to the remainder—those that flower on the previous season's growth but concurrently with, or later than, the development of the new. These cannot be cut back in the way prescribed for the previous group. To do so early would be to remove all the flowers; to do so later would be to rob the shoots of their best season of growth. Therefore such pruning as is done must be deferred until after flowering, and it must be a form of thinning rather than a process of shortening back.

The term 'thinning', as used in the present connection, implies the weeding out of all weakly, crowded, and superfluous shoots and the removal also, if necessary, of a proportion of the stronger ones. Many shrubs, such as the earlier flowering spiraeas, the shrubby loniceras, philadelphuses, and deutzias, have a natural tendency to thicken into a dense mass of twiggy growth. A judicious thinning-out, such as that just mentioned, not only promotes the development of a cleaner, stronger growth, and consequently finer flowers, but it often gives also a more graceful aspect to the plant. It need not necessarily be an annual operation, but the questions, how often? and how much? must be left to the pruner's judgement. The 'thinning-out' style of pruning may be applied more or less to nearly all flowering shrubs; but the shortening back style of pruning must only be adopted for those that have a full season of growth between the pruning and the next flowering season.

There are some shrubs, of which *Philadelphus* × *lemoinei* may be taken as an example, whose growths have the power of renewing themselves mainly from the base every year. This philadelphus flowers about midsummer, by which time the new shoots are 6 to 12 in. long. By cutting away the entire flowering shoots as soon as the blossoms are over, the plant is reduced to a cluster of new growths, many springing from near to its base. These now obtain the maximum of light and air, and during the season get to be 1½ to 2 ft long. Nearly the whole of this will produce flowers the following year, and is in turn cut away as soon as they are faded. By this treatment *P.* × *lemoinei*, which is naturally about 6 ft high, may be kept less than half as high, and be made to produce a very much larger crop of flowers—for the whole plant is made up of flowering wood. *Cytisus purpureus*, Crimson Rambler rose, and others of the *Rosa wichuraiana* or *R. multiflora* groups, can be treated in the same way.

CHAPTER VIII

CARE OF OLD TREES

One frequently sees, in parks and gardens especially, trees which, although aged and decrepit, are still precious because of their history and associations, or valued perhaps for their size and rarity. There can be no question that the term of years of many such trees is shortened by neglect and wrong treatment. The commonest sources of decay are starvation at the root, droughty summers, and fungoid parasites. For remedying the first the notes on TOPDRESSING (p. 68) should be consulted; the second, of course, is a question of water supply; but these two together do not hasten the end of trees so much as disease, due to the entry of parasitic fungi. The most important of all matters concerning the longevity of trees is the maintenance of a whole skin. But there are many ways in which it may be broken. Insects may bore through the bark, frost sometimes ruptures it, and winds break off the branches and twigs. The last is the commonest source of decay, augmented often enough in gardens by the practice of leaving stumps so long that the bark cannot grow over them, and by leaving unprotected surfaces. The raw or jagged surfaces afford a resting-place for moisture and fungus-spores, decay commences and gradually finds its way inwards, until the trunk is reached. But if branches or snags are sawn off as previously advised, and the wounds kept covered with a bituminous compound, the new bark commences to creep over the cut surface from both sides until, if it is not too large, it fills up to the middle, and forms a perfect covering for the wound, of which in time all evidences disappear.

Treatment of Cavities in Trees. From what has just been written it will be seen that the formation of cavities by decay in the branches and trunks of trees is to a great extent preventable. With regard to cavities that already exist, the following treatment is recommended. First remove all, or as much as possible, of the decayed wood, especially the soft, brown, crumbling wood, and the soppy mass found at the bottom. Sound dead wood that has become dry and hard does not matter. Then wash the surface of the wood with a solution of carbolic acid or with a wood preservative such as

'Cuprinol'. The carbolic acid solution is made by mixing one part of 'commercial' carbolic acid (liquid) with twenty parts of methylated spirit. After this has become dry, a good thick coating of a bituminous compound should be laid on. The object of this antiseptic treatment is to destroy the parasitic fungi and arrest, as far as possible, the decaying process. Cavities that have taken the form of pockets and hold water must be thoroughly drained; the bottom of the hole may be located by probing with a piece of stiff wire or a sharpened iron rod, and its situation marked on the outside of the trunk; a hole must now be bored with an auger from the outside upwards in a slanting direction to the bottom of the cavity, by means of which the moisture can escape and wet decayed matter can be extracted. After allowing it to drain and dry out the cavity or pocket must be filled up and made water-tight. The best stopping for small holes is cement, or for small round ones a plug of oak or other hard wood will do (as for the auger hole mentioned above).

The chief points are: the keeping out of moisture, and the provision of a surface over which the new bark may grow. If the tree is in a state of vigorous health, as many hollow trees are, the bark will in time close over the filling just as it will over the flat sawn surface where a branch has been removed. But unless some such surface is provided on which the new bark can set itself, it forms thickened rolls all round the rims of the hollow, and these, in hollows of large size, will never meet and close up.

For the successful filling of larger holes and cavities it is necessary to ensure that the area is properly cleaned out and prepared, also that it is larger on the inside than the external opening. Unless this is so, the filling will not stay in position.

With very large cavities, some reinforcement is needed and for this various methods and materials may be employed. Large-headed clout-nails can be driven in around the inner edges of the cavity and to them, crossing wires may be attached. Small-meshed wire netting can also be attached, and if there is need for extra stabilisation, metal rods or pieces of piping can be inserted.

After this preparation, the filling can be firmly packed into position, with the finished surface just below the bark layer, so that the filling should not in any way impede the growth of healing tissue. After the filling is set and perfectly hardened the finished surface should be treated with a bituminous dressing, or painted to conform with the natural colouring of the bark.

Materials for Filling. For many years the use of cement, and for large cavities, bricks and mortar, was employed, and the use of these solid, hard-setting fillings, while successful in many ways, did have certain disadvantages insomuch as they were rigid and did not allow flexibility. As a result, cracking and shrinkage at the edges of the filling occurred, permitting entry of moisture. Generally the use of cement and brick fillings or the cheaper commodity—concrete—is no longer recommended, except possibly for a large cavity at the base of the trunk or bole where movement due to wind-sway is more or less non-existent. Even so, cement or concrete fillings must be treated around the edges with a bituminous compound to fill in cracks caused by shrinkage.

Various plastic and bitumastic preparations, also synthetic rubberised compounds, make very good fillings but their use, especially for large fillings, is expensive. Cold asphalt of the type used for road repairs is satisfactory, but it is difficult to use in a large cavity. The problem is to compact a fairly large mass of it, and often, when used for a cavity having a vertical orifice, falling out will occur. The reason is that it is not possible to compact a layer more than an inch or so in thickness. Asphalt can, however, be used on top of a concrete or brick filling to exclude the entry of moisture, especially at the base of the tree.

To fill small holes or cavities a mixture of bitumen and clean sand makes a very good filler. It is prepared by mixing together 1 part bitumen to 2 parts sand. Hard-wood sawdust can be used instead of sand, but the mixing is not so easy, nor is the filling so durable when set. Provided it is firmly rammed into the hole, this mixture will make a water-tight seal because it does not shrink or crack. The finished surface should nevertheless be painted over with bitumen every two or three years to preserve the filling and ensure that it remains sound.

The advantage of bituminous compounds for tree surgery is that they are non-toxic. Gas tar or Stockholm tar, which in the past were widely used as a wound dressing, can do harm because of their toxicity. Some trees, of which catalpas and magnolias are examples, have sensitive bark and any toxic dressing applied to wounds can cause die-back of the bark, and delay healing.

Open Cavities. Decay in trees is not always extensive or deepseated, and where this is so, and the heart wood is not affected, there is an alternative to filling, which is known as the 'open cavity'.

This method of treatment is not new, and at Kew trees can be seen with open cavities which have remained more or less the same for forty years or more. A typical example is the large tree of *Ginkgo biloba* which has an open cavity in the main trunk.

The advantage of the open-cavity method is that once all dead wood and debris has been cleaned out and the basal part of the opening cut to a sloping angle so that water will drain away, treatment is reduced to a minimum. All that is necessary is to char the inner parts of the cavity with a blow-lamp and then treat the surface with bituminous compound to ensure that it is waterproof. After-treatment should consist of an annual dressing of bitumen and also the removal of any decaying leaves or other debris that may collect. If the shaping of the damaged area is correctly attended to in the first place, no difficulty will be experienced because water should drain out and the cavity remain clear.

Leaving the cavity open will not affect the stability of the tree because the injury will not have extended deep enough. Generally, if the cavity after cleaning out extends into the wood for more than 4 to 5 in., it should not be left open, but filled in the normal way.

The only real drawback to the open-cavity method is that if the area of damage is sizeable it can be unsightly and detract from the beauty of the tree. For this reason, and the fact that if situated at a height above eye level it is not so easy to watch its condition, the open cavity is not a popular method of treatment.

Supporting Heavy and Dangerous Branches. The dismemberment of large old trees whose limbs, having become unduly heavy, are at the mercy of strong winds, or a heavy fall of snow, may be prevented or deferred by staying the branches to one another or to the main trunk.

Various methods have been adopted, and for many years the usual method of doing it was to place an iron band or collar round each of the two branches that have to be connected and joining them together by means of a chain or iron rod. The iron bands were hinged on one side and connected on the other side with a screw-bolt, which also secured the connecting chain or rod. Apart from being cumbersome, the great defect of this system is that the iron band presses on the bark and tends to restrict the flow of sap, with the result that the branch soon begins to thicken above and below it. Unless the band is adjusted or removed it will cut in and become embedded. The remedy is, of course, to provide timely attention and either move the band up or down the branch, or readjust it to the increased girth of the branch, by easing the screw-bolt. The unfortunate thing is that this attention is more often than not neglected, with the result that the iron collars become hopelessly embedded in the limbs.

Although the support provided is efficient, it can be troublesome, and for this reason the method is seldom used today.

Equally out-of-date is the method of supporting limbs by connecting them with iron rods fixed through holes bored through the centre of each limb with an auger and secured by iron plates and nuts. This method, although providing good support, is difficult, because the boring of holes through large limbs is very arduous, particularly when it has to be accomplished at a height involving the use of ladders. The system, when fixed, does have the advantage of being trouble-free, and it will usually last as long as the rods and fittings do. The bark may in time grow over the plate and nut on the outside, but that is an advantage rather than otherwise.

Cable-bracing. This method of support has become popular in recent years and, in addition to providing adequate support, it is easier to assemble and also adjust. It is also very adaptable and has a number of uses, being equally suitable as a support to low branches as it is to limbs forming the main framework of a branching system.

Usually, one of two methods of fixing can be adopted. The first is by the use of screw-eye and hook bolts which are screwed into the limb or trunk after first drilling a small hole. To these bolts or screws, the required length of a flexible steel cable is attached by passing it through the eye or over the hook of the bolt, and then clamping it back on itself with dog-clips or clamp-bolts. Once secured, this method of fixing is permanent, but to allow for adjustment an awning screw is introduced at one end of the cable, between the eye-bolt.

The second method of fixing, which does not involve the use of screw hooks or eyes, is known as sling-fixing. It is very simple and only requires a number of hard-wood slats or battens cut into convenient lengths (about 9 in.) and slotted in the middle. A number of these, depending on the size of the limb or branch, are placed around it to prevent the cable from cutting into the bark. If the wood slats are treated with wood preservative, they will last for years. Once in the required position the slings are joined up by a length of cable using shackles, dog-grips, or clamping bolts, and also an awning screw to provide adjustment.

The use of flexible steel cable for supporting limbs and branches is without doubt far superior to any other method; also the method of fixing is less involved and not so exacting, yet at the same time providing adequate and secure support. What is equally important is that heavy limbs or branches can be fully supported and yet retain a certain flexibility, which is essential to allow for wind-sway, something of the utmost importance with large trees which are exposed to gale-force winds.

Although support to large trees is essential and quite often it must be provided in the interests of public safety, trees that are well trained in their early life will require but little artificial help, for Nature has endowed them with an enormous self-sustaining power. Trees with forking trunks and steep crotches, alluded to on page 84, provide the commonest instance of the need for artificial support.

As an alternative to the use of these artificial supports for heavy branches, there is often that of reducing their weight by pruning. It should, of course, only be resorted to when it will leave the contours of the tree unspoilt. (See notes on PRUNING.)

For further information on the care of trees reference to the following books can be made.

BIBLIOGRAPHY

DALLIMORE, W., *Pruning of Trees and Shrubs*. Dulau, Oxford, new ed. 1945.

EDLIN, H. L., *The Forester's Handbook*. Thames and Hudson, London, 1953.

HALLER, J. M., *Tree Care*. Macmillan, New York, 1957.

HARTIG, R., *Diseases of Trees*. Macmillan, London, 1894.

LE SUEUR, A. D. C., *The Care and Repair of Ornamental Trees*. Country Life, London, 2nd ed. 1949.

PEARCE, S. A., *Ornamental Trees*. Collingridge, London, 1961.

PEET, E., *Practical Tree Repair*. McBride, New York, 1942.

PIRONE, P. P., *Tree Maintenance*. Oxford University Press, New York, 3rd ed. 1959.

RANKIN, W. H., *Manual of Tree Diseases*. Macmillan, New York, 1918.

PART THREE

MISCELLANEOUS

CHAPTER IX

TAXONOMY AND NOMENCLATURE

Taxonomy. Taxonomy, or 'systematics' as it used to be more popularly known, may be defined as the study and practice of classification, a subject both more and less than a science which involves the definition of items and groups of items and their arrangement in categories according to a set plan. At the present time, the term taxonomy itself has an almost exclusively biological connotation, although there are signs that it is spreading into more general parlance. Allied to taxonomy from a practical point of view, are identification and nomenclature, and these are usually taken to be part of the taxonomist's stock-in-trade.

Classification is a basic and necessary human thought process, to aid memory and orderly thinking, and is one of the oldest and most elemental branches of biology. From pre-scientific times men have sought to distinguish the different kinds of plants and animals one from the next, as much for a variety of practical reasons as out of innate curiosity, and to group them according to particular characters or properties. In modern biological classification the individual classes or units, once they have been delimited, are termed **taxa** (singular: **taxon**) and are assigned appropriate rank in a hierarchical system of categories. The term taxon applies to each unit of whatever rank or degree of inclusiveness, so that taxa may be likened to boxes within boxes. The main ranks or levels in the hierarchy, up to the level of family, are shown at the top of page 90 (the most important being printed in capitals).

The Families of plants are grouped into Orders, the Orders into Classes, and so on to the topmost rank of Kingdom.

Early systems of classification emphasised the differences between plants in order to facilitate identification. The pioneer eighteenth-century taxonomist and nomenclaturist, Linnaeus, used as the basis of his so-called 'Sexual System' of classification two of the most constant and easily observable features of the flower, the number of stamens (male organs) and pistils (female organs). As such a system uses few characters and does not actually group together the plants most alike in most respects it is said to be artificial. Under the

FAMILY (formerly 'Natural Order'*)
  Subfamily
    Tribe
      Subtribe
        GENUS (plural, genera)
          Subgenus
            Section
              Series
                SPECIES (sp.)   ⎫
                  Subspecies (ssp.) ⎬ (singular and plural the same)
                    Variety (var.) (or, varietas; plural, varietates)
                      Form (f.) (or, forma; plural, formae)
                        Cultivar (cv.)

---

* Not to be confused with Order, the next higher rank.

'Sexual System' the genera *Azalea* (now a part of *Rhododendron*), *Rhododendron* and *Erica* (nowadays members of one family) turn up in different classes, *Azalea* among the borages, *Rhododendron* among the legumes, and *Erica* in company with the nasturtiums- and evening primroses! Influenced by the theory of evolution, modern taxonomy in contrast aims to express the degree and direction of *resemblances* between plants in the belief that in general these are to be interpreted as evidence of their common ancestry at some relatively recent or more distant time in the past. The differences between plants are interpreted as the observable effects at our point in time of continuing processes of evolution and diversification. The mechanism of diversification may, in outline, be envisaged as follows. During the course of many generations, individuals and populations within a group corresponding, let us say, to a single species, may be subjected to different environmental influences or pressures, favouring the survival and selection of strains naturally modified or adapted in various ways advantageous in their particular circumstances; as these strains disperse themselves interbreeding between them will probably occur more rarely because of spatial separation or geographical isolation; eventually distinct races may become discernible, although the individuals of different races may at first be fully interfertile if brought together artificially; ultimately the morphological dissimilarity of such races may become so pronounced and natural interbreeding between them so rare because of genetic, geographical or ecological barriers that they may be recognisable as distinct species. Both environmental circumstances and the capacity of plants to respond must be expected to vary, so that different groups of plants are today at many different stages of evolution and speciation. In evolutionary terms one may thus think of individuals and populations of more or less homogeneous individuals; geographical and ecological races (now often treated taxonomically as **subspecies**) which display all degrees of incipient speciation; 'mature', well-defined species occupying well-defined ranges; and relict or senescent species, usually very distinct or isolated systematically and representing survivors of groups which are dying out. The general pattern is obscured and complicated in various ways, as for example by natural or artificial hybridisation, and more especially by the behaviour of groups of plants which reproduce or are capable of reproducing by methods other than the normal sexual means, for instance by **apomixis** (as in species of *Rosa*, *Rubus* and *Sorbus*) where viable seeds form from unfertilised ovules. From all this it will be seen that the traditional method of classification inescapably has the severe limitation that it imposes a system of discrete and static categories, like the genus and species, on what is actually an unresolved and dynamic situation.

To appreciate this situation is to begin to understand the broadness with which genus, species and other taxonomic categories are defined, and the botanist's plight in face of legitimate difference of opinion over the status of particular taxa. In practice (as every plantsman knows) individual plants can be identified and individual species distinguished from one another with varying degrees of satisfaction, even when the uneven standard of taxonomic literature is frankly admitted! The uniqueness of every group of plants in its physical make-up, its evolutionary history, capacity for variation, geographical and ecological range, and so on, makes *exact* comparison with other groups impossible and no objective and overall definition of taxonomic categories such as the species practicable. (At the level of species the traditional criterion of interfertility between members of the same species and complete or partial intersterility or non-interbreeding in natural circumstances between members of different species, subject to many qualifications, may, however, still be regarded as fundamental.) Above the level of species, the categories can only be objectively defined in terms of their fixed relative order in the taxonomic hierarchy. In practice the level of the genus is as much defined subjectively by the practical convenience of a norm which corresponds with what may be described as an intelligent layman's appreciation of the different 'kinds' of plants, as expressed in vernacular names such as oak, elm and beech; by a desire for consistency so far as possible between one group and the next; and not least by tradition, by the need for stability in nomenclature, and by the convenience of having neither too many levels nor too many taxa at a particular level.

For variants of a lower order than species, taxonomists admit three main levels in the hierarchy, the *subspecies*, *varietas*, and *forma*. The rank of **subspecies** is usually reserved for variants of a distinctly racial nature, that is to say where variants replace one another in particular geographical location or environment (as on different soil types or at different altitude, for instance). A variant of a minor nature which may crop up anywhere in a population, such as a white-flowered form of a red-flowered species, is often treated as a **forma** (plural: **formae**); sometimes, however, *formae* can, like *subspecies*, be races, but on a more minor scale. The use of the remaining category, the variety or **varietas**, is a vexed problem. For one thing, the term variety belongs as much to the language of horticulture as to that of science, but its range of meaning is different in each. For this reason some botanists now try to use the Latin form *varietas* (plural: *varietates*) to distinguish it from the horticultural variety which has been renamed *'cultivar'*. To add to this ambiguity, botanists are unfortunately by no means unanimous in how they use the category *varietas*. Some (chiefly in North America) equate it with *subspecies*, some with *forma*, for yet others it lies between the two. Rarely is there a need to make divisions within a species at more than two levels, so that not uncommonly taxa that would be treated as *subspecies* and *varietates* by one authority would be the *varietates* and *formae* of another. The *subspecies* is not yet a familiar category to horticulturists, but its application is less liable to misunderstanding, and it remains to be seen whether the *varietas* will survive as a category or eventually become obsolete. The eventual application of the term **cultivar** to all horticultural varieties, that is to say variants which are of horticultural rather than botanical significance, seems well-assured. A chapter which discusses the rules governing the nomenclature of cultivars will be found following this chapter.

That there can be legitimate difference of opinion between experienced botanists as to the status and relationships of particular taxa has already been implied. The modern taxonomist is increasingly able, however, to bring to bear on classification the researches of workers in other botanical disciplines besides the traditional one of morphology (the study of the external form of the plant and its organs). Among the most productive of these newer botanical sciences are cytology (the study of cells and the chromosomes, bearers of the hereditary material), palynology (the study of pollen grains), plant chemistry, and experimental taxonomy or biosystematics (the study of living populations of plants in wild or artificial environments, which provides a means of distinguishing variation which is inherent in the genetic make-up of each plant from that which is induced by environmental factors during the life of an individual specimen). With this broadening basis of taxonomy there is in progress a revolution towards the more objective and scientific assessment of the nature and significance of resemblances and differences. Traditionally the experienced eye and intuition of the botanist have told him which potential classificatory characters are valuable and which less so or worthless, but by the examination of as wide as possible a range of characters and the comparison of these in a wide range of individuals, now greatly facilitated by electronic devices such as the computer, the element of choice and subjective error can be substantially reduced, though not wholly eliminated.

Nomenclature. We must now move on to deal with nomenclature, of which it cannot be too strongly stressed, taxonomy itself is altogether independent, since a classification can be made of any group of items, whether they be plants or anything else, without recourse to names. The naming of taxa is a separate procedure, though subject by international botanical convention to complex formulated rules; and names themselves are vehicles of communication, their purpose being to convey unambiguously the concept intended by those who originate them.

The **'binomial system'** of nomenclature used at the present day gained acceptance in the mid-eighteenth century when it was first consistently employed by Linnaeus. Each species is given a name or **binomial** consisting of two words: The **generic name** (a proper noun) followed by a qualifying adjective (or noun in apposition), the **specific epithet.** (As the same specific epithet may be used for quite different plants in different genera, specific epithets cannot stand on their own. They merely qualify generic names and are not in themselves names but *epithets*. Earlier it had been the usual practice to refer to plants by a succinct but nevertheless unwieldy descriptive phrase, prefaced by the generic name, as for example: '*Acer foliis tripartito-palmatis, laciniis utrinque emarginatis obtusis, cortice sulcato*' (Linnaeus, *Hortus Cliffortianus*, 1737), which is now *Acer campestre* Linn.

It is important to note that a binomial is more than just a 'handle' by which to refer to a particular species; it is not only a name but a terse classification as well, since the generic name tells the user to which others the species is related and is in a sense a code-word for the generic characters of the group. The serious disadvantage of this otherwise highly practical system is that the names themselves (and not only the subjective classification they reflect) are affected by taxonomic opinion, and instead of being fixed once and for all, must always be to a degree unstable.

It was perhaps inevitable that during the post-Linnaean evolution of the nomenclatural system differences of opinion should have arisen concerning the various conventions that were introduced, and it has been the aim of successive International Congresses during the last one hundred years (the first congress being that held in Paris in 1867) to standardise nomenclatural practice and so to stabilise plant names and prevent name changes other than those occasioned by changes of taxonomic opinion. Among the principles adopted and upheld by successive congresses were those of **priority**, giving precedence to the oldest available name or epithet published in accordance with the rules; the establishment of the original edition of Linnaeus's *Species Plantarum* (1753) as the first place where publication of binomials is to be considered valid; the establishment of a list of generic names to be 'conserved' as exceptions to the rule of priority because of their wide use in preference to older but less well-known names; the laying down of certain conditions for publication of names to be valid, such as the requirement that a Latin diagnosis accompany all names published after a certain date; and so forth. The most serious differences of opinion during the evolution of the rules have concerned the rigidity with which the principle of priority should be maintained. As has already been noted, an exception to the principle has been made in the case of certain generic names which are 'conserved'. In 1905 when the rule of priority was first officially waived for this purpose, however, an unofficial rule was already in existence which represented a major limitation to the application of the principle of priority to specific epithets. This was the so-called 'Kew Rule', practised chiefly by British and certain North American botanists. In any genus the correct epithet to be assigned to a particular species was, under this rule, the earliest published *in combination with the particular generic name*. Thus when a species was found to have been described independently in different genera it was not obligatory to use the earliest specific epithet if it were not already combined with the generic name accepted. The name of the popular *Hydrangea macrophylla* is a case in point. After the introduction of this species by Banks in 1789, this species was named *Hydrangea hortensis* by Sir J. E. Smith, and so it continued to be popularly known. Thunberg, having first collected the plant himself, had, however named it *Viburnum macrophyllum* in 1784. Under modern rules the epithet *macrophylla* therefore, has precedence, but under the 'Kew Rule' *hortensis* could be maintained.

The nomenclature adopted in early editions of the present book (and in the original volumes of the Index Kewensis and many other works) was according to the Kew Rule, and when the rule was abandoned in favour of the principle of priority it was of course necessary to change a very considerable number of well-known names, as in the case of the *Hydrangea* quoted above. A further unfortunate consequence has been that we have been obliged all too frequently to replace well-known epithets for particular species in favour of others more obscure, published earlier but overlooked until brought to light by bibliographical or taxonomic research. Sometimes the name of a well-known plant has had to be changed more than once, like that of the Douglas Fir. Carrière, who was first to place the Douglas Fir in a separate genus, adopted the specific epithet under which it was already well known in combination with a new generic name: *Pseudotsuga douglasii*. Applying the rule of priority, however, the name was changed to *Pseudotsuga taxifolia*, the epithet *taxifolia* having been published earlier than *douglasii*. For many years there was thus a choice of names according to one's views on priority. Subsequently an objection to the epithet *taxifolia* was found and the name *Pseudotsuga mucronata* enjoyed a brief reign. Then grounds were found for restoring *taxifolia* again, to be discredited by another means only a few years later and yet another epithet found, *menziesii*! On the basis of available evidence, *Pseudotsuga menziesii* is certainly the correct name at the time of writing, but for how long? Under the 'Kew Rule', *Pseudotsuga douglasii* would have been the only name from Carrière's time to the present day.

Rigid application of the rule of priority is to be defended however, as an objective means of dealing with alternative names and in general of ensuring that the specific epithet stays the same in whatever genus a species is put, as the option of an individual botanist to choose a new epithet when making a transfer is restricted to certain exceptional cases. Moreover, it is argued, there must come a time when all early epithets have been examined and no further name changes should be necessary by reason of the rule. Nevertheless there is a considerable body of botanical opinion in favour of instituting meanwhile some means of fixing or 'conserving' specific names as a compromise to prevent further aggravating name-changes involving plants of economic or horticultural importance. Inevitably this would be at the expense of the dissension which might be aroused over individual cases and of the necessity of evaluating the merits of a perhaps unending stream of names proposed for conservation. Experience of these disadvantages with the existing list of conserved generic names has taught nomenclaturists to exercise caution in accepting a comparable principle for specific names, but some progress in this direction has been made in recent years.

A particular taxon may be classified by different authorities at different ranks. Very often the same epithet can be used for a taxon whether it is treated, for instance, as a species or as a variety, but the priority of an epithet does not extend beyond that given by its date of publication at any particular rank. Consequently, the epithet that must be used for a taxon is normally the earliest available *at the chosen rank*. The Corsican Pine, for example, was first described as a species by Poiret in 1804, as *Pinus laricio*. Nowadays it is often treated as a variety (*varietas*) of *Pinus nigra* Arnold (1785), along with certain other European Pines. Regardless of the fact that it was not published until 1814 and then in combination, not with *P. nigra* but with *P. sylvestris*, the epithet *maritima*, being the earliest *at varietal rank*, must in these circumstances be adopted (*P. nigra* var. *maritima* (Aiton) Melville, based on *P. sylvestris* var. *maritima* Aiton).

Like the 'Kew Rule', another major issue in the development of the nomenclatural system has been the method by which the application of names should be controlled, and the introduction of the **'type method'**. Before the type method was formulated in the late nineteenth century and incorporated into the International Code of Botanical Nomenclature in 1930, it was the usual practice for the correct application of botanical names to be determined by their circumscription. Broadly speaking, this meant that the publishing author of a taxon would aim to leave no doubt to what group of plants he intended a name to apply, by means of the description he gave and usually by mentioning specimens he had seen. In normal cases, such a method might be adequate, but all too often complications could arise when it was found that the author had in fact included more than one recognisable taxon or element under one name. Some of the 'species' accepted by Linnaeus, for instance, have been found to be compounded of two or more. With such imprecision, differences of opinion could easily arise as to which of such taxa or elements the original name should properly apply. It was to bring precision and objectivity into nomenclature that the type method was eventually adopted. It provides that the names of taxa are to be based on nomenclatural types. The purpose of a nomenclatural type (which in the case of names of species and taxa of lower ranks is usually a specimen, but may be an illustration or a description) is to associate finally and incontrovertibly a particular name with a particular unique and indivisible individual plant or portion of a plant, in order that there can be no argument over the application of the name. There is no implication whatever that the chosen nomenclatural type is in any way representative of the range of individuals which may subsequently be considered to belong to the same taxon. Nomenclatural types thus typify in a *nomenclatural* and not a *taxonomic* sense; in other words, a nomenclatural type is not necessarily a 'typical' or average example of the mass of individuals which are given the same name. The name *Rosa banksiae*, for instance, was based on material of the double-flowered form, which came into cultivation long before the 'normal' single form. The importance of nomenclatural types is such that the International Code lays down that the nomenclatural type of each new taxon described must be cited, and strongly recommends that the type should be 'deposited in a permanent responsible institution' and be scrupulously conserved.

A phrase still frequently encountered in the literature of horticulture that is a source of confusion and misunderstanding because of the ambiguity of the word 'type' runs something like this: 'The var. (whatever it may be) differs from the type in the following characters . . . ' By 'type' in expressions of this nature the *typical variety* (*varietas*) or *type variety* is meant, not the nomenclatural type of the species, which is normally a single individual. In the days before the advent of the type method a species was sometimes thought of rather loosely as an entity distinct from its varieties, and the description of a species in a book such as this would not necessarily cover characters and variation exhibited by the named varieties. In a hierarchical system, however, all the varieties of a species are of course included taxonomically within the limits of the species, and all the individual plants of the species which are not to be identified with named varieties must be considered to belong to the same variety as the *nomenclatural type* of the species, i.e. to the typical or type variety.

Under the type method, names of all named varieties are based on types; the nomenclatural type of the typical variety will by definition be the same as that of the species. The nomenclature of the typical variety of a species, as well as that of the typical *forma* of a variety and so on, is governed by a hard and fast rule which states that in the name of a taxon which includes the nomenclatural type of the next higher taxon, the epithet of the lower taxon repeats that of the higher. The rule may be illustrated by reference to the example of *Pinus nigra* used earlier. For many years the Austrian Pine was known as *P. nigra* var. *austriaca*, but the nomenclatural type of *P. nigra* is in fact identifiable with the Austrian variety rather than with any of the others such as the Corsican (var. *maritima*). Regardless, therefore, of the prior publication of the epithet *austriaca*, the correct varietal epithet is *nigra*, and the name of the Austrian Pine is *P. nigra* var. *nigra*. Such epithets as *typica*, *genuina* and *normalis* which were used for a time for typical varieties are not now allowed.

Implied in all that has so far been said are two principles of nomenclature both more fundamental than the law of priority or the type method: That there can only be one correct name under a particular classification for any individual taxon and that the same name cannot correctly be applied to more than one taxon. For various reasons, however, a taxon may have been given more than one, sometimes many, different names, which are termed **synonyms**. In the relatively rare case when, for instance, through ignorance by one authority of the work of another, the names which are synonyms are based on the same identical nomenclatural type, they are nomenclatural synonyms; there is no possibility that they could apply to different taxa. More commonly, synonyms result from changes of classification, either through the union of taxa previously described as distinct, or by the change of rank or systematic position of a taxon.

Synonyms, then, are different names for the same taxon, and are unfortunately all too numerous. The opposite situation also not uncommonly arises when the same name has been proposed for two or more different taxa. Names which duplicate one another are termed **homonyms** and are subject to the law of priority, so that later homonyms must be rejected. The name *Spiraea corymbosa*, for instance, given by Roxburgh in 1832 to a Sino-Japanese species, must be rejected because it duplicates the same name given by Rafinesque to a North American species in 1814. The correct name of the Sino-Japanese species is *S. cantoniensis* Lour.; the North American species retains the name *S. corymbosa* Raf. The law of priority is, however, waived in the following circumstances to preclude the creation of homonyms: If a species is transferred to another genus and the transfer of the specific epithet would result in the new name being a homonym, a new epithet must be chosen for the species transferred, even if its present epithet is older than that already combined in the genus to which it is being transferred.

In the *Spiraea* example, Roxburgh used the descriptive epithet *corymbosa* in ignorance of Rafinesque's work. At the present day it is less excusable for a botanist to duplicate a name accidentally in this way when describing a new taxon. It sometimes happens, however, that a botanist writing a formal description of a taxon in a monographic work or a flora may unintentionally misapply a name because the material with which he is working is in fact misidentified. Such a misapplication though it may effectively duplicate the use of the name is not technically a homonym, as it was not the intention of the author to describe a new taxon. A case of a species with a misapplied name was "*Cotoneaster buxifolia*" of gardens. Grown for many years and figured under this name, the plant was not the true *C. buxifolia* of Wallich but something else (*C. prostrata* Baker).

A feature of modern nomenclatural practice which will concern users of this book for the first time in this edition is the '**double citation**' of authorities. It is laid down by the International Code that for a botanical name to be accurate and complete the name of the authority who first published it should be cited. (This has been done in previous editions.) A further rule adds that when a taxon is reclassified without change of epithet, the name of the original author must be cited in parentheses, followed by the name of the author who effected the alteration. A new name occasioned by such a reclassification is termed a **new combination** and the method of citing authorities referred to as 'double citation'. Some examples are given below. The original name is termed the **basionym** and must be cited, together with its place of publication, when a new combination based on it is made. The name *Chaenomeles japonica* (Thunberg) Lindley ex Spach was (when first published) a new combination which had as its basionym *Cydonia japonica* Thunberg. The name *Cotoneaster bacillaris* Lindley is the basionym of *Cotoneaster affinis* Lindley var. *bacillaris* (Lindley) Schneider.

The Code recommends but does not lay down that when a name has been proposed but not validly published by one author and is subsequently validly published and ascribed to him by another author, the name of the former author followed by the connecting word *ex* may be inserted before the name of the publishing author, as in the example (*Chaenomeles*) above. For brevity's sake, only the name of the publishing author (being the more important) is cited in this edition except in certain instances where it has seemed desirable to give the citation in full. Similarly, when one author has published a name and description in the work of another, only the name of the author who supplied the name and description is given here.

CHAPTER X

CULTIVARS AND THEIR NOMENCLATURE

The plants cultivated by Man are broadly of two kinds. On the one hand there are those which have been brought into cultivation from the wild but do not differ in any significant way from the parental stock. These bear in cultivation the names that are applied to the same taxa growing in nature and their nomenclature is governed by the rules of the Botanical Code. On the other hand, there are the variants of wild plants that have arisen in cultivation by selection, or hybridisation. For such man-made (or man-maintained) plants the term cultivar has been coined (abbreviated cv.) and their naming, for long a haphazard affair, is now subject to the International Code of Nomenclature for Cultivated Plants (here referred to for shortness as the Cultivar Code). The first edition of this Code, drawn up under the auspices of the Seventh International Botanical Congress (Stockholm, 1950) and the Thirteenth International Horticultural Congress (London, 1952), was published in 1953. The subsequent editions (1958, 1961) and the one now current (published in 1969) were drawn up by the International Commission for the Nomenclature of Cultivated Plants.

It is not necessary here to summarise those provisions of the Cultivar Code which govern the choice of names for new garden varieties, but certain of its articles are retroactive and have had to be taken into consideration in preparing the present revision. The application of these articles, and some of the problems encountered, must be discussed. The references are to the current (1961) edition of the Cultivar Code.

Article 29 of this Code rules that a cultivar name, when immediately following a botanical or common name, must be distinguished clearly from the latter, either by placing the prefix cv. before the cultivar name or in some other way, usually by placing the cultivar name in single quotation marks and/or distinguishing it from the botanical part of the name typographically, e.g. *Calluna vulgaris* 'Tib' or *C. vulgaris* cv. Tib, Lilac 'Mont Blanc' or Lilac cv. Mont

Blanc.* The name chosen for a new cultivar must now (as from 1st January 1959) be a 'fancy' name (*nom de fantaisie*), that is, an invented name markedly different from a botanical epithet.† This regulation finally puts an end to the practice of dubbing garden varieties with Latin epithets of botanical form—*nana, argentea, pendula, kewensis, veitchii*, etc. As must be explained later, this usage has led to an almost irremediable confusion in the nomenclature of woody cultivars, since, being of botanical form, they came to be treated according to the rules of botanical nomenclature. Many such names are, in fact, perfectly valid according to botanical rules but it is legitimate to treat the Latin epithets as cultivar names if the plants concerned are in fact cultivars and not wild variants. If this is the case then the Latin epithet is treated in exactly the same way as a 'fancy' name, e.g. *Fagus sylvatica* 'Rohanii', *F. sylvatica* 'Purpurea Pendula'.

* In this revision, cultivar names, when appearing in side-headings, are indicated both by the prefix cv. and by single quotation marks. The prefix cv. is needed as a counterpart to the botanical prefixes var. and f.; single quotation marks are added for further emphasis and because they are the commonest method of denoting a cultivar. Normally, however, it is quite unnecessary to use both devices, and the prefix cv. is dispensed with when cultivar names are mentioned in the running text, or where listed separately from botanical names.

† This rule, far from being new, simply reasserts Article 40 of De Candolle's *Lois de la Nomenclature Botanique*, adopted at the International Botanical Congress, Paris, 1867. It reads: 'Seedlings, half-breeds (*métis*) of unknown origin and sports should receive from horticulturalists fancy names (*noms de fantaisie*) in common language, as distinct as possible from the Latin names of species and varieties . . .'. Fancy names had, of course, long been used for florists' plants but the strict application of Article 40 of the Paris Code would have resulted in their being used in other groups (even the conifers!) where Latin epithets and phrase-names had long held sway. The Paris Code was not binding on horticulturalists, but it is interesting to note that it was received with enthusiasm by the *Gardeners' Chronicle*, and some pungent editorial comment on the excessive use of Latin by gardeners appeared in that periodical during 1868. For example: 'In the matter of nomenclature botanists are to blame from ignorance, nurserymen from the vicious habit some have of copying botanical usages in cases where they are not applicable' (page 78); and 'For our parts we simply contend for the principle that botanists' names and horticulturalists' names . . . should be as distinct in form as possible. Neither botanist nor horticulturalist should in this matter poach on the other's manor' (page 737).

The De Candolle rule was never strictly observed and a reactionary tendency set in early this century. The use of pseudobotanical epithets for plants of garden origin was permitted in the draft code adopted by the International Horticultural Congress of 1910 (*Journ. R.H.S.*, Vol. 37, pp. 140–151) and also in the appendix on garden nomenclature published in the 1935 edition of the International Rules of Botanical Nomenclature, which helps to explain why this practice has persisted until so recently. Botanists are apt to blame horticulturalists for the resulting confusion, but in the past they seem often to have turned a blind eye on the 'poaching' or even connived at it.

It is in the treatment of Latin-named cultivars that the present edition differs most markedly from previous ones, in which no distinction was made between a true botanical variety (varietas) and a garden variety (cultivar), although it was in most cases obvious enough from the context in which sense the prefix var. was intended. This was, until very recently, the general practice, though in some works, notably in Rehder's *Bibliography*, the lowly taxonomic status of variants of garden origin was emphasised by giving them the rank of botanical formae.

In the majority of instances the true status of a Latin-named variant is easily decided. For example *F. sylvatica* 'Rohanii' is the result of hybridisation in a garden between the purple beech and a cut-leaved beech; *Chamaecyparis lawsoniana* 'Fletcheri' derives fom a branch sport. The fact that these variants have been given botanical status is of no significance and the equivalent botanical names can be discarded.

There is, however, a hard core of cases that cannot be so easily disposed of. In the wild state, numerous woody species produce minor departures from the normal form in such characters as branching habit, form or colour of leaf, fruit- or flower-colour etc., and it is therefore only to be expected that similar variants should occur now and then in nursery seed-beds; indeed it would be surprising if they did not do so. These minor variants may not be particularly common, nor of great interest to taxonomic botanists, but none the less they are an expression of the genetic potentialities of the species and certainly they do not owe their origin to Man. There is the further difficulty that the origin of many variants grown in gardens is completely unknown. There is a well-known cut-leaved form of the common alder the name of which might be given as *A. glutinosa* f. *imperialis* (Lemaire) Kirchn. or 'cultivar-wise' as *A. glutinosa* 'Imperialis'. If the decision in this and numerous other similar cases depended on knowledge of the origin of the plant, then the task of applying the Cultivar Code would be impossible.

Fortunately this problem recedes once it is recognised that even if a pendulous, golden or cut-leaved seedling is a gift of Nature, the clone (see p. 113) deriving from it is man-made and therefore a cultivar. This argument can be taken further. If an individual plant of horticultural interest is discovered growing in the wild and is propagated vegetatively, either directly or after being moved bodily into a garden, then it is permitted to regard the resulting clone as a cultivar since it represents the artificial multiplication of an individual which 'if unmolested upon its native hills would quickly have passed away into the type from which it sprang' (Lindley in *Bot. Reg.*, under t. 822). There are many clones that have originated in this way, e.g. *Erica carnea* 'Springwood White' and *Calluna vulgaris* 'H. E. Beale', and, despite their wild origin, their status as cultivars is implicitly recognised in the latest (1966) edition of the Botanical Code (Article 28) where the examples given are *Phlox nivalis* 'Gladwyne' and, for good measure, *Phlox nivalis* 'Azure'. In the cases mentioned the clone bears a 'fancy' name, but in the interest of consistency the status of cultivar should also be given to plants which bear Latin epithets but originated in the same way, e.g. the Florence Court yew *Taxus baccata* 'Fastigiata' and many others (see further below).

It follows from the above discussion that in certain cases a name can be presented in two different ways according to the meaning intended. For example, in *Traité Général des Conifères* (1855, p. 207) Carrière published the name *Abies pectinata pendula* Hort., with particular reference to a plant that had arisen in a nursery seed-bed at Ville d'Avray some twenty years earlier. However, he adds that the same variant had been raised at other times and other places; and, although he did not mention it, such trees also occur in the wild. Thus the description can be taken as publication of the cultivar name 'Pendula' for the Ville d'Avray tree. But the name is also valid in a botanical sense and appears in Rehder's *Bibliography* as *A. alba* f. *pendula* (Carr.) Rehd., which is of general application to all pendulously branched trees of *A. alba*. Another example is provided by André's broom, for which the botanical name is *Cytisus scoparius* f. *andreanus* (Puissant) Zabel. The original account by Puissant constitutes valid publication of the basionym *Genista andreana*; but he states that the type plant was dug up, moved to a garden and propagated by approach-grafting—a treatment not generally accorded to nomenclatural types! Thus the epithet *andreanus* can also be used as a cultivar name ('Andreanus') for the clone descended from the type plant.

A comparable but slightly different case is *Erica vagans* 'St Keverne'. This a clone of wild origin which was subsequently given botanical status as *E. vagans* var. *kevernensis* Turrill. The question which name is correct does not arise, since both are correct in the appropriate context. 'St Keverne' is a clonal name for the descendants of a particular wild individual, whereas var. *kevernensis* is a collective botanical name which *could* be used for plants similar to 'St Keverne' but of independent origin, if such plants were found and thought worthy of taxonomic recognition.

Thus the prefix cv. (or single quotation marks), when used in association with a Latin epithet, is intended to indicate that the epithet is really the equivalent of a fancy name (i.e., one in a modern language). Among woody ornamentals a fancy name would almost invariably indicate a clone, and in the interests of uniformity it is obviously desirable that Latin epithets, when bearing the prefix cv., or contained in single quotation marks, should have the same meaning. In conformity with this principle the appropriate botanical name is used in this work wherever a variant, no matter how minor, is being discussed collectively, i.e., when reference is being made to plants, wild and cultivated, which share the general characters by which the taxon (usually a forma) is defined. But if the type of the taxon was a member of a clone, or the originator of a clone, then the Latin epithet, given 'cultivar-wise', is intended to indicate that clone.

The above considerations should make it clear why certain variants are treated under their botanical names in this revision, even though they are known to have arisen in cultivation. For reasons explained earlier in this chapter it is impossible, and indeed unscientific, to attempt to draw a hard line between the sports of the forest and hedgerow and the sports of the nursery. For clarity of nomenclature and rationality of discourse it is more important to recognise and maintain the distinctness between a collective name, which a plant bears by virtue of possessing the general characters by which the group is defined, and a clonal name. Confusion between these two kinds of name was the worst feature of the old system of garden nomenclature. The history of many cultivars is so obscure, the nomenclature so confused, and the original descriptions often so inadequate, that it cannot be claimed with any confidence that the principle stated above has been applied accurately in every instance. But at least the criteria adopted are objective and their application to particular cases challengeable on grounds of fact.

A difficult problem is presented by cultivars which have been propagated partly by vegetative means and partly by seeds. An example is the purple-leaved form of *Acer palmatum*. In giving the name of this variant as *A. palmatum* 'Atropurpureum' it is assumed that only vegetatively raised plants, true to type, are entitled to this cultivar name and that seedlings, which are very variable, should be regarded as non-authentic and sold for what they are. This is in accordance with British nursery practice. There are certain cases where it might be desirable to 'protect' an important clone from non-authentic seedlings by giving it a name in some modern language. See, for example, the discussion under *Taxus baccata* 'Fastigiata'.

Nomenclature. The rules governing the nomenclature of cultivars differ in some respects from those applicable to botanical categories, the nomenclature of which is, of course, governed by the Botanical Code. This raises some problems concerning the correct naming of cultivars that bear Latin names, since these were, until recently, treated as botanical taxa.

Under Article 27 (c) it is laid down that when a cultivar name may be chosen from two or more previously published botanical epithets in Latin form, the epithet chosen should be the one which best preserves established usage. There are, unfortunately, some cases where a clone no longer has an established name. For example, there is a well-known cut-leaved clone of the grey alder *A. incana* which appears in modern works, published since the Cultivar Code came into force, as either 'Laciniata', 'Acuminata' or 'Acutiloba'. In previous editions of this work it was called var. *incisa* Dippel but fortunately the name 'Incisa' is not available as a fourth possibility, since it is now realised that Dippel's variety was a different clone. Of the three rival epithets, *laciniata* is the only one which can be regarded as having been used over a long period as the garden name for this clone and is therefore adopted here as the cultivar name. Similar plants are to be found in the wild state and the name for these would be either *A. incana* f. *laciniata* (Loud.) Hylander or, if Rehder's *Bibliography* were followed, then *A. incana* f. *acutiloba* (Koch) Hallier.

The convention by which Latin-named cultivars were treated according to botanical rules has often resulted in a perfectly distinct clone being relegated to synonymy under the name of a clone of earlier origin, merely on the grounds that they were similar in a botanical sense. The following are examples:

(*a*) There was once a cultivar of *Arbutus unedo* known as *croomei* which when first introduced was hailed as being an improvement on the old *rubra*. But according to *botanical* criteria they are one and the same, with the result that *A. unedo croomei* was sunk into the syn-onymy of *A. unedo* var. *rubra* Aiton. If the true *croomei* can be found it should certainly be called *A. unedo* 'Croomei'.

(*b*) A number of different clones of pendulous beech were put into commerce in the last century, the earliest of which was named *F. sylvatica* var. *pendula* by Loudon, in reference to a form offered by Loddiges' nursery. Later clones received distinctive epithets—*remillyensis*, *borneyensis*, *miltonensis*, etc., but there was a tendency in gardens to call these variants *pendula remillyensis*, *pendula borneyensis*, etc. (this is how they appear in Schelle's *Handbuch der Laubholz-benennung*, 1907). But inevitably the second part of the name tended to be dropped. In Rehder's *Bibliography* all three names appear in the synonymy of *F. sylvatica* f. *pendula* (Loud.) Schelle, but this should not be taken as meaning that Rehder was so ignorant as to believe that all these epithets represented one clone. He was making a botanical statement, namely that the four pendulous beeches be-longed to the same group (forma), for which *pendula* was the earliest epithet. His view was that, if gardeners persisted in giving pseudo-botanical names to their clones, they must expect them to be treated according to botanical criteria. Indeed, the *Bibliography*, in which his views found their most comprehensive expression, may have helped to deliver the *coup de grâce* to the practice of giving Latin names to the oddments of seed-beds. By pushing it to its logical conclusion he exposed its essential fatuity. The cultivar names *F. sylvatica* 'Remillyensis' etc. should, of course, always be used if the original clone can be identified; the cultivar name 'Pendula' belongs only to the form distributed by Loddiges and should not be used for *any* pendulous beech.

The application of botanical rules to Latin-named cultivars has thus been a source of confusion, since formerly distinct clones came to be lumped under one name. The same situation also arose in another way. In the days when plants of garden origin were dubbed with descriptive epithets such as *nana*, *glauca*, etc. it was inevitable that similar but distinct plants came to bear the same epithet. In practice this did not matter much since there was nothing in such a name as, say, *Aucuba japonica longifolia* to imply that any particular clone was being offered. If a gardener bought this plant from William Bull of Chelsea he would get Bull's *longifolia*; if from Standish, then that firm's version. The retroactive application of the Cultivar Code in such cases often leads to a specious appearance of exactitude, since a descriptive epithet in single quotation marks implies the same precision of meaning as a 'fancy' name would have among florists' plants, which is far from always being the case. The solution is either to restrict the epithet to the clone which originally bore it, or, if that clone can no longer be identified, then to revert to the use of a horticultural trinomial, e.g. *Aucuba japonica longifolia*. Unfortunately these 'straight' trinomials, in which the status of the infraspecific variant is not indicated by a prefix, are not sanctioned by either the Botanical or the Cultivar Code, although still used in gardens for botanical varieties, where they are least appropriate. In the present revision a group of confused clones is treated under its botanical name, e.g. *Aucuba japonica* f. *longifolia*, but the cultivar name 'Longifolia' would be perfectly correct for the Veitchian form, which was the first to be named.

In botanical treatments of Latin-named cultivars the original 'varietal' name, if it consisted of more than one word, had to be shortened and often altered in form, since a true botanical epithet must, of course, consist of a single word. Sometimes the botanical epithet has displaced the original phrase-name in garden usage and if so, it is accepted in the present revision. But where the original garden name is still in use it is retained, e.g. *A. palmatum* 'Linearilobum Atropurpureum' and *Fagus sylvatica* 'Purpurea Pendula'; these names are to be preferred to 'Atrolineare' and 'Purpureo-pendula', which represent very inelegant attempts to reduce the garden name to a single botanical epithet.

There are cases where a cultivar received a 'fancy' name which was subsequently Latinised. The original name is revived in the present revision unless there are reasonable grounds for not so doing. Hence + *Crataegomespilus dardarii* 'Jules d'Asnières', not 'Asnieresii', *Ilex aquifolium* 'J. C. van Tol', not 'Polycarpa'. But the rendering *Acer platanoides* 'Stollii' is retained, since the original name 'Oekonomierath Stoll' is rather cumbrous (this is permissible under Article 35 of the Cultivar Code).

It may happen that a cultivar belongs botanically not to the typical variety ('type') of a species but to some other botanical variety that has been distinguished. Must the cultivar name in such cases be placed after the full botanical name? The Cultivar Code is not very explicit in this matter but the deduction to be drawn from Article 25 is that this is a matter for individual judgement. Common sense dictates that the cultivar name should be kept as near to the generic name as possible, both for shortness and to make the full name less subject to nomenclatural changes at the botanical level. A good example is provided by the clone once known as *Acer palmatum septemlobum elegans*. Under botanical rules the varietal epithet *septemlobum* has proved to be invalid and replaced by *heptalobum* (*A. palmatum* var. *heptalobum* Rehd.). This variety, although founded on cultivars, is said to occur in the wild. But if we turn to Ohwi's *Flora of Japan* we find that two wild varieties are recognised in addition to the typical one and that these are called var. *amoenum* and var. *matsumurae*; Rehder's var. *heptalobum* is ignored. Clearly then the taxonomy and nomenclature of the botanical varieties of *A. palmatum* is a controversial matter. But there is no need for the clone mentioned to be involved in it if the name is given simply as *A. palmatum* 'Elegans'.

Hybrids. Whereas the name of a cultivar deriving from a single species is usually placed after the specific name, the presentation of the names of hybrid cultivars is somewhat more complex, but essentially the same. It is not unusual, and perfectly in order, for the names of hybrid clones to be placed immediately after the generic name, e.g. *Ceanothus* 'Gloire de Versailles'. It is not desirable, nor necessary, to insert a multiplication sign in front of the latter. The multiplication sign should be used only in formulas, or as a prefix to a collective epithet of Latin form (see below).

It is often convenient and sometimes necessary to group inter-specific cultivars, and there are three principal ways of doing this. This first is by means of a formula, e.g. *Prunus campanulata* × *incisa* is a collective name for all hybrids between these two species. The clone 'Okame' belongs here and its name could be given in full as *P.* (*campanulata* × *incisa*) 'Okame', the words in brackets being equivalent to a specific epithet. However, the insertion of the formula is not necessary, since the clone is adequately distinguished if the name is given as *Prunus* 'Okame'.

The commonest and most familiar way of naming hybrid groups is by means of a botanical name of binomial form, with the insertion of a multiplication sign between the generic noun and the 'specific' epithet, e.g. *Cistus* × *florentinus* is a collective name for hybrids between *C. monspeliensis* and *salviifolius*. Such collective names of Latin form are subject to all the provisions of the Botanical Code, and this is so even if the hybrids are of garden origin or, indeed, even if the parent species are not in contact in the wild state and could therefore only hybridise if brought together in gardens. Under present-day rules, a collective name for an interspecific cross, if of Latin form, would have to be published in a scientific journal with a diagnosis in Latin. Before 1935, however, an adequate description in a modern language in the horticultural press was enough to constitute valid publication, with the result that many hybrid cultivars attained botanical status if they happened to have been given Latin names, as was often the case. For example, the collective names *Cytisus* × *dallimorei* and *Caryopteris* × *clandonensis* were both published in reference to single plants that were subsequently propagated vegetatively, and thus came to bear a dual meaning. *C.* × *clandonensis* is a collective name for hybrids between *C. incana* and *C. mongolica*, but in garden usage it meant the clone descended from the plant raised by the late Arthur Simmonds, which was selected for its hardiness. This ambiguity would have remained latent but for the fact that the original clone sets fertile seed and indeed produced self-sown seedlings; these, as Mr Simmonds himself pointed out, were not necessarily so hardy as the original. Furthermore, named clones of the same parentage emerged, with the result that an awkward contrast has to be made between *C.* × *clandonensis*, meaning the original clone, and *C.* × *clandonensis* 'Kew Blue', where the botanical name has its proper collective sense. Under the new rules of nomenclature this situation cannot arise, since the original cultivar of a hybrid group would receive its own distinctive cultivar name and the collective epithet for the group would assume its proper meaning from the start (Article 45). In the interests of clarity it has been necessary to restrict certain collective names to their proper meaning by adopting new cultivar names for the original clones. The name 'John Waterer' is already in use for the original clone of *Cotoneaster* × *watereri* and certain other new clonal names used here were published in 1969, e.g. 'Darley Dale' for the original clone of *Erica* × *darleyensis*. An alternative method of distinguishing the original cultivar of a hybrid group is to repeat the collective Latin epithet. For example, the name *Deutzia* × *rosea* 'Rosea' is perfectly correct for the hybrid cultivar which Lemoine originally put out as *D. gracilis rosea*. It is also appropriate, since all the other cultivars in the group bear Latin names, e.g. *D.* × *rosea* 'Carminea'. This method is, of course, only applicable where a collective epithet is founded on a cultivar and the original cultivar still exists.

A third device, generally used for the naming of rhododendron crosses, is to employ a name in some modern language, the collective significance of which may be indicated by prefixing it with the sign 'g.', an abbreviation of 'grex' (Latin for swarm or flock). This method will be discussed further under *Rhododendron* in Volume III. Whether it should be accepted in other woody genera is a question on which there appears to have been no authoritative ruling. Vernacular grex-names in other genera than *Rhododendron* are not recognised in this work.

GLOSSARY

Technical terms have been avoided as much as possible, but to avoid inconvenient length of phrase, especially in regard to shape of leaf and form of inflorescence, a few botanical terms have been employed. They are also necessary to define the parts of the flower and the particular kind of fruit. See also the glossary of nursery terms at the end of Chapter III; and the various definitions of taxonomic and nomenclatural terms given in Chapter VIII.

Abortive. Only partially developed.

Achene. A small, dry, single-seeded fruit not splitting when ripe.

Acuminate. Having a gradually tapered point.

Acute. Sharply pointed, but less gradually tapered than acuminate.

Adnate. United to a different organ, e.g. the filament of a stamen to the corolla (cf. *connate*).

Alternate. Not opposite to each other on the axis.

Androecium. The male part of a flower; the stamens considered collectively.

Anther. That part of the stamen carrying the pollen.

Apex. The end (applied to the termination of leaf, petal, etc.).

Apocarpous. With carpels free from one another.

Apomixis. A term for abnormal types of reproduction in which seed is produced without the union of male and female cells (gametes). A plant known to reproduce in this way is known as an *apomict.*

Appressed. Lying close to or against.

Aril. A fleshy outgrowth from the base of the seed, which it partly or wholly covers.

Auricle. An appendage or lobe shaped like an ear.

Awl-shaped. Narrow, and tapering from the base to a stiff point: subulate.

Axil. The angle formed on the upper side by the union of leaf-stalk and stem, or by the chief veins and midrib.

Axillary. Springing from an axil. Usually applied to an inflorescence arising at that part of a stem, as distinct from the end.

Basionym. See page 100.

Berry. A fruit whose seeds are not surrounded by a stony layer and are immersed in a pulpy or juicy substance enclosed by a skin.

Bisexual. Having both stamens and pistils: hermaphrodite: perfect.

112

Bract. A leaf-like organ or a degenerate leaf from whose axil the flower or inflorescence is produced.

Bullate. Puckered or blistered.

Calyx. The outer envelope of the flower composed of sepals (outside the petals). Often used in the same sense as 'calyx-tube' or receptacle.

Calyx-tube. Strictly, the tube of a calyx in which the sepals are united; also used in the same sense as 'receptacle' (q.v.).

Campanulate. Bell-shaped.

Capitate. Densely clustered into a head; head-like.

Capsule. A dry dehiscent fruit of two or more cells.

Carpel. A simple pistil or one part of a several-celled pistil.

Catkin. A slender, often tail-like, inflorescence, with scale-like bracts and stalkless flowers.

Caudate. Tail-like.

Chromosomes. Bodies contained within the cell-nuclei which bear the 'genetic code' that determines the inheritable characters of a living organism.

Ciliate. Fringed with hairs; usually applied to the margins of leaves or petals.

Circinate. Inwardly coiled upon itself.

Clone. A group of identical plants having their origin from a single plant by vegetative propagation.

Compound (composite). Made up of several parts or units, like a rose leaf or the flower-head of a daisy.

Cone. The fruit of pines, firs, spruces, etc., made up of overlapping scales.

Connate. United to a similar organ (e.g. petal to petal, or the base of a leaf to that of the opposite leaf).

Convolute. Rolled.

Cordate. (Of leaf-base) With two rounded lobes, separated by a sinus.

Corolla. The inner envelope of the flower composed of petals (inside the calyx).

Corymb. An inflorescence of flat or flattish shape, in which the stalks of the outer flowers are long enough to bring them to approximately the same level as the inner ones.

Crenate. Applied to leaf margins with rounded teeth.

Culm. The stem of a grass or bamboo.

Cultivar. The term '. . . denotes an assemblage of cultivated plants which is clearly distinguished by any characters (morphological, physiological, cytological, chemical, or others), and which, when reproduced (sexually or asexually), retains its distinguishing characters'. (*Code of Nomenclature for Cultivated Plants*. Article 10.)

See further in Chapter X.

Cuspidate. Abruptly tipped with a sharp, rigid point.

cv. Abbreviation of cultivar.

Cyme. A broad, flattish, flower-cluster, the inner or terminal flowers opening first, as in *Euonymus*.

Decurrent. As when the edges of the leaf are continued down the stem or petiole as raised lines or narrow wings.

Decussate. Applied to leaves arranged oppositely, but with one pair standing at right angles to the next pair (as in *Hebe*).

Dehiscent. Splitting open to release the contents.

Deltoid. Shaped like an equal-sided triangle.

Dentate. Prominently toothed, the teeth directed outwards, e.g. of leaf-margins.

Digitate. Applied to compound leaves, in which the leaflets arise from the same point at the end of the common stalk (as in horse-chestnut).

Dimorphic. Occurring in two forms on the same plant, e.g. leaves of many junipers, or applied to a species existing in two distinct forms, as *Colletia cruciata*.

Dioecious. Applied to plants which have male and female flowers borne on separate individuals.

Diploid. Having two sets of chromosomes in the nuclei of its body-cells, one set being contributed by the male gamete, the other by the female. A plant with more than two sets is *polyploid*; if the number of sets is four the plant is *tetraploid*. Plants with three sets of chromosomes are *triploid*; they often arise from the crossing of diploids and tetraploids and are usually sterile.

Disk. A development from the receptacle, sometimes nectar-secreting.

Distichous. Applied to leaves arranged oppositely, and superposed in two ranks.

Down. A covering of short, fine, soft hairs.

Drupe. A fruit in which the seed is enclosed by an inner hard stony layer and an outer fleshy layer (plum).

Eglandular. Destitute of glands.

Ellipsoid. Said of a solid body that is elliptical in outline.

Emarginate. Notched at the tip.

Endemic. Confined to a limited geographical region.

Entire. Not toothed or lobed (applied to leaf-margins, etc.).

Epicalyx. An involucre of bracts below the flower resembling an extra calyx.

Epiphyte. A plant that grows on other plants, drawing nourishment from organic residues (rotted leaves and bark, etc.) present on the host-plant, but not parasitic on it.

Exserted. Projecting beyond; sticking out.

Fasciated. Applied to stems or branchlets which form a broad, flat shoot, as though two or more stems or branchlets have become united side by side.

Fasciculate. Applied to a cluster of flowers each with its own stalk but all arising from the same point, say a leaf-axil.

Fastigiate. Of close erect growth, e.g. the Lombardy poplar.

Filament. The stalk of a stamen supporting the anther.

Fimbriate. With the margin bordered by long slender processes.

Follicle. A dehiscent fruit developed from a single pistil and dehiscing along one side only.

f. Abbreviation of *forma* (q.v.).

Forma. A botanical taxon lower in rank than a variety (*varietas*). See p. 92.

Free. Not united to another organ.

Gamopetalous. With petals more or less united.

Glabrous. Smooth, without hairs or down.

Gland. A protuberance on leaves, young shoots and parts of flowers, sometimes on hairs or bristles, often secreting and viscid.

Glaucous. Covered with a white or blue-white bloom.

Glume. A papery bract; usually applied to the sterile bracts found at the base of spikelet of a grass or bamboo.

Grex. A group of hybrid cultivars. This term, abbreviated g., is used most commonly in the naming of hybrids of *Rhododendron*, where it is customary to use vernacular ('fancy') names for hybrid groups. Thus g. Fabia (the Fabia grex) is the group-name for hybrids between *R. griersonianum* and *R. dichroanthum*.

Gynoecium. The female part of a flower (used most commonly where this consists of more than one pistil).

Habit. Manner of growth.

Hermaphrodite. With both sexes together, a complete flower with stamens and pistils both functional.

Hybrid. A plant resulting from a cross between two genetically dissimilar plants, usually belonging to two different species.

Imbricate. Overlapping like tiles.

Impressed. Sunk below the surface, like, e.g., the veins in a bullate leaf.

Incised. Deeply and irregularly cut.

Included. Not protruding.

Indehiscent. Used in reference to a fruit that does not open to release its seeds.

Indumentum. A hairy covering.

Inferior ovary. An ovary that lies below the level of insertion of the perianth. The tissues that surround the ovary, and on which the perianth is borne, are by some authorities regarded as an outgrowth from the receptacle, by others as the result of the growing together of the lower parts of the perianth and stamens. An ovary is termed *superior* if it is borne above the point of attachment of perianth and stamens. But intermediate conditions are to be found in some genera and families (see the introductory notes to *Prunus* and *Rosa*).

Inflorescence. The arrangement of the flowers.

Infraspecific. Used in reference to any taxon (q.v.) below the level of the species.

Inserted. Attached.

Internodes. The spaces on a branchlet between the joints or nodes.

Involucre. Two or more bracts united below an inflorescence.

Involute. When the edges of the leaves are rolled inwards.

Keel. The boat-shaped lowermost 'petal' of a flower of the Pea family formed by the fusion of two petals.

Laciniate. Cut into narrow segments.

Lamellate. (Of pith) Forming thin transverse plates.

Lanceolate. Shaped like a lance-head; applied to leaves several times longer than wide and broadest below the middle.

Latex. Milky sap.

Lemma. The lower of the two bracts immediately enclosing the flower of a grass or bamboo. The upper of the two is known as the *palea*.

Lenticel. A corky or wart-like protuberance on the surface of a shoot.

Lepidote. With a covering of scale-like hairs, as on the undersides of the leaves of many species of *Rhododendron*.

Limb. The expended portion of a petal, as distinct from its stalk or claw.

Linear. Applied to narrow leaves, petals, etc., several times longer than wide, with parallel margins.

Lip. Applied to the upper and lower divisions of a corolla, as in the Labiate family (lavender, salvia, etc.).

Lobes. The primary divisions of a simple leaf or other organ (leaf of sycamore).

Lobulate. Faintly lobed.

Lobule. A small lobe.

Locule. (Of ovary) Cell or compartment.

Loculicidal. Splitting down the middle of each cell of the fruit.

Midrib. The primary or central rib of a leaf; the prolongation of its stalk.

Monoecious. Applied to plants which have male and female flowers borne on the same individual.

Monotypic. Applied to a genus that contains a single species.

Mucro. A small abrupt point or tip.

Node. The joint of a branchlet; the place bearing bud or leaf.

Nutlet. A small dry one-seeded indehiscent fruit.

Oblanceolate. Inversely lanceolate, the broadest part being above the middle.

Oblate. Round, flattened top and bottom, broader than long.

Obovate. Inversely egg-shaped in outline, the broadest part being above the middle (see *ovate*).

Obovoid. Applied to solids having the shape of an egg in outline, the thickest end uppermost.

Odd-pinnate. (Of a pinnate leaf) Having a terminal leaflet.

Operculum. Defined in the introductory note to Eucalyptus.

Orbicular. Circular in outline.

Ovary. The part of the flower enclosing the ovules which ultimately develop into seeds; the lowest part of the pistil, as distinct from the style and stigma.

Ovate. Applied to flat objects having the outline of an egg, the widest part being below the middle. A common shape of leaf and petal.

Ovoid. Applied to solid objects having the outline of an egg. Common in fruits.

Ovule. The body within the ovary (usually one of many) which, after fertilisation, develops into a seed.

Palmate. Applied to leaves with radiating lobes, as in *Fatsia japonica*.

Panicle. A branched inflorescence strictly a branched raceme, as distinct from a simple raceme or spike.

Pappus. The limb of the calyx in the family Compositae, much divided or downy, to assist in the dispersion of the seed by wind.

Pedicel. The stalk of a flower.

Peduncle. The stalk of an inflorescence (below the lowermost flower).

Peltate. Applied to leaves which are attached to their stalks by the lower surface, not at the margin.

Perfect. Applied to flowers which have effective male and female organs, as opposed to unisexual or sterile.

Perianth. The envelope of the flower. Usually applied in practice to flowers which have only calyx or corolla, or in which the two are not distinguishable.

Petal. A division of the corolla; strictly only applicable when it is quite separate and distinct.

Petiole. The stalk of a leaf.

Phylloclade. A branch, more or less flattened and functioning as a leaf.

Phyllode. The flattened petiole or stalk of a leaf, resembling and functioning as a leaf-blade.

Pinnae. The leaflets of a pinnate leaf, or the primary divisions of a doubly pinnate one.

Pinnate. Applied to leaves composed of leaflets arranged along each side of a common stalk; feather-like.

Pistil. An ovary with its style(s) (if present) and stigma(s).

Pollen. A usually yellow powder borne in the anthers; the male or fertilising material.

Polygamous. Bearing both unisexual and bisexual flowers.

Polygamo-dioecious. Functionally dioecious, but also bearing a few bisexual flowers.

Polymorphic. Variable in habit (growth-form) or botanical characters.

Polyploid. See under *diploid.*

Pome. A fruit made up of several carpels enclosed in a thick layer of flesh, e.g. apple.

Procumbent. Trailing or lying flat but not rooting.

Pruinose. Covered with a waxy powder (bloom).

Pubescent. Covered with short soft hairs.

Pyramidal. (Of trees) Conical.

Raceme. An inflorescence in which the flowers are about equally stalked, and borne on a more or less elongated axis; the oldest flowers at the base, the youngest at the top.

Rachis. The common axis of a compound leaf, or raceme, spike, etc. on which the leaflets or flowers are borne.

Receptacle. The more or less enlarged end of a stem, on which the floral parts are borne. The term is also used for the cup or tube that surrounds the ovary (or ovaries) in such genera as *Prunus, Rosa* and *Eucalyptus,* although this is now considered by many authorities to derive mainly or partly from floral tissues and not to be receptacular in origin as once believed.

Reniform. Kidney-shaped.

Reticulate. Net-veined.

Retuse. Slightly notched at the rounded apex.

Revolute. With the margin rolled towards the underside.

Rhomboidal. Diamond- or lozenge-shaped.

Rugose. Wrinkled.

Samara. An indehiscent, winged fruit, as in the maples, ashes, elms, etc.

Scale. Applied to scarious bodies borne on various parts of plants; such as the enclosing parts of flower-buds, leaf-buds, acorn-cups, etc. The term is also applied to branched hairs in which the branches are united into a disk, e.g. the scales on the undersides of the leaves in the lepidote series of *Rhododendron,* or in the Elaeagnaceae.

Septicidal. Applied to a capsule that splits along the partitions.

Serrate. With forward-pointing saw-like teeth.

Sessile. Not stalked.

Simple. The opposite of compound.

Sinus. The recess ('bay') between two lobes or teeth.

Spathulate. Spoon-shaped.

Spike. An inflorescence with the flowers sessile along a simple undivided axis.

Spikelet. In grasses a small spike composed of one or more flowers enclosed by glumes.

Staminode. A sterile stamen; staminodes are sometimes petal-like and showy.

Standard. The broad upper petal of a flower of the Pea family.

Stellate. Starlike; hairs with several arms radiating horizontally.

Stigma. The point or surface of the pistil which receives the pollen.

Stipel. The stipule of a leaflet.

Stolon. A horizontal shoot which roots.

Stone. The inner part of a drupe, consisting of the hardened, innermost tissues of the ovary-wall and containing one or (more rarely) several seeds.

Striate. Marked with parallel longitudinal lines, grooves or ridges.

Style. The usually elongated part of the pistil between the ovary and the stigma.

Subulate. Awl-shaped, tapering from base to apex.

Syncarpous. Composed of two or more united carpels.

Synonym. See page 98.

Taxon. A unit of classification, such as a family, genus, species or variety. See page 89.

Taxonomy. See page 89.

Tepal. A petal-like segment; the term is used in the description of flowers where there is no differentiation into sepals and petals, e.g. *Calycanthus* (or the tulips).

Terete. Cylindrical, circular in transverse section.

Ternate. Arranged in threes; applied to leaves.

Tessellated. Having colours or surface divisions in regularly arranged squares or patches; chequered.

Testa. The outer coat of a seed.

Tetraploid. See under *diploid.*

Trifoliolate. Composed of three leaflets, e.g. leaf of Laburnum.

Triploid. See under *diploid.*

Truncate. Ending abruptly, as if cut off.

Umbel. An inflorescence in which a number of stalked flowers are clustered at the end of a common stalk.

Umbo. A conical projection, a boss.

Unisexual. Of one sex only, as distinct from hermaphrodite, bisexual and perfect.

Valvate. (Of buds) With the segments meeting by the edges but not overlapping (cf. *imbricate*).

Valve. One of the several parts into which a capsule splits as it dehisces.

var. Abbreviation of *varietas* (botanical variety).

Variety. According to context, this word may mean a botanical variety (*varietas*) or a garden variety (cultivar). See Chapters IX and X.

Veins. Ramifications of fibro-vascular bundles proceeding from the midrib and traversing the blade of a leaf or a petal.

Whorl. Applied to flowers or leaves borne in a circle round a stalk or branchlet.

Wing. A flat membranous expansion; one of the two lateral petals of a flower of the Pea family.

Woolly. Covered with long and soft hairs (chiefly on stems or leaves).

SELECT BIBLIOGRAPHY

The following is a list of the chief botanical and horticultural works of which use has been made in preparing the present work. It has been thought worth while to print it here as a guide to the most important literature dealing, in particular, with hardy trees and shrubs. It might of course, be indefinitely amplified, but will, nevertheless, serve to direct the attention of those who desire to make up a collection of works on this fascinating branch of natural history to the best and most useful of them. A number of modern works devoted to the floras of those parts of the temperate world which are especially rich in woody plants of horticultural interest have been included in the list. Works devoted to a single genus or part thereof have been omitted, but are mentioned in the introduction to the genus concerned. See also the specialised bibliographies at the ends of Chapters I and VIII.

ALLAN, H. H.—*Flora of New Zealand*, Vol. 1. Wellington, 1961. 8vo. liv + 1085 pp., 40 text-figures, and 4 maps.

ARNOLD-FOSTER, W.—*Shrubs for the Milder Counties.* London, 1948. 1 vol. 8vo, viii + 367 pp., and 41 plates.

BAKER, H. CLINTON.—*Illustrations of Conifers.* Hertford, 1909–13. 3 vols. 4to, 230 plates, with text.

BOOM, B. K.—*Nederlandse Dendrologie.* Ed. 5, Wageningen, 1965. 1 vol. 8vo, 456 pp., and numerous text-figures.

BRETSCHNEIDER, EMIL.—*History of European Botanical Discoveries in China.* St Petersburg, 1898; reprint, Leipzig, 1962. 2 vols. 8vo, 1167 pp.

BRITTON, NATHANIEL LORD, and JOHN A. SHAFER.—*North American Trees.* New York, 1908. 1 vol. 8vo, 904 pp., with 781 text-figures.

CARRIÈRE, ÉLIE ABEL.—*Traité général des Conifères.* Paris, 1855. 1 vol. 8vo, xv + 656 pp. Ed. 2. Paris, 1867. 1 vol. 8vo, xii + 910 pp.

CARTER, H. GILBERT.—*British Trees and Shrubs*, including those commonly planted. London, 1936. 1 vol. 8vo, 291 pp.

CHITTENDEN, F. J. (ed.).— *Conifers in Cultivation*: The Report of the Conifer Conference held by the Royal Horticultural Society, 1931. London, 1932. 1 vol. 8vo, 634 pp., and some plates.

CHITTENDEN, F. J. (ed.).—*Ornamental Flowering Trees and Shrubs*: Report of the Conference held by the Royal Horticultural Society, 1938. London, 1940. 1 vol. 8vo, 271 pp., and 80 plates.

COWAN, J. M. (ed.).—*The Journeys and Plant Introductions of George Forrest*. London, 1952. 1 vol. 8vo, xi + 252 pp., numerous plates, and one map.

COX, E. H. M.—*The Plant Introductions of Reginald Farrer*. London, 1930. 1 vol. 4to, ix + 113 pp., with 16 plates (12 coloured).

COX, E. H. M.—*Plant Hunting in China*. London, 1945. 1 vol. 8vo, 230 pp., 25 plates, and 3 maps.

COX, E. H. M. and P. A.—*Modern Shrubs*. London, 1958. 1 vol. 8vo, xii + 220 pp., 4 colour plates, and 21 text-figures.

COX, E. H. M. and P. A.—*Modern Trees*. London, 1961. 1 vol. 8vo, x + 185 pp., 4 colour plates, and 23 text-figures.

CURTIS, WINIFRED M.—*A Student's Flora of Tasmania*. Hobart, 1956– . 8vo. Parts 1 to 3 have been published, 661 pp., and numerous text-figures.

DALLIMORE, W.—*Holly, Yew and Box*. London and New York, 1908. 1 vol. 8vo, 284 pp., with 44 plates.

DALLIMORE, W., and JACKSON, A. B.—*A Handbook of Coniferae and Ginkgoaceae*. Ed. 4, revised by S. G. Harrison, London, 1966. 1 vol. 8vo, xix + 729 pp., 46 plates, and 131 text-figures.

DAME, LORIN L., and HENRY BROOKS.—*Handbook of the Trees of New England*. Boston, 1902. 1 vol. 8vo, xiv + 196 pp., with 87 plates.

DEN OUDEN, P., and BOOM, B. K.— *Manual of Cultivated Conifers*. The Hague, 1965. 1 vol. 4to, x + 526 pp., and numerous text-figures.

DIPPEL, LEOPOLD.—*Handbuch der Laubholzkunde*. Berlin, 1889–93. 3 vols. (parts) 8vo, xv + 1792 pp., and 831 figures.

DUHAMEL DU MONCEAU, HENRI LOUIS. *Traité des arbres et arbustes*. Paris, 1755. 2 vols. 4to; vol. i, lxii + 368 pp., and 139 plates; vol. ii, 387 pp., and 111 plates. A second edition of this work, edited by J. L. A. Loiseleur-Deslongchamps and Etienne Michel, with figures by P. J. Redouté and P. Bessa, was published at Paris, 1801–19. 7 vols. folio, with 488 plates. This fine work is often cited as 'Nouveau Duhamel'.

EASTWOOD, ALICE.—*A Handbook of the Trees of California*. San Francisco, 1905. 1 vol. 8vo, 86 pp., and 57 plates.

EDLIN, H. L.—*British Woodland Trees*. London, 1944. 1 vol. 8vo, 132 pp., with 133 plates and numerous text-figures.

ELWES, HENRY JOHN, and AUGUSTINE HENRY.—*The Trees of Great*

Britain and Ireland. Edinburgh, 1906–13. 7 vols. 4to, xxiv + 2022 pp., and 411 plates.

EMERSON, GEORGE BURRELL.—*Trees and Shrubs of Massachussetts.* Boston, 1846. 1 vol. 8vo, xv + 547 pp., and 17 plates. Ed. 2. Boston, 1875. 2 vols. 8vo; vol. i, xxii + 318 pp., and 79 plates; vol. ii, ix + 306 pp., and 64 plates.

FORBES, JAMES.—*Pinetum Woburnense; or, a Catalogue of the Coniferous Plants in the Collection of the Duke of Bedford at Woburn Abbey.* London, 1839. Large 8vo, 67 coloured plates, and 1 uncoloured.

GLEASON, H. A.—*Illustrated Flora of the Northeastern United States and Adjacent Canada* ('The New Britton and Brown'). New York, 1952. 3 vols. 4to; vol. i, lxxv + 482 pp.; vol. ii, 655 pp.; vol. iii, 595 pp., all with numerous text-figures.

GRAY, A.—*Manual of Botany.* Ed. 8, revised by M. L. Fernald, New York, 1950. 1 vol. 8vo, lxiv + 1632 pp.

HARLOW, W. M., and HARRAR, E. S.—*Textbook of Dendrology.* Ed. 4, New York, 1958. 1 vol. 8vo, ix + 561 pp., 236 text-figures, and numerous distribution maps.

HEGI, GUSTAV.—*Illustrierte Flora von Mitteleuropa.* Ed. 1, Munich, 1906–31. 7 vols. 4to. Ed. 2, Munich, 1936– . A richly illustrated work of which the second edition is in course of publication.

HEMSLEY, WM BOTTING.—*Handbook of hardy Trees, Shrubs, and Herbaceous Plants.* Based on the French work of Messrs Decaisne and Naudin. London, 1873. 1 vol. 8vo, xliii + 687 pp., and 264 text-figures.

HORNIBROOK, M.—*Dwarf and slow-growing Conifers.* London, 1923. 1 vol. 8vo. Ed. 2, 1938, 286 pp., and 39 plates.

JACKSON, A. B.—*Catalogue of the Trees and Shrubs at Westonbirt.* Oxford, 1927. 1 vol. 4to, viii + 206 pp., and 67 plates.

JACKSON, A. B.—*Catalogue of the Trees and Shrubs at Borde Hill, Sussex.* 1 vol. 8vo, viii + 284 pp., 8 plates, and one map.

JAY, B. A.—*Conifers in Britain: An Illustrated Guide to Identification.* London, 1952. 1 vol. 8vo, 47 pp., and 136 plates.

JEPSON, WILLIS LINN.—*The Silva of California.* Berkeley, 1910. 1 vol. 4to, with 85 plates, 3 maps, and 10 text-figures.

JEPSON, W. L.—*The Trees of California.* San Francisco, 1909. 1 vol. 8vo, 228 pp., with 117 figures.

KENT, ADOLPHUS H.—*Veitch's Manual of the Coniferae.* Chelsea, 1881. New Edition, Chelsea, 1900. 1 vol. 8vo, 562 pp., with about 160 text-figures.

KOCH, KARL.—*Dendrologie*. Erlangen, 1869–73. 8vo, Theil i, 735 pp.; Theil ii, 1089 pp.

KOEHNE, EMIL.—*Deutsche Dendrologie*. Stuttgart, 1893. 8vo, 601 pp., 100 text-figures.

KRÜSSMANN, GERD.—*Handbuch der Laubgehölze*. Berlin, 1960–2. 2 vols. 4to. Vol. i, vi + 495 pp., 164 plates and 305 text-figures; vol. ii, 608 pp., 220 plates, and 333 text-figures.

KRÜSSMANN, GERD.—*Die Nadelgehölze*. Ed. 2., Berlin, 1960. 1 vol. 8vo, 335 pp., and 419 text-figures.

LAVALLÉE, ALPHONSE.—*Arboretum Segrezianum*. Paris, 1880–5. 1 vol. 4to, iv + 121 pp., and 36 plates.

LAWSON, A. H.—*Bamboos. A Gardener's Guide to their Cultivation in Temperate Climates*. 8vo, 192 pp., 9 line drawings and 19 plates. London, 1968.

LI, HUI-LIN.—*Woody Flora of Taiwan*. Narberth, Pennsylvania, 1963. 1 vol. 8vo, x + 974 pp., and 371 text-figures.

LOUDON, JOHN CLAUDIUS.—*Arboretum et Fruticetum Britannicum; or, the Trees and Shrubs of Britain, native and foreign*. London, 1838. 8 vols. 8vo; 4 vols. of text, illustrated by about 2500 figures, and 4 vols. of plates.

LOUDON, J. C.—*An Encyclopedia of Trees and Shrubs*. An abridgement of the preceding. London, 1842. 8vo, lxxii + 1162 pp., 2109 text-figures. Re-issued in 1875.

MCMINN, H. E.—*An Illustrated Manual of California Shrubs*. Berkeley and Los Angeles, 1951. 1 vol. 8vo, xi + 663 pp., and 775 text-figures.

MAKINS, F. K.—*The Identification of Trees and Shrubs*. 1 vol. 8vo, 326 pp., including 128 pp. of diagrams. London, 1935.

MITFORD, ALGERNON BERTRAM FREEMAN (Lord Redesdale).—*The Bamboo Garden*. London, 1896. 1 vol. 8vo, xi + 224 pp., with 10 figures.

MONGREDIEN, AUGUSTUS.—*Trees and Shrubs for English Plantations*. London, 1870. 1 vol. 8vo, x + 388 pp., with 29 text-figures.

MOUILLEFERT, PIERRE.—*Traité des Arbres et Arbrisseaux forestiers*. Paris, 1892–8. 2 vols. (parts) of text (xvi + 1403 pp.), and 195 plates.

MUNZ, P. A.—*A California Flora*. Berkeley and Los Angeles, 1959. 1 vol. 8vo, 1681 pp.

MURRAY, ANDREW.—*The Pines and Firs of Japan*. London, 1863. 1 vol. 8vo, 124 pp., with 224 text-figures.

OHWI, J.—*Flora of Japan.* Washington, D.C., 1965. 1 vol. 4to, ix + 1067 pp., 17 plates, 17 text-figures, and one map.

RAVENSCROFT, EDWARD JAMES.—*The Pinetum Britannicum.* A descriptive account of hardy Coniferous trees cultivated in Britain (sometimes called 'Lawson's Pinetum Britannicum'). The botanical descriptions were contributed by J. Lindley, A. Murray, and M. T. Masters. Edinburgh and London, 1863–84. 3 vols. large folio, 331 pp. 53 plates, mostly coloured, and numerous text-figures.

REHDER, ALFRED.—*Manual of Cultivated Trees and Shrubs.* Ed. 2, New York, 1940; reprint 1956. 1 vol. 8vo, xxx + 996 pp.

REHDER, ALFRED.—*Bibliography of Cultivated Trees and Shrubs.* Jamaica Plain, 1949. 1 vol. 4to, xl + 825 pp.

ROGERS, CHAS. COLTMAN.—*Conifers and their Characteristics.* London, 1920. 1 vol. 8vo, ix + 333 pp. with numerous full-page figures.

SARGENT, CHARLES SPRAGUE.—*The Silva of North America.* A description of the trees which grow naturally in N. America, exclusive of Mexico. Boston and New York, 1891–1902. 14 vols. 4to, 704 plates, with text; Ed. 2, 1922, 1 vol. 8vo, xxiv + 910 pp., map, and 783 text-figures.

SARGENT, C. S.—*Manual of the Trees of North America* (exclusive of Mexico). Boston and New York, 1905. 1 vol. 8vo, xxiii + 826 pp., map, and 642 text-figures.

SARGENT, C. S.—*Forest Flora of Japan.* Boston and New York, 1894. 1 vol. 4to, 93 pp., and 26 plates.

SARGENT, C. S.—*Trees and Shrubs.* Illustrations and descriptions of new or little known ligneous plants. Boston and New York. 4to; vol. i, 1902–5, 217 pp., and 100 plates; vol. ii (completed 1913), 100 plates.

SARGENT, C. S.—*Plantae Wilsonianae.* An enumeration of the woody plants collected in W. China for the Arnold Arboretum during 1907, 1908, and 1910, by E. H. Wilson. Cambridge, Mass., 1911–17. 8vo. Nine parts, forming three volumes.

SCHNEIDER, CAMILLO KARL.—*Illustriertes Handbuch der Laubholzkunde.* Jena, 1904–12. 2 vols. 8vo, 1880 pp., with 1088 text-figures; index, 136 pp.

SHIRASAWA, HOMI.—*Inconographie des essences forestières du Japon.* Tokyo, 1900–8. 2 vols. folio, 120 coloured plates, text in 2 vols. 8vo. Paris, 1899 (in French).

THURSTON, EDGAR.—*Trees and Shrubs in Cornwall.* Cambridge, 1930. 1 vol. 8vo, xi + 288 pp., with 42 plates.

TUTIN, T. G., HEYWOOD, V. H. et al. (ed.).— *Flora Europaea*, Cambridge, 1964– . 4to. Vol. i, 1964, Lycopodiaceae to Platanaceae, xxxii + 464 pp., and 5 maps; Vol. ii, 1968, Rosaceae to Umbelliferae, xxvii + 455 pp., maps.

U.S. DEPARTMENT OF AGRICULTURE, FOREST SERVICE.—*Silvics of Forest Trees of the United States*. Washington, D.C., 1965. 1 vol. 4to, vi + 762 pp., with numerous text-figures and distribution maps.

WATSON, PETER WILLIAM.—*Dendrologia Britannica; or, Trees that will Live in the Open Air of Britain*. London, 1825. 2 vols. 8vo, 172 coloured plates.

WELCH, H. J.—*Dwarf Conifers*. London, 1966. 1 vol. 4to, 334 pp., 20 identifications plates, and 285 text figures.

WILSON, E. H.—*The Conifers and Taxads of Japan*. Cambridge, Mass., December 1916. 1 vol. 4to, 91 pp., and 59 plates.

WYMAN, DONALD.—*Shrubs and Vines for American Gardens*. New York, 1949. 1 vol. 8vo, 442 pp., numerous text-figures, and one map.

WYMAN, DONALD.—*Trees for American Gardens*. Ed. 2, New York, 1965. 1 vol. 8vo, viii + 502 pp., numerous text-figures, and one map.

APPROXIMATE METRIC EQUIVALENTS

$\frac{1}{32}$ in = 0·8 mm	$\frac{3}{4}$ in = 19·1 mm	4 in = 101 mm
$\frac{1}{16}$ = 1·6	$\frac{7}{8}$ = 22·2	5 = 127
$\frac{1}{8}$ = 3·2	1 = 25·4	6 = 152
$\frac{3}{16}$ = 4·8	$1\frac{1}{4}$ = 31·8	7 = 178
$\frac{5}{16}$ = 7·9	$1\frac{1}{2}$ = 38·1	8 = 203
$\frac{3}{8}$ = 9·5	$1\frac{3}{4}$ = 44·5	9 = 229
$\frac{7}{16}$ = 11·1	2 = 51	10 = 254
$\frac{1}{2}$ = 12·7	3 = 76	11 = 279
$\frac{5}{8}$ = 15·9		12 = 305

FEET TO METRES

2 ft = 0·61 m	12 ft = 3·66 m	60 ft = 18·3 m
3 = 0·91	15 = 4·57	70 = 21·3
4 = 1·22	20 = 6·10	80 = 24·4
5 = 1·52	25 = 7·62	90 = 27·4
6 = 1·83	30 = 9·15	100 = 30·5
7 = 2·13	35 = 10·67	110 = 33·5
8 = 2·44	40 = 12·20	120 = 36·6
9 = 2·74	45 = 13·72	130 = 39·6
10 = 3·05	50 = 15·2	140 = 42·7
11 = 3·55		150 = 45·7

ALTITUDES TO METRES

500 ft = 152 m	4,000 ft = 1,219 m
1,000 = 305	5,000 = 1,524
1,500 = 457	10,000 = 3,048
3,000 = 914	15,000 = 4,572

TEMPERATURES: °F TO °C

0 °F = −17·8 °C	45 °F = 7·2 °C
10 = −12·2	50 = 10·0
20 = −6·7	55 = 12·8
32 = 0·0	60 = 15·6
40 = 4·4	65 = 18·3
	70 = 21·1

TREE MEASUREMENTS

All measurements of girth were taken at 5 ft (1·52 m) unless otherwise stated.

PART FOUR

PLATES

LIST OF PLATES

1 ABELIA × GRANDIFLORA

2 ABELIOPHYLLUM DISTICHUM

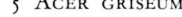

3 ABIES MAGNIFICA

4 ABUTILON MEGAPOTAMICUM VARIEGATUM   5 ACER GRISEUM

6 ACACIA DEALBATA

7 ACER PALMATUM DISSECTUM

8 ACER OPALUS at Kew

9 AESCULUS INDICA at Kew

10 Amelanchier asiatica

11 Alnus maximowiczii

12 ARALIA ELATA 'VARIEGATA'

13 ARBUTUS × ANDRACHNOIDES
at Kew

14 ARCTOSTAPHYLOS MANZANITA

15 ARISTOLOCHIA MACROPHYLLA
in fruit

16 ARUNDINARIA NITIDA

17 Berberis linearifolia

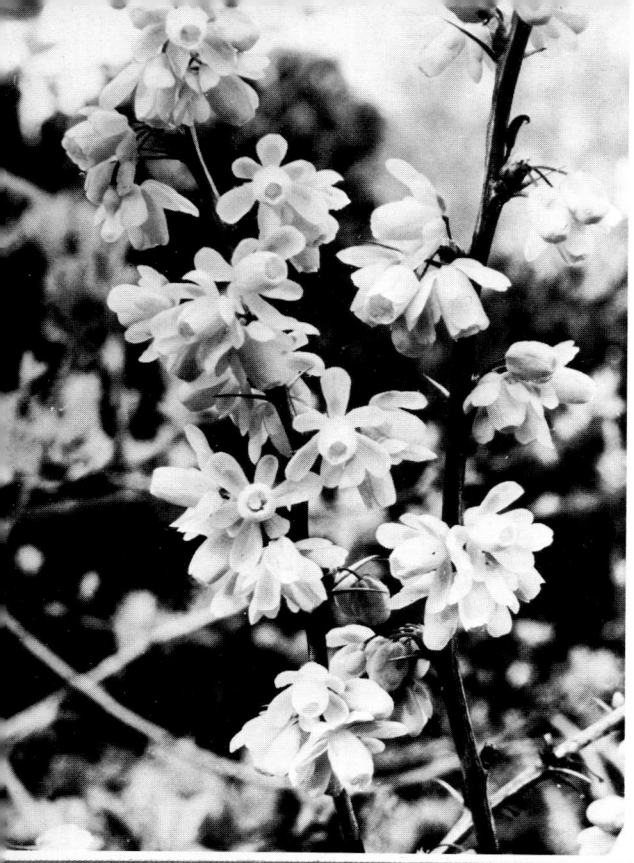

18 Berberis 'Sibbertoft Coral'

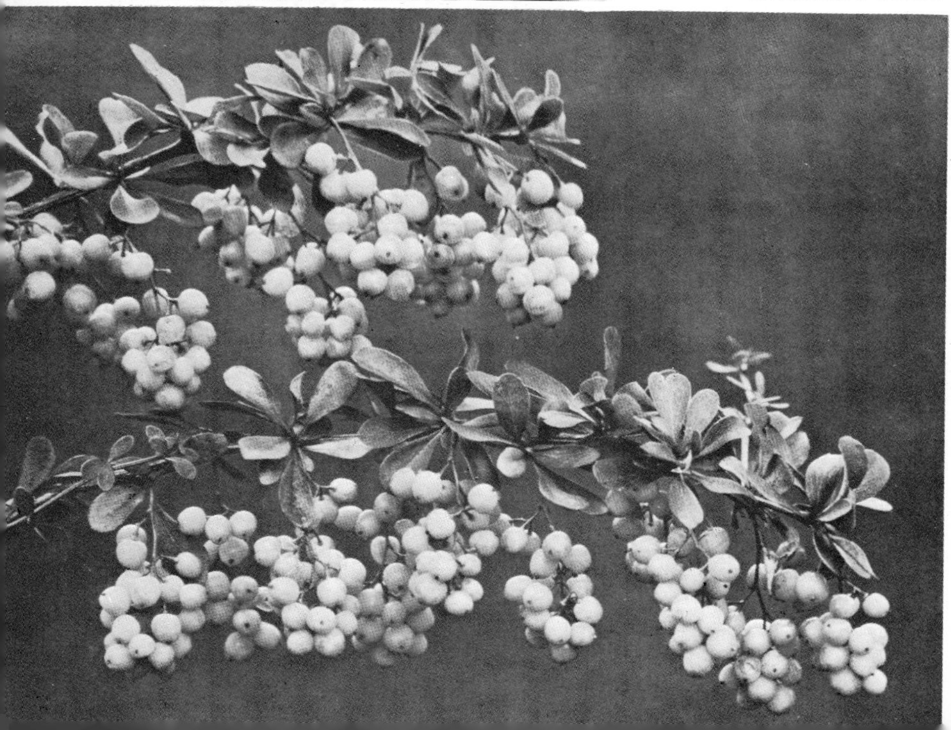

19 BETULA ALBO-SINENSIS at Werrington Park

20 BETULA JACQUEMONTII near Sonamarg, Kashmir

21 BIGNONIA CAPREOLATA

BUDDLEIA ALTERNIFOLIA at Wisley

23 BUDDLEIA CRISPA

24 Caesalpinia japonica

25 .Camellia reticulata. The Captain Rawes Camellia

26 Camellia saluenensis

27 Campsis grandiflora

28 Carpentaria californica

29 CARPINUS TURCZANINOWII at Highdown

30 Caryopteris × clandonensis

31 Cassiope lycopodioides

32 CASSIOPE FASTIGIATA in Bhutan

33 CATALPA BIGNONIOIDES at Kew

34 CASTANEA SATIVA 'ALBO-MARGINATA'

35 CEANOTHUS
'GLOIRE DE VERSAILLES'

36 CELASTRUS ORBICULATUS

37 Cedrus·libani

38 CERCIDIPHYLLUM JAPONICUM at Westonbirt

39 Cercis siliquastrum

40 Ceratostigma willmottianum

41 Chaenomeles speciosa 'Simonii'

42 Chamaecyparis formosensis

43 CHAMAECYPARIS LAWSONIANA. A group of garden varieties at Kew

44 CHIONANTHUS RETUSUS
at Highlands Park,
Rochester, New York

45 CHIMONANTHUS PRAECOX

46 Cistus × lusitanicus 'Decumbens'

47 Cistus × cyprius

48 Cladrastis sinensis at Kew

49 Clematis armandii
at the Savill Gardens

50 Clematis macropetala

51 Clematis montana var. rubens at Kew

52 CLEMATIS ORIENTALIS growing on *Hippophae rhamnoides* in the Himalaya

53 Clematis tangutica

54 Clethra delavayi

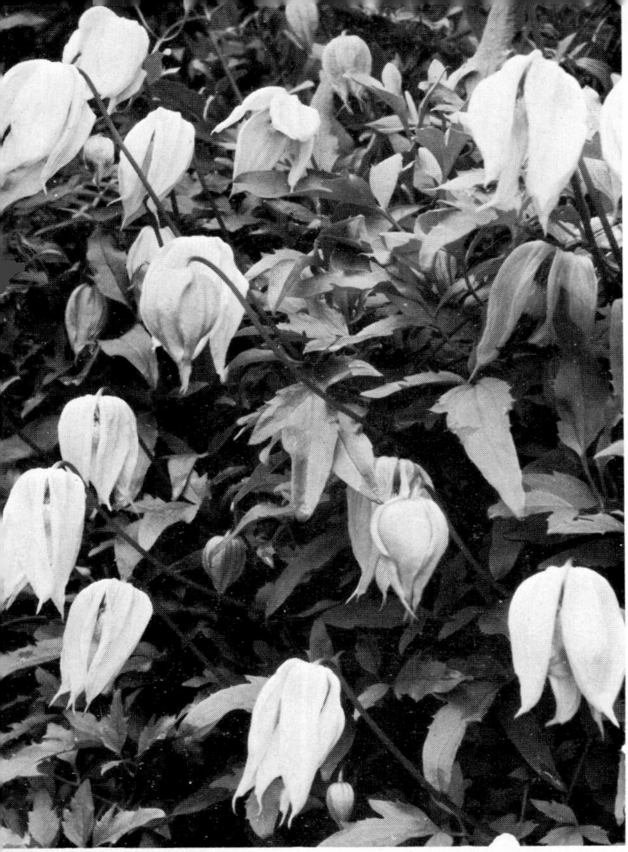

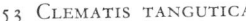

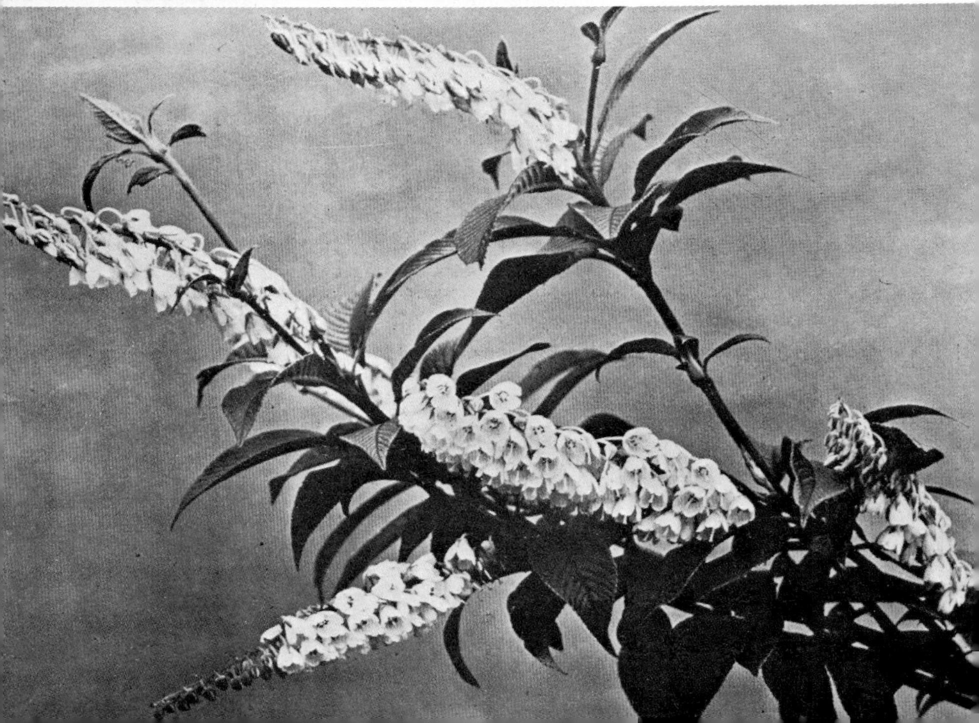

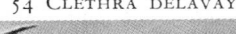

55 COLLETIA CRUCIATA

56 CORDYLINE AUSTRALIS in Cornwall

57 Convolvulus cneorum

58 Cornus kousa

59 Cornus chinensis

60 Cornus controversa 'Varieg

61 CORNUS FLORIDA

62 CORONILLA GLAUCA

63 Corylopsis sinensis

64 Corylopsis willmottiae

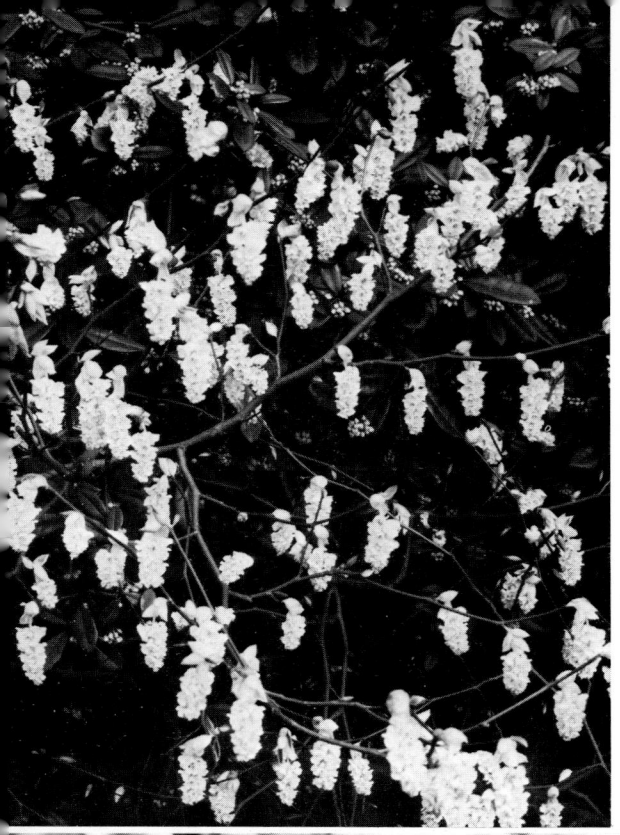

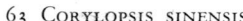

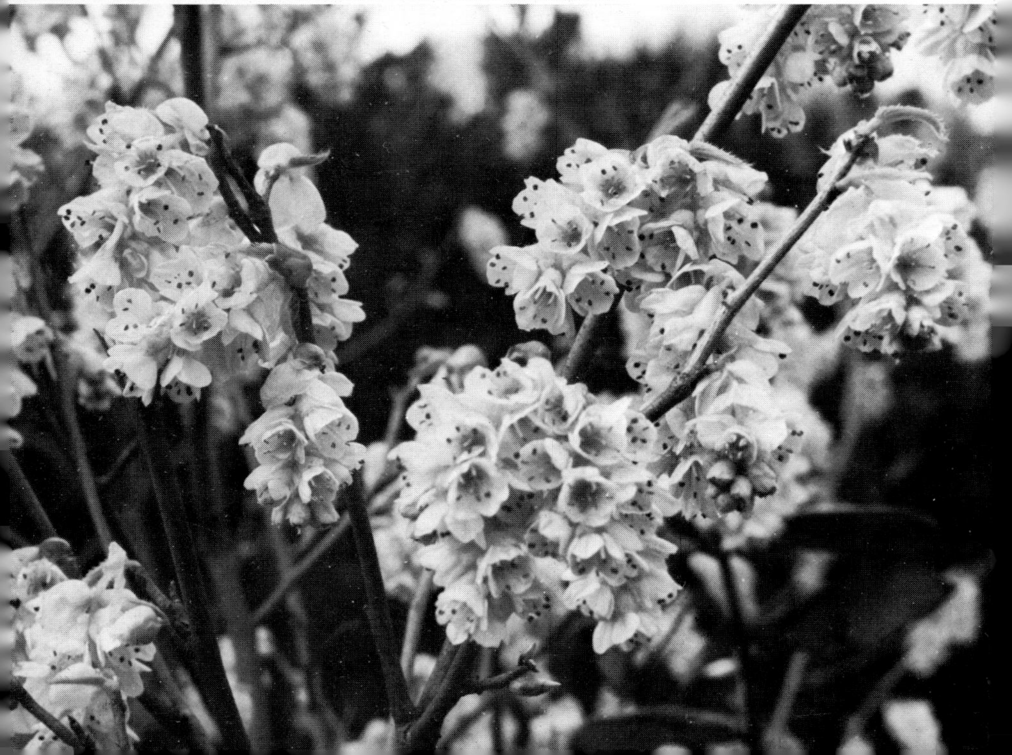

65 Cotinus coggygria

66 Cotoneaster multiflorus

67 Cotoneaster conspicuus

68 Crataegus phaenopyrum at K[...]

69 Crataegus mollis

70 Crataegus prunifolia
at Kew

71 Cryptomeria japonica

72 CUNNINGHAMIA LANCEOLATA. A photograph taken by E. H. Wilson southeast of Tatsien-lu in 1908

73　× Cupressocyparis leylandii at Kew

74 CYTISUS × KEWENSIS

75 CYTISUS × BEANII

76 Cytisus purpureus

77 Cytisus battandieri

PART FIVE

DESCRIPTIONS AND INDEX

ABELIA CAPRIFOLIACEAE

A genus of shrubs named in honour of Dr Clarke Abel, who first discovered *A. chinensis* whilst attached to Lord Amherst's embassy to China in 1816–17. About half a score species are at present in cultivation, which come from China, Japan, the Himalaya, and Mexico. Leaves opposite, or in threes; corolla tubular to bell-shaped; calyx composed of two to five sepals, which remain long on the plants after the corolla has fallen; stamens four.

With two or three exceptions, the abelias are scarcely hardy enough to succeed in the average climate of the British Isles unless wall protection be given; but provided the situation is warm enough, they are not in any way difficult to cultivate. They like an open, loamy soil, and can very easily be increased by means of cuttings made of half-ripened wood in July; these should be placed in pots of sandy soil, and plunged in a frame where there is a little bottom heat.

A. CHINENSIS R. Br.
A. rupestris Lindl.

A deciduous shrub 3 to 5 ft high, of spreading habit, the young branches covered with minute reddish down. Leaves ovate, pointed, tapered or rounded at the base, ¾ to 1½ in. long, ½ to 1 in. wide, toothed (sometimes obscurely so), downy at the base of the midrib beneath, and with few or many hairs scattered over the upper surface. Flowers white, fragrant, produced during summer and autumn in forking clusters from the terminal leaf-axils, the whole forming a short terminal panicle; the flowers are mostly in pairs on each stalk. Corolla ½ in. long, scarcely as wide, funnel-shaped, hairy inside and out. Calyx composed of five rosy-tinted, slightly downy sepals, each ¼ in. long and obovate. Stamens protruded. *Bot. Mag.*, n.s., t. 168.

Native of China, where it is widely spread; discovered in 1816–17 by Clarke Abel. On a sunny wall it will pass through most winters with little harm, but the true plant is rare in cultivation. Lindley's name *A. rupestris* has been used both for this species and for *A.* × *grandiflora*.

A. ENGLERIANA (Graebn.) Rehd.
Linnaea engleriana Graebn.

A deciduous shrub of bushy habit, 3 to 6 ft high, with brown, minutely downy young bark, afterwards glabrous and shining, ultimately peeling. Leaves oval-lanceolate, tapered at both ends, but more slenderly at the apex; ¾ to 1½ in. long, ⅓ to ⅝ in. wide; bright green and glabrous above, paler and glossy beneath, with scattered hairs on the midrib and veins; margins bristly-hairy; stalk ⅛ in. or less long. Flowers borne usually in pairs from the end of short lateral twigs; sepals two, narrowly oval, ⅓ in. long, minutely ciliated; corolla ⅝ in. long,

137

funnel-shaped, curved, minutely downy outside, rose-coloured. Stamens shorter than the corolla. Flowers from June onwards.

Native of Szechwan, China; originally discovered by Henry about 1888; introduced to cultivation twenty years later by Wilson when collecting for Harvard University. Flowered at Kew in 1911.

A. FLORIBUNDA Decne.

An evergreen shrub 6 to 10 ft high in a wild state, but frequently more on walls in this country; young shoots reddish, downy. Leaves ovate to roundish ovate, ¾ to 1¾ in. long, ½ to 1 in. broad, shallowly toothed, pointed, firm in

ABELIA FLORIBUNDA

texture; glossy green and glabrous on both surfaces, but paler beneath; hairy only on the margin; stalk ⅛ in. or less long. Flowers pendulous, rosy-red to magenta, produced in June at or near the end of short twigs which spring from the year-old wood. Corolla slenderly funnel-shaped, narrowing towards the base, 1½ to 2 in. long, nearly 1 in. wide at the mouth, where are five rounded, spreading lobes. Sepals five, green, linear-oval, ⅓ in. long. Stamens hairy. *Bot. Mag.*, t. 4316.

Native of Mexico on the Cordilleras of Oaxaca at 10,000 ft, also found in the neighbouring states of Veracruz and Puebla; introduced to Europe in 1841. This is the handsomest of the abelias that can be grown out-of-doors with us, but it needs the protection of a wall. At Kew, a plant growing against the wall of a greenhouse has flourished for many years and flowers well most seasons, but it is quite unable to live in the open unprotected. For a south wall this shrub, with its shining leaves and gay flowers, is most attractive. In the milder countries it will reach a height of 20 ft, but good specimens have become rare since the hard winters of 1961–3, when *A. floribunda* was killed or badly damaged nearly everywhere.

A. GRAEBNERIANA Rehd.

A deciduous shrub up to 10 ft high; young shoots nearly or quite glabrous. Leaves ovate, often rounded at the base, long and slenderly pointed, often rather conspicuously toothed; 1½ to 2¼ in. long, ¾ to 1⅜ in. wide; slightly downy on the midrib and with scattered hairs above, conspicuously downy beneath on the midrib and veins near the stalk; margins set with whitish hairs; stalk glabrous, ⅛ in. long. The leaves on the flowering twigs are much smaller and almost toothless. Flowers solitary on the stalk; corolla pink, yellow in the throat, 1 in. long, between funnel-shaped and bell-shaped. Sepals two, narrow oblong. Blossoms in June and July.

Native of Central China; introduced by Wilson in 1910. It is closely related to *A. engleriana*, but the leaves are normally larger and more conspicuously toothed, the flowers larger. *A. schumannii* is easily distinguished by its small, nearly or quite entire, blunt-ended leaves and deeper-coloured flowers.

cv. 'VEDRARIENSIS'.—Leaves larger than in the type and deeper green. Flowers larger, with a more prominent blotch in the throat.

A. × GRANDIFLORA (André) Rehd.   [PLATE I

A. rupestris grandiflora André; *A. chinensis* Hort., not R. Br.; *A. rupestris* Hort.

An evergreen shrub 3 to 6 ft high, with slender, arching branches clothed with minute down. Leaves of a brilliant dark green, ovate, pointed, 1 to 2½ in. long, half as wide, mostly more or less shallowly toothed; quite glabrous above, pale shining green beneath, downy only on the lower part of the midrib. Flowers slightly fragrant, produced from July to October at the end of the shoots of the year and in the leaf-axils; solitary to as many as four on a stalk. Corolla white tinged with pink, funnel-shaped, ¾ in. long, nearly as wide at the five-lobed mouth; throat hairy. Sepals two to five, ¾ in. long, but varying in width according to the number, the lower numbers being proportionately wider; they persist for several months, and are often of a purplish tinge.

A hybrid between *A. chinensis* and *A. uniflora* first described in 1886 from a plant raised from seed in the Rovelli nurseries, Pallanza, on Lake Maggiore; whether the plants cultivated today are from this or some other source is not known, since the cross may have occurred in other gardens. Like many hybrids, *A.* × *grandiflora* appears to have acquired a vigour and constitution superior to that of either of its parents. It is hardy at Kew in all but the severest winters, when it is cut to the ground; it is also the most ornamental of the really hardy kinds. The habit is graceful, the foliage a singularly brilliant green, and it is useful in blossoming so late in the season. The height given in the description is that which it normally attains; in mild gardens, and on walls, it may grow taller.

There is a variegated form in cultivation in which the greater part of the leaf-blade is pale green, irregularly streaked or marbled with darker green, especially along the midrib and main veins.

A. (× *grandiflora* × *schumannii*) 'EDWARD GOUCHER'.—This hybrid was raised at the Glenn Dale Plant Introduction Station, Maryland, U.S.A., in 1911, but only recently introduced to this country. In foliage it leans towards

A. × *grandiflora*, but the darker-coloured purple-pink flowers show the influence of *A. schumannii*, which it also resembles in having the sepals in pairs, not in threes, fours or fives as in *grandiflora*. The leaves are never so pubescent nor so wide as the largest leaves of *A. schumannii*. The barren shoots are distinctive in having the leaves in whorls of three. Mr H. G. Hillier, to whom we are indebted for this description, tells us that it is growing well in open shrubbery at Winchester.

A. SCHUMANNII (Graebn.) Rehd.

Linnaea schumannii Graebn.

A deciduous shrub with slender arching shoots that are downy when young and purplish. Leaves ovate, not or but little toothed, blunt or rounded at the apex, tapered at the base; ½ to 1¼ in. long, ¼ to ½ in. wide; downy along the mid-rib beneath. Flowers successively produced from June to August singly in the leaf-axils of short, leafy twigs springing from the joints of the previous year's growth. Corolla 1 in. or rather more long, rosy pink, minutely downy outside, broadly funnel-shaped, slightly bellied towards the base. Sepals two, oval or obovate, rounded at the end, ¼ in. long. Stamens downy at the base. *Bot. Mag.*, t. 8810.

Native of Central China; introduced by Wilson in 1910. In the open air at Kew it is rather tender and often cut back by winter cold, but it shoots up again in spring. It does not, therefore, reach any great size. It has a long blossoming season and flowers are often developed up to November. It is perhaps the handsomest of the E. Asiatic abelias.

Its nearest relative is *A. engleriana*, which is distinguished by its smaller flowers and larger, more slenderly pointed leaves. Another ally is *A. graebneriana* (q.v.).

A. LONGITUBA Rehd., with which *A. schumannii* has been confused in the *Botanical Magazine* (t. 8810), is perhaps not in cultivation.

A. SERRATA Sieb. & Zucc.

A deciduous shrub 3 to 5 ft high; young shoots very slender and minutely downy. Leaves ovate to ovate-lanceolate, sparsely toothed or not at all, tapered to a bluntish apex, wedge-shaped at the base; ½ to 1¾ in. long, ¼ to ⅝ in. wide; hairy on the midrib and with scattered hairs above, glabrous beneath except towards the base of the midrib. Flowers usually in pairs terminating short leafy twigs, opening in May and June. Corolla funnel-shaped, ½ to ⅝ in. long, tapered to a slender tube at the base, hairy outside, dullish white, sometimes yellowish or flesh-coloured. Sepals two.

Native of Japan; introduced by Charles Maries in 1879 from Mt Fuji, where he found it at altitudes of 2,000 ft and upwards. It is a widespread shrub in the main island of Japan and variable in such characters as the indumentum and toothing of the leaf. Of the varieties that have been described the most important is var. BUCHWALDII (Graebn.) Nakai, which has also been regarded as a distinct species. It has longer leaves than in the type and the flowers are over 1 in. long.

The plants from Maries' introduction seem to have been of little worth; in previous editions of this work they were described as small-flowered and unattractive. But the description of var. *buchwaldii* suggests that there are better forms still to be introduced.

A. SPATHULATA Sieb. & Zucc.

A deciduous shrub 3 or 4 ft high, much branched; twigs downy when young. Leaves oval-lanceolate, rhomboidal, or ovate; 1 to 2 in. long, ⅓ to 1 in. wide; unequally toothed; with scattered hairs above, and down on the nerves below; margins red when young. Flowers in pairs at the ends of short side twigs; corolla white with yellow in the throat, ¾ to 1 in. long, widely funnel-shaped. Sepals usually five, ¼ in. long, rosy, oblong-spathulate, slightly downy. Stamens shorter than corolla. *Bot. Mag.*, t. 6601.

Native of Japan; introduced by Maries in 1880. It is hardy in the milder parts of the southern counties and grew well at Leonardslee, near Horsham.

A. TRIFLORA R. Br.

A deciduous shrub or small tree of vigorous, erect habit, 8 to 12 ft high, sometimes more; young shoots furnished with reflexed bristles; bark of main stem pale, greyish and conspicuously corrugated. Leaves ovate-lanceolate to lanceolate, tapering more abruptly to the base than to the apex, 1½ to 3 in. long, ⅓ to 1 in. wide; dull dark green, paler beneath; more or less hairy on both surfaces and at the margins until late in the year when they become nearly or quite glabrous. Most of the leaves are neither toothed nor lobed, but the lowest leaves on the twigs are frequently deeply and sharply cut. Flowers fragrant, produced in June in erect clusters 2 in. across, terminating short twigs; often three flowers on a stalk. Corolla delicate rosy white, with a slender downy tube ⅝ in. long, expanding at the mouth into five rounded lobes, and there ⅓ in. across. Sepals five, persistent, reddish, very narrow and linear, ⅓ to ⅝ in. long, feathered with silky hairs. *Bot. Mag.*, t. 9131.

Native of the N.W. Himalaya. It was introduced in 1847 to Glasnevin and first flowered there in 1852. This is one of the hardiest of the abelias and has grown vigorously in the open at Kew for many years. When it flowers freely (which does not happen every year) it makes a pretty display, and remains interesting because of the curious persistent calyces surmounting the fruits. There is a fine example of this shrub in the Glasnevin Botanic Garden which is probably of the original introduction; it is about 16 ft high, with three stout stems, the thickest a foot in diameter. At Mount Usher, Co. Wicklow, Eire, it is 37 ft high, and it has reached 20 ft in Devon.

A. BUDDLEIOIDES W. W. Sm.—A native of S.W. China, closely allied to the preceding, from which it differs in its smaller leaves and in its sepals, which are only one half to one third as long as the corolla tube, with shorter and weaker marginal hairs. It is, or was, in cultivation under Yü 14481 and Forrest 10500.

A. umbellata (Graebn. & Buchw.) Rehd. *Linnaea umbellata* Graebn. & Buchw.—Like the preceding species, this belongs to the section *Zabelia*, in which the corolla is tubular with a flattened limb, the branchlets bristly and the petioles of the opposite leaves swollen and united, concealing the leaf-buds. Leaves glossy, elliptic to lanceolate, $1\frac{1}{4}$ to 3 in. long. Flowers white, four to seven on a single peduncle at the end of the lateral shoots. A native of Szechwan, introduced by Wilson. In the West-Hill nursery of Messrs Hillier it has made a spreading shoot about 6 ft high and 7 ft across. In the related A. zanderi (Graebn.) Rehd. the flowers are pink and the peduncles only two-flowered.

A. uniflora R. Br.

An evergreen shrub of spreading habit, 5 or 6 ft high, ultimately with arching branches; shoots slender, minutely downy when young. Leaves ovate, often with long, tapered points, rounded or tapered at the base, sparsely and shallowly toothed; 1 to 2 in. long, $\frac{1}{2}$ to 1 in. wide; dark glossy green and glabrous above, paler beneath and downy on the midrib. Flowers solitary, in pairs, or in threes in the terminal leaf-axils, produced from June onwards. Corolla white, blush-tinted, with orange markings in the throat; 1 in. long and the same in width across the mouth, where are five ovate lobes; it has much the shape of a miniature foxglove. Calyx of usually two sepals, persistent. *Bot. Mag.*, t. 4694.

Native of China; introduced by Fortune in 1845. It is one of the parents of *A.* × *grandiflora*, which owes to this species its hardiness and the brilliant green of its leaves, and which appears to have displaced it in gardens. It is no longer grown at Kew and seems to be quite lost to cultivation in this country but might still be found on the continent. It can be distinguished from *A.* × *grandiflora* by its larger corollas, marked orange in the throat, and by its calyx, which rarely has more than two sepals. *A. uniflora* was hardy in the south of England in all but the severest winters. Its flowers are the largest of the cultivated species, and being abundantly produced make a very pretty display.

ABELIOPHYLLUM   oleaceae

A genus related to *Forsythia*, containing the one species described below.

A. distichum Nakai   [plate 2

A deciduous shrub 3 ft or more high; young shoots glabrous, grooved on opposite sides, making them four-angled, slightly warted. Leaves opposite, in two ranks, simple, entire, ovate to oval, 2 to $3\frac{1}{2}$ in. long, slender-pointed, wedge-shaped or rounded at the base, hairy on both surfaces; stalk very short. Flowers white or faintly tinged with pink on opening, borne in axillary racemes $\frac{1}{2}$ to $1\frac{1}{2}$ in. long of three to fifteen; petals four, oblong, $\frac{3}{8}$ in. long, $\frac{1}{10}$ in. wide, notched at the apex; calyx $\frac{1}{8}$ in. long with four rounded, ciliate lobes; stamens two, anthers yellow, filaments $\frac{1}{12}$ in. long; calyx and flower-stalk glabrous, very darkly coloured. The fruit recalls that of an elm, being compressed, almost circular, and edged all around with a wing. *Bot. Mag.*, n.s., t. 10.

Native of Korea; introduced in 1924. It is a beautiful early-flowering shrub but comes from a region where, although the winters are much colder than here, the summers are decidedly hotter. For this reason, no doubt, it has not been generally successful as an open-ground plant but might be tried on a wall, as in the R.H.S. Garden at Wisley, where it will grow to 8 ft or more high. The wood deteriorates after a few seasons and should be renewed fairly frequently by pruning heavily immediately after flowering is over. It is propagated by cuttings of half-ripened wood, taken in July, or by layers.

ABIES   PINACEAE

A group of about forty species generally known as 'silver firs'. They are found in Europe, N. Africa, temperate Asia and on the American continent from Canada to Guatemala. They are mostly conical and very symmetrical in form, especially when young, and the finest are from 200 to 300 ft high. They produce their branches in whorls or tiers, one tier yearly. Leaves always linear or nearly so, from $\frac{1}{20}$ to $\frac{1}{8}$ in. wide, with invariably two bands of stomata beneath, occasionally lines of stomata above also; they are always attached to the shoot in a spiral arrangement, but by a twisting at the base are usually made to appear in two opposite sets, the green faces of all uppermost. Female cones always erect, in which respect they differ from those of *Picea* (the spruces), and from *Tsuga* (the hemlocks), both of which genera have been, and still are, often called "Abies". There is a simple way of distinguishing a fir (*Abies*) from a spruce by pulling off a living leaf from the shoots: in the firs the leaf breaks off sharply at the base where it joins the twig, but in the spruces (*Picea*) it tears away a little of the bark with it. Also, the leaves of the spruces are inserted on woody, peg-like projections which persist on the stems for many years after the leaves have fallen.

The cones are built up of a close spiral arrangement of overlapping, usually more or less fan-shaped scales, to the outer surface of which a bract is always attached. The length of this bract and whether or not it protrudes beyond the scale, affords a good distinguishing character between the species. Seeds are borne in pairs on the inner side of the scales, and are winged. The male flowers occur on branches separate from the females, and are borne on the under side of the branch; anthers highly coloured. On flowering and cone-bearing branches the leaves frequently alter much in character, becoming shorter, stiffer, sharper pointed, and more erect.

The silver firs are undoubtedly best suited in a moist climate where late spring frosts are rare. Nowhere in the British Isles, perhaps, do they, as a whole, succeed quite so well as in the Perthshire valleys. Where the rainfall is deficient, lack of moisture can to some extent be compensated for by a good deep soil. Whenever possible they should be raised from seeds, but of some sorts cuttings may be made to take root. The cuttings should always be taken from leading shoots, as distinct from lateral ones, which rarely develop a good leader. The best plan is to head back a plant, thus inducing it to make several shoots; these are then taken off with a slight heel of old wood attached, and placed singly in small pots of sandy soil in a gentle bottom heat. But both cuttings and grafts should only be resorted to when seeds are unobtainable. Several species, among them *alba*, *amabilis*, *magnifica*, *nordmanniana*, and *procera*, are subject in many places to attacks by aphides of the genus *Adelges*; gouty swellings on the branches and woolly patches on branches and trunk are a sign of their presence. The remedy, only practicable on young trees, is regular spraying with an emulsion of paraffin and soft soap or some modern aphicide.

A. ALBA Mill.   EUROPEAN SILVER FIR
A. pectinata DC.

A tree up to 150 ft high in Britain, with a trunk 5 to 6½ ft in thickness; young shoots brownish grey, covered with a short down; winter buds not resinous. Leaves usually in two opposite sets spreading horizontally, but occasionally with others on the upper side pointing forwards; ½ to 1⅓ in. long, the upper ranks of each set the smaller and scarcely half as long as the lower ones; $\frac{1}{16}$ to $\frac{1}{12}$ in. wide, notched at the blunt apex, dark glossy green above, with two white stomatic bands beneath. Cones 4½ to 6 in. long, 1½ to 2 in. wide; at first green, then reddish brown; the bracts protruded and reflexed. On cone-bearing branches the leaves become pointed, shorter, stiffer, and curved upwards.

Native of the mountains of Central and S. Europe; cultivated in Britain for more than three centuries. The common silver fir refuses to grow in the hot, dry, Lower Thames Valley, and does not thrive in many low-lying and frosty parts of the south of England. A generous rainfall and a situation reasonably free from late spring frosts are necessary for its success and, although not exacting as to soil, it is not suited to infertile sands and peats. In the moist valleys of Scotland it reaches magnificent proportions and there are numerous trees there exceeding 140 ft in height and 15 ft in girth. The silver fir is very patient of shade and for this reason was once much used for underplanting. Its susceptibility to aphis attack has restricted its use as a forestry tree in recent years, although interest is now reviving owing, partly, to its resistance to *Fomes*.

The tallest specimen measured in the British Isles grows by the roadside at Kilbride, Inveraray, Argyll, and is one of a group probably planted about 1680; in 1960 it measured about 180 ft in height and 20½ ft in girth. The following is only a selection of other notable specimens: Powis Castle, Montg., two trees *pl.* 1847, 162 × 11¾ ft and 150 × 8¾ ft (1954); Inveraray, Argyll, one on Loch Shira, 153 × 15½ ft, and another at Tom Breac, 151 × 19¾ ft (1955); Dunkeld,

Perths., 151 × 15¾ ft (1962); Alnwick Castle, Northumb., 137 × 17 ft and 142 × 16 ft (1956).

In southern England there are no specimens to compare with these, but an old tree at Highclere, Hants, now dying, stood at 146 × 13¼ ft when measured in 1955. There is another tall tree in Savernake Forest, about 145 ft high.

f. PENDULA (Carr.) Aschers. & Graebn.—Sports in which the main and secondary branches are in some degree pendulous occur fairly frequently in the wild and have been recorded from the Vosges, the Black Forest, and other parts. The cultivar name 'Pendula' belongs to a clone that originated in Godefroy's nursery in France before 1835 and may have been distributed in this country by Knight and Perry of Chelsea. There are examples of this sport at Tregrehan, Cornwall, and Endsleigh, Devon, probably of the same origin.

f. PYRAMIDALIS (Carr.) Voss—Branches ascending, making a fastigiate or pyramidal tree after the fashion of the Lombardy poplar. Trees of this kind were in cultivation in Britain in the middle of the last century, but their origin is unknown and none has been traced. This sport is very rare in the wild, but according to Carrière (*Traité des Conifères*, 1855) one was found in the department of Isères, France.

A. BORISII-REGIS Mattf. *A. alba* var. *acutifolia* Turrill—As Mattfeld defined it, this is a variable species, native of S. Bulgaria and N.E. Greece, which combines in various ways the characters of *A. alba* and *A. cephalonica*. In parts of its area it is in contact with one or other of these species, but in the Rhodope Range of Bulgaria, and on the Athos peninsula, it occurs in isolation from both. Mattfeld considered the species to be the product of hybridisation at the end of the Tertiary period, when *A. alba* migrated southward as the climate cooled with the onset of the Ice Age and met and crossed with *A. cephalonica*. However, the whole complex is in need of further study.

A. NEBRODENSIS (Lojac.) Mattei *A. alba* var. *nebrodensis* Lojac.—A close ally of *A. alba*, from which it differs in its resinous buds and shorter leaves. Extensive forests of this species once existed in N. Sicily in the Monti Nebrodi and Madonie. It is now almost extinct but attempts are being made to re-establish it. A few grafted plants are in cultivation.

A. AMABILIS Forbes   PACIFIC SILVER FIR

A tree up to 250 ft high in nature; bark on young or middle-aged trees whitish; young shoots downy; winter buds small, globose, very resinous. Leaves crowded at the sides and on the upper surface of the shoot, which they completely hide from above; ¾ to 1½ in. long, $\frac{1}{16}$ to $\frac{1}{12}$ in. wide, broadest towards the apex; the uppermost leaves are considerably the shorter, and point forwards, the lower ones spread horizontally; all are rich glossy green and deeply grooved above, vividly blue-white and with broad bands of stomata beneath; apex notched. Cones rich purple, 4 to 6 in. long, 2 to 2½ in. wide, tapering slightly towards the rounded top; bracts enclosed. *Bot. Mag.*, n.s., t. 306.

Native of S.E. Alaska, British Columbia, Washington, and Oregon; discovered by Douglas in 1825, introduced five years later. Later sendings were in 1851 and

1882. This beautiful fir, which in open situations clothes itself to the ground with gracefully drooping branches, has not been a success in British gardens. It seems to be short-lived in cultivation, trees from the original introduction being mostly dead by the turn of the century, although in its native habitat the Pacific silver fir reaches maturity at about 250 years. From his knowledge of existing specimens, A. F. Mitchell concludes: 'It can be miffy, scraggy and gaunt; or make luscious, vigorous, rich, symmetrical trees of superb shape, as at Benmore, Stanage Park, and Castlewellan.'

Some of the best specimens recorded by Mr Mitchell are: Doldowlod, Merioneth, 97 × 11 ft (1959); Killerton, Devon, *pl.* 1909, 96 × 8½ ft (1964); Benmore, Argyll, 86 × 7½ ft, growing fast (1964); Leonardslee, Sussex, 73 × 4½ ft (1962); Stanage Park, Radnor, 73 × 6¾ ft (1959); Castlewellan, Co. Down, 86 × 9½ ft (1966).

A. amabilis is sometimes confused with *A. nordmanniana*, which it resembles in several respects, notably in the arrangement of the leaves on the shoot; but the winter buds, looking like globes of resin, easily distinguish it, and the leaves have an odour like orange peel. See also *A. mariesii*.

A. BALSAMEA (L.) Mill.   BALSAM FIR
Pinus balsamea L.

A tree 60 to 80 ft high; young shoots downy; winter buds red, very resinous, roundish. Leaves on young trees in two opposite sets spreading horizontally; ½ to 1¼ in. long, $\frac{1}{20}$ to $\frac{1}{16}$ in. wide, the uppermost leaves much the shorter, rounded or notched at the apex, glossy green above, with a few broken lines of stomata near the tip; the under-surface with two narrow whitish bands each composed of four to eight lines of stomata. On cone-bearing shoots the leaves are often pointed (sometimes sharply) as well as rounded or slightly notched, and they are stiffer, broader ($\frac{1}{12}$ in. wide), and curved upwards rather than arranged in two sets. Cones 2½ to 3½ in. long, 1 to 1¼ in. wide, dark purple or olive-green, the bracts either quite enclosed within the scales or slightly exposed.

Native of Canada from Labrador to the Upper Yukon; south of the border it ranges into the Lake States and through New England into Virginia; introduced by Bishop Compton in 1697. It is among the biggest failures of firs in this country, for it is short-lived and becomes ungainly after twenty or so years. But when young it is an elegant tree and grows as well in south-eastern England as it does in Scotland. In previous editions, trees at Keillour, Perthshire, were mentioned; planted in 1830, some had attained a height of 60 ft by the end of the century but were even then falling into decrepitude. At the present time there are two small plots in Scotland; in one of these, at Kilmun in Argyllshire planted in 1930, the best is 45 × 2¼ ft (1964). In the south of England the few specimens range from 30 to 55 ft; the tree at Leonardslee, Sussex, although not among the tallest, is very shapely and slender. Ellen Willmott had a balsam fir in her famous garden at Great Warley, Essex.

The species is closely related to *A. fraseri*, under which the distinctions are referred to. It yields a transparent balsamic resin, known as Balm of Gilead or Canada Balsam, and is popular in parts of N. America as a Christmas tree.

f. HUDSONIA (Jacques) Fern. & Weatherby—A curious, very dwarf moun-
tain form rarely more than 2 ft high, which never bears cones. Leaves about $\frac{1}{4}$ in.
long. Found originally on the White Mountains of New Hampshire, U.S.A.

A. BRACTEATA (D. Don) Nutt.   SANTA LUCIA FIR
Pinus bracteata D. Don; *Abies venusta* (Dougl.) K. Koch; *Pinus venusta* Dougl.

A tree 100 to 150 ft high, of pyramidal form, but abruptly narrowed near
the top into a slender, steeple-like apex; young shoots pale green, perfectly
glabrous; winter buds $\frac{1}{2}$ to $\frac{3}{4}$ in. long, slenderly conical, the scales being loose,

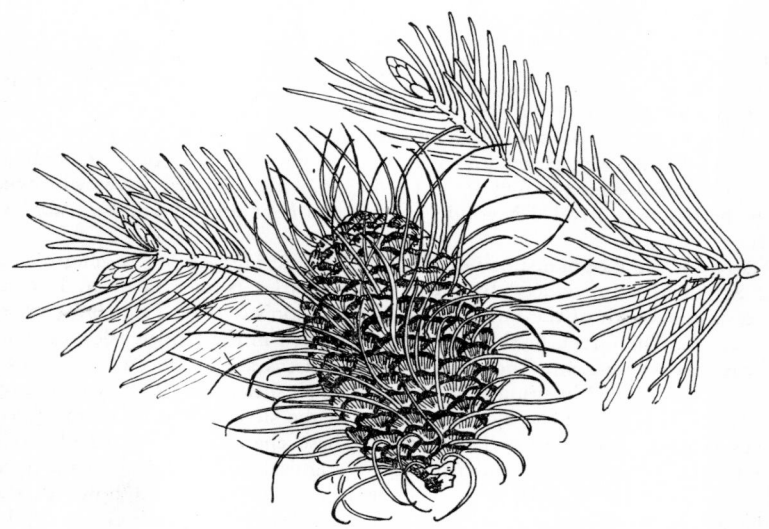

ABIES BRACTEATA

pale brown, non-resinous. Leaves flat, stiff, and spine-tipped; $1\frac{1}{4}$ to $2\frac{1}{4}$ in. long,
$\frac{1}{10}$ in. wide; dark shining green, with two blue-white bands of stomata beneath;
the leaves are aggregated into two sets, one each side of the shoot, leaving a
broad V-shaped opening between. Cones 3 to 4 in. long, 2 to $2\frac{1}{2}$ in. wide, egg-
shaped, purplish brown, each bract terminated by a slender, stiff, spine-tipped
point, 1 to 2 in. long. *Bot. Mag.*, t. 4740.

Native of, and confined to, the Santa Lucia Mountains, California; discovered
in 1832; introduced by W. Lobb in 1853. It is in several respects the most
remarkable of all firs: its pyramidal spire-topped shape and its buds are quite
unlike those of any other species; its spine-tipped, never notched, leaves are
comparable only with those of *A. cephalonica*; and, chief of all, the bayonet-like
terminations of the bracts projecting all round the cone are only seen in this
species. The tree generally is not a success, owing to its susceptibility to late

spring frosts, and appears to be rather short-lived, judging from the high casualty rate found by A. F. Mitchell among the trees mentioned by Elwes and Henry (1906–8) and in the R.H.S. Conifer Conference returns (1931). Best placed in a moist and sheltered position, with good air drainage.

The following are some of the larger specimens, and others whose planting dates are known: Eastnor Castle, Heref., 117 × 15¼ ft (1961); Bodnant, Denbigh, *pl.* 1891, 114 × 10½ ft (1966); University of Exeter, Devon, 105 × 11 and 85 × 11¾ ft (1967); Mells Park, Somerset, 97 × 8¾ ft (1966); Althorp, Northants, 96 × 9 ft (1964); Nymans, Sussex, *pl.* 1908, 64 × 5¼ ft (1957); Stanage Park, Radnor, *pl.* 1909, 72 × 6 ft (1959); Hergest Croft, Heref., *pl.* 1922, 56 × 4¾ ft (1961).

A. CEPHALONICA Loud.   GREEK FIR

A tree up to 120 ft high; young shoots smooth, shining brown; buds reddish, resinous. Leaves standing out nearly at right angles to, and all round the stem, but more densely above than below; the lower ones are the longer and all have the green surface uppermost; they are stiff, sharply pointed; ⅝ to 1⅛ in. long, 1/16 to 1/12 in. wide; rich glossy green above, and with two well-defined stomatic bands beneath. Cones 4 to 6 in. long, 1¼ to 1¾ in. wide, cylindric, velvety brown, with the bracts protruded beyond the scale and bent downward. *Bot. Mag.*, t. 8691.

Native of the mountains of Greece and of bordering parts of S. Yugoslavia and S. Albania; introduced by General Sir Charles Napier in 1824. For an interesting account of the introduction see Loudon's *Arb. et Frut. Brit.*, 1838, pp. 2325–9. The Greek fir thrives remarkably well in the British Isles, even in the east and south-east, although the biggest girths are produced in the west. Some care is needed in siting it, however, as it flushes early and may be cut by late frosts. It is one of the most distinctive of the silver firs in its sharp-tipped leaves standing out all round the shoot. These characters, with its glabrous shoots and resinous buds, render it easily recognisable, and distinguish it from all other firs except *A. pinsapo*, to which it is allied. In that species, however, the radial arrangement of the leaves is much more marked than in the Greek fir; the leaves are also shorter and the bracts of the cone are completely enclosed.

Two trees at Barton, Suffolk, 120 and 110 ft in height when measured by the late Maynard Greville in 1952, are probably from the seed sent by General Napier and planted there by his brother-in-law Sir Henry Bunbury, Bt. Other old trees of known planting date are: Stanage Castle, Radnor, *pl.* 1841, 80 × 12½ ft (1959), and Inveraray, Argyll, *pl.* 1849, 78 × 13½ ft (1955).

Among the tallest recorded are: Cortachy Castle, Angus, 118 × 14¼ ft and 110 × 17 ft (1962); Bodnant, Denbigh, *pl.* 1876, 117 × 10 ft (1957); Fulmodestone, Norfolk, 116 × 10½ ft (1959); Bicton, Devon, 113 × 12 ft (1959); Brinkburn Priory, Northumb., 112 × 13¼ ft (1958). There are many others of around 110 ft in height, well distributed over the country. The rapid growth of the Greek fir in middle years is shown by a tree at Wakehurst Place, Sussex, 25 × 1½ ft (1931) and 78 × 7½ ft (1964).

var. APOLLINIS (Link) Beissn. *A. apollinis* Link.—In this variety, described from Mt Parnassus, the leaves are more crowded on the upper side of the shoot, and more inclined to point forward; they are also thicker and more abruptly pointed, sometimes rounded, at the apex. But the Greek fir is variable in the wild state and intermediate forms are said to exist. Trees referable to this variety grow at Tilgate, Sussex; Warnham Court, Sussex; Hergest Croft, Heref.; and Haffield House, Heref.

A. CHENSIENSIS Van Tiegh.

A. ernestii (Rehd. & Wils.) Rehd.; *A. beissneriana* Rehd. & Wils., not Mott.

A tall tree, attaining 200 ft in W. Szechwan but apparently smaller in other parts of its range. Young shoots glabrous, rarely slightly hairy, yellow or yellowish grey. Leaves $\frac{1}{2}$ to $1\frac{3}{4}$ in. long, spreading slightly upward from the shoot or almost vertically, but with a V-shaped opening between the two ranks; they are pointed or blunt at the apex, or slightly emarginate, and with whitish or glaucous bands of stomata beneath. Cones cylindric to ovoid, 2 to $3\frac{3}{4}$ in. long, green at first but reddish brown when ripe, sessile or short-stalked. Bracts shorter than the scales and concealed by them.

Native of W. China; discovered in the Chin Ling Shan, Shensi province, by the Abbé David in 1872. In 1907 Wilson found in the Tapao Shan, W. Szechwan, a finer form of this fir which is sometimes treated as a distinct species (*A. ernestii*). *A. chensiensis* has a wide range in W. China from Shensi to the Burmese border and probably the majority of the trees in cultivation in this country are from Forrest's seed, collected in Yunnan. Plants sent out by Messrs Hillier around 1940 are almost certainly from seed distributed by the Sun Yat Sen University; they agreed so well with Wilson's specimens from the Tapao Shan that the late E. Hillier retained the name *A. ernestii* for them.

A. chensiensis is well-marked by its stout yellowish shoots and by its crowded leaves separated into two ranks by a V-shaped depression. It is very rare, however. The tallest authentic specimen traced is at Stanage Park, Radnor, 42 ft in 1959.

A. CILICICA (Ant. & Kotschy) Carr.

Pinus cilicica Ant. & Kotschy

A tree up to 100 ft high in a wild state, and already more than half as high in cultivation; buds non-resinous, the bud-scales ridged at the back and with free points; young shoots greyish brown, furnished with scattered, stiff, small bristles. Leaves $\frac{3}{4}$ to $1\frac{1}{4}$ in. long, $\frac{1}{16}$ to $\frac{1}{12}$ in. wide; notched, rounded, or pointed at the apex; rather pale bright green above, with two bands of stomata beneath. On strong shoots the leaves are spread equally all over the upper side of the branchlet, those in the middle being shorter, erect, and pointing forwards; on weak shoots they are in two opposite sets, with a narrow or wide V-shaped opening between. Cones cylindrical, about 7 or 8 in. long and 2 to $2\frac{1}{2}$ in. wide, reddish brown; the scales are of remarkable size, being $1\frac{3}{4}$ to 2 in. wide, 1 in. deep not including the claw at the base; bracts completely hidden.

Native of Asia Minor and Syria, and often associated in a wild state with the cedar of Lebanon; discovered in 1853, introduced one or two years subsequently.

Allied to *A. nordmanniana*, it differs in its paler, less dense foliage, and in the larger scales and enclosed bracts of the cones. It is subject to injury by late frosts and few good examples are known. A tree in the National Pinetum at Bedgebury grew rapidly to 92 × 7¼ ft (1964) but is now dying back. Others are: Adhurst St Mary, Hants, 73 × 7 ft (1964); Speech House, Glos., 64 × 7¼, growing fast but with many tops (1964); Smeaton Hepburn, E. Lothian, 62 × 5½ ft (1966); Wakehurst Place, Sussex, 58 × 5½ ft, forks at 3 ft (1964).

A. CONCOLOR (Gord.) Hildebrand   COLORADO FIR
Picea concolor Gord.

A tree 80 to 100 ft high in nature; young shoots yellowish, patched with minute down, or glabrous; buds very resinous, egg-shaped, rounded at the top. Leaves glaucous green, 1 to 3 in. long, $\frac{1}{12}$ to $\frac{1}{10}$ in. wide; tapered at the base, rounded (with sometimes a slight notch) at the apex; otherwise of even width, not grooved above. There are not very conspicuous lines of stomata on both surfaces; they cover the whole centre of the leaf above, but beneath they are in two bands. The leaves are mostly aggregated into two opposite sets, but on the upper side of the branchlet there are a number of leaves pointing upwards, and beneath some pointing downwards; the arrangement therefore is irregular, and the upper leaves are considerably the shorter. On cone-bearing shoots the leaves generally are shorter and stouter and curve upwards. Cones about 4 in. long, 1½ to 1¾ in. wide, of a rich plum colour, as I have seen them in Waterers' nursery at Knap Hill, turning brown with age; bracts enclosed by the scales.

Native of Colorado, Arizona, New Mexico, and Utah (but see var. *lowiana*); discovered in 1847 and introduced in 1872. It is one of the most beautiful of all conifers and grows almost as well in southern England as it does in the moister and cooler parts of the country. The best recorded are: Cragside, Northumb., 131 × 11½ ft (1958); Benmore, Argyll, 131 × 9½, 128 × 11¼, and 124 × 9¾ ft (1956); Blair Atholl, Perths., 127 × 9¾ ft (1955); Eridge Castle, Kent, 118 × 11¼ ft (1963). There are also big trees at Westonbirt and Batsford, Glos., and at Dropmore, Bucks.

f. VIOLACEA (A. Murr.) Beissn.—This name applies in general to trees with leaves of a particularly silvery-glaucous tinge; such forms occur in nature and in seed-beds.

cv. 'WATTEZII'.—Leaves silvery-yellow when young; of Dutch nursery origin.

var. LOWIANA (Gord.) Lemm. *A. lowiana* (Gord.) A. Murr.; *Picea lowiana* Gord.—As seen in gardens, this fir is well distinguished from cultivated specimens of *A. concolor* and indeed has long been grown as a distinct species. The distinguishing characters of the "*A. lowiana*" of reference books are found mainly in the foliage: the middle line of erect leaves seen in 'typical' *concolor* is absent, the leaves lying pectinately in one plane, or directed upward and outward in a V-shaped arrangement. It is also said to have a separate area of distribution, being confined to the ranges near the Pacific, from Oregon into the Sierra Nevada (cf. the distribution of *A. concolor*). However, American botanists are for the most part reluctant to concede even varietal status to this fir, preferring to regard it as a phase of *A. concolor*, included within the natural span of variation of that species. Here, following the Kew Hand-list, it is treated as a variety.

A. F. Mitchell of the Forestry Commission has observed that the trees cultivated in this country are of two forms. The first has a rectangular crown, is often forked, and has a dark, not markedly corky bark; its leaves recall *A. grandis*, being flatly arranged, long, and quite green. These are likely to have originated from Oregon.* The second form, probably from the Sierra Nevada, approaches *A. concolor* as seen in cultivation; it is conical-crowned, forks only at a great height, and has a thick, corky, paler brown bark; leaves partly assurgent, bluish green, with stomatal bands above.

This variety, if such it be, has attained a good height in cultivation. For the most part, the best specimens are in areas of high rainfall but the thriving tree in the National Pinetum, Bedgebury, Kent, suggests that it is a fairly amenable fir. This tree is of the second form described above; planted 1925 it measured 86 × 9 ft in 1965. Of this form the two best recorded are: Durris House, Kinc., 145 × 14¼ ft (1955), and Bodnant, Denbigh, *pl.* 1886, 133 × 11½ ft (1966). Others of 125 ft and over are at Dupplin, Perths.; Cragside, Northumb.; Oakley Park, Shrops.; and Westonbirt, Glos. The first form, with the *"grandis"* type of foliage (see above), is represented by trees of 115 ft and over at Rammerscales, Dumf.; Monk Hopton, Shrops.; and Brockhall, Northants. Two others of this form whose planting dates are known are: Youngsbury, Herts., *pl.* 1866, 108 × 7 ft; and Castle Milk, Dumf., *pl.* 1886, 113 × 9 ft (both 1966).

A. DELAVAYI Franch.

A. delavayi was discovered by the French missionary Delavay in the Tali Range, Yunnan, China, in 1884, but so far as is known it is not in cultivation in its typical state. It might, however, still be found if any trees survive from Forrest's 30975, collected in the type locality on his last expedition. The cultivated trees which descend from the seed collected by Wilson and were long known as *A. delavayi* (or *A. fabri*) are here treated under var. *fabri*.

var. FABRI (Mast.) D. R. Hunt *Keteleeria fabri* Mast.; *Abies fabri* Craib (as "faberi").—An evergreen tree up to 130 ft high in a wild state, with a trunk 8 to 16 ft in girth; young shoots minutely downy at first, yellowish to dark brown. Terminal winter buds ⅖ in. long, slightly resinous. Leaves dark green above, with two whitish bands of stomata in nine to eleven rows beneath; ½ to 1 in. long, $\frac{1}{12}$ in. wide in adult trees; 1¾ in. long in juvenile ones; rounded and occasionally very slightly notched at the end; margins distinctly recurved; the outer leaves are horizontal, the inner ones more or less erect. Male inflorescence 1¼ in. long by ¼ in. wide. Cone cylindrical, rounded at the top, about 3 in. long, 1¼ to 1¾ in. wide, dark blue or bluish black, the awl-shaped tips of the bracts protruding about ¼ in. and much decurved. *Bot. Mag.*, t. 9201.

Native of China in the western part of the province of Szechwan; discovered

---

* Cultivated trees considered to be hybrids between *A. concolor* and *A. grandis* have been reported from Belgium and Germany.

by the missionary Faber and introduced by Wilson from the Omei Shan and Wa Shan in 1903 and again in 1910. Wilson's firs were at first considered to be typical *A. delavayi* and distributed under that name. This view was first disputed by Craib (*Notes Edin. Bot. Gard.*, Vol. 11, 1918, pp. 278–9). From an examination of the original material and specimens collected by Forrest in the type locality and other parts of Yunnan he came to the conclusion that the trees found by Wilson were specifically distinct from *A. delavayi*. His judgement was based on certain differences in the leaves, notably the stronger recurving of the margins of the Yunnan specimens of *A. delavayi*. He therefore placed Wilson's fir in *A. fabri*, a species which he constructed partly from Wilson's material and partly from a specimen collected earlier in the same part of Szechwan and originally described as *Keteleeria fabri* by Masters. Other authorities considered that these characters are inconstant and unreliable, and treated *A. fabri* as a synonym of *A. delavayi*. The view adopted in the present revision is that, while *A. fabri* can scarcely be upheld as a species, it should, in the present state of our knowledge, be maintained as a distinct entity, with the rank of variety. A note on this matter has been published (D. R. Hunt, *Journ. R.H.S.*, Vol. 92, 1967, p. 263).

The following specimens have been recorded: Stourhead, Wilts., 68 × 3 ft (1961); East Bergholt Place, Suffolk, 58 × 3½ ft (1966); Abbotswood, Glos., *pl.* 1916, 47 × 2¾ and 43 × 3¾ ft (1966); Dawyck, Peebl., *pl.* 1918, 51 × 3½ ft (1961); Edinburgh Botanic Garden, from W. 4078, 44 × 4¾ ft (1968).

var. FAXONIANA (Rehd. & Wils.) A. B. Jacks. *A. faxoniana* Rehd. & Wils.— The characters that best distinguish this variety are: young lateral shoots densely clothed with a stiff, rust-coloured down; leaves spreading irregularly in two ranks with a broad and shallow V-shaped depression between; leaf-margins not or only slightly revolute. In cultivated specimens the leaves are much less white beneath than in the type and the other three varieties. This fir was discovered by Wilson in 1910 in N.W. Szechwan, where it grows 60 to 130 ft high, and introduced by him the same year; trees were raised from his W. 4060 (see E. L. Hillier in *Journ. R.H.S.*, Vol. 62, 1941, p. 410, where there is a detailed description of a tree raised from this number), and also from W. 4052 and 4070. It is now rare in cultivation; the Westonbirt trees, which reached the coning stage, no longer exist. The following are probably authentic: Abbotswood, Glos., *pl.* 1916, 44 × 3, 48 × 3 and 57 × 4 ft, the last unusual in having the leaves bright silver below (1966); Speech House, Glos., *pl.* 1916, 39 × 2½ ft (1959); Dawyck, Peebl., *pl.* 1918, 46 × 3 ft (1961). Plants from seed collected later by Rock may also be in cultivation.

var. FORRESTII (C. C. Rogers) A. B. Jacks. *A. forrestii* C. C. Rogers—A tree to 130 ft in the wild state; young shoots reddish brown, usually glabrous, sometimes with reddish hairs; winter buds densely resinous. Leaves dark glossy green above with two conspicuous bands of stomata beneath, ¾ to 1½ in. long (up to 2 in. on young trees), rounded or nearly truncate and distinctly notched at the apex; margins slightly recurved. They are arranged in two sets with a narrow V-shaped opening along the top, the lower leaves standing out at almost a right angle, the upper ones almost erect. Cones similar to those of the type and as beautifully coloured. *Bot. Mag.*, t. 9201.

Native of China in the province of Yunnan; discovered by Forrest in 1910 and introduced as typical *A. delavayi*. C. Coltman Rogers, who grew it in his collection at Stanage Park, was the first to recognise its distinctness and it was at his suggestion that the name *A. forrestii* was adopted. The full description was published by Craib in 1919. It is also in cultivation from later sendings by Forrest from other parts of Yunnan, to which it is apparently confined. It is distinguished from var. *fabri* by the brighter red-brown branchlets, thickly resinous buds, and by the notched leaves, with wider stomatic bands and plane, not recurved margins.

It is remarkably handsome in the young state, its long leaves being dark green above and curving upward to expose the almost pure white bands beneath. It grows vigorously but deteriorates rather quickly and seems to be short-lived and rather sensitive to drought. It is not at its best in the drier parts of southern England but on the whole the best trees are fairly widely spread. These are: Stanage Park, Radnor, 66 × 5¼ and 42 × 5 ft (1959); Werrington Park, Cornwall, 57 × 3½ and 54 × 5 ft (1966); Sidbury Manor, Devon, from 1922 seed, 47 × 3¾ ft (1959); Walcot Park, Shrops., 60 × 4¾ ft (1959); Tregullow, Redruth, Cornwall, 62 × 4¼ ft (1959); Cortachy Castle, Angus, 59 × 4¼ ft (1962). The tree at Lanarth, Cornwall, mentioned in previous editions, was also the one that provided the material for the figure in the *Botanical Magazine*; it died a few years later in the drought of 1933.

var. GEORGEI (Orr) Melville   *A. georgei* Orr—This variety is closely related to the preceding, but distinguished by the remarkable cones, with long, protruded bracts, prolonged at the apex into a pronounced tail. A less reliable character is the rusty-red pubescence of the young shoots. It was introduced, as *A. forrestii*, in 1922 (F. 22547) and trees from this sending first coned around 1939. It was not distinguished as a separate entity until about 1930 and the first seed to be distributed as *A. georgei* was collected by Forrest in 1931 (F. 30853), shortly before his death. This variety and var. *forrestii* are closely associated in the wild and both names commemorate George Forrest.

Trees from Forrest's seed are now around 35 to 45 ft in height. Most of these are in the north and west (Burnside, Forfar; Strathallan, Perths.; Lamellen, Cornwall; Hergest Croft, Heref.; Vivod, Denbigh). In the home counties there are examples at Blackmoor, Hants, and Borde Hill, Sussex.

A. FARGESII Franch.

A tree up to 120 ft high in the wild, with a trunk 15 ft in girth; winter buds resinous; young shoots red-brown or purplish, glabrous or clad with dark hairs, the latter condition being found on weak shoots. Leaves ¾ to 1½ in. long, spreading in two or more horizontal ranks, those on the upper side half as long as the lower ones; notched at the apex, dark green above with two white bands of stomata beneath, each made up of nine or ten lines. Cones 2 to 3½ in. long, purple or reddish brown, scarcely resinous, the slightly exposed portion of the bracts reflexed.

Originally discovered by Père Farges in E. Szechwan, China; Wilson introduced it from N.W. Hupeh, where, according to him, it was the commonest fir and remnants of old forests of it were still to be found. He also remarked that the trunks are of nearly uniform thickness for half their height and that the branches, though short, are very massive. Although Wilson first sent seed in 1901, and on two other occasions, this fir is extremely rare in Britain; the only specimen recorded is at Dawyck, Peebl., which first coned in 1940; it measured 53 × 2½ ft in 1961. It is hardy in the N.E. United States, and there are good specimens there in the Hunnewell Arboretum and other collections.

A. FIRMA Sieb. & Zucc.   JAPANESE FIR

A tree 120 to 150 ft high in nature; young shoots downy in the grooves between the bases of the leaves; buds small, very slightly or not resinous. Leaves aggregated into two opposite sets, spreading at about right angles to the shoot and leaving a broad, V-shaped opening along the upper side; they are deep glossy green above, with two not very conspicuous bands of stomata beneath; ⅝ to 1½ in. long, $\frac{1}{12}$ to ⅛ in. wide, very stiff, tapered somewhat towards both ends, the apex distinctly notched, leaving two sharp, slender points. Cones 3½ to 5 in. long, 1½ to 2 in. wide, brown; bracts exposed and not reflexed.

Native of Japan; introduced to England by John Gould Veitch in 1861. Sargent describes wild trees as the most beautiful of Japanese firs. The leaves are not invariably notched at the apex, and the notch is deepest in young plants. The tree at Pencarrow, Cornwall, referred to in previous editions as measuring 59 ft in 1908, was still a fine tree when seen in 1957; it then measured 88 × 10 ft. Others of good size are: Bicton, Devon, 94 × 8½ ft (1959); Westonbirt, Glos., in Silkwood, 78 × 9 ft (1963); Nymans, Sussex, 77 × 7¼ ft (1957); Borde Hill, Sussex, *pl.* 1890, 77 × 6½ and 76 × 6¾ ft (1961); Stourhead, Wilts, *pl.* 1911 (?), 72 × 7½ ft (1965).

A. FRASERI (Pursh) Poir.
Pinus fraseri Pursh

A tree 30 to 40, occasionally 70 ft high; young shoots covered with short reddish hairs; buds small, resinous. Leaves amongst the shortest in firs, ½ to 1 in. long, $\frac{1}{16}$ to $\frac{1}{12}$ in. wide; rounded and usually notched at the apex; dark glossy green above, with two broad, very white bands beneath, each composed of six to twelve rows of stomata. Cones 1½ to 2½ in. long, 1 to 1¼ in. wide, purple; bracts golden brown, much protruded, and bent downwards so as to hide the scales.

Native of the mountains of the S.E. United States, often forming forests at elevations of 4,000 to 6,000 ft. It was introduced by John Fraser, after whom it was named, about 1807. No silver fir ever introduced has proved of less value in English gardens than this, or shorter-lived; there is perhaps scarcely a good tree in the country, but, like *A. balsamea*, it is attractive when young. There are small examples at Westonbirt, Glos.; Crarae, Argyll; and in the National Pinetum, Bedgebury, Kent. It has been confused with *A. balsamea*, but in that species the bracts of the cone are very little or not at all protruded, the leaves have only four to eight lines of stomata in each band, and bear a few broken lines of stomata on the upper surface.

A. GRANDIS Lindl.   GIANT FIR

A tree 230 to 300 ft high in nature, with a trunk 4 to 5 ft thick; young shoots glossy, olive-green, not corrugated, minutely downy; winter buds small, conical, resinous, bluish. Leaves in two opposite sets, spreading flatly and horizontally, each set composed of two ranks, the upper ones much shorter than the lower; the leaves are ¾ to 2¼ in. long, $\frac{1}{16}$ to $\frac{1}{10}$ in. wide; the apex notched and rounded; dark shining green, with two broad white stomatic bands beneath. Cones cylindrical, 3 to 4 in. long, 1¼ to 1¾ in. wide, bright green; the bracts enclosed.

Native of western N. America from Vancouver Island to California; discovered by Douglas in 1825. It was introduced six or seven years later, but all the extant trees are from later sendings. Probably the largest silver fir in the world, it thrives exceedingly well in the moister parts of the British Isles and grows very quickly in deep, moist soil, often at a rate of 2 to 3 ft annually. Very distinct in the flat, comb-like arrangement of the leaves, it is in this respect most nearly approached by *A. concolor* var. *lowiana*, which in some of its forms is not easily distinguished from *A. grandis* in the field.

When this work was first published in 1914 the tallest specimens in the British Isles stood at around 90 to 100 ft; at the present time a tree would have to be near 150 ft to be outstanding. What the ultimate height in cultivation here will prove to be, only the next century will show. Some of the trees now 140 to 150 ft are still growing in height, while others have stopped; in either case girth continues to increase. Tops frequently blow out at 80–100 ft, but are replaced by many new leaders, which grow as fast as the old.

The following are some of the trees mentioned by Elwes and Henry (1908) and still extant today; at that time they were 90 to 98 ft in height and mostly 6½ to 8 ft in girth: Eridge Castle, Kent, *pl.* 1868, 152 × 14 ft (1963); Eastnor Castle, Heref., 144 × 14¼ ft (1961); Fonthill Abbey, Wilts, 149 × 12½ ft (1963). Another at Welford Park, Berks., *pl.* 1878, died recently and was felled; its measurement was 154 × 12 ft (1958).

Other examples, to mention only those of 150 ft or more in height, are: Leighton Hall, Montg., 170 × 11 ft (1966) and 159 × 9½ ft (1959); Ardkinglas, Argyll, 164 × 15¼ ft (1953); Inveraray, Argyll, on Loch Shira, 160 × 9¾ and 156 × 12¼ ft (1955); Taymouth Castle, Perths., 152 × 14¼ ft (1962); Batsford Park, Glos., 150 × 12¼ ft (1963).

A. HOLOPHYLLA Maxim.

A tree up to 150 ft high in the wild, with a trunk 12 ft in girth; winter buds slightly resinous; young shoots not downy, slightly grooved, yellowish grey. Leaves ¾ to 1¾ in. long, not notched at the tip but bluntish or abruptly pointed there; shining dark green above with the two stomatic bands beneath inconspicuously marked. Cone cylindrical, 4 to 5 in. long, green at first, pale brown when mature; bracts hidden.

Native of Manchuria and Korea; introduced to the United States from the latter country in 1905. E. H. Wilson, who saw it not uncommonly 100 ft in Korea, ranked it with *A. homolepis* for beauty as a garden tree, but in this country it has not lived up to his expectations and remains very rare. There are two trees at Westonbirt, the larger 44 × 3½ ft (1963); and three at Borde Hill, Sussex, the largest 61 × 3¾ ft (1968).

A. HOMOLEPIS Sieb. & Zucc.   NIKKO FIR
A. brachyphylla Maxim.

A tree 100, occasionally 130 ft high in Japan; young shoots without down, but corrugated with the wrinkled protuberances on which the leaves are seated, the groove between the leaf-bases being deep; buds resinous. Leaves ⅓ to 1⅛ in. long,

ABIES HOMOLEPIS

about 1/16 in. wide; slightly notched at the flattish apex, dark bright green above, with two broad, blue-white stomatic bands beneath. The undermost leaves are the longest, and they spread horizontally; above them each succeeding rank becomes smaller and more erect, leaving at last a very narrow, or scarcely perceptible V-shaped opening along the top. Cones 3 to 4 in. long, 1¼ to 1½ in. wide tapered at top and bottom, purple, finally brown; bracts quite enclosed. *Bot. Mag.*, t. 7114.

Native of Japan; introduced about 1870. This is one of the most thriving

and handsome of firs, and very hardy. It occasionally bears good crops of its
rich purple cones, and is then very beautiful. It is, perhaps, best distinguished
by the deeply corrugated branchlets, the grooves in which become deeper the
two following years, by the scaly bark of the trunk and the short, notched
leaves. A few of the best specimens on record are: Taymouth Castle, Perths.,
101 × 10¼ ft (1961); Westonbirt, Glos., *pl.* 1880, 87 × 7¼ ft (1966); Yester
House, E. Lothian, 88 × 8¾ ft (1955); Grayswood Hill, Surrey, *pl.* 1882,
82 × 8¼ and 82 × 7½ ft (1964); Bodnant, Denbigh, 87 × 7½ ft (1966).

A. KAWAKAMII (Hayata) Ito   FORMOSAN FIR
A. mariesii var. *kawakamii* Hayata

A tree of pyramidal shape 50 to 120 ft high in the wild; young shoots very
downy; terminal winter buds not resinous. Leaves ⅓ to ¾ in. long, ¹⁄₁₆ in. wide,
rounded and slightly notched at the apex; green on both surfaces, the stomata
being only faintly visible beneath. Cones violet-purple, resinous, cylindrical,
rounded at the top, 2½ to 3 in. long, 1½ in. wide, bracts hidden.

Native of Formosa, one of its localities on that island being Mt Morrison
at 12,000 ft altitude, another Mt Nitaka at 11,000 ft. Wilson, in a collector's
note made in 1918, describes the tree as up to 120 ft high, with a trunk 18 ft in
girth, the bark very pale grey. It appears to be most nearly related to *A. mariesii*,
differing according to Hayata, the leading authority on the flora of Formosa, in
having 'longer cylindrical cones and black seeds and seed-wings'. It appears to
be perfectly hardy but is uncommon in gardens. It first coned with the Earl of
Rosse at Birr Castle, Eire, where it is now 38 × 4¾ ft (1966). There are other
examples in the Chandlers Ford nursery of Messrs Hillier, at Westonbirt, Glos.,
and Crarae, Argyll.

A. KOREANA Wils.   KOREAN FIR

A tree up to 60 ft high in the wild; young shoots slightly downy at first,
then smooth and purplish; winter buds somewhat resinous; bark of old trees
rough and fissured. Leaves thickly set on the twig, ½ to ¾ in. long, ¹⁄₁₆ to ¹⁄₁₂ in.
wide; rounded or notched at the end which is the broadest part of the leaf, dark
green above, white beneath with stomata except for the thin green midrib.
Cones cylindric except for the slightly tapered apex, 2 to 3 in. long, 1 in. thick,
bright violet-purple; scales ⅝ in. wide with little more than the deflexed, mucronate tips of the bracts visible; seeds with a purplish wing ¼ in. wide. *Bot. Mag.*,
n.s., t. 40.

Native of S. Korea; first found by Père Faurie in 1907 on Quelpaert Island,
where it is abundant at 3,000 ft and over; introduced to France in 1908 and thence
to Kew in 1913; Wilson collected seed in 1917 and probably the plants now in
cultivation are mostly of this provenance (W. 9486). It is by nature a small bushy
tree of compact, pyramidal growth and produces its beautiful blue cones when
only 3 ft or so high. It is rather slow-growing but quite hardy. There are specimens in the National Pinetum, Bedgebury, Kent, of 15 and 20 ft. The best

recorded are: Borde Hill, Sussex, 33 × 2 ft (1961); Hergest Croft, Heref., *pl.* 1927, 32 × 3 ft (1961); and Wakehurst Place, Sussex, 26 × 2 ft (1964).

A. LASIOCARPA (Hook.) Nutt.   SUBALPINE FIR
Pinus lasiocarpa Hook.; *A. subalpina* Engelm.

In nature a tree to 100 ft, occasionally to 160 ft, with a greyish or chalky-white bark; young shoots finely downy; buds ovoid, resinous. Leaves arranged like those of *A. procera*, to 1½ in. long on lower branches, shorter and more inclined to be bunched and forward-pointing on upper branches; stomata on both surfaces. Cones dark purple, 2¼ to 4 in. long. *Bot. Mag.*, t. 9600.

A native of western N. America at high altitudes, where it often forms beautiful park-like stands in sub-alpine meadows. It is an elegant, slender tree but finds our climate too soft and does not thrive.

var. ARIZONICA (Merriam) Lemm. *A. arizonica* Merriam—Introduced in 1903. It has more glaucous leaves and owes its name, the corkbark fir, to its thick, corky, yellowish-white bark, and is found at high altitudes in the southern Rocky Mountains.

The name *A. lasiocarpa* is sometimes used erroneously for *A. concolor* var. *lowiana*.

A. MAGNIFICA A. Murr.   RED FIR   [PLATE 3

A tree to 180 ft in nature, occasionally over 200 ft, with a narrowly conical crown and reddish bark; young shoots furnished with a minute down; buds resinous at the top, more or less concealed by leaves. Leaves 1 to 1¾ in. long, $\frac{1}{12}$ in. wide; glaucous green, with stomata on all surfaces; blunt, but not notched at the apex, nor grooved along the upper surface. On old cone-bearing branches they are pointed, stiffer, shorter, and diamond-shaped in cross-section. The leaves are crowded on the top as much as on the sides of the shoot; those on the top have their bases flattened to, and nearly hiding the stem, then curve upwards. Cones 6 to 8 in. long, about half as wide, purple when young, afterwards brown; bracts enclosed (except in the variety mentioned below). *Bot. Mag.*, t. 8552.

Native of Oregon and California; introduced by Jeffrey in 1851. It is a strikingly elegant tree of slender conical shape and should be planted more widely. It is seen at its best in the cooler and rainier parts of the British Isles but some good specimens in the south of England (see below) suggest that it could be grown in a drier climate provided it is given a sheltered position and moist soil. However, it grows poorly in the Thames Valley and will not tolerate a polluted atmosphere. A. F. Mitchell has observed that it gains rapidly in girth in early years but appears to be rather short-lived (in nature the rate of growth is slower but the life-span 250 years or more). From *A. procera*, to which it is allied, it may be distinguished by its longer, never-grooved needles.

With but one exception the tallest extant specimens are all in Scotland: Blair Atholl, Perths., 116 × 10¼ ft (1955); Dunkeld, Perths., two on the Cathedral

Lawn, 115 × 9½ and 115 × 8¼ (1961), and another by Dunkeld House, 110 × 9¼ ft (1962); Glamis Castle, Angus, *pl.* 1864, 112 × 10½ ft (1955); Taymouth Castle, Perths., 110 × 9¾ and 101 × 10¼ ft (1961); Cragside, Northumb., 105 × 8½ ft (1958). In the south, the best recorded are: Borde Hill, Sussex, 80 × 7 ft (1961), an earlier measurement being 24 × 3 ft (1931); Hergest Croft, Heref., *pl.* 1917, 64 × 7¼ ft (1963); National Pinetum, Bedgebury, Kent, *pl.* 1925, 64 × 8 ft (1965).

var. SHASTENSIS Lemm.—Cones shorter and thicker, with the bracts conspicuously protruded.

A. MARIESII Mast.

A tree 40 to 50, occasionally 80 ft high, of compact, pyramidal form; young shoots very densely covered with red-brown down, which persists several years; buds small, globose, completely encased in resin. Leaves ⅓ to 1 in. long, $\frac{1}{12}$ in. wide; dark shining green and deeply grooved above; glaucous beneath, with two broad bands of stomata; apex rounded and notched. The lower ranks spread horizontally, whilst the upper and shorter ones point forward and completely hide the shoot. Cones 3 to 4 in. long, about 2 in. wide, rounded at the top, egg-shaped, purple when young; bracts hidden. *Bot. Mag.*, n.s., t. 45.

Native of Japan; introduced by Charles Maries from Mt Hakkoda in 1878, but the oldest plants in cultivation are from another source, perhaps the German nursery firm of Hesse. It is a handsome fir, with shining foliage, but slow-growing and very rare in cultivation. The best specimens known are: Dawyck, Peebl., *pl.* 1910, 55 × 5 ft (1966); Leonardslee, Sussex, 58 × 3 ft (1961); Grayswood Hill, Surrey, 55 × 3½ ft (1964).

It has been confused with *A. veitchii* and with the American *A. amabilis*, while the fir illustrated in *Bot. Mag.*, t. 8098, is not *A. mariesii* but *A. spectabilis*.

A. NEPHROLEPIS (Trautv.) Maxim.

A. sibirica var. *nephrolepis* Trautv.

A tree up to 80 ft high in the wild with a trunk 6 ft in girth; young shoots downy; winter buds not resinous. Leaves crowded above and spreading outwards from the twigs; ½ to 1¼ in. long, $\frac{1}{16}$ in. wide; slightly notched at the rounded apex; faintly lined beneath with stomatic bands. Cones violet-purple, cylindrical, 2 in. long, ¾ to 1 in. wide, the bracts two-thirds as long as the scales, only the thread-like tip exposed and pointing upwards.

Native of Manchuria, Korea, and N. China, originally described by Trautvetter as a variety of *A. sibirica* from specimens collected in the region of the Amur River. Wilson found it in Korea and Purdom in the province of Shan-si, N. China. It is evidently nearly related to *A. sibirica* and is considered by Wilson and Rehder to be the eastern Asiatic form of that species. It is rare in cultivation and of little ornamental value, but represented at Westonbirt, Glos. and a few other collections. Introduced in 1908.

f. CHLOROCARPA Wils.—A form with green cones, introduced by Wilson.

A. SIBIRICA Ledeb.—Native of Russia, where it covers vast tracts, from the Urals almost to the Pacific and from the Arctic Circle to the mountains of Central Asia. It was introduced in 1820 but, like so many trees adapted to very harsh climates, it does not thrive in this country and no examples of any note have been found. It differs from *A. nephrolepis* in its smooth bark, more downy shoots, and in the shorter cone-bracts, which are concealed by the scales. For another close ally, see *A. sachalinensis*.

A. NORDMANNIANA Spach   CAUCASIAN FIR

A tree described as reaching 200 ft in height in a wild state, with a trunk 4 to 5 ft in diameter; young shoots shining grey-brown, furnished with short stiff hairs; buds not resinous, ovoid. Leaves very densely arranged, mostly on the upper side of the shoot, the lower ones being the longer, and spreading horizontally; the upper ones shorter, and pointing forward; it is only on weak shoots that any indication of a two-ranked or V-shaped arrangement is seen. The leaves measure $\frac{3}{4}$ to $1\frac{1}{2}$ in. in length, $\frac{1}{16}$ to $\frac{1}{12}$ in. wide, apex rounded and

ABIES NORDMANNIANA

notched; very dark glossy green above, midrib sunken, two whitish stomatic bands beneath. Cones 5 or 6 in. long, 1¾ to 2 in. wide, cylindrical or tapered towards the top, reddish brown; scales 1¼ to 1¾ in. wide, ⅝ to ¾ in. deep; bracts conspicuously protruded and bent downwards. *Bot. Mag.*, t. 6992.

Native of the Caucasus and Asia Minor; discovered in 1836 and first distributed in Britain by Lawson of Edinburgh a few years later. It is undoubtedly one of the handsomest and, in most places, best-growing of the firs, although in some places very subject to the attacks of aphis. It thrives in very much the same conditions that suit *A. grandis* but tolerates more lime in the soil. In foliage it is not unlike the W. American *A. amabilis*, which has, however, more rounded and resinous buds, and cones with enclosed bracts. Botanically, it stands much closer to *A. alba*.

It is possible to mention only a few of the fine specimens in the British Isles: Oakley Park, Shrops., 132 × 9 ft (1960); Woodhouse, Devon, 126 × 8½ ft (1957); Taymouth Castle, Perths., 120 × 13 ft, a superb tree with very luxuriant foliage (1961); Benmore, Argyll, 120 × 9¾ ft (1964); Vivod, Denbigh, 117 × 7½ ft (1964); Moor Park, Shrops., 115 × 8¾ ft (1962); Durris House, Kinc., 114 × 12 ft (1955); Mells Park, Somerset, 113 × 9½ ft, with a very fine bole (1962); Boconnoc, Cornwall, 111 × 11¾ ft, a very fine tree (1957).

At Powerscourt, Co. Wicklow, Eire, there are large numbers in splendid vigour and size, planted in 1867. Of these the largest is 134 × 14¼ ft (1966).

cv. 'PENDULA'.—Branches pendulous; originated in Young's nursery, Milford, Surrey. A tree at Headfort, Co. Meath, Eire, probably belongs here. It was planted in 1916 and measures 60 × 4 ft (1966).

At Belladrum, Inverness-shire, there is a remarkable tree 102 ft high, making a fine, narrow, solid column and with incurved, twisted needles. It agrees with the description of 'Tortifolia' but is unlikely to be of that clone.

A. BORNMUELLERIANA Mattf.—A species allied to the preceding but with some of the characters of *A. cephalonica*, notably the resinous buds and glabrous shoots. It has been considered to be a hybrid between them, but if so, the crossing must have taken place in the distant past, since the two species are not in contact at the present time. It has a small range in N.W. Asia Minor, where it forms forests on the Bithynian Olympus. It is distinguished from *A. nordmanniana* by the characters mentioned, and from *A. cephalonica* by its emarginate leaves. There are examples of over 80 ft at Dropmore, Bucks., and Gordon Castle, Moray.

A. × INSIGNIS Carr. ex Bailly—This name covers the various hybrids that have arisen in cultivation between *A. nordmanniana* and *A. pinsapo*. The type form occurred spontaneously in a French nursery and was a seedling of *A. pinsapo*, but the same cross was made deliberately, also in France, using *A. nordmanniana* as the seed parent.

A. NUMIDICA Carr.   ALGERIAN FIR

A tree said to be 70 ft high in the wild state but already taller in cultivation; buds not, or very slightly, resinous; young shoots shining brown, glabrous.

Leaves arranged all round the shoot, but with those underneath mostly brought upwards into a horizontal position; on strong shoots the leaves on the upper side are erect or pointed backwards, but on weaker shoots there is a V-shaped opening formed by the separation of the leaves into two sets. Leaves $\frac{1}{2}$ to $\frac{3}{4}$ in. long, $\frac{1}{12}$ in. wide; rounded, or notched, or somewhat pointed at the apex; dark glossy green above, often with a grey patch near the apex made up of a few broken lines of stomata; lower surface with a conspicuous grey band of stomata each side of the midrib. Cones 5 to 7 in. long, $1\frac{1}{2}$ to $1\frac{3}{4}$ in. wide, cylindrical, brown.

Native of Mt Babor in Algeria, where it grows in association with *Cedrus atlantica*; discovered in 1861, and soon afterwards introduced. Vigorous plants are very distinct in the grey patch of stomata on the upper side of the leaf and in the dense array of thick, round-ended, or notched leaves all over the upper side of the shoot, the middle ones of which often point backwards. On weak shoots these characters are not so marked.

It is a handsome fir, and like its allies *A. pinsapo* and *cephalonica* grows well in the south and south-east and does not object to lime in the soil. The tallest on record are: Bicton, Devon, 95 × 9¼ ft (1959); Westonbirt, Glos., *pl.* 1910, 83 × 5¾ ft; another, *pl.* 1929, is 42 × 3¾ ft (1966); Borde Hill, Sussex, *pl.* 1907, 80 × 7¾ ft (1961); Necton Park, Norfolk, 75 × 7 ft (1952); Eridge Park, Kent, *pl.* 1892, 68 × 5 ft (1963); Pampisford, Cambs., 67 × 7¼ ft (1959).

A. PARDEI Gaussen—Trees growing in the Arboretum Les Barres, France, originally identified as *A. numidica*, have been described as *A. pardei*. Gaussen considered them to be near to *A. alba* and suggested that they might represent a form of that species found wild in Calabria. Other views are that they are *A. pinsapo* × *numidica*, or a form of *A.* × *insignis* (q.v. under *A. nordmanniana*). The origin of the trees is unknown.

A tree at Headfort, Co. Meath, Eire, is illustrated in *Bot. Mag.*, n.s., t. 272, as 'A. pinsapo var. vel hybrida'. It shows a mixture of the characters of *A. pinsapo* and *A. numidica*, recalling the latter in the arrangement of its leaves. It was bought of Veitch in 1912 and is 43 ft high (1966).

A. PINDROW Royle

A. webbiana var. *pindrow* (Royle) Brandis

A lofty tree with a trunk 6 to 8 ft in diameter; trees in this country of slender pyramidal form; young shoots glabrous, shining, yellowish grey; winter buds globose, very resinous, bluish at the base. Leaves narrowly linear, 1½ to 2¾ in. long, $\frac{1}{16}$ in. to $\frac{1}{12}$ in. wide; divided at the apex into two sharp unequal points; bright green above, and with two faintly defined stomatic bands beneath. The leaves are arranged on all sides of the shoot except underneath, the side ones spreading horizontally, the uppermost ones pointing forward. On young plants the leaves are sharply pointed and not divided at the apex. Cones 4½ to 7 in. long, 2½ to 3 in. wide, deep purple, then brown; bracts short and completely hidden.

Native of the W. Himalaya as far east as Kumaon. In the wild state it has been found over 200 ft high but in cultivation specimens of over 90 ft are rare. Although coming from a lower elevation than *A. spectabilis* and considered to be more tender, it has the advantage of starting into growth later, and thus more often escapes spring frosts. It is seen at its best in the milder, moister parts of the country, and is then extremely handsome. It has been associated as a variety with *A. spectabilis*, although two firs could scarcely be more distinct. The rough, downy shoots of *A. spectabilis*, its round-ended leaves vividly white beneath, and the more spreading habit, amply distinguish it.

By far the finest specimen recorded is one at Castle Leod, Ross, which measured 117 × 13¼ ft in 1966. Others of good size are: Tregrehan, Cornwall, 97 × 8½ ft (1965); Monk Coniston, Lancs., 90 × 9 ft (1957); Aldourie, Inv., 90 × 8½ ft (1956); Whittingehame, E. Lothian, 88 × 9 ft (1957); Inchmarlo, Kinc., 84 × 11½ ft (1956); Eastnor Castle, Heref., 82 × 5½ ft (1961). There are many dead or dying trees in collections, some of them around 80 ft in height.

var. BREVIFOLIA Dallim. & A. B. Jacks. *A. gamblei* Hickel—This variety differs in its reddish-brown, not grey branchlets (in which character it recalls *A. spectabilis*), and in its shorter leaves (1 to 1½ in. long), which are more rigid than in the type and pointed, not notched, at the apex. Such forms have been in cultivation since about 1860 and certainly derive from Himalayan seed. Hickel found a good match for this variety in a specimen collected in Garwhal province and raised the variety to specific status as *A. gamblei*, but it seems preferable to retain it as a variety until the pattern of variation shown by the two Himalayan firs in a wild state is better understood.

var. INTERMEDIA Henry—This variety was described from a tree growing at Eastnor Castle, Herefordshire, planted in 1870, which was thought by Henry to show characters intermediate between *A. pindrow* and *A. spectabilis*, but to be nearer to the former. Since these two firs overlap in the western Himalaya it is not unlikely that hybrids or intermediates might occur in nature. The actual tree from which Henry received the specimen cannot now be traced. Another intermediate, but nearer to *A. spectabilis*, was received from Rostrevor by the late Commander F. Gilliland of Brook House, Londonderry, and given an Award of Merit when a branch was shown at Vincent Square in 1944 (*Journ. R.H.S.*, Vol. 68, p. 310, and Vol. 69, p. 375). Mr David Gilliland tells us that the tree now measures 40 × 5¾ ft; it was most attractive when younger and fully furnished but is becoming progressively more ugly with age.

A. PINSAPO Boiss.   SPANISH FIR

A tree up to 100 ft high; young shoots glabrous, brown; buds reddish, resinous. Leaves densely arranged all round the branchlet (more equally than in any other fir, but still somewhat more densely above), and standing out stiffly from it at right angles; they are ½ to ¾ in. long, about 1/12 in. broad; thick, abruptly pointed or blunt at the apex, dark green with numerous faintly defined lines of stomata on both surfaces. Cones cylindric, with a tapered apex, 4 to 5 in. long, about 1½ in. wide, purplish brown; bracts small and completely enclosed.

Native of S.E. Spain, in the mountains about Ronda, always on limestone; discovered in 1837 and introduced to England two years later. It succeeds admirably in this country, whether the soil is calcareous or not. It is, perhaps, the most distinct and unmistakable of firs, especially in the short, blunt leaves being set about equally all round the branchlet. The best specimens lie for the most part outside the cooler and moister areas favoured by the majority of firs, as the following records show: Rhinefield, New Forest, Hants, 102 × 5¾ ft, forks from the base (1962), and another in Rhinefield Drive, 93 × 6¼ ft, on a fine single stem (1964); Bodnant, Denbigh, *pl.* 1876, 96 × 9¼ ft (1957); Eridge Castle, Kent, *pl.* 1886, 88 × 6¼ ft (1963); Poltimore, Devon, 89 × 10 ft (1964); Leonardslee, Sussex, 88 × 4½ ft (1958); Longleat, Wilts, 83 × 10¼ ft, fine bole (1963); Lydhurst, Sussex, 73 × 12 ft, single-stemmed to the top (1965); Dropmore, Bucks., two of the original introduction, *pl.* 1843, 84 × 7 and 75 × 7 ft (1964). The rate of growth in younger trees is shown by: Wakehurst Place, Sussex, *pl.* 1915, 57 × 4½ ft (1964).

f. GLAUCA (Carr.) Beissn.—Leaves of a glaucous hue; found wild with the type and common in the stands near Grazalema. It was originally described from a tree growing in a French nursery and the cultivar name 'Glauca' would belong only to the descendants of that tree by vegetative propagation.

A. × INSIGNIS. See under *A. nordmanniana*.

A. × VILMORINII Mast. (*A. pinsapo* × *cephalonica*).—This cross was made artificially by Henri de Vilmorin at Verrières, near Paris, in 1867, but hybrid seed is said to occur quite frequently where the two species grow together. There are examples in the National Pinetum, Bedgebury, Kent; Westonbirt, Glos.; Leonardslee, Sussex; and in the Chandlers Ford nursery of Messrs Hillier. Their heights range from 42 to 55 ft.

For '*A. pinsapo* var. vel hybrida', illustrated in *Bot. Mag.*, n.s., t. 272, see *A. numidica*.

A. MAROCANA Trabut—Native of Morocco, where it occupies a small area in the mountains south of Tetuan, at no great distance from the stands of *A. pinsapo* on the other side of the straits. It is said to be intermediate in its characters between that species and *A. numidica*. Probably not in cultivation in this country.

A. PROCERA Rehd. NOBLE FIR
A. nobilis (D. Don) Lindl., not *A. nobilis* Dietrich; *Pinus nobilis* D. Don.

A tree up to 240 ft high in nature, and already more than half that height in cultivation in Britain; young shoots clothed with a reddish-brown minute down; buds roundish, resinous, surrounded at the base by a collar of long-pointed scales free at the tips. Leaves ½ to 1⅓ in. long, 1/16 in. wide, distinctly grooved on the top, round at the apex, glaucous green, with stomata both above and below; the leaves are very densely arranged on the upper side and at the sides of the shoot, leaving it exposed only underneath; the upper leaves have their bases flattened to the shoot (completely hiding it), then curve abruptly upwards. Cones 6 to 10 in. long, 3 to 3½ in. wide, cylindrical, rounded at the top, of a rich brown-purple, with the green bracts conspicuously protruded and reflexed.

Native of Oregon, Washington, and California; discovered by Douglas in 1825 and introduced by him six years later on his second visit. No fir from western

N. America has succeeded better than this in certain parts of the country, and best of all in Scotland, where it regenerates naturally. It enjoys a moist climate and deep soil but will grow quite well in cold, exposed situations and in poor mountain peats. The larger trees in this country, and some younger ones, produce cones in great profusion. These cones are the largest among firs, and, standing stiffly erect, their size and rich colour render them very striking. Unfortunately the noble fir is subject to attacks by an aphis which induces gouty swellings on the shoots, but spraying with aphicide will keep the pest in check on young trees. This fir is most closely allied to *A. magnifica*, but has a more spreading crown and differs in its grooved leaves. Both are distinct from other firs in the crowded leaves on the upper side of the branchlets having their bases flattened against it. The noble fir varies in the intensity of its glaucous hue, forms most notable in this respect being distinguished as f. GLAUCA (Ravenscroft) Rehd.

The fine trees at Murthly Castle, Perthshire, were mentioned in previous editions; of these the tallest was felled in 1943, the best of those remaining being about 130 ft high. Trees of the original introduction by Douglas, and planted in 1835, grow at Chatsworth, Derbyshire, and Dropmore, Bucks. The tallest examples recorded, to mention only those of over 130 ft, are: Duncraig Castle, Ross, 150 × 11 ft (1961); Inveraray, Argyll, by Dubh Loch, *pl.* 1873, 147 × 10 and 136 × 7¼ ft (1953–4); Stourhead, Wilts, 140 × 12 ft (1965); Bolderwood, Hants, 138 × 13½ ft, a superb tree (1954); Dupplin Castle, Perths., 135 × 10 ft (1954); Benmore, Argyll, 133 × 9 ft (1956); Kirkennan, Kirkc., 132 × 10½ ft, fine bole (1954); Durris House, Kinc., 132 × 14¼ ft (1955); Cowdray Park, Sussex, 132 × 10 ft (1967); Castle Milk, Dumf., *pl.* 1884, 130 × 9½ ft (1954).

A. RECURVATA Mast.

An evergreen tree up to 120 ft high in a wild state, with a trunk up to 16 ft in girth; bark dark grey or reddish brown; young shoots without down, glossy, yellowish grey; winter buds ovoid, very resinous. Leaves ½ to 1½ in. long, very much recurved, sharply pointed on young trees, abruptly so on adult ones; lustrous green on both surfaces but paler beneath where are eight or nine faintly defined rows of stomata on each side of the midrib. Cones oblong-ovoid, 2 to 4 in. long, violet-purple at first, finally grey-brown, slightly resinous; bracts entirely hidden.

Native of W. Szechwan, China, where Wilson discovered it in the valley of the Min River in 1903 and introduced it to cultivation in 1910. This fir is very distinct on account of the strongly recurved, sharply pointed leaves, especially characteristic of young shoots. Wilson observes that 'this species is one of the most desirable of the family and was well worth a long journey to introduce it to cultivation'.

The tree in the Little Hall Pinetum mentioned in previous editions cannot now be traced but there are several thriving specimens in the country. The younger may be from seed collected by Rock in 1925; the oldest are from Wilson's introduction: Tilgate, Sussex, *pl.* 1913, 66 × 3¼ ft (1961); Wakehurst Place, Sussex, 58 × 2¾ and 46 × 1½ ft (1964), and another, *pl.* 1919, 40 × 2½ ft

(1964); Tilgate Forest Lodge, Sussex, 42 × 2 and 40 × 3 ft (1961); Westonbirt, Glos., 42 × 2½ ft (1965); Gordon Castle, Moray, 41 × 3¼ ft (1958).

A. RELIGIOSA (H.B.K.) Schlecht.   MEXICAN FIR
Pinus religiosa H.B.K.

A tree to about 150 ft in the wild, rarely more; bark smooth and greyish when young, becoming rough and plated; buds resinous; young shoots red-brown to purplish, more or less downy, especially when young. Leaves 1 to 1½ in. long, about ¹⁄₁₆ in. wide, apex usually pointed and rather horny, sometimes blunt or rounded, dark glossy green above, with two greyish bands of stomata beneath. Those on the lower side of the shoot spread horizontally, those on the upper side pointing forward and upward. Cones 4 to 6 in. long, cylindric but tapered at the apex, blue when young; bracts protruded and reflexed. *Bot. Mag.*, t. 6753.

Native of Mexico and Guatemala; introduced in 1838. In its typical form it is common in the mountains of north-western Mexico at 8,000 to 10,000 ft, sometimes higher. The forms found further to the south-west and in Guatemala are by some botanists regarded as specifically distinct from *A. religiosa*. The Mexican fir is very tender and, in the very mild parts where it grows well, is liable to damage from Atlantic gales once it reaches a good height; of the two famous trees at Fota near Cork, one blew down early this century and the other in 1930. Many other promising trees have suffered the same fate or lost their tops, and no specimen of any size has been recorded in recent years.

A. VEJARI Martinez—A rare species in nature, first described in 1942; native of N.E. Mexico at 9,000 to 10,000 ft. It differs from *A. religiosa* in its irregularly arranged leaves, with stomata on both sides, and in its shorter and squatter cones (to about 3½ in. long and 2 in. wide). Introduced in 1964 and therefore untried. Its main stands are in the state of Tamaulipas, where, according to Martinez, it covers an area of about 500 hectares and grows to over 100 ft high.

A. SACHALINENSIS (Schmidt) Mast.
A. veitchii var. *sachalinensis* Schmidt

A tree to 130 ft with a smooth, whitish bark; buds resinous; young shoots furrowed, greyish, hairy in the grooves. Leaves arranged as in *A. veitchii* but longer and narrower, 1¾ in. long, ¹⁄₂₀ in. wide, bright green above, with two bands of stomata below, each with seven or eight lines. Cones cylindrical, to 3½ in. long, with protruding, reflexed bracts.

Native of the northern island of Japan (Hokkaido), Sakhalin, and the Kuriles, allied to *A. sibirica* and *A. nephrolepis*. It was introduced in 1878 and, in spite of its being much subject to injury by late frosts, has grown well in some collections. The best recorded are: Dyffryn Park, Glam., 75 ft (1964); Wakehurst Place, Sussex, 74 × 4¾ ft (1965); Murthly Castle, Perths., 57 × 3¾ ft (1962); Stourhead, Wilts, 57 × 3 ft (1965); Borde Hill, Sussex, 50 × 1¾ ft (1957); Castle Milk, Dumf., *pl.* 1921, 50 × 4 ft (1966).

It is most likely to be confused with *A. nephrolepis* and *A. sibirica*, which it closely resembles in foliage but from which it differs in its grooved branchlets and in the exserted cone-bracts.

A. SPECTABILIS (D. Don) G. Don

Pinus spectabilis D. Don; *A. webbiana* Lindl.

A tree up to 150 ft high in nature, with a trunk 6 or 7 ft in diameter; young shoots very stout, rough, downy in the grooves between the leaf-bases; buds resinous. Leaves aggregated in two opposite sets so as to leave a V-shaped opening along the top, the lower ones on each side spreading horizontally; they are, individually, $1\frac{1}{4}$ to 2 in. long, $\frac{1}{12}$ to $\frac{1}{8}$ in. wide, linear, distinctly notched at the apex; dark green, glossy, and deeply grooved above, and with two broad, vividly blue-white bands of stomata beneath. Cones 5 or 6 in. long, 3 in. in diameter, violet-purple at first, ultimately brown. *Bot. Mag.*, t. 8098 as *A. mariesii*.

Native of the Himalaya from Afghanistan to Assam; in the western part of its range it overlaps with *A. pindrow* but occurs at a higher altitude than that species. The eastern populations (from Sikkim eastward) are said to be finer than the western and are sometimes regarded as a distinct species, *A. densa* Griff., but this name is usually relegated to synonymy under *A. spectabilis*.

The first successful introduction of this fir was in 1822 but the older extant specimens are of later date. It is a species that thrives best in the milder and moister parts of the British Isles, in positions not subject to late spring frosts. Where suited, it has grown well and many old trees remain. It is very distinct in its large, arched leaves, so vividly white beneath, and in its large, globose, very resinous buds, but it is as a young tree that it is most decorative. The following are some of the older and taller specimens on record: Dropmore, Bucks., *pl.* 1843, 95 × $4\frac{3}{4}$ ft (1961); Inveraray, Argyll, *pl.* 1876, 90 × $9\frac{1}{4}$ ft (1955); Castle Leod, Ross, 87 × 12 ft (1966); Albury Park, Surrey, *pl.* 1891, 80 × 4 ft (1961); Howick, Northumb., *pl.* 1841, 78 × 10 ft (1958).

var. BREVIFOLIA (Henry) Rehd. *A. webbiana* var. *brevifolia* Henry—A very distinct variety with grey branchlets, less prominently furrowed than in the type. Leaves much shorter, to $1\frac{1}{4}$ in. long, greyish beneath with two inconspicuous stomatic bands. It was described from a cultivated tree, raised from Himalayan seed in 1879. It is matched by wild specimens collected in the western Himalaya and may be the form assumed by *A. spectabilis* in that part of its range. The trees showing the characters of this variety are less spring-tender than the type and have reached a greater height in cultivation. Those recorded are: Taymouth Castle, Perths., *c.* 105 × $9\frac{1}{4}$ ft (1962); Tregrehan, Cornwall, 100 × $6\frac{1}{2}$ ft (1957); Dupplin Castle, Perths., 91 × $7\frac{1}{2}$ ft (1957); Castle Leod, Ross, 85 × $8\frac{1}{4}$ ft (1966).

A. SQUAMATA Mast.

An evergreen tree 60 to 120 ft high, with a trunk girthing 7 to 16 ft; terminal buds roundish, very resinous; young shoots covered with brownish down. Branches six or more years old become shaggy through the peeling off of the purplish-brown bark in thin papery layers, as occurs in several birches. Leaves ½ to 1 in. long, blunt or abruptly pointed, varying (according to Wilson) in the amount of glaucous colouring; stomatic lines eight or nine each side of the midrib and usually forming two whitish bands beneath. Cones violet-coloured, resinous, 2 to 2½ in. long, between cylindrical and egg-shaped; bracts showing only the recurved, pointed tips.

Native of W. Szechwan, China, 'in the wild country west of Tatien-lu', where it forms entire forests at between 12,000 and 14,000 ft altitude; discovered by Wilson in 1904, introduced by him in 1910. The most distinctive character of this silver fir is its peeling bark. It is very rare in cultivation, the only examples known being: Hergest Croft, Heref., pl. 1921, 44 × 2¾ ft and another slightly smaller (1961); Bicton, Devon, pl. 1920, 32 × 2¼ ft (1965); Stanage Park, Radnor, 34 × 1¾ ft (1950); Ripley Castle, Yorks., 34 × 2¾ ft (1958); Chandlers Ford nursery of Messrs Hillier, 27 × 1½ ft (1961); Dawyck, Peebl., pl. 1931, 27 × 1¾ ft (1966); Birr Castle, Co. Offaly, Eire, 37 × 3¼ ft (1966).

A. SUTCHUENENSIS (Franch.) Rehd. & Wils.

A. fargesii var. *sutchuenensis* Franch.

A tree ordinarily 80 to 100 ft high in the wild but sometimes 180 to 200 ft high as seen in the Upper Tebu country in S.W. Kansu, China, by J. F. Rock, who describes the bark as 'pale whitish brown'. Buds variable in shape, resinous, partly concealed by the leaves. Young shoots reddish brown, ordinarily glabrous, but weak shoots densely downy. Leaves on adult trees ½ to 1 in. long, bluntish, rounded or obscurely notched at the apex, glossy green above with two strips of stomatiferous lines beneath. The arrangement of the leaves on sterile shoots is not given in the original description but in cultivated specimens they are densely set on the shoot, pointing forward and outward and closely overlapping; on coning branches they curve upward. Cones ovoid-oblong, rounded at the top, 2 to 3 in. long and 1⅓ in. wide, purplish- or violet-black, not or very slightly resinous, with little more than the subulate, deflexed tips of the bracts showing.

This silver fir which, judging by Rock's account, must be one of the finest in the world, was first found by Purdom, in 1911, on the banks of the Tao River in Kansu. The species was described from his No. 805, thought by Rehder and Wilson to be the same as a specimen collected earlier by Père Farges in E. Szechwan, described as *A. fargesii* var. *sutchuenensis* by Franchet. It was also introduced by Purdom, and the trees at Dawyck and Hergest Croft are probably from his seed. The main introduction was in 1925, when seed collected by Rock was distributed by the Arnold Arboretum. In *A. fargesii*, with which it might be confused, the leaves on sterile shoots are longer and more outward pointing and the top of the main part of the bracts is exposed. A good field character is that in that species the leaves when crushed smell of orange, whereas in *A. sutchuenensis* they are unpleasantly pungent (E. L. Hillier in *Journ. R.H.S.*, Vol. 66, 1941, p. 434). It has also been confused with *A. delavayi* var. *faxoniana*, which, however, has downy shoots and larger cones.

The few specimens recorded are: Dawyck, Peebl., pl. 1924, 44 × 3½ ft (1966);

Hergest Croft, Heref., *pl.* 1923, 35 × 3 ft (1961); Wakehurst Place, Sussex, 28 × 1¼ ft (1964); Westonbirt, Glos., 28 × 1½ ft (1964). There are smaller examples at Burnside, Angus, and Blairquhan, Ayrs.

A. VEITCHII Lindl.

A tree 50 to 70 ft high; young shoots brown, furnished with a more or less scattered, minute down; buds globose, very resinous, purplish. Leaves ½ to 1⅜ in. long, 1⁄16 in. wide, the base tapered, the apex cut off straight and notched; dark glossy green and grooved above, vividly white with stomatic lines beneath. All the leaves point forwards, and most of them curve more or less upwards; a few occur underneath the shoot, but most of them are above it or at the sides. On lateral shoots growing erect or nearly erect, the leaves are arranged about equally round the twig. Cones cylindrical, 2 to 2½ in. long, about 1 in. wide; blue-purple at first.

Native of central and southern Japan; discovered by John Gould Veitch on Mt Fuji in 1860; introduced by Maries in 1879. Among silver firs this species is very distinct, on account of the narrow, truncate leaves, pointed forwards and curving upwards, and intensely blue-white beneath. The trunk is smooth even on old trees, and characteristically folded into wrinkles around the branch insertions. It is not a long-lived species; the tree at Murthly Castle, mentioned in previous editions (31 ft in 1906), had attained twice that height by 1931 but is now dead, as are many others planted at the end of the last century. The following are the best recorded: Westonbirt, Glos., *pl.* 1916, 76 × 3¾ ft (1966); Dawyck, Peebl., 70 × 5¼, 72 × 3¾ and 70 × 7 ft (1966); Benmore, Argyll, 69 × 4½ ft (1956); Borde Hill, Sussex, *pl.* 1890, 69 × 4¾ ft (1957); Murthly Castle, Perths., 71 × 4½ ft (1955).

ABUTILON MALVACEAE

A genus of about one hundred woody or herbaceous species, mostly tropical and sub-tropical in distribution. The cultivated species are soft-wooded plants, nearly all of them natives of Central and S. America, with showy flowers borne singly in the leaf-axils, or in small panicles. As is common in the Mallow family the numerous stamens are united into a tube which surrounds the gynoecium; the ovary has several chambers and the style is divided into as many arms as there are chambers; the calyx may be tubular and only shortly five-lobed, or divided to the base into five segments; petals five. The fruit is dry and splits into segments (schizocarps), each of which opens to release a few seeds.

A. vitifolium, *A. ochsenii* and two other species not described here are characterised by a type of style not seen elsewhere in the genus and are for this reason separated as a distinct section—*Corynabutilon*—or even as a distinct genus (Kearney in *Leafl. West. Bot.*, 5, p. 189, 1949).

A. MEGAPOTAMICUM St.-Hil. & Naud.   [PLATE 4
A. vexillarium Morr.

An evergreen shrub of lax, graceful habit, to 6 ft high. Leaves ovate, cordate at the base, 2 to 4 in. long, slender-pointed, coarsely toothed. Flowers pendulous, borne singly in the leaf-axils from April onwards; calyx inflated, rich red, about 1 in. long; corolla yellow, about ½ in. longer than the calyx. The stamens and stigmas form a club-shaped stalked cluster that stands out well beyond the corolla. *Bot. Mag.*, t. 5717.

Native of Brazil. Although by no means hardy, it will survive most winters on a warm, sheltered wall, and is certainly one of the most attractive subjects for such a situation. There is also a variegated form in which the leaves are prettily blotched and tessellated with bright yellow. Its hybrids with *A. pictum* are known as A. × MILLERI, of which several have been raised, with yellow flowers streaked with red; the leaves are longer than in *A. megapotamicum* and relatively narrower.

Although *A. megapotamicum* has no part in their make-up, certain other tender hybrids may be mentioned here which are sometimes grown out-of-doors in the milder parts. The main parents of this group are thought to be A. DARWINII (leaves about twice as long as wide, velvety) and A. STRIATUM (leaves almost as wide as long, glabrous), both with orange flowers, veined with red. Three of the best known in this miscellany are 'GOLDEN FLEECE', with rich yellow flowers; 'ASHFORD RED', with large flowers of a colour described as 'a deep shade of crushed strawberry'; and 'BOULE DE NEIGE', perhaps a hybrid of *A. insigne*, with white flowers; according to Thurston, it once reached a height of 13 ft in Cornwall.

A. VITIFOLIUM (Cav.) Presl
Sida vitifolia Cav.; *Corynabutilon vitifolium* (Cav.) Kearney

A soft-wooded shrub, or almost a tree, sometimes 15 to 30 ft high, more usually about half as high; young wood covered with a white down. Leaves alternate, long-stalked, three- or five-lobed, maple-like, heart-shaped at the base; varying much in size according to the vigour and age of the plant, but usually between 4 and 6 in. long, three-fourths as wide; each lobe ends in a drawn-out point, and is coarsely and unevenly toothed; both surfaces (but especially the lower one) covered with greyish tufted hairs. Flowers borne, three or four together, towards the end of a woolly stalk, 3 to 5 in. long, springing from the leaf-axils; each flower measures 2½ to 3 in. across, has five rounded petals of a beautiful pale, purplish blue, and is in form rather like the flower of a 'single' hollyhock. *Bot. Mag.*, t. 4227.

The flowers vary in colour, and in one form, to which the name ALBA has been given, they are snow-white. This usually comes true from seed, but occasionally the purplish-flowered form appears amongst the seedlings, just as seeds of the purplish one will sometimes produce the white one. In the clone 'VERONICA TENNANT' the large flowers are pale lavender in colour.

Native of Chile; first raised in Dublin in 1836 by Capt. Cottingham, an amateur gardener of the time, who had obtained seeds from its native country. It is not hardy in the open at Kew and is even uncertain against a wall there, but in the milder parts of the country few shrubs are more lovely during summer when it is in bloom. It is not a long-lived plant, and, as is not uncommon with soft-wooded shrubs that flower and bear seed so profusely, it is apt to die suddenly without apparent cause. Happily, its abundant seeds give a quick and easy

ABUTILON VITIFOLIUM

means of renewing the stock. It is most fortunately placed in some sheltered corner, such as in the angle of two walls, where it will develop into a loose, graceful shrub. It may also be grown on a wall, but in the milder parts of the country will stand on the open lawn.

A. OCHSENII (Phil.) Phil. *Anoda ochsenii* Phil.; *Corynabutilon ochsenii* (Phil.) Kearney—This near ally of *A. vitifolium* was introduced *c*. 1957 from Chile by E. B. Anderson. The parent plant grew in the garden of the late Sra Margharita Manns and was collected by her in Valdivia province. It differs from *A. vitifolium* in its much less hairy stems, leaves and peduncles and its smaller, deeper-coloured flowers borne singly or in pairs. The greener leaves and violet-blue flowers render it very distinct from the older species. It is not yet fully tested in cultivation, but judging from its performance in the winters of 1961–3 it is as hardy or even hardier. It is certainly a vigorous grower, likely to reach a height of at least 12 ft on a wall. It is figured in *Bot. Mag.*, n.s., t. 445.

ACACIA LEGUMINOSAE

A very large genus of trees and shrubs found in many tropical and warm temperate regions, but more especially in Australia and Africa. In Australia the acacias and eucalyptuses are the dominant genera of woody plants, and of the former there are now about 400 species recognised. The best known of them in this country is *A. dealbata*, the 'silver wattle', sprays of which are imported as 'mimosa' in winter from the south of France in great quantities to the London flower market.

The leaves of acacias are normally doubly pinnate, but in a large number of species this type of leaf disappears after the seedling stage and becomes reduced to a mere development of the leaf-stalk—what is known as a 'phyllode'. These phyllodes are of one piece, flat and leaf-like, often of considerable size, and perform the same functions as ordinary leaves.

The flowers of all cultivated acacias are of some shade of yellow, varying from bright to very pale, and they are borne either in ball-like clusters or in cylindrical ones like tiny bottle-brushes. The stamens constitute the most conspicuous feature of the blossom, which is very different in structure from the typical pea-like flower of the family.

The species selected for the descriptive notes that follow are the most important of those that are, or have been grown in the milder parts of the British Isles. They include the majority of those most valued by Australian gardeners and are a good representation of the genus as a whole. None is so hardy as to be quite exempt from the risk of severe damage or death in hard winters, but *A. dealbata*, the best-known and most widely grown of the acacias, comes through most winters in the south of England with wall protection and is common as an open-ground plant in S. Cornwall; many others might be tried on a sunny, sheltered wall, where, thanks to their rapid growth, they may give many seasons of flower before the next killing winter supervenes. It should be added that many of the species have a wide natural range and might yet yield hardier forms than those now in cultivation.

The acacias are easily raised from seed but selected forms must be increased by cuttings of half-ripened wood and struck with gentle bottom heat. They will grow in any good garden soil provided it is not excessively limy; *A. longifolia* and *A. rhetinodes* are known to be exceptionally lime-tolerant.

A. ARMATA R. Br.   KANGAROO THORN

An evergreen shrub 10 ft or more high, of densely bushy shape; young shoots ribbed and usually more or less (sometimes very) bristly. 'Leaves' (phyllodes) in the form generally cultivated closely set on the twigs, obliquely oblong or linear-oblong with a curved point; ½ to 1 in. long, ⅛ to ¼ in. wide; glabrous, dark green. Each joint of the twigs in the typical form is armed with a forked pair of needle-like spines ⅛ to ½ in. long which are really modified stipules, but these are often absent in cultivated forms. Flowers rich yellow, produced in balls ⅓ in. wide singly or in pairs, each ball on a slender stalk ⅓ to ¾ in. long. Pod 1½ to 2 in. long, ⅛ to ¼ in. wide, softly silky. *Bot. Mag.*, t. 1653.

Native of Australia where it is widespread, although absent from Tasmania; introduced in 1803. It is the best known and commonest of pot-grown or green-house acacias, requiring little winter heat and always flowering well in spring. It is cultivated out-of-doors, happiest against a wall, in various Cornish gardens. There are quite a number of forms in cultivation, varying chiefly in the size and shape of the phyllodes.

A. ACINACEA Lindl.—A closely allied species, differing mainly in its non-spiny stipules.

A. BAILEYANA F. v. Muell.   COOTAMUNDRA WATTLE

A small evergreen tree of slender graceful habit, with often pendulous branches, devoid of down in all its parts; young shoots glaucous. Leaves bipin-nate, 1¼ to 2 in. long, composed of four, six, or eight main divisions (pinnae), each ¾ to 1¼ in. long, on which the leaflets are pinnately arranged in pairs; leaflets linear, abruptly and obliquely pointed, ⅛ to ¼ in. long, $\frac{1}{20}$ in. wide, sixteen to forty on each of the pinnae, where they are almost or quite contiguous. All the parts of the leaf are of a beautiful pale glaucous hue. Racemes produced from the leaf-axils of the past season's shoots (which are often 1 to 2 ft long), each raceme 2½ to 4 in. long and bearing twenty to thirty flower-heads. Flowers rich bright yellow, crowded in globose heads or balls about ¼ in. wide, each ball on a stalk ⅛ to ¼ in. long. Pods 2 to 3 in. long, ½ in. wide. *Bot. Mag.*, t. 9309.

Native of New South Wales; introduced about 1888. This is undoubtedly one of the most beautiful of all acacias, combining with its exceptional elegance a vivid bluish whiteness of foliage and young shoot, and a wonderful profusion and beauty of blossom. It blooms early in the year. It is more tender than *A. dealbata* and will survive the average bad winter only in the mildest counties. A beautiful, round-headed tree once grew at Lanarth, Cornwall, which in May 1930 had a spread of 20 ft. At the present time there are good specimens in Eire, where it grows well at Mount Usher, Co. Wicklow, on a garden wall, and at Glenveagh, Co. Donegal, in a sheltered border.

A. DEALBATA Link   SILVER WATTLE, MIMOSA   [PLATE 6
A. decurrens var. *dealbata* (Link) F. v. Muell.

An evergreen tree occasionally 100 ft high in a wild state, with a trunk as much as 11 ft in girth; young shoots angled, clothed with fine white down. Leaves doubly pinnate, 3 to 5 in. long, the main divisions (pinnae) in usually fifteen to twenty pairs, each 1 to 1¼ in. long, and bearing thirty to fifty pairs of tiny linear leaflets, which are about ⅛ in. long and $\frac{1}{30}$ in. wide. All the parts of the leaves are covered with the same silvery down as the young shoots, but not so thickly. Flowers fragrant, produced in panicles of globose heads or balls, each panicle 3 to 4 in. long, each head ⅛ in. wide, yellow, opening (on outdoor plants) in late winter and early spring. Seed-pods blue-white, 2 to 3 in. long, $\frac{1}{4}$ to $\frac{1}{2}$ in. wide, flat.

Native of New South Wales, Victoria, and Tasmania; introduced from Tasmania in 1820. At Kew it has to be given cool greenhouse treatment but is successfully grown in many Irish, Cornish, and Devon gardens, also along the coasts of Sussex and Hampshire. At Abbotsbury, in Dorset, it reached 70 ft in height and produced good seed. Even as far east as Suffolk it has grown and flowered well in the open ground. Really severe winters like those of the early sixties will kill it or cut it to the ground over much of the country but it is, perhaps, our cool and cloudy summers that prevent it from developing its full beauty as a flowering shrub, abundant sun and heat being necessary if the wood is to ripen and produce the embryonic flowers. For this reason the silver wattle is most likely to prove a success in sunny coastal gardens, in a position protected from strong winds, but unfortunately it will not tolerate chalky soils.

It is remarkably beautiful on the French Riviera, especially about Cannes, whence it is that such large quantities of flowering branches are sent to Paris and London as 'mimosa'. The beautiful silvery, feathery foliage and clear yellow, fragrant flowers make a charming and perfectly beautiful combination.

A. DECURRENS (Wendl.) Willd. *Mimosa decurrens* Wendl.—Leaves less hairy, rich green, with the ultimate divisions more widely spaced. *A. dealbata* is sometimes considered to be a variety of this species, and certainly they are closely allied.

A. DIFFUSA Ker

A shrub sometimes attaining a height of 9 ft in the wild but more commonly of low and spreading habit; branches stiff and angular. Phyllodes rigid, linear, ending in a sharp point, slightly tapered at the base, straight or sickle-shaped, up to 1 in. long, sometimes more, and $\frac{1}{12}$ to $\frac{1}{8}$ in. wide. Flower-heads globular, bright yellow, on stalks up to 1 in. long, usually borne two or three together in each leaf-axil.

Native of Tasmania, Victoria, and New South Wales; introduced in 1818. The low-growing form of this species, introduced from Tasmania by Comber (No. 1446), has proved to be one of the hardiest of the acacias. It flowers well each spring on a wall outside the Temperate House at Kew, and survived the winter of 1962–3.

A. JUNIPERINA (Vent.) Willd. *Mimosa juniperina* Vent.—A small shrub to 3 ft or so, found in Tasmania in coastal heaths and in E. Australia. It is allied to the preceding but differs in its phyllodes, which are broadest at the base, and in its pale yellow flower-heads, borne singly in the leaf-axils.

A. LONGIFOLIA (Andr.) Willd.   SYDNEY GOLDEN WATTLE
Mimosa longifolia Andr.

An evergreen small tree or shrub 15 to 30 ft high, of vigorous growth; young shoots angular, usually glabrous. Phyllodes leaf-life, leathery, oblong-lanceolate, blunt or more or less pointed, tapered at the base; 3 to 6 in. long, $\frac{3}{8}$ to $\frac{3}{4}$ in. wide; dark green. Flowers bright yellow, produced from the axils of the phyllodes in cylindrical spikes $1\frac{1}{2}$ to 2 in. long, $\frac{1}{4}$ to $\frac{3}{8}$ in. wide. Pod 3 to 4 in. long, $\frac{1}{6}$ to $\frac{1}{3}$ in. wide. *Bot. Mag.*, tt. 1827, 2166.

Native of the Australian mainland, and (if interpreted in a wide sense) of Tasmania; introduced in 1792 and ever since a popular cool greenhouse shrub. It can usually be recognised by its large, narrowly oblong 'leaves' and its long, rather slender flower-spikes, which open in spring. It has been grown in many Cornish gardens, and the late Sir F. Stern once had a plant against his house at Highdown, Worthing, eventually killed by frost. It is one of the most lime-tolerant species, and for that reason used on the French Riviera as a stock for other species. It is popular as a street tree in California.

var. SOPHORAE (Labill.) F. v. Muell. *Mimosa sophorae* Labill.—Distinct in its spreading habit and short, broad phyllodes, often widest above the middle. It is found wild in Tasmania on sand dunes, and in S. and E. Australia; said to be very resistant to sea-winds. It is sometimes given specific rank as *A. sophorae* (Labill.) R. Br.

var. FLORIBUNDA (Vent.) F. v. Muell. *Mimosa floribunda* Vent.—Phyllodes very narrow, $\frac{1}{4}$ in. or less wide and 3 to 5 in. long, with prominent parallel veins.

A. MUCRONATA Willd.—This is best considered as an independent species, although it is closely allied to *A. longifolia*, and has been considered a variety of it. It is widespread in Tasmania and is also found on the mainland in Victoria. Typically, this species has very narrow phyllodes, to about $\frac{1}{5}$ in. wide at the most, with three to five rather prominent nerves; but in foliage characters it is very variable. *Bot. Mag.*, t. 2747.

A. MELANOXYLON R. Br.   BLACKWOOD

An evergreen tree reaching in a wild state heights of 60 to 80, sometimes 100 to 120 ft; young shoots angular, minutely downy. True leaves are comparatively rarely present on old trees, but in the juvenile state they are quite frequently mixed up with phyllodes. They are doubly pinnate, the leaflets oblong, shortly and abruptly pointed, and $\frac{1}{4}$ in. long. Phyllodes scimitar-shaped, tapered at both ends; $2\frac{1}{2}$ to $5\frac{1}{2}$ in. long, $\frac{3}{4}$ to $1\frac{1}{8}$ in. wide; with three to five prominent veins running lengthwise; minutely downy when young. Flowers yellow, produced in spring in globose heads $\frac{1}{4}$ in. wide; they occur, a few together, in axillary racemes. Pods flat, 2 to 4 in. long, $\frac{1}{3}$ in. wide, often much curved. *Bot. Mag.*, t. 1659.

Native of Tasmania and the southern parts of Australia; introduced from the former in 1808. It grows quite well in the open air in southern England from Dorset westward, in S.W. Scotland and in Ireland. At Abbotsbury, near Weymouth, it used to be 40 to 50 ft high; at Boslowick in Cornwall it reached 70 ft. At the present time there are no specimens of this size in England, so far as is known, but there are many flourishing trees in Eire. At Rossdohan in Co. Kerry the two best examples are 81 × 7$\frac{3}{4}$ and 80 × 6 ft (1966) with others of 50 ft; self-sown seedlings occur there. At Ilnacullin (Garinish Island), in Bantry Bay, Co. Cork, the best is 55 × 6 ft. In Scotland there are two examples at Brodick, Isle of Arran, about 25 ft high.

Although not so decorative in flower as the other acacias described here, it makes the finest tree. It yields a valuable timber, hard and close-grained, and has some value in forestry in the warmer parts of the world. It is naturalised in Madeira, where it is one of the commonest trees around Funchal.

A. PRAVISSIMA F. v. Muell.   OVENS WATTLE

A shrub or small tree to about 20 ft, of graceful habit, with slender, angled branchlets. Phyllodes set densely on the stem, ¼ to ½ in. long and wide, triangular-obovate or unequally four-angled; venation prominent. Flower-heads rich yellow, globular, only ⅛ in. or so wide, arranged in long compound racemes. Flowering time March to April.

Native of Victoria and New South Wales. There is a good example of this acacia at Ilnacullin (Garinish Island), Co. Cork, about 24 ft high. At Malahide Castle, near Dublin, it proved hardy in the winters of 1961–3 and is now some 12 ft high on a garden wall. It is remarkable for its very lop-sided phyllodes, set edgeways to the shoot.

A. CULTRIFORMIS G. Don KNIFE-LEAF WATTLE.—An allied species, distinguished by its silvery-grey, triangular phyllodes. It is probably very tender, but according to Thurston was once grown out-of-doors at St Michael's Mount. Native of New South Wales and Queensland. *Bot. Mag.*, n.s., t. 322.

A. PODALYRIIFOLIA G. Don QUEENSLAND SILVER WATTLE.—A very beautiful species growing to 10 ft high or more; shoots white-downy at first. Phyllodes silvery-glaucous, downy, oval to ovate, 1 to 1½ in. long, slightly oblique. Flower-heads fragrant, golden yellow, borne in winter and early spring in long racemes. It is fairly hardy in Cornwall and, with its various forms and hybrids, is much cultivated on the French Riviera. *Bot. Mag.*, t. 9604.

A. PULCHELLA R. Br.
A. hispidissima DC.

A much branched evergreen shrub or small tree of dense, very leafy habit; young shoots angular, downy or bristly. Leaves (there are no phyllodes) pinnate, ½ to 1 in. long, produced in pairs that are united at the base, each made up of four to eight pairs of leaflets; main-stalk downy or bristly. Leaflets oblong, rounded at the end, ⅛ to ¼ in. long, 1/16 in. wide; dull intense green, sometimes ciliate. At the base of the leaf-axil there is often a needle-like spine ¼ to ½ in. long. Flowers rich bright yellow, produced in balls ¼ to ½ in. wide, usually in pairs from the leaf-axils, each on a slender stalk ½ to 1 in. long. Pod 1 to 2 in. long, ⅛ in. wide, the margins thickened in the same way as those of common laburnum. *Bot. Mag.*, t. 4588.

Native of W. Australia in the Swan River region; introduced about 1803. It is one of the most beautiful of Australian acacias and flowers every spring in the greatest profusion.

A. RHETINODES Schlecht.

A shrub or small tree to 20 ft high, glabrous in all its parts, with angular branchlets. Phyllodes rather thin in texture, with a single main-vein and inconspicuous side-veins, linear to narrowly oblanceolate, 2½ to 5 in. long, ⅛ to ⅗ in. wide, tapered at the base, usually somewhat curved at the blunt or pointed apex. Flowers pale yellow, in small globular heads, borne six to twelve together in short axillary racemes; the phyllodes on the floral part of the shoots are sometimes shed, giving to it the appearance of a panicle of blossom. Pods up to 7 in. long, not constricted between the seeds. *Bot. Mag.*, t. 9177.

Native of Tasmania, Victoria, and S. Australia. From its habit of flowering off and on throughout the year it is in Australia sometimes called the four seasons wattle; even in this country flowers are borne from early spring into autumn. It is not one of the showiest acacias, but the combination of grey-green leaves and soft-yellow flowers is attractive; it is reputed to be one of the hardiest and is tolerant of lime. It grows well on a garden wall at Malahide Castle near Dublin. At Binstead, Isle of Wight, it reached 20 ft.

A. PYCNANTHA Benth. GOLDEN WATTLE.—A shrub or small tree to 25 ft. Phyllodes leathery but flexible, usually curved, 3 to 8 in. long, ⅛ to 1¾ in. wide. Flowers golden yellow, fragrant, in large heads arranged racemosely. Native of S. and E. Australia, absent from Tasmania. It reached 20 ft in N. Ireland and survived the winter of 1962–3 at the Slieve Donard nurseries, Co. Down. In Australia it is one of the showiest acacias but needs, perhaps, more summer heat and sun than our climate provides; if tried, it should be given a warm wall and is perhaps best planted in rather poor, sandy soil. It is very eucalyptus-like in its foliage.

A. RICEANA Henslow   RICE'S WATTLE

A very graceful evergreen small tree up to 30 ft high, with abundant slender, pendulous, angular, glabrous young shoots. Phyllodes solitary or two to four at each joint, linear or awl-shaped, spine-tipped; 1 to 2 in. long, 1/12 to ⅛ in. wide; dark green, often more or less curved. Flower-spikes very slender, axillary, arched or drooping, 1 to 2 in. long, bearing the flowers in small clusters ⅛ in. wide and about ¼ in. apart, pale clear yellow. Pod 2 to 3 in. long, ⅛ in. wide, downy. *Bot. Mag.*, t. 5835.

Native of the southern part of Tasmania and described by Sir Joseph Hooker as by far the most beautiful acacia of that island, where it grows on the banks of streams and resembles weeping willow. It was named in honour of Mr T. Spring-Rice, Chancellor of the Exchequer, 1835–9. Near London and farther north, where it has to be given winter protection, it is very attractive as a spring-flowering shrub for cool greenhouses, its slender habit adapting it for clothing pillars or training on the roof. Charles Williams grew it out-of-doors at Greenways, S. Devon, and it reached 20 to 30 ft in Cornish gardens such as Penjerrick, Carclew, and Bosahan.

Of the species with similar foliage treated here, *A. diffusa* and *juniperina* are distinguished by their spherical flower-heads and *A. verticillata* by the peculiar arrangement of its phyllodes.

A. VERTICILLATA (L'Hérit.) Willd.
Mimosa verticillata L'Hérit.

An evergreen shrub up to 30 ft high of dense habit; young shoots distinctly and angularly ridged, downy. Phyllodes mostly arranged in whorls (verticillate), usually about six in a whorl; linear, awl-shaped, prickly pointed; $\frac{1}{3}$ to $\frac{5}{8}$ in. long, $\frac{1}{20}$ to $\frac{1}{12}$ in. wide; dark green, not downy, with a prominent midrib. Flowers clear bright yellow, closely packed in bottle-brush-like spikes $\frac{1}{2}$ to $1\frac{1}{2}$ in. long and $\frac{1}{4}$ to $\frac{1}{3}$ in. wide, each spike springing from the axil of a phyllode on a downy stalk $\frac{1}{8}$ to $\frac{1}{2}$ in. long. Pods slender, $1\frac{1}{2}$ to 2 in. long, $\frac{1}{8}$ in. wide, often curved or even sickle-shaped, sprinkled with pale hairs. *Bot. Mag.*, t. 110.

Native of Australia (Victoria) and Tasmania; introduced by Sir Joseph Banks to Kew in 1780. There was once a very healthy plant at Lanarth in Cornwall, which reached a height of 20 ft and as much in spread, and bloomed in April and May. It is very beautiful every spring in the Australian House at Kew and is distinct among the acacias here described by the short prickly 'leaves' being arranged in whorls, but there are several other species in the genus that are similar in that respect.

ACANTHOPANAX   ARALIACEAE

A genus of trees and shrubs, now including *Eleutherococcus*, allied to *Aralia* and *Fatsia*. They have pithy, sometimes prickly or bristly stems; alternate leaves, consisting of three or five leaflets digitately arranged, or sometimes not completely divided, and only deeply lobed. Flowers in umbels, dull-coloured, followed by clusters of fruit very like those of the common ivy, being crowded in spherical clusters and inky black. In gardens, the members of this genus will be chiefly notable for their distinct and striking foliage—of a type very rare in hardy shrubs—and for their black fruits. A light warm, loamy soil suits them all, and they can be propagated by root-cuttings, sometimes by division or offsets. Some give seed freely.

The character which was relied on to distinguish Maximowicz's genus of *Eleutherococcus* from *Acanthopanax*, viz., the articulated (jointed) flower-stalk, is not really differentiative, and the two are now combined.

A. DIVARICATUS (Sieb. & Zucc.) Seem.
Panax divaricatum Sieb. & Zucc.

A deciduous shrub of thin open growth, up to 12 ft high; young shoots glabrous or downy, sometimes armed with a pair of broad-based spines about

¼ in. long at the joints. Leaves with normally five leaflets, sometimes reduced to three, borne on a downy main-stalk 1 to 3½ in. long. Leaflets obovate to oblanceolate, simply or doubly toothed, gradually tapered at the base to a very short stalk; 2 to 4½ in. long, ⅝ to 2 in. wide; dullish green and with tiny scattered bristles above, downy beneath. Flowers with brownish purple petals and yellowish anthers, very small, closely crowded in globose heads at or near the end of the leafy shoots. Each head is about 1 in. wide on a densely downy main-stalk rarely more than 1 in. long; individual flower-stalks covered with white down. Fruits black, ¼ in. wide, borne in a spherical head, 1½ in. in diameter, each surmounted by the slightly two-lobed style.

Native of Japan; described in 1845. Maries found it on the island of Yezo (Hokkaido) in 1880. I do not know if he introduced it for Messrs Veitch at the time, probably not, as he was there in August which is its flowering month, and too early for seeds. The first plant I saw at Kew was obtained from A. K. Bulley in 1898. As with other species its main features are its compound leaves and heads of black fruits. Its distinctive characters amongst the quinquefoliolate species are its two-lobed style, roughly downy leaves, and mossy stalk of the flower-heads.

A. GIRALDII Harms

A deciduous shrub 6 to 9 ft high; young shoots very dark green, densely covered with slender, bristle-like, mostly deflexed spines ⅛ to ¼ in. long. Leaves composed of three to five leaflets borne on a slender main-stalk 1½ to 3 in. long and occasionally prickly. Leaflets scarcely stalked, narrowly oval or oblanceolate, doubly toothed except near the base, slender pointed; 1 to 2½ in. long, ⅓ to ¾ in. wide; usually quite glabrous. Flowers small, greenish, crowded on a usually solitary umbel, each flower on a glabrous stalk ¼ to ½ in. long, the umbel itself on a main-stalk ¼ to ¾ in. long. Fruits black, ¼ to ⅓ in. wide, crowned with a very short but distinctly five-lobed style.

Native of Central and N. China, where Henry, Wilson, and Purdom collected it. Forrest also found it, or something very like it, more to the south-west (Nos. 10875 and 12585). It was introduced to cultivation in 1912. It resembles *A. senticosus* in the dense furnishing of decurved spines on the branchlets, but that species differs very much in its larger leaflets, larger much longer-stalked umbels, and longer unlobed style. *A. giraldii* is about the sparsest in its flowering of the cultivated species, the flower-heads being small and solitary. It grows well at Kew, the leafless shoots in winter being conspicuous on account of their thick covering of whitish spines. Flowers in July.

A. HENRYI (Oliver) Harms

Eleutherococcus henryi Oliver

A sturdy bush, said to become 10 ft high in a wild state, with rigid, pale brown branchlets, rough with minute bristles, and armed with broad sturdy spines, ⅛ in. long, straight or slightly decurved. Leaves composed of five leaflets on a stalk 1½ to 3 in. long, rough to the touch. Leaflets obovate or oval, 1½ to

3½ in. long, ¾ to 1½ in. wide; tapering nearly equally towards both ends, scarcely stalked; the margins finely and simply toothed; upper surface harsh, lower one more or less hairy. Flowers in a terminal cluster of umbels borne on a sturdy, slightly hairy stalk, 1 to 2 in. long; the terminal umbel the largest and earliest. Fruits inky black, oblong, ⅜ in. long, in globose umbels 2 in. across. *Bot. Mag.*, t. 8316.

Native of Central China; introduced by Wilson for Messrs Veitch in 1901, and first flowered at Coombe Wood four years later. It is an interesting but not showy shrub, although its foliage and spherical clusters of inky black fruit are striking; the latter remain long on the plants. It is a close ally of *A. simonii*, but the very different toothing of the leaflets of that species, the more decurved and slender spines, and its smoother branches distinguish it readily from the present one.

A. LASIOGYNE Harms

A deciduous shrub up to 15 or 20 ft high, of graceful habit, with wide-spreading, arching branches, young shoots grey, glabrous. Leaves made up of three leaflets borne on a glabrous slender stalk up to 2½ in. long. Leaflets stalkless or nearly so, without or nearly without teeth; the side ones obliquely ovate, middle one obovate or oval, pointed; 1½ to 2½ in. long; pale bright green and quite glabrous. Flowers white, borne in July in short-stalked umbels, each flower on a stalk ¼ to 5⁄16 in. long, covered with whitish down. Fruit black, egg-shaped or obovoid, 5⁄16 in. long, the calyx scar at the top downy; styles two, only united near the base, curving outwards.

Native of W. China; introduced to Kew from France in 1912. It succeeds very well at Kew, where there are handsome graceful bushes 12 ft high and as much in diameter. When well furnished with the black fruits they have an interesting appearance. On the whole it is one of the hardiest and most satisfactory of the hardy Araliads. It is distinct in its small, usually entire, glabrous leaflets and especially in the two styles (which adhere to the top of the fruit) being united only at the base and curving outwards. The plants at Kew have stout, broad-based spines ½ in. wide on the old branches, but the younger parts are unarmed.

A. LEUCORRHIZUS (Oliver) Harms
Eleutherococcus leucorrhizus Oliver

A deciduous shrub, probably 6 to 10 ft high, entirely devoid of down, sometimes unarmed, sometimes with small, slender, downward-pointing prickles at the joints. Leaves composed of three or five leaflets borne on a stalk 1 to 3 in. long; leaflets 2 to 4 in. long, ⅝ to 1¼ in. wide, lanceolate, slender-pointed, doubly toothed, tapering at the base to a stalk ⅛ to ⅜ in. long. Flowers produced in July in a terminal cluster of umbels, each umbel 1½ to 2 in. across, spherical, borne on a stalk 2 to 4 in. long. Each flower is small, greenish, on a slender stalk ½ to ¾ in. long. Fruits black, roundish oval, ¼ in. long, crowded in umbels over 2 in. across. *Bot. Mag.*, t. 8607.

Native of Central China; discovered by A. Henry; introduced by Wilson in 1901. This is one of the handsomest species in this genus; its habit is not so stiff as that of its near allies, and the large umbels of black fruit are effective. It has been confused with *A. simonii* (q.v.), but differs in being glabrous and in the arrangement and shape of the prickles; from *A. henryi* it differs in the same

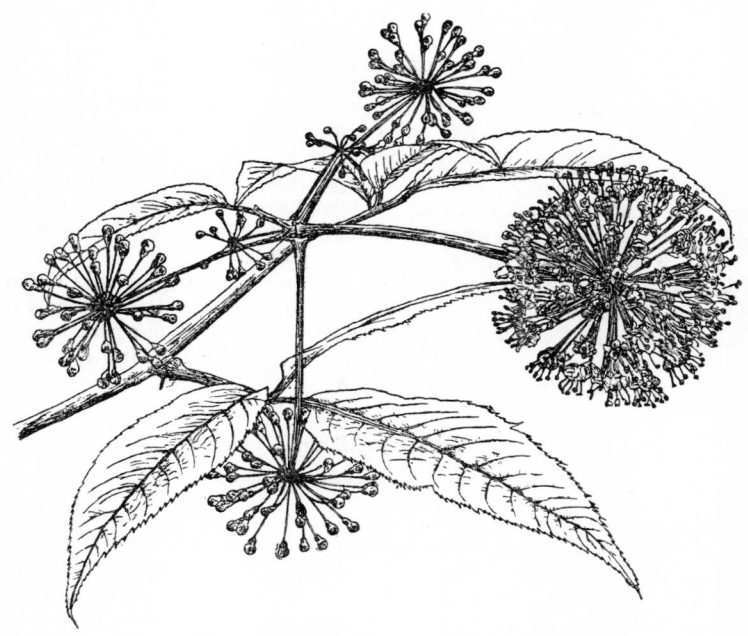

ACANTHOPANAX LEUCORRHIZUS

respects as well as in the toothing of the leaflets. The Chinese obtain a drug from the root.

var. SCABERULUS Harms & Rehd.—A deciduous bush 4 to 6 ft high; young shoots glabrous, usually unarmed except for some deflexed spines found occasionally at the joints. Leaves always composed of five leaflets, borne on a common stalk 1½ to 3½ in. long, which is either smooth or furnished with reflexed bristle-like spines. Leaflets oblanceolate to obovate, tapered at the base, slenderly pointed, doubly toothed; 1½ to 2½ in. long, ½ to 1½ in. wide; upper surface rough to the touch with short stiff hairs; lower surface downy on the midrib and chief veins beneath. Flowers yellowish green, produced during July in globose umbels about 1 in. wide. Fruits black, globose to oval, ¼ in. long.

Native of Hupeh and Szechwan, China; introduced for Messrs Veitch by Wilson in 1904 and again three years later for the Arnold Arboretum, Mass. From the glabrous type this variety differs in the smaller downy leaflets, in the often bristly leaf-stalks, and in the uniformly five-foliolate leaves. Another form in cultivation is:

var. FULVESCENS Harms & Rehd.—This has leaflets also downy beneath and rough above; but they are larger (up to 5 in. long by 2¼ in. wide), have no bristles on the leaf-stalks, the down beneath is yellowish, and, as in the type, the leaflets may be three to five to each leaf.

A. SCIADOPHYLLOIDES Franch. & Sav.

A shrub or small tree to 40 ft high, with grey-brown unarmed branches; young growths hairy. Leaflets five on a common stalk 3 to 11 in. long; terminal leaflets 4 to 6 in. long and 1¾ to 2¾ in. wide, the lateral ones smaller, obovate or elliptic to oblong, abruptly pointed at the apex, rounded or cuneate at the base, glabrous beneath except for axillary tufts of brown hairs; margins toothed. Umbels arranged in a large, loosely branched panicle borne in late summer on the wood of the season. Fruits globose, black-purple.

Native of Japan. John Gould Veitch, who saw it growing wild about a century ago in the mountains of Nikko and on Mt Hakkoda, later reported that 'its handsome foliage would impart a distinctive feature to our park scenery'; but there is no record of its having been introduced to Britain. It may however be in cultivation in Germany and the U.S.A.

A. SENTICOSUS (Maxim.) Harms
Eleutherococcus senticosus Maxim.

A deciduous shrub, usually 4 to 6 ft high, but said to become occasionally twice or thrice that height. Stems erect, scarcely branched, covered with stiff bristles. Leaves composed of three or five leaflets borne on a slender, sometimes bristly stalk 3 to 5 in. long. Leaflets oval, ovate, or slightly obovate, the side ones often oblique at the base; 2½ to 5 in. long, usually more than half as wide; finely toothed; upper surface dark glossy green, and furnished with stiff short hairs on the ribs and veins; paler underneath; stalk ⅓ in. or less long. Flowers numerous, in one or more globular umbels terminating the shoot; each umbel 1½ in. diameter, on a smooth slender stalk 2 to 3 in. long; flowers purplish yellow, very small, each on a stalk ½ to ¾ in. long; produced in July. Fruits subglobose, ⅓ in. wide.

Native of China; introduced to Kew in 1893. It is an interesting shrub with handsome foliage, remarkable for its bristly (scarcely prickly) stems, which distinguish it from all other hardy Araliads.

A. SESSILIFLORUS (Rupr. & Maxim.) Seem.
Panax sessiliflorum Rupr. & Maxim.

A deciduous shrub of vigorous habit, forming a large spreading bush up to 12 ft or more high, and twice as much wide; stems stout, very pithy, grey, scarcely or not armed. Leaves composed of three, sometimes five, leaflets on a common stalk 1½ to 2½ in. long; leaflets narrowly oval or obovate 2 to 5 in. long, about half as wide, the central one the largest; tapering at both ends, very short-stalked, irregularly toothed, almost or quite glabrous on both sides, but slightly harsh to the touch. Flowers produced in July and August, at the end of the shoot, packed closely in a globose, almost stalkless cluster 1 in. across, brown-purple with yellowish protruding stamens. Fruits in a spherical head, 1 to 1¼ in. across, inky black.

Native of Manchuria, China, and Korea, introduced to St Petersburg about 1860. It is one of the hardiest shrubs introduced from N. Asia, and one, fortunately, that is not enticed into premature growth by unseasonable winter warmth. Whilst its flowers have no beauty, the black fruits are rather striking, and the shrub itself is handsome. The finest specimen I have seen was in the Botanic Garden at Herrenhausen, Hanover; in 1908 this was 12 ft high and 21 ft in diameter—a broad-based pyramid of foliage. Propagated by seeds. The allied *A. divaricatus* (q.v.) is easily distinguished by its more downy character.

A. SETCHUENENSIS Diels

A deciduous shrub or small tree, up to 10 ft high, free from down in every part; stems with few or no prickles. Leaves composed of three leaflets borne on a stalk 1½ to 4 in. long. Leaflets dark green above, paler or slightly glaucous beneath; oblong to ovate, 2 to 5½ in. long, 1 to 2 in. wide, the margins finely toothed or almost entire; stalks ¼ to ½ in. long. Flowers in a panicle of about six spherical umbels borne at the end of the season's shoots during July; each umbel is 1 to 1½ in. across, the central terminal one the largest; they are borne on stalks of varying length (¾ to 3 in.), the whole panicle from 5 to 7 in. high. Fruits black.

Native of W. China; introduced by Wilson for Messrs Veitch about 1904. It is quite hardy and flowers in July. The absence of down from all parts of the plant and the trifoliolate leaves render it distinct.

A. SIEBOLDIANUS Makino

A. pentaphyllus (Sieb. & Zucc.) Marchal; *A. spinosus* Hort., not (L.f.) Miq.

A deciduous shrub of loose habit, 8 to 10 ft high, with erect stems and arching, slender branches, often armed with a spine at the base of each leaf-stalk or leaf-cluster; the whole plant without down. Leaves composed of three to (normally) five leaflets, borne on a slender common stalk 1½ to 3½ in. long; leaflets stalkless, obovate, 1 to 2½ in. long, ⅓ to 1 in. wide, toothed except towards the tapering base. Flowers very small, greenish white, produced during June and later, on a spherical umbel ¾ to 1 in. diameter, terminating a slender stalk 2 to 4 in. long. On the year-old wood the leaves are produced in clusters from the previous year's buds; it is from the centre of this cluster that the inflorescence is borne.

Native of China and Japan; introduced in 1874, but for long confined to cool greenhouses. It is quite hardy if given shelter from north and east, and a most elegant, handsome-foliaged shrub, although destitute of flower beauty. Still more pleasing is the garden variety cv. 'VARIEGATUS', whose leaflets are edged with a broad border of creamy white. This is one of the daintiest of variegated shrubs, hardy, but needing a sheltered position. Propagated by cuttings made of short, moderately firm shoots in heat; or of harder wood under a handlight. It was once known in gardens as *Panax quinquefolium variegatum*. Illustrated in *Flore des Serres*, tt. 2079–80 (1874).

A. SIMONII Schneid.

A deciduous shrub up to 10 ft. high, bushy; branches not downy, armed with stout, pale spines, pointing downwards. Leaves composed of five leaflets radiating from the end of a slender stalk 2 or 3 in. long, and often armed with a few slender prickles. Leaflets of different sizes; the terminal one the largest, sometimes 5 or 6 in. long and 1½ to 2 in. wide; the lower pair much smaller; all lanceolate, long-pointed, tapering at the base to a short stalk; sharply, somewhat coarsely toothed, the teeth set with one or two bristles; dark green, and furnished with scattered bristly hairs above, paler and similarly bristly beneath. Flowers in a terminal cluster of umbels, each umbel on a stalk 1 to 2 in. long. Fruits ¼ in. long, black, each on a slender glabrous stalk ½ in. long.

Native of China; first appeared in Europe in the nursery of Simon-Louis, near Metz (probably raised from seed collected by a French missionary), and also introduced by Wilson for the Veitch nurseries in 1901.

A. WARDII W. W. Sm.
A. ternatus Rehd.

A round-headed shrub up to 6 or 7 ft high; young shoots grey or brownish, not downy, unarmed or with a few spines in pairs below the leaf-stalk. Leaves trifoliolate; leaflets scarcely stalked, ovate to rhomboidal, pointed, tapered at the base (the two side ones often more or less obliquely so), sometimes with one or more coarse teeth, but usually entire; ⅞ to 1¾ in. long, ½ to ⅞ in. wide; dark green above, pale below, smooth and glossy on both surfaces; main-stalk ½ to 1¼ in. long. Flowers dull greenish white, quite small, produced in autumn in a terminal cluster of globose umbels, each on a glabrous slender stalk ½ to ¾ in. long. Fruits black-purple, roundish, compressed, $\frac{3}{16}$ in. long, crowned by two recurved free styles.

Native of Yunnan, China; raised by Maurice de Vilmorin from seed sent to him by the Abbé Monbeig about 1905, but first described from a specimen collected by Kingdon Ward a few years later. It flowers in autumn but I have not noticed that it has any special merit.

A. TRIFOLIATUS (L.) Voss *Xanthoxylum trifoliatum* L.—An allied species, differing in its climbing habit and in the stout, recurved spines that occur scattered on its stems, leaf-stalks and peduncles. It is a common thicket plant in E. Asia, ranging from the E. Himalaya to the Philippines.

ACER   Maple   ACERACEAE

A large and important genus composed chiefly of deciduous trees, some being of the largest size, many middle-sized or small, a few shrubby. The hardy species are widely spread over the three northern continents, the finest trees being natives of N. America. A large number come from E. Asia, many of which, however, are small trees.

The most constant and distinctive characters of the genus are the opposite leaves and the form of the fruits. Each fruit consists normally of two sections, known as samarae (commonly as 'keys'), attached to each other by their bases, and each 'key' consists of a nutlet, containing one, sometimes two, seeds, and a large, thin, membranous wing. These wings assist in the dispersal of the seed. The flowers are sometimes unisexual. The typical maple leaf is broad and flat, with five palmate lobes. But there is a great diversity of shape in the genus: some species have as many as eleven or thirteen lobes to each leaf, many have but three lobes, and there is a distinct group with leaves not lobed at all. Finally comes the section of maples with compound leaves consisting of three or five distinct leaflets, sometimes kept generically separate as *Negundo*.

Most of the maples have tamely coloured flowers, varying from yellow to greenish white; a few have purple flowers (like *A. circinatum*), and are very ornamental when in blossom; whilst others, like *A. opalus*, flower in early spring before the leaves expand, and although not highly coloured make, at that season especially, a pleasing display. Still, on the whole, the attractions of the maples generally are in the large or handsomely cut foliage, and in the red or yellow tints many of them assume in autumn.

Few trees are more easily cultivated than these, their chief requirements being a rich moist soil and a moderately sunny, or at any rate not unduly shaded, position. Some of the smaller species, however, like *A. rufinerve*, *A. capillipes*, and *A. argutum*, like their stems shaded. All the maples should, if possible, be raised from seeds; if grafting has to be resorted to, as for the numerous coloured-leaved and variously habited varieties, the scions should be worked on stocks of their own species.

The number of species of maple has so largely increased in this century by introductions from China that even the largest garden could not accommodate them all, though no other genus of hardy broad-leaved trees is so varied or has so many species that are worthy of cultivation. The following is a short selection:

Large and Medium-sized Trees: *A. cappadocicum* 'Aureum', 'Rubrum' and var. *sinicum*; *A. heldreichii*; *A. lobelii*; *A. monspessulanum*; *A. opalus*; *A. platanoides*, *A. p.* 'Goldsworth Purple', 'Crimson King' or 'Faasen's Black', *A. p.* 'Drummondii'; *A. pseudoplatanus* 'Atropurpureum' (syn. 'Purpureum Spaethii'); *A. rubrum*; *A. saccharum*; *A. saccharinum* (but the brittle wood makes it unsuitable for town-planting); *A. trautvetteri*; *A.* × *zoeschense*.

Small Trees and Shrubs: *A. argutum*; *A. circinatum*; *A. cissifolium*; *A. davidii*; *A. forrestii*; *A. griseum*; *A. grosseri* var. *hersii*; *A. japonicum*, *A. j.* 'Aureum' and 'Vitifolium'; *A. negundo* and its cultivars; *A. nikoense*; *A. palmatum* and its cultivars; *A. pensylvanicum*; *A. pseudoplatanus* 'Brilliantissimum'; *A. rufinerve*; *A. triflorum*.

A. ACUMINATUM Wall. ex D. Don (1825)
A. caudatum Wall., in part (1831)*

A small, deciduous tree with smooth, purplish young stems. Leaves three-lobed, or five-lobed with the basal pair of lobes very small; blades $3\frac{1}{2}$ to $5\frac{1}{2}$ in. long and about as wide, lobes triangular, prolonged at the apex into tail-like points which are often strikingly long and slender, sharply toothed, often doubly so, the midrib and main nerves of the under-surface covered at first with whitish or yellowish hairs but becoming glabrous except for hairs in the axils of the nerves near the base; leaf-stalks $1\frac{3}{4}$ to 4 in. long, covered with white down at first, later glabrous or remaining hairy near the apex. Male flowers in corymbs. Fruits in simple lax racemes 4 to 7 in. long, borne on pedicels $\frac{2}{5}$ to $1\frac{1}{2}$ in. long; wings of fruit diverging at an acute angle, $1\frac{1}{2}$ to $1\frac{3}{4}$ in long with the nutlet, $\frac{1}{3}$ to $\frac{1}{2}$ in. wide.

Native of the W. Himalaya from Kashmir to Kumaon; date of introduction uncertain. For the reasons explained in the note, this species has been much confused with *A. papilio* (*A. caudatum* sensu Rehder) but is distinguished from that species by the soon glabrous leaves, the corymbose male inflorescence, and by the fruits being borne in long, lax racemes on pedicels much longer than in *A. papilio*; the fruits are also larger, with less spreading wings.

Acer acuminatum is represented in the maple collection at Kew by a specimen 18 ft high, raised from seeds received under the name "*A. pentapomicum*".

*NOTE: *A. acuminatum* was described by David Don (*Prodr. Fl. Nepal.*, p. 249 (1825)) from a specimen collected at 'Sirinagur' by Kamroop, one of the native collectors employed by Nathaniel Wallich, who was for many years the Superintendent of the East India Company's Botanic Garden at Calcutta. Don took the name from one of Wallich's letters. The name *A. acuminatum* does not occur in the so-called Wallich Catalogue (the 'Numerical List' of the East India Company's herbarium which Wallich wrote), but under No. 1225 *Acer caudatum* there is material collected by Kamroop 'Ex alpibus Sirinagur', which agrees with *A. acuminatum*. Indeed, all the material under this number is *A. acuminatum* except for one sterile specimen which may be *A. papilio*. When Wallich came to describe his *A. caudatum* (*Pl. As. Rar.*, Vol. 2, p. 4, p. 28 and t. 132 (1831)), he cited the collections he had enumerated under No. 1225 and therefore *A. caudatum* Wall. consists, in part, of *A. acuminatum*.

A. ARGUTUM Maxim.

A small, deciduous, dioecious tree, with erect branches; young branchlets covered with a fine down. Leaves 2 to 4 in. long, as much wide, five-lobed, produced on long, slender stalks, the lobes ovate, long-pointed, with margins prettily double-toothed; lower surface downy, especially on the whitish veins.

Male flowers borne in clusters of racemes, before the leaves; female flowers on racemes borne singly in the axils of leafy shoots; they are greenish yellow and the racemes downy. Fruits on slender stalks to about ¾ in. long, ¼ in. wide, spreading horizontally.

Native of the mountain woods of Japan; introduced to England in 1881, for Messrs Veitch, by Maries. It is a maple of elegant appearance, with pale green leaves as prettily lobed and toothed as those of *A. palmatum*. The stalk of the inflorescence and that of the individual flower lengthens considerably as the fruits develop. The branches acquire a purplish-brown shade in winter. It grows best in a cool, moist situation, shielded from strong sun, which scorches the leaf-margins. There is a good example of this maple, about 30 ft high, at the Winkworth Arboretum, Godalming, Surrey.

A. BARBINERVE Maxim.

A small, deciduous, dioecious tree, sometimes a shrub; young shoots downy. Leaves five-lobed, roundish to ovate in main outline, slightly heart-shaped at the base, slender-pointed, sharply, coarsely and unevenly toothed, the niche between the lobes very narrow; 2 to 3½ in. long, almost or quite as wide; dark green and slightly downy when young above, softly downy beneath with conspicuous tufts in the vein-axils; stalk slender, often as long as the blade. Flowers yellowish, produced in April; those of the male tree in short clusters of four to six; those of the female tree on a raceme 2 in. long terminating a twin-leafed twig. Wings of the fruit ⅜ to ½ in. diameter spreading at an angle of about 120°, and, with the nutlet, making the whole fruit 1¼ to 1½ in. wide.

Native of S.E. Manchuria; introduced about 1890. It is akin to *A. argutum*, another unisexual maple, from which its more coarsely toothed leaves, its petals being narrowed to a stalk at the base, and its larger fruits distinguish it.

A. BUERGERIANUM Miq.
A. trifidum Hook. & Arn., not Thunb.

A deciduous, small tree, with distinctly three-lobed leaves 1½ to 3½ in. long, and about the same from tip to tip of the side lobes, which point forward, and are triangular and pointed; the leaf is distinctly three-nerved, and tapers to the rounded base; margins irregularly, sometimes obscurely, toothed; upper surface bright dark green, lower one dull and slightly glaucous. Except for a loose floss on the lower surface when quite young, which soon falls away, the leaf is glabrous; leaf-stalk slender, as long or longer than the blade. Flowers in a downy, umbel-like corymb, numerous, small. Fruit with keys ¾ to 1 in. long; the wings ¼ in. wide, parallel or connivent.

Native of China; originally described as *A. trifidum* from a specimen collected there in the eighteenth century. It is probably not a genuine native of Japan, but the present name is based on a tree cultivated in that country. It was introduced to Kew in 1896, where it thrives very well and grows quickly; the largest tree now in the collection is 36 × 3 ft (1967). It is rather uncommon in gardens but worthy of wider cultivation, for it is very distinct in its rich-green, rather ivy-like leaves, which are held long into the autumn without any change of colour. The leaves on wild trees are, however, rather variable in shape; some are entire or only faintly lobed, and such leaves appear to be the rule in the Formosan variety (var. FORMOSANUM (Hayata) Sasaki). In the polymorphism of its leaves *A. buergerianum* recalls *A. paxii*, but in that species they are evergreen. The degree to which this character is shown by cultivated trees seems to depend on the age of the specimen and even, perhaps, on the season.

var. TRINERVE (Dipp.) Rehd. *A. trinerve* Dipp.—Lateral lobes spreading, produced near the base of the leaf, margins of all three lobes coarsely toothed, underside of leaves glaucous. This is thought to be a juvenile form of the species and was introduced from Japan in the nineteenth century. According to Pax it was grown on the continent as a greenhouse plant under the name "*A. trifidum*". In shape, the leaves resemble those of *A. pilosum* and *A. pentapotamicum*.

A. CAMPBELLII Hook. f.

A deciduous tree 50 to 60 ft high, young shoots glabrous, reddish at first. Leaves 3 to 5 in. long, 4 to 7 in. wide, five- or seven-lobed with a slightly heart-shaped base; the lobes ovate, terminating in a slender tail-like point where they are sharply toothed (lower down they become indistinctly toothed or quite entire); green on both surfaces and glabrous except on the veins beneath when quite young, soon reduced to a few hairs where the blade joins the stalk; stalk reddish, $1\frac{1}{2}$ to 3 in. long. The flowers are borne at the end of leafy shoots in May on a slender panicle up to 6 in. long, sepals yellowish, petals white, stamens eight. Fruits glabrous, $1\frac{1}{2}$ to 2 in. across the wings, which spread at an angle of 150°.

Native of the Sikkim Himalaya up to 10,000 ft altitude; it was found and introduced by Sir Joseph Hooker during his Himalayan journeys (1847–51), and several times since, but owing to its tenderness has never become really established. At Caerhays Castle, Cornwall, there is a specimen of 43 × 2¾ ft (1966), and others at Trewithen in the same county and at Mount Usher, Co. Wicklow, Eire. Although certainly on the tender side, the strain now available may be hardier than the older introductions. A bushy specimen at Weston-birt attained a height of about 30 ft and survived the hard winters of the early sixties, but was recently smashed by a falling tree. The young foliage is beautifully tinted red.

A. FLABELLATUM Rehd.—This species is allied to *A. campbellii*, from which it differs in its leaves, which are deeply cordate at the base, the margins saw-toothed throughout, and the teeth acuminate but not bristle-tipped as in *A. campbellii* nor so fine. A further mark of distinction is that in *A. flabellatum* the floral disk and ovary are glabrous (hairy in *A. campbellii*). A native of China (Hupeh and Szechwan); probably introduced by Wilson in 1907. It is in cultivation at Caerhays Castle and Trewithen, Cornwall, and is probably hardy except in the coldest parts.

var. YUNNANENSE (Rehd.) Fang *A. campbellii* var. *yunnanense* Rehd.—A native of Yunnan, China, intermediate between *A. flabellatum* and *A. campbellii*, being nearer to the former in floral characters and to the latter in the bristle-tipped teeth of the leaf-margins. There is a specimen at Trewithen, Cornwall, raised from seeds collected by Forrest.

A. OSMASTONII Gamble—A deciduous tree said to attain 90 ft in the wild and found in the Sikkim Himalaya. It is intermediate in character between *A. campbellii* and *A. laevigatum*, differing from the former in its three-lobed leaves and less divergent fruit-keys, and from the latter in having the leaves lobed instead of entire, on longer petioles. It is, perhaps, a hybrid between the two species, but Gamble considered that it was too widely distributed for this to be a likely explanation.

A. CAMPESTRE L.   COMMON MAPLE

A deciduous, round-headed tree, usually between 20 and 35 ft in height, but occasionally over 70 ft. Leaves five-lobed, palmate, up to 4 in. across (usually 2 to 3 in.), somewhat less in length, downy beneath and at the edges; the stalk about as long as the blade, exuding a milky sap when broken. Flowers few, green, produced in small, and at first erect, corymbs. Fruits with horizontally spreading wings 1 in. or more long, ⅛ in. wide, usually downy.

Native of Europe, including Britain, and of the Near East and N. Africa. It is a common hedgerow tree in the south of England, with a preference for limy soils. Two varieties are found here: the commoner and typical one with downy fruits; and LEIOCARPUM (Opiz) Tausch, with glabrous ones.

When well grown, the common maple is a rather handsome, neatly shaped small tree, and may reach a substantial size in south-eastern England: at Mote Park, Maidstone, Kent it has attained 78 × 8¾ ft. Often enough, however, it is a mere bush in English hedgerows. It makes a close, neat hedge, and although not much used in England is popular on the continent for this purpose. The famous hedges in the gardens of the former summer palace of the Austrian Emperors at Schönbrunn, near Vienna, are largely formed of this maple—perpendicular walls of verdure 35 ft high. The wood is hard, with a fine grain.

On the continent the common maple is a more variable tree than it is with us. In some forms, found near the Mediterranean, it resembles *A. monspessulanum*, but the milky sap exuded by the leaf-stalks will always distinguish it from that species. A variety in cultivation is:

var. AUSTRIACUM (Tratt.) DC.—Leaves more leathery than in the type, the lobes more pointed and less indented; it occurs wild in S.E. Europe.

The following are the principal garden varieties:

cv. 'COMPACTUM'.—A dwarf bush of very close, compact growth, only a few feet high, and usually broader than it is high. Origin uncertain; first described in *Gartenflora*, Vol. 42, 1893, p. 329.

cv. 'POSTELENSE'.—Leaves golden yellow; very effective in springtime. The parent of this clone was found near Postel in Silesia, and put into commerce around 1896.

cv. 'PULVERULENTUM'.—Leaves speckled and flecked with white. The true clone of this name was in cultivation in the Muskau Arboretum in 1864, but its origin is unknown. Forms have also been described in which the leaves are more coarsely blotched with white.

cv. 'SCHWERINII'.—Leaves purple on first expanding, afterwards turning green. Distributed by Hesse's nurseries, Germany, before 1899.

A. DIVERGENS Pax *A. quinquelobum* K. Koch, not Gilib.—A shrub or small tree. Leaves five-lobed, less commonly three-lobed, 1¼ to 3 in. wide, truncate or slightly heart-shaped at the base, the lobes broad-ovate, bluntly pointed, entire, glabrous on both sides, dark green above, paler beneath. Wings of fruit spreading at a wide angle; keys about 1 in. long; nutlet flattened on both sides. Native of Asiatic Turkey. It was introduced to Kew in 1923, where there is a specimen of 20 × 1¾ ft (1966). There is a smaller example in the Knap Hill Nursery, Surrey.

A. CAPILLIPES Maxim.

A deciduous tree sometimes 30 to 35 ft high, the branchlets glabrous, red when young and becoming brown marked with longitudinal whitish stripes. Leaves reddish when young, three-lobed, 3 to 5 in. long, about three-fourths as wide, glabrous, doubly toothed, the terminal lobe triangular and larger than the side ones, but sometimes the sinuses are so shallow that the leaves are virtually unlobed and kite-shaped; veins and stalk usually red. Flowers greenish white, in drooping slender racemes 2½ to 4 in. long. Fruits glabrous, numerous, in drooping racemes; keys ½ to ¾ in. long; wings rounded at the end, ⅕ in. wide, spreading at an angle of 120° or almost horizontally.

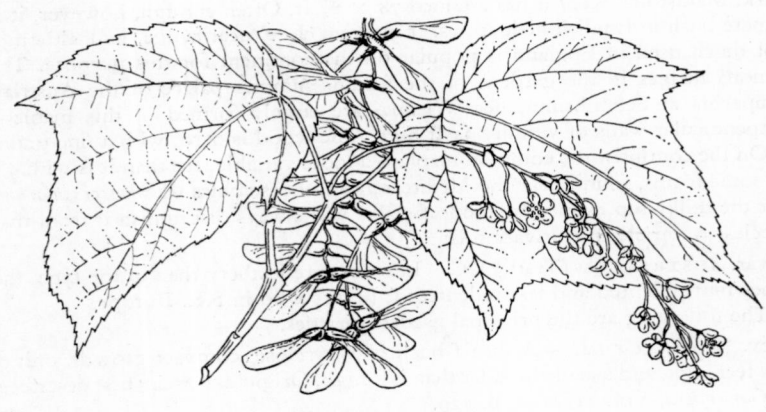

ACER CAPILLIPES

Native of Japan, introduced to cultivation by Prof. Sargent, who found fruiting trees in Japan in October 1892, and sent young trees to Kew a year or two later. It has proved hardy. It is one of the handsome group with striated branches including *A. pensylvanicum* and *A. rufinerve*, to both of which it is closely allied and bears much resemblance in shape of leaf, but is readily distinguished by the absence of rusty down from the undersides of the young leaves. The usually red petioles and the relatively long central lobe, extending about half-way towards the base of the leaf, also serve to distinguish it. In *A. rufinerve*, the side lobes arise nearer to the tip of the leaf, and the central lobe is rather short and stubby; also its young stems are distinctly glaucous. There is a fine specimen in the Winkworth Arboretum, Surrey.

A. CAPPADOCICUM Gleditsch

A. laetum C. A. Mey.; *A. pictum colchicum* Hort.

A deciduous tree up to 70 ft high, branchlets remaining green the second year. Leaves green on opening, five- or seven-lobed, heart-shaped at the base, 3 to 6 in. across, glabrous except for tufts of hairs in the axils of the veins; the lobes broadly triangular, but drawn out to a long tail-like point; leaf-stalk milky when broken. Flowers in corymbs about 2 in. long, yellow. Fruits with wings 1¼ to 1¾ in. long (twice to four times as long as the nutlets), spreading at a wide angle.

Native of the Caucasus and Asia Minor; introduced in 1838. There is much confusion between this maple and *A. mono* (formerly known as *A. pictum*) and many trees bearing the label "A. pictum" are really *cappadocicum*. The best means of distinguishing between the two (as seen in cultivation) is by the second-year wood; in *A. cappadocicum* this remains smooth and greenish or purplish, while in *A. mono* it becomes wrinkled or fissured and grey-brown. The typical form appears to be less common in cultivation than the garden variety 'Rubrum' (see below), but is represented at Kew by a tree of 45 × 2¾ ft (1966); the ultimate height in cultivation is probably around 60 ft.

cv. 'AUREUM'.—Leaves yellow in the spring, becoming green, and again yellow in the autumn. Once grown as "pictum aureum". Probably first distributed by Hesse's nurseries, Germany. There is an example at Kew 45 × 5 ft (1966) and another of about the same size at Westonbirt, Glos. but the tallest recorded grows in the West Dean Arboretum, Sussex, and measures 55 × 6¼ ft (1967).

cv. 'RUBRUM'.—Unfolding leaves blackish red; on young trees the leaves at the tips of the summer growths are bright red. An old garden form, propagated by grafting or layers; introduced to Britain in 1846 and probably first distributed by Booth's nurseries, Hamburg. It is commoner in cultivation than the normal form and more desirable. It has rarely exceeded 60 ft in cultivation but there are two trees at Westonbirt, near the Main Gate, one 75 × 7 ft and another, a sucker from this, 77 × 3¾ ft (1966). Similar forms are found wild in Dagestan on the western shores of the Caspian Sea, where, according to Van Volxem, they grow intermixed with the type, with all shades of difference between the two extremes; f. RUBRUM (Kitchn.) Rehd. is a collective name, referring to all such forms, wild or cultivated.

cv. 'TRICOLOR'.—Young leaves variegated red, pink, and cream. A branch sport from 'Rubrum'. (Carrière in *Rev. Hort.*, 1886, p. 371.)

A. cappadocicum, in its typical state, extends to the western shores of the Caspian and perhaps a little further east, into Persia. From there on, in the mountains of Persia, throughout the Himalaya, and in W. and Central China, it is represented by the following varieties:

var. CULTRATUM (Wall.) Bean *A. cultratum* Wall.—As defined by Pax in his monograph, this variety comprised all the eastern representatives of *A. cappadocicum* from Persia to China. The differentiating characters given by him were: leaves harder in texture than in the type, with only five lobes and truncate (not cordate) at the base; wings of fruit spreading horizontally. However, the Chinese part of this variety has been detached as:

var. SINICUM Rehd.—This differs from the Himalayan form in its smaller leaves, with narrower and longer lobes; introduced by Wilson and later by Forrest. This variety, at least as seen in cultivation, is remarkable for its bright red fruits. There are two specimens at Kew, measuring 31 × 2½ and 44 × 4¾ ft, and another in the garden of the late Sir Frederick Stern at Highdown, about 30 ft high. It was given an Award of Merit when shown from Kew in June 1958.

f. TRICAUDATUM (Rehd.) Rehd.—A form of var. *sinicum* in which the leaves have only three lobes; introduced by Wilson in 1901 and again in 1908 (W. 1358).

A. AMPLUM Rehd.—A small tree closely related to *A. cappadocicum* but with larger leaves (to 7 in. across), more broadly lobed. It was introduced by Wilson from W. Szechwan in 1901 and later by Forrest from Yunnan. A tree from the latter's sending is about 20 ft high at Messrs Hilliers' nurseries and there is another from the same source at Borde Hill, Sussex. It is 25 × 1¾ ft in the Glasnevin Botanic Garden. The var. TIENTAIENSE (Schneid.) Rehd. is also in cultivation; it differs from the type in its smaller, mostly three-lobed leaves, with narrower, longer lobes.

Other Chinese species belonging to the same group as *A. cappadocicum* are A. CATALPIFOLIUM Rehd., with almost unlobed leaves, and A. LONGIPES Franch. ex Rehd., which differs from *A. amplum* mainly in the downiness of the leaves.

A. CARPINIFOLIUM Sieb. & Zucc. HORNBEAM MAPLE

A deciduous tree, said to become 50 ft high in Japan, but in cultivation in this country scarcely more than half that height; branchlets dark, glabrous. Leaves oblong, usually from 3 to 4 in. long, 1¼ to 2 in. wide, not lobed, doubly toothed, densely covered when young, especially on the veins, with grey silky hairs, but becoming almost glabrous by autumn; veins parallel as in the hornbeam, in about twenty pairs; stalks from ¼ to ¾ in. long. Flowers green, borne on long slender stalks in a short umbel or raceme. Fruit with wings about ½ in. long, ¼ in. wide, the wings decurved in the shape of a bow.

Native of Japan; introduced in 1879 by Maries for Messrs Veitch. The resemblance the leaves bear to those of the hornbeam make this perhaps the most easily distinguished of maples. From the hornbeam their opposite arrangement, of course, at once distinguishes it even in the absence of fruit. This maple is quite hardy, and there was in 1913 a fine specimen then about 20 ft high in the

Coombe Wood nursery—the largest in Britain at that time. Even today there are few specimens of that size. The best recorded is at Coles, Privett, Hants, which is 30 ft high. There are smaller examples at Kew, Westonbirt, and other collections.

A. CAUDATUM *see* A. PAPILIO

A. CIRCINATUM Pursh   VINE MAPLE

A low, deciduous tree, often scarcely more than a shrub, but sometimes over 30 ft high; branchlets glabrous. Leaves seven- or nine-lobed, almost circular in general outline, but heart-shaped at the base, 3 to 5 in. wide, the lobes unequally or doubly toothed; lower surface hairy when young, but ultimately almost glabrous; stalks stout, 1 to 1½ in. long. Flowers in small corymbose clusters, each flower ½ in. across, the sepals reddish purple; petals smaller, dull white. Fruit with wings about 1½ in. long, ⅜ in. wide, spreading almost horizontally, red when young.

Native of western N. America from British Columbia south to California; introduced by Douglas in 1826. This maple is very distinct, and one of the most ornamental in its flowers. In April, when well in bloom, the wine-coloured sepals contrasting with the whitish petals make a very pretty display, especially as they are associated with conspicuous crimson bud-scales. Its leaves frequently die off in beautiful red and orange-coloured shades. If it is desirable that it should form a trunk, the lower branches should be pruned off as the tree grows in height until sufficient clean stem has been formed. But, allowed to grow in its natural way, it makes a low, wide-spreading bush of pleasing form, often with the lower branches laid on the ground and taking root there. Owing to this peculiarity it forms impenetrable thickets in a wild state. It is an admirable subject for a lawn in a small garden.

A. CISSIFOLIUM (Sieb. & Zucc.) K. Koch
Negundo cissifolium Sieb. & Zucc.

A deciduous tree of compact, rounded form, 30 ft or more high; branchlets downy. Leaf consisting of three leaflets borne on a slender common stalk 2 to 3 in. long, glabrous except for a few hairs at the junction of the stalks of the leaflets. Leaflets 2 to 3½ in. long, obovate, oval or ovate, the terminal part of each one coarsely and irregularly toothed; they are glabrous except for small tufts of down in the axils of the veins. Flowers minute, each on a stalk ⅛ to ¼ in. long, produced in May with the leaves, on very slender racemes 2 to 4 in. long, and downy. Fruit in long racemes; keys 1 in. long, glabrous; the wings obliquely ovate, ⅛ in. wide, diverging from each other at an angle of 60° or less.

Native of Japan; date of introduction uncertain, but before 1870. This interesting maple is one of the small number that bear compound leaves. Its nearest ally appears to be the American *A. negundo* but in that species the leaves are often composed of five leaflets, with the terminal one larger than the laterals, and the male flowers are borne in corymbs. *A. nikoense*, another Japanese species with compound leaves, is well distinguished from *A. cissifolium* by its upright habit, by the hairiness of the main leaf-stalk, of the undersides of the leaves and of the nutlets; flowers of both sexes are borne on the same tree, and in corymbs, not racemes.

It is an elegant species of mushroom-like habit, and the foliage turns red and yellow in the autumn. A position shaded from the strongest sun should be chosen, especially if the soil is on the dry side. The best-known specimens in the British Isles are at Westonbirt, Glos., in Morley, Mitchell, and Holford Drives, ranging from 25 to 31 ft in height (1966). At East Bergholt Place, Suffolk, it is 25 ft high in woodland (1966).

A. × CORIACEUM Tausch

A small deciduous tree with a rounded head of branches; branchlets glabrous. Leaves three-lobed, sometimes indistinctly five-lobed; 2 to 3 in. wide, somewhat less long, the stalk about as long as the blade; glabrous, deep glossy green, and rather leathery in texture, the base heart-shaped; lobes shallow and rounded, the side ones with occasionally one to three large teeth on the outer margin. Flowers in small corymbs, yellowish green, produced in April. Fruits glabrous; keys 1 in. long; wings $\frac{1}{3}$ in. wide, diverging at about 60°.

A hybrid between *A. pseudoplatanus* and *A. monspessulanum*. The tree in general aspect and leaf more resembles the Montpelier maple, but the influence of *A. pseudoplatanus* is evident in the larger leaf, and in the larger fruit with more divergent wings. It is neat and pleasing in habit, and retains its foliage until December or later. There is an example at Kew 24 × 4 ft and another at Westonbirt, Glos., 44 × 5½ ft (both 1966).

A. CRATAEGIFOLIUM Sieb. & Zucc.

A slender, deciduous tree of erect habit, up to 30 ft; branchlets purplish, glabrous. Leaves of variable shape, ovate with a truncate or heart-shaped base; 2 to 3 in. long, about half as wide; irregularly toothed, often three- or even five-lobed, the lobes shallow. When quite young there are tufts of hairs in the axils of the veins; otherwise they are quite glabrous. Flowers yellowish white, in erect inconspicuous racemes 1½ to 2 in. long, produced in April along with the young leaves. Fruit glabrous; keys ¾ to 1 in. long; wings ⅜ in. wide, spreading nearly horizontally.

Native of Japan; introduced in 1879 by Maries for Messrs Veitch. The bark is striped with white lines, as in others of the snake-bark group. The resemblance of the leaves to those of a hawthorn, suggested by the specific name, is a fanciful one. It is rarely seen under its correct label, but the short leaves, entire or shallowly three-lobed at the base, should distinguish it from its allies. There is a specimen at Westonbirt, Glos., measuring 36 × 1½ ft (1967).

cv. 'VEITCHII'.—Leaves handsomely marbled with rose and white.

A. × VEITCHII Schwer.—Not to be confused with the above, this maple was thought by Schwerin to be a hybrid between *A. crataegifolium* and *A. rufi-nerve*. If so, Veitch's statement that the seed came from N. China is unlikely to be correct; certainly nothing comparable has been found wild there. Branchlets greenish; leaves up to 3 in. long, leathery, green on both sides and soon glabrous, undivided, or with two short lobes near the base.

A. DAVIDII Franch.

A deciduous tree 30 to 50 ft high, with the younger bark green or purplish red becoming striped with white. Leaves glossy green, ovate, slightly heart-shaped at the base, unevenly toothed, 3 to 7 in. long, 1½ to 4 in. wide; veins prominent and parallel; covered with reddish down when young, each vein enlarging at the base where it joins the midrib and forming a minute pocket. Flowers yellowish, on slender, pendulous racemes 1½ to 2½ in. long, the female flowers on longer stalks and larger racemes than the males. Fruit glabrous; keys 1¼ in. long; wings ⅜ in. wide, spreading almost horizontally.

Native of China; described in 1888, but Maries had introduced it for Veitch in 1879 from the Ichang area, W. Hupeh; Wilson collected seed in the same locality in 1902 and later in other parts of Hupeh and Szechwan. *A. davidii* has a wide range in China and it was later introduced from further south, in Yunnan, by Forrest and Kingdon Ward. Two very distinct forms of *A. davidii* are grown in the Edinburgh Botanic Garden. One is of compact habit; the branches have short internodes, about 2½ in. long, and the leaves are up to 4½ in. long and 3 in. wide. This represents the Maries–Wilson provenance. The other tree derives from seed collected by Forrest in Yunnan; this is of loose open habit; the branches have internodes up to 4 in. long and the leaves are larger than in the other tree, being up to 7½ in. long by 5 in. wide (*Baileya*, Vol. 5, 1957, p. 141). The second tree is also distinct in its purplish young stems. This Forrest intro-duction is also represented at Kew and Westonbirt, and is sometimes seen in collections under the label *"A. forrestii"*. The confusion apparently arose through seeds and plants of this form having been distributed in error under the field number F. 22239, which properly belongs to an introduction of the true *A. forrestii*.

Although the leaves of *A. davidii* are normally quite unlobed, forms with small lobes near the base are represented in the Kew Herbarium; certainly on some cultivated trees a certain lobing is discernible. On the other hand, in the allied *A. grosseri* the usual lobes are sometimes absent or poorly developed. In that species, however, the leaf-margins are more finely toothed than in *A. davidii* and the leaves relatively wider, being roundish-ovate and almost as broad as long.

This interesting species is well represented at Westonbirt by specimens up to 48 ft high. The fine example near the junction of Mitchell and Morley Drives appears to be of the Maries or Wilson provenance: it has yellowish-green leaves which are folded upward along the line of the midrib, and a dense, rounded crown. It is strikingly distinct from the tree in the Nursery at Weston-birt which has flat, longer, more tapered leaves and a narrower and laxer habit. This is probably from Forrest's seed. At Kew there is a beautiful specimen, planted in 1923, received under the number F. 22239 (see above). This is in the *Acer* collection. Here, and at the western end of the Cedar Vista (near the Lake), there are trees raised from McLaren 250, with sparse, elegantly arching branches; others, from this number and from Yü 15041, are in the *Acer* collection, and there are similar specimens at Westonbirt. This beautiful form of *A. davidii* has acquired the misleading cultivar name 'Horizontale', which is likely to cause confusion with the botanical var. *horizontale*, described by Pax from a specimen collected in Shensi and distinguished from the type by the horizontally spreading fruit-wings. This variety was considered by Rehder to belong to *A. grosseri*.

A. DIABOLICUM K. Koch

A round-topped, deciduous tree about 30 ft high; branchlets covered with whitish hairs when young, becoming glabrous later. Leaves 4 to 7 in. wide and long, five-lobed, heart-shaped or almost truncate at the base, the lobes broadly ovate and with a few large teeth. When young, both surfaces, the margins and the leaf-stalk are thickly covered with whitish hairs; with age, these mostly fall away, but remain on the stalk, ribs and veins, and are scattered more or less over the lower surface. Flowers yellow, produced in April before the leaves in short pendulous corymbs from the joints of the previous year's wood; flower-stalk downy, 1 to 1½ in. long. Fruit with numerous whitish, stinging bristles on the nutlets and a few on the wings; keys 1¼ in. long; wings oval, ⅖ in. wide.

Native of Japan; introduced by Maries for Messrs Veitch in 1880. It is quite hardy, and is one of the biggest-leaved of hardy maples; but Prof. Sargent observes that it has no bright autumn colour, and is one of the least ornamental maples in Japan. The curious specific name is said to refer to the two horn-like, persistent styles attached to the inner side of the nutlets between the wings.

There is a specimen 45 × 3½ ft in the Main Drive at Westonbirt (1966).

f. PURPURASCENS (Franch. & Sav.) Rehd. *A. purpurascens* Franch. & Sav.— Flowers purple; unfolding leaves and young fruits also purple. This form is probably of Japanese garden origin and much to be preferred to the type. At Kew the foliage turns red in the autumn.

A. × DIECKII (Pax) Pax

A. lobelii var. *dieckii* Pax; *A. platanoides integrilobum* Zab.

A deciduous tree probably 60 ft high ultimately. Leaves three-, four-, or five-lobed, 3 to 7 in. (sometimes as much as 10 in.) wide; two-thirds as long, dark glossy green above, with tufts of brown hairs in the axils of the veins beneath; lobes broadly triangular, blunt-pointed, margins nearly always entire. Flowers yellow, in corymbs. Fruit glabrous; the keys 1½ to 1¾ in. long, spreading at a broad angle.

A hybrid, believed to have originated from *A. platanoides* and *A. lobelii*; introduced from the Zoeschen nursery to Kew in 1887. It was first sent out under the second synonym given above. The leaf-stalk exudes a milky sap when broken.

A. DISTYLUM Sieb. & Zucc.

A deciduous tree, probably 50 ft high eventually. Leaves ovate, deeply heart-shaped at the base, 4 to 6½ in. long, about three-fourths as wide, slender-pointed, quite glabrous except when young, the margin set with small teeth; leaf-stalk quite short, 1 to 1½ in. long. Flowers borne in a branching raceme, yellowish. Fruits glabrous, in erect racemes or corymbs; keys 1¼ in. long; wings ⅓ in. wide, ultimately spreading at an angle of about 100°.

Native of Japan; introduced by Veitch's nurseries in 1879. One of the original trees at Coombe Wood (Kingston, Surrey) reached 30 ft in height and used to produce fruit annually. It has never been common in gardens but the following examples are known: Wakehurst Place, Sussex, 35 × 2¼ ft (1964); Grayswood Hill, Surrey, 30 × 2 ft (1955); Westonbirt, Glos., three pl. 1936, the largest 28 × 1¼ ft (1966).

The leaves in shape are similar to those of a lime, but the resemblance is not very marked in the forms with rather oblong leaves sometimes seen in cultivation.

A. × DURETTII Pax

A deciduous tree 40 ft, perhaps more, high, with glabrous branchlets. Leaves 2 to 4 in. across, 2 to 3 in. long; bright green, and glabrous above except for a tuft of hairs at the base, hairy along the veins beneath; there are always three large triangular lobes, and these are usually supplemented by two small ones at the base; the margins irregularly toothed. Flowers greenish yellow, produced in May on hairy-stalked corymbs, 1½ to 3 in. long.

A maple of unknown origin, but related to A. × coriaceum, from which it differs in having down along the veins beneath. It is no doubt a hybrid between A. pseudoplatanus and one of the Opalus group.

A. ERIANTHUM Schwer.

A small deciduous tree with glabrous young shoots. Leaves five-, six-, or seven-lobed, truncate or slightly heart-shaped at the base; 2 to 4½ in. long, about as much wide; lobes ovate, sharply and unevenly toothed, each one tapering to a slender point; dark green and glabrous above, paler, net-veined and glabrous beneath except for conspicuous tufts of white down in the vein-axils; stalk slender, 1 to 4 in. long. Panicles terminal, slender, 3 to 4 in. long, ⅝ in. wide, the flowers crowded on the upper two-thirds. Flowers about ¼ in. wide, yellowish; calyx downy on the inside; petals glabrous, rather shorter than the sepals; stamens longer than either; ovary felted with yellowish wool. Fruits crowded in panicles 2 to 4 in. long, and 2½ to 3 in. wide; nutlets downy when young, finally almost glabrous, the wings spreading horizontally, each 1 in. long, ¼ to ⅜ in. wide.

Native of Szechwan and Hupeh; introduced by Wilson in 1907. This handsome maple is distinct in its slender flower-panicles, woolly ovary, and especially in the conspicuous white tufts of down sprinkled over the under-surface of the leaves. There is an example 28 ft high at Caerhays Castle, Cornwall, but it has remained uncommon in gardens and grows slowly. A specimen in the Edinburgh Botanic Garden, raised from W. 4428 and planted in 1911, measures 12 × 1 ft (1968).

A. FARGESII Rehd.
A. laevigatum fargesii Hort. Veitch.

A deciduous or partially evergreen tree up to 30 ft high, usually smaller; young shoots glabrous, slender, pink at first, then yellowish-green. Leaves narrowly oblong to lanceolate, slender-pointed, tapered or rounded at the base, mostly entire on adult trees, often more or less toothed on young ones; 2 to 4½ in. long, ½ to 1¼ in. wide; glabrous, pink when quite young, becoming light green on both surfaces; stalk ⅛ to ⅓ in. long. Flower-panicles red, 1½ to 2 in. long, 1 to 1¼ in. wide, glabrous, produced on short leafy shoots. Wings of fruit red, ½ to ¾ in. long, ¼ to ⅜ in. wide, rounded at the end, spreading at right (or wider) angles; nutlet egg-shaped to spherical, ⅙ in. long.

Native of Hupeh and Szechwan, China; introduced to the Coombe Wood nursery by Wilson in 1902. It is worth growing for the charming red young twigs and leaves. It is related to *A. oblongum*, but that species is well distinguished by its downy flower-stalks and the leaves being glaucous beneath. *A. fargesii* is on the tender side and best suited in the milder counties. Lord Rosse, who grows it at Birr Castle, Co. Offaly, Eire, finds it is always cut by ten degrees of frost.

A. LAEVIGATUM, with which Farges' maple has been associated as a variety, is a tender Himalayan as well as Chinese species. It belongs, like the others, to the group with narrow, mostly entire leaves that are red when young, but it differs from *A. fargesii* in its larger, distinctly net-veined leaves. *A. oblongum* is readily distinguished from both by the leaves being three-veined at the base. There is an example 28 × 1¾ ft at Mount Usher, Co. Wicklow, Eire (1966).

A. FORRESTII Diels

A deciduous tree up to 40 ft or more high in a wild state; young shoots purplish or red, glabrous. Leaves mostly three- (sometimes five-) lobed, slender-pointed, more or less heart-shaped at the base, finely toothed; side lobes triangular, divergent, sometimes much reduced on flowering shoots; 2 to 4½ in. long, 1 to 3 in. wide; smooth on both surfaces except for axil-tufts of down beneath; stalk 1 to 2½ in. long; chief veins webbed at the base. Flowers brownish green, produced with the leaves in May on slender racemes up to 4 in. long. Fruits glabrous, the wings ¼ in. wide, spreading almost horizontally and giving the whole fruit (with the nutlets) a spread of 1½ to 2 in.

Native of China; discovered by Forrest on the eastern flank of the Lichiang range in 1906 and introduced by him in the same year. Rehder and Wilson, in *Plantae Wilsonianae*, Vol. 3, p. 426, made *A. forrestii* a synonym of *A. laxiflorum*, but later Rehder withdrew this judgement and treated the two species as distinct in *Journ. Arn. Arb.*, Vol. 14, pp. 211–22, as does Fang in his monograph on

ACER FORRESTII

the Chinese maples. The key character by which *A. forrestii* may be distinguished from *laxiflorum* is that the leaves are glaucescent beneath and, except for tufts of down in the axillary pockets, glabrous; in the latter they are green beneath and downy on the veins, at least when young. There seems to be no other reliable character by which they may be distinguished and indeed the material in the Kew Herbarium suggests that the difference between them is slight.

A. forrestii is uncommon in cultivation. The largest specimens recorded are at Caerhays Castle, Cornwall, where there is one of 38 × 2¼ ft, dividing at 3½ ft, raised from Forrest 30631, and another 36 × 3¼ ft at 2 ft, from Forrest 28395 (both measured 1966). There is a smaller plant at Westonbirt in Mitchell Drive and others in Silkwood. *A. forrestii* is a handsome species with the characteristic snake-bark of its group; the branching is sparse but very graceful and the beautifully formed leaves, borne on red petioles, are of a rich green and held long into the autumn. It is rather tender when young.

A. WARDII W. W. Sm.—A native of Upper Burma and neighbouring parts of Yunnan and Tibet; discovered by Kingdon Ward in 1914; introduced by Forrest. It is a tender and little-known maple, more at home in section *Macrantha* with the snake-bark maples than near *A. sinense*, which Sir William Wright-Smith suggested as its nearest ally. The fine specimen at Trewithen, Cornwall, died recently from the effects of the 1962–3 winter but we are told by Mrs Johnstone that one cutting from it was struck.

A. FRANCHETII Pax

A deciduous tree 20 ft high, with glabrous branchlets. Leaves three-lobed or occasionally with two additional basal lobes; 3 to 6 in. long, and as much wide, the base slightly heart-shaped; lobes pointing forward, triangular, coarsely

T S—H

toothed; leaf-stalk often about as long as the blade. There are tufts of down in the vein-axils. Flowers yellowish green, in racemes 1 to 2 in. long from the joints of the previous season's wood; stalks downy. Fruit with slightly hairy nutlets; keys 2 in. long; wings ⅝ to ¾ in. wide, spreading at nearly right angles.

Native of Central China; introduced in 1901 for Messrs Veitch by Wilson. There is a tree in the Edinburgh Botanic Garden 17 ft high, raised from W. 337 and planted in 1908, which thrives and frequently fruits (1965). Two examples from Forrest's seed grow at Caerhays Castle, Cornwall. They measure 29 × 2½ and 32 × 2½ ft, with boles of 8 and 10 ft respectively (1966).

A. VILLOSUM Wall.—This is really the Himalayan equivalent of the preceding and so closely allied that it is difficult to find any reliable character by which they can be distinguished. If they were merged, it would be under the name *A. villosum*. It has been in cultivation off and on for more than a century and said to be fairly hardy. But much would depend on the source of the seed; West Himalayan forms are likely to be the hardiest. Cultivated specimens of *A. villosum* differ from *A. franchetii* in their larger leaves (up to 10 in. long and wide).

A. THOMSONII Miq. *A. villosum* var. *thomsonii* (Miq.) Hiern—This is very distinct from the preceding in its leaves. The additional basal lobes seen in the other two species are scarcely discernible, and the main side lobes are very short; keys up to 3 in. long. Native of the E. Himalaya. Seed from Sikkim distributed as "*A. villosum*" may produce this species. Probably tender.

A. GINNALA Maxim.   AMUR MAPLE
A. tataricum var. *ginnala* (Maxim.) Maxim.

A small tree, or large shrub of bushy habit; branchlets glabrous. Leaves up to 3½ in. long, 2½ in. wide, three-lobed, slightly heart-shaped or truncate at the base, margins angularly toothed; nearly, or quite glabrous on both surfaces, bright dark green above; the lobes are ovate, with the middle one much the longest; leaf-stalk and midrib reddish. Flowers yellowish white, in small panicles, very fragrant, appearing in May. Fruit glabrous; keys 1 in. long; wings ⅓ in. wide, nearly parallel.

Native of China, Manchuria, and Japan; first introduced by way of St Petersburg. This maple is nearly allied to *A. tataricum*, but differs markedly in the shape of the leaf. The foliage turns a beautiful red in early autumn, but often drops so soon after colouring that the effect is rather fleeting.

var. SEMENOWII (Reg. & Herd.) Pax *A. semenowii* Reg. & Herd.—A geographical form found farther to the west, in Turkestan. Its leaves are smaller, sometimes five-lobed, and the wings of the fruit are more divergent.

A. GIRALDII Pax

A deciduous tree to 40 ft high in cultivation, with a dark brown, peeling bark; young stems covered with a glaucous bloom. Leaves 4 to 5 in. long and slightly more wide, usually with three lobes, the central one broadly triangular, the lateral ones shorter, all tapered at the apex; sometimes five-lobed by the addition of two small lobes near the base; glabrous above, downy at first and prominently net-veined beneath; margins rather coarsely and remotely toothed. Flowers in corymbs. Wings of fruit almost parallel; keys to 2 in. long, with convex nutlets.

Native of China; discovered by the missionary Giraldi in Shensi; introduced by Forrest from Yunnan. It is rare in gardens but there is an example at Caerhays Castle, Cornwall, measuring 39 × 3 ft; others grow at Dawyck, Peebl., Hergest Croft, Heref., and at Birr Castle and Headfort, Eire.

A. CAESIUM Wall.—This is the Himalayan counterpart of *A. giraldii*. Leaves usually five-lobed, the lobes more tapered at the apex; margins more finely toothed; undersides not so prominently net-veined.

A. GLABRUM Torr.   ROCK MAPLE

A deciduous shrub or small tree, occasionally 30 to 40 ft high in a wild state; branches erect; branchlets quite glabrous. Leaves very variable in shape, usually three- but sometimes five-lobed; the lobes so deep sometimes that the leaf becomes trifoliolate, at other times quite shallow; 3 to 5 in. long and broad, coarsely toothed, quite glabrous on both surfaces; dark shining green above, pale beneath; stalk reddish, 1½ to 3 in. long. Flowers few, produced towards the end of April in clusters 1 to 2 in. long, greenish yellow, ¼ in. across. Fruit with incurved wings, each ¾ in. long, ⅜ to ½ in. wide, reddish when young.

Native of western N. America; introduced about 1884. It is very distinct because of its thin, lustrous leaves, quite devoid of any down. At Kew it is thriving well, the best being now 40 × 3 ft (1967). The trees are well marked by their upright, almost fastigiate branches.

A. GRANDIDENTATUM Nutt.

A deciduous tree, occasionally 30 to 40 ft high, usually much less; branchlets reddish and glabrous. Leaves three-lobed (or five-lobed with the basal pair of lobes much reduced), 2 to 4 in. across, heart-shaped at the base; lobes triangular or oblong, entire or with three secondary lobes; downy beneath, especially along the ribs; stalks reddish, glabrous. Flowers yellow, borne in drooping short-stalked clusters, appearing with the leaves. Fruit glabrous; keys 1 to 1¼ in. long; wings ¼ to ½ in. wide, diverging at about 60°.

Native of western N. America; originally discovered by Thos. Nuttall on the head-waters of the Columbia River in N. Montana, whence it extends southward to Arizona and New Mexico. It is represented in the Kew collection by plants received from Prof. Sargent in 1885, which was probably its first introduction to England. It is allied to the sugar maple (*A. saccharum*), and is treated as a subspecies of it by Murray (*Morris Arb. Bull.*, Vol. 18, p. 45, 1967). It represents that species on the western side of N. America.

A. GRISEUM (Franch.) Pax   [PLATE 5
A. nikoense var. *griseum* Franch.

A deciduous tree, up to 45 ft so far in cultivation, with a peeling bark; branch-lets woolly at first. Leaves composed of three leaflets on a downy stalk; terminal leaflet 2 to 2½ in. long, half as wide, oval-lanceolate, with three to five pairs of coarse teeth, short-stalked; side leaflets smaller, oblique at the base, stalkless; all very glaucous beneath. Flowers few or solitary, on pendulous downy stalks 1 in. long. Fruit with very downy nutlets and wings; each key 1¼ in. long; wings ½ in. wide, the pairs forming an angle of 60° to 90°.

Native of Central China; introduced by Wilson for Messrs Veitch in 1901. Among the trifoliolate group of maples this is very distinct, because of the large blunt teeth on the leaflets. Its nearest ally is *A. nikoense*, but in this the leaflets are twice as large and scarcely toothed. It is the most striking of the trifoliolate maples, especially on account of its peeling bark, which hangs on the stem in large loose flakes, revealing the orange-coloured newer bark within; also for the fine autumnal red or orange of its leaves.

A. griseum has thrived in cultivation but seems to be at its best in southern England. The tree planted in woodland by the late Charles Eley at East Bergholt Place, Suffolk, and illustrated in his *Twentieth Century Gardening*, is now (1966) 45 × 2¼ ft; the slender bole, he wrote, 'is as rigid as a column of steel'. At Hergest Croft, Heref., there is a tree about as high but larger in girth; this measured 43 × 5¼ ft in 1963. Specimens of over 30 ft are at Wakehurst Place, Sussex; Westonbirt and Abbotswood, Glos.; and Arley Castle, Worcs. The peeling bark is well shown in the group of many-stemmed trees at Hidcote, Glos. *A. griseum* grows well on chalk, as at Highdown near Worthing, where there is a tree 29 ft high, bought at the Veitch sale in 1912, as well as many seedlings from it. The best tree at Kew is 29 × 1¾ ft (1960).

A. griseum fruits freely but the seed has a very low germination rate—rarely more than 5% even when taken from a group of several trees—and there is no readily available stock on to which it might be grafted. Thus one of the most beautiful of all small trees has been rendered all too scarce in commerce.

A. GROSSERI Pax

A small tree to 20 ft in the wild state, or a many-stemmed shrub. Young shoots grey-green or yellowish but ultimately becoming striped after the fashion of the snake-bark group. Leaves roundish-ovate, 2 to 2½ in. long, 1½ to 2 in. wide, heart-shaped at the base, palmately three-veined, triangular-ovate in out-line, usually with two small, spreading, sharply acuminate lobes; margins sharply saw-toothed; undersides rusty-pubescent near the base but soon glabrous. Flowers in pendulous racemes. Wings of fruit curved, spreading at an obtuse angle or almost horizontally.

Native of China; discovered by the missionary Giraldi in Shensi and introduced to Kew from the Arnold Arboretum in 1927. In some of its forms *A. grosseri* has almost unlobed leaves, and is then difficult to distinguish from *A. davidii*. However, the toothing of the leaves is always sharper than in that species, and the leaves smaller and proportionately wider.

var. HERSII (Rehd.) Rehd. *A. hersii* Rehd.—Discovered by Hers in 1919 in Honan provi..ce; introduced by him to the Arnold Arboretum in 1923 and thence to Kew a few years later. From the type it differs mainly in the more distinct lobing of the leaves; the lateral lobes, borne above the middle of the leaf, are tapered at the apex into a long point.

For garden purposes there is little to choose between the type and the variety. Both colour red in the autumn and have the beautiful striped bark of their group. But in the colder winters of New England the variety has proved to be the hardier, and certainly, both in Britain and the United States, it is commoner in gardens than the type.

At Kew typical *A. grosseri* is represented by a specimen of 16 × ¾ ft, while var. *hersii* is 31 × 3½ ft (1967). There are several specimens of the variety at Westonbirt, the tallest, *pl.* 1936, 40 × 1½ ft (1966).

A. HELDREICHII Boiss.

A deciduous tree of medium height; branchlets glabrous dark red-brown, marked with pale oblong lenticels. Leaves 4 to 7 in. wide, not quite so long, five-lobed, the three terminal lobes reaching nearly to the base, the basal pair not so deep or sometimes absent; lobes oblong-lanceolate, coarsely toothed; there is a tuft of hairs at the base on the upper side, and brown wool along the principal veins beneath; otherwise the leaves are glabrous; rather glaucous beneath. Flowers yellow, produced at the end of May in short, broad corymbs. Fruits glabrous; the keys 1½ to 2 in. long; wings ⅝ in. wide, spreading at about 60°.

Native of the Balkan States and Greece; introduced about 1879. It is very distinct and striking in foliage, on account of the deep, comparatively narrow lobes. The leaves suggest a Virginia creeper, and are unlike any other of the large-leaved European maples. In depth of lobing they resemble *A. platanoides* 'Lorbergii', but the lobes themselves are quite differently shaped. *A. trautvetteri* bears some similarity to *A. heldreichii* but its leaves are not so deeply cleft. A handsome maple.

The description given above is strictly that of var. MACROPTERUM (Vis.) Pax, which appears to be less widely distributed than the type and perhaps linked to it by intermediates. The type is smaller in both leaf and fruit. *A. heldreichii* (typical) is 39 × 3½ ft at Kew (1966) and 45 × 4¾ at Edinburgh (1968); var. *macropterum* is 22 × 1 ft at Kew (1966) and 42 × 4 ft at Edinburgh (1968). The tallest specimen recorded, status uncertain, is at Hergest Croft, Heref., 65 × 7½ ft (1961).

A. HENRYI Pax

A deciduous tree 30 to 40 ft; branchlets downy at first, soon becoming smooth. Leaves composed of three leaflets borne on a slender common stalk 2 to 4 in. long; leaflets 2½ to 4 in. long, 1 to 1½ in. wide, oval, with a long drawn-out point, wedge-shaped at the base, entire or with a few large teeth; green on both surfaces and downy on the veins, especially beneath. Flowers in slender downy spikes, produced in May before the leaves from the naked joints of the previous year's wood. Fruits red when young, in racemes 6 to 9 in. long, each fruit very short-stalked, glabrous; keys ¾ to 1 in. long; wings divergent at a small angle.

Native of Central China; discovered by Henry, and introduced by Wilson in 1903 for Messrs Veitch. It belongs to the same group as *A. nikoense* and *cissifolium*, but differs from them and all other trifoliolate maples in the often entire margins of the leaflets and in the stalkless flowers. At Westonbirt the leaves turn a fine red before falling in autumn. The best tree there, *pl.* 1914, is 35 × 2 ft. Smaller trees are at: Abbotswood, Glos.; Killerton, Devon; and in the West Hill nursery of Messrs Hillier. In Eire there are examples at Birr Castle, Co. Offaly; Mount Usher, Co. Wicklow; and in the Glasnevin Botanic Garden, Dublin.

A. SUTCHUENENSE Franch.—This differs from *A. henryi* in its glabrous young shoots and more markedly toothed leaflets, and from *A. mandschuricum* in its more numerously flowered inflorescence and protruding stamens. It was discovered by Père Farges in N.E. Szechwan. Wilson collected specimens, but whether he ever introduced it to cultivation is not certain. The tree figured under the name by Veitch (*Journ. R.H.S.*, Vol. 29, figs. 93 and 96) is said by Rehder to be *A. henryi*.

A. HOOKERI Miq.

A deciduous tree 40 to 50 ft high; young shoots glabrous, red. Leaves not lobed, 3 to 6 in. long, half as wide, ovate with a heart-shaped base, the apex contracted, slender, tail-like, sharply toothed, glabrous; stalk slender, 1 to 2 in. long. Flowers ⅙ in. wide, borne on slender racemes about as long as the leaves, stalks thread-like, ⅓ in. long. Fruits with wings about ½ in. long, curved, spreading at angles of 90° to 120°.

Native of the E. Himalaya at altitudes of 9,000 to 10,000 ft. It is not hardy but has been grown successfully in Cornwall. The red young shoots are attractive and the fruits hang very elegantly.

A. × HYBRIDUM Spach

A tree ultimately 60 to 70 ft high; young shoots not downy, but with many pale warts. Leaves three-lobed, the lobes pointing forward, with rarely two additional, obscurely developed lobes at the base; 2 to 4½ in. wide, scarcely so long; dark dullish green and glabrous above, pale dull green beneath, with down only along the chief veins; irregularly and sparsely toothed; stalk not milky, glabrous, mostly shorter than the blade. Flowers yellowish, produced in May along with, or after, the leaves, in panicles or racemes 3 to 5 in. long. Fruit with keys ¾ to 1 in. long; the wings nearly parallel.

A hybrid of doubtful origin, but usually ascribed to *A. monspessulanum* crossed with *A. opalus*.

A. HYRCANUM Fisch. & Mey.

A deciduous tree 20 to 50 ft high. Leaves five-, more rarely three-lobed, 2 to 4 in. across, bright green above, paler, rather glaucous and glabrous beneath, except for a patch of down at the base and along the chief veins; stalk about as long as the blade. The three central lobes are parallel-sided, and each has several large, angular, blunt teeth; basal pair of lobes ovate. Flowers greenish yellow, produced during April in short-stalked corymbs. Fruit glabrous; keys ¾ to 1 in. long; wings nearly parallel, ¼ in. wide.

Native of S.E. Europe but represented in W. Asia by forms and varieties that differ to a greater or lesser degree from the plant described above. Even in S.E. Europe it is variable, and forms with small, leathery leaves found in Greece are sometimes regarded as a distinct species (*A.* REGINAE-AMALIAE Boiss.). *A. hyrcanum* is allied to *A. opalus*, but differs in the deeper and more angular lobing of the leaf. The form introduced is a slow-growing tree of neat shape. There are specimens 45 ft high at Westonbirt and in the University Parks, Oxford.

A. JAPONICUM Thunb.

A small, bushy, deciduous tree 20 to 30 ft (rarely 40 to 50 ft) in height; branchlets glabrous. Leaves 2 to 5 in. long and wide, roundish in the main, but seven- to eleven-lobed, the lobes ovate or lanceolate, long-pointed, sharply and irregularly toothed; there is a tuft of whitish hairs at the end of the downy leaf-stalk on the upper side, and the under-surface is furnished with whitish hairs on the ribs and in their axils. Flowers purplish red, produced in early April before the leaves in long-stalked clusters. Fruits at first hairy, then glabrous; keys ¾ to 1 in. long; wings ⅓ in. wide, spreading nearly or quite horizontally.

Native of Japan. It is best known in cultivation by its garden varieties, of which the following are the commonest:

cv. 'ACONITIFOLIUM'.—Lobes reaching to within ½ or ¼ in. of the end of the leaf-stalk, each lobe being again divided and sharply toothed; autumn colour crimson. It makes a rounded bush to 9 ft or even more. Also known as *A. j. laciniatum*, *A. j. parsonsii*, and *A. j. filicifolium*.

cv. 'AUREUM'.—Leaves wholly of a pale golden yellow, and very effective during the whole of the summer. There is an example in the Sunningdale Nurseries, Windlesham, about 20 ft high and 20 ft across.

cv. 'VITIFOLIUM'.—This variety contributes much to the autumn splendours of Westonbirt, where there are many large specimens. 'No maple gives a more brilliant or varied display of autumn colour, the central mass of foliage often remaining a vivid green, while the branches blaze into purple, crimson, scarlet and orange.' (A. B. Jackson, *Catalogue of the Trees and Shrubs at Westonbirt*.) It is for this quality that it is chiefly grown, but the leaves too are remarkable for their large size, being up to 6 in. long and wide. Of unknown origin, but described by Veitch in *Journ. R.H.S.*, Vol. 29, p. 334.

The typical *A. japonicum* often turns rich crimson in the autumn. The combination of characters which distinguish it from other maples are the numerous leaf-lobes, the downy leaf-stalk, and the glabrous young shoots.

A. PSEUDOSIEBOLDIANUM Komar.—Native of Manchuria, and also of Korea, where, according to Wilson, 'in autumn its foliage assumes wonderful tints of orange, scarlet and crimson and is reponsible for much of the autumn beauty of the forest'. It is allied to *A. japonicum*, but differs in its leaves, which have nine to eleven lobes, never as few as seven, as in that species; the lobes are lanceolate-oblong, narrower and more elongated.

A. SIEBOLDIANUM Miq.—Native of Japan. Also allied to *A. japonicum*, from which it differs in its yellow flowers and the downiness of the young shoots. There is an example at Kew 16 ft high, which colours yellow in the autumn.

A. LAXIFLORUM Pax

A small tree with glabrous young stems. Leaves membranaceous or somewhat leathery, rather narrowly oblongish-ovate, broadly cordate to rounded at the base, the apex gradually acuminate, prolonged into a tail-like point, 2 to 4 in. long, 1½ to 2 in. wide, margins finely saw-toothed and lobulate or with short lateral lobes near the base, rusty pubescent on the veins beneath at first, later glabrous. Flowers and young fruits usually reddish, borne on long lax racemes; wings of fruits spreading at about a right-angle.

A native of W. China, described by Pax from specimens collected by Pratt near Tatsien-lu (Kating-fu) and by Faber on Mt Omei. The taxonomic boundaries of this species are a matter of dispute and have expanded and contracted according to this or that interpretation. In *Plantae Wilsonanae*, Vol. 3, p. 426, Rehder placed *A. forrestii* under *A. laxiflorum* in synonymy and this judgement, subsequently retracted, was widely accepted and adopted in previous editions of this work. As a result, many trees grown under the label *A. laxiflorum* are really *A. forrestii*, now very properly accepted as a distinct species. Secondly, in the first volume of the work cited (p. 94, 1911), Rehder described a variety of *A. laxiflorum*, namely var. *longilobum*, differing from the type chiefly in the five-lobed leaves with the veins beneath covered with a dense, yellowish, floccose tomentum. In 1933, however, (*Journ. Arn. Arb.*, Vol. 14) Rehder placed this variety under *A. taronense* in synonymy, with the exclusion of Wilson's specimen W. 4108 (see below), which he transferred to the typical part of *A. laxiflorum*. Finally, the maples grown under the collector's number W. 4100 are not this species but fall well within the span of variation of *A. maximowiczii*. The corresponding herbarium specimen was in fact transferred to *A. maximowiczii* by Rehder in the article cited above.

With the exclusion of this alien material, *A. laxiflorum* becomes once again the species that Pax described (though the leaves are occasionally more lobed than in the type specimens). He placed it near to *A. davidii*, *A. hookeri* and *A. crataegifolium*, and it is perhaps most closely allied to the last of these, but differs in the larger, more finely toothed leaves and by the wings of the fruits spreading at about a right-angle (horizontal or widely spreading in *A. crataegifolium*). From the other two species it differs in its lobulate or slightly lobed leaves. Also, *A. hookeri* is a quite glabrous species, and *A. davidii* differs from *A. laxiflorum* in its much more coarsely toothed leaves, more abruptly acuminate at the apex.

There should be no possibility of confusing *A. laxiflorum* with *A. forrestii*, which has strongly three-veined and three-lobed leaves, glabrous beneath.

The true *A. laxiflorum* is rare in cultivation but represented at Trewithen, Cornwall, by two specimens 20 to 25 ft high (1968). These agree well with Pax's original description and figure. In Wilson 4108, as represented in the Edinburgh Botanic Garden, the leaves on the extension growths and young spurs are strongly three-lobed; on older, branched spurs they are less lobed but always strongly three-veined. The difference between this and the Trewithen trees is very striking, but it would appear to belong to *A. laxiflorum* as at present understood.

A. RUBESCENS Hayata—This rare maple is a native of Formosa (Taiwan), where it inhabits mountain forests at 6,000 to 8,000 ft and grows to 65 ft high; allied to *A. laxiflorum*; in cultivation at Trewithen from seed collected by Yashiroda some thirty years ago under his No. 109. Its closest ally is A. MORRI-SONENSE Hayata, another Formosan species, under which it is placed in synonymy by H. L. Li (*Woody Flora of Taiwan*, 1963).

A. LOBELII Ten.

A deciduous tree, ultimately 50 to 60 ft high, whose erect branches give it a narrow columnar form; young shoots glabrous, bluish grey. Leaves palmate, five-lobed, 4 to 7 in. wide, rather less in length (smaller leaves are often three-lobed); heart-shaped or truncate at the base, glabrous and dark green above, paler beneath, with tufts of hair in the axils of the veins; lobes ovate, ending in a long drawn-out point. Flowers in corymbs, yellow. Fruit glabrous, with keys 1 to 1¼ in. long; wings ⅓ in. wide, wide-spreading but not quite horizontal.

Native of S. Italy; said to have been introduced in 1683. This maple is closely allied to the Norway maple, and by some authorities is made a variety of it. It has the same inflorescence, fruits, and milky sap in the leaf-stalks. The erect narrow habit, however, at once distinguishes it, the cleft at the base of the leaves is not so deep, and the terminal lobes have not the few large teeth so frequently in the Norway maple; the young bark also is markedly striped. It is perhaps even more closely allied to *A. cappadocicum* which it resembles in the entire lobes of the leaves; but from which it differs in the leaves being darker green, three- to five-lobed (never seven-lobed as in *A. cappadocicum*), with the basal pair of lobes directed forward (not spreading horizontally) and in the glaucous, not green young stems. It is a handsome, well-marked, and vigorous tree. There is a tree of exceptional size at Westonbirt in the area known as Clay Island, *pl.* 1922, 73 × 5¼ ft (1966). Others of size are: Edinburgh Botanic Garden, 57 × 6¾ ft (1966); Borde Hill, Sussex, 60 × 8½ ft (1967); Birr Castle, Co. Offaly, Eire, *pl.* 1932, 60 × 3¾ ft (1966).

A. MACROPHYLLUM Pursh   OREGON MAPLE

A tree occasionally over 100 ft high, with a trunk 3 or 4 ft in diameter. In young trees the branches are erect, but become more spreading in older ones, forming eventually a compact, rounded head. Branchlets glabrous. Leaves probably the largest among maples, usually from 6 to 12 in. across, and cut more than half-way to the base into three or usually five lobes, each one being again cut into large, triangular minor lobes; ciliate; upper surface glossy green, lower one paler, with tufts of white hairs in the axils of the veins; leaf-stalk containing

ACER MACROPHYLLUM

milky sap. Flowers yellow, scented, produced in April on dense pendulous racemes 4 to 6 in. long, each flower $\frac{1}{8}$ in. across. Fruits covered with long, pale brown bristles; the wings nearly glabrous, $1\frac{1}{2}$ in. long, $\frac{1}{2}$ in. wide, diverging at about 90°.

Native of the coast regions of western N. America from S. Alaska to California. It was introduced by Douglas for the Horticultural Society in 1826 or 1827, but had been discovered by Archibald Menzies more than thirty years before. In many respects it is the noblest of maples, and it thrives well in many parts of the British Isles. Owing to the late growth of young trees during mild autumns, they are apt to be cut back in hard winters; but otherwise it is absolutely hardy at Kew, where there are several good specimens. On young trees the leaves are larger, but not so deeply lobed. It flowers and bears seed in great quantities some seasons, and the keys are very frequently in threes instead of the usual pairs. Owing to their hairiness and the great size of the wings, the fruits are particularly striking. The timber is highly valued in N.W. America for furniture and indoor work—more so than that of any other tree of those regions except conifers.

The largest specimens of this maple recorded in recent years are fairly well distributed over the British Isles: Westonbirt, Glos., 75 × 9¼ ft (1965); Kew, 67 × 8 ft (1963); Syon House, Middlesex, 65 × 5½ ft (1959); Dawyck, Peebl., 58 × 4¾ ft (1966); Tortworth, Glos., 47 × 6½ ft (1966); Hungerford Priory, Wilts, by the cross-roads, 45 × 6 ft (1956). In Ireland there are two large specimens at Trinity College, Dublin; one, in the New Quadrangle, is 50 × 9½ ft, the other, in the Main Quadrangle, 55 ft (estim.) × 10 ft (1966).

A. MANDSHURICUM Maxim.

A small, deciduous tree, sometimes a shrub. Leaves composed of three leaflets, on a stalk up to 4 in. long. Terminal leaflet 2 to 3½ in. long, 1 to 1¼ in. wide, lanceolate, pointed, saw-toothed, glabrous when mature except for hairs along the midrib; the side leaflets are rather smaller and shorter-stalked than the terminal one; main leaf-stalk often longer than the largest leaflet. Flowers greenish yellow, often produced in threes; stamens not protruding. Fruit glabrous, purplish when young; keys 1¼ to 1½ in. long; wings ½ in. wide, the pair forming an angle of about 90°.

Native of E. Siberia and Manchuria; trees in cultivation at Kew were received from St Petersburg in 1904. This maple is closely allied to *A. nikoense* and *A. sutchuenense*; the former differs in its hairy young leaves and flower-stalks, the latter in its many-flowered inflorescence and protruding stamens. It is very liable to injury by late spring frost. There is an example at Kew about 14 ft high and another of 22 ft, about twenty-five years planted, in the Chandlers Ford nursery of Messrs Hillier. Like many trees from continental N.E. Asia it is ill-adapted to our climate; in the hotter summers of New England it thrives and sets fertile seed.

A. MAXIMOWICZII Pax

A. urophyllum Maxim.; *A. laxiflorum* of some authors, in part, not Pax

A small tree with glabrous young stems, which are usually purplish red and gradually become striated after the fashion of the 'snake-bark' group. Leaves three- or five-lobed, ovate-oblong in general outline, 2 to 3 in. long, dark, slightly bluish green above, paler along the midrib and main nerves, whitish green beneath and quite glabrous on both sides except for prominent tufts of white hairs in the axils of the veins beneath; central lobe elongated, caudate-acuminate, lateral lobes shorter and usually acute or at least scarcely developed, basal lobes usually small and sometimes less finely tapered than the central one; margins double-toothed and incised. Flowers reddish, on rather stiff, short racemes. Fruit wings spreading at about a right-angle.

Native of W. China; described from specimens collected by Henry in W. Hupeh and by the Russian explorer Potanin in Kansu; introduced by Wilson from N.W. Szechwan under W. 4100 (as "*A. laxiflorum*"), from W. Hupeh (W. 4427) and possibly under other numbers. The leaves of this species are very variable in the degree of lobing, even on the same tree. Rock's specimens collected in Kansu are said by Rehder to be mostly three-lobed and certainly Wilson's 4100, from the borders between Szechwan and Kansu is less lobed than his W. 4427, which comes from much farther to the east and south.

A. maximowiczii is a very hardy species, very decorative in winter when young owing to its purplish red stems, but this character becomes less evident as the tree ages. It is in cultivation at Kew, in the Edinburgh Botanic Garden, at Westonbirt, in the Knap Hill Nursery, Surrey (from Westonbirt seed), and at Borde Hill, Sussex. Its nearest ally appears to be the Japanese *A. tschonoskii* but in that species the central and lateral lobes are more equal in size and more deeply incised; the basal lobes are usually well developed; and the veins beneath are covered with a rusty down when young. In the leaves of *A. forrestii* the central lobe is relatively shorter and broader than in *A. maximowiczii* and the margins are much more finely and regularly toothed. The leaves of *A. laxiflorum* are downy beneath when young, at least on the veins, and the prominent axillary tufts seen in *A. maximowiczii* are absent.

A. MICRANTHUM Sieb. & Zucc.

A small, deciduous tree, sometimes a shrub. Leaves five-lobed, 2 to 3½ in. long and wide, glabrous except for a tuft of hairs at the base, where the ribs join the stalk; base heart-shaped; lobes ovate with a long drawn-out point, deeply and handsomely toothed; leaf-stalk downy. Flowers greenish white, numerous, on slender racemes 1½ to 3 in. long, small (about ⅕ in. across). Fruits glabrous; keys ½ to 1 in. long; wings ¼ in. wide, rounded at the end, spreading at a wide angle.

Native of Japan; introduced about 1879. The foliage turns a bright red in autumn, and is very prettily cut. It belongs to the same group of maples as *A. rufinerve* and *A. capillipes*, but within that group its nearest ally is *A. tschonoskii*, from which it differs in its small flowers, which are also more numerous on each raceme than in the other species (ten or more).

A. MIYABEI Maxim.

A deciduous tree 30 to 40 ft high, with a trunk 12 to 18 in. in diameter, of rounded habit; branchlets at first minutely downy. Leaves 4 to 6 in. wide, not quite so long, deeply three-lobed, the lower pair of lobes usually again divided into two, but not deeply so; lobes ovate, with a long blunt apex, the margins cut into several large rounded teeth; stalks downy, as are also both surfaces, especially on the ribs and chief veins. On young trees the leaves are deeply notched at the base, but on older ones they are frequently truncate. Flowers yellow, downy, produced a few together each on a slender stalk in corymbs 2 to 3 in. long. Fruit with downy nutlets; keys ¾ to 1 in. long; wings ⅓ in. wide, slightly reflexed beyond the horizontal position.

Native of Japan; sent to Kew in 1895 by Prof. Sargent, who had discovered this rare tree in September 1892, in a new locality in Yezo. He records the incident in the *Forest Flora of Japan*, p. 29:

'We stopped quite by accident at Iwanigawa, a railroad junction in Yezo some 40 or 50 miles from Sapporo, and, having a few minutes on our hands, strolled out of the town to a small grove of trees. In this grove, occupying a piece of low ground on the borders of a small stream, and chiefly composed of Acer pictum, was A. Miyabei covered with fruit. The find was a lucky one, for Iwanigawa is a long way from the station where this maple had been discovered and mature fruit had not been seen before. From these trees I obtained later a supply of seeds, enough to make this maple common in the gardens of America and Europe.'

It is thriving well at Kew, where there is an example 37 × 2¼ ft, and is evidently well adapted for the English climate. Other specimens recorded are: Westonbirt, Glos., 46 × 3¼ ft (1966) and Batsford Park, Glos., 52 × 4 ft (1963). Of European maples *A. platanoides* is most closely related to it, and it has, like that species, milky juice in the leaf-stalks.

A. MONO Maxim.

A. pictum Thunb. 1784, not Thunb. 1783; *A. pictum* var. *mono* (Maxim.) Maxim.

A deciduous tree up to 60 ft in height, young shoots not downy, becoming grey and slightly fissured the second year. Leaves five- or seven-lobed, 3 to 6 in. across, and rather more in length, the lobes ovate-triangular, ending in a long, narrow apex, the lowest pair spreading outwards; the base of the leaf is heart-shaped, the margins not toothed; the stalk has a milky sap, and both surfaces are green and glabrous except for tufts of hairs in the vein-axils beneath. Flowers appearing in April or early May with the first leaves, greenish yellow, in corymbose racemes 2 to 3 in. long. Fruit with glabrous wings, about 1½ times as long as the nutlets, the pairs spreading almost horizontally or ascending; less commonly they are parallel and almost connivent (f. CONNIVENS (Nichols.) Rehd.); each key ¾ to 1¼ in. long.

Native of Japan, Manchuria, N. and Central China, and Pacific Russia; introduced by Maries from Japan in 1881 under Thunberg's name *A. pictum*, published in 1784. This cannot stand, since Thunberg had used it a year earlier for a plant that was not a maple at all but the member of the aralia family now known as *Kalopanax pictus* (*Acanthopanax ricinifolium*). Maximowicz's name is in any case much to be preferred: the type of *A. pictum* was in fact a garden tree with variegated leaves (hence the epithet chosen) and had the wings of the fruit connivent, although this form is not common in the wild state of the species. The typical *A. mono* was introduced in 1901 by Wilson, when collecting in China for the Veitch nurseries, but had reached cultivation on the continent some years earlier by way of St Petersburg.

A. mono is a handsome tree, resembling *A. cappadocicum* (q.v. for the differentiative character), but is rarer in cultivation; most trees going under the name "*A. pictum*" are really *A. cappadocicum*. In the wild state, *A. mono* varies somewhat in the size, shape and indumentum of the leaf.

f. AMBIGUUM (Dipp.) Rehd. *A. ambiguum* Dipp.—Leaves downy beneath, lobes five, the centre one triangular ovate and much longer than the laterals. Origin uncertain.

cv. 'MARMORATUM'.—Leaves powdered over with white dots and stains, some being more white than green. Described by Nicholson in *Gard. Chron.*, Vol. 16, 1881, p. 375, as *A. pictum marmoratum*. It was probably growing at Kew at that time but is no longer in the collection. In the same article, Nicholson described an *A. pictum variegatum*, but it is not clear whether the account was based on a living tree or on Thunberg's original figure of *A. pictum*, which, as pointed out above, was based on a garden tree with variegated leaves.

var. MAYRII (Schwer.) Nemoto *A. mayrii* Schwer.—A tree with smooth, white bark; branchlets usually glaucous and remaining smooth in their second year, as in *A. cappadocicum*, and then yellowish or brown. Leaves rounded, with very short, broad lobes. Native of Japan in Hokkaido and the northern part of the main island. Probably not in cultivation at present.

var. TRICUSPIS Rehd. *A. tenellum* Pax—A tree to 25 ft high. Leaves thin and papery, three-lobed (the smaller ones ovate, not lobed), 2 to 3 in. long and as much or a little more wide, base truncate or heart-shaped; lobes triangular, pointed or bluntish. Leaf-stalk slender, 1 to 3 in. long.

Native of Szechwan, China; discovered by Henry about 1888 and introduced by Wilson in 1901 under W. 863. It is a very distinct maple on account of its thin, smooth, cleanly cut, three-lobed leaves, whose long, slender stalks cause them to be restless as those of an aspen. It is rare in gardens. The late Sir Frederick Stern had a fine specimen at Highdown near Worthing; it was destroyed in a gale some years ago but is survived by several younger trees raised from its seed.

A. FULVESCENS Rehd.—A tree to 70 ft high in W. Szechwan, China. It differs from *A. mono* chiefly in its leaves, which are almost invariably three-lobed and clad beneath with a yellowish down that darkens to rust-coloured as they mature; branchlets dark brown and smooth the first year, silvery grey and roughish in the second. Introduced by Wilson in 1908, but so rare that the only specimen known to us is at Borde Hill, Sussex. This is 30 ft high, branching at 3 ft, where it is 3½ ft in girth. It makes a very handsome, bushy tree of mushroom-like habit.

A. MONSPESSULANUM   MONTPELIER MAPLE

A deciduous tree of dense, rounded habit, occasionally more than 50 ft (usually 20 to 30 ft) high, sometimes scarcely more than a shrub; branchlets glabrous. Leaves three-lobed, with a heart-shaped base; 1½ to 2½ in. wide, less in length; dark green and glossy above, paler below, soon quite glabrous on both surfaces, except for a tuft of down where the three prominent veins join the stalk, which is 1 to 2 in. long and has no milky sap. Flowers greenish yellow, borne on drooping slender stalks ¾ to over 1 in. long, in few-flowered corymbs or loose racemes. Fruit reddish, often very abundant, with wings ¾ to 1 in. long, ¼ to ½ in. wide, and pointing downwards, so that the inner edges nearly meet or even overlap.

Native of S. Europe and parts of Central Europe; also of N. Africa and the Near East; introduced, according to Aiton, in 1739. In general appearance this maple bears much resemblance to our native *A. campestre*, but is easily distinguished by its glabrous three-lobed leaves, without milky juice in the stalks. It is a small tree of neat and pleasing appearance, very suitable as an isolated specimen in a small garden. There are several fine examples in or near London, where this maple thrives well. The largest at Kew measures 45 × 5 ft (1965). Others are: West Ham Park, 46 × 6¼ ft (1956), and Kensington Gardens, 50 × 5¼ ft (1967). This maple is used as a hedge plant in the south of Europe.

A. NEGUNDO L.   BOX ELDER

A deciduous tree 40 to 70 ft high, with a trunk 2 to 3 ft. in diameter, forming a wide-spreading head of branches; branchlets glabrous. Leaves long-stalked, pinnate, 6 to 10 in. long, consisting of three or five leaflets. Leaflets ovate, 2 to 4 in. long, pointed, coarsely toothed towards the end; upper side bright green, glabrous; lower one slightly downy or eventually glabrous; the terminal leaflet often three-lobed or even trifoliolate. Flowers (male and female on separate trees) yellow-green, without petals, the male ones crowded in dense clusters on the previous year's shoots, each flower on a slender hairy stalk, 1 to 1½ in. long; the females in slender, drooping racemes. Fruit in pendent racemes, 4 to 8 in. long; each key 1 to 1½ in. long, with a wing ¼ to ⅓ in. wide, the pair forming an angle of 60° or less.

Native of N. America, where it is widely spread. According to Sargent it is most common in the Mississippi Valley, but reaches as far north as New York State, and as far west as the inland slopes of the Rocky Mountains. It was cultivated by Bishop Compton at Fulham in 1688. Although the typical form is by no means common, it is a handsome tree, especially when isolated on a lawn. It is one of the maples that yield sugar in America. There is a tree 45 × 8¼ ft at Kew but this is exceeded in height by one at Northerwood House, Hants, 52 × 3 ft (1963). In Späth's nursery, near Berlin, there was once a specimen 60 ft high and 6½ ft in girth of trunk.

cv. 'AURATUM'.—Leaflets wholly yellow; this variety is one of the best of golden-coloured trees, and retains its colour until autumn. Branchlets green with a white bloom. Späth's nurseries, 1891, where it arose as a sport from a variegated form known as 'Aureo-limbatum'. G. Krüssmann, in *Handbuch der Laubgehölze*, points out that this clone is not the same as 'Odessanum', as has commonly been assumed.

cv. 'AUREO-MARGINATUM'.—Leaflets marked as in the common variegated box elder but with yellow instead of white. Dieck's nurseries before 1885.

var. CALIFORNICUM (Torr. & Gray) Sarg.—Differs from the type in the dense covering of grey down beneath the leaves, and by the downy branchlets and fruits. Native of California. Forms intermediate between this variety and the type are said to occur in Arizona, Texas, Missouri, etc. This variety should not be confused with *A. negundo californicum* Hort. (var. *pseudo-californicum* Schwer.), which appears to be no more than a strain, in cultivation since before 1864, characterised by its great vigour and by having the young branchlets green, as in the type, but covered with a pruinose bloom, as in var. *violaceum*.

cv. 'CRISPUM'.—Leaflets curled, often deformed; shrubby. In cultivation before 1825. A male clone. See Loudon, *Arb. et Frut. Brit.*, Vol. 1, p. 460.

cv. 'ELEGANS'.—Leaves glossy green, with a broad margin of yellow; young growths with a bluish bloom. Apparently of French origin and put into commerce as *A. n. aureomarginatum elegans*.

cv. 'HETEROPHYLLUM'.—Leaflets reduced to a linear or lanceolate shape, and with more or less deeply cut margins. Späth's nurseries, 1883.

cv. 'ODESSANUM'.—Leaves golden yellow as in 'Auratum' (q.v.), but the branchlets densely downy; put into commerce by Rothe's nursery, Odessa, Russia, in 1890; in cultivation on the continent.

cv. 'VARIEGATUM'.—One of the commonest of variegated trees, once largely used in town gardens and grown in pots for the decoration of halls and large rooms. The leaflets have an irregular border of white, or are sometimes wholly white. It first appeared as a sport on the green-leaved type in a nursery at Toulouse in 1845, but trees of a large size appear to be very uncommon. It is female, and the fruits are variegated like the leaves.

var. VIOLACEUM (Kirchn.) Jäg.—Young branchlets purplish, covered with a glaucous bloom. Such forms are common in the Middle West of the United States.

A. NIKOENSE Maxim.

A deciduous tree up to 40 or 50 ft high in a wild state, with a trunk 12 to 18 in. in diameter and a round-topped habit; branchlets hairy. Leaves composed of three leaflets on a stout, very hairy main-stalk; terminal leaflet short-stalked, oval, 3 to 5 in. long, $1\frac{1}{2}$ to $2\frac{1}{2}$ in. wide; the side ones obliquely ovate, stalkless, and somewhat smaller; all are either entire at the margins or shallowly and sparsely toothed, and more or less hairy beneath. Flowers yellow, $\frac{1}{2}$ in. diameter, produced usually three together on drooping hairy stalks $\frac{3}{4}$ in. long. Fruit with thick, brown-felted nutlets; keys $1\frac{1}{2}$ to 2 in. long; wings $\frac{3}{4}$ in. broad, rounded, nearly parallel to each other, or diverging to 60° (in cultivation often not so large). *Bot. Mag.*, n.s., t. 387.

Native of Japan, where, according to Sargent, it is widely distributed, but not common; also of Central China. Introduced by Messrs Veitch in 1881, in whose nursery at Coombe Wood, Kingston-on-Thames, was one of the first trees raised from Maries' seeds, ultimately 30 ft high. Compared with many maples this is not a quick grower, which in small gardens may be counted an advantage, especially as the tree has a most interesting and distinct appearance at all times, and is very beautiful in autumn when the leaves turn rich red or yellow. The winter buds are long and pyramid-shaped, with overlapping scales. In wild specimens collected by Henry in Central China the leaflets are 7 in. long and 3 in. wide.

In cultivation, *A. nikoense* makes a small bushy tree or vase-shaped shrub. There are a number of examples at Westonbirt, of which the largest are: Mitchell Drive, 43 × 2¾ ft; Victory Glade, 42 × 3¼ and 40 × 3 ft (1966–7). Others recorded recently are: Hergest Croft, Heref., 35 × 5 ft at 2 ft (1960); East Bergholt Place, Suffolk, 30 × 2¼ ft (1966); Sheffield Park, Sussex, 30 × 2½ ft (1960).

A. OBLONGUM DC.

A sub-evergreen or deciduous tree, found both in the Himalaya and China. In the Himalaya it grows 50 ft in height, but plants from that region are too tender for our climate. In China it appears to be most frequently 20 to 25 ft high. It is a tree without down; the leaves hard and leathery in texture, normally oblong or oblong-ovate, 2 to 4 in. long, ¾ to 1½ in. wide; pointed at the apex, tapered or rounded at the base, normally neither lobed nor toothed; distinctly glaucous beneath. In the Himalayan form the leaves may be up to 6 or 7 in. long. Flowers in downy panicles. Fruits glabrous; keys about 1 in. long; the wings about ¼ in. wide.

Native of the Himalaya, W. and S. China; an allied species is found in Formosa. This species is variable in leaf; the venation may be quite pinnate or become three-veined by the proportionately stronger development of the basal pair of lateral veins. Young plants often bear distinctly three-lobed, sharply toothed leaves as well as the normal ones. Three-lobed leaves may also occur on adult trees and it was such a one that furnished the type of Henry's var. *trilobum*, but this condition seems to be part of the normal variation of the species.

A. oblongum was introduced from the Himalaya in 1824 and a hardier form by Wilson in 1901. A tree at Kew from this seed died, but another, bought from Veitch in 1908, and almost certainly also from Wilson seed, proved hardy and is now 22 ft high (1960).

var. CONCOLOR Pax—Leaves green on both sides.

var. LATIALATUM Pax—Wings of fruit broad, ½ in. wide, and almost semi-circular. Described from a tree that once grew in the Botanic Garden, Florence, but reported from the wild.

A. PAXII Franch. *A. oblongum* var. *biauritum* W. W. Sm.—Rehder concluded that this species is no more than a variety of *A. oblongum* and identified it with var. *biauritum*, founded on a specimen collected by Forrest in Yunnan. Fang, in his Monograph on the Chinese Aceraceae, agrees that they are identical but retains *A. paxii* as an independent species. It bears evergreen leaves, which are sometimes quite entire, but just as commonly three-lobed, and the two kinds of leaf may appear together on the same shoot. The lobes, sometimes no more than large teeth, are borne about midway up the leaf, which is broadly ovate to halberd-shaped, and up to about 2½ in. long, 1⅗ in. wide. The inflorescence is a corymbose panicle, as in *A. oblongum*. However, specimens of *A. paxii* in the Kew Herbarium have glabrous inflorescence branches (downy in the other species) and also show the following further marks of difference: *A. paxii* has longer petals and the nutlets of the fruit are rounded, while in *A. oblongum* they are more angular.

A. paxii was discovered by Père Delavay in Yunnan and is distributed over much of S. China. A plant grown at Kew under this name has survived recent hard winters but does not thrive. It agrees with *A. paxii* in its foliage, but in the absence of flower and fruit it cannot be identified with certainty.

A. buergerianum, at least in the normal wild form, resembles *A. paxii* in its polymorphic leaves, but these are deciduous.

A. OLIVERIANUM Pax

A deciduous tree from 12 to 30 ft high; branchlets glabrous and often purplish. Leaves five-lobed, 2½ to 4 in. wide, scarcely so long, truncate or slightly heart-shaped at the base; the lobes ovate, long-pointed, minutely, regularly and sharply toothed; glabrous except for down along the veins and in their axils. Flowers borne at the end of a slender-stalked corymb, 2 in. long. Fruit glabrous; keys 1 in. long; wings ⅖ in. wide, spreading nearly horizontally.

Native of Central China; discovered by Henry, and introduced by Wilson for Veitch in 1901 during his first expedition. It is allied to *A. sinense*, but differs in the smaller more finely and evenly toothed leaves, and in the corymbose inflorescence. In the last character, and in the shape of its leaves, it bears a strong resemblance to the typical form of *A. palmatum*. But, as seen in gardens, it is well distinguished by its stiffer, more glossy leaves. A closely related species— A. SERRULATUM Hayata—is found in the island of Formosa (Taiwan); it is common there in mountain forests to an altitude of 7,000 ft and makes a tree of up to 70 ft in height.

A. OPALUS Mill.   [PLATE 8
A. italum Lauth; *A. opulifolium* Vill.

A tree 30 to 65 ft high, of rounded habit, sometimes much smaller or even bushy; branchlets glabrous. Leaves 2½ to 4½ in. wide, somewhat less in length, shallowly five-lobed, heart-shaped at the base, irregularly toothed; dark green, glossy and glabrous above, paler and more or less downy beneath, especially along the chief veins and in their axils, occasionally quite glabrous; lobes angular. Flowers yellow, appearing in March, numerously crowded in short-stalked corymbs; each flower on a slender, glabrous, pendent stalk, 1 to 1½ in. long. Fruit glabrous; keys 1 to 1½ in. long; wings ⅖ in. wide, varying considerably in divergence.

Native of S. and Central Europe; introduced in 1752. It is one of the most ornamental of early-flowering trees, producing its blossoms regularly and in great abundance in March and April; they are of a clearer and more pronounced yellow than in most maples. There are several good specimens at Kew, the largest 50 × 6 ft (1965). At Westonbirt there are two off the Broad Drive, 60 × 7½ and 53 × 4½ ft (1966). There is much confusion in the nomenclature of this maple. It is very variable and some authorities have separated the following varieties from it as distinct species:

var. OBTUSATUM (Willd.) Henry *A. obtusatum* Willd.—Leaves on the whole larger than in the type, and up to 5½ in. wide, the lobes more rounded and the whole under-surface covered with a close down; flower-stalks hairy; fruit-wings not so large as in var. *tomentosum*. Native of Central and E. Europe. There is an old specimen at Kew 48 ft high, on a trunk measuring 9 ft in girth at 3 ft.

var. TOMENTOSUM (Tausch) Rehd. *A. opulifolium* var. *tomentosum* Tausch; *A. neapolitanum* Ten.; *A. opalus* var. *neapolitanum* (Ten.) Henry—Leaves up to 6 or 7 in. wide, covered with a pale felt beneath, the lobes quite shallow, especially the basal ones. Flower-stalks hairy, remaining so until the fruits ripen. Native of the country about Naples, where, like the type farther north in Italy, it is largely employed in vineyards as a support on which to train the vines. There is an example of this variety at Westonbirt, off the Broad Drive, measuring 64 × 6½ ft (1966).

A. ORIENTALE *see* A. SEMPERVIRENS

A. PALMATUM Thunb.
A. polymorphum Sieb. & Zucc.

A deciduous tree of rounded form, rarely seen more than 20 ft high in cultivation, but more than twice as high in a wild state; habit rounded, often wider than high; branchlets glabrous. Leaves palmately five- or seven-lobed, 2 to 3½ in. long and wide; the lobes ovate-lanceolate, cleft two-thirds of the way to the base of the blade, sharply double-toothed, glabrous on both surfaces except in the axils of the ribs beneath; green at first, becoming bronzed or purplish in autumn. Flowers in somewhat erect, glabrous, stalked umbels; small and purple. Fruit glabrous; keys about ½ in. long; wings ⅛ in. wide, much incurved, the pair forming a broad arch.

Native of Japan, whence it was introduced to England in 1820, and also of China and Korea. Having long been cultivated by the Japanese, it has produced an extraordinary number and variety of forms differing in colour and form of leaf. To many of them unwieldy Latin names have been given and all bearing such names have been elaborately classified by botanists. Only those best known in cultivation at the present time are described here. These are listed under what would appear to be the correct clonal name according to the provisions of the *International Code of Nomenclature for Cultivated Plants*.

cv. 'ATROPURPUREUM'.—Leaves rich reddish, five-lobed or partly seven-lobed by the development of irregular minor lobes at the base. There may be several clones under this name, but by rights it belongs to the one distributed by Van Houtte's nursery and illustrated in *Flore des Serres*, Vol. 12, 1857, t. 1273. Messrs Cripps used to sell seedlings as *A. p. purpureum*.

cv. 'AUREUM'.—Leaves five-lobed, yellow when young, becoming golden later.

DISSECTUM Group.—This group comprises a number of garden forms with seven, nine or eleven lobes to the leaf, reaching to the leaf-stalk, each lobe being in turn deeply and finely cut and each ultimate division finely toothed. The clones differ somewhat in the fineness of the cutting of the leaf, as well as in its colour. The botanical group-name var. *dissectum* (Thunb.) Miq., which is founded on a Japanese garden plant described by Thunberg as *A. dissectum* in 1805, embraces all these clones, whatever their leaf-colouring. The forms with coloured leaves are well enough distinguished, but the naming of the green-leaved clones has become confused. What is generally known as *A. p. dissectum* or *A. p. dissectum viride* appears to be the clone distributed by Van Houtte as *A. p. palmatifidum*, illustrated and described in *Flore des Serres*, Vol. 21, 1875, t. 2156–7. The form distributed in this country by Messrs Cripps as *A. p. palmatifidum* was, however, a different clone from this, distinguished by its very finely cut, fern-like foliage. Both the green-leaved clones make mushroom-headed bushes that may reach in time a height of 6 to 8 ft but usually seen smaller than this.   [PLATE 7

cv. 'DISSECTUM ATROPURPUREUM'.—Leaf-cutting of the Dissectum group, the leaves deep red; a dwarf, slow-growing bush of pendulous habit. This well-known garden clone is not the same as 'Ornatum', as has been suggested.

cv. 'DISSECTUM ROSEO-MARGINATUM'.—Leaves coloured as in 'Roseo-marginatum' but with the cutting of the Dissectum group. Also known, on the continent, as 'Friderici-Guillelmii'. *Rev. Hort.*, 1867, p. 391, and *Gard. Chron.*, Vol. 16, 1881, p. 137.

cv. 'ELEGANS'.—Leaves up to 5 in. long, seven-lobed almost to the base, the leaves deeply and prettily toothed. Also known as *A. p. septemlobum elegans.* There is a purple-leaved form of this—'ELEGANS PURPUREUM'.

var. HEPTALOBUM Rehd. var. *septemlobum* K. Koch.—A group-name for forms with larger leaves than in the typical variety, to 5 in. wide, usually seven-lobed, the lobes ovate-oblong, broadest about the middle, more finely toothed than in the type. Such forms are found wild in Japan. The clones 'Elegans', 'Rubrum', and 'Osakazuki' belong here. Selected forms of this variety are in commerce in which the autumn colour is brilliant crimson.

cv. 'LINEARILOBUM'.—Lobes of leaf narrow, reaching almost to the base, finely toothed but not cut, green. There is also a purple-leaved form of this—'LINEARILOBUM ATROPURPUREUM', also known as 'Atrolineare'.

cv. 'ORNATUM'.—Leaves cut as in the Dissectum group, dark red when young, bronzy green when mature. *Rev. Hort.*, 1867, pp. 300 and 391.

cv. 'OSAKAZUKI'.—Leaves as in 'Elegans'; autumn colour brilliant scarlet and orange.

cv. 'RETICULATUM'.—Veins of leaf green; the interspaces yellowish green. *Ill. Hort.*, Vol. 17, 1870, t. 18.

cv. 'RIBESIFOLIUM'.—Leaves green; the lobes cleft to the base and deeply and irregularly jagged at the edges. Also known as 'Shishigashira'.

cv. 'ROSEO-MARGINATUM'.—Lobes five, irregularly toothed, rosy at the edges. *Flore des Serres*, Vol. 15, 1864, t. 1566.

cv. 'RUBRUM'.—Leaves large, seven-lobed, rich purplish red when young, the colour fading to purplish green as the leaves mature. Also known as *A. p. septemlobum rubrum* and *A. p. septemlobum sanguineum*.

cv. 'SANGUINEUM'.—Leaves five-lobed, blood-red when young, later dark olive green. *Ill. Hort.*, Vol. 14, 1867, t. 526.

cv. 'SENKAKI'.—This variety, known as the coral-bark maple, is chiefly grown for its beautiful coral-red young stems, which retain their brilliance throughout the winter, but is almost as valuable for its prettily cut light-green leaves, which turn in autumn to a soft yellowish orange. The habit is erect and it will in time make a tall shrub. At Caerhays Castle, Cornwall, there is a fine group, the largest 34 × 1½ ft, in which even the old bark retains a pinkish tinge; normally, as the bark ages, and the summer growths become shorter, the winter colouring becomes less apparent, but could doubtless be renewed by heavy pruning. Mr Graham Thomas tells us that 'Senkaki' was introduced to England by T. H. Lowinsky and put into commerce by the Sunningdale Nurseries around 1920. It may, however, have been introduced independently to Ireland by Smith's Daisy Hill Nursery, Newry, Co. Down. Also known as 'Sango-kaku' and *A. p. cinnabarinum*.

cv. 'SESSILIFOLIUM'.—Once thought to be a distinct species. Leaf shortly stalked, green, often with three or more distinctly stalked leaflets. Its true origin was not suspected until a similar sport was found growing on ordinary *A. palmatum*. There are two examples at Westonbirt, Glos., about 50 ft high.

The typical *A. palmatum* and most of the green and purple varieties are quite hardy in the south of England. Yet they are not very frequently seen in good condition. Although tolerant of shade, they are best in a bright position sheltered on the north and east sides, and in a good loamy or peaty soil. Perhaps their greatest drawback is their susceptibility to late spring frosts; it is not unusual to see the young growths cut back once or twice in the spring, and whilst the vigorous green, purple, and red varieties recover, that is fatal to the permanent success of the more delicate forms with the most exquisite colouring and cutting. Cold, drying winds are also detrimental to the unfolding leaves of these more delicate forms. Another source of failure is due to their being grafted on strong, ill-fitting stocks. Several forms, hitherto failures, have been found to succeed on their own roots.

A. PAPILIO King
A. caudatum Wall. ex Rehd.

A deciduous tree with ash-grey, smooth young stems. Leaves five-lobed, blades 2¾ to 5 in. long and about as wide; lobes triangular-ovate, acuminate, coarsely and acutely saw-toothed or lobulate, with the teeth or lobulations themselves finely serrate, lower surface with a more or less persistent covering of yellowish brown or fawn-coloured hairs; leaf stalks 2⅘ to 3⅘ in. long, finely downy at first. Flowers in erect, spike-like panicles of perfect and staminate flowers, main axis of inflorescence, peduncles and pedicels all hairy. Fruiting racemes about 4 in. long; fruits on pedicels ⅙ to ¼ in. long; wings ascending, 1 to 1⅕ long with the nutlet and about ⅖ in. wide.

Native of the E. Himalaya and of Upper Burma, much confused with *A. acu-*

minatum and *A. pectinatum* (see under these species for the marks of difference). It is generally known as "*A. caudatum*" but, for the reasons explained in the note, this name must be rejected as ambiguous.

NOTE: The name *A. caudatum* starts from Wallich (*Pl. As. Rar.*, Vol. 2, p. 4, p. 28 and t. 132 (1831)). Wallich included under it two sets of herbarium material which he had previously regarded as representing two distinct species. These he had catalogued in the East India Company's Herbarium as *A. caudatum* (No. 1225) and *A. pectinatum* (No. 1226). In his account of *A. caudatum* Wallich made clear that he had come to regard this material as representing a single variable species—*A. caudatum*—and cited *A. pectinatum* as a synonym. In fact, his earlier judgement was the correct one. No. 1226 is a distinct species (*A. pectinatum*, q.v.); No. 1225 is, with one exception mentioned below, *A. acuminatum*, a species validly described by David Don some years earlier. Wallich's description of *A. caudatum* is clearly compounded of these two species. As for the specimen figured under t. 132, there is nothing to match it in the Kew Herbarium, but it is nearest to a specimen of *A. pectinatum* in Hooker's herbarium and is not *A. caudatum* as understood by Rehder (i.e. *A. papilio*). This confusion would have been resolved if Wallich had designated a type for *A. caudatum*, but he did not do so, and there is no way of deducing one from his account. Rehder, in Sargent's *Trees and Shrubs*, Vol. 1, p. 163 (1905), applied the name *A. caudatum* Wall. to *A. papilio*, but excluded Wallich's description of the staminate flowers (which refers to *A. acuminatum*) and the synonym *A. pectinatum*. But what is left of Wallich's *A. caudatum* is then impossible to identify. Nor did Rehder deal with the material upon which Wallich based his account; he makes no mention of the Nos. 1225 and 1226 and the only specimen he cited for *A. caudatum* is one collected by J. D. Hooker in Sikkim—and the only specimen of this group in Hooker's herbarium is *A. pectinatum*. It should be added that one of the collectings in the Wallich herbarium under No. 1225 seems to be *A. papilio*. It is sterile and mounted with a flowering specimen which is clearly *A. acuminatum*. Even if the sterile piece is really *A. papilio*, there is no reason to take it as the holotype of *A. caudatum* unless it be that it is the one specimen that might answer to Wallich's descriptions of the leaves; in fact it does not agree well with his description. It will therefore be evident that the name *A. caudatum* Wall. has been so confused that it is best abandoned. The valid name for *A. caudatum* sensu Rehder is *A. papilio* King (*Journ. As. Soc. Bengal*, Vol. 65, p. 115 (1896)).

A. PECTINATUM Wall. ex Pax

A. caudatum Wall., in part; *A. pectinatum* Wall., ex Nicholson, nom. illegit.*

A deciduous tree with smooth purplish or brownish to grey young shoots. Leaves three- to five-lobed, but when five-lobed the basal lobes are sometimes very small; blades 3 to $5\frac{3}{5}$ in. long and as much or slightly more wide, lobes triangular to ovate, acuminate to caudate, finely and sharply saw-toothed, often doubly so, the teeth furnished with bristly tips, midrib and veins on the lower surface covered at first with a mealy, rust-coloured indumentum, but later becoming more or less glabrous except in the axils of the nerves at the base. Flowers in spikes. Fruits in compact racemes $2\frac{3}{5}$ to 4 in. long, borne on short pedicels $\frac{1}{6}$ to $\frac{2}{5}$ in. long; keys widespreading (often horizontally), $\frac{4}{5}$ to 1 in. long, the wings $\frac{1}{5}$ to $\frac{2}{5}$ in. wide.

Native of the Himalaya from Nepal eastward, and of Upper Burma (possibly also of Yunnan). It has been much confused with *A. papilio* (*A. caudatum* sensu Rehder), from which it is readily distinguished by the fine, bristle-tipped teeth of the leaf-margins, by the mealy, rust-coloured indumentum of the under-surface of the young leaves, and by the racemose inflorescence (in *A. papilio* the inflorescence is a narrow panicle which becomes racemose only in the fruiting state). *A. pectinatum* is a little known species, but of considerable interest as the only Himalayan representative of the section *Macrantha*, to which the 'snake-bark' maples belong.

*NOTE: Wallich originally gave the name *A. pectinatum* to Nepal specimens which he catalogued under No. 1226 in the East India Company's Herbarium and also to material collected by Dr Govan at Sirmore. The last is under No. 1225 and is, in fact, *A. acumin-atum*. When he compiled the catalogue, Wallich was of the opinion that *A. pectinatum* and *A. caudatum* were distinct species, but when he published the latter he cited *A. pectinatum* as a synonym and remarked that he had come to regard them as belonging both to one variable species. Nicholson, who validly published the name *A. pectinatum* Wall. for No. 1226 (*Gard. Chron.*, n.s., Vol. 15, p. 365 (1881)), unfortunately transgressed the Code of Botanical Nomenclature by citing *A. acuminatum* as a synonym. Pax followed Nicholson in treating *A. pectinatum* as a distinct species (*Bot. Jahrb.*, Vol. 7, p. 249 (1885–6) and *Pflanzenreich*, Aceraceae, p. 67 (1902)) and since he did not introduce any extraneous element the name can start from him.

A. PENSYLVANICUM L.   MOOSEWOOD

A deciduous tree, sometimes 30 or more ft high, usually 15 to 20 ft, with rather erect branches. Young wood at first green, becoming reddish brown and, when older, beautifully striped with white jagged lines. Leaves up to 7 in. long, a little less wide, with three conspicuous, tapering, forward-pointing lobes at the terminal part; margins finely and sharply double-toothed; lower surface covered with minute reddish down when young, which mostly wears off towards the end of the season; stalks 1½ to 2 in. long, the enlarged bases of each pair clasping the shoot. Flowers yellow, produced in May on slender, pendulous racemes 4 to 6 in. long; each flower is ⅓ in. diameter, and borne on a stalk ¼ to ½ in. long. Fruit in pendent racemes, glabrous; wings ¾ in. long, each pair forming a crescent 1½ to 2 in. across.

Native of eastern N. America; introduced in 1755. This maple is remarkable chiefly for the exceedingly handsome striping of its younger branches and stem. For a long time it was the only species known in cultivation with this character, but during the past eighty years or so several species have been introduced from Japan and China showing the same colouring, of which *A. rufinerve, capillipes*, and *davidii* are the best known. These and certain other species are placed in the section *Macrantha*, in which the characteristic snake-bark is associated with other distinctive botanical characters, notably the racemose inflorescence. It is most likely to be confused with *A. rufinerve* (q.v. for the marks of difference).

A. pensylvanicum is not so common in gardens as it was before the introduction of its Asiatic allies but still very worthy of cultivation. The leaves, large and handsome at maturity, have a pinkish tinge on opening, and usually turn yellow in autumn. It remains one of the most distinct and desirable of maples. It has been planted along two rides in the Forestry Commission's plantations at Alice Holt, Surrey, and thrives very well there; although only twelve years planted, some are over 20 ft tall.

cv. 'ERYTHROCLADUM'.—In this variety the young shoot turns a bright crimson after the fall of the leaf. This, added to the other attractions of the species, makes this variety one of the most attractive of small hardy trees. There are examples at Knightshayes Court, Devon, and Maidwell Hall, Northants. Put into commerce by Späth's nurseries, Berlin, in 1904.

A. PENTAPHYLLUM Diels

This maple, which appears to be very rare in the wild state, was discovered by Joseph Rock in the valley of the Yalung, Szechwan, China, in July 1929, and introduced by him at the same time under his No. 17819. Plants were raised and distributed by Messrs Hillier but none have been traced, and the only known adult specimens outside China grow at the Strybing Arboretum, Golden Gate Park, San Francisco. Rock recorded it in his Field Notes as a tree to 30 ft high, with spreading branches and an ash-coloured bark. The leaves are digitately compound, with four to seven leaflets; main stalk reddish or brownish, $1\frac{3}{4}$ to $2\frac{2}{8}$ in. long; lowermost leaflets almost sessile, the upper ones on short stalks; they are glabrous, glaucous beneath, lanceolate, tapered at the base, blunt at the apex, the middle ones 3 in. long, $\frac{3}{5}$ in. wide. Flowers not seen. Fruits in lax corymbs; wings spreading at a wide angle, $\frac{4}{5}$ in. long; nutlets downy, $\frac{1}{5}$ in. wide.

It has been placed provisionally in Section *Trifoliata*, but differs from the other members of the section (of which *A. griseum* and *nikoense* are the most important) in having four to seven leaflets in each leaf.

A. PENTAPOTAMICUM J. L. Stewart

A small tree with a smooth greyish bark. Leaves three-lobed, $1\frac{1}{4}$ to 4 in. long, $2\frac{1}{2}$ to 6 in. wide, truncate or heart-shaped at the base, pale green on both sides, glabrous when mature except for axillary tufts of hairs on the veins beneath; lobes extending about half-way to the centre of the leaf, ovate, tapered at the apex, bluntly toothed. Flowers in short corymbs. Wings of fruit diverging at an acute angle; keys about 1 in. long; nutlets glabrous.

Native of the N.W. Himalaya, where it grows in dry, open woodland in the basins of almost all the great rivers from the Jhelam to the Sutlej—hence the epithet *pentapotamicum* (of the five rivers), which, owing to a misprint or slip of the pen, was given as "*pentapomicum*" in the original description. This species is perhaps not in cultivation, though the name is sometimes encountered on labels. The tree at Kew raised from seed purporting to be of this species proves to be *A. acuminatum* and this is also true of one at Borde Hill, received from a nursery. Others grown in Ireland as *A. pentapotamicum* are also not the true species.

A. pentapotamicum was placed by Pax in section *Spicata* but its affinities within this group are uncertain.

A. PILOSUM Maxim.

A deciduous tree with glabrous, angular young shoots. Leaves three-lobed, the lobes ovate-lanceolate, pointed, toothed or nearly entire, the lateral ones wide-spreading and forming a truncate or slightly heart-shaped base to the leaf; 1½ to 3 in. long, often rather more wide; glabrous, dark green with pale veins above, slightly glaucous and downy beneath, especially on the veins; stalk reddish, ¾ to 1½ in. long, downy. Flowers few in a cluster or short raceme; males and females in separate clusters. Fruit ¾ in. long, with downy nutlets and parallel, forward-pointing wings.

Native of N. China; discovered in Kansu by Dr Piasezki in 1875; introduced to the Arnold Arboretum in 1911 from the same province by W. Purdom, under whose No. 767 it may be in cultivation.

A. PLATANOIDES L.   NORWAY MAPLE

A deciduous tree from 60 to 70, occasionally over 90 ft high, with glabrous branchlets. Leaves five-lobed, heart-shaped at the base, 4 to 7 in. wide and about three-fourths as long in adult trees (in young vigorous specimens they are considerably larger); bright green on both surfaces, glabrous except for a tuft of hairs in the axils of the veins; stalks exuding a milky sap when broken. Flowers greenish yellow, ⅓ in. diameter, produced in April before the leaves in erect, branching corymbs. Fruit pendulous, on stalks 2 to 3 in. long; keys 1½ to 2 in. long, glabrous; the wings wide-spreading but not quite horizontal, ⅓ to ½ in. wide. Timber white, and fairly close and hard in grain.

Native of continental Europe, where it is widely spread in a wild state from Norway southwards; cultivated in England for centuries, but not a native. The Norway maple is one of the handsomest, hardiest, and most vigorous of introduced trees. Its leaves are thinner and brighter than those of common sycamore or of the plane, which they somewhat resemble. It is also more ornamental when in flower than most maples, and its leaves fade in autumn into various shades of red, brown, and yellow. It thrives in almost any soil, and even in the poor sandy soil at Kew grows rapidly. For forming a screen quickly it is preferable in many places to black Italian poplar, for although it does not grow so fast nor so big, it is a tree of better form and more interesting character. Easily increased by seeds, which are produced abundantly.

At Westonbirt there are five specimens of Norway maple over 70 ft in height and ranging from 8 to 10½ ft in girth; the tallest of these, in Mitchell Drive, measures 90 × 8 ft (1966). At Beauport Park, Sussex, there is a fine tree with a wide spread of branches measuring 70 ft in height and 11¾ ft in girth at 3 ft (1965). Like the sycamore, the Norway maple attains a large size in Scotland. There are examples of 82 × 10 ft at Dawyck, Peebl. (1966), and 73 × 10¼ ft at Keillour Castle, Perths. Few large trees have produced more varieties under cultivation. More than twenty have been named, and of them the following are the more distinct:

cv. 'AUREO-MARGINATUM'.—Leaves often three-lobed; lobes deep and long-pointed, margined with yellow. 'HETEROPHYLLUM VARIEGATUM' is similar.

cv. 'COLUMNARE'.—Leaves smaller and shallower-lobed than in the type; branches erect; habit columnar. Raised in the nursery of Simon-Louis at Plantières, near Metz, in 1855.

cv. 'CRIMSON KING'.—Leaves deep crimson-purple throughout the summer; a seedling of 'Schwedleri', raised by Messrs Barbier of Orleans and put into commerce around 1946. 'Crimson King' is the name under which it was patented in the U.S.A. See also 'Goldsworth Purple'.

cv. 'CUCULLATUM'.—Leaves long-stalked, fan-shaped, with seven or nine prominent veins instead of the usual five; base of leaf wedge-shaped or truncate, not heart-shaped. Of the same type as 'Laciniatum', but with the lobes not so long-pointed. Nicholson in *Gard. Chron.*, Vol. 15, 1881, p. 564. There is an example at Kew measuring 50 × 4¾ ft, received from Van Volxem's nurseries in 1879. Another at Westonbirt, Glos., in Silkwood, probably planted at about the same time, measures 75 × 7 ft (1968).

cv. 'DISSECTUM'.—Leaves slit back to the stalk into three lobes, the basal pair often cut again almost as deeply, and all the lobes divided into secondary lobes with long drawn-out points. A small, bushy tree. Introduced by Knight and Perry from Belgium in 1845 but no tree that can with any certainty be ascribed to this clone has been traced. Von Schwerin (*Gartenflora*, Vol. 42, 1893, p. 586) adds that the young wood is brown, the unfolding leaves brownish, later dark green. Another tree with the same shape of leaf is 'LORBERGII', put into commerce by Van Houtte around 1881. This makes a taller tree to 60 or 70 ft and according to Von Schwerin (op. cit.) also differs from 'Dissectum' in its yellowish young wood and in its lighter green leaves, with the tips of the lobes standing out from the plane of the leaf. There is an example of 'Lorbergii' at Westonbirt, in Silkwood.

cv. 'DRUMMONDII'.—Leaves very clearly variegated with white; the best of its class.

cv. 'FAASEN'S BLACK'.—Leaves dark purplish brown, glossy, folded upwards at the margins; young leaves not wrinkled. Autumn colour red. Raised at Herk-de-Stadt, Belgium, around 1936 and put into commerce by Faasen-Herkens, Telelen, Holland. For this information we are indebted to G. Krüssmann, *Handbuch der Laubgehölze*. See also 'Goldsworth Purple'.

cv. 'GLOBOSUM'.—A dwarf form; head of foliage wide-spreading, dense, and mop-headed. Origin unknown; first described by Nicholson in *Gard. Chron.*, Vol. 15, 1881, p. 564.

cv. 'GOLDSWORTH PURPLE'.—Leaves light reddish brown and wrinkled when young, becoming deep, dull, blackish purple and remaining so until autumn. The original plant was presented to the Royal Horticultural Society's Garden at Wisley around 1936-7 by a lady in whose garden it had apparently arisen as a self-sown seedling but whose name was, unfortunately, not recorded. It was put into commerce by the Goldsworth Nurseries of Messrs Slocock around 1949. The parent tree still grows at Wisley in Seven Acres. For this information we are indebted to Mr Brian Mulligan, Director of the University of Washington Arboretum, who was assistant to the Director at Wisley from 1936 to 1941.

This clone is very similar to 'Faasen's Black' and 'Crimson King', both of continental origin. It has not been possible to find authentic specimens of either, but they are said to differ from 'Goldsworth Purple' in having the young leaves less brightly coloured and the mature ones somewhat glossier. 'Faasen's Black' has the young leaves scarcely wrinkled and gives red autumn colour.

cv. 'Laciniatum'.—A smaller and more twiggy tree than the type, of more erect, narrow habit. Leaves tapering and wedge-shaped at the base, the lobes ending in long, often curved, claw-like points. The oldest of named varieties, figured in an Austrian work in 1792, and known as the eagle's claw maple. The plant described appears to be part of a clone for which the epithet *laciniatum* has the sanction of long usage; var. *laciniatum* as understood by Loudon (*Arb. et Frut. Brit.*, 1838, Vol. I, p. 449 and fig. 121) is not the true eagle's claw maple.

cv. 'Nanum'.—Of dwarf, pyramidal shape. Nicholson in *Gard. Chron.*, Vol. 15, 1881, p. 565. Also known as *A. pyramidale nanum*. There is a specimen at Kew received from Späth in 1900, measuring 23 × 1¾ ft.

cv. 'Palmatifidum'.—An ambiguous name, deriving from *A. p.* var. *palmatifidum* Tausch, which has been used for both 'Dissectum' and 'Lorbergii.'

cv. 'Reitenbachii'.—A less vigorous tree than 'Schwedleri'. Leaves reddish when young (red on the extension growths), later green but changing to dark red as autumn approaches; found on his estate by the German landowner Reitenbach and put into commerce by Van Houtte before 1874. According to Elwes it comes 'fairly true' from seed but the name should be used only for descendants of the original tree by vegetative propagation. The maple once grown on the Continent as *A. platanoides rubrum* is not the same as 'Reitenbachii.'

cv. 'Schwedleri'.—Leaves of a bright red when young, becoming green as they mature. A popular variety, beautiful in late April and May. Origin unknown; in cultivation 1869.

cv. 'Stollii'.—Leaves very large, up to 9 in. in diameter; lobes not deep, usually three and often entire. Späth's nurseries, 1888.

cv. 'Walderseei'.—Leaves densely speckled with white dots, so as to give a delicate grey appearance; lobing rather irregular. Put into commerce by Späth's nurseries, 1904.

A. pseudoplatanus L.   Sycamore

A deciduous tree of the largest size, reaching at its best a height of over 100 ft and a girth of trunk of 20 ft. Bark of the trunk pale, greyish, and peeling off in large flakes; branchlets glabrous. Leaves usually five-lobed (small ones on fruiting twigs often three-lobed), 4 to 7 in. across in adult trees (larger in young ones), heart-shaped at the base; the lobes ovate, coarsely toothed, dark green and glabrous above, paler and dull glaucous beneath, with pale brown hairs in the axils of the veins or, sometimes, along the whole length of the chief ones. Flowers in large drooping racemes, often branching at the base, yellowish green. Fruit on long, pendulous racemes; keys 1¼ to 2 in. long; wings glabrous, the two forming an angle of about 60°.

Native of Europe, but not considered to be a true native of Britain, where however, it has existed many centuries and has thoroughly established itself.

Judging by the way seedlings spring up in the wilder parts of Kew Gardens, it would seem that in course of time the place, if left to run wild, would become a forest of common sycamore. It is a peculiarly hardy tree, and one of the few that will stand the full force of salt-laden winds in exposed places near the sea. One may see it in many of the gardens on the sea-fronts of English watering-places, battered and stunted in growth, yet helping largely to form that first line of defence against the winds, the establishment of which is really the most important item in the seaside planting. When fully grown it is a magnificent tree of stately proportions, thriving better perhaps in the north of England and in Scotland (where it is known as the 'plane') than in the warmer south. Early in this century there was an ancient tree in the grounds of Scone Palace, near Perth, reputed to have been planted by Mary Queen of Scots. Although still alive, most of its upper growth had gone, but its trunk was more than 6 ft through. Mr R. F. Adam, Factor of the Scone Estate, tells us that what remained of this tree was blown down about 1940–1, at which time it was little more than an ivy-covered stump. He adds that the Queen planted a maple on precisely the same spot in 1967. H. J. Elwes, in *Trees of Great Britain and Ireland*, wrote (1908) that in Scotland 'I have seen none to surpass in size, shape and perfection the one which I figure . . . in front of Newbattle Abbey'. He gave the size as about 95 ft high by 16 ft 6 in. in girth at 5 ft. This noble tree still exists; its height, however, is 90 ft, and its girth, measured at an old 5 ft mark, is 16 ft 4 in. (1966).

Among English trees Elwes gave the palm to one at Studley Royal in York-shire, then (1908) 104 ft high and 17½ ft in girth. This tree has not been traced and the tallest now on record for England are two at Cobham Hall, Kent, measuring 110 × 19¼ and 96 × 14¼ ft (1965). Others of size are: Gwydyr Castle, Caer., 90 × 16¼ ft (1966); Biel, E. Lothian, 105 × 13½ ft (1967); Hagley Castle, Worcs., 90 × 15 ft (1966); and Holywell Hall, Lincs., 85 × 19½ ft (1966).

The foliage of the sycamore has no autumn beauty, decaying a dingy brown; it is frequently attacked by the tar-spot fungus *Rhytisma acerinum*, which causes yellow or pale spots to appear on the leaf-blade in June that turn black towards the fall of the leaf. The timber is white, and easily worked.

The sycamore has produced very many varieties and forms under cultivation, some as seedling variations, others as branch sports. It is not necessary to enumerate more than the most distinct of them.

cv. 'ATROPURPUREUM'.—Leaves dark green above, rich purple beneath. Späth's nurseries, 1883. Also known in the trade as 'Purpureum Spaethii'. Forms of this nature, but with the colouring less rich, have probably arisen many times and may breed more or less true from seed. The purple sycamore described by Loudon (as var. *purpureum*) was stated by him to have originated in Sander's nursery, Jersey, in 1828. The cultivar name 'Purpureum' would belong to the clonal descendants of this tree; the group name for sycamores of this sort is f. *purpureum* (Loud.) Rehd.

cv. 'AUCUBIFOLIUM'.—Leaves blotched with yellow like the common aucuba. It appeared among seedlings in the nursery of Little and Ballantyne at Carlisle, about 1876.

cv. 'BRILLIANTISSIMUM'.—A very handsome variety with leaves of a beautiful pinkish hue on unfolding; slow-growing. There is a good example at

Powis Castle near Welshpool, 21 ft high with 15 ft diameter of spread (*Journ. R.H.S.*, Oct. 1962).

cv. 'CORSTORPHINENSE'.—Leaves pale yellow when young, golden in early summer. The original tree grew at Corstorphine, near Edinburgh. James Baillie, second Lord Forrester, is said to have been murdered by his sister-in-law at the foot of this tree, 26th August 1679 (*Garden and Forest*, 1893, p. 202). What is probably the original tree still exists and measures 55 × 12¼ ft (1968). There is a specimen at Myddleton House, Enfield, Middlesex, 80 × 6 ft (1957), and another at Studley, Yorks., 60 × 5¾ ft (1966).

f. ERYTHROCARPUM (Carr.) Pax—Fruits red; said to be wild in the Alps of Bavaria, but the tree on which the name is founded arose in a French nursery (*Rev. Hort.*, 1864, p. 171) and the cultivar name 'Erythrocarpum' belongs to this clone. The Pilrig 'plane' has similarly coloured fruits, but they are smaller and on longer racemes than in 'Erythrocarpum'.

cv. 'EUCHLORUM'.—A vigorous form with large leaves and fruit; the keys are up to 2½ in. long and nearly 1 in. wide. Leaves dark green. Späth's nurseries, 1878. There is a fine specimen at East Bergholt Place, Suffolk, measuring 80 × 11 ft (1966).

cv. 'LEOPOLDII'.—Leaves stained with yellowish pink and purple. Originated in Belgium about 1860. Other forms of the same character are 'SIMON-LOUIS FRÈRES' and 'TRICOLOR'.

cv. 'PRINZ HANDJERY'.—Leaves suffused with yellow above, purple beneath. Very pretty when the leaves are quite young. It is slow-growing and makes a shrubby tree. Späth's nurseries 1883, or perhaps earlier. 'NIZETII' is similar.

var. TOMENTOSUM Tausch *A. p.* var. *villosum* Parl.—A variety found in Sicily, S. Italy, and Dalmatia. Leaves covered with down beneath; the margins more coarsely toothed. .

f. VARIEGATUM (West.) Rehd.—This name is of general application to the common variegated sycamores, with leaves blotched and striped with yellow or yellowish white. Such forms have been known since the early eighteenth century and have even been reported from the wild, but it is doubtful whether they have ever been propagated vegetatively. The plants offered by nurserymen in the later eighteenth and early nineteenth century under such names as "*variegatum*", "*albo-variegatum*", and "*foliis variegatis*" were most probably seedlings. The variegation of the leaf seems to have little effect on the vigour of the tree, judging from the many large specimens in the country. At Petersham Lodge, Richmond, there is one of 90 × 12½ ft (1956) and another of about the same height but 16½ ft in girth, at Guisborough Priory, Yorks. (1952). The tallest measured recently is at Linton Park, Kent, 80 × 13½ ft (1965).

cv. 'WORLEEI'.—Leaves rich yellow. A superior form of the Corstorphine sycamore, raised in Germany; leaf-stalks reddish.

A. × ROTUNDILOBUM Schwer.

A hybrid of uncertain origin, although cultivated in Europe for more than half a century. It is probably a cross between *A. monspessulanum* and *A. opalus* var. *obtusatum*, being intermediate in its various characters between those two maples. Leaves three-lobed, sometimes with two additional, indistinct lobes at the base; 2½ to 4 in. long and broad, reddish when young, smooth except for a little down at the base beneath; pale beneath, dark green above; lobes shallow, rounded; leaf-stalk not milky.

A. RUBRUM L.   RED MAPLE

A deciduous tree, occasionally over 100 ft high in America, with a trunk up to 13 ft in girth; and over 70 ft high in England, forming a rounded head of branches; bark greyish; branchlets glabrous, except when quite young. Leaves three- or five-lobed (the lobes pointed and somewhat triangular, the middle one usually the longest), from 2 to 5 in. wide, and often longer than broad, coarsely and unevenly toothed; upper surface dark green, glabrous, lower one blue-white and more or less downy, especially along the veins. Flowers appearing in March and early April in dense clusters before the leaves, at the joints of the previous year's wood, or on short spurs of still older wood, rich red, each flower on a reddish stalk at first quite short, but lengthening as the flower and fruit develop. Fruits on slender drooping stalks 2 to 3 in. long; wings about ¾ in. long, ¼ in. wide, dark dull red spreading at about 60°.

Native of eastern N. America, and already in cultivation in England by the middle of the seventeenth century. It is a handsome and fairly common tree. When the first edition of this work was published the largest in the country grew at Bagshot Park, Surrey, which measured 80 × 9½ ft (1907); the tallest there now is 65 × 10½ ft (1960). At Westonbirt there is a specimen of 73 × 4¾ ft in Willesley Drive and two others in the collection approaching that size. At Wakehurst Place it is 65 × 6½ ft (1966) and at Kew 52 × 5¾ ft (1960). The red maple is represented in the R.H.S. Gardens, Wisley, by an example 45 ft high, near the lake.

There is a considerable resemblance between this tree and *A. saccharinum*, and they are frequently confused. *A. rubrum*, however, is more compact and of slower growth; the leaves are not so much or so deeply cut, the down beneath them more fluffy, and the fruits are less than half as large. In the United States this maple produces most beautiful colour effects in autumn, the leaves turning scarlet and yellow. In this country it is not so good, but sometimes the leaves change to bright yellow, or dark brownish red, or occasionally red. It should be planted in a moist position.

cv. 'COLUMNARE'.—A pyramidal variety figured in *Garden and Forest*, 1894, p. 65, growing in private grounds at Flushing, New York, which was then 80 ft high. The figure is erroneously described as a form of sugar maple.

var. DRUMMONDII (Hook. & Arn.) Sarg. *A. drummondii* Hook & Arn.—Differs in the downy character of the young shoots, leaf-stalks, and under-surface of the leaves. Fruit and flowers bright scarlet, the former larger than in ordinary *A. rubrum*. Native of Arkansas, Texas, and Louisiana.

cv. 'SANGUINEUM'.—The original tree of this variety grew at the Jardin des Plantes, Paris. Its leaves are glaucous green beneath, somewhat more downy than in the type, the flowers brilliant red. The leaves are said to turn a rich red in the autumn but at Kew, where there is an example 55 ft high, they colour no better than in the type.

cv. 'SCHLESINGERI'.—A clone selected in the United States for its brilliant autumn colour. It was found by Prof. Sargent in the grounds of a Mr Schlesinger and put into commerce in Europe by Späth's nurseries in 1888.

A. PYCNANTHUM K. Koch *A. rubrum* var. *pycnanthum* (K. Koch) Mak.—A rare tree, found in wet places in the mountains of the northern part of the main island of Japan. It is a close ally of the American red maple, differing in the shallowly three-lobed leaves, which are glaucous and glabrous beneath; and in the almost erect fruit-wings. Probably not in cultivation in Britain.

A. RUFINERVE Sieb. & Zucc.

A deciduous tree 30 to 40 ft high, with smooth blue-white young shoots. Leaves 2½ to 5 in. long, three-lobed or obscurely five-lobed, truncate or heart-shaped at the base; terminal lobe triangular, larger than the side ones, margins finely and irregularly toothed; upper surface dark green, glabrous; lower one paler, with reddish down along the veins, conspicuous when the leaf is young, but largely falling away by autumn. Flowers in erect racemes about 3 in. long, each one on a stalk ⅛ to ¼ in. long; the common stalk covered with reddish down. Keys ½ to ¾ in. long, the nutlets at first covered with reddish down, afterwards glabrous; wings diverging at from 90° to 120°.

Native of Japan; introduced for Messrs Veitch's nurseries by Charles Maries about 1879. It is nearly allied to *A. pensylvanicum*, resembling it somewhat in shape of leaf, and in the handsome markings of the branches; but differing in the glaucous young shoots, and in the more conspicuous reddish down beneath the leaves. The glaucous young shoots are also a good field character by which to distinguish *A. rufinerve* from *A. capillipes* (q.v. for further marks of difference) and from *A. grosseri* var. *hersii*. The foliage sometimes dies off a rich crimson.

This attractive maple thrives very well in cultivation. There are specimens of 40 ft high or near at Kew and at Hergest Croft, Heref.; Westonbirt, Glos.; Coles, Privett, Hants; and in the Glasnevin Botanic Garden, Dublin.

f. ALBOLIMBATUM (Hook. f.) Schwer.—A beautiful maple, whose leaves have a broad margin (or sometimes the whole surface) entirely covered with spots of white. It was introduced by Standish of Ascot, some years before the type, and was first exhibited by him in 1869. *Bot. Mag.*, t. 5793. It is propagated by seed and very variable in its leaf-marking. There is a fine group in the Winkworth Arboretum, Godalming, Surrey.

A. SACCHARINUM L.   SILVER MAPLE

A. dasycarpum Ehrh.; *A. eriocarpum* Michx.

A deciduous tree 90 to 120 ft high, with a trunk 9 to 12 ft in girth in America and reaching the lesser of these dimensions under cultivation in Central Europe. The habit is extremely graceful, the tree forming a huge spreading, rounded head with the smaller branches and branchlets pendulous; bark light grey; branchlets glabrous. Leaves five-lobed (the lobes sharp-pointed and irregularly toothed), heart-shaped at the base, 4 to 6 (occasionally 8) in. long, about the same in width, glabrous and light green on the upper surface, white and minutely downy beneath. Flowers greenish yellow, without petals, opening long in advance of the leaves and produced in short dense clusters from the joints of the previous year's wood. Fruit on slender, pendulous stalks 1½ to 2 in. long, the wings round-ended, ½ to ¾ in. wide, spreading at a broad angle.

Native of eastern N. America; introduced in 1725. This maple is the fastest-growing of the American species, and a tree of great beauty in habit and foliage. A little wind will set the long pendulous branches swaying, and by revealing the silvery under-surface of the leaves makes it one of the brightest of tree pictures. In mild seasons it will flower as early as the elm, and, perhaps in consequence, rarely develops seeds freely with us. In N. America the seeds are ripe by May, and falling to the ground, germinate at once and produce several pairs of leaves before autumn. In middle Europe it is more freely planted than in England, and is perhaps the most striking of all deciduous trees in N. Central Germany. Unfortunately, owing to the rather brittle nature of the wood, it is not suitable for use as a street tree, and may suffer damage when in leaf if grown in positions where it is subjected to gusty winds; in open parkland it seems to give less trouble in this respect. The leaves fade into yellow or red before falling.

Few deciduous trees of N. America have fared better in cultivation in the British Isles than the silver maple. The tallest at Kew grows by the Japanese Gate and measures 92 × 10¾ ft (1965), but this is surpassed by a tree at Weston-birt, in Willesley Drive, 100 × 8 ft (1965). There are two specimens about 70 ft high in the Pinetum at the R.H.S. Garden, Wisley.

Raised from seed, this maple produces many slightly different forms, several of which have received distinctive names. The following are the most important:

cv. 'BORN'S GRACIOSA'.—A new variety, raised by the firm of Georg Born, Rosenheim, Germany, and in commerce on the continent. Leaves lobed almost to the middle, the segments narrow, deeply toothed or lobed; said to be a graceful and vigorous tree.

cv. 'CRISPUM'.—A close-growing variety with the leaves deeply lobed and the margins crinkled. Of American origin.

f. LACINIATUM (Carr.) Rehd.—A group name applying generally to forms in which the leaves are divided into deeper and narrower lobes than in the type. It is founded on *A. wagneri laciniatum*, described in *Rev. Hort.*, 1868, p. 387. "*A. wagneri*" is probably an error of *wageri*, from Sir Charles Wager, who introduced the silver maple. The best-known clone referable botanically to this group is 'Wieri' (q.v.).

cv. 'LUTESCENS'.—Leaves orange-yellow when young, later yellowish. Späth's nurseries, before 1883.

cv. 'PENDULUM'.—Branches pendulous. The tree which Nicholson had in mind when publishing this name (*Gard. Chron.*, Vol. 15, 1881) was distributed by Van Volxem's nurseries. It was in cultivation at Kew in his time but was removed many years ago.

cv. 'PYRAMIDALE'.—A form of broadly columnar habit. Späth's nurseries, 1885.

cv. 'WIERI'.—Branches pendulous; leaf-lobes narrow and sharply toothed. Founded in 1873 by D. B. Wier and put into commerce originally by the American firm of Ellwanger and Barry.

A. SACCHARUM Marsh.   SUGAR MAPLE

A. saccharinum Wangenh., not L.

A deciduous tree over 100 ft high in a wild state, with a trunk 9 to 12 ft in girth, forming a shapely rounded head of branches; branchlets glabrous. Leaves palmate, usually five-lobed, heart-shaped at the base, 4 to 6 in. wide; always downy in the axils of the chief veins beneath, but varying in different trees from glabrous to downy in other parts. Flowers without petals, greenish yellow, produced in clusters, each flower on a thread-like, hairy stalk more than 2 in. long. Fruit glabrous, wings 1 in. long, ¾ in. wide.

Native of eastern N. America; introduced, according to Aiton, in 1735, but not many fine specimens are to be found in this country. The most notable are in the Westonbirt collection, the finest there, and perhaps in the country, being in the Park, near the lodge, measuring 80 × 8 ft (1966). Others at Westonbirt are: Willesley Drive 70 × 4¾ ft; Circular Drive 63 × 5¾ and 65 × 4¾ ft (1966). In the grounds of Blenheim Palace, Oxon., there is a tree of 64 × 5¼ ft (1965). In Ireland the best recorded is at Mount Usher, Co. Wicklow, Eire, 62 × 7¼ ft (1966). In leaf, the sugar maple, especially in its more glabrous form, bears some resemblance to the Norway maple; but the sap of the sugar maple is watery, not milky as in the other.

The famous maple sugar of N. America is obtained almost solely from the sap of this tree. The State of Massachusetts alone used to supply more than half a million pounds annually. It is obtained by tapping the trees and collecting the juice, which is afterwards evaporated. As an ornamental tree in England this maple never seems to have been a great success, and although it appears to be quite hardy, does not grow quickly when young. In streets, and isolated in the meadows of New England, it is magnificent, and forms one of the chief elements in the glorious colour effects of autumn there, its leaves dying off into various shades of orange, gold, scarlet, and crimson, each tree, according to Emerson, retaining year after year its particular shades.

var. RUGELII (Pax) Rehd. *A. rugelii* Pax—A large tree with thin, three-lobed leaves; the lobes usually entire, triangular, pointed; lower surface rather glaucous and downy. Found wild from N. Carolina and Georgia to Missouri, being the common form of sugar maple in that region. The lower branches often bear leaves identical with those of the type. Introduced to Kew in 1908.

cv. 'TEMPLE'S UPRIGHT'.—A very striking form with a narrow columnar habit. Once known as *A. saccharum monumentale*.

A. BARBATUM Michx.—This species, known as the southern sugar maple, takes the place of *A. saccharum* in the coastal plain, from Virginia to Texas. It makes a smaller tree with a paler bark; leaves smaller, to 3 in. wide, usually downy beneath; lobes with entire or undulate margins. The name *A. floridanum* Pax has also been used for this species. It is in cultivation at the Glasnevin Botanic Garden, where there is a tree 25 ft high.

A. NIGRUM Michx. f. *A. saccharum* var. *nigrum* (Michx. f.) Britt.—Another close ally of the sugar maple, known as the black maple, and found growing with it in the northern states of eastern and central U.S.A. The marks of distinction are the darker, more furrowed bark, the darker and duller green leaves with rather drooping sides, and the shallower, more rounded toothing of the lobes. According to Sargent it may be distinguished at all seasons by the orange colour of the branchlets.

A. LEUCODERME Small *A. saccharum* var. *leucoderme* (Small) Sarg.—A small shrubby tree, rarely more than 25 ft high, with a pale grey or chalky white bark. It is closely allied to the sugar maple but comes from further south, being commonest, according to Sargent, in the more northern parts of Georgia and Alabama. Leaves three- or five-lobed, 2 to 3½ in. long and wide, the lobes triangular, with usually two large teeth; the base truncate or slightly heart-shaped; lower surface covered with whitish velvety down, especially where the five veins meet the leaf-stalk, which is glabrous. Introduced to Kew in 1902, when seed was received from Prof. Sargent. The specimen now in the collection measures 28 × 1¾ ft (1960). There is one at Westonbirt, Glos., measuring 51 × 2¾ ft (1967).

A. SEMPERVIRENS L.

A. orientale auct., not L.; *A. creticum* L.; *A. heterophyllum* Willd.

A deciduous shrub or small tree, rarely 30 to 35 ft high, most often a bush 8 to 15 ft high; branches usually glabrous, although in some wild Cretan specimens the young twigs are covered with a close down. Leaves of various shapes, sometimes ovate, sometimes three-lobed, ¾ to 2 in. long, the lobes rounded and blunt, but often scarcely apparent, bright green and quite glabrous on both surfaces, margins entire, or with shallow undulations, or occasionally with a few small teeth. Flowers in few-flowered corymbs less than 1 in. long, greenish yellow. Fruit with glabrous wings ½ in, or rather more long, ultimately parallel or at an angle of about 60°. This maple frequently retains its leaves up to Christmas or later.

Native of the E. Mediterranean; introduced in 1752. There was a tree in the garden of Syon House, Brentford, which in its prime was 32 ft high, and nearly 50 ft in spread of branches. The finest known at the present time grows at

Tregothnan in Cornwall, measuring 30 × 4¾ ft (1961). There is a thriving specimen at Grayswood Hill, Surrey, about 18 ft high, with a spreading crown (1967). Usually it is a mere bush a few feet in height, and very slow in growth. It is allied to *A. monspessulanum*, but has no tuft of down in the axils of the leaf-veins. Nicholson regarded *A. heterophyllum* as distinct from this species, but it has not been possible to detect any reliable difference. *A. sempervirens* is a variable species in the shape of its leaves, and Pax differentiates half a dozen forms, founded probably on dried specimens. But as leaves of several shapes are to be found on the same tree, this is probably an over-refinement.

A. SINENSE Pax

A deciduous tree from 12 to 30 ft high; young shoots glabrous. Leaves 3 to 6 in. long and wide, five-lobed, slightly heart-shaped or truncate at the base, rather glaucous beneath; lobes ovate, with long drawn-out points, irregularly and sparsely toothed. Occasionally the leaves are quite glabrous at maturity, but often they have tufts of yellowish hairs in the axils of the veins. Flowers numerous, in panicles 2 to 4 in. long, greenish white. Fruits glabrous, in pendulous panicles; keys 1¼ in. long; wings ⅖ in. wide, the pair forming an angle of about 120°.

var. CONCOLOR Pax—This differs in the wings of the fruit spreading horizontally, and in the leaf being somewhat larger and green beneath.

Native of Central China, and at one time represented in the Coombe Wood nursery by plants of the variety *concolor*, raised from seed introduced in 1901, by Wilson. The leaves are handsome, being of a reddish shade when young, afterwards turning a dark lustrous green. The true species is rare in cultivation and no longer grown at Kew.

A. SPICATUM Lam.   MOUNTAIN MAPLE

A deciduous, tall shrub, or small tree of bushy appearance, occasionally 25 ft high, with a short trunk; young shoots covered with grey down when young. Leaves three-lobed or sometimes five-lobed, 3 to 5 in. long, about the same wide, more or less heart-shaped at the base, coarsely toothed, covered with grey down beneath; lobes long-pointed. Flowers very small, produced in June on slender, erect racemes 3 to 6 in. long, greenish yellow, each flower on a slender stalk about ½ in. long. Fruit with wings about ¼ in. long, ⅜ in. wide, each pair somewhat horse-shoe shaped, glabrous, red.

Native of the E. United States and Canada; introduced by Archibald, Duke of Argyll, in 1750. This maple, handsome in its slender racemes of bright red fruits, and red and yellow autumn tints, is not now common. Its most distinctive characters are its densely flowered, erect, slender racemes, and coarsely toothed, three-lobed leaves. There are two specimens of this maple in

ACER SPICATUM

the Winkworth Arboretum, Godalming, Surrey, the taller 20 ft high (1967). A smaller example is in the Kew collection.

A. SYRIACUM Boiss. & Gaillardot

An evergreen small tree or shrub of bushy, rounded shape; all its parts free from down or hairs. Leaves of hard, leathery texture, varying in shape from ovate to distinctly three-lobed and obovate, entire on old plants, frequently toothed on young or vigorous ones; 1 to 3 in. long and wide; strongly three-veined; stalk ½ to 2 in. long. Flowers in small clusters terminating short side shoots. Wings of fruit ⅜ in. wide, diverging at an angle of about 60° and, including the globose nut, about 1 in. long.

Native of Syria, Lebanon, Palestine, and Cyprus, originally described in 1856. In its hard leathery leaves it suggests *A. orientale*, but that species is not so strictly evergreen and its leaves are smaller. It is quite hardy in this country and very distinct as one of the very few evergreen maples that can be grown outdoors.

A. TARONENSE Hand.-Mazz.

A. laxiflorum var. *longilobum* Rehd.

A small spreading tree with slender, glabrous branches which are greyish brown and somewhat pruinose at first, becoming reddish brown. Leaves broadly ovate in outline, 1¾ to 4 in. long and about as wide, cordate at the base, five-lobed; lobes triangular-ovate, tapered at the apex into tail-like points, the lateral lobes as long as the central one, the two basal lobes small, spreading, dark green above, veins beneath covered with a brown wool; margins densely doubly saw-toothed. Fruiting racemes 2 to 3¼ in. long, soon glabrous; fruits on slender pedicels about ⅕ in. long, with wings spreading at a right-angle or a little wider.

Native of Upper Burma, Yunnan and Szechwan; described in 1924 by the

Austrian botanist and plant explorer Handel-Mazzetti from specimens collected by him in the valley of the river Taron, a tributary of the Irrawaddy. The taxonomic boundaries of this species are unsettled and for this reason the above description is based on Handel-Mazzetti's original account. Taking all the material in the Kew Herbarium that is thought by Rehder, Fang or Murray to belong to *A. taronense* two distinct elements appear to be present. First, there are specimens from Szechwan originally included in *A. laxiflorum* var. *longilobum*. In these the leaf-margin is more or less sharply serrated but the teeth are not aristate; the sinuses are fairly deep; and basal lobes, though small, are discernible. The rest of the material, from farther south and west, has the lateral lobes generally more abruptly acuminate with much shallower obtuse sinuses between them and the marginal teeth bristle-tipped; basal lobes can rarely be seen.

A. taronense bears some resemblance to *A. rufinerve*. But the Szechwan specimens differ from that species in the relatively longer and narrower, more caudate central lobe, more acute teeth, and in having fruits with an ovate nutlet tapering into the wing (in *A. rufinerve* the nutlet is almost spherical and fairly sharply demarcated from the wing). The rest of the material under *A. taronense* is readily distinguished by the leaves being more oblong-ovate in outline and by their bristle-tipped teeth.

A. taronense was introduced to cultivation by seeds collected by Forrest on the Burma–Yunnan border in 1924 (F. 24264, distributed as "*A. rufinerve*"). There is a specimen under this number at Caerhays Castle, Cornwall, measuring 36 × 3 ft (1966).

A. TATARICUM L.

A deciduous shrub of bushy habit, or a small, wide-spreading tree up to 30 ft high; branchlets glabrous. Leaves in adult trees not lobed, or occasionally slightly so; broadly ovate, rounded or slightly heart-shaped at the base, from 2 to 3½ in. long, 1½ to 2½ in. wide; glabrous above, more or less downy on the veins beneath, the margin doubly and irregularly toothed. Flowers in erect panicles 2 to 3 in. long, greenish white, produced in May and June. Fruit with keys ¾ to more than 1 in. long; the wings ¼ in. wide, almost parallel, red in autumn.

Native of S.E. Europe, Asia Minor, etc.; introduced, according to Aiton, in 1759. This interesting maple is very distinct in foliage, the shape of the leaves suggesting *Holodiscus discolor* rather than the typical maple. This, however, applies to the plant in its adult state; young, vigorous trees show a distinct tendency to the palmate three- or five-lobed shape. It bears its fruits quite abundantly, and, being red in autumn, they often give a pleasing effect. The leaves expand early, and die off in yellow, or reddish-brown tints. Early this century there was a tree at Arley Castle, near Bewdley, 30 ft high, planted in 1820.

A. TEGMENTOSUM Maxim.

A deciduous tree 30 ft high; young shoots quite glabrous, pale bright green at first, becoming striped with pale lines later; buds stalked. Leaves of papery texture, mostly three-lobed, sometimes obscurely five-lobed, sometimes not lobed at all and merely ovate, doubly and rather jaggedly toothed, more or less heart-shaped at the base, the short points of the lobes pointing forward; 2½ to 6 in. long, from two-thirds to fully as much wide; dull green above, pale beneath, glabrous on both surfaces; stalk 1½ to 3½ in. long. Flowers in drooping racemes 3 to 4 in. long. Wings of the fruit together with the nutlet ¾ to 1 in. long, glabrous, spreading almost horizontally; each fruit on a slender stalk up to ⅜ in. long.

Native of Manchuria and Korea. According to Nicholson it was cultivated by Lavallée at Segrez in France in the seventies of last century. It has always been rare and there is no record of any large specimen; the best at Kew is 8 ft high. It belongs to the same group as *A. capillipes* and *A. rufinerve*; the latter is easily distinguished by the reddish down along the veins of the leaf beneath. In *A. capillipes* the young shoots and leaves are reddish and the fruit stalks longer.

A. TETRAMERUM Pax

A deciduous tree 20 to 30 ft high, with quite glabrous young shoots. Leaves ovate, coarsely toothed, sometimes lobed, 2 to 3½ in. long, two-thirds as wide, the apex long-pointed, the base tapering, covered with fine down beneath, and with tufts of whitish hairs in the vein-axils. Flowers yellow, the males three or five together in short corymbs, the females in short slender racemes, appearing with the leaves. Fruit glabrous; keys 1 to 1½ in. long; wings ¼ to ½ in. wide, diverging at an angle of about 60°.

A. tetramerum is founded on a specimen collected by Henry in Hupeh but has a wide range in E. Asia from Kansu and Shensi to Upper Burma and S.E. Tibet. Even within a limited area it varies in the shape and indentation of the leaves and in the degree of downiness of the undersides and a number of varieties have been made out of these differences. These are, however, not very clearly demarcated from each other or from the type and it is best to distinguish the various cultivated forms by their original collectors' numbers, where these are still known, rather than by a varietal epithet.

Wilson introduced this species on his first expedition to China in 1901, under W. 680, collected in Hupeh; this is the form originally distributed by Veitch. In 1910 he sent seed from W. Szechwan under W. 4102 and probably most of the trees labelled var. *betulifolium* are from this number. The species is also in cultivation from seed collected by Forrest (F. 30462, 30625, 29396 and 28596), but these forms are rarer than Wilson's in gardens.

A. tetramerum is a very elegant maple, decorative in winter with its reddish to purplish young stems which later become green and striated after the fashion of the snake-bark maples. It is, however, quite distinct from these botanically and is more closely allied to *A. argutum*, being, like it, a dioecious species.

There are a number of good specimens at Westonbirt. The largest are in Clay Island and Victory Glade, both on two stems and about 40 ft high. Forrest's 30462 is represented by two small trees in Mitchell Drive and others in Silkwood. A tree at Caerhays Castle, Cornwall, probably raised from W. 4102, is 32 ft high, on several stems.

A. STACHYOPHYLLUM Hiern—A small tree, closely related to the preceding, native of the E. Himalaya, Upper Burma, and parts of W. and S.W.
China. Leaves ovate, with unlobed doubly serrate margins and a long, curving
tip, downy beneath. Fruits larger than in *A. tetramerum* and the racemes often
branched; in cultivation from Kingdon Ward 10965 and Forrest 11252. This
species is rare in gardens but is quite hardy in woodland at Borde Hill, Sussex,
and is represented at Edinburgh by four specimens, the tallest 25 ft high. In
his Field Notes, Kingdon Ward records that in the Zayul region of the E. Himalaya 'drinking cups are made from its wood—the most expensive kind'.

The boundary between this species and *A. tetramerum* appears to be rather
uncertain.

A. TRAUTVETTERI Medwed.   RED-BUD MAPLE

A tree up to 50 ft in height, and 6 ft in girth of trunk; branchlets glabrous,
dark red at the fall of the leaf. Leaves deeply five-lobed, 4 to 8 in. wide, about
three-fourths as long, base heart-shaped; dark lustrous green and glabrous
above, pale and slightly glaucous beneath, with tufts of down in the axils of the
chief veins, especially at the base where they meet the leaf-stalk; margins
coarsely and angularly toothed. Flowers following the leaves, and produced in
glabrous, erect corymbs. Fruits downy on the nutlets when young, becoming
glabrous; wings 1¾ to 2 in. long, ½ to ¾ in. wide, parallel, or almost connivent,
sometimes overlapping. *Bot. Mag.*, t. 6697.

Native of the Caucasus, Asiatic Turkey and Persia; introduced to Van
Volxem's nursery in 1866. It is a handsome-foliaged tree, very striking in spring
with its brilliant crimson bud-scales and again in late summer when the large
fruit-wings take on a reddish hue. It has been much confused with *A. velutinum*,
but is distinguished by the wings of the fruit not spreading and by the marginal
teeth not pointing forwards. See also *A. heldreichii*.

A. TRIFLORUM Komar.

A deciduous tree 20 to 45 ft high in a wild state; young shoots slender, freely
covered with minute warts, soon without down. Leaves trifoliolate; leaflets
ovate to oval or oblong-lanceolate, entire or with a few very large teeth, tapered
towards both ends, the side ones scarcely stalked; 1½ to 3½ in. long, ½ to 1¼ in.
wide; upper surface, midrib and main veins beneath, as well as the leaf-stalk
(which is 1 to 2½ in. long), all more or less covered with pale hairs, especially
when young. Flowers in clusters of threes terminating short, usually two-leaved
shoots. Wings of the fruit 1 to 1¼ in. long, ⅜ to ⅝ in. wide, spreading at an angle
of about 120°; nutlets thick, ¼ to ⅜ in. long, covered with pale hairs; fruit-stalk
hairy, about ⅝ in. long.

Native of Manchuria and Korea; introduced in 1923. It is nearly related to
A. nikoense, especially in its hairy nutlets, but that species has much larger leaflets
and the wings of the fruit diverge at a much smaller angle. It is rare in cultivation and grows slowly, needing, perhaps, greater summer heat than our
climate can offer. There is a good example in the Chandlers Ford nursery which,

Mr Hillier tells us, 'gives consistently excellent autumn colour, being one of the best trees for this purpose in the nursery'; another, growing on chalk at Winchester, collapsed and died in the summer of 1966. There are two small trees in the Mitchell Drive at Westonbirt whose leaves die off brilliant crimson and another by Down Gate 35 ft high. The young shoots recall *A. griseum* but the mature bark is ash-brown, loose, and vertically fissured.

A. TRUNCATUM Bunge

A small, deciduous tree up to 25 ft in height; branchlets glabrous, often tinged with purple when young. Leaves five- occasionally seven-lobed, $2\frac{1}{2}$ to $4\frac{1}{2}$ in. wide, less in length, dark green above, paler below; glabrous on both surfaces; truncate or somewhat heart-shaped at the base; the lobes triangular; the two basal ones out-spreading, the three terminal ones often furnished with two large teeth; leaf-stalk containing milky juice. Flowers $\frac{1}{3}$ to $\frac{1}{2}$ in. across, greenish yellow, each on a slender stalk $\frac{1}{2}$ in. long, borne in erect, branching corymbs 3 in. wide. Fruits glabrous; wings $1\frac{1}{4}$ to $1\frac{1}{2}$ in. long, $\frac{1}{3}$ to $\frac{1}{2}$ in. wide, about half as long again as the nutlet, the pair forming an angle of about 90°.

Native of N. China, whence seed collected in the autumn of 1881 were sent by Dr Bretschneider to Kew, and germinated in the spring of the following year. It is allied to *A. mono*, but differs in the truncate base of the leaf, and in the larger flowers. It grows well and is quite hardy at Kew. In the maple collection at Birr Castle, Co. Offaly, Eire, it is 40 × 3 ft (1966).

A. TSCHONOSKII Maxim.

A small, deciduous tree 15 to 20 ft high, or a shrub; young shoots glabrous; winter buds stalked. Leaves 2 to 4 in. long and wide, deeply five-lobed, heart-shaped at the base, margins sharply double-toothed, bright green and glabrous above, paler beneath, with reddish hairs along the main veins when young, reduced to their axils when mature; lobes triangular, long-pointed; leaf-stalk half as long as the blade. Flowers on glabrous, short stalks, produced along with the leaves, eight to ten, in racemes. Fruits pale brown; keys 1 to $1\frac{1}{4}$ in. long; wings $\frac{2}{5}$ in. wide, incurved, and spreading at a wide angle.

Native of Japan, where it grows in sub-alpine forests in the northern part of the main island and in Hokkaido. The dying leaves turn a beautiful canary yellow. It is allied to *A. micranthum* (q.v. for the marks of difference). Introduced in 1902.

var. RUBRIPES Komar.—A native of N. Korea and N. China, differing from the type in the longer, more tapered lobes, the reddish leaf-stalks and young growth, and the more spreading wings of the fruit.

A. UKURUNDUENSE Trautv. & Mey.
A. caudatum var. *ukurunduense* (Trautv. & Mey.) Rehd.

A small tree or large shrub with downy branchlets. Leaves five-lobed (more rarely seven-lobed), 3 to 5 in. long and as much wide, cordate at the base, covered beneath with a yellowish down; lobes tapered at the apex, ovate or triangular, margins sharply toothed and incised. Flowers in upright, slightly compound, hairy racemes. Wings of fruit almost upright; keys slightly downy or glabrous, about ¾ in. long.

Native of the mountains of Japan and of N.E. Asia; date of introduction uncertain, but later than 1881. It is closely related to the east American *A. spicatum*, of which Maximowicz made it a variety; but in that species the leaves are usually only three-lobed.

A. MULTISERRATUM Maxim.   *A. caudatum* var. *multiserratum* (Maxim.) Rehd.; *A. erosum* Pax—A closely allied species and a common tree in China from Kansu to Yunnan; the chief point of distinction is that the leaves are nearly glabrous beneath at maturity. Introduced by Wilson in 1907, but rare in gardens.

These two maples are closely allied to a Himalayan species which Rehder refers to *A. caudatum* Wall. Unfortunately this is a very confused name and has been abandoned in this work in favour of *A. papilio* (q.v.).

A. NIPPONICUM Hara   *A. parviflorum* Franch. & Sav., not Ehrh.; *A. brevilobum* Hort. Hesse.—A rare species in the wild state, native of Japan, allied to *A. ukurunduense*. Leaves 4 to 6 in. long, slightly more wide, shallowly five-lobed, sharply double-toothed (in its ally the toothing is coarser and more irregular); veins beneath covered with a rusty down. Distributed by Hesse's nurseries as *A. brevilobum*. It is in cultivation at Dawyck, Peebl.

A. VELUTINUM Boiss.

A. insigne Boiss.

A large deciduous tree with glabrous branchlets. Leaves three- or five-lobed, 3 to 6 in. wide and the same or rather more long, truncate or slightly heart-shaped at the base, undersides covered with a dense, pale brown, velvety down; margins coarsely toothed, the teeth often rounded or blunt. Flowers in erect corymbose panicles, 3 to 4 in. long, appearing towards the end of May. Nutlets and wings of fruit downy, wings diverging at an angle of 90° to 120°.

The tree described is the typical form of *A. velutinum* and the one that is commonest both in the wild and in cultivation. The species does, however, vary in the degree of downiness of leaf and fruit. It was a form quite glabrous in these parts that Boissier described as *A. insigne*, and which is now distinguished as f. GLABRESCENS (Boiss. & Buhse) Rehd. Boissier had described *A. velutinum* in an earlier work, and this name has priority.

A native of the Caucasus and the mountains of N. Persia; introduced to cultivation by Van Volxem, along with *A. trautvetteri* and the variety described below. At Kew, where the tallest specimen is 20 ft high, *A. velutinum* is one of the latest of all trees to break into growth.

var. VANVOLXEMII (Mast.) Rehd.   *A. vanvolxemii* Mast.—Leaves larger than in the species, up to 8 in. across, somewhat glaucous beneath and downy only on the veins. Native of the Caucasus, where it was discovered and introduced to cultivation by Van Volxem, who sent it to Kew about 1873. There is a specimen at Kew 52 × 5½ ft (1960) and two at Westonbirt, one in Broad Drive, the other in Willesley Drive, measuring 71 × 6¾ ft (1967) and 66 × 6¾ ft (1965) respectively. This variety is also represented in the Edinburgh and Glasnevin Botanic Gardens.

A. WILSONII Rehd.

A deciduous tree probably 30 to 40 ft high; young shoots glabrous, slender, yellowish green. Leaves three-lobed; the lobes ovate, slender-pointed, directed forwards, reaching half-way to the base, mostly entire on adult trees, often more or less toothed on young ones; 2 to 4 in. long, about the same wide; glabrous, bright green above, dull beneath, with minute tufts of whitish down in the vein-axils; stalk 1 to 2 in. long, not milky. Flowers very small, greenish white, appearing with the young leaves in May in drooping panicles 2 to 3 in. long; flower-stalks slender, glabrous. Fruits brownish yellow, the wings spreading horizontally, 1 in. long, ⅜ in. wide, nutlet small, egg-shaped.

Native of China; discovered by Henry in Yunnan and again in 1900 by Wilson in Hupeh; introduced by the latter in 1907 when collecting for the Arnold Arboretum, under W. 233. A tree at Kew raised from this batch of seed is now 25 ft high. It grows slowly on chalk in Messrs Hilliers' nurseries at Winchester and is 15 ft high there. There is a good example at Horsewell House, Kingsbridge, and the species is also represented in the Westonbirt collection. It is far from common, however, but an elegant maple with slender branches and rich green leaves with deep, narrow lobes, attractively tinted when young.

A. × ZOESCHENSE Pax
A. neglectum Lange

A deciduous tree, which will probably ultimately attain a height of 50 ft and upwards; young branchlets minutely downy. Leaves 3 to 5½ in. wide, about three-fourths as long, five-lobed, heart-shaped at the base, dark green and shining above, paler and downy beneath, becoming glabrous later except for tufts in the axils of the veins; lobes ovate, with a long apex. Flowers in erect, corymbose panicles, 2 to 4 in. long. Fruits downy; keys 1¼ in. long; wings ⅓ in. wide, almost horizontal.

A maple of garden origin with an obvious affinity to *A. campestre*, especially in the five-lobed leaf having milky sap in the stalk and in the downy horizontally-spreading keys. The leaves, however, are larger, and the lobes more angular. It is probably a hybrid between that species and either *A. cappadocicum* or *A. lobelii*. There are two specimens at Kew, planted in 1871, one 55 × 6½ ft and the other slightly smaller (1965); at Westonbirt, Glos., planted 1929, it is 38 ft high; and at the Glasnevin Botanic Garden, Dublin, 45 × 4¾ ft (1966).

ACRADENIA RUTACEAE

The species described below is the sole member of the genus, which is endemic to Tasmania. The generic name refers to the glands at the summit of the carpels.

A. FRANKLINIAE Kippist

An evergreen shrub of bushy rounded habit up to 10 or 12 ft high in a wild state, sometimes with the habit of a small tree; young shoots thickly covered with minute grey down. Leaves opposite, of stiffish texture, trifoliolate; mainstalk $\frac{1}{8}$ to $\frac{1}{3}$ in. long. The three leaflets are stalkless, oblong to narrowly oval, rounded and shallowly toothed at the apex, tapered and entire towards the base; 1 to $2\frac{3}{4}$ in. long, $\frac{3}{8}$ to $\frac{5}{8}$ in. wide; dark green and slightly downy above, quite glabrous and paler bright green beneath with dark oil-glands freely scattered over the surface. Flowers white, $\frac{3}{8}$ to $\frac{1}{2}$ in. wide, borne in May in terminal corymbose clusters $1\frac{1}{2}$ to 2 in. across. Petals five, ovate, downy; sepals five, downy, $\frac{1}{12}$ in. long; stamens ten, glabrous; disk of ten glands, alternating with the stamens; ovary of five felted carpels united at the lower half, each with a gland at the top. *Bot. Mag.*, t. 9187.

Native of W. Tasmania, where it was discovered by Dr Milligan on the banks of the Franklin River, near Macquarie Harbour, in April 1842. It has since been found on the Gordon and Pieman rivers, which are of the same drainage area. Introduced to Kew in 1845. It just misses being hardy there and is grown in the Temperate House, but thrived for many years on a wall at Wakehurst Place, Sussex. At Rowallane, Co. Down, there are two specimens against a north-west to south-west wall: one is a vigorous plant 11 ft high, which flowers well most years and was undamaged in the winter of 1962–3; another, in a draughty corner, was damaged in that winter but has since recovered.

The specific name commemorates Lady Franklin, whose husband, Sir John, was Governor of Tasmania in 1842. They were travelling with Dr Milligan when the shrub was first discovered. The leaves have a slightly acrid but not unpleasant odour when crushed.

ACTINIDIA ACTINIDIACEAE

A genus of vigorous climbers inhabiting N. India, China, and Japan. They have simple, alternate leaves. Most, if not all, the species are polygamo-dioecious, i.e. they are functionally dioecious even though some of the flowers are hermaphrodite. The fruit is a fleshy berry. Given a good soil they are easily cultivated, and can be grown in the various situations suitable for vigorous climbers, such as on walls, pergolas, on rough poles, or, better than all for the more vigorous ones, on a worn-out tree, if such can be given up to them, which they can cover with tangled growth. All the species can be propagated by cuttings of moderately ripened wood placed in gentle heat. The genus has been reviewed by Hui-Lin Li in *Journ. Arnold Arboretum*, Vol. 33 (1952).

A. ARGUTA (Sieb. & Zucc.) Miq.
Trochostigma arguta Sieb. & Zucc.

An exceptionally vigorous climber, reaching in its native haunts the tops of large trees. Leaves dark lustrous green, 3 to 5 in. long, sometimes nearly as wide; broadly ovate or ovate-oblong, edged with unequal bristle-like teeth, the base rounded or sometimes heart-shaped; almost glabrous except for down on the veins and in their axils; stalk rose-coloured, sometimes bristly, $1\frac{1}{2}$ to 3 in. long. Flowers fragrant, produced in the leaf-axils, usually in clusters of three; each flower $\frac{3}{4}$ in. across, its stalk slender, and $\frac{1}{2}$ to $\frac{3}{4}$ in. long; sepals green, ovate-oblong, blunt; petals orbicular, white tinged with green, very concave and in-curved, giving the flower a rather globular shape; stamens numerous, with dark purple anthers; the ovary has a short, stout style at the top of which about twenty stigmas radiate like the spokes of a wheel. Fruit an oblong, many-seeded, fleshy, greenish-yellow berry, nearly 1 in. long, with an insipid flavour, but eaten by the Japanese. Pith of young branches chambered. *Bot. Mag.*, t. 7497 as *A. polygama*.

Native of China, Japan, and the Amur region. One of the strongest growing of the actinidias, this is also one of the hardiest. It flowers very well out-of-doors in numerous gardens in the south and west, and is hardy at Kew, flowering there in June and July. Although hermaphrodite as well as unisexual flowers are to be found on most plants, this species is effectively dioecious, a pollinator as well as a female plant being necessary if fruit is to be obtained.

var. CORDIFOLIA Dunn—Leaves ovate with a conspicuously heart-shaped base, more hairy than in the type; leaf-stalk purple. This, as well as the type, is sometimes grown in gardens as *A. volubilis*.

A. arguta is a very variable species. A. GIRALDII Diels, which is founded on Chinese specimens, differs from the type in its broader leaves and in other minor characters, and is distinct enough as seen in cultivation. But Li considers that it is part of the normal variation of *A. arguta*, into which he merges it in syn-onymy.

A. RUFA (Sieb. & Zucc.) Planch. *A. arguta* var. *rufa* (Sieb. & Zucc.) Maxim.—Native of Japan and Korea, differing from the above in having the inflorescence and sepals covered with rusty-brown hairs.

A. CALLOSA Lindl.

A deciduous climbing shrub up to 25 or 30 ft high; young shoots glabrous but becoming conspicuously marked with elongated lenticels; pith chambered. Leaves oval, ovate or oblong, finely and regularly toothed, with a short slender point and a rounded or wedge-shaped base; 3 to 5 in. long, $1\frac{1}{2}$ to $2\frac{1}{2}$ in. wide;

glabrous on both surfaces; stalk 1 to 2 in. long. Flowers white or creamy yellow, ½ to ⅘ in. wide, fragrant, solitary to as many as five together, borne on glabrous slender stalks; anthers yellow; ovary downy. Fruit egg-shaped to oblong, ¾ to 1 in. long, green tinged with red, spotted.

Native of N. India, described and named as long ago as 1836 by Lindley and found by such early collectors as Griffiths in Bhutan, Wallich in Nepal, and Hooker in Sikkim; also of W. China, where it has been collected by Henry and Forrest. S. T. Dunn, a leading authority on the genus, observes that it may be distinguished by its yellow anthers, downy ovary, and spotted fruits.

A number of species closely related to *A. callosa* have been described, but so far as is known, only one has been introduced. This is A. VENOSA Rehd., which differs from that species in the rusty down that covers the sepals and inflorescence, and the prominently net-veined leaves.

A. CHINENSIS Planch.

A functionally dioecious climbing shrub of vigorous growth; sterile branchets densely covered with shaggy reddish hairs; flowering shoots more downy.

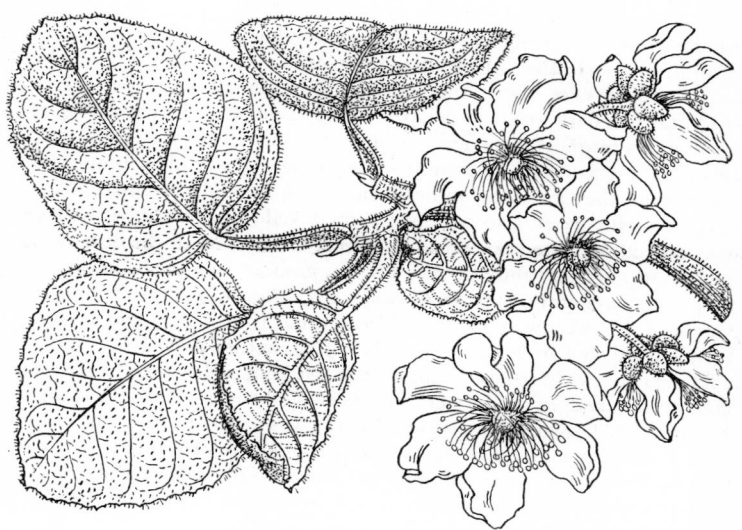

ACTINIDIA CHINENSIS

Leaves of the sterile shoots heart-shaped, pointed, from 5 to 8 in. long and from 4 to 7 in. wide; margins set with stiff hairs; upper surface dark green, slightly hairy; lower surface densely clothed with greyish tufted hairs, the midrib, veins, and stalk having larger reddish hairs like those of the young shoots. On the flowering shoots the leaves are shorter and proportionately broader, 2 to 4 in. long, 3 to 5 in. wide, somewhat orbicular, but deeply notched at the top and bottom. Flowers $1\frac{1}{2}$ in. across, at first white, then buff-yellow; produced on short branches from the year-old wood; calyx with five roundish woolly lobes; petals obovate; stamens very numerous. Fruit of the size and shape of a walnut, covered more or less with reddish-brown hairs, and of a very agreeable flavour. *Bot. Mag.*, t. 8538.

This remarkably handsome climber was first brought to the notice of Europeans by Robert Fortune in 1847, when he was travelling in China on behalf of the Royal Horticultural Society. It was later seen by Maries in Japan, but did not reach cultivation until 1900, when seeds were sent from China by Wilson, who had collected it in Hupeh. It is quite hardy and is succeeding well in England where it has borne fruit frequently. Although hermaphrodite forms may exist, fruit is only reliably produced if plants of the two sexes are grown close together. The 'chinese gooseberries' sometimes to be seen in greengrocers' shops are raised from named clones of *A. chinensis*, mainly in New Zealand. Some of these are available in the trade in this country. These fruits are also known as 'Kiwi berries'.

A. CORIACEA Dunn

A unisexual deciduous climber 20 to 25 ft high; young shoots glabrous, turning dark brown, freely spotted with small, whitish lenticels the second year; pith solid. Leaves leathery, lanceolate to oblanceolate, slenderly pointed at both ends, the margins set with rather remote, sharp, small teeth; 3 to $5\frac{1}{2}$ in. long, $\frac{3}{4}$ to $1\frac{3}{4}$ in. wide; dark green above, pale beneath, quite glabrous; stalk $\frac{3}{4}$ to $1\frac{1}{4}$ in. long. Flowers fragrant, produced in May and June singly or in pairs from the leaf-axils of the young wood or from separate short leafless branches of the previous year; they are deep, rather lurid red, $\frac{1}{2}$ in. wide; petals concave, $\frac{1}{4}$ in. long; sepals pale green, also concave; anthers yellow with reddish stalks; styles numerous, red, arranged cartwheel fashion at the summit of the downy balloon-shaped ovary. Fruit a white-dotted, brown, globose or egg-shaped berry, $\frac{3}{4}$ in. wide, juicy, containing many small seeds. *Bot. Mag.*, t. 9140—male plant.

Native of W. Szechwan, China; Wilson found it in Mupin and on Mt. Omei in 1904; introduced by him in 1908 (No. 932), and shown at Chelsea in 1921. The flowers are richly coloured but do not last long. It has proved rather tender in cultivation, and is no longer grown at Wakehurst Place, Sussex, nor at Rowallane, Co. Down—gardens in which it was stated in previous editions to have thrived. The cultivated plants were originally distributed as "*A. henryi*" and may still be grown under that name. The male plant figured in the *Botanical Magazine* has rather larger flowers and as many as four in a cluster.

A. HENRYI (Maxim.) Dunn
A. callosa var. *henryi* Maxim.

A tall climber with slightly ribbed young shoots, covered with stout, curly, reddish bristles; the year-old wood glabrous; pith chambered. Leaves ovate or ovate-oblong, heart-shaped or rounded at the base, taper-pointed, minutely toothed, 3 to 5 in. long, $1\frac{1}{2}$ to $2\frac{1}{2}$ in. wide; glaucous beneath, with a little down on the midrib and veins. Leaf-stalk ¾ to 1½ in. long, bristly when young. Flowers white, nearly ½ in. diameter, produced in the leaf-axils in short, rounded racemes, the stout main-stalk reddish bristly, the slender individual flower-stalks downy, ¼ to ½ in. long. Fruits cylindrical, ¾ to 1 in. long, ⅓ to ½ in. wide.

Native of Yunnan, in mountain forests at 5,000 to 6,000 ft; discovered by Henry; introduced by Wilson for the Arnold Arboretum, and sent thence to Kew in 1910.

A. KOLOMIKTA (Maxim. & Rupr.) Maxim.

A slender climber, growing 20 or more ft high. Leaves ovate-oblong, heart-shaped or sometimes rounded at the base, 3 to 6 in. long, the largest 3 to 4 in. wide; only slightly bristly above and beneath when quite young, the margins set with teeth of unequal size. The foliage is purplish when young, and later in the season is usually more or less variegated, sometimes the apex, sometimes half the leaf, and occasionally the whole leaf being white or pink. Flowers fragrant, produced one to three together, each ½ in. across; petals white, anthers yellow, stigmas sessile. Fruit not beaked. The chief merit of this climber is in its curious and often very striking leaf-colouring. It is perhaps, the weakest grower of all the actinidias, and supports 6 ft and upwards high are needed. The pith is brown and chambered (lamellate). Native of Manchuria, China and Japan, flowering in June; illustrated in *Bot. Mag.*, t. 9093. Its veins beneath and the leaf-stalk are slightly downy, but not so conspicuously bristly as in *A. polygama* (q.v.). There is a large and thriving specimen on a wall at Wisley in the R.H.S. Garden. The leaf-colouring is not fully developed on young plants and even adult plants may not show it if they are grown in too much shade.

A. MELANANDRA Franch.

A tall deciduous climber, with glabrous young shoots and chambered (lamellate) pith. Leaves oblong or narrowly oval, tapered or rounded at the base, slenderly often abruptly pointed, toothed; 2½ to 4 in. long, 1 to 1¾ in. wide; glabrous above, glaucous beneath, with tufts of brown down in the vein-axils; stalk 1 to 1½ in. long. Flowers unisexual, white, ¾ to 1 in. wide, females solitary, males three to seven in a short raceme; anthers purple. Fruit egg-shaped, 1 in. or rather more long, reddish brown covered with bloom. Blossoms in June.

Native of Hupeh and Szechwan, China; discovered in the latter province by the French missionary, Père Farges; introduced by Wilson in 1910. It is well distinguished by the glaucous under-surface of the leaves, which are glabrous except for the axil-tufts. It is quite hardy at Kew and has borne fruit there.

A. POLYGAMA (Sieb. & Zucc.) Maxim.   SILVER VINE
Trochostigma polygama Sieb. & Zucc.

A slender climber, forming in a wild state a large tangle of entwined stems 15 to 20 ft high. Leaves elliptical or ovate-oblong, pointed, 3 to 5 in. long, bristly toothed on the margin, and bristly on the veins, usually wedge-shaped, sometimes somewhat heart-shaped at the base; stalks bristly. Flowers fragrant, usually in threes (sometimes single or in pairs), ¾ in. diameter, white. Fruit beaked, 1½ in. long, ½ in. broad in the middle, narrowing at either end, canary yellow, translucent, soft and juicy, with a disagreeable flavour.

Native of Central Japan, and plentiful in the mountains there. As in *A. kolomikta*, sometimes the entire leaf, sometimes its terminal half, is white or yellowish, but it is a stronger grower. It is not, however, a tall climber like *A. arguta* and *A. chinensis*, but may be grown as a sort of thicket, if support be given at first. It is confused often with *A. kolomikta*, but differs in the usually tapered or rounded (instead of cordate) base of the leaf, in its white, solid (not chambered) pith, and in having the stigma on a short thick style. The plant, like several other species, has an extraordinary attraction for cats.

A. TETRAMERA Maxim.—Native of China, closely allied to the preceding and to *A. kolomikta*. It is distinguished by its narrowly ovate leaves, 1 to 1½ in. long, and by its flowers having four sepals and petals instead of the usual five.

A. PURPUREA Rehd.

A deciduous climbing shrub up to 25 ft high; young shoots mostly glabrous, without lenticels; pith chambered. Leaves oval, oblong or roundish, pointed, rounded at the base, toothed; 3 to 5 in. long; dull green and glabrous above, green and usually more or less downy on the midrib beneath; stalk 1 to 1½ in. long. Flowers white, ⅝ in. wide, the females solitary or in threes, the males mostly five or seven in a cluster. Fruit about 1 in. long, egg-shaped to oblong, purple. Blossoms in June.

Native of W. Szechwan and Yunnan, China; found by Henry, Wilson, and Forrest; introduced by Wilson in 1908. It is most closely related to *A. arguta*, which has larger, brighter green, more conspicuously toothed leaves and a greenish-yellow fruit.

ADENANDRA   RUTACEAE

A small genus of evergreen shrubs which, like the allied *Diosma*, *Coleonema*, etc. (not treated in this work), is endemic to S. Africa.

A. UNIFLORA (L.) Willd.
Diosma uniflora L.

A dwarf evergreen shrub 1 to 2 ft high, its slender erect stems being thickly clothed with leaves, six to ten to the inch. Leaves linear, pointed, tapered to the short stalk, not toothed; ⅓ to ¾ in. long, ⅛ in. or less wide; dark glossy green and smooth above, pale and dotted with translucent glands beneath; margins hairy, sometimes decurved. Flowers the size of half a crown, produced singly at the end of the shoots, several of which occur through branching near the summit; petals five, spreading, roundish-obovate, pure white with a streak of red down the middle of each; calyx of five sepals of the same size and shape as the leaves; their purplish-red colour adds to the beauty of the flower by showing in the gaps between the petals. Stamens ten; five fertile, five abortive. *Bot. Mag.*, t. 273.

Native of South Africa; originally introduced to Kew by Francis Masson in 1775. It is only hardy in the very mildest parts of the country; such as the rectory garden at Ludgvan, near Penzance, where it succeeded admirably and was made one of the features of the flower show at Truro in April or May. At the present time it thrives at Tresco Abbey in the Isles of Scilly and is also grown outdoors at Trengwainton, near Penzance. Except in such very favoured localities this delightful shrub would almost certainly succumb to winter cold or wet, and should, if attempted, be placed at the foot of a sheltered sunny wall.

ADENOCARPUS   LEGUMINOSAE

A genus of about ten species of deciduous or partly evergreen shrubs or small trees; leaves trifoliolate, small; flowers yellow, in terminal racemes; pod glandular, a character to which the generic name refers. The species are wild in the Mediterranean region and on the mountains of North Africa.

A. ANAGYRIFOLIUS Coss. & Balansa

A shrub of dense habit 3 to 6 ft high and wide; young shoots erect, slightly ribbed, glabrous or nearly so. Leaves trifoliolate, crowded, glaucous, main-stalk $\frac{1}{2}$ to $1\frac{1}{4}$ in. long, leaflets of equal size, sessile, oval to roundish or obovate, $\frac{1}{2}$ to $1\frac{1}{4}$ in. long, about two-thirds as wide, entire but frequently apiculate, glabrous. Flowers golden yellow, pea-shaped, $\frac{1}{2}$ in. long, densely set on quite erect, slender, terminal racemes 3 to 7 in. long by $1\frac{1}{2}$ in. wide; stalks and calyx silky hairy. Pods $1\frac{1}{2}$ to 2 in. long, $\frac{1}{4}$ in. wide, freely and conspicuously warted, carrying up to nine seeds.

Native of Morocco, on the slopes of the Main Atlas Range at 3,000–9,000 ft; introduced by E. K. Balls in 1936. It is a notable and very attractive shrub and was exhibited in flower by the late Sir Frederick Stern at Vincent Square on 21st June 1938 and given an Award of Merit. It grew for many years in his garden at Highdown but was almost exterminated in the winter of 1962–3, only one plant now remaining.

A. DECORTICANS Boiss.

A deciduous shrub of rather gaunt habit, sending out long horizontal branches, and reaching 8 to 10 ft in height in this country. Leaves trifoliolate, very crowded,

1 in. or less long; stalk very slender and downy, ¼ to ½ in. long. Leaflets ⅛ to ¾ in. in length, 1/16 in. wide, the margins usually rolled inwards. Flowers golden yellow, about the size and shape of common gorse, produced on the upper side of the branches in short, erect racemes, 1½ to 2½ in. long. Seed-pods 1½ to 2 in. long, ⅓ in. wide, pale, covered with conspicuous viscid glands. *Bot. Mag.*, n.s., t. 48.

Native of Spain, and only really hardy in the milder parts of Great Britain. At Kew it needs the protection of a wall, but has been grown in the open no

ADENOCARPUS DECORTICANS

farther from London than Grayswood Hill near Haslemere, where shrubs 6 to 8 ft high were laden in May and early June with golden blossom from end to end of their branches, making most gorgeous pictures. Like so many of its race, this shrub is not long-lived, and care should be taken to sow a few seeds occasionally (it produces them in great abundance), to renew the stock if needed. It should have the sunniest position available, and is suitable for a hot bank in gardens where it can thrive in the open. For colder localities a place on a south wall is necessary.

A. COMPLICATUS (L.) Gren. & Godr. *Spartium complicatum* L.—If understood in a wide sense, this is a very variable species, divided into local races, some of which have been given specific or varietal rank. A deciduous shrub, low and densely branched, more rarely erect; young branchlets downy or hairy, later glabrous and, in some forms, whitish. Leaves usually trifoliolate, with lanceolate or oblong-ovate leaflets usually folded lengthways, glabrous above, covered beneath with short appressed hairs. Flowers yellow, in terminal racemes of varying length; calyx glandular in the typical form but eglandular in some races, with unequal lips. Of wide distribution from Madeira through N. Africa and the Mediterranean region to the Near East; also reported from the region of the Italian lakes. *A. divaricatus* (L'Hérit.) Sweet and *A. parvifolius* DC. are synonyms of the type; the above description also includes *A. commutatus* DC. and *A. intermedius* DC.

A. HISPANICA (Lam.) DC.—Flowers usually larger than in *A. telonensis* or *A. complicatus* and longer stalked, borne in dense racemes. A native of Spain and Portugal.

A. TELONENSIS (Loisel.) Robert *Cytisus telonensis* Loisel.; *A. grandiflorus* Boiss.—Flowers larger than in *A. complicatus*, one to four together in short terminal racemes or heads; lower lip of calyx deeply toothed. A small, dense bush, native of the W. Mediterranean. According to Loudon it was introduced in 1800.

A. VISCOSUS (Willd.) Webb & Berth.

Genista viscosa Willd.; *A. frankenioides* Chois.; *A. anagyrus* Spreng.

A semi-evergreen shrub said to grow to 3 ft or so high in the wild state. Leaves trifoliolate, grey-green, sessile and set very densely on the shoots, hairy; leaflets linear-oblong. Flowers orange-yellow, in dense terminal racemes; calyx glandular and downy, the median tooth of the lower lip longer than the laterals. Pods densely glandular.

Native of the Canary Islands, mainly on Teneriffe. A closely allied species is A. FOLIOLOSUS (Ait.) DC. (*Cytisus foliolosus* Ait.), which is a native of the Grand Canary. It is a taller shrub, to about 10 ft high, distinguished botanically by having the calyx hairy but not glandular and the three teeth of its lower lip of equal length; the pods are only glandular when young.

A plant at Brodick in the Isle of Arran, labelled *A. foliolosus*, has not been examined in flower but appears to be *A. viscosus*. Planted in 1959, it has reached the remarkable stature of 14 ft high and 16 ft across (1966) and flowers and fruits well in most years.

AESCULUS HORSE-CHESTNUT, BUCKEYE
HIPPOCASTANACEAE

Deciduous trees and large shrubs found in all three northern continents. Leaves opposite, composed normally of five or seven leaflets (occasionally three or nine) radiating from the end of a long, slender stalk. Flowers borne in often large panicles at the end of the current season's growth; petals four or five. Fruits sometimes prickly, sometimes smooth, containing one or two large seeds. Several of the following species are commonly known under the generic name of PAVIA, the distinguishing characters being smooth fruits and four petals, as contrasted with the prickly fruits and five petals of true *Aesculus*. As in neither case are the characters invariably coexistent, the name *Pavia* has been dropped.

Few groups of woody plants are at once so well marked and so handsome as this. They all thrive well in the southern half of England, and most are hardy enough to succeed in any part of the country. All of them like a good deep soil, well drained but moist, and are easy to cultivate and transplant. For the multiplication of the species seeds are decidedly the best, but the hybrids and varieties of garden origin have to be propagated by budding. The common horse-chestnut is commonly used as a stock for all species, even such a small one as *A. pavia*, the result of which is an ungainly union of stock and scion and frequent ill-health. It may be used for *A.* × *carnea* (although that comes largely true from seed), and for its own numerous varieties, but for the other and smaller hybrids *A. flava* or *A. glabra* should be used as a stock. It should be mentioned that the buds selected are not those in the axils of the leaves, but the small, crowded buds at the base of the shoot nearest the old wood, which in ordinary circumstances remain dormant. Seeds of all the species should be planted as soon as they fall, and it is necessary to cover them only with about their own depth of soil. Kept dry during the winter, they lose much or sometimes all of their vitality.

In addition to the hybrids described below many others of natural origin in N. America have been identified, such as *A.* × *mississippiensis* Sarg. and *A.* × *bushii* Schneid. These hybrids are very confusing and difficult to distinguish and of little importance horticulturally.

A. ARGUTA Buckl.

A small tree or more commonly a low shrub, described by Sargent as having numerous small stems often made prostrate in autumn by the weight of the abundant fruits; shoots slender, downy. Leaves of seven or nine leaflets, which are elliptical to narrowly obovate, 3 to 6 in. long and often doubly toothed, usually more or less downy beneath at first. Flowers numerous in pyramidal panicles up to 6 or 8 in. long and half as wide at the base; petals pale yellow, nearly equal, oblong-obovate, each narrowed to a slender claw, downy outside; stamens usually seven, their stalks hairy; calyx bell-shaped, downy, pale yellow-green; ovary hairy. Fruit subglobose, one- to three-seeded; seeds chestnut-brown, 1 in. wide.

Native of E. Texas and an attractive hardy shrub, closely akin to *A. glabra*, but distinct in its dwarf habit and narrower longer-pointed leaflets. Discovered before 1860; introduced 1909. There is a specimen of 32 × 1½ ft in the Edinburgh Botanic Garden (1968).

A. CALIFORNICA (Spach) Nutt.

Calothyrsus californica Spach; *Pavia californica* (Spach) Hartw.

A tree with a short trunk and a low, spreading, rounded head of branches, considerably more in diameter than it is in height, or a large shrub; bark smooth; winter buds resinous. Leaves among the smallest in the genus, consisting usually of five (sometimes seven) narrowly oblong or oval, pointed, shallowly round-toothed, stalked leaflets, 2 to 4 in. long, downy when quite young, of a pale greyish green. Flowers fragrant, borne in dense, erect, cylindrical, downy panicles up to 6 or 8 in. long and 2 to 3 in. wide, white or faintly tinged with rose, the stamens protruding ½ in. beyond the petals. Fruit somewhat fig-shaped, swollen on one side, 2 to 3 in. long, ending in a point, the surface rough but not spiny. *Bot. Mag.*, t. 5077.

Native of California, where it is occasionally found from 30 to 40 ft high, but more often as a bush 10 to 15 ft high. It is perfectly hardy as a small tree at Kew,

AESCULUS CALIFORNICA

and thrives admirably there. The tree is very distinct on account of its habit, and its abundant foliage with a rather metallic hue. It flowers from June to August, and often shows the curious habit of developing a single flower at the top of the panicle first, which has formed a small fruit whilst the flowers immediately below it are still in bud. Introduced by W. Lobb about 1850, it first flowered in Messrs Veitch's Exeter nursery in 1858. There is an example at Kew by the Economic House; when it bears a full crop of flowers (and it does not do so every year) it is very striking owing to the contrast between the pure white or light rose panicles and the deep green foliage.

A. × CARNEA Hayne   RED HORSE-CHESTNUT

A tree of rounded form, 30 to 50 ft high in this country, but 60 to 80 ft high on the continent; winter buds slightly resinous. Leaves composed of five or seven leaflets, which are very like those of the common horse-chestnut, but smaller, darker green, and usually with a very short stalk. Flowers deep red on a panicle 6 to 8 in. high, 4 in. diameter; stamens slightly protruding. Fruit globose, slightly prickly, 1½ in. diameter.

Of the origin of the tree nothing certain is known. There is little doubt, however, that it is a hybrid between the common horse-chestnut and *A. pavia*, having the habit and foliage of the former, and the colour of the flowers and glandular-edged petals of the latter. It probably originated as a chance hybrid made by insects quite early in the nineteenth century, and had attained a considerable size before its distinctness was noticed. It was first distributed around 1820; the parent tree is thought to have grown in Germany and its original offspring were probably the products of budding or grafting.

The hybrid has proved to be of great scientific interest. About 1896 some half a dozen plants were raised from seed at Kew, which proved to be no different from ordinary *A. × carnea*, or from each other, except in the depth of colour of the flower. As was remarked in previous editions of this work, it is unusual for the progeny of a hybrid to resemble the parent so closely, but the reason is now understood and the original observations made at Kew have been confirmed by further experiment on a larger scale. The original *A. × carnea* must have been a diploid, with forty chromosomes, as in the parents. It was probably rather sterile, as is usually the case with hybrids between such distantly related species as *A. hippocastanum* and *A. pavia*, and would not have bred true even if fertile seed had been produced. But at some stage in the history of the clone (perhaps on the parent tree itself), spontaneous doubling of the chromosomes must have taken place, thus giving to each chromosome a matching partner and permitting the normal pairing that takes place in the flowering plants as a preliminary to reproduction. This phenomenon, of which many instances have been recorded, not only confers fertility on a previously sterile or partly sterile hybrid, but permits it to breed more or less true. Another well-known example is *Primula × kewensis*.

If the doubling of the chromosomes took place on the original parent tree— a possibility suggested above—then only part of it would have been tetraploid (i.e. with eighty chromosomes instead of the normal forty), and the scions would have given rise to diploid or tetraploid plants according to the branch from which they were taken. This might explain reports from the mid-nineteenth century that *A. × carnea* did *not* breed true, whereas the tree at Kew did so.

The trunk of this tree frequently becomes diseased when over 1 ft in diameter, and covered with ugly eruptions which ultimately decay and disintegrate into a sort of powder. According to Massee, there is no parasitic organism, animal or fungoid, present to cause this disease, which appears to be solely due to the abnormal development and ultimate rupture and death of the cells.

cv. 'BRIOTII'.—Raised from seed at Trianon in 1858; it is practically identical with the type, except that it has larger and more finely coloured panicles. Other named varieties are:

cv. 'Aureo-marginata'—Leaves margined yellow.

cv. 'Foliis Marginatis'.—A variegated form with a dark green border to the leaf, then an irregular band of yellow, the centre being pale green.

A garden variety with pendulous branches has also been described, but this character is common in some degree to most old trees.

A. chinensis Bunge Chinese Horse-chestnut

A tree 80 to 90 ft high; young shoots glabrous or minutely downy; winter buds resinous. Leaves composed of sometimes five, usually seven, leaflets, which are narrow-oblong or obovate, 5 to 8 in. long, about one-third as much wide, tapering to a fine point, shallowly and evenly toothed, the stalk $\frac{1}{6}$ to $\frac{5}{8}$ in. long. Panicle 8 to 14 in. long, and 2 to 4 in. wide at the base, narrowing gradually to the top, the basal one-fifth naked. Flowers on glabrous stalks, white, $\frac{1}{2}$ to $\frac{3}{4}$ in. across; petals four; stamens rather longer than the petals. Fruit truncate or slightly indented at the top, subglobose, 2 in. in diameter, rough, but not spiny.

Native of N. China, and although known to botanists for over seventy years was only introduced in 1912. It was collected near Pekin by Purdom, and from seeds sent by him to the Arnold Arboretum plants were raised and distributed. The tallest of these at Kew is now 33 × 1¾ ft (1966) and no longer suffers from late spring frosts, as it did when young. For many years A. turbinata was grown on the continent as A. chinensis, and even figured under that name, but the true plant is absolutely different.

A. wilsonii Rehd.—This tree was introduced by Wilson from Szechwan and Hupeh, China, in 1908. It was first considered to be A. chinensis, to which indeed it is very closely allied. It may be distinguished from A. chinensis as follows: Leaflets longer stalked, not generally so tapered at the base, but rounded or even slightly heart-shaped there; more downy at first beneath (but in both species becoming glabrous); veins more numerous (up to twenty-two pairs), forming at their junction with the midrib a more obtuse angle than in A. chinensis. Flower-stalks more downy. Fruit ovoid to pear-shaped, with a mucro at the apex, and, according to Rehder, with the husk only half as thick as in A. chinensis. Seed larger, with the scar (hilum) covering about one-third (one-half in A. chinensis). A. wilsonii has a more southern distribution. Racemes up to 16 in. long.

It flowered at Caerhays in June 1934. The tree there, raised from W. 200, is 48 ft high, with 48 ft diameter of spread (1966).

These two chestnuts, with A. indica, belong to a distinct section of the genus (Calothyrsus), but A. indica has broader panicles with less crowded, more erect branches, larger flowers, and broader petals.

A. + dallimorei Sealy

This interesting hybrid was brought to the notice of Kew by the late William Dallimore. He had observed that a tree of A. flava, growing near his home at Bidborough, Kent, bore a branch which in leaf and flower resembled the common horse-chestnut; the tree was grafted, and the branch in question had arisen from the union of stock and scion. It was described by J. R. Sealy in *Journ. R.H.S.*, Vol. 71, pp. 420–3 (Sept. 1956).

The leaves of *A. dallimorei* are of about the size of those of the common horse-chestnut, and resemble them further in having a rusty-red indumentum at the base of the leaflets and along the midribs of the undersides. In general shape the leaflets resemble those of neither parent, though the long tapering points recall *A. flava*, as does the white indumentum that covers the surface of the undersides *between* the main veins. The inflorescence resembles that of *A. hippocastanum* in general appearance. The flowers are intermediate, having four petals in two dissimilar pairs, the lower pair shorter but broader than the upper (in the horse-chestnut the petals are five in number, all of the same size; in *A. flava* the petals, although similar to those of *A. dallimorei* in number and shape, are more erect). As to colour, the majority of the flowers are white with red markings; but some suggest *A. flava* in having primrose-yellow or greenish-yellow petals with deeper markings at the base.

Sealy considers that *A. dallimorei* is most probably a graft-hybrid (periclinal chimaera) between *A. hippocastanum* and *A. flava*. And indeed this would be certain if the stock used was of the former species. There is, however, the possibility that the seedling stock onto which the scion of *A. flava* had been grafted was a sexual hybrid between the two species, in which case the anomalous branch could be explained as an outgrowth from the hybrid stock. Such a cross has, however, never been recorded, and, in Sealy's opinion, union of the tissues of stock and scion is the most likely explanation.

The original tree is in the care of the Kent County Council and its offspring are likely to make attractive ornamental trees, although a long time will elapse before they become generally available.

A. FLAVA Soland.*   SWEET OR YELLOW BUCKEYE

A. octandra Marsh.; *A. lutea* Wangenh.

A tree sometimes 90 ft high in N. America, with dark brown bark and non-resinous winter buds. Leaflets five or seven to each leaf, obovate or oval, 3 to 7 in. long, 1 to 3 in. wide, finely toothed, downy on the veins above and much more so over the whole under-surface; the down is frequently reddish

---

* The name *A. flava*, long used for this species, was superseded by *A. octandra* Marshall because the latter, published in 1785, antedated *A. flava*, which was cited from Aiton, *Hortus Kewensis*, 1789. Now although this work was not published until 1789, it is known to have been upwards of twenty years in preparation. The botanical work was by Jonas Dryander, who succeeded Daniel Solander as Banks' librarian when Solander died in 1782, and Dryander is known to have used MSS prepared by Solander. Now Mr B. L. Burtt, of the Royal Botanic Garden, Edinburgh, has drawn our attention to the fact that the name *A. flava* Solander was actually published in 1778 in a catalogue of the trees and shrubs growing in the Edinburgh Botanic Garden that year (*Cat. Arb. & Frut. Hort. Edin. Cres.* 1778, p. 3). The Catalogue seems to have been prepared by Dr John Hope, who was at that time Regius Keeper of the Edinburgh

brown. Flowers in an erect panicle up to 7 in. long, 2 to 3 in. wide, yellow; petals four; stamens shorter than and hidden by the petals. Fruit roundish oblique, 2 to 2½ in. long, smooth, carrying usually two seeds. It flowers in May and June.

Native of the United States from Pennsylvania to Tennessee and N. Georgia, and west into Ohio and Illinois; introduced in 1764. It thrives very well in the south of England, making a handsome round-headed tree, but attains greater dimensions on the continent. The tallest known when the first edition of this work was published grew at Syon House, Middlesex, and was nearing 70 ft in height. This tree no longer exists, and the tallest specimen known today is one at Kew, which measures 85 × 4 ft (1960). Others of good size are: Abbey Gardens, Bury St. Edmunds, 65 × 6½ ft (1962), and Much Hadham Rectory, Herts., 63 × 8¼ ft (1964).

f. VESTITA (Sarg.) Fern.—Leaflets beneath and young branchlets downy. Found wild in various localities.

f. VIRGINICA (Sarg.) Fern.—Flowers red, pink or cream. Found wild in W. Virginia.

A. × HYBRIDA DC.   *A. octandra* var. *hybrida* (DC.) Sarg.; *A. flava* var. *purpurascens* A. Gray; *A. octandra* var. *purpurascens* (A. Gray) Bean—A group of hybrids between *A. flava* and *A. pavia*, usually to be distinguished from the former by their bi-coloured or reddish flowers, which show the influence of the second parent in having glands as well as hairs on the margins of the petals. They are more tree-like than the hybrids of the *A.* × *mutabilis* group. De Candolle's type was taken from a tree growing in the Botanic Garden at Montpelier but the cross seems to have occurred several times in gardens and the seedlings and their progeny distributed under various names. The trees known as "*A. versicolor*" and "*A. lyonii*" probably belonged to this group but are little known today. *A. flava* var. *purpurascens* A. Gray is a wild form of the cross, with purplish-red flowers, found in the Alleghenies. Specimens of *A.* × *hybrida* measured recently are: Arley Castle, Worcs., 60 × 6 ft and Denman College, Berks., 58 × 6½ ft (both 1965).

A. GLABRA Willd.   OHIO BUCKEYE

A tree usually under 30 ft high, but sometimes up to 70 ft, with a trunk over 6 ft in girth; bark of the trunk rough, and much fissured. Leaves usually composed of five leaflets, which are 3 to 6 in. long, about one-third as wide; obovate or oval, with a long, tapering point, sharply toothed; downy when young, but becoming glabrous with age, except along the midrib and chief veins. Flowers

Botanic Garden, and he evidently received the name and diagnosis from Solander, to whom he may well have submitted material for identification. It is very pleasing to record here the restoration of a name given by one of the first botanists to work on the Kew collections, and, moreover, the man 'who reduced our garden plants to order and laid the foundations of the *Hortus Kewensis* of his friend Aiton' as his contemporary Sir James Edward Smith said (*Select. Corrsp. Linn. & Other Nat.* II. 3: 1821).

about 1 in. long, greenish yellow, in erect panicles 4 to 7 in. long, 2 to 3 in. wide; petals four; stamens ⅓ in. longer than the petals. Fruit 1 to 2 in. long, broadly obovoid, distinguished from other American buckeyes by prickles resembling those of common horse-chestnut, but much less prominent.

Native of the S.E. and Central United States. This tree is of handsome shape and foliage, but is the least attractive of the genus in its flowers. Often confused with *A. flava*, it is readily distinguished by its rougher bark, the less downy leaves, the longer outstanding stamens, and the prickly surfaced fruit. It flowers at the end of May and in early June. It grows well at Kew, where the largest specimen is now 56 × 6¾ ft (1967).

var. LEUCODERMIS Sarg.—Native of southern Missouri and Arkansas; best distinguished by its smooth, near-white bark, which only becomes scaly on old trees. Leaves glabrous.

var. MONTICOLA Sarg.—Differs in having six or seven leaflets and a more rounded fruit; found wild in Oklahoma.

f. PALLIDA (Willd.) Schelle *A. pallida* Willd.—Leaflets pubescent at maturity. Introduced to Britain in 1812. It is found wild in the Middle West.

var. SARGENTII Rehd. var. *arguta* Robins, in part; var. *buckleyi* Sarg.—A form with six or seven leaflets, also distinct in their longer, drawn out points and their doubly toothed margins. It does not reach so far eastward as the typical *A. glabra* and is found in Ohio and westward to Oklahoma. This variety has been confused by botanists with *A. arguta*.

A. GLAUCESCENS Sarg.

This is another usually shrubby species from the S.E. United States, also in cultivation, 6 to 10 ft high, but occasionally a small tree up to 30 ft high. Young shoots downy at first only; leaflets five, up to 8½ in. long, 2½ to 3½ in. wide, bright green and downy along the midrib above, rather glaucous and with axil-tufts of hairs beneath, leaf-stalk glabrous. Flowers each over 1 in. long, yellow; calyx bell-shaped, glandular on the margins; petals downy especially on the margins; stamens usually shorter than the petals. This species is closely akin to *A. flava*, the well-known 'sweet buckeye', which has also yellow flowers, but differs in its smaller, more downy leaves and leaf-stalks, and in the much larger fruits.

A. HIPPOCASTANUM L.   HORSE-CHESTNUT

A tree reaching over 100 ft in height, with a rounded, spreading head as much in diameter, and a trunk 15 ft or more in girth; winter buds very resinous. Leaves composed of five to seven leaflets, which are obovate, from 5 to 12 in. long, 2 to 5 in. wide, irregularly toothed, the terminal one the largest; the upper surface is glabrous, the lower one has patches of brown hairs in the axils of the veins, and short hairs thinly scattered over it. Panicles up to 12 in, high, and 4 in. through. Flowers with four or five petals, white with a patch of colour at the base, which is at first yellow, then red; stamens rather longer than the petals. Fruit spiny,

2½ in. across, containing one, sometimes two, of the well-known lustrous brown nuts.

The horse-chestnut is at once the best-known and the most beautiful of flowering trees of the largest size. The stately, spreading form of fully grown trees is appropriately accompanied by noble proportions and handsome shape of leaf, and by large, striking flower-clusters. An English park can afford no finer sight than a group of horse-chestnuts towards the end of May, when every branchlet carries its erect cone of white flowers. The history of the horse-chestnut is interesting. It reached Western Europe by way of Constantinople in 1576, when seeds were sent to the botanist Clusius at Vienna, and it had spread westwards to France and England early in the seventeenth century. For more than two hundred and fifty years its real native country was unknown. N. India was long regarded as its most probable home, and Loudon, as late as 1837, suggested N. America. Its real wild habitat is now definitely established as being much nearer home; namely, in the mountainous, uninhabited wilds of Northern Greece and Albania, where several observers have found it to be undoubtedly indigenous.

The economic value of the horse-chestnut is not great. The timber is soft and lacking in strength, and is chiefly employed in the manufacture of kitchen utensils, toys, and other articles for which durability is not of great importance. The nuts are abundantly produced, and are eaten by some animals, notably deer. I have noticed the deer in Bushey Park, at the time the nuts are falling, race eagerly for them as they drop to the ground. Loudon and others suggest various uses for them, but so far as I can learn there is no systematic demand for them. They have such an extraordinary fascination for boys in furnishing the material for the game of 'conkers' (conquerors), that the value of the species as a communal tree is in some districts seriously diminished by their efforts with sticks and stones to bring down the nuts before they naturally fall.

cv. 'BAUMANNII'.—A form with double flowers. According to A. N. Baumann, it was noticed by him as a sport on a tree of the ordinary type growing in the garden of a Mons. Duval, near Geneva, during the years 1819 to 1822. He sent grafts to his father's famous nursery at Bollwiller, in Alsace, whence it spread into cultivation. Its flowers last longer than those of the type, and as no nuts are formed the tree escapes the danger of injury just alluded to. For public places it is strongly recommended, and is the best of the garden varieties. It has also been called *A. h. flore pleno*.

cv. 'CRISPA'.—A tree of compact, rather pyramidal habit, with short, broad leaflets. Listed by Booth's nursery, Hamburg, 1838.

cv. 'DIGITATA'.—Leaflets short, narrow, often reduced to three, of linear shape; the main-stalk frequently very markedly winged. An old variety, no longer at Kew, said to have originated in France (var. *pumila* Dipp.).

cv. 'HENKELII'.—Leaflets smaller than in the type, with shreddy margins. The plant at Kew was bought from Henkel's nurseries in 1904. The *A. h. incisa* put into commerce by James Booth of Hamburg before 1838 was probably similar.

f. LACINIATA (Jacques) Schelle—Leaflets very narrow, deeply incised. There are several forms of this nature, of independent origin. The clonal name

'Laciniata' belongs to one found near Angers around 1844 and put into commerce by Leroy. Another was in commerce in Loudon's time as *A. h. aspleniifolia*. The form grown at Kew is an extraordinary curiosity of little beauty, whose leaflets are sometimes nine in number, but often reduced to the mere midrib with jagged remains of blade attached; it was received from Simon-Louis Frères in 1900.

cv. 'MEMMINGERI'.—Leaves pale greenish or greyish, yellow when they first expand. Of no merit. First described in 1855.

cv. 'PYRAMIDALIS'.—Branches growing upwards at an angle of 45° to the main stem. This would probably be useful as a street tree, and avoid to a large extent the drastic pruning so often practised to keep the ordinary form within bounds. There are two trees of this habit at Kew, apparently of the same clone. One was received from Späth in 1895 and the other from Transon in 1896.

cv. 'UMBRACULIFERA'.—A form with a low, dense, rounded head of branches. In cultivation since 1884, but origin unknown. A fine example grew earlier in this century in the nursery of Messrs Simon-Louis near Metz.

A form which breaks into leaf and flower ten to fourteen days in advance of the ordinary one was represented at Kew earlier this century by two large trees which no longer exist. The name under which they were listed—*A. h. praecox*—appears in the catalogue of James Booth and Sons, Hamburg, in 1838. There is, it should be added, still one tree at Kew, part of a row of thirty, that breaks into leaf a week or ten days earlier than the others, and also flowers earlier, but its origin is unknown.

Forms with white- or yellow-variegated leaves were in commerce in this country as early as 1775, but are only to be seen in old collections. One with yellow-blotched leaves was described in previous editions as 'a variety to be avoided'.

A. INDICA (Camb.) Hook.　　INDIAN HORSE-CHESTNUT

Pavia indica Wall. ex Camb.　　[PLATE 9]

A tree attaining a height of over 100 ft in N. India, often with a short, enormously thick trunk, the bark in old specimens peeling off in long strips; winter buds resinous. Leaves composed of usually seven leaflets, which are glabrous on both surfaces, shining dark green above; obovate to lanceolate, the central ones much the largest, sometimes 12 in. long, and 4 in. wide; toothed. Panicles erect, cylindrical, up to 12 or even 16 in. long, and 4 or 5 in. wide. Flowers 1 in. long, white; petals four, the upper and longer pair with a blotch of yellow and red at the base, the shorter pair flushed with pale rose; stamens standing out ¾ in. beyond the petals. Fruit rough, but not spiny, 2 to 3 in. long. *Bot. Mag.*, t. 5117.

Native of the N.W. Himalaya. One of the most magnificent of all temperate trees, and equalling the common horse-chestnut in beauty, it is remarkable that this species is still so little known in English gardens and parks. Although the young growths may be cut by late frosts in low-lying districts, it is quite winter-hardy and grows well in any good garden soil, including chalky ones. It does,

AESCULUS INDICA

however, appreciate generous moisture at the root, and will be slow to get away if planted in a dryish soil and exposed to full sun. At Kew there are two trees by the restaurant, planted 1888, the taller 50 × 7¼ ft (1966); they have fruited for many decades past and one of their seedlings, growing on chalk at Highdown near Worthing, is 40 ft high and in turn fruits well. Some good trees on record are: Wakehurst Place, Sussex, 56 × 7¼ ft (1966); Westonbirt, Glos.,

51 × 4¾ ft (1964); Tortworth, Glos., *pl.* 1890, 59 × 6¼ and 52 × 6¼ ft (1964). At Glendoick in E. Perthshire, there are two trees, about thirty-five years old, growing in 'a very cold and windy situation, which are about 28 ft high' (E. H. M. and P. Cox, *Modern Trees*, 1961).

A. indica was introduced in 1851 by Colonel Henry Bunbury and a seedling planted by his relative Sir Charles Bunbury at Barton in Suffolk had attained a height of 66 ft by 1904. Another plant there is known to have flowered in 1858, when only seven years old.

This chestnut flowers in June and July, and is, therefore, at least one month later than the common one—a great point in its favour. The unfolding leaves, too, are attractively tinted. It is best propagated from seed, which, however, quickly loses its vitality and, if not sown at once, should be over-wintered in moist soil or peat.

cv. 'SYDNEY PEARCE'.—A selected form, very free-flowering, with flowers more richly coloured than in the common run of seedlings and arranged in a denser spike. The parent tree grows at Kew, where it was planted around 1935. Scions have been distributed, but it will be many years before it is freely available. It was given an Award of Merit in 1967 (*Journ. R.H.S.*, Vol. 93, April 1968, pp. 182–3 and fig. 74).

A. × MUTABILIS (Spach) Schelle
Pavia mutabilis Spach

A group of hybrids thought to have originated from the crossing of *A. discolor* var. *mollis* (q.v. under *A. pavia*) and *A. neglecta* or its var. *georgiana*. The type was a garden tree, first described in 1834. The following forms of the cross are in commerce:

cv. 'HARBISONII'.—Undersides of leaves hairy when young and somewhat glaucous. Flowers bright red, in panicles 6 to 8 in. long, borne in May and June. A shrub of little garden value in the British Isles. It arose at the Arnold Arboretum among plants raised from wild seed of *A. neglecta* var. *georgiana*.

cv. 'INDUTA'.—This hybrid arose in Hesse's nurseries, Germany, and was originally known as *A. rosea nana*. Leaves hairy beneath; flowers pink, with yellow markings, borne in May and June more abundantly than in most of the American buckeyes. It makes a large shrub in time, and was given an Award of Merit when shown by the late Sir Henry Price, Wakehurst Place, Sussex, in 1959.

A. NEGLECTA Lindl.

The tree from which Lindley described this species in 1826 was imported from France as "*A. ohioensis*", an old name for *A. glabra*. Similar trees were in cultivation in Europe at that time and came to be known by Lindley's name. The origin of the seed from which the plant was raised is uncertain. But *A. neglecta* is very near in its botanical characters to a buckeye that grows wild in the south-eastern part of the United States, described by Sargent as *A. georgiana*. He found an even better match for it in some trees growing on the Du Pont estates near Delaware, said to have been raised from seed collected in the wild.

These he accepted as typical *A. neglecta* and placed *A. georgiana* under it as a variety—var. GEORGIANA (Sarg.) Sarg. *A. neglecta* is nearest to *A. flava*, but is of smaller stature and is distinguished by its downy (but not glandular) calyx and flower-stalks. In Lindley's type the flowers were yellow streaked with red. In the var. *georgiana* they are yellow or red.

The theory has been put forward that *A. neglecta* is a hybrid of *A. flava* but, if so, it is difficult to see what the other parent could be. *A. sylvatica* Bartram, the second parent suggested by Hardin in *Rhodora*, Vol. 59, pp. 185–203, is scarcely more than a bare name.

cv. 'ERYTHROBLASTOS'.—Unfolding leaves a vivid shrimp-pink; of German origin, first distributed by Späth's nurseries, reaching cultivation in this country a few years before 1935. 'The leaves start to unfold about the end of April, and are the most beautiful creamy pink colour, with bright carmine petioles. The plant is quite hardy but as late frosts will cut the young foliage it should be planted where the morning sun cannot get at it'. (R. C. H. Jenkinson in *The New Flora and Sylva*, Vol. 8, p. 59.) It was given an Award of Merit in 1962.

A. OCTANDRA *see* A. FLAVA

A. PARVIFLORA Walt.

A. macrostachya Michx.; *Pavia macrostachya* (Michx.) Loisel.

A shrub 8 to 15 ft high, usually broader than it is high, consisting of a crowd of slender stems, and spreading by means of sucker growths at the base. Rarely it forms a single trunk, and thus becomes a small tree. Leaves usually consisting of five, but sometimes seven, leaflets; each leaflet from 3 to 9 in. long, and 1¼ to 4 in. wide, obovate, tapering towards both ends, shallowly round-toothed, covered densely beneath with greyish down. Panicles cylindrical, erect, 8 to 12 in. long, 4 in. wide from the tips of the stamens. Flowers white; petals normally four, ½ in. long, the stamens thread-like and pinkish white, standing out fully an inch beyond them; anthers red. Fruit glabrous. *Bot. Mag.*, t. 2118.

Native of the S.E. United States; introduced by John Fraser in 1785. There are few shrubs about which more could be said in favour than this. It flowers freely in late July and August, at a time when few shrubs are in flower. It is of neat yet graceful habit, and it has a hardy, vigorous constitution. No better plant could be recommended as a lawn shrub, especially for places that are visited in August—such as many pleasure resorts. It rarely ripens seed in this country—only during such a hot, sunny season as that of 1911—but can be propagated by division. There is a specimen in the R.H.S. Garden at Wisley, near the Restaurant, about 10 ft high and 15 ft across (1967).

A. PAVIA L.   RED BUCKEYE

A shrub 8 to 12 ft or more high, with smooth branches and non-resinous buds. Leaves composed of five leaflets, which are 2 to 5 in. long, lanceolate, obovate or narrowly oblong, slightly downy beneath, especially in the vein-axils; irregularly, sharply, often doubly toothed. Flowers in panicles 3 to 6 in. long; each flower 1½ in. long, with the four petals glandular at the margins, which scarcely expand at all; stamens about the length of the petals. Fruit smooth. Blossoms in early June.

Native of the southern United States; introduced, according to Aiton, in 1711. It is one of the rarest of the genus in gardens. The plants once met with under the name were usually forms of *A.* × *hybrida*, and even these are rarely seen today. It was usually grafted as a standard on some other species, when it formed a round-headed small tree, with its lower branches pendulous. But the plants at present cultivated at Kew do not show this character. The flowers of the red buckeye are richly coloured, but owing to the petals keeping closed, do not make so fine a display as they otherwise would.

cv. 'ATROSANGUINEA'.—Flowers darker red than in the type.

cv. 'HUMILIS'.—A low, or even prostrate shrub, flowers red, in small panicles. In commerce by 1826 and figured as *A. humilis* Lindl. in *Bot. Reg.*, t. 1018. It is sometimes grafted as a standard or half-standard. Such, perhaps, were the trees once known as "*Pavia pendula*".

A. DISCOLOR Pursh.—This species is closely related to *A. pavia* but differs in the white down covering the leaf beneath. However, it is possible that the two species pass imperceptibly one into the other. The var. MOLLIS (Raf.) Sarg. (*A. austrina* Small) is more representative of the species than is typical *A. discolor*, which has red and yellow flowers and is rare; in var. *mollis*, which is commoner in the wild, they are red.

A. × PLANTIERENSIS André

A hybrid raised in the nursery of Messrs Simon-Louis Frères, at Plantières, near Metz, its parents no doubt *A. hippocastanum* and *A.* × *carnea*. The seed came from the former, so that it is (if the generally accepted parentage of *A.* × *carnea* be correct) three-fourths common horse-chestnut and one part the red buckeye (*A. pavia*). It shows the characters of both its parents in the leaf; the leaflets being stalkless, as in *A. hippocastanum*, yet showing the more strongly ridged and uneven surface of *A.* × *carnea*. In shape and size the panicle is like that of *A. hippocastanum*, but the whole flower is suffused with a charming shade of soft pink, which it inherits from the other parent. In habit and general appearance it is intermediate. It has flowered at Kew for many years past, and I consider it a very beautiful and desirable acquisition. It has developed no fruit at Kew, and I understand from Mr Jouin, of Plantières, that it does not bear seed in his nursery. For public places this is an advantage. It is still true (1966) that it has produced no fruit at Kew; the fact that it is a triploid explains this sterility.

A. SPLENDENS Sarg.

A deciduous shrub 9 to 12 ft high; young shoots slender and at first very finely downy. Leaves of five leaflets which are lanceolate or oblanceolate, slender-pointed, toothed; 4 to 6 in. long, 2 to 3½ in. wide; covered with a down beneath that is at first greyish, then rust-coloured, their stalks about ¼ in. long. Flowers 1½ in. long borne in pyramidal panicles 6 to 10 in. high, opening in May. Calyx tubular, bright red, ⅓ in. wide; petals scarlet. Fruit roundish to obovoid; seeds 1¼ in. wide, chestnut-brown.

Native of the S.E. United States. It is one of the smooth-fruited species and is related to *A. pavia*, which differs in the glabrous or nearly glabrous under-surface of the leaves. Sargent observes of *A. splendens* that its flowers are prob-ably the handsomest in the genus. At Kew this shrub has proved rather disap-pointing, its flowers being of a lacklustre scarlet, in narrow panicles.

A. TURBINATA Blume   JAPANESE HORSE-CHESTNUT

A tree 80 to 100 ft high in Japan, and said to have a trunk 20 ft in girth; winter buds very resinous. Leaves like those of *A. hippocastanum*, consisting of five to seven stalkless leaflets, but more regularly toothed and tapering more gradually at the apex. On the small plants at Kew they are obovate, and as much as 16 in. long and 6 in. wide, the whole leaf with its stalk 27 in. long. Panicles erect, 4 to 8 in. high, with a stalk half as long. Flowers ¾ in. across, creamy white, produced two or three weeks later than those of common horse-chestnut. Fruit without spines, but rough; broadly pear-shaped, 2 in. wide near the top, tapering to a short, warted stalk. *Bot. Mag.*, t. 8713.

Native of Japan up to 5,500 ft on the main island and in Hokkaido (Yezo). It is very similar in general appearance to *A. hippocastanum*, but hitherto has grown much more slowly. It is distinguishable by the different toothing of the leaf, still more so, of course, by the *pavia*-like fruits. Elwes says that the timber of this tree, although lacking strength, often shows a wavy figure, and is used in Japan for house fittings and articles of domestic use. As a tree for gardens and parks, it would seem to be inferior to the common horse-chestnut in all respects except in size of leaf. In that respect it is certainly the most striking of all. Young trees are curiously stiff and sturdy in habit.

The following specimens have been recorded: Westonbirt Arboretum, 70 × 5¼ and 65 × 3¾ ft (1967); Westonbirt House, *pl.* 1883, 55 × 6¾ ft (1967); Kew, *pl.* 1887, 47 × 5½ ft (1967). In Eire there are two sizeable trees at Headfort, Co. Meath, the larger 47 × 6¼ ft (1966).

AGAVE   AGAVACEAE

A genus of about 275 species (many differentiated by very minor charac-ters), ranging from the south-western part of the United States to S. America, but with its centre in Mexico, where more than one hundred species have been described. The leaves form a rosette springing from a root-stock or short trunk, and are commonly thick and leathery; in many species they are armed with formidable teeth and terminate with a horny spine; in length they vary from a mere 6 in. to the 7 ft or more attained in species like *A. atrovirens*. After a period of years—never so long as the one hundred suggested by the popular name "Century Plant"—an inflorescence grows out from the heart of the rosette and, nourished by water and nutrients stored in the leaves, develops with remarkable rapidity. In the larger species it attains, in the course of a few weeks, the dimensions of a good-sized tree, heights of 30 ft being not uncommon. The rosette that bears the inflorescence invariably dies after flowering, but in many species off-sets continue the life of the plant. The inflorescence is most commonly branched, but in a minority of species it is a simple spike.

Several species, notably *A. fourcrioides* and *A. sisalana*, are grown in the warmer parts of the world for their valuable fibre. The Mexican national drink *pulque* is fermented from the sap of several species, *A. atrovirens* being the most prized. The agaves played a vital role in the prehispanic civilisations of Central America, providing both paper and fibre as well as *pulque*.

Two species are or have been grown outdoors in the British Isles and proved fairly hardy.

A. PARRYI Engelm.

A stemless succulent plant, consisting mainly of a rosette of thick fleshy leaves usually 10 to 12 in. long, 3 to 4 in. wide, dull grey-green, glaucous when young, narrowing to a very stout black spine which is about 1 in. long and flattened or even grooved above. The horny margins are set, at $\frac{1}{2}$ to 1 in. apart, with small, narrowly triangular, often hooked teeth $\frac{1}{8}$ to $\frac{1}{5}$ in. long. Inflorescence perfectly erect, 8 to 12 ft high, the stem 2$\frac{1}{2}$ in. in diameter at the base, the flowers themselves being borne, candelabrum fashion, in a panicle at the top 3 ft long and 1 ft wide. Each flower is creamy white, about 2 in. long, the lower half consisting of the slender, spindle-shaped ovary, the upper half of the six-lobed perianth whose lobes are erect. Stamens conspicuously exserted, being about 1$\frac{1}{2}$ in. long and bearing anthers $\frac{5}{8}$ in. long.

Native of the W. United States from N. Arizona to S.E. New Mexico; also found in Chihuahua, Mexico; first collected in 1846, but introduced to cultivation in 1868 by C. C. Parry, who gathered seeds which were distributed under the present name. It proved quite hardy at Kew on a wall of the old T-range, but went when this was demolished. A sucker from the original plant is now grown under glass. E. A. Bowles had a plant in the open air at Myddleton House, Waltham Cross, for over thirty years. The plant can, of course, be recommended only to lovers of curiosities and as probably the hardiest species of a distinct and well-marked genus.

A. AMERICANA L.—A much larger species than the preceding, with leathery grey-green leaves 3 ft or more long, curving outward towards the apex; terminal spine brown, about 1 in. long; margins set with recurved teeth about $\frac{1}{5}$ in. long and $\frac{1}{2}$ to 2 in. apart. Flowers in a compound inflorescence to 25 ft high.

Probably a native of Mexico, but, if so, it is rare there and reports about its importance in that country refer to other species; introduced to Europe in 1561 and to Britain before 1800. It is now naturalised throughout most of the Mediterranean region and a familiar part of the landscape; further inland, it is established around some of the Italian Lakes. It has proved hardy on the south coast from Torquay westward, and in the Channel Islands and the Isles of Scilly. It flowered at Glendurgan, Cornwall, in 1964 and gardening literature of the past 150 years records many other instances. In a warm climate a young sucker should flower after ten to fifteen years of growth. Commonly known as the "American Aloe", but misleadingly so, for the aloes are members of the lily family and natives of Africa. Variegated forms of this species are also cultivated.

AILANTHUS SIMAROUBACEAE

A group of tall trees with alternate, pinnate leaves, found in temperate and tropical Asia. The flowers have no beauty, but the samaroid fruits are often richly coloured, and add much to the attractiveness of trees already very attractive in their fine, handsomely divided foliage. The species in cultivation thrive best in a rich, deep soil, and can be propagated by suckers from the root, by root-cuttings, and by grafting.

A. ALTISSIMA (Mill.) Swingle TREE OF HEAVEN

Toxicodendron altissimum Mill.; *A. glandulosa* Desf.

A large, deciduous, often unisexual tree, frequently 50 to 70 ft, rarely 100 ft high, with a trunk 2 to 3 ft in diameter, and a rounded head of branches. The older bark is marked with numerous grey fissures. Leaves pinnate, from 1 to 1½ ft long on adult trees (often twice as large on young ones), composed of fifteen to over thirty leaflets, foetid. Leaflets 3 to 6 in. long, ovate, pointed, widely cuneate to truncate or slightly retuse at the base; the margin entire except for one to three teeth on both sides near the base, each marked with a conspicuous gland; stalks ¼ to ¾ in. long. Flowers in terminal panicles, with male and female flowers as a rule on separate trees (but not always); greenish, the male ones evil-smelling. The fruit consists of one to three, sometimes five, keys like those of the ash, several hundreds of which are borne on large branching panicles 9 to 12 in. high and through. Each key (samara) is about 1½ in. long, ½ in. wide, flat, thin, narrow-oblong, tapering towards both ends, with one seed in the centre. The keys are reddish brown, and a tree in full fruit is handsome. They have a peculiar twist at each end, which causes them to revolve with great rapidity as they fall. They are thus much longer reaching the ground, and in even a slight movement of the air will be carried a considerable distance. This is no doubt a provision to help in the dissemination of the seeds.

Native of N. China; introduced by Peter Collinson in 1751. It is hardy over most parts of the British Isles, but apparently succeeds best in the south of

England. Few trees thrive so well in towns, but for planting there female trees should alone be used, owing to the objectionable odour of the male when in flower. For this purpose, the tree should be increased by root-cuttings taken from a female tree, as the sex of seedling plants cannot be determined until they are too big to transplant. Among pinnate-leaved trees of similar character, the ailanthus is easily recognised by the glandular teeth near the base of the leaflets. The generic name is derived from 'Ailanto', the native name for *A. moluccana*, signifying a tree tall enough to reach the skies. Hence also the popular name of 'Tree of Heaven'. It is very effectively used as a fine-foliaged plant in summer by cutting young trees back to the ground in spring, and reducing the young shoots to one. Treated in this way, and given good soil, leaves 4 ft long are produced.

The tallest specimen recorded recently in the British Isles grows at Endsleigh in Devon (95 × 9 ft in 1963). Others of size are: Selborne, Dorset, 82 × 12¼ ft (1964), Westonbirt, Glos., 80 × 8 ft (1967), St James's Park, London, 68 × 9 ft (1963).

cv. 'ERYTHROCARPA'.—Leaves darker than in the type; fruits red. Described by Carrière in *Rev. Hort.*, 1867, p. 419.

cv. 'PENDULIFOLIA'.—This has its branches erect as in the type, but the leaves, which are more than ordinarily long, hang downwards, rather than stand out horizontally as in the type. It also makes a bushier tree. It originated before 1889.

var. SUTCHUENENSIS (Dode) Rehd. & Wils. *A. sutchuenensis* Dode—This differs from the type in its glabrous, shining, reddish-brown young shoots, purplish leaf-stalks, also in the leaflets not being edged with fine hairs and wedge-shaped at the base. The winged fruits are 2 in. long, ½ in. wide. Originally found by Henry in Hupeh, afterwards by Farges in Szechwan. Introduced about 1897.

A. GIRALDII Dode—This species is of rather doubtful standing. Dode founded it on a specimen collected by Père Farges in E. Szechwan in 1893 and on young trees growing in French nurseries, raised from seed collected by French missionaries (probably by Farges himself and by Ducloux). The name chosen by Dode suggests that seed, or specimens, must also have been sent by the missionary Giraldi, who botanised in Shensi. Among the nurseries mentioned by Dode as having seedlings of this ailanthus was Messrs Chenault: but a tree at Kew received from that firm in 1907 as *A. glandulosa giraldii* has recently been examined and proves to differ in no botanical respect from *A. altissima* (*glandulosa*). This doubt has arisen too recently for it to have been possible to examine material from other cultivated trees.

A. giraldii is said to differ from *A. altissima* in leaves with larger, more numerous leaflets, more persistently downy on the undersides; longer panicles and larger fruits. The young wood is stated to be brown and the leaf-stalks purplish. In f. DUCLOUXII Rehd., the young wood is described as light orange; leaf-stalks green; leaves less downy beneath except on the veins.

A. VILMORINIANA Dode

A tree probably of the same dimensions and general aspect as *A. altissima*, but distinguished by the numerous soft spines which clothe the young branchlets.

Leaves pinnate, as large, or probably larger, than those of the previous species and very downy; the main stalk often of a rich red, and occasionally spiny like the branchlet. The inflorescence is sometimes 12 in. or more across, and the keys 2 in. long, with the twist resembling the propellers of an aeroplane even more marked. From this description it will be seen that this species, although similar to *A. altissima* in many respects (it has the same glandular teeth at the base of the leaflets), is on the whole quite distinct, especially in the spiny branchlets and very downy leaflets.

Native of Szechwan, W. China, whence seeds were sent to Maurice de Vilmorin by Père Farges, the missionary, in 1897. The parent of the older trees in Europe is at Les Barres, in France, where, when I first saw it, it had the spiny character of the branches well marked, but during a later visit I noticed the young shoots were becoming less spiny. It has been propagated by grafting on *A. altissima*. Wilson, who saw this species during his travels in W. China, remarks that the spininess of the young growths appears to be a juvenile character which disappears as the tree gets older. There are two specimens at Kew, one, *pl.* 1898, 52 × 5 ft, the other, *pl.* 1905, 52 × 5¼ (1967). Another in the West Dean Arboretum, Sussex, measures 65 × 4½ ft (1967).

AKEBIA LARDIZABALACEAE

A small genus of twining shrubs which produce male and female flowers on the same raceme; the former small, numerous; the latter few, large, and confined to the base. Neither is showy, for petals are absent, and the attractive part is three large sepals. The fruit is large and highly coloured, but not regularly produced in the British Isles. The two hardy species are attractive for their free growth and elegant foliage, and are useful for clothing pergolas, pillars, summer-houses, or for rambling over other shrubs or trees. They need but little training or tying, and the stems will fix themselves by twining round any wire, small branch, etc., with which they may come in contact. Their chief need in cultivation, after the provision of a suitable support, is a good loamy soil. They can be propagated by layers and by cuttings of the stems and roots. Layering is the least troublesome. Cuttings should be made from wood just getting firm, and placed in gentle heat. 'Akebia' is an adaptation of the Japanese name for these shrubs.

A. QUINATA (Houtt.) Decne.
Rajania quinata Houtt.

A twining shrub 30 to 40 ft in length, evergreen in mild winters and in warm localities, but losing its leaves where the conditions are more severe. Leaves with slender stalks 3 to 5 in. long, carrying normally five (sometimes three or four) radially arranged leaflets. Leaflets glabrous, oblong or obovate, distinctly notched at the apex, 1½ to 3 in. long, with stalks about ½ in. long. Flowers produced on slender, pendent racemes, very fragrant; males ¼ in. across, with pale purple, reflexed sepals, and occupying the terminal part of the raceme; females

AKEBIA QUINATA

(usually two) 1 to 1½ in. across, dark chocolate-purple, the sepals broadly elliptical and concave. Fruit 2½ to 4 in. long, in shape like a thick sausage, greyish violet or purplish in colour, containing numerous seeds immersed in white pulp. *Bot. Mag.*, t. 4864.

First introduced in 1845 from the Island of Chusan by Robert Fortune, this

climber has since been found to be native also of Japan, China, and Korea. It is perfectly hardy in a sheltered dell at Kew, but does not develop its handsome fruit out-of-doors. In the south-western counties it succeeds admirably, and is valued for the charming, spicy fragrance of its flowers, at times perceptible yards away from the plant, although even there the fruit is never abundantly borne. The failure to fruit would be understandable if, as is quite possibly the case, the individual plant is partly or wholly sterile to its own pollen and hence to that of any other plant of the same clone. The remedy would be to grow two or more plants known to be of diverse origin.

A. × PENTAPHYLLA (Mak.) Mak.—A hybrid between the two species of *Akebia* and intermediate between them. It occurs in the wild and is, of course, very likely to occur among seedlings raised in gardens where both species are grown. For an interesting account of deliberate cross-pollination see *Journ. R.H.S.*, Vol. 70, 1957, p. 215.

A. TRIFOLIATA (Thunb.) Koidzumi
Clematis trifoliata Thunb.; *A. lobata* Decne.

A deciduous, twining shrub of vigorous habit. Leaves glabrous, composed of three stalked leaflets, the stalk of the terminal one thrice the length of those of the lateral ones. Leaflets broadly ovate, 1½ to 4 in. long, the margins irregularly and shallowly lobed, the apex notched. Male and female flowers are borne on the same raceme, which is more or less pendulous and 3 to 5 in. long. Male flowers small, very numerous, ⅛ in. diameter, pale purple, and confined to the terminal part of the raceme. Female flowers basal and much larger, usually two in number, each about ¾ in. in diameter, the three concave sepals being dark lurid purple. The fruit is at first sausage-shaped, 3 to 5 in. long and 1½ to 2½ in. wide, pale violet; but when ripe it splits open from the base, revealing rows of black seeds embedded in white pulp. *Bot. Mag.*, t. 7485.

This remarkable and interesting climber was introduced to Kew in 1897, being a native of China and Japan. It has proved to be perfectly hardy and a luxuriant grower, but flowering as it does early in April, its blossoms are often destroyed by frost, and its remarkable and highly coloured fruits in consequence not often seen out-of-doors; but see the remarks under *A. quinata*.

ALANGIUM   ALANGIACEAE

Alangium, with about twenty species, mostly in the warmer parts of the Old World, is the only member of the family to which it gives its name. The position of this family among the flowering plants is a disputed question, but it appears to be most closely allied to Cornaceae and Nyssaceae.

A. PLATANIFOLIUM (Sieb. & Zucc.) Harms

Marlea platanifolia Sieb. & Zucc.

A deciduous shrub 6 ft or more high, with erect, zigzagged, but not much branched stems; branches very pithy and slightly downy; winter buds hairy. Leaves alternate, roundish or broadly ovate in main outline, 4 to 8 in. long, nearly as wide, with two to seven (usually three or five) large pointed lobes towards the apex; upper surface dark green, and smooth except for scattered hairs; lower surface covered with pale down; stalk 1 to 3 in. long. Flowers white, produced during June and July in a one- to four-flowered cyme from the leaf-axils of the current year's shoots; the common stalk is $\frac{1}{2}$ to $1\frac{1}{4}$ in. long and divides into two at the apex, the branches usually dividing again; flower-stalks $\frac{1}{4}$ to 1 in. long; the flowers are 1 to $1\frac{2}{5}$ in. long and have an inferior ovary about $\frac{1}{8}$ in. long and finely downy, which is surmounted by a narrow, finely toothed rim, which is the calyx; petals usually six, sometimes seven or eight, narrowly strap-shaped, cohering at first to form a narrowly tubular corolla but soon curving outward for over half their length, exposing the stamens and style; stamens as many as the petals, each attached to the base of a petal, filament $\frac{1}{3}$ to $\frac{2}{5}$ in. long and finely hairy, anthers very narrow, $\frac{2}{3}$ in. long; the style is smooth, about 1 in. long, its base surrounded by a subglobose, fleshy disk about $\frac{1}{12}$ in. long and bearing a shortly lobed, knob-shaped stigma. Fruit thinly fleshy (drupe-like), egg-shaped, about $\frac{1}{2}$ in. long, containing a single, bony stone.

Native of Japan, whence it was introduced by Maries for Messrs Veitch about 1879. It is also a native of China, where it was found in Hupeh by Henry. This shrub must be regarded more as a curiosity than as an ornament in gardens, although the large maple-like leaves are handsome. It has not proved really hardy at Kew and is no longer grown there, the soft pithy shoots being too often cut by winter cold.

ALBIZIA   LEGUMINOSAE

A genus of more than 100 species, all (save *A. occidentalis* of Mexico) confined to the Old World. It is closely related to *Acacia*, but differs in having the stamens united at the base. The generic name should be spelt with one z.

A. JULIBRISSIN (Willd.) Durazz.   PINK SIRIS

Acacia julibrissin Willd.

A deciduous tree 30 to 40 ft high, with angular glabrous branchlets. Leaves doubly pinnate, with from six to twelve pairs of main divisions (pinnae), each of which consists of twenty to thirty pairs of leaflets, the entire leaf being 9 to 18 in. long, half as wide. Each leaflet is $\frac{1}{3}$ to $\frac{1}{2}$ in. long, $\frac{1}{8}$ in. wide, oblong, oblique due to the blade developing only on the side of the midrib towards the base of the pinna. Flowers in a terminal cluster of dense heads each terminating a stalk of 1 to 2 in. long, the chief feature of the flower being the numerous thread-like pink stamens, 1 in. or more long, which give the flower-head the appearance of a brush. Pod about 5 in. wide, constricted between the seeds.

Native of the Near East, whence it was introduced in 1745; also common, cultivated or wild, in China and many other countries. It is now very well known in gardens in its juvenile state as an ornamental plant for subtropical bedding. For this purpose seeds are sown in heat in spring in pots, and the plants gradually hardened off by the end of May, then planted out in good soil. When the frosts come they are either destroyed, or potted up and housed in a cool greenhouse until the following spring. The species is not hardy at Kew in the open, but grows very well on a lofty wall, where its large, beautifully divided leaves give a very pleasing effect in the height of summer. In such a spot it is well to plant some other climber, preferably evergreen, to grow over the lower part of the wall beneath the albizia, which grows quickly in its younger stages and leaves its base naked.

Given a sunny wall, it will flower quite well if the summer is warm and the wood of the previous year well ripened, but it really needs a more continental climate than ours. A form introduced from Korea in 1918 is quite hardy in the open at the Arnold Arboretum, Mass., and has survived several zero frosts there. It is also of smaller, more spreading habit than the common form, with deeper-coloured stamens. Its ability to thrive in a climate with colder winters than ours can certainly be attributed to the better ripening of the wood; for a comparable case, see *Daphne genkwa*.

ALNUS ALDER BETULACEAE

The alders are deciduous trees and shrubs closely allied to, and only likely to be confounded with, the birches (*Betula*). Leaves with stipules, alternate, more or less toothed in all the cultivated species. Winter buds nearly always stalked. Male and female flowers borne on the same tree but on separate catkins. Male catkins long and slender, usually in clusters of two to six; the flowers small, with a four-lobed calyx, no petals, and usually four (sometimes one to three) stamens. Female catkins shorter, clustered, or rarely solitary, developing into woody, cone-like "fruits", correctly, 'strobiles', $\frac{1}{3}$ – 1$\frac{1}{4}$ in. long. The "seed" (the true fruit) is a minute, flattened nutlet, often with thin membranous wings at the sides. Apart from three species—*A. maritima*, *A. nepalensis*, and *A. nitida*—which flower in autumn, the cultivated alders form their catkins in the late summer and autumn; these expand the following spring, either very early before the leaf-buds begin to grow, or along with the leaves; the fruits develop during the summer and persist until the succeeding spring. From the alders the birches are distinguished by the fruits being longer, not woody, and falling to pieces (those of the alders falling whole), and the flowers of birches have never more than two stamens.

In gardens and parks the alders are chiefly valuable for growing in wet situations unsuited to the majority of trees. Some, however, such as *A. japonica, nitida, cordata,* and *firma,* succeed quite well in ordinary good soil. All are best propagated by seed except the garden varieties, which may be grafted on their respective types, or, better still, rooted from cuttings made as soon as the leaves fall, and put in sandy soil, as willow or poplar cuttings are—compared with which, however, they do not strike root so readily. The following is a selection of the best worth growing, irrespective of their use in damp places: *cordata, firma, nitida, rubra; glutinosa* 'Imperialis'; *incana* 'Laciniata' and 'Aurea'.

A. CORDATA Desf.   ITALIAN ALDER

A tree 80 ft high, of pyramidal habit; young shoots glabrous, viscid, angled; winter buds stalked. Leaves roundish to broadly ovate, usually deeply notched at the base, shortly and abruptly pointed or rounded at the apex, $1\frac{1}{2}$ to 4 in. long, from three-fourths to as much wide; finely and simply toothed; upper

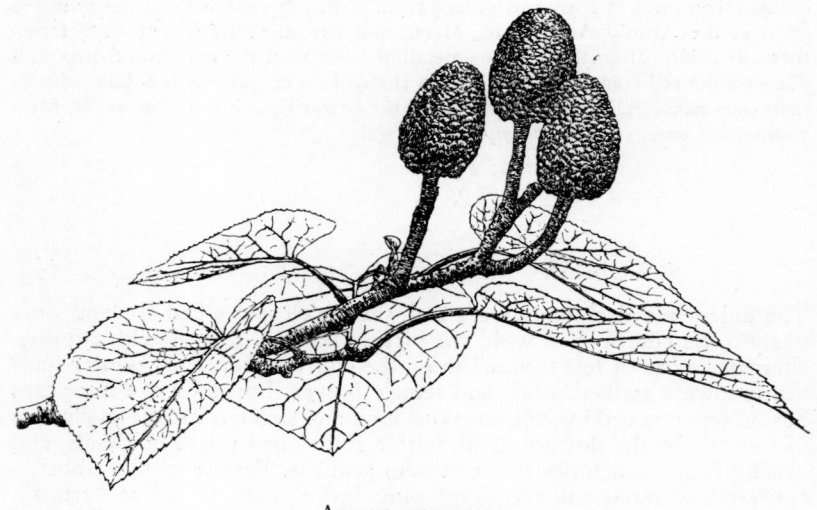

ALNUS CORDATA

surface glabrous, dark lustrous green; lower one paler and also glabrous, except for tufts of brownish down in the vein-axils; leaf-stalk slender, $\frac{1}{2}$ to $1\frac{1}{2}$ in. long, glabrous. Male catkins three to six, in a terminal zigzag raceme, each catkin 2 to 3 in. long, expanding in March. Fruit erect, egg-shaped, 1 to $1\frac{1}{4}$ in. long and $\frac{5}{8}$ to $\frac{3}{4}$ in. wide, mostly in threes. *Bot. Mag.,* t. 8658.

Native of Corsica and S. Italy; said to have been introduced in 1820. Undoubtedly one of the handsomest of the alders, this tree is not planted enough. Although it thrives on poor and dryish soil, and even on chalk, it is more at home near water. Its deeply heart-shaped, glistening leaves and large fruits (larger than those of any other species in cultivation) make it very distinct. From *A. subcordata* it is distinguished by its shorter male catkins, and by several other points mentioned under that species.

A fine pyramidal tree on the banks of the pond at Kew died in 1959, after attaining a height of about 70 ft. The tallest recorded in England grows at Westonbirt, Glos., and measured 90 × 8 ft in 1963, but this is almost equalled in height by a tree at Smeaton Hepburn, E. Lothian. There are several good specimens in Battersea Park, London.

A. CREMASTOGYNE Burk.

A tree 40 to 80 ft high, according to Wilson; young shoots soon becoming glabrous. Leaves usually distinctly obovate, sometimes nearly oval, tapered or somewhat rounded at the base, and shortly and abruptly pointed; margins set with small teeth; 2½ to 5½ in. long, 1½ to 3 in. wide; dark lustrous green, and glabrous above, paler beneath, with tufts of brown hairs in the vein-axils; veins in nine or ten pairs; stalk ¼ to ¾ in. long. Male catkins not yet seen. Fruits solitary, on axillary stalks 2 to 3½ in. long; oval, about ¾ in. long, ⅓ in. wide; "seed" with a broad thin wing.

Native of W. China; discovered by Henry in Szechwan, in 1899; introduced by Wilson in 1907. This species is very distinct from all other cultivated alders except *A. lanata* in its solitary, long-stalked fruits. The foliage, too, is distinct in its large size and dark, glabrous, glossy green appearance.

A. LANATA Duthie—Another alder found in W. China by Wilson, also with solitary fruits. It is very closely related to *A. cremastogyne*, but is easily recognised, especially when the foliage is young, by the dense brown woolly covering of the under-surface of the leaves, leaf-stalks, flower-stalks, and young shoots. Male catkins 2 to 3 in. long. Fruit-stalks 1¾ in long.

A. × ELLIPTICA Req.

A natural hybrid, between *A. glutinosa* and *A. cordata*, found in Corsica, on the banks of the river Salenzara, near its mouth. Leaves oval to roundish, 1½ to 3 in. long, 1 to 2½ in. wide; rounded at the apex, rounded or broadly wedge-shaped at the base, finely toothed; glossy dark green above, glabrous except for tufts of down in the vein-axils beneath. Male catkins slender, 3 to 4 in. long. Fruits ¾ to 1 in. long, ½ in. wide. There was once an example over 70 ft high on the banks of the lake at Kew. It was of unknown origin and grown as "*A cordifolia* var." until identified with the above by Prof. Henry. It is quite possible this particular tree may have originated as a hybrid under cultivation. It leant more to *A. cordata* than the other parent, but the leaves were never heart-shaped at the base, and rarely pointed; the fruits were not so large and broad, and the male catkins were longer.

A. FIRMA Sieb. & Zucc.

A. yasha Matsum.; *A. firma* var. *yasha* (Matsum.) Winkler

A small tree up to 30 ft high, of graceful habit, with long slender branches downy when young; winter buds not stalked. Leaves resembling those of a hornbeam, ovate-oblong to ovate-lanceolate, rounded or wedge-shaped at the base, more or less slender-pointed, finely toothed (often doubly so), 2 to 4½ in. long, 1 to 2 in. wide, with many parallel veins; upper surface with flattened hairs between the veins, lower one downy, especially on the midrib and veins; stalk hairy, ⅙ in. to ⅝ in. long. Male catkins often solitary or in pairs, 2 to 3 in. long, opening in March and April. Stalk of female inflorescence glandular-hairy. Fruits ½ to 1 in. long, oval.

Native of Japan. It is variable in the degree of downiness of the leaves beneath and of the young stems. The more downy forms are distinguished as var. HIRTELLA Franch. & Sav., which was introduced in 1894 as var. *yasha* and represents the species on the main island of Japan. Typical *A. firma* is said to be found only in Kyushu.

A. firma in the broad sense is common in the mountains of Japan and is also, as Sargent observes, largely planted on the margins of the fields of the Tokyo region to afford 'support for the poles on which the freshly cut rice is hung to dry'. It is represented at Kew by two trees planted in 1893, the taller 40 × 4 ft (1967).

var. MULTINERVIS Reg. *A. pendula* Matsum.—A very distinct variety, often given specific rank. Leaves long, with eighteen to twenty-four pairs of veins, conspicuously double-toothed; stalks short, ⅙ to ¼ in. long; fruits small, pendulous, little more than ½ in. long. This is the form originally introduced to Britain (1862).

var. SIEBOLDIANA (Matsum.) Winkler *A. sieboldiana* Matsum.—Branchlets glabrous, stout. Female catkins solitary. Native of the lower parts of the main island, commonest on the sea-coast.

A. GLUTINOSA (L.) Gaertn.   COMMON ALDER

Betula glutinosa L.

A tree 50 to 90 ft in height, with a trunk 5 to 12 ft in girth, of narrow, pyramidal habit; young shoots covered with minute glands, glutinous, not downy. Leaves broadly obovate, sometimes almost round, the base always more or less tapered, the apex rounded, and thus giving the leaf a pear-shaped outline; 1½ to 4 in. long, two-thirds to about as much wide; irregularly toothed except near the base; dark lustrous green, glabrous and glutinous above; pale green and with tufts of down in the vein-axils beneath; veins in six to eight pairs; stalk ½ to 1 in. long. Male catkins opening in March, usually three to five together, each 2 to 4 in. long. Fruit egg-shaped, ⅓ to ⅔ in. long, rather numerous in the cluster.

Native of Europe (including Britain), W. Asia, and N. Africa. The common alder has not much to recommend its being brought into the garden. It is abundant in a wild state, and the genus can be more effectively represented in gardens by selected varieties and such species as *A. cordata* and *A. nitida*. It is, at the same time, a very useful tree for planting in boggy places where few trees would thrive. The timber was once chiefly employed in the manufacture of the clogs so commonly used in the Lancashire mill towns. An ancient and humble, but honourable form of woodcraft was carried on where alders abound, especially in the north, by men who travelled from place to place, purchased the alder trees standing, felled them, then cut up the timber and roughly shaped it on the spot for clog-making.

There is a remarkable specimen of the common alder at Sandling Park, Kent, measuring 86 × 12¼ ft, with a smooth, round bole 45 ft in length to the first branch (1965).

Both *A. glutinosa* and *A. incana* (q.v.) are remarkable for the large number of cut-leaf forms which they have produced. These seem to be particularly common in Scandinavia and are reviewed by Nils Hylander in *Svensk Botanisk Tidskrift*, Vol. 51, part 2, 1957, with twenty-eight plates showing the extraordinary range of leaf-cutting that has been observed. The cultivated forms are also treated.

cv. 'AUREA'.—Leaves golden yellow. Raised in Vervaene's nursery, Ledeberg-les-Gand, about 1860. Not so vigorous as the type.

var. BARBATA (C. A. Mey.) Ledeb. *A. barbata* C. A. Mey.—Leaves oval or ovate, rounded at the base and either rounded or pointed at the apex, doubly toothed; 2 to 3½ in. long, 1½ to 2½ in. wide; dark glossy green above, downy beneath, especially on the veins and midrib; veins in eight to ten pairs; stalks 1 to ¾ in. long, downy. Native of the Caucasus and the mountains of Persia. It is distinguished from the type by the hairy shoots and leaves, and in the often pointed apex of the latter. It is represented at Kew by some small plants, the tree 30 ft by the lake, mentioned in previous editions, having died long ago.

cv. 'IMPERIALIS'.—Leaves deeply and pinnately lobed, the lobes lanceolate, slender, pointed, not toothed, reaching more than half-way to the midrib; stalks 1 to 1½ in. long. Often a thin, rather ungainly tree, never of great size. A well-known garden clone, in cultivation since before 1859.

f. INCISA (Willd.) Koehne *A. g.* var. *incisa* Willd.—Leaves small, usually less than 1 in. long, rounded or ovate in outline, deeply cut into broad, toothed lobes, or even right to the midrib. The plant once grown at Kew made a dwarf, compact bush and was probably of the clone distributed by Loddiges' Hackney nurseries, and by Booth's nurseries, Hamburg, Germany, as *A. glutinosa oxyacanthifolia*—the thorn-leaved alder. A form with similar leaves, but making a large shrub or small tree, has also been described and may represent a different clone. Elwes and Henry mentioned such a one at Barton, near Bury St Edmunds, 44 ft high and 2 ft 8 in. in girth.

The name *A. glutinosa incisa* has also been used, wrongly, for the clone 'Laciniata' (q.v.).

cv. 'LACINIATA'.—Similar to 'Imperialis', but not so deeply and narrowly lobed; lobes not toothed. In his review of the cut-leaf alders, Hylander accepts the statement made by Thouin (1819), and quoted by Loudon, that all the plants of this form descend from one grown in a garden near St Germain, 'where the stool still remains from which all the nurseries of Paris have been supplied with plants, and, probably all Europe'. It makes a tree of some size, and reached 70 ft at Syon Park, Middlesex.

It has been confused with f. *incisa*, but in that group the leaves are small and of rounded outline, with toothed lobes, whereas in 'Laciniata' the leaves are oblong and the lobes pointed and untoothed.

f. PYRAMIDALIS (Dipp.) Winkler—Branches erect. 'BIRKIANA' is a clone of this character, once distributed by Späth's nurseries.

f. QUERCIFOLIA (Willd.) Koehne—Upper part of the leaves with triangular, toothed lobes, the deepest not reaching more than one-third of the way to the midrib. Plants of this form were distributed early in the nineteenth century by Loddiges' nursery and are also found wild in Scandinavia.

cv. 'RUBRINERVIA'.—Leaves with red veins and stalks.

cv. 'SORBIFOLIA'.—Leaves oblong or oval, deeply cut into about six pairs of lobes, which are oblong and coarsely round-toothed, the sinuses often widest at the base. One of the most distinct of the cut-leaved sorts. The tree itself is not a strong grower, and is of rather lax habit. The plant described is almost certainly of the same clone as the one to which Dippel gave the name *A. g.* var. *sorbifolia* in 1892. Similar forms are found wild in Scandinavia and the group name for them all is f. LACERA (Mela) Mela (Hylander, op. cit.).

A. × PUBESCENS Tausch—A group-name for hybrids between *A. glutinosa* and *A. incana*, which are found fairly commonly where the two species meet. According to P. W. Ball in *Flora Europaea*, Vol. 1 (1964), such hybrids are usually characterised by downy young growths, leaves downy beneath, at least on the veins, blunt or shortly acuminate at the apex, and the female catkins shortly stalked (in the first parent they are stalked and in the second sessile).

A. HIRSUTA (Spach) Rupr.
A. incana var. *hirsuta* Spach; *A. tinctoria* Sarg.

A deciduous tree up to 65 ft high, with a trunk 6 ft in girth; young shoots hairy at first; winter buds egg-shaped, viscid, downy, purplish. Leaves broadly ovate, rounded to broadly wedge-shaped at the base, the apex shortly and slenderly pointed; shallowly lobed and doubly toothed; 2½ to 5 in. long, nearly as much wide; dark dull green and slightly downy above, glaucous and clothed more or less with reddish-brown down beneath, especially on the midrib and on the nine to twelve pairs of veins; stalk 1 to 1½ in. long. Fruits (strobiles) ¾ in. long, ½ in. wide, borne in clusters of two to six—usually three or four—on a main-stalk 1¾ in. long, individual fruit-stalks very short.

Native of Japan and Manchuria; originally introduced to the Coombe Wood nursery by Maries about 1879, and by Sargent from Japan in 1892. He found it in Hokkaido in moist ground, but usually at some distance from the banks of streams. This tree is related to *A. incana* more nearly than to any other alder, but is well distinguished by its larger leaves of rounder shape, and by its much larger fruits. It is a vigorous and handsome tree, sometimes found in gardens under the name "*A. incana hirsuta*". There is an example in the Edinburgh Botanic Garden measuring 46 × 4 ft (1968).

var. SIBIRICA (Spach) Schneid. *A. incana* var. *sibirica* Spach—This variety is distinguished by its young shoots being glabrous or near so, and the leaves downy only on the midrib and the veins beneath. In spite of its name, this variety occurs in Japan together with the type, as well as in continental N.E. Asia. There is a vigorous specimen in the Edinburgh Botanic Garden, planted in 1930, measuring 46 × 4¾ ft (1968).

A. MATSUMURAE Callier—A small tree, closely allied to the former, best distinguished by its leaves, which are obovate to orbicular, truncate or deeply notched at the apex, and almost glabrous beneath. Native of Japan. There is an example at Kew, planted in 1928, measuring 55 × 4¾ ft (1965).

A. INCANA (L.) Moench   GREY ALDER
Betula alnus var. *incana* L.

A tree 60 to 70 ft high, with a trunk occasionally 6 ft. in girth; young shoots covered with a short, grey down. Leaves ovate, oval, or occasionally obovate, rounded or wedge-shaped at the base, and with short, abrupt points; 2 to 4 in. long, 1¼ to 2¼ in. wide; the margins with six or more coarse teeth about the middle, these again being sharply toothed, the base entire; upper surface dull green covered with flattened down when young, lower surface grey with a close down, at least when young; veins in nine to twelve pairs; stalk ½ to ⅞ in. long, covered with minute down. Male catkins 2 to 4 in. long, usually three or four in a cluster, opening in February. Fruits ovoid, numerous, and rather densely clustered, ½ to ⅝ in. long.

Native of Europe and the Caucasus, not of Britain, but introduced in 1780. This alder is an exceptionally hardy tree, and useful for planting in cold, wet places. With the exception of *A. glutinosa*, it is the commonest of alders, but is more frequently represented in gardens by the various cut-leaved and coloured forms than by the type. From *A. glutinosa* in all its forms it is most obviously distinguished by the grey downy leaves and young shoots. The typical *A. glutinosa* is, of course, very distinct in the obovate, round-ended leaves, green and almost glabrous beneath.

The American form of *A. incana*, long known as *A. incana* var. *americana*, is now placed under *A. rugosa* (q.v.).

f. ANGUSTISSIMA Holmberg—Leaves cut to midrib or near it; lobes very narrow, usually toothed at the base and prolonged at the apex into thread-like points. This remarkable form has been found wild in several places in Scandinavia and is in cultivation in Sweden. It is illustrated in Hylander's monograph (for reference see *A. glutinosa*) in plates XXII to XXVI.

cv. 'AUREA'.—Leaves yellowish, downy beneath; young wood reddish yellow and remaining so through the winter; young catkins orange. 'RAMULIS COCCINEIS' (f. *coccinea* Callier) is similar, but has the leaves almost glabrous beneath; branchlets and buds a good red.

cv. 'LACINIATA'.—The handsomest of the cultivated cut-leaf alders, the blade being pinnately divided into six or eight pairs of narrow, lanceolate, toothed lobes, reaching two-thirds or more of the way to the midrib. Similar forms are found wild in Scandinavia and are referred by Hylander to *f. laciniata* (Loud.) Hylander. The nomenclature of the garden clone is very confused, but *A. incana laciniata* is the old horticultural name for it and the one under which it was given a first-class certificate in 1873; it should therefore be accepted as the clonal name. Botanical names under which it has been placed are: var. *acuminata* Reg.; var. *incisa* Bean (in previous editions); var. *pinnatifida* Dipp.; f. *acutiloba* (K. Koch) Hallier.

f. ORBICULARIS Callier—Leaves round-oval, under 2 in. in length; veins in about five pairs. Described from a plant found wild in Silesia.

cv. 'PENDULA'.—Branches weeping. Van der Bom's nursery, Holland, before 1903. Originally distributed as *A. i. pendula nova*.

cv. 'PINNATA'.—Leaves small, with blunt, toothed lobes which sometimes reach to the midrib. According to Hylander, the original plant described by Lundmark in 1790 (as *Betula pinnata*) was found at Lesjöfors in Värmland; it was propagated in the Uppsala Botanic Garden around 1800 and is the parent of all the cultivated trees. Similar forms have been found elsewhere in Scandinavia and are referable botanically to f. PINNATA (Lundmark) Willd. (syn. var. *incisa* Dipp.).

A. JAPONICA Sieb. & Zucc.

A pyramidal tree from 60 to 80 ft high; young shoots glabrous, or downy towards the base; buds stalked. Leaves lanceolate to narrowly ovate or oval, tapered at both ends, usually more slenderly at the apex; 2 to 5 in. long, $\frac{3}{4}$ to 2 in. wide, finely toothed, glabrous, dark glossy green; stalks downy, $\frac{1}{2}$ to 1 in. long. Male catkins opening in February or March, according to the warmth of the season, and produced in a terminal cluster of four to eight; each catkin erect, 2 to $3\frac{1}{2}$ in. long. Fruits oval, $\frac{3}{4}$ in. long.

Native of Japan and continental N.E. Asia, the true date of whose introduction is not recorded. Plants obtained from Lee's nursery had already reached the fruiting state at Kew in 1880. It is considered to have some relationship with the North American *A. maritima*, and has been regarded as a variety of it, but in the field it is quite distinct. It grows more than twice as high, has narrower, long-pointed leaves; and more than all, its habit of flowering in spring distinguishes it.

A. × SPAETHII Callier—A hybrid between *A. japonica* and *A. subcordata*, sent out by Späth of Berlin in 1908. Unfolding leaves, violet-purple.

A. MARITIMA (Marsh.) Nutt.
Betula-Alnus maritima Marsh.

A small tree, occasionally up to 30 ft high, with a trunk 1 to $1\frac{1}{2}$ ft in girth, but, according to Sargent, more often a shrub; young shoots at first downy, becoming glabrous later. Leaves obovate, sometimes oval or ovate, 2 to 4 in. long, $1\frac{1}{4}$ to $2\frac{1}{2}$ in. wide; wedge-shaped at the base, with short, broad points, the margins set with small, gland-tipped teeth; upper surface dark glossy green, glabrous; lower one dull, glabrous or with tufts of down in the vein-axils; stalks slightly downy, $\frac{1}{2}$ to $\frac{3}{4}$ in. long. Male flowers yellow, expanding in autumn on rough-stalked pendulous catkins $1\frac{1}{2}$ to $2\frac{1}{2}$ in. long, formed the same summer in the uppermost leaf-axils. Female catkins about $\frac{1}{6}$ in. long at the time of fertilisation, expanding and ripening the following year into egg-shaped fruits $\frac{5}{8}$ to $\frac{3}{4}$ in. long.

Native of Delaware and Maryland; usually found near water. It was raised from seed sent by Prof. Sargent to Kew in 1878, and a tree by the lake side succeeded well until 1895, when it succumbed—apparently to the great frosts of February of that year, the effect of which, no doubt, had been heightened by the low, wet situation in which it grew. Reintroduced in 1899, but not grown at Kew at the present time. Its habit of flowering in autumn distinguishes this species from all other cultivated alders except *A. nepalensis* and *A. nitida*.

A. MAXIMOWICZII Callier   [PLATE II
A. viridis var. *sibirica* Reg.

A deciduous tree up to 30 ft high, but more often a shrub; young shoots glabrous, older bark grey; buds sessile. Leaves broadly ovate, pointed, rounded or slightly heart-shaped at the base, the margins cut into numerous very fine, slender teeth, giving them a fringe-like appearance; 2 to 4 in. long, $1\frac{1}{2}$ to 3 in. wide; hairy when very young but glabrous later except for axil-tufts of down beneath; stalk $\frac{1}{2}$ to $1\frac{1}{4}$ in. long; veins in eight to eleven pairs, bright green on both surfaces. Male catkins 2 in. long; fruits egg-shaped or cylindrical, $\frac{5}{8}$ to $\frac{3}{4}$ in. long, borne on slender, glabrous stalks.

Native of Japan, where it is common on many of the higher mountains; introduced in 1914. It belongs to the same group of alders as *A. viridis*, but is distinguished by the often heart-shaped base of the leaves and their fringe-like toothing. Very hardy.

A. NEPALENSIS D. Don

A deciduous tree up to 50 or 60 ft high, with a silvery bark tinged with purple and yellow; young shoots thinly downy or glabrous. Leaves ovate to narrowly oval, slender-pointed, mostly tapered (sometimes rounded) at the base, shallowly toothed or almost entire; 3 to 7 in. long, 2 to 4 in. wide; dark glossy green and glabrous above; dull, paler, and loosely downy on the midrib and veins beneath, with tufts of down in the axils of the veins; stalk mostly $\frac{1}{4}$ to $\frac{3}{4}$ in. long; veins in ten to eighteen pairs. Male flowers borne in numerous slender catkins, each 3 to 6 in. long, $\frac{3}{16}$ in. wide, the whole forming a large, loose, drooping panicle; from ten to some scores of catkins may be borne in one panicle. Fruits egg-shaped or cylindrical, $\frac{1}{2}$ to 1 in. long, as many as ten or twelve packed on a short panicle.

Native of N. India and Yunnan; introduced around the year 1865, although possibly in cultivation before. It is common in the forests of the Temperate Himalaya, and Wilson observes that it is abundant in S.W. Yunnan, often forming pure stands. It has fine foliage, but its chief claim to beauty lies in the panicle of yellowish male flowers, which are borne in catkins not only rather long but often very numerous; they open towards autumn and must make a charming picture. Possibly the tree will be hardy only in the milder counties, but it should be well worth growing there. The bark is used for tanning in India. The only other autumn-flowering alders are *A. maritima* and *A. nitida*.

A. NITIDA (Spach) Endl.
Clethropsis nitida Spach

A tall tree, said to become 100 ft high in its native place, with a trunk 10 to 15 ft in girth; bark of trunk blackish and ultimately scaling; young twigs with a little loose down at first, soon quite glabrous. Leaves thin-textured, ovate to oval, 3 to 6 in. long, 2 to 3 in. wide, rounded or broadly wedge-shaped at the base, slender-pointed, coarsely toothed to almost entire; shining-green above, pale beneath, and glabrous except for tufts of down in the vein-axils; stalks ½ to 1 in. long, slightly downy. The male catkins open in September, and are produced as many as five together in a raceme, each catkin 4 to 6 in. long, ¼ in. in diameter, and pendulous. Fruits three to five together, erect, oblong, ¾ to 1¼ in. long.

Native of the N.W. Himalaya; introduced to Kew in 1882 through seed sent by R. E. Ellis. The trees then raised succeeded well but eventually died of some form of bacterial decay. A young tree planted in 1952 is now 30 ft high and growing well. Trees at the Forestry Commission's research station at Alice Holt, near Farnham, were planted at about the same time and have reached about the same height. It is at once distinguished from all other alders except *maritima* and *nepalensis* by flowering in autumn. The quadrangular scales on the bark are not developed on young trees.

A. ORIENTALIS Decne.

A deciduous tree up to 50 ft high; young shoots glabrous; winter buds stalked, glutinous. Leaves ovate to oval, coarsely and irregularly toothed; rounded, broadly wedge-shaped, or slightly heart-shaped at the base; 2½ to 4 in. long, 1 to 2½ in. wide; glossy green above and glabrous on both sides except for tufts of down in the vein-axils beneath; stalk ½ to 1 in. long, slender. Male catkins glutinous when young, usually three to five in a cluster. Fruits egg-shaped, ¾ to 1 in. long, ½ to ¾ in. wide, borne often in threes, sometimes solitary or in pairs.

Native of Syria, Cyprus, Cilicia, etc., on river banks; introduced from Cyprus to Kew in 1924, where a tree grew well, reaching a height of 45 ft and a girth of 3½ ft before it died some years ago. It is rarely to be seen in cultivation, but there is a good specimen in the Edinburgh Botanic Garden, 40 × 5½ ft (1968). Another grows in the Glasnevin Botanic Garden, Dublin, which measures 44 × 3½ ft (1966). It belongs to a handsome group of alders comprising *subcordata* and *cordata*, all with large fruits and large bright green, almost glabrous leaves. Botanists distinguish it from these by the absence of a wing to the seed. *A. cordata* has rounder, distinctly heart-shaped leaves, whilst those of *subcordata* are downy, especially along the midrib and chief veins beneath.

A. RHOMBIFOLIA Nutt.   WHITE ALDER

A tree 30 to 100 ft high, forming a thin, spreading, round-topped head of branches, pendulous at the ends; young branches at first covered with pale hairs which soon fall away. Leaves ovate, oval, or rounded, ordinarily 2 to 4 in. long, about two-thirds as wide; usually pointed (sometimes rounded) at the apex, tapered at the base, unevenly or doubly toothed; dark shining green (but at first very hairy) above; paler, yellowish, and permanently downy beneath. Male catkins two to seven in a cluster, opening on the naked shoots early in spring, each catkin 3 to 5 in. long; stamens two, rarely three. Fruits ⅓ to ¾ in. long, three to seven together.

Native of western N. America. The leaves occasionally approach the diamond shape indicated by the name, and on vigorous shoots are up to 5 in. long. According to Jepson, this alder keeps to streams which do not run dry, forming files of trees in mountain gorges which are 'to the traveller a reliable sign of water'. It is very rare in cultivation, the plant supplied for it in this country and on the continent being, as a rule, A. *rubra*.

A. RUBRA Bong.   RED ALDER
A. oregona Nutt.

A tree usually 40 to 50 ft, sometimes 80 ft high (Sargent), with a trunk 3 ft 6 in. in diameter, and a narrow pyramidal head of rather pendulous branches; young shoots angled, not downy; winter buds stalked, resinous. Leaves ovate or oval, 3 to 6 in. long, 2 to 4 in. wide, rounded or broadly wedge-shaped at the base, pointed, the margins decurved and with numerous small lobes or large teeth, each again unequally toothed; nerves parallel, reddish, in ten to fifteen pairs; upper surface dark green, lower one pale or greyish, covered at first with down which mostly falls away except on the nerves; stalk ½ to 1 in. long. Male catkins 4 to 6 in. long, ¼ in. wide, usually three to five in a cluster. Fruits ½ to ¾ in. long, barrel-shaped, three to six together.

Native of western N. America from Alaska to California; introduced some time previous to 1880, since when it has been grown at Kew. There are three in the collection, the largest 52 × 4½ ft (1967), and another in the Edinburgh Botanic Garden of about the same size. In Eire, there are good examples at Headfort, Co. Meath, and in the Glasnevin Botanic Garden, Dublin. It is a handsome and striking alder, both when in flower in March and when in full foliage later. Jepson observes that in some parts of California it forms 'pure groves of great beauty in bottom lands near the sea'.

A. RUGOSA (Du Roi) Spreng.   SPECKLED ALDER

A shrub or small tree to about 25 ft. Leaves 1½ to 4 in. long, oval or ovate, rounded or pointed at the apex, broadly obtuse or rounded at the base, sharply and unevenly double-toothed, glabrous above, downy or glabrous and pale green beneath. Male catkins up to 4 in. long, appearing before the leaves. Female catkins upright, ⅖ to ⅗ in. long.

Native of N. America from Newfoundland to British Columbia, also ranging southward on the eastern side of the continent to W. Virginia, Ohio, and Minnesota. It is a hardy shrub of no particular merit, but useful in cold, wet situations. Its close relationship to *A. incana*, the grey alder of the Old World, is most evident in the following variety:

var. AMERICANA (Reg.) Fern. *A. incana americana* Reg.; *A. incana* var. *glauca* Loud., not Ait.—Leaves glaucous beneath.

A. SERRULATA (Ait.) Willd. *Betula serrulata* Ait.—A closely allied species, differing chiefly in its leaves, which are usually broadest above the middle and have the margins set with fine, nearly regular teeth. It is confined to the eastern and north-central United States.

A. SINUATA (Reg.) Rydb.   SITKA ALDER
A. viridis var *sinuata* Reg.; *A. sitchensis* Sarg.

This tree is a native of western N. America, from the borders of the Arctic Ocean to Oregon. It was introduced to Kew in 1903 by Prof. Sargent, who described it as a tree sometimes 40 ft high, with a trunk 2 ft in girth, forming a narrow head of short and nearly horizontal branches; but sometimes a mere shrub, and forming thickets; young shoots finely downy at first, and very glandular. Leaves ovate, 3 to 6 in. long, $1\frac{1}{2}$ to 4 in. wide, rounded or broadly wedge-shaped at the base, pointed, doubly toothed; light green above, pale, very lustrous green beneath; glabrous or with hairs along the midrib, and tufts in the vein-axils; viscid when young; stalk stout, grooved, $\frac{1}{2}$ to $\frac{3}{4}$ in. long. Male catkins 4 to 5 in. long. Sargent distinguishes this species among American arborescent alders by the flowers opening with or after the leaves, by the female catkins being enclosed during the winter, and by the lustrous under-surface of the leaves. It is the Western American representative of *A. viridis*.

A. SUBCORDATA C. A. Mey.

A tree up to 60 ft high; young shoots downy, angled toward the end; buds stalked. Leaves ovate or oval, with a rounded or slightly heart-shaped base, and a short, abrupt point; 3 to 6 in. long, 2 to 4 in. wide; irregularly and often doubly toothed towards the apex, more finely so towards the base; dark green and almost glabrous above, paler and downy beneath, especially along the midrib and veins; primary veins in eight to ten pairs; stalk $\frac{3}{4}$ to over 1 in. long, downy. Male catkins in clusters of four or five, very slender, up to 6 in. long, expanding sometimes as early as December. Fruits $\frac{3}{4}$ to $1\frac{1}{8}$ in. long, nodding, solitary or up to as many as five together.

Native of the Caucasus and Persia; introduced, according to Loudon, in 1838, and raised that year from seed in the Birmingham Botanic Garden. It is a handsome, fine-foliaged alder, retaining its leaves until the end of November. There are two at Kew: one, *pl.* 1900, 62 × 5$\frac{3}{4}$ ft, the other, *pl.* 1923, 55 × 5$\frac{1}{4}$ ft (1967). *A. cordata* is the only other species with which it is likely to be confused, but that differs markedly in its glabrous shoots, its less downy, simply toothed, deeply cordate leaves, and larger fruits.

A. TENUIFOLIA Nutt.

A shrub or tree up to 30 ft high, with a trunk 1½ to 2 ft in girth; young shoots red, and covered at first with a fine down, glabrous by autumn; buds stalked, downy. Leaves oval or ovate, 2 to 4 in. long, two-thirds as wide, rounded or slightly heart-shaped at the base, pointed; veins in about ten pairs, each vein ending at the point of a toothed lobe; dark green above, with down on the midrib and nerves; paler green and more or less downy beneath; stalk ½ to 1 in. long, downy. Male catkins expanding in March in clusters of three or four, each 1½ to 2½ in. long. Fruits narrowly egg-shaped, ½ to ⅝ in. long, three to five in a cluster.

Native of western N. America, from British Columbia to California. It is, perhaps, most nearly allied to *A. rubra*, but the leaves are not greyish beneath, the male catkins are shorter, and the fruits smaller. According to Sargent, the wing of the seed in *A. tenuifolia* is reduced to a narrow border, whilst it is broad in *A. rubra*.

var. OCCIDENTALIS (Dipp.) Callier *A. occidentalis* Dipp.—This distinct variety was introduced to Europe by A. Purpus, and first cultivated at Zoeschen in Germany by Dr Dieck, from whom it came to Kew in 1889. The leaves are larger than in the type, and on young trees very large; at Kew they have been 7 in. long by 5 in. wide. Veins in ten to twelve pairs, the entire under-surface at first downy. Fruits ⅝ to ⅞ in. long. Native of British Columbia and Oregon.

A. VIRIDIS (Chaix) DC.   GREEN ALDER
Betula viridis Chaix; *A. alnobetula* K. Koch

A shrub 3 to 10 ft high, forming a cluster of erect stems; young branchlets viscid and usually glabrous. Leaves viscid, ovate, or roundish oval, 1 to 3½ in. long, ⅝ to 3 in. wide, unevenly and sharply toothed, rounded or broadly wedge-shaped at the base, mostly abruptly pointed; dark green and glabrous above, green and downy on the midrib and veins beneath; stalk about ⅓ in. long. Male catkins opening in April and May with the leaves, 2 to 3 in. long. Fruits ⅝ in. long, oval, slender-stalked, borne in loose racemes.

Native of the mountains of Central and S.E. Europe; introduced in 1820. The leaves are variable in the degree of hairiness, and forms markedly downy on both sides at maturity are named f. MOLLIS (Beck) Hegi. Several varieties have been distinguished, based on form and size of leaf etc., of which one of the most distinct is:

var. PUMILA Cesati *A. viridis* var. *brembana* (Rota) Callier; *A. brembana* Rota; *A. v.* var. *parvifolia* Reg.—A curiously dwarfed mountain state of *A. viridis*, growing 1 or 2 ft high, and forming little close mounds. Adult plants have leaves ½ to 1 in. long. This dwarfed condition, however, is merely due to the climate under which it exists. A plant introduced to Kew gradually lost its dwarf character and after twenty years was no longer distinguishable from ordinary *A. viridis*. Found on the Swiss Alps etc.

An alder very similar to *A. viridis* is found in North America. By some botanists it is included in that species and by others recognised as of specific rank under the name A. CRISPA (Ait.) Pursh. In *Bot. Mag.*, n.s., t. 382, the late Dr Turrill points out that there is no constant and reliable character by which the American plants may be distinguished from the European, but on the average they differ in their larger leaves on longer petioles and their larger fruits (strobiles). He considered that they should rank as a subspecies of *A. viridis* (subsp. *crispa* (Ait.) Turrill). The American green alder was first introduced in 1782. Both it and the European green alder are hardy and vigorous shrubs, of no special ornamental value, but useful for furnishing cold, damp spots.

The Siberian green alder—A. FRUTICOSA Rupr.—is also closely allied to *A. viridis*, and scarcely to be differentiated from it.

ALOYSIA VERBENACEAE

A genus of about twenty species, closely related to *Lippia*, in which it has been included. All are natives of the warmer parts of America from California to Chile.

A. TRIPHYLLA (L'Hérit.) LEMON-SCENTED VERBENA

Verbena triphyyla L'Hérit.; *Aloysia citrodora* Ortega ex Pers., nom. illegit.; *Lippia citrodora* (Ortega) H.B.K.

A deciduous shrub (naturally a small tree), reaching in the southern parts of the British Isles 10 to 15 ft or more in height; young shoots angular. Leaves mostly in threes, very fragrant, lance-shaped; usually 3 to 4 in. long, ½ to ⅞ in. wide; wedge-shaped at the base, taper-pointed, not toothed; both surfaces glandular, especially the upper one, pale green; margins set with appressed bristles. The veins are parallel, springing at right angles from the midrib. Flowers numerous, small, pale purple, produced in August in slender, terminal, stalked, downy panicles, 3 to 5 in. high; corolla tubular, ⅙ in. long, downy, as is also the cylindrical, toothed calyx.

Native of Chile; introduced in 1784. Near London this well-known shrub needs the protection of a wall, and is often grown in cold conservatories for the pleasant lemon-like scent of the leaves. In the Isle of Wight and the Channel Islands it becomes a large bush without any protection. Easily increased by summer cuttings.

ALYSSUM CRUCIFERAE

A genus of about 150 species of annuals, biennials and perennials, natives of the Old World. A few of them are true shrubs of dwarf habit and of these the species described is the best known in gardens. The genus is also represented in cultivation by a form of the polymorphic *A. murale* Waldst. & Kit., usually grown under the invalid name *A. argenteum* Vitm., but this scarcely qualifies as a woody plant, which is also true of the well-known *Alyssum saxatile*. The latter, with a few allied species, is better placed in the genus *Aurinia*, in which its correct name is *Aurinia saxatilis* (L.) Desv.

A. SPINOSUM L.

Ptilotrichum spinosum (L.) Boiss.

A spiny shrub of dense habit, with interlacing branches, 6 to 15 in. high, usually much more in diameter; young shoots covered with a close, silvery scurf; spines slender, $\frac{1}{8}$ to $\frac{5}{8}$ in. long. Leaves narrowly oblong to oblanceolate, tapered at the base, pointed or rounded at the apex, entire; $\frac{1}{2}$ to 2 in. long, $\frac{1}{16}$ in. or less wide; covered on both sides with silvery, star-like down. Flowers white or pale rose, fragrant, $\frac{3}{10}$ in. wide, numerous and closely packed in terminal umbellate racemes $\frac{3}{4}$ in. wide; petals four, obovate, tapered to the base. Pod circular to obovate, $\frac{1}{8}$ in. wide, glabrous, terminated by the persistent style.

Native of S.W. Europe and N. Africa, common in calcareous rocky places in S. France and Spain; introduced in 1683. It succeeds very well in full sunshine in rock gardens south of London, flowering in May and June.

AMELANCHIER SERVICEBERRY ROSACEAE

A genus of shrubs and small trees found wild in Europe, Asia, and most abundantly in N. America. The name is an adaptation of 'amelancier', an old name for *A. ovalis* in Savoy. The species are all deciduous, and have alternate, simple leaves, white flowers, and small black or purplish fruits, globose or pear-shaped, and containing five or ten seeds. The attractions of the amelanchiers are in the pure whiteness and abundance of the flowers, their graceful form, and in the fine shades of red, and sometimes yellow, the leaves assume before they fall.

Their cultivation is easy, as they will thrive in any soil that is not too dry and poor on the one hand, or water-logged on the other. They may be raised from seed, by layers, or by division. The practice of grafting them on the hawthorn, more common in Britain once than it is now, but still usual on the continent, should be strictly avoided.

Although *Amelanchier* is a small, compact genus there is considerable difficulty in distinguishing the American kinds, owing to the existence of forms intermediate between, or slightly differing from, the recognised types. The nomenclature, too, is extremely involved. The amelanchiers of N. America have been reviewed by G. N. Jones in *American Species of Amelanchier* (1946) and this work is largely followed in the present edition.

A. ARBOREA (Michx. f.) Fern.

Mespilus arborea Michx. f.; *A. canadensis* of many authors, not *A. canadensis* (L.) Med.

A tree 20 to 30 ft high in Britain, but occasionally over 40 ft high in a wild state; branches slender, the lower ones pendulous, forming in the open a wide-topped, rounded head. Leaves ovate or oval, rounded or heart-shaped at the base, pointed, saw-toothed, 1½ to 3 in. long, 1 to 1¾ in. wide; both surfaces clothed with white hairs when they expand, soon becoming quite glabrous and of firm texture. Flowers pure white, produced in April (usually when the leaves are less than half their full size), in erect clusters 2 to 3 in. long, terminating short lateral twigs; petals obovate or strap-shaped, ½ to ¾ in. long, ¼ in. wide. Fruit ripening in June, orange-shaped, ¼ to ⅓ in. wide, changing from green to red, finally to black-purple, dry and tasteless.

Native of the eastern and central United States from Maine to Florida and westward to Minnesota and Louisiana; owing to the confusion between this species and *A. laevis* the date of introduction is uncertain, but one or the other was introduced in 1746. From the time of the ripening of the fruit it is often called 'June-berry'. There are few more delightful small trees than this when seen at its best, which, at Kew, is usually about the second week in April; the whole tree then becomes sheeted with white. Unhappily, it is a very fleeting beauty, lasting, as a rule, less than a week. Its autumn beauty is more durable, and it is then one of the most striking of hardy trees, the foliage changing before it falls to a rich soft red; in some forms, however, to a clear bright yellow or orange-scarlet. See also *A. laevis*.

The name *A. canadensis* has had a chequered history. By early botanists it was used in a very wide sense, which included both *A. arborea* and *A. laevis*, as well as other related species. After the publication of Wiegand's monograph (1912) the name *A. canadensis* (L.) Med. was restricted to the species described above, but in 1941 Fernald (*Rhodora*, Vol. 43) pointed out that the *Mespilus canadensis* of Linnaeus is in fact the species which had been known as *A. oblongifolia* Roem., and it is for that species, which is rare in gardens, that the name *A. canadensis* (L.) Med. must be used. For the amelanchier described above, which is the *A. canadensis* of Rehder's *Manual* etc., the correct name under the rules of botanical nomenclature is *A. arborea*.

A. ASIATICA (Sieb. & Zucc.) Walp.   [PLATE 10

Aronia asiatica Sieb. & Zucc.; *A. canadensis* var. *japonica* Miq.

A deciduous tree, of very graceful habit, 15 to 40 ft high, branches slender. Leaves oval or ovate, pointed, 1½ to 3 in. long, half as much wide, sometimes nearly or wholly entire, but mostly toothed except at the base; covered when quite young with a loose floss which soon falls away, leaving both surfaces quite glabrous. Flowers on stalks ½ to ¾ in. long, in broad, erect racemes 1½ to 2½ in. long; white, fragrant; petals strap-shaped, ⅝ in. long. Fruit black-purple, about the size of a black currant.

Native of China, Korea, and Japan, introduced from the last-named country in 1865. The Chinese form, which is sometimes given varietal rank as var. SINICA Schneid., differs little from the type; it was introduced in 1920. It is not easy to distinguish *A. asiatica* from some of the forms of *A. arborea*, but at Kew it always flowers two or three weeks later (usually in mid-May, when the leaves are about full size), and the petals are uniformly strap-shaped. Also, the top of the ovary is woolly, while in *A. arborea* it is glabrous. A slender, elegant tree.

A. BARTRAMIANA (Tausch) Roem.

Pyrus bartramiana Tausch; *A. oligocarpa* Roem.

A low shrub usually 2 to 3 (rarely more than 6) ft high. Leaves oval or slightly ovate, 1 to 2 in. long, tapering towards both ends, sharply toothed nearly to the base, almost glabrous from the commencement, but with some loose floss on the surfaces and edges when expanding. Flowers pure white, ¾ to 1 in. across; solitary, in pairs, sometimes in threes or fours, on short lateral twigs, each flower on a slender stalk ½ to 1 in. long. Petals rounded, obovate, ¼ in. wide, broader in proportion to their length than in the other amelanchiers; top of ovary densely woolly. Fruit pear-shaped or oblong, dark purple, nearly ½ in. long, not so wide. *Bot. Mag.*, t. 8499.

Native of Canada, Newfoundland, and the northern United States, and the most northerly of the amelanchiers, inhabiting cold swamps and mountain bogs. It is extremely rare in cultivation, the plant usually supplied by nurserymen for this species being a form of *A. arborea*. It is easily distinguished by its few-flowered inflorescence and the rounded petals; and differs from all other species in cultivation by the prussic acid odour of the bark when bruised—like that of many cherries and almonds. A specimen in the R.H.S. Garden at Wisley has reached a height of 12 ft. It appears to be the true species.

A. CANADENSIS (L.) Med.

Mespilus canadensis L.; *A. oblongifolia* Roem.

A tall shrub with erect stems, spreading by means of sucker growths from the base; said to be sometimes a small tree to 25 ft high. Leaves very woolly when quite young, ultimately becoming glabrous; firm and rather leathery when mature, 1½ to 2½ in. long, ½ to 1¼ in. wide; elliptic to oblong, more rarely widest in the lower half, rounded (rarely cordate) at the base, finely and evenly toothed, though sometimes entire near the base. Racemes erect, compact, and remaining so in fruit, covered at first with a thick, loose floss, 2 or 3 in. long, carrying numerous white flowers, the petals of which are more distinctly and uniformly obovate than in *A. arborea* or *laevis* and somewhat shorter, being at the most $\frac{2}{5}$ in. long. Fruiting racemes with the lower pedicels $\frac{2}{5}$ to $\frac{4}{5}$ in. long. Fruit black and juicy, with the sepals erect or ascending. *Bot. Mag.*, t. 7619.

Native of eastern N. America, usually found in bogs and swamps, and of alder-like habit. It is allied to *A. arborea* and *laevis* but differs in the more obovate petals, the erect, more compact racemes, and the erect or ascending sepals on the fruit. The habit, too, is more fastigiate. As a shrubby amelanchier it is useful in gardens, forming in time a dense thicket. Easily increased by division in spring.

This species is better known as *A. oblongifolia*; for the *A. canadensis* of previous editions, see *A. arborea*, but some plants grown in gardens as "*A. canadensis*" may be *A. laevis*.

A. FLORIDA Lindl.

A. oxyodon Koehne; *A. alnifolia* of some authors, not Nutt.

A deciduous shrub, producing a thicket of erect stems to 10 ft or more high, or a small tree. Leaves roundish oval, 1 to 2 in. long, about two-thirds as wide, rounded at the apex, more rarely bluntly pointed, rounded or slightly heart-shaped at the base, glabrous, or slightly downy when young, margins coarsely toothed above the middle, more rarely in the lower half. Flowers white, about $\frac{3}{4}$ to $1\frac{1}{4}$ in. across, borne five to fifteen together in erect racemes, which are covered at first with a whitish down but soon glabrous; summit of ovary densely downy at flowering time but soon glabrous. Fruit black-purple, juicy and edible, glabrous. *Bot. Mag.*, t. 8611.

Native of western N. America from S.E. Alaska to W. Oregon and N.W. California; introduced by Douglas in 1826.

f. TOMENTOSA Sealy—Leaves glaucous, slightly downy or glabrous beneath; flower-stalks densely downy. *Bot. Mag.*, t. 9496.

The following related species from western N. America may be mentioned here:

A. ALNIFOLIA Nutt.—This species is closely allied to *A. florida* and the two have been much confused. According to Jones (op. cit.) it is best distinguished by its smaller flowers (to $\frac{4}{5}$ in. across); also, the leaves are usually rounder and thicker and the habit dwarfer. Its natural range lies further inland, in the Rocky Mountains. Another close relative is A. PALLIDA Greene, native of California, which differs from the two preceding species in the fine, persistent downiness of the leaves beneath; the leaves are also smaller and narrower and the racemes only four- to six-flowered. Much more distinct is:

A. CUSICKII Fern.—This is the largest-flowered of all the amelanchiers, the flowers being up to 2 in. across. It is a slenderly branched shrub 4 to 10 ft high; leaves quite glabrous even when young. It occupies a small area within the range of *A. alnifolia*. For a description of this species in its native habitat see B. O. Mulligan in *Journ. R.H.S.*, Vol. 73, 1948, p. 155.

A. UTAHENSIS Koehne—A very variable species inhabiting the drier parts of western N. America. It is unusual among the amelanchiers in having only two to four styles instead of the normal five. This peculiarity is also seen in *A. pallida*, but in that species the leaves are smaller, with nine pairs of veins at the most (eleven to thirteen in *A. utahensis*). This species has been introduced under various names from different parts of its range, e.g. *A. prunifolia* Greene, *A. rubescens* Greene, *A. purpusii* Koehne. These, however, are best considered (Jones, op. cit.) as states of *A. utahensis*.

A. LAEVIS Wieg.
A. canadensis of many authors, not *Mespilus canadensis* L.

A large shrub or small tree closely allied to *A. arborea* (q.v.) and, like that species, known erroneously as "*A. canadensis*" which name belongs properly to the species described in previous editions under the name *A. oblongifolia*. It is quite distinct from *A. arborea* by reason of the bronzy purple colour of the unfolding leaves and by their being almost or quite devoid of down almost from the beginning. In *A. arborea* both sides of the unfolding leaves are covered with white down. The fruit of *A. laevis* is black and sweet, that of *A. arborea* dry and tasteless. Other points of distinction are that in *A. laevis* the raceme is more lax, with the lower pedicels up to 2 in. long, and that the flowers are borne when the leaves are about half-grown.

A. laevis is found wild in the mountains of most of the eastern United States and extends into Canada as far as Newfoundland, where, however, it is reduced to shrubby dimensions. The comments on the garden value of *A. arborea* are equally applicable to this species, which is, however, considered to be the finer of the two, by reason of the bronzy colouring of the unfolding leaves and the more graceful racemes. It is a little later to flower.

A. × GRANDIFLORA Rehd.—A beautiful hybrid between *A. laevis* and *A. arborea* of which there are two forms in cultivation. The plant which Rehder took as the type was in cultivation in Europe as early as 1870 when the Simon-Louis nurseries listed it as *A. lancifolia*. Young leaves purplish, covered with a loose wool. Flowers larger than in *A. arborea* on longer, more slender racemes, tinged pink in the bud. The woolly young growths distinguish it from *A. laevis*. 'RUBESCENS', the other form of the cross, arose spontaneously in Seneca Park, Rochester, U.S.A., as a seedling of *A. arborea*. It is similar to the type, but the flowers are described as purplish pink in bud and tinged with pink when open.

Naturalised amelanchiers are fairly frequent on sandy heaths in Surrey and neighbouring counties. These have been referred to *A. laevis* and more recently to *A. confusa* Hylander. In *Flora Europaea*, Vol. 2 (1968), Franco gives *A. confusa* as a synonym of *A. × grandiflora* Rehd. (see above) and states that this hybrid is found naturalised in western Europe. So far as the British plants are concerned the position is obscure, however. Some specimens in the Kew Herbarium look like *A.* × *grandiflora*, others do not. Mr R. D. Meikle suggests that further investigation might well show that the British populations consist not of one species or hybrid but of a number of closely related species, their hybrids and back-crosses.

A. OVALIS Med.　　SNOWY MESPILUS

A. vulgaris Moench; *A. rotundifolia* (Lam.) Dum.-Cours.; *Crataegus rotundifolia* Lam.;
Mespilus amelanchier L.

A low tree 15 to 20 ft high, or more often a shrub. Leaves roundish oval, very downy and pure white beneath when young, becoming nearly or quite glabrous at maturity, 1 to 1½ in. long, ¾ to 1 in. wide; the margin sometimes quite entire, but usually more or less toothed, especially towards the apex. Racemes erect, carrying few but large white flowers often 1½ in. in diameter. Petals narrowly oblong; calyx covered with loose floss at first, its lobes triangular. Fruit at first red, then black, covered with a purplish bloom; about the size of a black currant, eatable but not very palatable.

Native of the mountains of Central and S. Europe; of unrecorded introduction, but in cultivation early in the eighteenth century. It has the largest individual flowers of all the amelanchiers commonly seen in cultivation, but not so large as in *A. cusickii* (q.v. under *A. florida*) or some forms of *A. sanguinea*. It is very beautiful in late April and early May.

var. CRETICA (Willd.) Bean　*A. vulgaris* var. *cretica* (Willd.) Boiss.　*A. cretica* (Willd.) DC.—A shrub covered with a close white down on leaf, young wood, calyx, and flower-stalk. Native of the E. Mediterranean.

var. INTEGRIFOLIA (Boiss. & Hohen.) Bean　*A. vulgaris* var. *integrifolia* (Boiss. & Hohen.) Boiss.—Leaves always entire.

A. SANGUINEA (Pursh) DC.

Pyrus sanguinea Pursh; *A. rotundifolia* Roem.

A deciduous shrub 3 to 10 ft high, straggling or erect, sometimes spreading by suckers and forming dense thickets of stems; or a small tree to 20 ft high. Leaves oval or oblong to almost rounded, 1 to 2¾ in. long, blunt or acute at the apex, densely downy beneath when unfolding, later glabrous, margins rather coarsely toothed almost to the base of the leaf. Flowers white, to about 1¼ in. wide, in loose racemes; top of ovary densely downy. Fruit juicy, purplish black, with a glaucous tinge.

Native of eastern N. America from S. Quebec to N. Carolina.

var. GRANDIFLORA (Wieg.) Rehd.　*A. sanguinea* f. *grandiflora* Wieg.　*A. amabilis* Wieg.—Flowers to 1¾ in. across, the lowermost on stalks up to 1⅗ in. long. Such forms are considered by Jones (op. cit.) to be part of the normal variation of the species.

A. GASPENSIS (Wieg.) Fern.　*A. sanguinea* var. *gaspensis* Wieg.—This species is confined to a small area of Canada around the St Lawrence estuary. It is unusual in bearing its flowers when the leaves are fully expanded; the leaves, too, are more rounded at the apex than in *A. sanguinea*, truncate at the base, and the flowers smaller, to ¾ in. wide at the most.

A. × SPICATA (Lam.) K. Koch

Crataegus spicata Lam.; *A. ovalis* Borkh., not Med.

A deciduous shrub increasing by sucker growths from the base and forming a thicket of stems 6 to 12 ft high; young shoots and under-surface of leaves downy when young. Leaves broadly oval, obovate, or ovate, toothed nearly to the base; 1 to 2¼ in. long. Flowers opening in late April and May on erect woolly-stalked racemes 2 in. long; white, the oblong petals ⅓ in. long, broadening towards the end. Fruit blue-black on stalks up to ½ in. long.

This amelanchier has been known in cultivation for over a century and is probably a hybrid between *A. canadensis* (*oblongifolia*) and *A. stolonifera*, between which it is intermediate in stature. The sepals crowning the fruit provide a distinction; in *canadensis* they are erect, in *stolonifera* they are recurved, but in × *spicata* they spread more or less horizontally.

Many American botanists consider that the *Crataegus spicata* of Lamarck is *not* the plant described above but the common dwarf amelanchier of eastern N. America (see under *A. stolonifera*) and accept the combination *A. spicata* (Lam.) K. Koch as the valid name for that species. If this view were correct (but it has been disputed), then some other name would have to be found for the plant of European gardens described above.

A. STOLONIFERA Wieg.

A deciduous shrub 4 to 6 ft high, increasing by underground suckers and forming a small thicket of stiff, erect stems. Leaves oval, sometimes inclined to ovate, finely toothed except towards the base where they are rounded or slightly heart-shaped; 1 to 2 in. long, ¾ to 1¼ in. wide; green when young, covered beneath for a short time with white down, soon nearly or completely glabrous; stalk ¼ to ⅝ in. long. Flowers white, produced on short, erect racemes; petals ⅓ in. long, broadening towards the rounded end. Fruit purplish black, glaucous, 'sweet, juicy and of good flavour, ripening in July' (Wiegand).

Native of eastern N. America from Newfoundland to Virginia, in non-calcareous soils. In the attractive but confusing group of suckering amelanchiers of its native region it is distinguished by the following group of characters: habit dwarf; leaves finely toothed; summit of ovary woolly.

A. HUMILIS Wieg.—This species is closely related to *A. stolonifera* but differs mainly in the more coarsely toothed leaves. The two species are merged by Jones (op. cit.) under the name *A. spicata* (Lam.) K. Koch, which in the present work is used in a different sense.

A. OBOVALIS (Michx.) Ashe *Mespilus canadensis* var. *obovalis* Michx.—A species of the coastal plain from Pennsylvania to Georgia. It resembles *A. stolonifera* in habit but bears its flowers early in spring on the leafless wood;

the glabrous ovary also serves to distinguish it. In the latter character and the erect sepals it recalls *A. canadensis* but is a dwarfer plant. So far as is known, it has not been introduced, and might prove tender.

× AMELASORBUS   ROSACEAE

In the rose family, hybrids between genera very dissimilar in outward aspect are not uncommon, and among them are the hybrids that have arisen between *Sorbus* and *Amelanchier*. In addition to the one described here, others have been reported from Europe but are apparently not in cultivation.

× A. JACKII Rehd.

A deciduous shrub to 9 ft high. Leaves 1¼ to 2¼ in. long (sometimes longer on extension growth), some entire, others showing the influence of *Sorbus* in being pinnately lobed, or even divided near the base into distinct leaflets. Flowers white, with oblong petals, about ⅘ in. across, borne in short panicles

× AMELASORBUS JACKII

(not racemes as in *Amelanchier*, nor corymbs as in *Sorbus*). Fruit subglobose, dark red, with a bluish bloom.

A hybrid between *Amelanchier alnifolia* Nutt. and *Sorbus scopulina* Greene, found wild in various localities in western N. America, where the two species are in contact. It is an interesting shrub, only recently brought into commerce in Britain, and surprisingly vigorous.

AMORPHA LEGUMINOSAE

A genus of shrubs exclusively native of N. America, with alternate pinnate leaves and elongated racemes of blue, purple, or white flowers. These plants belong to the pea-flowered group of Leguminosae, but the flowers, instead of having the normal five petals (namely, the standard petal, the two wing petals, and the two forming the keel), have but one—the standard. The flowers, however, are so crowded that the others are not missed. The two dwarf species—*canescens* and *nana*—are best adapted for gardens, although the foliage of *A. fruticosa* is very handsome. The two former can be increased by cuttings when seeds are not available, and *A. fruticosa* produces sucker growths from the base which can be removed with some roots attached. Besides the species more fully described below, there are in cultivation A. CALIFORNICA Torr. & Gr. (California) and A. VIRGATA Small (S.E. United States). Both resemble *A. fruticosa* in habit and general aspect, but *A. californica* has downy stems and leaf-stalks set with prickly glands, whilst *A. virgata* has broad leathery leaflets and twiggy branches.

A. CANESCENS Nutt. LEAD PLANT

A sub-shrubby plant 2 to 4 ft high, entirely covered with grey down. Stems erect, unbranched, springing from a woody base to which they largely die back every winter. Leaves pinnate, 2 to 3 in. long, composed of from ten to twenty pairs of leaflets and an odd one; leaflets ⅜ to ⅝ in. long, oblong or ovate, stalkless, extending the entire length of the main stalk; they are downy on both sides, but paler beneath. Flowers thickly crowded on cylindrical spikes, 3 to 6 in. long, produced from the leaf-axils near the apex of the shoot, and thus forming a large, leafy panicle 6 to 10 (sometimes 15 to 18) in. high. Each flower is about ¼ in. long, with a dull purplish-blue standard petal, and a grey downy calyx; they are borne close enough together to touch. Pod less than ¼ in. long, hairy, one-seeded. Anthers conspicuously orange-coloured. *Bot. Mag.*, t. 6618.

Native of eastern N. America; introduced in 1812. It flowers from late July to September, and only ripens seeds during very fine autumns. It may be increased by cuttings made of shoots too weak to flower, which must be rooted in gentle warmth. It makes a large deep root-stock, which enables it not only to withstand, but to thrive best in, hot, droughty seasons. It is an interesting and rather striking plant which is well suited for the front of a shrubbery. In a wild state it extends over a considerable latitude, and shows some variation in the grey tints of its stems and leaves, and especially in the size and openness of its inflorescence. The popular name of "lead plant" is founded on the belief which once prevailed that its presence in a wild state indicated the existence of lead ore beneath the soil.

A. FRUTICOSA L. FALSE INDIGO

A deciduous shrub 6 to 15 ft high, of spreading, rather ungainly habit, branches slightly grooved, either slightly downy or glabrous. Leaves pinnate, glabrous or somewhat downy, with thirteen to thirty-three leaflets, which are oval or oblong, ending in a bristle-like apex, and varying in length from 1 to 2 in.; there is a short, thread-like stipel at the base of each leaflet, and numerous transparent dots are scattered over the blade. Racemes slender, cylindrical, 4 to 6 in. long, more or less downy, or almost glabrous, produced at the end of the shoots of the year, and from the axils of the terminal leaves. Flowers ⅛ in. long, densely packed, purplish blue, with yellow anthers. Pod ⅛ in. long, very warty, one- or two-seeded.

Native of the southern United States; introduced to England in 1724, by, it is said, Mark Catesby, the author of the *Natural History of Carolina*. It exhibits under cultivation a certain amount of variation in the shape and size of the leaflets, in the number to each leaf, and especially in the degree of pubescence on various parts of the plant. This shrub flowers in July, when its slender racemes give a pretty effect; the foliage also is ornamental; yet it belongs to an inferior class of shrubs, and is perhaps best suited for rough shrubberies where it may be left to take care of itself. At Kew, in open ground, the shoots die back nearly their entire length, and they have to be pruned over every spring. It is a variable species and numerous natural and garden variants have been distinguished but are of no horticultural importance today. A. GLABRA Poir., an allied but more glabrous species, was in commerce early in the nineteenth century and is no doubt still to be seen in botanical collections.

A. NANA Nutt.
A. microphylla Pursh

A low, deciduous shrub about 2 ft high; stems branching, and having little or no down. Leaves pinnate, 2 to 4 in. long, with eight to thirteen pairs of leaflets and an odd one; leaflets ⅛ to ⅜ in. long, oval or obovate, nearly glabrous. Flowers purple, fragrant, very closely set in cylindrical terminal racemes 1 to 2 in. long. Pod one-seeded, ⅕ in. long, glandular.

Native of eastern and central N. America; introduced in 1811. Although somewhat similar to *A. canescens* in foliage, it is really very distinct. It is a true shrub, and has little or none of the grey down so conspicuous in *A. canescens*; its flower-spikes are also much shorter and not clustered. A rather dainty plant, but scarcely known in gardens nowadays.

AMPELOPSIS VITACEAE

A genus of some twenty species, natives of N. America and Asia, not represented in Europe. They are deciduous climbers which support themselves by tendrils and in this resemble *Vitis* but differ from *Parthenocissus*, in which the shoots are equipped with sticky pads that render the plants self-supporting on walls. The leaves are simple or compound and provide no differentiating characters. The flowers of *Ampelopsis* are, however, very distinct from those of *Vitis* in that the petals spread outward in orthodox fashion; in *Vitis* they are united at the tips to form a cap which falls as the flower opens. In the fruit there is no difference from *Vitis*; the name *Ampelopsis* derives from the Greek and means 'resembling the grape'.

The species described here all appeared in earlier editions under *Vitis*, but the genus *Ampelopsis* is by no means a new creation, having been founded by Michaux in 1803. Bentham and Hooker, in *Genera Plantarum*, interpreted *Vitis* in a very wide sense, including in it both *Ampelopsis* and the Linnaean genus *Cissus*, and their view has influenced garden nomenclature up to the present time, although it is no longer accepted by botanists. In the last edition of this work W. J. Bean retained this wide conception of *Vitis*, but in his contribution to *The Dictionary of Gardening* he adopted the system of classification first proposed by Planchon in 1887, which is the one that prevails at the present time and is followed in this revision.

All the species are of easy cultivation, provided the climate is warm enough for them. They like a good loamy soil and plenty of root room, although *A. brevipedunculata* var. *maximowiczii* (*Vitis heterophylla*) produces its blue fruits more abundantly with a restricted root run. The most inconvenient thing in their cultivation is the provision of suitable support. Best of all, perhaps, is a pergola on which the shoots can be trained and pruned back annually as much as is necessary. They can also be trained up posts, when, if the shoots are allowed to hang loosely, they are very elegant. All species are easily rooted from leafy cuttings of firm growth, made in July and August.

A. ACONITIFOLIA Bunge
Vitis aconitifolia (Bunge) Hance

A slender-stemmed, luxuriantly leafy, deciduous climber; young shoots glabrous. Leaves very variable in shape and size, composed either of three or five stalkless leaflets radiating from the end of a common stalk which is ½ to 2 in. long. The leaflets are lanceolate or diamond-shaped in general outline, but always deeply and coarsely toothed, and often conspicuously three- or five-lobed, the lobes reaching sometimes to the midrib. The entire leaf is 2 to 5 in. across, the leaflets 1 to 3 in. long, deep glossy green above, pale beneath, and glabrous on both sides except for small tufts of down in the vein-axils beneath. Flowers produced in August and September in numerous forked cymes. Fruits scarcely ¼ in. long, roundish-obovate, dull orange.

Native of China. Of the vines with compound leaves and deeply cut leaflets this is the hardiest and most luxuriant in growth. It can be trained up a tall post, which it will soon cover with a beautiful tangle. There has been some confusion in gardens between this species and *A. japonica*.

A. JAPONICA (Thunb.) Mak. *Paullinia japonica* Thunb.; *Vitis serjanaefolia*

TS—L

AMPELOPSIS ACONITIFOLIA

(Bunge) K. Koch—This is a native of China and Korea, cultivated in Japan, and quite distinct in foliage from *A. aconitifolia*. The leaflets are in threes or fives, and in the latter case are arranged pinnately on the common stalk (not all radiating from its ends as in the other). Another distinction is that the rhachis between the pairs of leaflets is winged. Sometimes the lowest pair of leaflets are themselves pinnately divided. In other respects the leaflets are dark green above, pale glossy green beneath, glabrous. Fruit ¼ in. wide, violet-blue. The plant has a tuberous root like a dahlia.

A. ARBOREA (L.) Koehne   PEPPER VINE
Vitis arborea L.; *A. bipinnata* Michx.

A deciduous climber, with slender, purplish, nearly or quite glabrous, somewhat angular, zigzag shoots, slightly marked with lenticels; tendrils slender, forked. Leaves 5 to 8 in. long, about as much wide, doubly (sometimes trebly) pinnate, and composed of numerous stalked leaflets, which are ovate, ½ to 1¾ in. long, ⅓ to 1¼ in. wide; sometimes lobed, always with very large, sharp, triangular teeth, the apex pointed, the base narrowly to broadly wedge-shaped; dark green and glabrous above; at first downy on the veins and in the vein-axils beneath, ultimately nearly or quite glabrous. Flowers in open, long-stalked cymes. Berries dark purple, about ⅓ in. in diameter.

Native of the southern United States; introduced in 1700, and quite hardy, although better against a wall than in the open. It is a very handsome climber when in vigorous growth, but although it flowers occasionally, rarely develops fruit with us. Perhaps partially or wholly evergreen in warmer climates. (See also *A. orientalis*.)

A. BODINIERI (Lévl. & Vant.) Rehd.

Vitis bodinieri Lévl. & Vant.; *Vitis micans* (Rehd.) Bean; *A. micans* Rehd.

A deciduous climbing vine up to 20 ft high; young shoots glabrous, purplish on the sunny side. Leaves roundish to triangular-ovate, three-lobed (often inconspicuously so), shallowly heart-shaped to truncate at the base, slenderly pointed, coarsely and triangularly toothed; 2½ to 5 in. long, glabrous on both sides, but of a glittering green above and pale or rather glaucous beneath; stalk purplish, 1½ to 3 in. long. Flowers crowded in a branching cluster at the end of a slender stalk 1 to 2 in. long. Fruits dark blue, flattened-globose, ⅕ in. wide.

Native of Hupeh and Szechwan, China; introduced by Wilson in 1900 to Veitch's Coombe Wood nursery. It was put in commerce by them as "*Vitis repens*". It is apparently one of the two plants once called "*Vitis flexuosa wilsonii*" but the charming little vine more generally grown under that name is a true *Vitis*, and correctly called *V. flexuosa* var. *parvifolia*. There is a vigorous plant of *A. bodinieri* on the vine pergola at Kew.

A. HUMULIFOLIA Bunge *Cissus davidiana* Carr.; *Vitis davidiana* (Carr.) Nichols.—An ally of the above, also native to China. It resembles *A. bodinieri* in its lustrous leaves, but these are of a brighter green, and usually three- or five-lobed, rarely unlobed, with rounded sinuses. Also distinguished by its fruit, which is pale yellow, changing partly or wholly to pale blue. It has been confused with *A. brevipedunculata*, but differs in its thicker and firmer leaves, which are whitish beneath. Introduced to cultivation by the French missionary David around 1865.

A. VITIFOLIA (Boiss.) Planch. *Cissus vitifolia* Boiss.; *Vitis persica* Boiss.— A native of S.W. Asia from Persia to Kashmir, allied to *A. bodinieri*, but differing in the absence of tendrils and other characters.

A. BREVIPEDUNCULATA (Maxim.) Trautv.

Cissus brevipedunculata Maxim.; *V. heterophylla* var. *cordata* Reg.; *A. heterophylla* var. *amurensis* Planch.

A vigorous climber with roughly hairy young shoots. Leaves distinctly three-, rarely five-lobed, the side lobes spreading and pointed; heart-shaped at the base; 2 to 6 in. long and wide, coarsely toothed, the teeth rounded, but ending in a minute abrupt point (mucro); dark green above with scattered short hairs at first; bristly hairy beneath; stalk from three-fourths to as long as the blade, very hairy, especially at first. Inflorescence hairy, once or twice forked, each fork terminated by a cymose flower-cluster. Fruit ¼ to ⅓ in. across, amethyst blue.

var. MAXIMOWICZII (Reg.) Rehd. *Vitis heterophylla* var. *maximowiczii* Reg.; *V. h.* var. *humulifolia* Hook. f.; *V. heterophylla* Thunb.; *Ampelopsis heterophylla* (Thunb.) Sieb. & Zucc., not Blume—This chiefly differs from the type in having the leaves beneath and the branchlets glabrous or only slightly downy when young. As seen in cultivation this variety (better known as *Vitis heterophylla*) is remarkable for the great variation in leaf-shape shown even by a single plant;

sometimes the leaves are broadly heart-shaped and not lobed at all, sometimes slightly three-lobed, sometimes deeply three- or five-lobed. *Bot. Mag.*, t. 5682.

A. brevipedunculata and var. *maximowiczii* have a wide range in E. Asia, being found in China, Korea, Japan, and the Russian Far East. The variety, at any rate in Japan, appears to grow intermingled with the type and may represent no more than a state of the species rather than a distinct entity.

The great beauty of these vines is in their blue fruits, and these are only produced when the plant is fully exposed to the sun. The best results, with either of the cultivated forms, are obtained by planting it against a south wall, where it has a rather restricted root run.

cv. 'CITRULLOIDES'.—Leaves deeply five-lobed, the central lobe narrowed near the middle and the base. In cultivation 1875.

cv. 'ELEGANS'.—Leaves handsomely splashed with pink and white, and the young shoots pink. It is too delicate to thrive away from a wall. Introduced by Siebold before 1847.

A. CHAFFANJONII (Lévl.) Rehd.
Vitis chaffanjonii Lévl.; *A. watsoniana* Wils.

A deciduous climber allied to *A. megalophylla*; leaves pinnate, up to 1 ft in length. Leaflets five or seven, oval or oblong, 1½ to 4½ in. long, ¾ to 2 in. wide; rounded or broadly tapered at the base, terminating in a long, slender point; sparsely toothed, lustrous green above, claret purple beneath, and, like the young shoots, perfectly smooth.

This vine was discovered in Western Hupeh, China, by Wilson and introduced in 1900. It was distributed by Messrs Veitch from the Coombe Wood nursery erroneously as "*V. leeoides*", and appeared as such in early editions of this work where, however, it was suggested that it might prove to be a new species. It differs from the true *A. leeoides* by its leaves being simply pinnate, never bipinnate. It does not seem to be very vigorous grown in an exposed position, but was very handsome trained up a pole in the Coombe Wood nursery. It succeeds well when grown on a south wall.

The true A. LEEOIDES (Maxim.) Planch., a native of Japan and Formosa, is probably not in cultivation.

A. CORDATA Michx.
Vitis indivisa Willd.

A vigorous deciduous climber; young bark warted, not or very slightly downy; tendrils forked, sometimes absent. Leaves roundish ovate, more or less heart-shaped at the base, shallowly but sharply toothed; glabrous or slightly downy along the veins and in the vein-axils beneath; 2 to 5 in. long, scarcely as wide; stalk often downy, shorter than the blade. Flowers on slender-stalked cymes 1½ to 3 in. broad. Fruits blue or greenish blue.

Native of the south-east and south central United States; introduced in 1803. It is quite hardy and grows vigorously at Kew, but has no special attraction.

The ends of the shoots are herbaceous and die back in winter, disarticulating at the nodes. Although the leaves have the typical *Vitis* shape, it is a true *Ampelopsis*, the sepals and petals being in fives, the latter separate and expanded, the bark not peeling.

A. DELAVAYANA Planch.
Vitis delavayana Franch. ex Bean

This species was introduced by Wilson for Messrs Veitch in 1900, and appears to be quite hardy and vigorous. It is a climber with hairy young stems, swollen at the joints. Leaves composed of three or five leaflets, the middle one of which is shortly stalked, narrowly oval, tapered at both ends, especially towards the point; side lobes stalkless, unequal at each side of the midrib, sometimes with a lobe on the lower side and oblique at the base. All are coarsely toothed, roughish above, downy (at least when young) on the veins beneath. Leaflets from 1½ to 4 in. long, ¾ to 1½ in. wide (larger on vigorous young plants). Fruits small, dark blue. Young shoots and leaf-stalks pinkish. Native of W. China.

A. MEGALOPHYLLA Diels & Gilg
Vitis megaphylla Veitch

A vigorous deciduous climber; young shoots rather glaucous, and, like the rest of the plant, quite glabrous. Leaves doubly pinnate (the upper and smaller ones simply pinnate), from 1½ to 2 ft, sometimes more, long, and nearly as wide. The larger ones are composed of seven or nine segments, the one or two lowest pairs of which are again pinnately divided. Leaflets of variable shape and size, but mostly ovate or ovate-oblong, deep green above, glaucous beneath; 2 to 6 in. long, 1 to 3 in. wide; coarsely toothed, each tooth terminated by a minute abrupt point. Flowers produced in August in a sparse, slenderly branched inflorescence, each branch terminating in a cyme. Fruit top-shaped, ¼ in. diameter, black. *Bot. Mag.*, t. 8537.

Native of W. China; introduced to France in 1894 by Maurice de Vilmorin, and by him distributed as *V. cantoniensis*—a different and probably not hardy vine. Wilson introduced *A. megalophylla* for Messrs Veitch in 1900, and from their nursery it was largely distributed. In some respects it is the most remarkable of all hardy vines. Its leaves are larger than those of any other in cultivation, suggesting at their biggest the leaves of *Aralia cordata*. Planted in good soil and trained up a lofty post (it should be 15 ft high), this vine provides a very striking effect. It made growths 8 to 10 ft long in one season in Veitch's Coombe Wood Nursery.

A. ORIENTALIS (Lam.) Planch.
Cissus orientalis Lam.

A laxly bushy, or sometimes climbing, deciduous shrub, with glabrous, slightly ribbed shoots. Leaves variable; often doubly trifoliolate (each of the three chief divisions being subdivided into three leaflets), sometimes simply pinnate, sometimes bipinnate. Leaflets ovate, diamond-shaped or obovate, tapered at the base; 1 to 3 in. long, ⅝ to 2 in. wide; the upper part coarsely toothed; dark dull green and glabrous above; paler, grey-green, also glabrous beneath, or with tiny tufts in the vein-axils. Flowers with the parts in fours, produced on long-stalked cymes. Fruit roundish, top-shaped, ¼ in. diameter, red.

Native of Asia Minor, Syria, etc., up to 5,000 ft on the mountains; introduced in 1818. It is, no doubt, closely allied, and very similar to the American *A. arborea*, but its foliage is coarser and not so distinctly bipinnate, and it falls sooner in autumn. The leaves are usually composed of nine leaflets (but sometimes eleven or fifteen), which are considerably larger on the average, and appear to be never downy on the veins beneath, as are frequently those of *A. arborea*. A handsome foliaged shrub, which used to fruit with Canon Ellacombe at Bitton, near Bath. He compared them to clusters of red currants.

ANAGYRIS   LEGUMINOSAE

A genus of two species; one, described here, native of the Mediterranean region, the other of the Canary Islands. It is the sole representative in Europe of the tribe Podalyriae, which has its centre in S. Africa and Australia. Among the papilionate genera, this group is distinguished by the combination of simple or palmate (not pinnate) leaves, and free stamens.

A. FOETIDA L.

A deciduous bush, or small tree, with alternate, trifoliolate leaves. Leaflets 1 to 2½ in. long, narrow oval, covered with fine down beneath, greyish green. Flowers pea-shaped, yellow, produced in short racemes on the growth of the previous year; each flower ¾ to 1 in. long, and but little expanded; calyx bell-shaped, downy and ciliated, green; petals yellow, the standard one hooded; wings narrow oblong. The racemes are 1½ to 3 in. long, and carry six to twenty flowers. Seed-pod 3 to 5 in. long, ½ to ¾ in. broad, pointed at both ends, curved like a scimitar, and containing three or four seeds.

Native of the countries bordering the Mediterranean Sea, and requiring at Kew the protection of a south wall—even there occasionally killed. The specific name refers to the unpleasant odour of the leaves, which is, however, only perceptible when they are crushed. The tree is known in the south of France as 'bois puant' on that account. The flowers are inodorous. In S. Europe they open in early spring, later in Britain.

ANDRACHNE   EUPHORBIACEAE

A group of plants belonging to the spurge family, of which two shrubby species are sometimes seen in cultivation. They have little beauty of flower or fruit, but are rather neat in habit. Leaves alternate. Flowers unisexual, produced in the leaf-axils of the current season's growth, small, green; the females solitary; males in axillary clusters. Fruit a dry capsule of three divisions, each division two-valved. There are about twelve species known, inhabiting both the New and Old Worlds, but the two following are the only shrubby ones I have seen in cultivation. Neither can be said to deserve a place in gardens except for its botanical interest. They thrive in ordinary loam in full sunshine, and can be increased by cuttings in August.

A. COLCHICA Boiss.

A native of the Caucasus, and a deciduous shrub about 3 ft high, of dense, erect habit, and with very slender, quite glabrous, leafy shoots, the terminal portions of which die back in winter. Leaves set about ¼ in. apart on the shoots, ovate, ⅓ to ¾ in. long, about half as wide, rounded at the base, blunt at the apex; quite glabrous, and with thickened, entire margins; dull green. Flowers ¼ in. across, on thread-like stalks ½ to ⅝ in. long, produced successively along the young shoots throughout the summer and early autumn. Fruit pale brown, ¼ in. across. Introduced to Kew, in 1900, from the Botanic Garden of Tiflis, but probably cultivated long previously.

A. PHYLLANTHOIDES (Nutt.) Muell.-Arg.
Lepidanthus phyllanthoides Nutt.

An erect, much-branched, deciduous shrub 1 to 3 ft high, its twigs angled, slightly downy, becoming glossy; slender, but not so slender as in *A. colchica*. Leaves obovate or oval, ½ to ¾ in. long, ⅓ to ½ in. wide, tapered or rounded at the base, bluntish or rounded at the apex, entire; quite glabrous or sparingly downy beneath, glossy green above; stalk 1/16 in. long. Flowers ¼ in. across, yellowish green, produced in summer and autumn. Fruits nearly globose.

Native of the S. Central United States. It is easily distinguished from the Caucasian species by its stouter, downy, angled branchlets, and its partially downy, shorter-stalked leaves, often broadest above the middle.

ANDROMEDA   ERICACEAE

As now understood, this genus contains only the two species described below. The name *Andromeda* has been extensively used for what are now considered to be distinct genera. Shrubs and trees described under this name in old works must be sought under *Oxydendrum*, *Lyonia*, and *Enkianthus*; and under the beautiful names *Cassandra*, *Cassiope*, *Leucothöe*, *Pieris*, and *Zenobia*, all published by David Don in 1834.

A. POLIFOLIA L.   BOG ROSEMARY

A low evergreen shrub rarely more than 1½ ft. high, whose slender, glabrous, wiry stems are clothed thickly with stiff, hard-textured leaves; young wood pinkish. Leaves linear-oblong, tapered at both ends, 1 to 1½ in. long, ⅛ to ⅓ in. wide, but made to appear narrower than they really are by the recurving of the margins; dark green above, glaucous or slightly felted beneath. Flowers produced in short, compact clusters at the end of the shoots during May and succeeding months, each flower on a stalk ¼ in. or less in length. The corolla is pink, ¼ in. long, pitcher-shaped, contracted towards the mouth, where are five small recurved teeth. Calyx five-lobed, the lobes triangular, glaucous.

Native of the colder parts of the northern hemisphere, mostly confined to mountains in the southern part of its range and found most commonly in peat or sphagnum bogs. It is an interesting and pretty shrub, requiring a damp peaty soil to thrive in. In the Thames Valley it succeeds better if the ground in which it is planted is covered with an inch or two of sphagnum moss, which acts as a sponge in conserving moisture.

Botanists have, for the most part, considered it unnecessary to distinguish the many slightly differing forms of this species in the natural state, though many of these, as shown by cultivated plants, were named in horticultural literature of the early nineteenth century. In Japan, which appears to be the main source of the plants now cultivated in British gardens, some of these names have been taken up by local botanists. For example, Nakai has adopted var. *minima* G. Don for dwarf plants of prostrate habit with narrow leaves; and var. *grandiflora* Lodd. for more robust plants with broader leaves, conspicuously glaucous beneath and larger, deeper-coloured flowers. However, such variants are certainly not confined to Japan: the two names mentioned are in fact founded on plants of European origin.

Certain other epithets current in gardens, such as *nana*, *compacta*, *congesta*, appear to derive from Japanese horticultural names and have no botanical standing, though some may represent clones. The Japanese garden plant known as *A. polifolia grandiflora compacta* is of compact habit, with abundant coral-pink flowers and glaucous, pea-green leaves (K. Wada, *Gard. Chron.*, May 15, 1965, p. 473). A plant similar to this was introduced from Japan between the wars and is usually grown as *compacta* or *nana compacta*, but the nomenclature is very confused. A beautiful white-flowered form collected in the mountains north of Tokyo was given an Award of Merit as *A. p. compacta alba* when shown by Roy Elliott, who introduced it, in 1959. Another white-flowered form was shown by Dr Giuseppi in 1934 as *A. p. congesta*.

A. GLAUCOPHYLLA Link—Leaves densely covered beneath with short, erect hairs; flower-stalks shorter than in *A. polifolia*. Native of N. America.

var. LATIFOLIA (Ait.) Rehd. *A. polifolia* var. *latifolia* Ait.; *A. canescens* Small—Leaves broader than in the type.

ANDROMEDA POLIFOLIA

ANOPTERUS   ESCALLONIACEAE

A genus of two species, one (described here) endemic to Tasmania, the other found on the Australian mainland. From *Escallonia* it differs chiefly in its flowers, with six to nine ovate petals and superior, single-chambered ovary; and in its winged seeds.

A. GLANDULOSA Labill.

An evergreen shrub or small tree, ultimately 20 to 40 ft high, of erect habit, with glabrous, stout young shoots. Leaves of leathery texture, crowded at the end of each year's twigs, narrowly obovate or oblanceolate, tapered towards both ends but more gradually towards the base, bluntish at the apex, edged with rather large, rounded teeth, each tooth tipped with a large gland; 2 to 5 in. long, ⅝ to 2 in. wide; dark glossy green above, pale beneath, glabrous on both sides; stalk ¼ to ¾ in. long. Flowers in terminal racemes 2 to 5 in. high, 1½ to 2 in. wide. Each flower is about ⅝ in. wide, cup-shaped, white or tinged with rose; petals six, concave, broadly obovate; calyx small, six-lobed, the triangular lobes toothed; stamens six, with flattened stalks tapered towards the yellow anthers. Fruit erect, slender, ½ in. long, ⅛ in wide, splitting when ripe into two halves which recurve outwards. *Bot. Mag.*, t. 4377.

Native of Tasmania; introduced to Kew about 1840. A very beautiful flowering evergreen with racemes suggesting those of *Clethra arborea*, but stiffer and with larger blossoms. It is not hardy in the London district, but succeeds in Devon, Cornwall, Isle of Wight, etc. It seems to have first flowered at Kew in winter (of course, under glass), but bloomed out-of-doors at Cann House, Devon, in May 1920. It has not, judging from the scarcity of thriving specimens, even in the milder parts, proved really successful in our climate. This is no doubt due in part to its tenderness but also in some measure 'to the difficulty in providing the exact conditions it needs. Besides a soft, moist atmosphere it would appear to require at least moderate shade and a soil rich in humus and of an acid or neutral nature'. (W. J. Bean in *New Flora and Sylva*, Vol. 7, pp. 14–15.)

ANTHYLLIS   LEGUMINOSAE

Three attractive shrubs belonging to this genus are cultivated in gardens— one unfortunately too tender to withstand our winters unprotected. The most distinctive botanical feature of the genus is the persistent calyx, which, after the petals fall, becomes more or less inflated and encloses the seed-pod. The flowers are aggregated in umbellate clusters. None of these shrubs needs a rich soil, but rather a warm, well-drained one, and abundant sunshine.

A. BARBA-JOVIS L.   JUPITER'S BEARD

An evergreen shrub growing 8 to 12 ft high on walls in this country; branchlets crooked, covered with appressed, silky hairs. Leaves pinnate, 1½ to 2 in. long, composed of nine to about nineteen leaflets. Leaflets linear-oblong, ⅓ to 1 in. long; covered with silvery hairs, especially beneath and at the edges, which towards the base are often incurved. Flowers pea-shaped, pale yellow, crowded in rounded heads at the end of short twigs; each head of flowers is ¾ to 1 in. across; calyx silky hairy, ¼ in. long.

Native of S.W. Europe and the Mediterranean region; cultivated in England since the middle of the seventeenth century. It is too tender to thrive in the open ground, but makes a charming shrub for a wall, where its sheen of silvery grey and (in May and June) clusters of yellow flowers are very effective. At Kew it is occasionally injured even growing against a wall. Seeds are said sometimes to ripen in this country, but the plant has, as a rule, to be increased by cuttings.

A. HERMANNIAE L.

A deciduous shrub of low, bushy habit, 1½ to 2 ft, perhaps more, high; branches crooked or zigzag, covered with short greyish down, and ending in a spine. Leaves simple (or occasionally trifoliolate), linear-obovate, ½ to 1 in. long, ⅛ in. or less wide, clothed more or less with silky hairs; apex rounded; base tapering. Flowers yellow, three to five together in axillary, very shortly stalked clusters, each flower about ⅓ in. long; calyx green, tubular, ⅛ in. long. *Bot. Mag.*, t. 2576.

Native of the Mediterranean region from Corsica eastwards to Turkey. It was in cultivation early in the eighteenth century, and is said to have been not uncommon up to the great frost of 1739–40, when most of the plants were destroyed. It is grown at Kew on a wall of the Herbaceous Ground and is quite hardy there. It has also been grown at Kew in the open ground and although occasionally injured on the upper growth in severe winters was never killed. It is a much-branched, twiggy bush of greyish aspect, flowering freely in June and July, and very pretty then. It is a suitable plant for a sunny place in the rock garden. As it rarely ripens its seeds here, it has to be increased by cuttings. They should be put in sandy soil under cloches in August.

A. MONTANA L.

A deciduous sub-shrub of more or less prostrate habit, with a woody base and root-stock, producing numerous erect stems 1½ to 4 in. high, the younger parts of which are covered with the membranous, hairy, densely sheathing bases of the leaves. Leaves pinnate, 1 to 3 in. long, consisting of eight to fifteen pairs of leaflets which are linear-oblong, pointed, ¼ to ½ in. long, 1/12 in. wide, stalkless, the upper surface covered with whitish hairs; not so hairy beneath; main-stalk hairy. Flowers produced in June, closely packed in a hemispherical head which is 1 to 1½ in. wide and borne at the top of an erect, hairy stalk 2 to 6 in. high. The corolla is pea-flower shaped, the standard petal ⅜ in. long and ¼ in. wide, rosy pink with a dark stain in the centre.

Native of the mountains of S. and S.E. Europe from Spain to the Balkan Peninsula, often on limestone; introduced according to Aiton in 1759. It is a neat and pleasing plant for a sunny spot in the rock garden and is quite hardy. The leaves in its native regions are usually whiter than under our duller skies, sometimes almost silvery. The species is found in its typical state only as far east as the Swiss Jura. Further east it is replaced by var. JACQUINII (Kern.) Beck, in which the flowers are paler, without the blotch on the standard, and the leaves covered with a thinner indumentum of appressed hairs. In the Maritime Alps and in N. Italy a form occurs distinguished as f. ATROPURPUREA Vukot., with smaller but more deeply coloured flowers.

APHANANTHE ULMACEAE

A small genus allied to *Celtis*, but differing in its invariably unisexual flowers. It is confined to E. Asia and Australia.

A. ASPERA (Thunb.) Planch.

Prunus aspera Thunb.; *Celtis muka* Sieb.; *Homoioceltis aspera* (Thunb.) Blume

A deciduous tree 60 to 70 ft high, allied, and similar in appearance to the nettle trees (*Celtis*); young shoots at first covered with flattened hairs, which mostly fall away before the leaves do. Leaves alternate, ovate, long- and taper-pointed; the base wedge-shaped, rounded, or (on very vigorous shoots) heart-shaped, often oblique; 1½ to 4 in. long, ⅓ to 2 in. wide; prominently parallel-veined, distinctly three-nerved at the base. When young both surfaces are densely covered with minute, flattened hairs which fall away from the upper surface, leaving it bright green and slightly rough, persisting more or less on the midrib and veins beneath; stalk ⅛ to ⅓ in. long. Flowers unisexual, very small, greenish; the males numerous, crowded in slender, stalked, cymose clusters at the base of the young side twigs; females solitary at the end. Fruit a roundish oval drupe, ¼ to ⅓ in. long, black-purple.

Native of Japan, Korea, and China; introduced to Kew from Japan in 1895. In their early years the trees made long succulent growths, frequently cut back in winter, but one of the original introduction has become established and is now 28 ft high. The species has little or no flower beauty and little claim to a place in any but botanic gardens.

ARALIA ARALIACEAE

A genus of about thirty species, some of them herbaceous, in E. Asia, Australia, and N. America.

A. ELATA (Miq.) Seem. JAPANESE ANGELICA TREE

Dimorphanthus elatus Miq.; *A. canescens* Sieb. & Zucc.; *A. chinensis* var. *mandshurica* (Maxim.) Rehd.

A deciduous tree 30 ft or more high, with a few stout branches; more often a shrub renewing itself by sucker growths from the base; young growths very thick (over 1 in. in diameter), pithy, and armed more or less with spines. Leaves doubly pinnate, often 3, sometimes 4 ft long, two-thirds as wide; composed of numerous ovate, taper-pointed, short-stalked leaflets, from 3 to 5 in. long, 2 to 3 in. wide, toothed; dark bright green and slightly hairy on the veins above, paler and always downy beneath, often much so, and especially on the midrib and veins; stalks somewhat prickly. Flowers small, whitish, produced in August and September in numerous globose umbels $\frac{3}{4}$ to $1\frac{1}{4}$ in. across, the whole forming a huge panicle 1 to 2 ft long and from half to nearly as much through; flower-stalks covered densely with down.

Native of Japan, Korea, Manchuria and the Russian Far East; introduced about 1830, and perhaps the finest of all hardy shrubs with foliage of its particular type. It is hardy enough in all but the coldest parts of the country, but still is seen at its best in the milder places. Near Falmouth there was a good specimen about 30 ft high, and as much in the spread of its branches, the main trunk 10 in. thick. In its ordinary shrubby state it makes an admirable ornament for a sheltered lawn, peculiarly effective at flowering time. Easily propagated by taking off small suckers or even pieces of root, potting them, and establishing them in heat.

cv. 'Aureo-variegata'.—Leaflets with a broad and irregular margin of golden yellow.

cv. 'Pyramidalis'.—Leaves rather smaller than in the type, and growing erect instead of spreading.

cv. 'Variegata'.—Leaflets irregularly margined, sometimes more than half covered, with creamy white; also known as *albo-marginata*. This form, and 'Aureo-variegata', are amongst the most effective and beautiful of all variegated shrubs. Both are increased by grafting on to the common form, but owing to their sparse production of suitable propagating material both remain rare and expensive.

[PLATE 12

The plant grown as *A. chinensis* var. *mandshurica* (Maxim.) Rehd. is now considered to belong to *A. elata* and to be not even varietally distinct from that species. It was probably introduced from Manchuria by Maximowicz around 1860–5, and is said to be hardier than the introduction from Japan.

A. elata was long grown in gardens as *A. chinensis* L., and not altogether wrongly so, for the two species are very closely allied, and if they were to be merged it would be under the latter name, which is by far the older.

A. CHINENSIS L.—This species has a wide range in China from Yunnan to Manchuria, where it overlaps with *A. elata*. It differs from that species in the following group of characters: stems less spiny; leaflets finely and closely toothed; main axis of inflorescence longer, producing an elongated, conical panicle (in *A. elata* the main axis is scarcely developed and the inflorescence umbrella-shaped). The leaflets of *A. chinensis* are usually sessile, but this is not an altogether reliable character.

In its typical form the species has the leaves downy beneath, and this is perhaps not in cultivation. But *A. chinensis* var. NUDA Nakai, with leaves glabrous beneath (except on the veins), was introduced from China to the Arnold Arboretum in 1919 and thence to Kew in 1926. The plant there died in 1952 and has not been replaced.

A. SPINOSA L. HERCULES' CLUB.—A native of the south-eastern United States, and very similar to *A. elata*. These two afford one of many instances of an extraordinary similarity between a plant native of N. America and another of N. Asia, which are yet not absolutely identical. In this case *A. spinosa* is distinguished by the leaflets being more glaucous beneath and much less downy, sometimes quite glabrous beneath, and by their being more distinctly stalked. The stems, too, are better armed with prickles. This American species is not so hardy and vigorous as the Asiatic one, and the two seen in juxtaposition are quite distinct. It is extremely rare in cultivation, but is represented in the Kew collection.

Although these species make finer foliage when grown in rich than in comparatively poor soil, the latter is, I think, to be preferred if healthy, long-lived plants are desired. In rich soil the wood, always soft and very pithy, becomes especially so, and renders the plants very liable to injury by winter cold.

ARAUCARIA   ARAUCARIACEAE

An important genus of conifers with some ten species in the southern hemisphere. It is represented in S. America by the species described below; and by *A. angustifolia* of S.E. Brazil and neighbouring parts of Argentina, known as the Parana pine. The other species are natives of Australia, New Guinea, and islands of the S.W. Pacific. Of the two Australian species, *A. bidwillii* and *A. cunninghamii*, the latter is an important forestry tree, and both are planted for ornament in frost-free climates. Still better known as a specimen tree is the Norfolk Island pine, *A. heterophylla* (*excelsa*), but this, too, is not hardy enough in Britain.

All the species are characterised by evergreen leaves which persist on the branches for many years; in the two S. American species, and in *A. bidwillii*, they are flat and broad, in the others more or less linear or awl-shaped. The former group is also distinguished by its larger cones.

The family Araucariaceae is a small one, comprising, besides *Araucaria*, only the genus *Agathis*, with some twenty closely allied species in New Zealand, the S.W. Pacific and Malesia. Of these the best known is the Kauri pine, *Agathis australis*, native of the northern extremity of the N. Island of New Zealand.

A. ARAUCANA (Mol.) K. Koch   CHILE PINE, MONKEY PUZZLE
Pinus araucana Mol.; *A. imbricata* Pavon

An evergreen tree 50 to 80 ft high, of pyramidal or rounded form, with an erect, cylindrical bole, $1\frac{1}{2}$ to $2\frac{1}{2}$ ft thick, all but the oldest parts prickly with living leaves or the remains of dead ones. Branches produced in regular tiers of five to seven. Leaves very uniform, ovate with a slender spine-tipped point, from 1 to 2 in. long, ½ to 1 in. wide; hard, rigid, and leathery; dark glossy green except at the paler-growing tips of the branches and with numerous stomatic lines on both surfaces. The leaves are arranged spirally on the branch, overlapping at the broad, stalkless base, and are very densely packed (about twenty-four to 1 in. of stem); they remain alive for ten to fifteen years, and then persist for an indefinite time dead. Male and female flowers are usually borne on separate trees, but not invariably; the former are produced on egg-shaped or cylindrical catkins 3 to 5 in. long, the scales lanceolate, densely packed, with the slender points reflexed, the pollen being shed in early July. The female cones take two seasons to develop; appearing in the spring of one year, and shedding their seeds in August or September of the next; they are globose, and usually 5 to 7 in. thick. Seeds conical, 1½ in. long, ¾ in. wide.

Native of Chile and Argentina; originally discovered about 1780, and introduced to England by Archibald Menzies in 1795. Menzies, when attached to Vancouver's voyage of survey, pocketed some nuts put on for dessert whilst he and the ship's officers were dining with the Governor of Chile. He sowed these nuts on board ship, and ultimately landed five plants, which proved to be the araucaria, alive in England. One of the five existed at Kew until 1892. The Chile pine, whilst hardy in most parts of the British Isles, attains its finest development in the softer, moister counties, and in good deep soil. It should always be raised from seeds, fertile ones of which are now regularly produced in several gardens. At Castle Kennedy I have seen seedling plants springing up naturally near the trees from which seeds had fallen. *Araucaria araucana* is of peculiar interest as the only conifer from south of the equator that attains to timber-producing size in the average climate of the British Isles. It becomes over 100 ft high and 7 ft in diameter of trunk in Chile, deriving its name from the Arauco province (inhabited by the Araucano Indians), where it was first found. In its general aspect, and especially as compared with ordinary types of northern vegetation, the Chile pine is the most remarkable hardy tree ever introduced to Britain. It should always be grown as an isolated tree, or in an isolated group, as it associates very badly with ordinary garden vegetation. It was first introduced in quantity to this country about 1839. In the *Gardeners' Chronicle* for 25th November 1843, Messrs Youell & Co. of Yarmouth offered 'fine robust plants four years old and 8 or 9 in. high' at £5 per 100. Messrs Veitch made a similar offer in May 1843, having raised 'many thousands from seed'.

The largest specimens of Chile pine in the British Isles stand at around 80 ft high and 9 to 12 ft in girth, but these dimensions are attained only in the moister parts. In the famous araucaria avenue at Bicton in Devon, planted in 1844, the biggest for height and girth measure 85 × 10½ and 78 × 12¼ ft respectively (1967). There is another fine avenue at Inishtioge, Co. Kilkenny, Eire, in which the largest tree measures 80 × 10 ft (1966). It is doubtful whether many wild trees exceed these dimensions, though individuals of over 100 ft have been recorded.

ARAUJIA   ASCLEPIADACEAE

A small genus of S. American climbing shrubs, natives mainly of Brazil and Uruguay.

A. SERICOFERA Brot.
Physianthus albens Mart.

An evergreen climber of very vigorous growth, the stems twining, covered with pale down when young. Leaves opposite, ovate-oblong, pointed, the base cut off squarely or broadly wedge-shaped; 2 to 4 in. long, ¾ to 2 in. broad; pale green, and clothed beneath with a pale minute felt; stalk ½ to 1¼ in. long. Flowers fragrant, borne two to eight together on racemes about 2 in. long, produced at the joints of the stem, not in either of the leaf-axils, but at the side between the leaf-stalks (the inflorescence is terminal, becoming lateral by sympodial growth of the stem). Corolla white, swollen at the base, the tube ½ in. long, ⅓ in. wide; opening at the top into five spreading lobes, and there 1 to 1¼ in. across. Calyx with five ovate lobes ⅓ in. long. Fruit a large grooved pod, 5 in. long, 2 to 3 in. wide at the base, tapering slightly towards the end; each seed with a tuft of silky hairs 1 in. or more long attached at the end. *Bot. Mag.*, t. 3201.

Native of S. America; introduced by Tweedie from Buenos Aires in 1830. It is not hardy at Kew, and even against a wall does not long survive, but at Pendell Court in Surrey it used to grow and flower. Where it is warm enough, as in the Channel Islands, it flowers and produces its curious large fruits freely. It likes a good loamy soil, and can be increased by cuttings as well as by seed. Flowers in late summer.

ARBUTUS   ERICACEAE

A group of evergreen trees and shrubs, of which three species are worth cultivating and hardy in the British Isles. They have alternate, leathery leaves, and bear their flowers in terminal panicles; corolla pitcher-shaped, white or pink; calyx five-lobed, persisting through the fruiting stage; stamens ten. The fruit is an edible but not very palatable drupe, roundish, orange-red, and very ornamental when ripe, enclosing numerous seeds.

The arbutuses are exceptionally attractive evergreens in their foliage, which is healthy dark green, and abundant, also ornamental in flower and fruit. *A. unedo*, *A. andrachne*, and *A.* × *andrachnoides* all thrive on limy soils, and may thus be included among the few ericaceous plants that can be grown where lime is present. But all succeed well in peaty or loamy soil. Wherever possible all the species should be raised from seed, but the named varieties have to be grafted on seedlings of *A. unedo*. They transplant rather badly, and are best grown in pots until finally planted out, which should be done as soon as possible.

A. ANDRACHNE L.

An evergreen tree 30 to 40 ft high in a wild state, but usually a shrub 10 to 20 ft high in Great Britain; young shoots glabrous; bark on older branches peeling and reddish brown. Leaves oval, usually 2 to 4 in. long, 1 to 2 in. wide, dark glossy green above, paler below, glabrous, toothed in young specimens and on very vigorous shoots, but entire in the adult normal state; stalks ½ to 1 in. long. Flowers produced during March and April in terminal, downy panicles, 2 to 4 in. long and wide; corolla pitcher-shaped, ¼ in. long, dull white, with five shallow, reflexed lobes at the contracted mouth; calyx lobes ovate, pointed; flower-stalks glandular-hairy. Fruit globose, ½ in. diameter, much smoother than that of *A. unedo*, orange red. *Bot. Mag.*, t. 2024.

Native of S.E. Europe, especially in the Eastern Mediterranean region; introduced from Smyrna in 1724. It is but little known in cultivation, nearly all the plants so-called being *A.* × *andrachnoides*. From *A. unedo* it is distinguished by its comparatively broader, toothless leaves and smooth shoots; and from *A. menziesii* by the leaves being less glaucous beneath, the smaller panicles, and the more compact habit.

A. × ANDRACHNOIDES Link   [PLATE 13
A. hybrida Ker-Gawler

A hybrid between *A. andrachne* and *A. unedo*, intermediate in many respects between the two, and very variable within the limits set by the parent species, sometimes leaning more to one species, sometimes more to the other. The leaf-stalks and young branches are glandular-hairy, but not so much so as in *A. unedo*; sometimes they show it only when quite young, and not very much even then. The leaves are toothed, rather glaucous beneath, and intermediate in size. Flowers produced in late autumn or in spring, in terminal, glandular-downy panicles, white, pitcher-shaped, ¼ in. long. Fruit not so rough nor so large as in *A. unedo*. *Bot. Reg.*, t. 619.

Found wild in Greece, where both the parent species occur, and said also to have been raised by Messrs Osborn of Fulham about 1800. On the whole it is the most useful as it is the commonest of the genus. Several of its finest forms have been given names, such as "magnifica", "photinaefolia", "rollissoni", all notable for their fine foliage and goodly sized trusses. As commonly seen in gardens it resembles *A. andrachne* in its bark but is distinct in the toothed leaves; in *A. unedo* the bark is rough and shreddy.

Perhaps the most beautiful specimen in the country grows at Bodnant, Denbigh; it is one of four, planted in 1905, and is about 30 ft high and as much in spread. 'I know of no tree whose aspect alters more readily with the changing vagaries of light and shade, breeze and calm. When the evening sun lights upon its leaves and vividly illuminates its branches the whole tree is a most lovely sight.' (Lord Aberconway in *Journ. R.H.S.*, Vol. 79, p. 184.) Other large specimens are: Kew, 35 × 4¼ ft at 1 ft (1967); Lytchett Heath, Dorset, *pl.* 1877, 30 × 4¼ ft at 4 ft; Highdown, Sussex, *pl.* 1924, 31 × 3¼ ft. This last tree, and another in the West Hill nursery of Messrs Hillier, proves that *A.* × *andrachnoides* grows well on chalk.

A. MENZIESII Pursh MADRONA
A. procera Douglas

An evergreen tree reaching in its native state heights of 20 to 100 ft, with a trunk 1 to 6 ft in thickness; in Britain it has not yet exceeded 60 ft in height, and is usually 20 to 30 ft. Young shoots glabrous; bark peeling, and, on the older branches and trunk, leaving the wood perfectly clean, and of a striking cinnamon colour. Leaves oval, 2 to 6 in. long, 1¼ to 3 in. wide; toothed on young plants or very vigorous shoots, but mostly with entire margins; dark glossy green above, glaucous or almost white beneath; stalk ½ to 1¼ in. long. Flowers

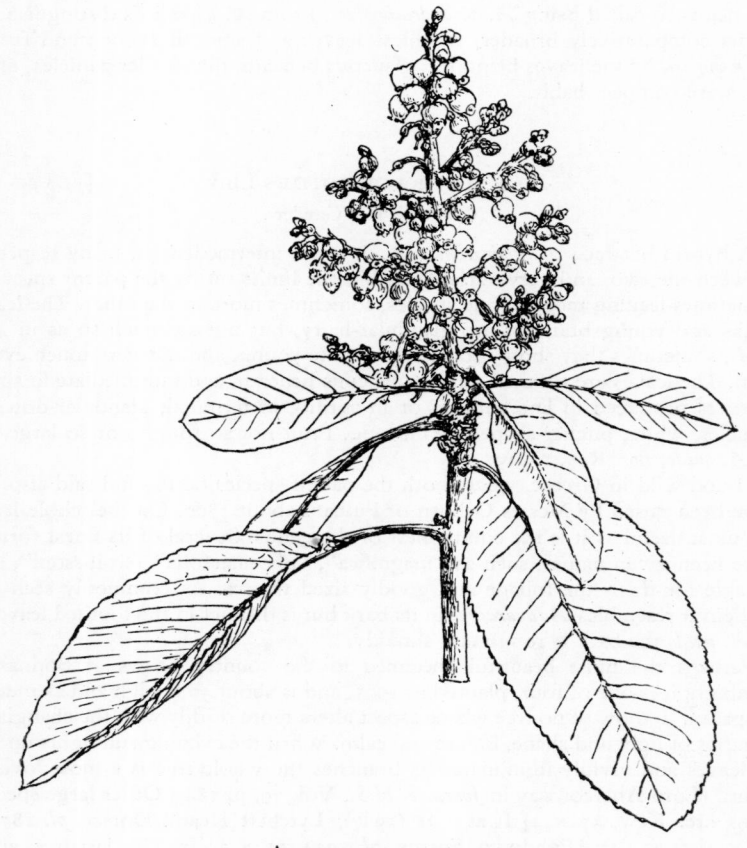

ARBUTUS MENZIESII

produced during May in a terminal pyramidal panicle, from 3 to 9 in. long and up to 6 in. wide; corolla pitcher-shaped, about ¼ in. long, dull white; flower-stalks downy; calyx small, greenish; fruit about the size of a large pea, orange-coloured. *Bot. Mag.*, n.s., t. 275.

Native of western N. America from British Columbia to the latitude of San Francisco; described from specimens collected by Menzies in 1792, when attached to Vancouver's voyage of discovery; introduced by Douglas in 1827. This is one of the most beautiful of all broad-leaved trees, and as seen at its best in the moist rich valleys of N. California is by far the noblest of all the heath family. It is especially noticeable for the perfectly smooth red branches. The fruit is rather variable in colour: in a tree at East Bergholt Place, from which a fruiting spray is figured in the *Botanical Magazine*, it is bright crimson. In the milder parts of Britain, it succeeds very well, and at Kew is perfectly hardy, except that in a young state the vigorous sappy shoots are apt to be cut back in winter. An old specimen at Kew died recently, perhaps as a result of the hard winter of 1962–3, but generally the species survived that winter with little damage. It should be propagated by imported seed, which is obtainable from American nurserymen and germinates well, if fresh. The young plants should as soon as possible be given a permanent place, as they transplant badly.

W. L. Jepson says that in N. California no other tree makes so strong an appeal to man's imagination as this, and that wherever it grows, 'the traveller, forester, hunter, artist, and botanist is held by the spell of its crown of flowers and masses of red fruits, its terra-cotta bark and burnished foliage'. It is far too rarely seen in cultivation. When once established it grows quickly; a tree at Kew raised from seed was in thirty years 29 ft high, with a trunk 3 ft 7 in. in girth.

The following are some of the finer specimens recorded in recent years: Bassett Wood, Hants, 60 × 5½ ft (1960); Chiltley Place, Liphook, Hants, 52 × 9½ ft (1961); East Bergholt Place, Suffolk, 45 × 3¾ and 40 × 4½ ft (1965), and a smaller tree in East Bergholt churchyard; Bodnant, Denbigh, 32 × 3¼ ft (1965). In Scotland there is a tree of about 25 ft in the Royal Botanic Garden, Edinburgh, and another of about the same size in a garden in Ferry Road. In Ireland the best so far recorded are: Castlewellan, 44 ft on two stems; and Fota, Co. Cork, Eire, *pl.* 1935, 43 × 5½ ft (1966).

A. UNEDO L.   STRAWBERRY TREE

An evergreen tree from 15 to 30 ft high, occasionally 40 ft in its native districts in Ireland, but usually a wide-topped small tree or a shrub in gardens; bark fibrous; young shoots glandular-hairy. Leaves glabrous, 2 to 4 in. long, ½ to 1¾ in. wide, narrowly oval or obovate, tapering towards both ends, toothed, dark shining green and leathery; stalk ¼ in. long, glandular. Flowers produced from October to December in drooping panicles 2 in. long and wide. Corolla white or pinkish, pitcher-shaped, ¼ in. long, with small, rounded, reflexed lobes at the mouth; calyx-lobes small, triangular, edged with minute hairs. Fruit globose, strawberry-like, ¾ in. across, orange-red, rough on the surface. It ripens during the autumn following the production of the flowers, at the same time as the succeeding crop of blossom is opening.

Native of the Mediterranean region and S.W. Ireland, especially on the islands and shores of the Lakes of Killarney, where it attains its largest dimensions. I have seen it wild also in Dalmatia (on calcareous ground), where, however, it was always scrub not more than 10 ft high. It is quite hardy in the warmer parts of England, and has withstood 30° of frost at Kew without injury. There is a large specimen growing in an exposed position in the nurseries of Messrs Waterer, Sons and Crisp at Bagshot, Surrey, which fruits well in most seasons and was quite undamaged in the winter of 1962–3. It is about 18 ft high and 30 ft in spread. *A. unedo* and its varieties are of especial value through flowering so late in the season.

cv. 'COMPACTA'.—A dwarf bush that does not flower freely.

f. INTEGERRIMA (Sims) Hegi—Leaves quite entire. The type was a cultivated plant, figured in *Bot. Mag.*, t. 2319, but similar forms occur in the wild.

f. RUBRA (Ait.) Rehd.—A red-flowered form of the strawberry tree was known to Philip Miller (*Gard. Dict.*, 1759) and named by Aiton in 1789 (*Hort. Kew.*, Vol. 3, p. 56). In the nineteenth century several forms were in cultivation (and may still be today), of which the best was considered to be 'Croomei'. This came into commerce before 1850 and was described as having flowers stained reddish pink and differing from the old *rubra* in its larger flowers and leaves, the latter more serrated. Mackay (*Flora Hibernica*, 1836) mentions a wild tree of f. *rubra* growing near Glengariff in Ireland, and doubtless similar plants occur throughout the range of the species. A red-flowered strawberry tree is figured in *Bot. Mag.*, n.s., t. 203. The form commonly seen in cultivation ('Croomei'?) is also more compact in habit than the type.

ARCTOSTAPHYLOS   ERICACEAE

A genus of evergreen shrubs, sometimes creeping, or small trees, all confined to western N. America and Mexico save one—*A. uva-ursi*—which ranges widely through the temperate parts of the N. hemisphere. The deciduous species once known as *Arctostaphylos alpina* is now placed in a separate genus (see *Arctous*). Leaves alternate, of leathery texture. Flowers urn-shaped (urceolate), ¼ in. or less long, narrowed at the mouth, where there are five small teeth; produced in short racemes or panicles. Fruit fleshy with four to ten bony nutlets. There is, however, a group of species in which the nutlets are united into a solid stone and the fruit drupe-like; these are, by some botanists, placed in separate genera—*Comarostaphylis* (with twenty-five species, mostly in Mexico) and *Xylococcus* (one species only).

All the following species are worthy of cultivation, but some are very rare in British gardens and others mentioned have yet to be introduced. Imported seeds from California are frequently difficult to get to germinate. The modern treatment is to immerse them in sulphuric acid; for further details see the article by Percy C. Everett in the *Journal of the California Horticultural Society*, April 1964. Immersion in boiling water for ten to twenty seconds or even longer is another possible remedy. Some of the California species germinate very freely after a bush-fire has swept over them, and Mr Everett has found that in the nursery germination can be hastened by burning straw or pine-needles over the seed-boxes, followed by stratification at 36–40° F. Most species, however, may be propagated by tip-cuttings.

A. ANDERSONII Gray   HEARTLEAF MANZANITA

An evergreen shrub, with spreading or erect branches, 3 to 12 ft high with a smooth, dark reddish-brown bark. Young growths covered with a dense down, intermixed with glandular hairs. Leaves ovate to oblong-ovate, 1¼ to 2¾ in. long, heart-shaped at the base and usually sessile, glabrous or downy or downy-glandular beneath. Flowers urceolate, ¼ in. long, pink or white, with glandular-hairy pedicels, arranged in a panicle and borne in spring; ovary glandular. Fruit globose, reddish brown, covered with a sticky down. *Bot. Mag.*, n.s., t. 280.

Native of California; introduced to the Royal Botanic Garden, Edinburgh, in 1934, by seed received from Mrs Lester Rowntree, who did so much to popularise the native shrubs of California. It grew well in front of the old planthouses, now demolished, where it reached a height of 14 ft and flowered and fruited in most years.

In the related A. AURICULATA Eastw., the leaves are auriculate at the base, downy but not glandular beneath, and grey-green in colour. Other allied species, probably not in cultivation in Britain, but said to be ornamental in flower and fruit, are: A. MORROENSIS Wieslander & Schreiber, and A. PAJAROENSIS Adams.

A. CANESCENS Eastw.   HOARY MANZANITA

An evergreen shrub to 7 ft high, with erect branches, or a low, spreading bush; bark smooth, dark reddish brown; branchlets white and downy (and also glandular in var. *sonomensis*). Leaves elliptic, oblong or obovate, 1¼ to 2 in. long, short-stalked, covered on both sides with a dense white down, later more or less glabrous. Flowers urn-shaped, white or pinkish, borne in spring in small, dense panicles; stalks and ovaries downy. Fruit globose, flattened at the apex, usually somewhat downy.

Native of California and Oregon; it is found in chaparral, but also grows in forests of Douglas fir and *Pinus ponderosa*. In the form introduced to Britain, it has proved one of the hardiest and most satisfactory of the taller species, and very decorative in spring when covered with its hoary young growth.

A. DIVERSIFOLIA Parry

Comarostaphylis diversifolia (Parry) Greene

An evergreen shrub or small tree 6 to 18 ft high; young shoots whitish with down. Leaves 1 to 2½ in. long, oval to oblong, the base tapered, the apex blunt to rounded, finely toothed, glabrous and shining above, white-downy beneath, margins revolute; stalk ¼ in. long. Flower white, ¼ in. across, borne on terminal pendulous racemes 3 to 4½ in. long; stalks and calyx downy, ovary densely hairy. Fruit red, berry-like, subglobose, ¼ in. wide, consisting of a three- to five-celled stone densely covered with pulpy granules.

Native of S. California; it was introduced to Kew before 1896 and flowered there in March and April, but is not in the collection at the present time. It is tender.

A. GLAUCA Lindl.　　BIGBERRY MANZANITA

An evergreen shrub 6 to 14 ft high, sometimes a small tree to 25 ft; bark smooth, reddish brown; branchlets pale green, glabrous and glaucous (but downy and sometimes glandular in var. *puberula* J. T. Howell). Leaves ovate to oblong-elliptic, to 1¾ in. long, truncate or slightly cordate at the base, on stalks to ⅓ in. long, greyish green and glabrous on both sides. Flowers urn-shaped, white or pinkish, borne in spring in broad, short, rather pendulous panicles. Fruit brownish, large for the genus (to ⅗ in. in diameter), with the nutlets united into a solid stone.

Native of S. California. A handsome species, but tender.

A. PRINGLEI var. DRUPACEA Parry—An erect, aromatic shrub to 14 ft high with densely hairy-glandular young branchlets. Leaves grey-green, to 1½ in. long, oblong-ovate to elliptic, finely glandular-downy on both sides. Flowers rose-coloured, in sessile racemes or panicles, on pink stalks and subtended by bracts of the same colour. Probably not in cultivation and perhaps tender, but its flowers are said to be among the most beautiful of the genus.

A. MANZANITA Parry　　MANZANITA　　[PLATE 14

An evergreen shrub 4 to 8 ft high in this country, but becoming a small tree 25 ft high in its native home; young shoots, inflorescence, leaf-stalks, and mid-ribs covered with dense down; bark peeling. Leaves ovate, heart-shaped or oval, 1¼ to 2½ in. long, ¾ to 1¾ in. wide, entire, thick and leathery; at first of a dull grey, afterwards bright grey-green, slightly downy when young; leaf-stalk stout, ⅓ to ½ in. long. Flowers produced in March and April in short terminal panicles about 1½ in. long and wide, lasting long in beauty. Corolla egg-shaped, about ¼ in. long, deep pink, with five small, rounded teeth at the nearly closed mouth; sepals whitish; flower-stalks slender, ¼ in. or less long. Fruit not seen in Britain, but described as a brownish-red, orange-shaped berry ⅓ to ½ in. wide. *Bot. Mag.*, t. 8128.

Native of California; introduced to Kew in 1897. This shrub requires a sunny position and a peaty, well-drained soil. Cuttings will not take root easily, at least a way has not yet been found, so far as I know, to make them do so. It is impatient of root disturbance, and should be given a permanent place early, and till then grown in pots. Its stiff, somewhat gaunt branches, red where not hidden by peeling bark; the rigid, hard, grey foliage; and the short, crowded flower-clusters, give this rare shrub a most distinct appearance. 'Manzanita', which has been selected for its specific name, is an old Spanish-Californian term for the bushy members of the genus generally.

A. PUNGENS H.B.K.—An allied species but with a more southerly distribution, distinguished by its smaller leaves (to 1¼ in. at the most in length and usually shorter) and smaller fruit (about ¼ in. wide). Flowers white, in compact racemes or panicles, the common stalks characteristically thickened towards the apex.

A. PATULA Greene   GREENLEAF MANZANITA

A spreading, much-branched evergreen shrub 3 to 7 ft high; stems with a bright red-brown bark, borne on a thickened root-stock from which the plant quickly regenerates after fires. Branchlets finely downy and usually glandular. Leaves bright green, broadly ovate or elliptic to almost round, 1 to 1¾ in. long, obtuse or rounded at the apex, rounded to slightly heart-shaped at the base, glabrous; leaf-stalks finely downy and glandular. Flowers pinkish or white, urn-shaped, about ¼ in. long, borne in corymbs or loose panicles; ovary glabrous. Fruit globose, flattened at the apex, dark brown to almost black.

Native of western N. America, where it grows in open coniferous forest dominated by *Pinus ponderosa* or *Abies amabilis*. In Britain, it has proved one of the most satisfactory of the larger manzanitas. A plant on the rock garden at Edinburgh, Dr Fletcher tells us, flourished for many years in an exposed position, until it was eventually blown over and failed to recover. The taller arctostaphylos, he adds, are not very wind-firm and do not take kindly to transplanting.

A. STANFORDIANA Parry

An erect evergreen shrub 3 to 6 ft high, with smooth, brown bark; branchlets glabrous. Leaves bright green, lustrous, narrowly ovate to lanceolate or oblanceolate, with a pointed apex and tapered base, 1 to 2¼ in. long, usually held erect, on stalks ⅛ to ¼ in. long. Flowers in lax terminal racemes or panicles, borne in spring; corolla pink, urn-shaped, about ¼ in. long. Fruit globose, bright red, flattened at the top, glabrous.

Native of California. By all accounts this is the most beautiful of the taller manzanitas, but by no means an easy plant to satisfy, even in Californian gardens. In the British Isles a position against a sunny wall, in very well-drained soil, is likely to suit it best. If tried, it might for good measure be associated with the equally beautiful but demanding *Ceanothus purpureus*, which should flower at the same time and grows on the same hillsides in Napa County, California. Both are safer in a neutral or slightly acid soil. Seed of *A. stanfordiana* requires pre-treatment in sulphuric acid if quick germination is to be obtained, but cuttings strike readily.

In subsp. HISPIDULA (Howell) Adams, the branchlets are glandular-hairy and the leaves dull green.

A. TOMENTOSA (Pursh) Lindl.   SHAGGY-BARKED MANZANITA
Arbutus tomentosa Pursh

An evergreen shrub of somewhat irregular habit, growing from 3 to 5 ft (probably more) high, with a shreddy bark; young wood clothed with dense hairs. Leaves oblong or ovate, rounded or slightly heart-shaped at the base, abruptly pointed, 1 to 2 in. long, ½ to 1 in. wide, not toothed, leathery, dull greyish green, downy above, thickly felted beneath; stalk ⅛ to ¼ in. long, hairy. Flowers produced from March to May, densely, in short, drooping racemes 1 to 2 in. long, from the end of the previous season's growth, and in the axils of one or two of the uppermost leaves. Corolla white, pitcher-shaped, ¼ in. long; sepals rounded, hairy on the margins; flower-stalks very hairy, ⅛ to ¼ in. long. Fruit a berry, brownish red, orange-shaped, ⅓ in. wide, downy. *Bot. Mag.*, t. 3320.

Native of the coast regions of California; discovered by Alexander Menzies about 1793 on the Monterey peninsula. It is a rare shrub, but was once grown successfully at Kew in peaty soil. Some plants grown as *A. tomentosa* have proved to be A. COLUMBIANA Piper, another hairy species, but distinguished by its smooth, not shaggy, bark and bright red fruits; it has a more northerly range, and extends into British Columbia.

Like *A. patula*, *A. tomentosa* develops a woody burl at the base from which new shoots are quickly produced if the plant is cut to the ground by fire—a peculiarity seen in other manzanitas not described here, and also in the species of *Eucalyptus* known as 'mallees'.

var. TRICHOCLADA (DC.) Munz—Branchlets glandular-hairy and often downy also; leaves and inflorescence glandular; found with the type.

A. UVA-URSI (L.) Spreng.   BEARBERRY
Arbutus uva-ursi L.

A trailing evergreen shrub, sending out long, slender, leafy branches, but rising only a few inches above the ground; young shoots glabrous or furnished with a minute down. Leaves leathery, obovate, rounded or retuse at the apex, with a long, tapering base, ½ to 1¼ in. long, ¼ to ½ in. wide; bright green on both sides; margins hairy when young, otherwise glabrous; stalk ¼ in. or less long. Flowers produced from April onwards in small, drooping, terminal clusters; corolla pitcher-shaped, ⅙ in. long, white or pink; ovary glabrous. Fruit globular, ¼ to ⅓ in. in diameter, red, smooth and shining.

Native of the cooler temperate regions of the northern hemisphere, both in the New and the Old Worlds, found in diverse soils and habitats. It is equally at home on limestone and siliceous rock and is a vigorous coloniser of screes, boulders, and freshly exposed soils. It is an inhabitant mainly of mountains and sub-arctic forest, but is also found in dry pine forest, as in N. Germany and the eastern coast of N. America. In California, the headquarters of the genus *Arctostaphylos*, it is said to be confined to the coast, its place in the mountains being taken by *A. nevadensis*.

The American plants differ in having the branchlets more persistently downy than in the Eurasiatic form, and are sometimes distinguished as var. COACTILIS Fern. & Macbr.

In gardens, the bearberry is useful for forming a low evergreen ground-cover, its spreading masses of green foliage and small pinkish flowers being always pleasing. It may also be planted on the top of upturned tree-roots, which it will eventually completely drape, or on the top of miniature declivities of the rock garden. It is easily propagated by cuttings.

A. × MEDIA Greene—The plant so named was found in the state of Washington and is thought to be a hybrid between *A. uva-ursi* and *A. columbiana*. It differs from the former in its larger leaves, downy beneath. Other plants have been found on the coast of western N. America, e.g. on Vancouver Island, which appear to be hybrids of this parentage.

A. NEVADENSIS Gray—A procumbent or prostrate shrub closely allied to *A. uva-ursi*. The main mark of difference is that the leaves have numerous stomata on both sides and a mucronate apex, whereas in *A. uva-ursi* the stomata

ARCTOSTAPHYLOS NEVADENSIS

are found only on the under-surface and the apex is blunt or retuse. It is a mountain plant of the Coast Range and the Sierra Nevada, California.

There are several other low-growing species in cultivation, all natives of California and best suited when trailing over rocks in full sun. In the following brief account mention is made only of those characters by which they may be distinguished from each other and from the preceding species.

A. HOOKERI G. Don—Branchlets downy. Leaves light lustrous green, shortly pointed or mucronate, with stomata on both surfaces, broadest below the middle (broadest above the middle in *A. nevadensis*). Fruit red. Confined to the coastal part of Monterey Co.

A. NUMMULARIA Gray—Usually prostrate or procumbent, but sometimes erect to 4 or 5 ft high. Branchlets downy. Leaves dark lustrous green, without stomata on the upper surface. Calyx lobes four, stamens eight; ovary downy. Fruit greenish. A coastal species.

A. MYRTIFOLIA Parry   *A. nummularia* var. *myrtifolia* (Parry) Jeps.—Branchlets with stiff hairs, some of them glandular. Calyx lobes four, stamens eight. Fruit greenish. An inland species, found in Amador and Calaveras counties.

A. PUMILA Nutt.—Branchlets downy. Leaves dull green, obovate, downy beneath, without stomata on the upper surface. Calyx lobes five, stamens ten. Fruit brown. Found only around Monterey Bay. It is tender.

The following species may not have been introduced as yet, but is worthy of trial:

A. EDMUNDSII J. T. Howell—A low shrub to about 2 ft high but eventually 10 ft or more across, with freely rooting stems. Branchlets with spreading hairs. Leaves about 1 in. long, ovate, elliptic or rounded, blunt and mucronate at the apex; upper surface without stomata. Flowers pink, in small compact inflorescences. Fruit brown. A recently described species, found only at the mouth of the Little Sur River, Monterey Co. This is by all accounts the finest of the dwarf manzanitas though probably tender.

ARCTOUS   ERICACEAE

A genus of one species (two or three in some interpretations), closely related to *Arctostaphylos*, but distinguished by the deciduous leaves.

A. ALPINUS (L.) Niedenzu

Arbutus alpina L.; *Arctostaphylos alpina* (L.) Spreng.

A low, procumbent, deciduous shrub a few inches high, shoots glabrous, reddish. Leaves obovate to oblanceolate, narrowed at the base to a slightly flattened stalk, often ciliate, ½ to 1¼ in. long, bright green, shallowly toothed. Flowers in terminal clusters of two to four; corolla urn-shaped, ⅛ in. long, with four or five small ciliate teeth; white tinged with pink; anthers chocolate-brown. Fruit a berry-like black-purple drupe about the size of a black currant.

Native of the northern latitudes of Europe, Asia, and N. America. It occurs in a good many mountainous places of Scotland, including Ben Nevis and

Ben Wyvis, Skye, Orkney, and Shetland. Its leaves often turn bright red in autumn. The best place for it is a cool damp spot in the rock garden.

var. RUBER Rehd. & Wils.—Fruits bright red. This variety is based on a plant found by Wilson in W. Szechwan, China, but similar forms have been reported from the mountains of western N. America.

ARDISIA   MYRSINACEAE

A large genus of evergreen trees and shrubs, mainly confined to tropical E. Asia and Central and S. America. The species described is the only one grown outdoors in this country, but A. PUSILLA A. DC., a shrub of similar habit and also native to Japan, may be of comparable hardiness.

A. JAPONICA (Thunb.) Blume
Bladhia japonica Thunb.

A low evergreen shrub 1 ft or rather more high, its erect clustered stems covered with dark, minute down when young. Leaves clustered in one or two whorls near the top of the stem; oval, 1½ to 3½ in. long, ¾ to 1½ in. wide; tapered at both ends, sharply toothed; bright dark green, and nearly or quite glabrous; stalks ¼ in. long, minutely downy. Flowers white, ½ in. across, star-shaped, with five narrow, ovate, pointed petals; the flowers occur singly or in twos or threes on short, downy stalks ½ to ¾ in. long, in the leaf-axils. They appear in August and September, and are followed by red (in one form white), globular berries, ¼ in. in diameter.

Native of China and Japan, and the only member of a large genus grown outside in this country. Its beauty is in the glossy foliage and bright fruits. It is suitable for the rock garden, in the south and west of England or Ireland, but is not wholly hardy at Kew. It first flowered in Knight's nursery at Chelsea in 1834.

ARISTOLOCHIA   ARISTOLOCHIACEAE

Although the most remarkable of the plants which constitute this genus are found in tropical countries, some half a dozen woody, climbing species can be grown in the open air in Britain which present so remarkable a flower-structure and are, withal, so vigorous in growth, that one or more of them ought to be seen in every garden. Leaves alternate, mostly heart-shaped. The flower has no corolla; the calyx (or perianth) is more or less tubular, curiously inflated, and bent so as to resemble a siphon or Dutch pipe. Some of the flowers of tropical aristolochias are fly-traps; the insect is attracted by a foetid odour, and enters the tube, which is clothed with hairs pointing downwards; these hairs offer no obstacle to the ingress of the fly, but effectually bar its return.

The hardy species like a good loamy soil, and can be increased by division or by cuttings. They are suitable for the various positions adapted for climbers.

A. ALTISSIMA Desf.

Chiefly of botanical interest, and not very hardy, this species is not common in gardens, although one sees it occasionally cultivated in the south and west country. By some botanists it is included in *A. sempervirens* L. (see below). It has smilax-like leaves, with three or five prominent veins, heart-shaped, 2 to 4 in. long, bright green, and quite glabrous, as are also the slender, six-ribbed stems. Flowers solitary, stalks slender 1 to 1½ in. long; perianth yellow-brown, striped with darker lines, 1½ in. long, bladder-like at the base, the upper part somewhat funnel-shaped, but doubled back on itself, expanding at the mouth into one ovate, oblique lobe. Seed-vessel oblong, 1¼ in. long, ¾ in. wide, minutely downy. *Bot. Mag.*, t. 6586.

Native of S.E. Europe, and N. Africa. At Kew it has to be grown against a wall, and even there in severe winters is cut to the ground. During the summer it sends up shoots 8 to 10 ft high, which flower from June to August. The form grown in the R.H.S. Garden, Wisley, Surrey, is completely hardy, however, and makes a useful ground cover.

A. SEMPERVIRENS L.—In its typical form, found on dry hillsides in Crete, this is a smaller and weaker plant than *A. altissima*, of prostrate or scrambling habit and, as seen in cultivation, with a purplish perianth. However, Davies and Khan (*Notes Roy. Bot. Gard. Edin.*, Vol. 23, 1961) consider that the two species cannot be kept apart, pointing out that in Crete and Cyprus every transition exists between them. They accordingly unite them under *A. sempervirens* L., as the older name.

A. CALIFORNICA Torr.

A vigorous, deciduous climber, with twining, downy stems, 10 ft or more high. Leaves heart-shaped, rounded or blunt-pointed at the apex, 3 to 8 in. long, nearly as wide; downy on both sides; stalk downy, 1 to 2 in. long. Flowers solitary on slender, downy stalks 1 in. long, with a tiny ovate bract at mid-length. Perianth tubular, inflated, about 2 in. long, bent double, about ¾ in. wide at the bend; downy, slightly contracted at the mouth, where are three slightly expanding lobes, dull purple.

Native of California; introduced to Kew in 1877 by Sir Joseph Hooker, who had collected it at Chico. In foliage it is similar to *A. tomentosa*, the leaves remaining downy until they fall, but not so markedly so. The flower, too, is less downy, larger, broader, and more inflated. *A. macrophylla* differs from both in its smooth flowers, with a large bract on the stalk.

A. DURIOR *see* A. MACROPHYLLA

A. HETEROPHYLLA Hemsl.

A rambling or climbing, half-woody, deciduous shrub, whose young shoots and leaves are covered with fine down; buds hairy. Leaves narrowly to broadly ovate, with a heart-shaped base, or sometimes with a shallow or prominent rounded lobe at each side near the base; pointed, 1½ to 4 in. long, ¾ to 2 in. wide, dull green; leaf-stalk ½ to 1 in. long. Flowers solitary on almost glabrous stalks 1½ to 2 in. long, which spring from the leaf-axils singly or in pairs, and are furnished near the base with a leaf-like, heart-shaped bract. The flower has the typical 'Dutchman's pipe' shape characteristic of the genus, the tube being about 2 in. long, yellow, downy, the terminal part sharply curved upwards; the orifice is ¼ in. in diameter, bright yellow inside. The spreading part of the flower is lurid purple, almost black, the lower lobe rounded, the two side ones given a pointed shape by the curling back of the margins. Flowers in June. Fruit 2 to 2½ in. long, 1 in. wide, six-ribbed.

Native of W. China; introduced by Wilson for Messrs Veitch in 1904. It was quite hardy in the Coombe Wood nursery at Kingston-on-Thames. The flowers are pretty and striking, and the plant a decided curiosity.

A. MACROPHYLLA Lam.   DUTCHMAN'S PIPE   [PLATE 15
A. durior sec. Rehd. in *Journ. Arn. Arb.*, Vol. 3, pp. 42–3 (1921), not Hill; *A. sipho* L'Hérit.

A vigorous, deciduous climber, with twining stems, 20 to 30 ft high; stems smooth, buds woolly. Leaves kidney-shaped or heart-shaped, pointed or blunt, 4 to 10 in. long, often almost as wide, downy beneath when young, afterwards almost or quite glabrous, pale green; leaf-stalk 1 to 3 in. long, smooth, or slightly downy near the blade. Flowers produced in June in pairs, often in pairs, each flower solitary on a flower-stalk 2 to 4 in. long, clasped by a roundish-oval bract on the lower third of its length. Perianth 1 to 1½ in. long, tubular inflated, bent like a siphon, and resembling a Dutch pipe; yellow-green outside; at the mouth the tube contracts to a small orifice, the three lobes spreading there into a flat, brown-purple border ½ to ¾ in. across. *Bot. Mag.*, t. 534.

Native of the eastern United States; sent to England first in 1783 by John Bartram of Philadelphia. This is the best-known of the genus in gardens, and is a handsome-foliaged climber; its flowers, although not highly coloured, are, like those of the other species, curiously and beautifully constructed. The plant may be used for covering pergolas, arbours, or pillars. Increased by division. The bark and more especially the root have an aromatic odour.

The late Dr Alfred Rehder thought that the plant described and figured by John Hill as *A. durior* might be this species but this is very doubtful and it is better to use the name *A. macrophylla* Lam., which antedates *A. sipho* L'Hérit.

A. MOUPINENSIS Franch.

A deciduous climber, of vigorous habit, with downy stems. Leaves heart-shaped, usually pointed at the apex, 2½ to 5 in. long, three-fourths as wide; covered beneath with down, slightly downy above; stalk 1 to 2 in. long, downy. Flowers solitary, produced in June from the joints of the stem, on slender, pendulous, slightly downy stalks about 2 in. long. Perianth 1½ in. long; tube inflated, ½ in. wide, somewhat flattened, downy, pale green, much bent back so as to expose the yellow mouth and three spreading lobes, which are yellow, dotted with purplish red, greenish towards the margin. Seed-vessel 3 in. long, 1¼ in. wide, with six ridges. *Bot. Mag.*, t. 8325.

Native of W. China; discovered by the Abbé David in 1886, but first introduced to cultivation by Wilson in 1903, and flowered in the Coombe Wood nursery in 1908. It appears to be quite hardy and, although not showy, is well worth growing for its prettily coloured, quaintly formed flowers.

A. TOMENTOSA Sims

A vigorous, deciduous climber 20 to 30 ft high, with very woolly young stems, leaves, and flowers. Leaves broadly ovate to roundish, heart-shaped at the base, mostly rounded at the apex; 3 to 8 in. long, often nearly as wide; dull pale green, only slightly downy above; leaf-stalk 1 to 3 in. long, woolly. Flowers solitary on a woolly stalk, which is 2 in. long, gradually thickening upwards. Perianth about 1½ in. long, tubular, inflated at the base, resembling a Dutch pipe, ¾ in. wide at the orifice, where it expands into three distinct lobes; the tubular part of the flower is greenish yellow, the throat dark brown, and the lobes yellowish. Flowers about midsummer. Fruits 2 in. long, cylindric, angled. *Bot. Mag.*, t. 1369.

Native of S.E. United States; introduced in 1799. Although not so frequently seen in gardens as *A. macrophylla*, it is a useful climber for similar positions. Its leaves do not run so large, and it is very distinct in its woolly parts, in the more deeply and distinctly three-lobed limb of the calyx, and in the absence of a bract on the flower-stalk.

ARISTOTELIA ELAEOCARPACEAE

A small genus of trees and shrubs, natives of S. America, New Zealand, Australia (including Tasmania), and the New Hebrides. The species described here are somewhat tender in our average climate, especially the

New Zealand ones, and are only seen at their best near the Atlantic seaboard. They are propagated by cuttings made of half-ripened wood and put in gentle bottom heat.

A. CHILENSIS (Mol.) Stuntz

Cornus chilensis Mol.; *A. macqui* L'Hérit.

An evergreen spreading shrub 6 to 10 ft high, considerably higher in the mildest counties. Leaves opposite and alternate on the same plant, ovate, usually from 2 to 5 in. long, shallowly toothed; dark lustrous green, almost glabrous except when young. Flowers in small, few-flowered cymes coming from the leaf-axils, or from the ends of short twigs; small (not more than ¼ in. across), greenish white. Male and female flowers appear on different plants. The fruit is about the size of a pea, at first purplish then black.

Native of Chile and Argentina, said to have been introduced in 1773 and certainly well known in gardens early in the nineteenth century. This shrub is best fitted for the warmer parts of the British Isles, where it forms a luxuriant but somewhat commonplace evergreen, and where the female plant bears fruit freely. At Kew it is cut back to the ground in all but the mildest winters, but sends up during the summer a crowd of thick, succulent, big-leaved shoots 3 or 4 ft high. In these circumstances it does not flower and has little interest, but on a wall it often flowers. The Chileans make a wine from the fruit, said to have medicinal properties. It is a common, weedy shrub of cleared forest and waste places.

cv. 'VARIEGATA'.—A form whose leaves are variegated with yellow; it is handsome where it thrives, but is more tender than the type.

A. PEDUNCULARIS (Labill.) Hook. f.

Elaeocarpus peduncularis Labill.; *Friesia peduncularis* (Labill.) DC.

An evergreen shrub of lax habit to 6 ft or more high, glabrous in all its parts. Leaves opposite or in threes, ovate to lanceolate or narrowly elliptic, to 3 in. long, toothed. Flowers borne singly in the leaf-axils (sometimes two or three together), pendulous on slender stalks up to ¾ in. long. Sepals four, green, lanceolate; petals four, white, ½ in. long, deeply three-lobed. Fruits heart-shaped, pink or red, black when ripe, up to ⅗ in. long. *Bot. Mag.*, t. 4246.

Native of Tasmania; introduced in 1818. The flowers, borne in May, are considerably larger than in the other species described, but are too sparse to make much display. This species is very rare in gardens but is probably no more tender than *A. chilensis*. Young plants are in cultivation in the R.H.S. Garden, Wisley.

A. SERRATA (J. R. & G. Forst.) W. R. B. Oliver

Dicera serrata J. R. & G. Forst., *A. racemosa* (A. Cunn.) Hook. f.

A small, deciduous tree of graceful form up to 25 ft high. Leaves 2 to 4 in. long, opposite or nearly so, ovate with a heart-shaped or rounded base, long-pointed, the margin cut up into deep, narrow, irregular teeth; the blade is thin and the stalk about half as long. All the younger parts of the plant are downy. Flowers in downy panicles from the leaf-axils; they are numerous but very small ($\frac{1}{6}$ in. across), rose-coloured; male and female flowers are on separate trees. Fruit a dark red or almost black berry, about the size of a pea.

Native of New Zealand, and only suitable for the milder and moister parts of the country, where it grows well. There are good specimens at Inverewe in Wester Ross, and at Castlewellan, Co. Down.

A. FRUTICOSA Hook. f.—Another New Zealand species, differing from the preceding in its leaves, which are leathery and not more than 1 in. long; and in its inflorescence, the flowers being borne singly or in few-flowered cymes. It is also a smaller plant, to 14 ft or so high.

Both species, like the Chilean one, are colonisers of felled forest and often hybridise where they meet. A. COLENSOI Hook. f. is thought to be the result of such a cross.

ARONIA   ROSACEAE

Three species of deciduous shrubs closely akin to *Sorbus* and natives of N. America. The flowers differ from *Sorbus* in always having five styles; leaves always simple and with glands on the upper side of the midrib. Calyx-lobes persisting at the top of the fruit. Fruits small, red or black. They can be propagated by cuttings or by seeds, sometimes also by division. Quite hardy, easily cultivated, and handsome.

A. ARBUTIFOLIA (L.) Pers.   RED CHOKEBERRY
Pyrus arbutifolia L.

A shrub of bushy, vigorous habit, from 5 to 10 ft high; branchlets covered with down, which persists over the winter. Leaves narrowly obovate or oval, tapering at both ends; $1\frac{1}{2}$ to $3\frac{1}{2}$ in. long, $\frac{1}{2}$ to $\frac{3}{4}$ in. wide; the margins set with even, black-tipped teeth; upper surface dark dull green, with dark glands along the midrib; lower surface covered with a thick grey felt, which remains until the leaf falls; stalk $\frac{1}{3}$ in. or less long. Flowers white or slightly rosy, about $\frac{1}{2}$ in. across, produced during late May in small corymbs. Fruit globular or rather pear-shaped, $\frac{1}{4}$ in. wide, bright red.

Native of eastern N. America; cultivated in England since 1700. It is a variable plant (Loudon describes some nine or ten forms), and has hybridised with *A. melanocarpa*. It is found under several names in gardens, and is confused with *A. melanocarpa*. That species, however, in its typical form, is well distinguished by its glabrous or nearly glabrous leaves and black fruits. The foliage of several forms of *A. arbutifolia*, especially one grown in nurseries as "erythrocarpa", turns a brilliant red before falling. The species is indeed worth growing for its autumn colour alone.

Between this species and *A. melanocarpa* comes A. PRUNIFOLIA (Marsh.) Rehd., also offered in nurseries under Spach's name "*floribunda*" and as the "purple-fruited chokeberry". It is intermediate between the other two species but, we are told by Dr Rehder, not a hybrid. The dark purple fruits furnish the best distinction.

cv. 'ERECTA'.—A form of narrowly fastigiate habit; leaves oblanceolate to oblong, dying off a bright crimson. Put into commerce by Messrs Marchant.

A. MELANOCARPA (Michx.) Ell.   BLACK CHOKEBERRY

Mespilus arbutifolia var. *melanocarpa* Michx.; *Pyrus melanocarpa* (Michx.) Willd.

A shrub 3 to 5 ft high, of bushy, flat-topped habit, producing sucker growths from the base; branchlets glabrous, or somewhat downy. Leaves obovate, from 1¼ to 3 in. long, from ¾ to 2 in. wide; usually short-pointed at the apex, always tapering at the base, finely and regularly toothed; the upper surface dark polished green and glabrous, except for dark glands on the midrib; lower surface paler, usually glabrous except when quite young, but occasionally downy throughout the season; stalk ¼ in. or less long. Flowers white, ⅓ to ½ in. across, produced towards the end of May in corymbs of six to twelve blossoms; calyx glabrous or downy, with triangular lobes. Fruit roundish, ⅓ to ½ in. across, black or black-purple. *Bot. Mag.*, t. 9052.

Native of eastern N. America, and cultivated in England probably for over two centuries. From the allied *A. arbutifolia* it is easily distinguished, that species having red fruit and dull leaves very woolly beneath. There is a form of *A. melanocarpa* which, in the more or less downy under-surface of the leaf and in the vinous red fruit approaches *A. arbutifolia*, but like the black-fruited, glabrous leaved type its fruits fall as soon as ripe (in September), whereas those of *A. arbutifolia* persist until mid-winter. *A. melanocarpa* flowers freely, and is a bright and pleasing shrub of neat habit.

var. ELATA Rehd.—A larger shrub in most respects, growing up to 10 ft high, with larger leaves of oblong-obovate shape and flowers and fruit also larger.

ARTEMISIA   COMPOSITAE

A large genus of shrubby and herbaceous plants with composite flowers, abundant in Europe, and especially in the dry, hot regions of western N. America, where they cover great plains and form what is known there as 'sage brush'. Most of them are of a more or less greyish tinge, and are notable for their strong, often agreeable odour. Some half-dozen shrubby species have at times been in cultivation, the two best of which are

A. abrotanum and *A. tridentata*. They need a sunny position, and a well-drained, not rich soil. Increased by cuttings.

A. ABROTANUM L.   SOUTHERNWOOD

A soft-wooded, semi-shrubby, fragrant plant about 3 ft high; stems erect, densely furnished with foliage, and covered at first with a grey down. Leaves downy, the terminal half doubly or trebly pinnate, the final divisions scarcely thicker than a thread; the entire leaf is from 1 to 2 in. long, $\frac{3}{4}$ to $1\frac{1}{2}$ in. wide, and dull green. Flower-heads dull yellow, $\frac{1}{6}$ in. across, nodding; produced during September and October in a tall, slender panicle 12 to 18 in. high, $1\frac{1}{2}$ to $2\frac{1}{2}$ in. through, terminating each shoot.

Native of S. Europe; cultivated in England since the sixteenth century. The flowers have little beauty, but the plant has always been a favourite in gardens, especially cottage gardens, for the sweet aromatic odour of its finely divided leaves. Village children were very fond of taking a sprig to school, and in the north of England the plant is often called "lad's love". It thrives in any soil, but likes a sunny, well-drained spot. Increased by cuttings taken any time during the summer, and placed either in gentle heat, or under a bell-glass in some sheltered corner. It flowers infrequently in most parts of Britain, and is valued solely for its fragrant sprigs.

A. ARBORESCENS L.

An evergreen shrub forming a cluster of erect, woody stems to about 4 ft high. Leaves and shoots covered with a close, silky, white down. Leaves cut into linear, bluntly tipped segments, those near the base of the stem distinctly stalked and trebly pinnate, the uppermost sessile and doubly or singly pinnate. Flower-heads bright yellow, globose, short-stalked, $\frac{1}{5}$ to $\frac{1}{3}$ in. wide, pendulous at first, later erect, arranged in a leafy, one-sided panicle; receptacles silky-hairy; achenes glandular.

Native of the Mediterranean, where it grows on cliffs and on rocky slopes near the coast; commonest in S. Italy and the Aegean, rarer in the western part of the basin. It is closely related to the common wormwood, *A. absinthium*, differing mainly in its larger flower-heads and in its non-glandular leaves, which lack the bitter principle characteristic of that species. It is tender but well worth attempting in mild, sunny gardens, best suited under a warm wall in well-drained soil.

A. PROCERA Willd.

A semi-woody plant of thin, erect habit, with pithy stems 6 to 8 ft high, glabrous or furnished with a little grey down. Leaves trebly pinnate, the final divisions thin and thread-like; the entire leaf is 2 to 3 in. long, and the same wide; dark green. Flower-heads nodding, $\frac{1}{8}$ in. across, yellowish green; produced in August in tall, slender panicles 12 to 20 in. long, the lower portion composed of racemes springing from the axils of the uppermost leaves.

Native of S.E. Europe and Asia Minor. Although rather elegant in late summer and autumn, when its tall stems are surmounted by their flower-panicles, the plant is of only third-rate value in gardens. It is quite hardy, and has lived outside for many years at Kew without protection. The leaves when crushed have a slightly pungent aroma.

A. TRIDENTATA Nutt.   SAGE BRUSH

An evergreen shrub of rather open habit 6 to 8 ft high; stems lax when young, clothed with shredding bark when old; young shoots and leaves covered with a dense, grey felt. Leaves of various sizes, crowded on the stems in clusters; wedge-shaped, tapering gradually from the apex (which is three-toothed and truncate) to the stalk; $\frac{1}{2}$ to $1\frac{3}{4}$ in. long, $\frac{1}{10}$ to $\frac{1}{4}$ in. wide at the apex. Flower-heads small, yellowish, $\frac{1}{4}$ in. long, supported by grey-felted bracts; produced in October in long, slender panicles, more or less arching or pendulous, and 12 to 18 in. long. No other hardy shrub in cultivation has a leaf similar to this in colour and shape.

Native of the western United States; introduced to Kew in 1895. When rubbed, the plant emits a strong but pleasant odour, which moisture of itself appears to release, for after a shower, or still more after a wet day, the air for several yards round a group of plants is filled with this aromatic scent. The species is usually a great favourite with those who cultivate it on this account. This shrub is one of those found in the dry alkaline districts of western N. America, which are known collectively as 'sage brush', and cover immense areas with a grey, monotonous vegetation. In our gardens it makes a very pleasing feature, not only for its fragrance, but also for the silvery grey foliage, which provides an agreeable contrast to ordinary green shrubs. It can be increased by cuttings made of half-ripened wood, and placed under a bell-glass in the propagating frame. But it does not take root with the readiness and certainty of most of its allies.

ARUNDINARIA*   BAMBOO   GRAMINEAE

Hardy bamboos have long been known in gardens under three generic names, viz., *Arundinaria*, *Bambusa* and *Phyllostachys*. Whilst most of the species of *Phyllostachys* are probably correctly placed, so much cannot be said for those put under *Bambusa* and *Arundinaria*, many of which had never been critically examined in flower at the time they were named. True species of *Bambusa*, perhaps with one exception, are not hardy in the British Isles; the exception—*B. glaucescens* Willd. (*B. nana* Roxb.) of which there are several attractive cultivars—might be grown in the open in sheltered positions in the south-west.

* Revised by Dr C. E. Hubbard.

As regards *Arundinaria*, American, Chinese and Japanese botanists have made extensive studies, in the field, of hardy bamboos during the past forty years, with the result that many species classified in the genus *Arundinaria* (*sensu lato*) have been referred to the following new genera:

CHIMONOBAMBUSA Makino—*A. marmorea*
PLEIOBLASTUS Nakai—*A. simonii*, *A. graminea*, *A. humilis*, etc.
PSEUDOSASA Makino—*A. japonica*
SASA Makino & Shibata—*A. palmata*, *A. ragamowskii*, *A. veitchii*, etc.
SEMIARUNDINARIA Makino—*A. fastuosa*
SINARUNDINARIA Nakai—*A. murielae*, *A. nitida*
TETRAGONOCALAMUS Nakai—*A. quadrangularis*

Also, the genus THAMNOCALAMUS Munro has been revived and to it are referred *A. falconeri* and *A. spathiflora*. With regard to the use of these generic names in this work, it has been decided to retain most species in *Arundinaria* as hitherto except for the three species *A. palmata*, *A. ragamowskii* and *A. veitchii*, which are referred to *Sasa* (q.v.). To assist those interested in the proposed division of the genus, the various new generic names are given prominently under the species concerned. The nomenclature of these hardy bamboos is still in an unsettled state, as some should probably be treated as cultivars, others are based on imperfect descriptions, while quite a number of species have not flowered, so that their precise generic position is uncertain. If the new classification were to be adopted only two species of *Arundinaria* hardy in Britain would be left in the genus, viz. *A. gigantea* (*A. macrosperma*) and *A. tecta*, both natives of the United States.

The following remarks concerning cultivation, etc., although placed under *Arundinaria*, are intended to apply to the hardy bamboos in general; other genera described in this work are *Chusquea*, *Phyllostachys*, *Sasa* and *Shibataea*.

The bamboos are really woody grasses, mostly characteristic of moist tropical and warm temperate regions, the species in cultivation being mainly from the Himalaya, temperate E. Asia (China, Japan, Korea and Formosa), the United States and the Andes of S. America (*Chusquea*). Although they are mere pygmies compared with the giants of equatorial regions, they have a special value in our gardens in introducing to them a form of vegetation not only of surpassing grace and beauty, but one of an absolutely distinct type.

Naturally they are evergreen, but in cold winters and in cold districts some of them lose much of, or all, their foliage. They have hollow stems divided into sections by a transverse woody layer at each node (or 'joint'), and the branches (from one to many) are produced at these joints, which are farthest apart about the middle of the stem. In the young state the stems are more or less encased in membranous, papery or coriaceous sheaths which in some species fall away, in others persist. At the ends of these stem-sheaths there is usually a leaf-like expansion known as the limb or blade and at the base of the latter often two lateral outgrowths known as auricles, which usually bear hairs or bristles. The stem-sheaths provide valuable distinguishing characters, differing in texture, whether hairless or hairy, in colour and whether spotted or blotched with a deeper coloration, also in shape and size, the presence or absence of auricles, the form of the auricular hairs and the shape and direction of the blade. They are most useful, when associated with other parts of the plant, for purposes of identification.

The leaf-blades of bamboos have a midrib supported on each side by from two to twenty more or less prominent secondary veins, between which again are thin, delicate veins of a third dimension, easily visible by holding the leaf between the eye and the light. In all but two of the species mentioned in these notes the thin veins are united by tiny cross-veins— easily seen with a lens by holding the leaf up to the light—which divide the space between each longitudinal vein into rectangular spaces of irregular size. Lord Redesdale made the interesting discovery that this tessellation of the veins is invariably characteristic of a really hardy bamboo; those that do not possess it are as invariably tender. This, however, does not mean that every bamboo with a tessellated venation is hardy. The leaf-blades are frequently narrowed to a short stalk at the base where they join the leaf-sheath, which is easily detached by pulling at the blade. At the junction of the sheath and blade many species bear a pair of lateral outgrowths—the auricles—which are usually fringed with few to several rough or smooth bristles. These auricles, like those of the stem-sheaths (see above), are useful distinguishing features.

In habit, bamboos are either tufted—i.e. they keep their stems in a close cluster and extend but slowly—or they spread by means of underground rhizomes, which may be short or long, giving rise to erect stems at intervals, which in some species push through the ground several feet away from the older stems (e.g. *Arundinaria anceps*).

The flowering of bamboos is a phenomenon of peculiar interest, but as the flowers have little bearing on the identification of those we cultivate, it is not necessary to enter into a definition of them here. On many of the sorts we grow they have never been seen in this country, nor, indeed, ever examined by botanists. For this reason they should be gathered and sent to a botanical institution for examination and, if necessary, preservation. It is only by recording instances of flowering that we shall be able to ascertain whether it occurs at more or less frequent intervals, and whether it is followed by the death of the individual plant. There is no doubt that the flowering of many bamboos is shortly and inevitably followed by their death: *Arundinaria falconeri* is an example. Others flower and although seriously crippled, in time recover: some of the *Phyllostachys* behave in this way. In a third group a small proportion of the stems flower, and although those particular stems die, the plant as a whole is unaffected; *Arundinaria viridistriata* (*A. auricoma*) is an example, plants of which can usually be found bearing a few spikelets at the tips of the stems. This is not a general (gregarious) flowering, however, but rather of a sporadic nature, isolated stems only bearing a few flowers. It should not be compared with flowering spread over several to many years and the final flowering and death of every stem and its branches such as occurred with *A. simonii* after blooming partially for at least twelve years; or with many plants of *A. fastuosa*, which flowered from 1957 to 1968 (or perhaps later) and finally died. It has been reported that the lives of bamboos (or of some of them) may be saved by cutting off all the stems close to the ground as soon as ever there is any indication that they are about to blossom. This is worth trying, although where the flowering is general it has usually been unsuccessful.

A curious circumstance in connection with the flowering of bamboos is the simultaneous flowering of all the plants of one species, although spread over great areas and growing under different conditions. Instances have been known where plants grown in English hothouses for many years have flowered (and died) during the same season as plants of identical species growing wild in the tropics. Hardy species in our gardens have behaved in the same way, flowering simultaneously all over the country as well as in other parts of the world, probably being derived from the same original introduction from the wild state; but the period of flowering appears to be longer and less clearly defined than in the case of wild species, and may extend over four or five years. Good examples of such flowering are *Phyllostachys nigra* and *P. aurea*, which flowered in various parts of Europe, S. America, Australia and New Zealand, and E. Asia during the same period of years.

CULTIVATION.—The most important item in the cultivation of the group as a whole is the provision of good shelter. Few plants we grow are less adapted to withstand cutting blasts from north and east than these. They need some position protected from those quarters, but open to the south and west. Nothing in our gardens is more lovely in form than a well-grown bamboo from midsummer to Christmas, but with the January and February frosts and the biting winds of March, many of them become seared and brown, and anything but pleasant objects. Adequate shelter from cold winds does much to prevent or defer this disfigurement.

As regards soil, they appear to thrive best in an open loam of fair quality; neither so sandy as to be poor, nor so clayey as to be heavy and cold. They also succeed well on a peaty formation. Being gross feeders they need abundant moisture, and are benefited by occasional mulchings with manure, leaf-soil or humus of any kind, particularly during dry springs and summers.

TRANSPLANTING AND PROPAGATION.—In the absence of seed—a very uncertain product in this country—propagation is effected by division. All disturbance at the root, whether for propagation or transplanting, is best deferred until May, or until the unfolding of new leaves indicates that root action has begun. Early autumn is also a good time, but from late autumn to early spring is the worst time to transplant. In order to divide some clumps of the tufted sorts it may be necessary to use a pickaxe, so hard and matted does the root system become; but from the running sorts pieces can be easily detached. To get a big stock quickly, a clump should be broken up into comparatively small pieces, which should be potted or planted thickly in a warm, moist greenhouse until re-established. In this case it is advisable to cut down the stems in proportion to the sacrifice of roots. Imported plants are safer if established in heat in this way before planting in the open ground.

For districts where the success of bamboos is problematical the following sorts are the best to experiment with: *Arundinaria anceps*, *A. fastuosa*, *A. japonica*, *A. nitida*; *Sasa palmata* (*Arundinaria palmata*), *S. tessellata* (*Arundinaria ragamowskii*); *Phyllostachys nigra* and *P. nigra* 'Henonis'.

ARUNDINARIA.—The most obvious distinctive characters of what we have been growing as *Arundinaria* are in the stems. These are round and straight, and develop the branches almost simultaneously from top to bottom, and, in the taller species, the branches at each joint are indefinite and numerous. The low, slender-stemmed, sparsely branched, very rhizomatous species included in previous editions under this genus, namely *A. veitchii*, *A. palmata* and *A. ragamowskii*, will be found in Vol. 3 under *Sasa*, the genus into which they have been separated by Japanese botanists.

The following species of *Arundinaria* are not treated in the present work: A. HOOKERIANA Munro (E. Himalaya), A. INTERMEDIA Munro (E. Himalaya) and A. KHASIANA Munro (Assam). They are not hardy at Kew but are grown in the open in the mildest parts of south-west England and of Ireland.

A. ANCEPS Mitf.   RINGAL
A. jaunsarensis Gamble

A graceful bamboo, with single culms arising at intervals from a long, creeping, scaly rhizome. Stems 10 to 15 ft or more high, about ½ in. in diameter; purplish at first, changing to brownish green; from 3 to 7 in. between the joints; branches purple, slender, forming dense clusters on the older stems. Stem-sheaths mottled within, hairy on the margin, truncate at the apex, with a narrow, falcate, bristly auricle on each side of the short, subulate blade. Leaf-sheath fringed with bristles and short hairs where it joins the base of the blade. Blades 1½ to 4 in. long, ¼ to ½ in. wide, brilliant green above, slightly glaucous beneath, edged with minute bristles on each margin. There are two or three secondary veins on each side of the midrib, and the tessellation is very minute, but quite distinct under a lens.

Native of the N.W. Himalaya; introduced by Col. Edmund Smyth from Garhwal, about 1865, and first cultivated at Elkington Hall, Lincolnshire. It is a handsome and graceful bamboo, spreading rapidly by means of underground rhizomes, sometimes becoming a nuisance when running under lawns or invading other plants. It is very hardy, and although it loses its leaves in severe winters its stems are rarely injured. It grows at elevations of 10,000 to 11,000 ft, and is said to flower and seed in its native home at intervals of twenty to twenty-five years, when vast fields of it die. A few plants flowered in the British Isles in 1910 and 1911, and in 1920; since 1957 flowering has been reported in various gardens, complete plants or isolated stems coming into bloom. These may be the forerunners of a general flowering, although the plants at Kew in 1967 showed no signs of flowering.

A. ANGUSTIFOLIA (Mitf.) H. de Lehaie

PLEIOBLASTUS ANGUSTIFOLIUS (Mitf.) Nakai; *Bambusa angustifolia* Mitf.; *B. vilmorinii* Hort.

Stems erect, 2 to 6 ft high, round, $\frac{1}{12}$ to $\frac{1}{5}$ in. in diameter, with a very small hollow up the centre; joints rather prominent, from 10 in. apart at the base to about 1 in. near the apex; branches slender, erect. Leaves $1\frac{1}{2}$ to 6 in. long, $\frac{1}{6}$ to $\frac{3}{4}$ in. wide, rounded at the base, long and slenderly pointed, glabrous, and of the same shade of brilliant green on both surfaces; bristle-toothed on one margin, minutely so on the other; secondary veins two to four each side the midrib; leaf-sheath with a tuft of erect hairs at the top, and smaller ones on the margin.

Native of Japan; introduced about 1895 by way of France. This bamboo spreads rapidly by means of underground rhizomes, and forms a dense thicket of slender, erect stems of various heights. Its distinguishing marks are in the narrowness of the leaves, their smoothness, and similarity of shade on both surfaces.

A. ARISTATA Gamble

THAMNOCALAMUS ARISTATUS (Gamble) E. G. Camus

Stems tufted, 8 to 12 ft or more high, $\frac{1}{3}$ to $\frac{3}{5}$ in. in diameter, at first glaucous green and white-scurfy, afterwards shining yellow; branches several at the joints, reddish. Stem-sheaths leaving a persistent cup-like base, straw-coloured, loose, with a ring of soft hairs at the base, sparsely stiffly hairy above, tipped with a short subulate blade. Leaf-blades in groups of two to three, oblong-lanceolate, $2\frac{1}{4}$ to $4\frac{1}{2}$ in. long, $\frac{2}{5}$ to $\frac{2}{3}$ in. wide, hairless or faintly hairy beneath, with three to five pairs of secondary nerves; leaf-sheaths bearing a few (six to eight) stiff purple bristles at the tip.

Native of the N.E. Himalaya (Sikkim and Bhutan), where it grows at elevations of 9,000 to 10,000 ft. Related to *A. spathiflora*, differing in size, habit, and in the structure of the spikelets. Suitable only for cultivation in the milder parts of the British Isles. It flowered in 1950-1.

A. CHINO (Franch. & Sav.) Makino

PLEIOBLASTUS CHINO (Franch. & Sav.) Nakai; *Bambusa chino* Franch. & Sav.; *Arundinaria simonii* var. *chino* (Franch. & Sav.) Makino; *Nipponocalamus chino* (Franch. & Sav.) Nakai

Stems rarely more than 2 to 6 ft high, slender, smooth, green, bearing one to three branches at the joints, with spreading, creeping rhizomes. Leaf-blades $1\frac{1}{2}$ to 8 in. long, $\frac{1}{6}$ to $\frac{5}{8}$ in. wide, hairless or slightly hairy beneath, with three to seven pairs of secondary veins.

Native of China, introduced to Japan and perhaps thence to Europe. Closely related to *A. simonii*, which has taller, stouter stems and mostly larger leaves.

cv. 'LAYDEKERI'.—Leaves dark green, mottled with dull yellow. Flowered in 1896 (*Arundinaria laydekeri* Bean; *Pleioblastus chino* var. *laydekeri* (Bean) Nakai).

A. CHRYSANTHA Mitf.
Sasa chrysantha (Mitf.) E. G. Camus

Stems 2 to 6 ft high, ⅛ to ⅙ in. diameter, dark green, round; joints 2 to 5½ in. apart, with several branches. Leaves 3 to 7 in. long, ½ to 1 in. broad, rounded at the base, rather abruptly tapered to a short, slender point, glabrous on both surfaces, minutely toothed at the margins. There is a tuft of long, silky hairs at the top of the leaf-sheath. Most of the leaves are quite green, but some are more or less striped with golden yellow like *A. viridistriata*. Secondary veins four to six each side the midrib.

Native of Japan; introduced in 1892, but a bamboo of no great attractiveness. The variegation is not abundant enough to give a colour effect, and the plant cannot be compared with *A. viridistriata* in this respect. It spreads rapidly by its underground rhizomes.

A. DISTICHA (Mitf.) Pfitzer
PLEIOBLASTUS DISTICHUS (Mitf.) Nakai; *Bambusa disticha* Mitf.; B. nana Hort.; *Sasa disticha* (Mitf.) E. G. Camus

A dwarf bamboo, with stems 1 to 3 ft high, very slender, zigzagged, green or purplish; joints ½ to 3½ in. apart, bearing solitary branches. Leaves arranged in two opposite rows, ¾ to 2¼ in. long, ⅙ to ⅓ in. wide, rounded at the base, pointed, bright green above, slightly glaucous beneath; both margins bristle-toothed, but one more than the other; secondary veins two or three each side the midrib; leaf-sheaths hairy on the margins.

Native of Japan; cultivated by Messrs Veitch in the 'seventies of last century, and probably introduced for them by John Gould Veitch during the previous decade. Its dwarf erect stems and tiny, distichously arranged leaves easily distinguish it from all other hardy bamboos. It was once known in gardens, erroneously, as "*Bambusa nana*".

This species was in flower at Wakehurst Place, Sussex, in 1967, a few 4 to 12 in. stems bearing one or two spikelets at their tips; this appears to be its first blooming in the British Isles, although the flowers may have been previously overlooked.

A. FALCATA Nees
CHIMONOBAMBUSA FALCATA (Nees) Nakai; *Bambusa gracilis* Hort.

Stems tufted, 10 to 15 ft high, glaucous when young, slender, round; the joints clothed with a velvety down, swollen, bearing numerous slender branches; stem-sheaths narrowed in the upper part to the ciliate, truncate tip, bearing a subulate recurved blade ½ to 2 in. long, ciliate on the margins especially when young, pale purple. Leaf-blades 2 to 6 in. long, ⅙ to ⅞ in. wide, narrowed at the base, tapering to a fine bristle-like tip, pubescent beneath when young, rather pale green, somewhat glaucous beneath; secondary veins two to five each side the midrib, not tesselated with cross-veinlets; leaf-sheaths striate, ending in a minutely hairy ring at the junction with the blade.

Native of the N.W. Himalaya at 4,000 to 7,000 ft (rarely higher), in damp oak forests. It is not a very hardy species, and is only suitable for the mildest parts of the kingdom. From all the bamboos here mentioned, except *A. falconeri*, it can be distinguished by the absence of cross-veinlets in the leaves. *A. falconeri* differs in having green or yellowish (not glaucous) stems with dark brown stains at the joints.

A. falcata flowers fairly frequently, being recorded in bloom in the British Isles in 1884–6, 1907–10, 1917–21, 1935–8, 1945 and 1951. Seed is fairly freely produced.

A. FALCONERI (Munro) Duthie

THAMNOCALAMUS FALCONERI Munro; *A. nobilis* Mitf.

Stems up to 25 ft long in the mildest parts of the kingdom, tufted, very slender, round, olive green, becoming yellowish, with a very distinct stain of purplish brown at the joints; the joints quite devoid of down; stem-sheaths purple, glabrous, except towards the top and at the margins. Leaves normally 2 to 4 in. long, about ⅓ in. wide, bright green, rather glaucous beneath, with purplish stalks and margins; secondary veins three or four each side the midrib, not tessellated with cross-veins; leaf-sheaths purplish, not hairy at the top. *Bot. Mag.*, t. 7947, as *A. nobilis*.

Native of the Himalaya; first introduced to England in 1847 by Col. E. Madden, who sent large quantities of seeds to Kew, which were distributed through Europe. These plants grew well where the climatic conditions were favourable, and flowered in 1875 and 1876. Every plant ultimately died, but from the seed they produced, a new generation was raised, which in its turn flowered between 1903 and 1908. The next general flowering occurred between 1929 and 1932 during which period plants flowered in Guernsey, in Cornwall (St Keverne) and in the Temperate House at Kew. From 1964 to 1967 flowering has taken place in English, Irish, Scottish and Welsh gardens, and in Guernsey.

A. falconeri produces its stems in a dense, crowded cluster, and does not spread by underground suckers. It is not very hardy, but in such places as Cornwall and the south-west of Ireland it is magnificent. At Kew it is killed to the ground every winter. The species has been much confused with *A. falcata*— an inferior bamboo, more tender, not so tall, and really very distinct in its glaucous stems with velvety joints, and in the long, tapered points of the stem-sheaths.

A. FASTUOSA (Mitf.) Makino

SEMIARUNDINARIA FASTUOSA (Mitf.) Makino; *Bambusa fastuosa* Mitf.; *Sasa fastuosa* (Mitf.) E. G. Camus

Stems up to 22 ft high, 1½ in. diameter at the base, perfectly erect, very hollow, dark green, round except at the upper internodes, which are flattened on one

side; branches short, very leafy. Stem-sheaths very large, up to 9 in. long by
4 in. wide at the base when spread out, purplish and at first downy outside,
beautifully glazed within; they fall off early. Leaves 4 to 8 in. long, ½ to 1 in.
wide, wedge-shaped at the base, long- and taper-pointed, dark lustrous green
above; one side the midrib beneath glaucous, the other greenish; margins
toothed; secondary veins four to six each side the midrib.

Native of Japan, where it is known as 'Narihira-dake'. Narihira, Lord Redesdale tells us, was the beautiful hero of one of the classic romances of Japan,
written in the eleventh century. Although in some respects this bamboo
resembles *A. simonii*, it is perfectly distinct and a superior plant. If not the most
graceful, it is the loftiest and stateliest of hardy species, differing from *A. simonii*
in the early fall of the stem-sheaths; in the short, crowded branches at each joint,
which give to each stem-growth a columnar appearance; and in the more tufted
habit. Although suckers do push through the ground good distances away from
the parent clump, it is not so rampant as *A. simonii*. Introduced in 1892, it commenced flowering in 1957; during the past eleven years blooming has taken place
in several gardens, many of the plants dying after flowering. It is very hardy,
and the foliage of no bamboo suffers less from winter cold.

A. GIGANTEA (Walt.) Chapm.   GIANT CANE

Arundo gigantea Walt.; *Arundinaria macrosperma* Michx.

Stems erect, 10 to 30 ft high, 1 to 3 in. in diameter at the base; unbranched
the first year, branching at the upper part the second. Stem-sheaths glabrous
except at the ciliate margins, fringed at the top. Leaves lanceolate, 4 to 15 in.
long, 1 to 1¼ in. wide, slenderly pointed, rounded at the base, finely toothed,
glabrous or slightly downy; veins in six to fourteen pairs; leaf-sheaths ciliate on
the margins, fimbriate at the tip.

This is the large cane reed of the S.E. United States, where it grows on river
banks and in swamps, forming extensive colonies in low woods, from Virginia
and Kentucky southward to Florida and Louisiana. The young culms are edible.
It is not established at Kew but should be hardy over a good part of the
south-west.

A. GRAMINEA (Bean) Makino

PLEIOBLASTUS GRAMINEUS (Bean) Nakai; *A. hindsii* var. *graminea* Bean

Stems up to 10 ft high, and about ¼ in. diameter, at first yellowish; the central
hollow very large, leaving only thin walls; joints 3 to 6 in. apart; ultimately very
densely branched and leafy towards the top, and forming besom-like masses.
Leaves the narrowest in proportion to their length of all hardy bamboos, being
4 to 9 in. long, but never, so far as I have observed, more than ½ in. wide;
secondary nerves two to four either side the midrib.

Native of Japan, where it is known as 'Taimin-chiku'; cultivated by Messrs
Veitch in 1877, and probably introduced by John Gould Veitch during the
previous decade. It forms thickets of stems of great density, but spreads rapidly,

and can be increased very quickly by division. In the earlier days of its cultivation in Britain I regarded it as a variety of *A. hindsii*, but in twenty years these two have assumed very different characters. *A. graminea* is a much more slender, leafy plant, hardier, and better for gardens; the leaves are only half as wide, and the secondary veins fewer. A few stems flowered in 1948 and others in 1965–7.

A. HINDSII Munro
PLEIOBLASTUS HINDSII (Munro) Nakai

Stems tufted, 8 to 10 ft high, round, quite erect, up to 1 in. diameter, dark olive green, at first covered with a waxy bloom; joints often 8 to 10 in. apart; central pipe large. Branches erect, forming dense clusters at each joint. Leaves mostly erect, dark green above, rather glaucous beneath, glabrous on the surfaces, but with numerous bristle-like teeth on one margin and a few scattered ones on the other; the longest are 8 to 9 in. long, the broadest ¾ to 1 in. wide, the average width from ¼ to ⅝ in., tapered at the base, the apex long, tail-like. Secondary veins four to six each side the midrib.

Native of Hong Kong; introduced to Japan and thence to Europe. It is doubtful whether the plant in cultivation is the same species as the Hong Kong bamboo. Munro described a narrow-leaved plant which may be the same as a bamboo which flowered on the Island in 1897 and again in 1909; its spikelets are, however, slightly different from those of the plants of British gardens, which flowered in 1910 and 1911. Until the group of bamboos comprising this species, *A. simonii*, *A. chino* and *A. graminea*, has been investigated the cultivated plant is best left under *A. hindsii*.

It is one of the least elegant of bamboos, similar in foliage to *A. graminea*, but less copiously leafy and with larger leaves. The stems and leaves are also stouter and darker green, the habit is less dense, and the plants do not 'run' so rapidly.

A. HUMILIS Mitf.
PLEIOBLASTUS HUMILIS (Mitf.) Nakai; *Bambusa nagashima* Hort.; *Arundinaria fortunei* var. *viridis* Hort.

A dwarf, rapidly spreading bamboo, 2 to 5 ft high as a rule, with a creeping rhizome; stems very slender, and with a minute hollow up the centre; stem-sheaths purplish at first. Leaves bright green on both sides, 2 to 7 in. long, ⅓ to ¾ in. wide, rounded at the base, slender-pointed; secondary veins three to five each side the midrib; leaf-sheaths with two clusters of bristles at the top.

A native of Japan, long grown in gardens as *A. fortunei* ('green form'). The true *A. fortunei* (now *A. variegata*) is well marked by its white-variegated leaves. I am, however, unable to see any real distinction between it and the *Bambusa nagashima* of French nurserymen; nor is there much to choose between these two and *A. chrysantha*, except the occasional variegation of the last. *A. humilis*, without possessing any special merit, forms pleasant masses of greenery from mid-summer onwards.

It flowered for the first time in 1964 at the tips of a few stems and has continued to do so since, but most of the stems remain in the vegetative state (1969).

A. JAPONICA Sieb. & Zucc.

PSEUDOSASA JAPONICA (Sieb. & Zucc.) Makino; *Bambusa metake* Sieb.;
Sasa japonica (Sieb. & Zucc.) Makino

Stems 10 to 12 ft high (5 or 6 ft more in the milder counties), round, very
hollow, erect, $\frac{1}{6}$ to $\frac{2}{3}$ in. diameter, with erect branches near the top, producing
only a few leaves the first year. Stem-sheaths nearly as long or longer than the
space between the joints, which is sometimes 8 in., very persistent, soon turning
pale brown, covered at first with flattened bristles; terminated when young by
an awl-shaped tongue up to 3 in. long, but only $\frac{1}{8}$ in. wide. Leaves 7 to 12 in.
long, $\frac{3}{4}$ to 2 in. wide, terminated by a long tail-like point; the upper surface
glossy dark green, rather glaucous beneath, except a strip about one-fourth of
its width near one margin, which is green. There are five to nine secondary
veins each side the midrib, minutely tessellated with cross-veinlets; one margin
is minutely, the other scarcely toothed.

Native of Japan; introduced by Von Siebold in 1850, and for long the only
bamboo commonly grown in British gardens. It is a very hardy and accommodating species, and a handsome evergreen, having larger leaves than any
other bamboo of its height and character that we can grow outside. It does not
spread quickly by underground suckers, but maintains a rather tufted habit. It
flowered in Europe between 1872 and 1874, and has been in flower in many
parts of the British Isles since about 1950. While all stems have flowered on some
plants, leading to their death, most plants have bloomed only on a few stems and
continue to produce vigorous new vegetative shoots.

A. MARMOREA (Mitf.) Makino

CHIMONOBAMBUSA MARMOREA (Mitf.) Makino; *Bambusa marmorea* Mitf.;
Arundinaria kokantsik Kurz

Stems round, slender, solid, erect, 3 to 5 ft high; purplish green, from $\frac{1}{8}$ to
$\frac{1}{4}$ in. thick at the base, almost hidden the first season by the clasping, persistent
sheaths, which are at first purplish, mottled conspicuously with pinkish grey,
turning grey-white with age. Branches erect, normally three at each joint, forming a dense but elegant, cylindrical mass of foliage; the branches, however, do
not develop until the second year, the tops of the slender, whip-like, leafless
stems of the first year standing out above the mass of foliage throughout the
winter. Leaves bright green, 2 to 5 in. long, $\frac{3}{8}$ in. to $\frac{1}{2}$ in. wide, with slender,
awl-like points; four or five secondary nerves each side the midrib; margins set
with minute bristles; leaf-sheath terminated by a tuft of pale curly bristles and
edged with small hairs.

Native of Japan; introduced to Ireland in 1889. A very pretty, well-marked
bamboo, distinguished by the marbled stem-sheaths, the stems remaining unbranched the first season, the absence of a pipe or hollow up the centre, and by
the apex of the leaf being constricted about $\frac{1}{2}$ in. from the tip. It spreads very
rapidly by underground suckers, forming luxuriant masses, but is liable to
injury by winter cold.

Flowering has been observed in most years on a few stems in well-established clumps, the first recorded being in 1909; the dark purple ovaries and developing seeds are exposed and protrude between the gaping lemma and palea, but soon fall.

cv. 'VARIEGATA'.—Leaves variegated with white; cultivated in Japan (*Chimonobambusa m.* cv. Variegata Ohwi; *C. m.* var. *variegata* Makino).

A. MURIELAE Gamble
SINARUNDINARIA MURIELAE (Gamble) Nakai

An evergreen bamboo 8 to 13 ft high, forming a dense thicket of stems erect and leafless the first year, afterwards becoming heavily laden with foliage and arching gracefully outwards. Stems ¼ to ⅖ in. in diameter, hollow, at first bright green, finally yellow. Stem-sheaths straw-coloured, 3 to 5 in. long, ½ to ¾ in. wide, rounded at the top where is a reflexed, awl-shaped tongue 1½ to 2½ in. long, glabrous except for minute hairs on the margin when young. Leaves 2½ to 4½ in. long, ⅖ to ⅗ in. wide, rounded at the base, tapering to a long slender apex, rich green and glabrous except for minute appressed bristles on both margins; secondary veins three or four each side the midrib; stalk ⅛ to ⅙ in. long. Leaf-sheath bristly where it joins its stalk.

Native of W. Hupeh, China, on uplands up to 10,000 ft altitude; discovered and introduced by Wilson in 1907 (No. 1462). A small plant was obtained from the Arnold Arboretum for Kew in 1913. This was easily propagated by division and afterwards distributed. Since then it has become well established in British gardens and has proved quite hardy. It more nearly resembles *A. nitida* than any other of the bamboos previously in cultivation and is equally beautiful and graceful. *A. nitida* is very distinct in its purple-black stems, purple stem-sheaths and smaller leaves. The specific name was given in honour of Muriel, daughter of the late E. H. Wilson.

A. NITIDA Mitf. [PLATE 16
SINARUNDINARIA NITIDA (Mitf.) Nakai

Stems up to 10 ft high, ⅜ in. in diameter, erect and leafless the first year, very dark purple, round and hollow, very crowded; branching the second season and becoming heavily laden with foliage at the top, then arching and very graceful. Stem-sheaths purplish, downy, measuring with the tongue at the apex 2 to 4 in. long, which is about the distance the stem joints are apart. Leaves 2 to 3½ in. long, ¼ to ⅜ in. wide, rounded at the base, finely pointed, vividly green above, somewhat glaucous beneath; secondary veins three or four each side the midrib, very faintly defined in the fresh leaf, but conspicuous enough in the dry; margins very minutely bristly on one side.

Native of Central and W. China; introduced by way of St Petersburg in 1889, and one of the very hardiest of bamboos. It withstood the bitter weather of February 1895 better than any other species, and scarcely lost a leaf; but this evergreen character appears to belong only to young plants. Since then, the same plants have often lost nearly all their leaves even in comparatively mild winters. The stems are never injured. This bamboo is of extraordinarily vigorous growth, sending up every year a crowd of new stems, which are erect and remain leafless except at the tips throughout the first winter; the second season the branches develop, and as the foliage increases in bulk the stems arch outwards, and the whole plant becomes an object of surpassing elegance.* It has to be mentioned that no bamboo is more susceptible to intense sunshine and dryness at the root, conditions whose presence is immediately indicated by the temporary curling up of the leaves. It should be given a semi-shaded spot, and abundant moisture. Easily distinguished from all other bamboos by its round, black-purple stems.

After some eighty years in cultivation, *A. nitida* presents an aged appearance in the clumps where it has been allowed to grow without division and replanting, but so far there are no signs of flowering in this desirable garden plant.

A. PUMILA Mitf.

PLEIOBLASTUS PUMILUS (Mitf.) Nakai; *A. variabilis* H. de Lehaie; *Bambusa pumila* Hort.

A dwarf species of tufted habit, with the few-branched stems as thick as a knitting-needle, and from 1 to 2 ft high; joints 2 to 6 in. apart. Stem-sheaths persistent, glabrous except at the base, where is a conspicuous ring of hairs. Leaves 2½ to 6 in. long, ⅓ to ⅞ in. wide, rounded at the base, narrowed often abruptly to a short slender point, dark green, and with minute hairs on both sides. Secondary veins four or five each side the midrib.

Native of Japan, and a neat little bamboo, but with no striking characters. It closely resembles *A. humilis,* but that species has mostly longer leaves with little or no hair on them, and their points are more gradually tapered.

A. QUADRANGULARIS (Fenzi) Makino   SQUARE-STEMMED BAMBOO

TETRAGONOCALAMUS QUADRANGULARIS (Fenzi) Makino; *Bambusa quadrangularis* Fenzi

Clumps rhizomatous; stems tufted, erect, mostly 6 to 12 ft high in cultivation (up to 20 or 30 ft high in the wild state), round when young and small, but distinctly four-sided when ½ in. or more thick (up to 1¼ in. thick in the wild state), rounded at the corners, thick-walled, with rather long internodes, rough, green, becoming brownish green; joints prominent, the lower bearing spine-like outgrowths or only aculeate; branches three from each joint, much divided and very slender; stem-sheaths firm, hairless. Leaf-blades narrowly lanceolate, acuminate, 4 to 8 in. long, ½ to 1 in. wide, rich green, minutely hairy when young, rough on both margins, with eight to fourteen pairs of secondary veins, tessellate.

Native of China and Formosa; introduced about 1892. This very distinct

* Mr Bean wrote in previous editions: 'If I were restricted to the cultivation of one bamboo, this would be my choice.' I feel sure that now he would have great difficulty in making the choice between it and the, to my mind, more attractive *A. murielae.* C. E. H.

bamboo is, unfortunately, not very hardy, and is killed to the ground at Kew during all but the mildest winters, although never outright. It is, no doubt, admirably adapted for the south-western counties, where its remarkable quadrangular stems and generally ornamental character would make it well worth cultivation. It runs freely, even at Kew, where the top growth is so frequently killed.

A. SIMONII (Carr.) A. & C. Rivière

PLEIOBLASTUS SIMONII (Carr.) Nakai; *Bambusa simonii* Carr.

Stems 12 to 24 ft high, round, very hollow, from 1 to 1¼ in. diameter at the base, the outer ones arching outwards, with slowly speading creeping rhizomes. Stem-sheaths rather persistent, the largest 8 to 10 in. long, purplish when young, hairy at the margins, very glazed within. Leaves narrow-oblong, broadly wedge-shaped at the base, with long, tapered points, 3 to 12 in. long, ⅓ to 1¼ in. wide, vivid green above, glaucous on one side of the midrib beneath, rather greener the other; secondary veins four to seven each side the midrib.

Native of China; introduced to France by M. Simon in 1862. A very vigorous bamboo, which spreads rapidly by means of its underground suckers, and, with the exception of *A. fastuosa* and *A. gigantea*, the tallest of our hardy sorts. It resembles the former, under which the distinctions are pointed out. *A. simonii* flowered all over the country between 1903 and 1905. For many years previous to those dates odd stems had flowered, and occasionally borne seed without any damage to the plants, but then came the flowering of the entire plants, none of which ever recovered. In gardens now *A. simonii* is only known by plants raised from the seed then obtained. These plants have been flowering on a few stems since 1948 and are continuing to flower in 1967, but there has so far been no general flowering such as took place in 1903–5.

cv. 'VARIEGATA'.—Some of the leaves striped with white, the leaves so marked being very small and narrow. The full-sized green leaves do not differ from those of the type. This variety has not yet flowered, except partially, in this country. It is of little value and tends to revert to the green form. (*A. simonii* var. *variegata* Hook. in *Bot. Mag.*, t. 7146; *A. simonii* var. *striata* Mitf.; *A. simonii* var. *albo-striata* Bean; *Bambusa albo-striata* Hort.)

A. SPATHIFLORA Trin.

THAMNOCALAMUS SPATHIFLORA (Trin.) Munro

An evergreen bamboo with erect, clustered stems that are 20 to 30 ft high in nature, yellowish brown, glabrous, ½ to 1 in. in diameter, much branched at the joints where, at the base of each, is a pale glaucous ring. Stem-sheaths rounded at the top except for an awl-shaped prolongation up to 2 in. long, not downy, ultimately straw-coloured, very smooth and glassy inside. Leaves 3 to 5 in. long, ¼ to ½ in. wide, finely pointed, tapered to a short stalk at the base, of thin, fine texture. Secondary veins three to five each side the midrib; still finer longitudinal veins between these secondary ones are joined by minute but (as seen through a lens) conspicuous cross-veins, thereby giving the tesselated venation characteristic of all really hardy bamboos. One margin of the leaf is minutely toothed. Leaf-sheaths ribbed, fringed at the apex.

Native of the N.W. Himalaya from 7,000 to 10,000 ft altitude; it flowered gregariously in 1882, from which seeding it was introduced. In general aspect of leaf and stem this bamboo most closely resembles *A. anceps* among hardy species, but its habit is tufted, whilst *A. anceps* spreads so rapidly by its underground stems that it is liable to become a nuisance. It may be distinguished from *A. aristata* by the absence of the hairy, spongy thickening at the apex of the leaf-sheath. *A. spathiflora* is quite hardy at Kew, where it is about 8 ft high. In warmer localities it will probably get to be at least twice as high. It is a very elegant plant and may be grown in semi-shaded spots. In its natural state it covers large areas, often as undergrowth beneath deodars and other conifers, the whole area of plants flowering simultaneously and dying after the ripening of the seed.

A. TECTA (Walt.) Muhl.　SMALL CANE, SWITCH CANE
A. macrosperma var. *tecta* Wood; *Arundo tecta* Walt.

Stems up to 7 ft high, cylindrical, hollow, branching at the upper joints with the branches slightly spreading. Stem-sheaths mostly as long as the internodes of the stem, persistent, fringed with hairs, and slightly downy when young, becoming glabrous. Leaves narrow-oblong, 5 to 10 in. long, ¾ to 1½ in. wide, downy beneath; secondary veins six or seven each side the midrib.

Native of the south-eastern United States, from Maryland to Illinois and southwards. It is by some authors regarded as a variety of *A. gigantea* (*macrosperma*), a taller species sometimes over 30 ft high, which inhabits the swamps and river-sides of the Southern States. Both species form dense, scarcely penetrable thickets, known as 'cane-brakes'. In the old slave days these canebrakes were of the greatest service to escaping negroes in affording shelter and hiding from their pursuers. As an ornamental bamboo for gardens, *A. tecta* is second-rate. It spreads by suckers, and has not been known to flower in this country.

A. TOOTSIK Makino
SINOBAMBUSA TOOTSIK (Makino) Makino; *Bambusa tootsik* Hort.

A bamboo of tufted habit, spreading by short rhizomes; stems cylindrical, up to 25 ft high and up to 3 or 4 in. thick, dark green, smooth, with at first prominent, hairy joints, pruinose below them, thick-walled; branches three at a joint, much divided and slender above; stem-sheaths soon falling, tough, sparsely hairy, or smooth and hairless except for a dense, conspicuous band of golden-brown or dark brown hairs at the base, narrowed upward and truncate at the tip, bearing there a linear or linear-lanceolate, sharply pointed blade, and two lateral auricles fringed with long, rigid, smooth bristles. Leaves clustered; blades narrowly lanceolate, 2 to 8 in. long, ⅓ to 1¼ in. wide, very finely pointed, narrowed at the base, green, with four to eight pairs of secondary nerves, prominently tessellate; leaf-sheaths ciliate, their terminal auricles fringed with rather long, rigid, erect bristles.

Native of China but long cultivated in Japan, where it is used as a hedge plant and for ornamental purposes. It is said to be a troublesome weed in Honolulu, dominating many acres of once native vegetation. It is distinguished from other species of *Arundinaria* by the dense band of brown hairs at the joints of the stems and bases of the sheaths. It is cultivated in the Temperate House at Kew and would only be suitable for the open in the mildest districts.

A. VAGANS Gamble

PLEIOBLASTUS VIRIDISTRIATUS var. VAGANS (Gamble) Nakai;
Bambusa pygmaea Hort.

The dwarfest of hardy bamboos, although the stems when drawn up in a dense mass will grow 2 ft high; they are bright green, about $\frac{1}{16}$ in. diameter, with a hollow up the centre which would only admit of a needle point; joints 1 to 4 in. apart. Leaves 2 to 5½ in. long, ⅓ to 1 in. wide, rounded at the base, rather abruptly narrowed at the apex to a slender point, sparsely hairy above, more so beneath. Secondary veins three to five each side the midrib.

Native of Japan. This little bamboo forms a low, dense carpet over the ground, and spreads with great rapidity. Because of its rampant habit it is not suited for borders or kept portions of the garden, but may be relegated to the wilder parts, where it will hold its own against the most vigorous of our native weeds. Among the dwarf creeping sorts with green leaves, the velvety under-surface of the leaves will best distinguish it.

A. VARIEGATA (Miq.) Makino

PLEIOBLASTUS VARIEGATUS (Miq.) Nakai; *Bambusa variegata* Miq.;
Arundinaria fortunei Rivière; *Sasa variegata* (Miq.) E. G. Camus

Stems up to 3½ ft high, very slender, the strongest only ⅛ in. diameter, the pipe up the centre very small; joints 1 to 6 in. apart; stem-sheaths persistent, hairy at the base. Leaves 2 to 7½ in. long, ¼ to 1 in. wide, rounded at the base, dark green copiously striped lengthwise with creamy white—sometimes it would be more correct to say 'white striped with green'; hairy on both surfaces, especially beneath; both margins toothed; leaf-sheaths hairy when young; secondary nerves three to five both sides the midrib.

Native of Japan; cultivated by Van Houtte of Ghent before 1863. This is the prettiest white variegated hardy bamboo we have, giving a very bright effect from late summer up to Christmas. It is of tufted habit, but spreads rapidly, and is easily increased by division. It has not yet flowered in cultivation.

A. VIRIDISTRIATA (Reg.) Makino

PLEIOBLASTUS VIRIDISTRIATUS (Reg.) Makino; *Bambusa viridistriata* Reg.;
B. fortunei aurea Hort.; *Arundinaria auricoma* Mitf.; *Sasa auricoma* (Mitf.) E. G. Camus

Stems tufted, 3 to 4 ft high, about as thick as a knitting-needle, slightly hollow, dark purplish green, from a creeping rhizome. Stem-sheaths persistent, edged with minute hairs. Leaves 3 to 8½ in. long, ⅓ to 1¼ in. wide, rounded, or even slightly heart-shaped at the base, fine-pointed, dark green always more or less striped with rich golden yellow. These yellow stripes vary in width and number, often the major part of the leaf is golden, with only thin lines of green. Secondary veins five to seven each side the midrib. The upper surface is at first minutely downy, and becomes rough to the touch with age; the lower surface remains velvety.

Native of Japan; cultivated since the 'seventies of last century, probably before, and long known as "*Bambusa fortunei aurea*". In its full late summer leafage it is a beautifully variegated plant, and quite distinct from all other dwarf bamboos. A few stems flower most years at Kew, but they are often hidden by the leaves of other shoots and consequently overlooked; flowering has also been observed in other gardens. The flowering shoots, bearing one to three spikelets at their tips, also have narrower and shorter leaves than usual. Up to 1969 there has been no general flowering of this attractive bamboo.

ASCYRUM   HYPERICACEAE

A small genus of N. American plants closely allied to *Hypericum*, but well distinguished by having four sepals and petals instead of five.

A. HYPERICOIDES L.   ST ANDREW'S CROSS

A low, decumbent, much-branched plant of semi-shrubby character, growing about 1 ft high; stems winged. Leaves opposite, ½ to 1 in. long, narrowly obovate, tapering at the base; stalkless. Flowers terminal, usually solitary or in threes, yellow, ½ to ¾ in. across; petals four, arranged in the form of a St Andrew's Cross; sepals four, in two pairs of unequal size, the larger ones almost as long as the petals.

Native of eastern United States; introduced in 1759. This species is grown in the rock garden at Kew, where it flowers from July to September; it likes a light, loamy soil, and can be increased by cuttings taken in July. It appears to be a rather delicate plant, or perhaps naturally short-lived, for which reason it is advisable to renew the stock from seed occasionally.

ASIMINA   ANNONACEAE

A genus of some eight species in eastern N. America, all small, tender shrubs except the one described here, which is of interest as the only member of the custard-apple family that can be grown outdoors in the British Isles.

A. TRILOBA (L.) Dun.   PAPAW
Annona triloba L.

A robust, deciduous shrub in this country, but developing into a small tree in the south-eastern United States. Leaves alternate, obovate, pointed, short-stalked, 4 to 8 in. long, glabrous except when quite young. Flowers produced singly on the wood of the previous year, during June. Calyx three-lobed; each lobe ½ in. long, ovate, downy outside. Petals six, of a dull lurid purple, the outer three much the larger, roundish, 1 in. long; the inner three half as large. Flower-stalk thick, often recurved, ½ to ¾ in. long, densely downy. Fruit bottle-shaped, 3 to 5 in. long, borne in whorls, containing when ripe a sweet, yellow, edible pulp. *Bot. Mag.*, t. 5854.

ASIMINA TRILOBA

Introduced from the south-eastern United States by Peter Collinson in 1736, this interesting shrub has never become common. Its foliage is striking, but the flowers although curious are not ornamental, and the fruit rarely develops in this country. It grows slowly, and one of the finest specimens in this country is, or was, at Claremont, a huge spreading bush 15 ft or so high. It thrives in a good loam, and propagation can be effected by layering; but seeds, procurable from American nurserymen, are preferable. The popular name papaw or pawpaw, although commonly used for this tree in the United States, properly belongs to the quite unrelated *Carica papaya*, a strange tree with a branchless, soft-wooded stem crowned by a tuft of leaves, under which are borne the delicious yellow-fleshed fruits.

ASTERANTHERA   GESNERIACEAE

Asteranthera is one of three genera of gesneriads found only in the temperate rain forests of Chile and neighbouring parts of Argentina, each consisting of a single species. The other two are *Mitraria* and *Sarmienta*, but from these it is very distinct in shape of flower and indeed might be taken for a columnea. Botanically, however, the three genera are grouped together in the *Mitrarïeae*, characterised by the disc at the base of the flower forming a continuous ring, not broken into separate, irregular glands as in the genus *Columnea*.

A. OVATA (Cav.) Hanst.
Columnea ovata Cav.

A creeping or climbing evergreen shrub which in nature inhabits the trunks of living trees and fallen timber, branching and rooting freely at the nodes. Stems slender, clad with whitish hairs. Leaves opposite, variable in shape but generally roundish, $\frac{1}{3}$ to $1\frac{1}{2}$ in. long, obtuse at the apex, covered with pale bristly hairs and edged with three to six coarse teeth; they are rather thick in texture where exposed to light but thinner in shade. Flowers rich raspberry-pink, borne singly in the leaf-axils at midsummer and later; corolla tubular at the base, spreading at the mouth, where it is about $1\frac{1}{2}$ in. wide. Anthers united into a star-shaped cluster—whence the name *Asteranthera*. *Bot. Mag.*, n.s., t. 15.

Native of the temperate forests of Chile and neighbouring parts of Argentina from about 40° S. to the Straits of Magellan; introduced by Comber in 1926. It inhabits the cooler and moister types of forest, where it is often to be found with *Desfontainia spinosa*. Here, thanks to the saturated atmosphere, it is able to grow in open and quite sunny places in the forest, forming dense mats on logs and tree-trunks and so profuse in flower that scarcely a leaf can be seen. In cultivation this delightful species has proved fairly hardy, but rather shy to flower, no doubt because the humid yet bright conditions that it demands are not easy to reproduce. Propagation is, however, so easy (by cuttings, or division) that experiment

ASTERANTHERA OVATA

would present no difficulties. A leafy soil is essential, and something to climb up or over. At Nymans in Sussex, where it has been cultivated since Comber first introduced it, it thrives on shady walls of both sandstone and brick. At Logan in Wigtownshire it is grown on the face of a peat wall. Dryness, at the root and in the air, are its chief enemies. It also thrives at Brodick, in the Isle of Arran.

ASTRAGALUS   LEGUMINOSAE

A very large genus of over 1,500 species in the temperate regions of the world, mostly of the northern hemisphere. For the most part they are herbaceous, but in arid climates take the form of dwarf, spiny shrubs.

A. MASSILIENSIS (Mill.) Lam.

Tragacantha massiliensis Mill.; *A. tragacantha* L., in part

A dwarf, deciduous, very spiny and much branched shrub of whitish aspect growing to about 1 ft high in the wild state. The old wood is completely covered with the closely set, sheathing bases of stiff, sharp spines 1 to 2½ in. long, which are really the persistent rhachises of the leaves become hard with age. These spines remain on the plant for many years and serve to protect the young leaves from browsing animals. Leaves pinnate, composed of six to twelve pairs of leaflets set on a spine-tipped rhachis; leaflets $\frac{1}{8}$ to $\frac{1}{4}$ in. long, oblong to elliptic, bluntly pointed, covered on both sides with silky hairs. The leaves are furnished with hairy stipules which are united to the petioles for about a third of their length. Flowers white, borne three to eight together in a raceme which is as

ASTRAGALUS MASSILIENSIS

long as or shorter than the leaves. Calyx tubular, about ¼ in. long, appressed-hairy, the teeth rather short, being at the most one-third the length of the tube; corollas peaflower-shaped, the standard ovate, about ⅜ in. long. Pods about ⅖ in. long, appressed-hairy, protruding from the persistent calyx.

A native of the north-west Mediterranean, found mostly in sandy or rocky places by the sea; probably introduced in 1640. It is suitable for a sunny ledge in the rock garden, in very well-drained soil.

This species is part of *A. tragacantha* L., but this name is best rejected as ambiguous, since Linnaeus included under it one, perhaps two, other distinct species. The identity of the plant that was described under this name in previous editions is uncertain, but the text figure agrees well with *A. massiliensis* and has therefore been retained.

A. SIRINICUS Ten.—This species is closely allied to *A. massiliensis*. It is usually of denser habit and at high altitudes and in exposed places forms hedgehog-like hummocks. The teeth of the calyx are relatively longer (up to one-half as long as the tube); hairs of calyx spreading. Flowers yellow or purplish. Pods with long rather spreading hairs, or almost glabrous. This species is of wider distribution than *A. massiliensis* (Corsica, Sardinia, Italian Apennines and parts of the Balkan peninsula) and is mainly an inhabitant of mountains. It is part of *A. tragacantha* as understood by some botanists.

A. ANGUSTIFOLIUS Lam.—A dense shrub, forming a hedgehog-like mound about 8 in. high. Leaflets in three to ten pairs, narrow-oblong, about ⅕ in. long, clad with silvery grey hairs at first, later more or less glabrous. Flowers creamy white, sometimes with a violet blotch at the tip of the keel, borne in July and August in almost sessile clusters of three to eight. Native of the Balkan peninsula and of Crete. A more attractive plant than the other two described, for a sunny, well-drained position in the rock garden. A. PUNGENS Willd., found in Greece, is closely related, but has longer-stalked clusters, with up to twelve flowers in each.

The three species described belong to the section *Melanocercis*, characterised by the spiny rachis and by the peculiar hairs, which are two-branched and keeled at the base, but lie appressed to the leaf or stem and have the appearance of single hairs attached by their centres.

ATHEROSPERMA   ATHEROSPERMATACEAE

A genus of one species, native to Australia. The family to which it belongs was formerly included in Monimiaceae and like that family has its main development in the southern hemisphere; it is also found in the W. African tropics, but is fairly closely allied to the Calycanthaceae of N. America and E. Asia, and more distantly to the magnolia and laurel families. The perianth in *Atherosperma*, as in other members of the family, is not divided into sepals and petals but consists of a single undifferentiated whorl of 'tepals', and the gynoecium consists of a number of distinct pistils, each with its own style. The family Atherospermataceae is otherwise represented outdoors in British gardens only by the genus *Laurelia*.

A. MOSCHATUM Labill.   BLACK SASSAFRAS

An evergreen tree to 100 ft high in the wild state, aromatic in all its parts. Leaves opposite, narrowly elliptic to lanceolate, 2 to 3 in. long, leathery, dark green above, greyish and glabrous or silky-hairy beneath, margins entire or with a few teeth. Flowers dioecious, creamy white, about 1 in. across with seven to ten tepals, borne singly in the leaf-axils; receptacle concave, silky-hairy inside and out; male flowers with about fifteen stamens; female flowers with several whorls of staminodes and numerous free pistils, each developing into a one-seeded fruit (achene). *Bot. Mag.*, n.s., t. 43.

Native of the temperate forests of Tasmania and S.E. Australia; introduced in 1824 and again by Comber in 1929. Although not common in cultivation, it is fairly hardy in a sheltered place. A specimen in woodland at the Edinburgh Botanic Garden is about 10 ft tall and flowers every year. At Caerhays Castle, Cornwall, it has reached 20 ft and there is another large specimen at Trewithen in the same county.

ATHROTAXIS   TAXODIACEAE

The three species which constitute this interesting genus of conifers are all natives of the mountains of Tasmania, and were all introduced about 1857. None is really tender and fair-sized specimens of all three are to be found in Sussex and Surrey, but they are better suited in the south-west and in Ireland, where their distinctness and beauty are very marked. Of the three, *A. selaginoides* seems to be the least hardy. Their nearest relatives are the sequoias of western N. America and *Cryptomeria japonica*.

They are small evergreen trees or shrubs with scale-like or awl-shaped leaves, closely and spirally arranged. The flower-catkins are unisexual, but both male and female are on the same tree. Cones woody, roundish, composed of eight to twenty scales, which are closely packed, tapered at the base and swollen at the top; the bract-scale is completely united with the ovule-bearing scale except at the apex, where it forms a spine-like tip. The cones ripen in one year; seeds winged.

A. CUPRESSOIDES D. Don

A tree of 20 to 50 ft; branchlets round and cord-like, the final subdivisions about ⅛ in. in diameter. Leaves scale-like, very closely flattened to the twig, blunt or rounded at the apex, the bases overlapping, the exposed part ⅛ to ⅙ in.

long, diamond-shaped, convex or somewhat keeled on the back, dark green. On the main branches the leaves are much larger, and sharply pointed. Ripe cones to ½ in. in diameter; scales rounded at the apex, with a short spiny point on the outer side.

Native of the mountains of central and western Tasmania at 3,000–4,000 ft.

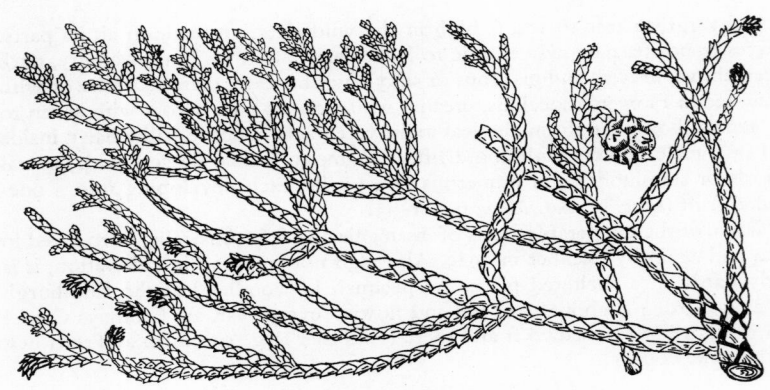

ATHROTAXIS CUPRESSOIDES

It is a small tree and not so valuable in Tasmanian forestry as *A. selaginoides*, besides being rarer. It is easily distinguished from the other two species by its very closely appressed leaves.

In the British Isles it has not grown so tall as the other two species. The best recorded are: Kilmacurragh, Co. Wicklow, Eire, a two-stemmed tree 45 × 5¼ + 3½ ft, and two others both 36 × 4½ ft (1966); Headfort, Co. Meath, Eire, *pl.* 1914, 30 × 3¼ ft (1966); Bicton, Devon, 30 × 2¼ ft (1957); Hergest Croft, Heref., 20 × 1¾ ft (1961); Leonardslee, Sussex, 20 × 1 ft (1960).

A. LAXIFOLIA Hook.
A. doniana Gordon

This rather puzzling species is in many respects intermediate between the other two, but nearer to *A. cupressoides*. It is said to be rare in nature, occurring only as isolated trees near one or other of its two allies, but showing no sign of hybridity (Winifred Curtis, *The Student's Flora of Tasmania*). It differs from *A. cupressoides* in the longer, much less appressed leaves, the points of which are sharp and incurved, but quite free. Branchlets round, slender, the final subdivisions (including the foliage) ⅙ in. wide (cf. *A. selaginoides*, in which they are much stouter); leaves ⅙ to ¼ in. long, ovate-lanceolate, keeled and thickened down the middle, with a sharp, rather hook-like point, inner surface with bands of stomata on each side the midrib. Cones about ⅜ in. wide; scales with a thin, acuminate process on the back near the apex.

A. laxifolia is the commonest of the three species in cultivation and has thrived the best, many specimens exceeding the maximum height of 40 ft said to be attained by wild trees. The following list is restricted to examples of 40 ft or above in height: Scorrier House, Cornwall, 63 × 7½ ft (1965); Tregrehan, Cornwall, 55 × 2¾ ft (1965); Trevarrick Hall, Cornwall, 50 × 5¼ ft (1965); Trewidden, Cornwall, 45 × 4¼ ft (1959); Lynhales, Heref., 41 × 5 ft (1961); Grayswood Hill, Surrey, 40 × 2½ ft (1955). In Ireland the only example above 40 ft so far recorded is at Kilmacurragh, Co. Wicklow, 50 ft high, on two stems, 6 and 5 ft in girth (1966).

A. SELAGINOIDES D. Don   KING WILLIAM PINE

A tree to 90 ft under optimum conditions but usually smaller, with a reddish-brown, furrowed, and somewhat fibrous bark, which is soft and spongy as in *Sequoiadendron giganteum*. It is very distinct from the other two species in its stout branchlets and in the size of the leaves, which are ¼ to ½ in. long, awl-shaped, ending in a sharp point, keeled at the back, hollowed inside, and with a band of white stomata each side the midrib. The leaves are incurved, but stand away from the twig at angles of 30° to 45°. The branchlets with their foliage are about ⅜ in. in diameter. Cones the largest of the three species, to ¾ in. or even more wide, the scales tapered towards the base, and with a thin, pointed, triangular apex. *Bot. Mag.*, t. 9639.

Native of western and south-western Tasmania, where it is found in the temperate rain-forest with *Nothofagus cunninghamii*, etc., or in eucalyptus wood-land, more rarely in small pure stands near the tree-line (*Forest Trees of Australia*, pp. 216–17). It is the most important of the three species, yielding a valuable timber resembling that of redwood, but mature trees have become rare in the wild. In cultivation it has proved the most tender of the three.

As with the other two species, the best examples in the Britsh Isles are to be found in Ireland and Cornwall, as the following records show: Tregrehan, Cornwall, 51 × 3½ ft (1965); Lamellen, Cornwall, 41 × 3 ft (1962); Killerton, Devon, 36 × 1¼ ft (1962); Scorrier House, Cornwall, 35 × 2¾ ft (1965); Wake-hurst Place, Sussex, 31 × 2¾ and 33 × 1 ft (1962). The following were all measured in Eire in 1966: Mount Usher, Co. Wicklow, 49 × 5, 43 × 2½, 41 × 3½, 39 × 4½ ft; Kilmacurragh, Co. Wicklow, 48 × 5¾ ft; Headfort, Co. Meath, *pl.* 1927, 32 × 2¾ and 27 × 2½ ft.

ATRAPHAXIS   POLYGONACEAE

Four or five species of *Atraphaxis* are sometimes grown, but they are scarcely known in gardens generally. They are amongst the few hardy woody representatives of the polygonum family, being lax-habited shrubs with alternate leaves, and pale, transparent, slender stipules that clasp the stem and terminate in a point at each side. The flowers have no petals, but four or five sepals prominently veined, the inner ones of which persist, keep their colour, and enlarge, ultimately surrounding the fruit.

Flower-stalks jointed. They are exclusively Old World plants, extending in a wild state from S.E. Europe to Central Asia. As they do not ripen seed in this country, at any rate commonly, they are best propagated by layers. A sunny position is best for them, and a well-drained sandy soil.

A. BILLARDIERI Spach

A deciduous, sometimes spiny shrub 1 to 2½ ft high of semi-prostrate growth; young shoots glabrous, pale grey. Leaves narrowly oval to lanceolate, entire, finely pointed, tapered towards the base; ⅛ to ⅓ in. long, $\frac{1}{12}$ to $\frac{3}{16}$ in. wide; green and quite glabrous, but distinctly net-veined; there is a distinct swollen joint on the very short stalk. Flowers produced in a rounded cluster about 1 in. wide during June at the end of short leafy twigs. Each flower is ultimately ¼ in. wide and is made up of five segments (or sepals), the two outer ones small and reflexed, the three inner ones roundish ovate or heart-shaped, ultimately ¼ in. long, rosy pink, erect, and hiding the stamens and ovary. Flower-stalk ⅛ to ¼ in. long, glabrous, slender, jointed midway. Fruit three-angled. *Bot. Mag.*, t. 8820.

Native of Greece, Asia Minor, and Syria; discovered by the French botanist Labillardière on the Lebanon Range about 1787. This very charming shrub has grown well in the rock garden at Kew and, as the sepals do not fall away but remain enclosing the fruit and retaining their glowing pink colour, it has a long season of beauty. It is essentially a sun-loving shrub and, growing naturally in regions with a hot dry summer, likes a well-drained soil. It is sometimes thorny like *A. spinosa*, but that species has only two of the large inner sepals and a two-edged fruit.

A. BUXIFOLIA (Bieb.) Jaub. & Spach
Polygonum crispulum Sims; *Polygonum buxifolium* Bieb.

A deciduous shrub 2 to 2½ ft high; branches not or slightly spiny, often decumbent; young wood pale, very minutely glandular. Leaves dull green obovate, oval, or roundish, ⅓ to ¾ in. long, from half to nearly as wide, glabrous, tapering at both ends, margins wavy and decurved; stalk ⅛ in. or less long with a pale, membranous, chaffy stipule at each side ¼ in. long. Flowers pinkish white, produced in June in racemes that are 1 to 1½ in. long; each flower is ⅓ in. diameter. Of the five divisions of the calyx, three remain, deepen in colour, and ultimately enclose the three-angled fruit. Flower-stalk slender, about ¼ in. long, jointed at about one-third of its length from the base. *Bot. Mag.*, t. 1065.

Native of the Caucasus, cultivated for more than a century in England, but not sufficiently showy to have ever become common. It is, nevertheless, interesting and pretty.

A. FRUTESCENS (L.) K. Koch
Polygonum frutescens L.; *A. lanceolata* Meissn.

A deciduous mostly unarmed shrub of straggling habit 1 to 2½ ft high; young wood glabrous, whitish. Leaves variable, linear-oblong or oblanceolate to lanceolate or oval; $\frac{1}{3}$ to $1\frac{1}{4}$ in. long, $\frac{1}{8}$ to $\frac{1}{3}$ in. wide; grey-green, wavy at the margin; stipules ending in long points. Flowers whitish, produced in slender, leafy racemes, from 1 to 3 in. long, at the end of short lateral twigs; flower-stalk jointed about midway; inner sepals becoming at the fruiting stage rounded, $\frac{1}{4}$ in. across, and ultimately rose-coloured.

Native of S.E. Europe and the Caucasus, to Siberia and Turkestan; introduced in 1770. It flowers in August, and long remains pretty, but, like the rest of the genus, has never attracted much notice in gardens.

var. VIRGATA Reg., found in Turkestan, has whiter and more slender twigs than the type.

A. MUSCHETOWII Krassn.

A. latifolia Koehne

A deciduous shrub 6 to 8 ft high, of open, lax, rather straggling habit; young stems smooth, pale; bark peeling. Leaves $\frac{3}{4}$ to $2\frac{1}{4}$ in. long, $\frac{1}{4}$ to $\frac{3}{4}$ in. wide; oblong or oval, tapered at both ends, margins wavy; glabrous, pale green; stalk very short; stipules pale, translucent, with two awl-shaped points, $\frac{1}{2}$ in. or more long. Flowers $\frac{1}{3}$ in. wide, white, with the anthers and ovary rose-coloured, produced in May and June in racemes 1 to $1\frac{1}{2}$ in. long, at the end of the previous year's

ATRAPHAXIS MUSCHETOWII

growth, when the young shoots are already several inches long; flower-stalk joined near the base. *Bot. Mag.*, t. 7435.

Native of the Thian Shan range of mountains in Central Asia, where it was discovered by Krassnov; introduced to Kew from St Petersburg in 1880. It is the strongest growing and perhaps the most ornamental of cultivated species of *Atraphaxis*, and distinct from the others in the large leaves.

A. SPINOSA L.

A low, deciduous, twiggy shrub of sprawling habit 1 to 2 ft high, and twice or thrice as wide; the slender branches often spine-tipped; young wood glabrous and whitish; bark loose. Leaves oval or obovate to roundish, $\frac{1}{4}$ to $\frac{1}{2}$ in. long, glabrous, blue-green. Flowers $\frac{1}{3}$ in. across, white, rosy-tinted, borne in small axillary clusters on short, spine-tipped, lateral twigs; sepals four, the two large inner ones roundish, veined, persisting and keeping their colour a long time, ultimately becoming flat, membranous, rounded, $\frac{1}{3}$ in. across, pressed close together with the two-edged fruit between them. It blossoms in August.

A widely spread species, native of W. Asia, S.E. Europe, the Near East, etc.; cultivated since early in the eighteenth century. In some of its drier native localities its leaves are very small. Very pretty and interesting in flower and fruit. Although sometimes confounded with *A. frutescens*, it is easily distinguished by its two-edged fruit, spiny branchlets, and smaller leaves.

ATRIPLEX   CHENOPODIACEAE

About half a dozen species of *Atriplex* are occasionally met with in gardens, the commonest and best being *A. halimus*. They belong to the goosefoot family, and are chiefly distinguished by the grey, whitish or silvery aspect of the foliage. The W. American species form part of the characteristic grey vegetation of the great alkaline and saline areas of that region. Leaves alternate or rarely opposite; flowers very small and quite unattractive. They need a light soil of moderate quality not enriched with manure, and a sunny position. They rarely bear fruit, and some do not even flower in cultivation. All should be tried in maritime localities. Increased easily by summer cuttings.

A. CANESCENS James   GREY SAGE BRUSH

An evergreen, unisexual shrub of sprawling habit 5 or 6 ft high, twice as much in diameter, of a light grey colour; leaves and young branches covered with a fine scurfy down. Leaves alternate, narrowly oblong, $\frac{3}{4}$ to 2 in. long, $\frac{1}{5}$ to $\frac{1}{3}$ in. wide, fleshy, bluntish at the apex, tapered at the base. Flowers yellowish, very small; produced during July in cylindrical, spiked clusters, both terminal and axillary, $\frac{1}{3}$ to 1 in. long; the whole forming a slender, tapered, leafy panicle 6 to 12 in. long. Fruit bracts $\frac{1}{2}$ in. long, deeply toothed.

Native of western N. America from British Columbia to Nebraska, and found in dry saline localities. It has long been cultivated at Kew, and is perfectly hardy. In no way showy in flower, it attracts notice and pleases many by its almost white appearance.

A. NUTTALLII S. Wats., with which the above has been confused in gardens, is quite a different plant. Its leaves are not very dissimilar, being ½ to 2 in. long, narrowly oblanceolate, often rounded at the apex, and grey; but the plant itself is low, and is shrubby only at the base, sending up erect, more or less annual stems, 1 to 3 ft high. The fruit bracts, too, are less than half as large as those of *A. canescens*, being ¼ in. or less long. Native of western N. America.

A. CONFERTIFOLIA (Torr.) S. Wats.
Obione confertifolia Torr.

A spreading, unisexual, sub-evergreen shrub 2 to 4 ft high; young branches and leaves covered with scurfy down, and the whole plant of a greyish-white aspect. Leaves alternate, obovate, sometimes ovate or lance-shaped; ⅓ to 1 in. long, ⅛ to ¼ in. wide; bluntish or rounded at the apex, tapered at the base. Flowers very small, yellowish green, crowded densely in the leaf-axils in small, stalkless, roundish clusters. It blossoms in June.

Native of western N. America from Oregon to New Mexico, and one of the characteristic inhabitants of the alkaline plains of that region. The male plant has, for some years, been cultivated in the rock garden at Kew; only attractive in its grey leaves.

A. HALIMUS L.   TREE PURSLANE

A vigorous, semi-evergreen shrub 4 to 8 ft high, of loose, bushy habit, the whole plant of a beautiful, silvery-grey aspect. Leaves alternate, ovate, rhomboidal or obovate; ½ to 2½ in. long, ¼ to 1 in. wide; tapered at both ends, minutely and abruptly pointed, covered with a fine silvery scurf. Panicle terminal, 6 to 12 in. long, produced in July, the flowers very small, greenish.

Native of S. Europe; cultivated since early in the seventeeenth century. This is certainly the most attractive of the purslanes in this country, producing a very striking, silvery effect when planted in a group, especially in association with dark-leaved shrubs. It is also one of the best seaside shrubs. It is very rarely seen in blossom with us, but that does not detract much from its value. Severe frosts injure it, but it springs out afresh and soon recovers. Sparrows are said to be fond of the leaves, but I have never noticed them touch the plants at Kew.

A. PORTULACOIDES L.   SEA PURSLANE
Halimione portulacoides (L.) Aellen

A low shrub of straggling habit 1 to 2 ft high, and of a greyish aspect; young shoots and leaves covered with a close scurf. Leaves opposite, obovate or oblong, $\frac{1}{8}$ to $\frac{1}{2}$ in. long, $\frac{1}{8}$ to $\frac{1}{3}$ in. wide, tapered at the base. Flowers very small, greenish, borne on a terminal panicle, composed of slender spikes, on which the flowers are arranged in small clusters.

Native of Europe, including Britain, where it is common on the shores. It has nothing to recommend it for the inland garden, for it is not so distinct and silvery as the other species here mentioned. But it is worthy of notice for planting in exposed positions near the sea, where almost anything that will grow is welcome. Flowers in August, and well distinguished from the other species in cultivation by its opposite leaves.

AUCUBA　　CORNACEAE

A genus of two or three Asiatic evergreen shrubs with opposite, leathery leaves; the sexes are on different plants, in which respect it differs from its allies the cornels (*Cornus*). The petals, calyx-lobes, and stamens are four to each flower; and the fruit is a large, oblong berry, scarlet or orange coloured.

A. CHINENSIS Benth.

The Chinese aucuba is a very variable shrub in regard to the shape of its leaves. One form (f. OBCORDATA Rehd.) has them wedge-shaped, tapering gradually from a broad truncate apex to the stalk; whilst in another (f. ANGUSTIFOLIA Rehd.) they are long and narrow, measuring 3 to 8 in. in length and $\frac{1}{2}$ to $1\frac{1}{2}$ in. in width. The average or typical form was introduced by Wilson in 1901. This has evergreen, oblong or oval, coarsely toothed leaves tapered towards both ends, 3 to 6 in. long, $1\frac{1}{2}$ to 3 in. wide; dull, dark, rather greyish green above, glaucous beneath. The Chinese aucuba is well distinguished from the common Japanese one by the coarser, sharper toothing of its leaves, by their markedly thicker texture, and especially by their duller, greyer hue. When in flower they may be distinguished by the petals being longer than those of *A. japonica* and drawn out at the apex into a slender tail. The red, egg-shaped fruits of both appear to be similar.

Native of Central and S. China, and of Formosa. It is not genuinely hardy at Kew and no longer in the collection.

A. JAPONICA Thunb.

A unisexual, evergreen shrub of rounded bushy form, 6 to 10 ft high, consisting of a thicket of erect or arching, little-branched stems. Branchlets stout, fleshy, quite glabrous and green, bud-scales hairy at the tips. Leaves opposite, leathery, narrowly oval; 3 to 8 in. long, $1\frac{1}{2}$ to 3 in. wide; glabrous, green and glossy on both surfaces, with usually a few large teeth towards the apex; stalk $\frac{1}{2}$ to 2 in. long. On the male plant the flowers are produced on an erect, terminal panicle, 2 to 4 in. long; each flower ⅛ in. across, with four (occasionally five) purplish petals; flower-stalks downy. Fruits only borne by the female plant, and produced in compact clusters 2 or 3 in. long, each berry roundish oval, ½ to ⅝ in. long, bright scarlet.

Native of Japan; introduced by John Graeffer in 1783. This first plant was the well-known yellow-spotted form ('Variegata') and was female. Owing to the absence of pollen it never set fertile fruit, but small, dry, abortive fruits were occasionally produced. In the decade 1856–66 many plants were introduced from Japan, and among these were male and female forms of the normal green-leaved aucuba. The first plant to be seen in full fruit was shown by Standish in 1864; it was a green-leaved female sent by Fortune in 1860, pollinated by a male, also green-leaved and introduced by him at the same time. Male plants were also brought home by J. G. Veitch from his Japanese visit and others, green and variegated, were introduced to Europe by Siebold and distributed in Britain chiefly by William Bull of Chelsea. A fruiting specimen of the old variegated clone was first figured in the *Floral Magazine* in 1866.

By the end of the century the aucubas, male and female, variegated and green, had become common garden evergreens, especially in the new suburbs, where they were valued for their great tolerance of a smoky atmosphere, and small plants in pots could be bought from costermongers' barrows in the streets of London.

Today the aucubas, like the monkey-puzzle, are out of favour, but the pendulum has swung too far. Green-leaved females make fine berrying shrubs, and the aucuba has one merit in greater degree than any other evergreen: this is its capability of thriving under the shade of trees. Even under a beech, lime or horse chestnut, where grass will not grow, it maintains a cheerful aspect. This means, of course, that it can not only manage without direct sunlight, but can fight its way against the roots of its big neighbours. To get fruit in abundance a moderately sunny spot is desirable, and of course plants of both sexes must be contiguous.

There are many slightly different forms of aucuba that have originated as sports or seedlings, and vary chiefly in size, shape and marking of leaf, also in the size and vigour of the shrub. The number of forms that were given Latin names and distributed was very large and the nomenclature is hopelessly confused. Many variegated forms which were given names are apt to revert to the common spotted form. Cuttings or even small branches, root with great freedom. The following varieties, most of them green-leaved, are a selection of those still in commerce:

cv. 'CRASSIFOLIA'.—A male form with large, green, leathery leaves. A female of the same kind—'MACROPHYLLA'—was introduced by Siebold and distributed in Britain by W. Bull.

cv. 'CROTONIFOLIA'.—Leaves large, finely speckled with yellow. One of the most distinctive of the variegated kinds. Female.

f. LONGIFOLIA (T. Moore) Schelle—This is the group-name for narrow-leaved forms of aucuba, of which a number were put into commerce a hundred years ago and have become confused. The cultivar name 'LONGIFOLIA' belongs to one shown by Veitch in 1862; leaves about 5 in. long, 1¼ in. wide, faintly toothed; sex not stated in the original description, but probably female. A similar plant, female, was introduced by Fortune and distributed by Standish; this was also called *longifolia* but was said to have broader leaves and longer teeth. A third, female, and again called *longifolia*, was introduced by Siebold and distributed here by William Bull. 'ANGUSTATA', another Siebold–Bull introduction, was male; and 'SALICIFOLIA', distributed by Standish, female.

cv. 'VARIEGATA'.—The original female variegated form, introduced in 1783 (see above); sometimes known as *A. j. maculata*, but the true 'MACULATA' was a male clone, with leaves blotched yellowish white, introduced by Siebold.

Forms with yellowish or whitish berries are also known.

A. HIMALAICA Hook. f. & Thoms.—In many respects this species is very similar to *A. japonica*, but it is certainly not so useful a shrub. I do not, indeed, think the true plant is in cultivation, and may possibly not be hardy. It has much narrower leaves, 5 to 8 in. long by 1 to 1½ in. wide, toothed much more finely and lower down the leaf than in the common aucuba; the quite young shoots, young leaves and especially the flower-stalks are hairy. The petals are more pointed; berry scarlet, ½ in. long.

Native of the eastern Himalaya at 5,000 to 9,000 ft, also of China. A plant in cultivation is sometimes called "himalaica", which is really the long, narrow-leaved form of green *A. japonica*.

AZARA   FLACOURTIACEAE

A genus of more or less tender shrubs, evergreen, and natives of Chile and Argentina. Leaves often apparently arranged in pairs at each joint of the branchlet, one of the pair much the smaller and really a stipule. The flowers have no petals, but abundant stamens, and are usually fragrant. *A. microphylla* may be grown in the open, but the others, except in the milder parts, require the protection of a south or west wall. All can be propagated by cuttings made of ripened wood placed in gentle heat. The name commemorates J. N. Azara, a Spanish scientist who was born in Aragon in 1731 and died in Paris in 1804.

A. DENTATA Ruiz & Pavon

An evergreen shrub 8 to 12 ft high, sometimes a low tree, with downy branchlets. Leaves alternate, ovate or oval, 1 to 1½ in. long, deep shining green above, very downy beneath, furnished with stipules; both the leaves and stipules are toothed. Flowers fragrant, borne on short, branching corymbs, the yellow stamens, as in *A. petiolaris*, giving the flower whatever beauty it possesses. A rather tender shrub, introduced from Chile about 1830. It is only hardy against a wall at Kew, and was killed or badly damaged in many gardens in the cold winters of 1961–3. It survived both at Edinburgh, however, and is 10 ft high there in a sheltered position. The leaves have a bitter taste.

A. SERRATA Ruiz & Pav.—This species, also a native of Chile, has been confused with the preceding. The true plant has downy branchlets like *A. dentata*, but the leaves are larger, not felted beneath, often nearly glabrous. The inflorescence too is very distinct, the flowers being arranged in a globose umbel borne at the end of a slender, downy stalk, up to 1½ in. long.

A. INTEGRIFOLIA Ruiz & Pavon

An evergreen bush or small tree ultimately 20 to 40 ft high; young shoots very downy. Leaves leathery, in apparent pairs or threes at each joint; the true leaves obovate, oval or somewhat diamond-shaped, usually toothless, bluntish or pointed, margins recurved; 1 to 2 in. long, ½ to 1 in. wide; glossy green, glabrous on both surfaces, veins raised on the under-surface; stalk ⅛ in. long, downy. The smaller 'leaves' (which are really leaf-like stipules) are rounder, ¼ to ⅝ in. long, very shortly stalked. Flowers fragrant, produced from January to March in the leaf-axils of the previous summer's shoots in shortly stalked, compact clusters ⅖ to ½ in. wide. The flower has no petals. Sepals four, $\frac{1}{12}$ in. long, oblong, dark purplish outside, woolly inside; stamens ⅛ to ⅕ in. long, numerous, rich yellow with very dark anthers. Leaves on young plants are often slightly toothed. Berries globose, ¼ in. wide, white stained with pale mauve. *Bot. Mag.*, t. 9620.

Native of Chile and neighbouring parts of Argentina; introduced in 1832 and again by Comber in 1925. From other species this is well distinguished by its leaves being normally without teeth. The flowers are abundant, and their fragrance is pleasing, though not strong. The ultimate height attained in the wild is given by Reiche as 10 ft and by Comber as 15 ft, but at Rostrevor, Co. Down, there was a specimen 32 ft high in 1930. Comber's form received an Award of Merit when shown from Nymans in 1934; the original plant no longer exists there, but a small replacement came through the winter of 1962–3 unharmed.

var. BROWNEAE (Phil.) Reiche *A. browneae* Phil.—This appears to differ chiefly from the type in the foliage. The largest leaves are up to 2¼ in. long by 1¼ in. wide, and the margins are often furnished with one to four teeth at each side towards the pointed apex. The leaves are of obovate outline, the lower part of the leaf very much tapered (cuneate). Native of the Cordilleras de Santiago; named in 1893 after Senora Marian Browne. It is rare, but is represented in the Glasnevin Botanic Garden by a specimen 6 ft high and 5 ft across.

cv. 'VARIEGATA'.—Leaves rather rounder than in the type, dark green in the centre, edged with pale pink that changes to creamy white; frequently toothed. Raised at Kew about 1870 and a good variegated shrub, no more tender than the type. There is an example in the National Trust garden at Overbecks, near Salcombe, Devon.

A. LANCEOLATA Hook. f.

An evergreen small tree or shrub up to 20 ft high; young shoots covered with a close, short, brownish down. Leaves lanceolate or narrowly oval, evenly and coarsely toothed, tapered about equally at both ends; $\frac{3}{4}$ to $2\frac{1}{2}$ in. long, $\frac{1}{4}$ to $\frac{5}{8}$ in. wide; bright green and glabrous on both surfaces; very shortly stalked. As in other species of this genus, a large, leaf-like stipule, $\frac{1}{4}$ to $\frac{1}{2}$ in. long, toothed and of orbicular to ovate outline, is attached to the base of each leaf, giving the impression that the leaves are in very unequal pairs. Both the leaves and stipules of cut-off shoots turn partially or wholly an inky black after a few days. Flowers small, produced during April in short corymbs of from four to seven blooms on a common-stalk about $\frac{1}{2}$ in. long; they are soft yellow, the conspicuous part being the stamens; there is a four-lobed calyx but no petals. The entire corymb is only 1 in. or less in diameter, but one is produced from most or all of the leaf-axils of the previous season's growth, the whole giving a charming effect; the

AZARA LANCEOLATA

flowers have a faint pleasant perfume and have downy stalks. Fruit globose, $\frac{5}{16}$ in. wide, of various shades of pale mauve to white, porcelain-like, the calyx persisting at the base, the style at the top. *Bot. Mag.*, t. 9374.

Native of Chile and some bordering parts of Argentina; first described and named by the younger Hooker in 1847; originally found by Charles Darwin on the Tres Montes peninsula in December 1834, whilst on the voyage of the *Beagle*. It was introduced, apparently for the first time, by H. F. Comber in 1926 and first flowered with Col. Messel at Nymans, Sussex, where Mr Comber's father, James Comber, was garden manager.

A. lanceolata ranges further south than the other species, but is confined to the cool temperate rain-forest, where atmospheric humidity is almost constantly high, and like so many southern hemisphere plants from such habitats, thrives best where the British climate is at its most oceanic. It is by no means so hardy as *A. microphylla*, but survived the cold winters of the early 'sixties in many gardens. It should be given a position sheltered from cold, drying winds, which quickly blacken the leaves. A very handsome evergreen in leaf, flower, and fruit and the most elegant of the azaras in habit.

A. MICROPHYLLA Hook. f.

An evergreen shrub or small tree, the branchlets covered with a very dense dark down, and arranged on the same plane in two opposite rows. Leaves shining dark green, small, very abundant, apparently in pairs, one of each pair being about thrice as large as the other; the true leaves are obovate, $\frac{1}{2}$ to 1 in. long, usually more or less toothed; the smaller 'leaves' (stipules) more rounded. Flowers tiny, numerous, fragrant, borne in clusters at the leaf-axils; sepals green, the more conspicuous stamens deep yellow. Fruit a small, red, globose berry.

Native of Chile and bordering parts of Argentina; introduced by Richard Pearce about 1861, when collecting for Veitch's nurseries. In nature it is a fairly faithful associate of the deciduous and hardy *Nothofagus obliqua*, which grows where the local climate is somewhat drier and less equable than it is in the region of the fully evergreen rain-forest. It is a delightful small tree which even at Belvoir in Leicestershire has reached nearly 20 ft in height, and considerably more in the west of England. The flowers open in February if the weather is mild, later if severe; and their vanilla-like fragrance is perceptible yards away from the bush.

Although not so hardy as to be altogether free of the danger of severe damage in such a winter as that of 1962–3, it will come through most winters unharmed or with nothing worse than the loss of the youngest growths. At Kew, a plant was cut to the ground in the exceptionally frosty February of 1895, but no damage of such severity has been experienced since then. Unlike most evergreens of the forests of the southern hemisphere, *A. microphylla* grows well in the eastern Midlands and in E. Anglia. It has, for example, thrived for many years in the nurseries of Messrs Nottcutt at Woodbridge, Suffolk, and Mr Maurice Mason tells us he has found it hardy in his garden near King's Lynn, Norfolk.

cv. 'VARIEGATA'.—Leaves unevenly and broadly edged with creamy white, making it one of the daintiest of variegated small trees. There is a fine example on a north-east wall at Rowallane, Co. Down, 22 ft high, now recovered from the damage suffered in 1962–3.

A. PETIOLARIS (D. Don) Johnston

Quillaya petiolaris D. Don; *Azara gilliesii* Hook. & Arn.

An evergreen shrub or small tree. Leaves holly-like, pointed, ovate or oval, 1½ to 3 in. long, with distant teeth, deep lustrous green, pale beneath, glabrous. Flowers densely crowded on racemes scarcely 1 in. long, springing from the axils of the leaves. Each flower is small, creamy yellow, the beauty of the raceme being due entirely to the numerous comparatively long stamens, which hide the remainder of the flower. *Bot. Mag.*, t. 5178. This charming shrub, a native of Chile, is the most ornamental of cultivated azaras in its blossoms, but is, unfortunately, not hardy enough to succeed in the open at Kew. Against a wall where it receives additional heat from a near-by stoke-hole, it flowers well every year in April and May. It is, however, more suited to the milder parts of the country. There are three old specimens in the Glasnevin Botanic Garden, Dublin, growing on walls, the tallest 12 ft high with a spread of about 9 ft. At Mount Usher, Co. Wicklow, it is 17 ft high.

BACCHARIS   COMPOSITAE

A large genus of shrubs, small trees, and herbaceous plants, found exclusively in the New World. With the exception of the two species here described, the introduced species are too tender for all but the mildest parts of the country. Leaves alternate. The flower-heads have no ray florets, and flowers of one sex only are found on a plant. The two following are easily accommodated in almost any soil, and are quite easily increased by summer cuttings. Many of the species have resinous secretions on the leaves and young wood, which give them, in the countries where they grow, a special value as firewood.

B. HALIMIFOLIA L.   BUSH GROUNDSEL

A deciduous, unisexual shrub, ultimately 12 ft high, and as much in diameter; of somewhat loose habit; young branches angular, glabrous. Leaves grey-green, alternate, very variable in shape and size, broadly obovate to narrowly oval, coarsely and unevenly toothed, except those on the flowering portion of the shoot, which are entire; 1 to 3 in. long, ¼ to 1½ in. wide, tapering at the base to a stalk ⅛ to ¼ in. long; both surfaces are freely sprinkled with resin dots, and rather viscid. Flower-heads produced in October in axillary, stalked clusters, about five in a cluster. The shoots of the year branch at the top into numerous short twigs furnished with untoothed leaves, from the axils of which the clusters of flower-heads are produced, so that the whole forms a large rounded or cylindrical leafy panicle 3 to 6 in. across. The blossom has little beauty, being of a dull white; but the numerous thistle-like heads of fruit of the female plant, with their silky white pappus, are rather striking.

Native of eastern N. America; introduced in 1683, but not ornamental enough to have ever become widely cultivated. It is hardy at Kew, and is a useful shrub for coast situations.

B. PATAGONICA Hook. & Arn.

An evergreen shrub, of somewhat open but stiff habit, with angled, viscid, rather scurfy twigs, densely furnished with leaves. Leaves obovate, rounded at the apex, tapering at the base, stalkless, ¼ to 1 in. long, half as wide; usually coarsely toothed towards the apex; deep green above, scurfy on both surfaces. Flower-heads stalkless or nearly so, produced singly in the leaf-axils, yellowish white, and of little beauty.

Native of Chile and Argentina in the region of the Straits of Magellan, etc. It has proved quite hardy at Kew, and is a rather interesting, small-leaved evergreen, growing 8 to 10 ft high there, probably considerably more in warmer districts. It blossoms in May, and this character as well as its stalkless, solitary flower-heads and evergreen leaves, make it very distinct from B. halimifolia. It can be increased by cuttings at almost any season.

BALLOTA LABIATAE

A genus of about twenty-five species of herbs and sub-shrubs, most of them natives of the Mediterranean region. One, however, is widespread in Europe including the British Isles, two or three are found in north-east tropical Africa, and one is S. African. Ballota pseudodictamnus, with white woolly leaves, is the most decorative of the genus, but is scarcely woody enough to qualify for treatment here.

B. FRUTESCENS (L.) Woods SHRUBBY HOREHOUND
Molucella frutescens L.; B. spinosa Link

A shrub 6 to 12 in. high of rounded bushy habit; young shoots very slender, downy, armed at each joint with a pair of slender, pale, mostly twin spines ¼ to ½ in. long. Leaves opposite, ovate, three- to nine-lobed or sometimes merely toothed, rounded or tapered at the base, pointed to rounded at the apex; ½ to 1 in. long, scarcely as wide; dull green, downy on both surfaces; stalk slender, ⅛ to ½ in. long. Flowers very shortly stalked, produced singly, in pairs, or in threes in the leaf-axils. Calyx narrowly funnel-shaped, ¼ in. long, ten-ribbed, downy, spreading at the mouth into five ovate slender-pointed lobes. Corolla white, two-lipped, the lower lip three-lobed, the upper lip densely covered with long white hairs. The whole flower is about ⅝ in. long and about ½ in. across the calyx-lobes, which stand out beyond the corolla. It blossoms in July and August.

Native of France in the Basses Alpes and Alpes Maritimes, also of Italy;

related to our native 'black horehound' (*B. nigra*). It is a long time since it was first cultivated in this country and Gerard seems to have grown it in his physic garden at Holborn in 1596. Its tenure, however, has always been uncertain and intermittent owing to its tenderness and lack of notable beauty. Its flowers, with the brush-like tuft of hairs on the corolla, are curious and interesting. It can only be grown in the warmer parts of the country and in the sunniest, sheltered spots.

BAUHINIA   LEGUMINOSAE

Bauhinia is a large and curious genus of about 150 species, chiefly found in tropical countries, most abundantly in Brazil and India. Usually they are climbers, some attaining to an enormous size. *B. vahlii*, an Indian species, is often 100 yards long, but others are simply bushy. The leaves constitute their most distinctive character, each one being either divided into two kidney-shaped lobes by a cleft of varying depth, or into two quite separate leaflets. From the base radiate several conspicuous veins. The flowers, usually in terminal clusters, have no resemblance to the typical pea-shape of the family, the five petals spreading in the fashion of an ordinary flower, although they are unequal in size. Stamens ten, usually some of them imperfect. Fruit a flat pod. The genus is most nearly related to *Cercis* amongst hardy trees. The name commemorates two brothers, John and Casper Bauhin, famous botanists of the sixteenth century, who worked in such close companionship that the twin leaflets were thought to symbolise their labours.

B. DENSIFLORA Franch.

A deciduous shrub of lax or semi-scandent habit growing 8 to 10 ft high. Leaves cleft to about one-third their depth, each half kidney-shaped, 1 to 2½ in. wide, ⅝ to 1½ in. long, glabrous above, downy beneath; leaf-stalk ½ to ¾ in. long. Flowers white, ½ in. wide, borne about six together on a short downy raceme; petals narrowly obovate.

Native of W. China; introduced by Forrest. Wilson saw it in flower at 3,000 to 4,000 ft altitude in Szechwan in June 1908, which is also its flowering time at Kew. It is neither a showy plant nor a very hardy one, but its foliage is unlike that of any other hardy tree or shrub. E. J. P. Magor flowered it at Lamellen, Cornwall, and it was grown for some years at Kew on a wall of the Temperate House, but is no longer in the collection. It likes a loamy soil and a sunny position.

BERBERIDOPSIS   FLACOURTIACEAE

A monotypic genus which owes its name to the character of the flower, in which the numerous perianth segments, as in *Berberis*, are not differentiated into distinct whorls of sepals and petals. In fact, the two genera are in no way related. *Berberidopsis*, at one time placed in the family Bixaceae, is now considered to belong to the Flacourtiaceae, together with *Azara, Idesia, Carrierea, Poliothyrsis, Xylosma*, and a few tropical and subtropical genera.

B. CORALLINA Hook. f.   CORAL PLANT

An evergreen, scandent shrub of remarkable beauty. Leaves alternate, ovate or heart-shaped, rather hard in texture, the apex and margins set with spiny teeth; dark green above, glaucous beneath, $1\frac{1}{2}$ to 4 in. long. Flowers produced in the axils of the uppermost leaves and in a terminal raceme, the whole forming a crowded group of pendent blossoms. Each flower is borne on a slender stalk, $1\frac{1}{2}$ to 2 in. long, deep red like the flower itself which is globose, $\frac{1}{2}$ in. across, composed of nine to fifteen petal-like segments, the outer ones of which are

BERBERIDOPSIS CORALLINA

small and spreading, the inner ones larger and concave, all of the deep fine red which pervades the whole inflorescence. *Bot. Mag.*, t. 5343.

Native of Chile, where it is said to be confined to the forests behind the port of Coronel, in Arauco province, and may by now be extinct even there; introduced by Richard Pearce in 1862. It is one of the most gorgeous of climbers but not completely hardy nor easy to suit. In favoured western gardens it can be trained up trees or allowed to ramble among shrubs, but elsewhere it needs the protection of a wall and must be carefully sited. A deep, moist soil is best, and a position where it is sheltered from drying winds and strong sun. A north wall is suitable so long as it is not exposed to winds from that quarter.

It commences to flower in July and continues in beauty for two or three months. The fruits form in this country, but do not usually produce good seed. Young plants can be raised from cuttings or layers. A little peaty soil should be put about the roots when first planted out but once established they will grow vigorously. This species will tolerate a slightly alkaline soil if peat is added, but is not really suited to chalky ones.

BERBERIS   Barberry   berberidaceae

A genus of deciduous and evergreen shrubs, now including nearly two hundred species. The hardy ones are natives of Europe, N. Asia, and the two Americas; the common barberry (*B. vulgaris*) extends to N. Africa—perhaps introduced. The leading characteristics of the genus are, the yellow wood, yellow flowers, and the three-parted character of the flowers; the sepals being six or nine, the petals six, and the stamens six. The fruit is an oblong or egg-shaped berry containing one to several seeds. The stamens are irritable, and if touched at the base with a fine-pointed instrument like a pin, they suddenly move from their sheltered position in the concavity of the petals, and close inwards on the pistil. The object of this interesting power is, no doubt, to secure cross-fertilisation. An insect in search of honey pushes itself or its proboscis into the flower, sets the stamens in action, and, becoming itself smeared with pollen grains, carries them away to another flower and deposits them on the pistil.

The morphology of the leaves and spines of barberry is interesting. In the true barberry group, the 'leaf', as we call it, is really the terminal leaflet of a pinnate leaf, the side ones of which are suppressed, and the tuft of leaves as a whole is a branch in which the internodes are suppressed. Then the spine (usually three-parted, but sometimes simple, sometimes much divided), in the axil of which the tuft of leaves is borne, is a metamorphosed pinnate leaf. An occasional reversion to the ancestral type reveals their true origin.

As ornamental shrubs the barberries have many good qualities and several of them are in the very first rank of garden plants. They prefer a warm, loamy soil, but are by no means fastidious. Seeds are, as a rule, freely borne, and afford the best and readiest means of propagation; but for those sorts which do not produce seed in this country, and for those also that do not come true from seed like the coloured-leaved varieties, cuttings, layers, or division of the plants must be resorted to. Cuttings should be made of fairly ripened wood, and put in sandy soil under a bell-glass or in cold frames.

The following is a selection of species and hybrids usually available in commerce:

Evergreen or semi-evergreen: *B. calliantha*; *candidula*; *darwinii*; *gagnepainii*; *hookeri*; *julianae* (or *sargentiana*); *linearifolia* (slightly tender); *pruinosa*; × *stenophylla* (the clones listed and also 'Autumnalis'); *valdiviana*; *verruculosa*.

Deciduous or nearly so: B. × *carminea* (clones listed); *dictyophylla*; *jamesiana*; *montana*; × *ottawensis* 'Superba'; × *rubrostilla* (clones listed); 'Sibbertoft Coral'; *temolaica*; *thunbergii* and cvs; *wilsoniae* and vars.

The major work on the genus is *Berberis and Mahonia* by L. W. A. Ahrendt, published as Vol. 57 (No. 369) of *The Journal of the Linnean Society* (Botany), 1961.

B. ACTINACANTHA Roem. & Schult.

A deciduous shrub 3 ft or sometimes more high, with rigid, crooked branchlets. The spines are very variable, some being the ordinary three-forked ones, so common in the genus; others are curiously flat and leaf-like, semi-circular or heart-shaped, the margins cut up into several long, triangular, spiny teeth. The spines on barberries, as has already been observed, are really modified leaves, and there is no species which shows their foliate character better than this. Leaves hard, rigid, not downy; variable in shape, and either obovate, oblong, or roundish; $\frac{1}{4}$ to $1\frac{1}{2}$ in. long, with a few large spiny teeth. Flowers sweetly fragrant, produced in short umbels or clusters, deep yellow, $\frac{2}{5}$ in. across. Fruit blue-black, $\frac{1}{3}$ in. long.

This remarkable barberry, common enough in a wild state on the mountains of Chile, and often introduced to cultivation, is still comparatively rare. It does not flower freely, and seldom produces fruit. It is well adapted for a sunny spot in the rock garden, but has more scientific interest than horticultural value.

B. AETNENSIS Presl

A deciduous, dwarf, stunted bush about 2 ft high, with crooked branches. Leaves small, $\frac{1}{4}$ to $\frac{3}{4}$ in. long, obovate, sometimes bristle-toothed, sometimes entire; spines three-parted, sometimes over 1 in. long. Flowers yellow, in short racemes $\frac{3}{4}$ to $1\frac{1}{4}$ in. long, carrying six to fifteen flowers. Fruit red.

Native of Sicily and Calabria, a scrubby bush inhabiting the mountains. It flowers in May and June, and is very pretty with its numerous closely set racemes. Suitable for the rock garden.

B. AGGREGATA Schneid.

B. geraldii Veitch

A deciduous shrub 3 to 5 ft high; young shoots angular, minutely downy, armed with slender, three-pronged spines $\frac{1}{3}$ to 1 in. long. Leaves clustered, obovate, $\frac{1}{3}$ to 1 in. long, spiny-toothed (often only sparsely), the base cuneate, the apex rounded; rather glaucescent beneath. Flowers pale yellow, $\frac{1}{4}$ in. across, densely packed in stalkless axillary panicles up to $1\frac{1}{2}$ in. long. Fruit roundish ovoid, nearly $\frac{1}{4}$ in. long, red with a bloom. *Bot. Mag.*, t. 8722.

Native of W. China, introduced by Wilson in 1908. It is an attractive species but has been largely displaced in gardens by its hybrid progeny (see *B.* × *carminea* and *B.* × *rubrostilla*). The seedling 'SIBBERTOFT CORAL', with large clusters of bright red berries, is near to *B. aggregata* in its botanical characters. For *B. aggregata* var. *prattii* and var. *recurvata*, see *B. prattii*. [PLATE 18

B. ARIDO-CALLIDA Ahrendt—This allied species was introduced by Farrer from Kansu half a century ago, but has never become established in gardens.

B. ANGULOSA Hook. f. & Thoms.

A deciduous shrub 4 ft or more high, with erect, grooved branchlets covered when young with a short, dark down. Leaves dark glossy green, clustered in the axils of stiff spines, which are sometimes single, but usually three- or five-branched, and up to $\frac{1}{2}$ in. long; the leaves are obovate, or narrowly wedge-shaped, 1 to $1\frac{1}{2}$ in. long, leathery, narrowing at the base to a very short stalk or none at all, the apex either rounded or pointed, often terminating in a short tooth; the slightly curled back margins are either entire, or have one to three spiny teeth at each side. Flowers solitary, on downy stalks $\frac{1}{2}$ to 1 in. long, or on short two- to four-flowered racemes; orange-yellow, globose, $\frac{1}{2}$ to $\frac{2}{3}$ in. across; outer sepals narrow oblong, inner ones twice as wide; petals obovate. Fruit elliptical, $\frac{2}{3}$ in. long, scarlet. *Bot. Mag.*, t. 7071.

Native of N. India; first discovered in Kumaon early in the nineteenth century, and in 1849 by Hooker in the Sikkim-Himalaya, at 11,000 to 13,000 ft. It is absolutely hardy at Kew, and although not one of the showiest barberries, is noteworthy for its unusually large flowers and berries. The latter are eatable, and, being less acid, are more palatable than most barberries.

B. CAPILLARIS Ahrendt   *B. ludlowii* var. *capillaris* (Ahrendt) Ahrendt— Closely allied to the preceding, but with the leaves grey-green above, grey beneath, the fruit narrower and the pedicels glabrous. Collected by Farrer in Burma in 1919 and, although named shortly afterwards, not described until 1941. Farrer's companion on that journey, Mr E. H. M. Cox, tells us that the species has been a failure in his garden in E. Perthshire. But in a milder climate it might make an attractive shrub, for, as Mr Cox wrote in *Farrer's Last Journey*, 'It is noticeable for the large size of the solitary flowers. They are rich yellow in colour and about the size of a shilling, while the fruit is scarlet and nearly as large as a cherry.'

B. PARISEPALA Ahrendt—This species differs only in minor botanical characters from *B. angulosa*, but grows taller and has a more easterly distribution in the Himalaya. It is in cultivation from Kingdon Ward's No. 8350, collected in the Mishmi Hills. The material for the plate in the *Botanical Magazine* (n.s., t. 119) was taken from a plant in the late Sir Frederick Stern's garden at Highdown. It breaks into leaf very late in the spring.

B. ARISTATA DC.
B. chitria Lindl.

There is some doubt concerning the identity of De Candolle's *B. aristata*. It would be beyond the scope of a general work such as this to explain or solve this involved problem, and indeed there is no necessity to do so, since all the plants that have been grown in gardens as "*B. aristata*" are referable to other, better defined species. Some are certainly *B. glaucocarpa* (q.v.), which is, at least in part, the barberry described under the name *B. aristata* in previous editions of this work. Other species that have been grown under that name, or been associated with it as varieties, are given short descriptions below. All belong to the subsection *Chitriae*.

B. CHITRIA Hort., and of *Bot. Reg.*, t. 729 (figure only), not Lindl.; *B. aristata* of many authors, not DC.*—A deciduous shrub up to 10 or 12 ft high, of spreading habit; young shoots finely downy, reddish brown the second year; spines very often simple but sometimes three-parted, ½ to 1 in. long. Leaves obovate to oval, often narrowly so, edged with fine teeth or almost toothless; 1 to 3 in. long, bright green on both sides. Flowers pale yellow, ⅜ in. wide, numerously borne in June and July on loose pendulous panicles up to 6 in. long. Fruits oval-oblong, dark red with a slight bloom on them, ⅓ to ½ in. long, with a conspicuous style.

Native of the Himalaya; introduced in 1823 and long believed to be the true *B. aristata* of De Candolle. It is a well-defined species, easily distinguished from its allies by its paniculate inflorescence with the flowers in groups of three, but unfortunately it lacks a valid name (see footnote).

B. CORIARIA Lindl. *B. aristata* var. *coriaria* (Lindl.) Schneid.; *B. aristata* var. *floribunda* (G. Don) Hook. f. & Thoms., in part.—A vigorous semi-deciduous shrub growing to 10 ft high; stems glabrous, pale yellow when mature; spines three-parted, about 1 in. long. Leaves obovate, ⅘ to 2 in. long and ⅓ to ⅘ in. wide, green above and below, margins entire. Inflorescence a stiff raceme with ten to twenty-five flowers. Fruit oblong, bright red, about ½ in. long, crowned by the short, persistent style. Native of the W. Himalaya and a fine fruiting shrub.

B. FLORIBUNDA G. Don *B. aristata* var. *floribunda* (G. Don) Hook. f. & Thoms., in part; *B. macrophylla* Hort.—This species somewhat resembles *B. coriaria*, from which it chiefly differs in its dark red, bloomy fruits. The cultivated plants were apparently first distributed by Späth's nursery, Berlin, about

---

* For the reasons pointed out by Dr Stapf under *Bot. Mag.*, t. 9102, *B. chitria* Lindl. is not a legitimate name for this species; it is, however, maintained here for the convenience of gardeners until a new name for it is published.

1905. Native of the Himalaya. Dr Ahrendt considers that most of the plants grown as "*B. aristata*" belong here.

B. SIKKIMENSIS (Schneid.) Ahrendt *B. chitria* var. *sikkimensis* Schneid.; *B. aristata* var. *micrantha* Hook. f. & Thoms., in part.—A semi-evergreen shrub to about 5 ft high. It is allied to *B. chitria*, from which it differs in the grooved stems, the smaller leaves and, most markedly, in the inflorescence, which is a condensed, umbel-like raceme. *Bot. Mag.*, n.s., t. 173. It is in cultivation at Kew and quite hardy there, though little known in gardens.

B. ASIATICA Roxb.

A strong-growing, vigorous evergreen shrub 12 ft or more high, branchlets very minutely downy, somewhat furrowed, yellowish. Leaves hard and leathery, 1½ to 3½ in. long, obovate, or sometimes nearly orbicular, tipped with a spiny tooth, the margin often entire, sometimes set with a few large, sharp teeth, dark green above, whitish beneath. Flowers yellow, in short corymbose racemes. Berries egg-shaped or nearly globular, red, then black covered with purplish bloom.

Native of the Himalaya; first introduced early in the nineteenth century, but still very rare. It is only suitable for Cornwall and similarly mild localities, and even there is sometimes affected by cold. It lived at Kew for a good many years on a sunny wall. It has been confused with other barberries and in particular with *B. glaucocarpa*, but the true species is well distinguished by the combination of rigid leaves, always white beneath, and a short inflorescence taking the form of a corymbose raceme.

B. ATROCARPA Schneid.

An evergreen shrub of bushy habit 5 or 6 ft high, its branchlets stiff, glabrous, armed with slender, stiff triple spines ½ to 1⅓ in. long. Leaves oblanceolate, tapering more gradually towards the base, often widest above the middle; 1½ to 3½ in. long, ¼ to ⅝ in. wide; not wavy at the margins but set there with sharp, bristle-like spines; dark, rather glossy green above, paler beneath and very smooth, the veins scarcely visible. Flowers in clusters of usually six to twelve, sometimes more, ¼ to ½ in. wide, yellow. Fruit described by Wilson as at first red, finally jet-black, without bloom. *Bot. Mag.*, t. 8857.

Native of W. Szechwan, China; introduced in 1909. A vigorous evergreen and an excellent hedging plant. It has been confused with *B. gagnepainii*, but as seen growing side by side the two are very distinct. The latter differs from *B. atrocarpa* in its leaves being very wavy, duller, and broadest below the middle, the stems more clustered, erect, and less branched. When first introduced it was thought to be *B. levis* Franch., but this species has yet to be introduced.

B. BEANIANA Schneid.

A deciduous shrub up to 8 ft high, of erect, rather dense growth; young shoots glabrous, reddish brown, becoming grey; spines three-forked, ½ to 1 in. long.

Leaves three to eight in a cluster at the joints, oval-lanceolate, spine-tipped, tapered at the base, toothed or sometimes entire, dark green above, rather glaucous beneath; ¾ to 2 in. long, ¼ to ½ in. wide. Flowers ¼ in. wide, deep yellow, produced in June ten to twenty together in cymose panicles, 1½ to 2 in. long. Fruit narrowly egg-shaped, ⅜ in. long, bright purple. *Bot. Mag.*, t. 8781.

Native of W. Szechwan, China; introduced by Wilson in 1904 (No. 1930). It is a handsome shrub producing a cluster of erect stems which arch outwards at the top, its beauty being greatest when bearing fruit. It was purchased in 1913 for Kew under the name "*B. veitchii*", but it has, of course, no close affinity with the true *B. veitchii* Schneid. I have noted that *B. beaniana* bears fruit more freely when three or four plants are growing close together, but this applies equally well to many shrubs grown for the beauty of their fruits.

B. BERGMANNIAE Schneid.

An evergreen shrub up to 10 ft high, of dense bushy habit; young shoots yellowish grey, angular, glabrous; spines three-pronged, each prong ½ to 1⅛ in. long. Leaves in clusters of up to five, obovate to oval, spiny toothed, tapering at the base to a very short stalk, of thick leathery texture, 1½ to 2 in. long. Flowers crowded as many as fifteen together in a cluster, each on a slender stalk ¼ to ½ in. long, yellow. Fruit oval, ⅛ in. long, black, covered with a blue-white bloom, the stalk reddish; style persisting at the top.

Native of W. China; introduced by Wilson in 1908. It has been compared with *B. pruinosa* especially in the vividly blue-white fruits, but that species has round, not angular, young shoots and its leaves are glaucous beneath. Related more nearly to *B. julianae*.

var. ACANTHOPHYLLA Schneid.—As seen growing at Kew this is a very striking barberry. The largest leaves are almost holly-like in appearance on account of the two to six large, conspicuous, triangular teeth on each margin; they are up to 2 in. long by ¾ in. wide. I should have thought it distinct enough to have deserved a specific name, but Dr Schneider observes that the red-stalked, blue-black fruits with two seeds closely resemble those of the type.

B. × WINTONENSIS Ahrendt

—A hybrid, with the preceding species as seed parent, which arose in the nurseries of Messrs Hillier, Winchester, about 1935. It is a hardy, compact evergreen, with narrower leaves than in the parent, flowering freely in February. The identity of the pollen parent is not known.

B. BUXIFOLIA Lam.
B. dulcis Sweet

A bush usually 6 to 10 ft high, of erect, stiff habit, partially evergreen in ordinary seasons, but losing most or all of its leaves during winters of unusual severity. Leaves leathery, even hard in texture, produced in tufts in the axils of stiff triple spines, or (near the end of the shoots) simple spines. Each leaf is ½ to 1 in. long, obovate or oblong, tapered at the base to a short stalk, spine-tipped but otherwise quite entire, glabrous. Flowers solitary on stalks ¾ to 1 in. long, amber yellow; one or two flowers spring from each tuft of leaves. Fruit globular or orange-shaped, dark purple. *Bot. Mag.*, t. 6505.

An old inhabitant of gardens, having been introduced about 1826 by Anderson, the botanical collector attached to Capt. King's expedition to survey the Magellan Straits. Seeds were sent to Low's nursery at Clapton, and a plant flowered there in 1831. It is the first of the true barberries to flower, its blossoms appearing early in April, sometimes in March. The berries are said to be used for conserves, etc., in Chile, where it extends from Tierra del Fuego to the latitude of Santiago; it is also found in Argentina. A fine example grew in the garden at Monreith, 13 ft high and 28 ft through.

cv. 'AUREO-MARGINATA'.—Leaves edged with golden yellow.

cv. 'NANA'.—A curious dwarf form of tufted habit, producing a thick mass of weak, unarmed stems rarely more than 18 in. high; leaves larger, rounder than in the type; flowers rarely seen. Described by Carrière in *Rev. Hort.*, 1867, p. 260, as *B. dulcis nana*.

B. CALLIANTHA Mulligan

An evergreen shrub of dwarf, compact growth, up to 3 ft high; shoots angled, armed with triple spines. Leaves elliptic or inclined to oval, 1 to 2½ in. long, ½ to ¾ in. wide, pointed, cuneate at the base, margins spiny-toothed, dark glossy green above, waxy white beneath; stalk $\frac{1}{10}$ to $\frac{1}{5}$ in. long. Flowers borne either solitary, in pairs, or in threes on short shoots bearing a terminal cluster of leaves,

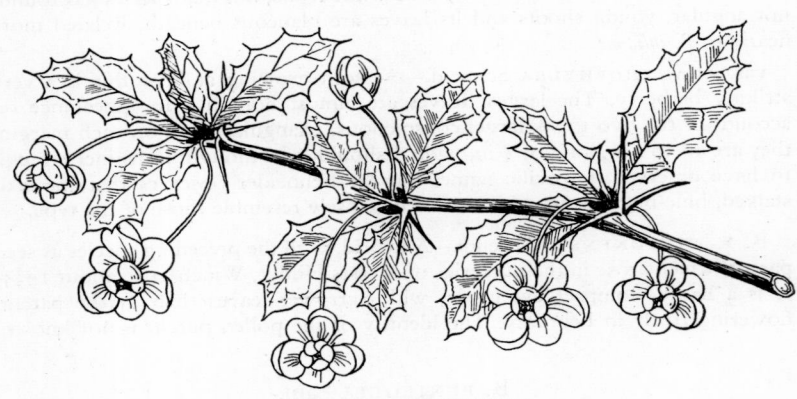

BERBERIS CALLIANTHA

each up to 1 in. across, pale to creamy yellow. Fruits egg-shaped to nearly oblong, up to about ⅝ in. long by ⅖ in. wide, blue-black but covered with a grey-white bloom.

Native of S.E. Tibet, discovered and introduced by Kingdon Ward in 1924. It belongs to the Wallichiana section of the genus which is commonly represented in gardens by *B. hookeri*. It flowers in May and is well marked by its large flowers and dwarf habit (Kingdon Ward found it 'growing in masses 1 ft high'). It was given an Award of Merit at Vincent Square, 19th May 1942.

B. × BRISTOLENSIS Ahrendt—A hybrid of B. *calliantha*, the other parent being in all probability B. *verruculosa*, which it resembles in having warty stems and solitary flowers. In leaf it is nearer to the first-named parent.

B. CANADENSIS Mill.

B. *angulizans* Massias

A deciduous shrub 3 to 6 ft high, with the branchlets not downy, but thickly covered with small, warty lenticels, and armed with three-parted spines. Leaves narrowly obovate, from 1 to 2½ in. long, tapering very gradually at the base, the apex rounded or acute, but always terminating in a short spine, the margin toothed, sometimes remotely so, sometimes almost entire, glabrous. Racemes 1 to 1½ in. long, bearing from six to fifteen yellow flowers. Fruit oval or nearly globose, red.

The specific name of this barberry is a misnomer, for it does not appear to be a native of any part of Canada, its real home being on the slopes of the Allegheny Mountains in Virginia, N. Carolina, etc., where it is most often found on the banks of mountain streams. In general appearance it is not unlike the Old World B. *vulgaris*, but it is not quite so attractive a shrub; it differs in its paler and more glaucous leaves, its smaller flowers, its shorter, almost corymbose racemes, and in its shorter, rounder fruit. It has been cultivated in this country since the middle of the eighteenth century, but is now rarely seen.

B. CANDIDULA Schneid.

B. *wallichiana* var. *pallida* Bois; B. *w. hypoleuca* Hort.

An evergreen, dwarf shrub of dense, hemispherical habit, probably never much more than 3 to 4 ft high; the branches rigidly arching, quite glabrous, bright brown, armed at each joint with a trio of stiff, sharp, pale brown spines, up to ⅝ in. long. Leaves produced in tufts in the axils of the spines, dark shining green above, vividly blue-white beneath; ½ to 1¼ in. long, ⅙ to ⅜ in. wide; oblong or narrowly oval, terminated by a minute, slender spine, and armed with a few similar ones on the recurved margins; very shortly stalked. Flowers bright yellow, somewhat globose, ⅝ in. across, solitary, on a slender stalk about ½ in. long. Fruit oval, covered with a purple bloom, ½ in. long.

Native of China; first collected by Farges, and raised in 1895 by M. Maurice de Vilmorin. It flowered in 1900, and was figured in the *Fruticetum Vilmorinianum*, p. 15, as "B. *wallichiana* var. *pallida*". It was later introduced by Wilson for the Veitch nurseries. It is most likely to be confused with B. *verruculosa*, but that species is of looser habit and the leaves are only glaucous beneath, not conspicuously white as in B. *candidula*. Its neat, dense habit and slow increase in size make it suitable for the rock garden, but it will in time attain a considerable spread—to 5 ft or even more.

B. × CARMINEA Ahrendt

Under this collective name Dr Ahrendt has grouped a number of named seedlings that show the influence of *B. aggregata* in their paniculate inflorescence and are probably the result of the chance crossing of that species with other Chinese barberries such as *B. wilsoniae* var. *subcauliata* and with members of the section *Angulosae* (*Journ. R.H.S.*, Vol. 67, p. 132). Here belong the tall and vigorous 'BARBAROSSA', 'BUCCANEER', and 'PIRATE KING': dwarfer in habit are 'BOUNTIFUL' and 'SPARKLER'. All are reliable berrying shrubs, in which the bright red fruits are enhanced by vivid autumn colour.

B. CHILLANENSIS (Schneid.) Sprague
B. montana var. *chillanensis* Schneid.

A deciduous shrub 5 to 15 ft high; young shoots greyish or greyish brown, minutely downy or glabrous; spines simple, three-pronged or absent, $\frac{1}{6}$ to $\frac{1}{3}$ in. long. Leaves very shortly stalked, narrowly obovate, mostly blunt or rounded at the apex; $\frac{1}{6}$ to $\frac{1}{2}$ in. long, $\frac{1}{12}$ to $\frac{1}{5}$ in. wide; quite entire. Flowers in fascicles, each $\frac{1}{2}$ in. wide and borne on a stalk $\frac{1}{5}$ to $\frac{2}{5}$ in. long; sepals yellow, petals pale orange coloured; stamens about as long as the petals. Fruit lemon-shaped, $\frac{1}{3}$ in. long, black, covered with purple bloom, the style prominently exposed at the end.

Native of the Chilean and Argentine Andes; discovered in the middle of the last century in the Cordillera of Chillan and first described by Schneider as a variety of *B. montana*, to which it is closely allied. Comber found it again in flower in January 1926, growing at 6,000 ft (415A), but the form he collected in seed grew at a lower altitude and was a taller plant, to 8 ft high (415). This differed from Schneider's type in having downy flower-stalks and more densely downy stems, and was distinguished by Sprague as var. HIRSUTIPES, which is thus the form in which the species is cultivated (*Bot. Mag.*, t. 9503). It is rare in gardens and not quite so fine a species as *B. montana*, for the flowers are smaller and more palely coloured.

B. CHRYSOSPHAERA Mulligan

A dwarf evergreen shrub; young shoots glabrous, tinged red, slightly grooved, armed with slender, three-pronged spines up to $\frac{1}{2}$ in. long. Leaves mostly oblanceolate but also narrowly oval, $\frac{1}{2}$ to $1\frac{1}{2}$ in. long, $\frac{1}{6}$ to $\frac{1}{2}$ in. wide, borne in clusters of three to seven in the axils of the spines, dark glossy green above, white beneath, margined with slender teeth. Flowers yellow, $\frac{1}{2}$ in. wide, borne singly from the axils of the clustered leaves in April and May, each on a slender stalk about 1 in. long. Fruits erect, blue-violet.

Native of S. Tibet, discovered and introduced by Kingdon Ward in 1933-4. It is closely related to *B. candidula* but has not the very distinctive close, compact, hemispherical shape of that species. It is an attractive plant for the rock garden or where space is restricted, and is quite hardy.

B. COMBERI Sprague & Sandw.

An evergreen shrub up to 4 ft high, of very stiff habit, increasing by sucker growths so that eventually one plant may become as much as 12 ft across; young shoots spineless, grey, glabrous. Leaves holly-like, stout, stiff, leathery, ovate-orbicular to oval, armed with two to six large triangular spine-tipped teeth and a terminal one; ¾ to 1½ in. long, ½ to 1¼ in. wide; perfectly glabrous, grey-green, or on young plants glaucous at first, becoming green and glossy by autumn; veins prominent beneath, especially the two lowest ones; leaf-stalk on seedling young plants ¼ in. long, much shorter on adult ones, distinctly jointed. Flowers apparently usually solitary in the leaf-axils, each on a stalk about $\frac{1}{10}$ in. long bearing several scales; about ½ in. wide, orange-yellow, fragrant. Sepals, petals, and stamens five.

Native of the Argentine Andes at 3,000 ft altitude; discovered in 1925 by H. F. Comber on the Cerro Lotena, and introduced by him. He records that it flowers profusely. It is a very distinct species, first in having no spines on the branchlets, their place being taken by foliage leaves, the short shoots in their axils being mostly without leaves and bearing flowers only; secondly in the parts of the flower being in fives (not the normal sixes). In general appearance it is also very distinct. Comber collected it in flower in the latter end of September, equivalent to our early April. He found it as a 'low-growing shrub 1 to 4 ft high in sheltered and exposed places on sandy, stony, and shaly soils'. The stamens, as in other barberries, are sensitive.

B. CONCINNA Hook. f.

A low, deciduous bush 3 ft high, of close, compact habit; branches furrowed. Leaves lustrous green above, white beneath, obovate, 1 in. or less long, tapering at the base to a short stalk, the margin armed with spiny teeth. Three spines, each ½ to ¾ in. long, guard the base of each tuft of leaves. Flowers solitary, on a slender stalk 1 to 1½ in. long, pendent, globose, deep yellow, ½ in. across. Berries oblong, fleshy, red, ½ to ¾ in. long. *Bot. Mag.*, t. 4744.

Native of the Sikkim-Himalaya at 12,000 to 13,000 ft; introduced to Kew by Sir Joseph Hooker about 1850. A very pretty barberry, and distinct through the vivid whiteness of the under-surface of the leaves. It is best propagated by seeds, which it produces most seasons.

B. (*concinna* × *calliantha*) 'CONCAL'.—This hybrid was raised by Capt. Collingwood Ingram, Benenden, Kent, and given an Award of Merit in 1948. It is a compact, semi-deciduous shrub with lemon-yellow flowers up to ¾ in. across.

A barberry collected by Kingdon Ward in 1924 under KW 6326 is near to *B. concinna* and was distributed under that name, but is given specific rank by Dr Ahrendt as B. TSANGPOENSIS. As a garden plant it differs in its lower and more spreading habit.

B. COXII Schneid.

A vigorous evergreen shrub to 7 ft high and eventually more across, with stout yellow-grey stems armed with flattened spines. Leaves elliptic to elliptic-ovate, about 2 in. long, leathery, glossy green above and glaucous grey beneath, with a few rather distant teeth. Flowers borne on stalks $\frac{1}{2}$ in. long, in clusters of three to six. Berries glaucous blue, about $\frac{1}{2}$ in. long.

Native of Upper Burma, introduced by Farrer from Hpimaw in 1919 and originally considered to be a form of *B. hookeri*, to which it is indeed closely related. It was recognised as a distinct species by Schneider and named by him after E. H. M. Cox, Farrer's companion in Burma and the founder and editor of the incomparable *New Flora and Sylva*, which ceased publication in 1940 but is still much read and consulted by plant-lovers. *B. coxii* is a fine evergreen, bushy and of good habit. Mr Cox tells us that the original plants at Glendoick, planted forty years ago, are now about 6 ft high and 14 ft across.

B. CRETICA L.

A low, sometimes prostrate, deciduous shrub; branches crooked, formidably armed with three-forked spines, each fork $\frac{1}{2}$ to $\frac{7}{8}$ in. long. Leaves small, obovate, pointed, averaging $\frac{1}{2}$ in. in length, mostly without teeth, sometimes slightly toothed. Flowers yellow, in short, few-flowered clusters. Berries globose, nearly black, with a bloom.

Native of the mountains of Crete and other islands of the Mediterranean. The leaves, spines, and flowers form a dense, crowded mass along the branches. It was introduced in 1703 but has always been rare in gardens.

B. DARWINII Hook.

An evergreen shrub of dense habit, from 6 to 12 ft high; branchlets covered with a dense, reddish-brown down. Leaves very dark, glossy green, stalkless, hard in texture, obovate, $\frac{3}{4}$ to $1\frac{1}{2}$ in. long, the apex three-spined, and with one to several spiny teeth down each side; they spring in tufts from the axils of short, multiple spines. Flowers on drooping racemes $1\frac{1}{2}$ to 2 in. long, each flower on a slender stalk longer than itself, deep golden or orange-coloured, tinged with red; petals elliptical notched at the tip. Fruit plum-coloured, roundish oval, the size of small peas. *Bot. Mag.*, t. 4590.

Native of Chile; first discovered by Charles Darwin in 1835, when attached as naturalist to the *Beagle* on her famous voyage. It was introduced in 1849 by William Lobb for Messrs Veitch, from the island of Chiloe. One of the finest of all evergreen shrubs, it is also perfectly hardy but prefers a not too dry soil and should be given a position sheltered from cutting winds; given these conditions *B. darwinii* will grow well even on chalky soils. It is in its greatest beauty, of course, during April and May, when laden with its profusion of golden blossom, but it is often very attractive also in early autumn, bearing a large crop of the bluish berries and occasionally a small crop of flowers. In mild and rainy parts of the country *B. darwinii* attains a great size. At Glenakil in Argyll there was a specimen 24 ft in diameter and 14 ft high; stem girth 4 ft 2 in.

B. darwinii should be raised from seed, which produces forms that vary somewhat in flower-colour and of these some have been selected and are in commerce as clones. Those known as *B. darwinii nana* and *B. d. prostrata*, although near to the species in their botanical characters, belong properly to its hybrid with *B. empetrifolia* (see *B.* × *stenophylla*). 'FLAME', raised by Messrs Marchant, also shows, though slightly, the influence of that species.

B. × ANTONIANA Ahrendt—An interesting hybrid between *B. darwinii* and *B. buxifolia* that arose in the Daisy Hill Nursery, Newry, Co. Down, and was originally distributed as *B. darwinii macrophylla*. The leaves recall the former species in colour and texture, but are almost entire. The flowers, borne singly, are almost ½ in. across.

For the hybrid between *B. darwinii* and *B. empetrifolia*, see *B.* × *stenophylla*.

B. DASYSTACHYA Maxim.

A deciduous shrub up to 12 ft high and more in diameter; young shoots grey the second and following years; spines often scarce, usually single, up to ⅝ in. long. Leaves minutely bristle-toothed, 1 to 2½ in. long, scarcely as wide, roundish elliptical, rounded at the apex, shortly tapered at the base to a slender stalk which is often 1 to 1½ in. long. Flowers opening in April and May, very closely packed, as many as forty together, on slender racemes 2½ in. long. The flower is small, globose, scarcely ¼ in. wide, lemon-yellow. Fruit egg-shaped, ¼ in. long, coral-red.

Native of Kansu, China, also probably of Szechwan; named by Maximowicz in 1877. The plants at present in cultivation all appear to have been introduced by Farrer, who describes the shrub as having 'arching sprays, hanging out tails of blossom all along, scented like *Lilium auratum*'. The finest plant I know of is in Mr Cox's garden at Glendoick, in the Tay valley below Perth. I saw it in June 1931, a noble bush 10 ft high and 15 ft in diameter; it had then passed out of bloom, but the shoots were thickly wreathed with naked flower-stalks; its largest leaves were fully 3 in. long. (This plant now measures 14 ft in height and 18 ft in spread—1965.)

This species is distinct in its long-stalked, roundish leaves and slender racemes of smallish flowers. It was given an Award of Merit on 20th April 1926, at Westminster, under the name "*kansuensis*". Very hardy.

B. DIAPHANA Maxim.

A deciduous shrub 2 to 3 ft high with glabrous stems, green when young, yellowish when mature, armed with stout three-pronged spines ½ to 1 in. long. Leaves ⅔ to 1 in. long, obovate to almost oblong, spiny-toothed, grey-green above with a prominent reticulate venation, grey beneath. Flowers ½ in. across, one to five in a cluster or condensed raceme. Berries bright red, about ½ in. long, ovoid, with a short style and containing six to ten seeds. *Bot. Mag.*, t. 8224.

Native of N.W. China. It is a decorative species, colouring well in the autumn. It was introduced to Kew at the end of the last century from the St Petersburg

Botanic Garden, to which seed had been sent from Kansu by the Russian explorer Przewalski.

B. AEMULANS Schneid.—This species is very near to *B. diaphana*, but grows to 6 ft high and has red or purplish-red young shoots. At Kew it grows very vigorously, and the long wand-like stems are very decorative in autumn after the leaves have fallen. Native of W. China, introduced by Wilson in 1908. *Bot. Mag.*, n.s., t. 179.

B. CIRCUMSERRATA Schneid.—This species was at first considered by Schneider to be a variety of *B. diaphana*, which it much resembles except in the leaves, which are more broadly rounded, and closely edged all round with slender bristle-like teeth. It was probably first introduced by Purdom, who collected it in the Tapai Shan, Shensi, in 1910–11.

B. DICTYONEURA Schneid.

A deciduous shrub to 5 ft high; young shoots green and glabrous, becoming grey and slightly warted. Spines three-parted, up to $\frac{4}{5}$ in. long. Leaves to $1\frac{1}{2}$ in. long, obovate, rounded at the apex, tapered at the base to a short stalk, prominently net-veined, dull grey-green above, yellow-green below, edged with numerous spiny teeth. Flowers up to $\frac{2}{5}$ in. across, borne six to fourteen together in a short raceme or more or less clustered. Berries usually egg-shaped, pink, $\frac{1}{3}$ in. long, with one or two seeds.

Native of China, introduced by Wilson in 1910 from the Min valley in W. Szechwan, under his No. 4633.

B. DICTYOPHYLLA Franch.

A graceful, deciduous bush up to 6 ft high, free from down on leaf and twig; with slender branches covered at first with a white bloom. Spines stout, three-pronged, to $1\frac{1}{4}$ in. long. Leaves $\frac{1}{2}$ to $\frac{4}{5}$ in. long, obovate, stalkless, green above, covered below with a white bloom, blunt at the apex, margins untoothed. Flowers usually borne singly in each cluster of leaves, to $\frac{2}{3}$ in. in diameter, of a soft, pale yellow. Berries red, with a white bloom.

Native of Yunnan and Szechwan, discovered by the French missionary Delavay in 1886 but not introduced until thirty years later, when Forrest sent seed under his F. 13224. His plants differ somewhat from the type and are referred by Dr Ahrendt to his var. CAMPYLOGYNA, characterised by a globose fruit tapered at the apex into a bent style (ovoid and style straight in the type), and the very short flower-stalks (in the type they are up to $\frac{3}{5}$ in. long). The type is also in cultivation, but less common. In either form it is a very striking barberry, the grey and white of its summer aspect turning in autumn to shades of red and gold. The flowers are exceptionally large for the genus, and in this it resembles *B. angulosa* and its nearer allies. It bears much resemblance to *B. temolaica*, but in that species the leaves are considerably longer (to almost 2 in.).

var. APPROXIMATA (Sprague) Rehd. *B. approximata* Sprague—This differs in its spiny-toothed leaves and smaller flowers; introduced into France from China by the French missionary Farges and thence to Kew in 1897. It was first grown as typical *B. dictyophylla* and was figured under that name in *Bot. Mag.*, t. 7833.

B. EMPETRIFOLIA Lam.

A low, evergreen shrub, rarely more than 12 to 18 in. high, with slender trailing branches in this country, but, as seen in Chile, often sturdier and more erect; young shoots red. Leaves ½ to 1 in. long, quite narrow (less than ⅛ in.), and made to look still narrower by the margins being curled down; the apex is spine-tipped. The leaves arise in tufts from the axils of simple, or three-parted spines, ¼ to ½ in. long. Flowers produced singly, or two together at each tuft, golden yellow. Fruit nearly black. Blossoms in mid-May.

Introduced from Chile in 1827 by Messrs Low, then nurserymen at Clapton. Quite distinct from any other barberry in leaf and habit, and the lowest-growing of them all, this little shrub is well worth a place in the rock garden. It is not common, but has played an important part in European horticulture in being one of the parents of the beautiful hybrid—*B. × stenophylla*. It was originally discovered by Commerson, the French traveller in South America.

B. FENDLERI A. Gray

A deciduous shrub up to 6 ft high, with stems and branches 'shining as if varnished'. Leaves glossy green, lanceolate, 1½ to 2 in. long, ⅜ to ½ in. wide; stalkless, toothed except at the base, produced in tufts of four or five. Flowers in six- to ten-flowered racemes 1½ to 2 in. long, each flower ⅓ in. across, the outer segments orange-coloured, the inner ones yellow. Fruit red.

Native of western N. America; first found by Mr Fendler near Santa Fé, New Mexico, and afterwards at the forks of the Rio Grande in S. Colorado. It is at present little known and does not appear to have any particular value for gardens. It is interesting, geographically, as the only West N. American representative of the true barberries, as distinct from Mahonias.

B. FRANCISCI-FERDINANDII Schneid.

An elegant deciduous shrub of rounded form up to 9 or 10 ft high; young shoots angled (especially vigorous virgin shoots), purplish; spines single on weak shoots, three-pronged and 1½ in. long on strong ones. Leaves obovate, oval, or oval-lanceolate, pointed, always tapering at the base to a stalk ¼ to ½ in. long, finely toothed, ¾ to 2½ in. long. Flowers yellow, ⅓ in. wide, produced in June on slender drooping racemes or panicles 3 to 5 in. long; individual flower-stalks ⅛ to ⅓ in. long. Fruit oval, ⅜ to ½ in. long, scarlet, two-seeded, borne as many as fifty on a panicle. *Bot. Mag.*, t. 9281.

Native of W. China; introduced by Wilson in 1900. Amongst the numerous species from the same region this is recognisable by the slender inflorescence (the slenderness due to the shortness of the flower-stalks) and the large pendulous bunches of scarlet berries. It is one of the most handsome of barberries, quite hardy and a good grower.

B. GAGNEPAINII Schneid.

B. acuminata Stapf, not Franch.

An evergreen shrub with clustered stems, free from down in all its parts, 6 to 8 ft high, the branches set with three-parted spines ½ to ¾ in. long. Leaves of firm texture, 1½ to 4 in. long, ¼ to ⅓ in. wide; linear-lanceolate, tapering to a fine point; dark dull green, the margins undulated and set with slender, forward-pointing teeth. Flowers in clusters of about six (sometimes ten or twelve) at each tuft of leaves, each flower on a slender stalk ½ to ¾ in. long, bright yellow, ½ in. across. Berries black, covered with blue bloom, oval, ⅓ to ⅝ in. long, ¼ in. wide. *Bot. Mag.*, t. 8185.

Native of Szechwan, China, introduced for Messrs Veitch by Wilson about 1904. This fine species is one of the most useful of Wilson's introductions from China, being evergreen, of compact, neat habit, and flowering abundantly. Allied to *B. hookeri*, it is of more graceful habit. The plant described above is the form commonly cultivated. It has longer leaves than in the type and has been distinguished by Dr Ahrendt as var. LANCEIFOLIA. It is quite hardy at Kew, and free growing. It flowers in late May. *Bot. Mag.*, n.s., t. 504.

cv. 'FERNSPRAY'.—A form with light green, crinkle-edged leaves, put into commerce by Messrs Jackman of Woking. It makes an elegant specimen to about 6 ft high and almost as much wide and is also recommended as a hedging plant.

B. × CHENAULTII Ahrendt—The typical form of this cross, which is *B. gagnepainii* × *verruculosa*, was raised by Chenault of Orleans around 1933 and put into commerce in this country by Messrs Hillier. It is a rather slow-growing shrub with arching branches and glossy leaves, but otherwise much resembles the first parent.

B. GLAUCOCARPA Stapf

B. coriacea Brandis, not St.-Hil.

A tall and vigorous deciduous shrub to 12 ft high of suckering habit and with glabrous pale yellow stems; spines mostly single, ⅕ to ⅖ in. long. Leaves 1¼ to 2½ in. long, ⅖ to 1 in. wide, oblanceolate to obovate, green on both sides, entire or with a few distant teeth. Flowers in a stiff, stout raceme ¾ to 1½ in. long. Fruits on short, stumpy stalks, oblong to globose, about ⅓ in. long, black but covered with a dense white bloom.

Native of the W. Himalaya. The type specimen was collected early in the last century and given by Brandis the name (never published) of *B. coriacea*, but it seems to have been cultivated as "*B. aristata*" or "*B. asiatica*". In 1926, Stapf (*Bot. Mag.*, t. 9102) remarked on its affinity to *B. lycium* and *B. lycioides* and gave it the name B. *glaucocarpa* (Brandis' name having been used earlier for another barberry); his description was later amplified by Dr Ahrendt.

It is not certain when and by whom it was first introduced, but it seems almost certain that it was this species and not the tender B. *asiatica* that was introduced (as Lindley records) by Sir Thomas Dyke-Acland in 1832 and used as a hedge-plant on his Killerton estates in Devon (and, we may reasonably infer, on his estates near Minehead as well). For it is B. *glaucocarpa*, so Mr Hadden informs us, that is today found in hedgerows between Porlock and Minehead and even around Cloutsham on Exmoor. This would also explain why it is still commoner in south-western gardens than it is elsewhere.

B. *glaucocarpa* has been confused with B. *aristata* and grown under that name. But it is well distinguished from the barberries of that group (section *Tinctoriae*) by its fruits, the ground colour being black, though masked with a heavy white bloom. In the *Tinctoriae* the fruits are red or purple. Its closest relationship is with B. *lycium* and other members of section *Asiaticae*.

B. GYALAICA Ahrendt

A deciduous shrub to 9 ft high, with arching, dark red stems. Spines yellow, single or three-parted, less than ½ in. long. The sessile leaves are elliptic, to ⅓ in. long, dull green above and greyish beneath. Flowers borne in July in dense panicles. Berries oblong to oval, about ⅓ in. long, black with a blue bloom. *Bot. Mag.*, n.s., t. 22.

This species was discovered by Kingdon Ward in 1924 in S.E. Tibet, on the Gyala Pass (KW 5962). On the same expedition he collected another new species —B. *johannis*—under KW 5936. The labels on the plants raised at Exbury were accidentally exchanged, with the result that the high praise accorded to KW 5936 by the late Lionel de Rothschild at the Tree and Shrub Conference of 1938 (*Report*, pp. 71–2) really belongs to B. *gyalaica*. As was pointed out by J. R. Sealy in his note accompanying the plate in the *Botanical Magazine*, the combination of red autumn foliage and dark-coloured berries that renders this species so striking is almost unique—for nearly all barberries that colour well in the autumn have red fruits. The paniculate inflorescence, though shared with B. *aggregata* and its allies, is also rare among the Old World barberries, although common in those of S. America. B. *gyalaica* grows vigorously, but Dr Ahrendt has found it somewhat tender in the climate of Oxfordshire.

B. SHERRIFFII Ahrendt—A closely related species, collected in S.E. Tibet in 1938 by Ludlow, Sherriff, and Taylor (LST 6629). It is quite hardy in the R.H.S. Garden at Wisley and very attractive in fruit. Another close ally of B. *gyalaica*—B. TAYLORII Ahrendt—was introduced by the same expedition (LST 7163).

B. HAKEOIDES (Hook. f.) Schneid.
B. *congestiflora* var. *hakeoides* Hook. f.

An evergreen shrub of loose, rather ungainly habit, as much as 12 ft high in favourable situations; branches erect, not downy, slightly furrowed and but little

branched. Leaves produced mostly in pairs, and very variable in size, ranging
from ½ to 2½ in. in length; usually almost orbicular, with a heart-shaped or
rounded base; thick and hard in texture, pale or slightly glaucous beneath, the
margins with spiny teeth, rarely entire. On the lower, bigger leaves of the branch
the stalks are as much as 1½ in. long, but towards the end of the branch the leaves
become smaller and the stalks shorter, until finally they are sessile. The leaves

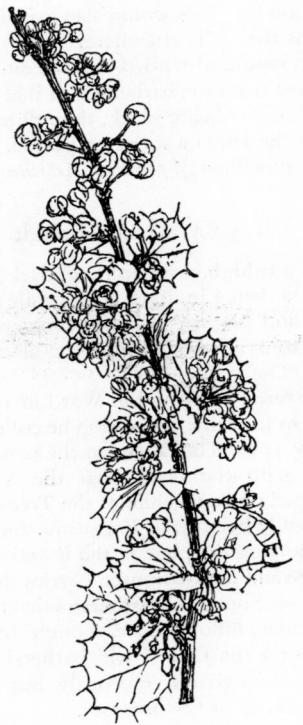

BERBERIS HAKEOIDES

and flowers spring from the axil of a small foliaceous, spiny leaf (which corresponds to the spines in other species), and this too becomes smaller as the
leaves decrease in size, until, near the apex of the shoot, leaves cease to be borne
and tiny spine-leaves alone remain. Flowers borne in April and May, on the
shoots of the previous summer in dense, round clusters, ½ to ⅜ in. across, from
the axil of each pair of leaves right to the leafless end of the branches; they
are bright golden yellow, ¼ in. across; sepals nine, concave; petals six, erect,
incurved, slightly notched. Fruit usually one-seeded, blue-black. *Bot. Mag.*,
t. 6770.

Native of Chile; discovered by Pearce, and introduced in 1861. In spite of its somewhat ungainly habit it is, when seen at its best, a shrub of striking beauty. There used to be a fine plant in the Coombe Wood nursery, the mother probably of all the plants in cultivation, but a still finer one was in Canon Ellacombe's garden at Bitton; this was growing against, but not on, a wall, and was 12 ft high. Still it is not amongst the hardiest of barberries, and at Kew is apt to become shabby during hard winters. It is usually propagated by grafting on *Mahonia aquifolium* or *B. vulgaris*, but owing to the habit of the stock producing suckers, layering would be preferable.

B. CONGESTIFLORA Gay, of which the above has been regarded as a variety, is in cultivation from seed collected by Comber in Valdivia province under his No. 973. It differs mainly in its thinner leaves, slightly downy stems, and more congested inflorescence. There are two specimens in the R.H.S. Garden at Wisley, in Seven Acres.

B. HETEROPHYLLA Juss.

A deciduous shrub 3 or 4 ft high, of straggling habit, with crooked, much-branched stems. Leaves of two kinds; the first kind ½ to 1 in. long, ⅛ to ¼ in. wide, narrowly obovate, rounded or spine-tipped at the apex, margins without teeth; second kind about the same in length but much wider in proportion, and with three or five large spiny teeth, altogether very much like a tiny holly leaf in form. The leaf-clusters spring from the axils of triple spines, each prong of which is ⅛ to ¾ in. long, and as they are often less than ½ in. apart on the branch-let, the shrub is formidably armed. Flowers solitary, on a stalk ⅓ in. long; orange-yellow, with sepals and petals so incurved as to make each flower a little ball. Berries about the size of peas, black, covered with blue bloom, but not often seen in this country.

Discovered originally on the Straits of Magellan by Commerson, but said also to occur wild in other parts of Chile and Argentina. It is a curious and very rare barberry, flowering at Kew in April. It produces sucker growths from the base, by which means it can be propagated. *B. ilicifolia* Forst., another species with holly-like leaves, bears some resemblance to this, but has short, many-flowered racemes.

B. HETEROPODA Schrenk

A deciduous shrub up to about 8 ft high, of loose, spreading habit; branchlets glossy, glabrous, brown, either armed with simple or three-parted spines 1 in. long, or unarmed. Leaves grey-green, broadly ovate or oval, rounded at the apex; the blade 1 to 1½ in. long, tapering at the base to a long, slender, reddish stalk, ⅔ to 1 in. long; margin sometimes almost or quite entire, more often set with fine teeth. Inflorescences drooping, long-stalked, three of which often issue from one tuft of leaves; one being large, racemose, with as many as fifteen flowers, the other two smaller, umbellate, with about three flowers. Each flower is on a slender stalk, fragrant, orange-yellow, opening in May. Fruit oblong or egg-shaped, ⅓ in. long, black, covered with blue bloom.

Native of Turkestan; introduced to Kew in 1886 from the St Petersburg Botanic Garden through Albert Regel. It is distinct by reason of its long, slender leaf-stalks, and long, drooping, many-flowered racemes, often flanked on either side by a few-flowered umbel.

B. HISPANICA Boiss. & Reut.

A deciduous shrub to 5 ft high, of open habit and with dark red stems. Spines three-parted or single, ½ to ¾ in. long. Leaves entire or with a few distant teeth, ⅓ to 1 in. long, ¼ to ½ in. wide, elliptic to obovate, with a tapering base. Flowers six to fifteen in a cluster or short raceme, orange-yellow. Berries ovoid, black and slightly glaucous, ¼ in. long.

Native of the mountains of S.E. Spain, Morocco, and Algeria. It has been regarded by some authorities as a variety or subspecies of *B. vulgaris*, but is very distinct from this in its blue-black fruits and red stems. By Dr Ahrendt it is placed in the section *Crataeginae*, together with *B. aetnensis* (q.v.) and the little-known *B. crataegina* of Asia Minor. The common barberry has its closest allies not in Europe, but in E. Asia.

B. HOOKERI Lem.

B. *wallichiana* Hook., not DC.

An evergreen shrub 3 to 5 ft high, producing a dense thicket of erect, angled stems, which branch near the top; young twigs not downy; spines usually three-forked, each fork slender, rigid, from ½ to 1 in. long. Leaves in tufts, lanceolate to obovate; 1 to 3 in. long, ½ to 1 in. wide; leathery, almost stalkless; dark green above, glaucous white beneath; the margins armed with slender teeth. Flowers solitary on their stalks, borne in clusters of three to six at each tuft of leaves; ⅝ in. across, pale yellow, the sepals tinged with red. Berries narrow, cylindrical, ½ in. long, tapering towards the end; black-purple, often remaining on the plant until the following spring. *Bot. Mag.*, t. 9153.

Native of the Himalaya. This shrub has been so much confused with B. WALLICHIANA of De Candolle, that it is hard to disentangle the histories of the two. The true *B. wallichiana* is probably not in cultivation; it differs from *B. hookeri* in the larger leaves (3 to 4¾ in. long), and especially in their veining; the veins branch out from the midrib, parallel with each other, but never reach the margin, becoming merged in a vein which runs parallel with it. In *B. hookeri*, the veins fork near the margin, but do not merge into one another. *B. hookeri* flowers in April and May, and as a rule is quite hardy.

var. VIRIDIS Schneid.—Leaves uniformly bright green beneath. Although a marked characteristic of some plants, the white under-surface of typical *B. hookeri* is not a wholly reliable distinctive character. I have seen young plants partly bright green and partly blue-white beneath.

The best way to increase this species and the above variety is by seed; they may be sown in shallow boxes or in pots, and the young plants pricked out the following years into nursery rows. Both the type and the variety *viridis*, which is the commoner in cultivation, are useful shrubs for planting in places where an evergreen is wanted that will keep fairly dwarf without pruning.

B. MANIPURANA Ahrendt—This plant has been long grown in gardens as "*B. hookeri* var. *latifolia*"—a name based on *B. wallichiana* var. *latifolia* Hook. f. & Thoms., which is not in cultivation. It has also been grown as "*B. knightii*" and "*B. xanthoxylon*". *B. manipurana* is a much taller and more robust shrub than *B. hookeri*, but not so hardy. It differs, too, in the considerably longer leaves (sometimes over 4 in.), which are glossy on both sides. It is a native of Manipur, whereas *B. hookeri* appears to be confined to the main Himalayan range.

B. HYPOKERINA Airy-Shaw

A glabrous, evergreen shrub, often 2 to 4 ft high and of stiff habit, but sometimes up to 8 ft. Leaves oblong-oval, up to 6 in. long and 2½ in. wide, very stiff and leathery, the margins formidably set with triangular spines up to ⅜ in. long, dark green above, brilliantly silvery-white beneath. Flowers pale yellow, ⅜ in. across, up to fifteen crowded in stalkless axillary clusters; individual stalks ½ to ¾ in. long. Fruit blue-purple, of the ordinary elliptical barberry shape, ⅜ in. long, pendent below the branches on their short stalks.

Native of Upper Burma, discovered and introduced by Kingdon Ward in 1926, and given an Award of Merit in June 1932. Its foliage is most striking, especially in size and in the vividly white under-surface. In a wild state it is said to grow best in shade along with rhododendrons, vacciniums, etc. It belongs to the *Wallichianae* section of the genus and got its Award as "*B. hookeri glauca*". Kingdon Ward, who describes it as a 'splendid shrub', found it at altitudes of 9,000 to 10,000 ft. Unfortunately, it has proved to be a sparsely branched shrub, of ungainly habit.

B. ILICIFOLIA Forst.

An evergreen, straggling bush, with deeply grooved branches; said to grow 8 ft high in Chile, but is not usually more than half as high in cultivation. Leaves holly-like, from 1 to 2 in. long, dark glossy green, obovate, with a few spiny teeth towards the apex. Flowers ⅔ to ¾ in. across, orange-yellow, densely crowded on short racemes. *Bot. Mag.*, t. 4308.

First introduced to Kew from S. Chile by Sir Joseph Hooker, whilst he was attached to Sir John Ross's Antarctic expedition, 1839–43, this striking barberry has always been one of the rarest in cultivation. It is probably better suited for the south-western maritime counties than inland ones. It was reintroduced about twenty years ago by Capt. Collingwood Ingram from Punta Arenas on the Straits of Magellan and received an Award of Merit when shown by him at Vincent Square in April 1962. The specimen bore flowers of brilliant orange-red between ½ and ¾ in. across, four to seven together in a sub-umbellate inflorescence. The plant sometimes found in gardens under the label "*B. ilicifolia*" is really the bi-generic hybrid × *Mahoberberis neubertii*.

B. INCRASSATA Ahrendt

An evergreen shrub of low growth; shoots glabrous, terete, reddish, thornless. Leaves elliptic-lanceolate, or narrowly oval, 2 to 5 in. long, ⅜ to 1 in. wide, strongly armed with stiff marginal teeth; stalkless, shining pale green beneath, borne singly and alternately on young shoots and in axillary clusters on older wood. Flowers $\frac{3}{8}$ to $\frac{1}{2}$ in. across, bright yellow, borne in short-stalked, dense clusters of fifteen to thirty; petals obovate. Fruit 'grape purple'.

Native of N. Burma, discovered by Kingdon Ward and introduced in 1931. It is a handsome foliage shrub belonging to the *Wallichianae* group and shows relationship with B. *insignis*, especially in the unarmed shoots. The foliage is particularly interesting for the pale green of the under-surface. It was first distinguished in the collection at Wisley but is not now in cultivation there. The specific name refers to the curious thickening upwards of the flower-stalks.

B. INSIGNIS Hook. f. & Thoms.

An evergreen shrub 5 or 6 ft high, with yellowish-grey, round young shoots which are usually unarmed. Leaves solitary or three at a joint, lanceolate to narrowly oval, slender-pointed, the margins set with short spiny teeth about $\frac{1}{8}$ in. apart; usually 3 to 5 in. long, 1 to $1\frac{3}{4}$ in. wide; dark shining green above, pale green and conspicuously veined beneath. Flowers fifteen to twenty-five clustered at one joint, each on a stalk about $\frac{1}{2}$ in. long, pale golden yellow. Fruit black, oval, $\frac{1}{3}$ in. long.

Native of the moist forests of Sikkim, E. Nepal, and Bhutan; introduced originally by Sir Joseph Hooker to Kew about 1850. In foliage it is one of the finest of barberries, but it is not one of the hardiest, although it survives ordinary winters at Kew without injury. It belongs to the same group as B. *hookeri*, but so distinct is it (1) in the size of its leaves (one of the largest amongst the true barberries as apart from the mahonias), which are often solitary at the joint, and (2) in the frequently entire absence of spines, that it is one of the most easily recognised in a difficult genus. There is a vigorous plant in the Edinburgh Botanic Garden 6 ft high and 12 ft across, raised from seed received from Darjeeling in 1923. Although the leaves are sometimes disfigured by frost, it is otherwise hardy and very free flowering. It also succeeds very well in the R.H.S. Garden at Wisley.

B. JAMESIANA Forr. & W. W. Sm.

A deciduous shrub found in a wild state 6 to 9 ft high; young shoots purple, slightly angled, armed with single or triple spines, $\frac{1}{3}$ to $1\frac{1}{4}$ in. long. Leaves in clusters of two to six; 1 to $2\frac{1}{4}$ in. long, $\frac{1}{2}$ to $1\frac{1}{2}$ in. wide; mostly obovate, rounded at the apex except for a short spine, tapering at the base to a short stalk; they are of firm texture, entire or minutely and sparsely toothed, and very distinctly net-veined. Flowers yellow, $\frac{1}{4}$ in. wide, produced in racemes 2 to 4 in. long, each flower on a stalk $\frac{1}{4}$ in. or so long. Fruits globose, scarlet, $\frac{3}{8}$ in. wide. *Bot. Mag.*, t. 9298.

Native of Yunnan, China; discovered in 1913 by Forrest and introduced by him. This is a very handsome and distinct barberry which has succeeded exceptionally well in the light soil of the Wisley Garden. Fine sprays of fruit, hung thickly along the branches in pendulous clusters, bright red, and of the shape and size of red currants, were exhibited at the Royal Horticultural Hall from Wisley on 20th October 1925, and obtained an Award of Merit. The attractiveness of the berries is enhanced by their transparency. The foliage turns a good red before falling. The seed distributed from Wisley produced forms of unequal quality but a particularly fine one, known as 'East Lodge', was given an Award of Merit when shown by W. B. Cranfield of Enfield, Middlesex, in 1947.

B. JOHANNIS Ahrendt

A deciduous shrub to 7 ft high, erect in some forms but in others of spreading habit. Stems slender and glabrous, with short and thin three-parted spines. Leaves less than 1 in. long, obovate and tapering to a short petiole, dull green above and greyish beneath, margins entire or with a few spines. Flowers borne in May in umbels or condensed racemes of three to seven flowers, the peduncle and individual flower-stalks coloured red. Berries bright red, narrow, with a waist near the middle and somewhat bent above it. *Bot. Mag.*, n.s., t. 57.

Native of S.E. Tibet; introduced by Kingdon Ward in 1924 (KW 5936) from Tumbatse, where he collected the famous *Primula florindae* in the same autumn. It is a vigorous and hardy shrub, which grows quickly from seed and is very decorative in late autumn. It has been confused with *B. gyalaica* (q.v.).

B. JULIANAE Schneid.

An evergreen shrub of dense habit, 8 to 10 ft high; young shoots yellowish, angled, armed with three-pronged spines which are up to 1½ in. long, stout and sharp. Leaves narrowly oval to oblanceolate, tapering to a short stalk, spiny-toothed; they are clustered as many as five together at a joint, each measuring 2 to 3 in. long, ⅓ to ½ in. wide. Flowers in clusters of as many as fifteen, each on a slender stalk ⅓ to ⅝ in. long, yellow, ¼ in. wide. Fruit ⅓ in. long, oval, black, covered with blue bloom, the conspicuous stalked style adhering at the end. *Bot. Mag.*, t. 9283, as "*B. xanthoxylon*".

Native of Central China; introduced by Wilson for Messrs Veitch in 1900 (No. 535). It is one of the hardiest of the evergreen barberries and makes a handsome erect bush. It has been confused with, and grown for, *B. sargentiana* in gardens, but that species has reddish young shoots, not angled, its fruits have not so much bloom on them nor is the terminal knob or style so conspicuous. There is a fine bush of *B. julianae* at Kew 10 ft high and 12 ft in diameter—a luxuriant rounded mass of foliage.

B. LEMPERGIANA Ahrendt—Related to *B. julianae* but with smaller, less toothed leaves and somewhat larger flowers. It occurs wild in Chekiang province, China, but the type is a plant raised by Messrs Hillier from seed sent to Dr Fritz Lemperg by the Nanking Botanic Garden. *Bot. Mag.*, n.s., t. 90.

B. KAWAKAMII Hayata

An evergreen, glabrous shrub up to 6 ft high and wide; shoots strongly ribbed or angled, pale brown; spines three-parted, ½ to 1 in. long, stiff. Leaves oval to narrowly oval, tapered to both ends, 1 to 2 in. long, ¼ to ¾ in. wide, edged with small, sharp teeth, conspicuously veined. Flowers rich yellow, ⅓ in. across, crowded in axillary, compact clusters of eight to twelve, opening in late March and April; stalks about ¼ in. long; petals five or six, notched at the rounded apex, giving the flowers a globose shape through being more or less concave; sepals very narrow, red at the back. Fruits oval, about ¼ in. long, dark blue. *Bot. Mag.*, t. 9622.

Native of Formosa; introduced by Wilson about 1918 and again by Yashiroda some twenty years later. It belongs to the *Wallichianae* group of barberries and being quite hardy, free and handsome in bloom, is well worth cultivating.

B. KOREANA Palib.

A deciduous, glabrous shrub up to 6 ft high, with grooved reddish young shoots. Spines on vigorous young shoots sometimes five-forked, with each fork curiously flattened, ovate, and nearly ¼ in. wide; from this type they grade down to slender single ones. Leaves 1 to 2⅘ in. long, obovate or oval, rounded at the apex, tapered to a stalk ¼ to ½ in. long; strongly veined beneath. Flowers yellow, borne in drooping racemes, 3 to 4 in. long, each flower on a slender stalk about ½ in. long. Fruits roundish egg-shaped, ¼ in. long, bright red.

Native of Korea, where, according to James H. Veitch, who visited that country in 1892, it is found often in quantity in hedgerows. The larger spines described above suggest those of the South American *B. actinacantha*, but are not always present. The leaves are large as barberries go and turn a good colour in autumn; the fruits also last long in colour.

B. LECOMTEI Schneid.
B. *thunbergii* var. *glabra* Franch.

A densely branched deciduous shrub to about 6 ft high with glabrous shoots, red when young, later grey. Spines thin, about ½ in. long, simple or three-parted. Leaves entire, oblanceolate, obovate, or lanceolate, ½ to 1½ in. long, blunt at the apex, tapering at the base into a very short stalk, dull grey-green above, greyish beneath. Flowers clustered, or in a short-stalked umbel or condensed raceme. Berries deep lustrous red, oblong to pear-shaped, about ⅖ in. long, without a style.

Native of China in Yunnan and S.W. Szechwan; discovered by the French missionary Delavay, and an old plant at Kew was probably raised from seed sent by him to France about 1885. It was later collected by Forrest and is in cultivation from his seed also. It closely resembles *B. thunbergii*.

B. THIBETICA Schneid.—This species is of little garden merit. It was introduced to Kew in 1903 by Maurice de Vilmorin, from seed collected by the French missionary Soulié on the borders of Yunnan and Tibet. It is related to the preceding, but the berries are bright red, larger, and bear a style; the leaves are prominently net-veined.

B. STEARNII Ahrendt—This species differs from B. *lecomtei* in its stylose fruit and from B. *thibetica* in the duller colouring of the fruit and the scarcely veined leaves. Dr Ahrendt remarks that it is decorative in spring, when the flower-buds are red and the young growth bright green, mottled with red. In cultivation from F. 29042.

B. LEPIDIFOLIA Ahrendt

A rather spreading shrub to 8 ft high, deciduous, but holding its leaves well into the winter. Stems glabrous, grooved, dark brown when mature, often without spines, which, where present, are simple. Leaves very narrow, never more than ⅕ in. wide, ⅔ to 2 in. long, dull green above, greyish beneath. Flowers small, borne in July, five to eight in an umbel about 1½ in. wide. Fruit ¼ in. long, black with a slight bloom.

Described from specimens collected by Forrest in the mountains between the rivers Yangtse and Mekong and in cultivation from his F. 23614. At Wisley, in the R.H.S. Garden, it has made a compact bush only 4 ft high.

B. LINEARIFOLIA Phil. [PLATE 17

An evergreen shrub of loose, erect habit, 4 to 8 ft high; young shoots ribbed, not downy, armed with three-forked spines ¼ to ⅝ in. long. Leaves arranged in clusters of three to six at each joint, linear, spine-tipped, tapered towards both ends, toothless; ¾ to 1¾ in. long, ¼ in. or less wide; dark shining green above, glaucous beneath, of leathery texture, scarcely stalked; margins recurved. Flowers clustered at the joints, four to six together, each on its own very slender red stalk ½ to 1¼ in. long; they are of a rich orange colour internally and of a beautiful apricot colour outside, and measure about ⅝ to ¾ in. across when open. Fruit black, covered with a blue bloom, egg-shaped, ½ in. long, terminated by the conspicuous style. *Bot. Mag.*, t. 9526.

Native of Chile; described by Philippi in 1856; introduced in 1927 by H. F. Comber, who found it at 3,400 ft altitude in shady moist woodland. Comber notes that it is 'one of the best', and, judging by small plants that flowered in less than three years from sowing the seed, that is a true estimate of its quality. The flowers are larger than those of B. *darwinii* and more richly coloured. It is of course very distinct from that barberry in its long, narrow, entire leaves. It appears to be very hardy, as two-year-old plants withstood the cold winter of 1928–9 out-of-doors at Kew without suffering in the least and flowered freely in April 1930. Clarence Elliott, who has seen it wild during his visits to Chile, speaks highly of its beauty. It seems remarkable that so excellent a shrub should have been overlooked so long, but I cannot find that it has been in cultivation before. A fine form was shown at the Horticultural Hall on 21st April 1931, by Lt-Col. Messel from his garden at Nymans and was given a First Class Certificate. It showed this species, both in the size and rich colour of its blooms, to be probably the finest of all the evergreen true barberries.

To the above account, first published in 1933, it is only necessary to add that in most gardens B. *linearifolia* came through the hard winters of the early sixties with little damage, and seems hardy enough in a position sheltered from cold, drying winds. It is tolerant of chalky soils.

B. × LOLOGENSIS Sandw.—A group-name for hybrids between B. *darwinii* and B. *linearifolia*. Comber found three plants near Lake Lolog in Argentina in 1927, growing with the parents, and introduced seed. The type is intermediate between the parents but favours *darwinii* more in foliage; the flowers are larger than in that species and have inherited some of the fine colouring of *linearifolia*. There appear to be forms intermediate between the type and both of the parents, judging from plants raised from Comber's seed. A selected form, raised by the late Sir Frederick Stern, is in commerce as 'HIGHDOWN'. He found that this hybrid, like B. *linearifolia*, grows well on chalk.

B. LYCIOIDES Stapf

A semi-deciduous, entirely glabrous shrub up to 10 ft, shoots terete, armed with simple and three-pronged spines up to ¾ in. long. Leaves in axillary clusters of four to six, up to 2½ in. long, ½ to ¾ in. wide, narrowly obovate to oblanceolate, the base cuneate, the apex shortly tapered to a small mucro; margins sparsely spiny to entire; slightly glaucous beneath. Flowers in two whorls of three, yellow, ⅖ in. wide, borne in pendulous racemes or sometimes panicles 2½ to 3½ in. long; calyx of three whorls of sepals. Fruits ovoid to ovoid-oblong, ⅜ in. long, black-purple, but coated freely with a blue-white, waxy bloom. *Bot. Mag.*, t. 9102.

Native of the N.W. Himalaya. It has been in cultivation since the early nineteenth century, but under other names such as B. *aristata*. It is hardy and beautiful both in flower and fruit.

B. LYCIUM Royle

A deciduous or semi-evergreen shrub, of spreading habit, 6 or 8 ft high; young shoots furnished with fine down. Leaves narrowly obovate, light green above, glaucous beneath, varying in length in each tuft from ¾ to 2 in. with a few teeth towards the apex, or with none, but always spine-tipped. Spines three-parted, ½ to ¾ in. long. Racemes 2 to 3 in. in length, carrying from twelve to thirty flowers, each ⅓ in. across, bright yellow. Berries ⅖ in. long, oblong, covered with a fine blue-purple bloom. *Bot. Mag.*, t. 7075.

Native of the Himalaya, and quite hardy at Kew, where it flowers in May and June. It was in cultivation there in 1853, and had probably been introduced by Sir Joseph Hooker a few years previously. This plant yields the drug known as 'Lycium', used for ages in inflammatory affections of the eyes. The beautiful purplish berries are eaten in N. India. It is a species distinct in the hard, pale green leaves, conspicuously net-veined above, glaucous beneath, and almost entire.

B. MITIFOLIA Stapf

A deciduous shrub 6 to 8 ft high, with angular, downy, grey young shoots, spines three-parted at the base of the shoot, single or absent towards the end,

½ to 1 in. long. Leaves oval to obovate, 1½ to 3 in. long, up to 1 in. wide; pointed or rounded at the apex, tapering to a stalk ½ in. or less long, usually more or less toothed, sometimes conspicuously so, sometimes entire; strongly veined beneath; green and downy on both sides, but especially so beneath. Flowers pale yellow, produced in May on cylindrical, downy, pendulous racemes 3 to 4 in. long, which are very slender on account of the shortness of the individual flower-stalks. Fruit blood-red, oval, ⅜ in. long, closely packed in pendulous clusters. *Bot. Mag.*, t. 9236.

Native of China; collected by Wilson in the mountains of W. Hupeh in 1901 and again in 1905. It was first considered by Schneider to be a form of *B. brachypoda* Maxim., under which name it was distributed by the Arnold Arboretum and given an Award of Merit when shown by Vicary Gibbs of Aldenham in 1923. For this reason it used to be known in gardens as "*B. brachypoda gibbsii*". It is one of the most easily recognised of barberries on account of the downy leaves and young shoots, and the slender racemes of flowers. Autumn colour red.

The true B. BRACHYPODA Maxim. comes from farther north, in the provinces of Kansu and Shensi. It was discovered by the Russian explorer Piasezski, to whom we owe the first knowledge of *Buddleia alternifolia*. It is more compact in habit than *B. mitifolia* and has berries of a brighter red, but is rare in cultivation. Another related species is B. GIRALDII Hesse, but this has leaves up to 4 in. in length, and considerably longer racemes. It comes from the same region as *B. brachypoda*, where it was discovered by the Italian missionary Giraldi, and distributed by Hesse's nurseries, Germany. It colours brilliantly in the autumn and the unfolding leaves, too, are tinged with red. Lastly there is B. GILGIANA Fedde, which is similar to *B. mitifolia* but has somewhat narrower leaves and red-brown or purple stems. It is rare in this country, but grown in the United States, where it is valued for its brilliant red fruits and autumn colour. Introduced by Purdom from the Tapai Shan, Shensi, in 1910–11. All these species are characterised by their spike-like racemes and downy young shoots; the leaves are also downy, at least beneath.

B. MONTANA Gay

A deciduous shrub up to 15 ft high in a wild state, its greyish, glabrous, angled branches armed with slender, simple or three-pronged spines ¼ to ½ in. long. Leaves produced in clusters of two to seven, obovate to oblanceolate, tapered to the very short stalk, bluntish or rounded at the apex, ½ to 1½ in. long, half or less than half as much wide, quite smooth and toothless. Flowers ¾ to ⅞ in. wide, yellow and pale orange, produced in May either in fascicles, each on its own stalk, or in slenderly stalked umbels, in either case of two to four blossoms. Fruit black, covered with a purple bloom, lemon-shaped, ¼ to ⅜ in. long, with the prominent stigma adhering at the end.

Native of the Chilean and Argentine Andes; described by Gay in 1845, but not, I think, established in cultivation until Comber sent home seeds during his Andean expedition of 1925–7. Judging by his wild specimens (No. 798), it must be a very beautiful barberry, especially the form with several flowers borne on a slender drooping main-stalk ½ to 1¼ in. long. The species varies a good deal in this matter of flower-stalks but Mr Comber tells me it is a very unstable character, dependent, he thinks, on such conditions as shade and altitude (Wilson found it to be the same with Japanese cherries).

To the above account, first published in 1933, it should be added that *B. montana* has proved a quite hardy shrub, with no objection to chalk. It is, however, of rather stiff habit, and inclined to become leggy with age. Whether Comber's No. 798 produced any plants that bear their flowers in umbels (see above) is not known for certain. But as usually seen in gardens *B. montana* has them in fascicles. They are strikingly large and jonquil-like. It is closely akin to *B. chillanensis* (q.v.), but that species differs in its downy, more slender stems and, as seen in cultivation, has smaller flowers.

B. MORRISONENSIS Hayata

A deciduous shrub described as growing up to 6 ft high in a wild state; young shoots often red, strongly angled, glabrous; spines three-parted, $\frac{1}{2}$ to $\frac{5}{8}$ in. long. Leaves in clusters of three to eight at each joint, $\frac{1}{2}$ to 1 in. long, obovate, rounded or pointed at the apex, the round-ended ones usually with bristle-like teeth on the margin, the pointed ones often entire; slightly glaucous beneath. Flowers pale yellow, produced during June in clusters of as many as five, each on a stalk $\frac{1}{2}$ to 1 in. long. Fruits globose-ovoid, $\frac{3}{8}$ in. long, bright red and somewhat translucent. *Bot. Mag.*, t. 9017.

Native of Formosa on mountains up to 13,000 ft altitude. First introduced to this country apparently by W. R. Price, who collected it on Mt Morrison in 1912 and raised it from seeds at Pen Moel, near Chepstow. It was collected by Wilson in October 1918, and seed was distributed by the Arnold Arboretum the following spring. From this seed the late Marquis of Headfort raised the plants from which the *Botanical Magazine* plate was prepared. It is a handsome barberry, especially in autumn, when, in addition to the beauty of its fruits, its foliage assumes brilliant shades of scarlet and gold. It is related to *B. diaphana*.

B. MUCRIFOLIA Ahrendt

A small deciduous shrub 10 in. to 2 ft high in the wild; stems yellowish or greyish, downy when young, angled and finely grooved. Spines slender, three-parted, up to $\frac{3}{4}$ in. long. Leaves narrow, elliptic to obovate, less than 1 in. long, glabrous, creamy green beneath; they bear a conspicuous spiny tip but are otherwise entire or (as seen on cultivated plants) with an occasional marginal tooth near the apex. Flowers solitary, about $\frac{1}{3}$ in. in diameter. Berries bright red, globose or somewhat elongated, about $\frac{1}{4}$ in. long, with a well-developed style.

This species was described by Dr Ahrendt in 1956 from specimens collected by Stainton, Sykes, and Williams in 1954 in Nepal, where they found it in open places on the mountain-sides between 9,000 and 14,000 ft. It is in cultivation from their 8111 (type) and also from seed collected by Polunin, Sykes, and Williams farther west in 1952 (PSW 5444). Plants raised from the latter were distributed by the late Miss Davenport Jones, Washfield Nurseries, Hawkhurst, Kent. It should make a neat miniature bush if grown in full sun, but the flowers are small and the fruits, though brightly coloured, are too sparse to make much display.

B. ORTHOBOTRYS Schneid.

B. vulgaris var. *brachybotrys* Hook. f.

A deciduous shrub up to 4 ft high, with dark, glabrous, young wood, armed with three-pronged slender spines up to ⅓ in. long. Leaves ½ to 1⅛ in. long, ⅛ to ½ in. wide, obovate or oblanceolate, mostly finely toothed, glabrous, and distinctly net-veined beneath. Flowers yellow, produced in May, five to twelve together in corymbose racemes scarcely 1 in. long. Fruits oval, red, ⅖ in. long.

Native of Kashmir, Afghanistan, etc. It was first found in the former country by T. Thomson and in the latter by Aitchison. As seen at Kew it is noticeable for the close arrangement of the leaf-clusters along the twigs. The clusters (made up of five to eight leaves) are scarcely half an inch apart. When in flower the twigs are almost hidden by blossom. The leaves are unusually small. A form distributed by Messrs Marchant differs from the type in its narrower leaves, covered beneath with a grey bloom, and has been distinguished by Dr Ahrendt as var. CANESCENS. It is a fine fruiting shrub, holding its red berries well into November.

B. POIRETII Schneid.

B. sinensis DC., in part

A very elegant deciduous shrub up to 5 or 6 ft high, with slender, pendulous branches; young shoots glabrous, somewhat angled, glossy; spines weak, sometimes three-parted at the base of the shoot, but mostly simple. Leaves green on

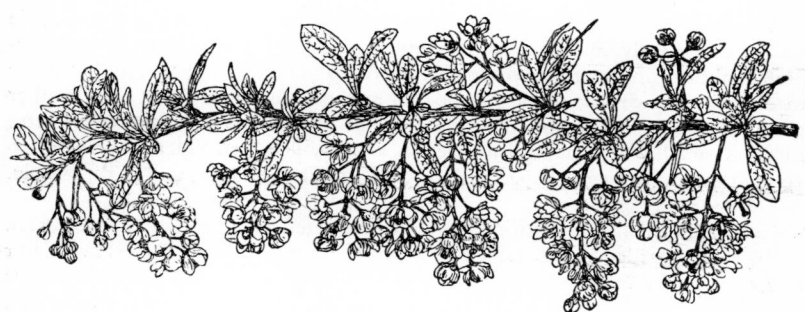

BERBERIS POIRETII

both surfaces, oblanceolate or narrowly obovate, ¾ to 2 in. long, ⅙ to ⅓ in. wide; on the flowering shoots they are smaller and without teeth, but on the sterile shoots are more or less toothed; sometimes rounded, sometimes spine-tipped. Racemes 2 to 3 in. long, one of them pendent from each leaf-cluster. Flowers pale yellow, ¼ in. diameter, each one borne on a thread-like stalk. Berries bright red, slender, nearly ½ in. long.

Native of N. China. The date of introduction is not certain, but it may be this species that was introduced to France by D'Incarville in the middle of the eighteenth century and thence to England. A specimen was collected near Peking by the Abbé David in 1862, but it is not certain whether he sent seed. It is one of the most attractive and graceful of deciduous barberries, flowering in remarkable profusion towards the end of May.

B. CHINENSIS Poir. *B. sinensis* DC., in part.—This species has been much confused with the preceding, to which it is related but from which it differs in its broader leaves and in its darker red berries, borne on stalks ¼ to ⅗ in. long (barely ⅕ in. long in *B. poiretii*). In spite of its name, this species is not a native of China but of Asia Minor and the Caucasus.

The name "*B. sinensis*" has been used for both the above species and also for *B. thunbergii*.

B. FORRESTII Ahrendt—A deciduous shrub to about 6 ft high with gracefully arching branches, which are unarmed or with only short, weak spines; young growths bright red. Leaves entire, oblong-obovate, to 2⅖ in. long, greyish above, grey-bloomy beneath. Flowers in umbellate racemes up to 5 in. long. Berries oblong-ovoid, ⅖ in. long, bright red. Native of Yunnan; introduced by Forrest around 1910 and first grown as B. PALLENS Franch., to which it is closely allied. Dr Ahrendt points out, however, that there is some confusion over the identity of Franchet's species and prefers to keep Forrest's plants separate from it.

B. PRATTII Schneid.
B. aggregata var. *prattii* (Schneid.) Schneid.

A deciduous shrub to 10 ft high; stems reddish and downy when young, pale yellow and nearly glabrous at maturity. Spines rather thin, single to three-parted, about ½ in. long. Leaves in clusters of up to ten, ⅖ to 1¼ in. long, obovate to oblong, rounded at the apex, tapered at the base into a short stalk, rather glossy green above, greyish beneath, margins entire or with a few spiny teeth. Flowers small, borne at midsummer in a many-flowered erect panicle up to 10 in. long. Berries egg-shaped, bright pink, about ¼ in. long, with a short style. *Bot. Mag.*, n.s., t. 286.

Native of China, in cultivation from seed collected by Wilson in W. Szechwan. It has been regarded as a variety of *B. aggregata*, from which it differs in its greater size and longer inflorescences. For a long time it was grown erroneously as *B. polyantha* (see below). It is a very fine species, remarkable for its large and abundant flower panicles. A particularly striking form was shown by E. H. M. Cox of Glendoick, Perthshire, in the autumn of 1953, when it received an Award of Merit. This plant is referred by Dr Ahrendt to var. *laxipendula* with which it agrees in its lax panicles and fruits larger than in the type, but, in fruit, the panicles are 6 to 12 in. in length. Mr Cox tells us: 'It comes into flower very late for a berberis, August, and the fruit does not colour before November. The best point, however, is the length of time the fruit hangs, till the end of January or early February; it is *never* touched by birds, however hard the weather. Our plants are from the original collection and are now 10 ft tall and about the same through, with very arching branches.'

var. LAXIPENDULA Ahrendt—Panicles somewhat pendulous, up to 4 in. long, usually less, and proportionately broader than in the type, and looser. Berries a little larger, with a longer style. Described from a plant growing at Kew, raised from Wilson 3152. Dr Ahrendt refers the A.M. plant (see above) to this variety.

var. RECURVATA Schneid.—This has the same garden value as the typical form, from which it differs only in its curved fruit stalks.

B. POLYANTHA Hemsl.—A semi-evergreen shrub 10 to 14 ft high, related to *B. prattii*, from which it differs in its dark red very narrowly ovoid fruits. It appears to be confined in a natural state to the region around Tatsienlu (Kangting) in W. Szechwan. It is also very rare in cultivation, the plants once grown under the name being *B. prattii*, but the true species is figured in *Bot. Mag.*, n.s., t. 236, from a plant growing at Maidwell Hall, Northants. The origin of the confusion between these two species is explained by Mr Sealy in the note accompanying this plate.

B. PRUINOSA Franch.

An evergreen shrub to 12 ft high; stems glabrous; spines three-parted, up to 1 in. long. Leaves three to five together in tufts, glabrous, leathery, 1 to 2½ in. long, oval or obovate, lustrous green above, often grey-white beneath, the apex and upper two-thirds set with slender, spiny teeth. Flowers variously arranged at each leaf-cluster, some being solitary on their stalks and in fascicles, others on an umbel 1 in. long; they are citron-yellow, and about the average size of barberry flowers. Fruit black, but covered with an abundant greyish bloom, ¼ in. long.

Introduced to France from Yunnan, China, by the Abbé Delavay in 1894, this species reached Kew three years later. It is a promising shrub, somewhat similar in general appearance to *B. glaucocarpa*, but quite distinct in the arrangement of its flowers. It commences to bloom at the end of April. It has reached a height of about 10 ft in the R.H.S. Garden at Wisley.

var. LONGIFOLIA Ahrendt—Leaves narrower than in the type, 2 to 3⅗ in. long, ⅖ to ⅘ in. wide. Berries slightly styled. Described from a cultivated plant which may, Dr Ahrendt suggests, be of hybrid origin.

B. REPLICATA W. W. Sm.

An evergreen shrub up to 4 or 5 ft high, with gracefully arching branches; devoid of down in all its parts; young shoots yellowish; spines three-parted, up to ⅝ in. long. Leaves in clusters of usually three to five, linear-oblong, made apparently narrower by the strongly recurved margins; spine-tipped and with a few teeth; 1 to 2 in. long; leathery, dark dull green above, whitish beneath. Flowers in clusters of three to ten, bright yellow, ¼ in. wide, each on its slender stalk ⅓ to ½ in. long. Fruit oblong, ⅜ in. long, red, finally purple-black. *Bot. Mag.*, t. 9076.

Native of S.W. Yunnan, China, in the valley of the Shweli river; discovered and introduced in 1917 by Forrest. This is a very pleasing evergreen in habit, in flower, and in fruit, easily recognised by its narrow leaves with recurved margins and whitish beneath—characters which distinguish it from its nearest ally, *B. sanguinea*. It appears to be quite hardy. The flowering season seems to be variable; the normal time apparently is April and May, but in a very mild winter and early spring it may bloom as soon as February.

B. TALIENSIS Schneid.—A dense evergreen shrub growing slowly to about 3 ft high. Leaves narrow, dark shining green; flowers greenish yellow in clusters of two to five. Fruits to ½ in. long, glaucous blue. It is closely allied to the preceding and was also introduced by Forrest.

B. × RUBROSTILLA Chittenden

This beautiful deciduous barberry was raised in the Royal Horticultural Society's garden at Wisley and was first exhibited on 7th November 1916 at the Horticultural Hall, Westminster, when it was awarded a First Class Certificate. It was raised from seed of *B. wilsoniae*, the result of hybridisation by insect agency with some other species, possibly *B. aggregata*. In foliage it bears considerable resemblance to *B. wilsoniae*, the leaves being oblanceolate, but they are, on the average, larger. Its remarkable beauty is in its fruits, which are borne two to four on a main-stalk ¼ in. long and hang from the branches in great profusion. Each berry is about ⅝ in. long, oblong-ovoid, and of a beautiful translucent coral-red.

Two excellent fruiting shrubs of the same type are 'CRAWLEYENSIS', raised by Messrs Cheal, with remarkably large fruits, and 'CHERRY RIPE', a seedling from it raised by Mrs Ahrendt of Stonefield, Watlington, Oxon., with almost round berries which are creamy white when young, becoming cherry-red. For other deciduous hybrids see *B. × carminea*.

B. SUBERECTA Ahrendt—A species of rather doubtful standing, raised by the late Harry White of Sunningdale Nurseries from seeds sent to him by the late J. C. Williams of Caerhays as "*B. dictyophylla* from the Tali Range" and said to have been collected by George Forrest in the period 1917–19. The plants were originally distributed as "the upright form of *B. rubrostilla*" and resemble that hybrid. Another species described from this batch of seed is *B. ambigua* Ahrendt.

B. SANGUINEA Franch.

An evergreen shrub 6 to 9 ft high, with glabrous, pale greyish branches armed with very slender three-forked spines, each fork up to 1½ in. long. Leaves in clusters of two to five, deep green, linear-lanceolate, tapering to a fine point, the margins armed with forward-pointing, spiny teeth; the leaf has a very short stalk, and is 1½ to 3 in. long and from ¼ to ⅖ in. wide. Flowers crowded in the leaf-axils at each joint, golden yellow, on reddish stalks of unequal length, the longest ¾ in. long. The outside of the sepals is reddish. Berries ⅜ in. long, scarlet, then blue-black.

Native of the mountains of Szechwan, China; discovered by the Abbé David in 1869 and first cultivated in Europe from seed sent by him to the garden of the Paris Museum; later raised by Maurice de Vilmorin from seed collected in all probability by the Abbé Farges. It is an elegant shrub; the specific name refers to the colour of the flower-stalks and sepals. The species is distinct in its narrow leaves and long, slender spines. I first saw it in 1904, in the nursery of Messrs Simon-Louis, near Metz, where it was apparently quite hardy.

A form introduced later by Wilson, and referred to *B. sanguinea* by Schneider, is considered by Dr Ahrendt to rank as a distinct species, which he has named B. PANLANENSIS. It differs in its smaller, more finely toothed leaves and larger greenish flowers, and was grown in gardens as *B. sanguinea* "*microphylla*". It is a slow-growing shrub of compact habit, to about 6 ft, with elegant foliage.

B. SARGENTIANA Schneid.

An evergreen shrub up to 6 ft high, forming thickets of erect stems; young shoots glabrous, reddish, becoming grey; armed with three-pronged spines that are ½ to 1¼ in. long, sharp and rigid, grooved beneath. Leaves narrowly elliptic or oblong-lanceolate, slender-pointed, 1½ to 5 in. long, ½ to 1¼ in. wide, edged with forward-pointing spiny teeth (sometimes double); dark green above, paler and distinctly veined on the undersides, quite glabrous on both surfaces. Flowers pale yellow, about ⅓ in. across, borne in stalkless clusters of two to six; petals broadly obovate, notched at the apex; individual flower-stalk up to ¾ in. long. Fruit black when ripe, broadly egg-shaped, ⅓ in. long.

Native of W. Hupeh, China; introduced by Wilson in 1907. It is allied to *B. hookeri* and similar in habit, but hardier. In the Arnold Arboretum it is described as the only evergreen barberry known to be hardy there. At Kew it has withstood, quite unaffected, weather which injured *B. hookeri*.

B. DUMICOLA Schneid.—This attractive species is closely related to the preceding but is smaller in stature, the flowers richer coloured and more numerous, and the berries bloomy.

B. SIBIRICA Pall.

A low, deciduous bush, usually 1½ to 2 ft high, with short, twiggy branches; young shoots glabrous, or minutely downy, angled; spines with three or five, sometimes nine or eleven, prongs, each ⅕ to ⅖ in. long, slender. Leaves produced in dense rosettes; small, obovate, ½ to 1 in. long, thin, with teeth directed outwards, and proportionately large. Flowers solitary, rarely in pairs, ½ in. across, bright yellow, drooping. Fruit dark red, obovoid, about ⅓ in. long.

Native of Siberia and Mongolia, where it grows in crevices of rocks and similar places. Resembling *B. aetnensis* in habit, it differs in its solitary flowers and much-divided spines. Pallas, the Russian traveller and naturalist, who introduced this shrub to cultivation in 1790, states that in Mongolia a decoction of the twigs is applied to the eyes as a charm, which recalls the virtues ascribed to *B. lycium* in eye affections by the natives of N. India.

B. SIEBOLDII Miq.

A deciduous shrub of rounded form, usually below 3 ft in height, with reddish branches armed with slender spines up to ½ in. long. Leaves thin, varying from narrowly obovate to oval, 1 to 2½ in. long, tapered at the base to a short stalk, the margins crowded with fine bristles. Flowers pale yellow, ⅓ in. across, in short umbel-like racemes. Fruit globose, about ⅕ in. across, yellowish red, shining as if glazed.

Native of Japan. It is an attractive small shrub of suckering habit, which colours well in the autumn if planted in a dry and sunny position. It is not common in cultivation, B. *regeliana* (q.v. under B. *vulgaris*) usually doing duty for it.

B. QUELPAERTENSIS Nakai—A native of Quelpaert Island (Cheju Do), which lies between Japan and Korea. It is closely allied to the preceding but Dr Ahrendt observes that in its yellow stems and more distinctly racemose inflorescence it tends towards B. *vulgaris*. It colours well in the autumn and the large crimson fruits are held from early autumn until the year's end. Introduced by Messrs Marchant.

B. DUBIA Schneid.—This native of Kansu and Mongolia is represented at Kew by an old plant of uncertain origin. It may have been raised from seed sent by the Russian explorer Przewalski to the St Petersburg Botanical Garden some ninety years ago. The species is related to B. *sieboldii*, but has coarsely spinose leaves and oblong berries.

B. SILVA-TAROUCANA Schneid.

A deciduous shrub up to 9 or 10 ft high; young shoots glabrous, distinctly grooved, reddish brown. Spines weak, single, ¼ in. or less long, often absent. Leaves obovate or oval, rounded at the end, tapering at the base to a slender stalk ¼ to 1 in. long; often without marginal teeth, sometimes with a few spiny teeth; blade ¾ to 2 in. long, ⅜ to 1 in. wide; distinctly net-veined and rather glaucous beneath. Flowers yellow, ¼ to ⅓ in. wide, produced eight to twelve together on racemes 1 to 2½ in. long, each on a slender stalk ¾ to ⅞ in. long. Fruit roundish egg-shaped, ⅖ in. long, scarlet.

Native of W. China; introduced to this country from the Arnold Arboretum in 1912, under the Wilson number 955. This barberry may usually be recognised by the following combination of characters: the long-stalked often toothless leaves; the weak, solitary, or often absent spines; and the rather long individual flower-stalks. It is quite hardy, grows freely, and has about the same garden value as B. *vulgaris*.

B. SOULIEANA Schneid.

B. *stenophylla* Hance, not Lindl.

An evergreen shrub up to 6 ft high, of stiff bushy habit; young shoots greyish, armed with yellowish, three-parted spines 1 to 1½ in. long, very stiff, hard and sharp. Leaves linear-oblong, narrowing towards the base, abruptly and sharply pointed, with ten to twelve slender teeth on each of the decurved margins; 1½ to 4 in. long, ¼ to ⅜ in. wide; veins indiscernible beneath. Flowers yellow, on stalks ⅓ in. or less in length, borne in clusters of about eight in the leaf-axils. Fruit globose, ¼ in. wide, black, covered with glaucous bloom, the conspicuous style adhering at the apex. Flowers in May.

Native of Central China; introduced to France in 1897, and first cultivated by Maurice de Vilmorin at Les Barres, afterwards put on sale by Lemoine of Nancy under the name of "*B. sanguinea*". It differs from the true *B. sanguinea* by its short flower-stalks and more formidable spines.

B. × STENOPHYLLA Lindl.

B. × *irwinii* Byhouwer

An evergreen bush 8 to 10 ft high, and as much through, consisting of a dense thicket of slender, interlacing stems arching towards the ends. Leaves numerous, in tufts about ⅓ in. apart on the shoots; hard, spine-tipped, 1 in. or so in length, ⅛ to ¼ in. wide, with incurved margins; deep green above, glaucous beneath. Flowers produced either in small fascicles or on short, few-flowered racemes, golden yellow, small, but very profusely borne. Berries globose, ¼ in. across, covered with blue-white bloom.

A hybrid which appeared in the nursery of Messrs Fisher & Holmes of Handsworth, near Sheffield, about 1860, its parents being *B. darwinii* and *B. empetrifolia*. It is perhaps the most beautiful and useful of all the barberries, and to the flower beauty of *B. darwinii* has united the greater hardiness of *B. empetrifolia*. The combination, moreover, has produced a grace of habit neither of the parents possesses. The bush forms an impenetrable mass of branches from out of which it throws every year slender, arching shoots 1 ft or more long. In the following April and May these are wreathed from end to end with rich golden-yellow flowers. A well-grown bush is one of the loveliest of all spring pictures, and is admirable in many positions; it makes a charming bush on a lawn, as a covering for a steep bank, and it may be used as a hedge plant, cutting it back immediately it has flowered. It is best propagated by cuttings put in very sandy soil under a bell-glass or in a frame in August. It ripens good seeds, but they rarely come true, reverting back more or less to one or other of the parents —generally to *B. darwinii*.

Many other forms of *B.* × *stenophylla* have been raised, which show the characters of the two parents in various combinations. The following is only a selection: 'COCCINEA' (dwarf, with prettily coloured buds and flowers); 'CORALLINA COMPACTA' and 'GRACILIS NANA' (both under 1 ft in height); 'CRAWLEY GEM' (prostrate, with wiry, arching branches, raised by Messrs Cheal); 'GRACILIS' (graceful habit, upright, to 4 ft high); 'PINK PEARL' (a sport with variegated leaves and round, pink flowers).

'IRWINII' was described as a distinct hybrid (*B.* × *irwinii* Byhouwer) but belongs to *B.* × *stenophylla*. It is a compact shrub to about 3 ft, inclining to *B. darwinii* in its foliage. Some other hybrids are near to *B. darwinii* and usually grown as varieties of that species, but all show to some degree the influence of

B. empetrifolia and belong properly to *B.* × *stenophylla*. Such are 'NANA' and 'PROSTRATA'.

B. SUBLEVIS W. W. Sm.

An evergreen shrub of sturdy habit from 5 to 7 ft high; shoots ribbed, glabrous, armed with three-pronged spines up to 1¼ in. long. Leaves varying from solitary to fascicles of six, 1½ to 3 in. long, ¼ to ½ in. wide, oblong-lanceolate, the base cuneate, the apex acute, spine-tipped, margins spiny, green beneath, glabrous. Flowers in close clusters of up to twelve, each on a slender stalk ½ to 1 in. long, fragrant, pale orange-yellow according to Forrest, ½ in. wide. Fruits small, deep red, ¼ in. or less long, narrowly oval.

Native of Yunnan, China, discovered by Forrest in 1912. It belongs to the *Wallichianae* section and has the characteristic dark green, more or less oblong leaves of that group. It was shown at Vincent Square on 9th March 1937 as "*B. wallichiana microcarpa*", carrying primrose-yellow flowers.

B. TEMOLAICA Ahrendt

A deciduous shrub to 8 ft high with stout, arching stems, glaucous when young but ageing to dark purple. Spines three-parted, about ⅖ in. long. Leaves oblong to obovate, ¾ to 1¾ in. long, tapered at the base into a very short stalk edged with a few spiny, spreading teeth or entire, dull glaucous green and slightly bloomy above, white beneath. Flowers solitary, pale yellow, on stalks about ½ in. long. Fruit red with a white bloom, egg-shaped to oblong, about ⅖ in. long.

This striking species was discovered by Kingdon Ward on the Temo La in the Tibetan province of Pome in 1924. It is also in cultivation (in its var. *artisepala* Ahrendt) from seed collected by Ludlow, Sherriff, and Taylor in the neighbouring Tsari district in 1938. It is an arresting sight in spring, when the blue and white of the young leaves and stems harmonise with the pale yellow flowers. It much resembles *B. dictyophylla* (q.v.) and is perhaps the finer shrub. The specific epithet is sometimes given wrongly as "*telomaica*".

B. temolaica, when first introduced, was quite widely distributed under the name "*B. mekongensis*" and may still be found under this label in older collections.

B. THUNBERGII DC.

A deciduous shrub, of very close, compact habit, from 3 to 8 ft high, with stiff, deeply grooved branches, and glabrous, reddish-brown bark. Leaves crowded in tufts along the branches (the tufts often ¼ to ½ in. apart), obovate or spathulate, ½ to 1¼ in. long, sometimes rounded at the apex, sometimes spine-tipped, never toothed. The thorns on the branches are about ½ in. long, almost invariably single, but occasionally three-pronged. Flowers ⅓ to ½ in. across, usually solitary in each tuft of leaves, but sometimes in pairs, each one borne on a slender stalk ½ in. long; sepals small, dull red; petals twice as long, pale yellow suffused with red. Berries bright red, ⅓ in. long. *Bot. Mag.*, t. 6646.

The first European to notice this barberry was Thunberg, who saw it in Japan in 1784, but it did not reach this country until about ninety years later. It has been found wild in China. Latterly it has become popular in gardens, owing to its neat, close habit, its handsome red fruits, but more than all for its brilliant red foliage in autumn. The flowers, although unusual in colour and freely borne, are not showy. In the suburbs of Boston, Mass., in the neighbourhood of the Arnold Arboretum, it thrives remarkably; I have measured bushes there 8 ft high and 15 ft across.

f. ATROPURPUREA (Chenault) Rehd.—Summer foliage in some shade of purplish or reddish brown. The original plant arose in the nursery of Messrs Renault (not Chenault) of Orleans around 1913 but was not distributed until about 1926. The raisers at first propagated this barberry vegetatively but later used seeds, by which means it seems to have been propagated ever since (Krüssmann in *Die Deutsche Baumschule*, Vol. 5, p. 143).

cv. 'ATROPURPUREA NANA'.—A bush with brownish red leaves, growing to about 2 ft high, raised by Messrs Van Eyck, Boskoop, Holland, 1942. A useful shrub for massing, which assorts well with heaths. It is a clone, and is also known as "Little Favourite".

var. MAXIMOWICZII (Reg.) Reg. *B. maximowiczii* Reg.—Branches more twiggy, with a purple bark. Leaves more purple, green beneath. The form distributed by Messrs Marchant has orange-red and yellow autumn colour.

cv. 'MINOR'.—A form of dwarf habit, with smaller leaves and flowers, which arose as a seedling in the Arnold Arboretum. Also known as *B. t. dawsonii.*

cv. 'ROSE GLOW'.—Leaves purple, variegated pink and white. Raised by Messrs Spaargen and Sons, Holland, around 1957 and introduced to this country in 1965.

In the United States, where *B. thunbergii* is more valued than it is here, a seed strain has been developed by Messrs Horvath of Mentor, Ohio, which is upright and intended for hedging (D. Wyman, *Shrubs and Vines for American Gardens*, 1961). It is known as *B. t. erecta*. The same firm has produced a very hardy hybrid between *B. thunbergii* and *B. julianae*, marketed as *B. mentorensis*.

B. TISCHLERI Schneid.

A deciduous shrub up to 8 or 12 ft high; young shoots reddish; spines three-pronged, yellowish, ½ to ¾ in. long. Leaves three to eight in a cluster, mostly obovate, usually finely and regularly toothed, but occasionally quite toothless; ½ to 2 in. long. Flowers yellow, three to ten on a drooping raceme 2 to 4 in. long, each on its slender stalk up to 1 in. long. Fruits oblong, ¾ in. long, red, covered with glaucous bloom, the style conspicuous at the end. Flowers in June.

Native of W. China; introduced by Wilson in 1904 under his W. 1731, but known earlier from specimens collected by the Russian explorer Potanin. It is quite hardy and a good grower, flowering and bearing fruit freely. It is related to *B. diaphana* but in that species the inflorescence is a fascicle or very condensed raceme with at the most five flowers. *B. consimilis* and *B. faxoniana* are related species, described by Schneider from plants growing in the Arnold Arboretum.

B. triacanthophora Fedde

An evergreen, glabrous shrub 5 to 6 ft high, of graceful spreading habit; young shoots round, reddish; spines three-parted, $\frac{5}{8}$ in. long. Leaves linear to oblanceolate, spine-tipped; 1 to 2 in. long, $\frac{1}{8}$ to $\frac{1}{4}$ in. wide; margins decurved, set with one to five slender teeth at each side; bright green above, more or less glaucous beneath. Flowers produced in clusters of usually three to five, each on its slender stalk $\frac{1}{2}$ to $1\frac{1}{8}$ in. long; very pale yellow or whitish, the petals tinged with red outside. Fruit oval, $\frac{1}{3}$ in. long, black, coated slightly with blue bloom.

Native of Central China; introduced by Wilson in 1907, or possibly earlier, as he collected specimens in W. Hupeh for Messrs Veitch in June 1900. It flowers with us in May and is quite hardy. The abundant spines and needle-tipped leaves render it very well armed. It varies in the glaucousness of the under-surface of the leaves. The colour of the flowers is rather indeterminate, but in habit of growth and as a fruit-bearer it is a handsome evergreen. It is closely akin to *B. sanguinea*, which is distinguished by its ribbed, yellowish-grey young shoots and shorter flower-stalks; also to *B. replicata*, which differs in its more strongly decurved leaf-margins, their more glaucous under-surface and shorter flower-stalks. It is also related to *B. gagnepainii*, but in that species the stems are yellowish and the leaves green beneath.

Dr Ahrendt has pointed out (*Gard. Chron.*, Vol. 105, p. 372, 1939) that what was distributed by Wisley as *B. triacanthophora* is not the true species, but a fine evergreen nonetheless. He has named these plants B. wisleyensis; they are, perhaps, hybrids with *B. gagnepainii* as the pollen parent.

B. tsarongensis Stapf

A deciduous, glabrous shrub 8 to 12 ft high; young shoots red turning to brown, armed with slender, simple or three-parted spines $\frac{1}{3}$ to $\frac{3}{4}$ in. long. Leaves in clusters usually of three to five, but varying from one to eight, $\frac{1}{2}$ to $1\frac{1}{8}$ in. long, mostly obovate to oblanceolate, rounded at the apex or pointed, entire or with one to four marginal spines often broad-based enough to constitute lobes. Flowers yellow, $\frac{1}{4}$ to $\frac{1}{3}$ in. wide in axillary clusters of up to eight; petals in two whorls of three, very concave; stalks slender, $\frac{1}{5}$ to $\frac{3}{5}$ in. long. Fruits ovoid, $\frac{3}{8}$ in. long, dark red, faintly bloomy. *Bot. Mag.*, t. 9332.

Native of N.W. Yunnan, China; introduced by Forrest in 1917. It flowered with the late Marquis of Headfort in May 1930, and is apparently quite hardy. The red young shoots and good crops of fruit are attractive.

B. umbellata G. Don

A deciduous or semi-evergreen shrub to 8 ft high; young growth red, maturing to reddish brown. Spines usually three-parted, up to $\frac{2}{3}$ in. long, but sometimes absent from parts of the stem. Leaves slightly lustrous above, waxy grey below, prominently net-veined on both sides, about $1\frac{1}{2}$ in. long and $\frac{3}{5}$ in. wide, obovate to oblanceolate, tapering abruptly to a short petiole; leaf-margins edged with spiny teeth. Flowers three to six together in a cluster on short umbellate raceme, borne in May. Berries oblong, $\frac{2}{5}$ in. long, dark red and bloomy. *Bot. Mag.*, n.s., t. 145.

Native of the Himalaya from Kumaon and Nepal. Although first described early in the nineteenth century this species long remained obscure; plants raised and distributed under the name usually proved to be some species of the Section *Tinctoriae*. However, around 1935 Dr Ahrendt, the well-known authority on the genus, received from Messrs Smith of Newry a plant which had originated from the German nursery firm of Späth. This proved to be the true species, and it is this plant that is figured in the *Botanical Magazine*.

B. VALDIVIANA Phil.

A sturdy evergreen shrub 8 to 12 ft high; shoots glabrous, formidably armed with stiff, three-pronged spines 1 to $1\frac{1}{2}$ in. long, but sometimes quite unarmed; spines grooved on the lower side. Leaves $\frac{3}{4}$ to 3 in. long, $\frac{1}{2}$ to $1\frac{1}{2}$ in. wide, oval to oval-oblong, the base cuneate to rounded, the apex abruptly narrowed to a mucro, varying from sparsely spiny-toothed to entire, glabrous, glossy; stalk $\frac{1}{4}$ in. or less long. Flowers saffron yellow, $\frac{3}{16}$ in. wide, borne twenty to thirty together densely on glabrous, pendulous racemes 1 to $1\frac{1}{2}$ in. long. Fruit roundish ovoid, $\frac{3}{16}$ in. long, purple, bloomy; stigma very prominent. *Bot. Mag.*, n.s., t. 139.

Native of Chile from Chillan to Valdivia province; described by Philippi in 1856. It was introduced to Kew in 1902, but the present stock is from seed collected by Clarence Elliott and the late Dr Gourlay near Temuco in 1929. Raised from their seed, it flowered in the Cambridge Botanic Garden in 1937 and was given an Award of Merit when shown by Lady Lawrence in 1939. Dr Gourlay had a plant 8 ft high in his garden at Cambridge; cut to the ground in the hard winter of 1946–7, it had by 1950 made a bush 6 ft high and as much wide. It was this plant that provided the material for the figure in the *Botanical*

BERBERIS VALDIVIANA

Magazine. It is very distinct in its usually unarmed, thick, leathery leaves and altogether a handsome evergreen that should be more widely grown.

B. VEITCHII Schneid.

B. *acuminata* Veitch, not Franch.

An evergreen shrub of open, spreading habit, with bright red young wood. Leaves two to four together in the axils of stout, three-parted spines, which are ¾ to 1 in. long; 3 to 6 in. long, narrowly lance-shaped, stalkless, glabrous, dark green; the margins cartilaginous, and armed with slender spiny teeth. Flowers brownish yellow, produced in clusters of four to eight from the leaf-axils of the previous year's shoots; each flower ¾ in. across, solitary on a slender stalk 1 to 1¼ in. long. Fruit oblong, nearly ½ in. long, black, covered with bluish bloom.

Discovered by the French missionary Delavay in Central China, in 1882, this fine barberry was not introduced to cultivation until 1900, when Wilson collected seeds in W. Hupeh. From these, plants were raised by Messrs Veitch at Coombe Wood, which flowered in 1904. The species is hardy, ornamental and distinct.

B. VERNAE Schneid.

B. *caroli* var. *hoanghensis* Schneid.

A deciduous shrub probably 6 to 10 ft high; young shoots grooved, glabrous, reddish brown by autumn; spines three-forked on the lower part of the shoot and ½ to 1⅛ in. long; at the terminal part of the shoot they are reduced to single, much smaller, needle-like spines. Leaves in clusters of about eight, varying in each cluster from ½ in. to 1¾ in. long and from ⅛ to ⅝ in. wide; oblanceolate or spathulate, rounded or abruptly pointed at the apex, tapered to the base; often quite entire, sometimes with a few bristle-like teeth, quite glabrous; stalks of the larger leaves ⅕ to ½ in. long. The inflorescence is a pendulous raceme 1 to 1¾ in. long, the flowers very crowded upon it, opening in May. They are bright yellow, small (about ⅙ in. wide), each borne on a stalk 1/12 to ⅛ in. long. Fruit salmon-red, globose, ⅕ in. wide. *Bot. Mag.*, t. 9089.

Native of Kansu and N.W. Szechwan, China; discovered in the former province by Purdom, introduced from the latter by Wilson in 1910 (No. 4022). It is a very distinct and pretty species. The pendent racemes come from each joint of the previous year's growth and are suspended along the shoot in a row. Although the flowers are small they are densely packed and brightly coloured and the effect is very graceful. The shrub is of vigorous growth and evidently very hardy. Wilson mentions having seen it in one place forming hedges. It is named in honour of Verna, daughter of Mr Berger, once of the La Mortola Garden, Ventimiglia. It reached a height of 8 ft and a spread of 12 ft at Headfort in Co. Meath.

B. VERRUCULOSA Hemsl. & Wils.

A sturdy, evergreen bush 4 to 6 ft high, very distinct on account of its branches being covered with dense, dark brown, tiny excrescences, which give the young bark a curiously rough surface. Stem-spines very slender, three-parted, ½ to ¾ in. long. Leaves dark lustrous green above, glaucous beneath; oval, tapering towards both ends; ½ to 1½ in. long, of leathery texture, margins recurved and set with a few spiny teeth. They are densely arranged in clusters or rosettes along the twigs. Flowers short-stalked, solitary or in small fascicles, golden yellow, ⅝ to ¾ in. across. Berries black covered with blue bloom, nearly ½ in. long, rather bottle-shaped. *Bot. Mag.*, t. 8454.

Discovered by Wilson in W. China and introduced by him in 1904. It makes a neat and compact evergreen, growing to about 6 ft high, and was given the Award of Garden Merit in 1929. It is closely related to *B. candidula* (q.v.).

B. VIRESCENS Hook. f.

An elegant, deciduous shrub 6 to 9 ft high; with glabrous, reddish-brown, shining branches, armed at each leaf-tuft with a slender, three-parted, or single spine up to ¾ in. long. Leaves ⅔ to 1¼ in. long, obovate, thin, pale but bright green; the apex rounded or tipped with a small spine, the margins toothed or entire. Flowers ⅓ in. diameter, pale greenish or sulphur yellow, and produced on slender, short stalks, either in panicles or short racemes. Berries slender, nearly ½ in. long, reddish, covered with bloom. *Bot. Mag.*, t. 7116.

Discovered by Sir Joseph Hooker, at an elevation of 9,000 ft, in Sikkim, in 1849, and introduced to Kew about the same time; this barberry was not given specific rank until described forty years after in the place quoted above. It is not one of the most attractive of barberries in regard to its flowers or fruit, but its habit is elegant, and the orange-red of its stems is pleasing in winter. There are two forms of this species at Kew, one, regarded as typical, with red fruits; the other, var. MACROCARPA Bean, with large black fruits ⅝ in. long. The latter is considered by Dr Ahrendt to be a distinct species, which he has described under the name B. PARAVIRESCENS.

B. VULGARIS L.   COMMON BARBERRY

A deciduous shrub, usually seen from 6 to 10 ft high, but occasionally more than twice as high; producing a crowded mass of stems erect at the base, branching and spreading outwards at the top into a graceful, arching, or pendulous form; branches greyish, grooved. Leaves in tufts from the axils of three-parted spines; thin, dull green, oval or obovate, 1 to 2 in. long, margined with fine teeth. Flowers in pendulous racemes 2 to 3 in. long, yellow. Berries egg-shaped, up to ½ in. long, bright red.

One of the best known of our native shrubs, the common barberry is found wild also over a large part of Europe, N. Africa, and temperate Asia. It was introduced to N. America, probably by early settlers, and is now naturalised there, more common in many places than the real American barberry (*B. canadensis*). It is one of the most attractive of all hardy shrubs, beautiful in blossom in May; perhaps even more so later in the year, when laden with heavy masses of coral-like berries. The berries are too acid to be palatable, even to birds, but at one time they were considered a wholesome delicacy, candied or preserved in sugar. According to the old herbalists the slightly acid leaves were once used to season meat with, and as a salad. A decoction of the bark and yellow wood was formerly celebrated as a remedy for jaundice. It is now discarded from the *Materia Medica*, but in many country places much faith in its virtues still exists.

In gardens, the barberry is useful on account of its accommodating nature and hardy constitution. It may be useful to fill up out-of-the-way corners or other such places, where its vigorous nature will enable it to grow and thrive, and hold its own without attention. But it is beautiful enough to deserve a more prominent position. It was planted at Kew on the top of the ha-ha wall that divides the gardens from the Thames, and nothing could be more beautiful than these plants in October, when the branches, drooping over the wall, were laden with masses of scarlet berries. But little now remains of this planting. Even on a lawn the common barberry will make a fine 'specimen' bush; more beautiful often than many rarer things so employed. The 'Cluster-cups' found on this barberry in spring and summer are the early condition of wheat rust (*Puccinia graminis*).

Innumerable varieties or minor forms of this barberry exist. No good purpose would be served by attempting to describe or even name them; a single sowing of seeds will sometimes produce variations quite as important, both botanically and horticulturally, as many of those to which long names have been given. The following deserve mention:

cv. 'ASPERMA'.—This remarkable variety produces berries without seeds and it is, in consequence, more valuable for preserves, etc., than the fertile type. The famous sweetmeats of Rouen, *confitures d'épine vinette*, are made from the fruits of this variety. It was grown in Britain from the seventeenth into the nineteenth century as a soft-fruit, and as a decorative berrying shrub was given an Award of Merit as late as 1937. It is said to bear larger and more abundant fruits than the type; the seedless fruits, according to early writers, are only produced on old plants. The earliest published name for this clone is *B. v. enuclea* (Weston, in *Flora Anglicana*, 1775) but the one given above is better known and to be preferred.

Loudon also mentions a sweet-fruited form of the common barberry under the name var. *dulcis*, said to occur in Austria.

cv. 'ATROPURPUREA'.—Leaves deep purple; one of the handsomest of wholly purple shrubs. The name is not appropriate to seedling plants, which came in various shades of purple and reddish purple.

cv. 'VARIEGATA'.—Leaves margined with yellow. Described by Nicholson in *Garden*, Vol. 35, 1889, p. 265. This is perhaps the same clone as 'Aureomarginata', a name published by Regel in 1869.

Forms of the common barberry with white or yellow fruits are known, but the black- and purple-fruited kinds mentioned in old literature probably belong not to *B. vulgaris* but to other species in which the berries are typically of that colour.

B. vulgaris is a parent of several garden hybrids, of which the following are the best known:

B. × LAXIFLORA Schrad.—To this group belong some garden plants that combine in various ways the characters of *B. vulgaris* and *B. chinensis* and are probably hybrids between them. According to Dr Ahrendt, the cultivar 'BRILLIANT' is of this parentage; he considers that, as a berrying shrub, it surpasses the common barberry and might replace it in gardens.

B. × OTTAWENSIS Schneid.—A group of hybrids between *B. vulgaris* and *B. thunbergii*, inclining towards the former in their yellow stems and brightly coloured berries but nearer to the latter in leaf and the clustered or umbel-like inflorescence. The original plants were the result of a deliberate cross made at the Ottawa Experimental Station early in this century, but similar hybrids have occurred spontaneously in gardens. Several forms have been named, of which the best known is 'SUPERBA', raised by the Dutch nursery firm of Ruys. It is a vigorous shrub with bronzy-red leaves, growing to 8 ft or so high; autumn colour crimson. Sometimes offered as "*B. thunbergii atropurpurea superba*".

B. AMURENSIS Rupr. *B. vulgaris* var. *amurensis* Reg.—This species, sometimes regarded as a geographical form of the common barberry, differs in the much larger leaves, which are often 3½ to 4 in. long, and 1½ to 2 in. wide, perhaps the largest of all true barberry leaves. They are thin in texture, as in *B. vulgaris*, but the toothing is proportionately closer and finer. Racemes 3 in. long, with flowers like those of *vulgaris* but rather larger, followed by large oblong berries. It has stouter stems than *vulgaris*, flowers rather earlier, and the petals are slightly notched. Native of Amurland.

B. REGELIANA Schneid. *B. amurensis* var. *japonica* Reg.—Undersides of the leaves grey, but otherwise much like *B. amurensis*. It has been confused with *B. sieboldii* but is a taller shrub than that species, with more angled branches, and the fruit is distinct in being of a bright rosy carmine, covered with a bluish bloom, and of oblong or oval shape.

B. WILSONIAE Hemsl.

An elegant, deciduous (sometimes partially evergreen) shrub 3 to 4 ft high, of spreading habit, and usually more in diameter; branches comparatively thin, reddish brown, slightly downy, armed with slender three-parted spines, ½ to ¾ in. long, and red when young. Leaves as a rule less than 1 in. long, mostly oblanceolate, and either rounded or sharply pointed at the apex, otherwise entire, or occasionally three-lobed at the apex; glabrous, conspicuously veined, grey-green above, somewhat glaucous beneath. Flowers small, pale yellow, borne two to six together in fascicles or short racemes. Berries roundish, coral- or salmon-red, somewhat translucent, borne very abundantly. *Bot. Mag.*, t. 8414.

Native of W. China; discovered and introduced about 1904 by E. H. Wilson, after whose wife it was named. This is one of the most charming introductions from W. China, of neat yet elegant habit, and most noteworthy for its prettily coloured, abundant berries and autumnal tints.

B. *wilsoniae* and its allies have contributed to the complex swarm of hybrids discussed under B. × *carminea* and B. × *rubrostilla*. Two seedlings which are near to the species in their botanical characters may be mentioned here. They are 'COMET', exceptionally profuse in berry, and the dwarf 'TOM THUMB', which makes a charming rock garden shrub, with vivid autumn foliage.

var. STAPFIANA (Schneid.) Schneid. B. *stapfiana* Schneid.—A shrub with gracefully arching branches, differing from the type in its taller growth (to about 5 ft high) and its glabrous twigs. Leaves oblanceolate, acute or obtuse or rounded at the apex, but always with a mucronate tip, $\frac{1}{2}$ to 1 in. long, $\frac{1}{12}$ to $\frac{3}{16}$ in. wide. Fruit ellipsoid. *Bot. Mag.*, t. 8701.

Native of W. China. According to Schneider's account it was introduced to Kew from Maurice de Vilmorin's collection at Les Barres, but there appears to have been an earlier introduction from St Petersburg in 1896, possibly from seed collected by Potanin in 1893. It is also in cultivation from Wilson's seed distributed by the Arnold Arboretum in 1909. A charming shrub of free, graceful growth.

var. SUBCAULIALATA (Schneid.) Schneid. B. *subcaulialata* Schneid.—This variety, like the preceding, differs from the type in the glabrous shoots, but the fruits are globose, ripening in November, and the leaves larger than in var. *stapfiana*. Introduced to the Vilmorin collection at Les Barres by the French missionary Soulié; and to this country by Wilson under W. 1267. The plants distributed by Veitch under the name B. *coryi* are usually considered to belong to var. *subcaulialata*. In 1938 Dr Yü re-introduced this variety; the very similar var. GUHTZUNICA (Ahrendt) Ahrendt was introduced by him at the same time.

B. YUNNANENSIS Franch.

A deciduous shrub 3 to 6 ft high, of dense, rounded habit, with grey, grooved branchlets, armed with three- or five-parted spines up to 1 in. long. Leaves obovate, sometimes almost orbicular, $\frac{3}{4}$ to $1\frac{1}{2}$ in. long, $\frac{1}{3}$ to $\frac{2}{3}$, rarely 1 in. wide, rounded or pointed at the apex, tapering to a stalk at the base; margins mostly entire on the flowering twigs, more often toothed on the sterile ones. Flowers pale yellow, three to eight in a cluster; $\frac{3}{4}$ in. across; flower-stalks slender, $\frac{3}{4}$ to $1\frac{1}{4}$ in. long. Berries oval, bright red, $\frac{1}{2}$ in. long.

Native of W. China; first discovered in Yunnan by Delavay in 1885, at an altitude of 10,000 ft. It reached cultivation by way of France, and was introduced to Kew in 1904. It is a pretty shrub, and is distinct in regard to the size of its flowers and fruit, both of which are amongst the largest in the genus. It is also one of the most beautiful in its autumn livery of crimson.

B. ZABELIANA Schneid.

A deciduous shrub of compact habit, attaining a height of 6 ft in the wild; stems pale yellow when mature. Leaves oblong-elliptic, 1 to 3 in. long, $\frac{3}{4}$ to $1\frac{1}{2}$ in.

wide, net-veined and green on both sides, but slightly glaucous beneath when young. Flowers rather small, in short, dense racemes. Berries oblong to obovoid, purple-red.

A native of Kashmir, where it forms thickets on open mountain-sides, and also of Afghanistan. It bears some resemblance to B. *vulgaris* but its closest affinity appears to be with such E. Asiatic species as B. *dasystachya*.

BERCHEMIA   RHAMNACEAE

A genus of deciduous, unarmed climbers or shrubs, with alternate leaves prominently and numerously parallel-veined. Flowers small, with five sepals and five petals, and not ornamental. Fruit fleshy, with a two-celled stone. Five species have been introduced: one American, the others Asiatic. They like a good, moist soil and can be propagated by cuttings. Allied to *Zizyphus* and *Paliurus*, both of which differ in having three-nerved leaves.

B. FLAVESCENS Brongn.

A climbing, deciduous shrub 6 to 10 ft high, the shoots slender, smooth or with dark outstanding hairs. Leaves 2 to 6 in. long, 1 to 2¾ in. wide, rounded or broadly tapered at the base, narrowed at the apex to a short tip, glabrous, and rather metallic green above, pale and either glabrous or with a slight down on the midrib and lower ribs beneath; ribs parallel, nine to sixteen pairs; stalk ½ to 1 in. long. Flowers white, ⅙ in. across, produced in pyramidal panicles 1½ to 4 in. long, terminal on the leafy shoots of the year; flower-stalks ⅛ to ⅙ in. long, either smooth or hairy. Fruit sausage-shaped, ⅓ in. long.

Native of the Himalaya, Tibet, and W. China; introduced from the last-named by Wilson in 1904 and appears to be quite hardy.

B. GIRALDIANA Schneid.

A deciduous scandent shrub up to 20 ft high, or dwarfer and of spreading habit, producing arching slender shoots several feet long in a season; young shoots glabrous, at first covered with a glaucous bloom, ultimately of a dark, shining, reddish brown. Leaves glabrous or slightly downy beneath, ovate-oblong, rounded, or slightly heart-shaped at the base, pointed, entire; 1 to 2½ in. long, ½ to 1½ in. wide; dark dull green above, rather glaucous beneath; veins in nine to thirteen pairs, parallel, running out to the margin unbranched; stalk ¼ to ¾ in. long. Flowers white, small, produced at the end of leafy shoots in a terminal pyramidal panicle, supplemented by smaller axillary ones, the whole 8 in. or more long. Fruits sausage-shaped, ⅓ in. long, at first red, finally black.

Native of China, in the provinces of Hupeh, Szechwan, and Shensi; discovered in the last-named by Giraldi. It is considered to be most nearly related to *B. racemosa*. It was introduced to Kew from Les Barres in France and is noticeable for its bright red-brown young shoots, graceful habit, and the numerous parallel veins of the leaves.

B. LINEATA DC.

A deciduous climbing shrub of elegant growth; young shoots finely downy. Leaves oval, often inclined to ovate, $\frac{1}{4}$ to $1\frac{1}{4}$ in. long, $\frac{1}{8}$ to $\frac{5}{8}$ in. wide, rounded at the base, often also at the apex except for the mucronate tip; dark green above, pale beneath, but distinctly and prettily marked with four to six parallel veins running out from the midrib to the margin; stalk very short. Flowers white, $\frac{3}{16}$ in. long, produced in terminal clusters and in the terminal leaf-axils of slender, lateral, often short twigs, each flower on a slender stalk $\frac{1}{8}$ to $\frac{1}{4}$ in. long; sepals erect, linear, enclosing the other parts. Fruit a cylindrical or oval drupe, $\frac{3}{16}$ to $\frac{1}{4}$ in. long, blue-black when ripe.

Native of China, Formosa, N. India. An elegant climber, very distinct in its abundant, parallel-veined leaves and its tiny blue fruits.

B. RACEMOSA Sieb. & Zucc.

A deciduous, twining shrub, with flexible, round, glabrous stems. Leaves ovate with a heart-shaped base, $1\frac{1}{2}$ to 3 in. long, half as much wide, entire, rather pale or glaucous beneath; veins in seven to nine pairs, parallel. Flowers in a terminal, pyramidal panicle 2 to 6 in. long; very small, greenish, produced in late summer. Fruit oblong, $\frac{1}{4}$ in. long, changing from green to red, then to black.

Native of Japan, where it forms a spreading, tangled shrub, rather than a genuine climber, but in cultivation it has reached a height of 40 ft when planted under trees. The foliage is neat and pretty, and when the plant is furnished with its handsome fruits it is both striking and attractive. But it does not produce them with regularity, and I have never seen it so good in this country as at Les Barres, in Central France, where it bears fruit abundantly. It is hardier and a better plant than *B. scandens*. A variegated form is in cultivation, whose leaves, especially towards the end of the shoot, are more creamy white than green.

B. SCANDENS (Hill) K. Koch   SUPPLE JACK
Rhamnus scandens Hill; *R. volubilis* L. f.; *B. volubilis* (L. f.) DC.

A deciduous climber, with glabrous, twining branches, growing 10 to 15 ft high (much higher in milder climates). Leaves glabrous, oval, $1\frac{1}{2}$ to 3 in. long, not heart-shaped but usually rounded, or broadly wedge-shaped at the base, the apex ending in a bristle-like point, the margins wavy; veins nine to twelve pairs. Flowers small, greenish white, arranged in racemes 1 to 2 in. long, terminating short, side twigs, and in a terminal panicle. Fruits oblong, ⅓ in. long, dark blue, or almost black.

Native of the southern United States; introduced in 1714. It does not fill an important place in English gardens, owing to its flowers having little beauty, and its fruits being rarely seen. From the commoner Japanese species it differs in the shape of the leaves, the more numerous veins, and in the smaller inflorescence. It is also a genuine climber, its stems twisting round each other, or anything of convenient size within reach. Not so hardy as *B. racemosa*.

BESCHORNERIA AMARYLLIDACEAE

A genus of about ten species, natives of Mexico, allied to *Furcraea* and *Agave*.

B. YUCCOIDES K. Koch

An evergreen plant with a low, thick, semi-woody stem or root-stock, bearing a rosette of radiating leaves in the same fashion as a yucca. Leaves stalkless, 1½ to 2½ ft long, 2 to 3½ in. wide, of somewhat lanceolate shape, sharply pointed, dilated at the sheathing base, rather glaucous, margins and under-surface rough. Flowers green, opening from June onwards on a stout, arching, red, branching scape, 4 to 6 ft long and 1 to 2 in. in diameter at the base. Towards the top the scape produces short drooping branches, each springing from the axil of a red bract and bearing three to five quite pendulous flowers. Each flower is about 2 in. long, the basal part consisting of a cylindrical ovary ¾ in. long, the terminal part of the cylinder-like perianth carrying six linear segments 1¼ in. long. Fruit fig-shaped, about 2 in. long. *Bot. Mag.*, t. 5203.

Native of Mexico; introduced some time previous to 1859, probably by Lord Ilchester. For a long time nothing was known of its origin, but early in the twentieth century the American botanist Pringle found it growing wild in the mountains above Pachuca, Mexico. It is not hardy at Kew but succeeds well nearer the south coast if planted at the foot of a south wall. Even at Cambridge, in the University Botanic Garden, planted against a greenhouse wall and covered every winter, it has borne flower-spikes 6 ft tall and is still grown there (1966). In the extreme south and west it is very fine and even grows well as far north as Inverewe in Wester Ross.

The flowers hang rather like fuchsias and their green colouring forms a not unpleasing contrast with the beautiful, rather rhubarb-like red of the main and secondary flower-stalks and bracts. It should be planted in good loam, well drained, and given the sunniest spot available. In its one known wild habitat it grows on a steep, rocky slope in a region where the winters are dry, which suggests that a soggy soil in winter may be as antagonistic to it as frost.

BETULA BIRCH BETULACEAE

The birches are deciduous trees and shrubs with alternate leaves and uni-sexual flowers produced on catkins, both male and female catkins being borne on the same tree. The male catkins are slender and pendulous, nearly always formed in autumn, but expanding in spring; the flower con-sists of a perianth and two stamens; they are produced in threes in the axil of a scale. Female catkins shorter, stiffer; the flowers consisting of an ovary with two styles, produced (also in threes) in the axil of a deciduous three-lobed scale. What is here (and commonly) called the seed, is really a tiny nut containing the true seed. It bears a transparent wing at each side, and usually the remains of the two styles at the top. The only other genus of trees with which the birches are likely to be confused are the alders, and they are readily distinguished by the persisting scales of the female catkin, which does not disintegrate like that of the birches, but falls away whole.

Two of the best-known features of the birches are the peculiar bark and frequently white trunks. The bark can often be separated in thin, papery layers, and being impervious to water, is used in other countries for canoe-building and for roofing. The timber, although not as a rule of the best, is put to various minor uses. Some of the Asiatic and American species, however, yield wood of considerable value. An aromatic prin-ciple pervades many of the birches, and a fragrant oil is obtained.

As garden trees the birches are chiefly valued for their striking trunks and graceful branches. The silvery-white trunk of the native *B. pendula*, the creamy-white to pinkish trunks of such species as *B. papyrifera*, *jacquemontii*, and *ermanii* provide some of the most delightful of winter effects. Just as striking, but more rarely seen in gardens, are the rich mahogany or cinnamon hues of the stems of *B. utilis* and *B. albo-sinensis*. The rugged trunks of *B. nigra* and *davurica* always attract attention, and the darker-coloured ones of *B. lutea* and *maximowiczii* are not without their charm. On the whole, no birch exceeds our native *B. pendula* in beauty, not only for its trunk, but in the singular lightness and delicate grace of its branching also. Most people will agree with the oft-quoted words of Coleridge, that it is

'most beautiful
Of forest trees, the Lady of the Woods.'

The young branches and twigs of many birches have a rich red-brown or orange-brown tint, which makes an admirable contrast in winter with such as have white trunks.

So far as I have seen, the birches thrive best on a deep, well-drained loam, and I do not know of any that object to it. But some species, like *B. pendula* and *populifolia*, are amongst the best trees for poor, sandy soils. The river birch, *B. nigra*, thrives well with its roots within reach of water, and is perhaps the handsomest birch to plant where the water-table is high. Others that will grow in such situations are *B. pubescens, nana, glandulosa,* and *pumila.*

Whenever possible the birches should be raised from seed, which most of them develop in plenty. It should be sown on the surface of fine soil, and not buried but simply pressed down. An old and good plan when the seed is sown out-of-doors is to cover it until it germinates with a thin layer of brushwood, which gives shade and shelter and protects it from interference by birds, etc.

The common birches are attacked by a gall-producing insect, *Phytoptus rudis,* which causes an abnormal swelling of the leaf-buds, and distorted, stunted growths.

B. ALBO-SINENSIS Burk. [PLATE 19

B. bhojpattra var. *sinensis* Franch.; *B. utilis* var. *sinensis* (Franch.) Winkler

A deciduous tree 60 to 90 ft high, with a trunk 6 to 11 ft in girth, the bark described by Wilson as 'bright orange to orange-red, peeling off in very thin sheets, each successive sheet covered with white glaucous bloom', young shoots slightly glandular, becoming dark brown and smooth except for scattered warts. Leaves ovate, slenderly pointed, rounded at the base, unevenly and jaggedly toothed, ultimately glabrous but hairy between the veins when young, 2 to 3 in. long, 1 to 1½ in. wide; veins in nine to fourteen pairs; stalk ¼ to ½ in. long, at first silky. Male catkins 1½ to 2½ in. long; female catkins 1 to 1½ in. long, ⅛ in. wide, produced usually solitarily, sometimes in pairs; scales of the female catkins three-lobed, glabrous; side lobes roundish; middle one linear-oblong, pointed, twice as long as, but narrower than the side lobes.

Native of W. China; introduced by Wilson in 1901 for Veitch, under W. 1157, collected in W. Hupeh, but the oldest trees appear to be from W. 4106, sent in 1910 from W. Szechwan. It is also in cultivation from later sendings by other collectors. This birch is well worth growing for its beautiful trunk. 'Its orange peeling papery bark, shining like burnished copper, leaves behind it a creamy, glaucous bloom that puts one in mind of a similar effect obtained from that rare maple *Acer griseum.*' (C. Coltman Rogers, *Journ. R.H.S.,* Vol. 53, Jan. 1928, p. 61.)

var. SEPTENTRIONALIS Schneid.—This variety was described from specimens collected by Wilson in the extreme west of Szechwan, in the Tapao Shan, and is also found in Shensi and Kansu. 'Bark orange-brown or orange to yellowish orange or orange-grey.... Singularly beautiful and makes the tree conspicuous in the forest' (Wilson). He introduced it from the type locality in 1908 under W. 900 and it is also in cultivation from seed collected by Purdom and by Rock. It is distinguished from the type by the following characters: leaves oblong-ovate rather than ovate; young shoots more distinctly glandular; leaves silky on the veins beneath and with prominent tufts of hair in the axils. It is possible that this variety merges into the type through intermediates.

B. albo-sinensis is closely allied to *B. utilis* but differs in its glabrous branchlets, and in its leaves, which are generally ovate-oblong, and hence narrower than in *B. utilis,* thinner in texture, with less prominent veins. In the type, the leaves are also glabrous beneath, but var. *septentrionalis* approaches *B. utilis* in having the veins silky beneath and glandular (but not hairy) branchlets.

This beautiful birch and its variety are not common in gardens but the following have been recorded (all measurements 1966): Werrington Park, Cornwall, from W. 4106, 50 × 5¾ ft at 3½ ft, on a short trunk, 42 × 3¾ ft, and 40 × 3½ ft; Westonbirt, Glos., one in the Circular Drive, *pl.* 1938, 39 × 1½ ft, and another in the Victory Glade, 61 × 3¼ ft; Bodnant, Denbigh, 50 × 3 ft, and another from Rock's seed, 35 × 3 ft; Caerhays Castle, Cornwall, 40 × 3½ ft at 4½ ft, on a short trunk, probably from W. 4106; Glendoick, Perths., a tree from Wilson's seed, about 35 ft high, on a clean 14-ft stem (blown down while this edition was in the press). In the Edinburgh Botanic Garden there are specimens 14 to 25 ft high under the following numbers: Forrest 19505, Yü 14547, Rock 15083 and 13648, and Purdom 752 (the last is var. *septentrionalis*).

B. CHINENSIS Maxim.

B. exalata S. Moore

A deciduous shrub usually up to 10 ft high, occasionally a small tree 12 to 30 ft high; bark greyish, young shoots silky-hairy. Leaves ovate, pointed, rounded at the base, jaggedly toothed; 1 to 2 in. long, half to two-thirds as much wide; veins in seven to ten pairs; upper surface dull dark green, sprinkled with silky hairs; silky-hairy beneath, mostly on the veins; stalk ⅙ to ¼ in. long, silky. Female catkins roundish oval, ½ to ¾ in. long, the scales of which are lanceolate in main outline but with three forward-pointing, narrow, linear lobes, the side ones much the shorter, all edged with minute hairs.

Native of N. China, Korea, and Japan; introduced to Kew from the Arnold Arboretum in 1920. It is shrubby in growth, about 11 ft high at Kew after thirty-five years, and it is as a shrub that it was often noted in a wild state by Wilson, Purdom, and other collectors. But a plant raised from W. 10707 has obtained 20 × 1½ ft in the Edinburgh Botanic Garden (1968). In addition to the neat, densely shrubby form, it is distinct on account of the very slender ciliate lobes of the scales of the seed-bearing catkins.

B. COERULEA-GRANDIS Blanch.   BLUE BIRCH

B. coerulea var. *grandis* Blanch.; *B. coerulea* var. *blanchardii* Sarg.

A small tree to about 35 ft high, with a white bark; young shoots warty and glabrous. Leaves 2 to 3 in. long, ovate to triangular-ovate, rounded, cuneate or truncate at the base, shortly tapered at the apex, sharply and irregularly toothed, dull green above, glabrous beneath, with up to eight pairs of veins. Female catkins cylindric, 1 to 1½ in. long and about ⅖ in. wide, short-stalked; lateral lobes of scales spreading, longer than the terminal one; wings of nutlets deeply notched.

A native of eastern N. America from Nova Scotia to Vermont. It resembles *B. populifolia*, but in that species the leaves are more finely tapered at the apex and the margins sharply double-toothed. There are two specimens of this birch at Westonbirt, planted in 1934, the taller 47 × 1¾ ft (1965) and another at Hergest Croft, Heref., 45 × 6 ft (1961).

B. × COERULEA Blanch.—The status of this tree is uncertain. It is agreed that it is of hybrid origin, with *B. populifolia* as one parent. The other parent is either *B. coerulea-grandis* or *B. papyrifera*. It differs from *B. populifolia* in having the undersides of the leaves hairy on the midrib and main veins, and from *B. coerulea-grandis* in its smaller leaves (to about 2¼ in. long), wedge-shaped at the base.

B. CORYLIFOLIA Reg. & Maxim.

A deciduous tree up to 60 or 70 ft high, with a greyish-white bark; young shoots glabrous except for a few hairs when quite young, dark purplish brown, with pale scattered warts. Leaves ovate-elliptical, often inclined to obovate, truncate to widely tapered at the base, pointed, coarsely and triangularly (sometimes doubly) toothed; 1½ to 3 in. long, 1 to 2 in. wide; glabrous above, slightly glaucous and silky-hairy on the midrib and veins beneath; veins in ten to thirteen pairs; stalk ⅛ to ⅝ in. long, silky-hairy when young. Male catkins slender, about 2 in. long. Female catkins 1½ to 2 in. long, ⅝ in. wide, cylindrical; scales deeply three-lobed, the lobes linear and erect, the middle one twice as long as the side ones, silky-hairy especially towards the tip. The seeds have narrow wings.

Native of the main island of Japan. There have been several birches grown in gardens under this name at different times, but most of them wrongly. Yet the true thing is very distinct, especially in the large, triangular, often incurved teeth of the leaves, their rather glaucous under-surface, and the very narrow ciliate lobes of the fruiting scales. Coming from high altitudes, it is very hardy. There is an authentic example at Edinburgh, raised from seed collected by Wilson for the Arnold Arboretum in 1914.

B. DAVURICA Pall.

A tree 60 ft or more high in nature, the trunk clothed with curling flakes of papery bark, giving it a curious, ragged appearance; bark at first warm brown; young shoots sparsely downy, thickly covered with glandular warts. Leaves ovate, 2 to 4 in. long, 1½ to 3 in. wide; broadly wedge-shaped or almost straight across at the base, pointed, coarsely and unequally toothed; dark green and glabrous above, downy beneath along the midrib. Veins six to eight pairs; leaf-stalk about ½ in. long.

Native of Manchuria, N. China, and Korea; introduced to Kew by Dr Bretschneider in 1882, but not a species of much promise, having a failing common to trees of this region in starting early into growth and being cut back by frost. In upland country it would, no doubt, thrive better. In the curious ruggedness of its bark it resembles *B. nigra*. The present example at Kew is twenty-five years old and about 25 ft high; it is reasonably hardy.

B. ERMANII Cham.

A tree said to become 100 ft high; bark of the trunk peeling, creamy or pinkish white; that of the branches orange-brown; young shoots not downy, but with numerous glandular warts; buds nearly ½ in. long, viscid, slender-pointed. Leaves broadly ovate, with a straight or slightly heart-shaped base, taper-pointed, coarsely triangular-toothed; 2 to 3 in. long, 1½ to 2¼ in. broad; freely specked with glands on both surfaces, and nearly glabrous except for hairs on the midrib, veins, and vein-axils beneath; veins in seven to eleven pairs; stalk ½ to 1 in. long, warted. Fruiting catkins barrel-shaped, 1 to 1¼ in. long, ½ to ⅝ in. wide, the three lobes of the scales broadest at the rounded ends.

A native of E. Asia from the Kamchatka peninsula through Pacific Russia to Korea, Japan, and Manchuria, and westward in Siberia as far as Lake Baikal. In favourable habitats it grows to 75 ft or more high, but becomes shrubby at high altitudes and near the northern end of its range, and is capable of colonising thin and poor soils—hence the Russian name for it, which means 'rock birch'. The bark varies in colour from white to grey or pale pinkish brown, and peels in thin sheets. According to Wilson, who studied this birch during his visit to Japan in 1914, it usually divides into several stems near the base, but develops a clean trunk and narrow crown when crowded.

This birch is extremely variable in shape, size, and toothing of leaf. The var. SUBCORDATA (Reg.) Koidz., as interpreted by Schneider, is really a miscellany of Japanese and mainland forms which have little in common except that they differ in one respect or another from the type. However, one variety (included by Schneider in var. *subcordata*) appears to be distinct. This is:

var. JAPONICA (Shirai) Koidz. *B. bhojpattra* var. *japonica* Shirai; *B. nikoense* Koidz.—Leaves triangular-ovate, with fourteen or fifteen pairs of veins, base more or less truncate. Scales of fruit-catkins with a narrow middle lobe and spreading lateral lobes. Found on the main island of Japan.

The first introduction of *B. ermanii*, towards the end of the last century, probably came from the mainland of N.E. Asia, and like so many plants from that region was very subject to injury by late frosts at Kew, owing to its early start into growth. A later introduction, probably from Japan, has proved hardier, and is represented at Kew by a specimen about 55 ft high. Perhaps the finest example of this species grows at Grayswood Hill, Surrey; it is 63 ft high and divides at the base, where it is 11½ ft in girth (1966); the provenance of the seed is not known.

B. COSTATA Trautv.—A native of N.E. Asia, bearing some resemblance to *B. ermanii* but differing in the narrower ovate leaves, which are also more markedly wedge-shaped (or rounded) at the base and longer-pointed at the apex; and in the ellipsoid to almost globular fruit-catkins. The leaves have ten to fourteen pairs of lateral veins, a character that further serves to distinguish this species from the continental forms of *B. ermanii*; Japanese representatives of *B. ermanii* may have up to fourteen or fifteen vein-pairs but differ from *B. costata* in the other characters mentioned.

B. FORRESTII (W. W. Sm.) Hand.-Mazz.

B. delavayi var. *forrestii* W. W. Sm.

A small tree to 40 or 50 ft, or a shrub, with a smooth, brown bark. Leaves with nine to fourteen pairs of veins, ovate or oblong-ovate, up to 3 in. long, obtuse or somewhat rounded at the apex, silky on the upper surface and on the veins beneath; leaf-stalk to ⅓ in. long. Fruiting catkins ⅘ to 1⅕ in. long; scales edged with silky hairs, the lateral lobes making a narrowly acute angle with the middle one and about one-third as long.

A native of Yunnan; discovered by Forrest in the Lichiang range in 1910. In the Edinburgh Botanic Garden there is an example 20 ft high from F. 15357, collected in 1918, and two others, 20 and 25 ft high, raised from seed sent by the Chinese collector Yü around 1937 (10561). These latter, Dr Fletcher tells us, are remarkable for their smooth, polished-looking, purplish-brown bark.

B. GLANDULOSA Michx.

A shrub procumbent at high elevations, rarely more than 4 ft high anywhere; young shoots not downy, but covered with glands. Leaves obovate to roundish- or kidney-shaped, usually ⅓ to ¾ in. (sometimes over 1 in.) long, green and glabrous both sides, conspicuously round-toothed; stalks up to ¼ in. long. Fruiting catkins erect, ½ to ¾ in. long.

Native of N. America, where it reaches across the continent at high latitudes and high altitudes; also of Greenland. It is closely allied to, and can only be confused with, B. *nana* (q.v.), but is abundantly distinct in its glandular-warted branchlets and longer-stalked leaves. It occupies similar moist positions in nature, and may be planted in similar positions in gardens.

B. GLANDULIFERA (Reg.) Butler B. *pumila* var. *glandulifera* Reg.—This closely allied species is distinguishable by its hairy, sparingly glandular branchlets. Native mainly of Canada.

B. GLOBISPICA Shirai

A deciduous tree to 70 ft high in the wild, with a greyish-white bark peeling in papery flakes; branchlets yellowish grey or greyish brown. Leaves broad ovate, 1¾ to 2¾ in. long, with eight to ten pairs of veins, abruptly tapered at the apex to a blunt point and with a wedge-shaped or rounded base; margins sharply and coarsely toothed; downy beneath on the midrib and main veins. Fruit-bearing catkins ovoid to globose, 1 to 1½ in. long; lobes of scales very narrow and edged with fine hairs, the lateral ones shorter by a half or a third than the middle lobe.

A rare birch, found here and there in the mountains of central Japan. It is scarcely known in cultivation in this country, but there are young trees at Kew, planted in 1957. It is well distinguished by the short, thick fruit-catkins.

B. GROSSA Sieb. & Zucc.   JAPANESE CHERRY BIRCH
B. *ulmifolia* Sieb. & Zucc.

A tree 50 to 70 ft high; young shoots slightly hairy, and with a few scattered, whitish lenticels; buds ovate, slender-pointed, of a pale shining green, not viscid. Leaves ovate-oblong, mostly heart-shaped, often unequal at the base, slenderly pointed, irregularly toothed, the teeth finely pointed and often incurved; 2 to 4 in. long, half as wide; dull green with flattened, silky hairs all over the upper surface, but confined to the veins and midrib beneath; the lower surface is also dotted with glands; veins in about twelve pairs; stalk ⅓ to ½ in. long, hairy. Fruiting catkins egg-shaped, ¾ in. long, ½ in. wide; scales downy, the middle lobe blunt, and about twice as long as the side ones.

Native of Japan; introduced to Kew in 1896. It was long grown under the name *B. ulmifolia*, but this species and *B. grossa* are now considered to be one and the same. Except for a certain liability to injury by late spring frost, it is apparently hardy, and is distinct in its leaf-buds and heart-shaped, many-ribbed leaves. The bark and twigs are aromatic, as in the allied American species *B. lenta* and *lutea*. A tree at Kew, *pl.* 1936, measures 39 × 2½ ft (1967). There is a group at Albury Park, Surrey, of which the largest is 45 × 3¼ ft.

B. HUMILIS Schrank

A shrub 2 to 9 ft high, young shoots hairy and glandular-warty. Leaves ovate, oval, or obovate, ½ to 1½ in. long, mostly tapered (sometimes rounded) at the base, pointed, irregularly and rather coarsely toothed (teeth triangular but often bluntish); both surfaces glabrous and green; veins in four or five pairs; stalk ¼ in. or less long. Fruiting catkins ⅓ to ⅝ in. long; scales with minute hairs on the margin, deeply three-lobed, the middle lobe usually thinner and larger than the side ones.

Native of high latitudes in Europe and Asia, or of higher altitudes in more southerly regions. This species and B. FRUTICOSA Pall. are very closely allied, and have often been united. The leaves of *B. fruticosa* are more tapered towards the apex, have usually five or six pairs of veins, and the toothing is finer, sharper, and more regular; the wings of the seed are also comparatively broader than in *humilis*. It is a native of N.E. Asia, inhabiting boggy places. Another close ally from the same region is B. MIDDENDORFII Trautv. & Mey., with more rounded leaves, pale yellowish green beneath.

B. JACQUEMONTII *see under* B. UTILIS

B. LENTA L.   SWEET BIRCH

A tree up to 70 or 80 ft high in a wild state; the bark of the trunk not peeling, dark, almost black; branchlets silky hairy when very young, soon becoming glabrous and shining brown. Leaves ovate or ovate-oblong, mostly heart-shaped at the base, pointed, 2½ to 6 in. long, 1½ to 3½ in. wide, toothed (often doubly so), dark glossy green and ultimately glabrous above, paler green and silky-hairy on the midrib and veins beneath; veins in ten to thirteen pairs; leaf-stalk ¼ to 1 in. long, hairy. Male catkins 2 to 3 in. long. Fruiting catkins 1 in. or rather more long, ½ in. in diameter, scarcely stalked; scales not downy, the lateral lobes rather wider than the middle one.

Native of eastern N. America, where it yields a valuable timber; introduced in 1759, according to Aiton. When bruised, the young bark has a sweet, aromatic taste and smell, and by distillation yields an aromatic oil. This birch is allied to *B. lutea*, but differs in the darker bark of the trunk, the sweeter-tasting young bark, and especially by the glabrous scales of the fruit catkin. In my experience it is not so well-doing a tree as *B. lutea* in this country.

B E T U L A   L E N T A

It is not common in cultivation in the British Isles, but there are specimens 45 to 50 ft high at Tortworth, Glos.; Dawyck, Peebl.; and Mount Usher, Co. Wicklow, Eire.

B. LUMINIFERA Winkler

B. alnoides var. *pyrifolia* Burk.

A tall tree, the younger branches bright reddish brown; young twigs covered more or less densely with pale hairs or down. Leaves ovate, $2\frac{1}{2}$ to 5 in. long, $1\frac{1}{2}$ to $3\frac{1}{2}$ in. wide, rounded or slightly heart-shaped at the base, pointed, unequally toothed, each tooth ending in an abrupt, slender point, ciliate, downy on both surfaces, dark dull green above, bright green beneath, covered with minute, lustrous resin-glands; veins nine to twelve; leaf-stalk $\frac{1}{2}$ to $\frac{3}{4}$ in. long, downy or nearly glabrous, reddish. The young, expanding leaves are of a pretty, red tinge. Fruiting catkins $1\frac{1}{2}$ to $3\frac{1}{2}$ in. long, cylindrical, $\frac{1}{4}$ in. diameter, borne singly; scales very small, the middle lobe several times larger than the side ones. Wings of fruit about as broad as the nutlet.

This species is closely allied to the Himalayan *B. alnoides* (see below), but is a native of W. China; discovered by the French missionary Farges in E. Szechwan and introduced by Wilson in 1901 and again in 1907. According to Wilson it is the common low-level birch in Szechwan and Hupeh, found up to an altitude of about 8,000 ft and rarely more than 65 ft in height. Trees at Kew grew well and were curiously distinct in the resinous sheen beneath the leaves, which became more apparent as the leaf dried. They varied considerably in the downiness of the young shoots. The last of these died in 1960 when 46 ft high.

B. ALNOIDES D. Don B. *acuminata* Wall., not Ehrh.—A tree to about 70 ft in the wild state, with a papery, greyish or brownish bark, peeling off in narrow, horizontal, silvery scrolls. A native of the Himalaya, longer known than B. *luminifera*, to which it is closely allied. It is reputed to be tender, but hardy forms might be found at the western end of its range in the Sutlej basin, where it ascends to 10,000 ft. It differs from B. *luminifera* in having the fruit-catkins in clusters of two or three.

B. CYLINDROSTACHYA Lindl. B. *alnoides* var. *cylindrostachya* (Lindl.) Winkler—A species closely allied to B. *alnoides*. According to Dr Bor (*Manual of Indian Forest Botany*) it is quite distinct in the field owing to its coppery brown bark, which peels in long vertical flakes and, in India, is confined to the eastern end of the Himalaya and the Naga Hills. It is also found in Burma and Yunnan.

The above three species are, however, little known and might prove on further investigation to be states of a single wide-ranging species. They are the representatives on the mainland of E. Asia of the section *Acuminatae*, characterised by the long ($1\frac{1}{2}$ to 4 in.), pendulous fruit-catkins, which, except in B. *luminifera*, are borne in clusters of two to four. The fourth, and best-known member of this group, is B. *maximowicziana* of Japan (q.v.).

B. LUTEA Michx.   YELLOW BIRCH
B. *alleghaniensis* Britt.

A tree up to 100 ft high in a wild state; bark of the trunk yellowish brown when newly revealed by the curling back of the outer layer; young wood more or less hairy the first summer. Leaves dull green, ovate or ovate-oblong, $2\frac{1}{2}$ to $4\frac{1}{2}$ in. long, half as wide; tapered, rounded, or heart-shaped at the base, pointed, doubly toothed; hairy on the margin, midrib, and chief veins, becoming glabrous above by the end of the season; veins in nine to twelve pairs. Fruiting catkins 1 to $1\frac{1}{2}$ in. long, erect, $\frac{3}{4}$ in. thick; scales conspicuously downy on the outside and margins, the lobes about equal size, oblong. The young bark has a bitter taste.

Native of eastern N. America; introduced in the latter half of the eighteenth century. It is a handsome birch, and might be more extensively planted. It is distinct in the colour of the newly exposed bark of the trunk. It is sometimes confused with B. *lenta*, under which the distinctions are pointed out.

This species is variable in the size and degree of downiness of the fruit-scales. Trees in which the scales are markedly long (more than $\frac{1}{3}$ in.) are sometimes distinguished as var. MACROLEPIS Fern.

In cultivation in the British Isles B. *lutea* has attained a height of around 45 ft. There are specimens of this size at Lanarth, Cornwall; Westonbirt, Glos.; and in other collections. The example at Kew, *pl.* 1934, measures 40 × $2\frac{1}{2}$ ft (1967).

B. MAXIMOWICZIANA Reg.

A tree 80 to 100 ft high; young shoots brown, warty, not downy; the bark of the older wood and trunk orange-brown, becoming ultimately grey or whitish.

Leaves heart-shaped, pointed, 3 to 6 in. long, three-fourths as wide; doubly toothed, dark green, downy at first, ultimately glabrous above, downy in the vein-axils beneath; veins in ten to twelve pairs; stalks 1 to 1¾ in. long. Male catkins 4 or 5 in. long. Fruiting catkins 2 to 2½ in. long, ⅛ in. wide, in racemes of two to four; scales glabrous, middle lobe longer and narrower than the side lobes. Seed-wings large. *Bot. Mag.*, t. 8337.

Native of Japan. There were several introductions of this birch at the end of the nineteenth century: to the Arnold Arboretum in 1893 and thence to Kew; by Veitch in 1888; and by Lemoine of Nancy, who supplied the tree at Grayswood Hill, planted in 1894. This fine birch is distinguished by the leaves being larger than those of any other species. I have measured them 7 in. long by 5 in. wide. The habit of young trees is rather open, and the branching stiff. It is a quick grower, very hardy, and altogether one of the best of its kind. Very distinct in its large leaves and racemose female catkins.

Good specimens of this birch are not common, but the following have been recorded: Kew, by Brentford Gate, *pl.* 1895, 40 × 2½ ft (1960); Westonbirt, Glos., off Mitchell Drive, 55 × 3 ft and 56 × 4 ft (1966); Leonardslee, Sussex, 58 × 3 ft (1961); Grayswood Hill, Surrey, *pl.* 1894, 57 × 6 ft (1964), and another about 60 ft high, six-stemmed from the base; Killerton, Devon, 60 × 5 ft (1960); Headfort, Co. Meath, Eire, 57 × 3¾ ft (1966).

B. MEDWEDIEWII Reg.

A large, spreading shrub growing in cultivation to about 15 ft in height and almost twice as much across; branchlets slightly hairy when young, with a few long lenticels. Winter buds very large and distinct, bright glossy green, narrowly ovoid and pointed, with ciliate scales; on vigorous shoots the buds are ½ in. long. Leaves ovate to roundish, 2 to 4 in. long, 1 to 3 in. wide; rounded or slightly heart-shaped at the base, pointed, irregularly toothed; dark green above, and glabrous or with a few hairs only on the midrib and the eight to eleven pairs of sunken veins, which are also slightly hairy beneath; stalk ¼ to ½ in. long, hairy. Fruit-catkins stalked, erect, 1 to 1½ in. long; scales ⅛ in. long, with some hairs on the margins, the middle lobe twice as long as the side ones. Seeds with narrow wings. *Bot. Mag.*, t. 9569.

Native of the Caucasus at sub-alpine elevations; introduced to Kew from Tiflis in 1897 and put into commerce by Späth of Berlin in 1906. It makes a handsome bush with alder-like leaves and is very striking in winter with its glossy, pale brown stems and large buds. The leaves usually die off a light yellow. The largest specimen recorded grows at Mount Usher in Co. Wicklow, Eire; it is 15 ft high and 27 ft across (1966). The specimen at Kew, referred to in the *Botanical Magazine* under the number cited, died in 1959; it was about 12 ft high and 15 ft across.

B. MEGRELICA Sosm.—This birch, also a native of the Caucasus, was described as late as 1930. It is allied to the preceding but differs in its tree-like habit and in its leaves, which are more ovate in shape, 1¼ to 3 in. long, ⅔ to 2½ in. wide, rounded to slightly heart-shaped at the base and gradually narrowed at the apex (but more rounded in outline on short shoots). Probably not yet introduced.

T S—P

B. NANA L.

A dwarf, neat-habited bush 2 to 4 ft high, branches erect, not warted, clothed the first two years with minute down. Leaves round or occasionally broader than long, never pointed, $\frac{1}{4}$ to $\frac{1}{2}$ in. diameter, conspicuously round-toothed except at the base; shining dark green above, prettily net-veined beneath, glabrous on both surfaces; veins in two to four pairs; stalk $\frac{1}{12}$ in. or less long, with a fringed stipule at each side. Fruiting catkins erect, $\frac{1}{3}$ in. long, shortly but distinctly stalked; scales glabrous, with lobes of about equal length, the middle one the broadest.

Native of northern latitudes in Europe (including N. Britain) and N. America, usually inhabiting moist places on mountains. In gardens it is useful for planting on the margins of streams and in moist places generally. Among shrubby birches it is distinguished by its round-toothed, orbicular leaves, and the absence of warts or glands on the shoots.

B. × INTERMEDIA Thomas   *B. alpestris* Fries.—Hybrids between *B. nana* and *B. pubescens*. In the typical form the leaves are larger than in *B. nana*, and more ovate, but retain much of the characteristic toothing of that species. Such hybrids are found in many parts of Europe where the two species are in contact.

B. NIGRA L.   RIVER BIRCH
B. rubra Michx.

A tree of pyramidal form 50 to 90 ft high, with a trunk often forked low down and, like the older branches, covered with large flakes of curling, blackish bark, which gives it a picturesque ruggedness of aspect seen in no other species except *B. davurica*; bark of young trees whitish; young shoots furnished with pale, round warts, and very downy. Leaves diamond-shaped to ovate, always wedge-shaped at the base, pointed, $1\frac{1}{2}$ to $3\frac{1}{2}$ in. long, $\frac{3}{4}$ to $2\frac{1}{2}$ in. wide, conspicuously double-toothed or small-lobed; glossy green above, glaucous beneath; downy only on the midrib and chief veins, finally glabrous above; veins in six to nine pairs; leaf-stalk downy, $\frac{1}{4}$ to $\frac{1}{2}$ in. long. Male catkins 2 to 3 in. long. Fruiting catkins 1 to $1\frac{1}{2}$ in. long, $\frac{1}{2}$ in. thick, erect; scales downy.

Native of the eastern United States; introduced by Peter Collinson in 1736. This is one of the most striking of birches, and its dark rugged trunk contrasts remarkably with those of our native and other white-barked species. Although the trunk is sometimes undivided, a characteristic feature of the tree, both wild and cultivated, is its division low down into two or three erect limbs. In the south-eastern United States this birch inhabits the banks of ponds and water-courses, often where the ground is inundated for several weeks at a time. Sargent remarks that the seeds ripen early in the summer, and fall when the water is at its lowest; they immediately germinate in the moist, rich soil, and thus secure a foothold by the time the waters return. It thrives quite well in ordinary soil; at Kew a tree reached a height of 60 ft far away from any water. At the present time there are examples 30 to 40 ft high by the lake in the R.H.S. Garden at Wisley, Surrey; in Windsor Great Park; in the Chandlers Ford nursery of

Messrs Hillier; and in the Winkworth Arboretum, Godalming, Surrey. A row of six has been planted in a street at Horsell, near Woking, Surrey, the tallest about 30 ft high.

B. OCCIDENTALIS Hook.

B. fontinalis Sarg.

A shrub up to 15 or 20 ft high, occasionally a tree twice as high, of elegant form; bark almost black, not peeling; young shoots resinous, warted. Leaves glandular, broadly ovate, rounded or slightly heart-shaped at the base, pointed, double-toothed; 1 to 2 in. long, $\frac{3}{4}$ to $1\frac{1}{2}$ in wide; dark dull green, slightly hairy above; paler and soon almost glabrous beneath; veins in three to five pairs; stalks $\frac{1}{4}$ to $\frac{1}{2}$ in. long, at first somewhat hairy, then glabrous. Male catkins up to 2 in. long. Fruiting catkins 1 to $1\frac{1}{4}$ in. long, the lobes of the scales about equal in size, slightly downy or glabrous.

Native of western N. America; introduced in 1897 to Kew, where it thrives very well and makes a graceful small tree. It is allied to *B. papyrifera*, but from the smaller-growing varieties of that species it is distinguished by the bark not separating into layers, and in being almost black. The very resinous young twigs and glandular young leaves also mark it.

The *B. occidentalis* of Sargent is *B. papyrifera* var. *commutata* (q.v.).

B. PAPYRIFERA Marsh.   PAPER BIRCH

B. papyracea Ait.

A tree 60 to 70 ft high, with a rather thin, open head of branches, sometimes pendulous at the ends. Bark of the trunk one of the whitest among birches, mostly very smooth, but coming away in thin, paper-like layers; young shoots warty, the hairs with which they are furnished when quite young soon falling away. Leaves ovate, rounded, sometimes heart-shaped at the base, slender-pointed; $1\frac{1}{2}$ to $3\frac{1}{2}$ in. long, two-thirds as wide; margins irregularly, often doubly toothed, and hairy; upper surface dull dark green, with scattered hairs; lower surface pale, downy in the axils of the veins, dotted with small black glands; veins in six to ten pairs; stalks up to 1 in. long. Male catkins up to 4 in. long. Fruiting catkins drooping, about $1\frac{1}{2}$ in. long, $\frac{1}{4}$ to $\frac{1}{3}$ in. thick; scales usually glabrous, the lateral lobes broader than the middle one.

Native of N. America, where it stretches right across the upper latitudes as far north as Labrador and Hudson's Bay, and south to Iowa and Nebraska; introduced in 1750. It is the most widely spread of all American birches, and the most useful tree of the inclement far north, providing the dwellers in those regions with fuel. The bark was used for roofing, to make drinking utensils, and especially canoes. In gardens it is valuable for the effect the vivid white trunk produces. In this respect it is not more attractive than our native white birch, nor has it the same delicate grace, its leaves being larger and less numerous; but the trunk remains white to a greater size. It varies very much, as might be expected from its wide distribution some trees have drooping branches, others erect.

The following are the largest paper birches recorded in recent years: Lydhurst, Sussex, 73 × 4¼ ft (1965); Woburn, Beds., 69 × 4¼ ft (1958); Tortworth, Glos., 69 × 5¼ ft, and two others of about the same size (1964); Hergest Croft, Heref., 60 × 4½ ft (1961).

var. COMMUTATA (Reg.) Fern. *B. lyalliana* Bean; *B. alba* subsp. *occidentalis* var. *commutata* Reg., *B. occidentalis* Sarg., not Hook.; *B. papyrifera* var. *occidentalis* Sarg.—There has been a good deal of confusion about this tree. The first synonym is the name under which it appeared in earlier editions of this work; the last is the one under which it will be found in the second edition of Sargent's *Manual of the Trees of N. America*. Sargent thought that this tree was *B. occidentalis* Hook., but Hooker's description clearly applies to the plants which Sargent named *B. fontinalis*, and it is for these that the name *B. occidentalis* must be used.

This variety is one of the very finest of birches, and reaches sometimes 120 ft in height; bark reddish brown to whitish, peeling. Young shoots warted, downy, yellowish brown. Leaves ovate with a rounded or heart-shaped base, ordinarily 3 to 4 in. long, but on young trees often over 5 in. long; hairy along the midrib and veins beneath; veins in seven to ten pairs. A native of British Columbia and Washington, inhabiting moist situations. There are two specimens of this birch in the Victory Glade at Westonbirt, the taller 58 × 3½ ft (1966); they were catalogued as *B. lyalliana*.

var. CORDIFOLIA (Reg.) Fern. *B. cordifolia* Reg.—A small tree or shrub found in Labrador, Newfoundland, and in the mountains of the E. United States. Leaves double-toothed, heart-shaped or truncate at the base. It is thought by some authorities to be a fertile hybrid between *B. papyrifera* and *B. lutea*.

var. HUMILIS (Reg.) Fern. & Raup *B. alba* subsp. *papyrifera* var. *humilis* Reg.; *B. neoalaskana* Sarg.; *B. papyrifera* var. *neoalaskana* (Sarg.) Raup—A tree 40 to 60 ft high, with the young shoots thickly covered with viscid warts, not downy. Leaves triangular-ovate, wedge-shaped or cut straight across at the base (heart-shaped on strong shoots), taper-pointed, 1½ to 3 in. long, 1 to 2 in. wide; coarsely and often doubly toothed; glossy dark green, viscid, and slightly hairy; stalks ½ to 1 in. long, reddish. Fruiting catkins 1 to 1¼ in. long; scales hairy on the margin only, the side lobes larger, rounder, and broader than the middle one. Native of Alaska, especially in the Yukon Valley; introduced in 1905. A tree sent to Kew by Prof. Sargent is thriving very well. It is in some respects like *B. occidentalis*, but differs in its thin, peeling, reddish-brown or dull white bark, and in the broader wing to the seeds. Sargent describes it as the common birch of the Yukon Valley. There is a slender, fast-growing specimen in the Edinburgh Botanic Garden, *pl.* 1951 and measuring 42 × 1½ ft (1968).

var. KENAICA (Evans) Henry *B. kenaica* Evans—Leaves 1½ to 2 in. long, ovate; irregularly, coarsely, often doubly toothed, tapered at the base; at first minutely downy above, becoming glabrous; veins in five or six pairs; stalk slender, ¾ to 1 in. long. The bark of the trunk is creamy white to reddish brown, and separates into layers. The tree grows 30 or 40 ft high, and is a native of the coast of Alaska. Introduced to Kew in 1891. It differs from the type in the fruit-scales being hairy on the margin, and in the smaller leaves.

var. SUBCORDATA (Rydb.) Sarg. *B. subcordata* Rydb.—A small tree with a silvery-grey or purplish-brown bark, found in British Columbia and adjoining parts of the United States, and thence eastward to Alberta, Montana, and Idaho. Leaves irregularly toothed or double-toothed, rounded to subcordate at the base, glabrous. Scales of fruiting catkins downy and ciliate.

B. PENDULA Roth   SILVER BIRCH

B. verrucosa Ehrh.; *B. alba* L., in part; *B. alba* var. *pendula* Ait.

A tree ordinarily from 40 to 60, occasionally over 100 ft high, with a silvery-white trunk; branches pendulous at the ends; young wood not downy, but furnished with glandular warts. Leaves broadly ovate, sometimes rather diamond-shaped; 1 to 2½ in. long, ¾ to 1½ in. wide; broadly wedge-shaped or truncate at the base, slenderly tapered at the apex, doubly toothed; not downy, but dotted with glands on both surfaces; stalk ½ to ¾ in. long. Fruiting catkins ¾ to 1¼ in. long, ¼ in. wide, cylindrical; scales glabrous except on the margin; middle lobe the smallest.

Native of Europe (including Britain), especially of high latitudes; also of parts of N. Asia. This birch, with *B. pubescens* (q.v.), forms the *B. alba* of Linnaeus, but most authorities now concur in separating them. The species is easily distinguished from *B. pubescens* by the warts on the young branchlets and by the absence of down on all the younger vegetative parts. In the latter respect it differs from all the other cultivated birches except *B. populifolia*. It is a more graceful tree than the downy birch and is found on drier soils. (For timber value etc. see *B. pubescens*.)

A study of the cut-leaved birches of Scandinavia, by Nils Hylander, was published in *Svensk Botanisk Tidskrift*, Vol. 51, part 2, 1957.

f. CRISPA (Reichb.) Holmberg *B. verrucosa* or *pendula* var. *laciniata* of many authors, not Wahl.—This form has been confused with 'Dalecarlica', but has the leaves more regularly and less deeply cut; the basal lobes are not so finely tapered and do not arch backwards at the ends. Found wild in several localities in Scandinavia.

cv. 'DALECARLICA'.—A very distinct tree, the leaves being lobed to within ⅛ to ¼ in. of the midrib, the lobes themselves lanceolate, coarsely toothed, and with long slender points, the ends of the basal lobes curving backwards; leaf-stalks 1 to 1¾ in. long. Branches and leaves pendulous and the whole tree very elegant. (*B. alba* var. *dalecarlica* L. f.; *B. a.* var. *laciniata* Wahl.; *B. pendula* f. *dalecarlica* (L. f.) Schneid.)

According to Hylander (op. cit.) the original tree, described by the younger Linnaeus in 1781, grew at Lilla Ornäs in the province of Dalarna (Dalecarlia), where it was first observed in 1767. It was destroyed in a storm in 1887 but graft-wood had been taken from it some years earlier and the offspring planted in the Experimental Garden at Stockholm. From these, and hence from the type-tree, all the true Ornäs birches are descended by vegetative propagation. The cultivar name 'Dalecarlica' should be reserved for this clone. The botanical group name *B. pendula* f. *dalecarlica* (L. f.) Schneid. is available for other trees of similar character, but in fact only one has since been observed in Sweden, in the province of Småland.

So far as is known the following specimens are of the true clone, which was introduced to Britain before 1885: Taymouth Castle, Perths., 90 × 5¼ ft, grafted at 1 ft (1961); Tittenhurst, Berks., 75 × 4½ and 69 × 4¼ ft, both grafted at 5–6 ft (1963); Sheffield Park, Sussex, *pl.* 1910, 65 × 3½ ft (1960); Madresfield Court, Worcs., 72 × 3¾ ft (1964); Royal Horticultural Society Gardens, Wisley, Surrey, 57 × 3¼ ft (1964).

cv. 'DENTATA VISCOSA'.—A bushy, small tree of close, twiggy habit; branchlets and leaves very viscid; leaves closely set on the twig, ¾ to 1½ in. long, coarsely double-toothed or even small-lobed; leaf-stalks ½ in. long. This tree is no longer grown at Kew and must be very rare or even non-existent in British gardens, but is to be seen in continental collections and should be re-introduced. It was first distributed by Chenault of Orleans around 1912 as *B. dentata viscosa pyramidalis.*

cv. 'ELEGANS'.—Branches hanging almost perpendicularly, leader erect. Bonamy's nursery, Toulouse, around 1866.

cv. 'FASTIGIATA'.—Branches erect-growing, the tree being of columnar habit and resembling a Lombardy poplar. First distributed by Simon-Louis Frères, before 1870. There is an example at Westonbirt, in Silkwood, measuring 71 × 3¼ ft (1964).

cv. 'GRACILIS'.—A small tree with finely cut leaves and drooping branches. The twigs are produced in clusters like elongated witches brooms. Origin unknown and perhaps not in cultivation here. There is a striking photograph of this birch in G. Krüssmann's *Handbuch der Laubgehölze*, plate 60.

f. OYCOWIENSIS (Besser) Schneid. *B. oycowiensis* Besser—A rare native of S.E. Poland, found in a few localities near Krakow. It bears three to four leaves on the flowering twigs (usually two in the type) and the leaves are more equally toothed. It is of shrubby habit.

cv. 'PURPUREA'.—Leaves deep purple. The purple birch arose among seedlings raised in his own garden by a worker in Transon's nursery, Orleans. He multiplied it by grafting and in 1873 sold the whole stock, which was apparently put into commerce under the epithets *atropurpurea* and *foliis purpureis.* But it was first described by André as *B. vulgaris purpurea* in *Ill. Hort.*, Vol. 19, p. 199 (1872). It is figured in *Rev. Hort. Belge*, Vol. 4, p. 185 (1878).

cv. 'TRISTIS'.—An elegant narrow-crowned tree with an erect leading shoot and drooping branches. Known since 1867. The same clone as 'Elegans'?

cv. 'YOUNGII'. YOUNG'S WEEPING BIRCH.—An elegant tree, good for small gardens. The branches are slender and perfectly pendulous, without a leading stem. If grafted on a high standard it makes a small mushroom-headed tree. If on its own stem it must be carefully trained.

B. OBSCURA A. Kotula—This birch is found wild in a number of localities in Poland and in parts of Russia and Czechoslovakia. It resembles the silver birch and has the same chromosome number, the main mark of difference being the bark, which is dark grey or blackish brown. The leaves are more rounded in outline, more consistently wedge-shaped at the base, and darker green.

B. × KOEHNEI Schneid.—This tree is of uncertain origin, but was thought by Schneider to be a hybrid between the silver birch and *B. papyrifera.* The type was grown in Späth's nurseries as "*B. cuspidata*". It is a graceful tree, which develops a white bark at an early age. There is an example 45 ft high in the Glasnevin Botanic Garden.

B. PLATYPHYLLA Sukatchev

B. mandschurica (Reg.) Nakai; *B. alba* subsp. *mandschurica* Reg.

B. platyphylla, in its typical form, is found on the mainland of N.E. Asia as far west as Mongolia and south to N. China. It is unlikely to be a success in the British Isles, where it is represented by its Japanese variety. From this variety, typical *B. platyphylla* differs chiefly in its leaves, which are glabrous beneath except for axillary tufts, and dotted with glands.

var. JAPONICA (Miq.) Hara *B. alba* var. *japonica* Miq.; *B. japonica* (Miq.) Winkler; *B. mandshurica* var. *japonica* (Miq.) Rehd. *B. pendula* var. *japonica* Rehd.; *B. verrucosa* var. *japonica* Henry—A deciduous tree up to 85 ft high in a wild state, with thin spreading branches and pure white bark on the trunk; young shoots slightly glandular-warty and either glabrous or slightly downy. Leaves 1½ to 3 in. long, downy or nearly glabrous, reddish. The young, expanding leaves are of a pretty, red tinge. Fruiting catkins 1½ to 3½ in. long, cylindrical, ¼ in. diameter, borne singly; scales very small, the middle lobe several times larger than the side ones. Nutlets with wings broader than themselves.

Native of Japan and the Okhotsk peninsula; in cultivation since 1887, probably before. Botanically, *B. platyphylla* is closely related to the silver birch (*B. pendula*) but this variety is easily distinguished from it by its larger, broader leaves, with axil-tufts beneath, their more numerous veins and usually single toothing. It thrives well in cultivation but I do not know that it has a greater value in the garden than our common silver birch. There is a large specimen of this birch at Tortworth, Glos., 72 × 5 ft (1965). At Westonbirt it is 46 × 2 ft in Holford Drive (1964).

var. SZECHUANICA (Schneid.) Rehd. *B. japonica* var. *szechuanica* Schneid.— Introduced by Wilson from W. Szechwan in 1908 (W. 983 and 4088); his specimens were at first treated by Schneider under the name *B. japonica* var. *mandshurica*. As seen in cultivation, Wilson's trees have rather bluish-green leaves and spreading crowns. The variety is easily distinguished from var. *japonica* by its leaves, which are dotted with glands beneath. It is a vigorous but rather graceless tree, with a silvery-white bark. 'This var. *szechuanica* is the only birch I know where the white comes off on the hands like old whitewash' (A. F. Mitchell). Examples recorded are: Kew, 39 × 2½ ft (1965); Westonbirt, Glos., in Mitchell Drive, 41 × 2¼ ft (1965); Tortworth, Glos., 58 × 4¾ ft (1966).

B. POPULIFOLIA Marsh. GREY BIRCH

A tree 20 to 40 ft high, with a rather thin, pyramidal head of branches, often pendulous at the ends; bark of the trunk grey-white, young shoots rough with many warts, not downy. Leaves broadly ovate or triangular, broadly wedge-shaped or truncate at the base, drawn out at the apex into a long, slender point;

2 to 3½ in. long, 1¼ to 2½ in. wide; glabrous and shining on both surfaces, glandular above; veins in six to nine pairs; leaf-stalk slender, dotted with black glands, ¾ to 1 in. long. Male catkins 2 to 3½ in. long. Fruiting catkins ¾ to 1¼ in. long, ¼ in. diameter; scales downy, with the side lobes broader and more rounded than the middle one.

Native of eastern N. America; introduced in 1750. The grey birch in its own region plays much the same part as its ally the white birch does in Europe. It occupies sterile and inclement regions, and is one of the first trees to find its way back to land stripped—either by man or by fire—of its original forest covering. It is short-lived, but according to Sargent performs a valuable function in acting as a nurse for the seedlings of more durable trees. It has little to recommend it for gardens except its interest, having no merit that our native birch does not possess in higher degree. This judgement applies to its behaviour in the British Isles; in its native climate its value as a garden tree may be greater. The longer stalk and drawn-out apex of the leaf, and the absence of down from the younger parts, amply distinguish it.

B. POTANINII Batal.
B. *wilsonii* Bean

A shrub 6 to 10 ft high; lower branches decumbent or prostrate; branchlets thickly clothed the first season with forward-pointing, somewhat appressed, pale brown hairs, glabrous and slightly warted the second season. Stipules triangular-ovate, silky. Leaves ovate, pointed, rounded or wedge-shaped at the base, irregularly, often doubly, toothed; ¾ to 1¾ in. long, ⅜ to 1 in. wide; veins deeply sunken and forming parallel grooves above, prominent beneath, in twelve to twenty-two pairs; dark green, becoming glabrous except on the hairy veins above, clothed beneath with long, brown, silky hairs, especially on the veins and midrib; leaf-stalk $\frac{1}{12}$ to ⅛ in. long, silky. Female catkins, ¾ in. long; scales three-lobed, $\frac{1}{10}$ in. long, the central lobe twice or more than twice as long as the rounded side-lobes, ciliate. Nutlet $\frac{1}{16}$ in. diameter, ovate-orbicular, the wing narrow, ciliate towards the end. Male catkins ½ in. long.

Native of W. China at altitudes of 7,000 to 9,000 ft. Introduced by Wilson in 1909, who describes it as often hanging down over cliffs. It is very distinct from other dwarf birches in its silky-hairy leaves with numerous veins.

B. PUBESCENS Ehrh.   DOWNY BIRCH
B. *alba* L., in part

A tree of small or medium size, occasionally 70 ft or more high; bark of trunk white, peeling off in papery layers, eventually dark and rugged at the base; young shoots downy, not warted. Leaves broadly ovate, 1½ to 2½ in. long, 1 to 2 in. wide; usually tapered, sometimes rounded or slightly heart-shaped at the base; pointed, coarsely toothed; upper surface thinly downy at first; lower one downy on the midrib and veins, sometimes only in the vein-axils, sometimes over the whole surface; veins in five to seven pairs; stalk more or less downy, ⅛ to ¾ in.

long. Fruiting catkins about 1 in. long; lobes of scale minutely downy, side ones rounded, terminal one ovate.

Native of Europe (including Britain) and N. Asia, and one of the two birches (the other is *B. pendula*) which make up the *B. alba* of Linnaeus. This is not so attractive a tree for the garden as *B. pendula*; its bark is darker, and its branching being more erect, it lacks the graceful, pendulous habit of that species. It affects moister places than *B. pendula*, and is especially abundant in Highland glens. Easily distinguished from typical *B. pendula* by its downy, not warted twigs.

It is a more variable species than *B. pendula* and in *Flora Europaea* is divided into three subspecies, of which two for certain occur in the British Isles:

subsp. PUBESCENS.—This is the typical downy birch, which is usually tree-like in habit, with downy young growths; leaves more than $1\frac{1}{4}$ in. long; wings of fruit as half as wide again as the nutlet.

subsp. CARPATICA (Willd.) Aschers. & Graebn.—Of more shrubby habit; young growths soon glabrous; leaves usually less than $1\frac{1}{4}$ in. long; wings of fruit as wide as the nutlet. Birches found in Scotland (referred to subsp. ODORATA in *Flora of the British Isles*) apparently belong here. Their young twigs and leaves are covered with resinous warts when young and are aromatic at that time; buds viscid. To this subspecies the *Flora Europaea* also refers var. MURITHII (Gaudin) Gremli, which is a dwarf tree up to 10 or 15 ft high, or a shrub, found in a few localities in Switzerland. It was discovered near Mauvoisin, Val de Bagne (Valais), and Dr Christ described it as a very pretty little tree. Var. PONTICA (Watson) Bean appears also to fall under this subspecies.

B. pubescens differs from *B. pendula* in having twice the number of chromosomes of that species ($2n = 56$). This difference restricts inter-breeding between the two species, and the first-generation crosses, when they occur, are sterile. The intermediates usually have the same chromosome number as *B. pubescens*, and must be hybrid swarms of complex origin (*Flora Europaea*).

The downy birch produces its seeds very freely and is, as a rule, one of the first trees to find its way back to deforested areas. Like the grey birch in N. America, it is sometimes useful in affording shelter for young timber trees of better class. The wood is of very little value in this country except for turnery and pulping. In Scandinavia, where it is used for veneers, the occasional tree is found in which the wood is beautifully grained and commands a high price. A fragrant oil is obtained from it which is used in the manufacture of russia leather. The bark is water-tight, and is used in the construction of roofs in Sweden, etc. Under certain conditions it is curiously indestructible. I have seen pieces unearthed during peat-cutting in the Highlands, which must have been buried some centuries, but were still quite silvery.

The following are the most important garden varieties:

cv. 'AUREA'.—Leaves yellow when young; shoots very downy.

cv. 'CRENATA NANA'.—A dwarf, round bush growing at the rate of 2 or 3 in. annually.

cv. 'URTICIFOLIA'.—A small tree whose leaves have a drawn-out apex, and are sharply double-toothed, very dull green, densely downy above when young. Fruiting catkins up to $1\frac{1}{2}$ in. long, and more slender than in *B. pubescens* itself. Loddiges' nursery 1836. Hylander considers that this clone may be

B. pendula × *pubescens* and that it was probably of garden origin. Similar nettle-leaved birches have, however, been reported from the wild. The Loddiges clone was later described under the name *B. virgultosa* Fries.

B. TURKESTANICA Litvin.—This is one of the numerous allies of *B. pubescens* found in the mountains of Central Asia. The young branchlets bear resinous glands as well as down; in the fruiting catkins the lobes of the scales are only about half as long as the central one (about the same length in *B. pubescens*).

B. PUMILA L.

An erect-habited shrub 2 to 9 (sometimes more) ft high; the young shoots downy or felted, but not warty. Leaves roundish, oval or obovate, ½ to 1½ in. long, pointed or bluntish at the apex, coarsely toothed, more or less downy on both sides, often thickly so; pale or greyish beneath; chief veins in five or six pairs, the smaller ones in between them finely netted; leaf-stalk ⅛ in. or less long. Fruiting catkins ½ to 1 in. long, middle lobe of scales longer than the side ones.

Native of eastern N. America, where it inhabits boggy places from Labrador to Ohio. It is only likely to be confused in gardens with *B. humilis* and *B. fruticosa*, both of which have warted, glandular branchlets. It has little merit in the garden.

B. RADDEANA Trautv.

A small tree or large shrub; young shoots clothed with a soft close down which persists into the second season, intermixed with which are a few pale warts; bark of adult trees silvery or pinkish grey. Leaves broadly ovate, pointed, rounded or slightly heart-shaped to broadly wedge-shaped at the base; coarsely and unequally toothed; 1½ to 2 in. long, two-thirds to quite as much wide; dullish dark green and slightly hairy above, hairy on the veins and in the vein-axils beneath; veins in about six or seven pairs; stalk ¼ to ½ in. long, hairy.

Native of the Caucasus, where it occurs at 5,000 to 6,500 ft altitude. First described in 1887, it was not, so far as I am aware, introduced to this country until 1924, when it was sent to Kew from Budapest. It is very hardy, of rather close growth, its most notable character in its juvenile state being the velvety clothing of down on the young shoots. Female catkins ovoid to elliptical, erect, twice as long as wide.

B. SCHMIDTII Reg.

A tree 60 to 100 ft high in the wild, with a stem 6 to 9 ft in girth; bark nearly black, falling off in thick, rather small plates of irregular shape; young shoots dark brown, warted, at first downy. Leaves ovate, slender-pointed, rounded or widely tapered at the base, finely but irregularly toothed; 1½ to 3 in. long, 1 to 1¾ in. wide; veins in nine to eleven pairs, slightly hairy above when young, more persistently so on the veins beneath; stalk $\frac{1}{6}$ to $\frac{1}{8}$ in. long, hairy. Male catkins $1\frac{1}{2}$ to $2\frac{1}{2}$ in. long; female catkins cylindrical, 1 to $1\frac{1}{4}$ in. long, $\frac{1}{8}$ in. wide, usually solitary, rarely in pairs, stiff and erect at the fruiting state; scales three-lobed, the lobes linear-oblong, pointed, ciliate, the middle one twice as long as the side ones.

Native of Japan, Korea, and Manchuria; named and described by Regel in 1865; introduced to this country in 1914 by Wilson. He says: 'This remarkable birch is rare in Japan and I saw it only on the wooded shores of Lake Chuzenji and in the ascent there from Nikko . . . it is a large tree with thick branches.' It may usually be recognised by its blackish bark, erect female catkins, short leaf-stalks and minutely toothed leaves. It is succeeding very well at Kew. The wood is too heavy to float in water.

The present example at Kew, which measures 32 × 2 ft and was planted in 1915, shows very well the striking black bark that characterises this species.

B. UTILIS D. Don   HIMALAYAN BIRCH
B. bhojpattra Wall.

A tree to 60 ft in the Himalaya, but reaching 100 ft in W. China (var. *prattii*). Bark variable in colour, peeling in horizontal, papery flakes; young shoots densely covered with grey down, becoming reddish brown. Leaves ovate, rounded at the base, pointed, 2 to $3\frac{1}{2}$ in. long, about two-thirds as wide, rather coarsely and irregularly toothed; upper surface dark green, with scattered down; lower surface pale, downy on the midrib and veins, the latter in nine to twelve pairs; leaf-stalk $\frac{3}{4}$ in. long, downy. Fruiting catkins $1\frac{1}{2}$ in. long, $\frac{1}{3}$ in. diameter, cylindrical; scales ciliate on the margins, three-lobed, the middle lobe considerably the longer, and round at the end; lateral lobes erect.

Native of the Himalaya and thence eastward and northward into China, where it passes over into the var. PRATTII Burkill, a rather indistinct variety in which the leaves are more downy beneath, the fruit-scales more ciliate at the margin, with spreading, not erect, lobes. This variety is found in W. Szechwan and Kansu, but the Himalayan type appears to extend as far as Yunnan. *B. utilis* was introduced from Sikkim in 1849 by Sir Joseph Hooker and from China by Wilson (W. 4035, 4087, and 4089) and by Forrest (F. 15381). The Himalayan provenance is said to be tender, but the Chinese trees have proved hardy enough and it is difficult to believe that all the Himalayan forms are tender.

B. utilis and var. *prattii* are represented in cultivation by trees 35 to 60 ft high at Westonbirt, Glos.; Hergest Croft, Heref.; Werrington Park, Cornwall; Youngsbury, Ware, Herts.; and Highdown, Sussex. The last-named was collected by George Fenwick-Owen on the frontier between China and Tibet in 1912. In one of the trees at Westonbirt, raised from F. 15381 and planted in 1924, the trunk is of a dark chocolate colour, with bands of purplish grey and mahogany; in another, it is reddish to orange-brown. The origin of the latter is uncertain, but in W. 4087 the bark is usually of that colour. In W. 4089 it is greyish (Coltman Rogers, *Journ. R.H.S.*, Vol. 53, 1928, p. 63). The beautiful specimen at Grayswood Hill, Haslemere, planted in 1882, was certainly raised from Himalayan seed and differs from the Chinese representatives of the species in its creamy-white bark slightly flushed with pink. It measures 40 × 4¾ ft (1968); cf. 30 × 2 ft (1906).

B. JACQUEMONTII Spach *B. bhojpattra* var. *jacquemontii* (Spach) Reg.; *B. utilis* var. *jacquemontii* (Spach) Winkler—This species is closely allied to *B. utilis*, which it replaces in the western part of the Himalaya. The two species appear to be linked by intermediates, but the western material in the Kew Herbarium is mostly distinguished from the eastern material by the following combination of characters: leaves more ovate, with seven to nine pairs of more widely spaced lateral veins, axillary tufts less prominent; male catkins longer and more slender; scales of fruit-catkins with a narrow, pointed central lobe which is marked longer than the lateral ones. The transition from *B. utilis* to *B. jacquemontii* appears to take place just west of Nepal, in the region known as Kumaon, and is probably gradual. [PLATE 20

Birches that agreed well with the type of *B. jacquemontii* were introduced to Kew from St Petersburg at the end of the last century but the provenance of the seed from which they were raised is not known. These trees died many years ago and no cultivated specimen is known to us that can be unequivocally referred to *B. jacquemontii*. The beautiful white-barked birches in the former botanic garden of Trinity College, Dublin, appear to lie on the borderline between the two species. They tend towards *B. jacquemontii* in some characters, but if over-riding weight were to be given to the number of pairs of lateral veins they would be referable to *B. utilis*, since these are around ten in number. The Dublin trees were raised from seed sent by Sir Joseph Hooker from Kew in 1881. Owing to the removal of the Botanic Garden to a new site they are probably doomed, but their offspring grow at Trinity College itself, at Mount Usher, Co. Wicklow, and at Castlewellan in N. Ireland. The tree in the Edinburgh Botanic Garden, which measures 43 × 3½ ft (1968) agrees fairly closely with the Dublin trees in its botanical characters and has a vividly white bark. It is considered to belong to *B. jacquemontii*.

It should be added that the bark of *B. jacquemontii* is not always white, nor even commonly so, though it seems to be usually pale-coloured; bark specimens in the Kew Herbarium range in colour from ochre-cream to ochre-brown or light pinkish brown. Equally, the bark of *B. utilis* is not necessarily always brown as in the Chinese trees. The bark-colour of *B. utilis* on the Gossain Than of Central Nepal, from which the type of that species came, is said to be creamy-white.

BIGNONIA   BIGNONIACEAE

As understood by Bentham and Hooker, *Bignonia* was a large genus of about 150 species; indeed, some of the early botanists included in it such bignoniaceous trees as *Catalpa* and *Paulownia*. In the drastic splitting of *Bignonia* carried out by Miers a century or so ago, even *B. capreolata*, described here, was transferred to *Doxantha*. However, it is now considered that this species should be regarded as the type species of the

Linnaean genus *Bignonia* and is the only species now recognised in that genus. It climbs by tendrils, a characteristic that easily distinguishes it from the allied *Campsis*.

B. CAPREOLATA L.   CROSS VINE   [PLATE 21

Doxantha capreolata (L.) Miers

An evergreen or semi-deciduous climber (according to climate), in nature ascending trees to a height of 40 to 50 ft; stems long, slender, glabrous except at the joints. Leaves opposite, composed of two leaflets on a common stalk ½ in. long, which is prolonged into a branched tendril. Leaflets oblong-lanceolate or ovate-lanceolate, 2 to 5 in. long, ½ to 2 in. wide; heart-shaped at the base, tapered at the apex, glabrous and deep green; stalk ½ in. long, hairy on the upper side. Flowers orange-red, clustered in the leaf-axils, each on a stalk 1 to 1¼ in. long. Corolla between tube- and funnel-shaped, 1½ to 2 in. long, 1¼ in. wide at the mouth, where it spreads into five ovate, rounded lobes. Calyx bell-shaped, ⅜ in. long, shallowly five-toothed. Pod about 6 in. long, slender, flattened. Blossoms in June. *Bot. Mag.*, t. 864.

Native of the south-eastern United States; introduced in 1710. In order to succeed near London this handsome climber must have a sheltered, sunny wall. The popular name refers to the cross-like appearance of the wood when cut through transversely.

In *Bot. Mag.*, t. 6501, a form is illustrated which differs from the type in its darker, red-purple flowers and longer, narrower leaves.

BILLARDIERA   PITTOSPORACEAE

A genus of a few evergreen Australian climbers, of which only the one described is grown outdoors in the British Isles. The name commemorates J. J. H. de Labillardière, a French botanist who travelled in Australia and published a work on its flora in Paris in 1804.

B. LONGIFLORA Labill.

A climbing, evergreen shrub up to 6 ft high, with slender, glabrous stems and narrow, lanceolate, entire leaves, 1 to 1½ in. long. Flowers solitary in the leaf-axils, each one on a slender stalk, ½ in. long, pendulous; the five petals are oblanceolate, ¾ in. long, free but not spreading, greenish yellow. Fruit an oblong-globular, dry capsule, of a beautiful dark blue, ¾ to 1 in. long. *Bot. Mag.*, t. 1507.

A native of Tasmania; introduced in 1810. This delightful climber is rather tender and needs a position where it is sheltered from cold winds and strong sun. It is at its best near the Atlantic seaboard, and grew very well at Rostrevor, Co. Down, as it does today at Inverewe and in many other mild gardens. In southern England it is best given the protection of a wall. It flowers freely in July and is then very pretty, but its greatest beauty comes in October and November, when the fruits acquire their charming colour. The fruit contains abundant seed, which germinates readily; it may also be increased by cuttings.

BILLARDIERA LONGIFLORA

Although the form commonly seen in cultivation has dark blue fruits, the colouring on wild plants is very variable, from shades of purple through rose to pure white. These various forms are said to breed more or less true from seed.

BOENNINGHAUSENIA   RUTACEAE

A genus allied to *Ruta* and *Dictamnus*, containing the one species described below (two or three in some interpretations). The name commemorates a German botanist, von Boenninghausen (1785–1864), who published botanical works in 1821 and 1824.

B. ALBIFLORA (Hook.) Reichenb.

Ruta albiflora Hook.

A deciduous sub-shrubby plant growing 1½ to 3 ft high, the younger parts herbaceous, without down on leaf or stem; young shoots hollow. Leaves alternate, doubly (sometimes trebly) pinnate; 3 to 6 in. long, not so wide, the lower half or third of the main-stalk naked. Leaflets (which vary from seven to eighty to a leaf) obovate or oval, rounded at the apex, entire, the largest ones nearly 1 in. long and ½ in. or more wide, the smallest ¼ in. long, dotted with translucent oil-glands, shortly stalked or stalkless. Flowers small, pure white, scarcely ½ in. wide, produced from August onwards in a loose panicle on the current season's growth and as much as 12 in. high by 8 in. wide. There are four oblong petals with rounded ends and yellow markings at the base. Calyx small, green, four-lobed. Stamens six, sometimes seven or eight, inserted at the base of a cup-shaped fleshy nectary, which is white with the margin divided into small blunt glandular yellowish processes and surrounds the base of a stalk on which the ovary is raised; lobes of ovary and stigma standing well out from the corolla. All these parts, even the petals, have glandular cells.

Native of E. Asia, where it is widely spread from the mountains of N. India to China and Japan. The plant, which is not strictly shrubby, is often found on

BOENNINGHAUSENIA ALBIFLORA

limestone and grows well on chalky soils. At one time it became rare in cultivation but is now (1966) well established in gardens and hardy enough against a sunny wall outside the Temperate House at Kew. Like the hardier fuchsias, it is cut to the ground every winter in most gardens and best covered each autumn with rough litter or weathered ashes. A well-drained soil is essential.

It is quite elegant, its foliage strongly suggesting a leguminous plant. When crushed the leaves give off a disagreeable odour. According to collectors' notes the flowers vary from pure to yellowish white in a wild state. The form in cultivation half a century ago is said to have grown to about 1½ ft only and was regarded by Farrer as a plant for the rock garden. As now seen in gardens it attains 3 ft or even more and in this connection it is of interest that Forrest gives 2 to 4 ft as the height of his F. 5093, collected in 1905 on the border between China and Burma. Forms found in dry places in Yunnan and S.W. Szechwan differ from the type in their sessile ovaries and star-shaped, not campanulate, flowers; they are sometimes recognised as a distinct species—B. sessilicarpa Lévl. The Japanese plants are sometimes split off as B. japonica (Miq.) Nakai, but the grounds for the distinction are not clear.

BOTRYOSTEGE   ERICACEAE

A genus of a single Japanese deciduous shrub, allied to *Tripetaleia* and, until recently, included in it. Stapf (*Kew Bulletin*, 1934, p. 192) placed

it in a genus of its own, distinguished from *Tripetaleia* by its simple, relatively few-flowered racemose inflorescence, its conspicuous leafy bracts, five free oblong sepals and sessile capsule (not borne on a distinct stalk as in the other genus).

B. BRACTEATA (Maxim.) Stapf
Tripetaleia bracteata Maxim.

A deciduous shrub 3 to 6 ft high, with glabrous, pale brown young shoots. Leaves alternate, obovate, tapered towards the base, mostly rounded at the apex or tapered to a short mucro, entire; 1 to 2 in. long, $\frac{3}{8}$ to 1 in. wide, quite glabrous on both surfaces; stalk $\frac{1}{8}$ in. or less long. Racemes erect, terminal on the current year's leafy twigs, slender, 3 to 6 in. long, bearing the flowers at intervals of $\frac{1}{4}$ to $\frac{1}{2}$ in., each on a slender stalk $\frac{1}{4}$ to $\frac{5}{8}$ in. long. Each flower springs from the axil of an oval or obovate, leafy, ciliate bract $\frac{1}{4}$ in. long and there are also smaller bracteoles on the individual flower-stalk. Petals white, tinged pink, usually three but sometimes four or even five, narrow-oblong, $\frac{3}{8}$ in. long, recurved at the end; sepals usually five, narrowly oval, $\frac{3}{16}$ in. long; stamens six. Style stout, standing out $\frac{3}{8}$ in. above the petals and strongly curved. Seed-vessel a dry, usually three-valved capsule, $\frac{1}{4}$ in. wide.

BOTRYOSTEGE BRACTEATA

Native of Japan. This shrub has been in intermittent cultivation at Kew and probably elsewhere during the last forty years, but it is quite uncommon. It was growing in the Arnold Arboretum in 1910. It flowered during July and August when grown at Kew and the copious racemes made it worth growing.

BOWKERIA   SCROPHULARIACEAE

A genus of some five species of evergreen shrubs, natives of S. Africa.

B. GERARDIANA Harvey
B. *triphylla* Hort., not Harvey

An evergreen shrub 8, 10, or more ft high; stems covered with fine grey hairs. Leaves stalkless, arranged in threes at each joint, 4 to 7 in. long, 1½ to 2¼ in. wide; ovate-lanceolate, toothed, long-pointed; dull green, somewhat downy on both surfaces. Flowers produced in August in lax, three- to ten-flowered cymes; the shaggy flower-stalks springing from the leaf-axils. Corolla pure white, ¾ in. across, similar to a calceolaria, two-lipped, flattened at the mouth of the tube to a broad slit; upper lip broadly two-lobed, lower one three-lobed. The inflorescence is very viscid. *Bot. Mag.*, t. 8021.

Native of Natal, and rare in cultivation. It has long been grown under glass at Kew, but my first knowledge of its existence in the open air was obtained in August 1903, when flowering shoots were sent to Kew from Mrs Gwytherne Williams' garden at Belvedere, St Lawrence, Isle of Wight. It is not only a beautiful shrub, but interesting as one of the comparatively few South African ones that can be grown outside in the south of England. It is, however, very tender and should not be attempted out-of-doors except in mild coastal gardens. A plant at Logan, Wigtownshire, reached 20 ft but was killed in the winter of 1961–2. The name under which it has been grown—"*B. triphylla*"—belongs to a plant apparently not in cultivation.

BRACHYGLOTTIS   COMPOSITAE

A genus of a single species, closely allied to *Senecio* and endemic to New Zealand.

B. REPANDA J. R. & G. Forst.

An evergreen shrub or small tree up to 20 ft high in a wild state; young shoots and leaf-stalks covered with a close, dull white felt. Leaves alternate, firm and rather leathery in texture; 4 to 12 in. long, 3 to 8 in. wide; ovate to oval, rounded or truncate at the base, pointed, the margin scalloped into large irregular lobes or teeth, the larger ones of which stand out one inch from the main body of the leaf; upper surface at first greyish, with a covering of down which eventually wears off, leaving it glabrous and dark glossy green tinged with purple, especially on the midrib; the under-surface is permanently clothed with a milk-white felt; stalk 2 to 5 in. long, stout. Flower-heads greenish white, individually small and about ⅛ in. long, but produced in huge terminal panicles sometimes 12 in. long, and 16 in. wide, much branched.

Native of the North and South Islands of New Zealand, and one of the most remarkable of the wonderful shrubby composites of that Dominion. It ranges up to 2,000 ft altitude and flowers from August to October. In England it flowers in early spring, sometimes so early as not to escape frost. It is hardy only in the milder parts of the country, and at Kew needs winter protection. The late Canon A. T. Boscawen grew it excellently at Ludgvan, near Penzance, and it is a common shrub in the Scilly Isles, especially on Tresco, where it finds a place in cottagers' gardens and is even planted as a wind-break. Put to that purpose, its leaves get too much torn and battered to leave them much beauty, but at its best it is a noble foliage plant. It does not appear to flower freely if given very generous treatment at the root, but that is no great loss. In a breeze the leaves reveal their white under-surface, which gives a very agreeable contrast to the dark shining green upper one.

This description is made from plants I have seen growing in this country, but it is possible some of them may be B. RANGIORA Buchanan, which Cheeseman regarded as a 'trivial variety of B. repanda from which it differs in no important character' but which has larger glossy leaves, whereas those of typical repanda are dull green. Allan, in *Flora of New Zealand* (1961), gives it as a variety (var. *rangiora* (Buchan.) Allan), but adds that the whole B. repanda complex needs further study. A purple-leaved form is also in cultivation.

BROUSSONETIA   MORACEAE

The broussonetias are closely allied to the mulberries, but are less woody, and the plants are unisexual. Two species are in cultivation, both from N.E. Asia. They have alternate leaves, and are rather rank-growing shrubs or small trees, deciduous, and with abundant pith in the young shoots. They grow well in any soil of moderate quality, and are easily increased by summer cuttings. These should be made in July or August, of short shoots with a heel of older wood attached. Female trees sometimes produce fruit under cultivation. Named after T. N. V. Broussonet, a French naturalist, 1761–1807.

B. KAZINOKI Sieb. & Zucc.

B. kaempferi Hort., not Sieb. & Zucc.; *B. sieboldii* Blume

A deciduous shrub 10 to 15 ft high, of open, spreading habit, with very pithy, purplish red young shoots, whose bark is slightly downy at first, soon quite glabrous. Leaves ovate, occasionally two- or three-lobed, rounded or slightly heart-shaped at the base, long and taper-pointed, toothed; extremely variable in size, three-nerved at the base; slightly downy when young, soon afterwards glabrous; upper surface rather rough. On strong growths they may be 6 to 10 in. long, 3 to 5 in. wide; on weaker shoots as small as 2 in. long; stalk ⅓ to ¾ in. long. Flowers of the male plant in clusters ½ in. long, on a slender, downy stalk about the same length; female flowers in a smaller, globose head, with long, slender, downy styles. Neither has any beauty. Fruits in a globose head, woolly.

Native of Japan and Korea. This species is distinguished from *B. papyrifera* by its glabrous young wood and leaves, by its shorter male inflorescence, and by the usually shorter leaf-stalks. It is not so striking or vigorous a shrub. It was once grown as "*B. kaempferi*"; the true species of that name is a dioecious, scrambling shrub found in the southern islands of Japan and in Formosa.

B. PAPYRIFERA (L.) Vent.   PAPER MULBERRY
Morus papyrifera L.

A coarse-growing, vigorous shrub, or a tree up to 50 ft high, forming a roundish, spreading head of branches; young wood thickly downy, soft and

BROUSSONETIA PAPYRIFERA (Male catkins)

pithy. Leaves very variable in size and form, ovate or variously lobed, often shaped like fig leaves; rounded, or more or less tapered at the base, pointed, toothed, three-nerved at the base; upper surface dull green and rough, lower surface densely woolly till they fall; stalk 1 to 4 in., long. Flowers of the male plant in cylindrical often curly, woolly catkins, 1½ to 3 in. long, ¼ in. wide; female flowers in ball-like heads ½ in. in diameter. Fruit red. *Bot. Mag.*, t. 2358.

Native of China and Japan; introduced early in the eighteenth century. It is now widely cultivated in Eastern countries; in Japan chiefly for the manufacture of paper from the bark, and in the Polynesian islands for the fibre, which is made into a cloth. Capt. Cook noticed in Otaheite that the finest and whitest cloth worn by the principal inhabitants was made from this material. In some of the Dalmatian towns, especially at Spalato (Split), I have seen it as a street tree of neat, rounded shape. The lobed leaves mostly occur on young vigorous trees, the unlobed ones on flowering specimens.

cv. 'CUCULLATA'.—A male tree with curious leaves whose margins are curled upwards, so as to give the leaf the shape of a boat.

cv. 'LACINIATA'.—In this remarkable variety, which is quite dwarf, the leaf is reduced to the stalk and the three main veins, the ends of which have each a small, narrow, variously shaped blade. The leaf has thus a trifoliolate aspect. When in foliage the whole shrub is a tangle of these slender leaf-stalks. I have not seen this variety in flower. Raised at Lyons around 1830-5 and also known as *B. p. dissecta*. 'BILLIARDII' is similar but more upright and vigorous; raised by a M. Billiard of Fontenay-aux-Roses. *Rev. Hort.*, 1866, p. 420, and 1878, p. 374.

Both the varieties here mentioned are merely curious freaks, but the type itself makes a handsome shrub; the male plant when freely furnished with its yellowish, drooping catkins is striking.

BRUCKENTHALIA   ERICACEAE

A monotypic genus related to *Erica*. Its corolla is wider at the mouth than in any hardy heath, and botanically it is distinguished from all members of that genus by having the stamens united with each other at the base and adnate to the corolla.

B. SPICULIFOLIA (Salisb.) Reichenb.

Erica spiculifolia Salisb.

A dwarf evergreen shrub about 9 in. high, forming dense tufts of erect, very leafy twigs, heath-like in appearance; branches slender, downy. Leaves spreading, much crowded, linear, ⅛ to ⅙ in. long, ending in a bristle; the margins recurved and more or less glandular-hairy; lower surface white, but nearly hidden by the recurved margins. Flowers densely packed in a terminal, erect raceme 1 in. or less long. Corolla bell-shaped, ⅛ in. long, with four rounded lobes, rosy; calyx similarly coloured but much smaller, and with pointed lobes. Stamens eight;

seed-vessel globular, with the style and calyx persisting; flower-stalk ⅛ in. long. *Bot. Mag.*, t. 8148.

Native of the mountains of E. Europe and Asia Minor, discovered by Sibthorp in 1802, near Bursa; introduced to Kew in 1888. It differs from hardy ericas in the open-mouthed corolla. Commencing to bloom early in June, it continues for about a month. It is a dainty little plant, not particularly showy, but suitable for a nook with peaty soil in the rock garden and quite hardy. It may be increased by seed, which it ripens freely, and by cuttings treated as advised for hardy heaths (see ERICA). The flower-colour of seedlings varies from pale to deep pink.

BRUCKENTHALIA SPICULIFOLIA

BRUNNICHIA POLYGONACEAE

A genus of a single species, native of N. America and allied to *Polygonum*. A West African species formerly included in *Brunnichia* is now separated as a distinct genus—*Afrobrunnichia*. The name commemorates M. T. Brunnich, a Scandinavian eighteenth-century naturalist.

B. CIRRHOSA Gaertn.

A deciduous climber growing 15 ft or more high, with slender, grooved stems, glabrous except at the joints, and supporting itself by means of forked tendrils terminating the branches. Leaves alternate, ovate, truncate or heart-shaped at the base, pointed; 2 to 4½ in. long, 1¼ to 2½ in. wide; not toothed, dark glossy green, almost or quite glabrous; stalk ½ to 1 in. long. Flowers small, greenish, arranged in clusters of two to five on slender terminal and axillary racemes 1½ to 6 in. long, the whole forming a loose panicle 12 to 18 in. high opening in July. Calyx persistent and surrounding the seed-vessel, enlarging and becoming leathery as the seed ripens; there is a wing ⅛ in. wide on one side extending down the flower-stalk, the whole ultimately about 1 in. long. Only a proportion of the flowers ripen seed and develop in this curious way. Seed deeply six-grooved.

Native of the south-eastern United States; introduced in 1787. This curious and interesting climber has not sufficient flower beauty to gain it much recognition in gardens, and although introduced so long ago, is very uncommon. It is perfectly hardy at Kew, where it has lived without protection in the open for more than seventy years. It somewhat resembles *Smilax* in leaf and growth.

BRYANTHUS   ERICACEAE

As now understood, the genus *Bryanthus* contains only the one species described here. Others once included in it are now placed in *Phyllodoce*, from which *Bryanthus* is distinguished by its rotate, four-lobed corolla and racemose inflorescence.

B. GMELINII D. Don

Andromeda bryantha L.; *Menziesia bryantha* (L.) Swartz; *B. musciformis* Nakai*

A low, prostrate, evergreen shrub. Leaves closely set on the slender stems, twenty or more to the inch, each ⅙ to ¼ in. long, 1/16 in. wide, linear, sparsely toothed and convex beneath. The flowers are borne on very slender, thread-like erect stalks 1 in. or more long which branch at the top into three or more parts, each part bearing a terminal flower. The flower is rosy pink about ¼ in. wide, with the calyx and corolla four-lobed; stamens eight.

Native of N.E. Asia, from Japan to the Behring Straits, long known to botanists. The date of its introduction is uncertain, but it is included in Don's *Gardener's Dictionary* (1834) and in Nicholson's *Dictionary of Gardening* (1885). The present stock was introduced shortly before 1940, when S. G. Fielder exhibited it at Vincent Square, but not in flower. It needs a cool position in peaty soil, but is

* The name *B. musciformis* Nakai was based on a supposed earlier name *Andromeda musciformis* Poiret. In fact, Poiret used for the species the Latin name *Andromeda bryantha* L. with the French name "Andromède musciforme", which has no standing in botanical nomenclature.

scarcely worth cultivating except to complete a collection of dwarf ericaceous species since, at least in the form introduced, it rarely flowers.

BUCKLEYA   SANTALACEAE

A genus of about four species, one N. American, the others E. Asiatic, living partly or wholly as parasites on the roots of other trees. The parasitic habit is characteristic of nearly all members of the Santalaceae, including our native representative *Thesium humifusum*, the bastard toad-flax.

B. DISTICHOPHYLLA (Nutt.) Torr.
Borya distichophylla Nutt.

A unisexual, deciduous, privet-like shrub 6 to 12 ft high, of lax, wide-spreading habit; young shoots downy. Leaves opposite or nearly so, arranged in two rows, lance-shaped or approaching ovate, rounded or broadly wedge-shaped at the base, long and taper-pointed; 1 to 2½ in. long, ⅓ to ⅞ in. wide; downy on the midrib and margins. Flowers small, greenish, terminal on young shoots; the males ⅛ in. across, in a small umbel; the females solitary, much larger than the males, ½ in. long, with four spreading, narrowly lanceolate bracts. Nuts hard, one-seeded, oblong, ¾ in. long, furrowed.

Native of N. Carolina and Tennessee; discovered by Nuttall in 1816; introduced to Kew in 1897. Naturally it is a parasite on the roots of other trees, mostly frequently *Tsuga canadensis*. Very little success has been attained in its cultivation here, although the seeds that are occasionally offered by nurserymen in the south-eastern United States germinate freely. A young plant parasitic on *Tsuga* lived for ten years at Kew, but usually there is a difficulty in getting it thoroughly attached to a host plant. Those who take an interest in remarkable plants of this kind may like to experiment with it. The seeds may be sown in pots under glass, and after germination planted near a host plant. They can live for some time on their own stored-up food. Other methods may be adopted, such as sowing seeds near the roots of *Tsuga* out-of-doors, protecting by a handlight at first. Perhaps this shrub needs more sun than it gets here, but is capable of withstanding intense frost. I remember a vigorous bush, 8 or 10 ft high, in the botanic garden of Harvard University, Cambridge, Mass., where the winter cold is much more intense than we experience here.

BUDDLEIA   LOGANIACEAE

The genus *Buddleia* was named in honour of the Rev. Adam Buddle, one-time vicar of Farnbridge, in Essex. The species are small trees and shrubs (rarely herbs) with often angled or winged stems and opposite, usually downy or woolly leaves; they are found in S. America, S. Africa, and E. Asia. In the cultivated species the flowers are produced in terminal and axillary racemes or panicles, on which they are grouped densely in close clusters, except in *B. globosa*, where they appear in globular heads. The calyx is bell-shaped, four- or five-toothed, or lobed; the corolla tubular, with four lobes, often withering on the stalk and persisting. Stamens four. Seed-vessel a capsule of two valves splitting from the top.

The buddleias, provided the climate is suitable for them, are easily cultivated. They all like a rich, loamy soil and a sunny position, and are easily propagated by cuttings of late summer growths, or by seeds. Those species which flower on the growths of the year may be pruned back in spring before growth commences. For *B. davidii* and its garden varieties this pruning is necessary in order to get strong shoots and panicles. The buddleias that flower on the previous season's wood may be lightly pruned after flowering.

Buddleias not described in the following notes are: B. ASIATICA Lour., a slender graceful shrub with long panicles of white, exquisitely fragrant flowers produced in winter and early spring. It is best regarded as a shrub for the cool greenhouse, though in the mildest parts it might be tried on a south or south-west wall. B. MADAGASCARIENSIS Lam., native of Madagascar, with terminal panicles of orange-yellow flowers and violet-coloured berries, is very tender but is grown on a wall at Trengwainton, near Penzance.

'MARGARET PIKE' is a hybrid between the above species, raised by A. V. Pike and given an Award of Merit in 1953 as a winter-flowering shrub for the cold greenhouse.

B. ALBIFLORA Hemsl.

B. hemsleyana Koehne

A strong-growing deciduous shrub, said by Wilson to attain a height of 12 ft in a wild state; branches erect, soon quite glabrous. Leaves narrow lanceolate, with a long tapered point and wedge-shaped base; 4 to 9 in. long, $\frac{1}{2}$ to $2\frac{1}{2}$ in. wide, toothed, dark green, and soon becoming glabrous above; covered beneath with a close, fine, silvery grey felt. Flowers fragrant, lilac (not white), with orange-coloured centres, produced from July onwards in slender, tapering panicles 8 to 18 in. long, 2 in. wide at the base, terminating the main shoots, with smaller ones on lateral shoots. Corolla-tube $\frac{1}{4}$ in. long; persisting as in other species until burst off by the swelling seed-vessel beneath it. Calyx glabrous, bell-shaped, with pointed narrow lobes.

Native of China; discovered by Henry, and introduced in 1900 by Wilson, who observes that it is fairly common on the shrub-clad mountains of Central China at 3,000 to 6,000 ft altitude. With the general aspect of *B. davidii*, it is not so good a shrub; the branchlets are not so square, the leaves are more distinctly stalked and the calyx differs in being glabrous.

B. hemsleyana Koehne, is no more than an inferior form of *B. albiflora*. It is only worth growing in collections. The flowers have not the orange-coloured eye seen in those of *albiflora* or *davidii*.

B. ALTERNIFOLIA Maxim. [PLATE 22

A deciduous shrub of very vigorous growth, or a small tree from 10 to 20 ft high, lax and widely branched, making pendulous shoots several feet long in one season. Young growths ribbed, at first furnished with minute scurfy down, soon becoming glabrous. Leaves alternate, entire, lanceolate, pointed, wedge-shaped at the base; 1½ to 4 in. long,¼ to ½ in. wide; dull dark green and glabrous above, glaucous or minutely scurfy beneath; stalk about ⅛ in. long. Flowers produced in June from the joints of the previous year's growth, densely crowded in clusters about 1 in. wide, often completely hiding the branch. Corolla bright lilac-purple, tubular at the base, dividing at the mouth into four rounded lobes and about $\frac{3}{16}$ in. wide there. Calyx tubular, ⅛ in. long, four-lobed, glaucous and scurfy like the flower-stalk, which is about as long as the calyx. *Bot. Mag.*, t. 9085.

Native of Kansu, China, described and named by Maximowicz in 1880, but introduced by W. Purdom and Reginald Farrer about 1915. This species is remarkably distinct from other cultivated buddleias in its alternate leaves. It is also singularly beautiful, flowering freely when a few years old and growing with great vigour. The flowers are fragrant, although not so much so as in some of the buddleias. I have seen no finer or handsomer specimen than one in the Royal Horticultural Society's Garden at Wisley, where it is a small tree. In the chalk garden at Highdown, near Worthing, it was, in May 1930, 16 ft high and wide, but, owing to the warmer climate, of looser, more diffuse branching than at Wisley. Farrer writes of it as seen in Kansu: 'a gracious, small-leaved, weeping willow when it is not in flower and a sheer waterfall of soft purple when it is'. I saw the Wisley tree in flower a few years ago and appreciated the aptitude of these comparisons. Whenever possible, it should be trained up into tree form. It likes a sunny position and a good loamy soil; easily increased by cuttings or by the root suckers it occasionally develops. It is one of the species that bears its flowers on wood made during the previous summer and should therefore *not* be spring-pruned.

The two plants referred to above still thrive (1966); the late Sir Frederick Stern told us that his was raised from the original seed (Farrer 100), which makes it more than half a century old.

cv. 'ARGENTEA'.—Leaves with appressed silky hairs, which give them a silvery sheen.

B. AURICULATA Benth.

An evergreen shrub of lax habit, 6 to 9 ft high (twice as high on a wall); young shoots slender, scurfy-downy at first, soon glabrous. Leaves opposite, lanceolate-oblong to ovate-oblong, slenderly pointed, tapered to rounded at the base, the terminal part more or less toothed; 2 to 4 in. long, ⅓ to 1 in. wide; dark dull green, glabrous and wrinkled above; white with a closely appressed felt and conspicuously veined beneath; stalks ¼ to ¾ in. long, with two auricles clasping the stem at the base of each pair. Flowers very fragrant, produced from September to January, crowded numerously in axillary and terminal panicles 1 to 2 in. long and about 1 in. wide. Corolla very downy, tubular, $\frac{1}{4}$ to $\frac{1}{3}$ in. long, $\frac{1}{12}$ in. wide, with four rounded lobes at the mouth, creamy white with yellow in the throat. Calyx grey-tomentose, $\frac{1}{16}$ in. long, with four pointed, triangular lobes. *Bot. Mag.*, t. 9409.

Native of S. Africa, where it is widely spread and where it seems first to have been collected by W. J. Burchell in 1813. The date of its introduction does not seem to be recorded. In a sheltered sunny nook at the foot of a wall at Kew it has survived in the open air for as long as ten years with a slight covering in severe weather. The present specimen was planted against a wall of the Temperate House in 1956. On a warm wall it has been successfully grown as far north as Northumberland. Planted fully in the open it would be killed off during most winters. In the west and on the south coast it is quite hardy save in exceptionally severe winters like that of 1962-3. Both out-of-doors and in greenhouses it is valued for the sweet fragrance of its blossom, which opens during the dullest months. It thrives in a light well-drained loamy soil, and as it flowers on the current season's growth can be pruned in early spring. Easily increased by summer cuttings.

B. CARYOPTERIDIFOLIA W. W. Sm.

This species was described from a flowering specimen collected by Forrest in Yunnan in 1913, but was not introduced on that occasion. The plants treated under the name *B. caryopteridifolia* in previous editions of this work were raised from seed sent by Forrest during his 1921-3 expedition and were cultivated in the Edinburgh Botanic Garden and in the late Sir Frederick Stern's garden at Highdown. However, H. F. Comber (*Notes Roy. Bot. Gard. Edin.*, Vol. 18, pp. 230-2, 1934) asserted that these plants were wrongly identified and referred to *B. truncatifolia* var. *glandulifera* (Lévl.) Marquand. In 1947, A. D. Cotton made a new species out of the Highdown plants—*B. sterniana*—and to it he also referred the plants at Edinburgh. Whether *B. sterniana* is really distinct from *B. caryopteridifolia* is debatable (see below). Assuming that it is, then it is doubtful whether the true *B. caryopteridifolia* is in cultivation. Mr Keenan of the Edinburgh Botanic Garden tells us that some of the plants which he has seen under that name are no more than forms of *B. crispa*.

B. STERNIANA Cotton—A deciduous shrub of rounded bushy shape, up to 8 or 10 ft high; young shoots, under-surface of leaves, flower-stalks and calyx, all covered with a thick and at first pure white wool. Leaves opposite; on young barren shoots they are ovate with a heart-shaped base, coarsely and unevenly toothed, 3 to 6 in. long, about half as wide, with golden-brown wool on the upper surface at first, later almost or quite glabrous; stalk 1 to 1½ in. long. On the second-year branchlets the leaves are much smaller and tapered at the base. Flowers fragrant, lavender-coloured, produced on slender panicles up to 3 in. long in spring or early summer from the previous season's growths. Corolla-tube $\frac{1}{4}$ in. long, downy, with four small, rounded lobes; calyx half as long as the corolla.

This species, which is probably a native of Yunnan, was described, as explained above, from cultivated plants previously considered to be B. *caryopteridifolia*. It might appear to be well distinguished from that species in bearing its flowers in spring on the previous season's wood, whereas B. *caryopteridifolia* was described as bearing its flowers terminally in early autumn. However, the buddleias of this group shows such variability in their inflorescence, as well as in their leaves, that the unwary botanist might easily make two or even more species out of specimens taken from a single plant. Mr Keenan tells us that at Edinburgh B. *sterniana* may flower in autumn as well as in spring, and suggests, tentatively, that this species and B. *caryopteridifolia* may, after all, be one and the same.

B. COLVILEI Hook. f. & Thoms.

A shrub or small tree 30 to 40 ft high in the Himalaya, of vigorous growth, producing long arching shoots in one season; all the younger parts of the plant are at first covered with red-brown wool. Leaves 3 to 10 in. long, $\frac{3}{4}$ to $2\frac{1}{2}$ in.

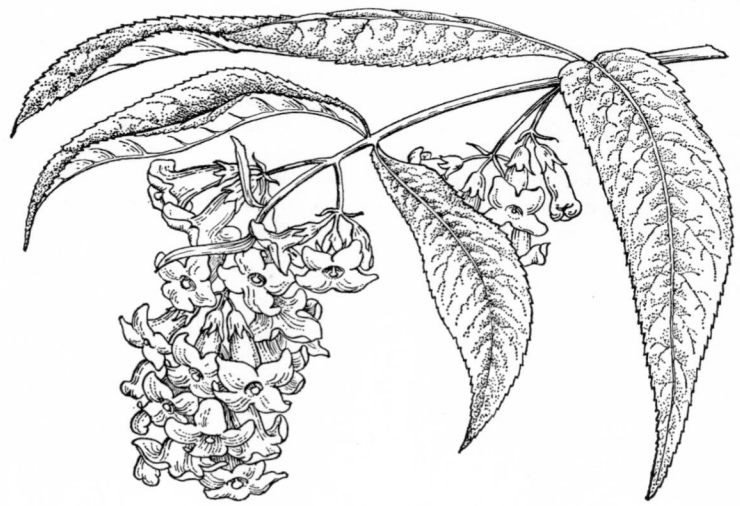

BUDDLEIA COLVILEI

wide; oval lance-shaped, shallowly toothed, tapered at both ends; dark green, at first downy above and felted beneath, but becoming nearly glabrous on both surfaces. Flowers produced in June in terminal pendulous panicles 6 to 8 in. long, about 3 in. wide. Corolla of a beautiful rose or crimson, white in the throat, the tube $\frac{3}{4}$ to 1 in. long, as much or more across the limb; the four lobes rounded, recurved. Calyx bell-shaped, with short lobes. *Bot. Mag.*, t. 7449.

Native of the Sikkim Himalaya, up to 12,000 ft; discovered by Sir Joseph Hooker in 1849. It first flowered with the late Mr W. E. Gumbleton at Belgrove, near Cork, in 1892. Although tender when young, mature plants have survived very hard winters even in the open ground. It is, however, best planted against a high wall, where the season's growths, on which the flowers are borne in the following summer, are more likely to ripen well and pass through the winter unharmed. This buddleia should not be pruned annually but may be kept within bounds by the removal of superfluous wood. No other buddleia capable of living out-of-doors in the British Isles has such large individual flowers, and it is undoubtedly the handsomest in the genus; Sir J. Hooker even said, 'the handsomest of all Himalayan shrubs'.

cv. 'KEWENSIS'.—This name has been given in gardens to the descendants of a plant that once grew in the Temperate House at Kew. Flowers a richer red than in the older cultivated form, the leaves a little narrower; the late Sir Frederick Stern also found it hardier when grown in the open ground at Highdown. Plants raised from seed collected in Bhutan by Ludlow, Sherriff, and Hicks have flowers of a similar hue (LSH 21281).

B. CRISPA Benth.   [PLATE 23

A deciduous shrub, of bushy habit, 6 to 12 ft high, more in diameter; the branchlets covered with a white or tawny, loose felt. Leaves lanceolate, 2 to 5 in. long, $\frac{3}{4}$ to $1\frac{3}{4}$ in. wide; slightly heart-shaped or cut nearly square at the base, tapering thence to the point, coarsely and angularly toothed, covered above, and more so below, with a whitish or tawny down; stalk $\frac{1}{4}$ to 1 in. long. Flowers fragrant, produced in June or later in a terminal panicle 3 in. high and 2 in. wide, formed of axillary whorls. Corolla lilac-coloured; the tube $\frac{1}{3}$ in. long, downy outside; the four-lobed limb about as much in diameter, white near the orifice of the tube. Calyx with erect, ovate lobes, woolly like the stem. *Bot. Mag.*, t. 4793.

Native of Afghanistan and the Himalaya, where it is occasionally a small tree; a similar but not identical plant is found in W. China. At Kew, a plant raised from seed sent home by Dr Aitchison from Afghanistan in 1879 proved perfectly hardy and grew there for more than thirty years without protection. This plant no longer exists, but later introductions have proved as hardy. It is seen at its best when grown on a wall, where it will flower continuously from June to the first frosts if pruned back in spring. It was given an Award of Merit in 1961. This species appeared in previous editions as *B. paniculata* Wall., which is probably not in cultivation.

B. DAVIDII Franch.
B. variabilis Hemsl.

A deciduous shrub, very variable in habit and flower, the largest forms 10 to 15 ft high and wide-spreading bushes of open growth; branchlets four-angled, downy. Leaves 4 to 12 in. long, 1 to 3 in. wide; lanceolate or linear-lanceolate, finely toothed, with very long, tapered points; dark green and soon becoming glabrous above, white-felted beneath; stalks very short. Flowers fragrant, arranged densely in short, rounded clusters on slender panicles 6 to 30 in. long, according to the vigour of the plant and the variety, and appearing from

July to October, or later. Corolla varying in colour from lilac to purple, orange-yellow at the mouth, the tube $\frac{1}{8}$ to $\frac{1}{3}$ in. long, the limb $\frac{1}{6}$ to $\frac{1}{3}$ in. wide, flower-stalks and calyx more or less felted. Seed-vessel smooth $\frac{1}{4}$ to $\frac{1}{3}$ in. long, cylindrical, pointed. *Bot. Mag.*, t. 7609.

Native of Central and W. China up to 9,000 ft; discovered by the French missionary David in 1869; specimens collected later by Henry were described by Hemsley under the name *B. variabilis*, under which it was long known in gardens. It was first introduced from Russia, no doubt from seed collected by one of the Russian explorers, but this was an inferior form, being of comparatively weak, low, semi-prostrate habit, poor in colour of flower. A second and much superior form was introduced to France in 1893 and was raised in the Jardin des Plantes, Paris, and by the nursery firm of Vilmorin. This introduction had a more erect habit and flowers in denser and longer panicles; it resembled var. *veitchiana*, later introduced by Wilson. It is from Wilson's seed, collected in Hupeh and Szechwan during the years 1900–8, that the garden varieties of the present day are descended. The following botanical varieties have been distinguished:

var. ALBA Rehd. & Wils.—Flowers white, leaves narrow. It occurs wild with the type.

var. MAGNIFICA (Wils.) Rehd. & Wils.—Flowers violet-purple, the divisions of the corolla reflexed at the margins. Similar in habit to var. *veitchiana*, but later to flower. Introduced by Wilson from W. Hupeh, where it occurs by stream-sides up to 6,500 ft.

var. NANHOENSIS (Chittenden) Rehd. *B. variabilis* var. *nanhoensis* Chittenden—A dwarf variety usually not more than 3 to 5 ft high, more compact in habit than the type; leaves smaller, panicles shorter. Introduced by Farrer from Kansu in 1914.

var. VEITCHIANA (Veitch) Rehd. *B. variabilis* var. *veitchiana* Veitch—A variety with arching branches; flowers in denser panicles than in the type and deeper-coloured, with a conspicuous orange eye. The earliest to bloom of Wilson's introductions from Hupeh.

var. WILSONII (Wils.) Rehd. & Wils.—Leaves long and tapering; flowers rosy lilac in lax panicles; corolla lobes more or less erect, with crinkled, reflexed margins.

Since 1945 many named clones have come into the trade in Britain, nearly all of them raised in the U.S.A. or on the continent, of which the following is a short selection:

'BLACK KNIGHT'.—Very dark purple.

'EMPIRE BLUE'.—Rich violet-blue with orange eye, upright growth.

'FASCINATING'.—Broad panicles of a vivid lilac-pink. Usually known as 'Fascination'.

'ROYAL RED'.—Rich purple-red.

'WHITE PROFUSION'.—White flowers followed by attractive russet-coloured seed heads.

There are two variegated forms in commerce—'VARIEGATED ROYAL RED' and 'HARLEQUIN'.

In its best forms *B. davidii* is one of the most effective of late summer-flowering shrubs, and a very popular one. Its flowers have a singular attraction for butterflies and this has increased its popularity. Possibly the way its seeds are carried off by the wind explains its existence in unexpected places. It is now thoroughly naturalised in waste places in the south of England and soon established itself on bombed sites in London after the last war.

The species in all its forms needs a good garden soil; the more robust its growth, the finer the flower-panicles. The previous year's growth should be pruned hard back every spring. Vigorous young plants treated in this way will make shoots 8 ft long in a season, terminated by panicles 2 to 2½ ft long. Growth should not, however, be forced by heavy feeding.

B. FALLOWIANA Balf. f. & W. W. Sm.

A deciduous shrub of vigorous, loose habit, 6 ft or more high; young shoots clothed with a dense white felt. Leaves lanceolate, wedge-shaped at the base, tapering to a long fine point, rather shallowly toothed, each tooth terminated by a short, abrupt, gland-tipped point; they vary much in size according to the vigour of the shoot, the largest being 8 to 10 in. long, 2½ to 3½ in. wide, the smallest 2½ in. long by 1 in. wide; upper surface at first clothed with white down, becoming dark green and less downy with age; lower surface clothed with dense, white felt, like the young shoots. Panicles terminal on the shoots of the current season, 8 to 15 in. long, 1 to 1¼ in. wide, densely crowded with very fragrant lavender-coloured flowers arranged in clusters on the main-stalk. Corolla ⅓ in. wide across the lobes, ⅜ in. long, the tube clothed with white felt outside; calyx ⅙ in. long, with sharp erect teeth, also felted. Blooms in late summer and autumn. *Bot. Mag.*, t. 9564.

Native of Yunnan, China. At Kew it is scarcely hardy enough for the open ground, so is given a place on a wall; if cut to the ground, however, it will grow again from the base and flower from the new growths. It is not so rampant in growth as *B. davidii* and is allied to *B. nivea*, but is distinct botanically in having the stamens inserted about the middle of the corolla tube; in *B. nivea* they are inserted immediately below the mouth.

var. ALBA Sabourin—Flowers white. These beautiful white-flowered forms of *B. fallowiana* seem to have arisen early in the twenties in more than one garden where seed of Forrest's sending was raised. Although, like the type, a little tender, they are, in all other respects, finer garden plants than any white-flowered form of *B. davidii*.

Two buddleias are in commerce which appear to be hybrids of *B. fallowiana*—perhaps with *B. davidii*, though this has not been verified. Both originated from the garden of the Earl of Stair at Lochinch, Wigtownshire, and both were originally distributed as typical *B. fallowiana*. One was put into commerce in the thirties by Messrs Marchant and the other by the Sunningdale Nurseries around 1954. Both are excellent garden plants, hardier and more vigorous than typical *B. fallowiana*. The hairy coating of the stems and leaves is not so dense as in the species, but sufficient to give to the plants a soft grey-green cast. The two forms differ in that Messrs Marchant's plant has flowers of a lavender blue, borne in erect spikes; in the Sunningdale form, which was named 'LOCHINCH' in 1959, the spikes droop at the tips and the flowers are of a mauver shade. It is likely that there are other clones of this hybrid in cultivation.

B. FARRERI Balf. f. & W. W. Sm.
B. *tibetica* var. *farreri* (Balf. f. & W. W. Sm.) Marquand.

A deciduous shrub 6 to 10 ft high; young shoots covered with a soft white felt. Uppermost leaves ovate with a shallowly heart-shaped base, those lower on the shoot truncate or more or less tapered at the base; pointed, coarsely and irregularly toothed at the margin; very variable in size according to the vigour of the plant, 3 to 12 in. long, 1½ to 4 in. wide; dull dark green and ultimately glabrous above, covered with white felt beneath; stalk up to 2 in. long, sometimes winged by an extension of the blade down each side. Flowers rose-lilac, produced in April in woolly-stalked inflorescences 1½ to 3 in. long from the terminal joints of the previous year's shoots, the whole forming a panicle up to 8 in. long. The corolla has a very slender tube ⅓ in. long; it is scarcely ¼ in. wide across the four rounded lobes; stamens inserted about the middle of the corolla tube. Calyx narrowly cylindrical, $\frac{3}{16}$ in. long, covered with white wool. *Bot. Mag.*, t. 9027.

Native of Kansu, China; introduced by Farrer in 1915. It has proved hardy in a sheltered nook at Kew and there are bushes 10 ft high and as much wide. Its flowers are liable to be injured by spring frosts and, being formed in autumn, may be lost in the bud-stage during hard winters. It can be grown on a wall or in a large pot out-of-doors during summer, autumn, and winter, taking it under cover to flower. It makes quite a pleasant picture but, so far as I have been able to observe, it has scarcely justified as yet in this country the somewhat ecstatic description given of it by its introducer. According to him it 'hugs only the very hottest and driest crevices, cliffs, walls, and banks down the most arid and torrid aspects of the Ha Shin Fang', from which it would appear to need all the warmth and direct sunlight we can give it. It is probable that lack of these may prevent it from ever making so beautiful a display with us as it does at home, although it sets flower freely after a hot summer. Like many plants from arid habitats, it is best suited in the eastern counties.

B. TIBETICA W. W. Sm.—A close ally of the preceding, from which it may be distinguished by the greyish indumentum that covers the upper surface of the leaves. Flowers purple, fading to white, borne in March–April in dense globose clusters. A native of Tibet, introduced by Lord Wigram in 1931 as "B. *hastata*". It is hardy, and more decorative as a garden specimen than B. *farreri* but, like it, flowers dangerously early in the spring. Its strikingly gaunt habit is well shown in the photograph reproduced in *Journ. R.H.S.*, Vol. 72, 1947, fig. 168.

The two buddleias described above are discussed by A. D. Cotton in *Journ. R.H.S.*, ibid., pp. 427–35.

B. FORRESTII Diels

A deciduous bush up to 10 ft high; shoots four-angled and, like the under-surface of the leaves, covered with a reddish-brown down. Leaves up to 9 or 12 in. long, by 3 in. wide; lanceolate, slender-pointed, tapered at the base, toothed; stalk ¼ to ½ in. long. Inflorescence cylindrical, 2 to 8 in. long, about 1 in. wide, made up of shortly stalked, few-flowered, closely packed clusters; it is terminal, supplemented by others from the axils of the top pairs of leaves; all the stalks very woolly. Flowers fragrant, described by Forrest as 'grey and maroon', 'reddish maroon', 'soft lavender rose', 'pale mauve, almost white'; from which it would seem that, like B. *davidii* (*variabilis*), it has a considerable range of colouring in even a wild state. Corolla ⅓ in. long, ⅛ in. wide across the lobes, more or less woolly outside; stamens inserted immediately below the mouth. Calyx ⅙ in. long, with four narrowly triangular lobes, more or less downy. Ovary downy, sometimes becoming smooth. *Bot. Mag.*, n.s., t. 93.

Native of S.W. China; discovered by Forrest in 1903 and introduced by him. It has been confused in gardens with B. *farreri*, with which it has no close kin-ship; that species flowers in spring from the joints of the previous year's growth, whilst B. *forrestii* flowers in late summer and autumn at the end of the current season's growth, in the same way as B. *davidii*. It is not very hardy in the open ground at Kew; and I have not yet seen it in a sufficiently attractive condition to justify a recommendation of it.

The description given above is of the typical form, but in downiness as well as in flower colour it varies a good deal, some forms approaching an almost glabrous state in branchlet, inflorescence, and ovary. The insertion of the sta-mens close to the mouth of the corolla, and the corolla being about twice as long as wide are (in association) the most distinctive characters. In the example now at Kew, which is figured in *Bot. Mag.*, n.s., t. 93, the lower surfaces of the leaves are covered with a thin, white indumentum and the stems are rounded, only rarely somewhat four-angled. It is grown on a wall of the Temperate House, where it is only cut in severe winters.

B. PTEROCAULIS A. B. Jacks. B. *longifolia* Gagnep, not H. B. K.—Another ally of B. *forrestii*, differing in its narrower corolla-tubes, longer inflorescences and larger leaves; introduced by Farrer from Upper Burma. It is in cultivation at Highdown but Sir Frederick Stern recorded, 'The flowers are a poor colour; it was only kept because Bean when staying here said I must keep it as it was the only one he had ever seen.'

B. GLOBOSA Hope

A partially evergreen, or, in hard winters, deciduous shrub 15 ft high in the open, still more on walls and in favoured places; of rather open, gaunt habit; stems angular, covered with a tawny, loose felt. Leaves lance-shaped, ordinarily 5 to 8 in. long, about one-fourth as wide (occasionally considerably larger), tapered at both ends, but more gradually towards the point; round-toothed, dark green and wrinkled but not downy above, covered beneath with a tawny felt; stalk ¼ in. or less long. Flowers fragrant, bright yellow, produced in June in balls ¾ in. diameter, eight or ten of these globose heads are arranged in a terminal panicle in opposite pairs, each on a stalk 1 to 1½ in. long; the whole panicle 6 to 8 in. long. *Bot. Mag.*, t. 174.

Native of Chile and Peru; introduced by the firm of Kennedy and Lee in 1774. This singularly handsome and striking shrub is hardy at Kew; only in exceptionally severe winters does it suffer injury. It is distinct among cultivated buddleias in the yellow of its flowers and their arrangement in globular heads.

B. HELIOPHILA W. W. Sm.

A deciduous shrub up to 10 ft high; young shoots circular in cross-section, covered with greyish wool. Leaves elliptic or lanceolate, rounded or tapered at the base, slender-pointed, toothless; 2½ to 5 in. long, 1 to 2 in. wide; soft with yellowish, ultimately greyish, wool beneath, almost glabrous above; stalk ¼ in. or less long. Panicles 3 to 6 in. long, 1½ to 2 in. wide, produced in May on short, often leafy, shoots springing from the preceding season's growths and made up of crowded short-stalked clusters of three to eight fragrant blossoms; flower-stalks woolly. Corolla rose-lavender, ½ in. long, downy outside, tube slender, orange-coloured in the throat; lobes rounded. Calyx $\frac{1}{10}$ in. long, very woolly, with triangular teeth. Ovary densely covered with white down. Stamens inserted midway down the corolla tube. *Bot. Mag.*, n.s., t. 193.

Native of Yunnan, China, found by Forrest in sunny, open situations on the Tali Range up to 10,000 ft altitude and introduced by him in 1913. In producing its flowers from the old wood in spring and early summer it resembles *B. farreri*, but that species is very different in the shape of the larger, coarsely toothed, long-stalked leaves. Occasionally, *B. heliophila* has a second flowering in autumn, when terminal panicles are produced on the season's growth, as in the summer-flowering buddleias. It flowers well at Caerhays in May. The material for the figure in the *Botanical Magazine* was provided by the late Charles Eley of East Bergholt Place, Suffolk.

B. JAPONICA Hemsl.

A deciduous shrub usually 3 to 5 ft high, open in habit, and sparsely branched; branches stiff, four-angled, the angles much winged. Leaves narrow-lanceolate, 3 to 8 in. long, 1 to 2 in. wide; minutely and sparsely toothed; dark green and glabrous above, at first tawny-felted beneath. Flowers crowded densely in terminal branched panicles, 4 to 8 in. long. Corolla pale lilac, woolly outside, the tube ½ in. long; the four lobes small. Calyx woolly, pitcher-shaped, with slender-pointed lobes; both calyx and corolla are persistent on the seed-vessels, which are egg-shaped, ¼ in. long, and very freely borne.

Native of Japan. This is not one of the best of the buddleias, although rather striking in autumn with the long, dense, drooping panicles of fruit. It bears these in such abundance that they appear to shorten the life of the shrub. At any rate, after a few years it becomes weak and thin in growth, and should be renewed (by seed rather than by cuttings). It has been cultivated on the continent as "*B. curviflora*", but is not the true plant of that name.

B. × INTERMEDIA (Carr.) Rehd.—The original plant appeared in France among seedlings of *B. japonica* and is thought to be a hybrid between *B. japonica* and *B. lindleyana*.

cv. 'INSIGNIS'.—This seedling of *B. japonica* is now thought to be a form of *B. × intermedia*. Described by Carrière in *Rev. Hort.*, 1878, p. 330, as *B. insignis* (*B. japonica* var. *insignis* (Carr.) Wils.). It is of more compact habit than *B. japonica*, with brighter-coloured flowers.

B. LINDLEYANA Fortune ex Lindl.

A deciduous shrub to 12 ft high on a wall, with glabrous four-angled stems. Leaves 4 to 8 in. long, ovate, tapered at the apex, pale green and almost glabrous beneath, margins almost untoothed. Flowers tubular, deep violet to lilac, about ¾ in. long and ⅓ in. wide at the mouth, covered on the outside with fine, short hairs; they are borne in July and August in terminal racemes 2 to 8 in. long.

A native of China, where it inhabits the hills and lower mountain slopes; introduced by Fortune in 1843 from a garden on the island of Chusan. Although somewhat tender it has grown well in many south-western gardens and attained a height of 12 ft in the Bath Botanic Garden. In the size and colouring of the individual flowers this is one of the most handsome of the genus, but so few are open at one time that it makes little display.

Wilson introduced var. SINUATODENTATA Hemsl., in which the leaves are wavy-toothed and more acuminate than in the type. An old plant from his seed has lived outdoors at the Glasnevin Botanic Garden for more than half a century.

B. NIVEA Duthie

A deciduous shrub 6 to 9 (perhaps more) ft high, with the young branchlets covered thickly with a pure white wool. Leaves of variable size, from the largest, 10 in. long by 4 in. wide, down to others 3 to 4 in. long and 1 in. wide; they are long-pointed, rounded at the base, angularly toothed except at the end; dark green and ultimately glabrous above except on the midrib; covered beneath with a thick wool, at first pure white, then tawny. Panicles branched, terminal on the main shoots, and supplemented by others at the end of short axillary branches. Each portion of the panicle is slender, ¾ to 1 in. in diameter, and 3 to 6 in. long. Flowers ¼ in. long, pale purple, only showing colour at the tip, the corolla-tube and calyx being covered with wool.

Native of China; discovered by Wilson in W. Szechwan, at altitudes around 7,000 to 8,000 ft, and introduced in 1901. It is a vigorous plant, but its chief attraction is the snowy covering of the leaves, shoots, and panicles. It flowers in August.

B. OFFICINALIS Maxim.

A deciduous or semi-evergreen shrub up to 9 ft high; young shoots at first indistinctly four-angled, clothed with a dense grey wool. Leaves narrowly lance-shaped, tapered towards both ends, but more gradually to the long fine point, mostly entire; 2½ to 6 in. long, ½ to 2 in. wide; dull dark green and slightly downy above, clothed with pale grey wool beneath; stalk ⅓ in. or less long. Flowers fragrant, produced in a terminal panicle 3 to 12 in. long, 2½ in. wide, composed of short-stalked racemes or cymes. Each flower is ⅜ in. wide, pale lilac with a yellow eye; corolla four-lobed, the slender tube ¼ in. long, hairy at the throat and downy outside. Calyx small, woolly, with short teeth. *Bot. Mag.*, t. 8401.

Native of Hupeh and Szechwan, China; named by Maximowicz in 1880, introduced to cultivation by Wilson in 1908. At Kew it has to be grown in pots and given greenhouse treatment from October onwards, as it is valuable in flowering for three months in midwinter. Hardy in Cornwall and similar mild localities, where it should be welcome on account of the season at which its delicate lilac, fragrant blossoms open. It is closely allied to B. *heliophila*, but in that species the leaves are almost sessile and the corollas up to ½ in. long.

B. SALVIIFOLIA (L.) Lam.
Lantana salvifolia L.

A partially evergreen shrub, described as 6 to 16 ft high in a wild state, with a stem 4 to 6 in. in diameter; young shoots long and slender, square, covered like the under-surface of the leaves, the flower-stalks and flowers themselves, with a whitish or brown-red down. Leaves stalkless or nearly so, lanceolate with a heart-shaped base, tapered thence gradually to the pointed apex, round-toothed; 1 to 3 in. long, ¼ to ⅝ in. wide (larger in warm climates), dull green and wrinkled like a sage leaf. Panicles born on the current season's growths in July, pyramidal, 3 to 6 in. long, 2 to 4 in. wide at the base. Corolla ⅓ in. long, woolly outside, lobes short; the colour of the part not covered with wool is white to pale lilac, with orange in the throat. Flowers fragrant.

Native of Africa from south-western Cape Province eastwards and northwards to Tanganyika. It was originally named *Lantana salvifolia* by Linnaeus and transferred to *Buddleia* by Lamarck in his *Encyclopaedia* in 1783, at which period it was in cultivation in the Jardin du Roi at Paris. It is remarkably hardy for a S. African shrub and has been grown out-of-doors without protection at Kew for twenty years, and occasionally flowered there. It is cut to the ground in severe weather but springs up again. The sage-like leaves distinguish it at once from all other cultivated buddleias. It is said to be the first shrub to reappear in the mountain forests of S. Africa after a fire. The wood is hard and was highly prized for making assegai shafts. As with other species, the flowers evidently vary in colour in a wild state; thus we have 'flowers orange and buff' (Barber); 'blossoms white' (Pegler); 'limb tinged with lilac above, throat deep orange' (Galpin). Sims in *Forest Flora of Cape Colony*, p. 277, says there is a pretty form with blue flowers.

B. STENOSTACHYA Rehd. & Wils.

A deciduous shrub up to 10 ft high; young shoots covered densely with a white wool. Leaves oblong-lanceolate, tapered at the base, long and slenderly pointed, generally slightly toothed, sometimes almost entire: 4 to 8 in. long,

$1\frac{1}{2}$ to $2\frac{1}{2}$ in. wide; dull green and slightly downy above, covered like the young shoots with white wool below; stalk about $\frac{1}{3}$ in. long. Panicles 6 to 18 in. long, about 1 in. wide, slenderly cylindrical, usually coming in threes from the end of the current season's growth in late summer and autumn, and composed of closely packed, few-flowered, shortly stalked cymes. Corolla $\frac{1}{3}$ in. long, about $\frac{1}{6}$ in. across the four roundish lobes, lilac-coloured, with orange in the throat, very downy inside and out. Calyx $\frac{1}{8}$ in. long, downy, with slender erect lobes. Stamens inserted between the middle and the apex of the corolla tube.

Native of W. Szechwan, China; discovered and introduced by Wilson in 1908. The species is cultivated in the Arnold Arboretum and plants under the name are grown in English gardens. It is notable for the slenderness of its long panicles. It resembles B. *nivea* in leaf, etc., but that species has a much shorter, pyramidal panicle and has the stamens close to the mouth of the corolla-tube.

B. × WEYERIANA Weyer

This is a hybrid raised in the autmn of 1914 by Mr Van de Weyer at Smedmore House, Corfe Castle, Dorset, by crossing B. *davidii* var. *magnifica* with B. *globosa*. A number of plants were raised from the seeds and they vary considerably; but most of them inherited from B. *globosa*, the seed parent, the ball-like flower-clusters arranged in panicles, and a more or less definite shade of yellow in the corolla. Two have been named: 'GOLDEN GLOW', with orange and yellow flowers shaded with pink and mauve. This is not only distinct from all the true species of *Buddleia* in the arrangement of the flowers, but has considerable beauty also. Another, not so good, is called 'MOONLIGHT', its flowers pale cream colour with deep orange-yellow in the throat. They flower from June onwards.

The shrubs themselves are very vigorous and hardy. The raiser's hope was to attain a buddleia combining the inflorescence of B. *davidii* with a clear yellow colour from B. *globosa*. In this he never succeeded; he raised one with flowers as in 'Moonlight', but 'fifty per cent better', but so far as is known this was never named or distributed.

BUMELIA   SAPOTACEAE

A genus of about twenty-five species of evergreen or deciduous shrubs and trees ranging from Virginia and Illinois into S. America. The species described are of interest as the only members of the Sapodilla family grown outside in the British Isles.

B. LYCIOIDES (L.) Pers.   SOUTHERN BUCKTHORN
Sideroxylon lycioides L.

A deciduous, small tree over 20 ft high in a wild state, but usually a shrub little more than half that height in cultivation; branchlets glabrous, and on young specimens usually armed with spines $\frac{3}{4}$ in. or less long. Leaves firm and rather hard in texture, varying in shape from narrow oval to obovate (the former shape more characteristic of young plants), 1 to 5 in. long, $\frac{1}{2}$ to $1\frac{1}{2}$ in. wide; always tapered to the base, pointed or rounded at the apex, not toothed, and quite glabrous except for a few silky hairs about the midrib beneath; conspicuously veined; stalk $\frac{1}{6}$ to $\frac{1}{3}$ in. long. Flowers $\frac{1}{8}$ in. in diameter, produced in August and September, each on a glabrous stalk $\frac{1}{2}$ in. or less long, crowded numerously in hemispherical clusters in the leaf-axils. Corolla white; calyx comparatively large, green. Fruit egg-shaped, $\frac{1}{2}$ in. long, black, rarely or never seen in this country.

Native of the south-eastern United States, and known in England since 1752, but not ornamental enough to be generally cultivated. It is quite hardy at Kew, but appears to be the only one of the genus of which so much can be said. The leaves on young sterile plants resemble those of a peach in size and shape. Several other species have at times been introduced, but they need at least the warmth of the south-western counties to thrive. Amongst them B. TENAX Willd., whose leaves are covered beneath with a tawny yellow, silky down; and B. LANUGINOSA (Michx.) Pers., with a more or less woolly down, are the most interesting. The latter is in cultivation in the Glasnevin Botanic Garden, but Dr Walsh tells us it has little to commend it as a garden plant.

BUPLEURUM   UMBELLIFERAE

A genus of about seventy-five species, most of them herbs and sub-shrubs. The one species described is of interest as the only shrubby member of the Umbelliferae that can be cultivated in the open air in Britain. Four herbaceous members of the same genus are natives of chalky districts in Britain and are known in country places as 'buplevers'.

B. FRUTICOSUM L.

An evergreen or semi-evergreen shrub, of lax habit, 5 to 8 ft high, with slender, not much divided branches, and glabrous, purplish young shoots. Leaves alternate, firm, narrowly obovate, stalkless, tapering at the base, rounded or with a short, bristle-like tip at the apex, entire; 2 to $3\frac{1}{2}$ in. long, $\frac{3}{4}$ to $1\frac{1}{2}$ in. wide; quite glabrous, and of a bluish green. Flowers small, yellow, produced in a terminal umbel 3 or 4 in. across. *Bot. Mag.*, n.s., t. 408.

Native of S. Europe and the Mediterranean region; introduced more than three hundred years ago. It is not completely hardy but grows and flowers well at Kew where protected by other shrubs. It has been grown there as a wall plant, where it reached a height of 10 ft. In most maritime districts and in the south-western counties it succeeds admirably, and its yellow flower-clusters and blue-green foliage make a very effective contrast. It flowers from July to September, and is propagated easily by cuttings. It is one of the best shrubs for planting on exposed cliffs near the sea, and is very well adapted for chalky districts.

BURSARIA   PITTOSPORACEAE

A genus of three or four species, natives of Australia. The generic name refers to the shape of the fruits.

B. SPINOSA Cav.

An evergreen, glabrous shrub 8 to 15 ft high, with both spiny and unarmed branches. Leaves alternate, obovate, $\frac{3}{4}$ to $1\frac{1}{2}$ in. long, $\frac{3}{16}$ to $\frac{3}{8}$ in. wide; notched or rounded at the apex, tapering towards the base, but scarcely stalked. Flowers produced in panicles that terminate the twigs towards the end of the branch, and vary in size according to the strength of the shoot that bears them, the largest 5 or 6 in. high by 3 to 4 in. through; each flower is about $\frac{1}{4}$ in. across, with narrow, white petals. Although the individual flower is so small, the entire bush makes a pretty display when in bloom, on account of its profusion. The fruit is a dry, flat, pouch-like capsule about $\frac{1}{3}$ in. across, reddish brown, resembling in shape that of common shepherd's purse. *Bot. Mag.*, t. 1767.

Native of New South Wales and Tasmania, and only suitable for the milder parts of the British Isles. In the vicarage garden at Bitton, near Bristol, it grew exceedingly well against a wall, flowering during August, when but few other shrubs are in bloom. The great crop of reddish fruits is also decidedly striking. This shrub can be increased by cuttings made of half-ripened wood placed in gentle heat. Flowers fragrant.

BUXUS   Box   BUXACEAE

Evergreen shrubs or trees, of which about thirty species are known, inhabiting all three continents of the Old World, also the W. Indies and Central America. The leaves are opposite, not toothed or lobed, leathery in texture, easily separated into two layers. Flowers unisexual, small and inconspicuous, produced in short dense clusters in the leaf-axils in spring, the males and females in the same cluster, the former the more numerous. They have no petals; but the male has four sepals and four stamens, the female six sepals and three pistils. Fruit a three-celled capsule, each valve two-horned; seeds black and shining. Wood of hard, bony texture.

The boxes succeed in almost any soil, and are often found wild on a limestone formation. They are useful for semi-shaded positions. Cuttings of all the cultivated species and varieties except *B. wallichiana* strike root freely.

B. BALEARICA Lam.   BALEARIC BOX

A shrub or small tree up to 30 ft high in the wild, densely branched; young stems square, and at first slightly downy. Leaves roundish oval to ovate-oblong;

¾ to 1½ in. long, ¼ to ¾ in. wide, wedge-shaped at the base, usually notched at the apex (or the terminal leaves sometimes minutely and abruptly pointed); thick and leathery, dark glossy green above, but not so shining as in *B. sempervirens*, pale green beneath; stalk slightly downy, $\frac{1}{12}$ in long. Flowers yellowish green, of no beauty; males shortly stalked.

Native of the Balearic Islands and the south-west of Spain. The species is easily distinguished from the common box by the duller, larger leaves, the thicker, more robust shoots, and the sturdier habit. The largest specimen I have seen in this country was at Kew, near the Temple of the Sun, and was about 24 ft high, its trunk 2½ ft in girth. It grew slowly, and was probably the oldest in the country. Loudon mentioned this tree, which once grew on the wall of a house, as being 13 ft high in 1836. Aiton gives 1780 as the date of its introduction. It was blown down during a storm in March 1916, the Temple of the Sun being destroyed at the same time. In the gardens of S. Europe this box takes the place that *B. sempervirens* occupies here.

B. HARLANDII Hance

A dwarf shrub 6 in. to 2 ft or so high; young branchlets slender, glabrous, or with a few short hairs near the nodes. Leaves oblanceolate to obovate-oblong, ½ to 1¼ in. long, ⅙ to ¼ in. wide, emarginate at the apex, very gradually tapered at the base. Staminate flowers stalked, the pistillate ones sessile; rudimentary ovary of the staminate flowers as long as the inner sepals; style of the pistillate flowers as long as the ovary (in *B. microphylla* and its varieties the style is only half as long as the ovary).

Native of Central and S. China, where it is found growing among rocks and stones in the beds of rivers and streams. The true species may not be in cultivation and would probably be tender, coming as it does from low elevations where the winters are mild. The plant grown in gardens as "*B. harlandii*" is not this species but a form of *B. microphylla* var. *sinica* and of uncertain origin. It was once grown in gardens as "*B chinensis*". The confusion seems to have arisen from the fact that on Hance's herbarium sheet there are two specimens—one the true *B. harlandii* and the other *B. microphylla* var. *sinica*.

B. MICROPHYLLA Sieb. & Zucc.

A dwarf shrub to about 3 ft high; stems square, glabrous. Leaves rather thin and membranous, ½ to ⅘ in. long, ⅙ to ⅓ in. wide, narrowly elliptic-oblong to oblanceolate, rounded or notched at the apex, tapered or cuneate at the base. Flowers as in *B. sempervirens*, but with the rudimentary ovary of the staminate flowers much larger than in that species (as long as the inner sepals). An inhabitant of Japanese gardens; whether it is also found wild in its typical state is a matter on which Japanese botanists are not agreed. It is a pleasing little box, which resembles some of the small forms of *B. sempervirens*, but its stems and leaves are quite glabrous.

B. microphylla, although described from a garden plant, was the first to be named in a group of closely related wild boxes which are widely distributed in

temperate E. Asia and usually considered as forming a single species of which
B. microphylla must be regarded as the nomenclatural type. The following
varieties are distinguished:

var. JAPONICA (Muell.-Arg.) Rehd. & Wils. *B. japonica* Muell.-Arg.—A
loose-habited shrub 3 to 6 ft high (more in the wild state); young stems glabrous,
winged. Leaves $\frac{1}{3}$ to 1 in. long, roundish obovate or inversely heart-shaped,
sometimes as broad as long, tapered at the base, rounded or notched at the apex,
smooth except for a slight down on the stalk when young. Native of Japan, and
perhaps the least ornamental of boxes. It has an ungainly habit, and has not the
healthy, vigorous aspect one associates with the genus. The roundish leaves,
winged stems, and the absence of down are its distinguishing features. It also
flowers more freely than any other species.

var. KOREANA Nakai—A dense shrub about 2 ft high; young stems and
leaf-stalks downy. Leaves to about $\frac{3}{5}$ in. long, obovate to elliptic-oblong, margins inrolled, venation scarcely visible on upper surface of leaves. Native of
Korea and parts of China, valued in the north-eastern U.S.A. for its great
hardiness.

var. RIPARIA (Mak.) Mak. *B. sempervirens* var. *riparia* Mak.—Native of
Japan, found on rocks by rivers in the mountains. Stems slender, often procumbent, leaves less than 1 in. long. This variety is said to be intermediate between
var. *japonica* and the type.

var. SINICA Rehd. & Wils.—A shrub 3 to 18 ft high in the wild state; young
stems downy. Leaves lustrous green, to $1\frac{2}{5}$ in. long, ovate to obovate, with the
venation visible on the upper surface of the leaf. Native of China, where it is
widespread. The "*B. harlandii*" of gardens belongs here; it is a dwarf form, perhaps of garden origin, growing to about 2 ft high, with leaves to $1\frac{1}{2}$ in. long and
barely $\frac{1}{4}$ in. wide.

B. SEMPERVIRENS L.   COMMON BOX

A spreading bush usually wider than it is high, or a small tree 15 to 20 (or
even 30) ft high; young stems square, slightly winged, minutely hairy. Leaves
ovate, oval or oblong, notched at the apex, $\frac{1}{2}$ to 1 in. long, about half as wide
(considerably larger in some of the garden forms); very dark green above, pale
below; shining on both sides; stalk very short, minutely hairy. Flowers produced
in April, pale green with yellow anthers; the staminate flowers bear a small
rudimentary pistil about half as long as the sepals. Seed-vessel $\frac{1}{3}$ in. long, with
six beaks.

Native of Europe, N. Africa, and W. Asia, and very probably indigenous to
Britain, although this is doubted by some authorities. The most famous site of
naturally grown box trees in England is Box Hill, near Dorking; but several
other place-names in England indicate a more extended habitat in former times.
It has been stated that £10,000 worth of box timber was taken from Box Hill
in 1815.

In gardens the box shares with the holly and the yew the distinction of being
the most useful (as distinct from the most beautiful) of hardy evergreens. Some
of the more pendulous forms make handsome lawn specimens, and the ordinary

type makes an admirable shelter, or a screen for hiding unsightly objects, especially in half-shaded places. Its use for topiary work is well known, also for planting in formal arrangements, where it is kept low and flat by clipping. For the latter purpose 'Suffruticosa', used so extensively for 'box-edging', is also employed. The adaptability of the ordinary form to pruning makes it useful in positions where space is strictly limited, for it can be kept permanently about 6 ft in height by a judicious removal of prominent shoots, and this without rendering it unduly formal.

Like the holly and the yew, the box was in earlier times associated with certain festivals and ceremonies. The wood is of a hard, almost bony consistence, and before wood-engraving became an almost lost art, was a favourite medium for the purpose. Large quantities were formerly imported from S.E. Europe and Persia. Even now, so useful is the wood, the world's supply is not equal to the demand, and has been partly replaced by Venezuelan box (*Gossipiospermum praecox*), though this species too is becoming scarce owing to over-exploitation.

Of numerous named varieties cultivated in gardens, some of which scarcely differ from each other, only the most distinct and readily available are described here. For some of the additional information included in this revision we are indebted to *An Account of the Cultivars of the Common Box Grown by Hillier and Sons*, by C. R. Lancaster. This study has since been published (*Gard. Chron.*, May 13, June 7 and 14, 1968).

cv. 'ARGENTEA'.—Leaves with a white border of varying depth; habit dense. Also incorrectly known as "Argenteo-variegata".

cv. 'AUREA PENDULA'.—Secondary branches pendulous. Leaves margined with, or almost wholly yellow.

cv. 'ELEGANTISSIMA'.—Leaves mostly smaller and narrower than in the type, some of them deformed, irregularly margined with creamy white; of neat, dense habit, to 6 ft high. Inclined to revert if closely and frequently clipped.

cv. 'HANDSWORTHENSIS'.—Habit vigorous, densely bushy, but somewhat erect. Leaves large and broad. Originated in the Handsworth nursery of Fisher, Son and Sibray, before 1872.

cv. 'LATIFOLIA BULLATA'.—Leaves ovate to orbicular, larger than in the type, bullate, dark green. A free-growing bush of spreading habit. There is an example at Kew 8 ft high and 10 ft across. Also known as 'Bullata'.

cv. 'LATIFOLIA MACROPHYLLA'.—Leaves ovate to orbicular, up to 1 in. long; habit spreading

cv. 'LONGIFOLIA'.—A dense, erect bush to 10 ft or more high; leaves to 1½ in. long but scarcely ½ in. wide, dark green. The name of this clone has recently and incorrectly been altered to "Angustifolia". It has nothing to do with either *B. angustifolia* Mill. nor with *B. sempervirens angustifolia* Kirchn.

cv. 'MYOSOTIFOLIA'.—A curious dwarf, very slow-growing variety, of dense, compact habit. Leaves green, very small, the largest about ½ in. long, ⅛ in. wide.

cv. 'MYRTIFOLIA'.—The box usually found under the name *B. s. myrtifolia* is of spreading habit and slow growth, with leaves ⅛ to ¾ in. long and up to ⅛ in. wide. Whether the plant so labelled at Kew, which is 15 ft high and as much through, belongs to this clone is not certain: perhaps so, since the myrtle-leaved box known to Loudon, though usually dwarf, grew quite large in favourable circumstances.

cv. 'PENDULA'.—A very elegant variety with pendent branches, but growing naturally into a small tree.

cv. 'PROSTRATA'.—A low, horizontally branched shrub, described by Dallimore (*Yew, Holly and Box*, 1908) as growing no more than a few feet high but covering a wide area of ground. In the West Hill nursery of Messrs Hillier it reached a height of 6 ft and a spread of 8 ft.

cv. 'ROSMARINIFOLIA'.—Leaves long and very narrow, $\frac{1}{6}$ to $\frac{1}{4}$ in. wide; dwarf.

cv. 'ROTUNDIFOLIA'.—Similar to 'Latifolia Macrophylla' but of stiff habit. The name adopted here appears to be the correct, or at least the established, name for the box described by Dallimore under the name *B. s. latifolia*.

cv. 'SALICIFOLIA ELATA'. Leaves a little shorter and narrower than in 'Longifolia', to $1\frac{1}{4}$ in. long and $\frac{1}{8}$ in. wide and of taller, more slender growth. It has reached 25 ft in height at Kew.

cv. 'SUFFRUTICOSA'.—For centuries this variety, distinguished by its dwarf habit and small obovate leaves, has been valued in formal gardening for making neat edgings to flower-beds, walks, etc. It can be kept a few inches high by persistent clipping, but left to itself as one may occasionally see it in old or neglected gardens, it becomes 4 or 5 ft high. It can be increased by division or by cuttings. It was described by Linnaeus as a species—*B. suffruticosa*.

B. WALLICHIANA Baill.   HIMALAYAN BOX

A shrub growing not more than 6 or 8 ft high in cultivation, but no doubt considerably taller in its native country; shoots very downy. Leaves 1 to $2\frac{1}{2}$ in. long, $\frac{1}{4}$ to $\frac{5}{8}$ in. wide; linear-lanceolate, tapered at both ends, dark green, not so glossy as *B. sempervirens*; the base of the leaf, the midrib, and the short stalk

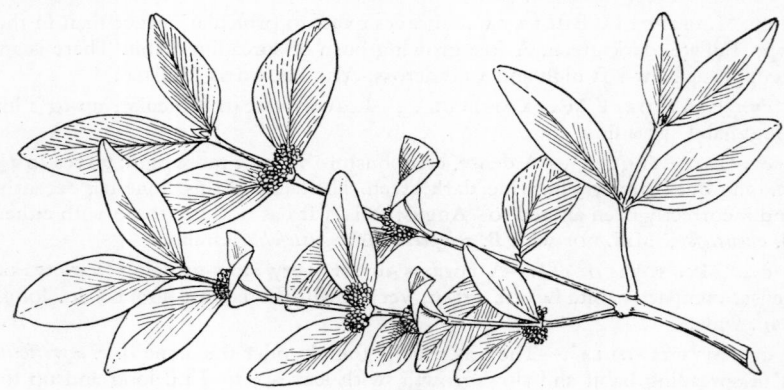

BUXUS WALLICHIANA

are all downy. Flowers in dense axillary clusters, opening in April, and only noticeable for the yellow anthers of the males.

Native of the north-western Himalaya; very rare in cultivation. Although it grows slowly it is perfectly hardy. A bush at Kew (which no longer exists) reached a height and spread of about 6 ft in fifty years or more. There is an example of about 8 ft high in the Edinburgh Botanic Garden. It is difficult to propagate by cuttings. This species is readily distinguished from B. *sempervirens* and B. *balearica* by the long, narrow leaves, blunt or pointed but not notched at the apex, and by the much more abundant down on the stems, which persists for more than a year. The timber is equal to, or greater in value than, that of the common box.

CAESALPINIA LEGUMINOSAE

Of the forty or so species of *Caesalpinia* known, two or three can be grown in the milder parts of the kingdom, but even as far south as Kew they need some shelter in the open air. Among hardy trees and shrubs they are most nearly allied to *Gymnocladus* and *Gleditsia*. The flowers are very dissimilar to those of the commoner pea-flowered type of Leguminosae, the petals being almost equal in size and shape. The other essential features are the tubular, five-toothed calyx, the ten free stamens, and the thick, compressed, leathery pod. Named after Andreas Caesalpini, an Italian botanist, 1519–1603.

C. GILLIESII (Hook.) Benth.
Poinciana gilliesii Hook.

A deciduous shrub or small tree, with slender erect branches; young shoots covered with gland-tipped hairs. Leaves doubly pinnate, about 8 in. long, composed of about nine to eleven pairs of primary divisions 1½ in. long, each of which carries numerous small, glabrous, oblong leaflets, about ¼ in. long and $\frac{1}{12}$ in. wide. Racemes terminal, stiffly erect, 1 ft or more long, carrying from thirty to forty flowers. Each flower is borne on a downy stalk, 1 in. or more long, the petals rich yellow, 1¼ in. long, forming a rather saucer-shaped corolla. Sepals ¾ in. long; stamens scarlet, 2½ to 3 in. long; pod 3 in. long, ⅝ in. wide. *Bot. Mag.*, t. 4006.

Native of the Argentine Republic, especially in the province of Mendoza; introduced in 1829, but too tender to have become generally cultivated. It succeeds quite well on a south wall at Kew, where it has grown 25 ft high, and flowered nearly every year in July and August. The plant now in the collection grows against a wall of the Temperate House. It has no chance at Kew in the open ground, but in a garden at Ryde, Isle of Wight, it succeeded admirably. The rich yellow flowers with long scarlet stamens give a singularly brilliant effect.

C. JAPONICA Sieb. & Zucc.   [PLATE 24

C. sepiaria var. *japonica* (Sieb. & Zucc.) Mak.

A deciduous, very thorny shrub, of straggling or scandent habit, not more than about 8 ft high when left to itself, but growing at least twice as high when trained up a wall. Branches not downy, armed with strong decurved thorns ¼ to ⅓ in. long. Leaves doubly pinnate, 12 in. or rather more long, each of the three to eight pairs of main divisions (pinnae) carrying six to ten pairs of leaflets; the common leaf-stalk is armed at each joint with one erect and two decurved prickles, and irregularly in between. Leaflets oblong or obovate, rounded at the apex; ½ to 1 in. long, ¼ to ½ in. wide; almost or quite glabrous. Racemes up to 12 in. long, 4 in. through, carrying twenty to over thirty flowers, each on a glabrous, slender stalk 1¼ in. long. Flowers canary yellow, 1¼ to 1½ in. across, the upper one of the five petals the smallest, and striped with red. Stamens ten, red, ⅝ in. long, forming a conspicuous cluster in the centre of the flower. Pod 3 in. long, 1 in. or more wide, flat, carrying six to nine seeds. *Bot. Mag.*, t. 8207.

Native of Japan and China; introduced by Messrs Veitch, who first flowered it in their Coombe Wood nursery in 1887. It succeeded well there on a sunny slope, and occasionally produced seed; but at Kew, in the open ground, it has always been a failure, although it may live for some years. It has grown well on a west wall, and in one of the bays outside the Temperate House. A plant on the potting shed in the R.H.S. Garden at Wisley flowers profusely. It was damaged in the winter of 1962–3 but has since recovered. There are few shrubs more beautiful either in leaf or flower, and it would be well worth growing in a sunny recess where it could be covered in winter. It is one of the most fiercely armed of all cultivated shrubs. Propagated by layers. Flowers in June and July. Nearly allied to this is:

C. SEPIARIA Roxb.—*C. japonica* is by many botanists considered to be a variety of this species, which differs in having very downy wood and less lax racemes. It is common throughout India and much used there as a hedging plant.

CALCEOLARIA   SCROPHULARIACEAE

This S. American genus, well known by its cultivated greenhouse races, commemorates F. Calceolari, an Italian botanist who lived in the sixteenth century. The plant described in previous editions under the name *C. violacea* is now placed in the small related genus *Jovellana*, distinguished by a corolla divided into almost equal erect 'lips', with flat or only slightly inrolled margins, and thus not showing the 'pouch' characteristic of the true calceolarias.

C. INTEGRIFOLIA Murr.

C. rugosa Ruiz & Pavon

An erect evergreen shrub of bushy habit, 4 ft high; young shoots semi-woody, clothed with a close velvety down. Leaves opposite, sage-like, oblong-ovate, tapered towards both ends, bluntish at the apex, minutely toothed; 2 to 3½ in. long, ¾ to 1½ in. wide; dull green and wrinkled above, with a soft, close, greyish felt beneath; stalkless. Flowers about ½ in. wide, with the characteristic 'pouch' of the genus, bright yellow, produced abundantly during the summer months in successive tiers on terminal corymbs that are 3 to 5 in. high, not so much wide. Calyx four-lobed, the lobes ovate, ⅛ in. long, felted like the slender flower-stalk. The inflorescence is borne on a clear stalk that is sometimes 6 to 9 in. long. *Bot. Mag.*, t. 2523.

Native of Chile; introduced in 1822 by the Horticultural Society. In most parts of the country this calceolaria needs protection, but in the south-western counties succeeds very well in the open ground, making there a very gay and attractive shrub. Near London it may be grown against a sunny wall, especially if covered with bracken or brushwood during severe frost. It likes a good, well-drained, loamy soil and is easily increased by cuttings in summer. Judging by wild specimens, it is very variable in leaf and flower; the description given above represents the form commonly grown in this country. Some are much more coarsely toothed, and one with narrower, smaller leaves is called var. ANGUSTIFOLIA Lindl.

CALDCLUVIA   CUNONIACEAE

A genus of a single species, endemic to the temperate forests of Chile and bordering parts of Argentina, belonging to the same family as *Wein-mannia*. It is named after Alexander Caldcleugh, to whom we owe our first knowledge of many Chilean plants.

C. PANICULATA (Cav.) D. Don

Weinmannia paniculata Cav.

An evergreen shrub or small tree to 15 or 20 ft. Leaves simple, oblong-lanceolate, tapered at both ends, 2 to 5 in. long, short-stalked, with sharply toothed margins and recalling, except in their thicker texture, the leaves of the sweet chestnut. The small white flowers are borne in June and July in axillary corymbs about 2 in. wide. Fruit a many-seeded leathery capsule.

This species is fairly common in the Chilean beech forests from Concepcion to the Rio Palena; it was introduced in 1832 and again by Comber in 1925. It is not so worthy a representative of its family as *Weinmannia trichosperma*, but a handsome evergreen. It is probably of the same order of hardiness as *Eucryphia cordifolia* and *Nothofagus dombeyi* and should succeed where these thrive. It grows well at Logan in Wigtownshire, but Mr Colledge tells us that it needs protection from wind.

CALLICARPA   VERBENACEAE

A genus of about forty species of shrubs or small trees found wild in N. and Central America, E. Asia, Australia, and Malaya. The name is given in reference to the beauty of the fruits, for which the following species are mainly cultivated. Leaves opposite.

C. BODINIERI Lévl.

C. giraldiana var. *subcanescens* Rehd.

An erect deciduous shrub 6 to 9 ft high; young shoots at first downy, soon becoming nearly or quite glabrous. Leaves narrowly oval or lanceolate, with a long slender point and tapered at the base, toothed; 2 to 5 in. long, 1 to $2\frac{1}{4}$ in. wide; dull dark green above, paler beneath, downy on both surfaces; stalk $\frac{1}{8}$ to $\frac{1}{2}$ in. long. Flowers numerously produced during July on the leafy shoots in close, rounded, axillary cymes $\frac{3}{4}$ to $1\frac{1}{2}$ in. wide, the stalks thickly furnished with star-like hairs. Each flower is about $\frac{3}{16}$ in. wide and $\frac{1}{6}$ in. long, the corolla lilac-coloured, with four rounded lobes; calyx bell-shaped with four short lobes, sprinkled with star-like hairs; anthers yellow. Fruit globose, $\frac{1}{8}$ to $\frac{1}{6}$ in. wide, pale bluish lilac, glossy.

Native of China in the provinces of Szechwan, Hupeh, Shensi; discovered by Henry in 1887. It was introduced to Germany at the end of the nineteenth century by the missionary Giraldi and distributed by Hesse's nurseries as *C. giraldiana*. Wilson introduced it to this country in 1907 from Szechwan and plants from his seed were also grown as *C. giraldiana*. However, some years elapsed before this name was validly published by Schneider, and in the meantime the same species had been described under the name *C. bodinieri*. It is variable in the degree of hairiness of leaf and inflorescence, and since the type chosen by Schneider differs markedly from that of *C. bodinieri* in this respect, it becomes:

var. GIRALDII (Rehd.) Rehd.   *C. giraldiana* Schneid.; *C. giraldii* Rehd.— Leaves glabrous above, glandular and thinly downy beneath; inflorescence also less downy than in the type. But some plants cultivated in this country under the name *C. giraldiana* may in fact be nearer to typical *C. bodinieri* than they are to the variety. *Bot. Mag.*, t. 8682.

So far as a climate like that of Kew is concerned *C. bodinieri* is the best calli-carpa for cultivation in the open. To get it at its best it requires generous treatment at the root and a sunny position. It frequently gives beautiful displays of fruit in October and November, and is perfectly hardy. Although the colour of the fruit is given above as pale bluish lilac, seedling plants at Kew bear berries that range in colour from lavender to rich purple. *C. japonica* is well distinguished from this species by its narrower glabrous leaves and glabrous flower-panicles. Both bear fruit more freely and surely when several seedling plants (or plants of different clones) are grown together. There is a white-fruited form in cultivation.

CALLICARPA BODINIERI var. GIRALDII

C. JAPONICA Thunb.

A deciduous shrub 3 to 5 ft high, with erect, semi-woody stems furnished at first with a pale tufted felt, which soon falls away. Leaves narrowly oval or ovate-lanceolate; 3 to 5 in. long, 1½ to 2 in. wide; tapering at both ends, often long and slender-pointed, the central part only toothed; almost or quite glabrous, with numerous yellowish glands beneath; stalk ⅙ to ⅓ in. long. Flowers pale pink, crowded in axillary cymes which are 1 to 1½ in. across, and expand in August. Fruit globular, about the size of peppercorns, violet.

Native of Japan. Although this plant lives in the open ground at Kew, and is only killed in very severe winters, it really needs some sheltered, sunny corner, such as the angle of a house facing south-west, to be seen at its best. As it flowers and fruits on the shoots of the year, a mere cutting back by frost does not matter; some such pruning is necessary. A loamy soil, not enriched, is best for it.

var. ANGUSTATA Rehd. *C. longifolia* Hemsl., not Lam.—A taller plant with lanceolate leaves, narrower than in the type (⅖ to 1⅕ in. wide). Native of China.

Closely allied to this species is C. DICHOTOMA (Lour.) K. Koch, a native of China and Japan, introduced by Fortune about 1857. It is not so hardy, and may be used as a greenhouse plant. It is not so vigorous a grower as *C. japonica*, but is of the same half-woody nature; it has thinner stems, and smaller leaves and berries, the latter deep lilac in colour, and about ⅛ in. across. Another species sometimes seen in gardens is:

C. AMERICANA L. FRENCH MULBERRY.—A shrub 3 to 6 ft high, with the flowers and fruits arranged as in *C. japonica*, the flowers bluish, the fruit violet, but very distinct in leaf and stem, both of which have more persistent down than in the Japanese species; the leaf, too, is much larger and broader, and 1½ to 4 in. in diameter. This species is native of the south-eastern and south-central United States, and is too tender for any but the mildest parts of the country.

C. MOLLIS Sieb. & Zucc.

A deciduous shrub 8 ft or more high, of erect habit; young shoots herbaceous, very thickly covered with down which persists until the following year. Leaves oval-lanceolate, slenderly pointed, rounded or tapered at the base, toothed; 2 to 4½ in. long, ⅝ to 1¾ in. wide; dull green and downy above, grey with thick, starry down beneath; stalk ¼ to ⅜ in. long. Flowers produced in the leaf-axils of the current season's growth in cymose clusters ½ to 1 in. wide on a main stalk ¼ to ⅜ in. long; corolla $\frac{3}{16}$ in. wide, four-lobed, light purplish rose; calyx ⅛ in. long with four awl-shaped lobes and, like the flower-stalk and the outside of the corolla, densely downy. Fruit globose, dullish violet-purple, $\frac{3}{16}$ in. wide.

Native of Japan and the Korean Archipelago. It was found by Richard Oldham, the Kew collector, in the latter habitat in 1861–3 and seeds were possibly sent home by him at the same time, as it is known to have been in cultivation a few years later. It is well distinguished by the dense covering of nearly all its parts with starry down. In a sheltered spot at Kew it is 8 ft high, but it is not so hardy or so handsome a shrub as *C. bodinieri*.

CALLISTEMON   MYRTACEAE

A genus of evergreen shrubs and small trees, natives of Australia, found mostly on the eastern side of the sub-continent and in Tasmania. The callistemons belong to the myrtle family, where they are associated with *Eucalyptus*, *Leptospermum*, *Metrosideros*, etc. in the subfamily Leptospermoideae, characterised by a dry, capsular fruit (not fleshy as in the 'true' myrtles and their allies). The genus is unmistakable and unlikely to be confused with any other except *Melaleuca*; but many of the species are poorly defined and in some instances grade into others by intermediates. All are alike in having entire, narrow leaves (round in cross-section in some species), hard in texture and with a prominent midrib. The flowers are in spikes; both sepals and petals are present, but are obscured by the long and very numerous red, yellowish, or greenish stamens, which give to the inflorescence the appearance of a bottle-brush; they are inserted on an ovoid or urn-shaped receptacle. The fruit is a woody capsule, fixed limpet-like to the branch and persisting for many years. A peculiarity of *Callistemon* (and of *Melaleuca*) is that the growing-point does not abort after flower production but grows on beyond the inflorescence to produce further stem, leaf, and, in due season, flower. The beautiful genus *Melaleuca* is too tender for inclusion in this work; it is distinguished from *Callistemon* by the arrangement of the stamens in several distinct clusters in each flower.

C. CITRINUS (Curt.) Skeels
Metrosideros citrina Curt.; *C. lanceolatus* (Sm.) DC.

A straggly shrub up to 15 ft high in the wild. Leaves $1\frac{1}{2}$ to $3\frac{1}{2}$ in. long, $\frac{1}{8}$ to $\frac{3}{4}$ in. wide, pointed at the apex; venation prominent. Inflorescence rather open, up to 4 in. long; stamens $\frac{3}{4}$ to 1 in. long, in some shade of red, with darker anthers.

Native of Australia on the coasts of New South Wales, Victoria, and Queensland; introduced by Sir Joseph Banks in 1788. It has long been grown as a cool greenhouse shrub, but is not suitable for outdoor cultivation except in mild gardens, and even there is best on a wall. The epithet '*citrinus*' refers to the fragrance of the leaves.

cv. 'SPLENDENS'.—A fine form with stamens of bright crimson, up to $1\frac{1}{2}$ in. long. It was raised at Kew from Australian seed (var. *splendens* Stapf, in *Bot. Mag.*, t. 9050).

The following species are allied to *C. citrinus* and somewhat hardier:

C. LINEARIS (Sm.) DC. *Metrosideros linearis* Sm.—A shrub to 7 ft high; young stems silky-hairy when young. Leaves linear, up to 5 in. long, not more than $\frac{1}{10}$ in. wide, channelled on the upper surface. Flower-spikes 3 to 5 in. long; stamens up to 1 in. long, crimson. Native of New South Wales.

C. RIGIDUS R. Br.—A shrub to 8 ft high; young stems slightly hairy when young. Leaves linear to linear-lanceolate, up to 6 in. long and $\frac{1}{4}$ in. wide, sharply pointed, not channelled. Flower-spikes dense, 3 to 4 in. long, stamens dark red, anthers dark brown. New South Wales and Queensland. A fine species, but reports that it is the hardiest of the red-flowered callistemons may perhaps refer to the next species, with which it has been confused in some gardens:

C. SUBULATUS Cheel—A small spreading shrub to about 4 ft high; young wood lustrous rich brown. Leaves glossy green on both sides, awl-shaped, $\frac{5}{8}$ to $1\frac{1}{2}$ in. long, $\frac{1}{8}$ to $\frac{1}{4}$ in. wide. Flower-spikes crimson, 2 to 3 in. long, $1\frac{1}{2}$ to 2 in. wide. Native of E. Victoria and New South Wales. *C. subulatus* has proved quite hardy at Wisley against a wall of the Alpine House. See also *C. rigidus* above.

C. SALIGNUS (Sm.) DC.
Metrosideros saligna Sm.

A small tree to 30 ft in the wild, with a papery bark; young stems silky-hairy. Leaves thin but firm in texture, linear to linear-lanceolate, tapered at both ends, 2 to $4\frac{1}{2}$ in. long and up to $\frac{1}{2}$ in. wide, red when unfolding, later dull green;

midrib prominent. Flower-spikes 2 to 3 in. long, with creamy or pale pink stamens (red or white in some cultivated forms).

Native of S.E. Australia, where it is found in coastal areas and swampy places. It is hardy on a wall in all but the coldest gardens, but in this country never makes so tall a plant as it does in the wild.

C. PALLIDUS (Bonpl.) DC. *Metrosideros pallida* Bonpl.—This species is nearly identical to the preceding and takes its place in Tasmania; it is also found in Victoria. Leaves narrow-elliptic to oblanceolate, $1\frac{1}{4}$ to $2\frac{1}{4}$ in. long, $\frac{1}{8}$ to $\frac{1}{2}$ in. wide, covered when young with a dense cobweb of silky hairs and then greyish pink in colour. Flower-spikes cream-coloured, $1\frac{1}{2}$ to $2\frac{1}{2}$ in. long.

C. SIEBERI DC. *C. pithyoides* Miq.—A shrub to about 15 ft in the wild with dark grey-brown stems. Leaves linear, thick and rigid, densely packed on the shoots, up to 1 in. long and $\frac{1}{10}$ in. wide. Flower-spikes narrow, $\frac{3}{4}$ to $1\frac{1}{2}$ in. long;

CALLISTEMON SIEBERI

stamens pale yellow. A native of the mountains of south-eastern Australia, known as the 'Alpine Bottlebrush'. It is perhaps the hardiest of the species cultivated in Britain. There is a handsome small specimen outside the Australian House at Kew, of dense habit, with dark, glossy leaves.

C. VIRIDIFLORUS (Sims) Sweet *Metrosideros viridiflora* Sims; *C. salignus* var. *viridiflorus* (Sims) F. v. Muell.—This species bears a close resemblance to *C. sieberi* and occupies similar habitats, but is confined to Tasmania. As in that species the small, rigid, sharply pointed leaves are densely set on the shoot, but the flower-spikes are greenish yellow. *Bot. Mag.*, t. 2602.

C. SPECIOSUS (Sims) DC.
Metrosideros speciosa Sims

A large shrub or small tree to 15 ft high with stout, red-brown branches densely furnished with stiff, leathery, linear-elliptic leaves, pointed at the apex, tapered to a narrow base, 3 to 5 in. long and $\frac{3}{8}$ to $\frac{1}{2}$ in. wide; venation prominent. Spikes dense, 4 to 6 in. long and $2\frac{1}{2}$ to 3 in. wide; stamens rich brilliant crimson with golden anthers, about 1 in. long, inserted on the rim of a cup-shaped receptacle which is densely white-hairy on the outside; sepals also hairy on the back. Fruit half-spherical, $\frac{1}{4}$ in. long and $\frac{1}{4}$ to $\frac{7}{16}$ in. wide. *Bot. Mag.*, t. 1761.

A native of W. Australia. It is at least the equal of *C. citrinus* in the beauty of its spikes. As seen in cultivation the leaves are usually of a rather glaucous grey-green, but this is apparently not a constant character of the species. Some plants in cultivation as "*C. speciosus*" are a form of *C. citrinus*.

C. PHOENICEUS Lindl.—Another W. Australian species, allied to the preceding. It is a rather diffuse shrub 3 to 8 ft high with slender branches that are brownish or reddish at first, later grey, rather loosely clad with linear or linear-elliptic leaves, acute at the apex, long-tapered at the base, $1\frac{1}{2}$ to $3\frac{1}{2}$ in. long and $\frac{3}{8}$ to $\frac{5}{8}$ in. wide. Inflorescence commonly 2 to $2\frac{1}{2}$ in. long but sometimes 3 to $3\frac{1}{2}$ in., and about 2 in. wide.; stamens rich crimson; receptacles $\frac{1}{8}$ in. long, glabrous like the sepals. Fruits deeply cupular to almost globose, $\frac{3}{16}$ in. long, $\frac{1}{4}$ in. across. Easily distinguished from *C. speciosus* by its slender branches, smaller leaves, inflorescences, and fruits, and by its glabrous receptacles and sepals. In the Edinburgh Botanic Garden a specimen of this species flourished in a sheltered border in front of the planthouses for more than twenty years.

CALLUNA ERICACEAE

A monotypic genus, differing from *Erica* in the large, coloured calyx with four tiny bracts at the base, forming an apparent outer calyx.

C. VULGARIS (L). Hull HEATHER, LING
Erica vulgaris L.

An evergreen shrub up to 3 ft high (usually from 9 to 24 in.), of staggling habit, much branched; branches densely leafy, and either downy or glabrous. Leaves opposite, arranged in four rows, giving a quadrangular shape to the twig, $\frac{1}{20}$ to $\frac{1}{10}$ in. long, closely packed and scale-like. Flowers in slender, one-sided racemes, 1 to 6, or as much as 12 in. long, purplish pink, varying in depth of shade in different plants. The calyx is the chief ornamental part of the flower, and consists of four nearly separate, narrowly oval sepals $\frac{3}{16}$ in. long; the corolla is about half as long. Stamens eight.

This is the shrub which covers so many thousands of acres of the moors and mountains of the north of England and Scotland, and makes them so beautiful in late summer and autumn. Among native woody plants it is the most abundant and covers the greatest area. In good soil it is apt to grow too quickly and become gaunt and bare, and short-lived; this can be remedied to some extent by cutting over the plants in early spring before growth recommences and removing all the old flower-stems. A poor soil, with peat mixed, keeps the plants dwarf and in better habit. The named varieties, of which there are many, are increased by cuttings or by division. They are useful for planting in masses on dry banks, which, with a little attention at first to weeding and perhaps watering, they will soon take complete possession of, giving beautiful patches of colour from July onwards for many years.

Bees are particularly fond of the flowers, and the honey they give is regarded as of special quality. In my native village in Yorkshire it used to be, and probably still is, the practice for the beehives of the cottagers to be laden on vans and taken every summer to the moors, ten or more miles away, for the bees to collect honey there from the heather. They were brought back in autumn. Branches of heather are much used in the north also for making besoms—in the same way that birch twigs are used in the south.

f. ALBA (West.) Braun-Blanquet var. *alba* (West.) G. Don; *E. vulgaris* var. *alba* West.—Flowers white. A fairly common variant.

var. HIRSUTA (Waitz) S. F. Gray *Erica vulgaris* var. *hirsuta* Waitz; *C. vulgaris* var. *tomentosa* G. Don; *C. vulgaris* var. *incana* Reichb.; *C. vulgaris* var. *hirsuta* f. *typica* Beijerinck—Stems and leaves clad with a greyish indumentum. Occasionally found wild with the type. The forma *typica* of Beijerinck was intended to distinguish the wild forms of var. *hirsuta* from the various cultivars which he classified under this variety.

Many clones have been named, some of them descending from wild plants and others of nursery origin. For a full account of these and for guidance on cultivation and arrangement the following works are recommended: F. J. Chapple, *The Heather Garden*, 1964; A. T. Johnson, *Hardy Heaths*, 1956; J. F. Letts, *Hardy Heaths and the Heather Garden*, 1966; D. Fyfe Maxwell and P. S. Patrick, *The English Heather Garden*, 1966. *The Heather Society*, founded in 1963, publishes a Year Book. For the following short selection from the cultivars we are indebted to *The Royal Horticultural Society*:

'ALBA JAE'.—White, very compact and erect, foliage bright medium green. 9 in. Aug.

'ALBA PLENA'.—Double white. Large flowers. Very free flowering. Compact, 8 in. Aug.

'ALPORTII'.—Bright crimson, in long erect spikes. 2 ft. Aug.

'AUGUST BEAUTY'.—White. Fairly compact, slightly spreading, vigorous. Foliage medium dark green. 11 in. July–Aug.

'AUREA'.—Soft mauve. Foliage gold in spring, green in summer, red in winter. Slender stems. 7 in. Late July–Aug.

'BARNETT ANLEY'.—Petunia Purple. Compact and erect, vigorous. Foliage fairly dark green. 1 ft. Aug.

'COUNTY WICKLOW'.—Clear pink, double in spikes. 3–6 in. long, of dense prostrate habit. Foliage dark green. 9 in. July–Sept.

'C. W. NIX'.—Dark crimson. Tall and graceful with feathery stems. 2 ft. Aug.–Sept.

'DRUM-RA'.—White. Compact and erect, vigorous. Foliage medium green. 11 in. Aug.

'ELSIE PURNELL'.—Amaranth Rose, double, on spikes 6½ in. long. Very vigorous and compact. 21 in. Aug.–Sept.

'FOXII NANA'.—Light purple, shy flowering. A good foliage plant forming dwarf, dense, compact cushions of deep green. 3–6 in. July–Oct.

'FRED J. CHAPPLE'.—Mallow Purple in spikes 4 in. long. Foliage medium green, but varying from gold, cream, and pink to copper; tips coral-pink. 10 in. Aug.–Sept.

'GOLD HAZE'.—Plentiful white flowers. A fine bright golden-yellow foliage plant, the colour persisting throughout the year. 7 in. Aug.–Sept.

'H. E. BEALE'—Silvery pink, double, large, in long spikes of strong branching open habit. 18 in. One of the best heathers, succeeding even on clay soil. Aug.–Oct.

'J. H. HAMILTON'.—Fuchsia Pink, fully double, on slender 6 to 10 in. high stems of semi-prostrate habit, making a dwarf mat of interlacing growth. 9–12 in. Aug.–Sept.

'JOAN SPARKES'.—Double pale pink, of trailing habit. 9 in. Aug.–Oct.

'MAIR'S VARIETY'.—Pure white in long spikes. Of upright branching growth. Foliage medium green. 2½ ft. Aug.–Sept.

'MULLION'.—Orchid Purple. Low and close-growing. Foliage medium green. 5 in. Aug.–Sept.

'MULTICOLOR'.—Phlox Purple. Of vigorous and spreading habit. Foliage medium green tipped golden and coral. 8–10 in. Late July–Aug.

'PETER SPARKES'.—Late flowering but similar in growth to 'H. E. Beale', of which it is stated to be a sport, but with flowers of a deeper pink. Aug.–Oct.

'ROBERT CHAPMAN'.—Rose Purple. Compact and fairly erect. Foliage green tinged yellow. Winter foliage medium green overlaid orange-red to scarlet. 8–10 in. Aug.-Sept.

'ROSALIND'.—Mallow Purple. Vigorous and erect. Foliage yellowish green. 10 in. Aug.–Sept.

'SERLEI'.—Pure white, freely produced on feathery branches, of rather tall and pyramidal habit, reaching a height of 2–3 ft. An excellent white heather of vigorous habit. Sept.–Nov.

'SERLEI AUREA'.—Similar to the above, with attractive golden foliage.

'TIB'.—Cyclamen Purple. Compact and erect, vigorous. Foliage dark green. 10 in. One of the first callunas to flower. July–Aug.

CALOPHACA   LEGUMINOSAE

A small genus of herbs and deciduous shrubs ranging from S. Russia to E. Asia.

C. WOLGARICA (L. f.) Fisch.

Cytisus wolgaricus L. f.

A deciduous shrub, said to become 6 ft high, but rarely more than half as high in this country; bark of branches downy when quite young, peeling when old. Leaves pinnate, 2 to 3 in. long, composed of eleven to seventeen leaflets. Leaflets oval to orbicular, ¼ to ½ in. long, the main-stalk of the leaf and the under-surface of the leaflets covered with down. Racemes produced from the leaf-axils of the current year's growth, 3 to 5 in. long, very downy, carrying four to nine flowers towards the end. Flowers yellow, pea-shaped, ¾ to 1 in. long, each on a stalk ⅓ in. long; calyx downy, ⅓ in. long, with slender pointed teeth. Pod ¾ to 1¼ in. long, cylindrical, covered with glandular hairs, one- or two-seeded. Blossoms in June and July.

Native of the south-eastern part of European Russia, in the regions of the rivers Volga (from which it takes its name) and Don. It is frequently found in arid places and on dry hillsides. Introduced in 1786. It is quite hardy in the south of England, but may need the protection of a wall in the north. It likes abundant sunshine, and during hot summers flowers profusely. It is only after such seasons that seeds ripen. As a rule it is grafted on standards of laburnum or caragana, when it forms a big, mop-headed plant with semi-pendent branches. Plants raised in that way are sometimes short-lived, but it is probably the best and easiest way, for plants raised from seed are not easy to rear. They are very liable to decay through damp during the winter, and should for two years be kept in pots, then planted out on a well-drained site. When grafted on the laburnum, no special precautions are needed.

C. GRANDIFLORA Reg.—Leaves with seventeen to twenty-five leaflets; racemes with ten to sixteen flowers. Pods to 1¾ in. long, less downy than in *C. wolgarica*. Native of Turkestan.

CALYCANTHUS   CALYCANTHACEAE

A genus of N. American shrubs with fragrant wood, three coming from the south-eastern United States, the other from California. They have opposite, deciduous leaves, minutely warted on the upper side. Flowers solitary on short, mostly two-leaved shoots of the year, or from the nodes of the previous year's growth. Sepals and petals numerous. Fruits hard, and shaped like a small fig, retaining the seeds for a long time. From the closely allied winter-sweets (*Chimonanthus*) these differ in their more numerous stamens and brown-purple or brown-red flowers produced on leafy shoots.

The species of *Calycanthus* are easily accommodated; they like a sunny position in order that the wood may ripen and flowers be freely borne. Any open, loamy, or peaty soil will suit them, provided it is sufficiently deep and moist. They are most easily propagated by layers in this country, where seeds do not usually ripen. Sucker growths are sent up from the base, and these sometimes afford opportunities for propagating by division. These shrubs flower from June to September.

C. FERTILIS Walt.
C. glaucus Willd.

A shrub of bushy habit, 6 ft or more high. Leaves 3 to 5 in. long, ovate or oval, acute or often acuminate; dark glossy green, and rough above, glaucous and slightly downy beneath. Flowers with little or no scent, 1½ to 2½ in. diameter, the strap-shaped sepals and petals chocolate-purple.

Native of the south-eastern United States, covering some of the same area as *C. floridus*, with which species it has been much confused. It was brought to England in 1806. The leaves of this species do not possess the aromatic odour so characteristic of the West American species, and the wood is only slightly fragrant. Summer leaf-buds concealed by base of leaf-stalk.

var. LAEVIGATUS (Willd.) Bean *C. laevigatus* Willd.—This shrub, by some considered a distinct species, chiefly differs from typical *C. fertilis* by the leaves being shining green and not downy beneath. Several intermediate forms exist.

cv. 'NANUS'.—A dwarf form with smaller leaves, which are green, not glaucous beneath.

C. FLORIDUS L.   CAROLINA ALLSPICE
C. sterilis Walt.

A deciduous shrub of rather straggling growth, ultimately 6 to 8 ft. or even more high. Leaves 3 to 5 in. long, oval, tapered at the base, rough to the touch and dark green above; soft, with a dense covering of short, pale down beneath. Flowers 2 in. or less in diameter, fragrant, produced June and July; sepals and petals strap-shaped, numerous, reddish purple, tinged with brown. *Bot. Mag.*, t. 503.

Native of the south-east United States, from Virginia southwards; first introduced to England by Mark Catesby, the author of the *Natural History of Carolina*, in 1726. According to old records the original plants were collected 'back of Charlestown', in S. Carolina. It is easily distinguished from the other species by the densely pubescent under-surface of the leaves. The leaves, wood, and roots have a pleasant, camphor-like fragrance, which is even more developed in the dried wood. The bark has been used as a substitute for cinnamon. Summer leaf-buds concealed.

C. MOHRII (Small) Pollard *Butneria mohrii* Small—This is a close ally of

CALYCANTHUS FLORIDUS

the above, but has ovate rather than oval leaves, rounded or somewhat heart-shaped at the base. Native of S. Tennessee and N. Alabama; distinguished under this name by Small and introduced in 1908. The *C. ovatus* of Aiton, in cultivation at Kew in 1789, may have belonged here or have been a form of *C. floridus.*

C. OCCIDENTALIS Hook. & Arn.   CALIFORNIAN ALLSPICE
C. macrophyllus Hort.

A loose habited, deciduous, aromatic shrub of stronger growth than the other species, and sometimes 12 ft high. Leaves the largest in the genus, varying from 3 to 8 in. in length, and in shape from heart-shaped and ovate to lanceolate; rough, dark green, and not downy above, paler and bright green beneath. Flowers 2 to 3 in. across; the sepals and petals purplish red, changing to a more tawny shade near the tips; rather unpleasantly scented. *Bot. Mag.*, t. 4808.

Native of California, where it commonly grows near the banks of streams; introduced by Douglas in 1831. This is the least desirable of the American allspices, being of rather ungainly habit. Its larger growth, foliage, and flowers distinguish it from the other species; as its leaves beneath are neither very downy like *floridus* nor glaucous like *fertilis*, it is only likely to be confused with the var. *laevigatus* of the latter. But both leaves and wood when bruised have a much stronger aromatic, spicy odour, and the flowers are paler, redder, larger, and longer-stalked. Summer leaf-buds exposed.

CAMELLIA   THEACEAE

A group of about eighty species of evergreen trees and shrubs widely distributed in Asia. Leaves alternate, toothed, short-stalked. Flowers usually showy, often solitary or two, never more than a few together, either clearly stalked with two to five bracteoles distinct from the five persistent sepals or appearing sessile because the short pedicel is completely covered by a series of overlapping, usually deciduous bud-scales which represent bracteoles and sepals; petals five to twelve, usually firmly united to the androecium and falling with it, but sometimes free; stamens numerous, the outer united for at least a short distance at the base and usually much higher to form a distinct fleshy tube. Seeds large and oily, soon decaying.

The genus was named by Linnaeus after George Joseph Kamel, a native of Moravia and a member of the Society of Jesus. He latinised his name into Camellus and under it wrote an account of the plants of the Island of Luzon in the Philippines, which he had visited. This account John Ray included as an appendix to his *Historia Plantarum*, published in London in 1704.

Until the introduction of *C. saluenensis*, hybrids were unknown, but once that species became established hybrids were raised between it and *C. japonica* and *C. cuspidata*, and the success of these crosses has led to a surfeit of crossing with each and every species and hybrid in cultivation. A comprehensive list of hybrids is given in the *American Camellia Year Book*, 1966, pp. 113–42, and see also pp. 203–27. *Camellia* has become a favoured genus, especially in the United States and Australia, and in addition to various regional and national Camellia societies, which publish journals—the largest being *The American Camellia Society*—there is now an *International Camellia Society* which publishes a journal, while the *Royal Horticultural Society* produces annually a Rhododendron and Camellia Year Book. The standard work on the species is: J. R. Sealy, *A Revision of the Genus Camellia*, London, 1958, illustrated with numerous line-drawings.

All the camellias prefer a peaty soil, but will thrive in a warm, open loam, especially if leaf-soil and a little peat be given them to start with, and so long as the soil is lime-free. They can be increased by stem and leaf-bud cuttings of half-ripened wood inserted in a mixture of sand and peat in a propagating frame. Bottom heat is desirable but not essential. *C. reticulata* is an exception and should be grafted onto seedlings of *C. japonica* of suitable size.

C. CUSPIDATA Veitch

Thea cuspidata Kochs

An evergreen bush 6 ft high, of erect, rather slender habit when young; young shoots glabrous. Leaves glabrous, narrow to broad elliptic or lanceolate-elliptic, rounded or wedge-shaped at the base, tapered gradually to a long, slender apex; 1⅛ to 3⅓ in. long, ⅝ to 1 in. wide; finely and shallowly toothed (the teeth gland-tipped); polished, dark, sometimes purplish green above; paler and covered with minute dots beneath; stalks ⅛ to ⅙ in. long, hairy at the margins. Flowers solitary at the end of short twigs or in the leaf-axils; pure white, 1½ in. across; pedicels ⅛ in. long with four bracteoles; calyx of five green triangular sepals $\frac{1}{2}$ in. across. Stamens erect in a dense cluster, $\frac{5}{8}$ in. long; anthers yellow. *Bot. Mag.*, t. 9277.

Native of W. China; introduced by Wilson to Veitch's Coombe Wood nursery in 1900. It is a bright-leaved hardy evergreen, with copper-tinted young leaves; it is not in the first rank as a flowering shrub, although quite pretty when well in flower. In cultivation it may reach a greater height than the 6 ft given in the description; Sir Giles Loder has it over 12 ft high at Leonardslee in Sussex,

CAMELLIA CUSPIDATA

where it is quite hardy. There is a plant almost as large in the R.H.S. Garden at Wisley.

C. (*cuspidata* × *saluenensis*) 'CORNISH SNOW'.—A very beautiful hybrid raised by J. C. Williams at Caerhays Castle, Cornwall. In general it resembles the former parent, but the flowers are larger and the white petals have a pink flush on the back. Other hybrids of the same parentage are in cultivation, 'MICHAEL', also raised at Caerhays, being one of the best.

C. FRATERNA Hance—A near relative of *C. cuspidata* but easily distinguished by the shoots, pedicels, and calyx being densely villose. It comes from E. China and is not likely to be hardy in any but the most sheltered gardens.

C. JAPONICA L.   COMMON CAMELLIA

An evergreen shrub or small tree 30 to 40 ft high, of much-branched habit. Leaves deep glossy green, ovate or oval, 3 to 4 in. long, tapering to a short point, shallow toothed, quite glabrous, specked with black or brown dots on the lower surface, and of firm, leathery texture. Flowers red, solitary at the end of the branchlets, stalkless, $2\frac{1}{2}$ to 4 in. across; petals normally five, but usually more in cultivated plants. Stamens numerous, united for a half to two-thirds of their length into a fleshy cup. Seeds $\frac{3}{4}$ to 1 in. long, half as wide; often flattened on several sides through compression.

Few exotic shrubs have filled a more important place in our greenhouses than the common camellia has in its time, but its merits as a hardy plant were not fully appreciated until this century. Whilst it is not adapted for exposed, windy positions, it is perfectly hardy near London in places where there is moderate shelter from north and east. At Kew it has withstood 31 degrees of frost without suffering in the least. It is, indeed, one of the most satisfactory of hardy ever-greens, there being no other except, perhaps, the laurels with quite the same lustrous black-green hue. This camellia is a native of Japan, the Korean Archi-pelago, and the Liu Kiu Islands. It is not found wild in China but has long been cultivated there as a garden plant. The oil expressed from the seeds is used by the Japanese women for dressing the hair.

The species first became known in Europe about the beginning of the eighteenth century, and many fine varieties were imported from China; in the half-century or so after the end of the Napoleonic wars many hundreds more were raised in Europe, first in England and later on the continent. As is generally known, these have flowers pure white, of various shades of red, deep scarlet, striped, and of various degrees of 'doubleness'. About the middle of the nine-teenth century the camellia had become perhaps the most popular of greenhouse flowers; its prim stiffness and solidity was not an inappropriate floral emblem of that period. But as the nineteenth century neared its close the popularity of the camellia declined. Its renaissance, now as an outdoor shrub, began in the period between the two world wars. The very hard winter of 1928–9 was, perhaps, the turning point, for it proved that the garden varieties of the common camellia are not only hardy, but among the hardiest of all evergreens. 'Their chief defect is the susceptibility of the flowers to injury by spring frost. A few degrees below freezing-point will discolour the petals so much that the blossom is robbed of all beauty. This undoubtedly detracts from the value of the Camellia in the open air. The best place of all for it is, no doubt, in thin woodland, where the trees are not so close together that their roots monopolise the ground entirely, yet whose branches are capable of providing shade and a certain amount of shelter. A canopy of even leafless branches will often mitigate the effect of short snaps of late frost and the evil effects of thawing by bright, early morning sunshine.

'For ordinary gardens, places that are sheltered on the east by either walls, trees or tall shrubs should, if possible, be chosen for Camellias. There at any rate they are protected from early morning sunshine. In spite of their capability of withstanding great cold they are not adapted for bleak, open, wind-swept sites. If no other place is available for them, they should be treated as wall plants, and, if given a western or north-western exposure, the chances of the flowers develop-ing their full beauty are all the more favourable.'*

In the open air *Camellia japonica* flowers from early to late spring and the best forms for out-of-doors are the semi-double and single red-flowered ones, which appear to open better than the very double ones, and to suffer less from late spring frosts. But any variety that has become too large for the greenhouse should be tried in the open air, for the sake of its foliage, if its flowers fail. It should be remembered that plants turned out of pots or tubs in which the roots

* Reprinted from an article by W. J. Bean in *The New Flora and Sylva*, Vol. 2, No. 2 (1930), by kind permission of Mr E. H. M. Cox.

have become matted require careful watering until the roots have spread into the surrounding ground. The single-flowered varieties may be propagated by cuttings made from firm wood about the end of June and placed in heat. It is best to treat them at first as cool greenhouse plants, as they grow more quickly. The fine double varieties are usually grafted on the cuttings of the single ones. For further information on the propagation of camellias the reader is referred to the article by P. Wiseman in *The Rhododendron and Camellia Year Book* for 1964, and by F. P. Knight, op. cit., 1956.

It would be impossible in a general work such as this to do even the scantiest justice to the numerous garden varieties of *C. japonica* now available in commerce. For the British gardener the best guide is the review by Charles Puddle and the late Francis Hanger published in *The Rhododendron and Camellia Year Book* for 1960 and 1961.

subsp. RUSTICANA (Honda) Kitamura *C. rusticana* Honda SNOW CAMELLIA.— This subspecies grows in the mountains of the north-western part of the main island of Japan (Honshu)—a region of long and snowy but not unduly harsh winters. Its southern limit is believed to lie around 30° N., while typical *C. japonica* is mostly found south of that line and never far above sea-level. In their more extreme forms the two races overlap, but generally subsp. *rusticana* can be distinguished by the following characters: petioles usually downy when young; involucre shorter (rarely as long as $\frac{4}{5}$ in., which is the lower limit in *C. japonica*); petals widely spread and adnate to the filaments of the outer stamens for only $\frac{1}{5}$ to $\frac{2}{5}$ in. approximately ($\frac{2}{5}$ to $\frac{3}{5}$ in. in *C. japonica*); filaments of stamens yellow, united only near their base (white or cream and high united into a tube in *C. japonica*). For further information see *The Rhododendron and Camellia Year Book*, 1956, pp. 84–9, and 1959, pp. 115–17.

C. HONGKONGENSIS Seem.—This species is definitely a greenhouse plant in this country. It is distinguished from *C. japonica* by its oblong, widely and minutely toothed leaves, persistent flower-bud scales, and hairy ovary. Indigenous in Hong Kong.

C. MALIFLORA Lindl.

An evergreen shrub of bushy shape up to 6 or 8 ft high (perhaps more); young shoots downy. Leaves oval-lanceolate, tapered to both ends, shallowly toothed, $1\frac{1}{2}$ to 2 in. long, $\frac{1}{2}$ to $1\frac{1}{4}$ in. wide, glossy blackish green, glabrous except on the midrib and short stalk. Flowers solitary, terminal, 1 to $1\frac{1}{2}$ in. across, opening in midwinter; petals numerous, soft rose-coloured; bracts very finely downy in the centre. *Bot. Mag.*, t. 2080; *Bot. Reg.*, t. 547.

The habitat of the plant from which this charming evergreen originated does not seem to be known, but it is no doubt Chinese. It is an excellent evergreen for a wall, even one partially shaded, where its flowers often open during the mild period that frequently precedes Christmas. It is easily recognised by its thin leaves and completely double flowers on short pedicels covered by bracteoles which grade into the sepals, and like them are green often with a red margin. The flowers fall off as a whole.

C. ROSIFLORA Hook.—Also unknown in a wild state and probably obtained originally from a Chinese nursery. It is closely allied to *C. maliflora* but has single rose-coloured flowers and thicker larger leaves 1⅘ to 3⅕ in. long, ⅘ to 1 in. wide and rather widely serrulate. *Bot. Mag.*, t. 5044. It was originally introduced into this country before 1858 and certainly persisted until 1900 and probably longer, but it seems to have been lost by 1935. It was re-introduced from Ceylon in 1956.

C. OLEIFERA Abel

An evergreen shrub of stiff habit, or a small tree, said to be up to 25 ft high in a wild state. Leaves stiff and leathery, often inclined to obovate, 1½ to 3 in. long, tapered to both ends, rather regularly toothed, glabrous except for the very short stalk which is occasionally hairy. Flowers mostly from the terminal leaf-axils, 2 to 2½ in. across, petals white, appearing from November to February; bud-scales downy to densely silky. Fruits about 1 in. long. *Bot. Mag.*, n.s., t. 221.

Native of China, long cultivated but nowadays often confounded with *C. sasanqua* which differs from *C. oleifera* in the thinner, blunter-pointed leaves, its much less downy flower-bud scales and smaller fruits. Both are hardy at Kew against a wall and both flower in winter. The species is widely grown in China for the oil—tea-oil—expressed from the seeds, which is of great commercial importance, this and tea-oil cake being used for toiletries and also in cooking.

C. RETICULATA Lindl. [PLATE 25

Amongst the camellias found and introduced by Forrest is one that proved to be the wild type of this species, which has been represented in English gardens since 1820 by a lovely cultivated form of Chinese gardens, with rose-coloured, semi-double flowers, further discussed below. The wild type flowered in March 1932, at Caerhays, and from a specimen kindly given to me by Mr J. C. Williams, supplemented with Forrest's wild material, the following description has been made.

An evergreen tree or shrub up to 35 ft high; young shoots greyish, glabrous; winter buds slender, ½ in. long. Leaves of leathery texture, elliptic or inclined to obovate, slenderly and often rather abruptly pointed, more or less tapered at the base, finely and regularly toothed; 2 to 4½ in. long, 1 to 2¼ in. wide; dark dull green, net-veined and glabrous. Flowers solitary, of a rich soft rosy red, sub-terminal, 3 in. wide; petals five to eight; sepals roundish ovate, silky outside; stamens very numerous, 1¼ in. long, the outer ones united at the lower half to form a tube, inner ones free; anthers yellow; ovary and base of styles downy, the latter 1¼ in. long and united nearly to the top. While the plant described above had dull green noticeably veined leaves like the forms with semi-double and double flowers long known in cultivation, Forrest also introduced single-flowered forms with leaves dark rather shining green above and bright green below. *Bot. Mag.*, t. 9397.

Native of Yunnan at altitudes of 6,000 to 9,000 ft. The broad elliptic, acute or shortly acuminate leaves, the large flower, and the velvety flower-bud scales distinguish this from all other species in cultivation. Some of the finer forms raised from Forrest's seed have been given clonal names, notably 'MARY WILLIAMS', raised at Caerhays, and 'TREWITHEN PINK'.

C. reticulata has been cultivated for many centuries by the Chinese and many distinct forms were evolved. Of these the first to be introduced was brought by Capt. Rawes of the East India Company in 1820, and is figured in *Bot. Mag.*, t. 2784 (1827); the second importation was by J. D. Parks for the London Horticultural Society in 1824 and it was from this plant that Lindley described *C. reticulata* (*Bot. Reg.*, t. 1078, 1827). The two introductions were very similar, both having beautiful semi-double, bright rose-coloured flowers about 6 in. across, but whether they are identical in the sense of being of the same clone is not certain. Mr Simmons, Assistant Curator of the Temperate Department at Kew, tells us that the old tree in the Temperate House, now about 23 ft high, may be of the Parks clone, but the evidence from the Kew Entry Books is not conclusive. The plate of Capt. Rawes' plant shows a flower in which normal and petaloid stamens are intermixed, while in that of Parks' plant all the stamens are normal; but the tree at Kew bears both types of flower on the same branch. Another early importation bears fully double flowers; it is known in gardens as 'ROBERT FORTUNE', but may already have been in cultivation when Fortune introduced it in 1843.

These early introductions came from gardens in the treaty ports. It was only quite recently that it became known that many other varieties of *C. reticulata* were to be found in gardens of cities deep in the interior of China, in the province of Yunnan. The story of the introduction of these from Kunming during the years 1948–50 is related by the late Ralph Peer in *Journ. R.H.S.*, Vol. 76, pp. 301–7. A complete set was presented by him to the Savill Gardens in 1956. For an account of the Kunming reticulatas see T. Yü, *Camellias and Magnolias*, 1950, and T. H. Findlay, *Rhododendron and Camellia Year Book*, 1964. Their hardiness is still untested, but the old clones and the wild forms although tender, survived the testing winters of 1961–3 as far east as Sussex in protected situations.

C. PITARDII Cohen Stuart—A near relative of *C. reticulata* from which it is distinguished by its more narrowly elliptic leaves 3⅗ to 5 in. long and 1 to 1⅗ in. wide, long acute to caudate at the apex and prominently serrulate. It is represented in cultivation by the var. YUNNANICA Sealy, which has the young branches hairy, the leaves more tapered to base and apex but not abruptly acuminate or caudate and less prominently toothed. Flowers light crimson, about 3 in. across, bud-scales downy to villose, petals five or six, stamens very numerous and united for over one-half to three-quarters their length; ovary densely hairy. Introduced by Forrest and by Major Lawrence Johnson. Native of Yunnan and S. Szechwan.

C. SALUENENSIS Stapf   [PLATE 26

An evergreen shrub 10 to 15 ft high, of very bushy, luxuriantly leafy habit; young shoots at first hairy. Leaves elliptic to elliptic-lanceolate, pointed, tapered at the base, very finely and regularly toothed, each tooth tipped with a black gland; 1½ to 2½ in. long, half as much wide; dark green above, paler beneath, glossy on both sides, glabrous except for hairs on the midrib beneath; stalk $\frac{1}{6}$ in. long, hairy. Flowers produced in early spring, singly or in pairs, from buds at the end of the previous summer's shoots; they are of a pale blush-pink with darker lines, the five petals 1 to $1\frac{1}{2}$ in. long, broadly wedge-shaped, notched. Fruit woody, 1 in. wide, carrying about three seeds, which have a flat side and are about $\frac{1}{2}$ in. wide.

Native of mid-west Yunnan, China, on the mountains between the Salween and Shweli rivers. It seems first to have been found by Forrest in 1917, and to have been introduced by him then or later. Apparently we owe its existence in cultivation to the late J. C. Williams, who grew several plants against a north wall at Caerhays. The plant was at first identified as *Thea* (*Camellia*) *speciosa*, Pitard, but the shrub to which that name was originally given proves to be a Gordonia; hence Dr Stapf's name that heads this note. The flowers evidently vary in colour in a wild state, as specimens collected by Forrest, with blossom described by him as 'white' and 'crimson', are included by Dr Stapf under this species. This camellia is generally hardy except in cold or exposed situations but may need protection at first. Its hybrids with *C. japonica* are hardier, see *C.* × *williamsii*. The plant figured in the *Botanical Magazine*, t. 9505, as *C. saluenensis* forma *macrophylla* is now known to be one of these hybrids.

C. SASANQUA Thunb.

An evergreen shrub or small tree. Leaves shining dark green, $1\frac{1}{2}$ to $3\frac{1}{2}$ in. long, one-third to half as much wide, obovate or narrowly oval, with rounded teeth on the margin. Flowers $1\frac{1}{2}$ to 2 in. across, white in a wild state, pale pink to deep rose in cultivated varieties, of which the Japanese have raised a considerable number, some with double flowers.

Native of Japan, where it is perhaps the most popular of all camellias, it was not introduced into Europe until 1896, the plants grown as *C. sasanqua* before that date being forms of the related *C. oleifera* imported from China by East India Company's captains in the period 1811–23. It flowers from autumn into early spring, and although quite as hardy in itself as *C. japonica*, it is more liable to have its flowers injured. It is therefore best grown on a wall, in a sunnier position than would be given to the japonica varieties. It thrives remarkably well in N. Italy, where bushes approaching 20 ft in height and not much less in diameter are of very close, dense habit. There is a large collection of sasanqua varieties in the gardens of the Villa Taranto on Lake Maggiore.

Several Japanese garden varieties have been introduced. Of these one of the best is 'NARUMI-GATA', with single flowers 4 in. across, white, tinged pink at the edges, opening October–November. It was given the Award of Merit in 1953 as *C. sasanqua* "var. *oleifera*". The similar 'FUKUZU-TSUMI' succeeds very well with N. G. Hadden at Porlock, Somerset. It flowers about a fortnight earlier.

C. SINENSIS (L.) O. Kuntze   TEA PLANT
Thea sinensis L.; *T. assamica* Mast.; *C. thea* Link; *C. theifera* Griff.

An evergreen shrub with lance-shaped, short-stalked leaves up to $4\frac{1}{2}$ in. in length, and about one-third as wide; glabrous, dull green, shallowly toothed.

Flowers fragrant, full white, 1 to 1½ in. across; one to three of them produced in the leaf-axils on stalks ½ in. long. Stamens very numerous, with yellow anthers.

Native of Yunnan, where it was found wild by Forrest and Rock at 7,000 to 9,000 ft altitude, the tea plant has been cultivated by the Chinese from time immemorial. It was introduced from China into Java and India about 1835 and into Ceylon a little later. In S. China, Indochina, Siam, Burma, and Assam, typical *C. sinensis* is replaced by a variety which grows into a tree over 50 ft high and has longer, thinner bluntly acuminate leaves. This is var. ASSAMICA (Mast.) Kitamura, and as it comes from tropical regions it is more suitable for growing in countries like Assam and Ceylon than the Chinese plant, much of the tea from these countries being in fact from var. *assamica* or its hybrids.

C. TALIENSIS (W. W. Sm.) Melchior

Thea taliensis W. W. Sm.

An evergreen shrub up to 10 ft high at least, probably more; shoots glabrous. Leaves oval to obovate, cuneate at the base, narrowed at the apex to a short acuminate or even tail-like point, rather regularly toothed, 3 to 6 in. long, 1½ to 3 in. wide, glabrous, dark dullish green; stalk up to 1½ in. long. Flowers 2 to 2½ in. across, one to three in the leaf-axils; petals eight to ten, white, rounded to broadly elliptical; sepals orbicular, ciliate; stamens very numerous, yellow, up to ¾ in. long; ovary densely furnished with whitish hairs; stalk ⅓ to ⅝ in. long. *Bot. Mag.*, t. 9684.

Native of Yunnan, China; introduced by Forrest from east of the Tali Lake in 1914. The globular flower-buds, which are white and get to be as large as cherries before bursting, add to the attractiveness of the plant. It is a close relative of the tea plant, *C. sinensis*, and like it has stout green flower-stalks with two or three caducous bracteoles and five persistent green sepals. This species is 10 ft high at Underway, Porlock, Somerset. Mr Hadden tells us that it came through the winter of 1962–3 unharmed and flowers freely in November and December in a favourable season.

C. TSAII Hu

A shrub to 15 ft high with moderately stout branches, tending to be pendulous, and more or less densely appressed hairy. Leaves oblong or lanceolate-oblong or oblong-elliptic, acuminate to caudate, mostly 2⅘ to 3⅘ in. long and ¾ to 1⅙ in. wide, serrulate, thin, deep shining green above, light green and sparsely villose along the midrib below. Flowers numerous on short green stalks which bear four or five persistent bracteoles; sepals five, small, rounded, and hairy; corolla white, about 1 in. across, of five petals strongly united to the stamens which are fused for one-third to one-half their length from the base into a tube; ovary glabrous.

Native of S.W. China, Burma, and Indochina, at 4,000 to 8,000 ft. It was introduced by Forrest in 1917–19 and 1924 and requires protection except in the mildest parts of the British Isles. It resembles *C. cuspidata* but is easily distinguished by its hairy branches, softer leaves, and longer pedicels. It was given an Award of Merit as a shrub for the cool greenhouse when shown from the Savill Gardens in February 1960.

C. × WILLIAMSII W. W. Sm.

Soon after *C. saluenensis* began to flower in this country it was crossed with *C. japonica*, notably by J. C. Williams at Caerhays and by Col. Stephenson Clarke at Borde Hill. The first plants raised at Caerhays were named 'J. C. WILLIAMS', 'ST EWE', and 'MARY CHRISTIAN', while those at Borde Hill were called 'DONATION' and 'SALUTATION'. These became widely known in the years 1940–7 and since then many more hybrids of the same parents have been raised and named. The first to flower is 'NOVEMBER PINK', raised at Caerhays, which starts to flower in early November and goes on to May. These hybrids are most floriferous, hardier than *C. saluenensis*, but as in that species the flowers fall when they are over, and do not have to be picked off as is so often the case with *C. japonica*. In general the hybrid favours *C. japonica* in vegetative characters, the branches being glabrous and the elliptic or broad elliptic leaves $2\frac{3}{5}$ to $3\frac{4}{5}$ in. long and $1\frac{1}{5}$ to $2\frac{1}{5}$ wide, shallowly serrulate, usually dark shining green above and bright shining green below, often with scattered brownish spots (cork-warts) which it inherits from its *japonica* parent. The flowers are more like those of *C. saluenensis*, 2 to 5 in. in diameter, single or semi-double, white flushed rose, or pale to deep rose, and as in that species the ovary is densely hairy, not glabrous as in *C. japonica*. An interesting form is 'C. F. COATES' which has the fish-tail leaves of its *japonica* parent.

C. 'LEONARD MESSEL' is a hybrid between *C. × williamsii* 'Mary Christian' and *C. reticulata*, raised at Nymans, Sussex, and given an Award of Merit when shown by the late Mrs Messel and the National Trust in 1958. It takes after the Captain Rawes camellia in the shape of its flowers but has the hardiness of the *C. × williamsii* hybrids, and is easily raised from cuttings. The flowers are deep pink and are borne over a long period (March to May).

CAMPHOROSMA CHENOPODIACEAE

A genus of about eight species ranging from the E. Mediterranean region to Central Asia, often on saline soils.

C. MONSPELIACA L.

An evergreen shrub up to 2 ft high, of grey, heath-like aspect; young shoots erect, slender, pale, woolly, giving off a camphor-like odour when crushed. Leaves $\frac{1}{6}$ to $\frac{1}{3}$ in. long, linear, covered with down; the larger ones arranged alternately, the smaller ones produced very numerously in axillary clusters $\frac{1}{8}$ to

T S—R

⅓ in. apart that really represent undeveloped shoots. Flowers very small, incon-spicuous, clustered in axillary tufts; there is no corolla, the flower consisting of a four-toothed calyx $\frac{1}{10}$ in. long, four stamens with protruded yellow anthers and a style with two reddish stigmas. Seeds black, shining.

Widely spread in nature from N. Africa and S. Europe to Central Asia. I have seen it near Spalato (Split) in Dalmatia, facing the Adriatic, as a low dense bush with slender erect young shoots. A more familiar habitat is Montpellier, from which it gets its specific name. The generic name refers to the camphor-like odour characteristic of the genus. The older physicians attributed to this shrub many medicinal virtues. The young shoots produce their flowers from July onwards and die back most of their length during winter. It would make a useful plant for sunny slopes at the warmer seaside resorts.

CAMPSIS   BIGNONIACEAE

A genus of two climbing species, one N. American, the other E. Asiatic, both hardy and both beautiful. They have been included in *Tecoma*, but as now understood, that genus is confined to the warmer parts of Central and S. America. The pinnate leaves are opposite, the flowers large trum-pet-shaped, coloured in rich shades of orange and scarlet. They should be planted against a sunny wall, *C. grandiflora* especially, and given a good loamy soil. *C. radicans* will cling of itself to walls or tree-trunks, but it is best to give additional support by nailing. When the allotted space is filled, both species should be pruned annually just as vines are pruned, i.e. cut back to within a few buds of the old wood. Except on rare occa-sions neither ripens seed in this country, but they can be propagated by cuttings in mist, or by layers.

C. GRANDIFLORA (Thunb.) K. Schum.   [PLATE 27

Bignonia grandiflora Thunb.; *Tecoma grandiflora* (Thunb.) Loisel.; *C. chinensis* (Lam.) Voss; *Bignonia chinensis* Lam.

A deciduous climber 20 to 30 or more ft high; stems glabrous. Leaves pinnate, composed of seven or nine leaflets, which are ovate, 1½ to 3 in. long, about half as wide, long-pointed, coarsely toothed, glabrous on both surfaces. Flowers in terminal, pendulous panicles of six or twelve, produced at the end of the current season's growth in August and later. Corolla deep orange and red, widely trumpet-mouthed, narrowing to a funnel-shaped tube; 2 to 3 in. long and wide, with five broad, rounded lobes. Calyx 1¼ in. long, bell-shaped, with five slender lance-shaped lobes ½ in. long. *Bot. Mag.*, t. 1398.

Native of China, long cultivated in Japan; introduced in 1800. Even more gorgeous than *C. radicans*, it is, unfortunately, not so hardy. It must have a sheltered sunny wall, and even there does not with us produce so wonderful a display as it does on the continent. It is easily distinguished from the better-known *radicans* by the panicled inflorescence, the broader mouth of the corolla, glabrous leaves, and the much more deeply lobed calyx.

cv. 'THUNBERGII'.—Tube of corolla shorter, and the lobes more reflexed; perhaps hardier. Introduced by Siebold in 1856 as *Tecoma thunbergii*; figured under that name in *Flore des Serres*, Vol. 12, p. 181, and described by Carrière in *Rev. Hort.*, 1876, p. 440.

C. × TAGLIABUANA (Vis.) Rehd. *Tecoma tagliabuana* Vis.; *T. grandiflora* var. *princei* Dipp.; *T. hybrida* Dipp.; *T. chinensis* var. *aurantiaca* Koehne—This name covers hybrids between the two species of *Campsis*. They cross readily and no doubt the first hybrids occurred early in the nineteenth century in those parts of the continent where the warm summers permit seed to ripen, but passed as variants of one or other of the two species. The first plant to be identified as a hybrid arose in the nursery of the Tagliabue brothers near Milan, and this is the type of the group. Later, many forms were distributed by French nurseries, of which the finest and best known is 'MME GALEN', which was put into commerce in 1889. It resembles *C. radicans* in having the leaves downy beneath, the other parent in its lax truss. It is beautifully figured in *Bot. Mag.*, n.s., t. 198, and further information will be found in the accompanying text.

C. RADICANS (L.) Seem.   TRUMPET VINE
Bignonia radicans L.; *Tecoma radicans* (L.) Juss.

A deciduous climber of vigorous habit forming a stout main stem, and growing at least 30 to 40 ft high; it climbs by means of aerial roots like an ivy; young stems glabrous. Leaves pinnate, 6 to 15 in. long, composed of seven to eleven leaflets, which are ovate, ¾ to 4 in. long, ¼ to 2 in. wide; coarsely and angularly toothed, with a long, often tail-like point; glabrous and dark green above, downy beneath, especially along the midrib and veins. Flowers produced in August and September, each on a short stout stalk, in a cluster at the end of the current season's growth, four to twelve flowers together. Corolla rich scarlet and orange, trumpet-shaped, 2½ to 3 in. long, 1½ in. wide at the mouth, where are five broad, short, rounded lobes. Calyx bell-shaped, ⅝ in. long, with triangular teeth. Pod spindle-shaped, stout, 5 in. long, ¾ in. wide in the middle.

Native of the south-eastern United States. The gorgeous beauty of this climber must early have attracted the notice of the first settlers, for it was cultivated in England in 1640. It can be planted against buildings, to which it will attach itself by aerial roots from the stems, but usually needs support from nails as well. Flowering as it does in late summer on the growths of the year, it should be pruned back every spring. It is hardy enough to be grown in the open ground at Kew, but the growths are so long that even pruned back annually it is of ungainly habit and unsuited for the open border. Very rarely, but sometimes after unusually hot summers, it develops its conspicuous brown pods, full of flattened seeds with silvery transparent wings.

CANTUA   POLEMONIACEAE

This small genus of S. American shrubs is one of the few woody members of the Phlox family. 'Cantua' is the Peruvian name for the species described.

C. BUXIFOLIA Juss.
C. dependens Pers.

An evergreen shrub of bushy habit growing 6 to 15 ft high in a wild state, all the parts more or less downy. The leaves are very variable in shape; on the leafy shoots they are 1 to 2 in. long, deeply lobed at the sides, dull green. On the flowering shoots they change to a much smaller size and become entire, box-like, and ½ to ¾ in. long. The blossoms come in pendulous clusters of four to eight at the end of the shoot. Flowers 3 in. long, the long tubular base bright rose, with streaks of a darker hue; at the mouth are five spreading lobes, rich red and giving a diameter of 1 to 1½ in.; they open in April and May. *Bot. Mag.*, t. 4582.

This gorgeous shrub is a native of the Peruvian Andes and in most parts of the country requires greenhouse conditions. In the extreme south and west it can, however, be grown on a wall. I remember to have seen it in Lord St Leven's garden on St Michael's Mount and at Tregye in Cornwall. It is very well worth trying in any likely place. A wall of 6 to 8 ft high would suit it.*

CARAGANA   LEGUMINOSAE

A genus of shrubs, one of which becomes occasionally a small tree, mostly natives of Central Asia, but distributed over the vast tract of land between the Caucasus and Japan. The leaves are alternate and pinnate, the leaflets being of even number, frequently four, but in *C. microphylla* occasionally eighteen or twenty to each leaf. The flower is pea-shaped, with the standard petal curled back at the sides. Most of the species are armed. In place of a terminal odd leaflet, the leaf-stalk has either a bristle or a short spine. In some species, after the leaflets fall the stalk remains, becomes woody, and is transformed into a slender spine which persists for years. The stipules frequently develop into a pair of spines also. Thus the caraganas may be armed (1) with single spines, or transformed leaf-stalks; (2) double spines, or stipules with the leaf-stalk fallen away; or (3) triple

---

* Reprinted from W. J. Bean, *Wall Shrubs and Hardy Climbers*, 1951, by kind permission of the publishers, Messrs Putnam.

spines where both leaf-stalk and stipules persist. But generally they are by no means so formidably armed under cultivation as they are in nature. Some of them inhabit dry, half-desert regions, and, as frequently happens with such plants introduced to a damp, comparatively sunless country, the spines are neither so long nor so numerous as in the wild state. What is there a spine often becomes a mere bristle with us.

Another distinctive character general to the caraganas is the curious arrested branches covered with scales. These commence from the joints of the year-old shoots, and produce a cluster of leaves and flowers every year, slowly increasing in length, but making no wood in the proper sense of the term.

Most of the kinds are of easy cultivation. The only ones that do not adapt themselves readily to the British climate are *C. jubata, gerardiana, spinosa*, and *tragacanthoides*, especially the two first. The others thrive in sunny places, and do not require a rich soil. They mostly produce seeds which germinate freely; those which do not can be grafted on *C. arborescens*, whilst *aurantiaca, pygmaea*, and the thinner-twigged ones can be increased by cuttings. The generic name is derived from 'caragan', the Mongolian name for *C. arborescens*.

C. ARBORESCENS Lam.   PEA-TREE

A deciduous shrub up to 15 and 20 ft high, of rather erect, sometimes almost fastigiate habit; by pruning away the lower branches and training up a leading shoot, it may be made to take the form of a small tree; bark on young branchlets slightly winged. Leaves 1½ to 3 in. long, equally pinnate, consisting usually of four to six pairs of leaflets (more on young or exceptionally vigorous shoots); leaflets oval or obovate, ⅓ to ⅝ in. long, becoming nearly or quite glabrous; the main-stalk ending in a bristle-like spine. Stipules linear, spine-tipped, developing ultimately into a pair of stiff spines at each joint, ¼ in. long. Flowers yellow, produced singly on thin, downy stalks from ½ to 1½ in. long, several coming from each of the enlarged scaly buds on the previous year's wood. Each flower is ⅝ to ⅞ in. long; calyx cup-shaped or tubular, five-toothed, with hairy margins; standard petal not expanded but curled backwards at the sides. Pod 1½ to 2 in. long on a slender stalk about the same length, smooth, cylindric, and carrying three or five oblong seeds, the calyx adhering at the base.

Native of Siberia and Mongolia; introduced in 1752. This is the commonest of the caraganas in gardens, and is a vigorous, free-growing shrub. Its long, sparsely branched shoots give it a distinct appearance, and although not one of the showiest of the broom family it is very pretty in early May, when the yellow flowers are associated with the tender green, almost fully formed leaves. It produces good seed in abundance. The species shows several different forms, especially in habit, of which the following are the most distinct.

cv. 'LORBERGII'.—A remarkable variety with very narrowly linear, pointed leaflets, 1/25 to 1/12 in. wide, ¼ to ¾ in. long. The wing-petals and the standard are also much narrowed. In flower beauty it is inferior to the type, but the remarkable foliage (resembling the ultimate divisions of a fennel leaf) makes it well worth growing. It was raised in Lorberg's nurseries, Germany, and introduced around 1906.

cv. 'NANA'.—A dwarf, stunted bush, with stiff, contorted branches which grow very slowly. It is usually grafted on the type, from which it does not differ in leaf and flower. A quaint-looking shrub.

cv. 'PENDULA'.—Branches stiffly pendent, but not ungraceful. This variety is usually grafted on standards of the type. Foliage and flower the same. Described by Carrière in *Flore des Serres*, Vol. 11, 1856, p. 165.

C. × SOPHORIFOLIA Tausch *C. cuneifolia* Dipp.; *C. arborescens* var. *cuneifolia* (Dipp.) Schneid.—Leaflets mostly in six pairs, to $\frac{3}{5}$ in. long, wedge-shaped at the base; pods of $\frac{4}{5}$ in. long. It has the aspect of a dwarf form of *C. arborescens*, but is a hybrid between that species and *C. microphylla*.

C. BOISII Schneid. *C. microphylla* var. *crasse-aculeata* Bois; *C. arborescens* var. *crasse-aculeata* (Bois) R. J. Moore—This was introduced to the collection of Maurice de Vilmorin by one of the French missionaries in China and is figured in the *Fruticetum Vilmorianum* (1904) under the first synonym. It differs from *C. arborescens* in the longer teeth of the calyx and in the downy ovary and young fruit. It has about the same garden value as *C. arborescens*.

C. FRUTICOSA (Pall.) Steud. *Robinia altagana* var. *fruticosa* Pall.; *C. redowskii* DC.—Allied to *C. arborescens* but with the stipules scarcely thorny, larger flowers and shorter pods (to $1\frac{1}{5}$ in. long). It is a shrub to about 6 ft high, native of Korea and the Amur region.

A caragana received at Kew in 1872 from Booth of Hamburg as *C. arborescens* var. *redowskii* is a remarkable shrub with long, serpentine branches, which will sometimes grow for several years without dividing. It thus acquires a thin and open, but not ungraceful habit, and is altogether a striking plant. It appears to be a form of *C. fruticosa*.

C. AURANTIACA Koehne

A deciduous shrub about 4 ft high, with graceful, ultimately pendulous leafy branches, long, slender, but little divided, and armed with triple spines. Leaves very shortly stalked, consisting of four narrow, linear leaflets, $\frac{1}{3}$ to $\frac{1}{2}$ in. long, $\frac{1}{8}$ in. wide. Flowers $\frac{3}{4}$ in. long, produced singly on a stalk $\frac{1}{4}$ in. long, orange-yellow; calyx $\frac{1}{16}$ in. long, bell-shaped, with five triangular, minutely ciliated teeth. Pod 1 to $1\frac{1}{2}$ in. long, glabrous, rather cylindrical, pointed, carrying four to six seeds.

Native of Central Asia; introduced in 1887 as a variety of *C. pygmaea*, of which it was at first regarded merely as a deeper-coloured form. It differs also in the more taper-pointed leaflets and in the shorter calyx. This and *C. pygmaea* are probably the prettiest of all caraganas. Its habit is graceful, and it blossoms with great profusion, the flowers hanging thickly from the underside of the branch in a long row, three or four to the inch. It blossoms in May and June, and can be easily propagated by late summer cuttings.

CARAGANA AURANTIACA

C. BREVISPINA Royle

A deciduous shrub up to 8 ft high, the young wood covered with fine down. Leaves pinnate; the common stalk (or rachis) is sharp-tipped, 1 to 3 in. long, remaining after the leaflets have fallen, and developing ultimately into a woody spine; stipules in the form of spines $\frac{1}{4}$ in. long. Leaflets ten to fourteen on each leaf, oblong or oblanceolate; $\frac{1}{3}$ to 1 in. long, $\frac{1}{16}$ to $\frac{1}{3}$ in. wide; covered when young with flattened silky hairs. Flowers yellow, about $\frac{3}{4}$ in. long, produced three or four together at the end of a common stalk 1 to 2 in. long. Calyx $\frac{1}{3}$ in. long, bell-shaped, with five narrow, fine-pointed teeth, downy. Pod 2 in. long, glabrous outside, woolly within.

Native of the north-western Himalaya at 5,000 to 9,000 ft elevation, distinguished from *arborescens* by the long, fine-pointed spines developed from the leaf-stalks, and by the several (not solitary) flowers on each stalk. It flowers in June. It is in cultivation in the R.H.S. Garden at Wisley from SSW 8135.

C. DECORTICANS Hemsl.

A deciduous shrub or small tree up to 15 or 18 ft high, densely branched, armed with spiny stipules ¼ in. long. Leaves 1 to 1½ in. long, pinnate in three to six pairs of leaflets which are oval or obovate, ¼ to ½ in. long, spine-tipped, with appressed hairs on both surfaces but especially beneath; main leaf-stalk, spine-tipped but deciduous. Flowers bright pale yellow, 1 in. long, each borne on a very slender downy stalk, ¾ in. long, jointed near the calyx; calyx bell-shaped, with a spiny-toothed, ciliate margin. Pod 1½ to 2 in. long.

Native of Afghanistan; discovered in 1879 by Dr Aitchison in the Kurrum Valley. It belongs to the same group as *C. arborescens* in having spiny persistent stipules and deciduous leaf-stalks, but the leaves and pods are shorter and the calyx has longer teeth. Aitchison observes that 'the bark is employed by the Afghans in the form of rings to slip over and hold the sheaths of their long knives in position in lieu of brasswork; the surface takes a good polish and when new resembles bronzed leather'. Flowers in June.

C. FRANCHETIANA Komar.
C. gerardiana var. *glabrescens* Franch.

A deciduous shrub originally collected in Yunnan, China, by the Abbé Delavay and made a variety of *C. gerardiana* by Franchet. It is, however, very distinct from that species in the young shoots having none of the shagginess seen in *C. gerardiana* and in the spines being set singly on the twigs half an inch apart instead of forming a thicket along the branches. These spines are really the persisting main-stalk of the leaves, enlarged, woody, stiff, and up to 2 in. long. Each leaf has eight or ten leaflets pinnately arranged; leaflets obovate, ¼ in. long, parallel-veined, silky-hairy beneath when young. Flowers 1 in. long, yellow; calyx cylindrical, ½ in. long, deeply triangular-lobed, downy; flower-stalk ¼ in. long, carrying three small bracts. Pod downy, 1¾ in. long.

The plants in cultivation were raised from seed collected by Forrest in Yunnan about 1913. Delavay found it in flower on 20th June 1885.

C. FRUTEX (L.) K. Koch
Robinia frutex L.; *C. frutescens* DC.

A deciduous shrub up to 10 ft in height, with long, often erect, supple branches, not much divided except near the ends. Leaves composed of two pairs of sessile leaflets, which are attached near the end of the common stalk, being themselves stalkless; they are obovate, rounded at the end, ½ to over 1 in. long, glabrous, dull green. Flowers bright yellow, ¾ to 1 in. long, produced singly on a stalk rather shorter than the corolla. Calyx ⅓ in. long, bell-shaped, glabrous. Pod 1½ in. long, ⅛ in. wide; cylindrical, glabrous.

In a wild state this species extends from the south of Russia to Central Asia. It was introduced in 1752. It is a pretty shrub in flower, and is often quite neat and graceful in habit, especially when 3 or 4 ft high, with its numerous thin twigs, rather pendulous. It is distinct in being unarmed and without down. Of several forms in cultivation the most distinct is var. MOLLIS (DC.) Schneid., with leaves downy on both sides; found wild in the Caucasus.

var. GRANDIFLORA Schneid. var. *macrantha* Rehd.—Flowers over 1 in. long, with a proportionately short calyx.

C. GERARDIANA (Graham) Benth.
Astragalus gerardianus Graham

A deciduous shrub, naturally of close, compact form, and from 2 to 4 ft high. Branches close-jointed, covered thickly with whitish, silky hairs. Leaves pinnate, 1½ to 2½ in. long, with four to six pairs of leaflets, the common stalk very downy, spine-tipped, remaining after the leaflets have fallen, and becoming eventually a rigid, slender spine. Leaflets oval or obovate with a bristle-like tip, ¼ to ½ in. long, silky-hairy. Stipules not spiny, but broad, thin and papery, ⅓ in. long. Flowers solitary on their very short stalks, pale yellow or nearly white, ¾ in. long; calyx hairy, cylindrical, ½ in. long. Pod hairy outside, downy within, about 1 in. long.

Native of the north-western Himalaya up to 13,000 ft. This shrub is remarkable for its long, slender spines, and the dense woolly covering, which gives the whole plant a greyish-white aspect. It is hardy at Kew, but I have never seen it in flower. Essentially a sun-lover, and coming from the dry inner valleys of N.W. India, it finds our climate too wet and dull. On the continent it thrives better. In Messrs Simon-Louis' nursery at Metz I have seen it in admirable health. It will probably be best suited in this country on a well-drained sunny ledge of the rock garden.

C. JUBATA (Pall.) Poir.
Robinia jubata Pall.

A deciduous, excessively spiny and hairy shrub 1 to 5, but sometimes 8 to 10 ft high, with thick branches completely covered with spines, woolly stipules, and leaflets. Leaves 1 to 2½ in. long, with four to eight pairs of leaflets. The leaf-stalk is downy when young, slender, spine-tipped, persisting after the leaflets have fallen, and hardening, the older branches thereby becoming thickly furnished with wiry-looking spines 1 to 2½ in. long. Leaflets oblong, ¼ to ¾ in. long, hairy; stipules ½ in. wide, each lobe ending in a stiff spine, the whole shaggy with long silky hairs. As the branch is completely covered with these overlapping stipules it has quite a padded appearance. Flowers solitary on short stalks, white, 1¼ in. long; calyx ½ in. long, hairy, with five narrowly triangular teeth. Pod ¾ in. long, hairy outside, glabrous within. Blossoms in April and May.

Native of Siberia and Mongolia; introduced from near Lake Baikal in 1796. This remarkable shrub comes from dry desert regions, where the summers are extremely hot and the winters extremely cold. In Great Britain it is most successfully grown at the foot of a warm, dry wall, in well-drained, light soil. The flowers are few and the shrub is not showy, yet it is worth growing as a curiosity.

C. MAXIMOWICZIANA Komarov

A densely branched, deciduous shrub of spreading habit, 4 to 6 ft high; young shoots slightly downy, afterwards armed with very slender spines $\frac{1}{2}$ to $\frac{3}{4}$ in. long, developed from the persistent main-stalks of the leaves. Leaflets four or six, pinnately arranged, linear-oblong, $\frac{3}{8}$ in. long, downy. Flowers solitary, very shortly stalked, yellow, 1 in. long; calyx cylindrical, $\frac{3}{8}$ in. long, with short triangular lobes, downy. Pod $\frac{3}{4}$ in. long, downy.

Native of W. Szechwan and Kansu, China, and of E. Tibet; collected by Père Soulié in 1893 at Tongolo, W. Szechwan, near the Tibetan border, but introduced to cultivation by E. H. Wilson, who saw it in flower in June 1908, and collected seed two years later. It is hardy in the Arnold Arboretum, Mass., and makes a handsome shrub there with bright green leaves and bright yellow flowers. It is related to *C. spinosa*, but that species has spines up to 2 in. in length and longer leaflets.

C. MICROPHYLLA Lam.

A deciduous shrub from 6 to 10 ft in height, wider than it is high, with light grey, silky young bark. Leaves pinnate, $1\frac{1}{2}$ to 3 in. long, composed of six to nine pairs of leaflets; main-stalk ending in a short spine, but not persistent; stipules spiny, $\frac{1}{6}$ in. long. Leaflets $\frac{1}{8}$ to $\frac{1}{3}$ in. long, oval or obovate, dull greyish green, silky-hairy at first, then glabrous. Flowers yellow, $\frac{3}{4}$ in. long, solitary on stalks rather shorter than the corolla; calyx $\frac{1}{3}$ in. long, cylindrical, with short, pointed teeth. Pod about $1\frac{1}{4}$ in. long, $\frac{1}{6}$ in. wide, compressed, glabrous or hairy.

Native of N. Central Asia from Siberia to China; introduced in 1789. It flowers in May and June, and is readily distinguished from all other species by the number and small size of its leaflets, the smallest scarcely $\frac{1}{8}$ in. long. It is a shrub of graceful habit, much wider than high (12 ft in diameter at Kew), the branches being long, slender, but little divided, and ultimately more or less pendent. Grafted on standards of *C. arborescens* it makes a small tree, but sucker growths from the stock are often troublesome. It is suitable as a specimen for a lawn.

C. OREOPHILA W. W. Sm.

A bushy deciduous shrub 3 to 4 ft high; young shoots clothed with soft white wool, which persists to the second year, becoming darker. Leaves equally pinnate, 1 to $1\frac{1}{2}$ in. long, made up of four to eight pairs of leaflets, the main-stalk stiff, woody, clothed with white wool except at the spiny tip, persisting and becoming transformed into a slender naked spine the second year. On the second-year and older shoots the leaves are borne in clusters and their main-stalk does not become spiny. Leaflets oval, pointed, $\frac{1}{4}$ to $\frac{3}{8}$ in. long, clothed with grey silky hairs on both surfaces. Flowers solitary on a stalk $\frac{3}{5}$ in. long, the corolla of the usual pea-flower shape, orange-coloured suffused with brown, about 1 in. long. Calyx tubular, with erect, awl-shaped teeth, about $\frac{1}{2}$ in. long, silky. Seed-pods $\frac{3}{4}$ to 1 in. long, woolly.

Native of W. China, discovered by Forrest in 'open alpine pasture on the mountains in the north-east of the Yangtze Bend'; introduced in 1913. It is a neat-looking shrub, interesting for the whiteness of its young shoots and leaves and closely related to *C. franchetiana*. Like all the caraganas it should be given as sunny a spot as possible.

C. PYGMAEA (L.) DC.
Robinia pygmaea L.

A deciduous shrub 3 to 4 ft high, similar in habit to *C. aurantiaca*, having long, slender, pendulous, or even prostrate branches. Leaves nearly stalkless, composed of four leaflets, each of which is ½ in. long, broadest near the apex, where it is about ⅛ in. wide, tapering thence towards the base; the apex has a short, wedge-shaped point. Flowers yellow, 1 in. long, produced in May and June at the joints of the previous season's shoots, each on its own stalk ⅓ in. long, and one flower from each joint; calyx ⅛ in. long, bell-shaped, triangular-toothed, edged with minute hairs; pod ¾ to 1¼ in. long, glabrous.

In a wild state this species extends over the region between the Caucasus and Siberia and Tibet; introduced in 1751. It is a very pretty plant when in flower, the blossoms being pendulous on their short stalks from the lower side of the branchlets. It is often grafted on standards of *C. arborescens*, but can quite well be struck from cuttings made of half-woody young twigs in July and placed in gentle heat. By growing it on its own roots, the ugly and often diseased union seen on grafted plants is avoided. It is nearly allied to *C. aurantiaca*, under which the differences are pointed out. Its slender, flexible shoots are used for tying in Siberia, and are said to be equal to osiers for that purpose.

C. GRANDIFLORA (Bieb.) DC. *C. pygmaea* var. *grandiflora* Dipp.—Flowers up to 1¼ in. long, the calyx longer, more swollen and unequal at the base; leaflets rather larger. Native of Armenia.

C. SINICA (Buc'hoz) Rehd.
Robinia sinica Buc'hoz; *C. chamlagu* Lam.

A deciduous shrub up to 5 ft high, with angular branches, and of rounded, bushy habit. Leaves composed of two unequal pairs of leaflets, the terminal pair the larger; the common stalk is sharp-tipped, and remains after the leaflets have fallen, but it does not develop into the formidable spine seen in *C. brevispina* or *gerardiana*; stipules ¼ to ⅓ in. long, becoming stiff spines. Leaflets very variable in size; in young plants as much as 1½ in. long and ¾ in. wide, usually obovate, but on old flowering shoots ¼ to ¾ in. long; glabrous and lustrous, rounded at the apex. Flower 1¼ in. long, solitary on its slender stalk ½ to ¾ in. long, reddish yellow. Calyx bell-shaped, nearly ½ in. long, with five short, triangular teeth. Pod 1½ in. long, slender, glabrous.

Native of N. China; introduced in 1773. It is distinct for its large, dark green, glossy, membranous leaflets, larger in a young state than those of any other cultivated caragana. The bruised bark smells like liquorice. Often grafted on standards of *C. arborescens*, it makes a handsome bushy-topped small tree. Flowers in May and June.

C. SPINOSA (L.) DC.
Robinia spinosa L.

A deciduous shrub 4 to 6 ft high, of rather gaunt habit, and with long, undivided, spiny branches, hairy when young. Leaves pinnate, composed of two to four pairs of leaflets, which are $\frac{1}{2}$ to $\frac{3}{4}$ in. long, $\frac{1}{8}$ to $\frac{1}{6}$ in. wide, nearly or quite glabrous; common stalk of leaf $\frac{1}{2}$ to $1\frac{1}{4}$ in. long, silky when young, sharp-tipped, remaining after the leaves have fallen, and developing into a rigid, slender spine. Stipules chaffy, lanceolate, $\frac{1}{4}$ in. long. Flowers very shortly stalked, nearly 1 in. long, bright yellow; calyx cylindrical, with short, triangular teeth. Pod $\frac{3}{4}$ in. long, glabrous.

Native of Siberia; introduced in 1775. This is a curious shrub of the same type as *C. jubata* and *gerardiana*, but not so formidably armed nor so downy. According to Pallas, the Russian botanist, in the neighbourhood of Pekin, where this shrub is plentiful, its branches are stuck in clay on the tops of walls to keep off trespassers, just as broken glass is used here. It is sometimes confused with *C. tragacanthoides*.

C. SUKIENSIS Schneid.

A deciduous shrub 5 ft or more high; young shoots pendulous, furnished with curly down. Leaves 1 to $1\frac{1}{2}$ in. long, pinnate; the main-stalk persistent, spine-tipped, hairy; leaflets ten to fourteen, $\frac{1}{4}$ to $\frac{1}{3}$ in. long, narrowly oblong-lanceolate, conspicuously parallel-veined, silky-hairy beneath. Flowers solitary, about 1 in. long, yellow; calyx tubular, $\frac{1}{4}$ in. long, hairy, lobes awl-shaped; stalk $\frac{1}{4}$ in. or less long. Pod $\frac{1}{2}$ to $\frac{3}{4}$ in. long, slightly downy.

Native of N.W. India; introduced in 1919 from Paris to Kew, where it flowered in June 1925. Most nearly akin to *C. gerardiana*, it is less shaggy on the young shoots and pods; as in that species the persistent, spine-tipped leaf-stalks provide its armature, but they are not so thickly massed on the branches. It is a graceful shrub, hardy enough to have passed through the trying winter of 1928–9 at Kew without injury but is no longer grown there, nor at Edinburgh, where it reached a height of 6 to 7 ft, but was lost during the 1939–45 war. It is, however, still in cultivation in the Glasnevin Botanic Garden, Dublin, and quite hardy there.

C. TRAGACANTHOIDES (Pall.) Poir.
Robinia tragacanthoides Pall.

A low, spreading, much-branched shrub 1 to $1\frac{1}{2}$ ft high. Branches very spiny, downy when young; spines (modified leaf-stalks) 1 to $1\frac{1}{2}$ in. long, slender; stipules narrow, $\frac{1}{8}$ in. long, scarcely spiny, silky. Leaves $\frac{3}{4}$ to $1\frac{1}{2}$ in. long, composed of three to five pairs of leaflets, which are rather variable in outline, oblanceolate, obovate or oblong, $\frac{1}{4}$ to $\frac{1}{2}$ in. in length, woolly. Flower $1\frac{1}{4}$ in. long, yellow, solitary on a downy stalk $\frac{1}{8}$ to $\frac{1}{4}$ in. long. Calyx $\frac{1}{2}$ in. long, bell-shaped, downy, and with short, triangular teeth. Pod 1 to $1\frac{1}{4}$ in. long, shaggy with silky hairs, the lower half enclosed by the persisting calyx.

Native of Tibet, N. China, Siberia; introduced in 1816. It is doubtful if the true plant is now in cultivation, the shrub commonly seen under the name being *C. spinosa*, which has smaller flowers and a glabrous pod and calyx. *C. tragacanthoides* is rather variable, some forms like var. VILLOSA Reg. having the young branches densely covered with shaggy grey hairs.

CARMICHAELIA   LEGUMINOSAE

A genus of shrubs in which some thirty-eight species are now recognised, of which fourteen were published by Simpson in 1945. All but one (found on Lord Howe Island) are natives of New Zealand. One of the most distinctive features of the genus is the very frequently flattened branches; another is the nearly always leafless condition of the shrubs at maturity; still another is the curious way in which the central part of the pod carrying the seeds falls out when quite ripe, leaving a sort of ring or empty framework. The carmichaelias make no great display of colour but they are pretty and very profuse in flower, and usually charmingly fragrant. The part played in the economy of most plants by leaves is, in this genus, largely performed by the green, flattened stems—not an uncommon occurrence in the broom family. *C. petriei* and *C. enysii* are apparently quite hardy; the other species described, with the exception of *C. grandiflora*, may need a sheltered spot close to a wall facing south or south-west.

C. AUSTRALIS R. Br.

A shrub 3 to 12 ft high in a wild state, of erect habit, much-branched; young shoots glabrous, flat, often leafless, ⅛ in. wide. In young seedling plants the leaves are 1 in. or more long and made up of three or five wedge-shaped leaflets notched at the end; in the adult state of the plants the leaves disappear altogether or become very much reduced and less than ¼ in. long. Flowers pale purple, scarcely $\frac{3}{16}$ in. long, crowded in short clusters of up to a dozen. Calyx bell-shaped, with small triangular teeth. Pod oval, ⅜ in. long, narrowed to a beak at the end, carrying one to four red seeds. *Bot. Mag.*, t. 8972.

The above description, taken from previous editions of this work, is of a plant, no longer at Kew, which grew well in a nook on the sunny side of a greenhouse, producing in June and July an amazing profusion of its pale purple flower-clusters. It was probably a plant of the old introduction, figured in *Bot. Mag.*, t. 912, and in cultivation since before 1823 as a greenhouse shrub. However, *C. australis* is a rather confused species and not recognised by Allan in *Flora of New Zealand* (1961), in which *C. australis* in the old sense is distributed among five species. Of these, the plant described above would appear to be nearest to the following two species:

C. EGMONTIANA (Ckn. & Allan) Simpson *C. Caustralis* var. *egmontiana*
Ckn. & Allan—This shrub is a native of the North Island of New Zealand where
it ascends to sub-alpine elevations on Mount Egmont and in the Pouakai Range.
From the plant described this differs in its narrower branchlets (normally about
$\frac{1}{12}$ in. wide); the shape of the pods is given as obliquely oblong. C. CUNNING-
HAMII Raoul is closely allied, but has wider branchlets ($\frac{1}{8}$ to $\frac{1}{6}$ in.) and oblong
to almost orbicular pods with one to two seeds, orange-red more or less mottled
with black. It is common in North Island at low elevations and doubtless more
tender than *C. egmontiana*.

C. ENYSII T. Kirk

A pygmy shrub 6 to 12 in. high, forming a tiny compact thicket of flat green
branches, which perform the functions of the almost entirely absent leaves.
Young shoots without down, ribbed, about $\frac{1}{16}$ in. wide. Flowers $\frac{3}{16}$ in. long,
solitary or a few together, bright violet; calyx bell-shaped with short teeth, the
lower part of it as well as the flower-stalk usually silky-downy. Pod flattened,
$\frac{1}{4}$ to $\frac{1}{3}$ in. long, roundish ovate, ending in a beak, usually one-seeded; seeds
black.

Native of the South Island of New Zealand, where it occurs up to an altitude
of 3,000 ft, but is rare and local; introduced to Kew in 1892. Cheeseman describes
the leaves of young plants as orbicular and notched at the end. The species is
quite hardy at Kew and flowers and bears seed there regularly. Whilst it must be
regarded chiefly as a curiosity it is worth the small space it requires in the rock
garden for its interest. Amongst the three or four species of similar dwarf stature
this is distinct in its one-seeded pods.

C. ORBICULATA Colenso *C. enysii* var. *orbiculata* (Colenso) Kirk—An allied
species differing in its broader branchlets (about $\frac{1}{8}$ in. wide) and olive-green,
black-mottled seeds. Native of the North Island.

C. FLAGELLIFORMIS Colenso

A deciduous or often leafless shrub 4 or 5 ft high, with numerous erect-
growing, slender, grooved branches, flattened or convex when young, round
when old. Leaves very small and inconspicuous, consisting of three or five tiny
leaflets, which are somewhat larger in young plants than in old ones. Flowers
purplish lilac, pea-shaped, produced in axillary downy racemes; there are from
one to three racemes at each joint of the twigs, and from three to seven flowers
in each raceme, the whole forming a short, dense cluster. The flowers, although
small (about $\frac{1}{8}$ in. long), are borne in extraordinary profusion. Pod $\frac{1}{4}$ to $\frac{1}{2}$ in.
long, nearly as wide, ending in a stout-pointed beak, and containing usually two
seeds, which are red, mottled with black.

Native of the North Island of New Zealand. Although not in cultivation at
Kew at the present time, it grew there for forty years or more in the open
ground, where, although slightly injured at the younger parts in severe winters,
it was on the whole quite hardy and produced both flowers and seed in abundance. The form now grown in gardens appears, however, to be tender. It is not

very showy or ornamental, but its flat erect branches give it a quaint and unusual aspect.

C. GRANDIFLORA (Benth.) Hook. f.
C. australis var. *grandiflora* Benth.

A deciduous, freely branching shrub up to 6 ft high; young shoots flattened, distinctly ribbed, glabrous, and leafy when young. Leaves (persisting until about midsummer) $\frac{1}{2}$ to $\frac{3}{4}$ in. long, made up of three or five leaflets which are glabrous, inversely heart-shaped, $\frac{3}{16}$ in. long. Flowers $\frac{1}{4}$ in. long, fragrant, pale purple veined with violet, produced five to twelve together in racemes up to 1 in. long; flower-stalks glabrous. Pod oblong, $\frac{1}{4}$ to $\frac{3}{8}$ in. long, narrowed at the end to a long beak and carrying two to four seeds, which are red, spotted with black.

Native of the South Island of New Zealand and found in mountainous districts up to 3,500 ft. A specimen preserved at Kew, collected by Dr Haast in October 1864, bears the note: 'Along the banks of the River Cameron, filling the air with delicious perfume.' The distinctive characters of the species are its leaf-bearing young shoots and the long-beaked, straw-coloured seed-pod, borne on an upright stalk, but in other respects it is variable: the form described above has glabrous flower-stalks, but in the type they are downy.

var. ALBA T. Kirk—Flowers white. Found wild near the Waimakariri glaciers.

The species flowers in June and July and ought, from the altitude at which it grows, to be reasonably hardy.

C. ODORATA Colenso

A shrub up to 10 ft high in a wild state; young shoots flattened, downy (especially towards the end), $\frac{1}{12}$ in. wide. Leaves pinnate, $\frac{1}{2}$ to 1 in. long; leaflets three to seven, each $\frac{1}{8}$ to $\frac{1}{4}$ in. long, wedge-shaped, notched at the end, downy, usually falling by early summer. Flowers $\frac{1}{8}$ to $\frac{1}{6}$ in. long, lilac-rose, fragrant, packed closely ten to twenty together on racemes $\frac{1}{2}$ to $\frac{3}{4}$ in. long; flower-stalk and calyx downy. Pod $\frac{1}{4}$ in. long, ovate, terminated by a slender beak, one- or two-seeded. *Bot. Mag.*, t. 9479.

Native of New Zealand, up to altitudes of 2,500 ft. It bears a wonderful profusion of blossom in June and July and the slender, pendulous branches give it a graceful shape. It needs a sunny, warm corner and shelter from north and east. The downy shoots and, early in the season, the pinnate downy leaves give distinctive characters. The leaves and leaflets of the larger dimensions given are only found on young seedling plants. There is a specimen 10 to 12 ft high on a wall in the Glasnevin Botanic Garden.

C. PETRIEI T. Kirk

A shrub described as stout, sparingly branched and from 2 to 6 ft high in a wild state. Young shoots without down, faintly ribbed, slightly flattened, but becoming almost round (terete) after the first year. Flowers $\frac{1}{6}$ in. long, violet-

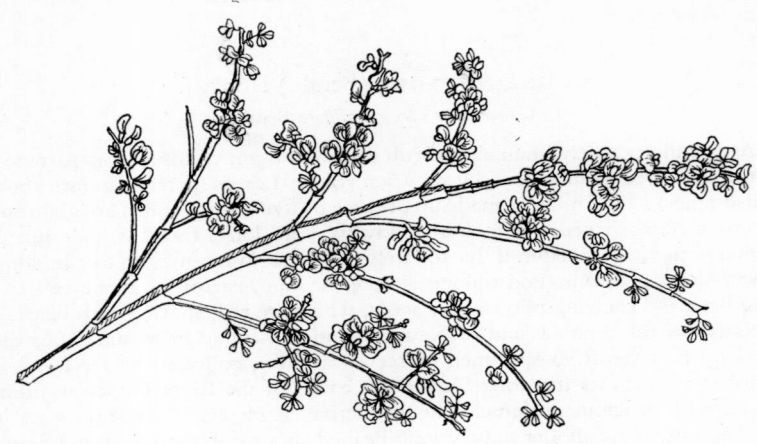

CARMICHAELIA ODORATA

purple, fragrant, produced in June and July, three to eight together on racemes
½ to 1 in. long; calyx and flower-stalks silky-downy, the former with short
triangular teeth. Pod ¼ to ⅖ in. long, stout, with usually two or three seeds.

Native of the South Island of New Zealand, up to 1,000 ft altitude. Its
distinctive characters are in the round (not flattened) branches, short thick pod,
and often thickly clustered downy racemes. It is not in cultivation at Kew, but
is reputed to be fairly hardy.

C. WILLIAMSII T. Kirk

A usually leafless shrub, much-branched, 3 to 8 ft high in a wild state. Branchlets ¼ to ½ in. wide, flat and thin, finely grooved, glabrous (or appressed-downy
when quite young only). Flowers large for this genus, being ¾ to 1 in. long,
broom-like, creamy yellow tinged with green; standard petal purple-stained at
the base, keel tipped with purple; they are sometimes solitary, but more often
two to six in a cluster are produced from the buds at the thin edge of the branchlet. Calyx slightly downy, obliquely tubular, ¼ in. long, green, with pointed
triangular lobes; flower-stalk ¼ in. long, downy. Pod thick, rounded, ¾ in. long,
with a distinct beak. *Bot. Mag.*, n.s., t. 70.

Native of New Zealand in the North Island, where it is described as rare and
local. Seeds were received at Kew from B. C. Aston in 1925, which had been
collected on the Hen and Chickens Island, and plants raised from them flowered
freely in the Temperate House, March 1928. The flowers were not 'yellowish
red', as described by Cheeseman, but greenish yellow. In comparison with other
carmichaelias in cultivation this is remarkable for the size of its flowers and for
the width of its thin, flat young shoots. It is only likely to be hardy in our mildest

counties; at Kew it has proved very tender when planted outside. Leaves, rarely seen except on young plants, are either simple or composed of three obovate or inversely heart-shaped leaflets.

CARPENTERIA   PHILADELPHACEAE

A genus of one species allied to *Philadelphus*, from which it differs in its evergreen leaves, single style and superior ovary.

C. CALIFORNICA Torr.   [PLATE 28

An evergreen shrub 6 to 15 ft high, of bushy habit and free growth, branchlets very pithy; young bark pale and minutely downy. Leaves opposite, lanceolate, 2 to 4½ in. long, ⅓ to 1 in. wide, tapering at both ends, not toothed, glabrous and bright green above, covered with a pale soft felt beneath; stalk ¼ in. long, or almost absent. Flowers fragrant, 2 to 3 in. in diameter, pure white, produced during June and July in a terminal cluster, three to seven flowers together; petals five, roundish; calyx downy, with five ovate, pointed lobes; stamens very numerous, their yellow anthers making a conspicuous centre to the flower. *Bot. Mag.*, t. 6911.

Native of California; discovered by Col. Fremont in the middle of the last century; introduced to Europe about 1880, and first flowered in this country by Miss Jekyll at Godalming in 1885. In places where it thrives, it is one of the most splendid acquisitions from the Californian flora. It is not hardy at Kew except against a wall, and under glass it is one of the most susceptible of all plants to injury by London fog. In the brighter, sunnier parts of England it is quite hardy on a warm wall in well-drained soil, always provided it is not softened by over-feeding. Even in the more continental climate of Cambridge-shire and East Anglia it succeeds and is hardy. At East Bergholt Place, Suffolk, it reached a height of 18 ft on a wall.

It is rather variable, and if raised from seed produces many worthless plants with rather narrow, watery-white petals. The finest forms have well-fashioned flowers almost 4 in. across with overlapping petals of good substance. These must be increased by cuttings, which root readily enough under mist, or by layering.

CARPINUS   HORNBEAM   CARPINACEAE

Some forty-five species of hornbeam are scattered over the temperate regions of the northern hemisphere, scarcely half of which are in cultivation. They are deciduous trees, rarely of the largest size, with zigzag twigs and alternate, conspicuously parallel-ribbed leaves. The flowers are unisexual, both sexes produced on the same tree, but on separate catkins. The pendulous male catkins come on the old wood; the females terminate the young shoots. The male flower consists of numerous stamens produced in the axil of a scale. The female inflorescence is stalked and at first erect, with the flowers in pairs in each deciduous scale; the single flower is subtended by a bract which is unequally lobed at the base and really a compound organ made up of a bract and two bractlets. In the fruiting stage the catkin elongates and becomes pendent, the seed being enclosed in a ribbed nut at the base of the enlarged bract and bractlets.

Hornbeams are hardy trees, and handsome, especially in summer when laden with pendent fruit clusters. As a park tree none is so valuable as our common hornbeam, but for gardens some of the Chinese and Japanese hornbeams are very attractive. They thrive in any good loam, and are at home on chalky soils. All the species should be raised from seed, but the rarer ones can be grafted on common hornbeam, as also must its own varieties be. There are two distinct sections of the genus:

1. CARPINUS proper.—Scales of male flowers ovate, scarcely stalked. Bracts of the fruiting catkins loosely overlapping, and so little infolded as to leave the nut exposed—*C. betulus*, etc. Veins in seven to fifteen pairs.

2. DISTEGOCARPUS.—Scales of male flowers narrower, stalked. Bracts of the fruiting catkins closely packed, overlapping, infolded at the base and surrounding the nut. Two of the species described belong to this section—*C. cordata* and *C. japonica*. Veins in fifteen to twenty-four pairs. At first glance these species might be confused with *Ostrya* (hop hornbeam) when in fruit, but in that genus the nut is completely enclosed in a bladder-like organ.

C. BETULUS L.   COMMON HORNBEAM

A tree 50 to 80 ft high, pyramidal when young, but ultimately forming a rounded or somewhat elongated head with the ends of the branches pendulous; trunk grey and often beautifully fluted; young shoots clothed more or less with pale hairs, which mostly soon fall away. Leaves oval or inclined to ovate, $1\frac{1}{2}$ to $3\frac{1}{2}$ in. long, 1 to 2 in. wide; the base rounded or heart-shaped, one side often longer than the other; short-pointed at the apex, unequally or doubly toothed; dark green and at first downy on the midrib above; under-surface more downy especially on the midrib and the ten to thirteen pairs of veins, both sides becoming nearly or quite glabrous by autumn; stalk $\frac{1}{4}$ to $\frac{1}{2}$ in. long. Male catkins $1\frac{1}{2}$ in. long. Fruiting catkins $1\frac{1}{2}$ to 3 in. long, furnished with large, conspicuous three-lobed bracts, the middle lobe 1 to $1\frac{1}{2}$ in. long, often toothed. They are produced in pairs facing each other, each with an ovate, ribbed nut at the base, $\frac{1}{4}$ in. long.

Native of Europe and Asia Minor; indigenous to the south-east and east of England. A well-grown hornbeam is one of our handsomest trees, the foliage turning yellow in autumn; more graceful than the beech, for which many people mistake it. It is, of course, distinct in the duller, more conspicuously toothed leaves, and in the ridged or fluted trunk, and the fruiting arrangement is quite different. The timber is hard, almost bony, and is valued for making those intricate parts of the pianoforte which convey the movement from the key to the hammer that strikes the strings. Elwes describes it as 'the hardest, heaviest, and toughest' of our native woods. In earlier times hornbeams were largely coppiced and pollarded for the supply of firewood, as may be seen by the old pollards that cover so much of Epping Forest. Sir J. E. Smith says that this tree formed the principal part of that and other forests which once lay to the north and east of London. The hornbeam is a useful hedge plant, and hedges of it may often be seen in old-established nurseries, planted originally for shelter. Nearly all the hedges in the R.H.S. Garden at Wisley are of hornbeam. In this clipped state it retains its dead leaves until spring, like the beech.

The common hornbeam thrives well at Kew, where the largest is 70 ft high, with a girth of 12¼ ft. The tallest recorded in recent years is one at Studley Royal, Yorks., 90 × 8½ ft (1958); this is perhaps the tree of which Elwes and Henry give a measurement of 75 × 6½ ft in 1908. A hornbeam in Bitton church-yard, Glos., was planted shortly after 1817 by the father of Canon Ellacombe (1822–1916), who became rector there and made a famous garden which is frequently mentioned in this work. It measures 60 × 10 ft (1959); Elwes and Henry give 65 × 8¼ ft as its dimensions in 1908.

cv. 'ASPLENIFOLIA'.—Leaves deeply and regularly double-toothed, the primary teeth large enough to be called lobes. See also 'Incisa'.

f. CARPINIZZA (Host) Neilr. *C. carpinizza* Host—A variety found in the south-eastern part of the range, e.g. in the Carpathians of Romania. It differs in the more distinctly heart-shaped base of the leaf and in the fewer (seven to nine) veins.

cv. 'COLUMNARIS'.—A rather slow-growing tree, densely branched and leaved; spire-like when young, later egg-shaped, always with a central leader. Put into commerce by Späth's nurseries, around 1891.

cv. 'FASTIGIATA'.—This is the now established name for a hornbeam previously known as *C. b. pyramidalis*. The trees commonly grown under these names appear to be all of one clone, faster growing than 'Columnaris', conical when young but becoming more open and rounded with age. Two trees at Kew, both planted in 1894 but received from different nurserymen (one from Croux and the other from Hesse) are almost of the same size and girth (56 × 6½ ft at 2 ft and 58 × 6¼ ft at 3 ft—1966). A similar tree at Westonbirt measures 47 × 8 ft at 1 ft (1966). It was planted in 1929. There are reports of trees of 'pyramidal' habit occurring in the wild both in France and Germany.

cv. 'HETEROPHYLLA'—Similar to 'Incisa', but with some of the leaves more or less normal. The two are sometimes regarded as one and the same, but Kirchner, who grew both (*Arb. Muscav.*, 1864), said they were distinct.

cv. 'HORIZONTALIS'.—Discovered growing wild by M. Jouin of the Simon-Louis establishment near Metz and described by him as flat-topped, like *Crataegus crus-galli*.

cv .'INCISA'.—With some similarity to 'Asplenifolia', this differs in having smaller and especially shorter leaves, coarsely and irregularly toothed, and only about six pairs of veins. There is little reason to doubt that this is an old clone, distributed early in the last century by Loddiges and by Booth of Hamburg (who had close trading relations) as *C. b. incisa* (or *foliis incisis*). It also agrees well enough with the original description of var. *incisa* by Aiton (*Hort. Kew.*, 1789). Sometimes known, though in our view wrongly, as 'Quercifolia' (q.v.). A further complication is that the name 'Incisa' has also been used for the clone described above as 'Asplenifolia', but the latter is certainly not the *incisa* of Aiton nor of Loudon.

cv. 'PENDULA'.—A weeping form; 'PENDULA DERVAESII' is still more elegant.

f. QUERCIFOLIA (Desf.) Schneid.—This name is founded on the var. *quercifolia* of Desfontaines, of which the description states merely that the leaves are oak-like. There are reports of trees in which some of the branchlets bear leaves which are smaller than in the type and with rounded lobes, and possibly it was such a tree that Desfontaines had in mind. The leaves of 'Incisa' (q.v.) are also somewhat oak-like, but the resemblance is to the leaves found on weak shoots of *Q. cerris* and the whole tree bears leaves of this type. The name *C. betulus* 'Quercifolia' (or *C. b. quercifolia*) has indeed been used, though wrongly it would seem, for 'Incisa'.

C. CAROLINIANA Walt.   AMERICAN HORNBEAM
C. americana Michx.

A small, bushy tree rarely 40 ft high, with a short, grey, fluted trunk; young shoots at first furnished with pale hairs. Leaves oval or ovate, 2 to 4 in. long, 1 to 2 in. wide; rounded or heart-shaped at the base, taper-pointed, sharply and often doubly toothed; covered with white silky hairs when quite young, becoming sparsely hairy above, downy on the midrib and vein-axils beneath; stalk $\frac{1}{4}$ to $\frac{1}{2}$ in. long, downy. Male catkins 1 to 1$\frac{1}{2}$ in. long. Fruiting clusters about 3 in. long; the bracts three-lobed, 1 to 1$\frac{1}{2}$ in. long; the middle lobe much the largest and nearly 1 in. wide, toothed (often on one side only).

Native of eastern N. America and Mexico; introduced in 1812. Although very similar to the European hornbeam it is not so fine a tree, growing more slowly and never attaining to so large a size. Its leaves turn a deeper, more orange-yellow, or even scarlet shade in autumn. In winter, the best distinction between the two species is afforded by the buds; these, in our native hornbeam, are slender and spindle-shaped, $\frac{1}{4}$ in. or more long, and like small beech buds, but they are egg-shaped and only $\frac{1}{8}$ in. long in the American one. The tallest example at Kew, planted in 1916, measures 40 × 2$\frac{1}{2}$ ft (1967); there are four others of about the same age, averaging 30 × 2 ft.

C. CORDATA Blume

A tree 40 to 50 ft high, with a scaly, furrowed bark; young shoots slightly hairy at first; terminal winter buds large, $\frac{5}{8}$ in. long. Leaves 2$\frac{1}{2}$ to 5$\frac{1}{2}$ in. long, 1$\frac{1}{2}$ to 3$\frac{1}{4}$ in. wide; taper-pointed, deeply heart-shaped at the base, unequally or doubly toothed; hairy on the midrib above, more so beneath; stalk $\frac{1}{2}$ to $\frac{3}{4}$ in. long. Male catkins 1 to 2 in. long, the scales linear, $\frac{1}{6}$ in. long, silky-hairy. Fruit-catkins 3 to 5 in. long, 1$\frac{1}{2}$ in. wide; the bracts closely overlapping, ovate, sparsely and sharply toothed, 1 to 1$\frac{1}{8}$ in. long, with one side doubled over. The nut is covered partly by this infolded portion, but more completely by a lobe of the bract attached to the base at the other side.

Native of Japan; introduced in 1879 by Maries for Veitch's nurseries. Sargent considered it to be the finest of the Japanese hornbeams but in this country it is of rather slow growth and not common. The best tree at Kew measures 29 × 1¾ ft. It is very distinct from its ally, *C. japonica*, in the large, deeply cordate leaves and big winter buds, but is similar in the curious way the nut is protected by basal portions of the bract infolding over it.

var. CHINENSIS Franch.--Native of E. Szechwan, China; introduced by Wilson in 1901. It differs from the Japanese type in having smaller, narrower leaves, and in the young shoots being more hairy.

C. EXIMIA Nakai

A deciduous tree up to 30 ft high, with a grey trunk 1 to 1½ ft in diameter. Leaves ovate to ovate-oblong, rounded or nearly truncate at the base, slender pointed, doubly toothed; 3 to 4 in. long, ¾ to 1¼ in. wide; veins in fourteen to sixteen pairs and silky-hairy beneath; upper surface downy. Fruiting catkin 2 to 3 in. long, 1¼ in. wide, the silky stalk 1½ to 2 in. long; bracts semi-ovate, 1½ in. long, ½ in. wide, with hairy veins. Nutlets dotted with glands, hairy at the top.

Native of Korea; introduced to Kew in 1925 from the Arnold Arboretum.

C. HENRYANA (Winkler) Winkler
C. tschonoskii var. *henryana* Winkler

A deciduous tree up to 60 ft high; young shoots clothed with silky hairs. Leaves narrowly ovate-lanceolate, mostly rounded or even slightly heart-shaped at the base, fine-pointed, simply or doubly toothed; 1½ to 3½ in. long, ⅝ to 1½ in. wide; glabrous above, silky-hairy on the midrib and veins beneath; veins in twelve to sixteen pairs; leaf-stalk ¼ to ⅜ in. long, very downy. Fruit-clusters up to 2 in. long, slender; the bracts obliquely ovate, coarsely toothed, ½ to ⅝ in. long; main-stalk silky-hairy. Nutlet dark brown, ovoid, six- to eight-ribbed, downy.

Native of Central and W. China; discovered by Henry, introduced by Wilson to the Arnold Arboretum in 1907, thence to Kew in 1912. It is very hardy, very leafy and vigorous there and makes a handsome tree 40 ft high with a girth of 2 ft (1967). It is one of the true hornbeams (as distinct from *Distegocarpus*) so that the nutlet is not covered by the bracts, but partly exposed.

C. JAPONICA Blume
Distegocarpus carpinus Sieb.

A tree 40 to 50 ft high, with wide-spreading branches, and scaly furrowed bark; young shoots first clothed with fine hairs. Leaves ovate, or inclined to oblong; 2 to 4½ in. long, ¾ to 1¾ in. wide; long and taper-pointed, mostly heart-shaped at the base, but sometimes rounded or wedge-shaped; sharply, sometimes double-toothed, but often with a large and a small tooth alternating; upper surface dark green, and downy only on the midrib, the twenty to twenty-four pairs of veins deeply impressed; lower surface downy on the veins, vein-axils, and midrib; stalk ¼ to ½ in. long, downy. Male catkin 1 to 2 in. long, with conspicuous, narrowly ovate, pointed scales ¼ in. long. Fruit-clusters 2 to 2½ in. long; the closely overlapping bracts ⅝ to ⅞ in. long, coarsely toothed, ovate, with

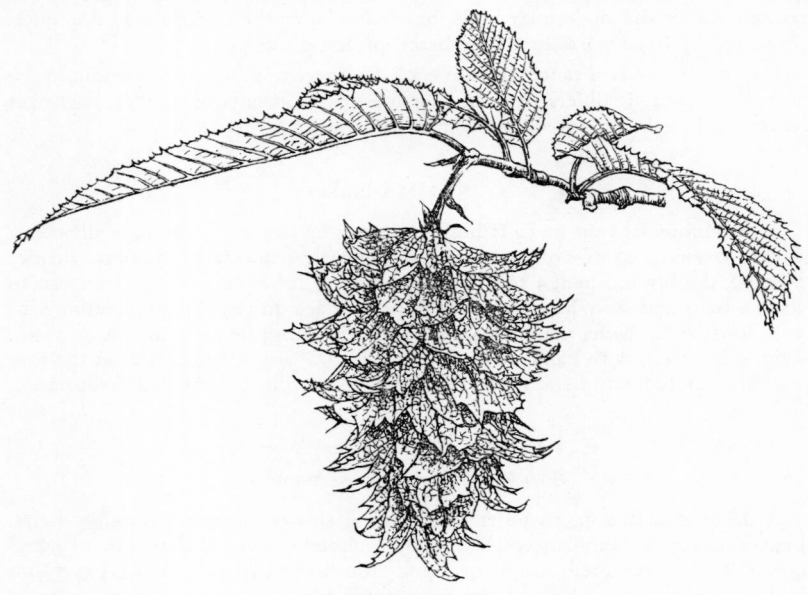

CARPINUS JAPONICA

the lower portion on one side doubled over. The nut is covered by a small roundish lobe on the opposite side, which is united to the bract at the base only; in *C. cordata* the equivalent lobe is larger and more completely united to the bract. *Bot. Mag.*, t. 8534.

Native of Japan; introduced in 1895. It makes, in a small state, a sturdy pyramidal tree, and is evidently very hardy. It is distinct and handsome-looking because of the numerous (up to twenty-four pairs), deeply impressed veins of the leaf. It is one of the species (see also *C. cordata*) regarded by some authorities as generically distinct from *Carpinus*, because of the infolded bases of the more crowded bracts of the fruit. There are two examples of this hornbeam at Kew, planted in 1895, the larger 35 ft high with a girth of 2½ ft at 3 ft (1967).

C. LAXIFLORA (Sieb. & Zucc.) Blume
Distegocarpus laxiflora Sieb. & Zucc.

A deciduous tree 45 to 50 ft high; young shoots at first silky-hairy, soon glabrous. Leaves ovate to oval, rounded or slightly heart-shaped at the base, abruptly narrowed to a long and slender point, doubly toothed; $1\frac{1}{2}$ to $3\frac{1}{2}$ in. long, 1 to $1\frac{1}{2}$ in. wide; glabrous except for a few silky hairs and axil-tufts of down beneath. Fruiting catkins loosely pendulous, 2 to 3 in. long, the bracts $\frac{1}{2}$ to $\frac{3}{4}$ in. long, usually three-lobed at the base, the middle lobe narrow and jagged on one side. Nutlets slightly dotted with resin.

Native of Japan; introduced in 1914, but not common in cultivation. Its distinctive points are the long slender apex of the leaf, the loose fruit raceme, and the small bracts with a long central lobe. A more common tree in gardens is the Chinese variety known as

var. MACROSTACHYA Oliver *C. fargesii* Franch.—This variety was discovered by Henry and introduced to Veitch's Coombe Wood nursery in 1900. It differs from the Japanese type in its bigger leaves (the larger ones 4 in. by 2 in.) and the often longer, stouter fruit-catkins up to 5 in. long by nearly 2 in. wide; the fruiting bracts are up to 1 in. in length. It is quite hardy and a good grower.

C. ORIENTALIS Mill.   ORIENTAL HORNBEAM
C. duinensis Scop.

A small tree, or a large shrub, sometimes found in a wild state as a scrubby bush; young shoots covered with fine silky down. Leaves ovate, 1 to 2 in. long, $\frac{1}{2}$ to 1 in. wide; rounded or slightly wedge-shaped at the base, pointed; sharply, regularly, and prettily double-toothed; veins in twelve to fifteen pairs; dark glossy green above, with silky down on both surfaces of the midrib; stalk hairy, $\frac{1}{8}$ to $\frac{1}{4}$ in. long. Male catkins $\frac{1}{2}$ to $\frac{3}{4}$ in. long. Fruit clusters $1\frac{3}{16}$ to $2\frac{3}{8}$ in.; bracts ovate, unequal-sided, $\frac{5}{8}$ to $\frac{7}{8}$ in. long, $\frac{1}{2}$ in. wide, coarsely and irregularly toothed, but not lobed. Nut $\frac{1}{8}$ in. long, exposed.

Native of S.E. Europe and Asia Minor; introduced in 1735 by P. Miller. It is abundant on some of the battlefields of the Crimea as low scrub, and, as I have been told by an officer who took part in the Crimean war, much impeded some of the advances of our men, made under cover of darkness. It has not much to commend it to the notice of planters in this country except as being an interesting rarity. The largest specimen at Kew, and probably in the country, is 50 ft high with a girth of $5\frac{3}{4}$ ft (1960). It was planted in 1878. In Finsbury Park, London, there is a specimen measuring 35 × $3\frac{3}{4}$ ft (1955).

Its small leaves and the unlobed bracts of the fruit clusters distinguish it from *C. betulus* and *C. caroliniana*.

C. TSCHONOSKII Maxim.
C. yedoensis Maxim.

A small tree whose young shoots are covered with hairs, many of which persist through the first winter. Leaves $1\frac{1}{2}$ to 3 in. long, $\frac{5}{8}$ to $1\frac{1}{2}$ in. wide, ovate, with a tapered point and a rounded base, unequally or doubly toothed; upper surface dark green, with flattened hairs on the midrib and between the nine to fifteen pairs of veins; lower surface hairy on the veins; stalk slender, downy, $\frac{1}{4}$ in. long. Fruit-clusters on silky stalks; the bracts $\frac{5}{8}$ to $\frac{3}{4}$ in. long, narrowly ovate, toothed on one side, silky-hairy, especially on the veins and at the base, where they become slightly boat-shaped, holding the ovoid nut in the hollow, but quite exposed.

Native of Japan and the north-eastern part of continental Asia; probably first introduced from Japan to the Darmstadt Botanic Garden in 1901. There are several examples at Kew planted around 1905, the largest of which measures 36 × 5½ ft (1967).

C. FARGESIANA Winkler—This species is closely allied to the preceding and has been confused with it. It was discovered by Farges in the mountains of E. Szechwan, China, and is best distinguished by the teeth of the leaves being blunt, not mucronate as they are in *C. tschonoskii.*

C. TURCZANINOWII Hance   [PLATE 29

A small tree to about 20 ft high in the wild state; young shoots slightly hairy. Leaves 1¼ to 2 in. long, ovate to broad-ovate, pointed, usually rounded at the base; margins double-toothed; dark green and soon becoming glabrous above, downy on the midribs and the veins beneath; stalk ⅓ to ½ in. long, downy; stipules narrowly linear, persistent during the winter. Fruit clusters 1 to 2 in. long; bracts ovate, unequal-sided, one side being sharply toothed, the other toothed only at the apex and with a small lobe at the base. Nut ovate, resin-dotted.

A native of N. China, where it is common in open woodland and scrub, and also of Japan; discovered by Turczaninow in 1831 but described from specimens collected ten years later by Kirilov. Farrer introduced it from Kansu in 1914 and trees from his seed are in cultivation at Highdown, Sussex, and at Kew. It makes a small, neat, bushy tree and colours rich brown and orange in the autumn. Mrs Farrer had at Ingleborough a shrubby pendulous form raised from the original seed; this is illustrated in *The New Flora and Sylva*, Vol. 3, fig. 99 (1931).

var. OVALIFOLIA Winkler *C. polyneura* Burk., in part, not Franch.—A tree to 30 ft high in the wild state. Leaves ovate to ovate-oblong, sharply but only occasionally double-toothed. Bracts of fruiting catkins not lobed at the base. A native of W. China, introduced to Kew by Henry in 1889 from E. Szechwan. A tree from this seed now measures 38 × 1¾ ft (1967). It was originally thought to be *C. polyneura* Franch.

CARRIEREA   FLACOURTIACEAE

A very small E. Asiatic genus in which four species have been described but of which only *C. calycina* has been introduced to cultivation. Its nearest allies among the hardy members of the family are *Idesia* and *Poliothyrsis.*

C. CALYCINA Franch.

A deciduous tree 20 to 30 ft (sometimes 40 ft) high, with a wide spreading head of branches; young shoots at first covered with minute down, reddish. Leaves alternate, ovate, with a tapered apex, rounded or cordate at the base, up to 5 in. long, half as wide; coarsely round toothed; glabrous, or nearly so, on both surfaces; with a stalk about one-third as long as the blade; at first reddish, then dark glossy green above, paler and also glossy beneath. The inflorescence is erect and rather candelabra-like and carries as many as ten blossoms, the five heart-shaped sepals of which form a cup-shaped flower $1\frac{1}{4}$ in. long and 1 in. wide; there are no petals, the centre of the flower being occupied by a large vase-shaped, downy ovary with yellow radiating stigmas at the top; the numerous stamens are short (about $\frac{1}{10}$ in. long) and surround the base of the ovary. The flowers are yellowish or greenish white, but one specimen collected by Wilson in Hupeh in 1900 he has marked as having them 'blush'. The fruit is a spindle-shaped capsule, downy, 3 to 4 in. long, $\frac{3}{4}$ in. wide at the middle, splitting into three narrowly lanceolate valves. Seeds winged. *Bot. Mag.*, n.s., t. 53.

Native of W. and Central China, at altitudes of 2,000 to 3,000 ft; introduced by Wilson in 1908. It first flowered in this country in the garden of Capt. and Mrs Desborough at Tulgey Wood, Broadstone, Dorset, in June 1929 and again the following year, but this specimen, which provided the material for the plate in the *Botanical Magazine*, died in 1931. Wilson considered this species to be of singular beauty of flower and a great acquisition to gardens should it prove hardy. It has, unfortunately, not lived up to its promise and has become very rare. In two other gardens where it is known to have reached the flowering stage —Bodnant in Denbighshire and Borde Hill, Sussex—it died during the last war or shortly after. At Kew, although apparently hardy, it died without flowering. The best specimen recorded grows at Birr Castle in Co. Offaly, Eire; this measures 38 × 2$\frac{3}{4}$ ft (1966).

CARYA   HICKORY   JUGLANDACEAE

Of the twenty or so species of hickory as yet recognised about half are in cultivation in the British Isles. They are all, save one, natives of eastern N. America. From its two allies, *Juglans* and *Pterocarya*, the genus is distinguished by its pith being solid, and not, as in the others, divided into thin transverse plates; and from *Juglans* in particular by the branched male inflorescences and four-valved fruit. The hickories are large, deciduous trees with pinnate leaves; the leaflets rather wide apart on a common stalk, themselves nearly or quite stalkless. Male flowers mostly in three-branched, slender catkins, produced either at the end of the previous year's shoots or at the base of the young ones of the current year; whilst the few-flowered, female inflorescence terminates the young shoot. Nut surrounded by a husk, which often thickens and becomes hard by the time the seed is ripe.

Considering their great beauty of foliage and stately habit—and there is scarcely any tree more striking than a well-grown young hickory—this genus is strangely uncommon in gardens. The reason appears to be their dislike of disturbance at the root, which makes them unsuited to ordinary nursery conditions. The frequent transplanting which is practised by good nurserymen to ensure success at the final removal of their stock is, in my experience, worse than useless with hickories. It induces a stunted, ultimately diseased condition, from which, at the best, it takes them long to recover. The great secret with hickories is to get them in their permanent places early. To anyone desirous of trying these fine trees I would recommend the following procedure. The best species to experiment with are *C. ovata, cordiformis, glabra*, and *tomentosa*. Nuts of these should be obtained in autumn from a reliable American seedsman as early as possible after they are ripe. During the winter they should be kept in a box of moist earth, either inside or out-of-doors. In spring the nuts may be placed singly in 6·in. pots, in a slightly heated frame or greenhouse. After they have germinated, all that is necessary is to protect them from frost until they are planted out about the end of May, if sufficient progress has been made. Caryas need a deep, loamy soil if they are to thrive permanently. Previous to planting the seedlings out, the ground should be well worked, and it is wise to put a couple together to anticipate failures; afterwards the weaker one can be removed. To avoid accidents each plant or plants should be enclosed by small-meshed wire-netting.

The object of all this trouble is to avoid the destruction of the tap-root, which is inevitable if ordinary nursery treatment be adopted. A young tree in deep loam, undisturbed, and with its tap-root preserved, will be a better tree in ten years than another treated in the ordinary way will be in twenty. This method, although the best, may not always be practicable. If perforce the seedlings have to be grown on for several years before planting in their final positions they should be grown in light soil and transplanted every year or two to induce a fibrous root system. Such trees will be more difficult to establish than they would have been if planted out in their first year of life, but at least are preferable to ones which have not received this attention.

C. AQUATICA (Michx. f.) Nutt.   WATER HICKORY
Juglans aquatica Michx. f.

A tree, usually small but occasionally 80 ft or more high in the wild, the bark of the trunk separating from it into long, loose, plate-like scales; young shoots at first coated with a loose, pale down. Leaves 9 to 15 in. long, made up of seven to thirteen leaflets, which are of narrow lanceolate shape with long tapered points, finely, often inconspicuously toothed, obliquely rounded or tapered at the base; 2½ to 5½ in. long, ½ to 1½ in. wide; at first covered with pale down which mostly falls away during the summer. Fruits egg-shaped, pointed, conspicuously four-winged, 1 to 1½ in. long; kernel bitter.

Native of the S.E. United States; discovered about the beginning of the nineteenth century. It inhabits low, swampy, often inundated places and, as it is associated in a wild state with *Liquidambar styraciflua* and *Taxodium distichum,* should, one would imagine, be as hardy as they are, but it is apparently not adapted to our climate. The long, unusually narrow leaflets make it distinct amongst the hickories.

C. BUCKLEYI Durand

A tree 30 to 50 ft high in the wild, the bark of the trunk nearly black, furrowed, not scaly; young shoots covered with reddish down. Leaves up to 1 ft or more long, made up of usually seven leaflets, the lower ones of which are smaller and lanceolate, the larger terminal ones oblanceolate; all pointed, tapered at the base, evenly and finely toothed; 3 to 6 in. long, ¾ to 2½ in. wide; downy on the veins beneath, scaly and with tufts of down in the vein-axils. Fruit (as figured by Sargent) nearly globose, 1½ in. wide.

Native of the S. Central United States; introduced to Kew from the Arnold Arboretum in 1924. It is very healthy but, like many hickories, grows slowly when young or after being transplanted. The leaves on young plants are larger than the dimensions given above.

var. ARKANSANA Sarg.—Fruit obovoid, rounded at the apex (the type has usually a pointed fruit). This also is in cultivation.

C. CORDIFORMIS (Wangenh.) K. Koch   BITTERNUT HICKORY
Juglans cordiformis Wangenh.; *C. amara* Nutt.

A tree up to 100 ft high; bark smooth on younger trees, later broken into shallow furrows and narrow, interlacing ridges; young shoots glabrous or soon becoming so; winter buds coated with bright yellow scales. Leaves 6 to 10 in. (occasionally 15 in.) long, composed usually of seven, but sometimes five or nine leaflets, the lowest pair of which are considerably smaller than the others. Leaflets lance-shaped, narrowly oval, oblong or obovate, tapered at both ends, sharply toothed; 2 to 6 in. long, ¾ to 2½ in. wide; glabrous above, downy at first below, especially along the midrib and veins; common stalk downy. Fruits usually in pairs or threes, pear-shaped to roundish, ¾ to 1½ in. long, with a thin, yellowish husk. Nut thin-shelled, with a bitter kernel. Male catkins usually in threes, 2½ to 3 in. long, downy.

Native of eastern N. America; introduced, according to Aiton, in 1766. Of all the cultivated hickories, this appears to be the hardiest and the best grower. It is easily distinguished from all the rest by the bright yellow winter buds.

The largest recorded in recent years are: Kew, by the Lion Gate, 84 × 5 ft (1963), another by the Main Gate, 89 × 5½ ft (1965) and others slightly smaller; Westonbirt, Glos., in the Main Drive, 86 × 4¾ ft (1964); Tortworth, Glos., 85 × 6¼ ft (1964); Hergest Croft, Heref., 70 × 4½ ft (1961); Bicton, Devon, 85 × 8¾ ft (1967).

C. GLABRA (Mill.) Sweet   PIGNUT HICKORY
Juglans glabra Mill.; *C. porcina* Nutt.

A tree to 100 ft high; bark grey, fissured, with interlacing ridges which are often scaly or ragged; young shoots glabrous. Leaves 8 to 12 in. long, composed of five or seven leaflets, the basal ones of which are ovate-lanceolate, the terminal ones much larger and more or less obovate; all taper-pointed, rounded or tapering at the base, sharply toothed; both surfaces glabrous except for some down along the midrib and veins, which mostly falls away by autumn. The large terminal leaflets are 5 to 7 in. long, and 2 to 3 in. wide, the lowest pair about one-third the size; common stalk glabrous. Male catkins 3 to 5 in. long, slightly scurfy. Fruit variable in shape and size, mostly rounded or pear-shaped, flattened or even sunk at the apex. Kernel of nut astringent.

Native of eastern N. America, as far to the north as Maine; introduced in 1799. This hickory thrives very well in England. Earlier this century there was a specimen 80 ft high at Kew, which often bore good crops of fruit. This is gone; the present example, by the Lion Gate, measures 52 × 4¼ (1963). There is a tree of about the same size in the Glasnevin Botanic Garden, Dublin.

C. ILLINOENSIS (Wangenh.) K. Koch   PECAN
Juglans illinoensis Wangenh.; *C. olivaeformis* Nutt.; *C. pecan* (Marsh.) Engl. & Graebn., not (Walt.) Nutt.

Little need be said of this tree, for it is ill adapted to our climate. Many times introduced to Kew, it usually lives only a few years. Young trees will make growths 12 or 15 in. long during the summer, but so badly ripened are they that unless the winter is very mild they are regularly cut back almost to the old wood. This renders them an easy prey to fungoid parasites, usually the 'coral-spot' fungus, and makes the species not worth cultivation. It is a native of the south-east and south-central United States, and is the most important of the hickories as a nut-bearing tree. It grows considerably over 100 ft high, and is distinct from all the cultivated species in the large number of leaflets—usually eleven to fifteen on each leaf. These are 2 to 6 in. long (sometimes more), curved like a scimitar, pointed, toothed. Fruits clustered, each 1 to 2½ in. long, about half as wide, oblong, pointed; the nut has a sweet-flavoured kernel. Perhaps the first tree in Europe grew in the Botanic Garden at Padua. Planted in 1760 it reached a height of about 100 ft but we are informed by the Curator, Dr Abrami, that it was blown down in 1920.

C. LACINIOSA (Michx. f.) Loud.   SHELLBARK HICKORY
Juglans laciniosa Michx. f.; *C. sulcata* Nutt.

A tree 100 to 120 ft high; bark separating from the trunk into broad plates often 3 or 4 ft long; young shoots at first downy; terminal winter bud 1 in. long. Leaves 12 to 22 in. long, composed of usually seven, sometimes nine, leaflets, the terminal ones of which are obovate, 4 to 8 in. long, 1½ to 2½ in. wide, the lower ones ovate and only one-third or one-fourth the size; all long and slender-pointed, toothed; glabrous, and glossy above, downy beneath. Male catkins 4 in. or more long. Fruit oblong, $2\frac{1}{2}$ in. long, 2 in. wide; nut four- or six-ridged.

Native of the eastern United States from New York and E. Pennsylvania southwards; introduced to England in 1804. The tree in Tortworth churchyard, Glos., mentioned in previous editions, now measures 60 × 5 ft (1964— 30 × $1\frac{3}{4}$ ft in 1905); no other sizeable specimen has been recorded. This species resembles the better-known *C. ovata* but usually has seven not five leaflets, which are downy beneath (glabrous in *C. ovata*). It resembles *C. tomentosa* in having leaves with usually seven leaflets, hairy beneath, but in that species the indumentum is woolly and persistent (merely downy in *C. laciniosa*) and glands are also present; also the bark of *C. tomentosa* is close, not shaggy, and the terminal winter buds are broadly ovoid (almost globose).

C. MYRISTICIFORMIS (Michx. f.) Nutt.   NUTMEG HICKORY
Juglans myristicaeformis Michx. f.

A tree 80 or more ft high in the wild, the bark of old trees broken irregularly into thin appressed plates; young shoots slender, covered with tiny yellowish glossy scales. Leaves 7 to 14 in. long, made up of five to eleven leaflets which are almost or quite stalkless, the terminal one the largest, of obovate outline, 3 to 5 in. long; the smaller side ones are of more lanceolate shape; all are finely, evenly, sharply toothed, slender-pointed, dull dark green and thinly scaly above, covered with silvery-white scales beneath. Male catkins in threes, $1\frac{1}{2}$ to 3 in. long. Nut oval or egg-shaped, 1 to $1\frac{1}{2}$ in. long.

Native of the S.E. United States; discovered in 1802 by the younger Michaux, the French botanist and traveller; introduced in 1911. It is described as a handsome tree in its native haunts, where it often occurs on limestone, but I know of small trees only in this country. Sargent observes that the 'lustrous undersurface of the leaves makes it perhaps the most beautiful of the hickories'. It is hardy but slow-growing at Kew. The popular name refers to the hard, furrowed, nutmeg-like shell of the nut.

C. CATHAYENSIS Sarg.—This species was discovered by F. N. Meyer in 1915 in the province of Chekiang, China, and is also reported from Kweichow. Its discovery was of particular interest in adding one more instance to those revealed in recent times of a genus previously thought to be confined to N. America, having a representative in China. Since then two other species have been discovered in Yunnan and Indo-China. Similar evidence of the remarkable affinity between the floras of China and eastern N. America is also provided by the following genera: *Decumaria, Liriodendron, Nyssa, Sassafras,* and *Symphoricarpos,* of all of which a single or two species have been found in China. The Chinese hickory is a tree up to 60 or 70 ft high, with leaves made up of five or seven leaflets. It is considered to be most nearly allied to *C. myristiciformis*.

C. OVALIS (Wangenh.) Sarg.   RED HICKORY
Juglans ovalis Wangenh.; *C. microcarpa* Nutt., in part

According to Sargent this is the most widely and generally distributed, also the most variable in its fruit, of all the hickories. It is most closely related to the pignut (*C. porcina*, now called *C. glabra*), but that species has a nut with a usually bitter, astringent kernel, whilst that of *C. ovalis* is sweet and edible. It is a tall tree, often well over 100 ft high, with young shoots at first scurfy and downy, afterwards glabrous. The leaves consist of five or seven leaflets, which are lanceolate to oblanceolate and obovate, the terminal one up to 6 in. long, the lower ones down to 3 in.; all are finely toothed and at first scurfy and downy like the young shoots.

Native of the eastern United States from New York south to Florida. It has apparently been in cultivation as "*C. microcarpa*" and "*C. porcina* var. *microcarpa*". The taxonomic position of this species is disputed. Some American botanists merge it into *C. glabra*; others consider it to be a hybrid between that species and *C. ovata*. Sargent made at least five varieties of this hickory, which is very variable in size and shape of nut. A tree at Kew introduced as *C. ovalis* var. *odorata* measures 72 × 5½ ft (1963).

C. OVATA (Mill.) K. Koch   SHAGBARK HICKORY
Juglans ovata Mill.; *C. alba* Nutt.

A tree 70 to 120 ft high in a wild state, very distinct in its loose grey bark, which comes away from the trunk in broad flakes 1 ft or more long, each flake attached by its middle; young shoots covered with pale down. Leaves 8 to 14 in. long (considerably more in young, vigorous trees), composed of five leaflets, the three upper ones of which are obovate, often very narrowly so, and considerably the largest; the lower pair ovate to ovate-lanceolate; all long-pointed and toothed, edged when young with a fringe of hairs; glabrous above, downy beneath when young, later glabrous. The leaflets vary much in size; in adult trees the three terminal ones are 5 to 7 in. long, 2 to 3 in. wide, with the lower pair less than half the size; but in young trees I have measured the terminal leaflet 12 in. long and 5 in. wide, with the other four in proportion. Male catkins in threes, 3 to 5 in. long, hairy. Fruit borne singly or in pairs, roundish, flattened at top and bottom, 1 to 2 in. long. Nut white, four-angled.

Native of eastern N. America, where it is spread over a large territory; introduced early in the seventeenth century. It thrives very well in England when young, and is one of the most striking of fine-foliaged trees. At Kew, the leaves turn a beautiful yellow in autumn. Of the hickories producing edible nuts, this is the most valuable in the United States, but it has no value in this respect in Britain. The largest tree noted by Elwes and Henry (1908) grew at Botley Hill, Hants; it was 75 × 5¼ ft and supposed to have been planted by W. Cobbett in 1820. What is probably the same tree is now about 85 ft high and 7¼ ft in girth (measurement by P. H. B. Gardner, 1967). There is a specimen at Albury Park, Surrey, 68 × 6 ft (1966).

C. ovata is best distinguished from other hickories by the combination of shaggy bark and leaves with five leaflets, glabrous beneath when mature.

C. × LANEYI Sarg.—A natural hybrid between *C. ovata* and *cordiformis* found wild in western New York.

C. TOMENTOSA (Poir.) Nutt. MOCKERNUT HICKORY

Juglans tomentosa Poir.; *C. alba* K. Koch, not Nutt.

A tree 50 to 60, occasionally 100 ft high; winter buds large, the terminal one broadly egg-shaped, pointed, ½ to ¾ in. long, and ½ in. or more wide; the inner scales covered with a soft pale felt; young shoots very downy, especially at first. Leaves fragrant, 8 to 12 in. (on very vigorous young trees 20 in.) long; composed usually of seven (sometimes five or nine) leaflets; terminal leaflet is 5 to 8 in. long, 2 to 4½ in. wide, obovate, wedge-shaped at the base; basal pair sometimes only 1½ to 2 in. long, ovate, rounded at the base; the middle pair or pairs are intermediate in size and shape; all taper-pointed, toothed, upper surface dark green, downy on the midrib; lower surface yellowish, and covered with starry down and glands; common stalk stellately downy. Male catkins 3 to 5 in. long, very downy. Fruit top-shaped or roundish.

Native of eastern N. America; rare in cultivation. The species is distinct in its large winter buds (it is sometimes called 'big-bud hickory') and in the fragrance of its foliage. This, of course, is most marked when the leaf is rubbed, but on dewy mornings in summer it can be perceived many yards away from the tree. The mockernut has been too much neglected in gardens, if only on this account. There is a fine specimen at Kew 70 ft high, remarkable for its stately habit and splendid foliage. Another grows at Sidbury Manor, Devon; planted in 1898, it is 68 ft high. Smaller trees grow at Westonbirt and Tortworth, Glos.; and in the University Parks, Oxford. This species resembles *C. cordiformis* in its bark but is easily distinguished by its terminal winter buds, which are brown, hairy and broadly ovate, with imbricate scales; in *C. cordiformis* they are bright yellow, scurfy, elongated, with two pairs of scales which do not overlap (valvate).

CARYOPTERIS   VERBENACEAE

A genus of about six species of deciduous shrubs, sub-shrubs and herbaceous plants confined in a wild state to E. Asia. The leaves are opposite, mostly more or less toothed, and deciduous. Easily grown in light loamy soil in full sunshine. Several are only semi-woody in this country and the summer growths are often well cut back in winter. Half-ripened cuttings strike root readily.

C. × CLANDONENSIS Simmonds   [PLATE 30

A group of hybrids deriving from *C. incana* × *mongolica*, of which the typical and original clone is:

cv. 'ARTHUR SIMMONDS'.—This hybrid was raised in the garden of the late Arthur Simmonds at West Clandon in Surrey. Leaves ovate-lanceolate, pointed, rounded at the base, entire or with a few teeth, 1 to 2 in. long, dull

green and wrinkled above, covered with close silvery down beneath. Flowers of
a lovely bright blue, especially the much-exposed anthers and corolla lobes.
Bot. Mag., n.s., t. 75.

On the whole this can probably be rated as the most attractive in the genus
and it is evidently quite hardy near London, flowering abundantly in September.
It makes a shapely, rounded, soft-wooded bush growing 2 ft high. It received
an Award of Merit at Vincent Square, 12th September 1933. It sets seed freely
but the seedlings are not necessarily as hardy or such good garden plants as
the parent. This and the other forms below should be pruned hard in spring.

cv. 'FERNDOWN'.—Leaves dark green and the flowers too of a deeper
colour than in 'Arthur Simmonds'. Raised by Messrs Stewart, Ferndown
Nurseries, Dorset.

cv. 'HEAVENLY BLUE'.—Habit more erect and compact than in 'Arthur
Simmonds'; of American origin.

cv. 'KEW BLUE'.—A seedling from 'Arthur Simmonds' with flowers of a
darker blue, raised at Kew about 1945. It has been distributed to the trade.

C. GLUTINOSA Rehd.

An erect shrub 3 to 5 ft high; young shoots downy. Leaves ½ to 1 in. long,
⅛ to ¼ in. wide, lanceolate, somewhat fleshy, dark green, glutinous and shining
above, mealy white with dark veins beneath; margins entire or occasionally with
a few triangular teeth; stalks short. Flowers blue, numerous in dense cymes from
the uppermost leaf-axils; corolla ¼ in. long, greyish downy outside, with a ring
of long white hairs at the mouth of the tube; ovary downy.

Native of China, especially in the Min River Valley in Western Szechwan,
where it was first noticed by E. H. Wilson when collecting for Messrs Veitch in
1903. It is most closely akin to *C. mongolica*, but is a taller shrub with the corolla
hairy at the mouth and viscid leaves. It is a handsome plant, blooming in
September.

C. INCANA (Houtt.) Miq.

Nepeta incana Houtt.; *C. mastacanthus* Schau.; *C. tangutica* Maxim.

A deciduous bush 3 to 5 ft high, of spreading habit; young stems semi-woody,
covered like the flower-stalks, leaf-stalks, and the underside of the leaves, with
a close grey felt. Leaves opposite, ovate; 1 to 3 in. long, ½ to 1¼ in. wide; the
base more or less broadly wedge-shaped, the apex blunt or pointed; coarsely
toothed, almost lobed, dull green and downy on the upper surface; stalk ¼ to
¾ in. long. Flowers bright violet-blue, produced during October in hemispherical
cymes from the axils of the uppermost leaves; main flower-stalk ¾ to 1½ in. long.
Corolla downy, tubular, ¼ in. long, with five lobes at the mouth; the four upper
ones ovate, the lower one larger, scoop-shaped, and fringed; stamens four, much
protruded; calyx funnel-shaped, with five-pointed teeth. *Bot. Mag.*, t. 6799.

Native of China and Japan; originally introduced in 1844 by Fortune, who
found it wild near Canton. It was at first treated as a greenhouse plant, and being
scarcely worth its room there, was eventually lost until re-introduced by Maries

in 1880. It is hardy at Kew in all but the hardest winters, and during a fine autumn makes a very pretty display. The leaves are pleasantly scented. It is increased with the greatest ease by means of soft cuttings in heat, and should be grown in an open, sandy soil, and given a sunny, sheltered position.

f. CANDICANS (Schneid.) Hara—A form with white flowers found wild in Japan. As grown in gardens, it is perhaps less hardy than the type.

C. *tangutica* was described by Maximowicz in 1881 from specimens collected by the Russian traveller Przewalski in Kansu, whence Farrer introduced it about 1915 under his number 305. Farrer's plants differ from C. *incana*, as seen in cultivation, in their smaller leaves and have the lip of the corolla less divided. They are also hardier and earlier to flower. However, C. *tangutica* is no longer considered to be a distinct species.

C. MONGOLICA Bunge

A deciduous shrub 2 to 3 ft high, of bushy habit; young shoots erect, clothed at first with a fine, close, grey down. Leaves opposite, linear or linear-lanceolate, not lobed or toothed; 1 to 1¾ in. long, ⅛ to ⅜ in. wide; greyish green, with a close, very minute down on both surfaces, more especially beneath. Flowers produced during July and August in cymes from the uppermost leaf-axils of the summer shoots. Each cyme is about 1½ in. long, slender-stalked, and carries six to nine flowers; the upper part of the stem thus becomes a kind of slender panicle sometimes 18 in. long. Each flower is about ½ in. long, with the large lobe (or 'lip') of the corolla much fringed, blue; calyx pale blue with five awl-shaped lobes; stamens (in two unequal pairs) similarly coloured, standing out ¼ in. beyond the corolla. *Bot. Mag.*, t. 9219.

Native of Mongolia and N. China. It flowered in France as long ago as 1844 and has been re-introduced on several occasions since then. This handsome species does not appear to be long-lived in this country. In its native habitat it experiences very cold winters but these are followed by summers much hotter than ours and, like many species from such regions, it does not take kindly to our softer, more equable climate. This, at any rate, would seem to be the reason why it has proved a failure in gardens where many genuinely tender plants thrive. It grew well for a time at Rowallane in Co. Down, as recorded in previous editions, but this plant died and the Hon. Mrs O'Neil tells us that it must be many years since the species has been cultivated there. It has been grown successfully in the Cambridge Botanic Garden, however, and it is, perhaps, in that part of England, and in E. Anglia, that it is likely to succeed best. This is true of many plants from more arid and more extreme climates than ours.

The typical form is distinct from all the other cultivated species in its toothless leaves, but in the var. SERRATA Maxim., they are sparsely and irregularly toothed. Still, both it and the type are readily distinguished by the narrowness of the leaves.

CASSIA   LEGUMINOSAE

Out of several hundred species of *Cassia* known (and they occur in all the warmer parts of the globe except Europe), only two are grown outside in Britain, and of these the first species is decidedly tender, while the second, though hardy, scarcely qualifies as a woody plant. *Cassia* belongs to the sub-family Caesalpinioideae, in which the petals are equal, or almost so, in size and shape. Stamens usually ten, but three or five of these may be absent, or reduced to staminodes. Leaves pinnate, with an even number of leaflets. The fruits of certain Near Eastern species are the senna pods of druggists; those of the beautiful Indian laburnum (*C. fistula*) attain a length of 2 or even 3 ft.

C. CORYMBOSA Lam.

A shrub to 5 or 6 ft high, glabrous in all its parts. Leaves with two or three pairs of leaflets, which are lanceolate to oblong-ovate, bluntly pointed at the apex, ¾ to 1½ in. long; a characteristic gland is found on the main-stalk between the lowermost pair of leaflets. Flowers rich yellow, borne in late summer in clusters of three to eight at the ends of axillary shoots; corolla somewhat cup-shaped, about 1 in. wide.

A native of N. Argentina and neighbouring parts of S. America, introduced in 1796. It is best known as a shrub for the cool greenhouse but has been grown successfully outside in many mild gardens; even there it is best on a sunny wall, as it needs abundant sunshine if it is to flower well and ripen its wood. It should be spurred back in spring before growth commences and may be propagated by cuttings of half-ripened wood.

C. MARYLANDICA L.   WILD SENNA

A semi-woody plant which sends up erect, pithy shoots 2 to 3 ft high each year, furnished with pinnate leaves 6 to 10 in. long, each composed of an even number of leaflets, usually seven to nine pairs. Leaflets 1 to 2½ in. long, oblong, the midrib terminating in a bristle. Racemes 2 to 3 in. long, terminal or springing from the axils of the leaves; the almost regular flowers crowded towards the end, ½ in. across; petals yellow, nearly alike; anthers a conspicuous dark purple. Pod 3 to 4 in. long, covered with grey hairs when young.

Native of the south-eastern United States; introduced to England in 1723. It flowers from the end of July until October, and is very handsome then. A sheltered position should be found for it, and, as it is not absolutely hardy in all winters, it is wise to cover the root-stock with a few inches of light litter in severe weather. It can be propagated by breaking up the old root-stock just as growth recommences in spring, and if the pieces can be given a mild bottom-heat and re-established in pots for planting out later, so much the better. But imported seeds can be obtained, and they, of course, give the best and simplest means of increase. The plant has certain cathartic properties resembling those of senna.

CASSINIA   COMPOSITAE

In our open grounds this genus is at present represented by four evergreen shrubs, introduced from New Zealand. Other species are found in Australia and S. Africa. They have a certain resemblance to the heaths in habit and in their small, crowded, narrow leaves, but bear their numerous tiny flowers (or rather flower-heads) in flattish terminal clusters. Such beauty as the flower-heads possess is given by the white, recurved tips of the inner bracts. The four species here included are very much alike in general appearance, and are not easily distinguished on paper. *C. fulvida*, however, the best and hardiest of the four, may generally be recognised in company with *leptophylla* by the yellowish cast of the upturned branch and the viscid leaves and twigs. *C. leptophylla* is grey-white instead of yellow, and not viscid. They can all be propagated easily by late summer cuttings, and will grow in a sandy loam or peaty soil. Even *C. fulvida*, the hardiest of the four, is apt to get browned in winter, and may need pruning back in spring.

C. FULVIDA Hook. f.
Diplopappus chrysophyllus Koehne

An evergreen, dense-habited shrub up to 6 ft in height, with erect branches, viscid when young, and clothed with a yellowish down. Leaves very crowded on the branches, $\frac{1}{6}$ to $\frac{1}{3}$ in. long, $\frac{1}{12}$ to $\frac{1}{6}$ in. wide; narrowly oblong-obovate, the margins recurved; dark green, glabrous and slightly viscid above, yellowish downy beneath. Flower-heads very small and numerous, white, forming terminal corymbs 1 to 3 in. across. Blossoms in July.

Native of New Zealand, where it occurs up to 3,500 ft. It is an interesting, rather heath-like shrub, with a tawny yellow aspect when the branches are bent over, but of no great value as an ornament. It is closely allied to *C. leptophylla*, differing chiefly in the yellow under-surface of the leaves, in the more glutinous character of the young branches, and in having no scales among the florets, or perhaps one or two only.

C. LEPTOPHYLLA (Forst. f.) R. Br.
Calea leptophylla Forst. f.

An evergreen, heath-like shrub 4 ft or more high, with erect, slender branchlets, not viscid, but clothed with a dense greyish down. Leaves $\frac{1}{8}$ to $\frac{1}{6}$ in. long, $\frac{1}{20}$ to $\frac{1}{16}$ in. wide, linear, or slightly wider towards the end; glabrous, dark green above, covered beneath with white or yellowish down. Flower-heads white, very small and numerous, forming terminal corymbs 1 to 2 in. across. Blossoms in August and September.

Native of New Zealand; very similar to *C. fulvida*, but the leaves paler beneath. The whole plant has a whiter cast. It differs also in having the disk (or receptacle) on which the florets are borne furnished with numerous scales; nor is it quite so hardy.

C. RETORTA DC.

An evergreen heath-like shrub 4 to 15 ft high; shoots white with down. Leaves very crowded, $\frac{1}{8}$ to $\frac{1}{5}$ in. long, narrowly oblong to narrowly obovate, almost stalkless, recurved, mostly glabrous above, densely covered beneath with white down. Flower-heads white, numerous in small terminal clusters $\frac{1}{3}$ to $\frac{1}{2}$ in. wide. Of the involucral bracts, the outer ones are the shorter and ovate-oblong, the inner ones narrowly oblong with blunt white tips.

Native of the North Island, New Zealand, commonest near the coast on sand dunes, etc. It is a pretty shrub and flowers in July, differing from other New Zealand species in the small flower-heads.

C. VAUVILLIERSII (Decne.) Hook. f.

Orothamnus vauvilliersii Decne.

An evergreen shrub 2 to 6 ft high, with erect branchlets, clothed with a tawny yellow, or yellowish white, down. Leaves $\frac{1}{4}$ to $\frac{1}{3}$ in. long, $\frac{1}{12}$ to $\frac{1}{8}$ in. wide; linear-obovate, round at the end, tapering at the base; dark green and glabrous above, of the same colour as the branches beneath; margins recurved. Flower-heads white, very small and numerous, in terminal rounded corymbs 1 to 2 in. across.

Native of New Zealand, and very similar in general aspect to *C. fulvida*, but with larger leaves, less bushy and more elongated shoots. The receptacle on which the florets are borne has numerous scales. In my experience this species does not flower very freely.

CASSIOPE   ERICACEAE

A group of some ten or twelve species of dwarf, evergreen shrubs, with a dense overlapping arrangement of the leaves similar to that of the common heather. Flowers solitary, bell-shaped, white or pink. They are found in Arctic or mountain regions of the northern hemisphere. None of the species here mentioned is very common, although they have long been known in gardens. They are capable of withstanding intense cold, but do not thrive particularly well in the open in the south of England; they need cooler and moister conditions, and miss more than anything their natural winter covering of snow. They are excited into premature growth by our mild winters and early spring, only to suffer by severe weather later in the year. For this reason *C. hypnoides* and *C. fastigiata* are frequently grown in cold frames in winter. They should have a peaty soil surfaced with sphagnum moss, and never be allowed to get dry at the root. The Botanic Garden of Edinburgh has long been famous for its success with these interesting and dainty plants. Propagated by layers and by cuttings. In the open they should have an airy but semi-shaded and damp position.

Since the last edition of this work was published, interest in this lovely but exacting genus has been stimulated by the introduction of *C. wardii* and the re-introduction, in improved form, of other Himalayan species. It has been sustained by the skill and enthusiasm of many gardeners, notably R. B. Cooke, who first flowered *C. wardii* and has raised several beautiful hybrids, and S. E. Lilley, who exhibited almost every cultivated species of *Cassiope* at Vincent Square in the spring of 1965. The latter is also the author of two valuable and well-illustrated articles on the genus: these will be found in the *Bulletin of the Alpine Gardening Society*, Vol. 29, pp. 72–85, and in the *Journal of the Royal Horticultural Society*, Vol. 90, pp. 302–5.

Two species of *Cassiope*—*C. hypnoides* and *stelleriana*—are by some authorities placed in the separate genus *Harrimanella*, distinguished from *Cassiope* by its alternate leaves and terminal flowers.

C. FASTIGIATA (Wall.) D. Don [PLATE 32
Andromeda fastigiata Wall.

A dwarf evergreen 6 to 12 in. high, forming dense tufts in the wild state; stems erect, squarish, densely clothed and completely hidden by four rows of closely overlapping leaves. Leaves stalkless, $\frac{3}{16}$ in. long, lance-shaped, deeply furrowed at the back, dark green, but with thin, silvery, membranous margins edged with fine hairs. Flowers produced in April and May singly from the leaf-axils. Corolla widely bell-shaped, $\frac{3}{8}$ in. across, white; calyx of five narrow, lance-shaped, pointed divisions; flower-stalk decurved, $\frac{1}{4}$ in. long, downy. *Bot. Mag.*, t. 4796.

Native of the Himalaya, common at elevations of 10,000 to 14,000 ft; introduced about 1849. It is similar in general aspect to the commoner *C. tetragona*, but its leaves are not so closely flattened to the stem, and its flowers are larger, wider, and more open-mouthed. It is the prettiest of the cassiopes.

A form with larger flowers was introduced by Ludlow and Sherriff from Bhutan in 1949.

C. HYPNOIDES (L.) D. Don
Andromeda hypnoides L.; *Harrimanella hypnoides* (L.) Cov.

A tiny evergreen, heather-like shrub from 1 to 3 in. high, with prostrate, slender stems completely covered with closely set leaves. Leaves $\frac{1}{8}$ in. long, linear, overlapping, somewhat erect, but not flattened against the stem. Flowers solitary on slender, erect, reddish stalks $\frac{1}{8}$ to $\frac{3}{4}$ in. long, produced at the end of the shoot; corolla nodding, white, bell-shaped, $\frac{1}{6}$ in. long, with five rather deep, rounded lobes; calyx red. Blossoms in April and May. *Bot. Mag.*, t. 2936.

Native of the Arctic and sub-Arctic parts of Europe and N. America, and of the mountain-tops of more southern latitudes; introduced in 1798.

C. LYCOPODIOIDES (Pall.) D. Don [PLATE 31

Andromeda lycopodioides Pall.

A prostrate evergreen shrub 1 to 3 in. high but 1 to 3 ft wide; shoots dense, slender, closely covered with tiny appressed ovate, glabrous leaves, and altogether (leaves with stem) only about $\frac{1}{12}$ in. wide. The leaves resemble those of *C. mertensiana* in having no groove down the back and thereby differ from those of *C. selaginoides*. Flowers pendent, solitary, axillary, white, bell-shaped and lily-of-the-valley-like, $\frac{1}{4}$ in. long, the stalks thread-like, $\frac{1}{2}$ to 1 in. long; opening in May and June, with sometimes a supplementary crop in autumn; stamens ten. *Bot. Mag.*, n.s., t. 298.

Native of high altitudes in Japan and thence northward to Alaska. A very beautiful little shrub, rare in cultivation, but occasionally offered by nurserymen. It likes cool, moist conditions, a peaty soil and shade during the middle of the day.

cv. 'RIGIDA'.—Larger in most of its parts, with the corolla more cylindrical and corolla lobes longer and proportionately narrower than in the type. Introduced from Japan around 1935. (*C. l.* var. *major* Stoker).

For the hybrid 'Muirhead', see *C. wardii. C. lycopodioides* has also crossed with *C. fastigiata* to give 'RANDLE COOKE' and 'BADENOCH'.

C. MERTENSIANA (Bong.) D. Don

Andromeda mertensiana Bong.; *A. cupressina* Hook.

A dwarf evergreen shrub 6 to 12 in. high, branches erect or spreading; young shoots not downy, completely hidden by the leaves. Leaves $\frac{3}{16}$ in. long, $\frac{1}{12}$ in. wide, without stalks, closely pressed to the shoot, tapering to a blunt apex; inner surface hollowed, outer surface ridged or keeled, thus giving a four-angled character to the twig which, leaves and all, is about $\frac{1}{8}$ in. wide. Flowers nodding, solitary on glabrous thread-like stalks, $\frac{1}{3}$ in. long, opening from the leaf-axils in April. Corolla cup-shaped, with five shallow reflexed lobes, $\frac{1}{4}$ in. wide, pure white; stamens very short, with white stalks; anthers brown, each prolonged at the back into a bristle; style glabrous, half as long as the corolla. Calyx of five sepals thickened at the base, $\frac{1}{10}$ in. long, pointed, jagged at the margins, often red or reddish.

Native of the mountains of western N. America, from California to Alaska. It is well distinguished from the common *C. tetragona* by the thick ridge down the back of the leaf, which in the other is grooved there. An interesting if not a showy shrub and quite hardy.

C. SELAGINOIDES Hook. f. & Thoms.

A dwarf evergreen shrub of tufted habit from 2 to 10 in. high. As in the other cassiopes, the stem is almost or quite hidden and the twig is made four-sided by the stalkless overlapping leaves tightly pressed to it. Leaves $\frac{1}{12}$ to $\frac{1}{8}$ in. long, of lanceolate shape, deeply grooved at the back, downy in the groove and on the margins. Flowers solitary on slender, hairy stalks ½ to 1 in. long, sometimes much shorter. Corolla nodding, pure glistening white, bell-shaped, ¼ to ⅜ in. long, five-lobed, the lobes triangular and slightly recurved. Sepals ⅛ in. long, pointed, with whitish membranous margins. Stamens shorter than the corolla, the stalks bearded and their anthers having each a bristle standing out at right-angles to the stalk.

Native of the Himalaya and China; originally discovered by the younger (Joseph) Hooker in 1849, in Sikkim, where it grows up to 13,000 ft altitude. Other collectors, including Wilson and Kingdon Ward, have found it in W. China and Tibet. Both these collectors note that it often grows under rhododendron bushes. Lt-Col. Messel flowered a plant at Nymans in 1928 that had been raised from Kingdon Ward's Tibetan seeds.

C. selaginoides is best adapted for a shady moist place in the rock garden where the soil is of a peaty nature. Its rather mossy flower-stalks are distinctive.

A beautiful and very distinct form of this species is LSE 13284, collected by Ludlow, Sherriff, and Elliott on the Deyang La in S.E. Tibet in 1947. It makes a graceful, diminutive bushlet about 8 in. high, with creamy white flowers, strikingly large for so small a plant and borne on long arching pedicels. It was given an Award of Merit in 1954.

A form is figured in *Bot. Mag.*, t. 9003b, which was only 1 in. high, the corolla ovoid, with small, scarcely recurved lobes. It was raised at Kew from seed received from Darjeeling and named var. *nana* by Stapf.

C. STELLERIANA (Pall.) DC.
Andromeda stelleriana Pall.; *Harrimanella stelleriana* (Pall.) Cov.

A dwarf, evergreen shrub of creeping habit, about 3 in. high, forming dense mats; shoots wiry, rooting freely. Leaves very small, erica-like, oblong, glabrous, spreading and not appressed as in other species. Flowers nodding and terminal on very short erect stalks; corolla creamy white, tinged pink, bell-shaped, ¼ to ⅜ in. diameter, four-lobed; stamens eight.

Native of the N. Pacific region from British Columbia to Japan; it was first described, figured and named by Pallas in 1789 under *Andromeda* and transferred to *Cassiope* by De Candolle in 1838, but not often seen in cultivation. It flowers very freely in April and was given an Award of Merit at Vincent Square in 1937. It is one of the most charming of dwarf Ericaceae and likes a moist, well-drained, peaty or open, lime-free soil and a sunny position. Admirable for the rock garden.

C. TETRAGONA (L.) D. Don
Andromeda tetragona L.

A dwarf, evergreen shrub growing 4 to 10 in. high in gardens; stems erect, much-branched, quite hidden on the younger parts by closely overlapping leaves. Leaves ⅙ in. long, arranged in four rows, so as to give the leaf-clothed stem a four-angled shape; stalkless, concave in front, each one closely appressed to the leaf above it; furrowed behind, slightly downy. Flowers sparsely borne at intervals along the younger parts of the stem during April and May, and produced singly from the leaf-axils. Corolla nodding, white tinged with red, bell-shaped, $\frac{1}{6}$ to $\frac{1}{4}$ in. long (occasionally longer), calyx of five ovate divisions, green tinged with red; flower-stalk decurved, about four to six times as long as the leaves. *Bot. Mag.*, t. 3181.

Native of the northern hemisphere, in Arctic and sub-Arctic regions; said to have been introduced from Lapland in 1810, and later from N. America. It differs from *C. fastigiata* in the smaller flowers, and in the leaves being without the silvery membranous margins, although slightly ciliated.

var. SAXIMONTANA (Small) Hitchcock *C. tetragona* subsp. *saximontana* (Small) Porsild.—Pedicels not more than two or three times the length of the leaves and often scarcely exceeding them, so that the flowers nestle against the leaves. As to the size of the flowers, they appear to be of about the same length as they normally are in the typical variety of *C. tetragona* (about $\frac{1}{5}$ in. long). A native of British Columbia, Alberta and S.E. Yukon; described by Small (as a species) from plants found by him on the summit of Mt Sulphur, near Banff.

C. (*tetragona* × *fastigiata*) 'EDINBURGH'.—This very free-flowering hybrid arose spontaneously in the Edinburgh Botanic Garden and was given an Award of Merit in 1957. The plant shown was about 7 in. high and 12 in. across and bore up to twelve open flowers near the tip of each stem.

C. WARDII Marquand

A dwarf evergreen shrub to about 8 in. high, with stout erect stems borne on horizontal primary branches which root freely where they touch the ground. The stems are clad with four rows of closely overlapping lanceolate leaves about $\frac{1}{5}$ in. long, furrowed at the back and edged with fine white hairs, but without the thin, hyaline margins characteristic of *C. fastigiata*. Flowers solitary, nodding, borne near the tips of the stems on short, hairy pedicels; calyx-lobes oblong, free to the base, more or less acute, tipped with red; corolla white, tinged with red inside at the base, broadly bell-shaped, about $\frac{3}{8}$ in. long, with five broadly triangular lobes, recurved at the tips. *Bot. Mag.*, n.s., t. 151.

C. wardii was discovered by Kingdon Ward in 1924 on the Temo La in the E. Himalaya but not introduced until 1938, when the Ludlow, Sherriff, and Taylor expedition collected seed under Namche Barwa, in the ranges enclosed by the Tsangpo bend. After the war it was again introduced by Ludlow and Sherriff, and is now well established in cultivation. It is closely allied to *C. fastigiata*, but in that species the leaves and sepals have thin, membranous margins, the leaves are more lustrous and the stems more slender. A hybrid between the two species has been raised by R. B. Cooke and named by him 'GEORGE TAYLOR'; it is interesting that it closely resembles a specimen collected by Sir George Taylor and his companions in 1938 and determined by Miss Muirhead as a hybrid of this parentage.

C. (lycopodioides × *wardii)* 'MUIRHEAD'.—This hybrid was raised by R. B. Cooke and given an Award of Merit in 1953. It resembles the former in its flexible, whip-cord branchlets and in bearing its flowers all along them—not concentrated near the tips as in *C. wardii.* The influence of this parent is shown in the more erect habit, larger flowers and hairy pedicels.

CASTANEA CHESTNUT FAGACEAE

There appear to be about ten species of chestnut known, but the number varies much in consequence of the varying conception of their specific limits. In any case they constitute a well-marked group of deciduous trees and shrubs, with alternate, parallel-ribbed, conspicuously toothed leaves, always approaching the oblong or narrow oval in shape. The leaves of all the chestnuts have a strong family resemblance; the only leaves anything like them in hardy trees occur in a few oaks. The unisexual flowers are produced in long, slender catkins from the leaf-axils of the young shoots during July. The lower catkins are entirely male; but from the axils of the later leaves there come shorter catkins, at the base of which one to three female flowers are borne. The flowers of all the chestnuts are pale yellow, and have little beauty of colour; but a tree well laden with catkins has a distinct appearance, the enjoyment of which to many people is spoilt by their heavy, unpleasant odour. The nuts are always enclosed in the well-known prickly burs.

The older botanists made *C. dentata* and *C. crenata* both forms of *C. sativa,* which may have led to their not being introduced, and to their present rarity. They are, however, distinct enough, especially as seen in the living state, although it is not easy to make the distinctions very clear on paper. It does not seem likely that any other than *C. sativa* will be of much value in Britain either for timber or nuts, although the variety 'Paragon', sometimes grown, is considered to have the 'blood' of *C. dentata* in it. The ordinary *C. sativa* varies extraordinarily in the size and quality of its nuts. There are numerous trees in Kew Gardens, some of which bear large, excellent nuts and others that never produce a nut worth eating. The merit of the better forms seems to be due largely to their being able to suppress all but one of the three or four nuts which each bur normally encloses. This enables the survivor to develop into a fine nut.

The chestnuts like a hot summer. Even during the driest and hottest seasons, like that of 1911, one rarely sees any of this genus suffering. They appear to thrive in any well-drained, loamy soil, even of moderate quality, but are said to be averse to calcareous soils. They should always be raised from seeds except in the case of the fine fruiting forms, which are grafted easily in spring on seedlings of the common sort.

C. ALNIFOLIA Nutt.

C. nana Muhl.

A deciduous shrub 1 to 2 ft high, with a creeping root-stock, growing naturally in small patches. Leaves oblong to oblong-obovate, often blunt at the apex, toothed; 2 to 6 in. long, ¾ to 2 in. wide; of stout texture, dark shining green and smooth above, covered beneath with rather tawny down; veins in twelve to sixteen pairs. Fruits solitary to three in a cluster, the husk covered with short spines. Nut solitary.

Native of the S.E. United States. Originally distinguished as a species by Nuttall in 1818, this afterwards became confused with *C. pumila*. It is, nevertheless, distinct in its dwarf habit, its often blunt-ended leaves whose down on the under-surface is not white as in *C. pumila*, and whose marginal teeth are more spreading and less bristle-like. The nuts also are said to be generally much larger but less abundant. It is interesting as the dwarfest of all chestnuts, yet inhabiting one of the warmest regions occupied by this genus. It grows chiefly on what the Americans call 'sandy pine-barrens', and it may not prove absolutely hardy with us.

C. CRENATA Sieb. & Zucc.   JAPANESE CHESTNUT

C. japonica Blume

A small tree, frequently less than 30 ft high, according to Sargent, but occasionally much larger; young shoots sometimes very downy, with the down persisting through the first winter, sometimes merely scaly. Leaves oblong-lanceolate, 3 to 7 in. long, 1¼ to 2 in. wide, heart-shaped or rounded at the base, pointed; the teeth small, with bristle-like points; lower surface covered with a close grey down; stalk ½ in. long, downy. Nuts like those of *C. sativa*.

Native of Japan; introduced in 1895, if not before, to Kew, where the species is thriving very well. This is a valuable food tree in Japan, and Sargent observes that he never saw chestnuts offered in such quantities for sale in Europe and America as there. He saw young trees 10 or 12 ft high fruiting freely. Ordinarily the nuts are smaller than those of the European tree, but from selected trees or varieties they are as large as the best European varieties.

C. DENTATA (Marsh.) Borkh.   AMERICAN CHESTNUT

Fagus-castanea dentata Marsh; C. americana Raf.

A tree occasionally 100 ft high in N. America, with the trunk and habit of the Spanish chestnut, but with, perhaps, scarcely so spreading a head; young shoots glabrous except for a dust-like scurf. Leaves dull green, narrowly oblong, tapering about equally at both ends, 6 to 9 in. long, 1¾ to 2 in. wide, coarsely toothed except at the base; both surfaces glabrous; stalk about ½ in. long. Catkins 6 to 8 in. long. Fruit as in the European species, consisting of a bur of numerous, branched, slender spines enclosing one to three nuts.

A native of eastern N. America, now on the verge of extinction by the chestnut blight, known to scientists as *Endothia parasitica*. The disease entered the U.S.A. from E. Asia at the end of the nineteenth century and spread so rapidly that today hardly a healthy mature tree remains. Trees killed to the ground frequently throw coppice shoots which for a time appear healthy and even bear fruit, but sooner or later these in their turn are overcome. So far, no resistant strain has been discovered and it now seems that the total extinction of the American chestnut is only a matter of time. The loss to the forests and landscapes where it once thrived is irreparable, but as a nut-bearing and timber tree its place may eventually be taken by hybrids between it and the Asiatic *C. crenata* and *C. mollissima*, or by selected forms of these species; both, and especially the former, are comparatively resistant to the disease.

The date of introduction of this species to Britain is not recorded. It is very rare in cultivation in this country, although a tree at Kew, now 50 ft high, thrives well. The leaves differ from those of *C. sativa* in the uniformly tapered base and in being narrower in proportion to their length. They are never clothed beneath with a close, thick down, as those of *C. sativa* and *C. crenata* often are. In the U.S.A. its fruit has been replaced by imports from Europe; they are smaller than those of the Spanish chestnut, but said to have a superior flavour.

C. HENRYI (Skan) Rehd. & Wils.

Castanopsis henryi Skan

A deciduous tree 60 to 80 ft high, its trunk 6 to 9 ft in girth; young shoots dark-coloured and quite glabrous. Leaves oblong-lanceolate, wedge-shaped at the base, tapered at the apex to a long slender point, the margin set with bristle-like teeth terminating the primary veins; 4 to 8 in. long, 1 to 2½ in. wide; green on both surfaces but rather paler below and quite glabrous except for a few whitish appressed hairs on the veins; veins in twelve to twenty pairs; stalk ¼ to 1 in. long, glabrous. Male catkins 4 in. or more long, solitary in the leaf-axils. Nut solitary in the husk, cone-shaped, ½ to ¾ in. wide at the base, enclosed in a prickly husk 1 in. wide. The fruits may be solitary or two or three in a cluster.

Native of China, where it is widely spread; according to Wilson it is common in the mountain woods of Hupeh and Szechwan. It was introduced by him to the Coombe Wood nursery in 1900, and a plant obtained from there is growing at Kew. Although hardy it does not promise to make a fine tree. The largest in the collection is forty-five years old and only 16 ft high. There is a larger specimen in the Edinburgh Botanic Garden measuring 37 × 3¼ ft (1968), with a smooth, shining bole.

C. MOLLISSIMA Blume   CHINESE CHESTNUT

C. bungeana Blume; *C. duclouxii* Dode; *C. hupehensis* Dode

A deciduous tree up to 60 ft high, with a trunk 6 ft in girth; young shoots furnished (often thinly) with comparatively long hairs or with short velvety down. Leaves oblong to oval, mostly rounded or heart-shaped at the base, tapered at the apex to a short slender point, the margins set with triangular or bristle-like teeth; 5 to 8 in. long, 2 to 3½ in. wide. The leaves vary much in regard to downiness, and according to Wilson there may be found on the same tree some nearly or quite glabrous, and others clothed beneath with a whitish felt; stalk $\frac{1}{4}$ to $\frac{1}{2}$ in. long, usually hairy. Male catkins 4 to 5 in. long. Nuts variable in size, in some forms being as large as the best class of Spanish chestnut. There are usually two or three in one husk, which is 2 in. wide and covered with straw-coloured spines and clothed with soft down.

Native of China, of which country it is the common chestnut, occurring as it does, wild or cultivated, from Peking to the far west. It is undoubtedly a native of Szechwan, where it is very common and whence Wilson introduced it to the Arnold Arboretum in 1908. Plants under his number 1141 are growing at Kew, and are quite hardy although slow and bushy in growth. The largest is now 28 ft high (1966). It had previously been introduced from Peking by Sargent in 1903. The earlier botanists confused it with *C. sativa*, the European chestnut, but it can usually be distinguished by the down and hairs on the young shoots. Its leaf-stalks in general are also shorter, being, even on large leaves, sometimes only $\frac{1}{4}$ in. long. The tree is valued in China for its edible nuts and as a source of fuel, which is obtained by a system of coppicing.

C. PUMILA (L.) Mill.   CHINQUAPIN
Fagus pumila L.

A deciduous shrub spreading by underground stems, or a small tree; young shoots covered with short hairs, which persist through the winter. Leaves oblong, inclined to oval and obovate, 3 to 5 in. long, 1 to 2 in. wide, pointed, wedge-shaped or rounded at the base, coarsely toothed; dark green and soon becoming glabrous above, but coated beneath with a persistent, greyish-white (at first quite white), close felt. Male catkins 4 in. or more long. Nut of good flavour, egg-shaped and not flattened, $\frac{3}{4}$ to 1 in. long, usually solitary in a bur $1\frac{1}{2}$ in. across.

Native of eastern N. America, where it is often known as the 'chinquapin'; introduced, according to Aiton, in 1699, but very rare in cultivation. There are shrubby examples at Kew which flower, but have never, in my experience, borne fruit. It probably needs a hotter summer than ours, as a small tree at Verrières, near Paris, often fruits freely. This chestnut is distinguished by its shrubby habit, and white under-surface of the leaf. In N. America a single plant often forms a thicket through its habit of spreading by suckers.

C. OZARKENSIS Ashe—A tree to 65 ft high. Leaves larger than in *C. pumila* (5 to 8 in. long), coarsely toothed, downy beneath. Fruit densely spiny. According to Sargent, it replaces *C. pumila* in the northern part of the Mississippi Basin.

C. × NEGLECTA Dode—A probable hybrid between the preceding and *C. dentata*. Leaves less downy beneath; fruits larger. Found wild in N. Carolina.

C. SEGUINII Dode—A Chinese species allied to *C. pumila* and identified with it by early botanists. It is common in thickets over much of the eastern and central parts of the country. Leaves glabrous beneath except on the veins; the husk contains three or more fruits.

CASTANEA PUMILA

C. SATIVA Mill.   SWEET, OR SPANISH CHESTNUT
C. *vesca* Gaertn.; C. *vulgaris* Lam.; *Fagus castanea* L.

A tree of the largest size, 100 ft or more high, with an enormous girth of trunk (sometimes 30 to 40 ft); young shoots at first covered with a minute down, or glabrous. Leaves oblong, with a narrowed, pointed apex, and a rounded, slightly heart-shaped or tapered base; coarsely toothed, 5 to 9 in. long, 2 to 3½ in. wide; stalk ½ to 1 in. long. When they first expand, they are covered beneath with a close felt which often rapidly falls away. Nuts red-brown, usually in twos or threes, enclosed in a globose, very prickly fruit or bur, 1½ to 2 in. across. They vary in size, according to the number in each bur, from ¾ to 1¼ in. across; sometimes there are four, sometimes only one, in a fruit.

Native of S. Europe, N. Africa, and Asia Minor. It is supposed to have been introduced to Britain by the Romans, and certainly existed in our islands previous to the Norman Conquest. It may be found springing up naturally in different parts of the country, and no foreign tree except perhaps the sycamore, can be said to have adapted itself better to our climate. In the south of Europe, where the nuts are much more esteemed as food than they are with us, numerous named varieties are in commerce. Of these 'Marron de Lyon', 'Gros Merle', and 'Paragon' are sometimes cultivated in England; they are propagated by grafting on seedlings of the common sort. In propagating the type itself, it is worth while to select the nuts from trees that bear them of good size. The sweet chestnut is intolerant of lime in the soil.

With us, however, the tree is grown chiefly as a park ornament, and for coppice. Certainly no tree gives greater distinction to a park or garden than an old, finely developed chestnut. For dry, hot soils no tree of its class is better adapted. At Kew, in shallow, sandy soil there are several fine specimens, one over 25 ft in girth of trunk. There are many splendid chestnuts scattered over the country. Perhaps the finest stand in the British Isles is the 'Chestnut Tole' at Godinton Park, Ashford, Kent. Here the tallest measure 118 × 11¾ ft and 116 × 16¼ ft. At the other end of the British Isles there are two remarkable trees at Castle Leod in Ross and Cromarty, planted in 1550, the larger of which measures 83 × 24¾ ft with a bole of 18 ft (1966; 76 × 21¾ ft in 1908). There are many large trees of exceptional girth at Shrublands Park, Ipswich. The timber much resembles oak, but is far from being as valuable, and very liable to 'shake' or split at the annual rings. Coffins made of it are frequently supplied as of genuine oak. The sweet chestnut has sported into a number of varieties, of which the following may be mentioned:

cv. 'ALBO-MARGINATA'.—Leaves margined with creamy white. 'Argenteo-marginata' is similar (perhaps the same clone). [PLATE 34

cv. 'ASPLENIFOLIA'.—Loudon's description reads: 'has the leaves cut into shreds, regularly or irregularly, and sometimes so as to appear like linear-lanceolate leaves' (*Arb. et Frut. Brit.*, p. 1984, 1838). Distributed by Loddiges nursery. Sports such as this one are reported to occur frequently and many were propagated and distributed in the last century under such names as *dissecta*, *dissecta nova*, *filipendula*, *linearifolia*, *heterophylla*, etc. In all of them the leaf-blade is much, but irregularly, narrowed, sometimes to ½ in. or less in width, but extraordinarily variable in form and length. A leaf found on a tree on Esher Common was 18 in. long, and in parts less than ¼ in. wide. These curious leaves are usually borne at the end of the summer shoot.

cv. 'AUREO-MARGINATA'.—Leaves similar to 'Albo-marginata', but with the margins yellow; very handsome.

cv. 'HOLTII'.—A tree of rather conical habit, cultivated at Kew from graft-wood received from a Mr Holt in 1907. The parent tree grew at Mount Maskell, Kent.

cv. 'LACINIATA'.—In this striking variety the teeth end in long, thread-like points. There is a large specimen at Westonbirt, Glos., in Silkwood. The name adopted here, although apparently the correct one, is usually given as a synonym of 'Asplenifolia', which has quite different leaves.

cv. 'PURPUREA'.—Leaves of large size (as much as 5 in. wide), purple when young, especially on the upper half, coppery in autumn. The original tree grew at Rostrevor.

cv. 'PYRAMIDALIS'.—Of rather conical habit.

The plant figured by Lavallée in his *Arboretum Segrezianum*, t. 33, as var.

pendulifolia is, apparently, *C. dentata*, the American chestnut, whose leaves have a more drooping pose than those of *C. sativa.*

CASTANOPSIS   FAGACEAE

A large genus of evergreen trees, natives of the warm temperate regions of eastern and southern Asia and allied to *Quercus* and *Castanea*. The fruit is entirely enclosed as in sweet chestnut, but the involucre splits irregularly, and, as in some species of oak, the fruit takes two years to ripen; as in *Castanea*, the male flower-spikes are upright. The well-known *Castanopsis chrysophylla* is now considered to represent a distinct genus—see *Chrysolepis*. With its departure, *Castanopsis* becomes a genus almost unrepresented in British gardens. In addition to the two species described here, *C. concolor* is in cultivation at Caerhays Castle, Cornwall, raised from seed collected by George Forrest in Yunnan, China (F. 24758).

C. CHRYSOPHYLLA *see* CHRYSOLEPIS CHRYSOPHYLLA

C. CUSPIDATA (Thunb.) Schottky
Quercus cuspidata Thunb.

A large tree in the forests of Japan, with elegant drooping branches; young shoots covered with scurfy hairs, later glabrous. Leaves leathery, ovate to oblong, 2 to 3½ in. long, ¾ to 1½ in. wide, tapered or somewhat rounded at the base, the apex drawn out into a slender, bluntly ended tip; margins undulately toothed near the apex or entire; upper surface dark, shining green, the lower paler and covered with fine scales which give it a metallic sheen. Acorns sessile, borne six to ten together on a common stalk; involucre more or less globose or ovoid, made up of several rows of downy scales, almost completely enclosing the nut and splitting into two or four valves.

Native of Japan, where it is common from Tokyo southward, and also of China; introduced by Maries for Veitch's nurseries in 1879. According to Siebold, acorns were successfully transported by him to Europe in 1830 by encasing them in clay. Although apparently quite hardy near London, it gives no promise of attaining its natural dimensions here. At Caerhays Castle in Cornwall it has made a tree measuring 37 × 3 ft, on a bole of 12 ft; on Garinish Island, Eire, it is represented by a large shrubby specimen 25 ft high, on two stems each 2½ ft in girth. But even at a smaller size it makes an elegant evergreen shrub.

cv. 'VARIEGATA'.—Leaves smaller than in the type, rarely more than 2 to 2½ in. long, with a broad regular margin of creamy yellow; sometimes the whole of one side of the midrib is of that colour. It is not so hardy as the green type, but was once used for greenhouse decoration. Introduced by Maries in 1879.

C. DELAVAYI Franch.

An evergreen tree up to 50 ft or more high in a wild state, free from down except for a sprinkling of scurfy stellate tomentum on shoot and leaf when they are quite young. Leaves stiff, leathery; elliptical, ovate or obovate; usually more or less abruptly tapered at the base; bluntish, rounded or pointed at the apex; coarsely toothed to merely wavy at the margin; 2 to 5 in. long, 1¼ to 3 in. wide; silvery-grey or whitish beneath; veins in six to eight pairs; stalk ¼ to ½ in. long. Male flowers yellow, borne on slender erect spikes 4 or 5 in. long. Female catkins about as long, bearing stalkless fruits which, when developed, are globose, about ½ in. wide, covered with stiff short spines, and containing usually one nut.

Native of W. China; discovered in Yunnan by the Abbé Delavay; introduced by Forrest in 1924. It is in cultivation at Caerhays Castle, Cornwall.

CATALPA   BIGNONIACEAE

Like many other genera of hardy trees and shrubs, the catalpas are found in both the Old and New Worlds. Although first made known to English cultivators from N. America in the form of *C. bignonioides* (which was introduced in 1726), the genus has been found in later times to be more abundantly represented in China, where four to six species occur. In the open ground the catalpas form low, wide-spreading, bushy-headed deciduous trees, a habit largely due, no doubt, to the shoots never forming a terminal bud. The young wood is stout, and very pithy. Leaves either opposite or in threes, large, long-stalked. Flowers produced in panicles, corymbs, or racemes at the end of the shoots of the year. Corolla bell-shaped at the base, with five spreading, frilled lobes; calyx two-lipped; stamens five, only two of which as a rule are fertile. Seed-vessel a very slender, cylindrical capsule 1 to 2 ft long, and ¼ to ½ in. diameter. Seeds numerous, flat, with a fringe of long, white hairs at each end.

Three Asiatic species have been introduced but none has proved superior to the American catalpas *C. bignonioides* and *speciosa*. These are undoubtedly among the most beautiful of all flowering trees and an isolated tree on a lawn is seen to exceptional advantage. The hybrid *C.* × *erubescens* 'Purpurea' also makes a very striking specimen. At the same time all the species are worth cultivation.

Catalpas like generous treatment at the root; a deep, moist loam is best, and an open, sunny, but not a bleak spot. Owing to the branches never forming a terminal bud and the annual bi- or tri-furcation this induces, it is advisable when the trees are young to train up a leader high enough to produce a trunk of the desired height, say 10 ft, when the tree may be left to assume the spreading habit natural to it. *C. bignonioides* thrives well in London, and for many years there have been fine specimens in Parliament Yard, Westminster. For propagation I would prefer seeds to any other means, believing that trees so raised are the longest-lived. But when these are unobtainable, and for distinct forms or coloured-leaved varieties, cuttings may be used. These should be made of the young leafy shoots as soon as they are moderately firm, and struck in mild bottom-heat.

The most recent treatment of the genus is by the Czechoslovak botanist Jiří Paclt in *Candollea*, 1952, pp. 241–85.

C. BIGNONIOIDES Walt. INDIAN BEAN, SOUTHERN CATALPA
C. syringaefolia Sims [PLATE 33

A tree 25 to 50 ft high, with a rounded, wide-spreading, much-branched head when grown apart from other trees. Leaves in adult trees broadly ovate, with a heart-shaped base; 4 to 10 in. long, 3 to 8 in. wide (in young trees considerably larger); with short, slender points, sometimes slightly lobed at the sides; light green and ultimately glabrous above, more or less clothed beneath, especially about the midrib and veins, with pale hairs; odour when crushed disagreeable; stalk half to three-fourths as long as the blade. Panicles broadly pyramidal, 8 to 10 in. long and wide, many-flowered. Corolla 1½ in. long and across, frilled at the margin, the tube bell-shaped; white with two ridges and two rows of yellow spots, and numerous purple spots on the tube and lower lobe. Fruit slender, 6 to 15 in. long, round, and about as thick as a lead pencil. *Bot. Mag.*, t. 1094.

Native of the eastern United States; introduced in 1726. It flowers at the end of July and in August, and is at that season the most beautiful of flowering trees. It is hardy, but is best adapted for the south of England. No large garden or park ought to be without one or more specimens, and young ones from seed ought to be always coming on to succeed the older ones, for the species is not particularly long-lived, and frequently declines when forty to fifty years of age. It bears fruit in hot seasons, and a tree densely hung with the long, pendent seed-pods has a curious aspect.

The best-known examples in Britain are those that grow in Palace Yard, Westminster, the largest of which measure 40 × 11 ft (1963). The tallest recorded are: Batsford Park, Glos., 60 × 4¾ ft (1963); Wakehurst Place, Sussex, 52 × 4½ ft (1966).

cv. 'AUREA'.—Those who admire yellow-leaved trees will not find a more striking one than this; its leaves are wholly of a rich yellow, which does not become dull or greenish as the season advances, but rather improves in colour. There are fine examples in the Sunningdale Nurseries, Windlesham, Surrey, and in the Jepson Gardens, Leamington Spa.

cv. 'KOEHNEI'.—Leaves yellowish green in the centre, with a wider margin of yellow.

cv. 'NANA'.—A dwarf form 3 to 6 ft high, bushy, with smaller leaves and said rarely or never to flower. Of French origin, around 1850. In the U.S.A. a dwarf form is top-grafted to make a small weeping specimen, but whether this is the same clone is not certain.

There is also a worthless variety with leaves blotched yellowish white.

C. BUNGEI C. A. Mey.

A tree 20 to 30 ft high, of bushy habit. Leaves 2 to $7\frac{1}{2}$ in. long, $1\frac{1}{2}$ to $4\frac{1}{2}$ in. wide; ovate or somewhat triangular, with a wedge-shaped or straightly cut base; sometimes entire, but often coarsely scalloped, so as to form one to six large teeth on each side, mostly on the lower half; quite glabrous at maturity; stalk half to two-thirds as long as the blade. Flowers not yet seen in this country, but described as 'white and purple'; they are produced three to twelve together in a flattish corymb. Corolla $1\frac{1}{2}$ in. long and wide.

Native of China, and evidently frequent in the neighbourhood of Peking. Although the true species was only introduced in 1905, through Prof. Sargent, plants under the name have long been in cultivation; these, however, are nearly always *C. bignonioides* 'Nana', but sometimes *C. ovata*. The true *C. bungei* is still very rare. Of its ornamental qualities little can yet be said, but as represented by dried specimens at Kew, the inflorescence is small. Its quite glabrous leaves distinguish it from other cultivated species except *C. fargesii* f. *duclouxii*. It is now in cultivation at Kew but grows poorly.

C. × ERUBESCENS Carr.

C. hybrida Spaeth; *C. teasii* Dode

The name *C. × erubescens* covers the various hybrids that have arisen in cultivation between the American southern catalpa *C. bignonioides* and the Chinese *C. ovata*. The type plant was described by Carrière in *Rev. Hort.*, 1869. It arose independently of 'J. C. Teas', but whether it was put into commerce is not known.

cv. 'HYBRIDA'.—Described by Späth in 1898 from a plant growing in his arboretum. He did not claim to have originated it and it is usually assumed that the plant belonged to the clone 'J. C. Teas'.

cv. 'J. C. TEAS'.—This—the best-known form of the cross—was raised by J. C. Teas at Bayville, Indiana, U.S.A. around 1874, from seed of *C. ovata*. The seed parent grew in the proximity of both *C. speciosa* and *C. bignonioides*, but it is now accepted that the pollen came from the latter species and not from *C. speciosa*, as stated in previous editions. The unfolding leaves are purplish, broad-ovate or slightly three-lobed, cordate, up to 12 in. long, downy beneath. Flowers white, stained with yellow and minutely spotted with purple, smaller than in *C. bignonioides*, but more numerous. In the central United States it has shown an extraordinary vigour: leaves over 2 ft wide, and panicles carrying over 300 flowers, have been produced. In Britain it is decidedly inferior to *C. bignonioides* as a flowering tree; the leaves, however, even here, are the largest in the genus. It flowers about the end of July into August and was introduced in 1891.

Large specimens of this hybrid recorded recently are: Hergest Croft, Heref., 58 × $7\frac{3}{4}$ ft (1963); Wakehurst Place, Sussex, 62 × $4\frac{3}{4}$ ft (1964); Crowholt, Farnham, Surrey, 50 × $8\frac{1}{2}$ ft (1963); Syon Park, Middx., 58 × $7\frac{3}{4}$ ft (1968).

cv. 'JAPONICA'.—This plant was put into commerce by Simon-Louis Frères about 1886. It was said to have come from Japan and was described by

Dode as a species—*C. japonica*. However, it is considered by Paclt (*Candollea*, 1952) to be a form of *C.* × *erubescens* and thus presumably of European garden origin. It is distinguished from *C. ovata* by its narrower, more compact and pyramidal inflorescence and its less markedly lobed leaves, of a clearer, more glossy green, and less downy. The flowers are fragrant, of a purer white than in *C. ovata*, dotted inside with violet. This is a vigorous and quick-growing tree.

cv. 'PURPUREA'.—Leaves and young shoots dark purple, almost black, when quite young. The colour largely disappears with age from the leaf-blade, but it always remains darker than in the type; the leaf-stalks retain it. This tree has long been considered a form of *C. ovata*, but is referred by Paclt to *C.* × *erubescens*. Its origin is uncertain, but it was probably raised in the Meehan nurseries near Philadelphia, U.S.A., before 1886. There is a fine specimen in the University Botanic Garden, Cambridge.

C. FARGESII Bureau
C. vestita Diels

A tree 30 to 60 ft high, the shoots, under-surface of the leaves, and inflorescences covered with velvety, branching hairs which mostly fall away by the end of the season. Leaves broadly ovate, straight or slightly heart-shaped at the base, long and taper-pointed, 3 to 6 in. long, 2 to 5 in. wide; stalk 1½ to 4 in. long. Flowers 1½ in. long and nearly as wide, pinkish, spotted in and round the throat with brownish red, and stained with yellow; produced seven to fifteen together in corymbs. Calyx velvety; corolla bell-shaped, with five rounded, frilled lobes, and about 1½ in. across. Seed-pod 12 to 18 in. long, very slender.

Native of W. China; introduced to France towards the end of last century. It was named from specimens collected by Père Farges in Szechwan, where it was also found by Henry. Wilson sent seed from Hupeh in 1901 and again in 1907.

f. DUCLOUXII (Dode) Gilmour *C. duclouxii* Dode; *C. sutchuenensis* Dode— This differs from the type chiefly in being destitute of stellate hairs; the shoots, leaves, and inflorescence are quite glabrous. Introduced by Wilson in 1907 under W. 640, but this seed was distributed as typical *C. fargesii*; also to Kew in 1908 from M. de Vilmorin. The f. *duclouxii* was given an Award of Merit when shown from Kew in 1934 and is figured in *Bot. Mag.*, t. 9458.

Although beautiful in flower, *C. fargesii* in both its forms makes a rather gaunt, narrow-crowned tree. The f. *duclouxii* in particular is of poor habit as seen in cultivation and seemingly short-lived.

C. OVATA G. Don
C. kaempferi Sieb.

A tree usually 20 to 30, sometimes 45 ft high, with a spreading head of branches as much or more in diameter. Leaves 5 to 10 in. long, and as much wide; broadly ovate with a heart-shaped base, often conspicuously three-lobed, each lobe with a short, slender point; pale green and at first finely downy above, permanently downy especially on the veins beneath; stalk 2 to 6 in. long. Panicles 4 to 10 in. high, narrowly pyramidal, produced in July and August. Corolla dull white stained with yellow and spotted with red inside, about 1 in. long and wide, the base bell-shaped; of the spreading lobes the lower one is the largest. Seed-vessel 12 in. long, ⅓ in. diameter. *Bot. Mag.*, t. 6611.

Native of China; introduced from Japan to Europe by Siebold in 1849. If not a native of Japan, it has for centuries been cultivated there; Kaempfer recorded it in 1693. From the two American species it is distinguished by its more conspicuously lobed leaves and smaller flowers, and from *C. bungei* by the larger, downy leaves and smaller flowers. It was also introduced by Wilson from its native habitat in China.

cv. 'FLAVESCENS'.—Flowers even smaller than in the type (about ¾ in. long and wide), the whole corolla suffused with yellow. The names "*wallichii*" and "*himalayensis*" by which it has been known would suggest a Himalayan origin, but no catalpa is known to be native to that region.

C. SPECIOSA Engelm.   WESTERN CATALPA

A tree sometimes over 100 ft high in a wild state, with a tall trunk 10 ft or more in circumference. Leaves inodorous, ovate, with a heart-shaped or rounded base, and a long, tapering point; 5 to 12 in. long, 3 to 8 in. wide; nearly or quite glabrous above when mature, covered beneath with pale brown down. Panicles about 6–8 in. long, rather more wide, with comparatively few flowers. Corolla white, 2 in. long and wide, the tube bell-shaped, the lobes spreading and frilled at the margin; the lower one with yellow spots and ridges as in *C. bignonioides*, but less freely spotted with purple. Seed-vessel 8 to 18 in. long, ½ in. or little more wide.

Native of the United States, found only west of the Alleghanies and extending further north in the Mississippi Basin than *C. bignonioides*; introduced in 1880. It differs from that species in its taller growth, its longer, more tapering, inodorous leaves, and in its flowers being larger, fewer in the panicles, and less profusely purple-spotted. At Kew it flowers well in July, two weeks in advance of the other, and promises to make a taller tree, of more upright habit. The largest in the collection measures 60 × 4¾ ft (1963). There is another in Radnor Gardens, Twickenham, measuring 55 × 9¾ ft (1967).

In the United States the timber of this tree is much valued on account of its extraordinary durability in contact with the ground and with moisture. Sargent mentions in the *Silva of North America*, Vol. vi, p. 90, a remarkable proof of this quality:

'The trunks of catalpa trees killed by the sinking and subsequent submersion of a large tract of land near New Madrid, Missouri, which followed the earthquake of August 1811, were standing and perfectly sound sixty-seven years later, although all their companions in the forest had disappeared long before.'

Gate posts, too, have been known to stand in perfect preservation fifty to one hundred years. Railway companies in the United States are now planting it largely, to provide a future supply of railway sleepers.

CATHAYA PINACEAE

A new genus of conifers, discovered by Chinese scientists in Kwangsi province in 1955. For the following account we are indebted to Mr David Hunt of the Kew Herbarium:

Two living species native to S.W. China have been described, *C. argyrophylla* Chun & Kuang and *C. nanchuanensis* Chun & Kuang, the second from vegetative material only, and consequently of doubtful status. Neither has been introduced and no material has been available for study. A third species, first described as a *Keteleeria*, was found some fifty years before in fossil deposits in Germany.

Evergreen trees with branchlets of two kinds; long shoots with spirally arranged leaves, lateral short shoots with more or less whorled leaves. Branchlets ribbed with the decurrent bases of the linear leaves, the point of leaf-insertion slightly raised, as in *Keteleeria* or *Pseudotsuga*. Pollen grains with air-sacs. Female cone-scales persistent, i.e. the cones not breaking up at maturity.

The dimorphic shoots should not be taken to imply a particularly close relationship between *Cathaya* and the larches, cedars, and pines, as the foliar spurs of *Cathaya* are not of the same order of structural specialisation as in these other groups, and are apparently sterile, whereas in the larches and cedars at least, it is the long shoots which are sterile. Furthermore, dimorphism of the shoots is a feature which appears to have arisen independently in quite unrelated groups of the Gymnospermae such as *Ginkgo*, *Phyllocladus*, and *Taxodium*. Rather, the general morphology of the leaves, shoots, and cones of *Cathaya* implies a close relationship with several genera of the *Abies* group, *Keteleeria* and *Pseudotsuga* in particular coming to mind. In a paper on the wood anatomy (Yatsenko-Khmelevsky and Budkevich, in *Journ. Bot. U.R.S.S.*, Vol. 43, pp. 477–80, 1958) general similarities with *Picea* and *Pseudotsuga* are shown (a comparison with *Keteleeria* does not appear to have been made) and Takhtajan is quoted as considering *Cathaya* nearest to *Picea*.

CEANOTHUS RHAMNACEAE

A well-marked genus of evergreen and deciduous shrubs or small trees, confined to N. America. They are peculiarly characteristic of the Pacific coast region, where they constitute a large part of that 'almost impenetrably dense brushwood called "chapparal", which covers the middle elevations of the coast range, and forms a distinct belt between the herbaceous vegetation of the foot-hills and the forest growth of the highest ridges and summits' (Greene). The flowers, usually of some shade of blue or white, are individually quite small, but they are so plentifully

borne in a crowd of fascicles or umbels, that they form as a whole a dense
and often showy panicle. Sepals and petals five, the latter of hooded form,
narrowing at the base to a slender stalk. The leaves afford useful distinguishing characters: one group has them opposite, the other alternate;
and the species of the latter group are again divisible according to the
veining, some having three more or less prominent veins, and some being
pinnate- or feather-veined.

The ceanothuses generally are somewhat tender, and, except where
noted, should be given the protection of a wall. They are, however, fast-
growing and flower well when young, so the loss of a mature plant is not
an irreparable tragedy. Most are easily multiplied by cuttings put in
during July and August in gentle heat and, where facilities are available,
it is a good practice, with these and many other easily struck, borderline
shrubs, to take precautionary cuttings each summer. With these reserves
to fall back on, the gardener can afford to be more adventurous and make
better use of the spells of mild or average winters.

The evergreen species and hybrids, when trained on a wall, should be
pruned after flowering by shortening the laterals to within two or three
buds of last year's stems; strong growths not needed for extending the
framework should be cut back. See also *C.* × *delilianus*.

The standard work on the genus is: M. Van Rensselaer and H. E.
McMinn, *Ceanothus*, published by the Santa Barbara Botanic Garden,
California (1942). This admirable study is unfortunately no longer in
print but the Californian species are treated in: H. E. McMinn, *An
Illustrated Manual of California Shrubs* (1951), and P. A. Munz, *A Cali-
fornia Flora* (1959).

C. AMERICANUS L.   NEW JERSEY TEA, REDROOT

A deciduous shrub about 3 ft high, with slightly downy or glabrous young
wood and reddish roots. Leaves alternate, ovate, sometimes broadly heart-
shaped; 2 to 3 in. long, ¾ to 2 in. wide; finely toothed, downy especially beneath,
with three conspicuous veins; leaf-stalks ¼ to ½ in. long. Flowers very small and
numerous, in a series of long-stalked, dense panicles proceeding from the axils
of the uppermost leaves of the current season's growth. The actual cluster of
flowers is 1 to 2 in. long, on a downy stalk about twice its own length, the
individual flower very tiny, less than ⅛ in. diameter, dull white, on a thread-like
stalk ⅛ in. long. Fruit dry, somewhat triangular, ⅕ in. wide. Flowers in June and
July. *Bot. Mag.*, t. 1479.

Native of the Eastern and Central States of N. America, and the oldest of the
genus in gardens, having been introduced to England in 1713. It is not often
seen true now, being largely superseded by the prettier and showier hybrids, of
which it is one of the parents. It requires no protection, and is, perhaps, the
hardiest in the genus. Its popular name is said to have arisen from the leaves
being used as a substitute for tea, especially during the American Revolutionary
war.

This species is somewhat variable in the natural state. Densely downy forms found in the Mississippi basin are sometimes given varietal status as var. PITCHERI Torr. & Gr.; smaller-leaved plants, with more numerous panicles, occur in the coastal plain and have been named var. INTERMEDIUS Torr. & Gr.

C. ARBOREUS Greene   CATALINA CEANOTHUS

A short-trunked, bushy evergreen tree 10 to 20, sometimes 30 ft high, with a trunk 1½ to 2½ ft in girth; bark scaling; young shoots densely downy. Leaves alternate, ovate or broadly oval, rounded or slightly heart-shaped at the base, rounded or shortly pointed at the apex, shallowly toothed, each tooth gland-tipped; 1¾ to 4 in. long, 1 to 2½ in. wide; dark bright green and minutely downy above, pale grey with a close felt (rarely glabrous) beneath; strongly three-veined; stalk downy, ⅓ to ¾ in. long. Flowers small (⅛ in. wide) pale blue, produced in pyramidal axillary panicles 3 to 4 in. long and 1½ to 2 in. wide, the main and secondary stalks grey downy. Seed-vessel black, ¼ in. wide.

Native of the islands off the coast of California: Santa Cruz, Santa Catalina, etc. It is one of the largest of the ceanothuses, exceeded in its dimensions only by C. thyrsiflorus. It has been grown at Kew against a south wall but was almost too large for such a position; certainly it is not a plant for a low wall; nor, being tender, is it really a suitable choice for the large space it needs, except in mild gardens. The flowers, which are borne in spring and more sparsely throughout the summer, vary from pale to deep blue. 'TREWITHEN BLUE' is a fine selection recently brought into commerce, with deeper blue flowers.

C. (arboreus × thyrsiflorus) 'TREASURE ISLAND'.—This hybrid, raised in California, is highly thought of there. Perhaps not introduced to Britain, but should prove hardier than C. arboreus.

C. 'BURKWOODII'

A hybrid between "C. floribundus" and C. 'Indigo' raised by Messrs Burkwood and Skipwith of Kingston-on-Thames. The first parent was presumably either a form of C. dentatus or C. × veitchianus, but owing to the confusion over the name "C. floribundus" its identity is uncertain. The second parent—'Indigo'—is a hybrid of the C. × delilianus group. This hybrid is therefore of particular interest as uniting in itself the two sections of the genus, viz. those that flower in spring on the growths of the preceding year (as in the evergreen Californian species) with those that flower in late summer and autumn on the growths of the current year (as in 'Indigo' and its parents and fellow hybrids).

An evergreen bush probably 5 or 6 ft high, richly leafy. Leaves rather shining green and glabrous above, greyish and downy beneath; oval, rounded at both ends, toothed, ½ to 1¼ in. long, about half as much wide. The chief veins are prominent beneath and number four or five each side the midrib, the basal pair usually the strongest and showing derivation from a species of the three-veined group. Flowers rich bright blue, in panicles 1 to 2½ in. long, opening from July to October. Each blossom is about ³⁄₁₆ in. wide, the petals ladle-shaped; stamens and style deeper blue than the petals; anthers pale yellow.

C. 'Autumnal Blue', raised by the same firm, is another hybrid of the same type but has *C. thyrsiflorus* as one of its parents. The leaves are larger than those of 'Burkwoodii', more glossy green, and quite distinctly three-veined. The flower trusses are larger and paler in colour.

Both these are distinct and beautiful acquisitions to late-flowering shrubs, and both, according to the raisers, have withstood 32° of frost uninjured, although growing without shelter in the lower Thames Valley. Like all their race, they should be given a sunny position. The Cory Cup, given to the best artificially raised hybrid of the year, was awarded to *C*. 'Burkwoodii' in 1930.

C. COERULEUS Lag.
C. azureus Desf.

A deciduous shrub up to 8 ft high; with the young wood, leaf-stalks, and flower-stalks, also the under-surface of the leaves, covered with a greyish down or felt. Leaves alternate, ovate, 1 to 2 in. long, toothed, thick and felted beneath in a wild state, thinner and less downy under cultivation here. Flowers of a deep blue, and arranged in dense clusters on the upper part of panicles 3 to 6 in. long, which appear in the leaf-axils towards the end of the current season's growth.

Native of Mexico, whence it was introduced in 1818, and of Guatemala. It is not thoroughly hardy at Kew except against a wall. One of the parents of the numerous race of garden hybrids (see *C*. × *delilianus*), its influence is always traceable in the fine blue flowers, the downy leaves, and often the tender constitution of its progeny. The typical plant, which flowers from July until the first frosts of autumn, is now uncommon.

C. CUNEATUS (Hook.) Nutt.   BUCK BRUSH
Rhamnus cuneatus Hook.

An evergreen shrub 4 to 6 ft high, of rather loose, straggling habit; twigs and leaves at first downy. Leaves entire, opposite, pinnate-veined, leathery in texture, obovate to elliptical, rounded or indented at the apex, tapered or rounded at the base, ¼ to 1 in. long, dull grey-green, paler beneath. Flowers dull white, or blue-tinted, produced on short axillary twigs, in short, dense, rounded corymbs, ½ to ¾ in. across.

Spread over the whole length of California in a wild state, this species is, in some parts, little better than a pest. A Californian writer (G. Hansen) observes that 'it clothes hillsides for miles and miles, and gives them a greyish green tint. Wherever man has done any cultivating, cleared an old wood road, cut a trail, ploughed a furrow in years past, or still keeps cultivating, this ceanothus follows him like a nettle or chickweed.' For gardens it has little to recommend it, except that it is one of the hardiest species, and flowers freely during May.

C. CYANEUS Eastw.

An evergreen shrub 4 to 10 ft high, or small tree 20 ft or more high; young shoots distinctly angular, bright green and quite glabrous except for a few scattered hairs when very young. Leaves alternate, ovate-elliptical, mostly bluntish or occasionally acute at the apex, rounded or broadly tapered at the base, toothed, each tooth gland-tipped; 1 to 2½ in. long, ⅓ to 1 in. wide; glittering green above, dull green beneath; glabrous except for a few hairs when very young; three-veined. Flowers of a lovely bright blue, each about ¼ in. across, opening in May and June and crowded in columnar panicles 2 to 5 in. long, 1 to 1½ in. wide, leafy at the base; main and secondary flower-stalks slightly downy, green, the individual flower-stalks glabrous and blue like the sepals and petals. Sepals incurved, the yellow-anthered stamens protruding between their turned-in margins; petals spoon-shaped, spreading.

Native of California; collected in San Diego county by Miss M. Phillbrook at 1,500 ft altitude in 1920. It was introduced to Kew in 1925, and a plant there was, in six years, over 20 ft high on a wall facing east; it is therefore a quick grower. The persistent, long-continued cold winds of the spring of 1932 injured many of its branchlets, and it will probably be seen at its best nearer the south coast. Miss Eastwood calls it 'certainly the loveliest of all the species of *Ceanothus*, with its large sprays of beautiful blue flowers'. This is very high praise but probably not undeserved. It is related to *C. thyrsiflorus* but the blossom is of a better blue than in any form of that species and the leaves are thinner. Miss Eastwood also observes that 'the seed pods, deeply three-lobed, not crested, yellowish, veiny, and glassy as if varnished' are distinctive. I saw a plant at Binstead, I. of W., 10 ft high in 1939.

'LA PRIMAVERA' is a beautiful hybrid from *C. cyaneus* raised in the Santa Barbara Botanic Garden about 1935; it flowers a month before *C. cyaneus*. The other parent is unknown. This plant has in turn given rise, by open pollination, to 'SIERRA BLUE' and 'MOUNTAIN HAZE', both raised by Lammerts in 1948 (*Journ. Calif. Hort.*, Vol. 9, p. 121).

C. × DELILIANUS Spach

Under this name it is convenient to group the so-called 'French' hybrids, which arose from the crossing of two deciduous species—the tender, blue-flowered *C. coeruleus* of Mexico (introduced to Europe in 1818) and the hardy, white-flowered *C. americanus*. In 1838, Loudon had suggested that this cross would be 'a very desirable acquisition', unaware that it had in fact been made some years earlier in France—the result being C. 'Delilianus' (syn. *C. arnouldii*). Following Rehder, we take this as the typical form of the hybrid group C. × *delilianus*, to which many beautiful additions were made, all by French breeders, during the ensuing decades of the nineteenth century.

C. × PALLIDUS Lindl.—The ceanothus so named by Lindley is thought to be the result of crossing *C. ovatus* (a white-flowered species closely allied to *C. americanus*) with 'Delilianus'. Some of the 'French hybrids', in particular those with rose-coloured flowers such as 'Marie Simon', may be the result of similar crosses (though a paler flower colour, due to the dilution of the *C. coeruleus* blood, might also be expected from back-crosses within the C. × *delilianus* group).

However, from the horticultural viewpoint the distinction between the

C. × *delilianus* and *C.* × *pallidus* is really of little moment. Together they form a most useful race of summer-flowering shrubs; all are deciduous and bear their flowers in panicles on the new wood. They must be hard pruned each spring in March or April, cutting back nearly to the base of the previous year's wood. The following is a selection:

'CERES'.—Lilac-pink flowers in large panicles.

'DELILIANUS'.—Flowers sky-blue.

'GLOIRE DE PLANTIÈRES'.—Dwarf-growing, deep blue flowers.

'GLOIRE DE VERSAILLES'.—Large panicles of powder-blue flowers. Perhaps the most widely cultivated of the group.   [PLATE 35

'HENRI DESFOSSE'.—Similar to 'Gloire de Versailles' but with deep blue flowers.

'INDIGO'.—The deepest blue of these hybrids but tender in some districts.

'LEON SIMON'.—Light blue flowers in clusters.

'MARIE SIMON'.—Rose-pink flowers. A pretty variety.

'PERLE ROSE'.—Bright carmine-rose flowers, but the colour is variable on some soils.

'TOPAZ'.—An excellent variety with rich indigo-blue flowers.

C. DENTATUS Torr. & Gr.

This evergreen shrub, one of the most popular ceanothuses in gardens, has by some authorities been regarded as a variety merely of *C. papillosus*. The leaves are alternate, $\frac{1}{5}$ to $\frac{1}{2}$ in. long (rarely as much as 1 in.), elliptic to narrowly oblong or linear, the margins decurved and set with gland-tipped teeth; the upper surface is dark, shiny green, and rather resinous; the under-surface covered with a close grey felt; venation pinnate. Flowers of a bright blue, in roundish clusters on short peduncles. From *C. papillosus* it differs in the absence of the warty excrescences on the leaves to which that species owes its name, and in its smaller leaves. But in the Redwood zone of the Santa Cruz Mountains, where the ranges of the two species overlap, intermediate forms are found. *C. dentatus* makes a charming wall plant, and in the milder counties is hardy in the open ground. The hybrid *C.* × *lobbianus* (q.v. under *C. thyrsiflorus*) is sometimes cultivated as "*dentatus*", but may be distinguished by its distinctly three-nerved leaves.

var. FLORIBUNDUS (Hook.) Trel. *C. floribundus* Hook.—Leaves usually broader and less revolute than in the type, and with scarcely glandular margins. Flowers borne in denser clusters on shorter peduncles. Such forms are reported to occur wild with the type.

In describing this variety, Trelease identified it with the *C. floribundus* of Hooker, a mysterious plant figured in the *Botanical Magazine*, t. 4806. It was raised at Veitch's nursery, Exeter, from seed collected by William Lobb in California around 1850, but exactly where is not known. From the gardener's point of view, this plant was distinguished not so much by its botanical characters as by the colouring of its flowers, which were of a particularly vivid shade of mazarine-blue. Not all plants falling botanically within the definition of

Trelease's var. *floribundus* would have this quality and indeed most plants grown under this name are said to be ordinary *C. dentatus* (E. E. Kemp in *Gard. Chron.*, 24th Aug. 1935). Others grown under this name are not forms of *C. dentatus* but *C. × veitchianus*. Whether any vegetative offspring of the Veitchian plant still exist is not certain.

The "*C. microphyllus*" of British gardens is a small-leaved form of *C. dentatus*. The true C. MICROPHYLLUS Michx. is a dwarf, heath-like shrub with white flowers, found in the sand-barrens and pine-woods of the south-eastern U.S.A.

C. FENDLERI A. Gray

A twiggy, deciduous shrub 4 to 6 ft high; with round, downy, spinose branchlets. Leaves alternate, linear-lanceolate to ovate, 1 in. or less long; three-veined, short-stalked, downy especially beneath; glandular-toothed towards the apex, or entire; of a dull grey-green. Flowers bluish white, in a cluster of umbels or fascicles at the end of the twigs, each cluster ½ to ¾ in. across; petals spoon-shaped, stamens with whitish stalks and yellow anthers. *Bot. Mag.*, t. 9264.

Native of the Rocky Mountains, from Colorado and New Mexico to Arizona, up to 8,000 ft. altitude. This ceanothus withstood the severe winter of 1908–9 better than any other W. American species, but it is one of the least showy, its foliage being dull and its flowers of an indeterminate hue. Introduced about 1898.

C. FOLIOSUS Parry

An evergreen shrub 1½ to 4 ft high, usually more in width, but often pro-cumbent or semi-prostrate; shoots downy, slender. Leaves one-veined, or some-what three-veined from the base, alternate, oval, ovate, or broadly oblong, tapered to both ends, ¼ to ¾ in long, the apex rounded or blunt, margins usually wavy, recurved and minutely toothed; teeth gland-tipped; dark green above, rather glaucous, downy or glabrous beneath but usually downy on the midrib and veins only; leaf-stalk very short. Often the principal leaves develop con-densed spurs in their axils, bearing clusters of smaller leaves. Flowers closely set in globose, terminal clusters, ⅓ to ½ in. wide, main-stalk ⅕ to ⅗ in. long (more rarely the clusters are grouped into a compound inflorescence up to 4 in. long); sepals and petals dark blue; filaments blue, anthers yellow. *Bot. Mag.*, t. 9540.

Native of California and a very pleasing shrub, usually compact and spreading, but according to Jepson, the Californian botanist, it may be found slender, erect, and 16 ft high in Mendocino county. It is a success at Kew both in the Rock Garden and against a wall. Blooms in May.

var. VINEATUS McMinn—A creeping or low, spreading shrub with rather larger leaves than in the type, found in various localities in Sonoma and Mendocino counties.

C. AUSTROMONTANUS Abrams—This species is now united with *C. foliosus* by leading authorities on the Californian flora. It was described from plants growing in the Cuyamaca Range in San Diego county, south of the main area of distribution of *C. foliosus*, and differs horticulturally in its low, spreading habit; leaves glossy and wavy-edged; flowers bright blue in small dense clusters. It seems, however, to be very near *C. foliosus* var. *vineatus*.

C. 'EDINBURGH'.—This ceanothus originated in the Edinburgh Botanic Garden around 1934 among seedlings of *C. austromontanus* and was distributed under that name. It is clearly a hybrid, with *C. griseus* (*C. thyrsiflorus* var. *griseus*) as one parent (E. Kemp in *Gard. Chron.*, 24th June 1961). Also known as "Edinensis".

C. 'ITALIAN SKIES'.—This ceanothus was raised by E. B. Anderson from seed of *C. foliosus* received from the University of Washington Arboretum, Seattle, U.S.A., in 1956. It makes a spreading bush with flowers of a brilliant blue arranged in dense, conical trusses 2 to 3 in. long. It appears to agree well with the seed parent in its botanical characters but the species of *Ceanothus* cross so readily in cultivation that it is perhaps preferable to treat this plant as an independent clone until its identity has been verified. It differs markedly from the form figured in the *Botanical Magazine* in having compound inflorescences, but this feature is accepted by McMinn as part of the normal variation of the species. Lord Morton has a fine specimen of 'Italian Skies' in his garden at Churt, Surrey, planted in 1964 and already 4 to 5 ft high and twice as wide.

C. GLORIOSUS J. T. Howell
C. prostratus var. *grandifolius* (Torr.) Jeps.

A prostrate or decumbent evergreen shrub to 1 ft high but 10 to 12 ft across, with long, stout, reddish-brown stems. Leaves opposite, ½ to 1½ in. long and up to 1 in. wide, elliptic to oblong, rounded at the apex, thick and leathery in texture, dark green above, paler beneath; margins edged with numerous teeth but sometimes entire towards the base; venation pinnate. Flowers deep blue to purple, borne in umbels on a short, stout peduncle.

A coastal species with a local distribution in California. According to McMinn, it is ground-hugging in full exposure but more upright away from the Pacific winds. In sheltered places inland, plants are found which grow to 6 ft high but otherwise resemble the type; they have been distinguished as var. EXALTATUS J. T. Howell. Related to *C. gloriosus* is C. MASONII, described by McMinn from plants he found growing on the Bolinas Ridge in Marin county. It has more erect and rigid stems than var. *exaltatus*, and smaller leaves.

C. IMPRESSUS Trel.
C. dentatus var. *impressus* (Trel.) Trel.

A low, spreading, densely branched shrub attaining in time a height and width of about 5 ft. Leaves alternate, ¼ to ½ in. long, elliptic to almost rounded, dark green and somewhat hairy above, deeply furrowed along the courses of the midrib and pinnately arranged veins; paler beneath, and hairy along the veins; margins revolute. Flowers deep blue in clusters about 1 in. long, borne in April and May.

A local species, confined to a few localities in the Californian counties of Santa Barbara and San Luis Obispo. It is closely related to *C. dentatus* but well distinguished by its impressed veins. Although described in 1888, this attractive species was not much cultivated until the Santa Barbara Botanic Garden recognised its merits and distributed it. It is one of the hardiest and most satisfactory of the evergreen species. Except in the milder parts it is best grown on a wall, where it may reach a height of 8 ft or even more.

var. NIPOMENSIS McMinn—Taller than the type (to 10 ft high), with lighter green, less furrowed and less revolute leaves.

C. (*impressus* × *thyrsiflorus* (?)) 'BURTONENSIS'.—A wild hybrid, believed to be of the parentage stated, of which a single plant was found on the Burton Mesa in 1941 and propagated in the Santa Barbara Botanic Garden; introduced to cultivation in Britain by F. P. Knight, Director of the R.H.S. Garden, in 1963. It appears to be very near to *C. impressus* but differs from the form of that species usually seen in cultivation in this country in its more rounded, often almost orbicular, glossy leaves. There is a specimen of this attractive ceanothus on the Laboratory wall in the R.H.S. Garden, Wisley.

C. INCANUS Torr. & Gr.

An evergreen shrub to 12 ft high, whose thorny branchlets are covered with a white bloom. Leaves alternate, ovate or broad-elliptic, ¾ to 2¼ in. long, rounded at the apex, rounded to slightly heart-shaped at the base, dull greyish green above, paler beneath, almost glabrous; margins entire or slightly toothed; three-veined. Flowers white, borne in May in branched clusters 1 to 3 in. long.

Native of California, where it inhabits open places in the moist Redwood belt of the coastal range. 'It is a spreading bush which in bloom has a lovely grey effect: cream-white flowers in stiff, spiraea-like spikes with a pearly tinge, downy leaves or pale green young foliage, all against a background of grey-white stems' (Lester Rowntree in *The New Flora and Sylva*, Vol. 5, p. 155).

C. INTEGERRIMUS Hook. & Arn.   DEER BRUSH

A deciduous or sub-evergreen shrub to 10 ft or more high, with roundish, slender branchlets, glabrous or hairy. Leaves alternate, variable in shape from oblong or elliptical to ovate or lanceolate, 1 to 3 in. long, pointed or blunt at the apex, rounded at the base, glabrous or somewhat downy above, commonly downy beneath, especially on the veins, more rarely glabrous; margins entire or toothed towards the apex; venation pinnate or three-veined, but the latter state is commoner. Flowers also rather variable in colour from white to several shades of pale blue, produced in compound racemes each 3 to 6 in. long, a large number of which at the end of each branch form a fine panicle of blossom 9 to 12 in. long and 3 to 4 in. broad. *Bot. Mag.*, t. 7640.

Native of California, where it was discovered by David Douglas in 1833, but not introduced until about twenty years later. It flowers in June, and is one of the most elegant wall plants of that season, producing its long, graceful panicles in great profusion. It needs the shelter of a wall. In the wild state it occurs throughout the length of California and shows considerable variation; the characters of the many varieties that have been distinguished are included in the above generalised description; they probably represent no more than states of one polymorphic species. *C. nevadensis* Kell. is now included in *C. integerrimus* as one of these varieties, viz. var. CALIFORNICUS (Kell.) Benson. It is commonest in the Sierra Nevada and has three-veined leaves; flowers commonly white.

C. MEGACARPUS Nutt.

An evergreen shrub up to 12 ft high; branches slender, finely downy when young. Leaves alternate, entire, obovate to oval, tapered at the base, rounded or notched at the apex, ½ to 1¼ in. long, glabrous above; the under-surface is finely and closely downy and prettily marked with numerous, closely set, parallel veins; stalk ⅛ in. or less long. Flowers white, ⅕ in. wide, produced in several umbels each about ½ in. wide on short twigs from late March to May; stalks glabrous, very slender. Fruit up to ⅜ in. wide, subglobose with a distinct rim and several horns.

Native of California, originally collected by Wm Lobb in the early fifties of last century. It needs wall protection, preferably south, in most parts of Britain and is about the earliest to flower in this country.

C. OVATUS Desf.

A deciduous shrub 2 to 3 ft high, with viscid, slightly downy young stems. Leaves alternate, narrow oval, 1 to 2½ in. long, ½ to 1 in. wide, bluntish or pointed at the apex, tapered or rounded at the base; glabrous and glossy, or slightly hairy beneath; stalk slender, ⅙ to ¼ in. long. Flowers white, produced in short-stalked, rounded clusters, the whole forming a loose panicle.

Native of S.E. and Central United States. It differs from *C. americanus* by its smoother, differently shaped leaves, never heart-shaped at the base, and shorter-stalked flower clusters. It flowers from June onwards, but the true plant is not common in gardens.

var. PUBESCENS (Torr. & Gr.) S. Wats.—This variety is similar to the type in habit, but the young shoots and the under-surface of the leaves are permanently downy.

C. PAPILLOSUS Torr. & Gr.

An evergreen shrub 4 to 15 ft high in the wild, with round, very downy young stems. Leaves alternate, pinnately veined, ½ to 2 in. long, ¼ to ½ in. wide, elliptic, oblong or linear, blunt or truncate at the apex, margins rolled towards the underside of the leaf (especially in dry habitats) and set with glandular teeth, the upper surface shining and furnished with conspicuous wart-like excrescences (papillae), which are also glandular. Flowers borne in May in terminal or axillary racemes 1 to 1½ in. long, on rather long, leafless peduncles, and of a delicate shade of blue. *Bot. Mag.*, t. 4815.

Discovered in 1833 by David Douglas in California; introduced by William Lobb about 1850. It is found in the Coast Range from just south of San Francisco to San Luis Obispo county, but attains its fullest development in the Santa Cruz Mountains, forming on the lower part of that range a densely branched shrub with very papillose leaves. Whilst this papillose surface of the leaves furnishes the most noticeable character of the species in its typical form, it does not appear to be a constant one. Higher up on the same mountains other ceanothuses appear with much smaller leaves, more decurved at the margins, and without papillae on the upper surface: the flowers too are a deeper blue. Some of these are difficult to distinguish from *C. dentatus*, which is also found here. It is, perhaps, from this area that Lobb introduced the plant that Hooker described as *C. floribundus* (see under *C. dentatus*).

var. ROWEANUS McMinn—Leaves narrower than in the type (less than $\frac{2}{5}$ in. wide), truncate or indented at the apex. Plants with these characters occur within the range of the species on dry slopes; but the type plants, which grow on Mount Tranquillon in Santa Barbara county, had the additional distinction that they were dwarf and compact in habit and made low, spreading bushes when brought into cultivation.

C. (*papillosus* × *rigidus*) 'DELIGHT'.—This is one of the hardiest of the hybrid ceanothuses. It is well suited to wall culture and a delightful feature when in full flower. There are large specimens at Kew which have withstood the rigour of winters over the past twenty years. It was raised by Messrs Burkwood and Skipwith and received an Award of Merit in 1933.

C. PARRYI Trel.

An evergreen shrub or small tree up to 18 ft high; young shoots angular, downy. Leaves oblong, inclined to oval, $\frac{1}{2}$ to $1\frac{1}{4}$ in. long, $\frac{1}{8}$ to $\frac{3}{8}$ in. wide, pinnately veined, apex blunt or rounded, rounded to tapered at the base, indistinctly toothed, cobwebby beneath; stalk quite short. Flowers blue, borne in simple or branched, downy panicles sparsely leafy at the base, up to 3 or 5 in. long, 1 to 2 in. wide, opening in late May and June. Capsules $\frac{1}{6}$ in. wide, globose, glabrous.

Native of California; apparently first collected by William Lobb in 1857. It is a fine, free-growing species, flowering very abundantly, and was given an Award of Merit when shown by Kew in 1944. It is quite hardy there as a wall plant, but needs good cultivation if it is to be seen at its best. Propagation by cuttings is not so easy as with other species and cuttings from a stock plant grown under glass will provide the best results.

C. PARVIFOLIUS (S. Wats.) Trel.
C. integerrimus var. *parvifolius* S. Wats.

A deciduous or semi-evergreen shrub 2 to 4 ft high; young shoots thin, flexible, quite glabrous. Leaves alternate, inconspicuously three-nerved, oblong, rounded at the end, broadly tapered to rounded at the base, quite entire; $\frac{1}{2}$ to

1 in. long, $\frac{3}{16}$ to $\frac{3}{8}$ in. wide; glabrous or nearly so on both surfaces. Flowers varying in shade from pale to deep blue, produced in panicles $\frac{1}{2}$ to $1\frac{1}{2}$ in. long; each flower is about $\frac{1}{10}$ in. wide, its stalk slender, $\frac{1}{4}$ to $\frac{3}{8}$ in. long.

Native of California, inhabiting mountain flats on the Sierra Nevada at 4,700 to 6,500 ft altitude. It is nearly related to *C. integerrimus* but differs in its dwarfer, often flat-topped habit, its blue flowers, much smaller leaves, and scarcely branched flower-panicles. It has been introduced and, coming from considerable elevations, should be hardy against a wall.

C. PROSTRATUS Benth.   SQUAW CARPET

An evergreen prostrate shrub, the branches in the natural state often taking root and forming a thick mat as much as 10 ft wide but only a few inches high; young shoots downy. Leaves opposite, of stout, thick texture, obovate to cuneate, coarsely toothed except at the tapered base, often with three spines near the apex only; $\frac{1}{3}$ to 1 in. long, $\frac{1}{5}$ to $\frac{1}{2}$ in. wide; green on both sides, varying from glabrous to downy beneath; stalk $\frac{1}{12}$ in. or less long. Flowers blue, $\frac{1}{8}$ in. wide, produced twelve to twenty together in clusters about 1 in. across at the end of short leafy shoots, each flower on a glabrous slender stalk $\frac{1}{3}$ to $\frac{1}{2}$ in. long. Fruit roundish oval with three conspicuous horns or excrescences on the top.

Native of western N. America from California to the State of Washington. Dried specimens are preserved at Kew that were collected in 1846 during Colonel Frémont's famous expedition to California. It is very distinct in the opposite, strongly toothed, holly-like leaves, one of its popular names being 'creeping holly'. More commonly it is known as 'squaw carpet' or 'Mahala mats'. It attains its most luxuriant growth on the eastern slope of the Oregon Cascades and in the Siskiyou Mountains, and has been described as one of the most showy and desirable of alpine shrubs. Forms with white and others with lavender-coloured flowers occur in a wild state. It should, of course, have a sunny place. Judging by the altitudes at which it grows it ought to be hardy with us; but in its early stages some protection in hard weather may be advisable.

C. PUMILUS Greene *C. prostratus* var. *profugus* Jeps.—This is essentially a very small-leaved extreme of *C. prostratus*, with leaves less than $\frac{1}{5}$ in. in width. It is common at high altitudes in the Siskiyou Mountains.

C. PURPUREUS Jeps.
C. jepsonii var. *purpureus* (Jeps.) Jeps.

An evergreen shrub $1\frac{1}{2}$ to 4 ft high, with rather stiff, reddish-brown stems. Leaves opposite, holly-like, pinnate-veined, broadly elliptic to rounded, $\frac{1}{2}$ to $\frac{3}{4}$ in. long, dark green and shining above, paler and thinly downy beneath; margins wavy, usually folded towards the upper surface of the leaf, set with spiny teeth. Flowers borne in April, deep blue or purple, in umbellate clusters. *Bot. Mag.*, n.s., t. 37.

This beautiful species is confined as a wild plant to one small area in Napa county, California, where Jepson discovered it at the end of the last century. It is not completely hardy at Kew but the late William Dallimore grew it successfully in his garden at Bidborough, near Tunbridge Wells, Kent, and it was his plant that provided the material for the figure in the *Botanical Magazine*. It is not easily reproduced by cuttings but seed, which it produces in abundance, affords a ready means of increase. It should be given a sunny position in well-drained soil.

CEANOTHUS PURPUREUS

C. JEPSONII Greene—This species is closely related to the preceding and has the same holly-like leaves. The main distinction is to be found in the seed-capsules: in *C. purpureus* the valves are horned near the apex, while in *C. jepsonii* they are ridged and wrinkled to the base. The flowers are blue or violet in the type, but more commonly white (var. ALBIFLORUS J. T. Howell). In cultivation this is a less satisfactory species than *C. purpureus*: the reason suggested by Van Rensselaer is that in nature it is confined to lead-rich, serpentine soils.

C. DIVERGENS Parry *C. prostratus* var. *divergens* (Parry) K. Brandegee—A near ally of *C. purpureus*, like it confined to one locality in Napa County, California. It is more lax in habit and the leaves less wavy at the margins. A plant of this species has lived for many years on the rock garden at the Edinburgh Botanic Garden.

C. RIGIDUS Nutt.

A densely branched evergreen shrub, usually low and spreading in the wild state but reaching 12 ft on a wall, with abundant foliage closely packed on short, stiff lateral branchlets. Leaves opposite, pinnate-veined, obovate to rounded in general outline, ⅛ to ½ in. long, wedge-shaped to rounded at the base, often truncate or retuse at the apex, dark glossy green above, minutely downy beneath, mostly toothed, at least near the apex, more rarely entire. Flowers bright blue to rich purplish blue, in sessile or short-stalked umbels. *Bot. Mag.*, t. 4664.

CEANOTHUS RIGIDUS

Native of California, found only on the Monterey peninsula, whence it was introduced by Hartweg for The Royal Horticultural Society in 1847. In the last edition of this work two forms of this species were described. One, which matches Nuttall's type, was shown by Miss Willmott in 1915 and became known as the 'Warley variety'; it has rather rounded, scarcely toothed leaves and short-stalked umbels. The other, commoner in gardens at that time, was introduced by Lobb sometime between 1849 and 1857, when collecting for Veitch's nurseries: it has narrower leaves, toothed near the apex, longer-stalked umbels and flowers of a paler shade. This form was distinguished by Sprague as var. *pallens*, but appears to fall within the limits of variability of typical *C. rigidus*.

This is one of the most beautiful of ceanothuses but, unfortunately, is also one of the tenderest. Against a wall at Kew it grows and flowers well every season, but in very hard winters is injured or killed even with that protection. It has no chance at all in the open. Like some other species, it is not long-lived, and the stock should be renewed occasionally by means of cuttings. It flowers from April to June, and will reach a height of 12 ft on a wall.

The following is a closely related species and indeed is part of *C. rigidus* as understood by Jepson:

C. RAMULOSUS (Greene) McMinn   *C. cuneatus* var. *ramulosus* Greene— Leaves usually less crowded than in *C. rigidus*; branchlets arching and more flexible. Flowers paler, in shades of lavender, pale blue, or white. This species has a wide distribution in the Coast Range, while *C. rigidus*, as now understood, is confined to the Monterey peninsula. McMinn (*Ceanothus*, 1942) considers that some plants grown in Britain as *C. rigidus* or var. *pallens* really belong to this species.

C. SANGUINEUS Pursh   OREGON TEA
C. oreganus Nutt.

A deciduous shrub up to 12 ft high; young shoots reddish or purplish, glabrous. Leaves alternate, distinctly three-ribbed, ovate or oval, mostly blunt or rounded at the apex, rounded or slightly heart-shaped at the base, the margin evenly set with bluntish teeth; $1\frac{1}{2}$ to $3\frac{1}{2}$ in. long, $\frac{3}{4}$ to $1\frac{3}{4}$ in. wide; dark green above, pale and more or less downy beneath; stalk $\frac{1}{2}$ to 1 in. long. Panicles $2\frac{1}{2}$ to $4\frac{1}{2}$ in. long, 1 in. wide, produced in late spring or early summer from side-buds at the ends of the previous season's growth. Flowers white, $\frac{1}{10}$ in. wide, each borne on a slender stalk $\frac{1}{4}$ to $\frac{1}{2}$ in. long; main and secondary flower-stalks thinly hairy. Fruit flattened-globose $\frac{1}{6}$ in. wide. *Bot. Mag.*, t. 5177.

Native of western N. America, where it is widely spread from British Columbia to California. It was first discovered and collected in 1806 by Capt. Lewis, the leader of the first expedition across North America. About twenty years later it was found by David Douglas, who described it as abundant in the valleys of the Rocky Mountains and as a shrub 4 to 10 ft high, flowering there in June. It was introduced by Wm Lobb about 1853 to Messrs Veitch's nursery at Exeter and first flowered with them in May 1859. The epithet *sanguineus* refers to the red young wood. In general appearance it is most like the eastern N. American species, *C. americanus* and *C. ovatus*, but both these differ in producing their flower panicles at and towards the end of the current year's growths. It is one of the hardier kinds.

C. SOREDIATUS Hook. & Arn.   JIM BRUSH

A dense evergreen shrub 3 to 8 ft high in the wild, sometimes taller; branchlets rigid, grey-green or purplish, clad with long hairs and rather spiny. Leaves alternate, three-veined, elliptic to ovate, acute at the apex, up to 1 in. long, dark green and lustrous above, undersides covered with long appressed hairs, especially on the veins; margins edged with glandular teeth. Flowers pale to deep blue, in small dense clusters.

Native of California, widely distributed in the Coast Range and common around San Francisco. Of recent introduction, this species is growing well at Glendoick in E. Perthshire and at Malahide Castle near Dublin. It bears a second crop of flowers in the autumn.

C. THYRSIFLORUS Esch.

An evergreen shrub or small tree 15 to 30 ft high in this country, but half as high again in a wild state. Young branchlets angled, slightly downy or glabrous. Leaves alternate, three-veined, glabrous and glossy green above; green and either glabrous or downy on the main veins beneath; glandular-toothed, ovate, ¾ to 1½ in. long; leaf-stalk about one-third the length of the blade. Flowers pale blue, in roundish stalked clusters 1 to 3 in. long, produced from the leaf-axils of the previous season's growth, and surmounted by the growing leafy shoots of the current season.

Native of California; introduced in 1837. According to Sargent it attains its greatest size in the redwood forests of the Santa Cruz Mountains. This is the hardiest of the taller-growing ceanothuses. At Kew, quite unprotected, and in an exposed position, it has grown 20 ft high, and withstood all but the severest winters uninjured; at Warley Place, in Essex, it has been 10 ft higher. Farther north it will make an admirable evergreen for walls. It flowers in May and June in great profusion, and is the most striking among the really hardy species. It exhibits considerable variation in a wild state, in stature, size of leaf, and in the colour of the flowers, which are sometimes almost white. The basal pair of veins extend almost to the apex of the leaf.

var. REPENS McMinn—A prostrate variety found on the coast north of San Francisco and in Monterey county. In cultivation it retains its low, spreading habit and has proved both hardy and vigorous.

C. GRISEUS (Trel.) McMinn *C. thyrsiflorus* var. *griseus* Trel.—Leaves broad-ovate to roundish, blunt at the apex, silky-hairy or downy beneath; margins usually undulate between the teeth. In other respects it resembles *C. thyrsiflorus*, but is perhaps more tender in the British climate. The form described in the last edition had pale lilac flowers, but the colouring on wild plants is said to be violet blue. A low-growing form of this species has been distinguished as var. HORIZONTALIS McMinn.

C. × LOBBIANUS Hook.—This plant is now thought to be a hybrid between *C. griseus* and *C. dentatus*. It was introduced by Lobb in the fifties of the last century and has since been found wild in the Monterey area. It is cultivated sometimes as *"dentatus"* and sometimes as *"veitchianus"*, from both of which its distinctly three-veined leaves distinguish it. Flowers bright blue, with blue downy stalks. *Bot. Mag.*, t. 4811.

C. 'CASCADE'.—This ceanothus is very near to *C. thyrsiflorus* and usually considered to be a form of it. A tall nearly hardy shrub with arching growths, capable of attaining 25 ft in height on a wall. Flowers powder-blue in panicles up to 3 in. long. Raised by Messrs Jackman and given an Award of Merit in 1946.

C. 'RUSSELLIANUS'.—Although often listed as a variety of *C. dentatus*, this ceanothus is probably a hybrid of similar parentage to *C.* × *lobbianus*. It is a vigorous shrub with small, glossy leaves, and exceptionally free-flowering.

C. 'SOUTHMEAD'.—Also akin to *C.* × *lobbianus*, this ceanothus was raised by Capt. C. K. Mooney and given an Award of Merit when shown by Lord Talbot de Malahide at Chelsea in 1964.

C. × VEITCHIANUS Hook.

An evergreen shrub 10 ft or more high, with green glossy leaves, which are obovate, wedge-shaped, rounded at the apex, glandular toothed, greyish beneath. Flowers in dense heads 1 to 2 in. long, bright deep blue. This plant was originally introduced from California by W. Lobb about 1853. It does not appear to have been found wild since, and is of somewhat uncertain relationship. It has been suggested that it is a hybrid between *C. thyrsiflorus* or *griseus* and some other species, probably *rigidus*; the pinnate veins of the leaf and the greyish under-surface support this view. There is often a suggestion of the triple nerves of *C. thyrsiflorus* at the base of the leaf. The identity of the plant is also clouded by Hooker's original description in the *Botanical Magazine*, t. 5127, which alludes to the branchlets as 'glabrous'; in his Latin diagnosis the ultimate ones are said to be downy as in his type specimen. It is fairly common in cultivation and a handsome wall shrub, indeed one of the most beautiful of its race; in the milder parts it is hardy in the open. It is all too often grown under an incorrect name—sometimes as "*C. dentatus*" and often as "*C. dentatus floribundus*". To add to the confusion, some plants grown as "*C. veitchianus*" are really *C.* × *lobbianus*.

C. VELUTINUS Hook.

An evergreen shrub 8 to 10 ft high (probably more in a wild state), with stout, glabrous branchlets. Leaves prominently three-veined, 1½ to 3 in. long, two-thirds as much wide; broadly ovate or roundish, often with a slightly heart-shaped base, finely toothed; very shiny and dark green above, downy and much paler beneath. Flowers dull white, crowded on stout panicles which are 4 to 5 in. long, and spring from the leaf-axils. *Bot. Mag.*, t. 5165.

Native of California; first discovered by Douglas; introduced by W. Lobb about 1853. Its most distinctive feature is its large, dark green foliage, so glossy as to appear varnished; the flowers are not very showy, and appear late in the season. It requires the protection of a wall.

var. LAEVIGATUS (Hook.) Torr. & Gr.—This, which has leaves quite glabrous, is represented by a plant growing on a wall at Kew. It flowers every year in October and November, and is at all times noticeable for its large, leathery, varnished green leaves, which, as in the type, are quite viscous during the summer, and have a distinct resinous odour.

C. × MENDOCINENSIS McMinn—A natural hybrid between *C. velutinus* var. *laevigatus* and *C. thyrsiflorus*, reported from Mendocino and neighbouring counties where the two species are in contact. Leaves ovate, to 2½ in. long and

CEANOTHUS VELUTINUS var. LAEVIGATUS

1 in. wide, glabrous, dark green and glossy above, glaucous beneath; three-veined. Flowers pale blue or lavender in almost sessile umbels arranged in racemes or panicles 2 to 4 in. long; common stalk and rachis glabrous. The same hybrid may have occurred in gardens.

CEDRELA   MELIACEAE

The species described here is the only hardy member of the important mahogany family, though the beautiful *Melia azedarach* is widely grown in climates not so very much warmer than ours. The genus *Cedrela* has its main distribution in the American tropics and is rarer in the Old World: *C. australis*, the Australian 'red cedar', is now usually placed in the related genus *Flindersia*. *C. odorata*, the 'Spanish cedar', yields an aromatic wood from which all cigar-boxes were once made.

   C. sinensis bears some resemblance to *Ailanthus altissima* in the related family Simaroubaceae; but in that species the leaflets bear glandular teeth near the base and the leaves lack the oniony smell that characterises the cedrela.

C. SINENSIS Juss.   CHINESE CEDAR

Ailanthus flavescens Carr.; *Toona sinensis* (Juss.) Roem.

A handsome deciduous tree reaching 60 to 70 ft in height in China, and at present more than half as high in Britain; young branchlets downy; old bark peeling off in long strips. Leaves pinnate, 1 to 2 ft long, composed of from five to twelve pairs of leaflets, often of even numbers on one leaf (paripinnate). Leaflets very shortly stalked, 2½ to 4 in. long, ovate-lanceolate, the apex drawn out into a long fine point, the base unequal at each side the midrib, ultimately nearly or quite glabrous. Flowers in terminal panicles 1 ft long, whitish, fragrant, short-stalked. Fruit a capsule about 1 in. long; seeds winged.

Although known to botanists since 1743, this tree was not introduced to Europe until 1862. It was at first called "*Ailanthus flavescens*", but is easily distinguished from true *Ailanthus* by the entire margins of the leaflets and the absence of glandular teeth there. It is a native of N. and W. China, and in the latter region many seeds were collected by Wilson on his last journey. As is the case with nearly all trees of timber-producing size, this is best raised from seed, but failing them, root-cuttings may be employed. It is said to thrive well in calcareous soils. The young shoots and leaves have an oniony taste and are boiled and eaten as a vegetable by the Chinese. By far the largest specimen recorded grows at Heligan, Cornwall, which measures 90 × 8¼ ft (1959). Others are: Nettlecombe, Somerset, 65 × 7½ ft (1959); Kew, *pl.* 1907, 52 × 6¼ ft (1965). The tree in the Berberis Dell at Kew first flowered in 1947.

CEDRUS   CEDAR   PINACEAE

A group of three, or, if the Cyprian cedar be regarded as more than a variety, four species of evergreen trees, forming a very homogeneous group. They are as closely allied to each other as they are markedly distinct from other coniferous trees. Sir Joseph Hooker and other authorities regarded them all as geographical forms of one species. In a recent study, Schwartz recognises two species: *C. deodara* and *C. libani*, which he subdivides into four subspecies, viz. subsp. *libani*, *stenocoma* (q.v. under *C. libani*), *brevifolia*, and *atlantica* (*Fedde's Repertorium*, Vol. 54 (1), p. 26). Most closely allied to them are the larches, deciduous though these are. Given space for lateral development, old cedars become flat-topped, and their branches grow horizontally. As in the larches and some other conifers, the branchlets are of two kinds: (1) leading ones, which grow considerably (at least several inches) during the summer, and bear the leaves singly and spirally arranged; and (2) short, spur-like ones, which lengthen a fraction of an inch only per annum, and have the leaves crowded in a dense tuft at the end. The latter kind are capable of developing into the former. Flowers of both sexes appear on the same tree, usually on the upper side of the branches. Males very densely set in erect, finger-shaped cones, 2 to 3 in. long, ½ to ⅝ in. wide, shedding clouds of yellow pollen when ripe. Females in stout, erect cones, purplish at first, ultimately 3 to 5 in. long, flat or depressed at the top, the scales broad and closely overlapping; seeds winged.

The cedars all like a deep loamy soil, well drained but moist. They are admirably adapted for growing as specimen trees on lawns, and for this purpose should be planted when not more than 4 to 6 ft high. It is necessary to propagate some of the garden varieties by grafting on their typical forms, but they are of little importance. Trees raised from seed will always grow better and give the greater pleasure.

The timber of all the cedars as produced on their native mountains is valuable, but as grown in our milder, softer climate, it is not so hard and durable. The timber of English-grown Lebanon cedar is sometimes handsomely grained, and may be used for indoor purposes.

C. ATLANTICA Manetti   ATLAS CEDAR

A tree up to 120 ft high, pyramidal when young, ultimately assuming, at least in a wild state, the flat-topped shape with horizontally spreading branches, characteristic of the cedar of Lebanon; young shoots downy. Leaves ½ to 1 in. long, needle-like, stouter than in *C. libani*, curved towards the tip; varying in colour from green to silvery. Cones 3 in. long, 1½ to 2 in. wide, cylindrical.

Native of Algeria and Morocco on the Atlas Mountains; introduced about 1840. This cedar is very hardy, and is thriving splendidly in various parts of the British Isles. At Kew, on dry, hot soil it grows more quickly and withstands London smoke better than either the Lebanon cedar or the deodar. This species is sometimes difficult to distinguish from the cedar of Lebanon. If large numbers of specimens are examined, they are distinct enough, since average differences then emerge which would not be apparent if only a few examples of each were to be compared. This explains why experts, when confronted by an individual tree, are sometimes in doubt in which species to place it. The Atlas cedar in youth and early maturity is characterised by a stiff habit and erect leader, but in age it assumes the flat-topped habit wrongly thought to be the perquisite of the cedar of Lebanon. In the Atlas cedar, the shoots are always downy, and more so than those of the Lebanon species. Its cones, too, do not taper above the middle so much.

The following are among the oldest and finest trees measured in recent years: Bowood, Wilts., 132 × 18½ ft (1957); Westonbirt House, Glos., from the original introduction, 102 × 15 ft at 4 ft (1967); Eastnor Castle, Heref., 110 × 16¾ ft (1961); Gask House, Perths., 110 × 14 ft (1962); Althorp, Northants, 107 × 13¼ ft (1964); Corsham Court, Wilts., 87 × 21 ft, a superb tree (1965); Bodnant, Denbigh, *pl*, 1876, 110 × 11¼ ft (1967).

cv. 'AUREA'.—Leaves of a yellowish colour. This is only propagated by grafting, and is not so vigorous as seedling trees. There are small examples of this at Little Hall, Kent (*pl.* 1907), and at Poltimore, Devon, 40–50 ft high.

f. GLAUCA Beissn.—Leaves of a more or less silvery hue; in the finest forms, named *argentea*, the whole tree is of a beautiful pale, grey-blue colour. Ordinary f. *glauca* can often be selected among batches of seedlings, and there is every gradation between it and what we regard as the green type—in nature as well as in gardens. This form is as common among the older trees as the green-leaved one. Among the largest recorded are: Bowood, Wilts., 105 × 16 ft (1957); Eastnor Castle, Heref., 102 × 13 ft, from the original introduction (1961); Pampisford, Cambs., 105 × 13¼ ft (1959); Bodnant, Denbigh, 105 × 10¾ ft (1957); Dropmore, Bucks., *pl.* 1843, 95 × 13 ft.

f. PENDULA (Carr.) Rehd.—Leader and branches pendulous. Such forms are known to occur in the wild but the origin of the cultivated trees is unknown. The fine example in the Glasnevin Botanic Garden, with light grey-glaucous leaves, was planted around 1875 (J. P. Fanning in *Gard. Chron.*, 27 July 1957). Two at Tittenhurst, Berks., resemble the Dublin tree in foliage, but are more sharply pendulous.

f. FASTIGIATA (Carr.) Rehd.—Branches ascending. Trees of this character grow at Grayswood Hill, Surrey, 63 × 7¼ ft (1965), and Chiltley Place, Liphook, Hants, 55 × 4¼ ft (1961). Elwes and Henry mention one at Tortworth, 50 ft high in 1908. The tree described by Carrière (*Rev. Hort.*, 1890, p. 32) was raised by Lalande of Nantes but it is unlikely that any of the trees mentioned, and certainly not the last, are of this origin.

C. DEODARA (Roxb.) G. Don   DEODAR
Pinus deodara Roxb.

A tree up to 250 ft high in a wild state, forming in age, like the Lebanon and Atlas cedars, a flat, spreading top where there is room for lateral expansion; of broadly pyramidal form when young. Leading shoot arching; branchlets pendulous at the ends, always downy. Leaves 1 to 1½ (occasionally 2) in. long, needle-like. Cones about 4 in. long, 3 in. wide, broadly egg-shaped, as yet infrequently borne with us.

Native of the Himalaya from E. Afghanistan to Garwhal; introduced by the Hon. Leslie Melville in 1831 but distributed in greater quantity in 1856. Whilst the deodar is less hardy than the other cedars, it is the most elegant in a young state. Few coniferous trees are, indeed, so graceful. It is on this account (as well as by its longer leaves) easily distinguished from the other two, which have more or less erect leading shoots and stiff branchlets. The young twigs of the deodar, too, are as a rule distinctly more downy. Like the other cedars, it varies considerably in the hue of its foliage, which usually is of a grey or glaucous green, becoming dark green on older trees.

The following 'varieties' have been made out of the variations seen in cultivated trees raised from wild seed:

var. ROBUSTA (Laws.) Carr. *Pinus deodara* var. *robusta* Laws.—Branchlets stouter, leaves longer and thicker, than in the type. First distributed by Lawson's nursery, Edinburgh, before 1851: var. CRASSIFOLIA Carr. was said to be similar, but with shorter needles and short, stiff branchlets.

var. VIRIDIS Carr.—Leaves more slender than in the preceding, dark green or bottle-green.

It is very doubtful whether the above names ever represented clones. A. F. Mitchell has observed that the commonest variant seen among cultivated trees (raised from wild seed of the earlier introductions) has olive-green, thick needles, pointing forward in half-opened bunches. Such trees are marked with an asterisk in the list of specimens.

The following specimens are known or believed to date from the original introduction in 1831: Walcot Park, Shrops., 110 × 12¾ ft (1959); Dropmore, Bucks., 99 × 12¼ ft (1961), and Bicton, Devon, 97 × 18 ft at 4 ft (1967). Others of large size recorded in recent years are: Bolderwood, Hants, 120 × 9¾ ft (1962); Redleaf, Kent, 106 × 13½ ft*; Bury Hill, Surrey, 114 × 12¾ ft (1954); Stourhead, Wilts., 105 × 14¼ ft (1965)*; Longleat, Wilts., 110 × 12¼ ft (1959); Whitfield, Heref., 110 × 14¼ ft (1963); Pitt House, Devon, 107 × 13¾ ft (1960).

C. LIBANI A. Richard   CEDAR OF LEBANON

C. *libanitica* Trew (a pre-Linnean name)   [PLATE 37

A tree 80 to 120 ft high and 4 to 8 ft in diameter of trunk, pyramidal when young, ultimately flat and spreading at the top, and developing huge horizontal branches; young shoots usually furnished with a minute down. Leaves ¾ to 1¼ in. long, needle-like, but thickest towards the end. Cones 3 to 5 in. long, 2 to 2½ in. wide, barrel-shaped.

Native of the Near East, best known from its historic stands in the Lebanon, but attaining its maximum development in the Cilician Taurus, Turkey, where it forms forests at 4,000 to 7,000 ft; further west it occurs in scattered stands almost as far as the Aegean. Introduced in the seventeenth century, probably between 1670 and 1680, perhaps earlier. Irrespective of its sacred and historical associations, no tree ever introduced to our islands has added more to the charm of gardens than the cedar of Lebanon. Its thick, stately trunk and noble crown of wide-spreading, horizontal branches give to it an air of distinction no other tree at present can rival, although in course of time, perhaps, the Atlas cedar assumes a similar form. The largest specimen on Mount Lebanon is over 40 ft in girth of trunk.

As noted in previous editions, the finest tree recorded by Elwes and Henry grew at Pains Hill near Cobham and measured 115 to 120 ft high with a girth of 26½ ft. This tree no longer exists, but others of good size remain there. The following list of recent measurements includes trees notable in height, girth, or length of bole and some others of which the planting date is known: Petworth, Sussex, 132 × 17½ ft (1961); Fort Belvedere, Windsor, *pl.* 1760, 110 × 18½ ft (1964); Sherborne Castle, Dorset, 120 × 19¾ ft (1963); Highclere, Hants, 122 × 25 ft (1955); Bowood, Wilts., 129 × 18½ ft (1957); Cobham Hall, Kent,

98 × 20½ ft (1965); Claremont, Esher, Surrey, 95 × 20¼ ft (1965); Peper Harrow, Surrey, *pl.* 1735, 90 × 24½ ft (1961); The Whittern, Heref., *pl.* 1810, 80 × 22¾ ft (1963); Dogmersfield Park, Hants, 126 × 16½ ft (1961); Wilton House, Wilts., 93 × 25 and 100 × 23½ ft (1961); Bayfordbury, Herts., *pl.* 1765, 90 × 23½ ft (1962); Powderham Castle, Devon, 92 × 21¼ ft (1963); Whitfield House, Heref., 85 × 22¼ ft (1963); Blenheim Palace, Oxon., 85 × 27 ft and 115 × 23¼ ft (1965).

As will be seen from the above list, the cedar of Lebanon thrives best in the warmer parts of the country; it likes a deep, loamy soil. From London, where the climate suits it admirably, it is excluded by atmospheric pollution, to which it is very sensitive.

f. ARGENTEA (Carr.) Beissn.—Leaves of a very glaucous hue. Reported to be found wild in the Cilician stands.

Both in the Atlas and Lebanon cedars one occasionally sees forms that lose all or most of their leaves in winter. They are usually stiff in habit, short-leaved and slow-growing. It is questionable whether these characters are not merely due to inferior vigour.

var. BREVIFOLIA Hook. f. *C. brevifolia* (Hook. f.) Henry CYPRUS CEDAR. —This differs from the Lebanon cedar in the shorter leaves (¼ to ½ in. long), and in the smaller cylindrical cones; first described in 1879; introduced to Kew two years later. The trees on the mountains of Cyprus average about 40 ft in height. In cultivation the following sizes have been recorded: National Pinetum, Bedgebury, *pl.* 1926, 44 × 2¾ ft (1967); Borde Hill, Sussex, 52 × 3 ft (1958); Wakehurst Place, Sussex, 47 × 2½ and 44 × 3¾ ft (1964); Bicton, Devon, 43 × 3¾ ft (1964); Windsor Great Park, 39 × 1¾ ft (1964). For further information on the Cyprus cedar see the article by J. E. Garfitt in *Quarterly Journal of Forestry*, Vol. 60, July 1966.

The Turkish representatives of *C. libani* are said to be of more columnar habit than those found in the Lebanon, and trees raised from seed collected in the Cilician Taurus in 1903 have proved hardier at the Arnold Arboretum than the true cedar of Lebanon. Schwarz, whose views on the Mediterranean cedars are mentioned in the introductory note, treats the Turkish cedar as a subspecies, but Coode and Cullen remark that the botanical characters he used to distinguish this from subsp. *libani* are not well correlated and consider that the two taxa can hardly be maintained as distinct (*Flora of Turkey*, Vol. 1, pp. 71–2, 1965). See also the note and photographs by P. H. Davis in *Journ. R.H.S.*, Vol. 74, p. 112, and figs. 39 and 40.

CELASTRUS CELASTRACEAE

Vigorous climbers, or shrubs of a loose, spreading habit, with alternate, deciduous leaves. Flowers small, greenish-yellow or white, of little beauty; in terminal or axillary clusters, with the sexes sometimes on separate plants. Fruit very handsome; usually a three-lobed capsule, which when ripe splits open, revealing its highly coloured inner surface and the fleshy covering of the seeds, also highly coloured and known as the aril. The climbing species are admirable for covering rough oak branches 10 to 15 ft high set in the ground, old trees, or for planting anywhere where the twining shoots may firmly attach themselves and secure the plant, yet at the same time allow many of the long, slender shoots to hang unrestrained in free air. No systematic pruning is required except such as is necessary out of considerations of space, and this should be done as soon as the fruits have fallen in winter. Seeds afford an abundant means of propagation, and the plants also layer very freely. All of them are gross feeders, and like a deep, loamy soil.

C. ANGULATUS Maxim.

C. *latifolius* Hemsl.

A deciduous, dioecious shrub of striking appearance and remarkable vigour; ultimately 10 ft high and 20 to 30 ft through, with strong, spreading branches marked with lenticels, becoming corky the second year; pith lamellate. Leaves much larger than in any other hardy species; from 4 to 8 in. long, by 2½ to 6 in. wide; broadly oval or almost orbicular, with a short, abrupt, blunt apex, shallow rounded teeth at the margin, and a short stalk from ½ to 1 in. long. Flowers small, greenish, produced in a terminal panicle 4 to 6 in. long and 2 in. wide. Fruit a roundish, obscurely three-sided capsule ½ in. across; when the valves of the capsule burst open, they show the orange-coloured inner surface and the bright red, fleshy covering of the seeds.

Native of the Hupeh province of China; introduced by Messrs Veitch in 1900. The dioecious character of the species is a disadvantage in gardens, as it is necessary to have two plants to obtain fruits, which with such large, spreading ones as this is not always convenient.

C. FLAGELLARIS Rupr.

A deciduous climber, with slender, hollow twining stems, ultimately 25 ft high; not downy, but armed with short, decurved, hooked spines, in pairs at each joint. Leaves rounded or oval, ¾ to 2¼ in. long, from two-thirds to nearly as wide, the base broadly wedge-shaped, the apex abruptly pointed, the margin set with bristle-like teeth, both sides bright green, and smooth except for minute roughnesses on the veins beneath; stalk up to 1¼ in. long. Flowers small and green; short-stalked, one to three together, axillary on short twigs of the previous year. Capsules orange-yellow; seed-coat red; seeds ripe in October.

Native of Manchuria and Korea; known to botany since 1857, but only introduced to Kew in 1906. It has axillary flowers and fruit like *C. orbiculatus*, but its stems are more slender and crowded, and in a young state at least much more spiny. It is quite distinct from that and other species in the comparatively very long leaf-stalk. It fruits at Kew but is not so handsome as *C. orbiculatus*.

C. GLAUCOPHYLLUS Rehd. & Wils.

A deciduous climber up to 20 ft high, devoid of down in all its parts, the young shoots assuming a brownish purple tinge during their second year. Leaves oval, or obovate, pointed, tapered at the base, edged with shallow incurved teeth; 2 to 4 in. long, 1 to 2½ in. wide; slightly glaucous above, distinctly so beneath; stalk ¼ to ½ in. long. Flowers green, small and inconspicuous, produced a few together in the leaf-axils and in short terminal racemes. Fruits at first egg-shaped, ⅜ in. long, with a short spine-like tip, yellow; when the three-parted outer shell splits, the scarlet-coated seeds are revealed. Pith lamellate.

Native of W. China; discovered by Wilson in 1904, introduced by him in 1908 (No. 952). This species is growing at Kew, but is one of the least vigorous of the celastruses. It does not appear much inclined to twine. Its most distinctive characters are the glaucousness of both sides of the leaves and the combination of terminal and axillary inflorescences. It may be confused with C. hypoleucus but the leaves of that species are even more glaucous beneath and longer stalked, its terminal racemes are up to 8 in. long, and the fruit-stalks are 1¼ in. (or three times as) long.

C. HOOKERI Prain

A deciduous climber up to 20 ft high; young shoots furnished with reddish down (most of which falls away by autumn) and whitish lenticels. Leaves oval to ovate, coarsely toothed, rounded or broadly wedge-shaped at the base, slender-pointed; 3 to 6 in. long, 1½ to 3 in. wide; downy on the midrib and more prominent veins beneath; stalk ¼ to ½ in. long. Flowers inconspicuous, produced in shortly stalked, axillary clusters; stamens glabrous. Fruits ¼ in. long, orange-coloured; seed-coat red.

Native of the Himalaya and China; introduced by Wilson from W. Szechwan (No. 1184) in 1908. The Chinese plant grows vigorously at Kew and is quite hardy there, producing occasionally good crops of its orange-coloured fruits which persist into the new year and are very attractive. The most easily detected distinctive character is the reddish down on the shoots and on the veins of the leaf beneath. It is the only cultivated celastrus with that character. The Himalayan plant (which may not be so hardy as the Chinese one) was long confused with C. STYLOSA Wall. until separated and named by Sir David Prain. C. stylosa is well distinguished by its downy stamens.

C. HYPOLEUCUS (Oliver) Loes.

Erythrospermum hypoleucum Oliver; C. hypoglaucus Hemsl.

A large, deciduous climber up to 20 ft, whose young shoots are covered with a purplish waxy bloom, not downy. Leaves oblong or obovate, glabrous, 4 to 6 in. long, 2 to 2½ in. wide; the apex contracted abruptly into a short point, dark green above, blue-white beneath, the margin toothed. Flowers produced in a long terminal raceme, and in the axils of the uppermost leaves; each flower ¼ in. across, yellowish. Fruit in racemes as much as 8 in. long, about the size of a large pea, green until the valves split open, then showing the yellow interior and the red covering of the seeds.

Native of the provinces of Hupeh and Szechwan in China; discovered by Henry, but introduced by Wilson for Messrs Veitch about 1900. It is hardy at Kew, and is a handsome and distinct climber, well marked by the glaucous under-surface of the leaves and the terminal inflorescence, but does not grow so vigorously as the other species.

C. LOESENERI Rehd. & Wils.

A deciduous climber up to 20 ft high, all the parts without down, producing long, twining young shoots. Leaves oval or broadly ovate, rounded or broadly wedge-shaped at the base, abruptly pointed; shallowly and distantly toothed; 2 to 5½ in. long, 1¼ to 3 in. wide; dull dark green above, very pale beneath; stalk ¼ to ½ in. long. Flowers greenish white, small, usually produced a few together in shortly stalked axillary cymes, rarely in terminal racemes. Fruits yellow, ⅓ in. wide; seed-coat red. Pith lamellate.

Native of Central China; discovered and introduced by Wilson (No. 503) in 1907. This species is very hardy at Kew and one of the most vigorous in the genus; it also has some of the largest leaves. *C. orbiculatus* is closely akin to it, but differs in its thinner, rounder leaves. The celastrus given an Award of Merit as "*C. loeseneri*" when shown in 1931 by the late Sir Frederick Stern later proved to be *C. orbiculatus*. Whether the true *C. loeseneri* is still in cultivation is not certain: the plants so labelled at Kew are not *C. orbiculatus* but their precise identity cannot be established until they flower and fruit.

C. ORBICULATUS Thunb.   [PLATE 36
C. articulatus Thunb.

A strong, vigorous climber, growing 30 to 40 ft high, young stems twining, armed with a pair of spines at each bud in a young state, almost obsolete later; pith solid. Leaves shallow-toothed, 2 to 5 in. long, variable in shape, but usually either obovate or nearly orbicular; with a long, slender apex, or a short, abrupt one, narrowing at the base to a stalk ¼ to 1 in. long. Flowers two to four together in small axillary cymes ½ in. long, each flower ⅙ in. across, green. The fruit is at first a green, pea-shaped, three-valved capsule; but when mature the valves open and turn back, revealing their golden-yellow inner surface and the shining scarlet-coated seeds within. *Bot. Mag.*, t. 9394.

This beautiful climber is widely spread over N.E. Asia, and seeds were first sent to Kew by Prof. Sargent in 1870 and by Dr Bretschneider from Peking in 1883. But the species is by no means so well known as it ought to be, for it is the most striking of all hardy climbers during November, December, and January. At that season each branch is furnished from end to end with hundreds of the brilliantly coloured fruits, which remain for at least two months in full beauty, each branch a wreath of gold and scarlet. Fortunately, the fruits appear to have no attractions for birds. The species is perfectly hardy, and planted in good loam soon makes a fine growth. It may be grown over a pyramid of rough oak branches, or better still, on some decrepit deciduous tree. Once attached to any support round which its stems can twine, it soon makes good its hold. *C. orbiculatus* is said to be completely dioecious in the wild state, but hermaphrodite clones are in commerce. A plant raised from seed may prove to be either wholly male and hence of no value except as a pollinator; or, if female, will not bear fruit without a partner of the opposite sex.

The name *Celastrus articulatus*, so long used for this species, was the result of a printing error on p. 97 of Thunberg's *Flora Japonica*, and *C. orbiculatus*, which appears on p. xlii of that work, is the correct name.

C. ROSTHORNIANUS Loes.

A deciduous scandent shrub up to 20 ft high, not downy in any part, young shoots very slender. Leaves shining green, oval-lanceolate to ovate, narrowly to broadly tapered at the base, pointed, finely toothed; 1½ to 3 in. long, 1 to 1½ in. wide; stalk about ¼ in. long. Fruits the size of a small pea, three- or four-valved, orange yellow; they are borne two or three together in the leaf-axils and have stalks ⅛ to ¼ in. long; seed-coat scarlet.

Native of W. China; introduced by Wilson in 1910 (No. 4187). As seen at Kew this is recognisable by its very slender, often pendulous, branches and shining leaves. It bears large crops of its handsome fruits which, after splitting, remain on the shoots until well into the new year, showing the red-coated seeds. Trained up stout stakes it makes a pleasing graceful thicket. Pith lamellate.

C. RUGOSUS Rehd. & Wils.

A deciduous climber up to 20 ft high; young shoots not downy but furnished thickly with tiny lenticels. Leaves oval or ovate, rather conspicuously toothed, broadly wedge-shaped to rounded at the base, contracted at the apex to a short point; 2½ to 5½ in. long; wrinkled, not downy above, and with small wart-like excrescences or down on the midrib and chief veins beneath; stalk ⅛ to ½ in. long. Flowers small, greenish; solitary, few in axillary clusters, or produced in a short terminal raceme. Fruit ⅓ in. wide, orange-yellow; seed-coat red.

Native of W. China; discovered by Wilson in 1904, introduced to Kew in 1911 (Nos. 1106, 4157). It is very hardy and vigorous, producing annually long shoots thickly set with tiny warts and occasionally fine crops of its handsome fruits. Its wrinkled leaves, very strongly veined beneath and frequently warted on the midrib, make it distinct. The pith is lamellate.

C. SCANDENS L.   STAFF TREE

A deciduous dioecious shrub with twining branches, climbing over trees, shrubs, hedges, etc., in a wild state; pith solid. Leaves ovate or obovate or broad-elliptical, 2 to 4 in. long, finely and irregularly toothed; the apex sharply pointed and either short and abrupt or long and tapering. Flowers in terminal racemes or panicles, small, yellowish white, of little beauty. Fruit in heavy, cylindrical masses 2 or 3 in. long, each fruit at first the size of a large pea with three valves, which eventually split open and show their orange-coloured inner surface, and at the same time expose the brilliant scarlet pulpy covering of the seeds. It is then an object of singular beauty.

Introduced by Peter Collinson in 1736, this climber has never become widely cultivated. Apparently it does not fruit with the freedom that renders it one of the most beautiful autumnal plants of the eastern United States, where it is a native. Most, if not all, plants are unisexual, so that one of each sex should be planted together to form one tangle. Visitors to Niagara Falls will recall the grace and beauty of this climber on Goat Island, where it is very abundant, and, along with *Vitis aestivalis*, gives an effect of almost tropical luxuriance.

C. VANIOTII (Lévl.) Rehd.
Sarauja vaniotii Lévl.; *C. spiciformis* Rehd. & Wils.

I do not know that the true plant of this name is in cultivation. It is a native of W. China and was discovered by Wilson in 1900, but he does not appear to have collected seed. The form in cultivation is known as:

var. LAEVIS (Rehd. & Wils.) Rehd. *C. spiciformis* var. *laevis* Rehd. & Wils.— A deciduous climber up to 20 ft high with glabrous young shoots. Leaves oval or ovate, rounded or broadly wedge-shaped at the base, slender-pointed; margins round-toothed, sometimes very closely and regularly so; 2 to 4½ in. long, 1½ to 3 in. wide; dark green above, paler beneath, glabrous on both sides; stalk ½ to ⅝ in. long. Flowers yellowish white, small, produced in slender, terminal panicles 3 to 5 in. long, often supplemented by clusters in the uppermost leaf-axils. Fruit ¼ in. wide, orange-yellow, three-valved; seed-coat dark brown, shining.

Native of W. Szechwan, China; introduced in 1911 to Kew (No. 1176, Wilson), where it has proved very hardy and vigorous. It resembles *C. hypoleucus* in its long, slender terminal inflorescence, but the leaves of that species are very glaucous beneath and the fruit-stalks are twice as long. The typical *C. vaniotii* apparently differs chiefly from this variety in its leaves being downy on the midrib and veins beneath.

CELTIS   NETTLE-TREES   ULMACEAE

A group of deciduous, unarmed trees, sometimes shrubs, allied to the elms, consisting of fifty to sixty species, a small proportion only of which are hardy. They are found in S.E. Europe, the Near East, N. America, and China. Leaves alternate, mostly three-veined, and unequal-sided at the base. The nettle-trees have no beauty of flower, these being small and greenish; the flowers are unisexual, but both sexes occur on the same tree, the male or pollen-bearing ones a few together in a cluster near the base of the new growths; the seed-bearing or female flowers solitary, or two or three together in the axils of the young leaves. Fruit a drupe, solitary on a slender stalk, one-seeded. The fruit affords the best distinction between the nettle-trees and the elms, the latter having dry, winged fruits.

As garden trees the species of *Celtis* make elegant and shapely specimens, yet of no particular merit or beauty, except that the leaves of several of them turn bright yellow in autumn. In warmer countries the timber is valuable, especially that of *C. australis*. The fruit of this species is sweet, and is said to have been the lotus of the ancients—that delicious fruit which constituted the food of the Lotophagi, and made those who ate it forget their own country (*Treasury of Botany*, i., p. 245). Other species have fruits edible in their native countries.

The nettle-trees like a good loamy soil and a well-drained position. They are best propagated by seeds, but when these are not obtainable grafting on stocks of *C. occidentalis* must be resorted to. Seeds of this species, if they do not ripen here, are always obtainable from American seedsmen.

There is little to distinguish the different cultivated species in a general way, except the leaves. Of those here dealt with, *C. glabrata* and *C. bungeana* are distinct in having no down on the leaves; *C. laevigata* is the only one with uniformly or nearly uniformly entire leaves; and *C. australis* has lanceolate, very downy leaves.

C. AUSTRALIS L.

A tree up to 50 or 70 ft high, with a grey, smooth, beech-like trunk, sometimes 10 ft. in girth; young shoots hairy. Leaves lanceolate or ovate-lanceolate, wedge-shaped at the base, rounded on vigorous shoots, the apex long-tapering, often tail-like, coarsely toothed; 2 to 5 in. long, ⅝ to 1½ in. wide; upper side covered with short, stiff hairs which partially fall away, leaving bases which roughen the surface; covered beneath with soft down; stalk downy, ¼ to ½ in. long. Fruit globose, ⅓ to ½ in. long, reddish then brown, on a very slender stalk about 1 in. long.

Native of S. Europe and the Orient; cultivated in England since the sixteenth century by Gerard and others, but never common. I have raised it several times from seed obtained from various places in S. Europe; but although it makes coarse growths 4 or 5 ft long during summer, these are cut back almost to the base by moderately severe frost. As this is repeated every winter, the base becomes stunted and diseased, and the trees rarely survive more than a few years.

A more recent introduction is hardier but grows very slowly. The large trees mentioned by Loudon in 1838 as being at Kew and elsewhere were probably some other species. What it lacks here, no doubt, is the ripening influences on the wood of its native sunshine. In the south of Europe it is believed to attain the age of one thousand years, and its timber is tough and valuable. In the suburbs of Italian and Dalmatian cities I have seen it as a pleasing small street tree, with neat, rounded heads and smooth, handsome trunks. There are fine specimens of this tree in the Botanic Garden, Madrid. The leaves of young seedling trees are often blotched quite conspicuously with yellow.

In the British Isles no examples of any size have been recorded. Elwes and Henry mention a tree at Hursley Park near Winchester, then (1908) of some

age and about 20 ft high; it still exists and is about 20 ft taller. The small tree
at Tortworth, Glos., also referred to by them, now measures 35 × 3 ft (1964).

C. BIONDII Pampan.

A deciduous tree up to 45 ft high, often a large shrub; young shoots rusty-
downy at first, becoming almost or quite glabrous by the end of the season.
Leaves ovate to narrowly oval, pointed (sometimes slenderly), tapered to
rounded at the base, more or less coarsely toothed towards the apex or toothless;
1½ to 4 in. long; downy at first but almost or quite glabrous by autumn; stalk
⅛ to ¼ in. long. Fruit solitary, in pairs or in threes, globose or slightly tapered
towards the top, orange-coloured, ¼ in. long. on a stalk about twice the length.

Native of Central China; in cultivation at Kew since 1902. It resembles C.
bungeana in its leaves being toothed above the middle only and in the short leaf-
stalks, but that species has black or purplish-black fruits. The tree at Kew, planted
in 1902, now measures 35 × 3½ ft (1967).

C. BUNGEANA Blume
C. davidiana Carr.

A tree 30 to 45 ft high, forming a rounded, bushy head; young shoots slightly
downy at first, becoming glabrous by autumn. Leaves ovate or ovate-lanceolate,
2 to 3½ in. long, 1 to 1¾ in. wide; rounded, unequal sided, and three-nerved at
the base; taper-pointed, with a few remote teeth towards the apex only, sometimes almost entire; dark glossy green and glabrous above, paler and glossy
beneath, with small tufts of down in the lower vein-axils; stalk ¼ to ⅓ in. long,
slightly downy. Fruits egg-shaped, black, on slender stalks ¾ in. long.

Native of N. China in mountainous regions; also found by Henry in the
mountains of Hupeh. It was introduced to Kew in 1882, by means of seed sent
by Dr Bretschneider, and collected on the hills north of Peking. It is extremely
rare in cultivation, but is a notable and handsome species, very distinct in its lustrous, almost glabrous leaves. (See also C. glabrata.)

C. SINENSIS Pers., is similar in the hard texture and very glossy upper
surface of its leaves to C. bungeana, but its young shoots are clothed with minute
hairs and the obliquely ovate leaves are conspicuously toothed towards the
apex. The two are closely akin. A native of China and Japan, introduced in
1910. A specimen at Kew, planted in 1923, now measures 35 × 4¼ ft (1967).

C. JESSOENSIS Koidz.—A tree to 70 ft high in Japan and Korea. It may be
distinguished from C. bungeana, to which it is related, by its sharply toothed
leaves, glaucous beneath and slightly downy, especially on the veins. It was
introduced to the Arnold Arboretum in 1892.

C. CAUCASICA Willd.

A medium-sized tree with a greyish trunk and limbs, and a bushy head of
branches; young shoots downy. Leaves obliquely ovate or ovate-lanceolate,

slenderly (often rather abruptly) pointed, coarsely toothed; 2½ to 4 in. long, broadly wedge-shaped at the base; upper surface covered when young with short, bristle-like hairs which mostly fall away, leaving it slightly rough; lower surface covered at first with softer down, most of which also falls away except on the midrib and veins; stalk downy, ¼ to ½ in. long. Fruit ⅓ in. diameter, yellow, borne on a slender stalk about 1 in. long.

Native of Afghanistan, N. India, Caucasus, etc.; raised at Kew from seed sent from Afghanistan by Dr Aitchison when he was attached to the Delimitation Commission (1884–5). It is very closely allied to *C. australis*, but is evidently a much hardier tree, and far better adapted for cultivation in the south of England. It differs from that species in its comparatively shorter, broader leaves with less drawn-out points, less downy, and usually more coarsely toothed.

C. GLABRATA Planch.

A small tree or shrub with a rounded head of branches; young shoots furnished at first with minute scattered down, becoming quite glabrous later. Leaves obliquely ovate; 1 to 2¼ in. long, ⅝ to 1⅜ in. wide; markedly unequal-sided at the base, being usually rounded on one side the stalk and tapered on the other; the apex pointed; margins set with large, incurved teeth except near the base; upper surface dark green, not downy, but covered with minute warts which render it rough; lower surface paler and smooth, except for scattered minute bristles on the veins, only visible under the lens. Fruits globose, reddish brown, ⅙ in. diameter, on stalks ½ to 1 in. long.

Native of the Caucasus and Asia Minor; introduced to Kew from Van Volxem's nursery in 1870. The species had no doubt been introduced to cultivation by Jean Van Volxem, who had collected plants in the Caucasus about ten years previously. It is distinct from the other species except *C. bungeana*, in its glabrous leaves, and from that species is distinguished by the conspicuous incurved teeth extending almost all round the margins. There is an example at Kew measuring 35 × 4½ ft (1967), *pl.* 1879.

C. TOURNEFORTII Lam.—A shrub or small tree to 20 ft high, related to the preceding but easily distinguished by its leaves, which are blue- or grey-green above, downy beneath, with broad, blunt teeth. Native of Sicily, the Balkans, Asia Minor, and the Crimea. Although introduced in the eighteenth century, it is little known in this country; on the continent, according to Krüssmann (*Handbuch der Laubholzkunde*, 1960), it makes a picturesque small tree and colours well in the autumn.

C. KORAIENSIS Nakai

A deciduous tree up to 40 ft high, or a bush; young shoots glabrous. Leaves usually more or less obovate, sometimes roundish or even oval, broadly tapered or rounded and oblique at the base; toothed at the sides, jaggedly and more coarsely toothed (almost lobed) at the broad apex, where the midrib often elongates into a slender, awl-shaped lobe; 2 to 5 in. long, 1¼ to 3 in. wide;

dullish dark green and glabrous above, strongly and longitudinally veined beneath, downy on the veins; stalk ⅛ to ¼ in. long. Fruit roundish oval, nearly ½ in. long, dull orange, borne on a stalk ⅝ to ¾ in. long.

Native of Korea, Manchuria and N. China; introduced to Kew in 1920. In a difficult genus, this is well distinguished by the shape of the leaves and the unusually large fruit. The end of the leaf (often its widest part) has a curiously jagged, bitten-off appearance, quite distinct from the leaves, so far as I have seen, of any other cultivated nettle-tree.

C. LABILIS Schneid.

A deciduous tree 40 to 60 ft high, its trunk 3 to 6 ft in girth, the bark smooth and pale grey; young shoots yellowish, densely downy. Leaves ovate to ovate-lanceolate, obliquely rounded at the base, the apex shortly but often slenderly pointed, rather coarsely toothed except towards the base; 1½ to 4 in. long, half as much wide; dark glossy green and slightly downy above, duller and paler beneath. The pale-coloured veins are downy and the rest of the under-surface thinly downy or glabrous; stalk ⅛ to ⅓ in. long, very downy. Fruit orange-coloured, smooth, globose, scarcely ⅓ in. wide, produced in pairs or threes; fruit-stalks downy, ¼ in. long.

Native of China in W. Hupeh and E. Szechwan; introduced by Wilson to the Arnold Arboretum in 1907 (No. 444), and to Kew the following year. Wilson remarks that it is easily recognised by the small, fruit-bearing branchlets dropping off in entirety when the fruits are ripe.

C. LAEVIGATA Willd.   SUGARBERRY
C. mississippiensis Bosc

A tree 60 to 80 ft high in its native country, with a trunk 6 to 9 ft in girth; young shoots soon glabrous. Leaves 3 in. long, 1¼ in. wide; lanceolate or oval-lanceolate; rounded or wedge-shaped, unequal and three-nerved at the base; long and taper-pointed; margins entire or nearly so; dark green, and soon quite glabrous above, paler beneath, with scattered hairs on the veins and tufts of down in the vein-axils; stalks at first downy then glabrous, ¼ to ½ in. long. Fruit egg-shaped, ¼ in. long, orange-red.

Native of the southern United States; very rare in cultivation. There are two trees at Kew, raised from seed sent by Prof. Sargent in 1877, which both now measure about 40 × 4¼ ft (1967). It is distinct from all other cultivated species by its leaves being without teeth or with only a few.

var. SMALLII (Beadle) Sarg. C. smallii Beadle—A smaller tree than the type, with sharply toothed leaves, found in the S.E. United States. There is an example at Kew measuring 45 × 4½ ft (1967).

C. OCCIDENTALIS L.   HACKBERRY

A tree normally 30 to 40 ft high in the wild state, but taller in the rich alluvial soils of the Mississippi Basin; bark grey, rough, with warty excrescences; young branchlets glabrous or downy. Leaves ovate-lanceolate to broadly ovate, rounded or heart-shaped at the base, taper-pointed, 2 to 4½ in. long, sharply toothed, smooth or scabrous above, downy on the midrib and the veins beneath. Fruit ⅓ in. across, globose, yellowish or reddish, finally dark purple when ripe, borne on a slender stalk ½ to ⅔ in. long

Native of the United States from the Atlantic to the Rocky Mountains, and of E. Canada. This tree is variable in regard to stature, foliage, form and colour of fruit, etc.; but these variations although great are not clearly correlated. East of the Appalachians it makes a small tree with broadly ovate leaves, more or less rounded at the base. This is the typical state, introduced in 1656. In var. CANINA (Raf.) Sarg., the leaves are more narrowly ovate and finely tapered at the apex. More distinct is:

var. CORDATA (Pers.) Willd. *C. o.* var. *crassifolia* (Lam.) Gray—This is chiefly distinguished by its invariably downy young shoots, and its often heart-shaped, much larger leaves (2 to 6 in. long, 1 to 3 in. wide), very rough on the upper surface. In cultivation this is a vigorous tree, making arching or pendulous shoots several feet long in a season, clothed with big leaves sometimes as much as 7 in. by 4½ in.

This variety is commonest west of the Appalachians. It also appears to be the form in which the species is most commonly seen in cultivation in Europe. It was introduced, according to Loudon, in 1812, but probably earlier.

C. PUMILA (Muhl.) Pursh *C. occidentalis* var. *pumila* Muhl.—A shrub or small tree to 15 ft high. Leaves smaller than in *C. occidentalis*, downy on both sides when young, later glabrous; margins almost untoothed. It ranges to the west (Colorado, Utah, etc.) and was introduced to Kew from the Arnold Arboretum in 1905.

C. RETICULATA Torr.

A small deciduous tree 30 to 40 ft high, sometimes shrubby; young shoots covered thickly with outstanding down. Leaves obliquely ovate, rounded or heart-shaped at the base, pointed, toothed except at the base, often entire on adult plants; 1½ to 4½ in. long, 1 to 3 in. wide; pale bright green, rough to the touch and with scarcely any down above; very downy on the midrib and veins, and conspicuously net-veined beneath; stalk ¼ to ⅔ in. long. Fruit globose, ⅓ in. wide, orange-red, borne on a slender downy stalk ⅓ to ½ in. long.

Native of the S.W. United States (Texas, etc.); originally described in 1828. On young trees introduced from the Arnold Arboretum in 1920, the leaves are more downy and more conspicuously toothed than in adult fruit-bearing specimens collected in the wild; the latter have leaves toothed only near the apex or are quite toothless. The strong venation of the leaves is a prominent characteristic of this tree.

CEPHALANTHUS RUBIACEAE

A genus of seventeen species scattered through N. and Central America, E. Asia, and Africa. Only the N. American species described here is cultivated in the British Isles and is one of the few hardy woody species in the family Rubiaceae; others are *Mitchella repens*, *Emmenopterys henryi*, and some of the coprosmas. By some authorities, *Cephalanthus* and nine other genera of Rubiaceae are grouped in a separate family—Naucleaceae.

C. OCCIDENTALIS L. BUTTONBUSH

A deciduous shrub from 3 to 6 ft, occasionally 10 to 15 ft high, with glabrous, shining, olive-green young stems. Leaves opposite, in pairs or in threes, oval or ovate, 2 to 5 in. long, about half or scarcely half as wide; tapering at both ends, glabrous and glossy dark green above, paler and slightly downy on the midrib and veins beneath; stalks ¼ to ¾ in. long. Flowers small, crowded in quite globular heads 1 to 1¼ in. across, or, including the projecting styles, ⅜ in. more; these heads are borne at the end of the shoot solitary or in fours, often supplemented by others in the uppermost leaf-axils. Corolla creamy white, with a slender tube and four rounded lobes; style very long.

Native of the eastern United States and Canada; introduced in 1735. It reaches from New Brunswick to Florida, and the same species is said to occur in Cuba. It is usually found in moist situations, and in cultivation is averse to dryness at the root; it thrives well in a peaty soil. Flowering in August, it is desirable on that account, and although not showy, is interesting as one of the few hardy shrubby plants in the large family to which it belongs. It possesses bitter, tonic properties similar to those of its ally, the cinchona (quinine) plant. It is best propagated from imported seeds, the plants so raised thriving better than those raised from cuttings or layers.

CEPHALOTAXUS CEPHALOTAXACEAE

A group of small evergreen trees and shrubs, all natives of E. Asia. They resemble the yews in the shape and general disposition of the foliage but most botanists consider them distinct enough to rank as a separate family—the Cephalotaxaceae. They have erect stems, from which the branches are borne in tiers, whilst the branchlets are both alternate and opposite. Flowers unisexual, the sexes nearly always on separate plants. Male flowers composed of four to six stamens, enclosed in a bract, produced in April and May in the axils of the leaves of the previous year's growth, and arranged in clusters of small globose heads. Female flowers composed of pairs of carpels in the axils of scales at the base of the branchlets. Fruits (seeds) olive-like with a fleshy coat surrounding an almond-shaped resinous kernel (seed). The members of this genus bear a considerable resemblance to the torreyas, but differ in the leaves being soft rather than prickly pointed, and in the flowers being crowded instead of solitary in each leaf-axil. Another point of difference is that in the torreyas the stomata are arranged in narrow sunken bands.

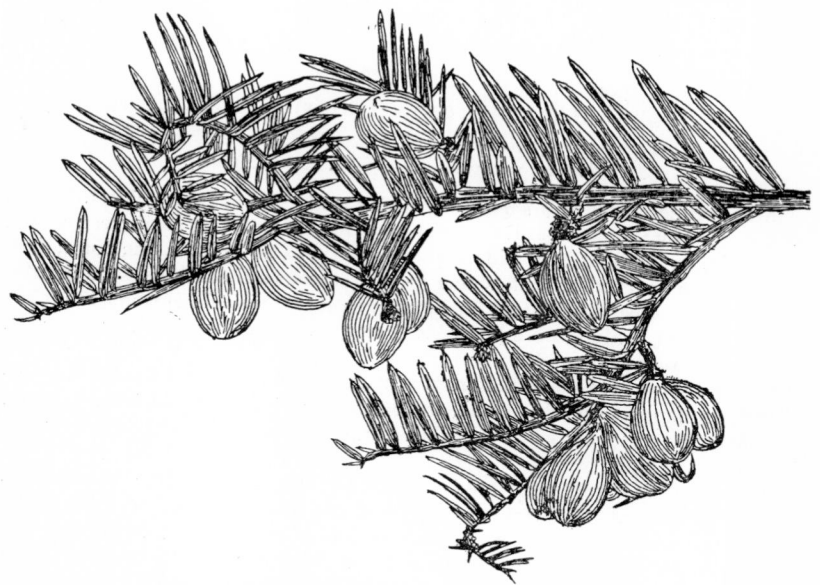

CEPHALOTAXUS HARRINGTONIA var. DRUPACEA

In gardens the species of *Cephalotaxus* are useful evergreens, especially for semi-shaded places, where they thrive better than in full sunshine. All those mentioned below are hardy and can be increased by cuttings, although seed should be preferred if obtainable. Female trees will sometimes develop fruit and infertile seed in the absence of pollen.

C. FORTUNI Hook.

A small tree with one or more erect stems giving off at intervals whorls of branches, and rarely seen more than 10 to 20 ft high in cultivation; branchlets forked. Leaves spreading in two opposite ranks, often almost horizontally, 2 to 3½ in. long, ⅛ in. or a little more wide; linear, tapering to a fine point, rich glossy green above, with two pale bands beneath, each composed of about twenty stomatic lines, and a green raised midrib. Male flowers in globose heads ¼ in. across. Fruit 1⅛ in. long, ¾ in. wide, oval, brown. *Bot. Mag.*, t. 4499.

Native of N. China; introduced by Robert Fortune in 1849. There is some difficulty in properly differentiating this from *C. harringtonia*, but it would seem to have longer, comparatively more slender leaves, farther apart on the branchlet, and with finer, longer points. The lines of stomata beneath are more numerous; the male flower-heads solitary or few on a stalk. Specimens gathered from the plants raised from Fortune's seed have more slender and less divided branchlets than *C. harringtonia*. I am inclined to think many of the so-called *C. fortuni* of the present day are really the other species. The true thing is a handsome and striking evergreen. The plants distributed in the last century as *C. "fortuni foemina"* are *C. harringtonia* var. *sinensis*.

C. HARRINGTONIA (Forbes) K. Koch

Taxus harringtonia Forbes; *C. pedunculata* Sieb. & Zucc.;
C. drupacea var. *pedunculata* (Sieb. & Zucc.) Miq.

A spreading shrub or a small tree, with mostly alternate branchlets. Leaves in two opposite ranks not all in the same plane, some being semi-erect; linear, ¾ to 2½ in. long, about ⅛ in. wide, rather abruptly narrowed to a fine point; dark green above, marked beneath with a broad glaucous strip each side the midrib, composed of fifteen to eighteen fine lines of stomata. Male flowers in a branched cluster ¾ to 1¼ in. long on a peduncle ¼ to 1 in. long. Fruit oval, or obovoid, about 1 in. long.

C. harringtonia was described from a male plant belonging to what was apparently a Japanese garden clone, introduced to Europe by Siebold in 1829. In cultivation it makes as a rule a rather low, spreading bush—the tallest at Kew is about 14 ft high.

C. harringtonia is very near in its characters to the wild Japanese cephalotaxus which Siebold and Zuccarini named *C. drupacea* and may indeed be part of the normal variation of that species. Unfortunately, the name *C. harringtonia* has priority, and if the two are to be regarded as at the most varietally distinct, which botanists now consider to be the case, then *C. drupacea* must take the subordinate position as:

var. DRUPACEA (Sieb. & Zucc.) Koidzumi *C. drupacea* Sieb. & Zucc.— This differs from the type only in its generally shorter leaves and more shortly stalked male aments. Native of Japan and Korea; introduced to Europe by Siebold in 1829. It is a rather handsome evergreen of yew-like character but bolder in foliage and not so densely furnished. *Bot. Mag.*, t. 8285.

cv. 'FASTIGIATA'.—A very interesting and distinct form, analogous in its mode of growth to the Irish Yew. The branches and branchlets are quite erect, sparsely divided, all the leaves being arranged spirally like those of the leading shoot of the type, and mostly decurved. The shrub is slow-growing, and of sturdy, columnar shape when young; useful for positions where a formal habit is desired. I have seen, however, large specimens in Italy and Dalmatia that assume a more open, spreading form (like old Irish yews), with a tendency to revert to the typical, distichous-leaved form at the base. Although long cultivated in Japan, this clone probably originated in Korea, as the Japanese name 'Chosen-maki' implies.

var. SINENSIS (Rehd. & Wils.) Rehd. *C. drupacea* var. *sinensis* Rehd. & Wils.; *C. sinensis* (Rehd. & Wils.) Li—This variety much resembles var. *drupacea* but has the leaves acuminate rather than abruptly mucronate. When collecting seed of *C. fortuni*, Fortune's Chinese collectors mixed it with seed taken from trees of this variety; the rogue plants were recognised as distinct when the seed was raised and were named "*C. fortuni foemina*" (see Fortune's own account of the confusion in *Gard. Chron.*, 1863, p. 1134).

cv. 'SPHAERALIS'.—A form with quite globular fruits described by Dr Masters from a tree growing in the garden of the Rev. J. Goring at Steyning, Sussex. (*Gard. Chron.*, 1884, p. 113 and fig. 23.)

C. OLIVERI Mast.

A Chinese species, first found on Mount Omei, in Szechwan, by the Rev. E. Faber, and in 1900 by Wilson, who sent home seeds. I only know of it as a low bush of sturdy habit, with flat, stiffly spreading branches. Leaves ¾ to 1 in. long, ⅛ to ⅙ in. wide; linear, curving slightly towards the end of the shoot, terminated abruptly in a short, stiff point; the base slightly the broadest part of the leaf, and truncate with rounded corners; the leaves are arranged on the twigs in two flat, quite horizontal ranks, very stiff, and so close together that the margins touch; dark green above, paler green at the margins and centre beneath, with two glaucous strips, each composed of about fifteen lines of stomata. Fruit (only seen in native specimens) egg-shaped, conspicuously tapered at the ends, 1¼ in. long, ¾ in. wide, borne on a stalk ½ in. long. A striking evergreen, especially in the close, stiff, comb-like arrangement of the leaves.

CERATOSTIGMA   PLUMBAGINACEAE

A genus consisting of about eight species of shrubs or herbaceous plants, the cultivated species of which come from China and the Himalaya. The generic name refers to the horn-like outgrowths on the stigma.

C. GRIFFITHII C. B. Clarke

A low, densely branched, evergreen shrub; young shoots covered with forwardly directed bristles. Leaves alternate, obovate, short-pointed, tapered at the base; ½ to 1¼ in. long, ¼ to ⅝ in. wide; dull green with purplish margins, covered on both surfaces with appressed bristles and (beneath especially) with tiny pale scales; margins bristly; stalk very short. Flowers produced from August onwards in terminal clusters ½ to 1 in. across; corolla bright blue; calyx tubular, ⅜ in. long, bristly, with five awl-shaped teeth.

Native of the E. Himalaya and Yunnan. It has been introduced from the latter province of China by Forrest, but is too tender to be grown satisfactorily in most parts of the kingdom. At Kew it suffers in severe weather, even against a wall. It is well distinguished from *C. willmottianum*, which has longer, more diamond-shaped, slender-pointed, less bristly leaves and less bristly shoots. To the inflorescences of both a spiky character is given by the erect, finely pointed bracts and teeth of the calyx.

C. MINUS Prain
C. polhillii Bulley

This species was first raised in this country by A. K. Bulley from seed sent to him by Polhill-Turner, a missionary stationed at Tatsien-lu, W. China, whose name it first bore in gardens. The first valid description of it was given in the *Journal of Botany*, 1906, p. 7, in an article on the genus by Sir David Prain, when it was named *C. minus*.

It is a deciduous shrub usually 1½ to 3 ft high, with obovate leaves rounded or blunt at the apex, tapered to a very short stalk, ¾ to 1½ in. long, scaly and with appressed bristles beneath, glabrous or nearly so above, bristly on the margins. The flowers are closely packed in terminal and axillary heads on which they open successively from late summer to October. Wilson, Forrest, and Kingdon Ward all describe them as 'bright blue', and the last-named says in addition 'calyx crimson'. The plants cultivated in the R.H.S. Garden at Wisley bear pale blue flowers. The inflorescence is furnished with spiky bracts like the other species.

The species is most nearly allied to *C. griffithii*, but that is very distinct by reason of the bristly character of the upper surface of the leaf. *C. willmottianum* is also bristly on both surfaces of its leaves, and they are lanceolate to rhomboid in shape and always tapered at the apex. Delavay first found *C. minus* in Yunnan about 1884, where Forrest also collected it later. Wilson saw it in Szechwan. In hardiness it is intermediate between the other two; that is to say it will be happiest in the sunny gardens of the south, and best planted against a wall.

C. WILLMOTTIANUM Stapf [PLATE 40

A deciduous shrub 2 to 4 ft high; young stems angled, sometimes purplish, furnished with forward-pointing bristles. Leaves alternate, stalkless, lanceolate to diamond shaped; 1 to 2 in. long, ⅓ to ¾ in. wide, bristly on both surfaces. Flowers closely packed in terminal heads, opening successively for three or four months in summer and autumn from the axils of slender lanceolate, pointed bracts which are ⅓ to ½ in. long, ¾ in. wide and edged with stiff bristles; the corolla has a slender, pale tube ¾ in. long and five spreading obovate lobes which are bright blue except at the base where they are white; anthers purple; calyx five-lobed, the lobes (or teeth) awl-shaped. *Bot. Mag.*, t. 8591.

Native of W. Szechwan, where Wilson found it in 1908 abundant in the semi-arid regions of the Min River valley. Miss Willmott raised two plants from his seed and from these the present stock in this country has mainly or wholly been derived. It is easily increased by late summer cuttings. It produces a long succession of prettily coloured flowers from July onwards. At Kew the semi-woody stems usually die to the ground, but a fresh crop springs up freely every year. In mild gardens, where the season's wood usually survives the winter, it should be pruned hard early in the spring. An attractive plant which needs a sunny position and grows well on chalky soils.

C. PLUMBAGINOIDES Bunge *Plumbago larpentae* Lindl.; *Valoradia plumbaginoides* (Bunge) Boiss.—This is the only other species much grown in the open air in this country. Being more herbaceous than shrubby, it scarcely comes within our province. It has brilliant blue flowers of a deeper hue than Miss Willmott's species and grows 1 to 1½ ft high only. The leaves differ in being larger, and obovate rather than lanceolate in outline and bristly at the margins only—the surfaces are glabrous or bear only a few scattered hairs. They often turn red in autumn and then make a striking background to the flowers, but in gardens with a short growing-season this species may prove a disappointment. Native of China; introduced in 1846 to Sir Geo. Larpent's garden at Roehampton. *Bot. Mag.*, n.s., t. 210.

CERCIDIPHYLLUM CERCIDIPHYLLACEAE

The position of *Cercidiphyllum* among the flowering plants has been the subject of much study and dispute and is still unsettled. The centre of the controversy lies in the inconspicuous apetalous female flower. The view that has long prevailed is that it consists of a calyx and a number of free carpels each with its own style and thus represents, though in a much-reduced and congested form, the same floral structure as is found in *Magnolia*, *Liriodendron*, and their allies. In this interpretation, *Cercidiphyllum* would belong to the Magnoliaceae, or constitute a small related family either on its own or as part, with *Trochodendron* and perhaps *Euptelea*, in the Trochodendraceae: but its affinities would lie, whatever its rank, within the Order Magnoliales. A quite contrary view is expressed by Swamy and Bailey (*Journ. Arn. Arb.*, Vol. 30, 1949, pp. 187–210), who hold that what other researchers have regarded as the female flower is really a congested inflorescence, made up of as many individual flowers as there are carpels in the other interpretation, and each subtended by a single bract. If this theory were correct, *Cercidiphyllum* would have to be regarded as a relic of some primitive type of flowering plant, not related to any other now living. This view has, however, been rejected by Dr Hutchinson (*The Genera of Flowering Plants*, Vol. 1, 1964), who recognises the distinctness of *Cercidiphyllum* by placing it in a separate family, the Cercidiphyllaceae, but within the Magnolia alliance, where it is 'perhaps most nearly related to the genus *Liriodendron*'.

C. JAPONICUM Sieb. & Zucc.   KATSURA TREE [PLATE 38

A deciduous tree of the largest size, often 100 ft high in its native state, with pendulous branches and a spirally twisted, furrowed trunk. The trunk is sometimes solitary, and 3 to 4 ft through, but more often the tree is made up of a group of several smaller stems. Leaves mostly opposite, but sometimes alternate towards the base of the shoot, broadly ovate or heart-shaped, 2 to 4 in. long, slightly scalloped on the margin, and glabrous except when young. The branch in its second year develops at each joint a short or almost obsolete twig, carrying a single leaf and flowers. The male and female flowers are borne on separate trees, but neither possesses any beauty; the males consist of a minute calyx and an indefinite number of stamens $\frac{1}{2}$ in. long; the females of four larger, but still very small, green, fringed sepals, and four to six carpels (but in another nterpretation these 'flowers' are inflorescences). The fruits are small pods, $\frac{1}{2}$ to $\frac{3}{4}$ in. long, borne usually two to four together on a short stalk.

This tree for a long time was thought to be confined to Japan, where it is the largest of deciduous trees, reaching its finest development in the island of Yezo; but Wilson found it in China in 1910. One tree, still living, but with its top fallen away, he found to be 55 ft in girth of trunk. The timber is light, straight-grained and yellowish, and is highly valued. The finest trees I have seen in Europe were in the Imperial Garden at Sans Souci, near Berlin, where there was, in 1908, a singularly elegant tree 30 ft high, with slender, spreading, arching branches. It succeeds equally well in the Royal Garden at Hanover. Still finer trees, but of denser habit, are in the Arnold Arboretum, Mass. It is very hardy and evidently likes a continental climate. At Kew, where it was introduced in 1881, it is not a success. Like so many other North Asiatic trees introduced to this country, it commences to grow early in spring, and its young shoots are almost invariably ruined by frost; sometimes even the second growths meet the same fate. The tree is very valuable where late spring frosts do not prevail. The generic name refers to the resemblance of the leaves to those of the Judas-tree (*Cercis*).

The following are among the finest examples of this tree recorded recently: Westonbirt, Glos., 61 × 3 + 2$\frac{3}{4}$ ft, 56 × 3$\frac{3}{4}$ ft and 58 × 3$\frac{1}{2}$ ft (1967); Lanarth, Cornwall, *pl.* 1908, 55 ft high on four stems, the thickest 3$\frac{3}{4}$ ft in girth and with a spread of 64 ft (1966); Ashbourne House, Co. Cork, Eire, 52 ft high on two stems each 4$\frac{3}{4}$ ft in girth (1966).

The Chinese form of this tree has been named var. SINENSE by Rehder and Wilson (see *Plantae Wilsonianae*, Vol. 1, p. 316). According to Wilson it differs from the Japanese type, which usually forms several trunks near the ground, in nearly always being confined to a single stem. The authors regard the leaf-stalk of var. *sinense* as shorter and the leaf itself not so markedly cordate as in the Japanese tree, but judging by a large series of specimens from both countries at Kew these differences are not very reliable. Wilson found trees up to 130 ft high and describes them as exceeding in girth and height all other deciduous, non-coniferous trees known from China.

In earlier editions of this work it was suggested that var. *sinense* turns red in the autumn and the Japanese type yellow, but now that the Chinese variety is better known it can be said with fair certainty that there is no difference between them in this respect. The autumn colouring of *C. japonicum* is in fact very variable both in tint and timing. The late Mark Fenwick, who planted many at Abbotswood in Gloucestershire, wrote (*Journ. R.H.S.*, Vol. 65, 1940, p. 167): 'One never knows when Cercidiphyllums are going to turn or what colour they will assume. Here they are seldom all red or all yellow, but generally assume shades of red, orange, pale yellow, pale pink, mauve and green.'

var. MAGNIFICUM Nakai *C. magnificum* (Nakai) Nakai—In this variety the leaves tend on the average to be larger than in the type, more rounded in outline and more cordate at the base; seeds slightly longer, winged at both ends. It makes a smaller tree than the type and differs too in its bark, which remains smooth until the tree is of some age. Native of the main island of Japan, where it occurs in scattered localities in the mountains; first described in 1920. There is a specimen about 25 ft high in Windsor Great Park and younger trees in the Kew collection.

CERCIS LEGUMINOSAE

The members of this genus, seven in number, constitute a very distinct and homogeneous group of hardy leguminous trees and shrubs whose resemblances to each other are as marked as are their differences from the other genera of the family Leguminosae. Their leaves furnish the most distinctive feature of the genus, being alternate, simple, entire, prominently five- or seven-nerved, broad and rounded, with a heart-shaped base, and from 2 to 6 in. long. The flowers in most of the species come in fasciculate clusters on wood one to many years old; but one Chinese species (*C. racemosa*) has them in racemes. The petals are nearly equal, but arranged somewhat after the fashion of a pea-shaped flower.

Few shrubs or small trees are more beautiful than the hardy species of *Cercis* at their best. They enjoy and merit generous conditions at the root, and succeed best in a deep, sandy loam, and should have as sunny a position as possible. Plants should be given a permanent position whilst still young, as the long, thick roots are liable to decay after the inevitable injury involved in transplanting old trees by ordinary means. Whatever transplanting is necessary should be done in May, and not until the expanding buds give some indication that active growth has recommenced. The most insidious enemy of these trees in my experience is the coral-spot fungus, for which drastic surgery is the only remedy; the affected branches should be cut back to undoubtedly healthy wood, and the wounds thoroughly covered with a protective dressing. The older and well-known species are propagated by seed, and this, of course, is preferable for all; but the newer species may be grafted on roots of *C. siliquastrum* or *C. canadensis*.

C. CANADENSIS L. REDBUD

A deciduous tree occasionally over 40 ft high in a wild state, more often a tall, spreading shrub in cultivation. Leaves broadly heart-shaped, pointed, 3 to 5 in. across, often wider than long; glabrous or thinly downy beneath. Flowers pale rose, $\frac{1}{2}$ in. long, each on a stalk as long as itself, produced in clusters (fascicles) of four to eight blossoms; calyx $\frac{1}{6}$ in. long, red. Pod about 3 in. long, $\frac{1}{2}$ in. wide, pink when fully grown, but rarely seen in this country. Flowers in May and June.

Native of the eastern and central United States, in some districts so plentiful as to make a conspicuous feature in the landscape when in flower. Although one of the most beautiful of N. American trees, it is not so striking in this country, and does not bear comparison with *C. siliquastrum* for beauty in our gardens. It is quite easily distinguished from that species by its leaves, which are thinner, brighter green, and pointed; the flowers are not so large.

f. ALBA Rehd.—Flowers white.

C. CHINENSIS Bunge　　CHINESE REDBUD

A tree sometimes 50 ft high in a wild state, with a trunk 3 to 4 ft in diameter, but in cultivation merely a shrub. Leaves heart-shaped, pointed, 3 to 5 in. long, nearly or quite as much wide, glossy green, and glabrous except for a few hairs beneath in the vein-axils. Flowers in close clusters of four to ten, pink, $\frac{3}{5}$ in. long. Pod $3\frac{1}{2}$ to 5 in. long, taper-pointed. Blossoms in May.

Native of China, and probably the largest of the genus. It is quite a failure in the open ground at Kew. It has flowered on a wall, but is evidently a plant better suited for climates with hotter summers than ours. There is a considerable resemblance between this tree and *C. canadensis*. Both have pointed, bright green leaves, quite distinct from *C. siliquastrum*. *C. chinensis* is distinguishable out of flower from *C. canadensis* by its larger, thinner stipules, and by the leaves being glossy beneath when quite young, those of *C. canadensis* being duller and more or less glaucous. The adult leaves appear also to be larger; there are some in the Kew Herbarium, gathered near Peking, $6\frac{1}{2}$ in. across. There is an example at Lanarth, in Cornwall, 20 ft high.

C. OCCIDENTALIS Gray　　WESTERN REDBUD

A deciduous shrub, or occasionally a small tree 15 ft high. Leaves roundish, heart-shaped, 2 to 3 in. across, glabrous. Flowers $\frac{1}{2}$ in. long, rose-coloured, produced on short stalks in clusters on the wood of the previous or earlier years. Pod 2 to $2\frac{1}{2}$ in. long, $\frac{2}{3}$ in. wide, glabrous.

Native of California, and quite distinct from the eastern *C. canadensis* in its leaves, which are rounded or notched at the apex, and are very similar in outline to those of the European Judas-tree, but of a vivid green. At Kew it thrives no better than *C. canadensis*. Nearly allied is C. RENIFORMIS S. Wats., from Texas and New Mexico, a slender tree sometimes 20 ft, rarely 40 ft high, with leaves downy beneath and pods larger than in *C. occidentalis*.

C. RACEMOSA Oliver

A deciduous tree up to 40 ft high, with downy young branchlets. Leaves heart-shaped, $2\frac{1}{2}$ to 5 in. long, 2 to 4 in. wide, glabrous and dark green above, paler and downy all over beneath, especially on the veins. Racemes up to 4 in. long, downy, carrying as many as thirty or forty flowers, which are under $\frac{1}{2}$ in. in length, rose-coloured. Pod 3 to 4 in. long, $\frac{3}{4}$ in. wide, flat, glabrous. *Bot. Mag.*, t. 9316.

Native of China, in the provinces of Hupeh and Szechwan. The beauty and distinctness of this species had been known to us ever since it was discovered by Henry about 1886, but it was not introduced until 1907, when Wilson collected seed for Harvard University. It is remarkably distinct from all other species in the comparatively long inflorescence; and the downy character of the young wood, leaf, and flower-stalk is also well marked. Wilson told me that this is one of the very best and most beautiful flowering trees he has introduced. Like the European Judas-tree it flowers on the naked wood, one to many years of age. It comes from 6,000 ft altitude in N.W. Hupeh. There is a fine tree at Borde Hill, Sussex, about 36 ft high (1967), and it is also very good at Highdown in the same county and at East Bergholt Place, Suffolk.

C. SILIQUASTRUM L.   JUDAS-TREE   [PLATE 39

A deciduous tree, usually of low, bushy habit, and below 25 ft in height, but occasionally forming a distinct trunk and reaching from 30 to 40 ft high; branchlets glabrous. Leaves roundish, with a heart-shaped base, sometimes pointed, but usually broad and rounded at the apex; from $2\frac{1}{2}$ to 4 in. across, somewhat less in length; they are quite glabrous, and of a well-marked glaucous green. Flowers produced in clusters from the joints of the old wood (even on the trunk of old trees), each flower on a slender stalk about $\frac{3}{4}$ in. long; they are bright purplish rose, and $\frac{1}{2}$ to $\frac{3}{4}$ in long. Pod 3 to 5 in. long, $\frac{5}{8}$ in. wide, flat, thin, red, eight- to twelve-seeded, remaining on the plants throughout the winter. *Bot. Mag.*, t. 1138.

Native of the East Mediterranean region and the Near East, probably not found in a wild state west of Dalmatia and Istria; known and cultivated in England for more than three hundred years. In Italy it is the most delightful tree flowering in April and May; with us, flowering a few weeks later, it is also one of the most beautiful and picturesque trees that can be found in gardens. It flowers in the leafless state, and the profusion of blossom gives at a distance the effect of a rosy-purple mist. A sun-loving tree, it is better suited for the south of England than the north. Nowhere does it thrive better than in the gardens of Cambridge. It should only be propagated from seeds which, although they do not come to perfection regularly in this country, can be easily and cheaply purchased. The popular name of 'Judas-tree' is derived from the legend that this was the tree upon which Judas went out and hanged himself after the great Betrayal. The largest tree at Kew was 40 ft high, with a trunk 4 ft 9 in. in girth. The flowers of the Judas-tree have a sweetish, acid taste, and are used as an ingredient in salads. They open in May.

The tree varies in the depth of shade of the flowers; Miller knew a form with flesh-coloured flowers. One with deeply coloured flowers was given the F.C.C. in 1944 when shown from Bodnant; the original tree there was planted in 1876 and is about 30 ft high. In f. ALBA (West.) Rehd., the flowers are white.

CERCOCARPUS　　ROSACEAE

Five or six species of this curious genus have been introduced, all found wild in western N. America. They are evergreen or sub-evergreen shrubs and small trees, with alternate leaves and small axillary flowers on short stalks, either solitary or in few-flowered clusters. They have no petals, but a five-lobed calyx, and numerous (fifteen to thirty) stamens. The most distinctive feature of the genus is the small, hard, slender fruit, terminated by the long, persistent style, which is plumed with long, white, silky hairs. The genus has been revised by F. L. Martin in *Brittonia*, Vol. 7, pp. 91–111 (1950).

C. BETULOIDES Torr. & Gr.

C. betulifolius Hook.; *C. parvifolius* var. *glaber* S. Wats.

An erect shrub or small tree to about 20 ft high with a smooth grey bark; young shoots more or less glabrous. Leaves obovate to ovate or broadly elliptic, about $\frac{1}{2}$ to 1 in. long, cuneate at the base, margins toothed in the upper half; dark green and glabrous above, paler and somewhat downy beneath; leaf-stalks $\frac{1}{8}$ to $\frac{1}{4}$ in. long. Flowers in clusters of two to three on short pedicels; flower-tube silky-hairy at first, later more or less glabrous. Fruits terminated by a plume-like style $1\frac{1}{2}$ to $4\frac{1}{4}$ in. long.

Native of western N. America from S.W. Oregon to Lower California. It is a common and variable species in which three varieties are recognised, differing from the type chiefly in their larger and differently shaped leaves. Of these the following is the most distinct:

var. TRASKIAE (Eastw.) Dunkle　*C. traskiae* Eastw.—Leaves leathery, thickly felted beneath, $1\frac{1}{5}$ to $2\frac{2}{5}$ in. long; flower-tube densely woolly on the outside. Found only on Sta Catalina Island.

C. betuloides is closely allied to *C. montanus* but differs in its grey, thin, flaky bark (not thick and fissured as in *C. montanus*), and taller, more robust habit.

C. INTRICATUS S. Wats.

An evergreen shrub up to 6 ft high, much and intricately branched; young shoots stiff, dark brown, downy; bark of the older parts ashy-grey. Leaves linear to narrowly lanceolate, made narrower by the decurved margins, wedge-shaped at the base, tapered at the apex to a short fine point, toothless; $\frac{1}{2}$ to $1\frac{1}{4}$ in. long, $\frac{1}{12}$ to $\frac{1}{4}$ in. wide; dark glossy green, at first hairy but becoming glabrous above; clothed with grey felt beneath and hairy on the midrib and veins; stalk $\frac{1}{16}$ in. long. Flowers (not seen by me on cultivated plants) described as stalkless, downy, $\frac{1}{6}$ in. wide and long; calyx-lobes five, triangular. Seed-vessels terminated by a slender feathery tail 1 to 2 in. long.

Native of western N. America, from Oregon to California and Nevada, Utah, and Arizona. Like the remainder of the species, the flower has no petals, and its chief ornamental quality is due to the tail of the fruit, which is clothed with white silky hairs. Of the other three species described, this is most nearly allied to *C. ledifolius*, both having toothless leaves. That species differs in habit, being slender and erect; this is bushy with spreading interlaced branches. The feathery tail is also longer in *C. ledifolius*.

C. LEDIFOLIUS Nutt.

A small, evergreen tree, sometimes 40 ft high, or a shrub, similar to *C. montanus* in flower and fruit, but very distinct in its foliage. Young shoots hairy; leaf somewhat resinous, lanceolate or narrow oblong, $\frac{1}{2}$ to $1\frac{1}{2}$ in. long, $\frac{1}{8}$ to $\frac{3}{8}$ in. wide; dark green and becoming glabrous above, downy beneath, the margins entire and decurved; the midrib is prominent, but the side veins are not conspicuous as in *C. montanus*. The fruits are terminated by the silky, plume-like style, 2 to 3 in. long, characteristic of the genus.

Native of western N. America, from Oregon south to New Mexico. It has been grown at Kew, where it is quite hardy, but is not at present in the collection. Flowers in June. Introduced about 1879.

C. MONTANUS Raf.
C. parvifolius Hook. & Arn., in part

An evergreen shrub of sparse habit up to 10 or 12 ft high, with thick, persistent bark; branchlets downy when young, becoming glabrous later. Leaves obovate, $\frac{1}{2}$ to $1\frac{1}{2}$ in. long, with a wedge-shaped base, and four to six pairs of prominent parallel veins, the apex coarsely toothed, the base entire; upper surface dull and clothed with silky hairs, becoming glabrous later; downy beneath, especially on the midrib and veins. Flowers produced during May, usually singly, sometimes in twos or threes, on a slender, downy stalk $\frac{1}{8}$ to $\frac{1}{2}$ in. long, from buds on the previous year's wood; each flower is about $\frac{1}{4}$ in. across, consisting chiefly of a cluster of stamens; calyx grey with down. Fruit $\frac{1}{3}$ in. long, $\frac{1}{12}$ in. wide, about the size of an oat grain, surmounted by a slender, twisted tail (the style), 2 to 4 in. long, clothed with fine, white, silky hairs.

Native of western N. America from Oregon to Lower California. This curious shrub has no beauty of flower, but is very remarkable for its long-tailed fruits. In California, where a great crop of them is borne, they give to the branches quite an ostrich feather-like appearance. It is perfectly hardy at Kew, and bears flowers and fruits there.

CESTRUM   SOLANACEAE

A genus of some 200 species of shrubs and small trees, natives of Central and S. America. Leaves alternate, entire. Flowers in cymes; corolla funnel- or pitcher-shaped, five-lobed at the mouth; fruit a berry. The species here described flower and winter well on walls in the milder parts; the hardiest, but least attractive, is *C. parqui*. All are easily increased by cuttings of half-ripened wood. A monograph of the genus by Pièrre Francey appeared in *Candollea*, Vol. 6, pp. 46–398 (1935) and Vol. 7, pp. 1–132 (1936).

C. ELEGANS (Brongn.) Schlecht.

Habrothamnus elegans Brongn.; *C. purpureum* (Lindl.) Standley

A large, evergreen shrub or small tree of loose, graceful, pendent growth; young shoots downy. Leaves 3 to 4 in. long, one-third as wide, entire, lanceolate, acuminate, the base rounded to cordate, dull deep green, downy. Flowers in dense, compound racemes; corolla rich purplish red, tubular, swelling upwards, ¾ in. long, but contracted at the mouth to five small triangular lobes. Fruit a grape-like, globose, deep red-purple berry, ¾ in. wide. *Bot. Mag.*, t. 5659.

Native of Mexico and a well-known cool-greenhouse shrub which has been in cultivation 100 years or more. It is hardy in the milder parts of Britain. I saw it beautifully in flower in Col. Stephenson-Clarke's garden at Binstead, Isle of Wight, in June 1939.

The species varies considerably in such characters as length and colour of corolla and size of berry. In var. LONGIFLORUM Francey the flowers are more than 1 in. long; in the garden clone 'Smithii', figured as var. *smithii* (Hort.) Bailey in *Bot. Mag.*, n.s., t. 249, they are pink.

C. FASCICULATUM (Schlecht.) Miers *Meyenia fasciculata* Schlecht.—It is mainly in its garden characters that this species differs from *C. elegans*; it is earlier flowering and has flowers of a purer shade of red in a more compact inflorescence. Botanically, it differs from that species in having the corolla downy or hairy on the outside. Native of Mexico. *Bot. Mag.*, t. 4183.

C. 'NEWELLII'.—A plant of garden origin, raised by a Mr Newell of Downham Market, Norfolk, shortly before 1880. Its parentage is unknown, but most probably it is a seedling of one or other of the two preceding species; it has flowers of a more vivid shade of crimson than either and was given an Award of Merit in 1951.

C. PARQUI L'Hérit.

A deciduous shrub 6 to 10 ft high, with quite glabrous young shoots and leaves. Leaves lanceolate to oval-lanceolate, pointed, tapered about equally at both ends or more abruptly towards the base, entire; 1½ to 5 in. long, ¾ to 2 in. wide; green on both sides; stalk up to ½ in. long. Flowers yellowish green, produced during June and July in a terminal cluster augmented by axillary ones, making altogether a panicle 4 to 6 in. long and slightly downy. Calyx tubular, $\frac{3}{16}$ in. long, downy, toothed, the teeth tipped with down. Corolla-tube $\frac{7}{8}$ in. long, slender, dividing at the top into five oblong spreading lobes that are downy behind and give the flower a diameter of nearly ½ in. Fruit egg-shaped, violet-brown, ⅜ in. long, the base cupped in the calyx. It is probably poisonous. *Bot. Mag.*, t. 1770.

Native of Chile; introduced in 1787. The plant figured in the *Botanical Magazine* flowered at Holland House, Kensington, about 1810. The flowers are not very pretty, but they are fragrant at night. The plant itself when touched has a rather heavy odour, like that of the haulm of garden peas. It is not fully hardy near London but will grow in a sunny sheltered nook of a building, especially if covered with a mat in very severe weather. Even if cut down to the ground it will usually break into growth again. The leaves are poisonous to cattle.

CHAENOMELES ROSACEAE

A genus of three species, natives of China and Japan, closely allied to *Cydonia*, in which genus they were once included. *Cydonia*, as now understood, comprises only the common quince—*Cydonia oblonga* Mill.—and, in the interpretation of some botanists, the rare tree described in previous editions under the name *Cydonia sinensis* Thouin. The latter has also been considered to belong to *Chaenomeles*, but it has certain characters that make it out of place in either genus and in this revision, following Schneider, it is placed in a genus of its own as *Pseudocydonia sinensis* (Thouin) Schneid.

Chaenomeles differs from *Cydonia* in its toothed leaves; in its calyx, which is glabrous outside and deciduous; and in the styles being united at the base. The leaves are deciduous, alternate, simple, and have large stipules. The flowers are in leafless clusters or solitary at the ends of leafy shoots. The fruit is apple-like, five-celled, and has many seeds in each cell. The fruits are fragrant and edible when cooked, but are excessively harsh and astringent in the raw state; like those of the common quince, they are used for making jellies and conserves. All like a sunny position and, while not particular as to soil, prefer a good well-drained loam. Propagation of the garden varieties is by cuttings of half-ripened wood taken in June or July, or by mound-layering; of the species, by seed.

Wall specimens are the better for regular pruning once a framework of branches has been established. Treatment consists in spurring back the branchlets after flowering; and, in late summer, the shortening of outward pointing growths and the removal of unwanted ones. Strong branches from the base should be trained in and old stems cut out—this can be done at any time.

The most recent study of the genus is by Claude Weber in *The Journal of the Arnold Arboretum*, Vol. 45, pp. 161–205 and 302–45 (1964), to which we are indebted for much of the information on the newer garden hybrids incorporated in this edition. For a Check List of cultivars by the same author see *Arnoldia*, Vol. 23, pp. 17–75.

C. CATHAYENSIS (Hemsl.) Schneid.

Cydonia cathayensis Hemsl.; *Chaenomeles lagenaria* var. *cathayensis* (Hemsl.) Rehd.; *Ch. cathayensis* var. *wilsonii* (Rehd.) Bean

A deciduous shrub of open habit, sparsely branched and more or less thorny. Branches tortuous, furnished with spiny spurs several inches long. Leaves short-stalked, lanceolate or linear-lanceolate, 3 to 5 in. long, finely toothed, pointed, tapering at the base; glabrous above, usually reddish downy beneath, at least when young. On the young growths of the year the stipules are large, broad, and leaf-like, oblique, 1 in. long, toothed. On year-old shoots the leaves are in tufts springing from the axil of a spine; stipules small. Flowers two or three together in sort clusters; each flower 1½ in. in diameter; petals white sometimes flushed with pink, round, overlapping, calyx ciliate. Stamens numerous, shorter than the petals. Fruit very large and heavy; 4 to 6 in. long, 2½ to 3½ in. wide; somewhat egg-shaped, but abruptly contracted near the base. Seed ⅜ in. long, wedge-shaped, pointed at one end.

Although this quince is probably a native of China, nothing appears to be definitely known of its habitat. Henry collected it in the province of Hupeh, China, but never undoubtedly wild. It has long been grown at Kew but its introduction is unrecorded. It is perfectly hardy and bears fruit freely, but this does not ripen always out-of-doors. Although not in any way showy, its habit is quaint, and the huge fruits stuck close to the branches have a curious and interesting appearance. There is a specimen of upright habit in the R.H.S. Garden at Wisley, about 15 ft high, which fruits abundantly. Increased by seeds.

C. JAPONICA (Thunb.) Spach

Pyrus japonica Thunb.; *Cydonia japonica* (Thunb.) Pers.; *Cydonia maulei* T. Moore; *Chaenomeles maulei* (T. Moore) Schneid.; *Pyrus maulei* (T. Moore) Mast.

A low, spreading, deciduous thorny shrub, usually under 3 ft in height, considerably more in width; branchlets very downy when young. Leaves 1 to 2 in. long, obovate or oval to almost orbicular, toothed, tapering at the base to a short stalk, quite glabrous; stipules large on the young growing shoots, ovate or broadly heart-shaped, ¼ to ¾ in. wide. Flowers in almost stalkless clusters from the joints of the year-old wood, very abundant, orange-red, scarlet or blood-red, 1½ in. across. Fruit apple-shaped, 1½ in. diameter, yellow stained with red on the sunny side, fragrant.

Native of Japan; introduced about 1869 by Messrs Maule of Bristol. It was at first considered to be a new species and was named *Cydonia maulei*. Many years passed before it was discovered that it was the species to which Thunberg had given the name *Pyrus japonica* in his *Flora Japonica* (1784), and that the plant grown for so long in gardens as "*Pyrus japonica*" or "*Cydonia japonica*" was quite another species, for which the correct name is *Chaenomeles speciosa* (q.v.).

This is one of the most charming of red-flowered dwarf shrubs, flowering from April to June, and when at its best, literally wreathing its branches with blossom. It bears fruits freely, and they are pleasantly coloured and scented in early winter; though harsh and acid when raw, they make an excellent conserve. Besides its dwarfer habit, it differs from its near ally, *C. speciosa*, in having minutely warted twigs, and more obovate or rounded, more coarsely toothed leaves.

f. ALBA (Nakai) Ohwi—Flowers white. This should not be confused with the garden variety 'Alba', which is now considered to belong to the hybrid group *C.* × *superba*.

var. ALPINA Maxim.—Plants dwarfer, with smaller leaves and flowers. This variety is not in cultivation. Plants raised from seed of dwarf specimens collected by Sargent in the mountains of Japan were at first considered to belong botanically to var. *alpina*. But in cultivation they did not retain the dwarfness of the wild parents, though remaining somewhat smaller than the plants from Maule's introduction to Britain. In Europe they were once grown under Lemoine's name *"Cydonia sargentii"*.

Following the introduction of *C. japonica* in 1869, many seedlings were raised from it, of various habit and colour, and distributed as varieties of *"Cydonia maulei"* (as it was then called). These, however, are now considered to be of hybrid origin, with *C. speciosa* as the other parent, and thus belong to the hybrid group *C.* × *superba* (q.v.).

C. × CLARKIANA Weber—This is the collective name for hybrids of the parentage *C. japonica* × *cathayensis*, first raised by the late W. B. Clarke of California. A few named forms of the cross have been distributed but are surpassed in garden value by the later *C.* × *californica* group (q.v. under *C.* × *superba*).

C. SPECIOSA (Sweet) Nakai

Cydonia speciosa Sweet; *Chaenomeles lagenaria* (Loisel.) Koidzumi; *Cydonia lagenaria* Loisel.; *Pyrus japonica* Sims, not Thunb.

A deciduous shrub of wide-spreading habit, forming a dense tangle of interlacing, more or less spiny branches, ultimately 10 ft high, and 20 ft in diameter; branchlets smooth and glabrous or slightly downy. Leaves 1½ to 3½ in. long, oval, tapering more gradually towards the base than towards the apex, evenly saw-toothed, dark glossy green above, paler beneath, quite glabrous on both surfaces; stipules large and conspicuous on the shoots of the year, as much as 1½ in. diameter, obliquely kidney-shaped and toothed. Flowers 1½ to 1¾ in. across, produced in clusters on the old wood, usually two to four on each cluster, scarlet to blood-red. Fruit stalkless, green-yellow, specked with small dots, 2 to 2½ in. long and wide, apple-shaped or pear-shaped, fragrant. *Bot. Mag.*, t. 692.

Native of China, long cultivated in Japan; introduced by Sir Jos. Banks to Kew in 1796, and for many years now one of the best-known and most admired of hardy shrubs. For more than a century it was known both to gardeners and to botanists as *Pyrus* or *Cydonia "japonica"* in the erroneous belief that it was the *Pyrus japonica* of Thunberg (see further under *C. japonica*). It sometimes commences to flower before Christmas, especially when grown on a wall, and is usually in blossom by February or March, continuing until June, or even later. Sometimes autumn flowers are produced in distinct racemes instead of the stalkless clusters usual to the species; in these cases the flowers are produced alternately on stalks 1 in. or more long, as many as half a dozen on each raceme. *C. speciosa* loves the sun, and flowers most freely planted against a south wall. Perhaps it is seen at its best in some sheltered sunny spot as a wide-spreading lawn shrub. It stands pruning well, summer pruning being best. Sometimes it is successfully used as a hedge plant.

According to Weber, the original introduction of *C. speciosa* in 1796 was probably sterile and propagated by vegetative means; but in 1830 Siebold brought from Japan a number of colour forms which, intercrossed, gave rise to further variants, large numbers of which were named and distributed by nurserymen in the last century. Further variation, both in colour and habit, followed on the introduction of *C. japonica* in 1896, and since then the hybrids between the two species (*C. × superba*) have come to predominate in gardens. In many instances it would be impossible, without botanical scrutiny, to decide whether a particular garden variety should be regarded as a colour form of *C. speciosa* or as one of its hybrids with *C. japonica* and for the gardener the problem is not of great importance. The following is a selection of those that can with reasonable certainty be ascribed to *C. speciosa*. All, unless otherwise stated, attain a height of 4 to 6 ft in the open ground, somewhat more on a wall:

'CARDINALIS'.—Flowers crimson-scarlet, about 1½ in. across; an old variety raised by Späth around 1885. Not to be confused with 'Cardinal', which is a form of *C. × californica*.

'FALCONNET CHARLET'.—A vigorous variety with double, salmon-pink flowers. Also known as 'Rosea Plena'.

'MOERLOOSII'.—Flowers large, white overlaid with pink and carmine. Raised in the mid-nineteenth century by Moerloos of Ledeberg, Belgium. Sometimes known incorrectly as 'Apple Blossom'.

'NIVALIS'.—A vigorous variety with pure white flowers raised by Lemoine about 1880 but still the best of its kind.

'PHYLIS MOORE'.—Flowers double, salmon-rose; owing to its sparse habit it is better grown on a wall. Raised by the Knap Hill nursery and named after the wife of Sir Frederick Moore, for many years Keeper of the Glasnevin Botanic Garden.

'RUBRA GRANDIFLORA'.—Flowers crimson, very large; habit low and spreading. An old variety, raised in Belgium.

'SIMONII'.—Low-growing, with deep red, semi-double flowers. [PLATE 41

'UMBILICATA'.—A vigorous variety introduced from Japan by Siebold in 1847; flowers deep pink.

C. × VILMORINIANA Weber *C. vedrariensis* Hort.—This cross between *C. speciosa* and *C. cathayensis* was first made in the Vilmorin nurseries in 1921. Later a hybrid of the same parentage arose spontaneously in the nursery of W. B. Clarke of San Jose, California, and was put into commerce as 'MOUNT EVEREST', followed by its seedling 'AFTERGLOW'. All are heavily armed shrubs reaching to about 8 ft high, with long, sharply toothed leaves and white flowers, flushed with pink.

C. × SUPERBA (Frahm) Rehd.

Soon after the introduction of *C. japonica* in 1869 spontaneous hybrids began to occur between it and *C. speciosa*, but their mixed parentage was not at first suspected and they were put into the trade as forms of "*Cydonia maulei*", which is the name under which *C. japonica* was first grown. The first of these to be recognised as a hybrid had been named var. *superba*, which by Rehder was made the type of the hybrid group *C.* × *superba* (Frahm) Rehd. To it belong many of the smaller chaenomeles grown in gardens at the present time.

Generally they are low, spreading shrubs to 4 or 5 ft high. In foliage they are intermediate between the two parents (leaves coarsely toothed in *C. japonica*, 1 to 2 in. long, obovate or rounded: finely toothed in *C. speciosa*, up to 3½ in. long, ovate or oblong). In the character of the shoots they incline towards *C. japonica* (downy and rough the first year, warty in the second; in *C. speciosa* the young growth is smooth and glabrous or only slightly downy and the second-year twigs are smooth also). Colour ranges through the whole gamut from white, pink, and crimson to various shades of orange and orange-scarlet. The following is a selection of some of the better-known forms:

'BOULE DE FEU'.—Flowers orange-scarlet; fruits bright yellow. This and its sister seedling 'Vermilion' are of interest as the first deliberate crosses between *C. speciosa* and *C. japonica*; they were raised by Barbier of Orleans in 1913.

'CORAL SEA'.—Flowers of the unusual and attractive shade known as Chinese Coral (HCC 614/1); it grows to about 3 ft high. 'YAEGAKI', a clone of Japanese origin, has flowers of the same colour, but they are double and the plant is of very dwarf habit.

'CRIMSON AND GOLD'.—A dense, spreading shrub to 3 ft high; flowers large, deep red, with golden anthers. Raised by W. B. Clarke of California and put into commerce in 1939. It is said to be invasive and suckering on some soils.

'KNAP HILL SCARLET'.—An old variety, raised by Anthony Waterer around 1870; of low, spreading habit; flowers large, brilliant red, very freely borne.

'ROWALLANE'.—Of low, spreading habit in the open ground, but makes a good wall plant. Flowers to 1½ in. across, brilliant crimson. Raised at Rowallane, Co. Down, in 1920.

C. × CALIFORNICA Weber—By crossing *C. cathayensis* with a form of *C.* × *superba*, the late W. B. Clarke of California founded a new hybrid group in which all three species of *Chaenomeles* are united. So far, according to Weber, the cross has not been repeated, the forms put into commerce being seedlings from the original cross and their offspring (some of which may be back-crosses). All so far distributed are erect spiny shrubs of stiff habit, with lanceolate leaves; the flowers are in shades of pink and rose red and remarkable for their size, which may be 2 in. across in some of the forms.

Some of the cultivars of *C.* × *californica* have been introduced to Kew, where they grow well both as lawn specimens and on walls, and bear handsome, bright yellow fruit. There are several named clones in commerce in the U.S.A., of which one of the finest is said to be 'CARDINAL'.

CHAMAEBATIA ROSACEAE

A genus of two species in California, belonging to the sub-family Rosoideae. Within this group it is distinguished by the tri-pinnatifid leaves and the five-petalled flowers with a single pistil borne in a funnel-to cup-shaped receptacle; fruit an achene.

C. FOLIOLOSA Benth.

A semi-evergreen shrub 2 to 3 ft high; young shoots, leaf-stalks and flower-stalks covered with grey down and stalked glands. Leaves fern-like, $1\frac{1}{2}$ to $2\frac{1}{2}$ in. long, ovate in main outline, but made up of countless tiny hairy leaflets $\frac{1}{16}$ in. long, tri-pinnately arranged. Flowers white, $\frac{1}{2}$ in. across, petals five; receptacle (calyx-tube) funnel-shaped to cup-shaped with five lanceolate lobes, the whole downy and glandular; stamens numerous, yellow; fruit dry, obovoid, enclosed by the calyx. The flowers are produced four to eight together on terminal slender-stalked corymbs 2 to 4 in. long and open in June and July. *Bot. Mag.*, t. 5171.

Native of California, one of its sites being the Big Tree Grove, Calaveras. It was discovered by Col. Frémont on the Sacramento Mountains in 1844 and collected there by Hartweg in 1848. Soon after Messrs Veitch imported living plants. It bears a strong resemblance to *Chamaebatiaria millefolium* and has a similar pleasant balsamic odour, but the fruit of that species divides longitudin-ally when ripe and its short-stalked flowers come numerously in terminal compound pyramidal panicles. *Chamaebatia foliolosa* is not so hardy as the chamaebatiaria and requires a sunny corner where the soil is light and well-drained; even then it is probably only suitable for the southern counties.

CHAMAEBATIARIA   ROSACEAE

This is one of several genera formerly included in *Spiraea*, from which it differs in its doubly pinnate leaves. It contains the one species described here.

C. MILLEFOLIUM (Torr.) Maxim.
Spiraea millefolium Torr.

A shrub 3 to 5 ft high, the erect branches covered with glandular down, sticky when young, and having a balsamic odour. Leaves 2 to $3\frac{1}{2}$ in. long, $\frac{1}{2}$ to 1 in. wide; doubly pinnate and very like those of the common milfoil, the ultimate subdivisions $\frac{1}{12}$ in. long, narrowly oblong, downy; common stalk slightly winged. Flowers white, $\frac{1}{3}$ to $\frac{1}{2}$ in. diameter, produced in erect, terminal branching panicles, 3 to 5 in. high; flower-stalks and calyx densely covered with tufted hairs; petals roundish, surrounding a cluster of yellow stamens. Flowers in July. *Bot. Mag.*, t. 7810.

Native of western N. America; first discovered in 1853 by Dr Bigelow; intro-duced to Kew in 1891. It occurs up to 10,000 ft altitude in California, and is

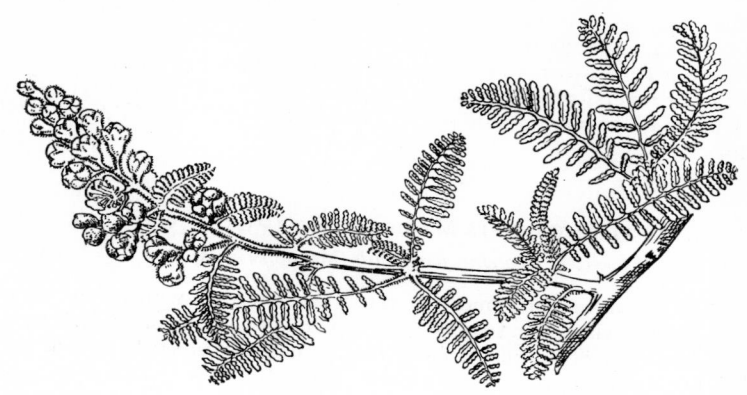

CHAMAEBATIARIA MILLEFOLIUM

quite hardy in the south of England, but likes a well-drained soil and as sunny a position as possible. The plant has a pungent aromatic odour.

CHAMAECYPARIS   CUPRESSACEAE

A genus of lofty evergreen trees allied to *Cupressus*, differing from it in their usually flattened sprays of branchlets, smaller cones usually ripening the first year, and by each cone-scale bearing only two, rarely three to five seeds. All save one—*C. thyoides* of eastern N. America—are natives of the lands bordering the Pacific Ocean, two in western N. America and the other three in Formosa and Japan. With the exception of *C. formosensis* all the species are hardy and comprise some of the very finest of ornamental evergreens. They like abundant moisture and a deep loamy soil, and can be increased by cuttings as well as by seeds.

The leaves of seedling and juvenile plants of *Chamaecyparis* (also of *Cupressus* and *Thuja*) are very different from those of adult trees, being needle-like or awl-like, up to ⅓ in. long and spreading. Individuals of some species show the remarkable characteristic of retaining this juvenile type of foliage permanently or, at any rate, for an indefinite period, and thereby have originated some very pretty garden trees. The juvenile form of *C. pisifera* known as 'Squarrosa' is so distinct from the type in its foliage that Siebold and Zuccarini (*Flora Japonica*, 1842) treated it as a distinct species of the genus *Retinispora* alongside the two wild Japanese cypresses, which also received their first descriptions in that work as *Retinispora pisifera* and *obtusa*. Later botanists transferred *R. pisifera* and *obtusa* to *Cupressus* or *Chamaecyparis*. As for *Retinispora squarrosa* its true nature was soon revealed through the raising of seedlings and the appearance of occasional reversion shoots with normal adult foliage. But in gardens the generic name, corrupted to *"Retinospora"*, continued to be used for the juvenile forms.

Some juvenile forms of more recent origin, having produced neither cones nor reversion shoots, still cannot be placed with certainty, either as to species or even to genus (see *C. obtusa* 'Sanderi' and *C. thyoides* 'Ericoides').

C. FORMOSENSIS Maxim.   FORMOSAN CYPRESS

Cupressus formosensis (Maxim.) Henry   [PLATE 42]

An evergreen tree sometimes 150 to nearly 200 ft high, with a trunk girthing over 60 ft; branches often swollen at their junction with the main stem. Branchlets arranged in horizontal fashion, the ultimate divisions flat, about $\frac{1}{16}$ in. wide. Leaves dull green on both surfaces, closely appressed to the stem in adult trees, about $\frac{1}{16}$ in. long, pointed; in young trees they are only appressed at the base, the more slender sharper points being quite free; the side leaves are keeled and boat-shaped, the front ones ovate and shorter. Cones $\frac{1}{3}$ in. wide, ellipsoid, with about ten scales; seeds with narrow wings.

Native of Formosa; first introduced by means of a single plant in 1910 by Admiral Sir Lewis Clinton-Baker to his brother's collection at Bayfordbury, Herts. The following year a quantity of seeds were received at Bayfordbury, from which a large number of plants were raised. The Formosan cypress may be regarded as one of the vegetable wonders of the world. Although considerably less in stature than the sequoias of California, it almost equals them in size of trunk, for trees girthing over 70 ft have been recorded. It appears to be most nearly related to *C. pisifera*, which differs in its globose cones, broadly winged seeds, and well-defined whitish patches beneath the sprays of foliage. H. J. Elwes visited Formosa in 1912 and, as indicating the extraordinary durability of the timber, mentions that he saw old, prostrate trunks of this cypress with trees growing on them that were 200 to 300 years old. He estimated the age of the largest trees as between 1,200 and 1,500 years.

The Formosan cypress is rather tender, at least when young. It would probably thrive best in a sheltered location in the milder and rainier parts of the country, wherever the summers are not too cool, but it is rather doubtful whether even there it will ever make a good tree. Specimens from the 1911 introduction now average about 38 ft in height and 3½ ft in girth and are to be found in the following collections: Nymans, Borde Hill, Tilgate, Wakehurst Place and Warnham Court, all in Sussex; Bicton, Devon; Stourhead, Wilts.; Hergest Croft, Heref.; and at Kew. In Eire there are examples at Fota and on Garinish Island, Co. Cork, and at Mount Usher, Co. Wicklow.

C. LAWSONIANA (A. Murr.) Parl.   LAWSON CYPRESS

Cupressus lawsoniana A. Murr.   [PLATE 43]

A tree frequently 200 ft high in a wild state, the trunk 7 ft or more in diameter above the buttressed base; bark reddish brown. As seen in cultivation it is a slenderly to broadly pyramidal tree, densely furnished to the ground with frond-like branches. The leaf-bearing branchlets are borne in two horizontally spreading ranks, usually more or less pendulous at the ends, the final subdivisions flattened, $\frac{1}{16}$ to $\frac{1}{12}$ in. wide. Leaves minute, scale-like, in four rows; the lateral leaves considerably the longer, those underneath usually glandular; they have minute, abrupt points. The foliage is extremely variable in shade, from deep green to a more or less glaucous green. Cones globose, glaucous (finally brown), $\frac{1}{3}$ in. diameter; scales eight. *Bot. Mag.*, t. 5581.

Native of western N. America in Oregon and California; introduced in 1854 to Lawson's nursery at Edinburgh. It is now the commonest and most valued of all cypresses, perhaps of all conifers, in gardens. It is very hardy, but likes a good loamy soil and a moist climate. In poor soils it is much benefited by artificial watering during dry periods, also by occasional supplies of manure water. In North America it yields a very valuable timber and is grown, though on a very small scale, as a forestry tree in this country.

The following are some of the outstanding specimens recorded recently to mention only those of 90 ft or more: Endsleigh, Devon, 119 × 9½ ft (1963); Rhinefield Drive, Hants, 103 × 12¾ ft and 101 × 8½ ft (1962); Inveraray, Argyll, 102 × 11¾ and 98 × 12 ft (1954–6); Penjerrick, Cornwall, 100 × 11 ft (1965); Blair Atholl, Perths., 99 × 9¼ ft (1955); Killerton, Devon, 92 × 9¾ ft (1960).

No conifer has produced so much variety in foliage and habit under cultivation. In almost any batch of seedlings a number of more or less differing forms may be observed. Some extraordinarily different varieties have been raised, so different that unless their origin were known they would be regarded as distinct species. These are best raised from cuttings which, taken in late summer, root readily—or they are easily grafted on seedlings. Such plants make nice trees, but have a tendency to produce several leads, at least in isolated positions. This, however, in the opinion of many may not detract from their beauty, and in any case may be obviated by cutting off the rival leaders as soon as noticed. Many of the named varieties are not worthy of distinction, and some with age have become indistinguishable from the type. The following are some of the most noteworthy:

cv. 'ALLUMII'.—Spire-like in habit; leaves very glaucous. There is a fine specimen at Wakehurst Place, Sussex, measuring 62 × 4½ ft.

cv. 'AUREA'.—Young shoots yellow the first summer, gradually becoming green. Of compact, bushy habit, becoming as broad as high. Raised by Waterer's nursery, Bagshot, Surrey, and given a F.C.C. in 1870.

cv. 'COLUMNARIS'.—Narrow columnar habit; branchlet stems erect, exposing the glaucous undersides of the leaves. Raised by Spek's nursery, Boskoop, Holland, and given the Award of Garden Merit in 1961. A tree presented by the raiser to the R.H.S. Garden, Wisley, planted in 1947, is now 17 ft high and 3 ft across at its widest (1967).

cv. 'ELEGANTISSIMA'.—Branchlets and foliage yellowish green. Raised by Barron's nursery near Derby around 1875 and still one of the best of its kind.

cv. 'ELLWOODII'.—Foliage juvenile, bluish green, as in 'Fletcheri'; of narrow, spire-like habit. Raised at Swanmore Park, Bishop's Waltham, where it originated as a seedling. It is of denser, more ascending habit than 'Fletcheri' and useful where a small tree is needed for vertical effect. It attains a height of 12 ft or more.

cv. 'ERECTA VIRIDIS'.—Of erect, columnar habit, green; perhaps the most striking columnar evergreen available for cultivation in the open air, but best in a young state, as it is apt to become naked or shabby at the base. Raised in the Knap Hill nursery in 1855.

cv. 'FILIFORMIS'.—In some respects this is the most striking and elegant, as well as the most distinct, of Lawson cypresses. It has a medium rate of growth, the branching is spiral (not two-ranked), and the terminal branchlets hang vertically, often 1 to 2 ft long, scarcely branched, cord-like, very dark green. Extremely effective as an isolated specimen.

cv. 'FLETCHERI'.—A form with juvenile leaves recalling those of a juniper or one of the "retinosporas", of a greyish, glaucous hue; habit conical, but broader and bushier than in 'Ellwoodii'. It arose as a branch sport in the Ottershaw nursery, Chertsey, and was put into commerce by Fletcher Bros., who showed it at Chelsea in 1913, when it received a First Class Certificate. Although slow-growing, it will attain in time a height of 35 ft or more.

cv. 'FORSTECKENSIS'.—A dense, globular bush with moss-like growths. Messrs Hillier have a plant at Winchester which is about thirty years old and is 3 ft high and 4 ft across.

cv. 'FRASERI'.—Similar to 'Allumii', but with darker foliage and of more slender habit.

cv. 'GRACILIS'.—A free, elegant form, the sprays pendulous, points of leaves usually spreading. Raised at the Knap Hill nursery before 1869. 'GRACILIS PENDULA' is more weeping.

cv. 'GREEN HEDGER'.—A denser form with bright green foliage raised by Messrs Jackman of Woking and very suitable for hedging.

cv. 'HILLIERI'.—A variety of great elegance with yellow young foliage, becoming yellowish green later in the season and finally soft green; branchlets slender, leaves slightly spreading. Habit dense, columnar.

cv. 'INTERTEXTA'.—Another very striking and elegant form; the branches decurved rather than turned up at the ends; branchlets weeping, the ultimate divisions stout and rather far apart. It is the stoutness and remoteness of the ultimate ramifications that give this variety its unique appearance. Of glaucous hue and vigorous growth. According to a letter to Kew from Lawson's of Edinburgh, it was raised in their nursery about 1869.

cv. 'KILMACURRAGH'.—Leaves rich green; habit columnar, resembling that of the Italian cypress. It bears the name of the once-famous Irish garden where it originated. The parent tree perhaps no longer exists but it was propagated before the garden fell into decay and is now well established in cultivation.

cv. 'LANEI'.—Habit narrowly columnar; branches spreading; sprays golden above, greenish yellow beneath. Yellower than 'Lutea', with the sprays more densely arranged. Raised by Lane's nurseries, Berkhamsted, about 1938.

cv. 'LUTEA'.—One of the yellowest of all the forms, the young growths being pale yellow changing to golden, and remaining so the first winter; habit stiff and closely pendulous. Rollison's nursery, Tooting, before 1873.

cv. 'MINIMA AUREA'.—A miniature form of conical habit, with golden foliage; ultimate height about 3 ft. Raised by Messrs Rogers of Chandlers Ford, Hants. 'Aurea Densa', raised by the same firm, is very similar (see H. J. Welsh, *Dwarf Conifers*, pp. 116–17).

cv. 'NANA'.—A dwarf, dense bush developing with age a conical form. Put into commerce by Dauvesse of Orleansi n 1861. 'MINIMA' is similar, but has a more rounded top; its branchlets tend to be arranged edgewise, as in *Thuja orientalis*.

cv. 'NIDIFORMIS'.—This variety arose in Rovelli's nursery, Pallanza, Lake Maggiore, and is thought by some authorities to be a hybrid between Lawson's cypress and *C. nootkatensis* (*C.* × *nidifera* Beissn.). It makes a low bush, with branches tending to the horizontal and drooping branchlets. 'TAM-ARISCIFOLIA' is very similar.

cv. 'PEMBURY BLUE'.—Leaves pale blue-grey in their first season, later green; of broadly conical habit. No other glaucous-leaved form of Lawson cypress has leaves of such a delicate shade. It was raised by Baggesen's nurseries, Pembury, Kent, and first distributed by Messrs Jackman.

cv. 'PENDULA'.—Branches horizontal but with the spray pendulous from underneath the branch, as in *C. nootkatensis* 'Pendula'. In 'PENDULA VERA', distributed by Hesse's nurseries around 1890, the branches as well as the branch-lets are pendulous.

cv. 'POTTENII'.—A medium-sized conical tree with dense, greyish-green foliage, partly juvenile. There is an example 39 ft high in the National Pinetum, Bedgebury.

cv. 'PYGMAEA ARGENTEA'.—A very slow-growing conifer of dense, rounded to conical habit; terminal branches white, the whole bush appearing white when the young growths are developing.

cv. 'SILVER QUEEN'.—Young foliage silvery white. There is a specimen at Kew measuring 67 × 3½ ft (1965).

cv. 'STEWARTII'.—Shoots rich yellow when young, changing to green. There is a specimen at Longleat, Wilts., measuring 58 × 6 ft (1963).

cv. 'TRIOMPF VAN BOSKOOP'.—Foliage steely blue; branches widely spaced. This well-known variety was raised at Boskoop around 1890. At Bicton, Devon, there is a specimen of 78 × 6¼ ft (1961).

cv. 'WESTERMANNII'.—Habit sturdy, pyramidal; ultimate branchlets pale yellow. Of Dutch origin, c. 1880.

cv. 'WISSELII'.—A curious, rather than beautiful form, of columnar habit, very dark and glaucous; the branchlets very short, and produced in crowded tufts. The plant is often too thinly furnished to be pleasing. Raised in Holland, 1888. At Nymans in Sussex there is a specimen planted in 1900, measuring 66 × 7¼ ft (1966), and another at Bicton, Devon, 79 × 11 ft (1967). There are two good specimens in the R.H.S. Garden, Wisley, about 50 ft high.

C. NOOTKATENSIS (D. Don) Spach   NOOTKA OR YELLOW
CYPRESS
Cupressus nootkatensis D. Don; *Thuyopsis borealis* Carr.

A tree 120 ft high, with a trunk 5 or 6 ft in diameter; as known in cultivation of rather slender, pyramidal form when young, becoming proportionately broader later; the smaller branches two-ranked, more or less pendulous; the ultimate division $\frac{1}{16}$ to $\frac{1}{12}$ in. wide, sometimes terete, more often four-angled, but broader than thick. Leaves in four ranks and of about equal size, $\frac{1}{12}$ to $\frac{1}{8}$ in. long, abruptly and sharply pointed, not often glandular, dark green. Cones $\frac{1}{3}$ to $\frac{1}{2}$ in. across, globose, rather glaucous, with usually four (sometimes six) scales that are furnished in the middle part with a triangular-pointed boss; ripening the second year.

Native of western N. America from Alaska to Oregon; discovered by Menzies in 1793, and introduced about 1853. It is, from a garden point of view, undoubtedly one of the finest and most desirable of the cypresses, growing rapidly, being very hardy, and almost invariably preserving a healthy, vigorous appearance. Nor does it seem fastidious as to soil. Of the other species it is most likely to be confused with Lawson's cypress, from which it may be distinguished by the following characters: leaves strongly pungent when crushed, with a median ridge and not marked with white on the under-surface; sprays rough to the touch; cone-scales with a prominent point; bark thin, and hence never deeply furrowed, even on old trees. From a distance the Nootka cypress is usually easy to distinguish by reason of its very pendulous sprays.

The Nootka cypress grows well over much of the British Isles but prefers a deep, moist soil and does not thrive on shallow chalky soils or poor peats. The following are a few of the best trees in the British Isles: Leonardslee, Sussex, 89 × 6¾ ft (1958); Linton Park, Kent, 86 × 7¼ ft (1965); Eridge Castle, Kent, 97 × 9½ ft (1963); Titness Park, Berks., 89 × 7½ ft (1957); Westonbirt, Glos., 90 × 10 ft (1965); Broxwood Court, Heref., 95 × 8¾ ft (1957); Dupplin Castle, Perths., 90 × 7¼ ft (1957); Castle Leod, Ross and Cromarty, 90 × 9½ ft (1966).

cv. 'COMPACTA'.—A dwarf form of dense habit.

cv. 'LUTEA'.—Young shoots yellow, finally green. A vigorous and handsome form. Wrongly called 'Aurea'.

cv. 'PENDULA'.—A very striking variety in which the trunk is erect, the primary branches about horizontal, and the leaf-bearing branchlets hanging as slender streamers from the lower side of the branches in a quite vertical line.

C. OBTUSA (Sieb. & Zucc.) Endl.   HINOKI CYPRESS
Retinispora obtusa Sieb. & Zucc.; *Cupressus obtusa* (Sieb. & Zucc.) K. Koch

A tree 100 to 120 ft high in Japan, with a reddish-brown trunk 3 or 4 ft in diameter. Branches horizontal or depressed, bearing the successive ramifications in two opposite horizontally spreading rows. The final leaf-bearing subdivisions are, leaves and all, about $\frac{1}{16}$ in. wide, and rather flattened. Leaves scale-like, not glandular, of two sizes, the lateral pairs the larger, about $\frac{1}{12}$ in. long, somewhat boat-shaped, clasping the smaller ones above and beneath; all are blunt, thick, and fleshy, rich green above, paler beneath. The margin of every leaf beneath is defined by a thin line of glaucous bloom, which gives a variegated appearance. Cones solitary on a short branch, $\frac{1}{3}$ in. diameter, brown; scales usually eight, the surface slightly hollowed towards the centre, where there is a small projection.

Native of Japan, and long cultivated there for its beauty and for its timber; introduced by John Gould Veitch in 1861. It yields the most valuable of Japanese timbers. As an ornamental tree in the British Isles it is very pleasing. It does not grow very fast, and the largest trees in the country are only about 70 to 80

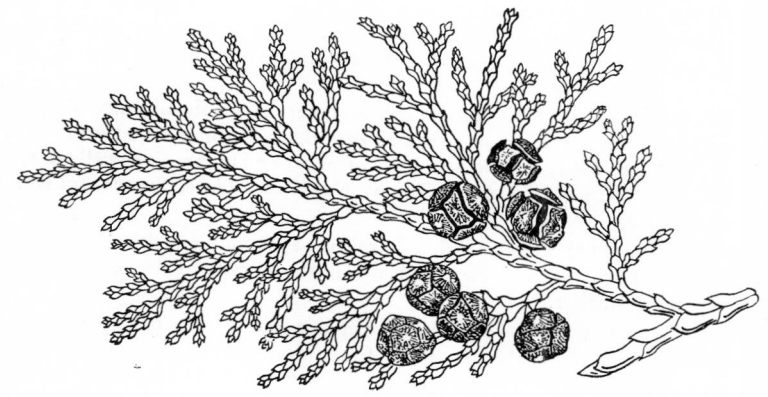

CHAMAECYPARIS OBTUSA

ft high, but well-grown specimens are very graceful in their soft feathery branching. It likes a good moist soil, but will not thrive where there is much lime. With age and on poor soils it is apt to get thin, but this can to some extent be remedied by clipping off the ends of the shoots to induce denser branching—a process it bears very well. It is one of the favourite subjects of the Japanese for dwarfing. It is well distinguished from *C. pisifera* and *C. lawsoniana* by its blunt, round-ended leaves, and the thin glaucous line just beyond the margins beneath.

The biggest specimen so far recorded in the British Isles grows near to the National Pinetum, Bedgebury, Kent; this is 83 ft high on two stems, the thickest $8\frac{1}{2}$ ft in girth (1966). The handsomest specimen found by A. F. Mitchell also grows in Kent; this is at Benenden, and measures 70 × $6\frac{1}{2}$ ft (1958). Others recorded are: Bicton, Devon, 71 × $7\frac{1}{4}$ ft (1957); Killerton, Devon, 68 × $7\frac{1}{2}$ ft (1964); Westonbirt, Glos., 67 × $4\frac{1}{2}$ ft (1963); Petworth House, Sussex, 77 × $4\frac{3}{4}$ ft (1961).

Numerous varieties are in cultivation, of which the following are the most important:

cv. 'AUREA'.—Young shoots golden yellow. A Japanese garden tree, introduced by Fortune in 1860. There is an example in the Italian Garden at Bicton, Devon, measuring 52 × 6 ft (1957).

cv. 'NANA'.—A very slow-growing bush, ultimately 3 ft or so high and more wide; leaves lustrous blackish green; sprays concave, arranged in horizontal tiers. Introduced from Japan by Siebold.

cv. 'NANA GRACILIS'.—One of the finest medium-dwarf conifers, growing 8 to 10 ft high; foliage blackish green. A tree of great individuality, with a rugged aspect.

cv. 'CRIPPSII'.—Coloured similarly to 'Aurea', but of a richer shade; very pleasing as a small tree of dense, very elegant habit. Raised by Cripps' nursery, Tunbridge Wells, around the turn of the century. The largest tree recorded was planted at Tilgate, Sussex, in 1905 and now measures 50 × 4¼ ft (1961). There are several other examples in the south of England approaching that size, e.g. Westonbirt, Glos., 42 × 2¾ ft (1966), and Nymans, Sussex, 44 × 3½ ft (1966).

cv. 'FILICOIDES'.—Habit dense; branching very close, the ultimate divisions short, much crowded, and not so flattened as in the type. Introduced from Japan by J. G. Veitch in 1861. An old specimen at Scorrier House, Cornwall, is 47 ft high with a girth of 4¼ ft (1959). One at Wakehurst Place, Sussex, measures 35 × 2½ ft (1964).

var. FORMOSANA (Hayata) Rehd.—A tree to 125 ft found in the northern and central part of Formosa. It differs from the Japanese type in the leaves, cones, and seeds being smaller.

cv. 'LYCOPODIOIDES'.—Branching irregular, not strictly in two rows, the ultimate branchlets much thicker, more four-sided, and less compressed than in the type. Like many Japanese plants, it was introduced almost simultaneously (in 1861) by Fortune and by J. G. Veitch. Although often stated to be of dwarf habit, there are specimens ranging from 37 to 46 ft in height at: Westonbirt, Glos.; Scorrier House, Coldrenick, and Tregrehan, Cornwall; Bicton, Devon; Nymans, Sussex; Linton Park, Kent; and Wansfell, Ambleside, Westm.

cv. 'SANDERI'.—A curious little shrub of rounded, dense habit, with stiff, spreading, awl-shaped leaves, ⅛ to ⅙ in. long, of a very glaucous blue tint, and borne in decussate pairs. It was put into cultivation by Sander's nursery as "*Juniperus sanderi*", but originated in Japan and does not appear to be a juniper. Masters and Beissner were both of the opinion that it is a juvenile state of *C. obtusa*.

cv. 'TETRAGONA AUREA'.—This has the branching of 'Filicoides', but the branchlets are thicker, more four-sided, and scarcely compressed. Young shoots yellow. Although slow-growing it is by no means dwarf as the following measurements show: Bicton, Devon, 36 × 2 ft (1967); Sindlesham, Berks., 30 × 1½ ft (1959); Nymans, Sussex, 29 × 3 ft (1966); Wakehurst Place, Sussex, 27 × 1½ ft (1965); Leonardslee, Sussex, 25 × 1¾ ft (1962). Its rate of growth is suggested by a tree in the National Pinetum, Bedgebury; planted in 1925 it measures 13 × ¾ ft (1966).

C. PISIFERA (Sieb. & Zucc.) Endl. SAWARA CYPRESS

Retinispora pisifera Sieb. & Zucc.; *Cupressus pisifera* (Sieb. & Zucc.) K. Koch

A tree 70 to 100, occasionally 120 to 150 ft high, with a trunk 3 to 5 ft in diameter. Branches arranged in two opposite horizontally spreading rows; branchlets flat, the ultimate divisions about $\frac{1}{16}$ in. wide. Leaves of about equal length, the lateral ones somewhat the larger ($\frac{1}{12}$ in. long), all with sharp, slender, free points; dark green above, green at the tips beneath, but with a broad patch of glaucous bloom at the base of each. Cones brown, about the size of a pea; scales ten or twelve, hollowed towards the centre, where is a minute projection.

Native of Japan; introduced at about the same time (1861) by J. G. Veitch and by Fortune. As a tree for gardens the typical *C. pisifera* is inferior to *C. obtusa*, from which it is readily distinguished by its sharply pointed leaves. It is more likely to be confused with some forms of *C. lawsoniana*, but the leaves of the American species are rarely so finely pointed, and those of the lateral ranks, as in *C. obtusa*, are conspicuously longer than the upper and lower ones. In habit *C. pisifera* is apt to be thin, especially in poor soils, but this may be improved by an occasional clipping over in spring, more especially when in a small state. An occasional application of manure water is also beneficial.

C. pisifera, in its typical state, is rather rare in gardens, but the following specimens have been recorded: Stourhead, Wilts., 63 × 6¾ ft (1965); Killerton, Devon, 73 × 7 ft (1964); Bicton, Devon, 76 × 5 ft (1967); Dropmore, Bucks., 70 ft on two stems, the larger 6¼ ft in girth (1961); Longleat, Wilts., 71 × 6¼ ft (1959); R.H.S. Garden, Wisley, 67 × 4¾ ft (1964); National Pinetum, Bedgebury, Kent, 63 × 6¼ ft (1966); Cowdray Park, Sussex, 77 × 7¼ ft (1967).

The numerous garden forms of *C. pisifera*, much commoner in cultivation than the type, may conveniently be classified into four groups:

1. In this group the cultivars bear normal foliage but differ from the type in colour of leaf or in habit. The best known are 'AUREA', with golden-yellow young sprays; introduced from Japan around 1860; and 'NANA', a neat, dome-shaped bush of small growth.

2. FILIFERA Group. In these forms the foliage is more or less of the adult kind but the lateral branching is much reduced, so that the main branchlets become elongated, terete, and cord-like. The typical form—'FILIFERA'—makes a low and wide tree, often a broadly pyramidal shrub only, its whole outer surface furnished with the slender, pendulous branches. In time it will grow to a considerable size; at Melbury, Dorset, it is 52 ft high. In 'FILIFERA AUREA' the young growths are golden; it is of slow growth, usually seen to 8 or 12 ft high at the most, but has attained 21 ft at Headfort in Ireland. 'FILIFERA NANA', with green leaves, is quite dwarf in its true form.

3. PLUMOSA Group. Persistently juvenile states of *C. pisifera* with awl-shaped leaves arranged in opposite pairs and standing out from the axis at an angle of about 45°. The typical green-leaved form 'PLUMOSA' ("*Retinospora plumosa*") makes a small bushy tree but is not so common in cultivation as 'PLUMOSA AUREA', with yellow young growths, introduced by Fortune in 1861. A specimen of this at Bicton, Devon, now dead, measured 78 × 5 ft (1957). Others

of 65 ft or over are at: Melbury, Dorset; Golden Grove, Carmarthen; Benenden Grange, Kent; The Hendre, Montg.; Lydhurst, Sussex.

4. SQUARROSA Group. These forms retain (usually permanently) an even more juvenile type of foliage and branching than the Plumosa group, and one characteristic of seedlings of the species. Normally, seedlings retain it for three or four months, when the plumosa type of foliage develops; the following year and the year after the typical adult form begins to appear. The typical form of this group, 'SQUARROSA' (*Retinispora squarrosa* Sieb. & Zucc.), is a very dense-habited bush of uniform silvery, glaucous hue, the branching very bushy, irregular, often lumpy. Leaves about ¼ in. long, narrow, flat, and pointed; glaucous on both sides, and standing out at angles of 45° to 90°. They are arranged in pairs or in threes, sometimes spirally, more often descussately. A very pleasing and striking small tree or bush. 'SQUARROSA SULPHUREA' has a distinctly yellowish hue, very marked when grown alongside the ordinary form. Both are apt to get thin with age, and are often improved by an occasional clipping. 'Squarrosa' reaches as great a height as the normal wild form. The tallest at Bicton, Devon, now dead, measured 81 × 7½ ft (1964). There is a good specimen in the R.H.S. Garden, Wisley, measuring 63 × 5 ft (1964).

Another member of this group is 'BOULEVARD' (*C. p. squarrosa cyano-viridis*), a very striking introduction from the U.S.A., with leaves grey-green above and vividly blue-white beneath; ultimate height unknown.

C. THYOIDES (L.) Britt., Sterns & Pogg.

Cupressus thyoides L.; *Ch. sphaeroidea* Spach; *Thuja sphaeroidea* Spreng.

A tree usually 20 to 50, but up to 70 or 80 ft high in a wild state, with a reddish-brown trunk 2 ft or more in diameter; of slender columnar form in a young state, and shortly branched. The smaller ramifications are flat, two-ranked, and somewhat fan-shaped; the branching as a whole is bushy, spiral, and irregular. The trees shed their effete branchlets in fan-shaped pieces, 1 to 3 in. long. Leaves in four ranks, the lateral ones usually longer than those above and beneath, which are marked with a conspicuous raised gland; they are $\frac{1}{16}$ to $\frac{1}{12}$ in. long, pointed, the lateral ones spreading at the tips; dull grey-green. Cones $\frac{1}{6}$ to $\frac{1}{4}$ in. in diameter, globose, very glaucous; scales six, each with a triangular boss in the centre.

Native of eastern N. America, usually found in cold, swampy, often inundated ground; introduced in the eighteenth century. This tree was more frequently cultivated in earlier times, before the Californian and Japanese cypresses were introduced, than it is now. It is not so striking as they are, but is worth growing for its neat columnar habit. Although a swamp tree in its native country it will thrive better here in ordinary, deep, moist soil. In New Jersey immense quantities of trunks of this tree have been found immersed in swamps, many of them, although buried for hundreds of years, perfectly sound and not at all water-logged. It is very distinct in its branching from any other chamaecyparis. There are specimens of this conifer in the National Pinetum, Bedgebury, Kent, the best measuring 40 × 5¼ ft (1957) and 46 × 4¼ ft (1964). A few others have been recorded, but none larger than these.

cv. 'KEWENSIS'.—Leaves glaucous; habit dense and broadly conical. Also known as 'Glauca'.

cv. 'ANDELYENSIS'.—A very distinct form of dwarf, close, pyramidal habit; the main branches erect, the smaller ones very short. Besides the ordinary type of adult foliage it has branches with the juvenile type of leaf, longer and more awl-shaped. It appears to have been raised in a nursery at Andelys, in N.W. France, about 1850 (*Retinispora leptoclada* Gord.).

cv. 'ERICOIDES'.—A dwarf, rather tender form with juvenile, needle-like leaves which originated in a French nursery in 1840 (*Retinispora ericoides* Gord.). But for the nurseryman's statement that it was a seedling of *C. thyoides* it would be difficult to decide even to what genus it belongs (very similar forms have been produced by species of *Thuja*).

C. HENRYAE Li—A tree to about 90 ft high, differing from *C. thyoides* in the following particulars: bark more shallowly fissured, with the ridges spirally twisted round the stem; branchlets less flattened; leaves lighter green, slightly longer and more appressed; juvenile leaves green beneath (not with two glaucous bands as in *C. thyoides*); cones larger, only slightly glaucous; seeds larger, with broader wings. A native of Florida and S. Alabama with its northern limit in Escambia county. It was described in 1962 (*Journ. Morris Arb.*, Vol. 13, pp. 43–6) and named after the late Mrs Henry of Gladwyne, Penn., who had long studied these trees, previously considered to be *C. thyoides*, and brought them to the notice of botanists. It has proved hardy in the U.S.A. as far north as Philadelphia.

CHAMAEDAPHNE   ERICACEAE

A genus with the one species described here. It is allied to *Leucothöe*, but the scaly undersides of the leaves distinguish it.

C. CALYCULATA (L.) Moench
Andromeda calyculata L.

An evergreen shrub, usually 2 or 3 (sometimes 4 or 5) ft high, with thin, wiry, branches, and a sparse, gaunt habit; young wood scaly. Leaves alternate, ¾ to 1¾ in. long, ⅜ to ¾ in. wide; obovate or narrowly oblong, shallowly toothed, but often only on the terminal half; both surfaces, but especially the lower one, covered with tiny scales. Flowers produced in March and April, singly in the axils of small leaves, at the terminal part, and on the lower side of the previous year's shoots, the whole forming a leafy raceme 2 to 4 in. long. The leaves associated with the flowers are much smaller than the ordinary ones described above, and become gradually smaller towards the end, where they are only ¼ in. or less in length. Corolla white, ¼ in. long, cylindrical, five-toothed at the mouth; calyx-lobes five, pointed, persistent, enclosing the base of the seed-vessel, which is a roundish, flattened capsule; flower-stalk scaly, $\frac{1}{8}$ in. long, with two bracteoles close beneath the calyx. *Bot. Mag.*, t. 1286.

Native of eastern N. America, whence it was introduced in 1748; also of N. Europe and N. Asia. It is a rather pretty shrub in flower, although not amongst the élite of the Ericaceae. A better plant for gardens is:

var. NANA (Lodd.) Rehd.—This grows 12 to 18 in. high, and forms a

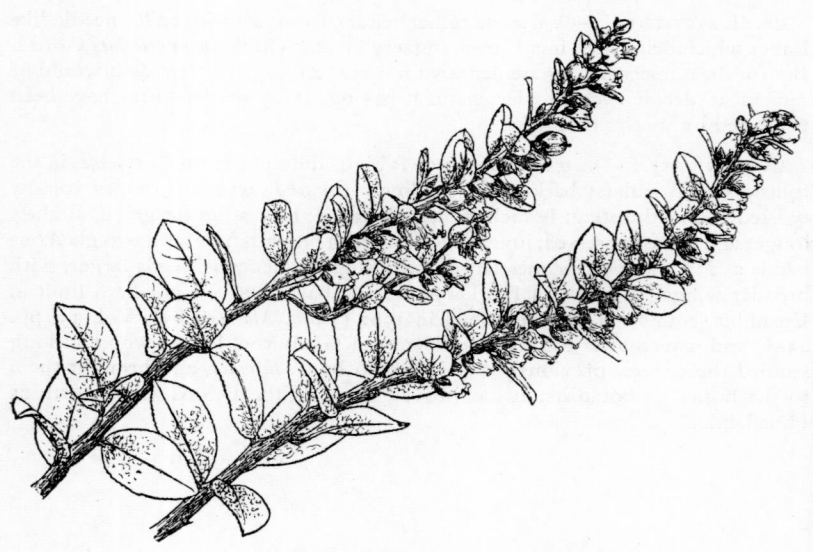

CHAMAEDAPHNE CALYCULATA var. NANA

dwarf, dense thicket, having a more twiggy habit and smaller leaves. It makes a pleasing small group. Both are propagated by cuttings or by seeds and thrive in a moist peaty soil.

CHAMAEROPS   PALMACEAE

A genus of one species and the only member of the Palm family native to Europe.

C. HUMILIS L.   DWARF FAN PALM

An evergreen shrub forming a dense cluster of growths close to the ground and giving a hemispherical mass of foliage; or a small tree with a stem 6 to 8 ft high, about 5 in. in diameter, clothed with stiff dark fibres near the top, and crowned with a rounded head of leaves. Leaves fan-shaped, of a greyish green, split nearly to the base into awl-shaped segments varying much in length. In starved wild specimens they may be only 4 in. long, but in cultivated ones 18 in. The basal part of the leaf is folded like a half-shut fan. The leaf-stalk also varies in length from a few inches to 3 or 4 ft, is flat above, rounded beneath, and armed (often formidably) with forward-pointing, stiff, sharp spines ⅛ to ½ in. long. In their young state the leaves are more or less furnished with a loose pale wool, especially at the back. The small yellow flowers are crowded on a stiff panicle 4 to 6 in. high, clasped at the base in the early stages by a large bract. *Bot. Mag.,* t. 2152.

This palm is not so hardy as *Trachycarpus fortunei* which has lived in perfect health at Kew in the open air for very many years, but it succeeds in S. Hants and S. Sussex and thence westwards. There are good examples in the public garden at Penzance and at Logan in Wigtownshire. Introduced in 1731 by Philip Miller.

It is interesting as the only palm native of Europe. At the present time it is most abundant, perhaps, in Spain, but it occurs also in Italy, Sardinia, Sicily, and across the Mediterranean on the coasts of Algeria and Morocco. At one time it was wild on the French Riviera, but it disappeared apparently about the middle of the nineteenth century and is now regarded as extinct there. Willdenow considered it existed in two varieties: one forming clean trunks (it has been stated sometimes 20 ft high), the other low and with clustered stems. Both types are found at Gibraltar and often a tall stem will have a cluster of dwarf growths at its base. The dwarf state may be due to starved, dry conditions at the root. It grows best in a loamy soil in a sheltered but sunny spot.

CHILIOTRICHUM   COMPOSITAE

A genus of one species in temperate S. America, closely allied to the Australasian genus *Olearia*.

C. DIFFUSUM (Forst.) O. Kuntze

Amellus diffusus Forst.; *C. amelloideum* Cass.; *C. amelloides* DC.; *C. rosmarinifolium* Lessing

An evergreen shrub 1 to 3 ft high in a wild state and 6 ft or more wide; young shoots often erect, clothed with white down. Leaves alternate, closely set together on the stems. In the form most widely cultivated in this country they are linear, stalkless; ¾ to 2 in. long, $\frac{1}{12}$ to ⅙ in. wide; grey with down above when young, more thickly covered beneath, becoming glabrous and dark green above; margins very much recurved; midrib deeply impressed. In the typical form, cultivated as "*C. amelloides diffusum*" the leaves differ in being wider and having a rust-coloured indumentum beneath. Flower-heads 1 to 2 in. wide, terminal, solitary on downy stalks 2 to 4 in. long; ray-florets about twelve, pure white, linear; disk-florets bright yellow. Bracts below the flower-heads (collectively known as the 'involucre') in four or five series, ovate-oblong, pointed, woolly, margined with hairs.

Native of southern S. America in the Andes of Chile and Argentina, descending to near sea-level around the Straits of Magellan, where it was discovered in 1774 during Cook's second voyage; also found on the Falkland Islands. The type of Lessing's *C. rosmarinifolium* was collected by Poeppig in the Chilean Andes and in this form Richard Pearce also found it when collecting for Veitch's nurseries. But it does not seem to have reached cultivation until Comber introduced it during his 1925–7 expedition. His form is a rosemary-like plant so far as the foliage goes, but its flowers are simply like enormous daisies. It needs a sunny, sheltered position and is likely to be seen at its best in mild coastal gardens. It has never been common, but is hardier and more beautiful than most of its allies, the olearias.

CHIMONANTHUS   CALYCANTHACEAE

Chimonanthus is the counterpart in China of the N. American genus *Calycanthus*. The leaves and wood lack, however, the spicy fragrance of that genus; the stamens are only five to six in number and the flowers are coloured yellow to white. *Calycanthus* has up to thirty stamens in each flower and the tepals are purplish brown. Three species of *Chimonanthus* are known, all natives of China.

C. PRAECOX (L.) Link   WINTER SWEET   [PLATE 45
Calycanthus praecox L.; *Ch. fragrans* Lindl.

A deciduous shrub, naturally about 8 ft high, and of compact, bushy habit but growing considerably higher on walls. Leaves rough to the touch above, but free from down except when quite young, and on the primary nerves; lanceolate with an acuminate apex, 2 to 5 in. long, dark lustrous green. Flowers exceedingly fragrant, produced at various times between November and March according to the weather, but in ordinary seasons at their best in December against a wall; they are solitary on very short stalks at the joints of the previous summer's shoots, ¾ to 1 in. across, the outer tepals of an almost transparent yellowish green, the inner ones smaller and purplish. Seeds produced in a stalked, gourd-shaped structure 1½ in. long, to the apex of which the stamens remain attached. *Bot. Mag.*, n.s., t. 184 (2).

cv. 'GRANDIFLORUS'.—Flowers a purer yellow and more showy than in the type, and as much as 1¾ in. across, but not so strongly fragrant. The leaves, too, are larger; I have seen them occasionally as much as 9 in. long and 4 in. wide. The shrub is of stronger growth; there used to be one 15 ft high at Warley Place. *Bot. Reg.*, t. 451; *Bot. Mag.*, n.s., t. 184 (3).

cv. 'LUTEUS'.—A variety known in gardens in the early part of the nineteenth century and described by Loudon. It differed in having the inner segments (tepals) yellow instead of purplish. Garden forms of this character have long been cultivated in China and Japan. The plant now grown as *C. praecox* 'Luteus' was probably introduced from Japan around 1930 and is unlikely to be the clone known to Loudon.

This delightful old shrub and its varieties have two strong claims to the notice of planters: it flowers in midwinter when very few other things are in bloom, and its blossoms diffuse around them one of the most pleasing of perfumes. A charming way to use cut sprays for indoor decoration is to associate them with sprays of *Mahonia aquifolium*. It is hardy, and frequently flowers in the open at Kew with great freedom. But usually (and always in cold localities) it is grown on a wall. It requires no pruning in the open, but on a wall an annual pruning is necessary. It should not be deferred much beyond February, so that the fullest possible length of time is allowed for the new growths to be made on which depend the next winter's crop of flowers. The pruning should consist of a shortening back of the stronger twigs, and the entire removal of the weaker and overcrowding ones. At the same time any re-tying that may be needed should be done, also the laying-in of new shoots in vacant places. Propagation is effected by layers and seeds; cuttings are extremely difficult to root.

C. praecox was introduced from China in 1766. C. NITENS Oliver, is an evergreen species with glabrous, shining oval-lanceolate leaves, 3 to 4 in. long. Flowers white, solitary, axillary, ¾ in. across. Found by Henry near Ichang, it has not yet been introduced, and is probably rare in a wild state. The third species, C. YUNNANENSIS W. W. Sm., was discovered in the Sungkwei Valley by Forrest at 6,000 to 7,000 ft altitude; probably not in cultivation.

CHIOGENES ERICACEAE

A genus of two species, natives one of N. America the other of Japan, allied to *Vaccinium* and *Gaylussacia*.

C. HISPIDULA (L.) Torr. & Gray CREEPING SNOWBERRY
Vaccinium hispidulum L.; *C. serpyllifolia* Salisb.; *Gaultheria hispidula* (L.) Muhl.

A creeping, evergreen shrub, the slender stems furnished with forward-pointing bristles. Leaves alternate, very abundant, ⅛ to ⅓ in. long, oval to nearly round, tapered at both ends, scarcely stalked; margins slightly decurved; glabrous and dark green above, pale beneath, and furnished with a few tiny, rust-coloured bristles. Flowers produced singly in the leaf-axils on short, decurved stalks; corolla ⅛ in. or less long, bell-shaped, deeply four-lobed, white; stamens eight; ovary half-inferior. Berry white, ⅓ in. across, roundish and rather bristly.

Native of N. America, from Newfoundland westward to British Columbia, and southward to N. Carolina; introduced in 1815. This plant is very rare in gardens, and the plant nearly always found under the name is one of the cranberries. These are nearly allied plants, but *Chiogenes* is abundantly distinct in leaf, flower, and especially the white berry. Out of flower the short, broad leaf and bristly young wood amply distinguish it. It has little garden value as an ornament, but is interesting. A moist, semi-boggy spot such as the cranberries love, should, if possible, be selected for it. The whole plant, including the berry, has an aromatic taste and odour, resembling that of *Gaultheria procumbens*. The Japanese species—*C. japonica* A. Gray—is closely allied to the American one. It is probably not in cultivation.

CHIONANTHUS   OLEACEAE

This is one of those interesting genera of plants represented, but very sparsely, in both the New and the Old Worlds. In this case one species is found in the eastern United States, the other in China. They belong to the olive family, and have opposite, deciduous leaves. The flowers are in panicles, their most remarkable feature being the four or five long, narrow, pure white petals, united quite at the base. Stamens two. The fruit is an egg-shaped or oblong drupe, containing usually one seed.

In gardens, although undeservedly neglected, the two species of *Chionanthus* are amongst the most attractive and distinguished of all hardy shrubs though neither flowers here with such profusion as in the eastern United States. They like a moist, loamy soil of good depth and quality, and a sunny position. *C. virginicus* is best propagated by seeds obtained from America, but both it and *C. retusus* can be raised from layers. The former is also grafted on the common and manna ashes, but plants so raised are neither so healthy nor so long-lived as those on their own roots. If *C. retusus* is not obtainable on its own roots, it might be grafted on seedlings of *C. virginicus*. Both of them are suitable as isolated specimens on lawns; they produce abundant fibres at the root, and transplant easily.

C. RETUSUS Lindl.   CHINESE FRINGE-TREE   [PLATE 44

A deciduous shrub in cultivation, but a small tree sometimes 30 to 40 ft high in China, of spreading, rounded habit; young shoots downy. Leaves variable in shape, usually oval, sometimes obovate, sometimes almost round; from 1 to 4 in. long, ¾ to 2 in. wide; rounded, notched, or blunt at the point, tapered at the base; shiny green above and downy on the midrib; downy more or less all over beneath, but especially on the midrib and veins; stalk ¼ to ½ in. long, downy. Flowers snow-white, produced during June and July in erect, cymose panicles terminating young shoots of the year, 2 to 3 in. high, and 2 to 4 in. wide. Each subdivision of the inflorescence carries normally three flowers, the four strap-shaped petals of which are ¾ in. long, ⅛ in. wide.

Native of China, where it is widely spread; introduced by Fortune in 1845, but apparently not established in gardens until reintroduced by Maries in 1879. It is easily distinguished from its American ally by flowering on the young

CHIONANTHUS RETUSUS

shoots of the year and by the erect, shorter, broader panicles. It is a shrub of the first rank, one traveller in China comparing it when in flower to a 'dome of soft, fleecy snow'.

C. VIRGINICUS L.   FRINGE-TREE

A deciduous shrub or small tree 10 to 20 or even 30 ft high; branchlets stout, stiff, downy when young. Leaves oblong, narrowly oval or obovate, always tapering at the base, usually at the apex; 2 to 8 in. long, rather less than half as wide, not toothed; bright green above and downy on the midrib, paler below, and downy especially on the veins; stalks downy, $\frac{1}{2}$ to 1 in. long. Flowers pure white, slightly fragrant; produced during June in very lax panicles 4 to 8 in. long; these panicles are crowded at the upper joints of the preceding year's growths, and form a dense, mop-like mass beneath the new growths. Each branch of the panicle bears three flowers, and springs from the axil of a leaf-like bract which is occasionally 1 to 1$\frac{1}{2}$ in. long at the base of the panicle, becoming smaller towards the end; the bracts persist to the fruiting stage. Petals four or five, each $\frac{3}{4}$ to 1$\frac{1}{4}$ in. long, $\frac{1}{16}$ to $\frac{1}{12}$ in. wide; calyx minute, with pointed lobes. Fruit roundish or egg-shaped, dark blue, $\frac{2}{3}$ in. long, borne on pendulous stalks.

Native of the eastern United States, from Pennsylvania southward; introduced in 1736. This is one of the most beautiful and striking of N. American shrubs, and is perfectly hardy in this country. I have never seen it flower so well here, however, as in Central Europe and in the United States, where the shrub in June is almost hidden in the profusion of pendent masses of blossom. There is nothing like it among flowering shrubs except its Asiatic ally.

var. MARITIMUS Pursh; var. *pubescens* Dipp.—More downy generally, but especially on the panicles.

CHOISYA   RUTACEAE

A genus of about seven species in Mexico and the S.W. United States, related to *Zanthoxylum*.

C. TERNATA H. B. K.   MEXICAN ORANGE FLOWER

An evergreen shrub, of rounded, bushy habit, 6 to 10 ft high; young shoots downy. Leaves opposite, 3 to 6 in. long, consisting nearly always of three leaflets, but occasionally two or four. Leaflets stalkless, obovate, 1$\frac{1}{2}$ to 3 in. long, about one-third as wide; rounded or blunt at the end, tapering to a common point of union at the end of a downy leaf-stalk 1 to 2 in. long; when crushed they have a strong, pungent, rather unpleasant odour, and held against the light will be seen to be pitted with numerous oil-glands. Flowers produced in a cluster of axillary corymbs at the end of the shoot, each corymb three- to six-flowered, with a slender, downy stalk 2 to 3 in. long. Flowers white, 1 to 1$\frac{1}{4}$ in. across, with five roundish oval petals; fragrant like hawthorn. *Bot. Mag.*, n.s., t. 318.

This fine evergreen is of interest as being one of the very few shrubs native of Mexico that are hardy near London. It survived practically uninjured the great frosts of February 1895 at Kew, also the trying winter of 1908–9. But for some constitutional reason it is often injured during spells of lesser cold, especially after the New Year. It was severely damaged in many gardens in the winters of 1961–3 but will usually come through winters of moderate severity without serious harm. Its normal flowering time may be considered April and May, but it often produces flowers more or less up to September. On a few occasions after a very mild November, it has been seen in full blossom in December. It should have an open but sheltered spot, and the soil may be a rather light loam.

CHOISYA TERNATA

It is better to encourage short, well-ripened growths rather than thick, sappy ones. Cuttings made of half-ripened wood root quickly placed in gentle heat; those of a little harder wood will take root in a cold frame.

CHORDOSPARTIUM   LEGUMINOSAE

A monotypic genus endemic to a few localities in the South Island of New Zealand. It may be distinguished from *Carmichaelia* by the combination of a many-flowered racemose inflorescence and a single-seeded indehiscent pod. In *Carmichaelia* some species have a similar inflorescence but in these the pod is dehiscent. In *Nothospartium*, another ally, the pod is many-seeded and jointed.

C. STEVENSONII Cheeseman

An almost leafless shrub or small tree, the latter occasionally 20 to 30 ft high, with a trunk 6 to 8 in. in diameter and slender pendulous branches. Young shoots long, slender, scarcely branched, $\frac{1}{16}$ to $\frac{1}{12}$ in. in diameter, minutely ribbed, not downy. Leaves are borne only on young plants and then persist only three or four months. Racemes cylindrical, $1\frac{1}{2}$ to $3\frac{1}{2}$ in. long, $\frac{5}{8}$ in. wide, sometimes solitary, sometimes in clusters of two to five; on these the flowers are closely packed a score or so to the inch. Flowers pea-flower-shaped, $\frac{1}{3}$ in. long, pale lilac, with darker lines on the standard petal; calyx and flower-stalks covered densely with a pale wool. Pod indehiscent, about $\frac{1}{5}$ in. long, carrying a single seed. *Bot. Mag.*, t. 9654.

Native of the South Island of New Zealand, confined to alluvial soils on the tributaries of the Clarence, Awatere, and Waitau Rivers; discovered in 1909 in the Seaward Kaikoura Range at 1,500 to 2,500 ft, near the mouth of the first-named river. Seed was sent to Kew in 1923 but it has never thrived there. The most suitable localities for cultivating this shrub are sunny spots on or near the south coast from Sussex westward. Mr Hillier, who had a good specimen in his private garden near Romsey, tells us that it is probably not long-lived in this country. His tree reached a height of about 7 ft and a spread of 4 or 5 ft, and was very striking in July when covered with its rosy-lilac flowers. The species was given an Award of Merit when shown from Exbury in 1943.

CHRYSOLEPIS   FAGACEAE

The species described below is better known as *Castanopsis chrysophylla*, but in a recent study (*Bot. Notiser*, Suppl. 2, p. 117, 1948) Hjelmqvist has pointed out that it is really as out-of-place in *Castanopsis* as it is in *Castanea*, in which genus Hooker first described it. He has accordingly created for it a new genus—*Chrysolepis*. Mr L. Forman of the Kew Herbarium, who has made a special study of the group, concurs. He tells us that the salient points which justify treating *Castanopsis chrysophylla* as a distinct genus are: 1. Each bur contains three nuts and is composed of seven spiny cupule-valves, five outside and around the nuts and two inside between the nuts and separating them from each other. 2. The cupule-valves are free from one another right from the start. 3. The fruits are triangular in section. The genus is further distinguished from *Castanopsis* by the female flowers being borne on the same catkins as the males, as in *Castanea*; in *Castanopsis* the spikes are unisexual.

C. CHRYSOPHYLLA (Hook.) Hjelmqvist   GOLDEN CHESTNUT
Castanea chrysophylla Hook.; *Castanopsis chrysophylla* (Hook.) DC.

An evergreen tree, described as occasionally over 100 ft high in California; but hitherto a small tree about 30 ft high, or a low, dense bush, in Britain; the young shoots and under-surface of the leaves covered with a beautiful, persistent, golden scurf. Leaves ovate, lanceolate, narrowly ovate or obovate, 1½ to 4 in. long, ½ to 1 in. wide, tapered at both ends, often long-pointed, not toothed,

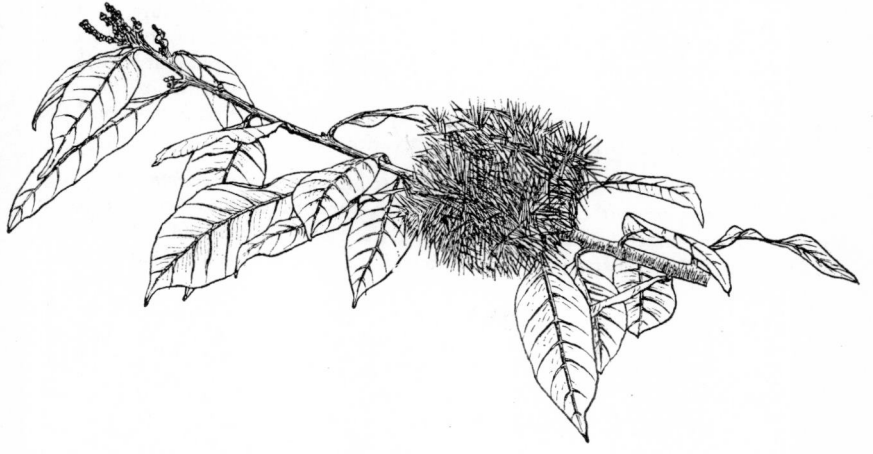

CHRYSOLEPIS CHRYSOPHYLLA

dark glossy green above; stalk ¼ in. long. Flowers unisexual; the males produced in erect, cylindrical catkins 1 to 1½ in. long, ¼ in. wide; the stamens numerous, yellow, slender. Female flowers produced at the base of the same catkin as the males in two opposite clusters of three to seven flowers, each ovary bearing three styles. Sometimes the female clusters are lacking and the catkins are wholly male. Fruit like that of a sweet chestnut, consisting of a bur 1 to 1½ in. in diameter, clothed with a mass of branched, slender spines, enclosing up to three small, pale brown, shining nuts, which are edible. *Bot. Mag.*, t. 4953.

Native of Oregon and California; introduced in 1844. The above description is based on cultivated English specimens, but in California, where it is sometimes 115 ft high, with a trunk 6 ft in diameter, the leaves are occasionally 6 in. long.

Although so long introduced, there are few large specimens in the country.

It is a species that ranges through a variety of climate and habitat and it might well be that if seed were introduced from a number of stands the resulting plants would differ very considerably in their response to the British climate. The largest specimen in the British Isles is probably the one at Leonardslee in Sussex, which was planted in 1908 and measures 53 × 4¾ ft (1962). There is a smaller tree, but a fine one, at Grayswood Hill, Surrey. In the Edinburgh Botanic Garden there are two trees which produce self-sown seedlings; one is 28 ft high, the other 20 ft high with a spread of 24 ft (1968).

Probably a deep, light and moist soil is best for this species. The trunk of the tree should not be exposed to full sunlight and its lower branches should not be cut away.

var. MINOR (Benth.)—A shrub or small tree to about 30 ft, found in the coastal ranges of California. It probably grades into the type; and it may be, as Henry thought, that some of the introductions to Britain belong to this variety.

cv. 'OBOVATA'.—This curious dwarf shrubby variety was raised by Messrs T. Smith & Son of Newry, Co. Down, from seeds obtained from N. America about 1914. The leaves are remarkably distinct in shape, being obovate, oval, or almost orbicular, always rounded or even flattish at the apex and only ½ to 1 in. long. They are yellow beneath when young, as in the type. A plant at Kew bore both male and female flowers in 1928 and developed prickly fruits of the same character as that figured here. It does not appear likely ever to get beyond the dwarf shrubby state. It is no longer in cultivation there.

C. SEMPERVIRENS (Kellogg) Hjelmqvist *Castanea sempervirens* Kellogg; *Castanopsis sempervirens* (Kellogg) Dudley—A shrubby species with a smooth bark and blunt-ended leaves, found inland in the Sierra Nevada of California and S. Oregon. There is a specimen at Edinburgh 12 ft high with a spread of 21 ft.

CHRYSOTHAMNUS   COMPOSITAE

A genus of about twelve species found in the drier parts of western N. America, once included in *Bigelowia*. The leaves of most species are aromatic and the stems of some yield a latex from which chrysil rubber is made. The heads are small, without ray-flowers, but usually united into large, showy paniculate or corymbose clusters. The involucral bracts are arranged in more or less vertical ranks, a character that distinguishes this genus from the related *Haplopappus*.

C. GRAVEOLENS (Nutt.) Greene
Chrysocoma graveolens Nutt.; *Bigelowia graveolens* (Nutt.) A. Gray

An evergreen shrub, 6 to 8 ft high, much branched; branches erect, and white when young. Leaves alternate, crowded on the branch, linear, 1 to 3 in. long,

⅛ in. wide or less, long-pointed, glabrous. Flower-heads bright yellow, very numerous, forming flattish corymbs 1 to 4 in. across; each head is composed of about five florets, each of which is very slender, tubular, ⅓ in. long, the pointed teeth of the corolla erect, the base slightly downy. When crushed the plant emits a not unpleasant, somewhat pungent odour. *Bot. Mag.*, t. 8155.

Native of western N. America, inhabiting dry situations. It is not hardy in the open at Kew, but thrives remarkably well on a south wall, where it flowers abundantly during the latter end of September and during October, producing heavy masses of corymbs often 9 to 12 in. across. It does not need a rich or heavy soil, but a well-drained, sandy loam, and all the sunshine possible. The above description is made from the plant at Kew, figured in the *Botanical Magazine*; but in a wild state the species is spread over a wide extent of country, and is said to vary much.

CHUSQUEA* GRAMINEAE

A genus of about forty species of evergreen bamboos, distributed from Mexico and the West Indies to Chile and Argentina. Many of the species from the Andes, especially those from high elevations and from Chile and Argentina, will probably prove hardy in the southern parts of the British Isles, but up to the present only one appears to be growing successfully in S. England. The hardy species are similar to *Arundinaria* in habit, having woody, cylindrical, jointed and solid or hollow stems, branching profusely at the joints, especially in the upper part, with flat, linear to lanceolate, stiff leaf-blades which finally disarticulate from their sheaths. *Chusquea* has a single fertile flower in each spikelet whereas in *Arundinaria* there are generally several to many flowers in each spikelet.

C. CULEOU E. Desv. COLIHUE, CULEU
C. andina Phil.

A bamboo 3 to 20 ft or more high, with green or at length yellow, solid, erect or slightly spreading stems, up to 1 in. thick at the base; branches in dense clusters, slender. Leaf-blades linear or linear-lanceolate, sharply pointed, shortly stalked, 1 to 2½ in. or more long, ⅙ to ⅓ in. wide, rigid, deep green, slightly hairy or hairless, five-veined, the midrib prominent beneath, mostly conspicuously tessellate; ligules blunt, up to 1/12 in. long.

Native of Argentina and Chile; introduced in 1926 by seed collected by H. F. Comber during his 1926–7 expedition to the Andes, and by L. Bridges in 1939 from the Magellan region. There are fine clumps of this graceful bamboo in several southern gardens, including those of the Royal Horticultural Society, Wisley, Surrey, and Hidcote, Gloucestershire.

* Contributed by Dr C. E. Hubbard.

It is possible that two other Chilean species of *Chusquea* are in cultivation, viz. C. CUMMINGII Nees, with solid, slender stems 6 to 10 ft high, lanceolate-linear leaf-blades 1 to 2 in. long and $\frac{1}{12}$ to $\frac{1}{4}$ in. wide, without tessellations; collected in the Andes by Clarence Elliott in 1927: and C. QUILA (Poir.) Kunth, with solid stems reaching 40 to 50 ft in height, narrowly lanceolate leaf-blades up to 5 in. long and $\frac{1}{2}$ in. wide, without tessellations; collected in the Andes in 1927 by H. F. Comber (no. 997) and in 1929 by Clarence Elliott (no. 576).

The above three species may be distinguished from the species of *Arundinaria* in cultivation by their solid culms and mostly few-veined leaf-blades.

CINNAMOMUM   LAURACEAE

A genus of some forty evergreen trees, natives of the warmer parts of E. Asia. In addition to *C. camphora* other species are of economic import-ance. The spice cinnamon is made from the shoots of *C. zeylanicum*, a native of Ceylon but now grown in many tropical regions. An inferior form is made from *C. cassia*, cultivated in China since the earliest historical times.

C. CAMPHORA (L.) Nees   CAMPHOR TREE
Laurus camphora L.

An evergreen tree of large size. Leaves alternate, oval or obovate, slender-pointed and tapered at the base; 3 to 6 in. long, 1½ to 3 in. wide; glabrous and shining, fragrant when crushed, firm and leathery in texture; stalk ¾ to 1¼ in. long. Usually the veins are in three or four pairs, and sometimes the lowest pair are so strongly developed as to give the leaf a three-ribbed character. Flowers greenish white, $\frac{1}{6}$ in. wide, produced in spring in axillary long-stalked panicles 2 to 3 in. long. *Bot. Mag.*, t. 2658.

A native of the southern part of Japan and of China and Formosa; introduced, according to Aiton, from Japan in 1727. It is only in the milder parts of the British Isles that the camphor tree can be grown in the open air. In 1920 it was 35 ft high in Lord Clinton's collection at Bicton in Devon and at Penjerrick in Cornwall it reached 50 ft. But neither of these trees now exists (1966) and none of such size has been found in any other garden. But the closely allied C. GLANDULIFERUM (Wall.) Meissn. is represented at Caerhays Castle, Corn-wall, by a specimen 27 ft high.

CISSUS   VITACEAE

A genus of about 250 deciduous and evergreen species almost wholly confined to tropical and subtropical regions. The majority are climbers, but some are inhabitants of desert regions, with succulent roots and herbaceous stems, or with stout, fleshy trunks. By far the best known member of the genus is the common house-plant *Cissus antarctica*, a native of New South Wales.

C. STRIATA Ruiz & Pavon
Vitis striata (Ruiz & Pavon) Miq.

An evergreen climber; young stems slender, angled, hairy and very leafy; tendrils thread-like. Leaves 1½ to 3 in. across, composed of five scarcely stalked leaflets, radiating from the end of a common stalk ¾ to 1½ in. long. Leaflets obovate or oblanceolate, ½ to 1½ in. long, ¼ to ¾ in. wide; tapered at the base, coarsely toothed towards the apex, each tooth tipped abruptly with a short gland; dark glossy green and glabrous on both surfaces. Flowers green, produced in small cymes. Fruits about the size and shape of small red currants, but of a reddish-purple colour.

Native of Chile and S. Brazil; introduced about 1878. Against a wall this survives all but the hardest winters, but is tender in the open. It is a very elegant plant, luxuriantly leafy, and with beautifully cut leaves. Tweedie, the Kew collector in S. America, called it the 'ivy of Uruguay', and says it covers the bushes with red berries in winter. It thrives very well in the south and west, and bore large crops of fruit at St Leonard's as long ago as 1885, but the berries were purplish rather than red. When cut down to the ground by frost it will often break up again the following summer, but on the whole it is only well adapted for the mildest counties.

CISTUS   ROCK ROSE   CISTACEAE

A genus of about twenty species, nearly allied to *Helianthemum*, but differing in having the seed-vessels five- or ten-celled, whilst in *Helianthemum* they are three-celled. Leaves opposite, evergreen. Flowers of a rose-like appearance, having five broadly wedge-shaped petals and very numerous stamens; sepals three to five. Seeds numerous. In a wild state the cistuses are found in the Mediterranean region, and are especially abundant in Spain and Portugal. The flowers usually last only a few hours in the morning, never more than a day, but a constant succession of them is maintained during sunny weather, making a fine display in June and July. None of the cistuses is yellow-flowered, but they very frequently have a patch of that colour at the base of each petal.

Although the number of true species is comparatively limited, they have hybridised freely. Some of the best are hybrids, such as × *cyprius*, × *purpureus*, and × *corbariensis*. These, and some others, will be found in their alphabetical position. Hybrids of lesser account are treated under one or other of the parents (see the Index to this volume). It must be emphasised that hybrid names in Latin such as *C.* × *skanbergii*, *C.* × *aguilari*, etc. are group-names that cover any form of the cross, whether it arose in the wild or in cultivation. It is purely accidental if such hybrids are represented in cultivation by a single clone. Some are, and all could be, grown in many slightly differing forms. Hybrids are likely to occur when plants are raised from seed in gardens where many species grow together. Numerous hybrids were raised artificially by Bornet at the Villa Thuret, Antibes, during the years 1860–75, and thanks to his researches it was established that many cistuses previously thought to be species were in fact hybrids. In the natural state, crossing between species is less likely to occur than in gardens since the various species tend to occupy different habitats or different geographical areas. However, some crosses are common in the wild: for example, Dansereau reports that, where *C. monspeliensis* and *C. salvifolius* are in contact, their hybrid (*C.* × *florentinus*) may make up ten per cent of the stand.

Unfortunately the rock roses with few exceptions are not genuinely hardy. They survive our mild winters, but many succumb in severe or even moderately hard ones. The great frosts of February 1895 killed all the cistuses at Kew except *C. laurifolius* and *C.* × *corbariensis*. The cold winters of 1961–3 confirmed the hardiness of these two, though the latter appears to be represented in cultivation by several clones, some less hardy than others. *C. parviflorus*, although not the most decorative of cistuses, has proved remarkably hardy. Others that survive well at Kew are *C.* × *cyprius* and 'Silver Pink' and to these might be added *C. ladanifer*, although in other gardens it is often reckoned as tender. They like a light, well-drained soil, and more than anything a position exposed to full sun, but otherwise sheltered, and something above the surrounding level. They never suffer from drought, and any dry, sunny bank will suit them. A covering of bracken or leafy branches in severe weather is a help, and will often save plants that would otherwise perish.

Propagation may be effected by seed or by cuttings, the latter being necessary for some of the hybrids which do not perfect seed. They are best taken in late summer, and struck in mild heat. Until planted out permanently, rock roses should be grown in pots, as they suffer badly from transplanting. Many of the species exude a fragrant gum, known as labdanum or ladanum, from the young stems and leaves. The most prolific source of this gum, which is used in perfumery and, at least at one time, in medicine, is *C. creticus*—a rather tender shrub. It is also got largely from *C. ladanifer*.

In the wild state, species of *Cistus* are hosts of the remarkable parasitic plant *Cytinus hypocistus*, which is the only European representative of the tropical and subtropical family Rafflesiaceae.

The genus *Cistus* was popular in gardens in the early nineteenth century: in Sweet's *Cistineae*, published 1825–30, 112 species, varieties, and hybrids are figured. Interest dwindled and its revival is largely due to Sir Oscar Warburg and his son, the late Dr Edmund Warburg. They travelled extensively in the cistus regions of Europe and N. Africa, and horticulture is indebted to them for a number of new varieties and hybrids which they introduced and propagated. Their note on the genus (*Journ. R.H.S.*, Vol. 55, pp. 1–52) is still of great value. The species of *Cistus* are reviewed by Dansereau in *Boissiera*, 1939, pp. 1–90.

C. ALBIDUS L.

A compact, bushy shrub, ultimately 5 or 6 ft high, if it survives long enough; young shoots, leaves, flower-stalks, and sepals covered with a dense, whitish, starry down. Leaves stalkless, oval, oblong or ovate, ¾ to 2 in. long, ⅛ to ¾ in. wide, rounded or blunt at the apex, three-nerved at the base, and strongly net-veined beneath. Flowers pale rosy lilac, with a patch of yellow at the base of each petal, about 2½ in. across, borne on a stalk ¾ to 1 in. long, and crowded three to eight together in a terminal cluster. Sepals five, broadly ovate, ¾ to ½ in. long.

Native of S.W. Europe and N. Africa; cultivated in 1640. It is one of the hardier sorts, and will survive all but our hardest winters. The epithet *albidus*, it should be noted, refers to the foliage, and not to the flowers. It has hybridised with and is closely allied to *C. crispus*, from which it differs in its flat, not undulated leaves, and its comparatively long-stalked flowers—those of *crispus* being almost stalkless.

f. ALBUS (Warb.) Dansereau—A form with pure white flowers found wild with the type.

C. × CANESCENS Sweet—A natural hybrid between *C. albidus* and *C. creticus* reported from Algeria but also occurring in gardens among seedlings of *C. albidus*. Leaves usually greener than in that species, narrower and more pointed. 'ALBUS' was raised by Sir Oscar Warburg from a pink form of *C. × canescens* which had been raised from seed of *C. albidus* f. *albus*.

C. × PULVERULENTUS Pourr. *C. × delilei* Burnat—A common hybrid between *C. albidus* and *C. crispus* found wild where they grow together, e.g. in France and the Iberian peninsula. Intermediate in character between the parents. The garden clone 'SUNSET' belongs here.

C. CLUSII Dun.

C. rosmarinifolius Pourr., in part, not All.

A dwarf shrub to about 1 ft high. Young shoots slender, hairy. Leaves linear, about 1 in. long, ⅛ to ¼ in. wide, with recurved margins, hairy on both sides. Flowers white with a yellow centre, about 1 in. across, borne in sparsely hairy clusters; sepals three to five, with ciliate margins.

Native of N. Africa; introduced before 1826. It is very distinct in its small flowers and narrow leaves, and is one of the hardiest species.

C. LIBANOTIS L. *C. bourgeanus* Coss.—A local species, found only in the Algarve and along the coast of S. Spain from the Portuguese border to Cadiz. It is related to the preceding but the inflorescence is glabrous and the sepals reddish.

C. × CORBARIENSIS Pourr.

A densely bushy, evergreen shrub 2 or 3 ft high, often more in width; young branches ¦glabrous, or with a very minute down. Leaves ovate, pointed, heart-shaped or rounded at the base, ¾ to 2 in. long, ⅓ to 1 in. wide; minutely toothed and wavy at the margin, each tooth crested with a tuft of minute hairs; net-veined, dull dark green above, paler beneath, both surfaces with starry down; stalks ¼ to ½ in. long, downy. Flowers 1½ in. across, white with a yellow stain at the base of the petals, produced in June at the end of short axillary shoots; there are from one to three flowers on each stalk, which is slender, stellately hairy, and about 3 in. long. Outer sepals heart-shaped, ⅓ in. long, hairy.

A natural hybrid between the Narbonne variety of *C. populifolius* and *C. salviifolius*, taking its name from Corbières, in the south of France. This is one of the hardiest and best of cistuses, and like many hybrids possesses a vigour and constitution superior to that of its parents. In the debacle of rather tender plants which followed the great frosts of February 1895, this cistus was one of those which survived at Kew, the other being *laurifolius*. It also survived the hard winters of 1961–3 in many gardens. There may be several forms of the cross in cultivation, differing somewhat in shape of leaf and perhaps in hardiness. Large groups of plants provide most pleasing displays from June onwards every year. The general aspect of the plant is that of a small-leaved *C. populifolius* of which it has been known as "var. *minor*".

C. CRETICUS L.

C. villosus L.; *C. incanus* auct., not L.; *C. polymorphus* Willk.

C. creticus L. (and not *C. villosus* L. nor *C. incanus* L.) is the valid name for a variable and taxonomically difficult species which occupies a wide range in the Mediterranean—indeed it is one of the most widespread and common of the cistuses in a wild state. Several attempts have been made to bring its manifold forms into an orderly system of subspecies and varieties, but with differing results. For garden purposes there is, in any case, nothing to be gained from following the botanists into this labyrinth. The following is a generalised description:

A much-branched, compact bush 2 to 4 ft high; young stems shaggy with long hairs, or downy with short stellate hairs (stems also glandular in some states, mostly in Crete and other parts of the E. Mediterranean). Leaves variable in shape from ovate to obovate or almost rounded, pointed to rounded at the apex, tapered at the base to a short, flat, broad stalk, usually swollen at the base and more or less connate with the stalk of the opposite leaf; hairy on both sides, but more so below; veins impressed; margins often wavy. Flowers in some shade between purple and rose, yellowish at the base of the petals; 2 to 2½ in. across; they are borne in a cymose cluster of three to five at the ends of the shoots. Flower-stalks and calyces closely downy to densely hairy and sometimes glandular; sepals broadly oval, with fine points.

Native of the Mediterranean region and (as pointed out above) very poly-morphic. The most distinct state is the glandular one (*C. creticus* L. in the narrow sense), in which the stems, the undersides of the leaves and the inflorescence exude an aromatic gum (the chief source of Gum ladanum). This, however, is not confined to Crete but is found in other parts of the E. Mediterranean. A glandular race is also found in Corsica. Owing to its variability, and the number of hybrids between it and other species that have appeared in cultivation, there

CISTUS CRETICUS

is considerable confusion in gardens as to its identity. It appears, however, to be tender in all its forms. From *C. albidus* and *C. crispus*, both of which have flowers of similar colouring, it differs in its pinnately veined leaves, whilst they are marked by leaves with three longitudinal veins.

C. CRISPUS L.

A compact, bushy shrub 2 ft high, much-branched; young shoots clothed with long white hairs. Leaves sessile, lance-shaped to narrowly oblong or ovate or oval, ½ to 1½ in. long, ¼ to ½ in. wide, pointed, three-nerved at the base, margins (especially of the lower leaves) much undulated; both surfaces rough through the deeply impressed veins, and densely coated with starry down. Flowers purplish red, about 1½ in. diameter, crowded in a terminal head, supplemented by smaller ones on short axillary branches; each flower is on a very hairy stalk, so short that it is almost hidden in the bracts; sepals five, ovate or lance-shaped, long-pointed, hairy. *Bot. Mag.*, t. 9306.

Native of S.W. Europe and N. Africa; said to have been introduced to England in 1656. It is one of the comparatively hardy species, and will survive moderately cold winters. Its short-stalked, richer red flowers, narrow, long-pointed sepals, and wavy-margined leaves distinguish it from the nearest ally, *C. albidus*.

C. × CRISPATUS Warb.—An artificial hybrid between *C. crispus* and *C. creticus* first raised at Antibes by Bornet. Sir Oscar Warburg had a form (from a repetition of the cross, also made at Antibes) which was a very attractive spreading shrub, with flowers of a good pink.

C. (*crispus* × *palhinhae*) 'ANNE PALMER'.—This cistus was raised by Capt. Collingwood Ingram, who in 1960 received for it the Reginald Cory Memorial Cup—an award given for the best man-made hybrid of the year (*Journ. R.H.S.*, Vol. 86, March 1961, fig. 39).

C. × CYPRIUS Lam.   [PLATE 47

An evergreen shrub of vigorous, bushy habit, up to 6 or 8 ft high; young branches clammy and shining with fragrant gum. Leaves narrow, lance-shaped, 1½ to 4 in. long, ⅓ to rather over 1 in. wide, wedge-shaped and three-nerved at the base, tapered to the apex, wavy at the margin, dark dull green above, grey with down beneath; stalk ⅛ to ½ in. long, the bases clasping the stem, shining and sticky with gum beneath, like the midrib. Both surfaces of the leaf are clammy. Flowers several (three to six) in a long-stalked cluster, terminating short side branches; each blossom about 3 in. across, white, with a conspicuous blood-red blotch near the base of each petal. Sepals three, yellowish, scaly, and, like the upper part of the flower-stalk, rather hairy. *Bot. Mag.*, t. 112.

The native country of this beautiful rock rose is generally given as Cyprus, but if, as is certainly the case, it is a hybrid between *C. ladanifer* and *C. laurifolius*, then the plant described by Lamarck cannot have originated in Cyprus, as *C. ladanifer* does not extend so far east. Hybrids between these two species (which are closely allied) are fairly common in France and the Iberian peninsula but the cultivated plants appear to be a clone, of unrecorded origin. Between the parents it is in many respects intermediate. It has the large, crimson-blotched flowers, the glabrous stems, and the scaly sepals of *C. ladanifer*, but the several flowers on a stalk and the broader-stalked leaves show the influence of *C. laurifolius*. In hardiness it is about intermediate, and is only injured by the very severest of winters. I consider it the most beautiful of all the cistuses we can grow out-of-doors. The leaves become metallic grey in autumn. For hot dry banks it is unsurpassed. The several flowers in a cluster are individually as beautiful as those of the solitary ones of *C. ladanifer*, and the shrub has much of the hardiness of *C. laurifolius*. Old plants assume a graceful, spreading habit. It thrives remarkably well in Notcutt's nursery at Woodbridge, in Suffolk.

var. ALBIFLORUS Verguin—Petals without a basal blotch.

C. × FLORENTINUS Lam.

An evergreen shrub 2 to 4 ft high, much-branched, not viscid, branchlets stellately downy when young. Leaves narrowly oval-lanceolate, wavy, pointed at the apex; 1 to 1¾ in. long, ¼ to ½ in. wide; upper surface dull green, roughish, net-veined beneath, the chief veins pinnately arranged; at first stellately downy above, covered beneath with a thin greyish wool. Flowers two to four on a stalk, white except for a blotch of yellow at the base of each petal; 1½ to 2 in. across. Sepals five, hairy, ovate, with a heart-shaped base and a slender, pointed apex.

A hybrid between *monspeliensis* and *salviifolius*, found wild in various parts of S. Europe and in Algiers. It is a useful plant although not among the hardiest. Intermediate between its parents, but somewhat variable, it has the same type of foliage as *C. monspeliensis*, but broader, whilst its flowers are larger and more like those of *C. salviifolius*. The stickiness of the young stems, seen in *monspeliensis*, is missing.

C. HIRSUTUS Lam.

A much-branched shrub up to 3 ft high, the shoots densely covered with down amidst which are numerous white outstanding hairs. Leaves stalkless, ovate-oblong, blunt at the apex, three-nerved and rounded at the base; 1 to 2½ in. long, ¼ to ¾ in. wide; very hairy, the hairs on the upper surface and at the margins long, whitish, simple; those beneath short, starry. Flowers 1½ in. diameter, white, with a yellow stain near the base of each petal; produced in a terminal cymose cluster. Sepals five, outer ones heart-shaped, ¾ in. long, with a broad base ½ in. wide, and a tapered point; inner ones ovate, smaller, all shaggy with white hairs.

Native of Spain and Portugal (it is not a native of France but has become naturalised there in Britanny near Landerneau); introduced about the middle of the seventeenth century. An almost hardy species, only injured in exceptionally severe winters. With *C. salviifolius* and *C. populifolius* it forms the group *Ledonia*, characterised by large, heart-shaped outer sepals. It is distinguished from the other two by its stalkless leaves.

var. PSILOSEPALUS (Sweet) Willk. *C. psilosepalus* Sweet—Leaves on short stalks; outer sepals glabrous on the back, with ciliate margins.

C. × LAXUS Ait. f.—A hybrid between *C. hirsutus* and *C. populifolius*. A shrub to about 4 ft high. Leaves ovate-lanceolate, hairy when young, three-veined at the base, short-stalked. Flowers white, about 2 in. wide; petals marked with yellow at the base; sepals five, hairy, cordate at the base. It occurs wild in Spain and Portugal and has also been raised in gardens. According to Aiton, it was cultivated in 1656 by John Tradescant. See also *C. × nigricans*.

C. × PLATYSEPALUS Sweet—A hybrid between *C. hirsutus* and *C. monspeliensis* which has been found wild in Portugal and also raised in gardens. It is intermediate between the parents, the leaves being less hairy than in *C. hirsutus* and ovate-lanceolate in shape. Abnormal forms which lack stamens have been reported.

C. LADANIFER* L.

An evergreen shrub 3 to 5 ft high, of erect, thin habit; branches very clammy with a shining resin. Leaves three-nerved, glutinous, linear-lanceolate, 1½ to 4 in. long, ¼ to ¾ in. wide; tapering gradually to both ends, scarcely stalked, the bases of each pair clasping the stem; dark green and glabrous above, covered beneath with a close grey felt. Flowers solitary at the end of slender side twigs, protected in the bud state by large bracts, white, with a fine blood-red blotch at the base of each petal, 3 to 4 in. across, the petals crimped at the margin. Sepals three, large, concave, covered with yellowish scales. Seed-vessel ten-valved.

Native of S. Europe and N. Africa; introduced in 1629. Near London this rock rose withstands frosts up to 20°, but is certainly not so hardy as C. × cyprius, nor so vigorous and bushy a plant. It is a beautiful species, especially the common crimson-blotched form, and has larger flowers than any other species we can cultivate out-of-doors. It differs from C. laurifolius in its narrow leaves, in the absence of hairs on the stem and flower-stalks, in the scaly sepals, and in the solitary flowers. (See also C. × cyprius.) There is a pure white, unspotted form of the species known as var. ALBIFLORUS (Dunal) Dansereau. It is said to be commoner in the wild than the blotched form.

var. PETIOLATUS Maire—Leaves shortly stalked; valves of capsule usually less than ten. This variety, native of N. Africa, also lacks the characteristic gum of the type. Dansereau considers that it may be the result of past hybridisation between C. ladanifer and C. laurifolius.

C. ladanifer, mostly in its blotched form, is the parent of most of the cistus hybrids commonly seen in gardens: see C. × cyprius, C. × lusitanicus, and C. × purpureus. The following are also cultivated:

C. × AGUILARI Pau—A hybrid between C. ladanifer and C. populifolius, found wild in the Iberian peninsula and in Morocco; introduced, in an unblotched form, by Sir O. Warburg. Leaves lanceolate, to 4 in. long, short-stalked, bright green above, paler below, three-nerved and strongly net-veined; margins closely undulate. It was collected in S. Spain and the second parent was C. populifolius var. lasiocalyx.

A blotched form of C. × aguilari—'MACULATUS'—was raised by Sir O. Warburg and received an Award of Merit in 1936. The parentage was given as C. ladanifer (blotched form) × C. populifolius var. lasiocalyx, but there is a possibility that C. × aguilari itself was the second parent (Gard. Chron., 26th March 1960, p. 187). It resembles the unspotted form in foliage, but the leaves are decidedly gummy, suggesting a stronger influence of C. ladanifer. Both forms

---

* This spelling of the specific epithet is to be preferred to the commoner rendering *ladaniferus*. Linnaeus treated *Cistus* as feminine and wrote the name of this species *Cistus ladanifera*. When *Cistus* is treated as a masculine noun, as it is generally, the epithet becomes *ladanifer*, in accordance with the rule of Latin grammar that compound adjectives ending in *-fer* and *-ger* take no termination in the nominative masculine.

of *C.* × *aguilari* are among the finest of cistuses, but not reliably hardy and apt to become top-heavy and blow over. Their flowers are of more substance than in most cistuses and the rippled leaves, of a cheerful green, render them very striking and decorative even when out of flower.

C. × HETIERI Verguin—A triple hybrid between *C. ladanifer, laurifolius,* and *monspeliensis.* An erect, free-flowering, and pleasing hardy shrub of garden origin, which has also been found wild in France.

C. × LORETII Rouy & Fouc.—A hybrid between *C. ladanifer* and *C. monspeliensis* which has been found wild and also raised in gardens. There is a spotted form in commerce with flowers about the size of those of *C. monspeliensis* and with linear-lanceolate leaves, intermediate between those of the parents. The plant once grown in gardens as "*C. loretii*" is *C.* × *lusitanicus* 'Decumbens'.

C. (*ladanifer* × *palhinhae*).—Shortly after introducing *C. palhinhae*, Capt. Ingram crossed it with a particularly fine (but tender) blotched form of *C. ladanifer* found by him in S.W. Spain in 1936. From the original cross and later seedlings from it he raised 'PALADIN' (Award of Merit 1946), 'PAT' (Award of Merit 1955), both with blotched flowers, and 'BLANCHE' (Award of Merit 1967), in which the flowers are unblotched. These hybrids, although rather tender, have the great merit of combining the beautiful flowers of *C. ladanifer* with a bushy and spreading habit of growth. This should render them more suitable for coastal gardens of the south and west than *C. ladanifer* and some of its other hybrids, which are inclined to become leggy, and to blow over in exposed positions.

C. × VERGUINII Coste & Soulie—A very rare natural hybrid between *C. ladanifer* and *C. salviifolius.* Flowers white, with a fine warm blotch. There is also an unblotched form in cultivation.

C. LAURIFOLIUS L.

An evergreen shrub 6 to 8 ft high, with stiff, erect, open branches, hairy and glutinous when young; bark peeling. Leaves ovate to ovate-lanceolate, 1½ to 3 in. long, ¾ to 1½ in. wide; rounded at the base, long and taper-pointed; three-nerved, the margins wavy; dark dull green and glabrous above, pale with a close down beneath, glutinous on both surfaces; stalk hairy, ½ to ¾ in. long, the bases of each pair meeting and clasping the stem. Flowers 2½ to 3 in. across, white, produced from midsummer onwards in hairy, erect, cymose panicles, 6 to 9 in. high, at the end of short side branches. Sepals three, ovate, pointed, very concave, hairy. Seed-vessel five-valved.

Native of S.W. Europe and the Mediterranean region; introduced in 1731. This is the hardiest and one of the best rock roses. Whilst not so showy as *C.* × *cyprius*, and of stiffer habit, it is capable of withstanding more intense cold. At Kew it has survived uninjured 32° of frost. Grown in the mass it makes a bold evergreen group, flowering profusely from June to August. On hot days the leaves and young stems give off a pleasant, aromatic, incense-like perfume. As a flowering evergreen for banks and places too dry for most evergreens it is particularly useful, but is, nevertheless, neglected in gardens. It should be increased by seed, which it produces in plenty.

var. ATLANTICUS Pitard—Native of Morocco. It differs from the type in its smaller leaves and less pointed sepals.

C. × GLAUCUS Pourr. C. × *recognitus* Rouy & Fouc.—A hybrid between C. *laurifolius* and C. *monspeliensis*. A shrub to about 4 ft high with linear-oblong to lanceolate leaves, viscid and dull green above, hairy beneath; flowers white, 1½ to 2 in. across in many-flowered clusters. Found wild in the south of France.

C. (*laurifolius* × *palhinhae*) 'ELMA'.—A floriferous and fairly hardy hybrid raised by Capt. Collingwood Ingram and given an Award of Merit in 1949. The flowers are numerous on each shoot as in the first parent, pure white and about 3½ in. across.

C. × LUSITANICUS Maund

A hybrid between C. *ladanifer* and C. *hirsutus* which has arisen in gardens and is also found wild in Portugal. There are two forms in cultivation of which the best known is:

cv. 'DECUMBENS'.—A spreading bush usually seen below 3 ft in height but taller in semi-shade; young stems gummy, sparsely hairy at first. Leaves stalkless, clammy, narrowly oblong-lanceolate to oblong-oblanceolate, bluntly pointed to rounded at the apex, 1 to 2½ in. long, ¼ to ¾ in. wide; three-nerved and clasping the stem at the base; upper surface dark green with a dull sheen, lower surface paler, with a few scattered hairs. Flowers white with a crimson blotch at the base of each petal, about 2½ in. across, borne in terminal clusters each of three to five flowers; sepals five, downy on the outside, clad within with silky hairs, especially near the edges. [PLATE 46]

The origin of this cistus is unknown but there can be little doubt that it is the plant figured and described in Maund's *The Botanic Garden*, Vol. 9, No. 733, fig. 3 (c. 1845) as C. *lusitanicus* var. *decumbens*. It is recorded that at Kew, it survived the great frosts of 1886. It was later confused with C. × *loretii* (q.v. under C. *ladanifer*) and this is the name under which it appeared in the first edition of this work and under which it was figured in the *Botanical Magazine*, t. 8490 (1913). It is only in the past thirty years or so that it has come to be known again by its correct name. C. × *lusitanicus* 'Decumbens' is one of the élite of cistuses, valuable for its low, spreading habit and for bearing its flowers freely over a long period. It is not reliably hardy, but should survive the average winter.

A second form of C. *ladanifer* × *hirsutus* is also in cultivation. It was once grown under the erroneous name of "C. *recognitus*", which is a synonym of C. × *glaucus*, a hybrid between C. *laurifolius* and C. *monspeliensis*. This cistus—now grown as typical C. *lusitanicus*—is easily distinguished from 'Decumbens' by the smaller and fainter blotch at the base of each petal. It also differs in its leaves, which are oblong-lanceolate, taper-pointed and lack the dull sheen which characterises the other cistus. Its habit, too, is more erect.

It should be pointed out that under the rules of botanical nomenclature the name *C.* × *lusitanicus* Maund is invalid, the same epithet having been used earlier by Philip Miller for some unidentified cistus. It is best retained, however, until a valid name is published.

C. MONSPELIENSIS L.

An evergreen shrub 2 to 4 ft high, with erect, much-divided branches, hairy and slightly viscid when young. Leaves stalkless, narrowly lance-shaped or linear, ¾ to 2 in. long, ⅛ to ½ in. wide; tapered at both ends, three-nerved, margins incurved; dark green, hairy and much wrinkled above; grey beneath with a close, starry down, as well as hairy on the midrib and nerves. Flowers white, about 1 in. wide, arranged in a compact head borne at the end of a slender, erect, shaggy stalk. All the branches are terminated by an inflorescence, the smaller side ones of three to six flowers, the terminal one of about twice as many. Sepals five, ovate, very hairy.

Native of S. Europe and N. Africa; cultivated here in the middle of the seventeenth century. From other hardy or nearly hardy species this is readily distinguished by its narrower leaves. It is not one of the hardiest sorts, and suffers in moderately severe winters. Where it survives it makes a neat bush, remarkably profuse in blossom.

C. × NIGRICANS Pourr.—This hybrid, believed to be *C. monspeliensis* × *C. populifolius*, was described by Rouy and Foucaud in *Flore de France*. Leaves lanceolate, tapered at the base to a short stalk, glabrous above, with an impressed, reticulate venation. Inflorescence a three- to six-flowered corymb; pedicels covered with a short down mixed with long, white hairs; sepals oval, heart-shaped at the base. A hybrid of this parentage would be difficult to distinguish from *C.* × *laxus*, also a hybrid of *C. populifolius* but with *C. hirsutus* as the other parent.

C. × SKANBERGII Lojac.—A very rare natural hybrid between *C. monspeliensis* and *C. parviflorus* described from a plant growing on the island of Lampedusa, later found by Atchley in Greece and introduced by him. It is an attractive fairly hardy cistus with grey-green foliage and small, beautiful pale pink flowers. *Bot. Mag.*, t. 9514.

C. ATCHLEYI Warb., nom. inedit.—The plant for which this name was proposed was found in 1929 by Shirley Atchley and Walter Ingwersen on Mt Smolikas in N. Greece at 1,500 to 2,000 ft. It appears to be closely related to *C. monspeliensis*, but its taxonomic status is still undecided.

C. × OBTUSIFOLIUS Sweet

An evergreen shrub of rounded, much-branched habit, 1½ to 2½ ft high; young shoots slender, covered with greyish starry down. Leaves almost or quite stalkless, oval or ovate-oblong, bluntish to rounded at the apex, tapered at the base; 1 to 2 in. long, ⅓ to ⅝ in. wide; dull grey green, starry-downy on both surfaces, more especially beneath, roughish above, margins slightly recurved. Flowers several in a cluster opening in June, white, about 1½ in. in diameter, each petal having a yellow stain at the base. Sepals green, ⅜ in. long, heart-shaped, pointed, hairy and fringed with hairs; flower-stalks grey with hairs.

This rock rose, originally named and described by Sweet about 1827, is a natural hybrid between *C. salviifolius* and *C. hirsutus* and shows its ancestry in the heart-shaped sepals and more or less three-veined leaves. The stalked leaves with pinnate veins and often solitary flowers of *C. salviifolius* distinguish it, and *C. hirsutus* is easily distinguished by its markedly three-veined, broad-based leaves. It is found wild in Portugal and is one of the hardier rock roses, growing well and flowering well in a sunny well-drained spot. Easily increased by late summer cuttings.

C. PALHINHAE Ingram

C. ladaniferus f. *latifolius* Daveau

A compact, evergreen, glutinous shrub about 1½ to 2 ft high, more in width, densely leafy; shoots glabrous. Leaves dark green, scarcely stalked, obovate, blunt or rounded at the apex, tapered from the middle downwards, 1½ to 2 in. long, about half as wide, pinnately veined, densely covered with white down beneath. Flowers solitary, pure satin-white, 3 to 4 in. wide, opening in May and June, sepals three, densely ciliate. *Bot. Mag.*, n.s., t. 157.

Native of Portugal, and introduced by Capt. Collingwood Ingram in 1939; it first flowered in 1943. It appears to be nearest in affinity to *C. ladanifer* and is certainly one of the finest species of the genus, its immense blossoms showing in great beauty against the dense, dark green foliage. The white under-surface of the leaves is very distinctive. It is confined in the natural state to the lime-stone promontory of Cape St Vincent in the Algarve, while *C. ladanifer*, which is common in this part of Portugal, stops short as soon as it meets the limestone (C. Ingram in *Journ. R.H.S.*, Vol. 77, 1952, p. 91). It is not completely hardy.

Using this species as a parent, Capt. Ingram has raised some fine hybrids—see under *C. crispus*, *ladanifer* and *laurifolius*.

C. PARVIFLORUS Lam.

C. complicatus Lam.

A shrub of compact habit, to about 3 ft high; young growths downy. Leaves ovate, pointed or rounded at the apex, up to 2½ in. long and 1¼ in. wide, on winged stalks; grey-green above, greener beneath and downy on both surfaces; three-nerved from the base with the reticulations impressed above and prominent beneath. Flowers about 1 in. across, clear rose-pink, in terminal and axillary heads; petals triangular ovate, not overlapping; sepals five, downy; stigma large, almost sessile.

Native of the E. Mediterranean, with its western outpost on Lampedusa Island, south of Sicily. It was in cultivation in Sweet's time and figured in his *Cistineae*, t. 14 (1826); another introduction was by Shirley Atchley from Greece around 1930. Botanically it is an interesting species. Its foliage and coloured flowers suggest affinity with such species as *C. crispus* and *C. creticus*, etc. But no other species has flowers of such a clear pink and the sessile stigma is a character otherwise found only among the white-flowered cistuses.

C. parviflorus, in the form now in commerce, has proved remarkably hardy and vigorous. During its short season of flower it makes a very pretty display and, with its healthy, almost blue-green young foliage, could serve as a foil to other plants during the rest of the season.

C. POPULIFOLIUS L.

An evergreen shrub 3 to 7 ft high, of vigorous growth; young shoots minutely downy and viscid. Leaves long-stalked, broadly ovate, with a deeply heart-shaped base, pointed; 1 to 3½ in. long, 1 to 2½ in. wide, prominently net-veined, ultimately glabrous; stalk ½ to 1 in. long, fringed with hairs. Flowers white, 2 in. across, with a yellow stain at the base of each petal, produced during June from the leaf-axils at the apex of the previous year's growth and beneath the new growth, in two- to five-flowered clusters; flower-stalk hairy, 2 to 3 in. long. Sepals five, the outer ones heart-shaped, ¾ in. long, ½ in. wide at the base; inner ones smaller.

Native of S.W. Europe; cultivated since 1656. It is quite distinct from all other cultivated species of rock rose in having leaves larger and longer-stalked than any. Whilst it will not withstand our hardest winters, it may still be included among the hardier species, and is well worth growing. The hardiest forms of this species are said to be those that grow in S.W. France around Narbonne. They have been given varietal status as var. NARBONNENSIS Willk., said to differ in the shorter-stalked flower-clusters and the smaller sepals, hairy only on the margin, but Sir O. Warburg doubted whether these characters are constant enough to warrant a variety being made out of them.

var. LASIOCALYX Willk.—A fine variety with larger flowers than the type but scarcely so hardy; found in S. Spain, S. Portugal, and Morocco.

C. × PURPUREUS Lam.

A bush of rounded habit 3 to 4 ft high, and as much through; young branches downy and resinous. Leaves oblong-lance-shaped to obovate; 1 to 2 in. long, ⅜ to ⅝ in. wide; blunt at the apex, tapering at the base but scarcely stalked, the bases clasping the stem; upper surface dull greyish green, the veins sunken; the lower one pale with starry down. Flowers 2½ to 3 in. across, reddish purple with a conspicuous dark red blotch at the base of each petal; the flowers are borne in terminal clusters of about three. Sepals ovate, with short slender points and covered with starry down.

This fine rock rose, by far the best of its colour in cultivation, is considered to be a hybrid between *C. creticus*, whence it gets its colour, and the spotted form of *C. ladanifer*, from which it derives its greater size and conspicuous blotches on the petals. It is only hardy through comparatively mild winters.

cv. 'BETTY TAUDEVIN'.—A seedling raised by Messrs Taudevin of Willaston, Cheshire. This cistus 'is noticeably hardier than the original. Though the leaves are narrower and less waved, the foliage is full in effect, and, as for the flowers, these are definitely a brighter shade, with the maroon blotch more clearly marked. Being smoother (less crinkled) in the petals they appear on the bush to be larger than those of the familiar type' (A. T. Johnson, 'The Gum Cistus', in *Journ. R.H.S.*, Vol. 77, July 1952, p. 249).

C. ROSMARINIFOLIUS *see* CISTUS CLUSI

C. SALVIIFOLIUS L.

An evergreen shrub about 2 ft high, of compact habit; the young stems, both surfaces of the leaves, and sepals covered with a soft coating of starry down. Leaves shortly stalked, oval to ovate-oblong, $\frac{1}{2}$ to $1\frac{1}{2}$ in. long, $\frac{1}{4}$ to 1 in. wide. Flowers white with a yellow stain at the base of each petal, $1\frac{1}{2}$ to $1\frac{3}{4}$ in. across, often solitary on their stalks. Sepals five, the outer ones heart-shaped, with fine points and $\frac{1}{2}$ in. long; inner ones smaller, ovate.

Widely spread over S. Europe along all the shores of the Mediterranean and in the foothills of the bordering ranges. It ascends to 4,000 ft in the Alpes Maritimes and is also found around the Italian Lakes. Cultivated since the middle of the sixteenth century, but not very hardy. Moderately severe winters kill or severely injure it. It is allied to *hirsutus* (q.v.), differing in the stalked leaves, the one- to three-flowered inflorescence and in the dense, starry down on the upper surface of the leaves and calyx. *C. salviifolius* has none of the large white hairs so conspicuous in *hirsutus*.

cv. 'PROSTRATUS'.—A low, spreading bush, growing to about 1 ft high; leaves smaller than in the type. Said to be hardier.

C. 'SILVER PINK'

This hybrid rock rose, raised by Messrs Hillier and Sons of Winchester, was first shown in public by them at the Horticultural Hall, Westminster, in flower on 17th July 1919, when it was given an Award of Merit. It is of neat, bushy shape, and Messrs Hillier observe that it never grows higher than about $2\frac{1}{2}$ ft. They consider it to have originated from *laurifolius* crossed with *creticus* (*villosus*). The leaves are of firm texture, lanceolate, 1 to 3 in. long, dark green above, greyish green beneath, whilst the flowers, each 3 in. wide, are of a clear 'silvery' pink with no suspicion of purple or magenta in the colouring. The centre is filled with a bunch of golden-yellow stamens. This very charming cistus is hardy if grown in a fairly rich, well-drained soil; on poor, acid soils it makes weak growth and is inclined to be tender. In this and in × *Halimiocistus wintonensis* (q.v.), Messrs Hillier have added two plants of great beauty and interest to gardens.

C. SYMPHYTIFOLIUS Lam.
C. vaginatus Ait.; *Rhodocistus berthelotianus* Spach

A shrub of rather open, straggling habit, 2 to 6 ft high according to situation; young stems sparsely clad with long hairs. Leaves oblong to oblong-elliptic,

1⅗ to 4 in. long, ⅗ to 2⅗ in. wide, pointed at the apex, tapered at the base into a short stalk; dark green above, with scattered hairs, somewhat tomentose beneath; margins plane or undulate. Flowers purplish pink, to 2 in. or a little more across, two to nine together in hairy panicles; sepals five, hairy, especially near the base; style to 1 in. long and always much longer than the stamens.

Native of the Canary Islands, mostly confined to the mountains above 1,500 ft; introduced early in the nineteenth century but, owing to its tenderness, uncommon in gardens. Some of the plants that are grown, or have been grown, as typical C. *symphytifolius* may belong to the following variety:

var. LEUCOPHYLLUS (Spach) Danserau *Rhodocistus berthelotianus* var. *leucophyllus* Spach; *C. candidissimus* Dun.; *C. ochreatus* Chr. Smith—Stems and leaves densely white-hairy.

C. OSBECKIIFOLIUS (Webb) Christ *Rhodocistus osbeckiifolius* Webb; *C. ochreatus* of some authors, not Chr. Smith.—Also a native of the Canary Islands, this species differs from the preceding in its thicker, smaller, and strongly three-nerved leaves. They are densely downy on both surfaces, with silky-haired petioles.

CLADOTHAMNUS   ERICACEAE

A monotypic genus allied to *Ledum, Tripetaleia,* and *Botryostege,* but distinguished by the combination of deciduous leaves, inflorescence of one to three flowers with ten stamens, conspicuous leafy bracts, five free linear-oblong sepals and a five-celled ovary.

C. PYROLIFLORUS Bongard

A deciduous shrub 3 to 6 ft (sometimes more) high, with erect angled stems and glabrous young shoots. Leaves alternate, oblanceolate or narrowly oval, 1 to 2 in. long, ¼ to ½ in. wide; tapered gradually to a stalkless base, abruptly narrowed to a point at the apex, entire, perfectly glabrous on both surfaces. Flowers produced in June, mostly solitary from the axils of the uppermost leaves and the end of the shoot, ¾ to 1 in. across. Sepals five, narrow oblong, persistent, green; petals five, spreading, broader and rather longer than the sepals, rosy in the centre, yellowish at the margins; stamens ten, spreading, the stalks flattened towards the base; style ⅜ in. long, decurved, persistent; flower-stalk ¼ to ½ in. long.

Native of Alaska, British Columbia, etc.; discovered in Sitka Island in 1828; introduced by T. Smith, of Newry. It is a neat shrub, suitable for a peaty situation in the rock garden.

CLADRASTIS   LEGUMINOSAE

A small genus of deciduous trees; one found in the United States, the others in China and Japan. The leaves are alternate, pinnate; the pea-shaped flowers in loose panicles; pods flattened. The shrub or small tree sometimes called *C. amurensis* is now usually placed in a separate genus— *Maackia*. The true *Cladrastis* is readily distinguished from *Maackia* on account of the swollen base of the leaf-stalks enclosing and hiding the buds; in *Maackia* they are exposed; the flowers of *Maackia*, too, are arranged closely in cylindrical racemes. The name of *Cladrastis* is derived from the Greek, and refers to the brittleness of the branches; this is characteristic of both the American and Asiatic species, but not of *Maackia*.

These trees thrive best when raised from seeds, but failing them, plants may be raised from root-cuttings. They like a loamy soil and a sunny position.

C. LUTEA (Michx.) K. Koch   YELLOW WOOD
Virgilia lutea Michx.; *C. tinctoria* Raf.

A tree occasionally 50 to 60 ft high, when drawn up by other trees, but usually 40 ft or less in the open, with a wide-spreading, rounded head of branches; trunk and limbs pale grey and glabrous; branchlets not downy. Leaves 8 to 12 in. long, pinnate, composed of usually seven or nine (sometimes five or eleven) leaflets, the base of their common stalk swollen and enclosing the bud; leaflets alternate, nearly or quite glabrous when mature, broadly oval, ovate or obovate, the terminal one the largest, and up to $4\frac{1}{2}$ in. long and $2\frac{3}{4}$ in. wide; basal pair of leaflets down to $1\frac{1}{2}$ in. long. Panicles terminal, 8 to 14 in. long, 4 to 6 in. wide at the base, pendulous. Flowers white, 1 to $1\frac{1}{4}$ in. long, produced on stalks scarcely half as long, slightly fragrant; standard petal $\frac{1}{2}$ to $\frac{3}{4}$ in. across, reflexed, with a pale yellow blotch at the base. Calyx bell-shaped, $\frac{5}{8}$ in. long, with five blunt teeth, and covered (like the flower-stalk) with minute down. Pod 3 to 4 in. long, $\frac{1}{2}$ in. wide, flat, with four to six seeds. *Bot. Mag.*, t. 7767.

Native of the south-east United States, most plentiful in Tennessee, although nowhere very common; introduced in 1812. This interesting tree does not flower regularly in this country, but is very distinct and handsome in its foliage, which turns bright yellow before falling, and in summer is of a beautifully vivid green and luxuriant aspect. The timber is hard, heavy, and close-grained, and when freshly cut is yellow. There is a good tree at Kew 35 ft high, with a head of branches 45 ft across. but the others mentioned in previous editions no longer exist. These were in the Knap Hill Nursery (45 ft) and at Syon House (60 ft). The best recorded recently are: Linton Park, Kent, 58 ft high (1956); Trent College, Notts., 30 × 3 ft at $2\frac{1}{2}$ ft (1962); Bath Botanic Garden, 30 × $2\frac{1}{4}$ ft. Propagated best by imported seeds. Blossoms in June.

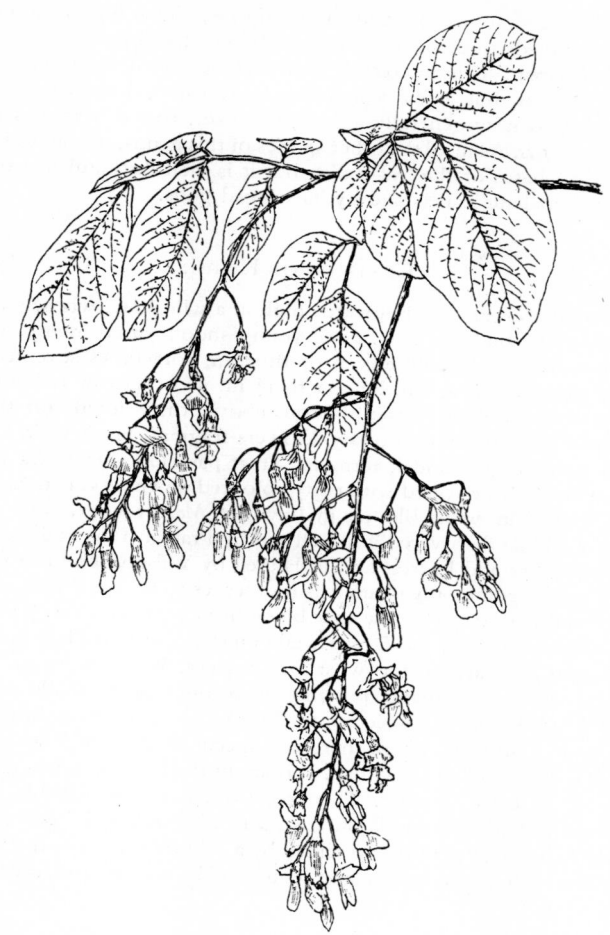

CLADRASTIS LUTEA

C. PLATYCARPA (Maxim.) Makino

Sophora platycarpa Maxim.; *Platyosprion platycarpum* (Maxim.) Maxim.

A deciduous tree, similar in habit and general appearance to *Sophora japonica*, branchlets glabrous, dark brown. Leaves pinnate, 8 to 10 in. long; leaflets in five and a half to seven and a half pairs, obliquely ovate, pointed; $1\frac{1}{2}$ to 4 in. long, 1 to $1\frac{1}{2}$ in. wide; bright green above, downy on the midrib and stalk, otherwise glabrous at maturity. Flowers white, pea-flower-shaped, $\frac{5}{8}$ in. long, produced on slender, downy stalks about $\frac{1}{4}$ in. long, in panicles 4 to 6 in. high, $2\frac{1}{2}$ to 4 in.

wide. Pod flat, 2 in. long, $\frac{1}{2}$ in. wide, tapered to a point at both ends and winged on the seams; seeds three or four, often only one developing.

Native of Japan. This interesting tree was described by Maximowicz as a species of *Sophora*, but a few years later he transferred it to a new genus—*Platyosprion*. It is now generally agreed, however, that this species is most at home in *Cladrastis*. As in all the other species of this genus, the buds are enclosed in the swollen bases of the leaf-stalks, but it is well distinguished from all of them by its stipellate leaflets and by its winged pods.

C. SINENSIS Hemsl.   [PLATE 48

A deciduous tree 50 ft and upwards high in a wild state, whose swollen leaf-bases enclose the buds as in *C. lutea*; young shoots rusty-downy at the base. Leaves composed of usually eleven or thirteen, sometimes seventeen leaflets, which are alternate, 3 to 5 in. long, 1 to 1$\frac{1}{2}$ in. wide; narrow oblong, pointed, tapered or rounded at the base; glabrous above, rusty-downy on the midrib, and glaucous beneath; stalks downy. Flowers fragrant, blush white, $\frac{1}{2}$ in. long, produced in large, pyramidal, terminal, erect panicles, sometimes 12 in. long and 9 in. wide. Calyx covered with rusty-coloured down. Pod flattened, smooth, 2 to 3 in. long, $\frac{1}{2}$ in. wide. Blooms in July. *Bot. Mag.*, t. 9043.

Native of China; discovered in Szechwan by Pratt in 1890 and later found in Yunnan by Henry and Forrest and in Hupeh by Wilson, who introduced it in 1901. It is not so commonly planted as it deserves to be, for it makes an elegant small tree and is one of the few that blossom in high summer. Three trees at Kew are about 20 ft high and flower well in most years in the latter part of July. It also flowers regularly in the West Hill nursery, Winchester, but Mr Hillier tells us this tree is now dying, possibly on account of the shallow chalky soil (though the species has no objection to chalk as such). It has attained its largest dimensions in Cornwall, where there is a specimen 40 ft high at Lanarth and another of a good size at Trewithen. It is about the last deciduous tree to break into growth in early summer. This tree furnishes a remarkable instance of geographical distribution. As is the case with *Chionanthus*, *Liriodendron*, *Gymnocladus*, and *Sassafras*, a genus represented by a solitary species in the New World and long known in gardens, was later reinforced by species from the Old World.

C. WILSONII Takeda

A deciduous tree 15 to 50 ft high in nature, its trunk sometimes 4 ft in girth; young shoots at first downy. Leaves pinnate, 9 to 13 in. long, composed of seven to eleven leaflets; main-stalk downy. Leaflets ovate to narrowly oval, pointed at the apex, wedge-shaped at the base, entire; 1$\frac{1}{2}$ to 3 in. long, $\frac{1}{2}$ to 1$\frac{1}{4}$ in. wide; dark green above, rather glaucous beneath, furnished when young with pale down, glabrous at maturity; stalk $\frac{1}{10}$ in. long, downy. The flowers (not yet seen on cultivated plants) are fragrant, white, about 1 in. long, of pea-flower character, and numerously borne on lax, terminal, broadly pyramidal panicles 5 to 8 in. long, the flower-stalks furnished with brownish down. Calyx downy, $\frac{1}{2}$ in. wide.

Native of W. Hupeh, China, where it was discovered by Wilson and introduced in 1907 to the Arnold Arboretum, whence a plant was obtained for Kew in 1910. There may be other plants in cultivation under Wilson's number 1102. It has been propagated at Kew by grafting on stocks of the American *C. lutea* but has scarcely spread into gardens. As in other species, the base of the leaf-stalk fits over the bud and completely hides it. The description given above of leaf and shoot is made from the tree at Kew, but on wild specimens collected in China the leaflets are fewer (seven to nine) and larger. It is nearly related to *C. sinensis*, which has a glabrous ovary and pod, larger panicles, and smaller flowers.

Apart from the yellow autumn colouring, this species has proved of no value in our climate and remains rare. The specimen in the R.H.S. Garden, Wisley, about 20 ft high, has yet to bear a flower.

CLEMATIS   RANUNCULACEAE

There are at present over two hundred species of *Clematis* known. They are spread more or less over all the great terrestrial regions, but the hardy ones are confined to Europe, N. Asia (especially China), and N. America. A New Zealand species, *C. paniculata* (*indivisa*), one of the most beautiful, is sometimes cultivated on walls in mild districts, but it is, strictly speaking, a greenhouse plant.

In habit, clematises vary from dwarf, herbaceous plants to woody climbers up to 60 or more feet high. The leaves are always in pairs at each joint, and are occasionally simple, but usually divided, consisting of the three, five, seven, nine, or perhaps fifteen leaflets. The climbing species support themselves by means of the leaf-stalks, which curl round any slender support available. In the absence of any such support they fasten on to each other, making an inextricable tangle. Whilst the clematises when in flower provide some of the most beautiful effects possible in gardens—excepting roses, they are our most extensive group of flowering climbers—the autumn and early winter effect is often deplorable. The leaves of many species do not fall off in autumn, but remain through much of the early winter black and unsightly. Nor are the early stages of decay enlivened by any bright colour.

Clematis belongs to the buttercup family, but is an anomalous member thereof, owing to the flowers having no petals. The showy, petal-like organs, usually four but up to eight in number, which give the flowers their chief decorative value, are sepals. There is one section of the genus, the *Atragene* section, sometimes kept up as a separate genus—which have between the sepals and stamens, one or more rows of petal-like organs which may be regarded as either petals or enlarged abortive stamens. There is considerable variation in the form of clematis blossoms. In the most popular forms, represented so abundantly in gardens by hybrids of

C. patens, florida, and *lanuginosa*; also by species like *montana* and *orientalis,* the sepals spread out nearly or quite to their full extent. In another section, of which *C. viorna* is the type, the sepals form a pitcher-shaped flower; that is, they are connivent at the margins, so that the flower is rounded and swollen at the base, but narrows to a contracted mouth. In the Series *Vitalbae,* the flowers are small, very numerous, and produced in panicles.

The seed-vessel, popularly known as the 'seed', and to botanists as the 'achene', is terminated by the persistent style, which in many species is from 1 to 2 in. long, and clothed with long silky hairs, so that a plant in full fruit is often a striking object. The juice of several species is acrid, and has an inflammatory effect on the skin.

CULTIVATION. The natural habit of the climbing sorts is mostly among small trees and shrubs, over which they run. The flowering portions of the plant are therefore exposed to full sunshine, whilst the main stem and lower parts of the plant are often in shade; this is a point that should not be overlooked in the cultivation of the more delicate species on posts and pillars. In such positions it is advisable to place the plant with its base on the northern side of its support. Otherwise, the plants delight in full sunshine.

They all like a deep, moist root-run and will not thrive on heavy clays or light sands unless the soil is carefully prepared. Whether they benefit from the addition of lime is a question on which leading growers are not agreed. It is certainly not essential and should not be applied in the neighbourhood of ericaceous plants.

The methods of pruning clematises depend on the position and space they are intended to occupy, and on their time and mode of flowering. Essentially there are three of these. 1. The early-flowering species like *montana* and *macropetala* must not be pruned in winter or early spring; whatever pruning is necessary should be done as soon as the flowers are past, and it should be done chiefly with relation to the space the plant is desired to occupy. *C. armandii* also flowers in spring on the previous year's wood, but is not so vigorous as the deciduous kinds and should never be pruned severely. 2. Many of the large-flowered hybrids bear their main crop of flowers in early summer on short shoots from the previous year's wood; these need little or no pruning but benefit from having the summer's growths carefully spaced and trained. Many in this group produce a second crop of flowers on these growths and, at the sacrifice of the first crop, may be pruned as in the next group, thus throwing all the energy of the plant into the late summer flowering. 3. In this group the flowers are borne on the season's growths from midsummer onwards. Some of the species and hybrids which belong here are herbaceous climbers or sub-shrubs and much or all of the summer's stems dies back naturally during the winter to ground-level or near it. It is desirable to remove as much of this dead growth as possible. The species and hybrids of section *Viorna, C. viticella,* etc. belong here. Others, however, do not die back, or lose only part of their growths in winter, and, if left unpruned, would form in a short time a heavy tangle at the top of their supports whilst they become quite naked at the base. With these it is a good plan to prune a proportion at least of the stems well back, so that in breaking into new growth they provide a furnishing for their supports near the ground. Or they may be pruned as a matter of course to about 3 ft above the ground, leaving only a few buds of the previous summer's growth.

The provision of support for clematises in gardens must remain a matter largely of discretion and opportunity. At Kew, where a collection of some forty to fifty species was at one time grown in close proximity, most of the climbing sorts were trained over untrimmed branches of oak or other wood stuck in the ground. Three or more of these were put in a bed, and the tops were fastened together so as to form a tent-like structure. The stronger species soon cover this when so grown, and in a few years a dense tangle of stems is formed which become almost self-supporting. For the species like *viorna* and *fusca*, which die back almost to the ground in winter, and send up shoots several feet long during the summer, ordinary pea-sticks are suitable. Pergolas, trellises, and arbours are of course admirable places for most species, and the stronger species may be used for covering the butts of trees and mounds.

An imitation of the natural conditions under which many of the clematises live should more frequently be attempted in gardens. They should be planted near shrubs, over which they can climb. Such shrubs should not be of great value, or very rank growers. William Robinson adopted this system in his garden at Gravetye, with happy results.

The leaves of *Clematis* vary much in size and form on the same plant, so that some of the descriptions in the following pages must in both respects be taken as approximate. It is also difficult in this genus to draw a line between the shrubby climbers and the herbaceous sorts.

Whilst many of the species and simpler hybrids described in the following pages are of great beauty, it has to be admitted that the interest taken in clematises at the present time is chiefly centred in the large-flowered races raised by intercrossing within the Viticella group—*C. lanuginosa, C. florida, C. patens,* and *C. viticella.* Under these species, and *C. × jackmanii,* the role that each has played in the formation of these hybrids is more particularly alluded to. For further information see: Christopher Lloyd, *Clematis* (1965); Ernest Markham, *The Large and Small Flowered Clematis* (1951); Spingarn, *The Large Flowered Clematis Hybrids* in the American publication *The National Horticultural Magazine,* 1935, pp. 64–94; W. E. Pennell in *Journ. R.H.S.,* Vol. 91, pp. 27–36; and the catalogues of leading growers.

The clematises, more especially the large-flowered hybrids, are subject to an affliction known as 'Clematis Wilt', which results in the rapid death of a shoot, frequently right down to the base. Affected plants are not killed outright and usually manage to produce a healthy shoot the next season, though this may in turn be attacked. Recent research by the Glasshouse Crops Research Institute indicates that a species of fungus is the probable cause of the disease; a full account of this work is given in their report for 1965. No definite control measures are known, but all dead shoots should be cut back to clean, living tissue, and the wounds, however small, should be painted with a good protective paint. Any new shoots which start to develop should be sprayed with a copper-containing fungicide, repeating two or three times at fortnightly intervals. For this information we are indebted to Miss Audrey Brooks, Plant Pathologist to the Royal Horticultural Society.

C. ACUTANGULA Hook. f. & Thoms.

A deciduous climbing shrub 12 to 15 ft high, perhaps more, with slender stems sharply angled, and very viscid when young; reddish purple. Leaves doubly pinnate, 6 to 9 in. long; the primary divisions are three-foliolate, or, in the case of the lower ones, often five-foliolate; leaflets ovate-lanceolate, 1 to 2 in. long, coarsely toothed or two- or three-lobed, glabrous and shining on both surfaces, and of a purplish tint; leaf-stalks ribbed, the bases of each pair flattened, expanded, and surrounding the stem. Inflorescences 1½ to 3 in. long, with usually five flower-buds, the terminal one of which opens first, and is often the only one to open. Flower bell-shaped, 1 in. wide, ⅝ in. long; sepals four, lilac-coloured, narrowly ovate, but much curled back at the points, which are downy. Stamens and styles clothed with silky down.

Native of the Himalaya and China; introduced from the latter by Wilson for Messrs Veitch about 1903. The only plant I have seen, and the one from which this description was made, grew in the Coombe Wood nursery, where it was a luxuriant grower and quite hardy, flowering in autumn.

C. AETHUSIFOLIA Turcz.

A deciduous climber, growing 5 or 6 ft high; stems slender, slightly ribbed, downy when quite young. Leaves 3 to 8 in. long, pinnately divided into three, five, or seven segments, which are themselves either deeply lobed or trifoliolate; the ultimate subdivisions varying from linear to obovate or oblong, ¼ to 1¼ in. long, coarsely and unequally toothed, downy. Flowers nodding, produced in August and September on erect, slender stalks 1 to 2 in. long, which come either singly from the joints of the stem, or three or five together at the end of short axillary branches, the whole terminal part of the shoot being transformed into a leafy panicle. Each flower is pale yellow, narrowly bell-shaped, ½ to ¾ in. long; the sepals narrow oblong. Seed-vessels with white feathery styles ⅝ in. long.

Native of N. China and Manchuria; introduced to Kew by way of St Petersburg about 1875. Although one of the smaller climbing clematises, it is a free grower, and forms a dense tangle of its slender stems. The finely divided foliage is very elegant. It blossoms in great profusion, the whole plant being covered with the little pendent bells, which, although not highly coloured, are pretty and graceful.

var. LATISECTA Maxim., is a form with leaf-divisions of the broader shape given above. *Bot. Mag.*, t. 6542.

C. AFOLIATA Buchan.

C. aphylla Colenso

A semi-scandent, unisexual shrub with slender, much-interlaced branches; twigs slender, slightly ribbed, glabrous, dark green. Leaves in the ordinary sense of the word are nearly always absent in adult plants, the blades being suppressed and leaving only the stalk, which is green, slender, and varies from ¾ to 4 in. in length. Sometimes in young plants, rarely in adult ones, three minute, ovate or triangular leaflets are produced. Flowers fragrant, greenish white, about 1 in. wide, borne singly on slender hairy stalks 1 to 2 in. long and produced in clusters of two to six from the axils of the leaf-stalks. Sepals four to six, lance-shaped, spreading, silky outside. Seed-vessel with silky style. *Bot. Mag.*, t. 8686.

Native of both islands of New Zealand, but more common and widely spread in the south. It was grown by Miss Willmott at the foot of a sunny wall at Warley, Essex, where it formed a dense mass of rush-like twigs and branches several feet long and blossomed in May. It was female. At Kew the present specimen has grown since 1956 on a wall of the Temperate House, and on the rock garden at Edinburgh there is a healthy plant growing in an exposed position. The late Canon Boscawen, who cultivated so many tender southern hemisphere species in his garden at the Ludgvan Rectory, Cornwall, planted this species there against a sunny wall, where it still flourishes. It is worth growing for the fragrance of its flowers and for its unusual aspect. Except in the maritime south and south-western counties, it will need some such protection as a sunny wall.

C. ALPINA (L.) Mill.

Atragene alpina L.

A deciduous climber 6 to 8 ft high, with glabrous, slightly ribbed stems, often much enlarged at the joints, through an agglomeration of buds there. Leaves 3 to 6 in. long, doubly ternate, being composed of nine leaflets arranged in three triplets; leaflets ovate-lanceolate, scarcely stalked, coarsely toothed, 1 to 2 in. long, one-third as wide, downy at the base. Flowers solitary, on stalks 3 to 4 in. long, nodding, produced along with the young leaves in April and May. Sepals four, blue of various shades, 1 to 1½ in. long, ⅓ to ½ in. wide, oblong; petals small, spoon-shaped, half as long as the sepals. Seed-vessels terminated by a silky style 1¼ to 1½ in. long, the whole forming a globular grey tuft, 2 in. or more across. *Bot. Mag.*, t. 530.

Native of N. Europe and N. Asia, also of the mountains of Central and S. Europe; introduced in 1792. It belongs to that section of the genus once kept separate as *Atragene*, because of the petal-like organs (staminodes) that come between sepals and stamens. They are not conspicuous, and the sepals make the chief decorative feature of the flower. As in *C. montana* and *macropetala*, the flowers are produced direct from axillary buds on the previous year's growth. A fine form of this species, with longer and more brightly coloured sepals, received an Award of Merit when shown at Vincent Square in May 1965 (*Journ. R.H.S.*, Vol. 91, p. 356). The correct name for this clone is 'FRANCES RIVIS'. Various other named forms are in commerce.

var. SIBIRICA (L.) Schneid. *Atragene sibirica* L.—Sepals yellowish white. Introduced in 1753. 'WHITE MOTH' is a selection with pure white sepals and numerous staminodes.

C. APIIFOLIA DC.

A vigorous, woody climber, deciduous, 12 to 15 ft high, with slightly downy, slender stems. Leaves mostly trifoliolate, but sometimes pinnate with the basal divisions trifoliolate; leaflets thin, broadly ovate to ovate-lanceolate, 1 to 3 in. long, heart-shaped to tapering at the base, deeply toothed, often three-lobed, nearly glabrous, except for hairs on the nerves beneath. Flowers dull white, ⅝ in. across, in axillary panicles 2 to 6 in. long, produced in September and October; sepals very downy outside, spreading; stamens glabrous. Seed-vessels with silky styles.

Native of China and Japan, cultivated at Kew for over seventy years. It is not one of the most attractive species, although a vigorous grower and flowering copiously. Allied to *C. vitalba*, it lacks the beauty of that species in fruit, at any rate in cultivation.

C. ARMANDII Franch.   [PLATE 49

An evergreen, woody climber, growing 20 to 30 ft high, stems minutely downy when quite young. Leaves composed of three leaflets, which are oblong-lanceolate to ovate, rounded or slightly heart-shaped at the base, pointed, not toothed, prominently three-veined, of a rich glossy green, and quite glabrous on both surfaces; they vary from 3 to 6 in. in length, and from 1 to 2½ in. in width; the main-stalk is 1½ to 4 in. long, the secondary ones ½ to 1 in. long and twisted. Flowers 2 to 2½ in. across, produced in April in dense axillary clusters, mostly three on a stalk; sepals four to seven, narrow oblong; about 1 in. long, ⅓ in. wide, pure or creamy white, changing to rose. The bases of the flower-stalks are surrounded by numerous bracts. *Bot. Mag.*, t. 8587.

Native of Central and W. China; introduced by Wilson for Messrs Veitch in 1900, and first flowered by them in their nursery at Coombe Wood. The plant described above is representative of the selected forms of *C. armandii* grown in gardens, of which 'APPLE BLOSSOM' is the best known. Rehder has pointed out that the wild species, as Franchet described it, has smaller flowers with less numerous sepals, borne on separate leafy peduncles. Garden plants with the characters given in the previous paragraph (flowers 2 to 2½ in. across, with four to seven sepals, borne in a sessile, leafless inflorescence of paniculate form) are by him distinguished as var. BIONDIANA (Pav.) Rehd.

In its selected forms this is a most beautiful clematis. It is not particularly hardy and succeeds best if allowed to grow freely on a sunny wall. No pruning is necessary or desirable unless it outgrows its allotted position. It also resents too close training; once the main framework of branches has been tied in the plant should be allowed to grow with the minimum of interference.

C. × AROMATICA Lenné & Koch

A presumed hybrid between *C. integrifolia* and *C. flammula*, and only woody at ground-level, dying back every winter. It grows 4 to 6 ft high, the stems slender, the leaves pinnate and mostly composed of five leaflets, which are oval or broadly ovate, unequal at the base, not toothed, and 1 to 2½ in. long. Flowers 1 to 1½ in. across, dark bluish violet, very fragrant, and produced on a slightly downy stalk about 2 in. long; sepals four, oblong, spreading fully, downy at the margins. Seed-vessels silky-hairy. It flowers from July to September, and is a valuable plant for grouping in the herbaceous border. Its origin is not precisely known, but the first place in which it was recorded as being in cultivation was the Royal Gardens of Sans Souci, about the middle of the nineteenth century. It is not a climber.

C. CAMPANIFLORA Brot.

A deciduous climber, growing 10 to 20 ft high, very vigorous; stems slender, slightly downy when young. Leaves composed normally of fifteen or twenty-one leaflets (that is, five or seven sets of three each), but irregular. Leaflets not toothed, but sometimes lobed, variable in shape, narrow-lanceolate, ovate and oval, up to 3 in. long, ultimately glabrous. Flowers solitary or several together at the end of a downy stalk 2 to 3 in. long, nodding, produced in July and August. Sepals four, woolly, oblong, pointed with the points recurved, ¾ in. long, half expanded; white tinged with violet. Seed-vessels roundish ovate, terminated by a slightly downy style less than ⅓ in. long.

Native of Portugal; introduced in 1810. A hardy species, very thriving in cultivation. The flowers are scarcely bell-shaped, as implied by the name, but rather bowl-shaped. The species is an ally of *C. viticella*.

C. CHINENSIS Retz.

A vigorous deciduous climber, the stems ribbed, glabrous except for some down at the nodes. Leaves pinnate, composed of five leaflets, the leaf-stalks curling round whatever support is available. Leaflets ovate or heart-shaped, three- or five-veined; 1½ to 3 in. long; minutely downy on the midrib, otherwise glabrous. Flowers fragrant, white, ½ to ¾ in. wide, produced numerously in cymose panicles springing from the leaf-axils in September and October. Sepals four, very narrow, downy on the margins. Seed-vessel covered with appressed hairs, each terminated by a slender style that is 1 to 1½ in. long and clothed with fine white hairs.

Native of Central and W. China and known to science since 1781, when it was described and figured by Retzius in his *Observationes Botanicae*, ii, t. 2. Wilson found it when collecting for Messrs Veitch in 1900 and introduced it then or soon after. Judging by its behaviour at Kew it is a vigorous grower and quite hardy, but often develops its flowers too late to escape autumn cold.

C. CHRYSOCOMA Franch.

A deciduous, semi-woody shrub 6 to 8 ft, perhaps more, high; young stems, leaves, leaf-stalks, and flower-stalks covered with a dense, brownish-yellow, shaggy down. Leaves trifoliolate; leaflets varying in shape from broadly ovate or rhomboidal to narrowly obovate; $\frac{1}{2}$ to $1\frac{3}{4}$ in. long, often as much wide, usually three-lobed, but sometimes merely coarsely and irregularly toothed. The two side leaflets are much smaller than (usually about half the size of) the terminal one. Common stalk 1 to 2 in. long, that of the terminal leaflet $\frac{1}{8}$ to $\frac{1}{4}$ in. long; the side leaflets are stalkless. Flowers white, tinged with pink, $1\frac{3}{4}$ in. diameter, produced singly on stalks $1\frac{1}{2}$ to 3 in. long, which spring from the joints of the previous year's wood. Sepals four, broadly oblong, with a short, abrupt point; stamens not downy, forming a cluster 1 in. across. Seed-vessels terminated by a style $\frac{3}{4}$ to $1\frac{1}{4}$ in. long, plumed with brownish golden hairs. *Bot. Mag.*, t. 8395.

Native of Yunnan, China; discovered by Delavay in 1884; introduced to Kew in 1910, by Maurice de Vilmorin. It is a very charming and pretty plant, distinct in its short, erect habit, and its covering of shaggy down. It is found on mountain slopes and summits at 7,000 to 9,000 ft, but is rather tender at Kew.

var. SERICEA Schneid. *C. spooneri* Rehd. & Wils.—In describing this plant as *C. spooneri*, Rehder and Wilson recognised its close relationship to *C. chrysocoma*, to which it is now attached as a variety. It resembles the type in its clothing of yellowish down, but appears to be more hardy and is a more genuine climber in our climate. *C. chrysocoma* has flowers not so large but often more numerous in each leaf-axil and it also continues after the normal blossoming season in June to flower on the current year's shoots, which var. *sericea* never does.

C. CIRRHOSA L.

C. balearica Pers., not Rich.

An evergreen climber, said to cover trees in its native country, but only a few feet high in the average climate of Britain; young stems silky-hairy. Leaves glossy beneath, broadly ovate with a heart-shaped base, or three-lobed, coarsely toothed, glabrous; $\frac{3}{4}$ to 2 in. long, $\frac{1}{2}$ to $1\frac{1}{2}$ in. wide; stalk $\frac{1}{2}$ to $1\frac{1}{2}$ in. long. Flower solitary or in pairs, on a stalk 1 to 2 in. long; sepals oval, dull white or cream-coloured, downy outside; the whole flower $1\frac{1}{2}$ to $2\frac{1}{2}$ in. across, produced in winter. Seed-vessels terminated by plumose styles $1\frac{1}{2}$ to 2 in. long, forming large, beautifully silky tassels. Blooms January to March. *Bot. Mag.*, t. 1070.

Native of the Mediterranean region; first discovered in Andalucia by the botanist Clusius in the latter half of the sixteenth century, and soon afterwards introduced to Britain. It appears to be hardier than var. *balearica*, but at Kew does not flower so well, nor has it the beautifully cut, bronzy foliage that is so attractive in its ally. The flowers are sometimes stained inside with narrow, irregular, reddish-purple spots (f. PURPURASCENS Willk.), or may be wholly red.

var. BALEARICA (Rich.) Willk. & Lange *C. balearica* Rich.; *C. calycina* Ait.— This variety differs from the type mainly in its finely divided, somewhat fern-like leaves, the larger ones deeply and doubly toothed, the smaller ones simply three- or five-lobed; they are 1½ to 3 in. long, the ultimate subdivisions linear and pointed. In summer the foliage is dark green, in winter it becomes bronzy purple. The flowers are produced from September to March. It reaches a height of 10 to 15 ft in this country.

Native of Majorca, Minorca, Corsica, etc.; introduced to Kew by way of Paris, in 1783. It is not so hardy as the type, but has lived out-of-doors at Kew merely trained up tree branches, flowering throughout the winter whenever the weather was mild. On account of its blossoming in midwinter, and the beauty of its finely cut foliage at that season, it is well worth a sunny, sheltered spot, although the flowers are not showy. It thrives well on a wall in the R.H.S. Garden at Wisley.

C. CONNATA DC.

A deciduous climber of vigorous habit, growing 20 ft or more high; stems only slightly ribbed, not downy. Leaves mostly consisting of three or five leaflets, which are bright green on both sides, sometimes three-lobed, but in the main ovate, with a heart-shaped base, and a long, fine point, coarsely toothed, 2 to 5 in. long, 1 to 3 in. wide, either glabrous or downy. The bases of the common stalks of each pair of leaves are flat, thin, and broad, and surround the stem. Flowers bell-shaped, slightly fragrant, produced in September and October in axillary panicles 4 or 5 in. long. Sepals soft yellow, oblong, ¾ to 1 in. long, pointed with the points turned back, finely downy inside. Seed-vessel surmounted by silky plumose styles, 1 to 1¼ in. long.

Native of the Himalaya up to 10,000 ft. It bears some resemblance to *C. rehderiana*, but its leaves are not silky, and are especially distinguished by the broad, flattened stalks at the base; the sepals, too, are not so distinctly ribbed. The flower is rather larger and not so fragrant. It is quite hardy at Kew in the open ground. The species varies considerably in the amount of down on the leaves and young stems, and in the size of the flattened expansions of the leaf-stalks.

C. CRISPA L.

A deciduous, half-woody climber, varying from 3 to 8 ft high. Leaves pinnate, consisting of three, five, or seven leaflets; these leaflets are themselves often trifoliolate or variously lobed, but not toothed, varying from lance-shaped to broadly ovate with a heart-shaped base, and from 1 to 3 in. long by ⅓ to 1½ in. wide, thin and glabrous. The larger leaves are altogether 6 to 8 in. long. Flowers solitary on stalks 1 to 3 in. long, fragrant; sepals 1¼ to 2 in. long, convergent below, spreading and separate towards the points, ⅓ to ½ in. wide, thin and wavy at the margins, partially downy at the back, bluish purple, nearly white at the margins. Seed-vessel either silky or becoming nearly glabrous. *Bot. Mag.*, t. 1892.

Native of the south-eastern United States; introduced in 1726. This is regarded as one of the *Viorna* group, but is amply distinguished by the upper half of the sepals expanding widely and being much broadened and wavy at the margin. It flowers from June to August.

C. × DURANDII O. Kuntze

A robust climber, growing 9 ft high, with stout stems. Leaves undivided, ovate, pointed, tapering or slightly heart-shaped at the base; 3 to 6 in. long, about half as wide, with three or five longitudinal veins, firm-textured, shining green, almost or quite glabrous; stalk 1 to 2 in. long. Flowers 3 to 4½ in. across, the sepals usually four (occasionally more), obovate, 1½ in. wide, wavy at the margins, dark blue-violet; stamens yellow. Seed-vessels with long silky tails.

A beautiful hybrid between *C. integrifolia* and (probably) *C. × jackmanii*, raised by Durand Frères of Lyons about 1870.

cv. 'PALLIDA'.—Flowers paler, violet-rose.

Both these are exceptionally desirable and flower from June to September.

C. × ERIOSTEMON Decne.

C. × eriostemon is the first name to be published for a hybrid between *C. integrifolia* and *C. viticella*. The typical form of the cross was raised in France and described in 1852, but is probably not in cultivation over here. Better known is:

cv. 'HENDERSONII'.—This form was raised by Henderson of St John's Wood about 1830, and is one of the most beautiful garden clematises. It is, however, scarcely woody enough to justify its inclusion in this work, dying back to the ground level each winter. The stems are slender, 6 to 8 ft high, the leaves pinnate, and the solitary, slightly perfumed flowers 2 to 2½ in. across, deep bluish purple, and borne on stalks 3 to 4 in. long. Sepals four, spreading ¾ in. wide. This clematis flowers most profusely from July to September, and if grown in a group, with the stems supported by stakes, makes a very gay display. The parentage of the plant as given above is deduced from its appearance, the habit and foliage resembling *C. viticella*, whilst the flower and feathery-tailed seed-vessel are those of *C. integrifolia*—a well-known herbaceous species.

cv. 'INTERMEDIA'.—This form of the cross is very handsome also, but taking more after *C. integrifolia* than 'Hendersonii' does. The flowers are bluish purple, 2½ in. across, and appear from July to September. The plant is sturdier and shorter than 'Hendersonii'.

C. FARGESII Franch.

This species is represented in cultivation by the following variety:

var. SOULIEI Finet & Gagnep.—A deciduous climber 20 ft high, with strongly ribbed, purplish, downy young shoots. Leaves up to 9 in. long, composed of five primary divisions each consisting of three leaflets; all the stalks downy. Leaflets ovate, pointed, wedge-shaped to truncate at the base, unevenly and coarsely toothed, sometimes three-lobed; 1 to 2 in. long, ½ to 1½ in. wide; the terminal one usually more than twice the size of the side ones, which are shortly stalked to stalkless; both surfaces downy, dullish green. Flowers up to 2½ in. wide, pure white, produced from the leaf-axils, singly or a few together on a main-stalk 3 to 6 in. long. Sepals six, obovate, ½ to ¾ in. wide, each with a short abrupt point; tinged with yellow and downy outside. Stamens with glabrous stalks and pale yellow anthers. Seed-vessel with a feathery style. *Bot. Mag.*, t. 8702.

Native of W. China; introduced by Wilson in 1911. It is quite hardy at Kew and grows freely. Whilst it does not make a great display at any one time the flowers are attractive in their pure whiteness and satiny texture and they continue to appear from June to September.

The true C. FARGESII Franch., which is perhaps not in cultivation in this country, is said to differ from var. *souliei* in having proportionately larger anthers in comparison with the filaments and in the leaflets being more rounded at the base and more downy.

C. FINETIANA Lévl. & Van.

C. pavoliniana Pamp.; *C. meyeniana* var. *pavoliniana* (Pamp.) Sprague

An evergreen climber without down on branch or leaf. Leaves made up of three leaflets borne on a common stalk 1½ to 3 in. long. Leaflets narrowly ovate, rounded or slightly heart-shaped at the base, tapering to a point, three-nerved, thin but rather leathery in texture; 2 to 4 in. long, 1¼ to 2 in. wide; dark, rather bright green. Flowers fragrant, 1 to 1½ in. wide, pure white but greenish at the back, produced in an inflorescence often of three blooms, but sometimes up to seven, from the leaf-axils; common stalk glabrous, 1½ to 2 in. long, individual ones shorter. Sepals four, lanceolate, pointed, spreading; stamens with smooth stalks much shorter than the sepals and yellow anthers. Seed-vessel hairy, with a brown feathery style. *Bot. Mag.*, t. 8655.

Native of Central to W. China; introduced in 1908 by Wilson, who reported it as very common in the glens and ravines around Ichang. It belongs to the group with three-veined leaves and white flowers, comprising C. *armandii*, *meyeniana*, and *uncinata*. It is well distinguished from C. *armandii* by the much smaller flowers; the numerously flowered panicles of C. *meyeniana* and its stamens being about as long as the sepals amply differentiate it; and the glabrous ovary of C. *uncinata* is a good distinction. C. *finetiana* has grown on a south wall for some years at Kew and it needs that amount of protection except in such places as Cornwall.

C. 'JEUNEANA' is a reputed hybrid between C. *finetiana* and C. *armandii* and was very beautiful as shown by Capt. Symons-Jeune at Westminster on 8th March 1921, when it was given a First Class Certificate. Flowers ¾ to 1 in. wide, produced in a cluster of three- or five-flowered axillary cymes; sometimes as many as thirty flowers come from a pair of leaf-axils. Sepals mostly five, oval lanceolate, 'silvery blush', pink underneath. The plant is possibly a form of the variable C. *armandi*. Flowers in June.

C. FLAMMULA L.

A climbing, deciduous plant, growing 10 ft or more high, forming at the top a heavy, bushy tangle, whilst it is comparatively naked and unfurnished below;

young stems glabrous. Leaves very variable in size and shape, but mostly composed of three or five leaflets, which are not toothed, but often two- or three-lobed and frequently trifoliolate; they are bright green on both sides and quite glabrous, varying in shape from narrowly lanceolate to almost round. Flowers pure white, delightfully fragrant, ¾ to 1 in. across, produced from August to October in loose panicles up to 1 ft in length. Seed-vessels oval, ¼ in. long, surmounted by a white-plumed style 1¼ in. long.

Native of S. Europe; cultivated in Britain since the sixteenth century. In the fragrance of its blossoms this clematis provides one of the greatest pleasures of the autumn garden. It is variously compared with the scent of almonds, vanilla, and hawthorn, and is perceptible some yards away from the plant.

C. × TRITERNATA DC. *C. violacea* A. DC. f.—This cross of *C. flammula* and *C. viticella* is represented in cultivation by:

cv. 'RUBRO-MARGINATA'.—Flowers 1 to 1½ in. across, sepals reddish violet, but white at the base. Their fragrance is equal to that of *C. flammula*, and they expand during the same period. One of the most charming of late summer-flowering climbers.

C. FLORIDA Thunb.

A deciduous, or semi-evergreen, shrubby climber, growing 8 to 12 ft high, with hard, wiry stems. Leaves 3 to 5 in. long, normally composed of three divisions, which are each again divided into three leaflets. Leaflets ovate to lanceolate, 1 to 2 in. long, mostly untoothed in the cultivated forms, but often coarsely toothed in the wild; glossy dark green above, more or less hairy beneath. Flowers 2½ to 3 in. across, solitary on downy stalks 3 to 4 in. long, that are furnished about the middle with a pair of stalkless, variously lobed, leaf-like bracts. Sepals from four to six, oval, pointed, fully spread, white or creamy white, with a greenish band down the back. Stamens spreading, dark (almost black) purple. Seed-vessels purplish, with silky tails. Flowers in June and July.

Native of China. It was first noticed by Thunberg in Japan, where it has long been grown in gardens; introduced in 1776. The wild ancestral form was found by Henry near Ichang in the Chinese province of Hupeh and later by Wilson in the same locality, but is probably not in cultivation. *C. florida* is closely allied to *C. patens* and the two are united by some authorities. But for garden purposes, *C. patens* is well distinguished in having no bracts to the flower-stalk and in the leaves consisting of three or five simple leaflets; in *C. florida* the leaves are doubly ternate.

cv. 'PLENA'.—Stamens transformed the same way as in 'Sieboldii' (see below), but white. A very old garden variety, commoner in nineteenth-century gardens than the single form, but now very rare.

cv. 'SIEBOLDII'.—In this variety the flowers are 'doubled' through the transformation of the stamens into petal-like organs. Whilst the sepals are white, the centre of the flower is purple. A cultivated Japanese variety introduced to England from Siebold's nursery in 1836. (var. *bicolor* Lindl.)

Whether *C. florida* is to be considered as one of the parents of the garden race of large-flowered clematises depends very much on the status of C. 'FORTUNEI'. This, like 'Sieboldii', is a double-flowered variety of Japanese gardens, with creamy white sepals and petaloid stamens, introduced by Fortune and much used by clematis breeders in the nineteenth century. It is usually regarded as a "variety" of *C. florida* but is placed by Rehder under *C. patens.*

In gardens it is still customary to distinguish a Florida group of large-flowered clematises—all double—but in no sense, either botanical or horticultural, can these be considered as varieties of *C. florida.* They are hybrids of complex origin some of which may have nothing or little of *C. florida* in their make-up. Thus the parentage of 'Belle of Woking' is C. (*lanuginosa* × *patens*) × 'Fortunei'. This clematis and others traditionally placed in the Florida group, such as 'Duchess of Edinburgh', require no pruning beyond the removal of the old flowering wood. This also applies to 'Sieboldii'.

C. FUSCA Turcz.

A semi-herbaceous climber 8 or 9 ft high, stems angled, downy when young. Leaves pinnate, 4 to 8 in. long, and composed mostly of five or seven leaflets, which are ovate with a rounded or heart-shaped base, and often long, tapering points, not toothed; glabrous or slightly downy beneath. Flowers solitary on stout stalks, which are ½ to 1 in. long, and thickly covered with reddish-brown hairs. The flower has the pitcher shape of the Viorna group, the sepals being ¾ to 1 in. long, the points recurved; outside they are reddish brown, woolly. Seed-vessels with tails about 1¼ in. long, plumed with yellowish-brown, silky hairs.

Native of N.E. Asia, from Asiatic Russia through Manchuria to the Kurile Islands. It is an interesting but not very ornamental plant, distinct in its group, because of the very short hairy flower-stalks, and the hairiness generally of the flower. It grows very well, and produces abundant seed.

C. GRACILIFOLIA Rehd. & Wils.

A deciduous climber up to 12 ft high; stems greyish, ribbed, clothed when young with appressed down. Leaves ternate or pinnate, consisting of three, five, or seven leaflets. Leaflets mostly ovate in main outline, but coarsely toothed or three-lobed, ½ to 1½ in. long; both stalk and blade slightly downy. Flowers white, 1½ to 2 in. wide, borne usually two to four together from the joints, each one on a downy slender stalk 1½ to 3 in. long. Sepals four, spreading, obovate, downy outside. Seed-vessel glabrous, with a feathery style nearly 1 in. long.

Native of W. China, where it was first found by Wilson in the province of Szechwan, afterwards by Purdom in Kansu, and by Forrest in Yunnan. Introduced by Wilson in 1910. It belongs to the same group as *C. chrysocoma* and *montana* (both of which have uniformly trifoliolate leaves) and is a graceful, free-blooming, hardy clematis. Flowers in June.

C. GRATA Wall.

The typical *C. grata* is a Himalayan species and may not be in cultivation. But in 1904 Wilson introduced to Veitch's Coombe Wood nursery a clematis which later proved to be a Chinese variety of the Himalayan plant. This is:

var. GRANDIDENTATA Rehd. & Wils.—A vigorous deciduous climber growing 30 ft high, with downy, ribbed stems. Leaves 6 in. or more long, composed of three or five leaflets; common stalk downy. Leaflets ovate, pointed, rounded or tapered at the base, the margins coarsely and unevenly set with triangular teeth; 1¼ to 3 in. long, the terminal one often deeply three-lobed and long-stalked, the basal pair with stalks ⅓ in. long; both surfaces, but especially the lower one, furnished with grey down. Panicles small, axillary and terminal, bearing the flowers in threes on the main-stalk or in threes on each of its branches. Sepals four or five, white, narrowly oblong, felted at the back. Flower 1 in. wide, opening in May and June. Seed-vessel glabrous, with a silky tail.

Native of W. Hupeh and Szechwan. This pleasing climber is related to *C. vitalba*, but differs from it in the glabrous or nearly glabrous inner face of the sepals but more downy leaflets. It grows vigorously and is perfectly hardy.

C. HERACLEIFOLIA DC.

C. tubulosa Turcz.

A semi-shrubby, deciduous plant, growing 2 to 3 ft high; stems ribbed, more or less downy, brownish red. Leaves composed of three leaflets, the terminal one much the largest, roundish ovate; shallowly, unequally, and sparsely bristly toothed; the base slightly heart-shaped, or almost cut off straight; from 2 to 5 in. long and wide; the side leaflets are similar in texture, etc., but are only half the size, and are scarcely stalked. Flowers ¾ to 1 in. long, produced from the joints of the stems of the year in dense short clusters, each flower on a downy stalk 1 in. or less in length. They are tubular at the lower half and swollen at the base, the four sepals curling outwards and backwards towards the end, deep blue outside, downy. The flowers are unisexual, but both sexes appear on one plant. Seed-vessels with feathered tails.

Native of Central and N. China; introduced in 1837; flowering from July to September. It is one of a group known as *Tubulosae*, whose four sepals close up and form a half-tubular flower of the same shape as hyacinths; to this group *C. stans* as well as other minor species belong. They are notable for the large leaves and robust, although semi-herbaceous growths.

var. DAVIDIANA (Verlot) Hemsl. *C. davidiana* Verlot.—This variety is somewhat taller than the type but similar in foliage and habit. The flowers are indigo-blue, the base tubular, but the four sepals spreading (not curled back as in the type) and also larger and longer. It is also distinct in being dioecious, male and female flowers being borne on separate plants. It is perhaps the most desirable of the section *Tubulosae*.

This variety was described (as *C. davidiana*) from plants raised from seed collected near Peking by Père David and sent by him to the Paris Museum in 1863. But the plant, from an English nursery, figured in *Bot. Mag.*, t. 4269

(Vol. 72, 1846) appears to belong to this variety; its provenance is unknown. The other form of the species figured in the *Botanical Magazine* (t. 6801) is the one that Decaisne described as *C. hookeri* and is presented under the name *C. tubulosa* var. *hookeri* (Decne.) Hook. f. The figure shows a plant with mauve flowers (light blue in t. 4269) but the characters by which Decaisne differentiated his *C. hookeri* were the herbaceous stems and precocious flowers, no mention being made of flower colour. The plant figured was received from the Segrez Arboretum and probably raised from seed sent by Père David.

Clematis 'CAMPANILE' and 'CÔTE D'AZUR' are very near to *C. heracleifolia* but are said to be seedlings of *C.* × *jouiniana*, its hybrid with *C. vitalba*. Both have flowers of azure blue, and self-supporting stems, but in the latter the flowers are of a deeper shade and the leaves glossier. *Clematis* 'CRÉPUSCULE' is a hybrid between *C. heracleifolia* and *C. stans*, raised by Lemoine.

C. INTEGRIFOLIA L.

Although usually classed as herbaceous, this species is a parent of three hybrids described in this work and therefore deserves mention. It is an erect, non-climbing herbaceous plant, sometimes becoming woody at the base, growing to about 4 ft high. Leaves stalkless, entire, ovate, up to $3\frac{1}{2}$ in. long and 2 in. wide, glabrous on both sides or slightly downy beneath. Flowers nodding, violet or blue, more rarely white, borne June to August singly, more rarely in twos or threes, at the ends of the shoots; pedicels about $1\frac{1}{2}$ in. long; sepals spreading, pointed at the apex, wavy and recurved at the margins, about 1 in. long.

A native mainly of the lower Danube basin, S.W. Russia (including the Caucasus) and Central Asia, long cultivated in gardens and of interest as the only European member of the section *Viorna*, with its nearest allies in N. America. It is a parent of the hybrids *C.* × *aromatica* (with *C. flammula*), *C.* × *eriostemon* (with *C. viticella*) and *C.* × *durandii* (probably with *C.* × *jackmanii*).

C. × JACKMANII T. Moore

In 1860 some plants were raised in the nursery of Messrs Jackman at Woking from seed of *C. lanuginosa* pollinated by *C. viticella* 'Atrorubens' and *C.* × *eriostemon* 'Hendersonii'. This batch flowered in 1862, and from it two forms were selected and put into commerce—one as *C. jackmanii* and the other as *C. rubro-violacea*. Since two pollen parents were used in making the cross, the precise parentage of the former, which is the type of the group *C.* × *jackmanii*, is not known for certain, but it is reasonable to assume that it is straight *C. lanuginosa* × *viticella*. It is still a valued garden plant today, with flowers 4 to 5 in. across, of a rich, velvety violet-purple.

The importance of the Jackmanii cross (a similar cross was made on the continent at about the same time) was that it united the genes of the European *C. viticella* with those of one of its E. Asiatic allies. The contribution of this species was: deepness of flower-colouring and the habit of flowering entirely on the season's growths as the days shorten. The Jackmanii group of hybrids is,

TS—Y

however, a complex race in the formation of which the other E. Asiatic species may have played a part and thus extends beyond the boundaries of *C. × jackmanii*. The hybrids of this group commence to flower in June or July and some are still gay in October if the weather remains open and sunny. They may be pruned to within a foot of the older stems each spring, being for the most part vigorous growers, and flowering on the shoots of the current year.

cv. 'SUPERBA'.—Similar to the original *C. × jackmanii* but with broader sepals of a more reddish purple, rich maroon when the flowers first expand. A very vigorous and beautiful clematis. It is of interest that 'MADAME GRANGÉ', raised in France before 1877, and bearing some resemblance to 'Superba', is known to have been a direct cross between *C. lanuginosa* and *C. viticella*. This cross was also made by the French nursery firm of Simon-Louis in 1861 and named by them *C. splendida*. The plants from this cross were said to resemble *C. × jackmanii* very closely, but the example figured in *Revue Horticole*, 1865, p. 70, has flowers of a redder purple.

C. × JOUINIANA Schneid.

A very vigorous, deciduous climber about 10 ft high, stems strongly ribbed and slightly downy. Leaves composed of three or five leaflets, which are more or less intermediate between those of *C. vitalba* and *heracleifolia*. Flowers in corymbs 4 to 6 in. long, springing from the leaf-axils towards the end of the shoot, the whole forming a large panicle 1 to 2 ft long. Sepals four, strap-shaped, pointed, ¾ in. long; at first yellowish white, finally suffused with lilac; half to fully expanded, but little recurved.

A hybrid between *C. vitalba* and *C. heracleifolia* var. *davidiana*, which is widely spread in gardens under the erroneous name of "*C. grata*". It is a quick-growing plant with perennial stems, and it flowers with great freedom from August to October. Very suitable for covering old tree-stumps or mounds. It was named after E. Jouin, manager of the Simon-Louis nurseries at Metz.

cv. 'MRS ROBERT BRYDON'.—Flowers pale lavender. It is perhaps nearer to *C. heracleifolia* than is the original *C. × jouiniana* but the stems are lax and need support. Raised in the U.S.A.

cv. 'PRAECOX'.—This variety starts to flower in late July or early August.

C. LANUGINOSA Lindl.

A deciduous climber, said to be only 6 ft high in nature. Leaves either simple or composed of three leaflets, which are heart-shaped at the base, pointed at the apex, up to 5 in. long by 3 in. wide, of thick texture, covered beneath with a thick, soft, grey wool, glabrous above; stalks 3 to 6 in. long, downy. Flowers 4 to 6 in. across, produced at the end of the shoots on woolly stalks which have no bracts. Sepals normally six, but often seven or eight; oval or obovate, over-lapping and fully expanded; very downy behind, varying in cultivated varieties from white to pale lilac. Seed-vessels with long silky tails.

This clematis was originally introduced to cultivation by Robt. Fortune, who

found it near Ningpo, China, in 1850. Although allied in a botanical sense to
C. patens and *C. florida*, it is amply distinct in its dwarfer habit, large flowers with
overlapping sepals, and the very woolly, often simple leaves and woolly flower-
stalks. Also, it bears its flowers successively from late spring into the autumn,

CLEMATIS × JOUINIANA

in contrast to the other two Asiatic allies, which, if left unpruned, bear their
main crop before midsummer. Although the species is very rare in cultivation,
if not extinct, there must be few large-flowered garden clematises that do not
have its blood in them. The first crosses using it as a parent were made by
Isaac Anderson-Henry and of these two, 'LAWSONIANA' and 'HENRYANA',

both with 'Fortunei' (see *C. florida*) as the pollen parent, are still in cultivation today.

The Lanuginosa group of clematises, as originally defined, comprised those hybrids which bear their flowers in succession on short lateral shoots from the current season's stems, from midsummer onwards. However, the distinction between this and the Florida and Patens groups was never well marked and has largely disappeared. Most of the group as now understood bear a crop of flowers in early summer and may be left unpruned; if pruned in spring the full flush will be had in mid- and late-summer.

C. LASIANDRA Maxim.

A vigorous, deciduous climber; stems slender, angled, viscid when young, sparsely hairy. Leaves ternate or doubly ternate, 3 to 8 in. long, composed of three or nine leaflets; when three they are often deeply three-lobed. Leaflets 2 to 4 in. long, ovate to lanceolate, the lateral ones of each trio oblique at the base; all with long, slender points, coarsely and irregularly toothed, sparsely downy and dark green above; paler, brighter and glabrous beneath. The base of the leaf-stalks and the nodes are hairy. Flowers usually in threes, in axillary cymes 1½ to 2 in. long; sepals downy, varying on different plants from white to dull slaty purple, oblong, the margins pressed together at the base, the points rolled back, forming a bell-shaped flower ½ in. long, stuffed with yellowish-white stamens thickly clothed with silky hairs. Fruit-heads composed of numerous ovate-lanceolate carpels, each with a long, feathery tail.

Native of Japan and China; introduced from the latter country by Wilson in 1900. It flowers in October. Not one of the most promising species.

C. LIGUSTICIFOLIA Torr. & Gr.

This little-known species, climbing to 20 ft, is a native of western N. America, and in the American floras is grouped with *C. virginiana*. It is easily distinguished from that species (which has trifoliolate leaves) by its five leaflets, the terminal one of which is deeply three-lobed or occasionally three-foliolate. It is, perhaps, more likely to be confounded with our native *C. vitalba* in foliage, but the plant is much less vigorous, and does not flower freely with us. Moreover, male and female flowers are confined to separate plants. They are white, fragrant, ¾ in. across, and produced in corymbose panicles, the sepals downy. Leaflets ovate, pointed, coarsely toothed, of firm texture, bright green and glabrous. Seed-vessels with feathery tails. Flowers in September.

var. CALIFORNICA S. Wats., has leaves downy or even velvety beneath.

C. MACROPETALA Ledeb.   [PLATE 50

A deciduous climber with slender angled stems, downy when young, more especially near the swollen joints. Leaves mostly bi-ternate, i.e., consisting of three main divisions, each having three leaflets—or nine in all; the whole leaf

3 to 6 in. long. Leaflets ovate to lance-shaped, pointed, rounded or tapered at the base, coarsely and irregularly toothed; ½ to 1½ in. long, ¼ to ¾ in. wide; nearly or quite glabrous except at the junction of the slender leaf-stalks. Flowers 2½ to 4 in. wide, produced from May or June onwards at the end of the shoots or at the joints, each on a slender stalk 3 in. or more long. Sepals four, blue or violet-blue; 1¼ to 2 in. long, ¼ to ⅓ in. wide; pointed. The centre of each flower is filled with a large number of petal-like segments decreasing in size towards the middle, the outer ones narrow, elliptic, pointed, and violet-blue like the sepals, the innermost of linear shape and almost white; all clothed with down. Stamens numerous, anthers pale yellow. Seed-vessels terminated by a slender, feathered style, 1½ in. long. *Bot. Mag.*, t. 9142.

Native of the province of Kansu, China, and of Siberia; first introduced by Purdom (No. 149), to the Coombe Wood nursery where it flowered in July, 1912; afterwards by Reginald Farrer (No. 315) about 1914. This beautiful climber belongs to the *Atragene* section of *Clematis*. Previous to its introduction this group was represented in gardens by only two species—*C. alpina* and *C. verticillaris*. These species are distinguished by the crowd of petal-like organs (staminodes) coming between the stamens and sepals. *C. macropetala* was collected about 1742 by d'Incarville in the mountainous country north of Peking, and it was named and first described by Ledebour in 1829 from a plant found in Siberia. It is closely akin to *C. alpina*, but the sepals are narrower, the petal-like organs longer, narrower and pointed (those of *C. alpina* being shorter, spathulate and blunt). *C. macropetala* is also later-flowering.

cv. 'MARKHAM'S PINK'.—Flowers rose-coloured, shaded with purple at the base.

cv. 'MAIDWELL HALL'.—A selection with flowers of a purer blue.

C. MAXIMOWICZIANA Fr. & Sav.

C. paniculata Thunb., not Gmel.; *C. dioscoreifolia* var. *robusta* (Carr.) Rehd.; *C. flammula* var. *robusta* Carr.

A very vigorous climber, growing 30 ft or more high, and forming a thick tangle; young stems slightly downy. Leaves composed of three or (usually) five leaflets, which are dark green on both sides, heart-shaped or ovate, 1 to 3 in. long, not lobed or toothed, nearly or quite glabrous, and comparatively long-stalked. The blades of the largest leaflets resemble in form and colour the leaves of the common lilac. Flowers scented like hawthorn, 1 in. or more across, produced during September and October in forked panicles, 3 to 4 in. long, from the axils of the current year's growth. Sepals four, white, oblong. Seed-vessels with grey feathered styles 1 to 1½ in. long, rarely seen in Britain.

Native of Japan; discovered by Thunberg, who lived in that country in the last quarter of the eighteenth century. He named it *C. paniculata*, under which name it has long been known in gardens, but this name had, unfortunately, been used a few years earlier for the New Zealand clematis better known as *C. indivisa*.

C. maximowicziana (*paniculata*) has never been largely planted in the British Isles, for, although hardy and vigorous enough, it rarely flowers with freedom, and usually too late in the season to develop well. In the eastern United States, on the other hand, it is one of the most beautiful and wonderful of climbing plants, producing its pure white flowers in marvellous profusion. In Britain it lacks, no doubt, sufficient summer sun to bring out its best qualities, and would be happiest against a south wall. It is an ally of *C. flammula*, but much more vigorous.

C. MEYENIANA Walp.

A vigorous evergreen climber 20 ft or more high; stems glabrous, wiry, purplish brown. Leaves made up of three leaflets on a main-stalk 2 to 4 in. long. Leaflets broadly ovate to lanceolate, shortly to slenderly pointed, heart-shaped or rounded at the base; 2 to 5 in. long, 1 to 3 in. wide; not toothed, distinctly three-veined, of leathery texture. Flowers 1 in. wide, produced numerously in large, lax panicles; the (normally) four sepals white, narrowly oblong, woolly at the margins, the anthers making a conspicuous yellow patch of colour in the centre. Styles of the seed-vessel 1¼ in. long, silky. *Bot. Mag.*, t. 7897.

Native of China, where it is widely spread from Hong Kong to Yunnan. There are evidently several forms of this clematis in a wild state, as one might, indeed, expect from its wide natural area. The plant figured in the *Botanical Magazine*, which may be regarded as typical, came to Kew from Hong Kong, and like its successors had to be given cool greenhouse treatment. Probably forms of more western origin would be hardier and in any case would succeed in our warmer counties in the open air. The species is of the same group as *C. armandii* but has smaller flowers; it makes a very fine display at Kew every year in the coolest section of the Temperate House, where it flowers during February and March and in advance of *C. armandii*. It is very closely allied to *C. finetiana*, which differs in its usually racemose or merely three-flowered inflorescence.

C. MONTANA DC.

A deciduous climber of vigorous habit, growing at least 20 ft high; stems glabrous except when quite young. Leaves composed of three leaflets on a common stalk 2 to 4 in. long; the leaflets short-stalked, ovate to lanceolate, pointed, variously and unequally toothed; 1 to 4 in. long, half as wide. Flowers solitary, pure white, 2 to 2½ in. across, each borne on a glabrous stalk 2 to 5 in. long. Sepals four, spreading, oval. Seed-vessel elliptical, glabrous, surmounted by a plumose style 1½ in. long.

Native of the Himalaya; introduced by Lady Amherst in 1831. It is quite hardy, and is undoubtedly one of the loveliest of all climbers. The flowers appear in May, and being produced singly on long stalks, can only be confused with the white variety of *C. alpina*, and that is not only very different in habit and vigour, but has the petal-like parts of the flower characteristic only of the *Atragene* section. *C. montana* is a valuable plant for covering arbours, pergolas, and especially verandas, where its long shoots can be allowed to hang down and form a sort of curtain.

CLEMATIS MONTANA var. RUBENS

cv. 'ELIZABETH'.—Flowers fragrant, large and light pink in colour.

f. GRANDIFLORA (Hook.) Rehd.—Flowers larger than in the type, up to 3 in. across.

var. RUBENS Kuntze—A Chinese variety introduced for Messrs Veitch by Wilson in 1900. It is very distinct, the foliage being similar in size and form to the type, but more downy and purplish, although not so markedly purple as the leaf-stalks and young stems. The flowers appear in June, rather later than those of the type, and are of a beautiful rosy red. The sepals are 1¼ in. long, ⅞ in. wide; flower-stalks hairy. The variety is probably the most beautiful and useful climber distributed in the twentieth century. It is hardier than the type and flowers with greater regularity. Easily increased by cuttings.   [PLATE 51

cv. 'TETRAROSE'.—A vigorous form with twice the normal number of chromosomes, raised in Holland. Flowers large, purplish pink.

var. WILSONII Sprague—This variety, figured in *Bot. Mag.*, t. 8365, has larger white flowers on downy stalks, 3 in. in diameter, and they appear in July and August. This habit of late flowering adds to its value. Native of Central China; Wilson, who introduced it, said it was the commonest form of the species in W. Szechwan. It was originally distributed by Veitch as "*C. repens*".

It should be noted that Wilson introduced another form of this variety which flowers at the normal time. It was further distinguished by its broadly obovate sepals and was for this reason given botanical rank as f. PLATYSEPALA Rehd. & Wils.

C. NANNOPHYLLA Maxim.

A deciduous shrub of erect, dense habit, growing 4 ft or more high and wide, young shoots slender, strongly ribbed, appressed grey-hairy. Leaves variable, ¾ to 2½ in. long, elegantly cut into usually three lobes or deeply, pinnately toothed, the parts narrow and sharply pointed; glabrous or nearly so. Flowers borne at the end of the branches, mostly solitary but sometimes in threes or, very rarely, in pairs. Each flower is ¾ to 1¼ in. wide, the four ovate or oval sepals each ⅓ to ½ in. wide with a brown centre and golden-yellow margins; style-clusters 1 in. across. *Bot. Mag.*, t. 9641.

Native of China, introduced from the province of Kansu by R. Farrer in 1914–15. It is a charming plant both in its elegantly cut leaves and the pretty, unusual colouring of its flowers. It frequently occurs wild under arid conditions. This species has always been rare in cultivation and now seems to have been lost altogether.

C. NAPAULENSIS DC.
C. forrestii W. W. Sm.

An evergreen climber up to 30 ft high; young shoots grooved, greyish. Leaves trifoliolate or quinquefoliolate; the latter found only on long barren shoots of the current season. Leaflets of thin texture, glabrous, ovate-lanceolate, pointed, either entire or with a few large teeth, or even three-lobed; 1½ to 3½ in. long, ½ to 1½ in. wide; the terminal one the largest. Flowers produced in winter, eight or ten together at the joints of the stem, each on its own stalk. Flower-stalk ¾ to 1½ in. long, furnished with a cup-shaped, downy bract ¼ in. long, and very downy between the bract and the sepals. Sepals four, ovate, creamy yellow, slightly spreading, ½ to 1 in. long, ⅙ in. wide, covered with silky down. Stamens very numerous, up to 1 in. long, purple. Seed-vessel with silky-white tails 1 in. or more long. *Bot. Mag.*, t. 9037.

Native of N. India and S.W. China. Forrest found it in the latter area in 1912 and it was named after him by Sir W. W. Smith. In 1925 (see *Botanical Magazine*, loc. cit.) Dr Stapf identified it with the Himalayan *C. napaulensis*. The chief beauty of the flower is in the purple stamens and anthers which are in admirable contrast with the creamy sepals. Botanically the species is related to *C. cirrhosa* in having a cup-shaped involucre or bract on the flower-stalk. It will no doubt be hardy in our warmer counties, but is as yet very rare. The figure in the *Botanical Magazine* was made from a plant growing at Caerhays Castle, Cornwall, where Forrest's form was first raised. It would no doubt be hardy in the warmer counties but elsewhere is best regarded as a cool greenhouse climber. As such it was given an Award of Merit when shown by Kew in November 1957. It bears its flowers through the winter under glass.

C. ORIENTALIS L.   [PLATE 52
C. graveolens Lindl.

A deciduous climber, growing 10 to 20 ft high; young stems ribbed and not downy. Leaves 6 to 8 in. long, pinnately divided, the primary divisions usually trifoliolate; leaflets with slender stalks 1 to 2 in. long, dull glaucous green, ovate or lanceolate, ½ to 2½ in. long, usually angularly toothed or deeply lobed, but sometimes entire, quite glabrous. Flowers yellow, slightly fragrant, 1½ to 2 in. across, produced during August and September singly on slender stalks 2 to

4 in. long (lengthening in fruit); sepals ovate, pointed, downy on the inside. Seed-vessel with slender, feathered styles $1\frac{1}{2}$ in. long, the whole forming a handsome globular tuft over 3 in. across.

In a wild state this clematis extends from the Caucasus and Persia to the Himalaya, N. China, and Manchuria; it accordingly varies considerably in minor points. The plant usually known as *C. graveolens* is a less glaucous form, the leaves slightly downy, the leaflets mostly larger. *C. orientalis* was introduced in 1731.

C. GLAUCA Willd. var. AKEBIOIDES (Maxim.) Rehd. & Wils. *C. orientalis* var. *akebioides* Maxim.—This has flowers $1\frac{1}{2}$ to $1\frac{3}{4}$ in. diameter, deep orange yellow. A handsome Chinese form introduced for Messrs Veitch by Wilson, which flowers late into October, and is more vigorous than the type. It differs from *C. orientalis* in having the sepals downy on the margins only.

A remarkable clematis of the *orientalis* alliance was introduced by Ludlow, Sherriff, and Elliott from the Himalaya in 1947, under LSE 13372, with thick, fleshy sepals that have been likened to orange-peel. It was given an Award of Merit when shown by Messrs Ingwersen in 1951.

C. PANICULATA Gmel.

C. indivisa Willd.

A vigorous evergreen climber festooning small trees and shrubs in a state of nature; young shoots ribbed and pubescent. Leaves of three leaflets borne on a common stalk $1\frac{1}{2}$ to 3 in. long. Leaflets ovate, blunt at the apex, rounded or slightly heart-shaped at the base, entire or sometimes lobed; $1\frac{1}{2}$ to 3 in. long, half to two-thirds as wide, glabrous, glossy green, each on a stalk $\frac{1}{3}$ to 1 in. long. Flowers unisexual, 2 to 4 in. wide on male plants, smaller in the female, produced in loose axillary panicles up to 1 ft long, each flower on a slender downy stalk which is from $1\frac{1}{2}$ to $4\frac{1}{2}$ in. long and has a pair of small bracts near the middle. Sepals usually six to eight, white, narrowly oblong, $\frac{1}{3}$ to $\frac{1}{2}$ in. wide. Stamens with yellow stalks and rose-coloured anthers. Seed-vessels downy, with a feathery tail 2 in. or more long.

Native of both islands of New Zealand, widely distributed and abundant; discovered during Capt. Cook's first voyage; first described by J. F. Gmelin in 1791 as *C. paniculata* but better known under the name Willdenow gave it— *C. indivisa*. For the Japanese clematis named *C. paniculata* by Thunberg in 1794 see *C. maximowicziana*. Introduced in 1840.

This beautiful climber is only hardy in the milder parts of the country and is probably seen at its best in Cornwall, where there is a fine specimen at Bosahan near Helston.

cv. 'LOBATA'.—This plant, figured in *Bot. Mag.*, t. 4398, has markedly lobed leaves but appears to fall within the normal span of variation of the type. At any rate, var. *lobata*, as Hooker named it, is not recognised by New Zealand botanists, who regard plants with lobed leaves as being a developmental stage towards the final state with entire leaves (Cheeseman in *Trans. New Zeal. Inst.*, Vol. 46, 1 (1914)). Since the plant is still in cultivation, and a good form, it is as well to maintain the name in cultivar form.

C. PATENS Morr. & Decne.
C. coerulea Lindl.

A deciduous climber, growing 8 to 12 ft high. Leaves composed of three or five leaflets with downy stalks; leaflets ovate-lanceolate; 2 to 4 in. long, $1\frac{1}{4}$ to $2\frac{1}{2}$ in. wide, pointed, glabrous above, downy beneath. Flowers solitary on downy stalks without bracts; 4 to 6 in. across; sepals six to eight, long-pointed, wide-spreading, and more separated from each other than in C. florida (q.v.). In the typical C. patens the flowers are said to be white, but this is probably not in cultivation now, and the cultivated forms of the Patens group vary from white tinged with violet to deep violet-blue. Seed-vessels with silky tails.

Commonly cultivated in, and probably a native of Japan, whence it was introduced to Europe in 1836 by Siebold, who had found it in a garden near Yokohama. Also native of China. Some authorities regard it as a variety of C. florida; the distinctions are pointed out under that species.

C. patens has made its contribution to the formation of the large-flowered clematis hybrids, but the type was probably less used by breeders than the Japanese garden variety 'STANDISHII', introduced by Fortune in 1861. This is usually placed under C. patens, but is considered by some authorities to be a hybrid between that species and C. florida. The clematises which are customarily classed together in the Patens group flower in early summer on short shoots from the previous year's wood and need no pruning apart from the removal of flowered growths.

C. PHLEBANTHA L.H.J.Williams

A shrub with trailing stems up to about 5 ft long, or an erect bush 1 to 2 ft high; young stems ribbed longitudinally and covered with a white wool, the older ones peeling in thin strips. Leaves opposite, imparipinnate, $\frac{3}{5}$ to 3 in. long, with a woolly rachis and petiole; leaflets five to nine, usually seven, about $\frac{3}{5}$ in. long and wide, sessile or nearly so, broadly cuneate at the base, the terminal leaflet five-lobed, the lateral ones mostly three-lobed, the lobes triangular or broadly so, acute, green and silky above, densely white-woolly beneath. Flowers hermaphrodite, borne, usually singly, in the leaf-axils towards the ends of the shoots, 1 to $1\frac{4}{5}$ in. in diameter; pedicels $\frac{4}{5}$ to $3\frac{1}{5}$ in. long, often furnished with a pair of simple or leaf-like and three-lobed bracts. Sepals five to seven, white, with reddish veins, elliptic to obovate, acute or slightly mucronate at the apex, $\frac{2}{5}$ to $\frac{4}{5}$ in. long, $\frac{1}{5}$ to $\frac{2}{5}$ in. wide. Anthers yellow, shorter than the filaments. Achenes hairy, terminated by the feathery persistent style.

Native of W. Nepal, where it inhabits cliffs and steep hillsides in the low-rainfall area north-west of the Dhaulagiri massif, at 9,800 to 12,200 ft; discovered by Polunin, Sykes and Williams during their expedition to Nepal in 1952 and introduced by them in the same year by means of seed collected at 9,400 ft under field number PSW 3436. It was described in Journ. R.H.S., Vol. 93, Aug. 1968, pp. 343–6, and to this account we are indebted for the particulars given here.

C. phlebantha was raised at Wisley from PSW 3436 and is represented there by two plants grown in the half-hardy house. If it proves hardy (and, perhaps more importantly, tolerant of our wet winters) it will be an attractive addition to the cultivated species, with its silvery foliage and prettily veined flowers. Grown outside, it will certainly need a well-drained soil and a sunny position. It belongs to sect. *Flammula* subsect. *Recta*.

C. DELAVAYI Franch.—This species resembles *C. phlebantha* in having pinnate leaves with the leaflets white tomentose beneath, but is easily distinguished by the shape and size of the leaflets and by the flowers being smaller and borne in terminal inflorescences. The leaflets are lanceolate to elliptic-ovate, acute, entire, about $\frac{1}{2}$ to $1\frac{2}{5}$ in. long, $\frac{1}{6}$ to $\frac{2}{5}$ in. (sometimes up to $\frac{2}{3}$ in.) wide. The flowers are up to $\frac{4}{5}$ in. wide. A native of China, introduced by Wilson from W. Szechwan. It is no longer in cultivation at Kew.

C. PITCHERI Torr. & Gray

A deciduous climber 12 or more ft high; young stems downy. Leaves pinnate, composed of three to seven leaflets, which are ovate, with a rounded or slightly heart-shaped base, sometimes two- or three-lobed, or even trifoliolate; 1 to 3 in. long, half as wide; strongly net-veined, and more or less downy beneath. The terminal leaflet is often reduced to a tendril. Flower solitary on a downy stalk, 2 to 4 in. long. Sepals purplish blue outside, $\frac{3}{4}$ to $1\frac{1}{4}$ in. long, the tapering points slightly reflexed, showing the greenish-yellow inner surface, margins downy; the margins of the sepals converge, giving the flower the urn or pitcher shape characteristic of the *Viorna* group to which this belongs. Seed-vessels almost circular, but narrowed at the top to a slightly downy (not feathery) style $\frac{3}{4}$ in. long.

Native of the Central United States; introduced to Kew in 1878. It has been confused in French periodicals with *C. texensis*, which differs not only in the colour of the flowers, but is, like another ally, *C. viorna*, distinguished by the plumed styles. *C. pitcheri* is the best of the *Viorna* group in gardens; the stems do not die back so much in winter as the others. It flowers from the end of May to September, never making any great display at one time.

C. QUINQUEFOLIATA Hutchins.

An evergreen climber with ribbed, downy stems. Leaves composed of five leaflets pinnately arranged, the main leaf-stalk 6 in. long. Leaflets lanceolate to ovate-lanceolate, rounded or heart-shaped at the base, bluntish or short-pointed at the end; 2 to 4 in. long, one-third as much wide; downy in the grooved midrib above, otherwise glabrous. Flowers produced during early autumn from the leaf-axils in cymes consisting of three, five, or seven flowers, each of which is $1\frac{1}{2}$ to 2 in. wide. Sepals four to six, milky white, narrowly oblong, $\frac{1}{6}$ to $\frac{1}{4}$ in. wide, downy beneath and especially at the margins; stamens very numerous, anthers yellow. Seed-vessel silky, terminated by a style 2 to 3 in. long and clothed with brownish-yellow, silky hairs.

Native of China in the provinces of Hupeh and Szechwan; discovered by

Henry, introduced by Wilson in 1900 and flowered in the Coombe Wood nursery in September 1906. It belongs to the same group as *C. armandii* and *C. meyeniana* but is well distinguished by its five-foliolate leaves. As seen at Coombe Wood it was a vigorous, quite ornamental climber, but does not appear to have spread in cultivation. Wilson commented on the strikingly handsome fulvous-hued styles of the fruits.

C. RANUNCULOIDES Franch.

An erect shrub 1 to 2 ft high in the open, but in hedges or on shrubs climbing 6 to 10 ft high; young stems grooved and angular, hairy to nearly glabrous. Leaves varying from trilobed to trifoliolate and quinquefoliolate, with the ovate or obovate leaflets $\frac{1}{2}$ to $2\frac{1}{2}$ in. long, coarsely toothed and usually more or less hairy, leaf-stalks from 2 to 6 in. long, often much curled. Flowers solitary in the leaf-axils or in few-flowered or terminal clusters, nodding on short, hairy, slender stalks; sepals purple to pale rose, oblong, $\frac{3}{8}$ in. long, much recurved, downy, three-ribbed on the back. Stamens $\frac{2}{5}$ in. long. Achenes compressed, $1\frac{1}{4}$ in. long, downy. *Bot. Mag.*, t. 9239.

Native of China; introduced in 1906 by Forrest from the Tali Range. At home it flowers from May to September, but in the Edinburgh Botanic Garden it has flowered as late as November. Often found in grassy situations and then only 1 to 2 ft high.

C. REHDERIANA Craib

C. nutans Hort., not Royle; *C. nutans* var. *thyrsoidea* Rehd. & Wils., in part; *C. buchananiana* Finet & Gagnep., not DC.

A deciduous climber up to 25 ft high, with angled, downy stems. Leaves pinnate, 6 to 9 in. long, consisting of usually seven or nine leaflets. Leaflets broadly ovate, pointed, heart-shaped at the base, often three-lobed, coarsely toothed; $1\frac{1}{2}$ to 3 in. long, about two-thirds as wide; more or less downy above, clothed with silky down and conspicuously veined beneath; stalk of leaflets 1 to $1\frac{1}{2}$ in. long, hairy. Flowers mostly nodding, fragrant like cowslips; borne on erect, downy, ribbed panicles 5 to 9 in. high from August to October. The four sepals are of a soft primrose yellow, ribbed, and form a bell-shaped perianth $\frac{1}{2}$ to $\frac{3}{4}$ in. long; their points are recurved, and they are velvety outside, glabrous within; stamens about as long as the sepals, thinly hairy their whole length. Seed-vessels orbicular-ovoid, downy, terminated by a silky style 1 in. long.

Native of W. China; introduced to France, in 1898, by Père Aubert from near Tatsien-lu, thence to Kew in 1904. Wilson introduced it from the same neighbourhood in 1908. It is one of the latest flowering clematises and is worthy of cultivation on that account, also for the sweet fragrance of its pretty blossoms. Its naming has been much confused. When first introduced it was called *C. buchaniana* by the French; then it was identified with *C. nutans*. Both these species are Himalayan, and probably not in cultivation. (For a fuller history of this species see the article by B. O. Mulligan in *Journ. R.H.S.*, Vol. 64, 1939, pp. 191–2.)

C. VEITCHIANA Craib, hitherto confused with the above under the name "*C. nutans*", differs in a number of characters. Its most noticeable distinction is in the leaves being doubly pinnate; the two or three lower primary divisions are usually trifoliolate. The leaflets, in consequence, are smaller and more numerous —often over twenty. Another distinction is that the bracts on the inflorescence are very small ($\frac{1}{8}$ to $\frac{1}{4}$ in. long) and awl-shaped, whereas in *C. rehderiana* they are much larger ($\frac{5}{8}$ to $\frac{3}{4}$ in. long), ovate or oval, sometimes deeply three-lobed. The flowers are rather smaller, but of the same shape and colour. Introduced from W. China by Wilson in 1904.

C. SERRATIFOLIA Rehd.

A deciduous climber, growing 10 ft high, with slender, glabrous, ribbed stems. Leaves doubly ternate, the leaflets ovate to lanceolate, $1\frac{1}{2}$ to 3 in. long, often oblique at the base, pointed, sharply toothed; thin in texture, quite glabrous, bright green; stalks $\frac{1}{2}$ to 1 in. long. Flowers produced singly, in pairs, or in threes from the leaf-axils in August and September. Sepals four, lanceolate or narrowly oblong, pointed, about 1 in. long, $\frac{1}{4}$ in. wide, soft yellow, downy inside and at the margins; stamens purple; seed-vessels with feathery styles 2 in. long.

Native of Korea; introduced about 1918. It is closely allied to *C. tangutica* but that species differs in its pinnate or doubly pinnate leaves. The flowers of *C. serratifolia* are smaller but borne more plentifully. An attractive addition to the clematises with yellow flowers.

C. SONGARICA Bunge

A semi-woody, scarcely climbing plant 4 or 5 ft high, with slender, furrowed, not downy stems. Leaves simple, lanceolate to linear; $1\frac{1}{2}$ to 4 in. long, $\frac{1}{4}$ to $1\frac{1}{4}$ in. wide; margins either entire or coarsely and angularly toothed, quite glabrous, and of a greyish or glaucous green, with three prominent veins; stalk $\frac{1}{2}$ to $1\frac{1}{4}$ in. long. Flowers yellowish white produced on stalked cymes 3 to 6 in. long, both axillary and terminal; each flower is $\frac{3}{4}$ to 1 in. across, on a slender stalk 1 to 2 in. long. Sepals downy outside, glabrous within. Seed-vessels with plumed styles.

Native of S. Siberia, Turkestan, Mongolia, and the region of the river Sungari, from which it takes its name; sent to Kew in 1880 by E. Regel of St Petersburg. Both entire leaves and leaves with jagged margins occur on the same plant, the former usually as basal leaves of flowering branches, springing from the axils of leaves of the latter type. The whole plant has a grey-green tinge similar to that of *C. orientalis*, but its simple leaves distinguish it.

C. STANS Sieb. & Zucc.

C. heracleifolia var. *stans* (Sieb. & Zucc.) Kuntze; *C. kousabotan* Decne.

A deciduous, sub-shrubby, or sometimes scandent plant, with stems up to 6 ft long, dying back nearly to the base in winter; stout, ribbed, covered with grey down. Leaves composed of three leaflets, broadly ovate, the terminal one three-lobed, all coarsely and sharply toothed, from 2 to 6 in. long, nearly as wide, downy on the stalks and on the strongly marked veins. Flowers produced on branched stalks 4 to 10 in. or more long, the flowers being clustered in the axils of leaf-like bracts. They are ¾ in. long and wide, tubular at the base, the sepals curled at the ends, nearly white. *Bot. Mag.*, t. 6810.

Native of Japan; introduced by Von Siebold to France about 1860. It belongs to the same group as *C. heracleifolia*, a group distinguished by tube-shaped, hyacinth-like flowers. In *C. stans* the plants may be male or female, or they may have flowers of both sexes on the one plant. The last (monoecious) form was once known as *C. kousabotan* Decne. *C. stans* is distinguished from *C. heracleifolia* by its laxer habit, more downy stems, and smaller flowers.

cv. 'LAVALLEI'.—A very strong-growing form with sweet-scented flowers of both sexes on the same plant (monoecious); flower-stalks up to 18 in. long; flowers ¾ in. long.

C. TANGUTICA (Maxim.) Korshinsky [PLATE 53
C. orientalis var. *tangutica* Maxim.

A species closely allied to, or perhaps a variety of, *C. orientalis*, growing 10 to 15 ft high; stems slightly downy. Leaves grey-green, like those of *C. orientalis*, but downy when young; leaflets raggedly toothed, and sometimes two- or three-lobed. Flowers rich yellow, solitary on downy stalks 3 to 6 in. long; sepals nearly 2 in. long, narrowly ovate, long and slenderly pointed, downy outside and at the edges. Seed-vessels crowned with long feathered styles. *Bot. Mag.*, t. 7710.

Native of Central Asia; introduced to Kew from St Petersburg in 1898. It was introduced again in 1911 from W. Kansu by Purdom; this form was raised at Wisley and seed from the plants there widely distributed from 1919 onward. It is the handsomest yellow-flowered clematis in cultivation, the finest flowers being about 4 in. across. It differs from *C. orientalis* in the larger flowers, downy stems, flower-stalks, etc. It is a superior autumnal flowering plant.

var. OBTUSIUSCULA Rehd. & Wils.—From the typical *C. tangutica* this variety is distinguished by its more woolly young shoots, leaf-stalks, and flower-stalks; by its smaller, more sparsely toothed leaflets; and by the shorter, blunt or scarcely pointed sepals 1 to 1¼ in. long. (In the typical *tangutica* the sepals have long slender points and are of greater length.) The flowers are rich yellow and solitary on stalks 3 to 4 in. long.

Native of W. Szechwan, China, at altitudes of 8,000 to 10,000 ft; introduced by Wilson in 1908. On the whole it is scarcely so handsome a plant as the type, although it possibly flowers more freely and grows more vigorously.

C. TEXENSIS Buckl.
C. coccinea Engelm.

A climbing, semi-herbaceous plant in this country, mostly dying back in winter, but several yards high in its native country. Leaves pinnate, glaucous, composed of four to eight leaflets, each of which has a stalk as long, or longer than its blade, the common stalk often ending in a sort of tendril. Leaflets ovate to roundish, or sometimes two- or three-lobed, mostly heart-shaped at the base, 1 to 3 in. long, with well-marked, netted veins; quite glabrous and not toothed. Flower solitary, on a ribbed stalk 5 to 6 in. long, pitcher-shaped, nodding; 1 in. long, ¾ in. wide at the base, much narrowed towards the mouth, of various shades of red from scarlet to purplish. Sepals thick, narrowly ovate, with the points slightly reflexed, downy at the margins. Seed-vessels ending in a feathery style, 1½ in. long. *Bot. Mag.*, t. 6594.

Native of Texas; discovered in 1850 and introduced in 1868. This species is rather tender, and needs some protection in winter. At Kew it lives outside, at the foot of a south wall. The flowers are variable in shade, but the rich red form in cultivation is unique in colour among cultivated species. Hybridised with the large-flowered varieties of the Patens and other groups it has given some very distinct and handsome varieties, such as 'GRAVETYE BEAUTY', 'COUNTESS OF ONSLOW', 'DUCHESS OF ALBANY' and 'ETOILE ROSE'. All are herbaceous or semi-woody climbers growing up to about 10 ft high, with small flowers in some shade of red, borne from June or July until late autumn. They are best grown as companions to wall shrubs, through which they will scramble harmlessly, but need a sunny position.

cv. 'MAJOR' has flowers up to 1½ in. long.

C. UNCINATA Benth.
C. leiocarpa Oliver

An evergreen climber 10 to 15 ft high, with glabrous, slender, grooved stems. Leaves with three or five primary divisions, each division trifoliolate; leaflets ovate to ovate-lanceolate, 2 to 4 in. long, pointed, glabrous, rather glaucous beneath. Flowers 1 in. wide, creamy white, numerously borne on leafless cymes, opening in summer; sepals narrow oblong; anthers linear, yellow.

Native of China, discovered by Champion in a ravine behind Mt Parker on Hong Kong in 1848. It is widespread in China and was found in Yunnan and Hupeh by Henry; introduced by Wilson in 1901. It is rather tender and needs the protection of a wall in most places. It thrives well in dry, chalky soil at Highdown in Sussex, scrambling over shrubs and into trees, and bearing scented flowers in June and July. The Highdown plants are referable to f. RETUSA Sprague (*Bot. Mag.*, t. 8633), which differs from the type in its leaves being blunt or notched at the apex and in its leafy inflorescences. This form was probably introduced together with the type.

C. × VEDRARIENSIS Vilm.
C. verrierensis Hort.

A vigorous deciduous climber probably 20 ft high, with ribbed, downy young shoots. Leaves composed of three leaflets borne on a downy common stalk 1 to 2 in. long. Leaflets shortly stalked, ovate, pointed, rounded or broadly wedge-shaped at the base, often three-lobed, always more or less coarsely toothed; 1 to 2½ in. long, ½ to 1½ in. wide, the terminal one always the largest; upper surface dull purplish green and furnished with pale hairs especially on the veins and midrib; lower surface paler and much more hairy, especially when young. Flowers springing from the leaf-axils on one-flowered, slender, hairy stalks up to 5 in. long. They are 2 to 2½ in. wide; the sepals four, sometimes five or six, spreading, roundish-oval with a short point, ¾ to 1 in. wide, delicate rose; the conspicuous cluster of stamens yellow.

A hybrid raised by Messrs Vilmorin at Verrières-le-Buisson, near Paris, from *C. montana* var. *rubens* crossed with *chrysocoma*. It was first exhibited by that firm in flower at the May meeting of the National Horticultural Society of France in 1914. It is quite hardy at Kew, where it grows and flowers well from May onwards. It inherits much of the downiness of *chrysocoma*, but the habit is that of *montana* var. *rubens*.

cv. 'ROSEA'.—A few years after making the cross described above, Vilmorin obtained pollen of the recently introduced *C. chrysocoma* var. *sericea* (then known as *C. spooneri*) and used it on both *C.* × *vedrariensis* and *C. montana* var. *rubens*. The products of these two crosses were very similar and were put into commerce under the confusing name of "*C. spooneri rosea*". Owing to the reduction of *C. spooneri* to the status of a variety of *C. chrysocoma*, these later crosses must also be regarded as forms of the group *C.* × *vedrariensis*. They are very near to typical *C.* × *vedrariensis* and equally fine.

C. VERTICILLARIS DC.   BELL RUE
Atragene americana Sims

A climbing shrub of the *Atragene* section 6 to 8 ft high; young stems slightly ribbed, glabrous, becoming much enlarged at the joints with age. Leaves ternate, being composed of three leaflets on a common stalk 2 to 3 in. long; leaflets ovate or heart-shaped, 1 to 2 in. long, coarsely toothed or entire, with a little loose down about the veins and stalks when young. Flower solitary on a stalk about 3 in. long, purple or purplish blue, 2 to 3 in. across. Sepals four, thin, lance-shaped, pointed, prominently veined, downy, especially at the margins; sepals about ⅝ in. long. Seed-vessel surmounted by a feathery style about 1½ in. long. *Bot. Mag.*, t. 887.

Native of eastern N. America; introduced in 1797. It is most nearly allied to the European *C. alpina*, producing its flowers in May from the joints of the previous year's wood, and having petals or petal-like organs between the sepals and stamens. It is, however, quite distinct in having but three leaflets to each leaf, and these have not the deep, handsome toothing of *C. alpina*. *C. verticillaris* is now very rare in gardens, as it is said to be also in a wild state.

C. KOREANA Komar.—Another member of the *Atragene* section, closely allied to the preceding. It is a trailing plant with leaflets coarsely and evenly toothed, the central one three-lobed or three-parted. Flowers dull violet in the type, yellow in f. LUTEA Rehd.

C. VIORNA L.

A half-woody climber 6 to 10 ft high. Leaves mostly pinnate; leaflets, usually five, of various sizes and shapes, the basal ones largest, mostly two- or three-lobed, or trifoliolate, often heart-shaped at the base, 1½ to 2 in. long and wide; the upper ones not lobed, ovate, ¾ to 1½ in. long; all of them without teeth and often glabrous. Flowers nodding, solitary on stiff stalks 2 or 3 in. long; sepals very thick and leathery, pointed, 1 to 1¼ in. long, dull reddish purple, greenish white or yellowish inside. The sepals touch and form a bell-shaped flower, slightly narrowed towards the mouth where the points are curved back. Seed-vessels with brownish feathery styles 1 in. long.

Native of the eastern United States, introduced in 1730. It is the type species of a group of Clematis whose converging sepals give an urn- or bell-shape to the flower. The stems die back in winter to the woody base of the plant. Although interesting and curious, this species is not particularly attractive.

C. VIRGINIANA L.

A deciduous, climbing shrub up to 20 ft high; young stems ribbed and almost without down. Leaves nearly always consisting of three leaflets (rarely five), which are ovate, rounded or heart-shaped at the base, coarsely and unequally toothed, borne on a common stalk 1½ to 3 in. long; each leaflet on its own stalk ¼ to ½ in. long, slightly downy when young. Flowers dull white, 1 to 1¼ in. across, produced in axillary panicles 3 to 6 in. long in August and September; sepals four, oblong, thin. Seed-vessels with silky, feathered styles, forming silvery heads about 2½ in. across.

Native of eastern N. America; introduced in 1767. It is but little grown outside botanic gardens, being inferior in vigour to our native species, and not so attractive as many others. It is allied most closely to C. vitalba, but is distinguished by its three-foliolate instead of five-foliolate leaves. Plants, too, are frequently unisexual.

C. VITALBA L.   TRAVELLER'S JOY, OLD MAN'S BEARD

A deciduous, climbing shrub, forming woody stems reaching ultimately, if support be available, 40 ft or more high, the older portions near the ground becoming in time as thick as a man's wrist; young stems ribbed and downy. Leaves very variable in size and length; from 3 to 10 in. long, composed of five leaflets pinnately arranged. Leaflets ovate with a heart-shaped or rounded base, or lance-shaped, 1 to 4 in. long, stalked, the lowest pair occasionally trifoliolate, coarsely toothed or almost entire, more or less downy. Flowers dull white, borne in panicles 3 to 5 in. long from the leaf-axils; each flower about ¾ in. in diameter, faintly almond-scented. Seed-vessels with long, plume-like styles, forming, when ripe, grey tufted balls very conspicuous in autumn and winter.

Native of Europe, and common in the south of England. Among our native climbers, it is the most vigorous and rapid in growth, making shoots several yards long in one season. It flowers from July to October, and its remarkable crop of silky fruits remain on the plants long after the leaves have fallen. It is of too aggressive a nature to be associated with valuable shrubs, which it would in time smother, but it has a charming effect in the wilder parts of the garden, where it may be allowed to wander over vigorous common shrubs or worn-out trees of little consequence. In such positions it gives a better idea than any other British plant of the *lianes* or 'bush ropes' of the tropics.

The popular name of 'old man's beard' refers of course to the silvery grey fruits. The French name, 'herbe aux gueux' (beggar's plant), originated from the use by beggars in Paris of the acrid juice of the plant to produce ulcerous wounds as a means of exciting pity. The pleasant name of 'traveller's joy', was apparently invented by Gerard, who says this clematis is 'esteemed for pleasure by reason of the goodly shadow and the pleasant *sent* or savour of its flowers. And because of its decking and adorning *waies* and hedges where people travel, thereupon have I named it Traveller's joy.'

C. VITICELLA L.

A deciduous, partially woody climber, growing 8 to 12 ft high; stems slender, ribbed, and slightly downy when young. Leaves 4 or 5 in. long, pinnate, with the primary divisions trifoliolate; leaflets not toothed, but frequently two- or three-lobed, lance-shaped to broadly ovate, ¾ to 2½ in. long. Flowers solitary on stalks 2 to 4 in. long, or several on a branched stalk; each 1½ in. across; sepals obovate, blue, purple, or rosy purple. Seed-vessels broad and short, with very small tails devoid of the feathery covering so common in *Clematis*. *Bot. Mag.*, t. 565.

Native of S. Europe; cultivated here since the sixteenth century. The type and the double-flowered form were grown in 1597 by Gerard, who says, 'they grow in my garden at Holborn and flourish exceedingly'. Many charming varieties have been raised in gardens, the double-flowered one just mentioned ('Plena') being one of the least attractive, owing to an excessive multiplication of the sepals, which gives the flower a heavy, lumpy aspect.

f. ALBIFLORA (O. Kuntze) Rehd.—Flowers white. It is found wild with the type. *C. viticella* var. *alba* of Carrière is a hybrid with *C. florida* as the other parent.

cv. 'NANA'.—A dwarf form about 3 ft high, described by Carrière in 1869.

cv. 'PLENA'.—The old double form with purplish flowers, described above. The name was first used by Weston in 1774 and should not be supplanted by 'Multiplex': the var. *multiplex* of G. Don was intended as a group-name for all the double-flowered kinds (he mentioned another with flesh-coloured flowers).

cv. 'RUBRA'.—The old red-flowered form of the species, known to Philip Miller, and so named by Weston in 1774, when it was on sale in London nurseries. Whether the *C. viticella rubra* of present-day gardens is the same clone is not known.

In addition there are several charming clematises which closely resemble *C. viticella* in flower and habit but probably have in them a touch of hybridity. Such are: 'ABUNDANCE', with small soft-purple flowers, veined deeper purple, raised by Markham; 'ALBA LUXURIANS', a white-flowered plant with dark anthers, probably raised at Veitch's Coombe Wood nursery; 'KERMESINA', with deep pure wine-red flowers, raised by Lemoine; 'ROYAL VELOURS', with purple, velvety sepals; and there are several others. The clematis known as *C. viticella venosa* is a hybrid, probably with *C. florida* as the other parent.

None of the forms and near related hybrids of *C. viticella* is genuinely shrubby in this country, the summer's growth dying back in winter nearly to the older stem. They should be cut back in February to the living part. All flower with great freedom from July to September.

CLEMATOCLETHRA ACTINIDIACEAE

A genus of deciduous climbers closely related to *Actinidia*, but differing in the flower having ten stamens and one style, whereas in *Actinidia* both stamens and styles are numerous; the pith, too, of *Actinidia* is sometimes lamellate but always continuous in *Clematoclethra*. About twenty-five species are known, all Asiatic. Wilson found eight of them in China. They are easily cultivated in free, loamy soil, but the introduced species are rather tender and need the shelter of a wall. Easily propagated by late summer cuttings in gentle bottom heat.

C. ACTINIDIOIDES Maxim.

A climber up to 40 ft or more high; young shoots glabrous. Leaves ovate to ovate-lanceolate, sometimes inclined to obovate, acuminate, rounded to cordate at the base, finely bristle-toothed; stalk 1 to 2 in. long, slender. Flowers ⅔ in. wide, axillary, solitary, in pairs, or in threes on stalks ½ to ¾ in. long; petals rounded, white faintly flushed with rose; sepals ciliate, broadly ovate to obovate or roundish. Fruit a nearly globose, black or purplish black berry, ¼ in. wide, seated on the calyx. *Bot. Mag.*, t. 9439.

Native of China, mainly in the provinces of Szechwan and Kansu; introduced in 1908. It was successfully grown and flowered by the late Lord Wakehurst in his garden near Ardingly in Sussex.

C. INTEGRIFOLIA Maxim. Introduced by Wilson from W. China in 1908, this is very near *C. actinidioides* and has, in fact, been made synonymous with it in the *Botanical Magazine*. The leaves are glabrous and glaucous beneath. It climbs 20 to 25 ft high, the flowers white and fragrant. Discovered by Potanin, the Russian traveller, in Kansu, in 1887. The name *integrifolia* does not entirely fit the plants now attributed to the species, for they have finely bristle-toothed leaves.

C. LASIOCLADA Maxim. has downy, not bristly, young shoots. The leaves are ovate, 2 to 4 in. long, bristle-toothed, and have tufts of down in the vein-axils beneath; stalks up to 2½ in. long. Flowers white, in cymes of two to seven blossoms. Fruit globose, ⅓ in. wide, black. This is a climber 20 to 25 ft high according to Wilson, who introduced it from W. China in 1908.

C. SCANDENS (Franch.) Maxim.

Clethra scandens Franch.

A climbing shrub which Wilson found up to 26 ft high, the younger shoots usually covered with a thick covering of brown bristles. Leaves oblong-lanceolate to ovate-lanceolate, pointed, rounded or tapered at the base, the margin thinly bristle-toothed; varying in size from 2 in. long by 1 in. wide to 5 in. long by 2¾ in. wide; bristly on the midrib above and beneath, also glaucous and downy beneath; stalk up to 1¼ in. long, bristly like the young wood. Flowers produced in June in the leaf-axils three to six together in short slender-stalked cymes; white, ⅓ in. wide, with five rounded oblong petals and five shorter ciliate sepals. Fruit a red, globose berry ⅓ in. wide, the calyx persisting at the base.

Native of W. China; introduced in 1908. This climber is hardy at Kew on a wall or sheltered by bushes. It was originally called "*Clethra scandens*" by Franchet in 1887—a strange aberration. To indicate its distinctness from clethras as previously known, he made for it a new section in the genus called *Clematoclethra*. This sectional name was afterwards adopted as the generic one by Maximowicz. It has of course no botanical relationship with either *Clethra* or *Clematis*.

CLERODENDRUM   VERBENACEAE

A large genus of shrubs and climbers, mostly tropical, only three species of which are hardy. Leaves opposite. Flowers in wide, cymose or corymbose clusters. Corolla slender-tubed, five-parted at the mouth. Calyx at first bell-shaped or inflated, persistent, becoming fleshy, with the sepals reflexed. Stamens four. Fruit fleshy, and highly coloured.

C. BUNGEI Steud.

C. *foetidum* Bunge

In the open air this species can scarcely be regarded as a shrub. It is killed back to the ground most winters, but sends up vigorous, erect, woody shoots during the summer 3 to 6 ft high, bearing large heart-shaped leaves 4 to 8 in. long and nearly as wide, coarsely toothed, downy on the veins. In August and September come the terminal rounded corymbs, each 4 to 5 in. across, densely packed with purple-red blossoms. *Bot. Mag.*, t. 4880.

Native of China; introduced by Fortune in 1844. It has lived for many years at the foot of a greenhouse wall at Kew, spreading rapidly by its suckers, and forming in summer a dense thicket of stems. It has proved hardy in an open position in the R.H.S. Garden, Wisley. Although the flowers are fragrant, the leaves when crushed emit a heavy nauseous odour. Easily increased by division in spring.

C. TRICHOTOMUM Thunb.

A deciduous, small tree 10 or 20 ft high, of bushy, rather sparse habit; branches very pithy, downy when young. Leaves variable in size, and considerably larger on young plants than on adult ones; in the latter they are ovate or oval, 4 to 9 in. long, 2 to 5 in. wide, occasionally toothed, soft, with scattered down beneath, and flaccid; stalks downy, 1 to 4 in. long. The lower leaves are sometimes deeply two- or three-lobed towards the apex. Flowers fragrant, produced from July to September in long-stalked cymes from the axils of the uppermost leaves, the whole forming an erect inflorescence 6 to 9 in. across. Corolla white,

CLERODENDRUM TRICHOTOMUM var. FARGESII in fruit

1 to 1½ in. across, the base tubular, expanding at the mouth into five spreading, oblong, narrow lobes. Calyx reddish, ½ in. long, inflated, five-angled, and five-lobed. Fruit bright blue, ultimately black, about the size of a pea, surrounded by the persistent crimson calyx whose lobes have become fleshy and spreading. *Bot. Mag.*, t. 6561.

Native of Japan and China, and a very handsome late summer-flowering tree. The leaves have a heavy unpleasant odour when crushed. It is quite hardy at Kew, and likes an open, loamy soil. The pithy branches are very apt to die back in winter. It is easily increased by root-cuttings, or by the young suckers which frequently spring from the roots.

var. FARGESII (Dode) Rehd. *C. fargesii* Dode—A vigorous, deciduous shrub, of very leafy habit; young wood greyish, almost glabrous. Leaves purple-red when quite young, afterwards glossy green on both sides, with scattered hairs on both surfaces. Calyx green, ovoid, conspicuously five-angled, and with five-pointed lobes, downy on the ridges. Fruit about the size of a pea, porcelain-blue, surrounded by the five fleshy, reflexed lobes of the persistent calyx which become pink with age.

Native of Szechwan, China; introduced to France by Père Farges, and first raised by Maurice de Vilmorin in 1898. It differs in the paler, more slender shoots; smaller, brighter green, less downy leaves; in the green, not red, young calyx; and paler blue fruits. It is inferior to the type in beauty, but is probably hardier and does not die back. The leaves have an unpleasant odour when crushed. It is not sharply marked off from typical C. *trichotomum* and is really no more than a phase of that variable species.

CLETHRA   CLETHRACEAE

From the closely related heath family the clethras are distinguished by having the five parts of the corolla so deeply divided that they appear to be separate petals. They are small trees or shrubs, all the hardy ones deciduous, but the tender ones all or mostly evergreen. Leaves alternate. Flowers white, fragrant, usually produced in racemes or panicles near the end of the shoot; stamens ten. Seed-vessel a capsule enclosed by the persistent calyx, and carrying many seeds.

Of the hardy species, three come from America, four from Eastern Asia. They all like a peaty soil, and are useful for flowering late in the season. Propagated by seeds, cuttings, and layers. The cuttings are best made in August, of side shoots 3 or 4 in. long, with a heel of older wood, and placed in gentle bottom heat.

C. ACUMINATA Michx.

A deciduous shrub under cultivation, but assuming the form of a small tree 20 ft high in a wild state; young wood downy. Leaves clustered at the ends of the shoots, oval, with a long tapering apex, 3 to 6 in. long, the base rounded or shortly tapered, toothed on the terminal part; lower surface downy; stalk ¼ to 1¼ in. long. Racemes 6 in. or more long, solitary, slender, cylindrical, terminal, hairy. Flowers white; petals ¼ in. long, not spreading; sepals downy, ovate, ribbed; stamens hairy at base; flower-stalk ⅛ in. long, downy.

Native of the south-eastern United States, found on cliffs and mountain-sides; introduced in 1806. It is the least hardy of the American species, but may be grown in the south of England. From C. *alnifolia* and C. *tomentosa* it is distinguished by the leaves being nearly always broadest below the middle, and crowded at the end of the twig. The racemes, too, are mostly solitary.

C. ALNIFOLIA L.   SWEET PEPPER-BUSH

A deciduous shrub, ultimately 8 or 9 ft high, with erect branches; young shoots covered with a very close, fine down. Leaves obovate or wedge-shaped; $1\frac{1}{2}$ to 4 in. long, $\frac{3}{4}$ to 2 in. wide; abruptly tapered at the apex, toothed except near the base, almost or quite glabrous except on the midrib and stalk, the latter being downy and $\frac{1}{8}$ to $\frac{3}{4}$ in. long. Flowers fragrant, $\frac{3}{8}$ in. across, thickly set on erect, cylindrical, downy racemes 2 to 6 in. long and $\frac{3}{4}$ in. wide, produced in August at the end of the current season's shoots and in the axils of their upper-most leaves. Petals white, obovate, rounded at the apex; sepals persistent, ovate, downy; stamens and style glabrous; flower-stalk $\frac{1}{8}$ in. long, downy.

Native of eastern N. America; introduced in 1731. A very handsome shrub, useful on account of its late flowering. It loves abundant moisture at the root. Propagated by layers or by separating the sucker growths at the base.

cv. 'PANICULATA'.—This form has terminal panicles (not merely clustered racemes) and is superior to the type. It is the best of all the clethras that can be grown out-of-doors, being quite hardy, a vigorous grower, and equal in flower beauty to *C. tomentosa*. Although described as a species—*C. paniculata*—by Aiton in 1789, and long grown as such or as a variety of *C. alnifolia*, it appears to be no more, in a botanical sense, than an extreme form of the species. How-ever, being horticulturally distinct and almost certainly a clone, it is treated here as a cultivar. Introduced in 1770.

cv. 'ROSEA'.—Buds deep pink; expanded flowers pinkish. Leaves glossy. Introduced 1906.

C. ARBOREA Ait.   LILY-OF-THE-VALLEY TREE

An evergreen small tree 20 to 25 ft high in Britain; young shoots reddish and at first hairy. Leaves oblanceolate, pointed, finely toothed, tapered towards both ends but more slenderly towards the base; 3 to 6 in. long, 1 to 2 in. wide; dark bright green and glabrous above, pale beneath with a hairy midrib and scattered hairs over the blade; stalk reddish, hairy, $\frac{1}{2}$ to $\frac{3}{4}$ in. long. Flowers fragrant, pure white, $\frac{1}{3}$ in. wide, produced in a terminal panicle made up of about half a dozen slender racemes 3 to 6 in. long, on which the blossoms are gracefully disposed, each on a stalk $\frac{1}{4}$ in. long. The petals are obovate, about $\frac{1}{4}$ in. long, and, being rather erect, give the flower a cupped shape. Calyx five-lobed, downy, the oval lobes $\frac{1}{8}$ in. long; ovary covered with erect, whitish bristles; main and secondary flower-stalks very downy. *Bot. Mag.*, t. 1057.

Native of Madeira, where it is known as the 'folhado'; introduced in 1784. It occurs wild in the woods and thickets of ravines at from 2,000 to 5,000 ft altitudes. This beautiful tree can only be grown with winter protection at Kew and in most other districts in this country. But it is cultivated in the open air in milder places in the British Isles. At Rossdohan in Co. Kerry, Eire, there is a remarkable specimen 51 ft high and 7 ft in girth at ground-level, and two others measuring 26 × 4 ft and 35 × $3\frac{1}{2}$ ft respectively (1966); on Garinish Island this species has reached 30 ft in height. Outside Eire, few examples comparable to these have been recorded in recent years but there is a healthy tree 18 ft high at

Brodick in the Isle of Arran, and one of 21 ft at Caerhays Castle, Cornwall. It flowers from August to October, and its beauty is so remarkable that it ought to be grown wherever possible. The flowers bear a superficial resemblance to those of the lily-of-the-valley, hence the popular name.

C. BARBINERVIS Sieb. & Zucc.

C. canescens Hort.

A deciduous shrub or small tree 6 to 10 ft high in cultivation, more bushy and less erect than the American species; young shoots at first sprinkled with a minute starry down. Leaves often clustered at the end of the twig, oval or obovate, more tapering at the base than at the apex; 2 to 5 in. long, 1 to 2¼ in. wide; hairy at first on both sides, but especially so on the midrib and nerves beneath, toothed; stalk ¼ to ¾ in. long. Flowers white, ⅓ in. across, produced from July to September in rather compact, terminal panicles 4 to 6 in. long, covered with white, starry down; calyx and seed-vessel hairy; stamens glabrous. *Bot. Mag.*, n.s., t. 398.

Native of Japan; introduced in 1870. It is a very pretty shrub where it thrives, but it is not so hardy as *C. alnifolia*, although it will survive all but the severest winters near London. It is quite hardy in the Wild Garden at Wisley, where there are two specimens about 10 ft high which came through the winter of 1962–3 unharmed.

C. DELAVAYI Franch.   [PLATE 54

A deciduous shrub or a tree up to 40 ft high; young shoots covered with star-shaped down. Leaves lanceolate, tapered towards both ends, slender-pointed, toothed; 2½ to 6 in. long, 1 to 2½ in. wide; rich green above, pale and very downy beneath; stalks ⅙ to ½ in. long. Inflorescence a terminal, solitary, one-sided raceme, 4 to 6 in. long, 1 to 1½ in. wide. Flowers white, tinged yellow, ½ in. wide, closely set on the raceme, each on a stalk ¼ to ½ in. long, opening in July. Calyx-lobes ovate, pointed, ⅛ in. long, felted with grey down, turning rose-coloured after the petals have dropped. Petals rounded and notched at the end, sufficiently erect to form a cup-shaped flower; stamens about half as long as the petals, slightly hairy; anthers brown; ovary grey with down. *Bot. Mag.*, t. 8970.

Native of Yunnan, China; discovered by Delavay in 1884; introduced by Forrest in 1913. I first saw it in flower in 1920, when the late Sir John Ross of Bladensburg sent it from his garden at Rostrevor, Co. Down, and was much impressed by its beauty. The racemes often take a more or less horizontal direction. Except for the evergreen *C. arborea* described above, this is probably the finest of all the clethras. It is unfortunately not quite hardy enough to grow out-of-doors at Kew, and after several trials has had to be relegated to a cool greenhouse. It thrives admirably in Sussex at Wakehurst Place, Nymans and Borde Hill, and at Minterne in Dorset. At Kilbryde in Northumberland, planted in 1927, it 'has given no trouble. Flowering in July adds greatly to its value and these last two rather wet summers seemed to have been to its liking' (R. B. Cooke in *Journ. R.H.S.*, Vol. 92, 1967, p. 85 and fig. 40).

On one of Forrest's wild specimens (12914) the leaves are 6 in. by 2¾ in. and the inflorescence 7 in. by nearly 2 in. It is at once distinguishable from *C. fargesii* and *C. monostachya* by its short stamens. In both those species they are longer than the petals.

C. FARGESII Franch.

A deciduous shrub found 10 to 15 ft high in a wild state; young shoots finely downy. Leaves lanceolate to oval-lanceolate, tapered to a long slender point, the base wedge-shaped or rounded; margins toothed; 2½ to 5 in. long, 1 to 1¾ in. wide; dark bright green and furnished at first with small, starry hairs above, finally glabrous; paler and more or less downy beneath, especially in the vein-axils; stalk ¼ to ¾ in. long, downy. Flowers fragrant, pure white, in a terminal cluster of slender racemes 6 to 10 in. long; both main and secondary flower-stalks very downy. The flowers are densely arranged on the raceme, each blossom about ¼ in. wide; calyx-lobes woolly, lanceolate with slender points, ⅛ in. long; stamens slightly downy towards the base; style glabrous.

Native of E. Szechwan and W. Hupeh, China, at from 4,000 to 7,800 ft; described in 1895 by Franchet, and five years later was found by Wilson when collecting for Messrs Veitch. It first flowered at Kew in July 1921, but gives one the impression that it would be better suited farther south. It is undoubtedly a beautiful clethra, and one specimen of Wilson's collecting has its terminal group of racemes forming an inflorescence close upon a foot long and 8 to 10 in. wide. It is related to *C. barbinervis* but that species has leaves broadest towards the apex, more densely and more persistently downy beneath; and its calyx-lobes are not slenderly pointed but rounded.

C. MONOSTACHYA Rehd. & Wils.

A deciduous shrub or small tree up to 10 ft high; young shoots at first sprinkled with star-like down. Leaves oval-lanceolate, much tapered at both ends but more slenderly towards the apex, saw-toothed; 3 to 5½ in. long, 1 to 2 in. wide; dark green and soon quite glabrous above, paler beneath, and with down tufted in the vein-axils and spread along the midrib; stalk ½ to 1 in. long. Flowers white, produced during July and August in a terminal raceme up to 8 in. long and 1 in. wide, the main and secondary flower-stalks densely clothed with starry down. The pure white petals are oblong, ¼ in. long, rounded or notched at the apex; calyx-lobes ovate, pointed, felted. Stamens a little longer than the petals, hairy at the base; style downy; seed-vessel ⅕ in. wide, downy.

Native of W. Szechwan, China; discovered by Wilson at 5,000 to 7,000 ft elevation and introduced by him to the Coombe Wood nursery in 1903. It is quite hardy. From *C. fargesii* it differs in having usually solitary racemes. That species with its clusters of long racemes would appear to be the finer one and it differs botanically from *C. monostachya* by its glabrous style.

C. TOMENTOSA Lam.
C. alnifolia var. pubescens Ait.

A deciduous shrub up to 6 or 8 ft high, branches erect; young shoots very downy. Leaves obovate 1½ to 4 in. long, ¾ to 2 in. wide, tapering to a very short stalk at the base, toothed on the terminal half, pointed; upper side with scattered

CLETHRA TOMENTOSA

short hairs, lower side felted with a thick, pale wool; veins in seven to ten pairs. Flowers fragrant, white, nearly ½ in. across, produced during September in erect, woolly racemes up to 6 in. long, either terminal or from the uppermost leaf-axils. Sepals woolly, ovate-oblong, $\frac{3}{16}$ in. long; stamens glabrous; style downy; flower-stalk woolly, ⅛ in. long. *Bot. Mag.*, t. 3743.

Native of the south-east United States; introduced in 1731. Closely akin to *C. alnifolia*, and sometimes regarded as a variety of it, it is distinguished by flowering a month later and by its greyish aspect due to the woolly covering of its various parts. Its flowers, too, are purer white, larger and more ornamental, and the style is downy. Its distribution in a wild state does not extend so far north as that of *C. alnifolia*, and it is not quite so hardy. At Kew, however, it does not suffer from cold.

CLEYERA THEACEAE

The genus *Cleyera*, named in honour of Dr Cleyer, a Dutch botanist, is a small genus of evergreen trees and shrubs from E. Asia. The calyx is five-parted, and there are five petals with numerous stamens slightly attached. The genus is nearly allied to *Eurya*, but differs in having chiefly bisexual flowers, those of *Eurya* being unisexual and found on different trees.

C. FORTUNEI Hook. f.

An evergreen shrub 5 to 6 ft or probably more high, with glabrous branchlets. Leaves 3 to 6 in. long, 1 to 1½ in. wide; tapering towards both ends, quite glabrous and entire, deep green in the middle with a yellow margin of varying width. Flowers produced singly or in pairs from the axils of the leaves, each one nearly ¾ in. across when fully open, the flower-stalk ½ in. long; petals pale yellow. *Bot. Mag.*, t. 7434.

C. fortunei was introduced from Japan by Robert Fortune about 1860, and was long grown in gardens, chiefly in cool greenhouses, as "*Eurya latifolia variegata*". It never appears to have flowered, or the fact of its doing so was not generally made known until 1894. In the September of that year it was exhibited in flower at Chiswick, and flowering specimens were sent to Kew about the same time, by Thomas Acton of Kilmacurragh. In this and other similarly situated gardens it may be grown without protection, but in colder localities wall protection is necessary. At Edinburgh, in the Royal Botanic Garden, it is reasonably hardy in a sheltered position. It has long been cultivated by the Japanese for its handsomely variegated leaves, but is probably a native of China. It is quite easily rooted from cuttings in gentle heat. No green-leaved form of the plant appears to be known, but it is certainly very near to *C. japonica* in its botanical characters. If considered to be a form of that species, as it is by some authorities, its correct name would be *C. japonica* 'Tricolor' (*C. japonica tricolor* Nicholson in *Dict. Gard.*, Vol. 1, 1885; *C. japonica f. tricolor* [Nichols.] Kobuski).

C. JAPONICA Thunb.

C. ochnacea DC.; *Eurya ochnacea* (DC.) Szysz.

An evergreen shrub or small tree to about 12 ft high, glabrous in all its parts. Leaves alternate, leathery, entire, narrow-oblong to ovate-oblong, $2\frac{3}{4}$ to 4 in. long, $\frac{4}{5}$ to $1\frac{3}{5}$ in. wide, bluntly pointed at the apex, narrowly wedge-shaped at the base, glossy deep green above, paler beneath; leaf-stalks to $\frac{4}{5}$ in. long. Flowers white to yellowish white, about $\frac{1}{2}$ in. across, borne singly or up to three together in each leaf-axil on the previous year's wood, or on short spurs; flower-stalks $\frac{2}{5}$ to $\frac{3}{5}$ in. long, with two small early deciduous bracteoles; sepals five, rounded, about $\frac{1}{8}$ in. long; petals rather fleshy, narrow-oblong; stamens numerous, anthers bearded; style with two or three stigmas. Fruit a pea-sized berry, red ripening to black.

Native of Japan, Formosa, Korea, China, Burma, Assam and of the Himalaya as far west as Nepal. As might be expected from so wide a distribution, the species is very variable. The plants in cultivation seem to fall under one or other of two varieties, namely:

var. JAPONICA *C. japonica* var. *kaempferiana* (DC.) Sealy; *C. ochnacea* var. *kaempferiana* DC.—This has relatively small leaves (blades mostly 2 to $2\frac{2}{5}$ in. by $\frac{7}{8}$ to $1\frac{1}{5}$ in. and petioles $\frac{1}{4}$ to $\frac{1}{3}$ in. long), shorter flower-stalks $\frac{1}{4}$ to $\frac{2}{5}$ (rarely $\frac{1}{2}$) in. long and a smaller calyx; this is native in Japan.

var. WALLICHIANA (DC.) Sealy *C. ochnacea* var. *wallichiana* DC.—This variety has longer leaves (blades $2\frac{2}{5}$ to $3\frac{2}{5}$ in. by $1\frac{1}{5}$ to $1\frac{3}{5}$ in. and petioles $\frac{1}{3}$ to $\frac{2}{5}$ in. long); flower-stalks $\frac{1}{2}$ to 1 in. long and calyx larger. Native of China and Nepal. *Bot. Mag.*, t. 9606.

C. japonica was once grown in greenhouses for its handsome evergreen foliage and fragrant flowers, which are borne in June–July, and for its long-lasting red fruits. The Japanese variety should be hardy in a sheltered position except in the coldest parts of the country. There are several plants in the Edinburgh Botanic Garden, some of them raised from seed sent by Forrest under field number 16080. Some plants grown as *C. japonica* or *ochnacea* may be *Eurya japonica*, which is easily distinguished by its rather inconspicuous unisexual flowers and toothed leaves. See also *Ternstroemia gymnanthera*.

CLIANTHUS LEGUMINOSAE

A genus of two species, one in New Zealand and the other (*C. formosus*) in Australia. The common name in New Zealand of 'parrot's bill' refers to the shape of the curved keel petals. The generic name is derived from the Greek and means 'glory flower'; and it is not so inappropriate.

C. PUNICEUS Banks & Soland.   GLORY PEA

An evergreen climbing shrub up to 20 ft high; young shoots furnished with minute appressed down. Leaves pinnate, 3 to 6 in. long, made up of from thirteen to twenty-five leaflets which are oblong, tapered at the base, rounded at the end; margins not toothed but slightly recurved; $\frac{1}{2}$ to $1\frac{1}{4}$ in. long, $\frac{1}{8}$ to $\frac{5}{16}$ in. wide, dark green above, paler and furnished with minute appressed down beneath; scarcely stalked. Racemes pendulous, produced from the leaf-axils during the

CLIANTHUS PUNICEUS

early summer months and carrying a number of flowers crowded at the end, the main-stalk being slender, zigzag, minutely downy and furnished with linear bracts $\frac{1}{8}$ in. long. Flowers constructed like those of the pea, the chief parts being the standard and keel petals, which are twice as long and several times larger than the wing petals. The standard petal is erect, bent back, $1\frac{1}{2}$ to 2 in. long, slender-pointed; the keel is canoe-shaped and 2 to $2\frac{1}{2}$ in. long; the whole of a brilliant red. Calyx bell-shaped with sharp teeth, downy, $\frac{1}{2}$ in. wide. Pod 3 in. long, $\frac{1}{2}$ in. wide. *Bot. Mag.*, t. 3584.

Native of New Zealand; introduced in 1831. This beautiful climber, attractive in its brilliantly coloured, curiously shaped flowers, and for its luxuriant and graceful foliage, is well suited for growing on walls in the milder parts of the kingdom, furnishing them with an admirable evergreen covering up to 8, 10, or even 12 ft high, and more in width. At Kew, although it survives soft winters, its tenure is uncertain and it is only really happy under glass. The plant loves an open, well-drained, sandy soil. Even in mild gardens it is rather short lived.

f. ALBUS Hort.—Flowers white. Such forms have been observed in the wild and are said to come true from seed. The cultivated plants are usually not so free-flowering and never so handsome as the red-blossomed type.

var. MAXIMUS (Col.) Kirk *C. maximus* Col.; var. *magnificus* Hort.—A larger plant, growing to 10 ft or more; leaflets longer than in the type; flowers darker, often with a dark blotch near the base. Found wild in the North Island from East Cape southward (Allan, *Flora of New Zealand*, 1961).

A spray with rose-coloured flowers was exhibited at Vincent Square by Lt-Col. E. W. Bolitho on 30th April 1940.

CLIFTONIA CYRILLACEAE

The genus (of which this is the only known species) commemorates Francis Clifton, F.R.S., a physician and friend of Sir Hans Sloane. He died in Jamaica in 1736. It belongs to a small family of which the only other species cultivated out-of-doors in the British Isles is *Cyrilla racemiflora*, also the only species of its genus. This is easily distinguished by its five stamens to each flower and axillary racemes. The family Cyrillaceae is allied to the Holly family (Aquifoliaceae), from which it differs in the racemose inflorescence and dry fruit.

C. MONOPHYLLA (Lam.) Sarg.
Ptelea monophylla Lam.; *C. ligustrina* (Willd.) Spreng.

An evergreen small tree or shrub with slender shoots; not downy in any part. Leaves alternate, narrowly oval to oblanceolate, not toothed, tapered to a usually blunt apex, more gradually to a scarcely noticeable stalk; 1 to $2\frac{1}{4}$ in. long, $\frac{3}{8}$ to $\frac{3}{4}$ in. wide; dark green, rather leathery. Flowers fragrant, white or pink, produced during spring in terminal cylindrical racemes $1\frac{1}{2}$ to $2\frac{1}{2}$ in. long, $\frac{5}{8}$ in. wide. Each flower is $\frac{1}{4}$ in. wide, with five obovate petals, and a small green calyx. Stamens ten. Ovary oblong with three or four angles and three or four cells; stigma slightly three- or four-lobed. Fruit dry, spongy, oval, $\frac{1}{4}$ in. long; with three or four wings running lengthwise. *Bot. Mag.*, t. 1625.

Native of the S.E. United States, discovered by W. Bartram in 1773; introduced probably by John Fraser about the beginning of the nineteenth century; it flowered and bore fruit in his son's nursery in Sloane Square and was figured from there in the *Botanical Magazine* in 1814. Sargent observes that under favourable conditions it will grow 40 to 50 ft high, but in cultivation I have only seen it as a small shrub. It cannot be considered really hardy at Kew, being much injured in cold winters. In suitable localities more to the south and west it is worth growing for its fragrant white flowers and curious, winged fruits. The latter caused it at first to be mistaken for a *Ptelea*. Seeds are offered by American nurserymen.

CNEORUM CNEORACEAE

A genus of two species found in the Canary Islands and around the shores of the Mediterranean (a Cuban plant is also included in *Cneorum* by some botanists). It is now placed in a family of its own, the Cneoraceae, the affinities of which are uncertain. In Engler's system it is placed near the Simaroubaceae, which would make it a fairly close ally of the very dissimilar *Ailanthus*. But in Dr Hutchinson's classification it appears in the Order Celastrales, near the Holly family (Aquifoliaceae). Another view is that the Cneoraceae are most nearly akin to the Zygophyllaceae. The generic name comes from the Greek 'kneoron', applied to some dwarf shrub resembling the olive and with acrid leaves (perhaps *Daphne gnidium*).

C. TRICOCCUM L.

A low, evergreen shrub 1 to 2 ft high, with erect, forking branches. Leaves alternate, greyish green, 1 to 2 in. long, rarely more than ⅓ in. wide, glabrous, terminating as a rule in a tiny, abrupt point. Flowers ⅓ in. in diameter, yellow, produced several together at the end of the branchlet and in the axils of the terminal leaves; petals three or four. Fruit brownish red, composed of three segments, each about the size of a small pea flattened on two sides; it has a fleshy covering, but is bony beneath.

Native of the Mediterranean region, and rather common along the French and Italian Riviera in dry positions. Among other places one may find it on the Cap d'Antibes, and on the hills behind Mentone. It is not hardy at Kew, but lives in the gardens of the south and west coasts. I have seen it flourishing in the garden of the late Mr Hiatt C. Baker at Almondsbury, near Bristol. It has been known in gardens since the last years of the eighteenth century, but owing no doubt to its lack of any striking beauty is rarely seen now. Easily increased by cuttings in a cold frame.

The second species of *Cneorum* is C. PULVERULENTUM Vent. of the Canary Islands. By some botanists it is placed in a separate genus—*Neochamaelea*—as *N. pulverulenta* (Vent.) Erdtm.

COCCULUS   MENISPERMACEAE

In the outdoor garden this genus is at present represented by three species, two of them climbers, the other an evergreen shrub. They are nearly allied to the 'moon-seeds' (*Menispermum*), but differ in having six petals and six stamens, whilst *Menispermum* has six to eight petals and twelve to twenty-four stamens and peltate leaves. The flowers are small, inconspicuous, and unisexual. The climbing species are of the easiest cultivation, growing in any soil of moderate quality, and easily propagated by division or pieces of root. They may be trained up rough branches of oak or supports of a similar nature. Their beauty, apart from the luxuriant foliage, is in their red or purplish-blue berries.

C. CAROLINUS (L.) DC.   CAROLINA MOONSEED

Menispermum carolinum L.; *Cebatha carolina* (L.) Britton

A climber 12 to 14 ft high with twining stems, naturally woody, but often herbaceous in Britain, downy. Leaves more or less heart-shaped or ovate, three- to seven-veined, rounded at the end, often obscurely lobed, 2 to 4½ in. long, with stalks nearly as long; clothed with pale down beneath, deep green, ultimately glabrous above. Flowers sometimes hermaphrodite, but usually unisexual, with the sexes on separate inflorescences, sometimes on separate plants, white; males on short, axillary panicles, each flower about ¼ in. across, with six sepals, petals, and stamens. Females in racemes, similar to the males as regards sepals and petals, but with abortive stamens and three to six pistils. Berries about the size of small peas, red when ripe.

Native of the S.E. United States. Although introduced in 1759, it has never become common. Flowers in July.

C. LAURIFOLIUS DC.

An evergreen shrub 10 ft or more high, sometimes a small tree, with lance-shaped, conspicuously three-ribbed leaves 5 to 8 in. long, about 2 in. wide, the stalks ¾ in. long; they are of a very glossy, varnished, dark green, giving to the shrub a very characteristic aspect. Flowers small, in axillary panicles. At Kew this plant can only be grown against a wall, where it lived for many years without injury. In the south of France and Italy it forms a picturesque spreading shrub or small tree. Native of the Himalaya.

C. TRILOBUS (Thunb.) DC.

Menispermum trilobum Thunb.; *C. thunbergii* DC.; *Cebatha orbiculata* O. Kuntze

A climbing, twining shrub 12 to 14 ft high with downy, naturally woody stems. Leaves 1½ to 4 in. long, ovate or heart-shaped, sometimes three- or five-lobed, rounded or pointed at the apex, downy beneath, especially when young, becoming glabrous (except on the nerves) and bright dark green above, prominently three- or five-nerved. Flowers in axillary clusters, expanding in August. Fruit spherical, ¼ in. diameter, black covered with a blue bloom, produced in clusters of six to twelve, ripe in October, and then rather handsome.

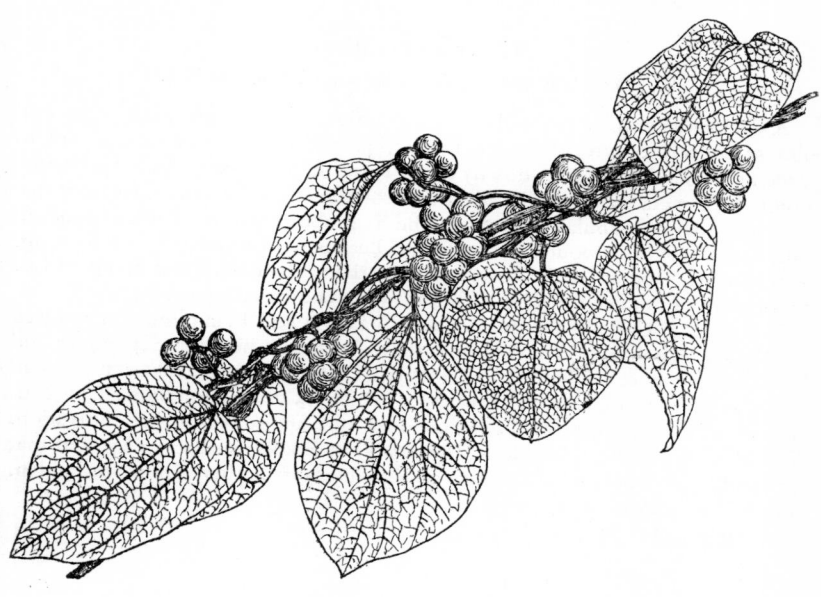

COCCULUS TRILOBUS

Plants at Kew bore a great crop in 1911, which seems to show they like abundant sunshine. *Bot. Mag.*, t. 8489.

Native of Japan, Korea, and China. The down, or small hairs, on the stems point downwards. The plant from which our figure was made was introduced to Kew from Japan by Prof. Sargent, but the species was in cultivation before 1870.

COLLETIA   RHAMNACEAE

This genus, named in honour of Philibert Collet, a French botanist (1643–1718), consists of about a dozen species, all natives of S. America. The following hardy ones have a curious—one of them a unique—appearance out-of-doors in this country. The smaller branches are really spines arranged oppositely, and there is very little or no leafage, especially on old plants. The most conspicuous part of the flower is the bell-shaped

TS—Z

or tubular calyx, the petals being very minute or absent. At Kew the three species described below are hardy in sheltered situations and grow well in a sandy, well-drained loam, flowering freely if given a sunny position. Propagation can be effected by means of cuttings.

C. ARMATA Miers

C. spinosa var. *armata* (Miers) Reiche; *C. valdiviana* Phil.

A deciduous shrub eventually 8 to 12 ft high, the younger parts consisting almost entirely of greyish-green, terete (i.e. circular in cross-section) spines which are usually distinctly downy and ½ to 1½ in. long, very rigid and sharply pointed. Flowers waxy, produced in twos or threes on the spines, fragrant like hawthorn, white, tubular, ⅛ in. long, the five lobes recurved; anthers standing out visibly from the mouth of the flower. Leaves when present ⅛ to ½ in. long, not so wide, tapered at the base, often toothed, glabrous. Fruit composed of three united roundish capsules each ⅛ in. wide and carrying a single seed.

Native of S. Chile in the provinces of Valdivia and Llanquihue; introduced by Messrs Veitch between 1880 and 1884. It flowers between September and December. It is closely allied to C. SPINOSA Lam., which, taken in a broad sense, is a very polymorphic species of which *C. armata* might well be considered a variety. Typical *C. spinosa* does not appear to be in cultivation. *C. armata* very much resembles *C. infausta* in its bodkin-shaped spines, but that species has no down on the spines or elsewhere, its anthers are more hidden, and it flowers from March to June.

cv. 'ROSEA'.—Flowers pale rose, deeper in bud.

C. CRUCIATA Gillies & Hook. [PLATE 55

C. bictoniensis Lindl.; *C. spinosa* Hort., not Lam.

A dimorphic shrub up to 10 ft high, armed with spines of two kinds; the one flat, triangular, rigid, frequently 1½ in. wide at the base; the other bodkin-shaped but flattish towards the base, sharply pointed, comparatively slender and from ½ to 1½ in. long. As a rule the adult plant has the larger, triangular spines only, but in very rare instances the two kinds are found on one plant (see *Gard. Chron.*, 2nd Sept. 1916, fig. 44). These spines, as in other species, are really branchlets producing leaves and flowers in the usual way; they are arranged in pairs, each pair set at right angles to the next. Leaves very small, scanty, or even absent, each one ¼ in. or so long, ovate, toothed. Flowers produced from below the spines singly, in pairs, or occasionally in clusters of four or six; they have no petals and the calyx is tubular, yellowish white, swollen at the base, divided at the mouth into five reflexed lobes; the whole flower and its stalk combined are little more than ¼ in. long. *Bot. Mag.*, t. 5033.

Native of Uruguay; introduced in 1824. This shrub, so uncommon of aspect, is one of the most grotesquely and formidably armed, as well as one of the most interesting of all hardy plants. In the warmer parts of the country it often flowers very freely and attractively in the autumn. It is quite hardy at Kew but is rather shy-flowering there except after fine, warm seasons. It is a curious fact that the plant with the normal flat triangular spines will sometimes, though very rarely, produce shoots with bodkin-like spines.

C. INFAUSTA N.E. Br.
C. spinosa Lindl., not Lam.

A deciduous shrub devoid of down in all its parts, growing up to 10 ft high. The younger parts of the plant consist almost wholly of terete spines ½ to 1 in. long, $\frac{1}{16}$ in. thick, very stiff and sharply pointed. Leaves (when present) ⅛ to ⅓ in. long, half or less than half as wide, pointed, often toothed. Flowers brownish or greenish white suffused with dull red, the tubular part ¼ in. long, the lobes pointed and recurved; they are produced, each on a short stalk, mostly from beneath the spines, from March to June. Anthers only half exposed at the mouth of the tube. *Bot. Mag.*, t. 3644.

Native of Chile; introduced in 1823. It is very like *C. armata* in general appearance, but that species is well marked by its downy spines, its more exposed anthers and autumnal flowering. The species is founded on a plant which flowered at Bicton, Devon, in March 1913. There is an example in the Edinburgh Botanic Garden, planted in 1920, which never flowers.

COLQUHOUNIA   LABIATAE

A genus of two or three species, natives of the Himalaya and S.E. Asia, named in honour of Sir Robert Colquhoun, Bart., 'a gentleman very conversant with the various branches of natural history' and at one time a patron of the Botanic Garden at Calcutta.

C. COCCINEA Wall.

A shrub of lax, open, straggly habit, up to 8 or 10 ft high, with obscurely four-angled, downy shoots and leaves very variable in size and shape. The latter range from 2 to 8 in. in length, 1 to 5 in. in width, and from lanceolate to heart-shaped in outline; dull green and downy above, grey or even whitish beneath with a felt-like down. Flowers produced on the shoots of the current season from August onwards to October in the axils of the terminal leaves and in whorls on a spike at the end of the shoot, the whole making a slender panicle of blossom sometimes one foot long. The corolla is scarlet or orange-red, funnel-shaped, 1 in. long, downy, ending in a conspicuously two-lipped mouth; the lower and larger lip is three-lobed and yellowish inside. Calyx funnel-shaped, ½ in. long, five-toothed, grey with down like the flower-stalks. The whole plant when crushed has a pleasant apple-like scent. *Bot. Mag.*, t. 4514; n.s., t. 115.

Native of the Himalaya, W. China and other parts of E. Asia; introduced before 1850. It is a rather variable species in such characters as the degree of denseness of the indumentum, and also in hardiness. One form, of uncertain origin, is usually grown as var. VESTITA (Prain) Wall., though it differs but little from the type. It is, however, fairly hardy and thrives at Borde Hill, Sussex, in a sheltered position in the open ground. A form with large trusses was introduced by Kingdon Ward from the Assam Himalaya in 1938. This is perhaps more tender but grows at Highdown, Sussex, on a south wall and is figured in *Bot. Mag.*, n.s., t. 115. All the forms so far introduced should live through ordinary winters if planted in some warm corner protected from north and east winds, especially if a mat can be thrown over the plant during very severe spells of cold.

COLUTEA   BLADDER SENNA   LEGUMINOSAE

A small genus of deciduous shrubs, natives of the Old World, with un-equally pinnate leaves and yellow, coppery, or reddish-brown, pea-shaped flowers borne in few-flowered racemes. The most distinctive character of the genus is the large, thin-walled, inflated pod, which, when half ripe, may be made to burst with a miniature report when squeezed. There is nothing similar among hardy Leguminosae, and among all hardy shrubs similar fruits occur only in *Staphylea* and *Koelreuteria*.

In gardens the coluteas do not figure largely; although the commonest species, *C. arborescens*, is sometimes seen in rough shrubberies. They all flower late, and over a long season, which is in their favour; and all except *C. istria* are of the easiest cultivation, thriving in any soil and any situation except a very shaded one. Those species that produce seeds are easily propagated by them, the others can be struck from cuttings made of half-ripened wood placed in gentle heat.

C. ARBORESCENS L.   COMMON BLADDER SENNA

A strong-growing, deciduous shrub up to 12 ft high, of bushy habit and copiously branched. Leaves 3 to 6 in. long; leaflets nine to thirteen, elliptic or broadly obovate with the apex notched, from ½ to 1 in. long, hairy beneath when young, becoming nearly or quite glabrous with age. Racemes axillary on the current season's growth, produced successively as the branches extend; 1½ to 4 in. long, carrying three to seven flowers towards the end. Flowers pea-shaped, yellow, ¾ in. long, borne on a downy stalk ¼ to ½ in. long; wing-petals rather shorter than the keel; calyx cup-shaped with triangular lobes. Pod inflated and bladder-like, about 3 in. long, 1 to 1½ in. wide, pointed, many-seeded.

Native of the Mediterranean region and S.E. Europe; cultivated for at least three hundred years in England. Few introduced shrubs have made themselves so thoroughly at home as this. It has taken possession of some of the railway banks in the suburbs of London, and will, indeed, grow in almost any position not water-logged where it has sufficient light. Its accommodating nature has made it, perhaps, despised in gardens, but it is quite pretty when in full bloom, and it lasts more or less from June until the frosts come. The inflated pods, which explode with a sharp report when squeezed, make the shrub very attractive to children. A group of plants can be kept to a neat shape and convenient size by pruning back the shoots almost to the old wood every winter, the flowers being borne on the shoots of the year. The abundant seeds render its increase easy.

cv. 'BULLATA'.—A dwarf form of dense habit, whose five or seven leaflets are small, rounded, and somewhat bullate.

cv. 'CRISPA'.—Low-growing; leaves wavy at the margin. (Kirchner in *Arb. Muscav.*, 1864).

C. CILICICA Boiss.
C. longialata Koehne

A deciduous shrub, similar in habit to *C. arborescens*. Leaves composed of nine to thirteen leaflets, which are obovate or oval, with a few flattened hairs beneath. Flowers yellow, produced three or five together in short racemes. Wing-petals longer than the keel.

Native of Asia Minor. Very similar to *C. arborescens* (of which it is perhaps only a geographical form) and to *C. melanocalyx*; it is chiefly distinguished from the former by the larger wing-petals, and from the latter by the unfelted calyx.

C. ISTRIA Mill.
C. halepica Lam.; *C. pocockii* Ait.

A deciduous shrub 3 to 5 ft high, much branched. Leaves composed of nine to fifteen leaflets, which are the smallest among cultivated coluteas, being $\frac{1}{4}$ to $\frac{2}{3}$ in. long, obovate or broadly oval, and furnished with white flattened hairs. Flowers borne two to five together towards the end of a raceme about 2 in. long. Each flower is $\frac{3}{4}$ in. long, coppery yellow, with a handsome standard petal $\frac{5}{8}$ in. across; wings as long as the keel. Pod 2 in. or more long.

Native of Asia Minor, and a similar or closely allied plant occurs in Abyssinia. It was first introduced in 1752, but the true plant has always been rare. It is, perhaps, not hardy enough to withstand our severest frosts. The small graceful foliage and handsome flowers make it at once distinct and handsome, and it has not the rank growth of the *arborescens* group. It is the earliest of the genus to flower, commencing in late May or early June, and continuing more or less for three months.

C. × MEDIA Willd.

A hybrid between *C. arborescens* and *C. orientalis*, given this name in 1809, at which time it was cultivated in the Botanic Garden of Berlin. It is a vigorous shrub of bushy habit very similar in general appearance to *C. arborescens*, the leaves consisting usually of eleven or thirteen leaflets, which are obovate, $\frac{1}{2}$ to

1 in. long, bluish green, downy beneath when young. The influence of C. *orientalis* is most in evidence in the colour of the flowers, which are of a brownish red or coppery hue, also in the longer, linear-lanceolate teeth of the calyx, as compared with the triangular lobes of *C. arborescens*. C. × *media* has a large inflated pod like *C. arborescens*, 3 in. long. This shrub is useful in the same situations as *C. arborescens*, and may be planted on dry banks. It was once grown in gardens under a variety of names, such as *C. arborescens rubra*, *C. purpurea*, etc.

C. MELANOCALYX Boiss.

A deciduous shrub very similar in general appearance to *C. arborescens*, differing chiefly in the calyx, which is longer (⅓ in. long), more tubular, with broader triangular teeth, and, like the stalk of the flower, clothed with a thick, very dark brown, velvety down. Petals yellow, the wings about as long as the keel. Leaflets seven to eleven, broadly elliptical, indented at the end.

Native of the mountains of Asia Minor; flowers from July to September.

C. ORIENTALIS Mill.
C. cruenta Ait.

A deciduous bush of rounded, close habit, up to 6 ft high, with rather erect branches, often marked with small black warts. Leaves pinnate, 3 to 4 in. long, composed usually of seven or nine leaflets which are broadly obovate or roundish, ¼ to ⅝ in. long, rounded at the end, tapered at the base; very glaucous, glabrous on both surfaces except when quite young. Flowers two to five, clustered towards the end of a raceme 1½ to 3 in. long, brownish red or copper-coloured, each ⅝ in. long, the rounded standard petal ½ in. across, with a yellow spot at the base; wings two-thirds as long as the keel. Calyx slightly hairy. Pod open at the end, 1½ in. long, glabrous.

Native of the Orient; introduced to England in 1710. It flowers from June to September, but never makes much display. It is more notable for its grey-white foliage.

C. PERSICA Boiss.

A deciduous shrub 6 to 8 ft high; young shoots glabrous, pale. Leaves pinnate, 1½ to 3 in. long, made up of five to eleven leaflets, which are obovate or obcordate, tapered to the base, broad at the apex and either rounded or indented there, ¼ to ½ in. long, glabrous or sparingly downy beneath. Racemes of three or four flowers, each about ¾ in. long, pure yellow, the wing-petals longer than the keel; calyx funnel-shaped with five sharp teeth. Pod inflated, glabrous, 1½ to 2 in. long, open at the end.

Native of Persia and Kurdistan. It resembles *C. orientalis* in foliage, although not so glaucous, and that species has brownish-red flowers. Baskets and panniers are made of its branchlets in Persia.

var. BUHSEI Boiss.—Pods furnished with appressed hairs; leaves and flowers somewhat larger.

COMPTONIA MYRICACEAE

A genus with the one species described here, related to our native sweet gale, *Myrica gale*. Indeed, it is merged into *Myrica* by some botanists, but differs in the two sexes usually occurring on the same plant, and in the ovary being surrounded by eight persistent scales, instead of two or four inconspicuous ones. It is also quite distinct from the myricas, or indeed any other hardy shrub, in general aspect.

The genus was named after Henry Compton, Bishop of London (1632–1713), a notable tree-lover of his time who planted extensively in the garden of Fulham Palace.

C. PEREGRINA (L.) Coult. SWEET FERN

Liquidambar (sic) *peregrina* L.; *C. peregrina* var. *tomentosa* Cheval.

A deciduous shrub 2 to 4 ft high, with slender, often erect branches, very hairy when young. Leaves alternate, linear-oblong, tapered at both ends, 2 to 4 in. long, $\frac{1}{3}$ to $\frac{5}{8}$ in. wide, the blade deeply cleft (almost to the midrib) into broad, oblique, rounded lobes, $\frac{1}{8}$ to $\frac{1}{4}$ in. wide; dark green, downy; stalk $\frac{1}{8}$ to $\frac{1}{4}$ in. long. Male catkins cylindrical, $\frac{3}{4}$ to 1 in. long, $\frac{1}{6}$ in. wide; closely set with

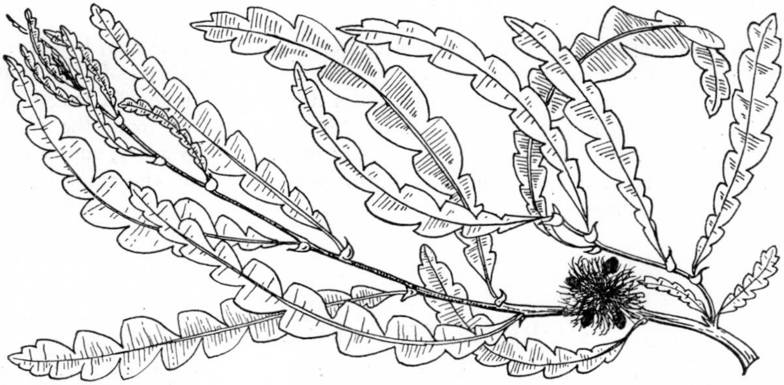

COMPTONIA PEREGRINA

downy, broadly triangular, long-pointed bracts. Female inflorescence globular, each ovary surrounded by eight awl-shaped, downy scales, which give the fruit-cluster a bur-like appearance. Nut egg-shaped, $\frac{1}{5}$ in. long, shining.

Native of eastern N. America; introduced in 1714, and long a favourite in gardens because of its beautifully cut, fern-like leaves, and pleasant bay-like scent. It likes a peaty soil and objects to lime.

var. ASPLENIFOLIA (L.) Fern. *Myrica asplenifolia* L. *Comptonia asplenifolia* (L.) Ait.—Branchlets only faintly downy; leaves smaller than in the type, almost glabrous. It is found in the coastal plain from Long Island to Virginia, while typical *C. peregrina*, in various degrees of downiness, is confined to the mountains. Probably most or all of the plants grown in gardens as *Comptonia asplenifolia* belong to typical *C. peregrina*, not to the variety.

CONVOLVULUS   CONVOLVULACEAE

In addition to the more familiar soft-stemmed species, *Convolvulus* contains a fair number of more or less woody plants, natives of the drier parts of S. Europe and W. Asia, with a few in the New World. Of these only the species described is widely cultivated.

C. CNEORUM L.   [PLATE 57

An evergreen, very leafy shrub 2 to 3 ft high, covered with silky hairs that give the entire younger part of the plant a beautiful silvery aspect. Leaves shortly stalked, alternate, narrowly oblong or oblanceolate, 1 to 2½ in. long, ⅛ to ½ in. wide, always tapered at the base, but either pointed or rounded at the apex. Flowers in a terminal umbel, but opening successively during the summer; they are of the trumpet-mouthed type common to 'morning glory', being 1¼ in. long, rather more across, of flimsy texture, white tinged with pink, yellow in the tube; calyx as long as the corolla-tube, silky. *Bot. Mag.*, t. 459.

Native of S. Europe; cultivated in England, according to Aiton, in 1640. It is not quite hardy near London except against a wall, but thrives in the south and west. There are five strips of silky hairs traversing the corolla lengthwise outside. The specific epithet chosen by Linnaeus derives from the Greek 'kneoron' (see introduction to the genus *Cneorum*). It needs a dry, sunny spot, and can be increased very readily by cuttings taken during the summer, and placed in gentle heat.

COPROSMA   RUBIACEAE

A genus of about ninety species found mainly in the lands bordering the S.W. Pacific from New Zealand (with about forty-five species) to Borneo; it is also represented in many of the smaller islands of the Pacific. They are shrubs, sometimes dwarf, more rarely trees, with evergreen, opposite leaves. The small, rather inconspicuous flowers have the petals united into a tube, with the stamens inserted on the corolla, and are prevailingly unisexual, the male and female flowers being borne on separate plants (dioecious). This characteristic limits their usefulness in gardens, since it is for the brightly coloured, fleshy fruits that they are grown. There is, however, much variability in this respect even within a single species: flowers of each sex may be found on one plant and even hermaphrodite flowers have been observed.

For the taxonomist, the New Zealand coprosmas are a very confusing group, owing to the readiness with which they hybridise in the wild and the various forms one and the same species may assume in response to the conditions of its habitat.

In addition to the species described here, mention must be made of C. LUCIDA J. R. & G. Forst., which is very tender but is sometimes grown outdoors in very mild gardens of the British Isles. It is a medium sized shrub with glossy green leaves up to 5 in. long and fruits of a vivid orange colour.

C. ACEROSA A. Cunn.

A low, evergreen shrub, whose prostrate wiry stems are covered with a minute down, and form a mass of interlacing twigs. Leaves opposite, either in pairs or in clusters, $\frac{1}{4}$ to $\frac{3}{4}$ in. long, about $\frac{1}{20}$ in. wide, linear, dark green, glabrous. Flowers unisexual; the males from one to four in a cluster, females solitary; both inconspicuous. Fruit globose and berry-like, $\frac{1}{6}$ to $\frac{1}{3}$ in. in diameter, of a pale, translucent blue.

Native of New Zealand, up to 4,000 ft. It is a fairly hardy shrub, surviving the winters at Kew, but finding more congenial conditions in milder places. I have seen it very charming in the botanic garden at Glasnevin and in other Irish gardens, where it bears fruit freely. There are two varieties in cultivation, viz.: var. BRUNNEA Kirk, with brown shoots, shorter branches, and more widely separate leaves—this is now given specific rank as C. brunnea (Kirk) Cheesem.; and var. ARENARIA Kirk, with yellow, more slender branches, and more closely set leaves. The former variety is said to fruit much the more freely in Ireland, and is more ornamental. It is suitable for the rock garden.

C. NITIDA Hook. f.

A densely branched shrub of variable habit: at high altitudes it forms dense, low masses but in more favourable situations is erect and may reach a height of 8 ft or more. Branches stiff, more or less glabrous. Leaves glossy and leathery, closely set on the stems, oblong-elliptic to lanceolate, $\frac{1}{6}$ to $\frac{4}{5}$ in. long. Flowers solitary at the end of short axillary spurs, male and female borne on separate plants. Fruits red or orange. A native of Tasmania and Victoria, where it is common in mountains above 2,500 ft; introduced by Comber in 1929. Mr Hadden of Porlock, who supplied the material for the figure in the *Botanical Magazine* (n.s., t. 88), tells us that his plants were killed many years ago in a hard winter.

C. PETRIEI Cheesem.

A dwarf plant with prostrate stems forming broad patches 2 to 3 in. high. The leaves are dark green, densely crowded, narrow oblong or obovate, $\frac{1}{8}$ to $\frac{1}{4}$ in. long, more or less hairy. Fruit ranging in colour from port-wine (var. ATROPURPUREA Ckn. & Allan) to various shades of blue, only borne in the presence of a male plant. A native of New Zealand, found in both islands to about 4,000 ft.

C. PSEUDOCUNEATA W. R. B. Oliver.—A shrub of variable habit, 10 ft tall in the forests but low and compact on open mountain-sides. Leaves thick and leathery, dark green, oblong or narrow-obovate, about $\frac{3}{4}$ in. long and up to $\frac{1}{4}$ in. wide. Fruits translucent, orange-red. Native of New Zealand, common near the tree-line in the mountains of South Island. According to Dr Philipson, this is 'one of the very finest of the sub-alpine shrubs of New Zealand', but he adds the warning: 'Quite apart from the need for unproductive male plants, the great majority of female plants are very loath to bear fruit. . . . However, the plant is so good at its best that it is worth taking trouble to obtain a good one' (*Rock Garden Plants*, p. 103).

C. PROPINQUA A. Cunn.

A shrub or small tree 6 to 20 ft high; shoots opposite, spreading often at nearly right angles to the stem, very slender, finely downy at first. Leaves opposite or in opposite clusters, linear, $\frac{1}{4}$ to $\frac{3}{5}$ in. long, $\frac{1}{12}$ to $\frac{1}{8}$ in. wide, scarcely stalked, curved, mostly blunt. Flowers of no beauty, axillary, solitary or two to four together; females with a four-toothed calyx, the corolla tubular, $\frac{1}{8}$ in. long, four-lobed; stamens absent. Male flowers with no calyx, corolla $\frac{1}{8}$ in. long, bell-shaped, four- or five-lobed; stamens four or five. Fruit a glabrous drupe $\frac{1}{4}$ in. long, pale blue to blue-black. *Bot. Mag.*, t. 9286.

Native of New Zealand, with a wide distribution from the North Island south to Stewart Island. Its chief attraction is in its fruits. It succeeded well with the late Lord Headfort at Kells, Co. Meath, and plants of Stewart Island should be pretty hardy in our average climate. It most frequently grows wild in damp places.

C. CUNNINGHAMII Hook. f., which is in commerce, is now thought to be part of a hybrid swarm between *C. propinqua* and *C. robusta*. It is an erect shrub with narrow, leathery leaves up to 2 in. long and pale yellow fruits. It is likely to be very tender.

C. PARVIFLORA Hook. f., was given an Award of Merit when shown from Exbury in 1945 but is not established in cultivation. It is related to *C. propinqua* but the fruits are purplish or (as in the form shown) white. It was at first considered to be *C. rigida*, and is discussed by the late Francis Hanger under that name in *Journ. R.H.S.*, Vol. 69, p. 291.

CORDYLINE   AGAVACEAE

A genus of about a dozen evergreen trees or shrubs with erect cylindrical stems, long narrow leaves more or less crowded at the top and small flowers produced very numerously in large panicles. The corolla (perianth) has six lobes; stamens six; fruit a globose berry containing black seeds. The species grown out-of-doors in Britain are natives of New Zealand and Norfolk Island; they are only hardy in the mildest counties. Besides the two species described below, which are the most commonly grown, C. BANKSII Hook. f., a shrub 10 to 20 ft high with leaves 3 to 6 ft long, and C. BAUERI Hook. f., of similar stature but with broader, shorter leaves (1½ to 2 ft by 2 to 2½ in.) and thinly arranged white flowers, are grown at Tresco Abbey in Scilly. The former is from New Zealand, the latter from Norfolk Island.

C. AUSTRALIS (Forst. f.) Hook. f.   CABBAGE TREE
Dracaena australis Forst. f.   [PLATE 56

An evergreen tree up to 40 ft high with an erect trunk usually unbranched for several, often a good many, feet up, then forking into several, sometimes fairly numerous, equally erect branches, each crowned with a dense rounded head of leaves. The branching usually commences after the plant has reached the flowering stage. Leaves sword-shaped, 1½ to 3 ft long, 1 to 2½ in. wide; pointed, of hardish texture; the midrib is obscure but there are numerous parallel veins running lengthwise. The upper leaves are more or less erect, the lower ones drooping. Panicles terminal, either erect or somewhat pendulous, 2 to 4 ft long, half as much wide, repeatedly branched, the ultimate divisions being cylindrical racemes about ½ in. wide upon which the creamy white fragrant flowers, each ¼ to ⅓ in. wide, are closely set. The six divisions of the perianth are narrow oblong; anthers yellow; berry white or bluish white, globose, ¼ in. wide; seeds black. *Bot. Mag.*, t. 5636.

Introduced in 1823 from New Zealand, where it is abundant on both islands and gives to their scenery one of its most characteristic features. In some of the gardens of Cornwall and W. Scotland it has also become familiar. So much is it at home there that numerous self-sown seedlings may often be seen. This is the case, for example, at Brodick in the Isle of Arran, where there are many trees, the tallest about 30 ft high. On the west coast of Scotland it grows as far north as Scourie, only 30 miles south of Cape Wrath. At Brodick specimens 10 ft high have been felled by mice, which eat out the pith in winter. Some of the best branched trees I have seen are in the public garden at Penzance. There appear to exist two forms of this cordyline which are differentiated by the persistence of the leaves. In one they drop cleanly away as they die, but in the other, after dying, they persist on the stem for many years, hanging down and hiding it. Whether this difference is merely an individual characteristic or is a racial one I do not know. At Kew all the various forms, some with variegated or reddish leaves, have to be given cool greenhouse treatment. The type itself is 40 ft high in the Temperate House and flowers annually.

C. INDIVISA (Forst. f.) Steud.
Dracaena indivisa Forst. f.

An evergreen tree with usually a single cylindrical, rarely branched stem up to 25 ft high, encircled by the scars of the fallen leaves. Leaves very numerous, forming a large head, 6 to 9 ft wide at the summit of the stem, the lower ones deflexed. Each leaf is from 3 to 6 ft long, 4 to 6 in. wide, at the middle, tapering to a long fine point, of hard texture, with prominent parallel veins running lengthwise; green, with often a distinct purplish tinge above, glaucous beneath; the midrib red or yellow. Panicles of flowers pendulous, 2 to 4 ft long, made up of numerous racemes; the main-stalk very thick, furnished with lanceolate bracts up to 6 in. long at the base, becoming smaller upwards. Racemes cylindrical, 4 to 6 in. long, 1 in. wide; closely packed with short-stalked flowers ⅓ in. wide. The six perianth lobes are much recurved, white suffused with green and lilac; anthers yellow; fruit a globose berry, purplish blue, ⅛ in. wide; seeds black, shining. *Bot. Mag.*, t. 9096.

Native of New Zealand; discovered in 1773 on Cook's second voyage. It is said to have been introduced to England about the middle of last century, but for many years other kinds of cordyline were grown in gardens under this name. (See for instance coloured plates in *Illustration Horticole*, Vols. 35 and 37.) I first saw the true plant, then about 6 ft high, in the late Mr Jonathan Rashleigh's garden at Menabilly in Cornwall in 1893, but at that time it was very rare. A few years later an importation of good seed made it much more plentiful in the gardens of Cornwall, Ireland, W. Scotland, etc., where it withstands ten degrees of frost without injury. At Logan in Wigtownshire there is a specimen about 15 ft high which flowers every second year and bears good crops of its attractive violet berries. It is also grown at Inverewe in Wester Ross and at Mount Stewart in Northern Ireland (1966).

It is a most imposing plant when once its leaves have attained their full size— and on vigorous young specimens they will be 7 or 8 in. wide. After a period of years it develops a clean stem but it is never more stately than just before the stem commences to become bare at the base, the leaves being then at their largest. It likes rich soil and should be planted in a permanent place early, as it does not like pot culture and requires very careful transplanting after it has attained a good size. At Kew it needs greenhouse treatment. It appears as yet to be shy-flowering, but that may alter as the plants get older.

COREMA   EMPETRACEAE

Two small, evergreen, heath-like shrubs, one native of S.W. Europe, the other of eastern N. America. They have short, slender leaves mostly in whorls of three, and flowers in terminal clusters, usually but not always unisexual, with the sexes on separate plants. Their only ally in gardens is the crowberry (*Empetrum*) from which the coremas are distinguished by the terminal inflorescence and three-seeded berries. Propagation and cultivation the same as for heaths.

C. ALBUM (L.) D. Don   PORTUGUESE CROWBERRY
Empetrum album L.

An evergreen shrub $1\frac{1}{2}$ to 2 ft high, erect in habit and heath-like; young shoots very downy. Leaves narrow linear, $\frac{1}{4}$ to $\frac{3}{8}$ in. long, blunt, the margins reflexed so as to leave only a narrow slit behind, dark green and soon becoming glabrous, mostly arranged in threes. Flowers in terminal clusters, stalkless and inconspicuous. The female plant bears globose white berries in clusters, each berry $\frac{1}{4}$ in. across.

Native of Portugal and Spain; introduced in 1774. It grows very well near London in sandy peat, and resembles its close ally Empetrum nigrum, but is taller and larger leaved, and the berry is white with only three seeds. A neat little evergreen, but not showy.

C. CONRADII (Torr.) Loud.   PLYMOUTH CROWBERRY
Empetrum conradii Torr.

An evergreen, heath-like shrub 6 to 20 in. high, forming spreading tufts; young branches nearly glabrous. Leaves narrow linear, $\frac{1}{8}$ to $\frac{1}{4}$ in. long, blunt, margins much curled back, often arranged in threes and very closely set; dark green. Flowers in terminal heads, the males conspicuous only for the long purplish stamens with brown anthers. Berry very small, and dark brown when ripe, containing usually three seeds.

Native of eastern N. America, usually in dry, sandy places; introduced in 1841. It is a rare shrub even in a wild state, and is found in only a comparatively few isolated places. Its most famous site is a few acres near Plymouth, Mass., where it is said to be very pretty in April, with its purple flowers. It has never become properly established in English gardens, although several times imported. It is not so robust a plant as C. album, from which it is easily distinguished by its small leaves and the almost glabrous branchlets.

CORIARIA   CORIARIACEAE

A small genus of shrubby and herbaceous plants whose affinities are doubtful. By Bentham and Hooker the family is placed near Anacardiaceae (Rhus, etc.), but other authorities regard it as more closely allied to Simaroubaceae (Ailanthus, etc.). The coriarias have simple, opposite, entire leaves; small flowers in racemes terminating the current season's growth, or produced from the joints of the previous season's wood. In some species male and female flowers are borne on separate and distinct racemes. Sepals and petals five; stamens ten; carpels five; one-seeded. The most interesting character of these plants is the persistence of the petals, which, as the fruit ripens, thicken and become juicy and more or less highly coloured, finally enclosing the fruit. It is to them that the plants owe most of their attractiveness. The leaves and fruits are mostly poisonous.

The coriarias are scarcely hardy enough to be seen at their best near London, being killed to the ground in severe winters. They are better adapted for more southern and western counties, where they bear fruit with greater certainty. They like a fairly good, loamy soil, and can be propagated by seed (which is preferable), or by cuttings made of half-ripened shoots.

C. JAPONICA A. Gray

A low, deciduous shrub with semi-herbaceous, pithy, four-angled branches, renewing itself by strong shoots from the base; it is rarely more than 2 ft high in this country. Leaves of variable size, 1 to $3\frac{1}{2}$ in. long on the secondary shoots, but half as large again on the first-year, sucker-like, basal ones; they are ovate-lanceolate, tapering to a long, fine point, prominently three-nerved, quite glabrous and entire, almost stalkless. Racemes produced two or three together from the joints of the year-old branches, $1\frac{1}{2}$ to $2\frac{1}{2}$ in. long, the male racemes shorter, more slender and drooping than the female ones, the flowers also smaller and inconspicuous. Petals of female flowers at first green, then thickening and becoming fleshy and turning bright coral red, ultimately purplish black; they and the fruit they enclose are $\frac{1}{5}$ in. across. *Bot. Mag.*, t. 7509.

Native of Japan; introduced to Kew in 1893, through Prof. Sargent. It is hardy at Kew, but not long-lived, and should be renewed occasionally by means of seeds or even cuttings. It is better adapted for a slightly warmer climate than that of London, and when seen at its best is extremely beautiful. It has been grown with particular success in the vicarage garden at Bitton.

C. MYRTIFOLIA L.   REDOUL

A deciduous shrub 4 to 6 ft high, of bushy habit, sending up from the base rather erect, angular, more or less four-sided stems, which the following year carry graceful, slender, twiggy shoots. Leaves opposite, in pairs, occasionally in threes; quite glabrous, entire, ovate, pointed, three-nerved, 1 to $2\frac{1}{2}$ in. long, very short-stalked, glaucous green. Flowers small, greenish, produced during the summer from the joints of the previous year's growths in racemes about 1 in. long. The petals, after becoming thick, fleshy, and juicy, turn black and shining; they and the fruit they enclose, $\frac{1}{4}$ in. across.

Native of the Mediterranean region, especially in the south of France, where it is often the first wild plant to reoccupy plots of ground abandoned from cultivation. It is fairly hardy in the London district, but is killed in very hard winters. When in full growth, which is rather late in the season, it is distinctly handsome in the graceful disposition of its glaucous leaves and branches. It flowers freely, but does not set fruit well in this country.

Both the leaves and fruits are poisonous, the latter especially so, producing, when eaten, convulsions similar to those caused by strychnine. Various animals, even goats, are sometimes poisoned by the leaves; the fruits, macerated in sweet water, make an excellent fly-poison. The leaves are rich in tannin, and are used for curing leather and for making ink; they also yield a black dye. Introduced to England in 1629.

C. NAPALENSIS Wall.

Naturally a deciduous shrub, with long spreading branches, but too tender to thrive well in the open air at Kew, where it is frequently cut to the ground during winter, and thus prevented from attaining anything like its natural size. Given the protection of glass it will grow 8 ft high. Leaves ovate or oblong, slightly heart-shaped, 3 or 4 in. long on the strong primary growths, much smaller on the branchlets, distinctly three-nerved, glabrous, entire. Flowers produced on year-old shoots in narrow, cylindrical racemes 1½ in. long, greenish yellow, the petals becoming in the fruiting stage much thickened, pulpy, and black-purple.

Native of the Himalaya and the Shan Hills, Upper Burma.

C. SINICA Maxim.

A deciduous shrub of thin spreading habit, said to be 18 ft high in a wild state and already 15 ft high in cultivation; young shoots squarish, warted, often growing 4 to 8 ft long in a season. Leaves oval or ovate, scarcely stalked, rounded at the base, shortly pointed, strongly three-veined, very variable in size, but averaging 2 to 3 in. long by half as much wide. Flowers borne in racemes 1 to 2 in. long, in pairs at each joint of the previous summer's growth; they have little beauty apart from the red anthers of the male flowers. The fruit (i.e. the fleshy persistent petals) is black.

Native of China, where it is very common in certain regions; introduced by Wilson in 1907. It is very nearly related to *C. napalensis*, but grows more strongly and is hardier. Comparing it with that species, Rehder and Wilson observe that 'the style of *C. sinica* is more slender, the rudimentary pistil and petals in the male flowers are much more minute (almost wanting) and the ripe carpels are smaller'. Wilson states that in Hupeh, where it is known as 'Ma-sang', the shoots are said to be poisonous to cattle. It is a shrub of coarse growth, and so far as I have seen has not the garden value of *terminalis* or *japonica*. The largest plant I know of is in the garden at South Lodge near Horsham. Its main stems are 3 or 4 in. thick.

C. TERMINALIS Hemsl.

This species can scarcely be termed a shrub. It forms a woody root-stock which sends up annual branching stems 2 to 4 ft long, and spreads by underground rhizomes. Leaves ovate, 1 to 3 in. long, usually five- or seven-nerved, occasionally nine-nerved; much the larger, broader, and rounder on the main stems. Flowers, male and female ones of which are produced on terminal racemes 6 to 9 in. long, are greenish at first, the petals of the female flowers thickening and becoming fleshy in the fruiting stage, and being then black or in one form, of a beautiful translucent yellow. Each fruit with its enveloping petals is nearly ½ in. across. *Bot. Mag.*, t. 8525.

Native of Sikkim, where it was collected by Sir Joseph Hooker, 1849–53; also of China and Tibet; introduced to England in 1897. This beautiful plant, which is distinct from the other cultivated coriarias in its invariably terminal inflorescence (borne on the shoots of the year) and more numerously veined leaves, is hardy at Kew, and fruits there annually. The yellow-fruited form is distinguished as var. XANTHOCARPA Rehd., and is found from Sikkim to Yunnan. Wilson introduced the form with black fruits from W. Szechwan in 1908.

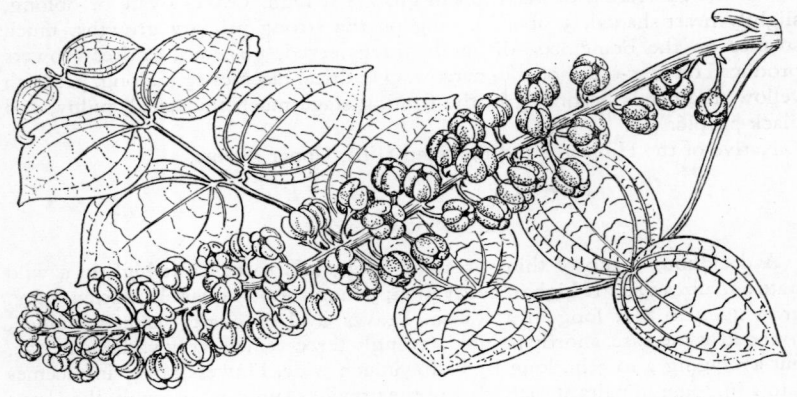

CORIARIA TERMINALIS

NOTE: In 1926 I had an interesting letter from the late Sir Herbert Maxwell who, writing from Monreith, Wigtownshire, said: 'You refer to the leaves and fruits of *Coriaria* as being "mostly poisonous" and we have scrupulously respected them as such; but a small grandson of mine, having with impunity devoured a branch of golden berries of *C. terminalis*, I would like to know whether anything definite is known about the properties of that species. I have tasted the fruit and found it agreeably sweet and juicy: if it were proved to be innocuous to human beings it would soon become popular as a beautiful dessert dish.'

I have not been able to find any definite pronouncement on the edibility or otherwise of the fruits of *Coriaria terminalis*, but from Sir Herbert's experience it would seem that they are harmless, at least in small quantities. The late W. Hancock, writing in 1896, says the fruits of *C. sinica* have almost exactly the same pleasant flavour as bilberries, and Forrest in a field note on the same species says 'fruit black, edible'.

In regard to the Indian species, *C. napalensis*, Sir George Watt writes, 'leaves said to act as a powerful poison when given in large doses; seeds stated sometimes to produce symptoms like tetanus', but goes on to say that he has seen horses eat the leaves without any injurious after-effects, and that the natives regularly eat the fruits, maintaining only that the seeds should be ejected.

There is no doubt at all about the deadly poisonous properties of *C. myrtifolia*. Much also has been written of the poisonous nature of *C. sarmentosa*, the 'toot-poison' of New Zealand (so-called from the Maori name for the plant—'tutu'—which is pronounced 'toot'). Cheeseman says that most parts of the plant are poisonous, especially the young shoots and seeds, but that the juice expressed from the fruits is innocuous.

It seems that, on the whole, the coriarias should be treated cautiously as food.

CORNUS CORNEL, DOGWOOD CORNACEAE

Trees or shrubs with usually deciduous opposite leaves, the only exceptions being *C. capitata*, more or less evergreen in mild districts; and *C. alternifolia* and *C. controversa*, both of which have alternate leaves. Flowers usually white, sometimes greenish or yellowish, always small, and produced in terminal corymbs or cymes, or clustered densely in heads; the parts of each flower are in fours. Fruit a drupe containing a two-celled stone. Many of the cornels are characterised by having the hairs of the leaf flattened to the surface and attached to it by their centres.

The species of *Cornus* treated in this work can conveniently be classified into four units, each of which should, in the opinion of some botanists, be given generic rank. The dismemberment of *Cornus* is not accepted in this work but in the following analysis the names of the segregate genera are given, together with their authors and synonymy.

1. Flowers borne in corymbose inflorescences which lack both bracts and bracteoles. This is the largest group and contains all the species described in this work except those mentioned by name under the other three groups. Considered as a genus, this group would take the name SWIDA Opiz (1838) (syn. *Cornus* L. emend. Hutch. (1948); *Thelycrania* (Dumort.) Fourr.). The generic name is also spelt '*Swyjda*' or '*Svida*'.

2. Flowers borne in dense umbels with a yellowish involucre which falls as the flowers open. Here belong *C. mas* and its allies, namely *C. officinalis* and *chinensis* from E. Asia and *C. sessilis* from western N. America. Although Linnaeus did not designate a type-species for the genus *Cornus*, the name had been restricted to *C. mas* by Opiz in 1838 and this species and its allies would therefore constitute the genus CORNUS in the narrow sense (syn. *Macrocarpium* Nakai).

3. Flowers in dense clusters, surrounded by large and conspicuous bracts. This group may be subdivided as follows:

   a) Fruits clustered but free from each other. Here belong *C. florida* and *nuttallii* (also the Mexican *C. urbaniana*).

   b) Fruits completely united into a fleshy compound fruit (syncarp). To this group, confined to E. and S.E. Asia, belong *C. capitata*, *C. kousa* and a few other species.

The correct name for this group, if considered to rank as a genus, would be BENTHAMIDIA Spach (1839) (syn. *Benthamia* Lindl. (1833), not Lindl. (1830), nor A. Rich. (1828); *Cynoxylon* Raf. ex Small (1903);* *Dendrobenthamia* Hutch. (1942)). If a further split were made, and the two sub-groups each given generic rank, then *C. florida* and its allies would retain the name *Benthamia* Spach and *C. capitata* and its allies would take the name *Dendrobenthamia* Hutch.

Species of osier-like habit, like *C. alba*, can be increased by cuttings of naked wood put in the open ground like willows, during the winter. Others with a stoloniferous habit can be propagated by offsets, and the rest by layers, when seed is not available. The following may be recommended as the best for general cultivation:

For Flower.—*C. mas*, *C. rugosa*, *C. racemosa*, *C. kousa*, *C. florida*, *C. nuttallii* (not for dry gardens), *C. capitata* (in mild localities).

For Colour of Leaf.—*C. alba* 'Spaethii', *C. alba* 'Elegantissima', *C. mas* 'Aurea Elegantissima'.

For Beauty of Stem.—*C. alba*, *C. alba* 'Sibirica', *C. stolonifera* 'Flaviramea'.

For Habit.—*C. controversa*, *C. macrophylla*, *C. rugosa*, *C. hessei*.

C. ALBA L.

C. sibirica Raf.; *C. tatarica* Mill.; *Swida alba* (L.) Opiz; *Thelycrania alba* (L.) Pojark.

A deciduous, wide-spreading shrub, producing a thicket of stems erect to prostrate; ultimately 10 ft high. Bark of the young shoots becoming in autumn and winter rich red. Leaves opposite, ovate to oval, rounded or wedge-shaped at the base, with short slender points; variable in size, but usually from 2 to 4½ in. long; dark green above, glaucous beneath, with minute flattened hairs on both sides; veins in about six pairs; stalks ⅓ to 1 in. long. Flowers small, yellowish white, in cymes 1½ to 2 in. across. Fruit whitish or tinted with blue, about the size of a pea. Stones longer than wide, flattened at each end.

Introduced from Siberia in 1741, and a native also of China. This is a rampant shrub, apt to smother anything less vigorous than itself growing near. It is therefore best adapted for forming an isolated mass on a spacious lawn, or on the banks of a pond, where its deep red stems are remarkably effective all through the winter. A number of varieties are in cultivation, of which the following form a representative set:

cv. 'ELEGANTISSIMA'.—Leaves with an irregular margin of creamy white, centre grey-green; winter-stems red. Also known as 'Sibirica Variegata'; both names are in use, but the one adopted here seems to be the better established, at least in this country. The epithet *argenteo-marginata* has been applied both to this clone and to 'Variegata', but is not a valid name for either.

cv. 'GOUCHAULTII'.—A variegated form, margined with yellow and stained with rose. It is duller than 'Spaethii', and with more green and rose in the centre. 'FROEBELII' and 'TRICOLOR' differ but little and are no better.

* Rafinesque published the name *Cynoxylon* in 1838 but it is a little uncertain whether he intended it to represent a genus or a subgenus; for this reason it is best passed over in favour of *Benthamidia*.

cv. 'KESSELRINGII'.—Branchlets dark brownish purple; unfolding leaves reddish.

cv. 'SIBIRICA'.—Not so rampant a grower as the type, the branches of a paler and brighter red; fruit bluish; leaves mostly more rounded and more shortly acuminate at the apex. The plants that correctly bear this name were put into commerce by Loddiges as "*Cornus sibirica*" and described by Loudon under the name *C. alba* var. *sibirica*. Unfortunately, some nineteenth-century botanists, believing that the *C. alba* of Linnaeus was the American red osier dogwood (properly *C. stolonifera*), used the name *C. alba* var. *sibirica* for the Siberian dogwood in general, which may explain why some of the plants in commerce as *C. alba sibirica* are typical *C. alba* and not the true 'Sibirica'.

The plants grown as "Westonbirt", "the Westonbirt dogwood" or *atrosanguinea* do not, judging from the trials at Wisley, differ in any way from the true 'Sibirica'. It is at present represented at Westonbirt only by a few plants in the home nursery; the common dogwood there is ordinary *C. alba*.

'Sibirica', being of rather weak constitution, should be grown in a damp, well-cultivated soil. The bark is most brightly coloured on the previous summer's growths and gradually darkens as spring approaches.

cv. 'SPAETHII'.—Undoubtedly the handsomest of all the variegated cornels, and perhaps the most effective of all deciduous, yellow-variegated shrubs in cultivation. A mass on a lawn has a most striking aspect all the summer through, for the plant has the great virtue of never having its foliage scorched by summer sun, although the major part of the leaf is bright yellow; nor does it become dull as the season advances, like many shrubs of this colour do. When visiting Späth's nursery at Rixdorf, near Berlin, many years ago, I was told that this remarkable shrub originated there on a stem of ordinary *Cornus alba*, on which had been grafted a scion of the variegated sort. The graft died, but just beneath the point of union a yellow variegated twig appeared, which was removed and propagated, and is the 'Spaethii' as we know it today. The bark is red in winter. The shrub does not need a very rich soil, and like the rest of the forms of *C. alba*, can be propagated by cuttings of leafless wood placed in the open ground in late autumn, or by late summer leafy shoots under glass. The outer branches can be easily layered.

cv. 'VARIEGATA'.—Leaves margined with creamy white. 'Elegantissima' is less vigorous and often preferable.

C. ALTERNIFOLIA L. f.

Swida alternifolia (L. f.) Small

A deciduous shrub, sometimes with a cluster of erect stems, sometimes a small tree 20 ft or so high in a wild state, flat-topped and with horizontal branches; young shoots glabrous. Leaves alternate, often aggregated at the end of the shoot, oval or ovate, tapered at both ends, the apex often slender-pointed; 2 to 5 in. long, 1 to 2½ in. wide; bright pale green and glabrous above, more or less glaucous and furnished with centrally attached flattened hairs beneath; stalk 1 to 2 in. long; veins in five or six pairs. Flowers yellowish white, small, numerous, of little beauty, produced during June in flattish cymes 2 to 2½ in.

across; flower-stalks downy. Fruit roundish, ¼ in. diameter, black with a blue bloom.

Native of eastern N. America; introduced in 1760. Although this species comes from as far north as New Brunswick and Nova Scotia, and therefore is capable of withstanding intense cold, it is not infrequently a failure in this country, probably owing to insufficiency of sunlight. Its alternate leaves distinguish it from all other cornels except *C. controversa*, which is a much larger tree with cymes twice as large, and leaves with usually one to three more pairs of veins.

cv. 'ARGENTEA'.—Leaves variegated with white; put into commerce by Temple and Beard, U.S.A., before 1900. This is one of the handsomest of variegated shrubs; as in the type, the branches are produced in tiers, making a spreading, flat-topped shrub.

C. AMOMUM Mill.
Swida amomum (Mill.) Small

A deciduous shrub of compact habit, up to 10 ft high; young bark downy, becoming purple. Leaves ovate, mostly rounded at the base, with short, abrupt points; 2 to 4 in. long, 1 to 2¼ in. wide; dark green and soon becoming glabrous above, paler and with silky down beneath, especially on the veins, the down often becoming rusty or tawny, stalks similarly downy, ¼ to ⅔ in. long; veins in four to seven pairs. Flowers small, yellowish white, produced in July in cymes 1½ to 2½ in. across. Fruit ¼ in. across, pale blue.

Native of eastern N. America; introduced in 1683. A shrub thriving well in our climate, but of no especial value. Its distinctive characters are its purple young wood with brown pith, the silky reddish down beneath the leaf, and the pale blue fruits.

C. OBLIQUA Raf. *C. purpusii* Koehne—A close ally of *C. amomum*, it is found in the same region. The leaves are narrower, glaucous and grey-white with down beneath (not rust-coloured), veins in about five pairs. Young shoots yellowish red to purplish. Fruit dull blue. Introduced about 1889, but perhaps in cultivation before as *C. amomum*. It is of looser, less compact habit than that species.

C. ASPERIFOLIA Michx.
C. microcarpa Nash; *Swida microcarpa* (Nash) Small

This species is represented in cultivation by the following variety:

var. DRUMMONDII (C. A. Mey.) Coult. & Evans *C. drummondii* C. A. Mey.— A deciduous shrub 10 to 15 ft high, or a small tree; twigs grey or reddish brown. Leaves ovate or oval, 2 to 4 in. long, about half as wide; slender-pointed, tapering or rounded at the base, upper surface dark green and rough, with minute, flattened, stiff hairs; lower surface pale and with thicker, softer down; veins in about five pairs; stalk ⅓ to ¾ in. long, grooved, downy. Flowers yellowish white, ¼ to ⅓ in. across, produced in rounded corymbs 1½ to 2½ in. in diameter;

petals narrowly oblong, calyx downy and with very minute teeth. Fruit round, white, ¼ in. across.

Native of the eastern and central United States, found occasionally as a tree nearly 50 ft high in Arkansas and Texas (Sargent). It reaches as far north as Lake Erie, and appears to be quite hardy near London. It has little, however, to recommend it as a garden shrub.

C. AUSTRALIS C. A. Mey.

C. sanguinea var. *australis* (C. A. Mey.) Koehne; *Thelycrania australis* (C. A. Mey.) Sanadze; *Swida australis* (C. A. Mey.) Pojark. ex Grossheim.

A deciduous shrub 6 to 12 ft high; young shoots minutely appressed-downy, green or purplish. Leaves oval, 1½ to 3½ in. long, about half as wide; sharply narrowed at the apex to a short point, tapered at the base, appressed-downy on both surfaces; veins in three or four pairs; stalk ½ in. or less long. Flowers white, in dense terminal clusters about 2 in. across; style club-shaped, as long as the stamens but shorter than the petals. Fruits ¼ in. wide.

Native of W. Asia, in cultivation since 1915. It is very hardy, but its only claim to special notice is in its autumnal red foliage.

C. BAILEYI Coult. & Evans

Swida baileyi (Coult. & Evans) Rydb.; *C. stolonifera* var. *baileyi* (Coult. & Evans) Drescher; *C. stolonifera* f. *baileyi* (Coult. & Evans) Rickett

An erect, deciduous shrub up to 10 ft high, with downy shoots turning reddish brown by winter. Leaves ovate or lanceolate, slender-pointed, rounded at the base; 2 to 5 in. long, 1 to 2½ in. wide; with minute flattened hairs above, and, when young, with a dense covering of woolly down as well as flattened hairs beneath; stalks slender, ½ to ¾ in. long. Flowers small, in woolly-stalked cymes 1 to 2 in. across. Fruit white, ⅛ in. across.

Native of eastern N. America; introduced in 1892. It has been much confused with *C. stolonifera*, from which it differs in the shoots and lower surface of the leaves being distinctly woolly, and in not being stoloniferous; the bark also is duller and browner. It is usually found on sandy shores, and is recommended for light soils.

C. CAPITATA Wall.   BENTHAM'S CORNEL

Benthamia fragifera Lindl.; *Dendrobenthamia capitata* (Wall.) Hutch; *Benthamidia capitata* (Wall.) Hara

An evergreen tree 30 to 40 or more ft high, of bushy habit, and, if allowed to develop without interference by other trees, wider than it is high; young shoots clad with flattened, grey down. Leaves leathery, opposite, narrow- to broad-elliptic, tapered at both ends; 2 to 5 in. long, ¾ to 1¾ in. wide; dull grey-green covered densely on both surfaces with minute flattened hairs; stalk ¼ to ¾ in. long. Flowers minute, inconspicuous, crowded in a hemispherical mass

½ in. across. The beauty of the inflorescence is in the four or six sulphur-yellow bracts that subtend the true flowers; these are obovate, 1½ to 2 in. long, ¾ to 1½ in. wide. Fruit a fleshy, strawberry-shaped, agglomerated crimson mass, 1 to 1½ in. across, in which many seeds are imbedded. *Bot. Mag.*, t. 4641.

Introduced from the Himalaya in 1825, and a native also of China. It is hopeless to attempt to grow this cornel unprotected near London, although it has lived many years against a wall at Kew, but rarely or never flowers there. One has to go to the Cornish gardens, or those of S.W. Ireland, to see this tree in its full splendour. The finest tree I have seen is at Fota, probably about 40 ft high, and 70 ft in diameter; but there are probably others in Cornwall quite as fine. When covered with pale yellow 'flowers', they provide one of the richest ornaments even those favoured gardens can display. In fruit, too, they are objects of great beauty, but often damaged by birds. The 'flowers' are at their best in June and July, and the fruits in October and November.

To the preceding, written in 1934, it may be added that the tree at Fota still exists; it is 36 ft high and the thickest of its many stems is 4½ ft in girth (1966). According to the catalogue presented to Kew by the Hon. Mrs Bell, this tree was 20 ft high in 1856 and must therefore certainly date from the original introduction in 1825. At Mount Usher there are two specimens both 47 ft high and about 5 ft in girth. In Britain the easternmost garden where it is known to flourish is Highdown, near Worthing, where there is a tree 22 ft in height raised from Chinese seed imported in 1937. In the Edinburgh Botanic Garden there is a specimen of the same provenance, 14 ft high with a spread of 12 ft. Remarkably for a Himalayan species, *C. capitata* stands exposure to sea winds very well in the coastal gardens of the west and south-west.

C. CONTROVERSA Hemsl.

C. brachypoda Hort, not C. A. Mey.; *Swida controversa* (Hemsl.) Sojak

A deciduous tree 30 to 50 ft high, with horizontal branches produced in tiers; young shoots glabrous or soon becoming so, and soon dark coloured. Leaves alternate, ovate or oval, rounded or somewhat wedge-shaped at the base, narrowed abruptly to a slender point; glabrous and dark glossy green above; glaucous beneath, and at first furnished with flattened hairs attached by their centres; veins in usually six to eight, sometimes nine pairs; blades 3 to 6 in. long, 2 to 3 in. wide; stalk 1 to 2 in. long. Flowers white, about ½ in. diameter, produced in June and July numerously in flattish cymes 3 to 7 in. across. Fruit blue-black, globose, ¼ in. diameter. *Bot. Mag.*, t. 8464.

Native of Japan, whence the cultivated plants originated, also of China and the Himalaya. This small tree, so distinct from all other cornels except the North American *C. alternifolia* in its alternate leaves, is of very elegant habit. It sends its slender branches out horizontally, and they are produced in a group at the end of each season's growth. When of sufficient age, it flowers freely. In some soils the leaves turn purple before falling. Even in winter this tree is very striking owing to its rich-red young wood and regularly forked branches. A specimen at Westonbirt, Glos., measures 45 × 4¾ ft and there is a finer one at Nymans, Sussex.

cv. 'VARIEGATA'.—This form appears to have been introduced by Veitch shortly before 1890 and was originally grown as *C. brachypoda variegata*. It has long, narrow, lanceolate leaves, rarely more than 1½ in. wide, often unequal-sided and more or less deformed, but strikingly variegated with an irregular, yellowish-white border; with the same elegant pose as the type. [PLATE 60

Although introduced around 1880 the name *C. controversa* was only given to it in 1909. Previously it had been known in England as "*C. brachypoda*", and on the continent as "*C. macrophylla*", in both cases erroneously, as these are synonymous terms for an opposite-leaved cornel (*C. macrophylla* Wall.—q.v.).

C. FLORIDA L.   FLOWERING DOGWOOD [PLATE 61
Cynoxylon floridum (L.) Raf. ex B. D. Jackson; *Benthamidia florida* Spach

A deciduous, wide-spreading, small tree 10 to 20 ft high in cultivation, but occasionally twice as high in some parts of its native habitat; young shoots soon becoming glabrous. Leaves opposite, broadly oval or ovate; 3 to 6 in. long, 1½ to 3 in. wide; rounded or tapered at the base, the apex with a short, abrupt, slender point; dark green and with scattered down above; pale, rather glaucous and downy beneath; stalk ¼ to ¾ in. long. Flowers insignificant, ¼ in. long, produced in a crowded head ½ in. across, green tipped with yellow. The real beauty of the plant is in the four bracts that form in autumn and enclose the flower-head during the winter, expanding in May. These bracts are inversely heart-shaped, the apex broad, rounded and notched, white, 1½ to 2 in. long, the whole forming a showy, corolla-like involucre 3 to 4 in. across, commonly called the 'flower'. *Bot. Mag.*, t. 526.

Native of the eastern United States, where it is generally distributed from Massachusetts southwards; introduced in the early part of the eighteenth century, and cultivated by Thos. Fairchild in his nursery at Hoxton in 1730. There is also evidence of its having been grown by Miller at Chelsea in 1739. Although really a very hardy shrub so far as its capability of supporting extreme cold is concerned, as is shown by its perfect health and robustness in the neigh-bourhood of Boston, Mass., it has never become generally cultivated in Britain. Through its susceptibility to spring frosts and the indifferent ripening of its wood in autumn, it is rarely seen in good health. It thrives best in south-eastern and eastern England in positions not subject to early autumn and late spring frosts; the damper, less sunny climate of the south-west does not suit it. After a fine summer the leaves change to glorious shades of red and crimson.

cv. 'CHEROKEE CHIEF'.—Bracts described as 'rich ruby-red'. Raised in the U.S.A. and patented in 1958.

cv. 'PENDULA'.—Branches rather stiffly pendulous. Meehan's nursery, Philadelphia, U.S.A., before 1880.

f. RUBRA (West.) Schelle—Bracts in some shade of pink or red. *Bot. Mag.*, t. 8315. Weston published this name (as var. *rubra*) in 1770, in reference to the wild red-bracted forms, of whose existence he was aware from American litera-ture (or from Miller's *Dictionary*). But there is no evidence that this form was cultivated in Britain until after 1889, in which year or thereabouts plants were received in Europe from Parsons of Flushing, New York (*Rev. Hort.*, 1894, p. 500). The variation in colouring shown by cultivated plants suggests, however, that there have been later introductions. Named clones are also available, of which one—'Cherokee Chief'—is mentioned above.

This form needs the same conditions as the type and, given them, flowers freely, though not as a young plant. There are several good specimens in the R.H.S. Garden at Wisley, up to 10 ft high.

cv. 'WHITE CLOUD'.—Bracts creamy white; said to be very floriferous. Raised in the U.S.A. and put into commerce there in 1948.

C. GLABRATA Benth.   WESTERN CORNEL
Swida glabrata (Benth.) Heller

A deciduous shrub up to 10 or 12 ft high, of bushy, densely twiggy habit; young shoots brown, glab**rous**. **Leaves** lanceolate, or narrowly oval, tapered at both ends; $1\frac{1}{4}$ to 3 in. long, $\frac{1}{8}$ to $1\frac{1}{4}$ in. wide; glossy green on both sides, and with minute, closely appressed hairs; slightly paler below; veins in three to five pairs; stalk slender, $\frac{1}{6}$ to $\frac{1}{2}$ in. long. Flowers dull white, in small cymes which are $1\frac{1}{4}$ in. or less in diameter. Fruit white or bluish white, $\frac{1}{5}$ in. wide.

Native of western N. America from Oregon to California. It has little beauty of flower, but is a neat-habited shrub of cheerful aspect, distinct in its small, abundant leaves, shining green on both sides. Introduced in 1894.

C. HEMSLEYI Schneid. & Wanger.
Swida hemsleyi (Schneid. & Wanger.) Sojak

A deciduous shrub up to 12 ft high or sometimes a small tree twice as tall; young shoots downy, becoming glabrous and red the second year. Leaves roundish-ovate; 2 to 3 in. long, 1 to 2 in. wide; rounded or slightly heart-shaped at the base, tapered abruptly at the apex to a short slender point; upper surface furnished with short stiff hairs, the lower one greyish white and covered with appressed hairs; midrib and veins darkened with rusty brown down; veins in six to eight pairs; stalk downy like the midrib, $\frac{1}{4}$ to $\frac{1}{2}$ in. long. Flowers small, white with blue anthers, in corymbs 2 to 3 in. across. Fruit globose, blue-black, $\frac{3}{16}$ in. wide.

Native of Hupeh, Szechwan, and other provinces of China. It is one of a crowd of similar cornels with small white flowers. The dark down on the midrib and veins is distinctive. Wilson found a tree 25 ft high with a trunk 1 ft in diameter. Flowers in July.

C. HESSEI Koehne
Swida hessei (Koehne) Sojak

A dwarf, very compact, slow-growing, deciduous shrub; dense in habit and apparently not likely to exceed 2 ft in height. Leaves opposite, crowded, oval-lanceolate, wedge-shaped at the base, slender pointed; 1 to $2\frac{1}{2}$ in. long, about one-third as wide; very dark, almost black-green above, glaucous beneath, both surfaces with flattened hairs; veins in three to five pairs. Flowers pinkish white, produced the summer through in cymes 1½ in. across. Fruit dingy bluish white, flattened globose, scarcely ¼ in. wide.

The native country of this very distinct little shrub does not appear to be known, but it is probably from N.E. Asia. It is quite unlike any other cornel in its dense, very leafy, compact habit and curiously dark foliage. It arose in Hesse's nurseries in a batch of crataegus seedlings raised from seed which they had received from the St Petersburg Botanic Garden.

C. KOUSA Hance [PLATE 58

Benthamia japonica Sieb. & Zucc.; *Dendrobenthamia kousa* (Hance) Hutch.; *Benthamidia japonica* (Sieb. & Zucc.) Hara

A deciduous shrub or small tree up to 20 ft in height, of bushy habit; young shoots glabrous. Leaves ovate sometimes broadly so with a slender point and wedge-shaped or rounded base, 1½ to 3 in. long, ¾ to 1¾ in. wide; margin undulated; both surfaces have minute, scattered hairs at first, becoming glabrous except for brown tufts in the vein-axils; stalk ⅛ to ¼ in. long. Flowers small and inconspicuous, produced in a round, button-like mass ⅜ in. across. The beauty of the shrub, as in *C. florida* and *C. nuttallii*, is in the bracts that accompany the inflorescence. These are four in number, lanceolate, slender-pointed, spreading; 1 to 2 in. long, ½ to ¾ in. wide; creamy white. The main-stalk is slender, glabrous, 2 to 2½ in. long. Fruit fleshy, strawberry-like in shape.

CORNUS KOUSA

Native of Japan, Korea, and Central China. The bracts and flowers are borne freely in May and June on short, lateral spurs at the end of a small two- or four-leaved twig and stand up erect in rows along the branches; they have a very striking and beautiful effect. Of the species that owe their beauty to their large showy bracts as distinct from the true flowers, this is the most promising for our climate. It is only likely to be confused in gardens with *C. florida*, its East American ally, but its long slender-pointed bracts readily distinguish it. Botanically it is more nearly allied to *C. capitata*, as is shown by the agglomerated fruits.

var. CHINENSIS Osborn—This variety was introduced from Hupeh, China, by Wilson in 1907 and plants were first received at Kew from the Arnold Arboretum in 1910. There does not seem to be any clear botanical distinction between it and the typical Japanese tree, but under cultivation it grows more freely and its flowers are larger than those of any form introduced from Japan. Both Henry and Wilson found it as a tree 30 ft high and the former notes that its fruit is sweet and edible. It blossoms in June, the petal-like bracts being lanceolate, 1½ to 2½ in. long, ¾ to 1 in. wide, at first green, gradually changing to pure white; they remain in good condition for several weeks, becoming creamy white and brownish in the end. As explained above, the true flowers are crowded in a button-like mass surrounded by four of these large white bracts. It blooms in great profusion, the horizontally growing branches being almost hidden by the erect inflorescences, on stalks from 2 to 3 in. long. The bracts evidently vary in shape on wild trees. A specimen collected by Wilson in Hupeh has them 2 in. long by 1⅝ in. wide. *Bot. Mag.*, t. 8833.

This beautiful flowering tree should be in every garden, being perfectly hardy, growing well in a rich, well-drained, loamy soil and blossoming at a season when most hardy trees and shrubs are out of flower. On account of its moderate size it is particularly suitable for small gardens or confined spaces. It should, however, have an at least moderately sunny place. Both the type and the variety, at least in some gardens, colour beautifully in the autumn; the red tinting of the leaves starts early and may last, increasing in brilliance, for a month before the leaves finally fall.

C. (*kousa* × *nuttallii*).—A self-sown seedling of *C. kousa*, which arose in the garden of N. G. Hadden, Porlock, Somerset, appears to be of this parentage.

C. MACROPHYLLA Wall.

C. brachypoda C. A. Mey.; *Swida macrophylla* (Wall.) Sojak

A deciduous tree 30 to 50 ft high; young shoots glabrous or nearly so. Leaves opposite, ovate to roundish or oblong, the base rounded or tapering, the apex with a slender, often tail-like point; 4 to 7 in. long, 2 to 3½ in. wide; bright green, and soon becoming glabrous above; glaucous beneath, and at first clothed with pale, flattened, minute hairs attached at their middle; veins in six to eight pairs; stalks ½ to 1¼ in. long. Flowers yellowish white, numerous, produced in terminal, somewhat rounded cymes 4 to 6 in. across; each flower ⅓ in. diameter; petals oblong; calyx minutely toothed, grey with minute down. Fruit globose, ¼ in. diameter, blue when ripe. Blossoms during July and August. *Bot. Mag.*, t. 8261.

Native of the Himalaya, whence it was introduced in 1827, China, and Japan. It is a handsome and striking small tree, chiefly noteworthy for its fine foliage;

the flowers, although profusely borne, are of too dull a white to be very effective. There was a tree approaching 40 ft in height in Coombe Wood nursery. Much confusion has existed between this species and *C. controversa* (q.v.).

C. MAS L.   CORNELIAN CHERRY
C. mascula L.

A deciduous shrub or small tree sometimes 25 ft high, of spreading, rather open habit; young branchlets covered with minute, flattened, greyish hairs. Leaves ovate, 1½ to 4 in. long, ¾ to 1½ in. wide (sometimes considerably larger on strong shoots); apex slender-pointed; base tapered or rounded; dark dull green, both surfaces furnished with centrally attached, flattened hairs; veins in three to five pairs; stalk ¼ in. or less long. Flowers ⅙ in. diameter, yellow, produced in February and March on the leafless stems in short-stalked umbels from the joints of the previous year's wood, each umbel about ¾ in. across, enclosed before opening in four downy, boat-shaped bracts. Fruit a bright red, oblong drupe ⅝ in. long, about ½ in. wide, indented at the apex, of good acid flavour. *Bot. Mag.*, t. 2675.

Native of Europe, cultivated for centuries in Britain. Before the introduction of the Japanese witch hazels the Cornelian cherry was the most effective of yellow-flowering shrubs in bloom as early as February. It is still one of the most valuable we have. As it is without foliage when in bloom, it is a great advantage if it can be associated with some evergreen, such as holly. The fruit is handsome, but not, in my experience, freely borne. The wood, although limited in quantity, has considerable value because of its tough, hard, durable nature. It was formerly, if not now, much used on the continent for small articles in domestic use. The fruit also used to be made into a rob (syrup) or preserve. The following varieties are in cultivation:

cv. 'AUREA ELEGANTISSIMA'.—Leaves prettily variegated, having a wide unequal border of yellow, some entirely yellow; others tinged with pink. This was given an F.C.C. when shown by Lee of Hammersmith in 1872 and probably originated with them.

f. NANA (Carr.) Schneid.—When he published the name var. *nana*, Carrière included under it two clones: one, making a small spherical bush, derived from a yellow-fruited form of the species; the other, similar in habit, had stouter shoots clad with short hairs and tinged red, especially near the leaf insertions.

cv. 'VARIEGATA'.—Similar to 'Aurea Elegantissima', but with creamy-white variegation.

There are also forms with yellow, purplish and white fruits, but these are not of much interest in this country, where the tree is shy-fruiting.

C. OFFICINALIS Sieb. & Zucc., is closely allied to *C. mas*; a Japanese and Korean species, it is seldom seen in gardens. It has the same yellow flowers and red fruits, but it differs in having in addition to the flat hairs attached by their centres, conspicuous patches of dense, rusty-coloured down beneath the leaves, in and near the vein-axils. It has also two additional (five to seven) pairs of veins to each leaf. When in flower it is not distinguishable from *C. mas*, except that the habit is perhaps coarser. It is occasionally 30 ft high in Japan.

C. CHINENSIS Wanger.—This is another E. Asiatic relative of *C. mas*, common in Central and S. China, collected several times by Henry. It is distinguished from *C. officinalis* by the whitish-grey indumentum of the under-surface of the leaves and from both species by its longer, more tapered sepals and the black fruits. For the late Frank Kingdon Ward, this species always called to memory the great Assam earthquake of 1950. Collecting near Rima, where the Tsargpo emerges from the Himalaya, his attention was caught by a dogwood that resembled *Cornus mas* but was 'taller, with a smooth, palm-like stem and much larger mops, composed of more numerous flowers, of a luminous sulphur-yellow'. A few days later the hillside on which he was camping was thrown into the river by the shock of the earthquake and he barely escaped with his life. However, seed of the Rima dogwood was collected and of the six plants raised, one survived and is the parent of those now in cultivation. The finest and best known specimen grows in the Temperate House at the Savill Gardens, where it has assumed the aspect of a tree of some tropical rain-forest, with leaves a foot long. Kingdon Ward's introduction is certainly tender, but worthy of trial in the milder and moister parts of the country.   [PLATE 59

C. MONBEIGII Hemsl.
Swida monbeigii (Hemsl.) Sojak

A deciduous shrub 12 to 20 ft high; young stems brown and at first furnished with scattered down, afterwards glabrous. Leaves opposite, varying from elliptic-ovate to orbicular-ovate, heart-shaped or rounded at the base, contracted to a slender point at the apex; 2½ to 4 in. long, 1¼ to 3½ in. wide; dull green and softly downy above, grey-white with a thicker softer down beneath; veins reddish, in six to nine pairs; stalk ½ to ¾ in. long. Flowers produced in June in a terminal cymose inflorescence 3 to 5 in. across, branched mostly thrice; each flower is about ½ in. wide; petals oblong-lanceolate, pointed; the flower-stalks, calyx, and outside the petals very downy. Fruit black, globose, ¼ in. wide.

Native of Yunnan, where it was discovered by Père Monbeig; introduced by Forrest from the Mekong–Salween divide in 1917. It is one of a large group of cornels of no particular merit from a garden point of view and is perhaps, better suited for thin woodland rather than the garden proper.

C. NUTTALLII Audubon   PACIFIC DOGWOOD
Cynoxylon nuttallii (Audubon) Shafer; *Benthamidia nuttallii* (Audubon) Moldenke

A deciduous tree up to 50 ft high, rarely 80 to 100 ft in a wild state, but often a shrub; young shoots minutely downy, becoming glabrous. Leaves oval or obovate, tapered at the base, short-pointed, 3 to 5 in. long, 1½ to 3 in. wide; downy on both sides, especially beneath; veins in five or six pairs; stalk ¼ to ½ in. long. Flowers very small, crowded into a dense head ¾ in. across, purple and green; surrounding them is a whorl of four to eight, commonly six, showy bracts which make what is commonly termed the 'flower'. These bracts are roundish oval or obovate, pointed, and from 1½ to 3 in. long, 1 to 2 in. wide, at first creamy, then white flushed with pink. The flower-head is formed the previous autumn, and is not enclosed by the bracts during winter, as in *C. florida*, but remains exposed, expanding with the bracts in May. *Bot. Mag.*, t. 8311.

Native of western N. America, where it is one of the most beautiful of flowering trees. In autumn, too, it is said to light up the forest by the yellow and scarlet of its decaying leaves. It is undoubtedly the noblest of the cornels, its 'flowers' sometimes 6 in. across; unfortunately it is not perfectly adapted to the colder parts of Great Britain, but succeeds in the southern counties. It flowers regularly every summer at Kew, but is not long-lived there. From many other gardens, even where the climate is more favourable than at Kew, there are reports that this species, while apparently in full vigour, suddenly deteriorates and eventually dies, although no more than twenty years or so planted. Perhaps the best proof that it is not well adapted to our climate is that no specimens remotely comparable to those of native trees have been recorded, although it was introduced a century and a quarter ago. This is no reason for not planting it, for it flowers well when quite young. But unless a better form is introduced, it is a species that must be counted as short-lived in British gardens.

C. nuttallii is variable in size of leaf and size of 'flower'. The leaves are generally from 2⅖ to 5 in. long and 1⅕ to 3⅗ in. wide, but a form is known with leaves 3⅘ to 7 in. long and 1⅗ to 3⅗ in. wide. The inflorescence ('flower') varies from 3⅕ to 6⅕ in. across.

C. OBLONGA Wall.

Swida oblonga (Wall.) Sojak

An evergreen shrub or small tree 10 to 20 ft high, with angular, very downy young shoots. Leaves opposite, narrowly oval, wedge-shaped at the base, slenderly pointed, entire; 1½ to 5 in. long, ½ to 1¾ in. wide; dark glossy green and clothed with appressed hairs above, dull grey beneath and downy, especially on the midrib; stalk ¼ to ¾ in. long, covered with the same yellowish-brown down that occurs on the young shoots and midrib of the leaves; veins five or six each side the midrib. Flowers white, in a terminal pyramidal panicle 3 in. high and wide, scented; each blossom is about ⅙ in. wide; flower-stalks and calyx downy. Fruit described as ovoid, ⅓ in. long.

Native of the Himalaya, Khasia Hills, Szechwan and Yunnan in China. It was originally described by Wallich in 1820 from Indian material. Henry discovered it in the two Chinese provinces mentioned. Although it is described by Loudon and said by him to have been introduced in 1818, it is very uncommon in cultivation now. It was grown by the late Lord Wakehurst at Wakehurst Place in Sussex, and it is from a flowering specimen he sent to me in October 1921 that the description given above was made. He had obtained his plant from Veitch's nursery at Coombe Wood some eight years previously, so that it had very probably been introduced by Wilson during his early journeys for that firm. The plant was 10 ft high and perfectly healthy in April 1931. A plant of similar size bloomed at Lanarth, December 1934.

This species must now be very rare in gardens. The specimen at Wakehurst mentioned above no longer exists and the one at Lanarth has not been traced.

C. OCCIDENTALIS Cov.

C. pubescens Nutt., not Willd. ex Schultes

A deciduous shrub 6 to 18 ft high in a wild state, with glabrous, purple branches. Leaves opposite, narrowly oval or ovate, $1\frac{1}{2}$ to 4 in. long, $\frac{3}{4}$ to 2 in. wide, tapered or somewhat rounded at the base, blunt or pointed, rarely slender at the apex; dark green and slightly hairy above; pale and woolly beneath. Flowers yellowish, crowded densely in compact, rounded, downy cymes about 2 in. across. Fruit white.

Native of British Columbia south to California; introduced in 1874. It blossoms towards the end of May and in June, and is pretty then. It is also distinct in its dark purplish branches and in its leaves, woolly beneath. It is allied to *C. stolonifera* and not easy to distinguish from it, owing to the existence of natural hybrids (or perhaps intermediates) between the two (see below).

C. × CALIFORNICA C. A. Mey. *C. torreyi* S. Wats.—According to Rickett in *North American Flora*, Vol. 28B, p. 305, much of the material hitherto placed under *C. pubescens* Nutt. and *C. torreyi* S. Wats. represents hybrids between *C. occidentalis* and *C. stolonifera*. It should be noted, however, that neither Jepson nor Rehder recognised the existence of these hybrids. The former (*Fl. Calif.*, Vol. 2, 1936, p. 677) treated *C. occidentalis* under the name *C. californica* C. A. Mey., and remarked that the intermediates (as he considered them to be) between this species and *C. stolonifera* made it difficult to draw a line between them. His suggestion that *C. californica* might best be treated as a variety of *C. stolonifera* was taken up by McMinn, who published the combination *C. stolonifera* var. *californica* (C. A. Mey.) McMinn.

C. PAUCINERVIS Hance

Swida paucinervis (Hance) Sojak

A deciduous shrub 6 ft or more high; young shoots angular, with very minute appressed hairs at first, becoming glabrous. Leaves narrowly oval; tapering about equally towards both ends; $1\frac{1}{2}$ to 4 in. long, $\frac{1}{2}$ to $1\frac{3}{4}$ in. wide with two or three pairs of prominent longitudinal veins, both surfaces covered with minute appressed hairs. Flowers white, $\frac{1}{3}$ in. across, produced in rounded hairy corymbs $2\frac{1}{2}$ to $3\frac{1}{2}$ in. across. Fruits black, globose, $\frac{1}{4}$ in. wide. The most distinctive character of this species is the narrow shape and few veins of its firm-textured leaves. The chief veins originate in pairs from the lower part of the midrib, and after curving outwards bend inwards again towards the top of the leaf. The shrub is pretty, and useful in flowering in late July and August. *Bot. Mag.*, t. 9197.

Native of W. and Central China; introduced by Wilson in 1907. It first flowered with the late Hon. Vicary Gibbs at Aldenham, in 1911.

C. RACEMOSA Lam.

C. candidissima Marsh.; *C. paniculata* L'Hérit.; *Swida racemosa* (Lam.) Moldenke

A much-branched, deciduous shrub 8 or 10 ft high, of bushy habit, with greyish bark; young shoots glabrous. Leaves opposite, ovate-lanceolate, wedge-shaped at the base, long and slender pointed, 1½ to 3½ in. long, half as wide; dark green above, pale or whitish beneath; both surfaces at first furnished with flattened, minute hairs, which largely fall away by autumn; veins in three or four pairs. Flowers small, white, borne in great profusion in June and July, in short cymose panicles about 2 in. wide, terminating every twig. Fruit white, roundish, but depressed at the top, ¼ in. diameter; the stalks bright red.

Native of the eastern and central United States; introduced in 1758. As a latish flowering shrub this cornel has much to recommend it, for it is usually laden with blossom shortly after midsummer. Unfortunately it does not set its fruit here with the freedom that makes it so attractive in the United States. It is neater and less rampant in growth than those of the *alba* and *stolonifera* groups.

Between *C. racemosa* and *C. obliqua* (see under *C. amomum*) there is a hybrid called C. × ARNOLDIANA Rehd. It originated in the Arnold Arboretum about the end of last century. Compared with *racemosa*, it is of more spreading habit; the year-old branches are purple; inflorescence less elongated; leaf downy beneath; fruit bluish. Introduced in 1907. (Sargent's *Trees and Shrubs*, t. 40).

C. STRICTA Lam. is closely related to *C. racemosa*, and has similar foliage. It differs in having purplish or reddish-brown twigs, and pale blue fruits. Native of the eastern U.S.A. from Virginia southwards; sometimes 16 ft high. *C. foemina* Mill. is an ambiguous name which has been used both for this species and for *C. racemosa*.

C. RUGOSA Lam.

C. circinata L'Hérit.; *Swida rugosa* (Lam.) Rydb.

A deciduous shrub 6 to 10 ft high, sometimes single-stemmed and like a small tree; young shoots green, warted, becoming purplish. Leaves roundish, inclined to ovate, abruptly pointed; 2½ to 5 in. long, nearly as wide; almost glabrous above, but covered beneath with a dense greyish wool; veins in six to eight pairs; stalk about ½ in. long. Flowers white, in slightly downy cymes 2 to 3 in. diameter. Fruit pale blue, about ¼ in. diameter.

Native of E. Canada and the United States; introduced in 1784. This species is very rarely seen in English gardens; but as I saw it, covered with flower in the Arnold Arboretum about mid-June, it was quite ornamental and had assumed the form of a miniature tree. Among the swarm of North American cornels this can be distinguished by its almost orbicular leaves, very downy beneath.

C. × SLAVINII Rehd., is a hybrid between *C. rugosa* and *C. stolonifera*, first noticed in Seneca Park, Rochester, New York, near the gorge of the Genesee River. The leaves are woolly beneath, and the young wood is purplish as in

C. rugosa, but the habit is more that of *C. stolonifera*, only more upright. Fruit bluish, rarely white. Leaves intermediate in shape. (See *Rhodora*, Vol. 12, p. 111.)

C. SANGUINEA L.   COMMON DOGWOOD
Swida sanguinea (L.) Opiz; *Thelycrania sanguinea* (L.) Fourret

A deciduous shrub 6 to 12 ft high, of erect habit; young shoots minutely downy, dull dark green. Leaves ovate, 1½ to 3 in. long, ¾ to 1¾ in. wide; tapered and rounded at the base, slender-pointed, furnished, especially when young, with pale scattered hairs on both surfaces, which are longer beneath than above; veins in three or four, sometimes five pairs; stalks ⅛ to ½ in. long. Flowers dull white, with a heavy odour, produced densely during June in downy cymes 1½ to 2 in. across; sepals and flower-stalks downy; petals about ¼ in. long. Fruit globose, purplish black, shining, ¼ in. wide, with a bitter taste.

Native of Europe, including the south of England, where it is abundant in some localities. It is a shrub of undistinguished character, its chief value being in the fine autumnal red of its leaves. The specific name applies to this and not to the young bark, which has nothing more than an occasional dark red tinge on the exposed side. The wood is tough and hard, and is used for making butchers' skewers and such like.

f. VIRIDISSIMA (Dieck) Schelle—Young stems green, remaining so the first winter; occurs wild with the type.

Variegated forms have been known since the eighteenth century, but none is of any garden value.

C. SESSILIS Torr.

Little is known in cultivation of this North Californian shrub, which in a wild state is 10 to 15 ft high, and was introduced in 1903. The young bark is greenish, and clothed with silky hairs; leaves shortly stalked, crowded at the end of the twigs; 1½ to 3 in. long, ovate, tapered at both ends, but more gradually towards the apex; nearly glabrous above, and with flattened hairs and tufts of down in the vein-axils beneath; veins in about four pairs. Flowers ¼ in. across, yellow, crowded in stalkless umbels, at first enclosed by four ovate bracts ⅓ in. long; flower-stalks silky, ⅓ in. long. Fruit oval, ½ in. long, dark purple. This shrub, producing its flowers, themselves stalked, in clusters without stalks, from the axils of four bracts and on leafless twigs, belongs to the same group as *C. mas* and *C. officinalis*.

C. STOLONIFERA Michx.   RED OSIER DOGWOOD
C. alba of many authors, not L.; *Swida stolonifera* (Michx.) Rydb.; *Thelycrania stolonifera* (Michx.) Pojark.

A vigorous deciduous shrub up to 8 ft high, suckering freely, and spreading by underground stems; bark of young shoots dark purplish red, glabrous. Leaves ovate, oval or oval-lanceolate, with long, tapered points; 2 to 5 in. long,

1 to 2½ in. wide; upper surface dark green, lower one glaucous, both with flattened hairs; veins in about five pairs; stalk ½ to 1 in. long. Flowers dull white, small, in cymes 1 to 2 in. across. Fruit white, globose, ⅕ in. across.

Native of N. America, reaching across the continent. It is closely allied to the Eurosiberian species C. alba and by some authors regarded as a subspecies of it. It differs in its stoloniferous habit, more abruptly pointed leaves, and in the stones of the fruits, which are as broad as high, and rounded at the base.

cv. 'FLAVIRAMEA'.—Bark of young shoots greenish yellow, and effective in winter, especially if associated with C. alba 'Sibirica'. Sent out by Späth in 1899.

C. WALTERI Wanger.

C. wilsoniana Hort., not Wanger.; Swida walteri (Wanger.) Sojak

A deciduous tree up to 35 or 40 ft high; young shoots finely downy at first only. Leaves oval, tapered at both ends, slender-pointed; 2 to 4½ in long, 1¼ to 2 in. wide; the dark green upper surface has fine appressed hairs, but they are much more abundant on the lower surface; veins in three to five pairs; stalk up to 1 in. long. Flowers ⅜ in. wide, white, produced during June in corymbs about 3 in. wide; style club-shaped; fruit globose, ¼ in. wide, black.

Native of Central and W. China; introduced by Wilson in 1907 under his number 1017. Without any special distinctiveness it is interesting as a tree cornel. It flowered and developed fruit at Abbotsbury, near Weymouth, in 1919. There is a specimen measuring 40 × 3 ft at Spetchley Park, Worcs., and another in the R.H.S. Garden, Wisley, about 25 ft high (1967).

COROKIA   CORNACEAE

A genus of four or five species of evergreen shrubs confined to New Zealand. They have alternate entire leaves and small yellow flowers; petals and stamens five. They are more or less tender and at Kew need wall protection but in milder climates, such as mid-Sussex and farther south and west, they make attractive features in the open ground. *Corokia* is adapted from the Maori name 'Korokia'.

C. BUDDLEIOIDES A. Cunn.

An evergreen shrub 6 to 8 ft high; young shoots slender and covered with a close, greyish-white felt which persists the second year. Leaves linear-lanceolate, tapering usually to a long, finely pointed apex, more abruptly tapered at the base; 1½ to 5 in. long, 3⁄16 to ⅝ in. wide; dark shining green and ultimately glabrous above, clothed beneath with a silvery white felt similar to that on the young shoots; stalk ⅛ to ¼ in. long. Flowers ½ in. wide, star-like in shape, produced during May on panicles 1 to 2 in. long that terminate short lateral shoots.

TS—AA

Petals five, bright yellow, downy outside, nearly $\frac{1}{4}$ in. long, $\frac{1}{16}$ in. wide, pointed; calyx small, top-shaped at the base with five pointed lobes, green covered with white down; stamens yellow. Each petal has a fringed appendage at the base. Fruit globose, blackish red, $\frac{1}{3}$ in. wide, covering the stone thinly. *Bot. Mag.*, t. 9019.

Native of the North Island of New Zealand; discovered by Allan Cunningham on the shore of the Bay of Islands in 1826. This species is very distinct amongst the corokias by reason of its slender, willow-like leaves and terminal panicles of flowers. Coming from the northern part of New Zealand, it is not so hardy as the better known *C. cotoneaster*. Still it succeeds in the warmer parts of the south and south-west.

C. COTONEASTER Raoul

A remarkable evergreen, but sparsely leaved shrub up to 8 ft in height forming a rounded bush; branches thin, exceedingly tortuous and interlaced

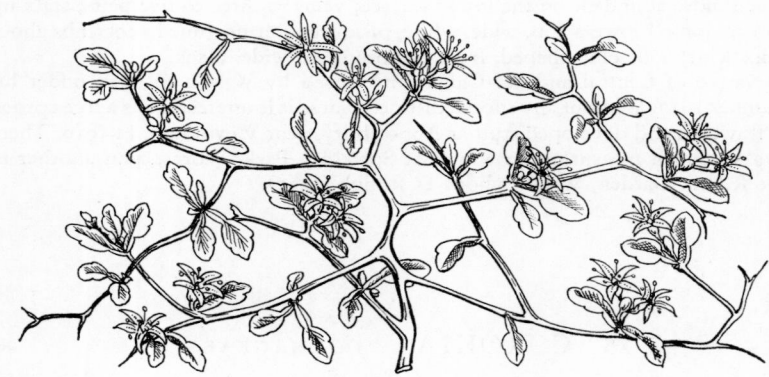

COROKIA COTONEASTER

somewhat rigid, and covered with white down when young, becoming almost black with age. Leaves alternate, $\frac{1}{2}$ to $\frac{3}{4}$ in. long (including the broad, flat stalk), roundish ovate or obovate, $\frac{1}{4}$ to $\frac{1}{2}$ in. wide, glabrous, and dark green above, covered beneath with a white felt. Flowers star-shaped, bright yellow, $\frac{1}{2}$ in. across, short-stalked, solitary, or as many as four in the leaf-axils; petals five, narrowly linear, pointed, silky at the back; calyx silky white, with five short, ovate lobes. Fruit red, round or oblong, $\frac{1}{4}$ to $\frac{1}{3}$ in. long. *Bot. Mag.*, t. 8425.

Native of New Zealand; introduced about 1875. At Kew this curious shrub needs the protection of a wall, where it thrives very well, and where its contorted branches, thin entangled twigs, and tiny spoon-shaped leaves are a perennial source of interest to visitors. It blossoms in May, and although not showy is decidedly pretty and interesting. The fruits have ripened in the vicarage garden at Bitton, and in shape and colour are not unlike small Cornelian cherries. At Castlewellan in Northern Ireland it has made a bush 8 ft high and 20 yds in circumference. With protection from cold winds it is hardy enough to be grown in the open ground except in the coldest parts of the country.

C. MACROCARPA T. Kirk

An evergreen shrub up to 20 ft high; young shoots stiffer and stouter than in the other species and, like the under-surface of the leaves and the flower-stalks, covered with silvery white felt. Leaves narrowly oval or oblong-lanceolate, tapered towards both ends; 2 to 4 in. long, ½ to 1 in. wide, rather leathery. Flowers yellow, ⅓ to ½ in. wide, produced in racemes ½ to 1½ in. long from the leaf-axils; petals narrow oblong. Fruit ⅓ in. long, broadish oblong, red. *Bot. Mag.*, t. 9168.

Native of, and confined to, Chatham Island. It is distinct from the other large-leaved species, *C. buddleioides*, in its axillary racemes of flowers and blunter-ended leaves. It has been grown, and flowered well, at both Wakehurst Place and Highdown, Sussex, but is not cultivated in either garden at present and must be reckoned as definitely tender.

C. VIRGATA Turrill

An evergreen shrub of twiggy, diffuse habit, probably 10 to 15 ft high; shoots slightly zigzagged, but not tortuous nor interlaced as in *C. cotoneaster*; clothed with a close white down when young. Leaves oblanceolate or rather spoon-shaped, tapered more abruptly to the pointed or rounded apex than at the slender base; ¼ to 1¾ in. long, ⅛ to ⅔ in. wide; dark glossy green and at first hairy above but soon nearly or quite glabrous, pure white beneath with closely appressed down; stalks never more than ⅛ in. long. Flowers borne during May in threes at or near the ends of the shoots; main-stalk ¼ in. long; individual stalks $\frac{1}{12}$ in. long, white like the under-surface of the leaves. Petals five, yellow, spreading, pointed, about ⅕ in. long; calyx funnel-shaped with five small triangular teeth, white outside; stamens five, alternate with the petals. Fruit an orange-yellow, egg-shaped berry ¼ in. long. *Bot. Mag.*, t. 8466.

Native of New Zealand; first described from a plant obtained by Kew in 1907 and grown in the Temperate House. It had been raised from a cutting sent from the office of the *Gardeners' Chronicle*. The species is on the border line of hardiness at Kew. Some fine bushes, 6 ft and upwards high, growing in a sheltered spot, bore fine crops of the orange-yellow fruit in 1928. They were cut to the ground during the ensuing hard winter, but broke into growth again from the base freely enough in 1929. Messrs Cheal of Crawley have informed me that it withstands hard winters there with comparatively little injury. Its white slender twigs and graceful form are very pleasing. Easily distinguished from the other three species by the size and shape of its leaves and its yellow fruits.

It is now considered that *C. virgata* is a hybrid between *C. buddleioides* and *C. cotoneaster*. These species cross readily in the wild wherever they grow together and plants are found in these hybrid swarms which match *C. virgata* fairly closely (Allan in *Flora of N.Z.*, 1961, p. 442). C. CHEESEMANII Carse is also a wild hybrid of the same parentage.

CORONILLA   LEGUMINOSAE

A genus of shrubs and herbaceous plants, two of the former being hardy in Britain and others half hardy. The distinctive features of the genus are the pinnate leaves, the umbellate arrangement of the pea-shaped flowers, the long-clawed petals, and the curious seed-pods. The last are slender, round, and separated into several one-seeded compartments defined by a constriction of the pod. The two hardy species are of easy cultivation liking a moderately rich, well-drained, loamy soil and a sunny position. They are propagated by cuttings, which may be struck either in a soft condition (when bottom heat should be given) or later, when the growths are more woody, under a bell-glass, in a cold frame.

C. EMEROIDES Boiss.

A deciduous shrub 4 or 5 ft high, with angled branches. Leaves in two opposite rows, pinnate, composed usually of seven leaflets; leaflets obovate, ¼ to ¾ in. long, with a few appressed hairs or quite glabrous. Flowers borne in an umbel at the end of a stalk 2 to 3 in. long, with from four to eight (more often five) flowers in the umbel; each flower ½ to ¾ in. long. Petals yellow, with a long claw; calyx ⅛ in. long, cup-shaped. Pod 2 to 3 in. long, slender, round and jointed, each segment containing one seed.

Native of Greece, Crete, and other parts of S. E. Europe, also Syria. It is nearly allied and very similar to the well-known *C. emerus*, in habit, leaf, colour and shape of flower. But it is distinguished by having seven instead of nine as the usual number of leaflets, by its longer-stalked umbels, and by the more numerous flowers in each. It commences to flower in May or June, and continues for several months.

C. EMERUS L.   SCORPION SENNA

A deciduous shrub 7 to 9 ft high, and as much through, of elegant habit. Branchlets angled, grooved, and glabrous. Leaves 1 to 2½ in. long, alternate, pinnate, distichous, composed usually of seven or nine leaflets, which are obovate, ⅓ to ¾ in. long, slightly downy when young. Flowers borne on slender stalks, 1 to 2 in. long, springing from the leaf-axils, and carrying not more than three flowers at the top. These are yellow, ¾ in. long, and distinct on account of the long claw to each petal; the standard petal has a reddish-brown line down the back. Pods 2 in. long, very slender, round, and jointed into several portions, each portion containing one seed. *Bot. Mag.*, t. 445.

Native of Central and S. Europe; cultivated in England for more than three centuries. This is a very pleasing, graceful hardy shrub, which begins to flower in May and continues until October. The popular name refers to the slender articulated seed-pod, which is compared to a scorpion's tail. It is very abundant, as an undergrowth in thin woodland, in some places along the French and Italian Riviera.

C. GLAUCA L. [PLATE 62

An evergreen shrub of dense habit and bushy, rounded form, up to 10 ft high; young shoots, leaves and inflorescence glabrous. Leaves very glaucous, pinnate, 1 to 1½ in. long, composed of five or seven leaflets, which are obovate, rounded or even indented at the apex, tapering to the base, shortly or not at all stalked; ¼ to ⅝ in. long. Stipules very small, awl-shaped. Flowers ½ in. long, rich yellow, borne as many as ten together in a dense umbellate cluster at the end of a common stalk 1 to 2 in. long; standard petal roundish, ½ in. long; individual flower-stalks scarcely ¼ in. long. Calyx cup-shaped with shallow triangular lobes. Pod 1½ in. long, ending in a slender tail, constricted between the three or four seeds. *Bot. Mag.*, t. 13.

Native of S. Europe; introduced in 1722. Although it suffers during hard winters, even against a wall, this shrub will usually survive in many parts of Britain with wall protection, even in Essex and Suffolk. In the winter of 1962–3 it was killed almost everywhere: in the previous winter, also a testing one, it was also killed or damaged in many gardens but quite unharmed at Kew. At Highdown near Worthing it is grown fully in the open and seeds itself freely. The flowers are fragrant in the daytime, but scentless at night; they are produced most freely from April to June, but in the south-west it flowers from late autumn onwards also. It requires full sunshine and grows well in a light, loamy soil.

cv. 'PYGMAEA'.—A very charming dwarf form of neat habit and rounded shape, usually 1½ to 2 ft high, flowering very freely in autumn.

There is also a pretty variegated form, not quite so hardy as the type.

C. JUNCEA L.

A curious shrub 2 to 3 ft high, with round, rush-like, somewhat hollow, zigzag, much-forked branches. Leaves ¾ to 1½ in. long, pinnate, composed of five or seven leaflets, which are narrow, oblong, ¼ to ½ in. long, the common stalk flattened. Flowers yellow, ⅓ in. long, arranged in often globose umbels produced from the leaf-axils, each umbel carrying six to twelve flowers. Seed-pods very slender, about 1 in. long.

Native of S. Europe; introduced, according to Aiton, in 1656, but always rare on account of its tenderness. It has succeeded against a wall in the Cambridge Botanic Garden, but except in some such warm corner its tenure is precarious.

C. VALENTINA L.
C. stipularis Lam.

An evergreen shrub 3 or 4 ft (perhaps more) high; young shoots, leaves and inflorescence glabrous. Leaves pinnate, 1¼ to 2 in. long, having usually seven, nine, or eleven leaflets, which are wedge-shaped, tapering from the broad truncate apex (which has a tiny mucro) to a very short stalk; ¼ to ¾ in. long,

¼ to ⅜ in. wide; bright green above, rather glaucous beneath. Flowers fragrant, borne in an umbellate cluster ten to fourteen together at the end of a common stalk that is 3 in. or more long; they are rich bright yellow, each about ½ in. long. Pod slender, curved, 1 to 1½ in. long, three- to six-seeded and constricted in the usual way between each seed. *Bot. Mag.*, t. 185.

Native of Spain eastwards to Dalmatia where I have seen it growing wild near Spalato (Split); cultivated in England in 1596. It is nearly related to *C. glauca* and is apparently much confused with it. *C. valentina* is the dwarfer shrub and the leaves have more (as many as eleven) leaflets. The stipules are markedly different, being rarely more than ⅛ in. long, narrow and pointed in *glauca*, whilst in *valentina* they are roundish or kidney-shaped and ¼ to ½ in. wide; young growing shoots are best for observing these differences as the stipules fall away later. It is on these large stipules that Lamarck's name (given above) was based. It flowers from May to July and is a most floriferous and charmingly fragrant bush, but not quite so hardy as *glauca*.

CORREA   RUTACEAE

A beautiful genus of about seven species of evergreen shrubs, natives of Australia and Tasmania. The showy flowers are borne singly or two to three together; calyx cup-shaped, truncate or toothed; petals four, more or less united into a bell-shaped or cylindrical tube; stamens eight. Fruit dry, splitting into four dehiscent parts. Forms of the very variable *C. reflexa* (*speciosa*) were once popular as pot plants for the cool greenhouse, all very tender. The species described here are not the showiest of the genus, but are perhaps hardier than the others.

C. BACKHOUSIANA Hook.

A densely branched shrub, attaining a height of 15 ft in the wild state, less in cultivation; branchlets greyish brown, slender, clad when young with stellate hairs. Leaves opposite, ovate-elliptic, rounded or blunt at the apex, rounded or slightly cordate at the base, ⅗ to 1⅖ in. long, margin entire, very dark green above, densely clad below with rust-coloured down; leaf-stalks ⅕ to ⅓ in. long. Flowers solitary or in few-flowered cymes, more or less pendulous; calyx cup-shaped, with the rim level all round or with four very shallow teeth; petals greenish yellow, rather thick, united into a funnel-shaped corolla about 1 in. long, with acute lobes; stamens eight, protruding beyond the mouth of the corolla; the four stamens inserted opposite the lobes have the filaments widened in the lower half, while in the other four they are of almost equal width throughout their length. *Bot. Mag.*, n.s., t. 289.

Native of Tasmania on the north and west coasts. It thrives very well at Tresco Abbey in the Isles of Scilly, where it is used as a hedging-plant, and has also been grown in other mild gardens, usually as "*C. speciosa*" or "*C. virens*".

It is closely allied to *C. reflexa* (*speciosa*) but the densely downy undersides of the leaves distinguish it.

C. LAWRENCIANA Hook.—This species, a native of Tasmania and Victoria, closely approaches the preceding in some of its forms, but may always be distinguished by the stamens, all eight of which are alike (cf. the description of *C. backhousiana* above). Being a montane species it is likely to prove hardier than the other Tasmanian correas. At Brodick Castle in the Isle of Arran it thrives very well; a plant 8 ft high and 6 ft across was damaged in a gale and removed in the spring of 1965, but young replacements are already flowering freely (1967).

CORYLOPSIS   HAMAMELIDACEAE

A small genus of deciduous shrubs and small trees from N.E. Asia with bristle-toothed leaves resembling those of the hazel (*Corylus*), hence the name. The flowers are pale (sometimes greenish) yellow, produced on the leafless shoots in short, pendent racemes; they are usually fragrant. The parts of the flower are in fives. Leaves alternate, plaited in the bud state, veins parallel, strong, proceeding from the midrib at an acute angle. Fruit a woody capsule. From its hardy allies—*Hamamelis* and *Parrotia*—the genus is very distinct. The raceme on which the flowers are borne is really a short branch. At the base there are a few thin, membranous, bract-like organs, which are not accompanied by flowers, but from the axils of which a leaf is developed after the flowers farther along the raceme have faded. By the time the seed vessels are ripe these leaves are fully developed. Seeds in all the known species black.

As garden shrubs the species of *Corylopsis* are not in the very first rank; at the same time the flowers have a soft beauty of their own, and they are among the earliest to open in spring. *C. spicata* was the first of the genus to be introduced and the best known, but others of more recent introduction are just as hardy if properly sited, and more graceful.

C. GLABRESCENS Franch. & Sav.

C. gotoana Mak.

A deciduous shrub up to 15 or 18 ft high, or even a small tree; young shoots brown, quite glabrous and slender. Leaves roundish ovate or obovate, short-pointed, more or less heart-shaped at the base, bristle-toothed; 2 to 4 in. long, $1\frac{1}{4}$ to 3 in. wide; slightly glaucous and with a few silky hairs beneath; stalks up to $\frac{3}{4}$ in. long; veins in seven to eleven pairs. Flowers pale yellow, fragrant, borne on drooping racemes 1 to $1\frac{1}{2}$ in. long in April; bracts boat-shaped, silky inside; flower-stalk glabrous; petals $\frac{1}{3}$ in. long, obovate; seed-vessel $\frac{1}{4}$ in. wide.

Native of the mountains of Japan; introduced to N. America in 1905 and to Kew in 1916. Rehder describes it as the hardiest in the genus, but most of the

Japanese and Chinese species are quite hardy in this country, except that the flowers and young shoots are liable to injury by late spring frosts. It produces its racemes freely enough, but, in comparison with most of the species, these are rather small and not so ornamental. Its distinctive combination of characters are the almost entire absence of down or hairs, the short racemes carrying eight to twelve flowers, and the petals being longer than broad. Although *C. gotoana* Mak. is given above as a synonym of *C. glabrescens* and is usually considered as such, it is maintained as a separate species by Ohwi in his *Flora of Japan* (1965). The distinctions he makes are:

C. glabrescens.—Leaves ovate-orbicular, with prominently awn-tipped teeth. Stamens about half as long as petals. Confined to Kyushu.

C. gotoana.—Leaves obovate to obovate-orbicular, with shortly awned teeth. Stamens nearly as long as petals. Main and southern islands.

If this distinction is made, the cultivated plants would probably be referable to *C. gotoana*.

C. GRIFFITHII Hemsl.

A shrub with very downy young wood. Leaves 3 to 4½ in. long, 2 to 3 in. wide, broadly ovate or roundish, more or less heart-shaped at the base, long-pointed, toothed; upper surface pale green, not downy, lower one downy, especially on veins and midrib; stalk 1 to 1½ in. long. Flowers pale primrose-yellow, very closely packed on pendulous spikes, 1½ to 2½ in. long, ¾ in. wide; basal bracts very thin, silky inside, oblong, ½ to 1 in. long, those of the flowers much smaller and silky both sides; anthers purplish red. *Bot. Mag.*, t. 6779.

Native of the Himalaya; introduced to Kew in 1879. One of the most orna-mental of *Corylopsis*, this is, unfortunately, not hardy enough to succeed without wall protection. It may be recommended for the south-western counties.

C. PAUCIFLORA Sieb. & Zucc.

A shrub of spreading habit 4 to 6 ft high; branches slender, glabrous. Leaves more or less broadly ovate, heart-shaped at the base, acutely pointed; 1½ to 3 in. long, 1 to 2 in. wide; with a few bristle-like teeth, glabrous and bright green above, somewhat silky beneath on the veins and margins; stalk slender, ⅓ to ¾ in. long. Flowers primrose-yellow, about ¾ in. across, produced two, sometimes three together on short spikes; basal bracts of spike pale green, thin, hairy inside. *Bot. Mag.*, t. 7736.

Native of Japan; introduced by Messrs Veitch. Although the spikes of this charming little shrub are shorter and fewer-flowered than in *C. spicata* and other species, the blossom itself is larger, more open, and more beautiful. The plant itself is not so hardy as *C. spicata*, and I have known it destroyed by severe cold; owing to its early growth also, spring frosts frequently pinch the young shoots. But given a cool, moist position, where it is protected from searing winds and late frost, it is quite hardy and grows quickly, flowering unfailingly every year. It delights in close woodland conditions and is intolerant of excessive sun, which stunts the plant and burns the edges of the leaves. Where well suited, there is no more delightful March-flowering shrub but unfortunately it does not thrive on chalky soils. It differs from the other hardy species in its large, open corollas and few-flowered inflorescence.

C. PLATYPETALA Rehd. & Wils.

A shrub said to reach 8 ft or so in the wild (but considerably more in cultivation), with slender branches and of erect habit; young shoots glandular-hairy at first, later glabrous. Leaves ovate to broadly ovate, more or less cordate at the base, shortly acuminate at the apex, up to 4 in. long, slightly silky-hairy when young, soon glabrous, dark green above and somewhat glaucous beneath; margins set with small bristle-like teeth; leaf-stalks slightly glandular. Flowers pale yellow, fragrant, in racemes 1 to 2 in. long, composed of eight to twenty flowers; bracts oblong, concave, clad with long hairs; calyx glabrous; petals hatchet-shaped, the blade being broader than long and clawed at the base; staminodes emarginate or truncate at the apex.

Native of W. China in the province of Hupeh; discovered by Wilson and introduced by him in 1907. The var. LEVIS Rehd. & Wils., introduced by Wilson in 1908 from W. Szechwan, differs chiefly in having the young growths and flower-stalks free of glands; mature growths brown.

This is a quite hardy species and has attained a considerable size in cultivation: there is a fine specimen at Trewithen in Cornwall, 20 ft high and 10 ft across; at Furzey near Lyndhurst, in the New Forest, it is even taller. If grown in full sun, the leaves of this species develop a glaucous, waxy bloom. It is allied to *C. willmottiae*, but in that species the staminodes are always deeply notched at the apex and the leaves downy beneath.

C. YUNNANENSIS Diels—This species was introduced by Forrest from the Lichiang Range of Yunnan, China, in 1906. It is allied to the preceding, but is not glandular in any part. Leaves downy on the veins beneath. Petals with an orbicular or obovate blade; calyx-lobes edged with fine hairs and slightly downy on the outside.

C. SINENSIS Hemsl.   [PLATE 63

A shrub 10 to 15 ft high in a wild state; young shoots downy and (like the leaf-stalks) more or less glandular. Leaves obovate-oblong, 2 to 3½ in. long, abruptly pointed, heart-shaped at the base, toothed, silky-felted beneath; stalk ¼ to ¾ in. long, very downy. Flowers pale primrose-yellow, fragrant, produced twelve to eighteen together during April in a drooping raceme 1½ to 2 in. long, each flower ⅓ in. long; petals orbicular, ⅙ in. diameter; anthers yellow; calyx greenish yellow with short rounded lobes; stipular bracts broader than long, concave, silky inside and at the margins, glabrous outside, yellow-green; floral bracts hairy both sides. Fruits globose, ⅓ in. diameter, hairy.

Native of Central and W. China; introduced by Wilson for Messrs Veitch about 1901. It appears to be closely allied to *C. griffithii*, but differs in the basal bracts of the inflorescence being broader and shorter, and in the yellow anthers.

C. spicata has differently shaped leaves, much more glaucous, and broadest below the middle. *C. sinensis* is quite hardy. At Coombe Wood (Kingston-on-Thames) it used to grow vigorously and flowered regularly in April.

C. SPICATA Sieb. & Zucc.

A wide-spreading bush up to 6 ft high, with crooked, flexible branches, clothed with silky down when young. Leaves broadly heart-shaped, pointed; 3 to 4 in. long, 2 to 3 in. wide; edged with minute bristle-like teeth; dull pale green above, glaucous and downy beneath; stalks woolly, $\frac{1}{2}$ to 1 in. long. Flowers yellow, six to twelve appearing on a drooping spike, the main stalk of which is very woolly, produced in March and April from the naked shoots of the previous summer. The base of the spike is occupied by several large, yellowish-green, ovate bracts, silky inside; on the terminal portion of the spike the bracts are much smaller, and in the axil of each one is a stalkless flower. Petals obovate, $\frac{1}{3}$ to $\frac{1}{2}$ in. long. Seed-vessels downy, top-shaped, $\frac{1}{3}$ in. long. *Bot. Mag.*, t. 5458.

Native of Japan; introduced by Messrs Veitch about 1863. The quiet beauty of this shrub would perhaps be little noticed two months later in the year, but being one of the earliest to blossom and often at its best in March, it becomes particularly welcome, especially as the soft yellow of its flowers is accompanied by a charming cowslip-like fragrance. The shrub itself is quite hardy, but the flowers are damaged by inclement weather. This species has had the longest tenure in gardens and is the one commonly seen in the older collections. But it is scarcely so graceful a shrub as more recently introduced species such as *C. willmottiae*, nor so suited to the small garden as *C. pauciflora*.

C. VEITCHIANA Bean

A shrub 5 to 6 ft high, of rounded, bushy habit; young shoots quite glabrous, reddish. Leaves oval or ovate, with a heart-shaped base; contracted at the apex to a short, slender point; 2 to 4 in. long, 1$\frac{1}{2}$ to 2 in. wide; purplish and sparingly silky-hairy beneath when young, somewhat glaucous and perfectly glabrous when fully grown; veins in six or seven pairs, the lowest pair giving off four to six nerves outwards; stalk about $\frac{1}{3}$ in. long. Flowers fragrant, primrose-yellow, produced in a nodding spike 1 to 2 in. long, $\frac{3}{4}$ in. wide. Basal bracts glabrous outside; floral bracts hairy outside. Anthers red-brown, distinctly protruded. Calyx-lobes short, rounded, hairy. Fruit at first densely hairy, about $\frac{1}{3}$ in. long. *Bot. Mag.*, t. 8349.

Introduced in 1900 by Wilson from Western Hupeh, China, and first raised in the Coombe Wood nursery. It flowers regularly in April but the blossoms are liable to be injured by late frosts. From *C. sinensis* it differs in its glabrous leaves and protruded red-brown anthers.

C. WILLMOTTIAE Rehd. & Wils.   [PLATE 64

A deciduous shrub 6 to 12 ft high; young shoots brown, not downy, but with numerous small lenticels; winter buds pale shining green, stalked. Leaves 2 to

4 in. long, oval, obovate or roundish ovate; truncate or slightly heart-shaped at the base, short-pointed; dark bright green and glabrous above; rather glaucous beneath and downy, especially on the midrib and veins; veins in seven to ten pairs. Flowers soft greenish yellow and fragrant. Calyx, ovary, and fruit glabrous. Seeds shining black. *Bot. Mag.*, n.s., t. 438.

Native of W. Szechwan, China; introduced by Wilson in 1909; first shown in flower at the Horticultural Hall, 5th March 1912, as "*C. multiflora*". The true plant of that name does not appear to be in cultivation. It was given an Award

CORYLOPSIS VEITCHIANA

of Merit on that occasion and an F.C.C. in 1965, when shown from Borde Hill, Sussex. A graceful and very floriferous species. It is allied to *C. sinensis* and some plants so labelled in gardens may be *C. willmottiae*. However, in that species the young branchlets are downy and the leaf-stalks densely so. See also *C. platypetala*.

C. WILSONII Hemsl.

A shrub or small tree, the branchlets at first furnished with stellate down. Leaves ovate or obovate; 3 to 5 in. long, 1¼ to 3 in. wide; abruptly contracted at the apex to a long narrow point, the base heart-shaped, the margin edged with bristle-like teeth; glaucous beneath, and glabrous on both sides when mature; stalk ¾ to 1¼ in. long. Flower-spike 2 to 3 in. long, the basal or stipular bracts roundish ovate, ¾ in. long, silky-hairy on both sides; flower bracts similar except for being smaller. Petals ¼ in. long, narrowly obovate, primrose-yellow. Fruits not downy.

Discovered in Central China and introduced to the Coombe Wood nursery in 1900. It differs from all other cultivated corylopsis in having the lower bracts hairy outside. In many other respects it resembles *C. veitchiana*.

CORYLUS   CORYLACEAE

The hazels are well-marked deciduous trees and shrubs, with alternate, toothed leaves. Male and female flowers are borne on the same plant. The pendulous male catkins are borne in clusters of two to five; each scale subtends a single flower with four to eight bifid stamens and two bracts. Female inflorescences bud-like, the upper scales each subtending a partial inflorescence of two flowers, each with a bract and two bractlets; ovary surmounted by two free styles, only the red tips of which protrude at flowering time. Fruit a nut, surrounded by a leafy involucre made up of the much enlarged bract and bractlets.

In gardens the hazels are chiefly known as bearing edible nuts, viz., cobnuts and filberts. The common species have not much to attract planters for ornament alone, although in February when they are freely hung with the graceful, slender, yellow, male catkins, they have that charm in great degree which even the humblest flower possesses to some extent at that early season. The female flowers, too, sometimes give a quite effective red haze in sunshine. *C. colurna* is a handsome tree, and the newer *C. chinensis* is of similar although possibly not so robust habit. *C. cornuta* and *C. sieboldiana* var. *mandschurica* have remarkable fruits. The attention of those who admire purple shrubs may be directed to *C. maxima* 'Purpurea'.

They all thrive well in a loamy soil, and are very suitable for chalky districts. The sorts grown for their fruit are most fertile on soil of moderate quality. In this country *C. colurna* needs some attention to ensure the formation of a good clean trunk by watching, and, if necessary, training up the leading shoot, and removing lower branches and suckers. As to propagation, most of the hardy sorts can be increased by taking off the suckers; if these do not form, layering should be adopted, and for the genuine species seed is usually obtainable. They bear transplanting well.

The species of *Corylus* are very much alike in leaf, and are best distinguished by habit and by the form of the husk.

C. AMERICANA Walt.

A shrub up to 8 or 10 ft high; young shoots glandular-hairy. Leaves broadly oval or ovate to roundish, coarsely, irregularly, or doubly toothed, heart-shaped or rounded at the base, pointed; 2 to 5 in. long, 1½ to 3½ in. wide; upper surface with scattered hairs, downy beneath; stalk ⅙ to ½ in. long, glandular-hairy. Male catkins 1½ to 3 in. long. Nut roundish, egg-shaped, about ½ in. long, slightly flattened and set in a husk (involucre), which is nearly double its length, downy, much and deeply toothed.

Native of eastern N. America; introduced in 1798. The American hazel is very similar in habit to *C. avellana*, but does not grow so high in this country. It is readily distinguished from it in fruit by the involucre being so much longer.

Compared with *C. avellana*, it is of no value as a nut-bearer in this country, and is scarcely needed except for botanical collections.

C. AVELLANA L.   HAZEL or COBNUT

A shrub 12 to 20 ft high, sometimes with the habit of a small tree, but usually forming a dense thicket of erect, much-branched stems, renewing itself by sucker growths from the base; young shoots glandular-downy. Leaves roundish or obovate, heart-shaped at the base, 2 to 4 in. long, 1½ to 3 in. wide; the lower half irregularly toothed, the terminal half often shallowly lobed as well as toothed; downy on both surfaces, but especially beneath; stalk glandular-hairy, ¼ to ½ in. long. Male catkins 1½ to 2½ in. long. Nut ¾ in. long, set in a husk about or scarcely as long as itself, the margins of which are cut into shallow, often toothed lobes.

Native of Europe (including Britain), W. Asia, and N. Africa. This is the hazel whose nuts are among those commonly eaten for dessert. It is really a shrub for the woodland rather than the garden, and on many properties a brake of it is grown for the sake of the nuts. In autumn, the hazel frequently turns a soft pleasing yellow, but its chief attraction as an ornamental shrub is in the abundance and earliness of its male catkins. These form in the autumn, and remain as short, dark, cylindrical bodies all the winter. About mid-February the anthers burst, and they then become a soft yellow; at that time a bush well in flower makes an attractive picture. The branches of the hazel are extremely supple, and on this account the shrub was in earlier times much used to form the pleached alleys or shaded walks in the vicinity of the old chateaux of France. The pliancy of hazel rods renders them useful for various purposes, such as hoops for crates, etc. The twigs are used by water-diviners. There are several varieties of hazel, most of them grown for the qualities of the nut. Those of interest as ornamental shrubs are as follows:

cv. 'AUREA'.—Leaves a poor yellow.

cv. 'CONTORTA'.—Twigs remarkably curled and twisted. This curious form was discovered about 1863, in a hedgerow at Frocester, in Gloucestershire (*Gard. Chron.*, 29th Sept. 1894, p. 380).

cv. 'FUSCO-RUBRA'.—This is of more recent origin than the purple variety of *C. maxima* and is not so coarse a grower. The purple of the leaves is not so heavy and dark. The name adopted here is preferable to "purpurea", since the *C. avellana* var. *purpurea* of Loudon is in fact the purple-leaved form of *C. maxima*.

cv. 'HETEROPHYLLA'.—Leaves smaller and more downy than in the type, and of oval outline. Their most distinctive character, and one which renders them very pretty, is the deep lobing all round the blade. These lobes are triangular and penetrate about one-third of the distance to the midrib, being themselves sharply toothed. In naming this form it is assumed that it belongs to the clone distributed by Loddiges' nursery around 1836 and described by Loudon (*Arb. et Frut. Brit.*, p. 2017).

cv. 'PENDULA'.—A weeping variety which, trained up to form a trunk or grafted high, makes a pretty small tree. It was introduced from France by Bull's nursery in 1869.

C. CHINENSIS Franch.   CHINESE HAZEL

C. colurna var. *chinensis* (Franch.) Burk.

Nearly allied to the Turkish hazel (*C. colurna*), this species may be distinguished by its darker-coloured, much more persistently glandular-downy young shoots, leaf-stalks, and midrib; by the leaf-margins being more finely and evenly toothed (not lobed as in *C. colurna*); and by the base being more unequally, if not so deeply heart-shaped. It was introduced by Wilson about 1900 from Hupeh, China, to the Coombe Wood nursery. Wilson told me he saw it up to 120 ft high in a wild state, and Henry several times collected it in Hupeh and Szechwan. It bore fruit for the first time at Kew in 1922; husk glabrous except for some minute down, constricted above the nut into a short recurved beak ¼ to ½ in. long, irregularly toothed at the end. Entire husk bottle-shaped, 1½ in. long, 1 in. wide. The leaves are up to 6 or 7 in. long, with as many as thirteen pairs of primary veins, downy on the veins beneath. The best specimens recorded in the British Isles are: Hergest Croft, Heref., 53 × 4¼ ft (1963), and Mount Usher, Co. Wicklow, Eire, 56 × 4½ ft (1966).

C. COLURNA L.   TURKISH HAZEL

A tree up to 70 or 80 ft high, with a trunk sometimes 7 ft or more in girth, covered with pale scaling bark; young shoots yellowish at first, glandular downy.

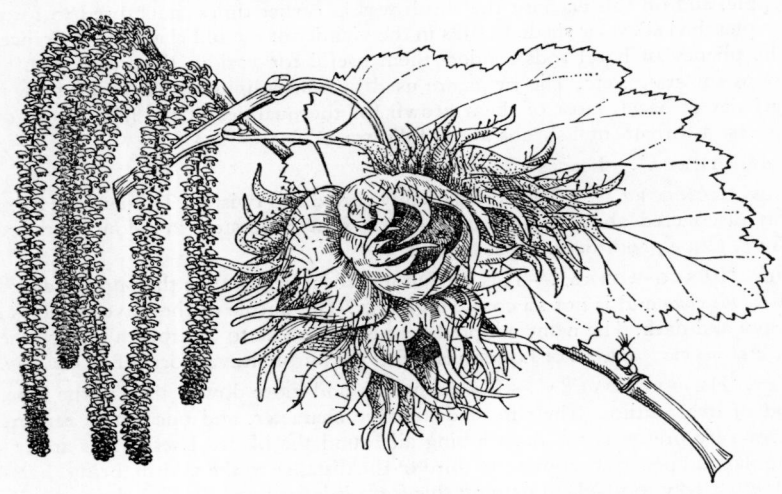

CORYLUS COLURNA

Leaves 2½ to 6 in. long, 2 to 4½ in. wide; broadly oval, obovate or ovate, pointed (sometimes abruptly) at the apex, heart-shaped at the base, coarsely double-toothed or almost lobed; upper side dark green, lower one downy along the midrib and veins; stalk ½ to 1 in. long, glandular-downy at first, afterwards glabrous. Male catkins 2 to 3 in. long. Nuts ½ to ⅝ in. diameter, the husk (involucre) in which it is set 1½ in. across, fringed with numerous narrow pointed lobes ½ to 1 in. long, covered with a fine down freely mixed with which are gland-tipped bristles. The nuts are closely clustered three or more together. *Bot. Mag.*, t. 9469.

Native of S.E. Europe and Asia Minor; introduced to England about the middle of the sixteenth century. There are some fine specimens in old English gardens, notably at Syon House, near Brentford, where there is an old specimen measuring 60 × 9¼ ft (1967). Others recorded recently are: Bicton, Devon, 55 × 11¼ ft at 1½ ft (1959); Oxford Parks, 58 × 8¼ ft (1965); Wakehurst Place, Sussex, 48 × 3½ ft and 45 × 3 ft (1964–5); Cambridge Botanic Garden, 45 ft with a spread of 66 ft (1967); Edinburgh Botanic Garden, 61 × 5¾ ft (1968).

The tree is well worth growing for its stately form, so remarkable for a hazel, and for its curiously enveloped nuts. It thrives very well in the hot summers and cold winters of Central Europe, and there usually has a short trunk with the bottom branches touching the ground, the whole tree forming a lofty pyramid. There are trees of this character at Schönbrunn, near Vienna. The height of these, 70 to 80 ft when this work was first published in 1914, is now over 100 ft. The tree in the Berggarten near Hanover, also mentioned in previous editions, died recently; the skeleton, which has been left *in situ*, shows a well-developed central stem with main branches springing from the base and almost equal to it in thickness.

C. JACQUEMONTII Decne. *C. lacera* Wall.—This is the Himalayan representative of *C. colurna*. It differs from that species chiefly in the husk of the nut having few or no glandular bristles mixed with the down, and in the leaves being more distinctly obovate and sharply lobed and toothed. It thrives well at Kew, where there is a specimen measuring 44 × 4½ ft (1960), which frequently bears good seed. Fruiting and flowering sprays from this tree are figured in *Bot. Mag.*, n.s., t. 391.

C. CORNUTA Marsh.
C. rostrata Ait.

A shrub 4 to 8 ft high, with erect, much-branched stems and slightly hairy young shoots. Leaves ovate, oval or obovate, heart-shaped at the base, usually pointed at the apex, closely and unevenly toothed, sometimes slightly lobed; 1½ to 4½ in. long, 1 to 3 in. wide; upper surface with scattered hairs at first, becoming glabrous; lower surface permanently downy on the midrib and veins; stalk ⅓ to ½ in. long. Male catkin 1 to 1¼ in. long. Nut about ½ in. long, the husk covered with a fine down mixed with which are numerous bristly hairs, the apex extended into a slender beak 1 to 1¼ in. beyond the nut.

Native of the eastern and central United States; introduced in 1745 by the then Duke of Argyll. It is rare in cultivation and has no value as a nut-bearing bush, but the long, drawn-out husk covered with bristles makes it interesting.

var. CALIFORNICA (A. DC.) Sharp *C. rostrata* var. *californica* A. DC.—

This differs chiefly in having the leaves more downy beneath, and the beak of the involucre shorter. Native of the western side of N. America.

C. HETEROPHYLLA Trautv.

A shrub or small tree up to 20 ft high; young shoots and leaf-stalks glandular-hairy. Leaves 2 to 4 in. long, variously shaped, often obovate, broadest near the apex, where they are cut off straight with the exception of a short, abrupt point; base often narrowed, always heart-shaped; unevenly toothed, often slightly lobed; downy beneath, especially on the midrib and veins. Nuts usually solitary or in pairs; the husk $\frac{3}{4}$ to 1 in. long, downy on the margin, cut into large triangular teeth $\frac{1}{6}$ to $\frac{1}{4}$ in. deep.

Native of Japan and China, where it appears to represent *C. avellana*, just as *C. americana* does in the New World. It is recognisable in fruit by the more regularly toothed husk. The leaves do not differ much, and some of identical shape are to be found on both species, but those of *C. avellana* are, in general, not so much lobed.

C. MAXIMA Mill.   FILBERT
C. tubulosa Willd.

A shrub of the same habit as *C. avellana*, but more robust, sometimes a tree 20 ft or more high; young shoots glandular-hairy. Leaves broadly obovate or roundish, heart-shaped at the base, usually with a short, slender, abrupt point; toothed all round the margin, doubly so on the upper half; 2 to 5 in. long, $1\frac{1}{2}$ to 4 in. wide; stalk glandular, $\frac{1}{4}$ to $\frac{1}{2}$ in. long. Male catkins 2 to 3 in. long. Nut ovate-oblong; the husk nearly twice the length of the nut, cut into numerous deep, narrow lobes.

Native of S. Europe, but not of Britain; introduced in 1759. It is the parent of the filberts of English orchards, distinguished from the hazel or cobnut by the husk protruding well beyond the nut, and quite enclosing and holding it. The nut itself is also longer and proportionately narrower. Several varieties are cultivated for their nuts, but the only one of an ornamental character worth mentioning is

cv. 'PURPUREA', whose leaves are of a dark purple. One of the most robust and effective shrubs of this colour. The catkins also are purple. *Bot. Mag.*, n.s., t. 268.

C. SIEBOLDIANA Blume

The hazel described in previous editions as *C. mandshurica* is now considered to be a variety of *C. sieboldiana*, viz.:

var. MANDSHURICA (Maxim. & Rupr.) Schneid. *C. mandshurica* Maxim. & Rupr.—A shrub up to 12 or 15 ft high, its largest leaves 5 or 6 in. long and 4 in. wide; ordinarily 3 or 4 in. long, roundish obovate, heart-shaped at the base, pointed, the terminal part doubly toothed or even shallowly lobed; stalk $\frac{1}{2}$ to

1 in. long. Nut conical, ½ in. long, the husk covered with pale brown bristles as well as down, and drawn out at the apex into a slender beak protruding 1¼ to 1½ in. beyond the nut and quite enclosing it.

Native of Manchuria and N. China; it was introduced to Kew in 1882 by Dr Bretschneider, and about ten years later by Prof. Sargent. It is quite hardy, and has borne good crops of its remarkable and handsome fruits. These occur in pendent clusters of three or four, the bases touching and the long beaks standing out horizontally. During the summer the husk is prettily suffused with purple. It is closely allied to and may be regarded as the Asiatic representative of *C. cornuta*, differing chiefly in the more distinctly lobed terminal portion of the leaves, which are also longer stalked, rounder, and broader.

C. SIEBOLDIANA itself, a native of Japan, has the same bristly hairy husk, but considerably shorter than either, and protruding beyond the nut ¾ in. only. It came into cultivation in 1904.

C. TIBETICA Batal.

C. ferox var. *tibetica* (Batal.) Franch.

A tree said to be 15 to 20 ft high in the wild, shoots glabrous, dark brown. Leaves broadly obovate or ovate, 2 to 5 in. long, 1¼ to 3 in. wide; heart-shaped or rounded at the base, the apex abruptly slender-pointed, unequally and sharply toothed; upper surface with flattened hairs on and between the nerves when young; lower surface slightly glaucous with silky hairs on the midrib and veins; stalk ½ to 1 in. long, silky-hairy, glandular on the upper side. Male catkins 2 to 3 in. long. Nuts in clusters of three to six, the husks covered with slender branching spines, the whole cluster forming a prickly ball like that of a sweet chestnut.

Native of China, and apparently widely spread in the regions bordering Tibet; introduced by Wilson for Messrs Veitch in 1901, but obtained in France by Maurice de Vilmorin three years previously. Its most distinctive character among cultivated hazels is the prickly burs that enclose the nut clusters. In this respect it is closely similar to C. FEROX Wall., a Himalayan species with narrower, more oblong, longer pointed leaves and less spiny·burs. Perhaps more tender and not in cultivation. There is a fine specimen of *C. tibetica* in the Glasnevin Botanic Garden which makes a narrow spire 48 ft high, with a trunk 3¼ ft in girth (1966).

COTINUS   ANACARDIACEAE

A genus of two species long included in *Rhus*, from which they are easily distinguished by their simple leaves and by their fruiting panicles having long, thread-like, plumose 'stalks', which are in fact the elongated pedicels of sterile flowers. One species is from Europe and Asia; the other from eastern N. America.

C. COGGYGRIA Scop.   VENETIAN SUMACH [PLATE 65

Rhus cotinus L.

A deciduous shrub, up to 15 ft high, of round, bushy habit, and often considerably wider than it is high; the branchlets glabrous. Leaves simple, glabrous, orbicular or obovate, rounded or slightly notched at the apex; 1½ to 3 in. long, with well-marked parallel veins and a stalk about half the length of the blade. Panicles loose, terminal, much-branched, many of the thread-like, final ramifications bearing no flower but developing a large number of silky hairs. During July the whole inflorescence (6 to 8 or more inches long and wide) turns a pale flesh colour, afterwards a smoky grey. Flowers few and small; fruit dry, prominently veined, one-seeded, ¼ in. across.

Native of Middle and S. Europe, extending eastwards to the Himalaya and China. In the late summer few hardy shrubs are more striking and beautiful than this. It produces its inflorescences so abundantly that the entire plant becomes covered with a filmy pinkish envelope. The leaves remain long on the plant, turning yellow or red before they fall. The wood is yellowish, and a good yellow dye is obtained from the twigs. Several popular names have been given to it besides the one quoted above, such as 'smoke plant', 'burning bush', and 'wig-tree', all in allusion to the characteristic inflorescence. This shrub, like its American ally, does not require a very rich soil, as it then grows too much and gives little flower.

cv. 'FLAME'.—Autumn colour brilliant orange-red.

cv. 'FOLIIS PURPUREIS'.—Leaves purplish when young, later green or purplish green; inflorescence usually pink. An old form, the predecessor and parent of the modern purple-leaved cultivars. It was possibly a seed-strain rather than a clone.

cv. 'NOTCUTT'S VARIETY'.—A selection from 'Foliis Purpureis' raised by Messrs Notcutt of Woodbridge, Suffolk, in 1915 and given an Award of Merit in 1921. Leaves dark maroon-purple; inflorescence purplish pink. Also known as 'Foliis Purpureis Notcutt's Variety' and 'Rubrifolius'. It was given the Award of Garden Merit in 1930 under the incorrect name *Rhus cotinus foliis purpureis* (see above); the epithet *atropurpureus* has also been wrongly applied to this clone. One of the finest of purple-leaved shrubs.

f. PURPUREUS (Dupuy-Jamin) Rehd. *Rhus cotinus* var. *purpureus* Dupuy-Jamin; *Rhus cotinus* var. *atropurpurea* Burvenich—Inflorescence in some shade of purplish pink; leaves green. In naming this variant, Dupuy-Jamin remarked (*Rev. Hort.*, 1870, p. 567) that it occurred fairly frequently when the species was raised from seed.

cv. 'ROYAL PURPLE'.—Leaves darker purple than in 'Notcutt's Variety'; also known as 'Kromhout' after the raisers Messrs Kromhout of Boskoop, Holland.

C. OBOVATUS Raf.

Rhus cotinoides Nutt.; *Cotinus americanus* Nutt.

A deciduous shrub or small tree, as much as 30 ft high in a wild state, its trunk 1 ft or more in diameter; in this country usually under 15 ft high, the young vigorous shoots and leaves often reddish purple. Leaves simple, obovate or oval, varying much in size according to the age and vigour of the plant, but ordinarily 2 to 5 in. long, rather more than half as wide; tapering to the stalk (which is ½ to 1½ in. long), but broad and rounded at the apex. In the female plant the flowers are borne on a large, sparse, terminal panicle, 6 to 12 in. long, three-fourths as wide. The larger proportion of the final ramifications of the inflorescence do not carry a flower, but are mere thread-like stalks clothed with fine hairs. Fruit ⅛ in. long, very sparsely produced. The male plant has the inflorescence better set with flowers.

This remarkable species is found in a few isolated localities in Tennessee, Alabama, and other south-eastern United States, but is nowhere common. First discovered by Nuttall in 1819, it did not reach this country until 1882, when it was sent to Kew by Prof. Sargent. In the beauty of its inflorescences it is very much inferior to *Cotinus coggygria*, but, on the other hand, it is one of the loveliest of all shrubs in autumn, its leaves turning to various shades of scarlet, claret colour, and orange before they fall. Disappointment has sometimes been caused by the failure of this shrub to colour as described, but this is nearly always due, so far as I have seen, to over-generous conditions at the root. In order to bring out its best colour, it should not be grown in rich or manured soil, which renders the growth too rank and coarse. The spring foliage is of a beautiful pinkish bronze. In a wild state it is said to be in danger of extinction; many large specimens have been cut down for the dye obtained from the wood, especially during the Civil War in N. America.

It has been confused with *C. coggygria* but may be distinguished by the leaves, which are silky-downy beneath when young, more obovate in shape, and wedge-shaped at the base.

COTONEASTER ROSACEAE

A group of shrubs or occasionally trees, both deciduous and evergreen, found most abundantly in the cool temperate regions of N. Asia, especially in China and the Himalaya. Others occur in Europe, and one is British. *C. microphyllus* is naturalised on the chalk downs near Ventnor, Isle of Wight, also in the counties of Gloucester and Somerset. Seeing how fond birds are of the fruit, it is curious that more naturalised species have not been found. They are closely allied to the thorns (*Crataegus*), but are easily distinguished by the always entire, not toothed nor lobed leaves, and by having no spines. The flowers are very uniform in size and colour, being nearly always ⅛ to ½ in. in diameter, and either pure white or rose-tinted. They are borne in clusters of varying size, from those of some species that are 2 or 3 in. across, to others with only two or three flowers in the cluster; still others have solitary flowers. The flowering time is mostly in May and June. Whilst some species are very pretty then, the cotoneasters generally are not showy in blossom. Apart from habit and foliage their greatest attraction is in their fruit. In the handsomest sorts this is brilliant red; in others it is yellowish or brownish, and in a considerable number it is black. They are either globose, egg-shaped, or oval, and vary little in size, averaging about ¼ in. in diameter, and contain two to five nutlets, each consisting of a seed surrounded by the hardened inner wall of the carpel.

The genus *Cotoneaster* is divided into two well-marked sections:

Sect. CHAENOPETALUM.—Petals spreading, more or less orbicular. Here belong: *C. dammeri*; *C. frigidus* and its allies; *C. microphyllus* and its allies; *C. multiflorus*; *C. pannosus* and its allies, of which *C. lacteus* is the most important; *C. racemiflorus*; *C. salicifolius* and its allies.

Sect. COTONEASTER.—Petals upright, inconspicuous and often tinged with red. Here belong all the other species, but few are widely cultivated in this country, the best known being: *C. adpressus*; *C. bullatus*; *C. dielsianus*; *C. distichus*; *C. franchetii*; *C. horizontalis*; *C. simonsii*. This section is usually but incorrectly called *Orthopetalum*.

No shrubs are more easily cultivated than these. They thrive in any soil that is not marshy or water-logged, and are very well adapted for poor soils. They can be propagated quite easily from cuttings made of half-ripened wood about July, and placed in gentle heat. Seeds, too, are plentiful, and can be used, but it is not advisable to use them in some cases, especially where it is desirable that the parent plant, for its brightly coloured fruit or special habit and foliage, should be propagated unchanged. The old practice of grafting them on hawthorn is indefensible. The note on the germination of crataegus seed applies also to the cotoneasters, though the proportion of species with hard-coated seeds is smaller. For a detailed study see: *Contributions of the Boyce Thompson Institute*, Vol. 6, pp. 323–38 (1934).

FIREBLIGHT. This destructive bacterial disease, which attacks apples, pears and their allies (Rosaceae, subfamily Pomoideae), first made its appearance in south-eastern England in 1956. There is so far no reliable cure for it beyond eradicating the affected plants or cutting out the diseased parts as soon as the onset of the disease is observed. Thanks to the control measures taken the spread of the disease has been checked but if it once took hold very serious losses to fruit growers would result. A number of ornamental plants common in gardens are subject to Fireblight and may become foci of infection from which the disease is spread to neighbouring orchards and commercial plantations.

Of the genera treated in this volume the main sources of infection are *Cotoneaster* and *Crataegus* but the following are also subject to the disease: *Amelanchier*, *Aronia*, *Chaenomeles*, and *Cydonia*. It is not possible here to give full particulars of the symptoms by which Fireblight can be diagnosed but danger signs are: blackening of the flowers; shrivelling of the foliage combined with the formation of wet-looking brown tissue immediately below the surface of the bark. For further information see the note in the *Journal of the Royal Horticultural Society*, Vol. 93, June 1968, pp. 228–33, and the leaflet published by the Plant Health Branch of the Ministry of Agriculture. Fireblight is a notifiable disease and anyone suspecting its presence should notify the local Plant Health Inspector, either directly or through the branch office of the Ministry of Agriculture. Owners in the Greater London area should write direct to the Ministry at Great Westminster House, Horseferry Road, London, S.W.1.

Between the purely evergreen and the strictly deciduous kinds there are others in which the persistence of the foliage during winter depends upon circumstances. They will retain their leaves in mild winters or warm localities, but lose them where the cold is greater. Vigorous young plants and those growing in good soil will also retain their foliage longer. The taller species from their beauty in fruit, grace of habit, and vigorous constitution, are admirable constituents of the tall shrubbery, but they are still better as isolated specimens on the lawn or in groups in thin woodland. The smaller species make useful and handsome coverings for sloping, sunny banks, whilst the dwarfest of all are very well adapted for the rock garden.

A selection of the best species etc. would include:

Tall Shrubs.—*C. affinis* var. *bacillaris*, *bullatus*, 'Cornubia', *frigidus*, *glaucophyllus* f. *serotinus*, *henryanus*, *lacteus*, *moupinensis*, *multiflorus*, *racemiflorus* var. *soongoricus*, *simonsii*, × *watereri* 'John Waterer'.

Medium and Dwarf.—*C. adpressus* var. *praecox*, *conspicuus*, *distichus*, *horizontalis*, *microphyllus*.

For rock garden.—*C. adpressus*, *congestus*, *microphyllus* var. *thymifolius*.

As a ground carpet.—*C. dammeri* and 'Skogholm', 'Hybridus Pendulus', *salicifolius* (dwarf clones).

Cotoneaster is, for the taxonomist, a genus of great complexity, rivalling in this respect other genera of the Rose family such as *Crataegus*, *Rubus*, *Sorbus*. These difficulties are due in part to the proneness of the cotoneasters to the 'pseudo-sexual' method of reproduction known as apomixis, by which seed is set without fertilisation and without the re-shuffling of genes that takes place as a preliminary to normal seed production. This process allows individual variants and hybrids to 'breed true' and leads to the formation of microspecies which satisfy most definitions of the classical species of taxonomists and yet may differ one from the other by the most minute differential characters. The treatment of apomicts is a difficult and controversial problem and for this reason it was thought inadvisable to make much use in the present revision of the valuable and interesting studies published on the continent in recent years. The most important are those by Gerhard Klotz, who published in 1957 a general survey of cotoneasters in cultivation (*Wiss. Z. Univ. Halle, Math.-Nat.*, Vol. 6, pp. 945–82), and in 1963 two papers on new or critical species in the *C. microphyllus* and *racemiflorus* groups (ibid., Vol. 12, pp. 753–86); and by K. E. Flinck and B. Hylmö (A List of Series and Species in the Genus *Cotoneaster*, *Bot. Notiser*, 1966, Vol. 119, Fasc. 3). A more conservative study is: Tse-Tsun Yü, 'Cotoneasters from the Eastern Himalaya' (*Bull. Brit. Mus., Bot. Ser.*, Vol. 5, No. 5, 1954).

In previous editions of this work the name *Cotoneaster* was, following the general custom, treated as a feminine noun. However, Medicus, who first published the name after 1753 (the date from which botanical nomenclature commences), treated it as masculine and this is in accordance with its derivation from *cotone* (quince) and *-aster* (a suffix meaning inferior, imperfect, or wild as contrasted with cultivated). The nouns *pinaster* and *oleaster*, of similar, derivation, are both masculine. The change of gender has been adopted in all modern works, so there is no alternative but to follow suit in the present edition.

C. ACUMINATUS Lindl.

A deciduous shrub 10 to 14 ft high, of erect habit; young shoots thickly covered with a pale brown wool. Leaves ovate-lanceolate, 1 to 2 in. long, about half as wide, long-pointed, dark green and silky-hairy above when young, paler and more hairy beneath; stalk $\frac{1}{4}$ in. or less long. Flowers more or less pink, $\frac{3}{8}$ in. across, produced in small clusters of rarely more than five, often of two or three, on short leafy twigs. Fruit red, $\frac{1}{3}$ in. long, oblong, thickening towards the top; downy near the apex; nutlets two.

Native of the Himalaya, up to 12,000 ft; first raised in this country by Loddiges of Hackney in 1820. The species, which is not much grown in gardens now, is allied to *C. simonsii*, but differs in its much larger, longer-pointed leaves. According to Brandis it often occurs as underwood in oak forests.

C. ACUTIFOLIUS Turcz.

C. pekinensis Zab.

A deciduous shrub of bushy habit 5 to 10 ft high, branches often pendulous; young twigs downy. Leaves pointed, ovate-lanceolate to oval, 1 to 2½ in. long, half as wide; dull green, and with scattered hairs above, paler and hairy beneath especially when young; veins in five or six pairs; stalk $\frac{1}{12}$ to $\frac{1}{8}$ in. long. Flowers white, three or more together in corymbs; stalks and calyx woolly, lobes of calyx triangular. Fruit reddish at first, finally black, $\frac{1}{3}$ in. diameter, glabrous; nutlets usually two.

Native of Mongolia, N. and W. China and the E. Himalaya. This is not one of the handsomest of cotoneasters, and is, perhaps, a poor form of *C. lucidus* (q.v.). There has been much confusion between the two, owing to *C. lucidus* also having been called *C. acutifolius*; but from that species the present one is distinguished by its dull green, not shining, more hairy leaves, and its woolly calyx and flower-stalks.

var. VILLOSULUS Rehd. & Wils. *C. villosulus* (Rehd. & Wils.) Flinck & Hylmö—Young shoots clothed with yellowish-grey loose hairs, becoming glabrous and purplish brown the second year. Leaves 1½ to 4½ in. long, ½ to 2¼ in. wide, larger and more drawn-out at the apex than in the type. Petals rose-tinted white. Fruit roundish pear-shaped, $\frac{2}{5}$ in. long, woolly, ultimately shining black. Native of the region from W. China to the E. Himalaya; introduced by Wilson from W. Hupeh in 1900. A very vigorous shrub.

C. TENUIPES Rehd. & Wils.—This cotoneaster, which was introduced by
Wilson from W. Szechwan, China, bears a close resemblance to the preceding
variety, but differs in its smaller leaves ($\frac{3}{5}$ to $1\frac{1}{5}$ in. long, more densely hairy
beneath).

C. ADPRESSUS Bois

C. horizontalis var. *adpressus* (Bois) Schneid.

A very dwarf, close-growing, rigidly branched, deciduous shrub, scarcely
more than 1 or $1\frac{1}{2}$ ft high, but spreading over the ground several yards in extent;
the branches pressing on the soil and taking root there; twigs downy. Leaves in
two opposite rows or irregularly arranged, broadly ovate or obovate, $\frac{1}{4}$ to $\frac{5}{8}$ in.
long, dullish green and glabrous on both sides, except for a few scattered hairs
beneath, wavy-margined and somewhat scoop-shaped. Flowers solitary or in
pairs, scarcely stalked, each one produced in the centre of a fascicle of leaves

COTONEASTER ADPRESSUS

from the year-old wood; petals white tipped with rose, but little expanded.
Fruit $\frac{1}{4}$ in. long, roundish, bright red, nutlets usually two.

Native of China; introduced to France about 1895; first raised and grown by
Maurice de Vilmorin at Les Barres (Loiret), where the original plant grew to
9 ft across. It is remarkable for its short, rigid branches, and close, prostrate
habit. It resembles *C. horizontalis*, and by some writers is regarded as a variety
of that species, but in general appearance and habit is quite distinct from that
or any other species. It is a very pleasing plant for the rock garden, or a border
of choice shrubs.

C. adpressus was later introduced again from W. Szechwan and more recently
cotoneasters closely resembling it have been found in the E. Himalaya,
S.E. Tibet and Upper Burma.

var. PRAECOX (Vilm.) Bois & Berthault *C. praecox* Vilm.; *C. nanshan* Vilm.;

C. nanchuanicus Reg.—A more vigorous plant than the type, growing to 2 ft or so high; leaves ½ to 1 in. long. Fruits ⅓ to ½ in. long, ripe in August. A charming dwarf shrub, remarkable for its large fruits. It was introduced from Szechwan by one of the French missionaries and originally raised, like the type, at Les Barres.

C. AFFINIS Lindl.

A deciduous shrub to about 15 ft high. Young shoots downy at first, later glabrous. Leaves mostly two-ranked, obovate, oblanceolate to elliptic, about 1¼ to 3¼ in. long, ⅗ to 1⅘ in. wide, acute or blunt at the apex, dull green above, downy or woolly beneath when young but becoming glabrous; leaf-stalks ⅕ to ⅖ in. long, downy at first. Flowers white, borne numerously in cymose clusters 1 to 2 in. across at the end of short axillary branchlets; inflorescence densely hairy in all its parts, but becoming partly glabrous. Fruit roundish, dark purplish brown to almost black, about ¼ in. across.

Native of the Himalaya; introduced in 1828. *C. affinis* is allied to *C. frigidus*, but well distinguished by the colour of the fruits. It is rarer in cultivation than the following variety:

var. BACILLARIS (Lindl.) Schneid. *C. bacillaris* Lindl.—A deciduous shrub to 15 ft high. Branches arching and often pendulous towards the end, the whole forming a wide-spreading mass more in diameter than in height. Botanically it differs from the type only in the less hairy inflorescence and leaf-undersides. The leaves are very variable in shape. Native of the Himalaya up to 10,000 ft. This is one of the most useful of cotoneasters, and one of the most graceful. It has been largely planted on the margins of the islands of the lake at Kew, where the branches overhang the water and have the elegance of a willow, with the added attractions of abundant flowers and fruits. As a flowering shrub, this is one of the prettiest in the genus, but its fruits have not the bright colour that gives to many cotoneasters their greatest charm. The wood is strong and elastic, and is valued in its native regions for making walking-sticks and spear-shafts.

C. AMBIGUUS Rehd. & Wils.

A deciduous shrub up to 6 or 10 ft high; young shoots clothed with short hairs, some of which persist until the following year; buds very hairy. Leaves oval, ovate or diamond-shaped, tapering to a slender point, wedge-shaped at the base; 1 to 2 in. long, ⅓ to 1 in. wide; at first hairy, ultimately nearly glabrous above, densely woolly beneath; veins in usually four pairs; stalk ⅛ in. or less long, woolly. Flowers in corymbs, five to ten together, each about ¼ in. wide, white; calyx and flower-stalk slightly downy; petals roundish obovate, ⅙ in. long; stamens fifteen to twenty. Fruit jet-black, shining, globose, ⅓ in. wide, downy at the top, containing two or three (rarely four or five) nutlets. *Bot. Mag.*, t. 9106.

Native of W. Szechwan, China; discovered and introduced by Wilson in 1903 (Wilson–Veitch number 1723). This cotoneaster is most closely related to

C. acutifolius, which is easily distinguished by its much less downy leaves, but more downy calyx. It was obtained for Kew from the Coombe Wood nursery and is quite hardy and bears fruit freely. I do not consider it in the front rank of cotoneasters, but this and the other black-fruited species make pleasing undergrowth for thin woodland and encourage bird-life. Flowers in June.

C. AMOENUS Wils.

A densely branched evergreen bush of spreading habit 3 to 5 ft high; young shoots slender but rigid, felted with grey wool. Leaves oval or ovate, tapered about equally to both ends, terminated by a fine point; $\frac{1}{3}$ to $\frac{3}{4}$ in. long, $\frac{1}{4}$ to $\frac{2}{5}$ in. wide; glossy green and with loose hairs above, clothed beneath with a thick, greyish wool; veins in two to four pairs; stalks $\frac{1}{12}$ to $\frac{1}{8}$ in. long. Flowers white, $\frac{1}{5}$ in. wide, borne in six- to ten-flowered corymbs; petals roundish; stamens twenty; calyx woolly, with triangular-ovate teeth. Fruit bright red, roundish obovoid (broadest above the middle), $\frac{1}{4}$ in. long, packed in umbel-like clusters at the end of short twigs that have sprung from the growths of the previous year.

Native of S.E. Yunnan, China; introduced by Wilson in 1899 to the Coombe Wood nursery. It is most closely allied to *C. franchetii* among older species, but is dwarfer and stiffer in habit, the leaves smaller, the berries a richer red, especially on the exposed side.

This is one of the few species introduced by Wilson from Yunnan. Wilson had arrived in China for the first time in 1899 and before proceeding to Hupeh he paid a visit to Szemao in S. Yunnan to seek the advice and guidance of Augustine Henry, who was then stationed there. Seeds of *Cotoneaster amoenus* and *harrovianus*, and plants of *Jasminum primulinum*, were collected during this visit, which was a prelude to his many fruitful journeys in Hupeh and Szechwan.

C. APICULATUS Rehd. & Wils.

A deciduous shrub up to 6 ft high; young shoots growing sometimes herring-bone fashion from the older ones, covered with yellowish down at first. Leaves orbicular, sometimes broadly obovate; they are usually apiculate (i.e. contracted at the apex to a minute point), but occasionally rounded or even notched there; $\frac{1}{4}$ to $\frac{3}{8}$ in. wide and long; upper surface glabrous, shining green, lower one slightly downy. Flowers solitary, white or pinkish. Fruit red, nearly globose, solitary, erect, $\frac{1}{4}$ in. wide.

Native of W. Szechwan, China; introduced in 1910. The true plant appears to be uncommon and, under Wilson's No. 4311, which belongs properly to this species, other species have been grown. It is one of the group to which *horizontalis* and *adpressus* belong. Flowers in June.

C. BULLATUS Bois

A deciduous shrub 10 to 12 ft (perhaps more) high, of rather spare habit; the branches few, long and arching, bark blackish brown covered with dark hairs when young. Leaves ovate or oblong; $1\frac{1}{2}$ to $3\frac{1}{2}$ in. long, about half as wide, pointed, dark green and slightly hairy above, paler and felted beneath with grey or yellowish down; between the veins the leaf-blade has a swollen (bullate) appearance; stalk $\frac{1}{12}$ in. long. Flowers in corymbs of from ten to thirty; each corymb 1 to 2 in. across, borne on short leafy branches; stalks downy. Petals rosy white, soon falling; calyx hairy, with short triangular lobes. Fruit brilliant red, pear-shaped or round, $\frac{1}{3}$ in. wide.

Native of W. China and Tibet; first cultivated in France about the year 1898, by Maurice de Vilmorin at Les Barres. It is undoubtedly one of the finest of the species introduced in this century. Of flower-beauty it has none, for it has rarely more than two or three flowers expanded on one cluster at a time, and the petals fall almost as soon as they open. But it is very handsome indeed in fruit, the clusters, many of them 2 in. across, being set on the shoot about 1 in. apart in opposite rows. Strictly the plant described above should be distinguished as *C. bullatus* f. *floribundus* (Stapf) Rehd. & Wils. (*C. moupinensis* f. *floribundus* Stapf, in *Bot. Mag.*, t. 8284). The plant that Bois took as the type of the species was greatly inferior in garden value, having up to twelve flowers only in each inflorescence and smaller fruits.

C. bullatus may also be in cultivation from seed collected in S.E. Tibet by Ludlow, Sherriff and Taylor (who found it as a tree up to 25 ft high—LST 6441), and by Kingdon Ward (KW 10906).

var. MACROPHYLLUS Rehd. & Wils. *C. rehderi* Pojark.—The leaves larger than in the type, being up to 6 in. long; calyx glabrous except on the margins. Discovered by Wilson in 1908 in W. Szechwan and in cultivation in the R.H.S. Garden, Wisley.

C. BUXIFOLIUS Lindl.

An evergreen shrub 1 or 2 ft high, its young shoots densely clothed with pale brownish down. Leaves oval or sometimes obovate, pointed, tapered at the base; $\frac{1}{4}$ to $\frac{1}{2}$ in. long, half as much wide; dull green and at first hairy above, densely clothed with tawny down beneath. Flowers two to seven together, white with pink anthers, calyx clothed with whitish hairs. Fruit red, obovoid, $\frac{1}{4}$ in. long.

Native of the Nilgiri Hills, India, where it has been described as a 'very scrubby little bush'. It differs from *C. prostratus* in its smaller, narrower, more closely downy leaves, more closely downy young shoots and in its smaller, hairy, more pear-shaped fruits.

The true species was introduced to Kew in 1919. The "*C. buxifolius*" of gardens is usually *C. prostratus* var. *lanatus*.

Cotoneasters closely related to *C. buxifolius* were found in China, in the mountains of Yunnan and Szechwan, by Delavay, Wilson, Forrest and Rock, but they are scarcely known in gardens here and their taxonomic status is uncertain. Wilson introduced a prostrate, rather glabrous plant which Rehder considered to belong to *C. buxifolius* f. *vellaeus* Franch. But Klotz refers it to C. ROCKII, a new species described by him in 1963 and founded on material collected by Rock.

C. CONGESTUS Baker

C. microphyllus var. *glacialis* Hook. f.; *C. pyrenaicus* Hort.

An evergreen shrub of low, compact, dense habit 1½ to 2½ ft high; young wood downy. Leaves oval or obovate, about ⅓ in. long, dull green above, whitish beneath with a few hairs at first, but becoming nearly or quite glabrous. Flowers solitary, ¼ in. across, pinkish white. Fruit bright red, round, ¼ in. diameter.

Native of the Himalaya up to 14,000 ft. This little evergreen has by some authorities been made a variety of *C. microphyllus*, which it may possibly be. But it is much more distinct from ordinary *C. microphyllus* than is *C. thymifolius*, especially in its habit, which, as Baker's name implies, is congested. Instead of its branches being spreading or prostrate, they are short, dense, often decurved, the whole forming a compact rounded mass. The dull green, paler leaves, not densely woolly beneath as in *C. microphyllus*, afford other distinctions. I have therefore retained the original name, and the one by which this plant is best known. It is a charming little evergreen for the rock garden, or for small borders of low shrubs where it runs no danger of being smothered by more aggressive plants.

In recent years similar cotoneasters have been collected in S.E. Tibet (e.g. Kingdon Ward 12386 and Ludlow, Sheriff and Elliott 15782).

C. CONSPICUUS Marquand　　[PLATE 67

C. conspicuus var. *decorus* Russell;* *C. microphyllus* var. *conspicuus* (Marquand) Yü; *C. permutatus* Klotz

An evergreen shrub of variable habit, usually seen as a prostrate or low, spreading shrub in the wild but, in some forms, reaching a height of 8 ft or so in cultivation; shoots villose. Leaves varying from ovate, oval and oblanceolate to linear-obovate, ⅙ to ¼ in. long, 1/12 to ¼ in. wide, glabrous and shining, black-green above, grey and woolly beneath. Flowers solitary, ⅜ to ½ in. wide; petals spreading, roundish, white, opening in May; anthers, dark red-purple. Fruit bright shining scarlet, globose to obovoid, ⅜ in. wide. *Bot. Mag.*, t. 9554.

Native of S.E. Tibet; discovered and introduced by Kingdon Ward in 1925 from Gyala on the Tsangpo River. The plant from which he took the seed grew pressed against a rock, but its offspring at Nymans in Sussex eventually reached a height of about 8 ft before dying of honey-fungus, and seedlings from them have reached a height of 6 ft in some gardens. On the other hand the plants at Exbury mentioned in previous editions have retained a low, spreading habit

* Marquand, in the absence of wild material, drew up the technical description of *C. conspicuus* from a cultivated plant. This was a prostrate form and had been raised in the U.S.A. from seed received from Exbury. It was this plant that Russell subsequently named var. *decorus*, which is therefore a superfluous name and a synonym of typical *C. conspicuus*. The fact that it has gained currency in gardens is due to the quite erroneous belief that it is the taller form that is the typical one. In fact, Marquand made it clear that he regarded both forms as part of the normal variation of the species. If a distinction were to be made between them, then it is the taller form which would require the distinguishing name. Indeed, Dr Klotz has given it specific rank as *C. permutatus*.

and at Wisley, on the rock-work opposite the greenhouses, there is a ground-hugging specimen which agrees well in habit with the wild parent plant. However, too much can be (indeed, has been) made of these differences, which may depend partly on situation. As usually seen in cultivation *C. conspicuus* is neither erect nor prostrate, but a low spreading shrub which builds up to a height of some 4 ft. A vigorous form was introduced more recently by Ludlow, Sherriff and Elliot (LSE 13310), which makes a mounded bush to about 8 ft high.

C. conspicuus ranks as one of the most valuable of the shrubby species as regards both flower and fruit. The berries are not attractive to birds and usually persist on the bush throughout the winter; the same is true in Tibet, where Kingdon Ward saw bushes still covered with fruit in mid-April.

C. COOPERI Marquand

A tall, deciduous shrub, shoots soon glabrous. Leaves elliptic-lanceolate, tapered to both ends, 2 to 4 in. long, ¼ to 1⅛ in. wide, glabrous above, at first covered beneath with grey-white hairs. Flowers small, ¼ in. across, white, borne in axillary and terminal, downy cymes on short, leafy side-shoots. Fruits obovoid, ⅖ in. long, dark purple.

Native of N. India, first collected in 1914 and named after R. E. Cooper of the Edinburgh Botanic Garden. It is very closely allied to *C. affinis* var. *bacillaris*.

var. MICROCARPA Marquand—Although undistinguishable in leaf and flower from the type, the fruits are smaller, more globose, and of a much redder purple. *Bot. Mag.*, t. 9478.

C. DAMMERI Schneid.

A prostrate, evergreen shrub, with slender creeping stems keeping close to the ground; young wood downy. Leaves obovate or oval, ¾ to 1¼ in. long, ¼ to ⅝ in. wide; margins incurved, apex usually rounded, downy on the lower surface when young, ultimately quite glabrous on both sides; stalk ⅛ to ¼ in. long; veins in four to six pairs. Flowers solitary, occasionally in pairs, on downy stalks ¼ in. long, pure white, ⅜ to ½ in. diameter; calyx downy, with broad triangular lobes. Fruit coral-red, globose or rather top-shaped, ¼ in. wide with usually five nutlets.

Native of Central China; found by Henry near Ichang, and introduced in 1900 by Wilson from W. Hupeh, where it occurs at 5,000 to 7,000 ft altitude. It is quite hardy, and is very distinct among cotoneasters for its perfectly prostrate habit. Its fruits are brightly coloured, and the plant has proved useful as an evergreen carpet-shrub, also for covering sunny slopes, as it is very vigorous. It occurs wild on heaths and rocky ground.

cv. 'MAJOR'.—A more vigorous form with leaves 1 to 1⅗ in. long. According to H. J. Grootendorst (*Dendroflora*, Vol. 3, p. 21) it is often found under the erroneous name *C. dammeri* 'Radicans'.

var. RADICANS Schneid.—Leaves longer-stalked than in the type (petioles to about ¼ in. long) and usually obovate; flowers on longer pedicels (to ⅗ in.

long). Some plants grown under this name are typical *C. dammeri*; others are *C. d.* 'Major' (see above).

C. 'SKOGHOLM'.—A vigorous form with prostrate or serpentine branches making mats up to about 1½ ft high. It is not free-fruiting, but makes a useful evergreen ground-cover. It is a seedling (possibly hybrid) of *C. dammeri*, raised in Sweden and put into commerce around 1950.

C. DIELSIANUS Pritz.
C. applanatus Duthie

A deciduous shrub 6 ft, perhaps more, high, with long, extremely slender, arching or quite pendulous branches; branchlets downy when young. Leaves ½ to 1½ in. long, ⅜ to 1 in. wide, ovate; hairy above when young, covered beneath with felt, at first white afterwards pale brown; veins prominent. Flowers pinkish, three to seven in a cluster, terminating side shoots 1 in. or so long; calyx and flower-stalk hairy, calyx lobes shallowly triangular. Fruit scarlet, round or rather pear-shaped, ¼ in. long; nutlets three or four.

Native of Central China; introduced for Messrs Veitch by Wilson in 1900. It flowers in June, and the fruit is in full colour in September and October; it is then one of the most effective of cotoneasters. The habit is singularly graceful, the long whip-like shoots spreading outwards and downwards in every direction. Duthie's name *C. applanatus* refers to the distichous arrangement of the branches of young plants, which gives them the appearance of a wall-trained tree.

var. ELEGANS Rehd. & Wils. *C. elegans* (Rehd. & Wils.) Flinck & Hylmö—Leaves thinner but more persistent than in the type and somewhat longer (to ⅗ in. long); fruits pendulous, orange-red. Introduced by Wilson from W. Szechwan in 1908.

C. DISTICHUS Lange
C. rotundifolius Wall. ex Baker, not Lindl.

A semi-evergreen or deciduous shrub 4 to 8 ft high, with stiff branches often arranged in two opposite rows; branchlets downy. Leaves usually in two rows, dark glossy green, ⅓ to ½ in. long, roundish, broadly ovate or oval, with a short, abrupt point; hairy on both sides when young, especially above, becoming glabrous later. Flowers white suffused with pink towards the centre, scarcely ½ in. diameter, produced usually singly, occasionally in pairs, on short lateral twigs; calyx almost glabrous. Fruit ½ in. long, scarcely so wide, broadest towards the top, tapering to a short stalk, bright scarlet-red.

Native of the Himalaya; introduced in 1825. In the beauty of its fruits this is the best of the dwarfer cotoneasters. They are not only among the largest and brightest coloured; they are usually very abundant, and remain on the plants throughout the winter until February or March. Whilst birds are quite keen for the fruits of *C. frigidus* at the first touch of cold, for some reason they leave those of this species alone. Although scarcely a true evergreen, it retains its leaves very late, especially in mild winters—often until March—and it rarely becomes quite bare. In mode of growth it bears a distinct resemblance to *C. horizontalis*, but it is not so low and flat as that quite deciduous species, its fruits are larger, and its calyx less downy. A group of a dozen plants makes a most pleasing winter picture.

This species is treated by some authorities under the name C. NITIDUS Jacques, which, as an earlier name, would have precedence over *C. distichus* if it could be established with certainty that it refers to the species described here. See also *C. prostratus*.

var. PARVIFOLIUS Yü—Leaves smaller than in the type, to about $\frac{1}{2}$ in. or a little more long; branches spreading horizontally. This may be in cultivation from KW 6788, or from Forrest's seed.

var. TONGOLENSIS Schneid.—Leaves thinly woolly above and densely brown-woolly beneath. This variety was described by Schneider from a specimen collected by Père Soulié in E. Tibet and was later found by Wilson in the vicinity of Kangting (Tatsien-lu) in W. Szechwan.

var. VERRUCULOSUS (Diels) Yü *C. verruculosus* Diels—Branches densely warted; stipules more persistent than in the type.

C. DIVARICATUS Rehd. & Wils.

A deciduous shrub up to 6 ft high, of spreading habit; young shoots clothed with greyish hairs, becoming the second year glabrous and reddish brown. Leaves roundish oval, sometimes ovate or obovate, tapered abruptly towards both ends, the apex mucronate; $\frac{1}{3}$ to 1 in. long, $\frac{1}{4}$ to $\frac{5}{8}$ in. wide (smaller on the flowering shoots); dark glossy green, and soon glabrous above, sparsely hairy beneath; veins in three or four pairs; leaf-stalk $\frac{1}{12}$ in. or less long. Flowers usually in threes at the end of short twigs, often supplemented by solitary ones in the axils of the terminal leaves, bright rose; calyx lobes triangular, they and the tube loosely woolly. Fruit red, egg-shaped, $\frac{1}{3}$ in. long, carrying usually two nutlets.

Native of W. Hupeh and W. Szechwan, China; first found by Henry in the latter province about 1887; introduced to the Coombe Wood nursery by Wilson in 1904. It is one of the handsomest in fruit of Chinese cotoneasters, and was given a First Class Certificate in the autumn of 1912.

C. FOVEOLATUS Rehd. & Wils.

A deciduous shrub 10 to 12 ft high; young shoots covered with yellowish grey, bristly hairs, becoming glabrous and greyish the second year. Leaves oval to ovate, slender-pointed, usually wedge-shaped (sometimes rounded) at the base; $1\frac{1}{2}$ to 4 in. long, $\frac{3}{4}$ to $1\frac{3}{4}$ in. wide; dull green and soon glabrous above, sparsely hairy beneath, more so on the midrib and veins; margins downy; veins in three to six pairs, the blade often puckered between them; stalk woolly, $\frac{1}{6}$ in. or less in length. Corymbs three- to seven-flowered, on a stalk about $\frac{1}{2}$ in. long, and hairy like the young wood; flowers $\frac{1}{3}$ in. wide; petals rose-tinted white; calyx tube woolly, the lobes triangular and woolly only on the margins. Fruit red, finally black, roundish, $\frac{1}{4}$ to $\frac{1}{3}$ in. wide, carrying usually three or four nutlets.

Native of W. Hupeh, China; introduced by Wilson in 1908. The foliage turns to bright scarlet and orange in autumn. The allied *C. moupinensis* (q.v.) also bears black fruits, but its inflorescences are many-flowered and its leaves have a strongly impressed venation.

C. FRANCHETII Bois

An evergreen shrub 8 to 10 ft high, with slender, gracefully arching branches, which the first year are covered with a dense, pale brown wool. Leaves oval, tapering towards both ends, from ¾ to 1¼ in. long, about half as wide, pointed; upper surface rather hairy when young, lustrous green later, lower surface covered with a thick, whitish, afterwards pale brown felt; stalk ⅛ in. or less long. Flowers borne in corymbs of five to fifteen flowers terminating short, lateral, leafy twigs; petals erect, white, touched with rose on the outside; calyx felted like the under-surface of the leaves. Fruit oblong, ¼ to ⅓ in. long; orange-scarlet; nutlets usually three. *Bot. Mag.*, t. 8571.

Native of Tibet and W. China; first raised in France about 1895, by Maurice de Vilmorin, from seed sent by the Abbé Soulié. It is a shrub of very elegant growth, whose fruits are freely borne, but lose in brilliancy by the greyish down, more or less dense, which covers them. It was at first confused with *C. pannosus* but the two species belong, in fact, to different subdivisions of the genus, so the resemblance is really superficial. The distinguishing characters may be defined as follows: leaves rather longer than in *pannosus*, but with stalks scarcely half as long, the upper surface somewhat lustrous; flowers not so numerous in each cluster, petals erect and rose-tinted; fruits larger, longer, and not of so deep a red. It flowers in May, and the fruit is ripe in October.

var. CINERASCENS Rehd.—Leaves larger, up to 1½ in. long, covered with a loose grey felt.

var. STERNIANUS Turrill *C. wardii* Hort., not W. W. Sm.—This variety differs from the type mainly in the shape of the fruit, which is obovoid to almost globose, not oblong. It was introduced by Farrer from Burma in 1919 and long grown in gardens as "*C. franchetii*" or, more commonly, as "*C. wardii*". It is figured in *Bot. Mag.*, n.s., t. 130, and discussed by the late Dr Turrill in the accompanying note. This variety is one of the finest of the taller cotoneasters, being very hardy and growing rapidly to a height of 6 ft or more. The older leaves frequently die off into bright orange shades just at the time that the fruits are in high colour. It was given the Award of Garden Merit in 1953.

C. WARDII W. W. Sm.—A native of S.E. Tibet, found by Kingdon Ward in 1913. It is perhaps not in cultivation, the plants grown as *wardii* being for the most part *C. franchetii* var. *sternianus*, from which it differs in its longer flowering branchlets, thinner leaves and in certain floral characters.

C. FRIGIDUS Wall.

A large, rounded, deciduous shrub 15 to 20 ft high, or a small tree; branchlets at first covered with pale down, becoming glabrous. Leaves 3 to 5 in. long,

1 to 2 in. wide; narrowly oval or obovate, deep dull green and glabrous above, pale and very woolly beneath when young, becoming almost glabrous by autumn. Flowers white, $\frac{1}{3}$ in. across, produced very numerously in flattish corymbs 2 in. or more across, terminating short leafy twigs; flower-stalks very woolly. Fruits in large clusters, each fruit about the size of a pea, rich bright red, with two nutlets.

Native of the Himalaya; introduced in 1824, and one of the most striking of all cotoneasters. The splendid clusters of 'berries' wreathing the branches make one of the most brilliant sights of autumn and early winter. The species is one of the most robust in the genus, making if left to itself a huge bush 20 ft high and as much through, consisting of numerous branching stems. But if kept to one stem when young and the lower branches removed, it will make a pretty round-headed tree with a well-shaped trunk. At Westonbirt, Glos., it has attained 40 ft in height. No hardy shrub more beautiful than this thrives in town gardens.

f. FRUCTU-LUTEO (Bean) Rehd.—Fruits yellowish or creamy white; rare and little known, but not so beautiful as the type.

cv. 'PENDULA'.—Branches pendulous; raised at Kew from seed obtained from Darjeeling in 1924.

cv. 'VICARII'.—An improved form raised by the late Hon. Vicary Gibbs at Aldenham.

C. frigidus has crossed spontaneously in gardens with *C. salicifolius* and its allies and some others of the Section *Chaenopetalum*. In this way some fine garden plants have arisen, of which the following are in commerce:

C. 'CORNUBIA'.—This is one of the very finest of the larger growing cotoneasters. It is a very spreading shrub up to 25 ft high and more in width, clothed to the ground with foliage. But by pruning and keeping it to one stem in the early stages, it may be made to develop a genuine tree-like form. The richly green, abundant leaves are 4 to 5 in. long, oval-lanceolate, pointed, glabrous above, slightly downy beneath. It bears enormous crops of brilliant red fruits and is not surpassed in that respect by any other cotoneaster. It received an Award of Merit in 1933 and a First Class Certificate three years later. It was raised at Exbury and is perhaps a hybrid between *C. frigidus* 'Vicarii' and a plant grown as "*C. glabratus*" which was probably itself a hybrid of *C. frigidus* with a member of the *C. salicifolius* group (*Orn. Fl. Trees & Shrubs*, R.H.S. Conf. Rep., 1940, pp. 74 and 77). Two forms of the cross were distributed but the name 'Cornubia' belongs to the one given the A.M. in 1933. The original plant at Exbury is 25 ft high and 20 ft across.

C. × CRISPII Exell—This hybrid arose from *C. frigidus* by open pollination in the nurseries of John Waterer and Sons. The other parent was thought by Exell to be *C. pannosus*, which it resembles in leaf, while tending to *C. frigidus* in its fruits.

C. (*frigidus × salicifolius*) 'EXBURIENSIS'.—A tall evergreen shrub of which the first parent was a yellow-fruited form of *C. frigidus*. Leaves narrowly lanceolate, to 5 in. long and 1 in. or a little more wide, with impressed veins.

Fruit pale yellow. 'ROTHSCHILDIANUS' is another form of the cross, rather weaker growing, with deeper yellow fruits.

C. 'HYBRIDUS PENDULUS'.—A vigorous shrub with slender, prostrate or arching branches which quickly makes a wide mat; if top-grafted, it makes a small weeping tree. Leaves medium green, slightly glossy, elliptic, acute, to about 3 in. long and 1 in. or slightly more wide. The red fruits are borne with great freedom in small cymes. The parentage and origin are both uncertain. Probably *C. frigidus* is one parent. The trailing habit suggests that *C. dammeri* might be the other, but another possibility is some species of the *C. salicifolius* group, in which prostrate seedlings have not infrequently occurred.

C. 'ST MONICA'.—A semi-evergreen shrub to about 15 ft high, with leaves to 6 in. long, bearing its fruit in long pendulous clusters. It was raised from *C. frigidus* at the Saint Monica Home, Bristol, and given an Award of Merit in 1933.

C. × WATERERI Exell—This fine shrub is a hybrid between *C. frigidus* and *C. henryanus*. It appeared as a chance seedling from *frigidus* in John Waterer and Son's nurseries at Bagshot and was described and named in 1928. Recently the clonal name 'JOHN WATERER' has been given to the original plant and its descendants by vegetative propagation, in order to distinguish them from seedlings and from other cotoneasters that might arise from the same parents. It is an evergreen or semi-evergreen shrub with narrowly elliptic leaves 1½ to 3 in. long, tapered about equally towards both ends, dark dull green, glabrous at maturity, veins about twelve each side the midrib. Fruits globose, scarlet, ¼ in. wide, borne in corymbose clusters 1½ to 2 in. across. *Bot. Mag.*, n.s., t. 282. Discussing this hybrid (loc. cit.) Dr Turrill remarked, 'On the whole, it seems that the characters of *C. henryanus* are strongly predominant in the supposed hybrid.' In view of this considered judgement it is scarcely correct to adopt *C. × watereri* as the group-name for hybrids between *C. frigidus* and *C. salicifolius*, as has been done by continental authorities. Doubtless the latter species and *C. henryanus* are near allies, but are generally held to be specifically distinct.

C. GLABRATUS Rehd. & Wils.

An evergreen shrub 10 ft or more high; young shoots usually purplish, soon quite glabrous. Leaves of leathery texture, mostly oblanceolate, sometimes narrowly elliptical, tapered towards both ends, oftenest more gradually towards the base; 2 to 4 in. long, ½ to 1½ in. wide; glabrous and bright green above, glaucous and soon glabrous beneath; stalk ¼ in. or less long. Flowers white, ¼ in. wide, borne in dense corymbs 1½ in. across, terminating short leafy shoots; calyx funnel-shaped, slightly downy like the flower-stalk; stamens twenty; styles two. Fruit rather small for this genus, red, globose.

Native of Szechwan, China; discovered by Wilson in 1906 and introduced in 1908 (No. 2185). It is nearly related to *C. salicifolius*, but the younger parts of that species are much more downy. The true species is perhaps rare in cultivation, the "*C. glabratus*" grown at Exbury and in other gardens, being, it is thought, a hybrid between *C. frigidus* and *C. salicifolius* (or one of its near allies).

TS—BB

C. GLAUCOPHYLLUS Franch.

A deciduous shrub of robust growth up to 10 ft high; shoots appressed downy at first. Leaves oval, often inclined to obovate, $1\frac{1}{2}$ to $2\frac{1}{2}$ in. long, the apex rounded, often with a small mucro projecting from the midrib, the base broadly tapered; firm in texture, dark green and glabrous above; stalk $\frac{1}{6}$ to $\frac{1}{4}$ in. long. Flowers white, $\frac{1}{4}$ in. across, crowded in corymbs $1\frac{1}{2}$ to 2 in. wide, that terminate short shoots, opening in July; petals rounded, spreading; calyx glabrous. Fruits globose, crimson, $\frac{1}{4}$ in. wide, containing two or three nutlets.

C. glaucophyllus was discovered by the French missionary Delavay in 1884, but the true species is rare in gardens, or perhaps not yet introduced. However, it is represented by a form which differs but little from Franchet's type. This is:

f. SEROTINUS (Hutchins.) Stapf C. serotinus Hutchins.—An evergreen shrub up to 30 ft high; young shoots covered (like the leaf-stalks and flower-stalks) with a close, tawny white down, becoming glabrous and dark brown later. Leaves oval, pointed, tapering at the base to a stalk $\frac{1}{4}$ in. long; 1 to 3 in. long, $\frac{5}{8}$ to $1\frac{1}{4}$ in. wide; dark green and glabrous above, pale and at first softly downy beneath, becoming quite glabrous. Flowers borne in July and August on corymbs 2 to 3 in. wide terminating short shoots which carry two or three leaves; they are white, $\frac{1}{4}$ in. wide; petals rounded; calyx covered with pale down; anthers reddish brown. Fruit bright red, obovoid, $\frac{1}{4}$ in. wide, containing two or three stones. Bot. Mag., t. 9171.

A native of W. China, introduced by Forrest from Yunnan in 1907 (F. 6754). Plants raised from his seed at Caerhays were in cultivation at Kew in 1914 but this cotoneaster first came into general notice on 13th January 1919, when fruit-bearing sprays were shown at Westminster by the Royal Horticultural Society from the Wisley garden under the name "C. glaucophyllus". However, when it was figured in the Botanical Magazine in the following year it was as a new species —C. serotinus Hutchins.—and under this name it was long grown in gardens. It was given its present status as a botanical form of C. glaucophyllus by Stapf, who pointed out (Bot. Mag., t. 9171) that it differed from the type mainly in its late-flowering season and unusual freedom in flowering; also in the fruits being glabrous and smaller and the leaves green beneath, not glaucous as in Delavay's specimen. It is a handsome shrub when bearing good crops of berries and they have the additional attraction of remaining on the shrubs until April. At Highdown, near Worthing, there is a plant 30 ft high and 30 ft in spread (1965).

var. MEIOPHYLLUS W. W. Sm.—Leaves smaller than in the type (to 1 in. long) and elliptic in shape rather than ovate, rounded at both ends.

var. VESTITUS W. W. Sm.—Leaves densely downy beneath; inflorescence also more downy than in the type. This and the preceding variety were described from specimens collected by Forrest in Yunnan in 1912.

C. HARROVIANUS Wils.

An evergreen shrub of loose, spreading habit, growing 6 ft in height, and more in diameter; young shoots at first covered with a pale down (which later falls away), afterwards becoming nearly or quite glabrous, glossy, and turning a dark purplish brown, almost black, on the side exposed to the sun. Leaves oval to obovate, wedge-shaped at the base, pointed at the apex, where the midrib is extended into a short bristle (or mucro); 1 to 2½ in. long, ½ to 1 in. wide; at first sparsely downy above, afterwards glabrous, and bright dark green, covered beneath with a pale yellowish-brown wool, which partially falls away by the end of the year; stalk ⅛ to ⅓ in. long. Flowers numerously and densely arranged in axillary and terminal corymbs about 1½ in. across; petals round, white; calyx and flower-stalk thickly coated with grey wool, the calyx lobes triangular and pointed. Stamens twenty, with reddish-purple anthers. Fruit red.

Native of Yunnan, China; discovered by Henry, introduced in 1899 by Wilson for Messrs Veitch, in honour of whose manager at the Coombe Wood nurseries, the late George Harrow, it was named. It is most nearly allied to *C. pannosus*, but has larger, more leathery leaves, and larger flower-clusters. One of the handsomest of cotoneasters in flower. For a note on the introduction of this species, see *C. amoenus*.

C. HEBEPHYLLUS Diels

A deciduous shrub 6 to 10 ft high, of graceful habit, or even a small tree 12 ft and upwards high; young shoots slender, at first downy, becoming glabrous and (the second year) purplish. Leaves on the barren shoots almost round with a bristle-like tip; 1 to 1½ in. long, scarcely so wide; glabrous above, loosely downy and rather glaucous beneath; stalk up to ¼ in. long. The leaves of the flower-bearing twigs are smaller and more oval. Flowers white with violet anthers, borne in May at the end of short leafy twigs in clusters of three to over a dozen. Fruit oval, ⅓ in. long, very dark red, usually containing one nutlet. *Bot. Mag.*, t. 9389.

Native of the region from Yunnan to the E. Himalaya; discovered by Forrest in Yunnan in 1904 and introduced some six years later. It is a free-growing shrub suitable for woodland.

var. FULVIDUS W. W. Sm.—Leaves clad beneath with a yellowish down, closer and thicker than in the type.

var. INCANUS W. W. Sm. *C. incanus* (W. W. Sm.) Klotz—Leaves covered beneath with a close, grey down.

C. MAJUSCULUS (W. W. Sm.) Klotz *C. hebephyllus* var. *majusculus* W. W. Sm.—Leaves larger than in the type, of stouter texture; fruits globose. It was first described as a variety of *C. hebephyllus* but seems distinct enough to rank as a species.

C. HENRYANUS (Schneid.) Rehd. & Wils.
C. rugosus var. *henryanus* Schneid.

An evergreen shrub 10 to 12 ft high, of sparse habit; the branches gracefully pendulous; young shoots hairy, becoming glabrous the second year, and of a dark purplish brown. Leaves 2 to 4½ in. long, about one-third as wide, narrowly oval or obovate, finely pointed, dark green, and somewhat rough to the touch above; covered beneath when young with a greyish wool which mostly falls away by the second season, that which remains becoming brown, and confined to the midrib and veins, the under-surface still remaining brownish white; veins in nine to twelve pairs; stalk ¼ to ½ in. long, hairy. Flowers white, produced about the middle of June in corymbs 2 to 2½ in. across, terminating leafy twigs less than 1 in. long, that spring from the axils of the still persisting leaves of the previous year; stamens twenty, with purple anthers; calyx and flower-stalks hairy. Fruit brownish crimson, egg-shaped, ¼ in. long with two or three nutlets.

Native of Central China; introduced by Wilson in 1901. A handsome and distinct evergreen, and probably the largest-leaved of cotoneasters with persistent leaves. It is allied to *C. salicifolius* and has been confused with it. In that species, however, the leaves are shorter and relatively narrower than in *C. henryanus*, and glabrous above even when young.

C. HORIZONTALIS Decne.

A deciduous shrub of low, flat habit, rarely more than 2 or 3 ft high in the open, the branches spreading quite horizontally, and increasing but slowly in height; branchlets covered with a thick brown wool, and produced in two opposite rows. Leaves roundish or broadly oval, from ¼ to ½ in. long, three-fourths as wide, shortly and abruptly pointed; dark glossy green above, glabrous, or with a few scattered hairs beneath. Flowers white, suffused with pink, about ¼ in. diameter, produced during May singly, or in pairs on short leafy twigs springing from the buds of the previous summer's wood; calyx woolly. Fruit globose, bright red, about ⅕ in. diameter, nutlets three.

Native of China; described from plants in the garden of the Paris Museum, raised from seed sent by the missionary Père David around 1870 and put into commerce in France in 1885. This is decidedly one of the prettiest and most distinct of cotoneasters. Its most striking characteristic is the opposite branching and low, horizontal habit. The leaves, although small, are so abundant as to be almost without intervening spaces; they remain long on the branches, and the shrub is often in full leaf in November. Then the lower ones of each shoot begin to fade off into various shades of orange and red, whilst the terminal part retains them green. By January the shrub, as a rule, has lost all its foliage, and its bare branches present a curious fish-bone-like appearance. The fruits are very bright, and often abundant, although smaller than in most of the species. In the open ground, where it has plenty of space to develop, this cotoneaster keeps low and flat, but it will grow much higher against a wall. In such a position there is a plant at Kew 10 ft high spreading over the wall, but keeping from actual contact with it. Increased easily by cuttings.

var. PERPUSILLUS Schneid. *C. perpusillus* (Schneid.) Flinck & Hylmö—A pleasing variety introduced by Wilson from W. Hupeh, China, in 1908. It differs from the typical plant in its smaller leaves which are ¼ in. or less in length. Wilson informed us that this variety is the common cotoneaster of the moorlands in its native home, being abundant in open rocky ground. He thought it may be merely a climatic form which under cultivation may revert to the type—as so often happens with depauperate forms. Up to the present, however, it is distinguishable.

cv. 'Saxatilis'.—Dwarfer than the type, with the 'fish-bone' habit of branching very well marked; it is also more prostrate and the leaves are smaller. Suitable for the rock garden but shy-fruiting. It was put into commerce by Messrs Hesse of Germany in 1950.

cv. 'Variegatus'.—Leaves edged with white. This is one of the most dainty of variegated shrubs. The low, flat, spreading nature of the growth shows up the variegation very effectively.

In his valuable survey of dwarf cotoneasters (*Dendroflora*, No. 3, 1966) H. J. Grootendorst also describes 'Robusta', a vigorous and free-fruiting form whose leaves colour well before falling. Put into commerce by Messrs Van Nes in 1954.

C. (*horizontalis* × *salicifolius* var. *floccosus*) 'Gracia' and 'Valkenburg'. —These two hybrids, with *horizontalis* as the pollen parent, were raised at Boskoop in 1951. Both are triploid and almost sterile, but the second is said to have some value as a semi-evergreen ground-cover. The cross is of interest in that it unites the two sections of the genus.

C. splendens Flinck & Hylmö—This species, described in 1964, was discovered and introduced to Sweden in 1934 by the Swedish botanist Dr Harry Smith from the region of Tatsien-lu (now called Kangting). It is described as an apomictic species allied to *C. dielsianus*, but differing in its lower growth, in its thinner, broadly ovate-elliptical to almost orbicular leaves with less impressed veins, and in its larger, lustrous, bright orange-red fruits. See also 'Sabrina'.

C. 'Sabrina'.—This cotoneaster arose as a self-sown seedling in the garden of N. G. Hadden, Porlock, and was given an Award of Merit in 1950. It appeared between two cotoneasters, of which one was *C. horizontalis*; the other was grown as "*C. pannosus*" but subsequently proved to be *C. franchetii* (P. F. Yeo in *Gard. Chron.*, April 21, 1962). In their account of *C. splendens* (see above) the authors remark that, judging from a herbarium specimen of Mr Hadden's plant, 'Sabrina' would appear to be identical with *C. splendens* and contend that it must have been raised from seed of this species, which has been in cultivation in a number of Scandinavian botanical gardens for some thirty years. This is both interesting and puzzling, since Mr Hadden assures us that his plant was, as stated, self-sown and in his opinion a hybrid between *C. horizontalis* and *C. franchetii*. Seedlings of *C. splendens* and 'Sabrina' are in cultivation in the University Botanic Garden, Cambridge. Dr Yeo tells us that the 'Sabrina' seedlings are uniform and seem to the eye to be very similar to those of *C. splendens*, though they are tending to produce 'herring-bone' branching, whereas *C. splendens* has the branches decussate. Until these plants come to maturity the question of the taxonomic position of 'Sabrina' (and of *C. splendens*) is best left in abeyance.

C. hupehensis Rehd. & Wils.

A deciduous shrub up to 6 ft high, of a spreading graceful habit due to its long arching shoots which, when young, are downy, becoming glabrous and purplish later. Leaves ovate or oval, mostly pointed but sometimes blunt at the apex, mostly rounded at the base; 1 to 1½ in. long, ½ to ¾ in. wide; glabrous and dark green above, greyish and thinly downy beneath; stalk ⅛ in. long. Flowers white, copiously produced in May on the upper side of the shoots in small clusters of six to twelve blossoms; flower-stalks ¼ to ½ in. long, downy like the calyx. Fruit bright red, globose, ⅓ to ½ in. wide, containing two nutlets. *Bot. Mag.,* n.s., t. 245.

Native of Hupeh and Szechwan, China; first found by Henry, introduced by Wilson in 1907. A hardy cotoneaster, handsome in regard to both flower and fruit as well as growth. Altogether one of the best of the newer Chinese species.

COTONEASTER HUPEHENSIS

It belongs to the same group as *C. frigidus* and *C. racemiflorus* with spreading white petals and large red fruit, but is distinct from both in the shape and size of the leaves.

C. INTEGERRIMUS Med.   COMMON COTONEASTER

Mespilus cotoneaster L.; *C. vulgaris* Lindl.

A deciduous shrub 4 to 7 ft high, of rounded, bushy habit; young wood woolly. Leaves ¾ to 1½ in. long, varying in outline from broadly ovate to almost round; sometimes pointed, sometimes rounded at the apex; glabrous or nearly so above, always densely grey-felted beneath; stalk ¼ in. or less long. Flowers white, rose-tinted, produced two to four together in short nodding clusters. Fruit round, ¼ in. across, red; nutlets two.

Native of Europe and N. Asia, and interesting as the only cotoneaster truly native of Britain. In 1783 it was discovered on the cliffs of Great Orme's Head, near Llandudno, by J. W. Griffith. This appears to be its only habitat in the British Isles, and even there it is now reduced to very few plants. I have spent a good deal of time wandering over the Head, but have never seen it there. (It has been seen in one or two places since these words were written but is now extremely rare. The latest specimen from this area in the Kew Herbarium is dated 1941.) The species flowers in April and May, but has little garden value. From its ally *C. tomentosus*, this differs in its glabrous calyx.

C. ROSEUS Edgew.—A native of Afghanistan and the N.W. Himalaya, related to the preceding, but distinguished by the glabrous undersides of the mature leaves.

C. LACTEUS W. W. Sm.

An evergreen shrub 8 to 12 ft high; young shoots at first covered with a dense white down which turns yellowish and falls away by winter, leaving them bare and reddish. Leaves obovate or broadly oval, usually pointed, sometimes rounded at the apex, always tapering at the base to a stalk which is ¼ in. or less long; 1¼ to 2¼ in. long, ¾ to 1¼ in. wide; dark green above, clothed beneath with thick white down which becomes yellowish with age but persists largely until the fall of the leaf; veins in six to nine pairs, very prominent. Flowers produced in corymbs 2 to 3 in. wide during late June and July, milky white. Fruits egg-shaped, $\frac{3}{16}$ in. long, ⅛ in. wide, red, with the downy calyx persisting at the top. *Bot. Mag.*, t. 9454.

Native of Yunnan, China; introduced by Forrest in 1913, under his No. 10419. It had previously been discovered by the Abbé Delavay. A plant raised from Forrest's seed bore a fine crop of fruits at Glasnevin in 1921, by which time it was 6 ft high and gave a fine effect. The species still flourishes in that garden and has been used to make a dense hedge 10 ft high. It belongs to the same group as *henryanus* and *salicifolius*, but the leaves are considerably broader in proportion to their length than they are in those two species. From *C. glaucophyllus*, another near ally, it differs in the stronger veining of the leaves, whose undersides are also more persistently downy than they are in any of the forms of that species. Some plants grown as *C. lacteus* may be *C. glaucophyllus f. serotinus*. It is a quite handsome shrub and a vigorous grower, but rather late in colouring its fruits.

C. LINDLEYI Steud.
C. nummularius Lindl., not Fisch.

A deciduous shrub 10 ft or more high, with long, slender young branches covered with down when young, but becoming bare towards the end of the summer, and of a very dark brown. Leaves roundish oval, or broadly ovate, 1 to 2½ in. long, ¾ to 1¾ in. broad, rounded at the base; the apex pointed, rounded, or even notched, but nearly always ending in a short bristle-like tip; dark green and sparsely hairy above when young, covered with pale greyish felt beneath; stalk ¼ in. or less long. Flowers white, in corymbs of five to twelve; calyx covered with a grey felt. Fruit black, roundish, about ¼ in. diameter.

Native of the north-western Himalaya; introduced in 1824. This is one of the taller and stronger-growing species, and was often grown in gardens as "*C. nummularius*". The true *C. nummularius* of Fischer is treated here as a variety of *C. racemiflorus*.

C. LUCIDUS Schlecht.

C. acutifolius Lindl., not Turcz.

A deciduous shrub of bushy habit 6 to 10 ft in height; young wood hairy. Leaves polished green and quite glabrous or nearly so above, sparsely hairy and paler beneath, ovate or oval, pointed; ¾ to 2 in. long, ½ to 1 in. wide. Flowers rosy white, produced from three to ten together in short corymbs with slightly hairy stalks; calyx woolly at the edges of the triangular teeth. Fruit black, globose, ⅓ to ⅖ in. wide, with three or four nutlets.

Native of Siberia and other parts of N. Asia. Long known in gardens, this species is but little cultivated now, although it is one of the handsomest of the black-fruited cotoneasters. From *C. acutifolius* Turcz., it differs in its glossy green leaves, its generally less hairy or downy character, and in its sturdier habit.

C. MELANOCARPUS Lodd.

A species with a wide range from Europe and W. Asia to Mongolia, and exceedingly variable. It is mostly represented in gardens by the following variety:

var. LAXIFLORUS (Lindl.) Schneid. *C. laxiflorus* Lindl.—A deciduous shrub, 4 to 8 ft high, of bushy habit; young wood downy. Leaves broadly oval or ovate, blunt or rounded at the apex, up to 1½ or 2 in. long, dark green and often hairy above when young, always greyish woolly beneath. Flowers pinkish white, borne in gracefully pendulous cymose panicles 1 to 2 in. long, some of the larger panicles carrying twenty to forty flowers; calyx glabrous. Fruit ¼ in. across, globose, black.

Native of Siberia; introduced to England from Vienna in 1826. Among the black-fruited cotoneasters this is distinguished by its comparatively large panicles of blossom, which give it quite a pretty aspect in May, and render it the most attractive of this group.

C. MICROPHYLLUS Lindl.

An evergreen shrub of low, spreading, or even prostrate habit, rarely more than 2 to 3 ft high unless trained. Branches often slender but rigid, woolly when young. Leaves ¼ to ½ in. long, half or less than half as wide; ovate or obovate, deep glossy green above, grey and woolly beneath, pointed, rounded or notched at the apex. Flowers white, ⅓ in. across, generally solitary (occasionally two or three). Fruit round, scarlet-red, ¼ in. in diameter.

Native of the Himalaya and S.W. China; introduced in 1824. This pleasing evergreen is a near relation of *C. prostratus* and of *C. conspicuus*. The former is, however, a more robust shrub with larger, broadly ovate to almost rounded leaves and a usually two- or three-flowered inflorescence. The latter (treated by Yü as a variety of the present species) may be distinguished by its narrow elliptic to oblong leaves, and the larger flowers and fruit. Another close ally is *C. congestus* (q.v. for the marks of distinction).

C. microphyllus makes a pretty covering for sloping banks, forming eventually

a dense, low thicket, though a really prostrate form of the more recently introduced *C. conspicuus* is to be preferred. Single plants make a pretty evergreen
furnishing for the rock garden, but where space is limited var. *thymifolius* or
C. congestus are more suitable.

var. COCHLEATUS (Franch.) Rehd. & Wils. *C. buxifolius* f. *cochleatus*
Franch. *C. cochleatus* (Franch.) Klotz—A more strictly prostrate and compact
variety with obovate or oval leaves rounded or notched at the apex, hairy
beneath like the shoots when quite young. Native of the Himalaya from Nepal
eastward, and of China. It was given an Award of Merit in 1931 for the beauty
of its brightly coloured fruits.

f. MELANOTRICHUS (Franch.) Hand.-Mazz. *C. buxifolius* f. *melanotrichus*
Franch.—Franchet made this *forma* out of a herbarium specimen on which the
leaves were covered beneath with black hairs. However, there is little doubt
that this peculiarity was simply due to a fungus. Plants in cultivation as "*C.
melanotrichus*" are either *C. microphyllus* or the var. *cochleatus*.

var. THYMIFOLIUS (Lindl.) Koehne *C. thymifolius* Lindl.—A dwarf or
prostrate close-habited shrub, with numerous rigid branches. Leaves narrower
than in the type, and made to appear more so by the curling under of the
margins. Besides being narrower, they also differ in being uniformly blunt at
the apex and broadest towards the end. Fruit and flower as in the type, but
smaller.

Native of the Himalaya at high elevations. In earlier editions the author
remarked that this plant, then treated as a species, was perhaps merely an
alpine form of *C. microphyllus*, smaller in all its parts, and the status it now
assumes is in conformity with that view. But his warning must be repeated—
that the close, tight, bright-leaved evergreen known in gardens as *C. thymifolius*
may not breed true from seed and should be propagated from cuttings.

C. MOUPINENSIS Franch.

A deciduous shrub up to 8 or 10 ft high; young shoots, under-surface of the
leaves and flower-stalks clothed with down. Leaves oval-lanceolate, pointed,
rounded or broadly wedge-shaped at the base; 2 to 4 in. long, $\frac{3}{4}$ to $1\frac{1}{2}$ in. wide;
strongly veined beneath. Flowers pinkish, borne in June in many-flowered
clusters, small and of little beauty. Fruit jet-black, obovoid or nearly globose,
$\frac{1}{4}$ to $\frac{1}{3}$ in. wide, containing four or five nutlets.

Native of W. Szechwan, China; introduced to this country from France in
1907. There has been much confusion in gardens between it and *C. bullatus*, but
the latter is a much handsomer shrub with abundant clusters of brilliant red
fruits. *C. moupinensis* is really nearer to the black-fruited *C. foveolatus*. Differences
between them are pointed out under *C. foveolatus* (q.v.), but it may be added
here that the leaves of *foveolatus* are much less prominently veined. In its bullate
leaves *C. moupinensis* closely resembles *C. bullatus*. It makes a fine spreading bush
12 ft or more through at Kew, and is excellent for woodland.

C. MULTIFLORUS Bunge   [PLATE 66
C. reflexus Carr.

A deciduous shrub or small tree 10 to 12 ft high; branches slender, pendulous
or arching, and glabrous except when quite young. Leaves thin in texture,
varying in shape from ovate and oval to roundish; ¾ to 2½ in. long, ½ to 1½ in.
wide; usually blunt or rounded at the end, hairy when quite young, but soon
becoming glabrous above; pale and often glabrous, never permanently woolly
beneath; stalk ¼ to ½ in. long. Flowers white, produced in branching clusters of
three to twelve or more, not pleasantly scented. Fruit round or pear-shaped, red.

A species of wide range in Asia, from the Caucasus through Central Asia and
W. Siberia to China; a variety (see below) is found in Spain. It was first discovered in Siberia, in the Altai Mountains, and introduced to Kew in 1837.
This is one of the most elegant of cotoneasters. There is a specimen at Kew
with a single well-formed trunk supporting a crown of pendulous or arching
branches; the whole 10 to 12 ft high. When the branches are wreathed with
abundant blossom in May and June, this tree makes a most charming picture.
The same species was later found in China by Wilson and other collectors.

var. CALOCARPUS Rehd. & Wils. *C. calocarpus* (Rehd. & Wils.) Flinck &
Hylmö—Leaves long and narrower than in the type; fruit larger. It was introduced by Wilson in 1908 and has proved to be a singularly beautiful fruit-
bearing shrub.

var. GRANATENSIS (Boiss.) Wenzig *C. granatensis* Boiss.—Widely separated
from the main range of the species, this variety is found on the slopes of the
Sierra Nevada, in S. Spain. It is near the type in its botanical characters, differing
in its more lax corymbs, somewhat hairy calyx, and more downy leaves.

C. NITENS Rehd. & Wils.

A deciduous shrub up to 6 ft high, of dense, leafy habit; young shoots slender,
bright brown, at first covered with tawny down. Leaves roundish oval, ½ to
⅞ in. long, ⅓ to ½ in. wide, pointed, tapered about equally towards both ends,
dark shining green above, slightly downy beneath, becoming almost glabrous;
stalk ¹⁄₁₂ in. long. Flowers pink, usually in threes, opening in June. Fruit egg-
shaped, ¼ to ⅓ in. long, purplish black, containing two nutlets.

Native of W. Szechwan, China; discovered and introduced by Wilson in 1910.
This species is distinguished by its dense habit and abundant lustrous leafage.
It is related to *C. divaricatus* but is scarcely so ornamental as that shrub, which
is well distinguished from it by its red fruits.

C. HARRYSMITHII Flinck & Hylmö—This recently described species was
introduced by the Swedish botanist Dr Harry Smith, who collected in W. China
1921–22 and 1934. It is allied to *C. nitens* but differs in the following particulars:
it is of weaker growth, with the branchlets arranged all in one plane; leaves
elliptic, with an acute to acuminate apex, clad on both sides with persistent
indumentum of soft hairs, about ⅗ in. long and a little more than half as wide;
flowers and fruits smaller.

C. NITIDIFOLIUS Marquand

A deciduous, densely leafy shrub of spreading habit 5 to 8 ft high; young shoots slender, covered with pale greyish hairs, afterwards brown. Leaves ovate-lanceolate to lanceolate, slender-pointed, tapered or sometimes nearly rounded at the base; 1½ to 2½ in. long, ⅝ to 1 in. wide; pale shining green and glabrous above, sparsely downy beneath; stalk ⅛ in. or less long. Flowers white, ¼ in. wide, four to nine in a short, terminal, cymose cluster; calyx very downy, the lobes triangular; flower-stalks short, hairy. Fruit subglobose to top-shaped, hairy at the summit, crimson, ¼ in. long, containing two to four nutlets.

Native of Yunnan, China; discovered and introduced in 1924 by Forrest from open thickets by streams on the Shweli–Salween divide at altitudes of 8,000 to 9,000 ft. It is quite unlike any other cotoneaster known to me in the curiously pale glittering green of the leaves, and may at once be picked out by that character in any collection of the genus.

C. OBSCURUS Rehd. & Wils.

A deciduous shrub up to 10 ft high, of spreading habit; young shoots covered with tawny down. Leaves oval to ovate-oblong, pointed, broadly wedge-shaped at the base; 1 to 1¾ in. long; dull green and furnished with tawny-down beneath; veins in four or five pairs; stalk ⅛ in. or less long. Flowers white tinged with pink, three to seven together in cymes on short side branches; calyx-lobes triangular, very downy. Fruit pear-shaped, ¼ to ⅓ in. long, dark red; nutlets usually three. Flowers in June.

Native of W. Szechwan, China; introduced by Wilson in 1910. It comes nearest perhaps to *C. acuminatus*, but that species is less downy beneath the leaves, and its brighter-coloured fruits have only two nutlets.

var. CORNIFOLIUS Rehd. & Wils.—This variety is distinguished by its larger leaves (up to 2¾ in. long) with five to seven pairs of more strongly marked veins; there are five nutlets in each fruit. It appears to be superior as a garden shrub to the type and seems to be the commoner in gardens.

C. GLOMERULATUS W. W. Sm.—This species resembles *C. obscurus* but has smaller leaves, covered beneath with a brown felt, more flowers to the inflorescence and smaller, brighter red fruits. Flinck and Hylmö, however, place it in the series *Glomerulati*, near to *C. nitidifolius* Marquand. It was discovered and introduced by Forrest.

C. PANNOSUS Franch.

An evergreen shrub of free and elegant habit 10 ft or more high; branches arching and slender, covered with whitish felt when young. Leaves oval, tapering towards both ends, ½ to 1 in. long, about half as wide; always dull green above, covered with whitish felt beneath; stalk up to ¼ in. long. Flowers ¼ to ⅜ in. across, borne in rounded corymbs of as many as fifteen or twenty; petals white, spreading; calyx woolly. Fruits scarcely ¼ in. long, dull red. *Bot. Mag.*, t. 8594.

Native of Yunnan, China, up to 9,000 ft altitude; raised in Paris in 1888, from seed sent there by the Abbé Delavay. Introduced to Kew in 1892. The differences between this species and *C. franchetii* have already been alluded to under that species. It is characterised by extreme elegance of habit, and by being very woolly on young bark, flower-stalk, calyx, and under-surface of leaves.

C. PROSTRATUS Baker

C. microphyllus var. *uva-ursi* Lindl.; *C. rotundifolius* Wall. ex Lindl.*

An evergreen shrub with arching branches growing to 5 ft high, sometimes procumbent or prostrate; stems hairy at first, later glabrous. Leaves arranged spirally on the stem, oval or obovate to roundish, ½ to ⅘ in. long, dark green and usually glabrous above, sparingly hairy beneath, sometimes rounded at the apex, sometimes with a short, abrupt point; stalk ¼ in. or less long. Flowers white, produced in clusters, usually two or three together, more rarely singly. Fruit red, rounded, ¼ in. or a little more in diameter, with two nutlets.

Native of the Himalaya from Kashmir eastwards; and of S.W. China; introduced, according to Loudon, in 1825. It is allied to *C. microphyllus* but differs in its larger, broadly ovate to roundish leaves and usually two- to three-flowered inflorescence, and makes a larger, more robust plant.

var. LANATUS (Jacques) *C. rotundifolius* var. *lanatus* (Jacques) Schneid.; *C. lanatus* Jacques; *C. buxifolius* Baker, not Lindl.; *C wheeleri* Hort.— In this variety the leaves are broad elliptic, densely hairy beneath; the cymes bear three to five flowers (up to eight on vigorous plants). In the form cultivated it is a very vigorous cotoneaster and one of the most useful, being pretty in habit, flower and fruit. It will grow to 10 ft high, forming a dense, impenetrable tangle of stems, from the main body of which stand out in every direction long, whip-like branches which give a very graceful and distinct effect. It is only necessary to tie the leading shoots to the fence until it is covered, and then leave the shrub to grow its own way; in this way it makes an admirable screen. This shrub used to be grown in gardens as "*C. buxifolius*" or "*C. wheeleri*", though some of the plants so named may be typical *C. prostratus*. The true *C. buxifolius* is quite a different species (q.v.).

C. RACEMIFLORUS (Desf.) K. Koch

Mespilus racemiflora Desf.; *C. fontanesii* Spach

A deciduous shrub up to 6 or 8 ft high, with slender branches, grey-felted when young, becoming glabrous and reddish brown later. Leaves oval or ovate,

* The name *C. rotundifolius* Lindl. admits of two interpretations. It is, in the majority of modern works, taken to refer to the species described here, which is an ally of *C. microphyllus*. But in previous editions of this work and, until recently, in the trade it was used for the species now more generally known as *C. distichus*, which is an ally of *C. horizontalis* and belongs to quite another section of the genus. Neither interpretation is indisputably correct or incorrect and, in view of this doubt, it seems better to reject the name *C. rotundifolius* as ambiguous. A note on this matter will be published elsewhere.

sometimes roundish, tapering towards the base, $\frac{1}{2}$ to $1\frac{1}{4}$ in. in length, dark green and ultimately glabrous above; grey-felted beneath. Flowers white, in clusters of four to twelve or more on felted stalks. Fruit roundish, bright red.

Native of N. Africa and of W. and Central Asia as far east as Turkestan; first described from plants growing in the Jardin de Plantes, Paris, in 1829 and introduced to Britain shortly thereafter. It is best known in cultivation by its Chinese varieties, introduced by Wilson. The attributions of the *Plantae Wilsonianae* are retained here; but his specimens have recently been re-studied by other botanists and their judgements are noted in due place.

var. MICROCARPUS Rehd. & Wils.—Fruits smaller than in the type or in var. *soongoricus*, ovoid, bright red; introduced by Wilson from W. Szechwan. In describing it, the authors remarked that it might represent a distinct species; if it were to rank as such, it would probably fall under *C. potaninii*, a species described in 1961 by the Russian botanist Poyarkova.

var. NUMMULARIUS (Fisch. & Mey.) Dipp. *C. nummularius* Fisch. & Mey.— A shrub of rather dwarf habit, 4 to 5 ft high, with more rounded leaves than in the type; native of Asia Minor and parts of Central Asia. It has been confused with the *C. nummularius* of Lindley, for which see *C. lindleyi*.

var. SOONGORICUS (Reg. & Herd.) Schneid. *C. fontanesii* var. *soongoricus* Reg. & Herd.; *C. soongoricus* (Reg. & Herd.) Popov—A native of Central Asia, first described from specimens collected in the region known as Dzungaria. Later, Wilson introduced a cotoneaster from W. Szechwan which was referred to this variety in *Plantae Wilsonianae*, but by the Russian botanist Poyarkova it is considered to be a distinct species—*C. tomentellus*. Wilson recorded it as common in arid river valleys and considered it to be one of the finest that he collected. In cultivation it has proved to be a graceful and exceptionally free-fruiting shrub, thriving even in dry, sandy soil. The Award of Merit was given in 1960 to a form with rose-coloured berries, shown by Maurice Mason of Kings Lynn, Norfolk.

A number of cotoneaster specimens collected in recent years in the E. Himalaya are referred to this variety by Yü and of these LSH 19632 has been introduced. This was found by Ludlow, Sherriff and Hicks in Bhutan in 1949 and has been given specific rank by Klotz (1963) as *C. LUDLOWII*.

var. VEITCHII Rehd. & Wils. *C. veitchii* (Rehd. & Wils.) Klotz—Leaves elliptic, sharply tapered at the apex, but chiefly distinguished from the type by its larger flowers (up to $\frac{3}{5}$ in. across) and by its larger fruit, which is more or less globose and up to $\frac{1}{2}$ in. wide. J. R. Sealy (*Bot. Mag.* under n.s., t. 245) considers that this variety has more affinity with *C. hupehensis* than with *C. racemiflorus*.

C. RHYTIDOPHYLLUS Rehd. & Wils.

An evergreen shrub up to 6 ft high, of graceful spreading habit; young shoots clothed at first with whitish down, which becomes tawny and mostly falls away before winter. Leaves of hard texture, oval-lanceolate, slender-pointed, tapered towards the base; $1\frac{1}{2}$ to $3\frac{1}{2}$ in. long, $\frac{1}{2}$ to $1\frac{1}{8}$ in. wide; dark glossy green, wrinkled and at first downy above; grey, woolly and strongly veined in five to ten pairs beneath; stalk about ⅛ in. long. Flowers white, borne ten to twelve together in corymbs about 1½ in. wide. Fruits pear-shaped, at first very downy, finally orange-red, ¼ in. long, containing three or four nutlets.

Native of W. Szechwan, China; discovered and introduced by Wilson in 1908. It is closely related to *C. henryanus*, but the leaves of that species have up to twelve pairs of veins, they are not so woolly beneath, and the fruits have only two or three seeds. Some plants cultivated under this name are really the common *C. henryanus*.

C. RUBENS W. W. Sm.

A deciduous shrub 2 to 4 ft high, of stout, flattish, spreading habit, irregularly branched; young shoots downy. Leaves roundish to broadly oval, ½ to 1 in. long, thinly hairy above at first, covered with pale yellowish wool beneath, obscurely mucronate; stalk scarcely discernible. Flowers solitary, almost stalkless, terminating short shoots, ⅜ in. wide, described by Forrest as 'red'; petals orbicular, ⅙ in. wide; calyx ovoid, appressed-downy; sepals ciliate; ovary densely woolly.

Native of Yunnan, China, discovered by Forrest in 1915. The late Mrs Gwendolen Anley, of Woking, showed a plant at Vincent Square in January 1935.

C. SALICIFOLIUS Franch.

An evergreen or semi-evergreen shrub up to 15 ft high, of spreading habit; young shoots downy. Leaves oval-oblong to ovate-lanceolate, 1½ to 3½ in. long, ⅓ to ¾ in. wide, rugose and glabrous above, downy and glaucous beneath; veins in five to twelve pairs, prominent. Flowers small, borne in very woolly corymbs up to 2 in. across. Fruit subglobose, ⅕ in. wide, bright red, carrying two or three nutlets.

var. FLOCCOSUS Rehd. & Wils. *C. floccosus* (Rehd. & Wils.) Flinck & Hylmö—Branchlets very slender, downy at first, but becoming glabrous and of a dark reddish brown by the end of the season. Leaves leathery, lanceolate or narrowly ovate, wedge-shaped at the base, tapering to a sharp point; ¾ to 2½ in. long, ¼ to ¾ in. wide; the upper surface glossy green, wrinkled, not downy; the lower one covered at first with silky white floss, some of which falls away by the end of the year, showing the grey-white surface beneath; veins in seven to fourteen pairs; leaf-stalk about ⅛ in. long. Corymbs about 1 in. wide, carrying nine to fifteen flowers at the end of short, three- or five-leaved twigs; stalks and calyx woolly, the teeth of the latter triangular. Fruit roundish, about ¼ in. diameter, bright red, containing usually three nutlets. *Bot. Mag.*, t. 8999.

Introduced by Wilson (No. 1133a) from W. China in 1908, and again in 1910. A very graceful, distinct, and attractive evergreen, highly recommended by its collector for the beauty of its fruit.

var. RUGOSUS (Pritz.) Rehd. & Wils. *C. rugosus* Pritz.—In this variety the leaves are larger, up to 3 in. long and 1⅛ in. wide, the veins numbering six to twelve pairs. The fruit is coral red, larger than in var. *floccosus*, and contains usually three nutlets. The plant is more vigorous, coarser looking, and with bigger leaves than var. *floccosus*, but in many respects similar.

Introduced by Wilson (No. 335) in 1907 from W. Hupeh, where he found it 9 ft high. *Bot. Mag.*, t. 8694.

In cultivation *C. salicifolius* has given rise to seedlings of procumbent or of low and spreading habit, several of which are in commerce, all raised on the continent: 'REPENS' (syn. 'Avondrood'), 'PARKTEPPICH' (both good for groundcover), 'GNOM' and others. 'HERBSTFEUER' (syn. 'Autumn Fire') was at one time considered to be a hybrid of the *C.* × *watereri* group but is now placed under *C. salicifolius* (Dr B. K. Boom in *Dendroflora*, Vol. 3, p. 11 (1966)). It is also of low, spreading but rather open habit and appears to breed more or less true from seed.

C. SIMONSII Baker

A deciduous, sometimes semi-evergreen shrub of erect, somewhat stiff habit, and up to 10 or 12 ft high; young branches covered with a dense, brown wool. Leaves arranged in opposite rows, ¾ to 1 in. long, ⅓ to ⅝ in. diameter; oval, roundish, or somewhat lozenge-shaped, tapering equally towards both ends; dark green, glossy and glabrous above except for scattered silky hairs when young, paler and hairy beneath; stalks less than ⅛ in. long. Flowers white, ⅓ in. diameter, produced usually two to four together on very short woolly stalks from small twigs. Fruit scarlet, ⅓ to ⅖ in. long; about the size and shape of common haws.

Native of the Khasi Hills, Assam. The introduction of this shrub is not recorded, and for a long time its origin was doubtful. Its native home was not known for certain until 1886, when it was discovered by C. B. Clarke at Lailankote, in the Khasi Hills. It had, no doubt, been introduced by, and named after, a Mr Simons, who had collected largely in the Khasi Hills many years previously. *C. simonsii* is a handsome vigorous shrub, very suitable for grouping in shrubberies, where it is well able to take care of itself, and for hedging. It differs from *distichus* in having more flowers in a cluster.

C. 'NEWRYENSIS'.—The status of this cotoneaster is rather uncertain. It has been regarded as a variety of *C. simonsii* or a hybrid between it and *C. franchetii*, but Flinck and Hylmö treat it as a species and place it near to *C. nitidifolius* and *C. glomerulatus*. It has a more arching habit than *C. simonsii* and larger leaves, woolly beneath. The fruits are borne in dense corymbose clusters. It appears to have been first distributed by Lemoine, who received it from the Daisy Hill nursery, Co. Down. (*C. newryensis* Lem.; *C. simonsii* var. *newryensis* (Lem.) Bean)

C. TOMENTOSUS Lindl.

A deciduous shrub of bushy habit up to 6 or 8 ft high, closely allied to *C. integerrimus* and differing chiefly in the rounder, larger leaves, the biggest of which are 2½ in. long and 1½ in. wide, slightly hairy above, very woolly beneath; stalk ⅛ to ¼ in. long. Flowers in short, nodding clusters, from three to six in each cluster, white; calyx very woolly; fruit red; nutlets three to five.

Native of the mountainous parts of Central and S. Europe; introduced in 1759. It can scarcely be regarded as more than a variety of *C. integerrimus*, although a rather superior one. The leaves are larger and more uniformly rounded at both ends, still not invariably so. The best distinction is afforded by the extremely woolly calyx and flower-stalk. (See also *C. zabelii.*)

C. TURBINATUS Craib

A vigorous evergreen shrub 10 ft or more high, of graceful habit; young shoots covered with fluffy grey down. Leaves narrowly oval, tapering about equally at both ends to a sharp point; ¾ to 2½ in. long, ⅜ to 1 in. wide; dark dull green above, covered beneath with a thick, grey-white felt. Flowers ¼ in. wide, white, with rose-coloured anthers, produced towards the end of July in hemispherical corymbs 1½ to 2½ in. across; flower-stalks and calyx covered with grey wool; petals round; calyx-lobes triangular-acuminate. Fruit pear-shaped, ¼ in. long, deep red, downy, ripe in October. *Bot. Mag.*, t. 8546.

Native of China; introduced to Kew in 1910 from de Vilmorin's collection at Les Barres. It is apparently perfectly hardy, and of rapid growth, remarkable and valuable among cotoneasters in flowering so late—six or eight weeks later than the majority, and a month later than any.

C. UNIFLORUS Bunge

This name has in gardens been given to several species of cotoneaster quite distinct from the true plant, most often to the evergreen *C. microphyllus*, with which it has nothing in common. The true *uniflorus* of Bunge is a deciduous shrub, found on the mountains of Siberia and Altai. It is, perhaps, only a dwarfed and depauperated *C. integerrimus*. In a wild state it is from a few inches to 2½ ft high, with thin, obovate or broadly oval leaves, ¾ to 1 in. long, glabrous above, downy when young beneath. Flowers usually solitary, sometimes in pairs; petals whitish, calyx glabrous. Fruit globose, red. This shrub is scarcely worth cultivating, and has probably no real claim to specific rank, but it differs from *C. integerrimus* in its dwarfer habit, its fewer flowers, and in the less woolly, smaller, narrower leaves.

C. ZABELII Schneid.

A deciduous shrub 6 to 9 ft high; young shoots covered with loose greyish hairs, becoming glabrous the second year, and dark brown. Leaves ½ to 1½ in. long, half to two-thirds as wide; variable in shape, but usually oval or ovate, mostly blunt to rounded at the apex, but sometimes pointed, the base rounded to truncate; dark dull green above, with loose, appressed hairs, clothed beneath with yellowish-grey felt; stalk ⅛ in. long, felted. Flowers in clusters of four to ten, small, rose-coloured; stamens twenty; flower-stalk and calyx felted. Fruit red, roundish pear-shaped, downy, ⅓ in. long; nutlets two.

Native of W. Hupeh, China; introduced in 1907 by Wilson, who described it as the common cotoneaster of the thickets of W. Hupeh. It is allied to *integerrimus* and *tomentosus*; from the former it differs in its felted calyx, and from both in the more numerously flowered inflorescences.

var. MINIATUS Rehd. & Wils. *C. miniatus* (Rehd. & Wils.) Flinck & Hylmö—Fruits smaller than in the type, light orange-scarlet. It is a denser plant, and the leaves turn yellow in autumn.

COWANIA   ROSACEAE

A genus of some four or five species of evergreen shrubs inhabiting the dry regions of North Mexico and the adjacent States of N. America. It was originally named by David Don in honour of James Cowan, a merchant who interested himself in the introduction of new plants, especially from Mexico and Peru. He died at Lima in 1823. *Cowania* belongs to the same group of the Rose family as *Fallugia* and *Cercocarpus*, distinguished by remarkable feathered styles terminating the seed-vessel similar to those that are so common in *Clematis*.

C. PLICATA D. Don
C. purpurea Zucc.

A stiff, much-branched evergreen up to 6 ft high with peeling bark; young shoots reddish, very glandular, covered at first with white appressed wool which soon falls off. Leaves ⅓ to 1 in. long, oblong or obovate with a tapering base, but deeply and pinnately five- to nine-lobed, covered with stalked glands; veins sunken above, prominent below; upper surface dark green, lower surface white with wool; margins decurved. Flowers solitary, very shortly stalked, terminal on short, leafy twigs, 1 to 1½ in. across, the rounded obovate petals rich rose; sepals glandular, reflexed; anthers yellow, the feathered styles shorter than in *C. stansburiana*. Bot. Mag., t. 8889–90.

Native of N. Mexico, first described and figured in Sweet's *British Flower Garden* in 1838 (vol. vii, t. 400). The plant depicted had been raised in a garden at Stamford Hill, where it blossomed in June 1837. It is a handsomer shrub than *C. stansburiana* and considering its great beauty and interest it would seem to be worth while to secure a consignment of seeds. It should succeed at the foot of a sunny wall grown in loam mixed with rubble of lime or mortar. It grows wild in limestone districts.

C. STANSBURIANA Torr.
C. mexicana var. *stansburiana* (Torr.) Jeps.

An aromatic evergreen shrub up to 6 ft high in a wild state, of stiff, sparse habit; young shoots thickly furnished with glands. Leaves alternate, mostly in clusters, three- or five-lobed, ¼ to ½ in. long; lobes linear with recurved margins, glandular above, covered with white down beneath, very stiff in texture. Flowers fragrant, solitary at the end of short twigs, ¾ in. wide, white or pale yellow;

petals five, obovate; calyx funnel-shaped at the base, with five lobes, glandular and downy like the flower-stalk; stamens numerous. Seed-vessels terminated by slender styles 1 to 1½ in. long, densely furnished with silky white hairs.

Native of the S.W. United States from Nevada, Utah, and Colorado to S. California, also of N. Mexico; discovered by Howard Stansbury in 1852 during his expedition to the great Salt Lake of Utah. This species and C. MEXICANA D. Don, are closely allied. Jepson, the Californian botanist, made it a variety of C. *mexicana*, and this status is accepted by Munz in *A California Flora* (1959). The calyx of C. *mexicana* is more bell-shaped than funnel-shaped. Both need the sunniest position that can be given them.

+ CRATAEGOMESPILUS   ROSACEAE

This name was devised to distinguish two deciduous trees, both of them chimaeras (graft hybrids) obtained by grafting the medlar (*Mespilus germanica*) on the hawthorn (*Crataegus monogyna*). They are trees of particular interest as affording evidence that Adam's story of the origin cf +*Laburnocytisus adamii* (q.v.) was not, as some people held, unbelievable. (Graft-hybrids have, as a matter of fact, been since obtained of set purpose, see *Kew Bulletin* 1911, p. 269.) The history of the two forms of *Crataegomespilus* is as follows: On a specimen of medlar grafted on a stock of hawthorn growing in the garden of Mr Dardar, at Bronvaux, near Metz, there was noticed a branch pushing from just beneath the graft which showed characters intermediate between those of the medlar and hawthorn. The leaves and fruits, although smaller, were those of the medlar, but the branches were spiny and the flowers in clusters, as in hawthorn. Plants raised from this branch are now known in gardens, and described below as +C. DARDARII.

Issuing from nearly the same place on Dardar's tree was another branch quite unlike the first; the leaves on this were lobed as in the hawthorn and the flowers also resembled those of that tree, but the leaves, shoots, and calyx were covered with grey wool, showing thereby the character of the medlar. The branch was propagated by grafting, and the plants so raised are now known, and described below, as +C. DARDARII 'Jules d'Asnières'. The same tree produced a third branch which at its base was purely hawthorn, but towards the extremity changed into 'Jules d'Asnières'. These branches were shown to E. Jouin of the Simon-Louis nursery, near Metz, about 1895, and he gave the first account of them in *Le Jardin*, Jan. 1899. The name *Crataegomespilus dardarii* was, however, first published in the *Revue Horticole* for 1899, p. 403, by Simon-Louis. In 1898 a grafted plant of +C. *dardarii* in the nursery of Messrs Simon-Louis of Plantières produced a branch of true medlar with the usual solitary flowers, whilst another branch was pure hawthorn. It will thus be seen that the behaviour of these graft-hybrids is very similar to that of +*Laburnocytisus adamii*.

The name *Crataegomespilus* has also been used for sexual hybrids between *Crataegus* and *Mespilus*. For these see ✕CRATAEMESPILUS.

+C. DARDARII Simon-Louis   BRONVAUX MEDLAR

A deciduous tree probably 15 to 20 ft high when fully grown, of pendulous habit; branchlets downy and more or less spiny. Leaves oblong, oval or ovate, 1½ to 4 in. long, ¾ to 1¾ in. wide; quite entire or more or less very finely toothed, downy on both sides; stalk ⅛ in. long. Flowers white, 1½ in. across, borne in

+ CRATAEGOMESPILUS DARDARII

corymbs as many as twelve together, each flower on a downy stalk ½ to 1 in. long; calyx with five narrow, pointed lobes ⅓ to ½ in. long, very downy. Fruit medlar-like, but smaller and in clusters.

A graft-hybrid between *Crataegus monogyna* and *Mespilus germanica*, but more nearly approaching the medlar (see above). On a tree at Kew which has flowered for several years past are three distinct types of growth. The bulk of the tree is +*C. dardarii*, as described above; but there are branches of 'Jules d'Asnières' (see below), and some of pure medlar, with its much larger leaves and solitary flowers and fruits. A tree at Aldenham produced a shoot and flowers of hawthorn.

cv. 'JULES D'ASNIÈRES'.—A small, deciduous, bushy-headed tree with pendulous branches, probably about 15 to 20 ft high ultimately. Shoots woolly, armed occasionally with hawthorn-like spines. Leaves varying in shape from obovate to broadly ovate; 1½ to 3 in. long, 1 to 1¾ in. wide; some entire, others deeply lobed like those of the hawthorn, mealy-looking when young, covered with soft down beneath. Flowers in corymbs, similar in form to those of the hawthorn, but larger and with a downy calyx; petals white, rose-tinted with age. Fruit oblong, brown, downy, about the size of those of the hawthorn. A beautiful flowering tree. For its history see the introductory note. The name 'Jules d'Asnières' is the one originally given to it by the raisers, and therefore to be preferred to 'Asnieresii'.

CRATAEGUS   HAWTHORN   ROSACEAE

The thorns in cultivation are deciduous trees or shrubs, nearly always more or less armed, sometimes very formidably, with spines. Some of the species from the southern United States and Mexico are inclined to be semi-evergreen. *Crataegus* is very sparsely represented in China, Japan, the Himalaya, and in western N. America. About a dozen species occur in Europe and Asia Minor. Most of the remainder are natives of eastern and central N. America, where an extraordinary number of beautiful species exist. A curious ignorance of the wealth of *Crataegus* in this area prevailed until the end of the last century. Sargent, dealing with the genus in his great *Silva of North America*, in 1892, described only fourteen species. Ten years later, in a supplement, the number increased to eighty-four. The number of so-called species of American thorns described and named up to the present is well over one thousand. The whole of them published up to about the year 1924 were listed and placed in their respective groups in the *Journal of the Arnold Arboretum*, Vol. 6, by E. J. Palmer. These groups number twenty-two. Palmer notes that the number of the stamens and the colour of their anthers furnish two of the most reliable characters for distinguishing species; the characteristics of the seeds (nutlets) and the venations of the leaves are also important.

It is scarcely credible that anything like so vast a number of genuine species exist there. A great many differ from each other scarcely more than garden varieties of apples do. At the present time, thanks to a growing understanding of the causes of the variation patterns seen in the American thorns a broader concept of the species is being adopted. Since 1925 the flow of new species from N. America has virtually dried up and many of those once recognised have been reduced to synonymy by Palmer (*Brittonia*, Vol. 5, pp. 471–90). In his treatment of the genus in the 'New Britton and Brown' (1952) the same author remarks that of the thousand and more species described from N. America 'many are now regarded as hybrids or as varieties of variable species'. In the area covered by that work he recognises 102 species as 'fully worthy of recognition as valid species'. A further sixty of more doubtful standing are also included.

It is evident that no work dealing with hardy trees and shrubs in general can, within ordinary and convenient limits, deal with more than a very small proportion of them. Even Dr Rehder of the Arnold Arboretum, Mass. (where are cultivated some six hundred "species" of *Crataegus*), has, in his comprehensive book on trees and shrubs cultivated in cool temperate N. America, given detailed consideration to less than thirty N. American species. There are in cultivation at Kew about 150 N. American species, but a monotonous proportion of them are what we should, in the old days, have lumped under *C. coccinea* or *mollis*. Certainly they have brought no increase of beauty into the genus anything like commensurate with their number. The genus can still quite adequately be represented in any garden by a selection from the species and varieties dealt with in these pages. Nor would it be justifiable to devote main entries to every one of the species included. Those of minor importance are given short treatment under some more important species in the same series or related series. These can be located by using the index in the present volume.

Leaves alternate, always toothed or lobed, often both; those of the vigorous non-flowering shoots of the year being usually much larger and broader at the base than those of the flowering shoots. They have also, as a rule, much larger and more persistent stipules. The stipules of *Crataegus*, however, vary so much, even on the same plant, that they do not afford very good differentiating characters. Flowers $\frac{1}{3}$ to $\frac{3}{4}$ in. in diameter; nearly always white, sometimes yellowish white, sometimes red in garden varieties; produced mostly in May and June, in flattish or rounded corymbs at the end of short, leafy shoots, which spring from the buds of the previous year's growths. In rare instances the flowers are solitary. Petals and calyx-lobes five; stamens five to twenty-five; styles one to five. Fruit a pome, consisting of a fleshy exterior, enclosing as many bony nutlets as there are styles. The fruits are of various colours, mostly red, but also black, yellow, and blue.

The nearest ally to *Crataegus* is *Cotoneaster*, which has, however, entire leaves and no thorns. *Mespilus* is also allied, but has large, solitary, scarcely stalked flowers, with long leaf-like lobes to the calyx. *Pyracantha*, included in *Crataegus* in many nineteenth-century works, differs in the evergreen leaves and in having consistently a five-styled flower and a fruit with always five nutlets.

The cultivation of the thorns presents no problems. They all like a loamy soil, and have no objection to lime. They are best raised from seeds, and trees so derived are better-growing and longer-lived than grafted ones. This applies especially to grafted trees of which stock and scion are of different species. It has long been the practice to graft the American thorns on C. *monogyna*, but although it is a longer business raising them from seed, it pays in the end. Named and selected forms have, perforce, to be increased by grafting; in that case stocks of the parent species should be selected.

As is the case with many temperate woody species, the seeds of the thorns require a period of after-ripening under cold and moist conditions before germination can take place; the optimum temperature is around 41°F. Species with hard seed-coats also need a period of warmth during which the bony outer-covering is softened by the attacks of soil organisms; this warm period must precede the cold one, since the after-ripening cannot begin until the seeds have been rendered permeable and the embryos have taken up water. The private grower is best advised to sow the seed in containers as early in the winter as possible; if germination does not take place in the following spring, it should do so a year later, though some species with very hard seed-coats may not germinate until the third year. If the species to be raised is known to be one which requires a preliminary warm period, sowing is best delayed until the late spring or early summer, since wintering will be ineffective in such cases until the seed-coats have softened. For the commercial grower who raises large numbers of plants in open-ground seed-beds it is clearly uneconomic to sow the seed until it is ready to germinate; it is therefore stratified in moist sand or peat for six or eighteen months, according to the species; the longer period is needed for the common hawthorn and many exotic species. Seed is extracted from the fruits by rotting or by macerating in water. For further information see *Contributions from the Boyce Thompson Institute*, Vol. 9, pp. 409–23, 1938, summarised in Barton and Crocker, *Twenty Years of Seed Research*, 1948, Chapters 6 and 8.

For the disease FIREBLIGHT, see the introductory note to *Cotoneaster*. The thorns do not transplant well if allowed to remain more than two or three years in a place. They like a good, well-drained soil, and the only pruning they need is the removal of overcrowding branches, and an encouragement of the leading shoot when young by removing rivals.

The thorns have two, frequently three, seasons of beauty—in flower, in fruit, and in the dying foliage. Few genera, indeed, supply so many charming lawn trees. Besides the garden forms of *oxyacantha* and *monogyna*, the following eleven thorns may be selected as specially worthy: *crus-galli*, ×*lavallei*, *macracantha*, *mollis*, *phaenopyrum*, *pinnatida* var. *major*, *prunifolia*, *punctata*, *tanacetifolia*, and *tomentosa* (*calpodendron*).

C. APIIFOLIA Michx.

A shrub or miniature tree in this country, with slender, downy young shoots; thorns 1 to 1½ in. long. Leaves triangular to kidney-shaped, the lower ones on the shoot deeply toothed, the upper ones deeply parallel-lobed as well as toothed; usually more or less hollowed at the base; 1 to 1¾ in. wide, not so long; bright green and almost or quite glabrous; stalk ½ to 1¼ in. long, slender. Flowers ¾ in. across; borne in May, each on a slender hairy stalk up to 1 in. long, in corymbs. Calyx-tube downy, the lobes glabrous; stamens twenty, anthers bright pink; styles one to three. Fruit scarlet, ⅓ in. long, oval.

Native of the southern United States; introduced early in the nineteenth century, but has frequently quite disappeared from cultivation. It is too tender for all but the milder parts of Britain, and although it may live for several years and flower, as it has done at Kew, I have never seen it bear fruit. It is very distinct in the shape and deep parallel lobing of the leaf.

C. APRICA Beadle

A small tree up to 20 ft high, or a shrub; branchlets zigzag, armed with thorns 1 to 1½ in. long; young shoots and leaves soon glabrous. Leaves broadly diamond-shaped, obovate, oval or even roundish, more or less tapered at the base, the upper half toothed and either pointed or rounded at the apex; lobed on strong barren shoots; ¾ to 2 in. long, nearly or quite as wide; stalks ¼ to ½ in. long, and, like the base of the leaf, very glandular. Flower ¾ in. diameter, white, produced three to six together on corymbs 1½ to 2 in. across; flower-stalk and calyx shaggy, calyx-lobes conspicuously glandular-toothed; stamens ten; anthers yellow; styles three to five. Fruit globose, ½ in. diameter, orange-red.

Native of the south-eastern United States; introduced in 1900. It belongs to the group of which *C. flava* is the type, but promises to be a much handsomer tree than that is. It flowers very freely, and its fruits are richly, if not very brightly coloured. It is marked by the very glandular leaf-bases, leaf-stalks, and inflorescence.

C. AZAROLUS L.   AZAROLE

C. aronia Bosc

A small, very slightly spiny tree up to 30 ft high; young shoots covered with fine down. Leaves wedge-shaped at the base, 1½ to 3 in. long, nearly as wide; obovate to rhomboidal, three- or five-lobed (sometimes almost to the midrib), lobes toothed at the end or sometimes entire; bright green, ultimately nearly glabrous above, downy beneath; stalk ½ to 1 in. long; stipules deeply toothed, cockscomb-shaped. Flowers white, about ½ in. across, produced during June in densely flowered corymbs 2 to 3 in. across; stamens twenty; style one or two (rarely three). Fruit up to ¾ or 1 in. diameter, globose, mostly orange or yellow, but varying to whitish or red, apple-like in flavour.

Native of S. Europe, N. Africa and the Near East; cultivated in England in the seventeenth century, but never, I think, very common—most of the trees so-called being either the var. *sinaica* or *C. laciniata*. The latter is different in general aspect, its leaves are thinner, and with narrower, deeper lobing as a rule, and the flowers have from three to five styles. The species is cultivated in S.E. Europe for its edible fruits, which vary much in size and colour.

var. SINAICA (Boiss.) Lange *C. sinaica* Boiss.; *C. maroccana* Lindl.—Leaves quite glabrous; fruit yellow or yellowish red. Native of the Near East; introduced in 1822. There is a specimen about 20 ft high in the Royal Victoria Park, Bath.

C. BRACHYACANTHA Sarg. & Engelm.   POMETTE BLEUE

A deciduous tree, described by Sargent as 40 to 50 ft high, forming a broad, compact, round-topped head; young shoots slightly downy at first, soon glabrous; thorns sturdy, ½ to 1 in. long. Leaves oval or ovate, 1 to 2 in. long, about half as wide, tapered at the base, shallowly round-toothed, glossy dark green, glabrous except on the upper surface when young. On vigorous barren shoots, the leaves are often of almost triangular shape, and truncate or even heart-shaped at the base, with stipules 1 in. long. Flowers small, the petals turning orange-coloured with age; flower-stalks and outside of calyx glabrous; calyx-lobes not toothed; stamens fifteen to twenty; styles three or five. Fruit roundish, bright blue, covered with a blue-white bloom, ⅓ to ½ in. across.

Native of the southern central United States; introduced in 1900. The most remarkable character of this thorn is the bright blue fruit. It belongs to Sargent's group *Brachyacanthae*, to which also belongs:

C. SALIGNA Greene—A native of Colorado, at 6,000–8,000 ft. Its glabrous reddish young shoots are armed with thorns ¾ in. or more long. Fruit globose, shining, $\frac{1}{4}$ in. across, red, finally blue-black. A tree 20 ft high, with firm-textured, deep green, smooth and glossy leaves up to 2 in. long and 1 in. wide, ovate-lanceolate or oval.

C. CHLOROSARCA Maxim.

A small, mostly unarmed tree, of pyramidal habit; young shoots stout, warted, slightly hairy at first, becoming by autumn deep brown-purple, with large, almost black buds. Leaves 2 to $3\frac{3}{4}$ in. long, nearly as wide at the base, triangular or broadly ovate, broadly wedge-shaped towards the stalk, rather shallowly seven- or nine-lobed, the lobes finely toothed, both sides hairy, the upper one becoming glabrous, very dark green; stalk $\frac{1}{3}$ to $\frac{3}{4}$ in. long; stipules gland-toothed. Flowers white, $\frac{1}{2}$ in. across; produced in corymbs 2 in. in diameter; outside of calyx and flower-stalks hairy; calyx-lobes minutely toothed; stamens twenty; styles five. Fruit black, $\frac{1}{2}$ in. diameter, flattened-globose.

Native of Manchuria and Japan; fairly common in gardens, where it is admired for the deep colouring of its branchlets. *C. chlorosarca* is only likely to be confused with *dsungarica* or *songorica*, which have also black fruit; it is distinguished from these by the shallower lobes of the leaves, their abrupter points, and finer teeth.

C. CHRYSOCARPA Ashe

A tree up to 20 ft high, with a wide-spreading head; young shoots at first more or less covered with loose white hairs which soon fall away, leaving them glabrous, shining brown; thorns up to 2 in. long. Leaves oval, diamond-shaped, or obovate; always wedge-shaped at the base, pointed at the apex, the upper half shallowly lobed, finely toothed, the teeth gland-tipped; 1 to 3 in. long, $\frac{3}{4}$ to 2 in. wide; at first downy above, becoming glabrous and glossy; hairy on the midrib and chief veins beneath; stalk $\frac{1}{2}$ to 1 in. long. Flowers white, $\frac{1}{2}$ to $\frac{3}{4}$ in. diameter, borne during May in corymbs 2 to 3 in. across; flower-stalks and calyx more or less shaggy with whitish hairs; stamens ten, anthers yellow; styles three or four. Fruit pendulous, red, rarely yellow, globose but rather flattened at the top, $\frac{1}{2}$ in. or less in diameter.

var. PHOENICEA Palmer *C. rotundifolia* Moench, not Lam.; *C. coccinea* var. *rotundifolia* (Moench) Sarg.—This distinct variety is quite glabrous except for slight down on the upper surface of the young leaves. Fruit lustrous red.

C. chrysocarpa is native of N. America from S.E. Canada to New York and westward into the Mississippi basin etc. The var. *phoenicea*, however, is confined to the eastern states. It is one of many species that have been grown as the *C. coccinea* of Linnaeus, and it was under this name that it appeared in previous editions of this work and in the first edition of Sargent's *Manual of the Trees and Shrubs of North America*. The name *C. coccinea* is now rejected as ambiguous, since Linnaeus applied it to two quite distinct species, now known as *C. pedicel-*

lata and *C. intricata*. Many other American thorns have been grown as *"C. coccinea"*, including *C. mollis*, *C. ellwangeriana* and *C. holmesiana*.

C. JACKII Sarg.—A small shrubby tree to about 10 ft high, confined to parts of Quebec province. Leaves oval to broadly ovate, sharply toothed, with shallow, indistinct lobes, truncate to broadly wedge-shaped at the base, 1 to 1½ in. long. Flowers with five to ten stamens and yellow anthers. Fruit dull red, juicy, broadly oblong to slightly egg-shaped, about ½ in. long, with two to three nutlets. Native of southern Quebec.

C. JONESIAE Sarg.—A tree to about 20 ft high, branchlets downy when young, becoming glossy orange-brown and armed with spines 2 to 3 in. long. Leaves broadly oval to obovate, up to 4 in. long, wedge-shaped at the base, sharply toothed and indented above the middle with pointed lobes; dark, glossy green above, downy beneath at least when young. Flowers up to 1 in. across; stamens ten with large rose-coloured anthers. Fruit bright red and juicy, ⅗ in. long, with two or three nutlets. Native of E. Canada and northern New England.

The following species, placed by Palmer in the series *Brainerdianeae*, may also be mentioned here:

C. DUNBARII Sarg.—A small shrubby tree to 15 ft high, with a dense, rounded crown. Leaves oval to ovate, shallowly lobed, hairy above when young, becoming dark glossy green. Flowers with ten stamens, anthers red, sepals edged with glandular teeth. Fruit with a thin flesh and three to four nutlets with cavities on the inner surface. Discovered by John Dunbar on the Genesee River, near Rochester, New York.

C. COCCINIOIDES Ashe

A round-headed tree to about 25 ft high, or a large shrub, with dark purple thorns 1½ to 2 in. long. Leaves triangular to ovate, truncate, rounded to slightly heart-shaped at the base, 2 to 2½ in. long and slightly less wide, with four to five pairs of pointed lobes, margins set with glandular teeth; they are rather thin, yellowish green, and almost glabrous even when young. Flowers ¾ in. wide, four to seven together in compact clusters; sepals with glandular teeth; stamens twenty, with red anthers. Fruit roundish, flattened at both ends, ⅗ in. across, juicy and bright red, with five nutlets.

A native of the Mississippi basin; introduced in 1883. According to Sargent, wild trees colour orange and scarlet in the autumn.

C. DILATATA Sarg. *C. coccinioides* var. *dilatata* (Sarg.) Eggl.—A tree up to 20 ft high, the leaves broadly ovate with an often rounded or cordate base, doubly toothed, glabrous when mature, 2½ in. long, almost as wide. Flowers white, large and as much as 1⅛ in. wide; stamens twenty with rose-coloured anthers; styles usually five; flower-stalks hairy. Fruits nearly globose, bright scarlet, about ¾ in. wide, ripening and falling early. Native of E. Canada and the eastern United States.

CRATAEGUS COCCINIOIDES

C. CRUS-GALLI L.   COCKSPUR THORN

A small, usually more or less flat-topped tree, with spreading, often horizontal branches; young shoots quite glabrous; thorns rigid, $1\frac{1}{2}$ to 3 in. long, ultimately twice as long, and branched. Leaves obovate, always tapered and without teeth towards the base, the apex toothed, rounded or abruptly pointed; 1 to 4 in. long, $\frac{1}{3}$ to $1\frac{1}{2}$ in. wide; dark glossy green and perfectly glabrous; stalk $\frac{1}{4}$ to $\frac{1}{2}$ in. long. Flowers white, $\frac{2}{3}$ in. across, produced in June on smooth-stalked corymbs 2 to 3 in. wide; stamens ten, anthers pink; styles usually two. Fruit nearly globose, $\frac{1}{2}$ in. diameter, deep red.

Native of eastern N. America; introduced in 1691. This beautiful and distinct thorn has much to recommend it. Its habit is striking and picturesque, it blossoms freely, its leaves change to brilliant scarlet in autumn, and its fruits, ripening in October and persisting until spring, make one of the brightest of early winter pictures. The species is, moreover, one of the hardiest and most thriving of its kind.

var. CAPILLATA Sarg.—Corymbs and flower-stalks furnished with down or short hairs.

var. PYRACANTHIFOLIA Ait.—Leaves oblong-lanceolate. Fruit smaller. Such variants are found in the wild state, intermingled with the type.

The following varieties are founded on variations seen in cultivated plants:

var. ARBUTIFOLIA Bean—Leaves obovate to oval, from $\frac{3}{4}$ to over 2 in. wide. In their size and to some degree their shape, this variety suggests *C. prunifolia* (q.v.), but it is quite free from down in all its parts, it has not more than ten stamens, and its fruits remain after the leaves. A handsome variety.

var. LINEARIS DC.—In the entire absence of down from this tree, it would appear to be a true *crus-galli* form intermediate between *arbutifolia* and *pyracanthifolia*.

var. SALICIFOLIA Ait.—Leaves narrower than in var. *pyracanthifolia*, oblanceolate; habit flat-topped.

C. BERBERIFOLIA Torr. & Gr.—A species related to *C. crus-galli* but amply distinguished by the downiness of the young parts and the yellow anthers. A native of the southern United States. It has been cultivated at Kew since 1878 and in spite of its southern habitat is quite hardy, although of no particular merit.

C. CANBYI Sarg.—A large shrub or small tree to 20 ft high, with a broad, open crown. In foliage it resembles *C. crus-galli* but the leaves are relatively broader, with their widest diameter near the middle. It also differs in the more lustrous fruit, with bright red flesh.

C. FONTANESIANA (Spach) Steud. *Mespilus fontanesiana* Spach; *C. olivacea* Sarg.—This species, introduced to Europe before 1830, differs from *C. crus-galli* chiefly in the thinner, yellowish-green leaves.

C. PERSISTENS Sarg.—A small tree closely resembling the cockspur thorn and perhaps a hybrid of it; it is not known in the wild state and its origin is uncertain. The leaves remain green well into the winter and the fruits remain long on the tree; it also differs from *C. crus-galli* in having flowers with twenty stamens. The glabrous undersides of the leaves distinguish it from *C.* × *lavallei*.

C. CUNEATA Sieb. & Zucc.

A twiggy shrub with slender, hairy, reddish young shoots; thorns about ¼ in. long, slender. Leaves obovate or somewhat spoon-shaped, much tapered and entire at the base, the apex rounded or abruptly tapered, slightly lobed and toothed; 1 to 2½ in. long, ½ to 1¼ in. wide; pale bright green, and soon quite glabrous above; slightly hairy beneath; stalk ½ in. long, or with the leaf-blade almost reaching to the base, hairy; stipules semi-heart-shaped, coarsely toothed, ½ in. long. Flowers white, ½ to ¾ in. across, produced during May and June in few-flowered corymbs; stalks hairy; stamens twenty; styles five, hairy at the base. Fruit globose or slightly pear-shaped, red, ½ to ⅝ in. diameter.

Native of Japan and Central China; long known in cultivation, but always rare. So far as I have seen, it has little to recommend it, although wild specimens show it to be a pretty bush in nature. I suspect it is spring tender.

C. × DIPPELIANA Lange

C. tanacetifolia var. *leeana* Loud.; *C. leeana* (Loud.) Bean; *C. celsiana* Dipp., not Bosc

The origin of the handsome thorn described here is not known for certain, but according to Loudon, who first described and figured it, it was believed to have originated in Lee's nursery at Hammersmith (*Arb. et Frut. Brit.*, p. 828). He records that it first flowered in 1836. The fact that it has to be called *C. × dippeliana* is simply due to a quirk of the rules of botanical nomenclature: Dippel (in 1893) identified this or some similar seedling (mistakenly) with the *C. celsiana* of Bosc, and Lange, in correcting the error, renamed it *C. dippeliana*. This name has priority over the more appropriate one of *C. leeana*, under which it was described in the first edition of this work.

   C. × dippeliana is a hybrid in whose origin one of the *orientalis* group of thorns has shared. The suggestion has been made that it is a hybrid between *tanacetifolia* and *punctata*, but it is difficult to see where the latter species is in evidence. Leaves 1½ to 3 in. long, ¾ to 2 in. wide; broadly ovate, sometimes obovate, with seven to eleven lobes reaching from one-third to half-way to the midrib; coarsely toothed; deep green and hairy at first above, becoming almost glabrous by the end of the season; more densely and permanently hairy beneath; stalk up to ⅝ in. long. Flowers ¾ to 1 in. diameter, white, produced very freely in mid-June; calyx and flower-stalk hairy like the young twigs; stamens eighteen to twenty-two. Fruit dull red, ½ to ⅝ in. across. No doubt closely allied to the tansy-leaved thorn, this is quite as handsome in flower, and it grows more robustly. The leaves are larger; the fruit smaller and red.

C. DOUGLASII Lindl.

C. rivularis Nutt.

   A tree 30 ft or more high, with a rounded head of branches; young shoots reddish brown, glabrous; thorns often absent; when present, ¾ to 1 in. long, stout. Leaves obovate to ovate, always tapered at the base, mostly pointed, sometimes rounded at the apex, upper part slightly lobed or double-toothed, or sometimes with two deep lobes near the base; 1½ to 4 in. long, 1 to 3 in. wide; dark glossy green and downy along the midrib above, ultimately quite glabrous below; stalk ½ to ¾ in. long. Flowers white, ½ in. diameter, produced during May in corymbs 2 in. across; calyx-tube and flower-stalk quite glabrous; calyx-lobes narrow, glandular-toothed or entire, downy inside; stamens twenty; styles two to five. Fruit black, ⅓ in. diameter, falling early.

   Native of N. America from Michigan to California and Oregon; introduced about 1828. It is one of the largest, but not, so far as I have seen, one of the most ornamental of thorns, its corymbs being rather small and its fruits ineffective.

C. DSUNGARICA Zab.

   A small tree, armed with spines ½ to ¾ in. long; young shoots glabrous, becoming bright purplish brown. Leaves of the barren shoots triangular, broadly wedge-shaped or cut almost straight across at the base, three- to seven-lobed, 1½ to 3¼ in. long and wide, the lowest pair of lobes large, spreading; leaves of the flowering shoots smaller, more ovate or diamond-shaped and tapered at the base, lobes sharply pointed and sparsely toothed; downy on both sides when quite young, soon becoming glabrous except in the vein-axils beneath; stalk ½ to

1⅜ in. long; stipules cockscomb-shaped, up to 1 in. diameter. Flowers white, ⅝ in. diameter, produced about the middle of May in corymbs 2 to 3 in. across; sepals and flower-stalks glabrous; stamens twenty; styles three to five; fruit globose, shining black, ½ in. in diameter, with three to five stones.

A handsome thorn native of Russian Central Asia. In foliage it much resembles *C. altaica* and *C. pinnatifida,* but its black fruits distinguish it from these and all of the Sanguinea group, except *C. chlorosarca* (*q.v.*). It is believed to be the product of hybridisation between *C. altaica* and the following species:

C. SONGORICA K. Koch *C. fischeri* Schneid.—A small tree or shrub, native of Russian Central Asia and bordering parts of China, also of Afghanistan and Persia. It closely resembles *C. dsungarica* but differs chiefly in the following particulars: leaves narrowly wedge-shaped at the base; inflorescence hairy; flowers with two or three styles; fruits purplish black, speckled, with two or three stones.

C. DUROBRIVENSIS Sarg.

A shrub 10 to 16 ft high, with glabrous young shoots; thorns 1½ to 2 in. long. Leaves broadly ovate, the base broadly wedge-shaped or rounded, the upper part sharply toothed, and cut up at each side into two or four triangular lobes ¼ to ½ in. deep; 1½ to 3 in. long, 1 to 2½ in. wide; quite glabrous on both surfaces except at first; stalk slender, glandular, up to 1⅛ in. long. Flowers white, ¾ to 1 in. across, stalks and outside of calyx glabrous; stamens twenty, anthers pink; styles five. Fruit globose, ⅝ in. diameter, dark shining crimson.

Discovered in May 1900 by J. Dunbar, on the banks of the Genesee River at Rochester, New York. Its flowers are amongst the largest in the genus, and the handsome fruits remain on the branches till midwinter. Sargent describes it as one of the most ornamental thorns of the northern United States. Introduced in 1901.

C. FLABELLATA (Spach) K. Koch
Mespilus flabellata Spach

A tree to 20 ft high with glabrous branchlets, armed with stout thorns. Leaves ovate to broad-ovate or rhombic, rounded to broadly wedge-shaped at the base, 1¼ to 2¾ in. long and almost as wide, with four to six pairs of sharply toothed, slender-pointed lobes, downy above and hairy on the veins beneath when young, later almost glabrous on both sides. Flowers in downy or hairy corymbs, with ten or fewer stamens; sepals toothed. Fruit crimson, ellipsoid, to ½ in. wide, with three to five nutlets.

In its typical state this species is confined to Quebec, but var. GRAYANA (Eggl.) Palmer, in which the flowers have twenty stamens and the fruit is more rounded, is of wider distribution. Both are very distinct in the fan-shaped, elegantly cut leaves. The species was introduced early in the nineteenth century (perhaps earlier to France).

C. MACROSPERMA var. ACUTILOBA (Sarg.) Eggl. *C. acutiloba* Sarg.— *C. macrosperma* is perhaps not in cultivation in its typical form, but the variety is an old inhabitant of European gardens, once grown as *"C. coccinea indentata"*. It has the leaves elegantly cut as in *C. flabellata* but may be distinguished by its glabrous corymbs and entire sepals.

C. FLAVA Ait.   YELLOW HAW

A tree 20 ft or more high, with glabrous young shoots; thorns about 1 in. long. Leaves obovate or diamond-shaped, always tapered and glandular at the base; pointed, sometimes three-lobed at the apex; doubly toothed; 1 to 2½ in. long, ½ to 1½ in. wide; glabrous on both sides; stalk ¼ to 1 in. long, glandular. Flowers white, ¾ in. diameter, produced in early June in corymbs of three to seven blossoms; flower-stalks glandular, glabrous (or at first somewhat downy); calyx glabrous, or downy only on the inner face, the lobes glandular; stamens ten to twenty; anthers purple. Fruit roundish, pear-shaped, greenish yellow, about ⅝ in. long.

Native almost certainly of eastern N. America, but not apparently known wild now in the form described by Aiton in 1789. A specimen from Bishop Good-enough's herbarium, dated 1781, is preserved at Kew, and is no doubt authentic, as it is ascribed to Solander, Aiton's coadjutor; this differs from the trees now cultivated at Kew by having about twenty stamens to each flower, and in being perfectly glabrous in flower and leaf. The species is of historical interest, and as being the type of a considerable group of thorns from the south-eastern United States; but in its few flowers and sparely borne, dull-coloured fruits it is one of the least ornamental.

C. HENRYI Dunn

A deciduous tree ultimately from 20 to 30 ft high, or often a shrub, quite without thorns; stipules semicordate, toothed, about ½ in. long. Leaves ovate-lanceolate or narrowly elliptical, unlobed and finely toothed on the flowering shoots, but occasionally three-lobed and more coarsely doubly-toothed on the barren ones; dark glossy green and (at first) furnished with short appressed hairs above, downy along the midrib and chief veins to nearly glabrous beneath; 1½ to 3 in. long by ⅝ to 1½ in. wide on the flowering shoots, 1 in. larger each way on the barren ones; stalk slender, ¼ to 1 in. long. Flowers creamy white, crowded in corymbs about 2 in. wide; stamens twenty; each flower ½ in. wide; flower-stalks glabrous. Fruit globose, dull red, ¾ in. wide, with five nutlets.

Native of Yunnan, China; discovered by Henry; introduced in 1909. A species distinct in its unarmed branches, narrow and ordinarily unlobed leaves, and five-stoned fruits. It is hardy at Kew and bears fruit there. Forrest collected it in Yunnan several times.

C. HETEROPHYLLA Flügge

A tree up to 20 ft high, forming a round dense head of branches; young shoots glabrous; not, or but little, armed. Leaves of two distinct types, viz.—(1) those of the barren shoots: diamond-shaped, tapered and entire at the base, the upper part sharply pointed, deeply lobed (after the fashion of *monogyna*), the lobes sharply and irregularly toothed; $1\frac{1}{2}$ to 3 in. long, $1\frac{1}{4}$ to $2\frac{1}{2}$ in. wide; stalk $\frac{1}{2}$ to $\frac{3}{4}$ in. long; (2) those of the flowering shoots: much smaller, oblong, obovate or oval, sometimes entire or with a few teeth at the apex only, sometimes the upper leaves of the shoot conspicuously three-lobed at the apex; 1 to $1\frac{1}{2}$ in. long, $\frac{1}{3}$ to $\frac{3}{4}$ in. wide. All the leaves are glossy dark green and quite glabrous. There are large, coarsely toothed stipules on the barren shoots, none on the flowering ones. Flowers white, $\frac{3}{4}$ in. across, borne during May and June in corymbs 2 to 3 in. across; flower-stalks and calyx glabrous; stamens fifteen to twenty, styles solitary. Fruit bright red, slenderly oval, $\frac{1}{2}$ to $\frac{5}{8}$ in. long.

Native of Armenia; cultivated since the beginning of the nineteenth century; not now very frequently seen, although there is an example about 30 ft high in the Royal Victoria Park, Bath. It is a beautiful thorn of the Oxyacantha group, bearing its large flowers and bright fruits freely. It is also one of the most distinct by reason of its variously shaped leaves, its long narrow fruits, and the absence of down from the younger parts.

C. INTRICATA Lange
C. coccinea L., in part

A shrub 3 to 12 ft high with spreading or upright branches armed with slender spines 1 to $1\frac{1}{2}$ in. long. Leaves thin, glabrous, ovate, rounded or wedge shaped at the base, $1\frac{1}{4}$ to $2\frac{1}{4}$ in. long, margins double-toothed, with shallow, pointed lobes; stalks slender, about 1 in. long. Corymb three- to seven-flowered; bracts and sepals glandular; stamens usually ten, with pale yellow or pinkish anthers. Fruit roundish to ellipsoid, reddish brown, with three to five nutlets. In var. STRAMINEA Palmer, the leaves are usually broadest near the middle, the anthers usually pink or purple and the fruit yellowish green to dull orange. Both are natives of eastern N. America.

C. LACINIATA Ucria
C. orientalis Bieb.; C. odoratissima Lindl.

A small, nearly unarmed tree 15 to 20 ft high, with a rounded or flattish, spreading head of branches, often pendulous at the ends; young branchlets at first covered with whitish hairs, many of which fall away by the end of the season. Leaves mostly triangular or lozenge-shaped; 1 to 2 in. long, nearly or quite as much wide; wedge-shaped to almost square at the base, more or less deeply cut (often nearly to the midrib) into five to nine narrow oblong lobes, which are themselves jaggedly toothed at the points; dark green above, grey beneath, downy on both sides; stalk $\frac{1}{4}$ to $\frac{3}{4}$ in. long; stipules $\frac{1}{3}$ in. across, with a few large teeth. Flowers $\frac{3}{4}$ in. across, white, produced in early June in corymbs of twelve or more blossoms; calyx and flower-stalks grey-woolly; stamens twenty. Fruit coral-red or yellowish red, $\frac{3}{4}$ in. diameter, globose, downy.

Native of the Orient; introduced in 1810. This beautiful thorn is much planted in the south of England, and is common in some of the London parks. Both in flower and fruit it is a charming tree.

C. HELDREICHII Boiss.—This species, a native of Greece, is closely allied to C. *laciniata (orientalis)*, from which it differs in its smaller leaves, $\frac{3}{5}$ to $2\frac{1}{5}$ in. long, with rounded, more or less entire lobes. There is an example about 12 ft high in the R.H.S. Garden at Wisley.

C. SCHRADERANA Ledeb. *C. orientalis* var. *sanguinea* Loud.; *C. tournefortii* Griseb.—Laxer than *C. laciniata (orientalis)* in habit, and with the lobes of the leaves somewhat broader. It is not so effective in fruit as that species, the fruits being of a dark dull or purplish red. Native of Greece and the Crimea.

C. × LAVALLEI Herincq ex Lav.

C. carrierei Vauvel ex Carr.

The tree on which this name is founded arose in the Segrez Arboretum, France, and was first described in 1880. Three years later Carrière published an account (*Rev. Hort.*, 1883, p. 108) of a very similar hawthorn, which was distributed, and long known as, *C. carrierei*. In a botanical sense this name must be regarded as a synonym of *C.* × *lavallei*, but it is desirable to preserve the name in cultivar form, in order to distinguish Carrière's plant from the Segrez form. Whether the latter was ever propagated and distributed is not known.

cv. 'CARRIEREI'.—A tree of sturdy, leafy habit up to 15 or 20 ft high; young shoots downy, sometimes retaining the down until the second season; thorns few, stout, 1 to $1\frac{1}{2}$ in. long. Leaves obovate or oval, tapered at both ends, $1\frac{1}{2}$ to $4\frac{1}{2}$ in. long, 1 to $2\frac{1}{2}$ in. wide; coarsely and irregularly toothed, glossy dark green above and soon glabrous except along the midrib; permanently downy beneath, especially on the midrib and veins; stalk $\frac{1}{4}$ to $\frac{3}{4}$ in. long. Flowers white, nearly 1 in. across, produced in June in erect corymbs about 3 in. in diameter. Flower-stalks and calyx very woolly, the lobes of the latter glandular-toothed, linear-lanceolate; stamens twenty; styles one to three. Fruits orange-red specked with brown, globose with a pear-shaped base, $\frac{3}{4}$ in. wide, persisting through the winter.

This fine thorn was said by Carrière (loc. cit.) to have originated in the Jardin des Plantes, Paris, from seed of *C. mexicana* (i.e. *C. stipulacea*). Certainly, it bears a strong resemblance to that species, which, however, has yellow fruit, not tapered where it joins the stalk, and its calyx-lobes are less conspicuously gland-toothed. The pollen parent is now generally thought to be *C. crus-galli*. It is one of the handsomest of all thorns, either in foliage, flower or fruit.

C. × GRIGNONENSIS Mouillef.—Another hybrid from *C. stipulacea*, which it resembles more closely than does *C.* × *lavallei*. It was first observed at Grignon in France in 1873 and probably originated there. It has much the same garden value as *C.* × *lavallei* 'Carrierei', which it resembles in the long persistent leaves and fruits but from which it differs in its glabrous shoots.

C. MACRACANTHA Loud.

A tree up to 15 ft or more high, and perhaps the most formidably armed of all thorns, the spines being sometimes 4 or 5 in. long, and very abundant; young shoots reddish brown, glabrous. Leaves roundish oval or obovate, 2 to 4 in. long, $1\frac{1}{2}$ to 3 in. wide; tapered more or less at the base, pointed at the apex, the upper part usually more or less lobed; sharply toothed; dark green, leathery, glabrous above except when young; remaining downy beneath, although finally only on the parallel veins (of which there are six or seven pairs) and the midrib; stalk $\frac{1}{4}$ to $\frac{3}{4}$ in. long. Flowers white, $\frac{3}{4}$ in. across, produced in May and June in corymbs 2 or 3 in. wide; flower-stalk either downy or not; calyx-lobes narrow, downy inside, glandular-toothed; stamens eight to ten, anthers yellow. Fruit globose, bright crimson, $\frac{1}{3}$ to $\frac{1}{2}$ in. diameter.

Native of eastern N. America; introduced in 1819. It is one of the most remarkable of all thorns in the extraordinary number and size of its thorns, even larger than in *C. crus-galli*. It is also one of the handsomest in fruit, a good grower, and very hardy. It differs from both *C. tomentosa* and *C. succulenta* in having not more than ten stamens, and yellow anthers. All three species are characterised by a longitudinal cavity on the inner side of the nutlets.

C. MOLLIS (Torr. & Gr.) Scheele [PLATE 69
C. coccinea var. *mollis* Torr. & Gr.

A tree up to 30 or 40 ft high, with a wide-spreading head of glabrous, grey branches; young branchlets covered with whitish hairs the first season; thorns 1 to 2 in. long. Leaves broadly ovate, rounded, truncate or heart-shaped at the base, pointed, with four to seven shallow lobes at each side, and very sharply glandular-toothed; 2 to $4\frac{1}{2}$ in. long, and nearly or quite as broad; both surfaces, but especially the lower one, downy, the upper becoming rather rough in the latter part of the season; stalk 1 to 2 in. long. Flowers white, 1 in. across; flower-stalks and calyx thickly coated with white hairs; calyx-lobes toothed and glandular, stamens about twenty; anthers pale yellow; styles four or five. Fruit subglobose, $\frac{3}{4}$ to 1 in. diameter, red, downy.

Native of the Central United States; long introduced, but much confused with *C. chrysocarpa*, a thorn with shoots soon glabrous, leaves more or less tapered at the base, flowers with only ten stamens, and fruit only $\frac{1}{2}$ in. across. *C. mollis* is also well distinguished by its larger leaves being always downy (very much so when young). As a flowering tree it is one of the most beautiful of thorns, and as a fruit-bearer is also handsome, but its fruits drop early (in September), a month or six weeks in front of those of *C. chrysocarpa*.

C. mollis is made the type of a group of American thorns by Sargent, which contains a number of very fine species, amongst which the following may be mentioned:

C. ARKANSANA Sarg. A tree 20 ft high, native of Arkansas; differing from *C. mollis* in the fruits being of longer, more oblong shape, and ripening in October; the leaves also are generally more tapered at the base. I saw a fine specimen in the Arnold Arboretum, and was struck by its great elegance of habit. Introduced in 1902. It is now considered to be part of the normal variation of *C. mollis*.

C. ARNOLDIANA Sarg.—A tree 15 to 20 ft high, native of Massachusetts and

TS—CC

Connecticut, with apparently a very local distribution. This species has only ten stamens to each flower. Introduced in 1901. It is a sturdy tree with a dense head of very thorny zigzag branches; thorns up to 3 in. long. It is thriving vigorously in this country. The fruit ripens in August.

C. SUBMOLLIS Sarg.—This differs from *C. mollis* in the flowers having only ten stamens. A tree 20 to 30 ft high, with broadly ovate, lobed and toothed leaves about 3 in. long, softly downy beneath. Flowers white, 1 in. wide, borne on very downy stalks; anthers pale yellow. Fruit broadly pear-shaped, ¾ in. long, bright orange-red, falling early. Native of the eastern United States; long in cultivation but confused with *C. mollis*. It was given an Award of Merit in 1953 when shown by Messrs Hilling of Chobham.

C. MONOGYNA Jacq.   COMMON HAWTHORN

The common hawthorn, as popularly known, consists of two very distinct forms now usually regarded as a separate species, viz., *C. monogyna* and *C. oxyacantha* (q.v.). *C. monogyna* is the commoner one, and is distinguished from the other by being, as a rule, a larger tree (up to 35 ft); its leaves are larger and more deeply three- to seven-lobed; its flowers have but one style, and its fruits but one stone. The fruit also is rounder and less elongated. It is, within its own limits, a very variable tree, and numerous named varieties are in cultivation. Many of these have little interest or value; the best and most distinct are noted below. Although the typical forms of *oxyacantha* and *monogyna* are absolutely distinct, they are united by others of an intermediate character, having flowers with one or more styles, and fruits with one or more stones. Some of the cultivars may belong to these intermediates, but to avoid complicating the nomenclature it seems best to retain them in the species they most resemble or under which they have customarily been placed. Those who regard the two as forms of a single species have much to support their view.

Crataegus monogyna, being more formidably armed than *C. oxyacantha*, is the one in common use for making hedges. On the whole, it may safely be said that no other tree or shrub is, in our climate, so good for the purpose. Easily raised, transplanting well when small, and bearing any amount of clipping, it fills a unique place in the English landscape in constituting tens of thousands of miles of hedgerow. Besides its efficacy as a hedge, due to its thorny nature and dense growth, it has in its rich, polished, green foliage much beauty as well, although well-kept hedges do not flower much, owing to the flowering wood being cut away in autumn.

The naturally grown hawthorn has a singular beauty of habit. It forms a comparatively slender trunk (1 to 2 ft in diameter, however, in old specimens), supporting a rounded head of dense branches gracefully pendulous at the ends. When in blossom no object of our waysides has greater beauty, and its charm is heightened by one of the sweetest of open-air perfumes. The flowers of the hawthorn open from the middle of May until early June. In accounting for its associations with the games and festivals of early May-time, we must remember that these grew up under the Old Style calendar, when 1st May occupied the same place in relation to the equinox that 13th May does at the present time. The hawthorn is very rarely in bloom on our present first of May.

cv. 'BIFLORA'. GLASTONBURY THORN.—This remarkable variety, besides bearing a crop of blossom at the ordinary season, flowers and produces young foliage in winter. The popular belief that it breaks into flower about Christmas Day has frequent support in fact, although much depends on the season. In the south and west of England, if November and December be mild, it will have some flowers open on Old Christmas Day (7th January). If those months are cold and the winter severe and long, the flowers may not expand until March or April. On the other hand, I have gathered flowers in November. The legend of the Glastonbury Thorn is, briefly, as follows:

Joseph of Arimathea, after the crucifixion of Christ, came to England to found Christianity. He went to Glastonbury, where, his exhortations having but little influence on the inhabitants, he prayed that a miracle might be performed in order that they might be convinced of the divine nature of his mission. God granted his prayer, for his staff, on being thrust into the ground, immediately burst into leaf and flower, although it was then Christmas Day. The wonder was thereafter repeated on every anniversary of that day.

An old tree grew in the vicinity of Glastonbury Abbey until about the beginning of the nineteenth century, to which popular belief attached this legend. The variety is worth growing, not only for the sake of the old legend, but because of its interest in flowering in midwinter. The flowers are not borne so abundantly as in May, but they have the true hawthorn fragrance, and this brings vividly to one's mind (as odours do), the most glorious season of the year. (*C. oxyacantha* var. *biflora* West.; *C. o.* var. *praecox* Loud.)

cv. 'FILICIFOLIA'.—Leaves broad, cuneate at the base, finely cut into curled segments (*Fl. des Serres*, Vol. 20, p. 51, and t. 2076, 1874). It is not the same clone as 'Pteridifolia' (Loudon, *Arb. et Frut. Brit.*, p. 865).

cv. 'FLEXUOSA'.—Branches 'twisted in a zig-zag manner'; distributed by Smith of Ayr and described by Loudon (*Arb. et Frut. Brit.*, p. 835).

cv. 'HORRIDA'.—Branches extremely thorny; forming conspicuous nests of thorns at the joints.

cv. 'INERMIS COMPACTA'.—Very dwarf and quite unarmed; a remarkable form, put into commerce by Späth's nurseries.

f. LACINIATA (Loud.) Dipp. *C. oxyacantha* var. *laciniata* Loud.—Leaves deeply cut, with irregularly toothed lobes; such variants occur wild with the type. The cultivar name 'Laciniata' would belong to the form of this nature distributed by Loddiges' nursery (Loudon, *Arb. et Frut. Brit.*, p. 830 and p. 865, fig. 603).

f. PENDULA (Loud.) Rehd. *C. oxyacantha* var. *pendula* Loud.—Branches pendulous. Such forms have arisen in seed-beds and have also been obtained by the grafting of wood taken from witches' brooms. The cultivar name would belong to a pendulous form distributed by Loddiges' nurseries around 1835.

cv. 'RAMULIS AUREIS'.—Branches yellow. Received at Kew in 1885 from Simon-Louis Frères. 'Xanthoclada', distributed by Späth, is possibly the same clone.

cv. 'REGINAE'.—A name given to the descendants of a tree which once grew in a garden near Edinburgh that belonged to the Regent Murray. Mary, Queen of Scots, was said to have spent many hours beneath it. It is, apparently, ordinary *C. monogyna*.

cv. 'SEMPERFLORENS'.—Blossoms continuously or at intervals from the ordinary time until August. It has tiny leaves ½ to 1 in. long, and slender branches, and is of shrubby habit and very slow-growing. A remarkably distinct dwarf variety. It was found in a seed-bed in Bruant's nursery, Poitiers—hence the old garden name "*C. bruantii*".

cv. 'SESTERIANA'.—Flowers double red.

f. STRICTA (Loud.) Zab. *C. oxyacantha* var. *stricta* Loud.—Branches erect. The cultivar name 'STRICTA' belongs to a clone that, according to Loudon, arose in Ronald's nursery at Brentford and was said by him to resemble the Lombardy poplar in habit. Such forms have been in commerce more recently, but whether they are of this clone or of independent origin is uncertain. There is a specimen in the R.H.S. Garden, Wisley, 25 ft high (1968).

There are also forms with yellowish and with variegated leaves.

C. NIGRA Waldst. & Kit.　　C. HUNGARIAN THORN

A tree 20 ft high, forming a rounded head of rather stiff branches; young shoots felted with a grey down, becoming smoother and purplish; thorns about ½ in. long, often almost absent. Leaves triangular to ovate, wedge-shaped to almost straight across at the base; 1½ to 4 in. long, usually two-thirds to quite as wide; seven- to eleven-lobed, the lower lobes reaching not more than half-way to the midrib, the upper ones shallower; sharply toothed, dull green, both surfaces downy; stalk rarely more than ¾ in. long, very downy; stipules sharply and coarsely toothed. Flowers white, turning rosy with age, ⅝ in. across, produced during May in rather small corymbs. Calyx and flower-stalks grey-hairy; stamens twenty; styles five. Fruit flattened globose, up to ½ in. diameter, shining black and soft.

Native of Hungary; introduced in 1819. Very distinct in its dense grey covering from other thorns, it is not, however, one of the most attractive. The inflorescences are too small and the foliage too far advanced at flowering time to make a good display.

C. OLIVERIANA [Dum.-Cours.] Bosc

Mespilus oliveriana Dum.-Cours.; *C. oxyacantha* var. *oliveriana* (Bosc) Lindl.; *C. pentagyna* var. *oliveriana* (Dum.-Cours.) Rehd.

A shapely small tree with the habit of the common hawthorn, but not so tall; young shoots grey, downy. Leaves 1 to 2 in. long, often as wide; three- or five-lobed, the basal lobes deep; grey with down on both sides, especially beneath, remaining downy until they fall, even on the upper side; stalks ½ to 1¼ in. long. Flowers white, ⅝ in. across, in compact corymbs about 2 in. across. Calyx and flower-stalk very woolly. Fruits about ¼ in. long, egg-shaped, black-purple, at first hairy, abundant.

Native of S.E. Europe. This rather striking thorn has by some authors been placed under *C. pentagyna*, to which it is, no doubt, closely allied. But, as represented at Kew, it differs plainly from it in the small fruits, in the deeper, more finely toothed lobes of the leaf, in the abundant and more persistent down, and in the entire or less deeply toothed stipules. It is, I think, undoubtedly the thorn mentioned by Loudon under the second synonym given above and figured by Lindley in *Bot. Reg.*, t. 1933.

C. ORIENTALIS *see* C. LACINIATA

C. OXYACANTHA L. emend. Jacq.*   HAWTHORN or MAY
C. oxyacanthoides Thuillier

A small thorny tree up to 15 or 20 ft high, with thorns 1 in. long. Leaves mostly obovate, three- or five-lobed, wedge-shaped at the base, the lobes rounded or pointed; toothed, dark glossy green, glabrous except when quite young; $\frac{1}{2}$ to $2\frac{1}{4}$ in. long, two-thirds to as much wide; stalks slender, $\frac{1}{4}$ to $\frac{3}{4}$ in. long. On strong, barren shoots the leaves are often more deeply lobed, and with large, gland-toothed stipules. Flowers white, $\frac{5}{8}$ in. diameter, produced during May six to twelve together in corymbs, the leaves at the time almost fully grown; calyx and flower-stalks glabrous; stamens about twenty, anthers red; styles two or three. Fruits roundish ovoid, $\frac{1}{4}$ to $\frac{3}{4}$ in. long, red, containing two, sometimes three stones.

Native of Europe, including Britain, and one of the two forms (now usually regarded as distinct species) known popularly as 'may' or 'hawthorn'. The other is *C. monogyna* (q.v.), which is best distinguished by having only one style and one stone in the fruit. Although *C. oxyacantha* has not broken up into so many varieties as *monogyna*, to it belong some of the very best garden forms of hawthorn. None make lovelier lawn trees.

f. AUREA (Loud.) Schneid. *C. oxyacantha* var. *xanthocarpa* (Roem.) Lange— Fruits yellow; occasionally found in the wild. In the first edition of this work, Loudon's *C. oxyacantha* var. *aurea* was transferred to *C. monogyna* but it has been assumed by most authorities that the yellow-fruited haw known to Loudon did indeed belong to *C. oxyacantha*. There is no evidence that a yellow-fruited form of *C. monogyna* has ever been in cultivation at Kew. For *C. monogyna fructu luteo* see 'François Rigaud'.

* The nomenclature of this species is involved. At an early date the name *C. oxyacantha* L. was used both for this species, which normally has two styles and fruits with two nutlets, and for the allied species with only one style and one nutlet. In 1775 the Austrian botanist Jacquin restricted *C. oxyacantha* L. to the former and gave the name *C. monogyna* to the one-styled species. However in 1946 J. E. Dandy (in *Rep. Bot. Exch. Club Br. Is.*, Vol. 12, p. 867) showed that none of the specimens seen by Linnaeus was the two-styled species, and that the name *C. oxyacantha* L. ought to have been used for the one-styled plant. The next available name—*C. oxyacanthoides* Thuill.—was therefore taken up for the two-styled species and *C. oxyacantha* L. abandoned as an ambiguous name. More recently, however, Prof. Franco has pointed out (in Fedde, *Rep. Sp. Nov.*, Vol. 74, p. 25) that there is yet another and older name for the two-styled species, namely *Mespilus laevigata* Poiret, published in 1798. If, then, the name *C. oxyacantha* must be abandoned, the correct name for this species would be *C. laevigata* (Poir.) DC.

cv. 'FRANÇOIS RIGAUD'.—Fruits yellow; branchlets yellowish. The tree at Kew was received from Bruant in 1894 as *C. "azarolus"* 'François Rigaud' but certainly does not belong to that species. It agrees with *C. oxyacantha* in its foliage but the flowers bear one or two styles and the fruits contain one or two nutlets, which suggests that it may be a hybrid with *C. monogyna*. This tree appeared in the old Kew Hand-lists as "*C. monogyna fructu luteo*".

cv. 'GIREOUDII'.—Late growths mottled with pink and white. Put into commerce by Späth in 1899. Mrs Stachan has a specimen of this variety in her garden near Cranleigh, Surrey, which has made a mound some 12 to 15 ft high and 40 to 45 ft in diameter.

cv. 'MASEKII'.—Flowers double, of a delicate rose. The origin of this variety is not known, but it was put into commerce by Späth in 1899.

cv. 'PAUL'S SCARLET'.—The best of all double-flowered red thorns. It originated about 1858 as a 'sport' on a tree of the double pink variety growing in the garden of Mr Christopher Boyd, near Waltham Cross. It was propagated by Wm. Paul and shown by him at the International Horticultural Exhibition of 1866 (*C. o. coccinea plena*; *C. o. paulii*).

cv. 'PLENA'.—Flowers double, white, changing to pink as they age. Culti-vated since the end of the eighteenth century and apparently a single clone. In 'Candida Plena', put into commerce by Späth in 1911, the flowers remain pure white.

cv. 'PUNICEA'.—Forms with rose-coloured flowers are occasionally found in the wild (see f. *rosea*) but in this clone they are crimson and the petals larger than in wild plants. It was raised in Scotland and distributed by Loddiges (*Bot. Cab.*, t. 1363, 1828).

cv. 'PUNICEA FLORE PLENO'.—According to Loudon (*Trees and Shrubs*, 1842) this thorn, with pink double flowers, was introduced from the continent in 1832. It is probably the parent of 'Paul's Scarlet'.

f. ROSEA (Willd.) Rehd.—Flowers tinted with rose. Such forms are fairly common in the wild.

C. × MORDENENSIS Boom—This name has been published recently for hybrids between *C. oxyacantha* and *C. succulenta*. The original form of the cross, named 'TOBA', was raised at the Morden Experimental Farm, Mani-toba, Canada, the first parent being 'Paul's Scarlet'. Leaves deeply two- to four-lobed, larger than in the first parent. Thorns shorter than in the second parent, inflorescence glabrous, sepals without glands. Flowers (of 'Toba') double, white, ageing to pink.

C. PEDICELLATA Sarg.

C. coccinea L., in part

A tree to 20 ft high with scaly, brown bark and a symmetrical crown of spreading or ascending branches; branchlets chestnut-brown, slightly hairy at first; spines to 2 in. long. Leaves broadly ovate, 3 to 4 in. long, rounded to broadly wedge-shaped at the base, rough to the touch above, glabrous beneath;

margins coarsely toothed, with four to five pairs of pointed lobes. Flowers white, borne in loose corymbs on long, thin, slightly downy stalks; stamens usually ten, their anthers rose-coloured. Fruit bright scarlet, pear-shaped to oblong, ¾ in. long, ripe in September. Native of eastern N. America. Its variety GLORIOSA Sarg., is one of the finest of all thorns as regards the size and colour of its fruits, which are larger and more lustrous than in the type. According to Sargent this variety is found wild near Rochester, New York, but is not common.

C. ELLWANGERIANA Sarg. *C. pedicellata* var. *ellwangeriana* (Sarg.) Eggl.— This thorn bears much resemblance to the preceding, differing chiefly in its hairy or downy inflorescence and the downiness of the leaf-stalks and the undersides of the leaves. However, it also bears a close resemblance to *C. submollis* Sarg., and *C. mollis* Scheele, but both those species have yellow anthers and the young leaves beneath, the leaf-stalks and inflorescences are tomentose, while the latter is further distinguished by its twenty, not ten, stamens. E. J. Palmer treats it as a variety of *C. pedicellata* but suggests that it might in fact be a hybrid between that species and a species of the *Molles* series. This is one of the most ornamental of the American thorns, especially when in fruit. It was given an Award of Merit in 1922 and is figured in *Bot. Mag.*, n.s., t. 105. The type-tree grew in the nursery of Ellwanger and Barry at Rochester, New York, but the species (if such it be) is of fairly wide distribution in north-eastern N. America.
Another ally of *C. pedicellata* is:

C. HOLMESIANA Ashe—A tree to about 30 ft; branches usually ascending, making a conical crown. Leaves ovate to ovate-oblong, relatively narrower than in *C. pedicellata*. Inflorescence glabrous (hairy in var. VILLIPES Ashe). Anthers pink or red, ten or fewer. Fruit pear-shaped to oblong, longer than wide. Native of eastern N. America. Introduced under its present name first in 1901, but probably in cultivation before as "*C. coccinea*".

C. PENTAGYNA Willd.

A small tree 15 to 20 ft high, with hairy young shoots; thorns few, ⅓ in. long. Leaves broadly tapered or nearly straight at the base, lobed; 1 to 3 in. long, nearly or quite as wide. On the barren shoots they are broadly ovate, the basal pair of lobes often deep; on the flowering shoots the leaves are narrower, diamond-shaped or obovate, with a more tapered base; all dark green and somewhat hairy above, paler and more hairy below, ultimately almost glabrous; stalk ½ to 1 in. long, stipules large, deeply toothed. Flowers white, ⅝ in. diameter, produced during May and June in rather lax corymbs 2 to 3 in. across. Calyx and flower-stalks clothed with grey down; stamens twenty, anthers red; styles four or five. Fruit black-purple, oval, ½ in. long.
Native of E. Europe. The group of thorns to which this belongs is somewhat doubtful in its inter-relationships. *C. melanocarpa* Bieb., and *C. oliveriana* Bosc, are included under it by Lange and others. (See note under *C. oliveriana*.) From *C. nigra* it differs in its less downy shoots and leaves, and in its oval fruits.

C. HIEMALIS Lange is supposed to be a hybrid between the above and *C. crus-galli*, and the way seedlings of *C. hiemalis* have reverted to a pure glabrousness like that of *crus-galli*, especially in the inflorescence, supports this theory.

C. PHAENOPYRUM L. f. (Med.)   WASHINGTON THORN
Mespilus phaenopyrum L. f.; *C. cordata* Ait.   [PLATE 68

An elegant tree up to 30 ft high, with a slender trunk supporting a dense, rounded head of leafy branches; young shoots slender, glabrous; thorns sharp, slender, up to 3 in. long, sometimes branched. Leaves triangular, broadly ovate, heart-shaped or slightly rounded at the base, pointed, often lobed towards the base, sharply toothed; 1 to 3 in. long, ¾ to 2¼ in. wide; of a vivid lustrous green, and glabrous except when first expanded; stalk up 1 in. long. Flowers white, ½ in. across, produced during July in terminal and axillary corymbs 2 to 3 in. wide. Calyx and flower-stalk quite glabrous; stamens twenty; anthers pink; styles two to five. Fruit scarlet, orange-shaped, ¼ in. diameter, persisting on the tree until spring.

Native of the south-eastern United States; introduced in 1738. This handsome species is one of the most distinct of all the thorns. It flowers the latest of all the better-known kinds, and its small, bright fruits are beautiful through the winter. The leaves die off in shades of scarlet and orange.

cv. 'FASTIGIATA'.—Of columnar habit.

C. PINNATIFIDA Bunge

A small tree up to 20 ft or more high; thorns absent or quite short; young shoots glabrous. Leaves wedge-shaped to straightly cut at the base, varying in general outline from broadly ovate and triangular to lozenge-shaped; 2 to 4 in. long, nearly as much to rather more in width, usually with a deep lobe reaching nearly to the midrib at the base on each side, the terminal portion being also lobed, but not so deeply; margins sharply, often doubly toothed, deep glossy green above, paler beneath, both sides downy along the midrib and chief veins; stalk 1 to 2¼ in. long, stipules cockscomb-shaped, coarsely toothed, often over 1 in. across. Flowers white, ¾ in. across, produced at the end of May and early in June on downy-stalked corymbs about 3 in. across; calyx hairy; stamens twenty; styles three or four. Fruit red, minutely dotted, and ⅝ in. diameter.

Native of N. China. Very distinct from all but its immediate allies in the long leaf-stalks and large leaves. The following variety is greatly to be preferred to the type as a garden tree:

var. MAJOR N. E. Br. *C. korolkowii* Schneid., not Henry—A tree up to 25 ft high, forming a dense, heavy, very leafy head of branches. It is really a very vigorous, large-leaved form of the type. The leaves are harder and thicker than in the type, and not so flat; 3 to 6 in. long and nearly as much wide; the lobes not so deep but broader; except for a slight hairiness along the midrib and larger veins, they are glabrous. They are of a rich dark lustrous green, the midrib, veins, and young wood tinged with red. Flowers like those of the type; calyx and flower-stalks downy. Fruits deep shining red, marked with minute dots, between pear-shaped and globose, 1 in. across, deeply hollowed at the top. When a tree is well furnished with the pendulous clusters of these large fruits it is remarkably handsome. This is, indeed, one of the most striking and effective of all the thorns. It is only slightly or not at all spiny. In October 1886, it was awarded a First Class Certificate by the Royal Horticultural Society, but had been in cultivation long previously. Native of N. China.

CRATAEGUS PINNATIFIDA var. MAJOR

var. PSILOSA Schneid.—The leaves of this variety are quite glabrous, and have deeper, narrower lobes than the type; flower-stalks and calyx also glabrous. Native of Amurland, Korea, etc., and like many trees of those regions, apt to start very early into growth, and suffer in consequence. Inferior to the type.

C. PRUINOSA (Wendl.) K. Koch

Mespilus pruinosa Wendl.

A tree up to 15 or 20 ft high, with horizontal branches; young twigs and leaves quite glabrous; thorns 1 to 1½ in. long. Leaves broadly ovate, broadly wedge-shaped to nearly truncate at the base, pointed at the apex, doubly and sharply toothed or triangular-lobed at the upper part; 1 to 2½ in. long, two-thirds to fully as wide; reddish when they unfold, becoming dark green above and glaucous beneath; stalks slender, ½ to 1¼ in. long. Flowers ¾ to 1 in. wide, borne in May in rather loose corymbs; flower-stalks and calyx quite smooth; stamens twenty; styles five. Fruit five-angled, ⅝ in. diameter, globose, at first apple-green covered with a purple bloom, finally dark red, shining, and much dotted.

Native of the southern United States, probably sometimes confused in gardens with *C. chrysocarpa*, from which it differs in the glaucous under-surface of the leaf, and the plum-coloured young fruits, also the thinner, longer leaf-stalks and flower-stalks.

C. PRUNIFOLIA (Lam.) Pers.   [PLATE 70

Mespilus prunifolia Lam.; *C. crus-galli* var. *prunifolia* (Lam.) Torr. & Gr.

Although undoubtedly related to the *crus-galli* group of thorns, this does not appear to have been found wild in N. America, although it has been suggested that a wild putative hybrid between *crus-galli* and *macracantha* is the same. This theory is supported by the shape of the nuts, which have hollows on the inner faces as in *macracantha*, only not so deep. Whatever its origin, *C. prunifolia* is one of the most admirable of all thorns. It is a tree up to 20 ft high, forming a rounded head of branches, wider than high, often reaching to the ground, and densely leafy; young shoots glabrous; spines rigid, sharp, $1\frac{1}{2}$ to 3 in. long. Leaves varying from roundish ovate or oval to obovate; $1\frac{1}{2}$ to $3\frac{1}{2}$ in. long, $1\frac{1}{2}$ to $2\frac{1}{2}$ in. wide; toothed nearly to the base, glabrous and brilliant dark green above; pale, dull and either glabrous or slightly downy on the midrib and veins beneath. The leaves turn a rich glowing crimson in autumn. Flowers $\frac{3}{4}$ in. diameter, produced during June in rounded corymbs with hairy stalks; calyx-lobes glandular-toothed, not downy; stamens ten to fifteen, anthers pink. Fruit rich red, $\frac{5}{8}$ in. long, globose, falling with the leaves in October. From *crus-galli* it is well distinguished by its wider leaves, hairy flower-stalks, and early falling fruit.

C. OVALIFOLIA (Hornemann) DC., differs in the following respects from *prunifolia*: leaves somewhat downy on both surfaces; stamens fifteen to eighteen; but there are intermediate forms.

C. SPLENDENS Lodd.—Loudon makes this synonymous with *C. crus-galli arbutifolia*, a quite glabrous tree, whereas all the trees I have seen under the name of *C. splendens* are simply *C. prunifolia* as described above, i.e. with invariably downy flower-stalks, and leaves glabrous, except sometimes on the chief veins beneath.

In *Dendroflora*, No. 4 (1967), p. 27, H. J. Grootendorst points out that the thorn offered by some nurseries in the Netherlands as *C. crus-galli* 'Splendens' is a clone of *C. prunifolia* distinguished by its very broad crown (the specimens at Kew by the Rose Garden are narrow-crowned, with pendulous branches).

C. PUNCTATA Jacq.

A tree 20 to 35 ft high, with a rounded head of often horizontal branches, more in diameter; trunk 10 to 20 in. through; branches more or less armed with spines 2 to 3 in. long; young shoots grey, hairy at first, then glabrous. Leaves broadly ovate, rounded or rather abruptly pointed at the apex, always tapered at the base; 2 to 4 in. long, $1\frac{1}{4}$ to $2\frac{3}{4}$ in. wide; toothed, the larger leaves of the barren shoots more or less lobed above the middle; veins parallel in five to ten pairs, deeply sunk above; upper surface dark green, both surfaces at first downy, afterwards almost or quite glabrous above, more persistently downy beneath; stalk $\frac{3}{4}$ in. or less long. Flowers white, $\frac{3}{4}$ in. diameter, opening early in June on corymbs up to 4 in. across; the calyx-tube, the inner surface of the narrow, almost entire lobes, and the flower-stalk hairy; stamens twenty; styles five. Fruit deep red, specked with pale dots; ¾ to 1 in. diameter, slightly pear-shaped or almost globose.

Native of eastern N. America; introduced in 1746. It is certainly one of the most attractive and well-doing of American thorns, giving great crops of its white blossom and crimson fruits. A tree at Aldenham, Herts., planted in 1845, attained a height of 33 ft, with a head of branches 40 ft across.

f. AUREA (Ait.) Rehd.—Fruits yellow. According to E. J. Palmer, yellow fruited trees occur wild with the type, becoming commoner northwards.

Forms have also been described in which the fruit is deep cherry-red and another in which it is red streaked with yellow near the base. In all forms of *C. punctata* the leaves are conspicuously parallel-veined and the fruits are marked by small pale dots. Leaves and fruits fall in October.

C. SANGUINEA Pall.

A small, mostly unarmed tree up to 20 ft high, young shoots slightly hairy at first, soon glabrous, and becoming of a deep shining brown-purple. Leaves diamond-shaped to ovate, always tapered at the base, with three, five, or seven shallowish lobes, sharply, sometimes doubly toothed; 2 to 3½ in. long, 1¼ to 2½ in. wide; slightly hairy on both sides, especially in the vein-axils beneath; stalk ¼ to ½ in. long; stipules semi-heart-shaped, coarsely toothed, ¾ in. across. Flowers white, ⅝ in. across, in dense corymbs; calyx and flower-stalks glabrous; stamens twenty, with purple anthers; styles ordinarily three. Fruit bright red, globose, scarcely ½ in. long.

Native of the vast region extending from S.E. Russia across Siberia; introduced early in the nineteenth century. It belongs to the same group as *altaica* and *chlorosarca*. The colour of its twigs is rather notable, but it is amongst the least desirable of thorns.

Closely allied to *C. sanguinea* is C. DAHURICA Koehne, also with branches of a deep brown-purple, but its leaves are smaller (rarely 2 in. long), scarcely or only finely lobed, almost glabrous. Fruit smaller, ¼ to ⅓ in. long, orange-red. Native of S.E. Siberia and Amurland, and, like many shrubs and trees of that region, starts early into growth. At Kew it blossoms at the end of April and early in May.

Occasionally seen in cultivation also is C. MAXIMOWICZII Schneid. (*C. sanguinea* var. *villosa* Maxim.), a species of the Sanguinea group, but very distinct in the bristly hairy flower-stalks, calyx, and young fruits—the last smooth and red when ripe. Amurland, N. Manchuria, etc.

Another species in this group is C. CHUNGTIENENSIS W. W. Sm., discovered by Forrest on the Chungtien Plateau, Yunnan, China, in 1913, and introduced by seed collected on the Yü-Hü expedition in 1937. It is in cultivation at Birr Castle, Co. Offaly, Eire, where, Lord Rosse tells us, it makes a dense-crowned tree and promises to reach a good size (Forrest described it as a shrub to about 20 ft high). It was described as differing from *C. sanguinea* in the smaller leaves, rounded to truncate at the base and in the stipules being edged with glandular teeth.

C. SPATHULATA Michx.

C. microcarpa Lindl.

A shrub or small tree, with a slender trunk and spreading branches; young shoots glabrous or soon becoming so, and reddish brown; thorns either absent or few. Leaves spoon-shaped, diamond-shaped, or obovate; often very distinctly three-lobed, the lobes coarsely round-toothed; apex blunt, the base narrowing to a long thin strip each side of the stalk; often with scattered down on both surfaces when young; the stalk, although apparently long, is really very short, owing to the extension of the blade in a narrow wing down each side. Excluding this, the leaves of the flowering shoots are ½ to 1 in. long, ⅜ to ⅝ in. wide; on the barren shoots 1 to 1½ in. long, nearly as much wide. Flowers white, ½ in. diameter, produced towards the end of June in corymbs 1½ in. across; stamens sixteen to twenty; styles two to five. Fruit $\frac{3}{16}$ in. in diameter, globose, coral-red.

Native of the south and south-eastern United States; introduced in 1806. It ripens its fruits late, not until October, and both they and the leaves remain on the plant until the New Year. This is one of the more tender thorns, and apt to suffer in severe winters. Distinct in its tiny fruits.

C. STIPULACEA Loud.

C. pubescens f. *stipulacea* (Loud.) Stapf

A small, usually unarmed tree probably 15 to 20 ft high; young shoots greyish at first with loose down, afterwards red-brown and roughish with minute warts. Leaves diamond-shaped, obovate or oval; wedge-shaped and entire at the base, the upper part pointed and doubly glandular-toothed; 1½ to 4 in. long, ¾ to 2 in. wide; usually much larger on the barren shoots and with large glandular-toothed stipules ¾ in. across; at first slightly downy, afterwards glabrous and dark green above; grey, dull, and persistently downy on the chief veins beneath; stalk about ⅓ in. long. Flowers white, ¾ in. across, produced in June in corymbs 2 to 2½ in. across; flower-stalks and calyx woolly, calyx-lobes slightly toothed or entire; stamens fifteen to twenty; styles two or three. Fruit yellowish, dotted, ¾ in. long, globose, persisting on the tree a long time. *Bot. Mag.*, t. 8589.

Native of elevated regions in Mexico; introduced by A. B. Lambert in 1824, and interesting as one of the few trees from that country that are hardy with us. It retains its leaves usually until the New Year. Sometimes known in gardens as *C. mexicana* DC.

C. SUCCULENTA Schrad.

A tree up to 20 ft high, with glabrous branchlets, becoming purplish brown by the end of the season; thorns 1½ to 2 in. long. Leaves roundish obovate, 2 to 3 in. long, 1¼ to 2½ in. wide, broadly wedge-shaped at the base, abruptly pointed, more or less lobed towards the apex, sharply toothed, at first downy beneath, soon glabrous; dark green and glossy above; veins parallel, in four to seven pairs. Flowers white, ¾ in. across, produced in early June in rounded corymbs,

3 in. or more across; flower-stalks hairy, and calyx usually so; stamens fifteen to twenty, anthers pink; styles two or three; fruit globose, bright red, ½ in. diameter.

Native of eastern N. America, and a close ally of *C. tomentosa*. It has the same deep longitudinal pits in the seeds (nutlets), but differs in the midrib and veins of the leaf being more deeply sunken on the upper side, and in the fruit being globose rather than oval, and of a deeper, brighter red. It is also a more vigorous and thorny tree.

C. TANACETIFOLIA (Lam.) Pers.

Mespilus tanacetifolia Lam.

A small, mostly unarmed tree up to 35 ft high, with erect branches and a trunk occasionally 5 ft in girth; young shoots clothed with a thick grey wool, which persists partially on year-old shoots. Leaves 1 to 2 in. long, nearly or quite as wide, tapered at the base; obovate or diamond-shaped in outline, but cut into five or seven parallel, narrow-oblong lobes, often reaching nearly to the midrib; the lobes more or less glandular-toothed, especially towards the points; both surfaces permanently hairy; stalk ⅛ to ¼ in. long; stipules large, curved, toothed. Flowers fragrant, white, 1 in. across, produced in mid-June in rounded clusters of six to eight blossoms; calyx covered with a pale grey felt; stamens twenty, with red anthers; styles five. Fruit globose, yellow, or suffused with red, partially downy, ¾ to 1 in. across, with the scent and somewhat the taste of the apple. Closely attached at and near the base are one or more deeply cut, moss-like bracts.

Native of Asia Minor, Syria, etc.; introduced in 1789. Belonging to the same group as *C. laciniata*, this handsome thorn is not common. *C. laciniata* often does duty for it, but the present tree can always be distinguished by the gland-toothed leaves and glandular laciniate bract, or bracts, attached at the base of the fruit. It is a slow-growing tree. There used to be a fine specimen at the entrance to Messrs Cunningham & Fraser's nursery at Edinburgh; another at Arley Castle, near Bewdley. At the present time there is a fine specimen in the Cambridge Botanic Garden, 28 ft high with a bole 2 ft in diameter and a spread of 24 ft (1965).

C. TOMENTOSA L.

C. calpodendron (Ehrh.) Med.

A small tree up to 15 ft high, with a rounded compact head of grey-barked branches, often very crooked; young shoots more or less downy; thorns infrequent, grey, 1 to 2 in. long. Leaves ovate to rhomboidal or obovate, pointed, wedge-shaped and entire at the base, the upper part coarsely double-toothed or lobed; 2 to 5 in. long, 1½ to 3 in. wide; parallel-veined, downy on both sides, especially beneath, the upper side becoming nearly or quite glabrous and dark green; stalk ½ to ¾ in. long. Flowers white, ⅝ in. diameter, borne in June in large, erect, loose corymbs 3 to 5 in. across; calyx and flower-stalk shaggy, calyx-lobes narrow, glandular-toothed; stamens sixteen to twenty, anthers pink; styles two to five. Fruits always erect, pear-shaped or oval, dull orange-coloured, ½ in. long.

Native of the eastern and central United States; introduced by Lee and Kennedy of Hammersmith in 1765. This is one of the most beautiful of American thorns when in flower, the upright corymbs being of unusual size. The leaves turn a brilliant orange or scarlet in autumn. Although on different plants the foliage varies in the amount of down it carries, the flower-stalks and calyx are always hairy.

C. UNIFLORA Muench.
C. parvifolia Ait.

A shrub or miniature tree, rarely more than 6 or 8 ft high, with hairy young shoots; thorns slender, up to 1¼ in. long. Leaves obovate, always tapered at the base, rounded or bluntish at the apex, rather coarsely (often doubly) round-toothed; 1 to 2 in. long, ½ to 1 in. wide; dark glossy green and with short scattered hairs above; pale, dull and downy on the midrib and veins beneath; stalk ⅙ in. or less long. Flowers creamy white, ½ to ¾ in. across; solitary or in pairs, occasionally in threes. Flower-stalk and calyx shaggy; calyx-lobes linear, conspicuously glandular-toothed; stamens about twenty, anthers whitish. Fruit pear-shaped to globose, about ½ in. long, yellow or greenish yellow, with the large calyx-lobes adhering at the top.

Native of the south-eastern United States; introduced early in the eighteenth century. It is an interesting and very distinct thorn, but in no way showy. Its small stature, often solitary flowers, and especially the long, persistent, prominently toothed calyx-lobes, distinguish it.

C. VAILIAE Britt., allied to *C. uniflora*, differs in the leaves being ovate or oval and pointed, in the longer leaf-stalks, in the two- to six-flowered corymbs, and in the more globose red fruit. Native of Virginia and N. Carolina.

C. VIRIDIS L.
C. arborescens Ell.

A tree 20 to 35 ft high; young shoots glabrous; thorns up to 1½ in. long, often absent. Leaves ovate or oval, always wedge-shaped at the base, the terminal part toothed, often shallowly lobed as well; 1½ to 3½ in. long, ¾ to 2½ in. wide; dark glossy green above, and when mature, quite glabrous, except for tufts of down in the vein-axils beneath; stalk ½ to 1½ in. long. Flowers white, ¾ in. across, borne in May and June in corymbs 1½ to 2 in. across. Flower-stalk and calyx glabrous, except that the lobes of the latter are sometimes downy inside; stamens twenty, anthers pale yellow; styles two to five. Fruit globose, ¼ to ⅓ in. diameter, bright red.

Native of the south-eastern United States. It grows well in cultivation, but is not one of the most attractive of thorns, the flowers, and especially the fruits not being abundant. It is the type species of a group of American thorns, one of which is:

C. NITIDA (Engelm.) Sarg. *C. viridis* var. *nitida* Engelm.—This differs in having ovate or narrowly obovate leaves; glandular-toothed calyx-lobes; fruit considerably larger, from broadly oval to globose, ⅝ in. long, covered with a glaucous bloom. S. United States.

C. WATTIANA Hemsl. & Lace

C. korolkowii L. Henry

A small tree, glabrous in all its parts, with lustrous, red-brown branchlets. Leaves ovate, 2 to 4 in. long and nearly as much wide, wedge-shaped or rounded at the base, lobed about half-way to the midrib and margined with short, triangular teeth. Flower-clusters about 3 in. across; stamens usually twenty, with pale yellow anthers. Fruit yellow to orange, roundish, about ½ in. wide, ripening in August but soon falling. Bot. Mag., t. 8818.

A native of Central Asia from the Altai Mountains to Baluchistan. It is an attractive species, showy in flower and fruit; the glossy-green leaves are among the largest in the genus.

C. ALTAICA (Loud.) Lange C. purpurea var. altaica Loud.—Another Central Asiatic species closely allied to the preceding. The leaves are more deeply lobed, the lowest pair reaching almost to the midrib. Fruit yellow, globose, about ⅖ in. across.

These two species have probably been confused with each other in gardens and both may have been grown as "C. korolkowii" or "C. sanguinea var. xanthocarpa". They resemble C. pinnatifida in foliage but in that species the leaves, flower-stalks and calyx are downy and the fruit is never yellow.

C. WILSONII Sarg.

A deciduous tree or shrub up to 20 or 25 ft high; young shoots furnished with pale hairs; spines very stout, ½ to 1 in. long. Leaves ovate in main outline, but shallowly lobed and finely toothed, broadly wedge-shaped or rounded at the base, pointed or blunt at the apex; 2 to 4 in. long, 1½ to 2½ in. wide; shining dark green above, loosely hairy in the vein-axils and on the veins beneath; stalk ½ to 1¼ in. long. On vigorous barren shoots the leaves are much more deeply lobed, approaching those of C. oxyacantha in this respect. Flowers white, produced in mid-June, crowded on corymbs 2½ in. wide, each flower about ½ in. wide; flower-stalks shaggy. Fruit red, shining, ⅖ in. long, ¼ in. wide.

Native of W. Hupeh, China; introduced by Wilson in 1907. It is an interesting species as representing in Asia the important group of American thorns to which C. tomentosa and C. macracantha belong. Hardy at Kew.

× CRATAEMESPILUS   ROSACEAE

Whereas the 'hybrids' treated under +Crataegomespilus are graft-chimaeras between species of Crataegus and Mespilus, the plants described here are of quite different origin and botanical standing, being normal sexual hybrids between the two genera. It has long been the practice to make the name *Crataegomespilus* do duty for both sorts of union, but modern rules of nomenclature demand, very reasonably, that they should be treated separately.

× C. GRANDIFLORA (Smith) E. G. Camus

Mespilus grandiflora Smith; *M. smithii* DC.; *M. lobata* Poir.; *Crataegomespilus grandiflora* (Smith) Bean

A deciduous tree up to 30 ft high, of rounded habit, the lower branches pendulous; branchlets downy. Leaves oval or obovate, 2 to 3½ in. long, half to two-thirds as wide; often with several angular lobes towards the end, these being most developed on the barren young shoots; margins finely toothed; both surfaces downy; stalk ¼ to ½ in. long, hairy. Flowers usually in pairs or threes, terminating short, leafy twigs; each flower 1 in. across, pure white, produced on a short, woolly stalk. Fruit ¾ in. in diameter, globular, yellowish brown, flesh mealy, tasting like that of a hawthorn, containing two hard stones.

The origin of this tree is unknown, but judging from Loudon's account it must have been introduced to Britain before 1800. It is a hybrid of the medlar, *Mespilus germanica*, the other parent being *C. oxyacantha* or *C. monogyna*, probably the former. It appears to be sterile, but flowers with the greatest freedom towards the end of May, and makes a picture of extreme beauty and elegance. It is a luxuriantly leafy tree of vigorous growth, an admirable ornament on a lawn.

× C. GILLOTII Beck ×*Crataegomespilus gillotii* (Beck) Rehd.—In 1875, Dr Gillot found some shrubs growing in a hedgerow by a ruined priory near Autun, Seine-et-Loire, which resembled the preceding but differed in their lobed, not toothed leaves and smaller flowers with two styles. The hawthorn parent of this hybrid is thought to be *C. monogyna*. Similar hybrids have been found in other parts of France.

CRINODENDRON   ELAEOCARPACEAE

A Chilean genus of two species, both evergreen shrubs or small trees, with alternate leaves, and solitary, bell- or urn-shaped flowers produced on pendulous, thickened stalks from the leaf-axils. They both delight in a cool, moist, peaty soil, or loam, and can be increased by cuttings of half ripened wood placed in a close frame with gentle bottom-heat. Excellent and attractive shrubs in the milder counties, they need protection near London.

C. HOOKERIANUM Gay

Tricuspidaria lanceolata Miq.; *T. dependens* Hort., not Ruiz & Pavon

An evergreen shrub or small tree up to 10 or 30 ft high, sometimes more, of a stiff, bushy growth; young wood felted with grey down. Leaves oblong-lanceolate, pointed; 1½ to 5 in. long, ½ to 1¼ in. wide; coarsely toothed except

CRINODENDRON HOOKERIANUM

towards the tapering base, dark green above and downy on the midrib, paler beneath and downy on the midrib and chief veins, stiff and hard in texture; stalk ⅓ in. or less long, downy. Flowers produced singly from the terminal leaf-axils each on a stout, stiff, downward-pointing stalk 2 to 3 in. long. Corolla urn-shaped, 1 to 1¼ in. long, rich crimson, very fleshy, grooved, toothed at the narrow mouth; calyx downy. *Bot. Mag.*, t. 7160.

Native of Chile in the provinces of Valdivia and Llanquihue and on the Island of Chiloe; introduced by William Lobb for Messrs Veitch in 1848, and for the same firm by Pearce about ten years later. It thrives best in such places as the Isle of Wight, Cornwall, Ireland, and the west of Scotland, and where it succeeds it is one of the most attractive of all shrubs. At Kilmacurragh, Co. Wicklow, it was 26 ft high. Perhaps the most remarkable specimen in the British Isles is at Brodick in the Isle of Arran. Planted around 1930, it measured 38 ft in height in 1965 and is still growing. At Mount Usher in Co. Wicklow there is an example 18 ft high. A plant on the east wall of the office of the National Pinetum, Bedgebury, Kent, has grown and flowered for years, in spite of setbacks in cold winters. It was planted by the late William Dallimore about 1927.

This species has the curious habit of pushing out its flower-stalks in autumn, but the flowers do not open until the following May. It likes a partially shaded spot; the leaves are often 'scorched' and brown at the margins when the plant stands fully exposed to sunshine or wind. It is better known in gardens as *Tricuspidaria lanceolata*, but the generic name *Crinodendron* has priority. It has also been grown as "*T. dependens*", which is a synonym of *C. patagua*.

C. PATAGUA Mol.

Tricuspidaria dependens Ruiz & Pavon; *C. dependens* (Ruiz & Pavon) Schneid.

An evergreen shrub or small tree, up to 30 ft high, the young shoots reddish and faintly downy. Leaves oval or ovate, 1 to 3 in. long, $\frac{1}{2}$ to $1\frac{1}{2}$ in. wide; shallowly and rather coarsely toothed, dark green and glabrous above, much paler beneath; stalk reddish, $\frac{1}{8}$ to $\frac{1}{4}$ in. long, slightly hairy. Flowers white, bell-shaped, $\frac{3}{4}$ in. long, produced singly on a pendulous stalk 1 to 2 in. long, from the leaf-axils. Corolla of five rather fleshy petals, which are three-toothed at the ends, downy at the margins, oblong. *Bot. Mag.*, t. 8115.

Native of Chile; introduced by H. J. Elwes in 1901. Its name was for a long time wrongly attached to its fellow species in gardens. It appears to thrive better than *C. hookerianum* as a wall shrub at Kew, but is considered to be more tender in the open in Ireland. It is certainly a much more rapid grower. On a wall at Kew it has stood quite uninjured for several winters, and blossoms freely in late summer. It is very distinct from *C. hookerianum* in its white, more bell-shaped flowers. Easily increased by cuttings.

CRYPTOMERIA　　TAXODIACEAE

A genus of one species in Japan and China, related to *Taxodium* and the redwoods (*Sequoia* and *Sequoiadendron*).

C. JAPONICA (L. f.) D. Don　　　　[PLATE 71

Cupressus japonica L. f.

An evergreen, pyramidal tree 100 to 180 ft high in Japan, with a trunk 3 to 7 ft in diameter, clothed with a thin reddish-brown bark which peels off in long, narrow strips. Leaves dagger-shaped, curved inwards towards the point, four-angled, $\frac{1}{4}$ to $\frac{3}{4}$ in. long, attached by their thickened bases to the branchlet on which they are closely and spirally set, all pointing forwards. Cones brown, globular, about $\frac{5}{8}$ in. in diameter, composed of from twenty to thirty scales, each bearing three to five seeds.

Native of China and Japan. Two geographical varieties are distinguished:

var. JAPONICA.—Branches straight and spreading; the leaves short, stout, dark green. Cone-scales with long acuminate processes, bracts also long-pointed; usually five seeds per scale. This is the typical variety.

var. SINENSIS Sieb.—Habit less dense than in the Japanese variety, with deflexed branches and longer, more slender terminal growths. Leaves longer and more slender, lighter green. Processes of cone-scales and tips of bracts shorter.

C. japonica was introduced to Kew in 1842, but not in quantity until 1844, when Fortune, then in the employ of the Horticultural Society, sent seeds from Shanghai. It was from a tree raised from this seed that Siebold described var. *sinensis*. The first direct introduction from Japan to this country appears to have been by Maries in 1879. But in 1853 Thomas Lobb obtained seed from trees in the Buitenzorg Botanic Garden, Java, to which they had been introduced by Siebold some thirty years earlier from Japan. Trees from this source have rather stiff, short branches, more tufted and bunchy at the ends, and not so elegant as the common form. They are usually distinguished as f. LOBBII (Carr.) Beissn.

In Japan, *C. japonica* has been used as a forestry tree from time immemorial and must have become subdivided into numerous strains adapted to local soils and climates and differing somewhat in leaf, habit etc. Many of the artificial forests are so ancient, and have acquired such a deceptively natural aspect, that it is not certain where in Japan this species is to be regarded as genuinely native. However, it is certainly wild on Yakushima and perhaps in parts of S. Japan.

Although one of the great timber trees of the world, and once used in Japan more than any other, it has not proved so generally fine a tree in this country as might have been expected, the best specimens being mostly in the milder and moister parts and ranging from 85 to 90 ft in height and 10 to 12 ft in girth. It likes a deep good soil, a sheltered position, and abundant rainfall. Some trees of above-average size recorded recently are: Fonthill, Wilts., 104 × 10¼ ft (1963) and 115 × 8½ ft (1965); Embley Park, Hants, 102 × 11½ ft (1961), a superb tree; Woodhouse, Devon, 117 × 8¾ ft (1957); Bicton, Devon, 110 × 10¼ ft (1965); Leaton Knolls, Shrops., 111 × 6¾ ft (1954); Redleaf, Kent, 100 × 10 ft (1963), with a fine bole; Northerwood House, Hants, 101 × 12¾ ft (1963); Leighton Hall, Montg., 103 × 11¼ ft (1960); Benmore, Argyll, 104 × 10¾ ft (1964); Endsleigh, Devon, 113 × 8½ ft (1963). In Ireland there is a tree with a fine bole at Fota, Co. Cork, 102 × 10½ ft (1966) and a handsome pair at Derreen, Co. Kerry, 95 × 13½ and 92 × 12¼ ft (1966).

The following are garden varieties:

cv. 'ARAUCARIOIDES'.—A shrub to about 7 ft high with long, thin, slender, pendulous branches, with densely set leaves. Introduced from Japan by Siebold, but similar forms may have arisen in Europe as branch-sports.

cv. 'ELEGANS'.—This, commonly known in gardens as *"Cryptomeria elegans"*, is a remarkable state, in which the foliage of the juvenile plant is retained permanently. The aspect of the tree is totally different from ordinary *C. japonica*, although the bark of the trunk has the same red-brown, peeling character. The leaves are on the whole larger, much softer, more slender, more spreading and wider apart on the branchlet than those of the type; they and the young shoots being a glaucous green in the summer, changing in autumn and winter to a bronzy red, very distinct, and remarkable among evergreens at that season. The leaves are reflexed at the tip, rather than incurved as in ordinary *C. japonica*. The whole tree is more bushy and dense than the type, and often falls over by its own weight; the trunks are very supple, and allow the crowns of trees 20 ft high to reach the ground without breaking. This form produces cones (rarely) which do not differ from those of the type. It bears pruning very well, and is often improved by it; if trees become top-heavy, they may be headed down far enough to become self-supporting. Introduced from Japan in 1861 by J. Gould Veitch. There is a dwarf dense-habited variety of it called 'ELEGANS NANA'.

cv. 'NANA'.—A dwarf form with stunted branches, of rather spreading habit, reaching eventually a height of about 5 ft; branchlets numerous, crowded and unequal. Leaves shorter and narrower than in the type, more densely set on the shoots. Introduced by Fortune.

cv. 'SPIRALIS'.—A dwarf form of remarkable dense habit, the leaves being much incurved and twisted, so that the branchlet often suggests wire rope. Judging by experience at Kew, it is apt to revert to the type. Webster, in *Hardy Coniferous Trees* (1896) used the name *C. j. spiralis* for what is clearly a different form, with the leaves 'so thickly and shortly set as to appear in a spiral manner throughout the entire length' of the shoot.

CUDRANIA   MORACEAE

A genus of about five species in E. Asia and the S.W. Pacific, related to *Morus* (mulberry), from which it is distinguished by having its female flowers in rounded clusters (not in catkins). Another close ally is *Maclura* (see below).

C. TRICUSPIDATA (Carr.) Lav.

Maclura tricuspidata Carr.

A deciduous shrub or small tree 20 ft high, with a dense, rounded head of thorny branches; young shoots quite glabrous. Leaves alternate, oval, obovate, or ovate; either entire or with three shallow rounded lobes, at the apex; 1½ to 4 in. long, ¾ to 2 in. wide; dark green, glabrous; stalk ¼ to ⅝ in. long, slightly downy. Flowers green, crowded in a little ball about ⅓ in. diameter, the sexes on different plants. The balls are produced during July, either singly or (usually) in pairs, from the leaf-axils of the current year's growth, each on a downy stalk ¼ in. long. The male tree only appears to be in cultivation, and a head of fruit has not yet been produced in this country; but it is an elliptical, hard, shining mass 1½ in. broad and 1 in. long, as seen in wild specimens.

Native of China, where it is widely spread; introduced to Britain in 1872. This tree, which is nearly allied to the Osage orange *Maclura pomifera*, but differs in flowering on the current season's growth, in its fewer-veined leaves, and very much in the fruits, is perfectly hardy, and flowers frequently at Kew. Its flowers are of no ornament, and the plant itself, although interesting both economically and botanically, has no special merit for the garden. Its leaves are much used

CUDRANIA TRICUSPIDATA

in China for feeding the silkworm on, being considered as good for this purpose as the mulberry.

CUNNINGHAMIA   PINACEAE

A genus of two, or possibly three species, natives of N.E. Asia, named after James Cunningham who originally found *C. lanceolata* on the Island of Chusan in 1701.

C. KONISHII Hayata

An evergreen tree of large size with reddish-brown bark. Leaves arranged on the twigs in two opposite sets on young trees, but evenly and spirally all round the shoot in mature ones. They are awl-shaped, slender-pointed, up to $1\frac{1}{8}$ in. long and $\frac{1}{8}$ in. wide at the base on young trees; $\frac{1}{3}$ to $\frac{3}{4}$ in. long and $\frac{1}{12}$ in. wide, stiffer, more leathery and not so slenderly pointed on adult ones; all minutely toothed. On adult trees the leaves have stomata on both surfaces but more abundantly underneath; on the juvenile trees in cultivation stomata occur on the under-surface only. Cones ovoid-conical, ¾ to 1 in. long, scarcely so much wide, the numerous scales ending in a hard, sharp spine.

Native of Formosa; first named in 1908 by Hayata from specimens collected by N. Konishi on Mt Randai at 7,000 ft altitude; introduced by Admiral Clinton-Baker in 1910. It differs from the well-known C. *lanceolata* by the leaves of adult trees being much smaller, in their standing out all round the branches, and in their having stomata on both surfaces in the adult state; they are said to persist on the branches for eight years instead of about five as in C. *lanceolata*. The cones, too, are considerably smaller. This species is rare in cultivation and does not thrive so well as C. *lanceolata*. There are examples of 15 to 30 ft in height at Sheffield Park, Sussex; Woburn, Beds.; Tregothnan, Cornwall; Borde Hill, Sussex; Castlewellan, Co. Down; and in Eire at Headfort, Co. Meath, and Mount Usher, Co. Wicklow.

C. KAWAKAMII Hayata—This species is of uncertain status. Hayata, who described it from trees found in Formosa, stated it was intermediate in all respects between the above and C. *lanceolata*. However, H. L. Li, in *Woody Plants of Taiwan* (1963), includes it in C. *konishii* in synonymy.

C. LANCEOLATA (Lamb.) Hook. [PLATE 62

Pinus lanceolata Lamb.; C. *sinensis* Rich.

An evergreen tree up to 150 ft high in a wild state, and up to two-thirds as high in Britain, with a scaling bark; young wood hidden on the upper side by the bases of the densely packed leaves, pale green and glabrous beneath. Leaves persistent about five years, springing equally from all round the stem, but twisted at the stalkless base so as to come into two opposite, spreading, horizontal ranks; they are linear-lanceolate, 1 to 2¼ in. long, $\frac{1}{12}$ to $\frac{3}{16}$ in. wide; minutely toothed, tapered to a long, fine point; dark glossy bluish green above, with a broad stomatic band beneath along each side the midrib. Cones roundish, rather broader than long, about 1½ in. wide; scales broadly ovate, with an abrupt, slender point, and irregularly toothed margins.

Native of China; introduced to Kew by William Kerr in 1804. In general appearance it bears considerable resemblance to the araucarias, especially to *A. angustifolia*, and it appears to be related to that genus. It represents one of the world's most ancient types of vegetation, a very similar plant being found in a fossil state.

The trees mentioned in previous editions as the best in the early years of this century still exist. They are: Killerton, Devon, about 68 × 4 ft (1913), now 79 × 7¾ ft (1959); Bicton, Devon, 56 × 4¾ ft (1908), now 102 × 7½ ft (1964); Pencarrow, Cornwall, *pl.* 1850, 40 × 4¾ ft (1908), now 79 × 8½ ft (1957); Claremont, Surrey, *pl.* 1819, 36 ft (1913), now 52 × 6¼ ft (1965). Other trees of size are: Trebah, Cornwall, 80 × 7¼ ft (1959), and Longleat, Wilts., 76 × 6¼ ft (1963). C. *lanceolata* reaches its best dimensions in the rainier parts of the country, but it has grown well in the National Pinetum in Kent where a tree planted in 1925 is now 47 ft high (1963); at Benenden, in the same county, there is a specimen 59 ft high.

× CUPRESSOCYPARIS CUPRESSACEAE

A genus of hybrids between *Cupressus* and *Chamaecyparis*, in which only one cross has so far been recorded—that between *C. macrocarpa* and *Ch. nootkatensis*.

× C. LEYLANDII (Dallim. & Jacks.) Dallim.   LEYLAND CYPRESS

Cupressus leylandii Dallim. & Jacks.   [PLATE 73

This cross between *Cupressus macrocarpa* and *Chamaecyparis nootkatensis* first occurred at Leighton Hall, near Welshpool, at that time the property of a Mr Naylor. In 1888 seed was sown there from a cone of Nootka cypress and of the seedlings six were seen to differ from the rest; they were, in fact, the result of cross-pollination by a tree of *Cupressus macrocarpa* growing nearby, although this was not appreciated until later. These six were taken by Naylor's brother-in-law, C. J. Leyland, and planted on his property, Haggerston Hall, Northumberland, in 1892–3. Five of these still exist and are the parents by vegetative propagation of × *C. leylandii*, Clones 1 to 5.

About 1911 the same cross was again raised at Leighton Hall, but this time *C. macrocarpa* was the seed parent and *Chamaecyparis nootkatensis* the pollinator; from this batch two seedlings were picked out and planted on the property. One of these (Clone 10) was blown down in 1955 but was propagated before its death; the other (Clone 11) still grows on the hill behind the house.

However, these trees did not come to the attention of botanists until 1925. Their hybrid origin and parentage was established by Dallimore and Jackson, who published a description in the Kew Bulletin in the following year, giving the hybrid the name *Cupressus × leylandii*. But the recognition of *Chamaecyparis* as a genus distinct from *Cupressus* necessitated the transfer of the Leyland cypress to the hybrid genus × *Cupressocyparis* and it first appeared under that name in the *Kew Hand-list of Conifers* in 1938.

To complete the story, it should be added that the same hybrid was again raised in a Dorset nursery around 1940; the two trees that resulted are the parents of Clones 20 and 21, both of which are in commerce and resemble Clone 11 ('Leighton Green') in habit and foliage.

The Leyland cypress is one of the most important tree introductions of recent times, having all the virtues for which *Cupressus macrocarpa* has been so widely planted and none of its vices. It is, in the first place, of very rapid growth, capable of making a fine specimen 55 to 60 ft high in twenty-five years. Like the Monterey cypress, it is resistant to sea-winds, but whereas the use of that species is restricted to the milder parts, the Leyland cypress inherits from its other parent the ability to resist the worst of our winters without damage and is likely to prove a reliable and fast-growing shelter-belt tree over much of the country. It also makes an excellent hedge plant; its ability to withstand restriction is shown by the flourishing dwarf hedges in the Arboretum nursery at Kew, planted in 1947, which have been kept by mechanical trimming to a height of 4 ft and show no resentment at such drastic treatment. Finally, it makes a fine specimen tree of columnar habit but it is to be hoped that gardeners will not be tempted by its rapid growth into using it to excess.

For the following descriptions of the main clones of Leyland cypress (and for much of the historical account) we are indebted to the study by H. Ovens, W. Blight and A. F. Mitchell in *Quarterly Journal of Forestry*, Vol. 53, Jan. 1964.

cv. 'HAGGERSTON GREY' (Clone 2).—Branchlets unevenly spaced, lying in two planes at right-angles and with side-shoots arranged irregularly round the axis; finest divisions also in more than one plane and circular in cross-section at the tips. This is the commonest of the clones in cultivation; in its system of branching it is nearer to the pollen parent *Cupressus macrocarpa*. The original tree at Haggerston Castle, planted in 1892, measured 72 × 5¾ ft in 1960 but has been outstripped by several of its offspring. Some of the tallest of these are: Bicton, Devon, 90 × 5¼ ft (1960); Wakehurst Place, Sussex, 77 × 5¾ ft (1964); R.H.S. Garden, Wisley, Surrey, 72 × 5½ ft (1964); Inveraray Castle, Argyll, 74 × 6¾ ft (1960).

cv. 'LEIGHTON GREEN' (Clone 11).—Leaves greener than in 'Haggerston Grey'; branchlets and their subdivisions mainly in one plane and thus recalling the pollen parent, *Chamaecyparis nootkatensis*. This form is also in commerce but large specimens are rarer in gardens, perhaps because it is somewhat difficult to strike. The original tree at Leighton Hall measured 95 × 9½ ft in 1968. Of its offspring some of the largest are: Wakehurst Place, Sussex, 63 × 6½ ft (1964); R.H.S. Garden, Wisley, Surrey, 64 × 5¾ ft (1964); Westonbirt Arboretum, Glos., *pl.* 1933, 62 × 4½ ft (1963).

Other clones which have received names are: 'GREEN SPIRE' (Clone 1) and 'NAYLOR'S BLUE' (Clone 10). The latter is only represented in cultivation by young plants, the parent having been blown down in 1955; it has the most glaucous foliage of the set and is the one that most closely resembles the Monterey cypress in general aspect.

The Leyland cypress must be propagated by cuttings taken from side growths in March before growth commences or in late summer from half-ripened growths; these should be about 3 in. long and struck in sand with slight bottom-heat. When used for a windbreak, it is essential that the plants should be young and whippy, with a healthy and freely developed root-system. Heavy plants, or those which have had their anchorage roots forced downwards by constriction in a pot, will not be wind-firm.

CUPRESSUS CYPRESS CUPRESSACEAE

A small genus of evergreen coniferous trees, natives of western N. America, Mexico, Guatemala, the Mediterranean region, the Himalaya and China. The leaves are always minute, scale-like and flattened to the branchlet, being superposed in four rows. The ultimate divisions of the branchlet are usually arranged irregularly, not in flattened sprays as in *Chamaecyparis* and most thujas. Flowers unisexual, both sexes on the same tree but in different catkins. Males composed of numerous short-stalked stamens; fruit a globose or elliptical cone composed of mushroom-shaped (peltate) scales with a 'boss' or enlargement in the centre; scales with numerous seeds (usually five or less in *Chamaecyparis*).

The hardiest of the cypresses are now considered to belong to the separate genus *Chamaecyparis*. Those that remain in *Cupressus* are nearly all somewhat tender in the average climate of Britain, the hardiest being *arizonica* and the allied *glabra*, *macnabiana* and *macrocarpa*, though *bakeri*, little known here at present, may prove to be as hardy as these or hardier. *C. lusitanica* is on the borderline, but is hardy as far east as Sussex and Surrey. They thrive in either loamy or peaty soil, well drained; and should be given a sheltered place, as they are subject to injury by wind, especially where they grow fast. Some species, notably *macrocarpa* and *sempervirens*, show two curiously diverse types of habit, viz., the horizontal-branched and the fastigiate, but most of them are, when young, of columnar or pyramidal form.

Most of the cypresses can be increased by means of cuttings, which, although probably not so good as seeds, still make good trees. All, if growing in poor soil, are benefited by applications of manure water or by top-dressings of manure. They are subject, especially in poor soils, and during a succession of dry seasons, to attacks by white scale insects. The best remedy is spraying with Malathion in March and April, when the young hatch out.

The North American species of *Cupressus* are studied by C. B. Wolf in *El Aliso*, Vol. 1, pp. 1-250 (1948).

C. ARIZONICA Greene   ARIZONA CYPRESS
C. arizonica var. *bonita* Lemm.

A tree to 75 ft in the wild state (sometimes taller in favoured localities); bark on young trees red, smooth, peeling in thin flakes, on mature trees dark brown, furrowed and fibrous. Leaves closely overlapping and scale-like, pale green to grey-green, more rarely blue-green, acutely pointed, about $\frac{1}{16}$ in. long; resin-pits usually inconspicuous and inactive. Branchlets irregularly arranged, the final subdivisions four-sided, $\frac{1}{20}$ in. in diameter. Cones short-stalked, globose, $\frac{3}{4}$ to 1 in. in diameter, glaucous; scales six (rarely eight), slightly rising towards the middle, where there is a pyramidal, pointed boss.

Native of the S.W. United States and N. Mexico (where it may intergrade with the closely allied *C. lusitanica*); discovered by Greene in 1880 in S.E. Arizona and also found in S.W. New Mexico. Most of the trees cultivated in Europe as *C. arizonica* or "var. *bonita*" belong to the following species, which is a close ally and not recognised by all authorities:

C. GLABRA Sudw. *C. arizonica* var. *bonita* Hort. and of many authors, not Lemm.—This species occupies parts of Arizona well to the west of *C. arizonica*, from Coconino Co. to the Mazatzal Mountains in Gila Co. It is a dense, bushy tree growing 45 to 60 ft high in the wild state, with a spreading crown and often lacking a central leader. The bark remains reddish, thin and smooth even on mature trees, and is shed in thin strips or plates (but becomes close on very old trees). The leaves are much greyer on the average than in *C. arizonica*, with conspicuous resin-secreting glands on the back. Some trees are strongly glaucous, especially when young and vigorous. The cones are usually larger than in *C. arizonica* and the seeds glaucous.

Many botanists have identified *C. glabra* with *C. arizonica* var. *bonita* Lemm., but C. B. Wolf has pointed out this variety differs in no respect from typical *C. arizonica*.

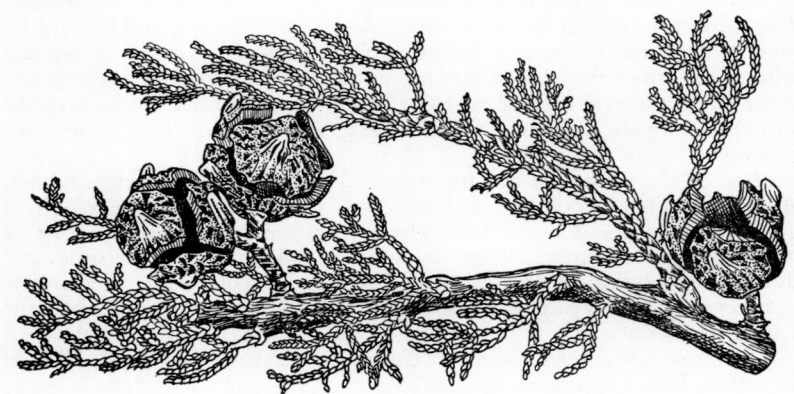

CUPRESSUS GLABRA

Owing to the confusion between the two species described above, the date of introduction of neither is known for certain. The seed sent by the Arnold Arboretum in 1882 is said to have been *C. arizonica* but may equally well have been *C. glabra*, which was described many years later. But the seed distributed by Purpus around 1890 was apparently collected in New Mexico, well within the range of *C. arizonica*. The trees cultivated in this country (most of which are probably *C. glabra*) are quite hardy and have reached heights of 60 to 75 ft and girths of 3¾ to 5 ft.

The beautiful form of the Arizona cypress so common in Italian gardens is usually known as *C. arizonica conica* (or *pyramidalis*). It is of narrowly conical habit, with blue-glaucous leaves. Although said to be tender in Central Europe it appears to be quite hardy in this country.

C. STEPHENSONII C. B. Wolf—This rare species is allied to *C. glabra* but is less glandular and with smaller leaves (about $\frac{1}{25}$ in. long). Confined to a small area in San Diego Co., California, and known as the Cuyamaca cypress.

C. CASHMERIANA Carr.

C. funebris var. *glauca* Mast.

A fine example of this remarkable cypress grows in the Temperate House at Kew, but when tried out-of-doors in even a very sheltered place, it has never recovered from the effects of the first winter. Its spray is perfectly pendulous, very glaucous, and flat, the branchlets hanging vertically in two opposite ranks. Leaves intermediate in character between the juvenile and adult states of the true cypresses; they are only $\frac{1}{16}$ to $\frac{1}{12}$ in. long, but are not scale-like, and have free, somewhat spreading points. Cones about $\frac{1}{2}$ in. diameter, globose; scales ten, with a triangular, hooked boss in the centre. This cypress is, no doubt, of Asiatic origin, but there appears to be no evidence that it is a native of Kashmir. Henry suggested it may be a juvenile state of *C. torulosa*. It is a tree of singular beauty both in form and colour. The finest tree in Europe is on Isola Madre, Lake Maggiore, Italy. Cones are freely borne by the tree at Kew, and young plants have been raised from the seed.

In the mildest parts it has proved tolerably hardy, but seems to need more summer heat than our climate can offer. The tallest example known is at Head-fort, Co. Meath, Eire; planted half a century ago it now measures 28 × 5 ft (1966). In Northern Ireland there is a specimen at Castlewellan measuring 22 × 1$\frac{3}{4}$ ft (1966), planted in 1946.

C. DUCLOUXIANA Hickel

A tall evergreen tree of elegant habit and densely twiggy; final subdivisions of the branches very slender and about $\frac{1}{32}$ in. in diameter. Leaves in the adult state closely appressed to the branches (free at the tips in young specimens) rather glaucous, about $\frac{1}{20}$ in. long, the exposed part diamond-shaped with a gland in the centre. Cones globose, $\frac{3}{4}$ to 1 in. wide before opening; scales about six, each $\frac{1}{2}$ in. wide, with a small boss in the centre; seeds reddish brown. *Bot. Mag.*, t. 9049.

Native of Yunnan, China; originally discovered by Delavay, the French missionary, subsequently by Monseigneur Ducloux, after whom it is named. It was originally introduced by Maurice de Vilmorin about 1905. It was at that time (following Franchet's identification) regarded as a Chinese form of *C. semper-virens*. It is closely related to that species but its twigs are more slender, the leaves smaller and more pointed, the cones smaller and with fewer scales, the seeds smaller and scarcely winged.

This species is rare in cultivation and the best specimens known are all in Eire. These are at Kilmacurragh and Mount Usher in Co. Wicklow and at Headfort in Co. Meath, and are between 30 and 40 ft in height. It is tender, when young at least and, in spite of several attempts, has never become established in the National Pinetum at Bedgebury.

C. FORBESII Jeps.   TECATE CYPRESS

A small tree, usually less than 30 ft high, with numerous ascending branches and very distinct from the other Californian cypresses (except *C. stephensonii*) in its smooth, lustrous, cherry-red or brown bark, which peels in thin flakes. Leaves light green; resin-pits absent or inconspicuous. Cones grey or brownish, globose, about 1 in. wide, with rather short umbos. Seeds dark brown. A native of S. California, with two separate locations, one in San Diego Co., and the other in Orange Co.; it extends, but scarcely, into Mexico. This cypress, of recent introduction, is allied to C. GUADALUPENSIS S. Wats., a species confined to the island of Guadelupe, which lies off the coast of Lower California. This makes a more massive tree than C. *forbesii*; the leaves are more glaucous; and the cones larger (to 1¾ in. wide). Both resemble C. *macrocarpa* in foliage and fruit, but are well distinguished by the smooth, peeling bark. There is a specimen of C. *guadalupensis* at Borde Hill, Sussex, about 50 ft high, which fruits regularly and shows very well the characteristic bark of this species.

C. FUNEBRIS Endl.   CHINESE WEEPING CYPRESS

A tree up to 70 ft high, of very characteristic habit, the trunk being erect and clothed with smooth brown bark, the branches horizontal or ascending, but furnished with vertically pendulous, slender sprays. The branchlets are in the same plane in two opposite ranks, with the final subdivisions much flattened, thin, and about $\frac{1}{20}$ in. wide. Leaves uniformly green, in four rows, $\frac{1}{12}$ to $\frac{1}{8}$ in. long, the terminal part of each triangular and tapered to a fine point; the lateral leaves have the points free and rather spreading, the upper and lower ones closely flattened. Cones $\frac{1}{3}$ to $\frac{1}{2}$ in. across, globose, borne on slender stalks $\frac{1}{8}$ to $\frac{1}{4}$ in. long; scales with a small boss in the centre.

Native of Central China, and now spread widely over that country in cultivation. First noticed by the members of Lord Macartney's mission to China in 1793, but introduced by Fortune in 1849. It is too tender for any but the mildest parts of the British Isles, and young trees have been killed time after time at Kew. It was grown in winter gardens for its elegant habit, and produces cones at an early age. The curiously dissimilar foliage of seedlings always attracts attention, the leaves in that state being in whorls of three or four, linear or awl-shaped, and $\frac{1}{4}$ to $\frac{1}{3}$ in. long; pale soft green. In its flat adult branchlets it bears some resemblance to *Chamaecyparis*, also in its small cones, and few seeds (three to five) to each scale. There are examples of 15 to 35 ft in height at: Killerton, Devon; the Bath Botanic Garden: and in Eire at Powerscourt; Mount Usher; and Kilmacurragh.

C. GOVENIANA Gord.

In the wild a small tree or large shrub, never more than about 25 ft high in its typical state, but taller in cultivation. The branchlets are more slender than in C. *macrocarpa*, clad with rich green foliage; as in that species they are arranged in four ranks, scale-like and flattened to the branch, but are somewhat smaller. The two species also resemble each other in having non-glandular leaves (cf. C. *macnabiana*, in which the leaves are pitted with sunken, resin-exuding glands). The cones are smaller than in C. *macrocarpa*, being $\frac{2}{5}$ to $\frac{3}{5}$ in. long, with six to ten scales and more or less globular in shape. Seed ripe in the second year, dark brown to almost black.

var. PYGMAEA Lemm. C. *pygmaea* (Lemm.) Sarg.—This variety is misleadingly named, being dwarf only on sterile soils; in favoured situations it develops a leading shoot and may attain a height of over 100 ft. The foliage is dull, dark green. Seeds lustrous black to dull brown.

C. *goveniana* is a very local species in the wild, found in the same part of Monterey Co. as the more famous C. *macrocarpa*, but farther inland. It was introduced from this locality by Hartweg in 1846. Var. *pygmaea* occurs much farther to the north, in Mendocino Co.

H. J. Elwes remarked (*The Trees of Great Britain and Ireland*) that C. *goveniana* appeared to be a short-lived tree; at that time (1910) it was represented in cultivation by specimens 40–50 ft high, some of them already going back; whether any of these remain today is doubtful—the researches of A. F. Mitchell have so far revealed none in Britain. At the present time all of the finest specimens of C. *goveniana* in this country are to be found at Wakehurst Place, Sussex, where there are altogether some twenty-five specimens, sixteen of which are over 50 ft high. The tallest is a narrowly columnar tree of 72 × 5¼ ft and there is one of similar habit almost as tall; another with a broad bushy crown is 63 × 7½ ft (1964). Other tall specimens grow at Bagshot Park, Surrey, and Woburn Abbey, Beds. There is a fine specimen in the R.H.S. Garden, Wisley, about 40 ft high.

C. ABRAMSIANA C.B. Wolf—A small bushy tree of conical habit found in a few localities in the Santa Cruz Mountains, California. It is intermediate between C. *sargentii* and C. *goveniana* in its botanical characters, but nearer to the latter, which it resembles in its bright, rich green foliage. The cones, however, are larger than in that species (over ⅗ in. long) and the seeds dull brown and glaucous.

C. SARGENTII Jeps.—This species is closely related to C. *goveniana*. It may be distinguished by its dull grey-green leaves, stouter branchlets and somewhat larger cones (¾ to 1 in. long). The seeds are lustrous brown, sometimes glaucous. It is a species of much wider range than C. *goveniana*, occurring here and there in the Coastal Range of California.

C. LUSITANICA Mill.   CEDAR OF GOA
C. lindleyi Klotzsch; *C. glauca* Lam.

A tree up to 100 ft high in the wild and almost as high in the British Isles, with wide-spreading branches and pendulous spray; the branching not two ranked, but spiral and irregular. Branchlets four-sided. Leaves in four rows, scale-like, 1/16 to 1/12 in. long, with the terminal part elongated, triangular, finely and sharply pointed, free at the tip. Cones very glaucous, and about the size of peas the first year; scales six or eight, with a conical, hooked crest in the centre; the cones become ½ in. in diameter, and shed their seeds the second year, and lose much of their glaucous hue. Seeds brown with conspicuous resinous warts. *Bot. Mag.*, t. 9434.

The native country of this cypress was long a matter of speculation. It appears to have been cultivated in England since the latter half of the seventeenth century, having been first introduced from Portugal; hence the epithet *lusitanica*. But it was never found wild either in Portugal or the Portuguese settlement of

Goa in Western India, in spite of its common name. It is now certain that it is a native of Mexico, and was, no doubt, introduced to the Peninsula by mariners or members of the religious fraternities, probably in the sixteenth century. The first direct introduction from Mexico was in the forties of the last century. The most celebrated plantation of *C. lusitanica* is at Busaco, in Portugal.

It should be added that Martinez (*Las Pinaceas Mexicanas*, 1963) does not recognise *C. lusitanica* as a native of Mexico. The native Mexican trees which most botanists now consider to belong to this species are treated by him under the name *C. lindleyi* Klotzsch.

For the northern and eastern parts of the country this tree is not suited. In southern England there are good specimens from Sussex westward, but it is in the south-west and in Ireland that it thrives the best. In England there are trees of 70 to 80 ft in height and 4½ to 6 ft in girth at Leonardslee and Wakehurst Place, Sussex; Blackmoor, Hants; Killerton, Devon; and The Hendre, Mon. (measured 1961–5). At Wisley there is a specimen about 45 ft high; it was untouched by the winter of 1962–3. The tallest known is an unhealthy tree at Bicton in Devon, which is 102 ft in height. In Ireland the best trees so far recorded are in the same height range as the English, but generally of larger girth. These are at Fota, Co. Cork; Inishtioge, Co. Kilkenny; Birr Castle, Co. Offaly (from seed collected by Coulter in Mexico in 1837); Mount Usher, Co. Wicklow; and, in Northern Ireland, at Castlewellan, Co. Down.

var. BENTHAMII (Endl.) Carr.   *C. benthamii* Endl.; *C. thurifera* Schlecht., not H. B. K.—Cones of this variety are identical with those of the type in colour, shape and size, but the branchlets are flattened and arranged in two opposite ranks, both on the same plane. Native of Mexico; introduced about 1838. According to Martinez, it has a restricted distribution, most of the stands being in the mountains N.E. of Pachuca. The name "*knightiana*" is sometimes given to a slightly more glaucous form; such forms, and others with yellowish green leaves, are found in the wild.

cv. 'FLAGILLIFERA'.—Shoots pendulous and whip-like, resembling *Chamaecyparis pisifera* 'Filifera'.

cv. 'GLAUCA PENDULA'.—A very beautiful, pendulous tree with glaucous foliage, put into commerce by Messrs Hillier around 1925. A plant at Rowallane, Co. Down, received from them in 1928, is now 36 ft high with a spreading crown 30 ft in diameter (1965). There is another specimen, probably from the same source, at Glendurgan, Cornwall.

C. MACNABIANA A. Murr.

A shrub or small bushy tree to 30 or 40 ft high; bark greyish, furrowed and fibrous. Branchlet systems forming flat sprays (though not constantly so), the ultimate divisions very slender and ⅛ to ¼ in. long. Leaves dark grey green, about $\frac{1}{20}$ in. long, scale-like, thick, convex and blunt, with a conspicuous resin-pit on the back. Cones short-stalked, globose, about ¾ in. across, rather glaucous at first, becoming brown or grey, scales usually six, rarely eight, those at the apex developing thickened, horn-like crests, those at the base with thin, recurved bosses. Seeds brown.

Native of California; discovered by Jeffrey in the Sierra Nevada in 1853, introduced by W. Murray the following year for Lawson's nursery, Edinburgh. It is now very rare in this country, and although apparently one of the hardiest of the true cypresses, appears to be short-lived under cultivation. It is one of the most easily recognised of a difficult group, first, by the resin-pit at the back of the leaf (quite conspicuous under the lens); second, by the prominent horn-like development on the upper scales of the cone. The foliage has a very pleasant aromatic fragrance.

This cypress has remained rare in gardens. There is an example at Wakehurst Place, Sussex, measuring 33 × 4½ ft at 1½ ft (1965), and others of about the same size in Eire at Birr Castle, Co. Offaly; and at Mount Usher and Powerscourt, Co. Wicklow.

C. BAKERI Jeps.—A tree to 50 ft high, closely allied to the preceding but with a reddish-brown bark which becomes grey with age but not furrowed. The branchlets are arranged all round the shoot, the ultimate divisions about ½ in. long and the leaves also somewhat longer (about $\frac{1}{12}$ in.). Cones smaller (about ¼ in. across). The Modoc cypress, as it is called, is confined to Shasta Co. and S.E. Siskiyou Co., where it grows at 4,000 to 6,000 ft.

subsp. MATTHEWSII C. B. Wolf—This makes a taller tree than typical C. bakeri; the ultimate divisions of the branchlets are longer and the cones larger (to $\frac{4}{5}$ in. across), with inconspicuous crests. It is found in the Siskiyou Mountains of California and Oregon and is known as the Siskiyou cypress.

C. bakeri and its subspecies have recently been introduced and promise to be more satisfactory in cultivation than C. macnabiana, coming as they do from considerably higher altitudes.

C. MACROCARPA Gord.   MONTEREY CYPRESS

C. lambertiana Gord.

A tree 60 to 90 ft high in cultivation, not more in a wild state; of pyramidal habit when young, becoming eventually flat-topped and with horizontal branches like a cedar of Lebanon. Branchlets much divided in an irregular (not two-ranked or horizontal) manner; the final ramifications terete or somewhat four-sided, $\frac{1}{20}$ in. thick. Leaves scale-like, $\frac{1}{16}$ in. long, uniform, closely flattened to the branchlet in four rows, overlapping each other at the base, the exposed part diamond-shaped, thick and rounded at the end. Cones oblong or globose, 1 to 1½ in. long, $\frac{2}{3}$ to 1 in. wide on short stout stalks; scales eight to fourteen, flattish, with a ridge-like projection in the centre. Seeds brown, minutely warted.

Native of California, where it is confined to two groves near the Pacific, south of Monterey. The larger, Cypress Point Grove, is 2 miles long and about a furlong wide; the other, Point Lobos Grove, is much smaller. The trees grow on the shore cliffs, and being undermined by the sea, occasionally fall into it. At this spot they appear as rugged veterans, identical in habit with the cedar of Lebanon. The species was introduced about 1838, and has proved to be one of the hardiest of the true cypresses. It succeeds much the best in warm maritime localities, but even in inland places like Kew it is over 80 ft high. When young it is more tender, and at this state is so distinct in general appearance as to show no apparent relationship to the adult type. The leaves are $\frac{1}{8}$ in. long, awl-shaped, with sharp, outwardly spreading points; the shoots much longer and more attenuated, the leaves well apart. As the plants increase in age, they gradually assume the adult state described above; but when, as they sometimes are in mild counties, used for hedges and clipped back annually, the young growths retain this juvenile type of foliage and branchlet. The young growths are sometimes distinctly lemon-scented.

The following are some of the largest specimens recorded recently in the British Isles, notable either for height or girth: Beauport, Sussex, 85 × 27 ft at 1 ft (1965); Bicton, Devon, 110 × 12 ft (1964), a fine tree; Northerwood House, Hants, 117 × 20½ ft at 3 ft (1963); Montacute House, Somerset, 117 × 22½ ft (1962), good bole; Melbury, Dorset, 117 × 18½ ft (1957); Watcombe, Torquay, 115 × 27¾ ft at 1 ft (1962); Mamhead, Devon, 105 × 16¾ ft (1963), a very shapely tree; Tregothnan, Cornwall, 120 × 19½ ft (1965), a very fine tree on an 8 ft bole.

cv. 'CRIPPSII'.—A juvenile state, with stiff branches.

f. FASTIGIATA (Carr.) Rehd. *C. lambertiana* var. *fastigiata* Carr.—Branches permanently erect-growing, giving a tree of columnar or fastigiate form. Such variants occur not uncommonly among seedlings.

cv. 'LUTEA'.—Young shoots and leaves of a beautiful yellow. Of the same kind, but with brighter golden foliage, are 'DONARD GOLD', raised by the Slieve Donard Nursery Co. in 1935; and 'GOLDCREST', raised by Messrs Treseder of Truro shortly after the second world war. As is the case with many golden-leaved conifers, none of these varieties develop their full colouring if grown in a shaded position.

cv. 'PYGMAEA'.—Very dwarf and dense in habit. Raised at Carshalton nursery.

C. SEMPERVIRENS L.   ITALIAN CYPRESS

A tree 80 to 150 ft high and 4 to 10 ft in girth of trunk in the Mediterranean region, its branching either horizontal or fastigiate, the bark thin; final sub-division of branchlets terete or squarish, $\frac{1}{30}$ to $\frac{1}{20}$ in. wide. Leaves scale-like, dark green, arranged in four rows, closely pressed to the twig or axis, over-lapping each other at their bases, the exposed part diamond-shaped, blunt at the apex. Cones globose to oblong, $\frac{3}{4}$ to $1\frac{1}{4}$ in. long; scales eight to fourteen, usually rising to a point in the middle, but sometimes flat or slightly hollowed, with a thin boss in the centre. Seeds not warted.

var. SEMPERVIRENS.—This is the typical variety, of fastigiate habit, usually known as var. *stricta* Ait., or as "*C. pyramidalis*". It is not known in the genuinely wild state but is widely distributed in the Mediterranean region and farther east as a cultivated and semi-naturalised tree. It is very variable and linked by intermediates to var. *horizontalis*. The very narrowly fastigiate forms are selections perpetuated by cuttings.

var. HORIZONTALIS (Mill.) Gord. *C. horizontalis* Mill.—Branches more or less horizontal. This is the state in which *C. sempervirens* is found as a wild tree in the Aegean and the Near East.

C. sempervirens is the 'cypress' of the ancients; cultivated in England for at least four centuries. It lives out-of-doors at Kew, but does not thrive there like *C. macrocarpa*, needing a warmer climate. This tenderness is more especially marked in young trees. There are fine examples scattered over the south and west parts of our islands. Wherever planted it likes shelter, and should be put out young. The erect-growing form is the most popular in this country, and is the tree whose tall, dark, columnar shape is so characteristic a feature of Italian gardens and cemeteries. It lives to be several hundreds of years old in S. Europe. In the Boboli Gardens, familiar to visitors to Florence, an avenue of cypresses is 300 years old, yet shows no evidence of decline. At Somma, in Lombardy, there grew what was, perhaps, the most famous tree in Europe. It was of the horizontal-branched kind and grew close to the Simplon road, which Napoleon is said to have diverted in order to save it. This tree, which was reputed to have been planted before the birth of Christ, was blown down in a storm on 2nd September 1944.

The wood of the Italian cypress is remarkably durable, and was much employed for making large chests for clothing, etc., in the Middle Ages, its odour, agreeable to human beings, keeping away moths. According to Loudon, the doors of St Peter's at Rome, made of this wood, stood for over 1,100 years, and were found to be perfectly sound on removal.

Among the cypresses, *C. sempervirens* is most closely allied to *C. macrocarpa*, but may usually be distinguished by the finer, more delicate spray and smaller leaves, also by the frequently shallow, pyramidal apex of the scales, and the smooth, not warted, seeds.

The largest specimens of *C. sempervirens* in the British Isles are around 55 to 70 ft in height. These are found at: Killerton, Devon; Penrhyn Castle, Caer.; Blackmoor, Hants; Nymans, Sussex; Nettlecombe, Somerset; Montacute House, Somerset; Mamhead, Devon; Blenheim Palace, Oxon.; Edinburgh Botanic Garden; Fota, Co. Cork, Eire. These are of rather open habit, but narrow spire-like specimens grow at Bodvean, Caer., and at Powerscourt in Eire. (All measurements 1955–66.)

C. TORULOSA D. Don   HIMALAYAN CYPRESS

A tree up to 150 ft high in the Himalaya, with horizontal branches, and bark peeling off in long strips. Branchlets arranged in opposite ranks, more or less drooping, the final subdivisions equally four-sided, about $\frac{1}{20}$ in. in diameter. Leaves of equal size, deep green, scale-like; overlapping at the base, the terminal part ovate, bluntish, incurved and thickened at the point, often grooved on the back. Cones purplish when young, globose, very shortly stalked, $\frac{1}{2}$ to $\frac{2}{3}$ in. in diameter; scales eight, rarely ten, each with a small central boss.

Discovered by Buchanan-Hamilton during his famous journey in Nepal, 1802–3; introduced in 1824. It is tender, and only seen to advantage in the southern and western counties. Specimens at Hewell Grange, Worcs., were mentioned in previous editions; the taller of two there, planted in 1866, measures

T S—D D

76 × 5½ ft (1963). At Nettlecombe in Somerset there are four trees, the tallest 92 ft high (1959). Others grow at Scorrier, Cornwall, and Keir House, Perths.

var. CORNEYANA (Knight and Perry) Carr.—In this variety the branchlets are arranged irregularly rather than in two opposite ranks, and they are more pendulous. It was distributed by Knight and Perry before 1850, but the origin of the seed is uncertain. There are examples of this variety at Kew; at Batsford Park, Glos.; and in Eire at Fota, Co. Cork, and Powerscourt, Co. Wicklow.

CYATHODES   EPACRIDACEAE

A genus of about fifteen species of evergreen shrubs, natives mainly of Australia and New Zealand, mostly small-leaved and rather heath-like in habit. Flowers small, usually solitary in the leaf-axils on short pedicels with numerous bracts, more rarely in short racemes; petals united into a tube on which the stamens are inserted, alternating with the corolla lobes. Fruit a fleshy drupe; stone with two to ten seeds. *Leucopogon*, treated as a distinct genus in the present work, is very closely allied to *Cyathodes* and has been united with it by H. H. Allan (*Flora of New Zealand*, 1961) so far as the New Zealand species are concerned.

C. COLENSOI (Hook. f.) Hook. f.
Leucopogon colensoi Hook. f.

A low shrub of heath-like habit up to 18 in. high. Leaves narrow-oblong, ⅕ to ⅓ in. long and up to ⅛ in. wide, glaucous grey above and often membranous towards the apex, undersides whitish with conspicuous, almost parallel veins; growth buds with numerous pinkish scales which remain for some time at the base of the young shoot. Flowers three to five in short racemes, borne in spring at the ends of the young growth; corolla tubular, about ¼ in. long, lobes densely hairy on the upper surface. Fruit white or red, about ⅛ in. wide.

A native of the mountains of New Zealand. It is one of the hardiest of the Epacris family, growing well though slowly in peaty soil and damaged only in the severest winters. Its fruits are rarely seen in this country but it is well worth growing for its attractive foliage and young growth.

C. EMPETRIFOLIA Hook. f.—A close ally of the preceding but of prostrate, straggling habit and with very narrow, linear leaves. The flowers are borne singly or in small clusters.

C. JUNIPERINA (J. R. & G. Forst.) Druce
Epacris juniperina J. R. & G. Forst.; *Cyathodes acerosa* (Gaertn.) R. Br.

An evergreen shrub of variable habit, sometimes found 15 ft or more high in the wild but more commonly low and spreading, 3 to 6 ft high; bark black. Leaves stiff and leathery, narrow-linear or linear-lanceolate, up to ¾ in. long and 1⁄12 in. wide, terminated by a sharp, rigid point, margins recurved, undersides glaucous. Flowers inconspicuous, borne singly in the leaf-axils. Fruit globose, about ¼ in. wide, usually some shade of pink or red, sometimes white.

Native of Australia (including Tasmania) and of New Zealand, better known in cultivation as *C. acerosa*, under which name it was once grown in greenhouses as a fruiting shrub. It is tender, but survives outside in the milder parts.

C. ROBUSTA Hook. f.—A native of Chatham Island, closely related to the preceding but distinguished by its blunt leaves. The fruits are somewhat larger and said to be more freely borne than in the other species.

CYDONIA   Quince   ROSACEAE

A genus which, as interpreted here, consists of only a single species—the common quince. For the three shrubby quinces described in previous editions under *Cydonia*, see *Chaenomeles*. A fifth species, the rare *Cydonia sinensis*, is best considered as constituting an independent genus and will be found under *Pseudocydonia*.

C. OBLONGA Mill.   COMMON QUINCE
Pyrus cydonia L.; *C. vulgaris* Pers.

A deciduous, thornless tree, 15 to 20 ft high, with crowded branches and a low quaint habit; young branchlets covered with greyish wool. Leaves ovate or elliptical, 2½ to 4 in. long, 1¾ to 2¼ in. wide, not toothed, dark green above, pale with a dense felt of grey wool beneath, especially when young; stipules hairy, glandular. Flowers 2 in. across, pink or white, each one solitary at the end of a short twig, produced during May. Fruit light golden yellow, pear-shaped, very fragrant.

The native country of the quince, like that of some other commonly cultivated plants, is not definitely known, but most probably it is wild only in parts of the Near East and Central Asia. It has been cultivated in the lands bordering the Mediterranean from time immemorial and has become naturalised in many parts; it was introduced to Britain at an early date.

cv. 'LUSITANICA'.—The Portuguese quince is more vigorous than the type, but not quite so hardy in Britain. The fruit is 4 in. long, 3½ in. wide at the thickest part, tapering thence to the stalk; skin deep yellow, covered with grey down. Flowers large, pale rose, and produced in sufficient abundance to make this variety the best worth growing for ornament. It was named *C. lusitanica* by Miller (*Gard. Dict.*, 1768).

cv. 'MALIFORMIS'.—The form of the quince that Miller took as the type of his *C. oblonga* bears pear-shaped fruits. In this form (*C. maliformis* Mill.) they are apple-shaped.

cv. 'VRANJA'.—This was introduced from and long grown near Vranja in

S. Serbia, Yugoslavia. The fruit is very fragrant, of a clear shining gold, and said to have a softer flesh than most quinces. 'BERECKI' is similar.

The fruit of the quince when raw is harsh and astringent, and unfit for food, but it has long been grown in orchards for flavouring apple-pies, ices, and

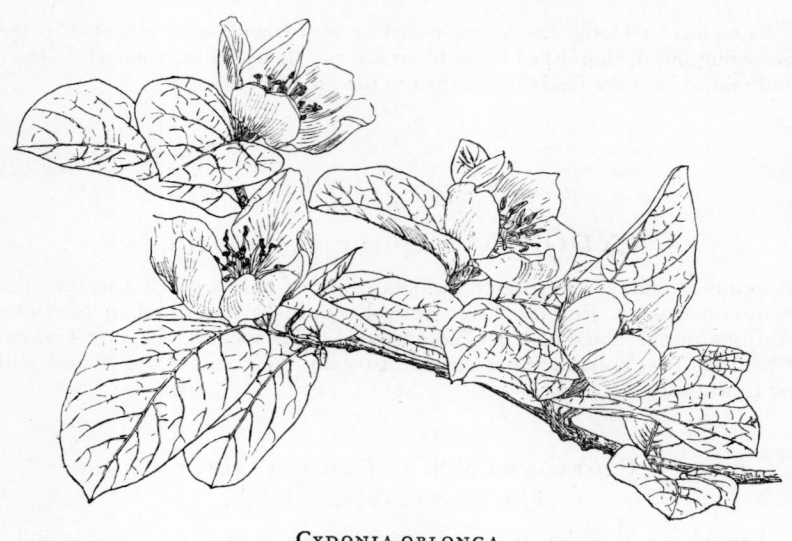

CYDONIA OBLONGA

various confections. The pear-shaped form is perhaps the handsomest of all hardy fruits. The quince is largely employed as a stock on which pears are grafted.

CYRILLA CYRILLACEAE

A genus of one variable and wide-ranging species (or a group of up to ten species in other interpretations), native of the New World from Virginia to northern S. America. The small family to which it belongs is allied to Aquifoliaceae and is also represented in gardens by *Cliftonia monophylla* (q.v.). The name commemorates Dominico Cirillo, an Italian physician (1739–99), at one time Professor of Botany at Naples.

C. RACEMIFLORA LEATHERWOOD

A deciduous shrub in this country, 4 ft or more high (a small tree in some parts of its native habitat), of spreading habit, free from down in all its parts; young shoots slender, very leafy. Leaves alternate, oblanceolate or obovate;

$1\frac{1}{2}$ to 4 in. long, $\frac{1}{2}$ to $1\frac{1}{4}$ in. wide; much tapered at the base, more abruptly so or rounded at the apex, dark lustrous green; stalks $\frac{1}{4}$ in. or less long. Flowers very small, numerous and white, crowded on slender cylindrical racemes 3 to 6 in. long, $\frac{1}{2}$ to $\frac{3}{4}$ in. wide; produced in late summer and autumn; the racemes appearing in a horizontal whorl at the base of the current season's growth. Fruit a roundish capsule $\frac{1}{12}$ in. long. *Bot. Mag.*, t. 2456.

This species, if interpreted in a broad sense, is native of N. America from Virginia to Texas, of the West Indies and of S. America as far south as Brazil. It was introduced to Britain in 1765, but had long disappeared until reimported about 1900. Only the form from the northern limits of its distribution, which is shrubby and deciduous, is hardy in the south of England; the more southern forms are evergreen, tree-like, and not hardy. There is a specimen of the former kind in the Wild Garden at Wisley. The profusion and curious arrangement of the racemes as well as the season at which they appear, give the species a certain distinction and merit. It thrives in a mixture of peat and loam.

CYTISUS   Broom   LEGUMINOSAE

A very important place is filled in gardens by the group of shrubs commonly classed together as 'brooms'. Of this group, which includes *Genista*, *Spartium*, etc., *Cytisus* is the most important genus. Its species are mostly quite deciduous, some are almost always leafless, and all are shrubby, varying in stature from 12 ft or more high, down to less than as many inches. The leaves are alternate, simple, or trifoliolate (sometimes both on the same plant). The flowers have the pea-flower shape characteristic of the family, and, with the exception of a few species, they are yellow. Fruit a pod. The genus is essentially a European one, but a few species extend eastward to Asia Minor, and others reach across the Mediterranean to N. Africa.

The affinities of the genus are with *Laburnum*, *Ulex*, and *Genista*. *Laburnum* is distinguished by the thickened or winged sutures (seams) of the pod; *Ulex* by the coloured calyx; but the distinctions between *Genista* and *Cytisus* are not so easily found. The most serviceable one is furnished by the seed. In *Cytisus* the outer coat of the seed has a wart-like excrescence near the hilum, which is technically known as the 'strophiole'. In *Genista* this is absent or rudimentary. A small group of species, of which the common broom *C. scoparius* is the best known, are by some botanists segregated as the genus SAROTHAMNUS. However, in addition to the taxonomic arguments against making this split, there is the practical one that many garden brooms derive from the crossing of the common broom with *C. multiflorus*. If the former were to be placed in *Sarothamnus*—and there is no obligation to do so—these brooms would have to be treated as bigeneric hybrids under the name × *Cytothamnus*. The section *Tubocytisus* (characterised by a tubular calyx) is also retained within *Cytisus* in the present revision, although by some authorities it is treated as a distinct genus under the name CHAMAECYTISUS. For a further discussion of the taxonomy of the *Cytisus–Genista* group, see the introductory note to *Genista* in vol. 2.

The species of *Cytisus* are easily cultivated. They like a fairly good, but not rich soil, and abundant sunshine. Whenever possible, they should be raised from seeds, but if these are not available cuttings and grafts can be used. Cuttings should be taken in August when the wood has become firm. Pieces from 1½ to 3 in. long may be used, always with a slight heel of older wood. They should be dibbled in very sandy soil under cloches, or in a frame, only uncovering to give water. They ought to push roots the following spring, and soon after can be potted in small pots, or, if vigorously rooted, planted out straight away in nursery beds, being careful to water and, if necessary, shade until established. The brooms do not transplant well after they have reached a good size, so it is wise to get them in their permanent places early.

Except for *C. battandieri* and *C. ingramii* no species of genuine importance or interest belonging to this genus has been introduced to gardens since the first publication of this work, the others now described having been in cultivation at or before that time. But a large number of varieties of garden origin have appeared, and continue to appear, which have added considerably to the importance of the genus as a contributor to ornamental hardy shrubs. Some of these are colour-forms of *C. scoparius*. The majority are members of a hybrid swarm stemming from *C.* × *dallimorei*. In recent years Dutch breeders have used *C.* × *praecox* as a parent: crossed with *C.* × *dallimorei* it has given 'ZEELANDIA' and, with *C.* 'Burkwoodii', 'HOLLANDIA'; 'DUKAAT' and 'FRISIA' are second-generation seedlings from these crosses. *C.* × *praecox* has also been crossed with *C.* × *beanii* and *C. ardoinii*. The next few decades are likely to see a stream of new hybrids of ever-increasing complexity and perhaps of dwarfer habit than the older sorts.

The following is a selection from those available in commerce, provided by the Royal Horticultural Society:

'BURKWOODII'.—Cerise and maroon-red. Vigorous and bushy.

'C. E. PEARSON'.—Rose, yellow and red.

'CORNISH CREAM'.—Cream and yellow. Bushy, open habit.

'DONARD SEEDLING'.—Mauve-pink and flame-red. Rather loose habit.

'ENCHANTRESS'.—Rose-pink and carmine. Of spreading bushy habit.

'FIREFLY'.—Yellow and rich mahogany-crimson. Bushy.

'GOLDFINCH'.—Crimson and yellow; pink and yellow wings.

'HOOKSTONE'.—Flowers lilac and orange.

'JOHNSON'S CRIMSON'.—Clear crimson. Graceful arching habit. Free flowering.

'KILLINEY RED'.—Flowers bright red. Dwarf, compact habit.

'KNAPHILL LEMON'.—Lemon-yellow flowers.

'LADY MOORE'.—Pinkish yellow and orange-flame. Loose, branching habit.

'LORD LAMBOURNE'.—Creamy-yellow and maroon-crimson. Branching and spreading.

'MINSTEAD'.—Fuchsia purple and white. Slender arching habit.

'ZEELANDIA'.—Pale lilac-pink and red. Long arching sprays.

C. ALBUS Hacq.

C. leucanthus Waldst. & Kit.; *C. schipkaensis* Dieck

A dwarf shrub of spreading habit 4 to 10 in. high, deciduous, with round hairy branchlets. Leaves trifoliolate, with a hairy main-stalk ¼ to ½ in. long; leaflets about ½ in. long, obovate or narrow elliptic, almost glabrous above, clothed beneath with appressed hairs. Flowers closely packed in a terminal cluster, yellowish white, six to ten in each cluster. The flower is ¾ in. long, but the petals do not expand fully through being clasped by the large hairy calyx ⅓ in. long. Pod ¾ in. long, compressed, shaggy, containing two to five seeds.

Native of south-east and east Central Europe and S. Poland; introduced about 1806, but was afterwards completely lost sight of in gardens; about 1890 it was again introduced from the Balkan Mountains, and having been found on the Shipka Pass, it was distributed from nurseries under the name of *C. schipkaensis*, without its identity with the old *leucanthus* being noticed. More recently, the rules of nomenclature have dictated that the name *C. albus* of Hacquet should be used for this species. For the broom long grown in gardens as "*C. albus*", see *C. multiflorus* (syn. *C. albus* Link, not Hacquet). It flowers best in June and July, but continues until October to produce odd clusters. It is not one of the prettiest of dwarf brooms, but flowers later than most of them. It may be used as a carpeting beneath thinly planted, taller shrubs, or in small patches in the rock garden. It belongs to the Supinus group.

C. ARDOINII Fournier

A low, decumbent, deciduous shrub 4 or 5 in. high, with round, shallowly grooved, hairy branches. Leaves trifoliolate, with a main-stalk ¼ in. long; leaflets obovate or oblong, ⅓ in. long, almost shaggy when young on both sides. Flowers golden yellow, produced in April and May, one to three (occasionally up to six) at each joint, on short hairy stalks, on the terminal part of the previous year's shoots. Each flower is about ½ in. long, with a short hairy calyx; the standard petal is orbicular and incurved at the edges. Pod ¾ to 1 in. long, hairy, containing one or two seeds.

Native of the Maritime Alps, where, according to Moggridge (*Flora of Mentone*, t. 58), it is extremely rare in a wild state owing to the plants being eaten over by grazing animals before the seeds have time to ripen. It was first discovered by Ardoino, after whom it is named, in 1847, but was apparently lost sight of until 1866, when it was found again by the Rev. Wm. Hawker and introduced to cultivation. It is a singularly pretty little shrub, one of the dwarfest of brooms, quite hardy, and flowers freely. Under cultivation it hybridises readily through insect agency if grown near other species. It is the seed parent of *C.* × *kewensis* and *C.* × *beanii*, as well as some other inferior unnamed kinds. It is a delightful rock garden plant, but if associated with other brooms should be raised from cuttings to be sure of coming true.

C. AUSTRIACUS L.

C. supinus subsp. *austriacus*. (L.) Briq.; *Chamaecytisus austriacus* (L.) Link

A species closely related to *C. supinus*, from which it differs in having the hairs of the stems, leaves and pods appressed; it is of more restricted range, occurring from Czechoslovakia and Hungary eastward to the Caucasus, while *C. supinus* extends westward as far as the Atlantic. It is usually represented in gardens by the following variety, which differs from the type in little but its more slender stems and narrower leaflets:

var. HEUFFELII (Griseb. & Schenk) Schneid. *C. heuffelii* Griseb. & Schenk; *Chamaecytisus heuffelii* (Griseb. & Schenk) Rothm.—A low, deciduous shrub with slender, erect, or arching branches covered with greyish appressed hairs. Leaves trifoliolate, with stalks $\frac{1}{3}$ in. long; leaflets $\frac{1}{2}$ to $\frac{3}{4}$ in. long, $\frac{1}{8}$ in. or less wide; linear oblong or linear obovate, covered with flattened hairs beneath; ultimately glabrous above. Flowers borne on the shoots of the year in a close terminal head, each $\frac{3}{4}$ in. long, with narrow, yellow petals, and a very hairy calyx which extends two-thirds the length of the flower. Pod 1 in. long, $\frac{3}{16}$ in. wide, covered with silky greyish hairs, and containing four to eight seeds.

Native of the Balkan peninsula and Danube basin. It has much the same garden value as *C. supinus* and should be pruned in the same manner.

Typical *C. austriacus* differs from the above in the following particulars: habit often procumbent; leaflets usually permanently hairy above; hairs of calyx spreading (appressed in var. *heuffelii*).

C. BATTANDIERI Maire   [PLATE 77

An unarmed deciduous shrub 15 ft or more high, of rather erect habit; young shoots stout, $\frac{1}{6}$ in. in diameter, covered with silky down. Leaves trifoliolate, with a main-stalk $1\frac{1}{2}$ to $2\frac{1}{2}$ in. long; stipules narrowly linear, $\frac{1}{4}$ to $\frac{3}{8}$ in. long, soon falling. Leaflets stalkless, obovate, tapered at the base; rounded, notched or mucronate at the apex; $1\frac{1}{2}$ to $3\frac{1}{2}$ in. long, 1 to $1\frac{1}{2}$ in. wide; both surfaces covered with silky white hairs giving them a silvery appearance. Racemes erect or curving upwards, about 5 in. long, terminating young leafy shoots, the flowers closely packed in a cylindrical mass on the upper half. Flowers fragrant, golden yellow, shortly stalked; calyx tubular, very silky, $\frac{1}{3}$ in. long, $\frac{1}{6}$ in. wide, with pointed narrowly triangular lobes; standard petal heart-shaped, $\frac{1}{2}$ in. wide, downy outside; wing petals and keel glabrous, nearly as long as the standard; stamens glabrous; ovary silvery downy, style incurved. Pods erect, stiff, $1\frac{1}{2}$ to 2 in. long, $\frac{1}{4}$ to $\frac{1}{3}$ in. wide, hairy, six- or seven-seeded. *Bot. Mag.*, t. 9528.

Native of Morocco on the middle Atlas Mountains at 5,000 to 6,000 ft altitude, where it flowers in June. It was named in 1915 and introduced to this country about 1922. It flowered at Kew under glass in 1928, and planted against a wall outside has never suffered from cold. It seems certain that it is quite hardy near London, for T. Hay grew it fully in the open in Hyde Park without protection. In June 1930, at six years old, when it had attained a height and diameter of 9 ft there, it flowered freely. It also blossomed with the late Sir Oscar Warburg at Boidier, near Epsom, where the garden is situated at 600 ft altitude, and in June 1932 a plant in the open air at Kew flowered beautifully.

In the last quarter century, *C. battandieri* has become a popular garden shrub. Its hardiness was amply proved in the winter of 1962–3 but, being of rather lax habit, it is perhaps seen at its best on a wall, where it will grow to 12 ft high; in the open ground it is more effective if several plants are grouped together. There is an old specimen in the R.H.S. Garden at Wilsey on Battleston Hill, 12 ft high and as much across (1968) which is completely hardy. Without attention *C. battandieri* deteriorates and should, especially if grown on a wall, be renewal-pruned by removing old, dishevelled growths after they have flowered and replacing them with younger growths springing from near the base. The same treatment, on a lesser scale, is successful when applied to open-ground plants. In the R.H.S. Garden, this broom only sets seed in warm summers; very occasionally a crop of self-sown seedlings is found.

In foliage *C. battandieri* is the most remarkable of all brooms, the leaflets being unusually large and the appressed silvery down giving the effect of shot silk; the sheen varies with the angle at which the leaf is held. It grows very vigorously and is a most beautiful addition to hardy shrubs. So distinct is it that a separate generic name, *Argyrocytisus*, has been suggested for it.

C. × BEANII Dallim. [PLATE 75

A deciduous, semi-prostrate shrub 6 to 18 in. high, twice or thrice as wide, with round, slightly grooved, slender branches, hairy when young, afterwards glabrous. Leaves simple, linear, about ½ in. long, hairy. Flowers produced singly, in pairs, or in threes at each joint of the previous summer's growth, deep golden yellow, forming charming sprays of blossom up to 1 ft in length. *Bot. Mag.*, n.s., t. 366.

A chance hybrid raised at Kew in 1900, and first noticed in a bed of seedlings of *C. ardoinii*. The pollen parent was evidently *C. purgans*, which it resembles in leaf and stem; its semi-prostrate habit it inherits from *C. ardoinii*. It flowers in May, and is then one of the prettiest of dwarf brooms; it is, however, at its best when two or three years old.

C. × DALLIMOREI Rolfe

× *Cytothamnus dallimorei* (Rolfe) Schneid.

A hybrid raised at Kew in 1900 by crossing *C. scoparius* 'Andreanus' (seed-bearer) with *C. multiflorus*. It is a tall shrub, perhaps 8 or 9 ft high, of thin, erect habit, suggesting that of *C. scoparius*; young wood ribbed. Leaves mostly trifoliolate, downy. Flowers about ⅝ in. long, the whole of the petals suffused with beautiful shades of rosy pink deepening on the wing petals to crimson;

the almost orbicular standard petal is $\frac{5}{8}$ in. long, darker outside than within, keel almost white. Calyx helmet-shaped, shining brown, slightly downy, $\frac{1}{4}$ in. long; flower-stalk $\frac{1}{4}$ in. long, downy. At each node the flowers are solitary or in pairs. *Bot. Mag.*, t. 8482.

This beautiful broom is quite distinct from any other in cultivation, and is the first hybrid broom raised by artificial cross-fertilisation, all its predecessors having originated as chance crosses made by insects. It is propagated by grafting on laburnum or by cuttings. The original hybrid (which should really be distinguished as *C.* × *dallimorei* 'William Dallimore') is less common now in gardens than formerly but still well worth growing for its beautiful flowers and for its historic interest as one of the parents of the modern race of garden brooms.

C. DECUMBENS (Durande) Spach
Spartium decumbens Durande

A prostrate shrub 4 to 6 in. high, with five-angled, sparsely hairy branches. Leaves simple, stalkless, $\frac{1}{4}$ to $\frac{3}{4}$ in. long, oblong or obovate, $\frac{1}{8}$ to $\frac{1}{6}$ in. wide; hairy, especially beneath. Flowers bright yellow, $\frac{1}{2}$ to $\frac{5}{8}$ in. long, produced singly, in pairs, or in threes from the joints of the preceding summer's shoots; the flower-stalks are $\frac{1}{8}$ to $\frac{1}{2}$ in. long, and the calyx $\frac{1}{6}$ in. long, both hairy. Pod $\frac{3}{4}$ to 1 in. long, hairy, three- or four-seeded. *Bot. Mag.*, t. 8230.

Native of S. Europe from France to Albania and Montenegro. This species is, perhaps, the most prostrate of all brooms in cultivation, lying as it does flat on the ground and only increasing in height by additional growths laid on the older ones. In May and June it is very gay with the bright but rich yellow flowers. It may be strongly recommended for the rock garden, especially for positions where it is in full sunlight. Said by Aiton to have been introduced in 1775, but now rare in gardens.

C. DEMISSUS Boiss.
C. hirsutus var. *demissus* (Boiss.) Halacsy

A deciduous shrub, low and spreading, usually not more than 3 or 4 in. above the ground; shoots very slender, densely and loosely grey-hairy. Leaves bright green, trifoliolate; leaflets oval, roundish or obovate, $\frac{1}{4}$ to $\frac{1}{2}$ in. long, $\frac{1}{12}$ to $\frac{1}{4}$ in. wide, hairy especially beneath. Flowers yellow, in clusters of two or three from the terminal leaf-axils, $\frac{3}{4}$ to $1\frac{1}{4}$ in. long; standard petal $\frac{1}{2}$ in. across, orbicular; notched; keel rich brown; calyx tubular, $\frac{1}{2}$ to $\frac{5}{8}$ in. long, hairy. Blooms in May.

Native of Greece and one of the most charming of dwarf brooms. Admirable for the rock garden. It grows on Mt Olympus at 7,000 to 8,000 ft altitude. The flowers are very large for this type of broom; they become reddish with age and the calyx is reddish. The late Dr Stoker grew it admirably in his garden north of London. Shown by G. P. Baker, Sevenoaks, at Vincent Square, 10th May 1932, it received an Award of Merit. It was originally described by Boissier in his *Flora Orientalis* in 1872 from specimens found about 1836 by Aucher-Eloy, whom Boissier describes as 'that hardy and courageous explorer whose adventurous travels in Greece, Macedonia, Asia Minor, etc., had for their sole motive his love of plants and science'. He discovered this cytisus on the slopes of Mt Olympus, where it has since been again collected by the late Dr Guiseppi.

C. DIFFUSUS (Willd.) Vis.

Genista diffusa Willd.

A deciduous shrub with a prostrate root-stock producing more or less erect, grooved, slender, soon glabrous young shoots from 3 to 10 in. long. Leaves simple, ¼ to ¾ in. long, oblong-lanceolate, pointed, glabrous. Flowers one to three in the leaf-axils, crowded to form leafy, slender racemes 6 in. or more long; corolla bright yellow, ⅜ in. long, glabrous. Pod ¾ in. long, glabrous or slightly hairy.

Native of S.E. Europe, often in calcareous regions. In May and June, when in flower, it is quite one of the most attractive dwarf brooms.

C. EMERIFLORUS Reichenb.

C. glabrescens Sart., not Shrank; *Genista glabrescens* (Sart). Briq.

A low, deciduous shrub of dense habit up to 3 ft high, with angled branchlets. Leaves trifoliolate with leaf-stalks ½ to 1 in. long; leaflets stalkless or nearly so,

CYTISUS EMERIFLORUS

obovate or oblong, ¼ to ½ in. long, clothed with silky hairs beneath. Flowers produced from the joints of the previous year's shoots, one to four, or occasionally more, at each joint; yellow. Each flower is about ½ in. long, on a hairy stalk of equal length. Pods 1 to 1½ in. long, ¼ in. wide, glabrous. *Bot. Mag.*, t. 8201.

Native of the mountains around Lakes Como and Garda, commonest on the

Grigna massif, where it ascends to 6,000 ft. This delightful shrub, which forms a neat, compact mass of branches, was introduced to Kew in 1896. It flowers in May, when the plant is almost hidden by blossom. It is worth a place in the rock garden, or wherever dainty plants can be accommodated without danger of being smothered by stronger-growing neighbours.

Although most authorities retain this species in *Cytisus* it is intermediate in certain respects between that genus and *Genista*, in which it was placed by Briquet.

C. FONTANESII Spach

Chronanthus biflorus (Desf.) Frodin & Heywood

An erect deciduous shrub 1 to 2 ft high, stems angled, glabrous, sometimes sparse and lanky or sometimes sturdy and crowded, internodes often ¾ to 1¼ in. apart. Leaves trifoliolate; leaflets linear, mostly ¼ to ½ in. long, $\frac{1}{16}$ in. or less wide, hairy, main-stalk very short. Flowers yellow, usually two to four at the tips of the shoots, shortly stalked; corolla ½ in. long, standard glabrous; calyx ⅛ in. long, membranous. Pod ⅝ in. to ¾ in. long; glabrous. Flowers in May.

Native of Spain, usually in calcareous districts. It is a curious shrub with very meagre foliage, giving the shoots a spartium-like appearance. It varies much in regard to pubescence: the type is regarded as quite or nearly glabrous, but in var. PLUMOSUS Boiss. most of the parts are very noticeably hairy. It appears also to be the more attractive.

C. GRANDIFLORUS (Brot.) DC. WOOLLY-PODDED BROOM

Spartium grandiflorum Brot.; *Genista grandiflora* (Brot.) Spach

A deciduous shrub 8 to 10 ft high, with much the same habit and general appearance as *C. scoparius*; leaflets and shoots clothed with silvery-grey hairs when quite young. Leaves consisting of three leaflets (or only one) which are ¼ to ½ in. long, oval, obovate or awl-shaped. Flowers solitary or in pairs, bright yellow, produced in May from the joints of the previous year's wood, each on a stalk ⅓ to ½ in. long. The keel petals are about 1 in. long, and the standard petal ¾ in. wide; calyx green, helmet-shaped, glabrous or slightly downy, ¼ in. long. Pod 1 in. long, ⅔ in. wide, pointed, compressed and covered with a thick grey wool.

Native of Spain and Portugal. Although this broom is said to have been introduced in 1816 and was mentioned by Loudon in 1837, it is now very rare in gardens. The only place I know of, to which it owes its existence in our gardens today, is the Sunningdale Nurseries at Windlesham, Surrey. There, according to the late H. White, it has been cultivated for a great many years as the 'woolly-podded broom', flowering and bearing seed freely. It is perfectly hardy at Kew. Related to common broom, it is conspicuously distinct in the long grey hairs with which the seed-pod is thickly covered. This broom must not be confused with the prostrate variety of *C. scoparius*, which is sometimes grown in gardens as "*C. grandiflorus*".

C. 'CHENISTON'.—This broom, raised by N. Hamilton-Smith and distributed by the Sunningdale Nurseries, appears to be a hybrid of *C. grandiflorus*, which it resembles in its silver-hairy pods. Flowers cream and apricot.

C. HIRSUTUS L.
Chamaecytisus hirsutus (L.) Link

A dwarf, more or less decumbent, deciduous shrub 1 to 3 ft high, with round slender stems covered when young with outstanding (not appressed) hairs. Leaves trifoliolate; leaflets oval, or broadly obovate, up to ⅜ in. long, half as much wide, under-surface shaggy. Flowers yellow, 1 in. or more long, produced in axillary clusters of two to four blossoms; standard petal stained with brown in the centre, roundish, and as much as ¾ in. across; calyx tubular, very hairy, ½ in. long. Pod 1 to 1½ in. long, flattened, shaggy. *Bot. Mag.*, t. 6819.

Native of S. Europe; introduced nearly two hundred years ago, but not often seen. It has been much confused with *supinus* and *ratisbonensis*; the former is, of course, quite distinct in its terminal inflorescence (but see the remarks under that species); the latter, which is the more closely allied, has the hairs on the various parts appressed.

var. HIRSUTISSIMUS (K. Koch) Boiss., is sometimes seen in gardens. It is a sturdier, more erect form found farther east than the type occurring in Asia Minor; the leaves, calyx, and pods are even more hirsute. Up to 3 or 4 ft high.

C. CILIATUS Wahlenb., is native in S.E. Europe and Turkey. It is sometimes made a variety of *hirsutus*, from which it differs chiefly in the pods being hairy only on the seams, or even almost glabrous. Habit and flower as in ordinary *C. hirsutus*. Introduced in 1817. C. FALCATUS Waldst. & Kit. is intermediate between this species and *C. hirsutus*, and perhaps a hybrid between them. Found wild in Central Europe.

C. INGRAMII Blakelock

A densely branched deciduous shrub up to 7 ft high. Branchlets appressed hairy when young, later glabrous. Leaves sessile or with a very short petiole, trifoliolate near the base of the shoot but entire towards the apex; leaflets about 1 in. long, ½ to ¾ in. wide, elliptic-oblong to obovate, blade glabrous above, the margins and undersides clad with appressed silky hairs. The large flowers are borne singly in the leaf-axils; calyx campanulate, two-lipped; standard cream-coloured, blotched brown within; wings and keel yellow. Fruit hairy, about 1¼ in. long. *Bot. Mag.*, n.s., t. 211.

This attractive broom was discovered by Capt. Collingwood Ingram in 1936 in N. Spain, between Corunna and Oviedo. In describing the species in the *Botanical Magazine*, Blakelock remarks that it bears some resemblance to *C. grandiflorus* in its large flowers and sessile leaves but is not (as that species is) a member of the section *Sarothamnus*; its nearest relative is *C. villosus*, a species of the W. Mediterranean. It is hardy in all but the severest winters and flowers in June.

C. × KEWENSIS Bean   [PLATE 74

A low, deciduous, perfectly procumbent shrub less than 1 ft high, but sometimes 6 ft across. Leaves sometimes simple, but usually trifoliolate, downy. Flowers produced in May singly, or two or three together, at each joint of the previous year's wood; they are each about ½ in. long, creamy white or pale sulphur-yellow, with a fine standard petal ½ in. across. *Bot. Mag.*, n.s., t. 299.

A hybrid between *C. ardoinii* (seed-bearer) and *C. multiflorus*, raised at Kew in 1891. For growing on shelves of the rock garden few dwarf shrubs are more beautiful. The flowers are rather larger than those of *C.* × *praecox*, but otherwise very similar.

C. MONSPESSULANUS L.   MONTPELIER BROOM

C. candicans (L.) DC.; *Genista candicans* L.; *Teline monspessulana* (L.) K. Koch

A shrub 6 ft or more high, with erect, very leafy branches; evergreen in mild winters. Branchlets conspicuously ridged, hairy when young. Leaves trifoliolate, short-stalked; leaflets obovate with a short, abrupt tip, ½ to ¾ in. long, glabrous above, hairy beneath. Flowers produced in early May in short racemes or short-stalked umbels, three to nine in each umbel, from the axils of the leaves; ½ in. long, bright yellow. Calyx ⅛ to ¼ in. long, bell-shaped, with unequal triangular teeth. Pod ½ to ¾ in. long, shaggy, three- to four-seeded. *Bot. Mag.*, t. 8685.

Native of S. Europe from France and Portugal to Dalmatia and Greece, also in N. Africa and Syria; cultivated in 1735, but never common on account of its tenderness. Although at Kew it survives winters of moderate severity it succumbs to 15° or 20° of frost, and is therefore really adapted for the mildest parts of our islands only. It has been introduced from N. India, being apparently naturalised in some parts there.

C. (monspessulanus × *racemosus)* 'PORLOCK'.—A beautiful and very floriferous hybrid raised by N. G. Hadden of Porlock. A specimen was received by Kew from Mr Hadden in 1922 and nine years later it received an Award of Merit when shown at the Chelsea Show, May 1931. It bears fragrant flowers in April and May and, though rather tender, grows quickly into a large shrub.

C. MULTIFLORUS (Ait.) Sweet

Spartium multiflorum Ait.; *C. albus* Link, not Hacq.

A tall broom, sometimes 10 or more ft high; branchlets very slender, round, slightly ribbed, downy when young; but little branched, and produced abundantly in besom-like masses. Leaves trifoliolate on the lower part of the shoot, simple towards the top; leaflets linear, silky, up to ½ in. long, or so small as to be scarcely noticeable. Flowers white, produced in May at the joints all along the previous summer's wood, singly, or two or three together; each flower ⅓ in. long on a stalk of equal length. Pods 1 in. long, hairy, with thickened seams, four- to six-seeded. *Bot. Mag.*, t. 8693.

Native of Spain and Portugal. This beautiful broom, the only really white one that is genuinely hardy, is one of the most useful of hardy shrubs. Easily raised from seed, and reaching its full beauty in three or four years, it is admirably adapted for planting in small groups in shrubberies in association with the sturdier evergreens. It does not rob other plants, although it soon out-tops most of them. Cultivated by Phillip Miller in 1752.

This species is better known in gardens as *C. albus*, the name given to it by Link in 1822, but Aiton several decades earlier had described it as *Spartium multiflorum* and his epithet must be used. Furthermore, Hacquet had earlier used the name *C. albus* for quite a different species (q.v.).

C. NIGRICANS L.

Lembotropis nigricans (L.) Griseb.

A deciduous shrub 3 to 5 ft high, with erect, round branches covered with appressed down. Leaves trifoliolate, with main-stalks ¼ to ¾ in. long; leaflets ½ to 1 in. long, obovate or oval, with scattered hairs beneath. Flowers yellow, in erect slender racemes, terminating the shoots of the year, and sometimes more than 1 ft long. Whilst the racemes are themselves leafless, they frequently extend into leafy growth above the flowers. Flowers crowded on the raceme, each one ⅓ to ½ in. long, and borne on a slender, rather shorter, hairy stalk. Calyx somewhat helmet-shaped, hairy. Pod 1 to 1½ in. long, ⅕ in. wide, hairy. *Bot. Mag.*, t. 8479.

Native of Central and S.E. Europe; introduced in 1730. This broom is very distinct among its kind, because of its long terminal racemes, which commence to open flowers in July, and continue until the end of August. Flowering as it does on the shoots of the current year, it should be pruned in spring before growth commences. It is wise also to remove the racemes when the flowers are over, so as to prevent excessive seed formation. A group of this broom in the front of a shrubbery is very effective but, although quite hardy, it is short-lived in some soils. The flowers turn black when dried, a peculiarity (not confined to this species) on which Linnaeus based the specific name.

C. PALMENSIS (Christ) Hutchins.   TAGASASTE

C. proliferus var. *palmensis* Christ

An evergreen shrub of slender lax habit, with long, thin, downy young shoots. Leaves of three leaflets, each of which is of narrowly elliptical or oblanceolate shape, very shortly stalked; ¾ to 1½ in. long, ⅙ to ⅜ in. wide; terminated by a short bristle-like tip; glabrous above, finely downy (not silky-hairy) beneath; common stalk ½ to 1 in. long, downy. Flowers white, opening from February to April, two to four in axillary clusters, ¾ in. long; calyx with triangular-lanceolate lobes, thickly downy like the flower-stalk. Pod 1½ in. long, ½ in. wide; seeds black, shining.

Native only of La Palma, one of the Canary Islands, where it is much valued as a fodder plant, especially during the long dry summer season. The plants are treated like osiers, being cut back annually and the young shoots given to mules

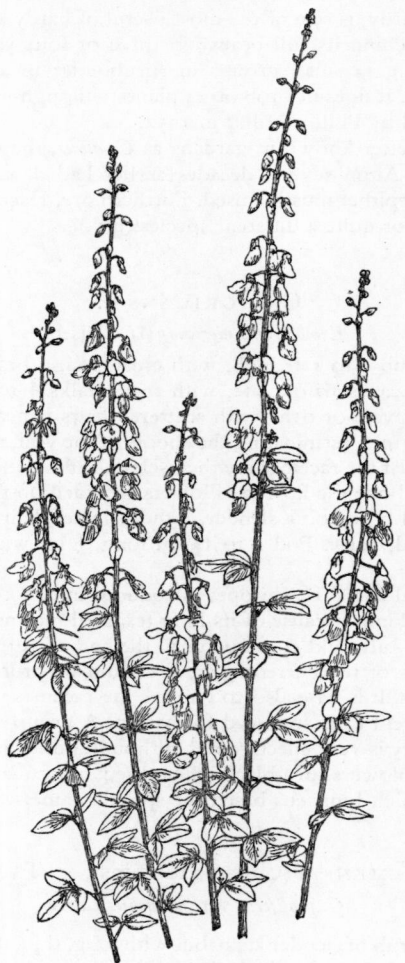

CYTISUS NIGRICANS

and cattle. Tagasaste, not being really hardy, is grown as a pillar plant in a cool greenhouse at Kew, where it is 15 ft high and flowers copiously every spring. It succeeds in a sunny spot or on a wall in the south and south-western counties, Isle of Wight, etc. Its long slender shoots wreathed with blossom are very graceful and beautiful.

It has been grown in several gardens as *C. proliferus* (q.v.), but the true plant of that name has its leaves densely silky-hairy beneath.

C. × PRAECOX Wheeler

A group of hybrid brooms derived from *C. purgans* crossed with *multiflorus*, of which the typical and original clone should be known as *C. × praecox* 'WARMINSTER'. This broom has the habit of *C. multiflorus*, but with denser and heavier masses of young branches. Leaves mostly simple, about ½ in. long, silky like the young shoots; soon falling. Flowers sulphur-yellow, produced in remarkable abundance in early May, and very beautiful then; but they have a heavy, rather unpleasant odour which renders the plant unsuitable for growing in large masses near the house. It ripens good seed, but the plants do not come true, reverting more or less to one or other parent. It can be increased easily from cuttings placed in sandy soil under cloches or in a cold frame during August. This fine broom first appeared among some seedlings of *C. purgans* in the nursery of Messrs Wheeler of Warminster about 1867. From its appearance it was surmised that it was a hybrid between that species and *C. multiflorus*, made through insect agency. The reversion of its seedlings to the white broom have since proved this to be true.

'Warminster' sets fertile seed, from which some named varieties have been raised. 'ALLGOLD', of Dutch origin, has deep yellow flowers and is slightly taller than the parent; 'GOLD SPEAR', raised in Germany in 1955 by G. Arends and first introduced to Britain in 1964, will probably prove to be rather smaller in habit than 'Warminster' of which, too, it is a seedling. The flowers are bright yellow, freely borne. In the older 'ALBUS', raised at the Daisy Hill nursery, they are white. For the use of the Warminster broom in recent hybridising, see the introductory note to *Cytisus*.

C. PROCUMBENS (Willd.) Spreng.

Genista procumbens Willd.; *C. kitaibelii* Vis., in part

A deciduous, very leafy shrub up to 1½ ft high, of prostrate habit, with slender arching young shoots 6 to 18 in. long covered with appressed hairs. Leaves simple, linear-oblong, or oblanceolate, pointed, ½ to 1¼ in. long, $\frac{1}{10}$ to $\frac{1}{6}$ in. wide, hairy on the margins and lower surface, often glabrous above. Flowers borne closely in the leaf-axils, either solitary, in pairs or in threes, bright yellow, ⅔ in. long, opening in May and June, and forming handsome, cylindrical leafy racemes 3 to 6 in. long; calyx silky-hairy. Pod up to 1 in. long by ¼ in. wide, shaggy with appressed hairs, carrying three or four seeds.

Native of the mountains of S.E. Europe, quite hardy, very floriferous and handsome, forming low patches several feet across. The late Fred Stoker grew it beautifully in his rock garden in Essex. It is near *C. decumbens* in affinity which differs in its outstanding pubescence. It was given an Award of Merit in 1948 when shown by R. E. Heath of Petts Wood, Kent.

C. PROLIFERUS L. f.   ESCABON

An evergreen shrub found wild only on the islands of Teneriffe and Gomera. It is very closely related to *palmensis*, which used to be regarded as a variety of it until given separate specific rank by Dr Hutchinson (see *Kew Bulletin*, 1918,

p. 21). It is of similarly lax habit and produces long, slender, downy stems. Leaves of three leaflets which are mostly of linear shape and narrower in proportion to their length than those of *C. palmensis*; the best distinction is provided by the covering of silky hairs (not mere down) beneath. Flowers white, 1 in. long, produced in clusters of four to seven towards the end of short, axillary, leaf-bearing shoots during April. Calyx ½ in. long, funnel-shaped, with narrow triangular lobes, very downy.

As with *C. palmensis*, the young shoots are highly valued as a fodder in the Canary Islands, the plants being cut back annually in the same way as osiers are. The endemic character of these and other brooms in the Canary Islands is very interesting. *C. proliferus* is wild only on Teneriffe and Gomera; *C. palmensis* and another species, *C. pallidus*, on La Palma; *C. perezii* on Grand Canary and Hierro; *C. stenopetalus* on La Palma, Gomera, and Hierro.

C. proliferus is grown in Cornwall, where it gets to be 12 or 15 ft high, the long slender shoots wreathed with flowers being very handsome in spring. A plant grown there as 'Miss Wingfield's Variety' is undoubtedly *C. proliferus*, but possibly an improved form. *C. palmensis* is also grown there under the name of *C. proliferus*.

C. perezii Hutchins., is in cultivation. It differs from *palmensis* and *proliferus* in having the leaflets silky-hairy on both sides, and in their being distinctly obovate, averaging 1¼ in. long by ⅜ in. wide. Known as 'Escabon de Canaria'.

C. PURGANS (L.) Spach
Genista purgans L.

A deciduous shrub, often nearly leafless, 3 or 4 ft high, of sturdy habit, forming a low, wide mass of rather rigid, erect, grooved branches. Leaves stalkless, narrowly obovate, ¼ to ½ in. long, clothed with appressed silvery hairs, and soon falling. Flowers produced in April and May, singly or in pairs from the joints of the preceding year's wood, deep golden yellow, each flower ½ in. long, on a somewhat shorter stalk. Pod ¾ to 1 in. long, hairy, three- or four-seeded. *Bot. Mag.*, t. 7618.

Native of France from the Loire southwards to Central Spain; long cultivated in English gardens (Philip Miller grew it in the Chelsea Physic Garden in the mid-eighteenth century). The exceptionally rich golden colour of its flowers makes this species well worth cultivation; it should have the sunniest possible position. Its foliage is a negligible quantity, but the numerous dark green branchlets give the effect of an evergreen. It can be increased in the usual way (see under *praecox*), but plants so raised are not so long-lived as seedlings. It is said to have purgative and emetic properties, but is poisonous in large quantity, and not used in medicine.

C. PURPUREUS Scop.   [PLATE 76
Chamaecytisus purpuseus (Scop.) Link

A low, deciduous shrub from 1 to 1½ ft high; branchlets glabrous or nearly so, well furnished with trifoliolate leaves. Leaflets obovate, ¼ to 1 in. long, stalkless themselves, but with a common stalk ¼ to 1 in. long; usually quite glabrous, dark green. Flowers purple, produced in May on the shoots of the preceding summer, one to three of them at each joint. Each flower is ¾ in. long; the calyx ⅓ to ½ in. long. Pod quite glabrous, 1 to 1½ in. long, containing three or four seeds. *Bot. Mag.*, t. 1176.

Native of the S. Alps and S.E. Europe; introduced in 1792. In the colour of its flowers it is one of the most distinct of brooms, and one of the most charming of dwarf shrubs. It makes an admirable cover for the ground beneath a group of taller, thinly planted shrubs. A good system of cultivating it is to cut out the flowering shoots as soon as the flowers have faded, leaving the young growths that always spring up from near the ground to form the flowering shoots for the following year. Seeds provide the best means of propagation, and a sufficient quantity of them should, of course, be left to ripen for the purpose.

f. ALBUS (Sweet) Zab.—A white-flowered form found wild near Bolzano and Trento and other parts of the Italian Tyrol.

A number of other colour variants have arisen in cultivation, with flowers in some shade of pink or of a richer purple than in the wild plant. An erect form is also known, and one with drooping branchlets.

C. RACEMOSUS *see* C. × SPACHIANUS

C. RATISBONENSIS Schaeffer

C. biflorus L'Hérit.; *C. ruthenicus* Woloszczak; *Chamaecytisus ratisbonensis* (Schaeffer) Rothm.

A procumbent or erect deciduous shrub 1 to 6 ft high; its round branches covered with short, greyish, appressed hairs. Leaves trifoliolate, on stalks ¼ to ¾ in. long; leaflets ¾ to 1¼ in. long, ¼ to ½ in. wide; covered beneath with appressed hairs, the margins silicate; upper surface glabrous except when young. Flowers produced during May, two to four together at each joint of the previous summer's wood; they are

CYTISUS PURPUREUS

bright yellow, 1 in. or more long, the standard petal roundish and ½ in. across, often spotted with red; calyx tubular, ½ in. long; pod 1 in. long, $\frac{3}{16}$ in. wide, both with appressed hairs. *Bot. Mag.*, t. 8661.

Native of Europe from Germany to west Russia, abundant in Hungary and the Balkan States. It is very hardy, and easily increased by the numerous seeds it bears; altogether a handsome and useful broom. It comes from the continent under a variety of names and in slightly differing forms, varying in stature and in the character of the down. C. ELONGATUS Waldstein, for instance, is a robust form with down of a more felted character mixed with outstanding hairs. Briquet makes it a variety of *C. hirsutus*, but that is well distinguished by its hairs not being appressed.

Another species in this group is C. ABSINTHIOIDES Janka, described from the mountains of Bulgaria. It differs from both the species described in its narrower leaflets, denser indumentum and shorter and broader pods. *Bot. Mag.*, n.s., t. 87.

C. ROCHELII Griseb. & Schenk
Chamaecytisus rochelii (Griseb. & Schenk) Rothm.

A deciduous shrub 3 to 4 ft high; shoots erect, terete, very hairy. Leaves trifoliolate; leaflets oblong-lanceolate to oblanceolate, ⅓ to 1¼ in. long, $\frac{1}{12}$ to ⅜ in. wide, tapered at the base, narrowed to a short point or bristle, appressed-hairy on both surfaces. Flowers ¾ in. long, aggregated at and near the summit of the leafy shoots, pale yellow spotted with brown; calyx and pod very hairy; standard petal downy outside. Blossoms in June and July.

Native of Central Europe. This is one of the group of brooms characterised by a tubular calyx to which *C. supinus* and *C. hirsutus* belong. It has no outstanding merit but is equally hardy.

C. SCOPARIUS (L.) Link   COMMON BROOM
Spartium scoparium L.; *Sarothamnus scoparius* (L.) K. Koch

A deciduous shrub up to 5 or 6 ft high in the open; twice as high when drawn up in shrubberies. Although the leaves fall in autumn, the plant, by the greenness of its branches, retains an evergreen aspect through the winter. Branchlets erect, straight, prominently angled, hairy when young. Leaves at the base of the shoot trifoliolate and stalked, those near the end stalkless and often reduced to one leaflet. Leaflets obovate, sometimes narrowly so, ¼ to ⅝ in. long, glabrous except beneath when quite young. Flowers a rich glowing yellow, 1 in. long, produced singly or in pairs from the joints of the year-old shoots in May; standard petal round, ¾ in. across; calyx glabrous. Pod 1½ to 2 in. long, hairy, especially on the margins.

Native of W. Europe, and the only cytisus native of the British Isles, over which it is widely spread. *C. scoparius* has been regarded as a distinct genus, *Sarothamnus* Wimmer, distinguished by a number of floral characters, of which the chief was the long, incurved, circinnate-convolute style. However, Bentham, in Bentham and Hooker f., *Genera Plantarum*, Vol. 1, p. 484 (1865), and in his *British Flora*, ed. 2, p. 110 (1866), reduced it to *Cytisus*, noting that there are species which 'show a gradual passage from the long spiral to the short and straight style'. In the *Genera Plantarum Sarothamnus* was treated as a section of *Cytisus*, and this was followed by Briquet in his *Études sur les Cytises des Alpes Maritimes* (1894), where he has eleven species in the section.

cv. 'ANDREANUS'.—Similar to the type in habit, foliage, and shape of flower, but with the wing petals of a rich brownish crimson, and the standard petal, though mainly yellow, stained and lined with the same colour. This beautiful and striking variety was discovered by Puissant growing wild in Normandy, about 1884. It succeeds best grafted on laburnum. It comes only partly true from seed, many of its progeny having flowers very poorly coloured as compared with the parent; but some distinct and improved forms have been obtained. One of the first to be put into commerce was 'FIREFLY', raised at the Daisy Hill nursery, Co. Down, around 1906. Directly, or through *C.* × *dallimorei* (q.v.), 'Andreanus' has played an important part in the formation of the garden brooms. Plants similar to it have been found elsewhere, for which the group-name is f. ANDREANUS (Puissant) Zab.

cv. 'PENDULUS'.—This variety is not only distinct because of its low prostrate habit (pendulous only when grafted on standards of laburnum), it is particularly showy because of the large size of its flowers. It appears to be a form of var. *prostratus* (see below).

var. PROSTRATUS (C. Bailey) A. B. Jacks. *Sarothamnus scoparius* subsp. *maritimus* (Rouy & Fouc.) Ulrich—Stems prostrate; leaves and young twigs densely silky-hairy. According to *Flora of the British Isles* (1962), where it is treated as a subspecies, it is found on cliffs in W. Cornwall and the Channel Islands, and breeds true. Similar plants are found on the continent on the North Sea coast and in the southern Alps.

f. SULPHUREUS (Goldring) Rehd. f. *ochroleucus* Zab.—Flowers sulphur-yellow; found occasionally in the wild state. The garden clone 'Moonlight' belongs here; it is also characterised by its dwarfer, flatter and more compact habit.

Whilst the ordinary broom, in spite of its great beauty, may be considered too common a shrub to deserve a place in the garden proper, it is admirable for semi-wild spots, dry banks, and such-like places. It is best increased by seed. For the propagation of the garden varieties see the introductory paragraphs on the genus.

C. SESSILIFOLIUS L.

A deciduous, bushy shrub 5 or 6 ft high, with ribbed, not downy branchlets. Leaves glabrous, trifoliolate, usually without stalks on the short flowering shoots, but with stalks up to ¾ in. long on the stronger, non-flowering ones. Leaflets very variable in shape, often obovate, but also oval, roundish, or oblate, from ¼ to ¾ in. long, pointed. Flowers four to ten, in short racemes terminating short side twigs of the year, bright yellow, ½ in. long, expanding in June. Pod 1¼ in. long, ⅓ in. wide, glabrous. *Bot. Mag.*, t. 255.

Native of S. Europe and N. Africa; introduced over three hundred years ago, and one of the most attractive of the later-flowering brooms. It is more appreciated on the continent than with us, and gives some of the brightest effects seen in German gardens in June.

C. × SPACHIANUS Webb

C. everestianus Carr.; *C. racemosus* Nichols., not Marnock

This well-known shrub is one of the most popular of greenhouse plants and small plants are common in florists' shops and are even sold in the streets from hawkers' barrows. It is only in the mildest parts of our islands that it can be grown out-of-doors, but where it thrives it is a very handsome plant. Nowhere, perhaps, did it succeed better than at Ludgvan Rectory near Penzance, but the gardens of S. Devon and Cornwall generally also grow it well. In these places it commences to bloom about the New Year and continues for several months.

It is an evergreen that gets to be 10 to 20 ft high, very leafy and luxuriant in habit. Its young shoots are hairy and somewhat ribbed. Leaves composed of three obovate leaflets $\frac{1}{3}$ to $\frac{3}{4}$ in. long, mostly rounded at the end, wedge-shaped at the base; they are scarcely stalked themselves but are borne on a common stalk about $\frac{1}{4}$ in. long; dark green and glabrous above and covered with silky appressed down beneath. Flowers in slender racemes 2 to 4 in. long, the main-stalk downy. Corolla of the usual pea-flowered shape, rich glowing yellow, about $\frac{1}{2}$ in. long. Calyx with five awl-shaped lobes, two larger than the others, all glistening with down; flower-stalk $\frac{1}{12}$ in. long.

The plant described above is representative of the "*C. racemosus*" of gardens and is believed to be a hybrid between *C. stenopetalus* and *C. canariensis*, for which the correct name is *C.* × *spachianus* (see further in note on p. 829). It has been in cultivation since before the middle of last century and is sometimes erroneously known as "*Genista fragrans*" and "*Cytisus fragrans*", both of which names are synonymous with *C. supranubius*.

cv. 'EVERESTIANUS'.—Flowers deeper coloured and habit dwarfer. Raised before 1862 and figured in *Rev. Hort.*, 1873, p. 390.

C. 'ELEGANS'.—The origin and status of this broom is uncertain, but it is usually considered to be a form of *C.* × *spachianus*. It is very distinct in its greyer, larger foliage (the leaflets being up to $1\frac{1}{2}$ or 2 in. long) and in the stronger growth. The individual flowers are also larger. A very beautiful shrub, in some respects finer than *C.* × *spachianus*. It flowers over a long season in spring. Being very difficult to increase by cuttings and not coming true from seed, it has to be grafted on *C.* × *spachianus*.

The two species mentioned above as the parents of *C.* × *spachianus* may be shortly described here:

C. STENOPETALUS (Webb) Christ *Teline stenopetala* Webb; *C. maderensis* sensu Briq., in part.—This species resembles *C.* × *spachianus* but differs in its larger leaflets (up to $1\frac{1}{2}$ in. long), on longer petioles. The var. MAGNI-FOLIOSUS O. Kuntze merely represents the extreme of the variation of the species in size of leaf and is scarcely worth distinguishing. *Bot. Mag.*, n.s., t. 327.

C. stenopetalus is allied to *C. maderensis* but differs in its indumentum of silvery grey (not rusty) hairs. Native of the Canary Islands on the islands of Palma,

Gomera and Hierro; it has also been collected on Teneriffe but appears to be rare there.

C. CANARIENSIS (L.) O. Kuntze *Genista canariensis* L.—This species differs from *C. stenopetalus* and from *C.* × *spachianus* in its very short-stalked to almost sessile leaves and its short, dense racemes of bright yellow flowers. In var. RAMOSISSIMUS (Poir.) Briq. the leaflets are very small, the racemes shorter and more numerous; this variety is also, like *C.* × *spachianus*, grown as a pot plant, often as "*Genista fragrans*". Native of the Canary Islands.

NOTE

Mrs Dingwall and Dr Gibbs of St Andrew's University, who are studying this group of *Cytisus*, find that *C. spachianus* is intermediate between *C. canariensis* and *C. stenopetalus* and may be a hybrid between them. That the *C. racemosus* of gardens is a hybrid between these two species was suggested as long ago as 1888 (Rolfe in *Gard. Chron.*, April 23, 1888) and is very probable.

C. × *spachianus* was described by P. B. Webb in 1845 (*Bot. Mag.*, t. 4195) from a plant raised in the Jardin du Roi, Paris, from seeds he had collected ten years earlier in the mountains of N.W. Teneriffe; he also sent seeds to Young and Penny, who had a nursery near his home at Godalming, Surrey. Of the two parents of *C.* × *spachianus*, *C. canariensis* is fairly common on Teneriffe. There are no old collections from this island in the Kew Herbarium either of *C. stenopetalus* or of *C.* × *spachianus* but there is evidence that both are, or were until recently, to be found there. Both were growing in the late Dr Perez's garden, Villa Oratava, Teneriffe, in 1911 and 1913, and there is a note from Dr Perez with specimens in the Kew Herbarium to the effect that *C.* × *spachianus* was said to have been introduced to the garden 'from near the forest of Agua Garcia, above Tacoronte, where two or three wild plants still exist'. The plants of *C. stenopetalus* in Dr Perez's garden originated from La Palma but also from Teneriffe. 'in heather earth brought from Agua Mansa (above Orotava)'. There is a specimen of *C. stenopetalus* in the Kew Herbarium collected by Eric Asplund in 1933 in the Orotava Valley, Teneriffe, at 800 metres, in the Barranco San Antonio.

The name *C. racemosus* was published by Marnock in 1837 (*Floricult. Mag.*, Vol. 2, p. 37 and t. 19). The figure shows a plant that closely resembles a large-leaved form of *C. stenopetalus* .It is not the *C. racemosus* of Nicholson and of gardens, which is *C. stenopetalus* × *canariensis*, i.e. *C.* × *spachianus*.

C. SUPINUS L.

C. capitatus Scop.; *Chamaecytisus supinus* (L.) Link

A deciduous shrub, 2 to 4 ft high, with round, erect, hairy branches. Leaves trifoliolate, with a main-stalk about ½ in. long; leaflets obovate or elliptical, very hairy beneath, ultimately glabrous above, ½ to 1 in. long. Flowers in a terminal cluster or umbel 2 in. across, each flower nearly 1 in. long, with bright yellow petals; calyx tubular, ½ in. long, very hairy. Pod 1½ in. long, ¼ in. wide, covered with shaggy, spreading hairs.

C. supinus is representative of a group of brooms that have their centre in the lands around the Black Sea and in the Danube basin but extend westward through much of Central and S. Europe as far as Spain; it is itself the most widespread of the group, being found over much of this area. All are characterised by a terminal umbel of flowers, a hairy, tubular calyx and hairy leaves and pods. *C. austriacus* and *C. albus* (*leucanthus*) also belong to this group and both have by some botanists been united with *C. supinus* into a large aggregate species with several subspecies and varieties. *C. austriacus* is very near to *C. supinus* but differs in having the hairs on the shoots and pods appressed; *C. albus* may be distinguished by its whitish or creamy flowers.

In the plant described, all the flowers are borne at the ends of the current season's growth, but in some forms there is an additional flowering in spring on short axillary shoots from the previous year's growth. Such plants, in their spring state, might be taken for *C. hirsutus*, but in that species all the flowers are borne in this way, while in *C. supinus* the spring flowering is only the prelude to the main flowering at the ends of the new growths.

C. supinus has some value in the garden, bearing its flowers in July and August and then intermittently until the frosts come. Whatever pruning is necessary should be done in spring before growth recommences, when the last-made shoots may, if desired, be cut back almost to the old wood.

C. SUPRANUBIUS (L. f.) O. Kuntze

Spartium supranubium L. f.; *C. fragrans* Lam.

A shrub 8 to 10 ft high, of broom-like habit; twigs stiff, stout, ribbed, clothed with white hairs at first, soon glabrous. Leaves of three leaflets, each $\frac{1}{6}$ to $\frac{1}{3}$ in. long, $\frac{1}{12}$ to $\frac{1}{8}$ in. wide, with a main-stalk of about the same length. Flowers fragrant, borne in May in axillary clusters on the previous season's shoots; they are milky white with a tinge of rose, $\frac{1}{2}$ in. long; standard petal roundish obovate, $\frac{1}{3}$ in. long; calyx and flower-stalk hairy. Seed-pod brown, 1 to $1\frac{1}{4}$ in. long. *Bot. Mag.*, t. 8509.

Native of the Canary Islands, and very abundant on the Peak of Teneriffe. It has been in cultivation at Kew but is too tender to withstand severe winters in the open there except on warm walls. It is, however, so beautiful and so distinct that it is much to be recommended for the milder parts of the British Isles. The numerous dark green branchlets resemble those of *Spartium junceum* and are much stouter than those of the common white broom—*C. multiflorus*. It has reached a height of 8 ft in the Glasnevin Botanic Garden, but was cut there by the winter of 1961–2. In the Edinburgh Botanic Garden it is fairly hardy in well-drained situations; one example has survived for twenty years on a dry bank.

C. TOMMASINII Vis.

Cytisanthus tommasinii (Vis.) Rothm.

A deciduous shrub, erect, about 2 ft high; young shoots very slender, appressed hairy. Leaves trifoliolate; leaflets $\frac{1}{3}$ to 1 in. long, $\frac{1}{12}$ to $\frac{1}{4}$ in. wide, oval-lanceolate to oval, tapered more to the base than to the short-pointed apex; central leaflets mostly obovate, at first appressed-hairy beneath. Flowers very shortly stalked in a terminal umbel; corolla yellow, $\frac{5}{8}$ to $\frac{3}{4}$ in. long, made narrow by the clasping, tubular, hairy calyx, $\frac{1}{2}$ in. long. Pod $\frac{3}{4}$ in. long, shaggy.

Native of E. Europe, quite frequent in the neighbourhood of Kotor in Dalmatia. It belongs to the confusing group of brooms centring round *C. supinus*.

C. × VERSICOLOR (Kirchn.) Dipp.

C. purpureus elongatus versicolor Kirchn.

A hybrid of which *C. purpureus* is one parent. The identity of the other parent is uncertain; it is now usually considered to be *C. hirsutus*, but *C. elongatus* has been suggested. It has inherited the characters and general aspect of *C. purpureus*, having glabrous stems and similar foliage, but is a sturdier, taller, and more rounded bush, 2 ft or more high. It differs from *C. purpureus* in having the flowers a distinct compromise between yellow and purple, and in having a quite hairy calyx. It has been known for about eighty years, and is a very desirable broom.

cv. 'HILLIERI'.—A hybrid between *C.* × *versicolor* and *C. hirsutus* var. *hirsutissimus*, raised by Messrs Hillier and put into commerce in 1933. It is a low shrub with arching branches and large yellow flowers flushed pale bronze, changing to buff-pink.

INDEX

As the general arrangement of this work is alphabetical it has not been considered necessary to index names which appear in their proper sequence. The following is an index of 'popular' or English names; of the more important synonyms which, in accordance with the usual practice, are given in italics; and of a number of trees and shrubs which are not described in their alphabetical order but under related plants.

The attention of the reader is called to the glossary of botanical terms on p. 112, and to the glossary of nursery terms on p. 54. The plates are listed on p. 131; the line drawings on pp. xix-xx.